The Canadian Oxford Paperback Thesaurus

Edited by
Robert Pontisso

Associate editors
Tom Howell
Heather Fitzgerald

Editor-in-chief, Canadian Dictionaries
Katherine Barber

OXFORD
UNIVERSITY PRESS

OXFORD
UNIVERSITY PRESS

70 Wynford Drive, Don Mills, Ontario M3C 1J9
www.oupcan.com

Oxford University Press is a department of the University of Oxford. It furthers the University
objective of excellence in research, scholarship, and education by publishing worldwide in

Oxford New York
Auckland Bangkok Buenos Aires Cape Town Chennai
Dar es Salaam Delhi Hong Kong Istanbul Karachi Kolkata
Kuala Lumpur Madrid Melbourne Mexico City Mumbai Nairobi
São Paulo Singapore Taipei Tokyo Toronto

Oxford is a registered trademark of Oxford University Press in the UK and in certain other
countries

Published in Canada
by Oxford University Press

Published by arrangement with Oxford University Press, Oxford. Based on the Oxford
Paperback Thesaurus—Second Edition © Oxford University Press, 2001

Statistics Canada information is used with the permission of the Minister of Industry, as
Minister responsible for Statistics Canada. Information on the availability of the wide range of
data from Statistics Canada can be obtained from Statistics Canada's Regional Offices, its
World Wide Web site at http://www.statcan.ca., and its toll-free access number 1-800-263-1136

National Library of Canada Cataloguing in Publication
Main entry under title:

The Canadian Oxford paperback thesaurus / edited by Robert Pontisso...[et al.].

ISBN 0-19-541795-X

1. English language — Canada — Synonyms and antonyms — Dictionaries.
2. Canadianisms. I. Pontisso, Robert, 1968–

PE3233.C35 2003   428′.00971′03   C2003-902294-3

1 2 3 4 – 06 05 04 03

This book is printed on permanent (acid-free) paper ∞.

Printed in Canada

Introduction

The *Canadian Oxford Paperback Thesaurus* marks the broadening of Oxford University Press's commitment to producing the most useful language tools for Canadian readers and writers. Designed as a companion to the *Canadian Oxford Dictionary* and the *Canadian Oxford Paperback Dictionary*, the thesaurus has been created using the same computational techniques and language data resources that went into producing its lexicographical predecessors. By carefully examining the English language as it is used by Canadians, the editors have been able to ensure that the included synonyms are wholly consistent with English usage in this country. Words or senses exclusive to Canadian English are explicitly marked with ♣.

Entries

The synonyms in each entry are grouped in numbered sets. Major synonym sets correspond roughly to different senses of the word in a dictionary, and are identifiable by example phrases or sentences. Many sets also contain finer distinctions, which are signalled by semicolons.

The synonyms in each set that are closest in meaning to the entry word are given first, usually starting with a "core synonym" in SMALL CAPITALS. Some sets have more than one core synonym if two synonyms are very close to the entry word but neither covers the whole sense; for example, at *audience*, both *spectators* and *listeners* are given as core synonyms. Two different core synonyms may also emphasize slightly different aspects of the meaning of the entry word. For example, at *prosperous*, the first core synonym given is *thriving*, followed by a group of words closely related to that aspect of its meaning, such as *flourishing* and *successful*. Then, after a semicolon, a second core synonym, *affluent*, is given, with an allied group of synonyms such as *wealthy* and *rich*.

Phrases and idiomatic expressions are provided in bold form at the end of the entry for their principal word. For example, *make do* and *make off* can be found with their synonyms at the end of the entry for *make*.

Most of the synonyms are part of standard English, but some are suitable only in certain contexts. These are grouped at the end of their synonym set and are given identifying labels, for example:

informal, e.g. *freebie*, *snappy*: the kind of vocabulary used in speech or informal writing.
literary, e.g. *beauteous, descry*.
historical, e.g. *privateer, intendant*: still used today, but only to refer to something that is no longer part of the modern world.
archaic, e.g. *hie, in sooth*: very old-fashioned language, not used today except for effect.

Basic opposite words are given for many entries, and most of these have entries of their own where a wider selection can be found.

Tables

Included in this thesaurus are 185 tables of word lists organized by category. Often a thesaurus entry will refer the reader to one of these boxes; at *bonspiel*, for example, the reader is directed to the table at *curling*, where more expressions related to this game can be found. Covering a wide range of topics, these tables are a valuable source of terminology and other information for those seeking to add detail to their work.

A Note of Caution

Using an unfamiliar word simply because it is listed in a thesaurus can be a disaster. To avoid inappropriate collocations or embarrassing malapropisms, users should look up unfamiliar words in a dictionary before employing them. One had better be aware of the connotations of *inveigle*, for example, before choosing it as a substitute for *persuade*. Although entries in the *Canadian Oxford Paperback Thesaurus* have been organized to facilitate the selection of the most appropriate synonyms, users should always have a good dictionary within arm's reach.

Major Features of the Thesaurus

Headword

Canadian synonym

Number and example, to distinguish different senses

Phrase

Superscript numbers distinguishing homonyms

Style label for headword

Specialized vocabulary

Regionalism

Combined synonym group standing for both *release* and *release mechanism*

Form of the entry word for which the following synonyms can be substituted

Pointer to other related entries where more synonyms can be found

Core synonym

Related words, prefixes, or suffixes

Brackets showing that the phrase they contain is one complete synonym

Style label for the following synonyms

Words meaning the opposite of the entry word; most have entries of their own, where a wider choice can be found

channel ▶ noun **1** *sailing the North Channel* STRAIT(S), sound, narrows, (sea) passage, (*Atlantic*) tickle ♣, snye ♣. **2** *the water ran down a channel* DUCT, gutter, conduit, trough, culvert, sluice, spillway, race, drain. **3** *a channel for their extraordinary energy* USE, medium, vehicle, way of harnessing; release (mechanism), safety valve, vent. **4** *a channel of communication* MEANS, medium, instrument, mechanism, agency, vehicle, route, avenue.

egg ▶ noun OVUM; gamete, germ cell; **(eggs)** roe, spawn, seed.
— RELATED TERMS: ovoid. *See also* EASTER EGG.

egg someone on URGE, goad, incite, provoke, push, drive, prod, prompt, induce, impel, spur on; encourage, exhort, motivate, galvanize.

stalk¹ ▶ noun *the stalk of a plant* STEM, shoot, trunk, stock, cane, bine, bent, haulm, straw, reed.
— RELATED TERMS: cauline.

stalk² ▶ verb **1** *a cat was stalking a rabbit* CREEP UP ON, trail, follow, shadow, track down, go after, be after, course, hunt; *informal* tail, still-hunt. **2** *she stalked out* STRUT, stride, march, flounce, storm, stomp, sweep.

unflappable ▶ adjective (*informal*) IMPERTURBABLE, unexcitable, cool, calm, {calm, cool, and collected}, self-controlled, cool-headed, level-headed; *informal* laid-back, Type-B.
— OPPOSITES: excitable.

voluntary ▶ adjective **1** *attendance is voluntary* OPTIONAL, discretionary, elective, non-compulsory, volitional; *Law* permissive. **2** *voluntary work* UNPAID, unsalaried, unwaged, for free, without charge, for nothing; honorary, volunteer; *Law* pro bono (publico).
— OPPOSITES: compulsory, paid.

Aa

aback

■ **take someone aback** SURPRISE, shock, stun, stagger, astound, astonish, startle, take by surprise; dumbfound, stop someone in their tracks; shake (up), jolt, throw, unnerve, disconcert, unsettle, bewilder; *informal* flabbergast, floor.

abandon ▶ **verb** **1** *the party abandoned policies that made it unelectable* RENOUNCE, relinquish, dispense with, disclaim, disown, disavow, discard, wash one's hands of; give up, drop, jettison, do away with, axe; *informal* ditch, dump, scrap, scrub, junk, deep-six; *formal* forswear. **2** *by that stage, she had abandoned painting* GIVE UP, stop, cease, drop, forgo, desist from, have done with, abstain from, discontinue, break off, refrain from, set aside; *informal* cut out, kick, pack in, quit; *formal* abjure. **3** *he abandoned his wife and children* DESERT, leave, leave high and dry, turn one's back on, cast aside, break (up) with; jilt, strand, leave stranded, leave in the lurch, throw over; *informal* walk out on, run out on, dump, ditch; *literary* forsake. **4** *the skipper gave the order to abandon ship* VACATE, leave, depart from, withdraw from, quit, evacuate. **5** *a vast expanse of territory was abandoned to the invaders* RELINQUISH, surrender, give up, cede, yield, leave. **6** *she abandoned herself to the sensuousness of the music* INDULGE IN, give way to, give oneself up to, yield to, lose oneself to/in.
— OPPOSITES: keep, retain, maintain, continue.
▶ **noun** *reckless abandon* UNINHIBITEDNESS, recklessness, lack of restraint, lack of inhibition, wildness, impulsiveness, impetuosity, immoderation, wantonness.
— OPPOSITES: self-control.

abandoned ▶ **adjective** **1** *an abandoned child* DESERTED, forsaken, cast aside/off; jilted, stranded, rejected; *informal* dumped, ditched. **2** *an abandoned tin mine* UNUSED, disused, neglected, idle; deserted, unoccupied, uninhabited, empty. **3** *a wild, abandoned dance* UNINHIBITED, reckless, unrestrained, wild, unbridled, impulsive, impetuous; immoderate, wanton.

abase ▶ **verb** HUMBLE, humiliate, belittle, demean, lower, degrade, debase, cheapen, discredit, bring low; (**abase oneself**) grovel, kowtow, bow and scrape, toady, fawn; *informal* crawl, suck up to someone, lick someone's boots.

abasement ▶ **noun** HUMILIATION, belittlement, lowering, degradation, debasement.

abashed ▶ **adjective** EMBARRASSED, ashamed, shamefaced, remorseful, conscience-stricken, mortified, humiliated, humbled, chagrined, crestfallen, sheepish, red-faced, blushing, put out of countenance, with one's tail between one's legs; taken aback, disconcerted, discomfited, fazed, floored, disturbed.

abate ▶ **verb** **1** *the storm had abated* SUBSIDE, die down/away/out, lessen, ease (off), let up, decrease, diminish, moderate, decline, fade, dwindle, recede, tail off, peter out, taper off, wane, ebb, weaken, come to an end; *archaic* remit. **2** *nothing abated his crusading*

zeal DECREASE, lessen, diminish, reduce, moderate, ease, soothe, dampen, calm, tone down, allay, temper.
— OPPOSITES: intensify, increase.

abatement ▶ **noun** **1** *the storm still rages with no sign of abatement* SUBSIDING, dying down/away/out, lessening, easing (off), let-up, decrease, moderation, decline, ebb. **2** *noise abatement* DECREASE, reduction, lowering.

abattoir ▶ **noun** SLAUGHTERHOUSE; *archaic* shambles.

abbey ▶ **noun** MONASTERY, CONVENT, priory, cloister, friary, nunnery; *historical* charterhouse; *rare* cenobium.

abbreviate ▶ **verb** SHORTEN, reduce, cut, contract, condense, compress, abridge, truncate, pare down, prune, shrink, telescope; summarize, abstract, précis, synopsize, digest, edit.
— OPPOSITES: lengthen, expand.

abbreviated ▶ **adjective** SHORTENED, reduced, cut, condensed, abridged, concise, compact, succinct; summary, thumbnail, capsule, synoptic; *formal* compendious.
— OPPOSITES: long.

abbreviation ▶ **noun** SHORTENED FORM, short form, contraction, acronym, initialism, symbol, diminutive; elision.

abdicate ▶ **verb** **1** *the king abdicated in 1936* RESIGN, retire, stand down, step down, bow out, renounce the throne; *archaic* demit. **2** *Ferdinand abdicated the throne* RESIGN FROM, relinquish, renounce, give up, surrender, vacate, cede; *Law* disclaim; *formal* abjure. **3** *the state abdicated all responsibility for their welfare* DISOWN, reject, renounce, give up, refuse, relinquish, repudiate, abandon, turn one's back on, wash one's hands of; forgo, waive; *formal* abjure; *literary* forsake.

abdication ▶ **noun** **1** *Edward VIII's abdication* RESIGNATION, retirement; relinquishment, renunciation, surrender; *formal* abjuration; *archaic* demission. **2** *an abdication of responsibility* DISOWNING, renunciation, rejection, refusal, relinquishment, repudiation, abandonment.

abdomen ▶ **noun** STOMACH, belly, gut, middle, intestines; *informal* tummy, tum, insides, guts, maw, breadbasket, pot, paunch.

abdominal ▶ **adjective** GASTRIC, intestinal, stomach, stomachic, enteric, duodenal, visceral, celiac, ventral.

abduct ▶ **verb** KIDNAP, carry off, seize, capture, run away/off with, make off with, spirit away, hold hostage, hold to ransom; *informal* snatch.

aberrant ▶ **adjective** DEVIANT, deviating, divergent, abnormal, atypical, anomalous, irregular, rogue; strange, odd, peculiar, uncommon, freakish; twisted, warped, perverted.
— OPPOSITES: normal, typical.

aberration ▶ **noun** *a statistical aberration* ANOMALY, deviation, departure from the norm, divergence, abnormality, irregularity, variation, freak, rarity, oddity, peculiarity, curiosity; mistake.

abet ▶ **verb** ASSIST, aid, help, lend a hand, support,

back, encourage; co-operate with, collaborate with, work with, collude with, be in collusion with, be hand in glove with, side with; second, endorse, sanction; promote, incite, champion, further, expedite, connive at.
— OPPOSITES: hinder.

abeyance ▶ noun SUSPENSION, a state of suspension, a state of uncertainty, remission; (**in abeyance**) pending, suspended, deferred, postponed, put off, put to one side, unresolved, up in the air; *informal* in cold storage, on ice, on the back burner.

abhor ▶ verb DETEST, hate, loathe, despise, execrate, regard with disgust, shrink from, recoil from, shudder at; *formal* abominate.
— OPPOSITES: love, admire.

abhorrence ▶ noun HATRED, loathing, detestation, execration, revulsion, abomination, disgust, repugnance, horror, odium, aversion.

abhorrent ▶ adjective DETESTABLE, hateful, loathsome, despicable, abominable, execrable, repellent, repugnant, repulsive, revolting, disgusting, distasteful, horrible, horrid, horrifying, awful, heinous, reprehensible, obnoxious, odious, nauseating, offensive, contemptible.
— OPPOSITES: admirable.

abide ▶ verb 1 *he expected everybody to abide by the rules* COMPLY WITH, obey, observe, follow, keep to, hold to, conform to, adhere to, stick to, hew to, stand by, act in accordance with, uphold, heed, accept, go along with, acknowledge, respect, defer to. 2 (*informal*) *I can't abide the smell of cigarettes* TOLERATE, bear, stand, put up with, endure, take, countenance; *informal* stomach; *formal* brook; *archaic* suffer. 3 *at least one memory will abide* CONTINUE, remain, survive, last, persist, stay, live on.
— OPPOSITES: flout, disobey.

abiding ▶ adjective ENDURING, lasting, persisting, long-lasting, lifelong, continuing, remaining, surviving, standing, durable, everlasting, perpetual, eternal, unending, constant, permanent, unchanging, steadfast, immutable.
— OPPOSITES: short-lived, ephemeral.

ability ▶ noun 1 *the ability to read and write* CAPACITY, capability, potential, potentiality, power, faculty, aptness, facility; wherewithal, means. 2 *the president's leadership ability* TALENT, skill, expertise, adeptness, aptitude, skilfulness, savoir faire, prowess, mastery, accomplishment; competence, proficiency; dexterity, adroitness, deftness, cleverness, flair, finesse, gift, knack, genius; qualification, resources; *informal* know-how.

abject ▶ adjective 1 *abject poverty* WRETCHED, miserable, hopeless, pathetic, pitiful, pitiable, piteous, sorry, woeful, lamentable, degrading, appalling, atrocious, awful. 2 *an abject sinner* CONTEMPTIBLE, base, low, vile, worthless, debased, degraded, despicable, ignominious, mean, unworthy, ignoble. 3 *an abject apology* OBSEQUIOUS, grovelling, fawning, toadyish, servile, cringing, sycophantic, submissive, craven.

abjure ▶ verb (*formal*) RENOUNCE, relinquish, reject, forgo, disavow, abandon, deny, repudiate, give up, wash one's hands of; eschew, abstain from, refrain from; *informal* kick, pack in; *Law* disaffirm; *literary* forsake; *formal* forswear, abnegate.

ablaze ▶ adjective 1 *several vehicles were ablaze* ON FIRE, alight, aflame, in flames, flaming, burning, fiery, blazing; *literary* afire, igneous. 2 *every window was*

ablaze with light LIT UP, alight, gleaming, glowing, aglow, illuminated, bright, shining, radiant, shimmering, sparkling, flashing, dazzling, luminous, incandescent. 3 *his eyes were ablaze with fury* PASSIONATE, impassioned, aroused, excited, stimulated, eager, animated, intense, ardent, fiery, fervent, frenzied.

able ▶ adjective 1 *he will soon be able to resume his duties* CAPABLE OF, competent to, equal to, up to, fit to, prepared to, qualified to; allowed to, free to, in a position to. 2 *an able student* INTELLIGENT, clever, talented, skilful, skilled, accomplished, gifted; proficient, apt, good, adroit, adept; capable, competent, efficient, effective.
— OPPOSITES: incompetent, incapable.

able-bodied ▶ adjective HEALTHY, FIT, in good health, robust, strong, sound, sturdy, vigorous, hardy, hale and hearty, athletic, muscular, strapping, burly, brawny, lusty; in good shape, in good trim, in fine fettle, fighting fit, as fit as a fiddle, as fit as a flea; *informal* husky; *dated* stalwart.
— OPPOSITES: infirm, frail, disabled.

abnegation ▶ noun (*formal*) 1 *a serious abnegation of their responsibilities* RENUNCIATION, rejection, refusal, abandonment, abdication, surrender, relinquishment, repudiation, denial; *formal* abjuration. 2 *people capable of abnegation and unselfishness* SELF-DENIAL, self-sacrifice, abstinence, temperance, continence, asceticism, austerity, abstemiousness.
— OPPOSITES: acceptance, self-indulgence.

abnormal ▶ adjective UNUSUAL, uncommon, atypical, untypical, non-typical, unrepresentative, rare, isolated, irregular, anomalous, deviant, divergent, aberrant, freak, freakish; STRANGE, odd, peculiar, curious, bizarre, weird, queer; eccentric, idiosyncratic, quirky; unexpected, unfamiliar, unconventional, surprising, unorthodox, singular, exceptional, extraordinary, out of the ordinary, out of the way; unnatural, perverse, perverted, twisted, warped, unhealthy, distorted; *informal* freaky.
— OPPOSITES: normal, typical, common.

abnormality ▶ noun 1 *born with a heart abnormality* MALFORMATION, deformity, irregularity, flaw, defect, anomaly. 2 *the abnormality of such behaviour* UNUSUALNESS, uncommonness, atypicality, irregularity, anomalousness, deviation, divergence, aberrance, aberration, freakishness; strangeness, oddness, peculiarity, unexpectedness, singularity.

abode ▶ noun HOME, house, place of residence, accommodation, seat; quarters, lodgings, domicile, rooms; address; *informal* pad, digs; *formal* dwelling, dwelling place, residence, habitation.

abolish ▶ verb PUT AN END TO, get rid of, scrap, end, stop, terminate, axe, eradicate, eliminate, exterminate, destroy, annihilate, stamp out, obliterate, wipe out, extinguish, quash, expunge, extirpate; annul, cancel, invalidate, negate, nullify, void, dissolve; rescind, repeal, revoke, overturn; discontinue, remove, excise, drop, jettison; *informal* do away with, ditch, junk, scrub, dump, chop, give something the chop; *formal* abrogate.
— OPPOSITES: retain, create.

abolition ▶ noun SCRAPPING, ending, termination, eradication, elimination, extermination, abolishment, destruction, annihilation, obliteration, extirpation; annulment, cancellation, invalidation, nullification, dissolution; revocation, repeal, discontinuation, removal; *formal* abrogation.

abominable ▸ **adjective** LOATHSOME, detestable, hateful, odious, obnoxious, despicable, contemptible, damnable, diabolical; disgusting, revolting, repellent, repulsive, offensive, repugnant, abhorrent, reprehensible, atrocious, horrifying, execrable, foul, vile, wretched, base, horrible, awful, dreadful, appalling, nauseating; horrid, nasty, disagreeable, unpleasant, distasteful; *informal* terrible, shocking, godawful; beastly; *dated* cursed, accursed.
– OPPOSITES: good, admirable.

abominate ▸ **verb** (*formal*) DETEST, loathe, hate, abhor, despise, execrate, shudder at, recoil from, shrink from, be repelled by.
– OPPOSITES: like, love.

abomination ▸ **noun 1** *in both wars, internment was an abomination* ATROCITY, disgrace, horror, obscenity, outrage, evil, crime, monstrosity, anathema, bane. **2** *an abomination of all kitsch* DETESTATION, loathing, hatred, aversion, antipathy, revulsion, repugnance, abhorrence, odium, execration, disgust, horror, hostility.
– OPPOSITES: liking, love.

aboriginal ▸ **adjective 1** *the area's aboriginal inhabitants* INDIGENOUS, native; original, earliest, first; ancient, primitive, primeval, primordial; *rare* autochthonous. **2** *Aboriginal soldiers serving in the Canadian Forces* NATIVE, indigenous, First Peoples, First Nations, Indian, Inuit, Metis.
▸ **noun** the social structure of the aboriginals NATIVE, aborigine, original inhabitant; *rare* autochthon, indigene.

abort ▸ **verb** *the crew aborted the takeoff* HALT, stop, end, axe, call off, cut short, discontinue, terminate, arrest, cancel, scrub; *informal* pull the plug on.

abortion ▸ **noun** TERMINATION, miscarriage.

abortive ▸ **adjective** UNSUCCESSFUL, failed, vain, thwarted, futile, useless, worthless, ineffective, ineffectual, to no effect, inefficacious, fruitless, unproductive, unavailing, to no avail, sterile, nugatory; *archaic* bootless.
– OPPOSITES: successful, fruitful.

abound ▸ **verb 1** *cafés and bars abound in the narrow streets* BE PLENTIFUL, be abundant, be numerous, proliferate, superabound, be thick on the ground; *informal* grow on trees. **2** *a stream which abounded with trout and eels* BE FULL OF, overflow with, teem with, be packed with, be crowded with, be thronged with, be alive with, be crawling with, be overrun by/with, swarm with, bristle with, be infested with, be thick with; *informal* be stuffed with, be jam-packed with, be chockablock with, be chock full of.

abounding ▸ **adjective** ABUNDANT, plentiful, superabundant, considerable, copious, ample, lavish, luxuriant, profuse, boundless, prolific, inexhaustible, generous; galore; *literary* plenteous.
– OPPOSITES: meagre, scanty.

about ▸ **preposition 1** *a book about needlecraft* REGARDING, concerning, with reference to, referring to, with regard to, with respect to, respecting, relating to, on, touching on, dealing with, relevant to, connected with, in connection with, on the subject of, in the matter of, apropos, re. **2** *two hundred people were milling about the room* AROUND, round, throughout, over, through, on every side of.
▸ **adverb 1** *there were babies crawling about in the grass* AROUND, here and there, to and fro, back and forth, from place to place, hither and thither, in all directions. **2** *I knew he was about somewhere* NEAR, nearby, around, hereabouts, not far off/away, close

by, in the vicinity, in the neighbourhood. **3** *the explosion caused about $15,000 worth of damage* APPROXIMATELY, roughly, around, round about, in the region of, circa, of the order of, something like; or so, or thereabouts, there or thereabouts, more or less, give or take a few, not far off; *informal* in the ballpark of. **4** *there's a lot of gossip about* AROUND, in circulation, in existence, current, going on, prevailing, prevalent, happening, in the air, abroad.
■ **about to** (JUST) GOING TO, ready to, all set to, preparing to, intending to, soon to; on the point of, on the verge of, on the brink of, within an ace of.

about-face ▸ **noun 1** *he saluted and did an about-face* VOLTE-FACE, turnaround, turnabout, U-turn; *informal* U-ey, one-eighty. **2** *the government was forced to make an about-face* VOLTE-FACE, U-turn, reversal, retraction, backtracking, swing, swerve; change of heart, change of mind, sea change.

above ▸ **preposition 1** *a tiny window above the door* OVER, higher (up) than; on top of, atop, on, upon. **2** *those above the rank of Colonel* SUPERIOR TO, senior to, over, higher (up) than, more powerful than; in charge of, commanding. **3** *you must be above suspicion* BEYOND, not liable to, not open to, not vulnerable to, out of reach of; immune to, exempt from. **4** *the Chinese valued pearls above gold* MORE THAN, over, before, rather than, in preference to, instead of. **5** *an increase above the rate of inflation* GREATER THAN, more than, higher than, exceeding, in excess of, over, over and above, beyond, surpassing, upwards of.
– OPPOSITES: below, under, beneath.
▸ **adverb 1** *in the darkness above, something moved* OVERHEAD, on/at the top, high up, on high, up above, (up) in the sky, high above one's head, aloft. **2** *the two cases described above* EARLIER, previously, before, formerly.
▸ **adjective** *the above example* PRECEDING, previous, earlier, former, foregoing, prior, above-stated, above-mentioned, aforementioned, aforesaid.
■ **above all** MOST IMPORTANTLY, before everything, beyond everything, first of all, most of all, chiefly, primarily, in the first place, first and foremost, mainly, principally, predominantly, especially, essentially, basically, in essence, at bottom; *informal* at the end of the day, when all is said and done.

above board ▸ **adjective** *the proceedings were completely above board* LEGITIMATE, lawful, legal, licit, honest, fair, open, frank, straight, overt, candid, forthright, unconcealed, trustworthy, unequivocal; *informal* legit, kosher, by the book, street legal, fair and square, square, on the level, on the up and up, upfront.
– OPPOSITES: dishonest, shady.

abrade ▸ **verb** WEAR AWAY, wear down, erode, scrape away, corrode, eat away at, gnaw away at.

abrasion ▸ **noun 1** *he had abrasions to his forehead* GRAZE, cut, scrape, scratch, gash, laceration, injury, contusion; sore, ulcer; *Medicine* trauma. **2** *the metal is resistant to abrasion* EROSION, wearing away/down, corrosion, scraping, scouring.

abrasive ▸ **adjective 1** *abrasive kitchen cleaners* CORROSIVE, corroding, erosive; caustic, harsh, scratching, coarse. **2** *her abrasive manner* CAUSTIC, cutting, biting, acerbic; rough, harsh, hard, tough, sharp, grating, curt, brusque, stern, severe; wounding, nasty, cruel, callous, insensitive, unfeeling, unsympathetic, inconsiderate.
– OPPOSITES: kind, gentle.

abreast ▸ **adverb 1** *they walked three abreast* IN A ROW, side by side, alongside, level, beside each other, shoulder to shoulder. **2** *try to keep abreast of current affairs* UP TO DATE WITH, up with, in touch with, informed about, acquainted with, knowledgeable about, conversant with, familiar with, au courant with, au fait with.

abridge ▶ verb SHORTEN, cut, cut short/down, curtail, truncate, trim, crop, clip, pare down, prune; abbreviate, condense, contract, compress, reduce, decrease, shrink; summarize, sum up, abstract, précis, synopsize, give a digest of, put in a nutshell, edit; *rare* epitomize.
– OPPOSITES: lengthen.

abridged ▶ adjective SHORTENED, cut, cut down, concise, condensed, abbreviated; summary, outline, thumbnail; bowdlerized, censored, expurgated; *informal* potted.

abridgement ▶ noun SUMMARY, abstract, synopsis, précis, outline, resumé, sketch, compendium, digest.

abroad ▶ adverb **1** *he regularly travels abroad* OVERSEAS, out of the country, to/in foreign parts, to/ in a foreign country/land. **2** *rumours were abroad* IN CIRCULATION, circulating, widely current, everywhere, in the air, {here, there, and everywhere}; about, around; at large.

abrogate ▶ verb *(formal)* REPEAL, revoke, rescind, repudiate, overturn, annul, *Law* disallow ♣, cancel, invalidate, nullify, void, negate, dissolve, countermand, declare null and void, discontinue; reverse, retract, remove, withdraw, abolish, put an end to, do away with, get rid of, end, stop, quash, scrap; *Law* disaffirm.
– OPPOSITES: institute, introduce.

abrogation ▶ noun *(formal)* REPEAL, revocation, repudiation, overturning, annulment, cancellation, invalidation, nullification, negation, dissolution, discontinuation; reversal, retraction, removal, withdrawal, abolition; *formal* rescission.

abrupt ▶ adjective **1** *an abrupt halt | an abrupt change of subject* SUDDEN, unexpected, without warning, unanticipated, unforeseen, precipitate, precipitous, surprising, startling; quick, swift, rapid, hurried, hasty, immediate, instantaneous. **2** *an abrupt manner* CURT, brusque, blunt, short, sharp, terse, crisp, gruff, rude, discourteous, uncivil, snappish, unceremonious, offhand, rough, harsh; bluff, no-nonsense, to the point; *informal* snappy. **3** *abrupt, epigrammatic paragraphs* DISJOINTED, jerky, uneven, disconnected, inelegant. **4** *an abrupt slope* STEEP, sheer, precipitous, bluff, sharp, sudden; perpendicular, vertical, dizzy, vertiginous.
– OPPOSITES: gradual, gentle.

abscess ▶ noun ULCER, ulceration, cyst, boil, blister, sore, pustule, carbuncle, pimple, wen, whitlow, canker; inflammation, infection, eruption.

abscond ▶ verb RUN AWAY, escape, bolt, flee, make off, take flight, take off, decamp; make a break for it, take to one's heels, make a quick getaway, beat a hasty retreat, run for it, make a run for it; disappear, vanish, slip away, split, steal away, sneak away; clear out, duck out, cut and run, skedaddle, skip, head for the hills, do a disappearing act, fly the coop, take French leave, vamoose; *informal* take a powder.

absence ▶ noun **1** *his absence from the office* NON-ATTENDANCE, non-appearance, absenteeism; TRUANCY, playing truant; leave, holiday, vacation, sabbatical. **2** *the absence of any other suitable candidate* LACK, want, non-existence, unavailability, deficiency, dearth; need.
– OPPOSITES: presence.

absent ▶ adjective **1** *she was absent from work* AWAY, off, out, non-attending, truant; off duty, on holiday, on leave; gone, missing, lacking, unavailable, non-existent; *informal* AWOL, playing hooky, *(Ont.)* skipping off ♣, *(West)* skipping out ♣. **2** *an absent look* DISTRACTED, preoccupied, inattentive, vague, absorbed, abstracted, unheeding, oblivious, distrait, absent-minded, dreamy, far away, in a world of one's own, lost in thought, in a brown study; blank, empty, vacant; *informal* miles away.
– OPPOSITES: present, attentive, alert.
▶ verb *Rose absented herself from the occasion* STAY AWAY, be absent, withdraw, retire, take one's leave, remove oneself.

absent-minded ▶ adjective FORGETFUL, distracted, preoccupied, inattentive, vague, abstracted, daydreaming, unheeding, oblivious, distrait, in a brown study, woolgathering; lost in thought, moony, pensive, thoughtful, brooding; *informal* scatterbrained, out of it, out to lunch, miles away, having a mind/memory like a sieve, spacey.

absolute ▶ adjective **1** *absolute silence | an absolute disgrace* COMPLETE, total, utter, out-and-out, outright, entire, perfect, pure, decided; thorough, thoroughgoing, undivided, unqualified, unadulterated, unalloyed, unmodified, unreserved; downright, undiluted, consummate, unmitigated; sheer, arrant, rank, dyed-in-the-wool. **2** *the absolute truth* DEFINITE, certain, positive, unconditional, categorical, unquestionable, incontrovertible, undoubted, unequivocal, decisive, conclusive, confirmed, infallible. **3** *absolute power* UNLIMITED, unrestricted, unrestrained, unbounded, boundless, infinite, ultimate, total, supreme, unconditional. **4** *an absolute monarch* AUTOCRATIC, despotic, dictatorial, tyrannical, tyrannous, absolutist, authoritarian, arbitrary, autonomous, sovereign, autarchic, omnipotent. **5** *absolute moral standards* UNIVERSAL, fixed, independent, non-relative, non-variable, absolutist.
– OPPOSITES: partial, qualified, limited, conditional.

absolutely ▶ adverb *you're absolutely right* COMPLETELY, totally, utterly, perfectly, entirely, wholly, fully, quite, thoroughly, unreservedly; definitely, certainly, positively, unconditionally, categorically, unquestionably, undoubtedly, without (a) doubt, without question, surely, unequivocally; exactly, precisely, decisively, conclusively, manifestly, in every way/respect, one hundred per cent, every inch, to the hilt; *informal* dead.
▶ exclamation *(informal)* 'Have I made myself clear?' 'Absolutely!' YES, indeed, of course, definitely, certainly, quite, without (a) doubt, without question, unquestionably; affirmative, by all means.

absolution ▶ noun FORGIVENESS, pardon, exoneration, remission, dispensation, indulgence, clemency, mercy; discharge, acquittal; freedom, deliverance, release; vindication; *formal* exculpation; *archaic* shrift.

absolve ▶ verb **1** *this fact does not absolve you from responsibility* EXONERATE, discharge, acquit, vindicate; release, relieve, liberate, free, deliver, clear, exempt, let off; *formal* exculpate. **2** *(Christianity)* *I absolve you of your sins* FORGIVE, pardon.
– OPPOSITES: blame, condemn.

absorb ▶ verb **1** *a sponge-like material which absorbs* water SOAK UP, suck up, draw up/in, take up/in, blot up, mop up, sop up. **2** *she absorbed the information in silence* ASSIMILATE, digest, take in. **3** *the company was absorbed into the new concern* INCORPORATE, assimilate, integrate, take in, subsume, include, co-opt, swallow up. **4** *these roles absorb most of his time and energy* USE (UP), consume, take up, occupy. **5** *she was totally absorbed in her book* ENGROSS, captivate, occupy, preoccupy, engage, rivet, grip, hold, interest, intrigue, immerse, involve, enthrall, spellbind, fascinate.

absorbent ▶ adjective POROUS, spongy, sponge-like, permeable, pervious, absorptive; *technical* spongiform.

absorbing ▶ adjective FASCINATING, interesting, captivating, gripping, engrossing, compelling, compulsive, enthralling, riveting, spellbinding, consuming, intriguing, thrilling, exciting; *informal* unputdownable.
– OPPOSITES: boring, uninteresting.

absorption ▶ noun **1** *the absorption of water* SOAKING UP, sucking up; *technical* osmosis. **2** *the company's absorption into a larger concern* INCORPORATION, assimilation, integration, inclusion. **3** *her total absorption in the music* INVOLVEMENT, immersion, raptness, engrossment, occupation, preoccupation, engagement, captivation, fascination, enthralment.

abstain ▶ verb **1** *Benjamin abstained from wine* REFRAIN, desist, hold back, forbear; give up, renounce, avoid, shun, eschew, forgo, go without, do without; refuse, decline; *informal* cut out; *formal* abjure. **2** *most pregnant women abstain, or drink very little* BE TEETOTAL, take the pledge; *informal* be on the wagon. **3** *262 voted against, 38 abstained* NOT VOTE, decline to vote.

abstemious ▶ adjective SELF-DENYING, temperate, abstinent, moderate, self-disciplined, restrained, self-restrained, sober, austere, ascetic, puritanical, Spartan, hair-shirt.
– OPPOSITES: self-indulgent.

abstinence ▶ noun SELF-DENIAL, self-restraint, self-abnegation; teetotalism, temperance, sobriety, forbearance, abstemiousness, abstention; chastity.

abstract ▶ adjective **1** *abstract concepts* THEORETICAL, conceptual, notional, intellectual, metaphysical, ideal, philosophical, academic; *rare* ideational. **2** *abstract art* NON-REPRESENTATIONAL, non-pictorial.
– OPPOSITES: actual, concrete.
▶ verb **1** *staff abstract material for an online database* SUMMARIZE, précis, abridge, condense, compress, shorten, cut down, abbreviate, synopsize; *rare* epitomize. **2** *he abstracted the art of tragedy from its context* EXTRACT, isolate, separate, detach.
▶ noun *an abstract of her speech* SUMMARY, synopsis, précis, resumé, outline, abridgement, digest, summation; wrap-up.

abstracted ▶ adjective ABSENT-MINDED, distracted, preoccupied, in a world of one's own, with one's head in the clouds, daydreaming, dreamy, inattentive, thoughtful, pensive, lost in thought, deep in thought, immersed in thought, woolgathering, in a brown study, musing, brooding, absent, oblivious, moony, distrait; *informal* miles away, out to lunch.
– OPPOSITES: attentive.

abstraction ▶ noun **1** *philosophical abstractions* CONCEPT, idea, notion, thought, theory, hypothesis. **2** *she sensed his momentary abstraction* ABSENT-MINDEDNESS, distraction, preoccupation, dreaminess, inattentiveness, inattention, woolgathering; thoughtfulness, pensiveness. **3** *the*

abstraction of metal from ore EXTRACTION, removal, separation.

abstruse ▶ adjective OBSCURE, arcane, esoteric, little known, recherché, rarefied, recondite, difficult, hard, puzzling, perplexing, cryptic, enigmatic, Delphic, complex, complicated, involved, over/above one's head, incomprehensible, unfathomable, impenetrable, mysterious.

absurd ▶ adjective PREPOSTEROUS, ridiculous, ludicrous, farcical, laughable, risible, idiotic, stupid, foolish, silly, inane, imbecilic, insane, hare-brained, cockamamie; nonsensical, unreasonable, irrational, illogical, nonsensical, incongruous, pointless, senseless; *informal* crazy, daft.
– OPPOSITES: reasonable, sensible.

absurdity ▶ noun PREPOSTEROUSNESS, ridiculousness, ludicrousness, incongruity, inappropriateness, risibility, idiocy, stupidity, foolishness, folly, silliness, inanity, insanity; unreasonableness, irrationality, illogicality, pointlessness, senselessness; *informal* craziness.

abundance ▶ noun PROFUSION, plentifulness, profuseness, copiousness, amplitude, lavishness, bountifulness, bounty; host, cornucopia, riot; plenty, quantities, scores, multitude; *informal* millions, sea, ocean(s), wealth, lot(s), heap(s), mass(es), stack(s), pile(s), load(s), bags, mountain(s), ton(s), slew, scads, oodles, gobs; *formal* plenitude.
– OPPOSITES: lack, scarcity.

abundant ▶ adjective *an abundant supply of food* PLENTIFUL, copious, ample, profuse, rich, lavish, abounding, liberal, generous, bountiful, large, huge, great, bumper, overflowing, prolific, teeming; in plenty, in abundance; *informal* galore; *literary* plenteous, bounteous.
– OPPOSITES: scarce, sparse.

abuse ▶ verb **1** *the judge abused his power* MISUSE, misapply, misemploy; exploit, take advantage of. **2** *he was accused of abusing children* MISTREAT, maltreat, ill-treat, treat badly; molest, interfere with, indecently assault, sexually abuse, sexually assault; injure, hurt, harm, damage. **3** *the referee was abused by players from both teams* INSULT, be rude to, swear at, curse, call someone names, taunt, badmouth, dis, shout at, revile, inveigh against, tear a strip off, give a tongue-lashing to, bawl out, vilify, slander, cast aspersions on.
▶ noun **1** *the abuse of power* MISUSE, misapplication, misemployment; exploitation. **2** *the abuse of children* MISTREATMENT, maltreatment, ill-treatment; molestation, interference, indecent assault, sexual abuse, sexual assault; injury, hurt, harm, damage. **3** *the scheme is open to administrative abuse* CORRUPTION, injustice, wrongdoing, wrong, misconduct, misdeed(s), offence(s), crime(s), sin(s). **4** *torrents of abuse* INSULTS, curses, jibes, expletives, swear words; swearing, cursing, name-calling; invective, vilification, vituperation, slander; *informal* trash talk; *archaic* contumely. **5** *alcohol abuse* ADDICTION, dependency, overuse, misuse, problems.

abusive ▶ adjective INSULTING, rude, vulgar, offensive, disparaging, belittling, derogatory, opprobrious, disrespectful, denigratory, uncomplimentary, censorious, pejorative, vituperative; defamatory, slanderous, libellous, scurrilous, blasphemous; *informal* bitchy; *archaic* contumelious.

abut ▶ verb ADJOIN, be adjacent to, butt against,

border, neighbour, join, touch, meet, reach, be contiguous with.

abysmal ▶ adjective (*informal*) *some of the teaching was abysmal* VERY BAD, dreadful, awful, terrible, frightful, atrocious, disgraceful, deplorable, shameful, hopeless, lamentable; *informal* rotten, appalling, crummy, pathetic, pitiful, woeful, useless, lousy, dire, the pits.

abyss ▶ noun CHASM, gorge, ravine, canyon, fissure, rift, crevasse, hole, gulf, pit, cavity, void, bottomless pit.

academic ▶ adjective **1** *an academic institution* EDUCATIONAL, scholastic, instructional, pedagogical. **2** *his academic turn of mind* SCHOLARLY, studious, literary, well-read, intellectual, clever, erudite, learned, educated, cultured, bookish, highbrow, pedantic, donnish, cerebral; *informal* brainy, inkhorn; *dated* lettered. **3** *the debate has been largely academic* THEORETICAL, conceptual, notional, philosophical, hypothetical, speculative, conjectural, suppositional; impractical, unrealistic, ivory-tower.
▶ noun *a group of Russian academics* SCHOLAR, lecturer, don, teacher, tutor, professor, fellow, man/woman of letters, bluestocking; *informal* egghead, bookworm; *formal* pedagogue.

academy ▶ noun **1** *studied at the academy for two years* EDUCATIONAL INSTITUTION, school, college, university, institute, seminary, conservatory, conservatoire. **2** *ideas pooh-poohed by the academy* ACADEMIA, academe, the academic world.

accede ▶ verb (*formal*) **1** *he acceded to the government's demands* AGREE TO, consent to, accept, assent to, acquiesce in, comply with, go along with, concur with, surrender to, yield to, give in to, give way to, defer to. **2** *Elizabeth I acceded to the throne in 1558* SUCCEED TO, come to, assume, inherit, take. **3** *Albania acceded to the IMF in 1990* JOIN, become a member of, sign up to.

accelerate ▶ verb **1** *the car accelerated down the hill* SPEED UP, go faster, gain momentum, increase speed, pick up speed, gather speed, put on a spurt. **2** *inflation started to accelerate* INCREASE, rise, go up, leap up, surge, escalate, spiral. **3** *the university accelerated the planning process* HASTEN, expedite, precipitate, speed up, quicken, make faster, step up, advance, further, forward, promote, give a boost to, stimulate, spur on; *informal* crank up, fast-track.
– OPPOSITES: decelerate, delay.

acceleration ▶ noun **1** *the acceleration of the industrial process* HASTENING, precipitation, speeding up, quickening, stepping up, advancement, furtherance, boost, stimulation, spur. **2** *an acceleration in the divorce rate* INCREASE, rise, leap, surge, escalation.

accelerator ▶ noun GAS PEDAL, gas.

accent ▶ noun **1** *a Newfoundland accent* PRONUNCIATION, intonation, enunciation, articulation, inflection, tone, modulation, cadence, timbre, manner of speaking, delivery; brogue, burr, drawl, twang. **2** *the accent is on the first syllable* STRESS, emphasis, accentuation, force, prominence; beat; *technical* ictus. **3** *the accent is on comfort* EMPHASIS, stress, priority, importance, prominence. **4** *an acute accent* MARK, diacritic, diacritical mark. *See table.*
▶ verb *fabrics which accent the background colours in the room* FOCUS ATTENTION ON, draw attention to, point up, underline, underscore, accentuate, highlight, spotlight, foreground, feature, play up, bring to the fore, heighten, stress, emphasize.

Accents & Diacritical Marks

acute (é)	grave (è)
breve (ĕ)	háček (č)
cedilla (ç)	macron (ē)
circumflex (ê)	tilde (ñ)
diaeresis (ë)	umlaut (ä)

accentuate ▶ verb FOCUS ATTENTION ON, draw attention to, point up, underline, underscore, accent, highlight, spotlight, foreground, feature, play up, bring to the fore, heighten, stress, emphasize.

accept ▶ verb **1** *she accepted a pen as a present* RECEIVE, take, get, gain, obtain, acquire. **2** *he accepted the job immediately* TAKE ON, undertake, assume, take responsibility for. **3** *she accepted an invitation to lunch* SAY YES TO, agree to. **4** *she was accepted as one of the family* WELCOME, receive, embrace, adopt. **5** *he accepted Ellen's explanation* BELIEVE, regard as true, give credence to, credit, trust; *informal* buy, swallow. **6** *we have agreed to accept his decision* GO ALONG WITH, agree to, consent to, acquiesce in, concur with, assent to, acknowledge, comply with, abide by, follow, adhere to, act in accordance with, defer to, yield to, surrender to, bow to, give in to, submit to, respect; *formal* accede to. **7** *she will just have to accept the consequences* TOLERATE, endure, put up with, bear, take, submit to, stomach, swallow; reconcile oneself to, resign oneself to, get used to, adjust to, learn to live with, make the best of; face up to.
– OPPOSITES: refuse, reject.

acceptable ▶ adjective **1** *an acceptable standard of living* SATISFACTORY, adequate, reasonable, quite good, fair, decent, good enough, sufficient, sufficiently good, fine, not bad, all right, average, tolerable, passable, middling, moderate; *informal* OK, jake, so-so, {comme ci, comme ça}, fair-to-middling. **2** *the risk had seemed acceptable at the time* BEARABLE, tolerable, allowable, admissible, sustainable, justifiable, defensible.

acceptance ▶ noun **1** *the acceptance of an award* RECEIPT, receiving, taking, obtaining. **2** *the acceptance of responsibility* UNDERTAKING, assumption. **3** *acceptances to an invitation* YES, affirmative reply, confirmation. **4** *her acceptance as one of the family* WELCOME, favourable reception, adoption. **5** *his acceptance of Matilda's explanation* BELIEF, credence, trust, faith. **6** *their acceptance of the decision* COMPLIANCE, acquiescence, agreement, consent, concurrence, assent, acknowledgement, adherence, deference, surrender, submission, respect, go-ahead, buy-in. **7** *the acceptance of pain* TOLERATION, endurance, forbearance.

accepted ▶ adjective RECOGNIZED, acknowledged, established, traditional, orthodox, sanctioned; usual, customary, common, current, normal, general, prevailing, accustomed, familiar, wonted, popular, expected, routine, standard, stock.

access ▶ noun **1** *the building has a side access* ENTRANCE, entry, way in, means of entry; approach, means of approach. **2** *they were denied access to the stadium* ADMISSION, admittance, entry, entrée, ingress, right of entry. **3** *students have access to a photocopier* (THE) USE OF, permission to use/visit.
▶ verb **1** *the program used to access the data* RETRIEVE, gain access to, obtain; read. **2** *you access the building from the south side* ENTER, approach, gain entry to.

accessible ▶ adjective **1** *the village is only accessible on foot | an easily accessible reference tool* REACHABLE, attainable, approachable; obtainable, available; *informal* get-at-able. **2** *his accessible style of writing* UNDERSTANDABLE, comprehensible, easy to understand, intelligible; *formal* exoteric. **3** *Professor Cooper is very accessible* APPROACHABLE, friendly, agreeable, obliging, congenial, affable, cordial, welcoming, easygoing, pleasant.

accession ▶ noun **1** *the Queen's accession to the throne* SUCCESSION, assumption, inheritance. **2** *accession to the Treaty of Rome was effected in 1971* ASSENT, consent, agreement; acceptance, acquiescence, compliance, concurrence. **3** *recent accessions to the museum* ADDITION, acquisition, new item, gift, purchase.

accessorize ▶ verb COMPLEMENT, enhance, set off, show off; go with, accompany; decorate, adorn, ornament, trim.

accessory ▶ noun **1** *camera accessories such as tripods and flashguns* ATTACHMENT, extra, addition, add-on, adjunct, appendage, appurtenance, fitment, supplement. **2** *fashion accessories* ADORNMENT, embellishment, ornament, ornamentation, decoration; frills, trimmings. **3** *she was charged as an accessory to murder* ACCOMPLICE, partner in crime, associate, collaborator, abettor, fellow conspirator, co-conspirator; henchman.
▶ adjective *an accessory gearbox* ADDITIONAL, extra, supplementary, supplemental, auxiliary, ancillary, secondary, subsidiary, reserve, add-on.

accident ▶ noun **1** *an accident at work* MISHAP, misadventure, unfortunate incident, mischance, misfortune, disaster, tragedy, catastrophe, calamity; *technical* casualty. **2** *she was injured in a highway accident* CRASH, collision, smash, bump, car crash; wreck; *informal* smash-up, pileup, fender-bender. **3** *it is no accident that there is a similarity between them* CHANCE, mere chance, coincidence, twist of fate, freak, hazard; fluke, bit of luck, serendipity; fate, fortuity, fortune, providence, happenstance.

accidental ▶ adjective **1** *an accidental meeting* FORTUITOUS, chance, adventitious, fluky, coincidental, casual, serendipitous, random; unexpected, unforeseen, unanticipated, unlooked-for, unintentional, unintended, inadvertent, unplanned, unpremeditated, unthinking, unwitting. **2** *the location is accidental and contributes nothing to the poem* INCIDENTAL, unimportant, by the way, by the by, supplementary, subsidiary, subordinate, secondary, accessory, peripheral, tangential, extraneous, extrinsic, irrelevant, non-essential, inessential.
– OPPOSITES: intentional, deliberate.

accident-prone ▶ adjective CLUMSY, bumbling, butterfingered, like a bull in a china shop, all thumbs.

acclaim ▶ verb *the booklet has been widely acclaimed by teachers* PRAISE, applaud, cheer, commend, approve, welcome, pay tribute to, speak highly of, eulogize, compliment, celebrate, sing the praises of, rave about, heap praise on, wax lyrical about, lionize, exalt, admire, hail, extol, honour, hymn; *informal* ballyhoo; *formal* laud.
– OPPOSITES: criticize.
▶ noun *she has won acclaim for her commitment to democracy* PRAISE, applause, cheers, ovation, tribute, accolade, acclamation, salutes, plaudits, bouquets; approval, approbation, admiration, congratulations,

commendation, kudos, welcome, homage; compliment, a pat on the back.
– OPPOSITES: criticism.

acclaimed ▶ adjective CELEBRATED, admired, highly rated, lionized, honoured, esteemed, exalted, well-thought-of, well received, acknowledged; eminent, great, renowned, distinguished, prestigious, illustrious, pre-eminent.

acclamation ▶ noun **1** *the proposal was received with considerable acclamation* PRAISE, applause, cheers, ovation, tribute, accolade, acclaim, salutes, plaudits, bouquets; approval, admiration, approbation, congratulations, commendation, homage; compliment, a pat on the back. **2** *(Cdn) she won re-election by acclamation* UNOPPOSED, without a ballot, without opposition, as the only candidate.

acclimatize ▶ verb ADJUST, adapt, accustom, accommodate, habituate, acculturate; get used, become inured, reconcile oneself, resign oneself; familiarize oneself; find one's feet, get one's bearings, become seasoned, become naturalized; acclimate.

accolade ▶ noun **1** *he received the accolade of knighthood* HONOUR, privilege, award, gift, title; prize, laurels, bays, palm. **2** *the hotel won a top accolade from the inspectors* TRIBUTE, commendation, praise, testimonial, compliment, pat on the back; salutes, plaudits, congratulations, bouquets, kudos; *informal* raves.

accommodate ▶ verb **1** *refugees were accommodated in army camps* LODGE, house, put up, billet, quarter, board, take in, shelter, give someone a roof over their head; harbour. **2** *the cottages accommodate up to six people* HOLD, take, have room for. **3** *our staff will make every effort to accommodate you* HELP, assist, aid, oblige; meet the needs/wants of, cater for, fit in with, satisfy. **4** *she tried to accommodate herself to her new situation* ADJUST, adapt, accustom, habituate, acclimatize, acculturate, get accustomed, get used, come to terms with; acclimate. **5** *the bank would be glad to accommodate you with a loan* PROVIDE, supply, furnish, grant.

accommodating ▶ adjective OBLIGING, co-operative, helpful, eager to help, adaptable, amenable, considerate, unselfish, generous, willing, compliant, kindly, hospitable, neighbourly, kind, friendly, pleasant, agreeable.

accommodation ▶ noun **1** *temporary accommodation* HOUSING, lodging(s), living quarters, quarters, rooms; place to stay, billet; shelter, a roof over one's head; *informal* digs, pad; *formal* abode, residence, place of residence, dwelling, dwelling place, habitation. **2** *lifeboat accommodation for 1,178 people* SPACE, room, seating; places. **3** *an accommodation between the two parties was reached* ARRANGEMENT, understanding, settlement, accord, deal, bargain, compromise. **4** *their accommodation to changing economic circumstances* ADJUSTMENT, adaptation, habituation, acclimatization, acculturation; inurement; acclimation.

accompaniment ▶ noun **1** *a musical accompaniment* BACKING, support, background, backup, soundtrack. **2** *the wine makes a superb accompaniment to cheese* COMPLEMENT, supplement, addition, adjunct, appendage, companion, accessory.

accompany ▶ verb **1** *I accompanied my brother to the audition* GO WITH, travel with, keep someone company, tag along with, hang out with, partner, escort, chaperone, attend, show, see, usher, conduct. **2** *the* *illness is often accompanied by nausea* OCCUR WITH, co-occur with, coexist with, go with, go together with, go hand in hand with, appear with, attend by. **3** *he accompanied the choir on the piano* BACK, play with, play for, support.

accomplice ▶ noun PARTNER IN CRIME, associate, accessory, abettor, confederate, collaborator, fellow conspirator; co-conspirator; henchman; *informal* sidekick.

accomplish ▶ verb FULFILL, achieve, succeed in, realize, attain, manage, bring about/off, carry out/ through, execute, effect, perform, do, discharge, complete, finish, consummate, conclude; *informal* pull off, nail; *formal* effectuate.

accomplished ▶ adjective EXPERT, skilled, skilful, masterly, successful, virtuoso, master, consummate, complete, proficient, talented, gifted, adept, adroit, deft, dexterous, able, good, competent, capable, efficient, experienced, seasoned, trained, practised, professional, polished, ready, apt; *informal* great, mean, nifty, crack, ace, wizard; *informal* crackerjack.

accomplishment ▶ noun **1** *the reduction of inflation was a remarkable accomplishment* ACHIEVEMENT, act, deed, exploit, performance, attainment, effort, feat, move, coup. **2** *a poet of considerable accomplishment* EXPERTISE, skill, skilfulness, talent, adeptness, adroitness, deftness, dexterity, ability, prowess, mastery, competence, capability, proficiency, aptitude, artistry, art; *informal* know-how.

accord ▶ verb **1** *the national assembly accorded him more power* GIVE, grant, present, award, vouchsafe; confer on, bestow on, vest in, invest with. **2** *his views accorded with mine* CORRESPOND, agree, tally, match, concur, be consistent, harmonize, be in harmony, be compatible, chime in, be in tune, correlate; conform to; *informal* square.
— OPPOSITES: withhold, disagree, differ.
▶ noun **1** *a peace accord* PACT, treaty, agreement, settlement, deal, entente, concordat, protocol, contract, convention. **2** *the two sides failed to reach accord* AGREEMENT, consensus, unanimity, harmony, unison, unity; *formal* concord.
■ **of one's own accord** VOLUNTARILY, of one's own free will, of one's own volition, by choice; willingly, freely, readily.
■ **with one accord** UNANIMOUSLY, in complete agreement, with one mind, without exception, as one, of one voice, to a man.

accordance ▶ noun *a ballot held in accordance with trade union rules* IN AGREEMENT WITH, in conformity with, in line with, true to, in the spirit of, observing, following, heeding.

according ▶ adjective **1** *she had a narrow escape, according to the doctors* AS STATED BY, as claimed by, on the authority of, in the opinion of. **2** *cook the rice according to the instructions* AS SPECIFIED BY, as per, in accordance with, in compliance with, in agreement with. **3** *salary will be fixed according to experience* IN PROPORTION TO, proportional to, commensurate with, in relation to, relative to, in line with, corresponding to.

accordingly ▶ adverb **1** *they appreciated the danger and acted accordingly* APPROPRIATELY, correspondingly, suitably. **2** *accordingly, he returned home to Kingston* THEREFORE, for that reason, consequently, so, as a result, as a consequence, in consequence, hence, thus, that being the case, ergo.

accordion ▶ noun SQUEEZEBOX, concertina, melodeon.

accost ▶ verb CONFRONT, call to, shout to, hail, address, speak to; approach, detain, stop, waylay; *informal* buttonhole, collar, bend someone's ear.

account ▶ noun **1** *an account of the extraordinary events* DESCRIPTION, report, version, story, narration, narrative, statement, explanation, exposition, delineation, portrayal, tale; chronicle, history, record, log; view, impression. **2** *the firm's quarterly accounts* FINANCIAL RECORD, ledger, balance sheet, financial statement; (**accounts**) books. **3** *I pay the account off in full each month* BILL, invoice, tally; debt, charges; *informal* tab. **4** *his background is of no account* IMPORTANCE, import, significance, consequence, substance, note; *formal* moment. **5** *efforts to keep our most important accounts happy* CLIENT, customer.
▶ verb *her visit could not be accounted a success* CONSIDER, regard as, reckon, hold to be, think, look on as, view as, see as, judge, adjudge, count, deem, rate.
■ **account for 1** *they must account for the delay* EXPLAIN, answer for, give reasons for, rationalize, justify. **2** *taxes account for much of the price of gasoline* CONSTITUTE, make up, form, compose, represent.
■ **on account of** BECAUSE OF, owing to, due to, as a consequence of, thanks to, by/in virtue of, in view of.
■ **on no account** NEVER, under no circumstances, not for any reason.

accountability ▶ noun RESPONSIBILITY, liability, answerability.

accountable ▶ adjective **1** *the government was held accountable for the food shortage* RESPONSIBLE, liable, answerable; to blame. **2** *the game's popularity is barely accountable* EXPLICABLE, explainable; understandable, comprehensible.

accountant ▶ noun BOOKKEEPER, comptroller, bean-counter; chartered accountant (CA), certified management accountant (CMA) ✧, certified general accountant (CGA) ✧.

accoutrements ▶ plural noun EQUIPMENT, paraphernalia, stuff, things, apparatus, tackle, kit, implements, material(s), rig, outfit, regalia, appurtenances, impedimenta, odds and ends, bits and pieces, trappings, accessories.

accredited ▶ adjective OFFICIAL, appointed, recognized, authorized, approved, certified, licensed.

accretion ▶ noun **1** *the accretion of sediments* ACCUMULATION, formation, collecting, cumulation, buildup, accrual; growth, increase. **2** *architectural accretions* ADDITION, extension, appendage, add-on, supplement.

accrue ▶ verb **1** *financial benefits will accrue from restructuring* RESULT, arise, follow, ensue; be caused by. **2** *interest is added to the account as it accrues* ACCUMULATE, collect, build up, mount up, grow, increase.

accumulate ▶ verb GATHER, collect, amass, stockpile, pile up, heap up, store (up), hoard, cumulate, lay in/up; increase, mass, multiply, accrue, snowball; run up.

accumulation ▶ noun MASS, buildup, pile, heap, stack, collection, stock, store, stockpile, reserve, hoard; amassing, gathering, cumulation, accrual, accretion.

accuracy ▶ noun CORRECTNESS, precision, preciseness, exactness, exactitude; factuality, literalness, fidelity, faithfulness, truth, truthfulness, veracity, closeness, authenticity, realism, verisimilitude.

accurate ▶ adjective **1** *accurate information* | *an accurate representation of the situation* CORRECT, precise, exact, right, error-free, perfect; FACTUAL, fact-based, literal, faithful, true, truthful, true to life, authentic, realistic; *informal* on the mark, bang on, on the money, on the button; *formal* veracious. **2** *an accurate shot* WELL-AIMED, on target, unerring, deadly, lethal, sure, true, on the mark.

accursed ▶ adjective **1** *(dated) that accursed woman* HATEFUL, detestable, loathsome, foul, abominable, damnable, odious, obnoxious, despicable, horrible, horrid, ghastly, awful, dreadful, terrible; annoying, irritating, vile, infuriating, exasperating; *informal* damned, damn, blasted, pesky, pestilential, infernal, beastly. **2** *(literary) he and his line are accursed* CURSED, damned, doomed, condemned, ill-fated, ill-omened, jinxed.
− OPPOSITES: pleasant, blessed.

accusation ▶ noun ALLEGATION, charge, claim, assertion, imputation; indictment, arraignment, incrimination, recrimination, inculpation; suit, lawsuit, impeachment; *informal* rap.

accuse ▶ verb **1** *four people were accused of assault* CHARGE WITH, indict for, arraign for; summons, cite, prefer charges against; impeach for. **2** *the companies were accused of causing job losses* BLAME FOR, lay/pin the blame on, hold responsible for, inculpate, hold accountable for; condemn for, criticize for, denounce for; *informal* lay at the door of, point the finger at.
− OPPOSITES: absolve, exonerate.

accustom ▶ verb ADAPT, adjust, acclimatize, habituate, accommodate, acculturate; reconcile oneself, become reconciled, get used to, come to terms with, learn to live with, become inured, acclimate.

accustomed ▶ adjective **1** *his accustomed lifestyle* CUSTOMARY, usual, normal, habitual, regular, routine, ordinary, typical, traditional, established, common, general; *literary* wonted. **2** *she's accustomed to hard work* USED TO, habituated to, acclimatized to, no stranger to, familiar with.

ace *(informal)* ▶ noun *a snowboarding ace* EXPERT, master, genius, virtuoso, maestro, adept, past master, doyen, champion, star; *informal* demon, hotshot, wizard, pro, whiz; *informal* maven, crackerjack.
− OPPOSITES: amateur.
▶ adjective *an ace tennis player* EXCELLENT, first-rate, first-class, marvellous, wonderful, magnificent, outstanding, superlative, formidable, virtuoso, masterly, expert, champion, consummate, skilful, adept; great, terrific, tremendous, superb, fantastic, sensational, fabulous, fab, crack, hotshot, A1, mean, demon, awesome, magic, top-top, top-notch; killer, blue-ribbon, blue-chip, brilliant; *slang* wicked.
− OPPOSITES: mediocre.

acerbic ▶ adjective SHARP, sarcastic, sardonic, mordant, trenchant, cutting, razor-edged, biting, stinging, searing, scathing, caustic, astringent, abrasive; *informal* snarky.

ache ▶ noun **1** *a stomach ache* PAIN, cramp, twinge, pang; gnawing, stabbing, stinging, smarting; soreness, tenderness, irritation, discomfort. **2** *the ache in her heart* SORROW, sadness, misery, grief, anguish, suffering, pain, agony, torture, hurt.
▶ verb **1** *my legs were aching* HURT, be sore, be painful, be in pain, pain, throb, pound, twinge; smart, burn. **2** *her heart ached for poor Philippa* GRIEVE, sorrow, be in distress, be miserable, be in anguish, bleed. **3** *I ached*

for her affection LONG, yearn, hunger, thirst, hanker, pine, itch; crave, desire.

achieve ▶ verb ATTAIN, reach, arrive at; realize, bring off/about, pull off, accomplish, carry off/out/ through, fulfill, execute, perform, engineer, conclude, complete, finish, consummate; earn, win, gain, acquire, obtain, score, come by, get, secure, clinch, net; *informal* wrap up, wangle, swing; *formal* effectuate.

achievement ▶ noun **1** *the achievement of a high rate of economic growth* ATTAINMENT, realization, accomplishment, fulfillment, implementation, execution, performance; conclusion, completion, close, consummation. **2** *they felt justifiably proud of their achievement* ACCOMPLISHMENT, attainment, feat, performance, undertaking, act, action, deed, effort, exploit, success, triumph; work, handiwork.

Achilles' heel ▶ noun WEAK SPOT, weak point, weak link, weakness, soft underbelly, shortcoming, failing, imperfection, flaw, defect, chink in one's armour; nemesis.
− OPPOSITES: strength.

acid ▶ adjective **1** *a slightly acid flavour* ACIDIC, SOUR, tart, bitter, sharp, acrid, pungent, acerbic, vinegary, acetic, acetous. **2** *acid remarks* ACERBIC, sarcastic, sharp, sardonic, scathing, cutting, razor-edged, biting, stinging, caustic, trenchant, mordant, bitter, acrimonious, astringent, harsh, abrasive, wounding, hurtful, unkind, vitriolic, venomous, waspish, spiteful, malicious; *informal* bitchy, catty; snarky.
− OPPOSITES: sweet, pleasant.

acknowledge ▶ verb **1** *the government acknowledged the need to begin talks* ADMIT, accept, grant, allow, concede, accede to, confess, own, recognize. **2** *he did not acknowledge Colin, but hurried past* GREET, salute, address; nod to, wave to, raise one's hat to, say hello to. **3** *Douglas was glad to acknowledge her help* EXPRESS GRATITUDE FOR, show appreciation for, thank someone for. **4** *nobody acknowledged my letters* ANSWER, reply to, respond to.
− OPPOSITES: reject, deny, ignore.

acknowledged ▶ adjective RECOGNIZED, accepted, approved, accredited, confirmed, declared, confessed, avowed.

acknowledgement ▶ noun **1** *acknowledgement of the need to take new initiatives* ACCEPTANCE, recognition, admission, concession, confession. **2** *a smile of acknowledgement* GREETING, welcome, salutation. **3** *she left without a word of acknowledgement* THANKS, gratitude, appreciation, recognition. **4** *I sent off the form, but there was no acknowledgement* ANSWER, reply, response.

acme ▶ noun PEAK, pinnacle, zenith, height, high point, crown, crest, summit, top, apex, apogee; climax, culmination.
− OPPOSITES: nadir.

acolyte ▶ noun ASSISTANT, helper, attendant, aide, minion, underling, lackey, henchman; follower, disciple, supporter, votary; *informal* sidekick, groupie, hanger-on.

acquaint ▶ verb *this exercise will acquaint students with land-use maps* FAMILIARIZE, make familiar, make aware of, inform of, advise of, apprise of, let know, get up to date; brief, prime; *informal* fill in on, clue in on.

acquaintance ▶ noun **1** *a business acquaintance* | *friends and acquaintances* CONTACT, associate, colleague; companion, neighbour. **2** *my acquaintance with George* ASSOCIATION, relationship, contact. **3** *the* *pupils had little acquaintance with the language* FAMILIARITY WITH, knowledge of, experience of, awareness of, understanding of, comprehension of, grasp of.

acquiesce ▶ verb *he acquiesced in the cover-up* ACCEPT, consent to, agree to, allow, concede, assent to, concur with, give the nod to; comply with, co-operate with, give in to, bow to, yield to, submit to; *informal* go along with.

acquiescence ▶ noun CONSENT, agreement, acceptance, concurrence, assent, leave; compliance, concession, co-operation, buy-in; submission.

acquiescent ▶ adjective COMPLIANT, co-operative, willing, obliging, agreeable, amenable, tractable, persuadable, pliant, unprotesting; submissive, self-effacing, unassertive, yielding, biddable, docile.

acquire ▶ verb OBTAIN, come by, get, receive, gain, earn, win, come into, be given; buy, purchase, procure, possess oneself of, secure, pick up, adopt; *informal* get one's hands on, get hold of, land, bag, cop, score.
– OPPOSITES: lose.

acquisition ▶ noun **1** *a new acquisition* PURCHASE, buy, gain, accession, addition, investment, possession. **2** *the acquisition of funds* OBTAINING, acquirement, gaining, earning, winning, procurement, collection.

acquisitive ▶ adjective GREEDY, covetous, avaricious, possessive, grasping, grabbing, predatory, avid, rapacious, mercenary, materialistic; *informal* money-grubbing.

acquisitiveness ▶ noun GREED, greediness, covetousness, cupidity, possessiveness, avarice, avidity, rapaciousness, rapacity, materialism; *informal* affluenza.

acquit ▶ verb **1** *the jury acquitted her* CLEAR, exonerate, find innocent, absolve; discharge, release, free, set free; *informal* let off (the hook); *formal* exculpate. **2** *the boys acquitted themselves well* BEHAVE, conduct oneself, perform, act; *formal* comport oneself.
– OPPOSITES: convict.

acquittal ▶ noun *the acquittal of the defendants* CLEARING, exoneration, absolution; discharge, release, freeing; *formal* exculpation.
– OPPOSITES: conviction.

acrid ▶ adjective PUNGENT, bitter, sharp, sour, tart, caustic, harsh, irritating, acid, acidic, vinegary, acetic, acetous; stinging, burning.

acrimonious ▶ adjective BITTER, angry, rancorous, caustic, acerbic, scathing, sarcastic, acid, harsh, sharp, cutting; virulent, spiteful, vicious, vitriolic, hostile, venomous, nasty, bad-tempered, ill-natured, mean, malign, malicious, malignant, waspish; *informal* bitchy, catty.

acrimony ▶ noun BITTERNESS, anger, rancour, resentment, ill feeling, ill will, bad blood, animosity, hostility, enmity, antagonism, waspishness, spleen, malice, spite, spitefulness, peevishness, venom.
– OPPOSITES: goodwill.

acrobat ▶ noun GYMNAST, tumbler, tightrope walker, wire walker, trapeze artist, aerialist; *rare* funambulist.

acrobatics ▶ plural noun **1** *staggering feats of acrobatics* GYMNASTICS, tumbling; agility; *rare* funambulism. **2** *the acrobatics required to negotiate an international contract* MENTAL AGILITY, skill, quick thinking, fancy footwork, alertness, inventiveness.

act ▶ verb **1** *the Government must act to remedy the* situation TAKE ACTION, take steps, take measures, move, react. **2** *he was acting on the orders of the party leader* FOLLOW, act in accordance with, obey, heed, comply with; fulfill, meet, discharge. **3** *a real estate agent acting for a prospective buyer* REPRESENT, act on behalf of; stand in for, fill in for, deputize for, take the place of. **4** *Alison began to act oddly* BEHAVE, conduct oneself, react; *formal* comport oneself. **5** *the scents act as a powerful aphrodisiac* OPERATE, work, function, serve. **6** *the drug acted directly on the blood vessels* AFFECT, have an effect on, work on; have an impact on, impact on, influence. **7** *he acted in a highly successful film* PERFORM, play a part, play-act, take part, appear; *informal* tread the boards, ham it up. **8** *we laughed, but most of us were just acting* PRETEND, play-act, put it on, fake it, feign it, dissemble, dissimulate.
▶ noun **1** *acts of kindness* | *a criminal act* DEED, action, feat, exploit, move, gesture, performance, undertaking, stunt, operation; achievement, accomplishment. **2** *the act raised the tax on tobacco* LAW, decree, statute, bill, act of Parliament, enactment, resolution, edict, dictum, ruling, measure; ordinance. **3** *the first act of the play* DIVISION, section, subsection, part, segment. **4** *a music hall act* PERFORMANCE, turn, routine, number, sketch, skit, shtick. **5** *it was all just an act* PRETENSE, show, front, facade, masquerade, charade, posture, pose, affectation, sham, fake; *informal* a put-on.
■ **act up** (*informal*) **1** *all children act up from time to time* MISBEHAVE, behave badly, get up to mischief, become unruly. **2** *the engine was acting up* MALFUNCTION, go wrong, be defective, be faulty; *informal* be on the blink/fritz.

acting ▶ noun *the theory and practice of acting* DRAMA, the theatre, the stage, the performing arts, thespianism, dramatics, dramaturgy, stagecraft, theatricals; *informal* treading the boards.
▶ adjective *the bank's acting governor* TEMPORARY, interim, caretaker, pro tem, pro tempore, provisional, stop-gap; deputy, stand-in, fill-in; *informal* pinch-hitting.
– OPPOSITES: permanent.

action ▶ noun **1** *there can be no excuse for their actions* DEED, act, move, undertaking, exploit, manoeuvre, endeavour, effort, exertion; behaviour, conduct, activity. **2** *the need for local community action* MEASURES, steps, activity, movement, work, operation. **3** *a man of action* ENERGY, vitality, vigour, forcefulness, drive, initiative, spirit, liveliness, vim, pep; activity; *informal* get-up-and-go. **4** *the action of hormones on the pancreas* EFFECT, influence, working; power. **5** *he missed all the action while he was away* EXCITEMENT, activity, happenings, events, incidents; *informal* goings-on. **6** *twenty-nine men died in the action* FIGHTING, hostilities, battle, conflict, combat, warfare; engagement, clash, encounter, skirmish. **7** *a civil action for damages* LAWSUIT, legal action, suit, case, prosecution, litigation, proceedings.

activate ▶ verb OPERATE, switch on, turn on, start (up), set going, trigger (off), set in motion, initiate, actuate, energize; trip.

active ▶ adjective **1** *despite her illness she remained active* ENERGETIC, lively, sprightly, spry, mobile, vigorous, vital, dynamic, sporty; busy, occupied; *informal* on the go. **2** *an active member of the union* HARD-WORKING, busy, industrious, diligent, tireless, contributing, effective, enterprising, involved, enthusiastic, keen, committed, devoted, zealous. **3** *the water mill was active until 1960* OPERATIVE,

working, functioning, functional, operating, operational, in action, in operation, running; live; *informal* up and running.
— OPPOSITES: listless, passive.

activist ▶ noun MILITANT, zealot, protester; radical, extremist.

activity ▶ noun **1** *there was a lot of activity in the area* BUSTLE, hustle and bustle, busyness, action, liveliness, movement, life, stir, flurry; happenings, occurrences, proceedings, events, incidents; *informal* toing and froing, comings and goings. **2** *a wide range of activities* PURSUIT, occupation, interest, hobby, pastime, recreation, diversion; venture, undertaking, enterprise, project, scheme, business, entertainment; act, action, deed, exploit.

actor, actress ▶ noun PERFORMER, player, thespian, trouper; film star, star, starlet, matinee idol; *informal* ham; lead, leading man, leading lady, stand-in.
— RELATED TERMS: histrionic.

actual ▶ adjective REAL, true, genuine, authentic, verified, attested, confirmed, definite, hard, plain, veritable; existing, existent, manifest, substantial, factual, de facto, bona fide; *informal* honest-to-goodness, real live.
— OPPOSITES: notional.

actuality ▶ noun *it's hard to tell actuality from fiction* REALITY, fact, truth, real life.
■ **in actuality** IN (ACTUAL) FACT, actually, really, in reality, in point of fact, in truth, if truth be told, to tell the truth; as a matter of fact; *archaic* in sooth.

actually ▶ adverb REALLY, in (actual) fact, in point of fact, as a matter of fact, in reality, in actuality, in truth, if truth be told, to tell the truth; literally; truly, indeed; *archaic* in sooth.

acumen ▶ noun ASTUTENESS, shrewdness, acuity, sharpness, sharp-wittedness, cleverness, smartness, brains; judgment, understanding, awareness, sense, common sense, canniness, discernment, wisdom, wit, sagacity, perspicacity, insight, perception, penetration; savvy, know-how, horse sense, smarts, street smarts.

acute ▶ adjective **1** *the acute food shortages* SEVERE, critical, drastic, dire, dreadful, terrible, awful, grave, bad, serious, desperate, dangerous. **2** *acute stomach pains* SHARP, severe, stabbing, piercing, excruciating, agonizing, racking, keen, shooting, searing. **3** *an acute mind* ASTUTE, shrewd, sharp, sharp-witted, razor-sharp, rapier-like, quick, quick-witted, agile, nimble, clever, intelligent, brilliant, keen, smart, canny, discerning, perceptive, perspicacious, penetrating, insightful, incisive, piercing, discriminating, sagacious, wise, judicious; *informal* on the ball, quick off the mark, quick on the uptake, streetwise, savvy. **4** *an acute sense of smell* KEEN, sharp, good, penetrating, discerning, sensitive.
— OPPOSITES: mild, dull.

acutely ▶ adverb EXTREMELY, exceedingly, very, markedly, severely, intensely, deeply, profoundly, keenly, painfully, desperately, tremendously, enormously, thoroughly, heartily; *informal* awfully, terribly; *slang* majorly.
— OPPOSITES: slightly.

adage ▶ noun SAYING, maxim, axiom, proverb, aphorism, apophthegm, saw, dictum, byword, precept, motto, truism, platitude, cliché, commonplace.

adamant ▶ adjective UNSHAKEABLE, immovable, inflexible, unwavering, unswerving, uncompromising, insistent, resolute, resolved, determined, firm, steadfast; stubborn, unrelenting, diehard, unyielding, unbending, rigid, obdurate, inexorable, intransigent, (dead) set.

adapt ▶ verb **1** *we've adapted the procedures to suit their needs* MODIFY, alter, change, adjust, readjust, convert, redesign, restyle, refashion, remodel, reshape, revamp, rework, rejig, redo, reconstruct, reorganize; customize, tailor; improve, amend, refine, tweak. **2** *he has adapted well to his new home* ADJUST, acclimatize oneself, acclimate, accommodate oneself, habituate oneself, become habituated, get used, orient oneself, reconcile oneself, come to terms, get one's bearings, find one's feet, acculturate, assimilate, blend in, fit in.

adaptable ▶ adjective **1** *competent and adaptable staff* FLEXIBLE, versatile, co-operative, accommodating, amenable. **2** *an adaptable piece of furniture* VERSATILE, modifiable, convertible, alterable, adjustable, changeable; multi-purpose, all-purpose.

adaptation ▶ noun **1** *an adaptation of a Friulian folk tale* ALTERATION, modification, redesign, remodelling, revamping, reworking, reconstruction, conversion. **2** *the cubs' adaptation to the zoo environment* ADJUSTMENT, acclimatization, acclimation, accommodation, habituation, acculturation, assimilation, integration.

add ▶ verb **1** *the back room was added in 1971 | add some more sugar to the mix* ATTACH, build on, join, append, affix, connect, annex; include, incorporate, throw/toss in; admix. **2** *they added up all the numbers* TOTAL, count (up), compute, calculate, reckon, tally, tot up. **3** *the subsidies added up to $1700* AMOUNT TO, come to, run to, make, total, equal, number. **4** *it all adds up to a deepening crisis* AMOUNT TO, constitute; signify, signal, mean, indicate, denote, point to, be evidence of, be symptomatic of; *informal* spell. **5** *her decision just added to his woe* INCREASE, magnify, amplify, augment, intensify, heighten, deepen; compound, reinforce; add fuel to the fire, fan the flames, rub salt on the wound. **6** *she added that she had every confidence in Laura* GO ON TO SAY, state further, continue, carry on.
— OPPOSITES: subtract.
■ **add up** (*informal*) *the situation just didn't add up* MAKE SENSE, stand to reason, hold up, hold water, ring true, be convincing.

addendum ▶ noun APPENDIX, codicil, postscript, afterword, tailpiece, rider, coda, supplement, *Law* adhesion ✦; adjunct, appendage, addition, add-on, attachment.

addict ▶ noun **1** *a heroin addict* ABUSER, user; *informal* junkie, druggie, stoner, -head, -freak, pill-popper, dope fiend. **2** (*informal*) *skiing addicts* ENTHUSIAST, fan, lover, devotee, aficionado; *informal* freak, buff, nut, fiend, bum, junkie, fanatic, maniac.

addicted ▶ adjective **1** *he was addicted to tranquilizers* DEPENDENT ON; *informal* hooked on, strung out on. **2** *she became addicted to the theatre* DEVOTED TO, obsessed with, fixated on, fanatical about, passionate about, a slave to; *informal* hooked on, mad about, crazy about, nuts about.

addiction ▶ noun **1** *his heroin addiction* DEPENDENCY, dependence, habit, problem. **2** *a slavish addiction to fashion* DEVOTION TO, dedication to, obsession with, infatuation with, passion for, love of, mania for, enslavement to.

addictive ▶ adjective HABIT-FORMING, addicting; compulsive.

addition ▶ noun **1** *the soil is improved by the addition of compost* ADDING, incorporation, inclusion, introduction. **2** *an addition to the existing regulations* SUPPLEMENT, adjunct, addendum, adhesion ✦, appendage, add-on, extra, attachment; rider, appurtenance.

■ **in addition 1** *the wind was frigid and, in addition, the sky threatened rain* ADDITIONALLY, as well, what's more, furthermore, moreover, also, into the bargain, to boot, likewise. **2** *eight cabinet members in addition to the Prime Minister* BESIDES, as well as, on top of, plus, over and above.

additional ▶ adjective EXTRA, added, supplementary, supplemental, further, auxiliary, ancillary; more, other, another, new, fresh; *informal* bonus.

additionally ▶ adverb ALSO, in addition, as well, too, besides, on top (of that), moreover, further, furthermore, what's more, over and above that, into the bargain, to boot, likewise; *archaic* withal.

additive ▶ noun ADDED INGREDIENT, addition; preservative, colouring.

addled ▶ adjective MUDDLED, confused, muzzy, fuddled, befuddled, dazed, disoriented, disorientated, fuzzy; *informal* woozy.

address ▶ noun **1** *the address on the envelope* inscription, superscription; directions, number. **2** *our officers arrived at the address* HOUSE, flat, apartment, home; *formal* residence, dwelling, dwelling place, habitation, abode, domicile. **3** *her address to board members* SPEECH, lecture, talk, monologue, dissertation, discourse, oration, peroration; *slang* spiel, chalk talk; sermon, homily, lesson; harangue.
▶ verb **1** *I addressed the envelope by hand* inscribe, superscribe. **2** *the preacher addressed a crowded congregation* TALK TO, give a talk to, speak to, make a speech to, give a lecture to, lecture, hold forth to; PREACH TO, give a sermon to; *informal* buttonhole, collar. **3** *the question of how to address one's parents-in-law* CALL, name, designate; speak to; *formal* denominate. **4** *correspondence should be addressed to the Personnel Department* DIRECT, send, forward, communicate, convey, route, remit. **5** *the minister failed to address the issue of subsidies* ATTEND TO, apply oneself to, tackle, see to, deal with, confront, come to grips with, get down to, turn one's hand to, take in hand, undertake, concentrate on, focus on, devote oneself to.

adduce ▶ verb *evidence adduced to support their argument* CITE, quote, name, mention, instance, point out, refer to; put forward, present, offer, advance, propose, proffer.

adept ▶ adjective *an adept negotiator* EXPERT, proficient, accomplished, skilful, talented, masterly, masterful, consummate, virtuoso; adroit, dexterous, deft, artful; brilliant, splendid, marvellous, formidable, outstanding, first-rate, first-class, excellent, fine; *informal* great, top-notch, tip-top, A1, ace, mean, hotshot, crack, nifty, deadly; *informal* crackerjack.
— OPPOSITES: inept.
▶ noun *figure skating adepts* EXPERT, past master, master, genius, maestro, doyen, virtuoso; *informal* wizard, demon, ace, hotshot, whiz, maven, crackerjack.
— OPPOSITES: amateur.

adequacy ▶ noun **1** *the adequacy of the existing services* SATISFACTORINESS, acceptability, acceptableness; sufficiency. **2** *he had deep misgivings about his own adequacy* CAPABILITY, competence, ability, aptitude, suitability; effectiveness, fitness; *formal* efficacy.

adequate ▶ adjective **1** *he lacked adequate financial resources* SUFFICIENT, enough, requisite. **2** *the company provides an adequate service* ACCEPTABLE, passable, reasonable, satisfactory, tolerable, fair, decent, quite good, pretty good, goodish, moderate, unexceptional, unremarkable, undistinguished, ordinary, average, not bad, all right, middling; *informal* OK, so-so, {comme ci, comme ça}, fair-to-middling, nothing to write home about. **3** *the workstations were small but seemed adequate to the task* EQUAL TO, up to, capable of, suitable for, able to do, fit for, sufficient for.

adhere ▶ verb **1** *a dollop of cream adhered to her nose* STICK (FAST), cohere, cling, bond, attach; be stuck, be fixed, be glued, be cemented. **2** *they adhere scrupulously to Judaic law* ABIDE BY, stick to, hold to, comply with, act in accordance with, conform to, submit to, hew to; follow, obey, heed, observe, respect, uphold, fulfill.
— OPPOSITES: flout, ignore.

adherent ▶ noun FOLLOWER, supporter, upholder, defender, advocate, disciple, votary, devotee, partisan, member, friend, stalwart; believer, true believer, worshipper, sectary.
— OPPOSITES: opponent.

adhesion ▶ noun *the adhesion of the gum strip to the paper fibres* STICKING, adherence.

adhesive ▶ noun *a spray adhesive* GLUE, fixative, gum, paste, cement, mucilage; *informal* stickum.
▶ adjective *adhesive paper* STICKY, tacky, gluey, gummed, stick-on, gooey; viscous, viscid; *technical* adherent.

adieu ▶ noun & exclamation GOODBYE, farewell, until we meet again; bye-bye, bye, cheers, ciao, au revoir, adios, sayonara, so long, ta-ta, cheerio, toodle-oo.

ad infinitum ▶ adverb FOREVER, for ever and ever, evermore, always, for all time, until the end of time, in perpetuity, until hell freezes over; perpetually, eternally, endlessly, interminably, unceasingly, unendingly, forevermore; *informal* until the cows come home, until kingdom come; *archaic* for aye.

adjacent ▶ adjective ADJOINING, neighbouring, next-door, abutting, contiguous, proximate; (**adjacent to**) close to, near, next to, by, by the side of, bordering on, beside, alongside, attached to, touching, cheek by jowl with.

adjoin ▶ verb BE NEXT TO, be adjacent to, border (on), abut, be contiguous with, communicate with, extend to; join, conjoin, connect with, touch, meet.

adjoining ▶ adjective CONNECTING, connected, interconnecting, adjacent, ensuite, neighbouring, bordering, next-door; contiguous, proximate; attached, touching.

adjourn ▶ verb **1** *the meeting was adjourned for lunch* SUSPEND, break off, discontinue, interrupt, prorogue, stay, recess. **2** *sentencing was adjourned until June 9* POSTPONE, put off/back, defer, delay, hold over, shelve. **3** *they adjourned to the sitting room for liqueurs* WITHDRAW, retire, retreat, take oneself; *formal* repair, remove; *literary* betake oneself.

adjournment ▶ noun SUSPENSION, discontinuation, interruption, postponement, deferment, deferral, stay, prorogation; break, pause, recess.

adjudge ▶ verb JUDGE, deem, find, pronounce,

proclaim, rule, hold, determine; consider, think, rate, reckon, perceive, regard as, view as, see as, believe to be.

adjudicate ▶ verb JUDGE, try, hear, examine, arbitrate, referee, umpire; pronounce on, give a ruling on, pass judgment on, decide, determine, settle, resolve.

adjudication ▶ noun JUDGMENT, decision, pronouncement, ruling, settlement, resolution, arbitration, finding, verdict, sentence; *Law* determination.

adjudicator ▶ noun JUDGE, arbitrator, arbiter; referee, umpire.

adjunct ▶ noun SUPPLEMENT, addition, extra, add-on, accessory, accompaniment, complement, appurtenance; attachment, appendage, addendum.
▶ adjective SUBORDINATE, auxiliary, assistant; temporary, provisional.

adjust ▶ verb **1** *Kate had adjusted to her new life* ADAPT, become accustomed, get used, accommodate, acclimatize, acclimate, orient oneself, reconcile oneself, habituate oneself, assimilate; come to terms with, fit in with, find one's feet in. **2** *he adjusted the harness* MODIFY, alter, regulate, tune, fine-tune, calibrate, balance; adapt, arrange, rearrange, change, rejig, rework, revamp, remodel, reshape, convert, tailor, improve, enhance, customize; repair, fix, correct, rectify, overhaul, put right; *informal* tweak.

adjustable ▶ adjective ALTERABLE, adaptable, modifiable, convertible, changeable, variable, multiway, versatile.

adjustment ▶ noun **1** *a period of adjustment* ADAPTATION, accommodation, acclimatization, acclimation, habituation, acculturation, naturalization, assimilation. **2** *they had to make some adjustments to their strategy* MODIFICATION, alteration, regulation, adaptation, rearrangement, change, reconstruction, customization, refinement; repair, correction, amendment, overhaul, improvement.

ad lib ▶ verb *she ad libbed half the speech* IMPROVISE, extemporize, speak impromptu, play it by ear, make it up as one goes along, wing it.
▶ adverb *she spoke ad lib* IMPROMPTU, extempore, without preparation, without rehearsal, extemporaneously; *informal* off the cuff, off the top of one's head; ad libitum.
▶ adjective *a live, ad-lib commentary* IMPROMPTU, extempore, extemporaneous, extemporary, improvised, unprepared, unrehearsed, unscripted; *informal* off-the-cuff, spur-of-the-moment.

administer ▶ verb **1** *the union is administered by a central executive* MANAGE, direct, control, operate, regulate, conduct, handle, run, organize, supervise, superintend, oversee, preside over, govern, rule, lead, head, steer; be in control of, be in charge of, be responsible for, be at the helm of; *informal* head up. **2** *the lifeboat crew administered first aid* DISPENSE, issue, give, provide, apply, allot, distribute, hand out, dole out, disburse. **3** *a gym shoe was used to administer punishment* INFLICT, mete out, deal out, deliver.

administration ▶ noun **1** *the day-to-day administration of the company* MANAGEMENT, direction, control, command, charge, conduct, operation, admin, running, leadership, government, governing, superintendence, supervision, regulation, overseeing. **2** *the previous Liberal administration* GOVERNMENT, cabinet, ministry, regime, executive, authority, directorate, council, leadership,

management; parliament, congress, senate; rule, term of office, incumbency. **3** *the administration of anti-inflammatory drugs* PROVISION, issuing, issuance, application, dispensing, dispensation, distribution, disbursement.

administrative ▶ adjective MANAGERIAL, management, directorial, executive, organizational, bureaucratic, supervisory, regulatory.

administrator ▶ noun MANAGER, director, executive, controller, head, chief, leader, governor, superintendent, supervisor; *informal* boss.

admirable ▶ adjective COMMENDABLE, praiseworthy, laudable, estimable, meritorious, creditable, exemplary, honourable, worthy, deserving, respectable, worthwhile, good, sterling, fine, masterly, great.
– OPPOSITES: deplorable.

admiration ▶ noun RESPECT, appreciation, (high) regard, esteem, veneration; commendation, acclaim, applause, praise, compliments, tributes, accolades, plaudits.
– OPPOSITES: scorn.

admire ▶ verb **1** *I admire your courage* ESTEEM, approve of, respect, think highly of, rate highly, hold in high regard, applaud, praise, commend, acclaim. **2** *we're just admiring your garden* DELIGHT IN, appreciate, take pleasure in.
– OPPOSITES: despise.

admirer ▶ noun *a great admirer of Morley Callaghan* FAN, devotee, enthusiast, aficionado; supporter, adherent, follower, disciple.

admissible ▶ adjective VALID, allowable, allowed, permissible, permitted, acceptable, satisfactory, justifiable, defensible, supportable, appropriate, well-founded, tenable, sound; legitimate, lawful, legal, licit; *informal* OK, kosher.

admission ▶ noun **1** *membership entitles you to free admission* ADMITTANCE, entry, entrance, right of entry, access, right of access, ingress; entrée. **2** *the admission was $8* ENTRANCE FEE, entry charge, cover (charge), ticket. **3** *a written admission of guilt* CONFESSION, acknowledgement, mea culpa, acceptance, concession, disclosure, divulgence.

admit ▶ verb **1** *he unlocked the door to admit her* LET IN, allow entry, permit entry, take in, usher in, show in, receive, welcome. **2** *she was admitted to the law program* ACCEPT, take on, receive, enrol, enlist, register, sign up. **3** *Paul admitted that he was angry* CONFESS, acknowledge, own, concede, grant, accept, allow; reveal, disclose, divulge; plead guilty, own up to, make a clean breast of.
– OPPOSITES: exclude, deny.

admittance ▶ noun ENTRY, right of entry, admission, entrance, access, right of access, ingress; entrée.
– OPPOSITES: exclusion.

admonish ▶ verb **1** *he was severely admonished by his father* REPRIMAND, rebuke, scold, reprove, reproach, upbraid, chastise, chide, berate, criticize, take to task, read the riot act to, haul over the coals; dress down, bawl out, rap over the knuckles, give someone hell; tear a strip off someone; chew out; *formal* castigate; *rare* reprehend. **2** *she admonished him to drink less* ADVISE, recommend, counsel, urge, exhort, bid, enjoin; caution, warn; *formal* adjure.

adolescence ▶ noun TEENAGE YEARS, teens, youth; pubescence, puberty.

adolescent ▶ noun *an awkward adolescent* TEENAGER,

youngster, young person, youth, boy, girl; juvenile, minor; *informal* teen, teeny-bopper.
▶ **adjective 1** *an adolescent boy* TEENAGE, pubescent, young; juvenile; *informal* teen, tween-ager. **2** *adolescent silliness* IMMATURE, childish, juvenile, infantile, puerile, jejune.
— OPPOSITES: adult, mature.

adopt ▶ verb **1** *the child was adopted by an American family* take as one's child, be adoptive parents to, take in, take care of. **2** *they adopted local customs* ESPOUSE, take on/up, embrace, assume; appropriate, arrogate. **3** *the people adopted him as their patron saint* CHOOSE, select, pick, vote for, elect, settle on, decide on, opt for; name, nominate, appoint.
— OPPOSITES: abandon.

adorable ▶ adjective LOVABLE, appealing, charming, cute, cuddly, sweet, enchanting, bewitching, captivating, engaging, endearing, dear, darling, delightful, lovely, beautiful, attractive, gorgeous, winsome, winning, fetching; *Scottish* bonny.
— OPPOSITES: hateful.

adoration ▶ noun **1** *the girl gazed at him with adoration* LOVE, devotion, care, fondness; admiration, high regard, awe, idolization, worship, hero-worship, adulation. **2** *our day of prayer and adoration* WORSHIP, glory, glorification, praise, thanksgiving, homage, exaltation, veneration, reverence.

adore ▶ verb **1** *he adored his mother* LOVE DEARLY, love, be devoted to, dote on, hold dear, cherish, treasure, prize, think the world of; admire, hold in high regard, look up to, idolize, worship; *informal* put on a pedestal. **2** *the people had come to pray and adore God* WORSHIP, glorify, praise, revere, reverence, exalt, extol, venerate, pay homage to; *formal* laud; *archaic* magnify. **3** (*informal*) *I adore oysters* LIKE, love, be very fond of, be very keen on, be partial to, have a weakness for; delight in, relish, savour; *informal* be crazy about, be wild about, have a thing about/for/ with, be hooked on.
— OPPOSITES: hate.

adorn ▶ verb DECORATE, embellish, ornament, enhance; beautify, prettify, grace, bedeck, deck (out), dress (up), trim, swathe, wreathe, festoon, garland, array, emblazon, titivate.
— OPPOSITES: disfigure.

adornment ▶ noun DECORATION, embellishment, ornamentation, ornament, enhancement; beautification, prettification; frill, accessory, doodad, fandangle, frippery; trimmings, finishing touches.

adrift ▶ adjective **1** *their empty boat was spotted adrift* DRIFTING, unmoored, unanchored. **2** *he was adrift in a strange country* LOST, off course; disoriented, confused, at sea; drifting, rootless, unsettled, directionless, aimless, purposeless, without purpose.

adroit ▶ adjective SKILFUL, adept, dexterous, deft, nimble, able, capable, skilled, expert, masterly, masterful, master, practised, handy, polished, slick, proficient, accomplished, gifted, talented; quick-witted, quick-thinking, clever, smart, sharp, cunning, wily, resourceful, astute, shrewd, canny; *informal* nifty, crack, mean, ace, A1, on the ball, savvy, crackerjack.
— OPPOSITES: inept, clumsy.

adroitness ▶ noun SKILL, skilfulness, prowess, expertise, adeptness, dexterity, deftness, nimbleness, ability, capability, mastery, proficiency, accomplishment, artistry, art, facility, aptitude, flair, finesse, talent; quick-wittedness, cleverness,

sharpness, cunning, astuteness, shrewdness, resourcefulness, savoir faire; *informal* know-how, savvy.

adulation ▶ noun HERO-WORSHIP, worship, idolization, adoration, admiration, veneration, awe, devotion, glorification, praise, flattery, blandishments.

adulatory ▶ adjective FLATTERING, complimentary, highly favourable, enthusiastic, glowing, rhapsodic, eulogistic, laudatory; fulsome, honeyed.
— OPPOSITES: disparaging.

adult ▶ adjective **1** *an adult woman* MATURE, grown-up, fully grown, full-grown, fully developed, of age, of full age. **2** *an adult movie* SEXUALLY EXPLICIT, pornographic, obscene, smutty, dirty, rude, erotic, sexy, suggestive, titillating; porn, porno, naughty, blue, X-rated, skin.

adulterate ▶ verb MAKE IMPURE, degrade, debase, spoil, taint, contaminate; doctor, tamper with, dilute, water down, weaken; bastardize, corrupt; *informal* cut, spike, lace, dope.
— OPPOSITES: purify.

adulterer ▶ noun cheat, cheater, two-timer.

adulterous ▶ adjective UNFAITHFUL, disloyal, untrue, inconstant, false, deceiving, deceitful, treacherous, illicit; extramarital; cheating, two-timing; extracurricular.
— OPPOSITES: faithful.

adultery ▶ noun INFIDELITY, unfaithfulness, falseness, disloyalty, cuckoldry, extramarital sex; affair, liaison, fling, amour; *informal* carrying-on, hanky-panky, two-timing, a bit on the side, fooling/ playing around.
— OPPOSITES: fidelity.

advance ▶ verb **1** *the battalion advanced rapidly* MOVE FORWARD, proceed, press on, push on, push forward, make progress, make headway, gain ground, approach, come closer, draw nearer, near. **2** *the court may advance the date of the hearing* BRING FORWARD, put forward, move forward. **3** *the move advanced his career* PROMOTE, further, help, aid, assist, boost, strengthen, improve, benefit, foster. **4** *our technology has advanced in the last few years* PROGRESS, make progress, make headway, develop, evolve, make strides, move forward (in leaps and bounds), move ahead; improve, thrive, flourish, prosper. **5** *the hypothesis I wish to advance in this article* PUT FORWARD, present, submit, suggest, propose, introduce, offer, adduce, moot. **6** *a relative advanced him some money* LEND, loan, put up, come up with.
— OPPOSITES: retreat, hinder, postpone, retract, borrow.
▶ noun **1** *the advance of the aggressors* PROGRESS, forward movement; approach. **2** *a significant medical advance* BREAKTHROUGH, development, step forward, step in the right direction, (quantum) leap; find, finding, discovery, invention. **3** *share prices showed significant advances* INCREASE, rise, upturn, upsurge, upswing, growth; *informal* hike. **4** *the writer is going to be given a huge advance* DOWN PAYMENT, retainer, prepayment, deposit, front money, money up front. **5** *unwelcome sexual advances* PASS, proposition.
▶ adjective **1** *an advance party of settlers* PRELIMINARY, sent (on) ahead, first, exploratory; pilot, test, trial. **2** *advance warning* EARLY, prior, beforehand.
■ **in advance** BEFOREHAND, before, ahead of time, earlier, previously; in readiness.

advanced ▶ adjective **1** *advanced manufacturing techniques* STATE-OF-THE-ART, new, modern, developed,

cutting-edge, leading-edge, up-to-date, up-to-the-minute, the newest, the latest; progressive, avant-garde, ahead of the times, pioneering, innovative, sophisticated. **2** *advanced further-education courses* HIGHER-LEVEL, higher.
− OPPOSITES: primitive.

advancement ▸ noun **1** *the advancement of computer technology* DEVELOPMENT, progress, evolution, growth, improvement, advance, furtherance; headway. **2** *employees must be offered opportunities for advancement* PROMOTION, preferment, career development, upgrading, a step up the ladder, progress, improvement, betterment, growth.

advantage ▸ noun **1** *the advantages of belonging to a union* BENEFIT, value, good point, strong point, asset, plus, bonus, boon, blessing, virtue; attraction, beauty, usefulness, helpfulness, convenience, advantageousness, profit. **2** *they appeared to be gaining the advantage over their opponents* UPPER HAND, edge, lead, whip hand, trump card; superiority, dominance, ascendancy, supremacy, power, mastery; *informal* inside track. **3** *there is no advantage to be gained from delaying the process* BENEFIT, profit, gain, good; *informal* mileage.
− OPPOSITES: disadvantage, drawback, detriment.

advantageous ▸ adjective **1** *an advantageous position* SUPERIOR, dominant, powerful; good, fortunate, lucky, favourable. **2** *the arrangement is advantageous to both sides* BENEFICIAL, of benefit, helpful, of assistance, useful, of use, of value, of service, profitable, fruitful; convenient, expedient, in everyone's interests.
− OPPOSITES: disadvantageous, detrimental.

advent ▸ noun ARRIVAL, appearance, emergence, materialization, occurrence, dawn, birth, rise, development; approach, coming.
− OPPOSITES: disappearance.

adventitious ▸ adjective *he felt that the conversation was not entirely adventitious* UNPLANNED, unpremeditated, accidental, chance, fortuitous, serendipitous, coincidental, casual, random.
− OPPOSITES: premeditated.

adventure ▸ noun **1** *they set off in search of adventure* EXCITEMENT, thrill, stimulation; risk, danger, hazard, peril, uncertainty, precariousness. **2** *her recent adventures in Italy* EXPLOIT, escapade, deed, feat, experience.

adventurer ▸ noun DAREDEVIL, hero, heroine, thrill-seeker; swashbuckler.

adventurous ▸ adjective **1** *an adventurous traveller* DARING, daredevil, intrepid, venturesome, bold, fearless, brave, unafraid, unshrinking, dauntless; *informal* gutsy, spunky. **2** *adventurous activities* RISKY, dangerous, perilous, hazardous, precarious, uncertain; exciting, thrilling.
− OPPOSITES: cautious.

adversary ▸ noun OPPONENT, rival, enemy, antagonist, combatant, challenger, contender, competitor, opposer; opposition, competition, foe.
− OPPOSITES: ally, supporter.

adverse ▸ adjective **1** *adverse weather conditions* UNFAVOURABLE, disadvantageous, inauspicious, unpropitious, unfortunate, unlucky, untimely, untoward. **2** *the drug's adverse side effects* HARMFUL, dangerous, injurious, detrimental, hurtful, negative, deleterious. **3** *an adverse response from the public* HOSTILE, UNFAVOURABLE, antagonistic, unfriendly,

ill-disposed, negative.
− OPPOSITES: favourable, auspicious, beneficial.

adversity ▸ noun MISFORTUNE, ill luck, bad luck, trouble, difficulty, hardship, distress, disaster, suffering, affliction, sorrow, misery, tribulation, woe, pain, trauma; mishap, misadventure, accident, upset, reverse, setback, crisis, catastrophe, tragedy, calamity, trial, cross, burden, blow; hard times, trials and tribulations; *informal* ill wind.

advertise ▸ verb PUBLICIZE, make public, make known, announce, broadcast, proclaim, trumpet, call attention to, bill, promulgate; promote, market, beat/bang the drum for, huckster; *informal* push, plug, hype, boost; *informal* ballyhoo, flack.

advertisement ▸ noun AD, announcement, notice; commercial, infomercial, promotion, endorsement, blurb, write-up; poster, leaflet, pamphlet, flyer, bill, handbill, handout, fact sheet, circular, bulletin, brochure, sign, placard, junk mail; *informal* plug, puff, bumph.

advice ▸ noun GUIDANCE, counselling, counsel, help, direction; information, recommendations, guidelines, suggestions, hints, tips, pointers, ideas, opinions, views, input, words of wisdom.

advisable ▸ adjective JUDICIOUS, desirable, preferable, well, best, sensible, prudent, proper, appropriate, apt, suitable, fitting, wise, recommended, suggested; expedient, politic, advantageous, beneficial, profitable, in one's (best) interests.

advise ▸ verb **1** *her grandmother advised her about marriage* COUNSEL, give guidance, guide, offer suggestions, give hints/tips/pointers. **2** *he advised caution* ADVOCATE, recommend, suggest, urge, encourage, enjoin. **3** *you will be advised of the requirements* INFORM, notify, give notice, apprise, warn, forewarn; acquaint with, make familiar with, make known to, keep posted, update about/on; *informal* fill in on.

adviser ▸ noun COUNSELLOR, mentor, guide, consultant, confidant, confidante; coach, teacher, tutor, guru.

advisory ▸ adjective CONSULTATIVE, advising.
− OPPOSITES: executive.

advocacy ▸ noun SUPPORT, backing, promotion, championing; recommendation, prescription.

advocate ▸ noun *an advocate of children's rights* CHAMPION, upholder, supporter, backer, promoter, proponent, exponent, spokesman, spokeswoman, spokesperson, campaigner, fighter, crusader; propagandist, apostle, apologist, booster, flag-bearer; *informal* libber.
− OPPOSITES: critic.
▸ verb *heart specialists advocate a diet low in cholesterol* RECOMMEND, prescribe, advise, urge; support, back, favour, espouse, endorse, uphold, subscribe to, champion, campaign on behalf of, speak for, argue for, lobby for, promote.

aegis ▸ noun PROTECTION, backing, support, patronage, sponsorship, charge, care, guidance, control, guardianship, trusteeship, agency, safeguarding, shelter, umbrella, aid, assistance, auspices.

aesthetic ▸ adjective ARTISTIC, tasteful, in good taste; graceful, elegant, exquisite, beautiful, attractive, pleasing, lovely.

afar ▸ adverb AT/TO A DISTANCE, far off, far away.

affable ▸ adjective FRIENDLY, amiable, genial,

congenial, cordial, warm, pleasant, nice, likeable, personable, charming, agreeable, sympathetic, simpatico, good-humoured, good-natured, jolly, kindly, kind, courteous, civil, gracious, approachable, accessible, amenable, sociable, hail-fellow-well-met, outgoing, gregarious, neighbourly.
– OPPOSITES: unfriendly.

affair ▶ noun **1** *what you do is your affair* BUSINESS, concern, matter, responsibility, province, preserve; problem, worry. **2** (**affairs**) *his financial affairs* TRANSACTIONS, concerns, matters, activities, dealings, undertakings, ventures, business. **3** *the board admitted responsibility for the affair* EVENT, incident, happening, occurrence, eventuality, episode; case, matter, business. **4** *his affair with Monica was over* RELATIONSHIP, love affair, affaire de coeur, romance, fling, flirtation, dalliance, liaison, involvement, intrigue, amour; *informal* hanky-panky.

affect[1] ▶ verb **1** *this development may have affected the judge's decision* HAVE AN EFFECT ON, influence, act on, work on, have an impact on, impact; change, alter, modify, transform, form, shape, sway, bias. **2** *he was visibly affected by the experience* MOVE, touch, make an impression on, hit (hard), tug at someone's heartstrings; UPSET, trouble, distress, disturb, agitate, shake (up). **3** *the disease affected his lungs* ATTACK, infect; hit, strike.

affect[2] ▶ verb **1** *he deliberately affected a republican stance* ASSUME, take on, adopt, embrace, espouse. **2** *Paul affected an air of injured innocence* PRETEND, feign, fake, simulate, make a show of, make a pretense of, sham; *informal* put on, make like.

affectation ▶ noun **1** *the affectations of a prima donna* PRETENSION, pretentiousness, affectedness, artificiality, posturing, posing; airs (and graces). **2** *an affectation of calm* FACADE, front, show, appearance, pretense, simulation, posture, pose.

affected ▶ adjective PRETENTIOUS, artificial, contrived, unnatural, stagy, studied, mannered, ostentatious; insincere, unconvincing, feigned, false, fake, sham, simulated; *informal* la-di-da, phony, pretend, put on.
– OPPOSITES: natural, unpretentious, genuine.

affecting ▶ adjective TOUCHING, moving, emotive, emotional; stirring, soul-stirring, heart-warming; poignant, pathetic, pitiful, piteous, tear-jerking, heart-rending, heartbreaking, disturbing, distressing, upsetting, sad, haunting.

affection ▶ noun FONDNESS, love, liking, tenderness, warmth, devotion, endearment, care, caring, attachment, friendship; warm feelings.

affectionate ▶ adjective LOVING, fond, adoring, devoted, caring, doting, tender, warm, warm-hearted, soft-hearted, friendly; demonstrative, cuddly; *informal* touchy-feely, lovey-dovey.
– OPPOSITES: cold.

affiliate ▶ verb ASSOCIATE WITH, unite with, combine with, join (up) with, join forces with, link up with, team up with, ally with, align with, band together with, federate with, amalgamate with, merge with; attach to, annex to, incorporate into, integrate into.
▶ noun PARTNER, branch, offshoot, subsidiary.

affiliated ▶ adjective ASSOCIATED, allied, related, federated, confederated, amalgamated, unified, connected, linked; in league, in partnership.

affiliation ▶ noun ASSOCIATION, connection, alliance, alignment, link, attachment, tie, relationship,

fellowship, partnership, coalition, union; amalgamation, incorporation, integration, federation, confederation.

affinity ▶ noun **1** *her affinity with animals and birds* EMPATHY, rapport, sympathy, accord, harmony, relationship, bond, fellow feeling, like-mindedness, closeness, understanding; liking, fondness; *informal* chemistry. **2** *the semantic affinity between the two words* SIMILARITY, resemblance, likeness, kinship, relationship, association, link, analogy, similitude, correspondence.
– OPPOSITES: aversion, dislike, dissimilarity.

affirm ▶ verb **1** *he affirmed that they would lend military assistance* DECLARE, state, assert, proclaim, pronounce, attest, swear, avow, guarantee, pledge, give an undertaking; *formal* aver. **2** *the referendum affirmed the republic's right to secede* UPHOLD, support, confirm, ratify, endorse, sanction.
– OPPOSITES: deny.

affirmation ▶ noun **1** *an affirmation of faith* DECLARATION, statement, assertion, proclamation, pronouncement, attestation; oath, avowal, guarantee, pledge; deposition; *formal* averment, asseveration. **2** *the poem ends with an affirmation of pastoral values* CONFIRMATION, ratification, endorsement.
– OPPOSITES: denial.

affirmative ▶ adjective *an affirmative answer* POSITIVE, assenting, consenting, corroborative, favourable.
– OPPOSITES: negative.
▶ noun *she took his grunt as an affirmative* AGREEMENT, acceptance, assent, acquiescence, concurrence; OK, yes, thumbs-up.
– OPPOSITES: disagreement.

affix ▶ verb **1** *he affixed a stamp to the envelope* STICK, glue, paste, gum; attach, fasten, fix; clip, tack, pin; tape. **2** (*formal*) *affix your signature to the document* APPEND, add, attach.
– OPPOSITES: detach.

afflict ▶ verb TROUBLE, burden, distress, cause suffering to, beset, harass, worry, oppress; torment, pester, plague, blight, bedevil, rack, smite, curse; *archaic* ail.

affliction ▶ noun **1** *a herb reputed to cure a variety of afflictions* DISORDER, disease, malady, complaint, ailment, illness, indisposition, handicap; scourge, plague, trouble. **2** *he bore his affliction with great dignity* SUFFERING, distress, pain, trouble, misery, wretchedness, hardship, misfortune, adversity, sorrow, torment, tribulation, woe.

affluent ▶ adjective WEALTHY, rich, prosperous, well off, moneyed, well-to-do; propertied, substantial, of means, of substance, plutocratic; *informal* well-heeled, rolling in it, made of money, filthy rich, stinking rich, loaded, on easy street; upper-class, upscale.
– OPPOSITES: poor, impoverished.

afford ▶ verb **1** *I can't afford a new car* PAY FOR, bear the expense of, have the money for, spare the price of. **2** *it took more time than he could afford* SPARE, allow (oneself). **3** *the rooftop terrace affords beautiful views* PROVIDE, supply, furnish, offer, give, make available, yield.

affront ▶ noun *an affront to public morality* INSULT, offence, indignity, slight, snub, put-down, provocation, injury; outrage, atrocity, scandal; *informal* slap in the face, kick in the teeth.
▶ verb *she was affronted by his familiarity* INSULT, offend,

mortify, provoke, pique, wound, hurt; put out, irk, displease, bother, rankle, vex, gall; outrage, scandalize, disgust; *informal* put someone's back up, needle.

aficionado ▶ noun CONNOISSEUR, expert, authority, specialist, pundit; enthusiast, devotee; *informal* fan, buff, freak, nut, fiend, bum, maniac, fanatic, addict, junkie.

aflame ▶ adjective BURNING, ablaze, alight, on fire, in flames, blazing; *literary* afire.

afloat ▶ adverb & adjective BUOYANT, floating, buoyed up, on/above the surface, (keeping one's head) above water.

afoot ▶ adjective & adverb GOING ON, happening, around, about, abroad, stirring, circulating, in circulation, at large, in the air/wind; brewing, looming, in the offing, on the horizon.

aforesaid ▶ adjective PREVIOUSLY MENTIONED, aforementioned, aforenamed; foregoing, preceding, earlier, previous; above.

afraid ▶ adjective 1 *they ran away because they were afraid* FRIGHTENED, scared, terrified, fearful, petrified, scared witless, scared to death, terror-stricken, terror-struck, frightened/scared out of one's wits, shaking in one's shoes, shaking like a leaf; intimidated, alarmed, panicky; faint-hearted, cowardly; *informal* scared stiff, in a cold sweat, spooked; chicken; *archaic* afeared, affrighted. 2 *don't be afraid to ask awkward questions* RELUCTANT, hesitant, unwilling, disinclined, loath, slow, chary, shy. 3 *I'm afraid that your daughter is ill* SORRY, sad, distressed, regretful, apologetic.
– RELATED TERMS: -phobe.
– OPPOSITES: brave, confident.

afresh ▶ adverb ANEW, again, over/once again, once more, another time.

after ▶ preposition 1 *she made a speech after the performance* FOLLOWING, subsequent to, at the close/end of, in the wake of; *formal* posterior to. 2 *Guy shut the door after them* BEHIND, following. 3 *after the way he treated my sister I never want to speak to him again* BECAUSE OF, as a result/consequence of, in view of, owing to, on account of. 4 *is he still going to marry her, after all that's happened?* DESPITE, in spite of, regardless of, notwithstanding. 5 *the policeman ran after him* IN PURSUIT OF, in someone's direction, following. 6 *I'm after information, and I'm willing to pay for it* IN SEARCH OF, in quest/pursuit of, trying to find, looking for. 7 *they asked after Dad* ABOUT, concerning, regarding, with regard/respect/reference to. 8 *the village was named after a Roman officer* IN HONOUR OF, as a tribute to.
– RELATED TERMS: post-.
– OPPOSITES: before, preceding.
▶ adverb 1 *soon after, we went to Madrid* LATER, afterwards, after this/that, subsequently. 2 *porters were following on after with their bags* BEHIND, in the rear, at the back, in someone's wake.
– OPPOSITES: previously, before, ahead, in front.
■ **after all** MOST IMPORTANTLY, above all, beyond everything, ultimately; *informal* when all's said and done, at the end of the day, when push comes to shove.

after-effect ▶ noun REPERCUSSION, aftermath, consequence; *Medicine* sequela.

afterlife ▶ noun LIFE AFTER DEATH, the next world, the hereafter, the afterworld, eternity, kingdom come; immortality.

aftermath ▶ noun REPERCUSSIONS, after-effects, consequences, effects, results, fruits; wake.

afternoon ▶ noun aft, p.m.

afterthought ▶ noun SECOND THOUGHT, parenthesis, postscript.

afterwards ▶ adverb LATER, later on, subsequently, then, next, after this/that, thereafter; at a later time/date, in due course.

again ▶ adverb 1 *her spirits lifted again* ONCE MORE, another time, afresh, anew. 2 *this can add half as much again to the price* EXTRA, in addition, additionally, on top. 3 *again, evidence was not always consistent* ALSO, furthermore; moreover, besides.
■ **again and again** REPEATEDLY, over and over (again), time and (time) again, many times, many a time; often, frequently, continually, constantly.

against ▶ preposition 1 *a number of delegates were against the motion* OPPOSED TO, in opposition to, hostile to, averse to, antagonistic towards, inimical to, unsympathetic to, resistant to, at odds with, in disagreement with, dead set against; *informal* anti. 2 *he was swimming against the tide* IN OPPOSITION TO, counter to, contrary to, in the opposite direction to. 3 *his age is against him* DISADVANTAGEOUS TO, unfavourable to, damaging to, detrimental to, prejudicial to, deleterious to, harmful to, injurious to, a drawback for. 4 *she leaned against the wall* TOUCHING, in contact with, up against, on.
– RELATED TERMS: anti-.
– OPPOSITES: in favour of, pro.

age ▶ noun 1 *he is 35 years of age* NUMBER OF YEARS, length of life; stage of life, generation, age group. 2 *her hearing had deteriorated with age* ELDERLINESS, old age, oldness, senescence, dotage, seniority, maturity; one's advancing/advanced/declining years; *literary* eld; *archaic* caducity. 3 *the Elizabethan age* ERA, epoch, period, time, eon. 4 *(informal) you haven't been in touch with me for ages* A LONG TIME, days/months/years on end, an eternity, an eon; *informal* ages and ages, donkey's years, a dog's age, a month of Sundays, forever.
▶ verb *Cabernet Sauvignon ages well | the experience has aged her* MATURE, mellow, ripen, season; grow/become/make old, (cause to) decline.

aged ▶ adjective ELDERLY, old, mature, older, senior, hoary, ancient, senescent, advanced in years, in one's dotage, long in the tooth, as old as the hills, past one's prime, not as young as one used to be, getting on, over the hill, no spring chicken.
– OPPOSITES: young.

agency ▶ noun 1 *an advertising agency* BUSINESS, organization, company, firm, office, bureau. 2 *the infection is caused by the agency of insects* ACTION, activity, means, effect, influence, force, power, vehicle, medium. 3 *regional policy was introduced through the agency of the Board of Trade* INTERVENTION, intercession, involvement, good offices; auspices, aegis.

agenda ▶ noun 1 *the next topic on the agenda* LIST OF ITEMS, schedule, program, timetable, itinerary, lineup, list, plan. 2 *their hidden agenda* PLAN, scheme, motive.

agent ▶ noun 1 *the sale was arranged through an agent* REPRESENTATIVE, emissary, envoy, go-between, proxy, negotiator, broker, spokesperson, spokesman, spokeswoman; *informal* rep. 2 *a travel agent* AGENCY, business, organization, company, firm, bureau. 3 *a CIA agent* SPY, secret agent, undercover agent, operative, fifth columnist, mole, Mata Hari; *informal* spook, G-man. 4 *the agents of destruction* PERFORMER, author, executor, perpetrator, producer, instrument, catalyst. **5** *a cleansing agent* MEDIUM, means, instrument, vehicle.

aggravate ▶ verb **1** *the new law could aggravate the situation* WORSEN, make worse, exacerbate, inflame, compound; add fuel to the fire/flames, add insult to injury, rub salt in the wound. **2** *(informal) you don't have to aggravate people to get what you want* ANNOY, irritate, exasperate, bother, put out, nettle, provoke, antagonize, get on someone's nerves, ruffle (someone's feathers), try someone's patience; *informal* peeve, needle, bug, miff, get under someone's skin; tick off.
– OPPOSITES: alleviate, improve.

aggravation ▶ noun **1** *the recession led to the aggravation of unemployment problems* WORSENING, exacerbation, compounding. **2** *(informal) it's not worth the aggravation* NUISANCE, annoyance, irritation, hassle, headache, trouble, difficulty, inconvenience, bother, pain, distress.

aggregate ▶ noun **1** *the specimen is an aggregate of rock and mineral fragments* COLLECTION, mass, agglomeration, conglomerate, assemblage; mixture, mix, combination, blend, accumulation; compound, alloy, amalgam. **2** *he won with an aggregate of 325* TOTAL, sum total, sum, grand total.
▶ adjective *an aggregate score* TOTAL, combined, gross, overall, composite.

aggression ▶ noun **1** *an act of aggression* HOSTILITY, aggressiveness, belligerence, bellicosity, force, violence; pugnacity, pugnaciousness, militancy, warmongering; attack, assault. **2** *he played the game with unceasing aggression* CONFIDENCE, self-confidence, boldness, determination, forcefulness, vigour, energy, zeal.

aggressive ▶ adjective **1** *aggressive and disruptive behaviour* VIOLENT, confrontational, antagonistic, truculent, pugnacious, macho, two-fisted; quarrelsome, argumentative. **2** *aggressive foreign policy* WARMONGERING, warlike, warring, belligerent, bellicose, hawkish, militaristic; offensive, expansionist. **3** *an aggressive promotional drive* ASSERTIVE, pushy, forceful, vigorous, energetic, dynamic; bold, audacious; *informal* in-your-face, feisty.
– OPPOSITES: peaceable, peaceful.

aggressor ▶ noun ATTACKER, assaulter, assailant; invader, instigator.

aggrieved ▶ adjective **1** *the manager looked aggrieved at the suggestion* RESENTFUL, affronted, indignant, disgruntled, discontented, upset, offended, piqued, riled, nettled, vexed, irked, irritated, annoyed, put out, chagrined; *informal* peeved, miffed, in a huff, sore, steamed. **2** *the aggrieved party* WRONGED, injured, mistreated, harmed.
– OPPOSITES: pleased.

aghast ▶ adjective HORRIFIED, appalled, dismayed, thunderstruck, stunned, shocked, staggered; *informal* flabbergasted.

agile ▶ adjective **1** *she was as agile as a monkey* NIMBLE, lithe, supple, limber, acrobatic, fleet-footed, light-footed, light on one's feet; *literary* fleet, lightsome. **2** *an agile mind* ALERT, sharp, acute, shrewd, astute, perceptive, quick-witted.
– OPPOSITES: clumsy, stiff.

agitate ▶ verb **1** *any mention of Clare agitates my grandmother* UPSET, perturb, fluster, ruffle, disconcert, unnerve, disquiet, disturb, distress, unsettle, unhinge; *informal* rattle, faze;

discombobulate. **2** *she agitated for the appointment of more women* CAMPAIGN, strive, battle, fight, struggle, push, press. **3** *agitate the water to disperse the oil* STIR, whisk, churn, beat.

agitated ▶ adjective UPSET, perturbed, flustered, ruffled, disconcerted, unnerved, unstrung, disquieted, disturbed, distressed, unsettled; nervous, jumpy, on edge, tense, keyed up; *informal* rattled, fazed, in a dither, in a flap, in a state, in a lather, steamed up, jittery, in a tizz/tizzy, discombobulated, hag-ridden.
– OPPOSITES: calm, relaxed.

agitator ▶ noun TROUBLEMAKER, rabble-rouser, agent provocateur, demagogue, incendiary; revolutionary, firebrand, rebel, insurgent, subversive; *informal* disturber.

agnostic ▶ noun SKEPTIC, doubter, doubting Thomas; unbeliever, non-believer.
– OPPOSITES: believer, theist.

ago ▶ adverb IN THE PAST, before, earlier, back, since, previously; *formal* heretofore.

agog ▶ adverb EAGER, excited, impatient, keen, anxious, avid, in suspense, on tenterhooks, on the edge of one's seat, on pins and needles, waiting with bated breath.

agonize ▶ verb WORRY, fret, fuss, brood, upset oneself, rack one's brains, wrestle with oneself, be worried/anxious, feel uneasy, exercise oneself; *informal* stew.

agonizing ▶ adjective EXCRUCIATING, harrowing, racking, searing, extremely painful, acute, severe, torturous, tormenting, piercing; *informal* hellish.

agony ▶ noun PAIN, hurt, suffering, torture, torment, anguish, affliction, trauma; pangs, throes.

agrarian ▶ adjective AGRICULTURAL, rural, rustic, pastoral, countryside, farming; *literary* georgic, sylvan, Arcadian.

agree ▶ verb **1** *I agree with you* CONCUR, be of the same mind/opinion, see eye to eye, be in sympathy, be united, be as one man. **2** *they had agreed to a ceasefire* CONSENT, assent, acquiesce, accept, approve, say yes, give one's approval, give the nod; *formal* accede. **3** *the plan and the drawing do not agree with each other* MATCH (UP), jibe, jive, accord, correspond, chime in, conform, coincide, fit, tally, be in harmony/agreement, harmonize, be consistent/equivalent; *informal* square. **4** *they agreed on a price* SETTLE, decide, arrive at, negotiate, reach an agreement, come to terms, strike a bargain, make a deal, shake hands.
– OPPOSITES: differ, contradict, reject.

agreeable ▶ adjective **1** *an agreeable atmosphere of rural tranquility* PLEASANT, pleasing, enjoyable, pleasurable, nice, to one's liking, appealing, charming, delightful. **2** *an agreeable fellow* LIKEABLE, charming, amiable, affable, pleasant, nice, friendly, good-natured, sociable, genial, congenial, simpatico. **3** *we should get together for a talk, if you're agreeable* WILLING, amenable, in accord/agreement.
– OPPOSITES: unpleasant.

agreement ▶ noun **1** *all heads nodded in agreement* ACCORD, concurrence, consensus; assent, consent, acquiescence, endorsement, buy-in. **2** *an agreement on military co-operation* CONTRACT, compact, treaty, covenant, pact, accord, concordat, protocol. **3** *there is some agreement between my view and that of the author* CORRESPONDENCE, consistency, compatibility, accord; similarity, resemblance, likeness, similitude.
– OPPOSITES: discord.

agricultural ▶ adjective **1** *an agricultural labourer* FARM, farming, agrarian; rural, rustic, pastoral, countryside; *literary* georgic, sylvan, Arcadian. **2** *agricultural land* FARMED, farm, agrarian, cultivated, tilled, horticultural.
– OPPOSITES: urban.

agriculture ▶ noun FARMING, cultivation, tillage, tilling, husbandry, land/farm management, horticulture; agribusiness, agronomy.
– RELATED TERMS: agri-, agro-.

aground ▶ adverb & adjective GROUNDED, ashore, beached, stuck, shipwrecked, high and dry, on the rocks, on the ground/bottom.

ahead ▶ adverb **1** *he peered ahead, but could see nothing* FORWARD(S), towards the front, frontwards, onward(s), along. **2** *he had ridden on ahead* IN FRONT, at the head, in the lead, at the fore, in the vanguard, in advance. **3** *she was preparing herself for what lay ahead* IN THE FUTURE, in time, in time to come, in the fullness of time, at a later date, after this, henceforth, later on, in due course, next. **4** *they are ahead by six points* LEADING, winning, in the lead, (out) in front, first, coming first.
– OPPOSITES: behind, at the back, in the past.

■ **ahead of 1** *Blanche went ahead of the others* IN FRONT OF, before. **2** *we have a demanding trip ahead of us* IN STORE FOR, waiting for. **3** *two months ahead of schedule* IN ADVANCE OF, before, earlier than.

aid ▶ noun **1** *with the aid of his colleagues he prepared a manifesto* ASSISTANCE, support, help, backing, co-operation; a helping hand. **2** *humanitarian aid* RELIEF, charity, financial assistance, donations, contributions, subsidies, handouts, subvention, succour; *historical* alms. **3** *a hospital aid* HELPER, assistant, girl/man Friday.
– OPPOSITES: hindrance.
▶ verb **1** *he provided an army to aid the King of England* HELP, assist, abet, come to someone's aid, give assistance, lend a hand, be of service; avail, succour, sustain. **2** *essences can aid restful sleep* FACILITATE, promote, encourage, help, further, boost; speed up, hasten, accelerate, expedite.
– OPPOSITES: hinder.

aide ▶ noun ASSISTANT, helper, adviser, right-hand man, man/girl Friday, adjutant, deputy, second-in-command, second; subordinate, junior, underling, acolyte.

ailing ▶ adjective **1** *his ailing mother* ILL, sick, unwell, sickly, poorly, weak, indisposed, in poor/bad health, infirm, debilitated, diseased, delicate, valetudinarian, below par, bedridden; *informal* laid up, under the weather. **2** *the country's ailing economy* FAILING, in poor condition, weak, poor, deficient.
– OPPOSITES: healthy.

ailment ▶ noun ILLNESS, disease, sickness, disorder, condition, affliction, malady, complaint, infirmity; *informal* bug, virus.

aim ▶ verb **1** *he aimed the rifle* POINT, direct, train, sight, line up. **2** *she aimed at the target* TAKE AIM, fix on, zero in on, draw a bead on. **3** *undergraduates aiming for a first degree* WORK TOWARDS, be after, set one's sights on, try for, strive for, aspire to, endeavour to achieve; *formal* essay. **4** *this system is aimed at the home entertainment market* TARGET, intend, destine, direct, design, tailor, market, pitch. **5** *we aim to give you the best possible service* INTEND, mean, have in mind/view; plan, resolve, propose, design.
▶ noun *our aim is to develop gymnasts to the top level* OBJECTIVE, object, goal, end, target, design, desire, desired result, intention, intent, plan, purpose, object of the exercise; ambition, aspiration, wish, dream, hope, raison d'être.

aimless ▶ adjective **1** *Flavia set out on an aimless walk* PURPOSELESS, goalless, without purpose, haphazard, wandering, without goal, desultory. **2** *aimless men standing outside the bars* UNOCCUPIED, idle, at a loose end; purposeless, undirected.
– OPPOSITES: purposeful.

air ▶ noun **1** *hundreds of birds hovered in the air* SKY, atmosphere; heavens, ether. **2** *open the windows to get some air into the room* BREEZE, draft, wind; breath/blast of air, gust of wind. **3** *an air of defiance* EXPRESSION, appearance, look, impression, aspect, aura, mien, countenance, manner, bearing, tone. **4** *putting on airs* AFFECTATIONS, pretension, pretentiousness, affectedness, posing, posturing, airs and graces. **5** *a traditional Scottish air* TUNE, melody, song; *literary* lay.
– RELATED TERMS: aerial, aero-.
▶ verb **1** *a chance to air your views* EXPRESS, voice, make public, ventilate, articulate, state, declare, give expression/voice to; have one's say. **2** *the windows were opened to air the room* VENTILATE, freshen, refresh, cool. **3** *the film was aired nationwide* BROADCAST, transmit, screen, show, televise, telecast.

airborne ▶ adjective FLYING, in flight, in the air, on the wing.

aircraft ▶ noun airplane, jet, helicopter, balloon, glider.

airily ▶ adverb LIGHTLY, breezily, flippantly, casually, nonchalantly, heedlessly, without consideration.
– OPPOSITES: seriously.

airplane ▶ noun *the airplane took off* AIRCRAFT, plane, airliner, (jumbo) jet, jetliner, bush plane, float plane, seaplane, crop-duster, water bomber; *dated* flying machine.

airport ▶ noun airfield, landing strip, airstrip, air terminal.

airtight ▶ adjective **1** *an airtight container* SEALED, hermetically sealed, closed/shut tight. **2** *an airtight alibi* INDISPUTABLE, unquestionable, incontrovertible, undeniable, incontestable, irrefutable, watertight, beyond dispute/question/doubt.

airy ▶ adjective **1** *the conservatory is light and airy* WELL VENTILATED, fresh; spacious, uncluttered; light, bright. **2** *an airy gesture* NONCHALANT, casual, breezy, flippant, insouciant, heedless. **3** *airy clouds* DELICATE, soft, fine, feathery, insubstantial.
– OPPOSITES: stuffy.

airy-fairy ▶ adjective (*informal*) IMPRACTICAL, unrealistic, idealistic, fanciful, blue-sky.
– OPPOSITES: practical.

aisle ▶ noun PASSAGE, passageway, gangway, walkway, corridor.

ajar ▶ adjective & adverb SLIGHTLY OPEN, half open.
– OPPOSITES: closed, wide open.

akin ▶ adjective SIMILAR, related, close, near, corresponding, comparable, equivalent; connected, alike, analogous.
– OPPOSITES: unlike.

alacrity ▶ noun EAGERNESS, readiness; enthusiasm, ardour, avidity, fervour, keenness; promptness, haste, swiftness, dispatch, speed.

alarm ▶ noun **1** *we spun around in alarm* FEAR, anxiety, apprehension, trepidation, nervousness, unease, distress, agitation, consternation, disquiet, perturbation, fright, panic. **2** *gave the alarm* WARNING, alert. **3** *a smoke alarm* SIREN, warning sound, danger/

distress signal; warning device, alarm bell; *archaic* tocsin.
— OPPOSITES: calmness, composure.
▶ **verb** *the news had alarmed her* FRIGHTEN, scare, panic, unnerve, distress, agitate, upset, disconcert, shock, dismay, disturb; *informal* rattle, spook, scare the living daylights out of.

alarming ▶ **adjective** FRIGHTENING, unnerving, shocking; distressing, upsetting, disconcerting, perturbing, worrisome, worrying, dismaying, disquieting, startling, disturbing; *informal* scary.
— OPPOSITES: reassuring.

alarmist ▶ **noun** SCAREMONGER, doomster, doomsayer, Cassandra, Chicken Little.
— OPPOSITES: optimist.

alas ▶ **exclamation** ALACK, oy vey, woe; unfortunately.

album ▶ **noun 1** SCRAPBOOK, register, collection, treasury. **2** RECORD, CD, recording, disc; LP, vinyl.

alchemy ▶ **noun** CHEMISTRY; magic, sorcery, witchcraft.

alcohol ▶ **noun** LIQUOR, intoxicating liquor, strong/alcoholic drink, drink, spirits; *informal* booze, hooch, the hard stuff, firewater, rotgut, moonshine, moose milk ✤, grog, tipple, the demon drink, the bottle, sauce, juice; *technical* ethyl alcohol, ethanol. *See table.*

alcoholic ▶ **adjective** *alcoholic drinks* INTOXICATING, inebriating, containing alcohol, fermented; strong, hard, stiff; *formal* spirituous.
▶ **noun** *he is an alcoholic* DIPSOMANIAC, drunk, drunkard, heavy/hard/serious drinker, problem drinker, alcohol-abuser, person with a drinking problem; tippler, sot, inebriate; *informal* boozer, lush, rubby ✤, alky, boozehound, dipso, juicer, soak, wino, barfly, sponge.

alcove ▶ **noun** RECESS, niche, nook, bay; arbour, bower.

alert ▶ **adjective 1** *police have asked neighbours to keep alert* VIGILANT, watchful, attentive, observant, wide awake, circumspect; on the lookout, on one's guard/toes, on the qui vive; *informal* heads-up, keeping one's eyes open/peeled, bright-eyed and bushy-tailed. **2** *mentally alert* QUICK-WITTED, sharp, bright, quick, keen, perceptive, wide awake, on one's toes; *informal* on the ball, quick on the uptake, all there, with it.
— OPPOSITES: inattentive.
▶ **noun 1** *a state of alert* VIGILANCE, watchfulness, attentiveness, alertness, circumspection. **2** *a flood alert* WARNING, notification, notice; siren, alarm, signal, danger/distress signal.
▶ **verb** *police were alerted by a phone call* WARN, notify, apprise, forewarn, put on one's guard, put on the qui vive; *informal* tip off, clue in.

alias ▶ **noun** *known under several aliases* ASSUMED NAME, false name, pseudonym, sobriquet, incognito; pen/stage name, nom de plume/guerre.
▶ **adverb** *Cassius Clay, alias Muhammed Ali* ALSO KNOWN AS, aka, also called, otherwise known as.

alibi ▶ **noun** *we've both got a good alibi for last night* DEFENCE, justification, explanation, reason; *informal* story, line.

alien ▶ **adjective 1** *an alien landscape* UNFAMILIAR, unknown, strange, peculiar; exotic, foreign. **2** *a vicious role alien to his nature* INCOMPATIBLE, opposed, conflicting, contrary, in conflict, at variance. **3** *alien beings* EXTRATERRESTRIAL, unearthly; Martian.
— OPPOSITES: native, familiar, earthly.
▶ **noun 1** *an illegal alien* FOREIGNER, non-native, immigrant, (*Atlantic*) come from away ✤, emigrant,

émigré. **2** *the alien's spaceship crashed* EXTRATERRESTRIAL, ET; Martian; *informal* little green man.

alienate ▶ **verb** *the controversial new book alienated long-time fans* ESTRANGE, divide, distance, put at a distance, isolate, cut off; set against, turn away, turn off, drive apart, marginalize, disunite, set at variance/odds, drive a wedge between.

alienation ▶ **verb** *my deep sense of alienation* ISOLATION, detachment, estrangement, distance, separation, division; cutting off, turning away.

alight[1] ▶ **verb 1** *he alighted from the train* GET OFF, step off, disembark, dismount, pile out; detrain, deplane. **2** *a swallow alighted on a branch* LAND, come to rest, settle, perch; *archaic* light.
— OPPOSITES: get on, board.

alight[2] ▶ **adjective 1** *the bales of hay were alight* BURNING, ablaze, aflame, on fire, in flames, blazing; *literary* afire. **2** *her face was alight with laughter* LIT UP, gleaming, glowing, aglow, ablaze, bright, shining, resplendent, radiant.

align ▶ **verb 1** *the desks are aligned in straight rows* LINE UP, put in order, put in rows/columns, straighten,

Alcoholic Spirits & Liqueurs

Whisky	Liqueurs
bourbon	absinthe
Canadian whisky	advocaat
Irish whiskey	amaretto
malt whisky	anisette
rye	Baileys*
Scotch whisky	Benedictine*
single malt	cassis
usquebaugh	Chartreuse*
whisky blanc ✤(*Que.*)	cherry brandy
	Cointreau*
Brandy	crème de cacao
applejack	crème de cassis
Armagnac	crème de menthe
Calvados	curaçao
cognac	Drambuie*
eau-de-vie	Frangelico*
grappa	Galliano*
kirsch	Grand Marnier*
marc	Kahlúa*
mirabelle	kümmel
slivovitz	maraschino
	ratafia
Gin	pastis
Hollands	Pernod*
London gin	sambuca
sloe gin	Southern Comfort*
	Tia Maria*
Rum	triple sec
screech ✤(*Nfld*)	
tafia	*See also* WINES *and*
	COCKTAILS & MIXED DRINKS.
Other Spirits	
alcool ✤(*Que.*)	*Proprietary term
aquavit	
arak	
grog	
schnapps	
tequila	
vodka;	
hooch	
moonshine	
rotgut	
white lightning	
swish ✤(*Atlantic*)	

place, position, situate, set, range. **2** *he aligned himself with the workers* ALLY, affiliate, associate, join, side, unite, combine, join forces, form an alliance, team up, band together, throw in one's lot, make common cause.

alike ► adjective *all the doors looked alike* SIMILAR, (much) the same, indistinguishable, identical, uniform, interchangeable, cut from the same cloth, like (two) peas in a pod, (like) Tweedledum and Tweedledee; *informal* much of a muchness.
– OPPOSITES: different.
► adverb *great minds think alike* SIMILARLY, (just) the same, in the same way/manner/fashion, equally, likewise, identically.

alimony ► noun FINANCIAL SUPPORT, maintenance, support; child support.

alive ► adjective **1** *he was last seen alive on Boxing Day* LIVING, live, breathing, animate, sentient; *informal* alive and kicking; *archaic* quick. **2** *the association has kept her dream alive* IN EXISTENCE, existing, existent; functioning, in operation; on the map. **3** *the thrills that kept him really alive* ANIMATED, lively, full of life, alert, active, energetic, vigorous, spry, sprightly, vital, vivacious, buoyant, exuberant, ebullient, zestful, spirited; *informal* full of beans, bright-eyed and bushy-tailed, chirpy, chipper, peppy, full of vim and vigour. **4** *the place was alive with mice* TEEMING, swarming, overrun, crawling, bristling, infested; crowded, packed; *informal* lousy.
– OPPOSITES: dead, inanimate, inactive, lethargic.

all ► adjective **1** *all the children went | all creatures need sleep* EACH OF, each/every one of, every single one of; every (single), each and every. **2** *the sun shone all week* THE WHOLE OF THE, every bit of the, the complete, the entire. **3** *in all honesty | with all speed* COMPLETE, entire, total, full; greatest (possible), maximum.
– RELATED TERMS: omni-, pan-, panto-.
– OPPOSITES: no, none of.
► pronoun **1** *all are welcome* EVERYONE, everybody, each/every person. **2** *all of the cups were broken* EACH ONE, the sum, the total, the whole lot. **3** *they took all of it* EVERYTHING, every part, the whole/total amount, the (whole) lot, the entirety.
– OPPOSITES: none, nobody, nothing.
► adverb *he was dressed all in black* COMPLETELY, fully, entirely, totally, wholly, absolutely, utterly; in every respect, in all respects, without reservation/exception.
– OPPOSITES: partly.

allay ► verb REDUCE, diminish, decrease, lessen, assuage, alleviate, ease, relieve, soothe, soften, calm, take the edge off.
– OPPOSITES: increase, intensify.

allegation ► noun CLAIM, assertion, charge, accusation, declaration, statement, contention, deposition, argument, affirmation, attestation, grievance; *formal* averment.

allege ► verb CLAIM, assert, charge, accuse, declare, state, contend, argue, affirm, maintain, attest, testify, swear; *formal* aver.

alleged ► adjective SUPPOSED, so-called, claimed, professed, purported, ostensible, putative, unproven.

allegedly ► adverb REPORTEDLY, supposedly, reputedly, purportedly, ostensibly, apparently, putatively, by all accounts, so the story goes.

allegiance ► noun LOYALTY, faithfulness, fidelity, obedience, homage, devotion; *historical* fealty; *formal*

troth.
– OPPOSITES: disloyalty, treachery.

allegorical ► adjective SYMBOLIC, metaphorical, figurative, representative, emblematic.

allegory ► noun PARABLE, analogy, metaphor, symbol, emblem.

allergic ► adjective **1** *she was allergic to nuts* HYPERSENSITIVE, sensitive, sensitized. **2** *an allergic reaction* ANAPHYLACTIC. **3** *(informal) Pat's allergic to tidying up* AVERSE, opposed, hostile, inimical, antagonistic, antipathetic, resistant, (dead) set against.

allergy ► noun **1** *an allergy to feathers* HYPERSENSITIVITY, sensitivity, allergic reaction; anaphylaxis. **2** *(informal) their allergy to free enterprise* AVERSION, antipathy, opposition, hostility, antagonism, dislike, distaste.

alleviate ► verb REDUCE, ease, relieve, take the edge off, deaden, dull, diminish, lessen, weaken, lighten, attenuate, mitigate, allay, assuage, palliate, damp, soothe, help, soften, temper.
– OPPOSITES: aggravate.

alley ► noun PASSAGE, passageway, alleyway, back alley, back lane, laneway ✚, backstreet, lane, path, pathway, walk, allée.

alliance ► noun **1** *a defensive alliance* ASSOCIATION, union, league, confederation, federation, confederacy, coalition, consortium, affiliation, partnership. **2** *an alliance between medicine and morality* RELATIONSHIP, affinity, association, connection.

allied ► adjective **1** *a group of allied nations* FEDERATED, confederated, associated, in alliance, in league, in partnership; unified, united, integrated. **2** *agricultural and allied industries* ASSOCIATED, related, connected, interconnected, linked; similar, like, comparable, equivalent.
– OPPOSITES: independent, unrelated.

all-important ► adjective VITAL, essential, indispensable, crucial, key, vitally important, of the utmost importance; critical, life-and-death, paramount, pre-eminent, high-priority; urgent, pressing, burning.
– OPPOSITES: inessential.

allocate ► verb ALLOT, assign, distribute, apportion, share out, portion out, dispense, deal out, dole out, give out, dish out, parcel out, ration out, divide out/up; *informal* divvy up.

allocation ► noun **1** *the efficient allocation of resources* ALLOTMENT, assignment, distribution, apportionment, sharing out, handing out, dealing out, doling out, giving out, dishing out, parcelling out, rationing out, dividing out/up; *informal* divvying up. **2** *our annual allocation of funds* ALLOWANCE, allotment, quota, share, ration, portion, grant, slice; *informal* cut.

allot ► verb ALLOCATE, assign, apportion, distribute, issue, grant; earmark for, designate for, set aside for; hand out, deal out, dish out, dole out, give out; *informal* divvy up.

allotment ► noun **1** *the allotment of shares by a company* ALLOCATION, assignment, distribution, apportionment, issuing, sharing out, handing out, dealing out, doling out, giving out, dishing out, parcelling out, rationing out, dividing out/up; *informal* divvying up. **2** *each member received an allotment of new shares* QUOTA, share, ration, grant, allocation, allowance, slice; *informal* cut.

all out ► adverb *I'm working all out to finish my novel* STRENUOUSLY, energetically, vigorously, hard, with all

one's might (and main), at full speed, in high gear, eagerly, enthusiastically, industriously, diligently, assiduously, sedulously, indefatigably; *informal* like mad, like crazy.
– OPPOSITES: lackadaisically.

▶ **adjective** *an all-out attack* STRENUOUS, energetic, vigorous, forceful, forcible; spirited, mettlesome, plucky, determined, resolute, unrestrained, aggressive, eager, keen, enthusiastic, zealous, ardent, fervent.
– OPPOSITES: half-hearted.

allow ▶ **verb 1** *the police allowed him to go home* PERMIT, let, authorize, give permission/authorization/leave, sanction, license, enable, entitle; consent, assent, give one's consent/assent/blessing, give the nod, acquiesce, agree, approve; tolerate, brook; *informal* give the go-ahead, give the thumbs up, OK, give the OK, give the green light; *formal* accede. **2** *allow an hour or so for driving* SET ASIDE, allocate, allot, earmark, designate, assign, leave. **3** *she allowed that all people had their funny little ways* ADMIT, acknowledge, recognize, agree, accept, concede, grant.
– OPPOSITES: prevent, forbid.

allowable ▶ **adjective** *the maximum allowable number of users* PERMISSIBLE, permitted, allowed, admissible, acceptable, legal, lawful, legitimate, licit, authorized, sanctioned, approved, in order; *informal* OK, legit.
– OPPOSITES: forbidden.

allowance ▶ **noun 1** *your baggage allowance* PERMITTED AMOUNT/QUANTITY, allocation, allotment, quota, share, ration, grant, limit, portion, slice. **2** *she spent her allowance on paperbacks* PAYMENT, pocket money, sum of money, contribution, grant, subsidy, stipend, maintenance, remittance, financial support, per diem. **3** *a tax allowance* CONCESSION, reduction, decrease, discount.
■ **make allowance(s) for 1** *you must make allowances for delays* TAKE INTO CONSIDERATION, take into account, bear in mind, have regard to, provide for, plan for, make plans for, get ready for, allow for, make provision for, make preparations for, prepare for. **2** *she made allowances for his faults* EXCUSE, make excuses for, forgive, pardon, overlook.

alloy ▶ **noun** MIXTURE, mix, amalgam, fusion, meld, blend, compound, combination, composite, union; *technical* admixture.

all-powerful ▶ **adjective** OMNIPOTENT, almighty, supreme, pre-eminent; dictatorial, despotic, totalitarian, autocratic.
– OPPOSITES: powerless.

all right ▶ **adjective 1** *the tea was all right* SATISFACTORY, acceptable, adequate, fairly good, passable, reasonable; *informal* so-so, {comme ci, comme ça}, OK, jake. **2** *are you all right?* UNHURT, uninjured, unharmed, unscathed, in one piece, safe (and sound); well, fine, alive and well, OK. **3** *it's all right for you to go now* PERMISSIBLE, permitted, allowed, allowable, admissible, acceptable, legal, lawful, legitimate, licit, authorized, sanctioned, approved, in order, OK, legit.
– OPPOSITES: unsatisfactory, hurt, forbidden.

▶ **adverb 1** *the system works all right* SATISFACTORILY, adequately, fairly well, passably, acceptably, reasonably; OK. **2** *it's him all right* DEFINITELY, certainly, unquestionably, undoubtedly, indubitably, undeniably, assuredly, for sure, without (a) doubt, beyond (any) doubt, beyond the shadow of a doubt; *archaic* in sooth, verily.

▶ **exclamation** *all right, I'll go* VERY WELL (THEN), right (then), fine, good, yes, agreed, wilco; *informal* OK, okey-dokey, roger.

allude ▶ **verb** REFER, touch on, suggest, hint, imply, mention (in passing), make an allusion to; *formal* advert.

allure ▶ **noun** *the allure of Paris* ATTRACTION, lure, draw, pull, appeal, allurement, enticement, temptation, charm, seduction, fascination.
▶ **verb** *will sponsors be allured by such opportunities?* ATTRACT, lure, entice, tempt, appeal to, captivate, draw, win over, charm, seduce, inveigle, beguile, fascinate, whet the appetite of, make someone's mouth water.
– OPPOSITES: repel.

alluring ▶ **adjective** ENTICING, tempting, attractive, appealing, inviting, captivating, fetching, seductive; enchanting, charming, fascinating; *informal* come-hither.

allusion ▶ **noun** REFERENCE, mention, suggestion, hint, intimation, comment, remark.

ally ▶ **noun** *close political allies* ASSOCIATE, colleague, friend, confederate, partner, supporter.
– OPPOSITES: enemy, opponent.

▶ **verb 1** *he allied his racing experience with business acumen* COMBINE, marry, couple, merge, amalgamate, join, fuse. **2** *the Catholic powers allied with Philip II* UNITE, combine, join (up), join forces, band together, team up, collaborate, side, align oneself, form an alliance, throw in one's lot, make common cause.
– OPPOSITES: split.

almanac ▶ **noun** YEARBOOK, calendar, register, annual; manual, handbook.

almighty ▶ **adjective 1** *I swear by almighty God* ALL-POWERFUL, omnipotent, supreme, pre-eminent. **2** (*informal*) *an almighty explosion* VERY GREAT, huge, enormous, immense, colossal, massive, prodigious, stupendous, tremendous, monumental, mammoth, vast, gigantic, giant, mighty, Herculean, epic; very loud, deafening, ear-splitting, ear-piercing, booming, thundering, thunderous; *informal* whopping, thumping, astronomical, mega, monster, humongous, jumbo, ginormous.
– OPPOSITES: powerless, insignificant.

almost ▶ **adverb** NEARLY, (just) about, more or less, practically, virtually, all but, as good as, close to, near, not quite, roughly, not far from/off, for all intents and purposes, approaching, bordering on, verging on; *informal* pretty near/much/well; *literary* well-nigh, nigh on.
– RELATED TERMS: quasi-.

alms ▶ **plural noun** GIFT(S), donation(s), handout(s), offering(s), charity, baksheesh, largesse.

aloft ▶ **adjective & adverb** UPWARDS, up, high, in(to) the air/sky, skyward, on high, overhead, heavenward, high up, up (above).
– OPPOSITES: down.

alone ▶ **adjective & adverb 1** *she was alone in the house* BY ONESELF, on one's own, all alone, solitary, single, singly, solo, solus; unescorted, partnerless, companionless, by one's lonesome. **2** *he managed alone* UNAIDED, unassisted, without help/assistance, single-handedly, solo, on one's own. **3** *she felt terribly alone* LONELY, isolated, solitary, deserted, abandoned, forsaken, forlorn, friendless. **4** *a house standing alone* APART, by itself/oneself, separate, detached, isolated. **5** *you alone can inspire me* ONLY, solely, just; and no one

else, and nothing else, no one but, nothing but.
— OPPOSITES: in company, with help, among others.

along ▶ preposition **1** *she walked along the corridor* DOWN, from one end —— to the other. **2** *trees grew along the river bank* BESIDE, by the side of, on the edge of, alongside. **3** *they'll stop along the way* ON, at a point on, in the course of.
▶ adverb **1** *Maurice moved along past the other exhibits* ONWARDS, on, ahead, forward(s), forth. **2** *I invited a friend along* AS COMPANY, with one, to accompany one, as a partner.
■ **along with** TOGETHER WITH, accompanying, accompanied by; at the same time as; as well as, in addition to, plus, besides.

aloof ▶ adjective DISTANT, detached, unfriendly, anti-social, unsociable, remote, unapproachable, formal, stiff, withdrawn, reserved, unforthcoming, uncommunicative, unsympathetic; *informal* standoffish.
— OPPOSITES: familiar, friendly.

aloud ▶ adverb AUDIBLY, out loud, for all to hear.
— OPPOSITES: silently.

alphabet ▶ noun ABC'S, letters, writing system, syllabary. *See table.*

Phonetic Alphabet

Alpha	November
Bravo	Oscar
Charlie	Papa
Delta	Quebec
Echo	Romeo
Foxtrot	Sierra
Golf	Tango
Hotel	Uniform
India	Victor
Juliet	Whisky
Kilo	X-ray
Lima	Yankee
Mike	Zulu

already ▶ adverb **1** *Anna had already suffered a great deal* BY THIS/THAT TIME, by now/then, thus/so far, before now/then, until now/then, up to now/then. **2** *is it 3 o'clock already?* AS EARLY AS THIS/THAT, as soon as this/that, so soon.

also ▶ adverb TOO, as well, besides, in addition, additionally, furthermore, further, moreover, into the bargain, on top (of that), what's more, to boot, equally; *informal* and all, likewise; *archaic* withal.

alter ▶ verb **1** *Eliot was persuaded to alter the passage* CHANGE, make changes to, make different, make alterations to, adjust, make adjustments to, adapt, amend, modify, revise, revamp, rework, redo, refine, vary, transform; *informal* tweak; *technical* permute. **2** *the state of affairs has altered* CHANGE, become different, undergo a (sea) change, adjust, adapt, transform, evolve.
— OPPOSITES: preserve, stay the same.

alteration ▶ noun CHANGE, adjustment, adaptation, modification, variation, revision, amendment, rearrangement, reordering, restyling, rejigging, reworking, revamping; sea change, transformation; *humorous* transmogrification.

altercation ▶ noun ARGUMENT, quarrel, squabble, fight, shouting match, disagreement, difference of opinion, falling-out, dispute, disputation, fracas, wrangle, blow-up, skirmish, run-in, war of words; *informal* tiff, scrap, spat, row, bust-up, rhubarb, broil.

alternate ▶ verb **1** *rows of trees alternate with dense shrub* BE INTERSPERSED, occur in turn/rotation, rotate, follow one another; take turns, take it in turns, work/act in sequence; oscillate, fluctuate. **2** *we could alternate the groups so that no one felt they had been left out* GIVE TURNS TO, take in turn, rotate, take in rotation; swap, exchange, interchange.
▶ adjective **1** *she attended on alternate days* EVERY OTHER, every second. **2** *place the leeks and noodles in alternate layers* ALTERNATING, interchanging, following in sequence, sequential, occurring in turns. **3** *an alternate player* ALTERNATIVE, other, another, second, different, substitute, replacement, deputy, relief, proxy, surrogate, cover, fill-in, stand-in, standby, emergency, reserve, backup, auxiliary, fallback, pinch-hitting.

alternative ▶ adjective **1** *an alternative route* DIFFERENT, other, another, second, possible, substitute, replacement, alternate; standby, emergency, reserve, backup, auxiliary, fallback. **2** *an alternative lifestyle* UNORTHODOX, unconventional, non-standard, unusual, uncommon, out of the ordinary, radical, revolutionary, nonconformist, avant-garde; *informal* off the wall, oddball, offbeat, way-out.
▶ noun *we have no alternative* OPTION, choice, other possibility; substitute, replacement.

alternatively ▶ adverb ON THE OTHER HAND, as an alternative, or; otherwise, instead, if not, then again, alternately.

although ▶ conjunction IN SPITE OF THE FACT THAT, despite the fact that, notwithstanding (the fact) that, even though/if, for all that, while, whilst.

altitude ▶ noun HEIGHT, elevation, distance above the sea/ground.

altogether ▶ adverb **1** *he wasn't altogether happy* COMPLETELY, totally, entirely, absolutely, wholly, fully, thoroughly, utterly, perfectly, one hundred per cent, in all respects. **2** *we have five offices altogether* IN ALL, all told, in toto. **3** *altogether it was a great evening* ON THE WHOLE, overall, all in all, all things considered, on balance, on average, for the most part, in the main, in general, generally, by and large.

altruistic ▶ adjective UNSELFISH, selfless, compassionate, kind, public-spirited; charitable, benevolent, beneficent, philanthropic, humanitarian; *literary* bounteous.

always ▶ adverb **1** *he's always late* EVERY TIME, each time, at all times, all the time, without fail, consistently, invariably, regularly, habitually, unfailingly. **2** *she's always complaining* CONTINUALLY, continuously, constantly, forever, perpetually, incessantly, ceaselessly, unceasingly, endlessly, the entire time; *informal* 24-7. **3** *the place will always be dear to me* FOREVER, for always, for good (and all), forevermore, for ever and ever, until the end of time, eternally, for eternity, until hell freezes over; *informal* for keeps, until the cows come home; *archaic* for aye. **4** *you can always take it back to the shop* AS A LAST RESORT, no matter what, in any event/case, come what may.
— OPPOSITES: never, seldom, sometimes.

amalgamate ▶ verb COMBINE, merge, unite, fuse, blend, meld; join (together), join forces, band (together), link (up), team up, go into partnership; *literary* commingle.
— OPPOSITES: separate.

amalgamation ▶ noun COMBINATION, union, blend, mixture, fusion, coalescence, synthesis, composite, amalgam.

amass ▶ verb GATHER, collect, assemble; accumulate, aggregate, stockpile, store (up), pile up, heap, cumulate, accrue, lay in/up, garner; *informal* stash (away).
— OPPOSITES: dissipate.

amateur ▶ noun **1** *the crew were all amateurs* NON-PROFESSIONAL, non-specialist, layman, layperson, greenhorn; dilettante. **2** *what a bunch of amateurs* BUNGLER, incompetent, bumbler.
— OPPOSITES: professional, expert.
▶ adjective **1** *an amateur sportsman* NON-PROFESSIONAL, non-specialist, lay; dilettante. **2** *their amateur efforts* INCOMPETENT, inept, unskilful, inexpert, amateurish, clumsy, maladroit, bumbling.

amatory ▶ adjective SEXUAL, amorous, romantic, sensual, passionate, erotic, sexy; *informal* randy, naughty.

amaze ▶ verb ASTONISH, astound, surprise, stun, stagger, shock, stupefy, awe, stop someone in their tracks, leave open-mouthed, leave aghast, take someone's breath away, dumbfound; *informal* bowl over, flabbergast, blow away; (**amazed**) thunderstruck, at a loss for words, speechless.

amazement ▶ noun ASTONISHMENT, surprise, shock, stupefaction, incredulity, disbelief, speechlessness, awe, wonder, wonderment.

amazing ▶ adjective ASTONISHING, astounding, surprising, stunning, staggering, shocking, startling, stupefying, breathtaking; awesome, awe-inspiring, sensational, remarkable, spectacular, stupendous, phenomenal, extraordinary, incredible, unbelievable; *informal* mind-blowing, jaw-dropping; *literary* wondrous.

ambassador ▶ noun **1** *the American ambassador* ENVOY, plenipotentiary, emissary, (papal) nuncio, representative, high commissioner, consul, consul general, diplomat; *archaic* legate. **2** *a great ambassador for the sport* CAMPAIGNER, representative, promoter, champion, supporter, backer, booster.

ambience ▶ noun ATMOSPHERE, air, aura, climate, mood, feel, feeling, character, quality, impression, flavour, look, tone; *informal* vibe(s).

ambiguity ▶ noun VAGUENESS, obscurity, abstruseness, doubtfulness, uncertainty; *formal* dubiety; ambivalence, equivocation, double meaning.

ambiguous ▶ adjective EQUIVOCAL, ambivalent, open to debate/argument, arguable, debatable; obscure, unclear, imprecise, vague, abstruse, doubtful, dubious, uncertain.
— OPPOSITES: clear.

ambit ▶ noun SCOPE, extent, range, breadth, width, reach, sweep; terms of reference, field of reference, jurisdiction; area, sphere, field, realm, domain, compass.

ambition ▶ noun **1** *young people with ambition* DRIVE, determination, enterprise, initiative, eagerness, motivation, resolve, enthusiasm, zeal, hunger, commitment, a sense of purpose; *informal* get-up-and-go. **2** *her ambition was to become a diplomat* ASPIRATION, intention, goal, aim, objective, object, purpose, intent, plan, desire, wish, design, target, dream.

ambitious ▶ adjective **1** *an energetic and ambitious politician* ASPIRING, determined, forceful, pushy, enterprising, motivated, enthusiastic, energetic, zealous, committed, purposeful, power-hungry; *informal* go-ahead, go-getting. **2** *he was ambitious to make it to the top* EAGER, determined, intent on, enthusiastic, anxious, hungry, impatient, striving. **3** *an ambitious task* DIFFICULT, exacting, demanding, formidable, challenging, hard, arduous, onerous, tough; *archaic* toilsome.
— OPPOSITES: laid-back.

ambivalent ▶ adjective EQUIVOCAL, uncertain, unsure, doubtful, indecisive, inconclusive, irresolute, of two minds, undecided, torn, in a quandary, on the fence, hesitating, wavering, vacillating, equivocating, blowing/running hot and cold; *informal* iffy.
— OPPOSITES: unequivocal, certain.

amble ▶ verb STROLL, saunter, wander, ramble, promenade, walk, go for a walk, take a walk; *informal* mosey, toddle, tootle; *formal* perambulate.

ambush ▶ noun *the soldiers were killed in an ambush* SURPRISE ATTACK, trap; *archaic* ambuscade.
▶ verb *twenty youths ambushed their patrol car* ATTACK BY SURPRISE, surprise, pounce on, fall upon, lay a trap for, set an ambush for, lie in wait for, waylay, bushwhack; *archaic* ambuscade.

ameliorate ▶ verb IMPROVE, make better, better, make improvements to, enhance, help, benefit, boost, amend; relieve, ease, mitigate; *informal* tweak, patch up.
— OPPOSITES: worsen.

amenable ▶ adjective **1** *an amenable child* CO-OPERATIVE, acquiescent, compliant, accommodating, obliging, biddable, manageable, controllable, governable, persuadable, tractable, responsive, pliant, malleable, complaisant, easily handled; *rare* persuasible. **2** *many cancers are amenable to treatment* SUSCEPTIBLE, receptive, responsive; *archaic* susceptive.
— OPPOSITES: uncooperative.

amend ▶ verb REVISE, alter, change, modify, qualify, adapt, adjust; edit, copy-edit, rewrite, redraft, rephrase, reword, rework, revamp.

amends ▶ plural noun
■ **make amends** COMPENSATE, recompense, redress, indemnify, make it up to; atone for, make up for, make good, expiate.

amenity ▶ noun *basic amenities* FACILITY, service, convenience, resource, appliance, aid, comfort, benefit, feature, advantage.

amiable ▶ adjective FRIENDLY, affable, amicable, cordial; warm, warm-hearted, good-natured, nice, pleasant, agreeable, likeable, genial, good-humoured, charming, easy to get on/along with, companionable, sociable, personable; *informal* chummy, simpatico.
— OPPOSITES: unfriendly, disagreeable.

amicable ▶ adjective FRIENDLY, good-natured, cordial, easy, easygoing, neighbourly, harmonious, co-operative, civilized.
— OPPOSITES: unfriendly.

amid ▶ preposition **1** *the jeep was concealed amid pine trees* IN THE MIDDLE OF, surrounded by, among, amongst; *literary* amidst, in the midst of. **2** *the truce collapsed amid fears of a revolt* AT A TIME OF, in an atmosphere of, against a background of; as a result of.

amiss ▶ adjective *an inspection revealed nothing amiss* WRONG, awry, faulty, out of order, defective, flawed, unsatisfactory, incorrect, not right; inappropriate, improper.
— OPPOSITES: right, in order.

■ **take something amiss** BE OFFENDED, take offence, be upset.

amity ▶ noun FRIENDSHIP, friendliness, harmony, harmoniousness, understanding, accord, co-operation, companionship, amicableness, goodwill, cordiality, warmth; *formal* concord.
— OPPOSITES: animosity, enmity.

ammunition ▶ noun *police seized arms and ammunition* BULLETS, shells, projectiles, missiles, rounds, shot, slugs, cartridges, munitions; *informal* ammo.

amnesty ▶ noun PARDON, pardoning, reprieve; grace; release, discharge.

amok
■ **run amok** GO BERSERK, get out of control, rampage, riot, run riot, go on the rampage, behave like a maniac, behave wildly/uncontrollably, become violent/destructive; *informal* raise hell.

among, amongst ▶ preposition **1** *you're among friends* SURROUNDED BY, in the company of, amid, in the middle of, with; *literary* amidst, in the midst of. **2** *a child was among the injured* INCLUDED IN, one/some of, in the group/number of. **3** *he distributed the proceeds among his creditors* BETWEEN, to each of. **4** *decide among yourselves* JOINTLY, mutually, together.
— RELATED TERMS: inter-.

amoral ▶ adjective UNPRINCIPLED, without standards/morals/scruples, unscrupulous, Machiavellian, unethical.
— OPPOSITES: principled.

amorous ▶ adjective ROMANTIC, lustful, sexual, erotic, amatory, ardent, passionate, impassioned; in love, enamoured, lovesick; *informal* lovey-dovey, kissy, smoochy, hot; randy.

amorphous ▶ adjective SHAPELESS, formless, structureless, indeterminate; vague, nebulous, indefinite.

amount ▶ noun QUANTITY, number, total, aggregate, sum, quota, group, size, mass, weight, volume, bulk, lot, quantum.
■ **the full amount** THE GRAND TOTAL, the total, the aggregate; *informal* the whole kit and caboodle, the whole shebang, the whole nine yards.
■ **amount to 1** *the bill amounted to $50* ADD UP TO, come to, run to, be, make, total. **2** *a result that amounted to complete failure* CONSTITUTE, be tantamount, come down, boil down; signify, signal, mean, indicate, suggest, denote, point to, be evidence, be symptomatic; *literary* betoken. **3** *her relationships had never amounted to anything significant* BECOME, grow/develop into, prove to be, turn out to be.

amphibian ▶ noun. *See table.*

Amphibians

axolotl	mud puppy
bullfrog	newt
cane toad	red-backed salamander
chorus frog	salamander
eft	spring peeper
frog	tiger salamander
Goliath frog	toad
horned toad	tree frog
leopard frog	tree toad
midwife toad	

ample ▶ adjective **1** *there is ample time for discussion* ENOUGH, sufficient, adequate, plenty of, more than enough, enough and to spare. **2** *an ample supply of wine* PLENTIFUL, abundant, copious, profuse, rich, lavish, liberal, generous, bountiful, bounteous, large, huge, great, bumper; *literary* plenteous.
— OPPOSITES: insufficient, meagre.

amplify ▶ verb **1** *amplified guitars screamed through the stadium* MAKE LOUDER, louden, turn up, magnify, intensify, increase, boost, step up, raise. **2** *these notes amplify our statement* EXPAND, enlarge upon, elaborate on, add to, supplement, develop, flesh out, add detail to, go into detail about.
— OPPOSITES: reduce, quieten.

amplitude ▶ noun MAGNITUDE, size, volume; extent, range, compass; breadth, width.

amputate ▶ verb CUT OFF, sever, remove (surgically), dismember, saw/chop off.

amulet ▶ noun LUCKY CHARM, charm, talisman, mojo, churinga, phylactery, fetish, mascot, totem, idol, juju.

amuse ▶ verb **1** *her annoyance simply amused him* ENTERTAIN, make laugh, delight, divert, cheer (up), please, charm, tickle; *informal* tickle pink, crack up. **2** *he amused himself by writing poetry* OCCUPY, engage, busy, employ, distract, absorb, engross, hold someone's attention; interest, entertain, divert.
— OPPOSITES: bore.

amusement ▶ noun **1** *we looked with amusement at the cartoon* MIRTH, merriment, light-heartedness, hilarity, glee, delight, gaiety, joviality, fun; enjoyment, pleasure, high spirits, cheerfulness. **2** *I read the book for amusement* ENTERTAINMENT, pleasure, leisure, relaxation, fun, enjoyment, interest, diversion; *informal* R and R; *archaic* disport. **3** *a wide range of amusements* ACTIVITY, entertainment, diversion; game, sport.

amusement park ▶ noun THEME PARK, fun park, exhibition, ex ✚, carnival, midway.

amusing ▶ adjective ENTERTAINING, funny, comical, humorous, light-hearted, jocular, witty, mirthful, hilarious, droll, diverting; laughable; *informal* wacky, side-splitting, rib-tickling.
— OPPOSITES: boring, solemn.

analogous ▶ adjective COMPARABLE, parallel, similar, like, akin, corresponding, related, kindred, equivalent.
— OPPOSITES: unrelated.

analogy ▶ noun SIMILARITY, parallel, correspondence, likeness, resemblance, correlation, relation, kinship, equivalence, similitude, metaphor, simile.
— OPPOSITES: dissimilarity.

analysis ▶ noun EXAMINATION, investigation, inspection, survey, study, scrutiny; exploration, probe, research, review, evaluation, interpretation, dissection.

analyst ▶ noun PSYCHOANALYST, psychiatrist, psychologist, psychotherapist, therapist; *informal* shrink.

analytical, analytic ▶ adjective SYSTEMATIC, logical, scientific, methodical, (well) organized, ordered, orderly, meticulous, rigorous; diagnostic.
— OPPOSITES: unsystematic.

analyze ▶ verb EXAMINE, inspect, survey, study, scrutinize, look over; investigate, explore, probe, research, go over (with a fine-tooth comb), review, evaluate, break down, dissect, anatomize.

anarchic ▶ adjective LAWLESS, without law and

order, in disorder/turmoil, unruly, chaotic, turbulent.
– OPPOSITES: ordered.

anarchist ▶ noun NIHILIST, insurgent, agitator, subversive, terrorist, revolutionary, revolutionist, insurrectionist.

anarchy ▶ noun LAWLESSNESS, nihilism, mobocracy, revolution, insurrection, disorder, chaos, mayhem, tumult, turmoil.
– OPPOSITES: government, order.

anathema ▶ noun *racial hatred was anathema to her* ABOMINATION, outrage, bane, bugbear, bête noire; ABHORRENT, hateful, repugnant, repellent, offensive.

anatomy ▶ noun BODILY STRUCTURE, makeup, composition, constitution, form, structure.

ancestor ▶ noun **1** *he could trace his ancestors back to a Loyalist* FOREBEAR, forefather, predecessor, antecedent, progenitor, primogenitor. **2** *the instrument is an ancestor of the lute* FORERUNNER, precursor, predecessor.
– OPPOSITES: descendant, successor.

ancestral ▶ adjective INHERITED, hereditary, familial.

ancestry ▶ noun ANCESTORS, forebears, forefathers, progenitors, antecedents; family tree; lineage, parentage, genealogy, descent, roots, stock, line.

anchor ▶ noun **1** *the anchor of the new coalition* MAINSTAY, cornerstone, linchpin, bulwark, foundation. **2** *a TV news anchor* PRESENTER, announcer, anchorman, anchorwoman, broadcaster.
▶ verb **1** *the ship was anchored in the bay* MOOR, berth, be at anchor; *archaic* harbour. **2** *the fish anchors itself to the coral* SECURE, fasten, attach, affix, fix.

ancient ▶ adjective **1** *in ancient times* OF LONG AGO, early, prehistoric, primeval, primordial, primitive; *literary* of yore; *archaic* foregone. **2** *an ancient custom* OLD, very old, age-old, archaic, time-worn, time-honoured, venerable. **3** *I feel positively ancient* OLD, aged, elderly, antiquated, decrepit, antediluvian, in one's dotage; old-fashioned, out of date, outmoded, obsolete, passé, démodé; *informal* horse-and-buggy.
– RELATED TERMS: archaeo-, palaeo-.
– OPPOSITES: recent, contemporary.

ancillary ▶ adjective ADDITIONAL, auxiliary, supporting, helping, extra, supplementary, accessory; *Medicine* adjuvant.
– RELATED TERMS: para-.

and ▶ conjunction TOGETHER WITH, along with, with, as well as, in addition to, also, too; besides, furthermore; *informal* plus.

android ▶ noun ROBOT, automaton, cyborg, droid, bot.

anecdote ▶ noun STORY, tale, narrative, incident; urban myth; *informal* yarn, chestnut.

anemic ▶ adjective **1** *his anemic face* COLOURLESS, bloodless, pale, pallid, wan, ashen, grey, sallow, pasty-faced, whey-faced, peaky, sickly, etiolated. **2** *an anemic description of her feelings* FEEBLE, weak, insipid, wishy-washy, vapid, bland; lame, tame, lacklustre, spiritless, languid, lifeless, ineffective, ineffectual, etiolated; *informal* pathetic.

anew ▶ adverb AGAIN, afresh, another time, once more/again, over again.

angel ▶ noun **1** *an angel appeared in the heavens* MESSENGER OF GOD, divine/heavenly messenger, divine being. **2** *she's an absolute angel* SAINT, paragon of virtue; gem, treasure, darling, dear; *informal* star.

3 (*informal*) *a financial angel* BACKER, sponsor, benefactor, fairy godmother, promoter, patron.
– OPPOSITES: devil.

angelic ▶ adjective **1** *angelic beings* DIVINE, heavenly, celestial, holy, seraphic, cherubic; spiritual. **2** *Sophie's angelic appearance* INNOCENT, pure, virtuous, good, saintly, wholesome; beautiful.
– OPPOSITES: demonic, infernal.

anger ▶ noun *his face was livid with anger* RAGE, vexation, exasperation, displeasure, crossness, irritation, irritability, indignation, pique; annoyance, fury, wrath, ire, outrage, irascibility, ill temper/humour; *informal* slow burn, aggravation; *literary* choler.
– RELATED TERMS: irascible.
– OPPOSITES: pleasure, good humour.
▶ verb *she was angered by his terse reply* INFURIATE, irritate, exasperate, irk, vex, peeve, madden, put out; enrage, incense, annoy; rub the wrong way; *informal* make someone's blood boil, get someone's back up, make someone see red, get someone's dander up, rattle someone's cage, make someone's hackles rise; aggravate, get someone, rile, tick off, cheese off, tee off, burn up.
– OPPOSITES: pacify, placate.

angle ▶ noun **1** *the wall is sloping at an angle of 33°* GRADIENT, slant, inclination. **2** *the angle of the roof* CORNER, intersection, point, apex. **3** *consider the problem from a different angle* PERSPECTIVE, point of view, viewpoint, standpoint, position, aspect, slant, direction.
▶ verb **1** *Anna angled her camera towards the tree* TILT, slant, direct, turn. **2** *angle your answer so that it is relevant* PRESENT, slant, orient, twist, bias. **3** *he was angling for an invitation* TRY TO GET, seek to obtain, fish for, hope for, be after.

anglophone ▶ noun ENGLISH-SPEAKER, Anglo, English Canadian.
▶ adjective ENGLISH-SPEAKING, English, Anglo, English Canadian.
– RELATED TERMS: francophone, allophone.

angry ▶ adjective **1** *Vivienne got angry* IRATE, mad, annoyed, cross, vexed, irritated, indignant, irked; furious, enraged, infuriated, in a temper, incensed, raging, fuming, seething, beside oneself, choleric, outraged; livid, apoplectic, hot under the collar, up in arms, in high dudgeon, foaming at the mouth, doing a slow burn, steamed up, in a lather, fit to be tied, seeing red, shirty; sore, bent out of shape, ticked off, teed off, cheesed off, PO'd; *literary* wrathful; *archaic* wroth. **2** *an angry debate* HEATED, passionate, stormy, 'lively'; bad-tempered, ill-tempered, ill-natured, acrimonious, bitter.
– OPPOSITES: pleased, good-humoured.
■ **get angry** LOSE ONE'S TEMPER, become enraged, go into a rage, go berserk, flare up; *informal* go crazy, go bananas, hit the roof, go through the roof, go up the wall, see red, go off the deep end, fly off the handle, blow one's top, blow a fuse/gasket, flip out, have a fit, foam at the mouth, explode, go ballistic, flip one's wig, blow one's stack, have a conniption.

angst ▶ noun ANXIETY, fear, apprehension, worry, foreboding, trepidation, malaise, disquiet, disquietude, unease, uneasiness.

anguish ▶ noun AGONY, pain, torment, torture, suffering, distress, angst, misery, sorrow, grief, heartache, desolation, despair; *literary* dolour.
– OPPOSITES: happiness.

angular ▶ adjective **1** *an angular shape*

SHARP-CORNERED, pointed, V-shaped, Y-shaped. **2** *an angular face* BONY, raw-boned, lean, spare, thin, skinny, gaunt.
− OPPOSITES: rounded, curving.

animal ▶ noun **1** *endangered animals* CREATURE, beast, living thing; *informal* critter, beastie; (**animals**) wildlife, fauna. **2** *the man was an animal* BRUTE, beast, monster, devil, demon, fiend; *informal* swine, bastard, pig.
− RELATED TERMS: ZOO-.
▶ adjective *a grunt of animal passion* CARNAL, fleshly, bodily, physical; brutish, beastly, bestial, unrefined, uncultured, coarse.

animate ▶ verb *a sense of excitement animated the whole school* ENLIVEN, vitalize, breathe (new) life into, energize, invigorate, revive, vivify, liven up; inspire, inspirit, exhilarate, thrill, excite, fire, arouse, rouse, quicken, stir; light a fire under.
− OPPOSITES: depress.
▶ adjective *an animate being* LIVING, alive, live, breathing; *archaic* quick.
− OPPOSITES: inanimate.

animated ▶ adjective LIVELY, spirited, high-spirited, energetic, full of life, excited, enthusiastic, eager, alive, active, vigorous, vibrant, vital, vivacious, buoyant, exuberant, ebullient, effervescent, bouncy, bubbly, perky; *informal* bright-eyed and bushy-tailed, bright and breezy, chirpy, chipper, peppy; heated.
− OPPOSITES: lethargic, lifeless.

animosity ▶ noun ANTIPATHY, hostility, friction, antagonism, acrimony, enmity, animus, bitterness, rancour, resentment, dislike, ill feeling/will, bad blood, hatred, hate, loathing; malice, spite, spitefulness.
− OPPOSITES: goodwill, friendship.

annals ▶ plural noun RECORDS, archives, chronicles, accounts, registers; *Law* muniments.

annex ▶ verb **1** *Charlemagne annexed northern Italy* TAKE OVER, take possession of, appropriate, seize, conquer, occupy. **2** *ten amendments were annexed to the constitution* ADD, append, attach, tack on, tag on.
▶ noun EXTENSION, addition; wing; ell.

annexation ▶ noun SEIZURE, occupation, invasion, conquest, takeover, appropriation.

annihilate ▶ verb DESTROY, wipe out, obliterate, wipe off the face of the earth; eliminate, liquidate, defeat.
− OPPOSITES: create.

anniversary ▶ noun JUBILEE, commemoration.

annotate ▶ verb COMMENT ON, add notes/footnotes to, gloss, interpret, mark up.

annotation ▶ noun NOTE, notation, comment, gloss, footnote; commentary, explanation, interpretation.

announce ▶ verb **1** *their financial results were announced* MAKE PUBLIC, make known, report, declare, divulge, state, give out, notify, publicize, broadcast, publish, advertise, circulate, proclaim, blazon. **2** *Victor announced the guests* INTRODUCE, present, name. **3** *strains of music announced her arrival* SIGNAL, indicate, give notice of, herald, proclaim; *literary* betoken.

announcement ▶ noun **1** *an announcement by the Minister* STATEMENT, report, declaration, proclamation, pronouncement, rescript; bulletin, communiqué. **2** *the announcement of the decision* DECLARATION, notification, reporting, publishing, broadcasting, proclamation; *archaic* annunciation.

announcer ▶ noun PRESENTER, anchorman,

anchorwoman, anchor, anchorperson; news reader, newscaster, broadcaster; host, master of ceremonies, MC, emcee.

annoy ▶ verb IRRITATE, vex, make angry/cross, anger, exasperate, irk, gall, pique, put out, antagonize, get on someone's nerves, get to, ruffle someone's feathers, make someone's hackles rise, nettle; rub the wrong way; *informal* aggravate, peeve, hassle, miff, rile, needle, frost, bug, get someone's goat, get someone's back up, get in someone's hair, give someone the gears ✦, drive mad/crazy/bananas, drive around the bend, drive up the wall, tee off, tick off, cheese off, burn up, rankle.
− OPPOSITES: please, gratify.

annoyance ▶ noun **1** *much to his annoyance, Louise didn't even notice* IRRITATION, exasperation, vexation, indignation, anger, displeasure, chagrin; *informal* aggravation. **2** *they found him an annoyance* NUISANCE, pest, bother, irritant, inconvenience, palaver; *informal* pain (in the neck), hassle; nudnik, burr under someone's saddle.

annoyed ▶ adjective IRRITATED, cross, angry, vexed, exasperated, irked, piqued, displeased, put out, disgruntled, chagrined, nettled, in a bad mood, in a temper; *informal* aggravated, peeved, frosted, miffed, riled; teed off, ticked off, cheesed off, sore, bent out of shape.

annoying ▶ adjective IRRITATING, infuriating, exasperating, maddening, trying, tiresome, troublesome, bothersome, nettlesome, obnoxious, irksome, vexing, cursed, vexatious, galling; *informal* aggravating, pesky.

annual ▶ adjective YEARLY, once-a-year; year-long, year-end, twelve-month.

annually ▶ adverb YEARLY, once a year, each year, per annum.

annul ▶ verb DECLARE INVALID, declare null and void, nullify, invalidate, void, disallow; repeal, reverse, rescind, revoke; *Law* vacate; *formal* abrogate; recall.
− OPPOSITES: restore, enact.

anoint ▶ verb *he was anointed and crowned* CONSECRATE, bless, ordain; *formal* hallow.

anomalous ▶ adjective ABNORMAL, atypical, irregular, aberrant, heteroclite, exceptional, freak, freakish, odd, bizarre, peculiar, unusual, out of the ordinary; deviant, mutant.
− OPPOSITES: normal, typical.

anomaly ▶ noun ODDITY, peculiarity, abnormality, irregularity, inconsistency, incongruity, aberration, quirk, rarity.

anonymous ▶ adjective **1** *an anonymous donor* UNNAMED, of unknown name, nameless, incognito, unidentified, unknown, secret. **2** *an anonymous letter* UNSIGNED, unattributed. **3** *an anonymous housing development* CHARACTERLESS, nondescript, impersonal, faceless.
− OPPOSITES: known, identified.

another ▶ adjective *have another drink* ONE MORE, a further, an additional.

answer ▶ noun **1** *her answer was unequivocal* REPLY, response, rejoinder, reaction; retort, riposte; *informal* comeback. **2** *a new filter is the answer* SOLUTION, remedy, key.
− OPPOSITES: question.
▶ verb **1** *Steve was about to answer* REPLY, respond, make a rejoinder, rejoin; retort, riposte, return. **2** *she has yet to answer the charges* REBUT, refute, defend oneself against. **3** *a man answering this description* MATCH, fit,

correspond to, be similar to. **4** *we're trying to answer the needs of our audience* SATISFY, meet, fulfill, fill, measure up to. **5** *I answer to the Commissioner* REPORT, work for/under, be subordinate, be accountable, be answerable, be responsible.

■ **answer back** RESPOND CHEEKILY, be cheeky, be impertinent, talk back, shoot back, cheek; *informal* sass.

■ **answer for 1** *he will answer for his crime* PAY FOR, be punished for, suffer for; make amends for, make reparation for, atone for. **2** *the government has a lot to answer for* BE ACCOUNTABLE FOR, be responsible for , be liable for, take the blame for; *informal* take the rap for.

answerable ▶ **adjective** ACCOUNTABLE, responsible, liable; subject.

ant ▶ **noun** EMMET, pismire.

antagonism ▶ **noun** HOSTILITY, friction, enmity, antipathy, animus, opposition, dissension, rivalry; acrimony, bitterness, rancour, resentment, animosity, aversion, dislike, ill feeling, ill will, bad blood.
– OPPOSITES: rapport, friendship.

antagonist ▶ **noun** ADVERSARY, opponent, enemy, foe, rival, competitor; (**antagonists**) opposition, competition.
– OPPOSITES: ally.

antagonistic ▶ **adjective 1** *he was antagonistic to the reforms* HOSTILE, against, (dead) set against, opposed, inimical, antipathetic, ill-disposed, resistant, in disagreement; *informal* anti. **2** *an antagonistic group of bystanders* HOSTILE, aggressive, belligerent, bellicose, pugnacious.
– OPPOSITES: pro.

antagonize ▶ **verb** AROUSE HOSTILITY IN, alienate; anger, annoy, provoke, vex, irritate; rub the wrong way; *informal* aggravate, rile, needle, rattle someone's cage, get someone's back up.
– OPPOSITES: pacify, placate.

antecedent ▶ **adjective** *antecedent events* PREVIOUS, earlier, prior, preceding, precursory, former, foregoing; *formal* anterior.
– OPPOSITES: subsequent.
▶ **noun 1** *her antecedents have been traced* ANCESTOR, forefather, forebear, progenitor, primogenitor; (**antecedents**) ancestry, family tree, lineage, genealogy, roots. **2** *the guitar's antecedent* PRECURSOR, forerunner, predecessor.
– OPPOSITES: descendant.

antedate ▶ **verb** PRECEDE, predate, come/go before.

antediluvian *her antediluvian attitudes* OUT OF DATE, outdated, outmoded, old-fashioned, antiquated, behind the times, passé.

antenna ▶ **noun** AERIAL, rabbit ears, mast, satellite dish.

anteroom ▶ **noun** ANTECHAMBER, vestibule, lobby, foyer; *Architecture* narthex.

anthem ▶ **noun** HYMN, song, chorale, psalm, paean.

anthology ▶ **noun** COLLECTION, selection, compendium, treasury, miscellany; *archaic* garland.

anticipate ▶ **verb 1** *we don't anticipate any trouble* EXPECT, foresee, predict, be prepared for, bargain on, reckon on; *informal* figure on. **2** *the defender must anticipate the attacker's moves* PRE-EMPT, forestall, second-guess; *informal* beat someone to the punch. **3** *a much-anticipated event* LOOK FORWARD TO, await, lick one's lips over.

anticipation ▶ **noun** *her eyes sparkled with*

anticipation EXPECTANCY, expectation, excitement, suspense.
■ **in anticipation of** IN THE EXPECTATION OF, in preparation for, ready for.

anticlimactic ▶ **adjective** BATHETIC, disappointing, dissatisfying.

anticlimax ▶ **noun** LETDOWN, disappointment, comedown, non-event; bathos.

antics ▶ **plural noun** CAPERS, pranks, larks, hijinks, frolicking, skylarking, foolery, tomfoolery.

antidote ▶ **noun 1** *the antidote to this poison* ANTITOXIN, antiserum, antivenin. **2** *laughter is a good antidote to stress* REMEDY, cure, nostrum.

antipathetic ▶ **adjective** HOSTILE, against, (dead) set against, opposed, antagonistic, ill-disposed, unsympathetic; *informal* anti, down on.
– OPPOSITES: pro.

antipathy ▶ **noun** HOSTILITY, antagonism, animosity, aversion, animus, enmity, dislike, distaste, hatred, hate, abhorrence, loathing.
– OPPOSITES: liking, affinity.

antiquated ▶ **adjective** OUTDATED, out of date, outmoded, outworn, old, stale, behind the times, old-fashioned, anachronistic, old-fangled, antediluvian, passé, démodé, obsolete; *informal* out of the ark, mouldy, horse-and-buggy.
– OPPOSITES: modern, up to date.

antique ▶ **noun** COLLECTOR'S ITEM, period piece, antiquity, heirloom.
▶ **adjective 1** *antique furniture* OLD, antiquarian, collectable, old-fashioned. **2** *statues of antique gods* ANCIENT, of long ago; *literary* of yore. **3** *antique work practices*. *See* ANTIQUATED.
– OPPOSITES: modern, state-of-the-art.

antiquity ▶ **noun 1** *the civilizations of antiquity* ANCIENT PAST, the ancient past, classical times, the distant past. **2** *Islamic antiquities* ANTIQUE, period piece, collector's item.

antiseptic ▶ **adjective 1** *an antiseptic substance* DISINFECTANT, germicidal, bactericidal, antibacterial, antibiotic. **2** *antiseptic bandages* STERILE, aseptic, germ-free, uncontaminated, disinfected. **3** *their antiseptic surroundings* CHARACTERLESS, colourless, soulless; clinical, institutional; dispassionate, detached.
– OPPOSITES: contaminated.
▶ **noun** DISINFECTANT, germicide, bactericide.

anti-social ▶ **adjective 1** *worrisome anti-social behaviour* SOCIOPATHIC, distasteful, disruptive, rebellious, misanthropic, asocial. **2** *I'm feeling a bit anti-social* UNSOCIABLE, unfriendly, uncommunicative, reclusive, withdrawn; standoffish.

antithesis ▶ **noun** (COMPLETE) OPPOSITE, converse, contrary, reverse, inverse, obverse, the flip side, the other side of the coin.

antithetical ▶ **adjective** (DIRECTLY) OPPOSED, contrasting, contrary, contradictory, conflicting, incompatible, irreconcilable, inconsistent, at variance/odds.
– OPPOSITES: identical, like.

antsy ▶ **adjective** AGITATED, anxious, fidgety, jumpy, fretful, restless, stir-crazy, wired.

anxiety ▶ **noun 1** *his anxiety grew* WORRY, concern, apprehension, apprehensiveness, uneasiness, unease, fearfulness, fear, disquiet, disquietude, inquietude, perturbation, agitation, angst, misgiving, nervousness, nerves, tension, tenseness; *informal* heebie-jeebies, butterflies (in one's stomach),

jitteriness, the jitters, twitchiness, collywobbles, jim-jams. **2** *an anxiety to please* EAGERNESS, keenness, desire.
– OPPOSITES: serenity.

anxious ▶ adjective **1** *her fever has us all a little anxious* WORRIED, concerned, apprehensive, fearful, uneasy, perturbed, troubled, bothered, disturbed, distressed, fretful, agitated, nervous, edgy, antsy, unquiet, on edge, tense, overwrought, worked up, keyed up, jumpy, worried sick, with one's stomach in knots, with one's heart in one's mouth; uptight, on tenterhooks, with butterflies in one's stomach, jittery, twitchy, in a stew/twitter/dither/lather/tizz/tizzy, het up; strung out, hag-ridden, having kittens; spooky, squirrelly. **2** *she was anxious for news* EAGER, keen, desirous, impatient.
– OPPOSITES: carefree, unconcerned.

any ▶ adjective **1** *is there any cake left?* SOME, a piece/part/bit of. **2** *it doesn't make any difference* THE SLIGHTEST BIT OF, a scrap/shred/jot/whit of, an iota of. **3** *any job will do* WHICHEVER, no matter which, never mind which; *informal* any old.
▶ pronoun *you don't know any of my friends* A SINGLE ONE, (even) one; anyone, anybody.
▶ adverb *is your father any better?* AT ALL, in the least, to any extent, in any degree.

anyhow ▶ adverb **1** *anyhow, it doesn't really matter. See* ANYWAY. **2** *her clothes were strewn about anyhow* HAPHAZARDLY, carelessly, heedlessly, negligently, in a muddle; *informal* all over the place.

anyway ▶ adverb ANYHOW, in any case/event, at any rate; however, be that as it may, regardless; *informal* anyways.

apace ▶ adverb *(literary)* QUICKLY, fast, swiftly, rapidly, speedily, briskly, without delay, post-haste, expeditiously.
– OPPOSITES: slowly.

apart ▶ adverb **1** *the villages are two miles apart* AWAY/DISTANT FROM EACH OTHER. **2** *Isabel stood apart* TO ONE SIDE, aside, separately, alone, by oneself/itself. **3** *his parents are living apart* SEPARATELY, independently, on one's own. **4** *the car was blown apart* TO PIECES/BITS, up; *literary* asunder.
■ **apart from** EXCEPT FOR, but for, aside from, with the exception of, excepting, excluding, bar, barring, besides, other than; *informal* outside of; *formal* save.

apartment ▶ noun **1** *a rented apartment* FLAT, penthouse, lodging. *See table.* **2** *the royal apartments* SUITE (OF ROOMS), rooms, living quarters, accommodation.

Apartments

bachelor ♣	penthouse
bachelorette ♣	pied-à-terre
bed-sitting room	studio apartment
efficiency unit ♣	suite
flat	walk-up
garden apartment	one-and-a-half ♣(Que.)
in-law suite	two-and-a-half ♣(Que.)
loft	three-and-a-half ♣(Que.)
maisonette	four-and-a-half ♣(Que.)
nanny suite	five-and-a-half ♣(Que.)

---

apathetic ▶ adjective UNINTERESTED, indifferent, unconcerned, unmoved, uninvolved, unemotional, emotionless, dispassionate, lukewarm, unmotivated, half-hearted; *informal* couldn't-care-less; *rare* Laodicean.

apathy ▶ noun INDIFFERENCE, lack of interest/enthusiasm/concern, unconcern, uninterestedness, unresponsiveness, impassivity, dispassion, lethargy, languor, ennui, acedia.
– OPPOSITES: enthusiasm, passion.

ape ▶ noun PRIMATE, simian; monkey; *technical* anthropoid. *See table at* PRIMATE.
▶ verb *he aped Barbara's accent* IMITATE, mimic, copy, parrot, do an impression of; *informal* take off, send up.

aperture ▶ noun OPENING, hole, gap, slit, slot, vent, crevice, chink, crack, interstice; *technical* orifice, foramen.

apex ▶ noun **1** *the apex of a pyramid* TIP, peak, summit, pinnacle, top, vertex. **2** *the apex of his career* CLIMAX, culmination; peak, top, pinnacle, zenith, acme, apogee, high(est) point, capstone.
– RELATED TERMS: apical.
– OPPOSITES: bottom, nadir.

aphorism ▶ noun SAYING, maxim, axiom, adage, epigram, dictum, gnome, proverb, saw, tag, apophthegm.

aphrodisiac ▶ noun LOVE POTION, philtre.

apiece ▶ adverb (FOR) EACH, respectively, per item, severally; *informal* a pop/throw, per.

aplenty ▶ adjective IN ABUNDANCE, in profusion, galore, in large quantities/numbers, by the dozen; *informal* by the truckload.

aplomb ▶ noun POISE, self-assurance, self-confidence, calmness, composure, collectedness, level-headedness, sang-froid, equilibrium, equanimity; *informal* unflappability.

apocalyptic ▶ adjective DOOMSDAY, doom-laden, ominous, portentous; catastrophic, momentous.

apocryphal ▶ adjective FICTITIOUS, made-up, untrue, fabricated, false, spurious; unverified, unauthenticated, unsubstantiated; bogus.
– OPPOSITES: authentic.

apologetic ▶ adjective REGRETFUL, sorry, contrite, remorseful, rueful, penitent, repentant; conscience-stricken, compunctious, shamefaced, ashamed.
– OPPOSITES: unrepentant.

apologia ▶ noun DEFENCE, justification, vindication, explanation; argument, case.

apologist ▶ noun DEFENDER, supporter, upholder, advocate, proponent, exponent, propagandist, champion, campaigner; *informal* cheerleader.
– OPPOSITES: critic.

apologize ▶ verb SAY SORRY, express regret, be apologetic, make an apology, ask forgiveness, ask for pardon, eat humble pie.

apology ▶ noun **1** *I owe you an apology* EXPRESSION OF REGRET, one's regrets. **2** *an apology for capitalism* DEFENCE, explanation, justification, apologia.

apostate ▶ noun DISSENTER, defector, backslider, turncoat; *archaic* heretic; *rare* tergiversator.
– OPPOSITES: follower.

apostle ▶ noun **1** *the 12 apostles* DISCIPLE, follower. **2** *the apostles of the Slavs* MISSIONARY, evangelist, proselytizer. **3** *an apostle of capitalism* ADVOCATE, apologist, proponent, exponent, promoter, supporter, upholder, champion, booster.

appall ▶ verb HORRIFY, shock, dismay, distress, outrage, scandalize; disgust, repel, revolt, sicken, nauseate, offend, make someone's blood run cold.

appalling ▶ adjective **1** *an appalling crime* SHOCKING, horrific, horrifying, horrible, terrible, awful, dreadful, ghastly, hideous, horrendous, frightful, atrocious, abominable, abhorrent, outrageous, gruesome, grisly, monstrous, heinous, egregious. **2** (*informal*) *your school work is appalling* BAD, dreadful, awful, terrible, frightful, atrocious, disgraceful, deplorable, hopeless, lamentable; *informal* rotten, crummy, pathetic, pitiful, woeful, useless, lousy, abysmal, dire.

apparatus ▶ noun **1** *laboratory apparatus* EQUIPMENT, gear, rig, tackle, gadgetry; appliance, instrument, machine, mechanism, device, contraption, gadget, gizmo, doohickey. **2** *the apparatus of government* STRUCTURE, system, framework, organization, network.

apparel ▶ noun (*formal*) CLOTHES, clothing, garments, dress, attire, wear, garb, getup; *informal* gear, togs, duds, threads; *archaic* raiment, habit, habiliments.

apparent ▶ adjective **1** *their relief was all too apparent* EVIDENT, plain, obvious, clear, manifest, visible, discernible, perceptible; unmistakable, crystal clear, palpable, patent, blatant, writ large; *informal* as plain as the nose on one's face, written all over one's face. **2** *his apparent lack of concern* SEEMING, ostensible, outward, superficial; supposed, alleged, professed.
— OPPOSITES: unclear.

apparently ▶ adverb SEEMINGLY, evidently, it seems/ appears (that), as far as one knows, by all accounts; ostensibly, outwardly, supposedly, on the face of it, so the story goes, so I'm told; allegedly, reputedly.

apparition ▶ noun *a monstrous apparition* GHOST, phantom, spectre, spirit, wraith; vision, hallucination; *informal* spook, chimera; *literary* phantasm, revenant, shade, visitant; *rare* eidolon.

appeal ▶ verb **1** *police are appealing for information* ASK URGENTLY/EARNESTLY, make an urgent/earnest request, call, make a plea, plead. **2** *Andrew appealed to me to help them* IMPLORE, beg, entreat, call on, plead with, exhort, ask, request, petition; *formal* adjure; *literary* beseech. **3** *the idea of travelling appealed to me* ATTRACT, be attractive to, interest, take someone's fancy, fascinate, tempt, entice, allure, lure, draw, whet someone's appetite.
▶ noun **1** *an appeal for help* PLEA, urgent/earnest request, entreaty, cry, call, petition, supplication, cri de coeur. **2** *the cultural appeal of the island* ATTRACTION, attractiveness, allure, charm; fascination, magnetism, drawing power, pull. **3** *the court allowed the appeal* RETRIAL, re-examination.

appealing ▶ adjective ATTRACTIVE, engaging, alluring, enchanting, captivating, bewitching, fascinating, tempting, enticing, seductive, irresistible, winning, winsome, charming, desirable.
— OPPOSITES: disagreeable, off-putting.

appear ▶ verb **1** *a cloud of dust appeared on the horizon* BECOME VISIBLE, come into view/sight, materialize, pop up. **2** *fundamental differences were beginning to appear* BE REVEALED, emerge, surface, manifest itself, become apparent/evident, come to light; arise, crop up. **3** (*informal*) *Bill still hadn't appeared* ARRIVE, turn up, put in an appearance, come, get here/there; *informal* show (up), roll in, pitch up, fetch up, blow in. **4** *they appeared to be completely devoted* SEEM, look, give the impression, come across as, strike someone as. **5** *the paperback edition didn't appear for two years* BECOME AVAILABLE, come on the market, go on sale, come out, be published, be produced. **6** *she appeared on Broadway* PERFORM, play, act.
— OPPOSITES: vanish.

appearance ▶ noun **1** *her dishevelled appearance*

LOOK(S), air, aspect, mien. **2** *they tried to maintain a respectable appearance* IMPRESSION, air, image, (outward) show; semblance, facade, veneer, front, pretense. **3** *the sudden appearance of her daughter* ARRIVAL, advent, coming, emergence, materialization. **4** *the appearance of these symptoms* OCCURRENCE, manifestation, development.

appease ▶ verb **1** *an attempt to appease his critics* CONCILIATE, placate, pacify, mollify, propitiate, reconcile, win over. **2** *I'd wasted a lot of money to appease my vanity* SATISFY, fulfill, gratify, indulge; assuage, relieve.
— OPPOSITES: provoke, inflame.

appeasement ▶ noun *a policy of appeasement* CONCILIATION, placation, concession, pacification, propitiation, reconciliation; fence-mending.
— OPPOSITES: provocation.

appellation ▶ noun (*formal*) NAME, title, designation, tag, sobriquet, byname, nickname, cognomen; *informal* moniker, handle; *formal* denomination.

append ▶ verb ADD, attach, affix, tack on, tag on; *formal* subjoin.

appendage ▶ noun **1** *I am not just an appendage to the family* ADDITION, attachment, adjunct, addendum, appurtenance, accessory. **2** *a pair of feathery appendages* PROTUBERANCE, projection; *technical* process.

appendix ▶ noun SUPPLEMENT, addendum, postscript, codicil; coda, epilogue, afterword, tailpiece, back matter; attachment.

appertain
■ **appertain to** PERTAIN TO, be pertinent to, apply to, relate to, concern, be concerned with, have to do with, be relevant to, have reference to, have a bearing on, bear on; regard.

appetite ▶ noun **1** *a walk sharpens the appetite* HUNGER, ravenousness, hungriness; taste, palate. **2** *my appetite for learning* CRAVING, longing, yearning, hankering, hunger, thirst, passion; enthusiasm, keenness, eagerness, desire; *informal* yen.

appetizer ▶ noun STARTER, first course, hors d'oeuvre, amuse-gueule, antipasto.

appetizing ▶ adjective **1** *an appetizing lunch* MOUTH-WATERING, inviting, tempting; tasty, delicious, flavourful, toothsome, delectable, succulent; *informal* scrumptious, yummy, delish, lip-smacking. **2** *the least appetizing part of election campaigns* APPEALING, attractive, inviting, alluring.
— OPPOSITES: bland, unappealing.

applaud ▶ verb **1** *the audience applauded* CLAP, give a standing ovation, put one's hands together; show one's appreciation; *informal* give someone a big hand. **2** *police have applauded the decision* PRAISE, commend, acclaim, salute, welcome, hail, celebrate, express admiration for, express approval of, look on with favour, approve of, sing the praises of, pay tribute to, speak highly of, take one's hat off to, express respect for.
— OPPOSITES: boo, criticize.

applause ▶ noun **1** *a massive round of applause* CLAPPING, hand clapping, (standing) ovation; acclamation. **2** *the museum's design won general applause* PRAISE, acclaim, acclamation, admiration, commendation, adulation, favour, approbation, approval, respect; compliments, accolades, tributes; *informal* props.

apple ▶ noun. *See table.*

Apples

Braeburn	Lodi
Bramley	McIntosh
codling	Melba ✤
Cortland	Mutsu
Cox's orange pippin	Newtown
crab	Norland
Crimson Beauty	Northern Spy
Crispin	Paula Red
Delicious	pippin
Duchess	Red Rome Beauty
Elstar	Rhode Island Greening
Empire	Royal Gala
Fameuse ✤	Sandow
Fuji	russet
Golden Delicious	Sinta
Golden Russet	Snow Apple ✤
Granny Smith	Spartan ✤
Gravenstein	Sunrise
greening	sweeting
Ida Red	Vista Bella
Jersey Mac	Winesap
Jonagold	Wolf River
Jonamac	Yellow Transparent ✤
Lobo	

appliance ▶ noun *domestic appliances* DEVICE, machine, instrument, gadget, contraption, apparatus, utensil, implement, tool, mechanism, contrivance, labour-saving device; *informal* gizmo. *See table.*

Kitchen Aids and Appliances

blender	icemaker
broiler	microwave
can opener	mixer
coffee maker	Mixmaster*
deep fryer	pastry blender
dicer	refrigerator
dishwasher	stove
food processor	toaster
garbage disposal	toaster oven
garburator ✤	waffle iron
hot plate	*Proprietary term.

applicable ▶ adjective *the laws applicable to the dispute* RELEVANT, appropriate, pertinent, appurtenant, apposite, germane, material, significant, related, connected; fitting, suitable, apt, befitting, to the point, useful, helpful.
– OPPOSITES: inappropriate, irrelevant.

applicant ▶ noun CANDIDATE, interviewee, competitor, contestant, contender, entrant; claimant, suppliant, supplicant, petitioner, postulant; prospective student/employee, job-seeker, job-hunter, auditioner.

application ▶ noun **1** *an application for a loan* REQUEST, appeal, petition, entreaty, plea, solicitation, supplication, requisition, suit, approach, claim, demand. **2** *the application of anti-inflation policies* IMPLEMENTATION, use, exercise, employment, utilization, practice, applying, discharge, execution, prosecution, enactment; *formal* praxis. **3** *the argument is clearest in its application to the theatre* RELEVANCE, relevancy, bearing, significance, pertinence, aptness, appositeness, germaneness, importance. **4** *the*

application of makeup PUTTING ON, rubbing in, applying. **5** *a smelly application to relieve muscle pain* OINTMENT, lotion, cream, rub, salve, emollient, preparation, liniment, embrocation, balm, unguent, poultice. **6** *a vector graphics application* PROGRAM, software, routine.

apply ▶ verb **1** *300 people applied for the job* PUT IN AN APPLICATION, put in, try, bid, appeal, petition, sue, register, audition; request, seek, solicit, claim, ask, try to obtain. **2** *the Act did not apply to Quebec* BE RELEVANT, have relevance, have a bearing, appertain, pertain, relate, concern, affect, involve, cover, deal with, touch; be pertinent, be appropriate, be significant. **3** *she applied some ointment* PUT ON, rub in, work in, spread, smear. **4** *a steady pressure should be applied* EXERT, administer, implement, use, exercise, employ, utilize, bring to bear.
■ **apply oneself** BE DILIGENT, be industrious, be assiduous, show commitment, show dedication; work hard, exert oneself, make an effort, try hard, do one's best, give one's all, buckle/hunker/knuckle down, put one's shoulder to the wheel, put one's nose to the grindstone; strive, endeavour, struggle, labour, toil; pay attention, commit oneself, devote oneself; persevere, persist; put one's back into it.

appoint ▶ verb **1** *he was appointed chairman* NOMINATE, name, designate, install as, commission, engage, co-opt; select, choose, elect, vote in; *Military* detail. **2** *the arbitrator shall appoint a date for the meeting* SPECIFY, determine, assign, designate, allot, set, fix, arrange, choose, decide on, establish, settle, ordain; prescribe, decree.
– OPPOSITES: reject.

appointed ▶ adjective **1** *at the appointed time* SCHEDULED, arranged, pre-arranged, specified, decided, agreed, determined, assigned, designated, allotted, set, fixed, chosen, established, settled, preordained, ordained, prescribed, decreed. **2** *a well-appointed room* FURNISHED, decorated, outfitted, fitted out, provided, supplied.

appointment ▶ noun **1** *a six o'clock appointment* MEETING, engagement, interview, arrangement, consultation, session; date, rendezvous, assignation; commitment, fixture. **2** *the appointment of directors* NOMINATION, naming, designation, installation, commissioning, engagement, co-option; selection, choosing, election, voting in; *Military* detailing. **3** *he held an appointment at the university* JOB, post, position, situation, employment, place, office; *dated* station.

apportion ▶ verb SHARE, divide, allocate, distribute, allot, assign, give out, hand out, mete out, deal out, dish out, dole out, parcel out; ration, measure out; split; *informal* divvy up.

apposite ▶ adjective APPROPRIATE, suitable, fitting, apt, befitting; relevant, pertinent, appurtenant, to the point, applicable, germane, material, congruous, felicitous; *formal* ad rem.
– OPPOSITES: inappropriate.

appraisal ▶ noun **1** *an objective appraisal of the book* ASSESSMENT, evaluation, estimation, judgment, rating, gauging, sizing up, summing-up, consideration. **2** *a free insurance appraisal* VALUATION, estimate, estimation, quotation, pricing; survey.

appraise ▶ verb **1** *they appraised their handiwork* ASSESS, evaluate, judge, rate, gauge, review, consider; *informal* size up. **2** *the goods were appraised at $1,800* VALUE, price, estimate, quote; survey.

appreciable ▶ adjective CONSIDERABLE, substantial, significant, sizeable, goodly, fair, reasonable,

marked; perceptible, noticeable, visible, discernible; *informal* tidy.
— OPPOSITES: negligible.

appreciate ▶ verb **1** *I'd appreciate your advice* BE GRATEFUL, be thankful, be obliged, be indebted, be in your debt, be appreciative. **2** *the college appreciated her greatly* VALUE, treasure, admire, respect, hold in high regard, think highly of, think much of. **3** *we appreciate your difficulty* RECOGNIZE, acknowledge, realize, know, be aware of, be conscious of, be sensitive to, understand, comprehend, grasp, fathom; *informal* be wise to. **4** *a home that will appreciate in value* INCREASE, gain, grow, rise, go up, escalate, soar, rocket.
— OPPOSITES: disparage, depreciate, decrease.

appreciation ▶ noun **1** *he showed his appreciation* GRATITUDE, thanks, gratefulness, thankfulness, recognition, sense of obligation. **2** *her appreciation of literature* VALUING, treasuring, admiration, respect, regard, esteem, high opinion. **3** *an appreciation of the difficulties involved* ACKNOWLEDGEMENT, recognition, realization, knowledge, awareness, consciousness, understanding, comprehension. **4** *a critical appreciation of the professor's work* REVIEW, critique, criticism, critical analysis, assessment, evaluation, judgment, rating.
— OPPOSITES: ingratitude, unawareness.

appreciative ▶ adjective **1** *we are appreciative of all your efforts* GRATEFUL, thankful, obliged, indebted, in someone's debt. **2** *an appreciative audience* SUPPORTIVE, encouraging, sympathetic, responsive; enthusiastic, admiring, approving, complimentary.
— OPPOSITES: ungrateful, disparaging.

apprehend ▶ verb **1** *the thieves were quickly apprehended* ARREST, catch, capture, seize; take prisoner, take into custody, detain, put in jail, put behind bars, imprison, incarcerate; *informal* bag, collar, nab, nail, run in, bust, pick up, pull in. **2** *they are slow to apprehend danger* APPRECIATE, recognize, discern, perceive, make out, take in, realize, grasp, understand, comprehend; *informal* get the picture.

apprehension ▶ noun **1** *he was filled with apprehension* ANXIETY, worry, unease, nervousness, nerves, misgivings, disquiet, concern, tension, trepidation, perturbation, consternation, angst, dread, alarm, fear, foreboding; *informal* butterflies, jitters, the willies, the creeps, the shivers, the heebie-jeebies, the jim-jams. **2** *the apprehension of a perpetrator* ARREST, capture, seizure; detention, imprisonment, incarceration; *informal* collar, nabbing, bagging, busting.
— OPPOSITES: confidence.

apprehensive ▶ adjective ANXIOUS, worried, uneasy, nervous, concerned, agitated, tense, afraid, scared, frightened, fearful; *informal* on tenterhooks.
— OPPOSITES: confident.

apprentice ▶ noun TRAINEE, learner, probationer, novice, beginner, starter, cadet; pupil, student; *informal* rookie, newbie, greenhorn; tenderfoot.
— OPPOSITES: veteran.
▶ verb *he learned the profession by apprenticing with Pratt's firm* INTERN, *Law* article ♣.

apprise ▶ verb INFORM, tell, notify, advise, brief, make aware, enlighten, update, keep posted; *informal* clue in, fill in, bring up to speed.

approach ▶ verb **1** *she approached the altar* MOVE TOWARDS, come/go towards, advance towards, inch towards, go/come/draw/move nearer, go/come/draw/move closer, near; close in, gain on; reach, arrive at.

2 *the trade deficit is approaching $20 million* BORDER ON, verge on, approximate, touch, nudge, near, come near to, come close to. **3** *she approached him about leaving his job* SPEAK TO, talk to; make advances, make overtures, make a proposal, sound out, proposition. **4** *he approached the problem in the best way* TACKLE, set about, address oneself to, undertake, get down to, launch into, embark on, go about, come to grips with.
— OPPOSITES: leave.
▶ noun **1** *a typical male approach* METHOD, procedure, technique, modus operandi, MO, style, way, manner; strategy, tactic, system, means. **2** *the dog barked at the approach of any intruder* ADVANCE, coming, nearing; arrival, appearance; advent. **3** *the approach to the castle* DRIVEWAY, drive, access road, road, avenue; way.

approachable ▶ adjective **1** *students found the staff approachable* FRIENDLY, welcoming, pleasant, agreeable, congenial, affable, cordial; obliging, communicative, helpful. **2** *the south landing is approachable by boat* ACCESSIBLE, attainable, reachable; *informal* get-at-able.
— OPPOSITES: aloof, inaccessible.

approbation ▶ noun APPROVAL, acceptance, endorsement, appreciation, respect, admiration, commendation, praise, congratulations, acclaim, esteem, applause; consent, go-ahead.
— OPPOSITES: criticism.

appropriate ▶ adjective *this isn't the appropriate time* SUITABLE, proper, fitting, apt, right; relevant, pertinent, apposite; convenient, opportune; seemly, befitting; *formal* ad rem; *archaic* meet.
— OPPOSITES: unsuitable.
▶ verb **1** *the barons appropriated church lands* SEIZE, commandeer, expropriate, annex, arrogate, sequestrate, sequester, take over, hijack; steal, take; *informal* swipe, nab, (*Nfld*) buck ♣, bag, pinch. **2** *his images have been appropriated by advertisers* PLAGIARIZE, copy; poach, steal, 'borrow'; *informal* rip off. **3** *we are appropriating funds for these expenses* ALLOCATE, assign, allot, earmark, set aside, devote, apportion.

approval ▶ noun **1** *their proposals went to the ministry for approval* ACCEPTANCE, agreement, consent, assent, permission, leave, the nod; rubber stamp, sanction, endorsement, ratification, authorization, validation; support, backing; *informal* the go-ahead, the green light, the OK, the thumbs up. **2** *Lily looked at him with approval* APPROBATION, appreciation, favour, liking, admiration, regard, esteem, respect, praise.
— OPPOSITES: refusal, dislike.

approve ▶ verb **1** *his boss doesn't approve of his lifestyle* AGREE WITH, endorse, support, back, uphold, subscribe to, recommend, advocate, be in favour of, favour, think well of, like, appreciate, go for, hold with, take kindly to; be pleased with, admire, applaud, praise. **2** *the government approved the proposals* ACCEPT, agree to, consent to, assent to, give one's blessing to, bless, rubber-stamp, give the nod; ratify, sanction, endorse, authorize, validate, pass; support, back; *informal* give the go-ahead, give the green light, give the OK, give the thumbs-up.
— OPPOSITES: condemn, refuse.

approximate ▶ adjective *approximate dimensions* ESTIMATED, rough, imprecise, inexact, indefinite, broad, loose; *informal* ballpark.
— OPPOSITES: precise.
▶ verb *the sound approximates that of a cow* RESEMBLE, be similar to, be not unlike; be/come close to, be/come near to, approach, border on, verge on.

approximately ▶ adverb ROUGHLY, about, around, circa, more or less, in the neighbourhood of, in the region of, of the order of, something like, round about, give or take (a few); near to, close to, nearly, almost, approaching; *informal* pushing, in the ballpark of.
− OPPOSITES: precisely.

approximation ▶ noun **1** *the figure is only an approximation* ESTIMATE, estimation, guess, rough calculation; *informal* guesstimate, ballpark figure. **2** *an approximation to the truth* SEMBLANCE, resemblance, likeness, similarity, correspondence.

appurtenances ▶ plural noun ACCESSORIES, trappings, appendages, accoutrements, equipment, paraphernalia, impedimenta, bits and pieces, things; *informal* stuff.

a priori ▶ adjective *a priori reasoning* THEORETICAL, deduced, deductive, inferred, postulated, suppositional.
− OPPOSITES: empirical, a posteriori.
▶ adverb *the results cannot be predicted a priori* THEORETICALLY, deductively, scientifically.

apron ▶ noun PINAFORE, overall; *informal* pinny; bib.

apropos ▶ preposition *he was asked a question apropos his resignation* WITH REFERENCE TO, with regard to, with respect to, regarding, concerning, on the subject of, connected with, about, re.
▶ adjective *the word 'conglomerate' was decidedly apropos* APPROPRIATE, pertinent, relevant, apposite, apt, applicable, suitable, germane, fitting, befitting, material; right on.
− OPPOSITES: inappropriate.
■ **apropos of nothing** IRRELEVANTLY, arbitrarily, at random, for no reason, illogically.

apt ▶ adjective **1** *a very apt description of how I felt* SUITABLE, fitting, appropriate, befitting, relevant, germane, applicable, apposite. **2** *they're apt to get a bit sloppy* INCLINED, given, likely, liable, disposed, predisposed, prone. **3** *an apt pupil* CLEVER, quick, bright, sharp, smart, intelligent, able, gifted, adept, astute.
− OPPOSITES: inappropriate, unlikely, slow.

aptitude ▶ noun TALENT, gift, flair, bent, skill, knack, facility, ability, proficiency, capability, potential, capacity, faculty, genius.

aquatic ▶ adjective MARINE, water, saltwater, freshwater, seawater, sea, oceanic, river; *technical* pelagic, thalassic.

aqueduct ▶ noun CONDUIT, race, channel, chute, watercourse, sluice, sluiceway, spillway.

aquiline ▶ adjective *an aquiline nose* HOOKED, curved, bent, angular, Roman; beak-like, beaky.

arable ▶ adjective FARMABLE, cultivable; fertile, productive.

arachnid ▶ noun. *See table at* SPIDER.

arbiter ▶ noun **1** *an arbiter between Moscow and Washington. See* ARBITRATOR. **2** *the great arbiter of fashion* AUTHORITY, judge, controller, director; master, expert, pundit.

arbitrary ▶ adjective **1** *an arbitrary decision* CAPRICIOUS, whimsical, random, chance, unpredictable; casual, wanton, unmotivated, motiveless, unreasoned, unsupported, irrational, illogical, groundless, unjustified; personal, discretionary, subjective. **2** *the arbitrary power of a prince* AUTOCRATIC, dictatorial, autarchic, undemocratic, despotic, tyrannical, authoritarian,

high-handed; absolute, uncontrolled, unlimited, unrestrained.
− OPPOSITES: reasoned, democratic.

arbitrate ▶ verb ADJUDICATE, judge, referee, umpire; mediate, conciliate, intervene, intercede; settle, decide, resolve, pass judgment.

arbitration ▶ noun ADJUDICATION, judgment, arbitrament; mediation, mediatorship, conciliation, settlement, intervention.

arbitrator ▶ noun ADJUDICATOR, arbiter, judge, referee, umpire; mediator, conciliator, intervenor, intercessor, go-between.

arbour ▶ noun BOWER, pergola; alcove, grotto, recess, gazebo.

arc ▶ noun *the arc of a circle* CURVE, arch, crescent, semicircle, half-moon; curvature, convexity.
▶ verb *I sent the ball arcing out over the river* CURL, curve; arch.

arcade ▶ noun **1** *a classical arcade* COLONNADE, gallery, cloister, loggia, portico, peristyle, stoa. **2** *playing hooky at the arcade* VIDEO ARCADE, video parlour, amusement arcade.

arcane ▶ adjective MYSTERIOUS, secret; enigmatic, esoteric, cryptic, obscure, abstruse, recondite, recherché, impenetrable, opaque.

arch¹ ▶ noun **1** *a stone arch* ARCHWAY, vault, span, dome. **2** *the arch of his spine* CURVE, bow, bend, arc, curvature, convexity; hunch, crook.
▶ verb *she arched her eyebrows* CURVE, arc.

arch² ▶ adjective *an arch grin* MISCHIEVOUS, teasing, saucy, knowing, playful, roguish, impish, cheeky, tongue-in-cheek.

arch- ▶ combining form *his arch-enemy* CHIEF, principal, foremost, leading, main, major, prime, premier, greatest, number-one.
− OPPOSITES: minor.

archaic ▶ adjective OBSOLETE, out of date, old-fashioned, outmoded, behind the times, bygone, anachronistic, antiquated, superannuated, antediluvian, olde worlde, old-fangled; ancient, old, extinct, defunct; prehistoric; *literary* of yore.
− OPPOSITES: modern.

archetypal ▶ adjective QUINTESSENTIAL, classic, most typical, representative, model, exemplary, textbook; stock, stereotypical, prototypical.
− OPPOSITES: atypical.

archetype ▶ noun QUINTESSENCE, essence, representative, model, embodiment, prototype, stereotype; original, pattern, standard, paradigm.

architect ▶ noun **1** *the architect of Durham Cathedral* DESIGNER, planner, draftsman. **2** *Andrew was the architect of the plan* ORIGINATOR, author, creator, founder, (founding) father; engineer, inventor, mastermind; *literary* begetter.

architecture ▶ noun **1** *modern architecture* BUILDING DESIGN, building style, planning, building, construction; *formal* architectonics. **2** *the architecture of a computer system* STRUCTURE, construction, organization, layout, design, build, anatomy, makeup; *informal* set-up.

archive ▶ noun **1** *she delved into the family archives* RECORDS, annals, chronicles, accounts; papers, documents, files; history; *Law* muniments. **2** *the national archive* RECORD OFFICE, registry, repository, depository, museum, chancery.
▶ verb *the videos are archived for future use* FILE, log, catalogue, document, record, register; store, cache.

arctic ▶ adjective **1** *Arctic waters* POLAR, far northern,

Architectural Styles

Art Deco	Ionic
Art Nouveau	Islamic
baroque	Jacobean
Bauhaus	medieval
beaux-arts	modernist
brutalist	Moorish
Byzantine	Moresque
Carolingian	Mozarabic
Château style ♣	neoclassical
Churrigueresque	neo-Gothic
cinquecento	Norman
classical	Palladian
colonial	Perpendicular
Corinthian	postmodernist
Decorated	Prairie Style
Doric	quattrocento
Early Christian	Queen Anne
Early English	Regency
Early Renaissance	Renaissance
Edwardian	rococo
Elizabethan	Roman
Empire	Romanesque
flamboyant	Saxon
functional	Spanish-Colonial
Georgian	Spanish-Mission
Gothic	Tudor
Gothic Revival	Tudorbethan
Greco-Roman	Tuscan
Grecian	vernacular
Greek Revival	Victorian Gothic
International Style	

boreal; *literary* hyperborean. **2** *arctic weather conditions* (BITTERLY) COLD, wintry, freezing, frozen, icy, glacial, hypothermic, gelid, sub-zero, polar, Siberian, bone-chilling.
– OPPOSITES: Antarctic, tropical.
▶ noun FAR NORTH, High Arctic, North Pole, Arctic Circle, North of Sixty ♣.
– OPPOSITES: Antarctic.

ardent ▶ adjective PASSIONATE, fervent, zealous, fervid, *literary* perfervid, wholehearted, vehement, intense, fierce, fiery; enthusiastic, keen, eager, avid, committed, dedicated.
– OPPOSITES: apathetic.

ardour ▶ noun PASSION, fervour, zeal, vehemence, intensity, verve, fire, emotion; enthusiasm, eagerness, avidity, gusto, keenness, dedication.

arduous ▶ adjective ONEROUS, taxing, difficult, hard, heavy, laborious, burdensome, strenuous, vigorous, back-breaking; demanding, tough, challenging, formidable; exhausting, tiring, punishing, gruelling; uphill, steep; *informal* killing; toilsome.
– OPPOSITES: easy.

area ▶ noun **1** *an inner-city area* DISTRICT, region, zone, sector, quarter, precinct; locality, locale, neighbourhood, parish, patch; tract, belt; *informal* neck of the woods, turf. **2** *specific areas of scientific knowledge* FIELD, sphere, discipline, realm, domain, sector, province, territory, line. **3** *the dining area* SECTION, space; place, room. **4** *the area of a circle* EXPANSE, extent, size, scope, compass; dimensions, proportions.

arena ▶ noun **1** *a hockey arena* STADIUM, rink, ice rink, ice pad ♣, ice palace ♣, *dated* hockey cushion ♣; amphitheatre, coliseum; sportsplex; ground, field, ring, pitch, court; bowl, park; *historical* circus. **2** *the political arena* SCENE, sphere, realm, province, domain, sector, forum, territory, world.

argot ▶ noun JARGON, slang, idiom, cant, parlance, vernacular, patois; dialect, speech, language; *informal* lingo.

arguable ▶ adjective **1** *he had an arguable claim for asylum* TENABLE, defendable, defensible, supportable, sustainable, plausible, able to hold water; reasonable, viable, acceptable. **2** *it is arguable whether these routes are worthwhile* DEBATABLE, questionable, open to question, controversial, contentious, doubtful, uncertain, moot.
– OPPOSITES: untenable, certain.

arguably ▶ adverb POSSIBLY, conceivably, feasibly, plausibly, probably, maybe, perhaps.

argue ▶ verb **1** *they argued that the government was to blame* CONTEND, assert, maintain, insist, hold, claim, reason, allege; *formal* aver, represent, opine. **2** *the children are always arguing* QUARREL, disagree, row, squabble, fall out, bicker, fight, wrangle, dispute, feud, have words, cross swords, lock horns, be at each other's throats; *informal* spat. **3** *it is hard to argue the point* DISPUTE, debate, discuss, controvert, deny, question.

argument ▶ noun **1** *he had an argument with Tony* QUARREL, disagreement, squabble, fight, dispute, wrangle, clash, altercation, feud, contretemps, disputation, falling-out; *informal* tiff, row, blow-up, rhubarb. **2** *arguments for the existence of God* REASONING, justification, explanation, rationalization; case, defence, vindication; evidence, reasons, grounds. **3** *the argument of the book* THEME, topic, subject matter; summary, synopsis, précis, gist, outline.

argumentative ▶ adjective QUARRELSOME, disputatious, captious, contrary, cantankerous, contentious; belligerent, bellicose, combative, antagonistic, truculent, pugnacious.

arid ▶ adjective **1** *an arid landscape* DRY, dried up, bone-dry, waterless, moistureless, parched, scorched, baked, thirsty, droughty, desert; BARREN, infertile. **2** *this town has an arid, empty feel* DREARY, dull, drab, dry, sterile, colourless, unstimulating, uninspiring, flat, boring, uninteresting, lifeless, emotionless, plain-vanilla.
– OPPOSITES: wet, fertile, vibrant.

arise ▶ verb **1** *many problems arose* COME TO LIGHT, become apparent, appear, emerge, crop up, turn up, surface, spring up; occur; *literary* befall, come to pass. **2** *injuries arising from defective products* RESULT, proceed, follow, ensue, stem, originate; be caused by. **3** *the beast arose* STAND UP, rise, get to one's feet, get up.

aristocracy ▶ noun NOBILITY, peerage, gentry, gentility, upper class, ruling class, elite, high society, establishment, haut monde; aristocrats, lords, ladies, peers (of the realm), nobles, noblemen, noblewomen; *informal* upper crust, top drawer, aristos.
– OPPOSITES: working class.

aristocrat ▶ noun NOBLEMAN, noblewoman, lord, lady, peer (of the realm), peeress, grandee; blueblood; *informal* aristo.
– OPPOSITES: commoner.

aristocratic ▶ adjective **1** *an aristocratic family* NOBLE, titled, upper-class, blue-blooded, high-born, well-born, elite; *informal* upper crust, top drawer. **2** *an aristocratic manner* REFINED, polished, courtly,

dignified, posh, decorous, gracious, fine; haughty, proud.
— OPPOSITES: working-class, vulgar.

arm ▶ noun **1** *an arm of the sea* INLET, creek, cove, fjord, bay; estuary, strait(s), sound, channel. **2** *the political arm of the group* BRANCH, section, department, division, wing, sector, detachment, offshoot, extension. **3** *the long arm of the law* REACH, power, authority, influence.
▶ verb *he armed himself with a revolver* EQUIP, provide, supply, furnish, issue, outfit, fit out.

armada ▶ noun FLEET, flotilla, squadron, navy.

armaments ▶ plural noun ARMS, weapons, weaponry, firearms, guns, ordnance, artillery, munitions, matériel, hardware.

armed forces ▶ plural noun MILITARY, service(s), army, navy, air force; troops, soldiers. *See also* CANADIAN FORCES. *For Canadian military ranks see table at* RANK.

armful ▶ noun ARMLOAD, yaffle ✤, bunch, load.

armistice ▶ noun TRUCE, ceasefire, peace, suspension of hostilities.

armour ▶ noun PROTECTIVE COVERING, armour plate, shield; chain mail, coat of mail, panoply; armoured vehicles, tanks; carapace.

armoured ▶ adjective ARMOUR-PLATED, steel-plated, ironclad; bulletproof, bombproof; reinforced, toughened.

armoury ▶ noun ARSENAL, arms depot, arms cache, ordnance depot, magazine, ammunition dump.

armpit ▶ noun **1** *wash your armpits* UNDERARM, pit; *technical* axilla. **2** *this town is a real armpit* DUMP, hole, hell, the pits.

arms ▶ plural noun **1** *the illegal export of arms* WEAPONS, weaponry, firearms, guns, ordnance, artillery, armaments, munitions, matériel. **2** *the family arms* CREST, emblem, coat of arms, heraldic device, insignia, escutcheon, shield.
— RELATED TERMS: heraldic.

army ▶ noun **1** *the invading army* ARMED FORCE, military force, land force, military, soldiery, infantry, militia; troops, soldiers; *archaic* host. *See also* CANADIAN FORCES. *For Canadian military ranks see table at* RANK. **2** *an army of tourists* CROWD, swarm, multitude, horde, mob, gang, throng, mass, flock, herd, pack.
— RELATED TERMS: military, martial.

aroma ▶ noun SCENT, fragrance, perfume, smell, bouquet, balm, nose, odour, whiff; *literary* redolence.

aromatic ▶ adjective FRAGRANT, scented, perfumed, fragranced, odorous; *literary* redolent.

around ▶ adverb **1** *there were houses scattered around* ON EVERY SIDE, on all sides, throughout, all over (the place), everywhere; about, here and there. **2** *he turned around* IN THE OPPOSITE DIRECTION, to face the other way, backwards, to the rear. **3** *there was no one around* NEARBY, near, about, close by, close (at hand), at hand, in the vicinity, at close range.
▶ preposition **1** *the palazzo is built around a courtyard* ON ALL SIDES OF, about, encircling, surrounding, enclosing. **2** *they drove around town* ABOUT, all over, in/to all parts of. **3** *around three miles* APPROXIMATELY, about, round about, circa, roughly, something like, more or less, in the region of, in the neighbourhood of, give or take (a few); nearly, close to, approaching; getting on for, in the ballpark of.

arouse ▶ verb **1** *they had aroused his suspicion* INDUCE, prompt, trigger, stir up, bring out, kindle, fire, spark off, provoke, engender, cause, foster; *literary* enkindle. **2** *his ability to arouse the masses* STIR UP, rouse,

galvanize, excite, electrify, stimulate, inspire, inspirit, move, fire up, whip up, get going, inflame, agitate, goad, incite. **3** *his touch aroused her* EXCITE, stimulate, titillate; *informal* turn on, get going, give a thrill to, light someone's fire. **4** *she was aroused from her sleep* WAKE (UP), awaken, bring to, rouse; *literary* waken.
— OPPOSITES: allay, pacify, turn off.

arraign ▶ verb **1** *he was arraigned for murder* INDICT, prosecute, put on trial, bring to trial, take to court, lay/prefer charges against, summons, cite; accuse of, charge with, incriminate; *archaic* inculpate. **2** *they bitterly arraigned the government* CRITICIZE, censure, impugn, attack, condemn, chastise, lambaste, rebuke, admonish, remonstrate with, take to task, berate, reproach; *informal* knock, slam, blast, lay into; castigate, excoriate.
— OPPOSITES: acquit, praise.

arrange ▶ verb **1** *she arranged the flowers* ORDER, set out, lay out, array, position, dispose, present, display, exhibit; group, sort, organize, tidy. **2** *they hoped to arrange a meeting* ORGANIZE, fix (up), plan, schedule, pencil in, contrive, settle on, decide, determine, agree. **3** *he arranged the piece for a full orchestra* ADAPT, set, score, orchestrate, transcribe, instrument.

arrangement ▶ noun **1** *the arrangement of the furniture* POSITIONING, disposition, order, presentation, display, grouping, organization, alignment. **2** *the arrangements for my trip* PREPARATION, plan, provision; planning, groundwork. **3** *we had an arrangement* AGREEMENT, deal, understanding, bargain, settlement, pact, modus vivendi. **4** *an arrangement of Beethoven's symphonies* ADAPTATION, orchestration, instrumentation.

arrant ▶ adjective *what arrant nonsense!* UTTER, complete, total, absolute, downright, outright, thorough, out-and-out, sheer, pure, unmitigated, unqualified; blatant, flagrant.

array ▶ noun **1** *a huge array of cars* RANGE, collection, selection, assortment, diversity, variety; arrangement, assemblage, lineup, formation; display, exhibition, exposition. **2** *she arrived in silken array* DRESS, attire, clothing, garb, garments; finery, apparel.
▶ verb **1** *a buffet was arrayed on the table* ARRANGE, assemble, group, order, place, position, set out, exhibit, lay out, dispose, display. **2** *he was arrayed in grey flannel* DRESS, attire, clothe, garb, deck (out), outfit, get up, turn out; *archaic* apparel.

arrears ▶ plural noun *rent arrears* MONEY OWING, outstanding payment(s), debt(s), liabilities, dues.
— OPPOSITES: credit.
■ **in arrears** BEHIND, behindhand, late, overdue, in the red, in debt.

arrest ▶ verb **1** *police arrested him for murder* APPREHEND, take into custody, take prisoner, imprison, incarcerate, detain, jail, put in jail; *informal* pick up, pull in, run in, pinch, bust, nab, collar. **2** *the spread of the disease can be arrested* STOP, halt, check, block, hinder, restrict, limit, inhibit, impede, curb; prevent, obstruct; *literary* stay. **3** *she tried to arrest his attention* ATTRACT, capture, catch, hold, engage; absorb, occupy, engross.
— OPPOSITES: release, start.
▶ noun **1** *a warrant for your arrest* DETENTION, apprehension, seizure, capture, takedown. **2** *a cardiac arrest* STOPPAGE, halt, interruption.

arresting ▶ adjective *an arresting image* STRIKING, eye-catching, conspicuous, engaging, engrossing,

fascinating, impressive, imposing, spectacular, dramatic, breathtaking, dazzling, stunning, awe-inspiring; remarkable, outstanding, distinctive.
— OPPOSITES: inconspicuous.

arrival ▶ noun **1** *they awaited Ruth's arrival* COMING, appearance, entrance, entry, approach. **2** *staff greeted the late arrivals* COMER, entrant, incomer; visitor, caller, guest.
— OPPOSITES: departure, end.

arrive ▶ verb **1** *more police arrived* COME, turn up, get here/there, make it, appear, enter, present oneself, come along, materialize; *informal* show (up), roll in/up, blow in, show one's face. **2** *we arrived at his house* REACH, get to, come to, make, make it to, gain, end up at; *informal* wind up at. **3** *they arrived at an agreement* REACH, achieve, attain, gain, accomplish; work out, draw up, put together, strike, settle on; *informal* clinch. **4** *the wedding finally arrived* HAPPEN, occur, take place, come about; present itself, crop up; *literary* come to pass. **5** *CD-ROMs arrived in the late eighties* EMERGE, appear, surface, come on the scene, dawn, be born, come into being, arise. **6** (*informal*) *their Rolls Royce proved that they had arrived* SUCCEED, be a success, do well, reach the top, make good, prosper, thrive; *informal* make it, make one's mark, do all right for oneself.
— OPPOSITES: depart, leave.

arrogant ▶ adjective HAUGHTY, conceited, self-important, egotistic, full of oneself, superior; overbearing, pompous, bumptious, presumptuous, imperious, overweening; proud, immodest; *informal* high and mighty, too big for one's britches/boots, big-headed, puffed-up; *rare* hubristic.
— OPPOSITES: modest.

arrogate ▶ verb ASSUME, take, claim, appropriate, seize, expropriate, wrest, usurp, commandeer.

arrow ▶ noun **1** *a bow and arrow* SHAFT, bolt, dart; *historical* quarrel. **2** *the arrow pointed right* POINTER, indicator, marker, needle.

arrow sash (*Cdn*) ▶ noun ceinture fléchée ✦, voyageur sash ✦, Assomption sash ✦.

arsenal ▶ noun **1** *Britain's nuclear arsenal* WEAPONS, weaponry, arms, armaments. **2** *mutineers broke into the arsenal* ARMOURY, arms depot, arms cache, ordnance depot, magazine, ammunition dump.

arson ▶ noun PYROMANIA, incendiarism, torching.

arsonist ▶ noun INCENDIARY, pyromaniac; *informal* firebug, pyro.

art ▶ noun **1** *the art of writing* SKILL, craft, technique, knack, facility, ability, know-how. **2** *she uses art to achieve her aims* CUNNING, artfulness, slyness, craftiness, guile; deceit, duplicity, artifice, wiles.

artful ▶ adjective **1** *artful politicians* SLY, crafty, cunning, wily, scheming, devious, Machiavellian, sneaky, tricky, conniving, designing, calculating; canny, shrewd; deceitful, duplicitous, disingenuous, underhanded; *informal* foxy, shifty; *archaic* subtle. **2** *artful precision* SKILFUL, clever, adept, adroit, skilled, expert.
— OPPOSITES: ingenuous.

article ▶ noun **1** *small household articles* ITEM, thing, object, artifact, commodity, product. **2** *an article in the paper* REPORT, account, story, write-up, feature, item, piece, column, review, commentary. **3** *the crucial article of the treaty* CLAUSE, section, subsection, point, item, paragraph, division, subdivision, part, portion.
▶ verb (*Cdn*) *Law* APPRENTICE.

Art Techniques and Media

acrylic painting	mezzotint
airbrushing	miniature painting
aquatint	montage
batik	mosaic
birchbark biting	mural painting
brass rubbing	oil painting
calligraphy	painting
cartooning	pastel
ceramics	photography
cloisonné	photogravure
collage	photomontage
colour print	pointillism
colour wash	screen printing
conté	sculpture
drawing	scumbling
dry-point	sgraffito
enamelling	silk painting
encaustic	silk-screen printing
engraving	sketching
etching	soapstone carving
finger painting	spray-painting
fresco	stained glass
gouache	stonecut
grisaille	tachism
illumination	tapestry
impasto	technical drawing
intaglio	tempera
lino cut	trompe l'oeil
lithography	tufting ✦
lost wax	watercolour
marbling	wood carving
marquetry	woodcut
metalwork	wood engraving

articulate ▶ adjective *an articulate speaker* ELOQUENT, fluent, effective, persuasive, lucid, expressive, silver-tongued; intelligible, comprehensible, understandable.
— OPPOSITES: unintelligible.
▶ verb *they were unable to articulate their emotions* EXPRESS, voice, vocalize, put in words, communicate, state; air, ventilate, vent, pour out; utter, say, speak, enunciate, pronounce; *informal* come out with.

articulated ▶ adjective HINGED, jointed, segmented; *technical* articulate.

artifact ▶ noun RELIC, article; handiwork.

artifice ▶ noun TRICKERY, deceit, deception, duplicity, guile, cunning, artfulness, wiliness, craftiness, slyness, chicanery; fraud, fraudulence.

artificial ▶ adjective **1** *artificial flowers* SYNTHETIC, fake, imitation, mock, ersatz, faux, substitute, replica, reproduction; man-made, manufactured, fabricated, inorganic; plastic; *informal* pretend, phony. **2** *an artificial smile* INSINCERE, feigned, false, unnatural, contrived, put-on, exaggerated, forced, laboured, strained, hollow; *informal* pretend, phony, bogus.
— OPPOSITES: natural, genuine.

artillery ▶ noun ORDNANCE, (big) guns, cannon(s); battery.

artisan ▶ noun CRAFTSMAN, craftswoman, craftsperson; skilled worker, technician; smith, wright, journeyman; *archaic* artificer.

artist ▶ noun **1** *a mural artist* DESIGNER, creator, originator, producer; old master. **2** *the surgeon is an artist with the knife* EXPERT, master, maestro, past

master, virtuoso, genius; *informal* pro, ace.
— OPPOSITES: novice.

artistic ▶ adjective **1** *he's very artistic* CREATIVE, imaginative, inventive, expressive; sensitive, perceptive, discerning; *informal* artsy. **2** *artistic touches* AESTHETIC, aesthetically pleasing, beautiful, attractive, fine; decorative, ornamental; tasteful, stylish, elegant, exquisite.
— OPPOSITES: unimaginative, inelegant.

artistry ▶ noun CREATIVE SKILL, creativity, art, skill, talent, genius, brilliance, flair, proficiency, virtuosity, finesse, style; craftsmanship, workmanship.

artless ▶ adjective NATURAL, ingenuous, naive, simple, innocent, childlike, guileless; candid, open, sincere, unaffected.
— OPPOSITES: scheming.

as ▶ conjunction **1** *she looked up as he entered the room* WHILE, just as, even as, (just) when, at the time that, at the moment that. **2** *we all felt as Frank did* IN THE (SAME) WAY THAT, the (same) way; *informal* like. **3** *do as you're told* WHAT, that which. **4** *they were free, as the case had not been proved* BECAUSE, since, seeing that/as, in view of the fact that, owing to the fact that; *informal* on account of; *literary* for. **5** *try as she did, she couldn't smile* THOUGH, although, even though, in spite of the fact that, despite the fact that, notwithstanding that, for all that, albeit, however. **6** *relatively short distances, as Fredericton to Saint John* SUCH AS, like, for instance, e.g., for example. **7** *I'm away a lot, as you know* WHICH, a fact which.
▶ preposition **1** *he was dressed as a policeman* LIKE, in the guise of, so as to appear to be. **2** *I'm speaking to you as your friend* IN THE ROLE OF, being, acting as.
■ **as for/as to** CONCERNING, with respect to, on the subject of, in the matter of, as regards, with regard to, regarding, with reference to, re, in re, apropos, vis-à-vis.
■ **as it were** SO TO SPEAK, in a manner of speaking, to some extent, so to say; *informal* sort of.
■ **as yet** SO FAR, thus far, yet, still, up till now, up to now.

ascend ▶ verb CLIMB, go up/upwards, move up/upwards, rise (up), clamber (up); mount, scale, conquer; take to the air, take off; rocket.
— OPPOSITES: descend.

ascendancy ▶ noun DOMINANCE, domination, supremacy, superiority, paramountcy, predominance, primacy, dominion, hegemony, authority, control, command, power, rule, sovereignty, lordship, leadership, influence.
— OPPOSITES: subordination.

ascendant ▶ adjective RISING (IN POWER), on the rise, on the way up, up-and-coming, flourishing, prospering, burgeoning.
— OPPOSITES: declining.

ascent ▶ noun **1** *the first ascent of the Matterhorn* CLIMB, scaling, conquest. **2** *a balloon ascent* RISE, climb, launch, takeoff, liftoff, blast-off. **3** *the ascent grew steeper* (UPWARD) SLOPE, incline, rise, upward gradient, inclination.
— OPPOSITES: descent, drop.

ascertain ▶ verb FIND OUT, discover, get to know, work out, make out, fathom, learn, deduce, divine, discern, see, understand, comprehend; establish, determine, verify, confirm; figure out.

ascetic ▶ adjective *an ascetic life* AUSTERE, self-denying, abstinent, abstemious, self-disciplined;

self-abnegating; simple, puritanical, monastic; reclusive, eremitic, hermitic; celibate, chaste.
— OPPOSITES: sybaritic.
▶ noun *a desert ascetic* ABSTAINER, puritan, recluse, hermit, anchorite, solitary; fakir, Sufi, dervish, sadhu; *archaic* eremite.
— OPPOSITES: sybarite.

ascribe ▶ verb ATTRIBUTE, assign, put down, accredit, credit, chalk up, impute; blame on, lay at the door of; connect with, associate with.

ash ▶ noun CINDERS, ashes, clinker.

ashamed ▶ adjective *I was too ashamed to return her call* SORRY, shamefaced, abashed, sheepish, guilty, contrite, remorseful, repentant, penitent, regretful, rueful, apologetic; embarrassed, mortified.
— OPPOSITES: proud, pleased.

ashen ▶ adjective PALE, wan, pasty, grey, ashy, colourless, pallid, anemic, white, waxen, ghostly, bloodless.

ashore ▶ adverb ON TO (THE) LAND, on to the shore, aground; shorewards, landwards; on the shore, on (dry) land.

aside ▶ adverb **1** *they stood aside* TO ONE SIDE, to the side, on one side; apart, away, separately. **2** *that aside, he seemed a nice man* APART, notwithstanding.
▶ noun *'Her parents died,' he said in an aside* WHISPERED REMARK, confidential remark, stage whisper; digression, incidental remark, obiter dictum.
■ **aside from** APART FROM, besides, in addition to, not counting, barring, other than, but (for), excluding, not including, except (for), excepting, leaving out, save (for).

asinine ▶ adjective STUPID, foolish, brainless, mindless, senseless, idiotic, imbecilic, ridiculous, ludicrous, absurd, nonsensical, fatuous, silly, inane, witless, empty-headed; *informal* halfwitted, dim-witted, dumb, moronic.
— OPPOSITES: intelligent, sensible.

ask ▶ verb **1** *he asked what time we opened* INQUIRE, query, want to know; question, interrogate, quiz. **2** *they want to ask a few questions* PUT (FORWARD), pose, raise, submit. **3** *don't be afraid to ask for advice* REQUEST, demand; solicit, seek, crave, apply, petition, call, appeal, beg, sue. **4** *let's ask them to dinner* INVITE, bid, summon, have someone over/round.
— OPPOSITES: answer.

askance ▶ adverb *they look askance at anything foreign* SUSPICIOUSLY, skeptically, cynically, mistrustfully, distrustfully, doubtfully, dubiously; disapprovingly, contemptuously, scornfully, disdainfully.
— OPPOSITES: approvingly.

askew ▶ adjective CROOKED, lopsided, tilted, angled, at an angle, skew, skewed, slanted, aslant, awry, oblique, out of true, to/on one side, uneven, off centre, asymmetrical; *informal* cockeyed, wonky.
— OPPOSITES: straight.

asleep ▶ adjective **1** *she was asleep in bed* SLEEPING, in a deep sleep, napping, catnapping, dozing, drowsing; *informal* snoozing, catching some Z's, zonked, flaked out, hibernating, dead to the world, comatose, in the land of Nod, in the arms of Morpheus; *literary* slumbering. **2** *my leg's asleep* NUMB, with no feeling, numbed, benumbed, dead, insensible.
— OPPOSITES: awake.

aspect ▶ noun **1** *the photos depict every aspect of life* FEATURE, facet, side, characteristic, particular, detail; angle, slant. **2** *his face had a sinister aspect* APPEARANCE, look, air, cast, mien, demeanour, expression; atmosphere, mood, quality, ambience, feeling.

asperity ▶ noun HARSHNESS, sharpness, abrasiveness, roughness, severity, acerbity, astringency, tartness, sarcasm.

aspersions

■ **cast aspersions on** VILIFY, disparage, denigrate, defame, run down, impugn, belittle, criticize, condemn, decry, denounce, pillory; malign, slander, libel, discredit; *informal* pull apart, throw mud at, knock, badmouth, dis.

asphalt ▶ noun TAR, pitch, paving, blacktop, tarmac.

asphyxiate ▶ verb CHOKE (TO DEATH), suffocate, smother, stifle; throttle, strangle.

aspiration ▶ noun DESIRE, hope, dream, wish, longing, yearning; aim, ambition, expectation, goal, target.

aspire ▶ verb DESIRE, hope, dream, long, yearn, set one's heart on, wish, want, be desirous of; aim, seek, pursue, set one's sights on.

aspiring ▶ adjective WOULD-BE, aspirant, hopeful, budding; potential, prospective, future; ambitious, determined, upwardly mobile; *informal* wannabe.

ass ▶ noun **1** *he rode on an ass* DONKEY, jackass, jenny; burro. **2** *(informal) don't be a silly ass* FOOL, idiot, dolt, simpleton, imbecile; dim-wit, halfwit, dim-bulb, dummy, dumdum, loon, jackass, cretin, jerk, fathead, blockhead, jughead, boob, bozo, numbskull, numbnuts, lummox, dunce, moron, meatball, doofus, ninny, nincompoop, dipstick, hoser ♣, lamebrain, chump, pea brain, thickhead, dumb-ass, wooden-head, pinhead, airhead, birdbrain; nitwit, twit, turkey, goofball, putz; *dated* tomfool, muttonhead. **3** *See* BUTTOCKS.

assail ▶ verb **1** *the army moved in to assail the enemy* ATTACK, assault, pounce on, set upon/about, fall on, charge, rush, storm; *informal* lay into, tear into, pitch into. **2** *she was assailed by doubts* PLAGUE, torment, rack, beset, dog, trouble, disturb, worry, bedevil, nag, vex. **3** *critics assailed the policy* CRITICIZE, censure, attack, condemn, pillory, revile; *informal* knock, slam.

assailant ▶ noun ATTACKER, mugger, assaulter.

assassin ▶ noun MURDERER, killer, gunman; executioner; *informal* hit man, hired gun; *dated* homicide.

assassinate ▶ verb MURDER, kill, slaughter; eliminate, execute, liquidate; *informal* hit, terminate, knock off; *literary* slay.

assassination ▶ noun MURDER, killing, slaughter, homicide; political execution, elimination; *informal* hit; *literary* slaying.

assault ▶ verb **1** *he assaulted a police officer* ATTACK, hit, strike, punch, beat up, thump; pummel, pound, batter; *informal* clout, wallop, belt, clobber, hammer, bop, sock, deck, slug, plug, lay into, do over, rough up; *literary* smite. **2** *they left to assault the hill* ATTACK, assail, pounce on, set upon, strike, fall on, swoop on, rush, storm, besiege. **3** *he first assaulted then murdered her* RAPE, sexually assault, molest, interfere with.
▶ noun **1** *he was charged with assault* BATTERY, violence; sexual assault, rape. **2** *an assault on the city* ATTACK, strike, onslaught, offensive, charge, push, thrust, invasion, bombardment, sortie, incursion, raid, blitz, campaign.

assay ▶ noun *new plate was brought for assay* EVALUATION, assessment, appraisal, analysis, examination, tests, inspection, scrutiny.
▶ verb *gold is assayed to determine its purity* EVALUATE,

assess, appraise, analyze, examine, test, inspect, scrutinize, probe.

assemblage ▶ noun COLLECTION, accumulation, conglomeration, gathering, group, grouping, cluster, aggregation, mass, number; assortment, selection, array, miscellany.

assemble ▶ verb **1** *a crowd had assembled* GATHER, collect, get together, congregate, convene, meet, muster, rally. **2** *he assembled the suspects* BRING/CALL TOGETHER, gather, collect, round up, marshal, muster, summon; *formal* convoke. **3** *how to assemble the kite* CONSTRUCT, build, fabricate, manufacture, erect, set up, put/piece together, connect, join.
— OPPOSITES: disperse, dismantle.

assembly ▶ noun **1** *an assembly of civil servants* GATHERING, meeting, congregation, convention, rally, convocation, assemblage, group, body, crowd, throng, company; *informal* get-together. **2** *the labour needed in car assembly* CONSTRUCTION, manufacture, building, fabrication, erection.

assent ▶ noun *they are likely to give their assent* AGREEMENT, acceptance, approval, approbation, consent, acquiescence, compliance, concurrence, the nod; sanction, endorsement, confirmation; permission, leave, blessing; *informal* the go-ahead, the green light, the OK, the thumbs up.
— OPPOSITES: dissent, refusal.
▶ verb *he assented to the change* AGREE TO, accept, approve, consent to, acquiesce in, concur in, give one's blessing to, give the nod; sanction, endorse, confirm; *informal* give the go-ahead, give the green light, give the OK, OK, give the thumbs up; *formal* accede to.
— OPPOSITES: refuse.

assert ▶ verb **1** *they asserted that all aboard were safe* DECLARE, maintain, contend, argue, state, claim, propound, proclaim, announce, pronounce, swear, insist, avow; *formal* aver, opine; *rare* asseverate. **2** *we find it difficult to assert our rights* INSIST ON, stand up for, uphold, defend, contend, establish, press/push for, stress.
■ **assert oneself** BEHAVE/SPEAK CONFIDENTLY, be assertive, put oneself forward, take a stand, make one's presence felt; *informal* put one's foot down.

assertion ▶ noun **1** *I questioned his assertion* DECLARATION, contention, statement, claim, opinion, proclamation, announcement, pronouncement, protestation, avowal; *formal* averment; *rare* asseveration. **2** *an assertion of the right to march* DEFENCE, upholding; insistence on.

assertive ▶ adjective CONFIDENT, self-confident, bold, decisive, assured, self-assured, self-possessed, forthright, firm, emphatic; authoritative, strong-willed, forceful, insistent, determined, commanding, pushy; *informal* feisty.
— OPPOSITES: timid.

assess ▶ verb **1** *we need more time to assess the situation* EVALUATE, judge, gauge, rate, estimate, appraise, consider, get the measure of, determine, analyze; *informal* size up. **2** *the damage was assessed at $5 million* VALUE, calculate, work out, determine, fix, cost, price, estimate.

assessment ▶ noun **1** *a teacher's assessment of the pupil's abilities* EVALUATION, judgment, rating, estimation, appraisal, analysis, opinion. **2** *some assessments valued the estate at $2 million* VALUATION, appraisal, calculation, costing, pricing, estimate.

asset ▶ noun **1** *he sees his age as an asset* BENEFIT,

advantage, blessing, good point, strong point, selling point, strength, forte, virtue, recommendation, attraction, resource, boon, merit, bonus, plus, pro. **2** *the seizure of all their assets* PROPERTY, resources, estate, holdings, possessions, effects, goods, valuables, belongings, chattels.
− OPPOSITES: liability.

assiduous ▶ adjective DILIGENT, careful, meticulous, thorough, sedulous, attentive, conscientious, punctilious, painstaking, rigorous, particular; persevering.

assign ▶ verb **1** *a young doctor was assigned the task* ALLOCATE, allot, give, set; charge with, entrust with. **2** *she was assigned to a new post* APPOINT, promote, delegate, commission, post, co-opt; select for, choose for, install in; *Military* detail. **3** *we assign large sums of money to travel budgets* EARMARK, designate, set aside, reserve, appropriate, allot, allocate, apportion. **4** *he assigned the opinion to the Prince* ASCRIBE, attribute, put down, accredit, credit, chalk up, impute; pin on, lay at the door of. **5** *he may assign the money to a third party* TRANSFER, make over, give, pass, hand over/down, convey, consign.

assignation ▶ noun RENDEZVOUS, date, appointment, meeting; *literary* tryst.

assignment ▶ noun **1** *I'm going to finish this assignment tonight* TASK, piece of work, job, duty, chore, mission, errand, undertaking, exercise, business, endeavour, enterprise; project, homework. **2** *the assignment of tasks* ALLOCATION, allotment, issuance, designation; sharing out, apportionment, distribution, handing out, dispensation. **3** *the assignment of property* TRANSFER, making over, giving, hand down, consignment; *Law* conveyance, devise, attornment.

assimilate ▶ verb **1** *the amount of information he can assimilate* ABSORB, take in, acquire, soak up, pick up, grasp, comprehend, understand, learn, master; digest, ingest. **2** *many tribes were assimilated by Turkic peoples* SUBSUME, incorporate, integrate, absorb, engulf, acculturate; co-opt, adopt, embrace, admit. **3** *after arriving it took us some time to assimilate* INTEGRATE, blend in.

assist ▶ verb **1** *I spend my time assisting the chef* HELP, aid, lend a (helping) hand to, oblige, accommodate, serve; collaborate with, work with; support, back (up), second; abet; *informal* pitch in with. **2** *the exchange rates assisted the firm's expansion* FACILITATE, aid, ease, expedite, spur, promote, boost, benefit, foster, encourage, stimulate, precipitate, accelerate, advance, further, forward.
− OPPOSITES: hinder, impede.

assistance ▶ noun HELP, aid, support, backing, reinforcement, succour, relief, TLC, intervention, co-operation, collaboration; a (helping) hand, a good turn; *informal* a break, a leg up; social security, benefits, the dole, pogey ♣.
− OPPOSITES: hindrance.

assistant ▶ noun *a photographer's assistant* HELPER, deputy, second-in-command, second, number two, right-hand man/woman, aide, attendant, mate, apprentice, junior, auxiliary, subordinate; hired hand, hired help, man/girl Friday; *informal* sidekick, gofer.

associate ▶ verb **1** *the colours that we associate with fire* LINK, connect, relate, identify, equate, bracket, set side by side. **2** *I was forced to associate with them* MIX, keep company, mingle, socialize, go around, rub shoulders, rub elbows, fraternize, consort, have

dealings; *informal* hobnob, hang out/around. **3** *the firm is associated with a local charity* AFFILIATE, align, connect, join, attach, team up, be in league, ally; merge, integrate, confederate.
▶ noun *his business associate* PARTNER, colleague, co-worker, workmate, comrade, ally, affiliate, confederate; connection, contact, acquaintance; collaborator; *informal* crony.

associated ▶ adjective *salaries and associated costs* RELATED, connected, linked, correlated, corresponding; attendant, accompanying, incidental.
− OPPOSITES: unrelated.

association ▶ noun **1** *a trade association* ALLIANCE, consortium, coalition, union, league, guild, syndicate, federation, confederation, confederacy, conglomerate, co-operative, partnership, affiliation, organization; club, society, congress. **2** *the association between language and nationalism* RELATIONSHIP, relation, interrelation, connection, interconnection, link, bond, union, tie, attachment, interdependence, affiliation.

Assomption sash (*Cdn*) ▶ noun ceinture fléchée ♣, voyageur sash ♣, arrow sash ♣.

assorted ▶ adjective VARIOUS, miscellaneous, mixed, varied, heterogeneous, varying, diverse, eclectic, multifarious, sundry; *literary* divers.

assortment ▶ noun MIXTURE, variety, array, mixed bag, mix, miscellany, selection, medley, diversity, ragbag, hodgepodge, mishmash, potpourri, salmagundi, farrago, gallimaufry, omnium gatherum.

assuage ▶ verb **1** *a pain that could never be assuaged* RELIEVE, ease, alleviate, soothe, mitigate, allay, palliate, abate, suppress, subdue; moderate, lessen, diminish, reduce. **2** *her hunger was quickly assuaged* SATISFY, gratify, appease, fulfill, indulge, relieve, slake, sate, satiate, quench, check.
− OPPOSITES: aggravate, intensify.

assume ▶ verb **1** *I assumed he wanted me to keep the book* PRESUME, suppose, take it (as given), take for granted, take as read, conjecture, surmise, conclude, deduce, infer, reckon, reason, think, fancy, believe, understand, gather, figure. **2** *he assumed a Southern accent* AFFECT, adopt, impersonate, put on, simulate, feign, fake. **3** *the disease may assume epidemic proportions* ACQUIRE, take on, come to have. **4** *they are to assume more responsibility* ACCEPT, shoulder, bear, undertake, take on/up, manage, handle, deal with. **5** *he assumed control of their finances* SEIZE, take (over), appropriate, commandeer, expropriate, hijack, wrest, arrogate, usurp.

assumed ▶ adjective *an assumed name* FALSE, fictitious, invented, made-up, fake, bogus, sham, spurious, make-believe, improvised, adopted; *informal* pretend, phony.
− OPPOSITES: genuine.

assumption ▶ noun **1** *an informed assumption* SUPPOSITION, presumption, belief, expectation, conjecture, speculation, surmise, guess, premise, hypothesis; conclusion, deduction, inference, illation, notion, impression. **2** *the assumption of power by revolutionaries* SEIZURE, arrogation, appropriation, expropriation, commandeering, confiscation, hijacking, wresting. **3** *the early assumption of community obligation* ACCEPTANCE, shouldering, tackling, undertaking.

assurance ▶ noun **1** *her calm assurance*

SELF-CONFIDENCE, confidence, self-assurance, self-possession, nerve, poise, aplomb, level-headedness; calmness, composure, sang-froid, equanimity; *informal* cool, unflappability. **2** *you have my assurance* WORD (OF HONOUR), promise, pledge, vow, avowal, oath, bond, undertaking, guarantee, commitment. **3** *there is no assurance of getting one's money back* GUARANTEE, certainty, certitude, surety, confidence, expectation.
– OPPOSITES: self-doubt, uncertainty.

assure ▸ verb **1** *we must assure him of our loyal support* REASSURE, convince, satisfy, persuade, guarantee, promise, tell; affirm, pledge, swear, vow. **2** *he wants to assure a favourable vote* ENSURE, secure, guarantee, seal, clinch, confirm; *informal* sew up.

assured ▸ adjective **1** *an assured demeanour* CONFIDENT, self-confident, self-assured, self-possessed, poised, phlegmatic, level-headed; calm, composed, equanimous, imperturbable, unruffled; *informal* unflappable, together. **2** *an assured supply of weapons* GUARANTEED, certain, sure, secure, reliable, dependable, sound; infallible, unfailing; *informal* sure-fire.
– OPPOSITES: doubtful, uncertain.

astonish ▸ verb AMAZE, astound, stagger, surprise, startle, stun, confound, dumbfound, strike dumb, boggle, stupefy, daze, shock, take aback, leave open-mouthed, leave aghast; *informal* flabbergast, blow away, bowl over, floor.

astonished ▸ adjective AMAZED, astounded, staggered, surprised, startled, stunned, thunderstruck, aghast, taken aback, dumbfounded, dumbstruck, stupefied, dazed, awestruck; *informal* flabbergasted, floored, blown away.

astonishing ▸ adjective AMAZING, astounding, staggering, surprising, breathtaking; remarkable, extraordinary, incredible, unbelievable, phenomenal; *informal* mind-boggling.

astonishment ▸ noun AMAZEMENT, surprise, stupefaction, incredulity, disbelief, speechlessness, awe, wonder, wonderment.

astound ▸ verb AMAZE, astonish, stagger, surprise, startle, stun, confound, dumbfound, boggle, stupefy, shock, daze, take aback, leave open-mouthed, leave aghast; *informal* flabbergast, blow away, bowl over, floor.

astounding ▸ adjective AMAZING, astonishing, staggering, surprising, breathtaking, remarkable, extraordinary, incredible, unbelievable, phenomenal; *informal* mind-boggling.

astral ▸ adjective STELLAR, sidereal.

astray ▸ adverb **1** *the shots went astray* OFF TARGET, wide of the mark, awry, off course; amiss. **2** *the older boys led him astray* INTO WRONGDOING, into error, into sin, into iniquity, away from the straight and narrow.

astride ▸ preposition & adverb STRADDLING.

astringent ▸ adjective **1** *the lotion has an astringent effect on pores* CONSTRICTING, constrictive, contracting; styptic. **2** *her astringent words* SEVERE, sharp, stern, harsh, acerbic, acidulous, caustic, mordant, trenchant; scathing, spiteful, cutting, incisive, waspish.

astrology ▸ noun HOROSCOPY; horoscopes.

astronaut ▸ noun SPACEMAN/WOMAN, cosmonaut, space traveller, space cadet.

astronomical ▸ adjective **1** *astronomical alignments* PLANETARY, stellar; celestial, astral. **2** *(informal) the sums he has paid are astronomical* HUGE, enormous, very

large, prodigious, monumental, colossal, vast, gigantic, massive; substantial, considerable, sizeable, hefty; inordinate; *informal* astronomic, whopping, humongous, ginormous.
– OPPOSITES: tiny.

astute ▸ adjective SHREWD, sharp, acute, adroit, quick, clever, crafty, intelligent, bright, smart, canny, intuitive, perceptive, insightful, incisive, sagacious, wise; *informal* on the ball, quick on the uptake, savvy; heads-up.
– OPPOSITES: stupid.

asunder ▸ adverb (*literary*) *the fabric of society may be torn asunder* APART, up, in two; to pieces, to shreds, to bits.

asylum ▸ noun **1** *he appealed for political asylum* REFUGE, sanctuary, shelter, safety, protection, security, immunity; a safe haven. **2** *he was confined to an asylum* PSYCHIATRIC HOSPITAL, mental hospital, mental institution, mental asylum; *informal* madhouse, loony bin, funny farm, nuthouse, bughouse; *dated* lunatic asylum; *archaic* bedlam.

asymmetrical ▸ adjective LOPSIDED, unsymmetrical, uneven, unbalanced, crooked, awry, askew, skew, misaligned; disproportionate, unequal, irregular; *informal* cockeyed, wonky.

atelier ▸ noun WORKSHOP, studio, workroom.

atheism ▸ noun NON-BELIEF, disbelief, unbelief, irreligion, skepticism, doubt, agnosticism; nihilism.

atheist ▸ noun NON-BELIEVER, disbeliever, unbeliever, skeptic, doubter, doubting Thomas, agnostic; nihilist.
– OPPOSITES: believer.

athlete ▸ noun SPORTSMAN, sportswoman, sportsperson; jock; Olympian; runner.

athletic ▸ adjective **1** *his athletic physique* MUSCULAR, muscly, sturdy, strapping, well-built, strong, powerful, robust, able-bodied, vigorous, hardy, lusty, hearty, brawny, burly, broad-shouldered, Herculean; FIT, in good shape, in trim; *informal* sporty, husky, hunky, beefy; *literary* thewy. **2** *athletic events* SPORTING, sports; Olympic. *See table at* TRACK AND FIELD.
– OPPOSITES: puny.

athletics ▸ plural noun SPORTS, sporting events, track and field events, track, games, races; contests; working out, exercising.

atmosphere ▸ noun **1** *the gases present in the atmosphere* AIR, aerospace; sky; *literary* the heavens, the firmament, the blue, the azure, the ether. *See table.* **2** *the hotel has a relaxed atmosphere* AMBIENCE, air, mood, feel, feeling, character, tone, tenor, aura, quality, undercurrent, flavour; *informal* vibe.

Layers of the Earth's Atmosphere

exosphere	stratosphere
ionosphere	thermosphere
mesosphere	troposphere
ozone layer	

atom ▸ noun **1** *they build tiny circuits atom by atom* PARTICLE, molecule, bit, piece, fragment, fraction. **2** *there wasn't an atom of truth in the allegations* GRAIN, iota, jot, whit, mite, scrap, shred, ounce, scintilla, trace, smidgen, modicum.

atone ▸ verb MAKE AMENDS, make reparation, make restitution, make up for, compensate, pay,

Subatomic Particles

antiparticle	neutrino
baryon	neutron
boson	photon
electron	pion/pi meson
fermion	positron
gluon	proton
hadron	quark
hyperon	string
kaon	tau particle
lepton	triton
meson	WIMP
muon	

recompense, expiate, redress, make good, offset; do penance.

atrocious ▶ **adjective 1** *atrocious cruelties* BRUTAL, barbaric, barbarous, savage, vicious, beastly; wicked, cruel, nasty, heinous, monstrous, vile, inhuman, black-hearted, fiendish, ghastly, horrible; abominable, outrageous, hateful, disgusting, despicable, contemptible, loathsome, odious, abhorrent, sickening, horrifying, unspeakable, execrable, egregious. **2** *the weather was atrocious* APPALLING, dreadful, terrible, very bad, unpleasant, miserable; *informal* abysmal, dire, rotten, lousy, godawful.
— OPPOSITES: admirable, superb.

atrocity ▶ **noun** ABOMINATION, cruelty, enormity, outrage, horror, monstrosity, obscenity, violation, crime, abuse; barbarity, barbarism, brutality, savagery, inhumanity, wickedness, evil, iniquity.

atrophy ▶ **verb** *muscles atrophy in microgravity* WASTE AWAY, become emaciated, wither, shrivel (up), shrink; decay, decline, deteriorate, degenerate, weaken.
— OPPOSITES: strengthen, flourish.
▶ **noun** *muscular atrophy* WASTING, emaciation, withering, shrivelling, shrinking; decay, decline, deterioration, degeneration, weakening, debilitation, enfeeblement.
— OPPOSITES: strengthening.

attach ▶ **verb 1** *a lead weight is attached to the cord* FASTEN, fix, affix, join, connect, link, couple, secure, make fast, tie, bind, chain; stick, adhere, glue, fuse; append. **2** *they attached importance to research* ASCRIBE, assign, attribute, accredit, impute. **3** *the medical officer attached to HQ* ASSIGN, appoint, allocate, second; *Military* detail.
— OPPOSITES: detach, separate.

attached ▶ **adjective 1** *I'm not interested in you — I'm attached* SPOKEN FOR, married, engaged, promised in marriage; going out, involved, seeing someone; *informal* hitched, spliced, shackled, going steady; *dated* betrothed; *formal* wed, wedded; *literary* affianced; *archaic* espoused. **2** *she was very attached to her brother* FOND OF, devoted to; *informal* mad about, crazy about.
— OPPOSITES: single.

attachment ▶ **noun 1** *he has a strong attachment to his mother* BOND, closeness, devotion, loyalty; fondness for, love for, affection for, feeling for; relationship with. **2** *the shower had a massage attachment* ACCESSORY, fitting, extension, add-on, appendage. **3** *the attachment of safety restraints* FIXING, fastening, linking, coupling, connection.

attack ▶ **verb 1** *Chris had been brutally attacked* ASSAULT, assail, set upon, beat up; batter, pummel, punch; *informal* do over, work over, rough up. **2** *they attacked along a 10-mile front* STRIKE, charge, pounce,

bombard, shell, blitz, strafe, fire, besiege. **3** *the clergy attacked government policies* CRITICIZE, censure, condemn, pillory, savage, revile, vilify; *informal* knock, slam, blast, bash, lay into. **4** *they have to attack the problem soon* ADDRESS, attend to, deal with, confront, apply oneself to, get to work on, undertake, embark on; *informal* get cracking on.
— OPPOSITES: defend, praise, protect.
▶ **noun 1** *the attack began at dawn* ASSAULT, onslaught, offensive, strike, blitz, raid, charge, rush, invasion, incursion. **2** *she wrote a hostile attack against him* CRITICISM, censure, rebuke, admonishment, reprimand; condemnation, denunciation, vilification; tirade, diatribe, polemic; *informal* roasting, caning, hatchet job. **3** *an asthmatic attack* FIT, seizure, spasm, convulsion, paroxysm, outburst, bout.
— OPPOSITES: defence, commendation.

attacker ▶ **noun** ASSAILANT, assaulter, aggressor; mugger, rapist, killer, murderer.

attain ▶ **verb** ACHIEVE, accomplish, reach, obtain, gain, procure, secure, get, hook, net, win, earn, acquire; realize, fulfill; *informal* clinch, bag, snag, wrap up.

attainable ▶ **adjective** ACHIEVABLE, obtainable, accessible, within reach, securable, realizable; practicable, workable, realistic, reasonable, viable, feasible, possible; *informal* doable, get-at-able.

attempt ▶ **verb** *I attempted to answer the question* TRY, strive, aim, venture, endeavour, seek, undertake, make an effort; have a go at, try one's hand at; *informal* go all out, bend over backwards, bust a gut, have a crack/shot/stab at, hazard; *formal* essay; *archaic* assay.
▶ **noun** *an attempt to improve the economy* EFFORT, endeavour, try, venture, trial; *informal* crack, go, bid, shot, stab; *formal* essay; *archaic* assay.

attend ▶ **verb 1** *they attended a carol service* BE PRESENT AT, sit in on, take part in; appear at, present oneself at, turn up at, visit, go to; *informal* show up at, show one's face at. **2** *he had not attended to the regulations* PAY ATTENTION, pay heed, be attentive, listen; concentrate, take note, bear in mind, take into consideration, heed, observe, mark. **3** *the wounded were attended to nearby* CARE FOR, look after, minister to, see to; tend, treat, nurse, help, aid, assist, succour; *informal* doctor. **4** *he attended to the boy's education* DEAL WITH, see to, manage, organize, sort out, handle, take care of, take charge of, take in hand, tackle. **5** *the princess was attended by an usher* ESCORT, accompany, chaperone, squire, guide, lead, conduct, usher, shepherd; assist, help, serve, wait on. **6** *her giddiness was attended with a fever* BE ACCOMPANIED BY, occur with, coexist with, be associated with, connected with, be linked with; be produced by, originate from/in, stem from, result from, arise from.
— OPPOSITES: miss, disregard, ignore, neglect.

attendance ▶ **noun 1** *please confirm your attendance* PRESENCE, appearance. **2** *attendance was dismal* TURNOUT, audience, house, gate, box office; crowd, congregation, gathering.
— OPPOSITES: absence.
■ **in attendance** PRESENT, here, there, at hand, available; assisting.

attendant ▶ **noun** STEWARD, waiter, waitress, garçon, porter, servant, waitperson, stewardess; escort, companion, retainer, aide, lady in waiting, equerry, chaperone; manservant, valet, butler, maidservant, maid, footman; busboy, houseman; lackey; gas jockey.

▸ **adjective** *new discoveries and the attendant excitement* ACCOMPANYING, associated, related, connected, concomitant, coincident; resultant, resulting, consequent.

attention ▸ **noun 1** *the issue needs further attention* CONSIDERATION, contemplation, deliberation, thought, study, observation, scrutiny, investigation, action. **2** *he tried to attract the attention of a policeman* AWARENESS, notice, observation, heed, regard, scrutiny, surveillance. **3** *adequate medical attention* CARE, treatment, ministration, succour, relief, aid, help, assistance. **4** *he was effusive in his attentions* OVERTURES, approaches, suit, wooing, courting; compliments, flattery; courtesy, politeness.

attentive ▸ **adjective 1** *a bright and attentive scholar* PERCEPTIVE, observant, alert, acute, aware, heedful, vigilant; intent, focused, committed, studious, diligent, conscientious, earnest; wary, watchful; *informal* not missing a trick, on the ball. **2** *the most attentive of husbands* CONSCIENTIOUS, considerate, thoughtful, kind, caring, solicitous, understanding, sympathetic, obliging, accommodating, courteous, gallant, chivalrous; dutiful, responsible.
– OPPOSITES: inconsiderate.

attenuated ▸ **adjective 1** *attenuated fingers* THIN, slender, narrow, slim, skinny, spindly, bony; *rare* attenuate. **2** *his muscle activity was much attenuated* WEAKENED, reduced, lessened, decreased, diminished, impaired.
– OPPOSITES: plump, broad, strengthened.

attest ▸ **verb** CERTIFY, corroborate, confirm, verify, substantiate, authenticate, evidence, demonstrate, show, prove; endorse, support, affirm, bear out, give credence to, vouch for; *formal* evince.
– OPPOSITES: disprove.

attic ▸ **noun** LOFT, garret.

attire ▸ **noun** *Thomas preferred formal attire* CLOTHING, clothes, garments, dress, wear, outfits, garb, costume; *informal* gear, duds, getup, threads; *formal* apparel; *archaic* raiment, habiliments.
▸ **verb** *she was attired in black crepe* DRESS (UP), clothe, garb, robe, array, costume, swathe, deck (out), turn out, fit out, trick out; *archaic* apparel, invest, habit.

attitude ▸ **noun 1** *you seem ambivalent in your attitude* VIEW, viewpoint, outlook, perspective, stance, standpoint, position, inclination, temper, orientation, approach, reaction; opinion, ideas, convictions, feelings, thinking. **2** *an attitude of prayer* POSITION, posture, pose, stance, bearing. **3** *hard rock with plenty of attitude* HOSTILITY, anger, venom, vitriol, rancour, spunk, spirit; *informal* 'tude.

attorney ▸ **noun** LAWYER, barrister and solicitor ♣, legal practitioner, legal professional, legal representative, member of the bar, counsel, Crown attorney/counsel/prosecutor ♣, Queen's counsel, QC, advocate; *informal* mouthpiece, ambulance chaser.

attract ▸ **verb 1** *positive ions are attracted to the negatively charged terminal* PULL, draw, magnetize. **2** *he was attracted by her smile* ENTICE, allure, lure, tempt, charm, win over, woo, engage, enthrall, enchant, entrance, captivate, beguile, bewitch, seduce.
– OPPOSITES: repel.

attraction ▸ **noun 1** *the stars are held together by gravitational attraction* PULL, draw; magnetism. **2** *she had lost whatever attraction she had ever had* APPEAL, attractiveness, desirability, seductiveness, seduction, allure, animal magnetism; charisma, charm, beauty, good looks, eye-appeal. **3** *the fair offers sideshows and* other attractions ENTERTAINMENT, activity, diversion, interest.
– OPPOSITES: repulsion.

attractive ▸ **adjective 1** *a more attractive career* APPEALING, inviting, tempting, irresistible; agreeable, pleasing, interesting. **2** *she has no idea how attractive she is* GOOD-LOOKING, beautiful, pretty, handsome, lovely, stunning, striking, arresting, gorgeous, prepossessing, fetching, captivating, bewitching, beguiling, engaging, charming, enchanting, enticing, appealing, delightful, winning, photogenic, telegenic; sexy, seductive, alluring, tantalizing, irresistible, ravishing, desirable; *informal* drop-dead gorgeous, foxy; *literary* beauteous; *archaic* comely, fair.
– OPPOSITES: uninviting, ugly.

attribute ▸ **verb** *they attributed their success to him* ASCRIBE, assign, accredit, credit, impute; put down, chalk up, hold responsible, blame, pin on; connect with, associate with.
▸ **noun 1** *he has all the attributes of a top player* QUALITY, characteristic, trait, feature, element, aspect, property, sign, hallmark, mark, distinction. **2** *the hourglass is the attribute of Father Time* SYMBOL, mark, sign, hallmark, trademark.

attrition ▸ **noun** WEARING DOWN/AWAY, weakening, debilitation, enfeebling, sapping, attenuation; abrasion, friction, erosion, corrosion, grinding, deterioration; gradual loss.

attune ▸ **verb** ACCUSTOM, adjust, adapt, acclimatize, condition, accommodate, assimilate; acclimate.

atypical ▸ **adjective** UNUSUAL, untypical, uncommon, unconventional, unorthodox, irregular, abnormal, anomalous, aberrant, deviant, unrepresentative; strange, odd, peculiar, bizarre, weird, queer, freakish, eccentric; exceptional, singular, unique, rare, out of the ordinary, extraordinary; *informal* funny, freaky.
– OPPOSITES: normal.

auburn ▸ **adjective** REDDISH-BROWN, red-brown, Titian (red), tawny, russet, chestnut, copper, coppery, rufous, rust.

au courant ▸ **adjective** UP TO DATE, au fait, in touch, familiar, at home, acquainted, conversant; abreast, apprised, in the know, well-informed, knowledgeable, well versed, enlightened; *informal* clued in, wise to, hip to; trendy.

audacious ▸ **adjective 1** *an audacious remark* IMPUDENT, impertinent, insolent, presumptuous, cheeky, irreverent, discourteous, disrespectful, insubordinate, ill-mannered, unmannerly, rude, brazen, shameless, pert, defiant, cocky, bold (as brass); *informal* fresh, lippy, mouthy, saucy, sassy, nervy; *archaic* contumelious. **2** *his audacious exploits* BOLD, daring, fearless, intrepid, brave, courageous, valiant, heroic, plucky; daredevil, devil-may-care, reckless, madcap; venturesome, mettlesome; *informal* gutsy, spunky, ballsy; *literary* temerarious.
– OPPOSITES: timid, polite.

audacity ▸ **noun 1** *he had the audacity to contradict me* IMPUDENCE, impertinence, insolence, presumption, cheek, bad manners, effrontery, nerve, gall, defiance, temerity; *informal* chutzpah, sass. **2** *a traveller of extraordinary audacity* BOLDNESS, daring, fearlessness, intrepidity, bravery, courage, heroism, pluck, grit; recklessness; spirit, mettle; *informal* guts, gutsiness, spunk, moxie.

audible ▸ **adjective** HEARABLE, perceptible,

discernible, detectable, appreciable; clear, distinct, loud.
— OPPOSITES: faint.

audience ► noun **1** *the audience applauded* SPECTATORS, LISTENERS, viewers, onlookers, patrons; crowd, throng, congregation, turnout; house, gallery, stalls. **2** *the radio station has a teenage audience* MARKET, PUBLIC, following, fans; listenership, viewership. **3** *an audience with the Pope* MEETING, consultation, conference, hearing, reception, interview; *informal* meet-and-greet.

audit ► noun *an audit of the party accounts* INSPECTION, examination, verification, scrutiny, probe, investigation, assessment, appraisal, evaluation, review, analysis; *informal* going-over, once-over.
► verb *we audited their accounts* INSPECT, examine, survey, go through, scrutinize, check, probe, vet, investigate, inquire into, assess, verify, appraise, evaluate, review, analyze, study; *informal* give something a/the once-over, give something a going-over.

audition ► noun TRYOUT, trial.

auditor ► noun ACCOUNTANT, bookkeeper, inspector.

auditorium ► noun THEATRE, hall, playhouse, assembly room; chamber, room, arena, stadium, gymnasium.

augment ► verb INCREASE, add to, supplement, top up, build up, enlarge, expand, extend, raise, multiply, swell, grow; magnify, amplify, escalate; improve, boost; *informal* up, jack up, hike up, bump up.
— OPPOSITES: decrease.

augur ► verb *these successes augur well for the future* BODE, portend, herald, be a sign, warn, forewarn, foreshadow, be an omen, presage, indicate, signify, signal, promise, threaten, spell, denote; predict, prophesy; *literary* betoken, foretoken, forebode.

augury ► noun OMEN, portent, sign, foretoken.

august ► adjective DISTINGUISHED, respected, eminent, venerable, hallowed, illustrious, prestigious, renowned, celebrated, honoured, acclaimed, esteemed, exalted; great, important, lofty, noble, imposing, impressive, awe-inspiring, stately, grand, dignified.

aura ► noun ATMOSPHERE, ambience, air, quality, character, mood, feeling, feel, flavour, tone, tenor; emanation; *informal* vibe.

auspices ► plural noun PATRONAGE, aegis, umbrella, protection, keeping, care; support, backing, guardianship, trusteeship, guidance, supervision.

auspicious ► adjective FAVOURABLE, propitious, promising, rosy, good, encouraging, opportune, timely, lucky, fortunate, providential, felicitous, advantageous.

austere ► adjective **1** *an outwardly austere man* SEVERE, stern, strict, harsh, steely, flinty, dour, grim, cold, frosty, unemotional, unfriendly; formal, stiff, reserved, aloof, forbidding; grave, solemn, serious, unsmiling, unsympathetic, unforgiving; hard, unyielding, unbending, inflexible; *informal* hard-boiled. **2** *an austere life* ASCETIC, self-denying, self-disciplined, non-indulgent, frugal, Spartan, puritanical, abstemious, abstinent, self-sacrificing, strict, temperate, sober, simple, restrained; celibate, chaste. **3** *the buildings were austere* PLAIN, simple, basic, functional, modest, unadorned, unembellished, unfussy, restrained; stark, bleak, bare, clinical, Spartan, ascetic; *informal* no frills, bare-bones.
— OPPOSITES: genial, immoderate, ornate.

austerity ► noun SEVERITY, strictness, seriousness, solemnity, gravity; frugality, thrift, economy, asceticism; self-discipline, abstinence, sobriety, restraint, chastity; starkness.

Australia ► noun *informal* OZ, Aussie, down under.

authentic ► adjective **1** *an authentic document* GENUINE, real, bona fide, true, veritable, simon-pure; legitimate, lawful, legal, valid; *informal* the real McCoy, the real thing, kosher. **2** *an authentic depiction of the situation* RELIABLE, dependable, trustworthy, authoritative, honest, faithful; accurate, factual, true, truthful; *formal* veridical, veracious.
— OPPOSITES: fake, unreliable.

authenticate ► verb **1** *the evidence will authenticate his claim* VERIFY, validate, prove, substantiate, corroborate, confirm, support, back up, attest to, give credence to. **2** *a mandate authenticated by the popular vote* VALIDATE, ratify, confirm, seal, sanction, endorse.

authenticity ► noun **1** *the authenticity of the painting* GENUINENESS, bona fides; legitimacy, legality, validity. **2** *the authenticity of this account* RELIABILITY, dependability, trustworthiness, credibility; accuracy, truth, veracity, fidelity.

author ► noun **1** *modern Canadian authors* WRITER, wordsmith; novelist, playwright, poet, essayist, biographer; columnist, reporter; bard; *informal* scribe, scribbler. **2** *the author of the peace plan* ORIGINATOR, creator, instigator, founder, father, architect, designer, deviser, producer; cause, agent.

authoritarian ► adjective *his authoritarian manner* AUTOCRATIC, dictatorial, despotic, tyrannical, draconian, oppressive, repressive, illiberal, undemocratic; disciplinarian, domineering, overbearing, high-handed, peremptory, imperious, strict, rigid, inflexible; *informal* bossy, iron-fisted.
— OPPOSITES: democratic, liberal.
► noun *the army is dominated by authoritarians* AUTOCRAT, despot, dictator, tyrant; disciplinarian, martinet.

authoritative ► adjective **1** *authoritative information* RELIABLE, dependable, trustworthy, sound, authentic, valid, attested, verifiable; accurate. **2** *the authoritative edition* DEFINITIVE, most reliable, best; authorized, accredited, recognized, accepted, approved, standard, canonical. **3** *his authoritative manner* ASSURED, confident, assertive; commanding, masterful, lordly; domineering, imperious, overbearing, authoritarian; *informal* bossy.
— OPPOSITES: unreliable, timid.

authority ► noun **1** *a rebellion against those in authority* POWER, jurisdiction, command, control, charge, dominance, rule, sovereignty, supremacy; influence; *informal* clout. **2** *the authority to arrest drug traffickers* AUTHORIZATION, right, power, mandate, prerogative, licence, permission. **3** *the authorities* OFFICIALS, officialdom; government, administration, establishment; police; *informal* the powers that be. **4** *an authority on the stock market* EXPERT, specialist, aficionado, pundit, guru, sage. **5** *on good authority* EVIDENCE, testimony, witness, attestation, word, avowal; *Law* deposition.

authorization ► noun PERMISSION, consent, leave, sanction, licence, dispensation, clearance, the nod; assent, agreement, approval, endorsement; authority, right, power, mandate; *informal* the go-ahead, the thumbs up, the OK, the green light.
— OPPOSITES: refusal.

authorize ► verb **1** *they authorized further action* SANCTION, permit, allow, approve, consent to, assent

to; ratify, endorse, validate; *informal* give the green light, give the go-ahead, OK, give the thumbs up. **2** *the troops were authorized to fire* EMPOWER, mandate, commission; entitle.
– OPPOSITES: forbid.

authorized ▶ adjective APPROVED, recognized, sanctioned; accredited, licensed, certified; official, lawful, legal, legitimate.
– OPPOSITES: unofficial.

autobiography ▶ noun MEMOIRS, life story, personal history.

autocracy ▶ noun ABSOLUTISM, totalitarianism, dictatorship, despotism, tyranny, monocracy, autarchy.
– OPPOSITES: democracy.

autocrat ▶ noun ABSOLUTE RULER, dictator, despot, tyrant.

autocratic ▶ adjective DESPOTIC, tyrannical, dictatorial, totalitarian, autarchic; undemocratic, one-party, monocratic; domineering, draconian, overbearing, high-handed, peremptory, imperious; harsh, rigid, inflexible, illiberal, oppressive, iron-fisted.

autograph ▶ noun *fans pestered him for his autograph* SIGNATURE; *informal* John Hancock.
▶ verb *Jack autographed copies of his book* SIGN.

automatic ▶ adjective **1** *automatic garage doors* MECHANIZED, mechanical, automated, computerized, electronic, robotic; self-activating. **2** *an automatic reaction* INSTINCTIVE, involuntary, unconscious, reflex, knee-jerk, instinctual, subconscious; spontaneous, impulsive, unthinking; mechanical; *informal* gut. **3** *he is the automatic choice for the team* INEVITABLE, unavoidable, inescapable, mandatory, compulsory; certain, definite, undoubted, assured.
– OPPOSITES: manual, deliberate.

automaton ▶ noun ROBOT, android, cyborg, droid, bot.

automobile ▶ noun CAR, auto, motor car; *informal* wheels; jalopy, lemon, beater, junker, clunker, tin Lizzie, rustbucket. *See table at* CAR.

autonomous ▶ adjective SELF-GOVERNING, self-ruling, self-determining, independent, sovereign, free.

autonomy ▶ noun SELF-GOVERNMENT, self-rule, home rule, self-determination, independence, sovereignty, freedom.

autopsy ▶ noun POST-MORTEM, PM, necropsy.

autumn ▶ noun FALL; twilight.

auxiliary ▶ adjective **1** *an auxiliary power source* ADDITIONAL, supplementary, supplemental, extra, spare, reserve, backup, emergency, fallback, other. **2** *auxiliary nursing staff* ANCILLARY, assistant, support.
▶ noun *a nursing auxiliary* ASSISTANT, helper, ancillary.

avail ▶ verb **1** *guests can avail themselves of the facilities* USE, take advantage of, utilize, employ. **2** *his arguments cannot avail him* HELP, aid, assist, benefit, profit, be of service.
▶ noun *(Cdn) living off the avails of prostitution* PROFITS, earnings, proceeds, revenue.
■ **to no avail** IN VAIN, without success, unsuccessfully, fruitlessly, for nothing.

available ▶ adjective **1** *refreshments will be available* OBTAINABLE, accessible, at/to hand, at one's disposal, handy, convenient; on sale, procurable; untaken, unengaged, unused; *informal* up for grabs, on tap, gettable. **2** *I'll see if he's available* FREE, unoccupied;

present, in attendance; contactable; unattached, single.
– OPPOSITES: busy, engaged.

avalanche ▶ noun **1** SNOWSLIDE. **2** *an avalanche of press comment* BARRAGE, volley, flood, deluge, torrent, tide, shower, wave.

avant-garde ▶ adjective INNOVATIVE, original, experimental, left-field, inventive, ahead of the times, cutting/leading/bleeding edge, new, modern, innovatory, advanced, forward-looking, state-of-the-art, trend-setting, pioneering, progressive, bohemian, groundbreaking, trail-blazing, revolutionary; unfamiliar, unorthodox, unconventional; *informal* offbeat, way-out.
– OPPOSITES: conservative.

avarice ▶ noun GREED, acquisitiveness, cupidity, covetousness, greediness, rapacity, materialism, mercenariness; *informal* money-grubbing, affluenza.
– OPPOSITES: generosity.

avenge ▶ verb REQUITE, punish, repay, pay back, revenge, take revenge for, exact/take vengeance, get even for, retaliate.

avenue ▶ noun **1** *tree-lined avenues* ROAD, street, drive, parade, boulevard, broadway, thoroughfare. **2** *possible avenues of research* LINE, path; method, approach.

average ▶ noun *the price is above the national average* MEAN, median, mode; norm, standard, rule, par.
▶ adjective **1** *the average temperature in May* MEAN, median, modal. **2** *a woman of average height* ORDINARY, standard, normal, typical, regular. **3** *a very average director* MEDIOCRE, second-rate, undistinguished, ordinary, middle-of-the-road, unexceptional, unexciting, unremarkable, unmemorable, indifferent, pedestrian, lacklustre, forgettable, amateurish; *informal* OK, so-so, {comme ci, comme ça}, fair-to-middling, no great shakes, underwhelming, plain-vanilla.
– OPPOSITES: outstanding, exceptional.
■ **on average** NORMALLY, usually, ordinarily, generally, in general, for the most part, as a rule, typically; overall, by and large, on the whole.

averse ▶ adjective OPPOSED, against, antipathetic, hostile, ill-disposed, resistant; disinclined, reluctant, unwilling, loath; *informal* anti.
– OPPOSITES: keen.

aversion ▶ noun DISLIKE, antipathy, distaste, abhorrence, hatred, odium, loathing, detestation, hostility; reluctance, unwillingness, disinclination.
– OPPOSITES: liking.

avert ▶ verb **1** *she averted her head* TURN ASIDE, turn away. **2** *an attempt to avert political chaos* PREVENT, avoid, stave off, ward off, forestall, preclude.

aviation ▶ noun FLIGHT, air travel, piloting.

aviator ▶ noun *(dated)* PILOT, airman/woman, flyer, fly boy, aviatrix, barnstormer.

avid ▶ adjective KEEN, eager, enthusiastic, ardent, passionate, zealous; devoted, dedicated, wholehearted, earnest.
– OPPOSITES: apathetic.

avoid ▶ verb **1** *I avoid situations that stress me out* KEEP/STAY AWAY FROM, steer clear of, give a wide berth to, fight shy of. **2** *he is trying to avoid responsibility* EVADE, dodge, sidestep, escape, run away from; *informal* duck, wriggle out of, get out of, cop out of. **3** *he swerved to avoid a check* DODGE, duck, get out of the way of. **4** *you've been avoiding me all evening* SHUN, stay away from, evade, keep one's distance, elude, hide from;

ignore, give the cold shoulder. **5** *he should avoid drinking alcohol* REFRAIN FROM, abstain from, desist from, eschew.
— OPPOSITES: confront, face up to, seek out.

avoidable ▶ adjective PREVENTABLE, stoppable, escapable.
— OPPOSITES: inescapable.

avow ▶ verb ASSERT, declare, state, maintain, swear, affirm, vow, insist; admit, confess, acknowledge; *formal* aver.

avowed ▶ adjective SELF-CONFESSED, self-declared, acknowledged, admitted; open, overt.

await ▶ verb **1** *Peter was awaiting news* WAIT FOR, expect, anticipate. **2** *many dangers await them* BE IN STORE FOR, lie ahead of, lie in wait for, be waiting for.

awake ▶ verb **1** *she awoke the following morning* WAKE (UP), awaken, stir, come to, come round; *literary* waken. **2** *the alarm awoke her at 7:30* WAKE (UP), awaken, rouse, arouse. **3** *it awoke our interest. See* AWAKEN sense 2. **4** *they finally awoke to the extent of the problem* REALIZE, become aware of, become conscious of; *informal* clue in to, get wise to.
▶ adjective **1** *she was still awake at 2:00* WAKEFUL, sleepless, restless, restive; *archaic* watchful. **2** *stay awake at all times* VIGILANT, alert, watchful, attentive, on guard. **3** *too few are awake to the dangers* AWARE OF, conscious of, mindful of, alert to; *formal* cognizant of; *informal* clued in to; *archaic* ware of.
— OPPOSITES: asleep, oblivious.

awaken ▶ verb **1** *I awakened early* | *the jolt awakened her. See* AWAKE senses 1, 2. **2** *he had awakened strong emotions in her* AROUSE, rouse, bring out, engender, evoke, incite, trigger, provoke, stir up, stimulate, animate, quicken, kindle; revive; *literary* enkindle.

Canadian Awards and Honours

Service
Order of Canada (Companion, Officer, Member)
Order of Military Merit (Commander, Officer, Member)
Cross of Valour
Star of Courage
Medal of Bravery

The Arts
Gémeaux (French-language television)
Gemini (English-language television)
Genie (filmmaking)
Giller Prize (literature)
Governor General's Award (literature)
Juno (music)

Sports
Allan Cup (senior amateur hockey)
Grey Cup (professional football)
Lou Marsh Trophy (athlete)
Mann Cup (senior amateur lacrosse)
Memorial Cup (major junior hockey)
Minto Cup (junior amateur lacrosse)
Stanley Cup (professional hockey)
Vanier Cup (university football)

---

award ▶ verb *the society awarded him a silver medal* GIVE, grant, accord, assign; confer on, bestow on, present to, endow with, decorate with.
▶ noun **1** *an award for high-quality service* PRIZE, trophy,

medal, decoration; reward. *See table*. **2** *a libel award* PAYMENT, settlement, compensation. **3** *the Arts Council gave him an award of $1,500* GRANT, scholarship, endowment; bursary.

aware ▶ adjective **1** *she is aware of the dangers* CONSCIOUS OF, mindful of, informed about, acquainted with, familiar with, alive to, alert to; *informal* clued in to, wise to, in the know about, hip to; *formal* cognizant of; *archaic* ware of. **2** *we need to be more environmentally aware* KNOWLEDGEABLE, enlightened, well-informed, au fait; *informal* clued in, tuned in, plugged in.
— OPPOSITES: ignorant.

awareness ▶ noun CONSCIOUSNESS, recognition, realization; understanding, grasp, appreciation, knowledge, insight; familiarity; *formal* cognizance.

awash ▶ adjective **1** *the road was awash* FLOODED, under water, submerged, submersed. **2** *the city was awash with journalists* INUNDATED, flooded, swamped, teeming, overflowing, overrun; *informal* knee-deep in, crawling with.

away ▶ adverb **1** *she began to walk away* OFF, from here, from there. **2** *stay away from the trouble* AT A DISTANCE FROM, apart from. **3** *Bernice pushed him away* ASIDE, off, to one side. **4** *we'll be away for two weeks* ELSEWHERE, abroad; gone, absent; on holiday, on vacation.

awe ▶ noun WONDER, wonderment; admiration, reverence, respect, esteem; dread, fear.

awed ▶ adjective *he spoke in an awed whisper* FILLED WITH WONDER, wonderstruck, awestruck, amazed, astonished, lost for words, open-mouthed; reverential.

awe-inspiring ▶ adjective. *See* AWESOME.

awesome ▶ adjective BREATHTAKING, awe-inspiring, magnificent, wonderful, amazing, stunning, staggering, imposing, stirring, impressive; formidable, fearsome, dreaded; *informal* mind-boggling, mind-blowing, jaw-dropping, excellent, marvellous; *literary* wondrous; *archaic* awful.
— OPPOSITES: unimpressive.

awestruck ▶ adjective AWED, wonderstruck, amazed, lost for words, open-mouthed; reverential, star-struck; terrified, afraid, fearful.

awful ▶ adjective **1** *the place smelled awful* DISGUSTING, horrible, terrible, dreadful, ghastly, nasty, vile, foul, revolting, repulsive, repugnant, odious, sickening, nauseating; *informal* yucky, gross, beastly. **2** *an awful book* TERRIBLE, atrocious, dreadful, frightful, execrable, abominable; inadequate, inferior, substandard, lamentable; *informal* crummy, pathetic, rotten, woeful, lousy, appalling, abysmal, dire. **3** *you look awful — go and lie down* ILL, unwell, sick, peaky, queasy, nauseous; poorly; *informal* rough, lousy, rotten, terrible, dreadful. **4** *I felt awful for getting so angry* REMORSEFUL, guilty, ashamed, contrite, sorry, regretful, repentant. **5** (*archaic*) *the awful sights of nature* AWE-INSPIRING, awesome, impressive; dread, fearful.
— OPPOSITES: wonderful.

awfully ▶ adverb **1** (*informal*) *an awfully nice man* VERY, extremely, really, immensely, exceedingly, thoroughly, dreadfully, exceptionally, remarkably, extraordinarily; *informal* terrifically, terribly, seriously, majorly, real, mighty, awful; *informal, dated* frightfully; *archaic* exceeding. **2** *we played awfully* VERY BADLY, terribly, poorly, dreadfully, atrociously, appallingly, execrably; *informal* abysmally, pitifully, diabolically.

awhile ▶ **adverb** FOR A MOMENT, for a (little) while, for a short time; *informal* for a bit.

awkward ▶ **adjective 1** *the box was awkward to carry* DIFFICULT, tricky; cumbersome, unwieldy. **2** *an awkward time* INCONVENIENT, inappropriate, inopportune, unseasonable, difficult. **3** *he put her in a very awkward position* EMBARRASSING, uncomfortable, unpleasant, delicate, tricky, problematic, troublesome, thorny; humiliating, compromising; *informal* sticky, dicey, hairy. **4** *she felt awkward alone with him* UNCOMFORTABLE, uneasy, tense, nervous, edgy, unquiet; self-conscious, embarrassed. **5** *his awkward movements* CLUMSY, ungainly, uncoordinated, graceless, inelegant, gauche, gawky, wooden, stiff; unskilful, maladroit, inept, blundering; *informal* clodhopping, ham-fisted, ham-handed, heavy-handed; *informal* all thumbs.
— OPPOSITES: easy, convenient, at ease, graceful.

awkwardness ▶ **noun 1** *the gesture betrayed his momentary awkwardness* EMBARRASSMENT, self-consciousness, discomfort, discomfiture, uneasiness, edginess, tension, nervousness. **2** *the adolescent awkwardness of his angular body* UNGAINLINESS, clumsiness, lack of coordination, gracelessness, inelegance, ineptness, gaucheness, gawkiness.

awning ▶ **noun** CANOPY, shade, marquee, sunshade, shelter, cover; blind.

awry ▶ **adjective 1** *something was awry* AMISS, wrong; *informal* up. **2** *his wig looked awry* ASKEW, crooked, lopsided, tilted, skewed, skew, to one side, off-centre, uneven; *informal* cockeyed, wonky.
— OPPOSITES: straight.

axe ▶ **noun** HATCHET, cleaver, tomahawk, adze, poleaxe, broadaxe; *historical* battleaxe, twibill.
▶ **verb 1** *the show was axed* CANCEL, withdraw, drop, scrap, discontinue, terminate, end; *informal* ditch, dump, pull the plug on. **2** *500 employees were axed* DISMISS, fire, make redundant, lay off, let go, discharge, get rid of; *informal* sack, give the sack, give marching orders, pink-slip.

axiom ▶ **noun** ACCEPTED TRUTH, general truth, dictum, truism, principle; maxim, adage, aphorism, apophthegm, gnome.

axis ▶ **noun 1** *the earth revolves on its axis* CENTRE LINE, vertical, horizontal. **2** *the Anglo-American axis* ALLIANCE, coalition, bloc, union, confederation, confederacy, league.

axle ▶ **noun** SHAFT, spindle, rod, arbor, mandrel, pivot.

azure ▶ **adjective** SKY-BLUE, bright blue, blue; *literary* cerulean.

Bb

babble ▶ verb **1** *Betty babbled away* PRATTLE, rattle on, gabble, chatter, jabber, twitter, go on, run on, prate, ramble, burble, blather, blether, gab, yak, yap, yabber, yatter, yammer, blabber, jaw, gas, shoot one's mouth off; natter, waffle, run off at the mouth. **2** *a brook babbled gently* BURBLE, murmur, gurgle, purl, tinkle; *literary* plash.
▶ noun *his inarticulate babble* PRATTLE, gabble, chatter, jabber, prating, rambling, blather, blether; *informal* gab, yabbering, yatter, natter.

babe ▶ noun **1** *(literary) a babe in arms. See* BABY *noun* sense 1. **2** *(informal) what a babe!* BEAUTY, hottie, looker, bombshell, belle, boy toy, heartthrob, hunk, knockout, fox, arm candy, eye-catcher, dish.

babel ▶ noun CLAMOUR, din, racket, confused noise, tumult, uproar, hubbub; babble, babbling, shouting, yelling, screaming; *informal* hullabaloo.

baby ▶ noun **1** *a newborn baby* INFANT, newborn, child, tot, little one; *literary* babe, babe in arms, suckling; papoose; *technical* neonate. **2** *don't be such a baby* SUCK, sissy, wimp, wuss, milquetoast, sook, *(Atlantic)* sooky baby ✤; pantywaist.
— RELATED TERMS: infantile.
▶ adjective *baby carrots* MINIATURE, mini, little, small, small-scale, scaled-down, toy, pocket, vest-pocket, midget, dwarf; *informal* teeny, teeny-weeny, teensy, teensy-weensy, itsy-bitsy, itty-bitty, little-bitty, bite-sized.
— OPPOSITES: large.
▶ verb *her aunt babied her* PAMPER, mollycoddle, spoil, cosset, coddle, indulge, overindulge, pet, nanny, pander to.

baby carriage ▶ noun STROLLER, baby buggy, pram.

babyish ▶ adjective CHILDISH, immature, infantile, juvenile, puerile, adolescent.
— OPPOSITES: mature.

bachelor party ▶ noun STAG, stag party.

back ▶ noun **1** *she's broken her back* SPINE, backbone, spinal column, vertebral column. **2** *the back of the house* REAR, rear side, other side; *Nautical* stern. **3** *the back of the line* END, tail end, rear end, tail, tag end. **4** *the back of a postcard* REVERSE, other side, underside; verso; *informal* flip side.
— RELATED TERMS: dorsal, lumbar.
— OPPOSITES: front, head, face.
▶ adverb **1** *he pushed his chair back* BACKWARDS, behind one, to one's rear, rearwards; away, off. **2** *a few months back* AGO, earlier, previously, before, in the past.
— OPPOSITES: forward.
▶ verb **1** *the government backed the initiative with $4 million* SPONSOR, finance, put up the money for, fund, subsidize, underwrite, be a patron of, act as guarantor of; *informal* foot the bill for, pick up the tab for; bankroll, stake. **2** *most people backed the idea* SUPPORT, endorse, sanction, approve of, give one's blessing to, smile on, favour, advocate, promote, uphold, champion; vote for, ally oneself with, stand behind, stick by, side with, be on the side of, defend, take up the cudgels for; second; *informal* throw one's weight behind. **3** *he backed the horse at 33–1* BET ON,

gamble on, stake money on. **4** *he backed away* REVERSE, draw back, step back, move backwards, back off, pull back, retreat, withdraw, give ground, backtrack, retrace one's steps, recede.
— OPPOSITES: oppose, advance.
▶ adjective **1** *the back seats* REAR, rearmost, backmost, hind, hindmost, hinder, posterior. **2** *a back copy* PAST, old, previous, earlier, former, out of date.
— OPPOSITES: front, future.
■ **back down** GIVE IN, concede defeat, surrender, yield, submit, climb down, concede, reconsider; backtrack, backpedal.
■ **back and forth** TO AND FRO, hither and thither, here and there.
■ **back out of** RENEGE ON, go back on, withdraw from, pull out of, retreat from, fail to honour, abandon, default on, repudiate, backpedal on.
■ **back something up** SUBSTANTIATE, corroborate, confirm, support, bear out, endorse, bolster, reinforce, lend weight to.
■ **back someone up** SUPPORT, stand by, give one's support to, side with, be on someone's side, take someone's side, take someone's part; vouch for.
■ **behind someone's back** SECRETLY, without someone's knowledge, on the sly, slyly, sneakily, covertly, surreptitiously, furtively.

backbiting ▶ noun MALICIOUS TALK, spiteful talk, slander, libel, defamation, abuse, character assassination, disparagement, denigration; slurs, aspersions; *informal* bitching, bitchiness, cattiness, mud-slinging, badmouthing, dissing.

backbone ▶ noun **1** *an injured backbone* SPINE, spinal column, vertebral column, vertebrae; back; *Anatomy* dorsum, rachis. **2** *infantry are the backbone of most armies* MAINSTAY, cornerstone, foundation, chief support, buttress, pillar, tower of strength. **3** *he has enough backbone to see us through* STRENGTH OF CHARACTER, strength of will, firmness, resolution, resolve, grit, true grit, determination, fortitude, mettle, spirit, intestinal fortitude; *informal* guts, spunk.
— RELATED TERMS: spinal.

back-breaking ▶ adjective GRUELLING, arduous, strenuous, onerous, punishing, crushing, demanding, exacting, taxing, crushing, draining; *informal* killing; *archaic* toilsome.
— OPPOSITES: easy.

backer ▶ noun **1** *the backers of the proposition* SUPPORTER, defender, advocate, promoter, proponent; seconder; booster. **2** *$3 million was provided by the project's backers* SPONSOR, investor, underwriter, financier, patron, benefactor, benefactress; *informal* angel.

backfire ▶ verb *Bernard's plan backfired* REBOUND, boomerang, come back; fail, miscarry, go wrong; *informal* blow up in someone's face.

background ▶ noun **1** *a background of palm trees* BACKDROP, backcloth, surrounding(s), setting, scene. **2** *students from many different backgrounds* SOCIAL CIRCUMSTANCES, family circumstances; environment,

class, culture, tradition; upbringing. **3** *her nursing background* EXPERIENCE, record, history, past, training, education, grounding, knowledge; backstory. **4** *the political background* CIRCUMSTANCES, context, conditions, situation, environment, milieu, scene, scenario.
— OPPOSITES: foreground.

■ **in the background** *maybe there was a sugar daddy in the background* BEHIND THE SCENES, out of the public eye, out of the spotlight, out of the limelight, backstage; inconspicuous, unobtrusive, unnoticed.

backhanded ▶ adjective INDIRECT, ambiguous, oblique, equivocal; double-edged, two-edged, left-handed; tongue-in-cheek.
— OPPOSITES: direct.

backing ▶ noun **1** *he has the backing of his colleagues* SUPPORT, help, assistance, aid; approval, endorsement, endorsation ♣, sanction, blessing. **2** *financial backing* SPONSORSHIP, funding, patronage; money, investment, funds, finance; grant, contribution, subsidy. **3** *musical backing* ACCOMPANIMENT; harmony, obbligato.

backlash ▶ noun ADVERSE REACTION, adverse response, counterblast, comeback, repercussion; retaliation, reprisal.

backlog ▶ noun ACCUMULATION, log-jam, pileup.

backpack ▶ noun KNAPSACK, rucksack, packsack, pack, day pack; (*Nfld*) nunny bag ♣.

backpedal ▶ verb *the government has backpedalled on its plans* CHANGE ONE'S MIND, backtrack, back down, climb down, (do an) about-face, reverse course, do a U-turn, renege, go back on, back out of, fail to honour, withdraw, take back, default on.

backslide ▶ verb *many things can cause dieters to backslide* RELAPSE, lapse, regress, weaken, lose one's resolve, give in to temptation, go astray, leave the straight and narrow, fall off the wagon.
— OPPOSITES: persevere.

backslider ▶ noun RECIDIVIST, apostate, fallen angel.

backtalk ▶ noun IMPUDENCE, impertinence, cheek, cheekiness, effrontery, insolence, rudeness; answering back, talking back; *informal* mouth, lip, sass, guff; *rare* contumely.

backtrack ▶ verb *the government backtracked when the poll results were released* BACKPEDAL, change one's mind, back down, reverse course, about-face, climb down.

backup ▶ noun HELP, support, assistance, aid; reinforcements, reserves, additional resources.

backward ▶ adjective **1** *a backward look* REARWARD, to/towards the rear, to/towards the back, behind one, reverse. **2** *the decision was a backward step* RETROGRADE, retrogressive, regressive, for the worse, in the wrong direction, downhill, negative. **3** *an economically backward country* UNDERDEVELOPED, undeveloped; primitive, unsophisticated, benighted. **4** *he was not backward in displaying his talents* HESITANT, reticent, reluctant; shy, diffident, bashful, timid; unwilling, afraid, loath, averse.
— OPPOSITES: forward, progressive, advanced, confident.

▶ adverb *the car rolled slowly backward. See* BACKWARDS.

backwards ▶ adverb **1** *Penny glanced backwards* TOWARDS THE REAR, rearwards, backward, behind one. **2** *count backwards from twenty to ten* IN REVERSE, in reverse order; *slang* ass-backwards, bass-ackwards.
— OPPOSITES: forwards.

backwash ▶ noun **1** *a ship's backwash* WAKE, wash, slipstream, **2** *the backwash of the Cuban missile crisis*

REPERCUSSIONS, reverberations, after-effects, aftermath, fallout.

backwater ▶ noun **1** *fishing in secret backwaters along the river* back channel ♣, snye ♣, bogan. **2** *living in a cultural backwater*, hinterland, wasteland, backwoods, jerkwater, backcountry, back concessions ♣, moose pasture ♣, boonies, boondocks.

backwoods ▶ plural noun THE BACK OF BEYOND, remote areas, the wilds, the bush, bush country, bushland, the hinterlands, a backwater; the backcountry, (*Ont. & Que.*) the back concessions ♣, the backlands; the middle of nowhere, the sticks, the boondocks; moose pasture ♣, the boonies.

backyard ▶ noun YARD, garden, dooryard; lawn, grass.

bacteria ▶ plural noun MICRO-ORGANISMS, microbes, germs, bacilli, pathogens, prokaryotes; *informal* bugs.

bad ▶ adjective **1** *bad workmanship* SUBSTANDARD, poor, inferior, second-rate, second-class, unsatisfactory, inadequate, unacceptable, not up to scratch, not up to par, deficient, imperfect, defective, faulty, shoddy, amateurish, careless, negligent, miserable, sorry; incompetent, inept, inexpert, ineffectual; awful, atrocious, appalling, execrable, deplorable, terrible, abysmal, godawful; *informal* crummy, rotten, pathetic, useless, woeful, bum, lousy, not up to snuff. **2** *the alcohol had a really bad effect on me* HARMFUL, damaging, detrimental, injurious, hurtful, inimical, destructive, ruinous, deleterious; unhealthy, unwholesome. **3** *the bad guys* WICKED, evil, sinful, immoral, morally wrong, corrupt, base, black-hearted, reprobate, amoral; criminal, villainous, nefarious, iniquitous, dishonest, dishonourable, unscrupulous, unprincipled; *informal* crooked, bent, dirty; *dated* dastardly. **4** *you bad girl!* BADLY BEHAVED, naughty, ill-behaved, disobedient, wayward, wilful, self-willed, defiant, unruly, insubordinate, undisciplined. **5** *bad news* UNPLEASANT, disagreeable, unwelcome; unfortunate, unlucky, unfavourable; terrible, dreadful, awful, grim, distressing. **6** *a bad time to arrive* INAUSPICIOUS, unfavourable, inopportune, unpropitious, unfortunate, disadvantageous, adverse, inappropriate, unsuitable, untoward. **7** *a bad accident* SEVERE, serious, grave, critical, acute; *formal* grievous. **8** *the meat's bad* ROTTEN, off, decayed, decomposed, decomposing, putrid, putrefied, mouldy, mouldering, sour, spoiled, rancid, rank, unfit for human consumption; (of an egg) addled, (of beer) skunky ♣. **9** *if you still feel bad, stay in bed. See* ILL *adjective* sense 1. **10** *a bad knee* INJURED, wounded, diseased. **11** *I felt bad about leaving them* GUILTY, conscience-stricken, remorseful, guilt-ridden, ashamed, contrite, sorry, full of regret, regretful, shamefaced. **12** *a bad cheque* INVALID, worthless; counterfeit, fake, false, bogus, fraudulent; *informal* phony, dud. **13** *bad language* OFFENSIVE, vulgar, crude, foul, obscene, rude, coarse, smutty, dirty, filthy, indecent, indecorous; blasphemous, profane.
— OPPOSITES: good, beneficial, virtuous, well-behaved, minor, slight, fresh, unrepentant.

■ **not bad** ALL RIGHT, adequate, good enough, reasonable, fair, decent, average, tolerable, acceptable, passable, middling, moderate, fine; *informal* OK, so-so, {comme ci, comme ça}, fair-to-middling, satisfactory.

badge ▶ noun **1** *a name badge* pin, brooch, button, emblem, crest. **2** *a badge of success* SIGN, symbol, indication, signal, mark; hallmark, trademark.

badger ► verb PESTER, harass, bother, plague, torment, hound, nag, chivvy, harry, keep on at, tease, go on at; *informal* hassle, bug, get on someone's case.

badly ► adverb **1** *the job had very been badly done* POORLY, incompetently, ineptly, inexpertly, inefficiently, imperfectly, deficiently, defectively, unsatisfactorily, inadequately, incorrectly, faultily, shoddily, amateurishly, carelessly, negligently; abominably; *informal* crummily, pitifully, woefully. **2** *try not to think badly of me* UNFAVOURABLY, ill, critically, disapprovingly. **3** *stop behaving badly* NAUGHTILY, disobediently, wilfully, reprehensibly, mischievously. **4** *he had been badly treated* CRUELLY, wickedly, unkindly, harshly, shamefully; unfairly, unjustly, wrongly, improperly. **5** *it turned out badly* UNSUCCESSFULLY, unfavourably, adversely, unfortunately, unhappily, unluckily. **6** *some of the victims are badly hurt* SEVERELY, seriously, gravely, acutely, critically; *formal* grievously. **7** *she badly needs help* DESPERATELY, sorely, intensely, seriously, very much, greatly, exceedingly.
– OPPOSITES: well, slightly.

bad-tempered ► adjective *See* IRRITABLE.

baffle ► verb PERPLEX, puzzle, bewilder, mystify, bemuse, confuse, confound; *informal* flummox, faze, stump, beat, fox, make someone scratch their head, be all Greek to, floor, discombobulate.
– OPPOSITES: enlighten.

baffling ► adjective PUZZLING, BEWILDERING, perplexing, mystifying, bemusing, confusing, unclear; inexplicable, incomprehensible, impenetrable, cryptic, opaque.
– OPPOSITES: clear, comprehensible.

bag ► noun **1** *I dug around in my bag for my lipstick* HANDBAG, purse, shoulder bag, clutch bag; sack, pouch; *historical* reticule. **2** *she began to unpack her bags* SUITCASE, case, valise, portmanteau, grip, overnighter; backpack, rucksack, knapsack, haversack, carryall, (*Nfld*) nunny-bag ✦, kit bag, duffel bag; satchel; (**bags**) luggage, baggage. **3** (*informal*) *mystery novels just aren't my bag* INTEREST, preoccupation, concern; *informal* thing.
► verb **1** *locals bagged the most fish* CATCH, land, capture, trap, snare, ensnare; kill, shoot. **2** *he bagged seven medals* GET, secure, obtain, acquire, pick up; win, achieve, attain; commandeer, grab, appropriate, take; *informal* get one's hands on, land, net.

baggage ► noun LUGGAGE, suitcases, cases, bags.

baggy ► adjective LOOSE-FITTING, loose, roomy, full, ample, voluminous, billowing; oversized, shapeless, ill-fitting, tent-like, sacklike.
– OPPOSITES: tight.

bail ► noun *he was released on bail* SURETY, security, assurance, indemnity, indemnification; bond, guarantee, pledge; *archaic* gage.
■ **bail out** *the pilot bailed out* EJECT, parachute to safety; desert, cop out.
■ **bail someone/something out** RESCUE, save, relieve; finance, help (out), assist, aid; *informal* save someone's bacon/neck/skin.

bait ► noun **1** *the fish let go of the bait* LURE, decoy, fly, troll, jig, plug. **2** *was she the bait to lure him into a trap?* ENTICEMENT, lure, decoy, snare, trap, siren, carrot, attraction, draw, magnet, incentive, temptation, inducement; *informal* come-on.
► verb *he was baited at school* TAUNT, tease, goad, pick on, torment, persecute, plague, harry, bother, harass, hound; *informal* needle.

bake ► verb **1** *bake the fish for 15–20 minutes* COOK, oven-bake, roast, dry-roast, pot-roast. **2** *the earth was baked by the sun* SCORCH, burn, sear, parch, dry (up), desiccate; broil.

balance ► noun **1** *I tripped and lost my balance* STABILITY, equilibrium, steadiness, footing. **2** *political balance in broadcasting* FAIRNESS, justice, impartiality, even-handedness, egalitarianism, equal opportunity; parity, equity, equilibrium, equipoise, evenness, symmetry, correspondence, uniformity, equality, equivalence, comparability. **3** *this stylistic development provides a balance to the rest of the work* COUNTERBALANCE, counterweight, stabilizer, compensation. **4** *the food was weighed on a balance* SCALE(S), weighing machine. **5** *the balance of the rent* REMAINDER, outstanding amount, rest, residue, difference, remaining part.
– OPPOSITES: instability.
► verb **1** *she balanced the book on her head* STEADY, stabilize, poise, level. **2** *he balanced his radical remarks with more familiar declarations* COUNTERBALANCE, balance out, offset, even out/up, counteract, compensate for, make up for. **3** *their income and expenditure do not balance* CORRESPOND, agree, tally, match up, concur, coincide, be in agreement, be consistent, equate, be equal. **4** *you need to balance cost against benefit* WEIGH, weigh up, compare, evaluate, consider, assess, appraise, judge.
■ **in the balance** UNCERTAIN, undetermined, unsettled, unresolved, unsure, pending, in limbo, up in the air, at a turning point, critical, at a critical stage, at a crisis.
■ **on balance** OVERALL, all in all, all things considered, taking everything into consideration/account, by and large, on average.

balanced ► adjective **1** *a balanced view* FAIR, equitable, just, unbiased, unprejudiced, objective, impartial, even-handed, dispassionate. **2** *a balanced diet* MIXED, varied; healthy, sensible. **3** *a balanced individual* LEVEL-HEADED, well-balanced, well-adjusted, mature, stable, sensible, practical, realistic, with both feet on the ground, pragmatic, reasonable, rational, sane, even-tempered, commonsensical, full of common sense; *informal* together.
– OPPOSITES: partial, unhealthy, neurotic.

balcony ► noun **1** *the balcony of the villa* veranda, terrace, balustrade, patio. **2** *the applause from the balcony* GALLERY, box, dress circle, peanut gallery, loges, gods; choir loft.

bald ► adjective **1** *a bald head* HAIRLESS, smooth, shaven, depilated; bald-headed; *informal* chrome-domed. **2** *a few bald bushes* LEAFLESS, bare, uncovered. **3** *the bald prairie* TREELESS, naked, barren. **4** *a bald statement* PLAIN, simple, unadorned, unvarnished, unembellished, undisguised, unveiled, stark, severe, austere, brutal, harsh; blunt, direct, forthright, plain-spoken, straight, straightforward, candid, honest, truthful, realistic, frank, outspoken; *informal* upfront.
– OPPOSITES: hairy, lush, vague.

balderdash ► noun. *See* NONSENSE sense 1.

baldness ► noun HAIR LOSS, hairlessness; *Medical* alopecia.

bale ► noun *a bale of cotton* BUNDLE, bunch, pack, package, parcel.

baleful ► adjective MENACING, threatening, unfriendly, hostile, antagonistic, evil, evil-intentioned, vindictive, malevolent, malicious, malignant, malign, sinister; harmful, injurious,

dangerous, destructive, noxious, pernicious, deadly, venomous, poisonous; *literary* malefic, maleficent.
— OPPOSITES: benevolent, friendly.

balk ▶ verb **1** *I balk at paying that much* BE UNWILLING TO, draw the line at, jib at, be reluctant to, hesitate over; eschew, resist, scruple to, refuse to, take exception to; draw back from, flinch from, shrink from, recoil from, demur from, not like to, hate to. **2** *they were balked by traffic* IMPEDE, obstruct, thwart, hinder, prevent, check, stop, curb, halt, bar, block, forestall, frustrate.
— OPPOSITES: accept, assist.

ball ▶ noun **1** *a ball of dough* SPHERE, globe, orb, globule, spherule, spheroid, ovoid. **2** *a musket ball* BULLET, pellet, slug, projectile. **3** *a fancy-dress ball* DANCE, dinner dance, masked ball, formal, grad ♣, prom, masquerade; hoedown, barn dance, hop, bop. **4** *everyone had a ball* GOOD TIME, blast, riot.

ballad ▶ noun SONG, folk song, shanty, ditty, canzone; poem, tale, saga.

ballast ▶ noun STABILIZER, counterbalance, counterweight.

ballet ▶ noun. *See table.*

Ballet Steps

arabesque	glissé
arabesque penchée	grand battement
attitude	grand jeté
balancé	jeté
ballonné	pas de basque
ballotté	pas de bourrée
batterie	pas de chat
bourreée	pas de cheval
brisé	petit battement
cabriole	petit jeté
cambré	piqué
chaîné	pirouette
changement	plié
chassé	port de bras
dégagé	promenade
demi-plié	relevé
développé	retiré
écarté	rond de jambe à terre
échappé	rond de jambe en l'aire
enchaînement	sauté
entrechat	saut de basque
failli	sissonne
fondu	soubresaut
fouetté	temps levé
frappé	tour en l'air
glissade	

ball hockey (*Cdn*) ▶ noun street hockey ♣, road hockey ♣.

balloon ▶ noun hot-air balloon, barrage balloon; airship, dirigible, Zeppelin, blimp.
▶ verb **1** *her long skirt ballooned in the wind* SWELL (OUT), puff out/up, bulge (out), bag, belly (out), fill (out), billow (out), distend. **2** *the company's debt has ballooned* INCREASE RAPIDLY, soar, rocket, shoot up, escalate, mount, surge, spiral, go through the roof, skyrocket.
— OPPOSITES: plummet.

ballot ▶ noun VOTE, poll, election, referendum, plebiscite, show of hands.

ballyhoo ▶ noun (*informal*) PUBLICITY, advertising, promotion, marketing, propaganda, push, puffery, buildup, boosting; fuss, excitement; *informal* hype, spiel, hullabaloo, splash.

ballyhooed ▶ adjective HYPED, promoted, praised, acclaimed.

balm ▶ noun **1** *a skin balm* OINTMENT, lotion, cream, salve, liniment, embrocation, rub, gel, emollient, unguent, balsam, moisturizer; *dated* pomade; *archaic* unction. **2** *balm for troubled spirits* RELIEF, comfort, ease, succour, consolation, cheer, solace.
— OPPOSITES: astringent, misery.

balmy ▶ adjective MILD, gentle, temperate, summery, calm, tranquil, clement, fine, pleasant, benign, soothing, soft.
— OPPOSITES: harsh, wintry.

baloney ▶ noun *that's a bunch of baloney* NONSENSE, hogwash, garbage, bunk, bull, guff, drivel, malarkey. *See also* NONSENSE.

bamboozle ▶ verb (*informal*). *See* TRICK *verb*.

ban ▶ verb **1** *smoking was banned* PROHIBIT, forbid, veto, proscribe, disallow, outlaw, make illegal, embargo, bar, debar, block, stop, suppress, interdict; *Law* enjoin, restrain. **2** *Gary was banned from the playground* EXCLUDE, banish, expel, eject, evict, drive out, force out, oust, remove, get rid of; *informal* boot out, kick out, turf out.
— OPPOSITES: permit, admit.
▶ noun **1** *a ban on smoking* PROHIBITION, veto, proscription, embargo, bar, suppression, stoppage, interdict, interdiction, moratorium, injunction. **2** *a ban from international competition* EXCLUSION, banishment, expulsion, ejection, eviction, removal.
— OPPOSITES: permission, admission.

banal ▶ adjective TRITE, hackneyed, clichéd, platitudinous, vapid, commonplace, ordinary, common, stock, conventional, stereotyped, overused, overdone, overworked, stale, worn out, time-worn, tired, threadbare, hoary, hack, unimaginative, humdrum, ho-hum, unoriginal, uninteresting, dull, trivial; *informal* old hat, corny, cornball, played out.
— OPPOSITES: original.

banality ▶ noun **1** *the banality of most sitcoms* TRITENESS, vapidity, staleness, unimaginativeness, lack of originality, prosaicness, dullness; *informal* corniness. **2** *they exchanged banalities* PLATITUDE, cliché, truism, commonplace, old chestnut, bromide.
— OPPOSITES: originality, epigram, witticism.

band ▶ noun **1** *a band round her waist* BELT, sash, girdle, strap, tape, ring, hoop, loop, circlet, circle, cord, tie, string, thong, ribbon, fillet, strip; *literary* cincture. **2** *the green band around his pullover* STRIPE, strip, streak, line, bar, belt, swathe; *technical* stria, striation. **3** *a band of robbers* GROUP, gang, mob, pack, troop, company, party, crew, body, working party, posse; team, side, lineup; association, society, club, circle, fellowship, partnership, guild, lodge, order, fraternity, confraternity, sodality, brotherhood, sisterhood, sorority, union, alliance, affiliation, institution, league, federation, clique, set, coterie; *informal* bunch. **4** *the band played on* (MUSICAL) GROUP, pop group, ensemble, orchestra; *informal* combo.
▶ verb *local people banded together* JOIN (UP), team up, join forces, pool resources, get together; amalgamate, unite, form an alliance, form an association, affiliate, federate.
— OPPOSITES: split up.

bandage ▶ noun *she had a bandage on her foot* DRESSING, covering, gauze, compress, plaster, tourniquet; *proprietary* Band-Aid, *proprietary* Tensor bandage ♣.
▶ verb *she bandaged my knee* BIND, bind up, dress, cover, wrap, swaddle, strap (up).

bandana ▶ noun HEAD SCARF, kerchief, babushka.

bandit ▶ noun *they were robbed by bandits* ROBBER, thief, outlaw, gunman, crook, mugger, gangster, raider, freebooter, hijacker, looter, marauder; *dated* desperado; *literary* brigand; *historical* rustler, highwayman, footpad, reaver.

bandy¹ ▶ adjective *bandy legs* BOWED, curved, bent; bow-legged, bandy-legged.
– OPPOSITES: straight.

bandy² ▶ verb **1** *lots of figures were bandied about* SPREAD (ABOUT/AROUND), put about, toss about, discuss, rumour, mention, repeat; *literary* bruit about/abroad. **2** *I'm not going to bandy words with you* EXCHANGE, swap, trade.

bane ▶ noun SCOURGE, plague, curse, blight, pest, nuisance, headache, nightmare, trial, hardship, cross to bear, burden, thorn in one's flesh/side, bitter pill, affliction, trouble, misery, woe, tribulation, misfortune, pain.

bang ▶ noun **1** *the door slammed with a bang* THUD, thump, bump, crack, crash, smack, boom, clang, clap, knock, tap, clunk, clonk; stamp, stomp, clump, clomp, blam, bam, kaboom, kapow, wham, whump, whomp; report, explosion, detonation. **2** *a nasty bang on the head* BLOW, knock, thump, bump, hit, smack, bonk, crack, bash, whack, thwack.
▶ verb **1** *he banged the table with his fist* HIT, strike, beat, thump, hammer, knock, rap, pound, thud, punch, bump, smack, slap, slam, welt, cuff, pummel, buffet, bash, whack, thwack, clobber, clout, clip, wallop, belt, bop, sock, lam, whomp, bust, slug, whale. **2** *fireworks banged in the air* GO BANG, thud, thump, boom, clap, pound, crack, crash, explode, detonate, burst, blow up.
▶ adverb *(informal) bang in the middle of town | bang on time* PRECISELY, exactly, right, directly, immediately, squarely, dead; promptly, prompt, dead on, sharp, on the dot; *informal* smack, slap, smack dab, plumb, on the button, on the nose, spang.

bangle ▶ noun BRACELET, wristlet, anklet, armlet.

banish ▶ verb **1** *he was banished for his crime* EXILE, expel, deport, eject, expatriate, ostracize, extradite, repatriate, transport; cast out, oust, evict, throw out, exclude, shut out, ban. **2** *he tried to banish his fear* DISPEL, dismiss, disperse, scatter, dissipate, drive away, chase away, shut out, quell, allay.
– OPPOSITES: admit, engender.

banister ▶ noun HANDRAIL, railing, rail; baluster; balustrade.

bank¹ ▶ noun **1** *the bank of the great river* EDGE, side, shore, coast, embankment, bankside, levee, border, verge, boundary, margin, rim, fringe; *literary* marge, skirt. **2** *a grassy bank* SLOPE, rise, incline, gradient, ramp; mound, ridge, hillock, hummock, knoll; bar, reef, shoal, shelf; accumulation, pile, heap, mass, drift. **3** *a bank of switches* ARRAY, row, line, tier, group, series.
– RELATED TERMS: riparian.
▶ verb **1** *they banked up the earth* PILE (UP), heap (up), stack (up); accumulate, amass, assemble, put together. **2** *the aircraft banked* TILT, LEAN, tip, slant, incline, angle, slope, list, camber, pitch, dip, cant.

bank² ▶ noun **1** *money in the bank* FINANCIAL INSTITUTION, merchant bank, savings bank, finance company, trust company, credit union, (Que.) caisse populaire ♣. **2** *a blood bank* STORE, reserve, accumulation, stock, stockpile, supply, pool, fund, cache, hoard, deposit; storehouse, reservoir, repository, depository.
▶ verb *I banked the money* DEPOSIT, pay in, invest, lay away.
■ **bank on** RELY ON, depend on, count on, place reliance on, bargain on, plan on, reckon on, calculate on; anticipate, expect; be confident of, be sure of, pin one's hopes/faith on, figure on.

bank machine ▶ noun AUTOMATED TELLER MACHINE, automated banking machine, ATM, ABM ♣, instant teller.

bankroll ▶ verb FINANCE, pay for, fund, subsidize, invest in.

bankrupt ▶ adjective **1** *the company was declared bankrupt* INSOLVENT, failed, ruined, in debt, owing money, in the red, in arrears, in receivership; *informal* bust, belly up, broke, cash-strapped, flat broke. **2** *this government is bankrupt of ideas* BEREFT, devoid, empty, destitute; completely lacking, without, in need of, wanting.
– OPPOSITES: solvent, teeming with.
▶ verb *the strike nearly bankrupted the union* RUIN, impoverish, reduce to penury/destitution, bring to ruin, bring someone to their knees, wipe out, break, beggar, pauperize.

bankruptcy ▶ noun *many companies were facing bankruptcy* INSOLVENCY, liquidation, failure, (financial) ruin, collapse, receivership.
– OPPOSITES: solvency.

banner ▶ noun **1** *students waved banners* SIGN, placard, poster, notice. **2** *banners fluttered above the troops* FLAG, standard, ensign, colour(s), pennant, banderole, guidon; *Nautical* burgee.

banquet ▶ noun FEAST, dinner; *informal* spread, scoff.
– OPPOSITES: snack.

banter ▶ noun *a brief exchange of banter* REPARTEE, witty conversation, raillery, wordplay, cut and thrust, kidding, ribbing, badinage, joshing.
▶ verb *sightseers were bantering with the guards* JOKE, jest, quip; *informal* josh, wisecrack.

baptism ▶ noun **1** *the baptism ceremony* CHRISTENING, naming. **2** *his baptism as a politician* INITIATION, debut, introduction, inauguration, launch, rite of passage.

baptize ▶ verb **1** *he was baptized as a baby* CHRISTEN. **2** *they were baptized into the church* ADMIT, initiate, enrol, recruit, convert. **3** *he was baptized Enoch* NAME, give the name, call, dub; *formal* denominate.

bar ▶ noun **1** *an iron bar* ROD, pole, stick, batten, shaft, rail, paling, spar, strut, crosspiece, beam. **2** *a bar of chocolate* BLOCK, slab, cake, tablet, brick, wedge, ingot. **3** *your drinks are on the bar* COUNTER, table, buffet, stand. **4** *she had a drink in a bar* TAVERN, booze can ♣, watering hole, pub, cocktail lounge, barroom, beer parlour ♣, beverage room ♣, taproom, (Que.) brasserie ♣, gin mill, after-hours club, lounge, parlour ♣, nightclub, brew pub, speakeasy, blind pig, barrelhouse, roadhouse, beer cellar, boîte, club, dive, hotel, inn, nineteenth hole, rathskeller, estaminet, cantina, bodega; singles bar, sports bar, sushi bar, oyster bar, wine bar, juice bar; public house, legion (hall); *historical* saloon, alehouse. **5** *a bar to promotion* OBSTACLE, impediment, hindrance, obstruction, block, hurdle, barrier, stumbling block. **6** *members of the Bar* LAWYERS, barristers, advocates, counsel, solicitors. **7** *the bar across the river mouth* SANDBANK, sandbar, shoal, shallow, reef.
– OPPOSITES: aid.
▶ verb **1** *they have barred the door* BOLT, lock, fasten,

secure, block, barricade, obstruct. **2** *I was barred from entering* PROHIBIT, debar, preclude, forbid, ban, interdict, inhibit; exclude, keep out; obstruct, hinder, block; *Law* enjoin.
— OPPOSITES: open, admit.
▶ **preposition** *everyone bar me. See* EXCEPT *preposition.*

barb ▶ **noun 1** *the hook has a nasty barb* SPIKE, prong, spur, thorn, needle, prickle, spine, quill. **2** *the barbs from his critics* INSULT, sneer, jibe, cutting remark, shaft, slight, brickbat, slur, jeer, taunt; **(barbs)** abuse, disparagement, scoffing, scorn, sarcasm, goading; *informal* dig, put-down.

barbarian ▶ **noun** *the city was besieged by barbarians* SAVAGE, heathen, brute, beast, wild man/woman; ruffian, thug, lout, vandal, boor, hoodlum, hooligan, low-life, Neanderthal, knuckle-dragger, troglodyte; philistine; *informal* roughneck.
▶ **adjective** *the barbarian hordes* SAVAGE, uncivilized, barbaric, primitive, heathen, vulgar, wild, brutish, Neanderthal.
— OPPOSITES: civilized.

barbaric ▶ **adjective** *barbaric crimes* BRUTAL, barbarous, brutish, bestial, savage, vicious, wicked, cruel, ruthless, merciless, villainous, murderous, heinous, monstrous, vile, inhuman, infernal, dark, fiendish, diabolical.
— OPPOSITES: civilized.

barbarity ▶ **noun** *the barbarity of slavery* BRUTALITY, brutalism, cruelty, bestiality, barbarism, barbarousness, savagery, viciousness, wickedness, villainy, baseness, inhumanity; atrocity.
— OPPOSITES: benevolence.

barbarous ▶ **adjective.** *See* BARBARIC.

barbecue ▶ **noun** COOKOUT, (*Que.*) mechoui ✦, wiener roast, corn roast; barbie, BBQ, grill, *proprietary* Hibachi, rotisserie, brazier.
▶ **verb** GRILL, spit-roast, broil, charbroil.

barbed ▶ **adjective** HURTFUL, wounding, cutting, stinging, mean, spiteful, nasty, cruel, vicious, unkind, snide, scathing, pointed, bitter, acid, caustic, sharp, vitriolic, venomous, poisonous, hostile, malicious, malevolent, vindictive; *informal* bitchy, catty.
— OPPOSITES: kindly.

barber ▶ **noun** HAIRDRESSER, haircutter, stylist, coiffeur, coiffeuse.

bard ▶ **noun** (*literary*). *See* POET.

bare ▶ **adjective 1** *he was bare to the waist* NAKED, unclothed, undressed, uncovered, stripped, having nothing on, nude, in the nude, stark naked; *informal* without a stitch on, buck-naked, butt-naked, mother-naked, in one's birthday suit, in the raw, in the altogether, in the buff, starkers. **2** *a bare room* EMPTY, unfurnished, cleared; stark, austere, Spartan, unadorned, unembellished, unornamented, plain. **3** *a cupboard bare of food* EMPTY, devoid, bereft; without, lacking, wanting, free from. **4** *a bare landscape* BARREN, bleak, exposed, desolate, stark, arid, desert, lunar; treeless, deforested, bald. **5** *the bare facts* BASIC, essential, fundamental, plain, straightforward, simple, pure, stark, bald, cold, hard, brutal, harsh. **6** *a bare minimum* MERE, no more than, simple; slim, slight, slender, paltry, minimum.
— OPPOSITES: clothed, furnished, embellished, lush.
▶ **verb** *he bared his arm* UNCOVER, strip, lay bare, undress, unclothe, denude, expose.
— OPPOSITES: cover.

barefaced ▶ **adjective** FLAGRANT, blatant, glaring,

obvious, undisguised, unconcealed, naked; shameless, unabashed, unashamed, impudent, audacious, unblushing, brazen.

barely ▶ **adverb** HARDLY, scarcely, just, only just, narrowly, by the skin of one's teeth, by a hair's breadth; almost not; *informal* by a whisker.
— OPPOSITES: easily.

bargain ▶ **noun 1** *this binder is a bargain at $1.98* GOOD BUY, (good) value for money, surprisingly cheap; *informal* steal, bargoon ✦, deal, giveaway, best buy. **2** *I'll make a bargain with you* AGREEMENT, arrangement, understanding, deal; contract, pact, compact; pledge, promise.
— OPPOSITES: rip-off.
▶ **verb** *they bargained over the contract* HAGGLE, negotiate, discuss terms, hold talks, deal, barter, dicker; *formal* treat.
■ **bargain for/on** EXPECT, anticipate, be prepared for, allow for, plan for, reckon with, take into account/consideration, contemplate, imagine, envisage, foresee, predict; count on, rely on, depend on, bank on, plan on, reckon on, figure on.
■ **in(to) the bargain** ALSO, as well, in addition, additionally, besides, on top of (that), over and above that, to boot, for good measure.

barge ▶ **noun** lighter, canal boat, wherry, scow.
▶ **verb** *he barged into us* PUSH, shove, force, elbow, shoulder, jostle, bulldoze, muscle.
■ **barge in** BURST IN, break in, butt in, cut in, interrupt, intrude, encroach; *informal* horn in.

bark[1] ▶ **noun** *the bark of a dog* WOOF, yap, yelp, bay.
▶ **verb 1** *the dog barked* WOOF, yap, yelp, bay. **2** *'Okay, outside!' he barked* SAY BRUSQUELY, say abruptly, say angrily, snap; shout, bawl, cry, yell, roar, bellow, thunder; *informal* holler.
— OPPOSITES: whisper.

bark[2] ▶ **noun** *the bark of a tree* RIND, skin, peel, covering; integument; cork; *technical* cortex.
— RELATED TERMS: corticate.

barn ▶ **noun** OUTBUILDING, shed, cowshed, shelter; stable, stall, outhouse; *archaic* grange, garner.

baron ▶ **noun 1** *he was created a baron* LORD, noble, nobleman, aristocrat, peer. **2** *a press baron* MAGNATE, tycoon, mogul, captain of industry, nabob, mandarin.

barracks ▶ **plural noun** GARRISON, camp, encampment, depot, billet, quarters, fort, cantonment.

barrage ▶ **noun 1** *an artillery barrage* BOMBARDMENT, cannonade; gunfire, shelling; salvo, volley, fusillade; *historical* broadside. **2** *a barrage of criticism* DELUGE, stream, storm, torrent, onslaught, flood, shower, spate, tide, avalanche, hail, blaze; abundance, mass, profusion.

barrel ▶ **noun** CASK, keg, butt, vat, tun, drum, hogshead, kilderkin, barrique, pipe; *historical* firkin.
— RELATED TERMS: cooper, stave, hoop.
▶ **verb** CHARGE, plow, stampede, rush, go headlong; zoom.

barren ▶ **adjective 1** *barren land* UNPRODUCTIVE, infertile, unfruitful, sterile, arid, desert. **2** (*archaic*) *a barren woman* INFERTILE, sterile, childless; *technical* infecund. **3** *a barren exchange of courtesies* POINTLESS, futile, worthless, profitless, valueless, unrewarding, purposeless, useless, vain, aimless, hollow, empty, vacuous, vapid.
— OPPOSITES: fertile.

Baseball Terms

Playing & Keeping Score		People	Field Locations & Equipment
assist	pinch hit	**People**	**Field Locations &**
at-bat	pitchout	batter	**Equipment**
balk	pop fly	designated hitter	ball field
base hit	pop-up	slugger	ballpark
blooper	popout	switch hitter	diamond
box score	put-out	baserunner	pitcher's mound
bouncer	roller	runner	home plate
bounder	rundown	fielder	first base
bunt	sacrifice fly	outfielder	second base
called strike	single	left fielder	third base
chopper	squeeze play	centre fielder	hot corner
inning	squibbler	right fielder	infield
dinger	steal	cut-off man	outfield
double	stolen base	infielder	baseline
double play	strike	shortstop	basepath
double steal	strikeout	catcher	foul line
earned run	strike zone	backcatcher ♣	alley
extra-base hit	Texas leaguer	backstop	dugout
fielder's choice	triple	pitcher	on-deck circle
fly ball	triple play	ace	batting cage
force play	walk	closer	ball
forceout		fireballer	bat
foul ball	**Pitches**	hurler	baseball cap/hat
foul tip	breaking ball	relief pitcher	baseball glove
grand slam	beanball	set-up man	
grounder	brushback	starter	**Similar Games**
groundout	changeup	stopper	box ball
hit	curve ball	bullpen	fastball ♣
hit and run	fadeaway	battery	fast pitch
home run	fastball	ballboy	kickball
homer	forkball	ballgirl	rounders
hopper	gopher ball	umpire	slo-pitch
intentional walk	knuckleball		softball
line drive	off-speed		stickball
loading the bases	screwball		stoopball
no-hitter	sinker		three-pitch ♣
passed ball	slider		T-ball
perfect game	spitball		wall ball
pickoff	split-fingered		
	wild pitch		

barricade ▶ noun *a barricade across the street* BARRIER, roadblock, blockade; obstacle, obstruction.
▶ verb *they barricaded the building* SEAL (UP), close up, block off, shut off/up; defend, protect, fortify, occupy.

barrier ▶ noun **1** *the barrier across the entrance* FENCE, railing, barricade, hurdle, bar, blockade, roadblock. **2** *a barrier to international trade* OBSTACLE, obstruction, hurdle, stumbling block, bar, block, impediment, hindrance, curb.

barring ▶ preposition EXCEPT FOR, with the exception of, excepting, in the absence of, if there is/are no, discounting, short of, apart from, but for, other than, aside from, excluding, omitting, leaving out, save for, saving; *informal* outside of.

bartender ▶ noun barkeep, barmaid, barman, beer slinger ♣, tapster; barista.

barter ▶ verb **1** *they bartered grain for salt* TRADE, swap, exchange, sell. **2** *you can barter for souvenirs* HAGGLE, bargain, negotiate, discuss terms, deal, dicker; *formal* treat.

base ▶ noun **1** *the base of the tower* FOUNDATION, bottom, foot, support, stand, pedestal, plinth. **2** *the system uses existing technology as its base* BASIS, foundation, bedrock, starting point, source, origin, root(s), core, key component, heart, backbone. **3** *the*

troops returned to their base HEADQUARTERS, camp, site, station, settlement, post, centre, starting point.
— OPPOSITES: top.
▶ verb **1** *he based his idea on a movie* FOUND, build, construct, form, ground, root; use as a basis; (**be based on**) derive from, spring from, stem from, originate in, have its origin in, issue from. **2** *the company was based in Laval* LOCATE, situate, position, install, station, site, establish; garrison.
▶ adjective *base motives* SORDID, ignoble, low, low-minded, mean, immoral, improper, unseemly, unscrupulous, unprincipled, dishonest, dishonourable, shameful, bad, wrong, evil, wicked, iniquitous, sinful.
— OPPOSITES: noble.

baseball ▶ noun ball. *See table.*

baseless ▶ adjective *baseless accusations* GROUNDLESS, unfounded, ill-founded, without foundation; unsubstantiated, unproven, unsupported, uncorroborated, unconfirmed, unverified, unattested; unjustified, unwarranted; speculative, conjectural; unsound, unreliable, spurious, specious, trumped up, fabricated, untrue.
— OPPOSITES: valid.

basement ▶ noun CELLAR, downstairs.

bash ▶ verb **1** *she bashed him with her stick* STRIKE, hit, beat, thump, slap, smack, bang, knock, batter, pound, pummel, wallop, clout, belt, whack, schmuck ♣, thwack, clobber, bop, sock, cold-cock; *archaic* smite. **2** *they bashed into one another* CRASH, run, bang, smash, slam, knock, bump; collide with, hit, meet head-on. **3** *bashing the government* CRITICIZE, censure, assail, attack, condemn, revile, denounce, rail against, cast aspersions on; *informal* pan, slam, hammer, lay into, pull to pieces, trash.
▶ noun **1** *a bash on the head* BLOW, rap, hit, knock, bang, slap, crack, thump, tap, wallop, clout, belt, whack, bonk, thwack, bop, sock; *archaic* smite. **2** *Harry's birthday bash. See* PARTY *noun* sense 1.

bashful ▶ adjective SHY, reserved, diffident, inhibited, retiring, reticent, reluctant, shrinking; hesitant, timid, apprehensive, nervous, wary demure, coy, blushing.
− OPPOSITES: bold, confident.

basic ▶ adjective **1** *basic human rights* FUNDAMENTAL, essential, primary, principal, cardinal, elementary, elemental, quintessential, intrinsic, central, pivotal, critical, key, focal; vital, necessary, indispensable. **2** *basic cooking facilities* PLAIN, simple, unsophisticated, straightforward, adequate; unadorned, undecorated, unornamented, without frills; Spartan, stark, severe, austere, limited, meagre, rudimentary, patchy, sketchy, minimal; unfussy, homely, homespun, meat-and-potatoes, bread-and-butter; rough (and ready), crude, makeshift.
− OPPOSITES: secondary, unimportant, elaborate.

basically ▶ adverb FUNDAMENTALLY, essentially, in essence; firstly, first of all, first and foremost, primarily; at heart, at bottom, au fond; principally, chiefly, above all, most of all, mostly, mainly, on the whole, by and large, substantially; intrinsically, inherently; *informal* at the end of the day, when all is said and done.

basics ▶ plural noun FUNDAMENTALS, essentials, rudiments, (first) principles, foundations, preliminaries, groundwork; essence, basis, core; *informal* nitty-gritty, brass tacks, nuts and bolts, meat and potatoes, bread and butter, ABC.

basin ▶ noun **1** *she poured water into the basin* BOWL, dish, pan; sink, washtub. **2** *a basin among low hills* VALLEY, hollow, dip, depression.

basis ▶ noun **1** *the basis of his method* FOUNDATION, support, base; reasoning, rationale, defence; reason, grounds, justification, motivation. **2** *the basis of discussion* STARTING POINT, base, point of departure, beginning, premise, fundamental point/principle, principal constituent, main ingredient, cornerstone, core, heart, thrust, essence, kernel, nub. **3** *on a part-time basis* FOOTING, condition, status, position; arrangement, system, method.

bask ▶ verb **1** *I basked in the sun* LAZE, lie, lounge, relax, sprawl, loll, wallow; sunbathe, sun oneself. **2** *she's basking in all the glory* REVEL, delight, luxuriate, wallow, take pleasure, rejoice, glory, indulge oneself; enjoy, relish, savour, lap up.

basket ▶ noun WICKERWORK BOX, hamper, creel, pannier, bushel.

basketball ▶ noun *See table.*

bass ▶ adjective LOW, deep, low-pitched, resonant, sonorous, rumbling, booming, resounding; baritone.
− OPPOSITES: high.

bastard ▶ noun **1** *(archaic) he had fathered a bastard* ILLEGITIMATE CHILD, child born out of wedlock, love child; *dated* by-blow; *archaic* natural child/son/daughter. **2** *(informal) he's a real bastard* SCOUNDREL, jerk, rascal, rogue, scamp, scalawag, miscreant, good-for-nothing, nogoodnik, reprobate, villain, low-life, beast, rat (fink), louse, swine, dog, skunk, heel, snake (in the grass); slimeball, son of a bitch, SOB, scumbag, scum-bucket, scuzzball, dirtbag, sleazeball, sleazebag; sleeveen; *dated* hound, cad; *archaic* blackguard, knave, varlet, whoreson.
▶ adjective **1** *(archaic) a bastard child* ILLEGITIMATE, born out of wedlock; *archaic* natural. **2** *a bastard socialism* ADULTERATED, alloyed, impure, inferior; hybrid, mongrel, patchwork.

bastardize ▶ verb ADULTERATE, corrupt, contaminate, weaken, dilute, taint, pollute, debase, distort.

bastion ▶ noun **1** *the town wall and bastions*

Basketball Terms

basketball	**Playing**
b-ball	air ball
hoops	alley-oop
	assist
Players	back door
cager	bank shot
centre	board
forward	coast-to-coast
guard	conversion
hoopster	double dribble
point guard	dribble
power forward	dunk
small forward	fadeaway
shooting guard	fallaway
	fast break
Court Positions and	field goal
Objects	foul shot
arc	free throw
backboard	full-court press
backcourt	goaltending
baseline	hook shot
basket	inbound
court	jump ball
downcourt	jumper
foul line	jumpshot
frontcourt	layup
half court	personal foul
high post	pick
hoop	pick-and-roll
iron	pivot
key	press
lane	rebound
low post	set shot
midcourt	shootaround
paint	skyhook
passing lane	slam
point	slam dunk
post	swish
shot clock	team foul
sideline	technical foul
three-point line	three
upcourt	three-pointer
	throw-in
	tip
	tip-in
	tipoff
	travelling
	trey
	triple-double

PROJECTION, outwork, breastwork, barbican; *Architecture* bartizan. **2** *a* bastion *of respectability* STRONGHOLD, bulwark, defender, support, supporter, guard, protection, protector, defence, prop, mainstay.

bat ▶ **verb** WHACK, thwack, back, rap, knock.

batch ▶ **noun** GROUP, quantity, lot, bunch, mass, cluster, raft, set, collection, bundle, pack; consignment, shipment.

bath ▶ **noun 1** *he lay soaking in the* bath BATHTUB, tub, hot tub, whirlpool, sauna, steam bath, Turkish bath; *proprietary* Jacuzzi. **2** *give it a* bath WASH, soak, cleansing, soaking, scrubbing, ablutions; dip; shower.

bathe ▶ **verb 1** *she bathed and dressed* HAVE/TAKE A BATH, wash; shower. **2** *I bathed in the local swimming pool* SWIM, go swimming, take a dip. **3** *they bathed his wounds* CLEAN, wash, rinse, wet, soak, immerse. **4** *the room was bathed in light* SUFFUSE, permeate, pervade, envelop, flood, cover, wash, fill.

bathing suit ▶ **noun** SWIMSUIT; bikini, swim trunks, monokini, maillot; swimwear.

bathos ▶ **noun** ANTICLIMAX, letdown, disappointment, disillusionment; absurdity; *informal* comedown.

bathroom ▶ **noun** *Excuse me, where's the bathroom?* WASHROOM, toilet, men's/ladies' room, restroom, lavatory, water closet, powder room, urinal, privy, latrine, commode, comfort station, WC, facilities; little girls'/boys' room, can, john, loo, biffy, throne room; *Nautical* head.

baton ▶ **noun 1** *the conductor's* baton STICK, rod, staff, wand. **2** *police* batons TRUNCHEON, club, billy club, cudgel, bludgeon, stick, nightstick, blackjack, mace, shillelagh.

battalion ▶ **noun 1** *an infantry* battalion regiment, brigade, force, division, squadron, squad, company, section, detachment, contingent, legion, corps, cohort. **2** *a* battalion *of supporters.* See CROWD *noun sense 1.*

batten ▶ **noun** *a timber* batten BAR, bolt, rail, shaft; board, strip.
▶ **verb** *Stephen was* battening *down the shutters* FASTEN, fix, secure, clamp, lash, make fast, nail, seal.

batter ▶ **verb** PUMMEL, pound, hit repeatedly, buffet, thrash, beat up, clobber, trounce, rain blows on; *informal* knock around/about, beat the living daylights out of, give someone a good hiding, lay into, lace into, do over, rough up.

battered ▶ **adjective** DAMAGED, shabby, run-down, worn out, beat-up, falling to pieces, falling apart, dilapidated, rickety, ramshackle, crumbling, the worse for wear, on its last legs; ABUSED.

battery ▶ **noun 1** *insert fresh* batteries CELL. **2** *a gun* battery EMPLACEMENT, artillery unit; cannonry, ordnance. **3** *a* battery *of equipment* ARRAY, series, set, bank, group, row, line, lineup, collection. **4** *a* battery *of tests* SERIES, sequence, cycle, string, succession. **5** *assault and* battery VIOLENCE, assault, mugging.

battle ▶ **noun 1** *he was killed in the* battle FIGHT, armed conflict, clash, struggle, skirmish, engagement, fray, duel; war, campaign, crusade; fighting, warfare, combat, action, hostilities; *informal* scrap, dogfight, shoot-out; brawl. See table. **2** *a power* battle *at the office* CONFLICT, clash, contest, competition, struggle, turf war; disagreement, argument, altercation, dispute, controversy, tug-of-war.
▶ **verb 1** *he has been* battling *against illness* FIGHT, combat, contend with; resist, withstand, stand up to,

confront; war, feud; struggle, strive, work. **2** *Mark* battled *his way to the bar* FORCE, push, elbow, shoulder, fight; struggle, labour.

Canadian Battles

Seven Years War	Boer War
Fort Beauséjour 1755	Leliefontein 1900
Plains of Abraham 1759	Paardeberg 1900
Restigouche 1760	**First World War**
Sainte-Foy 1760	Ypres 1915
War of 1812	Mount Sorrel 1916
Queenston Heights 1812	Somme 1916
Beaver Dams 1813	Hill 70 1917
Châteauguay 1813	Passchendaele 1917
Crysler's Farm 1813	Vimy Ridge 1917
Moraviantown 1813	Amiens 1918
Put-in-Bay 1813	Hindenburg Line 1918
Stoney Creek 1813	**Second World War**
Lundy's Lane 1814	Battle of the Atlantic 1939-1945
Plattsburgh 1814	Battle of Britain 1940
Rebellions of 1837	Hong Kong 1941
Saint-Denis 1837	Dieppe 1942
Saint-Eustache 1837	Ortona 1943
Fenian Raids	D-Day 1944
Ridgeway 1866	Hitler Line 1944
Northwest Rebellion	Normandy 1944
Batoche 1885	Scheldt Estuary 1944
Cut Knife 1885	Rhineland 1945
Duck Lake 1885	**Korean War**
Fish Creek 1885	Kap'yong 1951
Frenchman's Butte 1885	

battleaxe ▶ **noun 1** *a severe blow from a* battleaxe POLEAXE, axe, pike, halberd, tomahawk. **2** *(informal)* *she's a real* battleaxe. See HARRIDAN.

battle cry ▶ **noun 1** *the army's* battle cry WAR CRY, war whoop, rallying call/cry; rebel yell, banzai. **2** *the battle cry of the feminist movement* SLOGAN, motto, watchword, catchphrase, mantra.

battlefield ▶ **noun** BATTLEGROUND, field of battle, field of operations, combat zone, theatre (of war), front.

battlement ▶ **noun** CASTELLATION, crenellation, parapet, rampart, wall.

batty ▶ **adjective** *(informal).* See MAD *sense 1.*

bauble ▶ **noun** TRINKET, knick-knack, ornament, frippery, gewgaw, gimcrack, bibelot, kickshaw, tchotchke.

baulk ▶ **verb.** See BALK.

bawdy ▶ **adjective** RIBALD, indecent, risqué, racy, rude, spicy, sexy, suggestive, titillating, naughty, improper, indelicate, indecorous, off-colour, earthy, barnyard, broad, locker-room, Rabelaisian; pornographic, obscene, vulgar, crude, coarse, lewd, dirty, filthy, smutty, unseemly, salacious, prurient, lascivious, licentious, X-rated, blue, raunchy, nudge-nudge; *euphemistic* adult.
— OPPOSITES: clean, innocent.

bawl ▶ **verb 1** *'Come on!' he* bawled SHOUT, yell, roar, bellow, screech, scream, shriek, howl, whoop, bark, trumpet, thunder; *informal* yammer, holler. **2** *the children continued to* bawl CRY, sob, weep, shed tears, wail, whine, howl, squall, ululate.
— OPPOSITES: whisper.

■ **bawl someone out** *(informal).* See REPRIMAND.

bay¹ ▶ **noun** *ships were anchored in the* bay COVE, inlet, indentation, gulf, bight, basin, fjord, arm; natural harbour, anchorage.

bay² ▶ noun *there was a bay let into the wall* ALCOVE, recess, niche, nook, oriel, opening, hollow, cavity, inglenook; compartment.

bay³ ▶ verb HOWL, bark, yelp, yap, cry, bellow, roar.
■ **at bay** AT A DISTANCE, away, off, at arm's length.

bayonet ▶ noun *a man armed with a bayonet* sword, knife, blade, spear, lance, pike, javelin.

bazaar ▶ noun **1** *a Turkish bazaar* MARKET, marketplace, souk, mart, exchange. **2** *the church bazaar* RUMMAGE SALE, fair, carnival, garage sale, yard sale; fundraiser, charity event; flea market, swap meet.

be ▶ verb **1** *there was once a king* EXIST, have being, have existence; live, be alive, have life, breathe, draw breath, be extant. **2** *is there a doctor around here?* BE PRESENT, be around, be available, be near, be nearby, be at hand. **3** *the trial is tomorrow at half past one* OCCUR, happen, take place, come about, arise, crop up, transpire, fall, materialize, ensue; *literary* come to pass, befall, betide. **4** *the bed is over there* BE SITUATED, be located, be found, be present, be set, be positioned, be placed, be installed. **5** *it has been like this for hours* REMAIN, stay, last, continue, survive, endure, persist, prevail; wait, linger, hold on, hang on; *formal* obtain.

beach ▶ noun *a sandy beach* SEASIDE, seashore, shore, coast, waterfront, lakeshore, coastline, coastal region, littoral, seaboard, foreshore, water's edge; sands; *literary* strand.
▶ verb *they beached the boat* LAND, ground, strand, run aground, run ashore.

beached ▶ adjective STRANDED, grounded, aground, ashore, marooned, high and dry, stuck, washed up/ashore.

beacon ▶ noun LIGHTHOUSE, signal (light/fire), danger signal, bonfire, warning light/fire.

bead ▶ noun **1** *a string of beads* BALL, pellet, pill, globule, sphere, spheroid, oval, ovoid, orb, round; (**beads**) necklace, rosary, chaplet. **2** *beads of sweat* DROPLET, drop, blob, dot, dewdrop, teardrop.
■ **draw/get a bead on** AIM AT, fix on, focus on, zero in on, sight.

beak ▶ noun *a bird's beak* BILL, mandible.

beam ▶ noun **1** *an oak beam* JOIST, lintel, rafter, purlin; spar, girder, balk, timber, two-by-four, plank; support, strut; scantling, transom, stringer, collar beam, I-beam. **2** *a beam of light coming from the window* RAY, shaft, stream, streak, pencil, finger; flash, gleam, glow, glimmer, glint, flare. **3** *the beam on her face* GRIN, smile, happy expression, bright look.
— OPPOSITES: frown.
▶ verb **1** *the signal is beamed out* BROADCAST, transmit, relay, emit, send/put out, disseminate; direct, aim. **2** *the sun beamed down* SHINE, radiate, give off light, glare, gleam. **3** *he beamed broadly* GRIN, smile, smirk; *informal* be all smiles.
— OPPOSITES: frown.

beaming ▶ adjective **1** *his beaming face* GRINNING, smiling, laughing; cheerful, happy, radiant, glowing, sunny, joyful, elated, thrilled, delighted, overjoyed, rapturous, blissful. **2** *he greeted her with a beaming smile* BRIGHT, CHEERY, sparkling, flashing, brilliant, dazzling, intense, gleaming, radiant.
— OPPOSITES: frowning.

bear¹ ▶ verb **1** *I come bearing gifts* CARRY, bring, transport, move, convey, take, fetch, tote, lug.

2 *the bag bore my name* DISPLAY, exhibit, be marked with, show, carry, have. **3** *will it bear his weight?* SUPPORT, carry, hold up, prop up. **4** *they can't bear the cost alone* SUSTAIN, carry, support, shoulder, absorb, take on. **5** *she bore no grudge* HARBOUR, foster, entertain, cherish, nurse, nurture, brood over. **6** *such a solution does not bear close scrutiny* WITHSTAND, stand up to, stand, put up with, take, cope with, handle, sustain, accept. **7** *I can't bear having him around* ENDURE, tolerate, put up with, stand, abide, submit to, experience, undergo, go through, countenance, brave, weather, stomach, support; *informal* hack, swallow; *formal* brook; *archaic* suffer. **8** *she bore a son* GIVE BIRTH TO, bring forth, deliver, be delivered of, have, produce, spawn, birth; *informal* drop; *literary* beget. **9** *a shrub that bears yellow berries* PRODUCE, yield, give forth, give, grow, provide, supply. **10** *bear left at the junction* VEER, curve, swerve, fork, diverge, deviate, turn, bend.
■ **bear oneself** CONDUCT ONESELF, carry oneself, acquit oneself, act, behave, perform; *formal* comport oneself.
■ **bear down on** ADVANCE ON, close in on, move in on, converge on.
■ **bear fruit** YIELD RESULTS, get results, succeed, meet with success, be successful, be effective, be profitable, work, go as planned; *informal* pay off, come off, pan out, do the trick.
■ **bear something in mind** TAKE INTO ACCOUNT, take into consideration, remember, consider, be mindful, mind, mark, heed.
■ **bear on** BE RELEVANT TO, appertain to, pertain to, relate to, have a bearing on, have relevance to, apply to, be pertinent to.
■ **bear something out** CONFIRM, corroborate, substantiate, endorse, vindicate, give credence to, support, ratify, warrant, uphold, justify, prove, authenticate, verify.
■ **bear with** BE PATIENT WITH, show forbearance towards, make allowances for, tolerate, put up with, endure.
■ **bear witness/testimony to** TESTIFY TO, be evidence of, be proof of, attest to, evidence, prove, vouch for; demonstrate, show, establish, indicate, reveal, bespeak.

bear² ▶ noun. *See table.*
— RELATED TERMS: ursine.

Bears

American black bear	kermode bear
Asian black bear	Kodiak bear
brown bear	polar bear
cave bear (extinct)	Siberian brown bear
cinnamon bear	silvertip grizzly
giant panda	sloth bear
glacier bear	snow bear
grizzly bear	spirit bear
ice bear	sun bear

bearable ▶ adjective TOLERABLE, endurable, supportable, sustainable, sufferable.

beard ▶ noun *a black beard* FACIAL HAIR, whiskers, stubble, five o'clock shadow, bristles; goatee, imperial, Vandyke.
▶ verb *it was up to me to beard the bully* CONFRONT, face, challenge, brave, come face to face with, meet head on; defy, oppose, stand up against, dare, throw down the gauntlet to.

bearded ▶ adjective UNSHAVEN, whiskered, whiskery, bewhiskered; stubbly, bristly.
— OPPOSITES: clean-shaven.

bearer ▶ noun **1** *a lantern-bearer* CARRIER, porter. **2** *the bearer of bad news* MESSENGER, agent, conveyor, carrier, emissary. **3** *the bearer of the documents* HOLDER, possessor, owner.

bearing ▶ noun **1** *a man of military bearing* POSTURE, stance, carriage, gait, deportment; *formal* comportment. **2** *a rather regal bearing* DEMEANOUR, manner, air, aspect, attitude, behaviour, mien, style. **3** *this has no bearing on the matter* RELEVANCE, pertinence, connection, appositeness, germaneness, importance, significance, application. **4** *a bearing of 15°* DIRECTION, orientation, course, trajectory, heading, tack, path, line, run. **5** *he tormented her beyond bearing* ENDURANCE, tolerance, toleration. **6** *I lost my bearings* ORIENTATION, sense of direction; whereabouts, location, position.

beast ▶ noun **1** *the beasts of the forest* ANIMAL, creature, brute; *informal* critter, varmint. **2** *he is a cruel beast* MONSTER, brute, savage, barbarian, animal, swine, pig, ogre, fiend, demon, devil.
— RELATED TERMS: bestial.

beastly ▶ adjective **1** *politics is a beastly profession* AWFUL, horrible, rotten, nasty, foul, objectionable, unpleasant, disagreeable, offensive, vile, abominable, hateful, detestable, terrible, godawful. **2** *he was beastly to her* UNKIND, malicious, mean, nasty, unpleasant, unfriendly, spiteful, cruel, vicious, base, foul, malevolent, despicable, contemptible, horrible, horrid, rotten.
— OPPOSITES: pleasant, kind.

beat ▶ verb **1** *they were beaten with truncheons* HIT, strike, batter, thump, bang, hammer, punch, knock, thrash, pound, pummel, slap, smack, rain blows on; assault, attack, abuse; cudgel, club, birch; *informal* wallop, belt, bash, whack, thwack, clout, clobber, schmuck ♣, slug, tan, bop, sock, deck, plug, beat the living daylights out of, give someone a good hiding; *dated* chastise. **2** *the waves beat all along the shore* BREAK ON/AGAINST, dash against; lash, strike, lap, wash; splash, ripple, roll; *literary* plash, lave. **3** *the metal is beaten into a die* HAMMER, forge, form, shape, mould, work, stamp, fashion, model. **4** *her heart was still beating* PULSATE, pulse, palpitate, vibrate, throb; pump, pound, thump, thud, hammer, drum; pitter-patter. **5** *the eagle beat its wings* FLAP, flutter, thresh, thrash, wave, vibrate, oscillate. **6** *beat the cream into the mixture* WHISK, mix, blend, whip. **7** *she beat a path through the grass* TREAD, tramp, trample, wear, flatten, press down. **8** *the team they need to beat* DEFEAT, conquer, win against, get the better of, vanquish, trounce, rout, overpower, overcome, subdue; *informal* lick, thrash, whip, wipe the floor with, clobber, cream, shellac, skunk. **9** *he beat the record* SURPASS, exceed, better, improve on, go one better than, eclipse, transcend, top, trump, cap.
▶ noun **1** *the song has a good beat* RHYTHM, pulse, metre, time, measure, cadence; stress, accent. **2** *the beat of hooves* POUNDING, banging, thumping, thudding, booming, hammering, battering, crashing. **3** *the beat of her heart* PULSE, pulsating, vibration, throb, palpitation, reverberation; pounding, thump, thud, hammering, drumming; pitter-patter. **4** *a policeman on his beat* CIRCUIT, round, route, way, path.
▶ adjective (*informal*) *phew, I'm beat! See* EXHAUSTED sense 1.
■ **beat a (hasty) retreat.** *See* RETREAT verb sense 1.
■ **beat it** (*informal*). *See* RUN verb sense 2.

■ **beat someone up** ASSAULT, attack, mug, thrash, do over, work over, rough up, lay into, lace into, sail into, beat the living daylights out of, let someone have it, beat up on, knock about/around.

beaten ▶ adjective **1** *the beaten team* DEFEATED, losing, unsuccessful, conquered, bettered, vanquished, trounced, routed, overcome, overwhelmed, overpowered, overthrown, bested, subdued, quashed, crushed, broken, foiled, hapless, luckless; *informal* licked, thrashed, clobbered. **2** *a beaten dog* ABUSED, battered, maltreated, ill-treated, mistreated, misused, downtrodden; ASSAULTED, thumped, whacked, schmucked ♣, hit, thrashed, pummelled, smacked, drubbed; *informal* walloped, belted, bashed, clobbered, knocked about/around, roughed up. **3** *gradually stir in the beaten eggs* WHISKED, whipped, stirred, mixed, blended; frothy, foamy. **4** *a beaten path* TRODDEN, trampled; well-trodden, much trodden, well-used, much travelled, worn, well-worn.
— OPPOSITES: victorious, winning.
■ **off the beaten track** *we tried to find locations off the beaten track* OUT OF THE WAY, isolated, quiet, private, remote, unfrequented, outlying, secluded, hidden, backwoods, in the back of beyond, in the middle of nowhere, in the hinterlands; *informal* in the sticks.
— OPPOSITES: busy, popular.

beatific ▶ adjective **1** *a beatific smile* RAPTUROUS, joyful, ecstatic, seraphic, blissful, serene, happy, beaming. **2** *a beatific vision* BLESSED, exalted, sublime, heavenly, holy, divine, celestial, paradisical, glorious.

beatify ▶ verb CANONIZE, bless, sanctify, hallow, consecrate, make holy.

beatitude ▶ noun BLESSEDNESS, benediction, grace; bliss, ecstasy, exaltation, supreme happiness, divine joy/rapture; saintliness, sainthood.

beau ▶ noun (*dated*) **1** *Sally and her beau* BOYFRIEND, sweetheart, lover, darling, partner, significant other, escort, young man, admirer, suitor, main squeeze, boy toy. **2** *an eighteenth-century beau* DANDY, fop; *dated* swell, coxcomb, popinjay.

beautiful ▶ adjective ATTRACTIVE, pretty, handsome, good-looking, alluring, prepossessing; lovely, fair, charming, delightful, appealing, engaging, winsome; ravishing, gorgeous, stunning, arresting, glamorous, bewitching, beguiling; graceful, elegant, exquisite, aesthetic, artistic, decorative, magnificent; *informal* divine, drop-dead gorgeous, killer, cute, foxy; *formal* beauteous; *archaic* comely.
— OPPOSITES: ugly.

beautify ▶ verb ADORN, embellish, enhance, decorate, ornament, garnish, gild, smarten up, prettify, enrich, glamorize, spruce up, spiff up, deck (out), trick out, grace; *informal* get up, do up, tart up.
— OPPOSITES: spoil, uglify.

beauty ▶ noun **1** *the great beauty of the scenery* ATTRACTIVENESS, prettiness, good looks, comeliness, allure; loveliness, charm, appeal, eye-appeal, heavenliness; winsomeness, grace, elegance, exquisiteness; splendour, magnificence, grandeur, impressiveness, decorativeness; gorgeousness, glamour; *literary* beauteousness, pulchritude. **2** *she is a beauty* BEAUTIFUL WOMAN, belle, vision, Venus, goddess, beauty queen, picture; *informal* babe, hottie, looker, good looker, beaut, siren, doll, arm candy, lovely, stunner, knockout, bombshell, dish, cracker, peach, eyeful, fox, smasher. **3** *the beauty of this plan* ADVANTAGE, attraction, strength, benefit, boon, blessing, good thing, strong point, virtue, merit,

selling point.
— OPPOSITES: ugliness, drawback.

becalmed ▶ adjective MOTIONLESS, still, at a standstill, at a halt, unmoving, stuck.

because ▶ conjunction SINCE, as, in view of the fact that, inasmuch as, owing to the fact that, seeing that/ as; *informal* on account of, cuz; *literary* for.
— OPPOSITES: despite.
■ **because of** ON ACCOUNT OF, as a result of, as a consequence of, owing to, due to; thanks to, by/in virtue of; *formal* by reason of.

beckon ▶ verb **1** *the guard beckoned to Benny* GESTURE, signal, wave, gesticulate, motion. **2** *the countryside beckons you* ENTICE, invite, tempt, coax, lure, charm, attract, draw, call.

become ▶ verb **1** *she became rich* GROW, get, turn, come to be, get to be; *literary* wax. **2** *he became a tyrant* TURN INTO, change into, be transformed into, be converted into. **3** *he became Finance Minister* BE APPOINTED (AS), be assigned as, be nominated, be elected (as), be made. **4** *the dress becomes her* SUIT, flatter, look good on; set off, show to advantage; *informal* do something for. **5** *it ill becomes him to preach the gospel* BEFIT, suit, behoove.
■ **become of** HAPPEN TO, be the fate of, be the lot of, overtake; *literary* befall, betide.

becoming ▶ adjective FLATTERING, attractive, lovely, pretty, handsome, stylish, elegant, chic, fashionable, tasteful; *archaic* comely.

bed ▶ noun **1** *she got into bed* cot, cradle, crib, berth; brass bed, bunk bed, camp bed, canopy bed, captain's bed, daybed, feather bed; *proprietary* Hide-A-Bed, mate's bed, Murphy bed, sofa bed, spool bed, trundle bed, waterbed, divan, futon, four-poster; *informal* the sack, the hay. **2** *a flower bed* PATCH, plot, border, strip. **3** *built on a bed of stones* BASE, foundation, support, prop, substructure, substratum. **4** *a river bed* BOTTOM, floor, ground.
■ **go to bed** RETIRE, call it a day; go to sleep, have/take a nap, get some sleep; *informal* hit the sack, hit the hay, turn in, go to beddy-bye, crash out, catch forty winks, get some shut-eye, catch some zees.

bedaub ▶ verb (*literary*) SMEAR, daub, bespatter, spatter, splatter, cover, coat.

bedding ▶ noun BED LINEN, sheets and blankets; bedclothes; bedcovers, bedspread, covers; comforter, duvet.

bedeck ▶ verb DECORATE, adorn, ornament, embellish, furnish, garnish, trim, deck, grace, enrich, dress up, trick out; swathe, wreathe, festoon; *informal* get up.

bedevil ▶ verb AFFLICT, torment, beset, assail, beleaguer, plague, blight, rack, oppress, harry, curse, dog; harass, distress, trouble, worry, torture.

bedlam ▶ noun UPROAR, pandemonium, commotion, mayhem, confusion, disorder, chaos, anarchy, lawlessness; furor, upheaval, hubbub, hoopla, hurly-burly, turmoil, riot, ruckus, rumpus, tumult, hullabaloo, ructions.
— OPPOSITES: calm.

bedraggled ▶ adjective DISHEVELLED, disordered, untidy, unkempt, tousled, disarranged, in a mess, mussed.
— OPPOSITES: neat, clean, dry.

bedridden ▶ adjective CONFINED TO BED, sick in bed, laid up, immobilized, flat on one's back.

bedrock ▶ noun *the bedrock of our society* CORE, basis, base, foundation, roots, heart, backbone, principle, essence, nitty-gritty; *informal* nuts and bolts.

bedspread ▶ noun COMFORTER, coverlet, quilt, duvet, blanket; spread, bedcover; *dated* counterpane.

bee
— RELATED TERMS: apian.

beef ▶ noun **1** *there's plenty of beef on him* MUSCLE, brawn, bulk; strength, power. **2** *his beef was about the cost* COMPLAINT, criticism, objection, cavil, quibble, grievance, grumble, gripe, grouse.
▶ verb **1** *security was being beefed up* TOUGHEN UP, strengthen, build up, reinforce, consolidate, augment, improve. **2** *they're constantly beefing about the neighbour's dog* COMPLAIN, grumble, whine, carp, bitch, gripe, bellyache.

beefy ▶ adjective (*informal*) MUSCULAR, brawny, hefty, burly, hulking, strapping, well-built, solid, stalwart, strong, powerful, heavy, robust, sturdy, hunky, husky.
— OPPOSITES: puny.

beep ▶ noun & verb BLEEP, blip, honk.

beer ▶ noun ALE, brew, pint. *See* table.

Beer	
Types	**Containers and Vessels**
ale	
bitter	six-pack
bock	two-four ♣
brown ale	long neck
draft beer	tallboy
dry	stubby
Ice Beer*	mug
India pale ale	schooner
lager	stein
Pilsner	tankard
porter	Toby jug
stout	
wheat beer	**Other Names**
	barley sandwich ♣
	brewski
	cold one
	suds
	malt liquor
	*Proprietary term.

befall ▶ verb (*literary*) **1** *the same fate befell him* HAPPEN TO, overtake, come upon, be visited on. **2** *tell us what befell* HAPPEN, occur, take place, come about, transpire, materialize; ensue, follow, result; *informal* go down; *literary* come to pass, betide.

befitting ▶ preposition IN KEEPING WITH, as befits, appropriate to, fit for, suitable for, suited to, proper to, right for, compatible with, consistent with, in character with; *archaic* meet for.

before ▶ preposition **1** *he dressed up before going out* PRIOR TO, previous to, earlier than, preparatory to, in preparation for, preliminary to, in anticipation of, in expectation of; in advance of, ahead of, leading up to, on the eve of; *rare* anterior to. **2** *he appeared before the judge* IN FRONT OF, in the presence of, in the sight of. **3** *death before dishonour* IN PREFERENCE TO, rather than, sooner than.
— RELATED TERMS: pre-.
— OPPOSITES: after.
▶ adverb *she has ridden before* PREVIOUSLY, before now/ then, until now/then, up to now/then; earlier, formerly, hitherto, in the past, in days gone by; *formal*

heretofore.
— OPPOSITES: behind.

beforehand ▸ adverb IN ADVANCE, ahead of time, in readiness; before, before now/then, earlier (on), previously, already, sooner.
— OPPOSITES: afterwards.

befriend ▸ verb MAKE FRIENDS WITH, make a friend of; look after, help, protect, stand by.

befuddled ▸ adjective CONFUSED, muddled, addled, bewildered, disorientated, fazed, perplexed, dazed, dizzy, stupefied, groggy, muzzy, foggy, fuddled, fuzzy, dopey, woozy, befogged, mixed up, discombobulated.
— OPPOSITES: clear.

beg ▸ verb **1** he begged on the streets PANHANDLE, ask for money, seek charity, seek alms; informal sponge, cadge, scrounge, bum, mooch. **2** we begged for mercy ASK FOR, request, plead for, appeal for, call for, sue for, solicit, seek, press for. **3** he begged her not to go IMPLORE, entreat, plead with, appeal to, supplicate, pray to, importune; ask, request, call on, petition; literary beseech.

beget ▸ verb (literary) **1** he begat a son FATHER, sire, have, bring into the world, give life to, bring into being, spawn. **2** violence begets violence CAUSE, give rise to, lead to, result in, bring about, create, produce, generate, engender, spawn, occasion, bring on, precipitate, prompt, provoke, kindle, trigger, spark off, touch off, stir up, whip up, induce, inspire, promote; literary enkindle.

beggar ▸ noun **1** he never turned any beggar from his door PANHANDLER, mendicant, tramp, vagrant, vagabond, hobo; informal scrounger, sponger, cadger, freeloader, bum, moocher, mooch, schnorrer. **2** (informal) the lucky beggar! See PERSON.

begin ▸ verb **1** we began work START, commence, set about, go about, embark on, launch into, get down to, take up; initiate, set in motion, institute, inaugurate, get ahead with; informal get cracking on, get going on. **2** he began by saying hello OPEN, lead off, get underway, get going, get off the ground, start (off), go ahead, commence; informal start the ball rolling, kick off, get the show on the road, fire away, take the plunge. **3** when did the illness begin? APPEAR, arise, become apparent, make an appearance, spring up, crop up, turn up, come into existence, come into being, originate, start, commence, develop; literary come to pass.
— RELATED TERMS: incipient, inceptive, inchoate, embryonic.
— OPPOSITES: finish, end, disappear.

beginner ▸ noun NOVICE, newcomer, rookie, newbie, fledgling, neophyte, starter, (raw) recruit, apprentice, initiate, freshman, cub; tenderfoot, cheechako, new kid (on the block), greenhorn, tyro; postulant, novitiate.
— OPPOSITES: expert, veteran.

beginning ▸ noun **1** the beginning of socialism DAWN, birth, inception, conception, origination, genesis, emergence, rise, start, commencement, starting point, launch, onset, day one; informal kickoff. **2** the beginning of the article OPENING, introduction, start, first part, preamble, opening statement. **3** the therapy has its beginnings in China ORIGIN, source, roots, starting point, birthplace, cradle, spring, fountainhead; genesis, creation; literary fount, well spring.
— OPPOSITES: end, conclusion.

begrudge ▸ verb **1** she begrudged Brian his affluence ENVY, resent, grudge, be jealous of, be envious of. **2** don't begrudge the cost RESENT, feel aggrieved about, feel bitter about, be annoyed about, be resentful of, grudge, mind, object to, take exception to, regret.

beguile ▸ verb **1** she was beguiled by his beauty CHARM, attract, enchant, entrance, win over, woo, captivate, bewitch, spellbind, dazzle, hypnotize, mesmerize, seduce. **2** the program has been beguiling children for years ENTERTAIN, amuse, delight, please, occupy, absorb, engage, distract, divert, fascinate, enthrall, engross.
— OPPOSITES: repel, bore.

behalf
■ **on behalf of/on someone's behalf 1** I am writing on behalf of my client AS A REPRESENTATIVE OF, as a spokesperson for, for, in the name of, in place of, on the authority of, at the behest of. **2** a campaign on behalf of cycling IN THE INTERESTS OF, in support of, for, for the benefit of, for the good of, for the sake of.

behave ▸ verb **1** she behaved badly CONDUCT ONESELF, act, acquit oneself, bear oneself; formal comport oneself; archaic deport oneself. **2** the children behaved themselves ACT CORRECTLY, act properly, conduct oneself well, be well-behaved, be good; be polite, show good manners, mind one's manners.
— OPPOSITES: misbehave.

behaviour ▸ noun **1** his behaviour was inexcusable CONDUCT, deportment, bearing, actions, doings; manners, ways; formal comportment. **2** the behaviour of these organisms FUNCTIONING, action, performance, operation, working, reaction, response.

behead ▸ verb DECAPITATE, cut/chop/lop someone's head off, guillotine.

behest ▸ noun (literary) INSTRUCTION, requirement, demand, insistence, bidding, request, wish, desire, will; command, injunction, order, decree, ruling, directive; informal say-so.

behind ▸ preposition **1** he hid behind a tree AT THE BACK/REAR OF, beyond, on the far/other side of, in back of. **2** a guard ran behind him AFTER, following, at the back/rear of, hard on the heels of, in the wake of. **3** he was behind the bombings RESPONSIBLE FOR, at the bottom of, the cause of, the source of, the organizer of; to blame for, culpable of, guilty of. **4** we're behind you all the way SUPPORTING, backing, for, on the side of, in agreement with; financing; informal rooting for.
— OPPOSITES: in front of, ahead of.
▸ adverb **1** a man followed behind AFTER, afterwards, at the back/end, in the rear. **2** I looked behind OVER ONE'S SHOULDER, to/towards the back, to/towards the rear, backwards. **3** we're behind, so don't stop (RUNNING) LATE, behind schedule, behindhand, not on time, behind time. **4** he was behind with his subscription IN ARREARS, overdue; late, unpunctual, behindhand.
— OPPOSITES: in front, ahead.
▸ noun (informal) he sat on his behind. See BUTTOCKS.
■ **put something behind one** CONSIGN TO THE PAST, put down to experience, regard as water under the bridge, forget about, ignore.

behold ▸ verb (literary) no eyes beheld them SEE, observe, view, look at, watch, survey, witness, gaze at/upon, regard, contemplate, inspect, eye; catch sight of, glimpse, spot, spy, notice; informal clap eyes on, have/take a gander at, get a load of, eyeball; literary espy, descry.
▸ exclamation (archaic) behold, here I am! LOOK, see; archaic lo.

beholden ▸ adjective INDEBTED, in someone's debt,

obligated, under an obligation; grateful, owing a debt of gratitude.

behoove ► **verb 1** *it behooves me to go* BE INCUMBENT ON, be obligatory for, be required of, be expected of, be appropriate for. **2** *it ill behooves them to comment* BEFIT, become, suit.

beige ► **adjective** FAWN, pale brown, buff, sand, sandy, oatmeal, khaki, biscuit, coffee, coffee-coloured, café au lait, camel, ecru.

being ► **noun 1** *she is warmed by his very being* EXISTENCE, living, life, reality, actuality. **2** *God is alive in the being of man* SOUL, spirit, nature, essence, inner being, inner self, psyche; heart, bosom, breast; *Philosophy* quiddity, pneuma. **3** *an enlightened being* CREATURE, life form, living entity, living thing, (living) soul, individual, person, human (being).

belabour ► **verb** *don't belabour the point* OVER-ELABORATE, labour, dwell on, harp on about, hammer away at; overdo, overplay, over-dramatize, make too much of, place too much emphasis on; *informal* flog to death, drag out, make a big thing of, blow out of proportion.
– OPPOSITES: praise, understate.

belated ► **adjective** LATE, overdue, behindhand, behind time, behind schedule, delayed, tardy, unpunctual.
– OPPOSITES: early.

belch ► **verb 1** *onions make me belch* BURP. **2** *the furnace belched flames* EMIT, give off, give out, pour out, discharge, disgorge, spew out, spit out, vomit, gush, cough up.
► **noun** *he gave a loud belch* BURP; *formal* eructation.

beleaguered ► **adjective 1** *the beleaguered garrison* BESIEGED, under siege, blockaded, surrounded, encircled, beset, hemmed in, under attack. **2** *a beleaguered government* HARD-PRESSED, troubled, in difficulties, under pressure, under stress, with one's back to the wall, in a tight corner, in a tight spot, up against it; beset, assailed.

belie ► **verb** *his eyes belied his words* CONTRADICT, be at odds with, call into question, give the lie to, show/prove to be false, disprove, debunk, discredit, controvert, negative; *formal* confute.
– OPPOSITES: testify to, reveal.

belief ► **noun 1** *it's my belief that age is irrelevant* OPINION, view, conviction, judgment, thinking, way of thinking, idea, impression, theory, conclusion, notion. **2** *belief in God* FAITH, trust, reliance, confidence, credence. **3** *traditional beliefs* IDEOLOGY, principle, ethic, tenet, canon; doctrine, teaching, dogma, article of faith, creed, credo.
– OPPOSITES: disbelief, doubt.

believable ► **adjective** CREDIBLE, plausible, tenable, able to hold water, conceivable, likely, probable, possible, feasible, reasonable, with a ring of truth.
– OPPOSITES: inconceivable.

believe ► **verb 1** *I don't believe you* BE CONVINCED BY, trust, have confidence in, consider honest, consider truthful. **2** *do you believe that story?* REGARD AS TRUE, accept, be convinced by, give credence to, credit, trust, put confidence in; *informal* swallow, buy, go for. **3** *I believe he worked for you* THINK, be of the opinion that, have an idea that, imagine, suspect, suppose, assume, presume, take it, conjecture, surmise, conclude, deduce, understand, be given to understand, gather, fancy, guess, dare say; *informal* reckon, figure; *archaic* ween.
– OPPOSITES: doubt.

■ **believe in 1** *she believed in God* BE CONVINCED OF THE EXISTENCE OF, be sure of the existence of. **2** *I believe in lots of exercise* HAVE FAITH IN, pin one's faith on, trust in, have every confidence in, cling to, set (great) store by, value, be convinced by, be persuaded by; subscribe to, approve of; *informal* swear by.

believer ► **noun** DEVOTEE, adherent, disciple, follower, supporter.
– OPPOSITES: infidel, skeptic.

belittle ► **verb** DISPARAGE, denigrate, run down, deprecate, depreciate, downgrade, play down, trivialize, minimize, make light of, pooh-pooh, treat lightly, scoff at, sneer at; *formal* derogate; *rare* misprize.
– OPPOSITES: praise, magnify.

bellicose ► **adjective** BELLIGERENT, aggressive, hostile, warlike, warmongering, hawkish, antagonistic, pugnacious, truculent, confrontational, contentious, militant, combative; *informal* spoiling for a fight, scrappy.
– OPPOSITES: peaceable.

belligerent ► **adjective 1** *a belligerent attitude* HOSTILE, aggressive, threatening, antagonistic, warlike, warmongering, hawkish, pugnacious, bellicose, truculent, confrontational, contentious, militant, combative; *informal* spoiling for a fight, trigger-happy, scrappy. **2** *the belligerent states* WARRING, at war, combatant, fighting, battling.
– OPPOSITES: peaceable, neutral.

bellow ► **verb** *she bellowed in his ear* ROAR, shout, bawl, thunder, trumpet, boom, bark, yell, shriek, howl, scream; raise one's voice; *informal* holler.
– OPPOSITES: whisper.
► **noun** *a bellow of pain* ROAR, shout, bawl, bark, yell, yelp, shriek, howl, scream.
– OPPOSITES: whisper.

bellwether ► **noun** HARBINGER, herald, indicator.

belly ► **noun** *he scratched his belly* STOMACH, abdomen, paunch, middle, midriff, girth; *informal* tummy, tum, breadbasket, gut, guts, insides, pot, pot-belly, beer belly, Molson muscle ♣, spare tire.
► **verb** *her skirt bellied out* BILLOW (OUT), bulge (out), balloon (out), bag (out), fill (out); distend.
– OPPOSITES: sag, flap.

belong ► **verb 1** *the house belongs to his mother* BE OWNED BY, be the property of, be the possession of, be held by, be in the hands of. **2** *I belong to a trade union* BE A MEMBER OF, be in, be affiliated to, be allied to, be associated with, be linked to, be an adherent of. **3** *Italian belongs to the Romance language family* BE CLASSED, be classified, be categorized, be included, have a place, be located, be situated, be found, lie. **4** *she doesn't belong here* FIT IN, be suited to, have a rightful place, have a home; *informal* go, click.

belonging ► **noun** *a sense of belonging* AFFILIATION, acceptance, association, attachment, integration, closeness; rapport, fellow feeling, fellowship.
– OPPOSITES: alienation.

belongings ► **plural noun** POSSESSIONS, effects, worldly goods, assets, chattels, property; *informal* gear, tackle, kit, things, stuff.

beloved ► **adjective** *her beloved brother* DARLING, dear, dearest, precious, adored, much loved, cherished, treasured, prized, highly regarded, admired, esteemed, worshipped, revered, venerated, idolized.
– OPPOSITES: hated.
► **noun** *he watched his beloved* SWEETHEART, love, darling, dearest, lover, girlfriend, boyfriend, young lady,

young man, beau, lady friend; *informal* steady, main squeeze, swain; *archaic* paramour, doxy.

below ▶ **preposition 1** *the water rushed below them* BENEATH, under, underneath, further down than, lower than. **2** *the result is below average* LESS THAN, lower than, under, not as much as, smaller than. **3** *a captain is below a major* LOWER THAN, under, inferior to, subordinate to, subservient to.
— RELATED TERMS: hypo-, sub-.
— OPPOSITES: above, over, more than.
▶ **adverb 1** *I could see what was happening below* FURTHER DOWN, lower down, in a lower position, underneath, beneath. **2** *the statements below* UNDERNEATH, following, further on, at a later point.

belt ▶ **noun 1** *the belt of her coat* SASH, girdle, strap, cummerbund, band; *literary* cincture; *historical* baldric. **2** *farmers in the cotton belt* REGION, area, district, zone, sector, territory; tract, strip, stretch.
▶ **verb 1** *she belted them in* FASTEN, tie, bind; *literary* gird. **2** *(informal) a guy belted him in the face* HIT, strike, smack, slap, bang, beat, punch, thump, welt; *informal* clout, bash, whack, thwack, schmuck ♣, wallop, sock, slog, clobber, bop, lam, larrup, slug; *archaic* smite.
■ **below the belt** UNFAIR, unjust, unacceptable, inequitable; unethical, unprincipled, immoral, unscrupulous, unsporting, sneaky, dishonourable, dishonest, underhanded; *informal* lowdown, dirty.

bemoan ▶ **verb** LAMENT, bewail, mourn, grieve over, sorrow over, regret, cry over; deplore, complain about; *archaic* plain over.
— OPPOSITES: rejoice at, applaud.

bemused ▶ **adjective** BEWILDERED, confused, puzzled, perplexed, baffled, mystified, nonplussed, muddled, befuddled, dumbfounded, at sea, at a loss, taken aback, disoriented, disconcerted; *informal* flummoxed, bamboozled, clueless, fazed, discombobulated.

bench ▶ **noun 1** *he sat on a bench* PEW, stall, settle, seat; bleacher. **2** *a laboratory bench* WORKBENCH, work table, worktop, work surface, counter. **3** *the bench heard the evidence* JUDGES, magistrates, judiciary; court.
▶ **verb** *the coach benched him for two games* SIDELINE, sit out, cut.

benchmark ▶ **noun** STANDARD, point of reference, gauge, guide, guideline, guiding principle, norm, touchstone, yardstick, barometer, indicator, measure, model, exemplar, pattern, criterion, specification, convention.

bend ▶ **verb 1** *the frames can be bent to fit your face* CURVE, angle, hook, bow, arch, flex, crook, hump, warp, contort, distort, deform. **2** *the highway bent to the left* TURN, curve, incline, swing, veer, deviate, diverge, fork, change course, curl, loop. **3** *he bent down to tie his shoe* STOOP, bow, crouch, hunch, lean down/over. **4** *they want to bend me to their will* MOULD, shape, manipulate, direct, force, press, influence, incline, sway.
— OPPOSITES: straighten.
▶ **noun** *he came to a bend in the road* CURVE, turn, corner, jog, correction line ♣, kink, dogleg, oxbow, zigzag, angle, arc, crescent, twist, crook, deviation, deflection, loop, hairpin turn, hairpin.
— OPPOSITES: straight.
■ **bend over backwards** *(informal)* TRY ONE'S HARDEST, do one's best, do one's utmost, do all one can, give one's all, make every effort; *informal* do one's damnedest, go all out, pull out all the stops, bust a gut, move heaven and earth.

beneath ▶ **preposition 1** *we sat beneath the trees* UNDER, underneath, below, at the foot of, at the bottom of; lower than. **2** *the rank beneath theirs* INFERIOR TO, below, not so important as, lower in status than, subordinate to, subservient to. **3** *such an attitude was beneath her* UNWORTHY OF, unbecoming to, degrading to, below.
— OPPOSITES: above.
▶ **adverb** *sand with rock beneath* UNDERNEATH, below, further down, lower down.
— OPPOSITES: above.

benediction ▶ **noun 1** *the priest pronounced the benediction* BLESSING, prayer, invocation; grace, benedicite. **2** *filled with heavenly benediction* BLESSEDNESS, beatitude, bliss, grace.

benefactor, benefactress ▶ **noun** PATRON, supporter, backer, sponsor; donor, contributor, subscriber; *informal* angel.

beneficent ▶ **adjective** BENEVOLENT, charitable, altruistic, humanitarian, neighbourly, public-spirited, philanthropic; generous, kind, magnanimous, munificent, unselfish, unstinting, open-handed, liberal, lavish, bountiful; *literary* bounteous.
— OPPOSITES: unkind, mean.

beneficial ▶ **adjective** ADVANTAGEOUS, favourable, helpful, useful, of use, of benefit, of assistance, valuable, of value, profitable, rewarding, gainful.
— OPPOSITES: disadvantageous.

beneficiary ▶ **noun** HEIR, heiress, inheritor, legatee; recipient; *Law* devisee.

benefit ▶ **noun 1** *for the benefit of others* GOOD, sake, welfare, well-being, advantage, comfort, ease, convenience; help, aid, assistance, service; profit. **2** *the benefits of working for a large firm* ADVANTAGE, reward, merit, boon, blessing, virtue; bonus; value; *informal* perk; *formal* perquisite. **3** *state benefit* SOCIAL SECURITY PAYMENTS, baby bonus ♣, child (tax) benefit ♣, social assistance ♣, Spouse's Allowance ♣, Guaranteed Income Supplement ♣, *historical* family allowance ♣ (or mother's allowance ♣), northern allowance ♣, public assistance allowance, welfare, the dole; pogey ♣, employment insurance ♣, unemployment ♣, *(Atlantic)* stamps ♣; charity, donations, gifts, financial assistance.
— OPPOSITES: detriment, disadvantage.
▶ **verb 1** *the deal benefited them both* BE ADVANTAGEOUS TO, be beneficial to, be of advantage to, be to the advantage of, profit, do good to, be of service to, serve, be useful to, be of use to, be helpful to, be of help to, help, aid, assist, be of assistance to; better, improve, strengthen, boost, advance, further. **2** *they may benefit from the scheme* PROFIT, gain, reap benefits, reap reward, make money; make the most of, exploit, turn to one's advantage, put to good use, do well out of; *informal* cash in, make a killing.
— OPPOSITES: damage, suffer.

benevolence ▶ **noun** KINDNESS, kind-heartedness, big-heartedness, goodness, goodwill, charity, altruism, humanitarianism, compassion, philanthropy; generosity, magnanimity, munificence, unselfishness, open-handedness; beneficence; *literary* bounty, bounteousness.
— OPPOSITES: spite, miserliness.

benevolent ▶ **adjective 1** *a benevolent patriarch* KIND, kindly, kind-hearted, big-hearted, good-natured, good, benign, compassionate, caring, altruistic, humanitarian, philanthropic; generous,

magnanimous, munificent, unselfish, open-handed, beneficent; *literary* bounteous. **2** *a benevolent institution* CHARITABLE, non-profit, not-for-profit; *formal* eleemosynary.
— OPPOSITES: unkind, tight-fisted.

benign ▶ **adjective 1** *a benign grandfatherly role* KINDLY, kind, warm-hearted, good-natured, friendly, warm, affectionate, agreeable, genial, congenial, cordial, approachable, tender-hearted, gentle, sympathetic, compassionate, caring, well-disposed, benevolent. **2** *a benign climate* TEMPERATE, mild, gentle, balmy, soft, pleasant; healthy, wholesome, salubrious. **3** *(Medicine) a benign tumour* HARMLESS, non-malignant, non-cancerous; *Medicine* benignant.
— OPPOSITES: unfriendly, hostile, unhealthy, unfavourable, malignant.

bent ▶ **adjective** *the bucket had a bent handle* TWISTED, crooked, warped, contorted, deformed, misshapen, out of shape, irregular; bowed, arched, curved, angled, hooked, kinked; *informal* pretzelled.
▶ **noun** *an artistic bent* INCLINATION, leaning, tendency; talent, gift, flair, aptitude, facility, skill, capability, capacity; predisposition, disposition, instinct, orientation, predilection, proclivity, propensity.
■ **bent on** INTENT ON, determined on, set on, insistent on, resolved on, hell-bent on; committed to, single-minded about, obsessed with, fanatical about, fixated on.

bequeath ▶ **verb** LEAVE (IN ONE'S WILL), hand on/down, will, make over, pass on, entrust, grant, transfer; donate, give; endow on, bestow on, confer on; *Law* demise, devise, convey.

bequest ▶ **noun** LEGACY, inheritance, endowment, settlement; estate, heritage; bestowal; *Law* devise; *Law, dated* hereditament.

berate ▶ **verb** SCOLD, rebuke, reprimand, reproach, reprove, admonish, chide, criticize, upbraid, take to task, read someone the riot act, haul over the coals; tell off, give someone a talking-to, give someone what for, dress down, give someone a dressing-down, give someone a tongue-lashing, rap over the knuckles, bawl out, come down on, tear into, blast, tear a strip off; chew out, ream out, zing, take to the woodshed; castigate; *dated* call down, rate; *rare* reprehend.
— OPPOSITES: praise.

bereavement ▶ **noun** LOSS, deprivation, death in the family, passing (away); *formal* decease.

bereft ▶ **adjective** DEPRIVED, robbed, stripped, devoid, bankrupt; wanting, in need of, lacking, without; *informal* minus, sans, clean out of.

berry ▶ **noun** FRUIT. *See table.*

berserk ▶ **adjective** FRENZIED, raving, wild, out of control, amok, on the rampage, frantic, crazy, raging, insane, out of one's mind, hysterical, mad, crazed, maniacal, manic; *informal* bananas, bonkers, nuts, hyper, postal.

berth ▶ **noun 1** *a 4-berth cabin* BUNK, bed, cot, couch, hammock. **2** *the vessel left its berth* MOORING, dock, slip, anchorage; wharf, pier, jetty, quay.
▶ **verb** *they berthed at a jetty in Placentia Bay* DOCK, moor, land, tie up, make fast.
■ **give someone/something a wide berth** AVOID, shun, keep away from, stay away from, steer clear of, keep at arm's length, have nothing to do with; dodge, sidestep, circumvent, skirt round.

beseech ▶ **verb** *(literary)* IMPLORE, beg, entreat, plead with, appeal to, call on, supplicate, importune, pray to, ask, request, petition.

Berries

bakeapple	huckleberry
barberry	Juneberry
bearberry	lingonberry
bilberry	loganberry
black raspberry	lowbush blueberry
blackberry	lowbush cranberry
blackcurrant	marshberry ✦(Nfld)
blueberry	moss berry
bog cranberry	mountain cranberry
boysenberry	mulberry
bramble	nannyberry
buffalo berry	Oregon grape
bunchberry	partridgeberry
Cape gooseberry	raspberry
checkerberry	red-berry ✦(Nfld)
chokeberry	redcurrant
cloudberry	salmonberry
cowberry	saskatoon ✦(Prairies)
crackerberry	serviceberry
cranberry	shadberry
creeping snowberry	silverberry
crowberry	soapberry
currant	soopollalie
dewberry	squashberry
dogberry	strawberry
elderberry	tayberry
foxberry	teaberry
gooseberry	thimbleberry
hackberry	whortleberry
highbush blueberry	wineberry
highbush cranberry	

beset ▶ **verb 1** *he is beset by fears* PLAGUE, bedevil, assail, beleaguer, afflict, torment, rack, oppress, trouble, worry, harass, dog, harry. **2** *they were beset by enemy forces* SURROUND, besiege, hem in, shut in, fence in, box in, encircle, ring round.

beside ▶ **preposition 1** *Kate walked beside him* ALONGSIDE, by/at the side of, next to, parallel to, abreast of, at someone's elbow; adjacent to, next door to, cheek by jowl with; bordering, abutting, neighbouring. **2** *beside Paula, she felt clumsy* COMPARED WITH/TO, in comparison with/to, by comparison with, next to, against, contrasted with, in contrast to/with.
■ **beside oneself** DISTRAUGHT, overcome, out of one's mind, frantic, desperate, distracted, at one's wits' end, frenzied, wound up, worked up; hysterical, unhinged, mad, crazed.
■ **beside the point.** *See* POINT¹.

besides ▶ **preposition** *who did you ask besides Mary?* IN ADDITION TO, as well as, over and above, above and beyond, on top of; apart from, other than, aside from, but for, save for, not counting, excluding, not including, except, with the exception of, excepting, leaving aside; *informal* outside of.
▶ **adverb 1** *there's a lot more besides* IN ADDITION, as well, too, also, into the bargain, on top of that, to boot; *archaic* therewithal. **2** *besides, he's always late* FURTHERMORE, moreover, further; anyway, anyhow, in any case, be that as it may; *informal* what's more, anyways.

besiege ▶ **verb 1** *the English army besieged Leith* LAY SIEGE TO, beleaguer, blockade, surround; *archaic* invest. **2** *fans besieged his hotel* SURROUND, mob, crowd round, swarm round, throng round, ring round, encircle. **3** *guilt besieged him* OPPRESS, torment, torture, rack, plague, afflict, haunt, harrow, hound, beset, beleaguer, trouble, bedevil, prey on. **4** *he was besieged with requests* OVERWHELM, inundate, deluge, flood, swamp, snow under; bombard.

besmirch ▶ verb (*literary*) SULLY, tarnish, blacken, drag through the mud/mire, stain, taint, smear, disgrace, dishonour, bring discredit to, damage, ruin, slander, malign.
– OPPOSITES: honour, enhance.

besotted ▶ adjective INFATUATED, smitten, in love, head over heels in love, obsessed; doting on, greatly enamoured of; *informal* swept off one's feet by, crazy about, mad about, wild about, carrying a torch for, gaga about/for/over, struck on, gone on.

bespeak ▶ verb *a tree-lined road which bespoke money* INDICATE, be evidence of, be a sign of, denote, point to, testify to, evidence, reflect, demonstrate, show, manifest, display, signify; reveal, betray; *informal* spell; *literary* betoken.
– OPPOSITES: belie.

best ▶ adjective **1** *the best hotel in Fredericton* FINEST, greatest, top, foremost, leading, pre-eminent, premier, prime, first, chief, principal, supreme, of the highest quality, superlative, par excellence, unrivalled, second to none, without equal, nonpareil, unsurpassed, peerless, matchless, unparalleled, unbeaten, unbeatable, optimum, optimal, ultimate, incomparable, ideal, perfect; highest, record-breaking; *informal* star, number-one, a cut above the rest, top-drawer, the Cadillac/Rolls-Royce of. **2** *do whatever you think best* MOST ADVANTAGEOUS, most useful, most suitable, most fitting, most appropriate; most prudent, most sensible, most advisable.
– OPPOSITES: worst.
▶ adverb **1** *the best-dressed man* TO THE HIGHEST STANDARD, in the best way. **2** *the food he liked best* MOST, to the highest/greatest degree. **3** *this is best done at home* MOST ADVANTAGEOUSLY, most usefully, most suitably, most fittingly, most appropriately; most sensibly, most prudently, most wisely; better.
– OPPOSITES: worst, least.
▶ noun **1** *only the best will do* FINEST, choicest, top, cream, choice, prime, elite, crème de la crème, flower, jewel in the crown, nonpareil; *informal* tops, pick of the bunch. **2** *she dressed in her best* BEST CLOTHES, finery, Sunday best; *informal* glad rags. **3** *give her my best* BEST WISHES, regards, kind/kindest regards, greetings, compliments, felicitations, respects; love.
▶ verb (*informal*) *she was not to be bested* DEFEAT, beat, get the better of, outdo, outwit, outsmart, worst, be more than a match for, prevail over, vanquish, trounce, triumph over, surpass, outclass, outshine, put someone in the shade, overshadow, eclipse; *informal* lick.
■ **do one's best** DO ONE'S UTMOST, try one's hardest, make every effort, do all one can, give one's all; *informal* bend over backwards, do one's damnedest, go all out, pull out all the stops, bust a gut, break one's neck, move heaven and earth.
■ **had best** OUGHT TO, should.

bestial ▶ adjective *Stanley's bestial behaviour* SAVAGE, brutish, brutal, barbarous, barbaric, cruel, vicious, violent, inhuman, subhuman; depraved, degenerate, perverted, debauched, immoral, warped.
– OPPOSITES: civilized, humane.

bestir
■ **bestir oneself** EXERT ONESELF, make an effort, rouse oneself, get going, get moving, get on with it;

informal shake a leg, look lively, get cracking, get off one's backside.

bestow ▶ verb CONFER ON, grant, accord, afford, endow someone with, vest in, present, award, give, donate, entrust with, vouchsafe.

bestride ▶ verb **1** *the oil field bestrides the border* EXTEND ACROSS, lie on both sides of, straddle, span, bridge. **2** *he bestrode his horse* STRADDLE, sit/stand astride. **3** *Italy bestrode Europe in opera* DOMINATE, tower over/above.

bestseller ▶ noun great success, hit, smash (hit), blockbuster, chart-topper, chartbuster, megahit.
– OPPOSITES: failure, flop.

bestselling ▶ adjective VERY SUCCESSFUL, very popular, best-loved, number-one, chart-topping, hit.

bet ▶ verb **1** *he bet $10 on the favourite* WAGER, gamble, stake, risk, venture, hazard, chance; put/lay money, speculate. **2** (*informal*) *I bet it was your idea* BE CERTAIN, be sure, be convinced, be confident; expect, predict, forecast, guess.
▶ noun **1** *a $20 bet* WAGER, gamble, stake, ante, exactor ♣. **2** (*informal*) *my bet is that they'll lose* PREDICTION, forecast, guess; opinion, belief, feeling, view, theory. **3** (*informal*) *your best bet is to go early* OPTION, choice, alternative, course of action, plan.

bête noire ▶ noun BUGBEAR, a thorn in one's flesh/side, the bane of one's life, bugaboo, pain, pest.
– OPPOSITES: favourite.

betide ▶ verb (*literary*) HAPPEN, occur, take place, come about, transpire, arise, chance; result, ensue, follow, develop, supervene; *informal* go down; *formal* eventuate; *literary* come to pass, befall; *archaic* hap.

betoken ▶ verb (*literary*) **1** *a small gift betokening regret* INDICATE, be a sign of, be evidence of, evidence, manifest, mean, signify, denote, represent, show, demonstrate, bespeak. **2** *the blue sky betokened a day of good weather* FORETELL, signal, give notice of, herald, proclaim, prophesy, foreshadow, presage, be a harbinger of, portend, augur, be an omen of, be a sign of, be a warning of, warn of, bode; *literary* foretoken, forebode.

betray ▶ verb **1** *he betrayed his own brother* BE DISLOYAL TO, be unfaithful to, double-cross, cross, break faith with, inform on/against, give away, denounce, sell out, stab in the back, break one's promise to; *informal* rat on, fink on, sell down the river, squeal on, peach on, rat out, finger. **2** *he betrayed a secret* REVEAL, disclose, divulge, tell, give away, leak; unmask, expose, bring out into the open; let slip, let out, let drop, blurt out; *informal* blab, spill, kiss and tell.
– OPPOSITES: be loyal to, hide.

betrayal ▶ noun DISLOYALTY, treachery, bad faith, faithlessness, falseness, duplicity, deception, double-dealing; breach of faith, breach of trust, stab in the back; double-cross, sell-out; *literary* perfidy.
– OPPOSITES: loyalty.

betrayer ▶ noun TRAITOR, backstabber, Judas, double-crosser; renegade, quisling, double agent, collaborator, informer, mole, stool pigeon, stoolie; turncoat, defector; *informal* snake in the grass, rat, scab, fink.

betrothal ▶ noun (*dated*) ENGAGEMENT, marriage contract; *archaic* espousal.

betrothed ▶ adjective (*dated*) ENGAGED (TO BE MARRIED), promised/pledged in marriage; *literary* affianced; *archaic* plighted, espoused.
– OPPOSITES: unattached.

better ▶ adjective **1** *better facilities* SUPERIOR, finer, of

higher quality; preferable; *informal* a cut above, head and shoulders above, ahead of the pack/field. **2** *there couldn't be a better time* MORE ADVANTAGEOUS, more suitable, more fitting, more appropriate, more useful, more valuable, more desirable. **3** *are you better?* HEALTHIER, fitter, stronger; well, cured, healed, recovered; recovering, on the road to recovery, making progress, improving; *informal* on the mend.
— OPPOSITES: worse, inferior.
▶ **adverb 1** *I played better today* TO A HIGHER STANDARD, in a superior/finer way. **2** *this may suit you better* MORE, to a greater degree/extent. **3** *the money could be better spent* MORE WISELY, more sensibly, more suitably, more fittingly, more advantageously.
▶ **verb 1** *he bettered the record* SURPASS, improve on, beat, exceed, top, cap, trump, eclipse. **2** *refugees who want to better their lot* IMPROVE, ameliorate, raise, advance, further, lift, upgrade, enhance.
— OPPOSITES: worsen.

betterment ▶ **noun** IMPROVEMENT, amelioration, advancement, furtherance, upgrading, enhancement.

between ▶ **preposition 1** *Philip stood between his parents* IN THE SPACE SEPARATING, in the middle of, with one on either side; amid, amidst; *archaic* betwixt. **2** *the bond between her and her mother* CONNECTING, linking, joining; uniting, allying; among.
— RELATED TERMS: inter-.

bevel ▶ **noun** SLOPE, slant, angle, cant, mitre, chamfer.

beverage ▶ **noun** DRINK, liquid refreshment; *humorous* libation; *archaic* potation.

bevy ▶ **noun** GROUP, crowd, herd, flock, horde, army, galaxy, assemblage, throng, company, gathering, band, body, pack, covey; knot, cluster; bunch, gaggle, posse.

bewail ▶ **verb** LAMENT, bemoan, mourn, grieve over, sorrow over, cry over; deplore, complain about, wail about; *archaic* plain over.
— OPPOSITES: rejoice at, applaud.

beware ▶ **verb** BE ON YOUR GUARD, watch out, look out, be alert, be on the lookout, keep your eyes open/peeled, keep an eye out, keep a sharp lookout, be on the qui vive; take care, be careful, be cautious, watch your step, have a care; *Golf* fore.

bewilder ▶ **verb** BAFFLE, mystify, bemuse, perplex, puzzle, addle, confuse, confound; *informal* flummox, faze, stump, beat, fox, make someone scratch their head, be all Greek to, floor, discombobulate.
— OPPOSITES: enlighten.

bewildered ▶ **adjective** BAFFLED, mystified, bemused, perplexed, puzzled, confused, nonplussed, dumbfounded, at sea, at a loss, disorientated, taken aback; *informal* flummoxed, bamboozled; discombobulated.

bewitch ▶ **verb 1** *that evil woman bewitched him* CAST/PUT A SPELL ON, enchant; possess, curse, hex; *archaic* witch. **2** *we were bewitched by the surroundings* CAPTIVATE, enchant, entrance, enrapture, charm, beguile, delight, fascinate, enthrall.
— OPPOSITES: repel.

beyond ▶ **preposition 1** *beyond the trees* ON THE FAR SIDE OF, on the other side of, further away than, behind, past, after, over. **2** *inflation beyond 10 per cent* GREATER THAN, more than, exceeding, in excess of, above, over and above, above and beyond, upwards of. **3** *little beyond food was provided* APART FROM, except, other than, besides; *informal* outside of; *formal* save.

▶ **adverb** *a house with a garden beyond* FURTHER AWAY, further off.

bias ▶ **noun 1** *he accused the media of bias* PREJUDICE, partiality, partisanship, favouritism, unfairness, one-sidedness; bigotry, intolerance, discrimination, leaning, tendency, inclination, predilection. **2** *a dress cut on the bias* DIAGONAL, cross, slant, angle.
— OPPOSITES: impartiality.
▶ **verb** *this may have biased the result* PREJUDICE, influence, colour, sway, weight, predispose; distort, skew, slant.

biased ▶ **adjective** PREJUDICED, partial, partisan, one-sided, blinkered; bigoted, intolerant, discriminatory; distorted, warped, twisted, skewed.
— OPPOSITES: impartial.

Bible ▶ **noun 1** *he read the Bible* THE (HOLY) SCRIPTURES, Holy Writ, the Good Book, the Book of Books. *See the tables here and at* SCRIPTURE. **2** (*informal*) *the taxi driver's bible* HANDBOOK, manual, ABC's, companion, guide, vade mecum, primer.

bicker ▶ **verb** QUARREL, argue, squabble, wrangle, fight, disagree, dispute, spar, have words, be at each other's throats, lock horns; *informal* scrap, spat.
— OPPOSITES: agree.

bicycle ▶ **noun** CYCLE, bike, two-wheeler, mountain bike, ten-speed; *historical* penny farthing.

bid¹ ▶ **verb 1** *we bid $650 for the antique table* OFFER, make an offer of, put in a bid of, put up, tender, proffer, propose. **2** *she is bidding for a place on the Canadian team* TRY TO OBTAIN, try to get, make a pitch for, make a bid for.
▶ **noun 1** *a bid of $3,000* OFFER, tender, proposal. **2** *a bid to cut crime* ATTEMPT, effort, endeavour, try; *informal* crack, go, shot, stab; *formal* essay.

bid² ▶ **verb 1** *she bid him farewell* WISH; utter. **2** (*literary*) *I did as he bade me* ORDER, command, tell, instruct, direct, enjoin, charge. **3** (*literary*) *he bade his companions enter* INVITE TO, ask to, request to.

biddable ▶ **adjective** OBEDIENT, acquiescent, compliant, tractable, amenable, complaisant, co-operative, dutiful, submissive; *rare* persuasible.
— OPPOSITES: disobedient, uncooperative.

bidding ▶ **noun** COMMAND, order, instruction, decree, injunction, demand, mandate, direction, summons, call; wish, desire; request; *literary* behest; *archaic* hest.

bide
■ **bide one's time** WAIT, sit tight, stick around, hold on, hang around.

big ▶ **adjective 1** *a big building* LARGE, sizeable, substantial, great, huge, immense, enormous, extensive, colossal, massive, mammoth, vast, tremendous, gigantic, giant, monumental, mighty, gargantuan, elephantine, titanic, mountainous, Brobdingnagian; towering, tall, high, lofty; outsize, oversized; goodly; capacious, voluminous, spacious; king-size(d), man-size, family-size(d), economy-size(d); *informal* jumbo, whopping, thumping, bumper, mega, humongous, monster, astronomical, ginormous; *formal* commodious. **2** *clothing for big people* WELL-BUILT, sturdy, brawny, burly, broad-shouldered, muscular, muscly, rugged, Herculean, bulky, hulking, strapping, thickset, stocky, solid, hefty, large; tall, huge, gigantic; fat, stout, portly, plump, fleshy, paunchy, corpulent, obese, hunky, beefy, husky; full-figured, big-boned, buxom, zaftig, roly-poly, rotund, well-fed; *literary* thewy, stark. **3** *my big sister* ELDER, older; grown-up, adult, mature, grown. **4** *a big decision* IMPORTANT,

Books of the Christian Bible

The Old Testament	Song of Solomon/Song of Songs	The New Testament
Genesis	Wisdom of Solomon[1]	Matthew
Exodus	Ecclesiasticus/Sirach[1]	Mark
Leviticus	Isaiah	Luke
Numbers	Jeremiah	John
Deuteronomy	Lamentations	Acts of the Apostles
Joshua	Baruch[1]	Romans
Judges	Ezekiel	1 Corinthians
Ruth	Daniel	2 Corinthians
1 Samuel	(Prayer of Azariah and the Song	Galatians
2 Samuel	of the Three Children)[1]	Ephesians
1 Kings	(Susanna)[1]	Philippians
2 Kings	(Bel and the Dragon)[1]	Colossians
1 Chronicles	Hosea	1 Thessalonians
2 Chronicles	Joel	2 Thessalonians
Ezra	Amos	1 Timothy
Nehemiah	Obadiah	2 Timothy
Tobit[1]	Jonah	Titus
Judith[1]	Micah	Philemon
Esther	Nahum	Hebrews
(additions to Esther)[1]	Habakkuk	James
1 Maccabees[1]	Zephaniah	1 Peter
2 Maccabees[1]	Haggai	2 Peter
3 Maccabees[2]	Zechariah	1 John
Job	Malachi	2 John
Psalms	1 Esdras[2]	3 John
(Psalm 151)[2]	2 Esdras[3]	Jude
Proverbs	Prayer of Manasseh[2]	Revelation
Ecclesiastes		

[1] Accepted by Catholics and by Greek and Russian Orthodox but not by Protestants.
[2] Accepted by Greek and Russian Orthodox but not by Protestants and Catholics.
[3] Accepted by Russian Orthodox only.

significant, major, momentous, weighty, consequential, far-reaching, key, vital, critical, crucial. **5** (*informal*) *a big man in the government* POWERFUL, important, prominent, influential, high-powered, leading; major-league. **6** (*informal*) *she has big plans* AMBITIOUS, far-reaching, grandiose, on a grand scale. **7** *he's got a big heart* GENEROUS, kind, kindly, caring, compassionate, loving. **8** (*informal*) *east-coast bands are big across the country* POPULAR, successful, in demand, sought-after, all the rage; *informal* hot, in, cool, trendy, now, hip.
– OPPOSITES: small, minor, modest.
■ **too big for one's britches/boots** (*informal*) CONCEITED, full of oneself, cocky, arrogant, cocksure, above oneself, self-important, puffed-up; vain, self-satisfied, pleased with oneself, smug, complacent; *informal* big-headed; *literary* vainglorious.

big-headed ▶ adjective (*informal*) CONCEITED, full of oneself, cocky, arrogant, cocksure, above oneself, self-important; vain, self-satisfied, puffed-up, pleased with oneself, smug, complacent; *informal* too big for one's britches/boots; *literary* vainglorious.
– OPPOSITES: modest.

big-hearted ▶ adjective GENEROUS, magnanimous, munificent, open-handed, bountiful, unstinting, unselfish, altruistic, charitable, philanthropic, benevolent; kind, kindly, kind-hearted; *literary* bounteous.
– OPPOSITES: mean.

bigot ▶ noun CHAUVINIST, partisan, sectarian; racist, sexist, homophobe, dogmatist, jingoist.

bigoted ▶ adjective PREJUDICED, biased, partial, one-sided, sectarian, discriminatory; opinionated,

dogmatic, intolerant, narrow-minded, blinkered, illiberal; racist, sexist, chauvinistic, jingoistic; warped, twisted, distorted.
– OPPOSITES: open-minded.

bigwig ▶ noun (*informal*) VIP, important person, notable, dignitary, grandee; celebrity; *informal* somebody, heavyweight, big shot, big gun, big cheese, big fish, big kahuna, big wheel, top gun.
– OPPOSITES: nonentity.

bilious ▶ adjective **1** *I felt bilious* NAUSEOUS, sick, queasy, nauseated. **2** *his bilious disposition. See* IRRITABLE. **3** *a bilious green and pink colour scheme* NAUSEATING, sickly.
– OPPOSITES: well, good-humoured, muted.

bilk ▶ verb (*informal*). See SWINDLE *verb*.

bill[1] ▶ noun **1** *a bill for $60* INVOICE, account, statement, list of charges; check, tab; *archaic* reckoning, score. **2** *a parliamentary bill* DRAFT LAW, proposed piece of legislation, proposal. **3** *a $20 bill* BANKNOTE, note. **4** *he had been posting bills* POSTER, advertisement, ad, public notice, announcement; flyer, leaflet, handbill.
▶ verb **1** *please bill me for the work* INVOICE, charge, debit, send a statement to. **2** *the concert went ahead as billed* ADVERTISE, announce; schedule, program, timetable; slate. **3** *he was billed as the new Sean Connery* DESCRIBE, call, style, label, dub; promote, publicize, talk up, hype.

bill[2] ▶ noun *a bird's bill* BEAK; *technical* mandibles.

billet ▶ noun *the troops' billets* QUARTERS, rooms; accommodation, lodging, housing; barracks, cantonment.

▶ **verb** *two soldiers were billeted here* ACCOMMODATE, quarter, put up, lodge, house; station, garrison.

billow ▶ **noun** 1 *billows of smoke* CLOUD, mass. 2 *(archaic) the billows that break upon the shore* WAVE, roller, breaker.
▶ **verb** 1 *her dress billowed around her* PUFF UP/OUT, balloon (out), swell, fill (out), belly out. 2 *smoke billowed from the chimney* SWIRL, spiral, roll, undulate, eddy; pour, flow.

billowing ▶ **adjective** ROLLING, swirling, undulating, surging, heaving, billowy, swelling, rippling.

bin ▶ **noun** CONTAINER, receptacle, holder; drum, canister, box, caddy, can, crate, chest, tin.

bind ▶ **verb** 1 *they bound our hands and feet* TIE (UP), fasten (together), hold together, secure, make fast, attach; rope, strap, lash, fetter, truss, hog-tie, tether. 2 *the experience had bound them together* UNITE, join, bond, knit together, draw together, yoke together. 3 *we were bound by a rigid timetable* CONSTRAIN, restrict, restrain, trammel, tie hand and foot, tie down, fetter, shackle, hog-tie; hamper, hinder, inhibit. 4 *the edges are bound in a contrasting colour* TRIM, hem, edge, border, fringe; finish.
— OPPOSITES: untie, separate.
▶ **noun** *we're in a terrible bind* PREDICAMENT, difficult/ awkward situation, quandary, dilemma, plight, tight spot/situation/squeeze, Catch-22, fix, hole, cleft stick.

binder ▶ **noun** FOLDER, ring binder, three-ring binder; *proprietary* Duo-Tang ✦.

binding ▶ **adjective** IRREVOCABLE, unalterable, inescapable, unbreakable, contractual; compulsory, obligatory, mandatory, incumbent.

binge ▶ **noun** DRINKING BOUT, debauch; bender, booze-up, jag, toot; spree; *dated* souse; *literary* bacchanal, bacchanalia; *archaic* wassail.
▶ **verb** OVERINDULGE, overeat, gorge; *informal* pig out.

binoculars ▶ **plural noun** FIELD GLASSES.

biography ▶ **noun** LIFE STORY, life history, life, memoir; *informal* bio.

bird ▶ **noun** fowl; chick, fledgling, nestling; *informal* feathered friend, birdie; *technical* (**birds**) avifauna. *See table.*
— RELATED TERMS: avian, ornith-.

birth ▶ **noun** 1 *the birth of a child* CHILDBIRTH, delivery, nativity, birthing; blessed/happy event; *formal* parturition; *dated* confinement; *archaic* accouchement, childbed. 2 *the birth of science* BEGINNING(S), emergence, genesis, dawn, dawning, rise, start, onset, commencement. 3 *he is of noble birth* ANCESTRY, lineage, blood, descent, parentage, family, extraction, origin, genealogy, heritage, stock, kinship.
— RELATED TERMS: natal.
— OPPOSITES: death, demise, end.
■ **give birth to** HAVE, bear, produce, be delivered of, bring into the world; birth; *informal* drop; *dated* mother; *archaic* bring forth.

birthmark ▶ **noun** BEAUTY SPOT/MARK, mole, blemish, nevus.

birthright ▶ **noun** PATRIMONY, inheritance, heritage; right, due, prerogative, privilege; primogeniture.

birthstone ▶ **noun**. *See table.*

biscuit ▶ **noun** SCONE, tea biscuit ✦, (*Nfld*) tea bun ✦, bannock ✦, baking powder biscuit, (*Nfld*) bun ✦, (*Nfld*) pork bun ✦; SHIP'S BISCUIT, (*Nfld*) hard bread ✦, hardtack, water biscuit, soda biscuit, soda cracker, saltine; DOG BISCUIT.

Birds

blackbirds	nutcrackers
bluebirds	nuthatches
bobolinks	orioles
buntings	ovenbirds
bushtits	phoebes
cardinals	pigeons
catbirds	pipits
chaffinches	ravens
chickadees	redpolls
cowbirds	redstarts
creepers	robins
crossbills	sapsuckers
crows	shrikes
doves	siskins
dippers	skylarks
finches	sparrows
flickers	starlings
flycatchers	swallows
gnatcatchers	swifts
goatsuckers	tanagers
goldfinches	thrashers
grackles	thrush
grosbeaks	tits
hummingbirds	titmice
jays	towhees
juncos	veeries
kingbirds	vireos
kingfishers	wagtails
kinglets	warblers
larks	waxwings
longspurs	wheatears
magpies	whippoorwills
martins	woodpeckers
meadowlarks	wrens
mockingbirds	yellowthroats
nighthawks	

See also the tables at CHICKEN, CRANE, DUCK, GULL, PARROT, *and* RAPTOR.

Birthstones

Month	Birthstone
January	garnet
February	amethyst
March	aquamarine/bloodstone
April	diamond
May	emerald
June	pearl/moonstone
July	ruby
August	peridot/sardonyx
September	sapphire
October	opal/tourmaline
November	topaz
December	turquoise

bisect ▶ **verb** CUT IN HALF, halve, divide/cut/split in two, split down the middle; cross, intersect.

bishop ▶ **noun** diocesan, metropolitan, suffragan, eparch; *formal* prelate.
— RELATED TERMS: episcopal.

bishopric ▶ **noun** DIOCESE, see.

bit ▶ **noun** 1 *a bit of bread* PIECE, portion, segment, section, part; chunk, lump, hunk, slice; fragment, scrap, shred, crumb, grain, speck; spot, drop, pinch, dash, soupçon, modicum; morsel, mouthful, bite, sample; iota, jot, tittle, whit, atom, particle, trace,

touch, suggestion, hint, tinge; snippet, snatch, smidgen, tad. **2** *wait a bit* MOMENT, minute, second, (little) while; *informal* sec, jiffy.
— OPPOSITES: lot.

■ **a bit** SOMEWHAT, fairly, slightly, rather, quite, a little, moderately; *informal* pretty, sort of, kind of, kinda.

■ **bit by bit** GRADUALLY, little by little, in stages, step by step, piecemeal, slowly.

■ **in a bit** SOON, in a (little) while, in a second, in a minute, in a moment, shortly; *informal* in a jiffy, in two shakes, in a snap; *literary* ere long, anon.

bitch ► noun *(coarse slang)* **1** *she's such a bitch* WITCH, shrew, vixen, she-devil, hellcat, harridan, termagant, virago, harpy, cow, cat; *archaic* grimalkin. **2** *a bitch of a job* NIGHTMARE; *informal* bastard, bummer, ——from hell, stinker.

► verb *big men bitched about the price of oil* COMPLAIN, whine, grumble, grouse; *informal* whinge, moan, grouch, gripe.

bitchy ► adjective *(informal)*. See SPITEFUL.

bite ► verb **1** *the dog bit his arm* SINK ONE'S TEETH INTO, chew, munch, crunch, champ, tear at, snap at. **2** *the acid bites into the copper* CORRODE, eat into, eat away at, burn (into), etch, dissolve. **3** *a hundred or so retailers should bite* ACCEPT, agree, respond; be lured, be enticed, be tempted; take the bait.

► noun **1** *he took a bite of his sandwich* CHEW, munch, nibble, nip, snap. **2** *he ate it in two bites* MOUTHFUL, piece, bit, morsel. **3** *let's go out for a bite* SNACK, light meal, soupçon; refreshments; *informal* a little something. **4** *we came back from the picnic covered in insect bites* STING. **5** *the appetizer had a fiery bite* PIQUANCY, pungency, spiciness, strong flavour, tang, zest, sharpness, tartness; *informal* kick, punch, edge, zing.

biting ► adjective **1** *biting comments* VICIOUS, harsh, cruel, savage, cutting, sharp, bitter, scathing, caustic, acid, acrimonious, acerbic, stinging; vitriolic, hostile, spiteful, venomous, mean, nasty; *informal* bitchy, catty. **2** *the biting wind* FREEZING, icy, arctic, glacial; bitter, piercing, penetrating, raw, wintry.
— OPPOSITES: mild.

bitter ► adjective **1** *a bitter aftertaste* SHARP, acid, acidic, acrid, tart, sour, biting, unsweetened, vinegary; *technical* acerbic. **2** *a bitter woman* RESENTFUL, embittered, aggrieved, begrudging, rancorous, spiteful, jaundiced, ill-disposed, sullen, sour, churlish, morose, petulant, peevish, with a chip on one's shoulder. **3** *a bitter blow* PAINFUL, unpleasant, disagreeable, nasty, cruel, awful, distressing, upsetting, harrowing, heartbreaking, heart-rending, agonizing, traumatic, tragic, chilling; *formal* grievous. **4** *a bitter wind* FREEZING, icy, arctic, glacial; bitter, piercing, penetrating, raw, wintry. **5** *a bitter row* ACRIMONIOUS, virulent, angry, rancorous, spiteful, vicious, vitriolic, savage, ferocious, hate-filled, venomous, poisonous, acrid, nasty, ill-natured.
— OPPOSITES: sweet, magnanimous, content, welcome, warm, amicable.

bitterness ► noun **1** *the bitterness of the medicine* SHARPNESS, acidity, acridity, tartness, sourness, harshness; *technical* acerbity. **2** *there was no bitterness between them* RESENTMENT, rancour, indignation, grudge, spite, sullenness, sourness, churlishness, moroseness, petulance, pique, peevishness; ACRIMONY, hostility, malice, virulence, antipathy, antagonism, enmity, animus, friction, vitriol, hatred, loathing, venom, poison, nastiness, ill

feeling, ill will, bad blood. **3** *the bitterness of war* TRAUMA, pain, agony, grief; unpleasantness, disagreeableness, nastiness; heartache, heartbreak, distress, desolation, despair, tragedy.
— OPPOSITES: sweetness, magnanimity, contentment, warmth, goodwill.

bizarre ► adjective STRANGE, peculiar, odd, funny, curious, outlandish, outré, abnormal, eccentric, unconventional, unusual, unorthodox, queer, extraordinary; *informal* weird, wacky, oddball, way out, kooky, freaky, off the wall, offbeat.
— OPPOSITES: normal.

blabber ► verb *(informal)*. See BABBLE verb sense 1.

blabbermouth ► noun *(informal)* TALKER, chatterer, prattler, bigmouth, blatherskite; chatterbox, windbag, gasbag, motormouth.

black ► adjective **1** *a black horse* DARK, pitch-black, jet-black, coal-black, ebony, sable, inky. **2** *a black night* UNLIT, dark, starless, moonless, wan; *literary* tenebrous, Stygian. **3** *the blackest day of the war* TRAGIC, disastrous, calamitous, catastrophic, cataclysmic, fateful, wretched, woeful, awful, terrible; *formal* grievous. **4** *Mary was in a black mood* MISERABLE, unhappy, sad, wretched, broken-hearted, heartbroken, grief-stricken, grieving, sorrowful, sorrowing, anguished, desolate, despairing, disconsolate, downcast, dejected, sullen, cheerless, melancholy, morose, gloomy, glum, mournful, doleful, funereal, dismal, forlorn, woeful, abject; *informal* blue; *literary* dolorous. **5** *black humour* CYNICAL, macabre, weird, unhealthy, ghoulish, morbid, perverted, gruesome; *informal* sick. **6** *a black look*. See ANGRY sense 1. **7** *(archaic) a black deed*. See WICKED sense 1.
— OPPOSITES: white, clear, bright, joyful.

■ **black out** FAINT, lose consciousness, pass out, swoon; *informal* flake out, go out.

■ **black something out** DARKEN, shade, turn off the lights in; keep the light out of.

■ **in the black** IN CREDIT, in funds, debt-free, out of debt, solvent, financially sound, able to pay one's debts, creditworthy.

■ **black and white** **1** *a black-and-white picture* MONOCHROME, grey-scale. **2** *I wish to see the proposals in black and white* IN PRINT, printed, written down, set down, on paper, recorded, on record, documented. **3** *in black-and-white terms* CATEGORICAL, unequivocal, absolute, uncompromising, unconditional, unqualified, unambiguous, clear, clear-cut.

blackball ► verb REJECT, debar, bar, ban, vote against, blacklist, exclude, shut out; ostracize, expel.
— OPPOSITES: admit.

blacken ► verb **1** *they blackened their faces* BLACK, darken; dirty, make sooty, make smoky, stain, grime, soil. **2** *the sky blackened* GROW/BECOME BLACK, darken, dim, grow dim, cloud over. **3** *someone has blackened my name* SULLY, tarnish, besmirch, drag through the mud/mire, stain, taint, smear, disgrace, dishonour, bring discredit to, damage, ruin; slander, defame.
— OPPOSITES: whiten, clean, lighten, brighten, clear.

blacklist ► verb BOYCOTT, ostracize, blackball, spurn, avoid, embargo, steer clear of, ignore; stigmatize; refuse to employ.

black magic ► noun SORCERY, witchcraft, wizardry, necromancy, the black arts, devilry; malediction, voodoo, witching, witchery.

blackmail ► noun *he was accused of blackmail* EXTORTION; *informal* hush money; *formal* exaction.

► verb **1** *he was blackmailing the murderer* EXTORT MONEY FROM, threaten; *informal* demand hush money from.

2 *she blackmailed me to work for her* COERCE, pressurize, pressure, force; *informal* lean on, put the screws on, twist someone's arm.

blackout ▸ noun **1** *there must have been a blackout — all the clocks are blinking* POWER FAILURE, power outage, brownout. **2** *a news blackout* SUPPRESSION, silence, censorship, gag order, reporting restrictions. **3** *he had a blackout* FAINTING FIT, faint, loss of consciousness, passing out, swoon, collapse; *Medicine* syncope.

blah ▸ noun **(the blahs)** DOLDRUMS, low spirits, a blue funk, depression.
▸ adjective DULL, bland, unexciting, plain-vanilla; lethargic, unenthusiastic, listless, torpid.

blame ▸ verb **1** *he always blames others* HOLD RESPONSIBLE, hold accountable, condemn, accuse, find/consider guilty, assign fault/liability/guilt to, indict, point the finger at, finger, incriminate; *archaic* inculpate. **2** *they blame youth crime on unemployment* ASCRIBE TO, attribute to, impute to, lay at the door of, put down to; *informal* pin.
— OPPOSITES: absolve.
▸ noun *he was cleared of all blame* RESPONSIBILITY, guilt, accountability, liability, culpability, fault; the rap.

blameless ▸ adjective INNOCENT, guiltless, above reproach, irreproachable, unimpeachable, in the clear, exemplary, perfect, virtuous, pure, impeccable, faultless; *informal* squeaky clean.
— OPPOSITES: blameworthy.

blameworthy ▸ adjective CULPABLE, reprehensible, indefensible, inexcusable, guilty, criminal, delinquent, wrong, evil, wicked; to blame, at fault, reproachable, responsible, answerable, erring, errant, in the wrong.
— OPPOSITES: blameless.

blanch ▸ verb **1** *the moon blanches her hair* TURN PALE, whiten, lighten, wash out, fade, blench. **2** *his face blanched* PALE, turn pale, turn white, whiten, lose its colour, lighten, fade, blench. **3** *blanch the spinach leaves* SCALD, boil briefly.
— OPPOSITES: colour, darken.

bland ▸ adjective **1** *bland food* TASTELESS, flavourless, insipid, weak, watery, spiceless, wishy-washy. **2** *a bland film* UNINTERESTING, dull, boring, tedious, monotonous, dry, drab, dreary, wearisome; unexciting, unimaginative, uninspiring, uninspired, lacklustre, vapid, flat, stale, trite, blah, plain-vanilla, white-bread, banal, commonplace, humdrum, ho-hum, vacuous, wishy-washy. **3** *a bland expression* UNEMOTIONAL, emotionless, dispassionate, passionless, inexpressive, cool, impassive; expressionless, blank, wooden, stony, deadpan, hollow, undemonstrative, imperturbable.
— OPPOSITES: tangy, interesting, emotional.

blandishments ▸ plural noun FLATTERY, cajolery, coaxing, wheedling, persuasion, palaver, honeyed words, smooth talk, blarney, sweet talk, soft soap, buttering up, smarm.

blank ▸ adjective **1** *a blank sheet of paper* EMPTY, unmarked, unused, clear, free, bare, clean, plain. **2** *a blank face* EXPRESSIONLESS, deadpan, wooden, stony, impassive, unresponsive, poker-faced, vacuous, empty, glazed, fixed, lifeless, inscrutable. **3** *'What?' said Maxim, looking blank* BAFFLED, mystified, puzzled, perplexed, stumped, at a loss, stuck, bewildered, dumbfounded, nonplussed, bemused, lost, uncomprehending, at sea, confused; *informal* flummoxed, bamboozled. **4** *a blank refusal* OUTRIGHT, absolute, categorical, unqualified, complete, flat,

straight, positive, certain, explicit, unequivocal, clear, clear-cut.
— OPPOSITES: full, expressive, qualified.
▸ noun SPACE, gap, lacuna.

blanket ▸ noun *a blanket of cloud* COVERING, layer, coating, carpet, overlay, cloak, mantle, veil, pall, shroud. *See table.*
▸ adjective *blanket coverage* complete, total, comprehensive, overall, general, mass, umbrella, inclusive, all-inclusive, all-round, wholesale, outright, across-the-board, sweeping, indiscriminate, thorough; universal, international, worldwide, global, nationwide, countrywide, coast-to-coast.
— OPPOSITES: partial, piecemeal.
▸ verb *snow blanketed the mountains* COVER, coat, carpet, overlay; cloak, shroud, swathe, envelop; *literary* mantle.
— OPPOSITES: amplify.

Blankets

afghan	lap robe
blankie	point blanket ♣
buffalo robe	receiving blanket
button blanket	security blanket
Chilkat blanket	serape
duvet	space blanket
electric blanket	swansdown blanket
Hudson's Bay blanket ♣	throw

blare ▸ verb *sirens blared* BLAST, sound loudly, trumpet, bray, clamour, boom, blat, roar, thunder, bellow, resound.
— OPPOSITES: murmur.
▸ noun *the blare of the siren* BLAST, trumpeting, clamour, boom, roar, thunder, bellow, blat.
— OPPOSITES: murmur.

blaring ▸ adjective LOUD, noisy, deafening, strident; raucous, harsh, dissonant, discordant, cacophonous.

blarney ▸ noun **1** FLATTERY, honeyed words, smooth talk, blandishments, cajolery, coaxing, wheedling, persuasion, palaver, sweet talk, soft soap, smarm, buttering up; nonsense, baloney, hogwash, bunk, malarkey.

blasé ▸ adjective INDIFFERENT, unconcerned, uncaring, casual, nonchalant, offhand, uninterested, apathetic, unimpressed, unmoved, surfeited, jaded, unresponsive, phlegmatic; *informal* laid-back.
— OPPOSITES: concerned, responsive.

blaspheme ▸ verb SWEAR, curse, take the Lord's name in vain; *informal* cuss; *archaic* execrate.

blasphemous ▸ adjective SACRILEGIOUS, profane, irreligious, irreverent, impious, ungodly, godless.
— OPPOSITES: reverent.

blasphemy ▸ noun PROFANITY, sacrilege, irreligion, irreverence, taking the Lord's name in vain, swearing, curse, cursing, impiety, desecration; *archaic* execration.
— OPPOSITES: reverence.

blast ▸ noun **1** *the blast from the bomb* SHOCK WAVE, pressure wave. **2** *Friday's blast killed two people* EXPLOSION, detonation, discharge, burst. **3** *a sudden blast of cold air* GUST, rush, gale, squall, wind, draft, waft, puff. **4** *the shrill blast of the trumpets* BLARE, wail, roar, screech, shriek, hoot, honk, beep. **5** *we had a blast* GOOD TIME, ball, riot.
▸ verb **1** *bombers were blasting enemy airfields* BLOW UP, bomb, blow (to pieces), dynamite, shell, explode. **2** *guns were blasting away* FIRE, shoot, blaze, let fly,

discharge. **3** *he blasted his horn* HONK, beep, toot, sound. **4** *radios blasting out pop music* BLARE, boom, roar, thunder, bellow, pump, shriek, screech. **5** (*informal*) *the opposition blasted the government over the deal.* See BERATE.
■ **blast off** BE LAUNCHED, take off, lift off, leave the ground, become airborne, take to the air.

blasted ▶ **adjective** (*informal*). See DAMNED sense 2.

blast-off ▶ **noun** LAUNCH, liftoff, takeoff, ascent, firing.
– OPPOSITES: touchdown.

blatant ▶ **adjective** FLAGRANT, glaring, obvious, undisguised, unconcealed, open; shameless, barefaced, naked, unabashed, unashamed, unblushing, brazen.
– OPPOSITES: inconspicuous, shamefaced.

blather ▶ **verb** *he just blathered on* PRATTLE, babble, chatter, twitter, prate, go on, run on, rattle on, yap, jabber, maunder, ramble, burble, drivel, blabber, gab, yak, yatter, yammer, waffle, talk a blue streak.
▶ **noun** *mindless blather* PRATTLE, chatter, twitter, babble, prating, gabble, jabber, rambling; *informal* yatter, twaddle, gobbledegook.

blaze ▶ **noun 1** *firemen fought the blaze* FIRE, flames, conflagration, inferno, holocaust; forest fire, wildfire, bushfire. **2** *a blaze of light* GLARE, gleam, flash, burst, flare, streak, radiance, brilliance, beam.
▶ **verb 1** *the fire blazed for hours* BURN, be alight, be on fire, be in flames, flame. **2** *headlights blazed* SHINE, flash, flare, glare, gleam, glint, dazzle, glitter, glisten.

blazon ▶ **verb** *their name is blazoned across the sails* DISPLAY, exhibit, present, spread, emblazon, plaster; announce, proclaim.

bleach ▶ **verb** *the blinds had been bleached by the sun* TURN WHITE, whiten, turn pale, blanch, lighten, fade, decolorize, peroxide.
– OPPOSITES: darken.
▶ **noun** *a bottle of bleach* chlorine bleach; *proprietary* Javex ✦.

bleak ▶ **adjective 1** *a bleak landscape* BARE, exposed, desolate, stark, desert, lunar, open, empty, windswept; treeless, without vegetation, denuded. **2** *the future is bleak* UNPROMISING, unfavourable, unpropitious, inauspicious; discouraging, disheartening, depressing, dreary, dim, gloomy, black, dark, grim, hopeless, sombre. **3** *a bleak wind* COLD, bitter, biting, raw, freezing, icy.
– OPPOSITES: lush, promising.

bleary ▶ **adjective** BLURRED, blurry, unfocused; fogged, clouded, dull, misty, watery, rheumy; *archaic* blear.
– OPPOSITES: clear.

bleed ▶ **verb 1** *his arm was bleeding* LOSE BLOOD, hemorrhage. **2** *the doctor bled him* DRAW BLOOD FROM; *Medicine* exsanguinate; *archaic* phlebotomize. **3** *one colour bled into another* FLOW, run, seep, filter, percolate, leach. **4** *sap was bleeding from the trunk* FLOW, run, ooze, seep, exude, weep. **5** *the country was bled dry by poachers* DRAIN, sap, deplete, milk, exhaust. **6** *my heart bleeds for them* GRIEVE, ache, sorrow, mourn, lament, feel, suffer; sympathize with, pity.

blemish ▶ **noun 1** *not a blemish marred her skin* IMPERFECTION, flaw, defect, fault, deformity, discoloration, disfigurement; bruise, scar, pit, pock, pimple, blackhead, wart, scratch, cut, gash; mark, streak, spot, smear, speck, blotch, smudge, smut; birthmark, mole; *Medicine* stigma. **2** *the mayor's record*

is not without blemish DEFECT, fault, failing, flaw, imperfection, foible, vice; shortcoming, weakness, deficiency, limitation; taint, blot, stain, dishonour, disgrace.
– OPPOSITES: virtue.
▶ **verb 1** *nothing blemished the coast* MAR, spoil, impair, disfigure, blight, deface, mark, scar; ruin. **2** *his reign has been blemished by controversy* SULLY, tarnish, besmirch, blacken, blot, taint; spoil, mar, ruin, disgrace, damage, degrade, dishonour; *formal* vitiate.
– OPPOSITES: enhance.

blend ▶ **verb 1** *blend the ingredients until smooth* MIX, mingle, combine, merge, fuse, meld, coalesce, integrate, intermix; stir, whisk, fold in; *technical* admix; *literary* commingle. **2** *the new buildings blend with the older ones* HARMONIZE, go (well), fit (in), be in tune, be compatible; coordinate, match, complement.
▶ **noun** *a blend of bananas, raisins, and ginger* MIXTURE, mix, combination, amalgamation, amalgam, union, marriage, fusion, meld, synthesis, concoction; *technical* admixture.

bless ▶ **verb 1** *the chaplain blessed the couple* ASK/INVOKE GOD'S FAVOUR FOR, give a benediction for; CONSECRATE, sanctify, dedicate (to God), make holy, make sacred; *formal* hallow. **2** *bless the name of the Lord* PRAISE, worship, glorify, honour, exalt, pay homage to, venerate, reverence, hallow; *archaic* magnify. **3** *the gods blessed us with magical voices* ENDOW, bestow, furnish, accord, give, favour, grace; confer on; *literary* endue. **4** *I bless the day you came here* GIVE THANKS FOR, be grateful for, thank; appreciate.
– OPPOSITES: curse, trouble, rue, oppose.

blessed ▶ **adjective 1** *a blessed place* HOLY, sacred, hallowed, consecrated, sanctified; ordained, canonized, beatified. **2** *blessed are the meek* FAVOURED, fortunate, lucky, privileged, enviable, happy.
– OPPOSITES: cursed, wretched, unwelcome.

blessing ▶ **noun 1** *may God give us his blessing* PROTECTION, favour. **2** *a special blessing from the priest* BENEDICTION, invocation, prayer, intercession; grace. **3** *she gave the plan her blessing* SANCTION, endorsement, approval, approbation, favour, consent, assent, agreement; backing, support; *informal* the thumbs up, the OK, the nod. **4** *it was a blessing they didn't have far to go* GODSEND, boon, advantage, benefit, help, bonus, plus; stroke of luck, unmixed blessing, (lucky) break, windfall; *literary* benison.
– OPPOSITES: condemnation, affliction.

blight ▶ **noun 1** *potato blight* DISEASE, canker, infestation, fungus, mildew, mould. **2** *the blight of aircraft noise* AFFLICTION, scourge, bane, curse, plague, menace, misfortune, woe, trouble, ordeal, trial, nuisance, pest.
– OPPOSITES: blessing.
▶ **verb 1** *a tree blighted by leaf curl* INFECT, mildew; kill, destroy. **2** *scandal blighted the careers of several politicians* RUIN, wreck, spoil, mar, frustrate, disrupt, undo, end, scotch, destroy, shatter, devastate, demolish; *informal* mess up, foul up, stymie.

blind ▶ **adjective 1** *he has been blind since birth* SIGHTLESS, unsighted, visually impaired, visionless, unseeing; partially sighted, purblind; *informal* as blind as a bat. **2** *the government must be blind* IMPERCEPTIVE, unperceptive, insensitive, slow, obtuse, uncomprehending; stupid, unintelligent; *informal* dense, dim, thick, dumb, dopey, dozy. **3** *he was blind to her shortcomings* UNMINDFUL OF, mindless of, careless of, heedless of, oblivious to, insensible to,

unconcerned about, indifferent to. **4** *blind acceptance of conventional opinion* UNCRITICAL, unreasoned, unthinking, unconsidered, mindless, undiscerning, indiscriminate. **5** *a blind rage* IMPETUOUS, impulsive, uncontrolled, uncontrollable, wild, unrestrained, immoderate, intemperate, irrational, unbridled.
– OPPOSITES: sighted, perceptive, mindful, discerning.
▶ verb **1** *he was blinded in a car crash* MAKE BLIND, deprive of sight, render sightless; put someone's eyes out. **2** *he was blinded by his faith* DEPRIVE OF JUDGMENT, deprive of perception, deprive of reason, deprive of sense. **3** *they try to blind you with science* OVERAWE, intimidate, daunt, deter, discourage, cow, subdue, dismay; disquiet, discomfit, unsettle, disconcert; disorient, stun, stupefy, confuse, bewilder, bedazzle, confound, perplex, overwhelm; *informal* faze, psych out.
▶ noun **1** *a window blind* SCREEN, shade, sunshade, shutter, curtain, awning, canopy; louvres, jalousie. **2** *some crook had sent the card as a blind* DECEPTION, smokescreen, front, facade, cover, pretext, masquerade, feint, camouflage; trick, ploy, ruse, machination.

blindly ▶ adverb *they blindly followed Moscow policy* UNCRITICALLY, unthinkingly, mindlessly, indiscriminately.

blink ▶ verb **1** *his eyes did not blink* flutter, flicker, wink, bat. **2** *several red lights began to blink* FLASH, flicker, wink. **3** *no one even blinks at the estimated cost* BE SURPRISED, look twice; *informal* boggle. **4** *after a tense standoff, the union blinked* BACK DOWN, give in, knuckle under, submit, relent.

blinkered ▶ adjective NARROW-MINDED, inward-looking, parochial, provincial, insular, small-minded, close-minded, short-sighted; hidebound, illiberal, inflexible, entrenched, prejudiced.
– OPPOSITES: broad-minded.

bliss ▶ noun **1** *she gave a sigh of bliss* JOY, happiness, pleasure, delight, ecstasy, elation, rapture, euphoria. **2** *religions promise perfect bliss after death* BLESSEDNESS, benediction, beatitude, glory, heavenly joy, divine happiness; heaven, paradise.
– OPPOSITES: misery, hell.

blissful ▶ adjective ECSTATIC, happy, euphoric, joyful, elated, rapturous, delighted, thrilled, overjoyed, joyous, on cloud nine, in seventh heaven, over the moon, on top of the world.

blister ▶ noun **1** *a blister on each heel* bleb, vesicle, vesication; pustule, abscess. **2** *check for blisters in the roofing felt* BUBBLE, swelling, bulge, protuberance.

blistering ▶ adjective **1** *blistering heat* INTENSE, extreme, ferocious, fierce; SCORCHING, searing, blazing, burning, fiery; *informal* boiling, baking, roasting, sweltering. **2** *a blistering attack on the government* SAVAGE, vicious, fierce, bitter, harsh, scathing, devastating, caustic, searing, vitriolic. **3** *a blistering pace* VERY FAST, breakneck; *informal* blinding.
– OPPOSITES: mild, leisurely.

blithe ▶ adjective **1** *a blithe disregard for the rules* CASUAL, indifferent, unconcerned, unworried, untroubled, uncaring, careless, heedless, thoughtless; nonchalant, blasé. **2** *(literary) his blithe, smiling face* HAPPY, cheerful, jolly, merry, joyful, joyous, blissful, ecstatic, euphoric, elated; *dated* gay.
– OPPOSITES: thoughtful, sad.

blitz ▶ noun **1** *the 1940 blitz on London* BOMBARDMENT, bombing, onslaught, barrage; attack, assault, raid,

strike, blitzkrieg. **2** *an expensive new marketing blitz* CAMPAIGN, effort, operation, undertaking.

blizzard ▶ noun SNOWSTORM, whiteout, snow squall, flurry, snowfall, blowing snow, snow devil, gale.

bloated ▶ adjective SWOLLEN, distended, tumefied, bulging, inflated, enlarged, expanded, dilated, puffed (up).

blob ▶ noun **1** *a blob of cold gravy* DROP, droplet, globule, bead, bubble; *informal* glob. **2** *a blob of ink* SPOT, dab, blotch, blot, dot, smudge; *informal* splotch.

bloc ▶ noun ALLIANCE, coalition, federation, confederation, league, union, partnership, axis, body, association, group.

block ▶ noun **1** *a block of cheese* CHUNK, hunk, lump, wedge, cube, brick, slab, bar, piece. **2** *an apartment block* BUILDING, complex, structure, development. **3** *a block of shares* BATCH, group, set, quantity. **4** *a block to Third World development* OBSTACLE, bar, barrier, impediment, hindrance, check, hurdle, stumbling block, handicap, deterrent. **5** *a block in the pipe* BLOCKAGE, obstruction, stoppage, clog, congestion, occlusion, clot.
– OPPOSITES: aid.
▶ verb **1** *weeds can block drainage ditches* CLOG (UP), stop up, choke, plug, obstruct, gum up, dam up, congest, jam, close; *informal* gunge up; *technical* occlude. **2** *picket lines blocked access to the factory* HINDER, hamper, obstruct, impede, inhibit, restrict, limit; halt, stop, bar, check, prevent. **3** *he blocked a shot on the goal line* STOP, deflect, fend off, hold off, repel, parry, repulse.
– OPPOSITES: facilitate.
■ **block something off** CLOSE UP, shut off, seal off, barricade, bar, obstruct.
■ **block something out** *trees blocked out the light* CONCEAL, keep out, blot out, exclude, obliterate, blank out, stop.

blockade ▶ noun **1** *a naval blockade of the island* SIEGE; *rare* beseigement. **2** *they erected blockades in the streets* BARRICADE, barrier, roadblock; obstacle, obstruction.
▶ verb *rebels blockaded the capital* BARRICADE, block off, shut off, seal; BESIEGE, surround.

blockage ▶ noun OBSTRUCTION, stoppage, block, occlusion, clog, congestion.

blockhead ▶ noun *(informal).* See IDIOT.

blond, blonde ▶ adjective FAIR, light, yellow, flaxen, tow-coloured, golden, platinum, ash blond, strawberry blond, bottle blond, bleached, peroxide.
– OPPOSITES: dark.

blood ▶ noun **1** *he had lost too much blood* gore, vital fluid; *literary* lifeblood, ichor. **2** *a woman of noble blood* ANCESTRY, lineage, bloodline, descent, parentage, family, birth, extraction, origin, genealogy, heritage, stock, kinship.
– RELATED TERMS: hemal, hematic.

blood-curdling ▶ adjective TERRIFYING, frightening, bone-chilling, spine-chilling, chilling, hair-raising, horrifying, alarming; eerie, sinister, horrible; eldritch.

bloodless ▶ adjective **1** *a bloodless revolution* NON-VIOLENT, peaceful, peaceable, pacifist. **2** *his face was bloodless* ANEMIC, pale, wan, pallid, ashen, colourless, chalky, waxen, white, grey, pasty, drained, drawn, deathly. **3** *a bloodless production* FEEBLE, spiritless, lifeless, listless, half-hearted, unenthusiastic, lukewarm.
– OPPOSITES: bloody, ruddy, powerful.

bloodshed ▶ noun SLAUGHTER, massacre, killing, wounding; carnage, butchery, bloodletting, bloodbath; violence, fighting, warfare; *literary* slaying.

bloodthirsty ▶ adjective MURDEROUS, homicidal, violent, vicious, barbarous, barbaric, savage, brutal, cutthroat; fierce, ferocious, inhuman.

bloody ▶ adjective **1** *his bloody nose* BLEEDING. **2** *bloody medical waste* BLOODSTAINED, blood-soaked, gory; *archaic* sanguinary. **3** *a bloody civil war* VICIOUS, ferocious, savage, fierce, brutal, murderous, barbarous, gory; *archaic* sanguinary. **4** *a bloody nuisance!* See DAMNED sense 2.

bloom ▶ noun **1** *orchid blooms* FLOWER, blossom, floweret, floret. **2** *a girl in the bloom of youth* PRIME, perfection, acme, peak, height, heyday; salad days. **3** *the bloom of her skin* RADIANCE, lustre, sheen, glow, freshness; BLUSH, rosiness, pinkness, colour.
▶ verb **1** *the geraniums bloomed* FLOWER, blossom, open; mature. **2** *the children bloomed in the Laurentian air* FLOURISH, thrive, prosper, progress, burgeon; *informal* be in the pink.
− OPPOSITES: wither, decline.

blossom ▶ noun *pink blossoms* FLOWER, bloom, floweret, floret.
▶ verb **1** *the trilliums have blossomed* BLOOM, flower, open, unfold; mature. **2** *the whole region had blossomed* DEVELOP, grow, mature, progress, evolve; flourish, thrive, prosper, bloom, burgeon.
− OPPOSITES: fade, decline.
■ **in blossom** IN FLOWER, flowering, blossoming, blooming, in (full) bloom, abloom, open, out; *formal* inflorescence.

blot ▶ noun **1** *an ink blot* SPOT, dot, mark, blotch, smudge, patch, dab; *informal* splotch. **2** *the only blot on a clean campaign* BLEMISH, taint, stain, blight, flaw, fault; disgrace, dishonour.
▶ verb **1** *blot the excess water* SOAK UP, absorb, sponge up, mop up; dry up/out; dab, pat. **2** *he had blotted our name forever* TARNISH, taint, stain, blacken, sully, mar; dishonour, disgrace, besmirch.
− OPPOSITES: honour.
■ **blot something out 1** *Mary blotted out her picture* ERASE, obliterate, delete, efface, rub out, blank out, expunge, eradicate; cross out, strike out, wipe out. **2** *clouds were starting to blot out the stars* CONCEAL, hide, obscure, exclude, obliterate; shadow, eclipse.

blotch ▶ noun **1** *pink flowers with dark blotches* PATCH, smudge, dot, spot, blot, dab, daub; *informal* splotch. **2** *his face was covered in blotches* PATCH, mark, freckle, birthmark, discoloration, eruption, nevus.
▶ verb *her face was blotched and swollen* SPOT, mark, smudge, streak, blemish.

blotchy ▶ adjective MOTTLED, dappled, blotched, patchy, spotty, spotted, smudged, marked; *informal* splotchy.

blouse ▶ noun See table at SHIRT.

blow ▶ verb **1** *the icy wind blew around us* GUST, bluster, puff, blast, roar, rush, storm. **2** *his ship was blown on to the rocks* SWEEP, carry, toss, drive, push, force. **3** *leaves blew across the road* DRIFT, flutter, waft, float, glide, whirl, move. **4** *he blew a smoke ring* EXHALE, puff, breathe out; emit, expel, discharge, issue. **5** *he blew a trumpet* SOUND, blast, toot, pipe, trumpet; play. **6** *a rear tire had blown* BURST, explode, blow out, split, rupture, puncture. **7** (*informal*) *he blew his money on gambling* SQUANDER, waste, misspend, throw away, fritter away, go through, lose, lavish, dissipate, use up; spend recklessly; *informal* splurge. **8** (*informal*) *don't blow this opportunity* SPOIL, ruin, bungle, mess up,

fudge, muff; WASTE, lose, squander; *informal* botch, screw up, foul up. **9** *his cover was blown* EXPOSE, reveal, uncover, disclose, divulge, unveil, betray, leak.
▶ noun **1** *a blow on the head* KNOCK, BANG, hit, punch, thump, smack, crack, rap, karate chop; *informal* whack, thwack, bonk, bash, clout, sock, wallop. **2** *losing his wife must have been a blow* SHOCK, surprise, bombshell, thunderbolt, jolt; calamity, catastrophe, disaster, upset, setback. **3** *the harbour would offer protection in a blow* GALE, storm, tempest, hurricane; wind, breeze, gust, squall. **4** *a blow on the guard's whistle* TOOT, blast, blare; whistle.
■ **blow out 1** *the matches will not blow out in a strong wind* BE EXTINGUISHED, go out, be put out, stop burning. **2** *the front tire blew out.* See BLOW verb sense 6. **3** *the windows blew out* SHATTER, rupture, crack, smash, splinter, disintegrate; burst, explode, fly apart; *informal* bust.
■ **blow something out** EXTINGUISH, put out, snuff, douse, quench, smother.
■ **blow over** ABATE, subside, drop off, lessen, ease (off), let up, diminish, fade, dwindle, slacken, recede, tail off, peter out, pass, die down, fizzle out.
■ **blow up 1** *a truckload of shells blew up* EXPLODE, detonate, go off, ignite, erupt. **2** *he blows up at whoever's in his way* LOSE ONE'S TEMPER, get angry, rant and rave, go berserk, flare up, erupt; *informal* go mad, go crazy, go wild, hit the roof, fly off the handle. **3** *a crisis blew up* BREAK OUT, erupt, flare up, boil over; emerge, arise.
■ **blow something up 1** *they blew the plane up* BOMB, blast, destroy; explode, detonate. **2** *blow up the balloons* INFLATE, pump up, fill up, puff up, swell, expand. **3** *I blew the picture up on a photocopier* ENLARGE, magnify, expand, increase.
■ **blow out of proportion** EXAGGERATE, overstate, overstress, overestimate, magnify, amplify; aggrandize, embellish, elaborate.

blowout ▶ noun **1** *the steering is automatic in the event of blowouts* PUNCTURE, flat tire, burst tire; *informal* flat. **2** (*informal*) *this meal is our last real blowout* FEAST, banquet, celebration, party; *informal* shindig, whoop-up ✚, do, binge; *informal* bunfight. **3** *the game turned into a blowout* ROUT, whitewash, walkover, laugher, landslide.

blowsy ▶ adjective UNTIDY, sloppy, scruffy, messy, dishevelled, unkempt, frowzy, slovenly, raddled; coarse; RED-FACED, ruddy, florid.
− OPPOSITES: tidy, respectable.

blowy ▶ adjective WINDY, windswept, blustery, gusty, breezy; stormy, squally.
− OPPOSITES: still.

blubber[1] ▶ noun *whale blubber* FAT, fatty tissue; fatness, plumpness, bulk; beer belly, beer gut, Molson muscle ✚, paunch, flab.

blubber[2] ▶ verb (*informal*) *she started to blubber* CRY, sob, weep, snivel; *informal* boo-hoo.

bludgeon ▶ noun *hooligans wielding bludgeons* CUDGEL, club, stick, truncheon, baton; nightstick, billy club, blackjack.
▶ verb *he was bludgeoned to death* BATTER, cudgel, club, beat, thrash; clobber, pummel.

blue ▶ adjective **1** *bright blue eyes* sky blue, azure, cobalt, sapphire, navy, powder blue, midnight blue, Prussian blue, electric blue, indigo, royal blue, ice-blue, baby blue, air force blue, robin's egg blue, peacock blue, Oxford blue, Cambridge blue, ultramarine, aquamarine, steel blue, slate blue, cyan; *literary* cerulean. **2** (*informal*) *Mum was feeling a bit blue*

DEPRESSED, down, sad, unhappy, melancholy, miserable, gloomy, dejected, dispirited, downhearted, downcast, despondent, low, glum; *informal* down in the dumps.
— OPPOSITES: happy.

blue-collar ► **adjective** *blue-collar work* MANUAL, wage, industrial, factory.

blueprint ► **noun 1** *blueprints of the aircraft* PLAN, design, diagram, drawing, sketch, map, layout, representation. **2** *a blueprint for similar measures in other countries* MODEL, plan, template, framework, pattern, example, guide, prototype, pilot.

blues ► **plural noun** (*informal*) *a fit of blues* DEPRESSION, sadness, unhappiness, melancholy, misery, sorrow, gloom, dejection, despondency, despair; the doldrums, a blue funk.

bluff¹ ► **noun** *this threat was dismissed as a bluff* DECEPTION, front, subterfuge, pretense, posturing, sham, fake, deceit, feint, hoax, facade, fraud, charade; trick, ruse, scheme, machination; *informal* put-on.
► **verb 1** *they are bluffing to hide their guilt* PRETEND, sham, fake, feign, lie, hoax, pose, posture, masquerade, dissemble. **2** *I managed to bluff the board into believing me* DECEIVE, delude, mislead, trick, fool, hoodwink, dupe, hoax, beguile, gull; *informal* con, kid.

bluff² ► **adjective** *a bluff man* PLAIN-SPOKEN, straightforward, blunt, direct, no-nonsense, frank, open, candid, forthright, unequivocal; hearty, genial, good-natured; *informal* upfront.

bluff³ ► **noun 1** *an impregnable high bluff* CLIFF, promontory, headland, crag, bank, (*BC, Alta.,* & *North*) ramparts ✦, peak, escarpment, scarp. **2** *Cdn* (*Prairies*) *the bluffs of poplars* GROVE, copse, stand, thicket, wood, (*Atlantic*) droke ✦, clump.

blunder ► **noun** *he shook his head at his blunder* MISTAKE, error, gaffe, slip, oversight, faux pas, misstep, infelicity; *informal* botch, slip-up, boo-boo, blooper, boner, flub.
► **verb 1** *the government admitted it had blundered* MAKE A MISTAKE, err, miscalculate, bungle, trip up, be wrong; *informal* slip up, screw up, blow it, goof. **2** *she blundered down the steps* STUMBLE, lurch, stagger, flounder, struggle, fumble, grope.

blunt ► **adjective 1** *a blunt knife* UNSHARPENED, dull, worn, edgeless. **2** *the leaf is broad with a blunt tip* ROUNDED, flat, obtuse, stubby. **3** *a blunt message* STRAIGHTFORWARD, frank, plain-spoken, candid, direct, bluff, forthright, unequivocal; BRUSQUE, abrupt, curt, terse, bald, brutal, harsh; stark, unadorned, undisguised, unvarnished; *informal* upfront.
— OPPOSITES: sharp, pointed, subtle.
► **verb 1** *ebony blunts tools very rapidly* DULL, make less sharp. **2** *age hasn't blunted my passion for life* DULL, deaden, dampen, numb, weaken, sap, cool, temper, allay, abate; diminish, reduce, decrease, lessen, deplete.
— OPPOSITES: sharpen, intensify.

blur ► **verb 1** *tears blurred her vision* CLOUD, fog, obscure, dim, make hazy, unfocus, soften; *literary* bedim; *archaic* blear. **2** *movies blur the difference between villains and victims* OBSCURE, make vague, confuse, muddle, muddy, obfuscate, cloud, weaken.
— OPPOSITES: sharpen, focus.
► **noun** *a blur on the horizon* INDISTINCT SHAPE, smudge; haze, cloud, mist.

blurred ► **adjective** INDISTINCT, blurry, fuzzy, hazy,

misty, foggy, shadowy, faint; unclear, vague, indefinite, unfocused, obscure, nebulous.

blurt
■ **blurt something out** BURST OUT WITH, exclaim, call out; DIVULGE, disclose, reveal, betray, let slip, give away; *informal* blab, gush, let on, spill the beans, let the cat out of the bag.

blush ► **verb** *Joan blushed at the compliment* REDDEN, turn/go pink, turn/go red, flush, colour, burn up; feel shy, feel embarrassed.
► **noun** *a blush spread across his face* FLUSH, rosiness, pinkness, bloom, high colour.

bluster ► **verb 1** *he started blustering about the general election* RANT, rave, thunder, bellow, sound off; be overbearing; *informal* throw one's weight about/around. **2** *storms bluster in from the sea* BLAST, gust, storm, roar, rush.
► **noun** *his bluster turned to co-operation* RANTING, thundering, hectoring, bullying; bombast, bravado, bumptiousness, braggadocio.

blustery ► **adjective** STORMY, gusty, blowy, windy, squally, wild, tempestuous, turbulent; howling, roaring.
— OPPOSITES: calm.

board ► **noun 1** *a wooden board* PLANK, beam, panel, slat, batten, timber, lath. **2** *the board of directors* COMMITTEE, council, panel, directorate, commission, executive, group. **3** *your room and board will be free* FOOD, meals, provisions, refreshments, diet, table, bread, rations; keep, maintenance; *informal* grub, nosh, eats, chow, scoff.
► **verb 1** *he boarded the aircraft* GET ON, go aboard, enter, mount, ascend; embark, emplane, entrain; catch; *informal* hop on. **2** *a number of students boarded with them* LODGE, live, reside, be housed, room; *informal* put up. **3** *they run a facility for boarding dogs* ACCOMMODATE, lodge, take in, put up, house; keep, feed, cater for, billet.
■ **board something up/over** COVER UP/OVER, close up, shut up, seal.

board game ► **noun.** See table at GAME.

boast ► **verb 1** *his mother had been boasting about him* BRAG, crow, swagger, swank, gloat, show off; exaggerate, overstate; *informal* talk big, blow one's own horn, lay it on thick. **2** *the hotel boasts a fine restaurant* POSSESS, have, own, enjoy, pride oneself/itself on.
► **noun 1** *the government's main boast seemed undone* BRAG, self-praise; exaggeration, overstatement, grandiloquence, fanfaronade. **2** *the hall is the boast of the county* PRIDE, joy, wonder, delight, treasure, gem.

boastful ► **adjective** BRAGGING, swaggering, bumptious, puffed up, full of oneself; cocky, conceited, arrogant, egotistical; *informal* swanky, big-headed, blowhard; *literary* vainglorious.
— OPPOSITES: modest.

boat ► **noun** *a rowing boat* VESSEL, craft, watercraft, ship; *literary* keel, barque. See table.
► **verb** *they were out boating for hours* SAIL, yacht, paddle, row, cruise.

bob ► **verb** MOVE UP AND DOWN, bounce, toss, skip, dance, jounce, wobble, jiggle, joggle, jolt, jerk; NOD, incline, dip; wag, waggle.

bode ► **verb** AUGUR, portend, herald, be a sign of, warn of, foreshadow, be an omen of, presage, indicate, signify, promise, threaten, spell, denote, foretell; prophesy, predict; *literary* betoken, forebode.

bodily ► **adjective** *bodily sensations* PHYSICAL,

Boats

airboat	Gander Bay boat	multihull	torpedo boat
baidarka	gig	outboard	towboat
banker ♣(Nfld)	gondola	outrigger	trap boat
barge	gunboat	packet	trap skiff ♣(Atlantic)
bark	hooker	paddleboat	trimaran
barque	houseboat	pedal boat	tub
bateau ♣	hydrofoil	Peterhead ♣(North)	tugboat
bay boat ♣(Nfld)	hydroplane	pinnace	umiak
bully ♣(Nfld)	iceboat	pointer ♣	vaporetto
bumboat	ice canoe ♣	pontoon	water bus
by-boat ♣hist.	inflatable	prahu	watercraft
cabin cruiser	jack boat ♣(Nfld) hist.	pram	water taxi
canal boat	jet boat	punt	whaleboat
canoe	jigger	raft	wherry
Cape Islander ♣	johnboat	riverboat	yacht
catamaran	jolly	rodney ♣(Nfld)	yawl
catboat	keelboat	rowboat	York boat ♣hist.
coastal boat ♣(Nfld)	ketch	runabout	dragger
coble	lake boat ♣	sailboat	drifter
cockboat	lapstrake	sampan	gillnetter
cockle	launch	scow	seine boat
dinghy	lifeboat	scull	trawler
dory	lighter	shallop	troller;
dragon boat	log bronc ♣(BC)	shell	crabber
felucca	longboat	ship's boat	lobster boat
ferry	mission boat ♣(BC) hist.	skiff	scalloper
fishboat ♣(esp. BC)	monohull	skipjack	shrimper
fishing boat	motorboat	steamboat	*See also* CANOES, SHIPS *and*
flatboat	motorsailer	stern drive	SAILING VESSELS.

corporeal, corporal, somatic, fleshly; concrete, real, actual, tangible.
− OPPOSITES: spiritual, mental.

body ► noun **1** *the human body* FIGURE, frame, form, physique, anatomy, skeleton; soma; *informal* bod. **2** *he was hit by shrapnel in the head and body* TORSO, trunk. **3** *the bodies were exhumed* CORPSE, carcass, skeleton, remains; *informal* stiff; *Medicine* cadaver. **4** *the body of the article* MAIN PART, central part, core, heart. **5** *a body of water* EXPANSE, mass, area, stretch, tract, sweep, extent. **6** *a growing body of evidence* QUANTITY, amount, volume, collection, mass, corpus. **7** *the representative body of the employers* ASSOCIATION, organization, group, party, company, society, circle, syndicate, guild, corporation, contingent. **8** *add body to your hair* FULLNESS, thickness, substance, bounce, lift, shape.
■ **body and soul** COMPLETELY, entirely, totally, utterly, fully, thoroughly, wholeheartedly, unconditionally, to the hilt.

bodyguard ► noun guard, protector, guardian, defender.

bog ► noun MARSH, swamp, muskeg, mire, quagmire, morass, slough, fen, wetland, bogland.
■ **bogged down** MIRED, stuck, entangled, ensnared, embroiled; hampered, hindered, impeded, delayed, stalled, detained; swamped, overwhelmed.

boggle ► verb **1** *this data makes the mind boggle* MARVEL, wonder. **2** *this boggles my mind* BAFFLE, astonish, astound, amaze, stagger, overwhelm.

boggy ► adjective MARSHY, swampy, miry, fenny, muddy, waterlogged, wet, soggy, sodden, squelchy; spongy, heavy, sloughy.

bogus ► adjective FAKE, spurious, false, fraudulent, sham, deceptive; COUNTERFEIT, forged, feigned; make-believe, dummy, pseudo, phony, pretend, fictitious.
− OPPOSITES: genuine.

bohemian ► noun *he is an artist and a real bohemian* NONCONFORMIST, free spirit, dropout; hippie, beatnik, boho.
− OPPOSITES: conservative.
► adjective *a bohemian student life* UNCONVENTIONAL, nonconformist, unorthodox, avant-garde, irregular, alternative; artistic; *informal* boho, artsy, artsy-fartsy, way-out, offbeat.
− OPPOSITES: conventional.

boil[1] ► verb **1** *boil the potatoes* BRING TO A BOIL, simmer, parboil, poach; cook. **2** *the soup is boiling* SIMMER, bubble, stew. **3** *a huge cliff with the sea boiling below* CHURN, seethe, froth, foam; *literary* roil.
► noun bring the stock to a boil BOILING POINT.
■ **boil something down** CONDENSE, reduce, concentrate, thicken.
■ **boil down to** COME DOWN TO, amount to, add up to, be in essence.

boil[2] ► noun *a boil on her neck* SWELLING, SPOT, pimple, blister, pustule, eruption, carbuncle, wen, abscess, ulcer; *technical* furuncle.

boiling ► adjective **1** *boiling water* AT BOILING POINT, at 100 degrees centigrade; very hot, piping hot; bubbling. **2** *(informal) it was a boiling day* VERY HOT, scorching, blistering, sweltering, sultry, torrid; *informal* broiling, roasting, baking, sizzling.
− OPPOSITES: freezing.

boisterous ► adjective **1** *a boisterous game of handball* LIVELY, animated, exuberant, spirited, rambunctious; rowdy, unruly, wild, uproarious, unrestrained, undisciplined, uninhibited, uncontrolled, rough, disorderly, riotous, knockabout; noisy, loud, clamorous. **2** *a boisterous wind* BLUSTERY, gusty, windy, stormy, wild, squally, tempestuous; howling, roaring; *informal* blowy.
− OPPOSITES: restrained, calm.

bold ► adjective **1** *bold adventurers* DARING, intrepid,

brave, courageous, valiant, valorous, fearless, dauntless, audacious, daredevil; adventurous, heroic, plucky, spirited, confident, assured; *informal* gutsy, spunky, feisty. **2** *don't be bold* IMPUDENT, insolent, impertinent, brazen, brash, disrespectful, presumptuous, forward; cheeky, lippy, fresh. **3** *a bold pattern* STRIKING, vivid, bright, strong, eye-catching, prominent; gaudy, lurid, garish. **4** *departure times are in bold type* HEAVY, thick, pronounced.
— OPPOSITES: timid, pale.

bolster ▶ **verb** *a break would bolster her morale* STRENGTHEN, reinforce, boost, fortify, renew; support, sustain, buoy up, prop up, shore up, maintain, aid, help; augment, increase.
— OPPOSITES: undermine.

bolt ▶ **noun 1** *the bolt on the shed door* BAR, LOCK, catch, latch, fastener, deadbolt. **2** *nuts and bolts* RIVET, pin, peg, screw. **3** *a bolt whirred over my head* ARROW, quarrel, dart, shaft. **4** *a bolt of lightning* FLASH, thunderbolt, shaft, streak, burst, flare. **5** *Mark made a bolt for the door* DASH, dart, run, sprint, leap, bound. **6** *a bolt of cloth* ROLL, reel, spool; quantity, amount.
▶ **verb 1** *he bolted the door* LOCK, bar, latch, fasten, secure. **2** *the lid was bolted down* RIVET, pin, peg, screw; fasten, fix. **3** *Anna bolted from the room* DASH, dart, run, sprint, hurtle, career, rush, fly, shoot, bound; flee; *informal* tear, scoot, leg it. **4** *he bolted down his breakfast* GOBBLE, gulp, wolf, guzzle, devour; *informal* demolish, polish off, shovel down, scarf, snarf.
■ **a bolt from/out of the blue** SHOCK, surprise, bombshell, thunderbolt, revelation.
■ **bolt upright** STRAIGHT, rigidly, stiffly.

bomb ▶ **noun 1** *they saw bombs bursting on the runway* EXPLOSIVE, incendiary (device); missile, projectile; *dated* blockbuster, bombshell. **2** *countries with the bomb* NUCLEAR WEAPONS, nuclear bombs, atom bombs, A-bombs. **3** *their next film was a bomb* FAILURE, flop, megaflop, fiasco, bust, dud, washout, debacle, turkey, dog, clunker.
▶ **verb 1** *their headquarters were bombed* BOMBARD, blast, shell, blitz, strafe, pound; attack, assault; blow up, destroy, demolish, flatten, devastate. **2** *she bombed across the Prairies. See* SPEED *verb* sense 1. **3** *the film bombed at the box office* FAIL, flop, fall flat, founder.

bombard ▶ **verb 1** *gun batteries bombarded the islands* SHELL, pound, blitz, strafe, bomb; assail, attack, assault, batter, blast, pelt. **2** *we were bombarded with information* INUNDATE, swamp, flood, deluge, snow under; besiege, overwhelm.

bombastic ▶ **adjective** POMPOUS, blustering, turgid, verbose, orotund, high-flown, high-sounding, overwrought, pretentious, ostentatious, grandiloquent; *informal* highfalutin, puffed up; *rare* fustian.

bona fide ▶ **adjective** AUTHENTIC, genuine, real, true, actual; legal, legitimate, lawful, valid, proper; *informal* legit, the real McCoy.
— OPPOSITES: bogus.

bonanza ▶ **noun** WINDFALL, godsend, boon, blessing, bonus, stroke of luck, jackpot.

bond ▶ **noun 1** *the bond between her and her son* RELATIONSHIP, tie, link, friendship, fellowship, partnership, association, affiliation, alliance, attachment. **2** *the prisoner struggled with his bonds* CHAINS, fetters, shackles, manacles, irons, restraints. **3** *I've broken my bond* PROMISE, pledge, vow, oath, word (of honour), guarantee, assurance; agreement, contract, pact, bargain, deal.

▶ **verb** *the extensions are bonded to your hair* JOIN, fasten, fix, affix, attach, secure, bind, stick, fuse.

bondage ▶ **noun** SLAVERY, enslavement, servitude, subjugation, subjection, oppression, domination, exploitation, persecution; enthralment, thraldom; *historical* serfdom, vassalage.
— OPPOSITES: liberty.

bonehead ▶ **noun** See IDIOT.

bon mot ▶ **noun** WITTICISM, quip, pun, pleasantry, jest, joke; *informal* wisecrack, one-liner, sally.

bonspiel ▶ **noun** See table at CURLING.

bonus ▶ **noun 1** *the extra space is a real bonus* BENEFIT, advantage, boon, blessing, godsend, stroke of luck, asset, plus, pro, attraction, gravy. **2** *she's on a good salary and she gets a bonus* GRATUITY, gift, present, reward, prize; incentive, inducement, handout; *informal* perk, sweetener; *formal* perquisite.
— OPPOSITES: disadvantage.

bon vivant, bon viveur ▶ **noun** HEDONIST, pleasure-seeker, sensualist, sybarite, voluptuary; epicure, gourmet, gastronome.
— OPPOSITES: puritan.

bony ▶ **adjective** GAUNT, ANGULAR, skinny, thin, lean, spare, spindly, skin-and-bones, skeletal, emaciated, underweight; *informal* like a bag of bones.
— OPPOSITES: plump.

boo ▶ **verb** JEER, heckle, catcall, hiss, hector.

book ▶ **noun 1** *Nadine and Ian have recommended some good books* VOLUME, tome, publication, title; novel, storybook, anthology, treatise, manual; paperback, hardback, pocket book, e-book. **2** *he scribbled in his book* NOTEPAD, notebook, pad, memo pad, exercise book, scribbler ✚, workbook; logbook, ledger, journal, diary, scratch pad. **3** *the council has to balance its books* ACCOUNTS, records; account book, record book, ledger, balance sheet.
▶ **verb 1** *Bill and Veronica booked a table at the restaurant* RESERVE, make a reservation for, pre-arrange, order; *formal* bespeak. **2** *we booked a number of events in the Festival* ARRANGE, program, schedule, timetable, line up, pencil in, slate.
■ **by the book** ACCORDING TO THE RULES, within the law, lawfully, legally, legitimately; honestly, fairly; *informal* on the level, fair and square.

booking ▶ **noun** RESERVATION, pre-arrangement; appointment, date.

bookish ▶ **adjective** STUDIOUS, scholarly, academic, intellectual, highbrow, erudite, learned, lettered, educated, well-read, knowledgeable; cerebral, serious, earnest; pedantic.

booklet ▶ **noun** PAMPHLET, brochure, leaflet, handbill, flyer, fact sheet, tract, chapbook; folder, mailer.

boom ▶ **noun 1** *the boom of the thunder* REVERBERATION, resonance, thunder, echoing, crashing, drumming, pounding, roar, rumble, explosion. **2** *an unprecedented boom in sales* UPTURN, upsurge, upswing, increase, advance, growth, boost, escalation, improvement, spurt.
— OPPOSITES: slump.
▶ **verb 1** *thunder boomed overhead* REVERBERATE, resound, resonate; rumble, thunder, blare, echo; crash, roll, clap, explode, bang. **2** *a voice boomed at her* BELLOW, roar, thunder, shout, bawl; *informal* holler. **3** *the market continued to boom* FLOURISH, burgeon, thrive, prosper, progress, improve, pick up, expand, mushroom, snowball.
— OPPOSITES: whisper, slump.

boomerang ▶ verb BACKFIRE, recoil, reverse, rebound, come back, ricochet; be self-defeating; *informal* blow up in one's face.

booming ▶ adjective **1** *a booming voice* RESONANT, sonorous, ringing, resounding, reverberating, carrying, thunderous; strident, stentorian, strong, powerful. **2** *booming business* FLOURISHING, burgeoning, thriving, prospering, prosperous, successful, strong, buoyant; profitable, fruitful, lucrative, boffo; expanding.

boon ▶ noun *their help was such a boon* BLESSING, godsend, bonus, plus, benefit, advantage, help, aid, asset; stroke of luck, windfall.
— OPPOSITES: curse.

boondocks ▶ noun BACKWATER, boonies, hinterland, backwoods, backcountry, back concessions ✤, the sticks, the bush, middle of nowhere, moose pasture ✤, wasteland.

boor ▶ noun LOUT, oaf, ruffian, thug, yahoo, barbarian, Neanderthal, knuckle-dragger, brute, beast, lubber; *informal* clod, roughneck, troglodyte, pig, peasant.

boorish ▶ adjective COARSE, uncouth, rude, ill-bred, ill-mannered, uncivilized, unrefined, rough, thuggish, loutish, oafish, lubberly, lumpen; vulgar, unsavoury, gross, brutish, Neanderthal, knuckle-dragging; *informal* cloddish.
— OPPOSITES: refined.

boost ▶ noun **1** *a boost to one's morale* UPLIFT, lift, spur, encouragement, help, inspiration, stimulus. **2** *a boost in sales* INCREASE, expansion, upturn, upsurge, upswing, rise, escalation, improvement, advance, growth, boom; hike, jump.
— OPPOSITES: decrease.
▶ verb **1** *he phones her to boost her morale* IMPROVE, raise, uplift, increase, enhance, encourage, heighten, help, promote, foster, stimulate, invigorate, revitalize; *informal* buck up. **2** *they used advertising to boost sales* INCREASE, raise, escalate, improve, strengthen, inflate, push up, promote, advance, foster, stimulate, maximize; facilitate, help, assist, aid; jump-start; *informal* hike, bump up.
— OPPOSITES: decrease.

Boots

arctic boots	jackboots
balmorals	kamiks ✤
bluchers	larigans
booties	logans ✤(Nfld)
buskins	moon boots
caulk boots	mukluks
combat boots	rainboots
construction boots	roughout boots
cork boots ✤(BC)	rubber boots
cowboy boots	seaboots
desert boots	snow boots
duck boots	snowmobile boots ✤
gumboots	steel-toed boots
half-boots	top boots
Hessian boots	waders
hiking boots	wellingtons
hip boots	wellies
hip waders	workboots
hobnailed boots	

boot[1] ▶ noun *muddy boots. See table.*
▶ verb **1** *his shot was booted away by the goalkeeper* KICK,

punt; propel, drive. **2** *boot up your computer* START UP, fire up, reboot.
■ **boot someone out / give someone the boot** *(informal). See* DISMISS sense 1.

boot[2]
■ **to boot** AS WELL, also, too, besides, into the bargain, in addition, additionally, on top, what's more, moreover, furthermore, likewise; *informal* and all.

booth ▶ noun **1** *booths for different traders* STALL, stand, kiosk. **2** *a phone booth* CUBICLE, kiosk, box, enclosure.

bootleg ▶ adjective ILLEGAL, illicit, unlawful, unauthorized, unlicensed, pirated; contraband, smuggled, black-market.

bootlicker ▶ noun *(informal)* SYCOPHANT, brown-noser, browner ✤, toady, lickspittle, flatterer, flunky, lackey, yes-man, spaniel, doormat, stooge, cringer, suck ✤, suck-up.

booty ▶ noun LOOT, plunder, pillage, haul, spoils, stolen goods, ill-gotten gains, pickings; *informal* swag.

booze *(informal)* ▶ noun *fill him up with food and booze* ALCOHOL, alcoholic drink, liquor, drink, spirits, intoxicants; *informal* grog, firewater, rotgut, the hard stuff, the bottle, hooch, moonshine, moose milk ✤; juice, the sauce. *See table at* ALCOHOL.
▶ verb *he was out boozing with his buddies* DRINK, tipple, imbibe, indulge; *informal* hit the bottle, knock a few back, swill, chug; bend one's elbow.

boozer ▶ noun *(informal) he's a notorious boozer* DRINKER, drunk, drunkard, alcoholic, dipsomaniac, tippler, imbiber, bibber, sot, inebriate; *informal* lush, alky, rubby ✤, dipso, soak, boozehound, wino, sponge, barfly.

bop ▶ verb *(informal) they were bopping on the dance floor* DANCE; boogie, jive, groove, disco, rock, stomp; get down, hoof it, cut a/the rug.

bordello ▶ noun BROTHEL, whorehouse; *informal* cathouse; *euphemistic* massage parlour, body-rub parlour ✤; *archaic* bawdy house, house of ill fame, house of ill repute; *Law* disorderly house.

border ▶ noun **1** *the border of a medieval manuscript* EDGE, MARGIN, perimeter, circumference, periphery; rim, fringe, verge; sides. **2** *the Canada-US border* FRONTIER, boundary; forty-ninth parallel ✤, *(West)* Medicine Line ✤; borderline, perimeter; marches, bounds.
▶ verb **1** *the fields were bordered by hedges* SURROUND, enclose, encircle, circle, edge, fringe, bound, flank. **2** *the straps are bordered with gold braid* EDGE, fringe, hem; trim, pipe, finish. **3** *the property bordered on the provincial park* ADJOIN, abut, be next to, be adjacent to, be contiguous with; touch, join, meet, reach.
■ **border on** VERGE ON, approach, come close to, be comparable to, approximate to, be tantamount to, be similar to, resemble.

borderline ▶ noun *the borderline between old and antique* DIVIDING LINE, divide, division, demarcation line, line, cut-off point; threshold, margin, border, boundary.
▶ adjective *borderline cases* MARGINAL, uncertain, indefinite, unsettled, undecided, doubtful, indeterminate, unclassifiable, equivocal; questionable, debatable, controversial, contentious, problematic, ambiguous; *informal* iffy.

bore ▶ verb **1** *the television news bored Philip* STULTIFY, pall on, stupefy, weary, tire, fatigue, send to sleep, leave cold; bore to death, bore to tears; *informal* turn off. **2** *bore a hole in the ceiling* DRILL, pierce, perforate,

puncture, punch, cut; tunnel, burrow, mine, dig, gouge, sink.
▶ **noun** *you can be such a bore* TEDIOUS PERSON/THING, tiresome person/thing, dull person/thing, yawn, bother, nuisance, wet blanket.

boreal forest ▶ **noun** taiga.

boredom ▶ **noun** WEARINESS, ennui, apathy, unconcern; frustration, dissatisfaction, restlessness, restiveness, lethargy, lassitude; tedium, dullness, monotony, repetitiveness, flatness, dreariness; *informal* deadliness.

boring ▶ **adjective** TEDIOUS, dull, monotonous, repetitive, unrelieved, unvaried, unimaginative, uneventful; characterless, featureless, colourless, lifeless, insipid, uninteresting, unexciting, uninspiring, unstimulating; unreadable, unwatchable; jejune, flat, bland, dry, stale, tired, banal, lacklustre, stodgy, vapid, dreary, humdrum, mundane; mind-numbing, soul-destroying, wearisome, tiring, tiresome, irksome, trying, frustrating; *informal* deadly, ho-hum, samey, dullsville, dull as dishwater, plain-vanilla.

borrow ▶ **verb 1** *we borrowed a lot of money* take as a loan; lease, hire; *informal* cadge, scrounge, bum, mooch. **2** *(informal) they 'borrowed' all of his tools* TAKE, help oneself to, appropriate, commandeer, abscond with, carry off; steal, purloin; *informal* filch, rob, swipe, nab, rip off, lift, 'liberate', snaffle, pinch, knock off, heist, glom. **3** *adventurous chefs borrow foreign techniques* ADOPT, take on, acquire, embrace.
— OPPOSITES: lend.

bosom ▶ **noun 1** *the gown was set low over her bosom* BUST, chest; breasts, mammary glands, mammae; *informal* mammaries, boobs, knockers, bazooms. **2** *(literary) the family took Gill into its bosom* PROTECTION, shelter, safety, refuge; heart. **3** *love was kindled within his bosom* HEART, breast, soul, core, spirit.
▶ **adjective** *bosom friends* CLOSE, intimate, inseparable, faithful, constant, devoted; good, best, firm, favourite.

boss ▶ **noun** *the boss of a large company* HEAD, chief, director, president, principal, chief executive, chair, manager; supervisor, foreman, overseer, controller; employer, owner, proprietor, patron; *informal* number one, kingpin, boss man, top dog, bigwig, big cheese, head honcho, padrone, big kahuna.
▶ **verb** *you have no right to boss me around* ORDER AROUND, dictate to, lord it over, bully, push around, domineer, dominate, pressurize, browbeat; call the shots, lay down the law, bulldoze, walk all over, railroad.

bossy ▶ **adjective** DOMINEERING, pushy, overbearing, imperious, officious, high-handed, authoritarian, dictatorial, controlling; *informal* high and mighty.
— OPPOSITES: submissive.

botch ▶ **verb** *examiners botched the marking* BUNGLE, mismanage, mishandle, make a mess of, mess up, make a hash of, muff, fluff, foul up, screw up, flub.

bother ▶ **verb 1** *no one bothered her* DISTURB, trouble, inconvenience, pester, badger, harass, molest, plague, nag, hound, harry, annoy, upset, irritate, hassle, bug, give someone the gears ✦, get in someone's hair, get on someone's case, get under a someone's skin, ruffle someone's feathers, rag on, ride. **2** *the incident was too small to bother about* MIND, care, concern oneself, trouble oneself, worry oneself; *informal* give a damn, give a hoot. **3** *there was something bothering him* WORRY, trouble, concern, perturb, disturb, distract, disconcert, unnerve, fret, upset, distress, agitate, gnaw at, weigh down; *informal* rattle.

▶ **noun 1** *I don't want to put you to any bother* TROUBLE, effort, exertion, inconvenience, fuss, pains. **2** *the food was such a bother to cook* NUISANCE, hassle, pain (in the neck), headache, pest, palaver, rigmarole, job, trial, drag, chore, inconvenience, trouble, problem.

bothersome ▶ **adjective** ANNOYING, irritating, obnoxious, vexatious, maddening, exasperating; tedious, wearisome, tiresome; troublesome, trying, taxing, awkward, aggravating, pesky, pestilential.

bottle ▶ **noun 1** *a bottle of whisky* carafe, flask, decanter, canteen, vessel, pitcher, mickey ✦, twenty-six ✦, forty-ouncer ✦ (forty-pounder ✦), Texas mickey ✦, flagon, magnum, stubby, carboy, demijohn. **2** *(informal) a world blurred by the bottle. See* ALCOHOL.
■ **bottle something up** SUPPRESS, repress, restrain, withhold, hold in, rein in, inhibit, smother, stifle, contain, conceal, hide, cork, keep a lid on.

bottleneck ▶ **noun** TRAFFIC JAM, jam, congestion, tie-up, holdup, snarl-up, gridlock, log-jam, constriction, narrowing, restriction, obstruction, blockage, choke point.

bottom ▶ **noun 1** *the bottom of the stairs* FOOT, lowest part, lowest point, base; foundation, substructure, underpinning. **2** *the bottom of the car* UNDERSIDE, underneath, undersurface, undercarriage, underbelly. **3** *the bottom of Lake Ontario* FLOOR, bed. **4** *the bottom of the standings* LOWEST POSITION, lowest level. **5** *I enjoyed the horseback ride, except for my sore bottom* REAR (END), backside, seat, buttocks, rump, cheeks, behind, derrière, bum, butt, fanny, keister, tush, tail, buns, heinie, arse, ass; fundament, posterior, gluteus maximus, sit-upon, stern; *Anatomy* nates. **6** *police got to the bottom of the mystery* ORIGIN, cause, root, source, basis, foundation; heart, kernel; essence.
— OPPOSITES: top, surface.
▶ **adjective** *she sat on the bottom step* LOWEST, last, bottommost; *technical* basal.
— OPPOSITES: top.
■ **hit (rock) bottom** bottom out.

bottomless ▶ **adjective 1** *the bottomless pits of hell* FATHOMLESS, unfathomable, endless, infinite, immeasurable. **2** *George's appetite was bottomless* UNLIMITED, limitless, boundless, infinite, inexhaustible, endless, never-ending, everlasting; vast, huge, enormous.
— OPPOSITES: limited.

bottom line ▶ **noun 1** *how will the move affect our bottom line?* PROFIT, net, gain, earnings, return. **2** *the bottom line is passenger safety* CRUX, issue, essential/crucial/main point, heart of the matter, nub.

bough ▶ **noun** BRANCH, limb, arm, offshoot.

boulder ▶ **noun** ROCK, stone.

boulevard ▶ **noun** AVENUE, street, road, drive, thoroughfare, way.

bounce ▶ **verb 1** *the ball bounced* REBOUND, spring back, ricochet, jounce, carom; reflect. **2** *William bounced down the stairs* BOUND, leap, jump, spring, bob, hop, skip, trip, prance.
▶ **noun 1** *he reached the door in a single bounce* BOUND, leap, jump, spring, hop, skip. **2** *she had lost her bounce* VITALITY, vigour, energy, vivacity, liveliness, animation, sparkle, verve, spirit, enthusiasm, dynamism; cheerfulness, happiness, buoyancy, optimism; exuberance, ebullience; *informal* get-up-and-go, pep, zing.
■ **bounce back** RECOVER, revive, rally, pick up, be on

the mend; perk up, cheer up, brighten up, liven up; *informal* buck up.

bouncing ▶ adjective VIGOROUS, thriving, flourishing, blooming; HEALTHY, strong, robust, fit, in fine fettle; *informal* in the pink.

bouncy ▶ adjective **1** *a rather bouncy ride* BUMPY, jolting, jerky, jumpy, jarring, rough. **2** *she was always bouncy* LIVELY, energetic, perky, frisky, jaunty, dynamic, vital, vigorous, vibrant, animated, spirited, buoyant, bubbly, sparkling, vivacious; enthusiastic, ebullient, upbeat; *informal* peppy, zingy, chirpy.

bound[1] ▶ adjective **1** *he raised his bound ankles* TIED, chained, fettered, shackled, secured, tied up. **2** *she seemed bound to win* CERTAIN, sure, very likely, destined, fated, doomed. **3** *you're bound by the law to keep quiet* OBLIGATED, obliged, compelled, required, constrained, forced. **4** *the unrest was bound up with the region's economic stagnation* CONNECTED, linked, tied, united, allied.

bound[2] ▶ verb *hares bound in the fields* LEAP, jump, spring, bounce, hop; skip, bob, dance, prance, gambol, gallop.
▶ noun *he crossed the room with a single bound* LEAP, jump, spring, bounce, hop.

bound[3] ▶ verb **1** *corporate freedom is bounded by law* LIMIT, restrict, confine, circumscribe, demarcate, delimit. **2** *the garden is bounded by a hedge* ENCLOSE, surround, encircle, circle, border; close in/off, hem in.
■ **out of bounds** OFF LIMITS, restricted; forbidden, banned, proscribed, illegal, illicit, unlawful, unacceptable, taboo; *informal* no go.

boundary ▶ noun **1** *the boundary between Alberta and British Columbia* BORDER, frontier, borderline, partition; cutline ✦, fenceline. **2** *the boundary between art and advertising* DIVIDING LINE, divide, division, borderline, cut-off point. **3** *the boundary of his estate* BOUNDS, confines, limits, margins, edges, fringes; border, periphery, perimeter. **4** *the boundaries of accepted behaviour* LIMITS, parameters, bounds, confines; ambit, compass.

boundless ▶ adjective LIMITLESS, unlimited, unbounded, untold, immeasurable, abundant; inexhaustible, endless, infinite, interminable, unfailing, ceaseless, everlasting.
— OPPOSITES: limited.

bountiful ▶ adjective **1** *their bountiful patron* GENEROUS, magnanimous, munificent, open-handed, unselfish, unstinting, lavish; benevolent, beneficent, charitable. **2** *a bountiful supply of fresh food* ABUNDANT, plentiful, ample, copious, bumper, superabundant, inexhaustible, prolific, profuse; lavish, generous, handsome, rich; *informal* whopping; *literary* plenteous.
— OPPOSITES: mean, meagre.

bouquet ▶ noun **1** *her bridal bouquet* BUNCH OF FLOWERS, posy, nosegay, spray, corsage, boutonniere. **2** *bouquets go to Ann for a well-planned event* COMPLIMENT, commendation, tribute, accolade, praise, congratulations, applause. **3** *the Chardonnay has a fine bouquet* AROMA, nose, smell, fragrance, perfume, scent, odour.

bourgeois ▶ adjective **1** *a bourgeois family* MIDDLE-CLASS, propertied; CONVENTIONAL, conservative, conformist; provincial, suburban, small-town; *informal* white-bread. **2** *bourgeois decadence* CAPITALISTIC, materialistic, money-oriented, commercial.
— OPPOSITES: proletarian, communist.

▶ noun *a proud bourgeois* MEMBER OF THE MIDDLE CLASS, property owner.

bout ▶ noun **1** *a bout of dysentery* ATTACK, fit, spasm, paroxysm, convulsion, eruption, outburst; period, session, spell. **2** *he is fighting only his fifth bout* CONTEST, match, fight, prizefight, competition, event, meeting, fixture.

bovine ▶ adjective **1** *large, bovine eyes* COWLIKE, calflike, taurine. **2** *an expression of bovine amazement* STUPID, slow, ignorant, unintelligent, imperceptive, vacuous, mindless, witless, doltish, dumb, dense, dim, dim-witted, dopey, birdbrained, pea-brained, dozy.
▶ noun COW, heifer, bull, bullock, calf, ox, bison; beef.

bow[1] ▶ verb **1** *the officers bowed* INCLINE THE BODY, incline the head, nod, salaam, kowtow, curtsy, bob, genuflect. **2** *the government bowed to foreign pressure* YIELD, submit, give in, surrender, succumb, capitulate, defer, conform; comply with, accept, heed, observe.
▶ noun *a perfunctory bow* OBEISANCE, salaam, bob, curtsy, nod; *archaic* reverence.
■ **bow out** WITHDRAW, resign, retire, step down, pull out, back out; give up, quit, leave, pack it in.

bow[2] ▶ noun *the bow of the tanker* PROW, front, stem, nose, head, cutwater.

bow[3] ▶ noun **1** *she tied a bow in her hair* LOOP, knot; ribbon. **2** *he bent the rod into a bow* ARC, curve, bend; crescent, half-moon. **3** *an archer's bow* longbow, crossbow; *Archery* recurve.

bowdlerize ▶ verb EXPURGATE, censor, blue-pencil, cut, edit; sanitize, water down.

bowel ▶ noun **1** *a disorder of the bowels* INTESTINE(S), entrails, innards, small intestine, large intestine, colon; *informal* guts, insides, viscera. **2** *the bowels of the ship* INTERIOR, inside, core, belly; depths, recesses; *informal* innards.

bower ▶ noun *a rose-scented bower* ARBOUR, pergola, grotto, alcove, sanctuary; gazebo.

bowl ▶ noun **1** *she cracked two eggs into a bowl* DISH, basin, pot, crock, mortar; container, vessel, receptacle; *rare* jorum, porringer. **2** *the Hollywood Bowl* STADIUM, arena, amphitheatre, colosseum.
▶ verb
■ **bowl someone over 1** *the explosion bowled us over* KNOCK DOWN/OVER, fell, floor, prostrate. **2** *(informal)* *I have been bowled over by your generosity* OVERWHELM, astound, astonish, overawe, awe, dumbfound, stagger, stun, amaze, daze, shake, take aback, leave aghast, flabbergast, blow away.

bowling ▶ noun TENPIN, five-pin, bowls, lawn bowling, boules, bocce, carpet bowling.

box[1] ▶ noun *a box of cigars* CARTON, pack, packet; case, crate, chest, coffer, casket; container, receptacle.
▶ verb *Muriel boxed up his clothes* PACKAGE, pack, parcel, wrap, bundle, crate, bin.
■ **box something/someone in** HEM IN, fence in, close in, shut in; trap, confine, imprison, intern; surround, enclose, encircle, circle.

box[2] ▶ verb **1** *he began boxing professionally* FIGHT, prizefight, spar; brawl; *informal* scrap. **2** *he boxed my ears* STRIKE, smack, cuff, hit, thump, slap, swat, punch, jab, wallop, belt, bop, sock, clout, clobber, whack, slug, boff.

boxer ▶ noun FIGHTER, pugilist, prizefighter, kick-boxer; *informal* bruiser, scrapper.

boxing ▶ noun PUGILISM, the sweet science, fighting, sparring, fisticuffs; kick-boxing, prizefighting.

Boxing Weight Classes

Professional		Amateur	
Class	Weight Limit (lbs)	Class	Weight Limit (kg)
heavyweight	unlimited	superheavyweight	unlimited
cruiserweight	190	heavyweight	91
light heavyweight	175	light heavyweight	81
super middleweight	168	middleweight	75
middleweight	160	welterweight	69
junior/light middleweight (super welterweight)	154	light welterweight	64
welterweight	147	lightweight	60
junior/light welterweight (super lightweight)	140	featherweight	57
lightweight	135	bantamweight	54
junior lightweight (super featherweight)	130	flyweight	51
featherweight	126	light flyweight	48
junior featherweight (super bantamweight)	122	pinweight	45
bantamweight	118		
junior bantamweight (super flyweight)	115		
flyweight	112		
junior/light flyweight	108		
strawweight (mini flyweight, minimumweight)	105		

boy ▶ noun LAD, schoolboy, male child, youth, young man, laddie, stripling. *See also* CHILD.

boycott ▶ verb *they boycotted the elections* SPURN, snub, shun, avoid, abstain from, wash one's hands of, turn one's back on, reject, veto.
− OPPOSITES: support.
▶ noun *a boycott of imported lumber* BAN, veto, embargo, prohibition, sanction, restriction; avoidance, rejection, refusal.

boyfriend ▶ noun LOVER, sweetheart, beloved, darling, dearest, young man, man friend, man, guy, escort, suitor; PARTNER, significant other, companion, (main) squeeze, flame, steady, fancy man, toy boy, boy toy, sugar daddy; *literary* swain; *dated* beau; *archaic* paramour.

boyish ▶ adjective YOUTHFUL, young, childlike, adolescent, teenage; immature, juvenile, infantile, childish, babyish, puerile.

bozo ▶ noun *See* FOOL *noun* sense 1.

brace ▶ noun *the aquarium is supported by wooden braces* PROP, beam, joist, batten, rod, post, strut, stay, support, stanchion, bracket.
▶ verb **1** *the plane's wing is braced by a system of rods* SUPPORT, shore up, prop up, hold up, buttress, underpin; strengthen, reinforce. **2** *he braced his hand on the railing* STEADY, secure, stabilize, fix, poise; tense, tighten. **3** *brace yourself for disappointment* PREPARE, get ready, gear up, nerve, steel, galvanize, gird, strengthen, fortify; *informal* psych oneself up.

bracelet ▶ noun BANGLE, band, circlet, armlet, wristlet, anklet.

bracing ▶ adjective INVIGORATING, refreshing, stimulating, energizing, exhilarating, reviving, restorative, rejuvenating, revitalizing, rousing, fortifying, strengthening; FRESH, brisk, keen.

bracket ▶ noun **1** *each speaker is fixed on a separate bracket* SUPPORT, prop, stay, batten, joist; rest, mounting, rack, frame. **2** *put the words in brackets*

PARENTHESIS; *Printing* brace. **3** *a higher tax bracket* GROUP, category, grade, classification, set, division, order.

brackish ▶ adjective SLIGHTLY SALTY, saline, salt, briny.

brag ▶ verb BOAST, crow, swagger, swank, bluster, gloat, show off; blow one's own horn, sing one's own praises; *informal* talk big, lay it on thick.

braggart ▶ noun *he was a prodigious braggart and a liar* BOASTER, bragger, swaggerer, egotist; *informal* big head, loudmouth, show-off, showboat, blowhard.

braid ▶ noun *her hair is in braids* PLAIT, pigtail, twist; cornrows, dreadlocks.
▶ verb **1** *she began to braid her hair* PLAIT, entwine, intertwine, interweave, weave, twist, twine. **2** *the sleeves are braided in scarlet* TRIM, edge, border, pipe, hem, fringe.

brain ▶ noun **1** *the disease attacks certain cells in the brain* CEREBRUM, cerebral matter, encephalon. **2** *success requires brains as well as brawn* INTELLIGENCE, intellect, brainpower, IQ, cleverness, wit(s), reasoning, wisdom, acumen, discernment, judgment, understanding, sense, grey matter, savvy; smarts. **3** (*informal*) *Janice is the brains of the family* CLEVER PERSON, intellectual, intellect, thinker, mind, scholar; genius, Einstein; *informal* egghead, brainiac, rocket scientist.
− RELATED TERMS: cerebral, encephalic.
− OPPOSITES: dunce.

brainless ▶ adjective STUPID, FOOLISH, witless, unintelligent, ignorant, idiotic, simple-minded, slow-witted, feeble-minded, empty-headed, stunned ♣, dumb, halfwitted, brain-dead, moronic, cretinous, bubbleheaded, thick, dopey, dozy, birdbrained, pea-brained, dippy, wooden-headed, chowderheaded.
− OPPOSITES: clever.

brainteaser ▶ noun PUZZLE, problem, riddle, conundrum, poser, enigma, stumper.

brainwash ▶ verb INDOCTRINATE, condition, re-educate, persuade, influence.

brainy ▶ adjective (*informal*) CLEVER, intelligent, smart, bright, brilliant, gifted; intellectual, erudite, academic, scholarly, studious, bookish.
− OPPOSITES: stupid.

brake ▶ noun *a brake on research* CURB, check, restraint, restriction, constraint, control, limitation.
▶ verb *she braked at the traffic lights* SLOW (DOWN), decelerate, reduce speed, stop.
− OPPOSITES: accelerate.

branch ▶ noun **1** *the branches of a tree* BOUGH, limb, arm, offshoot. **2** *a branch of the river* TRIBUTARY, feeder, side stream, fork, side channel ✦, influent. **3** *the judicial branch of government* DIVISION, subdivision, section, subsection, subset, department, sector, part, side, wing. **4** *the corporation's New York branch* OFFICE, bureau, agency; subsidiary, affiliate, offshoot, satellite.
▶ verb **1** *the place where the road branches* FORK, bifurcate, divide, subdivide, split. **2** *narrow paths branched off the road* DIVERGE FROM, deviate from, split off from; fan out from, radiate from.
■ **branch out** EXPAND, open up, extend; diversify, broaden one's horizons.

brand ▶ noun **1** *a new brand of margarine* MAKE, line, label, marque; type, kind, sort, variety; trade name, trademark, proprietary name. **2** *her particular brand of humour* TYPE, kind, sort, variety, class, category, genre, style, ilk, stripe. **3** *the brand on a sheep* IDENTIFICATION, marker, earmark.
▶ verb **1** *the letter M was branded on each animal* MARK, stamp, burn, sear. **2** *the scene was branded on her brain* ENGRAVE, stamp, etch, imprint. **3** *the media branded us as communists* STIGMATIZE, mark out; denounce, discredit, vilify; label.

brandish ▶ verb FLOURISH, wave, shake, wield; swing, swish; display, flaunt, show off.

brandy ▶ noun applejack, Armagnac, Calvados, cognac, eau-de-vie, grappa, kirsch, marc, mirabelle, slivovitz.

brash ▶ adjective *a brash man* SELF-ASSERTIVE, pushy, cocksure, cocky, self-confident, arrogant, bold, audacious, brazen, bumptious, overweening, puffed-up; forward, impudent, insolent, rude.
− OPPOSITES: meek.

brassy ▶ adjective BRAZEN, forward, bold, self-assertive, pushy, cocksure, cocky, cheeky, saucy, brash; shameless, immodest; loud, vulgar, showy, ostentatious; *informal* flashy.
− OPPOSITES: demure.

brat ▶ noun RASCAL, wretch, imp, scamp, scapegrace; minx; *informal* monster, horror, whippersnapper.

bravado ▶ noun BOLDNESS, swaggering, bluster; machismo; boasting, bragging, bombast, braggadocio; *informal* showing off.

brave ▶ adjective **1** *they put up a brave fight* COURAGEOUS, valiant, valorous, intrepid, heroic, lion-hearted, bold, fearless, gallant, daring, plucky, audacious; unflinching, unshrinking, unafraid, dauntless, doughty, mettlesome, stout-hearted, spirited; *informal* game, gutsy, spunky. **2** (*literary*) *his medals made a brave show* SPLENDID, magnificent, impressive, fine, handsome.
− OPPOSITES: cowardly.
▶ noun (*dated*) *an Indian brave* WARRIOR, soldier, fighter.
▶ verb *fans braved freezing temperatures to see them play*

ENDURE, put up with, bear, withstand, weather, suffer, go through; face, confront, defy.

bravery ▶ noun COURAGE, pluck, valour, intrepidity, nerve, daring, fearlessness, audacity, boldness, dauntlessness, stout-heartedness, heroism; backbone, grit, true grit, spine, spirit, mettle; *informal* guts, balls, cojones, spunk.

bravo ▶ exclamation WELL DONE, congratulations, brava; encore; *informal* attaboy.

bravura ▶ noun *a display of bravura* SKILL, brilliance, virtuosity, expertise, artistry, talent, ability, flair, éclat, wizardry.
▶ adjective *a bravura performance* VIRTUOSO, masterly, outstanding, excellent, superb, brilliant, first-class; *informal* mean, ace, A1.

brawl ▶ noun *a drunken brawl* FIGHT, skirmish, scuffle, tussle, fray, melee, free-for-all, scrum; fisticuffs; *informal* scrap, dust-up, set-to, punch-up.
▶ verb *he ended up brawling with photographers* FIGHT, skirmish, scuffle, tussle, exchange blows, grapple, wrestle; *informal* scrap.

brawn ▶ noun PHYSICAL STRENGTH, muscle(s), burliness, huskiness, toughness, power, might; vigour, punch; *informal* beef, beefiness.

brawny ▶ adjective STRONG, muscular, muscly, well-built, powerful, mighty, Herculean, strapping, burly, sturdy, husky, rugged; hefty, solid; *informal* beefy, hunky.
− OPPOSITES: puny, weak.

bray ▶ verb **1** *a donkey brayed* NEIGH, whinny, hee-haw. **2** *Billy brayed with laughter* ROAR, bellow, trumpet.

brazen ▶ adjective *brazen defiance* BOLD, SHAMELESS, unashamed, unabashed, unembarrassed; defiant, impudent, impertinent, cheeky, saucy, insolent, in-your-face; barefaced, blatant, flagrant.
− OPPOSITES: timid.
■ **brazen it out** PUT ON A BOLD FRONT, stand one's ground, be defiant, be unrepentant, be unabashed.

breach ▶ noun **1** *a clear breach of the regulations* CONTRAVENTION, violation, infringement, infraction, transgression, neglect; *Law* delict. **2** *a breach between government and Church* RIFT, schism, division, gulf, chasm; disunion, estrangement, discord, dissension, disagreement; split, break, rupture, scission. **3** *a breach in the seawall* BREAK, rupture, split, crack, fracture; opening, gap, hole, fissure.
▶ verb **1** *the river breached its bank* BREAK (THROUGH), burst, rupture; *informal* bust. **2** *the changes breached union rules* BREAK, contravene, violate, infringe; defy, disobey, flout, fly in the face of; *Law* infract.

bread ▶ noun **1** *a slice of bread. See table.* **2** (*informal*) *his job puts bread on the table. See* FOOD *sense 1.* **3** (*informal*) *I hate doing this, but I need the bread. See* MONEY *sense 1.*

breadth ▶ noun **1** *a breadth of 100 metres* WIDTH, broadness, wideness, thickness; span; diameter. **2** *the breadth of his knowledge* RANGE, extent, scope, depth, reach, compass, scale, degree.

break ▶ verb **1** *the mirror broke* SHATTER, smash, crack, snap, fracture, fragment, splinter, fall to bits, fall to pieces; split, burst; *informal* bust. **2** *she had broken her leg* FRACTURE, crack. **3** *the bite had barely broken the skin* PIERCE, puncture, penetrate, perforate; cut. **4** *the coffee machine has broken* STOP WORKING, break down, give out, go wrong, malfunction, crash; *informal* go kaput, conk out, be on the blink/fritz, give up the ghost. **5** *traders who break the law* CONTRAVENE, violate, infringe, breach; defy, flout, disobey, fly in the face of. **6** *his concentration was broken* INTERRUPT, disturb,

Bread

bagel	loaf
baguette	matzo
bannock ✤	Montreal bagel ✤
black bread	multigrain bread
Boston brown bread	nan
breadcrumbs	panettone
bread stick	panino
brioche	paratha
brown bread	Parker House roll
bun	paska ✤
butterhorn	pita
Calabrese bread	pumpernickel
challah	puri
chapati	quick bread
ciabatta	raisin bread
cornbread	roll
cracked wheat bread	rusk
crescent roll	rye bread
croissant	Sally Lunn
croutons	sippet
crumpet	soda bread
egg bread	sourdough
English muffin	stollen
flatbread	stone-ground bread
focaccia	tea bread
French bread	toast
French stick	touton ✤(Nfld)
garlic bread	white bread
injera	whole grain bread
Italian bread	whole wheat bread
johnnycake	zwieback
kaiser (roll)	

interfere with. **7** *they broke for coffee* STOP, pause, have a rest, recess, take five. **8** *a pile of carpets broke his fall* CUSHION, soften the impact of, take the edge off. **9** *the film broke box-office records* EXCEED, surpass, beat, better, cap, top, outdo, outstrip, eclipse. **10** *habits are very difficult to break* GIVE UP, relinquish, drop; *informal* kick, shake, quit. **11** *the strategies used to break the union* DESTROY, crush, quash, defeat, vanquish, overcome, overpower, overwhelm, suppress, cripple; weaken, subdue, cow, undermine. **12** *her self-control finally broke* GIVE WAY, crack, cave in, yield, go to pieces. **13** *four thousand dollars wouldn't break him* BANKRUPT, ruin, pauperize. **14** *he tried to break the news gently* REVEAL, disclose, divulge, impart, tell; announce, release. **15** *he broke the encryption code* DECIPHER, decode, decrypt, unravel, work out; *informal* figure out. **16** *the day broke fair and cloudless* DAWN, begin, start, emerge, appear. **17** *a political scandal broke* ERUPT, break out. **18** *the weather broke* CHANGE, alter, shift. **19** *waves broke against the rocks* CRASH, dash, beat, pound, lash. **20** *her voice broke as she relived the experience* FALTER, quaver, quiver, tremble, shake.
— OPPOSITES: repair, keep, resume.
▶ **noun 1** *the magazine has been published without a break since 1950* INTERRUPTION, interval, gap, hiatus; discontinuation, suspension, disruption, cut-off; stop, stoppage, cessation. **2** *a break in the weather* CHANGE, alteration, variation. **3** *let's have a break* REST, respite, recess; stop, pause; interval, intermission; *informal* breather, time out, down time; coffee break, (Nfld) mug-up ✤. **4** *a weekend break* HOLIDAY, vacation, getaway. **5** *a break in diplomatic relations* RIFT, schism, split, breakup, severance, rupture. **6** *the actress got her first break in 1951* OPPORTUNITY, chance, opening.
■ **break away 1** *she attempted to break away from his*

grip ESCAPE, get away, run away, flee, make off; break free, break loose, get out of someone's clutches; *informal* cut and run. **2** *a group broke away from the main party* LEAVE, secede from, split off from, separate from, part company with, defect from, form a splinter group; *Politics* cross the floor.
■ **break down 1** *his van broke down.* See BREAK verb sense 4. **2** *pay negotiations broke down* FAIL, collapse, founder, fall through, disintegrate; *informal* fizzle out. **3** *Vicky broke down, sobbing loudly* BURST INTO TEARS; lose control, be overcome, go to pieces, crumble, disintegrate; *informal* crack up, lose it.
■ **break something down 1** *the police broke the door down* KNOCK DOWN, kick down, smash in, pull down, tear down, demolish. **2** *break big tasks down into smaller parts* DIVIDE, separate. **3** *graphs show how the information can be broken down* ANALYZE, categorize, classify, sort out, itemize, organize; dissect.
■ **break in 1** *thieves broke in and took her chequebook* COMMIT BURGLARY, break and enter; force one's way in. **2** *'I don't want to interfere,' Mrs. Hendry broke in* INTERRUPT, butt in, cut in, interject, interpose, intervene, chime in.
■ **break someone in** TRAIN, initiate; *informal* show someone the ropes.
■ **break into 1** *thieves broke into a house in Perth Street* BURGLE, burglarize, rob; force one's way into. **2** *Phil broke into the discussion* INTERRUPT, butt into, cut in on, intervene in. **3** *he broke into a song* BURST INTO, launch into.
■ **break off** SNAP OFF, come off, become detached, become separated.
■ **break something off 1** *I broke off a branch from the tree* SNAP OFF, pull off, sever, detach. **2** *they threatened to break off diplomatic relations* END, terminate, stop, cease, call a halt to, finish, dissolve; SUSPEND, discontinue; *informal* pull the plug on.
■ **break out 1** *he broke out of the detention centre* ESCAPE FROM, abscond from, flee from; get free. **2** *fighting broke out* FLARE UP, start suddenly, erupt, burst out.
■ **break up 1** *the meeting broke up* END, finish, stop, terminate; adjourn; recess. **2** *the crowd began to break up* DISPERSE, scatter, disband, part company. **3** *Danny and I broke up last year* SPLIT UP, separate, part (company); divorce. **4** *waiting for the ice to break up go out* ✤. **5** (*informal*) *the whole cast broke up* BURST OUT LAUGHING, crack up, dissolve into laughter.
■ **break something up 1** *police tried to break up the crowd* DISPERSE, scatter, disband. **2** *I'm not going to let you break up my marriage* WRECK, ruin, destroy.

breakable ▶ **adjective** FRAGILE, delicate, flimsy, destructible, brittle; *formal* frangible.

breakaway ▶ **adjective** *a breakaway group* SEPARATIST, secessionist, schismatic, splinter; rebel, renegade.

breakdown ▶ **noun 1** *the breakdown of the negotiations* FAILURE, collapse, disintegration, foundering. **2** *on the death of her father she suffered a breakdown* NERVOUS BREAKDOWN, collapse; *informal* crack-up. **3** *the breakdown of the computer system* MALFUNCTION, failure, crash. **4** *a breakdown of the figures* ANALYSIS, classification, examination, investigation, dissection.

breaker ▶ **noun** WAVE, roller, comber; *informal* (big) kahuna.

break-in ▶ **noun** BURGLARY, robbery, theft, raid, breaking and entering, break and enter; *informal* smash-and-grab.

breakneck ▶ adjective *the breakneck pace of change* EXTREMELY FAST, rapid, speedy, high-speed, lightning, whirlwind.

breakthrough ▶ noun ADVANCE, development, step forward, success, improvement; discovery, innovation, revolution; breakout.
— OPPOSITES: setback.

breakup ▶ noun **1** *the breakup of negotiations* END, dissolution; breakdown, failure, collapse, disintegration. **2** *their breakup was very amicable* SEPARATION, split, parting, divorce; estrangement, rift.

breakwater ▶ noun SEAWALL, jetty, (*Great Lakes*) breakwall ♣, mole, bulwark, groyne, pier.

breast ▶ noun **1** *a baby at her breast* mammary gland, mamma; (**breasts**) BOSOM(S), bust, chest; *informal* boobs, knockers, bazooms, hooters. **2** *feelings of frustration were rising up in his breast* HEART, bosom, soul, core.

breath ▶ noun **1** *I took a deep breath* INHALATION, inspiration, gulp of air; exhalation, expiration; *Medicine* respiration. **2** *a breath of wind* PUFF, waft, faint breeze. **3** *a breath of scandal* HINT, suggestion, trace, touch, whisper, murmur, suspicion, whiff, undertone. **4** (*archaic*) *there was no breath left in him* LIFE (FORCE).
— RELATED TERMS: respiratory.
■ **take someone's breath away** ASTONISH, astound, amaze, stun, startle, stagger, shock, take aback, dumbfound, jolt, shake up; awe, overawe, thrill, flabbergast, blow away, bowl over, stop someone in their tracks, leave someone speechless.
■ **bad breath** HALITOSIS.

breathe ▶ verb **1** *she breathed deeply* inhale and exhale, respire, draw breath; puff, pant, blow, gasp, wheeze, huff; *Medicine* inspire, expire. **2** *at least I'm still breathing* BE ALIVE, be living, live. **3** *she would breathe new life into his firm* INSTILL, infuse, inject, inspire, impart, imbue. **4** *'Together at last,' she breathed* WHISPER, murmur, purr, sigh, say.

breather ▶ noun BREAK, REST, respite, breathing space, pause, interval, recess.

breathless ▶ adjective **1** *Will arrived flushed and breathless* OUT OF BREATH, panting, puffing, gasping, wheezing, hyperventilating; winded, puffed out, short of breath. **2** *the crowd were breathless with anticipation* AGOG, open-mouthed, waiting with bated breath, on the edge of one's seat, on tenterhooks, in suspense; excited, impatient.

breathtaking ▶ adjective SPECTACULAR, magnificent, wonderful, awe-inspiring, awesome, astounding, astonishing, amazing, stunning, incredible; thrilling, exciting; *informal* sensational, out of this world, jaw-dropping; *literary* wondrous.

breed ▶ verb **1** *elephants breed readily in captivity* REPRODUCE, produce/bear/generate offspring, procreate, multiply, propagate; mate. **2** *she was born and bred in the village* BRING UP, rear, raise, nurture. **3** *the political system bred discontent* CAUSE, bring about, give rise to, lead to, produce, generate, foster, result in; stir up; *literary* beget.
▶ noun **1** *a breed of cow* VARIETY, stock, strain; type, kind, sort. **2** *a new breed of journalist* TYPE, kind, sort, variety, class, brand, genre, generation.

breeding ▶ noun **1** *individual birds pair for breeding* REPRODUCTION, procreation; mating. **2** *the breeding of rats* REARING, raising, nurturing. **3** *her aristocratic breeding* UPBRINGING, rearing; parentage, family, pedigree, blood, birth, ancestry. **4** *people of rank and breeding* (GOOD) MANNERS, gentility, refinement, cultivation, polish, urbanity; *informal* class.

breeze ▶ noun **1** *a breeze ruffled the leaves* GENTLE WIND, puff of air, gust, cat's paw; *Meteorology* light air; *literary* zephyr. **2** *getting your child in and out of the seat is a breeze* EASY TASK, child's play, nothing, piece of cake, cinch, snap, kids' stuff, cakewalk, five-finger exercise, duck soup.
▶ verb *Roger breezed into her office* SAUNTER, stroll, sail, cruise.

breezy ▶ adjective **1** *a bright, breezy day* WINDY, fresh, brisk, airy; blowy, blustery, gusty. **2** *his breezy manner* JAUNTY, CHEERFUL, cheery, brisk, carefree, easy, casual, relaxed, informal, light-hearted, lively, buoyant, blithe spirited, sunny, jovial; *informal* upbeat, bright-eyed and bushy-tailed; *dated* gay.

brevity ▶ noun **1** *the report is notable for its brevity* CONCISENESS, concision, succinctness, economy of language, pithiness, incisiveness, shortness, compactness. **2** *the brevity of human life* SHORTNESS, briefness, transience, ephemerality, impermanence.
— OPPOSITES: verbosity.

brew ▶ verb **1** *this beer is brewed in Guelph* FERMENT, make. **2** *I'll brew some tea* PREPARE, infuse, make, steep, stew. **3** *there's trouble brewing* DEVELOP, loom, threaten, impend, be imminent, be on the horizon, be in the offing.
▶ noun **1** *home brew* BEER, ale. **2** *a hot reviving brew* DRINK, beverage; tea, coffee. **3** *a dangerous brew of political turmoil and violent conflict* MIXTURE, mix, blend, combination, amalgam, mishmash, hodgepodge.

bribe ▶ verb *he used his wealth to bribe officials* BUY OFF, pay off, suborn; *informal* grease someone's palm, fix, square.
▶ noun *she accepted bribes* INDUCEMENT, incentive, payoff, kickback, payola, boodle, sweetener, sop.

bribery ▶ noun GRAFT, payola, palm-greasing, hush money.

bric-a-brac ▶ noun ORNAMENTS, knick-knacks, trinkets, bibelots, gewgaws, gimcracks, tchotchkes; bits and pieces, odds and ends, things, stuff, junk.

brick ▶ noun **1** *bricks and mortar* block, cinder block, firebrick, adobe, header, stretcher. **2** *a brick of ice cream* BLOCK, cube, bar, cake.

bridal ▶ adjective *the bridal party* WEDDING, nuptial, marriage, matrimonial, marital, conjugal.

bride ▶ noun WIFE, marriage partner; newlywed.

bridge ▶ noun **1** *a bridge over the river* VIADUCT, overpass, fixed link, aqueduct. *See* bridge. **2** *a bridge between rival groups* LINK, connection, bond, tie.
▶ verb **1** *a walkway bridged the motorway* SPAN, cross (over), extend across, traverse, arch over. **2** *an attempt to bridge the gap between cultures* JOIN, link, connect, unite; straddle; overcome, reconcile.

Types of Bridge

Bailey bridge	girder bridge
bascule bridge	skew bridge
cantilever bridge	suspension bridge
covered bridge	swing bridge
drawbridge	swinging bridge
floating bridge	trestle bridge
footbridge	

bridle ▶ noun *a horse's bridle* HARNESS, headgear; hackamore.
▶ verb **1** *she bridled at his tone* BRISTLE, take offence, take

umbrage, be affronted, be offended, get angry. **2** he *bridled his indignation* CURB, restrain, hold back, control, check, rein in/back; suppress, stifle; *informal* keep a/the lid on.

brief ▶ adjective **1** *a brief account* CONCISE, succinct, short, pithy, incisive, abridged, condensed, compressed, abbreviated, compact, thumbnail, capsule, potted; *formal* compendious. **2** *a brief visit* SHORT, flying, fleeting, hasty, hurried, quick, cursory, perfunctory; temporary, short-lived, momentary, transient; *informal* quickie. **3** *a pair of brief shorts* SKIMPY, scanty, short; revealing. **4** *the boss was rather brief with him* BRUSQUE, abrupt, curt, short, blunt, sharp.
– OPPOSITES: lengthy.
▶ noun **1** *a lawyer's brief* SUMMARY, case, argument, contention; dossier. **2** *a brief of our requirements* OUTLINE, summary, synopsis, précis, sketch, digest.
▶ verb *employees were briefed about the decision* INFORM, tell, update, notify, advise, apprise; prepare, prime, instruct; *informal* fill in, clue in, put in the picture.

briefcase ▶ noun ATTACHÉ (CASE), satchel, portfolio, dispatch case.

briefing ▶ noun *a press briefing* CONFERENCE, meeting, interview, backgrounder; orientation.

briefly ▶ adverb **1** *Henry paused briefly* MOMENTARILY, temporarily, for a moment, fleetingly. **2** *briefly, the plot is as follows* IN SHORT, in brief, to cut a long story short, in a word, in sum, in a nutshell, in essence.

briefs ▶ plural noun *See* UNDERWEAR.

brigade ▶ noun **1** *a brigade of soldiers* UNIT, contingent, battalion, regiment, division, squadron, company, platoon, section, corps, troop. **2** *the volunteer ambulance brigade* SQUAD, team, group, band, party, crew, force, outfit.

brigand ▶ noun (*literary*). *See* BANDIT.

bright ▶ adjective **1** *the bright surface of the metal* SHINING, brilliant, dazzling, beaming, glaring; sparkling, flashing, glittering, scintillating, gleaming, glowing, luminous, radiant; shiny, lustrous, glossy. **2** *a bright morning* SUNNY, sunshiny, cloudless, clear, fair, fine. **3** *bright crayons* VIVID, brilliant, intense, strong, bold, glowing, rich; gaudy, lurid, garish; COLOURFUL, vibrant; *dated* gay. **4** *a bright guitar sound* CLEAR, vibrant, pellucid; high-pitched. **5** *a bright young graduate* CLEVER, intelligent, quick-witted, smart, canny, astute, intuitive, perceptive; ingenious, resourceful; gifted, brilliant; *informal* brainy. **6** *a bright smile* HAPPY, cheerful, cheery, jolly, merry, sunny, beaming; lively, exuberant, buoyant, bubbly, bouncy, perky, chirpy; *dated* gay. **7** *a bright future* PROMISING, rosy, optimistic, hopeful, favourable, propitious, auspicious, encouraging, good, golden.
– OPPOSITES: dull, dark, stupid.
▶ adverb (*literary*) *the moon shone bright* BRIGHTLY, brilliantly, intensely.

brighten ▶ verb **1** *sunshine brightened the room* ILLUMINATE, light up, lighten, make bright, make brighter, cast/shed light on; *formal* illume. **2** *Sarah brightened up as she thought of Emily's words* CHEER UP, perk up, rally; be enlivened, feel heartened, be uplifted, be encouraged, take heart; *informal* buck up, pep up.

brilliance ▶ noun **1** *a philosopher of great brilliance* GENIUS, intelligence, wisdom, sagacity, intellect; talent, ability, prowess, skill, expertise, aptitude, flair, finesse, panache; greatness. **2** *the brilliance and beauty of Paris* SPLENDOUR, magnificence, grandeur, resplendence. **3** *the brilliance of the sunshine* BRIGHTNESS, vividness, intensity; sparkle, glitter, glittering, glow, blaze, luminosity, radiance.

brilliant ▶ adjective **1** *a brilliant student* BRIGHT, intelligent, clever, smart, astute, intellectual; gifted, talented, able, adept, skilful; elite, superior, first-class, first-rate, excellent; *informal* brainy. **2** *his brilliant career* SUPERB, glorious, illustrious, impressive, remarkable, exceptional. **3** *a shaft of brilliant light* BRIGHT, shining, blazing, dazzling, vivid, intense, gleaming, glaring, luminous, radiant; *literary* irradiant, coruscating. **4** *brilliant green* VIVID, intense, bright, bold, dazzling.
– OPPOSITES: stupid, bad, dark.

brim ▶ noun **1** *the brim of his hat* peak, visor, shield, shade; fringe. **2** *the cup was filled to its brim* RIM, lip, brink, edge.
▶ verb **1** *the pan was brimming with water* BE FULL (UP), be filled to the top; overflow, run over. **2** *a family brimming with hope* FULL OF, teeming with, awash in/with, chock full of, loaded with.

brimful ▶ adjective FULL (UP), brimming, filled/full to the brim, filled to capacity, overfull, running over; *informal* chock full.
– OPPOSITES: empty.

brindle, brindled ▶ adjective TAWNY, brownish, brown; DAPPLED, streaked, mottled, speckled, flecked, marbled.

bring ▶ verb **1** *he brought over a tray* CARRY, fetch, bear, take; convey, transport, tote; move, haul, shift, lug. **2** *Philip brought his bride to his mansion* ESCORT, conduct, guide, lead, usher, show, shepherd. **3** *the wind changed and brought rain* CAUSE, produce, create, generate, precipitate, lead to, give rise to, result in; stir up, whip up, promote; *literary* beget. **4** *the police contemplated bringing charges* PUT FORWARD, prefer, lay, submit, present, initiate, institute. **5** *this job brings him a regular salary* EARN, make, fetch, bring in, yield, net, gross, return, produce; command, attract.
■ **bring something about** *the affair that brought about her death* CAUSE, produce, give rise to, result in, lead to, occasion, bring to pass; provoke, generate, engender, precipitate; *formal* effectuate.
■ **bring someone (a)round 1** *she administered artificial respiration and brought him (a)round* WAKE UP, return to consciousness, rouse, bring to. **2** *we would have brought him (a)round, given time* PERSUADE, convince, talk round, win over, sway, influence.
■ **bring something back 1** *the smell brought back memories* REMIND ONE OF, put one in mind of, bring/call to mind, conjure up, evoke, summon up; take one back. **2** *bring back capital punishment* REINTRODUCE, reinstate, re-establish, revive, resurrect.
■ **bring someone down 1** *he was brought down by a clumsy challenge* TRIP, knock over/down; foul. **2** *I couldn't bear to bring her down* DEPRESS, sadden, upset, get down, dispirit, dishearten, discourage.
■ **bring something down 1** *we will bring down the price* DECREASE, reduce, lower, cut, drop; *informal* slash. **2** *the unrest brought down the government* UNSEAT, overturn, topple, overthrow, depose, oust.
■ **bring something forward** PROPOSE, suggest, advance, raise, table, present, move, submit, lodge.
■ **bring something in 1** *he brought in a private member's bill* INTRODUCE, launch, inaugurate, initiate, institute. **2** *the event brings in one million dollars each year. See* BRING *sense 5*.
■ **bring something off** ACHIEVE, accomplish, attain,

bring about, pull off, manage, realize, complete, finish; execute, perform, discharge; *formal* effectuate.

■ **bring something on**. See BRING SOMETHING ABOUT.

■ **bring something out 1** *they were bringing out a new magazine* LAUNCH, establish, begin, start, found, set up, instigate, inaugurate, market; publish, print, issue, produce. **2** *the shawl brings out the colour of your eyes* ACCENTUATE, highlight, emphasize, accent, set off.

■ **bring oneself to** *she could not bring herself to complain* FORCE ONESELF TO, make oneself, bear to.

■ **bring someone up** REAR, raise, care for, look after, nurture, provide for.

■ **bring something up** MENTION, allude to, touch on, raise, broach, introduce; voice, air, suggest, propose, submit, put forward, bring forward, table.

brink ▶ noun **1** *the brink of the abyss* EDGE, verge, margin, rim, lip; border, boundary, perimeter, periphery, limit(s). **2** *two countries on the brink of war* VERGE, threshold, point, edge.

brio ▶ noun VIGOUR, vivacity, gusto, verve, zest, enthusiasm, vitality, dynamism, animation, spirit, energy; *informal* pep, vim, get-up-and-go.

brisk ▶ adjective **1** *a brisk pace* QUICK, rapid, fast, swift, speedy, hurried; energetic, lively, vigorous. **2** *business was brisk at the bar* BUSY, bustling, lively, hectic; good. **3** *a brisk breeze* BRACING, fresh, crisp, invigorating, refreshing, stimulating, energizing; biting, keen, chilly, cold; *informal* nippy.
— OPPOSITES: slow, quiet.

bristle ▶ noun **1** *the bristles on his chin* HAIR, whisker; (**bristles**) stubble, five o'clock shadow; *Zoology* seta. **2** *a hedgehog's bristles* SPINE, prickle, quill, barb.
▶ verb **1** *the hair on the back of his neck bristled* RISE, stand up, stand on end; *literary* horripilate. **2** *she bristled at his tone* BRIDLE, take offence, take umbrage, be affronted, be offended; get angry, be irritated. **3** *the roof bristled with antennae* ABOUND, overflow, be full, be packed, be crowded, be jammed, be covered; *informal* be thick, be jam-packed, be chock full.

bristly ▶ adjective **1** *bristly little bushes* PRICKLY, spiky, thorny, scratchy, brambly. **2** *the bristly skin of his cheek* STUBBLY, hairy, fuzzy, unshaven, whiskered, whiskery; scratchy, rough, coarse, prickly; *Zoology* hispid.
— OPPOSITES: smooth.

brittle ▶ adjective **1** *glass is a brittle material* BREAKABLE, fragile, delicate; splintery; *formal* frangible. **2** *a brittle laugh* HARSH, hard, sharp, grating. **3** *a brittle young woman* EDGY, anxious, unstable, high-strung, tense, excitable, jumpy, skittish, neurotic; *informal* uptight.
— OPPOSITES: flexible, resilient, soft, relaxed.

broach ▶ verb **1** *I broached the matter with my parents* BRING UP, raise, introduce, talk about, mention, touch on, air. **2** *he broached a barrel of beer* PIERCE, puncture, tap; OPEN, uncork; *informal* crack open.

broad ▶ adjective **1** *a broad flight of steps* WIDE. **2** *the leaves are two inches broad* WIDE, across, in breadth, in width. **3** *a broad expanse of prairie* EXTENSIVE, vast, immense, great, spacious, expansive, sizeable, sweeping, rolling. **4** *a broad range of opportunities* COMPREHENSIVE, inclusive, extensive, wide, all-embracing, eclectic, unlimited. **5** *this report gives a broad outline* GENERAL, non-specific, unspecific, rough, approximate, basic; loose, vague. **6** *a broad hint* OBVIOUS, unsubtle, explicit, direct, plain, clear, straightforward, bald, patent, transparent, undisguised, overt. **7** *a broad Newfoundland accent* PRONOUNCED, noticeable, strong, thick. **8** *he was*

attacked in broad daylight FULL, complete, total; clear, bright.
— OPPOSITES: narrow, limited, detailed, subtle.

broadcast ▶ verb **1** *the show will be broadcast worldwide* TRANSMIT, relay, air, beam, show, televise, telecast, webcast, simulcast, cablecast, screen. **2** *the result was broadcast far and wide* REPORT, announce, publicize, proclaim; spread, circulate, air, blazon, trumpet.
▶ noun *radio and television broadcasts* PROGRAM, show, production, transmission, telecast, webcast, simulcast, screening.

broaden ▶ verb **1** *her smile broadened* WIDEN, expand, stretch (out), draw out, spread; deepen. **2** *the government tried to broaden its political base* EXPAND, enlarge, extend, widen, swell; increase, augment, add to, amplify; develop, enrich, build on.

broadly ▶ adverb **1** *the pattern is broadly similar for men and women* IN GENERAL, on the whole, as a rule, in the main, mainly, predominantly; loosely, roughly, approximately. **2** *he was smiling broadly now* WIDELY, openly.

broad-minded ▶ adjective LIBERAL, tolerant, open-minded, freethinking, progressive, permissive, unprejudiced, unbiased, unbigoted.
— OPPOSITES: intolerant.

broadside ▶ noun **1** (*historical*) *the gunners fired broadsides* SALVO, volley, cannonade, barrage, blast, fusillade. **2** *a broadside against the economic reforms* CRITICISM, censure, polemic, diatribe, tirade; attack, onslaught; *literary* philippic.

brochure ▶ noun BOOKLET, pamphlet, leaflet, flyer, handbill, catalogue, handout, prospectus, fact sheet, folder.

broil ▶ verb GRILL, toast, barbecue, bake; cook.

broiling ▶ adjective *the sweaty nights and broiling days* HOT, scorching, roasting, baking, boiling (hot), blistering, sweltering, parching, searing, blazing, sizzling, burning (hot), sultry, torrid, tropical, like an oven, like a furnace.
— OPPOSITES: cold, cool.

broke ▶ adjective PENNILESS, moneyless, bankrupt, insolvent, ruined, cleaned out, strapped (for cash), down-and-out, without a penny to one's name, without a (red) cent, without two nickels/pennies to rub together, flat broke, bust, hard up; poor, poverty-stricken, impoverished, impecunious, penurious, indigent, in penury, needy, destitute, as poor as a church mouse.

broken ▶ adjective **1** *a broken bottle* SMASHED, shattered, fragmented, splintered, crushed, snapped; in bits, in pieces; destroyed, disintegrated; cracked, split; *informal* in smithereens. **2** *a broken arm* FRACTURED, damaged, injured. **3** *this TV's broken* DAMAGED, faulty, defective, not working, malfunctioning, in disrepair, inoperative, out of order, broken-down, down; *informal* on the blink, on the fritz, kaput, bust, busted, conked out, acting up, done for, has had the biscuit ♣. **4** *broken skin* CUT, ruptured, punctured, perforated. **5** *a broken marriage* FAILED, ended. **6** *broken promises* FLOUTED, violated, infringed, contravened, disregarded, ignored, unkept. **7** *he was left a broken man* DEFEATED, beaten, subdued; DEMORALIZED, dispirited, discouraged, crushed, humbled; dishonoured, ruined. **8** *a night of broken sleep* INTERRUPTED, disturbed, fitful, disrupted, discontinuous, intermittent, unsettled, troubled. **9** *he pressed on over the broken ground* UNEVEN, rough,

irregular, bumpy; rutted, pitted. **10** *she spoke in broken English* HALTING, hesitating, disjointed, faltering, imperfect.
– OPPOSITES: whole, working, uninterrupted, smooth, perfect.

broken-down ▸ adjective **1** *a broken-down hotel* DILAPIDATED, run-down, ramshackle, tumbledown, in disrepair, beat-up, battered, crumbling, deteriorated, gone to rack and ruin; *informal* fleabag. **2** *a broken-down car* DEFECTIVE, broken, faulty; not working, malfunctioning, inoperative, non-functioning; *informal* kaput, conked out, done for, had the biscuit ♣.

broken-hearted ▸ adjective HEARTBROKEN, grief-stricken, desolate, devastated, despondent, inconsolable, disconsolate, miserable, depressed, melancholy, wretched, sorrowful, forlorn, heavy-hearted, woeful, doleful, downcast, woebegone, sad, down; *informal* down in the mouth; *literary* heartsick.
– OPPOSITES: overjoyed.

broker ▸ noun *a top Wall Street broker* DEALER, agent; middleman, intermediary, mediator; liaison; stockbroker, stockjobber.
▸ verb *an agreement brokered by the secretariat* ARRANGE, organize, orchestrate, work out, settle, clinch, bring about; negotiate, mediate.

bromide See PLATITUDE.

bronze ▸ noun *Canadian skaters won the bronze* BRONZE MEDAL, third prize.

brooch ▸ noun pin, clip, clasp, badge; *historical* fibula.

brood ▸ noun **1** *the bird flew to feed its brood* OFFSPRING, young, progeny; family, hatch, clutch. **2** *(informal) Gill was the youngest of the brood* FAMILY; children, offspring, youngsters, progeny; *informal* kids.
▸ verb **1** *once the eggs are laid the male broods them* INCUBATE, hatch. **2** *he slumped in his armchair, brooding* WORRY, fret, agonize, mope, sulk; think, ponder, contemplate, meditate, muse, ruminate.

brook ▸ noun *a babbling brook* STREAM, creek, streamlet, rivulet, rill, brooklet, runnel; bourn.
▸ verb *(formal) we brook no violence* TOLERATE, allow, stand, bear, abide, put up with, endure; accept, permit, countenance; *informal* stomach, stand for, hack; *archaic* suffer.

broom ▸ noun brush, birch broom, push broom, whisk broom, besom.

broth ▸ noun STOCK, bouillon, consommé, soup.

brothel ▸ noun WHOREHOUSE, bordello, massage parlour, body-rub parlour ♣, cathouse, bagnio; *Law* disorderly house; *archaic* bawdy house, house of ill fame, house of ill repute.

brother ▸ noun **1** *then Steve and his brother Dan showed up* SIBLING; *informal* bro. **2** *they were brothers in crime* COLLEAGUE, associate, partner, comrade, fellow, friend; *informal* pal, chum, mate. **3** *a brother of the Order* MONK, cleric, friar, religious, monastic.
– RELATED TERMS: fraternal.

brotherhood ▸ noun **1** *the ideals of justice and brotherhood* COMRADESHIP, fellowship, brotherliness, fraternalism, kinship; camaraderie, friendship. **2** *a masonic brotherhood* SOCIETY, fraternity, association, alliance, union, league, guild, order, body, community, club, lodge, circle.

brotherly ▸ adjective **1** *brotherly rivalry* FRATERNAL, sibling. **2** *brotherly love* FRIENDLY, comradely; affectionate, amicable, kind, devoted, loyal.

brow ▸ noun **1** *the doctor wiped his brow* FOREHEAD, temple; *Zoology* frons. **2** *heavy black brows* EYEBROW. **3** *the brow of the hill* SUMMIT, peak, top, crest, head, pinnacle, apex.

browbeat ▸ verb BULLY, hector, intimidate, force, coerce, compel, dragoon, bludgeon, pressure, pressurize, tyrannize, terrorize, menace; harass, harry, hound; *informal* bulldoze, railroad.

brown ▸ adjective *she has brown eyes* hazel, chocolate-coloured, coffee-coloured, cocoa-coloured, nut-brown; brunette; sepia, mahogany, umber, burnt sienna; beige, buff, tan, fawn, camel, café au lait, caramel, chestnut.

browse ▸ verb **1** *I browsed among the little shops* LOOK AROUND/ROUND, window-shop, peruse. **2** *she browsed through the newspaper* SCAN, skim, glance, look, peruse; thumb, leaf, flick; dip into. **3** *three cows were browsing in the meadow* GRAZE, feed, crop; ruminate. **4** *he spent hours online, just browsing* SURFING.

bruise ▸ noun *a bruise across her forehead* CONTUSION, lesion, mark, injury; swelling, lump, bump, welt.
▸ verb **1** *her face was badly bruised* injure, mark, discolour. **2** *every one of the apples is bruised* MARK, discolour, blemish; damage, spoil. **3** *Eric's ego was bruised* UPSET, offend, insult, affront, hurt, wound, injure, crush.

brunette ▸ adjective BROWN-HAIRED, dark, dark-haired.

brunt ▸ noun *(FULL)* FORCE, impact, shock, burden, pressure, weight; effect, repercussions, consequences.

brush ▸ noun **1** *a dustpan and brush* BROOM, sweeper, besom, whisk. **2** *he gave the seat a brush with his hand* CLEAN, sweep, wipe, dust. **3** *the brush of his lips against her cheek* TOUCH, stroke, skim, graze, nudge, contact; kiss. **4** *a brush with the law* ENCOUNTER, clash, confrontation, conflict, altercation, incident; *informal* run-in. **5** *the pheasant scampered into the brush* UNDERGROWTH, bushes, scrub, underwood, underbrush, brushland, brushwood, shrubs, (*Nfld*) tuckamore ♣, chaparral; thicket, copse.
▸ verb **1** *he spent his day brushing the floors* SWEEP, clean, buff, scrub. **2** *she brushed her hair* GROOM, comb, neaten, tidy, smooth, arrange, fix, do; curry. **3** *she felt his lips brush her cheek* TOUCH, stroke, caress, skim, sweep, graze, contact; kiss. **4** *she brushed a wisp of hair away* PUSH, move, sweep, clear.
■ **brush something aside** DISREGARD, ignore, dismiss, shrug off, wave aside; overlook, pay no attention to, take no notice of, neglect, forget about, turn a blind eye to; reject, spurn; laugh off, make light of, trivialize; *informal* pooh-pooh.
■ **brush someone off** REBUFF, dismiss, spurn, reject, slight, scorn, disdain; ignore, disregard, snub, cut, turn one's back on, give someone the cold shoulder, freeze out; jilt, cast aside, discard.
■ **brush up (on)** REVISE, read up, go over, relearn, cram, study; improve, sharpen (up), polish up; hone, refine, perfect; *informal* bone up.

brush-off ▸ noun REJECTION, dismissal, refusal, rebuff, repulse; snub, slight, cut, kiss-off; the axe, the boot, the gate, the sack.

brusque ▸ adjective CURT, abrupt, blunt, short, sharp, terse, peremptory, gruff, bluff; offhand, discourteous, impolite, rude; *informal* snappy.
– OPPOSITES: polite.

brutal ▸ adjective **1** *a brutal attack* SAVAGE, cruel, vicious, ferocious, brutish, barbaric, barbarous, wicked, murderous, bloodthirsty, cold-blooded,

callous, heartless, ruthless, merciless, sadistic; heinous, monstrous, abominable, atrocious. **2** *brutal honesty* UNSPARING, unstinting, unembellished, unvarnished, bald, naked, stark, blunt, direct, straightforward, frank, outspoken, forthright, plain-spoken; complete, total. **3** *(informal) a brutal haircut.* See BAD sense 1.
— OPPOSITES: gentle.

brute ▶ **noun** *a callous brute* SAVAGE, beast, monster, animal, barbarian, fiend, ogre; sadist; thug, lout, ruffian; *informal* swine, pig.
▶ **adjective** *brute strength* PHYSICAL, bodily; crude, violent.

bubble ▶ **noun** *the bubbles in his mineral water* GLOBULE, bead, blister; air pocket; (**bubbles**) sparkle, fizz, effervescence, froth, head.
▶ **verb 1** *this wine bubbled nicely on the tongue* SPARKLE, fizz, effervesce, foam, froth. **2** *the milk was bubbling above the flame* BOIL, simmer, seethe, gurgle. **3** *she was bubbling over with enthusiasm* OVERFLOW, brim over, be filled, gush.

bubbly ▶ **adjective 1** *a bubbly wine* SPARKLING, bubbling, fizzy, effervescent, gassy, aerated, carbonated; spumante, frothy, foamy. **2** *she was bubbly and full of life* VIVACIOUS, animated, ebullient, exuberant, lively, high-spirited, zestful; sparkling, bouncy, buoyant, carefree; merry, happy, cheerful, perky, sunny, bright; *informal* upbeat, chirpy.
— OPPOSITES: still, listless.
▶ **noun** *(informal) a bottle of bubbly* CHAMPAGNE, sparkling wine, spumante, cava; *informal* fizz.

buck ▶ **verb** *it takes guts to buck the system* RESIST, oppose, defy, fight, kick against.
■ **buck up** *(informal)* CHEER UP, perk up, take heart, pick up, bounce back.
■ **buck someone up** *(informal)* CHEER UP, buoy up, perk up, hearten, uplift, encourage, enliven, give someone a lift; *informal* pep up.

bucket ▶ **noun 1** *a bucket of cold water* PAIL, scuttle, can, tin, tub; ice bucket, wine cooler. **2** *(informal) everyone wept buckets* FLOODS, gallons, oceans.

buckle ▶ **noun** *a belt buckle* CLASP, clip, catch, hasp, fastener.
▶ **verb 1** *he buckled the belt around his waist* FASTEN, do up, hook, strap, secure, clasp, clip. **2** *the front axle buckled* WARP, bend, twist, curve, distort, contort, deform; bulge, arc, arch; crumple, collapse, give way.
■ **buckle down** GET (DOWN) TO WORK, set to work, get down to business; work hard, apply oneself, make an effort, be industrious, be diligent, focus.

bucolic ▶ **adjective** RUSTIC, rural, pastoral, country, countryside; *literary* Arcadian, sylvan, georgic.

bud ▶ **noun** *fresh buds* SPROUT, shoot, blossom; *Botany* plumule.
▶ **verb 1** *trees began to bud* SPROUT, shoot, germinate. **2** *a budding actor.* See BUDDING.

budding ▶ **adjective** PROMISING, up-and-coming, rising, in the making, aspiring, emerging, fledgling, developing, blossoming; *informal* would-be, wannabe.

buddy ▶ **noun** See CHUM.

budge ▶ **verb 1** *the horses wouldn't budge* MOVE, shift, stir, go. **2** *I couldn't budge the door* DISLODGE, shift, move, reposition. **3** *they refuse to budge on the issue* GIVE IN, give way, yield, change one's mind, acquiesce, compromise, do a U-turn.

budget ▶ **noun 1** *your budget for the week* FINANCIAL PLAN, forecast; accounts, statement, Blue Book ♣. **2** *a*

cut in the defence budget ALLOWANCE, allocation, quota; grant, award, funds, resources, capital.
▶ **verb 1** *we have to budget $7,000 for the work* ALLOCATE, allot, allow, earmark, designate, set aside. **2** *budget your finances* SCHEDULE, plan, cost, estimate; ration.
▶ **adjective** *a budget hotel* CHEAP, inexpensive, economy, affordable, low-cost, low-price, cut-rate, discount, bargain, down-market.
— OPPOSITES: expensive.

buff ▶ **adjective** *a plain buff envelope* BEIGE, yellowish, yellowish-brown, light brown, fawn, sandy, wheaten, biscuit, camel.
▶ **verb** *he buffed the glass* POLISH, burnish, shine, clean, rub.
▶ **noun** *(informal) a film buff* ENTHUSIAST, fan, devotee, lover, admirer; expert, aficionado, authority, pundit; *informal* freak, nut, fanatic, fiend, addict, junkie, bum.
■ **in the buff** *(informal). See* NAKED sense 1.

buffer ▶ **noun** *a buffer against market fluctuations* CUSHION, bulwark, shield, barrier, guard, safeguard.
▶ **verb** *she attempted to buffer the children from the troubles* SHIELD, protect, defend, cushion, insulate, screen, guard.

buffet¹ ▶ **noun 1** *a sumptuous buffet* COLD TABLE, self-service meal, smorgasbord. **2** *the plates are kept in the buffet* SIDEBOARD, cabinet, cupboard. **3** *a station buffet* CAFÉ, cafeteria, snack bar, lunch counter, luncheonette, canteen, restaurant.

buffet² ▶ **verb 1** *rough seas buffeted the coast* BATTER, pound, lash, strike, hit. **2** *he has been buffeted by bad publicity* AFFLICT, trouble, harm, burden, bother, beset, harass, assail, harry, plague, torment, blight, bedevil.

buffoon ▶ **noun** *they regarded him as a buffoon* FOOL, idiot, dunce, ignoramus, dummy, simpleton, jackass, chump, blockhead, jughead, boob, bozo, doofus, nincompoop, numbskull, numbnuts, dope, twit, nitwit, halfwit, birdbrain. *See also* ASS sense 2.

bug ▶ **noun 1** *bugs were crawling everywhere* INSECT, mite; *informal* creepy-crawly, beastie. **2** *(informal) a stomach bug* ILLNESS, ailment, disorder, infection, disease, sickness, complaint, upset, condition; bacterium, germ, virus. **3** *(informal) he caught the journalism bug* OBSESSION, enthusiasm, craze, fad, mania, passion, fixation. **4** *the bug planted on his phone* LISTENING DEVICE, hidden microphone, wire, wiretap, tap. **5** *a bug in the software* FAULT, error, defect, flaw; virus; *informal* glitch, gremlin.
▶ **verb 1** *her conversations were bugged* RECORD, eavesdrop on, spy on, overhear; wiretap, tap, monitor. **2** *(informal) she really bugs me. See* ANNOY.

bugbear ▶ **noun** PET HATE, bête noire, bogey, bugaboo; bane, irritation, vexation, thorn in one's flesh/side; nightmare, peeve, pain (in the neck), hang-up.

build ▶ **verb 1** *they were building a tree house* CONSTRUCT, erect, put up, assemble; make, form, create, fashion, model, shape. **2** *they are building a business strategy* ESTABLISH, found, set up, institute, inaugurate, initiate. **3** *the pressure was building* INCREASE, mount, intensify, escalate, grow, rise.
▶ **noun** *a man of slim build* PHYSIQUE, frame, body, figure, form, shape, stature, proportions; *informal* vital statistics.
■ **build something in/into** INCORPORATE IN/INTO, include in, absorb into, subsume into, assimilate into.
■ **build on** EXPAND ON, enlarge on, develop, elaborate,

flesh out, embellish, amplify; refine, improve, perfect.

■ **build up** INCREASE, grow, mount up, intensify, escalate; strengthen.

■ **build something up 1** *he built up a huge business* ESTABLISH, set up, found, institute, start, create; develop, expand, enlarge. **2** *she built up her stamina* BOOST, strengthen, increase, improve, augment, raise, enhance, swell; *informal* beef up. **3** *I have built up a collection of prints* ACCUMULATE, amass, collect, gather; stockpile, hoard.

builder ▶ **noun** CONSTRUCTOR, contractor, creator, maker; planner, architect, deviser, designer; CONSTRUCTION WORKER, bricklayer, labourer.

building ▶ **noun 1** *a brick building* STRUCTURE, construction, edifice, erection, pile; property, premises, establishment. **2** *the building of power stations* CONSTRUCTION, erection, fabrication, assembly.
− RELATED TERMS: tectonic.

buildup ▶ **noun 1** *the buildup of military strength* INCREASE, growth, expansion, escalation, development, proliferation. **2** *the buildup of carbon dioxide* ACCUMULATION, accretion. **3** *the buildup for the World Cup* PUBLICITY, promotion, advertising, marketing; *informal* hype, ballyhoo, brouhaha, to-do.

built-in ▶ **adjective 1** *a built-in cupboard* integrated, integral, incorporated. **2** *built-in advantages* INHERENT, intrinsic, inbuilt; essential, implicit, basic, fundamental, deep-rooted.

bulbous ▶ **adjective** BULGING, protuberant, round, fat, rotund; swollen, tumid, distended, bloated.

bulge ▶ **noun 1** *a bulge in the tire* SWELLING, bump, lump, protuberance, prominence, tumescence. **2** *(informal) a bulge in the population* SURGE, upsurge, rise, increase, escalation.
▶ **verb** *his eyes were bulging* SWELL, stick out, puff out, balloon (out), bug out, fill out, belly, distend, tumefy, intumesce; project, protrude, stand out.

bulk ▶ **noun 1** *the sheer bulk of the bags* SIZE, volume, dimensions, proportions, mass, scale, magnitude, immensity, vastness. **2** *the bulk of entrants were women* MAJORITY, main part, major part, lion's share, preponderance, generality; most, almost all.
− OPPOSITES: minority.

bulky ▶ **adjective** *bulky items of refuse* LARGE, big, huge, sizeable, substantial, massive; king-size, economy-size(d), outsize, oversized, considerable, voluminous; CUMBERSOME, unmanageable, unwieldy, ponderous, heavy, weighty; *informal* jumbo, whopping, hulking, humongous, ginormous.
− OPPOSITES: small, slight.

bulldoze ▶ **verb 1** *they plan to bulldoze the park* DEMOLISH, knock down, tear down, pull down, flatten, level, raze, clear. **2** *he bulldozed his way through* FORCE, push, shove, barge, elbow, shoulder, jostle, muscle; plunge, crash, sweep, bundle. **3** *(informal) she tends to bulldoze everyone* BULLY, hector, browbeat, intimidate, dragoon, domineer, pressurize, tyrannize, strong-arm, push around, walk all over; railroad, steamroller, lean on, boss.

bullet ▶ **noun** ball, shot, cartridge; *informal* slug; (**bullets**) lead, ammunition, ammo.

bulletin ▶ **noun 1** *a news bulletin* REPORT, dispatch, story, press release, newscast, flash; statement, announcement, message, communication, communiqué. **2** *the society's monthly bulletin* NEWSLETTER, proceedings; newspaper, magazine, digest, gazette, review, tipsheet.

bulletin board ▶ **noun** notice board, cork board, call board, message board; hoarding.

bullish ▶ **adjective** CONFIDENT, positive, assertive, self-assertive, assured, self-assured, bold, determined; optimistic, buoyant, sanguine; *informal* feisty, upbeat.

bully ▶ **noun** *the school bully* PERSECUTOR, oppressor, tyrant, tormentor, intimidator; tough guy, bully boy, thug.
▶ **verb 1** *the others bully him* PERSECUTE, oppress, tyrannize, browbeat, harass, torment, intimidate, strong-arm, dominate, bullyrag; *informal* push around. **2** *she was bullied into helping* COERCE, pressure, pressurize, press, push; force, compel; badger, goad, prod, browbeat, bludgeon, intimidate, dragoon, strong-arm; *informal* bulldoze, railroad, lean on.

bulwark ▶ **noun 1** *ancient bulwarks* WALL, rampart, fortification, parapet, stockade, palisade, barricade, embankment, earthwork. **2** *a bulwark of liberty* PROTECTOR, defender, protection, guard, defence, supporter, buttress; mainstay, bastion, stronghold.

bum ▶ **noun** *(informal)* **1** *I have a sore bum. See* BUTTOCKS. **2** *the bums sleeping on the sidewalk. See* TRAMP *noun* sense 1. **3** *you lazy bum* IDLER, loafer, slacker, good-for-nothing, ne'er-do-well, layabout, lounger, shirker; loser. **4** *(informal) a ski bum* ENTHUSIAST, fan, aficionado, lover, freak, nut, buff, fanatic, addict.
▶ **verb 1** *that summer he bummed around Montreal* LOAF, lounge, idle, moon, wander, drift, meander, dawdle; *informal* mooch, lallygag. **2** *they bummed money off him* BEG, borrow; *informal* scrounge, cadge, sponge, mooch.
▶ **adjective** *a bum deal* CRUMMY, rotten, pathetic, lousy, pitiful; BAD, poor, second-rate, tinpot, third-rate, second-class, unsatisfactory, inadequate, unacceptable; dreadful, awful, terrible, deplorable, lamentable.
− OPPOSITES: excellent.

bumbling ▶ **adjective** BLUNDERING, bungling, inept, clumsy, maladroit, awkward, muddled, klutzy; oafish, clodhopping, lumbering; botched, schlubby, ham-handed/fisted.
− OPPOSITES: efficient.

bump ▶ **noun 1** *I landed with a bump* BANG, crash, smash, smack, crack, jolt, thud, thump; *informal* whack, thwack, bash, bonk, wallop. **2** *a bump in the road* HUMP, lump, ridge, bulge, knob, protuberance; swelling.
▶ **verb 1** *cars bumped into each other* HIT, crash, smash, smack, slam, bang, knock, run, plow; ram, collide with, strike, impact. **2** *a cart bumping along the road* BOUNCE, jolt, jerk, rattle, shake. **3** *she got bumped in favour of a rookie* DISPLACE, demote, dislodge, supplant.
■ **bump into** *(informal)* MEET (BY CHANCE), encounter, run into/across, come across, chance on, happen on.

bumpkin ▶ **noun** YOKEL, peasant, provincial, rustic, country cousin, hayseed, hillbilly, hick, rube; (*Nfld*) baywop ♣, (*Nfld*) bayman ♣ (noddy ♣), culchie.

bumptious ▶ **adjective** SELF-IMPORTANT, conceited, arrogant, self-assertive, pushy, pompous, overbearing, cocky, swaggering; proud, haughty, overweening, egotistical; *informal* snooty, uppity.
− OPPOSITES: modest.

bumpy ▶ **adjective 1** *a bumpy road* UNEVEN, rough, rutted, rutty, pitted, potholed, holey; lumpy, rocky. **2** *a bumpy ride* BOUNCY, rough, uncomfortable,

jolting, lurching, jerky, jarring, bone-shaking.
— OPPOSITES: smooth.

bun ▶ noun ROLL, bread roll, kaiser, panino; (**buns**). See BUTTOCKS.

bunch ▶ noun **1** *a bunch of flowers* BOUQUET, posy, nosegay, spray, corsage; wreath, garland. **2** *a bunch of grapes* CLUSTER, clump, knot; group. **3** *we invited the whole bunch* GROUP, set, circle, company, collection, bevy, band; gang, crowd, load. **4** *a bunch of things* ASSORTMENT, bundle, collection; many, lots, load, an abundance, job lot.
▶ verb **1** *he bunched the reins in his hand* BUNDLE, clump, cluster, group, gather; pack. **2** *her skirt bunched at the waist* GATHER, ruffle, pucker, fold, pleat. **3** *the runners bunched up behind him* CLUSTER, huddle, gather, congregate, collect, amass, group, crowd.

bundle ▶ noun *a bundle of clothes* BUNCH, roll, clump, wad, parcel, sheaf, bale, bolt; package; pile, stack, heap, mass; *informal* load.
▶ verb **1** *she bundled up her things* TIE, pack, parcel, wrap, roll, fold, bind, bale, package. **2** *she was bundled in furs* WRAP, envelop, clothe, cover, muffle, swathe, swaddle, shroud, drape, enfold. **3** (*informal*) *he was bundled into a van* shove, push, thrust, manhandle, hurry, rush.

bungle ▶ verb MISHANDLE, mismanage, mess up, spoil, ruin, blunder; *informal* botch, muff, fluff, make a hash of, foul up, screw up, flub, goof up.

bungling ▶ adjective INCOMPETENT, blundering, amateurish, inept, unskilful, maladroit, clumsy, klutzy, awkward, bumbling; *informal* ham-handed/fisted.

bunk ▶ noun **1** *there were twelve bunks per dormitory* BERTH, cot, bed. **2** (*informal*) *the idea was sheer bunk*. See NONSENSE sense 1.

bunkum ▶ noun (*informal*). See NONSENSE sense 1.

buoy ▶ noun *a mooring buoy* FLOAT, (*Nfld*) keg ✚, marker, beacon; bell buoy, breeches buoy, dan buoy, nun-buoy, sonobuoy.
▶ verb *the party was buoyed by a by-election victory* CHEER (UP), hearten, rally, invigorate, uplift, lift, encourage, stimulate, inspirit; *informal* pep up, perk up, buck up.
— OPPOSITES: depress.

buoyant ▶ adjective **1** *a buoyant substance* ABLE TO FLOAT, floating, floatable. **2** *a buoyant mood* CHEERFUL, cheery, happy, light-hearted, carefree, bright, merry, joyful, bubbly, bouncy, sunny, jolly; lively, jaunty, high-spirited, perky; optimistic, confident, positive; *informal* peppy, upbeat.

burble ▶ verb **1** *two fountains were burbling outside* GURGLE, bubble, murmur, purr, whirr, drone, hum, rumble. **2** *he burbled on* PRATTLE, blather, blether, babble, gabble, prate, drivel, rattle, ramble, maunder, go on, run on; *informal* jabber, blabber, yammer, yatter, gab, waffle.

burden ▶ noun **1** *a financial burden* ENCUMBRANCE, strain, care, problem, worry, difficulty, trouble, millstone; RESPONSIBILITY, onus, charge, duty, obligation, liability. **2** *they shouldered their burdens* LOAD, weight, cargo, freight.
▶ verb LOAD, charge, weigh down, encumber, hamper; overload, overburden; OPPRESS, trouble, worry, harass, upset, distress; haunt, afflict, strain, stress, tax, overwhelm.

burdensome ▶ adjective ONEROUS, oppressive, troublesome, weighty, worrisome, stressful; vexatious, irksome, trying, difficult, arduous, strenuous, hard, back-breaking, laborious,

exhausting, tiring, taxing, demanding, punishing, gruelling.

bureau ▶ noun **1** *an oak bureau* DESK, writing table, secretaire, escritoire; chest of drawers, cabinet, dresser, commode, tallboy, highboy. **2** *the tourism bureau* AGENCY, service, office, business, company, firm; DEPARTMENT, division, branch, section.

bureaucracy ▶ noun **1** *the ranks of the bureaucracy* CIVIL SERVICE, government, administration; establishment, system, powers that be; ministries, authorities. **2** *unnecessary bureaucracy* RED TAPE, rules and regulations, protocol, officialdom, paperwork.

bureaucrat ▶ noun OFFICIAL, administrator, civil servant, functionary, mandarin; *derogatory* apparatchik, bean-counter, paper shuffler.

burgeon ▶ verb FLOURISH, thrive, prosper, improve, develop; expand, escalate, swell, grow, boom, mushroom, snowball, rocket.

burglar ▶ noun ROBBER, housebreaker, cat burglar, thief, raider, looter, safecracker, second-storey man; intruder, prowler; yegg.

burglary ▶ noun **1** *a sentence for burglary* HOUSEBREAKING, breaking and entering, theft, stealing, robbery, larceny, thievery, looting, pilferage. **2** *a series of burglaries* BREAK-IN, theft, robbery, raid; *informal* smash and grab, break and enter, heist.

burgle ▶ verb ROB, burglarize, loot, steal from, plunder, rifle, pillage; break into.

burial ▶ noun BURYING, interment, committal, entombment; funeral, obsequies; *formal* inhumation; *archaic* sepulture.
— RELATED TERMS: funerary, sepulchral.
— OPPOSITES: exhumation.

burial ground ▶ noun CEMETERY, graveyard, churchyard, necropolis; memorial park/garden; *informal* boneyard; *archaic* God's acre; *historical* potter's field.

burlap ▶ noun SACKCLOTH, gunny, (*Nfld*) brin ✚, Hessian.

burlesque ▶ noun PARODY, caricature, satire, lampoon, skit, farce; send-up, takeoff, spoof; striptease, strip.

burly ▶ adjective STRAPPING, well-built, sturdy, brawny, strong, muscular, muscly, thickset, blocky, big, hefty, bulky, stocky, stout, Herculean, hunky, beefy, husky, hulking.
— OPPOSITES: puny.

burn ▶ verb **1** *the coal was burning* BE ON FIRE, be alight, be ablaze, blaze, go up (in smoke), be in flames, be aflame, smoulder, glow. **2** *he burned the letters* SET FIRE TO, set on fire, set alight, set light to, light, ignite, touch off; incinerate; *informal* torch. **3** *I burned my dress with the iron* SCORCH, singe, sear, char, blacken, brand, sizzle; scald. **4** *her face burned* BE HOT, be warm, be feverish, be on fire; blush, redden, go red, flush, colour. **5** *she was burning with curiosity* BE CONSUMED, be eaten up, be obsessed, be tormented, be beside oneself. **6** *the energy they burn up* CONSUME, use up, expend, get/go through, eat up; dissipate.

burning ▶ adjective **1** *burning coals* BLAZING, flaming, fiery, ignited, glowing, red-hot, smouldering, igneous; raging, roaring. **2** *burning desert sands* EXTREMELY HOT, red-hot, fiery, blistering, scorching, searing, sweltering, torrid; *informal* baking, boiling (hot), broiling, roasting, sizzling. **3** *a burning desire* INTENSE, passionate, deep-seated, profound, wholehearted, strong, ardent, fervent, urgent, fierce, eager, frantic, consuming, uncontrollable. **4** *burning issues* IMPORTANT, crucial, significant, vital, essential, pivotal; urgent, pressing, compelling, critical.

burnish ▶ verb POLISH, shine, buff, rub, gloss.

burp ▶ verb BELCH.
▶ noun BELCH; *formal* eructation.

burrow ▶ noun *a rabbits' burrow* HOLE, tunnel, warren, dugout; lair, set, den, earth.
▶ verb *the mouse burrows a hole* TUNNEL, dig (out), excavate, grub, mine, bore, channel; hollow out, gouge out.

burst ▶ verb **1** *one balloon burst* SPLIT (OPEN), rupture, break, tear. **2** *a shell burst* EXPLODE, blow up, detonate, go off. **3** *smoke burst through the hole* BREAK, erupt, surge, gush, rush, stream, flow, pour, spill; spout, spurt, jet, spew. **4** *he burst into the room* BARGE, charge, plunge, plow, hurtle, career, careen, rush, dash, tear. **5** *they burst into tears* BREAK OUT IN, erupt in, have a fit of.
▶ noun **1** *mortar bursts* EXPLOSION, detonation, blast, eruption, bang. **2** *a burst of gunfire* VOLLEY, salvo, fusillade, barrage, discharge; hail, rain. **3** *a burst of activity* OUTBREAK, eruption, flare-up, blaze, attack, fit, rush, gale, storm, surge, upsurge, spurt.
■ **burst out** *'I don't care!' she burst out* EXCLAIM, blurt, cry, shout, yell; *dated* ejaculate.

bury ▶ verb **1** *the dead were buried* INTER, lay to rest, entomb; *informal* put six feet under; *literary* inhume. **2** *she buried her face in her hands* HIDE, conceal, cover, enfold, engulf, tuck, cup, sink. **3** *the bullet buried itself in the wood* EMBED, sink, implant, submerge; drive into. **4** *he buried himself in his work* ABSORB, engross, immerse, occupy, engage, busy, involve.
— OPPOSITES: exhume.

bus ▶ noun COACH, trolley, motorcoach, school bus, minibus, double-decker; *historical* omnibus.

bush ▶ noun **1** *a rose bush* SHRUB, brier; (**bushes**) undergrowth, shrubbery. **2** *out in the bush* WILDS, wilderness, forest, woodland, timberland, bush country, bushland; backwoods, hinterland(s), backcountry, backlands; *informal* the sticks, boondocks, (*Ont. & Que.*) the back concessions ♣, moose pasture ♣.

bush-league ▶ adjective *the bush-league event left her unimpressed* UNSOPHISTICATED, provincial, mediocre, inferior, uncouth; *informal* small-time, two-bit, rinky-dink.

bushy ▶ adjective THICK, shaggy, fuzzy, bristly, fluffy, woolly; luxuriant.
— OPPOSITES: sleek, wispy.

business ▶ noun **1** *he has to smile in his business* WORK, line of work, occupation, profession, career, employment, job, position; vocation, calling; field, sphere, trade, métier, craft; *informal* biz, racket, game. **2** *who do you do business with?* TRADE, trading, commerce, dealing, traffic, merchandising; dealings, transactions, negotiations. **3** *her own business* COMPANY, firm, concern, enterprise, venture, organization, operation, corporation, undertaking; office, agency, franchise, practice; *informal* outfit. **4** *none of your business* CONCERN, affair, responsibility, duty, function, obligation; problem; *informal* beeswax, bailiwick. **5** *an odd business* AFFAIR, matter, thing, case, circumstance, situation, event, incident, happening, occurrence; episode.
— RELATED TERMS: corporate.

businesslike ▶ adjective PROFESSIONAL, efficient, competent, methodical, disciplined, systematic,

orderly, organized, structured, practical, pragmatic, routine, slick.

businessman, businesswoman ▶ noun ENTREPRENEUR, business person, industrialist, manufacturer, tycoon, baron, magnate, executive, employer; dealer, trader, broker, merchant, buyer, seller, marketeer, merchandiser, vendor, retailer, supplier.

bust[1] ▶ noun **1** *her large bust* CHEST, bosom, breasts. **2** *a bust of Caesar* SCULPTURE, carving, effigy, statue; head and shoulders.

bust[2] (*informal*) ▶ verb **1** *I didn't mean to bust your DVD player* BREAK, smash, fracture, shatter, crack, disintegrate, snap; split, burst. **2** *he promised to bust the mafia* OVERTHROW, destroy, topple, bring down, ruin, break, overturn, overcome, defeat, get rid of, oust, dislodge. **3** *they were busted for drugs.* See ARREST verb sense 1. **4** *my apartment got busted.* See RAID verb sense 3.
■ **go bust** FAIL, collapse, fold, go under, founder; go bankrupt, go into receivership, go into liquidation, be wound up; *informal* crash, go broke, go belly up, flop, bomb.

bustle ▶ verb *people bustled about* RUSH, dash, hurry, scurry, scuttle, hustle, scamper, scramble; run, tear, charge; *informal* scoot, beetle, buzz, zoom.
▶ noun *the bustle of the market* ACTIVITY, action, liveliness, hustle and bustle, excitement; tumult, hubbub, whirl, commotion; *informal* toing and froing, comings and goings.

bustling ▶ adjective BUSY, crowded, swarming, teeming, thronged; buzzing, abuzz, hectic, lively.
— OPPOSITES: deserted.

busy ▶ adjective **1** *they are busy raising money* OCCUPIED (IN), engaged in, involved in, employed in, working at, hard at work (on); rushed off one's feet, hard-pressed, swamped, up to one's neck; on the job, absorbed, engrossed, immersed, preoccupied; *informal* (as) busy as a bee, on the go, hard at it. **2** *she is busy at the moment* UNAVAILABLE, engaged, occupied; working, in a meeting, on duty; *informal* tied up. **3** *the busy streets of Toronto* HECTIC, active, lively; crowded, bustling, abuzz, swarming, teeming, full, thronged. **4** *a busy design* ORNATE, over-elaborate, overblown, overwrought, overdone, fussy, cluttered, overworked.
— OPPOSITES: idle, free, quiet.
▶ verb *he busied himself with paperwork* OCCUPY, involve, engage, concern, absorb, engross, immerse, preoccupy; distract, divert.

busybody ▶ noun MEDDLER, interferer, mischief-maker, troublemaker; gossip, scandalmonger; eavesdropper; *informal* kibitzer, buttinsky, nosy parker, snoop, snooper, yenta.

but ▶ conjunction **1** *he stumbled but didn't fall* YET, nevertheless, nonetheless, even so, however, still, notwithstanding, despite that, in spite of that, for all that, all the same, just the same; though, although. **2** *this one's expensive but this one isn't* WHEREAS, conversely, but then, then again, on the other hand, by/in contrast, on the contrary.
▶ preposition *everyone but him* EXCEPT (FOR), apart from, other than, besides, aside from, with the exception of, bar, excepting, excluding, leaving out, save (for), saving.
▶ adverb *he is but a shadow of his former self* ONLY, just, simply, merely, no more than, nothing but; a mere.
■ **but for** EXCEPT FOR, if it were not for, were it not for, barring, notwithstanding.

butch ▶ adjective (*informal*) MASCULINE, manly;

mannish, manlike; *informal* macho.
— OPPOSITES: effeminate.

butcher ▶ noun **1** *a butcher's shop* MEAT SELLER, meat vendor, meat trader. **2** *a Nazi butcher* MURDERER, slaughterer, killer, assassin; *literary* slayer; *dated* cutthroat, homicide.
▶ verb **1** *the goat was butchered* SLAUGHTER, cut up, carve up, joint. **2** *they butchered 150 people* MASSACRE, murder, slaughter, kill, destroy, exterminate, assassinate; *literary* slay. **3** *the studio butchered the film* SPOIL, ruin, mutilate, mangle, mess up, wreck; *informal* make a hash of, screw up, botch.

butler ▶ noun MANSERVANT, servant, chamberlain, man, steward, major-domo, seneschal.

butt ▶ noun **1** *the butt of a joke* TARGET, victim, object, subject, dupe; laughingstock. **2** *the butt of a gun* STOCK, end, handle, hilt, haft, helve. **3** *a cigarette butt* STUB, end, tail end, stump, remnant. **4** (*informal*) *sitting on his butt*. See BUTTOCKS.
▶ verb **1** *the shop butts up against the house* ADJOIN, abut, be next to, be adjacent to, border (on), be connected to; join, touch. **2** *students butting everyone with their backpacks* RAM, headbutt, bunt; bump, buffet, push, shove.
■ **butt in** INTERRUPT, break in, cut in, chime in, interject, intervene, interfere, interpose; *informal* poke one's nose in, put one's oar in.

butter
■ **butter someone up** (*informal*) FLATTER, sweet-talk, curry favour with, court, wheedle, cajole, persuade, blarney, coax, compliment, get around, prevail on; be obsequious towards, be sycophantic towards, toady to, fawn on, make up to, play up to, ingratiate oneself with, suck up to, be all over, keep someone sweet, soft-soap.

butterfly ▶ noun **1** *an unfamiliar species of butterfly* LEPIDOPTERAN. *See table.* **2** *I had butterflies as I waited* NERVES, anxiety, the jitters.

Butterflies & Moths

Butterflies	Moths
admiral	burnet
argus	cinnabar
blue	clothes moth
cabbage butterfly	codling moth
comma butterfly	geometer moth
copper	gypsy moth
fritillary	hawk moth
hairstreak	leopard moth
monarch	luna moth
mourning cloak	silk moth
painted lady	sphinx moth
red admiral	tiger moth
ringlet	tortrix
satyrid	tussock moth
skipper	
sulphur	
swallowtail	
tortoiseshell	
white admiral	

buttocks ▶ plural noun REAR (END), backside, seat, bottom, rump, cheeks, behind, derrière, bum, butt, fanny, keister, tush, tail, buns, heinie, arse, ass, caboose; fundament, posterior, haunches, gluteus maximus, sit-upon, stern, wazoo; *Anatomy* nates.

button ▶ noun **1** *shirt buttons* FASTENER, stud, toggle; hook, catch, clasp, dome fastener, snap fastener, pin.

2 *press the button* SWITCH, knob, control; lever, handle; icon, box.

buttonhole ▶ verb (*informal*). See ACCOST.

buttress ▶ noun **1** *stone buttresses* PROP, support, abutment, brace, shore, pier, reinforcement, stanchion. **2** *a buttress against social collapse* SAFEGUARD, defence, protection, guard; support, prop; bulwark.
▶ verb *authority was buttressed by religion* STRENGTHEN, reinforce, fortify, support, bolster, shore up, underpin, cement, uphold, prop up, defend, sustain, back up.

buxom ▶ adjective LARGE-BREASTED, big-breasted, bosomy, big-bosomed; shapely, ample, plump, rounded, full-figured, voluptuous, curvaceous, Rubenesque; *informal* busty, built, stacked, chesty, well-endowed, curvy.

buy ▶ verb *they bought a new house* PURCHASE, acquire, obtain, get, pick up; take, procure, pay for; invest in; *informal* get hold of, snatch up, snap up, grab, score.
— OPPOSITES: sell.
▶ noun (*informal*) *a good buy* PURCHASE, investment, acquisition, gain; deal, value, bargain.

buyer ▶ noun PURCHASER, customer, consumer, shopper, investor.

buzz ▶ noun **1** *the buzz of the bees* HUM, humming, buzzing, murmur, drone, zizz. **2** *the buzz of the doorbell* RING, purr, note, tone, beep, bleep, warble, alarm, warning sound. **3** (*informal*) *give me a buzz*. See CALL *noun* sense 3. **4** (*informal*) *the buzz is that he's gone*. See RUMOUR. **5** (*informal*) *get a buzz out of flying* THRILL, stimulation, glow, tingle; *informal* kick, rush, high, charge.
▶ verb **1** *bees buzzed* HUM, drone, bumble, murmur, zizz. **2** *the intercom soon buzzed* PURR, warble, sound, ring, beep, bleep. **3** (*informal*) *he buzzed around the province* BUSTLE, scurry, scuttle, hurry, rush, race, dash, tear, chase; *informal* scoot, beetle, whiz, zoom, zip. **4** *the club is buzzing with excitement* HUM, throb, vibrate, pulse, bustle, be abuzz.
■ **buzz off** SCRAM, get lost, go away, take a hike, beat it, bug off, go fly a kite, go suck an egg, vamoose, be off, begone, fuddle duddle ♣.

by ▶ preposition **1** *I broke it by forcing the lid* THROUGH, as a result of, because of, by dint of, by way of, via, by means of; with the help of, with the aid of, by virtue of. **2** *be there by midday* NO LATER THAN, in good time for, at, before. **3** *a house by the lake* NEXT TO, beside, alongside, by/at the side of, adjacent to, side by side with; near, close to, neighbouring, adjoining, bordering, overlooking; connected to, contiguous with, attached to. **4** *go by the building* PAST, in front of, beyond. **5** *all right by me* ACCORDING TO, with, as far as —— is concerned.
▶ adverb *people hurried by* PAST, on, along.
■ **by and by** EVENTUALLY, ultimately, finally, in the end, one day, some day, sooner or later, in time, in a while, in the long run, in the fullness of time, in time to come, at length, in the future, in due course, over the long haul.
■ **by oneself** ALONE, on one's own, singly, separately, solitarily, unaccompanied, companionless, unattended, unescorted, solo; unaided, unassisted, without help, by one's own efforts, under one's own steam, independently, single-handed(ly), off one's own bat, on one's own initiative; *informal* by one's lonesome.

bye ▶ exclamation See GOODBYE.

bygone ▶ adjective PAST, former, olden, earlier,

previous, one-time, long-ago, of old, ancient, antiquated; departed, dead, extinct, defunct, out of date, outmoded; *literary* of yore.
— OPPOSITES: present, recent.

bylaw ▶ noun LOCAL LAW, regulation, rule.

bypass ▶ noun RING ROAD, detour, diversion, alternative route, shortcut.
▶ **verb 1** *bypass the farm* GO AROUND, go past, make a detour around; avoid. **2** *an attempt to bypass the problem* AVOID, evade, dodge, escape, elude, circumvent, get around, shortcut around, skirt, sidestep, steer clear of; *informal* duck. **3** *they bypassed the regulations* IGNORE, pass over, neglect, go over the head of; *informal* short-circuit.

by-product ▶ noun SIDE EFFECT, consequence, entailment, corollary; ramification, repercussion, spinoff, fallout; fruits.

bystander ▶ noun ONLOOKER, looker-on, passerby, non-participant, observer, spectator, eyewitness, witness, watcher, gawker; *informal* railbird, rubbernecker.

byword ▶ noun **1** *their office was a byword for delay* PERFECT EXAMPLE, classic case, model, exemplar, embodiment, incarnation, personification, epitome. **2** *reality was his byword* SLOGAN, motto, maxim, mantra, catchword, watchword, formula; middle name; proverb, adage, saying, dictum.

Cc

cab ► noun **1** *she hailed a cab* TAXI, taxicab, hack; rickshaw, calèche ♣, trishaw, pedicab. **2** *a truck driver's cab* (DRIVER'S) COMPARTMENT, cabin.

cabal ► noun CLIQUE, faction, coterie, cell, sect, camarilla, junta; lobby (group), pressure group, ginger group.

cabaret ► noun **1** *the evening's cabaret* ENTERTAINMENT, (floor) show, performance. **2** *the cabarets of Montreal* NIGHTCLUB, dinner theatre, club, boîte, café, nightspot, clip joint, honky-tonk.

cabin ► noun **1** *a cabin by the lake* COTTAGE, log cabin, shack, shanty, (*Nfld*) tilt ♣, hut; chalet; cabana; caboose ♣; *historical* camboose ♣. **2** *the driver's cabin* CAB, compartment.

cabinet ► noun **1** *a walnut cabinet* CUPBOARD, bureau, bookcase, chest of drawers, sideboard, buffet, dresser, credenza, highboy, tallboy, wardrobe, chiffonier, armoire, wall unit; china cabinet, file cabinet, medicine cabinet. **2** *a meeting of the new cabinet* SENIOR MINISTERS, ministry, council, executive, Privy Council.

cable ► noun **1** *a thick cable moored the ship* ROPE, cord, line, guy, wire; hawser, stay, bridle; choker. **2** *electric cables* WIRE, lead; power line, hydro line ♣, transmission line.

cache ► noun *a cache of arms* HOARD, store, stockpile, stock, supply, reserve; arsenal; *informal* stash.

cachet ► noun PRESTIGE, status, standing, clout, kudos, snob value, stature, pre-eminence, eminence; street credibility.

cackle ► verb **1** *the geese cackled at him* SQUAWK, cluck, gabble. **2** *Noel cackled with glee* LAUGH LOUDLY, guffaw, chortle, chuckle.

cacophonous ► adjective NOISY, loud, ear-splitting, raucous, discordant, dissonant, jarring, grating, inharmonious, unmelodious, unmusical, tuneless.
— OPPOSITES: harmonious.

cacophony ► noun DIN, racket, noise, clamour, discord, dissonance, discordance, uproar.

cad ► noun (*dated*) See JERK noun sense 3.

cadaver ► noun (*Medicine*) CORPSE, (dead) body, remains, carcass; *informal* stiff; *archaic* corse.

cadaverous ► adjective (DEATHLY) PALE, pallid, ashen, grey, whey-faced, sallow, wan, anemic, bloodless, etiolated, corpse-like, deathlike; bony, skeletal, emaciated, skin-and-bones, haggard, gaunt, drawn, pinched, hollow-cheeked, hollow-eyed; *informal* like a bag of bones, anorexic.
— OPPOSITES: rosy, plump.

cadence ► noun INTONATION, modulation, lilt, accent, inflection; rhythm, tempo, metre, beat, pulse; *Music* resolution.

cadge ► verb (*informal*) SCROUNGE, borrow; *informal* bum, mooch, sponge, touch someone for.

cadre ► noun CORPS, body, team, group, nucleus, core.

café ► noun COFFEE SHOP, coffee bar, tea room; bistro, brasserie, cafeteria; snack bar, buffet, diner, eatery.

cafeteria ► noun LUNCHROOM, luncheonette, lunch counter, caf ♣, cafetorium; snack bar, (*Que.*) casse-croûte ♣, buffet, canteen, café.

cage ► noun *animals in cages* ENCLOSURE, pen, pound; coop, hutch; birdcage, aviary, corral.
► verb *many animals are caged* CONFINE, shut in/up, pen, coop up, fence in, immure, impound, corral.

cagey ► adjective (*informal*) SECRETIVE, guarded, cautious, wary, noncommittal, tight-lipped, reticent, evasive; *informal* playing one's cards close to one's chest.
— OPPOSITES: open.

cahoots
■ **in cahoots** (*informal*) IN LEAGUE, colluding, in collusion, conspiring, collaborating, hand in glove, in bed.

cajole ► verb PERSUADE, wheedle, coax, talk into, prevail on, blarney, sweet-talk, butter up, soft-soap, seduce, inveigle.

cake ► noun **1** *chocolate cakes. See table.* **2** *a cake of soap* BAR, tablet, block, brick, slab, lump.
► verb **1** *boots caked with mud* COAT, encrust, plaster, cover. **2** *the blood was beginning to cake* CLOT, congeal, coagulate, solidify, set, inspissate.
■ **a piece of cake** See CINCH sense 1.

calamitous ► adjective DISASTROUS, catastrophic, cataclysmic, devastating, dire, tragic; *literary* direful.

calamity ► noun DISASTER, catastrophe, tragedy, cataclysm, adversity, tribulation, affliction, misfortune, misadventure.
— OPPOSITES: godsend.

calculate ► verb **1** *the interest is calculated on a daily basis* COMPUTE, work out, reckon, figure; add up/together, count up, tally, total, tote, tot up. **2** *his words were calculated to wound her* INTEND, mean, aim, design. **3** *we had calculated on a quiet Sunday* EXPECT, count, anticipate, reckon, bargain, figure.

calculated ► adjective DELIBERATE, premeditated, planned, pre-planned, preconceived, intentional, intended, wilful; *Law* prepense.
— OPPOSITES: unintentional.

calculating ► adjective CUNNING, crafty, wily, shrewd, sly, scheming, devious, designing, conniving, Machiavellian; *informal* foxy; *archaic* subtle.
— OPPOSITES: ingenuous.

calculation ► noun **1** *the calculation of the overall cost* COMPUTATION, reckoning, adding up, counting up, working out, figuring, totalling up, totting up. **2** *political calculations* ASSESSMENT, judgment; forecast, projection, prediction.

calendar ► noun ALMANAC, diary, schedule, agenda, program, annual, yearbook. *See also the table at* MONTH.

calibrate ► verb ADJUST, measure, set, graduate, correct.

calibre ► noun **1** *a man of his calibre* QUALITY, merit, distinction, stature, excellence, pre-eminence; ability, expertise, talent, capability, capacity, proficiency. **2** *questions about the calibre of the*

Cakes, Puddings, and Other Sweet Foods

angel food cake	honeycake
baba	hot cross bun
babka	jelly roll
baked Alaska	kuchen
bangbelly ♣(Nfld)	ladyfinger
Bavarian cream	layer cake
Black Forest cake/torte	loaf cake
blancmange	madeleine
blueberry	marble cake
buckle ♣(Maritimes)	matrimonial cake
bombe	milk pudding
Boston cream pie	mille feuille
bread pudding	mousse
brown Betty	Nanaimo bar
brownie	napoleon
Bundt cake	panettone
burfi	pastry
carrot cake	petit four
cassata	plum cake
charlotte	plum pudding
charlotte russe	poppy seed cake
cheesecake	pound cake
Chelsea bun	poutine ♣(NB)
chiffon cake	queen of puddings
Christmas cake	rice pudding
Christmas pudding	Sachertorte
cinnamon bun	semolina pudding
clafoutis	shortcake
cobbler	spice cake
coffee cake	sponge cake
cottage pudding	sticky bun
crisp	stollen
crumble	streusel
cupcake	summer pudding
dainties ♣(Prairies & NW Ont.)	Swiss roll
date square ♣	tapioca pudding
devil's food cake	tiramisù
Dobos torte	torte
duff	trifle
Dutch apple cake	upside-down cake
figgy duff ♣(Nfld)	vinarterta ♣
floating island	wedding cake
fruitcake	yule log
genoise	zabaglione
gingerbread	*See also* PIES, TARTS, & TURNOVERS *and* DOUGHNUTS & DEEP-FRIED SWEETS.

officiating STANDARD, level, quality. **3** *the calibre of a gun* BORE, diameter, gauge.

call ▶ verb **1** *'Wait for me!' she called* CRY (OUT), shout, yell, hail, bellow, roar, bawl, vociferate; *informal* holler. **2** *I'll call you tomorrow* PHONE, telephone, get someone on the phone, give someone a call, give someone a ring, give someone a buzz. **3** *dinner's ready — call the kids* SUMMON, send for, assemble, muster, invite, order. **4** *the prime minister called a meeting* CONVENE, summon, assemble; *formal* convoke. **5** *they called their son Liam* NAME, christen, baptize; designate, style, term, dub; *formal* denominate. **6** *yes, I would call him a friend* DESCRIBE as, regard as, look on as, consider to be.
▶ noun **1** *I heard calls from the auditorium* CRY, shout, yell, roar, scream, exclamation, vociferation; *informal* holler. **2** *the call of the loon* CRY, song, sound. **3** *I'll give you a call tomorrow* PHONE CALL, telephone call, ring;

informal buzz. **4** *he paid a call on Harold* VISIT, social call. **5** *a call for party unity* APPEAL, request, plea, entreaty. **6** *the last call for passengers on flight 701* SUMMONS, request. **7** *there's no call for expensive wine here* DEMAND, desire, market. **8** *the call of the sea* ATTRACTION, appeal, lure, allure, spell, pull, draw. **9** *it's your call* DECISION, ruling, judgment, verdict.
■ **call for** *desperate times call for desperate measures* REQUIRE, need, necessitate; justify, warrant.
■ **call something off** CANCEL, abandon, scrap, drop, axe, scrub, nix; end, terminate.
■ **call on 1** *I might call on her later* VISIT, pay a visit to, go and see, drop in on, pop in on, drop/pop/stop by, visit with. **2** *he called on the government to hold a plebiscite* APPEAL TO, ask, request, petition, urge, exhort. **3** *we are able to call on qualified staff* HAVE RECOURSE TO, avail oneself of, draw on, make use of.
■ **call the shots** BE IN CHARGE, be in control, be the boss, be at the helm/wheel, be in the driver's seat, pull the strings, run the show, rule the roost.
■ **call to mind** *this calls to mind the last constitutional debate* EVOKE, bring to mind, call up, conjure up.
■ **call someone up 1** *Roland called me up to ask me out.* See CALL *verb* sense 2. **2** *they called up the reservists* ENLIST, recruit, conscript; draft. **3** *he was called up from the minors* SELECT, pick, choose.
■ **on call** ON DUTY, on standby, available.

calligraphy ▶ noun HANDWRITING, script, penmanship, hand, pen.

calling ▶ noun PROFESSION, occupation, vocation, call, summons, career, work, employment, job, business, trade, craft, line (of work); *informal* bag; *archaic* employ.

callous ▶ adjective HEARTLESS, unfeeling, uncaring, cold, cold-hearted, hard, as hard as nails, hard-hearted, insensitive, lacking compassion, hardbitten, hard-nosed, hard-edged, unsympathetic.
— OPPOSITES: kind, compassionate.

callow ▶ adjective IMMATURE, inexperienced, juvenile, adolescent, naive, green, raw, untried, unworldly, unsophisticated; *informal* wet behind the ears.
— OPPOSITES: mature.

calm ▶ adjective **1** *she seemed very calm* SERENE, tranquil, relaxed, unruffled, unperturbed, unflustered, untroubled; equable, even-tempered; placid, unexcitable, unemotional, phlegmatic; composed, {calm, cool, and collected}, cool-headed, self-possessed; *informal* unflappable, unfazed, nonplussed. **2** *the night was calm* WINDLESS, still, tranquil, serene, (Nfld) civil ♣, quiet. **3** *the calm waters of the lake* TRANQUIL, still, smooth, (Nfld) civil ♣, glassy, like a millpond; *literary* stilly.
— OPPOSITES: excited, nervous, stormy.
▶ noun **1** *calm prevailed* TRANQUILLITY, stillness, calmness, quiet, quietness, quietude, peace, peacefulness. **2** *his usual calm deserted him* COMPOSURE, coolness, calmness, self-possession, sang-froid; serenity, tranquility, equanimity, equability, placidness, placidity; *informal* cool, unflappability.
▶ verb **1** *I tried to calm him down* SOOTHE, pacify, placate, mollify, appease, conciliate, quiet (down), relax. **2** *she forced herself to calm down* COMPOSE ONESELF, recover/regain one's composure, control oneself, pull oneself together, simmer down, cool down/off, take it easy; *informal* get a grip, keep one's shirt on, wind down, chill (out), cool one's jets, hang/stay loose, decompress.
— OPPOSITES: excite, upset.

calumny ▶ noun SLANDER, defamation (of character), character assassination, libel; vilification, traducement, obloquy, verbal abuse; *informal* mud-slinging, trash-talk; *rare* contumely.

camaraderie ▶ noun FRIENDSHIP, comradeship, fellowship, companionship, fraternity, conviviality; mutual support, team spirit, esprit de corps.

cameo ▶ noun BIT PART, vignette.

camouflage ▶ noun 1 *pieces of turf served for camouflage* DISGUISE, concealment, cover, screen. 2 *her indifference was merely camouflage* FACADE, (false) front, smokescreen, cover-up, mask, blind, screen, masquerade, dissimulation, pretense.
▶ verb *the van was camouflaged with branches* DISGUISE, hide, conceal, keep hidden, mask, screen, cover (up).

camp[1] ▶ noun 1 *a kids' camp* CAMPSITE, campground, encampment, bivouac. 2 *the liberal and conservative camps* FACTION, wing, group, lobby, caucus, bloc, party, coterie, sect, cabal.
▶ verb *they camped in a field* PITCH TENTS, set up camp, encamp, bivouac.

camp[2] (*informal*) ▶ adjective 1 *a highly camp actor* EFFEMINATE, effete, mincing; *informal* campy, limp-wristed. 2 *camp humour* EXAGGERATED, theatrical, affected; *informal* over the top, camped up.
– OPPOSITES: macho.
■ **camp it up** POSTURE, behave theatrically/affectedly, overact; *informal* ham it up.

campaign ▶ noun 1 *Napoleon's Russian campaign* MILITARY OPERATION(S), manoeuvre(s); crusade, war, battle, offensive, attack. 2 *the campaign to reduce vehicle emissions* CRUSADE, drive, push, struggle; operation, strategy, battle plan.
▶ verb 1 *they are campaigning for political reform* CRUSADE, fight, battle, push, press, strive, struggle, lobby. 2 *she campaigned as a political outsider* RUN/STAND FOR OFFICE, canvass, mainstreet ♣, barnstorm, electioneer, stump, go on the hustings, glad-hand.

campaigner ▶ noun ACTIVIST, fighter, crusader; champion, advocate, promoter; *informal* libber.

camper ▶ noun RECREATIONAL VEHICLE, RV, motorhome; *proprietary* Winnebago, trailer, house trailer, tent trailer, fifth wheel (trailer).

can ▶ noun TIN, canister, bin; garbage can, jerry can, oil can, spray can.
▶ verb FIRE, dismiss, axe, let go, lay off, sack.

Canada ▶ noun the Dominion, the True North, the Great White North, Johnny Canuck.

Canadian Forces ▶ plural noun Canadian Armed Forces ♣; Army, Land Forces Command ♣; Navy, Maritime Command ♣; Air Force, Air Command ♣.

canal ▶ noun 1 *barges chugged up the canal* INLAND WATERWAY, watercourse, channel. 2 *the ear canal* DUCT, tube, passage.

cancel ▶ verb 1 *the meeting was cancelled* CALL OFF, abandon, scrap, drop, axe, scrub, nix. 2 *his visa has been cancelled* ANNUL, invalidate, nullify, declare null and void, void; revoke, rescind, retract, countermand, withdraw; *Law* vacate. 3 *rising unemployment cancelled out earlier economic gains* NEUTRALIZE, counterbalance, counteract, balance (out), countervail, compensate for; negate, nullify, wipe out.

cancer ▶ noun 1 *most skin cancers are curable* MALIGNANT GROWTH, cancerous growth, tumour, malignancy; *technical* carcinoma, sarcoma, melanoma, lymphoma, myeloma. 2 *the cancer of slavery spread across the continent* EVIL, blight, scourge, poison, canker, plague; *archaic* pestilence.
– RELATED TERMS: carcinomatous, carcin-.

candid ▶ adjective 1 *his responses were remarkably candid* FRANK, outspoken, forthright, blunt, open, honest, truthful, sincere, direct, plain-spoken, straightforward, ingenuous, bluff; *informal* upfront, on the level, on the up and up. 2 *candid shots* UNPOSED, informal, uncontrived, impromptu, natural.
– OPPOSITES: guarded.

candidate ▶ noun *candidates should be computer-literate* (JOB) APPLICANT, job-seeker, interviewee; contender, contestant, nominee.

candle ▶ noun taper, sconce, votive candle; *archaic* glim.

candlestick ▶ noun CANDLE HOLDER, candelabra, menorah, flambeau.

candour ▶ noun FRANKNESS, openness, honesty, candidness, truthfulness, sincerity, forthrightness, directness, plain-spokenness, bluntness, straightforwardness, outspokenness; *informal* telling it like it is.

candy ▶ noun SWEET, confectionery, bonbon. See table.

Candy and Other Sweets

allsorts	jelly baby
bark	jelly bean
barley sugar	jujube
beernuts	kill
breath mint	kiss
brittle	knob ♣(Nfld)
bubble gum	lemon drop
butterscotch	licorice
candy cane	lollipop
candy corn	marshmallow
candy floss	mint
caramel	nob ♣(Nfld)
chewing gum	nougat
chocolate	peanut brittle
chocolate bar	peppermint
cotton candy	peppermint
dragée	knob ♣(Nfld)
drop	praline
fondant	saltwater taffy
fudge	spun sugar
gobstopper	sucker
gumdrop	sugar plum
gummi bear*	taffy
halvah	toffee
hard candy	Turkish delight
humbug	wine gum
jawbreaker	*Proprietary term.

cane ▶ noun 1 *a silver-topped cane* WALKING STICK, staff; alpenstock; crook, pikestaff. 2 *he was beaten with a cane* STICK, rod, birch; *historical* ferule.
▶ verb *Matthew was caned for bullying* BEAT, strike, hit, flog, thrash, lash, birch, flagellate; *informal* give someone a hiding, larrup, whale.

canine ▶ noun DOG, wolf, fox.
▶ adjective DOGLIKE, doggish; wolfish, wolflike, lupine; foxlike, vulpine.

canister ▶ noun CONTAINER, box, tin, can.

canker ▶ noun 1 *this plant is susceptible to canker* FUNGAL DISEASE, plant rot; blight. 2 *ear cankers* ULCER, ulceration, infection, sore, abscess. **3** *racism remains a canker. See* CANCER sense 2.

cannabis ▶ noun MARIJUANA, pot, hashish, hash, dope, grass, weed, Mary Jane, bud, bhang, hemp, kef, ganja, green, sinsemilla, skunkweed, locoweed; joint, reefer, doob, spliff.

cannibal ▶ noun MAN-EATER, people-eater.

cannon ▶ noun (MOUNTED) GUN, field gun, piece of artillery; mortar, howitzer; *historical* culverin, falconet.
▶ verb *the couple behind cannoned into us* COLLIDE WITH, hit, run into, crash into, plow into.

cannonade ▶ noun BOMBARDMENT, shelling, gunfire, artillery fire, barrage, pounding.

canny ▶ adjective SHREWD, astute, smart, sharp, sharp-witted, discerning, penetrating, discriminating, perceptive, perspicacious, wise, worldly-wise, sagacious; cunning, crafty, wily, as sharp as a tack, savvy; *dated* long-headed.
– OPPOSITES: foolish.

canoe ▶ noun *See table.*
▶ verb PADDLE, trip ♣.

Canoes

bastard canoe	dugout
(batard) ♣	express canoe ♣
birchbark	freight canoe ♣
Canadian canoe	Gander Bay boat ♣(Nfld)
canot du maître ♣	ice canoe ♣
Montreal canoe ♣	kayak
canot du nord ♣	outrigger
north canoe ♣	Peterborough canoe ♣
voyageur canoe ♣	pirogue
cedarstrip ♣	

canon ▶ noun **1** *the canons of fair play and equal opportunity* PRINCIPLE, rule, law, tenet, precept; standard, convention, criterion, measure. **2** *a set of ecclesiastical canons* LAW, decree, edict, statute, dictate, decretal. **3** *the Shakespeare canon* (LIST OF) WORKS, writings, oeuvre.

canonical ▶ adjective *the canonical method* RECOGNIZED, authoritative, authorized, accepted, sanctioned, approved, established, orthodox.
– OPPOSITES: unorthodox.

canonize ▶ verb BEATIFY, declare to be a saint; GLORIFY, deify, idolize.

canopy ▶ noun AWNING, shade, sunshade; marquee; baldachin, tester, chuppah.

cant[1] ▶ noun **1** *religious cant* HYPOCRISY, sanctimoniousness, sanctimony, pietism. **2** *thieves' cant* SLANG, jargon, idiom, argot, patois, speech, terminology, language; *informal* lingo, -speak, -ese.

cant[2] ▶ verb *the deck canted some twenty degrees* TILT, lean, slant, slope, incline; tip, list, bank, heel.
▶ noun *the cant of the walls* SLOPE, slant, tilt, angle, inclination.

cantankerous ▶ adjective BAD-TEMPERED, irascible, irritable, grumpy, grouchy, crotchety, tetchy, testy, crusty, curmudgeonly, ill-tempered, ill-humoured, ill-natured, peevish, cross, shirty, fractious, pettish, crabbed, crabby, prickly, touchy, snappish, snappy, chippy, cranky, ornery, bitchy.
– OPPOSITES: affable.

canteen ▶ noun **1** *a canteen of water* CONTAINER, flask, mickey ♣, bottle. **2** *the staff canteen* RESTAURANT, cafeteria, buffet, refectory, lunchroom, mess hall.

canvass ▶ verb **1** *he's canvassing for the Green Party* CAMPAIGN, electioneer, stump, mainstreet ♣, barnstorm, glad-hand. **2** *they promised to canvass all members* POLL, question, ask, survey, interview. **3** *they're canvassing support* SEEK, try to obtain.

canyon ▶ noun RAVINE, gorge, gully, defile, couloir; chasm, abyss, gulf, gulch, coulee.

cap ▶ noun **1** *his cap blew off in the wind. See the table at* HAT. **2** *a white plastic cap* LID, top, stopper, cork, bung. **3** *the cap on spending* (UPPER) LIMIT, ceiling; curb, check.
▶ verb **1** *mountains capped with snow* TOP, crown, cover, coat. **2** *his breakaway goal capped a great game* ROUND OFF, crown, top off, be a fitting climax to. **3** *they tried to cap each other's stories* BEAT, better, improve on, surpass, outdo, outshine, outstrip, top, upstage. **4** *budgets will be capped* SET A LIMIT ON, limit, restrict; curb, control, peg.

capability ▶ noun ABILITY, capacity, power, potential; competence, proficiency, adeptness, aptitude, faculty, wherewithal, experience, skill, skilfulness, talent, flair; *informal* know-how.

capable ▶ adjective *a very capable young woman* COMPETENT, able, efficient, effective, proficient, accomplished, adept, handy, experienced, skilful, skilled, talented, gifted; *informal* useful.
– OPPOSITES: incompetent.
■ **be capable of** *I'm quite capable of looking after myself* HAVE THE ABILITY TO, be equal to (the task of), be up to, have what it takes to.

capacious ▶ adjective ROOMY, spacious, ample, big, large, sizeable, generous; *formal* commodious.
– OPPOSITES: cramped, small.

capacity ▶ noun **1** *the capacity of the freezer* VOLUME, size, magnitude, dimensions, measurements, proportions. **2** *his capacity to inspire trust. See* CAPABILITY. **3** *in his capacity as Commander-in-Chief* POSITION, post, job, office; role, function.

cape[1] ▶ noun *a woollen cape* CLOAK, mantle, cope, wrap, stole, tippet, capelet, poncho, shawl; *historical* pelisse, mantelet.

cape[2] ▶ noun *the ship rounded the cape* HEADLAND, promontory, point, spit, head, foreland, horn, hook.

caper ▶ verb *children were capering about* SKIP, dance, romp, frisk, gambol, cavort, prance, frolic, leap, hop, jump, rollick.
▶ noun **1** *she did a little caper* DANCE, skip, hop, leap, jump. **2** (*informal*) *I'm too old for this kind of caper* STUNT, monkey business, escapade, prank, trick, mischief, foolery, tomfoolery, antics, hijinks, skylarking, lark, shenanigans.

capital ▶ noun **1** *Warsaw is the capital of Poland* FIRST CITY, seat of government, metropolis. **2** *she had enough capital to pull off the deal* MONEY, finance(s), funds, the wherewithal, the means, assets, wealth, resources, investment capital; *informal* cash, dough, bread, loot, bucks. **3** *he wrote the name in capitals* CAPITAL LETTERS, upper-case letters, block capitals; *informal* caps.

capitalism ▶ noun PRIVATE ENTERPRISE, free enterprise, the free market.
– OPPOSITES: communism.

capitalist ▶ noun FINANCIER, investor, industrialist; magnate, tycoon, entrepreneur, businessman, businesswoman.

capitalize ▶ verb *the capacity to capitalize new ventures* FINANCE, fund, underwrite, provide capital for, back; *informal* bankroll, stake, grubstake.
■ **capitalize on** TAKE ADVANTAGE OF, profit from, make the most of, exploit; *informal* cash in on.

capitulate ► verb SURRENDER, give in/up, yield, concede defeat, give up the struggle, submit, knuckle under; lay down one's arms, raise/show the white flag, throw in the towel/sponge.
— OPPOSITES: resist, hold out.

caprice ► noun **1** *his wife's caprices* WHIM, whimsy, vagary, fancy, fad, quirk, eccentricity, foible. **2** *the staff tired of his caprice* FICKLENESS, changeableness, volatility, capriciousness, unpredictability.

capricious ► adjective FICKLE, inconstant, changeable, variable, mercurial, volatile, unpredictable, temperamental; whimsical, fanciful, flighty, quirky, faddish.
— OPPOSITES: consistent.

capsize ► verb OVERTURN, turn over, turn upside down, upend, flip/tip/keel over, turn turtle; *Nautical* pitchpole; *archaic* overset.
— OPPOSITES: right.

capsule ► noun **1** *he swallowed a capsule* PILL, tablet, lozenge, pastille, drop; *informal* tab. **2** *a space capsule* MODULE, craft, probe.

captain ► noun **1** *the ship's captain* COMMANDER, master; *informal* skipper. **2** *the team's captain* LEADER, head; *informal* boss, skipper. **3** *a captain of industry* MAGNATE, tycoon, industrialist; chief, head, leader, principal; *informal* boss, number one, bigwig, big shot/gun/cheese/wheel/kahuna, honcho, top dog, top banana.
► verb *a vessel captained by a cutthroat* COMMAND, run, be in charge of, control, manage, govern; *informal* skipper.

caption ► noun TITLE, heading, wording, head, legend, subtitle; *proprietary* Surtitle, rubric, slogan.

captivate ► verb ENTHRALL, charm, enchant, bewitch, fascinate, beguile, entrance, enrapture, delight, attract, allure; engross, mesmerize, spellbind, hypnotize.
— OPPOSITES: repel, bore.

captive ► noun *release the captives* PRISONER, convict, detainee, inmate, abductee; prisoner of war, POW, internee; *informal* jailbird, yardbird, lifer.
► adjective *captive wild animals* CONFINED, caged, incarcerated, locked up; jailed, imprisoned, in prison, interned, detained, in captivity, under lock and key, behind bars.

captivity ► noun IMPRISONMENT, confinement, internment, incarceration, detention, custody.
— OPPOSITES: freedom.

capture ► verb **1** *the spy was captured in Moscow* CATCH, apprehend, seize, arrest; take prisoner/captive, imprison, detain, put/throw in jail, put behind bars, put under lock and key, incarcerate; *informal* nab, collar, bag, pick up. **2** *guerrillas captured a strategic district* OCCUPY, invade, conquer, seize, take (possession of). **3** *the music captured the atmosphere of a summer morning* EXPRESS, reproduce, represent, encapsulate. **4** *the tales of pirates captured the children's imaginations* ENGAGE, attract, catch, seize, hold.
— OPPOSITES: free.
► noun *he tried to evade capture* ARREST, apprehension, seizure, being taken prisoner/captive, imprisonment.

car ► noun **1** *he drove up in his car* AUTOMOBILE, auto, motor car; *informal* wheels, gas guzzler, jalopy, lemon, beater, junker, clunker, tin Lizzie, rustbucket. *See table.* **2** *the dining car* CARRIAGE, coach.

carafe ► noun FLASK, jug, pitcher, decanter, flagon.

caravan ► noun **1** *a refugee caravan* CONVOY, procession, column, train, cavalcade. **2** *a fishing*

Cars

compact	racing car
convertible	ragtop
coupe	roadster
dragster	runabout
four-by-four	sedan
four-door	soft top
GTi	sports car
hardtop	sport-utility vehicle
hatchback	station wagon
hearse	stretch limo
hot rod	stock car
jeep	subcompact
limousine	SUV
minivan	two-door
race car	

holiday in a caravan VAN, camper, trailer, RV, motorhome; *proprietary* Winnebago.

carbuncle ► noun BOIL, sore, abscess, pustule, wen; *technical* furuncle.

carcass ► noun *a lamb carcass* CORPSE, (dead) body, remains; *Medicine* cadaver; *informal* stiff, roadkill; *archaic* corse.

card ► noun **1** *a piece of stiff card* CARDBOARD, pasteboard, board, bristol board. **2** *I'll send her a card* GREETING CARD, postcard, hasty note ♣, notecard. **3** *she produced her card* IDENTIFICATION, ID, credentials, pass card, health card ♣, driver's licence; business card. **4** *she paid with her card* CREDIT CARD, debit card, bank card, cash card, charge card, affinity card, gold card, platinum card; Calling Card, phone card; *informal* plastic. **5** *the cards were dealt* PLAYING CARD; (**cards**) pack of cards. *See table.* **6** (*informal*) *he said she was a card* ECCENTRIC, character; JOKER, wit, wag, jester, clown, comedian; *informal* laugh, scream, hoot, riot, jokester.

Card Games

baccarat	lansquenet
beggar-thy-neighbour	monte
bezique	nap
blackjack	old maid
brag	pinochle
bridge	piquet
canasta	poker
chemin de fer	rouge-et-noir
contract bridge	rummy
coon-can	skat
crazy eights	snap
cribbage	solitaire
duplicate bridge/whist	solo
écarté	stook ♣(West)
euchre	stud poker
fan-tan	tarabish ♣(Cape Breton)
faro	three-card monte
five hundred	twenty-one
forty-five	war
gin rummy	whist
hearts	

cardinal ► adjective FUNDAMENTAL, basic, main, chief, primary, crucial, pivotal, prime, principal, paramount, pre-eminent, highest, key, essential.
— OPPOSITES: unimportant.

care ► noun **1** *the care of the child* SAFEKEEPING, supervision, custody, charge, protection, control,

responsibility; guardianship, wardship. **2** *handle with care* CAUTION, carefulness, heedfulness, heed, attention, attentiveness. **3** *she chose her words with care* DISCRETION, judiciousness, forethought, thought, regard, heed, mindfulness; accuracy, precision, discrimination. **4** *the cares of the day* WORRY, anxiety, trouble, concern, stress, pressure, strain; sorrow, woe, hardship. **5** *care for the elderly* HELP, aid, assistance, succour, support, TLC; concern, consideration, thought, regard, solicitude.
— OPPOSITES: neglect, carelessness.
▶ **verb** *the teachers didn't care about our work* BE CONCERNED, worry (oneself), trouble/concern oneself, bother, mind, be interested; *informal* give a damn/hoot/rap.
■ **care for 1** *he cares for his children* LOVE, be fond of, be devoted to, treasure, adore, dote on, think the world of, worship, idolize. **2** *would you care for a cup of coffee?* LIKE, want, desire, fancy, feel like. **3** *the hospice cares for the terminally ill* LOOK AFTER, take care of, tend, attend to, minister to, nurse; be responsible for, keep safe, keep an eye on.

careen ▶ **verb** *the car careened down the highway* RUSH, hurtle, career, streak, shoot, race, bolt, dash, speed, run, whiz, zoom, flash, blast, charge, fly, pelt, go like the wind, belt, scoot, tear, zip, whip, zap, go like a bat out of hell, bomb, hightail, hare, clip.

career ▶ **noun 1** *a business career* PROFESSION, occupation, job, vocation, calling, employment, line (of work), walk of life, métier. **2** *a checkered career* HISTORY, existence, life, course, passage, path.
▶ **adjective** *a career politician* PROFESSIONAL, permanent, full-time.
▶ **verb** *they careered down the hill. See* CAREEN.

carefree ▶ **adjective** UNWORRIED, untroubled, blithe, airy, nonchalant, insouciant, happy-go-lucky, free and easy, easygoing, relaxed, mellow, laid-back, loosey-goosey.
— OPPOSITES: careworn.

careful ▶ **adjective 1** *be careful when you go up the stairs* CAUTIOUS, heedful, alert, attentive, watchful, vigilant, wary, on guard, circumspect. **2** *careful consideration of the facts* ATTENTIVE, conscientious, painstaking, meticulous, diligent, deliberate, assiduous, sedulous, scrupulous, punctilious, methodical; *informal* persnickety.
— OPPOSITES: careless, extravagant.

careless ▶ **adjective 1** *careless motorists* INATTENTIVE, incautious, negligent, absent-minded, remiss; heedless, irresponsible, impetuous, reckless, foolhardy; cavalier, supercilious, devil-may-care. **2** *careless work* SHODDY, slapdash, slipshod, scrappy, slovenly, negligent, lax, slack, disorganized, hasty, hurried; *informal* sloppy, slap-happy. **3** *a careless remark* THOUGHTLESS, insensitive, indiscreet, unguarded, incautious, inadvertent. **4** *she carried on, careless of the time* HEEDLESS, unconcerned, indifferent, oblivious.
— OPPOSITES: careful, meticulous.

caress ▶ **verb** STROKE, touch, fondle, brush, pet, skim, nuzzle.

caretaker ▶ **noun** JANITOR, attendant, porter, custodian, concierge, superintendent, super, maintenance man.
▶ **adjective** *a caretaker government* TEMPORARY, short-term, provisional, substitute, acting, interim, pro tem, stand-in, fill-in, stop-gap.
— OPPOSITES: permanent.

careworn ▶ **adjective** WORRIED, anxious, strained, stressed, dispirited; drained, drawn, gaunt, haggard.
— OPPOSITES: carefree.

cargo ▶ **noun** FREIGHT, load, haul, consignment, delivery, shipment; goods, merchandise, payload, lading.

caricature ▶ **noun** *a caricature of the Prime Minister* CARTOON, parody, satire, lampoon, burlesque; *informal* send-up, takeoff.
▶ **verb** *she has turned to caricaturing her fellow actors* PARODY, satirize, lampoon, make fun of, burlesque, mimic; *informal* send up, take off.

caring ▶ **adjective** KIND, kind-hearted, warm-hearted, tender; concerned, attentive, thoughtful, solicitous, altruistic, considerate; affectionate, loving, doting, fond; sympathetic, understanding, compassionate, feeling.
— OPPOSITES: cruel.

carnage ▶ **noun** SLAUGHTER, massacre, mass murder, butchery, bloodbath, bloodletting, gore; holocaust, pogrom, ethnic cleansing.

carnal ▶ **adjective** SEXUAL, sensual, erotic, lustful, lascivious, libidinous, lecherous, licentious; physical, bodily, corporeal, fleshly.
— OPPOSITES: spiritual.

carnival ▶ **noun 1** *the town's carnival* FESTIVAL, fiesta, fete, gala, jamboree, celebration, fest. **2** *he worked at a carnival* FAIR, amusement park, fun fair, exhibition ✦, ex ✦, amusement show, circus, big top, midway.

carnivorous ▶ **adjective** MEAT-EATING, flesh-eating, predatory, —— of prey.
— OPPOSITES: herbivorous, vegetarian.

carol ▶ **noun** *children sang carols* CHRISTMAS SONG, hymn, canticle.

carouse ▶ **verb** DRINK AND MAKE MERRY, go on a drinking bout, go on a spree; revel, celebrate, roister; *informal* party, booze, go boozing, binge, go on a binge, go on a bender, paint the town red, rave, whoop it up; *archaic* wassail.

carp ▶ **verb** COMPLAIN, cavil, grumble, grouse, whine, bleat, nag; *informal* gripe, grouch, beef, bellyache, moan, bitch, whinge, kvetch.
— OPPOSITES: praise.

carpenter ▶ **noun** WOODWORKER, cabinet-maker.

carpet ▶ **noun 1** *a Turkish carpet* RUG, mat, matting, floor covering. *See table.* **2** *a carpet of wildflowers* COVERING, blanket, layer, cover, cloak, mantle.
▶ **verb** *the gravel was carpeted in moss* COVER, coat, overlay, overspread, blanket.

Carpets & Rugs

area rug	numdah
Aubusson	oriental
Axminster	Persian
bearskin	prayer rug
Berber	rag rug
braided rug	runner
broadloom	shag carpet
dhurrie	sheepskin rug
floor cloth	Turkish
hearth rug	twist
hooked rug	wall-to-wall
kilim	Wilton

carriage ▶ **noun 1** *a horse and carriage. See table.* **2** *a railway carriage* COACH, car, flatcar.

Horse-Drawn Carriages, Carts, and Wagons

barouche	fly
brougham	four-in-hand
buckboard	gig
buggy	hackney carriage
cab	hansom
cabriolet	jaunting car (*Ireland*)
calash	landau
calèche ✤	long car/cart ✤(*Nfld*)
carriole	phaeton
carryall	post-chaise
chaise	Red River cart ✤
chariot	sloven ✤(*Atlantic*)
chuckwagon	stagecoach
clarence	stanhope
coach	sulky
Conestoga wagon	surrey
coupe	tallyho
curricle	tilbury
democrat wagon	tonga (*India*)
dogcart	trap
dray	troika (*Russia*)
droshky (*Russia*)	tumbrel
ekka (*India*)	victoria
fiacre	wagonette

carrier ▶ **noun** BEARER, conveyor, transporter, shipper; courier, hauler, porter.

carry ▶ **verb** 1 *she carried the box into the kitchen* CONVEY, transfer, move, take, bring, bear, lug, tote, fetch, cart. 2 *a cruise operator carrying a million passengers a year* TRANSPORT, convey, move, handle. 3 *satellites carry the signal across the country* TRANSMIT, conduct, relay, communicate, convey, dispatch, beam. 4 *the dinghy can carry the weight of the baggage* SUPPORT, sustain, stand; prop up, shore up, bolster. 5 *managers carry most responsibility* BEAR, accept, assume, undertake, shoulder, take on (oneself). 6 *she was carrying twins* BE PREGNANT WITH, bear, expect; *technical* be gravid with. 7 *she carried herself with assurance* CONDUCT, bear, hold; act, behave, acquit; *formal* comport. 8 *a resolution was carried* APPROVE, vote for, accept, endorse, ratify, pass; agree to, assent to, rubber-stamp; *informal* OK, give the thumbs up to. 9 *I carried the whole audience* WIN OVER, sway, convince, persuade, influence; motivate, stimulate. 10 *today's paper carried an article on housing policy* PUBLISH, print, communicate, distribute; broadcast, transmit. 11 *we carry a wide range* SELL, stock, keep (in stock), offer, have (for sale), retail, supply. 12 *most toxins carry warnings* DISPLAY, bear, exhibit, show, be marked with. 13 *it carries a penalty of two years' imprisonment* ENTAIL, involve, result in, occasion, have as a consequence. 14 *his voice carried across the field* BE AUDIBLE, travel, reach.
■ **be/get carried away** LOSE SELF-CONTROL, get overexcited, go too far; *informal* flip, lose it.
■ **carry something off** *she carried off four awards* WIN, secure, gain, achieve, collect; *informal* land, net, bag, scoop.
■ **carry on** *they carried on arguing* CONTINUE, keep (on), go on; persist in, persevere in, stick with/at. 2 (*informal*) *she was carrying on with other men* HAVE AN AFFAIR, commit adultery, have a fling, play around, mess around, fool around. 3 (*informal*) *I was always carrying on* MISBEHAVE, behave badly, get up to mischief, cause trouble, get up to no good, be

naughty; clown about/around, fool about/around, mess around, act up.
■ **carry something on** *we carried on a conversation* ENGAGE IN, conduct, undertake, be involved in, carry out, perform.
■ **carry something out** 1 *operations were carried out in secret* CONDUCT, perform, implement, execute. 2 *I carried out my promise to her* FULFILL, carry through, honour, redeem, make good; keep, observe, abide by, comply with, adhere to, stick to, keep faith with.

cart ▶ **noun** 1 *a horse-drawn cart*. See table at CARRIAGE. 2 *carts lined up at the checkout* SHOPPING CART, bundle buggy, handcart, pushcart, trolley, barrow.
▶ **verb** (*informal*) *he had the wreckage carted away* TRANSPORT, convey, haul, move, shift, take; carry, lug.

carte blanche ▶ **noun** FREE REIN, a free hand, a blank cheque.

carton ▶ **noun** BOX, package, cardboard box, container, pack, packet; milk carton, drinking box ✤, juice box.

cartoon ▶ **noun** 1 *a cartoon of the Prime Minister* CARICATURE, parody, lampoon, satire; *informal* takeoff, send-up. 2 *he was reading cartoons* COMIC STRIP, comic, funnies, graphic novel. 3 *they watched cartoons on television* ANIMATED FILM, animation, toon, anime. 4 *detailed cartoons for a full-size portrait* SKETCH, rough, outline, preliminary drawing, underdrawing.

cartridge ▶ **noun** 1 *a toner cartridge* CASSETTE, canister, container, magazine. 2 *a rifle cartridge* BULLET, round, shell, charge, shot.

carve ▶ **verb** 1 *she carved horn handles* SCULPT, sculpture; cut, hew, whittle; form, shape, fashion. 2 *I carved my initials on the tree* ENGRAVE, etch, incise, score. 3 *he carved the roast chicken* SLICE, cut up, chop.
■ **carved in stone** UNALTERABLE, immutable, unchangeable, irreversible, irrevocable.
■ **carve something up** DIVIDE, partition, apportion, subdivide, split up, break up; share out, dole out; *informal* divvy up.

carving ▶ **noun** SCULPTURE, model, statue, statuette, figure, figurine.

cascade ▶ **noun** WATERFALL, cataract, falls, rapids, chute ✤, white water.
▶ **verb** *rain cascaded from the roof* POUR, gush, surge, spill, stream, flow, issue, spurt.

case¹ ▶ **noun** 1 *a classic case of overreaction* INSTANCE, occurrence, manifestation, demonstration, exposition, exhibition; example, illustration, specimen, sample, exemplification. 2 *if that is the case, I will have to find somebody else* SITUATION, position, state of affairs, the lay of the land; circumstances, conditions, facts, how things stand; *informal* score. 3 *the officers on the case* INVESTIGATION, inquiry, examination, exploration, probe, search, inquest. 4 *urgent cases* PATIENT, sick person, invalid, sufferer, victim. 5 *she lost her case* LAWSUIT, (legal) action, legal dispute, suit, trial, legal/judicial proceedings, litigation. 6 *a strong case* ARGUMENT, contention, reasoning, logic, defence, justification, vindication, exposition, thesis.

case² ▶ **noun** 1 *a cigarette case* CONTAINER, box, canister, receptacle, holder. 2 *a seed case* CASING, cover, covering, sheath, sheathing, envelope, sleeve, jacket, integument. 3 *a case of wine* CRATE, box, pack; two-four. 4 *a glass display case* CABINET, cupboard, buffet.
▶ **verb** (*informal*) *a thief casing the joint* RECONNOITRE, inspect, examine, survey, explore, check out.

cash ▶ noun **1** *a wallet stuffed with cash* MONEY, currency, hard cash; (bank) notes, coins, change, bills; *informal* dough, bread, loot, moolah, bucks, dinero, lucre. **2** *a lack of cash* FINANCE, money, resources, funds, assets, the means, the wherewithal.
– OPPOSITES: cheque, credit.
▶ verb *the bank cashed her cheque* EXCHANGE, change, convert into cash/money; honour, pay, accept.
■ **cash in on** TAKE ADVANTAGE OF, exploit, milk; make money from, profit from, make a killing from.

cashier ▶ noun *the cashier took the cheque* CHECKOUT GIRL/BOY/PERSON, clerk; bank clerk, teller, banker, treasurer, bursar, purser.

casing ▶ noun COVER, case, shell, envelope, sheath, sheathing, sleeve, jacket, housing.

casino ▶ noun GAMBLING HOUSE, gambling club, gambling den, gaming house.

cask ▶ noun BARREL, keg, butt, tun, vat, drum, hogshead; *historical* firkin.

casket ▶ noun **1** *a small casket* BOX, chest, case, container, receptacle. **2** *the casket of a dead soldier* COFFIN, sarcophagus; *informal* box; *humorous* wooden overcoat.

casserole ▶ noun *See table at* STEW.

cassette ▶ noun TAPE, video, cartridge; *dated* eight-track.

cast ▶ verb **1** *he cast the stone into the stream* THROW, toss, huck ✤, fling, pitch, hurl, lob, chuck. **2** *fishermen cast their nets* SPREAD, throw, open out. **3** *she cast a fearful glance over her shoulder* DIRECT, shoot, throw, send. **4** *each citizen cast a vote* REGISTER, record, enter, file, vote. **5** *the fire cast a soft light* EMIT, give off, send out, radiate. **6** *the figures cast shadows* FORM, create, produce; project, throw. **7** *the stags' antlers are cast each year* SHED, lose, discard, slough off. **8** *a figure cast by hand* MOULD, fashion, form, shape, model; sculpt, sculpture, forge. **9** *they were cast as extras* CHOOSE, select, pick, name, nominate.
▶ noun **1** *a cast of the writer's hand* MOULD, die, matrix, shape, casting, model. **2** *a cast of the dice* THROW, toss, fling, pitch, hurl, lob, chuck. **3** *an inquiring cast of mind* TYPE, sort, kind, character, variety, class, style, stamp, nature. **4** *the cast of 'The Barber of Seville'* ACTORS, performers, players, company, troupe; dramatis personae, characters.
■ **cast something aside** DISCARD, reject, throw away/out, get rid of, dispose of, abandon.

castaway ▶ adjective **1** *castaway sailors* SHIPWRECKED, wrecked, stranded, aground. **2** *castaway clothing* CAST-OFF, discarded, used, throwaway.

caste ▶ noun (SOCIAL) CLASS, social order, rank, level, stratum, echelon, status; *dated* estate, station.

castigate ▶ verb REPRIMAND, rebuke, admonish, chastise, chide, censure, upbraid, reprove, reproach, scold, berate, take to task, lambaste, give someone a piece of one's mind; *informal* haul/rake over the coals, tell off, give someone an earful, give someone a tongue-lashing, give someone a roasting, rap someone on the knuckles, slap someone's wrist, dress down, bawl out, give someone hell, blow up at, lay into, blast, zing, have a go at, tear a strip off of someone, give someone what for, chew out, ream out; *rare* reprehend.
– OPPOSITES: praise, commend.

castle ▶ noun FORTRESS, fort, stronghold, fortification, keep, citadel.

castrate ▶ verb NEUTER, geld, cut, desex, unsex, sterilize, fix, alter, doctor; *archaic* emasculate.

casual ▶ adjective **1** *a casual attitude to life* INDIFFERENT, apathetic, uncaring, unconcerned; lackadaisical, blasé, nonchalant, insouciant, offhand, flippant; easygoing, free and easy, blithe, carefree, devil-may-care; *informal* laid-back, loosey-goosey, Type-B. **2** *a casual remark* OFFHAND, spontaneous, unpremeditated, unthinking, unconsidered, impromptu, throwaway, unguarded; *informal* off-the-cuff. **3** *a casual glance* CURSORY, perfunctory, superficial, passing, fleeting; hasty, brief, quick. **4** *a casual acquaintance* SLIGHT, superficial. **5** *casual work* TEMPORARY, part-time, freelance, impermanent, irregular, occasional. **6** *casual sex* PROMISCUOUS, extramarital, free. **7** *a casual meeting changed his life* CHANCE, accidental, unplanned, unintended, unexpected, unforeseen, unanticipated, fortuitous, serendipitous, adventitious. **8** *a casual shirt* INFORMAL, comfortable, leisure, everyday; *informal* sporty. **9** *the inn's casual atmosphere* RELAXED, friendly, informal, unceremonious, easygoing, free and easy; *informal* laid-back.
– OPPOSITES: careful, planned, formal.

casualty ▶ noun VICTIM, fatality, loss, MIA; (**casualties**) dead and injured, missing (in action).

casuistry ▶ noun SOPHISTRY, specious reasoning, speciousness.

cat ▶ noun FELINE, tomcat, tom, kitten, mouser; *informal* pussy (cat), puss, kitty; *archaic* grimalkin. *See table.*

Cats

Domestic	Wild
Abyssinian cat	Bengal tiger
alley cat	bobcat
Angora	Canada lynx
Birman	caracal
Burmese cat	catamount
calico	cheetah
chinchilla	clouded leopard
ginger	cougar
Himalayan	eyra
longhair	jaguar
Maine Coon	jaguarundi
Manx	leopard
marmalade	lion
Persian	lynx
Rex	margay
Russian Blue	mountain lion
shorthair	ocelot
Siamese	panther
tabby	puma
tortoiseshell	Siberian tiger
	snow leopard
	tiger
	tiger cat
	wildcat

cataclysm ▶ noun DISASTER, catastrophe, calamity, tragedy, devastation, holocaust, ruin, ruination, upheaval, convulsion, apocalypse.

catacombs ▶ plural noun UNDERGROUND CEMETERY, crypt, vault, tomb, ossuary.

catalogue ▶ noun **1** *a library catalogue* DIRECTORY, register, index, list, listing, record, archive, inventory. **2** *a mail-order catalogue* BROCHURE, magalogue, mailer, wish book.
▶ verb *the collection is fully catalogued* CLASSIFY,

categorize, systematize, index, list, archive, make an inventory of, inventory, record, itemize.

catalyst ▸ noun STIMULUS, stimulation, spark, sparkplug, spur, incitement, impetus.

catapult ▸ verb *the boulder was catapulted into the sea* PROPEL, launch, hurl, fling, send flying, fire, blast, shoot.

cataract ▸ noun WATERFALL, cascade, falls, rapids, white water.

catastrophe ▸ noun DISASTER, calamity, cataclysm, holocaust, havoc, ruin, ruination, tragedy; adversity, blight, trouble, trial, tribulation.

catastrophic ▸ adjective DISASTROUS, calamitous, cataclysmic, apocalyptic, ruinous, tragic, fatal, dire, awful, terrible, dreadful.

catcall ▸ noun WHISTLE, boo, hiss, jeer, raspberry, taunt; (**catcalls**) scoffing, abuse, taunting, derision.

catch ▸ verb **1** *he caught the ball* SEIZE, grab, snatch, seize/grab/take hold of, grasp, grip, trap, clutch, clench; receive, get, intercept. **2** *we've caught the thief* CAPTURE, seize; apprehend, arrest, take prisoner/captive, take into custody; trap, snare, ensnare; net, hook, land; *informal* nab, collar, run in, bust. **3** *her heel caught in a hole* BECOME TRAPPED, become entangled, snag. **4** *she caught the last bus* BE IN TIME FOR, make, get; board, get on, step aboard. **5** *they were caught siphoning gas* DISCOVER, find, come upon/across, stumble on, chance on; surprise, catch red-handed, catch in the act. **6** *it caught his imagination* ENGAGE, capture, attract, draw, grab, grip, seize; hold, absorb, engross. **7** *she caught a trace of aftershave* PERCEIVE, notice, observe, discern, detect, note, make out. **8** *I couldn't catch what she was saying* HEAR, perceive, discern, make out; understand, comprehend, grasp, apprehend; *informal* get, get the drift of, figure out. **9** *it caught the flavour of the sixties* EVOKE, conjure up, call to mind, recall, encapsulate, capture. **10** *the blow caught her on the side of her face* HIT, strike, slap, smack, bang. **11** *he caught malaria* BECOME INFECTED WITH, contract, get, fall ill with, be taken ill with, develop, come down with, be struck down with. **12** *the kindling wouldn't catch* IGNITE, start burning, catch fire, kindle.
— OPPOSITES: drop, release, miss.
▸ noun **1** *he inspected the catch* HAUL, net, bag, yield. **2** *he secured the catch* LATCH, lock, fastener, clasp, hasp. **3** *it looks great, but there's a catch* SNAG, disadvantage, drawback, stumbling block, hitch, fly in the ointment, pitfall, complication, problem, hiccup, difficulty; trap, trick, snare.

■ **catch on 1** *radio soon caught on* BECOME POPULAR/FASHIONABLE, take off, boom, flourish, thrive. **2** *I caught on fast* UNDERSTAND, comprehend, learn, see the light; *informal* cotton on, latch on, get the picture/message, get wise.

■ **catch up to someone** DRAW LEVEL (WITH), reach; gain on, close in on.

catching ▸ adjective (*informal*) INFECTIOUS, contagious, communicable, transmittable, transmissible, infective.

catchphrase ▸ noun SAYING, quotation, quote, slogan, motto, catchword, watchword, byword, buzzword, tag (line), mantra.

catch-22 ▸ noun DILEMMA, quandary, chicken-and-egg problem, vicious circle.

catchy ▸ adjective MEMORABLE, unforgettable, haunting; appealing, popular; singable, melodious, tuneful.

categorical ▸ adjective UNQUALIFIED,

unconditional, unequivocal, absolute, explicit, express, unambiguous, definite, direct, downright, outright, emphatic, positive, point-blank, conclusive, without reservations, out-and-out.
— OPPOSITES: qualified, equivocal.

categorize ▸ verb CLASSIFY, class, group, grade, rate, designate; order, arrange, sort, rank; file, catalogue, list, index; typecast, pigeonhole, stereotype.

category ▸ noun CLASS, classification, group, grouping, bracket, heading, set; type, sort, kind, variety, species, breed, brand, make, model; grade, order, rank; *informal* pigeonhole.

cater ▸ verb **1** *we cater for vegetarians* PROVIDE FOOD FOR, feed, serve, cook for. **2** *a resort catering to older travellers* SERVE, provide for, meet the needs/wants of, accommodate; satisfy, indulge, pander to, gratify. **3** *he seemed to cater to all tastes* TAKE INTO ACCOUNT/CONSIDERATION, allow for, consider, bear in mind, make provision for, have regard for.

caterwaul ▸ verb HOWL, wail, bawl, cry, yell, scream, screech, yowl, ululate.

catharsis ▸ noun (EMOTIONAL) RELEASE, relief, release, venting; purging, purgation, purification, cleansing; *Psychoanalysis* abreaction.

catholic ▸ adjective UNIVERSAL, diverse, diversified, wide, broad, broad-based, eclectic, liberal, latitudinarian; comprehensive, all-encompassing, all-embracing, all-inclusive.
— OPPOSITES: narrow.

cattle ▸ plural noun COWS, bovines, oxen, bulls, cattle beasts; stock, livestock.
— RELATED TERMS: bovine. *See table.*

Cattle

Aberdeen Angus	Holstein
Alderney	Jersey
Ayrshire	kouprey
beefalo	Limousin
bison	longhorn
Brahma	ox
buffalo	plains bison
Charolais	Shorthorn
Galloway	Simmental
gaur	Texas Longhorn
gayal	wood bison
Guernsey	yak
Hereford	zebu
Highland cattle	

catty ▸ adjective (*informal*) *a catty remark. See* SPITEFUL.

caucus ▸ noun **1** *the Tory caucus* MEMBERS, party, faction, camp, bloc, group, set, band, ring, cabal, coterie, pressure group, ginger group. **2** *caucuses will be held in eleven states* MEETING, assembly, gathering, congress, conference, convention, rally, convocation.

cauldron ▸ noun POT, kettle.

cause ▸ noun **1** *the cause of the fire* SOURCE, root, origin, beginning(s), starting point; mainspring, base, basis, foundation, fountainhead; originator, author, creator, producer, agent. **2** *there is no cause for alarm* REASON, grounds, justification, call, need, necessity, occasion, excuse, pretext. **3** *the cause of human rights | a good cause* PRINCIPLE, ideal, belief, conviction; object, end, aim, objective, purpose, mission; charity. **4** *he went to plead his cause* CASE, suit,

lawsuit, action, dispute.
— RELATED TERMS: -genic, -facient.
— OPPOSITES: effect, result.

▶ **verb** *this disease can cause blindness* BRING ABOUT, give rise to, lead to, result in, create, produce, generate, engender, spawn, bring on, precipitate, prompt, provoke, trigger, make happen, induce, inspire, promote, foster; *literary* beget, enkindle.
— OPPOSITES: result from.

caustic ▶ **adjective** **1** *a caustic cleaner* CORROSIVE, corroding, abrasive, mordant, acid. **2** *a caustic comment* SARCASTIC, cutting, biting, mordant, sharp, bitter, scathing, derisive, sardonic, ironic, scornful, trenchant, acerbic, abrasive, vitriolic, acidulous.

caution ▶ **noun** **1** *proceed with caution* CARE, carefulness, heedfulness, heed, attention, attentiveness, alertness, watchfulness, vigilance, circumspection, discretion, prudence. **2** *a first offender may receive a caution* WARNING, admonishment, injunction; reprimand, rebuke, reproof, scolding, talking-to.
▶ **verb** ADVISE, warn, counsel; admonish, reprimand, rebuke, reprove, scold; *informal* give someone a talking-to.

cautious ▶ **adjective** CAREFUL, heedful, attentive, alert, watchful, vigilant, circumspect, prudent; cagey, canny.
— OPPOSITES: reckless.

cavalcade ▶ **noun** PROCESSION, parade, motorcade, cortège, march past.

cavalier ▶ **noun** (*archaic*) *foot soldiers and cavaliers* HORSEMAN, equestrian; cavalryman, trooper, knight.
▶ **adjective** *a cavalier disregard for danger* OFFHAND, indifferent, casual, dismissive, insouciant, unconcerned; supercilious, patronizing, condescending, disdainful, scornful, contemptuous; *informal* couldn't-care-less, devil-may-care.

cavalry ▶ **plural noun** MOUNTED TROOPS, cavalrymen, troopers, horse; *historical* dragoons, lancers, hussars.

cave ▶ **noun** CAVERN, grotto, underground chamber, pothole; cellar, vault, crypt.
— RELATED TERMS: speleology, speleologist; spelunking, spelunker.
■ **cave in 1** *the roof caved in* COLLAPSE, fall in/down, give (way), crumble, subside. **2** *the manager caved in to their demands* YIELD, surrender, capitulate, submit, give in, back down, make concessions, throw in the towel.

caveat ▶ **noun** WARNING, caution, admonition; proviso, condition, stipulation, provision, clause, rider, qualification.

caveman, cavewoman ▶ **noun** CAVE-DWELLER, troglodyte, primitive man/woman, prehistoric man/woman; Neanderthal.

cavern ▶ **noun** LARGE CAVE, grotto, underground chamber/gallery, vault.

cavernous ▶ **adjective** VAST, huge, large, immense, spacious, roomy, airy, capacious, voluminous, extensive, deep; hollow, gaping, yawning; *formal* commodious.
— OPPOSITES: small.

cavil ▶ **verb** COMPLAIN, carp, grumble, grouse, whine, bleat, quibble, niggle, gripe, grouch, beef, bellyache, moan, bitch, whinge, kick up a fuss, kvetch.

cavity ▶ **noun** SPACE, chamber, hollow, hole, pocket, pouch; cavern, aperture; socket, gap, crater, pit.

cavort ▶ **verb** SKIP, dance, romp, jig, caper, frisk, play/horse around, gambol, prance, frolic, lark;

bounce, trip, leap, jump, bound, spring, hop; roughhouse, rollick.

cease ▶ **verb** **1** *hostilities had ceased* COME TO AN END, come to a halt, end, halt, stop, conclude, terminate, finish, draw to a close, be over. **2** *they ceased all military activity* BRING TO AN END, bring to a halt, end, halt, stop, conclude, terminate, finish, wind up, discontinue, suspend, break off; *informal* leave off.
— OPPOSITES: start, continue.
■ **without cease** CONTINUOUSLY, incessantly, unendingly, unremittingly, without a pause/break, on and on.

ceasefire ▶ **noun** ARMISTICE, truce, peace, suspension of hostilities.

ceaseless ▶ **adjective** CONTINUAL, constant, continuous; incessant, unceasing, unending, endless, never-ending, interminable, non-stop, uninterrupted, unremitting, relentless, unrelenting, unrelieved, sustained, persistent, eternal, perpetual.
— OPPOSITES: intermittent.

cede ▶ **verb** SURRENDER, concede, relinquish, yield, part with, give up; hand over, deliver up, give over, make over, transfer; abandon, forgo, sacrifice; *literary* forsake.

ceiling ▶ **noun** UPPER LIMIT, maximum, limitation.

ceinture fléchée (*Cdn*) ▶ **noun** arrow sash ✦, voyageur sash ✦, Assomption sash ✦.

celebrate ▶ **verb** **1** *they were celebrating their wedding anniversary* COMMEMORATE, observe, mark, keep, honour, remember, memorialize. **2** *let's all celebrate!* ENJOY ONESELF, have fun, have a good time, have a party, revel, roister, carouse, make merry; *informal* party, go out on the town, paint the town red, whoop it up, make whoopee, live it up, have a ball. **3** *he was celebrated for his achievements* PRAISE, extol, glorify, eulogize, reverence, honour, pay tribute to; *formal* laud.

celebrated ▶ **adjective** ACCLAIMED, admired, highly rated, lionized, revered, honoured, esteemed, exalted, vaunted, well-thought-of, ballyhooed; eminent, great, distinguished, prestigious, illustrious, pre-eminent, estimable, notable, of note, of repute; *formal* lauded.
— OPPOSITES: unsung.

celebration ▶ **noun** **1** *the celebration of his 50th birthday* COMMEMORATION, observance, marking, keeping. **2** *a birthday celebration for Eriq and Liam* PARTY, gathering, festivities, festival, fete, carnival, gala, jamboree, function; *informal* do, bash, shindig, whoop-up ✦, rave, bunfight. **3** *the celebration of the Eucharist* OBSERVANCE, performance, officiation, solemnization.

celebrity ▶ **noun** **1** *a sports celebrity* FAMOUS PERSON, VIP, very important person, personality, (big) name, famous/household name, star, superstar, celeb, somebody, someone, megastar. **2** *his celebrity grew* FAME, prominence, renown, eminence, pre-eminence, stardom, popularity, distinction, note, notability, prestige, stature, repute, reputation.
— OPPOSITES: obscurity.

celestial ▶ **adjective** **1** *a celestial body* (IN) SPACE, heavenly, astronomical, extraterrestrial, stellar, astral, planetary. **2** *celestial beings* HEAVENLY, holy, saintly, divine, godly, godlike, ethereal, otherworldly; immortal, angelic, seraphic, cherubic.
— OPPOSITES: earthly, hellish.

celibate ▶ **adjective** UNMARRIED, single, unwed,

spouseless; chaste, virginal, virgin, maidenly, maiden, intact, abstinent, self-denying.

cell ▶ noun **1** *a prison cell* ROOM, cubicle, chamber; dungeon, oubliette, lock-up. **2** *each cell of the honeycomb* COMPARTMENT, cavity, hole, hollow, section. **3** *terrorist cells* UNIT, faction, arm, section, ring, coterie, group.

cellar ▶ noun BASEMENT, vault, underground room, lower ground floor, downstairs; cantina; crypt, undercroft.
– OPPOSITES: attic.

cement ▶ noun MORTAR, grout, concrete; ADHESIVE, glue, fixative, gum, paste; superglue; mucilage.
▶ verb *he cemented the sample to a microscope slide* STICK, bond; fasten, fix, affix, attach, secure, bind, glue, gum, paste.

cemetery ▶ noun GRAVEYARD, churchyard, burial ground, burying ground, necropolis, memorial park/garden; *informal* boneyard; *historical* potter's field; *archaic* God's acre.

censor ▶ noun *the film censors* EXPURGATOR, bowdlerizer; examiner, inspector, editor.
▶ verb *letters home were censored* CUT, delete parts of, make cuts in, blue-pencil; edit, expurgate, bowdlerize, sanitize; *informal* clean up.

censorious ▶ adjective HYPERCRITICAL, overcritical, fault-finding, disapproving, condemnatory, denunciatory, deprecatory, disparaging, reproachful, reproving, censuring, captious, carping, sitting in judgment.
– OPPOSITES: complimentary.

censure ▶ verb *he was censured for his conduct.* See REPRIMAND *verb.*
▶ noun *a note of censure* CONDEMNATION, criticism, attack, abuse; reprimand, rebuke, admonishment, reproof, upbraiding, disapproval, reproach, scolding, obloquy; *informal* flak, dressing-down, tongue-lashing; *formal* excoriation, castigation.
– OPPOSITES: approval.

central ▶ adjective **1** *occupying a central position* MIDDLE, centre, halfway, midway, mid, median, medial, mean; *Anatomy* mesial. **2** *central Winnipeg* INNER, innermost, middle, mid; downtown. **3** *their central campaign issue* MAIN, chief, principal, primary, leading, foremost, first, most important, predominant, dominant, key, crucial, vital, essential, basic, fundamental, core, prime, premier, paramount, major, overriding; *informal* number-one.
– OPPOSITES: side, outer, subordinate.

centralize ▶ verb CONCENTRATE, consolidate, amalgamate, condense, unify, streamline, focus, rationalize.
– OPPOSITES: devolve.

centre ▶ noun *the centre of the town* MIDDLE, nucleus, heart, core, hub; middle point, midpoint, halfway point, mean, median.
– OPPOSITES: edge.
▶ verb *the story centres on a doctor* FOCUS, concentrate, pivot, hinge, revolve, be based.

centrepiece ▶ noun HIGHLIGHT, main feature, high point, best part, climax; focus of attention, focal point, centre of attention/interest, magnet, cynosure.

ceramics ▶ plural noun POTTERY, pots, china.

cereal ▶ noun. *See table.*

cerebral ▶ adjective INTELLECTUAL, academic, rational, logical, analytical, scholarly; bookish, brainy.
– OPPOSITES: emotional.

Cereal Grains

arborio rice	milo
barley	oat
basmati rice	Patna rice
brown rice	pearl millet
buckwheat	Red Fife wheat
bulgur	rice
corn	rye
durra	sorghum
durum	spelt wheat
einkorn wheat	teff
emmer wheat	triticale
jowar	wheat
Marquis wheat	wild rice
millet	

ceremonial ▶ adjective *a ceremonial occasion* FORMAL, official, state, public; ritual, ritualistic, prescribed, stately, courtly, solemn.
– OPPOSITES: informal.

ceremonious ▶ adjective DIGNIFIED, majestic, imposing, impressive, solemn, ritualistic, stately, formal; courtly, regal, imperial, elegant, grand, glorious, splendid, magnificent, resplendent, portentous; *informal* starchy.

ceremony ▶ noun **1** *a wedding ceremony* RITUAL, rite, ceremonial, observance; service, sacrament, liturgy, worship, celebration. **2** *the new Queen was proclaimed with due ceremony* POMP, protocol, formalities, niceties, decorum, etiquette, punctilio, politesse.

certain ▶ adjective **1** *I'm certain he's guilty* SURE, confident, positive, convinced, in no doubt, satisfied, assured, persuaded. **2** *it is certain that more changes are in the offing* UNQUESTIONABLE, sure, definite, beyond question, not in doubt, indubitable, undeniable, irrefutable, indisputable; obvious, evident, recognized, confirmed, accepted, acknowledged, undisputed, undoubted, unquestioned. **3** *they are certain to win* SURE, very likely, bound, destined. **4** *certain defeat* INEVITABLE, assured, destined, predestined; unavoidable, inescapable, inexorable, ineluctable. **5** *there is no certain cure for this* RELIABLE, dependable, trustworthy, foolproof, tried and tested, effective, guaranteed, sure, unfailing, infallible; *informal* sure-fire, idiot-proof, goof-proof. **6** *a certain sum of money* DETERMINED, definite, fixed, established, precise. **7** *a certain lady* PARTICULAR, specific, individual, special. **8** *to a certain extent that is true* MODERATE, modest, medium, middling; limited, small.
– OPPOSITES: doubtful, possible, unlikely.

certainly ▶ adverb *this is certainly a forgery* UNQUESTIONABLY, surely, assuredly, definitely, beyond/without question, without doubt, indubitably, undeniably, irrefutably, indisputably; obviously, patently, evidently, plainly, clearly, unmistakably, undisputedly, undoubtedly; sure as shootin', for sure.
– OPPOSITES: possibly.
▶ exclamation *'May I have one?' 'Certainly.'* YES, definitely, absolutely, sure, by all means, indeed, of course, naturally; affirmative, OK, okay.

certainty ▶ noun **1** *she knew with certainty that he was telling the truth* CONFIDENCE, sureness, positiveness, conviction, certitude, assurance. **2** *he accepted defeat as a certainty* INEVITABILITY, foregone conclusion; *informal* sure thing, cert, dead cert, no-brainer.
– OPPOSITES: doubt, possibility.

certificate ▶ noun GUARANTEE, certification, document, authorization, registration, authentication, credentials, accreditation, licence, diploma.

certify ▶ verb 1 *the aircraft was certified as airworthy* VERIFY, guarantee, attest, validate, confirm, substantiate, endorse, vouch for, testify to; provide evidence, give proof, prove, demonstrate. 2 *a certified hospital* ACCREDIT, recognize, license, authorize, approve, warrant.

certitude ▶ noun CERTAINTY, confidence, sureness, positiveness, conviction, assurance.
— OPPOSITES: doubt.

cessation ▶ noun END, ending, termination, stopping, halting, ceasing, finish, finishing, stoppage, conclusion, winding up, discontinuation, abandonment, suspension, breaking off, cutting short.
— OPPOSITES: start, resumption.

chafe ▶ verb 1 *the collar chafed his neck* ABRADE, graze, rub against, gall, scrape, scratch; *Medicine* excoriate. 2 *material chafed by the rock* WEAR AWAY/DOWN, erode, abrade, scour, scrape away. 3 *the bank chafed at the restrictions* BE ANGRY, be annoyed, be irritated, fume, be exasperated, be frustrated.

chaff ▶ noun 1 *separating the chaff from the grain* HUSKS, hulls, pods, shells, bran, shucks. 2 *the proposals were so much chaff* GARBAGE, dross, rubbish, trash, junk, crap, schlock. 3 *good-natured chaff* BANTER, repartee, teasing, ragging, joking, jesting, raillery, badinage, wisecracks, witticism(s); *informal* kidding, ribbing; *formal* persiflage.
▶ verb *the pleasures of chaffing your buddies* TEASE, make fun of, poke fun at, make sport of; *informal* rib, razz, kid, josh, have on, pull someone's leg, yank/pull someone's chain, goof on.

chagrin ▶ noun ANNOYANCE, irritation, vexation, exasperation, displeasure, dissatisfaction, discontent; anger, rage, fury, wrath, indignation, resentment; embarrassment, mortification, humiliation, shame.
— OPPOSITES: delight.

chagrined ▶ adjective See ANNOYED.

chain ▶ noun 1 *he was held in chains* FETTERS, shackles, irons, leg irons, manacles, handcuffs; *informal* cuffs, bracelets; *historical* bilboes. 2 *a chain of events* SERIES, succession, string, sequence, train, course.
▶ verb *she chained her bicycle to the railings* SECURE, fasten, tie, tether, hitch; restrain, shackle, fetter, manacle, handcuff.

chair ▶ noun 1 *he sat down on a chair* SEAT. *See table.* 2 *the chair of the committee. See* CHAIRMAN.
▶ verb *she chairs the economic committee* PRESIDE OVER, take the chair of; lead, direct, run, manage, control, be in charge of.

chairman, chairwoman ▶ noun CHAIR, chairperson, president, leader, convener; spokesperson, spokesman, spokeswoman.

chalet ▶ noun LODGE, cabin, cottage.

chalk
— RELATED TERMS: calcareous.
■ **chalk something up 1** *he has chalked up another success* ACHIEVE, attain, accomplish, gain, earn, win, succeed in making, make, get, obtain, notch up, rack up. 2 *I forgot completely — chalk it up to age* ATTRIBUTE, assign, ascribe, put down; blame on, pin on, lay at the door of.

Chairs

Adirondack chair	ladderback
armchair	lawn chair
barber chair	lounge chair
bar stool	Morris chair
Boston rocker	Muskoka chair ♣
butterfly chair	platform rocker
button-back	pressback
cane chair	recliner
captain's chair	rocker
dentist's chair	rocking chair
dining chair	sidechair
chaise longue	stacking chair
deck chair	stool
director's chair	straight-backed chair
easy chair	swivel chair
fiddleback	Windsor chair
fighting chair	wingback
folding chair	*See also* SOFAS & COUCHES.
high chair	

chalky ▶ adjective 1 *chalky skin* PALE, bloodless, pallid, colourless, wan, ashen, white, pasty. 2 *chalky bits at the bottom of the glass* POWDERY, gritty, granular.

challenge ▶ noun 1 *he accepted the challenge* DARE, provocation; summons. 2 *a challenge to his leadership* TEST, questioning, dispute, stand, opposition, confrontation. 3 *it was proving quite a challenge* PROBLEM, difficult task, test, trial.
▶ verb 1 *we challenged their statistics* QUESTION, disagree with, dispute, take issue with, protest against, call into question, object to. 2 *he challenged one of my men to a duel* DARE, summon, throw down the gauntlet to, drop the gloves ♣. 3 *changes that would challenge them* TEST, tax, strain, make demands on; stretch, stimulate, inspire, excite.

challenging ▶ adjective DEMANDING, testing, taxing, exacting; stretching, exciting, stimulating, inspiring; difficult, tough, hard, formidable, onerous, arduous, strenuous, gruelling; *formal* exigent.
— OPPOSITES: easy, uninspiring.

chamber ▶ noun 1 *a debating chamber* ROOM, hall, assembly room, auditorium. 2 *(archaic) we slept safely in our chamber* BEDROOM, room; *literary* bower; *historical* boudoir; *archaic* bedchamber. 3 *the left chamber of the heart* COMPARTMENT, cavity; *Anatomy* auricle, ventricle.

champagne ▶ noun SPARKLING WINE; spumante, cava; *informal* bubbly, fizz.

champion ▶ noun 1 *the world champion* WINNER, titleholder, defending champion, gold medallist, titlist; prizewinner, victor; *informal* champ, number one, king. 2 *a champion of change* ADVOCATE, proponent, promoter, supporter, defender, upholder, backer, exponent; campaigner, lobbyist, crusader, apologist, booster, flag-bearer. 3 *(historical) the king's champion* KNIGHT, man-at-arms, warrior.
▶ verb *championing the rights of refugees* ADVOCATE, promote, defend, uphold, support, back, stand up for, take someone's part; campaign for, lobby for, fight for, crusade for, stick up for.
— OPPOSITES: oppose.

championship ▶ noun *Westmount won the championship* TITLE, crown, first place, palm.

chance ▶ noun 1 *there was a chance he might be released* POSSIBILITY, prospect, probability, likelihood, likeliness, expectation, anticipation; risk, threat, danger. 2 *I gave her a chance to answer* OPPORTUNITY, opening, occasion, turn, time, window (of

opportunity); *informal* shot, kick at the can/cat ✤.
3 *Nigel took an awful chance* RISK, gamble, venture,
speculation, long shot, shot in the dark. **4** *pure chance*
ACCIDENT, coincidence, serendipity, fate, destiny,
fortuity, providence, happenstance; good fortune,
(good) luck, fluke.
▶ **adjective** *a chance discovery* ACCIDENTAL, fortuitous,
adventitious, fluky, coincidental, serendipitous;
unintentional, unintended, inadvertent, unplanned.
− OPPOSITES: intentional.
▶ **verb 1** *I chanced to meet him* HAPPEN. **2** *she chanced
another look* RISK, hazard, venture, try; *formal* essay.
■ **by chance** FORTUITOUSLY, by accident, accidentally,
coincidentally, serendipitously; unintentionally,
inadvertently.
■ **chance on/upon** COME ACROSS/UPON, run across/
into, happen on, light on, stumble on, find by
chance, meet (by chance), bump into.

chancy ▶ **adjective** (*informal*) RISKY, unpredictable,
uncertain, precarious; unsafe, insecure, tricky,
high-risk, hazardous, perilous, parlous; *informal* dicey,
hairy.
− OPPOSITES: predictable.

change ▶ **verb 1** *this could change the face of television* |
things have changed ALTER, make/become different,
adjust, adapt, amend, modify, revise, refine; reshape,
refashion, redesign, restyle, revamp, rework,
remodel, reorganize, reorder; vary, transform,
transfigure, transmute, metamorphose, evolve;
informal tweak, doctor, rejig; *technical* permute. **2** *they've
changed places* EXCHANGE, substitute, swap, switch,
replace, alternate, interchange.
− OPPOSITES: preserve, keep.
▶ **noun 1** *a change of plan* ALTERATION, modification,
variation, revision, amendment, adjustment,
adaptation; remodelling, reshaping, rearrangement,
reordering, restyling, reworking; metamorphosis,
transformation, evolution, mutation; *informal*
transmogrification. **2** *a change of government*
EXCHANGE, substitution, swap, switch, changeover,
replacement, alternation, interchange. **3** *I don't have
any change* COINS, loose/small change, (hard) cash,
silver, specie.
■ **have a change of heart**. *See* HEART.

changeable ▶ **adjective 1** *the weather will be
changeable* | *changeable moods* VARIABLE, inconstant,
varying, changing, fluctuating, irregular; erratic,
inconsistent, unstable, unsettled, turbulent,
protean; fickle, capricious, temperamental, volatile,
mercurial, unpredictable, blowing hot and cold;
informal up and down. **2** *the colours are changeable*
ALTERABLE, adjustable, modifiable, variable, mutable,
exchangeable, interchangeable, replaceable.
− OPPOSITES: constant.

changeless ▶ **adjective** UNCHANGING, unvarying,
timeless, static, fixed, permanent, constant,
unchanged, consistent, uniform, undeviating;
stable, steady, unchangeable, unalterable, invariable,
immutable.
− OPPOSITES: variable.

channel ▶ **noun 1** *sailing the North Channel* STRAIT(S),
sound, narrows, (sea) passage, (*Atlantic*) tickle ✤,
snye ✤. **2** *the water ran down a channel* DUCT, gutter,
conduit, trough, culvert, sluice, spillway, race, drain.
3 *a channel for their extraordinary energy* USE, medium,
vehicle, way of harnessing; release (mechanism),
safety valve, vent. **4** *a channel of communication* MEANS,
medium, instrument, mechanism, agency, vehicle,
route, avenue.

▶ **verb 1** *she channelled out a groove* HOLLOW OUT, gouge
(out), cut (out). **2** *many countries channel their aid
through charities* CONVEY, transmit, conduct, direct,
guide, relay, pass on, transfer.

chant ▶ **noun 1** *the protesters' chants* SHOUT, cry,
(rallying) call, cheer, slogan. **2** *the melodious chant of
the monks* INCANTATION, intonation, singing, song,
plainsong, recitative.
▶ **verb 1** *protesters were chanting slogans* SHOUT, chorus,
repeat. **2** *the choir chanted Psalm 118* SING, intone,
incant.

chaos ▶ **noun** DISORDER, disarray, disorganization,
confusion, mayhem, bedlam, pandemonium, havoc,
turmoil, tumult, commotion, disruption, upheaval,
uproar, maelstrom; a muddle, a mess, a shambles, a
free-for-all; anarchy, lawlessness, entropy; *informal*
hullabaloo, hoopla, all hell broken loose.
− OPPOSITES: order.

chaotic ▶ **adjective** DISORDERLY, disordered, in
disorder, in chaos, in disarray, disorganized,
topsy-turvy, in pandemonium, in turmoil, in uproar;
in a muddle, in a mess, messy, in a shambles;
anarchic, lawless, shambolic.

chap¹ ▶ **verb** *my skin chapped in the wind* BECOME RAW,
become sore, become inflamed, chafe, crack.

chap² ▶ **noun** *he's a nice chap*. *See* GUY.

chaperone ▶ **noun** *two teachers attended as
chaperones* SUPERVISOR, companion, duenna, escort,
minder, den mother.
▶ **verb** *she was chaperoned by her mother* ACCOMPANY,
escort, attend, watch over, keep an eye on, protect,
mind.

chapped ▶ **adjective** DRY, cracked, rough.

chapter ▶ **noun 1** *the first chapter of the book* SECTION,
division, part, portion. **2** *a new chapter in our history*
PERIOD, phase, page, stage, epoch, era. **3** *the Ontario
chapter of the Canadian Bar Association* BRANCH, division,
subdivision, section, department, lodge, wing, arm.
4 *the cathedral chapter* GOVERNING BODY, council,
assembly, convocation, synod, consistory.

char ▶ **verb** SCORCH, burn, singe, sear, blacken;
informal toast.

character ▶ **noun 1** *a forceful character* | *the character
of a town* PERSONALITY, nature, disposition,
temperament, temper, mentality, makeup; features,
qualities, properties, traits; spirit, essence, identity,
ethos, complexion, tone, feel, feeling. **2** *a woman of
character* INTEGRITY, honour, moral strength/fibre,
rectitude, uprightness; fortitude, strength,
backbone, resolve, grit, willpower; *informal* guts,
gutsiness. **3** *a stain on his character* REPUTATION, (good)
name, standing, stature, position, status. **4** (*informal*) *a
bit of a character* ECCENTRIC, oddity, madcap, crank,
individualist, nonconformist, rare bird, oddball, free
spirit. **5** *a boorish character* PERSON, man, woman, soul,
creature, individual, customer; *informal* cookie. **6** *the
characters develop throughout the play* PERSONA, role,
part; (**characters**) dramatis personae. **7** *thirty
characters per line* LETTER, figure, symbol, sign, mark.

characteristic ▶ **noun** *interesting characteristics*
ATTRIBUTE, feature, (essential) quality, property, trait,
aspect, element, facet; mannerism, habit, custom,
idiosyncrasy, peculiarity, quirk, oddity, foible.
▶ **adjective** *his characteristic eloquence* TYPICAL, usual,
normal, predictable, habitual; distinctive, particular,
special, especial, peculiar, idiosyncratic, defining,
singular, unique.

characterize ▶ **verb 1** *the period was characterized by* *scientific advancement* DISTINGUISH, make distinctive, mark, typify, set apart. **2** *the women are characterized as prophets of doom* PORTRAY, depict, present, represent, describe; categorize, class, style, brand.

charade ► **noun** FARCE, pantomime, travesty, mockery, parody, pretense, act, masquerade.

charge ► **verb** **1** *he didn't charge much* ASK (IN PAYMENT), levy, demand, want, exact; bill, invoice. **2** *the subscription will be charged to your account* BILL, debit from, take from. **3** *two men were charged with theft* ACCUSE, indict, arraign; prosecute, try, put on trial, inculpate. **4** *they charged him with reforming the system* ENTRUST, burden, encumber, saddle, tax. **5** *the cavalry charged the tanks* ATTACK, storm, assault, assail, fall on, swoop on, descend on; *informal* lay into, tear into. **6** *we charged into the crowd* RUSH, storm, stampede, push, plow, launch oneself, go headlong, steam, barrel, zoom. **7** *his work was charged with energy* SUFFUSE, pervade, permeate, saturate, infuse, imbue, load, fill. **8** *I charge you to stop* ORDER, command, direct, instruct, enjoin; *formal* adjure; *literary* bid.
► **noun** **1** *all customers pay a charge* FEE, payment, price, tariff, amount, sum, fare, levy. **2** *he pleaded guilty to the charge* ACCUSATION, allegation, indictment, arraignment. **3** *an infantry charge* ATTACK, assault, offensive, onslaught, drive, push, thrust. **4** *the child was in her charge* CARE, protection, safekeeping, control; custody, guardianship, wardship; hands. **5** *his charge was to save the business* DUTY, responsibility, task, job, assignment, mission, function; *informal* marching orders. **6** *the safety of my charge* WARD, protege, dependant. **7** *the judge gave a careful charge to the jury* INSTRUCTION, direction, directive, order, command, dictate, exhortation. **8** (*informal*) *I get a real charge out of working hard* THRILL, tingle, glow; excitement, stimulation, enjoyment, pleasure; *informal* kick, buzz, rush.
■ **in charge of** RESPONSIBLE FOR, in control of, in command of, at the helm/wheel of; MANAGING, running, administering, directing, supervising, overseeing, controlling; *informal* running the show.

charisma ► **noun** CHARM, presence, (force of) personality, strength of character; magnetism, attractiveness, appeal, allure.

charismatic ► **adjective** CHARMING, fascinating, strong in character; magnetic, captivating, beguiling, attractive, appealing, alluring, winning.

charitable ► **adjective** **1** *charitable activities* PHILANTHROPIC, humanitarian, altruistic, benevolent, public-spirited; non-profit; *formal* eleemosynary. **2** *charitable people* BIG-HEARTED, generous, open-handed, free-handed, munificent, bountiful, beneficent; *literary* bounteous. **3** *he was charitable in his judgments* MAGNANIMOUS, generous, liberal, tolerant, easygoing, broad-minded, considerate, sympathetic, lenient, indulgent, forgiving, kind.

charity ► **noun** **1** *a children's charity* NON-PROFIT ORGANIZATION, voluntary organization, charitable institution; fund, trust, foundation. **2** *we don't need charity* FINANCIAL ASSISTANCE, aid, welfare, (financial) relief; handouts, gifts, presents, largesse; *historical* alms. **3** *his actions are motivated by charity* PHILANTHROPY, humanitarianism, humanity, altruism, public-spiritedness, social conscience, benevolence, beneficence, munificence. **4** *show a bit of charity* GOODWILL, compassion, consideration, concern, kindness, kind-heartedness, tenderness, tender-heartedness, sympathy, indulgence, tolerance, leniency, caritas; *literary* bounteousness.

charlatan ► **noun** QUACK, sham, fraud, fake, imposter, hoaxer, cheat, deceiver, double-dealer, (confidence) trickster, swindler, fraudster, mountebank, phony, shark, con man/artist, goniff, snake oil salesman; *dated* confidence man/woman.

charm ► **noun** **1** *people were captivated by her charm* ATTRACTIVENESS, beauty, glamour, loveliness; appeal, allure, desirability, seductiveness, magnetism, charisma. **2** *these traditions retain a lot of charm* APPEAL, drawing power, attraction, allure, fascination. **3** *magical charms* SPELL, incantation, conjuration, magic formula/word, mojo, hex. **4** *a lucky charm* TALISMAN, fetish, amulet, mascot, totem, juju.
► **verb** **1** *he charmed them with his singing* DELIGHT, please, win (over), attract, captivate, allure, lure, dazzle, fascinate, enchant, enthrall, enrapture, seduce, spellbind. **2** *he charmed his mother into agreeing* COAX, cajole, wheedle; *informal* sweet-talk, soft-soap; *archaic* blandish.

charming ► **adjective** DELIGHTFUL, pleasing, pleasant, agreeable, likeable, endearing, lovely, lovable, adorable, appealing, attractive, good-looking, prepossessing; alluring, delectable, ravishing, winning, winsome, fetching, captivating, enchanting, entrancing, fascinating, seductive; *informal* heavenly, divine, gorgeous, smashing, killer; *literary* beauteous; *archaic* fair, comely.
– OPPOSITES: repulsive.

chart ► **noun** **1** *check your ideal weight on the chart* GRAPH, table, diagram, histogram; bar chart, pie chart, flow chart; *Computing* graphic. **2** *the pop charts* TOP TWENTY, list, listing; *dated* hit parade.
► **verb** **1** *the changes were charted accurately* TABULATE, plot, graph, record, register, represent; make a chart/diagram of. **2** *the book charted his progress* FOLLOW, trace, outline, describe, detail, record, document, chronicle, log.

charter ► **noun** **1** *a Royal charter* AUTHORITY, authorization, sanction, dispensation, consent, permission; permit, licence, warrant, franchise. **2** *the UN Charter* CONSTITUTION, code, canon; fundamental principles, rules, laws. **3** *the charter of a yacht* HIRE, hiring, lease, leasing, rent, rental, renting; booking, reservation, reserving.
► **verb** *they chartered a bus* HIRE, lease, rent; book, reserve.

chary ► **adjective** WARY, cautious, circumspect, heedful, careful, on one's guard; distrustful, mistrustful, skeptical, suspicious, dubious, hesitant, reluctant, leery, canny, nervous, apprehensive, uneasy; *informal* cagey, iffy.

chase ► **verb** **1** *the cat chased the mouse* PURSUE, run after, give chase to, follow; hunt, track, trail; *informal* tail. **2** *chasing young girls* WOO, pursue, run after, make advances to, flirt with; *informal* chat up, come on to, hit on; *dated* court, romance, set one's cap at, make love to. **3** *she chased away the donkeys* DRIVE, send, scare; *informal* shoo, send packing. **4** *she chased away all thoughts of him* DISPEL, banish, dismiss, drive away, shut out, put out of one's mind.
► **noun** *they gave up the chase* PURSUIT, hunt, trail.

chasm ► **noun** **1** *a deep chasm* GORGE, abyss, canyon, ravine, gully, gulf, defile, couloir, crevasse, fissure, crevice, gulch, coulee. **2** *the chasm between their views* BREACH, gulf, rift; difference, separation, division, dissension, schism, scission.

chassis ► **noun** FRAMEWORK, frame, structure, substructure, shell, casing.

chaste ▶ adjective **1** *her determination to remain chaste* VIRGINAL, virgin, intact, maidenly, unmarried, unwed; celibate, abstinent, self-restrained, self-denying, continent; innocent, virtuous, pure (as the driven snow), sinless, undefiled, unsullied, immaculate; *literary* vestal. **2** *a chaste kiss on the cheek* NON-SEXUAL, platonic, innocent. **3** *the dark, chaste interior* PLAIN, simple, bare, unadorned, undecorated, unornamented, unembellished, functional, no-frills, austere.
— OPPOSITES: promiscuous, passionate.

chasten ▶ verb **1** *both men were chastened* SUBDUE, humble, cow, squash, deflate, abase, flatten, take down a peg or two, put someone in their place, cut down to size, settle someone's hash. **2** *(archaic) the Heaven that chastens us*. See CHASTISE.

chastise ▶ verb *the staff were chastised for arriving late* SCOLD, upbraid, berate, reprimand, reprove, rebuke, admonish, chide, censure, lambaste, castigate, lecture, give someone a piece of one's mind, give someone a tongue-lashing, take to task, haul over the coals; *informal* tell off, dress down, bawl out, blow up at, give someone an earful, give someone a roasting, come down on someone like a ton of bricks, have someone's guts for garters, slap someone's wrist, rap over the knuckles, give someone hell, tear a strip off someone, give someone what for, chew out, ream out, zing; *archaic* chasten; *rare* reprehend.
— OPPOSITES: praise.

chastity ▶ noun CELIBACY, chasteness, virginity, abstinence, self-restraint, self-denial, continence; innocence, purity, virtue, morality.

chat ▶ noun *I popped in for a chat* TALK, conversation, chit-chat, gossip, chatter, heart-to-heart, tête-à-tête; *informal* jaw, confab, chinwag, rap, bull session; *formal* confabulation, colloquy.
▶ verb *they chatted with their guests* TALK, gossip, chatter, speak, converse, engage in conversation, tittle-tattle, prattle, jabber, babble; *informal* gas, jaw, chew the fat, yap, yak, yabber, yatter, yammer, natter, shoot the breeze/bull, kibitz; *formal* confabulate.
■ **chat someone up** *(informal)* FLIRT WITH, make advances to; *informal* come on to; *dated* make love to, set one's cap at, romance.

chatter ▶ noun *she tired him with her chatter* CHAT, talk, gossip, chit-chat, jabbering, jabber, prattling, prattle, babbling, babble, tittle-tattle, blathering, blather; *informal* yabbering, yammering, yattering, yapping, jawing, chewing the fat, nattering; *formal* confabulation, colloquy.
▶ verb *they chattered excitedly*. See BLATHER *verb*.

chatterbox ▶ noun *(informal)* TALKER, chatterer, prattler; windbag, bigmouth, gasbag, blabbermouth, blatherskite, Chatty Cathy, motormouth.

chatty ▶ adjective **1** *he was a chatty person* TALKATIVE, communicative, expansive, unreserved, gossipy, gossiping, garrulous, loquacious, voluble, verbose; *informal* mouthy, talky, gabby, motor-mouthed. **2** *a chatty letter* CONVERSATIONAL, gossipy, informal, casual, familiar, friendly; *informal* newsy.
— OPPOSITES: taciturn.

chauvinist ▶ adjective *chauvinist sentiments* JINGOISTIC, chauvinistic, excessively patriotic, excessively nationalistic, flag-waving, xenophobic, racist, racialist, ethnocentric; bigoted, sexist, male chauvinist, anti-feminist, misogynist, woman-hating.
▶ noun *he's a chauvinist* SEXIST, bigot, anti-feminist, misogynist, woman-hater; *informal* male chauvinist pig.

cheap ▶ adjective **1** *cheap tickets* INEXPENSIVE, low-priced, low-cost, economical, competitive, affordable, reasonable, reasonably priced, budget, economy, bargain, down-market, cut-rate, reduced, discounted, discount, rock-bottom, giveaway, bargain-basement, low-end, dirt cheap, cheap like borscht ♣. **2** *cheap furniture* POOR-QUALITY, second-rate, third-rate, tinpot, substandard, low-grade, inferior, vulgar, shoddy, trashy, tawdry, meretricious, cheapjack, gimcrack, Brummagem, pinchbeck; *informal* rubbishy, chintzy, cheapo, junky, tacky, cheesy, ticky-tacky, kitsch, *(Que.)* kétaine ♣, two-bit, dime-store, schlocky. **3** *she was too cheap to contribute to the fund* MISERLY, stingy, parsimonious, tight-fisted, niggardly, chintzy, frugal, penny-pinching, cheese-paring. **4** *the cheap exploitation of suffering* DESPICABLE, contemptible, immoral, unscrupulous, unprincipled, unsavoury, distasteful, vulgar, ignoble, shameful. **5** *he made me feel cheap* ASHAMED, humiliated, mortified, debased, degraded.
— OPPOSITES: expensive.

cheapen ▶ verb **1** *Hetty never cheapened herself* DEMEAN, debase, degrade, lower, humble, devalue, abase, discredit, disgrace, dishonour, shame, humiliate, mortify, prostitute. **2** *cheapening the cost of exports* REDUCE, lower (in price), cut, mark down, discount; *informal* slash.

cheat ▶ verb **1** *customers were cheated* SWINDLE, defraud, deceive, trick, scam, dupe, hoodwink, double-cross, gull; *informal* rip off, con, fleece, shaft, hose, sting, bilk, diddle, rook, gyp, finagle, bamboozle, flim-flam, put one over on, pull a fast one on, sucker, stiff, hornswoggle; *formal* mulct; *literary* cozen. **2** *the boy cheated death* AVOID, escape, evade, elude, foil, frustrate, thwart. **3** *cheating husbands* COMMIT ADULTERY, be unfaithful, stray; *informal* two-time, play around; cuckold.
▶ noun **1** *a liar and a cheat* SWINDLER, cheater, fraudster, trickster, deceiver, hoaxer, double-dealer, double-crosser, sham, fraud, fake, charlatan, quack, crook, snake oil salesman, mountebank; *informal* con man/artist, scam artist, shark, sharper, phony, flim-flammer, bunco artist; *dated* confidence man, confidence woman. **2** *a sure cheat for generating cash* SWINDLE, fraud, deception, deceit, hoax, sham, trick, ruse; *informal* con.

check ▶ verb **1** *troops checked all vehicles | I checked her background* EXAMINE, inspect, look at/over, scrutinize, survey; study, investigate, research, probe, look into, inquire into; *informal* check out, give something a once-over. **2** *he checked that the gun was cocked* MAKE SURE, confirm, verify. **3** *two defeats checked their progress* HALT, stop, arrest, cut short; bar, obstruct, hamper, impede, inhibit, frustrate, foil, thwart, curb, block, stall, hold up, retard, delay, slow down; *literary* stay. **4** *her tears could not be checked* SUPPRESS, repress, restrain, control, curb, rein in, stifle, hold back, choke back; *informal* keep a lid on.
▶ noun **1** *a check of the records* EXAMINATION, inspection, scrutiny, perusal, study, investigation, probe, analysis; test, trial, monitoring; checkup; *informal* once-over, look-see. **2** *a check on the abuse of authority* CONTROL, restraint, constraint, curb, limitation. **3** *the waitress arrived with the check* BILL, account, invoice, statement, tab.
■ **check in** REPORT (ONE'S ARRIVAL), book in, sign in, register.

■ **check out** LEAVE, vacate, depart; pay the bill, settle up.

■ **check something out** (*informal*) **1** *the police checked out dozens of leads* INVESTIGATE, look into, inquire into, probe, research, examine, go over; assess, analyze, evaluate; follow up; *informal* give something a once-over, scope out. **2** *she checked herself out in the mirror* LOOK AT, survey, regard, inspect, contemplate; *informal* eyeball.

■ **keep something in check** CURB, restrain, hold back, keep a tight rein on, rein in/back; control, govern, master, suppress, stifle; *informal* keep a lid on.

checkered ▶ **adjective 1** *a checkered tablecloth* CHECKED, plaid, tartan, multicoloured, many-coloured. **2** *a checkered history* VARIED, mixed, up and down, full of ups and downs, vicissitudinous; unstable, irregular, erratic, inconstant.

checkout ▶ **noun** *we met her at the supermarket checkout* cash ✦, cash desk, customer service desk.

checkpoint ▶ **noun** *a roadside checkpoint* spot check, (*Alta.*) checkstop ✦, (*Ont.*) RIDE ✦, roadblock, inspection point/station.

checkup ▶ **noun** EXAMINATION, inspection, evaluation, analysis, survey, probe, test, appraisal; check, health check; *informal* once-over, going-over.

cheek ▶ **noun** *that's enough of your cheek!* IMPUDENCE, impertinence, insolence, audacity, cheekiness, presumption, effrontery, gall, pertness, impoliteness, disrespect, bad manners, overfamiliarity, cockiness; answering back, talking back; *informal* brass, lip, mouth, chutzpah, sass, sassiness, nerviness, back talk; *archaic* assumption.

cheeky ▶ **adjective** IMPUDENT, impertinent, insolent, presumptuous, audacious, forward, pert, bold (as brass), brassy, brazen, cocky, overfamiliar, discourteous, disrespectful, impolite, bad-mannered; *informal* lippy, mouthy, fresh, saucy, sassy, nervy. — OPPOSITES: respectful, polite.

cheep ▶ **verb** CHIRP, chirrup, twitter, tweet, peep, chitter, trill, warble, sing.

cheer ▶ **noun 1** *the cheers of the crowd* HURRAY, hurrah, whoop, bravo, shout, roar; hosanna, alleluia; (**cheers**) applause, acclamation, clamour, acclaim, ovation. **2** *a time of cheer* HAPPINESS, joy, joyousness, cheerfulness, cheeriness, gladness, merriment, gaiety, jubilation, jollity, jolliness, high spirits, joviality, jocularity, conviviality, light-heartedness; merrymaking, pleasure, rejoicing, revelry. **3** *Christmas cheer* FARE, food, foodstuffs, eatables, provender; drink, beverages; *informal* eats, nibbles, nosh, grub, chow; *formal* victuals, comestibles. — OPPOSITES: boo, sadness.
▶ **verb 1** *they cheered their team* APPLAUD, hail, salute, shout for, root for, hurrah, hurray, acclaim, clap; encourage, support; bring the house down, holler for, give someone a big hand, put one's hands together for. **2** *the bad weather did little to cheer me* RAISE SOMEONE'S SPIRITS, make happier, brighten, buoy up, enliven, exhilarate, hearten, gladden, uplift, perk up, boost, encourage, inspirit; *informal* buck up. — OPPOSITES: boo, depress.

■ **cheer someone on** ENCOURAGE, urge on, spur on, drive on, motivate, inspire, fire (up), inspirit, light a fire under.

■ **cheer up** PERK UP, brighten (up), become more cheerful, liven up, rally, revive, bounce back, take heart; *informal* buck up.

cheerful ▶ **adjective 1** *he arrived looking cheerful* HAPPY, jolly, merry, bright, glad, sunny, joyful, joyous, light-hearted, in good/high spirits, sparkling, bubbly, exuberant, buoyant, ebullient, elated, gleeful; gay, breezy, cheery, jaunty, animated, radiant, smiling; jovial, genial, good-humoured; carefree, unworried, untroubled, without a care in the world; *informal* upbeat, chipper, chirpy, peppy, bright-eyed and bushy-tailed, full of beans; *formal* blithe, jocund. **2** *a cheerful room* PLEASANT, attractive, agreeable, cheering, bright, sunny, happy, friendly, welcoming. — OPPOSITES: sad.

cheerless ▶ **adjective** GLOOMY, dreary, dull, dismal, bleak, drab, sombre, dark, dim, dingy, funereal, austere, stark, bare, comfortless, unwelcoming, uninviting; miserable, wretched, joyless, depressing, disheartening, dispiriting.

cheers ▶ **exclamation** (*informal*) *he raised his glass and said 'Cheers!'* HERE'S TO YOU, good health, your health, skol, prosit, salut, salute, l'chaim; *informal* bottoms up, down the hatch, here's mud in your eye, chin-chin.

cheery ▶ **adjective**. See CHEERFUL sense 1.

cheese ▶ **noun** See table.

■ **cheese off** See IRRITATE sense 1.

Cheeses

Asiago	havarti
Bel Paese*	jack cheese
blue cheese	Jarlsberg*
bocconcini	Leicester
Boursin	Limburger
brick	mascarpone
brie	Monterey Jack
Caerphilly	Montrachet
Cambozola*	mozzarella
Camembert	Muenster
cheddar	Migneron ✦
Cheshire	Oka ✦
chèvre	paneer
colby	Parmesan
cottage cheese	Parmigiano Reggiano
cream cheese	pecorino
curd cheese	Port Salut
Danish blue	processed cheese
Edam	provolone
Emmenthal	quark
Ermite ✦	ricotta
feta	Romano
fontina	Roquefort
Friulano	Stilton
fromage blanc	Swiss cheese
fromage frais	Taleggio
goat cheese	Tilsit
Gorgonzola	Wensleydale
Gouda	*Proprietary term.
Gruyère	

---

cheesy ▶ **adjective** CORNY, cornball, trite, tacky, cheap, tawdry.

chef ▶ **noun** COOK, food preparer; chef de cuisine, pastry chef, sous-chef, short-order cook, cordon bleu cook, cookie.

chemistry ▶ **noun** *there was a chemistry between them* AFFINITY, attraction, rapport, spark.

cheque ▶ **noun** DRAFT, bank draft; traveller's cheque, certified cheque, counter cheque.

cherish ▶ **verb 1** *a woman he could cherish* ADORE, hold dear, love, dote on, be devoted to, revere, esteem, admire; think the world of, set great store by, hold in high esteem; care for, tend to, look after, protect, preserve, keep safe. **2** *I cherish her letters* TREASURE, prize, value highly, hold dear. **3** *they cherished dreams of glory* HARBOUR, entertain, possess, hold (on to), cling to, keep in one's mind, foster, nurture.

cherub ▶ noun **1** *she was borne up to heaven by cherubs* ANGEL, seraph. **2** *a cherub of 18 months* BABY, infant, toddler, little angel, (tiny) tot; *literary* babe (in arms).

cherubic ▶ adjective ANGELIC, sweet, cute, adorable, appealing, lovable; innocent, seraphic, saintly.

chest ▶ noun **1** *a bullet wound in the chest* BREAST, upper body, torso, trunk; *technical* thorax. **2** *a matronly chest* BUST, bosom; breasts. **3** *an oak chest* BOX, case, casket, crate, trunk, coffer, strongbox.

– RELATED TERMS: pectoral, thoracic.

■ **get something off one's chest** (*informal*) CONFESS, disclose, divulge, reveal, make known, make public, make a clean breast of, bring into the open, tell all about, get a load off one's mind.

chesterfield ▶ noun COUCH, sofa, divan. *See table at* SOFA.

chest of drawers ▶ noun CABINET, dresser, bureau, highboy, tallboy, commode.

chesty ▶ adjective *See* BUXOM.

chew ▶ verb *Carolyn chewed a mouthful of toast* MASTICATE, munch, champ, crunch, nibble, gnaw, eat, consume; *formal* manducate.

■ **chew something over** MEDITATE ON, ruminate on, think about/over/through, mull over, consider, ponder on, deliberate on, reflect on, muse on, dwell on, give thought to, turn over in one's mind; brood over, puzzle over, rack one's brains about; *informal* kick around, bat around; *formal* cogitate about.

■ **chew the fat** (*informal*). *See* CHAT verb.

chic ▶ adjective STYLISH, elegant, sophisticated, dressy, smart; fashionable, high-fashion, in vogue, up-to-date, up-to-the-minute, contemporary, à la mode, chi-chi, au courant; dapper, dashing, trim; *informal* trendy, with it, happening, snappy, snazzy, modish, du jour, in, funky, natty, swish, fly, spiffy, kicky, tony.

– OPPOSITES: unfashionable.

chicanery ▶ noun TRICKERY, deception, deceit, deceitfulness, duplicity, dishonesty, deviousness, unscrupulousness, underhandedness, subterfuge, fraud, fraudulence, swindling, cheating, duping, hoodwinking, sharp practice; *informal* crookedness, monkey business, hanky-panky, shenanigans, skulduggery, monkeyshines; *archaic* management, knavery.

chicken ▶ noun *See table.*

chide ▶ verb SCOLD, chastise, upbraid, berate, reprimand, reprove, rebuke, admonish, censure, lambaste, lecture, give someone a piece of one's mind, take to task, haul over the coals; *informal* tell off, dress down, bawl out, blow up at, give someone an earful, give someone a roasting, give someone a tongue-lashing, come down on someone like a ton of bricks, have someone's guts for garters, tear a strip off, slap someone's wrist, rap over the knuckles, give someone hell, take to the woodshed, have a go at, give someone what for, chew out, ream out; *formal* castigate; *archaic* chasten; *rare* reprehend.

– OPPOSITES: praise.

chief ▶ noun **1** *a Native chief* LEADER, chieftain, grand chief, sachem, sagamore, head, headman, ruler, overlord, master, commander, seigneur, liege (lord), potentate, cacique. **2** *the chief of the central bank* HEAD,

Chickens and Ground Birds

Chickens	grouse
bantam	guinea fowl
brahma	hazel grouse
Cornish	Hungarian partridge
leghorn	partridge
Plymouth Rock	peafowl/peacock/peahen
Rhode Island Red	pheasant
Rock Cornish	prairie chicken
Sussex	ptarmigan
White Rock	quail
Wyandot	ringneck
	ring-necked pheasant
Other Ground Birds	rock ptarmigan
black grouse	ruffed grouse
blue grouse	sage grouse
bobwhite	sharp-tailed grouse
capercaillie	snow partridge
chicken	spruce grouse
chukar	tragopan
fool hen	turkey
francolin	willow grouse
grey partridge	willow ptarmigan

principal, chief executive (officer); CEO, president, chair, chairman, chairwoman, chairperson, governor, director, manager, manageress; employer, proprietor; *informal* big cheese, big shot, bigwig, skipper, numero uno, (head) honcho, boss, padrone. ▶ adjective **1** *the chief rabbi* HEAD, leading, principal, premier, highest, foremost, supreme, arch. **2** *their chief aim* MAIN, principal, most important, primary, prime, first, cardinal, central, key, crucial, essential, predominant, pre-eminent, paramount, overriding, number-one.

– RELATED TERMS: arch-.

– OPPOSITES: subordinate, minor.

chiefly ▶ adverb MAINLY, in the main, primarily, principally, predominantly, mostly, for the most part; usually, habitually, typically, commonly, generally, on the whole, largely, by and large, almost always.

child ▶ noun YOUNGSTER, little one, boy, girl; baby, newborn, infant, toddler; cherub, angel; schoolboy, schoolgirl; minor, junior, preteen; son, daughter, descendant; *informal* kid, kiddie, tot, tyke, young 'un, lad, rug rat, ankle-biter; *derogatory* brat, terrible two, guttersnipe, urchin, gamin, gamine; *literary* babe (in arms); (**children**) offspring, progeny, issue, brood, descendants.

– RELATED TERMS: pedo-.

childbirth ▶ noun LABOUR, delivery, giving birth, birthing, child-bearing; *formal* parturition; *dated* confinement; *literary* travail; *archaic* lying-in, accouchement, childbed.

– RELATED TERMS: obstetric, puerperal.

childhood ▶ noun YOUTH, early years/life, infancy, babyhood, boyhood, girlhood, pre-pubescence, minority; the springtime of life, one's salad days; *formal* nonage, juvenescence.

– OPPOSITES: adulthood.

childish ▶ adjective **1** *childish behaviour* IMMATURE, babyish, infantile, juvenile, puerile; silly, inane, jejune, foolish, irresponsible. **2** *a round childish face* CHILDLIKE, youthful, young, young-looking, girlish, boyish.

– OPPOSITES: mature, adult.

childlike ▶ adjective **1** *grandmother looked almost*

childlike YOUTHFUL, young, young-looking, girlish, boyish. **2** *geniuses tend to be rather childlike* INNOCENT, artless, guileless, unworldly, unsophisticated, naive, ingenuous, trusting, unsuspicious, unwary, credulous, gullible; unaffected, without airs, uninhibited, natural, spontaneous; *informal* wet behind the ears.

children ▶ **plural noun** *See* CHILD.

chill ▶ **noun 1** *a chill in the air* COLDNESS, chilliness, coolness, iciness, rawness, bitterness, nip. **2** *he had a chill* COLD, sniffles, shivers, flu/influenza, fever; *archaic* grippe. **3** *the chill in their relations* UNFRIENDLINESS, lack of warmth/understanding, chilliness, coldness, coolness.
— OPPOSITES: warmth.
▶ **verb 1** *the dessert is best chilled* MAKE COLD, make colder, cool (down/off); refrigerate, ice. **2** *his quiet tone chilled Ruth* SCARE, frighten, petrify, terrify, alarm; make someone's blood run cold, chill to the bone/marrow, make someone's flesh crawl; *informal* scare the pants off; *archaic* affright.
— OPPOSITES: warm.
▶ **adjective** *a chill wind* COLD, chilly, cool, fresh; wintry, frosty, icy, ice-cold, icy-cold, glacial, polar, arctic, raw, bitter, bitterly cold, biting, freezing, frigid, gelid, hypothermic; *informal* nippy.
■ **chill out** *(informal) a place to chill out. See* RELAX *sense 1*.

chilly ▶ **adjective 1** *the weather had turned chilly* COOL, cold, crisp, fresh, wintry, frosty, brisk, icy, ice-cold, icy-cold, chill, glacial, polar, arctic, raw, bitter, bitterly cold, freezing, frigid, gelid, hypothermic; *informal* nippy. **2** *a chilly reception* UNFRIENDLY, unwelcoming, cold, cool, frosty, gelid; *informal* standoffish, offish.
— OPPOSITES: warm.

chime ▶ **verb 1** *the bells began to chime* RING, peal, toll, sound; ding, dong, clang, boom, bong; *literary* knell. **2** *the clock chimed eight o'clock* STRIKE, sound.
▶ **noun** *the chimes of the bells* PEAL, pealing, ringing, carillon, toll, tolling; ding-dong, clanging, tintinnabulation; *literary* knell.
■ **chime in** *in 'Yes, you do that,' Doreen chimed in* INTERJECT, interpose, interrupt, butt in, cut in, join in.

chimera ▶ **noun** ILLUSION, fantasy, delusion, dream, daydream, pipe dream, figment, fancy, castle in the air, mirage.

chimney ▶ **noun** SMOKESTACK, stack; flue, funnel, vent, stovepipe.

china ▶ **noun 1** *a china cup* PORCELAIN. **2** *a table laid with the best china* DISHES, plates, cups and saucers, tableware, chinaware, dinner service, tea service, crockery.

chink ▶ **noun** *a chink in the curtains* OPENING, gap, space, hole, aperture, crack, fissure, crevice, cranny, cleft, split, slit, slot.
▶ **verb** *the glasses chinked* JINGLE, jangle, clink, tinkle.

chintzy ▶ **adjective** CHEAP, cheesy, shoddy, low-grade, low-end, second-rate, third-rate, kitschy, tacky, trashy, gimcrack.

chip ▶ **noun 1** *wood chips* FRAGMENT, sliver, splinter, shaving, paring, flake. **2** *a chip in the glass* NICK, crack, scratch, notch; flaw, fault. **3** *fish and chips* French fries, fries, home fries, frites, pommes frites. **4** *gambling chips* COUNTER, token, check.
▶ **verb 1** *a stone chipped my windshield* NICK, crack, scratch; damage. **2** *the plaster had chipped* BREAK (OFF), crack, crumble. **3** *chip the flint to the required shape* WHITTLE, hew, chisel, carve.

■ **chip away** *chipping away at their defences* erode, wear down, wear away, whittle down, corrode, gnaw away at.
■ **chip in** *parents and staff chipped in to raise the cash* CONTRIBUTE, make a contribution/donation, pay; *informal* fork out, shell out, cough up, kick in.

chipper ▶ **adjective** CHEERFUL, lively, perky, high-spirited, cheery, buoyant, sunny, bubbly.

chirp ▶ **verb** TWEET, twitter, cheep, peep, chitter, chirrup, chirr; sing, warble, trill.

chisel ▶ **verb** HEW, engrave, incise, score, chip, carve.

chit-chat ▶ **noun** *(informal)* SMALL TALK, chatter, gossip, chewing the fat, chat, chatting, prattle.

chivalrous ▶ **adjective 1** *his chivalrous treatment of women* GALLANT, gentlemanly, honourable, respectful, considerate; courteous, polite, gracious, well-mannered, mannerly; *archaic* gentle. **2** *chivalrous pursuits* KNIGHTLY, noble, chivalric; brave, courageous, bold, valiant, valorous, heroic, daring, intrepid.
— OPPOSITES: rude, cowardly.

chivalry ▶ **noun 1** *acts of chivalry* GALLANTRY, gentlemanliness, courtesy, courteousness, politeness, graciousness, mannerliness, good manners. **2** *the values of chivalry* KNIGHT ERRANTRY, courtly manners, knightliness, courtliness, nobility; bravery, courage, boldness, valour, heroism, daring, intrepidity; bushido.
— OPPOSITES: rudeness.

choice ▶ **noun 1** *it's your choice | freedom of choice* SELECTION, election, choosing, picking; decision, say, vote. **2** *you have no other choice* OPTION, alternative, possible course of action. **3** *an extensive choice of wines* RANGE, variety, selection, assortment. **4** *the critics' choice* PREFERENCE, selection, pick, favourite.
▶ **adjective** *choice plums* SUPERIOR, first-class, first-rate, prime, premier, grade A, best, finest, excellent, select, quality, high-quality, top, top-quality, high-grade, prize, fine, special; hand-picked, carefully chosen; *informal* tip-top, A1, top-notch, blue-ribbon, blue-chip.
— OPPOSITES: inferior.

choir ▶ **noun** SINGERS, chorus, chorale, choral society, voices, choristers, glee club.
— RELATED TERMS: choral.

choke ▶ **verb 1** *Christopher started to choke* GAG, retch, cough, fight for breath. **2** *thick dust choked her* SUFFOCATE, asphyxiate, smother, stifle. **3** *she had been choked to death* STRANGLE, throttle; asphyxiate, suffocate; *informal* strangulate. **4** *the eavestrough was choked with leaves* CLOG (UP), stop up, block, obstruct, plug, bung up; *technical* occlude. **5** *the leaders choked in the playoffs* UNDERACHIEVE, underperform, disappoint, lose, collapse, fall apart.
■ **choke something back** SUPPRESS, hold back, fight back, bite back, swallow, check, restrain, control, repress, smother, stifle; *informal* keep a lid on.

choleric ▶ **adjective** BAD-TEMPERED, irascible, irritable, angry, grumpy, grouchy, crotchety, tetchy, testy, cranky, crusty, cantankerous, curmudgeonly, ill-tempered, peevish, cross, fractious, crabbed, crabby, waspish, prickly, peppery, touchy, short-tempered; snappish, snappy, chippy, short-fused, ornery.
— OPPOSITES: good-natured, affable.

chomp ▶ **verb** MUNCH, crunch, champ, chew, bite.

choose ▶ **verb 1** *we chose a quiet country inn* SELECT, pick (out), opt for, settle on, decide on, fix on, take; appoint, name, nominate, vote for, elect. **2** *I'll stay as* long as I choose WISH, want, desire, feel/be inclined, please, like, see fit.

choosy ▶ adjective FUSSY, finicky, fastidious, over-particular, difficult/hard to please, demanding; informal picky, persnickety, pernickety.

chop ▶ verb **1** chop the potatoes into pieces CUT UP, cut into pieces, chop up, cube, dice, hash. **2** they were out back chopping wood CHOP UP, cut up, cut into pieces, hew, split. **3** four fingers were chopped off SEVER, cut off, hack off, slice off, lop off, saw off, shear off. **4** they chopped down large areas of rainforest CUT DOWN, fell, hack down, clear-cut, harvest. **5** their training courses were chopped CUT, axe, abolish, scrap, slash, cancel, terminate, ditch, dump, pull the plug on.

choppy ▶ adjective ROUGH, turbulent, heavy, heaving, stormy, tempestuous, squally; uneven.
— OPPOSITES: calm.

chore ▶ noun TASK, job, duty, errand; (domestic) work; joe job; drag, bore, pain.

chortle ▶ verb CHUCKLE, laugh, giggle, titter, tee-hee, snigger.

chorus ▶ noun **1** the chorus sang powerfully CHOIR, ensemble, choral group, choristers, (group of) singers, voices, glee club. **2** Nancy sang the chorus REFRAIN.
■ **in chorus** IN UNISON, together, simultaneously, as one, united; in concert, in harmony.

chosen ▶ adjective SELECTED, picked, appointed, elected, favoured, hand-picked.

christen ▶ verb **1** she was christened Sara BAPTIZE, name, give the name of, call. **2** a group who were christened 'The Magic Circle' CALL, name, dub, style, term, designate, label, nickname, give the name of; formal denominate.

chronic ▶ adjective **1** a chronic illness PERSISTENT, long-standing, long-term; incurable; Medicine immedicable. **2** chronic economic problems CONSTANT, continuing, ceaseless, unabating, unending, persistent, long-lasting; severe, serious, acute, grave, dire. **3** a chronic liar INVETERATE, hardened, dyed-in-the-wool, incorrigible; compulsive; informal pathological.
— OPPOSITES: acute, temporary.

chronicle ▶ noun a chronicle of the region's past RECORD, written account, history, annals, archive(s); log, diary, journal.
▶ verb the events that followed have been chronicled RECORD, put on record, write down, set down, document, register, report.

chronicler ▶ noun ANNALIST, historian, archivist, diarist, recorder, reporter.

chronological ▶ adjective SEQUENTIAL, consecutive, in sequence, in order (of time).

chubby ▶ adjective PLUMP, fat, rotund, portly, dumpy, chunky, well-upholstered, well-rounded; informal roly-poly, tubby, pudgy, blubbery, big-boned, full-figured; zaftig, corn-fed.
— OPPOSITES: skinny.

chuck ▶ verb (informal) **1** he chucked the letter onto the table THROW, toss, fling, hurl, pitch, cast, lob, huck ♣. **2** I chucked the old comics THROW AWAY/OUT, discard, dispose of, get rid of, dump, bin, scrap, jettison; informal ditch, junk, deep-six, trash. **3** Mary chucked him for another guy LEAVE, throw over, finish with, break off with, jilt; informal dump, ditch.

chuckle ▶ verb GIGGLE, chortle, titter, tee-hee, snicker, snigger.

chug ▶ verb GULP, guzzle, quaff, swig.

chum ▶ noun (informal) FRIEND, buddy, bud, pal; companion, sidekick, intimate; mate, playmate, classmate, schoolmate, workmate; crony; amigo, compadre.
— OPPOSITES: enemy, stranger.

chummy ▶ adjective (informal) FRIENDLY, on good terms, close, familiar, intimate; informal buddy-buddy, thick, matey, palsy-walsy.

chunk ▶ noun LUMP, hunk, wedge, block, slab, square, nugget, brick, cube, bar, cake, Nfld nug ♣.

chunky ▶ adjective **1** a chunky young man STOCKY, sturdy, thickset, heavily built, well-built, burly, bulky, brawny, solid, heavy. **2** a chunky sweater THICK, bulky, heavy-knit.
— OPPOSITES: slight, light.

church ▶ noun **1** a village church PLACE OF WORSHIP, house of God, house of worship; cathedral, minster, abbey, chapel, basilica; synagogue, mosque. **2** the Methodist Church DENOMINATION, ecclesial community; creed, faith.
— RELATED TERMS: ecclesiastical.

churchyard ▶ noun CEMETERY, graveyard, burial ground, burying ground, necropolis, memorial park/ garden; informal boneyard; historical potter's field; archaic God's acre.

churlish ▶ adjective RUDE, ill-mannered, ill-bred, discourteous, impolite, unmannerly, uncivil, unchivalrous; inconsiderate, uncharitable, surly, sullen.
— OPPOSITES: polite.

churn ▶ verb **1** village girls churned the milk STIR, agitate, beat, whip, whisk. **2** the sea churned HEAVE, boil, swirl, toss, seethe; literary roil. **3** the propellers churned up the water DISTURB, stir up, agitate; literary roil.
■ **churn something out** PRODUCE, make, turn out; informal crank out, bang out.

chute ▶ noun CHANNEL, slide, shaft, funnel, conduit; log chute ♣, timber slide ♣.

chutzpah ▶ noun AUDACITY, cheek, guts, nerve, boldness, temerity.

cigarette ▶ noun smoke, butt, cig, ciggie, cancer stick, coffin nail; rollie, filter tip.

cinch ▶ noun (informal) **1** it's a cinch EASY TASK, child's play, snap, walkover, laugher, piece of cake, picnic, breeze, kids' stuff, cakewalk, pushover, duck soup, five-finger exercise. **2** he was a cinch to take a prize CERTAINTY, sure thing, (dead) cert.
— OPPOSITES: challenge.

cinders ▶ plural noun ASHES, ash, embers.

cinema ▶ noun **1** the local cinema MOVIE THEATRE/ HOUSE, multiplex, cinematheque; historical nickelodeon. **2** Italian cinema FILMS, movies, pictures, motion pictures.

cipher ▶ noun **1** information in cipher CODE, secret writing. **2** working as a cipher NOBODY, nonentity, unimportant person, no-name.

circa ▶ preposition APPROXIMATELY, around, about, roughly, something like, of the order of, or so, or thereabouts, more or less, in the region of, in the ballpark of, give or take.
— OPPOSITES: exactly.

circle ▶ noun **1** a circle of gold stars RING, band, hoop, circlet; halo, disc; technical annulus. **2** her circle of friends GROUP, set, company, coterie, clique; crowd, band; informal gang, bunch, crew. **3** illustrious circles SPHERE, world, milieu; society.
▶ verb **1** seagulls circled above WHEEL, move round,

revolve, rotate, whirl, spiral. **2** *satellites circling the earth* GO ROUND, travel round, circumnavigate; orbit, revolve round. **3** *the abbey was circled by a wall* SURROUND, encircle, ring, enclose, encompass; *literary* gird.

circuit ▶ **noun 1** *two circuits of the course* LAP, turn, round, circle. **2** *a racing circuit* TRACK, racetrack, raceway, running track, course. **3** *the judge's circuit* TOUR (OF DUTY), rounds.

circuitous ▶ **adjective 1** *a circuitous route* ROUNDABOUT, indirect, winding, meandering, serpentine, tortuous. **2** *a circuitous discussion* INDIRECT, oblique, roundabout, circumlocutory, periphrastic.
— OPPOSITES: direct.

circular ▶ **adjective** *a circular window* ROUND, disc-shaped, ring-shaped, annular.
▶ **noun** *a free circular* LEAFLET, pamphlet, handbill, flyer, mailer, folder.

circulate ▶ **verb 1** *the news was widely circulated* SPREAD (ABOUT/AROUND), communicate, disseminate, make known, make public, broadcast, publicize, advertise, propagate, promulgate; distribute, give out, pass around. **2** *fresh air circulates freely* FLOW, course, move round. **3** *they circulated among their guests* SOCIALIZE, mingle.

circulation ▶ **noun 1** *the circulation of fresh air* FLOW, motion, movement, course, passage. **2** *the circulation of the information* DISSEMINATION, spreading, communication, transmission, making known, putting about; broadcasting, publication, propagation, promulgation; distribution, diffusion, issuance. **3** *the magazine had a large circulation* DISTRIBUTION, readership.

circumference ▶ **noun 1** *the circumference of the pit* PERIMETER, border, boundary; edge, rim, verge, margin, fringe; *literary* marge. **2** *the circumference of his arm* GIRTH, width.

circumlocution ▶ **noun** PERIPHRASIS, discursiveness, long-windedness, verbosity, verbiage, wordiness, prolixity, redundancy, pleonasm, tautology, repetitiveness, repetitiousness.

circumscribe ▶ **verb** RESTRICT, limit, keep within bounds, curb, confine, restrain; regulate, control.

circumspect ▶ **adjective** CAUTIOUS, wary, careful, chary, guarded, on one's guard; watchful, alert, attentive, heedful, vigilant, leery; *informal* cagey, playing one's cards close to one's chest.
— OPPOSITES: unguarded.

circumstances ▶ **plural noun 1** *favourable economic circumstances* SITUATION, conditions, state of affairs, position; (turn of) events, incidents, occurrences, happenings; factors, context, background, environment. **2** *Jane explained the circumstances to him* THE FACTS, the details, the particulars, how things stand, the lay of the land; *informal* what's what, the score. **3** *reduced circumstances* FINANCIAL POSITION, lot, lifestyle; resources, means, finances, income.

circumstantial ▶ **adjective 1** *they have only circumstantial evidence* INDIRECT, inferred, deduced, conjectural; inconclusive, unprovable. **2** *a circumstantial account* DETAILED, particularized, comprehensive, thorough, exhaustive; explicit, specific.

circumvent ▶ **verb** AVOID, get round/past, evade, bypass, sidestep, dodge; *informal* duck.

circus ▶ **noun 1** *the kids enjoyed the circus* CARNIVAL, big top, cirque. **2** *the meeting degenerated into a circus* TURMOIL, chaos, zoo, bedlam, mayhem, pandemonium.

cistern ▶ **noun** TANK, reservoir, container, butt.

citadel ▶ **noun** FORTRESS, fort, stronghold, fortification, castle.

citation ▶ **noun 1** *a citation from an eighteenth-century text* QUOTATION, quote, extract, excerpt, passage, line; reference, allusion. **2** *a citation for gallantry* COMMENDATION, (honourable) mention. **3** *(Law) a traffic citation* SUMMONS, subpoena, writ, court order.

cite ▶ **verb 1** *cite the passage in full* QUOTE, reproduce. **2** *he cited the case of Francis v. Perrin* REFER TO, make reference to, mention, allude to, adduce, instance; specify, name. **3** *he has been cited many times* COMMEND, pay tribute to, praise. **4** *(Law) the writ cited four of the signatories* SUMMON, summons, serve with a summons/ writ, subpoena.

citizen ▶ **noun 1** *a Canadian citizen* NATIONAL, subject, passport holder, native. **2** *the citizens of Calgary* INHABITANT, resident, native, townsman, townswoman, denizen; burgher; taxpayer, ratepayer.

city ▶ **noun** TOWN, municipality, metropolis, megalopolis, megacity; conurbation, urban area, metropolitan area, urban municipality; borough, township; *informal* big smoke, burg.
— RELATED TERMS: urban, civic.

civic ▶ **adjective** MUNICIPAL, city, town, urban, metropolitan; public, civil, community, local.

civil ▶ **adjective 1** *a civil marriage* SECULAR, non-religious, lay; *formal* laic. **2** *civil aviation* NON-MILITARY, civilian. **3** *a civil war* INTERNAL, domestic, interior, national. **4** *he behaved in a civil manner* POLITE, courteous, well-mannered, well-bred, chivalrous, gallant; cordial, genial, pleasant, affable; gentlemanly, ladylike.
— OPPOSITES: religious, military, international, rude.

civilian ▶ **noun** NON-COMBATANT, non-military person, ordinary/private citizen; *informal* civvy.

civility ▶ **noun 1** *he treated me with civility* COURTESY, courteousness, politeness, good manners, graciousness, consideration, respect, politesse, comity. **2** *she didn't waste time on civilities* POLITE REMARK, politeness, courtesy; formality.
— OPPOSITES: rudeness.

civilization ▶ **noun 1** *a higher stage of civilization* HUMAN DEVELOPMENT, advancement, progress, enlightenment, culture, refinement, sophistication. **2** *ancient civilizations* CULTURE, society, nation, people.

civilize ▶ **verb** ENLIGHTEN, edify, improve, educate, instruct, refine, cultivate, polish, socialize, humanize.

civilized ▶ **adjective** POLITE, courteous, well-mannered, civil, gentlemanly, ladylike, mannerly; cultured, cultivated, refined, polished, sophisticated; enlightened, educated, advanced, developed.
— OPPOSITES: rude, unsophisticated.

civil servant ▶ **noun** PUBLIC SERVANT, government official; bureaucrat, official, administrator, functionary; apparatchik, mandarin; bean-counter, paper shuffler.

clad ▶ **adjective** DRESSED, clothed, attired, got up, garbed, rigged out, togged out, costumed; wearing, sporting; *archaic* apparelled.

claim ▶ **verb 1** *Davies claimed that she was lying* ASSERT, declare, profess, maintain, state, hold, affirm, avow, argue, contend, allege; *formal* aver. **2** *no one claimed the*

items LAY CLAIM TO, assert ownership of, formally request. **3** *you can claim compensation* REQUEST, ask for, apply for; demand, exact. **4** *the fire claimed four lives* TAKE, cause/result in the loss of.
▶ noun **1** *her claim that she was unaware of the problem* ASSERTION, declaration, profession, affirmation, avowal, protestation; contention, allegation. **2** *a claim for damages* REQUEST, application; demand, petition. **3** *we have first claim on their assets* ENTITLEMENT TO, title to, right to.

claimant ▶ noun APPLICANT, candidate, supplicant; petitioner, plaintiff, litigant, appellant.

clairvoyance ▶ noun ESP, extrasensory perception, sixth sense, psychic powers, second sight; telepathy.

clairvoyant ▶ noun PSYCHIC, fortune teller, crystal-gazer; medium, spiritualist; telepath, mind-reader.
▶ adjective PSYCHIC, telepathic.

clam ▶ noun. *See table at* MOLLUSC.

clamber ▶ verb SCRAMBLE, climb, scrabble, scravel ✤, claw one's way.

clammy ▶ adjective **1** *his clammy hands* MOIST, damp, sweaty, sticky; slimy, slippery. **2** *the clammy atmosphere* DAMP, dank, wet; humid, close, muggy, heavy.
— OPPOSITES: dry.

clamorous ▶ adjective NOISY, loud, vocal, vociferous, raucous, rowdy; importunate, demanding, insistent, vehement.
— OPPOSITES: quiet.

clamour ▶ noun **1** *her voice rose above the clamour* DIN, racket, rumpus, loud noise, uproar, tumult, shouting, yelling, screaming, roaring; commotion, brouhaha, hue and cry, hubbub, hullabaloo, hoopla. **2** *the clamour for her resignation* DEMAND(S), call(s), urging. **3** *the clamour of protectionists* PROTESTS, complaints, outcry.
▶ verb **1** *clamouring crowds* YELL, shout loudly, bay, scream, roar. **2** *scientists are clamouring for a ban* DEMAND, call, press, push, lobby.

clamp ▶ noun BRACE, vice, press, clasp; *Music* capo (tasto); *Climbing* jumar.
▶ verb **1** *the sander is clamped on to the workbench* FASTEN, secure, fix, attach; screw, bolt. **2** *a pipe was clamped between his teeth* CLENCH, grip, hold, press, clasp.
■ **clamp down on** SUPPRESS, prevent, stop, put a stop/end to, stamp out; crack down on, limit, restrict, control, keep in check.

clampdown ▶ noun *(informal)* SUPPRESSION, prevention, stamping out; crackdown, restriction, restraint, curb, check.

clan ▶ noun **1** *the Macleod clan* GROUP OF FAMILIES; sept; family, house, dynasty, tribe; *Anthropology* sib, kinship group. **2** *a clan of art collectors* GROUP, set, circle, clique, coterie; crowd, band; *informal* gang, bunch.

clandestine ▶ adjective SECRET, covert, furtive, surreptitious, stealthy, cloak-and-dagger, hole-and-corner, closet, backstairs, backroom; hush-hush.

clang ▶ noun *the clang of the church bells* REVERBERATION, ringing, ring, ding-dong, bong, peal, chime, toll.
▶ verb *the huge bells clanged* REVERBERATE, resound, ring, bong, peal, ring, chime, toll.

clank ▶ noun *the clank of rusty chains* JANGLING, clanging, rattling, clinking, jingling; clang, jangle, rattle, clangour, clink, jingle.

▶ verb *I could hear the chain clanking* JANGLE, rattle, clink, clang, jingle.

clannish ▶ adjective CLIQUEY, cliquish, insular, exclusive; unfriendly, unwelcoming.

clap ▶ verb **1** *the audience clapped* APPLAUD, clap one's hands, give someone a round of applause, put one's hands together; *informal* give someone a big hand. **2** *he clapped Owen on the back* SLAP, strike, hit, smack, thump; pat; *informal* whack, thwack. **3** *the dove clapped its wings* FLAP, beat, flutter.
▶ noun **1** *everybody gave him a clap* ROUND OF APPLAUSE, handclap; *informal* hand. **2** *a clap on the shoulder* SLAP, blow, smack, thump; pat; *informal* whack, thwack. **3** *a clap of thunder* CRACK, crash, bang, boom; thunderclap.

claptrap ▶ noun *sentimental claptrap. See* NONSENSE sense 1.

clarify ▶ verb **1** *their report clarified the situation* MAKE CLEAR, shed/throw light on, elucidate, illuminate; EXPLAIN, explicate, define, spell out, clear up. **2** *clarified butter* PURIFY, refine; filter, fine.
— OPPOSITES: confuse.

clarity ▶ noun **1** *the clarity of his account* LUCIDITY, lucidness, clearness, coherence; *formal* perspicuity. **2** *the clarity of the image* SHARPNESS, clearness, crispness, definition. **3** *the crystal clarity of the water* LIMPIDITY, limpidness, clearness, transparency, translucence, pellucidity.
— OPPOSITES: vagueness, blurriness, opacity.

clash ▶ noun **1** *clashes between armed gangs* CONFRONTATION, skirmish, fight, battle, engagement, encounter, conflict. **2** *an angry clash* ARGUMENT, altercation, confrontation, shouting match; contretemps, quarrel, disagreement, dispute, run-in. **3** *a clash of tweeds and a striped shirt* MISMATCH, discordance, discord, lack of harmony. **4** *the clash of cymbals* STRIKING, bang, clang, crash.
▶ verb **1** *protesters clashed with police* FIGHT, skirmish, contend, come to blows, come into conflict; do battle. **2** *the prime minister clashed with union leaders* DISAGREE, differ, wrangle, dispute, cross swords, lock horns, be at loggerheads. **3** *her red scarf clashed with her coat* BE INCOMPATIBLE, not match, not go, be discordant. **4** *she clashed the cymbals together* BANG, strike, clang, crash.

clasp ▶ verb **1** *Ruth clasped his hand* GRASP, grip, clutch, hold tightly; take hold of, seize, grab. **2** *he clasped Joanne in his arms* EMBRACE, hug, enfold, fold, envelop; hold, squeeze.
▶ noun **1** *a gold clasp* FASTENER, fastening, catch, clip, pin; buckle, hasp. **2** *his tight clasp* EMBRACE, hug, cuddle; grip, grasp.

class ▶ noun **1** *a hotel of the first class* CATEGORY, grade, rating, classification, group, grouping. **2** *a new class of heart drug* KIND, sort, type, variety, genre, brand; species, genus, breed, strain, stripe. **3** *the middle class* SOCIAL DIVISION, social stratum, rank, level, echelon, group, grouping, income group; social status; *dated* estate; *archaic* condition. **4** *a math class* LESSON, period; seminar, tutorial, workshop, study group. **5** *(informal) a woman of class* STYLE, stylishness, elegance, chic, sophistication, taste, refinement, quality, excellence.
▶ verb *the 12-seater is classed as a commercial vehicle* CLASSIFY, categorize, group, grade; order, sort, codify; bracket, designate, label, pigeonhole.
▶ adjective *(informal) a class player* CLASSY, decent, gracious, respectable, noble.

classic ▶ adjective **1** *the classic work on the subject* DEFINITIVE, authoritative; outstanding, first-rate,

first-class, best, finest, excellent, superior, masterly. **2** *a classic example of Norman design* TYPICAL, archetypal, quintessential, vintage; model, representative, perfect, prime, textbook. **3** *a classic style* SIMPLE, elegant, understated; traditional, timeless, ageless.
– OPPOSITES: atypical.
▶ noun *a classic of the genre* DEFINITIVE EXAMPLE, model, epitome, paradigm, exemplar; great work, masterpiece.

classical ▶ adjective **1** *classical mythology* ancient Greek, Hellenic, Attic; Latin, ancient Roman. **2** *classical music* TRADITIONAL, long-established; serious, highbrow. **3** *a classical style* SIMPLE, pure, restrained, plain, austere; well-proportioned, harmonious, balanced, symmetrical, elegant.
– OPPOSITES: modern.

classification ▶ noun **1** *the classification of diseases* CATEGORIZATION, categorizing, classifying, grouping, grading, ranking, organization, sorting, codification, systematization. **2** *a series of classifications* CATEGORY, class, group, grouping, grade, grading, ranking, bracket.

classify ▶ verb *we can classify the students into two groups* CATEGORIZE, group, grade, rank, rate, order, organize, range, sort, type, codify, bracket, systematize, systemize; catalogue, list, file, index, lump.

classy ▶ adjective **1** *a classy hotel* STYLISH, high-class, superior, exclusive, chic, elegant, smart, sophisticated, upscale, upmarket, high-toned; *informal* posh, ritzy, plush, swanky. **2** *a classy organization* DECENT, gracious, respectable, noble.

clatter ▶ verb *the cups clattered on the tray* RATTLE, clank, clink, clunk, clang.

clause ▶ noun *a new clause in the treaty* SECTION, paragraph, article, subsection; stipulation, condition, proviso, rider.

claw ▶ noun **1** *a bird's claw* TALON, nail; *technical* unguis. **2** *a crab's claw* PINCER, nipper; *technical* chela.
▶ verb *her fingers clawed his shoulders* SCRATCH, lacerate, tear, rip, scrape, graze, scrob, dig into.

clay ▶ noun **1** *the soil is mainly clay* EARTH, soil, loam. **2** *potter's clay* argil, china clay, kaolin, adobe, ball clay, pug; fireclay.

clean ▶ adjective **1** *keep the wound clean* WASHED, scrubbed, cleansed, cleaned; spotless, unsoiled, unstained, unsullied, unblemished, immaculate, pristine, dirt-free; hygienic, sanitary, disinfected, sterilized, sterile, aseptic, decontaminated; laundered; *informal* squeaky clean, as clean as a whistle. **2** *a clean sheet of paper* BLANK, empty, clear, plain; unused, new, pristine, fresh, unmarked. **3** *clean air* PURE, clear, fresh, crisp, refreshing; unpolluted, uncontaminated. **4** *a clean life* VIRTUOUS, good, upright, upstanding; honourable, respectable, reputable, decent, righteous, moral, exemplary; innocent, pure, chaste; *informal* squeaky clean. **5** *the firm is clean* INNOCENT, guiltless, blameless, guilt-free, crime-free, above suspicion; *informal* squeaky clean. **6** *a good clean fight* FAIR, honest, sporting, sportsmanlike, honourable, according to the rules; *informal* on the level. **7** *(informal) they are trying to stay clean* SOBER, teetotal, dry, non-drinking; DRUG-FREE, off drugs; *informal* on the wagon. **8** *a clean cut* NEAT, smooth, crisp, straight, precise. **9** *a clean break* COMPLETE, thorough, total, absolute, conclusive, decisive, final, irrevocable. **10** *clean lines* SIMPLE,

elegant, graceful, streamlined, smooth.
– OPPOSITES: dirty, polluted.
▶ adverb *(informal) I clean forgot* COMPLETELY, entirely, totally, fully, quite, utterly, absolutely.
▶ verb **1** *Dad cleaned the windows* WASH, cleanse, wipe, sponge, scrub, mop, rinse, scour, swab, hose down, sluice (down), disinfect; *literary* lave. **2** *I got my clothes cleaned* LAUNDER, dry-clean. **3** *she cleaned the fish* GUT, draw, dress; *formal* eviscerate.
– OPPOSITES: dirty.
■ **clean someone out** *(informal)* BANKRUPT, ruin, make insolvent, make penniless, wipe out.
■ **come clean** *(informal)* TELL THE TRUTH, tell all, make a clean breast of it; confess, own up, admit guilt, admit to one's crimes/sins; *informal* fess up.

clean-cut ▶ adjective UPRIGHT, upstanding, respectable, clean-living, wholesome.

cleanse ▶ verb **1** *the wound was cleansed* CLEAN (UP), wash, bathe, rinse, disinfect. **2** *cleansing the environment of traces of lead* RID, clear, free, purify, purge.

clear ▶ adjective **1** *clear instructions* UNDERSTANDABLE, comprehensible, intelligible, plain, uncomplicated, explicit, lucid, coherent, simple, straightforward, unambiguous, clear-cut, crystal clear; *formal* perspicuous. **2** *a clear case of harassment* OBVIOUS, evident, plain, crystal clear; sure, definite, unmistakable, manifest, indisputable, patent, incontrovertible, irrefutable, beyond doubt, beyond question; palpable, visible, discernible, conspicuous, overt, blatant, glaring; as plain as day, as plain as the nose on one's face. **3** *clear water* TRANSPARENT, limpid, pellucid, translucent, crystal clear; unclouded. **4** *a clear blue sky* BRIGHT, cloudless, unclouded, without a cloud in the sky. **5** *her clear complexion* UNBLEMISHED, spot-free. **6** *Rosa's clear voice* DISTINCT, bell-like, as clear as a bell. **7** *the road was clear | a clear view* UNOBSTRUCTED, unblocked, passable, unrestricted, open, unhindered. **8** *a clear conscience* UNTROUBLED, undisturbed, unperturbed, unconcerned, having no qualms; peaceful, at peace, tranquil, serene, calm, easy. **9** *two clear days' notice* WHOLE, full, entire, complete.
– OPPOSITES: vague, opaque, cloudy, obstructed.
▶ adverb **1** *stand clear of the doors* AWAY FROM, apart from, at a (safe) distance from, out of contact with. **2** *Tommy's voice came loud and clear* DISTINCTLY, clearly, as clear as a bell, plainly, audibly. **3** *he has time to get clear away* COMPLETELY, entirely, fully, wholly, totally, utterly; *informal* clean.
▶ verb **1** *the sky cleared briefly* BRIGHTEN (UP), lighten, clear up, become bright/brighter/lighter, become fine/sunny. **2** *the drizzle had cleared* DISAPPEAR, go away, end; peter out, fade, wear off, decrease, lessen, diminish. **3** *together they cleared the table* EMPTY, unload, unburden, strip. **4** *clearing drains* UNBLOCK, unstop. **5** *staff cleared the building* EVACUATE, empty; leave. **6** *Karen cleared the dirty plates* REMOVE, take away, carry away, tidy away/up. **7** *I cleared the bar on my first attempt* GO OVER, pass over, sail over; jump (over), vault (over), leap (over), hurdle. **8** *he was cleared by an appeal court* ACQUIT, declare innocent, find not guilty; absolve, exonerate; *informal* let off (the hook); *formal* exculpate. **9** *I was cleared to work on the atomic project* AUTHORIZE, give permission, permit, allow, pass, accept, endorse, license, sanction, give approval/consent to; *informal* OK, okay, give the OK, give the thumbs up, give the green light, give the go-ahead. **10** *I cleared $50,000 profit* NET, make/realize a profit of,

take home, pocket; gain, earn, make, get, bring in, pull in.
■ **clear out** (*informal*). See LEAVE[1] sense 1.
■ **clear something out 1** *we cleared out the junk room* EMPTY (OUT); tidy (up), clear up. **2** *clear out the old equipment* GET RID OF, throw out/away, discard, dispose of, dump, scrap, jettison, chuck (out/away), deep-six, ditch, get shut of, trash.
■ **clear up**. See CLEAR *verb* sense 1.
■ **clear something up 1** *clear up the garden* TIDY (UP), put in order, straighten up, clean up, spruce up. **2** *we've cleared up the problem* SOLVE, resolve, straighten out, find an/the answer to; get to the bottom of, explain; *informal* crack, figure out, suss out.

clearance ▶ **noun 1** *slum clearance* REMOVAL, clearing, demolition. **2** *you must have clearance to enter* AUTHORIZATION, permission, consent, approval, blessing, leave, sanction, licence, dispensation, assent, agreement, endorsement; *informal* the green light, the go-ahead, the thumbs up, the OK, the say-so. **3** *the clearance of a debt* REPAYMENT, payment, paying (off), settling, discharge. **4** *there is plenty of clearance* SPACE, room (to spare), margin, leeway.

clear-cut ▶ **adjective** DEFINITE, distinct, clear, well-defined, precise, specific, explicit, unambiguous, unequivocal, black and white, cut and dried.
— OPPOSITES: vague.

clearing ▶ **noun** OPENING, glade.

clearly ▶ **adverb 1** *write clearly* INTELLIGIBLY, plainly, distinctly, comprehensibly, with clarity; legibly, audibly; *formal* perspicuously. **2** *clearly, substantial changes are needed* OBVIOUSLY, evidently, patently, unquestionably, undoubtedly, without doubt, indubitably, plainly, undeniably, incontrovertibly, irrefutably, doubtless, it goes without saying, needless to say.

cleave[1] ▶ **verb 1** *cleaving wood for the fire* SPLIT (OPEN), cut (up), hew, hack, chop up; *literary* rive. **2** *cleaving a path through the traffic* PLOW, drive, bulldoze, carve.

cleave[2]
■ **cleave to** (*literary*) **1** *her tongue clove to the roof of her mouth* STICK (FAST) TO, adhere to, be attached to. **2** *cleaving too closely to Moscow's line* ADHERE TO, hold to, abide by, be loyal/faithful to.

cleaver ▶ **noun** CHOPPER, hatchet, axe, knife; butcher's knife, kitchen knife.

cleft ▶ **noun 1** *a deep cleft in the rocks* SPLIT, slit, crack, fissure, crevice, rift, break, fracture, rent, breach. **2** *the cleft in his chin* DIMPLE.
▶ **adjective** *a cleft tail* SPLIT, divided, cloven, bifid.

clemency ▶ **noun** MERCY, mercifulness, leniency, mildness, indulgence, quarter; compassion, humanity, pity, sympathy.
— OPPOSITES: ruthlessness.

clench ▶ **verb 1** *he stood there clenching his hands* SQUEEZE TOGETHER, clamp together, close/shut tightly; make into a fist. **2** *he clenched the iron bar* GRIP, grasp, grab, clutch, clasp, hold tightly, seize, press, squeeze.

clergy ▶ **noun** CLERICS, clergymen, clergywomen, churchmen, churchwomen, priests, ecclesiastics, men/women of God; ministry, priesthood, holy orders, the church, the cloth.
— RELATED TERMS: clerical.
— OPPOSITES: laity.

clergyman, clergywoman ▶ **noun** CLERIC, priest, minister, preacher, pastor, vicar, rector, chaplain, father, ecclesiastic, bishop, parson, curate,

deacon, deaconess; churchman, churchwoman, man/woman of the cloth, man/woman of God; *informal* reverend, padre, Holy Joe, sky pilot.

clerical ▶ **adjective 1** *clerical jobs* OFFICE, desk, back-room; administrative, secretarial; white-collar. **2** *a clerical minister* ECCLESIASTICAL, church, priestly, religious, spiritual, sacerdotal; holy, divine.
— OPPOSITES: secular.

clerk ▶ **noun** OFFICE WORKER, clerical worker, administrator; bookkeeper; cashier, teller; *informal* pen-pusher, pencil-pusher, paper-shuffler; *historical* scrivener.

clever ▶ **adjective 1** *a clever young woman* INTELLIGENT, bright, smart, astute, sharp, quick-witted, shrewd; talented, gifted, brilliant, capable, able, competent, apt; educated, learned, knowledgeable, wise; *informal* brainy, savvy. **2** *a clever scheme* INGENIOUS, canny, cunning, crafty, artful, slick, neat. **3** *she was clever with her hands* SKILFUL, dexterous, adroit, adept, deft, nimble, handy; skilled, talented, gifted. **4** *a clever remark* WITTY, amusing, droll, humorous, funny.
— OPPOSITES: stupid.

cliché ▶ **noun** PLATITUDE, hackneyed phrase, commonplace, banality, old saying, maxim, truism, stock phrase, trite phrase; old chestnut.

click ▶ **noun** CLACK, snick, snap, pop, tick; clink.
▶ **verb 1** *cameras clicked* CLACK, snap, snick, tick, pop; clink. **2** (*informal*) *that night it clicked* BECOME CLEAR, fall into place, come home, make sense, dawn, register, get through, sink in. **3** (*informal*) *we just clicked* TAKE TO EACH OTHER, get along, be compatible, be like-minded, feel a rapport, see eye to eye; *informal* hit it off, get on like a house on fire, be on the same wavelength. **4** (*informal*) *this issue hasn't clicked with the voters* GO DOWN WELL, prove popular, be a hit, succeed.

client ▶ **noun** CUSTOMER, buyer, purchaser, shopper, consumer, user; patient; patron, regular; (**clients**) clientele, patronage, public, market; *Law* vendee.

cliff ▶ **noun** PRECIPICE, rock face, crag, bluff, ridge, escarpment, scar, scarp, ledge, (*BC*, *Alta.*, & *North*) rampart ✦, overhang.

climactic ▶ **adjective** FINAL, ending, closing, concluding, ultimate; exciting, thrilling, gripping, riveting, dramatic, hair-raising; crucial, decisive, critical.

climate ▶ **noun 1** *a mild climate* WEATHER CONDITIONS, weather; atmospheric conditions. **2** *they come from colder climates* REGION, area, zone, country, place; *literary* clime. **3** *the political climate* ATMOSPHERE, mood, feeling, ambience, tenor; tendency, ethos, attitude; milieu; *informal* vibe(s).

climax ▶ **noun** *the climax of his career* PEAK, pinnacle, height, high(est) point, top; acme, zenith; culmination, crowning point, crown, crest; highlight, high spot, high-water mark.
— OPPOSITES: nadir.
▶ **verb** *the event will climax with a concert* CULMINATE, peak, reach a pinnacle, come to a crescendo, come to a head.

climb ▶ **verb 1** *we climbed the hill* ASCEND, mount, scale, scramble up, clamber up, shinny up; go up, walk up; conquer, gain. **2** *the plane climbed* RISE, ascend, go up, gain altitude. **3** *the road climbs steeply* SLOPE UPWARDS, rise, go uphill, incline upwards. **4** *the shares climbed to $10.77* INCREASE, rise, go up, shoot up, soar, rocket. **5** *he climbed through the ranks* ADVANCE, rise, move up, progress, work one's way. **6** *he climbed*

out of his car CLAMBER, scramble; step.
— OPPOSITES: descend, drop, fall.
▶ **noun** *a steep climb* ASCENT, clamber.
— OPPOSITES: descent.
■ **climb down 1** *Sandy climbed down the ladder* DESCEND, go/come down, move down, shinny down. **2** *the Government had to climb down* BACK DOWN, admit defeat, surrender, capitulate, yield, give in, give way, submit; retreat, backtrack; eat one's words, eat humble pie, eat crow; do a U-turn.

clinch ▶ **verb 1** *he clinched the deal* SECURE, settle, conclude, close, pull off, bring off, complete, confirm, seal, finalize; *informal* sew up, wrap up. **2** *these findings clinched the matter* SETTLE, decide, determine; resolve; *informal* sort out. **3** *Westmount clinched the title* WIN, secure; be victorious, come first, triumph, prevail. **4** *the boxers clinched* GRAPPLE, wrestle, struggle, scuffle.
— OPPOSITES: lose.

cling ▶ **verb** *rice grains tend to cling together* STICK, adhere, hold, cohere, bond, bind.
■ **cling (on) to 1** *she clung to him* HOLD ON, clutch, grip, grasp, clasp, attach oneself to, hang on; embrace, hug. **2** *they clung to their beliefs* ADHERE TO, hold to, stick to, stand by, abide by, cherish, remain true to, have faith in; *informal* swear by, stick with.

clinic ▶ **noun** MEDICAL CENTRE, health centre, (*Que.*) CLSC ✦, nursing station ✦, (*Nfld*) cottage hospital ✦, outpatients' department, surgery, doctor's office.

clinical ▶ **adjective 1** *he seemed so clinical* DETACHED, impersonal, dispassionate, objective, uninvolved, distant, remote, aloof, removed, cold, indifferent, neutral, unsympathetic, unfeeling, unemotional. **2** *the room was clinical* PLAIN, simple, unadorned, unembellished, stark, austere, Spartan, bleak, bare; clean; functional, utilitarian, basic, institutional, impersonal, characterless.
— OPPOSITES: emotional, luxurious.

clink ▶ **verb** DING, ping, jingle, chink, tinkle.

clip¹ ▶ **noun 1** *a briefcase clip* FASTENER, clasp, hasp, catch, hook, buckle, lock. **2** *a mother-of-pearl clip* BROOCH, pin, badge. **3** *his clip was empty* MAGAZINE, cartridge, cylinder.
▶ **verb** *he clipped the pages together* FASTEN, attach, fix, join; pin, staple, tack.

clip² ▶ **verb 1** *I clipped the hedge* TRIM, prune, cut, snip, shorten, crop, shear, pare; lop; neaten, shape. **2** *clip the coupon below* REMOVE, cut out, snip out, tear out, detach. **3** *his trailer clipped a parked van* HIT, strike, touch, graze, glance off, run into. **4** *Mum clipped his ear* HIT, cuff, strike, smack, slap, box; *informal* clout, whack, wallop, clobber, sock.
▶ **noun 1** *I gave the dog a clip* TRIM, cut, crop, haircut; shear. **2** *a film clip* EXTRACT, excerpt, snippet, cutting, fragment; trailer. **3** (*informal*) *a clip round the ear* SMACK, cuff, slap, box; *informal* clout, whack, wallop, sock. **4** (*informal*) *the truck went at a good clip* SPEED, rate, pace, velocity; *informal* lick.
■ **clip someone's wings** RESTRICT SOMEONE'S FREEDOM, impose limits on, keep under control, stand in the way of; obstruct, impede, frustrate, thwart, fetter, hamstring, handcuff.

clipping ▶ **noun** CUTTING, snippet, extract, excerpt.

clique ▶ **noun** COTERIE, set, circle, ring, in-crowd, group; club, society, fraternity, sorority; cabal, caucus; *informal* gang.

cloak ▶ **noun 1** *the cloak over his shoulders* CAPE, poncho, shawl, burnoose, cope, robe, cowl, djellaba, domino, mantle, wrap, pelisse, serape, tippet; cassock, chasuble, pallium; *historical* cardinal. **2** *a cloak of secrecy* COVER, veil, mantle, shroud, screen, mask, shield, blanket.
▶ **verb** *a peak cloaked in mist* CONCEAL, hide, cover, veil, shroud, mask, obscure, cloud; envelop, swathe, surround.

clobber ▶ **verb** (*informal*) *I'll clobber him. See* HIT *verb* sense 1.

clock ▶ **noun** *a grandfather clock* TIMEPIECE, timekeeper, timer; chronometer, chronograph.
▶ **verb** (*informal*) **1** *we clocked up record exports* REGISTER, record, log, achieve, attain, accomplish, make; *informal* chalk up, bag. **2** *his fastball was clocked at 92 mph* TIME, measure.

clod ▶ **noun 1** *clods of earth* LUMP, clump, chunk, hunk. **2** (*informal*) *an insensitive clod. See* IDIOT.

clog ▶ **noun** *a wooden clog* sabot.
▶ **verb** *the pipes were clogged* BLOCK, obstruct, congest, jam, choke, bung up, plug, stop up, fill up, gunge up.

cloister ▶ **noun 1** *the convent cloisters* WALKWAY, covered walk, arcade, loggia, gallery. **2** *I was educated in the cloister* ABBEY, monastery, friary, convent, priory, nunnery.

cloistered ▶ **adjective** SECLUDED, sequestered, sheltered, protected, insulated; shut off, isolated, confined, incommunicado; solitary, monastic, reclusive.

close¹ ▶ **adjective 1** *the town is close to Joliette* NEAR, adjacent; in the vicinity of, in the neighbourhood of, within reach of; neighbouring, adjoining, abutting, alongside, on the doorstep, a stone's throw away, {a hop, skip and a jump from}; nearby, at hand, at close quarters; *informal* within spitting distance; *archaic* nigh. **2** *flying in close formation* DENSE, compact, tight, close-packed, packed, solid; crowded, cramped, congested. **3** *I was close to tears* NEAR, on the verge of, on the brink of, on the point of. **4** *a very close match* EVENLY MATCHED, even, with nothing to choose between them; neck and neck; *informal* even-steven(s). **5** *close relatives* IMMEDIATE, direct, near. **6** *close friends* INTIMATE, dear, bosom; close-knit, tight-knit, inseparable, attached, devoted, faithful; special, good, best, fast, firm; *informal* (as) thick as thieves. **7** *a close resemblance* STRONG, marked, distinct, pronounced. **8** *a close examination* CAREFUL, detailed, thorough, minute, searching, painstaking, meticulous, rigorous, scrupulous, conscientious; attentive, focused. **9** *keep a close eye on them* VIGILANT, watchful, keen, alert. **10** *a close translation* STRICT, faithful, exact, precise, literal; word for word, verbatim. **11** *the weather was close* HUMID, muggy, stuffy, airless, heavy, sticky, sultry, oppressive, stifling.
— OPPOSITES: far, distant, one-sided, slight, loose, fresh.

close² ▶ **verb 1** *she closed the door* SHUT, pull to, push to, slam; fasten, secure. **2** *close the hole* BLOCK (UP/OFF), stop up, plug, seal (up/off), shut up/off, cork, stopper, bung (up); clog (up), choke, obstruct. **3** *the enemy was closing fast* CATCH UP, creep up, near, approach, gain on someone. **4** *the gap is closing* NARROW, reduce, shrink, lessen, get smaller, diminish, contract. **5** *his arms closed around her* MEET, join, connect; form a circle. **6** *he closed the meeting* END, conclude, finish, terminate, wind up, break off, halt, discontinue, dissolve; adjourn, suspend. **7** *the factory is to close* SHUT DOWN, close down, cease production, cease trading, be wound up, go out of business, go bankrupt, go into

receivership, go into liquidation; *informal* fold, go bust. **8** *he closed a deal* CLINCH, settle, secure, seal, confirm, establish; transact, pull off; complete, conclude, fix, agree, finalize; *informal* wrap up.
— OPPOSITES: open, widen, begin.
▶ **noun** *the close of the talks* END, finish, conclusion, termination, cessation, completion, resolution, climax, denouement; *informal* outro.
— OPPOSITES: beginning.
■ **close down.** See CLOSE² verb sense 7.

closet ▶ **noun** *a clothes closet* CUPBOARD, wardrobe, cabinet, locker.
▶ **adjective** *a closet Sherlock Holmes fan* SECRET, covert, private; surreptitious, clandestine, underground, furtive.
▶ **verb** *David was closeted in his den* SHUT AWAY, sequester, seclude, cloister, confine, isolate.

closure ▶ **noun** CLOSING DOWN, shutdown, winding up; termination, discontinuation, cessation, finish, conclusion; failure; *informal* folding.

clot ▶ **noun** *blood clots* LUMP, clump, mass; thrombus, thrombosis, embolus; *informal* glob, gob.
▶ **verb** *the blood is likely to clot* COAGULATE, set, congeal, curdle, thicken, solidify.

cloth ▶ **noun 1** *a maker of cloth* FABRIC, material, textile(s), soft goods. **2** *a cloth to wipe the table* RAG, wipe, duster, sponge; flannel, towel.

clothe ▶ **verb 1** *they were clothed in silk* DRESS, attire, robe, garb, array, costume, swathe, deck (out), turn out, fit out, rig (out); *informal* get up; *archaic* apparel, habit, invest. **2** *a valley clothed in conifers* COVER, blanket, carpet; envelop, swathe.

clothes ▶ **plural noun** CLOTHING, garments, attire, garb, dress, wear, costume; *informal* gear, togs, duds, threads, getup; *formal* apparel; *archaic* raiment, habiliments, vestments.
— RELATED TERMS: sartorial.

clothing ▶ **noun.** See CLOTHES.

cloud ▶ **noun 1** *dark clouds* storm cloud, cloudbank, cloud cover; mackerel sky. *See table.* **2** *a cloud of exhaust smoke* MASS, billow; pall, mantle, blanket.
▶ **verb 1** *the sky clouded* BECOME CLOUDY, cloud over, become overcast, lower, blacken, darken. **2** *the sand is churned up, clouding the water* MAKE CLOUDY, make murky, dirty, darken, blacken. **3** *anger clouded my judgment* CONFUSE, muddle, obscure, fog, muddy, mar.
■ **on cloud nine** ECSTATIC, rapturous, joyful, elated, blissful, euphoric, in seventh heaven, walking on air, transported, in raptures, delighted, thrilled, overjoyed, over the moon, on top of the world, tickled pink.

Clouds

altocumulus	nimbostratus
altostratus	nimbus
anvil	rain cloud
chinook arch ♣	storm cloud
cirrocumulus	stratocirrus
cirrostratus	stratocumulus
cirrus	stratus
cumulonimbus	streamer
cumulus	thundercloud
funnel cloud	thunderhead
mare's tails	

cloudy ▶ **adjective 1** *a cloudy sky* OVERCAST, clouded; dark, grey, black, leaden, murky; sombre, dismal, heavy, gloomy; sunless, starless; hazy, misty, foggy. **2** *cloudy water* MURKY, muddy, milky, dirty, opaque, turbid. **3** *his eyes grew cloudy* TEARFUL, teary, weepy, lachrymose; moist, watery; misty, blurred.
— OPPOSITES: clear.

clout (*informal*) ▶ **noun 1** *a clout on the ear* SMACK, slap, thump, punch, blow, hit, cuff, box, clip; *informal* whack, wallop. **2** *her clout in the business world* INFLUENCE, power, weight, sway, leverage, control, say; dominance, authority; *informal* teeth, muscle.
▶ **verb** *he clouted me* HIT, strike, punch, smack, slap, cuff, thump, buffet; *informal* wallop, belt, whack, clobber, sock, bop,

cloven ▶ **adjective** SPLIT, divided, cleft.

clown ▶ **noun 1** *a circus clown* COMEDIAN; jester, fool, zany. **2** *the class clown* JOKER, comedian, comic, humorist, wag, wit, prankster, jester, buffoon; *informal* laugh, kidder, wisecracker. **3** *bureaucratic clowns* FOOL, idiot, dolt, ass, simpleton, ignoramus; bungler, blunderer; *informal* moron, meatball, bozo, jackass, chump, numbskull, numbnuts, nincompoop, halfwit, bonehead, knucklehead, fathead, birdbrain, twit, nitwit, twerp.
▶ **verb** *Harvey clowned around* FOOL AROUND/ABOUT, play the fool, play about/around, monkey about/around; joke, jest; *informal* mess about/around, lark (about/around), muck about/around, muck around/about.

cloying ▶ **adjective** SICKLY, syrupy, saccharine, over-sweet; sickening, nauseating; mawkish, sentimental, twee; *informal* over the top, mushy, slushy, sloppy, gooey, cheesy, corny, cornball, sappy.

club¹ ▶ **noun 1** *a canoeing club* SOCIETY, association, organization, institution, group, circle, band, body, ring, crew; alliance, league, union. **2** *the city has great clubs* NIGHTCLUB, disco, discotheque, bar. **3** *the top club in the league* TEAM, squad, side, lineup, franchise.

club² ▶ **noun** *a wooden club* CUDGEL, truncheon, bludgeon, baton, stick, mace, bat, blackjack, nightstick.
▶ **verb** *he was clubbed with an iron bar* CUDGEL, bludgeon, bash, beat, hit, strike, batter, belabour; *informal* clout, clobber.

clue ▶ **noun 1** *police are searching for clues* EVIDENCE, hint, information, indication, sign, signal, pointer, trace, indicator; lead, tip, tipoff. **2** *a crossword clue* QUESTION, problem, puzzle, riddle, poser, conundrum.
■ **clue someone in** (*informal*) INFORM, notify, make aware, prime; keep up to date, keep posted; *informal* tip off, give the lowdown, fill in on, put in the picture, put wise, keep up to speed.
■ **not have a clue** (*informal*) HAVE NO IDEA, be ignorant, not have an inkling; be baffled, be mystified, be at a loss; *informal* be clueless, not have the faintest/foggiest/ slightest.

clump ▶ **noun 1** *a clump of trees* CLUSTER, thicket, group, bunch, assemblage. **2** *a clump of earth* LUMP, clod, mass, wad, glob, gob.
▶ **verb 1** *galaxies clump together* CLUSTER, group, collect, gather, assemble, congregate, mass. **2** *they were clumping around upstairs* STAMP, stomp, clomp, tramp, lumber; thump, thud, bang; *informal* galumph.

clumsy ▶ **adjective 1** *she was terribly clumsy* AWKWARD, uncoordinated, ungainly, graceless, inelegant; inept, maladroit, unskilful, unhandy, accident-prone, like a bull in a china shop, all thumbs; *informal* ham-fisted, butterfingered, having two left feet, klutzy. **2** *a clumsy contraption* UNWIELDY, cumbersome, bulky, awkward. **3** *a clumsy remark* GAUCHE, awkward,

graceless; unsubtle, uncouth, boorish, crass; tactless, insensitive, thoughtless, undiplomatic, indelicate, ill-judged.
— OPPOSITES: graceful, elegant, tactful.

clunker (*informal*) ▶ noun FAILURE, flop, bust, dud, turkey; jalopy, lemon, beater, rustbucket.

cluster ▶ noun **1** *clusters of berries* BUNCH, clump, mass, knot, group, clump, bundle, truss. **2** *a cluster of spectators* CROWD, group, knot, huddle, bunch, throng, flock, pack, band; *informal* gang, gaggle.
▶ verb *they clustered around the television* CONGREGATE, gather, collect, group, assemble; huddle, crowd, flock.

clutch¹ ▶ verb *she clutched his arm* GRIP, grasp, clasp, cling to, hang on to, clench, hold.
■ **clutch at** REACH FOR, snatch at, make a grab for, catch at, (*Nfld*) scravel at ♣, claw at.

clutch² ▶ noun **1** *a clutch of eggs* GROUP, batch. **2** *a clutch of awards* GROUP, collection; raft, armful; *informal* load, bunch, ton.

clutches ▶ plural noun POWER, control, domination, command, rule, tyranny; hands, hold, grip, grasp, claws, jaws, tentacles; custody.

clutter ▶ noun **1** *a clutter of toys* MESS, jumble, litter, heap, tangle, muddle, hodgepodge. **2** *a desk full of clutter* DISORDER, chaos, disarray, untidiness, mess, confusion; litter, rubbish, junk.
▶ verb *the garden was cluttered with tools* LITTER, mess up, disarrange; be strewn, be scattered; *literary* bestrew.

coach¹ ▶ noun **1** *a journey by coach* BUS, minibus; *dated* omnibus. **2** *a railway coach* CAR, carriage, wagon, compartment, van, Pullman. **3** *a coach and horses* HORSE-DRAWN CARRIAGE, trap, hackney, hansom, gig, landau, brougham.

coach² ▶ noun *a football coach* INSTRUCTOR, trainer, manager; teacher, tutor, mentor, guru.
▶ verb *she coached Richard in math* INSTRUCT, teach, tutor, school, educate; drill; train.

coagulate ▶ verb CONGEAL, clot, thicken, jell; solidify, harden, set, dry.

coalesce ▶ verb MERGE, unite, join together, combine, fuse, mingle, blend; amalgamate, consolidate, integrate, homogenize, converge.

coalition ▶ noun ALLIANCE, union, partnership, bloc, caucus; federation, league, association, confederation, consortium, syndicate, combine; amalgamation, merger.

coarse ▶ adjective **1** *coarse blankets* ROUGH, scratchy, prickly, wiry. **2** *his coarse features* LARGE, rough, rough-hewn, heavy; ugly. **3** *a coarse boy* OAFISH, loutish, boorish, uncouth, rude, impolite, ill-mannered, uncivil; vulgar, common, rough, uncultured, crass. **4** *a coarse innuendo* VULGAR, crude, rude, off-colour, dirty, filthy, smutty, indelicate, improper, unseemly, crass, tasteless, lewd, prurient, blue, farmyard.
— OPPOSITES: soft, delicate, refined.

coarsen ▶ verb **1** *hands coarsened by work* ROUGHEN, toughen, harden. **2** *I had been coarsened by the army* DESENSITIZE, dehumanize; dull, deaden.
— OPPOSITES: soften, refine.

coast ▶ noun *the west coast* SEABOARD, coastal region, coastline, seashore, shore, foreshore, shoreline, seaside, waterfront, littoral; *literary* strand.
▶ verb *the car coasted down a hill* FREEWHEEL, cruise, taxi, drift, glide, sail.

coat ▶ noun **1** *a winter coat* OVERCOAT, jacket. *See table.* **2** *a dog's coat* FUR, hair, wool, fleece; hide, pelt, skin.

3 *a coat of paint* LAYER, covering, coating, skin, film, wash; plating, glaze, varnish, veneer, patina; deposit.
▶ verb *the tube was coated with wax* COVER, paint, glaze, varnish, wash; surface, veneer, laminate, plate, face; daub, smear, cake, plaster.

Coats & Jackets

Afghan	Mackinaw
amautik ♣(*North*)	matinee coat
atigi ♣(*North*)	mess jacket
bed jacket	Mother Hubbard ♣
blanket coat	Nehru jacket
blazer	Norfolk jacket
blouson	overcoat
bolero	parka
bomber jacket	pea jacket
boyfriend jacket	raglan
bush jacket ♣	rain jacket
capote	raincoat
car coat	redingote
cardigan	reefer
Chanel jacket	safari jacket
chesterfield	shell
cutaway	shirt jacket
dinner jacket	single-breasted
dolman	spencer
double-breasted	sports coat
doublet	sports jacket
dress coat	storm coat
duffle coat	suit coat
duster coat	sunburst ♣
frock coat	surcoat
greatcoat	surtout
happi	sweater coat
hockey jacket ♣	swing coat
Hudson's Bay blanket	tailcoat
coat ♣	topcoat
jean jacket	topper
jerkin	ulster
jibba	windbreaker
kangaroo jacket ♣	trench coat
lumberjack jacket	

coating ▶ noun. *See* COAT *noun sense 3.*

coax ▶ verb PERSUADE, wheedle, cajole, get around; beguile, seduce, inveigle, manoeuvre; *informal* sweet-talk, soft-soap, butter up, twist someone's arm.

cobble
■ **cobble something together** PREPARE ROUGHLY/HASTILY, make roughly/hastily, throw together; improvise, contrive, rig (up), whip up; *informal* rustle up.

cocaine ▶ noun COKE, crack, blow, freebase, nose candy, rock, snow.

cock ▶ noun ROOSTER, cockerel, capon.
▶ verb **1** *he cocked his head* TILT, tip, angle, incline, dip. **2** *she cocked her little finger* BEND, flex, crook, curve. **3** *the dog cocked its leg* LIFT, raise, hold up.

cockeyed ▶ adjective (*informal*) **1** *that picture is cockeyed* CROOKED, awry, askew, lopsided, tilted, off-centre, skewed, skew, misaligned, wonky. **2** *a cockeyed scheme* ABSURD, preposterous, ridiculous, ludicrous, farcical, laughable, cockamamie, risible, idiotic, stupid, foolish, silly, inane, imbecilic, half-baked, hare-brained; impractical, unfeasible, irrational, illogical, nonsensical, crazy, daft.

cockpit ▶ noun FLIGHT DECK, helm, control room; driver's seat.

cocksure ▶ adjective ARROGANT, conceited, overweening, overconfident, cocky, proud, vain, self-important, egotistical, presumptuous; smug, patronizing, pompous; *informal* high and mighty, puffed-up.
— OPPOSITES: modest.

cocktail ▶ noun. *See table.*

Cocktails & Mixed Drinks

Alcoholic	planter's punch
Alexander	punch
black velvet	red-eye ♣
B-52	rickey
Bloody Caesar ♣	rum and Coke
Bloody Mary	rusty nail
blueberry tea	rye and dry
boilermaker	rye and ginger
brown cow ♣	sangria
Caesar ♣	screwdriver
callibogus ♣(esp. Nfld)	shandy
caribou ♣(esp. Que.)	shrub
cobbler	sidecar
Collins	Singapore sling
cosmopolitan	sling
daiquiri	spritzer
gimlet	stinger
gin-and-it	swizzle
gin and tonic	syllabub
grasshopper	tequila sunrise
Harvey Wallbanger	toddy
highball	Tom Collins
kir	vodka and orange (juice)
Long Island ice tea	whisky sour
mai tai	White Russian
manhattan	wine cooler
margarita	zombie
martini	
mimosa	**Non-Alcoholic**
mint julep	mocktail
mulled wine	prairie oyster
old fashioned	Shirley Temple
pina colada	Virgin Mary
pink lady	*See also* WINES *and*
moose milk ♣	ALCOHOLIC SPIRITS & LIQUEURS.

cocky ▶ adjective ARROGANT, conceited, overweening, overconfident, cocksure, self-important, egotistical, presumptuous, boastful, self-assertive; bold, forward, insolent, cheeky, puffed-up.
— OPPOSITES: modest.

cocoon ▶ verb **1** *he cocooned her in a towel* WRAP, swathe, swaddle, muffle, cloak, enfold, envelop, cover, fold. **2** *he was cocooned in the university* PROTECT, shield, shelter, screen, cushion, insulate, isolate, cloister.

coddle ▶ verb PAMPER, cosset, mollycoddle; spoil, indulge, overindulge, pander to; baby, mother, wait on hand and foot.
— OPPOSITES: neglect.

code ▶ noun **1** *a secret code* CIPHER, key; hieroglyphics; cryptogram. **2** *a strict social code* MORALITY, convention, etiquette, protocol, value system. **3** *the penal code* LAW(S), rules, regulations; constitution, system.

codify ▶ verb SYSTEMATIZE, systemize, organize, arrange, order, structure; tabulate, catalogue, list, sort, index, classify, categorize, file, log.

coerce ▶ verb PRESSURE, pressurize, press, push, constrain; force, compel, oblige, browbeat, bludgeon, bully, threaten, intimidate, dragoon, twist someone's arm; *informal* railroad, squeeze, lean on.

coercion ▶ noun FORCE, compulsion, constraint, duress, oppression, enforcement, harassment, intimidation, threats, arm-twisting, pressure.

coffee ▶ noun *informal* joe, java. *See table.*

Coffee

black	Irish coffee
cappuccino	latte
café au lait	lungo
café noir	macchiato
decaf	mocha
double double	mochaccino
drip	percolated
espresso	Spanish coffee
instant	Turkish coffee

coffer ▶ noun **1** *every church had a coffer* STRONGBOX, money box, cash box, money chest, treasure chest, safe; casket, box. **2** *the government coffers* FUND(S), reserves, resources, money, finances, wealth, cash, capital, purse; treasury, exchequer; *informal* pork barrel.

coffin ▶ noun casket; sarcophagus; *informal* box; *humorous* wooden overcoat.

cogent ▶ adjective CONVINCING, compelling, strong, forceful, powerful, potent, weighty, effective; valid, sound, plausible, telling; impressive, persuasive, eloquent, credible, influential; conclusive, authoritative; logical, reasoned, rational, reasonable, lucid, coherent, clear.

cogitate ▶ verb *(formal)* THINK (ABOUT), contemplate, consider, mull over, meditate, muse, ponder, reflect, deliberate, ruminate; dwell on, brood on, chew over; *informal* put on one's thinking cap.

cognate ▶ adjective *(formal)* ASSOCIATED, related, connected, allied, linked; similar, like, alike, akin, kindred, comparable, parallel, corresponding, analogous.

cognition ▶ noun PERCEPTION, discernment, apprehension, learning, understanding, comprehension, insight; reasoning, thinking, thought.

cognizant ▶ adjective *(formal)*. *See* AWARE sense 1.

cohabit ▶ verb LIVE TOGETHER, live with; *informal* shack up (with); *dated* live in sin.

cohere ▶ verb **1** *the stories cohere into a convincing whole* STICK TOGETHER, hold together, be united, bind, fuse. **2** *this view does not cohere with others* BE CONSISTENT, hang together.

coherent ▶ adjective LOGICAL, reasoned, reasonable, rational, sound, cogent, consistent; clear, lucid, articulate; intelligible, comprehensible.
— OPPOSITES: muddled.

cohesion ▶ noun UNITY, togetherness, solidarity, bond, coherence; connection, linkage.

cohort ▶ noun **1** *a Roman army cohort* UNIT, force, corps, division, brigade, battalion, regiment, squadron, company, troop, contingent, legion, phalanx. **2** *the 1940–4 birth cohort of women* GROUP, grouping, category, class, set, division, batch, list; age group, generation. **3** *a party thrown by her departmental cohorts* COLLEAGUE, companion, associate, friend.

coil ▶ noun *coils of rope* LOOP, twist, turn, curl, convolution; spiral, helix, corkscrew.

▶ **verb** *he coiled her hair around his finger* WIND, loop, twist, curl, curve, bend, twine, entwine; spiral, corkscrew.

coin ▶ **noun 1** *coins in my pocket* penny, nickel, dime, quarter, loonie ♣ (loon ♣), toonie ♣; piece. **2** *large amounts of coin* COINAGE, coins, specie; (loose) change, small change, silver, copper(s), gold.
– RELATED TERMS: numismatic.
▶ **verb 1** *loonies were coined* MINT, stamp, strike, cast, punch, die, mould, forge, make. **2** *he coined the term* INVENT, create, make up, conceive, originate, think up, dream up.

coincide ▶ **verb 1** *the events coincided* OCCUR SIMULTANEOUSLY, happen together, be concurrent, concur, coexist. **2** *their interests do not always coincide* CORRESPOND, tally, agree, accord, concur, match, fit, be consistent, equate, harmonize, be compatible, dovetail, correlate; *informal* square.
– OPPOSITES: differ.

coincidence ▶ **noun 1** *too close to be mere coincidence* ACCIDENT, chance, serendipity, fortuity, providence, happenstance, fate; a fluke. **2** *the coincidence of inflation and unemployment* CO-OCCURRENCE, coexistence, conjunction, simultaneity, contemporaneity, concomitance. **3** *a coincidence of interests* CORRESPONDENCE, agreement, accord, concurrence, consistency, conformity, harmony, compatibility.

coincidental ▶ **adjective 1** *a coincidental resemblance* ACCIDENTAL, chance, fluky, random; fortuitous, adventitious, serendipitous; unexpected, unforeseen, unintentional, inadvertent, unplanned. **2** *the coincidental disappearance of the two men* SIMULTANEOUS, concurrent, coincident, contemporaneous, concomitant.

coitus ▶ **noun** (technical). See SEX noun sense 1.

cold ▶ **adjective 1** *a cold day* CHILLY, chill, cool, freezing, icy, snowy, wintry, frosty, frigid, gelid; bitter, biting, raw, bone-chilling, nippy, arctic. **2** *I'm very cold* CHILLY, chilled, cool, freezing, frozen, shivery, numb, benumbed; hypothermic. **3** *a cold reception* UNFRIENDLY, inhospitable, unwelcoming, forbidding, cool, frigid, frosty, glacial, lukewarm, indifferent, unfeeling, unemotional, formal, stiff.
– OPPOSITES: hot, warm.

cold-blooded ▶ **adjective** CRUEL, callous, sadistic, inhuman, inhumane, pitiless, merciless, ruthless, unforgiving, unfeeling, uncaring, heartless; savage, brutal, barbaric, barbarous; cold, cold-hearted, unemotional.

cold-hearted ▶ **adjective** UNFEELING, unloving, uncaring, unsympathetic, unemotional, unfriendly, uncharitable, unkind, insensitive; hard-hearted, stony-hearted, heartless, hard, cold.

collaborate ▶ **verb 1** *they collaborated on the project* CO-OPERATE, join forces, team up, band together, work together, participate, combine, ally; pool resources, put —— heads together. **2** *they collaborated with the enemy* COLLUDE, conspire, fraternize, co-operate, consort, sympathize; *informal* be in cahoots.

collaborator ▶ **noun 1** *his collaborator on the book* CO-WORKER, partner, associate, colleague, confederate; assistant. **2** *a wartime collaborator* QUISLING, fraternizer, collaborationist, colluder, (enemy) sympathizer; traitor, fifth columnist.

collapse ▶ **verb 1** *the roof collapsed* CAVE IN, fall in, subside, fall down, give (way), crumple, buckle, sag,

slump. **2** *he collapsed last night* FAINT, pass out, black out, lose consciousness, keel over, swoon; *informal* flake out, conk out. **3** *he collapsed in tears* BREAK DOWN, go to pieces, lose control, be overcome, crumble; *informal* crack up. **4** *peace talks collapsed* BREAK DOWN, fail, fall through, fold, founder, miscarry, come to grief, be unsuccessful; end; *informal* flop, fizzle out.
▶ **noun 1** *the collapse of the roof* CAVE-IN, subsidence. **2** *her collapse on stage* FAINTING FIT, faint, blackout, loss of consciousness, swoon; *Medicine* syncope. **3** *the collapse of the talks* BREAKDOWN, failure, disintegration; end. **4** *he suffered a collapse* (NERVOUS) BREAKDOWN, personal crisis, psychological trauma; *informal* crack-up.

collar ▶ **noun 1** *a shirt collar* NECKBAND, choker; *historical* ruff, gorget, bertha. **2** *a collar round the pipe* RING, band, collet, sleeve, flange.
▶ **verb** (*informal*) **1** *he collared a thief* APPREHEND, arrest, catch, capture, seize; take prisoner, take into custody, detain; *informal* nab, pinch, bust, pick up, pull in. **2** *she collared me in the street* ACCOST, waylay, hail, approach, detain, stop, halt, catch, confront, importune; *informal* buttonhole.

collate ▶ **verb 1** *the system is used to collate information* COLLECT, gather, accumulate, assemble; combine, aggregate, put together; arrange, organize. **2** *we must collate these two sources* COMPARE, contrast, set side by side, juxtapose, weigh against.

collateral ▶ **noun** SECURITY, surety, guarantee, guaranty, insurance, indemnity, indemnification; backing.

colleague ▶ **noun** CO-WORKER, fellow worker, workmate, teammate, associate, partner, collaborator, ally, confederate.

collect ▶ **verb 1** *he collected the rubbish* GATHER, accumulate, assemble; amass, stockpile, pile up, heap up, store (up), hoard, save; mass, accrue. **2** *a crowd collected in the square* GATHER, assemble, meet, muster, congregate, convene, converge, flock together. **3** *I must collect the children* FETCH, go/come to get, call for, meet. **4** *they collect money for charity* RAISE, appeal for, ask for, solicit; obtain, acquire, gather. **5** *he paused to collect himself* RECOVER, regain one's composure, pull oneself together, steady oneself; *informal* get a grip (on oneself). **6** *she collected her thoughts* MUSTER, summon (up), gather, get together, marshal.
– OPPOSITES: disperse, distribute.

collected ▶ **adjective** CALM, cool, self-possessed, self-controlled, composed, poised; serene, tranquil, relaxed, unruffled, unperturbed, untroubled; placid, quiet, sedate, phlegmatic; *informal* unfazed, nonplussed, together, laid-back.
– OPPOSITES: excited, hysterical.

collection ▶ **noun 1** *a collection of stolen items* HOARD, pile, heap, stack, stock, store, stockpile; accumulation, reserve, supply, bank, pool, fund, mine, reservoir. **2** *a collection of shoppers* GROUP, crowd, body, assemblage, gathering, throng; knot, cluster, multitude, bevy, party, band, horde, pack, flock, swarm, mob; *informal* gang, load, gaggle. **3** *a collection of Victorian dolls* SET, series; array, assortment. **4** *a collection of short stories* ANTHOLOGY, selection, compendium, treasury, compilation, miscellany, potpourri. **5** *a collection for the poor* DONATIONS, contributions, gifts, subscription(s); penny drive, loonie drive ♣; *historical* alms. **6** *a church collection* OFFERING, offertory, tithe.

collective ▶ **adjective** COMMON, shared, joint,

combined, mutual, communal, pooled; united, allied, co-operative, collaborative.
− OPPOSITES: individual.

college ▶ noun **1** *a college of technology* SCHOOL, academy, university, polytechnic, institute, seminary, conservatoire, conservatory. *See table at* SCHOOL. **2** *the college of physicians* ASSOCIATION, society, club, institute, body, fellowship, guild, lodge, order, fraternity, league, union, alliance.

collide ▶ verb **1** *the trains collided with each other* CRASH, hit, strike, impact, run into, bump into, meet head-on, cannon into, plow into, barrel into. **2** *in her work, politics and metaphysics collide* CONFLICT, clash; differ, diverge, disagree, be at odds, be incompatible.

collision ▶ noun **1** *a collision in the collector lanes* CRASH, accident, impact, smash, bump, hit, fender-bender, wreck, pileup. **2** *a collision between two ideas* CONFLICT, clash; disagreement, incompatibility, contradiction.

colloquial ▶ adjective INFORMAL, conversational, everyday, non-literary; unofficial, idiomatic, slangy, vernacular, popular, demotic.
− OPPOSITES: formal.

collusion ▶ noun *there has been collusion between the security forces and paramilitary groups* CONSPIRACY, connivance, complicity, intrigue, plotting, secret understanding, collaboration, scheming.

cologne ▶ noun SCENT, perfume, fragrance, eau de toilette; aftershave.

colonist ▶ noun SETTLER, colonizer, colonial, pioneer; immigrant, newcomer, homesteader.
− OPPOSITES: native.

colonize ▶ verb SETTLE (IN), people, populate; occupy, take over, seize, capture, subjugate.

colonnade ▶ noun ROW OF COLUMNS; portico, gallery, stoa, peristyle; arcade.

colony ▶ noun **1** *a French colony* SETTLEMENT, dependency, protectorate, satellite, territory, outpost, province. **2** *an artists' colony* COMMUNITY, commune; quarter, district, ghetto.

colossal ▶ adjective HUGE, massive, enormous, gigantic, giant, mammoth, vast, immense, monumental, prodigious, mountainous, titanic, towering, king-size(d), economy-size(d); *informal* monster, whopping, humongous, jumbo, ginormous.
− OPPOSITES: tiny.

colour ▶ noun **1** *the lights changed colour* HUE, shade, tint, tone, coloration. **2** *oil colour* PAINT, pigment, colourant, dye, stain, tint, wash. **3** *the colour in her cheeks* REDNESS, pinkness, rosiness, ruddiness, blush, flush, bloom. **4** *people of every colour* SKIN COLOURING, skin tone, colouring; race, ethnic group. **5** *anecdotes add colour to the text* VIVIDNESS, life, liveliness, vitality, excitement, interest, richness, zest, spice, piquancy, impact, force; *informal* oomph, pizzazz, punch, kick; *literary* salt. **6** *the regimental colours. See* FLAG[1] *noun.*
− RELATED TERMS: chromatic.
▶ verb **1** *the wood was coloured blue* TINT, dye, stain, paint, pigment, wash. **2** *she coloured* BLUSH, redden, go pink, go red, flush. **3** *the experience coloured her outlook* INFLUENCE, affect, taint, warp, skew, distort, bias, prejudice. **4** *they colour evidence to make a story saleable* EXAGGERATE, overstate, embroider, embellish, dramatize, enhance, varnish; falsify, misreport, manipulate.

colourful ▶ adjective **1** *a colourful picture* BRIGHTLY COLOURED, vivid, vibrant, brilliant, radiant, rich;

gaudy, glaring, garish; multicoloured, multicolour, rainbow, varicoloured, harlequin, polychromatic, psychedelic, neon, jazzy. **2** *a colourful account* VIVID, graphic, lively, animated, dramatic, fascinating, interesting, stimulating, scintillating, evocative.

colourless ▶ adjective **1** *a colourless liquid* UNCOLOURED, white, bleached; *literary* achromatic. **2** *her colourless face* PALE, pallid, wan, anemic, bloodless, ashen, white, waxen, pasty, peaky, sickly, drained, drawn, ghostly, deathly. **3** *a colourless personality* UNINTERESTING, dull, boring, tedious, dry, dreary; unexciting, bland, weak, insipid, vapid, vacuous, feeble, wishy-washy, lame, lifeless, spiritless, anemic, bloodless; nondescript, characterless, plain-vanilla.
− OPPOSITES: colourful, rosy.

column ▶ noun **1** *arches supported by massive columns* PILLAR, post, support, upright, baluster, pier, pile, pilaster, stanchion; obelisk, monolith; Doric, Ionic, Corinthian, Tuscan. **2** *a column in the paper* ARTICLE, piece, item, story, report, account, write-up, feature, review, notice, editorial. **3** *we walked in a column* LINE, file, queue, procession, train, cavalcade, convoy.

columnist ▶ noun WRITER, contributor, journalist, correspondent, newspaperman, newspaperwoman, newsman, newswoman; wordsmith, penman; critic, reviewer, commentator; *informal* scribbler, pencil-pusher, hack.

coma ▶ noun state of unconsciousness; *Medicine* persistent vegetative state.

comatose ▶ adjective **1** *he was comatose after the accident* UNCONSCIOUS, in a coma, insensible, insensate. **2** *(informal) she lay comatose in the sun* INERT, inactive, lethargic, sluggish, torpid, languid; somnolent, sleeping, dormant.

comb ▶ verb **1** *she combed her hair* GROOM, brush, untangle, smooth, straighten, neaten, tidy, arrange; curry. **2** *police combed the area* SEARCH, scour, explore, sweep, probe, hunt through, forage through, poke around/about in, go over, go over with a fine-tooth comb; leave no stone unturned.

combat ▶ noun *he was killed in combat* BATTLE, fighting, action, hostilities, conflict, war, warfare.
▶ verb *they tried to combat the disease* FIGHT, battle, tackle, attack, counter, resist, withstand; impede, block, thwart, inhibit; stop, halt, prevent, check, curb.

combatant ▶ noun **1** *a combatant in the war* FIGHTER, soldier, serviceman/woman, warrior, trooper. **2** *combatants in the computer market* CONTENDER, adversary, opponent, competitor, challenger, rival.
▶ adjective *combatant armies* WARRING, at war, opposing, belligerent, fighting, battling.

combative ▶ adjective PUGNACIOUS, aggressive, antagonistic, quarrelsome, argumentative, contentious, hostile, truculent, belligerent, bellicose, militant; *informal* spoiling for a fight.
− OPPOSITES: conciliatory.

combination ▶ noun **1** *a combination of ancient and modern* AMALGAMATION, amalgam, merge, blend, mixture, mix, fusion, marriage, coalition, integration, incorporation, synthesis, composite; *informal* combo. **2** *he acted in combination with his brother* CO-OPERATION, collaboration, association, union, partnership, league.

combine ▶ verb **1** *he combines comedy with tragedy* AMALGAMATE, integrate, incorporate, merge, mix, fuse, blend; bind, join, marry, unify. **2** *teachers combined to* *tackle the problem* CO-OPERATE, collaborate, join forces, get together, unite, team up, throw in one's lot; *informal* gang up.

combustible ▶ adjective INFLAMMABLE, flammable, incendiary, ignitable.

combustion ▶ noun BURNING; kindling, ignition.

come ▶ verb **1** *come and listen* MOVE NEARER, move closer, approach, advance, draw close/closer, draw near/nearer; proceed; *archaic* draw nigh. **2** *they came last night* ARRIVE, get here/there, make it, appear, come on the scene; approach, enter, turn up, come along, materialize; *informal* show (up), roll in/up, blow in, show one's face. **3** *they came to a stream* REACH, arrive at, get to, make it to, make, gain; come across, run across, happen on, chance on, come upon, stumble on; end up at, wind up at. **4** *the dress comes to her ankles* EXTEND, stretch, reach, come as far as. **5** *she comes from Italy* BE FROM, be a native of, hail from, originate in; live in, reside in. **6** *attacks came without warning* HAPPEN, occur, take place, come about, transpire, fall, present itself, crop up, materialize, arise, arrive, appear; ensue, follow; *literary* come to pass, befall. **7** *the car does not come in red* BE AVAILABLE, be for sale; be made, be produced.
– OPPOSITES: go, leave.

■ **come about** HAPPEN, occur, take place, transpire, fall; crop up, materialize, arise, arrive, appear, surface; ensue, follow; *literary* come to pass, befall.

■ **come across 1** *they came across his friends* MEET/ FIND BY CHANCE, meet, run into, run across, come upon, chance on, stumble on, happen on; discover, encounter, find, locate; *informal* bump into. **2** *the emotion comes across* BE COMMUNICATED, be perceived, get across, be clear, be understood, register, sink in, strike home. **3** *she came across as cool* SEEM, appear, look, sound, look to be.

■ **come along 1** *the puppies are coming along nicely* PROGRESS, develop, shape up; come on, turn out; improve, get better, pick up, rally, recover. **2** *Come along!* HURRY (UP), be quick, get a move on, come on, look lively, speed up, move faster; *informal* get moving, get cracking, step on it, move it, buck up, shake a leg, make it snappy; *dated* make haste.

■ **come apart** BREAK APART, break up, fall to bits, fall to pieces, disintegrate, come unstuck, separate, split, tear.

■ **come back** RETURN, get back, arrive home, come home; come again.

■ **come between** ALIENATE, estrange, separate, divide, split up, break up, disunite, set at odds.

■ **come by** OBTAIN, acquire, gain, get, find, pick up, procure, secure, buy, purchase; *informal* get one's hands on, get hold of, bag, score, swing.

■ **come down** DECIDE, conclude, settle; choose, opt, plump.

■ **come down on**. See REPRIMAND *verb*.

■ **come down to** AMOUNT TO, add up to, constitute, boil down to, be equivalent to.

■ **come down with** FALL ILL WITH, fall sick with, be taken ill with, show symptoms of, become infected with, get, catch, develop, contract, fall victim to.

■ **come forward** VOLUNTEER, offer one's services, make oneself available.

■ **come in** ENTER, gain admission, cross the threshold.

■ **come into** INHERIT, be left, be willed, be bequeathed.

■ **come in for** RECEIVE, experience, sustain, undergo,

go through, encounter, face, be subjected to, bear, suffer.

■ **come off** SUCCEED, work, turn out well, work out, go as planned, produce the desired result, get results.

■ **come on** PROGRESS, develop, shape up, take shape, come along, turn out; improve.

■ **come out 1** *it came out that he'd been to Rome* BECOME KNOWN, become apparent, come to light, emerge, transpire; get out, be discovered, be uncovered, be revealed, leak out, be disclosed. **2** *my book is coming out* BE PUBLISHED, be issued, be released, be brought out, be printed, go on sale. **3** *the flowers have come out* BLOOM, flower, open. **4** *it will come out all right* END, finish, conclude, work out, turn out; *informal* pan out. **5** *the MP came out voluntarily* come out of the closet, disclose one's homosexuality.

■ **come out with** UTTER, say, let out, blurt out, burst out with; issue, present.

■ **come round 1** *I came round to her view* BE CONVERTED, be won over (by), agree (with), change one's mind, be persuaded (by); give way, yield, relent. **2** *Friday the 13th comes round every few months* OCCUR, take place, happen, come up, crop up, arise; recur, reoccur, return, reappear. **3** *come round for a drink* VISIT, stop by, drop by/in/over, come over, pop in/over.

■ **come through 1** *we came through OK* SURVIVE, get through, ride out, weather, live through, pull through; withstand, stand up to, endure, surmount, overcome; *informal* stick out. **2** *you came through for us* HELP, be there.

■ **come to 1** *the bill came to $17.50* AMOUNT TO, add up to, run to, total, equal. **2** *I came to in a screaming ambulance* REGAIN CONSCIOUSNESS, come round, come to one's senses, recover, revive, awake, wake up.

■ **come up** ARISE, occur, happen, come about, transpire, emerge, surface, crop up, turn up, pop up.

■ **come up to 1** *he came up to his shoulder* REACH, come to, be as tall as, extend to. **2** *he never came up to her expectations* MEASURE UP TO, match up to, live up to, fulfill, satisfy, meet, equal, compare with; be good enough; *informal* hold a candle to.

■ **come up with** PRODUCE, devise, think up; propose, put forward, submit, suggest, recommend, advocate, introduce, moot.

comeback ▶ noun **1** *he made a determined comeback* RESURGENCE, recovery, return, rally, upturn. **2** (*informal*) *one of my best comebacks* RETORT, riposte, return, rejoinder; answer, reply, response.

comedian, comedienne ▶ noun **1** *a famous comedian* COMIC, comedienne, funny man/woman, humorist, gagster, stand-up. **2** *Dad was such a comedian* JOKER, jester, wit, wag, comic, wisecracker, jokester; prankster, clown, fool, buffoon; *informal* laugh, hoot, riot, case; *informal, dated* card.

comedown ▶ noun (*informal*) **1** *a bit of a comedown for a sergeant* LOSS OF STATUS, loss of face, humiliation, belittlement, demotion, degradation, disgrace. **2** *it's such a comedown after Christmas* ANTICLIMAX, letdown, disappointment, disillusionment, deflation, decline.

comedy ▶ noun **1** *he excels in comedy* LIGHT ENTERTAINMENT, comic play, comic film, farce, situation comedy, satire, pantomime, comic opera; burlesque, slapstick; *informal* sitcom. **2** *the comedy in their work* HUMOUR, fun, funny side, comical aspect, absurdity, drollness, farce.
– OPPOSITES: tragedy, gravity.

comely ▶ adjective (*archaic*). See ATTRACTIVE sense 2.

come-on ▶ noun (*informal*) INDUCEMENT, incentive,

attraction, lure, pull, draw, enticement, bait, carrot, temptation; fascination, charm, appeal, allure.

comeuppance ▶ noun (*informal*) JUST DESERTS, just punishment, due, retribution, requital, what's coming to one.

comfort ▶ noun **1** *travel in comfort* EASE, relaxation, repose, serenity, tranquility, contentment, coziness; luxury, opulence, prosperity; bed of roses. **2** *words of comfort* CONSOLATION, solace, condolence, sympathy, commiseration; support, reassurance, cheer.
▶ verb *a friend tried to comfort her* CONSOLE, solace, condole with, commiserate with, sympathize with; support, succour, ease, reassure, soothe, calm; cheer, hearten, uplift; *informal* buck up.
— OPPOSITES: distress, depress.

comfortable ▶ adjective **1** *a comfortable lifestyle* PLEASANT, free from hardship; affluent, well-to-do, luxurious, opulent. **2** *a comfortable room* COZY, snug, warm, pleasant, agreeable; restful, homelike, homely; *informal* comfy. **3** *comfortable clothes* LOOSE, loose-fitting, casual; *informal* comfy. **4** *a comfortable pace* LEISURELY, unhurried, relaxed, easy, gentle, sedate, undemanding, slow; *informal* laid-back. **5** *they feel comfortable with each other* AT EASE, relaxed, secure, safe, unworried, contented, happy.
— OPPOSITES: hard, Spartan, tense.

comforting ▶ adjective CONSOLING, sympathetic, compassionate, solicitous, tender, warm, caring, loving; supportive, reassuring, soothing, calming; cheering, heartening, encouraging.

comfortless ▶ adjective **1** *a comfortless house* GLOOMY, dreary, dismal, bleak, grim, sombre; joyless, cheerless, depressing, disheartening, dispiriting, unwelcoming, uninviting; austere, Spartan, institutional. **2** *he left her comfortless* MISERABLE, heartbroken, grief-stricken, unhappy, sad, distressed, desolate, devastated, inconsolable, disconsolate, downcast, downhearted, dejected, cheerless, depressed, melancholy, gloomy, glum; *informal* blue, down in the dumps, down in the mouth.
— OPPOSITES: cozy, happy.

comic ▶ adjective *a comic play* HUMOROUS, funny, droll, amusing, hilarious, uproarious; comical, farcical, silly, slapstick, zany; witty, jocular; *informal* priceless, side-splitting, rib-tickling; *informal, dated* killing.
— OPPOSITES: serious.
▶ noun **1** *a music hall comic* COMEDIAN, comedienne, funny man/woman, comedy actor/actress, humorist, wit; joker, clown; *informal* kidder, wisecracker. **2** *Tony read his comic* CARTOON, comic book, graphic novel; *informal* funny.

comical ▶ adjective **1** *he could be quite comical* FUNNY, comic, humorous, droll, witty, jocular, hilarious, amusing, diverting, entertaining; *informal* jokey, wacky, waggish, side-splitting, rib-tickling, priceless, a scream, a laugh; *informal, dated* killing, a card, a caution. **2** *they look comical in those suits* SILLY, absurd, ridiculous, laughable, risible, ludicrous, preposterous, foolish; *informal* wacky, crazy.
— OPPOSITES: sensible.

coming ▶ adjective *the coming election* FORTHCOMING, imminent, impending, approaching; future, expected, anticipated; close, at hand, in store, in the offing, in the pipeline, on the horizon, on the way; *informal* in the cards.
▶ noun *the coming of spring* APPROACH, advance, advent, arrival, appearance, emergence, onset.

command ▶ verb **1** *he commanded his men to retreat*

ORDER, tell, direct, instruct, call on, require; *literary* bid. **2** *Jones commanded a tank squadron* BE IN CHARGE OF, be in command of, be the leader of; head, lead, control, direct, manage, supervise, oversee; *informal* head up. **3** *they command great respect* RECEIVE, get, gain, secure.
▶ noun **1** *officers shouted commands* ORDER, instruction, directive, direction, commandment, injunction, decree, edict, demand, stipulation, requirement, exhortation, bidding, request. **2** *he had 160 men under his command* AUTHORITY, control, charge, power, direction, dominion, guidance; leadership, rule, government, management, supervision, jurisdiction. **3** *a brilliant command of Italian* KNOWLEDGE, mastery, grasp, comprehension, understanding.

commandeer ▶ verb SEIZE, take, requisition, appropriate, expropriate, sequestrate, sequester, confiscate, annex, take over, claim, pre-empt; hijack, arrogate, help oneself to; *informal* walk off with; *Law* distrain.

commander ▶ noun LEADER, head, chief, overseer, controller; commander-in-chief, C in C, commanding officer, CO, officer; *informal* boss, boss man, skipper, numero uno, number one, top dog, kingpin, head honcho, big kahuna.

commanding ▶ adjective **1** *a commanding position* DOMINANT, dominating, controlling, superior, powerful, prominent, advantageous, favourable. **2** *a commanding voice* AUTHORITATIVE, masterful, assertive, firm, emphatic, insistent, imperative; peremptory, imperious, dictatorial; *informal* bossy.

commemorate ▶ verb CELEBRATE, pay tribute to, pay homage to, honour, salute, toast; remember, recognize, acknowledge, observe, mark.

commemorative ▶ adjective MEMORIAL, remembrance; celebratory.

commence ▶ verb BEGIN, start; get the ball rolling, get going, get underway, get off the ground, set about, embark on, launch into, lead off; open, initiate, inaugurate; *informal* kick off, get the show on the road.
— OPPOSITES: conclude.

commencement ▶ noun **1** *the commencement of the festivities* BEGINNING, start, opening, outset, onset, launch, initiation, inception, origin; *informal* kickoff. **2** *commencement ceremonies* GRADUATION, convocation.

commend ▶ verb **1** *we should commend him* PRAISE, compliment, congratulate, applaud, salute, honour; sing the praises of, pay tribute to, take one's hat off to, pat on the back; *formal* laud. **2** *I commend her to you without reservation* RECOMMEND, suggest, propose; endorse, advocate, vouch for, speak for, support, back. **3** (*formal*) *I commend them to your care* ENTRUST, trust, deliver, commit, hand over, give, turn over, consign, assign.
— OPPOSITES: criticize.

commendable ▶ adjective ADMIRABLE, praiseworthy, creditable, laudable, estimable, meritorious, exemplary, noteworthy, honourable, respectable, fine, excellent.
— OPPOSITES: reprehensible.

commendation ▶ noun **1** *letters of commendation* PRAISE, congratulation, appreciation; acclaim, credit, recognition, respect, esteem, admiration, homage, tribute. **2** *a commendation for bravery* AWARD, accolade, prize, honour, (honourable) mention, citation.

commensurate ▶ adjective **1** *they had privileges but commensurate duties* EQUIVALENT, equal, corresponding, correspondent, comparable, proportionate, proportional. **2** *a salary commensurate with your qualifications* APPROPRIATE TO, in keeping with, in line with, consistent with, corresponding to, according to, relative to; dependent on, based on.

comment ▶ **noun 1** *their comments on her appearance* REMARK, observation, statement, utterance; pronouncement, judgment, reflection, opinion, view; criticism. **2** *a great deal of comment* DISCUSSION, debate; interest. **3** *a comment in the margin* NOTE, annotation, footnote, gloss, commentary, explanation.

▶ **verb 1** *they commented on the food* REMARK ON, speak about, talk about, discuss, mention. **2** *'It will soon be night,' he commented* REMARK, observe, reflect, say, state, declare, announce; interpose, interject.

commentary ▶ **noun 1** *the soccer commentary* NARRATION, description, account, report, review. **2** *textual commentary* EXPLANATION, elucidation, interpretation, exegesis, analysis; assessment, appraisal, criticism; notes, comments.

commentator ▶ **noun 1** *a television commentator* NARRATOR, announcer, presenter, anchor, anchorman, anchorwoman; reporter, journalist, newscaster, sportscaster; *informal* talking head. **2** *a political commentator* ANALYST, pundit, monitor, observer; writer, speaker.

commerce ▶ **noun 1** *industry and commerce* TRADE, trading, buying and selling, business, dealing, traffic; (financial) transactions, dealings. **2** *(dated) human commerce* RELATIONS, dealings, socializing, communication, association, contact, intercourse.

commercial ▶ **adjective 1** *a vessel built for commercial purposes* TRADE, trading, business, private enterprise, mercantile, sales. **2** *a commercial society* PROFIT-ORIENTATED, money-orientated, materialistic, mercenary.

▶ **noun** *a TV commercial* ADVERTISEMENT, promotion, display; *informal* ad, plug, infomercial.

commercialized ▶ **adjective** PROFIT-ORIENTATED, money-orientated, commercial, materialistic, mercenary.

commiserate ▶ **verb (commiserate with)** OFFER SYMPATHY TO, be sympathetic to, offer condolences to, condole with, sympathize with, empathize with, feel pity for, feel sorry for, feel for; comfort, console.

commiseration ▶ **noun** CONDOLENCE(S), sympathy, pity, comfort, solace, consolation; compassion, understanding.

commission ▶ **noun 1** *the dealer's commission* PERCENTAGE, brokerage, share, portion, dividend, premium, fee, consideration, bonus; *informal* cut, take, rake-off, slice. **2** *the commission of building a palace* TASK, employment, job, project, mission, assignment, undertaking; duty, charge, responsibility; *informal* marching orders. **3** *items made under royal commission* WARRANT, licence, sanction, authority. **4** *an independent commission* COMMITTEE, board, council, panel, directorate, delegation. **5** *the commission of an offence* PERPETRATION, committing, committal, execution.

▶ **verb 1** *he was commissioned to paint a portrait* ENGAGE, contract, charge, employ, hire, recruit, retain, appoint, enlist, book, sign up. **2** *they commissioned a sculpture* ORDER; authorize; *formal* bespeak.

■ **in commission** IN SERVICE, in use; working, functional, operative, up and running, in operation, in working order.

■ **out of commission** NOT IN SERVICE, not in use,

unserviceable; not working, inoperative, out of order, malfunctioning, broken, down.

commit ▶ **verb 1** *he committed a murder* CARRY OUT, do, perpetrate, engage in, enact, execute, effect, accomplish; be responsible for; *informal* pull off. **2** *she was committed to their care* ENTRUST, consign, assign, deliver, give, hand over, relinquish; *formal* commend. **3** *they committed themselves to the project* PLEDGE, devote, apply, give, dedicate. **4** *the judge committed him to prison* CONSIGN, send, deliver, confine. **5** *her husband had her committed* HOSPITALIZE, confine, institutionalize, put away; certify.

commitment ▶ **noun 1** *the pressure of his commitments* RESPONSIBILITY, obligation, duty, tie, liability; task; engagement, arrangement. **2** *her commitment to her students* DEDICATION, devotion, allegiance, loyalty, faithfulness, fidelity. **3** *he made a commitment* VOW, promise, pledge, oath; contract, pact, deal; decision, resolution.

committed ▶ **adjective** DEVOUT, devoted, dedicated, loyal, faithful, staunch, firm, steadfast, unwavering, wholehearted, keen, passionate, ardent, fervent, sworn, pledged; dutiful, diligent; *informal* card-carrying, hard-core, true blue.

— OPPOSITES: apathetic.

committee ▶ **noun** BOARD, council, brain trust.

commodious ▶ **adjective** *(formal)* ROOMY, capacious, spacious, ample, generous, sizeable, large, big, extensive.

— OPPOSITES: cramped.

commodity ▶ **noun** ITEM, material, product, article, object; import, export.

common ▶ **adjective 1** *the common folk* ORDINARY, normal, average, unexceptional; simple. **2** *a very common art form* USUAL, ordinary, familiar, regular, frequent, recurrent, everyday; standard, typical, conventional, stock, commonplace, run-of-the-mill; *informal* garden variety. **3** *a common belief* WIDESPREAD, general, universal, popular, mainstream, prevalent, prevailing, rife, established, conventional, traditional, orthodox, accepted. **4** *the common good* COLLECTIVE, communal, community, public, pooled, general; shared, combined. **5** *they are far too common* UNCOUTH, vulgar, coarse, rough, boorish, unladylike, ungentlemanly, ill-bred, uncivilized, unrefined, unsophisticated; lowly, low-born, low-class, inferior, proletarian, plebeian.

— OPPOSITES: unusual, rare, individual, refined.

commonly ▶ **adverb** OFTEN, frequently, regularly, repeatedly, time and (time) again, all the time, routinely, habitually, customarily, oftentimes; *informal* lots.

commonplace ▶ **adjective 1** *a commonplace writing style* ORDINARY, run-of-the-mill, unremarkable, unexceptional, average, mediocre, pedestrian, prosaic, lacklustre, dull, bland, uninteresting, mundane; hackneyed, trite, banal, clichéd, predictable, stale, tired, unoriginal; *informal* by-the-numbers, boilerplate, plain-vanilla, a dime a dozen, bush-league. **2** *a commonplace occurrence* COMMON, normal, usual, ordinary, familiar, routine, standard, everyday, daily, regular, frequent, habitual, typical.

— OPPOSITES: original, unusual.

▶ **noun 1** *early death was a commonplace* EVERYDAY EVENT, routine. **2** *a great store of commonplaces* PLATITUDE, cliché, truism, hackneyed phrase, trite phrase, old chestnut, banality; *dated* bromide.

common sense ▸ noun SENSIBLENESS, (good) sense, judgment, level-headedness, prudence, discernment, canniness, astuteness, shrewdness, wisdom, insight, perception, perspicacity; practicality, capability, resourcefulness, enterprise; *informal* horse sense, gumption, savvy, (street) smarts.
– OPPOSITES: folly.

commonsensical ▸ adjective SENSIBLE, reasonable, rational, prudent, smart, practical, realistic, level-headed.

commotion ▸ noun DISTURBANCE, uproar, tumult, rumpus, ruckus, brouhaha, hoopla, furor, hue and cry, fuss, foofaraw, stir, storm; turmoil, disorder, confusion, chaos, mayhem, havoc, pandemonium; unrest, fracas, riot, breach of the peace, donnybrook, ruction, ballyhoo, kerfuffle, hoo-ha, to-do, hullabaloo.

communal ▸ adjective **1** *the kitchen was communal* SHARED, joint, common. **2** *they farm on a communal basis* COLLECTIVE, co-operative, community, communalist, combined.
– OPPOSITES: private, individual.

commune ▸ noun *she lives in a commune* COLLECTIVE, co-operative, communal settlement, kibbutz.
▸ verb **1** *we pray to commune with God* COMMUNICATE, speak, talk, converse, interface. **2** *she likes to commune with nature* EMPATHIZE, identify, have a rapport, feel at one; relate to, feel close to.

communicable ▸ adjective CONTAGIOUS, INFECTIOUS, transmittable, transmissible, transferable, spreadable; *informal* catching.

communicate ▸ verb **1** *he communicated the news to his boss* CONVEY, tell, impart, relay, transmit, pass on, announce, report, recount, relate, present; divulge, disclose, mention; spread, disseminate, promulgate, broadcast. **2** *they communicate daily* BE IN TOUCH, be in contact, have dealings, interface, interact, commune, meet, liaise; talk, speak, converse; *informal* have a confab, powwow. **3** *explain how to communicate* GET ONE'S MESSAGE ACROSS, explain oneself, be understood, get through to someone. **4** *the disease is communicated easily* TRANSMIT, transfer, spread, carry, pass on. **5** *each bedroom communicates with a bathroom* CONNECT WITH, join up with, open on to, lead into.

communication ▸ noun **1** *the communication of news* TRANSMISSION, conveyance, divulgence, disclosure; dissemination, promulgation, broadcasting. **2** *there was no communication between them* CONTACT, dealings, relations, connection, association, socializing, intercourse; correspondence, dialogue, talk, conversation, discussion. **3** *an official communication* MESSAGE, statement, announcement, report, dispatch, communiqué, letter, bulletin, correspondence. **4** *road and rail communications* LINKS, connections; services, routes.

communicative ▸ adjective FORTHCOMING, expansive, expressive, unreserved, uninhibited, vocal, outgoing, frank, open, candid; talkative, chatty, loquacious; *informal* gabby.

communion ▸ noun **1** *a sense of communion with others* AFFINITY, fellowship, kinship, friendship, fellow feeling, togetherness, closeness, harmony, understanding, rapport, connection, communication, empathy, accord, unity. **2** *Christ's presence at Communion* EUCHARIST, Holy Communion, Lord's Supper, Mass.

communiqué ▸ noun OFFICIAL COMMUNICATION, press release, bulletin, message, missive, dispatch, statement, report, announcement, declaration, proclamation, advisory; *informal* memo.

communist ▸ noun & adjective COLLECTIVIST, leftist, (radical) socialist; Soviet, Bolshevik, Bolshevist, Marxist, Leninist, Trotskyist, Trotskyite, Maoist; *informal, derogatory* Commie, Bolshie, red, lefty.

community ▸ noun **1** *work done for the community* (GENERAL) PUBLIC, populace, people, citizenry, population, collective; residents, inhabitants, citizens. **2** *a suburban community* DISTRICT, region, zone, area, locality, locale, neighbourhood; *informal* neck of the woods, hood. **3** *concerns in the immigrant community* GROUP, body, set, circle, clique, faction; *informal* gang, bunch. **4** *a monastic community* BROTHERHOOD, sisterhood, fraternity, sorority, sodality; order, congregation, abbey, convent.

commute ▸ verb **1** *they commute by train* TRAVEL TO AND FROM WORK, travel to and fro, travel back and forth. **2** *his sentence was commuted* REDUCE, lessen, lighten, shorten, cut, attenuate, moderate. **3** *knight service was commuted for a payment* EXCHANGE, change, substitute, swap, trade, switch.
– OPPOSITES: increase.

commuter ▸ noun (DAILY) TRAVELLER, passenger; *informal* straphanger.

compact¹ ▸ adjective **1** *a compact rug* DENSE, close-packed, tightly packed; thick, tight, firm. **2** *a compact camera* SMALL, little, petite, miniature, mini, small-scale; *informal* teeny, teeny-weeny; little-bitty, itty-bitty; *Scottish* wee. **3** *her tale is compact* CONCISE, succinct, condensed, brief, pithy; short and sweet; *informal* snappy; *formal* compendious.
– OPPOSITES: loose, large, rambling.
▸ verb *the snow has been compacted* COMPRESS, condense, pack down, press down, tamp (down), flatten.

compact² ▸ noun *the warring states signed a compact* TREATY, pact, accord, agreement, contract, bargain, deal, settlement, covenant, concordat; pledge, promise, bond.

companion ▸ noun **1** *Harry and his companion* ASSOCIATE, partner, escort, compatriot, confederate; friend, intimate, confidant(e), comrade; *informal* pal, chum, crony, sidekick, mate, buddy, amigo, compadre. **2** *a lady's companion* ATTENDANT, aide, helper, assistant, valet, equerry, lady in waiting; chaperone; minder. **3** *the tape is a companion to the book* COMPLEMENT, counterpart, twin, match; accompaniment, supplement, addition, adjunct, accessory. **4** *The Gardener's Companion* HANDBOOK, manual, guide, reference book, ABC, primer, vade mecum; *informal* bible.

companionable ▸ adjective FRIENDLY, affable, cordial, genial, congenial, amiable, easygoing, good-natured, comradely; sociable, convivial, outgoing, gregarious; *informal* chummy, buddy-buddy, clubby.

companionship ▸ noun FRIENDSHIP, fellowship, closeness, togetherness, amity, intimacy, rapport, camaraderie, brotherhood, sisterhood; company, society, social contact.

company ▸ noun **1** *an oil company* FIRM, business, corporation, establishment, agency, office, bureau, institution, organization, concern, enterprise; conglomerate, consortium, syndicate, multinational; *informal* outfit. **2** *I enjoy his company* COMPANIONSHIP, friendship, fellowship, amity, camaraderie; society, association. **3** *I'm expecting company* GUESTS, house guests, visitors, callers,

people; someone. **4** *a company of poets* GROUP, crowd, party, band, assembly, cluster, flock, herd, troupe, throng, congregation; *informal* bunch, gang. **5** *a company of infantry* UNIT, section, detachment, troop, corps, squad, squadron, platoon, battalion, division.
– RELATED TERMS: corporate.

comparable ▸ adjective **1** *comparable incomes* SIMILAR, close, near, approximate, akin, equivalent, commensurate, proportional, proportionate; like, matching, homologous. **2** *nobody is comparable with him* EQUAL TO, as good as, in the same league as, able to hold a candle to, on a par with, on a level with; a match for.

comparative ▸ adjective RELATIVE.

compare ▸ verb **1** *we compared the data sets* CONTRAST, juxtapose, collate, differentiate, **2** *he was compared to Wagner* LIKEN, equate, analogize; class with, bracket with, set side by side with. **3** *the porcelain compares with Dresden's fine china* BE AS GOOD AS, be comparable to, bear comparison with, be the equal of, match up to, be on a par with, be in the same league as, come close to, hold a candle to, be not unlike; match, resemble, emulate, rival, approach.
■ **beyond compare** WITHOUT EQUAL, second to none, in a class of one's own; peerless, matchless, unmatched, incomparable, inimitable, supreme, outstanding, consummate, unique, singular, perfect.

comparison ▸ noun **1** *a comparison of the results* JUXTAPOSITION, collation, differentiation. **2** *there's no comparison between them* RESEMBLANCE, likeness, similarity, correspondence, correlation, parallel, parity, comparability.

compartment ▸ noun **1** *a secret compartment* SECTION, part, bay, recess, chamber, cavity; pocket. **2** *they put science and religion in separate compartments* DOMAIN, field, sphere, department; category, pigeonhole, bracket, group, set.

compartmentalize ▸ verb CATEGORIZE, pigeonhole, bracket, group, classify, characterize, stereotype, label, brand; sort, rank, rate.

compass ▸ noun SCOPE, range, extent, reach, span, breadth, ambit, limits, parameters, bounds.

compassion ▸ noun PITY, sympathy, empathy, fellow feeling, care, concern, solicitude, sensitivity, warmth, love, tenderness, mercy, leniency, tolerance, kindness, humanity, charity.
– OPPOSITES: indifference, cruelty.

compassionate ▸ adjective SYMPATHETIC, empathetic, understanding, caring, solicitous, sensitive, warm, loving; merciful, lenient, tolerant, considerate, kind, humane, charitable, big-hearted.

compatibility ▸ noun LIKE-MINDEDNESS, similarity, affinity, closeness, fellow feeling, harmony, rapport, empathy, sympathy.

compatible ▸ adjective **1** *they were never compatible* (WELL) SUITED, well-matched, like-minded, in tune, in harmony; reconcilable. **2** *her bruising is compatible with a fall* CONSISTENT, congruous, congruent; in keeping.

compatriot ▸ noun FELLOW COUNTRYMAN/WOMAN, countryman, countrywoman, fellow citizen.

compel ▸ verb **1** *he compelled them to leave their land* FORCE, pressure, press, push, urge; dragoon, browbeat, bully, intimidate, strong-arm; oblige, require, make; *informal* lean on, put the screws on. **2** *they can compel compliance* EXACT, extort, demand, insist on, force, necessitate.

compelling ▸ adjective **1** *a compelling performance* ENTHRALLING, captivating, gripping, riveting, spellbinding, mesmerizing, absorbing, irresistible. **2** *a compelling argument* CONVINCING, persuasive, cogent, irresistible, powerful, strong, weighty, plausible, credible, sound, valid, telling, conclusive, irrefutable, unanswerable.
– OPPOSITES: boring, weak.

compendious ▸ adjective *(formal)* SUCCINCT, pithy, short and to the point, concise, compact, condensed, compressed, abridged, summarized, synoptic, capsule; *informal* snappy.
– OPPOSITES: expanded.

compendium ▸ noun COLLECTION, compilation, anthology, treasury, digest; summary, synopsis, précis, outline.

compensate ▸ verb **1** *you must compensate for what you did* MAKE AMENDS, make up, make reparation, recompense, atone, requite, pay; expiate, make good, rectify. **2** *we agreed to compensate him for his loss* RECOMPENSE, repay, pay back, reimburse, remunerate, recoup, requite, indemnify. **3** *his flair compensated for his faults* BALANCE (OUT), counterbalance, counteract, offset, make up for, cancel out, neutralize, negative.

compensation ▸ noun RECOMPENSE, repayment, reimbursement, remuneration, requital, indemnification, indemnity, redress; damages; *informal* comp.

compete ▸ verb **1** *they competed in a tennis tournament* TAKE PART, participate, play, be a competitor, be involved; enter. **2** *they had to compete with other firms* CONTEND, vie, battle, wrangle, jockey, go head to head; strive against, pit oneself against; challenge, take on. **3** *no one can compete with Elaine* RIVAL, challenge, keep up with, keep pace with, compare with, match, be in the same league as, come near to, come close to, touch; *informal* hold a candle to.

competence ▸ noun **1** *my technical competence* CAPABILITY, ability, competency, proficiency, accomplishment, expertise, adeptness, skill, prowess, mastery, talent; *informal* savvy, know-how. **2** *the competence of the system* ADEQUACY, appropriateness, suitability, fitness; effectiveness; *formal* efficacy. **3** *matters within the competence of the courts* AUTHORITY, power, control, jurisdiction, ambit, scope.

competent ▸ adjective **1** *a competent carpenter* CAPABLE, able, proficient, adept, adroit, accomplished, complete, skilful, skilled, gifted, talented, expert; good, excellent; *informal* great, mean, wicked, nifty, ace. **2** *she spoke competent French* ADEQUATE, acceptable, satisfactory, reasonable, fair, decent, not bad, all right, average, tolerable, passable, moderate, middling; *informal* OK, okay, so-so, {comme ci, comme ça}. **3** *the court was not competent to hear the case* FIT, suitable, suited, appropriate; qualified, empowered, authorized.
– OPPOSITES: inadequate, unfit.

competition ▸ noun **1** *Stephanie won the competition* CONTEST, tournament, match, game, heat, fixture, event. **2** *I'm not interested in competition* RIVALRY, competitiveness, vying; conflict, feuding, fighting; *informal* keeping up with the Joneses. **3** *we must stay ahead of the competition* OPPOSITION, other side, field; enemy; challengers, opponents, rivals, adversaries; *literary* foe.

competitive ▸ adjective **1** *a competitive player* AMBITIOUS, zealous, keen, pushy, combative,

aggressive. **2** *a highly competitive industry* RUTHLESS, aggressive, fierce; *informal* dog-eat-dog, cutthroat. **3** *competitive prices* REASONABLE, moderate; low, inexpensive, cheap, budget, bargain, reduced, discount; rock-bottom, bargain-basement, down-market.
– OPPOSITES: apathetic, exorbitant.

competitor ▶ noun **1** *the competitors in the race* CONTESTANT, contender, challenger, participant, entrant; runner, player. **2** *our European competitors* RIVAL, challenger, opponent, adversary; competition, opposition.
– OPPOSITES: ally.

compilation ▶ noun COLLECTION, selection, anthology, treasury, compendium, album, corpus; potpourri.

compile ▶ verb ASSEMBLE, put together, make up, collate, compose, organize, arrange; gather, collect.

complacency ▶ noun SMUGNESS, self-satisfaction, self-congratulation, self-regard; gloating, triumph, pride; satisfaction, contentment.

complacent ▶ adjective SMUG, self-satisfied, self-congratulatory, self-regarding; gloating, triumphant, proud; pleased, satisfied, content, contented.

complain ▶ verb PROTEST, grumble, whine, bleat, carp, cavil, grouse, make a fuss; object, speak out, criticize, find fault; *informal* whinge, kick up a fuss, raise a stink, bellyache, moan, snivel, beef, bitch, sound off, gripe, kvetch.

complaint ▶ noun **1** *they lodged a complaint* PROTEST, objection, grievance, grouse, cavil, quibble, grumble; charge, accusation, criticism; *informal* beef, gripe, jeremiad, whinge; *Law* plaint. **2** *little cause for complaint* PROTESTATION, objection, exception, grievance, grumbling; criticism, fault-finding, condemnation, disapproval, dissatisfaction; *informal* whingeing, grousing, bellyaching, nitpicking. **3** *a kidney complaint* DISORDER, disease, infection, affliction, illness, ailment, sickness; condition, problem, upset, trouble.

complaisant ▶ adjective WILLING, acquiescent, agreeable, amenable, co-operative, accommodating, obliging; biddable, compliant, docile, obedient.

complement ▶ noun **1** *the perfect complement to the food* ACCOMPANIMENT, companion, addition, supplement, accessory, trimming. **2** *a full complement of lifeboats* AMOUNT, total, contingent, capacity, allowance, quota.
▶ verb *this sauce complements the dessert* ACCOMPANY, go with, round off, set off, suit, harmonize with; enhance, complete.

complementary ▶ adjective HARMONIOUS, compatible, corresponding, matching, twin; supportive, reciprocal, interdependent.
– OPPOSITES: incompatible.

complete ▶ adjective **1** *the complete interview* ENTIRE, whole, full, total; uncut, unabridged. **2** *their research was complete* FINISHED, ended, concluded, completed, finalized; accomplished, achieved, discharged, settled, done; *informal* wrapped up, sewn up, polished off. **3** *a complete fool* ABSOLUTE, out-and-out, utter, total, real, downright, thoroughgoing, veritable, prize, perfect, unqualified, unmitigated, sheer, arrant, full-out.
– OPPOSITES: partial, unfinished.
▶ verb **1** *he had to complete his training* FINISH, end, conclude, finalize, wind up; *informal* wrap up, sew up,

polish off. **2** *the outfit was completed with a veil* FINISH OFF, round off, top off, crown, cap, complement. **3** *complete the application form* FILL IN/OUT, answer.

completely ▶ adverb TOTALLY, entirely, wholly, thoroughly, fully, utterly, absolutely, perfectly, unreservedly, unconditionally, quite, altogether, downright; in every way, in every respect, one hundred per cent, every inch, to the hilt; *informal* dead, deadly, to the max.

completion ▶ noun REALIZATION, accomplishment, achievement, fulfillment, consummation, finalization, resolution; finish, end, conclusion, close, cessation.

complex ▶ adjective **1** *a complex situation* COMPLICATED, involved, intricate, convoluted, elaborate, impenetrable, Gordian; difficult, knotty, tricky, thorny, fiddly. **2** *a complex structure* COMPOUND, composite, multiplex.
– OPPOSITES: simple.
▶ noun **1** *a complex of roads* NETWORK, system, nexus, web, tissue; combination, aggregation. **2** *(informal) he had a complex about losing his hair* OBSESSION, fixation, preoccupation; neurosis; *informal* hang-up, thing, bee in one's bonnet.

complexion ▶ noun **1** *a pale complexion* SKIN, skin colour, skin tone; pigmentation. **2** *this puts an entirely new complexion on things* PERSPECTIVE, angle, slant, interpretation; appearance, light, look. **3** *governments of all complexions* TYPE, kind, sort; nature, character, stamp, ilk, kidney.

complexity ▶ noun COMPLICATION, problem, difficulty; twist, turn, intricacy.

compliance ▶ noun **1** *compliance with international law* OBEDIENCE TO, observance of, adherence to, conformity to, respect for. **2** *he mistook her silence for compliance* ACQUIESCENCE, agreement, assent, consent, acceptance; complaisance, pliability, docility, meekness, submission.
– OPPOSITES: violation, defiance.

compliant ▶ adjective ACQUIESCENT, amenable, biddable, tractable, complaisant, accommodating, co-operative; obedient, docile, malleable, pliable, submissive, tame, yielding, controllable, unresisting, persuadable, persuasible.
– OPPOSITES: recalcitrant.

complicate ▶ verb MAKE (MORE) DIFFICULT, make complicated, mix up, confuse, muddle; *informal* mess up, screw up, snarl up.
– OPPOSITES: simplify.

complicated ▶ adjective COMPLEX, intricate, involved, convoluted, tangled, impenetrable, knotty, tricky, thorny, labyrinthine, tortuous, Gordian; confusing, bewildering, perplexing, fiddly.
– OPPOSITES: straightforward.

complication ▶ noun **1** *a complication concerning ownership* DIFFICULTY, problem, obstacle, hurdle, stumbling block; drawback, snag, catch, hitch; *informal* fly in the ointment, headache, wrench in the works. **2** *the complication of life in our society* COMPLEXITY, complicatedness, intricacy, convolutedness.

complicity ▶ noun COLLUSION, involvement, collaboration, connivance; conspiracy; *informal* being in cahoots.

compliment ▶ noun **1** *an unexpected compliment* FLATTERING REMARK, tribute, accolade, commendation, bouquet, pat on the back; (**compliments**) praise, acclaim, admiration, flattery, blandishments, honeyed words. **2** *my compliments on your cooking*

CONGRATULATIONS, commendations, praise; *informal* props, kudos. **3** *Margaret sends her compliments* GREETINGS, regards, respects, good wishes, best wishes, salutations, felicitations.
– OPPOSITES: insult.

▶ **verb** *they complimented his performance* PRAISE, pay tribute to, speak highly/well of, flatter, wax lyrical about, make much of, commend, acclaim, applaud, salute, honour; congratulate, pat on the back.
– OPPOSITES: criticize.

complimentary ▶ **adjective 1** *complimentary remarks* FLATTERING, appreciative, congratulatory, admiring, approving, commendatory, favourable, glowing, adulatory; *informal* rave. **2** *complimentary tickets* FREE (OF CHARGE), gratis, for nothing; courtesy; *informal* on the house.
– OPPOSITES: derogatory.

comply ▶ **verb** *Myra complied with his wishes* ABIDE BY, observe, obey, adhere to, conform to, hew to, follow, respect; agree to, assent to, go along with, yield to, submit to, defer to; satisfy, fulfill.
– OPPOSITES: ignore, disobey.

component ▶ **noun** *the components of electronic devices* PART, piece, bit, element, constituent, ingredient, building block; unit, module, section.
▶ **adjective** *the molecule's component elements* CONSTITUENT, integral; basic, essential.

comport
■ **comport oneself** (*formal*) BEHAVE, conduct oneself, act, acquit oneself; *archaic* deport oneself.

compose ▶ **verb 1** *a poem composed by Shelley* WRITE, formulate, devise, make up, think up, produce, invent, concoct; pen, author, draft; score, orchestrate, choreograph. **2** *compose a still life* ORGANIZE, arrange, set out. **3** *the congress is composed of ten senators* MAKE UP, constitute, form.
■ **compose oneself** CALM DOWN, control oneself, regain one's composure, pull oneself together, collect oneself, steady oneself, keep one's head, relax; *informal* get a grip, keep one's cool, cool one's jets, decompress.

composed ▶ **adjective** CALM, collected, cool (as a cucumber), self-controlled, self-possessed; serene, tranquil, relaxed, at ease, unruffled, unperturbed, untroubled; equable, even-tempered, imperturbable; *informal* unflappable, together, laid-back.
– OPPOSITES: excited.

composer ▶ **noun** songwriter, melodist, symphonist, songster, writer; *informal* tunesmith, songsmith.

composite ▶ **adjective** *a composite structure* COMPOUND, complex; combined, blended, mixed.
▶ **noun** *a composite of plastic and metal* AMALGAMATION, amalgam, combination, compound, fusion, synthesis, mixture, blend; alloy.

composition ▶ **noun 1** *the composition of the council* MAKEUP, constitution, configuration, structure, formation, form, framework, fabric, anatomy, organization; *informal* set-up. **2** *a literary composition* WORK (OF ART), creation, opus, oeuvre, piece, arrangement. **3** *we all participated in the composition of the school song* WRITING, creation, formulation, invention, concoction, orchestration. **4** *a school composition* ESSAY, paper, study, piece of writing, theme. **5** *the composition of the painting* ARRANGEMENT, disposition, layout; proportions, balance, symmetry. **6** *an adhesive composition* MIXTURE, compound, amalgam, blend, mix.

compost ▶ **noun** FERTILIZER, mulch, manure, bone meal, fish meal, blood meal, guano; humus, peat; plant food, top-dressing.

composure ▶ **noun** SELF-CONTROL, self-possession, calm, equanimity, equilibrium, serenity, tranquility; aplomb, poise, presence of mind, sang-froid; imperturbability, placidness, impassivity; *informal* cool.

compound ▶ **noun 1** *a compound of two elements* AMALGAM, amalgamation, combination, composite, blend, mixture, mix, fusion, synthesis; alloy. **2** *they were contained in the compound* ENCLOSURE, pound, coop; estate, cloister.
▶ **adjective** *a compound substance* COMPOSITE, complex; blended, fused, combined.
– OPPOSITES: simple.
▶ **verb 1** *a smell compounded of dust and mould* BE COMPOSED OF, be made up of, be formed from. **2** *soap compounded with disinfectant* MIX, combine, blend, amalgamate, fuse, synthesize. **3** *his illness compounds their problems* AGGRAVATE, exacerbate, worsen, add to, augment, intensify, heighten, increase, magnify; complicate.
– OPPOSITES: alleviate.

comprehend ▶ **verb 1** *Katie couldn't comprehend his message* UNDERSTAND, grasp, take in, see, apprehend, follow, make sense of, fathom, get to the bottom of, unravel, decipher, interpret; *informal* work out, figure out, make heads or tails of, get one's head around, get the drift of, catch on to, get, twig, suss (out). **2** (*formal*) *a divine order comprehending all men* COMPRISE, include, encompass, embrace, involve, contain.
– OPPOSITES: exclude.

comprehensible ▶ **adjective** INTELLIGIBLE, understandable, accessible; lucid, coherent, clear, plain, explicit, unambiguous, straightforward, fathomable.
– OPPOSITES: opaque.

comprehension ▶ **noun** UNDERSTANDING, grasp, conception, apprehension, cognition, ken, knowledge, awareness, perception; interpretation.
– OPPOSITES: ignorance.

comprehensive ▶ **adjective** INCLUSIVE, all-inclusive, complete; thorough, full, extensive, all-embracing, exhaustive, detailed, in-depth, encyclopedic, universal, catholic; far-reaching, radical, sweeping, across the board, wholesale; broad, wide-ranging; *informal* wall-to-wall.
– OPPOSITES: limited.

compress ▶ **verb 1** *the skirt can be compressed into a bag* SQUEEZE, press, squash, crush, cram, jam, stuff; tamp, pack, compact; constrict; *informal* scrunch. **2** *the text was compressed* ABRIDGE, condense, shorten, cut, abbreviate, truncate; summarize, précis.
– OPPOSITES: expand.

comprise ▶ **verb 1** *the country comprises twenty states* CONSIST OF, be made up of, be composed of, contain, encompass, incorporate; include; *formal* comprehend. **2** (*informal*) *this breed comprises half the herd* MAKE UP, constitute, form, compose; account for.

compromise ▶ **noun 1** *they reached a compromise* AGREEMENT, understanding, settlement, terms, deal, trade-off, saw-off ♣, bargain; middle ground, happy medium, balance. **2** *a happy marriage needs compromise* GIVE AND TAKE, concession, co-operation.
– OPPOSITES: intransigence.
▶ **verb 1** *we compromised* MEET EACH OTHER HALFWAY, come to an understanding, make a deal, make concessions, saw off ♣, find a happy medium, strike

a balance; give and take. **2** *his actions could compromise his reputation* UNDERMINE, weaken, damage, harm; jeopardize, prejudice; discredit, dishonour, shame, embarrass.

compulsion ▶ noun **1** *he is under no compulsion to go* OBLIGATION, constraint, coercion, duress, pressure, intimidation. **2** *a compulsion to tell the truth* URGE, impulse, need, desire, drive; obsession, fixation, addiction; temptation.

compulsive ▶ adjective **1** *a compulsive desire* IRRESISTIBLE, uncontrollable, compelling, overwhelming, urgent; obsessive. **2** *compulsive eating* OBSESSIVE, obsessional, addictive, uncontrollable. **3** *a compulsive liar* INVETERATE, chronic, incorrigible, incurable, hardened, hopeless, persistent; obsessive, addicted, habitual; *informal* pathological. **4** *it's compulsive viewing* FASCINATING, compelling, gripping, riveting, engrossing, enthralling, captivating.

compulsory ▶ adjective OBLIGATORY, mandatory, required, requisite, necessary, essential; imperative, unavoidable, enforced, demanded, prescribed.
— OPPOSITES: optional.

compunction ▶ noun SCRUPLES, misgivings, qualms, worries, unease, uneasiness, doubts, reluctance, reservations; guilt, regret, contrition, self-reproach.

compute ▶ verb CALCULATE, work out, reckon, determine, evaluate, quantify; add up, count up, tally, total, totalize, tot up.

computer ▶ noun PERSONAL COMPUTER, PC, laptop, desktop, terminal; mainframe.

comrade ▶ noun COMPANION, friend; colleague, associate, partner, co-worker, workmate; *informal* pal, crony, mate, chum, buddy.

con (*informal*) ▶ verb. *we got conned. See* SWINDLE.
▶ noun **1** *an ex-con. See* CONVICT. **2** *a public relations con. See* SWINDLE.

con artist ▶ noun SWINDLER, fraud, cheater, scam artist, fraudster, goniff.

concatenation ▶ noun SERIES, sequence, succession, chain.

concave ▶ adjective INCURVED, curved inwards, hollow, depressed, sunken; indented, recessed.
— OPPOSITES: convex.

conceal ▶ verb **1** *clouds concealed the sun* HIDE, screen, cover, obscure, block out, blot out, mask, shroud, secrete. **2** *he concealed his true feelings* HIDE, cover up, disguise, mask, veil; keep secret, draw a veil over; suppress, repress, bottle up; *informal* keep a lid on, keep under one's hat.
— OPPOSITES: reveal, confess.

concealed ▶ adjective HIDDEN, not visible, out of sight, invisible, covered, disguised, camouflaged, obscured; private, secret.

concealment ▶ noun **1** *the concealment of his weapon* HIDING, secretion. **2** *the deliberate concealment of facts* SUPPRESSION, hiding, cover-up, hushing up; whitewash.

concede ▶ verb **1** *I had to concede that I'd overreacted* ADMIT, acknowledge, accept, allow, grant, recognize, own, confess; agree. **2** *he conceded the Auvergne to the king* SURRENDER, yield, give up, relinquish, cede, hand over.
— OPPOSITES: deny, retain.
■ **concede defeat** CAPITULATE, give in, give, surrender, yield, give up, submit, raise the white flag; back down, climb down, throw in the towel.

conceit ▶ noun **1** *his extraordinary conceit* VANITY, narcissism, conceitedness, egotism, self-admiration, self-regard; pride, arrogance, hubris, self-importance; self-satisfaction, smugness; *informal* big-headedness; *literary* vainglory. **2** *the conceits of Shakespeare's verse* IMAGE, imagery, metaphor, simile, trope. **3** *the conceit of time travel* IDEA, notion, fancy.
— OPPOSITES: humility.

conceited ▶ adjective VAIN, narcissistic, self-centred, egotistic, egotistical, egocentric; proud, arrogant, boastful, full of oneself, self-important, immodest, swaggering; self-satisfied, smug; supercilious, haughty, snobbish; *informal* big-headed, too big for one's britches, stuck-up, high and mighty, uppity, snotty; *literary* vainglorious.

conceivable ▶ adjective IMAGINABLE, possible; plausible, tenable, credible, believable, thinkable, feasible; understandable, comprehensible.

conceive ▶ verb **1** *they were unable to conceive* BECOME PREGNANT, become impregnated. **2** *the project was conceived in 1977* THINK UP, think of, dream up, devise, formulate, design, originate, create, develop; *informal* cook up, hatch. **3** *I can hardly conceive what it must be like* IMAGINE, envisage, visualize, picture, think, envision; grasp, appreciate, apprehend; *formal* ideate.

concentrate ▶ verb **1** *the government concentrated its efforts* FOCUS, direct, centre, centralize. **2** *she concentrated on the film* FOCUS ON, pay attention to, keep one's mind on, devote oneself to; be absorbed in, be engrossed in, be immersed in. **3** *troops concentrated on the horizon* COLLECT, gather, congregate, converge, mass, cluster, rally. **4** *the liquid is filtered and concentrated* CONDENSE, boil down, reduce, thicken.
— OPPOSITES: disperse, dilute.
▶ noun *a fruit concentrate* EXTRACT, decoction, distillation.

concentrated ▶ adjective **1** *a concentrated effort* STRENUOUS, concerted, intensive, intense; *informal* all-out. **2** *a concentrated solution* CONDENSED, reduced, evaporated, thickened; undiluted, strong.
— OPPOSITES: half-hearted, diluted.

concentration ▶ noun **1** *a task requiring concentration* CLOSE ATTENTION, attentiveness, application, single-mindedness, tunnel vision, absorption. **2** *the concentration of effort* FOCUSING, centralization. **3** *concentrations of seals* GATHERING, cluster, mass, congregation, assemblage.
— OPPOSITES: inattention.

concept ▶ noun IDEA, notion, conception, abstraction; theory, hypothesis; belief, conviction, opinion; image, impression, picture.

conception ▶ noun **1** *from conception until natural death* INCEPTION OF PREGNANCY, conceiving, fertilization, impregnation, insemination. **2** *the product's conception* INCEPTION, genesis, origination, creation, invention; beginning, origin. **3** *his original conception* PLAN, scheme, project, proposal; intention, aim, idea. **4** *my conception of democracy* IDEA, concept, notion, understanding, abstraction; theory, hypothesis; perception, image, impression. **5** *they had no conception of our problems* UNDERSTANDING, comprehension, appreciation, grasp, knowledge; idea, inkling; *informal* clue.

concern ▶ verb **1** *the report concerns the war* BE ABOUT, deal with, have to do with, cover; discuss, go into, examine, study, review, analyze; relate to, pertain to. **2** *that doesn't concern you* AFFECT, involve, be relevant to, apply to, have a bearing on, impact on; be important to, interest. **3** *I won't concern myself with your affairs* INVOLVE ONESELF IN, take an interest in, busy oneself with, devote one's time to, bother oneself with. **4** *one thing still concerns me* WORRY, disturb, trouble, bother, perturb, unsettle, make anxious.

▶ noun **1** *a voice full of concern* ANXIETY, worry, disquiet, apprehensiveness, unease, consternation. **2** *his concern for others* SOLICITUDE, consideration, care, sympathy, regard. **3** *housing is the concern of the council* RESPONSIBILITY, business, affair, charge, duty, job; province, preserve; problem, worry; *informal* bag, bailiwick. **4** *issues that are of concern to women* INTEREST, importance, relevance, significance. **5** *Aboriginal concerns* AFFAIR, issue, matter, question, consideration. **6** *a publishing concern* COMPANY, business, firm, organization, operation, corporation, establishment, house, office, agency; *informal* outfit.
– OPPOSITES: indifference.

concerned ▶ adjective **1** *her mother looked concerned* WORRIED, anxious, upset, perturbed, troubled, distressed, uneasy, apprehensive, agitated. **2** *he is concerned about your welfare* SOLICITOUS, caring; attentive to, considerate of. **3** *all concerned parties* INTERESTED, involved, affected; connected, related, implicated.

concerning ▶ preposition ABOUT, regarding, relating to, with reference to, referring to, with regard to, as regards, with respect to, respecting, dealing with, on the subject of, in connection with, re, apropos of.

concert ▶ noun MUSICAL PERFORMANCE, show, production, presentation; recital; *informal* gig.
■ **in concert** TOGETHER, jointly, in combination, in collaboration, in co-operation, in league, side by side; in unison.

concerted ▶ adjective **1** *make a concerted effort* STRENUOUS, vigorous, intensive, intense, concentrated; *informal* all-out. **2** *concerted action* JOINT, united, collaborative, collective, combined, co-operative.
– OPPOSITES: half-hearted, individual.

concession ▶ noun **1** *the government made several concessions* COMPROMISE, allowance, exception, sop. **2** *a concession of failure* ADMISSION, acknowledgement, acceptance, recognition, confession. **3** *the concession of territory* SURRENDER, relinquishment, sacrifice, handover. **4** *tax concessions* REDUCTION, cut, discount, deduction, decrease; rebate; *informal* break. **5** *a fast-food concession* STAND, kiosk, stall, counter, vendor. **6** *Cdn (Ont. & Que.) go east along the 6th Concession* ROAD, country road, highway. **7** *a logging concession* RIGHT, privilege; licence, permit, franchise, warrant, authorization.
– OPPOSITES: denial, acquisition.

concierge ▶ noun DOORKEEPER, doorman, porter, attendant, superintendent.

conciliate ▶ verb **1** *he tried to conciliate the peasantry* APPEASE, placate, pacify, mollify, assuage, soothe, humour, reconcile, win over, make peace with. **2** *he conciliated in the dispute* MEDIATE, act as peacemaker, arbitrate; pour oil on troubled waters.
– OPPOSITES: provoke.

conciliator ▶ noun PEACEMAKER, mediator, go-between, middleman, intermediary, intercessor; dove.
– OPPOSITES: troublemaker.

conciliatory ▶ adjective PROPITIATORY, placatory, appeasing, pacifying, mollifying, peacemaking.

concise ▶ adjective SUCCINCT, pithy, incisive, brief, short and to the point, short and sweet; abridged,

condensed, compressed, abbreviated, compact, capsule, potted; *informal* snappy.
– OPPOSITES: lengthy, wordy.

conclave ▶ noun (PRIVATE) MEETING, gathering, assembly, conference, council, summit; *informal* parley, powwow, get-together.

conclude ▶ verb **1** *the meeting concluded at ten* FINISH, end, draw to a close, be over, stop, cease. **2** *she concluded the press conference* BRING TO AN END, close, wind up, terminate, dissolve; round off; *informal* wrap up. **3** *an attempt to conclude a ceasefire* NEGOTIATE, broker, agree, come to terms on, settle, clinch, finalize, tie up; bring about, arrange, effect, engineer; *informal* sew up. **4** *I concluded that he was rather unpleasant* DEDUCE, infer, gather, judge, decide, conjecture, surmise, extrapolate, figure, reckon.
– OPPOSITES: commence.

conclusion ▶ noun **1** *the conclusion of his speech* END, ending, finish, close, termination, wind-up, cessation; culmination, denouement, peroration, coda; *informal* outro. **2** *the conclusion of a trade agreement* NEGOTIATION, brokering, settlement, completion, arrangement, resolution. **3** *his conclusions have been verified* DEDUCTION, inference, interpretation, illation, reasoning; opinion, judgment, verdict; assumption, presumption, supposition.
– OPPOSITES: beginning.
■ **in conclusion** FINALLY, in closing, to conclude, last but not least; to sum up, in short, to make a long story short.

conclusive ▶ adjective **1** *conclusive proof* INCONTROVERTIBLE, undeniable, indisputable, irrefutable, unquestionable, unassailable, convincing, certain, decisive, definitive, definite, positive, categorical, unequivocal; airtight, watertight. **2** *a conclusive win* EMPHATIC, resounding, convincing.
– OPPOSITES: unconvincing.

concoct ▶ verb **1** *he planned to concoct a dessert* PREPARE, make, assemble; *informal* fix, rustle up. **2** *this story she has concocted* MAKE UP, dream up, fabricate, invent, trump up; formulate, hatch, brew, cook up.

concoction ▶ noun **1** *a concoction containing gin and vodka* MIXTURE, brew, preparation, potion. **2** *a strange concoction of folky pop and Gregorian chant* BLEND, mixture, mix, combination, hybrid. **3** *her story is an improbable concoction* FABRICATION, invention, falsification; *informal* fairy tale.

concomitant ▶ adjective (*formal*) ATTENDANT, accompanying, associated, related, connected; resultant, consequent.
– OPPOSITES: unrelated.

concord ▶ noun *council meetings rarely ended in concord* AGREEMENT, harmony, accord, consensus, concurrence, unity.
– OPPOSITES: discord.

concourse ▶ noun **1** *the station concourse* ENTRANCE, foyer, lobby, hall. **2** (*formal*) *a vast concourse of onlookers* CROWD, group, gathering, assembly, body, company, throng, flock, mass.

concrete ▶ adjective **1** *concrete objects* SOLID, material, real, physical, tangible, palpable, substantial, visible, existing. **2** *concrete proof* DEFINITE, firm, positive, conclusive, definitive; real, genuine, bona fide.
– OPPOSITES: abstract, imaginary.

concubine ▶ noun (*archaic*) MISTRESS, kept woman,

hetaera; lover; *informal* bit on the side; *archaic* paramour.

concupiscence ▶ noun *See* LUST *noun sense 1.*

concur ▶ verb **1** *we concur with this view* AGREE, be in agreement, go along, fall in, be in sympathy; see eye to eye, be of the same mind, be of the same opinion. **2** *the two events concurred* COINCIDE, be simultaneous, be concurrent, coexist.
– OPPOSITES: disagree.

concurrent ▶ adjective **1** *nine concurrent life sentences* SIMULTANEOUS, coincident, contemporaneous, parallel. **2** *concurrent lines* CONVERGENT, converging, meeting, intersecting.

concussion ▶ noun **1** *he suffered a concussion* temporary unconsciousness; brain injury. **2** *the concussion of the blast* FORCE, impact, shock, jolt.

condemn ▶ verb **1** *he condemned the suspended players* CENSURE, criticize, denounce, revile, blame, chastise, berate, reprimand, rebuke, reprove, take to task, find fault with; *informal* slam, blast, lay into, tear a strip off of; *formal* castigate. **2** *he was condemned to death* SENTENCE; convict, find guilty. **3** *the house has been condemned* DECLARE UNFIT, declare unsafe. **4** *her mistake had condemned her* INCRIMINATE, implicate; *archaic* inculpate. **5** *his illness condemned him to a lonely life* DOOM, destine, damn; consign, assign.
– OPPOSITES: praise.

condemnation ▶ noun CENSURE, criticism, strictures, denunciation, vilification; reproof, disapproval; *informal* flak, (a) bad press; *formal* castigation.

condensation ▶ noun **1** *windows misty with condensation* MOISTURE, water droplets, steam. **2** *the condensation of the vapour* PRECIPITATION, liquefaction, deliquescence. **3** *a condensation of recent literature* ABRIDGEMENT, summary, synopsis, précis, digest. **4** *the condensation of the report* SHORTENING, abridgement, abbreviation, summarization.

condense ▶ verb **1** *the water vapour condenses* PRECIPITATE, liquefy, become liquid, deliquesce. **2** *he condensed the play* ABRIDGE, shorten, cut, abbreviate, compact; summarize, synopsize, précis; truncate, curtail.
– OPPOSITES: vaporize, expand.

condensed ▶ adjective **1** *a condensed text* ABRIDGED, shortened, cut, compressed, abbreviated, reduced, truncated, concise; outline, thumbnail, capsule; *informal* potted. **2** *condensed soup* CONCENTRATED, evaporated, reduced; strong, undiluted.
– OPPOSITES: diluted.

condescend ▶ verb **1** *don't condescend to your reader* PATRONIZE, talk down to, look down one's nose at, look down on, put down. **2** *he condescended to see us* DEIGN, stoop, descend, lower oneself, demean oneself; vouchsafe, see fit, consent.

condescending ▶ adjective PATRONIZING, supercilious, superior, snobbish, snobby, disdainful, lofty, haughty; *informal* snooty, stuck-up.

condition ▶ noun **1** *check the condition of your wiring* STATE, shape, order. **2** *they lived in appalling conditions* CIRCUMSTANCES, surroundings, environment, situation, set-up, setting, habitat. **3** *she was in top condition* FITNESS, health, form, shape, trim, fettle. **4** *a liver condition* DISORDER, problem, complaint, illness, disease, ailment, sickness, affliction, infection, upset. **5** *a condition of membership* STIPULATION, constraint, prerequisite, precondition, requirement, rule, term, specification, provision, proviso.

▶ verb **1** *their choices are conditioned by the economy* CONSTRAIN, control, govern, determine, decide; affect, touch, impact on; form, shape, guide, sway, bias. **2** *our minds are conditioned by habit* TRAIN, teach, educate, guide; accustom, adapt, habituate, mould, inure. **3** *condition the boards with water* TREAT, prepare, prime, temper, process, acclimatize, acclimate, season. **4** *a product to condition your skin* IMPROVE, nourish, tone (up), moisturize.

conditional ▶ adjective **1** *their approval is conditional on success* SUBJECT TO, dependent on, contingent on, based on, determined by, controlled by, tied to. **2** *a conditional offer* CONTINGENT, dependent, qualified, with reservations, limited, provisional, provisory.

condolences ▶ plural noun SYMPATHY, commiseration(s), compassion, pity, support, comfort, consolation, understanding.

condom ▶ noun CONTRACEPTIVE, prophylactic, sheath; *informal* rubber, safe, French safe ♣.

condone ▶ verb DISREGARD, accept, allow, let pass, turn a blind eye to, overlook, forget; forgive, pardon, excuse, let go.
– OPPOSITES: condemn.

conducive ▶ adjective FAVOURABLE, beneficial, advantageous, opportune, propitious, encouraging, promising, convenient, good, helpful, instrumental, productive, useful.
– OPPOSITES: unfavourable.

conduct ▶ noun **1** *they complained about her conduct* BEHAVIOUR, performance, demeanour; actions, activities, deeds, doings, exploits; habits, manners; *formal* comportment. **2** *the conduct of the elections* MANAGEMENT, running, direction, control, supervision, regulation, administration, organization, coordination, orchestration, handling.
▶ verb **1** *the election was conducted lawfully* MANAGE, direct, run, administer, organize, coordinate, orchestrate, handle, control, oversee, supervise, regulate, carry out/on. **2** *he was conducted through the corridors* ESCORT, guide, lead, usher, show; shepherd, see, bring, take, help. **3** *aluminum conducts heat* TRANSMIT, convey, carry, transfer, impart, channel, relay; disseminate, diffuse, radiate.
■ **conduct oneself** BEHAVE, act, acquit oneself, bear oneself; *formal* comport oneself.

conduit ▶ noun CHANNEL, duct, pipe, tube, gutter, trench, culvert, cut, sluice, spillway, flume, chute.

confectionery ▶ noun CANDY, sweets, chocolates, bonbons.

confederacy ▶ noun FEDERATION, confederation, alliance, league, association, coalition, consortium, syndicate, group, circle; bloc, axis.

confederate ▶ noun *he met his confederate in the street* ASSOCIATE, partner, accomplice, helper, assistant, ally, collaborator, colleague.

confederation ▶ noun ALLIANCE, league, confederacy, federation, association, coalition, consortium, conglomerate, co-operative, syndicate, group, circle; society, union.

confer ▶ verb **1** *she went to confer with her colleagues* CONSULT, talk, speak, converse, have a chat, have a tête-à-tête, parley; *informal* have a confab, powwow. **2** *she conferred a knighthood on him* BESTOW ON, present to, grant to, award to, decorate with, honour with, give to, endow with, extend to.

conference ▶ noun **1** *an international conference* CONGRESS, meeting, convention, seminar, colloquium, symposium, forum, summit. **2** *he* gathered them for a conference DISCUSSION, consultation, debate, talk, conversation, dialogue, chat, tête-à-tête, parley; informal confab; formal confabulation.

confess ▶ verb **1** he confessed that he had done it ADMIT, acknowledge, reveal, disclose, divulge, avow, declare, profess; own up, tell all. **2** they could not make him confess OWN UP, plead guilty, accept the blame; tell the truth, tell all, make a clean breast of it; informal come clean, spill the beans, let the cat out of the bag, get something off one's chest, let on, fess (up). **3** I confess I don't know ACKNOWLEDGE, admit, concede, grant, allow, own, declare, affirm.
– OPPOSITES: deny.

confession ▶ noun ADMISSION, acknowledgement, profession; revelation, disclosure, divulgence, avowal; guilty plea.

confidant, fem. **confidante** ▶ noun CLOSE FRIEND, bosom friend, best friend; intimate; informal buddy, chum, pal, crony, mate.

confide ▶ verb **1** he confided his fears to his mother REVEAL, disclose, divulge, lay bare, betray, impart, declare, intimate, uncover, expose, vouchsafe, tell; confess, admit, give away; informal blab, spill. **2** I need him to confide in OPEN ONE'S HEART TO, unburden oneself to, confess to, tell all to.

confidence ▶ noun **1** I have little confidence in these figures TRUST, belief, faith, credence, conviction. **2** she's brimming with confidence SELF-ASSURANCE, self-confidence, self-possession, assertiveness; poise, aplomb, phlegm; courage, boldness, mettle, nerve. **3** the girls exchanged confidences SECRET, confidentiality, intimacy.
– OPPOSITES: skepticism, doubt.

confident ▶ adjective **1** we are confident that business will improve OPTIMISTIC, hopeful, sanguine; sure, certain, positive, convinced, in no doubt, satisfied, assured, persuaded. **2** a confident young man SELF-ASSURED, assured, self-confident, positive, assertive, self-possessed, self-reliant, poised; cool-headed, phlegmatic, level-headed, unperturbed, imperturbable, unruffled, at ease; informal together, can-do.

confidential ▶ adjective **1** a confidential chat PRIVATE, personal, intimate, quiet; secret, sensitive, classified, restricted, unofficial, unrevealed, undisclosed, unpublished; informal hush-hush, mum; formal sub rosa; archaic privy. **2** a confidential friend TRUSTED, trustworthy, trusty, faithful, reliable, dependable; close, bosom, intimate.

confidentially ▶ adverb PRIVATELY, in private, in confidence, between ourselves/themselves, off the record, quietly, secretly, in secret, behind closed doors; between you and me and the gatepost; formal sub rosa.

configuration ▶ noun ARRANGEMENT, layout, geography, design, organization, order, grouping, positioning, disposition, alignment; shape, form, appearance, formation, structure, set-up, format.

confine ▶ verb **1** they were confined in the house ENCLOSE, incarcerate, imprison, intern, impound, hold captive, trap; shut in/up, keep, lock in/up, coop (up); fence in, hedge in, wall in/up. **2** he confined his remarks to the weather RESTRICT, limit.

confined ▶ adjective CRAMPED, constricted, restricted, limited, small, narrow, compact, tight, poky, uncomfortable, inadequate.
– OPPOSITES: roomy.

confinement ▶ noun **1** solitary confinement IMPRISONMENT, internment, incarceration, custody, captivity, detention, restraint; house arrest. **2** the confinement of an animal CAGING, enclosure; quarantine. **3** (dated) she went to hospital for her confinement LABOUR, delivery, birthing; birth, childbirth; formal parturition; archaic lying-in, childbed.

confines ▶ plural noun LIMITS, margins, extremities, edges, borders, boundaries, fringes, marches; periphery, perimeter.

confirm ▶ verb **1** records confirm the latest evidence CORROBORATE, verify, prove, validate, authenticate, substantiate, justify, vindicate; support, uphold, back up. **2** he confirmed that help was on the way AFFIRM, reaffirm, assert, assure someone, repeat; promise, guarantee. **3** his appointment was confirmed by the president RATIFY, validate, sanction, endorse, formalize, authorize, warrant, accredit, approve, accept.
– OPPOSITES: contradict, deny.

confirmation ▶ noun **1** independent confirmation of the deaths CORROBORATION, verification, proof, testimony, endorsement, authentication, substantiation, evidence. **2** confirmation of your appointment RATIFICATION, approval, authorization, validation, sanction, endorsement, formalization, accreditation, acceptance.

confirmed ▶ adjective ESTABLISHED, long-standing, committed, dyed-in-the-wool, through and through; staunch, loyal, faithful, devoted, dedicated, steadfast; habitual, compulsive, persistent; unapologetic, unashamed, inveterate, chronic, incurable; informal card-carrying.

confiscate ▶ verb IMPOUND, seize, commandeer, requisition, appropriate, expropriate, sequester, sequestrate, take (away); Law distrain.
– OPPOSITES: return.

confiscation ▶ noun SEIZURE, requisition, appropriation, expropriation, sequestration; Law distraint.

conflagration ▶ noun FIRE, blaze, flames, inferno, firestorm.

conflate ▶ verb MIX, blend, fuse, unite, integrate.

conflict ▶ noun **1** industrial conflicts DISPUTE, quarrel, squabble, disagreement, dissension, clash; discord, friction, strife, antagonism, hostility, disputation, contention; feud, schism. **2** the Vietnam conflict WAR, campaign, battle, fighting, (armed) confrontation, engagement, encounter, struggle, hostilities; warfare, combat. **3** a conflict between his business and domestic life CLASH, incompatibility, incongruity, friction; mismatch, variance, difference, divergence, contradiction, inconsistency.
– OPPOSITES: agreement, peace, harmony.
▶ verb their interests sometimes conflict CLASH, be incompatible, vary, be at odds, be in conflict, differ, diverge, disagree, contrast, collide.

conflicting ▶ adjective CONTRADICTORY, incompatible, inconsistent, irreconcilable, incongruous, contrary, opposite, opposing, antithetical, clashing, discordant, divergent; at odds.

confluence ▶ noun CONVERGENCE, meeting, junction.

conform ▶ verb **1** visitors have to conform to our rules COMPLY WITH, abide by, obey, observe, follow, keep to, hew to, stick to, adhere to, uphold, heed, accept, go along with, fall in with, respect, defer to; satisfy, meet, fulfill. **2** they refuse to conform FOLLOW

CONVENTION, be conventional, fit in, adapt, adjust, follow the crowd; comply, acquiesce, toe the line, follow the rules; submit, yield; *informal* play it by the book, play by the rules. **3** *goods must conform to their description* MATCH, fit, suit, answer, agree with, be like, correspond to, be consistent with, measure up to, tally with, square with.
– OPPOSITES: flout, rebel.

conformist ▶ noun TRADITIONALIST, conservative, stickler, formalist, diehard, reactionary; *informal* stick-in-the-mud, stuffed shirt.
– OPPOSITES: eccentric, rebel.

confound ▶ verb **1** *the figures confounded analysts* AMAZE, astonish, dumbfound, stagger, surprise, startle, stun, throw, shake, discompose, bewilder, bedazzle, baffle, mystify, bemuse, perplex, puzzle, confuse; take aback, shake up, catch off balance; *informal* flabbergast, blow someone's mind, blow away, flummox, faze, stump, beat, fox, discombobulate. **2** *he has always confounded expectations* CONTRADICT, counter, invalidate, negate, go against, quash, explode, demolish, shoot down, destroy, disprove; *informal* poke holes in.

confront ▶ verb **1** *Jones confronted the intruder* CHALLENGE, face (up to), come face to face with, meet, accost, waylay; stand up to, brave, beard, tackle; *informal* collar. **2** *the problems that confront us* TROUBLE, bother, burden, distress, worry, oppress, annoy, strain, stress, tax, torment, plague, blight, curse; face, beset. **3** *they must confront their problems* TACKLE, address, face, come to grips with, grapple with, take on, attend to, see to, deal with, take care of, handle, manage. **4** *she confronted him with the evidence* PRESENT, face.
– OPPOSITES: avoid.

confrontation ▶ noun CONFLICT, clash, fight, battle, encounter, faceoff, engagement, skirmish; hostilities, fighting; *informal* set-to, run-in, dust-up, showdown.

confuse ▶ verb **1** *don't confuse students with too much detail* BEWILDER, baffle, mystify, bemuse, perplex, puzzle, confound; *informal* flummox, faze, stump, fox, discombobulate, bedazzle. **2** *the authors have confused the issue* COMPLICATE, muddle, jumble, garble, blur, obscure, cloud. **3** *some confuse strokes with heart attacks* MIX UP, muddle up, confound; mistake for.
– OPPOSITES: enlighten, simplify.

confused ▶ adjective **1** *they are confused about what is going on* BEWILDERED, bemused, puzzled, perplexed, baffled, mystified, nonplussed, muddled, dumbfounded, at sea, at a loss, taken aback, disoriented, disconcerted; *informal* flummoxed, bamboozled, clueless, fazed, discombobulated. **2** *her confused elderly mother* DEMENTED, bewildered, muddled, addled, befuddled, disoriented, disorientated; unbalanced, unhinged; senile. **3** *a confused recollection* VAGUE, unclear, indistinct, imprecise, blurred, hazy, woolly, shadowy, dim; imperfect, sketchy. **4** *a confused mass of bones* DISORDERLY, disordered, disorganized, disarranged, out of order, untidy, muddled, jumbled, mixed up, chaotic, topsy-turvy; *informal* shambolic.
– OPPOSITES: lucid, clear, precise, neat.

confusing ▶ adjective BEWILDERING, baffling, unclear, perplexing, puzzling, mystifying, disconcerting; ambiguous, misleading, inconsistent, contradictory; unaccountable, inexplicable, impenetrable, unfathomable; complex, complicated.

confusion ▶ noun **1** *there is confusion about the new*

system UNCERTAINTY, incertitude, unsureness, doubt, ignorance; *formal* dubiety. **2** *she stared in confusion* BEWILDERMENT, bafflement, perplexity, puzzlement, mystification, befuddlement; shock, daze, wonder, wonderment, astonishment; *informal* bamboozlement, head-scratching, discombobulation. **3** *her life was in utter confusion* DISORDER, disarray, disorganization, untidiness, chaos, mayhem; turmoil, tumult, disruption, upheaval, uproar, hurly-burly, muddle, mess, shambles. **4** *a confusion of boxes* JUMBLE, muddle, mess, heap, tangle; *informal* shambles.
– OPPOSITES: certainty, order.

confute ▶ verb *(formal)* DISPROVE, contradict, controvert, refute, deny, rebut, belie, negate, invalidate, explode, discredit, debunk, quash; *informal* poke holes in; *formal* gainsay.
– OPPOSITES: prove.

congeal ▶ verb COAGULATE, clot, thicken, jell, cake, set, curdle.

congenial ▶ adjective **1** *very congenial people* LIKE-MINDED, compatible, kindred, well-suited; companionable, sociable, sympathetic, comradely, convivial, hospitable, genial, personable, agreeable, friendly, pleasant, likeable, amiable, nice, simpatico. **2** *a congenial environment* PLEASANT, pleasing, agreeable, enjoyable, pleasurable, nice, appealing, satisfying, gratifying, delightful, relaxing, welcoming, hospitable; suitable, well-suited, favourable.
– OPPOSITES: unpleasant.

congenital ▶ adjective **1** *congenital defects* INBORN, inherited, hereditary, innate, inbred, constitutional, inbuilt, natural, inherent. **2** *a congenital liar* INVETERATE, compulsive, persistent, chronic, regular, habitual, obsessive, confirmed; incurable, incorrigible, irredeemable, hopeless; unashamed, shameless, pathological.
– OPPOSITES: acquired.

congested ▶ adjective CROWDED, overcrowded, full, overflowing, packed, jammed, thronged, teeming, swarming; obstructed, blocked, clogged, choked; *informal* snarled up, gridlocked, jam-packed.
– OPPOSITES: clear.

congestion ▶ noun CROWDING, overcrowding; obstruction, blockage; traffic jam, bottleneck; *informal* snarl-up, gridlock.

conglomerate ▶ noun **1** *the conglomerate was broken up* CORPORATION, company, business, multinational, combine, group, consortium, partnership; firm. **2** *a conglomerate of disparate peoples* MIXTURE, mix, combination, amalgamation, union, marriage, fusion, composite, synthesis; miscellany, hodgepodge.
▶ adjective *a conglomerate mass* AGGREGATE, agglomerate, amassed, combined.
▶ verb *the debris conglomerated into planets* COALESCE, unite, join, combine, merge, fuse, consolidate, amalgamate, integrate, mingle, intermingle.

congratulate ▶ verb **1** *she congratulated him on his marriage* SEND ONE'S BEST WISHES, wish someone good luck, wish someone joy; drink someone's health, toast. **2** *they are to be congratulated* PRAISE, commend, applaud, salute, honour; pay tribute to, regard highly, pat on the back, take one's hat off to.
– OPPOSITES: criticize.

■ **congratulate oneself** TAKE PRIDE, feel proud, flatter oneself, pat oneself on the back; feel satisfaction, take pleasure, glory, bask, delight.

congratulations ▶ plural noun **1** *her congratulations*

on their wedding GOOD WISHES, best wishes, compliments, felicitations. **2** *you all deserve congratulations* PRAISE, commendation, applause, salutes, honour, acclaim, cheers; approval, admiration, compliments, bouquets, kudos, adulation; a pat on the back.
▶ **exclamation** *Congratulations! You did it!* BRAVO, brava, mazel tov, naches, kudos; *informal* attaboy/attagirl, congrats.

congregate ▶ **verb** ASSEMBLE, gather, collect, come together, convene, rally, rendezvous, muster, meet, cluster, group.
— OPPOSITES: disperse.

congregation ▶ **noun 1** *the chapel congregation* PARISHIONERS, parish, churchgoers, flock, faithful, followers, believers, fellowship, communicants, laity, brethren, membership; throng, company, assemblage, audience. **2** *congregations of birds* GATHERING, assembly, flock, swarm, bevy, pack, group, body, crowd, mass, multitude, horde, host, mob, throng.

congress ▶ **noun 1** *a congress of mathematicians* CONFERENCE, convention, seminar, colloquium, symposium, forum, meeting, assembly, gathering, rally, summit. **2** *elections for the new Congress* LEGISLATURE, legislative assembly, parliament, convocation, diet, council, senate, chamber, house.

congruence ▶ **noun** COMPATIBILITY, consistency, conformity, match, balance, consonance, congruity; agreement, accord, consensus, harmony, unity; *formal* concord.
— OPPOSITES: conflict.

conical ▶ **adjective** CONE-SHAPED, tapered, tapering, pointed, funnel-shaped; *formal* infundibular; *informal* pointy; *Zoology* conoid.

conjectural ▶ **adjective** SPECULATIVE, suppositional, theoretical, hypothetical, putative, notional; postulated, inferred, presumed, assumed, presupposed, tentative.

conjecture ▶ **noun** *the information is merely conjecture* SPECULATION, guesswork, surmise, fancy, presumption, assumption, theory, postulation, supposition; inference, extrapolation; *estimate; informal* guesstimate, a shot in the dark.
— OPPOSITES: fact.
▶ **verb** *I conjectured that the game was over* GUESS, speculate, surmise, infer, fancy, imagine, believe, think, suspect, presume, assume, hypothesize, suppose.
— OPPOSITES: know.

conjugal ▶ **adjective** MARITAL, matrimonial, nuptial, marriage, bridal; *Law* spousal; *literary* connubial.

conjunction ▶ **noun 1** *a theory that the Americas were formed by a conjunction of floating islands* COMING TOGETHER, convergence, union, confluence. **2** *a conjunction of planets* CO-OCCURRENCE, concurrence, coincidence, coexistence, simultaneity, contemporaneity, concomitance, synchronicity, synchrony.
■ **in conjunction with** TOGETHER WITH, along with, accompanying, accompanied by; as well as, in addition to, plus.

conjure ▶ **verb 1** *he conjured a cigarette out of the air* PRODUCE, make something appear, materialize, magic, summon. **2** *the picture that his words conjured up* BRING TO MIND, call to mind, evoke, summon up, recall, recreate; echo, allude to, suggest, awaken.

conjuring ▶ **noun** MAGIC, illusion, sleight of hand, legerdemain, prestidigitation.

conjuror ▶ **noun** MAGICIAN, illusionist, prestidigitator.

connect ▶ **verb 1** *electrodes were connected to the device* ATTACH, join, fasten, fix, affix, couple, link, secure, hitch; stick, adhere, fuse, pin, screw, bolt, clamp, clip, hook (up); add, append. **2** *rituals connected with Easter* ASSOCIATE, link, couple; identify, equate, bracket, relate to.

connection ▶ **noun 1** *the connection between commerce and art* LINK, relationship, relation, interconnection, interdependence, association; bond, tie, tie-in, correspondence, parallel, analogy. **2** *a poor connection in the plug* ATTACHMENT, joint, fastening, coupling. **3** *he has the right connections* CONTACT, friend, acquaintance, ally, colleague, associate; relation, relative, kin.
■ **in connection with** REGARDING, concerning, with reference to, with regard to, with respect to, respecting, relating to, in relation to, on, connected with, on the subject of, in the matter of, apropos, re.

conniption ▶ **noun** See FIT[2] sense 3.

connivance ▶ **noun** COLLUSION, complicity, collaboration, involvement, assistance; tacit consent, conspiracy, intrigue.

connive ▶ **verb** CONSPIRE, collude, collaborate, intrigue, be hand in glove, plot, scheme; *informal* be in cahoots.

conniving ▶ **adjective** SCHEMING, cunning, crafty, calculating, devious, wily, sly, tricky, artful, guileful; manipulative, Machiavellian, disingenuous, deceitful, underhanded, treacherous; *informal* foxy.

connoisseur ▶ **noun** EXPERT, authority, specialist, pundit, savant; arbiter of taste, aesthete; gourmet, epicure, gastronome; *informal* buff, maven.

connotation ▶ **noun** OVERTONE, undertone, undercurrent, implication, hidden meaning, nuance, hint, echo, vibrations, association, intimation, suggestion, suspicion, insinuation.

connote ▶ **verb** IMPLY, suggest, indicate, signify, hint at, give the impression of, smack of, be associated with, allude to.

conquer ▶ **verb 1** *the Franks conquered the Visigoths* DEFEAT, beat, vanquish, trounce, triumph over, be victorious over, get the better of, worst; overcome, overwhelm, overpower, overthrow, subdue, subjugate, quell, quash, crush, rout; *informal* lick, best, hammer, clobber, thrash, paste, demolish, annihilate, wipe the floor with, walk all over, make mincemeat of, massacre, slaughter, cream, shellac, skunk. **2** *Peru was conquered by Spain* SEIZE, take (over), appropriate, subjugate, capture, occupy, invade, annex, overrun. **3** *the first men to conquer Mount Everest* CLIMB, ascend, mount, scale, top, crest. **4** *the way to conquer fear* OVERCOME, get the better of, control, master, get a grip on, deal with, cope with, surmount, rise above, get over; quell, quash, beat, triumph over; *informal* lick.

conqueror ▶ **noun** VANQUISHER, conquistador; victor, winner, champion, conquering hero.

conquest ▶ **noun 1** *the conquest of the Aztecs* DEFEAT, vanquishment, annihilation, overthrow, subjugation, rout, mastery, crushing; victory over, triumph over. **2** *their conquest of the valley* SEIZURE, takeover, capture, occupation, invasion, acquisition, appropriation, subjugation, subjection. **3** *the conquest of Everest* ASCENT. **4** *she's his latest conquest* CATCH, acquisition, prize, slave; admirer, fan, worshipper; lover, boyfriend, girlfriend.

consanguinity ▶ noun *See* RELATIONSHIP sense 2.

conscience ▶ noun SENSE OF RIGHT AND WRONG, moral sense, inner voice; morals, standards, values, principles, ethics, beliefs; compunction, scruples, qualms.

conscience-stricken ▶ adjective GUILT-RIDDEN, remorseful, ashamed, shamefaced, apologetic, sorry; chastened, contrite, guilty, regretful, rueful, repentant, penitent, abashed, sheepish, compunctious.
— OPPOSITES: unrepentant.

conscientious ▶ adjective DILIGENT, industrious, punctilious, painstaking, sedulous, assiduous, dedicated, careful, meticulous, thorough, attentive, hard-working, studious, rigorous, particular; religious, strict.
— OPPOSITES: casual.

conscious ▶ adjective **1** *the patient was conscious* AWARE, awake, alert, responsive, sentient, compos mentis. **2** *he became conscious of people talking* AWARE OF, alert to, mindful of, sensible of; *formal* cognizant of. **3** *a conscious effort* DELIBERATE, intentional, intended, purposeful, purposive, knowing, considered, calculated, wilful, premeditated, planned, volitional.
— OPPOSITES: unaware.

conscript ▶ verb *they were conscripted into the army* CALL UP, enlist, recruit; *US* draft; *historical* press, impress.
▶ noun *an army conscript* compulsorily enlisted soldier, recruit; *US* draftee.
— OPPOSITES: volunteer.

consecrate ▶ verb SANCTIFY, bless, make holy, make sacred; dedicate to God, devote, reserve, set apart; anoint, ordain; *formal* hallow.

consecutive ▶ adjective SUCCESSIVE, succeeding, following, in succession, running, in a row, one after the other, back-to-back, continuous, straight, uninterrupted.

consensus ▶ noun **1** *there was consensus among delegates* AGREEMENT, harmony, concurrence, accord, unity, unanimity, solidarity; *formal* concord. **2** *the consensus was that they should act* GENERAL OPINION, majority opinion, common view.
— OPPOSITES: disagreement.

consent ▶ noun *the consent of all members* AGREEMENT, assent, acceptance, approval, approbation; permission, authorization, sanction, leave; backing, endorsement, support; *informal* go-ahead, thumbs up, green light, OK.
— OPPOSITES: dissent.
▶ verb *she consented to surgery* AGREE, assent, yield, give in, submit; allow, give permission for, sanction, accept, approve, go along with.
— OPPOSITES: forbid.

consequence ▶ noun **1** *a consequence of inflation* RESULT, upshot, outcome, effect, repercussion, ramification, corollary, concomitant, aftermath, after-effect; fruit(s), product, by-product, end result; *informal* payoff; *Medicine* sequela. **2** *the past is of no consequence* IMPORTANCE, import, significance, account, substance, note, mark, prominence, value, concern, interest; *formal* moment.
— OPPOSITES: cause.

consequent ▶ adjective RESULTING, resultant, ensuing, consequential; following, subsequent,

successive; attendant, accompanying, concomitant; collateral, associated, related.

consequential ▶ adjective **1** *a fire and the consequential smoke damage* RESULTING, resultant, ensuing, consequent; following, subsequent; attendant, accompanying, concomitant; collateral, associated, related. **2** *one of his more consequential initiatives* IMPORTANT, significant, major, momentous, weighty, material, appreciable, memorable, far-reaching, serious.
— OPPOSITES: insignificant.

consequently ▶ adverb AS A RESULT, as a consequence, so, thus, therefore, ergo, accordingly, hence, for this/that reason, because of this/that, on this/that account; inevitably, necessarily.

conservation ▶ noun PRESERVATION, protection, safeguarding, safekeeping; care, guardianship, husbandry, supervision; upkeep, maintenance, repair, restoration; ecology, environmentalism.

conservative ▶ adjective **1** *the conservative wing of the party* RIGHT-WING, reactionary, traditionalist; Tory, blue; *US* Republican; *informal* redneck. **2** *the conservative trade-union movement* TRADITIONALIST, traditional, conventional, orthodox, old-fashioned, dyed-in-the-wool, hidebound, unadventurous, set in one's ways; moderate, middle-of-the-road, buttoned-down; *informal* stick in the mud. **3** *a conservative suit* CONVENTIONAL, sober, modest, plain, unobtrusive, restrained, subtle, low-key, demure; *informal* square, straight. **4** *a conservative estimate* LOW, cautious, understated, moderate, reasonable.
— OPPOSITES: socialist, radical, ostentatious.
▶ noun *liberals and conservatives have found common ground* Tory ♣, right-winger, reactionary, rightist, diehard; *(Que.)* bleu ♣, Blue; *US* Republican.

conservatory ▶ noun **1** *a frost-free conservatory* SUMMER HOUSE, belvedere; glasshouse, greenhouse, hothouse. **2** *a teaching job at the conservatory* CONSERVATOIRE, music school, drama school.

conserve ▶ verb *fossil fuel should be conserved* PRESERVE, protect, save, safeguard, keep, look after; sustain, prolong, perpetuate; store, reserve, husband.
— OPPOSITES: squander.
▶ noun *cherry conserve* JAM, preserve, jelly, marmalade, fruit butter.

consider ▶ verb **1** *Isabel considered her choices* THINK ABOUT, contemplate, reflect on, examine, review; mull over, ponder, deliberate on, chew over, meditate on, ruminate on; assess, evaluate, appraise; *informal* size up. **2** *I consider him irresponsible* DEEM, think, believe, judge, adjudge, rate, count, find; regard as, hold to be, reckon to be, view as, see as. **3** *he considered the ceiling* LOOK AT, contemplate, observe, regard, survey, view, scrutinize, scan, examine, inspect; *informal* check out, eyeball. **4** *the inquiry will consider those issues* TAKE INTO CONSIDERATION, take account of, make allowances for, bear in mind, be mindful of, remember, mind, mark, respect, heed, note, make provision for.
— OPPOSITES: ignore.

considerable ▶ adjective **1** *a considerable amount of money* SIZEABLE, substantial, appreciable, significant, goodly, fair, hefty, handsome, decent, worthwhile; ample, plentiful, abundant, great, large, generous; *informal* tidy, not to be sneezed at. **2** *considerable success* MUCH, great, a lot of, lots of, a great deal of, plenty of, a fair amount of. **3** *a considerable player in the game of politics* DISTINGUISHED, noteworthy, important,

significant, prominent, eminent, influential, illustrious; renowned, celebrated, acclaimed.
– OPPOSITES: paltry, minor.

considerably ▶ adverb GREATLY, (very) much, a great deal, a lot, lots; significantly, substantially, appreciably, markedly, noticeably; *informal* plenty, seriously.

considerate ▶ adjective ATTENTIVE, thoughtful, solicitous, mindful, heedful; obliging, accommodating, helpful, co-operative, patient; kind, unselfish, compassionate, sympathetic, caring, charitable, altruistic, generous; polite, sensitive, tactful.

consideration ▶ noun 1 *your case needs careful consideration* THOUGHT, deliberation, reflection, contemplation, rumination, meditation; examination, inspection, scrutiny, analysis, discussion; attention, regard; *formal* cogitation. 2 *his health is the prime consideration* FACTOR, issue, matter, concern, detail, aspect, feature. 3 *firms should show more consideration* ATTENTIVENESS, concern, care, thoughtfulness, solicitude; kindness, understanding, respect, sensitivity, tact, discretion; compassion, charity, benevolence.
■ **take something into consideration** CONSIDER, give thought to, take into account, allow for, provide for, plan for, make provision for, accommodate, bargain for, reckon with; foresee, anticipate.

considering ▶ preposition *considering his size he was speedy* BEARING IN MIND, taking into consideration, taking into account, keeping in mind, in view of, in (the) light of.
▶ adverb (*informal*) *he'd been lucky, considering* ALL THINGS CONSIDERED, all in all, on the whole, at the end of the day, when all's said and done.

consign ▶ verb 1 *he was consigned to prison* SEND, deliver, hand over, turn over, sentence; confine in, imprison in, incarcerate in, lock up in; *informal* put away, put behind bars. 2 *the picture was consigned to the gallery* ASSIGN, allocate, place, put, remit, commit. 3 *the package was consigned by a local company* SEND (OFF), courier, dispatch, transmit, convey, mail, post, ship. 4 *I consigned her picture to the garbage can* DEPOSIT, commit, banish, relegate.

consignment ▶ adjective *a consignment clothing shop* SECOND-HAND, used, pre-owned, cast-off, hand-me-down.
▶ noun DELIVERY, shipment, load, boatload, truckload, cargo; batch; goods.

consist ▶ verb 1 *the exhibition consists of 180 drawings* BE COMPOSED, be made up, be formed; comprise, contain, include, incorporate. 2 *style consists in the choices that writers make* BE INHERENT, lie, reside, be present, be contained; be expressed by.

consistency ▶ noun 1 *the trend shows a degree of consistency* UNIFORMITY, constancy, regularity, evenness, steadiness, stability, equilibrium; dependability, reliability. 2 *mix until the batter is of pouring consistency* THICKNESS, density, viscosity, heaviness, texture; firmness, solidity.

consistent ▶ adjective 1 *consistent opinion-poll evidence* CONSTANT, regular, uniform, steady, stable, even, unchanging, undeviating, unfluctuating; dependable, reliable, predictable. 2 *her injuries were consistent with a knife attack* COMPATIBLE, congruous, consonant, in tune, in line, reconcilable; corresponding to, conforming to.
– OPPOSITES: irregular, incompatible.

consolation ▶ noun COMFORT, solace, sympathy, compassion, pity, commiseration, empathy; relief, help, (moral) support, encouragement, reassurance.

console[1] ▶ verb *she tried to console him* COMFORT, solace, condole with, sympathize with, commiserate with, show compassion for; help, support, cheer (up), hearten, encourage, reassure, soothe.
– OPPOSITES: upset.

console[2] ▶ noun *a digital console* CONTROL PANEL, instrument panel, dashboard, keyboard, keypad; *informal* dash.

consolidate ▶ verb 1 *we consolidated our position in the market* STRENGTHEN, secure, stabilize, reinforce, fortify; enhance, improve. 2 *consolidate the results into an action plan* COMBINE, unite, merge, integrate, amalgamate, fuse, synthesize, bring together, unify.

consonance ▶ noun AGREEMENT, accord, harmony, unison; compatibility, congruity, congruence; *formal* concord.

consonant
■ **consonant with** IN AGREEMENT WITH, consistent with, in accordance with, in harmony with, compatible with, congruous with, in tune with.

consort ▶ noun *the queen and her consort* (LIFE) PARTNER, companion, mate; spouse, husband, wife, helpmate.
▶ verb *he consorted with other women* ASSOCIATE, keep company, mix, go around, spend time, socialize, fraternize, have dealings; *informal* run around, hang around/out, be thick.

consortium ▶ noun ASSOCIATION, alliance, coalition, union, league, guild, syndicate, federation, confederation, confederacy, conglomerate, co-operative, combine, partnership, affiliation, organization; club, society, congress.

conspicuous ▶ adjective EASILY SEEN, clear, visible, noticeable, discernible, perceptible, detectable; obvious, manifest, evident, apparent, marked, pronounced, prominent, patent, crystal clear; striking, eye-catching, overt, blatant, writ large; distinct, recognizable, unmistakable, inescapable; *informal* as plain as the nose on one's face, standing/sticking out like a sore thumb.

conspiracy ▶ noun 1 *a conspiracy to manipulate the results* PLOT, scheme, plan, machination, ploy, trick, ruse, subterfuge; *informal* racket. 2 *conspiracy to commit murder* PLOTTING, collusion, intrigue, connivance, machination, collaboration; treason.

conspirator ▶ noun PLOTTER, schemer, intriguer, colluder, collaborator, conniver.

conspire ▶ verb 1 *they admitted conspiring to steal cars* PLOT, scheme, plan, intrigue, machinate, collude, connive, collaborate, work hand in glove; *informal* be in cahoots. 2 *circumstances conspired against them* ACT TOGETHER, work together, combine, unite, join forces; *informal* gang up.

constancy ▶ noun 1 *constancy between lovers* FIDELITY, faithfulness, loyalty, commitment, dedication, devotion; dependability, reliability, trustworthiness. 2 *the constancy of Henry's views* STEADFASTNESS, resolution, resolve, firmness, fixedness; determination, perseverance, tenacity, doggedness, staunchness, staying power, obstinacy. 3 *the constancy of their doubt* CONSISTENCY, permanence, persistence, durability, endurance; uniformity, immutability, regularity, stability, steadiness.

The 88 Constellations

Latin	English	Latin	English	Latin	English
Andromeda	Andromeda	Cygnus	The Swan	Orion	The Hunter
Antlia	The Air Pump	Delphinus	The Dolphin	Pavo	The Peacock
Apus	Bird of Paradise	Dorado	The Goldfish/	Pegasus	The Flying Horse
Aquarius	The Water		Swordfish	Perseus	Perseus
	Bearer/Carrier	Draco	The Dragon	Phoenix	The Firebird
Aquila	The Eagle	Equuleus	The Little Horse	Pictor	The Easel
Ara	The Altar	Eridanus	The River	Pisces	The Fishes
Aries	The Ram		Eridanus	Piscis	The Southern Fish
Auriga	The Charioteer	Fornax	The Furance	Austrinus	
Bootes	The Herdsman	Gemini	The Twins	Puppis	The Ship's Stern
Caelum	The Chisel	Grus	The Crane		or Poop Deck
Camelopardalis	The Giraffe	Hercules	Hercules	Pyxis	The Ship's
Cancer	The Crab	Horologium	The Clock		Compass
Canes Venatici	The Hunting Dogs	Hydra	The Sea Monster	Reticulum	The Net
Canis Major	The Big Dog	Hydrus	The Sea Serpent	Sagitta	The Arrow
Canis Minor	The Little Dog	Indus	The Indian	Sagittarius	The Archer
Capricornus	The Goat	Lacerta	The Lizard	Scorpius	The Scorpion
Carina	The Ship's Keel	Leo	The Lion	Sculptor	The Sculptor
Cassiopeia	Cassiopeia	Leo Minor	The Little Lion	Scutum	The Shield
Centaurus	The Centaur	Lepus	The Hare	Serpens Caput	The Serpent
Cepheus	Cepheus	Libra	The Scales/	Sextans	The Sextant
Cetus	The Whale		Balance	Taurus	The Bull
Chamaeleon	The Chameleon	Lupus	The Wolf	Telescopium	The Telescope
Circinus	The Compass	Lynx	The Lynx	Triangulum	The Triangle
Columba	The Dove	Lyra	The Harp/Lyre	Triangulum	The Southern
Coma Berenices	Berenice's Hair	Mensa	The Table	Australe	Triangle
Corona	The Southern	Microscopium	The Microscope	Tucana	The Toucan
Australis	Crown	Monoceros	The Unicorn	Ursa Major	The Great Bear
Corona	The Northern	Musca	The Fly	Ursa Minor	The Little Bear
Borealis	Crown	Norma	The Rule	Vela	The Sails
Corvus	The Crow/Raven	Octans	The Octant	Virgo	The Virgin
Crater	The Cup	Ophiuchus	The Serpent	Volans	The Flying Fish
Crux	The Cross		Bearer	Vulpecula	The Little Fox

constant ▶ adjective **1** *the constant background noise* CONTINUAL, continuous, persistent, sustained, round-the-clock; ceaseless, unceasing, perpetual, incessant, never-ending, eternal, endless, unabating, non-stop, unrelieved; interminable, unremitting, relentless. **2** *a constant speed* CONSISTENT, regular, steady, uniform, even, invariable, unvarying, unchanging, undeviating, unfluctuating. **3** *a constant friend* FAITHFUL, loyal, devoted, true, fast, firm, unswerving; steadfast, staunch, dependable, trustworthy, trusty, reliable, dedicated, committed. **4** *constant vigilance* STEADFAST, steady, resolute, determined, tenacious, dogged, unwavering, unflagging.
— OPPOSITES: fitful, variable, fickle.
▶ noun *dread of cancer has been a constant* UNCHANGING FACTOR, given.

constantly ▶ adverb ALWAYS, all the time, continually, continuously, persistently; round-the-clock, night and day, {morning, noon, and night}; endlessly, non-stop, incessantly, unceasingly, perpetually, eternally, forever; interminably, unremittingly, relentlessly; *informal* 24-7.
— OPPOSITES: occasionally.

constellation ▶ noun. *See table.*

consternation ▶ noun DISMAY, perturbation, distress, disquiet, discomposure; surprise, amazement, astonishment; alarm, panic, fear, fright, shock.
— OPPOSITES: satisfaction.

constituency ▶ noun *rumblings in the Premier's own constituency* riding ♣, electoral district, seat.

constituent ▶ adjective *constituent parts* COMPONENT, integral; elemental, basic, essential, inherent.
▶ noun **1** *MPs must listen to their constituents* VOTER, elector, member of a constituency. **2** *the constituents of tobacco* COMPONENT, ingredient, element; part, piece, bit, unit; section, portion.

constitute ▶ verb **1** *farmers constituted 10 per cent of the population* AMOUNT TO, add up to, account for, form, make up, compose. **2** *this constitutes a breach of copyright* BE EQUIVALENT TO, be, embody, be tantamount to, be regarded as. **3** *the courts were constituted in 1875* INAUGURATE, establish, initiate, found, create, set up, start, form, organize, develop; commission, charter, invest, appoint, install, empower.

constitution ▶ noun **1** *the constitution guarantees our rights* CHARTER, social code, law; bill of rights; rules, regulations, fundamental principles. **2** *the chemical constitution of the dye* COMPOSITION, makeup, structure, construction, arrangement, configuration, formation, anatomy. **3** *she has the constitution of an ox* HEALTH, physique, physical condition, shape, fettle.

constitutional ▶ adjective **1** *constitutional powers* LEGAL, lawful, legitimate, authorized, permitted; sanctioned, ratified, warranted, constituted, statutory, chartered, vested, official; by law. **2** *a constitutional weakness* INHERENT, intrinsic, innate, fundamental, essential, organic; congenital, inborn, inbred.
▶ noun (dated) *she went out for a constitutional.* See WALK noun sense 1.

constrain ▶ verb **1** *he felt constrained to explain* COMPEL, force, drive, impel, oblige, coerce, prevail on, require; press, push, pressure. **2** *prices were constrained by government controls* RESTRICT, limit, curb, check, restrain, contain, rein in, hold back, keep down.

constrained ▶ adjective UNNATURAL, awkward, self-conscious, forced, stilted, strained; restrained, reserved, reticent, guarded.
− OPPOSITES: relaxed.

constraint ▶ noun **1** *financial constraints* RESTRICTION, limitation, curb, check, restraint, control, damper, rein; hindrance, impediment, obstruction, handicap. **2** *they were able to talk without constraint* INHIBITION, uneasiness, embarrassment; restraint, reticence, guardedness, formality; self-consciousness, awkwardness, stiltedness.

constrict ▶ verb **1** *fat constricts the blood vessels* NARROW, make narrower, tighten, compress, contract, squeeze, strangle, strangulate; *archaic* straiten. **2** *fear of crime constricts many people's lives* RESTRICT, impede, limit, inhibit, obstruct, interfere with, hinder, hamper.
− OPPOSITES: expand, dilate.

constriction ▶ noun TIGHTNESS, pressure, compression, contraction, cramp; obstruction, blockage, impediment; *Medicine* stricture, stenosis.

construct ▶ verb **1** *a new high-rise was being constructed* BUILD, erect, put up, set up, raise, establish, assemble, manufacture, fabricate, create, make. **2** *he constructed a faultless argument* FORMULATE, form, put together, create, devise, design, compose, work out; fashion, mould, shape, frame.
− OPPOSITES: demolish.

construction ▶ noun **1** *the construction of a new airport* BUILDING, erection, putting up, setting up, establishment; assembly, manufacture, fabrication, creation. **2** *the station was a spectacular construction* STRUCTURE, building, edifice, pile. **3** *you could put an honest construction on their conduct* INTERPRETATION, reading, meaning, explanation, explication, construal; *informal* take, spin.

constructive ▶ adjective USEFUL, helpful, productive, positive, encouraging; practical, valuable, profitable, worthwhile.

construe ▶ verb INTERPRET, understand, read, see, take, take to mean, regard.

consul ▶ noun AMBASSADOR, diplomat, chargé d'affaires, attaché, envoy, emissary, plenipotentiary, (Que.) delegate-general ♣.

consult ▶ verb **1** *you need to consult a lawyer* SEEK ADVICE FROM, ask, take counsel from, call on/upon, speak to, turn to, have recourse to; *informal* pick someone's brains. **2** *the government must consult with interested parties* CONFER, have discussions, talk things over, exchange views, communicate, parley, deliberate; *informal* put their heads together. **3** *she consulted her diary* REFER TO, turn to, look at.

consultant ▶ noun ADVISER, expert, specialist, authority, pundit.

consultation ▶ noun **1** *the need for further consultation with industry* DISCUSSION, dialogue, discourse, debate, negotiation, deliberation. **2** *a 30-minute consultation* MEETING, talk, discussion, interview, audience, hearing; appointment, session; *formal* confabulation, colloquy.

consume ▶ verb **1** *vast amounts of food and drink were consumed* EAT, devour, ingest, swallow, gobble up, wolf down, guzzle, feast on, snack on; DRINK, gulp down, imbibe; *informal* tuck into, put away, polish off, dispose of, pig out on, down, swill, scarf (down/up), snarf (down/up). **2** *natural resources are being consumed at an alarming rate* USE (UP), utilize, expend; deplete, exhaust; waste, squander, drain, dissipate, fritter away. **3** *the fire consumed fifty houses* DESTROY, demolish, lay waste, wipe out, annihilate, devastate, gut, ruin, wreck. **4** *Carolyn was consumed with guilt* EAT UP, devour, obsess, grip, overwhelm; absorb, preoccupy.

consumer ▶ noun PURCHASER, buyer, customer, shopper; user, end-user; client, patron; (**the consumer** or **consumers**) the public, the market.

consuming ▶ adjective ABSORBING, compelling, compulsive, obsessive, overwhelming; intense, ardent, strong, powerful, burning, raging, fervid, profound, deep-seated.

consummate ▶ verb *the deal was finally consummated* COMPLETE, conclude, finish, accomplish, achieve; execute, carry out, perform; *informal* sew up, wrap up; *formal* effectuate.
▶ adjective *his consummate skill* | *a consummate politician* SUPREME, superb, superlative, superior, accomplished, expert, proficient, skilful, skilled, masterly, master, first-class, talented, gifted, polished, practised, perfect, ultimate; complete, total, utter, absolute, pure.

consumption ▶ noun **1** *food unfit for human consumption* EATING, drinking, ingestion. **2** *the consumption of fossil fuels* USE, using up, utilization, expending, depletion; waste, squandering, dissipation.

contact ▶ noun **1** *a disease transmitted through casual contact* TOUCH, touching; proximity, exposure. **2** *foreign diplomats were asked to avoid all contact with him* COMMUNICATION, correspondence, touch; association, connection, intercourse, relations, dealings; *archaic* traffic. **3** *he had many contacts in Germany* CONNECTION, acquaintance, associate, friend.
▶ verb *anyone with information should contact the police* GET IN TOUCH WITH, communicate with, make contact with, approach, notify; telephone, phone, call, speak to, talk to, write to, get hold of.

contagion ▶ noun (*dated*) DISEASE, infection, illness, plague, blight; *informal* bug, virus; *archaic* pestilence.

contagious ▶ adjective INFECTIOUS, communicable, transmittable, transmissible, spreadable; *informal* catching; *dated* infective.

contain ▶ verb **1** *the archive contains much unpublished material* INCLUDE, comprise, take in, incorporate, involve, encompass, embrace; consist of, be made up of, be composed of. **2** *the boat contained four people* HOLD, carry, accommodate, seat. **3** *he must contain his anger* RESTRAIN, curb, rein in, suppress, repress, stifle, subdue, quell, swallow, bottle up, hold in, keep in check; control, master.

container ▶ noun RECEPTACLE, vessel, canister, *proprietary* Tupperware, holder, repository, tote ♣.

contaminate ▶ verb POLLUTE, adulterate, defile, debase, corrupt, taint, infect, foul, spoil, soil, stain, sully; poison; *literary* befoul.
− OPPOSITES: purify.

contemplate ▶ verb **1** *she contemplated her image in the mirror* LOOK AT, view, regard, examine, inspect, observe, survey, study, scrutinize, scan, stare at, gaze at, eye. **2** *he contemplated his fate* THINK ABOUT, ponder, reflect on, consider, mull over, muse on, dwell on, deliberate over, meditate on, ruminate on, chew over, brood on/about, turn over in one's mind; *formal* cogitate. **3** *he was contemplating action for damages* CONSIDER, think about, have in mind, intend, propose; envisage, foresee.

contemplation ► noun **1** *the contemplation of beautiful objects* VIEWING, examination, inspection, observation, survey, study, scrutiny. **2** *the monks sat in quiet contemplation* THOUGHT, reflection, meditation, consideration, rumination, deliberation, reverie, introspection, brown study; *formal* cogitation, cerebration.

contemplative ► adjective THOUGHTFUL, pensive, reflective, meditative, musing, ruminative, introspective, brooding, deep/lost in thought, in a brown study.

contemporary ► adjective **1** *contemporary sources* OF THE TIME, of the day, contemporaneous, concurrent, coeval, coexisting, coexistent. **2** *contemporary society* MODERN, present-day, present, current, present-time. **3** *a very contemporary design* MODERN, up-to-date, up-to-the-minute, fashionable; modish, latest, recent; *informal* trendy, with it, du jour.
— OPPOSITES: old-fashioned, out of date.
► noun *Chaucer's contemporaries* PEER, fellow; *formal* compeer.

contempt ► noun **1** *she regarded him with contempt* SCORN, disdain, disrespect, scornfulness, contemptuousness, derision; disgust, loathing, hatred, abhorrence. **2** *he is guilty of contempt of court* DISRESPECT, disregard, slighting.
— OPPOSITES: respect.

contemptible ► adjective DESPICABLE, detestable, hateful, reprehensible, deplorable, unspeakable, disgraceful, shameful, ignominious, abject, low, mean, cowardly, unworthy, discreditable, petty, worthless, shabby, cheap, beyond contempt, beyond the pale, sordid; *archaic* scurvy.
— OPPOSITES: admirable.

contemptuous ► adjective SCORNFUL, disdainful, disrespectful, insulting, insolent, derisive, mocking, sneering, scoffing, withering, scathing, snide; condescending, supercilious, haughty, proud, superior, arrogant, dismissive, aloof; *informal* high and mighty, snotty, sniffy.
— OPPOSITES: respectful.

contend ► verb **1** *the pilot had to contend with torrential rain* COPE WITH, face, grapple with, deal with, take on, pit oneself against. **2** *three main groups were contending for power* COMPETE, vie, contest, fight, battle, tussle, go head to head; strive, struggle. **3** *he contends that the judge was wrong* ASSERT, maintain, hold, claim, argue, insist, state, declare, profess, affirm; allege; *formal* aver.

content[1] ► adjective *she seemed content with life* CONTENTED, satisfied, pleased, gratified, fulfilled, happy, cheerful, glad; unworried, untroubled, at ease, at peace, tranquil, serene.
— OPPOSITES: discontented, dissatisfied.
► verb *her reply seemed to content him* SATISFY, please; soothe, pacify, placate, appease, mollify.
► noun *a time of content*. See CONTENTMENT.

content[2] ► noun **1** *foods with a high fibre content* AMOUNT, proportion, quantity. **2** (**contents**) *the contents of a vegetarian sausage* CONSTITUENTS, ingredients, components, elements. **3** (**contents**) *the book's table of contents* CHAPTERS, sections, divisions. **4** *the content of the essay* SUBJECT MATTER, subject, theme, argument, thesis, message, thrust, substance, matter, material, text, ideas.

contented ► adjective *a contented man*. See CONTENT[1] adjective.

contention ► noun **1** *a point of contention* DISAGREEMENT, dispute, disputation, argument, discord, conflict, friction, strife, dissension, disharmony. **2** *we questioned the validity of his contention* ARGUMENT, claim, plea, submission, allegation, assertion, declaration; opinion, stand, position, view, belief, thesis, case.
— OPPOSITES: agreement.
■ **in contention** IN COMPETITION, competing, contesting, contending, vying; striving, struggling.

contentious ► adjective **1** *a contentious issue* CONTROVERSIAL, disputable, debatable, disputed, open to debate, vexed. **2** *a contentious debate* HEATED, vehement, fierce, violent, intense, impassioned. **3** *contentious people*. See QUARRELSOME.

contentment ► noun CONTENTEDNESS, content, satisfaction, gratification, fulfilment, happiness, pleasure, cheerfulness; ease, comfort, well-being, peace, equanimity, serenity, tranquillity.

contest ► noun **1** *a boxing contest* COMPETITION, match, tournament, game, meet, event, trial, bout, heat, tie, race. **2** *the contest for the party leadership* FIGHT, battle, tussle, struggle, competition, race.
► verb **1** *he intended to contest the seat* COMPETE FOR, contend for, vie for, fight for, try to win, go for, throw one's hat in the ring. **2** *we contested the decision* OPPOSE, object to, challenge, take a stand against, take issue with, question, call into question. **3** *the issues have been hotly contested* DEBATE, argue about, dispute, quarrel over.

contestant ► noun COMPETITOR, participant, player, contender, candidate, aspirant, hopeful, entrant.

context ► noun **1** *the wider historical context* CIRCUMSTANCES, conditions, factors, state of affairs, situation, background, scene, setting. **2** *a quote taken out of context* FRAME OF REFERENCE, contextual relationship; text, subject, theme, topic.

contiguous ► adjective ADJACENT, neighbouring, adjoining, bordering, next-door; abutting, connecting, touching, in contact, proximate.

continent ► adjective SELF-RESTRAINED, self-disciplined, abstemious, abstinent, self-denying, ascetic; chaste, celibate, monkish, monastic, virginal.
► noun LAND MASS.

contingency ► noun EVENTUALITY, (chance) event, incident, happening, occurrence, juncture, possibility, fortuity, accident, chance, emergency.

contingent ► adjective **1** *the merger is contingent on government approval* DEPENDENT ON, conditional on, subject to, determined by, hinging on, resting on. **2** *contingent events* CHANCE, accidental, fortuitous, possible, unforeseeable, unpredictable, random, haphazard.
► noun **1** *a contingent of Japanese businessmen* GROUP, party, body, band, company, cohort, deputation, delegation; *informal* bunch, gang. **2** *a contingent of soldiers* DETACHMENT, unit, group.

continual ► adjective **1** *a service disrupted by continual breakdowns* FREQUENT, repeated, constant, recurrent, recurring, regular. **2** *she was in continual pain* CONSTANT, continuous, unending, never-ending, unremitting, unabating, relentless, unrelenting, unrelieved, chronic, uninterrupted, unbroken, round-the-clock.
— OPPOSITES: occasional, temporary.

continually ► adverb **1** *security measures are*

continually updated and improved FREQUENTLY, regularly, repeatedly, recurrently, again and again, time and (time) again; constantly. **2** *patients were continually monitored* CONSTANTLY, continuously, round-the-clock, day and night, night and day, {morning, noon, and night}, without a break, non-stop; all the time, the entire time, always, forever, at every turn, incessantly, ceaselessly, endlessly, perpetually, eternally, 24-7.
— OPPOSITES: occasionally, sporadically.

continuance ▸ noun **1** *concerned with the continuance of life.* See CONTINUATION. **2** *the prosecution sought a continuance* ADJOURNMENT, postponement, deferment, stay.

continuation ▸ noun CARRYING ON, continuance, extension, prolongation, protraction, perpetuation.
— OPPOSITES: end.

continue ▸ verb **1** *he was unable to continue with his job* CARRY ON, proceed, pursue, go on, keep on, persist, press on, persevere, keep at; *informal* stick at, soldier on. **2** *discussions continued throughout the night* GO ON, carry on, last, extend, be prolonged, run on, drag on. **3** *we are keen to continue this relationship* MAINTAIN, keep up, sustain, keep going, keep alive, preserve. **4** *his willingness to continue in office* REMAIN, stay, carry on, keep going. **5** *we continued our conversation after supper* RESUME, pick up, take up, carry on with, return to, recommence.
— OPPOSITES: stop, break off.

continuing ▸ adjective ONGOING, continuous, sustained, persistent, steady, relentless, uninterrupted, unabating, unremitting, unrelieved, unceasing.
— OPPOSITES: sporadic.

continuity ▸ noun CONTINUOUSNESS, uninterruptedness, flow, progression.

continuous ▸ adjective CONTINUAL, uninterrupted, unbroken, constant, ceaseless, incessant, steady, sustained, solid, continuing, ongoing, unceasing, without a break, non-stop, round-the-clock, persistent, unremitting, relentless, unrelenting, unabating, unrelieved, without respite, endless, unending, never-ending, perpetual, everlasting, eternal, interminable; consecutive, running, without surcease.
— OPPOSITES: intermittent.

contort ▸ verb TWIST, bend out of shape, distort, misshape, warp, buckle, deform.

contour ▸ noun OUTLINE, shape, form; lines, curves, figure; silhouette, profile.

contraband ▸ noun **1** *contraband was suspected* SMUGGLING, illegal traffic, black marketeering, bootlegging; the black market. **2** *they confiscated the contraband* STOLEN GOODS, swag, bootleg.
▸ adjective *contraband goods* SMUGGLED, black-market, bootleg, under the counter, illegal, illicit, unlawful; prohibited, banned, proscribed, forbidden; *informal* hot.

contraceptive ▸ noun BIRTH CONTROL; prophylactic, condom, birth control pill, the pill, diaphragm, female condom, IUD, cervical cap, morning-after pill.

contract ▸ noun *a legally binding contract* AGREEMENT, commitment, arrangement, settlement, understanding, compact, covenant, bond; deal, bargain; *Law* indenture.
▸ verb **1** *the market for such goods began to contract* SHRINK, get smaller, decrease, diminish, reduce, dwindle, decline. **2** *her stomach muscles contracted* TIGHTEN, tense, flex, constrict, draw in, narrow. **3** *she contracted her brow* WRINKLE, knit, crease, purse, pucker. **4** *his name was soon contracted to 'Jack'* SHORTEN, abbreviate, cut, reduce; elide. **5** *the company contracted to rebuild the stadium* UNDERTAKE, pledge, promise, covenant, commit oneself, engage, agree, enter an agreement, make a deal. **6** *she contracted rubella* DEVELOP, catch, get, pick up, come down with, be struck down by, be stricken with, succumb to. **7** *he contracted a debt of $3,300* INCUR, run up.
— OPPOSITES: expand, relax, lengthen.
■ **contract something out** SUBCONTRACT, outsource, farm out.

contraction ▸ noun **1** *the contraction of the industry* SHRINKING, shrinkage, decline, decrease, diminution, dwindling. **2** *the contraction of muscles* TIGHTENING, tensing, flexing. **3** *my contractions started at midnight* LABOUR PAINS, labour; cramps. **4** *'goodbye' is a contraction of 'God be with you'* ABBREVIATION, short form, shortened form, elision, diminutive.

contradict ▸ verb **1** *he contradicted the government's account of the affair* DENY, refute, rebut, dispute, challenge, counter, controvert; *formal* gainsay. **2** *nobody dared to contradict him* ARGUE AGAINST, go against, challenge, oppose; *formal* gainsay. **3** *this research contradicts previous assertions* CONFLICT WITH, be at odds with, be at variance with, be inconsistent with, run counter to, disagree with.
— OPPOSITES: confirm, agree with.

contradiction ▸ noun **1** *the contradiction between his faith and his lifestyle* CONFLICT, clash, disagreement, opposition, inconsistency, mismatch, variance. **2** *a contradiction of his statement* DENIAL, refutation, rebuttal, countering.
— OPPOSITES: confirmation, agreement.

contradictory ▸ adjective OPPOSED, in opposition, opposite, antithetical, contrary, contrasting, conflicting, at variance, at odds, opposing, clashing, divergent, discrepant, different; inconsistent, incompatible, irreconcilable.

contraption ▸ noun DEVICE, gadget, apparatus, machine, appliance, mechanism, invention, contrivance; *informal* gizmo, widget, doohickey, dingus.

contrary ▸ adjective **1** *contrary views* OPPOSITE, opposing, opposed, contradictory, clashing, conflicting, antithetical, incompatible, irreconcilable. **2** *she was sulky and contrary* PERVERSE, awkward, difficult, uncooperative, unhelpful, obstructive, disobliging, recalcitrant, wilful, self-willed, stubborn, obstinate, defiant, mulish, pigheaded, intractable; *informal* cussed, balky, bloody-minded; *formal* refractory; *archaic* froward.
— OPPOSITES: compatible, accommodating.
▸ noun *in fact, the contrary is true* OPPOSITE, reverse, converse, antithesis.
■ **contrary to** IN CONFLICT WITH, against, at variance with, at odds with, in opposition to, counter to, incompatible with.

contrast ▸ noun **1** *the contrast between rural and urban trends* DIFFERENCE, dissimilarity, disparity, distinction, contradistinction, divergence, variance, variation, differentiation; contradiction, incongruity, opposition, polarity. **2** *Jane was a complete contrast to Sarah* OPPOSITE, antithesis; foil, complement.
— OPPOSITES: similarity.
▸ verb **1** *a view which contrasts with his earlier opinion*

DIFFER FROM, be at variance with, be contrary to, conflict with, go against, be at odds with, be in opposition to, disagree with, clash with. **2** *people contrasted her with her sister* COMPARE, set side by side, juxtapose; measure against; distinguish from, differentiate from.
– OPPOSITES: resemble, liken.

contravene ▶ verb **1** *he contravened several laws* BREAK, breach, violate, infringe; defy, disobey, flout. **2** *the prosecution contravened the rights of the individual* CONFLICT WITH, be in conflict with, be at odds with, be at variance with, run counter to.
– OPPOSITES: comply with.

contravention ▶ noun BREACH, violation, infringement, neglect, dereliction.

contretemps ▶ noun ARGUMENT, quarrel, squabble, disagreement, difference of opinion, dispute; *informal* tiff, set-to, run-in, spat, row.

contribute ▶ verb **1** *the government contributed a million dollars* GIVE, donate, put up, subscribe, hand out, grant, bestow, present, provide, supply, furnish; *informal* chip in, pitch in, fork out, shell out, cough up, kick in, ante up, pony up. **2** *an article contributed by Dr. Clouson* SUPPLY, provide, submit. **3** *numerous factors contribute to job satisfaction* PLAY A PART IN, be instrumental in, be a factor in, have a hand in, be conducive to, make for, lead to, cause.

contribution ▶ noun **1** *voluntary financial contributions* DONATION, gift, offering, present, handout, grant, subsidy, allowance, endowment, subscription; *formal* benefaction. **2** *contributions from local authors* ARTICLE, piece, story, item, chapter, paper, essay.

contributor ▶ noun **1** *the magazine's regular contributors* WRITER, columnist, correspondent. **2** *campaign contributors* DONOR, benefactor, subscriber, supporter, backer, patron, sponsor.

contrite ▶ adjective REMORSEFUL, repentant, penitent, regretful, sorry, apologetic, rueful, sheepish, hangdog, ashamed, chastened, shamefaced, conscience-stricken, guilt-ridden.

contrition ▶ noun REMORSE, remorsefulness, repentance, penitence, sorrow, sorrowfulness, regret, ruefulness, pangs of conscience; shame, guilt, compunction; *archaic* rue.

contrivance ▶ noun **1** *a mechanical contrivance* DEVICE, gadget, machine, appliance, contraption, apparatus, mechanism, implement, tool, invention; *informal* gizmo, widget, doohickey, dingus. **2** *her matchmaking contrivances* SCHEME, stratagem, tactic, manoeuvre, move, plan, ploy, gambit, wile, trick, ruse, plot, machination.

contrive ▶ verb BRING ABOUT, engineer, manufacture, orchestrate, stage-manage, create, devise, concoct, construct, plan, fabricate, plot, hatch; *informal* wangle, set up.

contrived ▶ adjective FORCED, strained, studied, artificial, affected, put-on, phony, pretended, false, feigned, fake, manufactured, unnatural; laboured, overdone, elaborate.
– OPPOSITES: natural.

control ▶ noun **1** *China retained control over the region* JURISDICTION, sway, power, authority, command, dominance, government, mastery, leadership, rule, sovereignty, supremacy, ascendancy; charge, management, direction, supervision, superintendence. **2** *strict import controls* RESTRAINT, constraint, limitation, restriction, check, curb,

brake, rein; regulation. **3** *her control deserted her* SELF-CONTROL, self-restraint, self-possession, composure, calmness; *informal* cool. **4** *easy-to-use controls* SWITCH, knob, button, dial, handle, lever. **5** *mission control* HEADQUARTERS, HQ, base, centre of operations, command post, nerve centre.
▶ verb **1** *one family had controlled the company since its formation* BE IN CHARGE OF, run, manage, direct, administer, head, preside over, supervise, superintend, steer; command, rule, govern, lead, dominate, hold sway over, be at the helm; *informal* head up, be in the driver's seat, run the show. **2** *she struggled to control her temper* RESTRAIN, keep in check, curb, check, contain, hold back, bridle, rein in, suppress, repress, master. **3** *public spending was controlled* LIMIT, restrict, curb, cap, constrain; *informal* put the brakes on.

controversial ▶ adjective CONTENTIOUS, disputed, at issue, disputable, debatable, arguable, vexed, tendentious; *informal* hot, hot-button.

controversy ▶ noun DISAGREEMENT, dispute, argument, debate, dissension, contention, disputation, altercation, wrangle, wrangling, quarrel, quarrelling, war of words, storm; cause célèbre, hot potato, minefield.

contusion ▶ noun BRUISE, discoloration, injury.

conundrum ▶ noun **1** *the conundrums facing policy-makers* PROBLEM, difficult question, difficulty, quandary, dilemma; *informal* poser. **2** *Roderick enjoyed conundrums and crosswords* RIDDLE, puzzle, word game; *informal* brainteaser.

convalesce ▶ verb RECUPERATE, get better, recover, get well, get back on one's feet.

convalescence ▶ noun RECUPERATION, recovery, return to health, rehabilitation, improvement.

convalescent ▶ adjective RECUPERATING, recovering, getting better, on the road to recovery, improving; *informal* on the mend.

convene ▶ verb **1** *he convened a secret meeting* SUMMON, call, call together, order; *formal* convoke. **2** *the committee convened for its final session* ASSEMBLE, gather, meet, come together, congregate.

convenience ▶ noun **1** *the convenience of the arrangement* EXPEDIENCE, advantage, propitiousness, timeliness; suitability, appropriateness. **2** *for convenience, the handset is wall-mounted* EASE OF USE, usability, usefulness, utility, serviceability, practicality. **3** *the kitchen has all the modern conveniences* APPLIANCE, (labour-saving) device, gadget, amenity; *informal* gizmo.

convenience store ▶ noun VARIETY STORE, corner store, (*Que.*) dep ✤ (depanneur ✤), milk store ✤, (*Ont.*) jug milk ✤, mini-mart, smoke shop, (*Cape Breton*) dairy ✤, confectionery.

convenient ▶ adjective **1** *a convenient time* SUITABLE, appropriate, fitting, fit, suited, opportune, timely, well-timed, favourable, advantageous, seasonable, expedient. **2** *a hotel that's convenient for public transit* NEAR (TO), close to, within easy reach of, well situated for, handy for, not far from, just round the corner from; *informal* a stone's throw from, within spitting distance of.

convent ▶ noun NUNNERY, priory, abbey, religious community.

convention ▶ noun **1** *social conventions* CUSTOM, usage, practice, tradition, way, habit, norm; rule, code, canon, punctilio; propriety, etiquette, protocol; *formal* praxis; (**conventions**) mores. **2** *a convention* *signed by 74 countries* AGREEMENT, accord, protocol, compact, pact, treaty, concordat, entente; contract, bargain, deal. **3** *the party's biennial convention* CONFERENCE, meeting, congress, assembly, gathering, summit, convocation, synod, conclave.

conventional ▶ adjective **1** *the conventional wisdom of the day* ORTHODOX, traditional, established, accepted, received, mainstream, prevailing, prevalent, accustomed, customary. **2** *a conventional railway* NORMAL, standard, regular, ordinary, usual, traditional, typical, common. **3** *a very conventional woman* CONSERVATIVE, traditional, traditionalist, conformist, bourgeois, old-fashioned, of the old school, small-town, suburban; *informal* straight, buttoned-down, square, stick-in-the-mud, fuddy-duddy. **4** *a conventional piece of work* UNORIGINAL, formulaic, predictable, stock, unadventurous, unremarkable; *informal* humdrum, run-of-the-mill.
— OPPOSITES: unorthodox, original.

converge ▶ verb **1** *the railway lines converge at Union Station* MEET, intersect, cross, connect, link up, coincide, join, unite, merge. **2** *5,000 protesters converged on Parliament Hill* CLOSE IN ON, bear down on, approach, move towards.
— OPPOSITES: diverge, leave.

conversant ▶ adjective FAMILIAR, acquainted, au fait, au courant, at home, well versed, well-informed, knowledgeable, informed, abreast, up-to-date, up to speed, in the loop; *formal* cognizant.

conversation ▶ noun DISCUSSION, talk, chat, gossip, tête-à-tête, heart-to-heart, exchange, dialogue; *informal* confab, jaw, chit-chat, chinwag, natter, gabfest; *formal* confabulation, colloquy.

conversational ▶ adjective **1** *conversational English* INFORMAL, chatty, relaxed, friendly; colloquial, idiomatic. **2** *a conversational man* TALKATIVE, chatty, communicative, forthcoming, expansive, loquacious, garrulous.

converse[1] ▶ verb *they conversed in low voices* TALK, speak, chat, have a conversation, discourse, communicate; *informal* chew the fat, jaw, natter, visit, shoot the breeze/bull; *formal* confabulate.

converse[2] ▶ noun *the converse is also true* OPPOSITE, reverse, obverse, contrary, antithesis, other side of the coin, flip side.

conversion ▶ noun **1** *the conversion of waste into energy* CHANGE, changing, transformation, metamorphosis, transfiguration, transmutation, sea change; *humorous* transmogrification. **2** *the conversion of the building* ADAPTATION, alteration, modification, reconstruction, rebuilding, redevelopment, redesign, renovation, rehabilitation. **3** *his religious conversion* REBIRTH, regeneration, reformation.

convert ▶ verb **1** *plants convert the sun's energy into chemical energy* CHANGE, turn, transform, metamorphose, transfigure, transmute; *humorous* transmogrify; *technical* permute. **2** *the factory was converted into lofts* ADAPT, turn, change, alter, modify, rebuild, reconstruct, redevelop, refashion, redesign, restyle, revamp, renovate, rehabilitate; *informal* do up, rehab. **3** *they sought to convert sinners* PROSELYTIZE, evangelize, bring to God, redeem, save, reform, re-educate, cause to see the light.
▶ noun *Christian converts* PROSELYTE, neophyte, new believer; *Christianity* catechumen.

convey ▶ verb **1** *taxis conveyed guests to the station* TRANSPORT, carry, bring, take, fetch, bear, move, ferry, shuttle, shift, transfer. **2** *he conveyed the information to me* COMMUNICATE, pass on, make known, impart, relay, transmit, send, hand on, relate, tell, reveal, disclose. **3** *it's impossible to convey how I felt* EXPRESS, communicate, get across/over, put across/over, indicate, say. **4** *he conveys an air of competence* PROJECT, exude, emit, emanate.

conveyance ▶ noun **1** *the conveyance of agricultural produce* TRANSPORTATION, transport, carriage, carrying, transfer, movement, delivery; haulage, portage, cartage, shipment. **2** *(formal) three-wheeled conveyances* VEHICLE, means/method of transport.

convict ▶ verb *he was convicted of sexual assault* FIND GUILTY, sentence.
— OPPOSITES: acquit.
▶ noun *two escaped convicts* PRISONER, inmate; criminal, offender, lawbreaker, felon; *informal* jailbird, con, crook, lifer, yardbird.

conviction ▶ noun **1** *his conviction for murder* DECLARATION OF GUILT, sentence, judgment. **2** *his political convictions* BELIEF, opinion, view, thought, persuasion, idea, position, stance, article of faith. **3** *she spoke with conviction* CERTAINTY, certitude, assurance, confidence, sureness, no shadow of a doubt.
— OPPOSITES: acquittal, uncertainty.

convince ▶ verb **1** *he convinced me that I was wrong* MAKE CERTAIN, persuade, satisfy, prove to; assure, put/set someone's mind at rest. **2** *I convinced her to marry me* PERSUADE, induce, prevail on, get, talk into, win over, cajole, inveigle.

convincing ▶ adjective **1** *a convincing argument* COGENT, persuasive, plausible, powerful, potent, strong, forceful, compelling, irresistible, telling, conclusive. **2** *a convincing 5-0 win* RESOUNDING, emphatic, decisive, conclusive.

convivial ▶ adjective FRIENDLY, genial, affable, amiable, congenial, agreeable, good-humoured, cordial, warm, sociable, outgoing, gregarious, companionable, clubby, hail-fellow-well-met, cheerful, jolly, jovial, lively; enjoyable, festive.

conviviality ▶ noun FRIENDLINESS, geniality, affability, amiability, bonhomie, congeniality, cordiality, warmth, good nature, sociability, gregariousness, cheerfulness, good cheer, joviality, jollity, gaiety, liveliness.

convocation ▶ noun **1** *the students gathered for their convocation* GRADUATION (CEREMONY), commencement; *informal* grad ♣. **2** *a convocation of church leaders* ASSEMBLY, gathering, meeting, conference, convention, congress, council, symposium, colloquium, conclave, synod.

convoke ▶ verb *(formal)* CONVENE, summon, call together, call.

convoluted ▶ adjective COMPLICATED, complex, involved, elaborate, serpentine, labyrinthine, tortuous, tangled, Byzantine; confused, confusing, bewildering, baffling.
— OPPOSITES: straightforward.

convolution ▶ noun **1** *crosses adorned with elaborate convolutions* TWIST, turn, coil, spiral, twirl, curl, helix, whorl, loop, curlicue; *Architecture* volute. **2** *the convolutions of the plot* COMPLEXITY, intricacy, complication, twist, turn, entanglement.

convoy ▶ noun *a convoy of vehicles* GROUP, fleet, cavalcade, motorcade, cortège, caravan, line, train.
▶ verb *the ship was convoyed by army gunboats* ESCORT, accompany, attend, flank; protect, defend, guard.

convulse ▶ verb SHAKE UNCONTROLLABLY, go into spasms, shudder, jerk, thrash about.

convulsion ▶ noun **1** *she had convulsions* FIT, seizure, paroxysm, spasm, attack; *Medicine* ictus. **2 (convulsions)** *the audience collapsed in convulsions* FITS OF LAUGHTER, paroxysms of laughter, uncontrollable laughter; *informal* hysterics. **3** *the political convulsions of the period* UPHEAVAL, eruption, cataclysm, turmoil, turbulence, tumult, disruption, agitation, disturbance, unrest, disorder.

convulsive ▶ adjective SPASMODIC, jerky, paroxysmal, violent, uncontrollable; *informal* herky-jerky.

cook ▶ verb **1** *Scott cooked dinner* PREPARE, make, put together; *informal* fix, rustle up. **2** (*informal*) *he's been cooking the books* FALSIFY, alter, doctor, tamper with, interfere with, massage, manipulate, fiddle. **3** (*informal*) *what's cooking? See* HAPPEN sense 1.
▶ noun CHEF, food preparer, short-order cook, pastry chef; chef de cuisine, sous-chef, cordon bleu cook; cookie.
■ **cook something up** (*informal*) CONCOCT, devise, contrive, fabricate, trump up, hatch, plot, plan, invent, make up, think up, dream up.

cookie ▶ noun. *See table.*

Cookies

amaretti	gingersnap
animal cracker	hermit
arrowroot	langue de chat
biscotti	macaroon
chocolate chip	oatmeal
cream cracker	praline
crescent	ratafia
crisp	refrigerator cookie
dainty	shortbread
digestive	snap
drop cookie	soda cracker
Fig Newton*	sugar cookie
Florentine	thimble cookie
fortune cookie	vanilla wafer
gingerbread	*Proprietary term.

cooking ▶ noun CUISINE, cookery, baking; food. *See table.*
— RELATED TERMS: culinary.

Cooking Methods

baking	microwaving
barbecuing	oven-roasting
blanching	pan-frying
boiling	parboiling
braising	pre-cooking
broiling	pressure-cooking
browning	roasting
caramelizing	sautéing
casseroling	scalding
charbroiling	searing
coddling	simmering
currying	slow-cooking
deep-frying	smoking
fricasseeing	spit-roasting
frying	steaming
griddling	stewing
grilling	stir-frying
marinating	toasting

cool ▶ adjective **1** *a cool breeze* CHILLY, chill, cold, bracing, brisk, crisp, fresh, refreshing, invigorating, nippy. **2** *a cool response* UNENTHUSIASTIC, lukewarm, tepid, indifferent, uninterested, apathetic, half-hearted; unfriendly, distant, remote, aloof, cold, chilly, frosty, unwelcoming, unresponsive, uncommunicative, undemonstrative, standoffish. **3** *his ability to keep cool in a crisis* CALM, {calm, cool, and collected}, composed, as cool as a cucumber, collected, cool-headed, level-headed, self-possessed, controlled, self-controlled, poised, serene, tranquil, unruffled, unperturbed, unmoved, untroubled, imperturbable, placid, phlegmatic; *informal* unflappable, together, laid-back. **4** *a cool lack of morality* BOLD, audacious, nerveless; brazen, shameless, unabashed. **5** (*informal*) *she thinks she's so cool* FASHIONABLE, stylish, chic, up-to-the-minute, sophisticated; *informal* trendy, funky, with it, hip, big, happening, groovy, phat, kicky, tony, fly. **6** (*informal*) *a cool song. See* EXCELLENT.
— OPPOSITES: warm, enthusiastic, agitated.
▶ noun **1** *the cool of the evening* CHILL, chilliness, coldness, coolness. **2** *Ken lost his cool* SELF-CONTROL, control, composure, self-possession, calmness, equilibrium, calm; aplomb, poise, sang-froid, presence of mind.
— OPPOSITES: warmth.
▶ verb **1** *cool the sauce in the fridge* CHILL, refrigerate. **2** *her reluctance did nothing to cool his interest* LESSEN, moderate, diminish, reduce, dampen. **3** *Simon's ardour had cooled* SUBSIDE, lessen, diminish, decrease, abate, moderate, die down, fade, dwindle, wane. **4** *after a while, she cooled off* CALM DOWN, recover/regain one's composure, compose oneself, control oneself, pull oneself together, simmer down.
— OPPOSITES: heat, inflame, intensify.
▶ exclamation EXCELLENT, awesome, great, neat, neat-o, groovy, far-out, funky, fab, right on, wicked, brilliant; *dated* keen, swell.

coop ▶ noun *a hen coop* PEN, run, cage, hutch, enclosure.
▶ verb *he hates being cooped up at home* CONFINE, shut in/up, cage (in), pen up/in, keep, detain, trap, incarcerate, immure.

co-operate ▶ verb **1** *police and social services co-operated in the operation* COLLABORATE, work together, work side by side, pull together, band together, join forces, team up, unite, combine, pool resources, make common cause, liaise. **2** *he was happy to co-operate* BE OF ASSISTANCE, assist, help, lend a hand, be of service, do one's bit; *informal* play ball.

co-operation ▶ noun **1** *co-operation between management and workers* COLLABORATION, joint action, combined effort, teamwork, partnership, coordination, liaison, association, synergy, give and take, compromise. **2** *thank you for your co-operation* ASSISTANCE, helpfulness, help, helping hand, aid.

co-operative ▶ adjective **1** *a co-operative effort* COLLABORATIVE, collective, combined, common, joint, shared, mutual, united, concerted, coordinated. **2** *pleasant and co-operative staff* HELPFUL, eager to help, glad to be of assistance, obliging, accommodating, willing, amenable, adaptable.
▶ noun *a housing co-operative | a farm co-operative* COMPLEX, co-op, commune, collective; joint venture, co-operative enterprise; credit union, caisse populaire ♣; pool, wheat pool ♣.

coordinate ▶ verb **1** *exhibitions coordinated by a team of international scholars* ORGANIZE, arrange, order, systematize, harmonize, correlate, synchronize, bring together, fit together, dovetail. **2** *care workers coordinate at a local level* CO-OPERATE, liaise, collaborate, work together, negotiate, communicate, be in contact. **3** *floral designs coordinate with the decor* MATCH, complement, set off; harmonize, blend, fit in, go.

cop (*informal*) ▶ **noun** *a traffic cop.* See POLICE OFFICER.
▶ **verb** *he tried to cop out of his responsibilities.* See AVOID sense 2.

cope ▶ **verb** **1** *she couldn't cope on her own* MANAGE, survive, subsist, look after oneself, fend for oneself, shift for oneself, carry on, get by/through, bear up, hold one's own, keep one's end up, keep one's head above water; *informal* make it, hack it. **2** *his inability to cope with the situation* DEAL WITH, handle, manage, address, face (up to), confront, tackle, come to grips with, get through, weather, come to terms with.

copious ▶ **adjective** ABUNDANT, superabundant, plentiful, ample, profuse, full, extensive, generous, bumper, lavish, fulsome, liberal, overflowing, in abundance, many, numerous; *informal* galore; *literary* plenteous.
– OPPOSITES: sparse.

copse ▶ **noun** THICKET, grove, wood, (*Prairies*) bluff ♣, (*Atlantic*) droke ♣, coppice, stand, bush, woodlot, clump, brake, brush; *archaic* hurst, holt, boscage.

copulate ▶ **verb**. See HAVE SEX at SEX.

copulation ▶ **noun**. See SEX sense 1.

copy ▶ **noun** **1** *a copy of the report* DUPLICATE, facsimile, photocopy, carbon (copy), mimeograph, mimeo; transcript; reprint; *proprietary* Xerox. **2** *a copy of a sketch by Leonardo da Vinci* REPLICA, reproduction, replication, print, imitation, likeness; counterfeit, forgery, fake; *informal* knock-off.
▶ **verb** **1** *each form had to be copied* DUPLICATE, photocopy, xerox, mimeograph, run off, reproduce. **2** *portraits copied from original paintings by Reynolds* REPRODUCE, replicate; forge, fake, counterfeit. **3** *their sound was copied by a lot of jazz players* IMITATE, reproduce, emulate, follow, echo, mirror, parrot, mimic, ape; plagiarize, steal; *informal* rip off.

coquettish ▶ **adjective** FLIRTATIOUS, flirty, provocative, seductive, inviting, kittenish, coy, arch, teasing, playful; *informal* come-hither, vampish.

cord ▶ **noun** STRING, thread, thong, lace, ribbon, strap, tape, tie, line, rope, cable, wire, ligature; twine, yarn, elastic, braid, braiding; babiche ♣, (*West*) shaganappi ♣.

cordial ▶ **adjective** *a cordial welcome* FRIENDLY, warm, genial, affable, amiable, pleasant, fond, affectionate, warm-hearted, good-natured, gracious, hospitable, welcoming, hearty.
▶ **noun** *fruit cordial* DRINK, juice, concentrate.

cordon ▶ **noun** *a cordon of 500 police* BARRIER, line, row, chain, ring, circle; picket line.
▶ **verb** *troops cordoned off the area* CLOSE OFF, shut off, seal off, fence off, separate off, isolate, enclose, surround.

core ▶ **noun** **1** *the earth's core* CENTRE, interior, middle, nucleus; recesses, bowels, depths; *informal* innards; *literary* midst. **2** *the core of the argument* HEART, heart of the matter, nucleus, nub, kernel, marrow, meat, essence, quintessence, crux, gist, pith, substance, basis, fundamentals; *informal* nitty-gritty, brass tacks, nuts and bolts.
▶ **adjective** *the core issue* CENTRAL, key, basic, fundamental, principal, primary, main, chief,

crucial, vital, essential; *informal* number-one.
– OPPOSITES: peripheral.

cork ▶ **noun** STOPPER, stop, plug, peg, spigot, spile.

corner ▶ **noun** **1** *the cart lurched around the corner* BEND, curve, crook, dog-leg; turn, turning, jog, junction, fork, intersection; hairpin turn. **2** *a charming corner of Italy* DISTRICT, region, area, section, quarter, part; *informal* neck of the woods. **3** *he found himself in a tight corner* PREDICAMENT, plight, tight spot, mess, can of worms, muddle, difficulty, problem, dilemma, quandary; *informal* pickle, jam, stew, fix, hole, hot water, bind.
▶ **verb** **1** *he was eventually cornered by police dogs* DRIVE INTO A CORNER, bring to bay, cut off, block off, trap, hem in, pen in, surround, enclose; capture, catch. **2** *crime syndicates have cornered the stolen car market* GAIN CONTROL OF, take over, control, dominate, monopolize; capture; *informal* sew up.

cornerstone ▶ **noun** FOUNDATION, basis, keystone, mainspring, mainstay, linchpin, bedrock, base, backbone, key, centrepiece, core, heart, centre, crux.

corner store ▶ **noun** CONVENIENCE STORE, variety store, (*Que.*) dep ♣ (depanneur ♣), milk store ♣, (*Ont.*) jug milk ♣, mini-mart, smoke shop, (*Cape Breton*) dairy ♣, confectionery .

cornucopia ▶ **noun** ABUNDANCE, profusion, plentifulness, profuseness, copiousness, amplitude, lavishness, bountifulness, bounty; host, riot, plethora; plenty, quantities, scores, multitude; *informal* millions, sea, ocean(s), wealth, lot(s), heap(s), mass(es), stack(s), pile(s), load(s), bags, mountain(s), ton(s), slew; *formal* plenitude.

corny ▶ **adjective** (*informal*) BANAL, trite, hackneyed, commonplace, clichéd, predictable, hoary, stereotyped, platitudinous, tired, stale, overworked, overused, well-worn; mawkish, sentimental, cloying, syrupy, sugary, saccharine, twee; *informal* cheesy, schmaltzy, mushy, slushy, sloppy, cutesy, soppy, cornball, hokey.

corollary ▶ **noun** CONSEQUENCE, (end) result, upshot, effect, repercussion, product, by-product, offshoot.

coronet ▶ **noun**. See CROWN *noun* sense 1.

corporal ▶ **adjective** See CORPOREAL.

corporation ▶ **noun** *the chairman of the corporation* COMPANY, firm, business, concern, operation, house, organization, agency, trust, partnership; conglomerate, group, chain, multinational; *informal* outfit, set-up.

corporeal ▶ **adjective** BODILY, fleshly, carnal, corporal, somatic, human, mortal, earthly, physical, material, tangible, concrete, real, actual.

corps ▶ **noun** *an army corps* UNIT, division, detachment, section, company, contingent, squad, squadron, regiment, battalion, brigade, platoon. **2** *a corps of trained engineers* GROUP, body, band, cohort, party, gang, pack; team, crew.

corpse ▶ **noun** DEAD BODY, body, carcass, skeleton, (mortal) remains; *informal* stiff; *Medicine* cadaver.
– RELATED TERMS: necro-.

corpulent ▶ **adjective** FAT, obese, overweight, plump, portly, stout, chubby, paunchy, beer-bellied, heavy, bulky, chunky, well-upholstered, well padded, well covered, meaty, fleshy, rotund, broad in the beam; *informal* tubby, pudgy, beefy, porky, roly-poly, blubbery, corn-fed; *rare* abdominous.
– OPPOSITES: thin.

corral ▶ **noun** *she was galloping a pony around the corral*

ENCLOSURE, pen, fold, compound, pound, stockade, paddock.
▶ verb **1** *the sheep and goats were corralled at night* ENCLOSE, confine, lock up, shut up, shut in, fence in, pen in, wall in, cage, cage in, coop up, mew up. **2** *she corralled some new volunteers* GET, capture, collect, pick up, round up.

correct ▶ adjective **1** *the correct answer* RIGHT, accurate, true, exact, precise, unerring, faithful, strict, faultless, flawless, error-free, perfect, word-perfect; *informal* on the mark, on the nail, bang on, (right) on the money, on the button. **2** *correct behaviour* PROPER, seemly, decorous, decent, respectable, right, suitable, fit, fitting, befitting, appropriate, apt; approved, accepted, conventional, customary, traditional, orthodox, comme il faut.
– OPPOSITES: wrong, improper.
▶ verb **1** *proofread your work and correct any mistakes* RECTIFY, put right, set right, right, amend, emend, remedy, repair. **2** *an attempt to correct the trade imbalance* COUNTERACT, offset, counterbalance, compensate for, make up for, neutralize. **3** *the thermostat needs correcting* ADJUST, regulate, fix, set, standardize, normalize, calibrate, fine-tune.

corrective ▶ adjective REMEDIAL, therapeutic, restorative, curative, reparative, rehabilitative.

correctly ▶ adverb **1** *the questions were answered correctly* ACCURATELY, right, unerringly, precisely, faultlessly, flawlessly, perfectly, without error; *dated* aright. **2** *she behaved correctly at all times* PROPERLY, decorously, with decorum, decently, suitably, fittingly, appropriately, well.

correlate ▶ verb **1** *postal codes correlate with geographic location* CORRESPOND, match, parallel, agree, tally, tie in, be consistent, be compatible, be consonant, coordinate, dovetail, relate, conform; *informal* square, jibe. **2** *good health is correlated with physical fitness* CONNECT, establish a relationship/connection between, associate, relate.
– OPPOSITES: contrast.

correlation ▶ noun CONNECTION, association, link, tie-in, tie-up, relation, relationship, interrelationship, interdependence, interaction, interconnection; correspondence, parallel.

correspond ▶ verb **1** *their policies do not correspond with their statements* CORRELATE, agree, be in agreement, be consistent, be compatible, be consonant, accord, be in tune, concur, coincide, tally, tie in, dovetail, fit in; match, parallel; *informal* square, jibe, jive. **2** *a rank corresponding to the Canadian rank of corporal* BE EQUIVALENT, be analogous, be comparable, equate. **3** *Debbie and I corresponded for years* EXCHANGE LETTERS, write, communicate, keep in touch/contact.

correspondence ▶ noun **1** *there is some correspondence between the two variables* CORRELATION, agreement, consistency, compatibility, consonance, conformity, similarity, resemblance, parallel, comparability, accord, concurrence, coincidence. **2** *his private correspondence* LETTERS, messages, missives, mail, post; communication. *See table at* LETTER.

correspondent ▶ noun *the paper's foreign correspondent* REPORTER, journalist, columnist, writer, contributor, newspaperman, newspaperwoman, commentator; *informal* stringer, newshound.
▶ adjective *a correspondent improvement in quality. See* CORRESPONDING.

corresponding ▶ adjective COMMENSURATE,

parallel, correspondent, matching, correlated, homologous, relative, proportional, proportionate, comparable, equivalent, analogous.

corridor ▶ noun PASSAGE, passageway, aisle, gangway, hall, hallway, gallery, arcade.

corroborate ▶ verb CONFIRM, verify, endorse, ratify, authenticate, validate, certify; support, back up, uphold, bear out, bear witness to, attest to, testify to, vouch for, give credence to, substantiate, sustain.
– OPPOSITES: contradict.

corrode ▶ verb **1** *the iron had corroded* RUST, become rusty, tarnish; wear away, disintegrate, crumble, perish, spoil; oxidize. **2** *acid corrodes buildings* WEAR AWAY, eat away (at), gnaw away (at), erode, abrade, consume, destroy.

corrosive ▶ adjective CAUSTIC, corroding, erosive, abrasive, burning, stinging; destructive, damaging, harmful, harsh.

corrugated ▶ adjective RIDGED, fluted, grooved, furrowed, crinkled, crinkly, puckered, creased, wrinkled, wrinkly, crumpled; *technical* striated.

corrupt ▶ adjective **1** *a corrupt official | corrupt practices* DISHONEST, unscrupulous, dishonourable, unprincipled, unethical, amoral, untrustworthy, venal, underhanded, double-dealing, fraudulent, bribable, criminal, illegal, unlawful, nefarious; *informal* crooked, shady, dirty, sleazy. **2** *the earth was corrupt in God's sight* IMMORAL, depraved, degenerate, reprobate, vice-ridden, perverted, debauched, dissolute, dissipated, bad, wicked, evil, base, sinful, ungodly, unholy, irreligious, profane, impious, impure; *informal* warped. **3** *a corrupt text* IMPURE, bastardized, debased, adulterated.
– OPPOSITES: honest, ethical, pure.
▶ verb **1** *a book that might corrupt its readers* DEPRAVE, pervert, debauch, degrade, warp, lead astray, defile, pollute, sully. **2** *the apostolic writings had been corrupted* ALTER, tamper with, interfere with, bastardize, debase, adulterate.

corruption ▶ noun **1** *political corruption* DISHONESTY, unscrupulousness, double-dealing, fraud, fraudulence, misconduct, crime, criminality, wrongdoing; bribery, venality, extortion, profiteering, jobbery, payola; *informal* graft, grift, crookedness, sleaze. **2** *fall into corruption* IMMORALITY, depravity, vice, degeneracy, perversion, debauchery, dissoluteness, decadence, wickedness, evil, sin, sinfulness, ungodliness; *formal* turpitude. **3** *these figures have been subject to corruption* ALTERATION, bastardization, debasement, adulteration.
– OPPOSITES: honesty, morality, purity.

corsair ▶ noun (*archaic*). *See* PIRATE *noun* sense 1.

corset ▶ noun GIRDLE, panty girdle, foundation (garment), corselette; *historical* stays.

cortège ▶ noun **1** *the funeral cortège* PROCESSION, parade, cavalcade, motorcade, convoy, caravan, train, column, file, line. **2** *the prince's cortège* ENTOURAGE, retinue, train, suite; attendants, companions, followers, retainers.

cosmetic ▶ adjective *most of the changes were merely cosmetic* SUPERFICIAL, surface, skin-deep, outward, exterior, external.
– OPPOSITES: fundamental.
▶ noun (**cosmetics**) *a new range of cosmetics* MAKEUP, beauty products, maquillage, face paint; *informal* war paint, paint.

cosmic ▶ adjective **1** *cosmic bodies* EXTRATERRESTRIAL, in space, from space. **2** *an epic of cosmic dimensions*

VAST, huge, immense, enormous, massive, colossal, prodigious, immeasurable, incalculable, unfathomable, fathomless, measureless, infinite, limitless, boundless.

cosmonaut ▶ noun ASTRONAUT, spaceman/woman, space traveller, space cadet.

cosmopolitan ▶ adjective **1** *the student body has a cosmopolitan character* MULTICULTURAL, multiracial, international, worldwide, global. **2** *a cosmopolitan audience* WORLDLY, worldly-wise, well travelled, experienced, unprovincial, cultivated, cultured, sophisticated, suave, urbane, glamorous, fashionable; *informal* jet-setting, cool, hip, stylish.

cosset ▶ verb PAMPER, indulge, overindulge, mollycoddle, coddle, baby, pet, mother, nanny, nursemaid, pander to, spoil; wait on someone hand and foot.

cost ▶ noun **1** *the cost of the equipment* PRICE, asking price, market price, selling price, unit price, fee, tariff, fare, toll, levy, charge, rental; value, valuation, quotation, rate, worth; *informal, humorous* damage. **2** *the human cost of the conflict* SACRIFICE, loss, expense, penalty, toll, price. **3** (**costs**) *we need to make $10,000 to cover our costs* EXPENSES, disbursements, overheads, running costs, operating costs, fixed costs; expenditure, spending, outlay.
▶ verb **1** *the chair costs $186* BE PRICED AT, sell for, be valued at, fetch, come to, amount to; *informal* set someone back, go for. **2** *the proposal has not yet been costed* PUT A PRICE ON, price, value, put a value on, put a figure on.

costly ▶ adjective **1** *costly machinery* EXPENSIVE, dear, high-priced, highly priced, overpriced; *informal* steep, pricey, costing an arm and a leg, costing the earth. **2** *a costly mistake* CATASTROPHIC, disastrous, calamitous, ruinous; damaging, harmful, injurious, deleterious, woeful, awful, terrible, dreadful; *formal* grievous.
— OPPOSITES: cheap.

costume ▶ noun (SET OF) CLOTHES, garments, robes, outfit, ensemble; dress, clothing, attire, garb, uniform, livery; *informal* getup, gear, togs, threads; *formal* apparel; *archaic* habit, habiliments, raiment.

coterie ▶ noun CLIQUE, set, circle, inner circle, crowd, in-crowd, band, community, gang.

cottage ▶ noun *summers up at Anna and Renzo's cottage* CABIN, lodge, (*Que.*) chalet ♣; shack, shanty; (*Cape Breton*) bungalow ♣, bunkhouse ♣, bunkie ♣, (*Que.*) country house ♣.

couch ▶ noun *she seated herself on the couch* SOFA, chesterfield ♣, divan, chaise longue, settee, love seat, settle, ottoman, daybed, davenport, studio couch. *See the table at* SOFA
▶ verb *his reply was couched in deferential terms* EXPRESS, phrase, word, frame, put, formulate, style, convey, say, state, utter.

cough ▶ verb *he coughed loudly* HACK, hawk, bark, clear one's throat, hem.
▶ noun *a loud cough* HACK, bark.
— RELATED TERMS: tussive.
■ **cough up** PAY (UP), come up with, hand over, dish out, part with; fork out, shell out, lay out, ante up, pony up.

council ▶ noun **1** *the town council* LOCAL AUTHORITY, municipal authority, local government, administration, executive, chamber, assembly, corporation. **2** *the Student Council* ADVISORY BODY, board, committee, brain trust, commission,

assembly, panel; synod, convocation. **3** *that evening, she held a family council meeting*, gathering, conference, conclave, assembly.

counsel ▶ noun **1** *his wise counsel* ADVICE, guidance, counselling, direction, information; hints, recommendations, suggestions, guidelines, tips, pointers, warnings. **2** *the counsel for the defence* LAWYER, barrister and solicitor ♣, barrister, advocate, attorney, counsellor(-at-law); Crown attorney/counsel/prosecutor ♣.
▶ verb *he counselled the team to withdraw from the deal* ADVISE, recommend, direct, advocate, encourage, urge, warn, caution; guide, give guidance.

counsellor ▶ noun ADVISER, consultant, guide, mentor; expert, specialist.

count ▶ verb **1** *Vern counted the money again* ADD UP, add together, reckon up, total, tally, calculate, compute, tot up; census; *formal* enumerate; *dated* cast up. **2** *a company with 250 employees, not counting overseas staff* INCLUDE, take into account, take account of, take into consideration, allow for. **3** *I count it a privilege to be asked* CONSIDER, think, feel, regard, look on as, view as, hold to be, judge, deem, account. **4** *it's your mother's feelings that count* MATTER, be of consequence, be of account, be significant, signify, be important, carry weight; *informal* cut any ice.
▶ noun **1** *at the last count, the committee had 57 members* CALCULATION, computation, reckoning, tally; *formal* enumeration. **2** *her white blood cell count* AMOUNT, number, total.
■ **count on/upon 1** *you can count on me* RELY ON, depend on, bank on, trust (in), be sure of, have (every) confidence in, believe in, put one's faith in, take for granted, take as read. **2** *they hadn't counted on his indomitable spirit* EXPECT, reckon on, anticipate, envisage, allow for, be prepared for, bargain for/on, figure on.
■ **down/out for the count** (*informal*). *See* UNCONSCIOUS *adjective* sense 1.

countenance ▶ noun *his strikingly handsome countenance* FACE, features, physiognomy, profile; (facial) expression, look, appearance, aspect, mien; *informal* mug, phiz, puss; *literary* visage, lineaments.
▶ verb *he would not countenance the use of force* TOLERATE, permit, allow, agree to, consent to, give one's blessing to, go along with, hold with, put up with, endure, stomach, swallow, stand for; *formal* brook.

counter[1] ▶ noun *a pile of counters* TOKEN, chip, disc, piece, man, marker, check.

counter[2] ▶ verb **1** *workers countered accusations of dishonesty* RESPOND TO, parry, hit back at, answer, retort to. **2** *the second argument is more difficult to counter* OPPOSE, dispute, argue against/with, contradict, controvert, negate, counteract; challenge, contest; *formal* gainsay, confute.
— OPPOSITES: support.
▶ adjective *a counter bid* OPPOSING, opposed, opposite.
■ **counter to** AGAINST, in opposition to, contrary to, at variance with, in defiance of, in contravention of, in conflict with, at odds with.

counteract ▶ verb **1** *new measures to counteract drug trafficking* PREVENT, thwart, frustrate, foil, impede, curb, hinder, hamper, check, put a stop/end to, defeat. **2** *a drug to counteract the side effects* OFFSET, counterbalance, balance (out), cancel out, even out, counterpoise, countervail, compensate for, make up for, remedy; neutralize, nullify, negate, invalidate.
— OPPOSITES: encourage, exacerbate.

counterbalance ▶ verb COMPENSATE FOR, make up

counterfeit ▶ adjective *counterfeit $100 bills* FAKE, faked, bogus, forged, imitation, spurious, substitute, ersatz, phony.
– OPPOSITES: genuine.
▶ noun *the notes were counterfeits* FAKE, forgery, copy, reproduction, imitation; fraud, sham; *informal* phony, knock-off.
– OPPOSITES: original.
▶ verb **1** *his signature was hard to counterfeit* FAKE, forge, copy, reproduce, imitate. **2** *he grew tired of counterfeiting interest* FEIGN, simulate, pretend, fake, sham.

countermand ▶ verb REVOKE, rescind, reverse, undo, repeal, retract, withdraw, quash, overturn, overrule, cancel, annul, invalidate, nullify, negate; *Law* disaffirm, discharge, vacate; *formal* abrogate.
– OPPOSITES: uphold.

counterpane ▶ noun (*dated*). See BEDSPREAD.

counterpart ▶ noun EQUIVALENT, opposite number, peer, equal, coequal, parallel, complement, analogue, match, twin, mate, fellow, brother, sister; *formal* compeer.

countless ▶ adjective INNUMERABLE, numerous, untold, legion, without number, numberless, unnumbered, limitless, multitudinous, incalculable; *informal* umpteen, no end of, a slew of, loads of, stacks of, heaps of, masses of, oodles of, zillions of, gazillions of; *literary* myriad.
– OPPOSITES: few.

countrified ▶ adjective RURAL, rustic, pastoral, bucolic, country; idyllic, unspoiled; *literary* Arcadian, sylvan, georgic.
– OPPOSITES: urban.

country ▶ noun **1** *foreign countries* NATION, (sovereign) state, kingdom, realm, principality, palatinate, duchy. *See table.* **2** *he risked his life for his country* HOMELAND, native land, fatherland, motherland, the land of one's fathers. **3** *the whole country took to the streets* PEOPLE, public, population, populace, citizenry, nation, body politic; electors, voters, taxpayers, grass roots; *informal* Joe Public, John Q. Public, Joe Blow, Joe Schmoe. **4** *thickly forested country* TERRAIN, land, territory, parts; landscape, scenery, setting, surroundings, environment. **5** *she hated living in the country* COUNTRYSIDE, greenbelt, great outdoors; provinces, rural areas. (*Ont. & Que.*) the back concessions ♣, backwoods, back of beyond, hinterland, bush, backcountry; *informal* sticks, middle of nowhere, boondocks, boonies; *Austral.* outback.
▶ adjective *country pursuits* RURAL, countryside, outdoor, rustic, pastoral, bucolic; *literary* sylvan, Arcadian, georgic.
– OPPOSITES: urban.

countryman, countrywoman ▶ noun **1** *the traditions of his countrymen* COMPATRIOT, fellow citizen. **2** *the countryman takes a great interest in the weather* COUNTRY DWELLER, country cousin, son/daughter of the soil, farmer; rustic, yokel, (country) bumpkin, peasant, provincial, hayseed, hick, hillbilly, rube; *archaic* swain.

countryside ▶ noun **1** *beautiful unspoiled countryside* LANDSCAPE, scenery, surroundings, setting, environment; country, terrain, land. **2** *I was brought up in the countryside. See* COUNTRY *noun sense 5.*

county ▶ noun *families from neighbouring counties*

REGION, province, administrative unit, territory, district, area.

coup ▶ noun **1** *a violent military coup* SEIZURE OF POWER, coup d'état, putsch, overthrow, takeover, deposition; (palace) revolution, rebellion, revolt, insurrection, mutiny, insurgence, uprising. **2** *a major publishing coup* SUCCESS, triumph, feat, accomplishment, achievement, scoop, master stroke, stroke of genius.

coup de grâce ▶ noun DEATH BLOW, finishing blow, killer, kiss of death; *informal* KO, kayo.

coup d'état ▶ noun. See COUP *sense 1.*

couple ▶ noun **1** *a couple of girls* PAIR, duo, twosome, two; *archaic* twain, brace. **2** *a honeymoon couple* HUSBAND AND WIFE, twosome, partners, lovers; *informal* item. **3** *I have a couple of things to do* SOME, a few, a handful, one or two.
▶ verb **1** *a sense of hope is coupled with a sense of loss* COMBINE, accompany, mix, incorporate, link, associate, connect, ally; add to, join to; *formal* conjoin. **2** *a cable is coupled to one of the wheels* CONNECT, attach, join, fasten, fix, link, secure, tie, bind, strap, rope, tether, truss, lash, hitch, yoke, chain, hook (up).
– OPPOSITES: detach.

coupon ▶ noun **1** *grocery coupons* VOUCHER, token, ticket; *informal* comp, rain check. **2** *fill in the coupon below* FORM, tear-off card.

courage ▶ noun BRAVERY, courageousness, pluck, pluckiness, valour, fearlessness, intrepidity, nerve, daring, audacity, boldness, grit, true grit, hardihood, heroism, gallantry; *informal* guts, spunk, moxie, cojones, balls, sand.
– OPPOSITES: cowardice.

courageous ▶ adjective BRAVE, plucky, fearless, valiant, valorous, intrepid, heroic, lion-hearted, bold, daring, daredevil, audacious, undaunted, unflinching, unshrinking, unafraid, dauntless, indomitable, doughty, mettlesome, venturesome, stout-hearted, gallant; *informal* game, gutsy, spunky, ballsy.
– OPPOSITES: cowardly.

courier ▶ noun **1** *the documents were sent by courier* MESSENGER, runner. **2** *a courier for the trip.* See GUIDE *noun sense 1.*

course ▶ noun **1** *the island was not far off our course* ROUTE, way, track, direction, tack, path, line, trail, trajectory, bearing, heading, orbit. **2** *the course of history* PROGRESSION, development, progress, advance, evolution, flow, movement, sequence, order, succession, rise, march, passage, passing. **3** *what is the best course to adopt?* PROCEDURE, plan (of action), course/line of action, MO, modus operandi, practice, approach, technique, way, means, policy, strategy, program; *formal* praxis. **4** *a waterlogged course* RACECOURSE, raceway, racetrack, track, ground. **5** *I'm taking a French course* PROGRAM/COURSE OF STUDY, curriculum, syllabus; classes, lectures, studies. **6** *a course of antibiotics* PROGRAM, series, sequence, system, schedule, regimen.
▶ verb *tears coursed down her cheeks* FLOW, pour, stream, run, rush, gush, cascade, flood, roll.
■ **in due course** AT THE APPROPRIATE TIME, when the time is ripe, in time, in the fullness of time, in the course of time, at a later date, by and by, sooner or later, in the end, eventually.
■ **of course** NATURALLY, as might be expected, as you/one would expect, needless to say, certainly, to be sure, as a matter of course, obviously, it goes without saying; *informal* natch.

Independent Countries of the World

Country	Capital	Country	Capital	Country	Capital
Afghanistan	Kabul	Estonia	Tallinn	Mozambique	Maputo
Albania	Tirana	Ethiopia	Addis Ababa	Myanmar (see Burma)	
Algeria	Algiers	Fiji	Suva	Namibia	Windhoek
Andorra	Andorra la Vella	Finland	Helsinki	Nauru	-
Angola	Luanda	France	Paris	Nepal	Kathmandu
Antigua and	St. John's	Gabon	Libreville	Netherlands, the	Amsterdam/
Barbuda		Gambia	Banjul		The Hague
Argentina	Buenos Aires	Georgia	Tbilisi	New Zealand	Wellington
Armenia	Yerevan	Germany	Berlin/Bonn	Nicaragua	Managua
Australia	Canberra	Ghana	Accra	Niger	Niamey
Austria	Vienna	Greece	Athens	Nigeria	Abuja
Azerbaijan	Baku	Grenada	St. George's	North Korea	Pyongyang
Bahamas	Nassau	Guatemala	Guatemala City	Norway	Oslo
Bahrain	Manama	Guinea	Conakry	Oman	Muscat
Bangladesh	Dhaka	Guinea-Bissau	Bissau	Pakistan	Islamabad
Barbados	Bridgetown	Guyana	Georgetown	Palau	Koror
Belarus	Minsk	Haiti	Port-au-Prince	Panama	Panama City
Belgium	Brussels	Honduras	Tegucigalpa	Papua New	Port Moresby
Belize	Belmopan	Hungary	Budapest	Guinea	
Benin	Porto Novo	Iceland	Reykjavik	Paraguay	Asunción
Bhutan	Thimphu	India	New Delhi	Peru	Lima
Bolivia	La Paz/Sucre	Indonesia	Djakarta	Philippines	Quezon City/
Bosnia and	Sarajevo	Iran	Tehran		Manila
Herzegovina		Iraq	Baghdad	Poland	Warsaw
Botswana	Gaborone	Ireland	Dublin	Portugal	Lisbon
Brazil	Brasilia	Israel	Jerusalem	Qatar	Doha
Brunei	Bandar Seri	Italy	Rome	Romania	Bucharest
	Begawan	Ivory Coast	Yamoussoukro	Russia	Moscow
Bulgaria	Sofia	Jamaica	Kingston	Rwanda	Kigali
Burkina Faso	Ouagadougou	Japan	Tokyo	St. Kitts and Nevis	Basseterre
Burma (Myanmar)	Rangoon	Jordan	Amman	St. Lucia	Castries
Burundi	Bujumbura	Kazakhstan	Astana	St. Vincent and	Kingstown
Cambodia	Phnom Penh	Kenya	Nairobi	the Grenadines	
Cameroon	Yaoundé	Kiribati	Bairiki	Samoa	Apia
Canada	Ottawa	Kuwait	Kuwait City	San Marino	San Marino
Cape Verde	Praia	Kyrgyzstan	Bishkek	São Tomé and	São Tomé
Central African	Bangui	Laos	Vientiane	Principe	
Republic		Latvia	Riga	Saudi Arabia	Riyadh
Chad	N'Djamena	Lebanon	Beirut	Senegal	Dakar
Chile	Santiago	Lesotho	Maseru	Serbia and	(see Yugoslavia)
China	Beijing	Liberia	Monrovia	Montenegro	
Colombia	Bogotá	Libya	Tripoli	Seychelles, the	Victoria
Comoros	Moroni	Liechtenstein	Vaduz	Sierra Leone	Freetown
Congo, Dem.Rep.	Kinshasa/	Lithuania	Vilnius	Singapore	Singapore
	Lubumbashi	Luxembourg	Luxembourg	Slovakia	Bratislava
Congo, Rep.	Brazzaville	Macedonia	Skopje	Slovenia	Ljubljana
Costa Rica	San José	Madagascar	Antananarivo	Solomon Islands	Honiara
Croatia	Zagreb	Malawi	Lilongwe/	Somalia	Mogadishu
Cuba	Havana		Blantyre	South Africa	Pretoria/
Cyprus	Nicosia	Malaysia	Kuala Lumpur		Cape Town
Czech Republic	Prague	Maldives	Male	South Korea	Seoul
Denmark	Copenhagen	Mali	Bamako	Spain	Madrid
Djibouti	Djibouti	Malta	Valletta	Sri Lanka	Colombo
Dominica	Roseau	Marshall Islands	Majuro	Sudan	Khartoum
Dominican	Santo	Mauritania	Nouakchott	Suriname	Paramaribo
Republic	Domingo	Mauritius	Port Louis	Swaziland	Mbabane
East Timor	Dili	Mexico	Mexico City	Sweden	Stockholm
Ecuador	Quito	Micronesia	Palikir	Switzerland	Berne
Egypt	Cairo	Moldova	Chişinău	Syria	Damascus
El Salvador	San Salvador	Monaco	-	Taiwan	Taipei
Equatorial Guinea	Malabo	Mongolia	Ulan Bator	Tajikistan	Dushanbe
Eritrea	Asmara	Morocco	Rabat	Tanzania	Dodoma

Independent Countries of the World (continued)

Country	Capital	Country	Capital	Country	Capital
Thailand	Bangkok	Uganda	Kampala	Vatican City	-
Togo	Lomé	Ukraine	Kiev	Venezuela	Caracas
Tonga	Nuku'alofa	United Arab	Abu Dhabi	Vietnam	Hanoi
Trinidad and	Port of Spain	Emirates		Western Samoa (see Samoa)	
Tobago		United Kingdom	London	Yemen	San'a
Tunisia	Tunis	United States	Washington	Yugoslavia	Belgrade
Turkey	Ankara	Uruguay	Montevideo	Zaire (see Congo, Dem.Rep.)	
Turkmenistan	Ashgabat	Uzbekistan	Tashkent	Zambia	Lusaka
Tuvalu	Funafuti	Vanuatu	Vila	Zimbabwe	Harare

court ▶ noun **1** *the court found him guilty* COURT OF LAW, law court, bench, bar, judicature, tribunal, chancery. **2** *the King's court* ROYAL HOUSEHOLD, retinue, entourage, train, suite, courtiers, attendants. **3** *she made her way to the queen's court* ROYAL RESIDENCE, palace, castle, château.
▶ verb **1** *a newspaper editor who was courted by senior politicians* CURRY FAVOUR WITH, cultivate, try to win over, make up to, ingratiate oneself with; *informal* suck up to, butter up. **2** *he was busily courting public attention* SEEK, pursue, go after, strive for, solicit. **3** *he has often courted controversy* RISK, invite, attract, bring on oneself. **4** *(dated)* *he's courting her sister* WOO, go out with, pursue, run after, chase; *informal* date, see, go steady with; *dated* set one's cap at, romance, seek the hand of.

courteous ▶ adjective POLITE, well-mannered, civil, respectful, well-behaved, well-bred, well-spoken, mannerly; gentlemanly, chivalrous, gallant; gracious, obliging, considerate, pleasant, cordial, urbane, polished, refined, courtly, civilized.
− OPPOSITES: rude.

courtesan ▶ noun *(archaic).* See PROSTITUTE noun.

courtesy ▶ noun POLITENESS, courteousness, good manners, civility, respect, respectfulness; chivalry, gallantry; graciousness, consideration, thought, thoughtfulness, cordiality, urbanity, courtliness.

courtier ▶ noun ATTENDANT, lord, lady, lady-in-waiting, steward, page, squire.

courtly ▶ adjective REFINED, polished, suave, cultivated, civilized, elegant, urbane, debonair; polite, civil, courteous, gracious, well-mannered, well-bred, chivalrous, gallant, gentlemanly, ladylike, aristocratic, dignified, decorous, formal, stately, ceremonious.
− OPPOSITES: uncouth.

courtship ▶ noun **1** *a whirlwind courtship* ROMANCE, (love) affair; engagement. **2** *his courtship of Emma* WOOING, courting, suit, pursuit.

courtyard ▶ noun QUADRANGLE, cloister, square, plaza, piazza, close, enclosure, yard; *informal* quad.

cove ▶ noun *a small sandy cove* BAY, inlet, fjord, anchorage.

covenant ▶ noun *a breach of the covenant* CONTRACT, agreement, undertaking, commitment, guarantee, warrant, pledge, promise, bond, indenture; pact, deal, settlement, arrangement, understanding.
▶ verb *the landlord covenants to repair the property* UNDERTAKE, contract, guarantee, pledge, promise, agree, engage, warrant, commit oneself, bind oneself.

cover ▶ verb **1** *she covered her face with a towel* PROTECT, shield, shelter; hide, conceal, veil. **2** *his car was covered in mud* CAKE, coat, encrust, plaster, smother, daub, bedaub. **3** *snow covered the fields* BLANKET, overlay,

overspread, carpet, coat; *literary* mantle. **4** *a course covering all aspects of the business* DEAL WITH, consider, take in, include, involve, comprise, incorporate, embrace. **5** *the trial was covered by several newspapers* REPORT ON, write about, describe, commentate on, publish/broadcast details of. **6** *he turned on the radio to cover the noise of the air conditioner* MASK, disguise, hide, camouflage, muffle, block out, stifle, smother. **7** *I'm covering for Jill* STAND IN FOR, fill in for, deputize for, take over from, relieve, take the place of, sit in for, understudy, hold the fort; *informal* sub for, pinch-hit for. **8** *can you make enough to cover your costs?* PAY (FOR), be enough for, fund, finance; pay back, make up for, offset. **9** *your home is covered against damage and loss* INSURE, protect, secure, underwrite, assure, indemnify. **10** *we covered ten miles each day* TRAVEL, journey, go, do, traverse.
− OPPOSITES: expose.
▶ noun **1** *a protective cover | a manhole cover. See* COVERING. **2** *a book cover* BINDING, jacket, dust jacket, dust cover, wrapper. **3** **(covers)** *she pulled the covers over her head* BEDCLOTHES, bedding, sheets, blankets. **4** *a thick cover of snow* COATING, coat, covering, layer, carpet, blanket, overlay, dusting, film, sheet, veneer, crust, skin, cloak, mantle, veil, pall, shroud. **5** *panicking onlookers ran for cover* SHELTER, protection, refuge, sanctuary, haven, hiding place. **6** *there is considerable game cover around the lake* UNDERGROWTH, vegetation, greenery, woodland, trees, bushes, brush, scrub, plants; covert, thicket, copse. **7** *the company was a cover for an international swindle* FRONT, facade, smokescreen, screen, blind, camouflage, disguise, mask, cloak. **8** *the bar charged a cover on Fridays* COVER CHARGE, entry charge, entrance fee, admission charge, price of admission.
■ **cover something up** CONCEAL, hide, keep secret/dark, hush up, draw a veil over, suppress, sweep under the carpet, gloss over; *informal* whitewash, keep a/the lid on.

coverage ▶ noun **1** *up-to-the-minute coverage of the situation* REPORTAGE, reporting, description, treatment, handling, presentation, investigation, commentary; reports, articles, pieces, stories, ink. **2** *your policy provides coverage against damage by fire* INSURANCE, protection, security, assurance, indemnification, indemnity, compensation.

covering ▶ noun **1** *a plastic covering* AWNING, canopy, tarpaulin, cowling, cowl, casing, housing; wrapping, wrapper, cover, envelope, sheath, sleeve, jacket, lid, top, cap. **2** *a covering of snow* LAYER, coating, coat, carpet, blanket, overlay, topping, dusting, film, sheet, veneer, crust, skin, cloak, mantle, veil.
▶ adjective *a covering letter* ACCOMPANYING, explanatory, introductory, prefatory.

coverlet ▶ noun BEDSPREAD, bedcover, cover, throw,

duvet, quilt, eiderdown, comforter; *dated* counterpane.

covert ▶ adjective SECRET, furtive, clandestine, surreptitious, stealthy, cloak-and-dagger, hole-and-corner, backstairs, backroom, hidden, under-the-table, concealed, private, undercover, underground; *informal* hush-hush.
— OPPOSITES: overt.

cover-up ▶ noun **1** *the aides were implicated in the cover-up* WHITEWASH, concealment, false front, facade, camouflage, disguise, mask, veneer, pretext. **2** *she pulled a cover-up over her swimsuit* DRESSING GOWN, bathrobe, robe, housecoat, wrapper.

covet ▶ verb DESIRE, yearn for, crave, have one's heart set on, want, wish for, long for, hanker after/for, hunger after/for, thirst for.

covetous ▶ adjective GRASPING, greedy, acquisitive, desirous, possessive, envious, green with envy, green-eyed.

covey ▶ noun GROUP, gang, troop, troupe, party, company, band, bevy, flock; knot, cluster; *informal* bunch, gaggle, posse, crew.

cow ▶ verb INTIMIDATE, daunt, browbeat, bully, tyrannize, scare, terrorize, frighten, dishearten, unnerve, subdue; *informal* psych out, bulldoze.

coward ▶ noun WEAKLING, milksop, namby-pamby, mouse; *informal* chicken, scaredy-cat, yellow-belly, sissy, sook, baby, (*Atlantic*) sooky baby ♣, candy-ass, milquetoast.
— OPPOSITES: hero.

cowardly ▶ adjective FAINT-HEARTED, lily-livered, spineless, chicken-hearted, craven, timid, timorous, fearful, pusillanimous; *informal* yellow, chicken, weak-kneed, gutless, yellow-bellied, wimpish, wimpy.
— OPPOSITES: brave.

cowboy ▶ noun *cowboys on horseback* CATTLEMAN, cowhand, cowman, cowherd, herder, herdsman, drover, stockman, rancher, gaucho, vaquero; *informal* cowpuncher, cowpoke, broncobuster; *dated* buckaroo.
▶ adjective *a cowboy pilot* MAVERICK, original, nonconformist, unorthodox, rebel, rebellious.

cower ▶ verb CRINGE, shrink, crouch, recoil, flinch, pull back, draw back, tremble, shake, quake, blench, quail, grovel.

coy ▶ adjective ARCH, simpering, coquettish, flirtatious, kittenish; demure, shy, modest, bashful, reticent, diffident, self-effacing, shrinking, timid.
— OPPOSITES: brazen.

cozen ▶ verb (*literary*). See TRICK verb.

cozy ▶ adjective **1** *a cozy country cottage* SNUG, comfortable, warm, homelike, homey, homely, welcoming; safe, sheltered, secure, down-home, homestyle; *informal* comfy, toasty, snug as a bug (in a rug). **2** *a cozy chat* INTIMATE, relaxed, informal, friendly.

crab ▶ noun. See table.

crabbed ▶ adjective **1** *her crabbed handwriting* CRAMPED, ill-formed, bad, illegible, unreadable, indecipherable, hieroglyphic; shaky, spidery. **2** *a crabbed old man.* See CRABBY.

crabby ▶ adjective IRRITABLE, cantankerous, irascible, bad-tempered, grumpy, grouchy, crotchety, tetchy, testy, crusty, curmudgeonly, ill-tempered, ill-humoured, peevish, cross, fractious, pettish, crabbed, prickly, waspish; *informal* snappish, snappy, chippy, shirty, cranky, ornery.
— OPPOSITES: affable.

crack ▶ noun **1** *a crack in the glass* SPLIT, break, chip, fracture, rupture; crazing. **2** *a crack between two rocks*

Crustaceans

barnacle	land crab
black tiger shrimp	langouste
blue crab	langoustine
brine shrimp	lobster
crab	Norway lobster
crawdad	prawn
crawfish	scampi
crayfish	shrimp
daphnia	snow crab
Dungeness crab	spider crab
fiddler crab	spiny lobster
hermit crab	squill
horseshoe crab	stone crab
king crab	tiger shrimp
krill	*See also the table at* MOLLUSC

SPACE, gap, crevice, fissure, cleft, breach, rift, cranny, chink, interstice. **3** *the crack of a rifle* BANG, report, explosion, detonation, pop; clap, crash. **4** *a crack on the head* BLOW, bang, hit, knock, rap, punch, thump, bump, smack, slap; *informal* bash, whack, thwack, clout, wallop, clip, bop. **5** (*informal*) *we'll have a crack at it* ATTEMPT, try; *informal* go, shot, stab, whack; *formal* essay. **6** (*informal*) *cheap cracks about her clothes* JOKE, witticism, quip; jibe, barb, taunt, sneer, insult; *informal* gag, wisecrack, funny, dig.
▶ verb **1** *the glass cracked in the heat* BREAK, split, fracture, rupture, snap. **2** *she cracked him across the forehead* HIT, strike, smack, slap, beat, thump, knock, rap, punch; *informal* bash, whack, thwack, clobber, clout, clip, wallop, belt, bop, sock, boff, bust, slug. **3** *the witnesses cracked* BREAK DOWN, give way, cave in, go to pieces, crumble, lose control, yield, succumb. **4** (*informal*) *the naval code proved harder to crack* DECIPHER, interpret, decode, break, solve, resolve, work out, find the key to; *informal* figure out, suss out.
▶ adjective *a crack shot* EXPERT, skilled, skilful, formidable, virtuoso, masterly, consummate, excellent, first-rate, first-class, marvellous, wonderful, magnificent, outstanding, superlative; deadly; *informal* great, superb, fantastic, ace, hotshot, mean, demon, brilliant, crackerjack, bang-up.
— OPPOSITES: incompetent.

■ **crack down on** SUPPRESS, prevent, stop, put a stop to, put an end to, stamp out, eliminate, eradicate; clamp down on, get tough on, come down hard on, limit, restrain, restrict, check, keep in check, control, keep under control.

■ **crack up** (*informal*) BREAK DOWN, have a breakdown, lose control, go to pieces, go out of one's mind, go mad; *informal* lose it, fall/come apart at the seams, go crazy, freak out.

cracked ▶ adjective **1** *a cracked cup* CHIPPED, broken, crazed, fractured, splintered, split; damaged, defective, flawed, imperfect. **2** (*informal*) *you're cracked!* See MAD sense 1.

crackle ▶ verb SIZZLE, fizz, hiss, crack, snap, sputter, crepitate.

cradle ▶ noun **1** *the baby's cradle* CRIB, bassinet, cot, rocker. **2** *the cradle of democracy* BIRTHPLACE, fount, fountainhead, source, spring, fountain, origin, place of origin, seat; *literary* wellspring.
▶ verb *she cradled his head in her arms* HOLD, support, pillow, cushion, shelter, protect; rest, prop (up).

craft ▶ noun **1** *a player with plenty of craft* SKILL, skilfulness, ability, capability, competence, art, talent, flair, artistry, dexterity, craftsmanship, expertise, proficiency, adroitness, adeptness, deftness, virtuosity. **2** *the historian's craft* ACTIVITY, occupation, profession, work, line of work, pursuit. **3** *she used craft to get what she wanted* CUNNING, craftiness, guile, wiliness, artfulness, deviousness, slyness, trickery, duplicity, dishonesty, deceit, deceitfulness, deception, intrigue, subterfuge; wiles, ploys, ruses, schemes, stratagems, tricks. **4** *a sailing craft* VESSEL, ship, boat; *literary* barque.

craftsman, craftswoman ▶ noun ARTISAN, artist, skilled worker; expert, master; *archaic* artificer.

craftsmanship ▶ noun WORKMANSHIP, artistry, craft, art, handiwork, work; skill, skilfulness, expertise, technique.

crafty ▶ adjective CUNNING, wily, guileful, artful, devious, sly, tricky, scheming, calculating, designing, sharp, shrewd, astute, canny; duplicitous, dishonest, deceitful; *informal* foxy.
– OPPOSITES: honest.

crag ▶ noun CLIFF, bluff, ridge, precipice, height, peak, tor, escarpment, scarp.

craggy ▶ adjective **1** *the craggy cliffs* STEEP, precipitous, sheer, perpendicular; rocky, rugged, ragged. **2** *his craggy face* RUGGED, rough-hewn, strong, manly; weather-beaten, weathered.

cram ▶ verb **1** *closets crammed with clothes* FILL, stuff, pack, jam, fill to overflowing, fill to the brim, overload; crowd, overcrowd. **2** *they all crammed into the car* CROWD, pack, pile, squash, squish, squeeze, wedge oneself, force one's way. **3** *he crammed his clothes into a suitcase* THRUST, push, shove, force, ram, jam, stuff, pack, pile, squash, compress, squeeze, wedge. **4** *most of the students are cramming for exams* STUDY, review, bone up.

cramp ▶ noun *stomach cramps* MUSCLE/MUSCULAR SPASM, pain, shooting pain, pang, stitch; *Medicine* hyperkinesis.
▶ verb *tighter rules will cramp economic growth* HINDER, impede, inhibit, hamper, constrain, hamstring, interfere with, restrict, limit, shackle; slow down, check, arrest, curb, retard.

cramped ▶ adjective **1** *cramped accommodation* CONFINED, uncomfortable, poky, restricted, constricted, small, tiny, narrow; crowded, packed, congested; *archaic* strait. **2** *cramped handwriting* SMALL, crabbed, illegible, unreadable, indecipherable, hieroglyphic.
– OPPOSITES: spacious.

crane ▶ noun **1** *the whooping crane.* See table. **2** *it was lifted by a crane* DERRICK, winch, hoist, davit, windlass; block and tackle.

cranium ▶ noun SKULL, head, braincase, brainpan.

crank[1] ▶ verb *you crank the engine by hand* START, turn (over), get going.
■ **crank something up** *(informal)* INCREASE, intensify, amplify, heighten, escalate, add to, augment, build up, expand, extend, raise; speed up, accelerate; up, jack up, hike up, step up, bump up, pump up.

crank[2] ▶ noun *they're nothing but a bunch of cranks* ECCENTRIC, oddity, madman/madwoman, lunatic; *informal* oddball, freak, weirdo, crackpot, loony, nut, nutcase, nutbar, head case, maniac, screwball, kook.

cranky ▶ adjective *the children were tired and cranky.* See CRABBY.

cranny ▶ noun CHINK, crack, crevice, slit, split, fissure, rift, cleft, opening, gap, aperture, cavity, hole, hollow, niche, corner, nook, interstice.

Shore Birds & Wading Birds

adjutant stork	marabou
avocet	moorhen
Baird's sandpiper	oystercatcher
beach bird	pectoral sandpiper
bittern	peewit
brolga	piping plover
cattle egret	plover
coot	rail
crane	red knot sandpiper
curlew	ringed plover
dotterel	ruff/reeve
dowitcher	sanderling
dunlin	sandhill crane
egret	sandpiper
flamingo	snipe
gallinule	sora
godwit	spoonbill
golden plover	stilt
great blue heron	stint
heron	stork
ibis	tattler
jabiru	turnstone
jacana	waterhen
killdeer	whimbrel
lapwing	whooping crane
least bittern	willet
limpkin	yellowlegs

See also the tables at DUCK *and* GULL.

crap ▶ noun **1** *he's talking crap.* See GARBAGE sense 2. **2** *pick up that crap.* See GARBAGE sense 1.

crash ▶ verb **1** *the car crashed into a tree* SMASH INTO, collide with, be in collision with, hit, strike, ram, cannon into/against, plow into, meet head-on, run into, impact. **2** *he crashed his car* SMASH, wreck, write off, total. **3** *waves crashed against the shore* DASH, batter, pound, lash, slam, be hurled. **4** *thunder crashed overhead* BOOM, crack, roll, clap, explode, bang, blast, blare, resound, reverberate, rumble, thunder, echo. **5** *(informal) his clothing company crashed* COLLAPSE, fold, fail, go under, go bankrupt, become insolvent, cease trading, go into receivership, go into liquidation, be wound up; *informal* go broke, go bust, go belly up.
▶ noun **1** *a crash on the highway* ACCIDENT, collision, smash, road traffic accident, derailment, wreck; *informal* pileup, rear-ender. **2** *a loud crash* BANG, smash, smack, crack, bump, thud, clatter, clunk, clonk, clang; report, detonation, explosion; noise, racket, clangour, din. **3** *the stock market crash* COLLAPSE, failure, bankruptcy.
▶ adjective *a crash course* INTENSIVE, concentrated, rapid, short; accelerated, immersion.

crass ▶ adjective STUPID, insensitive, mindless, thoughtless, witless, oafish, boorish, asinine, coarse, gross, graceless, tasteless, tactless, clumsy, heavy-handed, blundering; *informal* ignorant, pig-ignorant.
– OPPOSITES: intelligent.

crate ▶ noun CASE, packing case, chest, box; container, receptacle.

crater ▶ noun HOLLOW, bowl, basin, hole, cavity, depression; *Geology* caldera.

crave ▶ verb LONG FOR, yearn for, desire, want, wish for, hunger for, thirst for, sigh for, pine for, hanker after, covet, lust after, ache for, set one's heart on, dream of, be bent on; *informal* have a yen for, have a jones for, itch for, be dying for.

craven ▶ adjective COWARDLY, lily-livered, faint-hearted, chicken-hearted, spineless, timid, timorous, fearful, pusillanimous, weak, feeble; *informal* yellow, chicken, weak-kneed, gutless, yellow-bellied, wimpish; contemptible, abject, ignominious.
— OPPOSITES: brave.

craving ▶ noun LONGING, yearning, desire, want, wish, hankering, hunger, thirst, appetite, greed, lust, ache, need, urge; *informal* yen, itch, jones.

crawl ▶ verb **1** *they crawled under the table* CREEP, worm one's way, go on all fours, go on hands and knees, wriggle, slither, squirm, scrabble. **2** (*informal*) *I'm not going to go crawling to him* GROVEL TO, ingratiate oneself with, be obsequious to, kowtow to, pander to, toady to, truckle to, bow and scrape to, dance attendance on, curry favour with, make up to, fawn on/over; *informal* suck up to, lick someone's boots, butter up. **3** *the place was crawling with soldiers* BE FULL OF, overflow with, teem with, be packed with, be crowded with, be alive with, be overrun with, swarm with, be bristling with, be infested with, be thick with; *informal* be lousy with, be jam-packed with, be chockablock with, be chock full of.

craze ▶ noun FAD, fashion, trend, vogue, enthusiasm, mania, passion, rage, obsession, compulsion, fixation, fetish, fancy, taste, fascination, preoccupation; *informal* thing.

crazed ▶ adjective MAD, insane, out of one's mind, deranged, demented, certifiable, psychopathic, lunatic; wild, raving, berserk, manic, maniac, frenzied; *informal* crazy, mental, out of one's head, bushed ♣, raving mad, psycho. *See also* CRAZY sense 1.
— OPPOSITES: sane.

crazy ▶ adjective (*informal*) **1** *a crazy old man* MAD, insane, out of one's mind, deranged, demented, not in one's right mind, crazed, lunatic, non compos mentis, unhinged, mad as a hatter, bushed ♣, mad as a March hare; *informal* mental, nutty (as a fruitcake), off one's rocker, not right in the head, round the bend, raving mad, bats, batty, bonkers, cuckoo, loopy, wingy ♣, ditzy, spinny ♣, loony, bananas, loco, with a screw loose, touched, gaga, not all there, out to lunch, crackers, nutso, out of one's tree, meshuga, wacko, gonzo. **2** *Andrea had a crazy idea* STUPID, foolish, idiotic, silly, absurd, ridiculous, ludicrous, preposterous, farcical, laughable, risible, nonsensical, imbecilic, hare-brained, cockamamie, half-baked, impracticable, unworkable, ill-conceived, senseless; *informal* cockeyed, daft, kooky. **3** *he's crazy about her* PASSIONATE ABOUT, very keen on, enamoured of, infatuated with, smitten with, devoted to; very enthusiastic about, fanatical about; *informal* wild/mad/nuts about, hog-wild about, gone on.
— OPPOSITES: sane, sensible, apathetic.

creak ▶ verb SQUEAK, grate, rasp; groan, complain.

cream ▶ noun **1** *skin creams* LOTION, ointment, moisturizer, emollient, unguent, cosmetic; salve, rub, embrocation, balm, liniment. **2** *the cream of the crop* BEST, finest, pick, flower, crème de la crème, elite.
— OPPOSITES: dregs.
▶ adjective *a cream dress* OFF-WHITE, whitish, cream-coloured, creamy, ivory, yellowish-white, ecru.

creamy ▶ adjective **1** *a creamy paste* SMOOTH, thick, velvety, whipped; rich, buttery. **2** *creamy flowers*

OFF-WHITE, whitish, cream-coloured, cream, ivory, yellowish-white.
— OPPOSITES: lumpy.

crease ▶ noun **1** *pants with knife-edge creases* FOLD, line, ridge; pleat, tuck; furrow, groove, corrugation. **2** *the creases at the corners of her eyes* WRINKLE, line, crinkle, pucker; (**creases**) crow's feet.
▶ verb *her skirt was creased and stained* CRUMPLE, wrinkle, crinkle, line, scrunch up, rumple, ruck up.

create ▶ verb **1** *she has created a work of stunning originality* PRODUCE, generate, bring into being, make, fabricate, fashion, build, construct; design, devise, originate, frame, develop, shape, form, forge. **2** *regular socializing creates good team spirit* BRING ABOUT, give rise to, lead to, result in, cause, breed, generate, engender, produce, make for, promote, foster, sow the seeds of, contribute to. **3** *the governments planned to create a free-trade zone* ESTABLISH, found, initiate, institute, constitute, inaugurate, launch, set up, form, organize, develop.
— OPPOSITES: destroy.

creation ▶ noun **1** *the creation of a coalition government* ESTABLISHMENT, formation, foundation, initiation, institution, inauguration, constitution; production, generation, fabrication, fashioning, building, construction, origination, development. **2** *the whole of creation* THE WORLD, the universe, the cosmos; the living world, the natural world, nature, life, living things. **3** *Margaret Atwood's literary creations* WORK, work of art, production, opus, oeuvre; achievement, intellectual property; *informal* brainchild.
— OPPOSITES: destruction.

creative ▶ adjective INVENTIVE, imaginative, innovative, experimental, original; artistic, expressive, inspired, visionary; enterprising, resourceful.

creativity ▶ noun INVENTIVENESS, imagination, innovation, innovativeness, originality, individuality; artistry, inspiration, vision; enterprise, initiative, resourcefulness.

creator ▶ noun **1** *the creator of the series* AUTHOR, writer, designer, deviser, maker, producer; originator, inventor, architect, mastermind, prime mover; *literary* begetter. **2** *the Sabbath is kept to honour the Creator. See* GOD sense 1.

creature ▶ noun **1** *the earth and its creatures* ANIMAL, beast, brute; living thing, living being; *informal* critter, varmint. **2** *you're such a lazy creature!* PERSON, individual, human being, character, soul, wretch, customer; *informal* devil, beggar, sort, type. **3** *she was denounced as a creature of the Liberals* LACKEY, minion, hireling, servant, puppet, tool, cat's paw, pawn; *informal* stooge, yes-man, running dog.

credence ▶ noun **1** *the government placed little credence in the scheme* BELIEF, faith, trust, confidence, reliance. **2** *later reports lent credence to this view* CREDIBILITY, plausibility, believability; *archaic* credit.

credentials ▶ plural noun DOCUMENTS, documentation, papers, identity papers, bona fides, ID, ID card, identity card, passport, proof of identity; certificates, diplomas, certification, references.

credibility ▶ noun **1** *the whole tale lacks credibility* PLAUSIBILITY, believability, tenability, probability, feasibility, likelihood, credence; authority, cogency. **2** *the party lacked moral credibility* TRUSTWORTHINESS, reliability, dependability, integrity; reputation, status.

credible ▸ adjective BELIEVABLE, plausible, tenable, able to hold water, conceivable, likely, probable, possible, feasible, reasonable, with a ring of truth, persuasive.

credit ▸ noun **1** *he never got the credit he deserved* PRAISE, commendation, acclaim, acknowledgement, recognition, kudos, glory, esteem, respect, thanks, admiration, tributes, gratitude, appreciation; *informal* bouquets, brownie points, full marks. **2** *the speech did his credit no good in the House of Commons* REPUTATION, repute, image, (good) name, character, prestige, standing, status, estimation, credibility. **3** *(archaic) his theory has been given very little credit* CREDENCE, belief, faith, trust, reliance, confidence. **4** *she bought her new car on credit* LOAN, advance, (bridge) financing; installments; *informal* plastic.
▸ verb **1** *the wise will seldom credit all they hear* BELIEVE, accept, give credence to, trust, have faith in; *informal* buy, swallow, fall for, take something as gospel (truth). **2** *the scheme's success can be credited to the team's frugality* ASCRIBE, attribute, assign, accredit, chalk up, put down.

creditable ▸ adjective COMMENDABLE, praiseworthy, laudable, admirable, honourable, estimable, meritorious, worthy, deserving, respectable.
– OPPOSITES: deplorable.

credulous ▸ adjective GULLIBLE, naive, too trusting, easily taken in, impressionable, unsuspecting, unsuspicious, unwary, unquestioning; innocent, ingenuous, inexperienced, unsophisticated, unworldly, wide-eyed; *informal* born yesterday, wet behind the ears.
– OPPOSITES: suspicious.

creed ▸ noun **1** *people of many creeds and cultures* FAITH, religion, religious belief, religious persuasion, church, denomination, sect. **2** *his political creed* SYSTEM OF BELIEF, (set of) beliefs, principles, articles of faith, ideology, credo, doctrine, teaching, dogma, tenets, canons.

creek ▸ noun STREAM, river, brook, rivulet, freshet, runnel, rill, tributary, bourn, watercourse.
■ **up the creek** IN TROUBLE, in difficulty/difficulties, in a mess, in a predicament, in a pickle, in a jam, in a fix.

creep ▸ verb **1** *Tim crept out of the house* TIPTOE, steal, sneak, slip, slink, sidle, pad, edge, inch; skulk, prowl. **2** *(informal) they're always creeping to the boss* GROVEL TO, ingratiate oneself with, curry favour with, toady to, truckle to, kowtow to, bow and scrape to, pander to, fawn on/over, make up to; *informal* crawl to, suck up to, lick someone's boots, butter up, brown-nose to.
▸ noun. *he's such a creep!* See BASTARD noun sense 2.

creeper ▸ noun CLIMBING PLANT, trailing plant, trailer; vine, climber, rambler.

creeps
■ **give someone the creeps** *(informal)* REPEL, repulse, revolt, disgust, sicken, nauseate, make someone's flesh creep, make someone's skin crawl; scare, frighten, terrify, horrify; gross out, freak out, creep out.

creepy ▸ adjective *(informal)* FRIGHTENING, eerie, disturbing, sinister, weird, hair-raising, menacing, threatening, eldritch; *informal* spooky, scary, freaky.

crescent ▸ noun HALF-MOON, sickle-shape, lunula, lunette; arc, curve, bow.

crest ▸ noun **1** *the bird's crest* COMB, plume, tuft of feathers. **2** *the crest of the hill* SUMMIT, peak, top, tip, pinnacle, brow, crown, apex. **3** *the Winnipeg city crest*
INSIGNIA, regalia, badge, emblem, heraldic device, coat of arms, arms.

crestfallen ▸ adjective DOWNHEARTED, downcast, despondent, disappointed, disconsolate, disheartened, discouraged, dispirited, dejected, depressed, desolate, in the doldrums, sad, glum, gloomy, dismayed, doleful, miserable, unhappy, woebegone, forlorn; *informal* blue, bummed, in a blue funk, down in the mouth, down in the dumps.
– OPPOSITES: cheerful.

crevasse ▸ noun CHASM, abyss, fissure, cleft, crack, split, breach, rift, hole, cavity.

crevice ▸ noun CRACK, fissure, cleft, chink, interstice, cranny, nook, slit, split, rift, fracture, breach; opening, gap, hole.

crew ▸ noun **1** *the ship's crew* SAILORS, mariners, hands, ship's company, ship's complement. **2** *a crew of cameramen and sound engineers* TEAM, group, company, unit, corps, party, gang. **3** *(informal) they were a motley crew* CROWD, group, band, gang, mob, pack, troop, swarm, herd, posse, bunch, gaggle.

crib ▸ noun **1** *the baby's crib* CRADLE, cot, bassinet. **2** *the oxen's crib* MANGER, stall, feeding trough.
▸ verb *(informal) she cribbed the plot from a Shakespeare play* COPY, plagiarize, poach, appropriate, steal, 'borrow'; *informal* rip off, lift, pinch.

crick ▸ noun KINK, pinch, knot, strain, stiffness.

crime ▸ noun **1** *kidnapping is a very serious crime* OFFENCE, unlawful act, illegal act, felony, misdemeanour, misdeed, wrong; *informal* no-no. **2** *the increase in crime* LAW-BREAKING, delinquency, wrongdoing, criminality, misconduct, illegality, villainy; *informal* crookedness; *Law* malfeasance. **3** *a crime against humanity* SIN, evil, immoral act, wrong, atrocity, abomination, disgrace, outrage.

criminal ▸ noun *a convicted criminal* LAWBREAKER, offender, villain, delinquent, felon, convict, malefactor, wrongdoer, culprit, miscreant; thief, burglar, robber, armed robber, gunman, gangster, terrorist; *informal* crook, con, jailbird, hood, yardbird, perp; *Law* malfeasant.
▸ adjective **1** *criminal conduct* UNLAWFUL, illegal, illicit, lawless, felonious, delinquent, fraudulent, actionable, culpable; villainous, nefarious, corrupt, wrong, bad, evil, wicked, iniquitous; *informal* crooked; *Law* malfeasant. **2** *(informal) a criminal waste of taxpayer's money* DEPLORABLE, shameful, reprehensible, disgraceful, inexcusable, unforgivable, unconscionable, unpardonable, outrageous, monstrous, shocking, scandalous, wicked.
– OPPOSITES: lawful.

crimp ▸ verb PLEAT, flute, corrugate, ruffle, fold, crease, crinkle, pucker, gather; pinch, compress, press together, squeeze together.

crimped ▸ adjective *crimped blond hair* CURLY, wavy, curled, frizzy, ringlety.

cringe ▸ verb **1** *she cringed as he bellowed in her ear* COWER, shrink, recoil, shy away, flinch, blench, draw back; shake, tremble, quiver, quail, quake. **2** *it makes me cringe when I think of it* WINCE, shudder, squirm, feel embarrassed/mortified.

crinkle ▸ verb WRINKLE, crease, pucker, furrow, corrugate, line; rumple, scrunch up, ruck up.

crinkly ▸ adjective WRINKLED, wrinkly, crinkled, creased, crumpled, rumpled, crimped, corrugated, fluted, puckered, furrowed; wavy.

cripple ▸ verb **1** *the accident crippled her* DISABLE, paralyze, immobilize, lame, incapacitate, handicap, leave someone a paraplegic/quadriplegic. **2** *the company had been crippled by the recession* DEVASTATE, ruin, destroy, wipe out; paralyze, hamstring, bring to a standstill, put out of action, sideline, put out of business, bankrupt, break, bring someone to their knees.

crippled ▶ **adjective** DISABLED, paralyzed, incapacitated, physically handicapped, lame, immobilized, bedridden, in a wheelchair, paraplegic, quadriplegic; *euphemistic* physically challenged.

crisis ▶ **noun 1** *the situation had reached a crisis* CRITICAL POINT, turning point, crossroads, watershed, head, moment of truth, zero hour, point of no return, Rubicon, doomsday; *informal* crunch; *Medicine* climacteric. **2** *the current economic crisis* EMERGENCY, disaster, catastrophe, calamity; predicament, plight, mess, trouble, dire straits, difficulty, extremity.

crisp ▶ **adjective 1** *crisp bacon* CRUNCHY, crispy, brittle, crumbly, friable, breakable; firm, dry. **2** *a crisp autumn day* INVIGORATING, bracing, brisk, fresh, refreshing, exhilarating, tonic, energizing; cool, chill, chilly, cold, nippy. **3** *her answer was crisp* BRISK, decisive, businesslike, no-nonsense, incisive, to the point, matter of fact, brusque; terse, succinct, concise, brief, short, short and sweet, laconic, snappy. **4** *crisp white bed linen* SMOOTH, uncreased, ironed; starched.
– OPPOSITES: soft, sultry, rambling.

criterion ▶ **noun** STANDARD, specification, measure, gauge, test, scale, benchmark, yardstick, touchstone, barometer; principle, rule, law, canon.

critic ▶ **noun 1** *a literary critic* REVIEWER, commentator, evaluator, analyst, judge, pundit. **2** *critics of the government* DETRACTOR, attacker, fault-finder, back-seat driver, gadfly.

critical ▶ **adjective 1** *a highly critical report* CENSORIOUS, condemnatory, condemning, denunciatory, disparaging, disapproving, scathing, fault-finding, judgmental, accusatory, negative, unfavourable; *informal* nitpicking, picky. **2** *a critical essay* EVALUATIVE, analytical, interpretative, expository, explanatory. **3** *the situation is critical* GRAVE, serious, dangerous, risky, perilous, hazardous, precarious, touch-and-go, in the balance, uncertain, parlous, desperate, dire, acute, life-and-death. **4** *the choice of materials is critical for product safety* CRUCIAL, vital, essential, of the essence, all-important, paramount, fundamental, key, pivotal, decisive, deciding, climacteric.
– OPPOSITES: complimentary, unimportant.

criticism ▶ **noun 1** *she was stung by his criticism* CENSURE, condemnation, denunciation, disapproval, disparagement, opprobrium, fault-finding, attack, broadside, brickbats, potshot, stricture, recrimination; *informal* flak, bad press, panning, put down, knock, slam; *formal* excoriation. **2** *literary criticism* EVALUATION, assessment, appraisal, analysis, judgment; commentary, interpretation, explanation, explication, elucidation.

criticize ▶ **verb** FIND FAULT WITH, censure, denounce, condemn, attack, lambaste, pillory, rail against, inveigh against, arraign, cast aspersions on, pour scorn on, disparage, denigrate, give bad press to, run down; *informal* knock, pan, maul, slam, slag, roast, hammer, lay into, lace into, flay, crucify, take apart, pull to pieces, pick holes in, pummel, trash, nitpick; *formal* excoriate.
– OPPOSITES: praise.

critique ▶ **noun** ANALYSIS, evaluation, assessment, appraisal, appreciation, criticism, review, study, commentary, exposition, exegesis.

croak ▶ **verb** *'Thank you,' I croaked* RASP, squawk, caw, wheeze, gasp.

crock ▶ **noun 1** *a crock of honey* POT, jar; jug, pitcher, ewer; container, receptacle, vessel. **2** (**crocks**) *a pile of dirty crocks. See* CROCKERY. **3** (*informal*) *he's a bit of an old crock* INVALID, valetudinarian, senior (citizen); geriatric, dotard. **4** *his story was a total crock* LIE, falsehood, fib, made-up story, invention, fabrication, deception, (piece of) fiction; (little) white lie, half-truth; *informal* tall story/tale, whopper.

crockery ▶ **noun** DISHES, crocks, china, tableware; plates, bowls, cups, saucers.

crony ▶ **noun** (*informal*) FRIEND, companion, bosom friend, intimate, confidant(e), familiar, associate, accomplice, comrade; *informal* pal, chum, sidekick, partner in crime, mate, buddy, amigo, compadre; *archaic* compeer.

crook ▶ **noun 1** (*informal*) *a small-time crook* CRIMINAL, lawbreaker, offender, villain, delinquent, felon, convict, malefactor, culprit, wrongdoer; rogue, scoundrel, shyster, cheat, scam artist, swindler, racketeer, confidence trickster, snake oil salesman; thief, robber, burglar; *informal* shark, con man, con, jailbird, hood, yardbird; *Law* malfeasant. **2** *the crook of a tree branch* BEND, fork, curve, angle.
▶ **verb** *he crooked his finger and called the waiter* COCK, flex, bend, curve, curl.

crooked ▶ **adjective 1** *narrow, crooked streets* WINDING, twisting, zigzag, meandering, tortuous, serpentine. **2** *a crooked spine* BENT, twisted, misshapen, deformed, malformed, contorted, out of shape, wry, warped, bowed, distorted. **3** *the picture over the bed looked crooked* LOPSIDED, askew, awry, off-centre, uneven, out of line, asymmetrical, tilted, at an angle, aslant, slanting, cockeyed, wonky. **4** (*informal*) *a crooked cop / crooked deals* DISHONEST, unscrupulous, unprincipled, untrustworthy, corrupt, corruptible, venal; criminal, illegal, unlawful, nefarious, fraudulent, shady, dodgy.
– OPPOSITES: straight, honest.

croon ▶ **verb** SING SOFTLY, hum, warble, trill.

crop ▶ **noun 1** *some farmers lost their entire crop* HARVEST, year's growth, yield; fruits, produce. **2** *a bumper crop of mail* BATCH, lot, assortment, selection, collection, supply, intake. **3** *a rider's crop* WHIP, switch, cane, stick.
▶ **verb 1** *she's had her hair cropped* CUT SHORT, cut, clip, shear, shave, lop off, chop off, hack off; dock, bob. **2** *a flock of sheep were cropping the turf* GRAZE ON, browse on, feed on, nibble, eat. **3** *the hay was cropped several times this summer* HARVEST, reap, mow; gather (in), collect, pick, bring home.
■ **crop up** HAPPEN, occur, arise, turn up, spring up, pop up, emerge, materialize, surface, appear, come to light, present itself; *literary* come to pass, befall.

cross ▶ **noun 1** *a bronze cross* CRUCIFIX, rood. **2** *we all have our crosses to bear* BURDEN, trouble, worry, trial, tribulation, affliction, curse, bane, misfortune, adversity, hardship, vicissitude; millstone, albatross, thorn in one's flesh/side; misery, woe, pain, sorrow, suffering; *informal* hassle, headache. **3** *a cross between a yak and a cow* HYBRID, hybridization, cross-breed, half-breed; mongrel; mixture, amalgam, blend, combination.
▶ **verb 1** *they crossed the hills on foot* TRAVEL ACROSS, traverse, range over; negotiate, navigate, cover. **2** *a lake crossed by a fine stone bridge* SPAN, bridge; extend/

stretch across, pass over. **3** *the point where the two roads cross* INTERSECT, meet, join, connect, criss-cross. **4** *no one dared cross him* OPPOSE, resist, defy, obstruct, impede, hinder, hamper; contradict, argue with, quarrel with, stand up to, take a stand against, take issue with; *formal* gainsay. **5** *the breed was crossed with the similarly coloured Holstein* HYBRIDIZE, cross-breed, interbreed, cross-fertilize, cross-pollinate.

▶ **adjective** *Jane was getting cross* ANGRY, annoyed, irate, irritated, in a bad mood, vexed, irked, piqued, out of humour, put out, displeased; irritable, short-tempered, bad-tempered, snappish, snappy, crotchety, grouchy, grumpy, fractious, testy, tetchy, crabby, cranky, mad, hot under the collar, peeved, riled, on the warpath, up in arms, steamed up, shirty, sore, bent out of shape, teed off, ticked off, pissed off.
− OPPOSITES: pleased.

■ **cross something out** DELETE, strike out, ink out, score out, edit out, cancel, obliterate.

cross-examine ▶ **verb** INTERROGATE, question, cross-question, quiz, catechize, give someone the third degree; *informal* grill, pump, put someone through the wringer.

crossing ▶ **noun 1** *a busy road crossing* INTERSECTION, crossroads, junction, interchange; level crossing. **2** *a short ferry crossing* JOURNEY, passage, voyage, trip.

crosswise, crossways ▶ **adverb** DIAGONALLY, obliquely, transversely, aslant, at an angle, on the bias; cater-cornered, kitty-corner.

crotch ▶ **noun** GROIN; lap, genitals.

crotchety ▶ **adjective** BAD-TEMPERED, irascible, irritable, grumpy, grouchy, cantankerous, short-tempered, tetchy, testy, curmudgeonly, ill-tempered, ill-humoured, ill-natured, cross-grained, peevish, cross, fractious, pettish, waspish, crabbed, crabby, crusty, prickly, touchy, snappish, snappy, chippy, shirty, cranky, ornery.
− OPPOSITES: good-humoured.

crouch ▶ **verb** SQUAT, bend (down), hunker down, scrunch down, hunch over, stoop, kneel (down); duck, cower.

crow ▶ **verb 1** *a cock crowed* CRY, squawk, screech, caw, call. **2** *try to avoid crowing about your success* BOAST, brag, trumpet, swagger, swank, gloat, show off, preen oneself, sing one's own praises; *informal* talk big, blow one's own horn.

crowd ▶ **noun 1** *a crowd of people* THRONG, horde, mass, multitude, host, army, herd, flock, drove, swarm, sea, troupe, pack, press, crush, mob, rabble; collection, company, gathering, assembly, audience, assemblage, congregation; *informal* gaggle, bunch, gang, posse. **2** *she wanted to stand out from the crowd* MAJORITY, multitude, common people, populace, general public, masses, rank and file, hoi polloi; *informal* Joe Public, John Q. Public. **3** *he's been hanging round with a bad crowd* SET, group, circle, clique, coterie; camp; *informal* gang, crew, lot. **4** *the spectacle attracted a capacity crowd* AUDIENCE, spectators, listeners, viewers; house, turnout, attendance, gate; congregation.

▶ **verb 1** *reporters crowded around her* CLUSTER, flock, swarm, mill, throng, huddle, gather, assemble, congregate, converge; scrum ✦. **2** *the guests all crowded into the dining room* SURGE, push one's way, jostle, elbow one's way; squeeze, pile, cram. **3** *the beach was crowded with tourists* THRONG, pack, jam, cram, fill. **4** *stop crowding me* pressure; harass, hound, pester, harry, badger, nag; *informal* hassle, lean on.

crowded ▶ **adjective** PACKED, full, filled to capacity,

full to bursting, congested, overcrowded, overflowing, teeming, swarming, thronged, populous, overpopulated; busy; *informal* jam-packed, stuffed, chockablock, chock full, bursting at the seams, wall-to-wall, standing room only, SRO.
− OPPOSITES: deserted.

crown ▶ **noun 1** *a jewelled crown* CORONET, diadem, circlet, tiara; *literary* coronal. **2** *the world heavyweight crown* TITLE, award, accolade, distinction; trophy, cup, medal, plate, shield, belt, prize; laurels, bays, palm. **3** *he and his family were loyal servants of the Crown* MONARCH, sovereign, king, queen, emperor, empress; monarchy, royalty; *informal* royals. **4** *the crown of the hill* TOP, crest, summit, peak, pinnacle, tip, head, brow, apex.

▶ **verb 1** *David II was crowned in 1331* ENTHRONE, install; invest, induct. **2** *a teaching post at Harvard crowned his career* ROUND OFF, cap, be the climax of, be the culmination of, top off, consummate, perfect, complete, put the finishing touch(es) on/to. **3** *a steeple crowned by a gilded cross* TOP, cap, tip, head, surmount. **4** (*informal*) *someone crowned him with a poker. See* HIT *verb* sense 1.

crucial ▶ **adjective 1** *negotiations were at a crucial stage* PIVOTAL, critical, key, climacteric, decisive, deciding; life-and-death. **2** *confidentiality is crucial in this case* ALL-IMPORTANT, of the utmost importance, of the essence, critical, pre-eminent, paramount, essential, vital.
− OPPOSITES: unimportant.

crucify ▶ **verb 1** *two thieves were crucified with Jesus* NAIL TO A CROSS; execute, put to death, kill. **2** *she had been crucified by his departure* DEVASTATE, crush, shatter, cut to the quick, wound, pain, harrow, torture, torment, agonize. **3** (*informal*) *the fans would crucify us if we lost. See* CRITICIZE.

crude ▶ **adjective 1** *crude oil* UNREFINED, unpurified, unprocessed, untreated; unmilled, unpolished, coarse, raw, natural. **2** *a crude barricade* PRIMITIVE, simple, basic, homespun, rudimentary, rough, rough and ready, rough-hewn, make-do, makeshift, improvised, unfinished, jerry-rigged, jerry-built, slapdash; *dated* rude. **3** *crude jokes* VULGAR, rude, naughty, suggestive, bawdy, off-colour, indecent, obscene, offensive, lewd, salacious, licentious, ribald, coarse, uncouth, indelicate, tasteless, crass, smutty, dirty, filthy, scatological; *informal* blue.
− OPPOSITES: refined, sophisticated.

cruel ▶ **adjective 1** *a cruel man* BRUTAL, savage, inhuman, barbaric, barbarous, brutish, bloodthirsty, murderous, vicious, sadistic, wicked, evil, fiendish, diabolical, monstrous, abominable; callous, ruthless, merciless, pitiless, remorseless, uncaring, heartless, stony-hearted, hard-hearted, cold-blooded, cold-hearted, unfeeling, unkind, inhumane; *dated* dastardly; *literary* fell. **2** *her death was a cruel blow* HARSH, severe, bitter, harrowing, heartbreaking, heart-rending, painful, agonizing, traumatic; *formal* grievous.
− OPPOSITES: compassionate.

cruelty ▶ **noun** BRUTALITY, savagery, inhumanity, barbarity, barbarousness, brutishness, sadism, bloodthirstiness, viciousness, wickedness; lack of compassion, callousness, ruthlessness.

cruise ▶ **noun** *a cruise to the islands* BOAT TRIP, sea trip; voyage, journey.

▶ **verb 1** *she cruised across the Atlantic* SAIL, voyage, journey. **2** *a taxi cruised past* DRIVE SLOWLY, drift; *informal* mosey, toodle.

crumb ▶ noun FRAGMENT, bit, morsel, particle, speck, scrap, shred, sliver, atom, grain, trace, tinge, mite, iota, jot, whit, ounce, scintilla, soupçon; *informal* smidgen, tad, titch.

crumble ▶ verb DISINTEGRATE, fall apart, fall to pieces, fall down, break up, collapse, fragment; decay, fall into decay, deteriorate, degenerate, go to rack and ruin, decompose, rot, moulder, perish.

crumbly ▶ adjective BRITTLE, breakable, friable, powdery, granular; crisp, crispy.

crumple ▶ verb **1** *she crumpled the note in her fist* CRUSH, scrunch up, screw up, squash, squeeze. **2** *his pants were dirty and crumpled* CREASE, wrinkle, crinkle, rumple, ruck up. **3** *her resistance crumpled* COLLAPSE, give way, cave in, go to pieces, break down, crumble, be overcome.

crunch ▶ verb *she crunched the apple with relish* MUNCH, chomp, champ, bite into.
▶ noun *(informal) when the crunch comes, she'll be forced to choose* MOMENT OF TRUTH, critical point, crux, crisis, decision time, zero hour, point of no return; showdown.

crusade ▶ noun **1** *the medieval crusades* HOLY WAR; jihad. **2** *a crusade against crime* CAMPAIGN, drive, push, movement, effort, struggle; battle, war, offensive.
▶ verb *she likes crusading for the cause of the underdog* CAMPAIGN, fight, do battle, battle, take up arms, take up the cudgels, work, strive, struggle, agitate, lobby, champion, promote.

crusader ▶ noun CAMPAIGNER, fighter, champion, advocate; reformer.

crush ▶ verb **1** *essential oils are released when the herbs are crushed* SQUASH, squeeze, press, compress; pulp, mash, macerate, mangle; flatten, trample on, tread on; *informal* smush. **2** *your dress will get crushed* CREASE, crumple, rumple, wrinkle, crinkle, scrunch (up), ruck up. **3** *crush the cookies with a rolling pin* PULVERIZE, pound, grind, break up, smash, crumble; mill; *technical* comminute. **4** *he crushed her in his arms* HUG, squeeze, hold tight, embrace, enfold. **5** *the new regime crushed all popular uprisings* SUPPRESS, put down, quell, quash, stamp out, put an end to, overcome, overpower, defeat, triumph over, break, repress, subdue, extinguish. **6** *Alan was crushed by her words* MORTIFY, humiliate, abash, chagrin, deflate, flatten, demoralize, squash; devastate, shatter; *informal* shoot down in flames, knock the stuffing out of.
▶ noun **1** *the crush of people* CROWD, throng, horde, swarm, sea, mass, pack, press, mob. **2** *(informal) a teenage crush* INFATUATION, obsession, love, passion; *informal* puppy love.

crust ▶ noun COVERING, layer, coating, cover, coat, sheet, thickness, film, skin, topping; incrustation, scab.

crusty ▶ adjective **1** *crusty French bread* CRISP, crispy, well baked; crumbly, brittle, friable. **2** *a crusty old man* IRRITABLE, cantankerous, irascible, bad-tempered, ill-tempered, grumpy, grouchy, crotchety, short-tempered, tetchy, testy, crabby, curmudgeonly, peevish, cross, fractious, pettish, crabbed, prickly, waspish, peppery, cross-grained; *informal* snappish, snappy, chippy, cranky, ornery.
— OPPOSITES: soft, good-natured.

crux ▶ noun NUB, heart, essence, central point, main point, core, centre, nucleus, kernel; *informal* the bottom line.

cry ▶ verb **1** *Mandy started to cry* WEEP, shed tears, sob, wail, cry one's eyes out, bawl, howl, snivel, whimper,

squall, mewl, bleat; lament, grieve, mourn, keen; *informal* boo-hoo, blubber, turn on the waterworks; *literary* pule. **2** *'Wait!' he cried* CALL, shout, exclaim, sing out, yell, shriek, scream, screech, bawl, bellow, roar, vociferate, squeal, yelp, holler; *dated* ejaculate.
— OPPOSITES: laugh, whisper.
▶ noun **1** *Leonora had a good cry* SOB, weep, crying fit, crying jag. **2** *a cry of despair* CALL, shout, exclamation, yell, shriek, scream, screech, bawl, bellow, roar, howl, yowl, squeal, yelp, interjection, holler; *dated* ejaculation. **3** *they've issued a cry for help* APPEAL, plea, entreaty, cry from the heart, cri de cœur.
■ **cry off** *(informal)* BACK OUT, pull out, cancel, withdraw, beg off, excuse oneself, change one's mind; *informal* get cold feet, cop out.

crybaby ▶ noun wimp, suck ♣, sissy, mama's boy, sook, *Atlantic* sooky baby ♣, wuss, pantywaist.

crypt ▶ noun TOMB, vault, mausoleum, burial chamber, sepulchre, catacomb, ossuary, undercroft.

cryptic ▶ adjective ENIGMATIC, mysterious, confusing, mystifying, perplexing, puzzling, obscure, abstruse, arcane, oracular, Delphic, ambiguous, elliptical, oblique; *informal* as clear as mud.
— OPPOSITES: clear.

crystallize ▶ verb **1** *minerals crystallize at different temperatures* FORM CRYSTALS, solidify, harden. **2** *the idea crystallized in her mind* BECOME CLEAR, become definite, take shape, materialize, coalesce; *informal* jell.

cub ▶ noun **1** *a lioness and her cubs* (**cubs**) YOUNG, offspring, pups; *archaic* whelps. **2** *a cub reporter* TRAINEE, apprentice, probationer, novice, tyro, learner, beginner, tenderfoot; *informal* rookie, newbie, greenhorn.
— OPPOSITES: veteran.

cubbyhole ▶ noun SMALL ROOM, booth, cubicle, broom closet; den, snug, cubby.

cube ▶ noun **1** *a shape that was neither a cube nor a sphere* HEXAHEDRON, cuboid, parallelepiped. **2** *a cube of soap* BLOCK, lump, chunk, brick.

cuddle ▶ verb **1** *she picked up the baby and cuddled her* HUG, embrace, clasp, hold tight, hold/fold in one's arms, snuggle. **2** *the pair were kissing and cuddling* EMBRACE, hug, caress, pet, fondle; *informal* canoodle, smooch; *informal, dated* spoon, bill and coo. **3** *I cuddled up to him* SNUGGLE, nestle, curl, nuzzle, burrow against.

cuddly ▶ adjective HUGGABLE, soft, warm, cuddlesome, snuggly, cushy; plump, curvaceous, rounded, buxom; attractive, endearing, lovable, zaftig.

cudgel ▶ noun *a thick wooden cudgel* CLUB, bludgeon, stick, truncheon, baton, shillelagh, mace, blackjack, billy, nightstick.
▶ verb *she was cudgelled to death* BLUDGEON, club, beat, batter, bash.

cue ▶ noun SIGNAL, sign, indication, prompt, reminder; nod, word, gesture.

cuff ▶ verb *Chris cuffed him on the head* HIT, strike, slap, smack, thump, beat, punch; *informal* clout, wallop, belt, whack, thwack, bash, clobber, bop, sock, boff, slug; *archaic* smite.
■ **off the cuff** *(informal)* **1** *an off-the-cuff remark* IMPROMPTU, extempore, ad lib; unrehearsed, unscripted, unprepared, improvised, spontaneous, unplanned. **2** *I spoke off the cuff* WITHOUT PREPARATION, without rehearsal, impromptu, ad lib; *informal* off the top of one's head.

cuisine ▶ noun COOKING, cookery, food, dishes.

cul-de-sac ▶ noun DEAD END, no exit, blind alley.

cull ▶ verb **1** *anecdotes culled from Greek history* SELECT, choose, pick, take, obtain, glean. **2** *he sees culling deer as a necessity* KILL, slaughter, destroy, harvest.

culminate ▶ verb COME TO A CLIMAX, come to a head, peak, climax, reach a pinnacle; build up to, lead up to; end with, finish with, conclude with.

culmination ▶ noun CLIMAX, pinnacle, peak, high point, highest point, height, high-water mark, top, summit, crest, apex, zenith, crowning moment, apotheosis, apogee; consummation, completion, finish, conclusion.
— OPPOSITES: nadir.

culpability ▶ noun GUILT, blame, fault, responsibility, accountability, liability, answerability; guiltiness, blameworthiness.

culpable ▶ adjective TO BLAME, guilty, at fault, in the wrong, answerable, accountable, responsible, blameworthy, censurable.
— OPPOSITES: innocent.

culprit ▶ noun GUILTY PARTY, offender, wrongdoer, perpetrator, miscreant; criminal, malefactor, felon, lawbreaker, delinquent; *informal* baddy, crook, perp.

cult ▶ noun **1** *a religious cult* SECT, denomination, group, movement, church, persuasion, body, faction. **2** *the cult of youth in Hollywood* OBSESSION WITH, fixation on, mania for, passion for, idolization of, devotion to, worship of, veneration of.

cultivate ▶ verb **1** *the peasants cultivated the land* TILL, plow, dig, hoe, farm, work, fertilize, mulch, weed. **2** *they were encouraged to cultivate basic food crops* GROW, raise, rear, plant, sow. **3** *Tessa tried to cultivate her as a friend* win someone's friendship, woo, court, curry favour with, ingratiate oneself with; *informal* get in someone's good books, butter up, suck up to. **4** *he wants to cultivate his mind* IMPROVE, better, refine, elevate; educate, train, develop, enrich.

cultivated ▶ adjective CULTURED, educated, well-read, civilized, enlightened, discerning, discriminating, refined, polished; sophisticated, urbane, cosmopolitan.

cultural ▶ adjective **1** *cultural differences* ETHNIC, racial, folk; societal, lifestyle. **2** *cultural achievements* AESTHETIC, artistic, intellectual; educational, edifying, civilizing.

culture ▶ noun **1** *20th century popular culture* THE ARTS, the humanities, intellectual achievement; literature, music, painting, philosophy, the performing arts. **2** *a man of culture* INTELLECTUAL/ARTISTIC AWARENESS, education, cultivation, enlightenment, discernment, discrimination, good taste, taste, refinement, polish, sophistication. **3** *Afro-Caribbean culture* CIVILIZATION, society, way of life, lifestyle; customs, traditions, heritage, habits, ways, mores, values. **4** *the culture of crops* CULTIVATION, farming; agriculture, husbandry, agronomy.

cultured ▶ adjective CULTIVATED, intellectually/artistically aware, artistic, enlightened, civilized, educated, well-educated, well-read, well-informed, learned, knowledgeable, discerning, discriminating, refined, polished, sophisticated; *informal* artsy.
— OPPOSITES: ignorant.

culvert ▶ noun CHANNEL, conduit, watercourse, trough; drain, gutter, ditch.

cumbersome ▶ adjective **1** *a cumbersome diving suit* UNWIELDY, unmanageable, awkward, clumsy, inconvenient, incommodious; bulky, large, heavy,

hefty, weighty, burdensome; *informal* hulking, clunky. **2** *cumbersome procedures* COMPLICATED, complex, involved, inefficient, unwieldy, slow.
— OPPOSITES: manageable, straightforward.

cumulative ▶ adjective INCREASING, accumulative, growing, mounting; collective, aggregate, amassed.

cunning ▶ adjective *a cunning scheme* CRAFTY, wily, artful, guileful, devious, sly, scheming, designing, calculating, Machiavellian; shrewd, astute, clever, canny; deceitful, deceptive, duplicitous, foxy; *archaic* subtle.
— OPPOSITES: honest.
▶ noun *his political cunning* GUILE, craftiness, deviousness, slyness, trickery, duplicity; shrewdness, astuteness.

cup ▶ noun **1** *a cup and saucer* teacup, coffee cup, demitasse; mug; beaker; *historical* chalice. **2** *the winner was presented with a silver cup* TROPHY, award, prize.

cupboard ▶ noun CABINET, buffet, sideboard, dresser, armoire, credenza, chiffonier, closet, wardrobe, commode.

Cupid ▶ noun EROS, the god of love; amoretto.

cupidity ▶ noun GREED, avarice, avariciousness, acquisitiveness, covetousness, rapacity, materialism, Mammonism; *informal* money-grubbing.
— OPPOSITES: generosity.

cur ▶ noun **1** *a mangy cur* MONGREL, mutt, (Nfld) crackie ♣, tyke. **2** (*informal*) *Neil was beginning to feel like a cur. See* JERK *noun sense* 3.

curable ▶ adjective REMEDIABLE, treatable, medicable, operable.

curative ▶ adjective HEALING, therapeutic, medicinal, remedial, corrective, restorative, tonic, health-giving.

curb ▶ noun *a curb on public spending* RESTRAINT, restriction, check, brake, rein, control, limitation, limit, constraint; *informal* crackdown; *literary* trammel.
▶ verb *he tried to curb his temper* RESTRAIN, hold back/in, keep back, repress, suppress, fight back, bite back, keep in check, check, control, rein in, contain, bridle, subdue; *informal* keep a/the lid on.

curdle ▶ verb CLOT, coagulate, congeal, solidify, thicken; turn, sour, ferment.

cure ▶ verb **1** *he was cured of the disease* HEAL, restore to health, make well/better; *archaic* cleanse. **2** *economic equality cannot cure all social ills* RECTIFY, remedy, put/set right, right, fix, mend, repair, heal, make better; solve, sort out, be the answer/solution to; eliminate, end, put an end to. **3** *some farmers cured their own bacon* PRESERVE, smoke, salt, dry, pickle.
▶ noun **1** *a cure for cancer* REMEDY, medicine, medication, medicament, antidote, antiserum; treatment, therapy; *archaic* physic. **2** *interest rate cuts are not the cure for the problem* SOLUTION, answer, antidote, nostrum, panacea, cure-all; *informal* quick fix, magic bullet, silver bullet.

cure-all ▶ noun PANACEA, cure for all ills, sovereign remedy, heal-all, nostrum; *informal* magic/silver bullet.

curio ▶ noun TRINKET, knick-knack, bibelot, ornament, bauble; objet d'art, collector's item, rarity, curiosity, oddity, kickshaw, tchotchke.

curiosity ▶ noun **1** *his evasiveness roused my curiosity* INTEREST, spirit of inquiry, inquisitiveness. **2** *the shop is a treasure trove of curiosities. See* CURIO.

curious ▶ adjective **1** *she was curious to know what had happened* INTRIGUED, interested, eager/dying to know, agog; inquisitive. **2** *her curious behaviour* STRANGE, odd, peculiar, funny, unusual, bizarre, weird, eccentric,

queer, unexpected, unfamiliar, extraordinary, abnormal, out of the ordinary, anomalous, surprising, incongruous, unconventional, offbeat, unorthodox.
– OPPOSITES: uninterested, ordinary.

curl ▶ verb **1** *smoke curled up from his cigarette* SPIRAL, coil, wreathe, twirl, swirl; wind, curve, bend, twist (and turn), loop, meander, snake, corkscrew, zigzag. **2** *Ruth curled her arms around his neck* WIND, twine, entwine, wrap. **3** *she washed and curled my hair* CRIMP, perm, wave. **4** *they curled up together on the sofa* NESTLE, snuggle, cuddle.
▶ noun **1** *the tangled curls of her hair* RINGLET, corkscrew, kink, wave; kiss-curl. **2** *a curl of smoke* SPIRAL, coil, twirl, swirl, twist, corkscrew, curlicue, helix.

curling ▶ noun THE ROARING GAME; jam-pail curling. See table.

Curling Terms

Players	Items
lead	broom
second	brush
third (vice-skip)	button
skip	cock
spare	corn broom
sweeper	end
	extra end
Actions	granite
bite	guard
blank	hack
burn	hammer
cold draw	hog line
double takeout	home ice
draw	house
freeze	pebble
heading home	rock
hit and stay/stick	sheet
hit and roll	shot rock
in-turn	skip rock
out-turn	stone
peel	tee
raise	fast ice
rink	keen ice
sweep	swingy ice
takeout	
	Competitions
	Brier ♣
	bonspiel
	carspiel
	cashspiel
	Silver Broom ♣hist.

curly ▶ adjective WAVY, curling, curled, ringlety, crimped, permed, frizzy, kinky, corkscrew.
– OPPOSITES: straight.

curmudgeon ▶ noun See GROUCH.

currency ▶ noun **1** *foreign currency* MONEY, legal tender, cash, banknotes, bills, notes, coins, coinage, specie. **2** *a term which has gained new currency* PREVALENCE, circulation, exposure; acceptance, popularity.

current ▶ adjective **1** *current events* CONTEMPORARY, present-day, modern, present, contemporaneous; topical, in the news, live, burning. **2** *the idea is still current* PREVALENT, prevailing, common, accepted, in circulation, circulating, on everyone's lips, popular, widespread. **3** *a current driver's licence* VALID, usable,

up-to-date. **4** *the current prime minister* INCUMBENT, present, in office, in power; reigning.
– OPPOSITES: past, out of date, former.
▶ noun **1** *a current of air* FLOW, stream, backdraft, slipstream; airstream, thermal, updraft, draft; undercurrent, undertow, tide. **2** *the current of human life* COURSE, progress, progression, flow, tide, movement. **3** *the current of opinion* TREND, drift, direction, tendency.

curriculum ▶ noun SYLLABUS, course/program of study, subjects, modules.

curse ▶ noun **1** *she put a curse on him* MALEDICTION, the evil eye, hex, jinx; *formal* imprecation; *literary* anathema. **2** *the curse of racism* EVIL, blight, scourge, plague, cancer, canker, poison. **3** *the curse of unemployment* AFFLICTION, burden, cross to bear, bane. **4** *muffled curses* SWEAR WORD, expletive, oath, profanity, four-letter word, dirty word, obscenity, blasphemy; *informal* cuss, cuss word; *formal* imprecation.
▶ verb **1** *it seemed as if the family had been cursed* PUT A CURSE ON, put the evil eye on, anathematize, damn, hex, jinx; *archaic* imprecate. **2** *she was cursed with feelings of inadequacy* AFFLICT, trouble, plague, bedevil. **3** *drivers cursed and honked their horns* SWEAR, blaspheme, take the Lord's name in vain; *informal* cuss; *archaic* execrate.

cursed ▶ adjective **1** *a cursed city* UNDER A CURSE, damned, doomed, ill-fated, ill-starred, jinxed, blighted; *literary* accursed, star-crossed. **2** (*informal, dated*) *those cursed children.* See ANNOYING.

cursory ▶ adjective PERFUNCTORY, desultory, casual, superficial, token; hasty, quick, hurried, rapid, brief, passing, fleeting.
– OPPOSITES: thorough.

curt ▶ adjective TERSE, brusque, abrupt, clipped, blunt, short, monosyllabic, summary; snappish, snappy, sharp, tart; gruff, offhand, unceremonious, ungracious, rude, impolite, discourteous, uncivil.
– OPPOSITES: expansive.

curtail ▶ verb **1** *economic policies designed to curtail spending* REDUCE, cut, cut down, decrease, lessen, pare down, trim, retrench; restrict, limit, curb, rein in; *informal* slash. **2** *his visit was curtailed* SHORTEN, cut short, truncate.
– OPPOSITES: increase, lengthen.

curtain ▶ noun *he drew the curtains* DRAPE, drapery, window treatment, window hanging, screen, blind(s), shade; valance, topper, café curtain.
▶ verb *the bed was curtained off from the rest of the room* CONCEAL, hide, screen, shield; separate, isolate.

curtsy ▶ verb *she curtsied to the king* BEND ONE'S KNEE, drop/bob a curtsy.
▶ noun *she made a curtsy* BOB, obeisance.

curvaceous ▶ adjective SHAPELY, voluptuous, sexy, full-figured, buxom, full-bosomed, bosomy, Junoesque; cuddly; *informal* curvy, well endowed, pneumatic, busty, built, stacked.
– OPPOSITES: skinny.

curve ▶ noun *the serpentine curves of the river* BEND, turn, loop, curl, twist, hook; arc, arch, bow, undulation, curvature, meander.
– RELATED TERMS: sinuous.
▶ verb *the road curved back on itself* BEND, turn, loop, wind, meander, undulate, snake, spiral, twist, coil, curl; arc, arch.

curved ▶ adjective BENT, arched, bowed, crescent,

curving, wavy, sinuous, serpentine, meandering, undulating, curvilinear, curvy.
– OPPOSITES: straight.

cushion ▶ noun *a cushion against inflation* PROTECTION, buffer, shield, defence, bulwark.
▶ verb **1** *she cushioned her head on her arms* SUPPORT, cradle, prop (up), rest. **2** *to cushion the blow, wages and pensions were increased* SOFTEN, lessen, diminish, decrease, mitigate, temper, allay, alleviate, take the edge off, dull, deaden. **3** *residents are cushioned from the outside world* PROTECT, shield, shelter, cocoon.

cushy ▶ adjective *(informal) a cushy job* EASY, undemanding; comfortable, secure.
– OPPOSITES: difficult.

custodian ▶ noun **1** *the school custodian* CARETAKER, janitor, superintendent, super. **2** *the custodian of the relic* keeper, guardian, steward, protector.

custody ▶ noun *the parent who has custody of the child* CARE, guardianship, charge, keeping, safekeeping, wardship, responsibility, protection, tutelage; custodianship, trusteeship.
■ **in custody** IN PRISON, in jail, imprisoned, incarcerated, locked up, under lock and key, interned, detained; on remand; *informal* behind bars, doing time, inside; in closed custody ♣, in secure custody ♣, in open custody ♣.

custom ▶ noun **1** *his unfamiliarity with the local customs* TRADITION, practice, usage, observance, way, convention, formality, ceremony, ritual; sacred cow, unwritten rule; mores; *formal* praxis. **2** *it is our custom to visit the Ottawa valley in October* HABIT, practice, routine, way, wont; policy, rule.

customarily ▶ adverb USUALLY, traditionally, normally, as a rule, generally, ordinarily, commonly; habitually, routinely.
– OPPOSITES: occasionally.

customary ▶ adjective **1** *customary social practices* USUAL, traditional, normal, conventional, familiar, accepted, routine, established, time-honoured, regular, prevailing. **2** *her customary good sense* USUAL, accustomed, habitual, wonted.
– OPPOSITES: unusual.

customer ▶ noun CONSUMER, buyer, purchaser, patron, client, subscriber; shopper.

customs ▶ plural noun. *See* TAX *noun* sense 1.

cut ▶ verb **1** *the knife slipped and cut his finger* GASH, slash, lacerate, sever, slit, pierce, penetrate, wound, injure; scratch, graze, nick, incise, score; lance. **2** *cut the pepper into small pieces* CHOP, cut up, slice, dice, cube, mince; carve, hash. **3** *cut back the new growth to about half its length* TRIM, snip, clip, crop, barber, shear, shave; pare; prune, poll, lop, dock; mow. **4** *I went to cut some flowers* PICK, pluck, gather; *literary* cull. **5** *lettering had been cut into the stonework* CARVE, engrave, incise, etch, score; chisel, whittle. **6** *the government cut public spending* REDUCE, cut back/down on, decrease, lessen, retrench, trim, slim down; rationalize, downsize, lower, slash, chop. **7** *the text has been substantially cut* SHORTEN, abridge, condense, abbreviate, truncate; edit; bowdlerize, expurgate. **8** *you need to cut at least ten lines per page* DELETE, remove, take out, excise, blue-pencil, chop. **9** *oil supplies to the area had been cut* DISCONTINUE, break off, suspend, interrupt; stop, end, put an end to. **10** *the point where the line cuts the vertical axis* CROSS, intersect, bisect; meet, join. **11** *she was suspended for cutting classes* SKIP, miss, ditch, play truant from, (*Ont.*) skip off ♣, (*West*) skip out ♣, play hooky from.
▶ noun **1** *a cut on his jaw* GASH, slash, laceration,

incision, wound, injury; scratch, graze, nick. **2** *a cut of beef* JOINT, piece, section. **3** (*informal*) *the directors are demanding their cut* SHARE, portion, bit, quota, percentage; *informal* slice, piece of the pie, rake-off, piece of the action. **4** *his hair was in need of a cut* HAIRCUT, trim, clip, crop. **5** *a smart cut of the whip* BLOW, slash, stroke. **6** *he followed this with the unkindest cut of all* INSULT, slight, affront, slap in the face, jibe, barb, cutting remark, put-down, dig. **7** *a cut in interest rates* REDUCTION, cutback, decrease, lessening, rollback. **8** *the elegant cut of his jacket* STYLE, design; tailoring, lines, fit.
■ **cut back** *companies cut back on foreign investment* REDUCE, cut, cut down on, decrease, lessen, retrench, economize on, trim, slim down, scale down; rationalize, downsize, pull/draw in one's horns, tighten one's belt; *informal* slash.
■ **cut someone/something down 1** *24 hectares of trees were cut down* FELL, chop down, hack down, saw down, hew. **2** *he was cut down in his prime* KILL, slaughter, shoot down, mow down, gun down; *informal* take out, blow away; *literary* slay.
■ **cut and dried** DEFINITE, decided, settled, explicit, specific, precise, unambiguous, clear-cut, unequivocal, black and white, hard and fast.
■ **cut in** INTERRUPT, butt in, break in, interject, interpose, chime in.
■ **cut someone/something off 1** *they cut off his finger* SEVER, chop off, hack off; amputate. **2** *oil and gas supplies were cut off* DISCONTINUE, break off, disconnect, suspend; stop, end, bring to an end. **3** *a community cut off from the mainland by the flood waters* ISOLATE, separate, keep apart; seclude, closet, cloister, sequester.
■ **cut out** STOP WORKING, stop, fail, give out, break down; *informal* die, give up the ghost, conk out.
■ **cut someone/something out 1** *cut out all the diseased wood* REMOVE, take out, excise, extract; snip out, clip out. **2** *it's best to cut out alcohol altogether* GIVE UP, refrain from, abstain from, go without; *informal* quit, leave off, pack in, lay off, knock off. **3** *his mother cut him out of her will* EXCLUDE, leave out, omit, eliminate.
■ **cut something short** BREAK OFF, shorten, truncate, curtail, terminate, end, stop, abort, bring to an untimely end.
■ **cut someone short** INTERRUPT, cut off, butt in on, break in on.

cutback ▶ noun REDUCTION, cut, decrease; economy, saving, rollback.
– OPPOSITES: increase.

cute ▶ adjective **1** *a cute baby* ENDEARING, adorable, lovable, sweet, lovely, appealing, engaging, delightful, dear, darling, winning, winsome, attractive, pretty; *informal* cutesy, twee. **2** *a cute guy* GOOD-LOOKING, handsome, attractive, gorgeous.

cut-rate ▶ adjective CHEAP, marked down, reduced, discount, bargain.

cutthroat ▶ noun (*dated*) *a band of robbers and cutthroats* MURDERER, killer, assassin; *informal* hit-man.
▶ adjective *cutthroat competition between rival firms* RUTHLESS, merciless, fierce, intense, aggressive, dog-eat-dog.

cutting ▶ noun **1** *plant cuttings* SCION, slip; graft. **2** *fabric cuttings* PIECE, bit, fragment; trimming.
▶ adjective **1** *a cutting remark* HURTFUL, wounding, barbed, pointed, scathing, acerbic, mordant, caustic, acid, sarcastic, sardonic, snide, spiteful, malicious, mean, nasty, cruel, unkind; *informal* bitchy, catty,

snarky. **2** *cutting winter winds* ICY, icy-cold, freezing, arctic, Siberian, glacial, hypothermic, bitter, chilling, chilly, chill; biting, piercing, penetrating, raw, keen, sharp.
— OPPOSITES: friendly, warm.

cyber ▶ **adjective** ELECTRONIC, digital, wired, virtual, web, Internet, Net, online.

cycle ▶ **noun 1** *the cycle of birth, death, and rebirth* ROUND, rotation; pattern, rhythm. **2** *the painting is one of a cycle of seven* SERIES, sequence, succession, run; set.
▶ **verb** *Patrick cycled 10 miles each day* RIDE (A BICYCLE), bike, pedal.

cyclical ▶ **adjective** RECURRENT, recurring, regular, repeated; periodic, seasonal, circular.

cyclone ▶ **noun** HURRICANE, typhoon, tropical storm, storm, tornado, windstorm, whirlwind, tempest, twister, dust devil.

cynic ▶ **noun** SKEPTIC, doubter, doubting Thomas; pessimist, prophet of doom, doomsayer, Cassandra, Chicken Little.
— OPPOSITES: idealist, Pollyanna.

cynical ▶ **adjective** SKEPTICAL, doubtful, distrustful, suspicious, disbelieving; pessimistic, negative, world-weary, disillusioned, disenchanted, jaundiced, sardonic.
— OPPOSITES: idealistic.

cynicism ▶ **noun** SKEPTICISM, doubt, distrust, mistrust, suspicion, disbelief; pessimism, negativity, world-weariness, disenchantment.
— OPPOSITES: idealism.

cyst ▶ **noun** GROWTH, lump; abscess, wen, boil, carbuncle, polyp, humour.

Dd

dab ▶ verb *she dabbed disinfectant on the cut* PAT, press, touch, blot, mop, swab; daub, apply, wipe, stroke.
▶ noun 1 *a dab of glue* DROP, spot, smear, splash, speck, taste, trace, touch, hint, bit; *informal* smidgen, tad, lick. 2 *apply concealer with light dabs* PAT, touch, blot, wipe.

dabble ▶ verb 1 *they dabbled their feet in rock pools* SPLASH, dip, paddle, trail; immerse. 2 *he dabbled in politics* TOY WITH, dip into, flirt with, tinker with, trifle with, play with, dally with.

dabbler ▶ noun AMATEUR, dilettante, layman, layperson; trifler, non-professional, non-specialist.
— OPPOSITES: professional.

daemon ▶ noun NUMEN, genius (loci), attendant spirit, tutelary spirit, demon.

daft ▶ adjective 1 *a daft idea* ABSURD, preposterous, ridiculous, ludicrous, farcical, laughable; idiotic, stupid, foolish, silly, inane, fatuous, hare-brained, cockamamie, half-baked, crazy, cockeyed. 2 *are you daft?* SIMPLE-MINDED, stupid, idiotic, slow, witless, feeble-minded, empty-headed, vacuous, vapid; unhinged, insane, mad; *informal* thick, dim, dopey, dumb, dim-witted, halfwitted, birdbrained, pea-brained, slow on the uptake, soft in the head, brain-dead, not all there, touched, crazy, mental, nuts, batty, bonkers, crackers, dumb-ass.
— OPPOSITES: sensible.

daily ▶ adjective *a daily event* EVERYDAY, day-to-day, quotidian, diurnal, circadian.
▶ adverb *the museum is open daily* EVERY DAY, once a day, day after day, diurnally.

dainty ▶ adjective 1 *a dainty china cup* DELICATE, fine, neat, elegant, exquisite. 2 *a dainty morsel* TASTY, delicious, choice, palatable, luscious, mouth-watering, delectable, toothsome; appetizing, inviting, tempting; *informal* scrumptious, yummy, finger-licking, melt-in-your/the-mouth. 3 *a dainty eater* FASTIDIOUS, fussy, finicky, particular, discriminating; *informal* choosy, pernickety, persnickety, picky.
— OPPOSITES: unwieldy, unpalatable, undiscriminating.
▶ noun *homemade dainties* DELICACY, tidbit, fancy, luxury, treat; nibble, savoury, appetizer; confection, bonbon, goody, square; *archaic* sweetmeat.

dais ▶ noun PLATFORM, stage, podium, rostrum, stand, apron; soapbox.

dale ▶ noun VALLEY, vale; hollow, basin, gully, gorge, ravine, glen; *literary* dell.

dally ▶ verb 1 *don't dally on the way to work* DAWDLE, delay, loiter, linger, waste time; lag, trail, straggle, fall behind; amble, meander, drift; *informal* dilly-dally; *archaic* tarry. 2 *he likes dallying with film stars* TRIFLE, toy, amuse oneself, flirt, play fast and loose, philander, carry on, play around.
— OPPOSITES: hurry.

dam ▶ noun *the dam burst* BARRAGE, barrier, wall, embankment, barricade, obstruction.

▶ verb *the river was dammed* BLOCK (UP), obstruct, bung up, close; *technical* occlude.

damage ▶ noun 1 *did the thieves do any damage?* HARM, destruction, vandalism; injury, impairment, desecration, vitiation, detriment; ruin, havoc, devastation. 2 (*informal*) *what's the damage?* COST, price, expense, charge, total. 3 *she won $4,300 damages* COMPENSATION, recompense, restitution, redress, reparation(s); indemnification, indemnity.
▶ verb *the parcel had been damaged* HARM, deface, mutilate, mangle, impair, injure, disfigure, vandalize; tamper with, sabotage; ruin, destroy, wreck, trash; *formal* vitiate.
— OPPOSITES: repair.

damaging ▶ adjective HARMFUL, detrimental, injurious, hurtful, inimical, dangerous, destructive, ruinous, deleterious; bad, malign, adverse, undesirable, prejudicial, unfavourable; unhealthy, unwholesome.
— OPPOSITES: beneficial.

damn ▶ verb 1 *they were all damning him* CURSE, put the evil eye on, anathematize, hex, jinx. 2 *we are not going to damn the new product before we try it* CONDEMN, censure, criticize, attack, denounce, revile; find fault with, deprecate, disparage; *informal* slam, lay into, blast.
— OPPOSITES: bless, praise.
▶ noun (*informal*) *it's not worth a damn* JOT, whit, iota, rap, scrap, bit; *informal* hoot, two hoots.
▶ exclamation DARN, drat, shoot, blast, doggone, goddammit, hell, rats, bugger, geez, tarnation, sugar, fuddle duddle ✤, fiddlesticks.
■ **give a damn** CARE, mind, concern oneself, give a hoot.

damnable ▶ adjective *a damnable nuisance* UNPLEASANT, disagreeable, objectionable, horrible, horrid, awful, nasty, dreadful, terrible; annoying, irritating, maddening, exasperating; hateful, detestable, loathsome, abominable, beastly.

damned ▶ adjective 1 *damned souls* CURSED, doomed, lost, condemned to hell; anathematized; *literary* accursed. 2 (*informal*) *this damned car won't start* BLASTED, damn, damnable, Christly, confounded, rotten, wretched; *informal* blessed, bloody, jeezly ✤; *dated* accursed.

damning ▶ adjective INCRIMINATING, condemnatory, damnatory; damaging, derogatory; conclusive, strong.

damp ▶ adjective *her hair was damp* MOIST, moistened, wettish, dampened, dampish; humid, steamy, muggy, clammy, sweaty, sticky, dank, moisture-laden, wet, wetted, rainy, drizzly, showery, misty, foggy, vaporous, dewy.
— OPPOSITES: dry.
▶ noun *the damp in the air* MOISTURE, dampness, humidity, wetness, wet, water, condensation, steam, vapour; clamminess, dankness; rain, dew, drizzle, precipitation, spray; perspiration, sweat.
— OPPOSITES: dryness.

Dances

Dance Forms	Historical/Folk Dances	Social Dances	
ballet	allemande	barn dance	shuffle
ballroom	bolero	beguine	skank
belly dancing	bourrée	bird dance	slam dance
breakdancing	bourrée	boogaloo	snake dance
butoh	cachucha	bossa nova	stomp
cancan	cancan	butterfly ♣	strathspey
Celtic dancing	chaconne	cakewalk	tango
character dancing	clog dance	carioca	Tush Push
contra	contredanse	cha-cha	twist
Cossack dancing	cotillion	Charleston	two-step
dancesport	country dance	conga	Virginia reel
flamenco	courante	disco	waltz
folk dancing	czardas	eightsome reel	**Dancing Events**
Highland dancing	fan dance	foxtrot	ball
Irish dancing	fandango	hokey-pokey	barn dance
jazz	farandole	hustle	cotillion
Kathak	galliard	jig	grad ♣
line dancing	galop	jitterbug	hoedown
modern dance	gavotte	jive	prom
round dancing	habanera	lambada	rave
soft shoe	Highland fling	limbo	social ♣(Prairies)
square dancing	hopak	lindy (hop)	sock hop
step dance	hora	line dance	stag and doe ♣(Ont.)
swing	hornpipe	Macarena	tea dance
tap dance	hula	mambo	
Aboriginal Dances	ländler	merengue	
chicken scratch	lion dance	paso doble	
drum dance ♣	mazurka	pogo	
grass dance	minuet	polka	
hamatsa	morris dance	quickstep	
hoop dance	musette	reel	
rain dance	pavane	rumba	
Red River jig ♣	polonaise	salsa	
sun dance	quadrille	samba	
war dance	saraband	schottische	
	sword dance	shimmy	
	tarantella		

▶ **verb 1** *sweat damped his hair.* See DAMPEN sense 1. **2** *nothing damped my enthusiasm.* See DAMPEN sense 2.

dampen ▶ **verb 1** *the rain dampened her face* MOISTEN, damp, wet, dew, water; *literary* bedew. **2** *nothing could dampen her enthusiasm* LESSEN, decrease, diminish, reduce, moderate, damp, put a damper on, throw cold water on, cool, discourage; suppress, extinguish, quench, stifle, curb, limit, check, restrain, inhibit, deter.
– OPPOSITES: dry, heighten.

damper ▶ **noun** CURB, check, restraint, restriction, limit, limitation, constraint, rein, brake, control, impediment; chill, pall, gloom.

dampness ▶ **noun**. See DAMP noun.

damsel ▶ **noun** (*literary*). See GIRL sense 2.

dance ▶ **verb 1** *he danced with Katherine* sway, trip, twirl, whirl, pirouette, gyrate; *informal* bop, disco, rock, boogie, shake a leg, hoof it, cut a/the rug, trip the light fantastic, get down, mosh, groove. **2** *little girls danced around me* CAPER, cavort, frisk, frolic, skip, prance, gambol, jig; leap, jump, hop, bounce. **3** *flames danced in the fireplace* FLICKER, leap, dart, play, flit, quiver; twinkle, shimmer.
▶ **noun** *they met at a dance* BALL, masquerade, prom, hoedown, disco, (sock) hop. *See the tables here and at* BALLET.

dancer ▶ **noun** danseur, danseuse, ballerina, prima ballerina, premier danseur, danseur noble; *informal* hoofer.

dandle ▶ **verb** BOUNCE, jiggle, dance, rock.

dandy ▶ **noun** *he became something of a dandy* FOP, man about town, glamour boy, rake; *informal* sharp dresser, snappy dresser, trendy, dude, pretty boy; *informal, dated* swell; *dated* beau; *archaic* buck, coxcomb, popinjay.
▶ **adjective** (*informal*) *our trip was dandy.* See EXCELLENT.

danger ▶ **noun 1** *an element of danger* PERIL, hazard, risk, jeopardy; perilousness, riskiness, precariousness, uncertainty, instability, insecurity. **2** *that car is a danger on the roads* MENACE, hazard, threat, risk; death trap, widow-maker. **3** *a serious danger of fire* POSSIBILITY, chance, risk, probability, likelihood, fear, prospect.
– OPPOSITES: safety.

dangerous ▶ **adjective 1** *a dangerous animal* MENACING, threatening, treacherous; savage, wild, vicious, murderous, desperate. **2** *dangerous wiring* HAZARDOUS, perilous, risky, high-risk, unsafe, unpredictable, precarious, insecure, touch-and-go, chancy, treacherous; *informal* dicey, hairy.
– OPPOSITES: harmless, safe.

dangle ▶ **verb 1** *a chain dangled from his belt* HANG (DOWN), droop, swing, sway, wave, trail, stream. **2** *he dangled the keys* WAVE, swing, jiggle, brandish, flourish. **3** *he dangled money in front of the locals* OFFER, hold out; entice someone with, tempt someone with.

dangling ▶ adjective HANGING, drooping, droopy, suspended, pendulous, pendent, trailing, flowing, tumbling.

dank ▶ adjective DAMP, musty, chilly, clammy, moist, wet, unaired, humid.
— OPPOSITES: dry.

dapper ▶ adjective SMART, spruce, trim, debonair, neat, well-dressed, well-groomed, well turned out, elegant, chic, dashing; informal snazzy, snappy, natty, sharp, spiffy, fly.
— OPPOSITES: scruffy.

dapple ▶ verb DOT, spot, fleck, streak, speck, speckle, mottle, marble.

dappled ▶ adjective SPECKLED, blotched, blotchy, spotted, spotty, dotted, mottled, marbled, flecked, freckled; piebald, pied, brindle, pinto, tabby, calico; patchy, variegated; informal splotchy.

dare ▶ verb **1** nobody dared to say a word BE BRAVE ENOUGH, have the courage; venture, have the nerve, have the temerity, be so bold as, have the audacity; risk, hazard, take the liberty of, stick one's neck out, go out on a limb. **2** she dared him to go CHALLENGE, defy, invite, bid, provoke, goad; throw down the gauntlet.
▶ noun she accepted the dare CHALLENGE, provocation, goad; gauntlet, invitation.

daredevil ▶ noun a young daredevil crashed his car MADCAP, hothead, adventurer, thrill-seeker, exhibitionist, swashbuckler; stuntman; informal show-off.
▶ adjective a daredevil skydiver DARING, bold, audacious, intrepid, fearless, madcap, dauntless; heedless, reckless, rash, impulsive, impetuous, foolhardy, incautious, imprudent, harum-scarum.
— OPPOSITES: cowardly, cautious.

daring ▶ adjective a daring attack BOLD, audacious, intrepid, venturesome, fearless, brave, unafraid, undaunted, dauntless, valiant, valorous, heroic, dashing; madcap, rash, reckless, heedless; informal gutsy, spunky, ballsy.
▶ noun his sheer daring BOLDNESS, audacity, temerity, fearlessness, intrepidity, bravery, courage, valour, heroism, pluck, spirit, mettle; recklessness, rashness, foolhardiness; informal nerve, guts, spunk, grit, moxie, sand, balls.

dark ▶ adjective **1** a dark night BLACK, pitch-black, jet-black, inky; unlit, unilluminated; starless, moonless; dingy, gloomy, dusky, shadowy, shady; literary Stygian. **2** a dark secret MYSTERIOUS, secret, hidden, concealed, veiled, covert, clandestine; enigmatic, arcane, esoteric, obscure, abstruse, impenetrable, incomprehensible, cryptic. **3** dark hair BRUNETTE, dark brown, chestnut, sable, jet-black, ebony. **4** dark skin SWARTHY, dusky, olive, brown, black, ebony; tanned, bronzed. **5** dark days TRAGIC, disastrous, calamitous, catastrophic, cataclysmic; dire, awful, terrible, dreadful, horrible, horrendous, atrocious, nightmarish, harrowing; wretched, woeful. **6** dark thoughts GLOOMY, dismal, pessimistic, negative, downbeat, bleak, grim, fatalistic, black, sombre, despairing, despondent, hopeless, cheerless, melancholy, glum, grave, morose, mournful, doleful. **7** a dark look MOODY, brooding, sullen, dour, scowling, glowering, angry, forbidding, threatening, ominous. **8** dark deeds EVIL, wicked, sinful, immoral, bad, iniquitous, ungodly, unholy, base; vile, unspeakable, sinister, foul, monstrous, shocking, atrocious, abominable, hateful, despicable, odious, horrible, heinous, execrable, diabolical, fiendish, murderous, barbarous, black; sordid, degenerate, depraved;

dishonourable, dishonest, unscrupulous; informal lowdown, dirty, crooked, shady.
— OPPOSITES: bright, blond, pale, happy, good.
▶ noun **1** he's afraid of the dark DARKNESS, blackness, gloom, murkiness, shadow, shade; dusk, twilight, gloaming. **2** she went out after dark NIGHT, nighttime, darkness; nightfall, evening, twilight, sunset.
— OPPOSITES: light, day.
■ **in the dark** (informal) UNAWARE, ignorant, incognizant, oblivious, uninformed, unenlightened, unacquainted, unconversant.

darken ▶ verb **1** the sky darkened GROW DARK, blacken, dim, cloud over, lower; shade, fog. **2** his mood darkened BLACKEN, become angry, become annoyed; sadden, become gloomy, become unhappy, become depressed, become dejected, become dispirited, become troubled.

darkness ▶ noun **1** lights shone in the darkness DARK, blackness, gloom, dimness, murkiness, shadow, shade; dusk, twilight, gloaming. **2** darkness fell NIGHT, nighttime, dark. **3** the forces of darkness EVIL, wickedness, sin, iniquity, immorality; devilry, the Devil.

darling ▶ noun **1** good night, my darling DEAR, dearest, love, lover, sweetheart, sweet, beloved; informal honey, hon, angel, pet, sweetie, sugar, babe, baby, treasure. **2** the darling of the media FAVOURITE, pet, idol, hero, heroine; informal blue-eyed boy/girl.
▶ adjective **1** his darling wife DEAR, dearest, precious, adored, loved, beloved, cherished, treasured, esteemed, worshipped. **2** a darling little hat ADORABLE, appealing, charming, cute, sweet, enchanting, bewitching, endearing, dear, delightful, lovely, beautiful, attractive, gorgeous, fetching; Scottish bonny.

darn ▶ verb he was darning his socks MEND, repair, reinforce; sew up, stitch, patch.
▶ noun a sweater with darns in the elbows PATCH, repair, reinforcement, stitch.
▶ exclamation DAMN, drat, shoot, blast, doggone, goddammit, hell, rats, bugger, geez, tarnation, sugar, fuddle duddle ✦, fiddlesticks.

dart ▶ noun **1** a poisoned dart SMALL ARROW, flechette, missile, projectile. **2** she made a dart for the door DASH, rush, run, bolt, break, start, charge, sprint, bound, leap, dive; scurry, scamper, scramble.
▶ verb **1** Karl darted across the road DASH, rush, tear, run, bolt, fly, shoot, charge, race, sprint, bound, leap, dive, gallop, scurry, scamper, scramble; informal scoot. **2** he darted a glance at her DIRECT, cast, throw, shoot, send, flash.

dash ▶ verb **1** he dashed home RUSH, race, run, sprint, bolt, dart, gallop, career, charge, shoot, hurtle, careen, hare, fly, speed, zoom, scurry, scuttle, scamper; informal tear, belt, pelt, scoot, zip, whip, hotfoot it, leg it, bomb, barrel, beetle. **2** he dashed the glass to the ground HURL, smash, crash, slam, throw, toss, fling, pitch, cast, project, propel, send; informal chuck, heave, sling, peg, West huck ✦. **3** rain dashed against the walls BE HURLED, crash, smash; batter, strike, beat, pound, lash. **4** her hopes were dashed SHATTER, destroy, wreck, ruin, crush, devastate, demolish, blight, overturn, scotch, spoil, frustrate, thwart, check; informal blow a hole in, put paid to, scupper, scuttle.
— OPPOSITES: dawdle, raise.
▶ noun **1** a dash for the door RUSH, race, run, sprint, bolt, dart, leap, charge, bound, break; scramble. **2** a dash of salt PINCH, touch, sprinkle, taste, spot, drop, dab,

speck, smattering, sprinkling, splash, bit, modicum, little; *informal* smidgen, tad, lick. **3** *he led off with such dash* VERVE, style, flamboyance, gusto, zest, confidence, self-assurance, élan, flair, vigour, vivacity, sparkle, brio, panache, éclat, vitality, dynamism; *informal* pizzazz, pep, oomph.

dashing ▶ adjective **1** *a dashing pilot* DEBONAIR, devil-may-care, raffish, sporty, spirited, lively, dazzling, energetic, animated, exuberant, flamboyant, dynamic, bold, intrepid, daring, adventurous, plucky, swashbuckling; romantic, attractive, gallant. **2** *he looked exceptionally dashing* STYLISH, smart, elegant, chic, dapper, spruce, trim, debonair; fashionable, modish, voguish; *informal* trendy, with it, hip, sharp, snazzy, classy, natty, swish, fly, spiffy.

dastardly ▶ adjective (*dated*) WICKED, evil, heinous, villainous, diabolical, fiendish, barbarous, cruel, black, dark, rotten, vile, monstrous, abominable, despicable, degenerate, sordid; bad, base, mean, low, dishonourable, dishonest, unscrupulous, unprincipled; *informal* lowdown, dirty, shady, rascally, scoundrelly, crooked; beastly.
— OPPOSITES: noble.

data ▶ noun FACTS, figures, statistics, details, particulars, specifics; information, intelligence, material, input; *informal* info.

date ▶ noun **1** *the only date he has to remember* DAY (OF THE MONTH), occasion, time; year; anniversary. **2** *a later date is suggested for this piece* AGE, time, period, era, epoch, century, decade, year. **3** *a lunch date* APPOINTMENT, meeting, engagement, rendezvous, assignation; commitment. **4** (*informal*) *he's my date for tonight* PARTNER, escort, girlfriend, boyfriend, steady. ▶ verb **1** *the sculpture can be dated accurately* ASSIGN A DATE TO, ascertain the date of, put a date on. **2** *the building dates from the 16th century* WAS MADE IN, was built in, originates in, comes from, belongs to, goes back to. **3** *the best films don't date* BECOME OLD-FASHIONED, become outmoded, become dated, show its age. **4** (*informal*) *he's dating Jill* GO OUT WITH, take out, go around with, be involved with, see, woo, go steady with; *dated* court.
■ **to date** SO FAR, thus far, yet, as yet, up to now, till now, until now, up to the present (time), hitherto.

dated ▶ adjective OLD-FASHIONED, outdated, outmoded, passé, behind the times, archaic, obsolete, antiquated; unfashionable, unstylish, untrendy; crusty, olde worlde, prehistoric, antediluvian; *informal* old hat, out, uncool.
— OPPOSITES: modern.

daub ▶ verb *he daubed a rock with paint* SMEAR, bedaub, plaster, splash, spatter, splatter, cake, cover, smother, coat.
▶ noun *daubs of paint* SMEAR, smudge, splash, blot, spot, patch, blotch, splotch.

daughter ▶ noun FEMALE CHILD, girl.

daunt ▶ verb DISCOURAGE, deter, demoralize, put off, dishearten, dispirit; intimidate, abash, take aback, throw, cow, overawe, awe, frighten, scare, unman, dismay, disconcert, discompose, perturb, unsettle, unnerve; throw off balance; *informal* rattle, faze, shake up.
— OPPOSITES: hearten.

dauntless ▶ adjective FEARLESS, determined, resolute, indomitable, intrepid, doughty, plucky, spirited, mettlesome; undaunted, undismayed, unflinching, unshrinking, bold, audacious, valiant,

brave, courageous, daring; *informal* gutsy, spunky, feisty.

dawdle ▶ verb **1** *they dawdled over breakfast* LINGER, dally, take one's time, be slow, waste time, idle; delay, procrastinate, stall, dilly-dally, lallygag; *archaic* tarry. **2** *Ruth dawdled home* AMBLE, stroll, trail, walk slowly, move at a snail's pace; *informal* mosey, toodle.
— OPPOSITES: hurry.

dawn ▶ noun **1** *we got up at dawn* DAYBREAK, sunrise, first light, daylight, cock crow; first thing in the morning, sun-up. **2** *the dawn of civilization* BEGINNING, start, birth, inception, origination, genesis, emergence, advent, appearance, arrival, dawning, rise, origin, onset; unfolding, development, infancy; *informal* kickoff.
— OPPOSITES: dusk, end.
▶ verb **1** *Thursday dawned crisp and sunny* BEGIN, break, arrive, emerge. **2** *a bright new future has dawned* BEGIN, start, commence, be born, appear, arrive, emerge; arise, rise, break, unfold, develop. **3** *the reality dawned on him* OCCUR TO, come to, strike, hit, enter someone's mind, register with, enter someone's consciousness, cross someone's mind, suggest itself.
— OPPOSITES: end.

day ▶ noun **1** *I stayed for a day* TWENTY-FOUR-HOUR PERIOD, twenty-four hours. **2** *enjoy the beach during the day* DAYTIME, daylight; waking hours. **3** *the leading architect of the day* PERIOD, time, age, era, generation. **4** *in his day he had great influence* HEYDAY, prime, time; peak, height, zenith, ascendancy; youth, springtime, salad days.
— RELATED TERMS: diurnal.
— OPPOSITES: night, decline.
■ **day after day** REPEATEDLY, again and again, over and over (again), time and (time) again, frequently, often, time after time; {day in, day out}, night and day, all the time; persistently, recurrently, constantly, continuously, continually, relentlessly, regularly, habitually, unfailingly, always, oftentimes; *informal* 24-7; *literary* oft, oft-times.
■ **day by day 1** *day by day they were forced to retreat* GRADUALLY, slowly, progressively; bit by bit, inch by inch, little by little. **2** *they follow the news day by day* DAILY, every day, day after day; diurnally.
■ **day in, day out** See DAY AFTER DAY.

daybreak ▶ noun DAWN, crack of dawn, sunrise, first light, first thing in the morning, cock crow; daylight, sun-up.
— OPPOSITES: nightfall.

daydream ▶ noun **1** *she was lost in a daydream* REVERIE, trance, fantasy, vision, fancy, brown study; inattentiveness, woolgathering, preoccupation, absorption, self-absorption, absent-mindedness, abstraction. **2** *a big house was one of her daydreams* DREAM, pipe dream, fantasy, castle in the air, fond hope; wishful thinking; *informal* pie in the sky.
▶ verb *stop daydreaming!* DREAM, muse, stare into space; fantasize, build castles in the air.

daydreamer ▶ noun DREAMER, fantasist, fantasizer, romantic, wishful thinker, idealist; visionary, theorizer, Utopian, Walter Mitty.

daylight ▶ noun **1** *do the test in daylight* NATURAL LIGHT, sunlight. **2** *she only went there in daylight* DAYTIME, day; broad daylight. **3** *police moved in at daylight* DAWN, daybreak, break of day, crack of dawn, sunrise, first light, first thing in the morning, early morning, cock crow, sun-up.
— OPPOSITES: darkness, nighttime, nightfall.

day-to-day ▶ adjective REGULAR, everyday, daily,

routine, habitual, frequent, normal, standard, usual, typical.

daze ▶ verb 1 *he was dazed by his fall* STUN, stupefy; knock unconscious, knock out; *informal* knock the stuffing out of. 2 *she was dazed by the revelations* ASTOUND, amaze, astonish, startle, dumbfound, stupefy, overwhelm, stagger, shock, confound, bewilder, bedazzle, take aback, shake up; *informal* flabbergast, bowl over, blow away.
▶ noun *she is in a daze* STUPOR, trance, haze; spin, whirl, muddle, jumble.

dazzle ▶ verb 1 *she was dazzled by the headlights* BLIND TEMPORARILY, deprive of sight. 2 *I was dazzled by the exhibition* OVERWHELM, overcome, impress, move, stir, affect, touch, awe, overawe, leave speechless, take someone's breath away; spellbind, hypnotize; *informal* bowl over, blow away, knock out.
▶ noun 1 *dazzle can be a problem to sensitive eyes* GLARE, brightness, brilliance, shimmer, radiance, shine. 2 *the dazzle of the limelight* SPARKLE, glitter, brilliance, glory, splendour, magnificence, glamour; attraction, lure, allure, draw, appeal; *informal* razzle-dazzle, razzmatazz.

dazzling ▶ adjective 1 *the sunlight was dazzling* BRIGHT, blinding, glaring, brilliant. 2 *Jenny's dazzling performance* IMPRESSIVE, remarkable, extraordinary, outstanding, exceptional; incredible, amazing, astonishing, phenomenal, breathtaking, thrilling; excellent, wonderful, magnificent, marvellous, superb, first-rate, superlative, matchless; *informal* mind-blowing, out of this world, fabulous, bang-up, skookum, fab, super, sensational, ace, A1, cool, awesome, killer.

deactivate ▶ verb DISABLE, defuse, disarm, disconnect, inactivate, make inoperative, immobilize, stop, turnoff.

dead ▶ adjective 1 *my parents are dead* PASSED ON/ AWAY, expired, departed, gone, no more; late, lost, lamented; perished, fallen, slain, slaughtered, killed, murdered; lifeless, extinct; *informal* (as) dead as a doornail, six feet under, pushing up daisies; *formal* deceased; *euphemistic* with God, asleep. 2 *patches of dead ground* BARREN, lifeless, bare, desolate, sterile. 3 *a dead language* OBSOLETE, extinct, defunct, disused, abandoned, discarded, superseded, vanished, forgotten; archaic, antiquated, ancient; *literary* of yore. 4 *the phone was dead* NOT WORKING, out of order, inoperative, inactive, in disrepair, broken, malfunctioning, defective; *informal* kaput, conked out, on the blink/fritz, has had the biscuit ♣, bust. 5 *a dead leg* NUMB, numbed, deadened, desensitized, unfeeling; paralyzed, crippled, incapacitated, immobilized, frozen. 6 *she has dead eyes* EMOTIONLESS, unemotional, unfeeling, impassive, unresponsive, indifferent, dispassionate, inexpressive, wooden, stony, cold; deadpan, flat; blank, vacant. 7 *his affection for her was dead* EXTINGUISHED, quashed, stifled; finished, over, gone, no more; ancient history. 8 *a dead town* UNEVENTFUL, uninteresting, unexciting, uninspiring, dull, boring, flat, quiet, sleepy, slow, lacklustre, lifeless; *informal* one-horse, dullsville. 9 *dead silence* COMPLETE, absolute, total, utter, out-and-out, thorough, unmitigated. 10 *a dead shot* UNERRING, unfailing, impeccable, sure, true, accurate, precise; deadly, lethal, bang on.
— OPPOSITES: alive, fertile, modern, lively, poor.
▶ adverb 1 *he was dead serious* COMPLETELY, absolutely, totally, utterly, deadly, perfectly, entirely, quite, thoroughly; definitely, certainly, positively,

categorically, unquestionably, undoubtedly, surely; in every way, one hundred per cent. 2 *flares were seen dead ahead* DIRECTLY, exactly, precisely, immediately, right, straight, due, squarely; *informal* bang, smack dab. 3 *(informal) it's dead easy.* See VERY.

deadbeat ▶ noun *(informal)* LAYABOUT, loafer, idler, good-for-nothing, bum, sponger; *literary* wastrel.

deaden ▶ verb 1 *surgeons tried to deaden the pain* NUMB, dull, blunt, suppress; alleviate, mitigate, diminish, reduce, lessen, ease, soothe, relieve, assuage, kill. 2 *the wood panelling deadened any noise* MUFFLE, mute, smother, stifle, dull, dampen; silence, quieten, soften; cushion, buffer, absorb. 3 *laughing might deaden us to the moral issue* DESENSITIZE, numb, anaesthetize; harden (one's heart), toughen, inure.
— OPPOSITES: intensify, amplify, sensitize.

deadline ▶ noun TIME LIMIT, limit, finishing date, target date, cut-off point.

deadlock ▶ noun *the negotiations reached a deadlock* STALEMATE, impasse, standoff, saw-off ♣, log-jam; standstill, halt, (full) stop, dead end.

deadly ▶ adjective 1 *these drugs can be deadly* FATAL, lethal, mortal, death-dealing, life-threatening; dangerous, injurious, harmful, detrimental, deleterious, unhealthy; noxious, toxic, poisonous; *literary* deathly. 2 *deadly enemies* MORTAL, irreconcilable, implacable, unappeasable, unforgiving, remorseless, merciless, pitiless; bitter, hostile, antagonistic. 3 *deadly seriousness* INTENSE, great, marked, extreme. 4 *he was deadly pale* DEATHLY, ghostly, ashen, white, pallid, wan, pale; ghastly. 5 *his aim is deadly* UNERRING, unfailing, impeccable, perfect, flawless, faultless; sure, true, precise, accurate, exact, bang on. 6 *(informal) life here can be deadly.* See BORING.
— OPPOSITES: harmless, mild, inaccurate, exciting.
▶ adverb *deadly calm* COMPLETELY, absolutely, totally, utterly, perfectly, entirely, wholly, quite, dead, thoroughly; in every way, one hundred per cent, to the hilt.

deadpan ▶ adjective BLANK, expressionless, inexpressive, impassive, inscrutable, poker-faced, straight-faced, stony, wooden, vacant, fixed, lifeless.
— OPPOSITES: expressive.

deaf ▶ adjective 1 *she is deaf and blind* HARD OF HEARING, having impaired hearing; *informal* deaf as a post. 2 *she was deaf to their pleading* UNMOVED BY, untouched by, unaffected by, indifferent to, unresponsive to, unconcerned by; unaware of, oblivious to, incognizant of, impervious to.

deafen ▶ verb MAKE DEAF, deprive of hearing, impair someone's hearing.

deafening ▶ adjective VERY LOUD, very noisy, ear-splitting, overwhelming, almighty ♣, mighty, tremendous; booming, thunderous, roaring, resounding, resonant, reverberating.
— OPPOSITES: quiet.

deal ▶ noun *completion of the deal* AGREEMENT, understanding, pact, bargain, covenant, contract, treaty; arrangement, compromise, settlement; terms; transaction, sale, account; *Law* indenture.
▶ verb 1 *how to deal with difficult children* COPE WITH, handle, manage, treat, take care of, take charge of, take in hand, sort out, tackle, take on; control; act towards, behave towards. 2 *the article deals with advances in chemistry* CONCERN, be about, have to do with, discuss, consider, cover, pertain to; study, explore, investigate, examine, review, analyze. 3 *the company deals in high-tech goods* TRADE IN, buy and

sell; sell, purvey, supply, stock, market, merchandise; traffic, smuggle; *informal* push, flog. **4** *the cards were dealt* DISTRIBUTE, give out, share out, divide out, hand out, pass out, pass round, dole out, dispense, allocate; *informal* divvy up. **5** *the court dealt a blow to government reforms* DELIVER, administer, dispense, inflict, give, impose; aim.
■ **a great deal/a good deal** A LOT, a large amount, a fair amount, much, plenty; *informal* lots, loads, heaps, bags, masses, tons, stacks.

dealer ▶ noun **1** *an antique dealer* TRADER, merchant, salesman/woman, seller, vendor, purveyor, peddler, hawker; buyer, merchandiser, distributor, supplier, shopkeeper, retailer, wholesaler. **2** *a drug dealer* TRAFFICKER, supplier.

dealing ▶ noun **1** *dishonest dealing* BUSINESS METHODS, business practices, business, commerce, trading, transactions; behaviour, conduct, actions. **2** *Canada's dealings with China* RELATIONS, relationship, association, connections, contact, intercourse; negotiations, bargaining, transactions; trade, trading, business, commerce, traffic; *informal* truck, doings.

dean ▶ noun **1** *students must have the consent of the dean* FACULTY HEAD, department head, college head, provost, university official; chief, director, principal, president, governor. **2** *the dean of Canadian literature* DOYEN(NE), elder statesman, grande dame, grand old man, veteran.

dear ▶ adjective **1** *a dear friend* BELOVED, loved, adored, cherished, precious; esteemed, respected, worshipped; close, intimate, bosom, best. **2** *her pictures were too dear to part with* PRECIOUS, treasured, valued, prized, cherished, special. **3** *such a dear man* ENDEARING, adorable, lovable, appealing, engaging, charming, captivating, winsome, lovely, nice, pleasant, delightful, sweet, darling. **4** *the meals are rather dear* EXPENSIVE, costly, high-priced, overpriced, exorbitant, extortionate; *informal* pricey, steep, stiff.
— OPPOSITES: hated, disagreeable, cheap.
▶ noun **1** *don't worry, my dear* DARLING, dearest, love, beloved, sweetheart, sweet, precious, treasure; *informal* sweetie, sugar, honey, hon, baby, pet, sunshine. **2** *he's such a dear* LOVABLE PERSON; darling, sweetheart, pet, angel, gem, treasure, star.

dearly ▶ adverb **1** *I love my son dearly* VERY MUCH, a great deal, greatly, deeply, profoundly, extremely; fondly, devotedly, tenderly. **2** *our freedom has been bought dearly* AT GREAT COST, at a high price, with much suffering, with much sacrifice.

dearth ▶ noun LACK, scarcity, shortage, shortfall, want, deficiency, insufficiency, inadequacy, paucity, sparseness, scantiness, rareness; absence.
— OPPOSITES: surfeit.

death ▶ noun **1** *her father's death* DEMISE, dying, end, passing, loss of life; eternal rest, quietus; murder, assassination, execution, slaughter, massacre; *informal* curtains; *formal* decease; *archaic* expiry. **2** *the death of their dream* END, finish, termination, extinction, extinguishing, collapse, destruction, eradication, obliteration. **3** *Death gestured towards a grave* THE GRIM REAPER, the Dark Angel, the Angel of Death.
— OPPOSITES: life, birth.
■ **put someone to death** EXECUTE, hang, behead, guillotine, decapitate, electrocute, shoot, gas, crucify, stone; kill, murder, assassinate, eliminate, terminate, exterminate, destroy; *informal* bump off, polish off, do away with, do in, knock off, string up,

take out, croak, stiff, blow away, ice, rub out, waste, whack, smoke; *literary* slay.

deathless ▶ adjective IMMORTAL, undying, imperishable, indestructible; enduring, everlasting, eternal; timeless, ageless.
— OPPOSITES: mortal, ephemeral.

deathly ▶ adjective DEATHLIKE, deadly, ghostly, ghastly; ashen, chalky, white, pale, pallid, bloodless, wan, anemic, pasty.

debacle ▶ noun FIASCO, failure, catastrophe, disaster, mess, ruin; downfall, collapse, defeat; *informal* foul-up, screw-up, hash, botch, washout, snafu.

debar ▶ verb **1** *women were debarred from the club* EXCLUDE, ban, bar, disqualify, declare ineligible, preclude, shut out, lock out, keep out, reject, blackball. **2** *the unions were debarred from striking* PREVENT, prohibit, proscribe, disallow, ban, interdict, block, stop; forbid to; *Law* enjoin, estop.
— OPPOSITES: admit, allow.

debase ▶ verb **1** *the moral code has been debased* DEGRADE, devalue, demean, cheapen, prostitute, discredit, drag down, tarnish, blacken, blemish; disgrace, dishonour, shame; damage, harm, undermine. **2** *the added copper debases the silver* REDUCE IN VALUE, reduce in quality, depreciate; contaminate, adulterate, pollute, taint, sully, corrupt; dilute, alloy.
— OPPOSITES: enhance.

debatable ▶ adjective ARGUABLE, disputable, questionable, open to question, controversial, contentious; doubtful, dubious, uncertain, unsure, unclear, borderline, inconclusive, moot, unsettled, unresolved, unconfirmed, undetermined, undecided, up in the air, iffy.

debate ▶ noun *a debate on the reforms* DISCUSSION, discourse, parley; dialogue; argument, dispute, wrangle, war of words; argumentation, disputation, dissension, disagreement, contention, conflict; negotiations, talks; *informal* confab, powwow.
▶ verb **1** *MPs will debate our future* DISCUSS, talk over/through, talk about, thrash out, hash out, argue, dispute; *informal* kick around, bat around. **2** *he debated whether to call her* CONSIDER, think over/about, chew over, mull over, ponder, revolve, deliberate, contemplate, muse, meditate; *formal* cogitate.

debauch ▶ verb **1** *public morals have been debauched* CORRUPT, debase, deprave, warp, pervert, lead astray, ruin. **2** *(dated) he debauched many women* SEDUCE, deflower, defile, violate; *literary* ravish.

debauched ▶ adjective DISSOLUTE, dissipated, degenerate, corrupt, depraved, sinful, unprincipled, immoral; lascivious, lecherous, lewd, lustful, libidinous, licentious, promiscuous, loose, wanton, abandoned; decadent, profligate, intemperate, sybaritic.
— OPPOSITES: wholesome.

debauchery ▶ noun DISSIPATION, degeneracy, corruption, vice, depravity; immodesty, indecency, perversion, iniquity, wickedness, sinfulness, impropriety, immorality; lasciviousness, salaciousness, lechery, lewdness, lust, promiscuity, wantonness, profligacy; decadence, intemperance, sybaritism; *formal* turpitude.

debilitate ▶ verb WEAKEN, enfeeble, enervate, devitalize, sap, drain, exhaust, weary, fatigue, prostrate; undermine, impair, indispose, incapacitate, cripple, disable, paralyze, immobilize,

lay low; *informal* knock out, do in.
— OPPOSITES: invigorate.

debility ▶ noun FRAILTY, weakness, enfeeblement, enervation, devitalization, lassitude, exhaustion, weariness, fatigue, prostration; incapacity, indisposition, infirmity, illness, sickness, sickliness; *Medicine* asthenia.

debonair ▶ adjective SUAVE, urbane, sophisticated, cultured, self-possessed, self-assured, confident, charming, gracious, courteous, gallant, chivalrous, gentlemanly, refined, polished, well-bred, genteel, dignified, courtly; well-groomed, elegant, stylish, smart, dashing; *informal* smooth, sharp, cool, slick, fly.
— OPPOSITES: unsophisticated.

debrief ▶ verb REVIEW, discuss, examine; cross-examine, interview, interrogate, question, probe, sound out; *informal* grill, pump.

debris ▶ noun DETRITUS, refuse, rubbish, waste, litter, scrap, dross, chaff, flotsam and jetsam; rubble, wreckage; remains, scraps, dregs, trash, garbage, dreck, junk.

debt ▶ noun 1 *he couldn't pay his debts* BILL, account, dues, arrears, charges; financial obligation, outstanding payment, money owing; check, tab. 2 *his debt to the author* INDEBTEDNESS, obligation; gratitude, appreciation, thanks.
■ **in debt** OWING MONEY, in arrears, behind with payments, overdrawn; insolvent, bankrupt, ruined; *informal* in the red.
■ **in someone's debt** INDEBTED TO, beholden to, obliged to, duty-bound to, honour-bound to, obligated to; grateful, thankful, appreciative.

debtor ▶ noun BORROWER, mortgagor; bankrupt, insolvent, defaulter.
— OPPOSITES: creditor.

debunk ▶ verb EXPLODE, deflate, quash, discredit, disprove, contradict, controvert, invalidate, negate; challenge, call into question, poke holes in; *formal* confute.
— OPPOSITES: confirm.

debut ▶ noun FIRST APPEARANCE, first performance, launch, coming out, entrance, premiere, introduction, inception, inauguration; *informal* kickoff.

decadence ▶ noun 1 *the decadence of modern society* DISSIPATION, degeneracy, debauchery, corruption, depravity, vice, sin, moral decay, immorality; immoderateness, intemperance, licentiousness, self-indulgence, hedonism. 2 *the decadence of nations* DETERIORATION, fall, decay, degeneration, decline, degradation, retrogression.
— OPPOSITES: morality, rise.

decadent ▶ adjective 1 *decadent city life* DISSOLUTE, dissipated, degenerate, corrupt, depraved, sinful, unprincipled, immoral; licentious, abandoned, profligate, intemperate; sybaritic, hedonistic, pleasure-seeking, self-indulgent. 2 *the decadent empire* DECLINING, decaying, ebbing, degenerating, deteriorating.

decamp ▶ verb 1 *he decamped with the profits* ABSCOND, make off, run off/away, flee, bolt, take flight, disappear, vanish, steal away, sneak away, escape, make a run for it, leave, depart; *informal* split, scram, vamoose, cut and run, do a disappearing act, head for the hills, go AWOL, take a powder, go on the lam. 2 *(archaic) the armies decamped* STRIKE ONE'S TENTS, break camp, move on.

decant ▶ verb POUR OUT/OFF, draw off, siphon off, drain, tap; transfer.

decapitate ▶ verb BEHEAD, guillotine.

decay ▶ verb 1 *the corpses had decayed* DECOMPOSE, rot, putrefy, go bad, go off, spoil, fester, perish, deteriorate; degrade, break down, moulder, shrivel, wither. 2 *the cities continue to decay* DETERIORATE, degenerate, decline, go downhill, slump, slide, go to rack and ruin, go to seed; disintegrate, fall to pieces, fall into disrepair; fail, collapse; *informal* go to pot, go to the dogs, go into/down the toilet.
▶ noun 1 *signs of decay* DECOMPOSITION, putrefaction, festering; rot, mould, mildew, fungus. 2 *tooth decay* ROT, corrosion, decomposition; caries, cavities, holes. 3 *the decay of American values* DETERIORATION, degeneration, debasement, degradation, decline, weakening, atrophy; crumbling, disintegration, collapse.

decayed ▶ adjective DECOMPOSED, decomposing, rotten, putrescent, putrid, bad, off, spoiled, perished; mouldy, festering, fetid, rancid, rank; maggoty, wormy.

decaying ▶ adjective 1 *decaying fish* DECOMPOSING, decomposed, rotting, rotten, putrescent, putrid, bad, off, perished; mouldy, festering, fetid, rancid, rank; maggoty, wormy. 2 *a decaying city* DECLINING, degenerating, dying, crumbling; run-down, tumbledown, ramshackle, shabby, decrepit; in decline, in ruins, on the way out.

decease ▶ noun *(formal) her decease was imminent* DEATH, dying, demise, end, passing, loss of life, quietus; *informal* curtains, croaking, snuffing; *archaic* expiry.

deceased ▶ adjective *(formal)* DEAD, expired, departed, gone, no more, passed on/away; late, lost, lamented; perished, fallen, slain, slaughtered, killed, murdered; lifeless, extinct; *informal* (as) dead as a doornail, six feet under, pushing up daisies; *euphemistic* with God, asleep.

deceit ▶ noun 1 *her endless deceit* DECEPTION, deceitfulness, duplicity, double-dealing, fraud, cheating, trickery, chicanery, deviousness, slyness, wiliness, guile, bluff, lying, pretense, treachery; *informal* crookedness, monkey business, monkeyshines. 2 *their life is a deceit* SHAM, fraud, pretense, hoax, fake, blind, artifice; trick, stratagem, device, ruse, scheme, dodge, machination, deception, subterfuge; cheat, swindle; *informal* con, set-up, scam, flim-flam, bunco.
— OPPOSITES: honesty.

deceitful ▶ adjective 1 *a deceitful woman* DISHONEST, untruthful, mendacious, insincere, false, disingenuous, untrustworthy, unscrupulous, unprincipled, two-faced, duplicitous, double-dealing, underhanded, crafty, cunning, sly, scheming, calculating, treacherous, Machiavellian, sneaky, tricky, foxy, crooked. 2 *a deceitful allegation* FRAUDULENT, counterfeit, fabricated, invented, concocted, made up, trumped up, untrue, false, bogus, fake, spurious, fallacious, deceptive, misleading; *euphemistic* economical with the truth.

deceive ▶ verb 1 *she was deceived by a con man* SWINDLE, defraud, cheat, trick, hoodwink, hoax, dupe, take in, mislead, delude, fool, outwit, lead on, inveigle, beguile, double-cross, gull; *informal* con, bamboozle, do, gyp, diddle, rip off, shaft, pull a fast one on, take for a ride, pull the wool over someone's eyes, sucker, snooker, stiff. 2 *he deceived her with* *another woman* BE UNFAITHFUL TO, cheat on, betray, play someone false; *informal* two-time.

decelerate ▸ verb SLOW DOWN/UP, ease up, slack up, reduce speed, brake.

decency ▸ noun **1** *standards of taste and decency* PROPRIETY, decorum, good taste, respectability, dignity, correctness, good form, etiquette; morality, virtue, modesty, delicacy. **2** *he didn't have the decency to tell me* COURTESY, politeness, good manners, civility, respect; consideration, thoughtfulness, tact, diplomacy.

decent ▸ adjective **1** *a decent burial* PROPER, correct, appropriate, apt, fitting, suitable; respectable, dignified, decorous, seemly; nice, tasteful; conventional, accepted, standard, traditional, orthodox; comme il faut. **2** *a very decent fellow* HONOURABLE, honest, trustworthy, dependable; respectable, upright, clean-living, virtuous, good; obliging, helpful, accommodating, unselfish, generous, kind, thoughtful, considerate; neighbourly, hospitable, pleasant, agreeable, amiable. **3** *a job with decent pay* SATISFACTORY, reasonable, fair, acceptable, adequate, sufficient, ample; not bad, all right, tolerable, passable, suitable; *informal* OK, okay, up to snuff.
— OPPOSITES: unpleasant, unsatisfactory.

deception ▸ noun **1** *they obtained money by deception* DECEIT, deceitfulness, duplicity, double-dealing, fraud, cheating, trickery, chicanery, deviousness, slyness, wiliness, guile, bluff, lying, pretense, treachery; *informal* crookedness, monkey business, monkeyshines. **2** *it was all a deception* TRICK, deceit, sham, fraud, pretense, hoax, fake, blind, artifice; stratagem, device, ruse, scheme, dodge, machination, subterfuge; cheat, swindle; *informal* con, set-up, scam, flim-flam, bunco.

deceptive ▸ adjective **1** *distances are very deceptive* MISLEADING, illusory, illusionary, specious; ambiguous; distorted; *literary* illusive. **2** *deceptive practices* DECEITFUL, duplicitous, fraudulent, counterfeit, underhanded, cunning, crafty, sly, guileful, scheming, treacherous, Machiavellian; disingenuous, untrustworthy, unscrupulous, unprincipled, dishonest, insincere, false; *informal* crooked, sharp, shady, sneaky, tricky, foxy.

decide ▸ verb **1** *she decided to become a writer* RESOLVE, determine, make up one's mind, make a decision; elect, choose, opt, plan, aim, have the intention, have in mind, set one's sights on. **2** *research to decide a variety of questions* SETTLE, resolve, determine, work out, answer; *informal* sort out, figure out. **3** *the court is to decide the case* ADJUDICATE, arbitrate, adjudge, judge; hear, try, examine; sit in judgment on, pronounce on, give a verdict on, rule on.

decided ▸ adjective **1** *they have a decided advantage* DISTINCT, clear, marked, pronounced, obvious, striking, noticeable, unmistakable, patent, manifest; definite, certain, positive, emphatic, undeniable, indisputable, unquestionable; assured, guaranteed. **2** *he was very decided* DETERMINED, resolute, firm, strong-minded, strong-willed, emphatic, dead set, unwavering, unyielding, unbending, inflexible, unshakeable, unrelenting, obstinate, stubborn, rock-ribbed. **3** *our future is decided* SETTLED, established, resolved, determined, agreed, designated, chosen, ordained, prescribed; set, fixed; *informal* sewn up, wrapped up.

decidedly ▸ adverb DISTINCTLY, clearly, markedly, obviously, noticeably, unmistakably, patently,

manifestly; definitely, certainly, positively, absolutely, downright, undeniably, unquestionably; extremely, exceedingly, exceptionally, particularly, especially, very; *informal* terrifically, devilishly, ultra, mega, majorly, ever so, dead, real, mighty, awful.

deciding ▸ adjective DETERMINING, decisive, conclusive, key, pivotal, crucial, critical, significant, major, chief, principal, prime.

decipher ▸ verb **1** *he deciphered the code* DECODE, decrypt, break, work out, solve, interpret, unscramble, translate; make sense of, get to the bottom of, unravel; *informal* crack, figure out, suss (out). **2** *the writing was hard to decipher* MAKE OUT, discern, perceive, read, follow, fathom, make sense of, interpret, understand, comprehend, grasp.
— OPPOSITES: encode.

decision ▸ noun **1** *they came to a decision* RESOLUTION, conclusion, settlement, commitment, resolve, determination; choice, option, selection. **2** *the judge's decision* VERDICT, finding, ruling, recommendation; judgment, judgment call, pronouncement, adjudication, order, rule, resolve; findings, results; *Law* determination. **3** *his order had a ring of decision* DECISIVENESS, determination, resolution, resolve, firmness; strong-mindedness, purpose, purposefulness.

decisive ▸ adjective **1** *a decisive man* RESOLUTE, firm, strong-minded, strong-willed, determined; purposeful, forceful, dead set, unwavering, unyielding, unbending, inflexible, unshakeable, obstinate, stubborn, rock-ribbed. **2** *the decisive factor* DECIDING, conclusive, determining; key, pivotal, critical, crucial, significant, influential, major, chief, principal, prime.

deck ▸ verb **1** *the street was decked with streamers* DECORATE, bedeck, adorn, ornament, trim, trick out, garnish, cover, hang, festoon, garland, swathe, wreathe; embellish, beautify, prettify, enhance, grace, set off; *informal* get up, do up, tart up; *literary* bejewel, bedizen, caparison. **2** *Ingrid was decked out in blue* DRESS (UP), clothe, attire, garb, robe, drape, turn out, fit out, rig out, outfit, costume; *informal* doll up, get up, do up, gussy up. **3** *he got up from the table and decked me.* see HIT verb sense 1.
▸ noun *they were lounging on the deck* SUNDECK, balcony, veranda, porch, patio, terrace.

declaim ▸ verb **1** *a preacher declaiming from the pulpit* MAKE A SPEECH, give an address, give a lecture, deliver a sermon; speak, hold forth, orate, preach, lecture, sermonize, moralize; *informal* sound off, spout, speechify, preachify. **2** *they loved to hear him declaim poetry* RECITE, read aloud, read out loud, read out; deliver; *informal* spout. **3** *he declaimed against the evils of society* SPEAK OUT, rail, inveigh, fulminate, rage, thunder; rant, expostulate; condemn, criticize, attack, decry, disparage.

declamation ▸ noun SPEECH, address, lecture, sermon, homily, discourse, oration, recitation, disquisition; monologue.

declaration ▸ noun **1** *they issued a declaration* ANNOUNCEMENT, statement, communication, pronouncement, proclamation, communiqué, edict, advisory. **2** *the declaration of war* PROCLAMATION, notification, announcement, revelation, disclosure, broadcasting. **3** *a declaration of faith* ASSERTION, profession, affirmation, acknowledgment, revelation, disclosure, manifestation, confirmation, testimony, validation, certification, attestation; pledge, avowal, vow, oath, protestation.

declare ▶ verb **1** *she declared her political principles* PROCLAIM, announce, state, reveal, air, voice, articulate, express, vent, set forth, publicize, broadcast; *informal* come out with, shout from the rooftops. **2** *he declared that they were guilty* ASSERT, maintain, state, affirm, contend, argue, insist, hold, profess, claim, avow, swear; *formal* aver. **3** *his speech declared him to be a gentleman* SHOW TO BE, reveal as, confirm as, prove to be, attest to someone's being.

decline ▶ verb **1** *she declined all invitations* TURN DOWN, reject, brush aside, refuse, rebuff, spurn, repulse, dismiss; forgo, deny oneself, pass up; abstain from, say no; *informal* give the thumbs down to, give something a miss. **2** *the number of traders has declined* DECREASE, reduce, lessen, diminish, dwindle, contract, shrink, fall off, tail off; drop, fall, go down, slump, plummet; *informal* nosedive, take a header, crash. **3** *standards steadily declined* DETERIORATE, degenerate, decay, crumble, collapse, slump, slip, slide, go downhill, worsen; weaken, wane, ebb; *informal* go to pot, go to the dogs, go into/down the toilet.
− OPPOSITES: accept, increase, rise.
▶ noun **1** *a decline in profits* REDUCTION, decrease, downturn, downswing, devaluation, depreciation, diminution, ebb, drop, slump, plunge; *informal* nosedive, crash, toboggan slide ♣. **2** *forest decline* DETERIORATION, degeneration, degradation, shrinkage; death, decay.
■ **in decline** DECLINING, decaying, crumbling, collapsing, failing; disappearing, dying, moribund; *informal* on its last legs, on the way out.

decode ▶ verb DECIPHER, decrypt, work out, solve, interpret, translate; make sense of, get to the bottom of, unravel, unscramble, find the key to; *informal* crack, figure out, suss (out).

decompose ▶ verb **1** *the chemical prevents corpses decomposing* DECAY, rot, putrefy, go bad, go off, spoil, fester, perish, deteriorate; degrade, break down, moulder, shrivel, wither. **2** *some minerals decompose rapidly* BREAK UP, fragment, disintegrate, crumble, dissolve; break down, decay.

decomposition ▶ noun **1** *an advanced state of decomposition* DECAY, putrefaction, putrescence, putridity. **2** *the decomposition of granite* DISINTEGRATION, dissolution; breaking down, decay.

decompress ▶ verb **1** *decompress the files before opening them* EXPAND, restore, recover. **2** *you need to take a few minutes to decompress* CALM DOWN, relax, take it easy, wind down, chill (out), hang/stay loose.

decontaminate ▶ verb SANITIZE, sterilize, disinfect, clean, cleanse, purify; fumigate.

decor ▶ noun DECORATION, furnishing, ornamentation; colour scheme.

decorate ▶ verb **1** *the door was decorated with a wreath* ORNAMENT, adorn, trim, embellish, garnish, furnish, enhance, grace, prettify; festoon, garland, bedeck. **2** *he started to decorate his home* PAINT, WALLPAPER, paper; refurbish, furbish, renovate, redecorate; *informal* do up, spruce up, do over, fix up, give something a facelift. **3** *he was decorated for courage* GIVE A MEDAL TO, honour, cite, reward.

decoration ▶ noun **1** *a ceiling with rich decoration* ORNAMENTATION, adornment, trimming, embellishment, garnishing, gilding; beautification, prettification; enhancements, enrichments, frills, accessories, trimmings, finery, frippery. **2** *internal decoration. See* DECOR. **3** *a Christmas tree decoration* ORNAMENT, bauble, trinket, knick-knack, spangle;

trimming, tinsel. **4** *a decoration won on the battlefield* MEDAL, award, star, ribbon; laurel, trophy, prize.

decorative ▶ adjective ORNAMENTAL, embellishing, garnishing, fancy, ornate, attractive, pretty, showy.
− OPPOSITES: functional.

decorous ▶ adjective PROPER, seemly, decent, becoming, befitting, tasteful; correct, appropriate, suitable, fitting; tactful, polite, well-mannered, genteel, respectable; formal, restrained, modest, demure, gentlemanly, ladylike.
− OPPOSITES: unseemly.

decorum ▶ noun **1** *he had acted with decorum* PROPRIETY, seemliness, decency, good taste, correctness; politeness, courtesy, good manners; dignity, respectability, modesty, demureness. **2** *a breach of decorum* ETIQUETTE, protocol, good form, custom, convention; formalities, niceties, punctilios, politeness.
− OPPOSITES: impropriety.

decoy ▶ noun *a decoy to distract their attention* LURE, bait, red herring; enticement, inducement, temptation, attraction, carrot; snare, trap.
▶ verb *he was decoyed to the mainland* LURE, entice, allure, tempt; entrap, snare, trap.

decrease ▶ verb **1** *pollution levels decreased* LESSEN, reduce, drop, diminish, decline, dwindle, fall off; die down, abate, subside, tail off, ebb, wane; plummet, plunge. **2** *decrease the amount of fat in your body* REDUCE, lessen, lower, cut (back/down), curtail; slim down, tone down, deplete, minimize, slash.
− OPPOSITES: increase.
▶ noun *a decrease in crime* REDUCTION, drop, decline, downturn, cut, fall-off, cutback, diminution, ebb, wane.
− OPPOSITES: increase.

decree ▶ noun **1** *a presidential decree* ORDER, edict, command, commandment, mandate, proclamation, dictum, fiat; law, bylaw, statute, act, order-in-council, cabinet order ♣; formal ordinance. **2** *a court decree* JUDGMENT, verdict, adjudication, ruling, resolution, decision.
▶ verb *he decreed that a stadium should be built* ORDER, command, rule, dictate, pronounce, proclaim, ordain; direct, decide, determine.

decrepit ▶ adjective **1** *a decrepit old man* FEEBLE, infirm, weak, weakly, frail; disabled, incapacitated, crippled, doddering, tottering; old, elderly, aged, ancient, senile; *informal* past it, over the hill, no spring chicken. **2** *a decrepit house* DILAPIDATED, rickety, run-down, tumbledown, beat-up, ramshackle, derelict, ruined, in (a state of) disrepair, gone to rack and ruin; battered, decayed, crumbling, deteriorating.
− OPPOSITES: strong, sound.

decry ▶ verb DENOUNCE, condemn, criticize, censure, attack, rail against, run down, pillory, lambaste, vilify, revile; disparage, deprecate, cast aspersions on; *informal* slam, blast, knock.
− OPPOSITES: praise.

dedicate ▶ verb **1** *she dedicated her life to the sick* DEVOTE, commit, pledge, give, surrender, sacrifice; set aside, allocate, consign. **2** *a book dedicated to his muse* INSCRIBE, address; assign. **3** *the chapel was dedicated to the Virgin Mary* DEVOTE, assign; bless, consecrate, sanctify; formal hallow.

dedicated ▶ adjective **1** *a dedicated socialist* COMMITTED, devoted, staunch, firm, steadfast, resolute, unwavering, loyal, faithful, true,

dyed-in-the-wool; wholehearted, single-minded, enthusiastic, keen, earnest, zealous, ardent, passionate, fervent; *informal* card-carrying. **2** *data is accessed by a dedicated machine* EXCLUSIVE, custom built, customized.
− OPPOSITES: indifferent.

dedication ▶ noun **1** *sport requires dedication* COMMITMENT, application, diligence, industry, resolve, enthusiasm, zeal, conscientiousness, perseverance, persistence, tenacity, drive, staying power; hard work, effort. **2** *her dedication to the job* DEVOTION, commitment, loyalty, adherence, allegiance. **3** *the book has a dedication to her husband* INSCRIPTION, address, message. **4** *the dedication of the church* BLESSING, consecration, sanctification, benediction.
− OPPOSITES: apathy.

deduce ▶ verb CONCLUDE, reason, work out, infer; glean, divine, intuit, understand, assume, presume, conjecture, surmise, reckon; *informal* figure out, suss out.

deduct ▶ verb SUBTRACT, take away, take off, debit, dock, discount; abstract, remove, knock off.
− OPPOSITES: add.

deduction ▶ noun **1** *the deduction of tax* SUBTRACTION, removal, debit, abstraction. **2** *gross pay, before deductions* SUBTRACTION. **3** *she was right in her deduction* CONCLUSION, inference, supposition, hypothesis, assumption, presumption, illation; suspicion, conviction, belief, reasoning.

deed ▶ noun **1** *kindly deeds* ACT, action; feat, exploit, achievement, accomplishment, endeavour, undertaking, enterprise. **2** *unity must be established in deed and word* FACT, reality, actuality. **3** *a deed to the property* LEGAL DOCUMENT, contract, indenture, instrument.

deem ▶ verb CONSIDER, regard as, judge, adjudge, hold to be, view as, see as, take for, class as, count, find, esteem, suppose, reckon; think, believe, feel.

deep ▶ adjective **1** *a deep ravine* CAVERNOUS, yawning, gaping, huge, extensive; bottomless, fathomless, unfathomable. **2** *two inches deep* IN DEPTH, downwards, inwards, in vertical extent. **3** *deep affection* INTENSE, heartfelt, wholehearted, deep-seated, deep-rooted; sincere, genuine, earnest, enthusiastic, great. **4** *a deep sleep* SOUND, heavy, intense. **5** *a deep thinker* PROFOUND, serious, philosophical, complex, weighty; abstruse, esoteric, recondite, mysterious, obscure; intelligent, intellectual, learned, wise, scholarly; discerning, penetrating, perceptive, insightful. **6** *he was deep in concentration* RAPT, absorbed, engrossed, preoccupied, immersed, lost, gripped, intent, engaged. **7** *a deep mystery* OBSCURE, mysterious, secret, unfathomable, opaque, abstruse, recondite, esoteric, enigmatic, arcane; puzzling, baffling, mystifying, inexplicable. **8** *his deep voice* LOW-PITCHED, low, bass, rich, powerful, resonant, booming, sonorous. **9** *a deep red* DARK, intense, rich, strong, bold, warm.
− OPPOSITES: shallow, superficial, high, light.
▶ noun **1** (*literary*) *creatures of the deep* THE SEA, the ocean; *informal* the drink, the briny; *literary* the profound. **2** *the deep of night* THE MIDDLE, the midst; the depths, the dead, the thick.
▶ adverb **1** *I dug deep* FAR DOWN, way down, to a great depth. **2** *he brought them deep into woodland* FAR, a long way, a great distance.

deepen ▶ verb **1** *his love for her had deepened* GROW, increase, intensify, strengthen, heighten, amplify, augment; *informal* step up. **2** *they deepened the hole* DIG OUT, dig deeper, excavate.

deeply ▶ adverb PROFOUNDLY, greatly, enormously, extremely, very much; strongly, powerfully, intensely, keenly, acutely; thoroughly, completely, entirely; *informal* well, seriously, majorly.

deep-rooted ▶ adjective DEEP-SEATED, deep, profound, fundamental, basic; established, ingrained, entrenched, unshakeable, inveterate, inbuilt; secure; persistent, abiding, lingering.
− OPPOSITES: superficial.

deep-seated ▶ adjective. See DEEP-ROOTED.

deer ▶ noun buck, stag, hart; doe, hind. *See table.*
− RELATED TERMS: cervine.

Deer

axis	muntjac
barren ground caribou	musk deer
blacktail	Père David's deer
brocket	Peary caribou
caribou	red deer
chital	reindeer
deer	roe
elk	sika
fallow deer	wapiti
moose	whitetail
mule deer	woodland caribou
muley	

deface ▶ verb VANDALIZE, disfigure, mar, spoil, ruin, sully, damage, blight, impair, trash.

de facto ▶ adverb *the republic is de facto two states* IN PRACTICE, in effect, in fact, in reality, really, actually.
− OPPOSITES: de jure.
▶ adjective *de facto control* ACTUAL, real, effective.
− OPPOSITES: de jure.

defamation ▶ noun LIBEL, slander, calumny, character assassination, vilification; scandalmongering, malicious gossip, aspersions, muckraking, abuse; disparagement, denigration; smear, slur; *informal* mud-slinging.

defamatory ▶ adjective LIBELLOUS, slanderous, calumnious, scandalmongering, malicious, vicious, backbiting, muckraking; abusive, disparaging, denigratory, insulting; *informal* mud-slinging, bitchy, catty.

defame ▶ verb LIBEL, slander, malign, cast aspersions on, smear, traduce, give someone a bad name, run down, speak ill of, vilify, besmirch, stigmatize, disparage, denigrate, discredit, decry; *informal* do a hatchet job on, drag through the mud, slur; *informal* badmouth, dis; *formal* calumniate.
− OPPOSITES: compliment.

default ▶ noun **1** *the incidence of defaults on loans* NON-PAYMENT, failure to pay, bad debt. **2** *I became a teacher by default* INACTION, omission, lapse, neglect, negligence, disregard; absence, non-appearance.
▶ verb **1** *the customer defaulted* FAIL TO PAY, not pay, renege, back out; go back on one's word; *informal* welsh, bilk. **2** *the program will default to its own style* REVERT, select automatically.

defeat ▶ verb **1** *the army which defeated the Scots* BEAT, conquer, win against, triumph over, get the better of, vanquish, rout, trounce, overcome, overpower, crush, subdue; *informal* lick, thrash, whip, wipe the floor with, make mincemeat of, clobber, slaughter, demolish, cream, skunk, nose out. **2** *these complex plans defeat their purpose* THWART, frustrate, foil, ruin, scotch, debar, snooker, derail; obstruct, impede, hinder, hamper; *informal* put the kibosh on, put paid

to, stymie, scupper, scuttle. **3** *the motion was defeated* REJECT, overthrow, throw out, dismiss, outvote, turn down; *informal* give the thumbs down. **4** *how to make it work defeats me* BAFFLE, perplex, bewilder, mystify, bemuse, confuse, confound, throw; *informal* beat, flummox, faze, stump.
▶ **noun 1** *a crippling defeat* LOSS, conquest, vanquishment; rout, trouncing; downfall; *informal* thrashing, hiding, drubbing, licking, pasting, massacre, slaughter. **2** *the defeat of his plans* FAILURE, downfall, collapse, ruin; rejection, frustration, abortion, miscarriage; undoing, reverse.
– OPPOSITES: victory, success.

defeatist ▶ **adjective** *a defeatist attitude* PESSIMISTIC, fatalistic, negative, cynical, despondent, despairing, hopeless, bleak, gloomy.
– OPPOSITES: optimistic.
▶ **noun** PESSIMIST, fatalist, cynic, prophet of doom, doomster; misery, killjoy, worrier; *informal* quitter, wet blanket, worrywart.
– OPPOSITES: optimist.

defecate ▶ **verb** EXCRETE (FECES), have a bowel movement, have a BM, evacuate one's bowels, void excrement, relieve oneself, go to the bathroom/toilet; *informal* do/go number two, poo.

defect¹ ▶ **noun** *he spotted a defect in my work* FAULT, flaw, imperfection, deficiency, weakness, weak spot, inadequacy, shortcoming, limitation, failing; kink, deformity, blemish; mistake, error; *informal* glitch; *Computing* bug.

defect² ▶ **verb** *his chief intelligence officer defected* DESERT, change sides, turn traitor, rebel, renege; abscond, quit, jump ship, escape; break faith; secede from, revolt against; *Military* go AWOL; *Polit.* cross the floor; *literary* forsake.

defection ▶ **noun** DESERTION, absconding, decamping, flight; apostasy, secession; treason, betrayal, disloyalty; *literary* perfidy.

defective ▶ **adjective 1** *a defective seat belt* FAULTY, flawed, imperfect, shoddy, inoperative, malfunctioning, out of order, unsound; in disrepair, broken; *informal* on the blink, on the fritz. **2** *these methods are defective* LACKING, wanting, deficient, inadequate, insufficient.
– OPPOSITES: perfect.

defector ▶ **noun** DESERTER, turncoat, traitor, renegade, Judas, quisling; *informal* rat.

defence ▶ **noun 1** *the defence of the fortress* PROTECTION, guarding, security, fortification; resistance, deterrent. **2** *the enemy's defences* BARRICADE, fortification; fortress, keep, rampart, bulwark, bastion. **3** *he spoke in defence of his boss* VINDICATION, justification, support, advocacy, endorsement; apology, explanation, exoneration. **4** *more spending on defence* ARMAMENTS, weapons, weaponry, arms; the military, the armed forces. **5** *the prisoner's defence* VINDICATION, explanation, mitigation, justification, rationalization, excuse, alibi, reason; plea, pleading; testimony, declaration, case.

defenceless ▶ **adjective 1** *defenceless animals* VULNERABLE, helpless, powerless, impotent, weak, susceptible. **2** *the country is wholly defenceless* UNDEFENDED, unprotected, unguarded, unshielded, unarmed; vulnerable, assailable, exposed, insecure.
– OPPOSITES: resilient.

defend ▶ **verb 1** *a fort built to defend the border* PROTECT, guard, safeguard, secure, shield; fortify, garrison, barricade; uphold, support, watch over.

2 *he defended his policy* JUSTIFY, vindicate, argue for, support, make a case for, plead for; excuse, explain. **3** *the manager defended his players* SUPPORT, back, stand by, stick up for, stand up for, argue for, champion, endorse; *informal* throw one's weight behind.
– OPPOSITES: attack, criticize.

defendant ▶ **noun** ACCUSED, prisoner (at the bar); appellant, litigant, respondent; suspect.
– OPPOSITES: plaintiff.

defender ▶ **noun 1** *defenders of the environment* PROTECTOR, guard, guardian, preserver; custodian, watchdog, keeper, overseer. **2** *a defender of colonialism* SUPPORTER, upholder, backer, champion, advocate, apologist, proponent, exponent, promoter; adherent, believer. **3** *he passed two defenders and scored* DEFENCEMAN, backliner, blueliner, rearguard; defensive back, sweeper.

defensible ▶ **adjective 1** *a defensible attitude* JUSTIFIABLE, arguable, tenable, defendable, supportable; plausible, sound, sensible, reasonable, rational, logical; acceptable, valid, legitimate; excusable, pardonable, understandable. **2** *a defensible territory* SECURE, safe, fortified; invulnerable, impregnable, impenetrable, unassailable.
– OPPOSITES: untenable, vulnerable.

defensive ▶ **adjective 1** *troops in defensive positions* DEFENDING, protective; wary, watchful. **2** *a defensive response* SELF-JUSTIFYING, over-sensitive, prickly, paranoid, neurotic; *informal* uptight, twitchy.

defer¹ ▶ **verb** *the committee will defer their decision* POSTPONE, put off, delay, hold over/off, put back; shelve, suspend, stay, mothball, put over, table, take a rain check on; *informal* put on ice, put on the back burner, back-burner, put in cold storage.

defer² ▶ **verb** *they deferred to Joseph's judgment* YIELD, submit, give way, give in, surrender, capitulate, acquiesce; respect, honour.

deference ▶ **noun** RESPECT, respectfulness, dutifulness; submissiveness, submission, obedience, surrender, accession, capitulation, acquiescence, complaisance, obeisance.
– OPPOSITES: disrespect.

deferential ▶ **adjective** RESPECTFUL, humble, obsequious; dutiful, obedient, submissive, subservient, yielding, acquiescent, complaisant, compliant, tractable, biddable, docile.

deferment ▶ **noun** POSTPONEMENT, deferral, suspension, delay, adjournment, interruption, pause; respite, stay, moratorium, reprieve, grace.

defiance ▶ **noun** RESISTANCE, opposition, non-compliance, disobedience, insubordination, dissent, recalcitrance, subversion, rebellion; contempt, disregard, scorn, insolence, truculence.
– OPPOSITES: obedience.

defiant ▶ **adjective** INTRANSIGENT, resistant, obstinate, uncooperative, non-compliant, recalcitrant; obstreperous, truculent, dissenting, disobedient, insubordinate, subversive, rebellious, mutinous, feisty.
– OPPOSITES: co-operative.

deficiency ▶ **noun 1** *a vitamin deficiency* INSUFFICIENCY, lack, shortage, want, dearth, inadequacy, deficit, shortfall; scarcity, paucity, absence, deprivation, shortness. **2** *the team's big deficiency* DEFECT, fault, flaw, imperfection, weakness, weak point, inadequacy, shortcoming, limitation, failing.
– OPPOSITES: surplus, strength.

deficient ▶ adjective **1** *a diet deficient in vitamin A* LACKING, wanting, inadequate, insufficient, limited, poor, scant; short of/on, low in. **2** *deficient leadership* DEFECTIVE, faulty, flawed, inadequate, imperfect, shoddy, weak, inferior, unsound, substandard, second-rate, poor.

deficit ▶ noun SHORTFALL, deficiency, shortage, debt, arrears; negative amount, loss.
– OPPOSITES: surplus.

defile ▶ verb **1** *her capacity for love had been defiled* SPOIL, sully, mar, impair, debase, degrade; poison, taint, tarnish; destroy, ruin. **2** *the sacred bones were defiled* DESECRATE, profane, violate; contaminate, pollute, debase, degrade, dishonour. **3** *(archaic) she was defiled by a married man* RAPE, violate; *literary* ravish; *dated* deflower.
– OPPOSITES: sanctify.

definable ▶ adjective DETERMINABLE, ascertainable, known, definite, clear-cut, precise, exact, specific.

define ▶ verb **1** *the dictionary defines it succinctly* EXPLAIN, expound, interpret, elucidate, describe, clarify; give the meaning of, put into words. **2** *he defined the limits of the law* DETERMINE, establish, fix, specify, designate, decide, stipulate, set out; demarcate, delineate. **3** *the farm buildings defined against the fields* OUTLINE, delineate, silhouette.

definite ▶ adjective **1** *a definite answer* EXPLICIT, specific, express, precise, exact, clear-cut, direct, plain, outright; fixed, established, confirmed, concrete. **2** *definite evidence* CERTAIN, sure, positive, conclusive, decisive, firm, concrete, unambiguous, unequivocal, clear, unmistakable, proven; guaranteed, assured, cut and dried. **3** *she had a definite dislike for dogs* UNMISTAKABLE, unequivocal, unambiguous, certain, undisputed, decided, marked, distinct. **4** *a definite geographical area* FIXED, marked, demarcated, delimited, stipulated, particular.
– OPPOSITES: vague, ambiguous, indeterminate.

definitely ▶ adverb CERTAINLY, surely, for sure, unquestionably, without doubt, without question, undoubtedly, indubitably, positively, absolutely; undeniably, unmistakably, plainly, clearly, obviously, patently, palpably, transparently, unequivocally.

definition ▶ noun **1** *the definition of 'intelligence'* MEANING, denotation, sense; interpretation, explanation, elucidation, description, clarification, illustration. **2** *the definition of the picture* CLARITY, visibility, sharpness, crispness, acuteness; resolution, focus, contrast.

definitive ▶ adjective **1** *a definitive decision* CONCLUSIVE, final, ultimate; unconditional, unqualified, absolute, categorical, positive, definite. **2** *the definitive guide* AUTHORITATIVE, exhaustive, best, finest, consummate; classic, standard, recognized, accepted, official.

deflate ▶ verb **1** *he deflated the tires* LET DOWN, flatten, void; puncture. **2** *the balloon deflated* GO DOWN, collapse, shrink, contract. **3** *the news had deflated him* SUBDUE, humble, cow, chasten; dispirit, dismay, discourage, dishearten; squash, crush, bring down, take the wind out of someone's sails, knock the stuffing out of. **4** *the budget deflated the economy* REDUCE, slow down, diminish; devalue, depreciate, depress.
– OPPOSITES: inflate.

deflect ▶ verb **1** *she wanted to deflect attention from herself* TURN ASIDE/AWAY, divert, avert, sidetrack; distract, draw away; block, parry, fend off, stave off. **2** *the ball deflected off the wall* BOUNCE, glance, ricochet, carom; diverge, deviate, veer, swerve, slew.

deform ▶ verb DISFIGURE, bend out of shape, contort, buckle, warp; damage, impair.

deformed ▶ adjective MISSHAPEN, distorted, malformed, contorted, out of shape; twisted, crooked, warped, buckled, gnarled; crippled, humpbacked, hunchbacked, disfigured, grotesque; injured, damaged, mutilated, mangled.

deformity ▶ noun MALFORMATION, misshapenness, distortion, crookedness; imperfection, abnormality, irregularity; disfigurement; defect, flaw, blemish.

defraud ▶ verb SWINDLE, cheat, rob, embezzle; deceive, dupe, hoodwink, double-cross, trick; *informal* con, do, sting, diddle, rip off, shaft, bilk, rook, gyp, pull a fast one on, put one over on, sucker, snooker, stiff.

defray ▶ verb PAY (FOR), cover, meet, square, settle, clear, discharge.

deft ▶ adjective SKILFUL, adept, adroit, dexterous, agile, nimble, handy; able, capable, skilled, proficient, accomplished, expert, polished, slick, professional, masterly; clever, shrewd, astute, canny, sharp; *informal* nifty, neat.
– OPPOSITES: clumsy.

defunct ▶ adjective DISUSED, unused, inoperative, non-functioning, unusable, obsolete; no longer existing, discontinued; extinct.
– OPPOSITES: working, extant.

defuse ▶ verb **1** *he tried to defuse the grenade* DEACTIVATE, disarm, disable, make safe. **2** *an attempt to defuse the tension* REDUCE, lessen, diminish, lighten, relieve, ease, alleviate, moderate, mitigate.
– OPPOSITES: activate, intensify.

defy ▶ verb **1** *he defied local law* DISOBEY, go against, flout, fly in the face of, disregard, ignore; break, violate, contravene, breach, infringe. **2** *his actions defy belief* ELUDE, escape, defeat; frustrate, thwart, baffle. **3** *he glowered, defying her to mock him* CHALLENGE, dare.
– OPPOSITES: obey.

degeneracy ▶ noun CORRUPTION, decadence, moral decay, dissipation, dissolution, profligacy, vice, immorality, sin, sinfulness, ungodliness; debauchery; *formal* turpitude.

degenerate ▶ adjective **1** *a degenerate form of classicism* DEBASED, degraded, corrupt, impure; *formal* vitiated. **2** *her degenerate brother* CORRUPT, decadent, dissolute, dissipated, debauched, reprobate, profligate; sinful, ungodly, immoral, unprincipled, amoral, dishonourable, disreputable, unsavoury, sordid, low, ignoble.
– OPPOSITES: pure, moral.
▶ noun *a group of degenerates* REPROBATE, debauchee, profligate, libertine, roué.
▶ verb **1** *their quality of life had degenerated* DETERIORATE, decline, slip, slide, worsen, lapse, slump, go downhill, regress, retrogress; go to rack and ruin; *informal* go to pot, go to the dogs, hit the skids, go into/down the toilet. **2** *the muscles started to degenerate* WASTE (AWAY), atrophy, weaken.
– OPPOSITES: improve.

degradation ▶ noun **1** *poverty brings with it degradation* HUMILIATION, shame, loss of self-respect, abasement, indignity, ignominy. **2** *the degradation of women* DEMEANING, debasement, discrediting. **3** *the* *degradation of the tissues* DETERIORATION, degeneration, atrophy, decay; breakdown.

degrade ▸ verb **1** *prisons should not degrade prisoners* DEMEAN, debase, cheapen, devalue; shame, humiliate, humble, mortify, abase, dishonour; dehumanize, brutalize. **2** *the polymer will not degrade* BREAK DOWN, deteriorate, degenerate, decay.
− OPPOSITES: dignify.

degraded ▸ adjective **1** *I feel so degraded* HUMILIATED, demeaned, cheapened, cheap, ashamed. **2** *his degraded sensibilities* DEGENERATE, corrupt, depraved, dissolute, dissipated, debauched, immoral, base, sordid.
− OPPOSITES: proud, moral.

degrading ▸ adjective HUMILIATING, demeaning, shameful, mortifying, ignominious, undignified, inglorious, wretched.

degree ▸ noun **1** *to a high degree* LEVEL, standard, grade, mark; amount, extent, measure; magnitude, intensity, strength; proportion, ratio. **2** *she completed her degree in 3 years* DIPLOMA, academic program; baccalaureate, bachelor's, master's, doctorate, Ph.D.
■ **by degrees** GRADUALLY, little by little, bit by bit, inch by inch, step by step, slowly; piecemeal.
■ **to a degree** TO SOME EXTENT, to a certain extent, up to a point, somewhat.

dehydrate ▸ verb **1** *alcohol dehydrates the skin* DRY (OUT), desiccate, dehumidify, effloresce. **2** *frogs can dehydrate quickly* DRY UP/OUT, lose water.
− OPPOSITES: hydrate.

deify ▸ verb **1** *she was deified by the early Romans* WORSHIP, revere, venerate, reverence, hold sacred; immortalize. **2** *he was deified by the press* IDOLIZE, lionize, hero-worship, extol; idealize, glorify, aggrandize, put on a pedestal.
− OPPOSITES: demonize.

deign ▸ verb CONDESCEND, stoop, lower oneself, demean oneself, humble oneself; consent, vouchsafe; *informal* come down from one's high horse.

deity ▸ noun GOD, goddess, divine being, supreme being, divinity, immortal; creator, demiurge; godhead.

dejected ▸ adjective DOWNCAST, downhearted, despondent, disconsolate, dispirited, crestfallen, disheartened; depressed, crushed, desolate, heartbroken, in the doldrums, sad, unhappy, doleful, melancholy, miserable, woebegone, forlorn, wretched, glum, gloomy; *informal* blue, down in the mouth, down in the dumps, in a blue funk.
− OPPOSITES: cheerful.

de jure ▸ adverb & adjective BY RIGHT, rightfully, legally, according to the law; rightful, legal.
− OPPOSITES: de facto.

deke ▸ verb FEINT, fake, dodge, avoid, evade, duck, jink, swerve; dipsy-doodle, stickhandle.

delay ▸ verb **1** *we were delayed by the traffic* DETAIN, hold up, make late, slow up/down, bog down; hinder, hamper, impede, obstruct. **2** *they delayed no longer* LINGER, dally, drag one's feet, be slow, hold back, dawdle, waste time; procrastinate, stall, hang fire, mark time, temporize, hesitate, dither, shilly-shally, dilly-dally; *archaic* tarry. **3** *he may delay the cut in interest rates* POSTPONE, put off, defer, hold over, shelve, suspend, stay; reschedule, put over, push back, table; *informal* put on ice, back-burner, put on the back burner, put in cold storage.
− OPPOSITES: hurry, advance.
▸ noun **1** *drivers will face lengthy delays* HOLDUP, wait,

detainment; hindrance, impediment, obstruction, setback. **2** *the delay of his trial* POSTPONEMENT, deferral, deferment, stay, respite; adjournment. **3** *I set off without delay* PROCRASTINATION, stalling, hesitation, dithering, dallying, lallygagging, dawdling.

delectable ▸ adjective **1** *a delectable meal* DELICIOUS, mouth-watering, appetizing, flavourful, toothsome, palatable; succulent, luscious, tasty; *informal* scrumptious, delish, yummy, finger-licking, nummy, lip-smacking, melt-in-your/the-mouth. **2** *the delectable Ms. Davis* DELIGHTFUL, pleasant, lovely, captivating, charming, enchanting, appealing, beguiling; beautiful, attractive, ravishing, gorgeous, stunning, alluring, sexy, seductive, desirable, luscious; *informal* divine, heavenly, dreamy.
− OPPOSITES: unpalatable, unattractive.

delectation ▸ noun *(humorous)* ENJOYMENT, gratification, delight, pleasure, satisfaction, relish; entertainment, amusement, titillation.

delegate ▸ noun *trade union delegates* REPRESENTATIVE, envoy, emissary, commissioner, agent, deputy, commissary; spokesperson, spokesman/woman; ambassador, plenipotentiary.
▸ verb **1** *she must delegate routine tasks* ASSIGN, entrust, pass on, hand on/over, turn over, devolve, depute, transfer. **2** *they were delegated to negotiate with the States* AUTHORIZE, commission, depute, appoint, nominate, mandate, empower, charge, choose, designate, elect.

delegation ▸ noun **1** *the delegation from South Africa* DEPUTATION, legation, (diplomatic) mission, commission; delegates, representatives, envoys, emissaries, deputies; contingent. **2** *the delegation of tasks to others* ASSIGNMENT, entrusting, giving, devolution, deputation, transference.

delete ▸ verb REMOVE, cut out, take out, edit out, expunge, excise, eradicate, cancel; cross out, strike out, blue-pencil, ink out, scratch out, obliterate, white out; rub out, erase, efface, wipe out, blot out; *Printing* dele.
− OPPOSITES: add.

deleterious ▸ adjective HARMFUL, damaging, detrimental, injurious; adverse, disadvantageous, unfavourable, unfortunate, undesirable, bad.
− OPPOSITES: beneficial.

deliberate ▸ adjective **1** *a deliberate attempt to provoke him* INTENTIONAL, calculated, conscious, intended, planned, studied, knowing, wilful, purposeful, purposive, premeditated, pre-planned; voluntary, volitional. **2** *small, deliberate steps* CAREFUL, cautious; measured, regular, even, steady. **3** *a deliberate worker* METHODICAL, systematic, careful, painstaking, meticulous, thorough.
− OPPOSITES: accidental, hasty, careless.
▸ verb *she deliberated on his words* THINK ABOUT/OVER, ponder, consider, contemplate, reflect on, muse on, meditate on, ruminate on, mull over, give thought to, brood over, dwell on, think on.

deliberately ▸ adverb **1** *he deliberately hurt me* INTENTIONALLY, on purpose, purposely, by design, knowingly, wittingly, consciously, purposefully; wilfully; *Law* with malice aforethought. **2** *he walked deliberately down the aisle* CAREFULLY, cautiously, slowly, steadily, evenly.

deliberation ▸ noun **1** *after much deliberation, I accepted* THOUGHT, consideration, reflection, contemplation, meditation, rumination; *formal* cogitation. **2** *he replaced the glass with deliberation* CARE, carefulness, caution, steadiness.

delicacy ▸ noun **1** *the fabric's delicacy* FINENESS, exquisiteness, daintiness, airiness; flimsiness, gauziness, silkiness. **2** *the children's delicacy* SICKLINESS, ill health, frailty, fragility, weakness, debility; infirmity, valetudinarianism. **3** *the delicacy of the situation* DIFFICULTY, trickiness; sensitivity, ticklishness, awkwardness. **4** *treat this matter with delicacy* CARE, sensitivity, tact, discretion, diplomacy, subtlety, sensibility. **5** *an Australian delicacy* CHOICE FOOD, gourmet food, dainty, treat, luxury, specialty.

delicate ▸ adjective **1** *delicate embroidery* FINE, exquisite, intricate, dainty; flimsy, gauzy, filmy, floaty, diaphanous, wispy, insubstantial. **2** *a delicate shade of blue* SUBTLE, soft, muted; pastel, pale, light. **3** *delicate china cups* FRAGILE, breakable, frail; *formal* frangible. **4** *his wife is delicate* SICKLY, unhealthy, frail, feeble, weak, debilitated; unwell, infirm; *formal* valetudinarian. **5** *a delicate issue* DIFFICULT, tricky, sensitive, ticklish, awkward, problematic, touchy, prickly, thorny; embarrassing; *informal* sticky, dicey. **6** *the matter required delicate handling* CAREFUL, sensitive, tactful, diplomatic, discreet, kid-glove. **7** *his delicate palate* DISCRIMINATING, discerning; FASTIDIOUS, fussy, finicky, dainty; *informal* picky, choosy, pernickety, persnickety. **8** *a delicate mechanism* SENSITIVE, precision, precise.
− OPPOSITES: coarse, lurid, strong, robust, clumsy.

delicious ▸ adjective **1** *Ezio's delicious sausages* DELECTABLE, mouth-watering, appetizing, tasty, flavourful, toothsome, palatable; succulent, luscious; *informal* scrumptious, delish, yummy, finger-licking, nummy, lip-smacking, melt-in-your/the-mouth. **2** *a delicious languor stole over her* DELIGHTFUL, exquisite, lovely, pleasurable, pleasant; *informal* heavenly, divine.
− OPPOSITES: unpalatable, unpleasant.

delight ▸ verb **1** *her manners delighted him* PLEASE GREATLY, charm, enchant, captivate, entrance, thrill; gladden, gratify, appeal to; entertain, amuse, divert; *informal* send, tickle pink, bowl over. **2** *Meg delighted in his touch* TAKE PLEASURE, revel, luxuriate, wallow, glory; adore, love, relish, savour, lap up; *informal* get a kick out of, get a thrill out of, get a charge out of, dig.
− OPPOSITES: dismay, disgust, dislike.
▸ noun *she squealed with delight* PLEASURE, happiness, joy, glee, gladness; excitement, amusement; bliss, rapture, elation, euphoria.
− OPPOSITES: displeasure.

delighted ▸ adjective PLEASED, glad, happy, thrilled, overjoyed, ecstatic, elated; on cloud nine, walking on air, in seventh heaven, jumping for joy; enchanted, charmed; amused, diverted; gleeful; *informal* over the moon, tickled pink, as pleased as punch, on top of the world, blissed out, on a high.

delightful ▸ adjective **1** *a delightful evening* PLEASANT, lovely, pleasurable, enjoyable; amusing, entertaining, diverting; gratifying, satisfying; marvellous, wonderful, splendid, sublime, thrilling; *informal* great, super, fabulous, fab, terrific, heavenly, divine, grand, brilliant, peachy, ducky. **2** *the delightful Sally* CHARMING, enchanting, captivating, bewitching, appealing; sweet, endearing, cute, lovely, adorable, delectable, delicious, gorgeous, ravishing, beautiful, pretty; *informal* dreamy, divine.

delimit ▸ verb DETERMINE, establish, set, fix, demarcate, define, delineate.

delineate ▸ verb **1** *the aims of the study as delineated by the boss* DESCRIBE, set forth/out, present, outline, sketch, depict, represent; map out, define, specify, identify. **2** *a section delineated in red marker pen* OUTLINE, trace, block in, mark (out/off), delimit.

delinquency ▸ noun **1** *teenage delinquency* CRIME, wrongdoing, law-breaking, lawlessness, misconduct, misbehaviour; misdemeanours, offences, misdeeds. **2** *(formal) grave delinquency on the host's part* NEGLIGENCE, dereliction of duty, irresponsibility.

delinquent ▸ adjective **1** *delinquent teenagers* LAWLESS, law-breaking, criminal; errant, badly behaved, troublesome, difficult, unruly, disobedient, uncontrollable. **2** *(formal) delinquent parents face tough penalties* NEGLIGENT, neglectful, remiss, irresponsible, lax, slack, derelict.
− OPPOSITES: dutiful.
▸ noun *teenage delinquents* OFFENDER, wrongdoer, malefactor, lawbreaker, culprit, criminal; hooligan, vandal, mischief-maker, ruffian, hoodlum, low-life, punk; young offender.

delirious ▸ adjective **1** *she was delirious but had lucid intervals* INCOHERENT, raving, babbling, irrational; feverish, frenzied; deranged, demented, unhinged, mad, insane, out of one's mind. **2** *the crowd was delirious during the concert* ECSTATIC, euphoric, elated, thrilled, overjoyed, beside oneself, walking on air, on cloud nine, in seventh heaven, carried away, transported, rapturous, hysterical, wild, frenzied; *informal* blissed out, over the moon, on a high.

delirium ▸ noun **1** *she had fits of delirium* DERANGEMENT, dementia, madness, insanity; incoherence, irrationality, hysteria, feverishness, hallucination. **2** *the delirium of desire* ECSTASY, rapture, transports, wild emotion, passion, wildness, excitement, frenzy, feverishness, fever; euphoria, elation.
− OPPOSITES: lucidity.

deliver ▸ verb **1** *the parcel was delivered to his house* BRING, take, convey, carry, transport, courier; send, dispatch, remit. **2** *the money was delivered up to the official* HAND OVER, turn over, make over, sign over; surrender, give up, yield, cede; consign, commit, entrust, trust. **3** *he was delivered from his enemies* SAVE, rescue, free, liberate, release, extricate, emancipate, redeem. **4** *the court delivered its verdict* UTTER, give, make, read, broadcast; pronounce, announce, declare, proclaim, hand down, return, set forth. **5** *she delivered a deadly blow to his head* ADMINISTER, deal, inflict, give; *informal* land. **6** *he delivered the ball* LAUNCH, aim, pitch, hurl, throw, cast, lob. **7** *the trip delivered everything she wanted* PROVIDE, supply, furnish. **8** *we must deliver on our commitments* FULFILL, live up to, carry out, carry through, make good; *informal* deliver the goods. **9** *she returned home to deliver her child* GIVE BIRTH TO, bear, be delivered of, have, bring into the world; *informal* drop.

deliverance ▸ noun **1** *their deliverance from prison* LIBERATION, release, delivery, discharge, rescue, emancipation; salvation; *informal* bailout. **2** *the tone he adopted for such deliverances* UTTERANCE, statement, announcement, pronouncement, declaration, proclamation; lecture, speech.

delivery ▸ noun **1** *the delivery of the goods* CONVEYANCE, carriage, transportation, transport; distribution, dispatch, remittance; haulage, shipment. **2** *we get several deliveries a day* CONSIGNMENT, load, shipment. **3** *the midwife had assisted at four deliveries* BIRTH, childbirth; *formal* parturition. **4** *her delivery was stilted* SPEECH, pronunciation, enunciation, articulation, elocution, utterance, recitation, recital, execution.

delude ▶ verb MISLEAD, deceive, fool, take in, trick, dupe, hoodwink, gull, lead on; *informal* con, pull the wool over someone's eyes, lead up the garden path, take for a ride, sucker, snooker.

deluge ▶ noun **1** *homes were swept away by the deluge* FLOOD, torrent, spate. **2** *the deluge turned the field into a swamp* DOWNPOUR, torrential rain; thunderstorm, thundershower, rainstorm, cloudburst. **3** *a deluge of complaints* BARRAGE, volley; flood, torrent, avalanche, stream, spate, rush, outpouring, niagara.
▶ verb **1** *homes were deluged by the rains* FLOOD, inundate, submerge, swamp, drown. **2** *we have been deluged with calls* INUNDATE, overwhelm, overrun, flood, swamp, snow under, engulf, bombard.

delusion ▶ noun MISAPPREHENSION, misconception, misunderstanding, mistake, error, misinterpretation, misconstruction, misbelief; fallacy, illusion, fantasy.

deluxe ▶ adjective LUXURIOUS, luxury, sumptuous, palatial, opulent, lavish; grand, high-class, quality, exclusive, choice, fancy; expensive, costly, upscale, upmarket; high-end, top-line, top-notch, five-star; *informal* plush, posh, classy, ritzy, swanky, pricey, swank.
— OPPOSITES: basic, cheap.

delve ▶ verb **1** *she delved into her pocket* RUMMAGE, search, hunt, scrabble around, root about/around, ferret, fish about/around in, dig; go through, rifle through. **2** *we must delve deeper into the matter* INVESTIGATE, inquire, probe, explore, research, look into, go into.

demagogue ▶ noun RABBLE-ROUSER, (political) agitator, soapbox orator, firebrand, fomenter, provocateur; *informal* tub-thumper.

demand ▶ noun **1** *I gave in to her demands* REQUEST, call, command, order, dictate, ultimatum, stipulation. **2** *the demands of a young family* REQUIREMENT, need, desire, wish, want; claim, imposition. **3** *there is a big demand for such toys* MARKET, call, appetite, desire.
▶ verb **1** *workers demanded wage increases* CALL FOR, ask for, request, push for, hold out for; insist on, claim. **2** *Harvey demanded that I tell him the truth* ORDER, command, enjoin, urge; *literary* bid. **3** *'Where is she?' he demanded* ASK, inquire, question, interrogate; challenge. **4** *an activity demanding detailed knowledge* REQUIRE, need, necessitate, call for, involve, entail. **5** *they demanded complete anonymity* INSIST ON, stipulate, make a condition of; expect, look for.
■ **in demand** SOUGHT-AFTER, desired, coveted, wanted, requested; marketable, desirable, popular, all the rage, at a premium, big, trendy, hot.

demanding ▶ adjective **1** *a demanding task* DIFFICULT, challenging, taxing, exacting, tough, hard, onerous, burdensome, formidable; arduous, uphill, rigorous, gruelling, back-breaking, punishing. **2** *a demanding child* NAGGING, clamorous, importunate, insistent; trying, tiresome, hard to please.
— OPPOSITES: easy.

demarcate ▶ verb SEPARATE, divide, mark (out/off), delimit, delineate; bound.

demarcation ▶ noun **1** *clear demarcation of function* SEPARATION, distinction, differentiation, division, delimitation, definition. **2** *territorial demarcations* BOUNDARY, border, borderline, frontier; dividing line, divide.

demean ▶ verb DEBASE, lower, degrade, discredit, devalue; cheapen, abase, humble, humiliate, disgrace, dishonour.
— OPPOSITES: dignify.

demeaning ▶ adjective DEGRADING, humiliating, shameful, mortifying, abject, ignominious, undignified, inglorious.

demeanour ▶ noun MANNER, air, attitude, appearance, look; bearing, carriage; behaviour, conduct; *formal* comportment.

demented ▶ adjective MAD, insane, deranged, out of one's mind, crazed, lunatic, unbalanced, unhinged, disturbed, non compos mentis; *informal* crazy, mental, psycho, off one's rocker, nutty, round the bend, raving mad, batty, cuckoo, loopy, loony, bananas, screwy, touched, gaga, not all there, out to lunch, bonkers, crackers, cracked, bushed ♣, buggy, nutso, squirrelly, wacko.
— OPPOSITES: sane.

dementia ▶ noun MENTAL ILLNESS, madness, insanity, derangement, lunacy.

demise ▶ noun **1** *her tragic demise* DEATH, dying, passing, loss of life, end, quietus; *formal* decease; *archaic* expiry. **2** *the demise of the Ottoman empire* END, breakup, disintegration, fall, downfall, collapse.
— OPPOSITES: birth.

demobilize ▶ verb DISBAND, decommission, discharge, demilitarize; *informal* demob.

democracy ▶ noun REPRESENTATIVE GOVERNMENT, elective government; self-government, autonomy; republic, commonwealth.
— OPPOSITES: dictatorship.

democratic ▶ adjective ELECTED, representative, parliamentary, popular; egalitarian, classless; self-governing, autonomous, republican.

demolish ▶ verb **1** *they demolished the building* KNOCK DOWN, pull down, tear down, bring down, destroy, flatten, raze (to the ground), level, bulldoze, topple; blow up; dismantle, disassemble. **2** *he demolished her credibility* DESTROY, ruin, wreck; refute, disprove, discredit, overturn, explode; *informal* poke holes in. **3** *(informal) our team was demolished.* See TROUNCE. **4** *(informal) she demolished a bagel.* See DEVOUR sense 1.
— OPPOSITES: construct, strengthen.

demon ▶ noun **1** *the demons from hell* DEVIL, fiend, evil spirit; incubus, succubus. **2** *the man was a demon* MONSTER, ogre, fiend, devil, brute, savage, beast, barbarian, animal. **3** *she's a demon on the tennis court* PRO, ace, expert, genius, master, virtuoso, maestro, past master, marvel; star; *informal* hotshot, whiz, buff. **4** *the demon of creativity.* See DAEMON.
— OPPOSITES: angel, saint.

demonic, demoniac ▶ adjective **1** *demonic powers* DEVILISH, fiendish, diabolical, satanic, Mephistophelean, hellish, infernal; evil, wicked. **2** *the demonic intensity of his playing* FRENZIED, wild, feverish, frenetic, frantic, furious, manic, like one possessed.

demonstrable ▶ adjective VERIFIABLE, provable, attestable; verified, proven, confirmed; obvious, clear, clear-cut, evident, apparent, manifest, patent, distinct, noticeable; unmistakable, undeniable.

demonstrate ▶ verb **1** *his findings demonstrate that boys commit more crimes* SHOW, indicate, determine, establish, prove, confirm, verify, corroborate, substantiate. **2** *she was asked to demonstrate quilting* GIVE A DEMONSTRATION OF, show how something is done; display, show, illustrate, exemplify, demo. **3** *his work demonstrated an analytical ability* REVEAL, bespeak, indicate, signify, signal, denote, show, display, exhibit; bear witness to, testify to; imply, intimate, give away. **4** *they demonstrated against the Government* PROTEST, rally, march; stage a sit-in, picket, strike, walk out; mutiny, rebel.

demonstration ▶ noun **1** *a dubious demonstration of God's existence* PROOF, substantiation, confirmation, affirmation, corroboration, verification, validation; evidence, indication, witness, testament. **2** *a demonstration of woodcarving* EXHIBITION, presentation, display, exposition, teach-in, demo, expo. **3** *his paintings are a demonstration of his talent* MANIFESTATION, indication, sign, mark, token, embodiment; expression. **4** *an anti-racism demonstration* PROTEST, march, rally, lobby, sit-in; stoppage, strike, walkout, picket (line); *informal* demo.

demonstrative ▶ adjective **1** *a very demonstrative family* EXPRESSIVE, open, forthcoming, communicative, unreserved, emotional, effusive, gushing; affectionate, cuddly, loving, warm, friendly, approachable; *informal* touchy-feely, lovey-dovey, huggy. **2** *the successes are demonstrative of their skill* INDICATIVE, suggestive, illustrative. **3** *demonstrative evidence of his theorem* CONVINCING, definite, positive, telling, conclusive, certain, decisive; incontrovertible, irrefutable, undeniable, indisputable, unassailable.
− OPPOSITES: reserved, inconclusive.

demoralize ▶ verb DISHEARTEN, dispirit, deject, cast down, depress, dismay, daunt, discourage, unman, unnerve, crush, shake, throw, cow, subdue; break someone's spirit, knock the stuffing out of,
− OPPOSITES: hearten.

demoralized ▶ adjective DISPIRITED, disheartened, downhearted, dejected, downcast, low, depressed, despairing; disconsolate, crestfallen, disappointed, dismayed, daunted, discouraged; crushed, humbled, subdued.

demote ▶ verb DOWNGRADE, relegate, declass, reduce in rank; depose, unseat, displace, oust; *Military* cashier.
− OPPOSITES: promote.

demotic ▶ adjective POPULAR, vernacular, colloquial, idiomatic, vulgar, common; informal, everyday, slangy.
− OPPOSITES: formal.

demur ▶ verb *Steve demurred when the suggestion was made* OBJECT, take exception, take issue, protest, cavil, dissent; voice reservations, be unwilling, be reluctant, balk, think twice; drag one's heels, refuse; *informal* boggle, kick up a fuss.
▶ noun *they accepted without demur* OBJECTION, protest, protestation, complaint, dispute, dissent, opposition, resistance; reservation, hesitation, reluctance, disinclination; doubts, qualms, misgivings, second thoughts; a murmur, a word.

demure ▶ adjective MODEST, unassuming, meek, mild, reserved, retiring, quiet, shy, bashful, diffident, reticent, timid, shrinking, coy; decorous, decent, seemly, ladylike, respectable, proper, virtuous, pure, innocent, chaste; sober, sedate, staid, prim, goody-goody, straitlaced.
− OPPOSITES: brazen.

den ▶ noun **1** *the mink left its den* LAIR, set, earth, burrow, hole, dugout, covert, shelter, hiding place, hideout, hidey-hole. **2** *a notorious drinking den* HAUNT, site, hotbed, nest, pit, hole; *informal* joint, dive. **3** *he scribbled a letter in his den* STUDY, studio, library; family room, living room, rumpus room; sanctum, retreat, sanctuary, hideaway.

denial ▶ noun **1** *the reports met with a denial* CONTRADICTION, refutation, rebuttal, repudiation, disclaimer; negation, dissent. **2** *the denial of insurance to certain people* REFUSAL, withholding; rejection, rebuff, repulse, veto, turndown; *formal* declination. **3** *the denial of worldly values* RENUNCIATION, eschewal, repudiation, disavowal, rejection, abandonment; surrender, relinquishment.

denigrate ▶ verb DISPARAGE, belittle, deprecate, decry, cast aspersions on, criticize, attack; speak ill of, give someone a bad name, defame, slander, libel; run down, abuse, insult, revile, malign, vilify, slur; *informal* badmouth, dis, pull to pieces.
− OPPOSITES: extol.

denizen ▶ noun *(formal)* INHABITANT, resident, townsman/woman, native, local; occupier, occupant, dweller; *archaic* burgher.

denominate ▶ verb *(formal)* CALL, name, term, designate, style, dub, label, tag, entitle.

denomination ▶ noun **1** *a Christian denomination* RELIGIOUS GROUP, sect, cult, movement, body, branch, persuasion, order, school; Church. **2** *they demanded bills in small denominations* VALUE, unit, size.

denote ▶ verb **1** *the headdresses denoted warriors* DESIGNATE, indicate, be a mark of, signify, signal, symbolize, represent, mean; typify, characterize, distinguish, mark, identify. **2** *his manner denoted an inner strength* SUGGEST, point to, smack of, indicate, show, reveal, intimate, imply, convey, betray, bespeak, spell.

denouement ▶ noun **1** *the film's denouement* FINALE, final scene, epilogue, coda, end, ending, finish, close; culmination, climax, conclusion, solution. **2** *the debate had an unexpected denouement* OUTCOME, upshot, consequence, result, end; *informal* payoff.
− OPPOSITES: beginning, origin.

denounce ▶ verb **1** *the Pope denounced abortion* CONDEMN, criticize, attack, censure, decry, revile, vilify, discredit, damn, reject; proscribe; malign, rail against, run down, slur; *informal* knock, slam, hit out at, lay into; *formal* castigate. **2** *he was denounced as a traitor* EXPOSE, betray, inform on; incriminate, implicate, cite, name, accuse.
− OPPOSITES: praise.

dense ▶ adjective **1** *a dense forest* THICK, close-packed, tightly packed, closely set, close-set, crowded, compact, solid, tight; overgrown, jungly, impenetrable, impassable. **2** *dense smoke* THICK, heavy, opaque, soupy, murky, smoggy; concentrated, condensed. **3** *(informal) they were dense enough to believe me* STUPID, unintelligent, ignorant, brainless, mindless, foolish, slow, witless, simple-minded, empty-headed, stunned ♣, vacuous, vapid, idiotic, imbecilic; *informal* thick, dim, moronic, dumb, dopey, dozy, wooden-headed, lamebrained, birdbrained, pea-brained; daft.
− OPPOSITES: sparse, thin, clever.

density ▶ noun SOLIDITY, solidness, denseness, thickness, substance, mass; compactness, tightness, hardness.

dent ▶ noun **1** *I made a dent in his car* INDENTATION, dimple, dip, depression, hollow, crater, pit, trough. **2** *a nasty dent in their finances* REDUCTION, depletion, deduction, cut.
− OPPOSITES: increase.
▶ verb **1** *Jamie dented his bike* INDENT, mark, ding. **2** *the experience dented her confidence* DIMINISH, reduce, lessen,

shrink, weaken, erode, undermine, sap, shake, damage, impair.

dentist ▶ noun DENTAL SURGEON, orthodontist, periodontist.

denude ▶ verb STRIP, clear, deprive, bereave, rob; lay bare, uncover, expose; deforest, defoliate; *dated* divest.
— OPPOSITES: cover.

deny ▶ verb **1** *the report was denied by witnesses* CONTRADICT, repudiate, challenge, contest, oppose; disprove, debunk, explode, discredit, refute, rebut, invalidate, negate, nullify, quash; *informal* poke holes in; *formal* gainsay. **2** *he denied the request* REFUSE, turn down, reject, rebuff, repulse, decline, veto, dismiss; *informal* give the thumbs down to, give the red light to, nix. **3** *she had to deny her parents* RENOUNCE, eschew, repudiate, disavow, disown, wash one's hands of, reject, discard, cast aside, abandon, give up; *formal* forswear; *literary* forsake.
— OPPOSITES: confirm, accept.

deodorant ▶ noun *an underarm deodorant* ANTIPERSPIRANT, body spray, perfume, scent; *informal* roll-on.

deodorize ▶ verb FRESHEN, sweeten, purify, disinfect, sanitize, sterilize; fumigate, aerate, air, ventilate.

depart ▶ verb **1** *James departed after lunch* LEAVE, go (away), withdraw, absent oneself, abstract oneself, quit, exit, decamp, retreat, retire; make off, run off/away; set off/out, get underway, be on one's way; *informal* make tracks, clear off/out, take off, split. **2** *the budget departed from the norm* DEVIATE, diverge, digress, drift, stray, veer; differ, vary; contrast with.
— OPPOSITES: arrive.

departed ▶ adjective DEAD, expired, gone, no more, passed on/away; perished, fallen; *informal* six feet under, pushing up daisies; *formal* deceased; with God, asleep.

department ▶ noun **1** *the public health department* DIVISION, section, sector, unit, branch, arm, wing; office, bureau, agency, ministry. **2** *the food is Kay's department* DOMAIN, territory, province, area, line; responsibility, duty, function, business, affair, charge, task, concern; *informal* baby, bag, bailiwick.

departure ▶ noun **1** *he tried to delay her departure* LEAVING, going, leave-taking, withdrawal, exit, egress, retreat. **2** *a departure from the norm* DEVIATION, divergence, digression, shift; variation, change. **3** *an exciting departure for film-makers* CHANGE, innovation, novelty, rarity.

depend ▶ verb **1** *her career depends on a good reference* BE CONTINGENT ON, be conditional on, be dependent on, hinge on, hang on, rest on, rely on; be decided by. **2** *my family depends on me* RELY ON, lean on; count on, bank on, trust (in), have faith in, believe in; pin one's hopes on.

dependable ▶ adjective RELIABLE, trustworthy, trusty, faithful, loyal, unfailing, sure, steadfast, stable; honourable, sensible, responsible.

dependant ▶ noun CHILD, minor; ward, charge, protege; relative; (**dependants**) offspring, progeny.

dependence ▶ noun. *See* DEPENDENCY senses 1, 2, 3.

dependency ▶ noun **1** *her dependency on her husband* DEPENDENCE, reliance; need for. **2** *the association of retirement with dependency* HELPLESSNESS, dependence, weakness, defencelessness, vulnerability. **3** *drug dependency* ADDICTION, dependence, reliance; craving, compulsion, fixation, obsession; abuse.
— OPPOSITES: independence.

dependent ▶ adjective **1** *your placement is dependent on her decision* CONDITIONAL, contingent, based; subject to, determined by, influenced by. **2** *the army is dependent on volunteers* RELIANT ON, relying on, counting on; sustained by. **3** *she is dependent on drugs* ADDICTED TO, reliant on; *informal* hooked on. **4** *he is ill and dependent* RELIANT, needy; helpless, weak, infirm, invalid, incapable; debilitated, disabled.

depict ▶ verb **1** *the painting depicts the Last Supper* PORTRAY, represent, picture, illustrate, delineate, reproduce, render; draw, paint. **2** *the process depicted by Darwin's theory* DESCRIBE, detail, relate; present, set forth, set out, outline, delineate; represent, portray, characterize.

depiction ▶ noun **1** *a depiction of Aphrodite* PICTURE, painting, portrait, drawing, sketch, study, illustration; image, likeness. **2** *the film's depiction of women* PORTRAYAL, representation, presentation, characterization.

deplete ▶ verb EXHAUST, use up, consume, expend, drain, empty, milk; reduce, decrease, diminish; slim down, cut back.
— OPPOSITES: augment.

depletion ▶ noun EXHAUSTION, use, consumption, expenditure; reduction, decrease, diminution; impoverishment.

deplorable ▶ adjective **1** *your conduct is deplorable* DISGRACEFUL, shameful, dishonourable, unworthy, inexcusable, unpardonable, unforgivable; reprehensible, despicable, abominable, contemptible, execrable, heinous, beyond the pale. **2** *the garden is in a deplorable state* LAMENTABLE, regrettable, unfortunate, wretched, atrocious, awful, terrible, dreadful, diabolical; sorry, poor, inadequate; *informal* appalling, dire, abysmal, woeful, lousy; *formal* grievous.
— OPPOSITES: admirable.

deplore ▶ verb **1** *we deplore violence* ABHOR, find unacceptable, frown on, disapprove of, take a dim view of, take exception to; detest, despise; condemn, denounce. **2** *he deplored their lack of flair* REGRET, lament, mourn, rue, bemoan, bewail, complain about, grieve over, sigh over.
— OPPOSITES: applaud.

deploy ▶ verb **1** *forces were deployed at strategic points* POSITION, station, post, place, install, locate, situate, site, establish; base; distribute, dispose. **2** *she deployed all her skills* USE, utilize, employ, take advantage of, exploit; bring into service, call on, turn to, resort to.

deport ▶ verb **1** *they were fined and deported* EXPEL, banish, exile, transport, expatriate, extradite, repatriate; evict, oust, throw out; *informal* kick out, boot out, send packing, turf out. **2** *(archaic) he deported himself with dignity. See* BEHAVE sense 1.
— OPPOSITES: admit.

deportment ▶ noun *unprofessional deportment* BEHAVIOUR, conduct, performance; manners, practices, actions.

depose ▶ verb **1** *the president was deposed* OVERTHROW, unseat, dethrone, topple, remove, supplant, displace; dismiss, oust, drum out, throw out, expel, eject; *informal* chuck out, boot out, get rid of, show someone the door, turf out. **2** *(Law) a witness deposed that he had seen me* SWEAR, testify, attest, assert, declare, claim.

deposit ▶ noun **1** *a thick deposit of ash* ACCUMULATION, sediment; layer, covering, coating, blanket. **2** *a copper deposit* SEAM, vein, lode, layer, stratum, bed, pipe.

3 *they paid a deposit* DOWN PAYMENT, advance payment, prepayment, instalment, retainer, stake.
▶ **verb 1** *she deposited her books on the table* PUT (DOWN), place, set (down), unload, rest; drop; *informal* dump, park, plonk, plunk. **2** *the silt deposited by flood water* LEAVE (BEHIND), precipitate, dump; wash up, cast up. **3** *the gold was deposited at the bank* LODGE, bank, house, store, stow, put away; *informal* stash, squirrel away.

deposition ▶ **noun 1** *(Law) depositions from witnesses* STATEMENT, affidavit, attestation, affirmation, assertion; allegation, declaration; testimony, evidence; *rare* asseveration. **2** *the deposition of calcium* DEPOSITING, accumulation, buildup, precipitation.

depository ▶ **noun** REPOSITORY, cache, store, storeroom, storehouse, warehouse; vault, strongroom, safe, treasury; container, receptacle.

depot ▶ **noun 1** *the bus depot* TERMINAL, terminus, station, garage; headquarters, base. **2** *an arms depot* STOREHOUSE, warehouse, store, repository, depository, cache; arsenal, magazine, armoury, ammunition dump, drop-off.

deprave ▶ **verb** CORRUPT, lead astray, warp, subvert, pervert, debauch, debase, degrade, defile, sully, pollute.

depraved ▶ **adjective** CORRUPT, perverted, deviant, degenerate, debased, immoral, unprincipled; debauched, dissolute, licentious, lecherous, prurient, indecent, sordid; wicked, sinful, vile, iniquitous, nefarious; *informal* warped, twisted, pervy, sick.

depravity ▶ **noun** CORRUPTION, vice, perversion, deviance, degeneracy, immorality, debauchery, dissipation, profligacy, licentiousness, lechery, prurience, obscenity, indecency; wickedness, sin, iniquity; *formal* turpitude.

deprecate ▶ **verb 1** *the school deprecates this behaviour* DEPLORE, abhor, disapprove of, frown on, take a dim view of, take exception to, detest, despise; criticize, censure. **2** *he deprecates the value of television.* See DEPRECIATE sense 3.
— OPPOSITES: praise, overrate.

deprecatory ▶ **adjective 1** *deprecatory remarks* DISAPPROVING, censorious, critical, scathing, damning, condemnatory, denunciatory, disparaging, denigrating, derogatory, negative, unflattering; disdainful, derisive, snide. **2** *a deprecatory smile* APOLOGETIC, rueful, regretful, sorry, remorseful, contrite, penitent, repentant; shamefaced, sheepish.

depreciate ▶ **verb 1** *these cars will depreciate quickly* DECREASE IN VALUE, lose value, fall in price. **2** *the decision to depreciate property* DEVALUE, cheapen, reduce, lower in price, mark down, discount. **3** *they depreciate the importance of art* BELITTLE, disparage, denigrate, decry, deprecate, underrate, undervalue, underestimate, diminish, trivialize; disdain, sneer at, scoff at, scorn; *informal* knock, badmouth, sell short, pooh-pooh.

depreciation ▶ **noun** *we are concerned about the depreciation of house prices* DEVALUATION, devaluing, decrease in value, lowering in value, reduction in value, cheapening, markdown, reduction, decline, downturn, downswing, drop, slump, plunge, tumble, nosedive, crash.
— OPPOSITES: rise.

depredation ▶ **noun** PLUNDERING, plunder, looting, pillaging, robbery; devastation, destruction, damage, rape; ravages, raids.

depress ▶ **verb 1** *the news depressed him* SADDEN, dispirit, cast down, get down, dishearten, demoralize, crush, shake, desolate, weigh down, oppress; upset, distress, grieve, haunt, harrow; *informal* give someone the blues. **2** *new economic policies depressed sales* SLOW DOWN, reduce, lower, weaken, impair; limit, check, inhibit, restrict. **3** *foreign imports will depress domestic prices* REDUCE, lower, cut, cheapen, keep down, discount, deflate, depreciate, devalue, diminish, axe, slash. **4** *depress each lever in turn* PRESS, push, hold down; thumb, tap; operate, activate.
— OPPOSITES: encourage, raise.

depressant ▶ **noun** SEDATIVE, tranquilizer, calmative, sleeping pill, soporific, opiate, hypnotic; *informal* downer, trank; *proprietary* Valium, Quaaludes; *Medicine* neuroleptic.
— OPPOSITES: stimulant.

depressed ▶ **adjective 1** *he felt lonely and depressed* SAD, unhappy, miserable, gloomy, glum, melancholy, dejected, disconsolate, downhearted, downcast, down, despondent, dispirited, low, heavy-hearted, morose, dismal, desolate; tearful, upset; *informal* blue, down in the dumps, down in the mouth. **2** *a depressed economy* WEAK, enervated, devitalized, impaired; inactive, flat, slow, slack, sluggish, stagnant. **3** *depressed prices* REDUCED, low, cut, cheap, marked down, discounted, discount; *informal* slashed. **4** *a depressed part of town* POVERTY-STRICKEN, poor, disadvantaged, underprivileged, deprived, needy, distressed; run-down, slummy. **5** *a depressed hollow* SUNKEN, hollow, concave, indented, recessed.
— OPPOSITES: cheerful, strong, inflated, prosperous, raised.

depressing ▶ **adjective 1** *depressing thoughts* UPSETTING, distressing, painful, heartbreaking; dismal, bleak, black, sombre, gloomy, grave, unhappy, melancholy, sad; wretched, doleful; *informal* morbid, blue. **2** *a depressing room* GLOOMY, bleak, dreary, grim, drab, sombre, dark, dingy, funereal, cheerless, joyless, comfortless, uninviting.

depression ▶ **noun 1** *she sank into a depression* UNHAPPINESS, sadness, melancholy, melancholia, misery, sorrow, woe, gloom, despondency, low spirits, heavy heart, despair, desolation, hopelessness; upset, tearfulness; *informal* the dumps, the doldrums, the blues, a (blue) funk; *Psychiatry* dysthymia, seasonal affective disorder, SAD. **2** *an economic depression* RECESSION, slump, decline, downturn, standstill; stagnation; the Great Depression, the dirty thirties ✦, *Economics* stagflation. **3** *a depression in the ground* HOLLOW, indentation, dent, cavity, concavity, dip, pit, hole, sinkhole, trough, crater, basin, bowl.

deprivation ▶ **noun 1** *unemployment and deprivation* POVERTY, impoverishment, penury, privation, hardship, destitution; need, want, distress, indigence, beggary, ruin; straitened circumstances. **2** *deprivation of political rights* DISPOSSESSION, withholding, withdrawal, removal, divestment, expropriation, seizure, confiscation; denial, forfeiture, loss; absence, lack.
— OPPOSITES: wealth.

deprive ▶ **verb** DISPOSSESS, strip, divest, relieve, deny, rob; cheat out of; *informal* do out of.

deprived ▶ **adjective** DISADVANTAGED, underprivileged, poverty-stricken, impoverished, poor, destitute, needy, unable to make ends meet.

depth ▶ **noun 1** *the depth of the caves* DEEPNESS, distance downwards, distance inwards; drop, vertical

extent; *archaic* profundity. **2** *the depth of his knowledge* EXTENT, range, scope, breadth, width; magnitude, scale, degree. **3** *her lack of depth* PROFUNDITY, deepness, wisdom, understanding, intelligence, sagacity, discernment, penetration, insight, astuteness, acumen, shrewdness; *formal* perspicuity. **4** *a work of great depth* COMPLEXITY, intricacy; profundity, gravity, weight. **5** *depth of colour* INTENSITY, richness, deepness, vividness, strength, brilliance. **6** *the depths of the sea* DEEPEST PART, bottom, floor, bed; abyss.
− OPPOSITES: shallowness, triviality, surface.
■ **in depth** THOROUGHLY, extensively, comprehensively, rigorously, exhaustively, completely, fully; meticulously, scrupulously, painstakingly.

deputation ▶ noun DELEGATION, legation, commission, committee, (diplomatic) mission; contingent, group, party.

depute ▶ verb **1** *he was deputed to handle negotiations.* See DESIGNATE sense 1. **2** *the judge deputed smaller cases to others.* See DELEGATE verb sense 1.

deputize ▶ verb **1** *he deputized them to keep order in his absence* APPOINT (AS A DEPUTY), designate, delegate, commission, charge, empower, enable. **2** *he deputized as registrar* STAND IN, sit in, fill in, cover, substitute, replace, take someone's place, understudy, be a locum, relieve, take over; hold the fort, act for, act on behalf of; *informal* sub.

deputy ▶ noun *he handed over to his deputy* SECOND, second-in-command, number two; substitute, stand-in, fill-in, relief, understudy, locum tenens; representative, proxy, agent, spokesperson; *informal* sidekick, locum.
▶ adjective *her deputy editor* ASSISTANT, substitute, stand-in, acting, reserve, fill-in, caretaker, temporary, provisional, stop-gap, surrogate, interim; *informal* second-string.

deranged ▶ adjective INSANE, mad, disturbed, unbalanced, unhinged, unstable, irrational; crazed, demented, berserk, frenzied, lunatic, certifiable; non compos mentis; *informal* touched, crazy, mental, psycho.
− OPPOSITES: rational.

derelict ▶ adjective **1** *a derelict building* DILAPIDATED, ramshackle, run-down, tumbledown, in ruins, falling apart; rickety, creaky, deteriorating, crumbling; neglected, untended, gone to rack and ruin. **2** *a derelict airfield* DISUSED, abandoned, deserted, discarded, rejected, neglected, untended. **3** *he was derelict in his duty* NEGLIGENT, neglectful, remiss, lax, careless, sloppy, slipshod, slack, irresponsible, delinquent.
▶ noun *the derelicts who survive on the streets* TRAMP, vagrant, vagabond, down and out, homeless person, drifter; beggar, mendicant; outcast; *informal* bag lady, hobo, bum.

dereliction ▶ noun **1** *buildings were reclaimed from dereliction* DILAPIDATION, disrepair, deterioration, ruin, rack and ruin; abandonment, neglect, disuse. **2** *dereliction of duty* NEGLIGENCE, neglect, delinquency, failure; carelessness, laxity, sloppiness, slackness, irresponsibility; oversight, omission.

deride ▶ verb RIDICULE, mock, scoff at, jibe at, make fun of, poke fun at, laugh at, hold up to ridicule, pillory; disdain, disparage, denigrate, dismiss, slight; sneer at, scorn, insult; *informal* knock, pooh-pooh.
− OPPOSITES: praise.

de rigueur ▶ adjective **1** *straight hair was de rigueur* FASHIONABLE, in fashion, in vogue, modish, up to date, up-to-the-minute, all the rage, du jour, trendy, with it. **2** *an address is de rigueur for business cards* CUSTOMARY, standard, conventional, normal, orthodox, usual, comme il faut; compulsory, necessary, essential; *informal* done.

derision ▶ noun MOCKERY, ridicule, jeers, sneers, taunts; disdain, disparagement, denigration, disrespect, insults; scorn, contempt; lampooning, satire.

derisive ▶ adjective MOCKING, jeering, scoffing, teasing, derisory, snide, sneering; disdainful, scornful, contemptuous, taunting, insulting; scathing, sarcastic.

derisory ▶ adjective **1** *a derisory sum* INADEQUATE, insufficient, tiny, small; trifling, paltry, pitiful, miserly, miserable; negligible, token, nominal; ridiculous, laughable, ludicrous, preposterous, insulting; *informal* measly, stingy, lousy, pathetic, piddling, piffling, mingy. **2** *derisory calls from the crowd.* See DERISIVE.

derivation ▶ noun **1** *the derivation of theories from empirical observation* DERIVING, induction, deduction, inference; extraction, eliciting. **2** *the derivation of a word* ORIGIN, etymology, root, etymon, provenance, source; origination, beginning, foundation, basis, cause; development, evolution.

derivative ▶ adjective *her poetry was derivative* IMITATIVE, unoriginal, uninventive, unimaginative, uninspired; copied, plagiarized, plagiaristic, second-hand; trite, hackneyed, clichéd, stale, stock, banal; *informal* copycat, cribbed, old hat.
− OPPOSITES: original.
▶ noun *a derivative of opium* BY-PRODUCT, subsidiary product; spinoff.

derive ▶ verb **1** *he derives consolation from his poetry* OBTAIN, get, take, gain, acquire, procure, extract, attain, glean. **2** *'coffee' derives from the Turkish 'kahveh'* ORIGINATE IN, stem from, descend from, spring from, be taken from. **3** *his fortune derives from trade* ORIGINATE IN, be rooted in; stem from, come from, spring from, proceed from, issue from.

derogate ▶ verb (*formal*) **1** *his contribution was derogated by critics* DISPARAGE, denigrate, belittle, deprecate, deflate; decry, discredit, cast aspersions on, run down, criticize; defame, vilify, abuse, insult, attack, pour scorn on; *informal* drag through the mud, knock, slam, bash, badmouth, dis. **2** *the act would derogate from the king's majesty* DETRACT FROM, devalue, diminish, reduce, lessen, depreciate; demean, cheapen. **3** *behaviours which derogate from the norm* DEVIATE, diverge, depart, digress, stray; differ, vary; conflict with, be incompatible with.
− OPPOSITES: praise, increase.

derogatory ▶ adjective DISPARAGING, denigratory, deprecatory, disrespectful, demeaning; critical, pejorative, negative, unfavourable, uncomplimentary, unflattering, insulting; offensive, personal, abusive, rude, nasty, mean, hurtful; defamatory, slanderous, libellous; *informal* bitchy, catty.
− OPPOSITES: complimentary.

descend ▶ verb **1** *the plane started descending* GO DOWN, come down; drop, fall, sink, dive, plummet, plunge, nosedive. **2** *she descended the stairs* CLIMB DOWN, go down, come down. **3** *the road descends to a village* SLOPE, dip, slant, go down, fall away. **4** *she saw Herb descend from the bus* ALIGHT, disembark, get down, get off, dismount. **5** *they would not descend to such mean tricks* STOOP, lower oneself, demean oneself, debase

oneself; resort, be reduced, go as far as. **6** *the army descended into chaos* DEGENERATE, deteriorate, decline, sink, slide, fall. **7** *they descended on the spot* COME IN FORCE, arrive in hordes; attack, assail, assault, storm, invade, swoop on, charge. **8** *he is descended from a Flemish family* BE A DESCENDANT OF, originate from, issue from, spring from, derive from. **9** *his estates descended to his son* BE HANDED DOWN, be passed down; be inherited by.
− OPPOSITES: ascend, climb, board.

descendant ► noun SUCCESSOR, scion; heir; (**descendants**) offspring, progeny, family, lineage; *Law* issue; *archaic* seed, fruit of one's loins.
− OPPOSITES: ancestor.

descent ► noun **1** *the plane began its descent* DIVE, drop; fall, pitch, nosedive. **2** *their descent of the mountain* DOWNWARD CLIMB. **3** *a steep descent* SLOPE, incline, dip, drop, gradient, declivity, slant; hill. **4** *his descent into alcoholism* DECLINE, slide, fall, degeneration, deterioration, regression. **5** *she is of Italian descent* ANCESTRY, parentage, ancestors, family, antecedents; extraction, origin, derivation, birth; lineage, line, genealogy, heredity, stock, pedigree, blood, bloodline; roots, origins. **6** *the descent of property* INHERITANCE, succession. **7** *the sudden descent of the cavalry* ATTACK, assault, raid, onslaught, charge, thrust, push, drive, incursion, foray.

describe ► verb **1** *he described his experiences* REPORT, recount, relate, tell of, set out, chronicle; detail, catalogue, give a rundown of; explain, illustrate, discuss, comment on. **2** *she described him as a pathetic figure* DESIGNATE, pronounce, call, label, style, dub; characterize, class; portray, depict, brand, paint. **3** *the pen described a circle* DELINEATE, mark out, outline, trace, draw.

description ► noun **1** *a description of my travels* ACCOUNT, report, rendition, explanation, illustration; chronicle, narration, narrative, story, commentary; portrayal, portrait; details. **2** *the description of coal as 'bottled sunshine'* DESIGNATION, labelling, naming, dubbing, pronouncement; characterization, classification, branding; portrayal, depiction. **3** *vehicles of every description* SORT, variety, kind, type, category, order, breed, class, designation, specification, genre, genus, brand, make, character, ilk, stripe.

descriptive ► adjective ILLUSTRATIVE, expressive, graphic, detailed, lively, vivid, striking; explanatory, explicative.

descry ► verb (*literary*). See NOTICE verb.

desecrate ► verb VIOLATE, profane, defile, debase, degrade, dishonour; vandalize, damage, destroy, deface.

desert[1] ► verb **1** *his wife deserted him* ABANDON, leave, turn one's back on; throw over, jilt, break up with; leave high and dry, leave in the lurch, leave behind, strand; *informal* walk out on, run out on, drop, dump, ditch; *literary* forsake. **2** *his allies were deserting the cause* RENOUNCE, repudiate, relinquish, wash one's hands of, abandon, turn one's back on, betray, disavow; *formal* abjure; *literary* forsake. **3** *soldiers deserted in droves* ABSCOND, defect, turn away, make off, decamp, flee, turn tail, take French leave, depart, quit, jump ship; *Military* go AWOL.

desert[2] ► noun *an African desert* WASTELAND, wastes, wilderness, wilds, barren land; dust bowl.
► adjective **1** *desert conditions* ARID, dry, moistureless, parched; scorched; hot; barren, bare, stark, infertile, unfruitful, dehydrated, sterile. **2** *an uncharted desert island* UNINHABITED, empty, lonely, desolate, bleak; wild, uncultivated.
− OPPOSITES: fertile.

deserted ► adjective **1** *a deserted wife* ABANDONED, thrown over, jilted, cast aside; neglected, stranded, marooned, forlorn, bereft; *informal* dumped, ditched, dropped; *literary* forsaken. **2** *a deserted village* EMPTY, uninhabited, unoccupied, unpeopled, abandoned, evacuated, vacant, untenanted, tenantless, neglected; desolate, lonely, godforsaken.
− OPPOSITES: populous.

deserter ► noun ABSCONDER, runaway, fugitive, truant, escapee; renegade, defector, turncoat, traitor.

desertion ► noun **1** *his wife's desertion of him* ABANDONMENT, leaving, jilting. **2** *the desertion of the president's colleagues* DEFECTION; betrayal, renunciation, repudiation, apostasy; *formal* abjuration. **3** *soldiers were prosecuted for desertion* ABSCONDING, running away, truancy, going absent without leave, taking French leave, escape; defection, treason; *Military* going AWOL.

deserve ► verb MERIT, earn, warrant, rate, justify, be worthy of, be entitled to, have a right to, be qualified for.

deserved ► adjective WELL-EARNED, merited, warranted, justified, justifiable; rightful, due, right, just, fair, fitting, appropriate, suitable, proper, apt; *archaic* meet.

deserving ► adjective **1** *the deserving poor* WORTHY, meritorious, commendable, praiseworthy, admirable, estimable, creditable; respectable, decent, honourable, righteous. **2** *a lapse deserving punishment* MERITING, warranting, justifying, suitable for, worthy of.

desiccated ► adjective DRIED, dry, dehydrated, powdered.
− OPPOSITES: moist.

desideratum ► noun REQUIREMENT, prerequisite, need, indispensable thing, sine qua non, essential, requisite, necessary.

design ► noun **1** *a design for the offices* PLAN, blueprint, drawing, sketch, outline, map, plot, diagram, draft, representation, scheme, model. **2** *tableware with a gold design* PATTERN, motif, device; style, composition, makeup, layout, construction, shape, form. **3** *his design of reaching the top* INTENTION, aim, purpose, plan, intent, objective, object, goal, end, target; hope, desire, wish, dream, aspiration, ambition.
► verb **1** *the church was designed by Hicks* PLAN, outline, map out, draft, draw. **2** *they designed a new engine* INVENT, originate, create, think up, come up with, devise, formulate, conceive; make, produce, develop, fashion; *informal* dream up. **3** *this paper is designed to provoke discussion* INTEND, aim; devise, contrive, purpose, plan; tailor, fashion, adapt, gear; mean, destine.
■ **by design** DELIBERATELY, intentionally, on purpose, purposefully; knowingly, wittingly, consciously, calculatedly.

designate ► verb **1** *she designated her successor* APPOINT, nominate, depute, delegate; select, choose, pick, elect, name, identify, assign. **2** *the building was designated a historical site* CLASSIFY, class, label, tag; name, call, entitle, term, dub; *formal* denominate.

designation ► noun **1** *the designation of a leader* APPOINTMENT, nomination, naming, selection, election. **2** *the designation of wildlife preserves*

CLASSIFICATION, specification, definition, earmarking, pinpointing. **3** *the designation 'Generalissimo'* TITLE, name, epithet, tag; nickname, byname, sobriquet; *informal* moniker, handle; *formal* denomination, appellation.

designer ▶ noun **1** *a designer of office furniture* CREATOR, planner, deviser, inventor, originator; maker; architect, builder. **2** *young designers made the dress* COUTURIER, tailor, dressmaker.

designing ▶ adjective SCHEMING, calculating, conniving; cunning, crafty, artful, wily, devious, guileful, manipulative; treacherous, sly, underhanded, deceitful, double-dealing; *informal* crooked, foxy.

desirability ▶ noun **1** *the desirability of the property* APPEAL, attractiveness, allure; agreeableness, worth, excellence. **2** *they debated the desirability of gay marriage* ADVISABILITY, advantage, expedience, benefit, merit, value, profit, profitability. **3** *her obvious desirability* ATTRACTIVENESS, sexual attraction, beauty, good looks; charm, seductiveness; *informal* sexiness.

desirable ▶ adjective **1** *a desirable location* ATTRACTIVE, sought-after, in demand, popular, desired, covetable, coveted, enviable; appealing, agreeable, pleasant; valuable, good, excellent; *informal* to die for. **2** *it is desirable that they should meet* ADVANTAGEOUS, advisable, wise, sensible, recommendable; helpful, useful, beneficial, worthwhile, profitable, preferable. **3** *a very desirable woman* (SEXUALLY) ATTRACTIVE, beautiful, pretty, appealing; seductive, alluring, enchanting, beguiling, captivating, bewitching, irresistible; *informal* sexy, beddable.
— OPPOSITES: unattractive, unwise, ugly.

desire ▶ noun **1** *a desire to see the world* WISH, want, aspiration, fancy, inclination, impulse; yearning, longing, craving, hankering, hunger; eagerness, enthusiasm, determination; *informal* yen, itch, jones. **2** *his eyes glittered with desire* LUST, sexual attraction, passion, sensuality, sexuality; lasciviousness, lechery, salaciousness, libidinousness; *informal* the hots, raunchiness, horniness, randiness.
▶ verb **1** *they desired peace* WANT, wish for, long for, yearn for, crave, hanker after, be desperate for, be bent on, covet, aspire to; fancy; *informal* have a yen for, have a jones for, yen for, hanker after/for. **2** *she desired him* BE ATTRACTED TO, lust after, burn for, be infatuated by; *informal* fancy, have the hots for, have a crush on, be mad about, be crazy about.

desired ▶ adjective **1** *cut the cloth to the desired length* REQUIRED, necessary, proper, right, correct; appropriate, suitable; preferred, chosen, selected. **2** *the desired results* WISHED FOR, wanted, coveted; sought-after, longed for, yearned for.

desirous ▶ adjective EAGER, desiring, anxious, keen, craving, yearning, longing, hungry; ambitious, aspiring; covetous, envious; *informal* dying, itching.

desist ▶ verb ABSTAIN, refrain, forbear, hold back, keep; stop, cease, discontinue, suspend, give up, break off, drop, dispense with, eschew; *informal* lay off, give over, quit, pack in.
— OPPOSITES: continue.

desk ▶ noun WRITING TABLE, bureau, escritoire, secretaire, rolltop desk, carrel, workstation.

desolate ▶ adjective **1** *desolate moorlands* BLEAK, stark, bare, dismal, grim; wild, inhospitable; deserted, uninhabited, godforsaken, abandoned, unpeopled, untenanted, empty, barren; unfrequented, unvisited, isolated, remote. **2** *she is desolate* MISERABLE, despondent, depressed, disconsolate, devastated, despairing, inconsolable, broken-hearted, grief-stricken, crushed, bereft; sad, unhappy, downcast, down, dejected, forlorn, upset, distressed; *informal* blue, cut up.
— OPPOSITES: populous, joyful.
▶ verb **1** *droughts desolated the plains* DEVASTATE, ravage, ruin, lay waste to; level, raze, demolish, wipe out, obliterate. **2** *she was desolated by the loss of her husband* DISHEARTEN, depress, sadden, cast down, make miserable, weigh down, crush, upset, distress, devastate; *informal* shatter.

desolation ▶ noun **1** *the desolation of the Gobi desert* BLEAKNESS, starkness, barrenness, sterility; wildness; isolation, loneliness, remoteness. **2** *a feeling of utter desolation* MISERY, sadness, unhappiness, despondency, sorrow, depression, grief, woe; broken-heartedness, wretchedness, dejection, devastation, despair, anguish, distress.

despair ▶ noun HOPELESSNESS, disheartenment, discouragement, desperation, distress, anguish, unhappiness; despondency, depression, disconsolateness, melancholy, misery, wretchedness; defeatism, pessimism.
— OPPOSITES: hope, joy.
▶ verb LOSE HOPE, abandon hope, give up, lose heart, lose faith, be discouraged, be despondent, be demoralized, resign oneself; be pessimistic.

despairing ▶ adjective HOPELESS, in despair, dejected, depressed, despondent, disconsolate, gloomy, miserable, wretched, desolate, inconsolable; disheartened, discouraged, demoralized, devastated; suicidal; defeatist, pessimistic.

desperado ▶ noun *(dated)* BANDIT, criminal, outlaw, lawbreaker, villain, renegade; robber, cutthroat, gangster, pirate.

desperate ▶ adjective **1** *a desperate look* DESPAIRING, hopeless; anguished, distressed, wretched, desolate, forlorn, distraught, fraught; out of one's mind, at one's wits' end, beside oneself, at the end of one's rope/tether. **2** *a desperate attempt to escape* LAST-DITCH, last-gasp, eleventh-hour, do-or-die, final; frantic, frenzied, wild; futile, hopeless, doomed. **3** *a desperate shortage of teachers* GRAVE, serious, critical, acute, risky, precarious; dire, awful, terrible, dreadful; urgent, pressing, crucial, vital, drastic, extreme; *informal* chronic. **4** *they were desperate for food* IN GREAT NEED OF, urgently requiring, in want of; eager, longing, yearning, hungry, crying out; *informal* dying. **5** *a desperate act* VIOLENT, dangerous, lawless; reckless, rash, hasty, impetuous, foolhardy, incautious, hazardous, risky; do-or-die.

desperately ▶ adverb **1** *he screamed desperately for help* IN DESPERATION, in despair, despairingly, in anguish, in distress, wretchedly, hopelessly, desolately, forlornly. **2** *they are desperately ill* SERIOUSLY, critically, gravely, severely, acutely, dangerously, perilously; very, extremely, dreadfully; hopelessly, irretrievably; *informal* terribly. **3** *he desperately wanted to talk* URGENTLY, pressingly; intensely, eagerly.

desperation ▶ noun HOPELESSNESS, despair, distress; anguish, agony, torment, misery, wretchedness; discouragement, disheartenment.

despicable ▶ adjective CONTEMPTIBLE, loathsome, hateful, detestable, reprehensible, abhorrent, abominable, awful, heinous; odious, vile, low, mean, abject, shameful, ignominious, shabby, ignoble,

disreputable, discreditable, unworthy; *informal* dirty, rotten, lowdown, lousy; beastly; *archaic* scurvy.
— OPPOSITES: admirable.

despise ▶ verb DETEST, hate, loathe, abhor, execrate, deplore, dislike; scorn, disdain, look down on, deride, sneer at, revile; spurn, shun; *formal* abominate.
— OPPOSITES: adore.

despite ▶ preposition IN SPITE OF, notwithstanding, regardless of, in the face of, for all, even with.

despoil ▶ verb 1 *a village despoiled by invaders* PLUNDER, pillage, rob, ravage, raid, ransack, rape, loot, sack; devastate, lay waste, ruin. 2 *the thief despoiled him of all he had* ROB, strip, deprive, dispossess, denude, divest, relieve, clean out.

despondency ▶ noun HOPELESSNESS, despair, discouragement, low spirits, wretchedness; melancholy, gloom, misery, desolation, disappointment, disheartenment, dejection, sadness, unhappiness; *informal* the blues, heartache.

despondent ▶ adjective DISHEARTENED, discouraged, dispirited, downhearted, downcast, crestfallen, down, low, disconsolate, despairing, wretched; melancholy, gloomy, morose, dismal, woebegone, miserable, depressed, dejected, sad; *informal* blue, down in the mouth, down in the dumps.
— OPPOSITES: hopeful, cheerful.

despot ▶ noun TYRANT, oppressor, dictator, absolute ruler, totalitarian, autocrat; *informal* slave driver.

despotic ▶ adjective AUTOCRATIC, dictatorial, totalitarian, absolutist, undemocratic, unaccountable; one-party, autarchic, monocratic; tyrannical, tyrannous, oppressive, repressive, draconian, illiberal.
— OPPOSITES: democratic.

dessert ▶ noun SWEET, confection, second course, last course, sweet course.

destabilize ▶ verb UNDERMINE, weaken, damage, subvert, sabotage, unsettle, upset, disrupt.
— OPPOSITES: strengthen.

destination ▶ noun JOURNEY'S END, end of the line; terminus, stop, stopping place, port of call; goal, purpose, target, end.

destined ▶ adjective 1 *he is destined to lead a charmed life* FATED, ordained, predestined, meant; certain, sure, bound, assured, likely; doomed. 2 *computers destined for Pakistan* HEADING, bound, en route, scheduled; intended, meant, designed, designated, allotted, reserved.

destiny ▶ noun 1 *master of his own destiny* FUTURE, fate, fortune, doom; lot; *archaic* portion. 2 *she believed their meeting was destiny* FATE, providence; predestination; God's will, kismet, the stars; luck, fortune, chance; karma, serendipity.

destitute ▶ adjective 1 *she was left destitute* PENNILESS, poor, impoverished, poverty-stricken, impecunious, without a cent/penny (to one's name); needy, in straitened circumstances, distressed, badly off; *informal* hard up, (flat) broke, strapped (for cash), without two coins/cents/nickels to rub together, without a red cent, dirt poor. 2 *we were destitute of clothing* DEVOID, bereft, deprived, in need; lacking, without, deficient in, wanting.
— OPPOSITES: rich.

destroy ▶ verb 1 *their offices were destroyed by bombing* DEMOLISH, knock down, level, raze (to the ground), fell; wreck, ruin, shatter; blast, blow up, dynamite, explode, bomb. 2 *the new highway would destroy the conservation area* SPOIL, ruin, wreck, disfigure, blight,

mar, impair, deface, scar, injure, harm, devastate, damage, wreak havoc on; *informal* total. 3 *illness destroyed his career* WRECK, ruin, spoil, disrupt, undo, upset, put an end to, put a stop to, terminate, frustrate, blight, crush, quash, dash, scotch; devastate, demolish, scupper, scuttle, sabotage; *informal* mess up, muck up, foul up, put paid to, put the kibosh on, fry, do for, blow a hole in; throw a wrench in the works of; *archaic* bring to naught. 4 *the horse had to be destroyed* KILL, put down, put to sleep, slaughter, terminate, exterminate, euthanize. 5 *we had to destroy the enemy* ANNIHILATE, wipe out, obliterate, wipe off the face of the earth, eliminate, eradicate, liquidate, finish off, erase; kill, slaughter, massacre, exterminate; *informal* take out, rub out, snuff out, waste, fry, nuke, zap.
— OPPOSITES: build, preserve, raise, spare.

destruction ▶ noun 1 *the destruction by allied bombers* DEMOLITION, wrecking, ruination, blasting, bombing; wreckage, ruins. 2 *the destruction of the countryside* DEVASTATION, ruination, blighting, disfigurement, impairment, scarring, harm, desolation. 3 *the destruction of cattle* SLAUGHTER, killing, putting down, extermination, termination. 4 *the destruction of the enemies' forces* ANNIHILATION, obliteration, elimination, eradication, liquidation; killing, slaughter, massacre, extermination.

destructive ▶ adjective 1 *the most destructive war* DEVASTATING, ruinous, disastrous, catastrophic, calamitous, cataclysmic; harmful, damaging, detrimental, deleterious, injurious, crippling; violent, savage, fierce, brutal, deadly, lethal. 2 *destructive criticism* NEGATIVE, hostile, vicious, unfriendly; unhelpful, obstructive, discouraging.

desultory ▶ adjective CASUAL, cursory, superficial, token, perfunctory, half-hearted, lukewarm; random, aimless, erratic, unmethodical, unsystematic, chaotic, inconsistent, irregular, intermittent, sporadic, fitful.
— OPPOSITES: keen.

detach ▶ verb 1 *he detached the lamp from its bracket* UNFASTEN, disconnect, disengage, separate, uncouple, remove, loose, unhitch, unhook, free, pull off, cut off, break off. 2 *he detached himself from the crowd* FREE, separate, segregate; move away, split off; leave, abandon. 3 *he has detached himself from his family* DISSOCIATE, divorce, alienate, separate, segregate, isolate, cut off; break away, disaffiliate, defect; leave, quit, withdraw from, break with.
— OPPOSITES: attach, join.

detached ▶ adjective 1 *a detached collar* UNFASTENED, disconnected, separated, separate, loosened; untied, unhitched, undone, unhooked, unbuttoned; free, severed, cut off. 2 *a detached observer* DISPASSIONATE, disinterested, objective, uninvolved, outside, neutral, unbiased, unprejudiced, impartial, non-partisan; indifferent, aloof, remote, distant, impersonal; *informal* cool. 3 *a detached house* STANDING ALONE, separate.

detachment ▶ noun 1 *she looked on everything with detachment* OBJECTIVITY, dispassion, disinterest, open-mindedness, neutrality, impartiality; indifference, aloofness. 2 *a detachment of soldiers* UNIT, detail, squad, troop, contingent, outfit, task force, patrol, crew; platoon, company, corps, regiment, brigade, battalion. 3 *retinal detachment* LOOSENING, disconnection, disengagement, separation; removal. 4 *the RCMP detachment* STATION, headquarters, division.

detail ▶ noun 1 *the picture is correct in every detail*

PARTICULAR, respect, feature, characteristic, attribute, specific, aspect, facet, part, unit, component, constituent; fact, piece of information, point, element, circumstance, consideration. **2** *that's just a detail* UNIMPORTANT POINT, trivial fact, triviality, technicality, nicety, subtlety, trifle, fine point, incidental, inessential, nothing. **3** *records with a considerable degree of detail* PRECISION, exactness, accuracy, thoroughness, carefulness, scrupulousness, particularity. **4** *a guard detail* UNIT, detachment, squad, troop, contingent, outfit, task force, patrol. **5** *I got kitchen detail* DUTY, task, job, chore, charge, responsibility, assignment, function, mission, engagement, occupation, undertaking, errand.

▶ **verb 1** *the report details our objections* DESCRIBE, explain, expound, relate, catalogue, list, spell out, itemize, particularize, identify, specify; state, declare, present, set out, frame; cite, quote, instance, mention, name. **2** *troops were detailed to prevent their escape* ASSIGN, allocate, appoint, delegate, commission, charge; send, post; nominate, vote, elect, co-opt.

■ **in detail** THOROUGHLY, in depth, exhaustively, minutely, closely, meticulously, rigorously, scrupulously, painstakingly, carefully; completely, comprehensively, fully, extensively.

detailed ▶ adjective COMPREHENSIVE, full, complete, thorough, exhaustive, all-inclusive; elaborate, minute, intricate; explicit, specific, precise, exact, accurate, meticulous, painstaking; itemized, blow-by-blow.
– OPPOSITES: general.

detain ▶ verb **1** *they were detained for questioning* HOLD, take into custody, take (in), confine, imprison, lock up, put in jail, intern; arrest, apprehend, seize; *informal* pick up, run in, haul in, nab, collar. **2** *don't let me detain you* DELAY, hold up, make late, keep, slow up/down; hinder, hamper, impede, obstruct.
– OPPOSITES: release.

detect ▶ verb **1** *no one detected the smell of gas* NOTICE, perceive, discern, be aware of, note, make out, spot, recognize, distinguish, remark, identify, diagnose; catch, sense, see, smell, scent, taste. **2** *they are responsible for detecting fraud* DISCOVER, uncover, find out, turn up, unearth, dig up, root out, expose, reveal. **3** *the hackers were detected* CATCH, hunt down, track down, find, expose, reveal, unmask, smoke out; apprehend, arrest; *informal* nail.

detection ▶ noun **1** *the detection of methane* DISCERNMENT, perception, awareness, recognition, identification, diagnosis; sensing, sight, smelling, tasting. **2** *the detection of insider trading* DISCOVERY, uncovering, unearthing, exposure, revelation. **3** *he managed to escape detection* CAPTURE, identification, exposure; apprehension, arrest; notice.

detective ▶ noun INVESTIGATOR, private investigator, private detective, operative; *informal* private eye, PI, sleuth, snoop, shamus, gumshoe; *informal, dated* (private) dick.

detention ▶ noun CUSTODY, imprisonment, confinement, incarceration, internment, detainment, captivity; arrest, house arrest; quarantine; punishment, discipline.

deter ▶ verb **1** *the high cost deterred many* DISCOURAGE, dissuade, put off, scare off; dishearten, demoralize, daunt, intimidate. **2** *the presence of a guard deters crime* PREVENT, stop, avert, fend off, stave off, ward off,

block, halt, check; hinder, impede, hamper, obstruct, foil, forestall, counteract, inhibit, curb.
– OPPOSITES: encourage.

detergent ▶ noun *laundry detergent* CLEANER, cleanser, cleaning agent; soap, soap flakes, soap powder, dish soap, soft soap.

deteriorate ▶ verb **1** *his health deteriorated* WORSEN, decline, degenerate; fail, slump, slip, go downhill, wane, ebb; *informal* go to pot. **2** *these materials deteriorate if stored wrongly* DECAY, degrade, degenerate, break down, decompose, rot, go off, spoil, perish; break up, disintegrate, crumble, fall apart.
– OPPOSITES: improve.

deterioration ▶ noun **1** *a deterioration in market conditions* DECLINE, failure, drop, downturn, slump, *informal* toboggan slide ♣, slip, retrogression. **2** *deterioration of the main structure* DECAY, degradation, degeneration, breakdown, decomposition, rot; atrophy, weakening; breakup, disintegration, dilapidation; entropy.

determinate ▶ adjective FIXED, settled, specified, established, defined, explicit, known, determined, definitive, conclusive, express, precise, categorical, positive, definite.

determination ▶ noun **1** *it took great determination to win* RESOLUTION, resolve, willpower, strength of character, single-mindedness, purposefulness, intentness; staunchness, perseverance, persistence, tenacity, staying power; strong-mindedness, backbone, stubbornness, doggedness, obstinacy; spirit, courage, pluck, grit, stout-heartedness; *informal* guts, spunk, balls, moxie; *formal* pertinacity. **2** *the determination of the rent* SETTING, specification, settlement, designation, arrangement, establishment, prescription. **3** *the determination of the speed of light* CALCULATION, discovery, ascertainment, establishment, deduction, divination, diagnosis, discernment, verification, confirmation.

determine ▶ verb **1** *chromosomes determine the sex of the embryo* CONTROL, decide, regulate, direct, dictate, govern; affect, influence, mould. **2** *he determined to sell* RESOLVE, decide, make up one's mind, choose, elect, opt; *formal* purpose. **3** *the sum will be determined by an accountant* SPECIFY, set, fix, decide on, settle, assign, designate, arrange, choose, establish, ordain, prescribe, decree. **4** *determine the composition of the fibres* ASCERTAIN, find out, discover, learn, establish, calculate, work out, make out, deduce, diagnose, discern; check, verify, confirm; *informal* figure out.

determined ▶ adjective **1** *he was determined to have his way* INTENT ON, bent on, set on, insistent on, resolved to, firm about, committed to; single-minded about, obsessive about. **2** *a very determined man* RESOLUTE, purposeful, purposive, adamant, single-minded, unswerving, unwavering, undaunted, intent, insistent; steadfast, staunch, stalwart; persevering, persistent, indefatigable, tenacious; strong-minded, strong-willed, unshakeable, steely, four-square, dedicated, committed; stubborn, dogged, obstinate, inflexible, intransigent, unyielding, immovable, rock-ribbed; *formal* pertinacious.

determining ▶ adjective DECIDING, decisive, conclusive, final, definitive, key, pivotal, crucial, critical, major, chief, prime.

deterrent ▶ noun DISINCENTIVE, discouragement, damper, curb, check, restraint; obstacle, hindrance,

impediment, obstruction, block, barrier, inhibition.
— OPPOSITES: incentive.

detest ▸ verb ABHOR, hate, loathe, despise, shrink from, be unable to bear, find intolerable, dislike, disdain, have an aversion to; *formal* abominate.
— OPPOSITES: love.

detestable ▸ adjective ABHORRENT, hateful, loathsome, despicable, abominable, execrable, repellent, repugnant, repulsive, revolting, disgusting, distasteful, horrible, horrid, awful; heinous, reprehensible, obnoxious, odious, offensive, contemptible.

dethrone ▸ verb DEPOSE, unseat, oust, topple, overthrow, bring down, dislodge, displace, supplant, usurp, eject, drum out.
— OPPOSITES: crown.

detonate ▸ verb **1** *the charge detonated on impact* EXPLODE, go off, blow up, shatter, erupt; ignite; bang, blast, boom. **2** *they detonated the bomb* SET OFF, explode, discharge, let off, touch off, trigger; ignite, kindle.

detonation ▸ noun EXPLOSION, discharge, blowing up, ignition; blast, bang, report.

detour ▸ noun DIVERSION, circuitous route, indirect route, scenic route; bypass, ring road; digression, deviation, shortcut.

detract ▸ verb *my reservations should not detract from the book's excellence* BELITTLE, take away from, diminish, reduce, lessen, minimize, play down, trivialize, decry, depreciate, devalue, deprecate.

detractor ▸ noun CRITIC, disparager, denigrator, deprecator, belittler, attacker, fault-finder, backbiter; slanderer, libeller; *informal* knocker.

detriment ▸ noun HARM, damage, injury, hurt, impairment, loss, disadvantage, disservice, mischief.
— OPPOSITES: benefit.

detrimental ▸ adjective HARMFUL, damaging, injurious, hurtful, inimical, deleterious, destructive, ruinous, disastrous, bad, malign, adverse, undesirable, unfavourable, unfortunate; unhealthy, unwholesome.
— OPPOSITES: benign.

detritus ▸ noun DEBRIS, waste, refuse, rubbish, litter, scrap, flotsam and jetsam, rubble; remains, remnants, fragments, scraps, dregs, leavings, sweepings, dross, scum, trash, garbage; *informal* dreck.

devalue ▸ verb BELITTLE, depreciate, disparage, denigrate, decry, deprecate, treat lightly, discredit, underrate, undervalue, underestimate, deflate, diminish, trivialize, run down; *informal* knock, sell short, put down, badmouth, pooh-pooh, pick holes in.

devastate ▸ verb **1** *the city was devastated by an earthquake* DESTROY, ruin, wreck, lay waste, ravage, demolish, raze (to the ground), level, flatten; *informal* trash, total. **2** *he was devastated by the news* SHATTER, shock, stun, daze, dumbfound, traumatize, crush, overwhelm, overcome, distress.

devastating ▸ adjective **1** *a devastating cyclone* DESTRUCTIVE, ruinous, disastrous, catastrophic, calamitous, cataclysmic; harmful, damaging, injurious, detrimental; crippling, violent, savage, fierce, dangerous, fatal, deadly, lethal. **2** *devastating news* SHATTERING, shocking, traumatic, overwhelming, crushing, distressing, terrible. **3** (*informal*) *he presented devastating arguments* INCISIVE, highly effective, penetrating, cutting; withering,

blistering, searing, scathing, fierce, savage, stinging, biting, caustic, harsh, unsparing.

devastation ▸ noun **1** *the hurricane left a trail of devastation* DESTRUCTION, ruin, desolation, havoc, wreckage; ruins, ravages. **2** *the devastation of Prussia* DESTRUCTION, wrecking, ruination, despoliation; demolition, annihilation. **3** *the devastation you have caused the family* SHOCK, trauma, distress, stress, strain, pain, anguish, suffering, upset, agony, misery, heartache.

develop ▸ verb **1** *the industry developed rapidly* GROW, expand, spread; advance, progress, evolve, mature; prosper, thrive, flourish, blossom. **2** *a plan was developed* INITIATE, instigate, set in motion; originate, invent, form, establish, generate. **3** *children should develop their talents* EXPAND, augment, broaden, supplement, reinforce; enhance, refine, improve, polish, perfect. **4** *a fight developed* START, begin, emerge, erupt, break out, burst out, arise, break, unfold, happen. **5** *he developed the symptoms last week* FALL ILL WITH, be stricken with, succumb to; contract, catch, get, pick up, come down with, become infected with.

development ▸ noun **1** *the development of the firm* EVOLUTION, growth, maturation, expansion, enlargement, spread, progress; success. **2** *the development of an idea* FORMING, establishment, initiation, instigation, origination, invention, generation. **3** *keep abreast of developments* EVENT, occurrence, happening, circumstance, incident, situation, issue. **4** *a housing development* COMPLEX, site.

deviant ▸ adjective *deviant behaviour* ABERRANT, abnormal, atypical, anomalous, irregular, non-standard; nonconformist, perverse, uncommon, unusual; freakish, strange, odd, peculiar, bizarre, eccentric, idiosyncratic, unorthodox, exceptional; warped, perverted; *informal* kinky, quirky.
— OPPOSITES: normal.
▸ noun *we were seen as deviants* NONCONFORMIST, eccentric, maverick, individualist; outsider, misfit; *informal* oddball, weirdo, freak, screwball, kook, odd duck.

deviate ▸ verb DIVERGE, digress, drift, stray, slew, veer, swerve; get sidetracked, branch off; differ, vary, run counter to, contrast with.

deviation ▸ noun DIVERGENCE, digression, departure; difference, variation, variance; aberration, abnormality, irregularity, anomaly, inconsistency, discrepancy.

device ▸ noun **1** *a device for measuring pressure* IMPLEMENT, gadget, utensil, tool, appliance, apparatus, instrument, machine, mechanism, contrivance, contraption; *informal* gizmo, widget, doohickey. **2** *an ingenious legal device* PLOY, tactic, move, stratagem, scheme, plot, plan, trick, ruse, manoeuvre, machination, contrivance, expedient, dodge, wile. **3** *their shields bear his device* EMBLEM, symbol, logo, badge, crest, insignia, coat of arms, escutcheon, seal, mark, design, motif; monogram, hallmark, trademark.

devil ▸ noun **1** *God and the Devil* SATAN, Beelzebub, Lucifer, the Lord of the Flies, the Prince of Darkness; *informal* Old Nick. **2** *they drove out the devils from their bodies* EVIL SPIRIT, demon, fiend, bogie; *informal* spook. **3** *look what the cruel devil has done* BRUTE, beast, monster, fiend; villain, sadist, barbarian, ogre. **4** *he's a naughty little devil* RASCAL, rogue, imp, fiend, monkey, wretch; *informal* monster, horror, scamp, tyke, varmint. **5** (*informal*) *the poor devils looked ill*

WRETCH, unfortunate, creature, soul, person, fellow; *informal* thing, beggar.

devilish ▶ adjective **1** *a devilish grin* DIABOLICAL, fiendish, demonic, satanic, demoniac, demoniacal; hellish, infernal; MISCHIEVOUS, wicked, impish, roguish. **2** *a devilish job* DIFFICULT, tricky, ticklish, troublesome, thorny, awkward, problematic.

devil-may-care ▶ adjective RECKLESS, rash, incautious, heedless, impetuous, impulsive, daredevil, hot-headed, wild, foolhardy, audacious, nonchalant, casual, breezy, flippant, insouciant, happy-go-lucky, easygoing, unworried, untroubled, unconcerned, harum-scarum.

devilment ▶ noun. *See* DEVILRY sense 2.

devilry, deviltry ▶ noun **1** *some devilry was afoot* WICKEDNESS, evil, sin, iniquity, vileness, badness, wrongdoing, dishonesty, unscrupulousness, villainy, delinquency, devilishness, fiendishness; *informal* crookedness, shadiness. **2** *she had a perverse sense of devilry* MISCHIEF, mischievousness, naughtiness, badness, perversity, impishness; misbehaviour, troublemaking, misconduct; pranks, tricks, roguery, devilment; *informal* monkey business, shenanigans. **3** *they dabbled in devilry* BLACK MAGIC, sorcery, witchcraft, wizardry, necromancy, enchantment, incantation; the supernatural, occultism, the occult, the black arts, divination, voodoo, witchery, mojo.

devious ▶ adjective **1** *the devious ways in which they bent the rules* UNDERHANDED, deceitful, dishonest, dishonourable, unethical, unprincipled, immoral, unscrupulous, fraudulent, dubious, unfair, treacherous, duplicitous; crafty, cunning, calculating, artful, conniving, scheming, sly, wily; sneaky, furtive, secret, clandestine, surreptitious, covert, snide; *informal* crooked, shady, dirty, lowdown. **2** *a devious route around the coast* CIRCUITOUS, roundabout, indirect, meandering, winding, tortuous.

devise ▶ verb CONCEIVE, think up, dream up, work out, formulate, concoct; design, invent, coin, originate; compose, construct, fabricate, create, produce, develop; discover, hit on; hatch, contrive; *informal* cook up.

devitalize ▶ verb WEAKEN, enfeeble, debilitate, enervate, sap, drain, tax, exhaust, weary, tire (out), fatigue, wear out, prostrate; indispose, incapacitate, lay low; *informal* knock out, do in, whack, bush, frazzle, poop.
— OPPOSITES: strengthen.

devoid ▶ adjective FREE, empty, vacant, bereft, denuded, deprived, destitute, bankrupt; **(devoid of)** lacking, without, wanting; *informal* minus.

devolution ▶ noun DECENTRALIZATION, delegation; redistribution, transfer; surrender, relinquishment.

devolve ▶ verb DELEGATE, depute, pass (down/on), download ♣, hand down/over/on, transfer, transmit, assign, consign, convey, entrust, turn over, give, cede, surrender, relinquish, deliver; bestow, grant.

devote ▶ verb ALLOCATE, assign, allot, commit, give (over), apportion, consign, pledge; dedicate, consecrate; set aside, earmark, reserve, designate.

devoted ▶ adjective LOYAL, faithful, true, staunch, steadfast, constant, committed, dedicated, devout; fond, loving, affectionate, caring, admiring.

devotee ▶ noun **1** *a devotee of rock music* ENTHUSIAST, fan, lover, aficionado, admirer; *informal* buff, bum, freak, nut, fiend, fanatic, addict, maniac. **2** *devotees thronged the temple* FOLLOWER, adherent, supporter, advocate, disciple, votary, member, stalwart, fanatic, zealot; believer, worshipper.

devotion ▶ noun **1** *her devotion to her husband* LOYALTY, faithfulness, fidelity, constancy, commitment, adherence, allegiance, dedication; fondness, love, admiration, affection, care. **2** *a life of devotion* DEVOUTNESS, piety, religiousness, spirituality, godliness, holiness, sanctity. **3** *morning devotions* (RELIGIOUS) WORSHIP, religious observance; prayers; prayer meeting, church service.

devotional ▶ adjective RELIGIOUS, sacred, spiritual, divine, church, ecclesiastical.
— OPPOSITES: secular.

devour ▶ verb **1** *he devoured his meal* EAT HUNGRILY, eat greedily, gobble (up/down), guzzle, gulp (down), bolt (down), gorge oneself on, wolf (down), feast on, consume, eat up; *informal* demolish, dispose of, make short work of, polish off, shovel down, stuff oneself with, pig out on, put away; *informal* scarf. **2** *flames devoured the house* CONSUME, engulf, envelop; destroy, demolish, lay waste, devastate; gut, ravage, ruin, wreck. **3** *he was devoured by remorse* AFFLICT, plague, bedevil, trouble, harrow, rack; consume, swallow up, overcome, overwhelm.

devout ▶ adjective **1** *a devout Christian* PIOUS, religious, devoted, dedicated, reverent, God-fearing; holy, godly, saintly, faithful, dutiful, righteous, churchgoing, orthodox. **2** *a devout hockey fan* DEDICATED, devoted, committed, loyal, faithful, staunch, genuine, firm, steadfast, unwavering, sincere, wholehearted, keen, enthusiastic, zealous, passionate, ardent, fervent, active, sworn, pledged; *informal* card-carrying, true blue.

dewy ▶ adjective **1** *walking on the dewy grass in the morning* MOIST, damp, wet. **2** *dewy innocence. See* DEWY-EYED.

dewy-eyed ▶ adjective SENTIMENTAL, nostalgic, wistful, romantic, maudlin, misty-eyed; trusting, trustful, naive, dewy, innocent, childlike.

dexterity ▶ noun **1** *painting china demanded dexterity* DEFTNESS, adeptness, adroitness, agility, nimbleness, handiness, ability, talent, skill, proficiency, expertise, experience, efficiency, mastery, delicacy, knack, artistry, finesse. **2** *his political dexterity* SHREWDNESS, astuteness, acumen, acuity, intelligence, ingenuity, inventiveness, cleverness, smartness; canniness, sense, discernment, insight, understanding, penetration, perception, perspicacity, discrimination; cunning, artfulness, craftiness; *informal* horse sense, savvy, street smarts.

dexterous ▶ adjective **1** *a dexterous flick of the wrist* DEFT, adept, adroit, agile, nimble, neat, handy, able, capable, skilful, skilled, proficient, expert, practised, polished; efficient, effortless, slick, professional, masterly; *informal* nifty, mean, ace. **2** *his dexterous accounting abilities* SHREWD, ingenious, inventive, clever, intelligent, brilliant, smart, sharp, acute, astute, canny, intuitive, discerning, perceptive, insightful, incisive, judicious; cunning, artful, crafty, wily; *informal* on the ball, quick off the mark, quick on the uptake, brainy, savvy.
— OPPOSITES: clumsy, stupid.

diabolical, diabolic ▶ adjective *his diabolical skill* DEVILISH, fiendish, satanic, demonic, demoniacal, hellish, infernal, evil, wicked, ungodly, unholy.

diacritic ▶ noun. *See table at* ACCENT.

diadem ▶ noun CROWN, coronet, tiara, circlet, chaplet; *literary* coronal.

diagnose ▶ verb IDENTIFY, determine, distinguish, recognize, detect, pinpoint.

diagnosis ▶ noun **1** *the diagnosis of celiac disease* IDENTIFICATION, detection, recognition, determination, discovery, pinpointing. **2** *the results confirmed his diagnosis* OPINION, judgment, verdict, conclusion.

diagonal ▶ adjective CROSSWISE, crossways, slanting, slanted, aslant, oblique, angled, at an angle; cater-cornered, kitty-cornered.

diagram ▶ noun DRAWING, line drawing, sketch, representation, draft, illustration, picture, plan, outline, delineation, figure; *Computing* graphic.

diagrammatic ▶ adjective GRAPHIC, graphical, representational, representative, schematic, simplified.

dial ▶ verb PHONE, telephone, call, make/place a call (to); *informal* buzz, get on the blower, get someone on the horn.

dialect ▶ noun REGIONAL LANGUAGE, local language, local speech, vernacular, patois, idiom; regionalisms, localisms; *informal* lingo.

dialectic ▶ noun DISCUSSION, debate, dialogue, logical argument, reasoning, argumentation, polemics; *formal* ratiocination.

dialogue ▶ noun **1** *a book consisting of a series of dialogues* CONVERSATION, talk, discussion, interchange, discourse; chat, tête-à-tête, heart-to-heart; *informal* confab, chinwag; *formal* colloquy, confabulation. **2** *they called for a serious political dialogue* DISCUSSION, exchange, debate, exchange of views, talk, consultation, conference, parley; talks, negotiations; *informal* powwow, skull session.

diameter ▶ noun BREADTH, width, thickness; calibre, bore, gauge.

diametrical, diametric ▶ adjective DIRECT, absolute, complete, exact, extreme, polar, antipodal.

diaphanous ▶ adjective SHEER, fine, delicate, light, thin, insubstantial, floaty, flimsy, filmy, silken, chiffony, gossamer, gossamer-thin, gauzy; translucent, transparent, see-through.
— OPPOSITES: thick, opaque.

diarrhea ▶ noun loose stools; *informal* the runs, the trots, squitters, the squirts, Delhi belly, Montezuma's revenge, turista; *archaic* the flux.
— OPPOSITES: constipation.

diary ▶ noun **1** *he put the date in his diary* APPOINTMENT BOOK, engagement book, (personal) organizer, daybook, PDA; *proprietary* Filofax. **2** *her World War II diaries* JOURNAL, memoir, chronicle, log, logbook, history, annal, record.

diatribe ▶ noun TIRADE, harangue, onslaught, attack, polemic, denunciation, broadside, fulmination, condemnation, censure, criticism; *informal* blast; *literary* philippic.

dicey ▶ adjective (*informal*) RISKY, uncertain, unpredictable, touch-and-go, precarious, unsafe, dangerous, fraught with danger, hazardous, perilous, high-risk, difficult; *informal* chancy, hairy, iffy, gnarly.
— OPPOSITES: safe.

dichotomy ▶ noun CONTRAST, difference, polarity, conflict; gulf, chasm, division, separation, split; *rare* contrariety.

dicker ▶ verb NEGOTIATE, haggle, bargain, barter.

dictate ▶ verb **1** *the president's attempts to dictate policy* PRESCRIBE, lay down, impose, set down, order, command, decree, ordain, direct, determine, decide,

control, govern. **2** *you are in no position to dictate to me* GIVE ORDERS TO, order about/around, lord it over; lay down the law; *informal* boss about/around, push around/about, throw one's weight about/around. **3** *choice is often dictated by availability* DETERMINE, control, govern, decide, influence, affect.
▶ noun *the dictates of his superior* ORDER, command, commandment, decree, edict, ruling, dictum, diktat, directive, direction, instruction, pronouncement, mandate, requirement, stipulation, injunction, demand; *formal* ordinance; *literary* behest.

dictator ▶ noun AUTOCRAT, absolute ruler, despot, tyrant, oppressor, autarch.

dictatorial ▶ adjective **1** *a dictatorial regime* AUTOCRATIC, undemocratic, totalitarian, authoritarian, autarchic, despotic, tyrannical, tyrannous, absolute, unrestricted, unlimited, unaccountable, arbitrary; *informal* iron-fisted. **2** *his dictatorial manner* DOMINEERING, autocratic, authoritarian, oppressive, imperious, officious, overweening, overbearing, peremptory, dogmatic, high and mighty; severe, strict; *informal* bossy, high-handed.
— OPPOSITES: democratic, meek.

dictatorship ▶ noun ABSOLUTE RULE, undemocratic rule, despotism, tyranny, autocracy, autarchy, authoritarianism, totalitarianism, Fascism; oppression, repression.
— OPPOSITES: democracy.

diction ▶ noun **1** *his careful diction* ENUNCIATION, articulation, elocution, locution, pronunciation, speech, intonation, inflection; delivery. **2** *her diction was archaic* PHRASEOLOGY, phrasing, turn of phrase, wording, language, usage, vocabulary, terminology, expressions, idioms.

dictionary ▶ noun LEXICON, wordbook, word list, glossary, thesaurus.
— RELATED TERMS: lexicographic.

dictum ▶ noun **1** *he received the head's dictum with evident reluctance* PRONOUNCEMENT, proclamation, direction, injunction, dictate, command, commandment, order, decree, edict, mandate, diktat. **2** *the old dictum 'might is right'* SAYING, maxim, axiom, proverb, adage, aphorism, saw, precept, epigram, motto, truism, commonplace, platitude; expression, phrase, tag.

didactic ▶ adjective INSTRUCTIVE, instructional, educational, educative, informative, informational, edifying, improving, preceptive, pedagogic, moralistic.

diddly-squat ▶ noun NOTHING, zero, zilch, zip, nada, squat, bubkes.

die ▶ verb **1** *her father died last year* PASS AWAY, pass on, lose one's life, expire, breathe one's last, meet one's end, meet one's death, lay down one's life, perish, go the way of all flesh, go to one's last resting place, go to meet one's maker, cross the great divide, slip away; *informal* give up the ghost, kick the bucket, croak, buy it, turn up one's toes, cash in one's chips, shuffle off this mortal coil, bite the big one, check out, buy the farm; *archaic* depart this life. **2** *the wind had died down* ABATE, subside, drop, lessen, ease (off), let up, moderate, fade, dwindle, peter out, wane, ebb, relent, weaken; melt away, dissolve, vanish, disappear; *archaic* remit. **3** (*informal*) *the engine died* FAIL, cut out, give out, stop, break down, stop working; *informal* conk out, go kaput, give up the ghost. **4** (*informal*) *she's dying to meet you* LONG, yearn, burn,

ache; *informal* itch.
− OPPOSITES: live, intensify.

diehard ► **adjective** HARDLINE, reactionary, ultra-conservative, conservative, traditionalist, dyed-in-the-wool, intransigent, inflexible, uncompromising, rigid, entrenched, set in one's ways; staunch, steadfast.

diet[1] ► **noun** *health problems related to your diet* SELECTION OF FOOD, food, foodstuffs; *informal* grub, nosh.
► **verb** *she dieted for most of her life* BE ON A DIET, eat sparingly; lose weight, watch one's weight, reduce, slenderize.

diet[2] ► **noun** *the diet's lower house* LEGISLATIVE ASSEMBLY, legislature, parliament, congress, senate, council, assembly.

differ ► **verb** 1 *the second set of data differed from the first* CONTRAST WITH, be different from, be dissimilar to, be unlike, vary from, diverge from, deviate from, conflict with, run counter to, be incompatible with, be at odds with, go against, contradict. 2 *the two sides differed over this issue* DISAGREE, conflict, be at variance/odds, be in dispute, not see eye to eye.
− OPPOSITES: resemble, agree.

difference ► **noun** 1 *the difference between the two sets of data* DISSIMILARITY, contrast, distinction, differentiation, variance, variation, divergence, disparity, deviation, polarity, gulf, gap, imbalance, contradiction, contradistinction. 2 *we've had our differences in the past* DISAGREEMENT, difference of opinion, dispute, argument, quarrel, wrangle, contretemps, altercation; *informal* tiff, set-to, run-in, spat, row. 3 *I am willing to pay the difference* BALANCE, remainder, rest, remaining amount, residue.
− OPPOSITES: similarity.

different ► **adjective** 1 *people with different lifestyles* DISSIMILAR, unalike, unlike, contrasting, contrastive, divergent, differing, varying, disparate; poles apart, incompatible, mismatched, conflicting, clashing. 2 *suddenly everything in her life was different* CHANGED, altered, transformed, new, unfamiliar, unknown, strange. 3 *two different occasions* DISTINCT, separate, individual, discrete, independent. 4 (*informal*) *he wanted to try something different* UNUSUAL, out of the ordinary, unfamiliar, novel, new, fresh, original, unconventional, exotic, uncommon.
− OPPOSITES: similar, related, ordinary.

differential ► **adjective** (*technical*) 1 *the differential achievements of boys and girls* DIFFERENT, dissimilar, contrasting, unalike, divergent, disparate, contrastive. 2 *the differential features between benign and malignant tumours* DISTINCTIVE, distinguishing.
− OPPOSITES: similar.

differentiate ► **verb** 1 *he was unable to differentiate between fantasy and reality* DISTINGUISH, discriminate, make/draw a distinction, tell the difference, tell apart. 2 *this differentiates their business from all other booksellers* MAKE DIFFERENT, distinguish, set apart, single out, separate, mark off.

differentiation ► **noun** DISTINCTION, distinctness, difference; separation, demarcation, delimitation.

difficult ► **adjective** 1 *a very difficult job* HARD, strenuous, arduous, laborious, tough, onerous, burdensome, demanding, punishing, gruelling, back-breaking, exhausting, tiring, fatiguing, wearisome; *informal* hellish, killing; *archaic* toilsome. 2 *she found math very difficult* HARD, complicated, complex, involved, impenetrable, unfathomable,

over/above one's head, beyond one, puzzling, baffling, perplexing, confusing, mystifying; problematic, intricate, knotty, thorny, ticklish. 3 *a difficult child* TROUBLESOME, tiresome, trying, exasperating, awkward, demanding, perverse, contrary, recalcitrant, unmanageable, obstreperous, unaccommodating, unhelpful, uncooperative, disobliging; hard to please, fussy, finicky; *formal* refractory. 4 *you've come at a difficult time* INCONVENIENT, awkward, inopportune, unfavourable, unfortunate, inappropriate, unsuitable, untimely, ill-timed. 5 *the family has been through very difficult times* BAD, tough, grim, dark, black, hard, adverse, distressing; straitened.
− OPPOSITES: easy, simple, accommodating.

difficulty ► **noun** 1 *the difficulty of balancing motherhood with a career* STRAIN, trouble, problems, toil, struggle, laboriousness, arduousness; *informal* hassle, stress. 2 *practical difficulties* PROBLEM, complication, snag, hitch, pitfall, handicap, impediment, hindrance, obstacle, hurdle, stumbling block, obstruction, barrier; *informal* fly in the ointment, headache, hiccup, wrench in the works; growing pains. 3 *Charles got into difficulties* TROUBLE, predicament, plight, hard times, dire straits; quandary, dilemma; *informal* deep water, a fix, a jam, a spot, a scrape, a stew, a hole, a pickle.
− OPPOSITES: ease.

diffidence ► **noun** SHYNESS, bashfulness, modesty, self-effacement, meekness, unassertiveness, timidity, humility, hesitancy, reticence, insecurity, self-doubt, uncertainty, self-consciousness.

diffident ► **adjective** SHY, bashful, modest, self-effacing, unassuming, meek, unconfident, unassertive, timid, timorous, humble, shrinking, reticent, hesitant, insecure, self-doubting, doubtful, uncertain, unsure, self-conscious; *informal* mousy.
− OPPOSITES: confident.

diffuse ► **verb** *such ideas were diffused widely in the 1970s* SPREAD, spread around, send out, disseminate, scatter, disperse, distribute, put about, circulate, communicate, purvey, propagate, transmit, broadcast, promulgate.
► **adjective** 1 *a diffuse community centred on the church* SPREAD OUT, scattered, dispersed, diasporic. 2 *a diffuse narrative* VERBOSE, wordy, prolix, long-winded, long-drawn-out, discursive, rambling, wandering, meandering, maundering, digressive, circuitous, roundabout, circumlocutory, periphrastic; *informal* waffly.

diffusion ► **noun** SPREAD, dissemination, scattering, dispersal, diaspora, distribution, circulation, propagation, transmission, broadcasting, promulgation.

dig ► **verb** 1 *she began to dig the heavy clay soil* TURN OVER, work, break up; till, harrow, plow, shovel. 2 *he took a spade and dug a hole* EXCAVATE, dig out, quarry, hollow out, scoop out, gouge out; cut, bore, tunnel, burrow, mine. 3 *the bodies were hastily dug up* EXHUME, disinter, unearth. 4 *Winnie dug her elbow into his ribs* POKE, prod, jab, stab, shove, ram, push, thrust, drive. 5 *he'd been digging into my past* DELVE, probe, search, inquire, look, investigate, research, examine, scrutinize, check up on; *informal* check out. 6 *I dug up some disturbing information* UNCOVER, discover, find (out), unearth, dredge up, root out, ferret out, turn up, reveal, bring to light, expose. 7 (*informal, dated*) *I dig talking with him. See* ENJOY *verb sense 1.*
► **noun** 1 *a dig in the ribs* POKE, prod, jab, stab, shove,

push. **2** (*informal*) *they're always making digs at each other* SNIDE REMARK, cutting remark, jibe, jeer, taunt, sneer, insult, barb, insinuation; *informal* wisecrack, crack, put-down.

digest ▶ verb *Liz digested this information* ASSIMILATE, absorb, take in, understand, comprehend, grasp; consider, think about, reflect on, ponder, contemplate, mull over.
▶ noun *a digest of their findings* SUMMARY, synopsis, abstract, précis, resumé, summation; compilation; *informal* wrap-up.

digit ▶ noun **1** *the door code has ten digits* NUMERAL, number, figure, integer. **2** *we wanted to warm our frozen digits* FINGER, thumb, toe; extremity.

dignified ▶ adjective STATELY, noble, courtly, majestic, distinguished, proud, august, lofty, exalted, regal, lordly, imposing, impressive, grand; solemn, serious, grave, formal, proper, ceremonious, decorous, reserved, composed, sedate.

dignify ▶ verb ENNOBLE, enhance, distinguish, add distinction to, honour, grace, exalt, magnify, glorify, elevate.

dignitary ▶ noun WORTHY, personage, VIP, grandee, notable, pillar of society, luminary, leading light, big name; *informal* heavyweight, bigwig, top brass, top dog, big gun, big shot, big cheese, big chief, supremo, big wheel, big kahuna, big enchilada, top banana.

dignity ▶ noun **1** *the dignity of the proceedings* STATELINESS, nobility, majesty, regality, courtliness, augustness, loftiness, lordliness, grandeur; solemnity, gravity, gravitas, formality, decorum, propriety, sedateness. **2** *he had lost his dignity* SELF-RESPECT, pride, self-esteem, self-worth.

digress ▶ verb DEVIATE, go off on a tangent, get off the subject, get sidetracked, lose the thread, turn aside/away, depart, drift, stray, wander.

digression ▶ noun DEVIATION, detour, diversion, departure, divergence, excursus; aside, incidental remark.

digs ▶ plural noun (*informal*) LODGINGS, (living) quarters, rooms, accommodation; house, home; *informal* pad, place; *formal* abode, dwelling, dwelling place, residence, domicile, habitation.

dike ▶ noun EMBANKMENT, (*Maritimes*) aboiteau ✦, levee; ditch, trench, gutter.

dilapidated ▶ adjective RUN-DOWN, tumbledown, ramshackle, broken-down, in disrepair, shabby, battered, beat-up, rickety, shaky, unsound, crumbling, in ruins, ruined, decayed, decaying, decrepit; neglected, uncared-for, untended, the worse for wear, falling to pieces, falling apart, gone to rack and ruin, gone to seed.

dilate ▶ verb **1** *her nostrils dilated* ENLARGE, widen, expand, distend. **2** *Diane dilated on the joys of her married life* EXPATIATE, expound, enlarge, elaborate, speak/write at length.
– OPPOSITES: contract.

dilatory ▶ adjective **1** *he had been dilatory in appointing an executor* SLOW, tardy, unhurried, sluggish, sluggardly, snail-like, lazy. **2** *dilatory procedural tactics* DELAYING, stalling, temporizing, procrastinating, time-wasting, Fabian, filibustering.
– OPPOSITES: fast.

dilemma ▶ noun QUANDARY, predicament, Catch-22, vicious circle, plight, mess, muddle; difficulty, problem, trouble, perplexity, confusion, conflict; *informal* no-win situation, fix, tight spot/corner, can of worms.

dilettante ▶ noun DABBLER, amateur, non-professional, non-specialist, layman, layperson.
– OPPOSITES: professional.

diligence ▶ noun CONSCIENTIOUSNESS, assiduousness, assiduity, hard work, application, concentration, effort, care, industriousness, rigour, meticulousness, thoroughness; perseverance, persistence, tenacity, dedication, commitment, tirelessness, indefatigability, doggedness.

diligent ▶ adjective INDUSTRIOUS, hard-working, assiduous, conscientious, particular, punctilious, meticulous, painstaking, rigorous, careful, thorough, sedulous, earnest; persevering, persistent, tenacious, zealous, dedicated, committed, unflagging, untiring, tireless, indefatigable, dogged; *archaic* laborious.
– OPPOSITES: lazy.

dilly ▶ noun *a dilly of a traffic jam. See* HUMDINGER.

dilly-dally ▶ verb (*informal*) WASTE TIME, dally, dawdle, loiter, linger, take one's time, delay, temporize, stall, procrastinate, pussyfoot around, drag one's feet; dither, hesitate, falter, vacillate, waver, hem/hum and haw; *informal* shilly-shally, lallygag, let the grass grow under one's feet; *archaic* tarry.
– OPPOSITES: hurry.

dilute ▶ verb **1** *strong bleach can be diluted with water* MAKE WEAKER, weaken, water down; thin out, thin; doctor, adulterate; *informal* cut. **2** *the original plans have been diluted* WEAKEN, moderate, tone down, water down.
▶ adjective *a dilute acid. See* DILUTED.

diluted ▶ adjective WEAK, dilute, thin, watered down, watery; adulterated.
– OPPOSITES: concentrated.

dim ▶ adjective **1** *the dim light* FAINT, weak, feeble, soft, pale, dull, subdued, muted. **2** *long dim corridors* DARK, badly lit, ill-lit, dingy, dismal, gloomy, murky; *literary* tenebrous. **3** *a dim figure* INDISTINCT, ill-defined, unclear, vague, shadowy, nebulous, obscured, blurred, blurry, fuzzy. **4** *dim memories* VAGUE, imprecise, imperfect, unclear, indistinct, sketchy, hazy, blurred, shadowy. **5** (*informal*) *is she a bit dim? See* STUPID sense 1. **6** *their prospects for the future looked dim* GLOOMY, unpromising, unfavourable, discouraging, disheartening, depressing, dispiriting, hopeless.
– OPPOSITES: bright, distinct, encouraging.
▶ verb **1** *the lights were dimmed* TURN DOWN, lower, soften, subdue, mute; *literary* bedim. **2** *my memories have not dimmed with time* FADE, become vague, dwindle, blur. **3** *the fighting dimmed hopes of peace* DIMINISH, reduce, lessen, weaken, undermine.
– OPPOSITES: brighten, sharpen, intensify.

dimension ▶ noun **1** *the dimensions of the room* SIZE, measurements, proportions, extent; length, width, breadth, depth, area, volume, capacity; footage, acreage. **2** *the dimension of the problem* SIZE, scale, extent, scope, magnitude; importance, significance. **3** *the cultural dimensions of the problem* ASPECT, feature, element, facet, side.

diminish ▶ verb **1** *the pain will gradually diminish* DECREASE, lessen, decline, reduce, subside, die down, abate, dwindle, fade, slacken off, moderate, let up, ebb, wane, recede, die away/out, peter out; *archaic* remit. **2** *new legislation diminished the courts' authority* REDUCE, decrease, lessen, curtail, cut, cut down/back, constrict, restrict, limit, curb, check; weaken, blunt, erode, undermine, sap. **3** *she lost no opportunity to diminish him* BELITTLE, disparage, denigrate, defame,

Dinosaurs

saurichians (lizard-hipped)		ornithischians (bird-hipped)		
theropods (two-footed carnivores)	sauropods (large, four-footed herbivores)	marginocephalia (horned or thick-skulled herbivores)	ornithopoda (bird-footed herbivores)	thyreophora (armoured herbivores)
albertosaurus	apatosaurus	chasmosaurus	camptosaurus	ankylosaurus
allosaurus	(brontosaurus)	pachycephalosaurus	dryosaurus	kentrosaurus
compsognathus	brachiosaurus	protoceratops	edmontosaurus	stegosaurus
deinonychus	camarasaurus	stegoceras	hypsilophodon	
dilophosaurus	diplodocus	triceratops	iguanodon	
giganotosaurus	seismosaurus		parasaurolophus	
megalosaurus	supersaurus		saurolophus	
oviraptor	titanosaurus			
spinosaurus	ultrasaurus			
troodon				
tyrannosaurus rex				
utahraptor				
velociraptor				

deprecate, rundown; decry, demean, cheapen, devalue; *formal* derogate.
— OPPOSITES: increase.

diminution ▶ noun REDUCTION, decrease, lessening, decline, dwindling, moderation, fading, fade-out, weakening, ebb.

diminutive ▶ adjective TINY, small, little, petite, elfin, minute, miniature, mini, minuscule, compact, pocket, toy, midget, undersized, short; *informal* teeny, weeny, teeny-weeny, teensy-weensy, itty-bitty, itsy-bitsy, baby, pint-sized, knee-high to a grasshopper, little-bitty; *Scottish* wee.
— OPPOSITES: enormous.

dimple ▶ noun INDENTATION, hollow, cleft.

dim-wit ▶ noun (*informal*). See FOOL noun sense 1.

dim-witted ▶ adjective (*informal*). See STUPID senses 1, 2.

din ▶ noun *he shouted above the din* NOISE, racket, rumpus, ruckus, cacophony, babel, hubbub, tumult, uproar, commotion, clatter; shouting, yelling, screaming, caterwauling, clamour, clangour, outcry; *informal* hullabaloo.
— OPPOSITES: silence.
▶ verb 1 *she had had the evils of drink dinned into her* INSTILL, inculcate, drive, drum, hammer, drill, ingrain; indoctrinate, brainwash. 2 *the sound dinning in my ears* BLARE, blast, clang, clatter, crash, clamour.

dine ▶ verb 1 *we dined at a restaurant* HAVE DINNER, have supper, eat; *dated* sup, break bread. 2 *they dined on lobster* EAT, feed on, feast on, banquet on, partake of; *informal* tuck into, chow down on.

diner ▶ noun SMALL RESTAURANT, eatery, café, cafeteria, truck stop; *informal* greasy spoon.

dinghy ▶ noun BOAT, lifeboat; *proprietary* Zodiac. See also table at BOAT.

dingy ▶ adjective GLOOMY, dark, dull, badly/poorly lit, murky, dim, dismal, dreary, drab, sombre, grim, cheerless; dirty, grimy, shabby, faded, worn, dowdy, seedy, run-down; *informal* grungy.
— OPPOSITES: bright.

dinky ▶ adjective (*informal*) TRIFLING, trivial, insignificant, unimportant, negligible, of no account.

dinner ▶ noun EVENING MEAL, supper, main meal; lunch, midday meal; feast, banquet, dinner party; *informal* spread; *humorous* din-dins; *formal* repast.
— RELATED TERMS: prandial.

dinosaur ▶ *See table.*

diocese ▶ noun BISHOPRIC, see, eparchy.

dip ▶ verb 1 *he dipped a rag in the water* IMMERSE, submerge, plunge, duck, dunk, lower, sink. 2 *the sun dipped below the horizon* SINK, set, drop, go/drop down, fall, descend; disappear, vanish. 3 *the president's popularity has dipped* DECREASE, fall, drop, fall off, decline, diminish, dwindle, slump, plummet, plunge. 4 *the road dipped* SLOPE DOWN, descend, go down; drop away, fall, sink. 5 *you might have to dip into your savings* DRAW ON, use, make use of, have recourse to, spend. 6 *an interesting book to dip into* BROWSE THROUGH, skim through, look through, flick through, glance at, peruse, run one's eye over.
— OPPOSITES: rise, increase.
▶ noun 1 *a relaxing dip in the pool* SWIM, bathe; paddle. 2 *give the fish a ten-minute dip in a salt bath* IMMERSION, plunge, ducking, dunking. 3 *chicken satay with peanut dip* SAUCE, relish, dressing. 4 *the hedge at the bottom of the dip* SLOPE, incline, decline, descent; hollow, concavity, depression, basin, indentation. 5 *a dip in sales* DECREASE, fall, drop, downturn, decline, falling-off, slump, reduction, diminution, ebb.

diploma ▶ noun CERTIFICATE, parchment; degree, accreditation, qualification, licence.

diplomacy ▶ noun 1 *diplomacy failed to win them independence* STATESMANSHIP, statecraft, negotiation(s), discussion(s), talks, dialogue; international relations, foreign affairs. 2 *Jack's quiet diplomacy* TACT, tactfulness, sensitivity, discretion, subtlety, finesse, delicacy, savoir faire, politeness, thoughtfulness, care, judiciousness, prudence.

diplomat ▶ noun AMBASSADOR, attaché, consul, chargé d'affaires, envoy, nuncio, emissary, plenipotentiary, (*Que.*) delegate-general ✦; *archaic* legate.

diplomatic ▶ adjective 1 *diplomatic activity* AMBASSADORIAL, consular. 2 *he tried to be diplomatic* TACTFUL, sensitive, subtle, delicate, polite, discreet, thoughtful, careful, judicious, prudent, politic,

clever, skilful.
— OPPOSITES: tactless.

dippy ▶ adjective STUPID, FOOLISH, witless, unintelligent, ignorant, idiotic, simple-minded, slow-witted, feeble-minded, empty-headed, stunned ♣, dumb, halfwitted, spinny, brain-dead, moronic, thick, dopey, dozy.

dipstick ▶ noun See IDIOT.

dipsy-doodle ▶ verb DEKE, feint, stickhandle, dodge, twist and turn, jink.

dire ▶ adjective **1** *the dire economic situation* TERRIBLE, dreadful, appalling, frightful, awful, atrocious, grim, alarming; grave, serious, disastrous, calamitous, ruinous, hopeless, irretrievable, wretched, desperate, parlous; *formal* grievous. **2** *he was in dire need of help* URGENT, desperate, pressing, crying, sore, grave, serious, extreme, acute, drastic. **3** *dire warnings of fuel shortages* OMINOUS, gloomy, grim, dismal, unpropitious, inauspicious, unfavourable, pessimistic.

direct ▶ adjective **1** *the most direct route* STRAIGHT, undeviating, unswerving; shortest, quickest. **2** *a direct flight* NON-STOP, unbroken, uninterrupted, through. **3** *he is very direct* FRANK, candid, straightforward, honest, open, blunt, plain-spoken, outspoken, forthright, downright, no-nonsense, matter-of-fact, not afraid to call a spade a spade; *informal* upfront. **4** *direct contact with the president* FACE TO FACE, personal, immediate, first-hand. **5** *a direct quotation* VERBATIM, word for word, to the letter, faithful, exact, precise, accurate, correct. **6** *the direct opposite* EXACT, absolute, complete, diametrical.
▶ verb **1** *an economic elite directed the nation's affairs* MANAGE, govern, run, administer, control, conduct, handle, be in charge/control of, preside over, lead, head, rule, be at the helm of; supervise, superintend, oversee, regulate, orchestrate, coordinate; *informal* run the show, call the shots, be in the driver's seat. **2** *was that remark directed at me?* AIM AT, target at, address to, intend for, mean for, design for. **3** *a man in uniform directed them to the hall* GIVE DIRECTIONS, show the way, guide, lead, conduct, accompany, usher, escort. **4** *the judge directed the jury to return a not guilty verdict* INSTRUCT, tell, command, order, charge, require; *literary* bid.

direction ▶ noun **1** *a northerly direction* WAY, route, course, line, run, bearing, orientation. **2** *the direction of my research* ORIENTATION, inclination, leaning, tendency, bent, bias, preference; drift, tack, attitude, tone, tenor, mood, current, trend. **3** *his direction of the project* ADMINISTRATION, management, conduct, handling, running, supervision, superintendence, regulation, orchestration; control, command, rule, leadership, guidance. **4** *explicit directions about nursing care* INSTRUCTION, order, command, prescription, rule, regulation, requirement.

directive ▶ noun INSTRUCTION, direction, command, order, charge, injunction, prescription, rule, ruling, regulation, law, dictate, decree, dictum, edict, mandate, fiat; *formal* ordinance.

directly ▶ adverb **1** *they flew directly to New York* STRAIGHT, right, as the crow flies, by a direct route. **2** *I went directly after breakfast* IMMEDIATELY, at once, instantly, right away, straight away, post-haste, without delay, without hesitation, forthwith; quickly, speedily, promptly; *informal* pronto. **3** *the houses directly opposite* EXACTLY, right, immediately; diametrically; *informal* bang. **4** *she spoke simply and*

directly FRANKLY, candidly, openly, bluntly, forthrightly, without beating around the bush.

director ▶ noun ADMINISTRATOR, manager, chairman, chairwoman, chairperson, chair, head, chief, principal, leader, governor, president; managing director, chief executive (officer), CEO; supervisor, controller, overseer; *informal* boss, kingpin, top dog, head honcho, numero uno.

directory ▶ noun INDEX, list, listing, register, catalogue, record, archive, inventory.

dirge ▶ noun ELEGY, lament, threnody, requiem, dead march; *Irish* keen.

dirt ▶ noun **1** *his face was streaked with dirt* GRIME, filth; dust, soot, smut; muck, mud, mire, sludge, slime, ooze, dross; smudges, stains; *informal* crud, yuck, grunge, gunge. **2** *the packed dirt of the road* EARTH, mud, loam, clay, silt; ground. **3** *(informal) dog dirt*. See EXCREMENT. **4** *(informal) they tried to dig up dirt on the President* SCANDAL, gossip, revelations, rumour(s); information.

dirty ▶ adjective **1** *a dirty sweatshirt | dirty water* SOILED, grimy, grubby, filthy, mucky, stained, unwashed, greasy, smeared, smeary, spotted, smudged, cloudy, muddy, dusty, sooty; unclean, sullied, impure, tarnished, polluted, contaminated, defiled, foul, unhygienic, unsanitary; *informal* cruddy, yucky, icky, grotty, grungy; *literary* befouled, besmirched, begrimed. **2** *a dirty joke* INDECENT, obscene, rude, naughty, vulgar, smutty, coarse, crude, filthy, bawdy, suggestive, ribald, racy, salacious, risqué, offensive, off-colour, lewd, pornographic, explicit, X-rated; *informal* blue, XXX; *euphemistic* adult. **3** *dirty tricks* DISHONEST, deceitful, unscrupulous, dishonourable, unsporting, ungentlemanly, below the belt, unfair, unethical, unprincipled; crooked, double-dealing, underhanded, sly, crafty, devious, sneaky. **4** *(informal) a dirty cheat* DESPICABLE, contemptible, hateful, vile, low, mean, unworthy, worthless, beyond contempt, sordid; *informal* rotten; *archaic* scurvy. **5** *a dirty look* MALEVOLENT, resentful, hostile, black, dark; angry, cross, indignant, annoyed, disapproving; *informal* peeved. **6** *dirty weather* UNPLEASANT, nasty, foul, inclement, bad; rough, stormy, squally, gusty, windy, blowy, rainy; murky, overcast, lowering.
— OPPOSITES: clean, innocent, honourable, pleasant.
▶ verb *the dog had dirtied her dress* SOIL, stain, muddy, blacken, mess up, mark, spatter, bespatter, smudge, smear, splatter; sully, pollute, foul, defile; *literary* befoul, besmirch, begrime.
— OPPOSITES: clean.

disability ▶ noun HANDICAP, disablement, incapacity, impairment, infirmity, defect, abnormality; condition, disorder, affliction.

disable ▶ verb **1** *an injury that could disable somebody for life* INCAPACITATE, put out of action, debilitate; handicap, cripple, lame, maim, immobilize, paralyze. **2** *the bomb squad disabled the device* DEACTIVATE, defuse, disarm. **3** *he was disabled from holding public office* DISQUALIFY, prevent, preclude.

disabled ▶ adjective **1** *a disabled athlete* HANDICAPPED, incapacitated; debilitated, infirm, out of action; crippled, lame, paralyzed, immobilized, bedridden, paraplegic, quadriplegic, in a wheelchair; *euphemistic* physically challenged, differently abled. **2** *a disabled cargo ship* BROKEN DOWN, out of service, out of commission, wrecked.
— OPPOSITES: able-bodied, functioning.

disabuse ▶ verb DISILLUSION, undeceive, set straight,

open someone's eyes, correct, enlighten, disenchant, shatter someone's illusions.

disadvantage ▶ noun DRAWBACK, snag, downside, stumbling block, fly in the ointment, catch, hindrance, obstacle, impediment; flaw, defect, weakness, fault, handicap, con, trouble, difficulty, problem, complication, nuisance; informal minus, wrench in the works.
− OPPOSITES: benefit.

disadvantaged ▶ adjective DEPRIVED, underprivileged, depressed, in need, needy, poor, impoverished, indigent, hard up.

disadvantageous ▶ adjective UNFAVOURABLE, adverse, unfortunate, unlucky, bad; detrimental, prejudicial, deleterious, harmful, damaging, injurious, hurtful; inconvenient, inopportune, ill-timed, untimely, inexpedient.

disaffected ▶ adjective DISSATISFIED, disgruntled, discontented, malcontent, frustrated, alienated; disloyal, rebellious, mutinous, seditious, dissident, up in arms; hostile, antagonistic, unfriendly.
− OPPOSITES: contented.

disagree ▶ verb **1** no one was willing to disagree with him TAKE ISSUE, challenge, contradict, oppose; be at variance/odds, not see eye to eye, differ, dissent, be in dispute, debate, argue, quarrel, wrangle, clash, be at loggerheads, cross swords, lock horns; formal gainsay. **2** their accounts disagree on details DIFFER, be dissimilar, be different, vary, diverge; contradict each other, conflict, clash, contrast. **3** the spicy food disagreed with her MAKE ILL, make unwell, nauseate, sicken, upset.

disagreeable ▶ adjective **1** a disagreeable smell UNPLEASANT, displeasing, nasty, offensive, off-putting, obnoxious, objectionable, horrible, horrid, dreadful, frightful, abominable, odious, repugnant, repulsive, repellent, revolting, disgusting, foul, vile, nauseating, sickening, unpalatable. **2** a disagreeable man BAD-TEMPERED, ill-tempered, curmudgeonly, cross, crabbed, irritable, grumpy, peevish, sullen, prickly; unfriendly, unpleasant, nasty, mean, mean-spirited, ill-natured, rude, surly, discourteous, impolite, brusque, abrupt, churlish, disobliging.
− OPPOSITES: pleasant.

disagreement ▶ noun **1** there was some disagreement over possible solutions DISSENT, dispute, difference of opinion, variance, controversy, discord, contention, division. **2** a heated disagreement ARGUMENT, debate, quarrel, wrangle, squabble, falling-out, altercation, dispute, disputation, war of words, contretemps; informal tiff, set-to, blow-up, spat, row. **3** the disagreement between the results of the two assessments DIFFERENCE, dissimilarity, variation, variance, discrepancy, disparity, divergence, deviation, nonconformity; incompatibility, contradiction, conflict, clash, contrast.

disallow ▶ verb REJECT, refuse, dismiss, say no to; ban, bar, block, debar, forbid, prohibit; cancel, invalidate, overrule, quash, overturn, countermand, reverse, throw out, set aside; informal give the thumbs down to, veto, nix.

disappear ▶ verb **1** by 4 o'clock the mist had disappeared VANISH, pass from sight, be lost to view/sight, recede from view; fade (away), melt away, clear, dissolve, disperse, evaporate, dematerialize; literary evanesce. **2** this way of life has disappeared DIE OUT, die, cease to exist, come to an end, end, pass away, pass into oblivion, perish, vanish.
− OPPOSITES: materialize.

disappoint ▶ verb **1** I'm sorry to have disappointed you LET DOWN, fail, dissatisfy, dash someone's hopes; upset, dismay, sadden, disenchant, disillusion, shatter someone's illusions, disabuse. **2** his hopes were disappointed THWART, frustrate, foil, dash, put a/the damper on; informal throw cold water on.
− OPPOSITES: fulfill.

disappointed ▶ adjective UPSET, saddened, let down, cast down, disheartened, downhearted, downcast, depressed, dispirited, discouraged, despondent, dismayed, crestfallen, distressed, chagrined; disenchanted, disillusioned; displeased, discontented, dissatisfied, frustrated, disgruntled; informal choked, bummed (out), miffed, cut up.
− OPPOSITES: pleased.

disappointing ▶ adjective REGRETTABLE, unfortunate, sorry, discouraging, disheartening, dispiriting, depressing, dismaying, upsetting, saddening; unsatisfactory; informal not all it's cracked up to be.

disappointment ▶ noun **1** she tried to hide her disappointment SADNESS, regret, dismay, sorrow; dispiritedness, despondency, distress, chagrin; disenchantment, disillusionment; displeasure, dissatisfaction, disgruntlement. **2** the trip was a bit of a disappointment LETDOWN, non-event, anticlimax, washout; informal bummer.
− OPPOSITES: satisfaction.

disapprobation ▶ noun. See DISAPPROVAL.

disapproval ▶ noun DISAPPROBATION, objection, dislike; dissatisfaction, disfavour, displeasure, distaste; criticism, censure, condemnation, denunciation, deprecation; informal the thumbs down.

disapprove ▶ verb **1** he disapproved of gamblers OBJECT TO, have a poor opinion of, look down one's nose at, take exception to, dislike, take a dim view of, look askance at, frown on, be against, not believe in; deplore, criticize, censure, condemn, denounce, decry, deprecate. **2** the board disapproved the plan REJECT, veto, refuse, turn down, disallow, throw out, dismiss, rule against; informal nix.

disapproving ▶ adjective REPROACHFUL, reproving, critical, censorious, condemnatory, condemning, disparaging, denigratory, deprecatory, unfavourable; dissatisfied, displeased, hostile.

disarm ▶ verb **1** the UN must disarm the country DEMILITARIZE, demobilize. **2** the militia refused to disarm LAY DOWN ONE'S ARMS, demilitarize; literary beat swords into ploughshares. **3** police disarmed the bomb DEFUSE, disable, deactivate, put out of action, make harmless. **4** the warmth in his voice disarmed her WIN OVER, charm, persuade, thaw; mollify, appease, placate, pacify, conciliate, propitiate.

disarmament ▶ noun DEMILITARIZATION, demobilization, decommissioning; arms reduction, arms limitation, arms control; the zero option.

disarming ▶ adjective WINNING, charming, irresistible, persuasive, beguiling, conciliatory, mollifying.

disarrange ▶ verb DISORDER, throw into disarray/disorder, put out of place, disorganize, disturb, displace; mess up, make untidy, make a mess of, jumble, mix up, muddle, turn upside-down, scatter; dishevel, tousle, rumple; informal turn topsy-turvy, make a shambles of, muss up.

disarray ▶ noun the room was in disarray DISORDER, confusion, chaos, untidiness, disorganization,

dishevelment, mess, muddle, clutter, jumble, tangle, shambles.
— OPPOSITES: tidiness.

disassemble ▶ **verb** DISMANTLE, take apart, take to pieces, take to bits, deconstruct, break up, strip down.

disassociate ▶ **verb** See DISSOCIATE verb.

disaster ▶ **noun 1** *a railway disaster* CATASTROPHE, calamity, cataclysm, tragedy, act of God, holocaust; accident. **2** *a string of personal disasters* MISFORTUNE, mishap, misadventure, mischance, setback, reversal, stroke of bad luck, blow. **3** (*informal*) *the film was a disaster* FAILURE, fiasco, catastrophe, debacle; *informal* flop, megaflop, dud, bomb, washout, dog, turkey, dead loss.
— OPPOSITES: success.

disastrous ▶ **adjective** CATASTROPHIC, calamitous, cataclysmic, tragic; devastating, ruinous, harmful, dire, terrible, awful, shocking, appalling, dreadful; black, dark, unfortunate, unlucky, ill-fated, ill-starred, inauspicious; *formal* grievous.

disavow ▶ **verb** DENY, disclaim, disown, wash one's hands of, repudiate, reject, renounce.

disavowal ▶ **noun** DENIAL, rejection, repudiation, renunciation, disclaimer.

disband ▶ **verb** BREAK UP, disperse, demobilize, dissolve, scatter, separate, go separate ways, part company.
— OPPOSITES: assemble.

disbelief ▶ **noun 1** *she stared at him in disbelief* INCREDULITY, astonishment, amazement, surprise, incredulousness; skepticism, doubt, doubtfulness, dubiousness; cynicism, suspicion, distrust, mistrust; *formal* dubiety. **2** *I'll burn in hell for my disbelief* ATHEISM, non-belief, unbelief, godlessness, irreligion, agnosticism, nihilism.

disbelieve ▶ **verb** NOT BELIEVE, give no credence to, discredit, discount, doubt, distrust, mistrust, be incredulous, be unconvinced; reject, repudiate, question, challenge; *informal* take with a pinch of salt.

disbeliever ▶ **noun** UNBELIEVER, non-believer, atheist, nihilist; skeptic, doubter, agnostic, doubting Thomas, cynic.

disbelieving ▶ **adjective** INCREDULOUS, doubtful, dubious, unconvinced; distrustful, mistrustful, suspicious, cynical, skeptical.

disburden ▶ **verb** RELIEVE, free, liberate, unburden, disencumber, discharge, excuse, absolve.

disburse ▶ **verb** PAY OUT, spend, expend, dole out, dish out, hand out, part with, donate, give; *informal* fork out/over, shell out, lay out, ante up, pony up.

disc, disk ▶ **noun 1** *the sun was a huge scarlet disc* CIRCLE, round, saucer, discus, ring, coin. **2** *computer disks. See* DISK *sense* 1. **3** (*dated*) *an old Stones disc* RECORD, album, LP, vinyl.

discard ▶ **verb** DISPOSE OF, throw away/out, get rid of, toss out, jettison, scrap, dispense with, cast aside/off, throw on the scrap heap; reject, repudiate, abandon, drop, have done with, shed; *informal* chuck (away/out), dump, ditch, junk, get shut of, trash, deep-six.
— OPPOSITES: keep.

discern ▶ **verb** PERCEIVE, make out, pick out, detect, recognize, notice, observe, see, spot; identify, determine, distinguish; *literary* descry, espy.

discernible ▶ **adjective** VISIBLE, detectable, noticeable, perceptible, observable, distinguishable, recognizable, identifiable; apparent, evident,

distinct, appreciable, clear, obvious, manifest, conspicuous.

discerning ▶ **adjective** DISCRIMINATING, judicious, shrewd, clever, astute, intelligent, sharp, selective, sophisticated, tasteful, sensitive, perceptive, percipient, perspicacious, wise, aware, knowing.

discharge ▶ **verb 1** *he was discharged from the post* DISMISS, eject, expel, throw out, give someone notice, make redundant; release, let go, fire, terminate; *Military* cashier; *informal* sack, give someone the sack, boot out, give someone the boot, turf out, give someone their marching orders, show someone the door, send packing, pink-slip, give some the (old) heave-ho. **2** *he was discharged from prison* RELEASE, free, set free, let go, liberate, let out. **3** *oil is routinely discharged from ships* SEND OUT, release, eject, let out, pour out, void, give off. **4** *the swelling will burst and discharge pus* EMIT, exude, ooze, leak. **5** *he accidentally discharged the gun* FIRE, shoot, let off; set off, trigger, explode, detonate. **6** *the ferry was discharging passengers* UNLOAD, off-load, put off; remove. **7** *they discharged their duties efficiently* CARRY OUT, perform, execute, conduct, do; fulfill, accomplish, achieve, complete. **8** *the executor must discharge the funeral expenses* PAY, pay off, settle, clear, honour, meet, liquidate, defray, make good; *informal* square.
— OPPOSITES: recruit, imprison, absorb.

▶ **noun 1** *his discharge from the service* DISMISSAL, release, removal, ejection, expulsion; *Military* cashiering; *informal* the sack, the boot, the axe, a/the pink slip. **2** *her discharge from prison* RELEASE, liberation. **3** *a discharge of diesel oil into the river* LEAK, leakage, emission, release, flow. **4** *a watery discharge from the eyes* EMISSION, secretion, excretion, seepage, suppuration; pus, matter; *Medicine* exudate. **5** *a single discharge of his gun* SHOT, firing, blast; explosion, detonation. **6** *the discharge of their duties* CARRYING OUT, performance, performing, execution, conduct; fulfillment, accomplishment, completion. **7** *the discharge of all debts* PAYMENT, repayment, settlement, clearance, meeting, liquidation.

disciple ▶ **noun 1** *the disciples of Jesus* APOSTLE, follower. **2** *a disciple of Rousseau* FOLLOWER, adherent, believer, admirer, devotee, acolyte, votary; pupil, student, learner; upholder, supporter, advocate, proponent, apologist.

disciplinarian ▶ **noun** MARTINET, hard taskmaster, authoritarian, stickler for discipline; tyrant, despot, ramrod; *informal* slave-driver.

discipline ▶ **noun 1** *a lack of proper parental discipline* CONTROL, training, teaching, instruction, regulation, direction, order, authority, rule, strictness, a firm hand; routine, regimen, drill, drilling. **2** *he was able to maintain discipline among his men* GOOD BEHAVIOUR, orderliness, control, obedience; self-control, self-discipline, self-government, self-restraint. **3** *sociology is a fairly new discipline* FIELD (OF STUDY), branch of knowledge, subject, area; specialty.

▶ **verb 1** *she had disciplined herself to ignore the pain* TRAIN, drill, teach, school, coach; regiment. **2** *she learned to discipline her emotions* CONTROL, restrain, regulate, govern, keep in check, check, curb, keep a tight rein on, rein in, bridle, tame, bring into line. **3** *he was disciplined by management* PUNISH, penalize, bring to book; reprimand, rebuke, reprove, chastise, upbraid; *informal* dress down, give someone a dressing-down, rap on/over the knuckles, give someone a roasting, call/have up on the carpet; *formal* castigate.

disc jockey, disk jockey ▶ noun DJ, deejay, mixmaster, turntablist, (Man.) music man ⬇.

disclaimer ▶ noun **1** *a disclaimer of responsibility* DENIAL, refusal, rejection. **2** *(Law) a deed of disclaimer* RENUNCIATION, relinquishment, resignation, abdication; repudiation, abjuration, disavowal.
— OPPOSITES: acceptance, acknowledgement.

disclose ▶ verb **1** *the information must not be disclosed to anyone* REVEAL, make known, divulge, tell, impart, communicate, pass on, vouchsafe; release, make public, broadcast, publish, report, unveil; leak, betray, let slip, let drop, give away; *informal* let on, blab, spill the beans, let the cat out of the bag; *archaic* discover, unbosom. **2** *exploratory surgery disclosed an aneurysm* UNCOVER, reveal, show, expose, bring to light.
— OPPOSITES: conceal.

disclosure ▶ noun **1** *she was embarrassed by this unexpected disclosure* REVELATION, declaration, announcement, news, report; leak. **2** *the disclosure of official information* PUBLISHING, broadcasting; revelation, communication, release, uncovering, unveiling, exposure, exposé; leakage.

discoloration ▶ noun STAIN, mark, streak, spot, blotch, tarnishing; blemish, flaw, defect, bruise, contusion; birthmark, nevus; liver spot, age spot; *informal* splotch.

discolour ▶ verb STAIN, mark, soil, dirty, streak, smear, spot, tarnish, sully, spoil, mar, blemish; blacken, char; fade, bleach.

discoloured ▶ adjective STAINED, marked, spotted, dirty, soiled, tarnished, blackened; bleached, faded, yellowed.

discombobulate ▶ verb See DISCOMFIT.

discomfit ▶ verb EMBARRASS, abash, disconcert, discompose, discomfort, take aback, unsettle, unnerve, put someone off their stroke/game, ruffle, confuse, fluster, agitate, disorientate, upset, disturb, perturb, distress; chagrin, mortify; *informal* faze, rattle, discombobulate.

discomfiture ▶ noun EMBARRASSMENT, unease, uneasiness, awkwardness, discomfort, discomposure, abashment, confusion, agitation, nervousness, disorientation, perturbation, distress; chagrin, mortification, shame, humiliation; *informal* discombobulation.

discomfort ▶ noun **1** *abdominal discomfort* PAIN, aches and pains, soreness, tenderness, irritation, stiffness; ache, twinge, pang, throb, cramp. **2** *the discomforts of life at sea* INCONVENIENCE, difficulty, bother, nuisance, vexation, drawback, disadvantage, trouble, problem, trial, tribulation, hardship; *informal* hassle. **3** *Ruth flushed and Thomas noticed her discomfort* EMBARRASSMENT, discomfiture, unease, uneasiness, awkwardness, discomposure, confusion, nervousness, perturbation, distress, anxiety; chagrin, mortification, shame, humiliation.
▶ verb *his purpose was to discomfort the Prime Minister. See* DISCOMFIT.

discomposure ▶ noun AGITATION, discomfiture, discomfort, uneasiness, unease, confusion, disorientation, perturbation, distress, nervousness; anxiety, worry, consternation, disquiet, disquietude; embarrassment, abashment, chagrin, loss of face; *informal* discombobulation.

disconcert ▶ verb UNSETTLE, discomfit, throw/catch off balance, take aback, rattle, unnerve, disorient, perturb, disturb, perplex, confuse,

bewilder, baffle, fluster, ruffle, shake, upset, agitate, worry, dismay, surprise, take by surprise, startle, put someone off (their stroke/game), distract; *informal* throw, faze, discombobulate.

disconcerting ▶ adjective UNSETTLING, unnerving, discomfiting, disturbing, perturbing, troubling, upsetting, worrying, alarming, distracting, off-putting; confusing, bewildering, perplexing.

disconnect ▶ verb **1** *the trucks were disconnected from the train* DETACH, disengage, uncouple, decouple, unhook, unhitch, undo, unfasten, unyoke. **2** *she felt as if she were disconnected from the real world* SEPARATE, cut off, divorce, sever, isolate, divide, part, disengage, dissociate, disassociate, remove. **3** *an engineer disconnected the appliance* DEACTIVATE, shut off, turn off, switch off, unplug.
— OPPOSITES: attach.

disconnected ▶ adjective **1** *a world that seemed disconnected from reality* DETACHED, separate, separated, divorced, cut off, isolated, dissociated, disengaged; apart. **2** *a disconnected narrative* DISJOINTED, incoherent, garbled, confused, jumbled, mixed up, rambling, wandering, disorganized, uncoordinated, ill-thought-out.

disconsolate ▶ adjective SAD, unhappy, doleful, woebegone, dejected, downcast, downhearted, despondent, dispirited, crestfallen, cast down, depressed, down, disappointed, disheartened, discouraged, demoralized, low-spirited, forlorn, in the doldrums, melancholy, miserable, long-faced, glum, gloomy; *informal* blue, choked, down in the mouth, down in the dumps, in a blue funk; *literary* dolorous.
— OPPOSITES: cheerful.

discontent ▶ noun DISSATISFACTION, disaffection, discontentment, discontentedness, disgruntlement, grievances, unhappiness, displeasure, bad feelings, resentment, envy; restlessness, unrest, uneasiness, unease, frustration, irritation, annoyance; *informal* a chip on one's shoulder.
— OPPOSITES: satisfaction.

discontented ▶ adjective DISSATISFIED, disgruntled, fed up, disaffected, discontent, malcontent, unhappy, aggrieved, displeased, resentful, envious; restless, frustrated, irritated, annoyed; *informal* fed up (to the teeth), hacked off, cheesed off, teed off, ticked off.
— OPPOSITES: satisfied.

discontinue ▶ verb STOP, end, terminate, put an end to, put a stop to, wind up, finish, call a halt to, cancel, drop, abandon, dispense with, do away with, get rid of, axe, abolish; suspend, interrupt, break off, withdraw; *informal* cut, pull the plug on, scrap, nix.

discontinuity ▶ noun DISCONNECTEDNESS, disconnection, break, disruption, interruption, disjointedness.

discontinuous ▶ adjective INTERMITTENT, sporadic, broken, fitful, interrupted, on and off, disrupted, erratic, disconnected.

discord ▶ noun **1** *stress resulting from family discord* STRIFE, conflict, friction, hostility, antagonism, antipathy, enmity, bad feeling, ill feeling, bad blood, argument, quarrelling, squabbling, bickering, wrangling, feuding, contention, disagreement, dissension, dispute, difference of opinion, disunity, division, opposition; infighting. **2** *the music faded in discord* DISSONANCE, discordance, disharmony, cacophony.

— OPPOSITES: accord, harmony.

discordant ▶ adjective **1** *the messages from Washington and Ottawa were discordant* DIFFERENT, in disagreement, at variance, at odds, divergent, discrepant, contradictory, contrary, in conflict, conflicting, opposite, opposed, opposing, clashing; incompatible, inconsistent, irreconcilable. **2** *discordant sounds* INHARMONIOUS, tuneless, off-key, dissonant, harsh, jarring, grating, jangling, jangly, strident, shrill, screeching, screechy, cacophonous; sharp, flat.

— OPPOSITES: harmonious.

discount ▶ noun *students get a 10 per cent discount* REDUCTION, deduction, markdown, price cut, cut, rebate.

▶ verb **1** *I'd heard rumours, but discounted them* DISREGARD, pay no attention to, take no notice of, take no account of, dismiss, ignore, overlook, disbelieve, reject; *informal* take with a pinch of salt, pooh-pooh. **2** *the actual price is discounted in many stores* REDUCE, mark down, cut, lower; *informal* knock down. **3** *top Banff hotels discounted 20 per cent off published room rates* DEDUCT, take off, rebate; *informal* knock off, slash.

— OPPOSITES: believe, increase.

discourage ▶ verb **1** *we want to discourage children from smoking* DETER, dissuade, disincline, put off, talk out of; advise against, urge against; *archaic* discountenance. **2** *she was discouraged by his hostile tone* DISHEARTEN, dispirit, demoralize, cast down, depress, disappoint, dash someone's hopes; put off, unnerve, daunt, intimidate, cow, crush. **3** *he sought to discourage further conversation* PREVENT, stop, put a stop to, avert, fend off, stave off, ward off; inhibit, hinder, check, curb, put a damper on, throw cold water on.

— OPPOSITES: encourage.

discouraged ▶ adjective DISHEARTENED, dispirited, demoralized, deflated, disappointed, let down, disconsolate, despondent, dejected, cast down, downcast, depressed, crestfallen, dismayed, low-spirited, gloomy, glum, pessimistic, unenthusiastic; put off, daunted, intimidated, cowed, crushed; *informal* down in the mouth, down in the dumps, unenthused, bummed.

discouraging ▶ adjective DEPRESSING, demoralizing, disheartening, dispiriting, disappointing, gloomy, off-putting; unfavourable, unpromising, inauspicious.

— OPPOSITES: encouraging.

discourse ▶ noun **1** *they prolonged their discourse outside the door* DISCUSSION, conversation, talk, dialogue, conference, debate, consultation; parley, powwow, chat, confab; *formal* confabulation, colloquy. **2** *a discourse on critical theory* ESSAY, treatise, dissertation, paper, study, critique, monograph, disquisition, tract; lecture, address, speech, oration; sermon, homily.

▶ verb **1** *he discoursed at length on his favourite topic* HOLD FORTH, expatiate, pontificate; talk, give a talk, give a speech, lecture, sermonize, preach; *informal* spout, sound off; *formal* perorate. **2** *Edward was discoursing with his friends* CONVERSE, talk, speak, debate, confer, consult, parley, chat.

discourteous ▶ adjective RUDE, impolite, ill-mannered, bad-mannered, disrespectful, uncivil, unmannerly, unchivalrous, ungentlemanly, unladylike, ill-bred, churlish, boorish, crass, ungracious, graceless, uncouth; insolent, impudent, cheeky, audacious, presumptuous; curt, brusque,

blunt, offhand, unceremonious, short, sharp; ignorant.

— OPPOSITES: polite.

discourtesy ▶ noun RUDENESS, impoliteness, bad manners, incivility, disrespect, ungraciousness, churlishness, boorishness, ill breeding, uncouthness, crassness; insolence, impudence, impertinence; curtness, brusqueness, abruptness.

discover ▶ verb **1** *firemen discovered a body in the debris* FIND, locate, come across/upon, stumble on, chance on, light on, bring to light, uncover, unearth, turn up; track down. **2** *eventually, I discovered the truth* FIND OUT, learn, realize, recognize, fathom, see, ascertain, work out, dig up/out, ferret out, root out; *informal* figure out, twig (to), dope out, suss out. **3** *scientists discovered a new way of dating fossil crustaceans* HIT ON, come up with, invent, originate, devise, design, contrive, conceive of; pioneer, develop.

discoverer ▶ noun ORIGINATOR, inventor, creator, deviser, designer; pioneer, explorer.

discovery ▶ noun **1** *the discovery of the body* FINDING, location, uncovering, unearthing. **2** *the discovery that she was pregnant* REALIZATION, recognition; revelation, disclosure. **3** *the discovery of new drugs* INVENTION, origination, devising; pioneering. **4** *he failed to take out a patent on his discoveries* FIND, finding; invention, breakthrough, innovation.

discredit ▶ verb **1** *an attempt to discredit him and his company* BRING INTO DISREPUTE, disgrace, dishonour, damage the reputation of, blacken the name of, put/ show in a bad light, reflect badly on, compromise, stigmatize, smear, tarnish, taint, slur. **2** *that theory has been discredited* DISPROVE, invalidate, explode, refute; *informal* debunk, poke holes in; *formal* confute.

▶ noun **1** *crimes which brought discredit on the administration* DISHONOUR, disrepute, disgrace, shame, humiliation, ignominy, infamy, notoriety; censure, blame, reproach, opprobrium; stigma; *dated* disesteem. **2** *the ships were a discredit to the country* DISGRACE, source of shame, reproach.

— OPPOSITES: honour, glory.

discreditable ▶ adjective DISHONOURABLE, reprehensible, shameful, deplorable, disgraceful, disreputable, blameworthy, ignoble, shabby, objectionable, regrettable, unacceptable, unworthy.

— OPPOSITES: praiseworthy.

discreet ▶ adjective **1** *discreet inquiries* CAREFUL, circumspect, cautious, wary, chary, guarded; tactful, diplomatic, prudent, judicious, strategic, politic, delicate, sensitive, kid-glove. **2** *discreet lighting* UNOBTRUSIVE, inconspicuous, subtle, low-key, understated, subdued, muted, soft, restrained.

discrepancy ▶ noun DIFFERENCE, disparity, variance, variation, deviation, divergence, disagreement, inconsistency, dissimilarity, mismatch, discordance, incompatibility, conflict.

— OPPOSITES: correspondence.

discrete ▶ adjective SEPARATE, distinct, individual, detached, unattached, disconnected, discontinuous, disjunct, disjoined.

— OPPOSITES: connected.

discretion ▶ noun **1** *you can rely on his discretion* CIRCUMSPECTION, carefulness, caution, wariness, chariness, guardedness; TACT, tactfulness, diplomacy, delicacy, sensitivity, prudence, judiciousness. **2** *his sentence would be determined at the discretion of the court*

CHOICE, option, preference, disposition, volition; pleasure, liking, wish, will, inclination, desire.

discretionary ► **adjective** OPTIONAL, voluntary, at one's discretion, elective.
– OPPOSITES: compulsory.

discriminate ► **verb 1** *he cannot discriminate between fact and fiction* DIFFERENTIATE, distinguish, draw a distinction, tell the difference, tell apart; separate, separate the sheep from the goats, separate the wheat from the chaff. **2** *existing employment policies discriminate against women* BE BIASED, be prejudiced; treat differently, treat unfairly, put at a disadvantage, single out; victimize.

discriminating ► **adjective** *she had discriminating tastes* DISCERNING, perceptive, astute, shrewd, judicious, perspicacious, insightful, keen; selective, fastidious, tasteful, refined, sensitive, cultivated, cultured, artistic, aesthetic.
– OPPOSITES: indiscriminate.

discrimination ► **noun 1** *racial discrimination* PREJUDICE, bias, bigotry, intolerance, narrow-mindedness, unfairness, inequity, favouritism, one-sidedness, partisanship; sexism, chauvinism, misogyny, racism, racialism, anti-Semitism, heterosexism, ageism, classism; (*in S. Africa, historical*) apartheid. **2** *a bland man with no discrimination* DISCERNMENT, judgment, perception, perceptiveness, perspicacity, acumen, astuteness, shrewdness, judiciousness, insight; selectivity, (good) taste, fastidiousness, refinement, sensitivity, cultivation, culture.
– OPPOSITES: impartiality.

discriminatory ► **adjective** PREJUDICIAL, biased, prejudiced, preferential, unfair, unjust, invidious, inequitable, weighted, one-sided, partisan; sexist, chauvinistic, chauvinist, racist, racialist, anti-Semitic, ageist, classist.
– OPPOSITES: impartial.

discursive ► **adjective 1** *dull, discursive prose* RAMBLING, digressive, meandering, wandering, maundering, diffuse, long, lengthy, wordy, verbose, long-winded, prolix; circuitous, roundabout, circumlocutory; *informal* waffly. **2** *an elegant discursive style* FLUENT, flowing, fluid, eloquent, expansive.
– OPPOSITES: concise, terse.

discuss ► **verb 1** *I discussed the matter with my wife* TALK OVER, talk about, talk through, converse about, debate, confer about, deliberate about, chew over, consider, consider the pros and cons of, thrash out; *informal* kick around, hash out, bat around. **2** *chapter three discusses this topic in detail* EXAMINE, explore, study, analyze, go into, deal with, treat, consider, concern itself with, tackle.

discussion ► **noun 1** *a long discussion with her husband* CONVERSATION, talk, dialogue, discourse, conference, debate, exchange of views, consultation, deliberation; powwow, chat, tête-à-tête, heart-to-heart, huddle; negotiations, parley; *informal* confab, chit-chat, rap (session), skull session, bull session; *formal* confabulation, colloquy. **2** *the book's candid discussion of sexual matters* EXAMINATION, exploration, analysis, study; treatment, consideration.

disdain ► **noun** *she looked at him with disdain* CONTEMPT, scorn, scornfulness, contemptuousness, derision, disrespect; disparagement, condescension, superciliousness, hauteur, haughtiness, arrogance, snobbishness, indifference, distaste, dislike, disgust.
– OPPOSITES: respect.

► **verb 1** *she disdained such vulgar exhibitionism* SCORN, deride, pour scorn on, regard with contempt, sneer at, sniff at, curl one's lip at, look down one's nose at, look down on; despise; *informal* turn up one's nose at, pooh-pooh. **2** *she disdained his invitation* SPURN, reject, refuse, rebuff, disregard, ignore, snub; decline, turn down, brush aside.

disdainful ► **adjective** CONTEMPTUOUS, scornful, derisive, sneering, withering, slighting, disparaging, disrespectful, condescending, patronizing, supercilious, haughty, superior, arrogant, proud, snobbish, lordly, aloof, indifferent, dismissive; *informal* high and mighty, hoity-toity, sniffy, snotty; *archaic* contumelious.
– OPPOSITES: respectful.

disease ► **noun** ILLNESS, sickness, ill health; infection, ailment, malady, disorder, complaint, affliction, condition, indisposition, upset, problem, trouble, infirmity, disability, defect, abnormality; pestilence, plague, cancer, canker, blight; *informal* bug, virus. *dated* contagion.
– RELATED TERMS: pathological.

diseased ► **adjective** UNHEALTHY, ill, sick, unwell, ailing, sickly, unsound; infected, septic, contaminated, blighted, rotten, bad, abnormal.

disembark ► **verb** GET OFF, step off, leave, pile out; go ashore, debark, detrain, deplane; land, arrive, alight.

disembodied ► **adjective** BODILESS, incorporeal, discarnate, spiritual; intangible, insubstantial, impalpable; ghostly, spectral, phantom, wraithlike.

disembowel ► **verb** GUT, draw, remove the guts from; *formal* eviscerate.

disenchanted ► **adjective** DISILLUSIONED, disappointed, disabused, let down, fed up, dissatisfied, discontented; cynical, soured, jaundiced, sick, indifferent, blasé.

disenchantment ► **noun** DISILLUSIONMENT, disappointment, dissatisfaction, discontent, discontentedness, rude awakening; cynicism.

disengage ► **verb 1** *I disengaged his hand from mine* REMOVE, detach, disentangle, extricate, separate, release, free, loosen, loose, disconnect, unfasten, unclasp, uncouple, undo, unhook, unhitch, untie, unyoke. **2** *UN forces disengaged from the country* WITHDRAW, leave, pull out of, quit, retreat from.
– OPPOSITES: attach, enter.

disentangle ► **verb 1** *Allen was disentangling a coil of rope* UNTANGLE, unravel, untwist, unwind, undo, untie, straighten out, smooth out; comb. **2** *he disentangled his fingers from her hair* EXTRICATE, extract, free, remove, disengage, untwine, release, loosen, detach, unfasten, unclasp, disconnect.

disfavour ► **noun** DISAPPROVAL, disapprobation; dislike, displeasure, distaste, dissatisfaction, low opinion; *dated* disesteem.

disfigure ► **verb** MAR, spoil, deface, scar, blemish, uglify; damage, injure, impair, blight, mutilate, deform, maim, ruin; vandalize.
– OPPOSITES: adorn.

disfigurement ► **noun 1** *the disfigurement of Victorian buildings* DEFACEMENT, spoiling, scarring, uglification, mutilation, damage, vandalizing, ruin. **2** *a permanent facial disfigurement* BLEMISH, flaw, defect, imperfection, discoloration, blotch; scar, pockmark; deformity, malformation, abnormality, injury, wound.

disgorge ► **verb 1** *the combine disgorged a stream of* *grain* POUR OUT, discharge, eject, throw out, emit, expel, spit out, spew out, belch forth, spout; vomit, regurgitate. **2** *they were made to disgorge all the profits* SURRENDER, relinquish, hand over, give up, turn over, yield; *informal* cough up, fork over.

disgrace ▶ noun **1** *he brought disgrace on the family* DISHONOUR, shame, discredit, ignominy, degradation, disrepute, ill-repute, infamy, scandal, stigma, opprobrium, obloquy, condemnation, vilification, contempt, disrespect; humiliation, embarrassment, loss of face; *dated* disesteem. **2** *the unemployment figures are a disgrace* SCANDAL, outrage; discredit, reproach, affront, insult; stain, blemish, blot, black mark; *informal* crime, sin.
— OPPOSITES: honour.

▶ verb **1** *you have disgraced the family name* BRING SHAME ON, shame, dishonour, discredit, bring into disrepute, degrade, debase, defame, stigmatize, taint, sully, tarnish, besmirch, stain, blacken, drag through the mud/mire. **2** *he was publicly disgraced* DISCREDIT, dishonour, stigmatize; humiliate, cause to lose face, chasten, humble, demean, put someone in their place, take down a peg or two, cut down to size.
— OPPOSITES: honour.

■ **in disgrace** OUT OF FAVOUR, unpopular, under a cloud, disgraced; *informal* in someone's bad/black books, in the doghouse.

disgraceful ▶ adjective SHAMEFUL, shocking, scandalous, deplorable, despicable, contemptible, beyond contempt, beyond the pale, dishonourable, discreditable, reprehensible, base, mean, low, blameworthy, unworthy, ignoble, shabby, inglorious, outrageous, abominable, atrocious, appalling, dreadful, terrible, disgusting, shameless, vile, odious, monstrous, heinous, iniquitous, unspeakable, loathsome, sordid, nefarious; *archaic* scurvy.
— OPPOSITES: admirable.

disgruntled ▶ adjective DISSATISFIED, discontented, aggrieved, resentful, fed up, displeased, unhappy, disappointed, disaffected; angry, irate, annoyed, cross, exasperated, indignant, vexed, irritated, piqued, irked, put out, peeved, miffed, bummed, aggravated, hacked off, riled, peed off, PO'd, hot under the collar, in a huff, cheesed off, shirty, sore, teed off, ticked off.

disguise ▶ verb *his controlled voice disguised his true feelings* CAMOUFLAGE, conceal, hide, cover up, dissemble, mask, screen, shroud, veil, cloak; gloss over, put up a smokescreen.
— OPPOSITES: expose.

■ **disguise oneself as** DRESS UP AS, pretend to be, pass oneself of as, impersonate, pose as; *formal* personate.

disguised ▶ adjective IN DISGUISE, camouflaged; incognito, under cover.

disgust ▶ noun *a look of disgust* REVULSION, repugnance, aversion, distaste, nausea, abhorrence, loathing, detestation, odium, horror; contempt, outrage.
— OPPOSITES: delight.

▶ verb **1** *the hospital food disgusted me* REVOLT, repel, repulse, sicken, nauseate, turn someone's stomach, make someone's gorge rise; *informal* turn off, gross out. **2** *Toby's behaviour disgusted her* OUTRAGE, shock, horrify, appall, scandalize, offend.

disgusting ▶ adjective **1** *the food was disgusting* REVOLTING, repellent, repulsive, sickening, nauseating, stomach-churning, stomach-turning,

off-putting, unpalatable, distasteful, foul, nasty, vomitous; *informal* yucky, icky, gross. **2** *I find racism disgusting* ABHORRENT, loathsome, offensive, appalling, outrageous, objectionable, shocking, horrifying, scandalous, monstrous, unspeakable, shameful, vile, odious, obnoxious, detestable, hateful, sickening, contemptible, despicable, deplorable, abominable, beyond the pale; *informal* gross, ghastly, sick.
— OPPOSITES: delicious, appealing.

dish ▶ noun **1** *a china dish* BOWL, plate, platter, salver, paten; container, receptacle, casserole, tureen; *archaic* trencher, charger; *historical* porringer. **2** *vegetarian dishes* RECIPE, meal, course; (**dishes**) food, fare. **3** (*informal*) *she's quite a dish. See* BEAUTY *sense 2.*

■ **dish something out** DISTRIBUTE, dispense, issue, hand out/around, give out, pass out/around; deal out, dole out, share out, allocate, allot, apportion.

■ **dish something up** SERVE (UP), spoon out, ladle out, scoop out.

disharmony ▶ noun DISCORD, friction, strife, conflict, hostility, acrimony, bad blood, bad feeling, enmity, dissension, disagreement, feuding, quarrelling; disunity, disunity, division, divisiveness.

dishearten ▶ verb DISCOURAGE, dispirit, demoralize, cast down, depress, disappoint, dismay, dash someone's hopes; put off, deter, unnerve, daunt, intimidate, cow, crush.
— OPPOSITES: encourage.

disheartened ▶ adjective DISCOURAGED, dispirited, demoralized, deflated, disappointed, let down, disconsolate, despondent, dejected, cast down, downcast, depressed, crestfallen, dismayed, low-spirited, gloomy, glum, pessimistic, unenthusiastic; daunted, intimidated, cowed, crushed; *informal* down in the mouth, down in the dumps, unenthused.

dishevelled ▶ adjective UNTIDY, unkempt, scruffy, messy, in a mess, disordered, disarranged, rumpled, bedraggled; uncombed, tousled, tangled, tangly, knotted, knotty, shaggy, straggly, windswept, wind-blown, wild; slovenly, slatternly, blowsy, frowzy, mussed (up), mussy.
— OPPOSITES: tidy.

dishonest ▶ adjective FRAUDULENT, corrupt, swindling, cheating, double-dealing; underhanded, crafty, cunning, devious, treacherous, unfair, unjust, dirty, unethical, immoral, dishonourable, untrustworthy, unscrupulous, unprincipled, amoral; criminal, illegal, unlawful; false, untruthful, deceitful, deceiving, lying, mendacious; *informal* crooked, shady, tricky, sharp, shifty, hinky; *literary* perfidious.

dishonesty ▶ noun FRAUD, fraudulence, sharp practice, corruption, cheating, chicanery, double-dealing, deceit, deception, duplicity, lying, falseness, falsity, falsehood, untruthfulness; craft, cunning, trickery, artifice, underhandedness, subterfuge, skulduggery, treachery, untrustworthiness, unscrupulousness, criminality, misconduct; *informal* crookedness, dirty tricks, shenanigans; *literary* perfidy.
— OPPOSITES: probity.

dishonour ▶ noun *the incident brought dishonour upon the police profession* DISGRACE, shame, discredit, humiliation, degradation, ignominy, scandal, infamy, disrepute, ill repute, loss of face, disfavour, ill favour, debasement, opprobrium, obloquy; stigma; *dated* disesteem.

▶ verb *his family name has been dishonoured* DISGRACE, shame, discredit, bring into disrepute, humiliate, degrade, debase, lower, cheapen, drag down, drag through the mud, blacken the name of, give a bad name to; sully, stain, taint, besmirch, smear, mar, blot, stigmatize.

dishonourable ▶ adjective DISGRACEFUL, shameful, disreputable, discreditable, degrading, ignominious, ignoble, blameworthy, contemptible, despicable, reprehensible, shabby, shoddy, sordid, sorry, base, low, improper, unseemly, unworthy; unprincipled, unscrupulous, corrupt, untrustworthy, treacherous, traitorous; *informal* shady, dirty; *literary* perfidious; *archaic* scurvy.

disillusion ▶ verb DISABUSE, enlighten, set straight, open someone's eyes; disenchant, shatter someone's illusions, disappoint, make sadder and wiser.
– OPPOSITES: deceive.

disillusioned ▶ adjective DISENCHANTED, disabused, disappointed, let down, discouraged; cynical, sour, negative, world-weary.

disincentive ▶ noun DETERRENT, discouragement, damper, brake, curb, check, restraint, inhibitor; obstacle, impediment, hindrance, obstruction, block, barrier.

disinclination ▶ noun RELUCTANCE, unwillingness, lack of enthusiasm, indisposition, hesitancy; aversion, dislike, distaste; objection, demur, resistance, opposition.
– OPPOSITES: enthusiasm.

disinclined ▶ adjective RELUCTANT, unwilling, unenthusiastic, unprepared, indisposed, ill-disposed, not in the mood, hesitant; loath, averse, antipathetic, resistant, opposed.
– OPPOSITES: willing.

disinfect ▶ verb STERILIZE, sanitize, clean, cleanse, purify, decontaminate; fumigate.
– OPPOSITES: contaminate.

disinfectant ▶ noun ANTISEPTIC, germicide, sterilizer, cleanser, decontaminant; fumigant.

disingenuous ▶ adjective INSINCERE, dishonest, untruthful, false, deceitful, duplicitous, lying, mendacious; hypocritical.

disinherit ▶ verb CUT SOMEONE OUT OF ONE'S WILL, cut off, dispossess; disown, repudiate, reject, cast off/ aside, wash one's hands of, have nothing more to do with, turn one's back on; *informal* cut off without a penny.

disintegrate ▶ verb BREAK UP, break apart, fall apart, fall to pieces, fragment, fracture, shatter, splinter; explode, blow up, blow apart, fly apart; crumble, deteriorate, decay, decompose, rot, moulder, perish, dissolve, collapse, go to rack and ruin, degenerate; *informal* bust, be smashed to smithereens.

disinter ▶ verb EXHUME, unearth, dig up, disentomb.

disinterest ▶ noun **1** *scholarly disinterest* IMPARTIALITY, neutrality, objectivity, detachment, disinterestedness, lack of bias, lack of prejudice; open-mindedness, fairness, fair-mindedness, equity, balance, even-handedness. **2** *he looked at us with complete disinterest* INDIFFERENCE, lack of interest, unconcern, impassivity; boredom, apathy.
– OPPOSITES: bias.

disinterested ▶ adjective **1** *disinterested advice* UNBIASED, unprejudiced, impartial, neutral, non-partisan, detached, uninvolved, objective, dispassionate, impersonal, clinical; open-minded,

fair, just, equitable, balanced, even-handed, with no axe to grind. **2** *he looked at her with disinterested eyes* UNINTERESTED, indifferent, incurious, uncurious, unconcerned, unmoved, unresponsive, impassive, passive, detached, unenthusiastic, lukewarm, bored, apathetic; *informal* couldn't-care-less.

disjointed ▶ adjective UNCONNECTED, disconnected, disunited, discontinuous, fragmented, disorganized, disordered, muddled, mixed up, jumbled, garbled, incoherent, confused; rambling, wandering.

disk, disc ▶ noun **1** DISKETTE, floppy disk, floppy; hard disk, zip disk, CD, CD-ROM, DVD; *proprietary* Mini Disc. **2** *shape it into the form of a disc. See* DISC sense 1.

dislike ▶ verb *a man she had always disliked* FIND DISTASTEFUL, regard with distaste, be averse to, have an aversion to, have no liking/taste for, disapprove of, object to, take exception to; hate, detest, loathe, abhor, despise, be unable to bear/stand, shrink from, shudder at, find repellent; *informal* be unable to stomach; *formal* abominate.
▶ noun *she viewed the other woman with dislike* DISTASTE, aversion, disfavour, disapproval, disapprobation, enmity, animosity, hostility, antipathy, antagonism; hate, hatred, detestation, loathing, disgust, repugnance, abhorrence, disdain, contempt.

dislocate ▶ verb **1** *she dislocated her hip* PUT OUT OF JOINT; *informal* put out; *Medicine* luxate. **2** *trade was dislocated by a famine* DISRUPT, disturb, throw into disarray, throw into confusion, play havoc with, interfere with, disorganize, upset, disorder; *informal* mess up.

dislodge ▶ verb **1** *replace any stones you dislodge* DISPLACE, knock out of place/position, move, shift; knock over, upset. **2** *economic sanctions failed to dislodge the dictator* REMOVE, force out, drive out, oust, eject, get rid of, evict, unseat, depose, topple, drum out; *informal* kick out, boot out, turf out.

disloyal ▶ adjective UNFAITHFUL, faithless, false, false-hearted, untrue, inconstant, untrustworthy, unreliable, undependable, fickle; treacherous, traitorous, subversive, seditious, unpatriotic, deceitful; dissident, renegade; adulterous; *informal* backstabbing, two-timing; *literary* perfidious.

disloyalty ▶ noun UNFAITHFULNESS, infidelity, inconstancy, faithlessness, fickleness, unreliability, untrustworthiness, betrayal, falseness, duplicity, double-dealing, treachery, treason, subversion, sedition, dissidence; adultery; *informal* back-stabbing, two-timing; *literary* perfidy, perfidiousness.

dismal ▶ adjective **1** *a dismal look* GLOOMY, glum, melancholy, morose, doleful, woebegone, forlorn, dejected, depressed, dispirited, downcast, despondent, disconsolate, miserable, sad, unhappy, sorrowful, desolate, wretched; *informal* blue, down in the dumps/mouth; *literary* dolorous. **2** *a dismal hall* DINGY, dim, dark, gloomy, dreary, drab, dull, bleak, cheerless, depressing, uninviting, unwelcoming. **3** *(informal) a dismal performance. See* POOR sense 2.
– OPPOSITES: cheerful, bright.

dismantle ▶ verb TAKE APART, take to pieces/bits, pull apart, pull to pieces, disassemble, break up, strip (down); knock down, pull down, demolish.
– OPPOSITES: assemble, build.

dismay ▶ verb *he was dismayed by the change in his friend* APPALL, horrify, shock, shake (up); disconcert, take aback, alarm, unnerve, unsettle, throw off

balance, discompose; disturb, upset, distress; *informal* rattle, faze.
— OPPOSITES: encourage, please.
▶ **noun** *they greeted his decision with dismay* ALARM, shock, surprise, consternation, concern, perturbation, disquiet, discomposure, distress.
— OPPOSITES: pleasure, relief.

dismember ▶ **verb** DISJOINT, joint; pull apart, cut up, chop up, butcher.

dismiss ▶ **verb 1** *the president dismissed five ministers* GIVE SOMEONE THEIR NOTICE, get rid of, discharge, terminate; lay off, make redundant, sack, give someone the sack, fire, boot out, give someone the boot/elbow/push, give someone their marching orders, show someone the door, can, pink-slip; *Military* cashier. **2** *the guards were dismissed* SEND AWAY, let go; disband, dissolve, discharge. **3** *he dismissed all morbid thoughts* BANISH, set aside, disregard, shrug off, put out of one's mind; reject, deny, repudiate, spurn.
— OPPOSITES: engage.

dismissal ▶ **noun 1** *the threat of dismissal* TERMINATION, discharge, one's notice; redundancy, laying off; *informal* the sack, sacking, firing, the boot, the axe, one's marching orders, the chop, the pink slip; *Military* cashiering. **2** *a condescending dismissal* REJECTION, repudiation, repulse, non-acceptance; *informal* kiss-off.
— OPPOSITES: recruitment.

dismissive ▶ **adjective** CONTEMPTUOUS, disdainful, scornful, sneering, snide, disparaging, negative; *informal* sniffy.
— OPPOSITES: admiring.

dismount ▶ **verb 1** *the cyclist dismounted* ALIGHT, get off/down. **2** *he was already dismounted* UNSEAT, dislodge, throw, unhorse.

disobedient ▶ **adjective** INSUBORDINATE, unruly, wayward, badly behaved, naughty, delinquent, disruptive, troublesome, rebellious, defiant, mutinous, recalcitrant, uncooperative, truculent, wilful, intractable, obstreperous; *archaic* contumacious.

disobey ▶ **verb** DEFY, go against, flout, contravene, infringe, transgress, violate; disregard, ignore, pay no heed to.

disobliging ▶ **adjective** UNHELPFUL, uncooperative, unaccommodating, unreasonable, awkward, difficult; discourteous, uncivil, unfriendly.
— OPPOSITES: helpful.

disorder ▶ **noun 1** *he hates disorder* UNTIDINESS, disorderliness, mess, disarray, chaos, confusion; clutter, jumble; a muddle, a shambles. **2** *incidents of public disorder* UNREST, disturbance, disruption, upheaval, turmoil, mayhem, pandemonium; violence, fighting, rioting, lawlessness, anarchy; breach of the peace, fracas, rumpus, ruckus, melee. **3** *a blood disorder* DISEASE, infection, complaint, condition, affliction, malady, sickness, illness, ailment, infirmity, irregularity.
— OPPOSITES: tidiness, peace.

disordered ▶ **adjective 1** *her grey hair was disordered* UNTIDY, unkempt, messy, in a mess, mussed (up), mussy; disorganized, chaotic, confused, jumbled, muddled, shambolic. **2** *a disordered digestive system* DYSFUNCTIONAL, disturbed, unsettled, unbalanced, upset.

disorderly ▶ **adjective 1** *a disorderly desk* UNTIDY, disorganized, messy, cluttered; in disarray, in a mess, in a jumble, in a muddle, at sixes and sevens; *informal*

shambolic, like a bomb went off. **2** *disorderly behaviour* UNRULY, boisterous, rough, rowdy, wild, riotous; disruptive, troublesome, undisciplined, lawless, unmanageable, uncontrollable, out of hand, out of control.
— OPPOSITES: tidy, peaceful.

disorganized ▶ **adjective 1** *a disorganized tool box* DISORDERLY, disordered, unorganized, jumbled, muddled, untidy, messy, chaotic, topsy-turvy, haphazard, ragtag; in disorder, in disarray, in a mess, in a muddle, in a shambles, shambolic. **2** *muddled and disorganized* UNMETHODICAL, unsystematic, undisciplined, badly organized, inefficient; haphazard, careless, slapdash; *informal* sloppy, hit-and-miss.
— OPPOSITES: orderly.

disoriented ▶ **adjective** CONFUSED, bewildered, at sea; lost, adrift, off-course, having lost one's bearings; *informal* not knowing whether one is coming or going.

disown ▶ **verb** REJECT, cast off/aside, abandon, renounce, deny; turn one's back on, wash one's hands of, have nothing more to do with; *literary* forsake.

disparage ▶ **verb** BELITTLE, denigrate, deprecate, trivialize, make light of, undervalue, underrate, play down; ridicule, deride, mock, scorn, scoff at, sneer at; run down, defame, discredit, speak badly of, cast aspersions on, impugn, vilify, traduce, criticize, slur; *informal* pick holes in, knock, slam, pan, badmouth, dis, pooh-pooh; *formal* calumniate, derogate.
— OPPOSITES: praise, overrate.

disparaging ▶ **adjective** DEROGATORY, deprecatory, denigratory, belittling; critical, scathing, negative, unfavourable, uncomplimentary, uncharitable; contemptuous, scornful, snide, disdainful; *informal* bitchy, catty; *archaic* contumelious.
— OPPOSITES: complimentary.

disparate ▶ **adjective** CONTRASTING, different, differing, dissimilar, unalike, poles apart; varying, various, diverse, diversified, heterogeneous, distinct, separate, divergent; *literary* divers.
— OPPOSITES: homogen(e)ous.

disparity ▶ **noun** DISCREPANCY, inconsistency, imbalance; variance, variation, divergence, gap, gulf; difference, dissimilarity, contrast.
— OPPOSITES: similarity.

dispassionate ▶ **adjective 1** *a calm, dispassionate manner* UNEMOTIONAL, emotionless, impassive, cool, calm, {calm, cool, and collected}, unruffled, unperturbed, composed, self-possessed, self-controlled, unexcitable; *informal* laid-back. **2** *a dispassionate analysis* OBJECTIVE, detached, neutral, disinterested, impartial, non-partisan, unbiased, unprejudiced; scientific, analytical.
— OPPOSITES: emotional, biased.

dispatch ▶ **verb 1** *all the messages were dispatched* SEND (OFF), post, mail, forward, transmit, email. **2** *the business was dispatched in the morning* DEAL WITH, finish, conclude, settle, discharge, perform; expedite, push through; *informal* make short work of. **3** *the good guy dispatched a host of villains* KILL, put to death, take/end the life of; slaughter, butcher, massacre, wipe out, exterminate, eliminate; murder, assassinate, execute; *informal* bump off, do in, do away with, take out, blow away, ice, rub out, waste; *literary* slay.
▶ **noun 1** *files ready for dispatch* SENDING, posting, mailing, emailing. **2** *efficiency and dispatch* PROMPTNESS, speed, speediness, swiftness, rapidity, briskness, haste, hastiness; *literary* fleetness, celerity.

3 *the latest dispatch from the front* COMMUNICATION, communiqué, bulletin, report, statement, letter, message; news, intelligence; *informal* memo, info, story, lowdown, scoop; *literary* tidings. **4** *the capture and dispatch of the wolf* KILLING, slaughter, massacre, extermination, elimination; murder, assassination, execution; *literary* slaying.

dispel ▶ verb BANISH, eliminate, drive away/off, get rid of; relieve, allay, ease, quell.

dispensable ▶ adjective EXPENDABLE, disposable, replaceable, inessential, non-essential; unnecessary, redundant, superfluous, surplus to requirements.

dispensation ▶ noun **1** *the dispensation of supplies* DISTRIBUTION, supply, supplying, issue, issuing, handing out, doling out, dishing out, sharing out, dividing out; division, allocation, allotment, apportionment. **2** *the dispensation of justice* ADMINISTRATION, administering, delivery, discharge, dealing out, meting out. **3** *a dispensation from the Pope* EXEMPTION, immunity, exception, exoneration, reprieve, remission. **4** *the new constitutional dispensation* SYSTEM, order, arrangement, organization.

dispense ▶ verb **1** *servants dispensed the drinks* DISTRIBUTE, pass round, hand out, dole out, dish out, share out; allocate, supply, allot, apportion. **2** *the soldiers dispensed summary justice* ADMINISTER, deliver, issue, discharge, deal out, mete out. **3** *dispensing medicines* PREPARE, make up; supply, provide, sell. **4** *the Pope dispensed him from his impediment* EXEMPT, excuse, except, release, let off, reprieve, absolve.
■ **dispense with 1** *let's dispense with the formalities* WAIVE, omit, drop, leave out, forgo; do away with, give something a miss. **2** *he dispensed with his crutches* GET RID OF, throw away/out, dispose of, discard; manage without, cope without; *informal* ditch, scrap, dump, deep-six, chuck out/away, get shut of.

disperse ▶ verb **1** *the crowd began to disperse | police dispersed the demonstrators* BREAK UP, split up, disband, scatter, leave, go their separate ways; drive away/off, chase away. **2** *the fog finally dispersed* DISSIPATE, dissolve, melt away, fade away, clear, lift. **3** *seeds dispersed by birds* SCATTER, disseminate, distribute, spread, broadcast.
— OPPOSITES: assemble, gather.

dispirited ▶ adjective DISHEARTENED, discouraged, demoralized, downcast, low, low-spirited, dejected, downhearted, depressed, disconsolate.
— OPPOSITES: heartened.

dispiriting ▶ adjective DISHEARTENING, depressing, discouraging, daunting, demoralizing.

displace ▶ verb **1** *roof tiles displaced by gales* DISLODGE, dislocate, move, shift, reposition; move out of place, knock out of place/position. **2** *the minister was displaced* DEPOSE, dislodge, unseat, remove (from office), dismiss, eject, oust, expel, force out, drive out; overthrow, topple, bring down; *informal* boot out, give someone the boot, show someone the door, turf out, bump. **3** *English displaced the local language* REPLACE, take the place of, supplant, supersede.
— OPPOSITES: replace, reinstate.

display ▶ noun **1** *a display of lights* EXHIBITION, exposition, array, arrangement, presentation, demonstration; spectacle, show, parade, pageant. **2** *they vied to outdo each other in display* OSTENTATION, showiness, extravagance, flamboyance, lavishness, splendour; *informal* swank, flashiness, glitziness. **3** *his display of concern* MANIFESTATION, expression, show.
▶ verb **1** *the paintings are displayed in the art gallery*

EXHIBIT, show, put on show/view; arrange, array, present, lay out, set out. **2** *the play displays his many theatrical talents* SHOW OFF, parade, flaunt, reveal; publicize, make known, call/draw attention to. **3** *she displayed a caustic sense of humour* MANIFEST, show evidence of, reveal; demonstrate, show; *formal* evince.
— OPPOSITES: conceal.

displease ▶ verb ANNOY, irritate, anger, irk, vex, pique, gall, nettle; put out, upset, aggravate, peeve, needle, bug, rile, miff; *informal* hack off, tee off, tick off, piss off.

displeasure ▶ noun ANNOYANCE, irritation, crossness, anger, vexation, pique, rancour; dissatisfaction, discontent, discontentedness, disgruntlement, disapproval; *informal* aggravation.
— OPPOSITES: satisfaction.

disposable ▶ adjective **1** *disposable plates* THROWAWAY, expendable, single-use. **2** *disposable income* AVAILABLE, usable, spendable.

disposal ▶ noun **1** *garbage ready for disposal* THROWING AWAY, discarding, jettisoning, scrapping, recycling; *informal* dumping, ditching, chucking (out/away), deep-sixing. **2** *the disposal of the troops in two lines* ARRANGEMENT, arranging, positioning, placement, lining up, disposition, grouping.
■ **at someone's disposal** FOR USE BY, in reserve for, in the hands of, in the possession of.

dispose ▶ verb **1** *he disposed the pictures in sequence* ARRANGE, place, put, position, array, set up, form; marshal, gather, group. **2** *the experience disposed him to be kind* INCLINE, encourage, persuade, predispose, make willing, prompt, lead, motivate, sway, influence.
■ **dispose of 1** *the waste was disposed of* THROW AWAY/OUT, get rid of, discard, jettison, scrap, junk; *informal* dump, ditch, chuck (out/away), get shut of, trash, deep-six. **2** *he disposed of all his assets* PART WITH, give away, hand over, deliver up, transfer; sell, auction; *informal* get shut of. **3** (*informal*) *she disposed of a fourth cake.* See CONSUME sense 1. **4** (*informal*) *he robbed her and then disposed of her.* See KILL verb sense 1.

disposed ▶ adjective **1** *they are philanthropically disposed* INCLINED, predisposed, minded. **2** *we are not disposed to argue* WILLING, inclined, prepared, ready, minded, in the mood. **3** *he was disposed to be cruel* LIABLE, apt, inclined, likely, predisposed, prone, tending; capable of.

disposition ▶ noun **1** *a nervous disposition* TEMPERAMENT, nature, character, constitution, makeup, mentality. **2** *his disposition to generosity* INCLINATION, tendency, proneness, propensity, proclivity. **3** *the disposition of the armed forces* ARRANGEMENT, positioning, placement, configuration; set-up, lineup, layout, array; marshalling, mustering, grouping; *Military* dressing. **4** (*Law*) *the disposition of the company's property* DISTRIBUTION, disposal, allocation, transfer; sale, auction.

dispossess ▶ verb DIVEST, strip, rob, cheat out of, deprive; *informal* do out of.

disproportionate ▶ adjective OUT OF PROPORTION TO, not appropriate to, inappropriate to, not commensurate with, incommensurate with, relatively too large/small for; inordinate, unreasonable, excessive, undue.

disprove ▶ verb REFUTE, prove false, rebut, falsify, debunk, negate, invalidate, contradict, confound, controvert, negative, discredit; *informal* poke holes in, blow out of the water, shoot down; *formal* confute, gainsay.

disputable ▶ adjective DEBATABLE, open to debate/question, arguable, contestable, moot, questionable, doubtful; *informal* iffy.

disputation ▶ noun DEBATE, discussion, dispute, argument, arguing, altercation, dissension, disagreement, controversy; polemics.

dispute ▶ noun **1** *a subject of dispute* DEBATE, discussion, disputation, argument, controversy, disagreement, quarrelling, dissension, conflict, friction, strife, discord. **2** *they have settled their dispute* QUARREL, argument, altercation, squabble, falling-out, disagreement, difference of opinion, clash, wrangle; *informal* tiff, spat, blow-up, scrap, row, rhubarb.
— OPPOSITES: agreement.
▶ verb **1** *George disputed with him* DEBATE, discuss, exchange views; quarrel, argue, disagree, clash, fall out, wrangle, bicker, squabble; *informal* have words, have a tiff/spat. **2** *they disputed his proposals* CHALLENGE, contest, question, call into question, impugn, quibble over, contradict, controvert, argue about, disagree with, take issue with; *formal* gainsay.
— OPPOSITES: accept.

disqualified ▶ adjective BANNED, barred, debarred; ineligible.
— OPPOSITES: allowed.

disquiet ▶ noun *grave public disquiet* UNEASE, uneasiness, worry, anxiety, anxiousness, concern, disquietude; perturbation, consternation, upset, malaise, angst; agitation, restlessness, fretfulness; *informal* jitteriness.
— OPPOSITES: calm.
▶ verb *I was disquieted by the news* PERTURB, agitate, upset, disturb, unnerve, unsettle, discompose, disconcert; make uneasy, worry, make anxious; trouble, concern, make fretful, make restless.

disquisition ▶ noun ESSAY, dissertation, treatise, paper, tract, article; discussion, lecture, address, presentation, speech, talk.

disregard ▶ verb *Annie disregarded the remark* IGNORE, take no notice of, pay no attention/heed to; overlook, turn a blind eye to, turn a deaf ear to, shut one's eyes to, gloss over, brush aside, shrug off; *informal* sneeze at.
— OPPOSITES: heed.
▶ noun *blithe disregard for the rules* INDIFFERENCE, non-observance, inattention, heedlessness, neglect.
— OPPOSITES: attention.

disrepair ▶ noun DILAPIDATION, decrepitude, shabbiness, collapse, ruin; abandonment, neglect, disuse.

disreputable ▶ adjective **1** *he fell into disreputable company* OF BAD REPUTATION, infamous, notorious, louche; dishonourable, dishonest, untrustworthy, unwholesome, villainous, corrupt, immoral; unsavoury, slippery, seedy, sleazy; *informal* crooked, shady, shifty, dodgy. **2** *filthy and disreputable* SCRUFFY, shabby, down-at-the-heel(s), seedy, untidy, unkempt, dishevelled.
— OPPOSITES: respectable, smart.

disrepute ▶ noun DISGRACE, shame, dishonour, infamy, notoriety, ignominy, bad reputation; humiliation, discredit, ill repute, low esteem, opprobrium, obloquy.
— OPPOSITES: honour.

disrespect ▶ noun **1** *disrespect for authority* CONTEMPT, lack of respect, scorn, disregard, disdain. **2** *he meant no disrespect to anybody* DISCOURTESY, rudeness, impoliteness, incivility, ill/bad manners; insolence, impudence, impertinence.
— OPPOSITES: esteem.

disrespectful ▶ adjective DISCOURTEOUS, rude, impolite, uncivil, ill-mannered, bad-mannered; insolent, impudent, impertinent, cheeky, flippant, insubordinate.
— OPPOSITES: polite.

disrobe ▶ verb UNDRESS, strip, take off one's clothes, remove one's clothes.

disrupt ▶ verb **1** *the strike disrupted public transit* THROW INTO CONFUSION/DISORDER/DISARRAY, cause confusion/turmoil in, play havoc with; disturb, interfere with, upset, unsettle; obstruct, impede, hold up, delay, interrupt, suspend; *informal* throw a wrench into the works of. **2** *the explosion disrupted the walls of the crater* DISTORT, damage, buckle, warp; shatter; *literary* sunder.

disruptive ▶ adjective TROUBLESOME, unruly, badly behaved, rowdy, disorderly, undisciplined, wild; unmanageable, uncontrollable, uncooperative, out of control/hand, obstreperous, truculent; *formal* refractory.
— OPPOSITES: well-behaved.

dissatisfaction ▶ noun DISCONTENT, discontentment, disaffection, disquiet, unhappiness, malaise, disgruntlement, vexation, annoyance, irritation, anger; disapproval, disapprobation, disfavour, displeasure.

dissatisfied ▶ adjective DISCONTENTED, malcontent, unsatisfied, disappointed, disaffected, unhappy, displeased; disgruntled, aggrieved, vexed, annoyed, irritated, angry, exasperated, fed up; *informal* cheesed off.
— OPPOSITES: contented.

dissect ▶ verb **1** *the body was dissected* ANATOMIZE, cut up/open, dismember; vivisect. **2** *the text of the gospels was dissected* ANALYZE, examine, study, scrutinize, pore over, investigate, go over with a fine-tooth comb.

dissection ▶ noun **1** *the dissection of corpses* CUTTING UP/OPEN, dismemberment; autopsy, post-mortem, necropsy, anatomy, vivisection. **2** *a thorough dissection of their policies* ANALYSIS, examination, study, scrutiny, investigation; evaluation, assessment.

dissemble ▶ verb DISSIMULATE, pretend, feign, act, masquerade, sham, fake, bluff, posture, hide one's feelings, put on a false front.

dissembler ▶ noun LIAR, dissimulator; imposter, humbug, bluffer, fraud, actor, hoaxer, charlatan.

disseminate ▶ verb SPREAD, circulate, distribute, disperse, promulgate, propagate, publicize, communicate, pass on, put about, make known.

dissension ▶ noun DISAGREEMENT, difference of opinion, dispute, dissent, conflict, friction, strife, discord, antagonism, infighting; argument, debate, controversy, disputation, contention.

dissent ▶ verb *two members dissented* DIFFER, disagree, demur, fail to agree, be at variance/odds, take issue; decline/refuse to support, protest, object, dispute, challenge, quibble.
— OPPOSITES: agree, accept.
▶ noun *murmurs of dissent* DISAGREEMENT, difference of opinion, argument, dispute; disapproval, objection, protest, opposition, defiance; conflict, friction, strife, infighting.
— OPPOSITES: agreement.

dissenter ▶ noun DISSIDENT, objector, protester, disputant; rebel, renegade, maverick, independent; apostate, heretic.

dissertation ▶ noun ESSAY, thesis, treatise, paper, study, discourse, disquisition, tract, monograph.

disservice ▶ noun UNKINDNESS, bad/ill turn, disfavour; injury, harm, hurt, damage, wrong, injustice.
— OPPOSITES: favour.

dissidence ▶ noun DISAGREEMENT, dissent, discord, discontent; opposition, resistance, protest, sedition.

dissident ▶ noun *a jailed dissident* DISSENTER, objector, protester; rebel, revolutionary, recusant, subversive, agitator, insurgent, insurrectionist, refusenik.
— OPPOSITES: conformist.
▶ adjective *dissident intellectuals* DISSENTING, disagreeing; opposing, objecting, protesting, rebellious, rebelling, revolutionary, recusant, nonconformist, dissentient.
— OPPOSITES: conforming.

dissimilar ▶ adjective DIFFERENT, differing, unalike, variant, diverse, divergent, heterogeneous, disparate, unrelated, distinct, contrasting; *literary* divers.

dissimilarity ▶ noun DIFFERENCE(S), variance, diversity, heterogeneity, disparateness, disparity, distinctness, contrast, non-uniformity, divergence.

dissimulate ▶ verb PRETEND, deceive, feign, act, dissemble, masquerade, pose, posture, sham, fake, bluff, hide one's feelings, be dishonest, put on a false front, lie.

dissimulation ▶ noun PRETENSE, dissembling, deceit, dishonesty, duplicity, lying, guile, subterfuge, feigning, shamming, faking, bluff, bluffing, posturing, hypocrisy.

dissipate ▶ verb **1** *his anger dissipated* DISAPPEAR, vanish, evaporate, dissolve, melt away, melt into thin air, be dispelled; disperse, scatter; *literary* evanesce. **2** *he dissipated his fortune* SQUANDER, fritter (away), misspend, waste, be prodigal with, spend recklessly/freely, spend like water; expend, use up, consume, run through, go through (like water); *informal* blow, splurge.

dissipated ▶ adjective DISSOLUTE, debauched, decadent, intemperate, profligate, self-indulgent, wild, depraved; licentious, promiscuous; drunken.
— OPPOSITES: ascetic.

dissipation ▶ noun **1** *drunken dissipation* DEBAUCHERY, decadence, dissoluteness, dissolution, intemperance, excess, profligacy, self-indulgence, wildness; depravity, degeneracy; licentiousness, promiscuity; drunkenness. **2** *the dissipation of our mineral wealth* SQUANDERING, frittering (away), waste, misspending; expenditure, draining, depletion.
— OPPOSITES: asceticism.

dissociate ▶ verb *the word 'spiritual' has become dissociated from religion* SEPARATE, detach, disconnect, sever, cut off, divorce; isolate, alienate, disassociate.
— OPPOSITES: relate.
■ **dissociate oneself from 1** *he dissociated himself from the Church* BREAK AWAY FROM, end relations with, sever connections with; withdraw from, quit, leave, disaffiliate from, resign from, pull out of, drop out of, defect from. **2** *he dissociated himself from the statement* DISOWN, reject, disagree with, distance oneself from.

dissociation ▶ noun SEPARATION, disconnection,

detachment, severance, divorce, split; segregation, division; *literary* sundering.
— OPPOSITES: union.

dissolute ▶ adjective DISSIPATED, debauched, decadent, intemperate, profligate, self-indulgent, wild, depraved; licentious, promiscuous; drunken.
— OPPOSITES: ascetic.

dissolution ▶ noun **1** *the dissolution of parliament* CESSATION, conclusion, end, ending, termination, winding up/down, discontinuation, suspension, disbanding; prorogation, recess. **2** *(technical) the dissolution of a polymer in a solvent* DISSOLVING, liquefaction, melting, deliquescence; breaking up, decomposition, disintegration. **3** *the dissolution of the empire* DISINTEGRATION, breaking up; decay, collapse, demise, extinction. **4** *a life of dissolution. See* DISSIPATION sense 1.

dissolve ▶ verb **1** *sugar dissolves in water* GO INTO SOLUTION, break down; liquefy, deliquesce, disintegrate. **2** *his hopes dissolved* DISAPPEAR, vanish, melt away, evaporate, disperse, dissipate, disintegrate; dwindle, fade (away), wither; *literary* evanesce. **3** *the crowd dissolved* DISPERSE, disband, break up, scatter, go in different directions. **4** *the assembly was dissolved* DISBAND, disestablish, bring to an end, end, terminate, discontinue, close down, wind up/down, suspend; prorogue, adjourn. **5** *their marriage was dissolved* ANNUL, nullify, void, invalidate, overturn, revoke.
■ **dissolve into/in** *she dissolved into tears* BURST INTO, break (down) into, be overcome with.

dissonant ▶ adjective **1** *dissonant sounds* INHARMONIOUS, discordant, unmelodious, atonal, off-key, cacophonous. **2** *dissonant colours* INCONGRUOUS, anomalous, clashing; disparate, different, dissimilar.
— OPPOSITES: harmonious.

dissuade ▶ verb DISCOURAGE, deter, prevent, divert, stop; talk out of, persuade against, advise against, argue out of.
— OPPOSITES: encourage.

distance ▶ noun **1** *they measured the distance* INTERVAL, space, span, gap, extent; length, width, breadth, depth; range, reach. **2** *our perception of distance* REMOTENESS; closeness. **3** *there is a distance between them* ALOOFNESS, remoteness, detachment, unfriendliness; reserve, reticence, restraint, formality; *informal* standoffishness.
▶ verb *he distanced himself from her* WITHDRAW, detach, separate, dissociate, disassociate, isolate, put at a distance.
■ **in the distance** FAR AWAY/OFF, afar, just in view; on the horizon; *archaic* yonder.

distant ▶ adjective **1** *distant parts of the world* FARAWAY, far-off, far-flung, remote, out of the way, outlying. **2** *the distant past* LONG AGO, bygone, olden; ancient, prehistoric; *literary* of yore. **3** *half a mile distant* AWAY, off, apart. **4** *a distant memory* VAGUE, faint, dim, indistinct, unclear, indefinite, sketchy, hazy. **5** *a distant family connection* REMOTE, indirect, slight. **6** *father was always distant* ALOOF, reserved, remote, detached, unapproachable; withdrawn, reticent, taciturn, uncommunicative, undemonstrative, unforthcoming, unresponsive, unfriendly; *informal* standoffish. **7** *a distant look in his eyes* DISTRACTED, absent-minded, faraway, detached, distrait, vague; *informal* spacey.
— OPPOSITES: near, close, recent.

distaste ▶ noun DISLIKE, aversion, disinclination,

disapproval, disapprobation, disdain, repugnance, hatred, loathing.
– OPPOSITES: liking.

distasteful ► adjective **1** *distasteful behaviour* UNPLEASANT, disagreeable, displeasing, undesirable; objectionable, offensive, unsavoury, unpalatable, obnoxious; disgusting, repellent, repulsive, revolting, repugnant, abhorrent, loathsome, vile. **2** *their eggs are distasteful to predators* UNPALATABLE, unsavoury, unappetizing, inedible, disgusting.
– OPPOSITES: agreeable, tasty.

distended ► adjective SWOLLEN, bloated, dilated, engorged, enlarged, inflated, expanded, extended, bulging, protuberant.

distill ► verb **1** *the water was distilled* PURIFY, refine, filter, treat, process; evaporate and condense. **2** *oil distilled from marjoram* EXTRACT, press out, squeeze out, express. **3** *whisky is distilled from barley* BREW, ferment. **4** *the solvent is distilled to leave the oil* BOIL DOWN, reduce, concentrate, condense; purify, refine.

distinct ► adjective **1** *two distinct categories* DISCRETE, separate, different, unconnected; precise, specific, distinctive, individual, contrasting. **2** *the tail has distinct black tips* CLEAR, well-defined, unmistakable, easily distinguishable; recognizable, visible, obvious, pronounced, prominent, striking.
– OPPOSITES: overlapping, indefinite.

distinction ► noun **1** *class distinctions* DIFFERENCE, contrast, dissimilarity, variance, variation; division, differentiation, dividing line, gulf, gap. **2** *a painter of distinction* IMPORTANCE, significance, note, consequence; renown, fame, celebrity, prominence, eminence, pre-eminence, repute, reputation; merit, worth, greatness, excellence, quality. **3** *he had served with distinction* HONOUR, credit, excellence, merit.
– OPPOSITES: similarity, mediocrity.

distinctive ► adjective DISTINGUISHING, characteristic, typical, individual, particular, peculiar, unique, exclusive, special.
– OPPOSITES: common.

distinctly ► adverb **1** *there's something distinctly odd about him* DECIDEDLY, markedly, definitely; clearly, noticeably, obviously, plainly, evidently, unmistakably, manifestly, patently. **2** *Laura spoke quite distinctly* CLEARLY, plainly, intelligibly, audibly, unambiguously.

distinguish ► verb **1** *distinguishing reality from fantasy* DIFFERENTIATE, tell apart, discriminate between, tell the difference between. **2** *he could distinguish shapes in the dark* DISCERN, see, perceive, make out; detect, recognize, identify; *literary* descry, espy. **3** *this is what distinguishes history from other disciplines* SEPARATE, set apart, make distinctive, make different; single out, mark off, characterize.
■ **distinguish oneself** ATTAIN DISTINCTION, be successful, bring fame/honour to oneself, become famous.

distinguishable ► adjective DISCERNIBLE, recognizable, identifiable, detectable.

distinguished ► adjective EMINENT, famous, renowned, prominent, well-known; esteemed, respected, illustrious, acclaimed, celebrated, great; notable, important, influential.
– OPPOSITES: unknown, obscure.

distinguishing ► adjective DISTINCTIVE, differentiating, characteristic, typical, peculiar, singular, unique.

distorted ► adjective **1** *a distorted face* TWISTED, warped, contorted, buckled, deformed, malformed, misshapen, disfigured, crooked, awry, out of shape. **2** *a distorted version* MISREPRESENTED, perverted, twisted, falsified, misreported, misstated, garbled, inaccurate; biased, prejudiced, slanted, coloured, loaded, weighted, altered, changed.

distract ► verb DIVERT, sidetrack, draw away, disturb, put off.

distracted ► adjective **1** *she seemed distracted today* PREOCCUPIED, inattentive, vague, abstracted, distrait; absent-minded, faraway, in a world of one's own; bemused, confused, bewildered; troubled, harassed, worried, anxious; *informal* miles away, not with it. **2** *she was distracted with worry* CRAZED, mad, insane, wild, out of one's head, crazy.
– OPPOSITES: attentive.

distracting ► adjective DISTURBING, unsettling, intrusive, disconcerting, bothersome, off-putting.

distraction ► noun **1** *a distraction from the real issues* DIVERSION, interruption, disturbance, interference, hindrance. **2** *frivolous distractions* AMUSEMENT, entertainment, diversion, recreation, leisure pursuit, divertissement. **3** *he was driven to distraction* FRENZY, hysteria, mental distress, madness, insanity, mania; agitation, perturbation.

distrait ► adjective DISTRACTED, preoccupied, absorbed, abstracted, distant, faraway; absent-minded, vague, inattentive, in a brown study, woolgathering, with one's head in the clouds, in a world of one's own; *informal* miles away, not with it, spaced out.
– OPPOSITES: alert.

distraught ► adjective WORRIED, upset, distressed, fraught; overcome, overwrought, beside oneself, out of one's mind, desperate, hysterical, worked up, at one's wits' end; *informal* in a state, unglued.

distress ► noun **1** *she concealed her distress* ANGUISH, suffering, pain, agony, torment, heartache, heartbreak; misery, wretchedness, sorrow, grief, woe, sadness, unhappiness, desolation, despair. **2** *a ship in distress* DANGER, peril, difficulty, trouble, jeopardy, risk. **3** *the poor in distress* HARDSHIP, adversity, poverty, deprivation, privation, destitution, indigence, impoverishment, penury, need, dire straits.
– OPPOSITES: happiness, safety, prosperity.
► verb *he was distressed by the trial* CAUSE ANGUISH/SUFFERING TO, pain, upset, make miserable; trouble, worry, bother, perturb, disturb, disquiet, agitate, harrow, torment; *informal* cut up.
– OPPOSITES: calm, please.

distressing ► adjective UPSETTING, worrying, disturbing, disquieting, painful, traumatic, agonizing, harrowing; sad, saddening, heartbreaking, heart-rending.
– OPPOSITES: comforting.

distribute ► verb **1** *the proceeds were distributed among his creditors* GIVE OUT, deal out, dole out, dish out, hand out/around; allocate, allot, apportion, share out, divide out/up, parcel out. **2** *the newsletter is distributed free* CIRCULATE, issue, hand out, deliver. **3** *a hundred and thirty different species are distributed worldwide* DISPERSE, scatter, spread.
– OPPOSITES: collect.

distribution ► noun **1** *the distribution of charity* GIVING OUT, dealing out, doling out, handing out/around, issue, issuing, dispensation; allocation, allotment, apportioning, sharing out, dividing up/

out, parcelling out. **2** *the geographical distribution of plants* DISPERSAL, dissemination, spread; placement, position, location, disposition. **3** *centres of food distribution* SUPPLY, supplying, delivery, transport, transportation. **4** *the statistical distribution of the problem* FREQUENCY, prevalence, incidence, commonness.

district ▶ noun NEIGHBOURHOOD, area, region, locality, locale, community, quarter, sector, zone, territory; ward; *informal* neck of the woods.

distrust ▶ noun *the general distrust of authority* MISTRUST, suspicion, wariness, chariness, leeriness, lack of trust, lack of confidence; skepticism, doubt, doubtfulness, cynicism; misgivings, qualms, disbelief; *formal* dubiety.
▶ verb *Louise distrusted him* MISTRUST, be suspicious of, be wary/chary of, be leery of, regard with suspicion, suspect; be skeptical of, have doubts about, doubt, be unsure of/about, have misgivings about, wonder about, disbelieve (in).

disturb ▶ verb *let's go somewhere where we won't be disturbed* INTERRUPT, intrude on, butt in on, barge in on; distract, disrupt, bother, trouble, pester, harass; *informal* hassle. **2** *don't disturb his papers* DISARRANGE, muddle, rearrange, disorganize, disorder, mix up, interfere with, throw into disorder/confusion, turn upside down. **3** *waters disturbed by winds* AGITATE, churn up, stir up; *literary* roil. **4** *he wasn't disturbed by the allegations* PERTURB, trouble, concern, worry, upset; agitate, fluster, discomfit, disconcert, dismay, distress, discompose, unsettle, ruffle.

disturbance ▶ noun **1** *we are concerned about the disturbance to local residents* DISRUPTION, distraction, interference; bother, trouble, inconvenience, upset, annoyance, irritation, intrusion, harassment, hassle. **2** *disturbances among the peasantry* RIOT, fracas, upheaval, brawl, street fight, melee, free-for-all, ruckus, rumpus, rumble, ruction. **3** *emotional disturbance* TROUBLE, perturbation, distress, worry, upset, agitation, discomposure, discomfiture; neurosis, illness, sickness, disorder, complaint.

disturbed ▶ adjective **1** *disturbed sleep* DISRUPTED, interrupted, fitful, intermittent, broken. **2** *the children seemed disturbed* TROUBLED, distressed, upset, distraught; unbalanced, unstable, disordered, dysfunctional, maladjusted, neurotic, unhinged; *informal* screwed up, mixed up.

disturbing ▶ adjective WORRYING, perturbing, troubling, upsetting; distressing, discomfiting, disconcerting, disquieting, unsettling, dismaying, alarming, frightening.

disunion ▶ noun BREAKING UP, separation, dissolution, partition.
— OPPOSITES: federation.

disunite ▶ verb BREAK UP, separate, divide, split up, partition, dismantle; *literary* sunder.
— OPPOSITES: unify.

disunity ▶ noun DISAGREEMENT, dissent, dissension, argument, arguing, quarrelling, feuding; conflict, strife, friction, discord.

disuse ▶ noun NON-USE, non-employment, lack of use; neglect, abandonment, desertion, obsolescence; *formal* desuetude.

disused ▶ adjective UNUSED, no longer in use, unemployed, idle; abandoned, deserted, vacated, unoccupied, uninhabited.

ditch ▶ noun *she rescued a cat from the ditch* TRENCH, trough, channel, dike, drain, gutter, gully, watercourse, conduit; *Archaeology* fosse.
▶ verb **1** *they started ditching the coastal areas* DIG A DITCH IN, trench, excavate, drain. **2** *(informal) she ditched her old curtains* THROW OUT, throw away, discard, get rid of, dispose of, do away with, deep-six, shed; abandon, drop, shelve, scrap, jettison, throw on the scrap heap; *informal* dump, junk, get shut of, chuck (away/out), pull the plug on, trash. **3** *(informal) she ditched her husband. See* ABANDON *verb* sense 3.

dither ▶ verb HESITATE, falter, waver, vacillate, change one's mind, be of two minds, be indecisive, be undecided; *informal* shilly-shally, dilly-dally.

ditzy, ditsy ▶ adjective SILLY, foolish, giddy, dizzy, spinny ✦, light-headed, scatty, scatterbrained, feather-brained, hare-brained, empty-headed, stunned ✦, vacuous, stupid, brainless; skittish, flighty, fickle, capricious, whimsical, inconstant; *informal* dippy, dopey.

diurnal ▶ adjective DAILY, everyday, quotidian, occurring every/each day.

divan ▶ noun SETTEE, sofa, couch, chesterfield; sofa bed, daybed, studio couch.

dive ▶ verb **1** *they dived into the clear water | the plane was diving towards the ground* PLUNGE, nosedive, jump headfirst; bellyflop; plummet, fall, drop, pitch, dive-bomb. **2** *the islanders dive for oysters* SWIM UNDER WATER; snorkel, scuba dive. **3** *they dove for cover* LEAP, jump, lunge, launch oneself, throw oneself, go headlong, duck.
▶ noun **1** *a dive into the pool* PLUNGE, swan dive, nosedive, jump, bellyflop; plummet, fall, drop, swoop, pitch. **2** *a sideways dive* LUNGE, spring, jump, leap. **3** *(informal) John got into a fight in some dive* SLEAZY BAR/NIGHTCLUB, seedy bar/nightclub, drinking den; *informal* drinking joint, hole.

diverge ▶ verb **1** *the two roads diverged* SEPARATE, part, fork, divide, split, bifurcate, go in different directions. **2** *areas where our views diverge* DIFFER, be different, be dissimilar; disagree, be at variance/odds, conflict, clash. **3** *he diverged from his script* DEVIATE, digress, depart, veer, stray; stray from the point, get off the subject.
— OPPOSITES: converge, agree.

divergence ▶ noun **1** *the divergence of the human and ape lineages* SEPARATION, dividing, parting, forking, bifurcation. **2** *a marked political divergence* DIFFERENCE, dissimilarity, variance, disparity; disagreement, incompatibility, mismatch. **3** *divergence from standard behaviour* DEVIATION, digression, departure, shift, straying; variation, change, alteration.

divergent ▶ adjective DIFFERING, varying, different, dissimilar, unlike, disparate, contrasting, contrastive; conflicting, incompatible, contradictory, at odds, at variance.
— OPPOSITES: similar.

divers ▶ adjective *(literary)* SEVERAL, many, numerous, multiple, manifold, multifarious, multitudinous; sundry, miscellaneous, assorted, various; *literary* myriad.

diverse ▶ adjective VARIOUS, sundry, manifold, multiple; varied, varying, miscellaneous, assorted, mixed, diversified, divergent, heterogeneous, a mixed bag of; different, differing, distinct, unlike, dissimilar; *literary* divers, myriad.

diversify ▶ verb **1** *farmers looking for ways to diversify* BRANCH OUT, expand, extend operations. **2** *a plan* aimed at diversifying the economy VARY, bring variety to; modify, alter, change, transform; expand, enlarge.

diversion ▶ noun **1** the diversion of 19 rivers RE-ROUTING, redirection, deflection, deviation, divergence. **2** traffic diversions DETOUR, bypass, deviation, alternative route. **3** the noise created a diversion DISTRACTION, disturbance, smokescreen, feint, deke. **4** a city full of diversions ENTERTAINMENT, amusement, pastime, delight, divertissement; fun, recreation, rest and relaxation, pleasure; informal R and R; dated sport.

diversity ▶ noun VARIETY, miscellany, assortment, mixture, mix, mélange, range, array, multiplicity; variation, variance, diversification, heterogeneity, difference, contrast.
— OPPOSITES: uniformity.

divert ▶ verb **1** a plan to divert the Fraser River RE-ROUTE, redirect, change the course of, deflect, channel. **2** he diverted her from her studies DISTRACT, sidetrack, disturb, draw away, be a distraction, put off. **3** the story diverted them AMUSE, entertain, distract, delight, enchant, interest, fascinate, absorb, engross, rivet, grip, hold the attention of.

diverting ▶ adjective ENTERTAINING, amusing, enjoyable, pleasing, agreeable, delightful, appealing; interesting, fascinating, intriguing, absorbing, riveting, compelling; humorous, funny, witty, comical.
— OPPOSITES: boring.

divest ▶ verb DEPRIVE, strip, dispossess, rob, cheat/ trick out of.

divide ▶ verb **1** he divided his estate into four SPLIT (UP), cut up, carve up; dissect, bisect, halve, quarter; literary sunder. **2** a curtain divided her cabin from the galley SEPARATE, segregate, partition, screen off, section off, split off. **3** the stairs divide at the mezzanine DIVERGE, separate, part, branch (off), fork, split (in two), bifurcate. **4** Jack divided up the cash SHARE OUT, allocate, allot, apportion, portion out, ration out, parcel out, deal out, dole out, dish out, distribute, dispense; informal divvy up. **5** he aimed to divide his opponents DISUNITE, drive apart, break up, split up, set at variance/odds; separate, isolate, estrange, alienate; literary tear asunder. **6** living things are divided into three categories CLASSIFY, sort (out), categorize, order, group, grade, rank.
— RELATED TERMS: schizo-.
— OPPOSITES: unify, join, converge.
▶ noun the sectarian divide BREACH, gulf, gap, split; borderline, boundary, dividing line.

dividend ▶ noun **1** an annual dividend SHARE, portion, premium, return, gain, profit, commission; informal cut, rake-off. **2** the research will produce dividends in the future BENEFIT, advantage, gain; bonus, extra, plus.

divination ▶ noun FORTUNE TELLING, divining, prophecy, prediction, soothsaying, augury; clairvoyance, second sight.
— RELATED TERMS: mantic, -mancy.

divine ▶ adjective **1** a divine being GODLY, angelic, seraphic, saintly, beatific; heavenly, celestial, supernal, holy. **2** divine worship RELIGIOUS, holy, sacred, sanctified, consecrated, blessed, devotional. **3** (informal) this food is divine. See EXCELLENT.
— OPPOSITES: mortal.
▶ noun (dated) puritan divines THEOLOGIAN, clergyman, clergywoman, member of the clergy, churchman, churchwoman, cleric, minister, man/woman of the cloth, preacher, priest; informal reverend.
▶ verb **1** Fergus divined how afraid she was GUESS,

surmise, conjecture, deduce, infer; discern, intuit, perceive, recognize, see, realize, appreciate, understand, grasp, comprehend; informal figure (out), savvy, twig, suss (out). **2** they divined that this was an auspicious day FORETELL, predict, prophesy, forecast, foresee, prognosticate.

diviner ▶ noun FORTUNE TELLER, clairvoyant, psychic, seer, soothsayer, prognosticator, prophesier, oracle, sibyl, crystal-gazer.

divinity ▶ noun **1** they denied Christ's divinity DIVINE NATURE, godliness, deity, godhead, holiness. **2** the study of divinity THEOLOGY, religious studies, religion; scripture. **3** a female divinity DEITY, god, goddess, divine/supreme being.

division ▶ noun **1** the division of the island | cell division DIVIDING (UP), breaking up, breakup, carving up, splitting, dissection, bisection; partitioning, separation, segregation. **2** the division of his estates SHARING OUT, dividing up, parcelling out, dishing out, allocation, allotment, apportionment; splitting up, carving up; informal divvying up. **3** the division between nomadic and urban cultures DIVIDING LINE, divide, boundary, borderline, border, demarcation line. **4** each class is divided into nine divisions SECTION, subsection, subdivision, category, class, group, grouping, set, subset, family. **5** an independent division of the company DEPARTMENT, branch, arm, wing, sector, section, subsection, subdivision, subsidiary. **6** the causes of social division DISUNITY, disunion, conflict, discord, disagreement, dissension, disaffection, estrangement, alienation, isolation.

divisive ▶ adjective ALIENATING, estranging, isolating, schismatic.
— OPPOSITES: unifying.

divorce ▶ noun **1** she wants a divorce DISSOLUTION, annulment, (official) separation. **2** a growing divorce between the church and people SEPARATION, division, split, disunity, estrangement, alienation; schism, gulf, chasm.
— OPPOSITES: marriage, unity.
▶ verb **1** her parents have divorced DISSOLVE ONE'S MARRIAGE, annul one's marriage, end one's marriage, get a divorce. **2** religion cannot be divorced from morality SEPARATE, disconnect, divide, dissociate, disassociate, detach, isolate, alienate, set apart, cut off.

divulge ▶ verb DISCLOSE, reveal, tell, communicate, pass on, publish, broadcast, proclaim; expose, uncover, make public, give away, let slip; informal spill the beans about, let on about, let the cat out of the bag about.
— OPPOSITES: conceal.

divvy ▶ verb See DIVIDE verb sense 4.

dizzy ▶ adjective **1** she felt dizzy GIDDY, light-headed, faint, unsteady, shaky, muzzy, wobbly; informal woozy. **2** dizzy heights CAUSING DIZZINESS, causing giddiness, vertiginous. **3** (informal) a dizzy blond. See DITZY.

do ▶ verb **1** she does most of the manual work CARRY OUT, undertake, discharge, execute, perform, accomplish, achieve; bring about/off, engineer; informal pull off; formal effectuate. **2** they can do as they please ACT, behave, conduct oneself, acquit oneself; formal comport oneself. **3** regular coffee will do SUFFICE, be adequate, be satisfactory, fill/fit the bill, serve one's purpose, meet one's needs. **4** the boys will do the dinner PREPARE, make, get ready, see to, arrange, organize, be responsible for, be in charge of; informal fix. **5** the company are doing a new range | a portrait I am doing MAKE, create, produce, turn out, design, manufacture; paint, draw, sketch; informal knock off.

6 *each room was done in a different colour* DECORATE, furnish, ornament, deck out, trick out; *informal* do up. **7** *her maid did her hair* STYLE, arrange, adjust; brush, comb, wash, dry, cut; *informal* fix. **8** *I am doing a show to raise money* PUT ON, present, produce; perform in, act in, take part in, participate in. **9** *you've done me a favour* GRANT, pay, render, give. **10** *show me how to do these equations* WORK OUT, figure out, calculate; solve, resolve. **11** *she's doing archaeology* STUDY, learn, take a course in. **12** *what does he do?* HAVE AS A JOB, have as a profession, be employed at, earn a living at. **13** *he is doing well at college* GET ON/ALONG, progress, fare, manage, cope; succeed, prosper. **14** *he was doing 25 km/h over the speed limit* DRIVE AT, travel at, move at. **15** *the cyclists do 30 miles per day* TRAVEL (OVER), journey, cover, traverse, achieve, notch up, log; *informal* chalk up. **16** *(informal) we're doing Scotland this summer* VISIT, tour, sightsee in.

▶ **noun** *(informal) he invited us to a grand do* PARTY, reception, gathering, celebration, function, social event/occasion, social, soiree; *informal* bash, shindig, *(Atlantic)* time ✚, bunfight.

■ **do away with 1** *they want to do away with the old customs* ABOLISH, get rid of, discard, remove, eliminate, discontinue, stop, end, terminate, put an end/stop to, dispense with, drop, abandon, give up; *informal* scrap, ditch, dump, deep-six. **2** *(informal) she tried to do away with her husband. See* KILL *verb* sense 1.

■ **do someone/something down** *(informal)* BELITTLE, disparage, denigrate, run down, deprecate, cast aspersions on, discredit, vilify, defame, criticize, malign, slur; *informal* have a go at, hit out at, knock, slam, pan, badmouth, dis.

■ **do someone/something in** *(informal)* **1** *the poor devil's been done in. See* KILL *verb* sense 1. **2** *the long walk home did me in* WEAR OUT, tire out, exhaust, fatigue, weary, overtire, drain; *informal* shatter, take it out of. **3** *I did my back in* INJURE, hurt, damage.

■ **do someone out of something** *(informal)* SWINDLE OUT OF, cheat out of, trick out of, deprive of; *informal* con out of, diddle out of.

■ **do something up 1** *she did her bootlace up* FASTEN, tie (up), lace, knot; make fast, secure. **2** *(informal) he's had his house done up* RENOVATE, refurbish, refit, redecorate, decorate, revamp, make over, modernize, improve, spruce up, smarten up; *informal* give something a facelift, rehab.

■ **do without** FORGO, dispense with, abstain from, refrain from, eschew, give up, cut out, renounce, manage without; *formal* forswear.

docile ▶ **adjective** COMPLIANT, obedient, pliant, dutiful, submissive, deferential, unassertive, co-operative, amenable, accommodating, biddable, malleable.
— OPPOSITES: disobedient, wilful.

dock¹ ▶ **noun** *his boat was moored at the dock* HARBOUR, marina, port, anchorage; wharf, quay, pier, jetty, landing stage.
▶ **verb** *the ship docked* MOOR, berth, put in, tie up, anchor.

dock² ▶ **verb** **1** *they docked the money from his salary* DEDUCT, subtract, remove, debit, take off/away, garnishee; *informal* knock off. **2** *workers had their pay docked* REDUCE, cut, decrease. **3** *the dog's tail was docked* CUT OFF, cut short, shorten, crop, lop; remove, amputate, detach, sever, chop off, take off.

docket ▶ **noun** **1** *he opened a new docket for the account* FILE, dossier, folder. **2** *I looked my name up on the docket* LIST, index; schedule, agenda, program, timetable.

▶ **verb** *docket the package* DOCUMENT, record, register; label, tag, tab, mark.

doctor ▶ **noun** *Claudio went to see a doctor* PHYSICIAN, medical practitioner, clinician; general practitioner, GP, consultant, registrar, medical officer, MD, medic, intern; *informal* doc, medico, quack, sawbones; *historical* saddlebag ✚. *See table.*
▶ **verb** **1** *(informal) he doctored their wounds* TREAT, medicate, cure, heal; tend, attend to, minister to, care for, nurse. **2** *he doctored Stephen's drink* ADULTERATE, contaminate, tamper with, lace; *informal* spike, dope. **3** *the reports have been doctored* FALSIFY, tamper with, interfere with, alter, change; forge, fake; *informal* cook, fiddle with.

Doctors

allergist	neonatologist
anaesthetist	neurologist
cardiologist	neurosurgeon
chiropractor	obstetrician
clinician	oncologist
consulting physician	ophthalmologist
dentist	orthodontist
dermatologist	orthopaedist
endocrinologist	pathologist
eye doctor	pediatrician
family doctor	podiatrist
gastroenterologist	proctologist
general practitioner	psychiatrist
geriatrician	radiologist
GP	resident
gynecologist	specialist
hematologist	surgeon
internist	urologist

doctrinaire ▶ **adjective** DOGMATIC, rigid, inflexible, uncompromising; authoritarian, intolerant, fanatical, zealous, extreme.

doctrine ▶ **noun** CREED, credo, dogma, belief, teaching, ideology; tenet, maxim, canon, principle, precept.

document ▶ **noun** *their lawyer drew up a document* (OFFICIAL/LEGAL) PAPER, certificate, deed, contract, legal agreement; *Law* instrument, indenture.
▶ **verb** *many aspects of school life have been documented* RECORD, register, report, log, chronicle, archive, put on record, write down; detail, note, describe.

documentary ▶ **adjective** **1** *documentary evidence* RECORDED, documented, registered, written, chronicled, archived, on record/paper, in writing. **2** *a documentary film* FACTUAL, non-fictional.
▶ **noun** *a documentary about rural Saskatchewan* FACTUAL PROGRAM/FILM; program, film, broadcast.

dodder ▶ **verb** TOTTER, teeter, toddle, hobble, shuffle, shamble, falter.

doddery ▶ **adjective** TOTTERING, tottery, staggering, shuffling, shambling, faltering, shaky, unsteady, wobbly; feeble, frail, weak.

dodge ▶ **verb** **1** *she dodged into a telephone booth* DART, bolt, dive, lunge, leap, spring. **2** *he could easily dodge the two cops* ELUDE, evade, avoid, escape, run away from, lose, shake (off), jink; *informal* give someone the slip, dipsy-doodle around ✚, ditch. **3** *the minister tried to dodge the debate* AVOID, evade, get out of, back out of, sidestep, do an end run; *informal* duck, wriggle out of.
▶ **noun** **1** *a dodge to the right* DART, bolt, dive, lunge, leap, spring. **2** *a clever dodge | a tax dodge* RUSE, ploy, scheme, tactic, stratagem, subterfuge, trick, hoax,

wile, cheat, deception, blind; swindle, fraud; *informal* scam, con (trick), bunco, grift.

doer ▶ noun **1** *the doer of unspeakable deeds* PERFORMER, perpetrator, executor, accomplisher, agent. **2** *Daniel is a thinker more than a doer* WORKER, organizer, man/woman of action; *informal* mover and shaker, busy bee.

doff ▶ verb (*literary*) TAKE OFF, remove, strip off, pull off; raise, lift, tip; *dated* divest oneself of.
— OPPOSITES: don.

dog ▶ noun **1** *she went for a walk with her dog* HOUND, canine, mongrel, cur, (*Nfld*) crackie ✦; pup, puppy; *informal* doggy, pooch. **2** (*informal*) *you black-hearted dog!* See JERK noun sense 3. **3** (*informal*) *you're a lucky dog!* See FELLOW sense 1.
▶ verb **1** *they dogged him the length of the country* PURSUE, follow, track, trail, shadow, hound; *informal* tail. **2** *the scheme was dogged by bad weather* PLAGUE, beset, bedevil, beleaguer, blight, trouble.

Breeds of Dog

affenpinscher	keeshond
Airedale	kelpie
Akita	Kerry blue terrier
Australian cattle dog	King Charles spaniel
Australian terrier	Labrador retriever
basenji	Lakeland terrier
basset hound	Lhasa Apso
beagle	malamute
bearded collie	Maltese terrier
Bedlington terrier	mastiff
Bernese mountain dog	Newfoundland
bichon frise	Nova Scotia duck tolling
bloodhound	retriever
border collie	Old English sheepdog
border terrier	papillon
borzoi	Pekingese
Boston terrier	pointer
Bouvier des Flandres	Pomeranian
boxer	poodle
Brittany spaniel	pug
bulldog	Rottweiler
bull terrier	rough collie
chihuahua	St. Bernard
chow chow	Saluki
cockapoo	Samoyed
cocker spaniel	schipperke
collie	schnauzer
coonhound	Scottish terrier
corgi	Sealyham terrier
dachshund	Shar-Pei
Dalmatian	sheepdog
Doberman pinscher	Shetland sheepdog
English setter	Shih Tzu
fox terrier	Siberian husky
Gordon setter	spitz
Great Dane	springer spaniel
greyhound	Staffordshire bull
griffon	terrier
husky	staghound
Irish setter	Sussex spaniel
Irish terrier	Weimaraner
Irish wolfhound	whippet
Jack Russell terrier	wolfhound
	See also WOLF.

dogged ▶ adjective TENACIOUS, determined, resolute, resolved, purposeful, persistent, persevering, single-minded, tireless; strong-willed, steadfast, staunch; *formal* pertinacious.
— OPPOSITES: half-hearted.

dogma ▶ noun TEACHING, belief, tenet, principle, precept, maxim, article of faith, canon; creed, credo, set of beliefs, doctrine, ideology.

dogmatic ▶ adjective OPINIONATED, peremptory, assertive, insistent, emphatic, adamant, doctrinaire, authoritarian, imperious, dictatorial, uncompromising, unyielding, inflexible, rigid.

doing ▶ noun **1** *the doing of the act constitutes the offence* PERFORMANCE, performing, carrying out, execution, implementation, implementing, achievement, accomplishment, realization, completion; *formal* effectuation. **2** *an account of his doings in Yellowknife* EXPLOIT, activity, act, action, deed, feat, achievement, accomplishment; *informal* caper. **3** *that would take some doing* EFFORT, exertion, (hard) work, application, labour, toil, struggle.

do-it-yourself ▶ adjective SELF-BUILD, DIY.

doldrums ▶ plural noun *winter doldrums* DEPRESSION, melancholy, gloom, gloominess, downheartedness, dejection, despondency, low spirits, despair; inertia, apathy, listlessness, blahs, a blue funk, blues.
■ **in the doldrums** INACTIVE, quiet, slow, slack, sluggish, stagnant.

dole ▶ noun **1** (*dated*) *the customary dole was a tumblerful of rice* HANDOUT, charity; gift, donation; *historical* alms. **2** (*informal*) *he was on the dole* UNEMPLOYMENT BENEFIT, social security, welfare, pogey ✦, EI ✦, UI, (*Atlantic*) stamps ✦.
■ **dole something out** DEAL OUT, share out, divide up, allocate, allot, distribute, dispense, hand out, give out, dish out/up, divvy up.

doleful ▶ adjective MOURNFUL, woeful, sorrowful, sad, unhappy, depressed, gloomy, morose, melancholy, miserable, forlorn, wretched, woebegone, despondent, dejected, disconsolate, downcast, crestfallen, downhearted; *informal* blue, down in the mouth/dumps; *literary* dolorous, heartsick.
— OPPOSITES: cheerful.

doll ▶ noun **1** *the child was hugging a doll* FIGURE, figurine, action figure, model; toy, plaything; *informal* dolly. **2** (*informal*) *she was quite a doll.* See BEAUTY sense 2.
■ **doll oneself up** (*informal*) DRESS UP; *informal* get/do oneself up, dress up to the nines, put on one's glad rags, tart oneself up.

dollop (*informal*) ▶ noun BLOB, gobbet, lump, ball; *informal* glob.

dolorous ▶ adjective (*literary*). See DOLEFUL.

dolour ▶ noun (*literary*). See MISERY sense 1.

dolt ▶ noun. See IDIOT.

doltish ▶ adjective. See STUPID sense 1.

domain ▶ noun **1** *they extended their domain* REALM, kingdom, empire, dominion, province, territory, land. **2** *the domain of art* FIELD, area, sphere, discipline, province, world.

dome ▶ noun CUPOLA, vault, arched roof.

domestic ▶ adjective **1** *domestic commitments* FAMILY, home, household. **2** *he was not at all domestic* HOUSEWIFELY, domesticated. **3** *small domestic animals* DOMESTICATED, tame, pet, household. **4** *the domestic car industry* NATIONAL, state, home, internal. **5** *domestic plants* NATIVE, indigenous.
▶ noun *they worked as domestics* SERVANT, domestic worker/help, maid, housemaid, cleaner, cleaning lady, housekeeper.

domesticated ▶ adjective **1** *domesticated animals*

TAME, tamed, pet, domestic, trained. **2** *domesticated crops* CULTIVATED, naturalized. **3** *I'm quite domesticated really* home-loving, homey, housewifely.
— OPPOSITES: wild.

domicile *(formal)* ▶ noun *changes of domicile* RESIDENCE, home, house, address, residency, lodging, accommodation; *informal* digs; *formal* dwelling (place), abode, habitation.
▶ verb *he is now domiciled in Australia* SETTLE, live, make one's home, take up residence; move to, emigrate to.

dominance ▶ noun SUPREMACY, superiority, ascendancy, pre-eminence, predominance, domination, dominion, mastery, power, authority, rule, command, control, sway; *literary* puissance.

dominant ▶ adjective **1** *the dominant classes* PRESIDING, ruling, governing, controlling, commanding, ascendant, supreme, authoritative. **2** *he has a dominant personality* ASSERTIVE, authoritative, forceful, domineering, commanding, controlling, pushy. **3** *the dominant issues in psychology* MAIN, principal, prime, premier, chief, foremost, primary, predominant, paramount, prominent; central, key, crucial, core; *informal* number-one.
— OPPOSITES: subservient.

dominate ▶ verb **1** *the Russians dominated Iran in the nineteenth century* CONTROL, influence, exercise control over, command, be in command of, be in charge of, rule, govern, direct, have ascendancy over, have mastery over; *informal* head up, be in the driver's seat, be at the helm, rule the roost, wear the pants, have someone in one's hip pocket; *literary* sway. **2** *it dominates the sports scene* PREDOMINATE, prevail, reign, be prevalent, be paramount, be pre-eminent; *informal* kick butt. **3** *the village is dominated by the viaduct* OVERLOOK, command, tower above/over, loom over.

domination ▶ noun RULE, government, sovereignty, control, command, authority, power, dominion, dominance, mastery, supremacy, superiority, ascendancy, sway.

domineer ▶ verb BROWBEAT, bully, intimidate, push around/about, order about/around, lord it over; dictate to, be overbearing, have under one's thumb, rule with a rod of iron; *informal* boss about/around, walk all over.

domineering ▶ adjective OVERBEARING, authoritarian, imperious, high-handed, autocratic; masterful, dictatorial, despotic, oppressive, iron-fisted, strict, harsh, bossy.

dominion ▶ noun **1** *France had dominion over Laos* SUPREMACY, ascendancy, dominance, domination, superiority, predominance, pre-eminence, hegemony, authority, mastery, control, command, power, sway, rule, government, jurisdiction, sovereignty, suzerainty. **2** *a British dominion* DEPENDENCY, colony, protectorate, territory, province, possession; *historical* tributary.

don ▶ verb *he donned an overcoat* PUT ON, get dressed in, dress (oneself) in, get into, slip into/on.

donate ▶ verb GIVE, give/make a donation of, contribute, make a contribution of, gift, pledge, grant, bestow; *informal* chip in, pitch in, kick in.

donation ▶ noun GIFT, contribution, present, pledge, handout, grant, offering; *formal* benefaction; *historical* alms.

done ▶ adjective **1** *the job is done* FINISHED, ended, concluded, complete, completed, accomplished, achieved, fulfilled, discharged, executed; *informal* wrapped up, sewn up, polished off. **2** *is the meat done?*

COOKED (THROUGH), ready. **3** *those days are done* OVER (AND DONE WITH), at an end, finished, ended, concluded, terminated, no more, dead, gone, in the past. **4** *(informal) that's just not done* PROPER, seemly, decent, respectable, right, correct, in order, fitting, appropriate, acceptable, the done thing.
— OPPOSITES: incomplete, underdone, ongoing.
■ **be/have done with** BE/HAVE FINISHED WITH, be through with, want no more to do with.
■ **done for** *(informal)* RUINED, finished, destroyed, undone, doomed, lost; *informal* washed-up, done like dinner ✦, has had the biscuit ✦.

done deal ▶ noun FAIT ACCOMPLI.

Don Juan ▶ noun WOMANIZER, philanderer, Romeo, Casanova, Lothario, flirt, ladies' man, playboy, seducer, rake, roué, libertine; *informal* skirt chaser, lady-killer, wolf.

donkey ▶ noun **1** *the cart was drawn by a donkey* ASS, jackass, jenny; mule, hinny, burro. **2** *(informal) you silly donkey! See* FOOL *noun* sense 1.
— RELATED TERMS: asinine.

donnish ▶ adjective SCHOLARLY, studious, academic, bookish, intellectual, learned, highbrow; *informal* egghead; *dated* lettered.

donor ▶ noun GIVER, contributor, benefactor, benefactress; supporter, backer, patron, sponsor, friend, member; *informal* angel.

donut ▶ noun *See table at* DOUGHNUT.

doohickey ▶ noun THING, so-and so, whatever it's called; *informal* whatsit, whatnot, doodad, thingy, thingummy, thingamajig, thingamabob, what's-its-name, whatchamacallit, whatchacallit.

doom ▶ noun **1** *his impending doom* DESTRUCTION, downfall, ruin, ruination; extinction, annihilation, death. **2** *(archaic) the day of doom* JUDGMENT DAY, the Last Judgment, doomsday, Armageddon.
▶ verb *we were doomed to fail* DESTINE, fate, predestine, preordain, foredoom, mean; condemn, sentence.

doomed ▶ adjective ILL-FATED, ill-starred, cursed, jinxed, foredoomed, damned; *literary* star-crossed.

door ▶ noun DOORWAY, portal, opening, entrance, entry, exit.
■ **out of doors** OUTSIDE, outdoors, in/into the open air, alfresco.

doorman ▶ noun DOORKEEPER, commissionaire, concierge.

dope ▶ noun *(informal)* **1** *he was caught smuggling dope* (ILLEGAL) DRUGS, narcotics; cannabis, heroin, cocaine. **2** *what a dope! See* FOOL *noun* sense 1. **3** *give me the dope on Mr. Dixon. See* INTELLIGENCE *sense* 2.
▶ verb **1** *the horse was doped* DRUG, administer drugs/ narcotics to, tamper with, interfere with; sedate. **2** *they doped his drink* ADD DRUGS TO, tamper with, adulterate, contaminate, lace; *informal* spike, doctor.

dopey ▶ adjective *(informal)* STUPEFIED, confused, muddled, befuddled, disorientated, groggy, muzzy; *informal* woozy, not with it.
— OPPOSITES: alert.

dormant ▶ adjective ASLEEP, sleeping, resting; INACTIVE, passive, inert, latent, quiescent.
— OPPOSITES: awake, active.

dose ▶ noun MEASURE, measurement, portion, dosage, shot; *informal* hit, fix.

dossier ▶ noun FILE, report, case history; account, notes, document(s), documentation, data, information, evidence.

dot ▶ noun *a pattern of tiny dots* SPOT, speck, fleck, speckle; full stop, decimal point, period, pixel.

▶ **verb 1** *spots of rain dotted his shirt* SPOT, fleck, mark, stipple, freckle, sprinkle; *literary* bestrew, besprinkle. **2** *the streets are dotted with restaurants* SCATTER, pepper, sprinkle, strew.
■ **on the dot** *(informal)* PRECISELY, exactly, sharp, prompt, dead on, on the stroke of ——; *informal* bang on, on the button, on the nose.

dotage ▶ **noun** DECLINING YEARS, winter/autumn of one's life; advanced years, old age; *literary* eld.

dot-com ▶ **noun** ONLINE RETAILER, e-business, e-tailer, online business, clicks and mortar, pure play.

dote
■ **dote on** ADORE, love dearly, be devoted to, idolize, treasure, cherish, worship, hold dear; indulge, spoil, pamper.

doting ▶ **adjective** ADORING, loving, besotted, infatuated; affectionate, fond, devoted, caring; uxorious.

dotty ▶ **adjective** *(informal)*. See MAD sense 1.

double ▶ **adjective 1** *a double garage* | *double yellow lines* DUAL, duplex, twin, binary, duplicate, in pairs, coupled, twofold. **2** *a double helping* DOUBLED, twofold. **3** *a double meaning* AMBIGUOUS, equivocal, dual, two-edged, double-edged, ambivalent, cryptic, enigmatic. **4** *a double life* DECEITFUL, double-dealing, two-faced, dual; hypocritical, false, duplicitous, insincere, deceiving, dissembling, dishonest.
— RELATED TERMS: di-, diplo-.
— OPPOSITES: single, unambiguous.
▶ **adverb** *we had to pay double* TWICE (OVER), twice the amount, doubly.
▶ **noun 1** *if it's not her, it's her double* LOOK-ALIKE, twin, clone, duplicate, exact likeness, replica, copy, facsimile, doppelgänger; *informal* spitting image, dead ringer. **2** *she used a double for the stunts* STAND-IN, substitute.
▶ **verb 1** *they doubled his salary* MULTIPLY BY TWO, increase twofold. **2** *the bottom sheet had been doubled up* FOLD (BACK/UP/DOWN/OVER/UNDER), turn back/up/down/over/under, tuck back/up/down/under. **3** *the kitchen doubles as a dining room* FUNCTION, do, (also) serve.
■ **at/on the double** VERY QUICKLY, as fast as one's legs can carry one, at a run, at a gallop, fast, swiftly, rapidly, speedily, at full speed, at full tilt, as fast as possible; *informal* like (greased) lightning, like the wind, like a bat out of hell, lickety-split, PDQ (pretty damn quick).

double-cross ▶ **verb** BETRAY, cheat, defraud, trick, hoodwink, mislead, deceive, swindle, be disloyal to, be unfaithful to, play false; *informal* sell down the river.

double-dealing ▶ **noun** DUPLICITY, treachery, betrayal, double-crossing, unfaithfulness, untrustworthiness, infidelity, bad faith, disloyalty, breach of trust, fraud, underhandedness, cheating, dishonesty, deceit, deceitfulness, deception, falseness; *informal* crookedness.
— OPPOSITES: honesty.

double entendre ▶ **noun** AMBIGUITY, double meaning, innuendo, play on words.

doublespeak ▶ **noun** EQUIVOCATING, evasion, dodging, beating about the bush, pussyfooting (around); jargon, double-talk, gibberish, gobbledegook; *informal* -speak, -ese, -babble.

doubly ▶ **adverb** TWICE AS, in double measure, even more, especially, extra.

doubt ▶ **noun 1** *there was some doubt as to the caller's identity* UNCERTAINTY, unsureness, indecision, hesitation, dubiousness, suspicion, confusion; queries, questions; *formal* dubiety. **2** *a weak leader racked by doubt* INDECISION, hesitation, uncertainty, insecurity, unease, uneasiness, apprehension; hesitancy, vacillation, irresolution. **3** *there is doubt about their motives* SKEPTICISM, distrust, mistrust, doubtfulness, suspicion, cynicism, uneasiness, apprehension, wariness, chariness, leeriness; reservations, misgivings, suspicions; *formal* dubiety.
— OPPOSITES: certainty, conviction.
▶ **verb 1** *they doubted my story* DISBELIEVE, distrust, mistrust, suspect, have doubts about, be suspicious of, have misgivings about, have qualms about, feel uneasy about, feel apprehensive about, query, question, challenge. **2** *I doubt whether he will come* THINK SOMETHING UNLIKELY, have (one's) doubts about, question, query, be dubious. **3** *stop doubting and believe!* BE UNDECIDED, have doubts, be irresolute, be ambivalent, be doubtful, be unsure, be uncertain, be of two minds, hesitate, shilly-shally, waver, vacillate.
— OPPOSITES: trust.
■ **in doubt 1** *the issue was in doubt* DOUBTFUL, uncertain, open to question, unconfirmed, unknown, undecided, unresolved, in the balance, up in the air; *informal* iffy. **2** *if you are in doubt, ask for advice* IRRESOLUTE, hesitant, vacillating, dithering, wavering, ambivalent; doubtful, unsure, uncertain, of two minds, shilly-shallying, undecided, in a quandary/dilemma; *informal* sitting on the fence.
■ **no doubt** DOUBTLESS, undoubtedly, indubitably, doubtlessly, without (a) doubt; unquestionably, undeniably, incontrovertibly, irrefutably; unequivocally, clearly, plainly, obviously, patently.

doubter ▶ **noun** SKEPTIC, doubting Thomas, non-believer, unbeliever, disbeliever, cynic, scoffer, questioner, challenger, dissenter.
— OPPOSITES: believer.

doubtful ▶ **adjective 1** *I was doubtful about going* IRRESOLUTE, hesitant, vacillating, dithering, wavering, in doubt, unsure, uncertain, of two minds, shilly-shallying, undecided, in a quandary/dilemma, blowing hot and cold. **2** *it is doubtful whether he will come* IN DOUBT, uncertain, open to question, unsure, unconfirmed, not definite, unknown, undecided, unresolved, debatable, in the balance, up in the air; *informal* iffy. **3** *the whole trip is looking rather doubtful* UNLIKELY, improbable, dubious, impossible. **4** *they are doubtful of the methods used* DISTRUSTFUL, mistrustful, suspicious, wary, chary, leery, apprehensive; skeptical, unsure, ambivalent, dubious, cynical. **5** *this decision is of doubtful validity* QUESTIONABLE, arguable, debatable, controversial, contentious; *informal* iffy.
— OPPOSITES: confident, certain, probable, trusting.

doubtless ▶ **adverb** UNDOUBTEDLY, indubitably, doubtlessly, no doubt; unquestionably, indisputably, undeniably, incontrovertibly, irrefutably; certainly, surely, of course, indeed.

doughnut ▶ **noun**. See table.

doughty ▶ **adjective** FEARLESS, dauntless, determined, resolute, indomitable, intrepid, plucky, spirited, bold, valiant, brave, stout-hearted, courageous; *informal* gutsy, spunky, feisty, ballsy.

dour ▶ **adjective** STERN, unsmiling, unfriendly, severe, forbidding, gruff, surly, grim, sullen, solemn, austere, stony.
— OPPOSITES: cheerful, friendly.

douse ▶ **verb 1** *a mob doused the thieves with gas* DRENCH, soak, saturate, wet, splash, slosh. **2** *a guard*

Doughnuts & Deep-Fried Sweets

Beaver Tail* ♣(esp. E. Ont.)	glazed
beignet	jambuster ♣(Man. & NW Ont.)
bismarck ♣	jelly doughnut
Burlington bun ♣(NS)	long john
cake doughnut	paczki
churro	Persian ♣(NW Ont.)
crostoli	raised doughnut
cruller	touton ♣(Nfld)
Dutchie	twist
fritter	*Proprietary term.

doused the flames EXTINGUISH, put out, quench, smother, snuff (out).

dovetail ▶ **verb 1** *the ends of the logs were dovetailed* JOINT, join, fit together, splice, mortise, tenon. **2** *this will dovetail well with the company's existing activities* FIT IN, go together, be consistent, match, conform, harmonize, be in tune, correspond; *informal* square, jibe.

dowdy ▶ **adjective** UNFASHIONABLE, frumpy, old-fashioned, outmoded, out-of-date, inelegant, shabby, frowzy.
— OPPOSITES: fashionable.

down[1] ▶ **adverb 1** *they went down in the elevator* TOWARDS A LOWER POSITION, downwards, downstairs. **2** *she fell down* TO THE GROUND/FLOOR, over.
— OPPOSITES: up.
▶ **preposition 1** *the elevator plunged down the shaft* TO A LOWER POSITION IN, to the bottom of. **2** *I walked down the street* ALONG, to the other end of, from one end of —— to the other. **3** *down the years* THROUGHOUT, through, during.
▶ **adjective 1** *I'm feeling a bit down* DEPRESSED, sad, unhappy, melancholy, miserable, wretched, sorrowful, gloomy, dejected, downhearted, despondent, dispirited, low; *informal* blue, down in the dumps/mouth. **2** *the computer is down* NOT WORKING, inoperative, malfunctioning, out of order, broken; not in service, out of action, out of commission; *informal* conked out, bust, (gone) kaput, on the fritz, on the blink.
— OPPOSITES: elated, working.
▶ **verb** (*informal*) **1** *anti-aircraft missiles downed the fighter jet* KNOCK DOWN/OVER, knock to the ground, bring down, topple; *informal* deck, floor, flatten. **2** *he downed his beer* DRINK (UP/DOWN), gulp (down), guzzle, quaff, drain, chugalug, toss off, slug, finish off; *informal* knock back, put away, scarf (down/up), snarf (down/up).
▶ **noun** *the ups and downs of running a business* SETBACKS, upsets, reverses, reversals, mishaps, vicissitudes; *informal* glitches.
■ **be down on** (*informal*) DISAPPROVE OF, be against, feel antagonism to, be hostile to, feel ill will towards; *informal* have it in for, be down with.

down[2] ▶ **noun** *goose down* SOFT FEATHERS, fine hair; fluff, fuzz, floss, lint.

down-and-out ▶ **adjective** DESTITUTE, poverty-stricken, impoverished, penniless, insolvent, impecunious; needy, in straitened circumstances, distressed, badly off; homeless, on the streets, vagrant, sleeping rough; *informal* hard up, (flat) broke, strapped (for cash), without two coins/cents to rub

together, without a red cent, on skid row.
— OPPOSITES: wealthy.
▶ **noun** POOR PERSON, pauper, indigent; beggar, homeless person, panhandler, vagrant, tramp, drifter, derelict, vagabond, hobo; *informal* have-not, bag lady, bum.

down-at-the-heel, down-at-heel ▶ **adjective 1** *the resort looks down-at-the-heels* RUN-DOWN, dilapidated, neglected, uncared-for; seedy, insalubrious, squalid, slummy, wretched; *informal* scruffy, scuzzy, flea-bitten; grotty, shacky. **2** *a down-at-the-heels labourer* SCRUFFY, shabby, ragged, tattered, mangy, sorry; unkempt, bedraggled, dishevelled, ungroomed, seedy, untidy, slovenly; *informal* tatty, scuzzy, grungy; grotty, raggedy.
— OPPOSITES: smart.

downbeat ▶ **adjective** *the mood is decidedly downbeat* PESSIMISTIC, gloomy, negative, defeatist, cynical, bleak, fatalistic, dark, black; despairing, despondent, depressed, dejected, demoralized, hopeless, melancholy, glum.

downcast ▶ **adjective** DESPONDENT, disheartened, discouraged, dispirited, downhearted, crestfallen, down, low, disconsolate, despairing; sad, melancholy, gloomy, glum, morose, doleful, dismal, woebegone, miserable, depressed, dejected; *informal* blue, down in the mouth, down in the dumps.
— OPPOSITES: elated.

downfall ▶ **noun** UNDOING, ruin, ruination; defeat, conquest, deposition, overthrow; nemesis, destruction, annihilation, elimination; end, collapse, fall, crash, failure; debasement, degradation, disgrace; Waterloo.
— OPPOSITES: rise.

downgrade ▶ **verb 1** *plans to downgrade three workers* DEMOTE, lower, reduce/lower in rank; relegate. **2** *I won't downgrade their achievement* DISPARAGE, denigrate, detract from, run down, belittle; *informal* badmouth, dis.
— OPPOSITES: promote, praise.

downhearted ▶ **adjective** DESPONDENT, disheartened, discouraged, dispirited, downcast, crestfallen, down, low, disconsolate, wretched; melancholy, gloomy, glum, morose, doleful, dismal, woebegone, miserable, depressed, dejected, sorrowful, sad; *informal* blue, down in the mouth, down in the dumps.
— OPPOSITES: elated.

download ▶ **verb 1** *I downloaded a new version of my browser* LOAD, copy, transfer, upload. **2** (*Cdn*) *the province has downloaded 5,100 km of highways onto municipalities* SHIFTED RESPONSIBILITY/COSTS TO, relegate, transfer, unload, off-load, consign, dump.

downpour ▶ **noun** RAINSTORM, cloudburst, deluge, shower; thunderstorm, thundershower; torrential/pouring rain.

downright ▶ **adjective 1** *downright lies* COMPLETE, total, absolute, utter, thorough, out-and-out, outright, sheer, arrant, pure, real, veritable, categorical, unmitigated, unadulterated, unalloyed, unequivocal. **2** *her downright attitude. See* FORTHRIGHT.
▶ **adverb** *that's downright dangerous* THOROUGHLY, utterly, positively, profoundly, really, completely, totally, entirely; unquestionably, undeniably, in every respect, through and through; *informal* plain.

downside ▶ **noun** DRAWBACK, disadvantage, snag, stumbling block, catch, pitfall, fly in the ointment; handicap, limitation, trouble, difficulty, problem,

complication, nuisance; hindrance; weak spot/point; *informal* minus.
— OPPOSITES: advantage.

down-to-earth ▶ adjective PRACTICAL, sensible, realistic, matter-of-fact, responsible, reasonable, rational, logical, balanced, sober, pragmatic, level-headed, commonsensical, sane.
— OPPOSITES: idealistic.

downtown ▶ noun CITY CENTRE, (central) business district, urban core; inner city, concrete jungle.
▶ adjective CENTRAL, metropolitan, metro, urban; uptown, midtown.

downtrodden ▶ adjective OPPRESSED, subjugated, persecuted, repressed, tyrannized, crushed, enslaved, exploited, victimized, bullied; disadvantaged, underprivileged, powerless, helpless; abused, maltreated.

downward ▶ adjective DESCENDING, downhill, falling, sinking, dipping; earthbound, earthward.

downy ▶ adjective SOFT, velvety, smooth, fleecy, fluffy, fuzzy, feathery, furry, woolly, silky.

dowry ▶ noun MARRIAGE SETTLEMENT, (marriage) portion; *archaic* dot.

doze ▶ verb CATNAP, nap, drowse, sleep lightly, rest; *informal* snooze, snatch/catch forty winks, get some shut-eye, catch some zees; *literary* slumber.
▶ noun CATNAP, nap, siesta, light sleep, drowse, rest; *informal* snooze, forty winks; *literary* slumber.
■ **doze off** FALL ASLEEP, go to sleep, drop off; *informal* nod off, drift off, sack out, flake out, conk out.

dozy ▶ adjective DROWSY, sleepy, half asleep, somnolent; lethargic, listless, enervated, inactive, languid, weary, tired, fatigued, logy, heavy-eyed; *informal* dopey, yawny.

drab ▶ adjective **1** *a drab interior* COLOURLESS, grey, dull, washed out, muted, lacklustre; dingy, dreary, dismal, cheerless, gloomy, sombre. **2** *a drab existence* UNINTERESTING, dull, boring, tedious, monotonous, dry, dreary; unexciting, unimaginative, uninspiring, insipid, lacklustre, flat, stale, wishy-washy, colourless; lame, tired, sterile, anemic, barren, tame; middle-of-the-road, run-of-the-mill, mediocre, nondescript, characterless, mundane, unremarkable, humdrum, plain-vanilla.
— OPPOSITES: bright, cheerful, interesting.

draconian ▶ adjective HARSH, severe, strict, extreme, drastic, stringent, tough; cruel, oppressive, ruthless, relentless, punitive; authoritarian, despotic, tyrannical, repressive.
— OPPOSITES: lenient.

draft¹ ▶ noun **1** *the draft of his speech* PRELIMINARY VERSION, rough outline, plan, skeleton, abstract; main points, bare bones. **2** *a draft of the building* PLAN, blueprint, design, diagram, drawing, sketch, map, layout, representation. **3** *a bank draft* CHEQUE, order, money order, bill of exchange.

draft² ▶ noun **1** *the draft made Robyn shiver* CURRENT OF AIR, rush of air; waft, wind, breeze, gust, puff, blast; *informal* blow. **2** *a deep draft of beer* GULP, drink, swallow, mouthful, slug; *informal* swig, swill.

drag ▶ verb **1** *she dragged the chair backwards* HAUL, pull, tug, heave, lug, draw; trail, trawl, tow; *informal* yank. **2** *the day dragged* BECOME TEDIOUS, pass slowly, creep along, hang heavy, wear on, go on too long, go on and on.
▶ noun **1** *the drag of the air brakes* PULL, resistance, tug. **2** (*informal*) *work can be a drag* BORE, nuisance, bother,

trouble, pest, annoyance, trial, chore, vexation; *informal* pain (in the neck), headache, hassle.
■ **drag on** PERSIST, continue, go on, carry on, extend, run on, be protracted, endure, prevail.
■ **drag something out** PROLONG, protract, draw out, spin out, string out, extend, lengthen, carry on, keep going, continue.

dragoon ▶ noun (*historical*) *the dragoons charged* CAVALRYMAN, mounted soldier; *historical* knight, chevalier, hussar; *archaic* cavalier.
▶ verb *he dragooned his friends into participating* COERCE, pressure, press, push; force, compel, impel; hound, harass, nag, harry, badger, goad, pester; browbeat, bludgeon, bully, twist someone's arm, strong-arm, railroad.

drag queen ▶ noun See TRANSVESTITE.

drain ▶ verb **1** *a valve for draining the tank* EMPTY (OUT), void, clear (out), evacuate, unload. **2** *drain off any surplus liquid* DRAW OFF, extract, withdraw, remove, siphon off, pour out, pour off; milk, bleed, tap, void, filter, discharge. **3** *the water drained away to the sea* FLOW, pour, trickle, stream, run, rush, gush, flood, surge; leak, ooze, seep, dribble, issue, filter, bleed, leach. **4** *more people would just drain our resources* USE UP, exhaust, deplete, consume, expend, get through, sap, strain, tax; milk, bleed. **5** *he drained his drink* DRINK (UP/DOWN), gulp (down), guzzle, quaff, down, imbibe, swallow, finish off, toss off, slug; *informal* swig, swill (down), polish off, knock back, put away.
— OPPOSITES: fill.
▶ noun **1** *the drain filled with water* SEWER, channel, conduit, ditch, culvert, duct, pipe, gutter, trough; sluice, spillway, race, flume, chute. **2** *a drain on the battery* STRAIN, pressure, burden, load, tax, demand.

dram ▶ noun DRINK, nip, tot, sip, drop, finger, splash, little, spot, taste.

drama ▶ noun **1** *a television drama* PLAY, show, piece, theatrical work, dramatization. **2** *he is studying drama* ACTING, the theatre, the stage, the performing arts, dramatic art, stagecraft. **3** *she liked to create a drama* INCIDENT, scene, spectacle, crisis; excitement, thrill, sensation; disturbance, commotion, turmoil; dramatics, theatrics.

dramatic ▶ adjective **1** *dramatic art* THEATRICAL, theatric, thespian, stage, dramaturgical; *formal* histrionic. **2** *a dramatic increase* CONSIDERABLE, substantial, sizeable, goodly, fair, marked, noticeable, measurable, perceptible, obvious, appreciable; significant, notable, noteworthy, remarkable, extraordinary, exceptional, phenomenal; *informal* tidy. **3** *there were dramatic scenes in the city* EXCITING, stirring, action-packed, sensational, spectacular; startling, unexpected, tense, gripping, riveting, fascinating, thrilling, hair-raising; rousing, lively, electrifying, impassioned, moving. **4** *dramatic headlands* STRIKING, impressive, imposing, spectacular, breathtaking, dazzling, sensational, awesome, awe-inspiring, remarkable, outstanding, incredible, phenomenal. **5** *a dramatic gesture* EXAGGERATED, theatrical, ostentatious, actressy, stagy, showy, splashy, melodramatic, overdone, histrionic, affected, mannered, artificial; *informal* hammy, ham, campy.
— OPPOSITES: insignificant, boring.

dramatist ▶ noun PLAYWRIGHT, writer, scriptwriter, screenwriter, scenarist, dramaturge.

dramatize ▶ verb **1** *the novel was dramatized* TURN INTO A PLAY/FILM, adapt for the stage/screen. **2** *the tabloids dramatized the event* EXAGGERATE, overdo, overstate, hyperbolize, magnify, amplify, inflate; sensationalize, embroider, colour, aggrandize, embellish, elaborate; *informal* blow up (out of all proportion).

drape ▶ verb **1** *she draped a shawl around her* WRAP, wind, swathe, sling, hang. **2** *the chair was draped with dirty laundry* COVER, envelop, swathe, shroud, deck, festoon, overlay, cloak, wind, enfold, sheathe. **3** *he draped one leg over the arm of his chair* DANGLE, hang, suspend, droop, drop.

drastic ▶ adjective EXTREME, serious, desperate, radical, far-reaching, momentous, substantial; heavy, severe, harsh, rigorous; oppressive, draconian.
– OPPOSITES: moderate.

draw ▶ verb **1** *he drew the house* SKETCH, make a drawing (of), delineate, outline, draft, rough out, illustrate, render, represent, trace; portray, depict. **2** *she drew her chair closer to the fire* PULL, haul, drag, tug, heave, lug, trail, tow; *informal* yank. **3** *the train drew into the station* MOVE, go, come, proceed, progress, travel, advance, pass, drive; inch, roll, glide, cruise; forge, sweep; back. **4** *she drew the curtains* CLOSE, shut, pull to, lower; open, part, pull back, pull open, fling open, raise. **5** *he drew some fluid off the knee joint* DRAIN, extract, withdraw, remove, suck, pump, siphon, milk, bleed, tap. **6** *he drew his gun* PULL OUT, take out, produce, fish out, extract, withdraw; unsheathe. **7** *I drew on my line of credit* WITHDRAW, take out. **8** *while I draw breath* BREATHE IN, inhale, inspire, respire. **9** *she was drawing huge audiences* ATTRACT, interest, win, capture, catch, engage, lure, entice; absorb, occupy, rivet, engross, fascinate, mesmerize, spellbind, captivate, enthrall, grip. **10** *what conclusion can we draw?* DEDUCE, infer, conclude, derive, gather, glean.
▶ noun **1** *she won the Christmas draw* RAFFLE, lottery, sweepstake, sweep, ballot, lotto. **2** *the match ended in a draw* TIE, dead heat, stalemate, saw-off ♣. **3** *the draw of the city* ATTRACTION, lure, allure, pull, appeal, glamour, enticement, temptation, charm, seduction, fascination, magnetism.
■ **draw on** CALL ON, have recourse to, avail oneself of, turn to, look to, fall back on, rely on, exploit, use, employ, utilize, bring into play.
■ **draw something out 1** *he drew out a gun. See* DRAW verb sense 6. **2** *they always drew out their goodbyes* PROLONG, protract, drag out, spin out, string out, extend, lengthen.
■ **draw someone out** ENCOURAGE TO TALK, put at ease.
■ **draw up** STOP, pull up, halt, come to a standstill, brake, park; arrive.
■ **draw something up 1** *we drew up a list* COMPOSE, formulate, frame, write down, draft, prepare, think up, devise, work out; create, invent, design. **2** *he drew up his forces in battle array* ARRANGE, marshal, muster, assemble, group, order, range, rank, line up, dispose, position, array.

drawback ▶ noun DISADVANTAGE, snag, downside, stumbling block, catch, hitch, pitfall, fly in the ointment; weak spot/point, weakness, imperfection; handicap, limitation, trouble, difficulty, problem, complication; hindrance, obstacle, impediment, obstruction, inconvenience, discouragement, deterrent; *informal* minus, hiccup, wrench in the works.
– OPPOSITES: benefit.

drawing ▶ noun SKETCH, picture, illustration, representation, portrayal, delineation, depiction,

composition, study; diagram, outline, design, plan.
– RELATED TERMS: graphic.

drawl ▶ verb SAY SLOWLY, speak slowly; drone.

drawn ▶ adjective *she looked pale and drawn* PINCHED, haggard, drained, wan, hollow-cheeked; fatigued, tired, exhausted; tense, stressed, strained, worried, anxious, harassed, fraught; *informal* hassled.

dread ▶ verb *I used to dread going to school* FEAR, be afraid of, worry about, be anxious about, have forebodings about; be terrified by, tremble/shudder at, shrink from, quail from, flinch from; *informal* get cold feet about.
▶ noun *she was filled with dread* FEAR, apprehension, trepidation, anxiety, worry, concern, foreboding, disquiet, unease, angst; fright, panic, alarm; terror, horror; *informal* the jitters, the creeps, the shivers, the heebie-jeebies, the jim-jams.
– OPPOSITES: confidence.
▶ adjective *the dread disease* AWFUL, frightful, terrible, horrible, dreadful; feared, frightening, alarming, terrifying, dire, dreaded.

dreadful ▶ adjective **1** *a dreadful accident* TERRIBLE, frightful, horrible, grim, awful, dire; horrifying, alarming, shocking, distressing, appalling, harrowing; ghastly, fearful, horrendous; tragic, calamitous; *formal* grievous. **2** *a dreadful meal* UNPLEASANT, disagreeable, nasty; frightful, shocking, awful, abysmal, atrocious, disgraceful, deplorable, very bad, repugnant; poor, inadequate, inferior, unsatisfactory, distasteful; *informal* pathetic, woeful, crummy, rotten, sorry, third-rate, lousy, godawful. **3** *you're a dreadful flirt* OUTRAGEOUS, shocking, inordinate, immoderate, unrestrained.
– OPPOSITES: pleasant, agreeable.

dreadfully ▶ adverb **1** *I'm dreadfully hungry* EXTREMELY, very, really, exceedingly, tremendously, exceptionally, extraordinarily; decidedly, most, particularly; *informal* terrifically, terribly, desperately, awfully, devilishly, mega, seriously, majorly, ever so, real, mighty, awful; *informal, dated* frightfully. **2** *she missed James dreadfully* VERY MUCH, much, lots, a lot, a great deal, intensely, desperately. **3** *the company performed dreadfully* TERRIBLY, awfully, very badly, atrociously, appallingly, abominably, poorly; *informal* abysmally, pitifully.

dream ▶ noun **1** *I awoke from my dreams* REM sleep; nightmare; vision, fantasy, hallucination. **2** *she went around in a dream* DAYDREAM, reverie, trance, daze, stupor, haze. **3** *he realized his childhood dream* AMBITION, aspiration, hope; goal, aim, objective, grail, intention, intent, target; desire, wish, yearning; daydream, fantasy, pipe dream. **4** *he's an absolute dream* DELIGHT, joy, marvel, wonder, gem, treasure; beauty, vision.
▶ verb **1** *she dreamed of her own funeral* HAVE A DREAM, have a nightmare. **2** *I dreamt of making the Olympic team* FANTASIZE ABOUT, daydream about; WISH FOR, hope for, long for, yearn for, hanker after, set one's heart on; aspire to, aim for, set one's sights on. **3** *she's always dreaming* DAYDREAM, be in a trance, be lost in thought, be preoccupied, be abstracted, stare into space, muse, be in la-la land. **4** *I wouldn't dream of being late* THINK, consider, contemplate, conceive.
▶ adjective *his dream home* IDEAL, perfect, fantasy.
■ **dream something up** THINK UP, invent, concoct, devise, hatch, contrive, create, work out, come up with; *informal* cook up.

dreamer ▶ noun FANTASIST, daydreamer; romantic,

sentimentalist, idealist, wishful thinker, Don Quixote; Utopian, visionary.
— OPPOSITES: realist.

dreamland ▶ noun **1** *I drift off to dreamland* SLEEP; *humorous* the land of Nod. **2** *they must be living in dreamland* THE LAND OF MAKE-BELIEVE, fairyland, cloudland, la-la land, never-never land, paradise, Utopia, heaven, Shangri-La.

dreamlike ▶ adjective UNREAL, illusory, imaginary, unsubstantial, chimerical, ethereal, phantasmagorical, trance-like; surreal; nightmarish, Kafkaesque; hazy, shadowy, faint, indistinct, unclear; *literary* illusive.

dreamy ▶ adjective **1** *a dreamy expression* DAYDREAMING, dreaming; pensive, thoughtful, reflective, meditative, ruminative; lost in thought, preoccupied, distracted, rapt, inattentive, woolgathering, vague, absorbed, absent-minded, with one's head in the clouds, in a world of one's own; *informal* miles away. **2** *he was dreamy as a child* IDEALISTIC, romantic, starry-eyed, impractical, unrealistic, Utopian, quixotic, airy-fairy. **3** *a dreamy recollection* DREAMLIKE, vague, dim, hazy, shadowy, faint, indistinct, unclear. **4** *(informal) the prince was really dreamy* ATTRACTIVE, handsome, good-looking, appealing, lovely, delightful; *informal* heavenly, divine, gorgeous, hot, cute.
— OPPOSITES: alert, practical, clear, ugly.

dreary ▶ adjective **1** *a dreary day at school* DULL, drab, uninteresting, flat, tedious, wearisome, boring, unexciting, unstimulating, uninspiring, soul-destroying; humdrum, monotonous, uneventful, unremarkable, featureless, ho-hum. **2** *she thought of dreary things* SAD, miserable, depressing, gloomy, sombre, grave, mournful, melancholic, joyless, cheerless. **3** *a dreary day* GLOOMY, dismal, dull, dark, dingy, murky, overcast; depressing, sombre.
— OPPOSITES: exciting, cheerful, bright.

dregs ▶ plural noun **1** *the dregs from a bottle of wine* SEDIMENT, deposit, residue, accumulation, sludge, lees, grounds, remains; *technical* residuum. **2** *the dregs of humanity* SCUM, refuse, riff-raff, outcasts, deadbeats; the underclass, the untouchables, the lowest of the low, the great unwashed, the hoi polloi; *informal* trash.

drench ▶ verb SOAK, saturate, wet through, permeate, douse, souse; drown, swamp, inundate, flood; steep, bathe.

dress ▶ verb **1** *he dressed quickly* PUT ON CLOTHES, clothe oneself, get dressed. **2** *she was dressed in a suit* CLOTHE, attire, garb, deck out, trick out, costume, array, robe; *informal* get up, doll up. **3** *they dress for dinner every day* WEAR FORMAL CLOTHES, wear evening dress, dress up. **4** *she enjoyed dressing the tree* DECORATE, trim, deck, adorn, ornament, embellish, beautify, prettify; festoon, garland, garnish. **5** *they dressed his wounds* BANDAGE, cover, bind, wrap, swathe; doctor, care for. **6** *she had to dress the chicken* PREPARE, get ready; clean. **7** *the field was dressed with manure* FERTILIZE, enrich, manure, mulch, compost, top-dress. **8** *he dressed Michelle's hair* STYLE, groom, arrange, do; comb, brush; preen, primp; *informal* fix. **9** *(Military) the battalion dressed its ranks* LINE UP, align, straighten, arrange, order, dispose; fall in.
▶ noun **1** *a long blue dress* frock, gown, robe, shift. See table. **2** *fancy dress* CLOTHES, clothing, garments, attire; costume, outfit, ensemble, garb; *informal* gear,

getup, togs, duds, glad rags, threads, Sunday best; *formal* apparel; *archaic* raiment.
— RELATED TERMS: sartorial.
■ **dress down** DRESS INFORMALLY, dress casually.
■ **dress someone down** *(informal).* See REPRIMAND verb.
■ **dress up 1** *Angela loved dressing up* DRESS SMARTLY, dress formally, wear evening dress; *informal* doll oneself up, put on one's glad rags, gussy oneself up. **2** *Hugh dressed up as Santa Claus* DISGUISE ONESELF, dress; put on fancy dress, put on a costume.
■ **dress something up** PRESENT, represent, portray, depict, characterize; embellish, enhance, touch up, embroider.

Dresses

A-line dress	off-the-shoulder dress
baby doll	pinafore
ballgown	polonaise
caftan	sari
chemise	sarong
cheongsam	sheath
coat dress	shift
cocktail dress	shirt-dress
dirndl	shirtwaist
empire dress	skimmer
evening dress/gown	slip dress
gown	smocked dress
granny dress	strapless dress
housedress	sundress
jingle dress	tank dress
jumper	tea gown
little black dress	tube dress
maternity dress	tunic
Mother Hubbard	wedding dress/gown
muumuu	

---

dressing ▶ noun **1** *salad dressing* SAUCE, relish, condiment, dip. See table at SAUCE. **2** *they put fresh dressings on her burns* BANDAGE, covering, plaster, gauze, lint, compress; *proprietary* Band-Aid. **3** *a dressing of fertilizer* FERTILIZER, mulch; manure, compost, dung, bone meal, blood meal, fish meal, guano; top-dressing.

dressmaker ▶ noun TAILOR, seamstress, needlewoman; clothier; couturier, designer.
— RELATED TERMS: sartorial.

dressy ▶ adjective SMART, formal; elaborate, ornate; stylish, elegant, chic, fashionable, fancy, black-tie; *informal* snappy, snazzy, natty, trendy, gussied up.
— OPPOSITES: casual.

dribble ▶ verb **1** *the baby started to dribble* DROOL, slaver, slobber, salivate, drivel. **2** *rainwater dribbled down her face* TRICKLE, drip, fall, drizzle; ooze, seep.
▶ noun **1** *there was dribble on his chin* SALIVA, spittle, spit, slaver, slobber, drool. **2** *a dribble of sweat* TRICKLE, drip, driblet, stream, drizzle; drop, splash.

dried ▶ adjective DEHYDRATED, desiccated, dry, dried up, moistureless.

drift ▶ verb **1** *his raft drifted down the river* BE CARRIED, be borne; float, bob, waft, meander. **2** *the guests drifted away* WANDER, meander, stray, putter, dawdle. **3** *don't allow your attention to drift* STRAY, digress, deviate, diverge, veer, get sidetracked. **4** *snow drifted over the path* PILE UP, bank up, heap up, accumulate, gather, amass.
▶ noun **1** *a drift from the country to urban areas* MOVEMENT, shift, flow, transfer, relocation, gravitation. **2** *the pilot had not noticed any drift*

DEVIATION, digression. **3** *he caught her drift* GIST, essence, meaning, sense, substance, significance; thrust, import, tenor; implication, intention; direction, course. **4** *a drift of deep snow* PILE, heap, bank, mound, mass, accumulation.

drifter ▶ noun WANDERER, traveller, transient, roamer, itinerant, tramp, vagabond, vagrant, hobo, bum.

drill ▶ noun **1** *a hydraulic drill* DRILLING TOOL, boring tool, auger, (brace and) bit, gimlet, awl, bradawl. **2** *they learned military drills* TRAINING, instruction, coaching, teaching; (physical) exercises, workout. **3** *Estelle knew the drill* PROCEDURE, routine, practice, regimen, program, schedule; method, system.
▶ verb **1** *drill the piece of wood* BORE A HOLE IN, make a hole in; bore, pierce, puncture, perforate. **2** *a sergeant drilling new recruits* TRAIN, instruct, coach, teach, discipline; exercise, put someone through their paces. **3** *his mother had drilled politeness into him* INSTILL, hammer, drive, drum, din, implant, ingrain; teach, indoctrinate, brainwash.

drink ▶ verb **1** *she drank her coffee* SWALLOW, gulp down, quaff, guzzle, imbibe, sip, consume; drain, toss off, slug; *informal* swig, down, knock back, put away, swill, chug. **2** *he never drank* DRINK ALCOHOL, tipple, indulge; carouse; *informal* hit the bottle, booze, knock a few back, get tanked up, go on a bender, bend one's elbow. **3** *let's drink to success* TOAST, salute.
▶ noun **1** *he took a sip of his drink* BEVERAGE, liquid refreshment; dram, bracer, nightcap, nip, tot; pint; *humorous* libation; *archaic* potation. *See table at* COCKTAIL. **2** *she turned to drink* ALCOHOL, liquor, alcoholic drink; *informal* booze, hooch, the hard stuff, firewater, rotgut, moonshine, moose milk ♣, the bottle, the sauce, grog, Dutch courage. **3** *she took a drink of her wine* SWALLOW, gulp, sip, draft, slug; *informal* swig, swill. **4** *a drink of orange juice* GLASS, cup, mug. **5** (*informal*) *he fell into the drink* THE SEA, the ocean, the water; *informal* the briny, Davy Jones's locker; *literary* the deep.
■ **drink something in** ABSORB, assimilate, digest, ingest, take in; be rapt in, be lost in, be fascinated by, pay close attention to.

drinkable ▶ adjective POTABLE, fit to drink, palatable; pure, clean, safe, unpolluted, untainted, uncontaminated.

drinker ▶ noun DRUNKARD, drunk, inebriate, imbiber, bibber, tippler, sot; alcoholic, dipsomaniac; *informal* boozer, soak, lush, rubby ♣, wino, alky, sponge, barfly; *archaic* toper.
— OPPOSITES: teetotaller.

drip ▶ verb **1** *there was a tap dripping* DRIBBLE, drop, leak. **2** *sweat dripped from his chin* DROP, dribble, trickle, drizzle, run, splash, plop; leak, emanate, issue.
▶ noun **1** *a bucket to catch the drips* DROP, dribble, spot, trickle, splash. **2** (*informal*) *that drip who fancies you* WEAKLING, ninny, milksop, namby-pamby, crybaby, suck ♣, softie, doormat, milquetoast; *informal* wimp, weed, sissy, wuss, candy-ass, pantywaist, *Atlantic* sooky baby ♣.

drive ▶ verb **1** *I can't drive a car* OPERATE, handle, manage; pilot, steer. **2** *he drove to the police station* TRAVEL BY CAR, motor. **3** *I'll drive you to the airport* CHAUFFEUR, run, give someone a lift/ride, take, ferry, transport, convey, carry. **4** *the engine drives the front wheels* POWER, propel, move, push. **5** *he drove a nail into the board* HAMMER, screw, ram, sink, plunge, thrust, propel, knock. **6** *she drove her cattle to market* IMPEL,

urge; herd, round up, shepherd. **7** *a desperate mother driven to crime* FORCE, compel, prompt, precipitate; oblige, coerce, pressure, goad, spur, prod. **8** *he drove his staff extremely hard* WORK, push, tax, exert.
▶ noun **1** *an afternoon drive* EXCURSION, outing, trip, jaunt, tour; ride, run, journey; *informal* spin. **2** *the house has a long drive* DRIVEWAY, approach, access road. **3** *sexual drive* URGE, appetite, desire, need; impulse, instinct. **4** *she lacked the drive to succeed* MOTIVATION, ambition, single-mindedness, willpower, dedication, doggedness, tenacity; enthusiasm, zeal, commitment, aggression, spirit; energy, vigour, verve, vitality, pep; *informal* get-up-and-go. **5** *an anti-corruption drive* CAMPAIGN, crusade, movement, effort, push, appeal.
■ **drive at** SUGGEST, imply, hint at, allude to, intimate, insinuate, indicate; refer to, mean, intend; *informal* get at.

drivel ▶ noun *he was talking complete drivel* NONSENSE, twaddle, claptrap, balderdash, gibberish, rubbish, mumbo-jumbo, garbage; *informal* poppycock, piffle, tripe, bull, hogwash, baloney, codswallop, flapdoodle, jive, guff, bushwa; *informal, dated* tommyrot, bunkum.
▶ verb *you always drivel on* TALK NONSENSE, talk rubbish, babble, ramble, gibber, blather, blether, prattle, gabble, waffle.

driver ▶ verb MOTORIST, chauffeur; pilot, operator.

driving ▶ adjective *the party's driving force* MOVING, motivating, dynamic, stimulating, energetic, inspirational.

drizzle ▶ noun **1** *they shivered in the drizzle* FINE RAIN, light shower, spray, mist. **2** *a drizzle of sour cream* TRICKLE, dribble, drip, stream, rivulet; sprinkle, sprinkling.
▶ verb **1** *it's beginning to drizzle* RAIN LIGHTLY, shower, spot, spit, sprinkle. **2** *drizzle the cream over the fruit* TRICKLE, drip, dribble, pour, splash, sprinkle.

droll ▶ adjective FUNNY, humorous, amusing, comic, comical, mirthful, hilarious; clownish, farcical, zany, quirky; jocular, light-hearted, facetious, witty, whimsical, wry, tongue-in-cheek; *informal* waggish, wacky, side-splitting, rib-tickling.
— OPPOSITES: serious.

drone ▶ verb **1** *a plane droned overhead* HUM, buzz, whirr, vibrate, murmur, rumble, purr. **2** *he droned on about right and wrong* SPEAK BORINGLY, go on and on, talk at length; intone, pontificate; *informal* spout, sound off, jaw, spiel, speechify.
▶ noun **1** *the drone of aircraft taking off* HUM, buzz, whirr, vibration, murmur, purr. **2** *drones supported by taxpayers' money* HANGER-ON, parasite, leech, passenger, bottom-feeder; idler, loafer, layabout, good-for-nothing, do-nothing; *informal* lazybones, scrounger, sponger, freeloader, slacker.

drool ▶ verb *after the stroke he was continually drooling* SALIVATE, dribble, slaver, slobber.
▶ noun *a fine trickle of drool* SALIVA, spit, spittle, dribble, slaver, slobber.

droop ▶ verb **1** *the dog's tail is drooping* HANG (DOWN), dangle, sag, flop; wilt, sink, slump, drop. **2** *his eyelids were drooping* CLOSE, shut, fall. **3** *the news made her droop* BE DESPONDENT, lose heart, give up hope, become dispirited, become dejected; flag, languish, wilt.

droopy ▶ adjective **1** *the plant was looking droopy* HANGING (DOWN), dangling, falling, dropping, draped; bent, bowed, stooping; sagging, flopping, wilting. **2** *after he left she felt droopy* DESPONDENT, dejected, depressed, down, sad, unhappy, melancholy, miserable, gloomy, dispirited, downhearted, downcast, low, glum; *informal* down in the dumps.

drop ▶ verb **1** *Eric dropped the box* LET FALL, let go of, lose one's grip on; release, unhand, relinquish. **2** *water drops from the cave roof* DRIP, fall, dribble, trickle, run, plop, leak. **3** *a plane dropped out of the sky* FALL, descend, plunge, plummet, dive, nosedive, tumble, pitch. **4** *she dropped to her knees* FALL, sink, collapse, slump, tumble. **5** (*informal*) *I was so tired I thought I would drop* COLLAPSE, faint, pass out, black out, swoon, keel over, conk out. **6** *the track dropped from the ridge* SLOPE DOWNWARDS, slant downwards, descend, go down, fall away, sink, dip. **7** *the exchange rate dropped* DECREASE, lessen, reduce, diminish, depreciate; fall, decline, dwindle, sink, slump, plunge, plummet. **8** *you can drop algebra if you wish* GIVE UP, finish with, withdraw from; discontinue, end, stop, cease, halt; abandon, forgo, relinquish, dispense with, have done with; *informal* pack in, quit. **9** *he was dropped from the team* EXCLUDE, discard, expel, oust, throw out, leave out; dismiss, discharge, let go; *informal* boot out, kick out, turf out. **10** *he dropped his unsuitable friends* ABANDON, desert, throw over; renounce, disown, turn one's back on, wash one's hands of; reject, give up, cast off; neglect, shun; *literary* forsake. **11** *he dropped all reference to compensation* OMIT, leave out, eliminate, take out, miss out, delete, cut, erase. **12** *the taxi dropped her off* DELIVER, bring, take, convey, carry, transport; leave, unload. **13** *drop the gun on the ground* PUT, place, deposit, set, lay, leave; *informal* pop, plonk. **14** *she dropped names* MENTION, refer to, hint at; bring up, raise, broach, introduce; show off. **15** *the team has yet to drop a point* LOSE, concede, give away.
— OPPOSITES: lift, rise, increase, keep, win.
▶ noun **1** *a drop of water* DROPLET, blob, globule, bead, bubble, tear, dot; *informal* glob. **2** *it needs a drop of oil* SMALL AMOUNT, little, bit, dash, spot; dribble, driblet, sprinkle, trickle, splash; dab, speck, smattering, sprinkling, modicum; *informal* smidgen, tad. **3** *a cough drop* CANDY, lozenge, pastille, bonbon. **4** *a small drop in profits* DECREASE, reduction, decline, fall-off, downturn, slump; cut, cutback, curtailment; depreciation. **5** *I walked to the edge of the drop* CLIFF, abyss, chasm, gorge, gully, precipice; slope, descent, incline.
— OPPOSITES: increase.
■ **drop back/behind** FALL BACK/BEHIND, get left behind, lag behind; straggle, linger, dawdle, dally, hang back, loiter, bring/take up the rear, dilly-dally.
■ **drop off 1** *trade dropped off sharply. See* DROP *verb* sense 7. **2** *she kept dropping off* FALL ASLEEP, doze (off), nap, catnap, drowse; *informal* nod off, drift off, snooze, take forty winks.
■ **drop out of** *he dropped out of his studies. See* DROP *verb* sense 8.

dropout ▶ noun **1** *a high school dropout* QUITTER; idler, layabout, loafer, deadbeat, delinquent, burnout. **2** *a sixties dropout* NONCONFORMIST, hippie, beatnik, bohemian, free spirit, rebel; *informal* oddball, eccentric.

droppings ▶ plural noun EXCREMENT, excreta, feces, stools, dung, ordure, manure; *informal* poo.

dross ▶ noun RUBBISH, junk; debris, chaff, detritus, flotsam and jetsam, garbage, trash, dreck.

drought ▶ noun DRY SPELL, lack of rain, shortage of water; *historical* the dirty thirties ✦.

drove ▶ noun **1** *a drove of cattle* HERD, flock, pack.

2 *they came in droves* CROWD, swarm, horde, multitude, mob, throng, host, mass, army, herd.

drown ▶ verb **1** *he nearly drowned* SUFFOCATE IN WATER, inhale water; go to a watery grave. **2** *the valleys were drowned* FLOOD, submerge, immerse, inundate, deluge, swamp, engulf. **3** *his voice was drowned out by the music* MAKE INAUDIBLE, overpower, overwhelm, override; muffle, deaden, stifle, extinguish.

drowse ▶ verb *they like to drowse in the sun* DOZE, nap, catnap, rest; *informal* snooze, get forty winks, get some shut-eye, catch some zees.
▶ noun *she had been woken from her drowse* DOZE, light sleep, nap, catnap, rest, siesta; *informal* snooze, forty winks, shut-eye.

drowsy ▶ adjective **1** *the tablet made her drowsy* SLEEPY, dozy, groggy, somnolent; tired, weary, fatigued, exhausted, yawning, nodding; lethargic, sluggish, torpid, listless, languid; *informal* snoozy, dopey, yawny, dead beat, all in, dog-tired, bone-weary. **2** *a drowsy afternoon* SOPORIFIC, sleep-inducing, sleepy, somniferous; narcotic, sedative, tranquilizing; lulling, soothing.
— OPPOSITES: alert, invigorating.

drubbing ▶ noun **1** *I gave him a good drubbing* BEATING, thrashing, walloping, thumping, battering, pounding, pummelling, slapping, punching, pelting; *informal* hammering, licking, clobbering, belting, bashing, pasting, tanning, hiding, kicking. **2** (*informal*) *Edmonton's 3-0 drubbing by Ottawa. See* DEFEAT *noun* sense 1.

drudge ▶ noun *a household drudge* MENIAL WORKER, slave, lackey, servant, labourer, worker, cog; *informal* gofer, runner, bottle-washer, joe-boy, serf.
▶ verb (*archaic*) *he drudged in the fields. See* TOIL *verb* sense 1.

drudgery ▶ noun HARD WORK, menial work, donkey work, toil, labour; chores.

drug ▶ noun **1** *drugs prescribed by doctors* MEDICINE, medication, medicament, pharmaceutical; remedy, cure, antidote. **2** *she was under the influence of drugs* NARCOTIC, stimulant, hallucinogen; *informal* dope.
▶ verb **1** *he was drugged* ANAESTHETIZE, narcotize; poison; knock out, stupefy; *informal* dope. **2** *she drugged his coffee* ADD DRUGS TO, tamper with, adulterate, contaminate, lace, poison; *informal* dope, spike, doctor.

drug addict ▶ noun. *See* ADDICT sense 1.

drugged ▶ adjective STUPEFIED, insensible, befuddled; delirious, hallucinating, narcotized; anaesthetized, knocked out; *informal* stoned, high (as a kite), doped, tripping, spaced out, wasted, wrecked, impaired ✦.
— OPPOSITES: sober.

drum ▶ noun **1** *the beat of a drum* percussion instrument; bongo, tom-tom, snare drum, kettledrum, bodhran; *historical* tambour. **2** *the steady drum of raindrops* BEAT, rhythm, patter, tap, pounding, thump, thud, rattle, pitter-patter, pit-a-pat, rat-a-tat, thrum. **3** *a drum of radioactive waste* CANISTER, barrel, cylinder, tank, bin, can; container.
▶ verb **1** *she drummed her fingers on the desk* TAP, beat, rap, thud, thump; tattoo, thrum. **2** *the rules were drummed into us at school* INSTILL, drive, din, hammer, drill, implant, ingrain, inculcate.
■ **drum someone out** EXPEL, dismiss, throw out, oust; drive out, get rid of; exclude, banish; *informal* give someone the boot, boot out, kick out, give someone their marching orders, show someone the door, send packing.

■ **drum something up** ROUND UP, gather, collect; summon, attract; canvass, solicit, petition.

drunk ▶ adjective INTOXICATED, inebriated, inebriate, impaired ✦, drunken, tipsy, under the influence; *informal* plastered, smashed, bombed, sloshed, sozzled, sauced, lubricated, well-oiled, wrecked, juiced, blasted, stinko, blitzed, half-cut, fried, wasted, hopped up, gassed, polluted, pissed, tanked (up), soaked, out of one's head/skull, loaded, trashed, hammered, soused, buzzed, befuddled, besotted, pickled, pixilated, canned, cockeyed, blotto, blind drunk, roaring drunk, dead drunk, punch-drunk, ripped, stewed, tight, merry, the worse for wear, far gone, pie-eyed, in one's cups, three sheets to the wind; *literary* crapulous.
– OPPOSITES: sober.
▶ noun DRUNKARD, inebriate, drinker, tippler, imbiber, sot; heavy drinker, problem drinker, alcoholic, dipsomaniac; *informal* boozer, soak, lush, rubby ✦, wino, alky, sponge, barfly; *archaic* toper.
– OPPOSITES: teetotaller.

drunken ▶ adjective **1** *drunken revellers.* See DRUNK adjective. **2** *a drunken all-night party* DEBAUCHED, dissipated, carousing, roistering, intemperate, unrestrained, uninhibited, abandoned; bacchanalian, Bacchic; *informal* boozy.

drunkenness ▶ noun INTOXICATION, inebriation, insobriety, tipsiness, impairment; intemperance, overindulgence, debauchery; heavy drinking, alcoholism, dipsomania.

dry ▶ adjective **1** *the dry desert* ARID, parched, droughty, scorched, baked; waterless, moistureless, rainless; dehydrated, desiccated, thirsty, bone dry. **2** *dry leaves* PARCHED, dried, withered, shrivelled, wilted, wizened; crisp, crispy, brittle; dehydrated, desiccated. **3** *the buns were dry* HARD, stale, old, past its best; off. **4** *a dry well* WATERLESS, empty. **5** *I'm really dry* THIRSTY, dehydrated; *informal* parched, gasping. **6** *it was dry work* THIRSTY, thirst-making; hot; strenuous, arduous. **7** *dry toast* UNBUTTERED, butterless, plain. **8** *the dry facts* BARE, simple, basic, fundamental, stark, bald, hard, straightforward. **9** *a dry debate* DULL, uninteresting, boring, unexciting, tedious, tiresome, wearisome, dreary, monotonous; unimaginative, sterile, flat, bland, lacklustre, stodgy, prosaic, humdrum, mundane; *informal* deadly. **10** *a dry sense of humour* WRY, subtle, laconic, sharp; ironic, sardonic, sarcastic, cynical; satirical, mocking, droll; *informal* waggish. **11** *a dry response to his cordial advance* UNEMOTIONAL, indifferent, impassive, cool, cold, emotionless; reserved, restrained, impersonal, formal, stiff, wooden. **12** *this is a dry state* TEETOTAL, prohibitionist, alcohol-free, non-drinking, abstinent, sober; *informal* on the wagon. **13** *dry white wine* CRISP, sharp, piquant, tart, bitter.
– OPPOSITES: wet, moist, fresh, lively, emotional, sweet.
▶ verb **1** *the sun dried the ground* PARCH, scorch, bake; dehydrate, desiccate, dehumidify. **2** *dry the leaves completely* DEHYDRATE, desiccate; wither, shrivel. **3** *he dried the dishes* TOWEL, rub; mop up, blot up, soak up, absorb. **4** *she dried her eyes* WIPE, rub, dab. **5** *methods of drying meat* DESICCATE, dehydrate; preserve, cure, smoke.
– OPPOSITES: moisten.
■ **dry out** GIVE UP DRINKING, give up alcohol, become a teetotaller, go on the wagon.
■ **dry up** *investment may dry up* DWINDLE, subside, peter

out, wane, taper off, ebb, come to a halt/end, run out, give out, disappear, vanish.

dual ▶ adjective DOUBLE, twofold, binary; duplicate, twin, matching, paired, coupled.
– OPPOSITES: single.

dub ▶ verb **1** *he was dubbed 'the world's sexiest man'* NICKNAME, call, name, label, christen, term, tag, entitle, style; designate, characterize, nominate; *formal* denominate. **2** *she dubbed a new knight* KNIGHT, invest.

dubiety ▶ noun *(formal)* DOUBTFULNESS, uncertainty, unsureness, incertitude; ambiguity, ambivalence, confusion; hesitancy, doubt.

dubious ▶ adjective **1** *I was rather dubious about the idea* DOUBTFUL, uncertain, unsure, hesitant; undecided, indefinite, unresolved, up in the air; vacillating, irresolute; skeptical, suspicious; *informal* iffy. **2** *dubious business practices* SUSPICIOUS, suspect, untrustworthy, unreliable, questionable; *informal* shady, fishy, hinky.
– OPPOSITES: certain, trustworthy.

duck¹ ▶ noun *male*: drake; *female*: duck; *young*: duckling. See table.

Water Birds

Ducks, Geese & Swans	
baldpate	ruddy duck
barnacle goose	sawbill
black duck	scaup
black swan	scoter
blue goose	shoveller
brant	smew
bufflehead	snow goose
Canada goose	surf scoter
canvasback	swan
common eider	teal
common merganser	trumpeter swan
eider	tundra swan
gadwall	white-winged scoter
garganey	whooping swan
goldeneye	widgeon
grey goose	wood duck
greylag	
harlequin duck	**Loons**
king eider	Arctic loon
lord and lady ✦	common loon
mallard	great northern diver
mandarin duck	Pacific loon
merganser	red-throated loon
mute swan	yellow-billed loon
oldsquaw	
pintail	**Grebes**
red-breasted merganser	grebe
redhead	helldiver
	horned grebe
	red-necked grebe
	See also the tables at CRANE *and* GULL.

duck² ▶ verb **1** *he ducked behind the wall* BOB DOWN, bend (down), stoop (down), crouch (down), squat (down), hunch down, hunker down; cower, cringe. **2** *she was ducked in the river* DIP, dunk, plunge, immerse, submerge, lower, sink. **3** *(informal) they cannot duck the issue forever* SHIRK, dodge, evade, avoid, elude, escape, back out of, shun, eschew, sidestep, bypass, circumvent; *informal* cop out of, get out of, wriggle out of, dipsy-doodle around.

duct ▶ noun TUBE, channel, canal, vessel; conduit,

culvert; pipe, pipeline, outlet, inlet, flue, shaft, vent; *Anatomy* ductus.

ductile ▸ adjective **1** *ductile metals* PLIABLE, pliant, flexible, supple, plastic, tensile; soft, malleable, workable, bendable; *informal* bendy. **2** *a way to make people ductile* DOCILE, obedient, submissive, meek, mild, lamblike; willing, accommodating, amenable, co-operative, compliant, malleable, tractable, biddable, persuadable.
— OPPOSITES: brittle, intransigent.

dud ▸ noun *their new product is a dud* FAILURE, flop, letdown, disappointment; *informal* washout, lemon, no-hoper, non-starter, dead loss, clunker.
— OPPOSITES: success.
▸ adjective **1** *a dud typewriter* DEFECTIVE, faulty, unsound, inoperative, broken, malfunctioning; *informal* bust, busted, kaput, conked out. **2** *a dud $50 bill* COUNTERFEIT, fraudulent, forged, fake, faked, false, bogus; invalid, worthless; *informal* phony.
— OPPOSITES: sound, genuine.

dude ▸ noun See FELLOW sense 1.

dudgeon
■ **in high dudgeon** INDIGNANTLY, resentfully, angrily, furiously; in a temper, in anger, with displeasure; *informal* in a huff, seeing red.

due ▸ adjective **1** *their fees were due* OWING, owed, payable; outstanding, overdue, unpaid, unsettled, undischarged, delinquent. **2** *the chancellor's statement is due today* EXPECTED, anticipated, scheduled for, awaited; required. **3** *the respect due to a great artist* DESERVED BY, merited by, warranted by; appropriate to, fit for, fitting for, right for, proper to. **4** *he drove without due care* PROPER, correct, rightful, suitable, appropriate, apt; adequate, sufficient, enough, satisfactory, requisite.
▸ noun **1** *he attracts more criticism than is his due* RIGHTFUL TREATMENT, fair treatment, just punishment; right, entitlement; just deserts; *informal* comeuppance. **2** *members have paid their dues* FEE, subscription, charge; payment, contribution.
▸ adverb *he hiked due north* DIRECTLY, straight, exactly, precisely, dead.
■ **due to 1** *her death was due to an infection* ATTRIBUTABLE TO, caused by, ascribed to, because of, put down to. **2** *the train was cancelled due to staff shortages* BECAUSE OF, owing to, on account of, as a consequence of, as a result of, thanks to, in view of; *formal* by reason of.

duel ▸ noun **1** *he was killed in a duel* SINGLE COMBAT; (sword) fight, confrontation, faceoff, shoot-out. **2** *a snooker duel* CONTEST, match, game, meet, encounter.
▸ verb *they duelled with swords* FIGHT A DUEL, fight, battle, combat, contend.

dulcet ▸ adjective SWEET, soothing, mellow, honeyed, mellifluous, euphonious, pleasant, agreeable; melodious, melodic, lilting, lyrical, silvery, golden.
— OPPOSITES: harsh.

dull ▸ adjective **1** *a dull novel* UNINTERESTING, boring, tedious, monotonous, unrelieved, unvaried, unimaginative, uneventful; characterless, featureless, colourless, lifeless, insipid, unexciting, uninspiring, unstimulating, jejune, flat, bland, dry, stale, tired, banal, lacklustre, ho-hum, stodgy, dreary, humdrum, mundane; mind-numbing, soul-destroying, wearisome, tiring, tiresome, irksome, deadly, samey, dullsville. **2** *a dull morning* OVERCAST, cloudy, gloomy, dark, dismal, dreary, sombre, grey, murky, sunless. **3** *dull colours* DRAB,

dreary, sombre, dark, subdued, muted, lacklustre, faded, washed out, muddy, dingy. **4** *a dull sound* MUFFLED, muted, quiet, soft, faint, indistinct; stifled, suppressed. **5** *the chisel became dull* BLUNT, unsharpened, edgeless, worn down. **6** *a rather dull child* UNINTELLIGENT, stupid, slow, witless, vacuous, empty-headed, stunned ♣, brainless, mindless, foolish, idiotic; *informal* dense, dim, moronic, halfwitted, thick, dumb, dopey, dozy, bovine, slow on the uptake, wooden-headed, fat-headed. **7** *her cold made her feel dull* SLUGGISH, lethargic, enervated, listless, languid, torpid, slow, sleepy, drowsy, weary, tired, fatigued; apathetic; *informal* dozy, dopey, yawny, logy.
— OPPOSITES: interesting, bright, loud, resonant, sharp, clever.
▸ verb **1** *the pain was dulled by drugs* LESSEN, decrease, diminish, reduce, dampen, blunt, deaden, allay, ease, soothe, assuage, alleviate. **2** *sleep dulled her mind* NUMB, benumb, deaden, desensitize, stupefy, daze. **3** *rain dulled the sky* DARKEN, blacken, dim, veil, obscure, shadow, fog. **4** *the sombre atmosphere dulled her spirit* DAMPEN, lower, depress, crush, sap, extinguish, smother, stifle.
— OPPOSITES: intensify, enliven, enhance, brighten.

dullard ▸ noun IDIOT, fool, stupid person, simpleton, ignoramus, oaf, dunce, dolt; *informal* duffer, moron, cretin, imbecile, nincompoop, dope, chump, nitwit, numbnuts, fathead, dumbo, dumdum, donkey, wally, doofus, goof, bozo, dummy, zombie.

duly ▸ adverb **1** *the document was duly signed* PROPERLY, correctly, appropriately, suitably, fittingly. **2** *he duly arrived to collect Alice* AT THE RIGHT TIME, on time, punctually.

dumb ▸ adjective **1** *she stood dumb while he shouted* MUTE, speechless, tongue-tied, silent, at a loss for words; taciturn, uncommunicative, untalkative, tight-lipped, close-mouthed; *informal* mum. **2** *(informal) he is not as dumb as you'd think* STUPID, unintelligent, ignorant, dense, brainless, mindless, foolish, slow, dull, simple, empty-headed, stunned ♣, vacuous, vapid, idiotic, half-baked, imbecilic, bovine; *informal* thick, dim, moronic, dopey, dozy, thick-headed, fat-headed, birdbrained, pea-brained; daft.
— OPPOSITES: clever.

dumbfound ▸ verb ASTONISH, astound, amaze, stagger, surprise, startle, stun, confound, stupefy, daze, take aback, stop someone in their tracks, strike dumb, leave open-mouthed, leave aghast; *informal* flabbergast, floor, bowl over.

dumbfounded ▸ adjective ASTONISHED, astounded, amazed, staggered, surprised, startled, stunned, confounded, nonplussed, stupefied, dazed, dumbstruck, open-mouthed, speechless, thunderstruck; taken aback, disconcerted; *informal* flabbergasted, flummoxed, bowled over, blown away, floored.

dummy ▸ noun **1** *a shop-window dummy* MANNEQUIN, model, figure. **2** *the book is just a dummy* MOCK-UP, imitation, likeness, look-alike, representation, substitute, sample; replica, reproduction; counterfeit, sham, fake, forgery; *informal* dupe. **3** *(informal) you're a dummy. See IDIOT.
▸ adjective *a dummy attack on the airfield* SIMULATED, feigned, pretended, practice, trial, mock, make-believe; *informal* pretend, phony, virtual.
— OPPOSITES: real.

dump ▸ noun **1** *take the garbage to the dump* TRANSFER

STATION, garbage dump, (*West*) nuisance grounds ✤, landfill site, rubbish heap, dumping ground; dustheap, slag heap. **2** (*informal*) *the house is a dump* HOVEL, shack, slum; mess; hole, pigsty.
▶ verb **1** *he dumped his bag on the table* PUT DOWN, set down, deposit, place, unload; drop, throw down; *informal* stick, park, plonk, plunk. **2** *they will dump asbestos at the site* DISPOSE OF, get rid of, throw away/ out, discard, jettison; *informal* ditch, junk, deep-six. **3** (*informal*) *he dumped her* ABANDON, desert, leave, jilt, break up with, finish with, throw over; *informal* walk out on, rat on, drop, ditch.

dumpling ▶ noun PEROGY, won ton, knish, matzo ball, doughboy, (*NB*) poutine ✤, varenyky, potsticker, gnocchi, kreplach.

dumps
■ **down in the dumps** (*informal*) UNHAPPY, sad, depressed, gloomy, glum, melancholy, miserable, dejected, despondent, dispirited, downhearted, downcast, down, low, heavy-hearted, dismal, desolate; tearful, upset, blue, down in the mouth.

dumpy ▶ adjective SHORT, squat, stubby; PLUMP, stout, chubby, chunky, portly, fat, bulky, tubby, roly-poly, pudgy, porky.
– OPPOSITES: tall, slender.

dun[1] ▶ adjective *a dun cow* GREYISH-BROWN, brownish, mousy, muddy, khaki, umber.

dun[2] ▶ verb *you can't dun me for her debts* IMPORTUNE, press, plague, pester, nag, harass, hound, badger, hassle, bug.

dunce ▶ noun FOOL, idiot, stupid person, simpleton, ignoramus, dullard; *informal* dummy, dumbo, thickhead, nitwit, dim-wit, dim-bulb, halfwit, moron, cretin, imbecile, dope, duffer, boob, chump, numbskull, numbnuts, nincompoop, fathead, airhead, birdbrain, pea-brain, ninny, ass, doofus, goof, meatball, schmuck, bozo, lummox.
– OPPOSITES: genius.

dune ▶ noun BANK, mound, hillock, hummock, knoll, ridge, heap, drift.

dung ▶ noun MANURE, muck; excrement, feces, droppings, scat, ordure, cow-pies, cow patties, cow flops, horse buns, horse apples, road apples, turds.

dungeon ▶ noun UNDERGROUND PRISON, oubliette; cell, jail, lock-up.

duo ▶ noun TWOSOME, pair, couple.

dupe ▶ verb *they were duped by a con man* DECEIVE, trick, hoodwink, hoax, swindle, defraud, cheat, double-cross; gull, mislead, take in, fool, inveigle; *informal* con, do, rip off, diddle, shaft, bilk, rook, pull the wool over someone's eyes, pull a fast one on, sucker, snooker.
▶ noun *an innocent dupe in her game* VICTIM, gull, pawn, puppet, instrument; fool, innocent; *informal* sucker, chump, stooge, sitting duck, fall guy, pigeon, patsy, sap.

duplicate ▶ noun *a duplicate of the invoice* COPY, carbon copy, photocopy, facsimile, reprint; replica, reproduction, clone; *informal* dupe; *proprietary* Xerox.
▶ adjective *duplicate keys* MATCHING, identical, twin, corresponding, equivalent.
▶ verb **1** *she will duplicate the newsletter* COPY, photocopy, xerox, mimeograph, reproduce, replicate, reprint, run off. **2** *a feat difficult to duplicate* REPEAT, do again, redo, replicate.

duplicity ▶ noun DECEITFULNESS, deceit, deception, double-dealing, underhandedness, dishonesty, fraud, trickery, sharp practice, chicanery, trickery, subterfuge, skulduggery, treachery; *informal* crookedness, shadiness, dirty tricks, shenanigans, monkey business; *literary* perfidy.
– OPPOSITES: honesty.

durability ▶ noun IMPERISHABILITY, durableness, longevity; resilience, strength, sturdiness, toughness, robustness.
– OPPOSITES: fragility.

durable ▶ adjective **1** *durable carpets* HARD-WEARING, long-lasting, heavy-duty, industrial-strength, tough, resistant, imperishable, indestructible, strong, sturdy. **2** *a durable peace* LASTING, long-lasting, long-term, enduring, persistent, abiding; stable, secure, firm, deep-rooted, permanent, undying, everlasting.
– OPPOSITES: delicate, short-lived.

duration ▶ noun FULL LENGTH, time, time span, time scale, period, term, span, fullness, length, extent, continuation.

duress ▶ noun COERCION, compulsion, force, pressure, intimidation, constraint; threats; *informal* arm-twisting.

during ▶ conjunction THROUGHOUT, through, in, in the course of, for the time of.

dusk ▶ noun TWILIGHT, nightfall, sunset, sundown, evening, (*Nfld*) duckish ✤, close of day; semi-darkness, gloom, murkiness; *literary* gloaming, eventide.
– OPPOSITES: dawn.

dusky ▶ adjective **1** *the dusky countryside* SHADOWY, dark, dim, gloomy, murky, shady; unlit, unilluminated; sunless, moonless. **2** (*dated*) *a dusky complexion* DARK-SKINNED, dark, olive-skinned, swarthy, ebony, black; tanned, bronzed, coppery, brown.
– OPPOSITES: bright, fair.

dust ▶ noun **1** *the desk was covered in dust* DIRT, grime, filth, smut, soot; fine powder. **2** *they fought in the dust* EARTH, soil, dirt; ground.
▶ verb **1** *she dusted her mantelpiece* WIPE, clean, brush, sweep, mop. **2** *dust the cake with icing sugar* SPRINKLE, scatter, powder, dredge, sift, cover, strew.

dust-up ▶ noun (*informal*). See SCRAP[2] noun.

dusty ▶ adjective **1** *the floor was dusty* DIRTY, grimy, grubby, unclean, soiled, mucky, sooty; undusted; *informal* grungy, cruddy; grotty. **2** *dusty sandstone* POWDERY, crumbly, chalky, friable; granular, gritty, sandy. **3** *a dusty pink* MUTED, dull, faded, pale, pastel, subtle; greyish, darkish, dirty.
– OPPOSITES: clean, bright.

dutiful ▶ adjective CONSCIENTIOUS, responsible, dedicated, devoted, attentive; obedient, compliant, submissive, biddable; deferential, reverent, reverential, respectful, good.
– OPPOSITES: remiss.

duty ▶ noun **1** *she was free of any duty* RESPONSIBILITY, obligation, commitment; allegiance, loyalty, faithfulness, fidelity, homage. **2** *it was his duty to attend the king* JOB, task, assignment, mission, function, charge, place, role, responsibility, obligation; *dated* office. **3** *the duty was raised on alcohol* TAX, levy, tariff, excise, toll, fee, payment, rate, countervail ✤; dues.
■ **off duty** NOT WORKING, at leisure, on holiday, on leave, off (work), free.
■ **on duty** WORKING, at work, busy, occupied, engaged; *informal* on the job.

dwarf ▶ noun **1** SMALL PERSON, short person; midget, pygmy, manikin, homunculus. **2** *the wizard captured* *the dwarf* GNOME, goblin, hobgoblin, troll, imp, elf, brownie, leprechaun.

▶ **adjective** *dwarf conifers* MINIATURE, small, little, tiny, toy, pocket, diminutive, baby, pygmy, stunted, undersized, undersize; *informal* mini, teeny, teeny-weeny, itsy-bitsy, pint-sized, little-bitty; *Scottish* wee.
– OPPOSITES: giant.

▶ **verb 1** *the buildings dwarf the trees* DOMINATE, tower over, loom over, overshadow, overtop. **2** *her progress was dwarfed by her sister's success* OVERSHADOW, outshine, surpass, exceed, outclass, outstrip, outdo, top, trump, transcend; diminish, minimize.

dwell ▶ **verb** *(formal)* *gypsies dwell in these caves* RESIDE, live, be settled, be housed, lodge, stay; *informal* put up; *formal* abide, be domiciled.

■ **dwell on** LINGER OVER, mull over, muse on, brood about/over, think about; be preoccupied by, be obsessed by, eat one's heart out over; harp on about, discuss at length.

dwelling ▶ **noun** *(formal)* RESIDENCE, home, house, accommodation, lodging place; lodgings, quarters, rooms; *informal* place, pad, digs; *formal* abode, domicile, habitation.

dwindle ▶ **verb 1** *the population dwindled* DIMINISH, decrease, reduce, lessen, shrink; fall off, tail off, drop, fall, slump, plummet; disappear, vanish, die out; *informal* nosedive. **2** *her career dwindled* DECLINE, deteriorate, fail, slip, slide, fade, go downhill, go to rack and ruin; *informal* go to pot, go to the dogs, hit the skids, go down the toilet/tubes/drain.
– OPPOSITES: increase, flourish.

dye ▶ **noun** *a blue dye* COLOURANT, colouring, colour, dyestuff, pigment, tint, stain, wash.

▶ **verb** *the gloves were dyed* COLOUR, tint, pigment, stain, wash.

dyed-in-the-wool ▶ **adjective** INVETERATE, confirmed, entrenched, established, long-standing,

deep-rooted, diehard; complete, absolute, thorough, thoroughgoing, out-and-out, true blue; firm, unshakeable, staunch, steadfast, committed, devoted, dedicated, loyal, unswerving, full bore; *informal* card-carrying.

dying ▶ **adjective 1** *his dying aunt* TERMINALLY ILL, at death's door, on one's deathbed, near death, fading fast, expiring, moribund, not long for this world, in extremis; *informal* on one's last legs, having one foot in the grave. **2** *a dying art form* DECLINING, vanishing, fading, ebbing, waning; *informal* on the way out. **3** *her dying words* FINAL, last; deathbed.
– OPPOSITES: thriving, first.

▶ **noun** *he took her dying very hard* DEATH, demise, passing, loss of life, quietus; *formal* decease.

dynamic ▶ **adjective** ENERGETIC, spirited, active, lively, zestful, vital, vigorous, forceful, powerful, positive; high-powered, aggressive, bold, enterprising; magnetic, passionate, fiery, high-octane; *informal* go-getting, peppy, full of get-up-and-go, full of vim and vigour, gutsy, spunky, feisty, go-ahead.
– OPPOSITES: half-hearted.

dynamism ▶ **noun** ENERGY, spirit, liveliness, zestfulness, vitality, vigour, forcefulness, power, potency, positivity; aggression, drive, ambition, enterprise; magnetism, passion, fire; *informal* pep, get-up-and-go, vim and vigour, guts, feistiness, gumption.

dynasty ▶ **noun** BLOODLINE, line, ancestral line, lineage, house, family, ancestry, descent, succession, genealogy, family tree; regime, rule, reign, empire, sovereignty.

dyspeptic ▶ **adjective** BAD-TEMPERED, short-tempered, irritable, snappish, testy, tetchy, touchy, crabby, crotchety, grouchy, cantankerous, peevish, cross, disagreeable, waspish, prickly; *informal* snappy, on a short fuse, cranky, ornery.

Ee

each ▶ **pronoun** *there are 47 books and each must be read* EVERY ONE, each one, each and every one, all, the whole lot.
▶ **adjective** *he visited each month* EVERY, each and every, every single.
▶ **adverb** *they gave $10 each* APIECE, per person, per capita, from each, individually, respectively, severally.

eager ▶ **adjective** **1** *small eager faces* KEEN, enthusiastic, avid, fervent, ardent, motivated, wholehearted, dedicated, committed, earnest; *informal* mad keen, gung-ho. **2** *we were eager for news* ANXIOUS, impatient, longing, yearning, wishing, hoping, hopeful; desirous of, hankering after; on the edge of one's seat, on tenterhooks, on pins and needles; *informal* itching, gagging, dying.
— OPPOSITES: apathetic.

eagerness ▶ **noun** KEENNESS, enthusiasm, avidity, fervour, zeal, wholeheartedness, earnestness, commitment, dedication; impatience, desire, longing, yearning, hunger, appetite, ambition, yen.

eagle ▶ **noun**. *See table at* RAPTOR.
— RELATED TERMS: aquiline.

ear ▶ **noun** **1** *an infection of the ear* inner ear, middle ear, outer ear. **2** *he had the ear of the president* ATTENTION, notice, heed, regard, consideration. **3** *he has an ear for a good song* APPRECIATION, discrimination, perception.
— RELATED TERMS: aural, auricular, oto-.
■ **play it by ear** IMPROVISE, extemporize, ad lib; make it up as one goes along, think on one's feet, wing it, fly by the seat of one's pants.

early ▶ **adjective** **1** *early copies of the book* ADVANCE, forward; initial, preliminary, first; pilot, trial. **2** *an early death* UNTIMELY, premature, unseasonable, before time. **3** *early man* PRIMITIVE, ancient, prehistoric, primeval; *literary* of yore. **4** *an early official statement* PROMPT, timely, quick, speedy, rapid, fast.
— OPPOSITES: late, modern, overdue.
▶ **adverb 1** *Rachel has to get up early* IN THE EARLY MORNING; at dawn, at daybreak, at cock crow. **2** *they hoped to leave school early* BEFORE THE USUAL TIME; prematurely, too soon, ahead of time, ahead of schedule.
— OPPOSITES: late.

earmark ▶ **verb** *the cash had been earmarked for the firm* SET ASIDE, keep (back), reserve; designate, assign, mark; allocate, allot, devote, pledge, give over.
▶ **noun** *he has all the earmarks of a leader* CHARACTERISTICS, attribute, feature, hallmark, quality.

earn ▶ **verb 1** *they earned $20,000* BE PAID, take home, gross, net; receive, get, make, obtain, collect, bring in; *informal* pocket, bank, rake in. **2** *he has earned their trust* DESERVE, merit, warrant, justify, be worthy of; gain, win, secure, establish, obtain, procure, get, acquire; *informal* clinch.
— OPPOSITES: lose.

earnest ▶ **adjective 1** *he is dreadfully earnest* SERIOUS, solemn, grave, sober, humourless, staid, intense; committed, dedicated, keen, diligent, zealous; thoughtful, cerebral, deep, profound. **2** *earnest prayer* DEVOUT, heartfelt, wholehearted, sincere, impassioned, fervent, ardent, intense, urgent.
— OPPOSITES: frivolous, half-hearted.
■ **in earnest 1** *we are in earnest about stopping crime* SERIOUS, sincere, wholehearted, genuine; committed, firm, resolute, determined. **2** *he started writing in earnest* ZEALOUSLY, purposefully, determinedly, resolutely; passionately, wholeheartedly.

earnestly ▶ **adverb** SERIOUSLY, solemnly, gravely, intently; sincerely, resolutely, firmly, ardently, fervently, eagerly.

earnings ▶ **plural noun** INCOME, wages, salary, stipend, pay, payment, fees; revenue, yield, profit, takings, proceeds, avails ♣, dividends, return, remuneration.

earth ▶ **noun 1** *the moon orbits the earth* WORLD, globe, planet. **2** *a trembling of the earth* LAND, ground, terra firma; floor. **3** *he plowed the earth* SOIL, clay, loam; dirt, sod, turf; ground. **4** *the earth rejoiced* HUMANITY, humankind, mankind, (all) people; *humorous* earthlings. **5** *the fox's earth* DEN, lair, set, burrow, warren, hole; retreat, shelter, hideout, hideaway; *informal* hidey-hole.
— RELATED TERMS: terrestrial, telluric.

earthenware ▶ **noun** POTTERY, crockery, stoneware; china, porcelain; pots.

earthly ▶ **adjective 1** *the earthly environment* TERRESTRIAL, telluric. **2** *the promise of earthly delights* WORLDLY, temporal, mortal, human; material; carnal, fleshly, bodily, physical, corporeal, sensual. **3** (*informal*) *there is no earthly explanation for this* FEASIBLE, possible, likely, conceivable, imaginable.
— OPPOSITES: extraterrestrial, heavenly.

earthquake ▶ **noun** (EARTH) TREMOR, shock, foreshock, aftershock, convulsion, seismic activity; *informal* quake.
— RELATED TERMS: seismic.

earthy ▶ **adjective 1** *an earthy smell* SOIL-LIKE, dirt-like. **2** *she was a simple, earthy girl* DOWN-TO-EARTH, unsophisticated, unrefined, simple, plain, unpretentious, natural. **3** *Emma's earthy language* BAWDY, ribald, off-colour, racy, rude, vulgar, lewd, crude, foul, coarse, uncouth, unseemly, indelicate, indecent, obscene, barnyard; *informal* blue, locker-room.

ease ▶ **noun 1** *he defeated them all with ease* EFFORTLESSNESS, no trouble, simplicity; deftness, adroitness, proficiency, mastery. **2** *his ease of manner* NATURALNESS, casualness, informality, amiability, affability; unconcern, composure, nonchalance, insouciance. **3** *he couldn't find any ease* PEACE, calm, tranquility, serenity; repose, restfulness, quiet, security, comfort. **4** *a life of ease* AFFLUENCE, wealth, prosperity, luxury, plenty; comfort, contentment, enjoyment, well-being.
— OPPOSITES: difficulty, formality, trouble, hardship.
▶ **verb 1** *the alcohol eased his pain* RELIEVE, alleviate, mitigate, soothe, palliate, moderate, dull, deaden,

numb; reduce, lighten, diminish. **2** *the rain eased off* ABATE, subside, die down, let up, slack off, diminish, lessen, peter out, relent, come to an end. **3** *work helped to ease her mind* CALM, quieten, pacify, soothe, comfort, console; hearten, gladden, uplift, encourage. **4** *we want to ease their adjustment* FACILITATE, expedite, assist, help, aid, advance, further, forward, simplify. **5** *he eased out the cork* GUIDE, manoeuvre, inch, edge; slide, slip, squeeze.
— OPPOSITES: aggravate, worsen, hinder.
■ **at ease/at one's ease** RELAXED, calm, serene, tranquil, unworried, contented, content, happy; comfortable.

easily ► **adverb 1** *she won the race easily* EFFORTLESSLY, comfortably, simply; with ease, without difficulty, without a hitch, smoothly; skilfully, deftly, smartly; *informal* no sweat, hands down. **2** *he's easily the best* UNDOUBTEDLY, without doubt, without question, indisputably, undeniably, definitely, certainly, clearly, obviously, patently; by far, far and away, by a mile.

east ► **adjective** EASTERN, easterly, eastward, oriental.

Easter egg ► **noun** chocolate egg, Ukrainian Easter egg, pysanka ♣, Fabergé egg.

easy ► **adjective 1** *the task was very easy* UNCOMPLICATED, undemanding, unchallenging, effortless, painless, trouble-free, facile, simple, straightforward, elementary, plain sailing; *informal* easy as pie, a piece of cake, child's play, kids' stuff, a cinch, no sweat, a breeze, smooth sailing, duck soup, a snap. **2** *easy babies* DOCILE, manageable, amenable, tractable, compliant, pliant, acquiescent, obliging, co-operative, easygoing. **3** *an easy target* VULNERABLE, susceptible, defenceless; naive, gullible, trusting. **4** *Dave's easy manner* NATURAL, casual, informal, unceremonious, unreserved, uninhibited, unaffected, easygoing, amiable, affable, genial, good-humoured; carefree, nonchalant, unconcerned, laid-back. **5** *an easy life* CALM, tranquil, serene, quiet, peaceful, untroubled, contented, relaxed, comfortable, secure, safe; *informal* cushy. **6** *an easy pace* LEISURELY, unhurried, comfortable, undemanding, easygoing, gentle, sedate, moderate, steady. **7** (*informal*) *people think she's easy* PROMISCUOUS, unchaste, loose, wanton, abandoned, licentious, debauched; *informal* sluttish, slutty, whorish.
— OPPOSITES: difficult, demanding, formal, chaste.

easygoing ► **adjective** RELAXED, even-tempered, placid, mellow, mild, happy-go-lucky, carefree, free and easy, nonchalant, insouciant, imperturbable; amiable, considerate, undemanding, patient, tolerant, lenient, broad-minded, understanding; good-natured, pleasant, agreeable; *informal* laid-back, unflappable, Type-B.
— OPPOSITES: intolerant.

eat ► **verb 1** *we ate a hearty breakfast* CONSUME, devour, ingest, partake of; gobble (up/down), bolt (down), wolf (down), swallow, chew, munch, chomp; *informal* guzzle, nosh, put away, chow down on, tuck into, demolish, dispose of, polish off, pig out on, scarf, snarf. **2** *we ate at a local restaurant* HAVE A MEAL, consume food, feed, snack; breakfast, lunch, dine; feast, banquet; graze, nosh; *archaic* sup. **3** *acidic water can eat away at pipes* ERODE, corrode, wear away/down/through, burn through, consume, dissolve, disintegrate, crumble, decay; damage, destroy.

eatable ► **adjective** EDIBLE, palatable, digestible; fit to eat, fit for consumption.

eatery ► **noun** See table at RESTAURANT.

eats ► **plural noun** (*informal*) FOOD, sustenance, nourishment, fare; eatables, snacks, tidbits, nosh, grub, chow, chuck.

eavesdrop ► **verb** LISTEN IN, spy; monitor, tap, wiretap, record, overhear, snoop, bug, wire.

ebb ► **verb 1** *the tide ebbed* RECEDE, go out, retreat, flow back, fall back/away, subside. **2** *his courage began to ebb* DIMINISH, dwindle, wane, fade away, peter out, decline, flag, let up, decrease, weaken, disappear.
— OPPOSITES: increase.
► **noun 1** *the ebb of the tide* RECEDING, retreat, subsiding. **2** *the ebb of the fighting* ABATEMENT, subsiding, easing, dying down, de-escalation, decrease, decline, diminution.

ebony ► **adjective** BLACK, jet-black, pitch-black, coal-black, sable, inky, sooty, raven, dark.

ebullience ► **noun** EXUBERANCE, buoyancy, cheerfulness, cheeriness, merriment, jollity, sunniness, jauntiness, light-heartedness, high spirits, elation, euphoria, jubilation; animation, sparkle, vivacity, enthusiasm, perkiness; *informal* chirpiness, bounciness, pep.

ebullient ► **adjective** EXUBERANT, buoyant, cheerful, joyful, cheery, merry, jolly, sunny, jaunty, light-hearted, elated; animated, sparkling, vivacious, irrepressible; *informal* bubbly, bouncy, peppy, upbeat, chirpy, smiley, full of beans; *dated* gay.
— OPPOSITES: depressed.

eccentric ► **adjective** *eccentric behaviour* UNCONVENTIONAL, uncommon, abnormal, irregular, aberrant, anomalous, odd, queer, strange, peculiar, weird, bizarre, outlandish, freakish, extraordinary; idiosyncratic, quirky, nonconformist, outré; *informal* way out, offbeat, freaky, oddball, wacky, kooky.
— OPPOSITES: conventional.
► **noun** *he was something of an eccentric* ODDITY, odd fellow, character, individualist, individual, free spirit; misfit; *informal* oddball, odd duck, weirdo, freak, nut, head case, crank, wacko, kook, screwball, crackpot.

eccentricity ► **noun** UNCONVENTIONALITY, singularity, oddness, strangeness, weirdness, quirkiness, freakishness; peculiarity, foible, idiosyncrasy, caprice, whimsy, quirk; *informal* nuttiness, screwiness, freakiness, kookiness.

ecclesiastic ► **noun** *a high ecclesiastic* CLERGYMAN, clergywoman, priest, churchman/woman, man/woman of the cloth, man/woman of God, cleric, minister, pastor, preacher, chaplain, father; bishop, vicar, rector, parson, curate, deacon; monk, nun, religious, friar, sister, brother; *informal* reverend, padre, Holy Joe, sky pilot, Bible-thumper.
► **adjective** *ecclesiastic embroidery.* See ECCLESIASTICAL.

ecclesiastical ► **adjective** PRIESTLY, ministerial, clerical, ecclesiastic, canonical, sacerdotal; church, churchly, religious, spiritual, holy, divine; *informal* churchy.

echelon ► **noun** LEVEL, rank, grade, step, rung, tier, position, order.

echo ► **noun 1** *a faint echo of my shout* REVERBERATION, reflection, ringing, repetition, repeat. **2** *the scene she described was an echo of the photograph* DUPLICATE, copy, replica, imitation, mirror image, double, match, parallel; *informal* look-alike, spitting image, dead ringer. **3** *a faint echo of their love* TRACE, vestige, remnant, ghost, memory, recollection, remembrance; reminder, sign, mark, token, indication, suggestion, hint; evidence.

▶ **verb 1** *his laughter echoed around the room* REVERBERATE, resonate, resound, reflect, ring, vibrate. **2** *Bill echoed Rex's words* REPEAT, restate, reiterate; copy, imitate, parrot, mimic; reproduce, recite, quote, regurgitate; *informal* recap.

éclat ▶ **noun** STYLE, flamboyance, confidence, élan, dash, flair, vigour, gusto, verve, zest, sparkle, brio, panache, dynamism, spirit; *informal* pizzazz, pep, oomph.

eclectic ▶ **adjective** WIDE-RANGING, broad-based, extensive, comprehensive, encyclopedic; varied, diverse, catholic, all-embracing, multi-faceted, multifarious, heterogeneous, miscellaneous, assorted.

eclipse ▶ **noun 1** *the eclipse of the sun* BLOTTING OUT, blocking, covering, obscuring, concealing, darkening; *Astronomy* occultation. **2** *the eclipse of the empire* DECLINE, fall, failure, decay, deterioration, degeneration, weakening, collapse.
▶ **verb 1** *the sun was eclipsed by the moon* BLOT OUT, block, cover, obscure, hide, conceal, obliterate, darken; shade; *Astronomy* occult. **2** *the system was eclipsed by new methods* OUTSHINE, overshadow, surpass, exceed, outclass, outstrip, outdo, top, trump, transcend, upstage.

economic ▶ **adjective 1** *economic reform* FINANCIAL, monetary, budgetary, fiscal; commercial. **2** *the firm cannot remain economic. See* PROFITABLE *sense 1.* **3** *an economic alternative to carpeting* CHEAP, inexpensive, low-cost, budget, economy, economical, cut-rate, discount, bargain.
— OPPOSITES: unprofitable, expensive.

economical ▶ **adjective 1** *an economical car* CHEAP, inexpensive, low-cost, budget, economy, economic; cut-rate, discount, bargain. **2** *a very economical shopper* THRIFTY, provident, prudent, sensible, frugal, sparing, abstemious; mean, parsimonious, penny-pinching, miserly, stingy.
— OPPOSITES: expensive, spendthrift.

economize ▶ **verb** SAVE (MONEY), cut costs; cut back, make cutbacks, retrench, budget, make economies, be thrifty, be frugal, scrimp, cut corners, tighten one's belt, watch the/your pennies.

economy ▶ **noun 1** *the nation's economy* WEALTH, (financial) resources; financial system, financial management. **2** *one can combine good living with economy* THRIFT, thriftiness, providence, prudence, careful budgeting, economizing, saving, scrimping, restraint, frugality, abstemiousness.
— OPPOSITES: extravagance.

ecstasy ▶ **noun** RAPTURE, bliss, elation, euphoria, transports, rhapsodies; joy, jubilation, exultation.
— OPPOSITES: misery.

ecstatic ▶ **adjective** ENRAPTURED, elated, in raptures, euphoric, rapturous, joyful, overjoyed, blissful; on cloud nine, in seventh heaven, beside oneself with joy, jumping for joy, delighted, thrilled, exultant; *informal* over the moon, on top of the world, blissed out.

ecumenical ▶ **adjective** NON-DENOMINATIONAL, universal, catholic, latitudinarian, all-embracing, all-inclusive.
— OPPOSITES: denominational.

eddy ▶ **noun** *small eddies at the river's edge* SWIRL, whirlpool, vortex, maelstrom.
▶ **verb** *cold air eddied around her* SWIRL, whirl, spiral, wind, circulate, twist; flow, ripple, stream, surge, billow.

edge ▶ **noun 1** *the edge of the lake* BORDER, boundary, extremity, fringe, margin, side; lip, rim, brim, brink, verge; perimeter, circumference, periphery, limits, bounds. **2** *she had an edge in her voice* SHARPNESS, severity, bite, sting, asperity, acerbity, acidity, trenchancy; sarcasm, acrimony, malice, spite, venom. **3** *they have an edge over their rivals* ADVANTAGE, lead, head start, the whip hand, the upper hand; superiority, dominance, ascendancy, supremacy, primacy; *informal* inside track.
— OPPOSITES: middle, disadvantage.
▶ **verb 1** *poplars edged the orchard* BORDER, fringe, verge, skirt; surround, enclose, encircle, circle, encompass, bound. **2** *a nightie edged with lace* TRIM, pipe, band, decorate, finish; border, fringe; bind, hem. **3** *he edged closer to the fire* CREEP, inch, work one's way, pick one's way, ease oneself; sidle, steal, slink.
■ **on edge** TENSE, nervous, edgy, anxious, apprehensive, uneasy, unsettled; twitchy, jumpy, keyed up, restive, skittish, neurotic, insecure; *informal* uptight, wired, strung out.

edgy ▶ **adjective 1** *everyone was edgy as the deadline approached* TENSE, nervous, on edge, anxious, apprehensive, uneasy, unsettled; twitchy, jumpy, keyed up, restive, skittish, neurotic, insecure; irritable, touchy, tetchy, testy, crotchety, prickly; *informal* uptight, snappy, strung out. **2** *an edgy new novel* CUTTING-EDGE, on-the-edge, fringe, avant-garde, innovative, original, offbeat; gritty.
— OPPOSITES: calm, conventional.

edible ▶ **adjective** SAFE TO EAT, fit for human consumption, wholesome, good to eat; consumable, digestible, palatable; *formal* comestible.

edict ▶ **noun** DECREE, order, command, commandment, mandate, proclamation, pronouncement, dictate, fiat, promulgation; law, statute, act, bill, ruling, injunction; *formal* ordinance.

edification ▶ **noun** (*formal*) EDUCATION, instruction, tuition, teaching, training, tutelage, guidance; enlightenment, cultivation, information; improvement, development.

edifice ▶ **noun** BUILDING, structure, construction, erection, pile, complex; property, development, premises.

edify ▶ **verb** (*formal*) EDUCATE, instruct, teach, school, tutor, train, guide; enlighten, inform, cultivate, develop, improve, better.

edit ▶ **verb 1** *she edited the text* CORRECT, check, copy-edit, improve, emend, polish; modify, adapt, revise, rewrite, reword, rework, redraft; shorten, condense, cut, abridge; *informal* clean up, blue-pencil. **2** *this volume was edited by a consultant* SELECT, choose, assemble, organize, put together. **3** *he edited the Globe and Mail* BE THE EDITOR OF, direct, run, manage, head, lead, supervise, oversee, preside over; *informal* be the boss of.

edition ▶ **noun** ISSUE, number, volume, impression, publication; version, revision.

educate ▶ **verb** TEACH, school, tutor, instruct, coach, train, drill; guide, inform, enlighten; inculcate, indoctrinate; *formal* edify.

educated ▶ **adjective** INFORMED, literate, schooled, tutored, well-read, learned, knowledgeable, enlightened; intellectual, academic, erudite, scholarly, cultivated, cultured; *dated* lettered.

education ▶ **noun 1** *the education of young children* TEACHING, schooling, tuition, tutoring, instruction, coaching, training, tutelage, guidance;

indoctrination, inculcation, enlightenment; *formal* edification. **2** *a woman of some education* LEARNING, knowledge, literacy, scholarship, enlightenment.
— RELATED TERMS: pedagogic.

educational ▶ **adjective 1** *a stuffy educational establishment* ACADEMIC, scholastic, school, learning, teaching, pedagogic, instructional. **2** *an educational experience* INSTRUCTIVE, instructional, educative, informative, illuminating, pedagogic, enlightening, didactic, heuristic; *formal* edifying.

educative ▶ **adjective.** *See* EDUCATIONAL *sense 2.*

educator ▶ **noun** TEACHER, tutor, instructor, schoolteacher, schoolmaster, schoolmistress, schoolmarm; educationalist, educationist; lecturer, professor; guide, mentor, guru; *formal* pedagogue; *archaic* schoolman.

eerie ▶ **adjective** UNCANNY, sinister, ghostly, unnatural, unearthly, supernatural, otherworldly; strange, abnormal, odd, weird, freakish; creepy, scary, spooky, freaky, frightening; bone-chilling, spine-chilling, hair-raising, blood-curdling, terrifying.

efface ▶ **verb 1** *the words were effaced by the rain* ERASE, eradicate, expunge, blot out, rub out, wipe out, remove, eliminate; delete, cancel, obliterate. **2** *he attempted to efface himself* MAKE ONESELF INCONSPICUOUS, keep out of sight, keep out of the limelight, lie low, keep a low profile, withdraw.

effect ▶ **noun 1** *the effect of these changes* RESULT, consequence, upshot, outcome, repercussions, ramifications; end result, conclusion, culmination, corollary, concomitant, aftermath; fruit(s), product, by-product, payoff; *Medicine* sequela. **2** *the effect of the drug* IMPACT, action, effectiveness, influence; power, potency, strength; success; *formal* efficacy. **3** *the new rules come into effect tomorrow* FORCE, operation, enforcement, implementation, effectiveness; validity, lawfulness, legality, legitimacy. **4** *some words to that effect* SENSE, meaning, theme, drift, import, intent, intention, tenor, significance, message; gist, essence, spirit. **5** *the dead man's effects* BELONGINGS, possessions, (worldly) goods, chattels; property, paraphernalia; *informal* gear, tackle, things, stuff.
— OPPOSITES: cause.
▶ **verb** *they effected many changes* ACHIEVE, accomplish, carry out, realize, manage, bring off, execute, conduct, engineer, perform, do, perpetrate, discharge, complete, consummate; cause, bring about, create, produce, make; provoke, occasion, generate, engender, actuate, initiate; *formal* effectuate.
■ **in effect** REALLY, in reality, in truth, in (actual) fact, effectively, essentially, in essence, practically, to all intents and purposes, all but, as good as, more or less, almost, nearly, just about; *informal* pretty much; *literary* well-nigh, nigh on.
■ **take effect 1** *these measures will take effect in May* COME INTO FORCE, come into operation, become operative, begin, become valid, become law, apply, be applied. **2** *the drug started to take effect* WORK, act, be effective, produce results.

effective ▶ **adjective 1** *an effective treatment* SUCCESSFUL, effectual, potent, powerful; helpful, beneficial, advantageous, valuable, useful; *formal* efficacious. **2** *a more effective argument* CONVINCING, compelling, strong, forceful, potent, weighty, sound, valid; impressive, persuasive, plausible, credible, authoritative; logical, reasonable, lucid, coherent, cogent, eloquent; *formal* efficacious. **3** *the new law will*

be effective next week OPERATIVE, in force, in effect; valid, official, lawful, legal, binding; *Law* effectual. **4** *Korea was under effective Japanese control* VIRTUAL, practical, essential, actual, implicit, tacit.
— OPPOSITES: weak, invalid, theoretical.

effectiveness ▶ **noun** SUCCESS, productiveness, potency, power; benefit, advantage, value, virtue, usefulness; *formal* efficacy.

effectual ▶ **adjective 1** *effectual political action* EFFECTIVE, successful, productive, constructive; worthwhile, helpful, beneficial, advantageous, valuable, useful; *formal* efficacious. **2** *(Law) an effectual document* VALID, authentic, bona fide, genuine, official; lawful, legal, legitimate, (legally) binding, contractual.

effeminate ▶ **adjective** WOMANISH, effete, foppish, unmanly, feminine; *informal* camp, campy, flaming.
— OPPOSITES: manly.

effervescence ▶ **noun 1** *wines of uniform effervescence* FIZZ, fizziness, sparkle, gassiness, carbonation, aeration, bubbliness. **2** *his cheeky effervescence* VIVACITY, liveliness, animation, high spirits, ebullience, exuberance, buoyancy, sparkle, gaiety, jollity, cheerfulness, perkiness, breeziness, enthusiasm, irrepressibility, vitality, zest, energy, dynamism, pep, bounce, spunk.

effervescent ▶ **adjective 1** *an effervescent drink* FIZZY, sparkling, carbonated, aerated, gassy, bubbly. **2** *effervescent young people* VIVACIOUS, lively, animated, high-spirited, bubbly, ebullient, buoyant, sparkling, scintillating, light-hearted, jaunty, happy, jolly, cheery, cheerful, perky, sunny, enthusiastic, irrepressible, vital, zestful, energetic, dynamic; *informal* bright-eyed and bushy-tailed, peppy, bouncy, upbeat, chirpy, full of beans.
— OPPOSITES: still, depressed.

effete ▶ **adjective 1** *effete trendies* AFFECTED, pretentious, precious, mannered, over-refined; ineffectual; *informal* la-di-da. **2** *an effete young man* EFFEMINATE, unmanly, girlish, feminine; soft, timid, cowardly, lily-livered, spineless, pusillanimous; *informal* sissy, wimpish, wimpy. **3** *the fabric of society is effete* WEAK, enfeebled, enervated, worn out, exhausted, finished, drained, spent, powerless, ineffectual.
— OPPOSITES: manly, powerful.

efficacious ▶ **adjective** *(formal)* EFFECTIVE, effectual, successful, productive, constructive, potent; helpful, beneficial, advantageous, valuable, useful.

efficacy ▶ **noun** *(formal)* EFFECTIVENESS, success, productiveness, potency, power; benefit, advantage, value, virtue, usefulness.

efficiency ▶ **noun 1** *we need to make changes to improve efficiency* ORGANIZATION, order, orderliness, regulation, coherence; productivity, effectiveness. **2** *I compliment you on your efficiency* COMPETENCE, capability, ability, proficiency, adeptness, expertise, professionalism, skill, effectiveness.

efficient ▶ **adjective 1** *efficient techniques* ORGANIZED, methodical, systematic, logical, orderly, businesslike, streamlined, productive, effective, cost-effective, labour-saving. **2** *an efficient secretary* COMPETENT, capable, able, proficient, adept, skilful, skilled, effective, productive, organized, businesslike.
— OPPOSITES: disorganized, incompetent.

effigy ▶ **noun** STATUE, statuette, sculpture, model, dummy, figurine; likeness, image; bust.

effluent ▶ noun (LIQUID) WASTE, sewage, waste water, effluvium, outflow, discharge, emission.

effort ▶ noun **1** *they made an effort to work together* ATTEMPT, try, endeavour; *informal* crack, shot, stab; *formal* essay. **2** *his score was a fine effort* ACHIEVEMENT, accomplishment, attainment, result, feat; undertaking, enterprise, work; triumph, success, coup. **3** *the job requires little effort* EXERTION, energy, work, endeavour, application, labour, power, muscle, toil, strain; *informal* sweat, elbow grease.

effortless ▶ adjective EASY, undemanding, unchallenging, painless, simple, uncomplicated, straightforward, elementary; fluent, natural; *informal* as easy as pie, child's play, kids' stuff, a cinch, no sweat, a breeze, duck soup, a snap.
— OPPOSITES: difficult.

effrontery ▶ noun IMPUDENCE, impertinence, cheek, insolence, cockiness, audacity, temerity, presumption, nerve, gall, shamelessness, impoliteness, disrespect, bad manners; *informal* brass, face, chutzpah, sauce, sass.

effusion ▶ noun **1** *an effusion of poisonous gas* OUTFLOW, outpouring, rush, current, flood, deluge, emission, discharge, emanation; spurt, surge, jet, stream, torrent, gush, flow. **2** *reporters' flamboyant effusions* OUTBURST, outpouring, gushing, rhapsody; wordiness, verbiage.

effusive ▶ adjective GUSHING, gushy, unrestrained, extravagant, fulsome, demonstrative, lavish, enthusiastic, lyrical; expansive, wordy, verbose, over the top.
— OPPOSITES: restrained.

egg ▶ noun OVUM; gamete, germ cell; (**eggs**) roe, spawn, seed.
— RELATED TERMS: ovoid. *See also* EASTER EGG.
■ **egg someone on** URGE, goad, incite, provoke, push, drive, prod, prompt, induce, impel, spur on; encourage, exhort, motivate, galvanize.

egghead ▶ noun (*informal*) INTELLECTUAL, thinker, academic, scholar, sage; bookworm, highbrow; expert, genius, mastermind; *informal* brain, whiz, brainiac, rocket scientist.
— OPPOSITES: dunce.

ego ▶ noun SELF-ESTEEM, self-importance, self-worth, self-respect, self-image, self-confidence.

egocentric ▶ adjective SELF-CENTRED, egomaniacal, egoistic, egotistic, self-interested, selfish, self-seeking, self-absorbed, narcissistic, vain, self-important.
— OPPOSITES: altruistic.

egotism, egoism ▶ noun SELF-CENTREDNESS, egomania, egocentricity, self-interest, selfishness, self-seeking, self-serving, self-regard, self-love, narcissism, self-admiration, vanity, conceit, self-importance; boastfulness.

egotist, egoist ▶ noun SELF-SEEKER, egocentric, egomaniac, narcissist; boaster, braggart; *informal* show-off, big head, showboat.

egotistic, egoistic ▶ adjective SELF-CENTRED, selfish, egocentric, egomaniacal, self-interested, self-seeking, self-absorbed, narcissistic, vain, conceited, self-important; boastful.

egregious ▶ adjective SHOCKING, appalling, terrible, awful, horrendous, frightful, atrocious, abominable, abhorrent, outrageous; monstrous, heinous, dire, unspeakable, shameful, unforgivable, intolerable, dreadful; *formal* grievous.
— OPPOSITES: marvellous.

egress ▶ noun **1** *the egress from the gallery was blocked* EXIT, way out, escape route. **2** *a means of egress* DEPARTURE, exit, withdrawal, retreat, exodus; escape.
— OPPOSITES: entrance.

eh ▶ exclamation (*informal*) KNOW WHAT I MEAN, get it, see, understand, capisce, get/catch my drift, okay, right.

eight ▶ cardinal number OCTET, octuplets; *technical* octad.
— RELATED TERMS: octo-.

ejaculate ▶ verb **1** EMIT SEMEN, climax, orgasm; *informal* come. **2** (*dated*) 'What?' he ejaculated EXCLAIM, cry out, call out, yell, blurt out, come out with.

ejaculation ▶ noun **1** *the ejaculation of fluid* EMISSION, ejection, discharge, release, expulsion. **2** *premature ejaculation* EMISSION OF SEMEN, climax, orgasm. **3** (*dated*) *the conversation consisted of ejaculations* EXCLAMATION, interjection; call, shout, yell.

eject ▶ verb **1** *the volcano ejected ash* EMIT, spew out, discharge, give off, send out, belch, vent; expel, release, disgorge, spout, vomit, throw up. **2** *the pilot had time to eject* BAIL OUT, escape, get out. **3** *they were ejected from the hall* EXPEL, throw out, turn out, cast out, remove, oust; evict, banish; *informal* chuck out, kick out, turf out, boot out, give someone the bum's rush. **4** *he was ejected from his post* DISMISS, remove, discharge, oust, expel, axe, throw out, force out, drive out; *informal* sack, fire, send packing, boot out, chuck out, kick out, give someone their marching orders, show someone the door; turf out.
— OPPOSITES: admit, appoint.

ejection ▶ noun **1** *the ejection of electrons* EMISSION, discharge, expulsion, release; elimination. **2** *their ejection from the grounds* EXPULSION, removal; eviction, banishment, exile. **3** *his ejection from office* DISMISSAL, removal, discharge, expulsion.

eke ▶ verb *I had to eke out my remaining funds* HUSBAND, use sparingly, be thrifty with, be frugal with, be sparing with, use economically; *informal* go easy on.
— OPPOSITES: squander.
■ **eke out a living** SUBSIST, survive, get by, scrape by, make ends meet, keep body and soul together, keep the wolf from the door, keep one's head above water.

elaborate ▶ adjective **1** *an elaborate plan* COMPLICATED, complex, intricate, involved; detailed, painstaking, careful; tortuous, convoluted, serpentine, Byzantine. **2** *an elaborate plasterwork ceiling* ORNATE, decorated, embellished, adorned, ornamented, fancy, fussy, busy, ostentatious, extravagant, showy, baroque, rococo, florid; *informal* fancy-dancy, fancy-schmancy.
— OPPOSITES: simple, plain.
▶ verb *both sides refused to elaborate on their reasons* EXPAND ON, enlarge on, add to, flesh out, put flesh on the bones of, add detail to, expatiate on; develop, fill out, embellish, embroider, enhance, amplify.

élan ▶ noun FLAIR, style, panache, confidence, dash, éclat; energy, vigour, vitality, liveliness, brio, esprit, animation, vivacity, zest, verve, spirit, pep, sparkle, enthusiasm, gusto, eagerness, feeling, fire; *informal* pizzazz, zing, zip, vim, oomph.

elapse ▶ verb PASS, go by/past, wear on, slip by/away/past, roll by/past, slide by/past, steal by/past, tick by/past.

elastic ▶ adjective **1** *elastic material* STRETCHY, elasticized, stretchable, springy, flexible, pliant, pliable, supple, yielding, plastic, resilient. **2** *an elastic concept of nationality* ADAPTABLE, flexible, adjustable,

accommodating, variable, fluid, versatile.
— OPPOSITES: rigid.
▶ noun RUBBER BAND, elastic band, scrunchie.

elasticity ▶ noun 1 *the skin's natural elasticity* STRETCHINESS, flexibility, pliancy, suppleness, plasticity, resilience, springiness, give. 2 *the elasticity of the term* ADAPTABILITY, flexibility, adjustability, fluidity, versatility.

elated ▶ adjective THRILLED, delighted, overjoyed, ecstatic, euphoric, very happy, joyous, gleeful, jubilant, beside oneself, exultant, rapturous, in raptures, walking on air, on cloud nine, in seventh heaven, jumping for joy, in transports of delight; *informal* on top of the world, over the moon, on a high, tickled pink.
— OPPOSITES: miserable.

elation ▶ noun EUPHORIA, ecstasy, happiness, delight, transports of delight, joy, joyousness, glee, jubilation, exultation, bliss, rapture.

elbow ▶ verb *he elbowed his way through the crowd* PUSH, shove, force, shoulder, jostle, barge, muscle, bulldoze.

elbow room ▶ noun ROOM TO MANOEUVRE/MOVE, room, space, breathing space, personal space, scope, opportunity, freedom, play, free rein, licence, latitude, leeway.

elder ▶ adjective *his elder brother* OLDER, senior, big.
▶ noun *the native elders* LEADER, senior figure, patriarch, father.

elderly ▶ adjective *her elderly mother* AGED, old, advanced in years, aging, long in the tooth, past one's prime; grey-haired, grizzled, hoary; in one's dotage, decrepit, doddering, doddery, senescent; *informal* getting on, past it, over the hill, no spring chicken.
— OPPOSITES: youthful.
▶ noun (**the elderly**) OLD PEOPLE, senior citizens, (old-age) pensioners, retired people; geriatrics, seniors, retirees, golden agers; *informal* oldies, oldsters, geezer, blue-hair.

elect ▶ verb 1 *a new president was elected* VOTE FOR, VOTE IN, return, cast one's vote for; acclaim ♣; choose, pick, select. 2 *she elected to stay behind* CHOOSE, decide, opt, vote.
▶ adjective *the president elect* FUTURE, -to-be, designate, chosen, elected, coming, next, appointed.
▶ noun (**the elect**) THE CHOSEN, the elite, the favoured; the crème de la crème.

election ▶ noun BALLOT, vote, popular vote, ballot box; poll(s); acclamation ♣, by-election; *US* primary.
— RELATED TERMS: psephology.

electioneer ▶ verb CAMPAIGN, canvass, go on the hustings, mainstreet ♣, glad-hand.

elector ▶ noun VOTER, member of the electorate, constituent.

electric ▶ adjective 1 *an electric kettle* ELECTRIC-POWERED, electrically operated, battery-operated. 2 *the atmosphere was electric* EXCITING, charged, electrifying, thrilling, heady, dramatic, intoxicating, dynamic, stimulating, galvanizing, rousing, stirring, moving, tense, knife-edge, explosive, volatile.

electricity ▶ noun POWER, electric power, energy, current, static; hydro ♣.

electrify ▶ verb EXCITE, thrill, stimulate, arouse, rouse, inspire, stir (up), exhilarate, intoxicate, galvanize, move, fire (with enthusiasm), fire someone's imagination, invigorate, animate, startle;

jolt, shock, light a fire under; *informal* give someone a thrill, give someone a charge.

elegance ▶ noun 1 *he was attracted by her elegance* STYLE, stylishness, grace, gracefulness, taste, tastefulness, sophistication; refinement, dignity, beauty, poise, charm, culture; suaveness, urbanity, panache. 2 *the elegance of the idea* NEATNESS, simplicity; ingenuity, cleverness, inventiveness.

elegant ▶ adjective 1 *an elegant black outfit* STYLISH, graceful, tasteful, sophisticated, classic, chic, smart, fashionable, modish; refined, dignified, poised, beautiful, lovely, charming, artistic, aesthetic; cultivated, polished, cultured; dashing, debonair, suave, urbane. 2 *an elegant solution* NEAT, simple, effective; ingenious, clever, deft, intelligent, inventive.
— OPPOSITES: gauche.

elegiac ▶ adjective MOURNFUL, melancholic, melancholy, plaintive, sorrowful, sad, lamenting, doleful; funereal, dirge-like; nostalgic, valedictory, poignant; *literary* dolorous.
— OPPOSITES: cheerful.

elegy ▶ noun LAMENT, requiem, threnody, dirge; *literary* plaint; *Irish* keen.

element ▶ noun 1 *an essential element of the game* COMPONENT, constituent, part, section, portion, piece, segment, bit; aspect, factor, feature, facet, ingredient, strand, detail, point; member, unit, module, item. 2 *there is an element of truth in this stereotype* TRACE, touch, hint, smattering, soupçon. 3 (**elements**) *the elements of political science* BASICS, essentials, principles, first principles; foundations, fundamentals, rudiments; *informal* nuts and bolts, ABC's. 4 *I braved the elements* THE WEATHER, the climate, meteorological conditions, atmospheric conditions; the wind, the rain, the snow.

elemental ▶ adjective 1 *the elemental principles of accounting* BASIC, primary, fundamental, essential, root, underlying; rudimentary. 2 *elemental forces* NATURAL, atmospheric, meteorological, environmental, climatic.

elementary ▶ adjective 1 *an elementary astronomy course* BASIC, rudimentary, fundamental; preparatory, introductory, initiatory, entry-level; *informal* 101. 2 *a lot of the work is elementary* EASY, simple, straightforward, uncomplicated, undemanding, painless, child's play, plain sailing; *informal* as easy as pie, as easy as ABC, a piece of cake, no sweat, kids' stuff.
— OPPOSITES: advanced, difficult.

elephant ▶ noun PACHYDERM, mammoth; jumbo.

elephantine ▶ adjective ENORMOUS, huge, gigantic, very big, massive, giant, immense, tremendous, colossal, mammoth, gargantuan, vast, prodigious, monumental, titanic; hulking, bulky, heavy, weighty, ponderous, lumbering; *informal* jumbo, whopping, humongous, monster, ginormous.
— OPPOSITES: tiny.

elevate ▶ verb 1 *we need a breeze to elevate the kite* RAISE, lift (up), raise up/aloft, upraise; hoist, hike up, haul up. 2 *he was elevated to Senior Writer* PROMOTE, upgrade, advance, move up, raise, prefer; ennoble, exalt, aggrandize; *informal* move up the ladder.
— OPPOSITES: lower, demote.

elevated ▶ adjective 1 *an elevated motorway* RAISED, upraised, high up, aloft; overhead. 2 *elevated language* LOFTY, grand, exalted, fine, sublime; inflated, pompous, bombastic, orotund. 3 *the gentry's elevated*

Chemical Elements

Element	Symbol	Atomic Number	Element	Symbol	Atomic Number	Element	Symbol	Atomic Number
actinium	Ac	89	hafnium	Hf	72	promethium	Pm	61
aluminum	Al	13	hassium	Hs	108	protactinium	Pa	91
americium	Am	95	helium	He	2	radium	Ra	88
antimony	Sb	51	holmium	Ho	67	radon	Rn	86
argon	Ar	18	hydrogen	H	1	rhenium	Re	75
arsenic	As	33	indium	In	49	rhodium	Rh	45
astatine	At	85	iodine	I	53	rubidium	Rb	37
barium	Ba	56	iridium	Ir	77	ruthenium	Ru	44
berkelium	Bk	97	iron	Fe	26	rutherfordium	Rf	104
beryllium	Be	4	krypton	Kr	36	samarium	Sm	62
bismuth	Bi	83	lanthanum	La	57	scandium	Sc	21
bohrium	Bh	107	lawrencium	Lr	103	seaborgium	Sg	106
boron	B	5	lead	Pb	82	selenium	Se	34
bromine	Br	35	lithium	Li	3	silicon	Si	14
cadmium	Cd	48	lutetium	Lu	71	silver	Ag	47
calcium	Ca	20	magnesium	Mg	12	sodium	Na	11
californium	Cf	98	manganese	Mn	25	strontium	Sr	38
carbon	C	6	meitnerium	Mt	109	sulphur	S	16
cerium	Ce	58	mendelevium	Md	101	tantalum	Ta	73
cesium	Cs	55	mercury	Hg	80	technetium	Tc	43
chlorine	Cl	17	molybdenum	Mo	42	tellurium	Te	52
chromium	Cr	24	neodymium	Nd	60	terbium	Tb	65
cobalt	Co	27	neon	Ne	10	thallium	Tl	81
copper	Cu	29	neptunium	Np	93	thorium	Th	90
curium	Cm	96	nickel	Ni	28	thulium	Tm	69
dubnium	Db	105	niobium	Nb	41	tin	Sn	50
dysprosium	Dy	66	nitrogen	N	7	titanium	Ti	22
einsteinium	Es	99	nobelium	No	102	tungsten	W	74
erbium	Er	68	osmium	Os	76	uranium	U	92
europium	Eu	63	oxygen	O	8	vanadium	V	23
fermium	Fm	100	palladium	Pd	46	xenon	Xe	54
fluorine	F	9	phosphorus	P	15	ytterbium	Yb	70
francium	Fr	87	platinum	Pt	78	yttrium	Y	39
gadolinium	Gd	64	plutonium	Pu	94	zinc	Zn	30
gallium	Ga	31	polonium	Po	84	zirconium	Zr	40
germanium	Ge	32	potassium	K	19			
gold	Au	79	praseodymium	Pr	59			

status HIGH, higher, high-ranking, of high standing, lofty, superior, exalted, eminent; grand, noble.
– OPPOSITES: lowly.

elevation ▶ noun **1** *his elevation to the directorship* PROMOTION, upgrading, advancement, advance, preferment, aggrandizement; ennoblement; *informal* step up the ladder. **2** *1500 to 3000 metres in elevation* ALTITUDE, height. **3** *elevations in excess of 3000 metres* HEIGHT, hill, mountain, mount; *formal* eminence. **4** *elevation of thought* GRANDEUR, greatness, nobility, loftiness, majesty, sublimity.

elevator ▶ noun **1** LIFT, *Mining* cage; dumb waiter. **2** *elevators on the prairie landscape* GRAIN ELEVATOR, country elevator ♣, primary elevator, terminal elevator, prairie sentinel ♣.

elf ▶ noun PIXIE, fairy, sprite, imp, brownie; dwarf, gnome, goblin, hobgoblin; leprechaun, puck, troll.

elfin ▶ adjective ELF-LIKE, elfish, elvish, pixie-like; puckish, impish, playful, mischievous; dainty, delicate, small, petite, slight, little, tiny, diminutive.

elicit ▶ verb OBTAIN, draw out, extract, bring out, evoke, call forth, bring forth, induce, prompt, generate, engender, trigger, provoke; *formal* educe.

eligible ▶ adjective **1** *those people eligible to vote* ENTITLED, permitted, allowed, qualified, able. **2** *an eligible bachelor* DESIRABLE, suitable; available, single, unmarried, unattached, unwed.

eliminate ▶ verb **1** *a policy that would eliminate inflation* REMOVE, get rid of, put an end to, do away with, end, stop, terminate, eradicate, destroy, annihilate, stamp out, wipe out, extinguish. **2** *he was eliminated in the first round of competition* KNOCK OUT, beat; exclude, rule out, disqualify.

elite ▶ noun BEST, pick, cream, crème de la crème, flower, nonpareil, elect; high society, jet set, beautiful people, beau monde, haut monde, glitterati; aristocracy, nobility, upper class.
– OPPOSITES: dregs.

elixir ▶ noun POTION, concoction, brew, philtre, decoction, mixture; medicine, tincture; extract, essence, concentrate, distillate, distillation; *literary* draft.

elliptical ▶ adjective **1** *an elliptical shape* OVAL, egg-shaped, elliptic, ovate, ovoid, oviform, ellipsoidal. **2** *elliptical phraseology* CRYPTIC, abstruse, ambiguous, obscure, oblique, Delphic; terse, concise, succinct, compact, economic, laconic, sparing, abridged.

elocution ▶ noun PRONUNCIATION, enunciation, articulation, diction, speech, intonation, vocalization, modulation; phrasing, delivery, public speaking.

elongate ▶ verb **1** *an exercise that elongates the muscles*

LENGTHEN, extend, stretch (out). **2** *the high notes were elongated* PROLONG, protract, draw out, sustain.
— OPPOSITES: shorten.

eloquence ▶ noun FLUENCY, articulateness, expressiveness, silver tongue, persuasiveness, forcefulness, power, potency, effectiveness; oratory, rhetoric, grandiloquence, magniloquence; *informal* gift of the gab, way with words.

eloquent ▶ adjective **1** *an eloquent speaker* FLUENT, articulate, expressive, silver-tongued; persuasive, strong, forceful, powerful, potent, well expressed, effective, lucid, vivid, graphic; smooth-tongued, glib. **2** *her glance was more eloquent than words* EXPRESSIVE, meaningful, suggestive, revealing, telling, significant, indicative.
— OPPOSITES: inarticulate.

elsewhere ▶ adverb SOMEWHERE ELSE, in/at/to another place, in/at/to a different place, hence; not here, not present, absent, away, abroad, out.
— OPPOSITES: here.

elucidate ▶ verb EXPLAIN, make clear, illuminate, throw/shed light on, clarify, clear up, sort out, unravel, spell out; interpret, explicate; gloss.
— OPPOSITES: confuse.

elucidation ▶ noun EXPLANATION, clarification, illumination; interpretation, explication; gloss.

elude ▶ verb EVADE, avoid, get away from, dodge, escape from, run (away) from; lose, shake off, give the slip to, slip away from, throw off the scent; *informal* slip through someone's fingers, slip through the net.

elusive ▶ adjective **1** *her elusive husband* DIFFICULT TO FIND; evasive, slippery; *informal* always on the move. **2** *an elusive quality* INDEFINABLE, intangible, impalpable, ambiguous.

Elysian ▶ adjective HEAVENLY, paradisal, paradisiacal, celestial, divine; *literary* empyrean.

Elysium ▶ noun *(Greek Mythology)* HEAVEN, paradise, the Elysian fields; eternity, the afterlife, the next world, the hereafter; *Scandinavian Mythology* Valhalla; *Classical Mythology* the Islands of the Blessed; *Arthurian Legend* Avalon.

emaciated ▶ adjective THIN, skeletal, bony, gaunt, wasted; scrawny, skinny, scraggy, skin and bones, raw-boned, stick-like, waiflike; starved, underfed, undernourished, underweight, half-starved; cadaverous, shrivelled, shrunken, withered; *informal* anorexic, like a bag of bones.
— OPPOSITES: fat.

email ▶ noun ELECTRONIC MAIL, webmail, text messaging; correspondence, communication, message, mail, memo, letter.
▶ verb SEND, transmit, forward, mail.

emanate ▶ verb **1** *warmth emanated from the fireplace* ISSUE, spread, radiate, be sent forth/out. **2** *the proposals emanated from a committee* ORIGINATE, stem, derive, proceed, spring, issue, emerge, flow, come. **3** *he emanated an air of power* EXUDE, emit, radiate, give off/out, send out/forth.

emanation ▶ noun **1** *an emanation of his tortured personality* PRODUCT, consequence, result, fruit. **2** *radon gas emanation* DISCHARGE, emission, radiation, effusion, outflow, outpouring, flow, leak; *technical* efflux.

emancipate ▶ verb FREE, liberate, set free, release, deliver, discharge; unchain, unfetter, unshackle, untie, unyoke; *rare* disenthral.
— OPPOSITES: enslave.

emancipated ▶ adjective LIBERATED, independent, unconstrained, uninhibited; free.

emasculate ▶ verb **1** *the Opposition emasculated the committee's proposal* WEAKEN, enfeeble, debilitate, erode, undermine, cripple; remove the sting from, pull the teeth out of; *informal* water down. **2** *(archaic) young ganders should be emasculated at three months.* See CASTRATE.

embalm ▶ verb **1** *his body had been embalmed* PRESERVE, mummify, lay out. **2** *the poem ought to embalm his memory* PRESERVE, conserve, enshrine, immortalize.

embankment ▶ noun BANK, mound, ridge, earthwork, causeway, barrier, levee, dam, dike.

embargo ▶ noun *an embargo on oil sales* BAN, bar, prohibition, stoppage, interdict, proscription, veto, moratorium; restriction, restraint, block, barrier, impediment, obstruction; boycott.
▶ verb *arms sales were embargoed* BAN, bar, prohibit, stop, interdict, debar, proscribe, outlaw; restrict, restrain, block, obstruct; boycott.
— OPPOSITES: allow.

embark ▶ verb **1** *they embarked on their honeymoon cruise yesterday* BOARD SHIP, go on board, go aboard; *informal* hop on, jump on. **2** *he embarked on a new career* BEGIN, start, commence, undertake, set about, take up, turn one's hand to, get down to; enter into, venture into, launch into, plunge into, engage in, settle down to; *informal* get cracking on, get going on, have a go/crack/shot at.

embarrass ▶ verb MORTIFY, shame, put someone to shame, humiliate, abash, chagrin, make uncomfortable, make self-conscious; discomfit, disconcert, discompose, upset, distress; *informal* show up, discombobulate.

embarrassed ▶ adjective MORTIFIED, red-faced, blushing, abashed, shamed, ashamed, shamefaced, humiliated, chagrined, awkward, self-conscious, uncomfortable, sheepish; discomfited, disconcerted, upset, discomposed, flustered, agitated, distressed; shy, bashful, tongue-tied; *informal* with egg on one's face, wishing the earth would swallow one up.

embarrassing ▶ adjective HUMILIATING, shaming, shameful, mortifying, ignominious; awkward, uncomfortable, compromising; disconcerting, discomfiting, upsetting, distressing.

embarrassment ▶ noun **1** *he was scarlet with embarrassment* MORTIFICATION, humiliation, shame, shamefacedness, chagrin, awkwardness, self-consciousness, sheepishness, discomfort, discomfiture, discomposure, agitation, distress; shyness, bashfulness. **2** *his current financial embarrassment* DIFFICULTY, predicament, plight, problem, mess, imbroglio; *informal* bind, jam, pickle, fix, scrape. **3** *an embarrassment of riches* SURPLUS, excess, overabundance, superabundance, glut, surfeit, superfluity; abundance, profusion, plethora.

embassy ▶ noun **1** *the Italian embassy* CONSULATE, legation. **2** *(historical) the king sent an embassy to the rebels* ENVOY, representative, delegate, emissary; delegation, deputation, legation, (diplomatic) mission.

embed, imbed ▶ verb IMPLANT, plant, set, fix, lodge, root, insert, place; sink, drive in, hammer in, ram in.

embellish ▶ verb **1** *weapons embellished with precious metal* DECORATE, adorn, ornament; beautify, enhance, grace; trim, garnish, gild; deck, bedeck, festoon, emblazon; *literary* bejewel, bedizen. **2** *the legend was* *embellished in later retellings* ELABORATE, embroider, expand on, exaggerate.

embellishment ▶ noun **1** *architectural embellishments* DECORATION, ornamentation, adornment; beautification, enhancement, trimming, trim, garnishing, gilding. **2** *we wanted the truth, not romantic embellishments* ELABORATION, addition, exaggeration.

ember ▶ noun GLOWING COAL, live coal; cinder; (**embers**) ashes, residue.

embezzle ▶ verb MISAPPROPRIATE, steal, thieve, pilfer, purloin, appropriate, defraud someone of, siphon off, pocket, help oneself to; have one's hand in the till, abstract; *informal* rob, rip off, skim, line one's pockets, pinch.

embezzlement ▶ noun MISAPPROPRIATION, theft, stealing, robbery, thieving, pilfering, purloining, pilferage, appropriation, swindling; fraud, larceny.

embittered ▶ adjective BITTER, resentful, rancorous, jaundiced, aggrieved, sour, frustrated, dissatisfied, alienated, disaffected.

emblazon ▶ verb **1** *shirts emblazoned with the company name* ADORN, decorate, ornament, embellish; inscribe. **2** *a flag with a hammer and sickle emblazoned on it* DISPLAY, depict, show.

emblem ▶ noun SYMBOL, representation, token, image, figure, mark, sign; crest, badge, device, insignia, stamp, seal, heraldic device, coat of arms, shield; logo, trademark, brand. *See table.*

Canadian Floral Emblems

BC	Pacific dogwood
Alberta	wild rose
Saskatchewan	prairie lily
Manitoba	prairie crocus
Ontario	trillium
Quebec	blue flag iris
New Brunswick	purple violet
Nova Scotia	mayflower
Prince Edward Island	lady's slipper
Newfoundland and Labrador	pitcher plant
Yukon	fireweed
NWT	mountain avens
Nunavut	purple saxifrage

emblematic, emblematical ▶ adjective **1** *a situation emblematic of the industrialized twentieth century* SYMBOLIC, representative, demonstrative, suggestive, indicative. **2** *emblematic works of art* ALLEGORICAL, symbolic, metaphorical, parabolic, figurative.

embodiment ▶ noun PERSONIFICATION, incarnation, realization, manifestation, avatar, expression, representation, actualization, symbol, symbolization, materialization; paradigm, epitome, paragon, soul, model; type, essence, quintessence, exemplification, example, exemplar, ideal; *formal* reification.

embody ▶ verb **1** *he embodies the spirit of industrial capitalism* PERSONIFY, realize, manifest, symbolize, represent, express, concretize, incarnate, epitomize, stand for, typify, exemplify; *formal* reify, hypostatize. **2** *the changes embodied in the gun control legislation* INCORPORATE, include, contain, encompass; assimilate, consolidate, integrate, organize, systematize; combine.

embolden ▶ verb FORTIFY, make brave/braver, encourage, hearten, strengthen, brace, stiffen the

resolve of, lift the morale of; rouse, stir, stimulate, cheer, rally, fire, animate, inspirit, invigorate; *informal* buck up.
– OPPOSITES: dishearten.

embrace ▶ verb **1** *he embraced her warmly* HUG, take/ hold in one's arms, hold, cuddle, clasp to one's bosom, clasp, squeeze, clutch; caress; enfold, enclasp, encircle, envelop, entwine oneself around; *informal* canoodle, clinch. **2** *most provinces have embraced the concept* WELCOME, welcome with open arms, accept, take up, take to one's heart, adopt; espouse, support, back, champion. **3** *the faculty embraces a wide range of departments* INCLUDE, take in, comprise, contain, incorporate, encompass, cover, involve, embody, subsume, comprehend.
▶ noun *a fond embrace* HUG, cuddle, squeeze, clinch, caress, clasp; bear hug.

embrocation ▶ noun OINTMENT, lotion, cream, rub, salve, emollient, liniment, balm, unguent.

embroider ▶ verb **1** *a cushion embroidered with a pattern of golden keys* SEW, stitch; decorate, adorn, ornament, embellish. **2** *she embroidered her stories with colourful detail* ELABORATE, embellish, enlarge on, exaggerate, touch up, dress up, gild, colour; *informal* jazz up.

embroidery ▶ noun **1** *the girls were taught embroidery* NEEDLEWORK, needlepoint, needlecraft, sewing, tatting, crewel work, tapestry. **2** *fanciful embroidery of the facts* ELABORATION, embellishment, adornment, ornamentation, colouring, enhancement; exaggeration, overstatement, hyperbole.

embroil ▶ verb INVOLVE, entangle, ensnare, enmesh, catch up, mix up, bog down, mire.

embryo ▶ noun **1** *a human embryo* FETUS, fertilized egg, unborn child/baby, zygote. **2** *the embryo of a capitalist economy* GERM, nucleus, seed; rudimentary version, rudiments, basics, beginning, start.

embryonic ▶ adjective **1** *an embryonic chick* FETAL, unborn, unhatched; in utero. **2** *an embryonic pro-democracy movement* RUDIMENTARY, undeveloped, unformed, immature, incomplete, incipient, inchoate; fledgling, budding, nascent, emerging, developing, early, germinal.
– OPPOSITES: mature.

emcee ▶ noun MASTER OF CEREMONIES, MC, host, hostess, ringmaster, chairman.

emend ▶ verb CORRECT, rectify, repair, fix; improve, enhance, polish, refine, amend; edit, rewrite, revise, copy-edit, redraft, recast, rephrase, reword, rework, alter, change, modify; *rare* redact.

emerge ▶ verb **1** *a policeman emerged from the alley* COME OUT, appear, come into view, become visible, surface, materialize, manifest oneself, issue, come forth. **2** *several unexpected facts emerged* BECOME KNOWN, become apparent, be revealed, come to light, come out, turn up, transpire, unfold, prove to be the case.

emergence ▶ noun APPEARANCE, arrival, coming, materialization; advent, inception, dawn, birth, origination, start, development, rise.

emergency ▶ noun **1** *a military emergency* CRISIS, urgent situation, extremity, exigency; accident, disaster, catastrophe, calamity; difficulty, plight, predicament, danger. **2** *they took her to emergency* emergency room/department, emerg ♣, ER.
▶ adjective **1** *an emergency meeting* URGENT, crisis; impromptu, extraordinary. **2** *emergency supplies* RESERVE, standby, backup, fallback, in reserve.

emergent ▶ adjective EMERGING, developing, rising,

dawning, budding, embryonic, infant, fledgling, nascent, incipient, inchoate.

emigrate ▶ verb MOVE ABROAD, move overseas, leave one's country, migrate; relocate, resettle; defect.
– OPPOSITES: immigrate.

emigration ▶ noun MOVING ABROAD, moving overseas, expatriation, migration; exodus, diaspora; relocation, resettling; brain drain; defection.

eminence ▶ noun 1 *his eminence as a scientist* FAME, celebrity, illustriousness, distinction, renown, pre-eminence, notability, greatness, prestige, importance, reputation, repute, note; prominence, superiority, stature, standing. 2 *various legal eminences* IMPORTANT PERSON, dignitary, luminary, worthy, grandee, notable, notability, personage, leading light, VIP; *informal* somebody, someone, big shot, big gun, heavyweight. 3 *(formal) the hotel's eminence above the sea* ELEVATION, height, rise.

eminent ▶ adjective 1 *an eminent man of letters* ILLUSTRIOUS, distinguished, renowned, esteemed, pre-eminent, notable, noteworthy, great, prestigious, important, influential, outstanding, noted, of note; famous, celebrated, prominent, well-known, lionized, acclaimed, exalted, revered, august, venerable. 2 *the eminent reasonableness of their claims* OBVIOUS, clear, conspicuous, marked, singular, signal; total, complete, utter, absolute, thorough, perfect, downright, sheer.
– OPPOSITES: unknown.

eminently ▶ adverb VERY, greatly, highly, exceedingly, extremely, particularly, exceptionally, supremely, uniquely; obviously, clearly, conspicuously, markedly, singularly, signally, outstandingly, strikingly, notably, surpassingly; totally, completely, utterly, absolutely, thoroughly, perfectly, downright.

emissary ▶ noun ENVOY, ambassador, delegate, attaché, consul, plenipotentiary; agent, representative, deputy; messenger, courier; nuncio.

emission ▶ noun DISCHARGE, release, outpouring, outflow, leak, excretion, secretion, ejection; emanation, radiation, effusion, ejaculation, disgorgement, issuance.

emit ▶ verb 1 *the hydrocarbons emitted from vehicle exhausts* DISCHARGE, release, give out/off, pour out, send forth, throw out, void, vent, issue; leak, ooze, excrete, disgorge, secrete, eject, ejaculate; spout, belch, spew out; emanate, radiate, exude. 2 *he emitted a loud cry* UTTER, voice, let out, produce, give vent to, come out with, vocalize.
– OPPOSITES: absorb.

emollient ▶ adjective *a rich emollient shampoo* MOISTURIZING, soothing, softening.
▶ noun *she applied an emollient* MOISTURIZER, cream, lotion, oil, rub, salve, unguent, balm; *technical* humectant.

emolument ▶ noun *(formal)* SALARY, pay, payment, wage(s), earnings, allowance, stipend, honorarium, reward, premium; fee, charge, consideration; income, profit, gain, return.

emotion ▶ noun 1 *she was good at hiding her emotions* FEELING, sentiment; reaction, response. 2 *overcome by emotion, she turned away* PASSION, strength of feeling, warmth of feeling. 3 *responses based purely on emotion* INSTINCT, intuition, gut feeling; sentiment, the heart.

emotional ▶ adjective 1 *an emotional young man* PASSIONATE, hot-blooded, ardent, fervent, excitable, temperamental, melodramatic, tempestuous;

demonstrative, responsive, tender, loving, feeling, sentimental, sensitive. 2 *he paid an emotional tribute to his wife* POIGNANT, moving, touching, affecting, powerful, stirring, emotive, heart-rending, heart-warming, impassioned, dramatic; haunting, pathetic, sentimental; *informal* tear-jerking. 3 *during the speech we all became a little emotional* TEARFUL, lachrymose, teary-eyed, sad, choked up, weepy.
– OPPOSITES: unfeeling.

emotionless ▶ adjective UNEMOTIONAL, unfeeling, dispassionate, passionless, unexpressive, inexpressive, cool, cold, cold-blooded, impassive, indifferent, detached, remote, aloof; toneless, flat, dead, expressionless, blank, wooden, stony, deadpan, vacant, poker-faced.

emotive ▶ adjective 1 *a highly emotive book.* See EMOTIONAL sense 2. 2 *an emotive issue* CONTROVERSIAL, contentious, inflammatory; sensitive, delicate, difficult, problematic, touchy, awkward, prickly, ticklish.

empathize ▶ verb IDENTIFY, sympathize, be in sympathy, understand, share someone's feelings, be in tune; be on the same wavelength as, talk the same language as; relate to, feel for, have insight into; *informal* put oneself in someone else's shoes.

emperor ▶ noun RULER, sovereign, king, monarch, potentate; *historical* czar, kaiser, mikado, khan.
– RELATED TERMS: imperial.

emphasis ▶ noun 1 *the curriculum gave more emphasis to reading and writing* PROMINENCE, importance, significance, value; stress, weight, accent, attention, priority, pre-eminence, urgency, force. 2 *the emphasis is on the word 'little'* STRESS, accent, accentuation, weight, prominence; beat; *Prosody* ictus.

emphasize ▶ verb STRESS, underline, highlight, focus attention on, point up, lay stress on, draw attention to, spotlight, foreground, play up, make a point of; bring to the fore, insist on, belabour; accent, accentuate, underscore; *informal* press home, rub it in.
– OPPOSITES: understate.

emphatic ▶ adjective 1 *an emphatic denial* VEHEMENT, firm, wholehearted, forceful, forcible, energetic, vigorous, direct, assertive, insistent; certain, definite, out-and-out, one hundred per cent; decided, determined, categorical, unqualified, unconditional, unequivocal, unambiguous, absolute, explicit, downright, outright, clear. 2 *an emphatic victory* CONCLUSIVE, decisive, decided, unmistakable; resounding, telling; *informal* thundering.
– OPPOSITES: hesitant, narrow.

empire ▶ noun 1 *the Ottoman Empire* KINGDOM, realm, domain, territory, imperium; commonwealth; power, world power, superpower. 2 *a worldwide shipping empire* ORGANIZATION, corporation, multinational, conglomerate, consortium, company, business, firm, operation. 3 *his dream of empire* POWER, rule, ascendancy, supremacy, command, control, authority, sway, dominance, domination, dominion.
– RELATED TERMS: imperial.

empirical ▶ adjective EXPERIENTIAL, practical, heuristic, first-hand, hands-on; observed, seen, demonstrable.
– OPPOSITES: theoretical.

employ ▶ verb 1 *she employed a chauffeur* HIRE, engage, recruit, take on, secure the services of, sign up, sign, put on the payroll, enrol, appoint; retain, contract; indenture, apprentice. 2 *Julio was employed in carving a stone figure* OCCUPY, engage, involve, keep

busy, tie up; absorb, engross, immerse. **3** *the team employed subtle psychological tactics* USE, utilize, make use of, avail oneself of; apply, exercise, practise, put into practice, exert, bring into play, bring to bear; draw on, resort to, turn to, have recourse to.
— OPPOSITES: dismiss.

employed ▶ adjective WORKING, in work, in employment, holding down a job; earning, waged, breadwinning.

employee ▶ noun WORKER, member of staff, staffer; blue-collar worker, white-collar worker, workman, labourer, (hired) hand; wage earner; *informal* desk jockey; (**employees**) personnel, staff, workforce, human resources.

employer ▶ noun **1** *his employer gave him a glowing reference* MANAGER, boss, proprietor, director, chief, head man, head woman; *informal* boss man, skipper; padrone. **2** *the largest private sector employer in Saskatchewan* COMPANY, firm, business, organization, manufacturer.

employment ▶ noun **1** *she found employment as a clerk* WORK, labour, service; job, post, position, situation, occupation, profession, trade, métier, business, line, line of work, calling, vocation, craft, pursuit; *archaic* employ. **2** *the employment of children* HIRING, hire, engagement, taking on; apprenticing. **3** *the employment of nuclear weapons* USE, utilization, application, exercise.

emporium ▶ noun STORE, shop, outlet, retail outlet, superstore, megastore, department store, chain store, big box store, supermarket, hypermarket; establishment.

empower ▶ verb **1** *the act empowered police to arrest dissenters* AUTHORIZE, entitle, permit, allow, license, sanction, warrant, commission, delegate, qualify, enable, equip. **2** *movements to empower the poor* EMANCIPATE, unshackle, set free, liberate.
— OPPOSITES: forbid.

empress ▶ noun RULER, sovereign, queen, monarch, potentate; *historical* czarina.

emptiness ▶ noun *she had filled an emptiness in his life* VOID, vacuum, empty space, vacuity, gap, vacancy, hole, lack.

empty ▶ adjective **1** *an empty house* VACANT, unoccupied, uninhabited, untenanted, bare, desolate, deserted, abandoned; clear, free. **2** *an empty threat* MEANINGLESS, hollow, idle, vain, futile, worthless, useless, nugatory, insubstantial, ineffective, ineffectual. **3** *without her my life is empty* FUTILE, pointless, purposeless, worthless, meaningless, valueless, of no value, useless, of no use, aimless, senseless, hollow, barren, insignificant, inconsequential, trivial. **4** *his eyes were empty* BLANK, expressionless, vacant, deadpan, wooden, stony, impassive, absent, glazed, fixed, lifeless, emotionless, unresponsive.
— OPPOSITES: full, serious, worthwhile.
▶ verb **1** *I emptied the dishwasher* UNLOAD, unpack, void; clear, evacuate. **2** *he emptied out the contents of the case* REMOVE, take out, extract, tip out, pour out, dump out.
— OPPOSITES: fill.

empty-headed ▶ adjective STUPID, foolish, silly, unintelligent, idiotic, brainless, witless, vacuous, stunned ♣, vapid, feather-brained, birdbrained, hare-brained, scatterbrained, scatty, thoughtless, imbecilic; *informal* halfwitted, dumb, dim, airheaded, brain-dead, dippy, dizzy, dopey, dozy, spinny ♣,

flaky, soft in the head, slow on the uptake, ditsy, dumb-ass.
— OPPOSITES: intelligent.

empyrean (*literary*) ▶ adjective *the empyrean regions* HEAVENLY, celestial, ethereal; upper.
▶ noun (**the empyrean**) HEAVEN, the heavens, the sky, the upper regions, the stratosphere; *literary* the ether, the wide blue yonder, the firmament, the welkin.

emulate ▶ verb IMITATE, copy, mirror, echo, follow, model oneself on, take a leaf out of someone's book; match, equal, parallel, be on a par with, be in the same league as, come close to; compete with, contend with, rival, surpass.

enable ▶ verb ALLOW, permit, let, give the means to, equip, empower, make able, fit; make possible, facilitate; authorize, entitle, qualify; *formal* capacitate.
— OPPOSITES: prevent.

enact ▶ verb **1** *the Charter was enacted in 1982* PASS, make law, legislate; approve, ratify, sanction, authorize; impose, lay down, bring down. **2** *members of the church enacted a nativity play* ACT OUT, act, perform, appear in, stage, mount, put on, present.
— OPPOSITES: repeal.

enactment ▶ noun **1** *the enactment of a Bill of Rights* PASSING; ratification, sanction, approval, authorization; imposition. **2** *parliamentary enactments* ACT, law, bylaw, ruling, rule, regulation, statute, measure; *formal* ordinance; (**enactments**) legislation.

enamel ▶ noun COATING, lacquer, varnish, glaze, finish.

enamoured ▶ adjective IN LOVE, infatuated, besotted, smitten, captivated, enchanted, fascinated, bewitched, beguiled; keen on, taken with; *informal* mad about, crazy about, wild about, dotty about, bowled over by, struck on, hot on/for, sweet on, carrying a torch for, moonstruck; *literary* ensorcelled by.

encampment ▶ noun CAMP, military camp, bivouac, cantonment; campsite, camping ground; tents.

encapsulate ▶ verb **1** *their conclusions are encapsulated in one sentence* SUMMARIZE, sum up, give the gist of, put in a nutshell; capture, express. **2** *seeds encapsulated in resin* ENCLOSE, encase, contain, envelop, enfold, sheath, cocoon, surround.

enchant ▶ verb CAPTIVATE, charm, delight, enrapture, entrance, enthrall, beguile, bewitch, spellbind, fascinate, hypnotize, mesmerize, rivet, grip, transfix; *informal* bowl someone over.
— OPPOSITES: bore.

enchanter ▶ noun WIZARD, witch, sorcerer, warlock, magician, necromancer, magus; witch doctor, medicine man, shaman; *archaic* mage; *rare* thaumaturge.

enchanting ▶ adjective CAPTIVATING, charming, delightful, bewitching, beguiling, adorable, lovely, attractive, appealing, engaging, winning, fetching, winsome, alluring, disarming, seductive, irresistible, fascinating; *dated* taking.

enchantment ▶ noun **1** *a race of giants skilled in enchantment* MAGIC, witchcraft, sorcery, wizardry, necromancy; charms, spells, incantations, mojo; *rare* thaumaturgy. **2** *the enchantment of the garden by moonlight* ALLURE, delight, charm, beauty, attractiveness, appeal, fascination, irresistibility, magnetism, pull, draw, lure. **3** *being with him was sheer enchantment* BLISS, ecstasy, heaven, rapture, joy.

enchantress ▶ noun WITCH, sorceress, magician, fairy; Circe, siren.

encircle ▶ verb SURROUND, enclose, circle, girdle, ring, encompass; close in, shut in, fence in, wall in, hem in, confine; *literary* gird, engirdle.

enclose ▶ verb **1** *tall trees enclosed the garden* SURROUND, circle, ring, girdle, encompass, encircle; confine, close in, shut in, corral, fence in, wall in, hedge in, hem in; *literary* gird, engirdle. **2** *please enclose a stamped addressed envelope* INCLUDE, insert, put in; send.

enclosure ▶ noun PADDOCK, fold, pen, compound, stockade, ring, yard; sty, coop, corral.

encomium ▶ noun *(formal)* EULOGY, panegyric, paean, accolade, tribute, testimonial; praise, acclaim, acclamation, homage.

encompass ▶ verb COVER, embrace, include, incorporate, take in, contain, comprise, involve, deal with, range across; *formal* comprehend.

encounter ▶ verb **1** *I encountered a teacher I used to know* MEET, meet by chance, run into, come across/upon, stumble across/on, chance on, happen on; *informal* bump into. **2** *we encountered a slight problem* EXPERIENCE, hit, run into, come up against, face, be faced with, confront.
▶ noun **1** *an unexpected encounter* MEETING, chance meeting. **2** *a violent encounter between police and demonstrators* BATTLE, fight, clash, confrontation, struggle, skirmish, engagement; *informal* run-in, set-to, dust-up, scrap.

encourage ▶ verb **1** *the players were encouraged by the crowd's response* HEARTEN, cheer, buoy up, uplift, inspire, motivate, spur on, stir, stir up, fire up, stimulate, invigorate, vitalize, revitalize, embolden, fortify, rally; *informal* buck up, pep up, give a shot in the arm to. **2** *she had encouraged him to go* PERSUADE, coax, urge, press, push, pressure, pressurize, prod, goad, egg on, prompt, influence, sway; *informal* put ideas into one's head. **3** *the Provincial Government must encourage local businesses* SUPPORT, back, champion, promote, further, foster, nurture, cultivate, strengthen, stimulate; help, assist, aid, boost, fuel.
— OPPOSITES: discourage, dissuade, hinder.

encouragement ▶ noun **1** *she needed a bit of encouragement* HEARTENING, cheering up, inspiration, motivation, stimulation, fortification; support, morale-boosting, a boost, a shot in the arm. **2** *they required no encouragement to get back to work* PERSUASION, coaxing, urging, pep talk, pressure, prodding, prompting; spur, goad, inducement, incentive, bait, motive; *informal* carrot. **3** *the encouragement of foreign investment* SUPPORT, backing, championship, championing, sponsoring, promotion, furtherance, furthering, fostering, nurture, cultivation; help, assistance, boosterism.

encouraging ▶ adjective **1** *an encouraging start* PROMISING, hopeful, auspicious, propitious, favourable, bright, rosy; heartening, reassuring, cheering, comforting, welcome, pleasing, gratifying. **2** *my parents were very encouraging* SUPPORTIVE, understanding, helpful; positive, responsive, enthusiastic.

encroach ▶ verb INTRUDE, trespass, impinge, obtrude, impose oneself, invade, infiltrate, interrupt, infringe, violate, interfere with, disturb;

tread/step on someone's toes; *informal* horn in on, muscle in on; *archaic* entrench on.

encroachment ▶ noun INTRUSION, trespass, invasion, infiltration, incursion, infringement, impingement.

encumber ▶ verb **1** *her movements were encumbered by her heavy skirts* HAMPER, hinder, obstruct, impede, cramp, inhibit, restrict, limit, constrain, restrain, bog down, retard, slow (down); inconvenience, disadvantage, handicap. **2** *they are encumbered with debt* BURDEN, load, weigh down, saddle; overwhelm, tax, stress, strain, overload, overburden.

encumbrance ▶ noun **1** *he soon found the old equipment a great encumbrance* HINDRANCE, obstruction, obstacle, impediment, constraint, handicap, inconvenience, nuisance, disadvantage, drawback; *literary* trammel; *archaic* cumber. **2** *she knew she was an encumbrance to him* BURDEN, responsibility, obligation, liability, weight, load, stress, strain, pressure, trouble, worry; millstone, albatross, cross to bear; *informal* ball and chain.

encyclopedic ▶ adjective COMPREHENSIVE, complete, thorough, thoroughgoing, full, exhaustive, in-depth, wide-ranging, all-inclusive, all-embracing, all-encompassing, universal, vast; *formal* compendious.

end ▶ noun **1** *the end of the road* EXTREMITY, furthermost part, limit; margin, edge, border, boundary, periphery; point, tip, tail end, tag end, terminus. **2** *the end of the novel* CONCLUSION, termination, ending, finish, close, resolution, climax, finale, culmination, denouement; epilogue, coda, peroration. **3** *wealth is a means and not an end in itself* AIM, goal, purpose, objective, object, holy grail, target; intention, intent, design, motive; aspiration, wish, desire, ambition. **4** *the commercial end of the business* ASPECT, side, section, area, field, part, portion, segment, province. **5** *his end might come at any time* DEATH, dying, demise, passing, expiry, quietus; doom, extinction, annihilation, extermination, destruction; downfall, ruin, ruination, Waterloo; *informal* curtains, final decease.
— OPPOSITES: beginning.
▶ verb **1** *the show ended with a wedding scene* FINISH, conclude, terminate, come to an end, draw to a close, close, stop, cease; culminate, climax, build up to, lead up to, come to a head. **2** *she ended their relationship* BREAK OFF, call off, bring to an end, put an end to, stop, finish, terminate, discontinue, curtail; dissolve, cancel, annul; *informal* can, axe.
— OPPOSITES: begin.

endanger ▶ verb IMPERIL, jeopardize, risk, put at risk, put in danger, expose to danger; threaten, pose a threat to, be a danger to, be detrimental to, damage, injure, harm; *archaic* peril.

endearing ▶ adjective LOVABLE, adorable, cute, sweet, dear, delightful, lovely, charming, appealing, attractive, engaging, winning, captivating, enchanting, beguiling, winsome.

endearment ▶ noun **1** *his murmured endearments* TERM OF AFFECTION, term of endearment, pet name; **(endearments)** sweet nothings, sweet talk. **2** *he spoke to her without endearment* AFFECTION, fondness, tenderness, feeling, sentiment, warmth, love, liking, care.

endeavour ▶ verb *the company endeavoured to expand its activities* TRY, attempt, seek, undertake, aspire, aim, set out; strive, struggle, labour, toil, work, exert oneself, apply oneself, do one's best, do one's utmost, give one's all, be at pains; *informal* have a go/shot/stab, give something one's best shot, do one's damnedest, go all out, bend over backwards; *formal* essay.

▶ **noun 1** *an endeavour to build a more buoyant economy* ATTEMPT, try, bid, effort, venture; *informal* go, crack, shot, stab, bash; *formal* essay. **2** *several days of endeavour* EFFORT, exertion, striving, struggling, labouring, toil, struggle, labour, hard work, application, industry; pains; *informal* sweat, {blood, sweat, and tears}, elbow grease; *literary* travail. **3** *an extremely unwise endeavour* UNDERTAKING, enterprise, venture, exercise, activity, exploit, deed, act, action, move; scheme, plan, project; *informal* caper.

ending ▶ noun END, finish, close, closing, conclusion, resolution, summing-up, denouement, finale; cessation, stopping, termination, discontinuation; *informal* outro.
— OPPOSITES: beginning.

endless ▶ adjective **1** *a woman with endless energy* UNLIMITED, limitless, infinite, inexhaustible, boundless, unbounded, untold, immeasurable, measureless, incalculable; abundant, abounding, great; bottomless, ceaseless, unceasing, unending, without end, everlasting, constant, continuous, continual, interminable, unfading, unfailing, perpetual, eternal, enduring, lasting. **2** *as children we played endless games* COUNTLESS, innumerable, untold, legion, numberless, unnumbered, numerous, very many, manifold, multitudinous, multifarious; a great number of, infinite numbers of, a multitude of; *informal* umpteen, no end of, loads of, stacks of, heaps of, masses of, oodles of, scads of, zillions of, gazillions of; *literary* myriad, divers.
— OPPOSITES: limited, few.

endorse ▶ verb **1** *endorse a product* SUPPORT, back, agree with, approve (of), favour, subscribe to, recommend, champion, stick up for, uphold, affirm, sanction; *informal* throw one's weight behind, okay. **2** *endorse a cheque* COUNTERSIGN, sign, autograph, authenticate.
— OPPOSITES: oppose.

endorsement ▶ noun SUPPORT, backing, approval, endorsation ♣, seal of approval, agreement, recommendation, championship, patronage, affirmation, sanction; *informal* buy-in.

endow ▶ verb **1** *the CEO endowed a hospital for sick kids* FINANCE, fund, pay for, provide for, subsidize, support financially, settle money on; establish, found, set up, institute. **2** *nature endowed fish with gills* PROVIDE, supply, furnish, equip, invest, favour, bless, grace, gift; give, bestow; *literary* endue.

endowment ▶ noun **1** *the endowment of a Chair of Botany* FUNDING, financing, subsidizing; establishment, foundation, institution. **2** *her will contained a generous endowment* BEQUEST, legacy, inheritance; gift, present, grant, award, donation, contribution, subsidy, settlement; *formal* benefaction. **3** *his natural endowments* QUALITY, characteristic, feature, attribute, facility, faculty, ability, talent, gift, strength, aptitude, capability, capacity.

endurable ▶ adjective BEARABLE, tolerable, supportable, manageable, sustainable.
— OPPOSITES: unbearable.

endurance ▶ noun **1** *she pushed him beyond the limit of his endurance* TOLERATION, tolerance, sufferance, forbearance, patience, acceptance, resignation, stoicism. **2** *the race is a test of endurance* STAMINA, staying power, fortitude, perseverance, persistence,

tenacity, doggedness, grit, indefatigability, resolution, determination; *formal* pertinacity.

endure ▶ verb **1** *he endured years of pain* UNDERGO, go through, live through, experience, meet, encounter; cope with, deal with, face, suffer, tolerate, put up with, brave, bear, withstand, sustain, weather. **2** *I cannot endure such behaviour* TOLERATE, bear, put up with, suffer, take, abide; *informal* hack, stand for, stomach, swallow, hold with; *formal* brook. **3** *our love will endure forever* LAST, live, live on, go on, survive, abide, continue, persist, persevere, remain, stay.
— OPPOSITES: fade.

enduring ▶ adjective LASTING, long-lasting, abiding, durable, continuing, persisting, eternal, perennial, permanent, unending, everlasting; constant, stable, steady, steadfast, fixed, firm, unwavering, unfaltering, unchanging; *literary* amaranthine.
— OPPOSITES: short-lived.

enemy ▶ noun OPPONENT, adversary, rival, antagonist, combatant, challenger, competitor, opposer, opposition, competition, other side, foe.
— OPPOSITES: ally.

energetic ▶ adjective **1** *an energetic teacher* ACTIVE, lively, dynamic, zestful, spirited, animated, vital, vibrant, bouncy, bubbly, exuberant, ebullient, perky, frisky, sprightly, tireless, indefatigable, enthusiastic; *informal* peppy, feisty, full of beans, bright-eyed and bushy-tailed. **2** *energetic exercises* VIGOROUS, strenuous, brisk; hard, arduous, demanding, taxing, tough, rigorous. **3** *an energetic advertising campaign* FORCEFUL, vigorous, high-powered, all-out, determined, bold, powerful, potent; intensive, hard-hitting, pulling no punches, aggressive, high-octane; *informal* punchy, in-your-face.
— OPPOSITES: lethargic, gentle, half-hearted.

energize ▶ verb **1** *people are energized by his ideas* ENLIVEN, liven up, animate, vitalize, invigorate, perk up, excite, electrify, stimulate, stir up, fire up, rouse, motivate, move, drive, spur on, encourage, galvanize; *informal* pep up, buck up, jump-start, kick-start, give a shot in the arm to, turbocharge. **2** *floor sensors energized by standing passengers* ACTIVATE, trigger, trip, operate, actuate, switch on, turn on, start, start up, power.

energy ▶ noun VITALITY, vigour, life, liveliness, animation, vivacity, spirit, spiritedness, verve, enthusiasm, zest, vibrancy, spark, sparkle, effervescence, ebullience, exuberance, buoyancy, sprightliness; strength, stamina, forcefulness, power, dynamism, drive, fire, passion, ardour, zeal; *informal* zip, zing, pep, pizzazz, punch, bounce, oomph, moxie, mojo, go, get-up-and-go, vim and vigour, feistiness.

enervate ▶ verb EXHAUST, tire, fatigue, weary, wear out, devitalize, drain, sap, weaken, enfeeble, debilitate, incapacitate, prostrate; *informal* knock out, do in, shatter.
— OPPOSITES: invigorate.

enervation ▶ noun FATIGUE, exhaustion, tiredness, weariness, lassitude, weakness, feebleness, debilitation, indisposition, prostration.

enfeeble ▶ verb WEAKEN, debilitate, incapacitate, indispose, lay low; drain, sap, exhaust, tire, fatigue, devitalize.
— OPPOSITES: strengthen.

enfold ▶ verb **1** *the summit was enfolded in white cloud* ENVELOP, engulf, sheathe, swathe, swaddle, cocoon, shroud, veil, cloak, drape, cover; surround, enclose, encase, encircle; *literary* enshroud, mantle. **2** *he enfolded her in his arms* CLASP, hold, fold, wrap, squeeze, clutch, gather; embrace, hug, cuddle; *literary* embosom.

enforce ▶ verb **1** *the sheriff enforced the law* IMPOSE, apply, administer, implement, bring to bear, discharge, execute, prosecute. **2** *they cannot enforce co-operation between the parties* FORCE, compel, coerce, exact, extort; *archaic* constrain.

enforced ▶ adjective COMPULSORY, obligatory, mandatory, involuntary, forced, imposed, required, requisite, stipulated, prescribed, contractual, binding, necessary, unavoidable, inescapable.
— OPPOSITES: voluntary.

enfranchise ▶ verb **1** *women were enfranchised in Manitoba in 1916* GIVE THE VOTE TO, give/grant suffrage to. **2** *(historical) he enfranchised his slaves* EMANCIPATE, liberate, free, set free, release; unchain, unyoke, unfetter, unshackle.

engage ▶ verb **1** *tasks which engage children's interest* CAPTURE, catch, arrest, grab, snag, draw, attract, gain, win, hold, grip, captivate, engross, absorb, occupy. **2** *he engaged a nursemaid to do the job* EMPLOY, hire, recruit, take on, secure the services of, put on the payroll, enrol, appoint. **3** *he engaged to pay them $10,000* CONTRACT, promise, agree, pledge, vow, covenant, commit oneself, bind oneself, undertake, enter into an agreement. **4** *the chance to engage in many social activities* PARTICIPATE IN, take part in, join in, become involved in, go in for, partake in/of, share in, play a part/role in; have a hand in, be a party to, enter into. **5** *infantry units engaged the enemy* FIGHT, do battle with, wage war on/against, attack, take on, set upon, clash with, skirmish with; encounter, meet.
— OPPOSITES: lose, dismiss.

engaged ▶ adjective **1** *he's otherwise engaged* BUSY, occupied, unavailable; *informal* tied up. **2** *she's engaged to an American guy* promised/pledged in marriage; attached; *informal* spoken for; *dated* betrothed; *literary* affianced; *archaic* plighted, espoused.
— OPPOSITES: free, unattached.

engagement ▶ noun **1** *they broke off their engagement* MARRIAGE CONTRACT; *dated* betrothal; *archaic* espousal. **2** *a social engagement* APPOINTMENT, meeting, arrangement, commitment, date, assignation, rendezvous; *literary* tryst. **3** *the first engagement of the war* BATTLE, fight, clash, confrontation, encounter, conflict, skirmish; warfare, action, combat, hostilities; *informal* dogfight.

engaging ▶ adjective **1** *an engaging young person* CHARMING, appealing, attractive, pretty, delightful, lovely, pleasing, pleasant, agreeable, likeable, winsome, enchanting, captivating. **2** *an engaging story* INTERESTING, engrossing, gripping, involving, absorbing, fascinating.
— OPPOSITES: unappealing, boring.

engender ▶ verb **1** *his works engendered considerable controversy* CAUSE, be the cause of, give rise to, bring about, occasion, lead to, result in, produce, create, generate, arouse, rouse, inspire, provoke, prompt, kindle, trigger, spark, stir up, whip up, induce, incite, instigate, foment; *literary* beget, enkindle. **2** *(archaic) he engendered six children* FATHER, sire, bring into the world, spawn, breed; *literary* beget.

engine ▶ noun **1** *a power-generating engine* MOTOR, machine, mechanism; jet, turbojet, turboprop, turbofan, turbine, generator. **2** *the main engine of change* CAUSE, agent, instrument, originator, initiator, generator. **3** *(historical) engines of war* DEVICE,

contraption, apparatus, machine, appliance, mechanism, implement, instrument, tool.

engineer ▶ noun **1** *a structural engineer* designer, planner, builder. *See table.* **2** *the ship's engineer* OPERATOR, driver, controller. **3** *the prime engineer of the approach* ORIGINATOR, deviser, designer, architect, inventor, developer, creator; mastermind.
▶ verb *he engineered a takeover deal* BRING ABOUT, arrange, pull off, bring off, contrive, manoeuvre, manipulate, negotiate, organize, orchestrate, choreograph, mount, stage, mastermind, originate, manage, stage-manage, coordinate, control, superintend, direct, conduct; *informal* wangle.

Branches of Engineering

aerospace engineering	genetic engineering
agricultural engineering	geotechnical engineering
bioengineering	human engineering
chemical engineering	industrial engineering
civil engineering	knowledge engineering
electrical engineering	mechanical engineering
electronic engineering	nuclear engineering
environmental engineering	structural engineering

engrained ▶ adjective. *See* INGRAINED.

engrave ▶ verb **1** *my name was engraved on the ring* CARVE, inscribe, cut (in), incise, chisel, chase, score, notch, etch, imprint, impress. **2** *the image was engraved in his memory* FIX, set, imprint, stamp, brand, impress, embed, etch.

engraving ▶ noun ETCHING, print, impression, lithograph; plate, dry point, woodcut, linocut.

engross ▶ verb ABSORB, engage, rivet, grip, hold, interest, involve, occupy, preoccupy; fascinate, captivate, enthrall, intrigue.

engrossed ▶ adjective ABSORBED, involved, interested, engaged, occupied, preoccupied, immersed, caught up, riveted, gripped, rapt, fascinated, intent, captivated, enthralled, intrigued.

engrossing ▶ adjective ABSORBING, interesting, riveting, gripping, captivating, compelling, compulsive, fascinating, intriguing, enthralling, engaging; *informal* unputdownable.

engulf ▶ verb INUNDATE, flood, deluge, immerse, swamp, swallow up, submerge; bury, envelop, overwhelm.

enhance ▶ verb INCREASE, add to, intensify, heighten, magnify, amplify, inflate, strengthen, build up, supplement, augment, boost, raise, lift, elevate, exalt; improve, enrich, complement.
— OPPOSITES: diminish.

enigma ▶ noun MYSTERY, puzzle, riddle, conundrum, paradox, problem, quandary; a closed book; *informal* poser.

enigmatic ▶ adjective MYSTERIOUS, inscrutable, puzzling, mystifying, baffling, perplexing, impenetrable, unfathomable, sphinx-like, Delphic, oracular; cryptic, elliptical, ambiguous, equivocal, paradoxical, obscure, oblique, secret.

enjoin ▶ verb URGE, encourage, admonish, press; instruct, direct, require, order, command, tell, call on, demand, charge; *formal* adjure; *literary* bid.

enjoy ▶ verb **1** *he enjoys playing the piano* LIKE, love, be fond of, be entertained by, take pleasure in, be keen on, delight in, appreciate, relish, revel in, adore, lap

up, savour, luxuriate in, bask in; *informal* get a kick out of, get a thrill out of, dig. **2** *she had always enjoyed good health* BENEFIT FROM, have the benefit of; be blessed with, be favoured with, be endowed with, be possessed of, possess, own, boast.
− OPPOSITES: dislike, lack.

■ **enjoy oneself** HAVE FUN, have a good time, have the time of one's life; make merry, celebrate, revel, disport; *informal* party, groove, love life, have a ball, have a whale of a time, whoop it up, let one's hair down.

enjoyable ▶ adjective ENTERTAINING, amusing, agreeable, pleasurable, diverting, engaging, delightful, to one's liking, pleasant, congenial, convivial, lovely, fine, good, great, delicious, delectable, satisfying, gratifying; marvellous, wonderful, magnificent, splendid; *informal* super, fantastic, fabulous, fab, terrific, magic, groovy, killer.

enjoyment ▶ noun PLEASURE, fun, entertainment, amusement, diversion, recreation, relaxation; delight, happiness, merriment, joy, gaiety, jollity; satisfaction, gratification, liking, relish, gusto; *humorous* delectation.

enlarge ▶ verb **1** *they enlarged the scope of their research* EXTEND, expand, grow, add to, amplify, augment, magnify, build up, supplement; widen, broaden, stretch, lengthen; elongate, deepen, thicken. **2** *the lymph glands had enlarged* SWELL, distend, bloat, bulge, dilate, tumefy, blow up, puff up, balloon. **3** *he enlarged on this subject* ELABORATE ON, expand on, add to, build on, flesh out, add detail to; expatiate on; develop, fill out, embellish, embroider.
− OPPOSITES: reduce, shrink.

enlargement ▶ noun EXPANSION, extension, growth, amplification, augmentation, addition, magnification, widening, broadening, lengthening; elongation, deepening, thickening; swelling, distension, dilation.

enlighten ▶ verb INFORM, tell, make aware, open someone's eyes, notify, illuminate, apprise, brief, update, bring up to date; disabuse, set straight; *informal* put in the picture, clue in, fill in, put wise, bring up to speed.

enlightened ▶ adjective INFORMED, well-informed, aware, sophisticated, advanced, developed, liberal, open-minded, broad-minded, educated, knowledgeable, wise; civilized, refined, cultured, cultivated.
− OPPOSITES: benighted.

enlightenment ▶ noun INSIGHT, understanding, awareness, wisdom, education, learning, knowledge; illumination, awakening, instruction, teaching; sophistication, advancement, development, open-mindedness, broad-mindedness; culture, refinement, cultivation, civilization.

enlist ▶ verb **1** *he enlisted in the cadets* JOIN UP, join, enrol in, sign up for, volunteer for. **2** *he was enlisted in the army* RECRUIT, call up, enrol, sign up; conscript; draft, induct; *archaic* levy. **3** *he enlisted the help of a friend* OBTAIN, engage, secure, win, get, procure.

enliven ▶ verb **1** *a meeting enlivened by her wit and vivacity* LIVEN UP, spice up, add spice to, ginger up, vitalize, leaven; *informal* perk up, pep up. **2** *the visit had enlivened my mother* CHEER UP, brighten up, liven up, raise someone's spirits, uplift, gladden, buoy up, animate, vivify, vitalize, invigorate, restore, revive, refresh, rejuvenate, stimulate, rouse, boost, exhilarate, light a fire under; *informal* perk up, buck up, pep up.

en masse ▶ adverb (ALL) TOGETHER, as a group, as one, en bloc, as a whole, wholesale; unanimously, with one voice.

enmesh ▶ verb EMBROIL, entangle, ensnare, snare, trap, entrap, ensnarl, involve, catch up, mix up, bog down, mire.

enmity ▶ noun HOSTILITY, animosity, antagonism, friction, antipathy, animus, acrimony, bitterness, rancour, resentment, aversion, ill feeling, bad feeling, ill will, bad blood, hatred, hate, loathing, odium; malice, spite, spitefulness, venom, malevolence.
− OPPOSITES: friendship.

ennoble ▶ verb DIGNIFY, honour, exalt, elevate, raise, enhance, add dignity to, distinguish; magnify, glorify, aggrandize.
− OPPOSITES: demean.

ennui ▶ noun BOREDOM, tedium, listlessness, lethargy, lassitude, languor, weariness, enervation; malaise, dissatisfaction, melancholy, depression, world-weariness, Weltschmerz.

enormity ▶ noun **1** *the enormity of the task* IMMENSITY, hugeness; size, extent, magnitude, greatness. **2** *the enormity of his crimes* WICKEDNESS, evil, vileness, baseness, depravity; outrageousness, monstrousness, hideousness, heinousness, horror, atrocity; villainy, cruelty, inhumanity, mercilessness, brutality, savagery, viciousness. **3** *the enormities of the regime* OUTRAGE, horror, evil, atrocity, barbarity, abomination, monstrosity, obscenity, iniquity; crime, sin, violation, wrong, offence, disgrace, injustice, abuse.

enormous ▶ adjective HUGE, vast, immense, gigantic, very big, great, giant, massive, colossal, mammoth, tremendous, mighty, monumental, epic, prodigious, mountainous, king-size(d), economy-size(d), titanic, towering, elephantine, gargantuan, Brobdingnagian; *informal* mega, monster, whopping, humongous, jumbo, astronomical, ginormous.
− OPPOSITES: tiny.

enormously ▶ adverb **1** *an enormously important factor* VERY, extremely, really, exceedingly, exceptionally, tremendously, immensely, hugely; singularly, particularly, eminently; *informal* terrifically, awfully, seriously, desperately, ultra, damn, damned, darn, darned; real, mighty. **2** *prices vary enormously* CONSIDERABLY, greatly, widely, very much, a great deal, a lot.
− OPPOSITES: slightly.

enough ▶ adjective *they had enough food* SUFFICIENT, adequate, ample, the necessary; *informal* plenty of.
− OPPOSITES: insufficient.
▶ pronoun *there's enough for everyone* SUFFICIENT, plenty, a sufficient amount, an adequate amount, as much as necessary; a sufficiency, an ample supply; one's fill.

en passant ▶ adverb IN PASSING, incidentally, by the way, parenthetically, while on the subject, apropos.

enquire ▶ verb. *See* INQUIRE.

enquiring ▶ adjective. *See* INQUIRING.

enquiry ▶ noun. *See* INQUIRY.

enrage ▶ verb ANGER, infuriate, incense, madden, inflame; antagonize, provoke, exasperate; *informal* drive mad/crazy, drive up the wall, make someone see red, make someone's blood boil, make someone's hackles rise, get someone's back up, get someone's

dander up; *informal* tick off, piss off, burn up.
— OPPOSITES: placate.

enraged ▶ adjective FURIOUS, infuriated, very angry, irate, incensed, raging, incandescent, fuming, ranting, raving, seething, beside oneself; *informal* mad, hopping mad, wild, livid, boiling, apoplectic, hot under the collar, on the warpath, foaming at the mouth, steamed up, fit to be tied, PO'd; *literary* wrathful.
— OPPOSITES: calm.

enrapture ▶ verb DELIGHT, enchant, captivate, charm, enthrall, entrance, bewitch, beguile, transport, thrill, excite, exhilarate, intoxicate, take someone's breath away; *informal* bowl someone over, blow someone's mind; *literary* ravish.

enrich ▶ verb ENHANCE, improve, better, add to, augment; supplement, complement; boost, elevate, raise, lift, refine.
— OPPOSITES: spoil.

enrol ▶ verb **1** *they both enrolled for the course* REGISTER, sign on/up, put one's name down, apply, volunteer; enter, join. **2** *280 new members were enrolled* ACCEPT, admit, take on, register, sign on/up, recruit, engage; empanel.

en route ▶ adverb ON THE WAY, in transit, during the journey, along/on the road, on the move; coming, going, proceeding, travelling.

ensconce ▶ verb SETTLE, install, plant, position, seat, sit, sit down; establish, nestle; hide away, tuck away; *informal* park, plonk.

ensemble ▶ noun **1** *a Bulgarian folk ensemble* GROUP, band; company, troupe, cast, chorus, corps; *informal* combo. **2** *the buildings present a charming provincial ensemble* WHOLE, entity, unit, body, set, combination, composite, package; sum, total, totality, entirety, aggregate. **3** *a pink and black ensemble* OUTFIT, costume, suit; separates, coordinates; *informal* getup.

enshrine ▶ verb PRESERVE, entrench, set down, lay down, set in stone, embody, incorporate, contain, include, treasure, immortalize, cherish.

enshroud ▶ verb *(literary)* ENVELOP, veil, shroud, swathe, cloak, cloud, enfold, surround, bury; cover, conceal, obscure, blot out, hide, mask; *literary* mantle.

ensign ▶ noun FLAG, standard, colour(s), banner, pennant, pennon, streamer, banderole.

enslave ▶ verb SUBJUGATE, suppress, tyrannize, oppress, dominate, exploit, persecute; *rare* enthrall, bind, yoke; disenfranchise.
— OPPOSITES: liberate, emancipate.

enslavement ▶ noun SLAVERY, servitude, bondage, forced labour; exploitation, oppression, bonds, chains, fetters, shackles, yoke; *historical* thraldom.
— OPPOSITES: liberation.

ensnare ▶ verb CAPTURE, catch, trap, entrap, snare, net; entangle, embroil, enmesh.

ensue ▶ verb RESULT, follow, develop, proceed, succeed, emerge, stem, arise, derive, issue; occur, happen, take place, come next/after, transpire, supervene; *formal* eventuate; *literary* come to pass, befall.

ensure ▶ verb **1** *ensure that the surface is completely clean* MAKE SURE, make certain, see to it; check, confirm, establish, verify. **2** *legislation to ensure equal opportunities for all* SECURE, guarantee, assure, certify, safeguard, set the seal on, clinch, entrench.

entail ▶ verb INVOLVE, necessitate, require, need, demand, call for; mean, imply; cause, produce, result in, lead to, give rise to, occasion.

entangle ▶ verb **1** *their parachutes became entangled* TWIST, intertwine, entwine, tangle, ravel, snarl, knot, coil, mat. **2** *the fish are easily entangled in fine nets* CATCH, capture, trap, snare, ensnare, entrap, enmesh. **3** *he was entangled in a lawsuit* INVOLVE, implicate, embroil, mix up, catch up, bog down, mire.

entanglement ▶ noun **1** *their entanglement in the war* INVOLVEMENT, embroilment. **2** *romantic entanglements* AFFAIR, relationship, love affair, romance, amour, fling, dalliance, liaison, involvement, intrigue; complication.

entente ▶ noun UNDERSTANDING, agreement, arrangement, entente cordiale, settlement, deal; alliance, treaty, pact, accord, convention, concordat.

enter ▶ verb **1** *police entered the house from the side* GO IN/INTO, come in/into, get in/into, set foot in, cross the threshold of, gain access to, infiltrate, access. **2** *a bullet entered his chest* PENETRATE, pierce, puncture, perforate; *literary* transpierce. **3** *he entered politics in 1979* GET INVOLVED IN, join, throw oneself into, engage in, embark on, take up; participate in, take part in, play a part/role in, contribute to. **4** *the planning entered a new phase* REACH, move into, get to, begin, start, commence. **5** *they entered the military at eighteen* JOIN, become a member of, enrol in/for, enlist in, volunteer for, sign up for; take up. **6** *she entered a cooking competition* GO IN FOR, put one's name down for, register for, enrol for, sign on/up for; compete in, take part in, participate in. **7** *the cashier entered the details in a ledger* RECORD, write, set down, put down, take down, note, jot down; put on record, minute, register, log. **8** *please enter your password* KEY (IN), type (in), tap in. **9** *(Law) he entered a plea of guilty* SUBMIT, register, lodge, record, file, put forward, present.
— OPPOSITES: leave.

enterprise ▶ noun **1** *a joint enterprise* UNDERTAKING, endeavour, venture, exercise, activity, operation, task, business, proceeding; project, scheme, plan, program, campaign. **2** *we want candidates with enterprise* INITIATIVE, resourcefulness, imagination, entrepreneurialism, ingenuity, inventiveness, originality, creativity; quick-wittedness, cleverness; enthusiasm, dynamism, drive, ambition, energy; boldness, daring, courage, leadership; *informal* gumption, get-up-and-go, oomph. **3** *a profit-making enterprise* BUSINESS, company, firm, venture, organization, operation, concern, corporation, establishment, partnership; *informal* outfit, set-up.

enterprising ▶ adjective RESOURCEFUL, entrepreneurial, imaginative, ingenious, inventive, creative; quick-witted, clever, bright, sharp, sharp-witted; enthusiastic, dynamic, proactive, ambitious, energetic; bold, daring, courageous, adventurous; *informal* go-ahead, take-charge, self-motivated.
— OPPOSITES: unimaginative.

entertain ▶ verb **1** *she wrote plays to entertain them* AMUSE, divert, delight, please, charm, cheer, interest; *informal* bring the house down; engage, occupy, absorb, engross. **2** *he entertains foreign visitors* RECEIVE, host, play host/hostess to, invite (round/over), throw a party for; wine and dine, feast, cater for, feed, treat, welcome, fete. **3** *we don't entertain much* RECEIVE GUESTS, have people round/over, have company, hold/throw a party. **4** *I would never entertain such an idea* CONSIDER, give consideration to, contemplate, think about, give thought to; countenance, tolerate, support; *formal* brook.
— OPPOSITES: bore, reject.

entertainer ▶ noun PERFORMER, artiste, artist.

entertaining ▶ adjective DELIGHTFUL, enjoyable, diverting, amusing, pleasing, agreeable, appealing, engaging, interesting, fascinating, absorbing, compelling; humorous, funny, comical; *informal* fun.

entertainment ▶ noun **1** *he read for entertainment* AMUSEMENT, pleasure, leisure, recreation, relaxation, fun, enjoyment, interest, diversion. **2** *an entertainment for the emperor* SHOW, performance, presentation, production, extravaganza, spectacle, pageant, mind candy.

enthrall ▶ verb CAPTIVATE, charm, enchant, bewitch, fascinate, beguile, entrance, delight; win, ensnare, absorb, engross, rivet, grip, transfix, hypnotize, mesmerize, spellbind.
— OPPOSITES: bore.

enthralling ▶ adjective FASCINATING, entrancing, enchanting, bewitching, captivating, charming, beguiling, delightful; absorbing, engrossing, compelling, riveting, gripping, exciting, spellbinding; *informal* unputdownable.

enthuse ▶ verb **1** *I enthused about the idea* RAVE, be enthusiastic, gush, wax lyrical, be effusive, get all worked up, rhapsodize; praise to the skies, extol; *informal* go wild/mad/crazy, ballyhoo. **2** *he enthuses people* MOTIVATE, inspire, stimulate, encourage, spur (on), galvanize, rouse, excite, stir (up), fire, inspirit.

enthusiasm ▶ noun **1** *she worked with enthusiasm* EAGERNESS, keenness, ardour, fervour, passion, zeal, zest, gusto, energy, verve, vigour, vehemence, fire, spirit, avidity; wholeheartedness, commitment, willingness, devotion, earnestness; *informal* get-up-and-go. **2** *he responded to the proposal with enthusiasm* INTEREST, admiration, approval, support, encouragement. **3** *they put their enthusiasms to good use* INTEREST, passion, obsession, mania; inclination, preference, penchant, predilection, fancy; pastime, hobby, recreation, pursuit.
— OPPOSITES: apathy.

enthusiast ▶ noun FAN, devotee, aficionado, lover, admirer, follower; expert, connoisseur, authority, pundit; *informal* buff, bum, freak, fanatic, nut, fiend, addict, maniac; geek, keener ♣, eager beaver.

enthusiastic ▶ adjective EAGER, keen, avid, ardent, fervent, passionate, ebullient, zealous, vehement; excited, wholehearted, committed, devoted, fanatical, earnest; *informal* hog-wild, can-do, gung-ho, rah-rah.

entice ▶ verb TEMPT, lure, allure, attract, appeal to; invite, persuade, convince, beguile, coax, woo, court; seduce, lead on; *informal* sweet-talk.

enticement ▶ noun LURE, temptation, allure, attraction, appeal, draw, pull, bait; charm, seduction, fascination; *informal* come-on.

enticing ▶ adjective TEMPTING, alluring, attractive, appealing, inviting, seductive, beguiling, charming; magnetic, irresistible.

entire ▶ adjective **1** *I devoted my entire life to him* WHOLE, complete, total, full; undivided. **2** *only one of the vases is entire* INTACT, unbroken, undamaged, unimpaired, unscathed, unspoiled, perfect, in one piece. **3** *they are in entire agreement* ABSOLUTE, total, utter, out-and-out, thorough, wholehearted; unqualified, unreserved, outright.
— OPPOSITES: partial, broken.

entirely ▶ adverb **1** *that's entirely out of the question* ABSOLUTELY, completely, totally, wholly, utterly, quite; altogether, in every respect, thoroughly,

downright, one hundred per ~~~; charitable purposes SOLELY, only, *entirely for* merely, just, alone. *purely,*

entirety ▶ noun WHOLE, total, ~~totality,~~ sum total.
— OPPOSITES: part.
■ **in its entirety** COMPLETELY, entirely, wholly; in every respect, in every way, ~~fully,~~ per cent, all the way, every inch, to the ~~red core;~~ *informal* holus-bolus.

entitle ▶ verb **1** *this pass entitles you to visit th~* QUALIFY, make eligible, authorize, allow, enable, empower. **2** *a chapter entitled 'Come~ Tragedy'* TITLE, name, call, label, head, designate, *formal* denominate.

entitlement ▶ noun *their entitlement to benefits* RIGH, prerogative, claim; permission, dispensation, privilege.

entity ▶ noun **1** *a single entity* BEING, creature, individual, organism, life form; person; body, object, article, thing. **2** *the distinction between entity and nonentity* EXISTENCE, being; life, living, animation; substance, essence, reality, actuality.

entomb ▶ verb INTER, lay to rest, bury; *informal* plant; *literary* inhume, sepulchre.

entourage ▶ noun RETINUE, escort, cortège, train, suite; court, staff, bodyguard; attendants, companions, retainers; *informal* posse.

entrails ▶ plural noun INTESTINES, bowels, guts, viscera, internal organs, vital organs; offal; *informal* insides, innards.

entrance¹ ▶ noun **1** *the main entrance* ENTRY, way in, entryway, entranceway, access, approach; door, portal, gate; opening, mouth; entrance hall, foyer, lobby, porch. **2** *the entrance of Mrs. Salter* APPEARANCE, arrival, entry, ingress, coming. **3** *he was refused entrance* ADMISSION, admittance, (right of) entry, access, ingress.
— OPPOSITES: exit, departure.

entrance² ▶ verb **1** *I was entranced by her beauty* ENCHANT, bewitch, beguile, captivate, mesmerize, hypnotize, spellbind; enthrall, engross, absorb, fascinate; stun, stupefy, overpower, electrify; charm, dazzle, delight; *informal* bowl over, knock out. **2** *Orpheus entranced the wild beasts* CAST A SPELL ON, bewitch, hex, spellbind, hypnotize, mesmerize.

entrance fee ▶ noun ADMISSION, cover charge, entry charge, ticket.

entrant ▶ noun **1** *university entrants* NEW MEMBER, new arrival, beginner, newcomer, freshman, recruit; novice, neophyte, tenderfoot, greenhorn; *informal* rookie, newbie. **2** *a prize will be awarded to the best entrant* COMPETITOR, contestant, contender, participant; candidate, applicant.

entrap ▶ verb **1** *fishing lines can entrap wildlife* TRAP, snare, snag, ensnare, entangle, enmesh; catch, capture. **2** *he was entrapped by an undercover policeman* ENTICE, lure, inveigle; bait, decoy, trap; lead on, trick, deceive, dupe, hoodwink, sting; *informal* set up, frame.

entreat ▶ verb IMPLORE, beg, plead with, pray, ask, request; bid, enjoin, appeal to, call on, petition, solicit, importune; *literary* beseech.

entreaty ▶ noun PLEA, appeal, request, petition; suit, application, claim; solicitation, supplication; prayer.

entree ▶ noun **1** *there are a dozen entrees on the menu* MAIN COURSE, main dish. **2** *an excellent entree into the profession* (MEANS OF) ENTRY, entrance, ingress; route, path, avenue, way, key, passport; *informal* in.

ent

······verb ESTABLISH, settle, lodge, set, root, **en**·· embed, seat; enshrine; *informal* dig in

/ed ▶ **adjective** INGRAINED, established, **l**, fixed, firm, deep-seated, deep-rooted; able, indelible, ineradicable, inexorable.

/reneur ▶ **noun** BUSINESSMAN/WOMAN, /riser, speculator, tycoon, magnate, mogul; r, trader; promoter, impresario; *informal* eler-dealer, whiz kid, mover and shaker, getter, high flyer, hustler, idea man/person.

tropy ▶ **noun** DETERIORATION, degeneration, rumbling, decline, degradation, decomposition, breaking down, collapse; disorder, chaos.

entrust ▶ **verb** 1 *he was entrusted with the task* CHARGE, invest, endow; burden, encumber, saddle. 2 *the powers entrusted to the Finance Minister* ASSIGN, confer on, bestow on, vest in, consign; delegate, depute, devolve; give, grant, vouchsafe. 3 *she entrusted them to the hospital* HAND OVER, give custody of, turn over, commit, consign, deliver; *formal* commend.

entry ▶ **noun** 1 *my moment of entry* APPEARANCE, arrival, entrance, ingress, coming. 2 *the entry to the building. See* ENTRANCE¹ sense 1. 3 *he was refused entry* ADMISSION, admittance, entrance, access, ingress. 4 *entries in the cash book* ITEM, record, note, listing; memo, memorandum; account. 5 *data entry* RECORDING, archiving, logging, documentation, capture, keying. 6 *we must pick a winner from the entries* CONTESTANT, competitor, contender, entrant, participant; candidate, applicant; submission, entry form, application.
— OPPOSITES: departure, exit.

entry-level ▶ **adjective** INTRODUCTORY, elementary, basic, first, starter, junior.

entwine ▶ **verb** WIND ROUND, twist round, coil round; weave, intertwine, interlace, interweave; entangle, tangle; twine, braid, plait, wreathe, knit.

enumerate ▶ **verb** 1 *he enumerated four objectives* LIST, itemize, set out, give; cite, name, specify, identify, spell out, detail, particularize. 2 *they enumerated voters* CALCULATE, compute, count, add up, tally, total, number, quantify; reckon, work out, tot up.

enunciate ▶ **verb** 1 *she enunciated each word slowly* PRONOUNCE, articulate; say, speak, utter, voice, vocalize, sound. 2 *a document enunciating the policy* EXPRESS, state, put into words, declare, profess, set forth, assert, air; put forward, air, proclaim.

envelop ▶ **verb** SURROUND, cover, enfold, engulf, encircle, encompass, cocoon, sheathe, swathe, enclose; cloak, screen, shield, veil, shroud.

envelope ▶ **noun** WRAPPER, wrapping, sleeve, cover, covering, casing, package.

enviable ▶ **adjective** DESIRABLE, desired, favoured, sought-after, admirable, covetable, attractive; fortunate, lucky; *informal* to die for.

envious ▶ **adjective** JEALOUS, covetous, desirous, grudging, begrudging, resentful; bitter.

environment ▶ **noun** 1 *birds from many environments* HABITAT, territory, domain; surroundings, environs, conditions. 2 *the hospital environment* SITUATION, SETTING, milieu, background, backdrop, scene, location; context, framework; sphere, world, realm; ambience, atmosphere. 3 *the impact of pesticides on the environment* THE NATURAL WORLD, nature, the earth, the planet, the ecosystem, the biosphere, Mother Nature; wildlife, flora and fauna, the countryside.

environmentalist ▶ **noun** CONSERVATIONIST, preservationist, ecologist, nature-lover; *informal* tree hugger, green, greenie.

environs ▶ **plural noun** SURROUNDINGS, surrounding area, vicinity, purlieu; locality, neighbourhood, district, region; precincts.

envisage ▶ **verb** IMAGINE, contemplate, visualize, envision, picture; conceive of, think of; foresee.

envision ▶ **verb** 1 *it was envisioned that the hospital would open soon* PLAN, envisage, predict, forecast, foresee, anticipate, expect; intend, mean. 2 *he envisioned a big shiny condominium* VISUALIZE, imagine, envisage, picture; conceive of, dream of, think of, see.

envoy ▶ **noun** AMBASSADOR, emissary, diplomat, consul, attaché, chargé d'affaires, plenipotentiary; nuncio; representative, delegate, proxy, surrogate, liaison, spokesperson; agent, intermediary, mediator; *informal* go-between; *historical* legate.

envy ▶ **noun** 1 *a pang of envy* JEALOUSY, covetousness; resentment, bitterness, discontent; the green-eyed monster. 2 *the firm is the envy of Europe* FINEST, best, pride, top, cream, jewel, flower, leading light, the crème de la crème.
▶ **verb** 1 *I admired and envied her* BE ENVIOUS OF, be jealous of; begrudge, be resentful of. 2 *we envied her lifestyle* COVET, desire, aspire to, wish for, want, long for, yearn for, hanker after, crave.

eon ▶ **noun** AGE, eternity, era; epoch.

ephemeral ▶ **adjective** TRANSITORY, transient, fleeting, passing, short-lived, momentary, brief, short; temporary, impermanent, short-term; fly-by-night.
— OPPOSITES: permanent.

epic ▶ **noun** 1 *the epics of Homer* HEROIC POEM; story, saga, legend, romance, chronicle, myth, fable, tale. 2 *a big Hollywood epic* long film; *informal* blockbuster.
▶ **adjective** 1 *a traditional epic poem* HEROIC, long, grand, monumental, Homeric, Miltonian. 2 *their epic journey* AMBITIOUS, heroic, grand, great, Herculean; very long, monumental; adventurous.

epicure ▶ **noun** GOURMET, gastronome, gourmand, connoisseur; *informal* foodie.

epicurean ▶ **noun** HEDONIST, sensualist, pleasure-seeker, sybarite, voluptuary, bon vivant, bon viveur; epicure, gourmet, gastronome, connoisseur, gourmand.
▶ **adjective** HEDONISTIC, sensualist, pleasure-seeking, self-indulgent, good-time, sybaritic, voluptuary, lotus-eating; decadent, unrestrained, extravagant, intemperate; immoderate; gluttonous, gourmandizing.

epidemic ▶ **noun** 1 *an epidemic of typhoid* OUTBREAK, plague, pandemic, epizootic. 2 *a joyriding epidemic* SPATE, rash, wave, eruption, outbreak, craze; flood, torrent; upsurge, upturn, increase, growth, rise.
▶ **adjective** *the craze is now epidemic* RIFE, rampant, widespread, wide-ranging, extensive, pervasive; global, universal, ubiquitous; endemic, pandemic, epizootic.

epigram ▶ **noun** WITTICISM, quip, jest, pun, bon mot; saying, maxim, adage, aphorism, apophthegm, epigraph; *informal* one-liner, wisecrack, (old) chestnut.

epigrammatic ▶ **adjective** CONCISE, succinct, pithy, aphoristic; incisive, short and sweet; witty, clever, quick-witted, piquant, sharp, gnomic, laconic; *informal* snappy.
— OPPOSITES: expansive.

epilogue ▶ **noun** AFTERWORD, postscript, PS, coda,

codicil, appendix, tailpiece, supplement, addendum, postlude, rider, back matter; conclusion.
– OPPOSITES: prologue.

episode ▸ noun **1** *the best episode of his career* INCIDENT, event, occurrence, happening; occasion, experience, adventure, exploit; matter, affair, thing; interlude, chapter. **2** *the final episode of the series* INSTALMENT, chapter, passage; part, portion, section, component; program, show. **3** *an episode of illness* PERIOD, spell, bout, attack, phase; *informal* patch.

episodic ▸ adjective **1** *episodic wheezing* INTERMITTENT, sporadic, periodic, fitful, irregular, spasmodic, occasional. **2** *an episodic account of the war* IN EPISODES, in instalments, in sections, in parts.
– OPPOSITES: continuous.

epistle ▸ noun (*formal*) LETTER, missive, communication, dispatch, note, line; news, correspondence.

epitaph ▸ noun ELEGY, commemoration, obituary; inscription, legend.

epithet ▸ noun SOBRIQUET, nickname, byname, title, name, label, tag; description, designation; *informal* moniker, handle; *formal* appellation, denomination.

epitome ▸ noun PERSONIFICATION, embodiment, incarnation, paragon; essence, quintessence, archetype, paradigm; exemplar, model, soul, example; height.

epitomize ▸ verb EMBODY, encapsulate, typify, exemplify, represent, manifest, symbolize, illustrate, sum up; personify; *formal* reify.

epoch ▸ noun ERA, age, period, time, span, stage; eon.

equable ▸ adjective **1** *an equable man* EVEN-TEMPERED, calm, composed, collected, self-possessed, relaxed, easygoing; nonchalant, insouciant, mellow, mild, tranquil, placid, stable, level-headed; imperturbable, unexcitable, untroubled, well-balanced, serene; *informal* unflappable, together, laid-back. **2** *an equable climate* STABLE, constant, uniform, unvarying, consistent, unchanging, changeless; moderate, temperate, (*Nfld*) civil ♣.
– OPPOSITES: temperamental, extreme.

equal ▸ adjective **1** *lines of equal length* IDENTICAL, uniform, alike, like, the same, equivalent; matching, even, comparable, similar, corresponding. **2** *fares equal to a month's wages* EQUIVALENT, identical, amounting; proportionate; commensurate (with), on a par (with). **3** *equal treatment before the law* UNBIASED, impartial, non-partisan, fair, just, equitable; unprejudiced, non-discriminatory, egalitarian; neutral, objective, disinterested. **4** *an equal contest* EVENLY MATCHED, even, balanced, level; on a par, on an equal footing; *informal* fifty-fifty, neck and neck.
– OPPOSITES: different, discriminatory.
▸ noun *they did not treat him as their equal* EQUIVALENT, peer, fellow, coequal, like; counterpart, match, parallel.
▸ verb **1** *two plus two equals four* BE EQUAL TO, be equivalent to, be the same as; come to, amount to, make, total, add up to. **2** *he equalled the world record* MATCH, reach, parallel, be level with, measure up to. **3** *the fable equals that of any other poet* BE AS GOOD AS, be a match for, measure up to, equate with; be in the same league as, rival, compete with.
■ **equal to** CAPABLE OF, fit for, up to, good/strong enough for; suitable for, suited to, appropriate for.

equality ▸ noun **1** *we promote equality for women*

FAIRNESS, equal rights, equal opportunities, equity, egalitarianism; impartiality, even-handedness; justice. **2** *equality between supply and demand* PARITY, similarity, comparability, correspondence; likeness, resemblance; uniformity, evenness, balance, equilibrium, consistency, homogeneity, agreement, congruence, symmetry.

equalize ▸ verb **1** *attempts to equalize their earnings* MAKE EQUAL, make even, even out/up, level, regularize, standardize, balance, square, match; bring into line. **2** *the Sens equalized in the second period* EVEN THE SCORE, tie the score.

equanimity ▸ noun COMPOSURE, calm, level-headedness, self-possession, cool-headedness, presence of mind; serenity, tranquility, phlegm, imperturbability, equilibrium; poise, assurance, self-confidence, aplomb, sang-froid, nerve; *informal* cool.
– OPPOSITES: anxiety.

equate ▸ verb **1** *he equates criticism with treachery* IDENTIFY, compare, liken, associate, connect, link, relate, class, bracket. **2** *the rent equates to $24 per square foot* CORRESPOND, be equivalent, amount; equal. **3** *moves to equate supply and demand* EQUALIZE, balance, even out/up, level, square, tally, match; make equal, make even, make equivalent.

equation ▸ noun **1** *a quadratic equation* MATHEMATICAL PROBLEM, sum, calculation, question. **2** *the equation of success with riches* IDENTIFICATION, association, connection, matching; equivalence, correspondence, agreement, comparison. **3** *other factors came into the equation* SITUATION, problem, case, question; quandary, predicament.

equatorial ▸ adjective TROPICAL, hot, humid, sultry.
– OPPOSITES: polar.

equestrian ▸ adjective *an equestrian statue* ON HORSEBACK, mounted, riding.
▸ noun *tracks for equestrians* (HORSEBACK) RIDER, horseman, horsewoman, jockey.

equilibrium ▸ noun **1** *the equilibrium of the economy* BALANCE, symmetry, equipoise, parity, equality; stability. **2** *his equilibrium was never shaken* COMPOSURE, calm, equanimity, sang-froid; level-headedness, cool-headedness, imperturbability, poise, presence of mind; self-possession, self-command; impassivity, placidity, tranquility, serenity; *informal* cool.
– OPPOSITES: imbalance, agitation.

equip ▸ verb **1** *the boat was equipped with a flare gun* PROVIDE, furnish, supply, issue, stock, provision, arm, endow, rig. **2** *the course will equip them for the workplace* PREPARE, qualify, suit, train, ready.

equipment ▸ noun APPARATUS, paraphernalia, articles, appliances, impedimenta; tools, utensils, implements, instruments, hardware, gadgets, gadgetry; stuff, things; kit, tackle, rig, equipage, (*Nfld*) fit-out ♣; resources, supplies; trappings, appurtenances, accoutrements; *informal* gear; *Military* matériel, baggage.

equitable ▸ adjective FAIR, just, impartial, even-handed, unbiased, unprejudiced, egalitarian; disinterested, objective, neutral, non-partisan, open-minded; *informal* fair and square.
– OPPOSITES: unfair.

equity ▸ noun **1** *the equity of Finnish society* FAIRNESS, justness, impartiality, egalitarianism; objectivity, balance, open-mindedness. **2** *he owns 25% of the equity in the property* VALUE, worth; ownership, rights, proprietorship.

equivalence ▶ noun EQUALITY, sameness, interchangeability, comparability, correspondence; uniformity, similarity, likeness, nearness.

equivalent ▶ adjective *a degree or equivalent qualification* EQUAL, identical; similar, comparable, corresponding, analogous, homologous, commensurate, parallel, synonymous; approximate, near.
▶ noun *Denmark's equivalent of Frank magazine* COUNTERPART, parallel, alternative, match, analogue, twin, opposite number; equal, peer; version.

equivocal ▶ adjective AMBIGUOUS, indefinite, noncommittal, vague, imprecise, inexact, inexplicit, hazy; unclear, cryptic, enigmatic, pettifogging; ambivalent, uncertain, unsure, indecisive.
− OPPOSITES: definite.

equivocate ▶ verb PREVARICATE, be evasive, be noncommittal, be vague, be ambiguous, dodge the question, beat around the bush, hedge, pussyfoot around; vacillate, shilly-shally, waver; temporize, hesitate, stall, hem and haw, sit on the fence; *rare* tergiversate.

era ▶ noun EPOCH, age, period, phase, time, span, eon; generation.

eradicate ▶ verb ELIMINATE, get rid of, remove, obliterate; exterminate, destroy, annihilate, kill, wipe out; abolish, stamp out, extinguish, quash; erase, efface, excise, expunge, expel; *informal* zap, nuke, clean house, wave goodbye to.

erase ▶ verb **1** *they erased his name from all lists* DELETE, rub out, wipe off, blot out, cancel; efface, expunge, excise, remove, obliterate, eliminate, cut. **2** *the old differences in style were erased* DESTROY, wipe out, obliterate, eradicate, abolish, stamp out, quash.

erect ▶ adjective **1** *she held her body erect* UPRIGHT, straight, vertical, perpendicular; standing. **2** *an erect penis* ENGORGED, enlarged, swollen, tumescent; hard, stiff, rigid. **3** *the dog's fur was erect* BRISTLING, standing on end, upright.
− OPPOSITES: bent, flaccid, flat.
▶ verb BUILD, construct, put up; assemble, put together, fabricate.
− OPPOSITES: demolish, dismantle, lower.

erection ▶ noun **1** *the erection of a house* CONSTRUCTION, building, assembly, fabrication, elevation. **2** *a bleak concrete erection* BUILDING, structure, edifice, construction, pile. **3** ERECT PENIS, phallus; tumescence.

ergo ▶ adverb THEREFORE, consequently, so, as a result, hence, thus, accordingly, for that reason, that being the case, on that account; *formal* whence; *archaic* wherefore.

ergonomic ▶ adjective WELL-DESIGNED, usable, user-friendly; comfortable, safe.

erode ▶ verb WEAR AWAY/DOWN, abrade, grind down, crumble; weather; eat away at, dissolve, corrode, rot, decay; undermine, weaken, deteriorate, destroy.

erosion ▶ noun WEARING AWAY, abrasion, attrition; weathering; dissolution, corrosion, decay; deterioration, disintegration, destruction.

erotic ▶ adjective SEXY, sexually arousing, sexually stimulating, titillating, suggestive; pornographic, sexually explicit, lewd, smutty, hard-core, soft-core, dirty, racy, risqué, ribald, naughty; sexual, sensual, amatory; seductive, alluring, tantalizing; *informal* blue, X-rated, steamy, raunchy; *euphemistic* adult.

err ▶ verb MAKE A MISTAKE, be wrong, be in error, be mistaken, blunder, fumble, be incorrect, miscalculate, get it wrong; sin, lapse; *informal* slip up, screw up, foul up, goof, make a boo-boo, drop the ball, bark up the wrong tree.

errand ▶ noun TASK, job, chore, assignment; collection, delivery; mission, undertaking.

errant ▶ adjective **1** *he fined the errant councillors* OFFENDING, guilty, culpable, misbehaving, delinquent, law-breaking; troublesome, unruly, wayward, disobedient. **2** *(archaic)* *a knight errant* TRAVELLING, wandering, itinerant, roaming, roving, voyaging.
− OPPOSITES: innocent.

erratic ▶ adjective UNPREDICTABLE, inconsistent, changeable, variable, inconstant, irregular, fitful, unstable, turbulent, unsettled, changing, varying, fluctuating, mutable; unreliable, undependable, volatile, spasmodic, mercurial, capricious, fickle, temperamental, moody.
− OPPOSITES: consistent.

erring ▶ adjective OFFENDING, guilty, culpable, misbehaving, errant, delinquent, law-breaking, aberrant, deviant.

erroneous ▶ adjective WRONG, incorrect, mistaken, in error, inaccurate, untrue, false, fallacious; unsound, specious, faulty, flawed; *informal* way out, full of holes.
− OPPOSITES: correct.

error ▶ noun MISTAKE, inaccuracy, miscalculation, blunder, oversight; fallacy, misconception, delusion; misprint, erratum; *informal* slip-up, boo-boo, goof.
■ **in error** WRONGLY, by mistake, mistakenly, incorrectly; accidentally, by accident, inadvertently, unintentionally, by chance.

ersatz ▶ adjective ARTIFICIAL, substitute, imitation, synthetic, fake, false, mock, simulated; pseudo, sham, bogus, spurious, counterfeit; manufactured, man-made; *informal* phony, wannabe.
− OPPOSITES: genuine.

erstwhile ▶ adjective FORMER, old, past, one-time, sometime, ex-, late, then; previous; *formal* quondam.
− OPPOSITES: present.

erudite ▶ adjective LEARNED, scholarly, educated, knowledgeable, well-read, well-informed, intellectual; intelligent, clever, academic, literary; bookish, highbrow, sophisticated, cerebral; *informal* brainy; *dated* lettered.
− OPPOSITES: ignorant.

erupt ▶ verb **1** *the volcano erupted* EMIT LAVA, become active, flare up; explode. **2** *fighting erupted* BREAK OUT, flare up, start suddenly; ensue, arise, happen. **3** *a boil erupted on her temple* APPEAR, break out, flare up, come to a head, suppurate, emerge.

eruption ▶ noun **1** *a volcanic eruption* DISCHARGE, ejection, emission; explosion. **2** *an eruption of violence* OUTBREAK, flare-up, upsurge, outburst, explosion; wave, spate. **3** *a skin eruption* RASH, outbreak, breakout, inflammation.

escalate ▶ verb **1** *prices have escalated* INCREASE RAPIDLY, soar, rocket, shoot up, mount, spiral, climb, go up, inflate; *informal* go through the roof, skyrocket. **2** *the dispute escalated* GROW, develop, mushroom, increase, heighten, intensify, accelerate.
− OPPOSITES: plunge, shrink.

escalation ▶ noun **1** *an escalation in oil prices* INCREASE, rise, hike, growth, leap, upsurge, upturn, climb. **2** *an escalation of the conflict* INTENSIFICATION, aggravation, exacerbation, magnification, amplification, augmentation; expansion, buildup; deterioration.

escapade ▶ noun EXPLOIT, stunt, caper, antic(s), spree, shenanigan, hijinks; adventure, venture, mission; deed, feat, trial, experience; incident, occurrence, event.

escape ▶ verb **1** *he escaped from prison* RUN AWAY/OFF, get out, break out, break free, make a break for it, bolt, flee, take flight, make off, take off, abscond, take to one's heels, make one's getaway, make a run for it; disappear, vanish, slip away, sneak away; *informal* cut and run, skedaddle, vamoose, fly the coop, take French leave, go on the lam. **2** *he escaped his pursuers* GET AWAY FROM, escape from, elude, avoid, dodge, shake off; *informal* give someone the slip. **3** *they escaped injury* evade, dodge, elude, miss, cheat, sidestep, circumvent, steer clear of; *informal* duck. **4** *lethal gas escaped* LEAK (OUT), seep (out), discharge, emanate, issue, flow (out), pour (out), gush (out), spurt (out), spew (out).
▶ noun **1** *his escape from prison* GETAWAY, breakout, jailbreak, bolt, flight; disappearance, vanishing act. **2** *a narrow escape from death* AVOIDANCE OF, evasion of, circumvention of. **3** *a gas escape* LEAK, leakage, spill, seepage, discharge, effusion, emanation, outflow, outpouring; gush, stream, spurt. **4** *an escape from boredom* DISTRACTION, diversion.

escapee ▶ noun RUNAWAY, escaper, absconder; jailbreaker, fugitive; truant; deserter, defector.

escapism ▶ noun FANTASY, fantasizing, daydreaming, daydreams, reverie; imagination, flight(s) of fancy, pipe dreams, wishful thinking, woolgathering; *informal* pie in the sky.
− OPPOSITES: realism.

eschew ▶ verb ABSTAIN FROM, refrain from, give up, forgo, shun, renounce, steer clear of, have nothing to do with, fight shy of; relinquish, reject, disavow, abandon, spurn, wash one's hands of, drop; *informal* kick, pack in; *formal* forswear, abjure.

escort ▶ noun **1** *a police escort* GUARD, bodyguard, protector, minder, attendant, chaperone; entourage, retinue, cortège; protection, defence, convoy. **2** *her escort for the evening* COMPANION, partner; *informal* date. **3** *an agency dealing with escorts* PAID COMPANION, hostess, geisha; gigolo.
▶ verb CONDUCT, accompany, guide, lead, usher, shepherd, bring, take; drive, walk.

esoteric ▶ adjective ABSTRUSE, obscure, arcane, recherché, rarefied, recondite, abstract; enigmatic, inscrutable, cryptic, Delphic; complex, complicated, incomprehensible, opaque, impenetrable, mysterious.

especial ▶ adjective **1** *especial care is required* PARTICULAR, (extra) special, superior, exceptional, extraordinary; unusual, out of the ordinary, uncommon, remarkable, singular. **2** *her especial brand of charm* DISTINCTIVE, individual, special, particular, distinct, peculiar, personal, own, unique, specific.

especially ▶ adverb **1** *complaints poured in, especially from Toronto* MAINLY, mostly, chiefly, principally, largely; substantially, particularly, primarily, generally, usually, typically. **2** *a committee especially for the purpose* EXPRESSLY, specially, specifically, exclusively, just, particularly, explicitly. **3** *he is especially talented* EXCEPTIONALLY, particularly, specially, very, extremely, singularly, strikingly, distinctly, unusually, extraordinarily, uncommonly, uniquely, remarkably, outstandingly, really; *informal* seriously, majorly.

espionage ▶ noun SPYING, infiltration; eavesdropping, surveillance, reconnaissance, intelligence, undercover work.

espousal ▶ noun ADOPTION, embracing, acceptance; support, championship, encouragement, defence; sponsorship, promotion, endorsement, advocacy, approval.

espouse ▶ verb ADOPT, embrace, take up, accept, welcome; support, back, champion, favour, prefer, encourage; promote, endorse, advocate.
− OPPOSITES: reject.

espy ▶ verb (*literary*) CATCH SIGHT OF, glimpse, see, spot, spy, notice, observe, discern, pick out, detect; *literary* behold.

essay ▶ noun **1** *he wrote an essay* ARTICLE, composition, study, paper, dissertation, thesis, discourse, treatise, disquisition, monograph; commentary, critique, theme. **2** (*formal*) *his first essay in telecommunications* ATTEMPT, effort, endeavour, try, venture, trial, experiment, undertaking.

essence ▶ noun **1** *the very essence of economics* QUINTESSENCE, soul, spirit, nature; core, heart, crux, nucleus, substance; principle, fundamental quality, sum and substance, warp and woof, reality, actuality; *informal* nitty-gritty. **2** *essence of ginger* EXTRACT, concentrate, distillate, elixir, decoction, juice, tincture; scent, perfume, oil.
■ **in essence** ESSENTIALLY, basically, fundamentally, primarily, principally, chiefly, predominantly, substantially; above all, first and foremost; effectively, virtually, to all intents and purposes; intrinsically, inherently.
■ **of the essence**. See ESSENTIAL *adjective* sense 1.

essential ▶ adjective **1** *it is essential to remove the paint* CRUCIAL, necessary, key, vital, indispensable, important, all-important, of the essence, critical, imperative, mandatory, compulsory, obligatory; urgent, pressing, paramount, pre-eminent, high-priority, non-negotiable. **2** *the essential simplicity of his style* BASIC, inherent, fundamental, quintessential, intrinsic, underlying, characteristic, innate, primary, elementary, elemental; central, pivotal, vital.
− OPPOSITES: unimportant, optional, secondary.
▶ noun **1** *an essential for broadcasters* NECESSITY, prerequisite, requisite, requirement, need; condition, precondition, stipulation; sine qua non; *informal* must. **2** *the essentials of the job* FUNDAMENTALS, basics, rudiments, first principles, foundations, bedrock; essence, basis, core, kernel, crux, sine qua non; *informal* nitty-gritty, brass tacks, nuts and bolts, meat and potatoes.

establish ▶ verb **1** *they established an office in Moscow* SET UP, start, initiate, institute, form, found, create, inaugurate; build, construct, install. **2** *evidence to establish his guilt* PROVE, demonstrate, show, indicate, signal, exhibit, manifest, attest to, evidence, determine, confirm, verify, certify, substantiate.

established ▶ adjective **1** *established practice* ACCEPTED, traditional, orthodox, habitual, set, fixed, official; usual, customary, common, normal, general, prevailing, accustomed, familiar, expected, routine, typical, conventional, standard. **2** *an established composer* WELL-KNOWN, recognized, esteemed, respected, famous, prominent, noted, renowned.

establishment ▶ noun **1** *the establishment of a democracy* FOUNDATION, institution, formation, inception, creation, installation; inauguration, start, initiation. **2** *a dressmaking establishment* BUSINESS, firm, company, concern, enterprise, venture, organization, operation; factory, plant, store, shop, office, practice; *informal* outfit, set-up. **3** *educational establishments* INSTITUTION, place, premises, foundation, institute. **4** *they dare to poke fun at the Establishment* THE AUTHORITIES, the powers that be, the system, the ruling class; the hierarchy, oligarchy; *informal* Big Brother; *historical* Château Clique ✦, Family Compact ✦.

estate ▶ **noun 1** *the lord's estate* PROPERTY, grounds, garden(s), park, parkland, land(s), landholding, manor, territory; *historical* seigneury ✦. **2** *a coffee estate* PLANTATION, farm, holding; forest, vineyard; ranch. **3** *he left an estate worth $610,000* ASSETS, capital, wealth, riches, fortune; property, effects, possessions, belongings; *Law* goods and chattels.

esteem ▶ **noun** *she was held in high esteem* RESPECT, admiration, acclaim, approbation, appreciation, favour, recognition, honour, reverence; estimation, regard, opinion.
▶ **verb 1** *such ceramics are highly esteemed* RESPECT, ADMIRE, value, regard, acclaim, appreciate, like, prize, treasure, favour, revere. **2** *(formal) I would esteem it a favour if you could speak to him.* See DEEM.

estimate ▶ **verb 1** *estimate the cost* CALCULATE ROUGHLY, approximate, guess; evaluate, judge, gauge, reckon, rate, determine; *informal* guesstimate, ballpark. **2** *we estimate it to be worth $50,000* CONSIDER, believe, reckon, deem, judge, rate, gauge.
▶ **noun 1** *an estimate of the cost* ROUGH CALCULATION, approximation, estimation, rough guess; costing, quotation, valuation, evaluation; *informal* guesstimate. **2** *his estimate of Paul's integrity* EVALUATION, estimation, judgment, rating, appraisal, opinion, view.

estimation ▶ **noun 1** *an estimation of economic growth* ESTIMATE, approximation, rough calculation, rough guess, evaluation; *informal* guesstimate, ballpark figure. **2** *she rated highly in Janice's estimation* ASSESSMENT, evaluation, judgment, perception; esteem, opinion, view.

estrange ▶ **verb** ALIENATE, antagonize, turn away, drive away, distance; sever, set at odds with, drive a wedge between.

estrangement ▶ **noun** ALIENATION, antagonism, antipathy, disaffection, hostility, unfriendliness; variance, difference; parting, separation, divorce, breakup, split, breach, schism.

estuary ▶ **noun** (RIVER) MOUTH, delta, (*BC*) slough ✦.

et cetera ▶ **adverb** AND SO ON, and so forth, and the rest, and/or the like, and suchlike, among others, et al., etc.; *informal* and what have you, and whatnot, and on and on, yada yada yada.

etch ▶ **verb** ENGRAVE, carve, inscribe, incise, chase, score, print, mark.

etching ▶ **noun** ENGRAVING, print, impression, block, plate; woodcut, linocut.

eternal ▶ **adjective 1** *eternal happiness* EVERLASTING, never-ending, endless, perpetual, undying, immortal, abiding, permanent, enduring, infinite, boundless, timeless; amaranthine. **2** *eternal vigilance* CONSTANT, continual, continuous, perpetual, persistent, sustained, unremitting, relentless, unrelieved, uninterrupted, unbroken, never-ending, non-stop, round-the-clock, endless, ceaseless.
— OPPOSITES: transient, intermittent.

eternally ▶ **adverb 1** *I shall be eternally grateful*

FOREVER, permanently, perpetually, (for) evermore, for ever and ever, for eternity, in perpetuity, enduringly; forevermore; *informal* until the cows come home; *archaic* for aye. **2** *the drummer is eternally complaining* CONSTANTLY, continually, continuously, always, all the time, persistently, repeatedly, regularly; day and night, non-stop; endlessly, incessantly, perpetually; interminably, relentlessly; *informal* 24-7.

eternity ▶ **noun 1** *the memory will remain for eternity* EVER, all time, perpetuity. **2** *(Theology) souls destined for eternity* THE AFTERLIFE, everlasting life, life after death, the hereafter, the afterworld, the next world; heaven, paradise, immortality. **3** *(informal) I waited an eternity for you* A LONG TIME, an age, ages, a lifetime; hours, years, eons; forever; *informal* donkey's years, a month of Sundays, a coon's age.

ethereal ▶ **adjective** DELICATE, exquisite, dainty, elegant, graceful; fragile, airy, fine, subtle; unearthly.
— OPPOSITES: substantial, earthly.

ethical ▶ **adjective 1** *an ethical dilemma* MORAL, social, behavioural. **2** *an ethical investment policy* MORAL, right-minded, principled, irreproachable; righteous, high-minded, virtuous, good, morally correct; clean, lawful, just, honourable, reputable, respectable, noble, worthy; praiseworthy, commendable, admirable, laudable; whiter than white, saintly, impeccable, politically correct; *informal* squeaky clean, PC.

ethics ▶ **plural noun** MORAL CODE, morals, morality, values, rights and wrongs, principles, ideals, standards (of behaviour), value system, virtues.

ethnic ▶ **adjective** RACIAL, race-related, ethnological; cultural, national, tribal, ancestral, traditional.

ethos ▶ **noun** SPIRIT, character, atmosphere, climate, mood, feeling, tenor, essence; disposition, rationale, morality, moral code, value system, principles, standards, ethics.

etiquette ▶ **noun** PROTOCOL, manners, accepted behaviour, rules of conduct, decorum, good form; courtesy, propriety, formalities, niceties, punctilios; custom, convention; netiquette; *informal* the done thing; *formal* politesse.

etymology ▶ **noun** DERIVATION, word history, development, origin, source.

eulogize ▶ **verb** EXTOL, acclaim, sing the praises of, praise to the skies, wax lyrical about, rhapsodize about, rave about, enthuse about, ballyhoo, hype.
— OPPOSITES: criticize.

eulogy ▶ **noun** ACCOLADE, panegyric, paean, tribute, compliment, commendation; praise, acclaim; plaudits, bouquets; *formal* encomium.
— OPPOSITES: attack.

euphemism ▶ **noun** POLITE TERM, indirect term, circumlocution, substitute, alternative, understatement, genteelism.

euphemistic ▶ **adjective** POLITE, substitute, mild, understated, indirect, neutral, evasive; diplomatic, inoffensive, genteel; periphrastic, circumlocutory, mealy-mouthed.

euphonious ▶ **adjective** PLEASANT-SOUNDING, sweet-sounding, mellow, mellifluous, dulcet, sweet, honeyed, lyrical, silvery, golden, lilting, soothing; harmonious, melodious; *informal* easy on the ear.
— OPPOSITES: cacophonous.

euphoria ▶ **noun** ELATION, happiness, joy, delight,

glee; excitement, exhilaration, jubilation, exultation; ecstasy, bliss, rapture.
— OPPOSITES: misery.

euphoric ▶ adjective ELATED, happy, joyful, delighted, gleeful; excited, exhilarated, jubilant, exultant; ecstatic, blissful, rapturous, transported, on cloud nine, in seventh heaven; *informal* on top of the world, over the moon, on a high.

eureka ▶ exclamation BINGO, I've got it, I know, that's it.

euthanasia ▶ noun MERCY KILLING, assisted suicide.

evacuate ▶ verb **1** *local residents were evacuated* REMOVE, clear, move out, take away, shift. **2** *they evacuated the bombed town* LEAVE, vacate, abandon, desert, move out of, quit, withdraw from, retreat from, decamp from, flee, depart from, escape from. **3** *police evacuated the area* CLEAR, empty. **4** *patients couldn't evacuate their bowels* EMPTY (OUT), void, open, move, purge; defecate. **5** *he evacuated the contents of his stomach* EXPEL, eject, discharge, excrete, void, empty (out), vomit up.

evade ▶ verb **1** *they evaded the guards* ELUDE, avoid, dodge, escape (from), steer clear of, keep at arm's length, sidestep; lose, leave behind, shake off; *informal* give someone the slip. **2** *he evaded the question* AVOID, dodge, sidestep, bypass, shirk, hedge, skirt round, fudge, be evasive about; *informal* duck.
— OPPOSITES: confront.

evaluate ▶ verb ASSESS, judge, gauge, rate, estimate, appraise, analyze, examine, get the measure of; *informal* size up, check out.

evaluation ▶ noun ASSESSMENT, appraisal, judgment, gauging, rating, estimation, consideration; analysis, examination, test, review.

evanescent ▶ adjective (*literary*) VANISHING, fading, evaporating, melting away, disappearing; ephemeral, fleeting, short-lived, short-term, transitory, transient, fugitive, temporary.
— OPPOSITES: permanent.

evangelical ▶ adjective **1** *evangelical Christianity* SCRIPTURAL, biblical; fundamentalist. **2** *an evangelical preacher* EVANGELISTIC, evangelizing, missionary, crusading, proselytizing; *informal* Bible-thumping.

evangelist ▶ noun PREACHER, missionary, gospeller, proselytizer, crusader; *informal* Bible-thumper.

evangelistic ▶ adjective. See EVANGELICAL sense 2.

evangelize ▶ verb CONVERT, proselytize, redeem, save, preach to, recruit; act as a missionary, missionize, crusade, campaign.

evaporate ▶ verb **1** *the water evaporated* VAPORIZE, become vapour, volatilize; dry up. **2** *the rock salt was washed and evaporated* DRY OUT, dehydrate, desiccate, dehumidify. **3** *the feeling has evaporated* END, pass (away), fizzle out, peter out, wear off, vanish, fade, disappear, dissolve, melt away.
— OPPOSITES: condense, wet, materialize.

evasion ▶ noun **1** *the evasion of immigration control* AVOIDANCE, elusion, circumvention, dodging, sidestepping. **2** *she grew tired of all the evasion* PREVARICATION, evasiveness, beating around the bush, hedging, pussyfooting, hemming and hawing, equivocation, vagueness, temporization; *rare* tergiversation.

evasive ▶ adjective EQUIVOCAL, prevaricating, elusive, ambiguous, noncommittal, vague, inexplicit, unclear; roundabout, indirect; *informal* cagey, shifty, slippery.

eve ▶ noun **1** *the eve of the election* DAY BEFORE, evening

before, night before; the run-up to. **2** (*literary*) *a winter's eve* EVENING, night; *literary* eventide.
— OPPOSITES: morning.

even ▶ adjective **1** *an even surface* FLAT, smooth, uniform, featureless; unbroken, undamaged; level, plane. **2** *an even temperature* UNIFORM, constant, steady, stable, consistent, unvarying, unchanging, regular. **3** *they all have an even chance* EQUAL, the same, identical, like, alike, similar, comparable, parallel. **4** *the score was even* TIED, drawn, level, all square, balanced; neck and neck; *informal* even-steven(s). **5** *an even disposition* EVEN-TEMPERED, balanced, stable, equable, placid, calm, composed, poised, cool, relaxed, easy, imperturbable, unexcitable, unruffled, untroubled; *informal* together, laid-back, unflappable.
— OPPOSITES: bumpy, irregular, unequal, moody.
▶ verb **1** *the canal bottom was evened out* FLATTEN, level (off/out), smooth (off/out), plane; make uniform, make regular. **2** *even out the portions* EQUALIZE, make equal, balance, square; standardize, regularize, homogenize.
▶ adverb **1** *it got even colder* STILL, yet, more, all the more. **2** *even the best hitters missed the ball* SURPRISINGLY, unexpectedly, paradoxically. **3** *she is afraid, even ashamed, to ask for help* INDEED, you could say, veritably, in truth, actually, or rather; *dated* nay. **4** *she couldn't even afford food* SO MUCH AS.
■ **even as** WHILE, whilst, as, just as, at the very time that, during the time that.
■ **even so** NEVERTHELESS, nonetheless, all the same, just the same, anyway, anyhow, still, yet, however, notwithstanding, despite that, in spite of that, for all that, be that as it may, in any event, at any rate; *informal* anyhoo, anyways.
■ **get even** HAVE ONE'S REVENGE, avenge oneself, take vengeance, even the score, settle the score, hit back, give as good as one gets, pay someone back, repay someone, reciprocate, retaliate, take reprisals, exact retribution; give someone their just deserts; *informal* get one's own back, give someone a taste of their own medicine, settle someone's hash; *literary* be revenged.

even-handed ▶ adjective FAIR, just, equitable, impartial, unbiased, unprejudiced, non-partisan, non-discriminatory; disinterested, detached, objective, neutral.
— OPPOSITES: biased.

evening ▶ noun NIGHT, late afternoon, end of day, close of day; twilight, dusk, nightfall, sunset, sundown; *literary* eve.

event ▶ noun **1** *an annual event* OCCURRENCE, happening, proceeding, incident, affair, circumstance, occasion, phenomenon; function, gathering; *informal* bash. **2** *the team lost the event* COMPETITION, contest, tournament, round, heat, match, fixture; race, game, bout.
■ **in any event/at all events** REGARDLESS, whatever happens, come what may, no matter what, at any rate, in any case, anyhow, anyway, even so, still, nevertheless, nonetheless; *informal* anyways, anyhoo.
■ **in the event** AS IT TURNED OUT, as it happened, in the end; as a result, as a consequence.

even-tempered ▶ adjective SERENE, calm, composed, tranquil, relaxed, easygoing, mellow, unworried, untroubled, unruffled, imperturbable, placid, equable, stable, level-headed; *informal* unflappable, together, laid-back.
— OPPOSITES: excitable.

eventful ▶ adjective BUSY, action-packed, full, lively,

active, hectic, strenuous; momentous, significant, important, historic, consequential, fateful.
— OPPOSITES: dull.

eventual ▶ adjective FINAL, ultimate, concluding, closing, end; resulting, ensuing, consequent, subsequent.

eventuality ▶ noun EVENT, incident, occurrence, happening, development, phenomenon, situation, circumstance, case, contingency, chance, likelihood, possibility, probability; outcome, result.

eventually ▶ adverb IN THE END, in due course, by and by, in time, after some time, after a bit, finally, at last, over the long haul; ultimately, in the long run, at the end of the day, one day, some day, sometime, at some point, sooner or later.

eventuate ▶ verb (formal) **1** you never know what might eventuate. See HAPPEN sense 1. **2** the fight eventuated in his death RESULT IN, end in, lead to, give rise to, bring about, cause.

ever ▶ adverb **1** the best I've ever done AT ANY TIME, at any point, on any occasion, under any circumstances, on any account; up till now, until now. **2** he was ever the optimist ALWAYS, forever, eternally, until hell freezes over, until the cows come home. **3** an ever increasing rate of crime CONTINUALLY, constantly, always, endlessly, perpetually, incessantly, unremittingly. **4** will she ever learn? AT ALL, in any way.

everlasting ▶ adjective **1** everlasting love ETERNAL, endless, never-ending, perpetual, undying, abiding, enduring, infinite, boundless, timeless. **2** his everlasting complaints CONSTANT, continual, continuous, persistent, relentless, unrelieved, uninterrupted, unabating, endless, interminable, never-ending, non-stop, incessant.
— OPPOSITES: transient, occasional.

every ▶ adjective **1** he exercised every day EACH, each and every, every single. **2** we make every effort to satisfy our clients ALL POSSIBLE, the utmost.

everybody ▶ pronoun EVERYONE, every person, each person, all, one and all, all and sundry, the whole world, the public; informal {every Tom, Dick, and Harry}, every man jack.

everyday ▶ adjective **1** the everyday demands of a baby DAILY, day-to-day, quotidian. **2** everyday drugs like acetaminophen COMMONPLACE, ordinary, common, usual, regular, familiar, conventional, run-of-the-mill, standard, stock; household, domestic; informal garden variety.
— OPPOSITES: unusual.

everyone ▶ pronoun See EVERYBODY.

everything ▶ pronoun EACH ITEM, each thing, every single thing, the (whole) lot; all; informal the whole kit and caboodle, the whole shebang, the whole schmear, the whole ball of wax, the whole nine yards.
— OPPOSITES: nothing.

everywhere ▶ adverb ALL OVER, all around, ubiquitously, in every nook and cranny, far and wide, near and far, high and low, {here, there, and everywhere}; throughout the land, the world over, worldwide, globally; informal all over the place, everyplace, all over the map.
— OPPOSITES: nowhere.

evict ▶ verb EXPEL, eject, oust, remove, dislodge, turn out, throw out, drive out; dispossess, expropriate; informal chuck out, kick out, boot out, bounce, give someone the (old) heave-ho, throw someone out on their ear, turf out, give someone the bum's rush, give someone their walking papers.

eviction ▶ noun EXPULSION, ejection, ousting, removal, dislodgement, displacement, banishment; dispossession, expropriation; Law ouster.

evidence ▶ noun **1** they found evidence of his plotting PROOF, confirmation, verification, substantiation, corroboration, affirmation, attestation. **2** the court accepted her evidence TESTIMONY, statement, attestation, declaration, avowal, submission, claim, contention, allegation; Law deposition, representation, affidavit. **3** evidence of a struggle SIGNS, indications, pointers, marks, traces, suggestions, hints; manifestation.
▶ verb the rise of racism is evidenced here INDICATE, show, reveal, display, exhibit, manifest; testify to, confirm, prove, substantiate, endorse, bear out; formal evince.
— OPPOSITES: disprove.
■ in evidence NOTICEABLE, conspicuous, obvious, perceptible, visible, on view, on display, plain to see; palpable, tangible, unmistakable, undisguised, prominent, striking, glaring; informal as plain as the nose on your face, sticking out like a sore thumb, staring someone in the face.

evident ▶ adjective OBVIOUS, apparent, noticeable, conspicuous, perceptible, visible, discernible, clear, clear-cut, plain, manifest, patent; palpable, tangible, distinct, pronounced, marked, striking, glaring, blatant; unmistakable, indisputable; informal as plain as the nose on your face, as clear as a sore thumb, as clear as day.

evidently ▶ adverb **1** he was evidently dismayed OBVIOUSLY, clearly, plainly, visibly, manifestly, patently, distinctly, markedly; unmistakably, undeniably, undoubtedly. **2** evidently, she believed herself superior SEEMINGLY, apparently, as far as one can tell, from all appearances, on the face of it; it seems (that), it appears (that).

evil ▶ adjective **1** an evil deed WICKED, bad, wrong, immoral, sinful, foul, vile, dishonourable, corrupt, iniquitous, depraved, reprobate, villainous, nefarious, vicious, malicious; malevolent, sinister, demonic, devilish, diabolical, fiendish, dark; monstrous, shocking, despicable, atrocious, heinous, odious, contemptible, horrible, execrable; informal lowdown, dirty. **2** an evil spirit CRUEL, mischievous, pernicious, malignant, malign, baleful, vicious; destructive, harmful, hurtful, injurious, detrimental, deleterious, inimical, bad, ruinous. **3** an evil smell UNPLEASANT, disagreeable, nasty, horrible, foul, disgusting, filthy, vile, noxious.
— OPPOSITES: good, beneficial, pleasant.
▶ noun **1** the evil in our midst WICKEDNESS, bad, badness, wrongdoing, sin, ill, immorality, vice, iniquity, degeneracy, corruption, depravity, villainy, nefariousness, malevolence; devil; formal turpitude. **2** nothing but evil would ensue HARM, pain, misery, sorrow, suffering, trouble, disaster, misfortune, catastrophe, affliction, woe, hardship. **3** the evils of war ABOMINATION, atrocity, obscenity, outrage, enormity, crime, monstrosity, barbarity.

evince ▶ verb (formal) REVEAL, show, make plain, manifest, indicate, display, exhibit, demonstrate, evidence, attest to; convey, communicate, proclaim, bespeak; informal ooze.
— OPPOSITES: conceal.

eviscerate ▶ verb (formal) DISEMBOWEL, gut, draw, dress.

evocative ▶ adjective REMINISCENT, suggestive, redolent; expressive, vivid, graphic, powerful, haunting, moving, poignant.

evoke ▶ verb BRING TO MIND, put one in mind of, conjure up, summon (up), invoke, elicit, induce, kindle, stimulate, stir up, awaken, arouse, call forth; recall, echo, capture.

evolution ▶ noun **1** *the evolution of Bolshevism* DEVELOPMENT, advancement, growth, rise, progress, expansion, unfolding; transformation, adaptation, modification, revision. **2** *his interest in evolution* DARWINISM, natural selection.

evolve ▶ verb DEVELOP, progress, advance; mature, grow, expand, spread; alter, change, transform, adapt, metamorphose; *humorous* transmogrify.

exacerbate ▶ verb AGGRAVATE, worsen, inflame, compound; intensify, increase, heighten, magnify, add to, amplify, augment; *informal* add fuel to the fire/ flames.
– OPPOSITES: reduce.

exact ▶ adjective **1** *an exact description* PRECISE, accurate, correct, faithful, close, true; literal, strict, faultless, perfect, impeccable; explicit, detailed, minute, meticulous, thorough; *informal* on the nail, on the mark, bang on, on the money, on the button. **2** *an exact manager* CAREFUL, meticulous, painstaking, punctilious, conscientious, scrupulous, exacting; methodical, organized, orderly.
– OPPOSITES: inaccurate, careless.
▶ verb **1** *she exacted high standards from them* DEMAND, require, insist on, request, impose, expect; extract, compel, force, squeeze. **2** *they exacted a terrible vengeance on him* INFLICT, impose, administer, apply.

exacting ▶ adjective **1** *an exacting training routine* DEMANDING, stringent, testing, challenging, onerous, arduous, laborious, taxing, gruelling, punishing, hard, tough. **2** *an exacting boss* STRICT, stern, severe, firm, demanding, tough, harsh; inflexible, uncompromising, unyielding, unsparing; *informal* persnickety.
– OPPOSITES: easy, easygoing.

exactly ▶ adverb **1** *it's exactly as I expected it to be* PRECISELY, entirely, absolutely, completely, totally, just, quite, in every way, in every respect, one hundred per cent, every inch; *informal* to a T, on the money. **2** *write the quotation out exactly* ACCURATELY, precisely, correctly, unerringly, faultlessly, perfectly; verbatim, word for word, letter for letter, to the letter, faithfully.
▶ exclamation *'She escaped?' 'Exactly.'* PRECISELY, yes, that's right, just so, quite (so), indeed, absolutely; *informal* you got it.
■ **not exactly** BY NO MEANS, not at all, in no way, certainly not; not really.

exaggerate ▶ verb OVERSTATE, overemphasize, overestimate, magnify, amplify, aggrandize, inflate; embellish, embroider, elaborate, overplay, dramatize; hyperbolize, stretch the truth; *informal* lay it on thick, make a mountain out of a molehill, blow out of all proportion, blow up, make a big thing of.
– OPPOSITES: understate.

exaggerated ▶ adjective OVERSTATED, inflated, magnified, amplified, aggrandized, excessive; hyperbolic, elaborate, overdone, overplayed, overblown, over-dramatized, melodramatic, sensational; *informal* over the top.

exaggeration ▶ noun OVERSTATEMENT, overemphasis, magnification, amplification, aggrandizement; dramatization, elaboration, embellishment, embroidery, hyperbole, overkill; gilding the lily.

exalt ▶ verb **1** *they exalted their hero* EXTOL, praise, acclaim, esteem; pay homage to, revere, venerate, worship, lionize, idolize, look up to; *informal* put on a pedestal, laud. **2** *this power exalts the peasant* ELEVATE, promote, raise, advance, upgrade, ennoble, dignify, aggrandize. **3** *his works exalt the emotions* UPLIFT, elevate, inspire, excite, stimulate, enliven, exhilarate.
– OPPOSITES: disparage, lower, depress.

exaltation ▶ noun **1** *a heart full of exaltation* ELATION, joy, rapture, ecstasy, bliss, happiness, delight, gladness. **2** *their exaltation of Shakespeare* PRAISE, acclamation, reverence, veneration, worship, adoration, idolization, lionization.

exalted ▶ adjective **1** *his exalted office* HIGH, high-ranking, elevated, superior, lofty, eminent, prestigious, illustrious, distinguished, esteemed. **2** *his exalted aims* NOBLE, lofty, high-minded, elevated; inflated, pretentious. **3** *she felt spiritually exalted* ELATED, exultant, jubilant, joyful, rapturous, ecstatic, blissful, transported, happy, exuberant, exhilarated; *informal* high.

exam ▶ noun TEST, examination, assessment, quiz; paper, term paper, oral.

examination ▶ noun **1** *artifacts spread out for examination* SCRUTINY, inspection, perusal, study, investigation, consideration, analysis, appraisal, evaluation. **2** *a medical examination* INSPECTION, checkup, assessment, appraisal; probe, test, scan; *informal* once-over, overhaul. **3** *a school examination* TEST, exam, quiz, assessment; paper, oral, mid-term. **4** *(Law) the examination of witnesses* INTERROGATION, questioning, cross-examination, inquisition.

examine ▶ verb **1** *they examined the bank records* INSPECT, scrutinize, investigate, look at, study, scan, sift (through), probe, appraise, analyze, review, survey; *informal* check out. **2** *students were examined after a year* TEST, quiz, question; assess, appraise. **3** *(Law) name the witnesses to be examined* INTERROGATE, question, quiz, cross-examine; catechize, give the third degree to, probe, sound out; *informal* grill, pump.

examiner ▶ noun ASSESSOR, questioner, interviewer, tester, appraiser, marker, inspector; auditor, analyst; adjudicator, judge, scrutineer.

example ▶ noun **1** *a fine example of Chinese porcelain* SPECIMEN, sample, exemplar, exemplification, instance, case, illustration, case in point. **2** *we must follow their example* PRECEDENT, lead, model, pattern, exemplar, ideal, standard, template, paradigm; role model, object lesson. **3** *he was hanged as an example to others* WARNING, caution, lesson, deterrent, admonition; moral.
■ **for example** FOR INSTANCE, e.g., by way of illustration, such as, as, like; in particular, case in point, namely, viz, to wit.

exasperate ▶ verb INFURIATE, incense, anger, annoy, irritate, madden, enrage, antagonize, provoke, irk, vex, get on someone's nerves, ruffle someone's feathers, rub the wrong way; *informal* aggravate, rile, bug, needle, get someone's back up, get someone's goat, tee off, tick off.
– OPPOSITES: please.

exasperating ▶ adjective INFURIATING, annoying, irritating, maddening, provoking, irksome, vexatious, trying, displeasing; *informal* aggravating.

exasperation ▶ noun IRRITATION, annoyance, vexation, anger, fury, rage, ill humour, crossness, tetchiness, testiness; disgruntlement, discontent, displeasure, chagrin; *informal* aggravation.

excavate ▶ verb **1** *she excavated a narrow tunnel* DIG (OUT), bore, hollow out, scoop out; burrow, tunnel, sink, gouge. **2** *numerous artifacts have been excavated* UNEARTH, dig up, uncover, reveal; disinter, exhume.

excavation ▶ noun **1** *the excavation of a grave* UNEARTHING, digging up; disinterment, exhumation. **2** *the excavation of a moat* DIGGING, hollowing out, boring, channelling. **3** *implements found in the excavations* HOLE, pit, trench, trough; archaeological site.

exceed ▶ verb **1** *the cost will exceed $400* BE MORE THAN, be greater than, be over, go beyond, overreach, top. **2** *Brazil exceeds the US in fertile land* SURPASS, outdo, outstrip, outshine, outclass, transcend, top, cap, beat, excel, better, eclipse, overshadow; *informal* best, leave standing, be head and shoulders above.

exceedingly ▶ adverb EXTREMELY, exceptionally, especially, tremendously, very, really, truly, awfully, seriously, totally, completely; *formal* most; *informal* mega, ultra, real, mighty; *archaic* exceeding.

excel ▶ verb **1** *he excelled at football* SHINE, be excellent, be outstanding, be skilful, be talented, be pre-eminent, reign supreme; stand out, be the best, be unparalleled, be unequalled, be second to none, be unsurpassed. **2** *she excelled him in her work* SURPASS, outdo, outshine, outclass, outstrip, beat, top, transcend, exceed, better, pass, eclipse, overshadow; *informal* best, be head and shoulders above, be a cut above.

excellence ▶ noun DISTINCTION, quality, superiority, brilliance, greatness, merit, calibre, eminence, pre-eminence, supremacy; skill, talent, virtuosity, accomplishment, mastery.

excellent ▶ adjective VERY GOOD, superb, outstanding, exceptional, marvellous, wonderful, magnificent; pre-eminent, perfect, matchless, unbeatable, peerless, supreme, divine, prime, first-rate, first-class, superlative, splendid, fine, beautiful, exemplary, dandy; *informal* A1, ace, great, terrific, tremendous, fantastic, fabulous, splendiferous, fab, top-notch, blue-ribbon, blue-chip, bang-up, skookum, class, awesome, magic, wicked, mean, cool, out of this world, hunky-dory, A-OK, brilliant, killer.
— OPPOSITES: inferior.

except ▶ preposition *every day except Monday* EXCLUDING, not including, excepting, omitting, not counting, but, besides, apart from, aside from, barring, bar, other than, saving; with the exception of, save for; *informal* outside of.
— OPPOSITES: including.
▶ verb *lawyers are all crooks, present company excepted* EXCLUDE, omit, leave out, count out, disregard; exempt.
— OPPOSITES: include.

exception ▶ noun *this case is an exception* ANOMALY, irregularity, deviation, special case, isolated example, peculiarity, abnormality, oddity; misfit, aberration; *informal* freak; bad apple.
■ **take exception** OBJECT, take offence, take umbrage, demur, disagree; resent, argue against, protest against, oppose, complain about, shudder at; *informal* kick up a fuss, raise a stink.
■ **with the exception of.** See EXCEPT preposition.

exceptionable ▶ adjective *(formal).* See OBJECTIONABLE.

exceptional ▶ adjective **1** *the drought was exceptional* UNUSUAL, uncommon, abnormal, atypical, extraordinary, out of the ordinary, rare,

unprecedented, unexpected, surprising; strange, odd, freakish, anomalous, peculiar, weird; *informal* freaky, something else. **2** *her exceptional ability* OUTSTANDING, extraordinary, remarkable, special, excellent, phenomenal, prodigious; unequalled, unparalleled, unsurpassed, peerless, matchless, nonpareil, first-rate, first-class; *informal* A1, top-notch.
— OPPOSITES: normal, average.

exceptionally ▶ adverb **1** *it was exceptionally cold* UNUSUALLY, uncommonly, abnormally, atypically, extraordinarily, unexpectedly, surprisingly; strangely, oddly; *informal* weirdly, freakily. **2** *an exceptionally acute mind* EXCEEDINGLY, outstandingly, extraordinarily, remarkably, especially, phenomenally, prodigiously.

excerpt ▶ noun EXTRACT, part, section, piece, portion, snippet, clip, bit, sample; reading, citation, quotation, quote, line, passage.
▶ verb QUOTE, extract, cite.

excess ▶ noun **1** *an excess of calcium* SURPLUS, surfeit, overabundance, superabundance, superfluity, glut; too much. **2** *the excess is turned into fat* REMAINDER, rest, residue; leftovers, remnants; surplus, extra, difference. **3** *a life of excess* OVERINDULGENCE, intemperance, immoderation, profligacy, lavishness, extravagance, decadence, self-indulgence.
— OPPOSITES: lack, restraint.
▶ adjective *excess skin oils* SURPLUS, superfluous, redundant, unwanted, unneeded, excessive; extra.
■ **in excess of** MORE THAN, over, above, upwards of, beyond.

excessive ▶ adjective **1** *excessive alcohol consumption* IMMODERATE, intemperate, imprudent, overindulgent, unrestrained, uncontrolled, lavish, extravagant; superfluous. **2** *the cost is excessive* EXORBITANT, extortionate, unreasonable, outrageous, undue, uncalled for, extreme, inordinate, unwarranted, disproportionate; too much, de trop; *informal* over the top.

excessively ▶ adverb INORDINATELY, unduly, unnecessarily, unreasonably, ridiculously, overly; very, extremely, exceedingly, exceptionally, impossibly; immoderately, intemperately, too much, ad nauseam.

exchange ▶ noun **1** *the exchange of ideas* INTERCHANGE, trade, trading, swapping, traffic, trafficking. **2** *a broker on the exchange* STOCK EXCHANGE, money market, bourse. **3** *an acrimonious exchange* CONVERSATION, dialogue, talk, discussion, chat; debate, argument, altercation, row; *formal* confabulation, colloquy.
▶ verb *we exchanged shirts* TRADE, swap, switch, change, interchange.
■ **exchange blows** FIGHT, brawl, scuffle, tussle; *informal* scrap, have a set-to.
■ **exchange words** ARGUE, quarrel, squabble, have an argument/disagreement; *informal* have a slanging match.

excise¹ ▶ noun *the excise on spirits* DUTY, tax, levy, tariff.

excise² ▶ verb **1** *the tumours were excised* CUT OUT/OFF/ AWAY, take out, extract, remove; *technical* resect. **2** *all unnecessary detail should be excised* DELETE, cross out/ through, strike out, score out, cancel, put a line through; erase, scratch; *informal* ditch, nix; *Computing, informal* kill; *Printing* dele.

excitable ▶ adjective TEMPERAMENTAL, mercurial, volatile, emotional, sensitive, high-strung, unstable,

nervous, tense, edgy, jumpy, twitchy, uneasy, neurotic; *informal* uptight, wired.
– OPPOSITES: placid.

excite ▶ verb **1** *the prospect of a holiday excited me* THRILL, exhilarate, animate, enliven, rouse, stir, stimulate, galvanize, electrify, inspirit; *informal* buck up, pep up, ginger up, give someone a buzz/kick, give someone a charge. **2** *she wore a chiffon nightgown to excite him* AROUSE (SEXUALLY), stimulate, titillate, inflame; *informal* turn someone on, get someone going. **3** *his clothes excited envy* PROVOKE, stir up, rouse, arouse, kindle, trigger (off), spark off, incite, cause; *literary* enkindle.
– OPPOSITES: bore, depress.

excited ▶ adjective **1** *they were excited about the prospect* THRILLED, exhilarated, animated, enlivened, electrified; enraptured, intoxicated, feverish, enthusiastic; *informal* high (as a kite), fired up. **2** (SEXUALLY) AROUSED, stimulated, titillated, inflamed; *informal* turned on, hot, horny, sexed up.

excitement ▶ noun **1** *the excitement of seeing a leopard in the wild* THRILL, pleasure, delight, joy; *informal* kick, buzz, charge, high. **2** *excitement in her eyes* EXHILARATION, elation, animation, enthusiasm, eagerness, anticipation, feverishness; *informal* pep, vim, zing. **3** (SEXUAL) AROUSAL, passion, stimulation, titillation.

exciting ▶ adjective **1** *an exciting story* THRILLING, exhilarating, action-packed, stirring, rousing, stimulating, intoxicating, electrifying, invigorating; gripping, compelling, powerful, dramatic. **2** (SEXUALLY) AROUSING, (sexually) stimulating, titillating, erotic, sexual, sexy; *informal* raunchy, steamy.

exclaim ▶ verb CRY (OUT), declare, blurt out; call (out), shout, yell; *dated* ejaculate.

exclamation ▶ noun CRY, call, shout, yell, interjection.

exclude ▶ verb **1** *women were excluded from many scientific societies* KEEP OUT, deny access to, shut out, debar, disbar, bar, ban, prohibit, ostracized. **2** *the clause excluded any judicial review* ELIMINATE, rule out, preclude, foreclose; *formal* except. **3** *the price excludes postage* BE EXCLUSIVE OF, not include. **4** *he excluded his name from the list* LEAVE OUT/OFF, omit, miss out.
– OPPOSITES: admit, include.

exclusive ▶ adjective **1** *an exclusive club* SELECT, chic, high-class, elite, fashionable, stylish, elegant, premier, grade A; expensive, upscale, upmarket, high-toned; *informal* posh, ritzy, classy, tony. **2** *a room for your exclusive use* SOLE, unshared, unique, only, individual, personal, private. **3** *prices exclusive of GST* NOT INCLUDING, excluding, leaving out, omitting, excepting. **4** *mutually exclusive alternatives* INCOMPATIBLE, irreconcilable.
– OPPOSITES: inclusive.
▶ noun *a six-page exclusive* SCOOP, exposé, special.

excoriate ▶ verb **1** (*Medicine*) *the skin had been excoriated* ABRADE, rub away/raw, scrape, scratch, chafe; strip away, skin. **2** (*formal*) *he was excoriated in the press. See* CRITICIZE.

excrement ▶ noun FECES, excreta, stools, droppings; waste matter, ordure, dung, dirt, turds; *informal* poo, poop, caca.
– RELATED TERMS: copro-, scato-.

excrescence ▶ noun **1** *an excrescence on his leg* GROWTH, lump, swelling, nodule, outgrowth. **2** *the*

new buildings were an excrescence EYESORE, blot on the landscape, monstrosity.

excrete ▶ verb EXPEL, pass, void, discharge, eject, evacuate; defecate, urinate.
– OPPOSITES: ingest.

excruciating ▶ adjective AGONIZING, severe, acute, intense, violent, racking, searing, piercing, stabbing, raging; unbearable, unendurable; *informal* splitting, killing.

excursion ▶ noun TRIP, outing, jaunt, expedition, journey, tour; day trip/out, side trip, drive, run, ride; *informal* junket, spin, sortie.

excusable ▶ adjective FORGIVABLE, pardonable, defensible, justifiable; venial.
– OPPOSITES: unforgivable.

excuse ▶ verb **1** *eventually she excused him* FORGIVE, pardon, absolve, exonerate, acquit; *informal* let someone off (the hook); *formal* exculpate. **2** *such conduct can never be excused* JUSTIFY, defend, condone, vindicate; forgive, overlook, disregard, ignore, tolerate, sanction. **3** *she has been excused from her duties* LET OFF, release, relieve, exempt, absolve, free.
– OPPOSITES: punish, blame, condemn.
▶ noun **1** *that's no excuse for stealing* JUSTIFICATION, defence, reason, explanation, mitigating circumstances, mitigation, vindication. **2** *an excuse to get away* PRETEXT, ostensible reason, pretense; *informal* story, alibi. **3** (*informal*) *that pathetic excuse for a man!* TRAVESTY OF, poor specimen of; *informal* apology for.

execrable ▶ adjective APPALLING, atrocious, lamentable, egregious, awful, dreadful, terrible; disgusting, deplorable, disgraceful, frightful, reprehensible, abhorrent, loathsome, odious, hateful, vile, abysmal, lousy, godawful.
– OPPOSITES: admirable.

execute ▶ verb **1** *he was convicted and executed* PUT TO DEATH, kill; hang, behead, guillotine, electrocute, send to the (electric) chair, shoot, put before a firing squad; *informal* string up, fry. **2** *the corporation executed a series of financial deals* CARRY OUT, accomplish, bring off/about, achieve, complete, engineer, conduct; *informal* pull off; *formal* effectuate. **3** *a well-executed act* PERFORM, present, render; stage.

execution ▶ noun **1** *the execution of the plan* IMPLEMENTATION, carrying out, accomplishment, bringing off/about, engineering, attainment, realization. **2** *the execution of the play* PERFORMANCE, presentation, rendition, rendering, staging. **3** *thousands were sentenced to execution* CAPITAL PUNISHMENT, the death penalty; the gibbet, the gallows, the noose, the rope, the scaffold, the guillotine, the firing squad, the (electric) chair.

executioner ▶ noun HANGMAN; *historical* headsman.

executive ▶ adjective *executive powers* ADMINISTRATIVE, decision-making, managerial; law-making.
▶ noun **1** *top-level bank executives* CHIEF, head, director, senior official, senior manager, CEO, chief executive officer; *informal* boss, exec, suit, big cheese. **2** *the executive has increased in number* ADMINISTRATION, management, directorate; government, legislative body.

exegesis ▶ noun INTERPRETATION, explanation, exposition, explication.

exemplar ▶ noun EPITOME, perfect example, paragon, ideal, exemplification, textbook example, embodiment; essence, quintessence; paradigm, model, role model, template.

exemplary ▸ adjective **1** *her exemplary behaviour* PERFECT, ideal, model, faultless, flawless, impeccable, irreproachable; excellent, outstanding, admirable, commendable, laudable, above/beyond reproach; textbook. **2** *exemplary jail sentences* DETERRENT, cautionary, warning, admonitory; *rare* monitory. **3** *her works are exemplary of cutting-edge feminism* REPRESENTATIVE, illustrative, characteristic, typical.
– OPPOSITES: deplorable.

exemplify ▸ verb **1** *this story exemplifies current trends* TYPIFY, epitomize, be a typical example of, represent, be representative of, symbolize. **2** *he exemplified his point with an anecdote* ILLUSTRATE, give an example of, demonstrate.

exempt ▸ adjective *they are exempt from all charges* FREE, not liable/subject, exempted, excepted, excused, absolved.
– OPPOSITES: subject to.
▸ verb *he had been exempted from military service* EXCUSE, free, release, exclude, give/grant immunity, spare, absolve; *informal* let off (the hook), grandfather.

exemption ▸ noun IMMUNITY, exception, dispensation, indemnity, exclusion, freedom, release, relief, absolution.

exercise ▸ noun **1** *exercise improves your heart* PHYSICAL ACTIVITY, a workout, working-out; gymnastics, sports, games, physical education, phys. ed., physical training, aerobics, body conditioning, calisthenics. **2** *Mr. Nixon's translation exercises* TASK, piece of work, problem, assignment, activity; *Music* étude. **3** *the exercise of professional skill* USE, utilization, employment; practice, application. **4** *military exercises* MANOEUVRES, operations; war games.
▸ verb **1** *she exercised every day* WORK OUT, do exercises, train; *informal* pump iron. **2** *he must learn to exercise patience* USE, employ, make use of, utilize; practise, apply.

exert ▸ verb **1** *he exerted considerable pressure on me* BRING TO BEAR, apply, exercise, employ, use, utilize, deploy. **2** *Geoff had been exerting himself* STRIVE, try hard, make an/every effort, endeavour, do one's best/utmost, give one's all, push oneself, drive oneself, work hard; *informal* go all out, pull out all the stops, bend/lean over backwards, do one's damnedest, do one's darnedest, move heaven and earth, bust one's chops.

exertion ▸ noun **1** *she was panting with the exertion* EFFORT, strain, struggle, toil, endeavour, hard work, labour; *literary* travail. **2** *the exertion of pressure* USE, application, exercise, employment, utilization.

exhale ▸ verb **1** *she exhaled her cigarette smoke* BREATHE OUT, blow out, puff out. **2** *the jungle exhaled mists of early morning* GIVE OFF, emanate, send forth, emit.
– OPPOSITES: inhale.

exhaust ▸ verb **1** *the effort had exhausted him* TIRE (OUT), wear out, overtire, fatigue, weary, drain, run someone into the ground; *informal* do in, take it out of one, wipe out, knock out, burn out, poop, tucker out. **2** *the country has exhausted its reserves* USE UP, run through, go through, consume, finish, deplete, spend, empty, drain, run out of; *informal* blow. **3** *we've exhausted the subject* TREAT THOROUGHLY, do to death, overwork.
– OPPOSITES: invigorate, replenish.

exhausted ▸ adjective **1** *I worked until I was exhausted* TIRED OUT, worn out, weary, dog-tired, bone-tired, ready to drop, drained, fatigued, enervated; *informal* done in, all in, dead beat, bushed, zonked, bagged, knocked out, wiped out, burned out,

whacked (out), pooped, tuckered out, tapped out, fried, whipped. **2** *exhausted reserves* USED UP, consumed, finished, spent, depleted; empty, drained.

exhausting ▸ adjective TIRING, wearying, taxing, fatiguing, wearing, enervating, draining; arduous, strenuous, onerous, demanding, gruelling; *informal* killing, murderous.

exhaustion ▸ noun **1** *sheer exhaustion forced Mona to give up* EXTREME TIREDNESS, overtiredness, fatigue, weariness, burnout. **2** *the exhaustion of fuel reserves* CONSUMPTION, depletion, using up, expenditure; draining, emptying.

exhaustive ▸ adjective COMPREHENSIVE, all-inclusive, complete, full, full-scale, encyclopedic, sweeping, thorough, in-depth; detailed, meticulous, painstaking.
– OPPOSITES: perfunctory.

exhibit ▸ verb **1** *the paintings were exhibited at Joyner's* PUT ON DISPLAY/SHOW, display, show, put on public view, showcase; set out, lay out, array, arrange. **2** *Luke exhibited signs of jealousy* SHOW, reveal, display, manifest; express, indicate, demonstrate, present; *formal* evince.
▸ noun **1** *exhibit A is a handwritten letter* OBJECT, item, piece, showpiece; display; evidence. **2** *people flocked to the exhibit. See* EXHIBITION sense 1.

exhibition ▸ noun **1** *an exhibition of Inuit sculpture* (PUBLIC) DISPLAY, show, showing, presentation, demonstration, exposition, showcase, exhibit. **2** *a convincing exhibition of concern* DISPLAY, show, demonstration, manifestation, expression.

exhibitionist ▸ noun POSTURER, poser, self-publicist; extrovert; *informal* show-off, showboat.

exhilarate ▸ verb THRILL, excite, intoxicate, elate, delight, enliven, animate, invigorate, energize, vitalize, stimulate; *informal* give someone a thrill/buzz, give someone a charge.

exhilaration ▸ noun ELATION, euphoria, exultation, exaltation, joy, happiness, delight, joyousness, jubilation, rapture, ecstasy, bliss.

exhort ▸ verb URGE, encourage, call on, enjoin, charge, press; bid, appeal to, entreat, implore, beg; *formal* adjure; *literary* beseech.

exhortation ▸ noun **1** *no amount of exhortation had any effect* URGING, encouragement, persuasion, pressure; warning. **2** *the government's exhortations to voters* ENTREATY, appeal, call, charge, injunction; admonition, warning.

exhume ▸ verb DISINTER, dig up, unearth.
– OPPOSITES: bury.

exigency ▸ noun **1** *the exigencies of the continuing war* NEED, demand, requirement, necessity. **2** *financial exigency* URGENCY, crisis, difficulty, pressure.

exiguous ▸ adjective (*formal*) MEAGRE, inadequate, insufficient, small, scanty, paltry, negligible, modest, deficient, miserly, niggardly, beggarly; *informal* measly, stingy, piddling.
– OPPOSITES: ample, generous.

exile ▸ noun **1** *his exile from the land of his birth* BANISHMENT, expulsion, expatriation, deportation. **2** *political exiles* ÉMIGRÉ, expatriate; displaced person, refugee, deportee; *informal* expat; *historical* DP.
▸ verb *he was exiled from his country* EXPEL, banish, expatriate, deport, drive out, throw out, outlaw.

exist ▸ verb **1** *animals existing in the distant past* LIVE, be alive, be living; be; happen. **2** *the liberal climate that existed during his presidency* PREVAIL, occur, be found, be in existence; be the case. **3** *she had to exist on a low* *income* SURVIVE, subsist, live, support oneself; manage, make do, get by, scrape by, make ends meet.

existence ▸ noun **1** *the industry's continued existence* ACTUALITY, being, existing, reality; survival, continuation. **2** *her suburban existence* WAY OF LIFE/ LIVING, life, lifestyle.

■ **in existence** *See* EXISTENT.

existent ▸ adjective IN EXISTENCE, alive, existing, living, extant; surviving, remaining, undestroyed.

exit ▸ noun **1** *the fire exit* WAY OUT, door, egress, escape route; doorway, gate, gateway, portal. **2** *take the second exit* TURNING, turnoff, turn, junction. **3** *his sudden exit* DEPARTURE, leaving, withdrawal, going, decamping, retreat; flight, exodus, escape.

– OPPOSITES: entrance, arrival.

▸ verb *the doctor had just exited* LEAVE, go (out), depart, withdraw, retreat.

– OPPOSITES: enter.

exodus ▸ noun MASS DEPARTURE, withdrawal, evacuation, leaving; migration, emigration; flight, escape, fleeing.

exonerate ▸ verb **1** *the inquiry exonerated them* ABSOLVE, clear, acquit, find innocent, discharge; *formal* exculpate. **2** *the Pope exonerated the king from his oath* RELEASE, discharge, free, liberate; excuse, exempt, except, dispense; *informal* let off.

– OPPOSITES: convict.

exorbitant ▸ adjective EXTORTIONATE, excessively high, excessive, prohibitive, outrageous, unreasonable, inflated, unconscionable, huge, enormous; *informal* steep, stiff, sky-high, over the top, rip-off.

– OPPOSITES: reasonable.

exorcist ▸ noun GHOSTBUSTER.

exorcize ▸ verb **1** *exorcizing an evil spirit* DRIVE OUT, cast out, expel. **2** *they exorcized the house* PURIFY, cleanse, purge.

exotic ▸ adjective **1** *exotic birds* FOREIGN, non-native, tropical. **2** *exotic places* FOREIGN, faraway, far-off, far-flung, distant. **3** *Linda's exotic appearance* STRIKING, colourful, eye-catching, flamboyant; unusual, unconventional, out of the ordinary, foreign-looking, extravagant, outlandish, orchidaceous; *informal* offbeat, off the wall.

– OPPOSITES: native, nearby, conventional.

expand ▸ verb **1** *metals expand when heated* INCREASE IN SIZE, become larger, enlarge; swell, dilate, inflate; lengthen, stretch, thicken, fill out. **2** *the company is expanding* GROW, become/make larger, become/make bigger, increase in size/scope, upsize; extend, augment, broaden, widen, develop, diversify, build up; branch out, spread, proliferate. **3** *the minister expanded on the proposals* ELABORATE ON, enlarge on, go into detail about, flesh out, develop, expatiate on. **4** *she expanded and flourished* RELAX, unbend, become relaxed, grow friendlier, loosen up.

– OPPOSITES: shrink, contract.

expanse ▸ noun AREA, stretch, sweep, tract, swathe, belt, region; sea, carpet, blanket, sheet.

expansion ▸ noun **1** *expansion and contraction* ENLARGEMENT, increase in size, swelling, dilation; lengthening, elongation, stretching, thickening. **2** *the expansion of the company* GROWTH, increase in size, enlargement, extension, development; spread, proliferation, multiplication. **3** *an expansion of a lecture given last year* ELABORATION, enlargement, amplification, development.

– OPPOSITES: contraction.

expansive ▸ adjective **1** *expansive moorland* EXTENSIVE, sweeping, rolling. **2** *expansive coverage* WIDE-RANGING, extensive, broad, wide, comprehensive, thorough, full-scale. **3** *Bethany became engagingly expansive* COMMUNICATIVE, forthcoming, sociable, friendly, outgoing, affable, chatty, talkative, garrulous, effusive, loquacious, voluble.

expatiate ▸ verb SPEAK/WRITE AT LENGTH, go into detail, expound, dwell, dilate, expand, enlarge, elaborate; *formal* perorate.

expatriate ▸ noun *expatriates working overseas* EMIGRANT, non-native, émigré, migrant; *informal* expat.

– OPPOSITES: national.

▸ adjective *expatriate workers* EMIGRANT, living abroad, non-native, foreign, émigré; *informal* expat.

– OPPOSITES: indigenous.

▸ verb *he was expatriated* EXILE, deport, banish, expel.

expect ▸ verb **1** *I expect she'll be late* SUPPOSE, presume, think, believe, imagine, assume, surmise; *informal* guess, reckon, figure. **2** *a 10 per cent rise was expected* ANTICIPATE, await, look for, hope for, look forward to; contemplate, bargain for/on, bank on; predict, forecast, envisage, envision. **3** *we expect total loyalty* REQUIRE, ask for, call for, want, insist on, demand.

expectancy ▸ noun **1** *feverish expectancy* ANTICIPATION, expectation, eagerness, excitement. **2** *life expectancy* LIKELIHOOD, probability, outlook, prospect.

expectant ▸ adjective **1** *expectant fans* EAGER, excited, agog, waiting with bated breath, hopeful; in suspense, on tenterhooks. **2** *an expectant mother* PREGNANT; *informal* expecting, preggers, with a bun in the oven; *technical* gravid; *dated* in the family way; *archaic* with child.

expectation ▸ noun **1** *her expectations were unrealistic* SUPPOSITION, assumption, presumption, conjecture, surmise, calculation, prediction, hope. **2** *tense with expectation* ANTICIPATION, expectancy, eagerness, excitement, suspense.

expecting ▸ adjective (*informal*). *See* EXPECTANT sense 2.

expedient ▸ adjective *a politically expedient strategy* CONVENIENT, advantageous, in one's own interests, useful, of use, beneficial, of benefit, helpful; practical, pragmatic, politic, prudent, wise, judicious, sensible.

▸ noun *a temporary expedient* MEASURE, means, method, stratagem, scheme, plan, move, tactic, manoeuvre, device, contrivance, ploy, machination, dodge.

expedite ▸ verb SPEED UP, accelerate, hurry, hasten, step up, quicken, precipitate, dispatch; advance, facilitate, ease, make easier, further, promote, aid, push through, urge on, boost, stimulate, spur on, help along, catalyze, fast-track.

– OPPOSITES: delay.

expedition ▸ noun **1** *an expedition to the South Pole* JOURNEY, voyage, tour, odyssey; exploration, safari, trek, hike. **2** (*informal*) *a shopping expedition* TRIP, excursion, outing, jaunt. **3** *all members of the expedition* GROUP, team, party, crew, band, squad.

expeditious ▸ adjective SPEEDY, swift, quick, rapid, fast, brisk, efficient; prompt, punctual, immediate, instant; *literary* fleet.

– OPPOSITES: slow.

expel ▸ verb **1** *she was expelled from her party* THROW OUT, eject, bar, ban, debar, drum out, oust, remove, get rid of, dismiss; *Military* cashier; *informal* chuck out, sling out, kick/boot out, turf out, give someone the

bum's rush. **2** *he was expelled from the country* BANISH, exile, deport, evict, expatriate, drive out, throw out. **3** *Dolly expelled a hiss* LET OUT, discharge, eject, issue, send forth.
− OPPOSITES: admit.

expend ▶ verb **1** *they had already expended $75,000* SPEND, pay out, disburse, dole out, dish out, get through, waste, fritter (away); *informal* fork out, shell out, lay out, cough up, blow, splurge, ante up. **2** *children expend a lot of energy* USE (UP), utilize, consume, eat up, deplete, get through, burn through.
− OPPOSITES: save, conserve.

expendable ▶ adjective **1** *an accountant decided he was expendable* DISPENSABLE, replaceable, non-essential, inessential, unnecessary, unneeded, not required, superfluous, disposable. **2** *an expendable satellite launcher* DISPOSABLE, throwaway, single-use.
− OPPOSITES: indispensable.

expenditure ▶ noun **1** *the expenditure of funds* SPENDING, paying out, outlay, use, disbursement, doling out, waste, wasting, frittering (away), dissipation. **2** *reducing public expenditure* COSTS, spending, payments, expenses, overheads.
− OPPOSITES: saving, income.

expense ▶ noun **1** *Nigel resented the expense* COST, price, charge, outlay, fee, tariff, levy, payment; *informal, humorous* damage. **2** *regular expenses* OVERHEAD, cost, outlay, expenditure, charge, bill, payment. **3** *tax cuts come at the expense of social programs* SACRIFICE, cost, loss.

expensive ▶ adjective COSTLY, dear, high-priced, overpriced, exorbitant, extortionate; *informal* steep, pricey, costing an arm and a leg, big-ticket, costing the earth.
− OPPOSITES: cheap, economical.

experience ▶ noun **1** *qualifications and experience* SKILL, (practical) knowledge, understanding; background, record, history; maturity, worldliness, sophistication; *informal* know-how. **2** *an enjoyable experience* INCIDENT, occurrence, event, happening, episode; adventure, exploit, escapade. **3** *his first experience of business* INVOLVEMENT IN, participation in, contact with, acquaintance with, exposure to, observation of, awareness of, insight into.
▶ verb *some policemen experience harassment* UNDERGO, encounter, meet, come into contact with, come across, come up against, face, be faced with.

experienced ▶ adjective **1** *an experienced pilot* KNOWLEDGEABLE, skilful, skilled, expert, accomplished, adept, adroit, master, consummate; proficient, trained, competent, capable, well trained, well versed; seasoned, practised, mature, veteran. **2** *she deluded herself that she was experienced* WORLDLY (WISE), sophisticated, suave, urbane, mature, knowing; *informal* streetwise, street smart.
− OPPOSITES: novice, naive.

experiment ▶ noun **1** *carrying out experiments* TEST, investigation, trial, examination, observation; assessment, evaluation, appraisal, analysis, study. **2** *these results have been established by experiment* RESEARCH, experimentation, observation, analysis, testing.
− RELATED TERMS: empirical.
▶ verb *they experimented with new ideas* CONDUCT EXPERIMENTS, carry out trials/tests, conduct research; test, trial, do tests on, try out, assess, appraise, evaluate.

experimental ▶ adjective **1** *the experimental stage* EXPLORATORY, investigational, trial, test, pilot; speculative, conjectural, hypothetical, tentative, preliminary, untested, untried. **2** *experimental music* INNOVATIVE, innovatory, new, original, radical, avant-garde, cutting-edge, alternative, unorthodox, unconventional; *informal* way-out.

expert ▶ noun *she is a yogic flying expert* SPECIALIST, authority, pundit; adept, maestro, virtuoso, (past) master, wizard; connoisseur, aficionado; *informal* ace, buff, pro, techie, whiz, hotshot, maven, crackerjack.
▶ adjective *an expert chess player* SKILFUL, skilled, adept, accomplished, talented, fine; master, masterly, brilliant, virtuoso, magnificent, outstanding, great, exceptional, excellent, first-class, first-rate, superb; proficient, good, able, capable, experienced, practised, knowledgeable; *informal* ace, crack, mean.
− OPPOSITES: incompetent.

expertise ▶ noun SKILL, skilfulness, expertness, prowess, proficiency, competence; knowledge, mastery, ability, aptitude, facility, capability; *informal* know-how.

expiate ▶ verb ATONE FOR, make amends for, make up for, do penance for, pay for, redress, redeem, offset, make good.

expire ▶ verb **1** *my contract has expired* RUN OUT, become invalid, become void, lapse; END, finish, stop, come to an end, terminate. **2** *the spot where he expired* DIE, pass away/on, breathe one's last; *informal* kick the bucket, bite the dust, croak, buy it, buy the farm; *dated* depart this life. **3** *(technical) afterwards the breath is expired* BREATHE OUT, exhale, blow out, expel.

expiry ▶ noun **1** *the expiry of the lease* LAPSE, expiration. **2** *the expiry of her term of office* END, finish, termination, conclusion. **3** *(archaic) the sad expiry of their friend* DEATH, demise, passing (away/on), dying; *formal* decease.

explain ▶ verb **1** *a technician explained the procedure* DESCRIBE, give an explanation of, make clear/intelligible, spell out, put into words; elucidate, expound, explicate, clarify, throw/shed light on; gloss, interpret. **2** *nothing could explain his new-found wealth* ACCOUNT FOR, give an explanation for, give a reason for; justify, give a justification for, give an excuse for, vindicate, legitimize.

explanation ▶ noun **1** *an explanation of the ideas contained in the essay* CLARIFICATION, simplification; description, report, statement; elucidation, exposition, expounding, explication; gloss, interpretation, commentary, exegesis. **2** *I owe you an explanation* ACCOUNT, reason; justification, excuse, alibi, defence, vindication, story, answers.

explanatory ▶ adjective EXPLAINING, descriptive, describing, illustrative, interpretive, instructive, expository.

expletive ▶ noun SWEAR WORD, obscenity, profanity, oath, curse, four-letter word, dirty word; *informal* cuss word, cuss; *formal* imprecation; (**expletives**) bad language, foul language, strong language, swearing.

explicable ▶ adjective EXPLAINABLE, understandable, comprehensible, accountable, intelligible, interpretable.

explicate ▶ verb EXPLAIN, make explicit, clarify, make plain/clear, spell out, untangle; interpret, translate, elucidate, expound, illuminate, throw light on.

explicit ▶ adjective **1** *explicit instructions* CLEAR, plain, straightforward, crystal clear, easily understandable; precise, exact, specific, unequivocal, unambiguous; detailed, comprehensive, exhaustive. **2** *sexually explicit material* GRAPHIC, uncensored, candid, full-frontal, hard-core. – OPPOSITES: vague.

explode ▶ verb **1** *a bomb has exploded* BLOW UP, detonate, go off, burst (apart), fly apart, erupt. **2** *exploding the first atomic device* DETONATE, set off, let off, discharge. **3** *he exploded in anger* LOSE ONE'S TEMPER, blow up, get angry, become enraged, get mad; *informal* fly off the handle, hit the roof, blow one's cool/top/stack, go wild, go bananas, go ballistic, see red, go off the deep end, go crackers, go postal. **4** *the city's exploding population* INCREASE SUDDENLY/RAPIDLY, mushroom, snowball, escalate, multiply, burgeon, rocket. **5** *exploding the myths about men* DISPROVE, refute, rebut, invalidate, negate, negative, controvert, repudiate, discredit, debunk, dispel, belie, give the lie to; *informal* poke holes in, blow out of the water; *formal* confute. – OPPOSITES: defuse.

exploit ▶ verb **1** *we should exploit this new technology* UTILIZE, harness, use, make use of, turn/put to good use, make the most of, capitalize on, benefit from; *informal* cash in on. **2** *exploiting the workers* TAKE ADVANTAGE OF, abuse, impose on, treat unfairly, misuse, ill-treat; *informal* walk (all) over, take for a ride, rip off.
▶ noun *his exploits brought him notoriety* FEAT, deed, act, adventure, stunt, escapade; achievement, accomplishment, attainment; *informal* lark, caper.

exploitation ▶ noun **1** *the exploitation of mineral resources* UTILIZATION, use, making use of, making the most of, capitalization on; *informal* cashing in on. **2** *the exploitation of the poor* TAKING ADVANTAGE, abuse, misuse, ill-treatment, unfair treatment, oppression.

exploration ▶ noun **1** *the exploration of space* INVESTIGATION, study, survey, research, inspection, examination, scrutiny, observation; consideration, analysis, review. **2** *explorations into the mountains* EXPEDITION, trip, journey, voyage; *archaic* peregrination; (**explorations**) travels.

exploratory ▶ adjective INVESTIGATIVE, investigational, explorative, probing, fact-finding, experimental, trial, tentative, test, preliminary, provisional.

explore ▶ verb **1** *they explored all the possibilities* INVESTIGATE, look into, consider; examine, research, survey, scrutinize, study, review, go over with a fine-tooth comb; *informal* check out. **2** *explore Nunavut!* TRAVEL OVER/IN/THROUGH, tour, range over; survey, take a look at, inspect, investigate, reconnoitre, wander through.

explorer ▶ noun TRAVELLER, discoverer, voyager, adventurer; surveyor, scout, prospector.

explosion ▶ noun **1** *Edward heard the explosion* DETONATION, eruption, blowing up; bang, blast, boom, kaboom. **2** *an explosion of anger* OUTBURST, flare-up, outbreak, eruption, storm, rush, surge; fit, paroxysm, attack. **3** *the explosion of human populations* SUDDEN/RAPID INCREASE, mushrooming, snowballing, escalation, multiplication, burgeoning, rocketing.

explosive ▶ adjective **1** *explosive gases* VOLATILE, inflammable, flammable, combustible, incendiary. **2** *Biff's explosive temper* FIERY, stormy, violent, volatile, angry, passionate, tempestuous, turbulent, touchy, irascible, hot-headed, short-tempered. **3** *an explosive situation* TENSE, (highly) charged, overwrought; dangerous, perilous, hazardous, sensitive, delicate,

unstable, volatile. **4** *explosive population growth* SUDDEN, dramatic, rapid; mushrooming, snowballing, escalating, rocketing, accelerating.
▶ noun *stocks of explosives* BOMB, incendiary (device).

exponent ▶ noun ADVOCATE, supporter, proponent, upholder, backer, defender, champion; promoter, propagandist, campaigner, fighter, crusader, enthusiast, apologist; *informal* cheerleader, booster. – OPPOSITES: critic, opponent.

export ▶ verb **1** *exporting raw materials* SELL OVERSEAS/ABROAD, send/ship overseas/abroad, trade internationally. **2** *she is trying to export her ideas to Japan* TRANSMIT, spread, disseminate, circulate, communicate, pass on; *literary* bruit about/abroad. – OPPOSITES: import.

expose ▶ verb **1** *at low tide the sands are exposed* REVEAL, uncover, lay bare. **2** *he was exposed to asbestos* MAKE VULNERABLE, subject, lay open, put at risk, put in jeopardy. **3** *they were exposed to liberal ideas* INTRODUCE TO, bring into contact with, make aware of, familiarize with, acquaint with. **4** *he was exposed as a liar* UNCOVER, reveal, unveil, unmask, detect, find out; discover, bring to light, bring into the open, make known; denounce, condemn; *informal* spill the beans on, blow the whistle on. – OPPOSITES: cover.
■ **expose oneself** *informal* flash.

exposé ▶ noun REVELATION, disclosure, exposure; report, feature, piece, column; *informal* tell-all, scoop. – OPPOSITES: cover-up.

exposed ▶ adjective UNPROTECTED, unsheltered, open to the elements/weather; vulnerable, defenceless, undefended. – OPPOSITES: sheltered.

exposition ▶ noun **1** *a lucid exposition* EXPLANATION, description, elucidation, explication, interpretation; account, commentary, appraisal, assessment, discussion, exegesis. **2** *the exposition will feature 200 exhibits* EXHIBITION, (trade) fair, show, expo, display, presentation, demonstration, exhibit.

expository ▶ adjective EXPLANATORY, descriptive, describing, explicatory, explicative, interpretative, exegetical.

expostulate ▶ verb REMONSTRATE, disagree, argue, take issue, protest, reason, express disagreement, raise objections, rail.

exposure ▶ noun **1** *the exposure of the lizard's vivid blue tongue* REVEALING, revelation, uncovering, baring, laying bare. **2** *exposure to harmful chemicals* SUBJECTION, vulnerability, laying open. **3** *suffering from exposure* HYPOTHERMIA, cold, frostbite. **4** *exposure to great literature* INTRODUCTION TO, experience of, contact with, familiarity with, acquaintance with, awareness of. **5** *the exposure of a banking scandal* UNCOVERING, revelation, disclosure, unveiling, unmasking, discovery, detection; denunciation, condemnation. **6** *we're getting a lot of exposure* PUBLICITY, coverage, publicizing, advertising, public interest/attention, media interest/attention, ink; *informal* hype, face time. **7** *a southern exposure* OUTLOOK, aspect, view; position, setting, location.

expound ▶ verb **1** *he expounded his theories* PRESENT, put forward, set forth, propose, propound; explain, give an explanation of, detail, spell out, describe. **2** *a treatise expounding Chomsky's theories* EXPLAIN, interpret, explicate, elucidate; comment on, give a commentary on.
■ **expound on** ELABORATE ON, expand on, expatiate on, discuss at length.

express¹ ▶ verb **1** *community leaders expressed their anger* COMMUNICATE, convey, indicate, show, demonstrate, reveal, make manifest, put across/over, get across/over; articulate, put into words, utter, voice, give voice to; state, assert, proclaim, profess, air, make public, give vent to; *formal* evince. **2** *all the juice is expressed* SQUEEZE OUT, press out, extract.

■ **express oneself** COMMUNICATE ONE'S THOUGHTS/ OPINIONS/VIEWS, put thoughts into words, speak one's mind, say what's on one's mind.

express² ▶ adjective *an express bus* RAPID, swift, fast, quick, speedy, high-speed; non-stop, direct.
– OPPOSITES: slow.

express³ ▶ adjective **1** *an express reference to confidential matters* EXPLICIT, clear, direct, obvious, plain, distinct, unambiguous, unequivocal; specific, precise, crystal clear, certain, categorical. **2** *one express purpose* SOLE, specific, particular, exclusive, specified, fixed.
– OPPOSITES: implied.

expression ▶ noun **1** *the free expression of opposition views* UTTERANCE, uttering, voicing, pronouncement, declaration, articulation, assertion, setting forth; dissemination, circulation, communication, spreading, promulgation. **2** *an expression of sympathy* INDICATION, demonstration, show, exhibition, token; communication, illustration, revelation. **3** *an expression of harassed fatigue* LOOK, appearance, air, manner, countenance, mien. **4** *a time-worn expression* IDIOM, phrase, idiomatic expression; proverb, saying, adage, maxim, axiom, aphorism, saw, motto, platitude, cliché. **5** *these pieces are very different in expression* EMOTION, feeling, spirit, passion, intensity; style, intonation, tone. **6** *essential oils obtained by expression* SQUEEZING, pressing, extraction, extracting.

expressionless ▶ adjective **1** *his face was expressionless* INSCRUTABLE, deadpan, poker-faced; blank, vacant, emotionless, unemotional, inexpressive; glazed, stony, wooden, impassive. **2** *a flat, expressionless tone* DULL, dry, toneless, monotonous, boring, tedious, flat, wooden, unmodulated, unvarying, devoid of feeling/emotion.
– OPPOSITES: expressive, lively.

expressive ▶ adjective **1** *an expressive shrug* ELOQUENT, meaningful, demonstrative, suggestive. **2** *an expressive song* EMOTIONAL, full of emotion/feeling, passionate, poignant, moving, stirring, evocative, powerful, emotionally charged. **3** *his diction is very expressive of his upbringing* INDICATIVE, demonstrative, revealing.
– OPPOSITES: expressionless, unemotional.

expressly ▶ adverb **1** *he was expressly forbidden to discuss the matter* EXPLICITLY, clearly, directly, plainly, distinctly, unambiguously, unequivocally; absolutely, specifically, categorically, pointedly, emphatically. **2** *a machine expressly built for spraying paint* SOLELY, specifically, particularly, specially, exclusively, just, only, explicitly.

expropriate ▶ verb SEIZE, take (away/over), appropriate, take possession of, requisition, commandeer, claim, acquire, sequestrate, confiscate; *Law* distrain.

expulsion ▶ noun **1** *expulsion from the party* REMOVAL, debarment, dismissal, exclusion, discharge, ejection, drumming out. **2** *the expulsion of bodily wastes* DISCHARGE, ejection, excretion, voiding, evacuation, elimination, passing.
– OPPOSITES: admission.

expunge ▶ verb ERASE, remove, delete, rub out, wipe out, efface; cross out, strike out, blot out, destroy, obliterate, scratch, eradicate, eliminate, deep-six.

expurgate ▶ verb CENSOR, bowdlerize, blue-pencil, cut, edit; clean up, sanitize, make acceptable, make palatable, water down, tame.

exquisite ▶ adjective **1** *exquisite antique glass* BEAUTIFUL, lovely, elegant, fine; magnificent, superb, excellent, wonderful, ornate, well-crafted, well-made, perfect; delicate, fragile, dainty, subtle. **2** *exquisite taste* DISCRIMINATING, discerning, sensitive, selective, fastidious; refined, cultivated, cultured, educated. **3** *exquisite agony* INTENSE, acute, keen, piercing, sharp, severe, racking, excruciating, agonizing, harrowing, searing; unbearable, unendurable.

extant ▶ adjective STILL EXISTING, in existence, existent, surviving, remaining, undestroyed.

extemporary, extemporaneous ▶ adjective *See* EXTEMPORE.

extempore ▶ adjective *an extempore speech* IMPROMPTU, spontaneous, unscripted, ad lib, extemporary, extemporaneous; improvised, unrehearsed, unplanned, unprepared, off the top of one's head; *informal* off-the-cuff; *formal* ad libitum.
– OPPOSITES: rehearsed.
▶ adverb *he was speaking extempore* SPONTANEOUSLY, extemporaneously, ad lib, without preparation, without rehearsal, off the top of one's head; *informal* off the cuff; *formal* ad libitum.

extemporize ▶ verb IMPROVISE, ad lib, play it by ear, think on one's feet; *informal* wing it, fly by the seat of one's pants.

extend ▶ verb **1** *he attempted to extend his dominions* EXPAND, enlarge, increase, make larger/bigger; lengthen, widen, broaden. **2** *the garden extends down to the road* CONTINUE, carry on, run on, stretch (out), reach, lead. **3** *we have extended our range of services* WIDEN, expand, broaden; augment, supplement, increase, add to, enhance, develop. **4** *extending the life of parliament* PROLONG, lengthen, increase; stretch out, protract, spin out, string out. **5** *extend your arms and legs* STRETCH OUT, spread out, reach out, straighten out. **6** *he extended a hand in greeting* HOLD OUT, reach out, hold forth; offer, give, outstretch, proffer. **7** *we wish to extend our thanks to Mr. Bayes* OFFER, proffer, give, grant, bestow, accord.
– OPPOSITES: reduce, narrow, shorten.
■ **extend to** INCLUDE, take in, incorporate, encompass.

extended ▶ adjective PROLONGED, protracted, long-lasting, long-drawn-out, spun out, long, dragged out, strung out, lengthy; *informal* marathon.

extension ▶ noun **1** *they are planning a new extension* ADDITION, add-on, adjunct, annex, wing, supplementary building, ell. **2** *an extension of knowledge* EXPANSION, increase, enlargement, widening, broadening, deepening; augmentation, enhancement, development, growth, continuation. **3** *an extension of opening hours* PROLONGATION, lengthening, increase. **4** *I need an extension on my essay* POSTPONEMENT, more/extra time, deferral, delay.

extensive ▶ adjective **1** *a mansion with extensive grounds* LARGE, large-scale, sizeable, substantial, considerable, ample, expansive, great, vast. **2** *extensive knowledge* COMPREHENSIVE, thorough, exhaustive; broad, wide, wide-ranging, catholic, eclectic.

extent ▶ noun **1** *two acres in extent* AREA, size, expanse, length; proportions, dimensions. **2** *the full extent of her father's illness* DEGREE, scale, level, magnitude, scope; size, breadth, width, reach, range.

extenuate ▶ verb EXCUSE, mitigate, palliate, make allowances/excuses for, defend, vindicate, justify; diminish, lessen, moderate, qualify, play down.

extenuating ▶ adjective MITIGATING, excusing, exonerative, palliative, justifying, justificatory, vindicating; *formal* exculpatory.

exterior ▶ adjective *the exterior walls* OUTER, outside, outermost, outward, external.
– RELATED TERMS: ecto-, exo-.
– OPPOSITES: interior.
▶ noun *the exterior of the building* OUTSIDE, outer surface, external surface, outward appearance, facade.

exterminate ▶ verb KILL, put to death, take/end the life of, dispatch; slaughter, butcher, massacre, wipe out, eliminate, eradicate, annihilate; murder, assassinate, execute, slay; *informal* do away with, bump off, do in, take out, blow away, ice, rub out, waste.

extermination ▶ noun KILLING, murder, assassination, putting to death, execution, dispatch, slaughter, massacre, liquidation, elimination, eradication, annihilation, slaying.

external ▶ adjective **1** *an external wall* OUTER, outside, outermost, outward, exterior. **2** *an external examiner* OUTSIDE, independent, non-resident, from elsewhere.
– RELATED TERMS: ecto-, exo-.
– OPPOSITES: internal, in-house.

extinct ▶ adjective **1** *an extinct species* VANISHED, lost, died out, no longer existing, no longer extant, wiped out, destroyed, gone. **2** *an extinct volcano* INACTIVE.
– OPPOSITES: extant, dormant.

extinction ▶ noun DYING OUT, disappearance, vanishing; extermination, destruction, elimination, eradication, annihilation.

extinguish ▶ verb **1** *the fire was extinguished* DOUSE, put out, (*Nfld*) dout ✤, stamp out, smother, beat out. **2** *all hope was extinguished* DESTROY, end, finish off, put an end to, bring to an end, terminate, remove, annihilate, wipe out, erase, eliminate, eradicate, obliterate; *informal* take out, rub out.
– OPPOSITES: light.

extirpate ▶ verb WEED OUT, destroy, eradicate, stamp out, root out, wipe out, eliminate, suppress, crush, put down, put an end to, get rid of.

extol ▶ verb PRAISE ENTHUSIASTICALLY, go into raptures about/over, wax lyrical about, sing the praises of, praise to the skies, acclaim, exalt, eulogize, adulate, rhapsodize over, rave about, enthuse about/over; *informal* go wild about, go on about, ballyhoo; *formal* laud; *archaic* panegyrize.
– OPPOSITES: criticize.

extort ▶ verb FORCE, extract, exact, wring, wrest, screw, squeeze, obtain by threat(s), blackmail someone for; *informal* put the bite on someone for; soak, rook.

extortion ▶ noun BLACKMAIL, shakedown; *formal* exaction.

extortionate ▶ adjective *extortionate prices* EXORBITANT, excessively high, excessive, outrageous, unreasonable, inordinate, inflated, exacting, harsh, severe, oppressive; *informal* over the top; grasping, bloodsucking, avaricious, greedy, money-grubbing.

extortionist ▶ noun RACKETEER, extortioner, extorter, blackmailer; *informal* bloodsucker, vampire.

extra ▶ adjective *extra income* ADDITIONAL, more, added, supplementary, further, auxiliary, ancillary, subsidiary, secondary, bonus.
▶ adverb **1** *working extra hard* EXCEPTIONALLY, particularly, specially, especially, very, extremely; unusually, extraordinarily, uncommonly, remarkably, outstandingly, amazingly, incredibly, really, awfully, terribly; *informal* seriously, mucho, majorly. **2** *we charge extra for cheese* IN ADDITION, additionally, as well, also, too, besides, on top (of that); *archaic* withal.
▶ noun **1** *an optional extra* ADDITION, supplement, adjunct, addendum, add-on, bonus. **2** *a film extra* WALK-ON, supernumerary, spear carrier, super.

extract ▶ verb **1** *he extracted the cigarette butt* TAKE OUT, draw out, pull out, remove, withdraw; free, release, extricate. **2** *extracting money* WREST, exact, wring, screw, squeeze, obtain by force/threats, extort, blackmail someone for; *informal* put the bite on someone for. **3** *the roots are crushed to extract the juice* SQUEEZE OUT, express, press out, obtain. **4** *the figures are extracted from the report* EXCERPT, select, reproduce, copy, take. **5** *ideas extracted from a variety of theories* DERIVE, develop, evolve, deduce, infer, obtain; *formal* educe.
– OPPOSITES: insert.
▶ noun **1** *an extract from his article* EXCERPT, passage, citation, quotation; (**excerpts**) analects. **2** *an extract of the ginseng root* DECOCTION, distillation, distillate, abstraction, concentrate, essence, juice.

extraction ▶ noun **1** *the extraction of gall bladder stones* REMOVAL, taking out, drawing out, pulling out, withdrawal; freeing, release, extrication. **2** *the extraction of grape juice* SQUEEZING, expressing, pressing, obtaining. **3** *a man of Irish extraction* DESCENT, ancestry, parentage, ancestors, family, antecedents; lineage, line, origin, derivation, birth; genealogy, heredity, stock, pedigree, blood, bloodline; roots, origins.
– OPPOSITES: insertion.

extradite ▶ verb DEPORT, send, ship, deliver, hand over; repatriate.

extradition ▶ noun DEPORTATION, repatriation, expulsion.

extraneous ▶ adjective **1** *extraneous considerations* IRRELEVANT, immaterial, beside the point, unrelated, unconnected, inapposite, inapplicable, superfluous. **2** *extraneous noise* EXTERNAL, outside, exterior.

extraordinary ▶ adjective **1** *an extraordinary coincidence* REMARKABLE, exceptional, amazing, astonishing, astounding, sensational, stunning, incredible, unbelievable, phenomenal; striking, outstanding, momentous, impressive, singular, memorable, unforgettable, unique, noteworthy; out of the ordinary, unusual, uncommon, rare, surprising; *informal* fantastic, terrific, tremendous, stupendous, awesome; *literary* wondrous. **2** *extraordinary speed* VERY GREAT, tremendous, enormous, immense, prodigious, stupendous, monumental.

extraterrestrial ▶ noun & adjective *See* ALIEN.

extravagance ▶ noun **1** *a fit of extravagance* PROFLIGACY, improvidence, wastefulness, prodigality, lavishness. **2** *the costliest brands are an extravagance* LUXURY, indulgence, self-indulgence, treat, extra, non-essential. **3** *the extravagance of the decor* ORNATENESS, elaborateness, embellishment, ornamentation; ostentation, over-elaborateness, excessiveness, exaggeration, outrageousness, immoderation, excess.

extravagant ▶ **adjective 1** *an extravagant lifestyle* SPENDTHRIFT, profligate, improvident, wasteful, prodigal, lavish. **2** *extravagant gifts* EXPENSIVE, costly, lavish, high-priced, high-cost; valuable, precious; *informal* pricey, costing the earth. **3** *extravagant prices* EXORBITANT, extortionate, excessive, high, unreasonable. **4** *extravagant praise* EXCESSIVE, immoderate, exaggerated, gushing, unrestrained, effusive, fulsome. **5** *decorated in an extravagant style* ORNATE, elaborate, decorated, ornamented, fancy; over-elaborate, gaudy, garish, ostentatious, exaggerated, baroque, rococo; *informal* lavish, flashy, glitzy.
— OPPOSITES: thrifty, cheap, plain.

extravaganza ▶ **noun** SPECTACULAR, display, spectacle, show, pageant, gala; blowout, barnburner.

extreme ▶ **adjective 1** *extreme danger* UTMOST, very great, greatest (possible), maximum, maximal, highest, supreme, great, acute, enormous, severe, high, exceptional, extraordinary. **2** *extreme measures* DRASTIC, serious, desperate, dire, radical, far-reaching, momentous, consequential; heavy, sharp, severe, austere, harsh, tough, strict, rigorous, oppressive, draconian. **3** *extreme views* RADICAL, extremist, immoderate, fanatical, revolutionary, rebel, subversive, militant, far-right, far-left. **4** *extreme sports* DANGEROUS, hazardous, risky, high-risk, adventurous. **5** *the extreme north* FURTHEST, farthest, furthermost, far, very, utmost; *archaic* outmost.
— RELATED TERMS: ultra-.
— OPPOSITES: slight, moderate.
▶ **noun 1** *the two extremes* OPPOSITE, antithesis, side of the coin, (opposite) pole, antipode. **2** *this attitude is taken to its extreme in the following quote* LIMIT, extremity, highest/greatest degree, maximum, height, top, zenith, peak, ne plus ultra.
■ **in the extreme.** See EXTREMELY.

extremely ▶ **adverb** VERY, exceedingly, exceptionally, especially, extraordinarily, in the extreme, tremendously, immensely, vastly, hugely, intensely, acutely, singularly, uncommonly, unusually, decidedly, particularly, supremely, highly, remarkably, really, truly, mightily; *informal* terrifically, awfully, terribly, devilishly, majorly, seriously, mega, ultra, damn, damned, ever so, real, mighty, awful, way, darned, gosh-darn; *archaic* exceeding.
— OPPOSITES: slightly.

extremist ▶ **noun** FANATIC, radical, zealot, fundamentalist, hard-liner, militant, activist; *informal* ultra.
— OPPOSITES: moderate.

extremity ▶ **noun 1** *the eastern extremity* LIMIT, end, edge, side, farthest point, boundary, border, frontier; perimeter, periphery, margin; *literary* bourn, marge. **2** *she lost feeling in her extremities* FINGERS AND TOES, hands and feet, limbs. **3** *the extremity of the violence* INTENSITY, magnitude, acuteness, ferocity, vehemence, fierceness, violence, severity, seriousness, strength, power, powerfulness, vigour, force, forcefulness. **4** *in extremity he will send for her* DIRE STRAITS, trouble, difficulty, hard times, hardship, adversity, misfortune, distress; crisis, emergency, disaster, catastrophe, calamity; predicament, plight, mess, dilemma; *informal* fix,

pickle, jam, spot, bind, hole, sticky situation, hot/deep water.

extricate ▶ **verb** EXTRACT, free, release, disentangle, get out, remove, withdraw, disengage; *informal* get someone/oneself off the hook.

extrinsic ▶ **adjective** EXTERNAL, extraneous, exterior, outside, outward.
— OPPOSITES: intrinsic.

extrovert ▶ **noun** *like most extroverts he was unhappy inside* OUTGOING PERSON, sociable person, socializer, life of the party.
— OPPOSITES: introvert.
▶ **adjective** *Raj's extrovert personality* OUTGOING, extroverted, sociable, gregarious, genial, affable, friendly, unreserved.
— OPPOSITES: introverted.

extrude ▶ **verb** FORCE OUT, thrust out, express, eject, expel, release, emit.

exuberant ▶ **adjective 1** *exuberant guests dancing on the terrace* EBULLIENT, buoyant, cheerful, jaunty, light-hearted, high-spirited, exhilarated, excited, elated, exultant, euphoric, joyful, cheery, merry, jubilant, vivacious, enthusiastic, irrepressible, energetic, animated, full of life, lively, vigorous; *informal* bubbly, bouncy, chipper, chirpy, full of beans; *literary* blithe. **2** *an exuberant coating of mosses* LUXURIANT, lush, rich, dense, thick, abundant, profuse, plentiful, prolific. **3** *an exuberant welcome* EFFUSIVE, extravagant, fulsome, expansive, gushing, gushy, demonstrative.
— OPPOSITES: gloomy, restrained.

exude ▶ **verb 1** *milkweed exudes a milky sap* GIVE OFF/OUT, discharge, release, emit, issue; ooze, weep, secrete, excrete. **2** *slime exudes from the fungus* OOZE, seep, issue, escape, discharge, flow, leak. **3** *he exuded self-confidence* EMANATE, radiate, ooze, emit; display, show, evince, exhibit, manifest, transmit, embody.

exult ▶ **verb 1** *her opponents exulted when she left* REJOICE, be joyful, be happy, be delighted, be elated, be ecstatic, be overjoyed, be jubilant, be rapturous, be in raptures, be thrilled, jump for joy, be on cloud nine, be in seventh heaven; celebrate, cheer; *informal* be over the moon, be on top of the world; *literary* joy; *archaic* jubilate. **2** *he exulted in his triumph* REJOICE AT/IN, take delight in, find/take pleasure in, find joy in, enjoy, revel in, glory in, delight in, relish, savour; be/feel proud of, congratulate oneself on, pat oneself on the back.
— OPPOSITES: sorrow.

exultant ▶ **adjective** JUBILANT, thrilled, triumphant, delighted, exhilarated, happy, overjoyed, joyous, joyful, gleeful, excited, rejoicing, ecstatic, euphoric, elated, rapturous, in raptures, enraptured, on cloud nine, in seventh heaven; *informal* over the moon, jumping for joy.

exultation ▶ **noun** JUBILATION, rejoicing, happiness, pleasure, joy, gladness, delight, glee, elation, cheer, euphoria, exhilaration, delirium, ecstasy, rapture, exuberance.

eye ▶ **noun 1** *he rubbed his eyes* EYEBALL; *informal* peeper, baby blues; *literary* orb. **2** *sharp eyes* EYESIGHT, vision, sight, powers of observation, (visual) perception. **3** *an eye for a bargain* APPRECIATION, awareness, alertness, perception, consciousness, feeling, instinct, intuition, nose. **4** *his watchful eye* WATCH, observance, gaze, stare, regard; observation, surveillance, vigilance, contemplation, scrutiny. **5** *to desert was despicable in their eyes* OPINION, (way of) thinking, mind,

view, viewpoint, attitude, standpoint, perspective, belief, judgment, assessment, analysis, estimation. **6** *the eye of a needle* HOLE, opening, aperture, eyelet, slit, slot. **7** *the eye of the storm* CENTRE, middle, heart, core, hub, thick.
− RELATED TERMS: ocular, ophthalmic.

▶ **verb** LOOK AT, observe, view, gaze at, stare at, regard, contemplate, survey, scrutinize, consider, glance at; watch, keep an eye on, keep under observation; ogle, leer at, make eyes at; *informal* have/take a gander at, check out, size up, eyeball; *literary* behold.

■ **lay/set/clap eyes on** (*informal*) SEE, observe, notice, spot, spy, catch sight of, glimpse, catch/get a glimpse of; *literary* behold, espy, descry.

■ **see eye to eye** AGREE, concur, be in agreement, be of the same mind/opinion, be in accord, think as one; be on the same wavelength, get on/along.

eye candy ▶ **noun** VISUAL FEAST, eyeful; gloss, tinsel, veneer, decoration, glitter, flamboyance, gaudiness, splendour; ritz, glitz, garishness, razzle-dazzle, razzmatazz; sight for sore eyes.

eye-catching   ▶ **adjective** STRIKING, arresting, conspicuous, dramatic, impressive, spectacular, breathtaking, dazzling, amazing, stunning, sensational, remarkable, distinctive, unusual, out of the ordinary.

eyelash ▶ **noun** LASH; *Anatomy* cilium.

eyesight ▶ **noun** SIGHT, vision, faculty of sight, ability to see, (visual) perception.

eyesore   ▶ **noun** MONSTROSITY, blot (on the landscape), mess, scar, blight, disfigurement, blemish, ugly sight.

eyewitness ▶ **noun** OBSERVER, onlooker, witness, bystander, spectator, watcher, viewer, passerby, gawker; *literary* beholder.

Ff

Fabrics

acetate	cretonne	knit	prunella
acid-washed	crinoline	lace	ramie
acrylic	Dacron*	lamé	rayon
alpaca	damask	lawn	russet
angora	denim	leno	sackcloth
astrakhan	dimity	Lincoln green	samite
baize	drill	linen	sateen
Balbriggan	drugget	loden	satin
barathea	duck	Lurex*	saxony
batik	duffle	Lycra*	seersucker
batiste	dungaree	Mackinaw	serge
Bedford cord	dupion	mackintosh	shantung
bengaline	faille	madras	sharkskin
bombazine	felt	melton	silk
bouclé	fishnet	merino	slub
brilliantine	flannel	mohair	spandex
broadcloth	flannelette	moiré	stroud
brocade	fleece	mouflon	suede
buckram	foulard	mousseline	swansdown
buckskin	gabardine	muslin	taffeta
bunting	gauze	nainsook	tarpaulin
burlap	gingham	nankeen	tartan
byssus	Gore-Tex*	Naugahyde*	tattersall
calico	grasscloth	nylon	terry cloth
cambric	grenadine	oilcloth	ticking
camel hair	grogram	organdy	toile
canvas	grosgrain	organza	towelling
cashmere	gunny	Orlon*	tricot
cavalry twill	haircloth	ottoman	tulle
challis	Harris tweed*	oxford cloth	tweed
chambray	herringbone	paisley	twill
charmeuse	hopsack	panne	Ultrasuede*
chenille	horsehair	pashmina	veiling
chiffon	huckaback	peau de soie	velour
chino	ikat	percale	velvet
chintz	jaconet	piqué	velveteen
ciré	jacquard	plaid	vicuña
cloqué	jean	plissé	Viyella*
Cordura*	jersey	plush	voile
corduroy	kente	polar fleece	webbing
cotton	kersey	polycotton	whipcord
crape	kerseymere	polyester	wool
crash	khadi	pongee	worsted
crepe	khaki	poplin	zephyr
			*Proprietary term.

fable ▶ noun **1** *the fable of the wary fox* MORAL TALE, parable, allegory. **2** *the fables of ancient Greece* MYTH, legend, saga, epic, folk tale, folk story, fairy tale, mythos, folklore, mythology.

fabled ▶ adjective **1** *a fabled god-giant of Finnish myth* LEGENDARY, mythical, mythic, mythological, fabulous, folkloric, fairy-tale; fictitious, fantastic, imaginary, imagined, made up. **2** *the fabled quality of French wine* CELEBRATED, renowned, famed, famous, well-known, legendary, prized, noted, notable, acclaimed, esteemed, prestigious, of repute, of high standing.

fabric ▶ noun **1** *the finest silk fabric* CLOTH, material, textile, tissue. *See table.* **2** *the fabric of society* STRUCTURE, infrastructure, framework, frame, form, composition, construction, foundations, warp and woof.

fabricate ▶ verb **1** *he fabricated research data* FALSIFY, fake, counterfeit, cook; invent, make up. **2** *fabricating a pack of lies* CONCOCT, make up, dream up, invent, trump up; *informal* cook up. **3** *you will have to fabricate an exhaust system* MAKE, create, manufacture, produce; construct, build, assemble, put together, form, fashion.

fabrication ▶ noun **1** *the story was a complete fabrication* INVENTION, concoction, (piece of) fiction, falsehood, lie, untruth, falsehood, fib, myth, made-up story, fairy story/tale, cock-and-bull story; white lie, half-truth, exaggeration; *informal* tall tale, whopper. **2** *the lintels are galvanized after fabrication* MANUFACTURE, creation, production; construction, building, assembly, forming, fashioning.

fabulous ▶ adjective **1** *fabulous wealth* TREMENDOUS, stupendous, prodigious, phenomenal, remarkable, exceptional; astounding, amazing, fantastic, breathtaking, staggering, unthinkable, unimaginable, incredible, unbelievable, unheard of, untold, undreamed of, beyond one's wildest dreams; *informal* mind-boggling, mind-blowing, jaw-dropping. **2** (*informal*) *we had a fabulous time.* See EXCELLENT. **3** *a fabulous horse-like beast* MYTHICAL, legendary, mythic, mythological, fabled, folkloric, fairy-tale; fictitious, imaginary, imagined, made up.

facade ▶ noun **1** *a half-timbered facade* FRONT, frontage, face, elevation, exterior, outside. **2** *a facade of bonhomie* SHOW, front, appearance, pretense, simulation, affectation, semblance, illusion, act, masquerade, charade, mask, cloak, veil, veneer.

face ▶ noun **1** *a beautiful face* COUNTENANCE, physiognomy, features; *informal* mug, phiz; puss; *literary* visage; *archaic* front. **2** *her face grew sad* (FACIAL) EXPRESSION, look, appearance, air, manner, bearing, countenance, mien. **3** *he made a face at the sourness of the drink* GRIMACE, scowl, wry face, wince, frown, glower, pout, moue. **4** *a cube has six faces* SIDE, aspect, flank, surface, plane, facet, wall, elevation. **5** *a watch face* DIAL, display. **6** *changing the face of the industry* (OUTWARD) APPEARANCE, aspect, nature, image. **7** *he put on a brave face* FRONT, show, display, act, appearance, facade, exterior, mask, masquerade, pretense, pose, veneer. **8** *criticism should never cause the recipient to lose face* RESPECT, honour, esteem, regard, admiration, approbation, acclaim, approval, favour, appreciation, popularity, prestige, standing, status, dignity; self-respect, self-esteem.
— RELATED TERMS: facial.
▶ verb **1** *the hotel faces the sea* LOOK OUT ON, front on to, look towards, be facing, look over/across, overlook, give on to, be opposite (to). **2** *you'll just have to face facts* ACCEPT, become reconciled to, get used to, become accustomed to, adjust to, acclimatize oneself to; learn to live with, cope with, deal with, come to terms with, become resigned to. **3** *he faces a humiliating rejection* BE CONFRONTED BY, be faced with, encounter, experience, come into contact with, come up against. **4** *the problems facing our police force* BESET, worry, distress, trouble, bother, confront; harass, oppress, vex, irritate, exasperate, strain, stress, tax; torment, plague, blight, bedevil, curse; *formal* discommode. **5** *he faced the challenge boldly* BRAVE, face up to, encounter, meet (head-on), confront; oppose, resist, withstand. **6** *a wall faced with flint* COVER, clad, veneer, overlay, surface, dress, put a facing on, laminate, coat, line.
■ **face to face** FACING (EACH OTHER), opposite (each other), across from each other.
■ **on the face of it** OSTENSIBLY, to all appearances, to all intents and purposes, at first glance, on the surface, superficially; apparently, seemingly, outwardly, it seems (that), it would seem (that), it appears (that), it would appear (that), as far as one can see/tell, by all accounts.

face cloth ▶ noun WASHCLOTH, washrag, terry cloth.

faceless ▶ adjective ANONYMOUS, unknown, nameless; characterless, nondescript, undistinguished, featureless.

facelift ▶ noun **1** *she's planning to have a facelift* COSMETIC SURGERY, plastic surgery, nip and tuck. **2** (*informal*) *the theatre is reopening after a facelift* RENOVATION, redecoration, refurbishment, revamp, revamping, makeover, reconditioning, overhauling, modernization, restoration, repair, redevelopment, rebuilding, reconstruction, refit.

facet ▶ noun **1** *the many facets of the gem* SURFACE, face, side, plane. **2** *other facets of his character* ASPECT, feature, side, dimension, characteristic, detail, point, ingredient, strand; component, constituent, element.

facetious ▶ adjective FLIPPANT, flip, glib, frivolous, tongue-in-cheek, ironic, sardonic, joking, jokey, jocular, playful, sportive, teasing, mischievous; witty, amusing, funny, droll, comic, comical, light-hearted, jocose.
— OPPOSITES: serious.

facile ▶ adjective **1** *a facile explanation* SIMPLISTIC, superficial, oversimplified; shallow, glib, jejune, naive; dime-store. **2** *he achieved a facile victory* EFFORTLESS, easy, undemanding, unexacting, painless, trouble-free.

facilitate ▶ verb MAKE EASY/EASIER, ease, make possible, make smooth/smoother, smooth the way for; enable, assist, help (along), aid, oil the wheels of, expedite, speed up, accelerate, forward, advance, promote, further, encourage, catalyze/be a catalyst for.
— OPPOSITES: impede.

facility ▶ noun **1** *parking facilities* PROVISION, space, means, potential, equipment. **2** *the facilities consisted of an old wooden outhouse* WASHROOM, toilet, restroom, bathroom. **3** *a wealth of local facilities* AMENITY, resource, service, advantage, convenience, benefit. **4** *a medical facility* ESTABLISHMENT, centre, place, station, location, premises, site, post, base; *informal* joint, outfit, set-up. **5** *his facility for drawing* APTITUDE, talent, gift, flair, bent, skill, knack, genius; ability, proficiency, competence, capability, capacity, faculty; expertness, adeptness, prowess, mastery, artistry.

facing ▶ noun **1** *green velvet facings* COVERING, trimming, lining, interfacing. **2** *brick facing on a concrete core* SIDING, facade, cladding, veneer, skin, surface, front, coating, covering, dressing, overlay, lamination, plating.

facsimile ▶ noun COPY, reproduction, duplicate, photocopy, replica, likeness, carbon copy, print, reprint, printout, offprint, fax; *proprietary* Xerox; *dated* photostat, mimeograph.
— OPPOSITES: original.

fact ▶ noun **1** *it is a fact that the water is polluted* REALITY, actuality, certainty; truth, verity, gospel. **2** *every fact was double-checked* DETAIL, piece of information, particular, item, specific, element, point, factor, feature, characteristic, ingredient, circumstance, aspect, facet; (**facts**) information. **3** *an accessory after the fact* EVENT, happening, occurrence, incident, act, deed.
— OPPOSITES: lie, fiction.
■ **in fact** ACTUALLY, in actuality, in actual fact, really, in reality, in point of fact, as a matter of fact, as it happens, in truth, to tell the truth; *archaic* in sooth, verily.

faction ▶ noun **1** *a faction of the Liberal Party* CLIQUE, coterie, caucus, cabal, bloc, camp, group, grouping, sector, section, wing, arm, branch, set; ginger group, pressure group. **2** *the council was split by faction* INFIGHTING, dissension, dissent, dispute, discord, strife, conflict, friction, argument, disagreement, controversy, quarrelling, wrangling, bickering, squabbling, disharmony, disunity, schism.

factious ▶ adjective DIVIDED, split, schismatic, discordant, conflicting, argumentative, disagreeing, disputatious, quarrelling, quarrelsome, clashing, warring, at loggerheads, at odds, rebellious, mutinous.
− OPPOSITES: harmonious.

factitious ▶ adjective BOGUS, fake, specious, false, counterfeit, fraudulent, spurious, sham, mock, feigned, affected, pretended, contrived, engineered, inauthentic, ersatz; *informal* phony, pseudo, pretend.
− OPPOSITES: genuine.

factor ▶ noun ELEMENT, part, component, ingredient, strand, constituent, point, detail, item, feature, facet, aspect, characteristic, consideration, influence, circumstance.

factory ▶ noun PLANT, works, yard, mill, workshop, shop.

factotum ▶ noun HANDYMAN, jack of all trades, man/girl Friday, all-rounder, gofer; *informal* (Mr.) Fix-It, odd-job man.

factual ▶ adjective TRUTHFUL, true, accurate, authentic, historical, genuine, fact-based; true-to-life, correct, exact, honest, faithful, literal, verbatim, word for word, well-documented, unbiased, objective, unvarnished; *formal* veridical.
− OPPOSITES: fictitious.

faculty ▶ noun **1** *the faculty of speech* POWER, capability, capacity, facility, wherewithal, means; **(faculties)** senses, wits, reason, intelligence. **2** *an unusual faculty for unearthing contributors* ABILITY, proficiency, competence, capability, potential, capacity, facility; aptitude, talent, gift, flair, bent, skill, knack, genius; expertise, expertness, adeptness, adroitness, dexterity, prowess, mastery, artistry. **3** *the arts faculty* DEPARTMENT, school, division, section. **4** *conflict between students and faculty* STAFF, teachers, professors, instructors.

fad ▶ noun CRAZE, vogue, trend, fashion, mode, enthusiasm, passion, obsession, mania, rage, compulsion, fixation, fetish, fancy, whim, fascination; *informal* thing.

fade ▶ verb **1** *the paintwork has faded* BECOME PALE, become bleached, become washed out, lose colour, discolour; grow dull, grow dim, lose lustre. **2** *sunlight had faded the picture* BLEACH, wash out, make pale, blanch, whiten. **3** *remove the flower heads as they fade* WITHER, wilt, droop, shrivel, die. **4** *the afternoon light began to fade* (GROW) DIM, grow faint, fail, dwindle, die away, wane, disappear, vanish, decline, melt away; *literary* evanesce. **5** *the Communist movement was fading away* DECLINE, die out, diminish, deteriorate, decay, crumble, collapse, fail, fall, sink, slump, go downhill; *informal* go to pot, go to the dogs; *archaic* retrograde.
− OPPOSITES: brighten, increase.

fagged ▶ adjective *(informal)* EXHAUSTED, tired (out), worn out, fatigued, weary, drained, washed out; *informal* done in, all in, dead beat, dead on one's feet, bushed, tuckered, pooped.

fail ▶ verb **1** *the enterprise had failed* BE UNSUCCESSFUL, not succeed, fall through, fall flat, collapse, founder, backfire, meet with disaster, come to nothing/naught; *informal* flop, bomb. **2** *he failed his examination* FLUNK, botch, be unsuccessful in, not pass; not make the grade; screw up, bungle, blow. **3** *his friends had failed him* LET DOWN, disappoint; desert, abandon, betray, be disloyal to; *literary* forsake. **4** *the crops failed* DIE, wither; be deficient, be insufficient, be inadequate. **5** *the daylight failed* FADE, dim, die away, wane, disappear, vanish. **6** *the ventilation system failed* BREAK (DOWN), stop working, cut out, crash; malfunction, go wrong, develop a fault; *informal* conk out, go on the blink/fritz. **7** *Joe's health was failing* DETERIORATE, degenerate, decline, fade, wane, ebb. **8** *900 businesses are failing a week* COLLAPSE, crash, go under, go bankrupt, go into receivership, go into liquidation, cease trading, be wound up; *informal* fold, flop, go bust, go broke, go belly-up.
− OPPOSITES: succeed, pass, thrive, work.

■ **without fail** WITHOUT EXCEPTION, unfailingly, regularly, invariably, predictably, conscientiously, religiously, whatever happened.

failing ▶ noun *Deborah accepted him despite his failings* FAULT, shortcoming, weakness, imperfection, defect, flaw, frailty, foible, idiosyncrasy, vice.
− OPPOSITES: strength.

▶ preposition *failing financial assistance, you will be bankrupt* IN THE ABSENCE OF, lacking, barring, absent, without.

failure ▶ noun **1** *the failure of the assassination attempt* LACK OF SUCCESS, non-fulfilment, defeat, collapse, foundering. **2** *all his schemes had been a failure* FIASCO, debacle, catastrophe, disaster; *informal* flop, megaflop, washout, dead loss, snafu, clinker, dud, flame-out, no-go. **3** *she was regarded as a failure* LOSER, underachiever, ne'er-do-well, disappointment; *informal* no-hoper, dead loss, dud, write-off. **4** *a failure in duty* NEGLIGENCE, dereliction; omission, oversight. **5** *a crop failure* INADEQUACY, insufficiency, deficiency. **6** *the failure of the camera* BREAKING DOWN, breakdown, malfunction; crash. **7** *company failures* COLLAPSE, crash, bankruptcy, insolvency, liquidation, closure.
− OPPOSITES: success.

faint ▶ adjective **1** *a faint mark* INDISTINCT, vague, unclear, indefinite, ill-defined, imperceptible, unobtrusive; pale, light, faded. **2** *a faint cry* QUIET, muted, muffled, stifled, feeble, weak, whispered, murmured, indistinct; low, soft, gentle. **3** *a faint possibility* SLIGHT, slender, slim, small, tiny, negligible, remote, vague, unlikely, improbable; *informal* minuscule. **4** *faint praise* UNENTHUSIASTIC, half-hearted, weak, feeble. **5** *I suddenly felt faint* DIZZY, giddy, light-headed, unsteady; *informal* woozy.
− OPPOSITES: clear, loud, strong.

▶ verb *she thought he would faint* PASS OUT, lose consciousness, black out, keel over, swoon; *informal* flake out, conk out, go out like a light.

▶ noun *a dead faint* BLACKOUT, fainting fit, loss of consciousness, swoon; *Medicine* syncope.

faint-hearted ▶ adjective TIMID, timorous, nervous, easily scared, fearful, afraid; cowardly, craven, spineless, pusillanimous, lily-livered; *informal* chicken, chicken-hearted, yellow-bellied, gutless, sissy, wimpy, wimpish.
− OPPOSITES: brave.

faintly ▶ adverb **1** *Maria called his name faintly* INDISTINCTLY, softly, gently, weakly; in a murmur, in a low voice. **2** *he looked faintly bewildered* SLIGHTLY, vaguely, somewhat, quite, fairly, rather, a

little, a bit, a touch, a shade; *informal* sort of, kind of, kinda.
– OPPOSITES: loudly, extremely.

fair¹ ▶ adjective **1** *the courts were generally fair* JUST, equitable, honest, upright, honourable, trustworthy; impartial, unbiased, unprejudiced, non-partisan, neutral, even-handed; lawful, legal, legitimate; *informal* legit, on the level; on the up and up. **2** *fair weather* FINE, dry, bright, clear, sunny, cloudless; warm, balmy, clement, benign, pleasant. **3** *fair winds* FAVOURABLE, advantageous, benign; on one's side, in one's favour. **4** *fair hair* BLOND(E), yellowish, golden, flaxen, light, light brown, ash blond; fair-haired, light-haired, golden-haired. **5** *Hermione's fair skin* PALE, light, light-coloured, white, creamy. **6** *(archaic) the fair maiden's heart. See* BEAUTIFUL. **7** *the restaurant was fair* REASONABLE, passable, tolerable, satisfactory, acceptable, respectable, decent, all right, good enough, pretty good, not bad, average, middling; *informal* OK, so-so, {comme ci, comme ça}.
– OPPOSITES: inclement, unfavourable, dark.

■ **fair and square** HONESTLY, fairly, without cheating, without foul play, by the book; lawfully, legally, legitimately; *informal* on the level, on the up and up.

fair² ▶ noun **1** *a country fair* CARNIVAL, ex ✤, festival, exhibition; midway. **2** *an antiques fair* MARKET, bazaar, mart, exchange, sale; *archaic* emporium. **3** *a new art fair* EXHIBITION, exhibit, display, show, presentation, exposition.

fairly ▶ adverb **1** *all pupils were treated fairly* JUSTLY, equitably, impartially, without bias, without prejudice, even-handedly; lawfully, legally, legitimately; by the book; equally, the same. **2** *the pipes are in fairly good condition* REASONABLY, passably, tolerably, adequately, moderately, quite, relatively, comparatively; *informal* pretty, kind of, kinda, sort of.

fair-minded ▶ adjective FAIR, just, even-handed, equitable, impartial, non-partisan, unbiased, unprejudiced; honest, honourable, trustworthy, upright, decent; *informal* on the level; on the up and up.

fairy ▶ noun SPRITE, pixie, elf, imp, brownie, puck, leprechaun; *literary* faerie, fay.

fairy tale, fairy story ▶ noun **1** *the film was inspired by a fairy tale* FOLK TALE, folk story, traditional story, myth, legend, fantasy, fable. **2** *(informal) she accused him of telling fairy tales* (WHITE) LIE, fib, half-truth, untruth, falsehood, tall tale, story, fabrication, invention, fiction; *informal* whopper, cock-and-bull story.

fait accompli ▶ noun DONE DEAL.

faith ▶ noun **1** *he justified his boss's faith in him* TRUST, belief, confidence, conviction; optimism, hopefulness, hope. **2** *she gave her life for her faith* RELIGION, church, sect, denomination, (religious) persuasion, (religious) belief, ideology, creed, teaching, doctrine.
– OPPOSITES: mistrust.

■ **break faith with** BE DISLOYAL TO, be unfaithful to, be untrue to, betray, play someone false, break one's promise to, fail, let down; double-cross, deceive, cheat, stab in the back.

■ **keep faith with** BE LOYAL TO, be faithful to, be true to, stand by, stick by, keep one's promise to.

faithful ▶ adjective **1** *his faithful assistant* LOYAL, constant, true, devoted, true-blue, unswerving, staunch, steadfast, dedicated, committed, trusty, trustworthy, dependable, reliable. **2** *a faithful copy*

ACCURATE, precise, exact, errorless, unerring, faultless, true, close, strict; realistic, authentic; *informal* on the mark, on the nail, bang on, on the money.
– OPPOSITES: inaccurate.

faithless ▶ adjective **1** *her faithless lover* UNFAITHFUL, disloyal, inconstant, false, untrue, adulterous, traitorous; fickle, flighty, untrustworthy, unreliable, undependable; deceitful, two-faced, double-crossing; *informal* cheating, two-timing, backstabbing; *literary* perfidious. **2** *a faithless society* UNBELIEVING, non-believing, irreligious, disbelieving, agnostic, atheistic; pagan, heathen.

fake ▶ noun **1** *the sculpture was a fake* FORGERY, counterfeit, copy, pirate(d) copy, sham, fraud, hoax, imitation, mock-up, dummy, reproduction, knock-off; *informal* phony, rip-off, dupe. **2** *that doctor is a fake* CHARLATAN, fraud, fraudster, phony, mountebank, sham, quack, humbug, imposter, hoaxer, cheat, (confidence) trickster; con man, con artist, scam artist.
▶ adjective **1** *fake $50 bills* COUNTERFEIT, forged, fraudulent, sham, imitation, pirate(d), false, bogus; invalid, inauthentic; *informal* phony, dud. **2** *fake diamonds* IMITATION, artificial, synthetic, simulated, reproduction, replica, ersatz, faux, man-made, dummy, false, mock, bogus; *informal* pretend, phony, pseudo. **3** *a fake accent* FEIGNED, faked, put-on, assumed, invented, affected, pseudo; unconvincing, artificial, mock; *informal* phony.
– OPPOSITES: genuine, authentic.
▶ verb **1** *the certificate was faked* FORGE, counterfeit, falsify, mock up, copy, pirate, reproduce, replicate; doctor, alter, tamper with. **2** *she faked a yawn* FEIGN, pretend, simulate, put on, affect. **3** *he faked left and scored with the goalie out of position* DEKE, feint; dipsy-doodle.

fall ▶ verb **1** *bombs began to fall* DROP, descend, come down, go down; plummet, plunge, sink, dive, tumble; cascade. **2** *he tripped and fell* TOPPLE OVER, tumble over, keel over, fall down/over, go head over heels, go headlong, collapse, take a spill, pitch forward; trip (over), stumble, slip; *informal* come a cropper, face plant. **3** *the river began to fall* SUBSIDE, recede, ebb, flow back, fall away, go down, sink. **4** *inflation will fall* DECREASE, decline, diminish, fall off, drop off, lessen, dwindle; plummet, plunge, slump, sink; depreciate, cheapen, devalue; *informal* go through the floor, nosedive, take a header, crash. **5** *the Mogul empire fell* DECLINE, deteriorate, degenerate, go downhill, go to rack and ruin; decay, wither, fade, fail; *informal* go to the dogs, go to pot, go down the toilet. **6** *those who fell in the war* DIE, perish, lose one's life, be killed, be slain, be lost, meet one's death; *informal* bite the dust, croak, buy it, buy the farm. **7** *the town fell to the barbarians* SURRENDER, yield, submit, give in, capitulate, succumb; be taken by, be defeated by, be conquered by, be overwhelmed by. **8** *Easter falls on April 23rd* OCCUR, take place, happen, come about; arise; *literary* come to pass. **9** *night fell* COME, arrive, appear, arise, materialize. **10** *she fell ill* BECOME, grow, get, turn. **11** *more tasks may fall to him* BE THE RESPONSIBILITY OF, be the duty of, be borne by, be one's job; come someone's way.
– OPPOSITES: rise, flood, increase, flourish.
▶ noun **1** *an accidental fall* TUMBLE, trip, spill, topple, slip; collapse; *informal* nosedive, face plant, header, cropper. **2** *a fall in sales* DECLINE, fall-off, drop, decrease, cut, dip, reduction, downswing; plummet,

plunge, slump; *informal* nosedive, toboggan slide ♣, crash. **3** *the fall of the Roman Empire* DOWNFALL, collapse, ruin, ruination, failure, decline, deterioration, degeneration; destruction, overthrow, demise. **4** *the fall of the city* SURRENDER, capitulation, yielding, submission; defeat. **5** *a steep fall down to the ocean* DESCENT, declivity, slope, slant, incline, downgrade. **6** *the fall of man* SIN, wrongdoing, transgression, error, offence, lapse, fall from grace. **7** *rafting trips below the falls* WATERFALL, cascade, cataract; rapids, white water.
— OPPOSITES: increase, rise, ascent.

■ **fall apart** FALL/COME TO PIECES, fall/come to bits, come apart (at the seams); disintegrate, fragment, break up, break apart, crumble, decay, perish; *informal* bust.

■ **fall asleep** DOZE OFF, drop off, go to sleep; *informal* nod off, go off, drift off, crash (out), flake out, conk out, go out like a light, sack out.

■ **fall away** SLOPE (DOWN), slant down, go down, drop (away), descend, dip, sink, plunge.

■ **fall back** RETREAT, withdraw, back off, draw back, pull away, pull away, move away.

■ **fall back on** RESORT TO, turn to, look to, call on, have recourse to; rely on, depend on, lean on.

■ **fall behind 1** *the other walkers fell behind* LAG (BEHIND), trail (behind), be left behind, drop back, bring up the rear; straggle, dally, dawdle, hang back. **2** *they fell behind on their payments* GET INTO DEBT, get into arrears, default, be in the red.

■ **fall for 1** *she fell for John* FALL IN LOVE WITH, become infatuated with, lose one's heart to, take a fancy to, be smitten by, be attracted to; *informal* have the hots for. **2** *she won't fall for that trick* BE DECEIVED BY, be duped by, be fooled by, be taken in by, believe, trust, be convinced by; *informal* go for, buy, swallow (hook, line, and sinker).

■ **fall in 1** *the roof fell in* COLLAPSE, cave in, crash in, fall down; give way, crumble, disintegrate. **2** *the troops fell in* GET IN FORMATION, get in line, line up, take one's position.

■ **fall in with** GET INVOLVED WITH, take up with, join up with, go around with, string along with, make friends with; *informal* hang (out) with.

■ **fall off** *See* FALL *verb* sense 4.

■ **fall on** ATTACK, assail, assault, fly at, set about, set upon; pounce upon, ambush, surprise, rush, storm, charge; *informal* jump, lay into, pitch into, beat someone up, have a go at.

■ **fall out** QUARREL, argue, row, fight, squabble, bicker, have words, disagree, be at odds, clash, wrangle, cross swords, lock horns, be at loggerheads, be at each other's throats; *informal* scrap.

■ **fall short of** FAIL TO MEET, fail to reach, fail to live up to; be deficient, be inadequate, be insufficient, be wanting, be lacking, disappoint; *informal* not come up to scratch/snuff.

■ **fall through** FAIL, be unsuccessful, come to nothing, miscarry, abort, go awry, collapse, founder, come to grief; *informal* fizzle out, flop, fold, come a cropper, go down like a lead balloon.

fallacious ▶ **adjective** ERRONEOUS, false, untrue, wrong, incorrect, flawed, inaccurate, mistaken, misinformed, misguided; specious, spurious, bogus, fictitious, fabricated, made up; groundless, unfounded, ill-founded, unproven, unsupported, uncorroborated; *informal* phony, full of holes.
— OPPOSITES: correct.

fallacy ▶ **noun** MISCONCEPTION, misbelief, delusion, mistaken impression, error, misapprehension,

misinterpretation, misconstruction, mistake; untruth, inconsistency, myth.

fallback ▶ **noun & adjective** BACKUP, reserve, contingency, auxiliary, spare.

fallen ▶ **adjective 1** *fallen heroes* DEAD, perished, killed, slain, slaughtered, murdered; lost, late, lamented, departed, gone; *formal* deceased. **2** (*dated*) *fallen women* IMMORAL, loose, promiscuous, unchaste, sinful, impure, sullied, tainted, dishonoured, ruined.

fallible ▶ **adjective** ERROR-PRONE, errant, liable to err, open to error; imperfect, flawed, weak.

fallout ▶ **noun** *the fallout from the scandal led to her resignation* REPERCUSSION, reverberation, aftermath, effect, consequence.

fallow ▶ **adjective 1** *fallow farmland* UNCULTIVATED, unplowed, untilled, unplanted, unsown; unused, dormant, resting, empty, bare. **2** *a fallow trading period* INACTIVE, dormant, quiet, slack, slow, stagnant; barren, unproductive.
— OPPOSITES: cultivated, busy.

false ▶ **adjective 1** *a false report* INCORRECT, untrue, wrong, erroneous, fallacious, flawed, distorted, inaccurate, imprecise; untruthful, fictitious, concocted, fabricated, invented, made up, trumped up, unfounded, spurious; counterfeit, forged, fraudulent. **2** *a false friend* FAITHLESS, unfaithful, disloyal, untrue, inconstant, treacherous, traitorous, two-faced, double-crossing, deceitful, dishonest, duplicitous, untrustworthy, unreliable; untruthful; *informal* cheating, two-timing, back-stabbing; *literary* perfidious. **3** *false pearls* FAKE, artificial, imitation, synthetic, simulated, reproduction, replica, ersatz, faux, man-made, dummy, mock; *informal* phony, pretend, pseudo.
— OPPOSITES: correct, truthful, faithful, genuine.

falsehood ▶ **noun 1** *a downright falsehood* LIE, untruth, fib, falsification, fabrication, invention, fiction, story, cock-and-bull story, flight of fancy; half truth; *informal* tall story, tall tale, fairy tale, whopper. **2** *he accused me of falsehood* LYING, mendacity, untruthfulness, fibbing, fabrication, invention, perjury, telling stories; deceit, deception, pretense, artifice, double-crossing, treachery; *literary* perfidy.
— OPPOSITES: truth, honesty.

falsify ▶ **verb 1** *she falsified the accounts* FORGE, fake, counterfeit, fabricate; alter, change, doctor, tamper with, fudge, manipulate, adulterate, corrupt, misrepresent, misreport, distort, warp, embellish, embroider; *informal* cook. **2** *the theory is falsified by the evidence* DISPROVE, refute, rebut, deny, debunk, negate, negative, invalidate, contradict, controvert, confound, demolish, discredit; *informal* poke holes in, blow out of the water; *formal* confute, gainsay.

falsity ▶ **noun** UNTRUTHFULNESS, untruth, fallaciousness, falseness, falsehood, fictitiousness, inaccuracy; mendacity, fabrication, dishonesty, deceit.

falter ▶ **verb 1** *the government faltered* HESITATE, delay, drag one's feet, stall; waver, vacillate, waffle, be indecisive, be irresolute, blow hot and cold, hem and haw; *informal* sit on the fence, dilly-dally, shilly-shally. **2** *she faltered over his name* STAMMER, stutter, stumble; hesitate, flounder. **3** *the economy was faltering* STRUGGLE, stumble, flounder, be in difficulty.

fame ▶ **noun** RENOWN, celebrity, stardom, popularity, prominence; note, distinction, esteem, importance, account, consequence, greatness, eminence,

prestige, stature, repute; notoriety, infamy.
— OPPOSITES: obscurity.

famed ▶ adjective FAMOUS, celebrated, well-known, prominent, noted, notable, renowned, respected, esteemed, acclaimed; notorious, infamous.
— OPPOSITES: unknown.

familiar ▶ adjective **1** *a familiar task* WELL-KNOWN, recognized, accustomed; common, commonplace, everyday, day-to-day, ordinary, habitual, usual, customary, routine, standard, stock, mundane, run-of-the-mill; *literary* wonted. **2** *are you familiar with the subject?* ACQUAINTED, conversant, versed, knowledgeable, well-informed; skilled, proficient; at home with, no stranger to, au fait with, au courant with; *informal* up on, in the know about. **3** *a familiar atmosphere* INFORMAL, casual, relaxed, easy, comfortable; friendly, unceremonious, unreserved, open, natural, unpretentious. **4** *he is too familiar with the teachers* PRESUMPTUOUS, overfamiliar, disrespectful, forward, bold, impudent, impertinent.
— OPPOSITES: formal.

familiarity ▶ noun **1** *her familiarity with Asian politics* ACQUAINTANCE WITH, awareness of, experience of, insight into, knowledge of, understanding of, comprehension of, grasp of, skill in, proficiency in. **2** *she was affronted by his familiarity* PRESUMPTION, overfamiliarity, presumptuousness, forwardness, boldness, audacity, cheek, impudence, impertinence, disrespect; liberties. **3** *our familiarity allows us to tease each other* CLOSENESS, intimacy, attachment, affinity, friendliness, friendship, amity; *informal* chumminess.

familiarize ▶ verb MAKE CONVERSANT, make familiar, acquaint; accustom to, habituate to, instruct in, teach in, educate in, school in, prime in, introduce to; brief; *informal* put in the picture about, give the lowdown on, fill in on.

family ▶ noun **1** *I met his family* RELATIVES, relations, (next of) kin, kinsfolk, kindred, one's (own) flesh and blood, nearest and dearest, people, connections; extended family, in-laws; clan, tribe; *informal* folks. **2** *he had the right kind of family* ANCESTRY, parentage, pedigree, genealogy, background, family tree, descent, lineage, bloodline, blood, extraction, stock; forebears, forefathers, antecedents, roots, origins. **3** *she is married with a family* CHILDREN, little ones, youngsters; offspring, progeny, descendants, scions, heirs; brood; *Law* issue; *informal* kids, kiddies, tots. **4** *the weaver bird family* TAXONOMIC GROUP, order, class, genus, species; stock, strain, line; *Zoology* phylum.

family tree ▶ noun ANCESTRY, genealogy, descent, lineage, line, bloodline, pedigree, background, extraction, derivation; family, dynasty, house; forebears, forefathers, antecedents, roots, origins.

famine ▶ noun *a nation threatened by famine* FOOD SHORTAGES, scarcity of food; starvation, malnutrition.
— OPPOSITES: plenty.

famished ▶ adjective RAVENOUS, hungry, starving, starved, empty, unfed; *informal* peckish.
— OPPOSITES: full.

famous ▶ adjective WELL KNOWN, prominent, famed, popular, renowned, noted, eminent, distinguished, esteemed, celebrated, respected; of distinction, of repute; illustrious, acclaimed, great, legendary, lionized; having one's name in lights; notorious, infamous.
— OPPOSITES: unknown.

fan[1] ▶ noun *a ceiling fan* VENTILATOR, blower, air conditioner.
▶ verb **1** *she fanned her face* COOL, aerate, ventilate; freshen, refresh. **2** *they fanned public fears* INTENSIFY, increase, agitate, inflame, exacerbate; stimulate, stir up, whip up, fuel, kindle, spark, arouse. **3** *the police squad fanned out* SPREAD, branch; outspread.

fan[2] ▶ noun *a basketball fan* ENTHUSIAST, devotee, admirer, lover; supporter, follower, disciple, adherent, zealot; expert, connoisseur, aficionado; *informal* buff, bum, fiend, freak, nut, addict, junkie, fanatic, groupie.

fanatic ▶ noun **1** *a religious fanatic* ZEALOT, extremist, militant, dogmatist, devotee, adherent; sectarian, bigot, partisan, radical, diehard; *informal* maniac. **2** *(informal) a hockey fanatic. See* FAN[2].

fanatical ▶ adjective **1** *they are fanatical about their faith* ZEALOUS, extremist, extreme, militant, dogmatic, radical, diehard; intolerant, single-minded, blinkered, inflexible, uncompromising, hard-core. **2** *he was fanatical about tidiness* ENTHUSIASTIC, eager, keen, fervent, ardent, passionate; obsessive, obsessed, fixated, compulsive; *informal* wild, gung-ho, nuts, crazy, hog-wild.

fancier ▶ noun *a pigeon fancier* ENTHUSIAST, lover, hobbyist; expert, connoisseur, aficionado; *informal* buff.

fanciful ▶ adjective **1** *a fanciful story* FANTASTIC, far-fetched, unbelievable, extravagant; ridiculous, absurd, preposterous; imaginary, made-up, make-believe, mythical, fabulous; *informal* tall, hard to swallow. **2** *a fanciful girl* IMAGINATIVE, inventive; whimsical, impractical, dreamy, quixotic; out of touch with reality, in a world of one's own. **3** *a fanciful building* ORNATE, exotic, fancy, imaginative, extravagant, fantastic; curious, bizarre, eccentric, unusual.
— OPPOSITES: literal, practical.

fancy ▶ verb **1** *she fancied him. See* LIKE sense 1. **2** *I fancied I could see lights* THINK, imagine, believe, be of the opinion, be under the impression; reckon.
▶ adjective *fancy clothes* ELABORATE, ornate, ornamental, decorative, adorned, embellished, intricate; ostentatious, showy, flamboyant; luxurious, lavish, extravagant, expensive; *informal* flashy, jazzy, ritzy, snazzy, posh, classy; fancy-schmancy.
— OPPOSITES: plain.
▶ noun *she took a fancy to you* LIKING, taste, inclination; urge, wish, whim, impulse, notion, whimsy, hankering, craving; *informal* yen, itch.

fanfare ▶ noun **1** *a fanfare announced her arrival* TRUMPET CALL, flourish, fanfaronade; *archaic* trump. **2** *the project was greeted with great fanfare* FUSS, commotion, show, display, ostentation, flashiness, pageantry, splendour; *informal* ballyhoo, hype, pizzazz, razzle-dazzle, glitz.

fantasize ▶ verb DAYDREAM, dream, muse, make-believe, pretend, imagine; build castles in the air, build castles in Spain, live in a dream world.

fantastic ▶ adjective **1** *a fantastic car* MARVELLOUS, wonderful, sensational, outstanding, superb, super, excellent, first-rate, first-class, dazzling, out of this world, breathtaking; *informal* great, terrific, fabulous, ace, magic, cool, wicked, awesome, brilliant, killer. **2** *a fantastic notion* FANCIFUL, extravagant, extraordinary, irrational, wild, absurd, far-fetched, nonsensical, incredible, unbelievable, unthinkable, implausible, improbable, unlikely, doubtful, dubious; strange, peculiar, odd, queer, weird,

eccentric, whimsical, capricious; visionary, romantic; *informal* crazy, cockeyed, off the wall. **3** *fantastic shapes* STRANGE, weird, bizarre, outlandish, queer, peculiar, grotesque, freakish, surreal, exotic; elaborate, ornate, intricate. **4** *his fantastic accuracy* TREMENDOUS, remarkable, great, terrific, impressive, outstanding, phenomenal.
— OPPOSITES: rational, ordinary.

fantasy ▶ noun **1** *a mix of fantasy and realism* IMAGINATION, fancy, invention, make-believe; creativity, vision; daydreaming, reverie. **2** *his fantasy about being famous* DREAM, daydream, pipe dream, fanciful notion, wish; fond hope, chimera, delusion, illusion; *informal* pie in the sky.
— OPPOSITES: realism.

far ▶ adverb **1** *we walked far that afternoon* A LONG WAY, a great distance, a good way; afar. **2** *her charm far outweighs any flaws* MUCH, considerably, markedly, immeasurably, greatly, significantly, substantially, appreciably, noticeably; to a great extent, by a long way, by far, by a mile, easily.
— OPPOSITES: near.

▶ adjective **1** *far places* DISTANT, faraway, far-off, remote, out of the way, far-flung, outlying. **2** *the far side of the campus* FURTHER, more distant; opposite.
— OPPOSITES: near.

■ **by far** BY A GREAT AMOUNT, by a good deal, by a long way, by a mile, far and away; undoubtedly, without doubt, without question, positively, absolutely, easily; significantly, substantially, appreciably, much.

■ **far and away.** See BY FAR.

■ **far and near** EVERYWHERE, {here, there, and everywhere}, far and wide, all over (the world), throughout the land, worldwide; *informal* all over the place; all over the map.

■ **far and wide.** See FAR AND NEAR.

■ **far from** *staff were far from happy* NOT, not at all, nowhere near; the opposite of, anything but.

■ **go far** BE SUCCESSFUL, succeed, prosper, flourish, thrive, get on (in the world), make good, set the world on fire; *informal* make a name for oneself, make one's mark, go places, do all right for oneself, find a place in the sun.

■ **go too far** GO TO EXTREMES, go overboard, overdo it.

■ **so far 1** *nobody has noticed so far* UNTIL NOW, up to now, up to this point, as yet, thus far, hitherto, up to the present, to date. **2** *his liberalism only extends so far* TO A CERTAIN EXTENT, up to a point, to a degree, within reason, within limits.

faraway ▶ adjective **1** *faraway places* DISTANT, far off, far, remote, far-flung, outlying; obscure, out of the way, off the beaten track. **2** *a faraway look in her eyes* DREAMY, daydreaming, abstracted, absent-minded, distracted, preoccupied, vague; lost in thought, somewhere else, not with us, in a world of one's own; *informal* miles away.
— OPPOSITES: nearby.

farce ▶ noun **1** *the stories approach farce* SLAPSTICK (COMEDY), burlesque, vaudeville, buffoonery. **2** *the trial was a farce* MOCKERY, travesty, absurdity, sham, pretense, masquerade, charade, joke, waste of time; *informal* shambles.
— OPPOSITES: tragedy.

farcical ▶ adjective **1** *the idea is farcical* RIDICULOUS, preposterous, ludicrous, absurd, laughable, risible, nonsensical; senseless, pointless, useless; silly, foolish, idiotic, stupid, hare-brained, cockamamie; *informal* crazy, daft. **2** *farcical goings-on* MADCAP, zany,

slapstick, comic, comical, clownish, amusing; hilarious, uproarious; *informal* wacky.

fare ▶ noun **1** *we paid the fare* TICKET PRICE, transport cost; price, cost, charge, fee, toll, tariff. **2** *the taxi picked up a fare* PASSENGER, traveller, customer. **3** *they eat simple fare* FOOD, meals, sustenance, nourishment, nutriment, foodstuffs, provender, eatables, provisions; cooking, cuisine; diet, table; *informal* grub, nosh, eats, chow; *informal* scoff; *formal* comestibles, victuals. **4** *typical Hollywood fare* wares, produce, menu.

▶ verb *how are you faring?* GET ON, get along, cope, manage, do, muddle through/along, survive; *informal* make out.

farewell ▶ exclamation *farewell to Nova Scotia* GOODBYE, so long, adieu; au revoir, bye, bye-bye, cheerio, see you (later), later, later skater, cheers; ciao, adios, sayonara; bon voyage; *informal, dated* toodle-oo.

▶ noun *an emotional farewell* GOODBYE, valediction, adieu; leave-taking, parting, departure; send-off.

far-fetched ▶ adjective IMPROBABLE, unlikely, implausible, unconvincing, dubious, doubtful, incredible, unbelievable, unthinkable; contrived, fanciful, unrealistic, ridiculous, absurd, preposterous; *informal* hard to swallow, fishy.
— OPPOSITES: likely.

farm ▶ noun *a farm of 100 acres* RANCH, farmstead, plantation, estate, family farm, hobby farm; farmland, market garden, river lot ✦, long lot ✦.

▶ verb **1** *he farmed locally* WORK THE LAND, be a farmer, cultivate the land; rear livestock. **2** *they farm the land* CULTIVATE, till, work, plow, dig, plant. **3** *the family farms sheep* BREED, rear, keep, raise, tend.

■ **farm something out** CONTRACT OUT, outsource, subcontract, delegate.

farmer ▶ noun AGRICULTURALIST, agronomist, rancher, smallholder, peasant; farmhand, *historical* habitant ✦, grazier; *slang* stubble-jumper ✦.

farming ▶ noun AGRICULTURE, cultivation, ranching, land management, farm management; husbandry; agronomy, agribusiness.

far out ▶ adjective *(informal).* See UNCONVENTIONAL.

farrago ▶ noun HODGEPODGE, mishmash, ragbag, potpourri, jumble, mess, confusion, mélange, gallimaufry, hash, assortment, miscellany, mixture, conglomeration, medley.

far-reaching ▶ adjective EXTENSIVE, wide-ranging, comprehensive, widespread, all-embracing, overarching, across the board, sweeping, blanket, wholesale; important, significant, radical, major, consequential.
— OPPOSITES: limited.

far-sighted ▶ adjective PRESCIENT, visionary, percipient, shrewd, discerning, judicious, canny, prudent.

farther ▶ adjective. See FURTHER adjective 1.

farthest ▶ adjective. See FURTHEST.

fascinate ▶ verb INTEREST, captivate, engross, absorb, enchant, enthrall, entrance, transfix, rivet, mesmerize, engage, compel; lure, tempt, entice, draw; charm, attract, intrigue, divert, entertain.
— OPPOSITES: bore.

fascinating ▶ adjective INTERESTING, captivating, engrossing, absorbing, enchanting, enthralling, spellbinding, riveting, engaging, compelling, compulsive, gripping, thrilling, alluring, tempting, irresistible; charming, attractive, intriguing, diverting, entertaining.

fascination ▸ noun INTEREST, preoccupation, passion, obsession, compulsion; allure, lure, charm, attraction, intrigue, appeal, pull, draw.

fascism ▸ noun AUTHORITARIANISM, totalitarianism, dictatorship, despotism, autocracy; Nazism, rightism; nationalism, xenophobia, racism, anti-Semitism; jingoism, isolationism; neo-fascism, neo-Nazism.

fascist ▸ noun *he was branded a fascist* AUTHORITARIAN, totalitarian, autocrat, extreme right-winger, rightist; Nazi, blackshirt; nationalist, xenophobe, racist, anti-Semite, jingoist; neo-fascist, neo-Nazi.
 — OPPOSITES: liberal.
▸ adjective *a fascist regime* AUTHORITARIAN, totalitarian, dictatorial, despotic, autocratic, undemocratic, illiberal; Nazi, extreme right-wing, rightist, militarist; nationalist(ic), xenophobic, racist, jingoistic.
 — OPPOSITES: democratic.

fashion ▸ noun **1** *the fashion for tight clothes* VOGUE, trend, craze, rage, mania, fad; style, look; tendency, convention, custom, practice; *informal* thing. **2** *the world of fashion* CLOTHES, clothing design, couture; the garment industry; *informal* the rag trade. **3** *it needs to be run in a sensible fashion* MANNER, way, method, mode, style; system, approach.
▸ verb *the model was fashioned from lead* CONSTRUCT, build, make, manufacture, fabricate, tailor, contrive; cast, shape, form, mould, sculpt; forge, hew.
 ■ **after a fashion** TO A CERTAIN EXTENT, in a way, somehow (or other), in a manner of speaking, in its way.
 ■ **in fashion** FASHIONABLE, in vogue, up-to-date, up-to-the-minute, all the rage, chic, à la mode; *informal* trendy, with it, cool, in, in the thing, hot, big, hip, happening, now, sharp, groovy, tony, fly.
 ■ **out of fashion** UNFASHIONABLE, dated, old-fashioned, out of date, outdated, outmoded, behind the times; unstylish, untrendy, unpopular, passé, démodé; *informal* old hat, out, square, uncool.

fashionable ▸ adjective IN VOGUE, voguish, in fashion, popular, up-to-date, up-to-the-minute, modern, all the rage, du jour, modish, à la mode, trend-setting; stylish, chic; *informal* trendy, classy, with it, cool, in, the in thing, hot, big, hip, happening, now, sharp, groovy, snazzy, spiffy, tony, fly.

fast¹ ▸ adjective **1** *a fast pace* SPEEDY, quick, swift, rapid; fast-moving, fast-paced, high-speed, turbo, sporty; accelerated, express, blistering, breakneck, pell-mell; hasty, hurried; *informal* nippy, zippy, blinding, supersonic; *literary* fleet. **2** *he held the door fast* SECURE, fastened, tight, firm, closed, shut, to; immovable, unbudgeable. **3** *a fast colour* INDELIBLE, lasting, permanent, stable. **4** *fast friends* LOYAL, devoted, faithful, firm, steadfast, staunch, true, bosom, inseparable; constant, enduring, unswerving. **5** *a fast woman* PROMISCUOUS, licentious, dissolute, debauched, impure, unchaste, wanton, abandoned, of easy virtue; sluttish, whorish; intemperate, immoderate, shameless, sinful, immoral; *informal* easy, tarty; *dated* loose.
 — OPPOSITES: slow, loose, temporary, chaste.
▸ adverb **1** *she drove fast* QUICKLY, rapidly, swiftly, speedily, briskly, at speed, at full tilt; hastily, hurriedly, in a hurry, post-haste, pell-mell; like a shot, like a flash, on the double, at the speed of light;

informal lickety-split, PDQ (pretty damn quick), nippily, like (greased) lightning, hell for leather, like mad, like the wind, like a bat out of hell; *literary* apace. **2** *his wheels were stuck fast* SECURELY, firmly, immovably, fixedly. **3** *he's fast asleep* DEEPLY, sound, completely. **4** *she lived fast and dangerously* WILDLY, dissolutely, intemperately, immoderately, recklessly, self-indulgently, extravagantly.
 — OPPOSITES: slowly.

fast² ▸ verb *we must fast and pray* EAT NOTHING, abstain from food, refrain from eating, go without food, go hungry, starve oneself; go on a hunger strike.
 — OPPOSITES: eat.
▸ noun *a five-day fast* PERIOD OF FASTING, period of abstinence; hunger strike; diet.
 — OPPOSITES: feast.

fasten ▸ verb **1** *he fastened the door* BOLT, lock, secure, make fast, chain, seal. **2** *they fastened splints to his leg* ATTACH, fix, affix, clip, pin, tack; stick, bond, join. **3** *he fastened his horse to a tree* TIE (UP), bind, tether, truss, fetter, lash, hitch, anchor, strap, rope. **4** *the dress fastens at the front* BUTTON (UP), zip (up), do up, close. **5** *his gaze fastened on me* FOCUS, fix, be riveted, concentrate, zero in, zoom in, direct at. **6** *blame had been fastened on the underling* ASCRIBE TO, attribute to, assign to, chalk up to; pin on, lay at the door of. **7** *critics fastened on the end of the report* SINGLE OUT, concentrate on, focus on, pick out, fix on, seize on.
 — OPPOSITES: unlock, remove, open, untie, undo.

fastener ▸ noun BUTTON, clasp, strap, tie, buckle, zipper, catch, dome fastener, snap, hook and eye; *proprietary* Velcro.

fastidious ▸ adjective SCRUPULOUS, punctilious, painstaking, meticulous; perfectionist, fussy, finicky, over-particular; critical, overcritical, hypercritical, hard to please, exacting, demanding; *informal* pernickety, persnickety, nitpicking, choosy, picky, anal.
 — OPPOSITES: lax.

fat ▸ adjective **1** *a fat man* PLUMP, stout, overweight, large, chubby, portly, flabby, paunchy, pot-bellied, beer-bellied, meaty, of ample proportions, heavy-set; obese, corpulent, fleshy, gross; *informal* plus-sized, big-boned, tubby, roly-poly, well-upholstered, beefy, porky, blubbery, chunky, pudgy. **2** *fat bacon* FATTY, greasy, oily, oleaginous; *formal* pinguid. **3** *a fat book* THICK, big, chunky, bulky, substantial, voluminous, long. **4** (*informal*) *a fat salary* LARGE, substantial, sizeable, considerable; generous, lucrative.
 — OPPOSITES: thin, lean, small.
▸ noun **1** *exercises to burn away the fat* FATTY TISSUE, adipose tissue, cellulite; blubber; flab, spare tire, love handles. **2** *eggs in sizzling fat* COOKING OIL, grease; lard, suet, butter, margarine.

fatal ▸ adjective **1** *a fatal disease* DEADLY, lethal, mortal, death-dealing; terminal, incurable, untreatable, inoperable, malignant; *literary* deathly. **2** *a fatal mistake* DISASTROUS, devastating, ruinous, catastrophic, calamitous, dire; costly; *formal* grievous.
 — OPPOSITES: harmless, beneficial.

fatalism ▸ noun PASSIVE ACCEPTANCE, resignation, stoicism.

fatality ▸ noun DEATH, casualty, mortality; victim; fatal accident.

fate ▸ noun **1** *what has fate in store for me?* DESTINY, providence, the stars, chance, luck, serendipity, fortune, kismet, karma. **2** *my fate was in their hands* FUTURE, destiny, outcome, end, lot. **3** *a similar fate would befall other killers* DEATH, demise, end;

retribution, sentence. **4** *the Fates will decide* the weird sisters, the Parcae, the Moirai.

▶ verb *his daughter was fated to face the same problem* BE PREDESTINED, be preordained, be destined, be meant, be doomed; be sure, be certain, be bound, be guaranteed.

fateful ▶ adjective **1** *that fateful day* DECISIVE, critical, crucial, pivotal; momentous, important, key, significant, historic, portentous. **2** *their fateful defeat in 1812* DISASTROUS, ruinous, calamitous, devastating, tragic, terrible.
– OPPOSITES: unimportant.

father ▶ noun **1** *his mother and father* DAD; daddy, pop, pa, dada, papa; old man, patriarch, paterfamilias. **2** (*literary*) *the religion of my fathers* ANCESTOR, forefather, forebear, predecessor, antecedent, progenitor, primogenitor. **3** *the father of democracy* ORIGINATOR, initiator, founder, inventor, creator, maker, author, architect. **4** *the city fathers* LEADER, elder, patriarch, official. **5** *our heavenly Father* GOD, Lord (God). **6** *pray for me, Father* PRIEST, pastor, parson, clergyman, cleric, minister, preacher; *informal* reverend, padre.
– RELATED TERMS: paternal, patri-.
– OPPOSITES: child, mother, descendant.

▶ verb PARENT, be the father of, bring into the world, spawn, sire, breed; *literary* beget; *archaic* engender.

fatherland ▶ noun NATIVE LAND, native country, homeland, mother country, motherland, land of one's birth.

fatherly ▶ adjective PATERNAL, fatherlike; protective, supportive, encouraging, affectionate, caring, sympathetic, indulgent.

fathom ▶ verb **1** *Charlotte tried to fathom her cat's expression* UNDERSTAND, comprehend, work out, make sense of, grasp, divine, puzzle out, get to the bottom of; interpret, decipher, decode; *informal* make head or tail of, crack, twig, suss (out). **2** *fathoming the ocean* MEASURE THE DEPTH OF, sound, plumb.

fatigue ▶ noun TIREDNESS, weariness, exhaustion, enervation, prostration.
– OPPOSITES: energy.

▶ verb *the troops were fatigued* TIRE (OUT), exhaust, wear out, drain, weary, wash out, overtire, prostrate, enervate; *informal* knock out, take it out of, do in, whack, poop, bush, wear to a frazzle.
– OPPOSITES: invigorate.

fatness ▶ noun PLUMPNESS, stoutness, heaviness, chubbiness, portliness, rotundity, flabbiness, paunchiness; obesity, corpulence; *informal* tubbiness, pudginess.
– OPPOSITES: thinness.

fatten ▶ verb **1** *fattening livestock* MAKE FAT/FATTER, feed (up), build up. **2** *we're sending her home to fatten up* PUT ON WEIGHT, gain weight, get heavier, grow fatter, fill out.
– OPPOSITES: slim.

fatty ▶ adjective GREASY, oily, fat, oleaginous; high-fat.
– OPPOSITES: lean.

fatuous ▶ adjective SILLY, foolish, stupid, inane, idiotic, vacuous, asinine; pointless, senseless, ridiculous, ludicrous, absurd; *informal* dumb, daft.
– OPPOSITES: sensible.

fault ▶ noun **1** *he has his faults* DEFECT, failing, imperfection, flaw, blemish, shortcoming, weakness, frailty, foible, vice. **2** *engineers have located the fault* DEFECT, flaw, imperfection, bug; error, mistake, inaccuracy; *informal* glitch, gremlin. **3** *it was not my*

fault RESPONSIBILITY, liability, culpability, blameworthiness, guilt. **4** *don't blame one child for another's faults* MISDEED, wrongdoing, offence, misdemeanour, misconduct, indiscretion, peccadillo, transgression; *informal* no-no.
– OPPOSITES: merit, strength.

▶ verb *you couldn't fault any of the players* FIND FAULT WITH, criticize, attack, censure, condemn, reproach, complain about, quibble about, moan about; *informal* knock, slam, gripe about, beef about, pick holes in.
■ **at fault** TO BLAME, blameworthy, culpable; responsible, guilty, in the wrong.
■ **to a fault** EXCESSIVELY, unduly, immoderately, overly, needlessly.

fault-finding ▶ noun CRITICISM, captiousness, cavilling, quibbling; complaining, grumbling, carping, moaning; *informal* nitpicking, griping, grousing, bellyaching.
– OPPOSITES: praise.

faultless ▶ adjective PERFECT, flawless, without fault, error-free, impeccable, accurate, precise, exact, correct, exemplary.
– OPPOSITES: flawed.

faulty ▶ adjective **1** *a faulty electric blanket* MALFUNCTIONING, broken, damaged, defective, not working, out of order; *informal* on the blink, acting up, kaput, bust, on the fritz. **2** *her logic is faulty* DEFECTIVE, flawed, unsound, inaccurate, incorrect, erroneous, fallacious, wrong.
– RELATED TERMS: dys-.
– OPPOSITES: working, sound.

fauna ▶ noun WILDLIFE, animals, living creatures.

faux pas ▶ noun GAFFE, blunder, mistake, indiscretion, impropriety, solecism, barbarism; *informal* boo-boo, blooper.

favour ▶ noun **1** *will you do me a favour?* SERVICE, good turn, good deed, (act of) kindness, courtesy. **2** *she looked on him with favour* APPROVAL, approbation, goodwill, kindness, benevolence. **3** *they showed favour to one of the players* FAVOURITISM, bias, partiality, partisanship. **4** *you shall receive the king's favour* PATRONAGE, backing, support, assistance.
– OPPOSITES: disservice, disapproval.

▶ verb **1** *she favours the modest option* PREFER, lean towards, opt for, tend towards, be in favour of; approve (of), advocate, support, **2** *he favours his son over his daughter* TREAT PARTIALLY, be biased towards, prefer. **3** *the conditions favoured the other team* BENEFIT, advantage, help, assist, aid, be of service to, do a favour for. **4** *he favoured Lucy with a smile* OBLIGE, honour, gratify, humour, indulge.
– OPPOSITES: oppose, dislike, hinder.
■ **in favour of** ON THE SIDE OF, pro, (all) for, giving support to, approving of, sympathetic to.

favourable ▶ adjective **1** *a favourable assessment of his ability* APPROVING, commendatory, complimentary, flattering, glowing, enthusiastic; good, pleasing, positive; *informal* rave. **2** *conditions are favourable* ADVANTAGEOUS, beneficial, in one's favour, good, right, suitable, fitting, appropriate; propitious, auspicious, promising, encouraging. **3** *a favourable reply* POSITIVE, affirmative, assenting, agreeing, approving; encouraging, reassuring.
– OPPOSITES: critical, disadvantageous, negative.

favourably ▶ adverb POSITIVELY, approvingly, sympathetically, enthusiastically, appreciatively.

favoured ▶ adjective PREFERRED, favourite, recommended, chosen, choice.

favourite ▶ adjective *his favourite aunt* BEST-LOVED, most-liked, favoured, dearest; preferred, chosen, choice.
▶ noun **1** *Brutus was Caesar's favourite* (FIRST) CHOICE, pick, preference, pet, darling, the apple of one's eye; *informal* blue-eyed boy/girl, golden boy/girl, fair-haired boy/girl. **2** *the favourite fell at the first fence* FRONT-RUNNER, top seed, expected winner.

favouritism ▶ noun PARTIALITY, partisanship, preferential treatment, favour, prejudice, bias, inequality, unfairness, discrimination.

fawn ▶ verb *they were fawning over the President* BE OBSEQUIOUS TO, be sycophantic to, curry favour with, flatter, play up to, crawl to, ingratiate oneself with, dance attendance on; *informal* suck up to, be all over, brown-nose, toady.

fawning ▶ adjective OBSEQUIOUS, servile, sycophantic, flattering, ingratiating, unctuous, oleaginous, grovelling, crawling; *informal* bootlicking, smarmy, sucky, brown-nosing, toadying.

faze ▶ verb DISCONCERT, perturb, disturb, unnerve, unsettle, daunt, disorientate, put off, throw (off), rattle.

fear ▶ noun **1** *she felt fear at entering the house* TERROR, fright, fearfulness, horror, alarm, panic, agitation, trepidation, dread, consternation, dismay, distress; anxiety, worry, angst, unease, uneasiness, apprehension, apprehensiveness, nervousness, nerves, perturbation, foreboding; *informal* the creeps, the shivers, the willies, the heebie-jeebies, jitteriness, twitchiness, butterflies (in the stomach). **2** *she overcame her fears* PHOBIA, aversion, antipathy, dread, bugbear, bogey, nightmare, horror, terror; anxiety, neurosis; *informal* hang-up. **3** *there's no fear of me leaving you alone* LIKELIHOOD, likeliness, prospect, possibility, chance, probability; risk, danger.
▶ verb **1** *she feared her husband* BE AFRAID OF, be fearful of, be scared of, be apprehensive of, dread, live in fear of, be terrified of; be anxious about, worry about, feel apprehensive about. **2** *he fears heights* HAVE A PHOBIA ABOUT, have a horror of, take fright at. **3** *he feared to tell them* BE TOO AFRAID, be too scared, hesitate, dare not. **4** *they feared for his health* WORRY ABOUT, feel anxious about, feel concerned about, have anxieties about. **5** (*archaic*) *all who fear the Lord* STAND IN AWE OF, revere, reverence, venerate, respect. **6** *I fear that you may be right* SUSPECT, have a (sneaking) suspicion, be inclined to think, be afraid, have a hunch, think it likely.

fearful ▶ adjective **1** *they are fearful of being overheard* AFRAID, frightened, scared (stiff), scared to death, terrified, petrified; alarmed, panicky, nervous, tense, apprehensive, uneasy, worried (sick), anxious; *informal* jittery, jumpy. **2** *the guards were fearful* NERVOUS, trembling, quaking, cowed, daunted; timid, timorous, faint-hearted; *informal* jittery, jumpy, twitchy, keyed up, in a cold sweat, a bundle of nerves, having kittens; *informal* spooked. **3** *a fearful accident* HORRIFIC, terrible, dreadful, awful, appalling, frightful, ghastly, horrible, horrifying, horrendous, terribly bad, shocking, atrocious, abominable, hideous, monstrous, gruesome.

fearfully ▶ adverb *she opened the door fearfully* APPREHENSIVELY, uneasily, nervously, timidly, timorously, hesitantly, with one's heart in one's mouth.

fearless ▶ adjective BOLD, brave, courageous, intrepid, valiant, valorous, gallant, plucky, lion-hearted, heroic, daring, audacious, indomitable,

doughty; unafraid, undaunted, unflinching; *informal* gutsy, spunky, ballsy, feisty.
— OPPOSITES: timid, cowardly.

fearsome ▶ adjective FRIGHTENING, scary, horrifying, terrifying, menacing, chilling, spine-chilling, hair-raising, alarming, unnerving, daunting, formidable, forbidding, dismaying, disquieting, disturbing.

feasible ▶ adjective PRACTICABLE, practical, workable, achievable, attainable, realizable, viable, realistic, sensible, reasonable, within reason; suitable, possible, expedient; *informal* doable.
— OPPOSITES: impractical.

feast ▶ noun **1** *a wedding feast* BANQUET, celebration meal, (*Que.*) mechoui ✦, lavish dinner, (*Atlantic*) scoff ✦; treat, entertainment; revels, festivities; *informal* blowout, spread, bunfight. **2** *the feast of St. Stephen* (RELIGIOUS) FESTIVAL, feast day, saint's day, holy day, holiday. **3** *a feast for the eyes* TREAT, delight, joy, pleasure.
▶ verb **1** *they feasted on lobster* GORGE ON, dine on, eat one's fill of, overindulge in, binge on; eat, devour, consume, partake of; *informal* stuff one's face with, stuff oneself with, pig out on, chow down on. **2** *they feasted the deputation* HOLD A BANQUET FOR, throw a feast/party for, wine and dine, entertain lavishly, regale, treat, fete.

feat ▶ noun ACHIEVEMENT, accomplishment, attainment, coup, triumph; undertaking, enterprise, venture, operation, exercise, endeavour, effort, performance, exploit.

feather ▶ noun PLUME, quill, flight feather, tail feather; *Ornithology* covert, plumule; (**feathers**) plumage, feathering, down.

feature ▶ noun **1** *a typical feature of French music* CHARACTERISTIC, attribute, quality, property, trait, hallmark, trademark; aspect, facet, factor, ingredient, component, element, theme; peculiarity, idiosyncrasy, quirk. **2** *her delicate features* FACE, countenance, physiognomy; *informal* mug, kisser, phiz; puss, pan; *literary* visage, lineaments. **3** *she made a feature of her garden sculptures* CENTREPIECE, (special) attraction, highlight, focal point, focus (of attention). **4** *she writes features at the newspaper* ARTICLE, piece, item, report, story, column, review, commentary, write-up. **5** *tonight's feature at the movie theatre* FILM, movie, flick, pic; main show, main event, star turn.
▶ verb **1** *the CBC is featuring a week of live concerts* PRESENT, promote, make a feature of, give prominence to, focus attention on, spotlight, highlight. **2** *she is to feature in a major advertising campaign* STAR, appear, participate, play a part.

febrile ▶ adjective FEVERISH, hot, burning, flushed, sweating; *informal* having a temperature.

feces ▶ plural noun EXCREMENT, bodily waste, waste matter, ordure, dung, manure; excreta, stools, droppings; dirt, filth, muck, mess, night soil; *informal* poo, pooh, doo-doo, turds, poop, caca.
— RELATED TERMS: copro-.

feckless ▶ adjective USELESS, worthless, incompetent, inept, good-for-nothing, ne'er-do-well; lazy, idle, slothful, indolent, shiftless; *informal* no-good, no-account.

fecund ▶ adjective FERTILE, fruitful, productive, high-yielding; rich, lush, flourishing, thriving.
— OPPOSITES: barren.

federal ▶ adjective CONFEDERATE, federated,

federative; combined, allied, united, amalgamated, integrated.

federal government ▶ noun Ottawa, the feds, Parliament.

federate ▶ verb CONFEDERATE, combine, unite, unify, merge, amalgamate, integrate, join (up), band together, team up.

federation ▶ noun CONFEDERATION, confederacy, league; combination, alliance, coalition, union, syndicate, guild, consortium, partnership, co-operative, association, amalgamation; informal federacy.

fed up ▶ adjective SICK AND TIRED, weary, tired, sick, have had it up to here, have had enough.

fee ▶ noun PAYMENT, wage, salary, allowance; price, cost, charge, tariff, rate, amount, sum, figure; (**fees**) remuneration, dues, earnings, pay; formal emolument.

feeble ▶ adjective **1** he was very old and feeble WEAK, weakly, weakened, frail, infirm, delicate, sickly, ailing, unwell, poorly, enfeebled, enervated, debilitated, incapacitated, decrepit, etiolated. **2** a feeble argument INEFFECTIVE, ineffectual, inadequate, unconvincing, implausible, unsatisfactory, poor, weak, flimsy. **3** he's too feeble to stand up to his boss COWARDLY, craven, faint-hearted, spineless, spiritless, lily-livered, chinless; timid, timorous, fearful, unassertive, weak, ineffectual, wishy-washy; informal wimpy, sissy, sissified, gutless, chicken. **4** a feeble light FAINT, dim, weak, pale, soft, subdued, muted.
— OPPOSITES: strong, brave.

feeble-minded ▶ adjective STUPID, idiotic, imbecilic, foolish, witless, doltish, empty-headed, vacuous; informal halfwitted, moronic, dumb, dim, dopey, dozy, dippy; daft.
— OPPOSITES: clever, gifted.

feed ▶ verb **1** feed the kids GIVE FOOD TO, provide (food) for, cater for, cook for. **2** feed the baby SUCKLE, nurse, breastfeed, bottle-feed. **3** too many cows feeding in a small area GRAZE, browse, crop, pasture; eat, consume food, chow down. **4** the birds feed on a varied diet LIVE ON/OFF, exist on, subsist on, eat, consume. **5** feeding one's self-esteem STRENGTHEN, fortify, support, bolster, reinforce, boost, fuel, encourage. **6** she fed secrets to the Russians SUPPLY, provide, give, deliver, furnish, issue, pass on.
▶ noun feed for goats and sheep FODDER, food, forage, pasturage, herbage, provender; formal comestibles.

feedback ▶ noun RESPONSE, reaction, comments, criticism; reception, reviews.

feel ▶ verb **1** she felt the fabric TOUCH, stroke, caress, fondle, finger, thumb, handle. **2** she felt a breeze on her back PERCEIVE, sense, detect, discern, notice, be aware of, be conscious of. **3** you will not feel any pain EXPERIENCE, undergo, go through, bear, endure, suffer. **4** he felt his way towards the door GROPE, fumble, scrabble, pick. **5** feel the temperature of the water TEST, try (out), check, assess. **6** he feels that he should go to the meeting BELIEVE, think, consider (it right), be of the opinion, hold, maintain, judge; informal reckon, figure. **7** I feel that he is only biding his time SENSE, have a (funny) feeling, get the impression, have a hunch, intuit. **8** the air feels damp SEEM, appear, strike one as.
▶ noun **1** the divers worked by feel (SENSE OF) TOUCH, tactile sense, feeling (one's way). **2** the feel of the paper TEXTURE, surface, finish; weight, thickness, consistency, quality. **3** the feel of a room ATMOSPHERE, ambience, aura, mood, feeling, air, impression, character, tenor, spirit, flavour; informal vibrations, vibes. **4** a feel for languages APTITUDE, knack, flair, bent, talent, gift, faculty, ability.
■ **feel for** SYMPATHIZE WITH, be sorry for, pity, feel pity for, feel sympathy for, feel compassion for, be moved by; commiserate with, condole with.
■ **feel like** WANT, would like, wish for, desire, fancy, feel in need of, long for; informal yen for, be dying for.

feeler ▶ noun **1** the fish has two feelers on its head ANTENNA, tentacle, tactile/sensory organ; Zoology antennule. **2** the minister put out feelers TENTATIVE INQUIRY/PROPOSAL, advance, approach, overture, probe.

feel-good ▶ adjective HEARTWARMING, uplifting, positive, warm and fuzzy, sentimental, soft-hearted, mawkish, touchy-feely.

feeling ▶ noun **1** assess the fabric by feeling (SENSE OF) TOUCH, feel, tactile sense, using one's hands. **2** a feeling of nausea SENSATION, sense, consciousness. **3** I had a feeling that I would win (SNEAKING) SUSPICION, notion, inkling, hunch, funny feeling, feeling in one's bones, fancy, idea; presentiment, premonition; informal gut feeling. **4** the strength of her feeling LOVE, affection, fondness, tenderness, warmth, warmness, emotion, sentiment; passion, ardour, desire. **5** a rush of feeling COMPASSION, sympathy, empathy, fellow feeling, concern, solicitude, solicitousness, tenderness, love; pity, sorrow, commiseration. **6** he had hurt her feelings SENSIBILITIES, sensitivities, self-esteem, pride. **7** my feeling is that it is true OPINION, belief, view, impression, intuition, instinct, hunch, estimation, guess. **8** a feeling of peace ATMOSPHERE, ambience, aura, air, feel, mood, impression, spirit, quality, flavour; informal vibrations, vibes.
▶ adjective a feeling man SENSITIVE, warm, warm-hearted, tender, tender-hearted, caring, sympathetic, kind, compassionate, understanding, thoughtful.

feign ▶ verb **1** she lay still and feigned sleep SIMULATE, fake, sham, affect, give the appearance of, make a pretense of. **2** he's not really ill, he's only feigning PRETEND, put it on, fake, sham, bluff, masquerade, play-act; informal kid.

feigned ▶ adjective PRETENDED, simulated, affected, artificial, insincere, put-on, fake, false, sham; informal pretend, phony.
— OPPOSITES: sincere.

feint ▶ noun BLUFF, blind, ruse, deception, subterfuge, hoax, trick, ploy, device, dodge, sham, pretense, cover, smokescreen, distraction, contrivance; deke; informal red herring.

feisty ▶ adjective SPIRITED, spunky, plucky, gutsy, ballsy.

felicitations ▶ plural noun CONGRATULATIONS, good/best wishes, (kind) regards, blessings, compliments, respects.

felicitous ▶ adjective **1** his nickname was particularly felicitous APT, well-chosen, fitting, suitable, appropriate, apposite, pertinent, germane, relevant. **2** the room's only felicitous feature FAVOURABLE, advantageous, good, pleasing.
— OPPOSITES: inappropriate, unfortunate.

felicity ▶ noun **1** domestic felicity HAPPINESS, joy, joyfulness, joyousness, bliss, delight, cheerfulness; contentedness, satisfaction, pleasure. **2** David expressed his feelings with his customary felicity ELOQUENCE, aptness, appropriateness, suitability,

suitableness, applicability, fitness, relevance, pertinence.
— OPPOSITES: unhappiness, inappropriateness.

feline ▶ adjective *she moved with feline grace* CATLIKE, graceful, sleek, sinuous.
▶ noun *her pet feline* CAT, kitten; *informal* puss, pussy (cat), kitty (cat); *archaic* grimalkin.

fell[1] ▶ verb **1** *all the dead sycamores had to be felled* CUT DOWN, chop down, hack down, saw down, clear. **2** *she felled him with one punch* KNOCK DOWN/OVER, knock to the ground, strike down, bring down, bring to the ground, prostrate; knock out, knock unconscious; *informal* deck, floor, flatten, down, lay out, KO.

fell[2] ▶ adjective *(literary) a fell intent* MURDEROUS, savage, violent, vicious, fierce, ferocious, barbarous, barbaric, monstrous, cruel, ruthless; *archaic* sanguinary.
■ **at/in one fell swoop** ALL AT ONCE, together, at the same time, in one go.

fellow ▶ noun **1** *(informal) he's a decent sort of fellow* MAN, boy; person, individual, soul; *informal* guy, character, customer, joe, devil, bastard, (esp. *Atlantic*) buddy ♣; chap, dude, hombre; *dated* dog. **2** *he exchanged glances with his fellows* COMPANION, friend, comrade, partner, associate, co-worker, colleague; peer, equal, contemporary, confrere; *informal* chum, pal, buddy.
■ **fellow feeling** SYMPATHY, empathy, feeling, compassion, care, concern, solicitude, solicitousness, warmth, tenderness, (brotherly) love; pity, sorrow, commiseration.

fellowship ▶ noun **1** *a community bound together in fellowship* COMPANIONSHIP, companionability, sociability, comradeship, camaraderie, friendship, mutual support; togetherness, solidarity; *informal* chumminess. **2** *the church fellowship* ASSOCIATION, society, club, league, union, guild, affiliation, alliance, fraternity, confraternity, brotherhood, sorority, sodality, benevolent society.

felon ▶ noun CONVICT, crook, criminal, outlaw, malefactor, wrongdoer; *informal* con.

felony ▶ noun *See* CRIME sense 1.

female ▶ adjective *female attributes* FEMININE, womanly, ladylike.
— OPPOSITES: male.
▶ noun *the author was a female. See* WOMAN sense 1.
— RELATED TERMS: gyneco-.

feminine ▶ adjective **1** *a very feminine young woman* WOMANLY, ladylike, girlish, girly. **2** *he seemed slightly feminine* EFFEMINATE, womanish, unmanly, effete, epicene; *informal* sissy, wimpy.
— OPPOSITES: masculine, manly.

femininity ▶ noun WOMANLINESS, feminineness, womanly/feminine qualities.

feminism ▶ noun THE WOMEN'S MOVEMENT, the feminist movement, women's liberation, female emancipation, women's rights, girl power; *informal* women's lib.

femme fatale ▶ noun SEDUCTRESS, temptress, siren; *informal* vamp, man-eater, home wrecker.

fen ▶ noun MARSH, marshland, salt marsh, fenland, wetland, muskeg, (peat) bog, swamp, swampland.

fence ▶ noun **1** *a gap in the fence* BARRIER, paling, railing, fencing, enclosure, barricade, stockade, palisade, fenceline. **2** *(informal) a fence dealing mainly in jewellery* RECEIVER (OF STOLEN GOODS), dealer.
▶ verb **1** *they fenced off many acres* ENCLOSE, surround, circumscribe, encircle, circle, encompass; *archaic* compass. **2** *he fenced in his chickens* CONFINE, pen in,

coop up, shut in/up, separate off; enclose, surround, corral. **3** *she fences as a hobby* SWORD-FIGHT; duel.
■ **(sitting) on the fence** *(informal)* UNDECIDED, uncommitted, uncertain, unsure, vacillating, wavering, dithering, hesitant, doubtful, ambivalent, of two minds, in a quandary, hemming and hawing, wishy-washy; neutral, impartial, non-partisan, open-minded.

fend ▶ verb *they were unable to fend off the invasion* WARD OFF, head off, stave off, hold off, repel, repulse, resist, fight off, defend oneself against, prevent, stop, block, intercept, hold back.
■ **fend for oneself** TAKE CARE OF ONESELF, look after oneself, provide for oneself, manage (by oneself), cope alone, stand on one's own two feet.

fender ▶ noun MUDGUARD, guard; *informal* bumper.

feral ▶ adjective **1** *feral dogs* WILD, untamed, untameable, undomesticated, untrained. **2** *a feral snarl* FIERCE, ferocious, vicious, savage, predatory, menacing, bloodthirsty.
— OPPOSITES: tame, pet.

ferment ▶ verb **1** *the beer continues to ferment* UNDERGO FERMENTATION, brew; effervesce, fizz, foam, froth. **2** *an environment that ferments disorder* CAUSE, bring about, give rise to, generate, engender, spawn, instigate, provoke, incite, excite, stir up, whip up, foment; *literary* beget, enkindle.
▶ noun FEVER, furor, frenzy, tumult, storm, rumpus; turmoil, upheaval, unrest, disquiet, uproar, agitation, turbulence, disruption, confusion, disorder, chaos, mayhem; *informal* kerfuffle, hoo-ha, to-do.

ferocious ▶ adjective **1** *ferocious animals* FIERCE, savage, wild, predatory, aggressive, dangerous. **2** *a ferocious attack* BRUTAL, vicious, violent, bloody, barbaric, savage, sadistic, ruthless, cruel, merciless, heartless, bloodthirsty, murderous; *literary* fell. **3** *(informal) a ferocious headache* INTENSE, strong, powerful, fierce, severe, extreme, acute, unbearable, raging; *informal* hellish.
— OPPOSITES: gentle, mild.

ferocity ▶ noun SAVAGERY, brutality, barbarity, fierceness, violence, bloodthirstiness, murderousness; ruthlessness, cruelty, pitilessness, mercilessness, heartlessness.

ferret ▶ verb **1** *she ferreted in her handbag* RUMMAGE, feel around, grope around, forage around, fish about/around, poke about/around; search through, hunt through, rifle through. **2** *ferreting out misdemeanours* UNEARTH, uncover, discover, detect, search out, bring to light, track down, dig up, root out, nose out, snoop around for.

ferry ▶ noun PASSENGER BOAT/SHIP, ferry boat, car ferry; ship, boat, vessel; *historical* packet (boat).
▶ verb TRANSPORT, convey, carry, ship, run, take, bring, shuttle.

fertile ▶ adjective **1** *the soil is fertile* FECUND, fruitful, productive, high-yielding, rich, lush. **2** *fertile couples* ABLE TO CONCEIVE, able to have children; *technical* fecund. **3** *a fertile brain* IMAGINATIVE, inventive, innovative, creative, visionary, original, ingenious; productive, prolific.
— OPPOSITES: barren.

fertilization ▶ noun CONCEPTION, impregnation, insemination; pollination, propagation.

fertilize ▶ verb **1** *the field was fertilized* FEED, mulch, compost, green manure, manure, dress, top-dress, add fertilizer to. **2** *these orchids are fertilized by insects* POLLINATE, cross-pollinate, cross-fertilize, fecundate.

fertilizer ▶ **noun** MANURE, plant food, compost, (*Maritimes*) mussel mud ✦, dressing, top dressing, dung.

fervent ▶ **adjective** IMPASSIONED, passionate, intense, vehement, ardent, sincere, fervid, heartfelt; enthusiastic, zealous, fanatical, wholehearted, avid, eager, keen, committed, dedicated, devout; *informal* mad keen; *literary* perfervid.
— OPPOSITES: apathetic.

fervid ▶ **adjective** FERVENT, ardent, passionate, impassioned, intense, vehement, wholehearted, heartfelt, sincere, earnest; *literary* perfervid.

fervour ▶ **noun** PASSION, ardour, intensity, zeal, vehemence, emotion, warmth, earnestness, avidity, eagerness, keenness, enthusiasm, excitement, animation, vigour, energy, fire, spirit, zest, fervency.
— OPPOSITES: apathy.

fester ▶ **verb** **1** *his deep wound festered* SUPPURATE, become septic, become infected, form pus, weep; *Medicine* be purulent; *archaic* rankle. **2** *the garbage festered* ROT, moulder, decay, decompose, putrefy, go bad/off, spoil, deteriorate. **3** *their resentment festered* RANKLE, eat/gnaw away, brew, smoulder.

festival ▶ **noun** **1** *the town's fall festival* FAIR, carnival, fiesta, jamboree, celebrations, festivities, fest. **2** *fasting precedes the festival* HOLY DAY, feast day, saint's day, commemoration, day of observance.

festive ▶ **adjective** JOLLY, merry, joyous, joyful, happy, jovial, light-hearted, cheerful, jubilant, convivial, high-spirited, mirthful, uproarious; celebratory, holiday, carnival; Christmassy; *archaic* festal.

festivity ▶ **noun** **1** *food plays an important part in the festivities* CELEBRATION, festival, entertainment, party, jamboree; merrymaking, feasting, revelry, jollification; revels, fun and games; *informal* bash, shindig, (*Atlantic*) time ✦, shindy, bunfight. **2** *the festivity of Canada Day* JUBILATION, merriment, gaiety, cheerfulness, cheer, joyfulness, jollity, conviviality, high spirits, revelry.

festoon ▶ **noun** *festoons of paper flowers* GARLAND, chain, lei, swathe, swag, loop.
▶ **verb** *the room was festooned with streamers* DECORATE, adorn, ornament, trim, deck (out), hang, loop, drape, swathe, garland, wreathe, bedeck; *informal* do up/out, get up, trick out; *literary* bedizen.

fetch ▶ **verb** **1** *he went to fetch a doctor* (GO AND) GET, go for, call for, summon, pick up, collect, bring, carry, convey, transport. **2** *the land could fetch a million dollars* SELL FOR, bring in, raise, realize, yield, make, command, cost, be priced at; *informal* go for, set one back, pull in.
■ **fetch up** (*informal*) END UP, finish up, turn up, appear, materialize, find itself; *informal* wind up, show up.

fetching ▶ **adjective** ATTRACTIVE, appealing, sweet, pretty, good-looking, lovely, delightful, charming, prepossessing, captivating, enchanting, irresistible; *Scottish* bonny; *informal* divine, heavenly; killer; *archaic* comely, fair.

fete ▶ **noun** GALA (DAY), bazaar, fair, festival, fiesta, jubilee, carnival; fundraiser, charity event.

fetid ▶ **adjective** STINKING, smelly, foul-smelling, malodorous, reeking, pungent, acrid, high, rank, foul, noxious, humming; *informal* funky; *literary*

noisome, miasmic, miasmal.
— OPPOSITES: fragrant.

fetish ▶ **noun** **1** *he developed a rubber fetish* FIXATION, obsession, compulsion, mania; weakness, fancy, fascination, fad; *informal* thing, hang-up. **2** *an African fetish* JUJU, talisman, charm, amulet; totem, idol, image, effigy.

fetter ▶ **verb** **1** *the captive was fettered* SHACKLE, manacle, handcuff, clap in irons, put in chains, chain (up); *informal* cuff; *literary* enfetter. **2** *these obligations fetter the company's powers* RESTRICT, restrain, constrain, limit, hinder, hamper, impede, obstruct, hamstring, inhibit, check, curb, trammel; *informal* hog-tie.

fetters ▶ **plural noun** SHACKLES, manacles, handcuffs, irons, leg irons, chains, restraints; *informal* cuffs, bracelets; *historical* bilboes.

fettle ▶ **noun** SHAPE, trim, (physical) fitness, (state of) health; condition, form, (state of) repair, (working) order.

fetus ▶ **noun** EMBRYO, unborn baby/child.

feud ▶ **noun** *tribal feuds* VENDETTA, conflict; rivalry, hostility, enmity, strife, discord; quarrel, argument, falling-out.
▶ **verb** *he feuded with his teammates* QUARREL, fight, argue, bicker, squabble, fall out, dispute, clash, differ, be at odds; *informal* scrap.

fever ▶ **noun** **1** *he developed a fever* FEVERISHNESS, high temperature, febrility; *Medicine* pyrexia; *informal* temperature. **2** *a fever of excitement* FERMENT, frenzy, furor; ecstasy, rapture. **3** *Stanley Cup fever* EXCITEMENT, frenzy, agitation, passion.
— RELATED TERMS: febrile.

fevered ▶ **adjective** **1** *her fevered brow* FEVERISH, febrile, hot, burning. **2** *a fevered imagination* EXCITED, agitated, frenzied, overwrought, fervid.

feverish ▶ **adjective** **1** *she's really feverish* FEBRILE, fevered, hot, burning; *informal* having a temperature. **2** *feverish excitement* FRENZIED, frenetic, hectic, agitated, excited, restless, nervous, worked up, overwrought, frantic, furious, hysterical, wild, uncontrolled, unrestrained.

few ▶ **adjective** **1** *police are revealing few details* NOT MANY, hardly any, scarcely any; a small number of, a small amount of, one or two, a handful of; little. **2** *comforts here are few* SCARCE, scant, meagre, insufficient, in short supply; thin on the ground, few and far between, infrequent, uncommon, rare; negligible.
— OPPOSITES: many, plentiful.
■ **a few** A SMALL NUMBER, a handful, one or two, a couple, two or three; not many, hardly any.

fiancée, masc. **fiancé** ▶ **noun** BETROTHED, wife-to-be, husband-to-be, bride-to-be, future wife/ husband, prospective spouse; *informal* intended.

fiasco ▶ **noun** FAILURE, disaster, catastrophe, debacle, shambles, farce, mess, wreck; *informal* flop, washout, snafu.
— OPPOSITES: success.

fiat ▶ **noun** DECREE, edict, order, command, commandment, injunction, proclamation, mandate, dictum, diktat.

fib ▶ **noun** *you're telling a fib* LIE, untruth, falsehood, made-up story, invention, fabrication, deception, (piece of) fiction; (little) white lie, half-truth; *informal* tall story/tale, whopper.
— OPPOSITES: truth.

fibre ▶ **noun** **1** *fibres from the murderer's sweater*

THREAD, strand, filament; *technical* fibril. **2** *natural fibres* MATERIAL, cloth, fabric. **3** *fibre in the diet* ROUGHAGE, bulk.

fickle ▶ adjective CAPRICIOUS, changeable, variable, volatile, mercurial; inconstant, undependable, unsteady, unfaithful, faithless, flighty, giddy, skittish; fair-weather; *technical* labile; *literary* mutable.
– OPPOSITES: constant.

fiction ▶ noun **1** *the popularity of Canadian fiction* NOVELS, stories, (creative) writing, (prose) literature; *informal* lit. **2** *the president dismissed the allegation as absolute fiction* FABRICATION, invention, lies, fibs, untruth, falsehood, fantasy, nonsense.
– OPPOSITES: fact.

fictional ▶ adjective FICTITIOUS, fictive, invented, imaginary, made up, make-believe, unreal, fabricated, mythical.
– OPPOSITES: real.

fictitious ▶ adjective **1** *a fictitious name* FALSE, fake, fabricated, sham; bogus, spurious, assumed, affected, adopted, feigned, invented, made up; *informal* pretend, phony. **2** *a fictitious character. See* FICTIONAL.
– OPPOSITES: genuine.

fiddle (*informal*) ▶ noun *she played the fiddle* VIOLIN, viola.
▶ verb **1** *he fiddled with a coaster* FIDGET, play, toy, twiddle, fuss, fool about/around; finger, thumb, handle; *informal* mess about/around, muck about/ around. **2** *he fiddled with the dials* ADJUST, tinker, play about/around, meddle, interfere. **3** *fiddling the figures* FALSIFY, manipulate, massage, rig, distort, misrepresent, doctor, alter, tamper with, interfere with; *informal* fix, flim-flam, cook (the books).

fidelity ▶ noun **1** *fidelity to her husband* FAITHFULNESS, loyalty, constancy; true-heartedness, trustworthiness, dependability, reliability; *formal* troth. **2** *fidelity to your king* LOYALTY, allegiance, obedience; *historical* homage, fealty. **3** *the fidelity of the reproduction* ACCURACY, exactness, precision, preciseness, correctness; strictness, closeness, faithfulness, authenticity.
– OPPOSITES: disloyalty.

fidget ▶ verb **1** *the audience began to fidget* MOVE RESTLESSLY, wriggle, squirm, twitch, jiggle, shuffle, be agitated; *informal* be jittery. **2** *she fidgeted with her scarf* PLAY, fuss, toy, twiddle, fool about/around; *informal* fiddle, mess about/around.
▶ noun **1** *his convulsive fidgets* TWITCH, wriggle, squirm, jiggle, shuffle, tic, spasm. **2** *what a fidget you are!* FLIBBERTIGIBBET, restless person, bundle of nerves.

fidgety ▶ adjective RESTLESS, restive, on edge, uneasy, antsy, nervous, keyed up, anxious, agitated; *informal* jittery, twitchy.

field ▶ noun **1** *a large plowed field* MEADOW, pasture, paddock, grassland, pasture land; *literary* lea, sward; *archaic* glebe. **2** *a soccer field* PITCH, ground, sports field, playing field, recreation ground. **3** *the field of biotechnology* AREA, sphere, discipline, province, department, domain, sector, branch, subject; *informal* bailiwick. **4** *your field of vision* SCOPE, range, sweep, reach, extent. **5** *she is well ahead of the field* COMPETITORS, entrants, competition; applicants, candidates, possibles.
▶ verb **1** *she fielded the ball* CATCH, stop, retrieve; return, throw back. **2** *fielding an ineligible player* PUT IN THE TEAM, send out, play; ice. **3** *they can field an army of about one million* DEPLOY, position, range, dispose. **4** *he fielded some awkward questions* DEAL WITH, handle, cope with, answer, reply to, respond to.
▶ adjective **1** *field experience* PRACTICAL, hands-on,

applied, experiential, empirical. **2** *field artillery* MOBILE, portable, transportable, movable, manoeuvrable, light.
– OPPOSITES: theoretical.

fiend ▶ noun **1** *a fiend had taken possession of him* DEMON, devil, evil spirit, bogie; *informal* spook. **2** *a fiend bent on global evildoing* VILLAIN, beast, brute, barbarian, monster, ogre, sadist, evildoer, swine. **3** (*informal*) *a drug fiend* ADDICT, abuser, user; *informal* junkie, —— head/freak. **4** (*informal*) *a fitness fiend* ENTHUSIAST, maniac; devotee, fan, lover, fanatic, addict, buff, freak, nut.

fiendish ▶ adjective **1** *a fiendish torturer* WICKED, cruel, vicious, evil, malevolent, villainous; brutal, savage, barbaric, barbarous, inhuman, murderous, ruthless, merciless; *dated* dastardly. **2** *a fiendish plot* CUNNING, clever, ingenious, crafty, canny, wily, devious, shrewd; *informal* sneaky. **3** *a fiendish puzzle* DIFFICULT, complex, challenging, complicated, intricate, involved, knotty, thorny, tricky.

fierce ▶ adjective **1** *a fierce black mastiff* FEROCIOUS, savage, vicious, aggressive. **2** *fierce competition* AGGRESSIVE, cutthroat, competitive; keen, intense, strong, relentless. **3** *fierce, murderous jealousy* INTENSE, powerful, vehement, passionate, impassioned, fervent, fervid, ardent. **4** *a fierce wind* POWERFUL, strong, violent, forceful; stormy, blustery, gusty, tempestuous. **5** *a fierce pain* SEVERE, extreme, intense, acute, awful, dreadful; excruciating, agonizing, piercing.
– OPPOSITES: gentle, mild.

fiery ▶ adjective **1** *the fiery breath of dragons* BURNING, blazing, flaming; on fire, ablaze, igneous; *literary* afire. **2** *a fiery red* BRIGHT, brilliant, vivid, intense, deep, rich. **3** *her fiery spirit* PASSIONATE, impassioned, ardent, fervent, fervid, spirited; quick-tempered, volatile, explosive, aggressive, determined, resolute.

fiesta ▶ noun FESTIVAL, carnival, holiday, celebration, party.

fight ▶ verb **1** *two men were fighting* BRAWL, exchange blows, attack/assault each other, hit/punch each other; struggle, grapple, wrestle; *informal* scrap, have a dust-up, have a set-to, roughhouse, engage in fisticuffs. **2** *they fought in the First World War* (DO) BATTLE, go to war, take up arms, be a soldier; engage, meet, clash, skirmish. **3** *a war fought for freedom* ENGAGE IN, wage, conduct, prosecute, undertake. **4** *they are always fighting* QUARREL, argue, row, bicker, squabble, fall out, have a row/fight, wrangle, be at odds, disagree, differ, have words, bandy words, be at each other's throats, be at loggerheads; *informal* scrap. **5** *fighting against wage reductions* CAMPAIGN, strive, battle, struggle, contend, crusade, agitate, lobby, push, press. **6** *they will fight the decision* OPPOSE, contest, contend with, confront, challenge, combat, dispute, quarrel with, argue against/with, strive against, struggle against. **7** *Tyler fought the urge to stick his tongue out* REPRESS, restrain, suppress, stifle, smother, hold back, fight back, keep in check, curb, control, rein in, choke back; *informal* keep the lid on.
▶ noun **1** *a fight outside a club* BRAWL, fracas, melee, rumpus, skirmish, sparring match, struggle, scuffle, altercation, scrum, clash, disturbance; fisticuffs; *informal* scrap, dust-up, set-to, shindy, shindig, punch-up, donnybrook. **2** *a heavyweight fight* BOXING MATCH, bout, match. **3** *Japan's fight against Russia* BATTLE, engagement, clash, conflict, struggle; war, campaign, crusade, action, hostilities. **4** *a fight with my girlfriend* ARGUMENT, quarrel, squabble, row,

wrangle, disagreement, falling-out, contretemps, altercation, dispute; *informal* tiff, spat, scrap, slanging match, cat fight, bust-up, blow-up. **5** *their fight for control of the company* STRUGGLE, battle, campaign, push, effort. **6** *she had no fight left in her* WILL TO RESIST, resistance, spirit, courage, pluck, pluckiness, grit, strength, backbone, determination, resolution, resolve, resoluteness, aggression, aggressiveness; *informal* guts, spunk, sand, moxie.

■ **fight back 1** *fight back against the oppressors* RETALIATE, counter-attack, strike back, hit back, respond, reciprocate, return fire, give tit for tat. **2** *Russ fought back tears.* See FIGHT *verb* sense 7.

■ **fight someone/something off** REPEL, repulse, beat off/back, ward off, fend off, keep/hold at bay, drive away/back, force back.

■ **fight shy of** FLINCH FROM, demur from, recoil from; have misgivings about, have qualms about, be averse to, be chary of, be loath to, be reluctant to, be disinclined to, be afraid to, hesitate to, balk at; *informal* boggle at.

fighter ▶ **noun 1** *a guerrilla fighter* SOLDIER, fighting man/woman, warrior, combatant, serviceman, servicewoman, trooper, mercenary; *archaic* man-at-arms. **2** *the fighter was knocked to the ground* BOXER, pugilist, prizefighter; wrestler; *informal* scrapper, pug. **3** *enemy fighters* WARPLANE, armed aircraft.

fighting ▶ **adjective** *a fighting man* VIOLENT, combative, aggressive, pugnacious, truculent, belligerent, bellicose, scrappy.
— OPPOSITES: peaceful.
▶ **noun** *200 were injured in the fighting* VIOLENCE, hostilities, conflict, action, combat; warfare, war, battles, skirmishing, rioting.
— OPPOSITES: peace.

figment ▶ **noun** INVENTION, creation, fabrication; hallucination, illusion, delusion, fancy, vision.

figurative ▶ **adjective** METAPHORICAL, non-literal, symbolic, allegorical, representative, emblematic.
— OPPOSITES: literal.

figure ▶ **noun 1** *the production figure* STATISTIC, number, quantity, amount, level, total, sum; **(figures)** data, information. **2** *the second figure was 9* DIGIT, numeral, numerical symbol. **3** *he can't put a figure on it* PRICE, cost, amount, value, valuation. **4** *I'm good with figures* ARITHMETIC, mathematics, math, calculations, computation, numbers. **5** *her petite figure* PHYSIQUE, build, frame, body, proportions, shape, form. **6** *a dark figure emerged* SILHOUETTE, outline, shape, form. **7** *a figure of authority* PERSON, personage, individual, man, woman, character, personality; representative, embodiment, personification, epitome. **8** *life-size figures* HUMAN REPRESENTATION, effigy, model, statue. **9** *geometrical figures* SHAPE, pattern, design, motif. **10** *see figure 4* DIAGRAM, illustration, drawing, picture, plate.
▶ **verb 1** *a beast figuring in Egyptian legend* FEATURE, appear, be featured, be mentioned, be referred to, have prominence, crop up. **2** *a way to figure the values* CALCULATE, work out, total, reckon, compute, determine, assess, put a figure on, crunch the numbers, tot up. **3** *(informal) I figured that I didn't have a chance* SUPPOSE, think, believe, consider, expect, take it, suspect, sense; assume, dare say, conclude, take it as read, presume, deduce, infer, extrapolate, gather, guess. **4** *'Charlotte's late.' 'That figures.'* MAKE SENSE, seem reasonable, stand to reason, be expected, be logical, follow, ring true.

■ **figure on** *they figured on paying about $100* PLAN ON, count on, rely on, bank on, bargain on, depend on, pin one's hopes on; anticipate, expect to.

■ **figure something out** *he tried to figure out how to switch on the lamp* WORK OUT, fathom, puzzle out, decipher, ascertain, make sense of, think through, get to the bottom of; understand, comprehend, see, grasp, get the hang of, get the drift of; *informal* twig, crack.

figurehead ▶ **noun 1** *the president was just a figurehead* TITULAR HEAD, nominal leader, leader in name only, front man, cipher, token, mouthpiece, puppet, instrument. **2** *the figurehead on the Titanic* CARVING, bust, sculpture, image, statue.

figure skating ▶ **noun** *See Table.*

Figure Skating Terms

Axel	Mohawk
camel spin	over-rotation
carnival ♣	pairs skating
Choctaw	toe pick
compulsory figures	precision skating
death spiral	triple
flip	double
flying	quad
free skate	Salchow
ice dancing	serpentine
ice queen	sit spin
ice show	spin
kiss-and-cry	spread-eagle
lift	toe loop
loop	twizzle
Lutz	walley

filament ▶ **noun** FIBRE, thread, strand; *technical* fibril.

file[1] ▶ **noun 1** *he opened the file* FOLDER, portfolio, binder, *proprietary* Duo-Tang ♣, document case. **2** *we have files on all the major companies* DOSSIER, document, record, report; data, information, documentation, annals, archives. **3** *the computer file was searched* DATA, document, text. **4** *the minister needed updating on the unity file* DOSSIER, department, front.
▶ **verb 1** *file the documents correctly* CATEGORIZE, classify, organize, put in place/order, order, arrange, catalogue, record, store, archive. **2** *Debbie has filed for divorce* APPLY, register, ask. **3** *two women have filed a civil suit against him* BRING, press, lodge, place; *formal* prefer.

file[2] ▶ **noun** *a file of boys* LINE, column, row, string, chain, procession, queue.
▶ **verb** *we filed out into the car park* WALK IN A LINE, march, parade, troop.

file[3] ▶ **verb** *she filed her nails* SMOOTH, buff, rub (down), polish, shape; scrape, abrade, rasp, sandpaper.

filial ▶ **adjective** DUTIFUL, devoted, compliant, respectful, affectionate, loving.

filibuster ▶ **noun** *many hours in committee are characterized by filibuster* STONEWALLING, delaying tactics, procrastination, obstruction, temporizing.
▶ **verb** *the opposition are filibustering* WASTE TIME, stall, play for time, stonewall, sandbag, procrastinate, buy time, employ delaying tactics, rag the puck ♣.

filigree ▶ **noun** TRACERY, fretwork, latticework, scrollwork, lacework, quilling.

fill ▶ **verb 1** *he filled a bowl with cereal* MAKE/BECOME FULL, fill up, fill to the brim, top up, charge. **2** *guests filled the parlour* CROWD INTO, throng, pack (into), occupy, squeeze into, cram (into); overcrowd, overfill. **3** *he began filling his shelves* STOCK, pack, load, supply,

replenish, restock, refill. **4** *fill all the holes with a wood-repair compound* BLOCK UP, stop (up), plug, seal, caulk. **5** *the perfume filled the room* PERVADE, permeate, suffuse, be diffused through, penetrate, infuse, perfume. **6** *he was going to fill a government post* OCCUPY, hold, take up; *informal* hold down. **7** *we had just filled a big order* CARRY OUT, complete, fulfill, execute, discharge.
– OPPOSITES: empty.

■ **fill in** SUBSTITUTE, deputize, stand in, cover, take over, act as stand-in, take the place of; *informal* sub, step into someone's shoes/boots, pinch-hit.

■ **fill someone in** INFORM OF, advise of, tell about, acquaint with, apprise of, brief on, update with; *informal* put in the picture about, bring up to speed on.

■ **fill something in** See FILL SOMETHING OUT sense 2.

■ **fill out** GROW FATTER, become plumper, flesh out, put on/gain weight, get heavier.

■ **fill something out 1** *this account needs to be filled out* EXPAND, enlarge, add to, elaborate on, flesh out; supplement, extend, develop, amplify. **2** *he filled out the forms* COMPLETE, answer, fill in.

filling ► noun *filling for cushions* STUFFING, padding, wadding, filler.
► adjective *a filling meal* SUBSTANTIAL, hearty, ample, satisfying, square; heavy, stodgy.

fillip ► noun *their support provided a fillip to her campaign* STIMULUS, stimulation, boost, incentive, impetus; tonic, spur, push, aid, help; *informal* shot in the arm.

film ► noun **1** *a film of sweat* LAYER, coat, coating, covering, cover, sheet, patina, overlay. **2** *Emma was watching a film* MOVIE, picture, feature (film), motion picture; *informal* flick, pic; *dated* moving picture, talkie. **3** *she would like to work in film* CINEMA, movies, the pictures.
– RELATED TERMS: cinematic.
► verb **1** *he immediately filmed the next scene* RECORD (ON FILM), shoot, capture on film, video. **2** *his eyes had filmed over* CLOUD, mist, haze; become blurred, blur; *archaic* blear.

film star ► noun (FILM) ACTOR/ACTRESS, movie star, leading man/woman, leading lady, lead; celebrity, star, starlet, matinee idol, superstar; *informal* celeb.

filmy ► adjective DIAPHANOUS, transparent, see-through, translucent, sheer, gossamer; delicate, fine, light, thin, silky.
– OPPOSITES: thick, opaque.

filter ► noun *a carbon filter* STRAINER, sifter; riddle; gauze, netting.
► verb **1** *the farmers filter the water* SIEVE, strain, sift, filtrate, clarify, purify, refine, treat. **2** *the rain had filtered through her jacket* SEEP, percolate, leak, trickle, ooze.

filth ► noun **1** *stagnant pools of filth* DIRT, muck, grime, mud, mire, sludge, slime, ooze; excrement, excreta, dung, manure, ordure, sewage; rubbish, refuse, dross; pollution, contamination, filthiness, uncleanness, foulness, nastiness, garbage, crud, grunge, gunge, trash. **2** *I felt sick after reading that filth* PORNOGRAPHY, pornographic literature/films, dirty books, smut, obscenity, indecency; *informal* porn, porno.

filthy ► adjective **1** *the room was filthy* DIRTY, mucky, grimy, muddy, muddied, slimy, unclean; foul, squalid, sordid, nasty, soiled, sullied; polluted, contaminated, unhygienic, unsanitary; *informal* cruddy, grungy; grotty; *literary* besmirched; *formal* feculent. **2** *his face was filthy* UNWASHED, unclean, dirty, grimy, smeared,

grubby, muddy, mucky, black, blackened, stained; *literary* begrimed. **3** *filthy jokes* OBSCENE, indecent, dirty, smutty, rude, improper, coarse, bawdy, vulgar, lewd, racy, raw, off-colour, earthy, barnyard, locker-room, ribald, risqué, 'adult', pornographic, explicit; *informal* blue, porn, porno, X-rated. **4** *you filthy brute!* DESPICABLE, contemptible, nasty, low, base, mean, vile, obnoxious; *informal* dirty (rotten), lowdown, no-good. **5** *he was in a filthy mood* BAD, foul, bad-tempered, ill-tempered, irritable, grumpy, grouchy, cross, fractious, peevish; *informal* snappish, snappy, shirty, cranky, ornery.
– OPPOSITES: clean.
► adverb *filthy rich* VERY, extremely, tremendously, immensely, remarkably, excessively, exceedingly; *informal* stinking, awfully, terribly, seriously, mega, majorly, ultra, damn.

final ► adjective **1** *the final year of study* LAST, closing, concluding, finishing, end, terminating, ultimate, eventual. **2** *their decisions are final* IRREVOCABLE, unalterable, absolute, conclusive, irrefutable, incontrovertible, indisputable, unchallengeable, binding.
– OPPOSITES: first, provisional.
► noun *the Stanley Cup final* DECIDER, clincher, final game/match.
– OPPOSITES: qualifier.

finale ► noun CLIMAX, culmination; end, ending, finish, close, conclusion, termination; denouement, last act, final scene.
– OPPOSITES: beginning.

finality ► noun CONCLUSIVENESS, decisiveness, decision, definiteness, definitiveness, certainty, certitude; irrevocability, irrefutability.

finalize ► verb CONCLUDE, complete, clinch, settle, work out, secure, wrap up, wind up, put the finishing touches to; reach an agreement on, agree on, come to terms on; *informal* sew up.

finally ► adverb **1** *she finally got her man to the altar* EVENTUALLY, ultimately, in the end, after a long time, at (long) last; in the long run, in the fullness of time. **2** *finally, wrap the ribbon round the edge* LASTLY, last, in conclusion, to conclude, to end. **3** *this should finally dispel that common misconception* CONCLUSIVELY, irrevocably, decisively, definitively, for ever, for good, once and for all.

finance ► noun **1** *he knows about finance* FINANCIAL AFFAIRS, money matters, fiscal matters, economics, money management, commerce, business, investment. **2** *short-term finance* FUNDS, assets, money, capital, resources, cash, reserves, revenue, income; funding, backing, sponsorship.
► verb *the project was financed by grants* FUND, pay for, back, capitalize, endow, subsidize, invest in; underwrite, guarantee, sponsor, support, bankroll.

financial ► adjective MONETARY, money, economic, pecuniary, fiscal, banking, commercial, business, investment.

financier ► noun INVESTOR, speculator, banker, capitalist, industrialist, businessman, businesswoman, stockbroker; *informal* money man, backer.

find ► verb **1** *I found the book I wanted* LOCATE, spot, pinpoint, unearth, obtain; search out, nose out, track down, root out; come across/upon, run across/into, chance on, light on, happen on, stumble on, encounter; *informal* bump into; *literary* espy. **2** *they have found a cure for rabies* DISCOVER, invent, come up with, hit on. **3** *the police found her purse* RETRIEVE, recover, get

back, regain, repossess. **4** *I hope you find peace* OBTAIN, acquire, get, procure, come by, secure, gain, earn, achieve, attain. **5** *I found the courage to speak* SUMMON (UP), gather, muster (up), screw up, call up. **6** *caffeine is found in coffee and tea* BE (PRESENT), occur, exist, be existent, appear. **7** *you'll find that it's a lively area* DISCOVER, become aware, realize, observe, notice, note, perceive, learn. **8** *I find their decision strange* CONSIDER, think, believe to be, feel to be, look on as, view as, see as, judge, deem, regard as. **9** *he was found guilty* JUDGE, adjudge, adjudicate, deem, rule, declare, pronounce. **10** *her barb found its mark* ARRIVE AT, reach, attain, achieve; hit, strike.
— OPPOSITES: lose.

▶ **noun 1** *an archaeological find* DISCOVERY, acquisition, asset. **2** *this table is a real find* GOOD BUY, bargain; godsend, boon.

■ **find out** DISCOVER, become aware, learn, detect, discern, perceive, observe, notice, note, get/come to know, realize; bring to light, reveal, expose, unearth, disclose; *informal* figure out, cotton on, catch on, tumble, get wise, savvy, twig.

finding ▶ **noun 1** *the finding of the leak* DISCOVERY, location, locating, detection, detecting, uncovering. **2** *the tribunal's findings* CONCLUSION, decision, verdict, pronouncement, judgment, ruling, rule, decree, order, recommendation, resolve; *Law* determination.

fine[1] ▶ **adjective 1** *fine wines* EXCELLENT, first-class, first-rate, great, exceptional, outstanding, quality, superior, splendid, magnificent, exquisite, choice, select, prime, supreme, superb, wonderful, superlative, of high quality, second to none; *informal* A1, top-notch, blue-ribbon, blue-chip, splendiferous. **2** *a fine citizen* WORTHY, admirable, praiseworthy, laudable, estimable, upright, upstanding, respectable. **3** *the initiative is fine, but it's not enough on its own* ALL RIGHT, acceptable, suitable, good (enough), passable, satisfactory, adequate, reasonable, tolerable; *informal* OK. **4** *I feel fine* IN GOOD HEALTH, well, healthy, all right, (fighting) fit, as fit as a fiddle, blooming, thriving, in good shape/condition, in fine fettle; *informal* OK, in the pink. **5** *a fine day* FAIR, dry, bright, clear, sunny, without a cloud in the sky, warm, balmy, summery. **6** *a fine old house* IMPRESSIVE, imposing, striking, splendid, grand, majestic, magnificent, stately. **7** *fine clothes* ELEGANT, stylish, expensive, smart, chic, fashionable; fancy, sumptuous, lavish, opulent; *informal* flashy, swanky, ritzy, plush. **8** *a fine mind* KEEN, quick, alert, sharp, bright, brilliant, astute, clever, intelligent, perspicacious. **9** *fine china* DELICATE, fragile, dainty. **10** *fine hair* THIN, light, delicate, wispy, fly-away. **11** *a fine point* SHARP, keen, acute, sharpened, razor-sharp. **12** *fine material* SHEER, light, lightweight, thin, flimsy; diaphanous, filmy, gossamer, silky, transparent, translucent, see-through. **13** *fine sand* FINE-GRAINED, powdery, powdered, dusty, ground, crushed; *technical* comminuted. **14** *fine detailed work* INTRICATE, delicate, detailed, elaborate, dainty, meticulous. **15** *a fine distinction* SUBTLE, ultra-fine, nice, hair-splitting, nitpicking. **16** *people's finer feelings* ELEVATED, lofty, exalted, noble; refined, sensitive, cultivated, cultured, civilized, sophisticated. **17** *fine taste* DISCERNING, discriminating, refined, cultivated, cultured, critical.
— OPPOSITES: poor, unsatisfactory, ill, inclement, thick, coarse.

▶ **adverb** (*informal*) *you're doing fine* WELL, all right, not

badly, satisfactorily, adequately, nicely, tolerably; *informal* OK, good.
— OPPOSITES: badly.

▶ **verb 1** *it can be fined right down to the required shape* THIN, make/become thin, narrow, taper, attenuate. **2** *additives for fining wine* CLARIFY, clear, purify, refine, filter.

fine[2] ▶ **noun** *heavy fines* (FINANCIAL) PENALTY, sanction, fee, charge.

▶ **verb** *they were fined for breaking environmental laws* PENALIZE, impose a fine on, charge.

finery ▶ **noun** REGALIA, best clothes, (Sunday) best; *informal* glad rags.

finesse ▶ **noun 1** *masterly finesse* SKILL, skilfulness, expertise, subtlety, flair, panache, élan, polish, artistry, virtuosity, mastery. **2** *a modicum of finesse* TACT, tactfulness, discretion, diplomacy, delicacy, sensitivity, perceptiveness, savoir faire. **3** *a clever finesse* WINNING MOVE, trick, stratagem, ruse, manoeuvre, artifice, machination.

finger ▶ **noun** *he wagged his finger at the cat* DIGIT, thumb, index finger, forefinger; *informal* pinkie.
— RELATED TERMS: digital.

▶ **verb 1** *she fingered her brooch uneasily* TOUCH, feel, handle, stroke, rub, caress, fondle, toy with, play (about/around) with, fiddle with. **2** *no one fingered the culprit* IDENTIFY, recognize, pick out, spot; inform on, point the finger at; *informal* rat on, squeal on, tell on, blow the whistle on, snitch on, peach on.

finicky ▶ **adjective** FUSSY, fastidious, punctilious, over-particular, difficult, exacting, demanding; *informal* picky, choosy, pernickety, persnickety; *archaic* nice.

finish ▶ **verb 1** *Mrs. Porter had just finished the task* COMPLETE, end, conclude, stop, cease, terminate, bring to a conclusion/end/close, wind up; crown, cap, round off, put the finishing touches to; accomplish, discharge, carry out, do, get done, fulfill; *informal* wrap up, sew up, polish off. **2** *Sarah has finished school* LEAVE, give up, drop; stop, discontinue, have done with, complete; *informal* pack in, quit. **3** *Hitch finished his dinner* CONSUME, eat, devour, drink, finish off, polish off, gulp (down); use (up), exhaust, empty, drain, get through, run through; *informal* down. **4** *the program has finished* END, come to an end, stop, conclude, come to a conclusion/end/close, cease. **5** *some items were finished in a black lacquer* VARNISH, lacquer, veneer, coat, stain, wax, shellac, enamel, glaze.
— OPPOSITES: start, begin, continue.

▶ **noun 1** *the finish of filming* END, ending, completion, conclusion, close, closing, cessation, termination; final part/stage, finale, denouement; *informal* sewing up, polishing off. **2** *a gallop to the finish* FINISHING LINE/POST, tape. **3** *an antiquated paint finish* VENEER, lacquer, lamination, glaze, coating, covering; surface, texture.
— OPPOSITES: start, beginning.

■ **finish someone/something off 1** *the executioners finished them off* KILL, take/end the life of, execute, terminate, exterminate, liquidate, get rid of; *informal* wipe out, do in, bump off, take out, dispose of, do away with, ice, rub out, waste. **2** *financial difficulties finished off the business* OVERWHELM, overcome, defeat, get the better of, worst, bring down; *informal* drive to the wall, best.

finished ▶ **adjective 1** *the finished job* COMPLETED, concluded, terminated, over (and done with), at an end; accomplished, executed, discharged, fulfilled, done; *informal* wrapped up, sewn up, polished off;

formal effectuated. **2** *a finished performance* ACCOMPLISHED, polished, flawless, faultless, perfect; expert, proficient, masterly, impeccable, virtuoso, skilful, skilled, professional. **3** *he was finished* RUINED, defeated, beaten, wrecked, doomed, bankrupt, broken; *informal* washed up, through, done like dinner ♣, has had the biscuit ♣.
— OPPOSITES: incomplete.

finite ► **adjective** LIMITED, restricted, determinate, fixed.

fire ► **noun 1** *a fire broke out* BLAZE, conflagration, inferno; flames, burning, combustion; forest fire, wildfire, brush fire. **2** *he lacked fire* DYNAMISM, energy, vigour, animation, vitality, vibrancy, exuberance, zest, élan; passion, ardour, zeal, spirit, verve, vivacity, vivaciousness; enthusiasm, eagerness, gusto, fervour, fervency; *informal* pep, vim, go, get-up-and-go, oomph. **3** *rapid machine-gun fire* GUNFIRE, firing, flak, bombardment. **4** *they directed their fire at the prime minister* CRITICISM, censure, condemnation, denunciation, opprobrium, admonishments, brickbats; hostility, antagonism, animosity; *informal* flak.
— RELATED TERMS: pyro-.
► **verb 1** *howitzers firing shells* LAUNCH, shoot, discharge, let fly with. **2** *someone fired a gun* SHOOT, discharge, let off, set off. **3** *(informal) he was fired* DISMISS, discharge, give someone their notice, lay off, let go, get rid of, axe, cashier; *informal* sack, give someone the sack, boot out, give someone the boot, make redundant, give someone their marching orders, pink-slip. **4** *the engine fired* START, get started, get going. **5** *the stories fired my imagination* STIMULATE, stir up, excite, awaken, arouse, rouse, inflame, animate, inspire, motivate.
■ **catch fire** IGNITE, catch light, burst into flames, go up in flames.
■ **on fire 1** *the restaurant was on fire* BURNING, alight, ablaze, blazing, aflame, in flames; *literary* afire. **2** *she was on fire with passion* ARDENT, passionate, fervent, excited, eager, enthusiastic.

firearm ► **noun** GUN, weapon, rifle, pistol, handgun, revolver; *informal* shooter, piece, heat.

firebrand ► **noun** RADICAL, revolutionary, agitator, rabble-rouser, incendiary, subversive, troublemaker.

fireproof ► **adjective** NON-FLAMMABLE, incombustible, fire resistant, flame resistant, flame retardant, heatproof.
— OPPOSITES: inflammable.

fireworks ► **plural noun 1** *celebratory fireworks downtown* PYROTECHNICS, firecrackers. **2** *his stubbornness has produced some fireworks* UPROAR, trouble, mayhem, fuss; tantrums, hysterics.

firm¹ ► **adjective 1** *the ground is fairly firm* HARD, solid, unyielding, resistant; solidified, hardened, compacted, compressed, dense, stiff, rigid, frozen, set. **2** *firm foundations* SECURE, secured, stable, steady, strong, fixed, fast, set, taut, tight; immovable, irremovable, stationary, motionless. **3** *a firm handshake* STRONG, vigorous, sturdy, forceful. **4** *I was very firm about what I wanted | a firm supporter* RESOLUTE, determined, decided, resolved, steadfast; adamant, emphatic, insistent, single-minded, in earnest, whole-hearted; unfaltering, unwavering, unflinching, unswerving, unbending; hardline, committed, dyed-in-the-wool. **5** *firm friends* CLOSE, good, intimate, inseparable, dear, special, fast; constant, devoted, loving, faithful, long-standing, steady, steadfast, rock-steady. **6** *firm plans* DEFINITE,

fixed, settled, decided, established, confirmed, agreed; unalterable, unchangeable, irreversible.
— OPPOSITES: soft, unstable, limp, indefinite.

firm² ► **noun** *an accounting firm* COMPANY, business, concern, enterprise, organization, corporation, conglomerate, office, bureau, agency, consortium; *informal* outfit, set-up.

firmament ► **noun** *(literary)* THE SKY, heaven; the heavens, the skies; *literary* the empyrean, the welkin.

first ► **adjective 1** *the first chapter* EARLIEST, initial, opening, introductory. **2** *first principles* FUNDAMENTAL, basic, rudimentary, primary; key, cardinal, central, chief, vital, essential. **3** *our first priority* FOREMOST, principal, highest, greatest, paramount, top, uppermost, prime, chief, leading, main, major; overriding, predominant, prevailing, central, core, dominant; *informal* number-one. **4** *first prize* TOP, best, prime, premier, winner's, winning.
— OPPOSITES: last, closing.
► **adverb 1** *the room they had first entered* AT FIRST, to begin with, first of all, at the outset, initially. **2** *she would eat first* BEFORE ANYTHING ELSE, first and foremost, now. **3** *she wouldn't go—she'd die first!* IN PREFERENCE, sooner, rather.
► **noun** *it was a first for both of us* NOVELTY, new experience; unknown territory.

first aid ► **noun** CARE, treatment, help, medical attention, assistance, ministrations.

first-class ► **adjective** SUPERIOR, first-rate, high-quality, top-quality, high-grade, five-star; prime, premier, premium, grade A, best, finest, select, exclusive, excellent, superb; *informal* A1, top-notch, blue-ribbon, blue-chip.
— OPPOSITES: poor.

first-hand ► **adjective** DIRECT, immediate, personal, hands-on, experiential, empirical, eye-witness.
— OPPOSITES: vicarious, indirect.

first name ► **noun** FORENAME, given name, Christian name.
— OPPOSITES: surname.

First Peoples ► **plural noun** NATIVE PEOPLES, Native Canadians, Native Americans, Aboriginal Peoples, Indigenous Peoples; First Nations, Indians, Inuit, Metis. *See table.*

first-rate ► **adjective** TOP-QUALITY, high-quality, top-grade, first-class, second to none, fine; superlative, excellent, superb, outstanding, exceptional, exemplary, marvellous, magnificent, splendid; *informal* top-notch, blue-ribbon, blue-chip, ace, A1, super, great, terrific, tremendous, bang-up, skookum, fantastic, killer.

fiscal ► **adjective** TAX, budgetary; financial, economic, monetary, money.

fish ► **verb 1** *some people were fishing in the lake* GO FISHING, angle, cast, trawl, troll, seine. **2** *she fished for her purse* SEARCH, delve, look, hunt; grope, fumble, ferret (about/around), root about/around, rummage (about/around/round). **3** *I'm not fishing for compliments* TRY TO GET, seek to obtain, solicit, angle, aim, hope, cast about/around/round, be after.
■ **fish someone/something out** PULL OUT, haul out, remove, extricate, extract, retrieve; rescue from, save from.

fisherman ► **noun** ANGLER, fisher, rod, fisheries worker.

fishing ► **noun** ANGLING, trawling, trolling, seining, ice fishing, catching fish.

fishy ► **adjective 1** *a fishy smell* FISHLIKE, piscine.

First Peoples' Languages

Algonquian	**Abenaki**	**Delaware/Munsee**
	Blackfoot	**Maliseet/Malecite/Wuastukwiuk**
	Blood/Kainai	**Mi'kmaq/Micmac**
	Peigan/Piegan	**Ojibwa/Anishinabe/Chippewa**
	Siksika	Algonquin/Algonkin
	Cree	Mississauga
	Attikamek	Odawa
	Innu/Montagnais-Naskapi	Oji-Cree
	Moose Cree	Saulteaux/Salteaux
	Plains Cree	**Potawatomi**
	Swampy Cree	
	Woods Cree	
Athapaskan/ Dene	**Beaver/Dunne-Za**	**South Slavey**
	Carrier	**Dogrib**
	Babine	**Gwich'in/Kutchin/Loucheux**
	Wet'suwet'en	**Han**
	Tsilhqot'in/Chilcotin	**Kaska**
	Chipewyan	**Sarcee/Tsuu T'ina**
	North Slavey/Sahtu Dene	**Sekani**
	Bear Lake	**Tagish**
	Hare	**Tahltan**
	Mountain	**Tutchone**
Haidan	**Haida**	
Iroquoian/ Haudenosaunee	**Cayuga**	**Seneca**
	Mohawk	**Tuscarora**
	Oneida	**Huron/Wendat**
	Onondaga	
Kutenaian	**Kutenay/Kootenay/Ktunaxa Kinbasket**	
Salishan	**Comox**	**Okanagan**
	Halkomelem	**Sechelt**
	Cowichan	**Shuswap/Secwepemc**
	Sne Nay Muxw	**Squamish**
	Chilliwack	**Straits**
	Matsqui	Saanich
	Sto:lo	Songhee/Lekwammen
	Lillooet/Stl'atl'imx	**Thompson/Nlaka'pamux**
	Nuxalk/Bella Coola	
Siouan	**Assiniboine**	**Stoney**
	Dakota/Santee	
Tlingit	**Inland Tlingit**	
Tsimshian	**Nass-Gitksan**	**Coast Tsimshian**
	Gitksan	
	Nisga'a/Nishga	
Wakashan	**Heiltsuk/Bella Bella**	**Nuu-cha-nulth/Nootka**
	Haisla	Ahousaht
	Kwakwala/Kwagiulth/Kwakiutl	Hesquiaht
	Lekwiltok	Nitinat/Ditidaht
Inuit	**Inuktitut**	
	Inuinnaqtun	
	Inuvialuktun	
	Inuttut	

Fish

albacore	cobia	koi	salmon
alewife	cod	lamprey	sand lance
amberjack	coelacanth	lancetfish	sardine
anchovy	conner ♣	largemouth	sawfish
anemone fish	crappie	ling	sculpin
angelfish	croaker	ling cod	sea bass
anglerfish	cusk	lunge	sea bream
barbel	dace	lungfish	sea raven
barbotte ♣	damselfish	mackerel	sea robin
bass	darter	mahi mahi	shark
billfish	devil ray	manta	skate
black bass	doré	marlin	skipjack tuna
black cod	dorado	minnow	smelt
blenny	eel	molly	snapper
blowfish	eelpout	moray eel	sole
blueback	electric eel	mudcat	spadefish
bluefin tuna	eulachon	muskellunge	squawfish
bluefish	eutherian	muskie	squirrel fish
bluegill	fighting fish	northern pike	stingray
bonito	flatfish	parrotfish	striped bass
Boston bluefish	flounder	perch	sturgeon
bowfin	flying fish	pickerel	sunfish
bream	frogfish	pike	swordfish
bucketmouth	gaspereau	pilchard	swordtail
buffalo fish	goby	pilotfish	tilapia
burbot	goldeye	piranha	tilefish
butterfish	goldfish	plaice	tommycod
butterfly fish	greenling	pollock	trout
candlefish	grey mullet	puffer fish	tuna
capelin	grouper	pumpkinseed	turbot
carp	guppy	ray	walleye
catfish	haddock	red snapper	whitefish
chain pickerel	hake	rock bass	Winnipeg goldeye
channel cat	halibut	roughy	*See also* SALMON & TROUT.
characin	harlequin fish	sablefish	*See also* SHARKS.
chub	herring	sailfish	

2 *round fishy eyes* EXPRESSIONLESS, inexpressive, vacant, lacklustre, glassy. **3** *(informal) there was something fishy going on* SUSPICIOUS, questionable, dubious, doubtful, suspect; odd, queer, peculiar, strange; *informal* funny, shady, crooked, sketchy.

fission ▶ noun SPLITTING, division, dividing, rupture, breaking, severance.
— OPPOSITES: fusion.

fissure ▶ noun OPENING, crevice, crack, cleft, breach, crevasse, chasm; break, fracture, fault, rift, rupture, split.

fist ▶ noun CLENCHED HAND; *informal* duke, mitt.

fit¹ ▶ adjective **1** *fit for human habitation | he is a fit subject for such a book* SUITABLE, good enough; relevant, pertinent, apt, appropriate, suited, apposite, fitting; *archaic* meet. **2** *is he fit to look after a child?* COMPETENT, able, capable; ready, prepared, qualified, trained, equipped. **3** *(informal) you look fit to commit murder!* READY, prepared, all set, in a fit state, likely, about; *informal* psyched up. **4** *he looked tanned and fit* HEALTHY, well, in good health, in (good) shape, in (good) trim, in good condition, fighting fit, as fit as a fiddle/flea; athletic, muscular, well-built, strong, robust, hale and hearty, in the pink.
— OPPOSITES: unsuitable, incapable, unwell.

▶ verb **1** *have your carpets fitted professionally* LAY, position, place, put in place/position, fix. **2** *cameras fitted with a backlight button* EQUIP, provide, supply, fit out, furnish. **3** *concrete slabs were fitted together* JOIN, connect, put together, piece together, attach, unite,

link, slot. **4** *a sentence that fits her crimes* MATCH, suit, be appropriate to, correspond to, tally with, go with, accord with, correlate to, be congruous with, be congruent with, be consonant with. **5** *an MA fits you for a professional career* QUALIFY, prepare, make ready, train, groom.

▶ noun *the degree of fit between a school's philosophy and practice* CORRELATION, correspondence, agreement, consistency, equivalence, match, similarity, compatibility, concurrence.

■ **fit in** CONFORM, be in harmony, blend in, be in line, be assimilated into.

■ **fit someone/something out/up** EQUIP, provide, supply, furnish, kit out, rig out.

fit² ▶ noun **1** *an epileptic fit* CONVULSION, spasm, paroxysm, seizure, attack; *Medicine* ictus. **2** *a fit of the giggles* OUTBREAK, outburst, attack, bout, spell. **3** *my mother would have a fit if she knew* TANTRUM, fit of temper, outburst of anger/rage, frenzy; *informal* blowout, hissy fit, conniption (fit).

■ **in/by fits and starts** SPASMODICALLY, intermittently, sporadically, erratically, irregularly, fitfully, haphazardly.

fitful ▶ adjective INTERMITTENT, sporadic, spasmodic, broken, disturbed, disrupted, patchy, irregular, uneven, unsettled; *informal* herky-jerky.

fitness ▶ noun **1** *ringette requires tremendous fitness* GOOD HEALTH, strength, robustness, vigour, athleticism, toughness, physical fitness, muscularity; good condition, good shape, well-being.

2 *his fitness for active service* SUITABILITY, capability, competence, ability, aptitude; readiness, preparedness, eligibility.

fitted ► adjective *a fitted sheet* SHAPED, contoured, fitting tightly/well.

fitting ► noun **1** *bathroom fittings* FURNISHINGS, furniture, fixtures, equipment, appointments, appurtenances. **2** *the fitting of catalytic converters* INSTALLATION, installing, putting in, fixing.

► adjective *a fitting conclusion* APT, appropriate, suitable, apposite; fit, proper, right, seemly, correct; *archaic* meet.

– OPPOSITES: unsuitable.

five ► cardinal number QUINTET, fivesome; quintuplets; *technical* pentad.

– RELATED TERMS: quin-, quinque-, penta-.

fix ► verb **1** *he fixed my washing machine* REPAIR, mend, put right, put to rights, get working, restore (to working order); overhaul, service, renovate, recondition. **2** *signs were fixed to lamp posts* FASTEN, attach, affix, secure; join, connect, couple, link; install, implant, embed; stick, glue, pin, nail, screw, bolt, clamp, clip. **3** *his words are fixed in my memory* STICK, lodge, embed, burned, branded. **4** *his eyes were fixed on the ground* FOCUS, direct, level, point, train. **5** (*informal*) *Laura was fixing her hair* ARRANGE, put in order, adjust; style, groom, comb, brush; *informal* do. **6** (*informal*) *Chris will fix supper* PREPARE, cook, make, get; *informal* rustle up, whip up. **7** *let's fix a date for the meeting* DECIDE ON, select, choose, resolve on; determine, settle, set, arrange, establish, allot; designate, name, appoint, specify. **8** *chemicals are used to fix the dye* MAKE PERMANENT, make fast, set. **9** (*informal*) *the fight was fixed* RIG, arrange fraudulently; tamper with, influence; *informal* fiddle. **10** (*informal*) *don't tell anybody, or I'll fix you!* GET ONE'S REVENGE ON, avenge oneself on, get even with, get back at, take reprisals against, punish, deal with; sort someone out. **11** *the cat has been fixed* CASTRATE, neuter, geld, spay, desex, sterilize; *informal* doctor, alter.

► noun (*informal*) **1** *they are in a bit of a fix* PREDICAMENT, plight, difficulty, awkward situation, corner, tight spot; mess, mare's nest, dire straits; *informal* pickle, jam, hole, scrape, bind, sticky situation. **2** *he needed his fix* DOSE; *informal* hit. **3** *a quick fix for the coal industry* SOLUTION, answer, resolution, way out, remedy, cure, placebo; *informal* magic bullet, band-aid solution. **4** *the result was a complete fix* FRAUD, swindle, trick, charade, sham; *informal* set-up, fiddle.

■ **fix someone up** (*informal*) PROVIDE, supply, furnish.

■ **fix something up** ORGANIZE, arrange, make arrangements for, sort out.

fixated ► adjective OBSESSED, preoccupied, obsessive; focussed, keen, gripped, engrossed, immersed, wrapped up, enthusiastic, fanatical; *informal* hooked, wild, nuts, crazy.

fixation ► noun OBSESSION, preoccupation, mania, addiction, compulsion; *informal* thing, bug, craze, fad.

fixed ► adjective **1** *there are fixed ropes on the rock face* FASTENED, secure, fast, firm; riveted, moored, anchored. **2** *a fixed period of time* PREDETERMINED, set, established, arranged, specified, decided, agreed, determined, confirmed, prescribed, allotted; definite, defined, explicit, precise.

fixture ► noun **1** *fixtures and fittings* FIXED APPLIANCE, installation, unit. **2** *she's a fixture at the bar* RESIDENT, lifer, permanent feature, part of the furniture.

fizz ► verb EFFERVESCE, sparkle, bubble, froth; *literary* spume.

► noun **1** *the fizz in champagne* EFFERVESCENCE, sparkle, fizziness, bubbles, bubbliness, gassiness, carbonation, froth. **2** (*informal*) *their set is a little lacking in fizz* EBULLIENCE, exuberance, liveliness, life, vivacity, animation, vigour, energy, verve, dash, spirit, sparkle, zest, fire; *informal* pizzazz, pep, zip, oomph. **3** *the fizz of the static* CRACKLE, crackling, buzz, buzzing, hiss, hissing, white noise; *literary* susurration.

fizzle ► verb *the loudspeaker fizzled* CRACKLE, buzz, hiss, fizz, crepitate.

► noun **1** *electric fizzle.* See FIZZ *noun* sense 3. **2** *the whole thing turned out to be a fizzle* FAILURE, fiasco, debacle, disaster; *informal* flop, washout, letdown, dead loss, snafu.

■ **fizzle out** PETER OUT, die off, ease off, cool off, flatline; tail off, wither away, wind down.

fizzy ► adjective EFFERVESCENT, sparkling, carbonated, gassy, bubbly, frothy; spumante, frizzante.

– OPPOSITES: still, flat.

flab ► noun (*informal*) FAT, excessive weight, fatness, plumpness, lard; paunch, pot-belly, beer gut, Molson muscle ♣.

flabbergast ► verb (*informal*). See ASTONISH.

flabby ► adjective **1** *his flabby stomach* SOFT, loose, flaccid, slack, untoned, drooping, sagging. **2** *a flabby child* FAT, fleshy, overweight, plump, chubby, portly, rotund, broad in the beam, of ample proportions, obese, corpulent; *informal* tubby, roly-poly, well-upholstered.

– OPPOSITES: firm, thin.

flaccid ► adjective **1** *a flaccid muscle* SOFT, loose, flabby, slack, lax; drooping, sagging. **2** *his play seemed flaccid* LACKLUSTRE, lifeless, listless, uninspiring, unanimated, tame, dull, vapid.

– OPPOSITES: firm, spirited.

flag¹ ► noun *he raised the flag* BANNER, standard, ensign, pennant, banderole, streamer, jack, gonfalon; colours; Maple Leaf ♣, Red Ensign ♣, Stars and Stripes, Old Glory, Union Jack, Jolly Roger.

– RELATED TERMS: vexillary.

► verb *flag the misspelled words* INDICATE, identify, point out, mark, label, tag, highlight.

■ **flag someone/something down** HAIL, wave down, signal to stop, stop, halt.

flag² ► verb **1** *they were flagging towards the finish* TIRE, grow tired/weary, weaken, grow weak, wilt, droop, fade, run out of steam. **2** *my energy flags in the afternoon* FADE, decline, wane, ebb, diminish, decrease, lessen, dwindle; wither, melt away, peter out, die away/down.

– OPPOSITES: revive.

flagellate ► verb FLOG, whip, beat, scourge, lash, birch, strap, belt, cane, thrash, horsewhip, tan/whip someone's hide, give someone a hiding.

flagrant ► adjective BLATANT, glaring, obvious, overt, conspicuous, barefaced, shameless, brazen, undisguised, unconcealed; outrageous, scandalous, shocking, disgraceful, dreadful, terrible, gross.

flagship ► adjective TOP-OF-THE-LINE, topline, premium, prime, leading, champion, best, top.

flagstone ► noun PAVING SLAB, paving stone, slab, flag.

flail ► verb **1** *he fell headlong, his arms flailing* WAVE, swing, thrash about, flap about. **2** *I was flailing about in the water* FLOUNDER, struggle, thrash, writhe, splash. **3** *he flailed their shoulders with his cane* THRASH, beat, strike, flog, whip, lash, scourge, cane; *informal* wallop, whack.

flair ▶ noun **1** *a flair for publicity* APTITUDE, talent, gift, instinct, (natural) ability, facility, skill, bent, feel, knack. **2** *she dressed with flair* STYLE, stylishness, panache, dash, élan, poise, elegance; (good) taste, discernment, discrimination; *informal* class, pizzazz.

flak ▶ noun **1** *my aircraft had been damaged by flak* ANTI-AIRCRAFT FIRE, shelling, gunfire; bombardment, barrage, salvo, volley. **2** (*informal*) *he has come in for a lot of flak* CRITICISM, censure, disapproval, disapprobation, hostility, complaints; opprobrium, obloquy, calumny, vilification, abuse, brickbats; *formal* castigation, excoriation.

flake¹ ▶ noun **1** *flakes of pastry* SLIVER, wafer, shaving, paring; chip, scale; fragment, scrap, shred; *technical* lamina. **2** *Geoff can be such a flake* DITZ, space cadet, airhead, fool, scatterbrain.
▶ verb *the paint was flaking* PEEL (OFF), chip, blister, come off (in layers).

flake²
■ **flake out** (*informal*) *she flaked out in her chair* FALL ASLEEP, go to sleep, drop off; collapse, faint, pass out, lose consciousness, black out, swoon; *informal* conk out, nod off, sack out.

flaky ▶ adjective **1** *flaky skin* FLAKING, peeling, scaly, blistering, scabrous. **2** *a flaky person* FOOLISH, silly, frivolous, flighty, spinny ♣, spacey, new-agey, hippy-dippy, airy-fairy.

flamboyant ▶ adjective **1** *her flamboyant personality* EXUBERANT, confident, lively, animated, vibrant, vivacious. **2** *a flamboyant cravat* COLOURFUL, brightly coloured, bright, vibrant, vivid; dazzling, eye-catching, bold; showy, ostentatious, gaudy, garish, lurid, loud; *informal* jazzy, flashy. **3** *a flamboyant architectural style* ELABORATE, ornate, fancy; baroque, rococo.
— OPPOSITES: restrained.

flame ▶ noun **1** *a sheet of flames* FIRE, blaze, conflagration, inferno. **2** *the flames of her anger* PASSION, warmth, ardour, fervour, fervency, fire, intensity. **3** (*informal*) *an old flame* SWEETHEART, boyfriend, girlfriend, lover, partner; *informal* beau; *dated* steady.
▶ verb **1** *logs crackled and flamed* BURN, blaze, be ablaze, be alight, be on fire, be in flames, be aflame. **2** *Erica's cheeks flamed* BECOME RED, go red, blush, flush, redden, grow pink/crimson/scarlet, colour, glow.
— OPPOSITES: extinguish.
■ **in flames** ON FIRE, burning, alight, flaming, blazing, ignited; *literary* afire.

flame-proof ▶ adjective NON-FLAMMABLE, non-inflammable, flame-resistant, fire-resistant, flame-retardant.
— OPPOSITES: flammable.

flaming ▶ adjective **1** *a flaming bonfire* BLAZING, ablaze, burning, on fire, in flames, aflame; *literary* afire. **2** *flaming hair* BRIGHT, brilliant, vivid; red, reddish-orange, ginger, titian. **3** *a flaming row* FURIOUS, violent, vehement, frenzied, angry, passionate. **4** *in a flaming temper* FURIOUS, enraged, fuming, seething, incensed, infuriated, angry, raging, livid; *literary* wrathful.

flammable ▶ adjective INFLAMMABLE, burnable, combustible.

flank ▶ noun **1** *the horse's flanks* SIDE, haunch, quarter, thigh. **2** *the southern flank of the army* SIDE, wing.
▶ verb *the garden is flanked by two rivers* EDGE, bound, line, border, fringe.

flap ▶ verb **1** *the mallards flapped their wings* BEAT, flutter, agitate, wave, wag, swing. **2** *the flag flapped in the breeze* FLUTTER, fly, blow, swing, sway, ripple, stir.
▶ noun **1** *pockets with buttoned flaps* FOLD, overlap, covering. **2** *a few flaps of the wing* FLUTTER, fluttering, beat, beating, waving. **3** (*informal*) *I'm in a desperate flap* PANIC, fluster, state, dither, twitter, stew, tizzy. **4** (*informal*) *she created a flap with her controversial statement* FUSS, commotion, stir, hubbub, storm, uproar; controversy, brouhaha, furor; *informal* to-do, ballyhoo, hoo-ha, kerfuffle.

flare ▶ noun **1** *the flare of the match* BLAZE, flash, dazzle, burst, flicker. **2** *a flare set off by the crew* DISTRESS SIGNAL, rocket, Very light, beacon, light, signal. **3** *a flare of anger* BURST, rush, eruption, explosion, spasm, access.
▶ verb **1** *the match flared* BLAZE, flash, flare up, flame, burn; glow, flicker. **2** *her nostrils flared* SPREAD, broaden, widen; dilate.
■ **flare up 1** *the wooden houses flared up like matchsticks* BURN, blaze, go up in flames. **2** *his injury has flared up again* RECUR, reoccur, reappear; break out, start suddenly, erupt. **3** *I flared up at him* LOSE ONE'S TEMPER, become enraged, fly into a temper, go berserk; *informal* blow one's top, fly off the handle, go mad, go bananas, hit the roof, go off the deep end, flip out, explode, have a fit, go crackers, flip one's wig, blow one's stack, go ballistic, go postal, have a conniption fit.

flash ▶ verb **1** *a torch flashed* LIGHT UP, shine, flare, blaze, gleam, glint, sparkle, burn; blink, wink, flicker, shimmer, twinkle, glimmer, glisten, scintillate; *literary* glister, coruscate. **2** (*informal*) *he was flashing his money around* SHOW OFF, flaunt, flourish, display, parade. **3** (*informal*) *he flashed at me* EXPOSE ONESELF. **4** *racing cars flashed past* ZOOM, streak, tear, shoot, dash, dart, fly, whistle, hurtle, careen, rush, bolt, race, speed, career, whiz, whoosh, buzz; *informal* belt, zap, bomb; barrel.
▶ noun **1** *a flash of light* FLARE, blaze, burst; gleam, glint, sparkle, flicker, shimmer, twinkle, glimmer. **2** *a basic uniform with no flashes* EMBLEM, insignia, badge; stripe, bar, chevron, brevet, wings. **3** *a sudden flash of inspiration* BURST, outburst, wave, rush, surge, flush.
▶ adjective (*informal*) *a flash sports car. See* FLASHY.
■ **in/like a flash** INSTANTLY, suddenly, abruptly, immediately, all of a sudden; quickly, rapidly, swiftly, speedily; in an instant/moment, in a (split) second, in a trice, in the blink of an eye; *informal* in a jiffy.

flashy ▶ adjective (*informal*) OSTENTATIOUS, flamboyant, showy, conspicuous, extravagant, expensive; vulgar, tasteless, brash, lurid, garish, loud, gaudy; *informal* snazzy, fancy, swanky, flash, jazzy, glitzy.
— OPPOSITES: understated.

flask ▶ noun BOTTLE, container; hip flask, mickey ♣, vacuum flask; *proprietary* Thermos.

flat ▶ adjective **1** *a flat surface* LEVEL, horizontal; smooth, even, uniform, regular, plane. **2** *the sea was flat* CALM, still, pacific, tranquil, glassy, undisturbed, without waves, like a millpond. **3** *a flat wooden box* SHALLOW, low-sided. **4** *flat sandals* LOW, low-heeled, without heels. **5** *the teacher's flat voice* MONOTONOUS, toneless, droning, boring, dull, tedious, uninteresting, unexciting, soporific; bland, dreary, colourless, featureless, emotionless, expressionless,

lifeless, spiritless, lacklustre, plain-vanilla. **6** *he felt flat and weary* DEPRESSED, dejected, dispirited, despondent, downhearted, disheartened, low, low-spirited, down, unhappy, blue; without energy, enervated, sapped, weary, tired out, worn out, exhausted, drained; *informal* down in the dumps. **7** *the market was flat* SLOW, inactive, sluggish, slack, quiet, depressed. **8** *a flat tire* DEFLATED, punctured, burst. **9** *a flat fee* FIXED, set, regular, unchanging, unvarying, invariable. **10** *a flat denial* OUTRIGHT, direct, absolute, definite, positive, straight, plain, explicit; firm, resolute, adamant, assertive, emphatic, categorical, unconditional, unqualified, unequivocal.
— OPPOSITES: vertical, uneven.
▶ **adverb 1** *she lay down flat on the floor* STRETCHED OUT, outstretched, spread-eagled, sprawling, prone, supine, prostrate, recumbent. **2** (*informal*) *she turned me down flat* OUTRIGHT, absolutely, firmly, resolutely, adamantly, emphatically, insistently, categorically, unconditionally, unequivocally.
▶ **noun** TIDAL FLATS, mud flats, (*Nfld*) landwash ♣, tideland, intertidal area.
■ **flat out** HARD, as hard as possible, for all one's worth, to the full/limit, all out; at full speed, as fast as possible, at full tilt, full bore, full throttle, in high gear; *informal* like crazy, like mad, like the wind, firing on all cylinders, like a bat out of hell.

flatten ▶ **verb 1** *Flynn flattened the crumpled paper* MAKE/BECOME FLAT, make/become even, smooth (out/off), level (out/off). **2** *the cows flattened the grass* COMPRESS, press down, crush, squash, compact, trample. **3** *tornadoes can flatten buildings in seconds* DEMOLISH, raze (to the ground), tear down, knock down, destroy, wreck, schmuck ♣, devastate, obliterate, total. **4** (*informal*) *Griff flattened him with a single punch* KNOCK DOWN/OVER, knock to the ground, fell, prostrate; *informal* floor, deck, schmuck ♣.

flatter ▶ **verb 1** *it amused him to flatter her* COMPLIMENT, praise, express admiration for, say nice things about, fawn over; cajole, humour, flannel, blarney; *informal* sweet-talk, soft-soap, brown-nose, butter up, play up to, slobber over; *formal* laud. **2** *I was flattered to be asked* HONOUR, gratify, please, delight; *informal* tickle pink. **3** *a hairstyle that flattered her* SUIT, become, look good on, go well with; *informal* do something for.
— OPPOSITES: insult, offend.

flatterer ▶ **noun** SYCOPHANT, bootlicker, brown-noser, browner ♣, toady, lickspittle, flunky, lackey, yes-man, doormat, stooge, cringer, suck ♣, suck-up.

flattering ▶ **adjective 1** *flattering remarks* COMPLIMENTARY, praising, favourable, commending, admiring, applauding, appreciative, good; fulsome, honeyed, sugary, cajoling, flannelling, silver-tongued, honey-tongued; fawning, oily, obsequious, ingratiating, servile, sycophantic; *informal* sweet-talking, soft-soaping, crawling, bootlicking; *formal* encomiastic. **2** *it was very flattering to be nominated* PLEASING, gratifying, honouring, gladdening. **3** *her most flattering dress* BECOMING, enhancing.

flattery ▶ **noun** PRAISE, adulation, compliments, blandishments, honeyed words; fawning, blarney, cajolery; *formal* encomium; *informal* sweet talk, soft soap, snow job, buttering up, toadying.

flatulence ▶ **noun 1** *medications that help with flatulence* (INTESTINAL) GAS, wind; *informal* farting, tooting; *formal* flatus. **2** *the flatulence of his latest*

recordings POMPOSITY, pompousness, pretension, pretentiousness, grandiloquence, bombast, turgidity.

flaunt ▶ **verb** SHOW OFF, display ostentatiously, make a (great) show of, put on show/display, parade; brag about, crow about, vaunt; *informal* flash.

flavour ▶ **noun 1** *the flavour of prosciutto* TASTE, savour, tang. **2** *salami can give extra flavour* FLAVOURING, seasoning, tastiness, tang, relish, bite, piquancy, pungency, spice, spiciness, zest; *informal* zing, zip. **3** *a strong international flavour* CHARACTER, quality, feel, feeling, ambience, atmosphere, aura, air, mood, tone; spirit, essence, nature. **4** *this excerpt will give a flavour of the report* IMPRESSION, suggestion, hint, taste.
— RELATED TERMS: gustative, gustatory.
▶ **verb** *spices for flavouring food* ADD FLAVOUR TO, add flavouring to, season, spice (up), add piquancy to, ginger up, enrich; *informal* pep up.
■ **flavour of the month** (*informal*) ALL THE RAGE, the latest thing, the fashion, in vogue; *informal* hot, in.

flavouring ▶ **noun 1** *this cheese is often combined with other flavourings* SEASONING, spice, herb, additive; condiment, dressing. **2** *vanilla flavouring* EXTRACT, flavour, essence, concentrate, distillate.

flaw ▶ **noun** DEFECT, blemish, fault, imperfection, deficiency, weakness, weak spot/point/link, inadequacy, shortcoming, limitation, failing, foible; *literary* hamartia; *Computing* bug; *informal* glitch.
— OPPOSITES: strength.

flawed ▶ **adjective 1** *a flawed mirror* FAULTY, defective, unsound, imperfect; broken, cracked, torn, scratched, deformed, distorted, warped, buckled. **2** *the findings were flawed* UNSOUND, defective, faulty, distorted, inaccurate, incorrect, erroneous, imprecise, fallacious, misleading.
— OPPOSITES: flawless, sound.

flawless ▶ **adjective** PERFECT, unblemished, unmarked, unimpaired; whole, intact, sound, unbroken, undamaged, mint, pristine; impeccable, immaculate, consummate, accurate, correct, faultless, error-free, unerring; exemplary, model, ideal, copybook; *theology* inerrant.
— OPPOSITES: flawed.

flay ▶ **verb 1** *the saint was flayed alive* SKIN, strip the skin off; *Medicine* excoriate. **2** *he flayed his critics. See* CRITICIZE.

fleck ▶ **noun** *flecks of pale blue* SPOT, mark, dot, speck, speckle, freckle, patch, smudge, streak, blotch, dab; *informal* splotch; *rare* macula.
▶ **verb** *the deer's flanks were flecked with white* SPOT, mark, dot, speckle, bespeckle, freckle, stipple, stud, bestud, blotch, mottle, streak, splash, spatter, bespatter, scatter, sprinkle; *informal* splotch.

fledgling ▶ **noun** *a woodpecker fledgling* CHICK, baby bird, nestling.
▶ **adjective** *fledgling industries* EMERGING, emergent, sunrise, dawning, embryonic, infant, nascent; developing, in the making, budding, up-and-coming, rising.
— OPPOSITES: declining, mature.

flee ▶ **verb 1** *she fled to her room* RUN (AWAY/OFF), run for it, make a run for it, dash, take flight, be gone, make off, take off, take to one's heels, make a break for it, bolt, beat a (hasty) retreat, make a quick exit, make one's getaway, escape; *informal* clear off/out, vamoose, skedaddle, split, leg it, turn tail, scram, light out, cut out, peel out; *archaic* fly. **2** *they fled the* *country* RUN AWAY FROM, leave hastily, escape from; *informal* skip; *archaic* fly.

fleece ▶ noun *a sheep's fleece* WOOL, coat.
▶ verb (*informal*) *we were fleeced by a scalper*. See SWINDLE *verb*.

fleecy ▶ adjective FLUFFY, woolly, downy, soft, fuzzy, furry, velvety, shaggy; *technical* floccose, pilose.
— OPPOSITES: coarse.

fleet[1] ▶ noun *the fleet set sail* NAVY, naval force, (naval) task force, armada, flotilla, squadron, convoy.

fleet[2] ▶ adjective (*literary*) *as fleet as a greyhound* NIMBLE, agile, lithe, lissome, acrobatic, supple, light-footed, light on one's feet, spry, sprightly; quick, fast, swift, rapid, speedy, brisk, smart; *informal* nippy, zippy, twinkle-toed.

fleeting ▶ adjective BRIEF, short, short-lived, quick, momentary, cursory, transient, ephemeral, fugitive, passing, transitory; *literary* evanescent.
— OPPOSITES: lasting.

flesh ▶ noun **1** *you need more flesh on your bones* MUSCLE, meat, tissue, brawn; *informal* beef. **2** *she carries too much flesh* FAT, weight; *Anatomy* adipose tissue; *informal* blubber, flab. **3** *a fruit with juicy flesh* PULP, soft part, marrow, meat. **4** *the pleasures of the flesh* THE BODY, human nature, physicality, carnality, animality; sensuality, sexuality.
— RELATED TERMS: carn-.
■ **one's (own) flesh and blood** FAMILY, relative(s), relation(s), blood relation(s), kin, kinsfolk, kinsman, kinsmen, kinswoman, kinswomen, kindred, nearest and dearest, people; *informal* folks.
■ **flesh out** PUT ON WEIGHT, gain weight, get heavier, grow fat/fatter, fatten up, get fat, fill out.
■ **flesh something out** EXPAND (ON), elaborate on, add to, build on, add flesh to, put flesh on (the bones of), add detail to, expatiate on, supplement, reinforce, augment, fill out, enlarge on.
■ **in the flesh** IN PERSON, before one's (very) eyes, in front of one; in real life, live; physically, bodily, in bodily/human form, incarnate.

fleshly ▶ adjective CARNAL, physical, animal, bestial; sexual, sensual, erotic, lustful.
— OPPOSITES: spiritual, noble.

fleshy ▶ adjective PLUMP, chubby, portly, fat, obese, overweight, stout, corpulent, heavy-set, paunchy, well padded, well covered, well-upholstered, rotund; *informal* tubby, pudgy, beefy, porky, roly-poly, blubbery, corn-fed.
— OPPOSITES: thin.

flex ▶ verb **1** *you must flex your elbow* BEND, crook, hook, cock, angle, double up. **2** *Rachel flexed her cramped muscles* TIGHTEN, tauten, tense (up), tension, contract.
— OPPOSITES: straighten, relax.

flexibility ▶ noun **1** *the flexibility of wood* PLIABILITY, suppleness, pliancy, plasticity; elasticity, stretchiness, springiness, spring, resilience, bounce; *informal* give. **2** *the flexibility of a mixed portfolio* ADAPTABILITY, adjustability, variability, versatility, open-endedness, freedom, latitude. **3** *the flexibility shown by the local authority* CO-OPERATION, amenability, accommodation, tolerance, willingness to compromise.
— OPPOSITES: rigidity, inflexibility, intransigence.

flexible ▶ adjective **1** *flexible tubing* PLIABLE, supple, bendable, pliant, plastic; elastic, stretchy, whippy, springy, resilient, bouncy; *informal* bendy. **2** *a flexible arrangement* ADAPTABLE, adjustable, variable, versatile, open-ended, open, free. **3** *the need to be flexible towards*

tenants ACCOMMODATING, amenable, willing to compromise, co-operative, tolerant, easygoing.
— OPPOSITES: rigid, inflexible, intransigent.

flick ▶ noun *a flick of the wrist* JERK, snap, flip, whisk.
▶ verb **1** *he flicked the switch* CLICK, snap, flip, jerk. **2** *the horse flicked its tail* SWISH, twitch, wave, wag, waggle, shake.
■ **flick through** THUMB (THROUGH), leaf through, flip through, skim through, scan, look through, browse through, dip into, glance at/through, peruse, run one's eye over.

flicker ▶ verb **1** *the lights flickered* GLIMMER, glint, flare, dance, gutter; twinkle, sparkle, blink, wink, flash, scintillate; *literary* glister, coruscate. **2** *his eyelids flickered* FLUTTER, quiver, tremble, shiver, shudder, spasm, jerk, twitch.

flight ▶ noun **1** *the history of flight* AVIATION, flying, air transport, aerial navigation, aeronautics. **2** *a flight to Rome* PLANE TRIP/JOURNEY, air trip, trip/journey by air. **3** *the flight of a baseball* TRAJECTORY, path through the air, track, orbit. **4** *a flight of birds* FLOCK, skein, covey, swarm, cloud. **5** *his headlong flight from home* ESCAPE, getaway, hasty departure, exit, exodus, decamping, breakout, bolt, disappearance. **6** *a flight of stairs* STAIRCASE, set of steps/stairs.
■ **put someone to flight** CHASE AWAY/OFF, drive back/away/off/out, scatter (to the four winds), disperse, repel, repulse, rout, stampede, scare off; *informal* send packing.
■ **take flight** FLEE, run (away/off), run for it, make a run for it, be gone, make off, take off, take to one's heels, make a break for it, bolt, beat a (hasty) retreat, make a quick exit, make one's getaway, escape; *informal* beat it, clear off/out, vamoose, skedaddle, split, leg it, turn tail, scram, light out, bug out, cut out, peel out; *archaic* fly.

flighty ▶ adjective FICKLE, inconstant, mercurial, whimsical, capricious, skittish, volatile, impulsive; irresponsible, giddy, reckless, wild, careless, thoughtless.
— OPPOSITES: steady, responsible.

flimsy ▶ adjective **1** *a flimsy building* INSUBSTANTIAL, fragile, breakable, frail, shaky, unstable, wobbly, tottery, rickety, ramshackle, makeshift; jerry-built, badly built, shoddy, chintzy, gimcrack. **2** *a flimsy garment* THIN, light, fine, filmy, floaty, diaphanous, sheer, delicate, insubstantial, wispy, gossamer, gauzy. **3** *flimsy evidence* WEAK, feeble, poor, inadequate, insufficient, thin, unsubstantial, unconvincing, implausible, unsatisfactory.
— OPPOSITES: sturdy, thick, sound.

flinch ▶ verb **1** *he flinched at the noise* WINCE, start, shudder, quiver, jerk, shy. **2** *she never flinched from her duty* SHRINK FROM, recoil from, shy away from, swerve from, demur from; dodge, evade, avoid, duck, balk at, jib at, quail at, fight shy of.

fling ▶ verb *he flung the axe into the river* THROW, toss, huck ✤, sling, hurl, cast, pitch, lob; *informal* chuck, heave, buzz.
▶ noun **1** *a birthday fling* GOOD TIME, spree, bit of fun, night on the town; fun and games, revels, larks; *informal* binge. **2** *she had a brief fling with him* AFFAIR, love affair, relationship, romance, affaire (de cœur), amour, flirtation, dalliance, liaison, entanglement, involvement, attachment.

flip ▶ verb **1** *the wave flipped the dinghy over* | *the plane flipped on to its back* OVERTURN, turn over, tip over, roll (over), upturn, capsize; upend, invert, knock over; keel over, topple over, turn turtle; *archaic* overset. **2** *he* *flipped the key through the air* THROW, flick, toss, fling, sling, pitch, cast, spin, lob; *informal* chuck; *dated* shy. **3** *I flipped the transmitter switch* FLICK, click, snap.

■ **flip through** THUMB (THROUGH), leaf through, flick through, skim through, scan, look through, browse through, dip into, glance at/through, peruse, run one's eye over.

flip-flop ▶ **noun** ABOUT-FACE, U-turn, volte-face, reversal, turnaround, one-eighty, change of heart, U-ey.

flippancy ▶ **noun** FRIVOLITY, levity, facetiousness; disrespect, irreverence, cheek, impudence, impertinence; sauce, sassiness; *dated* waggery.
— OPPOSITES: seriousness, respect.

flippant ▶ **adjective** FRIVOLOUS, facetious, tongue-in-cheek; disrespectful, irreverent, cheeky, impudent, impertinent; *informal* flip, waggish.
— OPPOSITES: serious, respectful.

flirt ▶ **verb 1** *it amused him to flirt with her* TRIFLE WITH, toy with, tease, lead on. **2** *those conservatives who flirted with fascism* DABBLE IN, toy with, trifle with, amuse oneself with, play with, tinker with, dip into, scratch the surface of. **3** *he is flirting with danger* DICE WITH, court, risk, not fear.
▶ **noun** *Anna was quite a flirt* TEASE, trifler, philanderer, coquette, heartbreaker.

flirtation ▶ **noun** COQUETRY, teasing, trifling.

flirtatious ▶ **adjective** COQUETTISH, flirty, kittenish, teasing.

flit ▶ **verb** DART, dance, skip, play, dash, trip, flutter, bob, bounce.

float ▶ **verb** *oil floats on water* STAY AFLOAT, stay on the surface, be buoyant, be buoyed up. **2** *the balloon floated in the air* HOVER, levitate, be suspended, hang, defy gravity. **3** *a cloud floated across the moon* DRIFT, glide, sail, slip, slide, waft. **4** *they have just floated that idea* SUGGEST, put forward, come up with, submit, moot, propose, advance, test the popularity of; *informal* run something up the flagpole (to see who salutes). **5** *the company was floated on the TSE* LAUNCH, get going, get off the ground, offer, sell, introduce.
— OPPOSITES: sink, rush, withdraw.

floating ▶ **adjective 1** *floating seaweed* BUOYANT, on the surface, afloat, drifting. **2** *floating helium balloons* HOVERING, levitating, suspended, hanging, defying gravity. **3** *floating voters* UNCOMMITTED, undecided, of two minds, torn, split, uncertain, unsure, wavering, vacillating, indecisive, blowing hot and cold, undeclared; *informal* sitting on the fence. **4** *a floating population* UNSETTLED, transient, temporary, variable, fluctuating; migrant, wandering, nomadic, on the move, migratory, travelling, drifting, roving, roaming, itinerant, vagabond. **5** *a floating exchange rate* VARIABLE, changeable, changing, fluid, fluctuating.
— OPPOSITES: sunken, grounded, committed, settled, fixed.

flock ▶ **noun 1** *a flock of sheep* HERD, drove. **2** *a flock of birds* FLIGHT, congregation, covey, clutch. **3** *flocks of people* CROWD, throng, horde, mob, rabble, mass, multitude, host, army, pack, swarm, sea; *informal* gaggle.
▶ **verb 1** *people flocked around McCartney* GATHER, collect, congregate, assemble, converge, mass, crowd, throng, cluster, swarm. **2** *tourists flock to the place* STREAM, go in large numbers, swarm, crowd, troop.

floe ▶ **noun** ICE FLOE, (ice) pan, iceberg, ice cake, (*Atlantic*) clumper ♣.

flog ▶ **verb** *the thief was flogged* WHIP, scourge, flagellate, lash, birch, switch, cane, thrash, beat, tan/whip someone's hide.

flood ▶ **noun 1** *a flood warning* INUNDATION, swamping, deluge, high water; torrent, overflow, flash flood, freshet, spate. **2** *a flood of tears* OUTPOURING, torrent, rush, stream, gush, surge, cascade. **3** *a flood of complaints* SUCCESSION, series, string, chain; barrage, volley, battery; avalanche, torrent, stream, tide, spate, storm, shower, cascade.
— OPPOSITES: trickle.
▶ **verb 1** *the whole town was flooded* INUNDATE, swamp, deluge, immerse, submerge, drown, engulf. **2** *the river could flood* OVERFLOW, burst its banks, brim over, run over. **3** *imports are flooding the domestic market* GLUT, swamp, saturate, oversupply. **4** *refugees flooded in* POUR, stream, flow, surge, swarm, pile, crowd.
— OPPOSITES: trickle.

floodgate ▶ **noun** SLUICE, watergate, penstock, caisson; lock, dam, weir.

floor ▶ **noun 1** *he sat on the floor* GROUND, flooring. **2** *the second floor* STOREY, level, deck, tier.
▶ **verb 1** *he floored his attacker* KNOCK DOWN, knock over, bring down, fell, prostrate; *informal* lay out. **2** (*informal*) *the question floored him* BAFFLE, defeat, confound, perplex, puzzle, mystify; *informal* beat, flummox, stump, fox.

flop ▶ **verb 1** *he flopped into a chair* COLLAPSE, slump, crumple, subside, sink, drop. **2** *his hair flopped over his eyes* HANG (DOWN), dangle, droop, sag, loll. **3** (*informal*) *the play flopped* BE UNSUCCESSFUL, fail, not work, fall flat, founder, misfire, backfire, be a disappointment, do badly, lose money, be a disaster; *informal* bomb, tank, flame out, come a cropper, bite the dust, blow up in someone's face.
— OPPOSITES: succeed.
▶ **noun** (*informal*) *the play was a flop* FAILURE, disaster, debacle, catastrophe, loser; *informal* washout, also-ran, dog, lemon, non-starter, clinker, turkey.
— OPPOSITES: success.

floppy ▶ **adjective** LIMP, flaccid, slack, flabby, relaxed; drooping, droopy; loose, flowing.
— OPPOSITES: erect, stiff.

florid ▶ **adjective 1** *a florid complexion* RUDDY, red, red-faced, rosy, rosy-cheeked, pink; flushed, blushing, high-coloured; *archaic* sanguine. **2** *florid plasterwork* ORNATE, fancy, elaborate, embellished, curlicued, extravagant, flamboyant, baroque, rococo, fussy, busy. **3** *florid prose* FLOWERY, flamboyant, high-flown, high-sounding, grandiloquent, ornate, fancy, bombastic, elaborate, turgid, pleonastic; *informal* highfalutin; *rare* fustian.
— OPPOSITES: pale, plain.

flotsam ▶ **noun** WRECKAGE, cargo, remains; debris, detritus, waste, dross, refuse, scrap, trash, garbage, rubbish; *informal* dreck, junk.

flounce[1] ▶ **verb** *she flounced off to her room* STORM, stride angrily, sweep, stomp, stamp, march, strut, stalk.

flounce[2] ▶ **noun** *a lace flounce* FRILL, ruffle, ruff, peplum, jabot, furbelow, ruche.

flounder ▶ **verb 1** *people were floundering in the water* STRUGGLE, thrash, flail, twist and turn, splash, stagger, stumble, reel, lurch, blunder, squirm, writhe. **2** *she floundered, not knowing quite what to say* STRUGGLE, be out of one's depth, have difficulty, be confounded, be confused; *informal* scratch one's head, be flummoxed, be clueless, be foxed, be fazed, be

floored, be beaten. **3** *more firms are floundering* STRUGGLE FINANCIALLY, be in dire straits, face financial ruin, be in difficulties, face bankruptcy/insolvency.
− OPPOSITES: prosper.

flourish ▶ verb **1** *ferns flourish in the shade* GROW, thrive, prosper, do well, burgeon, increase, multiply, proliferate; spring up, shoot up, bloom, blossom, bear fruit, burst forth, run riot. **2** *the arts flourished* THRIVE, prosper, bloom, be in good health, be vigorous, be in its heyday; progress, make progress, advance, make headway, develop, improve; evolve, make strides, move forward (in leaps and bounds), expand; *informal* be in the pink, go places, go great guns, get somewhere. **3** *he flourished the sword at them* BRANDISH, wave, flaunt, wield; swing, twirl, swish; display, exhibit, flaunt, show off.
− OPPOSITES: die, wither, decline.

flout ▶ verb DEFY, refuse to obey, disobey, break, violate, fail to comply with, fail to observe, contravene, infringe, breach, commit a breach of, transgress against; ignore, disregard.
− OPPOSITES: observe.

flow ▶ verb **1** *the water flowed down the channel* RUN, course, glide, drift, circulate; trickle, seep, ooze, dribble, drip, drizzle, spill; stream, swirl, surge, sweep, gush, cascade, pour, roll, rush. **2** *many questions flow from today's announcement* RESULT, proceed, arise, follow, ensue, derive, stem, accrue; originate, emanate, spring, emerge; be caused by, be brought about by, be produced by, be consequent on.
▶ noun *a good flow of water* MOVEMENT, motion, current, flux, circulation; trickle, ooze, percolation, drip; stream, swirl, surge, gush, rush, spate, tide.

flower ▶ noun **1** *blue flowers* BLOOM, blossom, floweret, floret. *See table.* **2** *the flower of the nation's youth* BEST, finest, pick, choice, cream, the crème de la crème, elite.
− RELATED TERMS: floral, flor-.
− OPPOSITES: dregs.

Parts of Flowers

androecium	peduncle
anther	perianth
bract	petal
calyx	placenta
capitulum	pollen
carpel	rachis
catkin	receptacle
corolla	sepal
corymb	spadix
cyme	spathe
filament	spike
floret	spikelet
glume	spur
gynoecium	stamen
involucre	stigma
nectary	style
ovary	tassel
ovule	tepal
palea	torus
panicle	umbel
pedicel	whorl

flowery ▶ adjective **1** *flowery fabrics* FLORAL, flower-patterned. **2** *flowery language* FLORID, flamboyant, ornate, fancy, convoluted; high-flown, high-sounding, magniloquent, grandiloquent, baroque, orotund, overblown, pleonastic; *informal*

highfalutin, purple, fancy-dancy, fancy-schmancy; *rare* fustian.
− OPPOSITES: plain.

flowing ▶ adjective **1** *long flowing hair* LOOSE, free, unconfined, draping. **2** *the new model will have soft, flowing lines* SLEEK, streamlined, aerodynamic, smooth, clean; elegant, graceful; *technical* faired. **3** *he writes in an easy, flowing style* FLUENT, fluid, free-flowing, effortless, easy, natural, smooth.
− OPPOSITES: stiff, curly, jagged, halting.

fluctuate ▶ verb VARY, change, differ, shift, alter, waver, swing, oscillate, alternate, rise and fall, go up and down, see-saw, yo-yo, be unstable.

fluctuation ▶ noun VARIATION, change, shift, alteration, swing, movement, oscillation, alternation, rise and fall, see-sawing, yo-yoing, instability, unsteadiness.
− OPPOSITES: stability.

flue ▶ noun DUCT, tube, shaft, vent, pipe, passage, channel, conduit; funnel, chimney, smokestack.

fluent ▶ adjective **1** *a fluent speech* ARTICULATE, eloquent, expressive, communicative, coherent, cogent, illuminating, vivid, well-written/spoken. **2** *fluent in French* ARTICULATE; (**be fluent in**) have a (good) command of. **3** *a very fluent running style* FREE-FLOWING, smooth, effortless, easy, natural, fluid; graceful, elegant; regular, rhythmic.
− OPPOSITES: inarticulate, jerky.

fluff ▶ noun **1** *fluff on his sleeve* FUZZ, lint, dust, dustballs, dust bunnies. **2** (*informal*) *he only made a few fluffs* MISTAKE, error, slip, missteps, flub, slip of the tongue; wrong note, slip-up; *formal* lapsus linguae.
▶ verb (*informal*) *Penney fluffed the shot* | *he fluffed his only line* FUMBLE, make a mess of, bungle, miss, deliver badly, muddle up, forget; *informal* mess up, make a hash of, botch, foul up, screw up, flub, goof up.
− OPPOSITES: succeed in.

fluffy ▶ adjective FLEECY, woolly, fuzzy, hairy, feathery, downy, furry; soft.
− OPPOSITES: rough.

fluid ▶ noun *the fluid seeps up the tube* LIQUID, watery substance, solution; GAS, gaseous substance, vapour.
− OPPOSITES: solid.
▶ adjective **1** *a fluid substance* FREE-FLOWING; liquid, liquefied, melted, molten, runny, running; gaseous, gassy. **2** *his plans were still fluid* ADAPTABLE, flexible, adjustable, open-ended, open, open to change, changeable, variable. **3** *the fluid state of affairs* FLUCTUATING, changeable, subject/likely to change, (ever-)shifting, inconstant; unstable, unsettled, turbulent, volatile, mercurial, protean. **4** *he stood up in one fluid movement* SMOOTH, fluent, flowing, effortless, easy, continuous, seamless; graceful, elegant.
− OPPOSITES: solid, firm, static, jerky.

fluke ▶ noun CHANCE, coincidence, accident, twist of fate; piece of luck, stroke of good luck/fortune, serendipity.

fluky ▶ adjective LUCKY, fortunate, providential, timely, opportune, serendipitous, expedient, heaven-sent, auspicious, propitious, felicitous; chance, fortuitous, accidental, unintended.
− OPPOSITES: planned.

flummox ▶ verb (*informal*) BAFFLE, perplex, puzzle, bewilder, mystify, bemuse, confuse, confound; *informal* faze, stump, beat, fox, be all Greek to, floor, discombobulate.

flunky ▶ noun **1** *a flunky brought us drinks* LIVERIED

SERVANT, lackey, steward, butler, footman, valet, attendant, page. **2** *government flunkies searched his offices* MINION, lackey, hireling, subordinate, underling, servant; creature, instrument, cat's paw; *informal* stooge, gofer.

flurried ▶ **adjective** AGITATED, flustered, ruffled, in a panic, worked up, beside oneself, overwrought, perturbed, frantic; *informal* in a flap, in a state, in a twitter, in a fluster, in a dither, in a tizzy.
— OPPOSITES: calm.

flurry ▶ **noun 1** *snow flurries* SWIRL, whirl, eddy, billow, blizzard, shower, gust. **2** *a flurry of activity* BURST, outbreak, spurt, fit, spell, bout, rash, eruption; fuss, stir, bustle, hubbub, commotion, disturbance, furor; *informal* to-do, flap. **3** *a flurry of imports* SPATE, wave, flood, deluge, torrent, stream, tide, avalanche; series, succession, string, outbreak, rash, explosion, run, rush.
— OPPOSITES: dearth, trickle.

flush¹ ▶ **verb 1** *Shane flushed in embarrassment* BLUSH, redden, go pink, go red, go crimson, go scarlet, colour (up). **2** *fruit helps to flush toxins from the body* RINSE, wash, sluice, swill, cleanse, clean. **3** *they flushed out the snipers* DRIVE, chase, force, dislodge, expel, frighten, scare.
— OPPOSITES: pale.
▶ **noun 1** *a flush crept over her face* BLUSH, reddening, high colour, colour, rosiness, pinkness, ruddiness, bloom. **2** *the flush of youth* BLOOM, glow, freshness, radiance, vigour, rush.
— OPPOSITES: paleness.

flush² ▶ **adjective** (*informal*) **1** *the company was flush with cash* WELL SUPPLIED, well provided, well stocked, replete, overflowing, bursting, brimful, brimming, loaded, overloaded, teeming, stuffed, swarming, thick, solid; full of, abounding in, rich in, abundant in; *informal* awash, jam-packed, chock full of. **2** *the years when cash was flush* PLENTIFUL, abundant, in abundance, copious, ample, profuse, superabundant; *informal* galore; *literary* plenteous, bounteous.
— OPPOSITES: lacking, low (on).

flushed ▶ **adjective 1** *flushed faces* RED, pink, ruddy, glowing, reddish, pinkish, rosy, florid, high-coloured, healthy-looking, aglow, burning, feverish; blushing, red-faced, embarrassed, shamefaced. **2** *flushed with success* ELATED, excited, thrilled, exhilarated, happy, delighted, overjoyed, joyous, gleeful, jubilant, exultant, ecstatic, euphoric, rapturous; *informal* blissed out, over the moon, high, on a high.
— OPPOSITES: pale, dismayed.

fluster ▶ **verb** *she was flustered by his presence* UNSETTLE, make nervous, unnerve, agitate, ruffle, upset, bother, put on edge, disquiet, disturb, worry, perturb, disconcert, confuse, throw off balance, confound; *informal* rattle, faze, put into a flap, throw into a tizzy, discombobulate.
— OPPOSITES: calm.
▶ **noun** *I was in a terrible fluster* STATE OF AGITATION, state of anxiety, nervous state, panic, frenzy, fret; *informal* dither, flap, tizz, tizzy, twitter, state, sweat.
— OPPOSITES: state of calm.

fluted ▶ **adjective** GROOVED, channelled, furrowed, ribbed, corrugated, ridged.
— OPPOSITES: smooth, plain.

flutter ▶ **verb 1** *butterflies fluttered around* FLIT, hover, flitter, dance. **2** *a tern was fluttering its wings* FLAP, move up and down, beat, quiver, agitate, vibrate, whiffle. **3** *she fluttered her eyelashes* FLICKER, bat. **4** *flags fluttered* FLAP, wave, ripple, undulate, quiver; fly. **5** *her heart fluttered* BEAT WEAKLY, beat irregularly, palpitate, miss/skip a beat, quiver, go pit-a-pat; *Medicine* exhibit arrhythmia.
▶ **noun 1** *the flutter of wings* BEATING, flapping, quivering, agitation, vibrating. **2** *a flutter of dark eyelashes* FLICKER, bat. **3** *the flutter of the flags* FLAPPING, waving, rippling. **4** *a flutter of nervousness* TREMOR, wave, rush, surge, flash, stab, flush, tremble, quiver, shiver, frisson, chill, thrill, tingle, shudder, ripple, flicker.

flux ▶ **noun** CONTINUOUS CHANGE, changeability, variability, inconstancy, fluidity, instability, unsteadiness, fluctuation, variation, shift, movement, oscillation, alternation, rise and fall, see-sawing, yo-yoing.
— OPPOSITES: stability.

fly ▶ **verb 1** *a bird flew overhead* TRAVEL THROUGH THE AIR, wing its way, wing, glide, soar, wheel; hover, hang; take wing, take to the air, mount. **2** *they flew to Paris* TRAVEL BY PLANE/AIR, jet. **3** *military planes flew in food supplies* TRANSPORT BY PLANE/AIR, airlift, lift, jet. **4** *he could fly a plane* PILOT, operate, control, manoeuvre, steer. **5** *the ship was flying a red flag* DISPLAY, show, exhibit, bear; have hoisted, have run up. **6** *flags flew in the town* FLUTTER, flap, wave. **7** *doesn't time fly?* GO QUICKLY, fly by/past, pass swiftly, slip past, rush past. **8** *the runners flew by. See* SPEED *verb* sense 1. **9** (*archaic*) *the beaten army had to fly. See* FLEE sense 1.
■ **fly at** ATTACK, assault, pounce on, set upon, set about, let fly at, turn on, round on, lash out at, hit out at, belabour, fall on; *informal* lay into, tear into, lace into, sail into, pitch into, wade into, let someone have it, jump, have a go at, light into.
■ **let fly. See** LET.

fly-by-night ▶ **adjective 1** *a fly-by-night character* UNRELIABLE, undependable, untrustworthy, disreputable; DISHONEST, deceitful, dubious, unscrupulous; *informal* iffy, shady, sketchy, shifty, slippery, crooked; bent. **2** *fly-by-night business enterprises* SHORT-LIVED, ephemeral, superficial, fleeting.
— OPPOSITES: honest, reliable.

flyer, flier ▶ **noun 1** *frequent flyers* AIR TRAVELLER, air passenger, airline customer, jet-setter. **2** *flyers killed in the war* PILOT, airman, airwoman; *dated* aviator, aeronaut. **3** *flyers promoting a new coffee bar* HANDBILL, bill, handout, leaflet, circular, advertisement, junk mail.

flying ▶ **adjective 1** *a flying beetle* WINGED; AIRBORNE, in the air, in flight. **2** *a flying visit* BRIEF, short, lightning, fleeting, hasty, rushed, hurried, quick, whistle-stop, cursory, perfunctory; *informal* quickie.
— OPPOSITES: long.

foam ▶ **noun** *the foam on the waves* FROTH, spume, surf; fizz, effervescence, bubbles, head; lather, suds.
▶ **verb** *the water foamed* FROTH, spume, fizz, effervesce, bubble; lather, ferment, rise; boil, seethe, simmer.

foamy ▶ **adjective** FROTHY, foaming, spumy, bubbly, aerated, bubbling, sudsy; whipped, whisked.

focus ▶ **noun 1** *schools are a focus of community life* CENTRE, focal point, central point, centre of attention, hub, pivot, nucleus, heart, cornerstone, linchpin, cynosure. **2** *the focus is on helping people* EMPHASIS, accent, priority, attention, concentration. **3** *the main focus of this chapter* SUBJECT, theme, concern, subject matter, topic, issue, thesis, point, thread; substance, essence, gist, matter. **4** *the*

resulting light beams are brought to a focus at the eyepiece FOCAL POINT, point of convergence.
▶ **verb 1** *she focused her binoculars on the tower* BRING INTO FOCUS; aim, point, turn. **2** *the investigation will focus on areas of social need* CONCENTRATE, centre, zero in, zoom in; address itself to, pay attention to, pinpoint, revolve around, have as its starting point.
■ **in focus** SHARP, crisp, distinct, clear, well-defined, well focused.
■ **out of focus** BLURRED, unfocused, indistinct, blurry, fuzzy, hazy, misty, cloudy, lacking definition, nebulous.

foe ▶ **noun** ENEMY, adversary, opponent, rival, antagonist, combatant, challenger, competitor, opposer, opposition, competition, other side.
− OPPOSITES: friend.

fog ▶ **noun** MIST, smog, murk, haze, ice fog; *archaic* sea smoke; *literary* brume, fume.
▶ **verb 1** *the windshield fogged up* | *his breath fogged the glass* STEAM UP, mist over, cloud over, film over, make/become misty. **2** *his brain was fogged with sleep* MUDDLE, daze, stupefy, fuddle, befuddle, bewilder, confuse, befog; *literary* bedim, becloud.
− OPPOSITES: demist, clear.

foggy ▶ **adjective 1** *the weather was foggy* MISTY, smoggy, hazy, (*Nfld*) mauzy ♣, murky. **2** *she was foggy with sleep* | *a foggy memory* MUDDLED, fuddled, befuddled, confused, at sea, bewildered, dazed, stupefied, numb, groggy, fuzzy, bleary; dark, dim, hazy, shadowy, cloudy, blurred, obscure, vague, indistinct, unclear; *informal* dopey, woolly, woozy, out of it.
− OPPOSITES: clear.

foible ▶ **noun** WEAKNESS, failing, shortcoming, flaw, imperfection, blemish, fault, defect, limitation; quirk, kink, idiosyncrasy, eccentricity, peculiarity.
− OPPOSITES: strength.

foil¹ ▶ **verb** *their escape attempt was foiled* THWART, frustrate, counter, balk, impede, obstruct, hamper, euchre, hinder, snooker, cripple, scotch, derail, scupper, scuttle, smash; stop, block, prevent, defeat; *informal* do for, put paid to, stymie, cook someone's goose.
− OPPOSITES: assist.

foil² ▶ **noun** *the wine was a perfect foil to pasta* CONTRAST, complement, antithesis, relief.

foist ▶ **verb** IMPOSE, force, thrust, off-load, unload, dump, palm off, fob off; pass off, get rid of; saddle someone with, land someone with, lumber someone with.

fold¹ ▶ **verb 1** *I folded the cloth* DOUBLE (OVER/UP), crease, turn under/up/over, bend; tuck, gather, pleat. **2** *fold the cream into the chocolate mixture* MIX, blend, stir gently, incorporate. **3** *he folded her in his arms* ENFOLD, wrap, envelop; take, gather, clasp, squeeze, clutch; embrace, hug, cuddle, cradle. **4** *the firm folded last year* FAIL, collapse, founder; go bankrupt, become insolvent, cease trading, go into receivership, go into liquidation, be wound up, be closed (down), be shut (down); *informal* crash, go bust, go broke, go under, go belly up.
▶ **noun** *there was a fold in the paper* CREASE, wrinkle, crinkle, pucker, furrow; pleat, gather.

fold² ▶ **noun 1** *the sheep were in their fold* ENCLOSURE, pen, paddock, pound, compound, ring, corral; sheepfold. **2** *they welcomed Joe back into the fold* COMMUNITY, group, body, company, mass, flock, congregation, assembly.

folder ▶ **noun** FILE, binder, ring binder, *proprietary* Duo-Tang ♣, portfolio, document case, envelope, sleeve, wallet.

foliage ▶ **noun** LEAVES, leafage; greenery, vegetation, verdure.

folk ▶ **noun** (*informal*) **1** *the local folk* PEOPLE, individuals, {men, women, and children}, (living) souls, mortals; citizenry, inhabitants, residents, populace, population; *formal* denizens. **2** *my folks came from the north* PARENTS, RELATIVES, relations, blood relations, family, nearest and dearest, people, kinsfolk, kinsmen, kinswomen, kin, kith and kin, kindred, flesh and blood.

folklore ▶ **noun** MYTHOLOGY, lore, oral history, tradition, folk tradition; legends, fables, myths, folk tales, folk stories, old wives' tales; mythos.

follow ▶ **verb 1** *we'll let the others follow* COME BEHIND, come after, go behind, go after, walk behind. **2** *he was expected to follow his father in the business* SUCCEED, replace, take the place of, take over from; *informal* step into someone's shoes, fill someone's shoes/boots. **3** *people used to follow the band around* ACCOMPANY, go along with, go around with, travel with, escort, attend, trail around with, string along with; *informal* tag along with. **4** *the KGB man followed her everywhere* SHADOW, trail, stalk, track, dog, hound; *informal* tail. **5** *follow the instructions* OBEY, comply with, conform to, adhere to, stick to, keep to, hew to, act in accordance with, abide by, observe, heed, pay attention to. **6** *penalties may follow from such behaviour* RESULT, arise, be a consequence of, be caused by, be brought about by, be a result of, come after, develop, ensue, emanate, issue, proceed, spring, flow, originate, stem. **7** *I couldn't follow what he said* UNDERSTAND, comprehend, apprehend, take in, grasp, fathom, appreciate, see; *informal* make head or tail of, get, figure out, savvy, get one's head around, get one's mind around, get the drift of. **8** *she followed her mentor in her poetic style* IMITATE, copy, mimic, ape, reproduce, mirror, echo; emulate, take as a pattern, take as an example, take as a model, adopt the style of, model oneself on, take a leaf out of someone's book. **9** *he follows the Flames* BE A FAN OF, be a supporter of, support, be a follower of, be an admirer of, be a devotee of, be devoted to.
− OPPOSITES: lead, flout, misunderstand.
■ **follow something through** COMPLETE, bring to completion, see something through; continue with, carry on with, keep on with, keep going with, stay with; *informal* stick something out.
■ **follow something up** INVESTIGATE, research, look into, dig into, delve into, make inquiries into, inquire about, ask questions about, pursue, chase up; *informal* check out, scope out.

follower ▶ **noun 1** *the president's closest followers* ACOLYTE, assistant, attendant, companion, henchman, minion, lackey, servant; *informal* hanger-on, sidekick. **2** *a follower of Christ* DISCIPLE, apostle, supporter, defender, champion; believer, true believer, worshipper. **3** *followers of Arctic sports* FAN, enthusiast, admirer, devotee, lover, supporter, adherent.
− OPPOSITES: leader, opponent.

following ▶ **noun** *his devoted following* ADMIRERS, supporters, backers, fans, adherents, devotees, advocates, patrons, public, audience, circle, retinue, train.
− OPPOSITES: opposition.
▶ **adjective 1** *the following day* NEXT, ensuing,

succeeding, subsequent. **2** *the following questions below,* further on; these; *formal* hereunder, hereinafter.
– OPPOSITES: preceding, aforementioned.

folly ▸ noun FOOLISHNESS, foolhardiness, stupidity, idiocy, lunacy, madness, rashness, recklessness, imprudence, injudiciousness, irresponsibility, thoughtlessness, indiscretion; *informal* craziness.
– OPPOSITES: wisdom.

foment ▸ verb INSTIGATE, incite, provoke, agitate, excite, stir up, whip up, encourage, urge, fan the flames of.

fond ▸ adjective **1** *she was fond of dancing* KEEN ON, partial to, addicted to, enthusiastic about, passionate about; attached to, attracted to, enamoured of, in love with, having a soft spot for; *informal* into, hooked on, gone on, sweet on, struck on. **2** *her fond husband* ADORING, devoted, doting, loving, caring, affectionate, warm, tender, kind, attentive, uxorious. **3** *a fond hope* UNREALISTIC, naive, foolish, over-optimistic, deluded, delusory, absurd, vain, Panglossian.
– OPPOSITES: indifferent, unfeeling, realistic.

fondle ▸ verb CARESS, stroke, pat, pet, finger, tickle, play with; maul, molest; *informal* paw, grope, feel up, touch up, cop a feel of.

fondness ▸ noun **1** *they look at each other with such fondness* AFFECTION, love, liking, warmth, tenderness, kindness, devotion, endearment, attachment, friendliness. **2** *a fondness for spicy food* LIKING, love, taste, partiality, keenness, inclination, penchant, predilection, relish, passion, appetite; weakness, soft spot; *informal* thing, yen, jones.
– OPPOSITES: hatred.

food ▸ noun **1** *French food* NOURISHMENT, sustenance, nutriment, fare, daily bread; cooking, cuisine; foodstuffs, edibles, (*Nfld*) prog ♣, provender, refreshments, meals, provisions, rations; solids; *informal* eats, eatables, nosh, grub, chow, nibbles, scoff, chuck; *formal* comestibles; *literary* viands; *dated* victuals; *archaic* commons, meat, aliment. **2** *food for the cattle* FODDER, feed, provender, forage.
– RELATED TERMS: alimentary, culinary.

foodie ▸ noun (*informal*) GOURMET, epicure, gastronome, gourmand.

fool ▸ noun **1** *you've acted like a complete fool* IDIOT, ass, halfwit, blockhead, jughead, dunce, dolt, dullard, simpleton, clod, dope, hoser ♣, ninny, nincompoop, silly, silly-billy, chump, dim-wit, dipstick, dim-bulb, goober, coot, goon, dumbo, dummy, ditz, dumdum, fathead, numbskull, numbnuts, dunderhead, thickhead, airhead, flake, lamebrain, zombie, cretin, moron, gimp, nerd, imbecile, pea-brain, birdbrain, jerk, donkey, noodle, nitwit, twit, goat, dork, twerp, schmuck, bozo, boob, turkey, schlep, chowderhead, dumbhead, goofball, goof, goofus, galoot, lummox, klutz, putz, schlemiel, sap, meatball. **2** *she made a fool of me* LAUGHINGSTOCK, dupe, butt, gull, figure of fun; *informal* stooge, sucker, fall guy, sap. **3** (*historical*) *the fool in King James's court* JESTER, court jester, clown, buffoon, joker, zany.
▸ verb **1** *he'd been fooled by a schoolboy* DECEIVE, trick, hoax, dupe, take in, mislead, delude, hoodwink, sucker, bluff, gull; swindle, defraud, cheat, double-cross; *informal* con, bamboozle, pull a fast one on, take for a ride, pull the wool over someone's eyes, put one over on, have on, diddle, fiddle, sting, shaft, snooker, stiff, euchre, hornswoggle; *literary* cozen. **2** *I'm not fooling, I promise* PRETEND, make believe,

feign, put on an act, act, sham, fake; joke, jest; *informal* kid; have someone on.
■ **fool around 1** *someone's been fooling around with the controls* FIDDLE, play (about/around), toy, trifle, meddle, tamper, interfere, monkey around; *informal* mess around, muck about/around. **2** (*informal*) *my husband's been fooling around* PHILANDER, womanize, flirt, have an affair, commit adultery, cheat; *informal* play around, mess around, carry on, play the field, sleep around.

foolery ▸ noun CLOWNING, fooling, tomfoolery, buffoonery, silliness, foolishness, stupidity, idiocy; antics, capers; *informal* larks, shenanigans, didoes; *archaic* harlequinade.

foolhardy ▸ adjective RECKLESS, rash, irresponsible, impulsive, hot-headed, impetuous, bullheaded, daredevil, devil-may-care, madcap, hare-brained, precipitate, hasty, overhasty; *literary* temerarious.
– OPPOSITES: prudent.

foolish ▸ adjective STUPID, silly, idiotic, witless, brainless, mindless, unintelligent, thoughtless, half-baked, imprudent, incautious, injudicious, unwise; ill-advised, ill-considered, impolitic, rash, reckless, foolhardy, daft; *informal* dumb, dim, dim-witted, halfwitted, thick, hare-brained, crack-brained, crackpot, pea-brained, wooden-headed, dumb-ass, chowderheaded.
– OPPOSITES: sensible, wise.

foolishness ▸ noun FOLLY, stupidity, idiocy, imbecility, silliness, inanity, thoughtlessness, imprudence, injudiciousness, lack of caution/foresight/sense, irresponsibility, indiscretion, foolhardiness, rashness, recklessness.
– OPPOSITES: sense, wisdom.

foolproof ▸ adjective INFALLIBLE, dependable, reliable, trustworthy, certain, sure, guaranteed, safe, sound, tried and tested; watertight, airtight, flawless, perfect; *informal* sure-fire, idiot-proof, goof-proof; *formal* efficacious.
– OPPOSITES: flawed.

foot ▸ noun **1** *my feet hurt informal* tootsies, trotters, dogs. **2** *the animal's foot* paw, hoof, trotter, pad. **3** *the foot of the hill* BOTTOM, base, lowest part; end; foundation.
– RELATED TERMS: pedi-, -pod(e).
■ **foot the bill** (*informal*) PAY (THE BILL), settle up; *informal* pick up the tab, pick up the check, cough up, fork out, shell out.

football ▸ noun *football season* Canadian football ♣, American football, gridiron, pigskin, flag football, touch football; Association football, soccer; rugby, Australian Rules. *See table.*

footing ▸ noun **1** *Natalie lost her footing* FOOTHOLD, toehold, grip, purchase. **2** *a solid financial footing* BASIS, base, foundation. **3** *on an equal footing* STANDING, status, position; condition, arrangement, basis; relationship, terms.

footling ▸ adjective TRIVIAL, trifling, petty, insignificant, inconsequential, picayune, unimportant, minor, small, time-wasting; *informal* piddling, fiddling.
– OPPOSITES: important, large.

footnote ▸ noun NOTE, marginal note, annotation, comment, gloss; aside, incidental remark, digression.

footprint ▸ noun FOOTMARK, footstep, mark, impression; pug, slot; (**footprints**) track(s), spoor.

footstep ▸ noun **1** *he heard a footstep* FOOTFALL, step,

Football Terms

Plays	Player Positions
aerial	back
audible	blocker
blitz	bookend
bootleg	centre
buck	cornerback
buttonhook	defensive back
carry	designated import ✦
chop block	end
clip	flanker
complete	free safety
conversion	fullback
convert ✦	guard
down	halfback
draw play	import ✦
drive	linebacker
drop kick	lineman
end run	non-import ✦
fair catch	nose tackle
(US)	quarterback
field goal	receiver
flea-flicker	safety
forward pass	secondary
fumble	slotback
Hail Mary	tackle
hand-off	tailback
huddle	tight end
incomplete	wideout
lateral	wide receiver
major ✦	wingback
pass rush	split end
pitchout	
place kick	**On-Field Locations and Objects**
play-action	backfield
punt	coffin corner
quarterback sneak	end zone
return	gridiron
reverse	hash marks
rouge ✦	line of scrimmage
run-and-shoot	pigskin
rush	pocket
sack	secondary
safety (touch) ✦	uprights
scrimmage	
shotgun	**Championships**
single point ✦	bowl game
snap	Grey Cup ✦
sweep	Superbowl
touchdown	Vanier Cup ✦

tread, stomp, stamp. **2** *footsteps in the sand* FOOTPRINT, footmark, mark, impression; (**footsteps**) track(s), spoor.

footwear ▶ noun BOOTS AND SHOES, footgear.

fop ▶ noun DANDY, poseur, man about town; *informal* snappy dresser, trendoid, hipster; *archaic* coxcomb, popinjay.

foppish ▶ adjective DANDYISH, dandified, dapper, dressy; affected, preening, vain; effeminate, girly, mincing; *informal* natty, sissy, camp, campy.

forage ▶ verb HUNT, search, look, rummage around, ferret, root about/around, scratch about/around, nose around/about, scavenge.
▶ noun **1** *forage for the horses* FODDER, feed, food, provender. **2** *a nightly forage for food* HUNT, search, look, quest, rummage, scavenge.

foray ▶ noun RAID, attack, assault, incursion, swoop,

strike, onslaught, sortie, sally, push, thrust; *archaic* onset.

forbear ▶ verb REFRAIN, abstain, desist, keep, restrain oneself, stop oneself, hold back, withhold; resist the temptation to; eschew, avoid, decline to.
— OPPOSITES: persist.

forbearance ▶ noun TOLERANCE, patience, resignation, endurance, fortitude, stoicism; leniency, clemency, indulgence; restraint, self-restraint, self-control.

forbearing ▶ adjective PATIENT, tolerant, easygoing, lenient, clement, forgiving, understanding, accommodating, indulgent; long-suffering, resigned, stoic; restrained, self-controlled.
— OPPOSITES: impatient, intolerant.

forbid ▶ verb PROHIBIT, ban, outlaw, make illegal, veto, proscribe, disallow, embargo, bar, debar, interdict; *Law* enjoin, restrain.
— OPPOSITES: permit.

forbidding ▶ adjective **1** *a forbidding manner* HOSTILE, unwelcoming, unfriendly, off-putting, unsympathetic, unapproachable, grim, stern, hard, tough, frosty. **2** *the dark castle looked forbidding* THREATENING, ominous, menacing, sinister, brooding, daunting, formidable, fearsome, frightening, chilling, disturbing, disquieting.
— OPPOSITES: friendly, inviting.

force ▶ noun **1** *he pushed with all his force* STRENGTH, power, energy, might, effort, exertion; impact, pressure, weight, impetus. **2** *they used force to achieve their aims* COERCION, compulsion, constraint, duress, oppression, harassment, intimidation, threats; *informal* arm-twisting, bullying tactics. **3** *the force of the argument* COGENCY, potency, weight, effectiveness, soundness, validity, strength, power, significance, influence, authority; *informal* punch; *formal* efficacy. **4** *a force for good* AGENCY, power, influence, instrument, vehicle, means. **5** *a peace-keeping force* BODY, body of people, group, outfit, party, team; detachment, unit, squad; *informal* bunch.
— OPPOSITES: weakness.
▶ verb **1** *he was forced to pay* COMPEL, coerce, make, constrain, oblige, impel, drive, pressurize, pressure, press, push, press-gang, bully, dragoon, bludgeon; *informal* put the screws on, lean on, twist someone's arm. **2** *the door had to be forced* BREAK OPEN, burst open, knock down, smash down, kick in. **3** *water was forced through a hole* PROPEL, push, thrust, shove, drive, press, pump. **4** *they forced a confession out of the kids* EXTRACT, elicit, exact, extort, wrest, wring, drag, screw, squeeze.
■ **in force 1** *the law is now in force* EFFECTIVE, in operation, operative, operational, in action, valid. **2** *her fans were out in force* IN GREAT NUMBERS, in hordes, in full strength.

forced ▶ adjective **1** *forced entry* VIOLENT, forcible. **2** *forced repatriation* ENFORCED, forcible, compulsory, obligatory, mandatory, involuntary, imposed, required, stipulated, dictated, ordained, prescribed. **3** *a forced smile* STRAINED, unnatural, artificial, false, feigned, simulated, contrived, laboured, stilted, studied, mannered, affected, unconvincing, insincere, hollow; *informal* phony, pretend, put on.
— OPPOSITES: voluntary, natural.

forceful ▶ adjective **1** *a forceful personality* DYNAMIC, energetic, assertive, authoritative, vigorous, powerful, strong, pushy, driving, determined, insistent, commanding, dominant, domineering; *informal* bossy, in-your-face, go-ahead, feisty. **2** *a forceful*

argument COGENT, convincing, compelling, strong, powerful, potent, weighty, effective, well-founded, telling, persuasive, irresistible, eloquent, coherent.
− OPPOSITES: weak, submissive, unconvincing.

forcible ▶ adjective **1** *forcible entry* FORCED, violent. **2** *forcible repatriation. See* FORCED *sense 2.*

ford ▶ noun *a ford across the Khutzeymateen* CROSSING PLACE, crossing; shallow place.
▶ verb *we tried to ford the river* CROSS, traverse; wade across, walk across, drive across, travel across, make it across, make one's way across.

forebear ▶ noun ANCESTOR, forefather, antecedent, progenitor, primogenitor.
− OPPOSITES: descendant.

forebode ▶ verb (*literary*) PRESAGE, augur, portend, herald, warn of, forewarn of, foreshadow, be an omen of, indicate, signify, signal, promise, threaten, spell, denote; *literary* betoken, foretoken.

foreboding ▶ noun **1** *a feeling of foreboding* APPREHENSION, anxiety, trepidation, disquiet, unease, uneasiness, misgiving, suspicion, worry, fear, fearfulness, dread, alarm; *informal* the willies, the heebie-jeebies, the jitters, the creeps, the jim-jams. **2** *their forebodings proved justified* PREMONITION, presentiment, bad feeling, sneaking suspicion, funny feeling, intuition; *archaic* presage.
− OPPOSITES: calm.

forecast ▶ verb *they forecast record profits* PREDICT, prophesy, prognosticate, foretell, foresee, forewarn of.
▶ noun *a gloomy forecast* PREDICTION, prophecy, forewarning, prognostication, augury, divination, prognosis.

forefather ▶ noun FOREBEAR, ancestor, antecedent, progenitor, primogenitor.
− OPPOSITES: descendant.

forefront ▶ noun VANGUARD, van, spearhead, head, lead, front, fore, front line, cutting edge, avant-garde.
− OPPOSITES: rear, background.

forego ▶ verb. *See* FORGO.

foregoing ▶ adjective PRECEDING, aforesaid, aforementioned, previously mentioned, earlier, above; previous, prior, antecedent.
− OPPOSITES: following.

foregone
■ **a foregone conclusion** CERTAINTY, inevitability, matter of course, predictable result; *informal* sure thing, cert, dead cert, no-brainer.

foreground ▶ noun **1** *the foreground of the picture* FRONT, fore. **2** *in the foreground of the political drama* FOREFRONT, vanguard, van, spearhead, head, lead, front, fore, front line, cutting edge.

forehead ▶ noun BROW, temple.
− RELATED TERMS: frontal, metopic.

foreign ▶ adjective **1** *foreign branches of Canadian banks* OVERSEAS, exotic, distant, external, alien, non-native. **2** *the concept is very foreign to us* UNFAMILIAR, unknown, unheard of, strange, alien; novel, new.
− RELATED TERMS: xeno-.
− OPPOSITES: domestic, native, familiar.

foreigner ▶ noun ALIEN, non-native, stranger, outsider, (*Atlantic*) come from away ✦; immigrant, landed immigrant ✦, refugee, settler, newcomer.
− OPPOSITES: native.

foreman, forewoman ▶ noun SUPERVISOR, overseer, superintendent, team leader; foreperson; captain; ramrod, straw boss.

foremost ▶ adjective LEADING, principal, premier, prime, top, top-level, greatest, best, supreme, pre-eminent, outstanding, most important, most prominent, most influential, most illustrious, most notable; ranking, number-one, star.
− OPPOSITES: minor.

forerunner ▶ noun **1** *archosaurs were the forerunners of dinosaurs* PREDECESSOR, precursor, antecedent, ancestor, forebear; prototype. **2** *a headache may be the forerunner of other complaints* PRELUDE, herald, harbinger, precursor, sign, signal, indication, warning.
− OPPOSITES: descendant.

foresee ▶ verb ANTICIPATE, predict, forecast, expect, envisage, envision, see; foretell, prophesy, prognosticate; *literary* foreknow.

foreshadow ▶ verb SIGNAL, indicate, signify, mean, be a sign of, suggest, herald, be a harbinger of, warn of, portend, prefigure, presage, promise, point to, anticipate; *informal* spell; *literary* forebode, foretoken, betoken; *archaic* foreshow.

foresight ▶ noun FORETHOUGHT, planning, far-sightedness, vision, anticipation, prudence, care, caution, precaution, readiness, preparedness.
− OPPOSITES: hindsight.

forest ▶ noun WOOD(S), woodland, timberland, trees, bush, plantation; jungle, rainforest, pinewood; *archaic* greenwood; taiga, boreal forest, Carolinian forest, Acadian forest.
− RELATED TERMS: sylvan.

forestall ▶ verb PRE-EMPT, get in before, steal a march on; anticipate, second-guess; nip in the bud, thwart, frustrate, foil, stave off, ward off, fend off, avert, preclude, obviate, prevent; *informal* beat someone to it.

forestry ▶ noun FOREST MANAGEMENT, tree growing, agroforestry; *technical* arboriculture, silviculture.

foretaste ▶ noun SAMPLE, taster, taste, preview, specimen, example, teaser; indication, suggestion, hint, whiff; warning, forewarning, omen.

foretell ▶ verb **1** *the locals can foretell a storm* PREDICT, forecast, prophesy, prognosticate; foresee, anticipate, envisage, envision, see. **2** *dreams can foretell the future* INDICATE, foreshadow, prefigure, anticipate, warn of, point to, signal, portend, augur, presage, be an omen of; *literary* forebode, foretoken, betoken; *archaic* foreshow.

forethought ▶ noun ANTICIPATION, planning, forward planning, provision, precaution, prudence, care, caution; foresight, far-sightedness, vision.
− OPPOSITES: impulse, recklessness.

forever ▶ adverb **1** *their love would last forever* FOR ALWAYS, evermore, for ever and ever, for good, for all time, until the end of time, until hell freezes over, eternally, forevermore, perpetually, in perpetuity; *informal* until the cows come home, until kingdom come; *archaic* for aye. **2** *he was forever banging into things* ALWAYS, continually, constantly, perpetually, incessantly, endlessly, persistently, repeatedly, regularly; non-stop, day and night, {morning, noon, and night}; all the time, the entire time; *informal* 24-7.
− OPPOSITES: never, occasionally.

forewarn ▶ verb WARN, warn in advance, give advance warning, give fair warning, give notice, apprise, inform; alert, caution, put someone on their guard; *informal* tip off.

forewarning ▶ noun OMEN, sign, indication, portent, presage, warning, harbinger, foreshadowing, augury, signal, promise, threat, hint, straw in the wind, writing on the wall, canary in the coal mine; *literary* foretoken.

foreword ▶ noun PREFACE, introduction, prologue, preamble; *informal* intro, lead-in; *formal* exordium, prolegomenon, proem.
– OPPOSITES: conclusion.

forfeit ▶ verb *latecomers will forfeit their places* LOSE, be deprived of, surrender, relinquish, sacrifice, give up, yield, renounce, forgo; *informal* pass up, lose out on.
– OPPOSITES: retain.
▶ noun *they are liable to a forfeit* PENALTY, sanction, punishment, penance; fine; confiscation, loss, relinquishment, forfeiture, surrender; *Law* sequestration.

forge¹ ▶ verb **1** *smiths forged swords* HAMMER OUT, beat into shape, fashion. **2** *they forged a partnership* BUILD, construct, form, create, establish, set up. **3** *he forged her signature* FAKE, falsify, counterfeit, copy, imitate, reproduce, replicate, simulate.

forge² ▶ verb *they forged through swamps* ADVANCE STEADILY, advance gradually, press on, push on, soldier on, march on, push forward, make progress, make headway.
■ **forge ahead** ADVANCE RAPIDLY, progress quickly, make rapid progress, increase speed.

forged ▶ adjective FAKE, faked, false, counterfeit, imitation, copied, pirate(d); sham, bogus; *informal* phony, dud.
– OPPOSITES: genuine.

forgery ▶ noun **1** *guilty of forgery* COUNTERFEITING, falsification, faking, copying, pirating. **2** *the painting was a forgery* FAKE, counterfeit, fraud, sham, imitation, replica, copy, pirate copy; *informal* phony.

forget ▶ verb **1** *he forgot where he was* FAIL TO REMEMBER, fail to recall, fail to think of; *informal* disremember. **2** *I never forget my briefcase* LEAVE BEHIND, fail to take/bring. **3** *I forgot to close the door* NEGLECT, fail, omit. **4** *you can forget that idea* STOP THINKING ABOUT, put out of one's mind, shut out, blank out, pay no heed to, not worry about, ignore, overlook, take no notice of; abandon, say goodbye to, deep-six.
– OPPOSITES: remember.
■ **forget oneself** MISBEHAVE, behave badly, be naughty, be disobedient, get up to mischief, get up to no good; be bad-mannered, be rude; *informal* carry on, act up.

forgetful ▶ adjective **1** *I'm so forgetful these days* ABSENT-MINDED, amnesic, amnesiac, vague, disorganized, dreamy, abstracted, with a mind/ memory like a sieve; *informal* scatterbrained, scatty. **2** *forgetful of the time* HEEDLESS, careless, unmindful; inattentive to, negligent about, oblivious to, unconcerned about, indifferent to, not bothered about.
– OPPOSITES: reliable, heedful.

forgetfulness ▶ noun **1** *his excuse was forgetfulness* ABSENT-MINDEDNESS, amnesia, poor memory, a lapse of memory, vagueness, abstraction; *informal* scattiness. **2** *a forgetfulness of duty* NEGLECT, heedlessness, carelessness, disregard; inattention, obliviousness, lack of concern, indifference.
– OPPOSITES: reliability, heed.

forgivable ▶ adjective PARDONABLE, excusable, condonable, understandable, tolerable, permissible, allowable, justifiable.

forgive ▶ verb **1** *she would not forgive him* PARDON, excuse, exonerate, absolve; make allowances for, feel no resentment/malice towards, harbour no grudge

against, bury the hatchet with; let bygones be bygones; *informal* let off (the hook); *formal* exculpate. **2** *you must forgive his rude conduct* EXCUSE, overlook, disregard, ignore, pass over, make allowances for, allow; turn a blind eye to, turn a deaf ear to, wink at, indulge, tolerate.
– OPPOSITES: blame, resent, punish.

forgiveness ▶ noun PARDON, absolution, exoneration, remission, dispensation, indulgence, clemency, mercy; reprieve, amnesty; *archaic* shrift.
– OPPOSITES: mercilessness, punishment.

forgiving ▶ adjective MERCIFUL, lenient, compassionate, magnanimous, humane, soft-hearted, forbearing, tolerant, indulgent, understanding.
– OPPOSITES: merciless, vindictive.

forgo, forego ▶ verb DO WITHOUT, go without, give up, waive, renounce, surrender, relinquish, part with, drop, sacrifice, abstain from, refrain from, eschew, cut out; *informal* swear off; *formal* forswear, abjure.
– OPPOSITES: keep.

forgotten ▶ adjective UNREMEMBERED, out of mind, past recollection, beyond/past recall, consigned to oblivion; left behind; neglected, overlooked, ignored, disregarded, unrecognized.
– OPPOSITES: remembered.

fork ▶ verb SPLIT, branch (off), divide, subdivide, separate, part, diverge, go in different directions, bifurcate; *technical* divaricate, ramify.

forked ▶ adjective SPLIT, branching, branched, bifurcate(d), Y-shaped, V-shaped, pronged, divided; *technical* divaricate.
– OPPOSITES: straight.

forlorn ▶ adjective **1** *he sounded forlorn* UNHAPPY, sad, miserable, sorrowful, dejected, despondent, disconsolate, wretched, abject, down, downcast, dispirited, downhearted, crestfallen, depressed, melancholy, gloomy, glum, mournful, despairing, doleful, woebegone; *informal* blue, down in the mouth, down in the dumps; *rare* lachrymose. **2** *a forlorn garden* DESOLATE, deserted, abandoned, forsaken, forgotten, neglected. **3** *a forlorn attempt* HOPELESS, vain, with no chance of success; useless, futile, pointless, purposeless, unavailing, nugatory; *archaic* bootless.
– OPPOSITES: happy, cared for, hopeful, sure-fire.

form ▶ noun **1** *the general form of the landscape* | *form is less important than content* SHAPE, configuration, formation, structure, construction, arrangement, appearance, exterior, outline, format, layout, design. **2** *the human form* BODY, shape, figure, stature, build, frame, physique, anatomy; *informal* vital statistics. **3** *the infection takes different forms* MANIFESTATION, appearance, embodiment, incarnation, semblance, shape, guise. **4** *sponsorship is a form of advertising* KIND, sort, type, class, classification, category, variety, genre, brand, style; species, genus, family. **5** *put the mixture into a form* MOULD, cast, shape, matrix, die. **6** *what is the form here?* ETIQUETTE, social practice, custom, usage, use, modus operandi, habit, wont, protocol, procedure, rules, convention, tradition, fashion, style; *formal* praxis. **7** *you have to fill in a form* QUESTIONNAIRE, document, coupon, paper, sheet. **8** *in top form* FITNESS, condition, fettle, shape, trim, health.
– OPPOSITES: content.
▶ verb **1** *the pads are formed from mild steel* MAKE, construct, build, manufacture, fabricate, assemble,

put together; create, produce, concoct, devise, contrive, frame, fashion, shape. **2** *he formed a plan* FORMULATE, devise, conceive, work out, think up, lay, draw up, put together, produce, fashion, concoct, forge, hatch, incubate, develop; *informal* dream up. **3** *they plan to form a company* SET UP, establish, found, launch, float, create, bring into being, institute, start (up), get going, initiate, bring about, inaugurate. **4** *a mist was forming* MATERIALIZE, come into being/ existence, crystallize, emerge, spring up, develop; take shape, appear, loom, show up, become visible. **5** *the horse may form bad habits* ACQUIRE, develop, get, pick up, contract, slip into, get into. **6** *the warriors formed themselves into a diamond pattern* ARRANGE, draw up, line up, assemble, organize, sort, order, range, array, dispose, marshal, deploy. **7** *the parts of society form an integrated whole* CONSTITUTE, make, make up, compose, add up to. **8** *the city formed a natural meeting point* CONSTITUTE, serve as, act as, function as, perform the function of, do duty for, make. **9** *teachers form the minds of children* DEVELOP, mould, shape, train, teach, instruct, educate, school, drill, discipline, prime, prepare, guide, direct, inform, enlighten, inculcate, indoctrinate, edify.
– OPPOSITES: dissolve, disappear, break.
■ **good form** GOOD MANNERS, manners, polite behaviour, correct behaviour, convention, etiquette, protocol; *informal* the done thing.

formal ▶ adjective **1** *a formal dinner* CEREMONIAL, ceremonious, ritualistic, ritual, conventional, traditional; stately, courtly, solemn, dignified; elaborate, ornate, dressy; black-tie. **2** *a very formal manner* ALOOF, reserved, remote, detached, unapproachable; stiff, prim, stuffy, staid, ceremonious, correct, proper, decorous, conventional, precise, exact, punctilious, unbending, inflexible, straitlaced; *informal* buttoned-down, standoffish. **3** *a formal garden* SYMMETRICAL, regular, orderly, arranged, methodical, systematic. **4** *formal permission* OFFICIAL, legal, authorized, approved, validated, certified, endorsed, documented, sanctioned, licensed, recognized, authoritative. **5** *formal education* CONVENTIONAL, mainstream; school, institutional.
– OPPOSITES: informal, casual, colloquial, unofficial.

formality ▶ noun **1** *the formality of the occasion* CEREMONY, ceremoniousness, ritual, conventionality, red tape, protocol, decorum; stateliness, courtliness, solemnity. **2** *his formality was off-putting* ALOOFNESS, reserve, remoteness, detachment, unapproachability; stiffness, primness, stuffiness, staidness, correctness, decorum, punctiliousness, inflexibility; *informal* standoffishness. **3** *we keep the formalities to a minimum* OFFICIAL PROCEDURE, bureaucracy, red tape, paperwork. **4** *the medical examination is just a formality* ROUTINE, routine practice, normal procedure.
– OPPOSITES: informality.

format ▶ noun DESIGN, style, presentation, appearance, look; form, shape, size; arrangement, plan, structure, scheme, composition, configuration.

formation ▶ noun **1** *the formation of the island's sand ridges* EMERGENCE, coming into being, genesis, development, evolution, shaping, origination. **2** *the formation of a new government* ESTABLISHMENT, setting up, start, initiation, institution, foundation, inception, creation, inauguration, launch, flotation. **3** *the aircraft were flying in tight formation* CONFIGURATION, arrangement, pattern, array, alignment, positioning, disposition, order.
– OPPOSITES: destruction, disappearance, dissolution.

formative ▶ adjective **1** *at a formative stage* DEVELOPMENTAL, developing, growing, malleable, impressionable, susceptible. **2** *a formative influence* DETERMINING, controlling, influential, guiding, decisive, forming, shaping, determinative.

former ▶ adjective **1** *the former bishop* ONE-TIME, erstwhile, sometime, ex-, late; PREVIOUS, foregoing, preceding, earlier, prior, past, last. **2** *in former times* EARLIER, old, past, bygone, olden, long-ago, gone by, long past, of old; *literary* of yore. **3** *the former of the two* FIRST-MENTIONED, first.
– OPPOSITES: future, next, latter.

formerly ▶ adverb PREVIOUSLY, earlier, before, until now/then, hitherto, née, once, once upon a time, at one time, in the past; *formal* heretofore.

formidable ▶ adjective **1** *a formidable curved dagger* INTIMIDATING, forbidding, daunting, disturbing, alarming, frightening, disquieting, brooding, awesome, fearsome, ominous, foreboding, sinister, menacing, threatening, dangerous. **2** *a formidable task* ONEROUS, arduous, taxing, difficult, hard, heavy, laborious, burdensome, strenuous, back-breaking, uphill, Herculean, monumental, colossal; demanding, tough, challenging, exacting; *formal* exigent; *archaic* toilsome. **3** *a formidable pianist* CAPABLE, able, proficient, adept, adroit, accomplished, seasoned, skilful, skilled, gifted, talented, masterly, virtuoso, expert, knowledgeable, qualified; impressive, powerful, mighty, terrific, tremendous, great, complete, redoubtable; *informal* mean, wicked, deadly, nifty, crack, ace, magic, crackerjack.
– OPPOSITES: pleasant-looking, comforting, easy, poor, weak.

formless ▶ adjective SHAPELESS, amorphous, unshaped, indeterminate; structureless, unstructured.
– OPPOSITES: shaped, definite.

formula ▶ noun **1** *a legal formula* FORM OF WORDS, set expression, phrase, saying, aphorism. **2** *a peace formula* RECIPE, prescription, blueprint, plan, method, procedure, technique, system; template. **3** *a formula for removing grease* PREPARATION, concoction, mixture, compound, creation, substance.

formulaic ▶ adjective CONVENTIONAL, stock, unoriginal, stereotypical, uninspired, clichéd, paint-by-number.

formulate ▶ verb **1** *the miners formulated a plan* DEVISE, conceive, work out, think up, lay, draw up, put together, form, produce, fashion, concoct, contrive, forge, hatch, prepare, develop; *informal* dream up. **2** *this is how Marx formulated his question* EXPRESS, phrase, word, put into words, frame, couch, put, articulate, convey, say, state, utter.

fornication ▶ noun *(formal)* EXTRAMARITAL SEX, extramarital relations, adultery, infidelity, unfaithfulness, cuckoldry; premarital sex; *informal* hanky-panky, a bit on the side.

forsake ▶ verb *(literary)* **1** *he forsook his wife* ABANDON, desert, leave, leave high and dry, turn one's back on, cast aside, break (up) with; jilt, strand, leave stranded, leave in the lurch, throw over; *informal* walk out on, run out on, dump, ditch, can. **2** *I won't forsake my vegetarian principles* RENOUNCE, abandon,

relinquish, dispense with, disclaim, disown, disavow, discard, wash one's hands of; give up, drop, jettison, do away with, axe; *informal* ditch, scrap, scrub, junk; *formal* forswear.
— OPPOSITES: keep to, adopt.

forswear ▶ verb (*formal*) RENOUNCE, relinquish, reject, forgo, disavow, abandon, deny, repudiate, give up, wash one's hands of; eschew, abstain from, refrain from; *informal* kick, pack in, quit, swear off; *Law* disaffirm; *literary* forsake; *formal* abjure, abnegate.
— OPPOSITES: adhere to, persist with, take up.

fort ▶ noun FORTRESS, castle, citadel, blockhouse, stronghold, redoubt, fortification, bastion; fastness.

forte ▶ noun STRENGTH, strong point, specialty, strong suit, talent, special ability, skill, bent, gift, métier; *informal* thing.
— OPPOSITES: weakness.

forth ▶ adverb **1** *smoke billowed forth* OUT, outside, away, off, ahead, forward, into view; into existence. **2** *from that day forth* ONWARDS, onward, on, forward; for ever, into eternity; until now.

forthcoming ▶ adjective **1** *forthcoming events* IMMINENT, impending, coming, upcoming, approaching, future; close, (close) at hand, in store, in the wind, in the air, in the offing, in the pipeline, on the horizon, on the way, on us, about to happen. **2** *no reply was forthcoming* AVAILABLE, ready, at hand, accessible, obtainable, at someone's disposal, obtained, given, vouchsafed to someone; *informal* up for grabs, on tap. **3** *he was not very forthcoming about himself* COMMUNICATIVE, talkative, chatty, loquacious, vocal; expansive, expressive, unreserved, uninhibited, outgoing, frank, open, candid; *informal* gabby.
— OPPOSITES: past, current, unavailable, uncommunicative.

forthright ▶ adjective FRANK, direct, straightforward, honest, candid, open, sincere, outspoken, straight, blunt, plain-spoken, no-nonsense, downright, bluff, matter-of-fact, to the point; *informal* upfront.
— OPPOSITES: secretive, evasive.

forthwith ▶ adverb IMMEDIATELY, at once, instantly, directly, right away, straight away, post-haste, without delay, without hesitation; quickly, speedily, promptly; *informal* pronto.
— OPPOSITES: sometime.

fortification ▶ noun RAMPART, wall, defence, bulwark, palisade, stockade, redoubt, earthwork, bastion, parapet, barricade.

fortify ▶ verb **1** *the knights fortified their citadel* BUILD DEFENCES ROUND, strengthen, secure, protect. **2** *the wall had been fortified* STRENGTHEN, reinforce, toughen, consolidate, bolster, shore up, brace, buttress. **3** *I'll have a drink to fortify me* INVIGORATE, strengthen, energize, enliven, liven up, animate, vitalize, rejuvenate, restore, revive, refresh; *informal* pep up, buck up, give a shot in the arm to.
— OPPOSITES: weaken, sedate, subdue.

fortitude ▶ noun COURAGE, bravery, endurance, resilience, mettle, moral fibre, strength of mind, strength of character, strong-mindedness, backbone, spirit, grit, true grit, doughtiness, steadfastness; *informal* guts.
— OPPOSITES: faint-heartedness.

fortress ▶ noun FORT, castle, citadel, blockhouse, stronghold, redoubt, fortification, bastion; fastness.

fortuitous ▶ adjective **1** *a fortuitous resemblance* CHANCE, adventitious, unexpected, unanticipated, unpredictable, unforeseen, unlooked-for, serendipitous, casual, incidental, coincidental, random, accidental, inadvertent, unintentional, unintended, unplanned, unpremeditated. **2** *the Habs were saved by a fortuitous rebound* LUCKY, fluky, fortunate, providential, advantageous, timely, opportune, serendipitous, heaven-sent.
— OPPOSITES: predictable, unlucky.

fortunate ▶ adjective **1** *he was fortunate that the punishment was so slight* LUCKY, favoured, blessed, blessed with good luck, in luck, having a charmed life, charmed; *informal* sitting pretty. **2** *in a fortunate position* FAVOURABLE, advantageous, providential, auspicious, welcome, heaven-sent, beneficial, propitious, fortuitous, opportune, happy, felicitous. **3** *the society gives generously to less fortunate people* WEALTHY, rich, affluent, prosperous, well off, moneyed, well-to-do, well-heeled, opulent, comfortable; favoured, privileged.
— OPPOSITES: unfortunate, unfavourable, underprivileged.

fortunately ▶ adverb LUCKILY, by good luck, by good fortune, as luck would have it, propitiously; mercifully, thankfully; thank goodness, thank God, thank heavens, thank the stars.

fortune ▶ noun **1** *fortune favoured him* CHANCE, accident, coincidence, serendipity, destiny, fortuity, providence, happenstance. **2** *a change of fortune* LUCK, fate, destiny, predestination, the stars, serendipity, karma, kismet, lot. **3** *an upswing in the team's fortunes* CIRCUMSTANCES, state of affairs, condition, position, situation; plight, predicament. **4** *he made his fortune in steel* WEALTH, riches, substance, property, assets, resources, means, possessions, treasure, estate. **5** (*informal*) *this dress cost a fortune* HUGE AMOUNT, vast sum, king's ransom, millions, billions; *informal* small fortune, mint, bundle, pile, wad, arm and a leg, pretty penny, tidy sum, killing, big money, big bucks, gazillions, megabucks, top dollar.
— OPPOSITES: pittance.

fortune teller ▶ noun CLAIRVOYANT, crystal-gazer, psychic, prophet, seer, oracle, soothsayer, augur, diviner, sibyl; palmist, palm-reader.

forum ▶ noun **1** *forums were held for staff to air grievances* MEETING, assembly, gathering, rally, conference, seminar, convention, symposium, colloquium, caucus; *informal* get-together; *formal* colloquy. **2** *a forum for discussion* SETTING, place, scene, context, stage, framework, backdrop; medium, means, apparatus, auspices. **3** *the Roman forum* PUBLIC MEETING PLACE, marketplace, agora.

forward ▶ adverb **1** *the traffic moved forward* AHEAD, forwards, onwards, onward, on, further. **2** *the winner stepped forward* TOWARDS THE FRONT, out, forth, into view. **3** *from that day forward* ONWARD, onwards, on, forth; for ever, into eternity; until now.
— OPPOSITES: backwards.

▶ adjective **1** *in a forward direction* MOVING FORWARDS, moving ahead, onward, advancing, progressing, progressive. **2** *the fortress served as the Austrian army's forward base against the Russians* FRONT, advance, foremost, head, leading, frontal. **3** *forward planning* FUTURE, forward-looking, for the future, prospective. **4** *the girls seemed very forward* BOLD, BRAZEN, brazen-faced, barefaced, brash, shameless, immodest, audacious, daring, presumptuous, familiar, overfamiliar, pert; *informal* fresh.
— OPPOSITES: backward, rear, late, shy.

▶ **verb 1** *my mother forwarded me your email* SEND ON, mail on, redirect, re-address, pass on. **2** *the goods were forwarded by sea* SEND, dispatch, transmit, carry, convey, deliver, ship.

forward-looking ▶ **adjective** PROGRESSIVE, enlightened, dynamic, pushing, bold, enterprising, ambitious, pioneering, innovative, modern, avant-garde, positive, reforming, radical; *informal* go-ahead, go-getting.
– OPPOSITES: backward-looking.

forwards ▶ **adverb**. *See* FORWARD *adverb*.

fossil ▶ **noun** PETRIFIED REMAINS, petrified impression, remnant, relic.

fossilized ▶ **adjective 1** *fossilized remains* petrified, ossified. **2** *a fossilized idea* ARCHAIC, antiquated, antediluvian, old-fashioned, quaint, outdated, outmoded, behind the times, anachronistic, stuck in time; *informal* prehistoric.

foster ▶ **verb 1** *he fostered the arts* ENCOURAGE, promote, further, stimulate, advance, forward, cultivate, nurture, strengthen, enrich; help, aid, abet, assist, contribute to, support, back, be a patron of. **2** *they started fostering children* BRING UP, rear, raise, care for, take care of, look after, nurture, provide for; mother, parent.
– OPPOSITES: neglect, suppress.

foul ▶ **adjective 1** *a foul stench* DISGUSTING, revolting, repulsive, repugnant, abhorrent, loathsome, offensive, sickening, nauseating, nauseous, stomach-churning, stomach-turning, distasteful, obnoxious, objectionable, odious, noxious, vomitous; *informal* ghastly, gruesome, gross, putrid, yucky, skanky, beastly; *literary* miasmic, noisome, mephitic. **2** *a foul mess* DIRTY, filthy, mucky, grimy, grubby, muddy, muddied, unclean, unwashed; squalid, sordid, soiled, sullied, scummy; rotten, defiled, decaying, putrid, putrefied, smelly, fetid; *informal* cruddy, yucky, icky, grotty; *rare* feculent. **3** *he had been foul to her* UNKIND, malicious, mean, nasty, unpleasant, unfriendly, spiteful, cruel, vicious, base, malevolent, despicable, contemptible; *informal* horrible, horrid, rotten; beastly. **4** *foul weather* INCLEMENT, unpleasant, disagreeable, bad; rough, stormy, squally, gusty, windy, blustery, wild, blowy, rainy, wet. **5** *foul drinking water* CONTAMINATED, polluted, infected, tainted, impure, filthy, dirty, unclean; *rare* feculent. **6** *a foul deed* EVIL, wicked, bad, wrong, immoral, sinful, vile, dishonourable, corrupt, iniquitous, depraved, villainous, nefarious, vicious, malicious; malevolent, sinister, demonic, devilish, diabolical, fiendish, dark; monstrous, shocking, despicable, atrocious, heinous, odious, contemptible, horrible, execrable; *informal* lowdown, dirty. **7** *foul language* VULGAR, crude, coarse, filthy, dirty, obscene, indecent, indelicate, naughty, lewd, smutty, ribald, salacious, scatological, offensive, abusive. **8** *a foul tackle* ILLEGAL; unfair, unsporting, unsportsmanlike, below the belt, dirty.
– OPPOSITES: pleasant, kind, fair, clean, righteous, mild, fair.
▶ **verb 1** *the river had been fouled with waste* DIRTY, infect, pollute, contaminate, poison, taint, sully, soil, stain, blacken, muddy, splash, spatter, smear, blight, defile, make filthy. **2** *the vessel had fouled her nets* TANGLE UP, entangle, snarl, catch, entwine, enmesh, twist.
– OPPOSITES: clean up, disentangle.

foul-mouthed ▶ **adjective** VULGAR, crude, coarse; obscene, rude, smutty, dirty, filthy, indecent,

indelicate, offensive, lewd, X-rated, scatological, foul, abusive.

found ▶ **verb 1** *she founded her company in 2002* ESTABLISH, set up, start (up), begin, get going, institute, inaugurate, launch, float, form, create, bring into being, originate, develop. **2** *they founded a new city* BUILD, construct, erect, put up; plan, lay plans for. **3** *their relationship was founded on trust* BASE, build, construct; ground in, root in; rest, hinge, depend.
– OPPOSITES: dissolve, liquidate, abandon, demolish.

foundation ▶ **noun 1** *the foundations of a building* FOOTING, foot, base, substructure, infrastructure, underpinning; bottom, bedrock, substratum. **2** *the report has a scientific foundation* BASIS, starting point, base, point of departure, beginning, premise; principles, fundamentals, rudiments; cornerstone, core, heart, thrust, essence, kernel. **3** *there was no foundation for the claim* JUSTIFICATION, grounds, defence, reason, rationale, cause, basis, motive, excuse, call, pretext, provocation. **4** *an educational foundation* ENDOWED INSTITUTION, charitable body, funding agency, source of funds, endowment.

founder¹ ▶ **noun** *the founder of modern physics* ORIGINATOR, creator, (founding) father, prime mover, architect, engineer, designer, developer, pioneer, author, planner, inventor, mastermind; *literary* begetter.

founder² ▶ **verb 1** *the ship foundered* SINK, go to the bottom, go down, be lost at sea. **2** *the scheme foundered* FAIL, be unsuccessful, not succeed, fall flat, fall through, collapse, backfire, meet with disaster, come to nothing/naught; *informal* flatline, flop, bomb. **3** *their horses foundered in the river bed* STUMBLE, trip, trip up, lose one's balance, lose/miss one's footing, slip, stagger, lurch, totter, fall, tumble, topple, sprawl, collapse.
– OPPOSITES: succeed.

foundling ▶ **noun** ABANDONED INFANT, waif, stray, orphan, outcast.

fountain ▶ **noun 1** *a fountain of water* JET, spray, spout, spurt, well, fount, cascade. **2** *a fountain of knowledge* SOURCE, fount, well; reservoir, fund, mass, mine.

four ▶ **cardinal number** QUARTET, foursome, tetralogy, quadruplets; *technical* tetrad; *rare* quadrumvirate.
– RELATED TERMS: quadri-, tetra-.

fox ▶ **noun**. *See table at* WOLF.
– RELATED TERMS: vulpine.

foxy ▶ **adjective** (*informal*) **1** *a foxy character* CRAFTY, wily, artful, guileful, devious, sly, scheming, designing, calculating, Machiavellian; shrewd, astute, clever, canny; deceitful, deceptive, duplicitous; *archaic* subtle. **2** *a foxy lady* SEXY, sexually attractive, hot, cute, seductive, luscious, toothsome.

foyer ▶ **noun** ENTRANCE HALL, hall, hallway, entrance, entry, entranceway, entryway, porch, reception area, atrium, concourse, lobby, narthex.

fracas ▶ **noun** DISTURBANCE, brawl, melee, rumpus, skirmish, struggle, scuffle, scrum, clash, fisticuffs, altercation; *informal* scrap, dust-up, set-to, shindy, shindig, punch-up, donnybrook, bust-up.

fraction ▶ **noun 1** *a fraction of the population* PART, subdivision, division, portion, segment, slice, section, sector; proportion, percentage, ratio, measure. **2** *only a fraction of the collection* TINY PART, fragment, snippet, snatch, smattering, selection. **3** *he moved a fraction closer* TINY AMOUNT, little, bit, touch,

soupçon, trifle, mite, shade, jot; *informal* smidgen, smidge, tad, titch.
− OPPOSITES: whole.

fractious ▸ adjective **1** *fractious children* GRUMPY, bad-tempered, irascible, irritable, crotchety, grouchy, cantankerous, short-tempered, tetchy, testy, curmudgeonly, ill-tempered, ill-humoured, peevish, cross, waspish, crabbed, crabby, crusty, prickly, touchy; *informal* snappish, snappy, chippy, shirty, cranky, rangy, ornery. **2** *the fractious opposition party* WAYWARD, unruly, uncontrollable, unmanageable, out of hand, obstreperous, difficult, headstrong, recalcitrant, intractable; disobedient, insubordinate, disruptive, disorderly, undisciplined; contrary, wilful; *formal* refractory; *archaic* contumacious.
− OPPOSITES: contented, affable, dutiful.

fracture ▸ noun **1** *the risk of vertebral fracture* BREAKING, breakage, cracking, fragmentation, splintering, rupture. **2** *tiny fractures in the rock* CRACK, split, fissure, crevice, break, rupture, breach, rift, cleft, chink, interstice; crazing.
▸ verb *the glass fractured* BREAK, crack, shatter, splinter, split, rupture; *informal* bust.

fragile ▸ adjective **1** *fragile porcelain* BREAKABLE, easily broken; delicate, dainty, fine, flimsy; eggshell; *formal* frangible. **2** *the fragile ceasefire* TENUOUS, shaky, insecure, unreliable, vulnerable, flimsy. **3** *she is still very fragile* WEAK, delicate, frail, debilitated; ill, unwell, ailing, poorly, sickly, infirm, enfeebled.
− OPPOSITES: strong, durable, robust.

fragment ▸ noun **1** *meteorite fragments* PIECE, bit, particle, speck; chip, shard, sliver, splinter; shaving, paring, snippet, scrap, offcut, flake, shred, wisp, morsel. **2** *a fragment of conversation* SNATCH, snippet, scrap, bit.
▸ verb *explosions caused the granite to fragment* BREAK UP, break, break into pieces, crack open/apart, shatter, splinter, fracture; disintegrate, fall to pieces, fall apart.

fragmentary ▸ adjective INCOMPLETE, fragmented, disconnected, disjointed, broken, discontinuous, piecemeal, scrappy, bitty, sketchy, uneven, patchy.

fragrance ▸ noun **1** *the fragrance of spring flowers* SWEET SMELL, scent, perfume, bouquet; aroma, redolence, nose. **2** *a bottle of fragrance* PERFUME, scent, eau de toilette, toilet water; eau de cologne, cologne; aftershave.

fragrant ▸ adjective SWEET-SCENTED, sweet-smelling, scented, perfumed, aromatic, perfumy; *literary* redolent.
− OPPOSITES: smelly.

frail ▸ adjective **1** *a frail old lady* WEAK, delicate, feeble, enfeebled, debilitated; infirm, ill, ailing, unwell, sickly, poorly, in poor health. **2** *a frail structure* FRAGILE, breakable, easily damaged, delicate, flimsy, insubstantial, unsteady, unstable, rickety; *formal* frangible.
− OPPOSITES: strong, robust.

frailty ▸ noun **1** *the frailty of old age* INFIRMITY, weakness, enfeeblement, debility; fragility, delicacy; ill health, sickliness. **2** *his many frailties* WEAKNESS, fallibility; weak point, flaw, imperfection, defect, failing, fault, shortcoming, deficiency, inadequacy, limitation.
− OPPOSITES: strength.

frame ▸ noun **1** *a tubular metal frame* FRAMEWORK, structure, substructure, skeleton, chassis, shell, casing, body, bodywork; support, scaffolding,

foundation, infrastructure. **2** *his tall, slender frame* BODY, figure, form, shape, physique, build, size, proportions. **3** *a picture frame* SETTING, mount, mounting.
▸ verb **1** *he had the picture framed* MOUNT, set in a frame. **2** *the legislators who frame the regulations* FORMULATE, draw up, draft, plan, shape, compose, put together, form, devise, create, establish, conceive, think up, originate; *informal* dream up.
■ **frame of mind** MOOD, state of mind, humour, temper, disposition.

frame-up ▸ noun (*informal*) CONSPIRACY, plot; trick, trap, entrapment; *informal* put-up job, set-up.

framework ▸ noun **1** *a metal framework* FRAME, substructure, infrastructure, structure, skeleton, chassis, shell, body, bodywork; support, scaffolding, foundation. **2** *the framework of society* STRUCTURE, shape, fabric, order, scheme, system, organization, construction, configuration, composition, warp and woof; *informal* makeup.

franchise ▸ noun **1** *the extension of the franchise to women* SUFFRAGE, the vote, the right to vote, voting rights, enfranchisement. **2** *the company lost its TV franchise* WARRANT, charter, licence, permit, authorization, permission, sanction, privilege.

francophone ▸ noun FRENCH-SPEAKER, French-Canadian ✦, Franco.
▸ adjective FRENCH-SPEAKING, franco, French, French-Canadian ✦.
− RELATED TERMS: anglophone, allophone.

frank ▸ adjective **1** *he was quite frank with me* CANDID, direct, forthright, plain, plain-spoken, straight, straightforward, explicit, to the point, matter-of-fact; open, honest, truthful, sincere; outspoken, bluff, blunt, unsparing, not afraid to call a spade a spade; *informal* upfront. **2** *she looked at the child with frank admiration* OPEN, undisguised, unconcealed, naked, unmistakable, clear, obvious, transparent, patent, manifest, evident, perceptible, palpable; blatant, barefaced, flagrant.
− OPPOSITES: evasive.

frankly ▸ adverb **1** *frankly, I couldn't care less* TO BE FRANK, to be honest, to tell you the truth, to be truthful, in all honesty, as it happens. **2** *he stated the case quite frankly* CANDIDLY, directly, plainly, straightforwardly, forthrightly, openly, honestly, without beating about the bush, without mincing one's words, without prevarication, point-blank; bluntly, outspokenly, with no holds barred.

frantic ▸ adjective PANIC-STRICKEN, panicky, beside oneself, at one's wits' end, distraught, overwrought, worked up, agitated, distressed; frenzied, wild, frenetic, fraught, feverish, hysterical, desperate; *informal* in a state, in a tizzy/tizz, wound up, het up, in a flap, tearing one's hair out.
− OPPOSITES: calm.

fraternity ▸ noun **1** *a spirit of fraternity* BROTHERHOOD, fellowship, kinship, friendship, (mutual) support, solidarity, community, union, togetherness; sisterhood. **2** *the teaching fraternity* PROFESSION, body of workers; band, group, set, circle. **3** *a college fraternity* SOCIETY, club, association; group, set.

fraternize ▸ verb ASSOCIATE, mix, consort, socialize, keep company, rub elbows; *informal* hang around, hang out, run around, hobnob, be thick with.

fraud ▸ noun **1** *he was arrested for fraud* FRAUDULENCE, cheating, swindling, embezzlement, deceit, deception, double-dealing, chicanery, sharp practice. **2** *social insurance frauds* SWINDLE, racket, deception, trick, cheat, hoax; *informal* scam, con, con trick, rip-off, sting, gyp, fiddle, bunco, hustle, grift. **3** *they exposed him as a fraud* IMPOSTER, fake, sham, charlatan, quack, mountebank; swindler, goniff, snake oil salesman, fraudster, racketeer, cheat, confidence trickster; *informal* phony, con man, con artist, scam artist.

fraudulent ▶ adjective DISHONEST, cheating, swindling, corrupt, criminal, illegal, unlawful, illicit; deceitful, double-dealing, duplicitous, dishonourable, unscrupulous, unprincipled; *informal* crooked, shady, dirty.
— OPPOSITES: honest.

fraught ▶ adjective **1** *their world is fraught with danger* FULL OF, filled with, rife with; attended by, accompanied by. **2** *she sounded a bit fraught* ANXIOUS, worried, stressed, upset, distraught, overwrought, worked up, antsy, agitated, distressed, distracted, desperate, frantic, panic-stricken, panic-struck, panicky; beside oneself, at one's wits' end, at the end of one's tether/rope; *informal* wound up, in a state, in a flap, in a cold sweat, tearing one's hair out, having kittens.

fray[1] ▶ verb **1** *cheap fabric soon frays* UNRAVEL, wear, wear thin, wear out/through, become worn. **2** *her nerves were frayed* STRAIN, tax, overtax, put on edge.

fray[2] ▶ noun *two men started the fray* BATTLE, fight, engagement, conflict, clash, skirmish, altercation, tussle, struggle, scuffle, melee, brawl, fracas; *informal* scrap, dust-up, set-to, punch-up, bust-up.

frayed ▶ adjective **1** *a frayed shirt collar* WORN, well-worn, threadbare, tattered, ragged, holey, moth-eaten, in holes, the worse for wear; *informal* tatty, raggedy, dog-eared. **2** *his frayed nerves* STRAINED, fraught, tense, edgy, stressed.

freak ▶ noun **1** *a genetically engineered freak* ABERRATION, abnormality, irregularity, oddity; monster, monstrosity, mutant; freak of nature. **2** *the accident was a complete freak* ANOMALY, aberration, rarity, oddity, unusual occurrence; fluke, twist of fate. **3** *(informal) they were dismissed as a bunch of freaks* ODDITY, eccentric, misfit, crank, lunatic; *informal* oddball, weirdo, nutcase, nut, wacko, kook. **4** *(informal) a fitness freak* ENTHUSIAST, fan, devotee, lover, aficionado; *informal* fiend, nut, fanatic, addict, maniac.
▶ adjective *a freak storm | a freak result* UNUSUAL, anomalous, aberrant, atypical, unrepresentative, irregular, fluky, exceptional, unaccountable, bizarre, queer, peculiar, odd, freakish; unpredictable, unforeseeable, unexpected, unanticipated, surprising; rare, singular, isolated.
— OPPOSITES: normal.
▶ verb *(informal) he freaked out* GO CRAZY, go mad, go out of one's mind, go to pieces, crack, snap, lose control; panic, become hysterical; *informal* lose it, lose one's cool, crack up, go ape, go postal.

freakish ▶ adjective *freakish weather. See* FREAK *adjective*.

freaky ▶ adjective *(informal). See* ODD *senses 1, 2.*

freckle ▶ noun SPECKLE, fleck, dot, spot, mole, blotch, macula.

free ▶ adjective **1** *admission is free* WITHOUT CHARGE, free of charge, for nothing; complimentary, gratis; *informal* for free, on the house. **2** *she was free of any pressures* UNENCUMBERED BY, unaffected by, clear of, without, rid of; exempt from, not liable to, safe from, immune from, excused from; *informal* sans, minus. **3** *I'm*

free this afternoon UNOCCUPIED, not busy, available, between appointments; off duty, off work, off; on vacation, on holiday, on leave; at leisure, with time on one's hands, with time to spare. **4** *the bathroom's free now* VACANT, empty, available, unoccupied, not taken, not in use. **5** *a citizen of a proud free nation* INDEPENDENT, self-governing, self-governed, self-ruling, self-determining, non-aligned, sovereign, autonomous; democratic. **6** *the killer is still free* ON THE LOOSE, at liberty, at large; loose, unconfined, unbound, untied, unchained, untethered, unshackled, unfettered, unrestrained. **7** *you are free to leave* ALLOWED, permitted; ABLE TO, in a position to, capable of. **8** *the free flow of water* UNIMPEDED, unobstructed, unrestricted, unhampered, clear, open, unblocked. **9** *she was free with her money* GENEROUS, liberal, open-handed, unstinting, bountiful; lavish, extravagant, prodigal. **10** *his free and hearty manner* FRANK, open, candid, direct, plain-spoken; unrestrained, unconstrained, free and easy, uninhibited.
— OPPOSITES: busy, occupied, captive, mean.
▶ verb **1** *three of the hostages were freed* RELEASE, set free, let go, liberate, discharge, deliver; set loose, let loose, turn loose, untie, unchain, unfetter, unshackle, unleash; *literary* disenthral. **2** *the victims were freed by firefighters* EXTRICATE, release, get out, pull out, pull free; rescue, set free. **3** *they wish to be freed from all legal ties* EXEMPT, except, excuse, relieve, unburden, disburden.
— OPPOSITES: confine, trap.
■ **free and easy** EASYGOING, relaxed, casual, informal, unceremonious, unforced, natural, open, spontaneous, uninhibited, friendly; tolerant, liberal; *informal* laid-back.
■ **a free hand** FREE REIN, carte blanche, freedom, liberty, licence, latitude, leeway, a blank cheque.

freebooter ▶ noun PIRATE, marauder, raider; bandit, robber; adventurer, swashbuckler; *historical* privateer; *archaic* buccaneer, corsair.

freedom ▶ noun **1** *a desperate bid for freedom* LIBERTY, liberation, release, deliverance, delivery, discharge; *literary* disenthralment; *historical* manumission. **2** *national revolution was the only path to freedom* INDEPENDENCE, self-government, self-determination, self rule, home rule, sovereignty, non-alignment, autonomy; democracy. **3** *freedom from local political accountability* EXEMPTION, immunity, dispensation; impunity. **4** *patients have more freedom to choose who treats them* RIGHT, entitlement, privilege, prerogative; scope, latitude, leeway, flexibility, space, breathing space, room, elbow room; licence, leave, free rein, a free hand, carte blanche, a blank cheque.

free-for-all ▶ noun BRAWL, fight, scuffle, tussle, struggle, confrontation, clash, altercation, fray, fracas, melee, rumpus, disturbance; breach of the peace; *informal* dust-up, scrap, set-to, shindy, punch-up, bust-up.

freelance ▶ adjective SELF-EMPLOYED, independent, contract.

freethinker ▶ noun NONCONFORMIST, individualist, independent, maverick; agnostic, atheist, non-believer, unbeliever.
— OPPOSITES: conformist.

free will ▶ noun SELF-DETERMINATION, freedom of choice, autonomy, liberty, independence.
■ **of one's own free will** VOLUNTARILY, willingly, readily, freely, without reluctance, without

compulsion, of one's own accord, of one's own volition, of one's own choosing.

freeze ▶ **verb 1** *the stream had frozen* ICE OVER, ice up, solidify. **2** *my fingers froze* become frozen, become frostbitten, (Nfld) burn ✦. **3** *the campers stifled in summer and froze in winter* BE VERY COLD, be numb with cold, turn blue with cold, shiver, be chilled to the bone/marrow. **4** *she froze in horror* STOP DEAD, stop in one's tracks, stop, stand (stock) still, go rigid, become motionless, become paralyzed. **5** *the prices of basic foodstuffs were frozen* FIX, hold, peg, set; limit, restrict, cap, confine, regulate; hold/keep down.
– OPPOSITES: thaw.
■ **freeze someone out** (informal) EXCLUDE, leave out, shut out, cut out, ignore, ostracize, spurn, snub, shun, turn one's back on, cold-shoulder, give someone the cold shoulder, leave out in the cold.

freezing ▶ **adjective 1** *a freezing wind* BITTER, bitterly cold, icy, chill, frosty, glacial, wintry, sub-zero, hypothermic; raw, biting, piercing, bone-chilling, penetrating, cutting, numbing; arctic, polar, Siberian. **2** *you must be freezing* FROZEN, extremely cold, numb with cold, chilled to the bone/marrow, frozen stiff, shivery, shivering; informal frozen to death.
– OPPOSITES: balmy, hot.

freezing rain ▶ **noun** sleet, ice storm ✦, (esp. Nfld) glitter storm ✦, (Atlantic) silver thaw ✦.

freight ▶ **noun 1** *freight carried by rail* GOODS, cargo, load, consignment, delivery, shipment; merchandise. **2** *our reliance on air freight* TRANSPORTATION, transport, conveyance, carriage, portage, haulage.

French-Canadian ▶ **noun** Francophone, Franco-Canadian, franco, Canadien, Canadienne; Acadian, Québécois, Québécoise, Franco-Ontarian, Franco-Manitoban, Fransaskois, Franco-Albertan, Franco-Columbian; historical habitant; pure laine.

french fries ▶ **noun** FRIES, french-fried potatoes, pommes frites, frites, home fries, chips, buffalo chips, shoestring potatoes, matchstick potatoes, poutine ✦.

frenetic ▶ **adjective** FRANTIC, wild, frenzied, hectic, fraught, feverish, fevered, mad, manic, hyperactive, energetic, intense, amped-up, fast and furious, turbulent, tumultuous.
– OPPOSITES: calm.

frenzied ▶ **adjective** FRANTIC, wild, frenetic, hectic, fraught, feverish, fevered, mad, crazed, manic, intense, furious, uncontrolled, out of control.
– OPPOSITES: calm.

frenzy ▶ **noun 1** *the crowd whipped her into a frenzy* HYSTERIA, madness, mania, delirium, feverishness, fever, wildness, agitation, turmoil, tumult; wild excitement, euphoria, elation, ecstasy. **2** *a frenzy of anger* FIT, paroxysm, spasm, bout.

frequency ▶ **noun** RATE OF OCCURRENCE, incidence, amount, commonness, prevalence; Statistics distribution.

frequent ▶ **adjective 1** *frequent bouts of chest infection* RECURRENT, recurring, repeated, periodic, continual, one after another, successive; many, numerous, lots of, several. **2** *a frequent business traveller* HABITUAL, regular.
– OPPOSITES: occasional.
▶ **verb** *he frequented chic nightclubs* VISIT, patronize, spend time in, visit regularly, be a regular visitor to, haunt; informal hang out in.

frequenter ▶ **noun** HABITUÉ, patron, regular, regular visitor, regular customer, regular client, familiar face.

frequently ▶ **adverb** REGULARLY, often, very often, all the time, habitually, customarily, routinely; many times, a lot, many a time, lots of times, again and again, time and again, over and over again, repeatedly, recurrently, continually, oftentimes; literary oft, oft-times.

fresh ▶ **adjective 1** *fresh fruit* NEWLY PICKED, garden-fresh, crisp, unwilted; raw, natural, unprocessed. **2** *a fresh sheet of paper* CLEAN, blank, empty, clear, white; unused, new, pristine, unmarked, untouched. **3** *a fresh approach* NEW, recent, latest, up-to-date, modern, modernistic, ultra-modern, newfangled; original, novel, different, innovative, unusual, unconventional, unorthodox; radical, revolutionary; informal offbeat. **4** *fresh recruits* YOUNG, youthful; new, inexperienced, naive, untrained, unqualified, untried; raw; informal wet behind the ears. **5** *he felt fresh and happy to be alive* REFRESHED, rested, restored, revived; (as) fresh as a daisy, energetic, vigorous, invigorated, full of vim and vigour, lively, vibrant, spry, sprightly, bright, alert, perky; informal full of beans, raring to go, bright-eyed and bushy-tailed, chirpy, chipper. **6** *her fresh complexion* HEALTHY, healthy-looking, clear, bright, youthful, blooming, glowing, unblemished; fair, rosy, rosy-cheeked, pink, ruddy. **7** *the night air was fresh* COOL, crisp, refreshing, invigorating, tonic; pure, clean, clear, uncontaminated, untainted. **8** *a fresh wind* CHILLY, chill, cool, cold, brisk, bracing, invigorating; strong; informal nippy. **9** (informal) *don't get fresh with me* IMPUDENT, sassy, saucy, brazen, shameless, forward, bold, cheeky, impertinent, insolent, presumptuous, disrespectful, rude, pert, (as) bold as brass; informal lippy, mouthy.
– OPPOSITES: stale, old, tired, warm.

freshen ▶ **verb 1** *this will freshen your breath* REFRESH, deodorize, cleanse; revitalize, restore. **2** *she went to freshen up before dinner* WASH, bathe, shower; tidy oneself (up), spruce oneself up, smarten oneself up, groom oneself, primp oneself, wash up; informal titivate oneself, doll oneself up, tart oneself up; formal, humorous perform one's ablutions. **3** *the waitress freshened their coffee* REFILL, top up, fill up, replenish.

freshman, freshwoman ▶ **noun** NEW STUDENT, first-year student, frosh, (esp. Ont.) niner ✦, undergraduate; newcomer, new recruit, probationer; beginner, learner, novice, tenderfoot; informal underprad, rookie, greenhorn.

fret ▶ **verb 1** *she was fretting about Jonathan* WORRY, be anxious, feel uneasy, be distressed, be upset, upset oneself, concern oneself; agonize, sigh, pine, brood, eat one's heart out. **2** *his absence began to fret her* TROUBLE, bother, concern, perturb, disturb, disquiet, disconcert, distress, upset, alarm, panic, agitate; informal eat away at.

fretful ▶ **adjective** DISTRESSED, upset, miserable, unsettled, uneasy, ill at ease, uncomfortable, edgy, agitated, worked up, tense, stressed, restive, fidgety, antsy; querulous, irritable, cross, fractious, peevish, petulant, out of sorts, bad-tempered, irascible, grumpy, crotchety, captious, testy, tetchy, cranky, het up, uptight, twitchy, crabby.

friable ▶ **adjective** CRUMBLY, easily crumbled, powdery, dusty, chalky, soft; dry, crisp, brittle.

friar ▶ **noun** MONK, brother, religious, cenobite, contemplative; prior, abbot.

friction ▸ noun **1** *a lubrication system which reduces friction* ABRASION, rubbing, chafing, grating, rasping, scraping; resistance, drag. **2** *there was considerable friction between father and son* DISCORD, strife, conflict, disagreement, dissension, dissent, infighting, opposition, contention, dispute, disputation, arguing, argument, quarrelling, bickering, squabbling, wrangling, fighting, feuding, rivalry; hostility, animosity, antipathy, enmity, antagonism, resentment, acrimony, bitterness, bad feeling, ill feeling, ill will, bad blood.
— OPPOSITES: harmony.

friend ▸ noun **1** *a close friend* COMPANION, soul mate, intimate, confidante, confidant, familiar, alter ego, second self, playmate, playfellow, classmate, schoolmate, workmate; ally, associate; sister, brother; best friend, kindred spirit, bosom buddy, bosom friend; *informal* pal, chum, sidekick, crony, main man, mate, buddy, bud, amigo, compadre, homeboy, homegirl, homie; *archaic* compeer. **2** *the friends of the National Ballet* PATRON, backer, supporter, benefactor, benefactress, sponsor; well-wisher, defender, champion; *informal* angel.
— OPPOSITES: enemy.

friendless ▸ adjective ALONE, all alone, by oneself, solitary, lonely, with no one to turn to, lone, without friends, companionless, unbefriended, unpopular, unwanted, unloved, abandoned, rejected, forsaken, shunned, spurned, forlorn, lonesome.
— OPPOSITES: popular.

friendliness ▸ noun AFFABILITY, amiability, geniality, congeniality, bonhomie, cordiality, good nature, good humour, warmth, affection, demonstrativeness, conviviality, joviality, companionability, sociability, gregariousness, camaraderie, neighbourliness, hospitableness, approachability, accessibility, openness, kindness, kindliness, sympathy, amenability, benevolence.

friendly ▸ adjective **1** *a friendly woman* AFFABLE, amiable, genial, congenial, cordial, warm, affectionate, demonstrative, convivial, companionable, sociable, gregarious, outgoing, comradely, neighbourly, hospitable, approachable, easy to get on with, accessible, communicative, open, unreserved, easygoing, good-natured, kindly, benign, amenable, agreeable, obliging, sympathetic, well-disposed, benevolent; *informal* chummy, clubby, buddy-buddy. **2** *friendly conversation* AMICABLE, congenial, cordial, pleasant, easy, relaxed, casual, informal, unceremonious; close, intimate, familiar. **3** *a friendly wind swept the boat to the shore* FAVOURABLE, advantageous, helpful; lucky, providential. **4** *a kid-friendly hotel* COMPATIBLE, suited, adapted, appropriate.
— OPPOSITES: hostile.

friendship ▸ noun **1** *lasting friendships* RELATIONSHIP, close relationship, attachment, mutual attachment, association, bond, tie, link, union. **2** *old ties of love and friendship* AMITY, camaraderie, friendliness, comradeship, companionship, fellowship, fellow feeling, closeness, affinity, rapport, understanding, harmony, unity; intimacy, mutual affection.
— OPPOSITES: enmity.

fright ▸ noun **1** *she was paralyzed with fright* FEAR, fearfulness, terror, horror, alarm, panic, dread, trepidation, dismay, nervousness, apprehension, apprehensiveness, perturbation, disquiet; *informal* jitteriness, twitchiness. **2** *the experience gave everyone a fright* SCARE, shock, surprise, turn, jolt, start; the

shivers, the shakes; *informal* the jitters, the heebie-jeebies, the willies, the creeps, the collywobbles, a cold sweat, butterflies (in one's stomach). **3** *(informal) she looked an absolute fright* UGLY SIGHT, eyesore, monstrosity; *informal* mess, sight, state, blot on the landscape.

frighten ▸ verb SCARE, startle, alarm, terrify, petrify, shock, chill, panic, shake, disturb, dismay, unnerve, unman, intimidate, terrorize, cow, daunt; strike terror into, put the fear of God into, chill someone to the bone/marrow, make someone's blood run cold; *informal* scare the living daylights out of, scare stiff, scare someone out of their wits, scare witless, scare to death, scare the pants off, spook, make someone's hair stand on end, make someone jump out of their skin, give someone the heebie-jeebies, make someone's hair curl, scare the bejesus out of; *archaic* affright.

frightening ▸ adjective TERRIFYING, horrifying, alarming, startling, white-knuckle, chilling, spine-chilling, hair-raising, blood-curdling, bone-chilling, disturbing, unnerving, intimidating, daunting, dismaying, upsetting, harrowing, traumatic; eerie, sinister, fearsome, nightmarish, macabre, menacing; eldritch; *informal* scary, spooky, creepy, hairy.

frightful ▸ adjective HORRIBLE, horrific, ghastly, horrendous, serious, awful, dreadful, terrible, nasty, grim, dire, unspeakable; alarming, shocking, terrifying, harrowing, appalling, fearful; hideous, gruesome, grisly; *informal* horrid; *formal* grievous.

frigid ▸ adjective **1** *a frigid January night* VERY COLD, bitterly cold, bitter, freezing, frozen, frosty, icy, gelid, chilly, chill, wintry, bleak, sub-zero, arctic, Siberian, bone-chilling, polar, glacial, hypothermic; *informal* nippy. **2** *frigid politeness* STIFF, formal, stony, wooden, unemotional, passionless, unfeeling, indifferent, unresponsive, unenthusiastic, austere, distant, aloof, remote, reserved, unapproachable; frosty, cold, icy, cool, unsmiling, forbidding, unfriendly, unwelcoming, hostile; *informal* offish, standoffish.
— OPPOSITES: hot, friendly.

frill ▸ noun **1** *a full skirt with a wide frill* RUFFLE, flounce, ruff, furbelow, jabot, peplum, ruche, ruching, fringe; *archaic* purfle. **2** *a comfortable apartment with no frills* OSTENTATION, ornamentation, decoration, embellishment, fanciness, fuss, chi-chi, gilding, excess; trimmings, extras, additions, non-essentials, luxuries, extravagances, superfluities.

frilly ▸ adjective RUFFLED, flounced, frilled, crimped, ruched, trimmed, lacy, frothy; fancy, ornate; *informal* fancy-dancy, fancy-schmancy.

fringe ▸ noun **1** *the city's northern fringe* PERIMETER, periphery, border, borderline, margin, rim, outer edge, edge, extremity, limit; outer limits, limits, borders, bounds, outskirts; *literary* marge. **2** *blue curtains with a yellow fringe* EDGING, edge, border, trimming, frill, flounce, ruffle; tassels; *archaic* purfle.
— OPPOSITES: middle.
▸ adjective *fringe theatre* UNCONVENTIONAL, unorthodox, alternative, avant-garde, experimental, innovative, left-field, innovatory, radical, extreme; peripheral; off-off Broadway; *informal* offbeat, way out.
— OPPOSITES: mainstream.
▸ verb **1** *a robe of gold, fringed with black velvet* TRIM, edge, hem, border, bind, braid; decorate, adorn, ornament, embellish, finish; *archaic* purfle. **2** *the lake is fringed by a belt of trees* BORDER, edge, bound, skirt, line,

surround, enclose, encircle, circle, girdle, encompass, ring; *literary* gird.

fringe benefit ▶ **noun** EXTRA, added extra, additional benefit, privilege, bonus; *informal* perk; *formal* perquisite.

frippery ▶ **noun 1** *a functional building with not a hint of frippery* OSTENTATION, showiness, embellishment, adornment, ornamentation, ornament, decoration, trimming, gilding, prettification, gingerbread; finery, frou-frou; *informal* bells and whistles. **2** *stalls full of fripperies* TRINKET, bauble, knick-knack, gewgaw, gimcrack, bibelot, ornament, novelty, trifle, kickshaw, tchotchke; *archaic* gaud.

frisk ▶ **verb 1** *the spaniels frisked around my ankles* FROLIC, gambol, cavort, caper, scamper, skip, dance, romp, trip, prance, leap, spring, hop, jump, bounce. **2** *the officer frisked him* SEARCH, check, inspect.

frisky ▶ **adjective** LIVELY, bouncy, bubbly, perky, active, energetic, animated, zestful, full of vim and vigour; playful, coltish, skittish, spirited, high-spirited, in high spirits, exuberant; *informal* full of beans, zippy, peppy, bright-eyed and bushy-tailed; *literary* frolicsome.

fritter ▶ **verb** SQUANDER, waste, misuse, misspend, dissipate; overspend, spend like water, be prodigal with, run through, get through; *informal* blow, splurge, pour/chuck something down the drain.
— OPPOSITES: save.

frivolity ▶ **noun** LIGHT-HEARTEDNESS, levity, joking, jocularity, gaiety, fun, frivolousness, silliness, foolishness, flightiness, skittishness; superficiality, shallowness, flippancy, vacuity, empty-headedness.

frivolous ▶ **adjective 1** *a frivolous girl* SKITTISH, flighty, giddy, silly, foolish, superficial, shallow, light-minded, irresponsible, thoughtless, feather-brained, empty-headed, pea-brained, birdbrained, vacuous, vapid; *informal* dizzy, dippy, ditsy, flaky. **2** *frivolous remarks* FLIPPANT, glib, facetious, joking, jokey, light-hearted; fatuous, inane, senseless, thoughtless; *informal* flip. **3** *new rules to stop frivolous lawsuits* TIME-WASTING, pointless, trivial, trifling, minor, petty, insignificant, unimportant.
— OPPOSITES: sensible, serious.

frizzle¹ ▶ **verb** *a hamburger frizzled in the pan* SIZZLE, crackle, fizz, hiss, spit, sputter, crack, snap; fry, cook.

frizzle² ▶ **verb** *their hair was powdered and frizzled* CURL, coil, crimp, crinkle, kink, wave, frizz.
— OPPOSITES: straighten.

frizzy ▶ **adjective** CURLY, curled, corkscrew, ringlety, crimped, crinkly, kinky, frizzed; permed.
— OPPOSITES: straight.

frog ▶ **noun** See table at AMPHIBIAN.

frolic ▶ **verb** *children frolicked on the sand* PLAY, amuse oneself, romp, disport oneself, frisk, gambol, cavort, caper, cut capers, scamper, skip, dance, prance, leap about, jump about; *dated* sport.
▶ **noun** *the youngsters enjoyed their frolic* ANTIC, caper, game, romp, escapade; (**frolics**) fun (and games), hijinks, merrymaking, amusement, skylarking.

frolicsome ▶ **adjective** *(literary)* PLAYFUL, frisky, fun-loving, jolly, merry, gleeful, light-hearted, exuberant, high-spirited, spirited, lively, perky, skittish, coltish, kittenish; mischievous, impish, roguish; *informal* peppy, zippy, full of beans.

front ▶ **noun 1** *the front of the boat* FORE, foremost part, forepart, anterior, forefront, nose, head; bow, prow; foreground. **2** *a shop front* FRONTAGE, face, facing, facade; window. **3** *the battlefield surgeons who work at* the front FRONT LINE, firing line, vanguard, van; trenches. **4** *the front of the line-up* HEAD, beginning, start, top, lead. **5** *she kept up a brave front* APPEARANCE, air, face, manner, demeanour, bearing, pose, exterior, veneer, (outward) show, act, pretense, affectation. **6** *the shop was a front for his real business* COVER, cover-up, false front, blind, disguise, facade, mask, cloak, screen, smokescreen, camouflage.
— OPPOSITES: rear, back.
▶ **adjective** *the front runners* LEADING, lead, first, foremost; in first place.
— OPPOSITES: last.
▶ **verb** *the houses fronted on a reservoir* OVERLOOK, look out on/over, face (towards), lie opposite (to); have a view of, command a view of.
■ **in front** AHEAD, to/at the fore, at the head, up ahead, in the vanguard, in the van, in the lead, leading, coming first; *informal* up front.

frontier ▶ **noun** BORDER, boundary, borderline, dividing line, demarcation line; perimeter, limit, edge, rim, bounds.

frost ▶ **noun 1** *bushes covered with frost* ICE CRYSTALS, ice, rime, verglas; hoarfrost, ground frost, black frost, (*Atlantic*) silver thaw ✦; *informal* Jack Frost; *archaic* hoar. **2** *there was frost in his tone* COLDNESS, coolness, frostiness, ice, iciness, frigidity; hostility, unfriendliness, stiffness, aloofness; *informal* standoffishness.

frosty ▶ **adjective 1** *a frosty morning* FREEZING, cold, icy-cold, bitter, bitterly cold, chill, wintry, frigid, glacial, hypothermic, arctic; frozen, icy, gelid; *informal* nippy; *literary* rimy. **2** *her frosty gaze* COLD, frigid, icy, glacial, unfriendly, inhospitable, unwelcoming, forbidding, hostile, stony, stern, steely, hard.

froth ▶ **noun** *the froth on top of the beer* FOAM, head; bubbles, frothiness, fizz, effervescence; lather, suds; scum; *literary* spume.
▶ **verb** *the liquid frothed up* BUBBLE, fizz, effervesce, foam, lather, churn, seethe; *literary* spume.

frothy ▶ **adjective 1** *a frothy liquid* FOAMING, foamy, bubbling, bubbly, fizzy, sparkling, effervescent, gassy, carbonated; sudsy; *literary* spumy. **2** *a frothy daytime talk show* LIGHTWEIGHT, light, superficial, shallow, slight, insubstantial, trivial, trifling, frivolous.

frown ▶ **verb 1** *she frowned at him* SCOWL, glower, glare, lower, make a face, look daggers, give someone a black look; knit/furrow one's brows; *informal* give someone a dirty look. **2** *public displays of affection were frowned on* DISAPPROVE OF, view with disfavour, dislike, look askance at, not take kindly to, take a dim view of, take exception to, have a low opinion of.
— OPPOSITES: smile.

frowzy ▶ **adjective 1** *a frowzy old biddy* SCRUFFY, unkempt, untidy, messy, dishevelled, slovenly, slatternly, bedraggled, down-at-the-heels, badly dressed, dowdy, raggedy. **2** *a frowzy room* DINGY, gloomy, dull, drab, dark, dim; stuffy, close, musty, stale, stifling; shabby, seedy, run-down.

frozen ▶ **adjective 1** *the frozen ground* ICY, ice-covered, ice-bound, frosty, frosted, gelid; frozen solid, hard, (as) hard as iron; *literary* rimy. **2** *his hands were frozen* FREEZING, icy, very cold, chilled to the bone/marrow, numb, numbed, frozen stiff, frostbitten; *informal* frozen to death.
— OPPOSITES: boiling.

frugal ▶ **adjective 1** *a hard-working, frugal woman* THRIFTY, economical, careful, cautious, prudent,

provident, unwasteful, sparing, scrimping; abstemious, abstinent, austere, self-denying, ascetic, monkish, Spartan; parsimonious, miserly, niggardly, cheese-paring, penny-pinching, close-fisted; *informal* tight-fisted, tight, stingy. **2** *their frugal breakfast* MEAGRE, scanty, scant, paltry, skimpy; plain, simple, Spartan, inexpensive, cheap, economical.
– OPPOSITES: extravagant, lavish.

fruit ▸ **noun 1** *fruit for dessert. See table.* **2** *the fruits of their labours* REWARD, benefit, profit, product, return, yield, legacy, issue; result, outcome, upshot, consequence, effect.

Edible Fruits

acerola	lemon
ackee	lime
anchovy pear	loquat
apple	mango
apricot	mangosteen
avocado	medlar
banana	melon
baobab	myrobalan
beach plum	nectarine
berry	olive
blood orange	orange
breadfruit	papaya
carambola	passion fruit
chayote	pawpaw
cherry	peach
cherry plum	pear
citron	persimmon
clementine	pineapple
coconut	plantain
cranberry	plum
custard apple	pomegranate
damson	quince
date	shaddock
fig	soursop
grape	star apple
grapefruit	star fruit
grenadilla	tangelo
guava	tangerine
jackfruit	tomatillo
kiwi	Ugli fruit*
kumquat	watermelon

See also BERRY.

*Proprietary term.

fruitful ▸ **adjective 1** *a fruitful tree* FERTILE, fecund, prolific, high-yielding; fruit-bearing, fruiting. **2** *fruitful discussions* PRODUCTIVE, constructive, useful, of use, worthwhile, helpful, beneficial, valuable, rewarding, profitable, advantageous, gainful, successful, effective, effectual, well-spent.
– OPPOSITES: barren, futile.

fruition ▸ **noun** FULFILLMENT, realization, actualization, materialization, achievement, attainment, accomplishment, resolution; success, completion, consummation, conclusion, close, finish, perfection, maturity, maturation, ripening; ripeness; implementation, execution, performance.

fruitless ▸ **adjective** FUTILE, vain, in vain, to no avail, to no effect, idle; pointless, useless, worthless, wasted, hollow; ineffectual, ineffective, inefficacious; unproductive, unrewarding, frustrating, profitless, unsuccessful, unavailing, barren, for naught; abortive; *archaic* bootless.
– OPPOSITES: productive.

frumpy ▸ **adjective** DOWDY, frumpish, unfashionable, old-fashioned; drab, dull, homely, shabby, scruffy.
– OPPOSITES: fashionable.

frustrate ▸ **verb 1** *his plans were frustrated* THWART, defeat, foil, block, stop, put a stop to, counter, spoil, check, balk, disappoint, forestall, dash, scotch, quash, crush, derail, snooker; obstruct, impede, hamper, hinder, hamstring, stand in the way of, spike someone's guns; *informal* stymie, foul up, screw up, put the kibosh on, do for; *informal* scupper, scuttle. **2** *the delays frustrated her* EXASPERATE, infuriate, annoy, anger, vex, irritate, irk, try someone's patience; disappoint, discontent, dissatisfy, discourage, dishearten, dispirit; *informal* aggravate, bug, miff.
– OPPOSITES: help, facilitate.

frustration ▸ **noun 1** *he clenched his fists in frustration* EXASPERATION, annoyance, anger, vexation, irritation; disappointment, dissatisfaction, discontentment, discontent; *informal* aggravation. **2** *the frustration of her attempts to introduce changes* THWARTING, defeat, prevention, foiling, blocking, spoiling, circumvention, forestalling, disappointment, derailment; obstruction, hampering, hindering; failure, collapse.

fry ▸ **verb** COOK, sauté, sear, brown, sizzle, frizzle, pan-fry, deep-fry.

fuddled ▸ **adjective** STUPEFIED, addled, befuddled, confused, muddled, bewildered, dazed, stunned, muzzy, groggy, foggy, fuzzy, vague, disorientated, disoriented, at sea; *informal* dopey, woozy, fazed, not with it, discombobulated.

fuddy-duddy ▸ **noun** (*informal*) (OLD) FOGEY, conservative, traditionalist, conformist; fossil, dinosaur, troglodyte, mossback, museum piece, stick-in-the-mud, square, stuffed shirt, dodo.

fudge ▸ **verb 1** *the minister tried to fudge the issue* EVADE, avoid, dodge, skirt, duck, gloss over; hedge, prevaricate, vacillate, be noncommittal, stall, beat around the bush, equivocate, hem and haw; *informal* cop out, sit on the fence; *rare* tergiversate. **2** *the government has been fudging figures* ADJUST, manipulate, massage, put a spin on, juggle, misrepresent, misreport, bend; tamper with, tinker with, interfere with, doctor, falsify, distort; *informal* cook, fiddle with.
▸ **noun** *the latest proposals are a fudge* COMPROMISE, cover-up; spin, casuistry, sophistry; *informal* cop-out.

fuel ▸ **noun 1** *the car ran out of fuel* GAS, gasoline, diesel, petroleum, propane; power source. **2** *she added more fuel to the fire* FIREWOOD, wood, kindling, (Nfld) splits ♣, logs; coal, coke, anthracite; oil, paraffin, kerosene, propane, lighter fluid; heat source. **3** *we need fuel to keep our bodies going* NOURISHMENT, food, sustenance, nutriment, nutrition. **4** *his antics added fuel to the opposition's cause* ENCOURAGEMENT, ammunition, stimulus, incentive; provocation, goading.
▸ **verb 1** *power stations fuelled by low-grade coal* POWER, fire, charge. **2** *the rumours fuelled anxiety among opposition backbenchers* FAN, feed, stoke up, inflame, intensify, stimulate, encourage, provoke, incite, whip up; sustain, keep alive.

fugitive ▸ **noun** *a hunted fugitive* ESCAPEE, runaway, deserter, absconder; refugee.
▸ **adjective 1** *a fugitive criminal* ESCAPED, runaway, on the run, on the loose, at large; wanted; *informal* AWOL, on the lam. **2** *the fugitive nature of life* FLEETING, transient, transitory, ephemeral, fading, momentary, short-lived, short, brief, passing,

impermanent, here today and gone tomorrow; *literary* evanescent.

fulfill ▶ verb **1** *she fulfilled a lifelong ambition to visit Israel* ACHIEVE, attain, realize, actualize, make happen, succeed in, bring to completion, bring to fruition, satisfy. **2** *she failed to fulfil her duties* CARRY OUT, perform, accomplish, execute, do, discharge, conduct; complete, finish, conclude, perfect. **3** *they fulfilled the criteria* MEET, satisfy, comply with, conform to, fill, answer.

fulfilled ▶ adjective SATISFIED, content, contented, happy, pleased; serene, placid, untroubled, at ease, at peace.
– OPPOSITES: discontented.

full ▶ adjective **1** *her glass was full* FILLED, filled up, filled to capacity, filled to the brim, brimming, brimful. **2** *streets full of people* CROWDED, packed, crammed, congested; teeming, swarming, thick, thronged, overcrowded, overrun; abounding, bursting, overflowing; *informal* jam-packed, wall-to-wall, stuffed, chockablock, chock full, bursting at the seams, packed to the gunwales, awash. **3** *all the seats were full* OCCUPIED, taken, in use, unavailable. **4** *I'm full* REPLETE, full up, satisfied, well-fed, sated, satiated, surfeited, gorged, glutted; *informal* stuffed. **5** *she'd had a full life* EVENTFUL, interesting, exciting, lively, action-packed, busy, energetic, active. **6** *a full list of available facilities* COMPREHENSIVE, thorough, exhaustive, all-inclusive, all-encompassing, all-embracing, in depth; complete, entire, whole, unabridged, uncut. **7** *a fire engine driven at full speed* MAXIMUM, top, greatest, highest. **8** *she had a full figure* PLUMP, well-rounded, rounded, buxom, shapely, ample, curvaceous, voluptuous, womanly, Junoesque; *informal* busty, curvy, well-upholstered, well-endowed, zaftig. **9** *a full skirt* LOOSE-FITTING, loose, baggy, voluminous, roomy, capacious, billowing. **10** *his full baritone voice* RESONANT, rich, sonorous, deep, vibrant, full-bodied, strong, fruity, clear. **11** *the full flavour of a Bordeaux* RICH, intense, full-bodied, strong, deep.
– OPPOSITES: empty, hungry, selective, thin.
▶ adverb **1** *she looked full into his face* DIRECTLY, right, straight, squarely, square, dead, point-blank; *informal* bang, plumb. **2** *you knew full well I was leaving* VERY, perfectly, quite; *informal* darn, damn, damned, bloody, darned.
■ **in full** IN ITS ENTIRETY, in toto, in total, unabridged, uncut; *informal* holus-bolus.
■ **to the full** FULLY, thoroughly, completely, to the utmost, to the limit, to the maximum, for all one's worth.

full-blooded ▶ adjective UNCOMPROMISING, all-out, out and out, committed, vigorous, strenuous, intense; full-blown, unrestrained, uncontrolled, unbridled, hard-hitting, pulling no punches.
– OPPOSITES: half-hearted.

full-blown ▶ adjective FULLY DEVELOPED, full-scale, full-blooded, fully fledged, complete, total, thorough, entire; advanced.

full-bodied ▶ adjective FULL-FLAVOURED, flavourful, full of flavour, rich, mellow, fruity, robust, strong, well-matured.
– OPPOSITES: tasteless.

full-grown ▶ adjective ADULT, mature, grown-up, of age; fully grown, fully developed, fully fledged, in one's prime, in full bloom, ripe.
– OPPOSITES: infant.

fullness ▶ noun **1** *the fullness of the information they* provide COMPREHENSIVENESS, completeness, thoroughness, exhaustiveness, all-inclusiveness. **2** *the fullness of her body* PLUMPNESS, roundedness, roundness, shapeliness, curvaceousness, voluptuousness, womanliness; *informal* curviness. **3** *the recording has a fullness and warmth* RESONANCE, richness, intensity, depth, vibrancy, strength, clarity, three-dimensionality.
■ **in the fullness of time** IN DUE COURSE, when the time is ripe, eventually, in time, in time to come, one day, some day, sooner or later; ultimately, finally, in the end.

full-scale ▶ adjective **1** *a full-scale model* FULL-SIZE, life-size. **2** *a full-scale public inquiry* THOROUGH, comprehensive, extensive, exhaustive, complete, all-out, all-encompassing, all-inclusive, all-embracing, thoroughgoing, wide-ranging, sweeping, in-depth, far-reaching.
– OPPOSITES: small-scale.

fully ▶ adverb **1** *I fully agree with him* COMPLETELY, entirely, wholly, totally, quite, utterly, perfectly, altogether, thoroughly, in all respects, in every respect, without reservation, without exception, to the hilt. **2** *fully two minutes must have passed* AT LEAST, no less than, no fewer than, easily, without exaggeration.
– OPPOSITES: partly, nearly.

fully fledged ▶ adjective TRAINED, qualified, proficient, experienced; mature, fully developed, full-grown.
– OPPOSITES: novice.

fulminate ▶ verb PROTEST, rail, rage, rant, thunder, storm, vociferate, declaim, inveigh, speak out, make/take a stand; denounce, decry, condemn, criticize, censure, disparage, attack, execrate; *informal* mouth off about; *formal* excoriate.

fulmination ▶ noun PROTEST, objection, complaint, rant, tirade, diatribe, harangue, invective, railing, obloquy; denunciation, condemnation, criticism, censure, attack, broadside, brickbats; *formal* excoriation; *literary* philippic.

fulsome ▶ adjective EXCESSIVE, extravagant, overdone, immoderate, inordinate, over-appreciative, flattering, adulatory, fawning, unctuous, ingratiating, cloying, saccharine; enthusiastic, effusive, rapturous, glowing, gushing, profuse, generous, lavish; *informal* over the top, smarmy.

fumble ▶ verb **1** *she fumbled for her keys* GROPE, fish, search blindly, scrabble around. **2** *he fumbled about in the dark* STUMBLE, blunder, flounder, lumber, stagger, totter, lurch; feel one's way, grope one's way. **3** *the quarterback fumbled the ball* MISS, drop, mishandle, bobble. **4** *she fumbled her lines* MESS UP, make a mess of, bungle, mismanage, mishandle, spoil; *informal* make a hash of, fluff, botch, muff, flub.
▶ noun *a fumble from the goaltender* SLIP, mistake, error, gaffe; *informal* slip-up, boo-boo.

fume ▶ noun **1** *a fire giving off toxic fumes* SMOKE, vapour, gas, effluvium; exhaust; pollution. **2** *stale wine fumes* SMELL, odour, stink, reek, stench, fetor, funk; *literary* miasma.
▶ verb **1** *fragments of lava were fuming and sizzling* EMIT SMOKE, emit gas, smoke; *archaic* reek. **2** *Elsa was still fuming at his arrogance* BE FURIOUS, be enraged, be very angry, seethe, be livid, be incensed, boil, be beside oneself, spit; rage, rant and rave; *informal* be hot under the collar, foam at the mouth, see red.

fumigate ▶ **verb** DISINFECT, purify, sterilize, sanitize, decontaminate, cleanse, clean out.
— OPPOSITES: soil.

fun ▶ **noun** **1** *I joined in with the fun* ENJOYMENT, entertainment, amusement, pleasure; jollification, merrymaking; recreation, diversion, leisure, relaxation; good time, great time; *informal* R and R (rest and recreation), living it up, a ball, beer and skittles. **2** *she's full of fun* MERRIMENT, cheerfulness, cheeriness, jollity, joviality, jocularity, high spirits, gaiety, mirth, laughter, hilarity, glee, gladness, light-heartedness, levity. **3** *he became a figure of fun* RIDICULE, derision, mockery, laughter, scorn, contempt, jeering, sneering, jibing, teasing, taunting.
— OPPOSITES: boredom, misery.
▶ **adjective** (*informal*) *a fun evening* ENJOYABLE, entertaining, amusing, diverting, pleasurable, pleasing, agreeable, interesting.
■ **in fun** PLAYFUL, in jest, as a joke, tongue in cheek, light-hearted, for a laugh, teasing.
■ **make fun of** TEASE, poke fun at, chaff, ridicule, mock, laugh at, taunt, jeer at, scoff at, deride; parody, lampoon, caricature, satirize; *informal* rib, kid, have on, pull someone's leg, send up, rag on, razz.

function ▶ **noun** **1** *the main function of the machine* PURPOSE, task, use, role. **2** *my function was to select and train the recruits* RESPONSIBILITY, duty, role, concern, province, activity, assignment, obligation, charge; task, job, mission, undertaking, commission; capacity, post, situation, office, occupation, employment, business. **3** *a function attended by local dignitaries* SOCIAL EVENT, party, social occasion, affair, gathering, reception, soiree, jamboree, gala, meet-and-greet, levee; *informal* do, bash, shindig, shindy, (*Atlantic*) time ♣.
▶ **verb** **1** *the electrical system had ceased to function* WORK, go, run, be in working/running order, operate, be operative. **2** *the museum functions as an educational centre* ACT, serve, operate; perform, work, play the role of, do duty as.

functional ▶ **adjective** **1** *a small functional kitchen* PRACTICAL, useful, utilitarian, utility, workaday, serviceable; minimalist, plain, simple, basic, modest, unadorned, unostentatious, no-frills, without frills; impersonal, characterless, soulless, institutional, clinical. **2** *the machine is now fully functional* WORKING, in working order, functioning, in service, in use; going, running, operative, operating, in operation, in commission, in action; *informal* up and running.

functionary ▶ **noun** OFFICIAL, office-holder, public servant, civil servant, bureaucrat, administrator, apparatchik, bean-counter.

fund ▶ **noun** **1** *an emergency fund for refugees* COLLECTION, kitty, reserve, pool, purse; endowment, foundation, trust, grant, investment; savings, nest egg; *informal* stash. **2** *I was very short of funds* MONEY, cash, ready money; wealth, means, assets, resources, savings, capital, reserves, the wherewithal; *informal* dough, bread, loot. **3** *his fund of stories* STOCK, store, supply, accumulation, collection, bank, pool; mine, reservoir, storehouse, treasury, treasure house, hoard, repository; *informal* pork barrel.
▶ **verb** *the agency was funded by Ottawa* FINANCE, pay for, back, capitalize, sponsor, put up the money for, subsidize, underwrite, endow, support, maintain; *informal* foot the bill for, pick up the tab for, bankroll, stake.

fundamental ▶ **adjective** BASIC, underlying, core, foundational, rudimentary, elemental, elementary, basal, root; primary, prime, cardinal, first, principal, chief, key, central, vital, essential, important, indispensable, necessary, crucial, pivotal, critical; structural, organic, constitutional, inherent, intrinsic.
— OPPOSITES: secondary, unimportant.

fundamentally ▶ **adverb** *she was, fundamentally, a good person* ESSENTIALLY, in essence, basically, at heart, at bottom, deep down, au fond; primarily, above all, first and foremost, first of all; *informal* at the end of the day, when all is said and done, when you get right down to it.

fundamentals ▶ **plural noun** BASICS, essentials, rudiments, foundations, basic principles, first principles, preliminaries; crux, crux of the matter, heart of the matter, warp and woof, essence, core, heart, base, bedrock; *informal* nuts and bolts, nitty-gritty, brass tacks, ABC, meat and potatoes.

fundraiser ▶ **noun** **1** *she worked as a party fundraiser* Politics bagman ♣. **2** *we helped organize the fundraiser* bazaar, bake sale, fowl supper ♣, fall supper ♣, pancake breakfast, box social, strawberry social, gala; walkathon, skate-a-thon ♣.

funeral ▶ **noun** **1** *he'd attended a funeral* BURIAL, interment, entombment, committal, inhumation, laying to rest; cremation; obsequies, last offices, memorial service; *archaic* sepulture. **2** (*informal*) *ignore my advice if you like — it's your funeral* RESPONSIBILITY, problem, worry, concern, business, affair; *informal* headache.

funereal ▶ **adjective** **1** *the funereal atmosphere* SOMBRE, gloomy, melancholy, lugubrious, sepulchral, miserable, doleful, woeful, sad, sorrowful, cheerless, joyless, bleak, dismal, depressing, dreary; grave, solemn, serious; *literary* dolorous. **2** *funereal colours* DARK, black, drab.
— OPPOSITES: cheerful.

fungus ▶ **noun** MUSHROOM, toadstool; mould, mildew, rust; *Biology* saprophyte.
— RELATED TERMS: myco-

funk ▶ **noun** *he was in a funk because his wife ran out on him* DEPRESSION, bad mood, low, the dumps, the doldrums, blue funk.

funky ▶ **adjective** **1** *Shannah liked funky music* GROOVY, bluesy, jazzy, syncopated. **2** *funky clothing* COOL, trendy, fashionable, hip, supercool. **3** *funky smell* UNPLEASANT, smelly, weird.

funnel ▶ **noun** **1** *fluid was poured through the funnel* TUBE, pipe, channel, conduit. **2** *smoke poured from the ship's funnels* CHIMNEY, flue, vent.
▶ **verb** *the money was funnelled back into the forestry industry* CHANNEL, feed, direct, pump, convey, move, pass; pour, filter, trickle down.

funny ▶ **adjective** **1** *a very funny film* AMUSING, humorous, witty, comic, comical, droll, facetious, jocular, jokey; hilarious, hysterical, riotous, uproarious; entertaining, diverting, sparkling, scintillating; silly, farcical, slapstick; *informal* side-splitting, rib-tickling, laugh-a-minute, wacky, zany, waggish, off the wall, a scream, rich, priceless; *informal, dated* killing. **2** *a funny coincidence* STRANGE, peculiar, odd, queer, weird, bizarre, curious, freakish, freak, quirky; mysterious, mystifying, puzzling, perplexing; unusual, uncommon, anomalous, irregular, abnormal, exceptional, singular, out of the ordinary, extraordinary. **3** *there's something funny about him* SUSPICIOUS, suspect,

dubious, untrustworthy, questionable; *informal* shady, sketchy, fishy.
– OPPOSITES: serious, unsurprising, trustworthy.

fur ▶ noun HAIR, wool; coat, fleece, pelt; *Zoology* pelage.

furious ▶ adjective **1** *she was furious when she learned about it* ENRAGED, infuriated, very angry, irate, incensed, raging, incandescent, fuming, ranting, raving, seething, beside oneself, outraged; *informal* mad, hopping mad, wild, livid, boiling, apoplectic, hot under the collar, on the warpath, foaming at the mouth, steamed up, fit to be tied; *literary* wrathful. **2** *a furious debate* HEATED, hot, passionate, fiery, 'lively'; fierce, vehement, violent, wild, unrestrained, tumultuous, turbulent, tempestuous, stormy.
– OPPOSITES: calm.

furnish ▶ verb **1** *the bedrooms are elegantly furnished* FIT OUT, provide with furniture, appoint, outfit. **2** *grooms furnished us with horses for our journey* SUPPLY, provide, equip, provision, issue, kit out, present, give, offer, afford, purvey, bestow; *informal* fix up.

furniture ▶ noun FURNISHINGS, fittings, movables, appointments, effects; *Law* chattels; *informal* stuff, things.

furor ▶ noun COMMOTION, uproar, outcry, fuss, upset, brouhaha, foofaraw, palaver, pother, tempest, agitation, pandemonium, disturbance, hubbub, rumpus, tumult, turmoil; stir, excitement; *informal* song and dance, to-do, hoo-ha, hullabaloo, ballyhoo, kerfuffle, flap, stink.

furrow ▶ noun **1** *furrows in a plowed field* GROOVE, trench, rut, trough, channel, hollow. **2** *the furrows on either side of her mouth* WRINKLE, line, crease, crinkle, crow's foot, corrugation.
▶ verb *his brow furrowed* WRINKLE, crease, line, crinkle, pucker, screw up, scrunch up, corrugate.

furry ▶ adjective COVERED WITH FUR, hairy, downy, fleecy, soft, fluffy, fuzzy, woolly.

further ▶ adverb *further, it gave him an excellent excuse not to attend* FURTHERMORE, moreover, what's more, also, additionally, in addition, besides, as well, too, to boot, on top of that, over and above that, into the bargain, by the same token; *archaic* withal.
▶ adjective **1** *the further side of the field* MORE DISTANT, more remote, remoter, further away/off, farther (away/off); far, other, opposite. **2** *further information* ADDITIONAL, more, extra, supplementary, supplemental, other; new, fresh.
▶ verb *an attempt to further his career* PROMOTE, advance, forward, develop, facilitate, aid, assist, help, help along, lend a hand to, abet; expedite, hasten, speed up, catalyze, accelerate, step up, spur on, oil the wheels of, give a push to, boost, encourage, cultivate, nurture, foster.
– OPPOSITES: impede.

furtherance ▶ noun PROMOTION, furthering, advancement, forwarding, development, facilitation, aiding, assisting, helping, abetting; hastening, acceleration, boosting, encouragement, cultivation, nurturing, fostering.
– OPPOSITES: hindrance.

furthermore ▶ adverb MOREOVER, further, what's more, also, additionally, in addition, besides, as well, too, to boot, on top of that, over and above that, into the bargain, by the same token; *archaic* withal.

furthest ▶ adjective MOST DISTANT, most remote, remotest, furthest/farthest away, farthest, furthermost, farthermost; outlying, outer, outermost, extreme, uttermost, ultimate; *archaic* outmost.
– OPPOSITES: nearest.

furtive ▶ adjective SECRETIVE, secret, surreptitious, clandestine, hidden, covert, conspiratorial, cloak-and-dagger, hole-and-corner, backstairs, backroom, sly, sneaky, under-the-table; sidelong, sideways, oblique, indirect; *informal* hush-hush, shifty.
– OPPOSITES: open.

fur trader ▶ noun trader, coureur de bois ✦, free trader ✦, factor ✦; trapper, (*Nfld*) furrier ✦; engagé ✦; voyageur ✦, homme du nord ✦, Northman ✦, northwester ✦; wintering partner ✦.

fury ▶ noun **1** *she exploded with fury* RAGE, anger, wrath, outrage, spleen, temper; crossness, indignation, umbrage, annoyance, exasperation; *literary* ire, choler. **2** *the fury of the storm* FIERCENESS, ferocity, violence, turbulence, tempestuousness, savagery; severity, intensity, vehemence, force, forcefulness, power, strength. **3** *she turned on her mother like a fury* VIRAGO, hellcat, termagant, spitfire, vixen, shrew, harridan, dragon, gorgon; (**Furies**) *Greek Mythology* Eumenides.
– OPPOSITES: good humour, mildness.

fuse ▶ verb **1** *a band which fuses rap with rock* COMBINE, amalgamate, put together, join, unite, marry, blend, merge, meld, mingle, integrate, intermix, intermingle, synthesize; coalesce, compound, alloy; *technical* admix; *literary* commingle. **2** *metal fused to a base of coloured glass* BOND, stick, bind, weld, solder; melt, smelt.
– OPPOSITES: separate.

fusillade ▶ noun SALVO, volley, barrage, bombardment, cannonade, battery, burst, blast, hail, shower, rain, stream; *historical* broadside.

fusion ▶ noun BLEND, blending, combination, amalgamation, joining, union, marrying, bonding, merging, melding, mingling, integration, intermixture, intermingling, synthesis; coalescence.

fuss ▶ noun **1** *what's all the fuss about?* ADO, excitement, agitation, pother, stir, commotion, confusion, disturbance, brouhaha, uproar, furor, palaver, foofaraw, tempest in a teapot, much ado about nothing; bother, fluster, flurry, bustle; *informal* hoo-ha, to-do, ballyhoo, song and dance, performance, pantomime, kerfuffle. **2** *they settled in with very little fuss* BOTHER, trouble, inconvenience, effort, exertion, labour; *informal* hassle. **3** *he didn't put up a fuss* PROTEST, complaint, objection, grumble, grouse; *informal* gripe.
▶ verb *he was still fussing about his clothes* WORRY, fret, be anxious, be agitated, make a big thing out of; make a mountain out of a molehill; *informal* flap, be in a tizzy, be in a stew, make a meal of.

fuss-budget ▶ noun (*informal*) FUSSY PERSON, worrier, perfectionist, stickler, grumbler; *informal* nitpicker, old woman, fuss, fusspot.

fussy ▶ adjective **1** *he's very fussy about what he eats* FINICKY, particular, over-particular, fastidious, discriminating, selective, dainty; hard to please, difficult, exacting, demanding; faddish; *informal* pernickety, persnickety, choosy, picky. **2** *a fussy, frilly bridal gown* OVER-ELABORATE, over-decorated, ornate, fancy, overdone; busy, cluttered.

fusty ▶ adjective **1** *the room smelt fusty* STALE, musty, dusty; stuffy, airless, unventilated; damp, mildewed, mildewy. **2** *a fusty conservative* OLD-FASHIONED, out of

date, outdated, behind the times, antediluvian, backward-looking; fogeyish; *informal* square, uncool.
— OPPOSITES: fresh.

futile ▶ adjective FRUITLESS, vain, pointless, useless, ineffectual, ineffective, inefficacious, to no effect, of no use, in vain, to no avail, unavailing; unsuccessful, failed, thwarted; unproductive, barren, unprofitable, abortive; impotent, hollow, empty, forlorn, idle, hopeless; *archaic* bootless.
— OPPOSITES: useful.

futility ▶ noun FRUITLESSNESS, pointlessness, uselessness, vanity, ineffectiveness, inefficacy; failure, barrenness, unprofitability; impotence, hollowness, emptiness, forlornness, hopelessness.

future ▶ noun **1** *his plans for the future* TIME TO COME, time ahead; what lies ahead, coming times. **2** *she knew her future lay in acting* DESTINY, fate, fortune; prospects, expectations, chances.

— OPPOSITES: past.
▶ adjective **1** *a future date* LATER, to come, following, ensuing, succeeding, subsequent, coming. **2** *his future wife* TO BE, destined; intended, planned, prospective.
■ **in future** FROM NOW ON, after this, in the future, from this day forward, hence, henceforward, subsequently, in time to come, down the road; *formal* hereafter.

fuzz ▶ noun *the soft fuzz on his cheeks* HAIR, down; fur, fluff, fleeciness; *informal* peach fuzz.

fuzzy ▶ adjective **1** *her fuzzy hair* FRIZZY, fluffy, woolly; downy, soft. **2** *a fuzzy picture* BLURRY, blurred, indistinct, unclear, bleary, misty, distorted, out of focus, unfocused, lacking definition, nebulous; ill-defined, indefinite, vague, hazy, imprecise, inexact, loose, woolly. **3** *my mind was fuzzy* CONFUSED, muddled, addled, fuddled, befuddled, groggy, disoriented, disorientated, mixed up, fazed, foggy, dizzy, stupefied, benumbed.

Gg

gab (*informal*) ▶ **verb** *they were all gabbing away like crazy* CHATTER, chitter-chatter, chat, talk, gossip, gabble, babble, prattle, jabber, blather, blab; *informal* yak, yackety-yak, yabber, yatter, yammer, blabber, blah-blah, jaw, gas, mouth off, natter, run off at the mouth.
■ **the gift of the gab** ELOQUENCE, fluency, expressiveness, a silver tongue; persuasiveness; *informal* a way with words, blarney.

gabble ▶ **verb** *he gabbled on in a panicky way* JABBER, babble, prattle, rattle, blabber, gibber, blab, drivel, twitter, splutter.
▶ **noun** *the boozy gabble of the crowd* JABBERING, babbling, chattering, gibbering, babble, chatter, rambling.

gabby ▶ **adjective** (*informal*). See TALKATIVE.

gad ▶ **verb** (*informal*) *she's been gadding about in Europe* GALLIVANT, traipse around, flit around, run around, travel around, roam (around).

gadabout ▶ **noun** (*informal*) PLEASURE-SEEKER; traveller, globetrotter, wanderer, drifter.

gadget ▶ **noun** APPLIANCE, apparatus, instrument, implement, tool, utensil, contrivance, contraption, machine, mechanism, device, labour-saving device, convenience, invention; *informal* gizmo, widget.

gaffe ▶ **noun** BLUNDER, mistake, error, slip, faux pas, indiscretion, impropriety, miscalculation, gaucherie, solecism; *informal* slip-up, howler, boo-boo, fluff, flub, blooper, goof.

gag¹ ▶ **verb 1** *a dirty rag was used to gag her mouth* SMOTHER, block, plug, stifle, stop up, muffle. **2** *the government tried to gag its critics* SILENCE, muzzle, mute, muffle, suppress, stifle; censor, curb, check, restrain, fetter, shackle, restrict. **3** *the stench made her gag* RETCH, heave, dry-heave.
▶ **noun** *his scream was muffled by the gag* MUZZLE, tie, restraint.

gag² ▶ **noun** (*informal*) *a film full of lame gags* JOKE, jest, witticism, quip, pun, play on words, double entendre; practical joke, stunt, lark; *informal* crack, wisecrack, one-liner.

gaiety ▶ **noun 1** *I was struck by her gaiety* CHEERFULNESS, light-heartedness, happiness, merriment, glee, gladness, joy, joie de vivre, joyfulness, joyousness, delight, high spirits, good spirits, good humour, cheeriness, jollity, mirth, joviality, exuberance, elation; liveliness, vivacity, animation, effervescence, sprightliness, zest, zestfulness; *informal* chirpiness, bounce, pep; *literary* blitheness. **2** *the hotel restaurant was a scene of gaiety* MERRYMAKING, festivity, fun, fun and games, frolics, revelry, jollification, celebration, pleasure; *informal* partying.
— OPPOSITES: misery.

gaily ▶ **adverb 1** *she skipped gaily along the path* MERRILY, cheerfully, cheerily, happily, joyfully, joyously, blithely, jauntily, gleefully. **2** *gaily painted boats* BRIGHTLY, colourfully, brilliantly.

gain ▶ **verb 1** *he gained a scholarship to the college* OBTAIN, get, secure, acquire, come by, procure, attain, achieve, earn, win, garner, capture, clinch, pick up, carry off, reap; *informal* land, net, bag, scoop, wangle, swing, walk away/off with. **2** *they stood to gain from the deal* PROFIT, make money, reap benefits, benefit, do well out of; *informal* make a killing, milk. **3** *the dog gained weight* PUT ON, increase in. **4** *the others were gaining on us* CATCH UP WITH/ON, catch someone up, catch, close (in) on, near. **5** *we gained the ridge* REACH, arrive at, get to, come to, make, attain, set foot on; *informal* hit.
— OPPOSITES: lose.
▶ **noun 1** *his gain from the deal* PROFIT, advantage, benefit, reward; percentage, takings, yield, return, winnings, receipts, proceeds, dividend, interest; *informal* pickings, cut, take, rake-off, slice, piece of the pie. **2** *a price gain of 7.5 per cent* INCREASE, rise, increment, augmentation, addition.
— OPPOSITES: loss, decrease.
■ **gain time** PLAY FOR TIME, stall, procrastinate, delay, temporize, hold back, hang back, hang fire, dally, drag one's feet.

gainful ▶ **adjective** PROFITABLE, paid, well-paid, remunerative, lucrative, money-making; rewarding, fruitful, worthwhile, useful, productive, constructive, beneficial, advantageous, valuable.

gainsay ▶ **verb** (*formal*) DENY, dispute, disagree with, argue with, dissent from, contradict, repudiate, challenge, oppose, contest, counter, controvert, refute, rebut; *formal* confute.
— OPPOSITES: confirm.

gait ▶ **noun** WALK, step, stride, pace, tread, bearing, carriage; *formal* comportment.

gala ▶ **noun** *the annual summer gala* FETE, fair, festival, carnival, pageant, jubilee, jamboree, party, garden party, celebration, whoop-up ✦; festivities.
▶ **adjective** *a gala occasion* FESTIVE, celebratory, merry, joyous, joyful; diverting, entertaining, enjoyable, spectacular.

galaxy ▶ **noun** STAR SYSTEM, solar system, constellation; stars, heavens.

gale ▶ **noun 1** *a howling gale* WINDSTORM, strong wind, high wind, hurricane, tornado, cyclone, whirlwind; storm, blizzard, squall, tempest, typhoon. **2** *gales of laughter* PEAL, howl, hoot, shriek, scream, roar; outburst, burst, fit, paroxysm, explosion.

gall¹ ▶ **noun 1** *she had the gall to ask for money* EFFRONTERY, impudence, impertinence, cheek, cheekiness, insolence, audacity, temerity, presumption, cockiness, nerve, shamelessness, disrespect, bad manners; *informal* face, chutzpah; sauce, sass. **2** *scholarly gall was poured on this work* BITTERNESS, resentment, rancour, bile, spleen, malice, spite, spitefulness, malignity, venom, vitriol, poison.

gall² ▶ **noun 1** *this was a gall that she frequently had to endure* IRRITATION, irritant, annoyance, vexation, nuisance, provocation, bother, torment, plague, thorn in one's side/flesh; *informal* aggravation, bore, headache, hassle, pain, pain in the neck, pain in the butt. **2** *a bay horse with a gall on its side* SORE, ulcer, ulceration; abrasion, scrape, scratch, graze, chafe.

▶ **verb** *it galled him that he had to wake early* IRRITATE, annoy, vex, anger, infuriate, exasperate, irk, pique, nettle, put out, displease, antagonize, get on someone's nerves, make someone's hackles rise, rub the wrong way; *informal* aggravate, peeve, miff, rile, needle, get (to), bug, get someone's goat, get/put someone's back up, get someone's dander up, drive mad/crazy, drive round the bend/twist, drive up the wall, tee off, tick off, rankle.

gallant ▶ **adjective 1** *his gallant countrymen* BRAVE, courageous, valiant, valorous, bold, plucky, daring, fearless, intrepid, heroic, lion-hearted, stout-hearted, doughty, mettlesome, dauntless, undaunted, unflinching, unafraid; *informal* gutsy, spunky. **2** *her gallant companion* CHIVALROUS, princely, gentlemanly, honourable, courteous, polite, mannerly, attentive, respectful, gracious, considerate, thoughtful.
— OPPOSITES: cowardly, discourteous.

gallantry ▶ **noun 1** *he received medals for gallantry* BRAVERY, courage, courageousness, valour, pluck, pluckiness, nerve, daring, boldness, fearlessness, dauntlessness, intrepidity, heroism, mettle, grit, stout-heartedness; *informal* guts, spunk, moxie. **2** *she acknowledged his selfless gallantry* CHIVALRY, chivalrousness, gentlemanliness, courtesy, courteousness, politeness, good manners, attentiveness, graciousness, respectfulness, respect.

gallery ▶ **noun 1** *the art gallery* MUSEUM; exhibition room, display room. **2** *they sat up in the gallery* BALCONY, circle, dress circle, loges; *informal* gods. **3** *a long gallery with doors along each side* PASSAGE, passageway, corridor, walkway, arcade.

galling ▶ **adjective** ANNOYING, irritating, vexing, vexatious, infuriating, maddening, irksome, provoking, exasperating, trying, tiresome, troublesome, bothersome, displeasing, disagreeable; *informal* aggravating.

gallivant ▶ **verb** FLIT, jaunt, run; roam, wander, travel, rove; *informal* gad.

gallop ▶ **verb** *Paul galloped across the clearing* RUSH, race, run, sprint, bolt, dart, dash, career, charge, shoot, hurtle, careen, hare, fly, speed, zoom, streak; *informal* tear, belt, pelt, scoot, zip, whip, hotfoot it, hightail it, bomb, barrel.
— OPPOSITES: amble.

gallows ▶ **plural noun 1** *the wooden gallows* GIBBET, scaffold, gallows tree. **2** *they were condemned to the gallows* HANGING, being hanged, the noose, the rope, the gibbet, the scaffold, execution.

galore ▶ **adjective** APLENTY, in abundance, in profusion, in great quantities, in large numbers, by the dozen; to spare; everywhere, all over (the place); *informal* by the truckload.

galoshes ▶ **plural noun** OVERSHOES, rubbers, toe rubbers ✦, gumshoes.

galvanize ▶ **verb** JOLT, shock, startle, impel, stir, spur, prod, urge, motivate, stimulate, electrify, excite, rouse, arouse, awaken; invigorate, fire, animate, vitalize, energize, exhilarate, thrill, catalyze, inspire, light a fire under; *informal* give someone a shot in the arm.

gambit ▶ **noun** STRATAGEM, scheme, plan, tactic, manoeuvre, move, course/line of action, device; machination, ruse, trick, ploy, wangle.

gamble ▶ **verb 1** *he started to gamble more often* BET, place/lay a bet on something, stake money on

something, back the horses, game; *informal* play the ponies. **2** *investors are gambling that the pound will fall* TAKE A CHANCE, take a risk, take a flier; *informal* stick one's neck out, go out on a limb.

▶ **noun 1** *his grandfather enjoyed a gamble* BET, wager, speculation; game of chance. **2** *I took a gamble and it paid off* RISK, chance, hazard, shot in the dark, leap of faith; pig in a poke, pot luck.

gambol ▶ **verb** FROLIC, frisk, cavort, caper, skip, dance, romp, prance, leap, hop, jump, spring, bound, bounce; play; *dated* sport.

Children's Games

bingo	kick the can
blind man's bluff	King of the Castle
British bulldog	leapfrog
broken telephone	marbles
bumper shining ✦(Man. & Sask.)	monkey in the middle
catch	murderball
cat's cradle	musical chairs
conkers	nicky nicky nine door ✦
cops and robbers	patty cake
cowboys and Indians	peekaboo
dodge ball	pin the tail on the
double dutch	donkey
dreidel	post office
duck, duck, goose	Red Rover
follow-the-leader	ring-around-the-rosie
four-square	Simon Says
hangman	skipping
hide-and-seek	tag
hopscotch	tic-tac-toe
I spy	tiddlywinks
jumpsies ✦	twenty questions

Table Games and Board Games

air hockey	go
backgammon	kriegspiel
bagatelle	Monopoly*
billiards	pachisi
checkers	pinball
chess	Scrabble*
Chinese checkers	snakes and ladders
crokinole ✦	table-top hockey
dominoes	Trivial Pursuit*
foosball	*Proprietary term.

game ▶ **noun 1** *Andrew and his friends invented a new game* PASTIME, diversion, entertainment, amusement, distraction, divertissement, recreation, sport, activity. *See tables.* **2** *the team hasn't lost a game all season* MATCH, contest, tournament, meet; final, play-off. **3** *I spoiled his little game* SCHEME, plot, ploy, stratagem, strategy, gambit, cunning plan, tactics, trick, device, manoeuvre, wile, dodge, ruse, machination, contrivance, subterfuge; prank, practical joke; *informal* scam; *archaic* shift. **4** *he lived off fish and game* WILD ANIMALS, wild fowl, big game, country food ✦.

▶ **adjective 1** *they weren't game enough to join in* BRAVE, courageous, plucky, bold, daring, intrepid, valiant, stout-hearted, mettlesome; fearless, dauntless, undaunted, unflinching; *informal* gutsy, spunky. **2** *I need a bit of help — are you game?* WILLING, prepared,

ready, disposed, of a mind; eager, keen, enthusiastic, up for it.
▶ **verb** *they were drinking and gaming all evening* GAMBLE, bet, place/lay bets.

gamin, fem. **gamine** ▶ noun (*dated*) URCHIN, ragamuffin, waif, stray; *derogatory* guttersnipe.

gamut ▶ noun RANGE, spectrum, span, scope, sweep, compass, area, breadth, reach, extent, catalogue, scale; variety.

gang ▶ noun **1** *a gang of teenagers* BAND, group, crowd, pack, horde, throng, mob, herd, swarm, troop, cluster; company, gathering; *informal* posse, bunch, gaggle, load. **2** (*informal*) *Shania was one of our gang* CIRCLE, social circle, social set, group, clique, in-crowd, coterie, cabal, lot, ring; *informal* crew, rat pack. **3** *a gang of workmen* CREW, team, group, squad, shift, detachment, unit.
▶ **verb** *they all ganged up to put me down* CONSPIRE, co-operate, collude, work together, act together, combine, join forces, team up, get together, unite, ally.

gangling, gangly ▶ adjective LANKY, rangy, tall, thin, skinny, spindly, stringy, bony, angular, scrawny, spare; awkward, uncoordinated, ungainly, gawky, inelegant, graceless, ungraceful; *dated* spindle-shanked.
– OPPOSITES: squat.

gangster ▶ noun HOODLUM, gang member, racketeer, robber, ruffian, thug, tough, villain, lawbreaker, criminal; gunman; Mafioso; *informal* mobster, crook, low-life, hit man, hood; *dated* desperado.

gap ▶ noun **1** *a gap in the shutters* OPENING, aperture, space, breach, chink, slit, slot, vent, crack, crevice, cranny, cavity, hole, orifice, interstice, perforation, break, fracture, rift, rent, fissure, cleft, divide. **2** *a gap between meetings* PAUSE, intermission, interval, interlude, break, breathing space, breather, respite, hiatus, recess. **3** *a gap in our records* OMISSION, blank, lacuna, void, vacuity. **4** *the gap between rich and poor* CHASM, gulf, rift, split, separation, breach; contrast, difference, disparity, divergence, imbalance.

gape ▶ verb **1** *she gaped at him in astonishment* STARE, stare open-mouthed, stare in wonder, goggle, gaze, ogle; *informal* rubberneck, gawk. **2** *a padded coat which gaped at every seam* OPEN WIDE, open up, yawn; part, split.

gaping ▶ adjective *a gaping hole* CAVERNOUS, yawning, wide, broad; vast, huge, enormous, immense, extensive.

garage ▶ noun **1** *he let them park in his garage* CAR PORT, lock-up, (*Ont.*) drive shed ✥. **2** *she took her car to the garage* SERVICE STATION, gas station. **3** *a new bus garage was to be built* DEPOT, terminus, terminal, base, headquarters; bus station.

garage sale ▶ noun YARD SALE, lawn sale, street sale; rummage sale.

garb ▶ noun *men and women in riding garb* CLOTHES, clothing, garments, attire, dress, costume, outfit, wear, uniform, livery, regalia; *informal* gear, getup, togs, duds; *formal* apparel; *archaic* raiment, habiliment, vestments.
▶ **verb** *both men were garbed in black* DRESS, clothe, attire, fit out, turn out, deck (out), kit out, costume, robe; *informal* get up; *archaic* apparel.

garbage ▶ noun **1** *the garbage is taken to landfill sites* TRASH, refuse, waste, detritus, litter, junk, scrap; scraps, leftovers, remains, slops, rubbish. **2** *most of what he says is garbage* NONSENSE, balderdash, claptrap,

twaddle, blather; dross, rubbish; *informal* hogwash, baloney, tripe, jive, bilge, bull, bunk, poppycock, piffle, dreck, codswallop, bunkum.

garble ▶ verb MIX UP, muddle, jumble, confuse, obscure, distort, scramble; misstate, misquote, misreport, misrepresent, mistranslate, misinterpret, misconstrue, twist.

garden ▶ noun YARD, plot; flower bed, lawn.
– RELATED TERMS: horticultural.
■ **lead someone up the garden path** (*informal*) DECEIVE, mislead, delude, hoodwink, dupe, trick, entrap, beguile, take in, fool, pull the wool over someone's eyes, gull; *informal* con, pull a fast one on, string along, take for a ride, put one over on.

gardening ▶ noun HORTICULTURE, yardwork, landscaping.

gargantuan ▶ adjective HUGE, enormous, vast, gigantic, very big, giant, massive, colossal, mammoth, immense, mighty, monumental, mountainous, titanic, towering, tremendous, elephantine, king-size(d), economy-size(d), prodigious; *informal* mega, monster, whopping, humongous, jumbo, ginormous.
– OPPOSITES: tiny.

garish ▶ adjective GAUDY, lurid, loud, harsh, glaring, violent, showy, glittering, brassy, brash; tasteless, in bad taste, tawdry, vulgar, unattractive, bilious; *informal* flash, flashy, tacky, tinselly, neon.
– OPPOSITES: drab.

garland ▶ noun *a garland of flowers* FESTOON, lei, wreath, ring, circle, swag; coronet, crown, coronal, chaplet, ring.
▶ **verb** *gardens garlanded with coloured lights* FESTOON, wreathe, swathe, hang; adorn, ornament, embellish, decorate, deck, trim, dress, bedeck, array; *literary* bedizen.

garment ▶ noun ITEM OF CLOTHING, article of clothing; (**garments**) clothes, clothing, dress, garb, outfit, costume, attire; *informal* get-up, gear, togs, duds, threads; *formal* apparel.

garner ▶ verb *Edward garnered ideas from his travels* GATHER, collect, accumulate, amass, get (together), assemble, reap.

garnish ▶ verb *garnish the dish with chopped parsley* DECORATE, adorn, ornament, trim, dress, embellish; enhance, grace, beautify, prettify, add the finishing touch to.
▶ noun *keep a few sprigs for a garnish* DECORATION, adornment, trim, trimming, ornament, ornamentation, embellishment, enhancement, finishing touch; *Cooking* chiffonade.

garret ▶ noun LOFT, attic, mansard.

garrison ▶ noun **1** *the enemy garrison had been burned alive* TROOPS, militia, soldiers, forces; armed force, military detachment, unit, platoon, brigade, squadron, battalion, corps. **2** *forces from three garrisons* FORTRESS, fort, fortification, stronghold, citadel, camp, encampment, cantonment, command post, base, station; barracks.
▶ **verb** *French infantry garrisoned the town* DEFEND, guard, protect, barricade, shield, secure; man, occupy. **2** *troops were garrisoned in various regions* STATION, post, put on duty, deploy, assign, install; base, site, place, position; billet.

garrulous ▶ adjective **1** *a garrulous old man* TALKATIVE, loquacious, voluble, verbose, chatty, chattering, gossipy; effusive, expansive, forthcoming, conversational, communicative;

informal mouthy, gabby, gassy, windy, having the gift of the gab, motor-mouthed. **2** *his garrulous reminiscences* LONG-WINDED, wordy, verbose, prolix, long, lengthy, rambling, wandering, maundering, meandering, digressive, diffuse, discursive; gossipy, chatty; *informal* windy, gassy.
— OPPOSITES: taciturn, concise.

gas ▶ noun FUEL, gasoline; *informal* juice.

gash ▶ noun *a gash on his forehead* LACERATION, cut, wound, injury, slash, tear, incision; slit, split, rip, rent; scratch, scrape, abrasion; *Medicine* lesion.
▶ verb *he gashed his hand on some broken glass* LACERATE, cut (open), wound, injure, hurt, slash, tear, gouge, puncture, slit, split, rend; scratch, scrape, graze, abrade.

gasoline ▶ noun GAS, fuel; diesel, unleaded gas, (*Prairies*) purple gas ♣; *informal* juice.

gasp ▶ verb **1** *I gasped in surprise* CATCH ONE'S BREATH, draw in one's breath, gulp; exclaim, cry (out). **2** *she collapsed on the ground, gasping* PANT, puff, wheeze, breathe hard, choke, fight for breath.
▶ noun *a gasp of dismay* GULP; exclamation, cry; sharp inhalation.

gas station ▶ noun service station, gas bar ♣, filling station, gasoline station, self-serve.

gastric ▶ adjective *gastric pain* STOMACH, intestinal, enteric, duodenal, celiac, abdominal, ventral.

gate ▶ noun GATEWAY, doorway, entrance, entryway; exit, egress, opening; door, portal; barrier, turnstile.

gather ▶ verb **1** *we gathered in the hotel lobby* CONGREGATE, assemble, meet, collect, come/get together, convene, muster, rally, converge; cluster together, crowd, mass, flock together. **2** *she gathered her family together* SUMMON, call together, bring together, assemble, convene, rally, round up, muster, marshal. **3** *knick-knacks he had gathered over the years* COLLECT, accumulate, amass, garner, accrue; store, stockpile, hoard, put by/away, lay by/in; *informal* stash away, squirrel away. **4** *they gathered corn from the fields* HARVEST, reap, crop; pick, pluck; collect. **5** *the show soon gathered a fanatical following* ATTRACT, draw, pull, pull in, collect, pick up. **6** *I gather that environmentalism is the hot issue* UNDERSTAND, be given to understand, believe, be led to believe, think, conclude, deduce, infer, assume, take it, surmise, fancy; hear, hear tell, learn, discover. **7** *he gathered her to his chest* CLASP, clutch, pull, embrace, enfold, hold, hug, cuddle, squeeze; *literary* embosom. **8** *his tunic was gathered at the waist* PLEAT, shirr, pucker, tuck, fold, ruffle.
— OPPOSITES: disperse.

gathering ▶ noun **1** *she rose to address the gathering* ASSEMBLY, meeting, convention, rally, turnout, congress, convocation, conclave, council, synod, forum; congregation, audience, crowd, group, throng, mass, multitude; *informal* get-together; *formal* concourse. **2** *the gathering of data for a future book* COLLECTING, collection, garnering, amassing, compilation, accumulation, accrual, cumulation, building up.

gauche ▶ adjective AWKWARD, gawky, inelegant, graceless, ungraceful, ungainly, maladroit, klutzy, inept; lacking in social grace(s), unsophisticated, uncultured, uncultivated, unrefined, raw, inexperienced, unworldly.
— OPPOSITES: elegant, sophisticated.

gaudy ▶ adjective GARISH, lurid, loud, over-bright, glaring, harsh, violent, showy, glittering, brassy,

ostentatious; tasteless, in bad taste, tawdry, vulgar, unattractive, bilious; *informal* flash, flashy, tacky, kitschy, tinselly, (*Que.*) kétaine ♣.
— OPPOSITES: drab, tasteful.

gauge ▶ noun **1** *the temperature gauge* MEASURING DEVICE, measuring instrument, meter, measure; indicator, dial, scale, display. **2** *exports are an important gauge of economic activity* MEASURE, indicator, barometer, point of reference, guide, guideline, touchstone, yardstick, benchmark, criterion, test, litmus test. **3** *guitar strings of a different gauge* SIZE, diameter, thickness, width, breadth; measure, capacity, magnitude; bore, calibre.
▶ verb **1** *astronomers can gauge the star's intrinsic brightness* MEASURE, calculate, compute, work out, determine, ascertain; count, weigh, quantify, put a figure on, pin down. **2** *it is difficult to gauge how effective the ban was* ASSESS, evaluate, determine, estimate, form an opinion of, appraise, get the measure of, judge, guess; *informal* guesstimate, size up.

gaunt ▶ adjective **1** *a gaunt, greying man* HAGGARD, drawn, thin, lean, skinny, spindly, spare, bony, angular, raw-boned, pinched, hollow-cheeked, scrawny, scraggy, as thin as a rake, cadaverous, skeletal, emaciated, skin-and-bones; wasted, withered, etiolated; *informal* like a bag of bones; *dated* spindle-shanked. **2** *the gaunt ruin of the dark tower* BLEAK, stark, desolate, bare, gloomy, dismal, sombre, grim, stern, harsh, forbidding, uninviting, cheerless.
— OPPOSITES: plump.

gauzy ▶ adjective TRANSLUCENT, transparent, sheer, see-through, fine, delicate, flimsy, filmy, gossamer, diaphanous, chiffony, wispy, thin, light, insubstantial, floaty.
— OPPOSITES: opaque, thick.

gawk ▶ verb (*informal*) GAPE, goggle, gaze, ogle, stare, stare open-mouthed; *informal* rubberneck.

gawky ▶ adjective AWKWARD, ungainly, gangling, gauche, maladroit, clumsy, klutzy, inelegant, uncoordinated, graceless, ungraceful; unconfident, unsophisticated.
— OPPOSITES: graceful.

gay ▶ adjective **1** *gay men and women* HOMOSEXUAL, lesbian; *informal* queer, camp, pink, lavender, dykey, flaming. **2** (*dated*) *her children all looked chubby and gay.* See CHEERFUL sense 1.
— OPPOSITES: heterosexual, gloomy.
▶ noun See HOMOSEXUAL.

gaze ▶ verb *he gazed at her* STARE, look fixedly, gape, goggle, eye, look, study, scrutinize, take a good look; ogle, leer; *informal* gawk, rubberneck, eyeball.
▶ noun *her piercing gaze* STARE, fixed look, gape; regard, inspection, scrutiny.

gazebo ▶ noun SUMMER HOUSE, pavilion, belvedere; arbour, bower.

gazette ▶ noun NEWSPAPER, paper, journal, periodical, organ, newsletter, bulletin; *informal* rag.

gear ▶ noun (*informal*) **1** *his fishing gear* EQUIPMENT, apparatus, paraphernalia, articles, appliances, impedimenta; tools, utensils, implements, instruments, gadgets; stuff, things; kit, rig, tackle, (*Nfld*) fit-out ♣, odds and ends, bits and pieces, trappings, appurtenances, accoutrements, regalia; *archaic* equipage. **2** *I'll go back to my hotel and pick up my gear* BELONGINGS, possessions, effects, personal effects, property, paraphernalia, odds and ends, bits and pieces, bags, baggage; *Law* chattels; *informal* things, stuff, kit. **3** *police in riot gear* CLOTHES, clothing, garments, outfits, attire, garb; dress, wear; *informal* togs, duds, getup, kit, threads; *formal* apparel.

gel ▶ verb. See JELL.

gelatinous ▶ adjective JELLY-LIKE, glutinous, viscous, viscid, mucilaginous, sticky, gluey, gummy, slimy; *informal* gooey, gunky.

geld ▶ verb CASTRATE, neuter, desex, fix, alter, doctor.

gem ▶ noun **1** *rubies and other gems* JEWEL, stone, precious stone, semi-precious stone; solitaire, brilliant, cabochon; *archaic* bijou. See table. **2** *the gem of the collection* BEST, finest, pride, prize, treasure, flower, pearl, the jewel in the crown; pick, choice, cream, the crème de la crème, elite, acme; *informal* one in a million, the bee's knees.

Gemstones

agate	hyacinth
alexandrite	jacinth
almandine	jade
amber	jasper
amethyst	jet
aquamarine	lapis lazuli
beryl	malachite
bloodstone	marcasite
cairngorm	moss agate
carbuncle	onyx
carnelian	opal
cat's-eye	peridot
chalcedony	pyrope
chrysolite	rose quartz
chrysoprase	ruby
citrine	sapphire
corundum	sardonyx
demantoid	sunstone
diamond	tiger's eye
emerald	topaz
fire-opal	tourmaline
garnet	turquoise
girasol	vermeil
greenstone	zircon

genealogy ▶ noun LINEAGE, line (of descent), family tree, bloodline; pedigree, ancestry, extraction, heritage, parentage, birth, family, dynasty, house, stock, blood, roots.

general ▶ adjective **1** *this is suitable for general use* WIDESPREAD, common, extensive, universal, wide, popular, public, mainstream; established, conventional, traditional, orthodox, accepted. **2** *a general pay increase* COMPREHENSIVE, overall, across the board, blanket, umbrella, mass, wholesale, sweeping, broad-ranging, inclusive, company-wide; universal, global, worldwide, nationwide. **3** *general knowledge* MISCELLANEOUS, mixed, assorted, diversified, composite, heterogeneous, eclectic. **4** *the general practice* USUAL, customary, habitual, traditional, normal, conventional, typical, standard, regular; familiar, accepted, prevailing, routine, run-of-the-mill, established, everyday, ordinary, common. **5** *a general description* BROAD, imprecise, inexact, rough, loose, approximate, unspecific, vague, woolly, indefinite; *informal* ballpark.
− OPPOSITES: restricted, localized, specialist, exceptional, detailed.

generality ▶ noun **1** *the debate has moved on from generalities* GENERALIZATION, general statement, general principle, sweeping statement; abstraction, extrapolation. **2** *the generality of this principle* UNIVERSALITY, comprehensiveness, all-inclusiveness, broadness.
− OPPOSITES: specific.

generally ▶ adverb **1** *summers were generally hot* NORMALLY, in general, as a rule, by and large, more often than not, almost always, mainly, mostly, for the most part, predominantly, on the whole; usually, habitually, customarily, typically, ordinarily, commonly. **2** *popular opinion veers generally to the left* OVERALL, in general terms, generally speaking, all in all, broadly, on average, basically, effectively. **3** *the method was generally accepted* WIDELY, commonly, extensively, universally, popularly.

generate ▶ verb **1** *moves to generate extra business* CAUSE, give rise to, lead to, result in, bring about, create, make, produce, engender, spawn, precipitate, prompt, provoke, trigger, spark off, stir up, induce, promote, foster. **2** *captive animals may not generate offspring* PROCREATE, breed, father, sire, mother, spawn, create, produce, have; *literary* beget; *archaic* engender.

generation ▶ noun **1** *people of the same generation* AGE, age group, peer group. **2** *generations ago* AGES, years, eons, a long time, an eternity; *informal* donkey's years. **3** *the next generation of computers* CROP, batch, wave, range. **4** *the generation of novel ideas* CREATION, production, initiation, origination, inception, inspiration. **5** *human generation* PROCREATION, reproduction, breeding; creation.

generator ▶ noun ENGINE, dynamo, alternator, magneto, cell, turbine, turbocharger, pump, windmill.

generic ▶ adjective **1** *a generic term for two separate offences* GENERAL, common, collective, non-specific, inclusive, all-encompassing, broad, comprehensive, blanket, umbrella. **2** *generic drugs are cheaper than brand-name ones* UNBRANDED, non-proprietary, no-name.
− OPPOSITES: specific.

generosity ▶ noun **1** *the generosity of our host* LIBERALITY, lavishness, magnanimity, munificence, open-handedness, free-handedness, unselfishness; kindness, benevolence, altruism, charity, big-heartedness, goodness; *literary* bounteousness. **2** *the generosity of the food portions* ABUNDANCE, plentifulness, copiousness, lavishness, liberality, largeness.

generous ▶ adjective **1** *she is generous with money* LIBERAL, lavish, magnanimous, munificent, giving, open-handed, free-handed, bountiful, unselfish, ungrudging, free, indulgent, prodigal; *literary* bounteous. **2** *it was generous of them to offer* MAGNANIMOUS, kind, benevolent, altruistic, charitable, noble, big-hearted, honourable, good; unselfish, self-sacrificing. **3** *a generous amount of fabric* LAVISH, plentiful, copious, ample, liberal, large, great, abundant, profuse, bumper, opulent, prolific; *informal* galore.
− OPPOSITES: mean, selfish, meagre.

genesis ▶ noun **1** *the hatred had its genesis in something dark* ORIGIN, source, root, beginning, start. **2** *the genesis of neurosis* FORMATION, development, evolution, emergence, inception, origination, creation, formulation, propagation.

genial ▶ adjective FRIENDLY, affable, cordial, amiable, warm, easygoing, approachable, sympathetic; good-natured, good-humoured, cheerful; neighbourly, hospitable, companionable, comradely,

Geological Ages

	Geological Age		Years ago
Precambrian	Archean eon		4,000-2,500 million
	Proterozoic eon		2,500-570 million
Phanerozoic	Paleozoic era	Cambrian period	570-510 million
		Ordovician period	510-439 million
		Silurian period	439-409 million
		Devonian period	409-363 million
		Carboniferous period — Mississippian	363-323 million
		Pennsylvanian	323-290 million
		Permian period	290-245 million
	Mesozoic era	Triassic period	245-208 million
		Jurassic period	208-146 million
		Cretaceous period	146-65 million
	Cenozoic era	Tertiary period — Paleocene epoch	65-56.5 million
		Eocene epoch	56.5-35.4 million
		Oligocene epoch	35.4-23.3 million
		Miocene epoch	23.3-5.2 million
		Pliocene epoch	5.2-1.64 million
		Quaternary period — Pleistocene epoch	1,640,000-10,000
		Holocene epoch	10,000-

sociable, convivial, outgoing, gregarious; *informal* chummy.
— OPPOSITES: unfriendly.

genitals ▶ plural noun PRIVATE PARTS, genitalia, sexual organs, reproductive organs, pudenda; crotch, groin, nether regions; *informal* naughty bits, privates.

genius ▶ noun **1** *the world knew of his genius* BRILLIANCE, intelligence, intellect, ability, cleverness, brains, erudition, wisdom, fine mind; artistry, flair. **2** *she has a genius for organization* TALENT, gift, flair, aptitude, facility, knack, bent, ability, expertise, capacity, faculty; strength, forte, brilliance, skill, artistry. **3** *he is a genius* BRILLIANT PERSON, gifted person, mastermind, Einstein, intellectual, great intellect, brain, mind; prodigy; *informal* egghead, bright spark, brainiac, rocket scientist.
— OPPOSITES: stupidity, dunce.

genocide ▶ noun MASS MURDER, mass homicide, massacre; annihilation, extermination, elimination, liquidation, eradication, decimation, butchery, bloodletting; pogrom, ethnic cleansing, holocaust.

genre ▶ noun CATEGORY, class, classification, group, set, list; type, sort, kind, breed, variety, style, model, school, stamp, cast, ilk.

genteel ▶ adjective REFINED, respectable, decorous, mannerly, well-mannered, courteous, polite, proper, correct, seemly; well-bred, cultured, sophisticated, ladylike, gentlemanly, dignified, gracious; affected.
— OPPOSITES: uncouth.

gentility ▶ noun REFINEMENT, distinction, breeding, sophistication; respectability, punctiliousness, decorum, good manners, politeness, civility, courtesy, graciousness, correctness; affectation, ostentation.

gentle ▶ adjective **1** *his manner was gentle* KIND, tender, sympathetic, considerate, understanding, compassionate, benevolent, good-natured; humane, lenient, merciful, clement; mild, placid, serene, sweet-tempered. **2** *a gentle breeze* LIGHT, soft. **3** *a gentle slope* GRADUAL, slight, easy. **4** (*archaic*) *a woman of gentle birth*. See NOBLE adjective sense 1.
— OPPOSITES: brutal, strong, steep, low.

gentleman ▶ noun MAN; nobleman; *informal* gent; *archaic* cavalier.

gentlemanly ▶ adjective CHIVALROUS, gallant, honourable, noble, courteous, civil, mannerly, polite, gracious, considerate, thoughtful; well-bred, cultivated, cultured, refined, suave, urbane.
— OPPOSITES: rude.

gentry ▶ noun UPPER CLASSES, privileged classes, elite, high society, haut monde, smart set; establishment, aristocracy; *informal* upper crust, top drawer.

genuine ▶ adjective **1** *a genuine Picasso* AUTHENTIC, real, actual, original, bona fide, true, veritable; attested, undisputed; *informal* the real McCoy, honest-to-goodness/God, the real thing, kosher. **2** *a very genuine person* SINCERE, honest, truthful, straightforward, direct, frank, candid, open; artless, natural, unaffected; *informal* straight, upfront, on the level, on the up and up.
— OPPOSITES: bogus, insincere.

genus ▶ noun **1** (*Biology*) *a large genus of plants* subdivision, division, group, subfamily. **2** *a new genus of music* TYPE, sort, kind, genre, style, variety, category, class; breed, brand, family, stamp, cast, ilk.

geography ▶ noun. See table.

Branches of Geography

biogeography	hypsography
cartography	meteorology
climatology	oceanography
demography	orography
geology	physical geography
geomorphology	political geography
geopolitics	seismology
glaciology	topography
human geography	volcanology
hydrology	

geology *See tables here and at* ROCK[2].

germ ▶ noun **1** *this detergent kills germs* MICROBE, micro-organism, bacillus, bacterium, virus; *informal* bug. **2** *a fertilized germ* EMBRYO, bud; seed, spore, ovule; egg, ovum. **3** *the germ of an idea* START, beginning(s), seed, embryo, bud, root, rudiment; origin, source, potential; core, nucleus, kernel, essence.

germane ▶ adjective RELEVANT, pertinent, applicable, apposite, material; apropos, to the point, appropriate, apt, fitting, suitable; connected, related, akin.
— OPPOSITES: irrelevant.

germinate ▶ verb **1** *the grain is allowed to germinate* SPROUT, shoot (up), bud; develop, grow, spring up; *dated* vegetate. **2** *the idea began to germinate* DEVELOP, take root, grow, incubate, emerge, evolve, mature, expand, advance, progress.

gestation ▶ noun **1** *a gestation of thirty days* PREGNANCY, incubation; development, maturation. **2** *the law underwent a period of gestation* DEVELOPMENT, evolution, formation, emergence, origination.

gesticulate ▶ verb GESTURE, signal, motion, wave, sign.

gesticulation ▶ noun GESTURING, gesture, hand movement, signals, signs; wave, indication; body language.

gesture ▶ noun **1** *a gesture of surrender* SIGNAL, sign, motion, indication, gesticulation; show. **2** *a symbolic gesture* ACTION, act, deed, move.
▶ verb *he gestured to her* SIGNAL, motion, gesticulate, wave, indicate, give a sign.

get ▶ verb **1** *where did you get that hat?* ACQUIRE, obtain, come by, receive, gain, earn, win, come into, take possession of, be given; buy, purchase, procure, secure; gather, collect, pick up, hook, net, land; achieve, attain; *informal* get one's hands on, get one's mitts on, get hold of, grab, bag, score. **2** *I got your letter* RECEIVE, be sent, be in receipt of, be given. **3** *your tea's getting cold* BECOME, grow, turn, go. **4** *get the children from school* FETCH, collect, go for, call for, pick up, bring, deliver, convey, ferry, transport. **5** *the chairman gets $650,000 a year* EARN, be paid, take home, bring in, make, receive, collect, gross; *informal* pocket, bank, rake in, net, bag. **6** *have the police got their man?* APPREHEND, catch, arrest, capture, seize; take prisoner, take into custody, detain, put in jail, put behind bars, imprison, incarcerate; *informal* collar, grab, nab, nail, run in, pinch, bust, pick up, pull in. **7** *I got a taxi* TRAVEL BY/ON/IN; take, catch, use. **8** *she got the flu* SUCCUMB TO, develop, go/come down with, sicken for, fall victim to, be struck down with, be afflicted by/with, become infected with, catch, contract, fall ill with, be taken ill with; *informal* take ill with. **9** *I got a pain in my arm* EXPERIENCE, suffer, be afflicted with, sustain, feel, have. **10** *I got him on the radio* CONTACT, get in touch with, communicate with, make contact with, reach; phone, call, radio; speak to, talk to; *informal* get hold of. **11** *I didn't get what he said* HEAR, discern, distinguish, make out, perceive, follow, take in. **12** *I don't get the joke* UNDERSTAND, comprehend, grasp, see, fathom, follow, perceive, apprehend, unravel, decipher; *informal* get the drift of, catch on to, latch on to, figure out, twig. **13** *we got there early* ARRIVE, reach, come, make it, turn up, appear, come on the scene, approach, enter, present oneself, come along, materialize, show one's face; *informal* show (up), roll in/up, blow in. **14** *we got her to go* PERSUADE, induce, prevail on, influence; wheedle into, talk into, cajole into. **15** *I'd like to get to meet him* CONTRIVE, arrange, find a way, manage; succeed in, organize; *informal* work it, fix it. **16** *I'll get supper*

PREPARE, get ready, cook, make, assemble, muster, concoct; *informal* fix, rustle up. **17** (*informal*) *I'll get him for that* TAKE REVENGE ON, exact/wreak revenge on, get one's revenge on, avenge oneself on, take vengeance on, get even with, pay back, get back at, exact retribution on, give someone their just deserts. **18** *He scratched his head. 'You've got me there.'* BAFFLE, perplex, puzzle, bewilder, mystify, bemuse, confuse, confound; *informal* flummox, faze, stump, beat, fox, discombobulate. **19** *what gets me is how neurotic she is* ANNOY, irritate, exasperate, anger, irk, vex, provoke, incense, infuriate, madden, try someone's patience, ruffle someone's feathers; *informal* aggravate, peeve, miff, rile, get to, needle, hack off, get someone's back up, get on someone's nerves, get someone's goat, drive mad, make someone see red, tee off, tick off.
— OPPOSITES: give, send, leave.

■ **get about** MOVE ABOUT, move around, travel.

■ **get something across** COMMUNICATE, get over, impart, convey, transmit, make clear, express.

■ **get ahead** PROSPER, flourish, thrive, do well; succeed, make it, advance, get on in the world, go up in the world, make good, become rich; *informal* go places, get somewhere, make the big time.

■ **get along 1** *does he get along with his family?* BE FRIENDLY, be compatible, get on; agree, see eye to eye, concur, be in accord; *informal* hit it off, be on the same wavelength. **2** *she was getting along well at school* FARE, manage, progress, advance, get on, get by, do, cope; succeed.

■ **get around** TRAVEL, circulate, socialize, do the rounds.

■ **get at 1** *it's difficult to get at the pipes* ACCESS, get to, reach, touch. **2** *she had been got at by enemy agents* CORRUPT, suborn, influence, bribe, buy off, pay off; *informal* fix, square. **3** (*informal*) *what are you getting at?* IMPLY, suggest, intimate, insinuate, hint, mean, drive at, allude to.

■ **get away** ESCAPE, run away/off, break out, break free, break loose, bolt, flee, take flight, make off, take off, decamp, abscond, make a run for it; slip away, sneak away; *informal* cut and run, skedaddle, do a disappearing act.

■ **get away with** ESCAPE BLAME FOR, escape punishment for.

■ **get back** RETURN, come home, come back.

■ **get something back** RETRIEVE, regain, win back, recover, recoup, reclaim, repossess, recapture, redeem; find (again), trace.

■ **get back at** TAKE REVENGE ON, exact/wreak revenge on, avenge oneself on, take vengeance on, get even with, pay back, retaliate on/against, exact retribution on, give someone their just deserts.

■ **get by** MANAGE, cope, survive, exist, subsist, muddle through/along, scrape by, make ends meet, make do, keep the wolf from the door; *informal* make out.

■ **get someone down** DEPRESS, sadden, make unhappy, make gloomy, dispirit, dishearten, demoralize, discourage, crush, weigh down, oppress; upset, distress; *informal* give someone the blues, make someone fed up.

■ **get lost** SCRAM, buzz off, go away, take a hike, beat it, bug off, go fly a kite, go suck an egg, vamoose, be off, begone, fuddle duddle ✤.

■ **get off 1** *Sally got off the bus* ALIGHT (FROM), step off, dismount (from), descend (from), disembark (from), leave, exit. **2** (*informal*) *he was arrested but got off* ESCAPE PUNISHMENT, be acquitted, be absolved, be cleared, be exonerated.

■ **get on 1** *we got on the train* BOARD, enter, step

aboard, climb on, mount, ascend, catch; *informal* hop on, jump on. **2** *how are you getting on?* FARE, manage, progress, get along, do, cope, get by, survive, muddle through/along; succeed, prosper; *informal* make out. **3** *she got on with her job* CONTINUE, proceed, go ahead, carry on, go on, press on, persist, persevere; keep at; *informal* stick with/at. **4** *we don't get on.* See GET ALONG sense 1.

■ **get out 1** *the prisoners got out.* See GET AWAY. **2** *the news got out* BECOME KNOWN, become common knowledge, come to light, emerge, transpire; come out, be uncovered, be revealed, be divulged, be disseminated, be disclosed, be reported, be released, leak out.

■ **get out of** EVADE, dodge, shirk, avoid, escape, sidestep; *informal* duck (out of), wriggle out of, cop out of.

■ **get over 1** *I just got over the flu* RECOVER FROM, recuperate from, get better after, shrug off, survive. **2** *we tried to get over this problem* OVERCOME, surmount, get the better of, master, get round, find an/the answer to, get a grip on, deal with, cope with, sort out, take care of, crack, rise above; *informal* lick.

■ **get something over.** See GET SOMETHING ACROSS.

■ **get round someone** CAJOLE, persuade, wheedle, coax, prevail on, win over, bring round, sway, beguile, charm, inveigle, influence, woo; *informal* sweet-talk, soft-soap, butter up, twist someone's arm.

■ **get together 1** *get together the best writers* COLLECT, gather, assemble, bring together, rally, muster, marshal, congregate, convene, amass; *formal* convoke. **2** *we must get together soon* MEET (UP), rendezvous, see each other, socialize.

■ **get up** GET OUT OF BED, rise, stir, rouse oneself; *informal* surface; *formal* arise.

■ **get someone up** (*informal*) DRESS, clothe, attire, garb, fit out, turn out, deck (out), trick out/up, costume, array, robe; *informal* doll up; *archaic* apparel.

getaway ▶ noun ESCAPE, breakout, bolt for freedom, flight; disappearance, vanishing act.

get-together ▶ noun PARTY, meeting, gathering, social event, social; *informal* do, bash, bunfight.

get-up ▶ noun (*informal*) OUTFIT, clothes, costume, ensemble, suit, clothing, dress, attire, garments, garb; *informal* gear, togs, duds, threads; *formal* apparel.

get-up-and-go ▶ noun (*informal*) DRIVE, initiative, enterprise, enthusiasm, eagerness, ambition, motivation, dynamism, energy, gusto, vim, vigour, vitality, verve, fire, fervour, zeal, commitment, spirit; *informal* gumption, oomph, pep.
— OPPOSITES: apathy.

ghastly ▶ adjective **1** *a ghastly stabbing* TERRIBLE, horrible, grim, awful, dire; frightening, terrifying, horrifying, alarming; distressing, shocking, appalling, harrowing; dreadful, frightful, horrendous, monstrous, gruesome, grisly. **2** (*informal*) *a ghastly building* UNPLEASANT, objectionable, disagreeable, distasteful, awful, terrible, dreadful, detestable, insufferable, vile, horrible, horrid. **3** *a ghastly pallor* PALE, white, pallid, pasty, wan, bloodless, peaky, ashen, grey, waxy, blanched, drained, pinched, green, sickly, like death warmed over, ghostly.
— OPPOSITES: pleasant, charming.

ghost ▶ noun **1** *his ghost haunts the crypt* SPECTRE, phantom, wraith, spirit, presence; apparition; *informal* spook. See also the table at SPIRIT. **2** *the ghost of a smile* TRACE, hint, suggestion, impression, suspicion, tinge; glimmer, semblance, shadow, whisper.

ghostly ▶ adjective SPECTRAL, ghostlike, phantom, wraithlike, phantasmal, phantasmic; unearthly, unnatural, supernatural; insubstantial, shadowy; eerie, weird, uncanny; frightening, spine-chilling, hair-raising, blood-curdling, bone-chilling, terrifying, chilling, sinister; *informal* creepy, scary, spooky.

ghoulish ▶ adjective MACABRE, grisly, gruesome, grotesque, ghastly; unhealthy, horrible, unwholesome.

giant ▶ noun *the forest giant had died* COLOSSUS, behemoth, Brobdingnagian, mammoth, monster, leviathan, titan; giantess; *informal* jumbo, whopper.
— OPPOSITES: dwarf.
▶ adjective *a giant balloon* HUGE, colossal, massive, enormous, gigantic, very big, mammoth, vast, immense, monumental, mountainous, titanic, towering, elephantine, king-size(d), economy-size(d), gargantuan, Brobdingnagian; substantial, hefty; *informal* mega, monster, whopping, humongous, jumbo, hulking, bumper, ginormous.
— OPPOSITES: miniature.

gibber ▶ verb PRATTLE, babble, ramble, drivel, jabber, gabble, burble, twitter, mutter, mumble; *informal* yammer, blabber, jibber-jabber, blather, blether.

gibberish ▶ noun NONSENSE, garbage, balderdash, blather, blether, rubbish, drivel, gobbledegook, mumbo-jumbo, tripe, hogwash, baloney, bilge, bull, bunk, guff, eyewash, piffle, twaddle, poppycock, codswallop.

gibe ▶ noun & verb. See JIBE.

giddy ▶ adjective **1** *she felt giddy* DIZZY, light-headed, faint, weak, vertiginous; unsteady, shaky, wobbly, reeling; *informal* woozy. **2** *she was young and giddy* FLIGHTY, silly, frivolous, skittish, irresponsible, flippant, whimsical, capricious; feather-brained, scatty, thoughtless, heedless, carefree; *informal* dippy, ditsy, ditzy, flaky, spinny ♣.
— OPPOSITES: steady, sensible.

gift ▶ noun **1** *he gave the staff a gift* PRESENT, handout, donation, offering, bestowal, bonus, award, endowment; tip, gratuity, baksheesh; largesse; *informal* freebie, perk; *formal* benefaction. **2** *a gift for melody* TALENT, flair, aptitude, facility, knack, bent, ability, expertise, capacity, capability, faculty; endowment, strength, genius, brilliance, skill, artistry.
▶ verb *he gifted a composition to the orchestra* PRESENT, give, bestow, confer, donate, endow, award, accord, grant; hand over, make over.

gifted ▶ adjective TALENTED, skilful, skilled, accomplished, expert, consummate, master(ly), virtuoso, first-rate, able, apt, adept, proficient; intelligent, clever, bright, brilliant; precocious; *informal* crack, top-notch, ace.
— OPPOSITES: inept.

gift wrap ▶ noun WRAPPING PAPER, packaging, tissue paper.

gigantic ▶ adjective HUGE, enormous, vast, extensive, very big, very large, giant, massive, colossal, mammoth, immense, monumental, mountainous, titanic, towering, elephantine, king-size(d), economy-size(d), gargantuan; *informal* mega, monster, whopping, humongous, jumbo, hulking, bumper, ginormous.
— OPPOSITES: tiny.

giggle ▶ verb *he giggled at the picture* TITTER, snigger, snicker, tee-hee, chuckle, chortle, laugh.

▶ **noun** *she suppressed a giggle* TITTER, snigger, snicker, tee-hee, chuckle, chortle, laugh.

gigolo ▶ **noun** PLAYBOY, (male) escort; admirer, lover; *informal* toy boy.

gild ▶ **verb 1** *she gilded the picture frame* GOLD-PLATE; cover with gold, paint gold. **2** *he tends to gild the truth* ELABORATE, embellish, embroider; camouflage, disguise, dress up, colour, exaggerate, expand on; *informal* jazz up.

gimcrack ▶ **adjective** SHODDY, jerry-built, flimsy, insubstantial, thrown together, makeshift; inferior, poor-quality, second-rate, cheap, cheapjack, catchpenny, tawdry, kitschy, chintzy, trashy, dime-store; tacky, (*Que.*) kétaine ♣, junky, cheapo, rubbishy, schlocky.

gimmick ▶ **noun** PUBLICITY STUNT, contrivance, scheme, stratagem, ploy; *informal* shtick.

gingerly ▶ **adverb** CAUTIOUSLY, carefully, with care, warily, charily, circumspectly, delicately; heedfully, watchfully, vigilantly, attentively; hesitantly, timidly.
— OPPOSITES: recklessly.

gird ▶ **verb 1** *the island was girded by rocks* SURROUND, enclose, encircle, circle, encompass, border, bound, edge, skirt, fringe; close in, confine. **2** *they girded themselves for war* PREPARE, get ready, gear up; nerve, steel, galvanize, brace, fortify; *informal* psych oneself up.

girdle ▶ **noun 1** *her stockings were held up by her girdle* CORSET, corselet, foundation garment, panty girdle; truss. **2** *a diamond-studded girdle* BELT, sash, cummerbund, waistband, strap, band, girth, cord.
▶ **verb** *a garden girdled the house* SURROUND, enclose, encircle, circle, encompass, circumscribe, border, bound, skirt, edge; (*literary*) gird.

girl ▶ **noun 1** *a five-year-old girl* FEMALE CHILD, daughter; schoolgirl; *Scottish* lass, lassie. *See also* CHILD. **2** *he settled down with a nice girl* YOUNG WOMAN, young lady, miss, mademoiselle; *Scottish* lass, lassie; *informal* chick, gal, grrrl, babe; *literary* maid, damsel, ingenue. **3** *his girl left him. See* GIRLFRIEND.

girlfriend ▶ **noun** SWEETHEART, lover, partner, significant other, main squeeze, girl, woman; fiancée; *informal* steady; *dated* lady (friend), lady love, betrothed; *archaic* leman.

girlish ▶ **adjective** GIRLY, youthful, childlike, childish, immature; feminine.

girth ▶ **noun 1** *a tree ten feet in girth* CIRCUMFERENCE, perimeter; width, breadth. **2** *he tied the towel around his girth* STOMACH, midriff, middle, abdomen, belly, gut; *informal* tummy, tum. **3** *a horse's girth* cinch.

gist ▶ **noun** ESSENCE, substance, central theme, heart of the matter, nub, kernel, marrow, meat, burden, crux; thrust, drift, sense, meaning, significance, import; *informal* nitty-gritty.

give ▶ **verb 1** *she gave them $2000* PRESENT WITH, provide with, supply with, furnish with, let someone have; hand (over), offer, proffer; award, grant, bestow, accord, confer, make over; donate, contribute, put up. **2** *can I give him a message?* CONVEY, pass on, impart, communicate, transmit; send, deliver, relay; tell. **3** *a baby given into their care* ENTRUST, commit, consign, assign; *formal* commend. **4** *she gave her life for them* SACRIFICE, give up, relinquish; devote, dedicate. **5** *he gave her time to think* ALLOW, permit, grant, accord; offer. **6** *this leaflet gives our opening times* SHOW, display, set out, indicate, detail, list. **7** *they gave no further trouble* CAUSE, make, create, occasion. **8** *garlic gives*

flavour PRODUCE, yield, afford, impart, lend. **9** *she gave a party* ORGANIZE, arrange, lay on, throw, host, hold, have, provide. **10** *Dominic gave a bow* PERFORM, execute, make, do. **11** *she gave a shout* UTTER, let out, emit, produce, make. **12** *he gave Larry a beating* ADMINISTER, deliver, deal, inflict, impose. **13** *the door gave* GIVE WAY, cave in, collapse, break, fall apart; bend, buckle.
— OPPOSITES: receive, take.
▶ **noun** (*informal*) *there isn't enough give in the jacket* ELASTICITY, flexibility, stretch, stretchiness; slack, play.
■ **give someone away** BETRAY, inform on; *informal* split on, rat on, peach on, blow the whistle on, sell down the river, rat out, finger.
■ **give something away** REVEAL, disclose, divulge, let slip, leak, let out.
■ **give in** CAPITULATE, concede defeat, admit defeat, give up, surrender, yield, submit, back down, give way, defer, relent, throw in the towel/sponge.
■ **give something off/out** EMIT, produce, send out, throw out; discharge, release, exude, vent.
■ **give out** RUN OUT, be used up, be consumed, be exhausted, be depleted; fail, flag; dry up.
■ **give something out** DISTRIBUTE, issue, hand out, pass round, dispense; dole out, dish out, mete out; allocate, allot, share out.
■ **give up.** *See* GIVE IN.
■ **give something up** STOP, cease, discontinue, desist from, abstain from, cut out, renounce, forgo; resign from, stand down from; *informal* quit, kick, swear off, leave off, pack in, lay off.

give and take ▶ **noun** COMPROMISE, concession; co-operation, saw-off ♣, reciprocity, teamwork, interplay.

given ▶ **adjective 1** *a given number of years* SPECIFIED, stated, designated, set, particular, specific; prescribed, agreed, appointed, pre-arranged, predetermined. **2** *she was given to fits of temper* PRONE, liable, inclined, disposed, predisposed, apt, likely.
— OPPOSITES: unspecified.
▶ **preposition** *given the issue's complexity, a summary is difficult* CONSIDERING, in view of, bearing in mind, in the light of; assuming.
▶ **noun** *his aggression is taken as a given* ESTABLISHED FACT, reality, certainty.

giver ▶ **noun** DONOR, contributor, donator, benefactor, benefactress, provider; supporter, backer, patron, sponsor, subscriber.

glacial ▶ **adjective 1** *glacial conditions* FREEZING, cold, icy, ice-cold, sub-zero, frozen, gelid, wintry; arctic, polar, Siberian, hypothermic; bitter, biting, raw, chill. **2** *Beverly's tone was glacial* UNFRIENDLY, hostile, unwelcoming; frosty, icy, cold, chilly. **3** *they proceeded at a glacial pace* SLOW, lugubrious, unhurried, leisurely, steady, sedate, slow-moving, plodding, dawdling, sluggish, sluggardly, lead-footed.
— OPPOSITES: tropical, hot, friendly.

glacier ▶ **noun** ICEFIELD.

glad ▶ **adjective 1** *I'm really glad you're coming* PLEASED, happy, delighted, thrilled, overjoyed, elated, gleeful, gratified, grateful, thankful; *informal* tickled pink, over the moon. **2** *I'd be glad to help* WILLING, eager, happy, pleased, delighted; ready, prepared. **3** *glad tidings* PLEASING, welcome, happy, joyful, cheering, heartening, gratifying.
— OPPOSITES: dismayed, reluctant, distressing.

gladden ▶ **verb** DELIGHT, please, make happy, elate; cheer (up), hearten, buoy up, give someone a lift,

uplift; gratify; *informal* give someone a kick, tickle someone pink, buck up.
— OPPOSITES: sadden.

gladly ▶ adverb WITH PLEASURE, happily, cheerfully; willingly, readily, eagerly, freely, ungrudgingly; *archaic* fain, lief.

glamorous ▶ adjective **1** *a glamorous woman* BEAUTIFUL, attractive, lovely, bewitching, enchanting, beguiling; elegant, chic, stylish, fashionable; charming, charismatic, appealing, alluring, seductive; *informal* classy, glam. **2** *a glamorous lifestyle* EXCITING, thrilling, stimulating; dazzling, glittering, glossy, colourful, exotic; *informal* ritzy, glitzy, jet-setting.
— OPPOSITES: dowdy, dull.

glamour ▶ noun *she had undeniable glamour* BEAUTY, allure, attractiveness; elegance, chic, style; charisma, charm, magnetism, desirability. **2** *the glamour of show business* ALLURE, attraction, fascination, charm, magic, romance, mystique, exoticism, spell; excitement, thrill; glitter, the bright lights; *informal* glitz, glam, tinsel.

glance ▶ verb **1** *Rachel glanced at him* LOOK BRIEFLY, look quickly, peek, peep; glimpse; *informal* have a gander. **2** *I glanced through the report* READ QUICKLY, scan, skim, leaf, flick, flip, thumb, browse; dip into. **3** *a bullet glanced off the ice* RICOCHET, rebound, be deflected, bounce; graze, clip. **4** *sunlight glanced off her hair* REFLECT, flash, gleam, glint, glitter, glisten, glimmer, shimmer.
▶ noun *a glance at his watch* PEEK, peep, brief look, quick look, glimpse; *informal* gander.
■ **at first glance** ON THE FACE OF IT, on the surface, at first sight, to the casual eye, to all appearances; apparently, seemingly, outwardly, superficially, it would seem, it appears, as far as one can see/tell, by all accounts.

glare ▶ verb **1** *she glared at him* SCOWL, glower, stare angrily, look daggers, frown, lower, give someone a black look, look threateningly; *informal* give someone a dirty look. **2** *the sun glared out of the sky* BLAZE, beam, shine brightly, be dazzling, be blinding.
▶ noun **1** *a cold glare* SCOWL, glower, angry stare, frown, black look, threatening look; *informal* dirty look. **2** *the harsh glare of the lights* BLAZE, dazzle, shine, beam; radiance, brilliance, luminescence.

glaring ▶ adjective **1** *glaring lights* DAZZLING, blinding, blazing, strong, bright, harsh. **2** *a glaring omission* OBVIOUS, conspicuous, unmistakable, inescapable, unmissable, striking; flagrant, blatant, outrageous, gross; overt, patent, transparent, manifest; *informal* standing/sticking out like a sore thumb.
— OPPOSITES: soft, minor.

glass ▶ noun **1** *a glass of water* TUMBLER, drinking vessel; flute, schooner, balloon, goblet, chalice. **2** *we sell china and glass* GLASSWARE, stemware, crystal, crystalware.
— RELATED TERMS: vitreous.

glasses ▶ plural noun SPECTACLES, eyeglasses, eyewear; *informal* specs; bifocals.

glasshouse ▶ noun GREENHOUSE, hothouse, conservatory.

glassy ▶ adjective **1** *the glassy surface of the lake* SMOOTH, mirror-like, gleaming, shiny, glossy, polished, vitreous; slippery, icy; clear, transparent, translucent; calm, still, flat. **2** *a glassy stare* EXPRESSIONLESS, glazed, blank, vacant, fixed, motionless; emotionless, impassive, lifeless, wooden, vacuous.
— OPPOSITES: rough, expressive.

glaze ▶ verb **1** *the pots are glazed when dry* VARNISH, enamel, lacquer, japan, shellac, paint; gloss. **2** *pastry glazed with caramel* COVER, coat; ice, frost. **3** *his eyes glazed over* BECOME GLASSY, go blank; mist over, film over.
▶ noun **1** *pottery with a blue glaze* VARNISH, enamel, lacquer, finish, coating; lustre, shine, gloss. **2** *a cake with an apricot glaze* COATING, topping; icing, frosting.

gleam ▶ verb SHINE, glimmer, glint, glitter, shimmer, sparkle, twinkle, flicker, wink, glisten, flash; *literary* glister.
▶ noun **1** *a gleam of light* GLIMMER, glint, shimmer, twinkle, sparkle, flicker, flash; beam, ray, shaft. **2** *the gleam of brass* SHINE, lustre, gloss, sheen; glint, glitter, glimmer, sparkle; brilliance, radiance, glow; *literary* glister. **3** *a gleam of hope* GLIMMER, flicker, ray, spark, trace, suggestion, hint, sign.

glean ▶ verb OBTAIN, get, take, draw, derive, extract, cull, garner, gather; learn, find out.

glee ▶ noun DELIGHT, pleasure, happiness, joy, gladness, elation, euphoria; amusement, mirth, merriment; excitement, gaiety, exuberance; relish, triumph, jubilation, satisfaction, gratification.
— OPPOSITES: disappointment.

gleeful ▶ adjective DELIGHTED, pleased, joyful, happy, glad, overjoyed, elated, euphoric; amused, mirthful, merry, exuberant; jubilant; *informal* over the moon.

glib ▶ adjective SLICK, pat, smooth-talking, fast-talking, silver-tongued, smooth, urbane, disingenuous, insincere, facile, shallow, superficial, flippant; *informal* flip, sweet-talking.
— OPPOSITES: sincere.

glide ▶ verb **1** *a gondola glided past* SLIDE, slip, sail, float, drift, flow; coast, freewheel, roll; skim, skate. **2** *seagulls gliding over the waves* SOAR, wheel, plane; fly. **3** *he glided out of the door* SLIP, steal, slink.

glimmer ▶ verb *moonlight glimmered on the lawn* GLEAM, shine, glint, flicker, shimmer, glisten, glow, twinkle, sparkle, glitter, wink, flash; *literary* glister.
▶ noun **1** *a glimmer of light* GLEAM, glint, flicker, shimmer, glow, twinkle, sparkle, flash, ray. **2** *a glimmer of hope* GLEAM, flicker, ray, trace, sign, suggestion, hint.

glimpse ▶ noun *a glimpse of her face* BRIEF LOOK, quick look; glance, peek, peep; sight, sighting.
▶ verb *he glimpsed a figure* CATCH SIGHT OF, notice, discern, spot, spy, sight, pick out, make out; *literary* espy, descry.

glint ▶ verb *the diamond glinted* SHINE, gleam, catch the light, glitter, sparkle, twinkle, wink, glimmer, shimmer, glisten, flash; *literary* glister.
▶ noun *the glint of the silver* GLITTER, gleam, sparkle, twinkle, glimmer, flash.

glisten ▶ verb SHINE, sparkle, twinkle, glint, glitter, glimmer, shimmer, wink, flash; *literary* glister.

glitter ▶ verb *crystal glittered in the candlelight* SHINE, sparkle, twinkle, glint, gleam, shimmer, glimmer, wink, flash, catch the light; *literary* glister.
▶ noun **1** *the glitter of light on the water* SPARKLE, twinkle, glint, gleam, shimmer, glimmer, flicker, flash; brilliance, luminescence. **2** *the glitter of show business* GLAMOUR, excitement, thrills, attraction, appeal; dazzle; *informal* razzle-dazzle, razzmatazz, glitz, ritziness.

gloat ▶ verb DELIGHT, relish, take great pleasure,

revel, rejoice, glory, exult, triumph, crow; boast, brag, be smug, congratulate oneself, preen oneself, pat oneself on the back; rub one's hands together; *informal* rub it in.

global ▶ adjective **1** *the global economy* WORLDWIDE, international, world, intercontinental. **2** *a global view of the problem* COMPREHENSIVE, overall, general, all-inclusive, all-encompassing, encyclopedic, universal, blanket; broad, far-reaching, extensive, sweeping.

globalize ▶ verb INTERNATIONALIZE, go global, expand worldwide.

globe ▶ noun **1** *every corner of the globe* WORLD, earth, planet. **2** *the sun is a globe* SPHERE, orb, ball, spheroid, round.

globular ▶ adjective SPHERICAL, spheric, spheroidal, round, globe-shaped, ball-shaped, orb-shaped, rounded, bulbous.

globule ▶ noun DROPLET, drop, bead, tear, ball, bubble, pearl; *informal* blob, glob.

gloom ▶ noun **1** *she peered into the gloom* DARKNESS, dark, dimness, blackness, murkiness, shadows, shade; dusk, twilight, gloaming. **2** *his gloom deepened* DESPONDENCY, depression, dejection, melancholy, melancholia, downheartedness, unhappiness, sadness, glumness, gloominess, misery, sorrow, woe, wretchedness; despair, pessimism, hopelessness; *informal* the blues, the dumps.
— OPPOSITES: light, happiness.

gloomy ▶ adjective **1** *a gloomy room* DARK, shadowy, sunless, dim, sombre, dingy, dismal, dreary, murky, unwelcoming, cheerless, comfortless, funereal; *literary* Stygian. **2** *Joanna looked gloomy* DESPONDENT, downcast, downhearted, dejected, dispirited, disheartened, discouraged, demoralized, crestfallen; depressed, desolate, low, sad, unhappy, glum, melancholy, miserable, woebegone, mournful, forlorn, morose; *informal* blue, down in the mouth, down in the dumps. **3** *gloomy forecasts about the economy* PESSIMISTIC, depressing, downbeat, disheartening, disappointing; unfavourable, bleak, bad, black, sombre, grim, cheerless, hopeless.
— OPPOSITES: bright, cheerful, optimistic.

glorify ▶ verb **1** *they gather to glorify their god* PRAISE, extol, exalt, worship, revere, reverence, venerate, pay homage to, honour, adore, thank, give thanks to; *formal* laud; *archaic* magnify. **2** *a poem to glorify the memory of the dead* ENNOBLE, exalt, elevate, dignify, enhance, augment, promote; praise, celebrate, honour, extol, lionize, acclaim, applaud, hail; glamorize, idealize, romanticize, enshrine, immortalize; *formal* laud.
— OPPOSITES: dishonour.

glorious ▶ adjective **1** *a glorious victory* ILLUSTRIOUS, celebrated, famous, acclaimed, distinguished, honoured; outstanding, great, magnificent, noble, triumphant. **2** *glorious views* WONDERFUL, marvellous, magnificent, superb, sublime, spectacular, lovely, fine, delightful; *informal* super, great, stunning, fantastic, terrific, tremendous, sensational, heavenly, divine, gorgeous, fabulous, fab, awesome, ace, killer; *literary* wondrous, beauteous.
— OPPOSITES: undistinguished, horrid.

glory ▶ noun **1** *a sport that won him glory* RENOWN, fame, prestige, honour, distinction, kudos, eminence, acclaim, praise; celebrity, recognition, reputation; *informal* bouquets. **2** *glory be to God* PRAISE, worship, adoration, veneration, honour, reverence, exaltation, homage, thanksgiving, thanks. **3** *a house restored to its former glory* MAGNIFICENCE, splendour, resplendence, grandeur, majesty, greatness, nobility; opulence, beauty, elegance. **4** *the glories of Vermont* WONDER, beauty, delight, marvel, phenomenon; sight, spectacle.
— OPPOSITES: shame, obscurity, modesty.
▶ verb *we gloried in our independence* TAKE PLEASURE IN, revel in, rejoice in, delight in; relish, savour; congratulate oneself on, be proud of, boast about, bask; *informal* get a kick out of, get a thrill out of, kvell.

gloss¹ ▶ noun **1** *the gloss of her hair* SHINE, sheen, lustre, gleam, patina, brilliance, shimmer. **2** *beneath the gloss of success* FACADE, veneer, surface, show, camouflage, disguise, mask, smokescreen; window dressing.
▶ verb **1** *she glossed her lips* MAKE GLOSSY, shine; glaze, polish, burnish. **2** *he tried to gloss over his problems* CONCEAL, cover up, hide, disguise, mask, veil; shrug off, brush aside, play down, minimize, understate, make light of; *informal* brush under the carpet.

gloss² ▶ noun *glosses in the margin* EXPLANATION, interpretation, exegesis, explication, elucidation; annotation, note, footnote, commentary, comment, rubric; translation, definition; *historical* scholium.
▶ verb *difficult words are glossed in a footnote* EXPLAIN, interpret, explicate, define, elucidate; annotate; translate, paraphrase.

glossy ▶ adjective **1** *a glossy wooden floor* SHINY, gleaming, lustrous, brilliant, shimmering, glistening, satiny, sheeny, smooth, glassy; polished, lacquered, glazed. **2** *a glossy magazine* EXPENSIVE, high-quality; stylish, fashionable, glamorous; attractive, artistic, upmarket, coffee-table; *informal* classy, ritzy, glitzy.
— OPPOSITES: dull, cheap.

glove ▶ noun MITTEN, mitt, gauntlet. *See table.*

Gloves and Mitts

buff	data glove
dogskin	surgical glove
deerskin	hockey gloves
kid	blocker
gauntlet	trapper
nipper ◆*(Atlantic)*	boxing gloves
oven mitt	baseball glove/mitt
garbage mitt ◆*(Man.)*	catcher's mitt

glow ▶ verb **1** *lights glowed from the windows* SHINE, radiate, gleam, glimmer, flicker, flare; luminesce. **2** *a fire glowed in the hearth* RADIATE HEAT, smoulder, burn. **3** *she glowed with embarrassment* FLUSH, blush, redden, colour (up), go pink, go scarlet; burn. **4** *she glowed with pride* TINGLE, thrill; beam.
▶ noun **1** *the glow of the fire* RADIANCE, light, shine, gleam, glimmer, incandescence, luminescence; warmth, heat. **2** *a glow spread over her face* FLUSH, blush, rosiness, pinkness, redness, high colour; bloom, radiance. **3** *a warm glow deep inside her* HAPPINESS, contentment, pleasure, satisfaction; *informal* warm fuzzy.
— OPPOSITES: pallor.

glower ▶ verb *she glowered at him* SCOWL, glare, look daggers, frown, lower, give a someone black look; *informal* give someone a dirty look.
▶ noun *the glower on his face* SCOWL, glare, frown, black look; *informal* dirty look.

glowing ▶ adjective **1** *glowing coals* BRIGHT, shining, radiant, glimmering, flickering, twinkling, incandescent, luminous, luminescent; lit (up), lighted, illuminated, ablaze; aglow, smouldering. **2** *his glowing cheeks* ROSY, pink, red, flushed, blushing; radiant, blooming, ruddy, florid; hot, burning. **3** *glowing colours* VIVID, vibrant, bright, brilliant, rich, intense, strong, radiant, warm. **4** *a glowing report* COMPLIMENTARY, favourable, enthusiastic, positive, commendatory, admiring, lionizing, rapturous, rhapsodic, adulatory; fulsome; *informal* rave.

glue ▶ noun *a tube of glue* ADHESIVE, fixative, gum, paste, cement; epoxy (resin), size, mucilage, stickum. ▶ verb **1** *the planks were glued together* STICK, gum, paste; affix, fix, cement, bond. **2** *(informal) she was glued to the television* BE RIVETED TO, be gripped by, be hypnotized by, be mesmerized by.

glum ▶ adjective GLOOMY, downcast, downhearted, dejected, despondent, crestfallen, disheartened; depressed, desolate, unhappy, doleful, melancholy, miserable, woebegone, mournful, forlorn, in the doldrums, morose; *informal* blue, down in the mouth, in a blue funk, down in the dumps.
— OPPOSITES: cheerful.

glut ▶ noun *a glut of cars* SURPLUS, excess, surfeit, superfluity, overabundance, superabundance, oversupply, plethora.
— OPPOSITES: dearth.
▶ verb *the factories are glutted* OVERLOAD, cram full, overfill, oversupply, saturate, flood, inundate, deluge, swamp, congest; *informal* stuff.

glutinous ▶ adjective STICKY, viscous, viscid, tacky, gluey, gummy, treacly; adhesive; *informal* gooey, cloggy, gloppy.

glutton ▶ noun GOURMAND, overeater, big eater, gorger, gobbler; *informal* (greedy) pig, guzzler.

gluttonous ▶ adjective GREEDY, gourmandizing, voracious, insatiable, wolfish; *informal* piggish, piggy.

gluttony ▶ noun GREED, greediness, overeating, gourmandism, gourmandizing, voracity, insatiability; *informal* piggishness.

gnarled ▶ adjective **1** *a gnarled tree trunk* KNOBBLY, knotty, knotted, gnarly, lumpy, bumpy, nodular; twisted, bent, crooked, distorted, contorted. **2** *gnarled hands* TWISTED, bent, misshapen; arthritic; rough, wrinkled, wizened.

gnash ▶ verb GRIND, grate, rasp, grit.

gnaw ▶ verb **1** *the dog gnawed at a bone* CHEW, champ, chomp, bite, munch, crunch; nibble, worry. **2** *the pressures are gnawing away their independence* ERODE, wear away, wear down, eat away (at); consume, devour. **3** *the doubts gnawed at her* NAG, plague, torment, torture, trouble, distress, worry, haunt, oppress, burden, hang over, bother, fret; niggle.

go ▶ verb **1** *he's gone into town* MOVE, proceed, make one's way, advance, progress, pass; walk, travel, journey; *literary* betake oneself. **2** *the road goes to Prince Rupert* EXTEND, stretch, reach; lead. **3** *the money will go to charity* BE GIVEN, be donated, be granted, be presented, be awarded; be devoted; be handed (over). **4** *it's time to go* LEAVE, depart, take oneself off, go away, withdraw, absent oneself, make an exit, exit; set off, start out, get underway, be on one's way; decamp, retreat, retire, make off, clear out, run off/away, flee, make a move; *informal* make tracks, push off, beat it, take off, skedaddle, scram, split, scoot. **5** *three years go by* PASS, elapse, slip by/past, roll by/past, tick away; fly by/past. **6** *a golden age that has gone for good* DISAPPEAR, vanish, be no more, be over, run its course, fade away;

finish, end, cease. **7** *all our money had gone* BE USED UP, be spent, be exhausted, be consumed, be drained, be depleted. **8** *I'd like to see my grandchildren before I go* DIE, pass away, pass on, lose one's life, expire, breathe one's last, perish, go to meet one's maker; *informal* give up the ghost, kick the bucket, croak, buy it, bite the big one, buy the farm, check out; *archaic* decease, depart this life. **9** *the bridge went suddenly* COLLAPSE, give way, fall down, cave in, crumble, disintegrate. **10** *his hair had gone grey* BECOME, get, turn, grow. **11** *he heard the bell go* MAKE A SOUND, sound, reverberate, resound; ring, chime, peal, toll, clang. **12** *everything went well* TURN OUT, work out, develop, come out; result, end (up); *informal* pan out. **13** *those colours don't go* MATCH, be harmonious, harmonize, blend, be suited, be complementary, coordinate, be compatible. **14** *my car won't go* FUNCTION, work, run, operate. **15** *where does the cutlery go?* BELONG, be kept. **16** *this all goes to prove my point* CONTRIBUTE, help, serve; incline, tend.
— OPPOSITES: arrive, come, return, clash.
▶ noun **1** *her second go* ATTEMPT, try, effort, bid, endeavour; *informal* shot, stab, crack, bash, whirl, whack; *formal* essay. **2** *he has plenty of go in him* ENERGY, vigour, vitality, life, liveliness, spirit, verve, enthusiasm, zest, vibrancy, sparkle; stamina, dynamism, drive, push, determination; *informal* pep, punch, oomph, get-up-and-go.
■ **go about** SET ABOUT, begin, embark on, start, commence, address oneself to, get down to, get to work on, get going on, undertake; approach, tackle, attack; *informal* get cracking on/with.
■ **go along with** AGREE TO/WITH, fall in with, comply with, co-operate with, acquiesce in, assent to, follow; submit to, yield to, defer to.
■ **go away.** See GO verb sense 4.
■ **go back on** RENEGE ON, break, fail to honour, default on, repudiate, retract; do an about-face; *informal* cop out (of), rat on.
■ **go by** *we have to go by his decision* OBEY, abide by, comply with, keep to, conform to, follow, heed, defer to, respect.
■ **go down 1** *the ship went down* SINK, founder, go under. **2** *interest rates are going down* DECREASE, get lower, fall, drop, decline; plummet, plunge, slump. **3** *(informal) they went down in the first round* LOSE, be beaten, be defeated, come to grief. **4** *his name will go down in history* BE REMEMBERED, be recorded, be commemorated, be immortalized.
■ **go far** BE SUCCESSFUL, succeed, be a success, do well, get on, get somewhere, get ahead, make good; *informal* make a name for oneself, set the world, make one's mark.
■ **go for 1** *I went for the tuna* CHOOSE, pick, opt for, select, decide on, settle on. **2** *the dog went for her* ATTACK, assault, hit, strike, beat up, assail, set upon, rush at, lash out at; *informal* lay into, rough up, have a go at, beat up on. **3** *she goes for younger men* BE ATTRACTED TO, like, fancy; prefer, favour, choose; *informal* have a thing about.
■ **go in for** TAKE PART IN, participate in, engage in, get involved in, join in, enter into, undertake; practise, pursue; espouse, adopt, embrace.
■ **go into** INVESTIGATE, examine, inquire into, look into, research, probe, explore, delve into; consider, review, analyze.
■ **go off 1** *the bomb went off* EXPLODE, detonate, blow up. **2** *the milk's gone off* GO BAD, go stale, go sour, turn, spoil, go rancid; decompose, go mouldy.
■ **go on 1** *the lecture went on for hours* LAST, continue, carry on, run on, proceed; endure, persist; take. **2** *she*

Gods & Goddesses

Greek	Hypnos	Roman	Scandinavian	Egyptian
Aeolus	Iris	Aesculapius	Aegir	Amun/Ammon
Amphitrite	Momus	Aurora	the Aesir	Anubis
Aphrodite	Nemesis	Bellona	Asgard	Apis
Apollo (Phoebus)	Nereus	Ceres	Balder	Bastet
Ares	Oceanus	Cupid	Frey	Bes
Artemis	Orpheus	Diana	Freya	Hathor
Asclepius	Pan	Faunus	Frigga	Horus
Athena	Paris	Flora	Hel	Isis
Cronus	Persephone	Fortuna	Loki	Khonsu
Demeter	Phaethon	Juno	the Norns	Maat
Dionysus	Philemon	Jupiter	Odin	Mut
Eos	Pluto	Luna	Thor	Nut
Eros	Poseidon	Maia	Tyr	Osiris
Gaia	Priapus	Mars	the Vanir	Ptah
Hebe	Proteus	Mercury		Ra
Hecate	Selene	Minerva	**Middle Eastern**	Sekhmet
Helios	Serapis	Mithras	Assur	Seth
Hephaestus	Tartarus	Morpheus	Astarte	Thoth
Hera	Tethys	Neptune	Ishtar	
Hermes	Themis	Orcus	Marduk	
Hestia	Tyche	Saturn	Tammuz	
Hygeia	Uranus	Venus	Tiamat	
Hymen	Victory	Vesta	Baal	
	Zeus	Vulcan		

went on about the sea TALK AT LENGTH, ramble, rattle on, chatter, prattle, gabble, blether, blather, twitter; *informal* gab, yak, yabber, yatter, natter, waffle, run off at the mouth, mouth off. **3** *I'm not sure what went on* HAPPEN, take place, occur, transpire, go down; *literary* come to pass, betide.

■ **go out 1** *the lights went out* BE TURNED OFF, be extinguished; stop burning. **2** *he's going out with Kate* SEE, date, take out, be someone's boyfriend/girlfriend, be involved with, go with, court, woo, go steady with.

■ **go over 1** *go over the figures* EXAMINE, study, scrutinize, inspect, look at/over, scan, check; analyze, appraise, review. **2** *we are going over our lines* REHEARSE, practise, read through, run through.

■ **go round 1** *the wheels were going round* SPIN, revolve, turn, rotate, whirl. **2** *a nasty rumour going round* BE SPREAD, be circulated, be put about, circulate, pass round, be broadcast.

■ **go through 1** *the terrible things she has gone through* UNDERGO, experience, face, suffer, be subjected to, live through, endure, brave, bear, tolerate, withstand, put up with, weather. **2** *she went through hundreds of dollars* SPEND, use up, run through, get through, expend, deplete, burn up; waste, squander, fritter away. **3** *she went through Sue's bag* SEARCH, look, hunt, rummage, rifle; *informal* frisk. **4** *I have to go through the report* EXAMINE, study, scrutinize, inspect, look over, scan, check; analyze, appraise, review. **5** *the deal has gone through* BE COMPLETED, be concluded, be brought off; be approved, be signed, be rubber-stamped, be given the green light.

■ **go under** GO BANKRUPT, cease trading, go into receivership, go into liquidation, become insolvent, be liquidated, be wound up, be shut (down); fail; *informal* go broke, go belly up, fold.

■ **go without 1** *I went without breakfast* ABSTAIN FROM, refrain from, forgo, do without, deny oneself. **2** *the children did not go without* BE DEPRIVED, be in want, go short, go hungry, be in need.

goad ▶ **noun 1** *he applied his goad to the cows* PROD, spike, staff, crook, rod. **2** *a goad to political change* STIMULUS, incentive, encouragement, inducement, fillip, spur, prod, prompt, catalyst; motive, motivation.
▶ **verb** *we were goaded into action* PROVOKE, spur, prod, egg on, hound, badger, incite, rouse, stir, move, stimulate, motivate, prompt, induce, encourage, urge, inspire; impel, pressure, dragoon.

go-ahead (*informal*) ▶ **noun** *they gave the go-ahead for the scheme* PERMISSION, consent, leave, licence, dispensation, warrant, clearance; authorization, assent, agreement, approval, endorsement, sanction, blessing, the nod; *informal* the thumbs up, the OK, the green light.
▶ **adjective** *go-ahead companies* ENTERPRISING, resourceful, innovative, ingenious, original, creative; progressive, pioneering, modern, forward-looking, enlightened; enthusiastic, ambitious, entrepreneurial, high-powered; bold, daring, audacious, adventurous, dynamic; *informal* go-getting.

goal ▶ **noun** OBJECTIVE, aim, end, target, design, intention, intent, plan, purpose; (holy) grail; ambition, aspiration, wish, dream, brass ring, desire, hope.

goaltender ▶ **noun** GOALKEEPER, goalie, netminder, backstop.

goat ▶ **noun 1** *a herd of goats* billy (goat), nanny (goat), kid. **2** *be careful of that old goat* LECHER, libertine, womanizer, seducer, Don Juan, Casanova, Lothario, Romeo; pervert, debauchee, rake; *informal* lech, dirty old man, lady-killer, wolf.
– RELATED TERMS: caprine.

gobble ▶ **verb** GUZZLE, bolt, gulp, devour, wolf, cram, gorge (oneself) on; *informal* tuck into, put away, demolish, polish off, shovel down, stuff one's face (with), pig out (on); *informal* scoff, scarf (down/up).

gobbledegook ▶ **noun** (*informal*) GIBBERISH, claptrap, nonsense, rubbish, balderdash, mumbo-jumbo, blather, blether, garbage; *informal* drivel, tripe, hogwash, baloney, bilge, bull, bunk, bafflegab, guff, eyewash, piffle, twaddle, poppycock, phooey, hooey, codswallop; bushwa.

go-between ▸ **noun** INTERMEDIARY, middleman, agent, broker, liaison, contact; negotiator, interceder, intercessor, mediator.

goblet ▸ **noun** WINE GLASS, chalice; glass, beaker, tumbler, cup.

goblin ▸ **noun** HOBGOBLIN, gnome, dwarf, troll, imp, elf, brownie, fairy, pixie, leprechaun.

god ▸ **noun 1** *a gift from God* THE LORD, the Almighty, the Creator, the Maker, the Godhead; Allah, Jehovah, Yahweh; (God) the Father, (God) the Son, the Holy Ghost/Spirit, the Holy Trinity; the Great Spirit, Gitchi Manitou; *humorous* the Man Upstairs. **2** *sacrifices to appease the gods* DEITY, goddess, divine being, celestial being, divinity, immortal, avatar. **3** *wooden gods* IDOL, graven image, icon, totem, talisman, fetish, juju.

godforsaken ▸ **adjective** WRETCHED, miserable, dreary, dismal, depressing, grim, cheerless, bleak, desolate, gloomy; deserted, neglected, isolated, remote, backward.
– OPPOSITES: charming.

godless ▸ **adjective 1** *a godless society* ATHEISTIC, unbelieving, agnostic, skeptical, heretical, faithless, irreligious, ungodly, unholy, impious, profane; infidel, heathen, idolatrous, pagan; satanic, devilish. **2** *godless pleasures* IMMORAL, wicked, sinful, wrong, evil, bad, iniquitous, corrupt; irreligious, sacrilegious, profane, blasphemous, impious; depraved, degenerate, debauched, perverted, decadent; impure.
– OPPOSITES: religious, virtuous.

godlike ▸ **adjective** DIVINE, godly, superhuman; angelic, seraphic; spiritual, heavenly, celestial; sacred, holy, saintly.

godly ▸ **adjective** RELIGIOUS, devout, pious, reverent, believing, God-fearing, saintly, holy, prayerful, spiritual, churchgoing.
– OPPOSITES: irreligious.

godsend ▸ **noun** BOON, blessing, bonus, plus, benefit, advantage, help, aid, asset; stroke of luck, windfall, manna (from heaven).
– OPPOSITES: curse.

go-getter ▸ **noun** ACHIEVER, high flyer, success story, high achiever, man/woman of action; bigwig, mover and shaker, wheeler-dealer, hustler.

goggle ▸ **verb** STARE, gape, gaze, ogle; *informal* gawk, rubberneck.

goings-on ▸ **plural noun** EVENTS, happenings, affairs, business; mischief, misbehaviour, misconduct, funny business; *informal* monkey business, hanky-panky, shenanigans.

gold ▸ **noun 1** *she won the gold* GOLD MEDAL, first prize. **2** *he struck gold* PAY DIRT, jackpot, bull's eye.
– RELATED TERMS: auric, aurous.

golden ▸ **adjective 1** *her golden hair* BLOND(E), yellow, fair, flaxen, tow-coloured. **2** *a golden time* SUCCESSFUL, prosperous, flourishing, thriving; favourable, providential, lucky, fortunate; happy, joyful, glorious. **3** *a golden opportunity* EXCELLENT, fine, superb, splendid; special, unique; favourable, opportune, promising, bright, full of promise; advantageous, profitable, valuable, providential. **4** *the golden girl of tennis* FAVOURITE, favoured, popular, admired, beloved, pet; acclaimed, applauded, praised; brilliant, consummate, gifted; *informal*

blue-eyed; *formal* lauded.
– OPPOSITES: dark, unhappy.

golf ▸ **noun**. *See table*.

Golf Terms

Scoring	On a Golf Course
ace	tee
hole-in-one	divot
double eagle	fairway
albatross	rough
eagle	green
birdie	dogleg
par	fringe
bogey	collar
double-bogey	apron
dormie	pin
halve	flag
handicap	flagstick
penalty	stick
match play	lip
stroke play	cup
bye	hole
	bunker
Shots	hazard
approach	sand trap
putt	water hazard
drive	trap
bisque	back nine
gimme	front nine
loft	turn
chip shot	gallery
pitch shot	leaderboard
cut	nineteenth hole
duff	green fee
fat	greenskeeper
flier	links
recovery	foursome
run-up	caddy
stroke	card
short game	golf bag
carry	golf ball
address	golf cart
backswing	
honour	**Types of Club**
waggle	brassie
mulligan	driver
draw	iron
fade	long iron
lag	short iron
hook	jigger
duck hook	putter
pull	sand wedge
shank	wedge
slice	wood
fore!	
	Related Activities
Ball Position	driving range
lie	miniature golf
pin-high	mini-putt ♣
stymie	minigolf
	snow golf

gone ▸ **adjective 1** *I wasn't gone long* AWAY, absent, off, out; missing, unavailable. **2** *those days are gone* PAST, over (and done with), no more, done, finished, ended; forgotten, dead and buried. **3** *the milk's all gone* USED UP, consumed, finished, spent, depleted; at an end. **4** *an aunt of mine, long since gone* DEAD, expired, departed, no more, passed on/away; late, lost, lamented; perished, fallen; defunct, extinct; *informal*

six feet under, pushing up daisies; *formal* deceased; *euphemistic* with God, asleep, at peace.
– OPPOSITES: present, here, alive.

goo ▸ noun (*informal*) STICKY SUBSTANCE, ooze, sludge, muck; *informal* gunk, crud, gloop, gunge, glop.

good ▸ adjective **1** *a good product* FINE, superior, quality; excellent, superb, outstanding, magnificent, exceptional, marvellous, wonderful, first-rate, first-class, sterling; satisfactory, acceptable, up to scratch, up to standard, not bad, all right; *informal* great, OK, A1, jake, hunky-dory, ace, terrific, fantastic, fabulous, fab, top-notch, blue-chip, blue-ribbon, bang-up, skookum, killer, class, awesome, wicked; smashing, brilliant. **2** *a good person* VIRTUOUS, righteous, upright, upstanding, moral, ethical, high-minded, principled; exemplary, law-abiding, irreproachable, blameless, guiltless, unimpeachable, honourable, scrupulous, reputable, decent, respectable, noble, trustworthy; meritorious, praiseworthy, admirable; whiter than white, saintly, saintlike, angelic; *informal* squeaky clean. **3** *the children are good at school* WELL-BEHAVED, obedient, dutiful, polite, courteous, respectful, deferential, compliant. **4** *a good thing to do* RIGHT, correct, proper, decorous, seemly; appropriate, fitting, apt, suitable; convenient, expedient, favourable, opportune, felicitous, timely. **5** *a good driver* CAPABLE, able, proficient, adept, adroit, accomplished, skilful, skilled, talented, masterly, virtuoso, expert; *informal* great, mean, wicked, nifty, ace, crackerjack. **6** *a good friend* CLOSE, intimate, dear, bosom, special, best, firm, valued, treasured; loving, devoted, loyal, faithful, constant, reliable, dependable, trustworthy, trusty, true, unfailing, staunch. **7** *the dogs are in good condition* HEALTHY, fine, sound, tip-top, hale and hearty, fit, robust, sturdy, strong, vigorous. **8** *a good time was had by all* ENJOYABLE, pleasant, agreeable, pleasurable, delightful, great, nice, lovely; amusing, diverting, jolly, merry, lively; *informal* super, fantastic, fabulous, fab, terrific, grand, brilliant, killer, peachy, ducky. **9** *it was good of you to come* KIND, kind-hearted, good-hearted, generous, charitable, magnanimous, gracious; altruistic, unselfish, selfless. **10** *a good time to call* CONVENIENT, suitable, appropriate, fitting, fit; opportune, timely, favourable, advantageous, expedient, felicitous, happy, providential. **11** *bananas are good for you* WHOLESOME, healthy, healthful, nourishing, nutritious, nutritional, beneficial, salubrious. **12** *are these eggs good?* EDIBLE, safe to eat, fit for human consumption; fresh, wholesome, consumable; *formal* comestible. **13** *good food* DELICIOUS, tasty, mouth-watering, appetizing, flavourful, delectable, toothsome, palatable; succulent, luscious; *informal* scrumptious, delish, yummy, lip-smacking, finger-licking, nummy, melt-in-your/the-mouth. **14** *a good reason* VALID, genuine, authentic, legitimate, sound, bona fide; convincing, persuasive, telling, potent, cogent, compelling. **15** *we waited a good hour* WHOLE, full, entire, complete, solid. **16** *a good number of them* CONSIDERABLE, sizeable, substantial, appreciable, significant; goodly, fair, reasonable; plentiful, abundant, great, large, generous; *informal* tidy. **17** *wear your good clothes* BEST, smart, smartest, finest, nicest; special, party, Sunday, formal, dressy. **18** *good weather* FINE, fair, dry; bright, clear, sunny, cloudless; calm, windless; warm, mild, balmy, clement, pleasant, nice.
– OPPOSITES: bad, wicked, naughty, poor, terrible, inconvenient, small, scruffy.

▸ noun **1** *issues of good and evil* VIRTUE, righteousness, goodness, morality, integrity, rectitude; honesty, truth, honour, probity; propriety, worthiness, merit; blamelessness, purity. **2** *it's all for your good* BENEFIT, advantage, profit, gain, interest, welfare, well-being; enjoyment, comfort, ease, convenience; help, aid, assistance, service; behalf.
– OPPOSITES: wickedness, disadvantage.

▸ exclamation *good, that's settled* FINE, very well, all right, right, right then, yes, agreed; *informal* okay, OK, okey-dokey, roger.

■ **for good** *those days are gone for good* FOREVER, permanently, for always, (for) evermore, for ever and ever, for eternity, never to return, forevermore; *informal* for keeps, until the cows come home, until hell freezes over; *archaic* for aye.

■ **make good** SUCCEED, be successful, be a success, do well, get ahead, reach the top; prosper, flourish, thrive; *informal* make it, make the grade, make a name for oneself, make one's mark, get somewhere, arrive.

■ **make something good 1** *he promised to make good any damage* REPAIR, mend, fix, put right, see to; restore, remedy, rectify. **2** *they made good their escape* EFFECT, conduct, perform, implement, execute, carry out; achieve, accomplish, succeed in, realize, attain, engineer, bring about, bring off. **3** *he will make good his promise* FULFILL, carry out, implement, discharge, honour, redeem; keep, observe, abide by, comply with, stick to, heed, follow, be bound by, live up to, stand by, adhere to.

goodbye ▸ exclamation FAREWELL, adieu, au revoir, ciao, adios; bye, bye-bye, so long, see you (later), later (skater), sayonara; bon voyage; cheers; *informal, dated* toodle-oo.
▸ noun PARTING, leave-taking, send-off.

good-for-nothing ▸ adjective *a good-for-nothing layabout* USELESS, worthless, incompetent, inefficient, inept, ne'er-do-well; lazy, idle, slothful, indolent, shiftless; *informal* no-good, lousy.
– OPPOSITES: worthy.
▸ noun *lazy good-for-nothings* NE'ER-DO-WELL, layabout, do-nothing, idler, loafer, lounger, sluggard, shirker, underachiever; *informal* slacker, lazybones, couch potato.

good-humoured ▸ adjective GENIAL, affable, cordial, friendly, amiable, easygoing, approachable, good-natured, cheerful, cheery; companionable, comradely, sociable, convivial; *informal* chummy, clubby.
– OPPOSITES: grumpy.

good-looking ▸ adjective ATTRACTIVE, beautiful, pretty, handsome, lovely, stunning, striking, arresting, gorgeous, prepossessing, fetching, captivating, bewitching, beguiling, engaging, charming, enchanting, appealing, delightful; sexy, seductive, alluring, tantalizing, irresistible, ravishing, desirable; *Scottish* bonny; *informal* hot, easy on the eye, drop-dead gorgeous, cute, foxy, bodacious; *literary* beauteous; *archaic* comely, fair.
– OPPOSITES: ugly.

goodly ▸ adjective LARGE, largish, sizeable, substantial, considerable, respectable, significant, decent, generous, handsome; *informal* tidy, serious.
– OPPOSITES: paltry.

good-natured ▸ adjective WARM-HEARTED, friendly, amiable; neighbourly, benevolent, kind, kind-hearted, generous, unselfish, considerate, thoughtful, obliging, helpful, supportive, charitable;

understanding, sympathetic, easygoing, accommodating.
— OPPOSITES: malicious.

goodness ▶ noun **1** *he had some goodness in him* VIRTUE, good, righteousness, morality, integrity, rectitude; honesty, truth, truthfulness, honour, probity; propriety, decency, respectability, nobility, worthiness, worth, merit, trustworthiness; blamelessness, purity. **2** *the neighbour's goodness towards us* KINDNESS, kindliness, tender-heartedness, humanity, mildness, benevolence, graciousness; tenderness, warmth, affection, love, goodwill; sympathy, compassion, care, concern, understanding, tolerance, generosity, charity, leniency, clemency, magnanimity. **3** *slow cooking retains the food's goodness* NUTRITIONAL VALUE, nutrients, wholesomeness, nourishment.

goods ▶ plural noun **1** *he dispatched the goods* MERCHANDISE, wares, stock, commodities, produce, products, articles; imports, exports. **2** *the dead woman's goods* PROPERTY, possessions, effects, chattels, valuables; *informal* things, stuff, junk, gear, kit, bits and pieces.

good-tempered ▶ adjective EQUABLE, even-tempered, imperturbable; unruffled, unflustered, untroubled, well-balanced; easygoing, mellow, mild, calm, relaxed, cool, at ease; placid, stable, level-headed; cheerful, upbeat; *informal* unflappable, laid-back.
— OPPOSITES: moody.

goodwill ▶ noun BENEVOLENCE, compassion, goodness, kindness, consideration, charity; co-operation, collaboration; friendliness, amity, thoughtfulness, decency, sympathy, understanding, neighbourliness.
— OPPOSITES: hostility.

goody-goody ▶ adjective *(informal)* SELF-RIGHTEOUS, sanctimonious, pious; prim and proper, straitlaced, prudish, priggish, puritanical, moralistic; *informal* square.

gooey ▶ adjective *(informal)* **1** *a gooey mess* STICKY, viscous, viscid; gluey, tacky, gummy, treacly, syrupy; *informal* icky, gloppy. **2** *a gooey movie* SENTIMENTAL, mawkish, cloying, sickly, saccharine, sugary, syrupy; romantic, twee; *informal* slushy, sloppy, mushy, schmaltzy, lovey-dovey, cheesy, corny, soppy; cornball, sappy.

goof ▶ verb BLUNDER, err, mess up, fluff, flub, slip up, make a mistake.
▶ noun FOOL, idiot, goofball, nitwit, turkey, noodle, dumbo. *See also* FOOL.
■ **goof off** MESS ABOUT, fool around, clown, act up, play the fool.

goose ▶ noun gander, gosling. *See table at* DUCK.

gore[1] ▶ noun *the book's gratuitous gore* BLOOD, bloodiness; bloodshed, slaughter, carnage, butchery.

gore[2] ▶ verb *he was gored by a bull* PIERCE, stab, stick, impale, spear, horn.

gorge ▶ noun *the river runs through a gorge* RAVINE, canyon, gully, defile, couloir; chasm, gulf; gulch, coulee.
▶ verb **1** *they gorged themselves on cakes* STUFF, cram, fill; glut, satiate, overindulge, overfill; *informal* pig out on. **2** *vultures gorged on the flesh* DEVOUR, guzzle, gobble, gulp (down), wolf; *informal* tuck into, demolish, polish off, scoff (down), down, stuff one's face (with); scarf (down/up).

gorgeous ▶ adjective **1** *a gorgeous woman* GOOD-LOOKING, attractive, beautiful, pretty, handsome, lovely, stunning, striking, arresting, prepossessing, fetching, captivating, bewitching, charming, enchanting, appealing, delightful; sexy, seductive, alluring, tantalizing, irresistible, ravishing, desirable; *Scottish* bonny; *informal* hot, easy on the eye, drop-dead gorgeous, cute, foxy, bodacious; *literary* beauteous; *archaic* comely, fair. **2** *a gorgeous view* SPECTACULAR, splendid, superb, wonderful, grand, impressive, awe-inspiring, awesome, amazing, stunning, breathtaking, incredible; *informal* sensational, fabulous, fantastic. **3** *gorgeous uniforms* RESPLENDENT, magnificent, sumptuous, luxurious, elegant, opulent; dazzling, brilliant.
— OPPOSITES: ugly, drab.

gory ▶ adjective **1** *a gory ritual slaughter* GRISLY, gruesome, violent, bloody, brutal, savage; ghastly, frightful, horrid, fearful, hideous, macabre, horrible, horrific; shocking, appalling, monstrous, unspeakable; *informal* blood-and-guts. **2** *gory pieces of flesh* BLOODY, bloodstained, bloodsoaked.

gospel ▶ noun **1** *the Gospel according to John* CHRISTIAN TEACHING, Christian doctrine, Christ's teaching; the word of God, the good news, the New Testament. **2** *don't treat this as gospel* THE TRUTH; fact, actual fact, reality, actuality, factuality, the case, a certainty. **3** *her gospel of non-violence* DOCTRINE, dogma, teaching, principle, ethic, creed, credo, ideology, ideal; belief, tenet, canon.

gossamer ▶ noun *her dress swirled like gossamer* COBWEBS; silk, gauze, chiffon.
▶ adjective *a gossamer veil* GAUZY, gossamery, fine, diaphanous, delicate, filmy, floaty, chiffony, cobwebby, wispy, thin, light, insubstantial, flimsy; translucent, transparent, see-through, sheer.

gossip ▶ noun **1** *tell me all the gossip* TITTLE-TATTLE, tattle, rumour(s), whispers, canards, tidbits; scandal, hearsay; *informal* chit, buzz, scuttlebutt; loose lips. **2** *she's such a gossip* SCANDALMONGER, gossipmonger, tattler, busybody, muckraker, flibbertigibbet.
▶ verb **1** *she gossiped about his wife* SPREAD RUMOURS, spread gossip, tittle-tattle, tattle, talk, whisper, tell tales; *informal* dish the dirt. **2** *people sat around gossiping* CHAT, talk, converse, speak to each other, discuss things; *informal* gas, chew the fat, jaw, yak, yap, natter, chinwag; shoot the breeze, shoot the bull; *formal* confabulate.

gouge ▶ verb SCOOP OUT, hollow out, excavate; cut (out), dig (out), scrape (out), scratch (out).

gourmand ▶ noun GLUTTON, overeater, big eater, gobbler, gorger; *informal* (greedy) pig, guzzler.

gourmet ▶ noun GASTRONOME, epicure, epicurean; connoisseur; *informal* foodie.

govern ▶ verb **1** *he governs the province* RULE, preside over, reign over, control, be in charge of, command, lead, dominate; run, head, administer, manage, regulate, oversee, supervise; *informal* be in the driver's seat. **2** *the rules governing social behaviour* DETERMINE, decide, control, regulate, direct, rule, dictate, shape; affect, influence, sway, act on, mould, modify, impact on.

governess ▶ noun TUTOR, duenna; teacher.

government ▶ noun **1** *the government announced cuts* ADMINISTRATION, executive, regime, authority, powers that be, directorate, council, leadership; cabinet, ministry, Ottawa; *informal* feds. **2** *her job was the government of the country* RULE, governing, running, leadership, control, administration, regulation, management, supervision.

governor ▸ noun LEADER, ruler, chief, head; *historical* intendant; premier, president, viceroy, chancellor; administrator, principal, director, chairperson, chair, superintendent, commissioner, controller; *informal* boss.

gown ▸ noun DRESS, frock, shift, robe.

grab ▸ verb **1** *Jessica grabbed his arm* SEIZE, grasp, snatch, take hold of, grip, clasp, clutch, glom on to; take. **2** (*informal*) *I'll grab another drink* OBTAIN, acquire, get; buy, purchase, procure, secure, snap up; gather, collect, garner; achieve, attain; *informal* get one's hands on, get one's mitts on, get hold of, bag, score, nab.
▸ noun *she made a grab for his gun* LUNGE, snatch.
■ **up for grabs** (*informal*) AVAILABLE, obtainable, to be had, for the taking; for sale, on the market; *informal* for the asking, on tap, gettable.

grace ▸ noun **1** *the grace of a ballerina* ELEGANCE, poise, gracefulness, finesse; suppleness, agility, nimbleness, light-footedness. **2** *he had the grace to look sheepish* COURTESY, decency, (good) manners, politeness, decorum, respect, tact. **3** *she fell from grace* FAVOUR, approval, approbation, acceptance, esteem, regard, respect; goodwill. **4** *he lived there by grace of the king* FAVOUR, goodwill, generosity, kindness, indulgence; *formal* benefaction. **5** *they have five days' grace to decide* DEFERMENT, deferral, postponement, suspension, adjournment, delay, pause; respite, stay, moratorium, reprieve. **6** *say grace* BLESSING, thanksgiving, benediction.
— OPPOSITES: inelegance, effrontery, disfavour.
▸ verb **1** *the occasion was graced by the president* DIGNIFY, distinguish, honour, favour; enhance, ennoble, glorify, elevate, aggrandize, upgrade. **2** *a mosaic graced the floor* ADORN, embellish, decorate, ornament, enhance; beautify, prettify, enrich, bedeck.

graceful ▸ adjective ELEGANT, fluid, fluent, natural, neat; agile, supple, nimble, light-footed.

graceless ▸ adjective GAUCHE, maladroit, inept, awkward, unsure, unpolished, unsophisticated, uncultured, unrefined; clumsy, ungainly, ungraceful, inelegant, uncoordinated, gawky, gangling, bumbling; tactless, thoughtless, inconsiderate; *informal* ham-handed, ham-fisted, klutzy.

gracious ▸ adjective **1** *a gracious hostess* COURTEOUS, polite, civil, chivalrous, well-mannered, mannerly, decorous; tactful, diplomatic; kind, benevolent, considerate, thoughtful, obliging, accommodating, indulgent, magnanimous; friendly, amiable, cordial, hospitable. **2** *gracious colonial buildings* ELEGANT, stylish, tasteful, graceful; comfortable, luxurious, sumptuous, opulent, grand, high-class; *informal* swanky, plush. **3** *God's gracious intervention* MERCIFUL, compassionate, kind; forgiving, lenient, clement, forbearing, humane, tender-hearted, sympathetic; indulgent, generous, magnanimous, benign, benevolent.
— OPPOSITES: rude, crude, cruel.

gradation ▸ noun **1** *a gradation of ability* RANGE, scale, spectrum, span; progression, hierarchy, ladder, pecking order. **2** *a number of gradations* LEVEL, grade, rank, position, status, stage, standard, echelon, rung, step, notch; class, stratum, group, grouping, set.

grade ▸ noun **1** *a higher grade of steel* CATEGORY, set, class, classification, grouping, group, bracket. **2** *his*

job is of the lowest grade RANK, level, echelon, standing, position, class, status, order; step, rung, stratum, tier. **3** *she got the best grades in the class* MARK, score; assessment, evaluation, appraisal. **4** *he's in grade 5* YEAR; class. **5** *a steep grade. See* GRADIENT.
▸ verb **1** *eggs are graded by size* CLASSIFY, class, categorize, bracket, sort, group, arrange, pigeonhole; rank, evaluate, rate, value. **2** *the essays have been graded* ASSESS, mark, score, judge, evaluate, appraise. **3** *the colours grade into one another* BLEND, shade, merge, pass.
■ **make the grade** (*informal*) QUALIFY, be up to scratch, be up to snuff, come up to standard, pass, pass muster, measure up; succeed, win through; cut it, cut the mustard.

gradient ▸ noun **1** *a steep gradient* SLOPE, incline, hill, rise, ramp, bank; declivity, grade. **2** *the gradient of the line* STEEPNESS, angle, slant, slope, inclination.

gradual ▸ adjective **1** *a gradual transition* SLOW, measured, unhurried, cautious; piecemeal, step-by-step, progressive, continuous, systematic, steady. **2** *a gradual slope* GENTLE, moderate, slight, easy.
— OPPOSITES: abrupt, steep.

gradually ▸ adverb SLOWLY, slowly but surely, cautiously, gently, gingerly; piecemeal, little by little, bit by bit, inch by inch, by degrees; progressively, systematically; regularly, steadily.

graduate ▸ verb **1** *he wants to teach when he graduates* pass one's exams, get one's degree, complete/finish one's studies. **2** *she wants to graduate to serious drama* PROGRESS, advance, move up. **3** *a thermometer graduated in Fahrenheit* CALIBRATE, mark off, measure out, grade.

graduation ▸ noun GRADUATION CEREMONY, commencement, convocation, grad ✦.

graffiti ▸ noun STREET ART, spray-painting, inscriptions, drawings; defacement, vandalism.

graft¹ ▸ noun **1** *grafts may die from lack of water* SCION, cutting, shoot, offshoot, bud, sprout, sprig. **2** *a skin graft* TRANSPLANT, implant.
▸ verb **1** *graft a bud onto the stem* AFFIX, join, insert, splice. **2** *tissue is grafted on to the cornea* TRANSPLANT, implant. **3** *a mansion grafted on to a farmhouse* ATTACH, add, join.

graft² ▸ noun *sweeping measures to curb official graft* CORRUPTION, bribery, dishonesty, deceit, fraud, unlawful practices, illegal means, payola; *informal* palm-greasing, hush money, kickbacks, crookedness, sharp practices.
— OPPOSITES: honesty.

grain ▸ noun **1** *the local farmers grow grain* CEREAL, cereal crops. *See table at* CEREAL. **2** *a grain of wheat* KERNEL, seed, grist. **3** *grains of sand* GRANULE, particle, speck, mote, mite; bit, piece; scrap, crumb, fragment, morsel. **4** *a grain of truth* TRACE, hint, tinge, suggestion, shadow; bit, soupçon; scintilla, ounce, iota, jot, whit, scrap, sheed; *informal* smidgen, smidge, tad. **5** *the grain of the timber* TEXTURE, surface, finish; weave, pattern.

grain elevator ▸ noun elevator, country elevator ✦, primary elevator, terminal elevator, prairie sentinel ✦, cathedral of the prairies.

grammar ▸ noun SYNTAX, sentence structure, rules of language, morphology; linguistics.

grammatical ▸ adjective **1** *the grammatical structure of a sentence* SYNTACTIC, morphological; linguistic. **2** *a* *grammatical sentence* WELL-FORMED, correct, proper; acceptable, allowable.

grand ▸ adjective **1** *a grand hotel* MAGNIFICENT, imposing, impressive, awe-inspiring, splendid, resplendent, majestic, monumental; palatial, stately, large; luxurious, sumptuous, lavish, opulent, upmarket, upscale; *informal* fancy, posh, plush, classy, swanky, five-star. **2** *a grand scheme* AMBITIOUS, bold, epic, big, extravagant. **3** *a grand old lady* AUGUST, distinguished, illustrious, eminent, esteemed, honoured, venerable, dignified, respectable; pre-eminent, prominent, notable, renowned, celebrated, famous; aristocratic, noble, regal, blue-blooded, high-born, patrician; *informal* upper-crust. **4** *a grand total of $2,000* COMPLETE, comprehensive, all-inclusive, inclusive; final. **5** *the grand staircase* MAIN, principal, central, prime; biggest, largest. **6** (*informal*) *you're doing a grand job* EXCELLENT, very good, marvellous, first-class, first-rate, wonderful, outstanding, sterling, fine, splendid, superb, terrific, fabulous, great, super, ace, killer; smashing, brilliant.
— OPPOSITES: inferior, humble, minor, poor.
▸ noun (*informal*) *a cheque for ten grand* THOUSAND DOLLARS; *informal* thou, K; G, gee.

grandeur ▸ noun SPLENDOUR, magnificence, impressiveness, glory, resplendence, majesty, greatness; stateliness, pomp, ceremony.

grandfather ▸ noun **1** *his grandfather lives here informal* grandad, grandpa, gramps, grampy, grandaddy, poppa, zeda, opa. **2** *the grandfather of modern liberalism* FOUNDER, inventor, originator, creator, initiator; father, founding father, pioneer. **3** *our pioneering grandfathers* FOREFATHER, forebear, ancestor, progenitor, antecedent.
▸ verb *some smokers have been grandfathered* EXEMPT, excuse, free, exclude, grant immunity, spare, absolve; *informal* let off (the hook).

grandiloquent ▸ adjective POMPOUS, bombastic, magniloquent, pretentious, ostentatious, high-flown, orotund, florid, flowery; overwrought, overblown, overdone; *informal* highfalutin, purple.
— OPPOSITES: understated.

grandiose ▸ adjective **1** *the court's grandiose facade* MAGNIFICENT, impressive, grand, imposing, awe-inspiring, splendid, resplendent, majestic, glorious, elaborate; palatial, stately, luxurious, opulent; *informal* plush, swanky, flash. **2** *a grandiose plan* AMBITIOUS, bold, over-ambitious, extravagant, high-flown, flamboyant; *informal* over the top.
— OPPOSITES: humble, modest.

grandmother ▸ noun *informal* grandma, granny, gran, nan, nana, gramma; baba, bubbe, oma.

granola ▸ noun CEREAL, trail mix, nuts and raisins, gorp.
▸ adjective HIPPIE, folkie, bohemian, flower-child, Birkenstocked, back-to-the-earth, tree-hugging, environmentalist, liberal.

grant ▸ verb **1** *he granted them leave of absence* ALLOW, accord, permit, afford, vouchsafe. **2** *he granted them $20,000* GIVE, award, bestow on, confer on, present with, provide with, endow with, supply with. **3** *I grant that the difference is not absolute* ADMIT, accept, concede, yield, allow, appreciate, recognize, acknowledge, confess; agree.
— OPPOSITES: refuse, deny.
▸ noun *a grant from the council* ENDOWMENT, subvention, award, donation, bursary, allowance, subsidy, contribution, handout, allocation, gift; scholarship.

granular ▸ adjective POWDER, powdered, powdery, grainy, granulated, gritty.

granulated ▸ adjective POWDERED, crushed, crumbled, ground, minced, grated, pulverized; particulate.

granule ▸ noun GRAIN, particle, fragment, bit, crumb, morsel, mote, speck.

graph ▸ noun *use graphs to analyze your data* CHART, diagram; histogram, bar chart, pie chart, scatter diagram.
▸ verb *we graphed the new prices* PLOT, trace, draw up, delineate.

graphic ▸ adjective **1** *a graphic representation of language* VISUAL, symbolic, pictorial, illustrative, diagrammatic; drawn, written. **2** *a graphic account* VIVID, explicit, expressive, detailed; uninhibited, powerful, colourful, rich, lurid, shocking; realistic, descriptive, illustrative; telling, effective.
— OPPOSITES: vague.
▸ noun (*Computing*) *this printer's good enough for graphics* PICTURE, illustration, image, (visual) art; diagram, graph, chart.

grapple ▸ verb **1** *the policemen grappled with him* WRESTLE, struggle, tussle; brawl, fight, scuffle, battle. **2** *he grappled his prey* SEIZE, grab, catch (hold of), take hold of, grasp. **3** *she is grappling with her problems* TACKLE, confront, face, deal with, cope with, come to grips with; apply oneself to, devote oneself to.

grasp ▸ verb **1** *she grasped his hands* GRIP, clutch, clasp, hold, clench; catch, seize, grab, snatch, latch on to. **2** *everybody grasped the important points* UNDERSTAND, comprehend, follow, take in, perceive, see, apprehend, assimilate, absorb; *informal* get, catch on to, figure out, get one's head around, take on board, twig. **3** *he grasped the opportunity* TAKE ADVANTAGE OF, act on; seize, leap at, snatch, jump at, pounce on.
— OPPOSITES: release, overlook.
▸ noun **1** *his grasp on her hand* GRIP, hold; clutch, clasp, clench. **2** *his domineering mother's grasp* CONTROL, power, clutches, command, domination, rule, tyranny. **3** *a prize lay within their grasp* REACH, scope, power, limits, range; sights. **4** *your grasp of history* UNDERSTANDING, comprehension, perception, apprehension, awareness, grip, knowledge; mastery, command.

grasping ▸ adjective AVARICIOUS, acquisitive, greedy, rapacious, mercenary, materialistic; mean, miserly, parsimonious, niggardly, hoarding, selfish, possessive, close; *informal* tight-fisted, tight, stingy, money-grubbing, cheap, grabby.

grass ▸ noun TURF, sod; lawn, green; prairie wool ♣.

grassroots ▸ adjective *a grassroots movement* POPULAR, bottom-up, non-hierarchical, rank-and-file.

grate ▸ verb **1** *she grated the cheese* SHRED, pulverize, mince, grind, granulate, crush, crumble. **2** *her bones grated together* GRIND, rub, rasp, scrape, jar, grit, creak. **3** *the tune grates slightly* IRRITATE, set someone's teeth on edge, jar; annoy, nettle, chafe, fret; *informal* aggravate, get on someone's nerves, get under someone's skin, get someone's goat.

grateful ▸ adjective *we were all grateful to Rita* THANKFUL, appreciative; indebted, obliged, obligated, in your debt, beholden.

gratification ▸ noun SATISFACTION, fulfillment, indulgence, relief, appeasement; pleasure, enjoyment, relish.

gratify ▸ verb **1** *it gratified him to be seen with her*

PLEASE, gladden, make happy, delight, make someone feel good, satisfy; *informal* tickle pink, give someone a kick, buck up. **2** *he gratified her desires* SATISFY, fulfill, indulge, comply with, pander to, cater to, give in to, satiate, feed, accommodate.
– OPPOSITES: displease, frustrate.

grating¹ ▶ adjective **1** *the chair made a grating noise* SCRAPING, scratching, grinding, rasping, jarring. **2** *a grating voice* HARSH, raucous, strident, piercing, shrill, screechy; discordant, cacophonous; hoarse, rough, gravelly. **3** *it's written in grating language* IRRITATING, annoying, infuriating, irksome, maddening, displeasing, tiresome; jarring, unsuitable, inappropriate; *informal* aggravating.
– OPPOSITES: harmonious, pleasing, appropriate.

grating² ▶ noun *a strong iron grating* GRID, grate, grille, lattice, trellis, mesh.

gratis ▶ adverb FREE (OF CHARGE), without charge, for nothing, at no cost, gratuitously; *informal* on the house, for free.

gratitude ▶ noun GRATEFULNESS, thankfulness, thanks, appreciation, indebtedness; recognition, acknowledgement, credit.

gratuitous ▶ adjective UNJUSTIFIED, uncalled for, unwarranted, unprovoked, undue; indefensible, unjustifiable; needless, unnecessary, inessential, unmerited, groundless, senseless, wanton, indiscriminate; excessive, immoderate, inordinate, inappropriate.
– OPPOSITES: necessary.

gratuity ▶ noun TIP, baksheesh, gift, present, donation, reward, handout; bonus, extra.

grave¹ ▶ noun *she left flowers at his grave* TOMB, gravesite, sepulchre, vault, burial chamber, mausoleum, crypt; last resting place.

grave² ▶ adjective **1** *a grave matter* SERIOUS, important, weighty, profound, significant, momentous; critical, acute, urgent, pressing; dire, terrible, awful, dreadful; *formal* exigent. **2** *Jackie looked grave* SOLEMN, serious, sober, unsmiling, grim, sombre; severe, stern, dour.
– OPPOSITES: trivial, cheerful.

gravel ▶ noun PEBBLES, stones, shingle, grit, aggregate.

gravelly ▶ adjective **1** *a gravelly beach* SHINGLY, pebbly, stony, gritty. **2** *his gravelly voice* HUSKY, gruff, throaty, deep, croaky, rasping, grating, harsh, rough.

gravestone ▶ noun HEADSTONE, tombstone, stone, monument, memorial.

graveyard ▶ noun CEMETERY, churchyard, burial ground, burying ground, necropolis, columbarium, memorial park/garden; *informal* boneyard; *historical* potter's field.

gravitas ▶ noun DIGNITY, seriousness, solemnity, gravity, sobriety; authority, weightiness.
– OPPOSITES: frivolity.

gravitate ▶ verb MOVE, head, drift, be drawn, be attracted; tend, lean, incline.

gravity ▶ noun **1** *the gravity of the situation* SERIOUSNESS, importance, significance, weight, consequence, magnitude; acuteness, urgency, exigence; awfulness, dreadfulness; *formal* moment. **2** *the gravity of his demeanour* SOLEMNITY, seriousness, sombreness, sobriety, soberness, severity, grimness, humourlessness, dourness; gloominess.

graze¹ ▶ verb *the deer grazed* FEED, eat, crop, nibble, browse.

graze² ▶ verb **1** *she grazed her knuckles on the box* SCRAPE, abrade, skin, scratch, chafe, bark, scuff, rasp; cut, nick. **2** *his shot grazed the far post* TOUCH, brush, shave, skim, kiss, scrape, clip, glance off.
▶ noun *grazes on the skin* SCRATCH, scrape, abrasion, cut; *Medicine* trauma.

grease ▶ noun **1** *engines covered in grease* OIL, lubricant, lubricator, lubrication. **2** *the kitchen was filmed with grease* FAT, oil, cooking oil, animal fat; lard, suet. **3** *his hair was smothered with grease* GEL, lotion, cream, brilliantine; *proprietary* Brylcreem.
▶ verb *grease a baking dish* LUBRICATE, oil, smear/coat/spray with oil, butter.

greasy ▶ adjective **1** *a greasy supper* FATTY, oily, buttery, oleaginous; *formal* pinguid. **2** *greasy hair* OILY. **3** *the pole was very greasy* SLIPPERY, slick, slimy, slithery, oily; *informal* slippy. **4** *a greasy little man* INGRATIATING, obsequious, sycophantic, fawning, toadying, grovelling; effusive, gushing, gushy; unctuous, oily; *informal* smarmy, slimy, bootlicking, sucky.
– OPPOSITES: lean, dry.

great ▶ adjective **1** *they showed great interest* CONSIDERABLE, substantial, significant, appreciable, special, serious; exceptional, extraordinary. **2** *a great expanse of water* LARGE, big, extensive, expansive, broad, wide, sizeable, ample; vast, immense, huge, enormous, massive; *informal* humongous, whopping, ginormous. **3** *you great fool!* ABSOLUTE, total, utter, out-and-out, downright, thoroughgoing, complete; perfect, positive, prize, sheer, arrant, unqualified, consummate, veritable. **4** *great writers* PROMINENT, eminent, important, distinguished, illustrious, celebrated, honoured, acclaimed, admired, esteemed, revered, renowned, notable, famous, famed, well-known; leading, top, major, principal, first-rate, matchless, peerless, star. **5** *the country is now a great power* POWERFUL, dominant, influential, strong, potent, formidable, redoubtable; leading, important, foremost, major, chief, principal. **6** *a great castle* MAGNIFICENT, imposing, impressive, awe-inspiring, grand, splendid, majestic, sumptuous, resplendent. **7** *a great sportsman* EXPERT, skilful, skilled, adept, accomplished, talented, fine, masterly, master, brilliant, virtuoso, marvellous, outstanding, first-class, superb; *informal* crack, ace, A1, class. **8** *a great fan of rugby* ENTHUSIASTIC, eager, keen, zealous, devoted, ardent, fanatical, passionate, dedicated, committed. **9** *we had a great time* ENJOYABLE, delightful, lovely, pleasant, congenial; exciting, thrilling; excellent, marvellous, wonderful, fine, splendid, very good; *informal* terrific, fantastic, fabulous, splendiferous, fab, super, grand, cool, hunky-dory, killer, swell.
– OPPOSITES: little, small, minor, modest, poor, unenthusiastic, bad.

greatly ▶ adverb VERY MUCH, considerably, substantially, appreciably, significantly, markedly, sizeably, seriously, materially, profoundly, enormously, vastly, immensely, tremendously, mightily, abundantly, extremely, exceedingly; *informal* plenty, majorly.
– OPPOSITES: slightly.

greatness ▶ noun **1** *a child destined for greatness* EMINENCE, distinction, illustriousness, repute, high standing; importance, significance; celebrity, fame, prominence, renown. **2** *her greatness as a writer* GENIUS, prowess, talent, expertise, mastery, artistry, virtuosity, skill, proficiency; flair, finesse; calibre, distinction.

greed, greediness ▸ noun **1** *human greed* AVARICE, cupidity, acquisitiveness, covetousness, rapacity; materialism, mercenariness; *informal* money-grubbing, affluenza. **2** *her mouth watered with greed* GLUTTONY, hunger, voracity, insatiability; gourmandism, intemperance, overeating, self-indulgence; *informal* piggishness. **3** *their greed for power* DESIRE, appetite, hunger, thirst, craving, longing, lust, yearning, hankering; avidity, eagerness; *informal* yen, itch.
— OPPOSITES: generosity, temperance, indifference.

greedy ▸ adjective **1** *a greedy eater* GLUTTONOUS, ravenous, voracious, intemperate, self-indulgent, insatiable, wolfish; *informal* piggish, piggy. **2** *a greedy capitalist* AVARICIOUS, acquisitive, covetous, grasping, materialistic, mercenary, possessive; *informal* money-grubbing, money-grabbing, grabby. **3** *she is greedy for an award* EAGER, avid, hungry, craving, longing, yearning, hankering; impatient, anxious; *informal* dying, itching.

green ▸ adjective **1** *a green scarf* viridescent; olive, jade, pea green, emerald, lime green, bottle green, sea green; *literary* virescent, glaucous. **2** *a green island* VERDANT, grassy, leafy, verdurous. **3** *he promotes Green issues* ENVIRONMENTAL, ecological, conservation, eco-. **4** *a green alternative to diesel* ENVIRONMENTALLY FRIENDLY, non-polluting, ecological; ozone-friendly. **5** *green bananas* UNRIPE, immature. **6** *green timber* UNSEASONED, not aged, unfinished; pliable, supple. **7** *the new lieutenant was very green* INEXPERIENCED, unversed, callow, immature; new, raw, unseasoned, untried; inexpert, untrained, unqualified, ignorant; simple, unsophisticated, unpolished; naive, innocent, ingenuous, credulous, gullible, unworldly; *informal* wet behind the ears, born yesterday. **8** *he went green* PALE, wan, pallid, ashen, ashen-faced, pasty, pasty-faced, grey, whitish, washed out, whey-faced, waxen, waxy, blanched, drained, pinched, sallow; sickly, nauseous, ill, sick, unhealthy.
— OPPOSITES: barren, dry, experienced, ruddy.
▸ noun **1** *a canopy of green over the road* FOLIAGE, greenery, plants, leaves, leafage, vegetation. **2** *a village green* PARK, common, grassy area, lawn, sward. **3** *eat your greens* VEGETABLES, leaf vegetables, salad; *informal* veg, veggies. **4** *Greens are against multinationals* ENVIRONMENTALIST, conservationist, preservationist, nature-lover, eco-activist; *informal* tree hugger, greenie.

greenery ▸ noun FOLIAGE, vegetation, plants, green, leaves, leafage, undergrowth, underbrush, plant life, flora, herbage, verdure.

greenhorn ▸ noun (*informal*). See NOVICE sense 1.

greenhouse ▸ noun HOTHOUSE, glasshouse, conservatory.

green light ▸ noun *he was given the green light to implement his proposals* AUTHORIZATION, permission, approval, assent, consent, sanction; leave, clearance, warranty, agreement, imprimatur, one's blessing, the seal/stamp of approval, the rubber stamp, the nod; authority, licence, dispensation, empowerment, freedom, liberty; *informal* the OK, the go-ahead, the thumbs up, the say-so.
— OPPOSITES: the red light, refusal.

greet ▸ verb **1** *she greeted Hank cheerily* SAY HELLO TO, address, salute, hail, halloo; welcome, meet, receive. **2** *the decision was greeted with outrage* RECEIVE, acknowledge, respond to, react to, take.

greeting ▸ noun **1** *he shouted a greeting* HELLO, salute, salutation, address; welcome; acknowledgement.

2 *birthday greetings* BEST WISHES, good wishes, congratulations, felicitations; compliments, regards, respects.
— OPPOSITES: farewell.

gregarious ▸ adjective **1** *he was fun-loving and gregarious* SOCIABLE, company-loving, convivial, companionable, outgoing, friendly, affable, amiable, genial, warm, comradely; *informal* chummy. **2** *gregarious fish* SOCIAL, living in groups.
— OPPOSITES: unsociable.

grey ▸ adjective **1** *a grey suit* silvery, silver-grey, gunmetal, slate, charcoal, smoky. **2** *his grey hair* WHITE, silver, hoary. **3** *a grey day* CLOUDY, overcast, dull, sunless, gloomy, dreary, dismal, sombre, bleak, murky. **4** *her face looked grey* ASHEN, wan, pale, pasty, pallid, colourless, bloodless, white, waxen; sickly, peaky, drained, drawn, deathly. **5** *the grey daily routine* CHARACTERLESS, colourless, nondescript, insipid, jejune, unremarkable, flat, bland, dry, stale; dull, uninteresting, boring, tedious, monotonous.
— OPPOSITES: sunny, ruddy, lively.
▸ verb *the population greyed* AGE, grow old, mature.

grid ▸ noun **1** *a metal grid* GRATING, mesh, grille, gauze, lattice. **2** *the grid of streets* NETWORK, matrix, reticulation.

grief ▸ noun **1** *he was overcome with grief* SORROW, misery, sadness, anguish, pain, distress, heartache, heartbreak, agony, torment, affliction, suffering, woe, desolation, dejection, despair; mourning, mournfulness, bereavement, lamentation; *literary* dolour, dole. **2** (*informal*) *the police gave me loads of grief* TROUBLE, annoyance, bother, irritation, vexation, harassment; *informal* aggravation, hassle.
— OPPOSITES: joy.
■ **come to grief** FAIL, meet with disaster, miscarry, go wrong, go awry, fall through, fall flat, founder, come to nothing, come to naught; *informal* come unstuck, come a cropper, flop.

grief-stricken ▸ adjective SORROWFUL, sorrowing, miserable, sad, heartbroken, broken-hearted, anguished, pained, distressed, tormented, suffering, woeful, doleful, desolate, despairing, devastated, upset, inconsolable, wretched; mourning, grieving, mournful, bereaved, lamenting; *literary* dolorous, heartsick.
— OPPOSITES: joyful.

grievance ▸ noun **1** *social and economic grievances* INJUSTICE, wrong, injury, ill, unfairness; affront, insult, indignity. **2** *students voiced their grievances* COMPLAINT, criticism, objection, grumble, grouse; ill feeling, bad feeling, resentment, bitterness, pique; *informal* gripe, whinge, moan, grouch, niggle, beef, bone to pick.

grieve ▸ verb **1** *she grieved for her father* MOURN, lament, sorrow, be sorrowful; cry, sob, weep, shed tears, keen, weep and wail, beat one's breast. **2** *it grieved me to leave her* SADDEN, upset, distress, pain, hurt, wound, break someone's heart, make someone's heart bleed.
— OPPOSITES: rejoice, please.

grievous (*formal*) ▸ adjective **1** *his death was a grievous blow* SERIOUS, severe, grave, bad, critical, dreadful, terrible, awful, crushing, calamitous; painful, agonizing, traumatic, wounding, damaging, injurious; sharp, acute. **2** *a grievous sin* HEINOUS, grave, deplorable, shocking, appalling, atrocious, gross, dreadful, egregious, iniquitous.
— OPPOSITES: slight, trivial.

grim ▸ adjective **1** *his grim expression* STERN,

forbidding, uninviting, unsmiling, dour, formidable, harsh, steely, flinty, stony; cross, churlish, surly, sour, ill-tempered; fierce, ferocious, threatening, menacing, implacable, ruthless, merciless. **2** *grim humour* BLACK, dark, mirthless, bleak, cynical. **3** *the asylum holds some grim secrets* DREADFUL, dire, ghastly, horrible, horrendous, horrid, terrible, awful, appalling, frightful, shocking, unspeakable, grisly, gruesome, hideous, macabre; depressing, distressing, upsetting, worrying, unpleasant. **4** *a grim little hovel* BLEAK, dreary, dismal, dingy, wretched, miserable, depressing, cheerless, comfortless, joyless, gloomy, uninviting; *informal* godawful. **5** *grim determination* RESOLUTE, determined, firm, decided, steadfast, dead set; obstinate, stubborn, obdurate, unyielding, intractable, uncompromising, unshakeable, unrelenting, relentless, dogged, tenacious.
– OPPOSITES: amiable, pleasant.

grimace ▶ **noun** *his mouth twisted into a grimace* SCOWL, frown, sneer; face.
▶ **verb** *Nina grimaced at Joe* SCOWL, frown, sneer, glower, lower; make a face, make faces, pull a face.
– OPPOSITES: smile.

grime ▶ **noun** *her skirt was smeared with grime* DIRT, filth, mud, mire, smut, soot, dust; *informal* muck, crud, gunge.
▶ **verb** *concrete grimed by diesel exhaust* BLACKEN, dirty, stain, soil; *literary* begrime, besmirch.

grimy ▶ **adjective** DIRTY, grubby, mucky, soiled, stained, smeared, filthy, smutty, sooty, dusty, muddy; *informal* yucky, cruddy, grotty; *literary* besmirched, begrimed.
– OPPOSITES: clean.

grin ▶ **verb** *Liam grinned at us* SMILE, smile broadly, beam, smile from ear to ear, grin like a Cheshire cat; smirk; *informal* be all smiles.
▶ **noun** *a silly grin* SMILE, broad smile; smirk.
– OPPOSITES: frown, scowl.

grind ▶ **verb** **1** *the sandstone is ground into powder* CRUSH, pound, pulverize, mill, granulate, crumble, smash, press; *technical* triturate, comminute. **2** *a knife being ground on a wheel* SHARPEN, whet, hone, file, strop; smooth, polish, sand, sandpaper. **3** *one tectonic plate grinds against another* RUB, grate, scrape, rasp.
▶ **noun** *the daily grind* DRUDGERY, toil, hard work, labour, donkey work, exertion, chores, slog; *informal* sweat; *literary* travail.
■ **grind away** LABOUR, toil, work hard, slave (away), work one's fingers to the bone, work like a dog; *informal* slog, plug away, beaver away; *literary* travail; *archaic* drudge.
■ **grind someone down** OPPRESS, crush, persecute, tyrannize, ill-treat, maltreat.

grip ▶ **verb** **1** *she gripped the edge of the table* GRASP, clutch, hold, clasp, take hold of, clench, grab, seize, cling to; squeeze, press, glom on to. **2** *Harry was gripped by a sneezing fit* AFFLICT, affect, take over, beset, rack, convulse. **3** *we were gripped by the drama* ENGROSS, enthrall, absorb, rivet, spellbind, hold spellbound, bewitch, fascinate, hold, mesmerize, enrapture; interest.
– OPPOSITES: release.
▶ **noun** **1** *a tight grip* GRASP, hold. **2** *the wheels lost their grip on the road* TRACTION, purchase, friction, adhesion, resistance. **3** *he was in the grip of an obsession* CONTROL, power, hold, stranglehold, chokehold, clutches, command, mastery, influence. **4** *I had a pretty good grip on the situation* UNDERSTANDING,

comprehension, grasp, perception, awareness, apprehension, conception; *formal* cognizance. **5** *a leather grip* TRAVELLING BAG, bag, overnight bag, flight bag, kit bag.
■ **come to grips with** DEAL WITH, cope with, handle, grasp, tackle, undertake, take on, grapple with, face, face up to, confront.

gripe (*informal*) ▶ **verb** *he's always griping about something* COMPLAIN, grumble, grouse, protest, whine, bleat; *informal* moan, bellyache, beef, bitch, whinge, kvetch.
▶ **noun** *employees' gripes* COMPLAINT, grumble, grouse, grievance, objection; cavil, quibble, niggle; *informal* moan, beef, whinge, kvetch.

gripping ▶ **adjective** ENGROSSING, enthralling, absorbing, riveting, captivating, spellbinding, bewitching, fascinating, compulsive, compelling, mesmerizing; thrilling, exciting, action-packed, dramatic, stimulating; *informal* unputdownable, page-turning.
– OPPOSITES: boring.

grisly ▶ **adjective** GRUESOME, ghastly, frightful, horrid, horrifying, fearful, hideous, macabre, spine-chilling, horrible, horrendous, grim, awful, dire, dreadful, terrible, horrific, shocking, appalling, abominable, loathsome, abhorrent, odious, monstrous, unspeakable, disgusting, repulsive, repugnant, revolting, repellent, sickening; *informal* gross.

gristly ▶ **adjective** STRINGY, sinewy, fibrous; tough, leathery, chewy.

grit ▶ **noun** **1** *the grit from the paths* SAND, dust, dirt; gravel, pebbles, stones, shingle. **2** *the true grit of a seasoned campaigner* COURAGE, bravery, pluck, mettle, backbone, spirit, strength of character, strength of will, moral fibre, steel, nerve, fortitude, toughness, hardiness, resolve, resolution, determination, tenacity, perseverance, endurance; *informal* guts, spunk.
▶ **verb** *Gina gritted her teeth* CLENCH, clamp together, shut tightly; grind, gnash.

gritty ▶ **adjective** **1** *a gritty floor* SANDY, gravelly, pebbly, stony; powdery, dusty. **2** *a gritty performance* COURAGEOUS, brave, plucky, mettlesome, stout-hearted, valiant, bold, spirited, intrepid, tough, determined, resolute, purposeful, dogged, tenacious; *informal* gutsy, spunky, feisty. **3** *a gritty look at urban life* REALISTIC, uncompromising, tough, true-to-life, unidealized, graphic, sordid.

grizzled ▶ **adjective** GREY, greying, silver, silvery, snowy, white, salt-and-pepper; grey-haired, hoary.

groan ▶ **verb** **1** *she groaned and rubbed her stomach* MOAN, whimper, cry, call out. **2** *they were groaning about the management* COMPLAIN, grumble, grouse; *informal* moan, niggle, beef, bellyache, bitch, gripe. **3** *the old wooden door groaned* CREAK, squeak; grate, rasp.
▶ **noun** **1** *a groan of anguish* MOAN, cry, whimper. **2** *their moans and groans* COMPLAINT, grumble, grouse, objection, protest, grievance; *informal* grouch, moan, beef, gripe. **3** *the groan of the elevator* CREAKING, creak, squeak, grating, grinding.

grocery store ▶ **noun** SUPERMARKET, convenience store, corner store, food store, market, groceteria, grocer, greengrocer.

groggy ▶ **adjective** DAZED, muzzy, stupefied, in a stupor, befuddled, fuddled, dizzy, disoriented, disorientated, punch-drunk, shaky, unsteady, wobbly, weak, faint; *informal* dopey, woozy, not with it.

groin ▶ noun CROTCH, genitals.
— RELATED TERMS: inguinal.

groom ▶ verb **1** *she groomed her pony* CURRY, brush, comb, clean, rub down. **2** *his dark hair was carefully groomed* BRUSH, comb, arrange, do; tidy, spruce up, smarten up, preen, primp; *informal* fix. **3** *they were groomed for stardom* PREPARE, prime, ready, condition, tailor; coach, train, instruct, drill, teach, school.
▶ noun **1** *a groom took his horse* STABLE HAND, stableman, stable lad, stable boy, stable girl; *historical* equerry. **2** *the bride and groom* BRIDEGROOM; newly-married man, newlywed.

groove ▶ noun FURROW, channel, trench, trough, canal, gouge, hollow, indentation, rut, gutter, cutting, cut, fissure; *Carpentry* rabbet.

grooved ▶ adjective FURROWED, fluted, corrugated, ribbed, ridged.

grope ▶ verb **1** *she groped for her glasses* FUMBLE, scrabble, fish, ferret, rummage, feel, search, hunt. **2** *(informal) one of the men started groping her* FONDLE, touch; *informal* paw, maul, feel up, touch up.

gross ▶ adjective **1** *the child was pale and gross* OBESE, corpulent, overweight, fat, big, large, fleshy, flabby, portly, bloated; *informal* porky, pudgy, tubby, blubbery, roly-poly. **2** *men of gross natures* BOORISH, coarse, vulgar, loutish, oafish, thuggish, brutish, philistine, uncouth, crass, common, unrefined, unsophisticated, uncultured, uncultivated; *informal* cloddish. **3** *(informal) the place smelled gross* DISGUSTING, repellent, repulsive, abhorrent, loathsome, foul, nasty, obnoxious, sickening, nauseating, stomach-churning, unpalatable; vomitous; *informal* yucky, icky, gut-churning. **4** *a gross distortion of the truth* FLAGRANT, blatant, glaring, obvious, overt, naked, barefaced, shameless, brazen, audacious, undisguised, unconcealed, patent, transparent, manifest, palpable; out and out, utter, complete. **5** *their gross income* TOTAL, whole, entire, complete, full, overall, combined, aggregate; before deductions, before tax, pre-tax.
— OPPOSITES: slender, refined, pleasant, net.
▶ verb *she grosses over a million dollars a year* EARN, make, bring in, take, get, receive, collect; *informal* rake in.

grotesque ▶ adjective **1** *a grotesque creature* MALFORMED, deformed, misshapen, misproportioned, distorted, twisted, gnarled, mangled, mutilated; ugly, unsightly, monstrous, hideous, freakish, unnatural, abnormal, strange, odd, peculiar; *informal* weird, freaky. **2** *grotesque mismanagement of funds* OUTRAGEOUS, monstrous, shocking, appalling, preposterous, ridiculous, ludicrous, farcical, unbelievable, incredible.
— OPPOSITES: normal.

grotto ▶ noun CAVE, cavern, hollow; pothole, underground chamber.

grouch ▶ noun *(informal) an ill-mannered grouch* GRUMBLER, complainer, moaner, curmudgeon; *informal* grump, sourpuss, whiner, sorehead, kvetch.
▶ verb *(informal) there's not a lot to grouch about* GRUMBLE, complain, grouse, whine, bleat, carp, cavil; *informal* moan, whinge, gripe, beef, bellyache, bitch, sound off, kvetch.

grouchy ▶ adjective GRUMPY, cross, irritable, bad-tempered, crotchety, crabby, crabbed, cantankerous, curmudgeonly, testy, tetchy, huffy, owly, snappish, waspish, prickly; *informal* snappy, cranky.

ground ▶ noun **1** *she collapsed on the ground* FLOOR, earth, terra firma; flooring; *informal* deck. **2** *the soggy ground* EARTH, soil, dirt, clay, loam, turf, clod, sod; land, terrain. **3** *the mansion's grounds* ESTATE, gardens, lawns, park, parkland, land, acres, property, surroundings, holding, territory; *archaic* demesne. **4** *grounds for dismissal* REASON, cause, basis, base, foundation, justification, rationale, argument, premise, occasion, excuse, pretext, motive, motivation. **5** *coffee grounds* SEDIMENT, precipitate, settlings, dregs, lees, deposit, residue.
▶ verb **1** *the boat grounded on a mud bank* RUN AGROUND, run ashore, beach, land. **2** *an assertion grounded on results of several studies* BASE, found, establish, root, build, construct, form. **3** *they were grounded in classics and history* INSTRUCT, coach, teach, tutor, educate, school, train, drill, prime, prepare; familiarize with, acquaint with.
■ **hold one's ground** STAND FIRM, stand fast, make a stand, stick to one's guns, dig in one's heels.
■ **gain ground** ADVANCE, progress, make headway; catch up, close in.

groundbreaking ▶ adjective See INNOVATIVE.

groundless ▶ adjective BASELESS, without basis, without foundation, ill-founded, unfounded, unsupported, uncorroborated, unproven, empty, idle, unsubstantiated, unwarranted, unjustified, unjustifiable, without cause, without reason, without justification, unreasonable, irrational, illogical, misguided.

groundswell ▶ noun UPSURGE, surge, rise, increase, escalation, outbreak, outburst, wave, upwelling.

groundwork ▶ noun PRELIMINARY WORK, preliminaries, preparations, spadework, legwork, donkey work; planning, arrangements, organization, homework; basics, essentials, fundamentals, underpinning, foundation.

group ▶ noun **1** *the exhibits were divided into three distinct groups* CATEGORY, class, classification, grouping, set, lot, batch, bracket, type, sort, kind, variety, family, species, genus, breed; grade, grading, rank, status. **2** *a group of tourists* CROWD, party, body, band, company, gathering, congregation, assembly, collection, cluster, flock, pack, troop, gang; *informal* bunch, pile. **3** *a coup attempt by a group within the parliament* FACTION, division, section, clique, coterie, circle, set, ring, camp, bloc, caucus, cabal, fringe movement, splinter group. **4** *the women's group* ASSOCIATION, club, society, league, guild, circle, union, sorority, fraternity. **5** *a small group of trees* CLUSTER, knot, collection, mass, clump. **6** *a local singing group* BAND, ensemble, act; *informal* lineup, combo, outfit.
▶ verb **1** *patients were grouped according to their symptoms* CATEGORIZE, classify, class, catalogue, sort, bracket, pigeonhole, grade, rate, rank; prioritize, triage. **2** *wooden chairs were grouped round the table* PLACE, arrange, assemble, organize, range, line up, dispose. **3** *the two parties grouped together* UNITE, join together/up, team up, gang up, join forces, get together, ally, form an alliance, affiliate, combine, marry, merge, pool resources; collaborate, work together, pull together, co-operate.

grouse ▶ verb *she groused about the food* GRUMBLE, complain, protest, whine, bleat, carp, cavil, make a fuss; *informal* moan, bellyache, gripe, beef, bitch, grouch, sound off, kvetch.
▶ noun *our biggest grouse was about the noise* GRUMBLE, complaint, grievance, objection, cavil, quibble; *informal* moan, beef, gripe, grouch.

grove ▶ noun COPSE, woods, wood, thicket, bush, stand, woodlot, (*Prairies*) bluff ✦, (*Atlantic*) droke ✦, coppice; orchard, plantation; *archaic* hurst, holt.

grovel ▶ verb **1** *George grovelled at his feet* PROSTRATE ONESELF, lie, kneel, cringe. **2** *she was not going to grovel to him* BE OBSEQUIOUS, fawn on, kowtow, bow and scrape, toady, truckle, abase oneself, humble oneself; curry favour with, flatter, dance attendance on, make up to, play up to, ingratiate oneself with; *informal* crawl, creep, suck up to, lick someone's boots.

grow ▶ verb **1** *the boys had grown* GET BIGGER, get taller, get larger, increase in size. **2** *sales and profits continue to grow* INCREASE, swell, multiply, snowball, mushroom, balloon, build up, mount up, pile up; *informal* skyrocket. **3** *flowers grew among the rocks* SPROUT, germinate, shoot up, spring up, develop, bud, burst forth, bloom, flourish, thrive, run riot, burgeon. **4** *he grew vegetables* CULTIVATE, produce, propagate, raise, rear, nurture, tend; farm. **5** *the family business grew* EXPAND, extend, develop, progress, make progress; flourish, thrive, burgeon, prosper, succeed, boom. **6** *the modern fable grew from an ancient myth* ORIGINATE, stem, spring, arise, emerge, issue; develop, evolve. **7** *Leonora grew bored* BECOME, get, turn, begin to feel.
— OPPOSITES: shrink, decline.

growl ▶ verb SNARL, bark, yap, bay.

grown-up ▶ noun *she wanted to be treated like a grown-up* ADULT, (grown) woman, (grown) man, mature woman, mature man.
— OPPOSITES: child.
▶ adjective *she has two grown-up daughters* ADULT, mature, of age; fully grown, full-grown, fully developed.

growth ▶ noun **1** *population growth* INCREASE, expansion, augmentation, proliferation, multiplication, enlargement, mushrooming, snowballing, rise, escalation, buildup. **2** *the growth of plants* DEVELOPMENT, maturation, growing, germination, sprouting; blooming. **3** *the marked growth of local enterprises* EXPANSION, extension, development, progress, advance, advancement, headway, spread; rise, success, boom, upturn, upswing. **4** *a growth on his jaw* TUMOUR, malignancy, cancer; lump, excrescence, outgrowth, swelling, nodule; cyst, polyp.
— OPPOSITES: decrease, decline.

grub ▶ noun **1** *a small black grub* LARVA; maggot; caterpillar. **2** (*informal*) *pub grub. See* FOOD sense 1.
▶ verb **1** *they grubbed up the old weeds* DIG UP, unearth, uproot, root up/out, pull up/out, tear out. **2** *he began grubbing about in the bin* RUMMAGE, search, hunt, delve, dig, scrabble, ferret, root, rifle, fish, poke.

grubby ▶ adjective DIRTY, grimy, filthy, mucky, unwashed, stained, soiled, smeared, spotted, muddy, dusty, sooty; unhygienic, unsanitary; *informal* cruddy, yucky, grotty; *literary* befouled, begrimed.
— OPPOSITES: clean.

grudge ▶ noun *a former employee with a grudge* GRIEVANCE, resentment, bitterness, rancour, pique, umbrage, dissatisfaction, disgruntlement, bad feelings, hard feelings, ill feelings, ill will, animosity, antipathy, antagonism, enmity, animus; *informal* a chip on one's shoulder.
▶ verb BEGRUDGE, resent, feel aggrieved about, be resentful of, mind, object to, take exception to, take umbrage at.

grudging ▶ adjective RELUCTANT, unwilling, forced, half-hearted, unenthusiastic, hesitant; begrudging, resentful.
— OPPOSITES: eager.

gruelling ▶ adjective EXHAUSTING, tiring, fatiguing, wearying, taxing, draining, debilitating; demanding, exacting, difficult, hard, arduous, strenuous, laborious, back-breaking, harsh, severe, stiff, stressful, punishing, crippling; *informal* killing, murderous, hellish.

gruesome ▶ adjective GRISLY, ghastly, frightful, horrid, horrifying, hideous, horrible, horrendous, grim, awful, dire, dreadful, terrible, horrific, shocking, appalling, disgusting, repulsive, repugnant, revolting, repellent, sickening; loathsome, abhorrent, odious, monstrous, unspeakable; *informal* sick, gross.
— OPPOSITES: pleasant.

gruff ▶ adjective **1** *a gruff reply | his gruff exterior* ABRUPT, brusque, curt, short, blunt, bluff, no-nonsense; laconic, taciturn; surly, churlish, grumpy, crotchety, curmudgeonly, crabby, crabbed, cross, bad-tempered, short-tempered, ill-natured, crusty, tetchy, bearish, ungracious, unceremonious; *informal* grouchy. **2** *a gruff voice* ROUGH, guttural, throaty, gravelly, husky, croaking, rasping, raspy, growly, hoarse, harsh; low, thick.
— OPPOSITES: friendly, soft.

grumble ▶ verb *they grumbled about the disruption* COMPLAIN, grouse, whine, mutter, bleat, carp, cavil, protest, make a fuss; *informal* moan, bellyache, beef, bitch, grouch, sound off, gripe, whinge, kvetch.
▶ noun *his customers' grumbles* COMPLAINT, grievance, protest, cavil, quibble, criticism, grouse; *informal* grouch, moan, beef, bitch, gripe.

grumpy ▶ adjective BAD-TEMPERED, crabby, ill-tempered, short-tempered, crotchety, tetchy, testy, waspish, prickly, touchy, irritable, irascible, crusty, cantankerous, curmudgeonly, bearish, surly, ill-natured, churlish, ill-humoured, peevish, cross, fractious, disagreeable, pettish; *informal* grouchy, snappy, snappish, shirty, cranky, ornery.
— OPPOSITES: good-humoured.

guarantee ▶ noun **1** *all repairs have a one-year guarantee* WARRANTY. **2** *a guarantee that the hospital will stay open* PROMISE, assurance, word (of honour), pledge, vow, oath, bond, commitment, covenant. **3** *banks usually demand a personal guarantee for loans* COLLATERAL, security, surety, guaranty, earnest.
▶ verb **1** *he agreed to guarantee the loan* UNDERWRITE, put up collateral for. **2** *can you guarantee he wasn't involved?* PROMISE, swear, swear to the fact, pledge, vow, undertake, give one's word, give an assurance, give an undertaking, take an oath.

guard ▶ verb **1** *infantry guarded the barricaded bridge* PROTECT, stand guard over, watch over, keep an eye on; cover, patrol, police, defend, shield, safeguard, keep safe, secure. **2** *the prisoners were guarded by armed men* KEEP UNDER SURVEILLANCE, keep under guard, keep watch over, mind. **3** *forest wardens must guard against poachers* BEWARE OF, keep watch for, be alert to, keep an eye out for, be on the alert/lookout for.
▶ noun **1** *border guards* SENTRY, sentinel, security guard, (night) watchman; protector, defender, guardian; lookout, watch; garrison. **2** *her prison guard* WARDER, warden, keeper; jailer; *informal* screw; *archaic* turnkey. **3** *he let his guard slip and they escaped* VIGILANCE, vigil, watch, surveillance, watchfulness, caution, heed, attention, care, wariness. **4** *a metal*

guard SAFETY GUARD, safety device, protective device, shield, screen, fender; bumper, buffer.

■ **off (one's) guard** UNPREPARED, unready, inattentive, unwary, with one's defences down, cold, unsuspecting; *informal* napping, asleep at the wheel.

■ **on one's guard** VIGILANT, alert, on the alert, wary, watchful, cautious, careful, heedful, chary, circumspect, on the lookout, on the qui vive, on one's toes, prepared, ready, wide awake, attentive, observant, keeping one's eyes peeled; *informal* keeping a weather eye out.

guarded ▶ adjective CAUTIOUS, careful, circumspect, wary, chary, on one's guard, reluctant, reticent, noncommittal, restrained, reserved; *informal* cagey.

guardian ▶ noun PROTECTOR, defender, preserver, custodian, warden, guard, keeper; conservator, curator, caretaker, steward, trustee.
— RELATED TERMS: tutelary.

guerrilla ▶ noun FREEDOM FIGHTER, irregular, member of the resistance, partisan; rebel, radical, revolutionary, revolutionist; terrorist.

guess ▶ verb **1** *he guessed she was about 40* ESTIMATE, hazard a guess, reckon, gauge, judge, calculate; hypothesize, postulate, predict, speculate, conjecture, surmise; *informal* guesstimate. **2** *(informal) I guess I owe you an apology* SUPPOSE, think, imagine, expect, suspect, dare say; *informal* reckon, figure.
▶ noun *my guess was right* HYPOTHESIS, theory, prediction, postulation, conjecture, surmise, estimate, belief, opinion, reckoning, judgment, supposition, speculation, suspicion, impression, feeling; *informal* guesstimate, shot in the dark.

guesswork ▶ noun GUESSING, conjecture, surmise, supposition, assumptions, presumptions, speculation, hypothesizing, theorizing, prediction; approximations, rough calculations; hunches; *informal* guesstimates.

guest ▶ noun **1** *I have two guests coming to dinner* VISITOR, house guest, caller; company; *archaic* visitant. **2** *hotel guests* PATRON, client, visitor, boarder, lodger, roomer.
— OPPOSITES: host.
▶ adjective *a guest speaker* INVITED, featured, special.

guest house ▶ noun BOARDING HOUSE, bed and breakfast, B&B, hotel; pension.

guff ▶ noun *(informal)*. See NONSENSE sense 1.

guffaw ▶ verb ROAR WITH LAUGHTER, laugh heartily/loudly, roar, bellow, cackle.

guidance ▶ noun **1** *she looked to her father for guidance* ADVICE, counsel, direction, instruction, enlightenment, information; recommendations, suggestions, tips, hints, pointers, guidelines. **2** *work continued under the guidance of a project supervisor* DIRECTION, control, leadership, management, supervision, superintendence, charge; handling, conduct, running, overseeing.

guide ▶ noun **1** *our guide took us back to the hotel* ESCORT, attendant, tour guide, docent, cicerone; usher, chaperone; *historical* dragoman. **2** *she is an inspiration and a guide* ADVISER, mentor, counsellor; guru. **3** *the light acted as a guide for shipping* POINTER, marker, indicator, signpost, mark, landmark; guiding light, sign, signal, beacon. **4** *the techniques outlined are meant as a guide* MODEL, pattern, blueprint, template, example, exemplar; standard, touchstone, measure, benchmark, yardstick, gauge. **5** *a pocket guide to the Cariboo*. See GUIDEBOOK.
▶ verb **1** *he guided her to her seat* LEAD, lead the way,

conduct, show, show someone the way, usher, shepherd, direct, steer, pilot, escort, accompany, attend; see, take, help, assist. **2** *the chairperson must guide the meeting* DIRECT, steer, control, manage, command, lead, conduct, run, be in charge of, have control of, pilot, govern, preside over, superintend, supervise, oversee; handle, regulate. **3** *he was always there to guide me* ADVISE, counsel, give advice to, direct, give direction to.

guidebook ▶ noun GUIDE, travel guide, travelogue, vade mecum; companion, handbook, directory; *informal* bible.

guideline ▶ noun RECOMMENDATION, instruction, direction, suggestion, advice; regulation, rule, principle, guiding principle; standard, criterion, measure, gauge, yardstick, benchmark, touchstone; procedure, parameter.

guild ▶ noun ASSOCIATION, society, union, league, organization, company, co-operative, fellowship, club, order, lodge, brotherhood, fraternity, sisterhood, sorority.

guile ▶ noun CUNNING, craftiness, craft, artfulness, art, artifice, wiliness, slyness, deviousness; wiles, ploys, schemes, stratagems, manoeuvres, tricks, subterfuges, ruses; deception, deceit, duplicity, underhandedness, double-dealing, trickery.
— OPPOSITES: honesty.

guileless ▶ adjective ARTLESS, ingenuous, naive, open, genuine, natural, simple, childlike, innocent, unsophisticated, unworldly, unsuspicious, trustful, trusting; honest, truthful, sincere, straightforward.
— OPPOSITES: scheming.

guilt ▶ noun **1** *the proof of his guilt* CULPABILITY, guiltiness, blameworthiness; wrongdoing, wrong, criminality, misconduct, sin. **2** *a terrible feeling of guilt* SELF-REPROACH, self-condemnation, shame, a guilty conscience, pangs of conscience; remorse, remorsefulness, regret, contrition, contriteness, compunction.
— OPPOSITES: innocence.

guiltless ▶ adjective INNOCENT, blameless, not to blame, without fault, above reproach, above suspicion, in the clear, unimpeachable, irreproachable, faultless, sinless, spotless, immaculate, unsullied, uncorrupted, undefiled, untainted, unblemished, untarnished, impeccable; *informal* squeaky clean, whiter than white, as pure as the driven snow.
— OPPOSITES: guilty.

guilty ▶ adjective **1** *the guilty party* CULPABLE, to blame, at fault, in the wrong, blameworthy, responsible; erring, errant, delinquent, offending, sinful, criminal; *archaic* peccant. **2** *I still feel guilty about it* ASHAMED, guilt-ridden, conscience-stricken, remorseful, sorry, contrite, repentant, penitent, regretful, rueful, abashed, shamefaced, sheepish, hangdog; in sackcloth and ashes.
— OPPOSITES: innocent, unrepentant.

guise ▶ noun **1** *the god appeared in the guise of a swan* LIKENESS, outward appearance, appearance, semblance, form, shape, image; disguise. **2** *additional sums paid under the guise of consultancy fees* PRETENSE, disguise, front, facade, cover, blind, screen, smokescreen.

gulf ▶ noun **1** *our ship sailed into the gulf* INLET, bay, bight, cove, fjord, estuary, sound. **2** *the ice gave way and a gulf widened slowly* HOLE, crevasse, fissure, cleft, split, rift, pit, cavity, chasm, abyss, void; ravine, gorge, canyon, gully. **3** *a growing gulf between rich and poor* DIVIDE, division, separation, gap, breach, rift, split, chasm, abyss; difference, contrast, polarity.

gull ▸ noun *See table.*

▸ **verb** HOODWINK, fool, dupe, deceive, delude, hoax, trick, mislead, lead on, take in, swindle, cheat, double-cross; *informal* pull the wool over someone's eyes, pull a fast one on, put one over on, bamboozle, con, sucker, snooker; *literary* cozen.

Seabirds & Penguins

Seabirds	murrelet
ancient murrelet	noddy ✦
Arctic tern	northern fulmar
Atlantic puffin	northern gannet
auk	parasitic jaeger
auklet	pelagic cormorant
baccalieu bird ✦	pelican
bawk ✦	petrel
black guillemot	pigeon guillemot
black tern	pomarine jaeger
black-footed albatross	prion
Bonaparte's gull	puffin
booby ✦	razorbill
bull bird ✦	ring-billed gull
Cassin's auklet	Ross's gull
common murre	Sabine's gull
cormorant	sea pigeon
crow duck	sea swallow
double-crested	seagull
cormorant	shag
dovekie	shearwater
Franklin's gull	skimmer
frigate bird	skua
fulmar	sooty shearwater
gannet	storm petrel
glaucous gull	tern
glaucous-winged gull	ticklace ✦
greater shearwater	tropic bird
guillemot	turr ✦
gull	white pelican
herring gull	
jaeger	**Penguins**
kittiwake	Adélie penguin
little auk	emperor penguin
Manx shearwater	gentoo
marbled murrelet	king penguin
mew gull	rockhopper
Mother Carey's chicken	*See also the tables at* DUCK
murre	*and* CRANE

gullet ▸ noun ESOPHAGUS, throat, maw, pharynx; crop, craw; *archaic* throttle, gorge.

gullible ▸ adjective CREDULOUS, naive, over-trusting, over-trustful, easily deceived, easily taken in, exploitable, dupable, impressionable, unsuspecting, unsuspicious, unwary, ingenuous, innocent, inexperienced, unworldly, green; *informal* wet behind the ears, born yesterday.
— OPPOSITES: suspicious.

gully ▸ noun **1** *a steep icy gully* RAVINE, canyon, gorge, pass, defile, couloir, gulch, coulee, draw. **2** *water runs from the drainpipe into a gully* CHANNEL, conduit, trench, ditch, drain, culvert, cut, gutter.

gulp ▸ verb **1** *she gulped her juice* SWALLOW, quaff, swill down, down; *informal* swig, (Nfld) glutch ✦, knock back, chug, chugalug. **2** *he gulped down the rest of his meal* GOBBLE, guzzle, devour, bolt, wolf, cram, stuff; *informal*

put away, demolish, polish off, shovel down, scoff. **3** *Lisa gulped back her tears* CHOKE BACK, fight back, hold back/in, suppress, stifle, smother.
— OPPOSITES: sip.

▸ **noun** *a gulp of cold beer* MOUTHFUL, swallow, draft, (Nfld) glutch ✦; *informal* swig.

gum ▸ noun *photographs stuck down with gum* GLUE, adhesive, fixative, paste, epoxy resin, mucilage.

▸ **verb** *the receipts were gummed into a book* STICK, glue, paste; fix, affix, attach, fasten.

■ **gum something up** CLOG (UP), choke (up), stop up, plug; obstruct; *informal* bung up, gunge up; *technical* occlude.

gummy ▸ adjective STICKY, tacky, gluey, adhesive, resinous, viscous, viscid, glutinous, mucilaginous; *informal* gooey.

gumption ▸ noun (*informal*) INITIATIVE, resourcefulness, enterprise, ingenuity, imagination; astuteness, shrewdness, acumen, sense, common sense, wit, mother wit, practicality; spirit, backbone, pluck, mettle, nerve, courage, wherewithal; *informal* get-up-and-go, spunk, oomph, moxie, savvy, horse sense, (street) smarts.

gun ▸ noun FIREARM, pistol, revolver, rifle, shotgun, carbine, automatic, handgun, semi-automatic, machine gun, Kalashnikov, Uzi; weapon; *informal* shooter, piece.

gunfire ▸ noun GUNSHOTS, shots, shooting, firing, sniping; artillery fire, strafing, shelling; tracer fire.

gunman ▸ noun ARMED ROBBER, gangster, terrorist; sniper, gunfighter; assassin, murderer, killer; *informal* hit man, hired gun, gunslinger, mobster, shootist, hood.

gurgle ▸ verb *the water swirled and gurgled* BABBLE, burble, tinkle, bubble, ripple, murmur, purl, splash; *literary* plash.

▸ **noun** *the gurgle of a small brook* BABBLING, tinkling, bubbling, rippling, trickling, murmur, murmuring, purling, splashing; *literary* plashing.

guru ▸ noun **1** *a Hindu guru and mystic* SPIRITUAL TEACHER, teacher, tutor, sage, mentor, spiritual leader, leader, master; *Hinduism* swami, maharishi. **2** *a management guru* EXPERT, authority, pundit, leading light, master, specialist; *informal* whiz.
— OPPOSITES: disciple.

gush ▸ verb **1** *water gushed through the weir* SURGE, burst, spout, spurt, jet, stream, rush, pour, spill, well out, cascade, flood; flow, run, issue. **2** *everyone gushed about the script* ENTHUSE, rave, be enthusiastic, be effusive, rhapsodize, go into raptures, wax lyrical, praise to the skies; *informal* go mad/wild/crazy.

▸ **noun** *a gush of water* SURGE, stream, spurt, jet, spout, outpouring, outflow, burst, rush, cascade, flood, torrent; *technical* efflux.

gushing, gushy ▸ adjective EFFUSIVE, enthusiastic, over-enthusiastic, unrestrained, extravagant, lavish, fulsome, rhapsodic, lyrical; *informal* over the top.
— OPPOSITES: restrained.

gust ▸ noun **1** *a sudden gust of wind* FLURRY, blast, puff, blow, rush; squall. **2** *gusts of laughter* OUTBURST, burst, eruption, fit, paroxysm; gale, peal, howl, hoot, shriek, roar.

▸ **verb** *wind gusted around the chimneys* BLOW, bluster, flurry, roar.

gusto ▸ noun ENTHUSIASM, relish, appetite, enjoyment, delight, glee, pleasure, satisfaction, appreciation, liking; zest, zeal, fervour, verve, keenness, avidity.

— OPPOSITES: apathy, distaste.

gusty ▸ adjective BLUSTERY, windy, breezy; squally, stormy, tempestuous, wild, turbulent; *informal* blowy.

— OPPOSITES: calm.

gut ▸ noun **1** *he had an ache in his gut* STOMACH, belly, abdomen, solar plexus; intestines, bowels; *informal* tummy, tum, insides, innards. **2** *fish heads and guts* ENTRAILS; intestines, viscera; offal, gurry; *informal* insides, innards. **3** (*informal*) *Nicola had the guts to say what she felt* COURAGE, bravery, backbone, nerve, pluck, spirit, boldness, audacity, daring, grit, fearlessness, feistiness, toughness, determination; *informal* spunk, moxie.

— RELATED TERMS: visceral, enteric.

▸ adjective (*informal*) *a gut feeling* INSTINCTIVE, instinctual, intuitive, deep-seated; knee-jerk, automatic, involuntary, spontaneous, unthinking, visceral.

▸ verb **1** *clean, scale, and gut the trout* REMOVE THE GUTS FROM, disembowel, draw; *formal* eviscerate. **2** *the church was gutted by fire* DEVASTATE, destroy, demolish, wipe out, lay waste, ravage, consume, ruin, wreck.

gutless ▸ adjective (*informal*). *See* COWARDLY.

gutsy ▸ adjective (*informal*) BRAVE, courageous, plucky, bold, daring, fearless, adventurous, audacious, valiant, intrepid, heroic, lion-hearted, undaunted, unflinching, unshrinking, unafraid, dauntless, indomitable, doughty, stout-hearted; spirited, determined, resolute; *informal* spunky, gutty, feisty, ballsy.

gutter ▸ noun DRAIN, sluice, sluiceway, culvert, spillway, sewer; channel, conduit, pipe; eavestrough ♣, rain gutter; trough, trench, ditch, furrow, cut.

guttural ▸ adjective THROATY, husky, gruff, gravelly, growly, growling, croaky, croaking, harsh, rough, rasping, raspy; deep, low, thick.

guy ▸ noun (*informal*) *he's a handsome guy* MAN, fellow, gentleman; youth, boy; *informal* lad, fella, (esp. *Atlantic*) buddy ♣, geezer, gent, dude, joe, Joe Blow, Joe Schmoe, hombre, schmo.

guzzle ▸ verb *she guzzled down the orange juice* GULP DOWN, swallow, quaff, down, swill; *informal* knock back, swig, slug.

gym ▸ noun **1** *she exercised at the local gym* GYMNASIUM, health club, fitness centre, recreation centre, rec centre, spa. **2** *gym was his least favourite class* PHYSICAL EDUCATION, phys. ed., gymnastics.

Gymnastic Events

balance beam	power tumbling
balls	rhythmic
clubs	ribbons
floor exercise	rings
hoops	sports aerobics
horizontal bar	trampoline
parallel bars	uneven bars
pommel horse	vault

gypsy, gipsy ▸ noun ROMANY, Rom, traveller, nomad, rover, roamer, wanderer.

gyrate ▸ verb ROTATE, revolve, wheel, turn round, whirl, circle, pirouette, twirl, swirl, spin, swivel.

Hh

habit ▶ noun **1** *it was his habit to go for a run every morning* CUSTOM, practice, routine, wont, pattern, convention, way, norm, tradition, matter of course, rule, usage. **2** *her many irritating habits* MANNERISM, way, quirk, foible, trick, trait, idiosyncrasy, peculiarity, singularity, oddity, eccentricity, feature; tendency, propensity, inclination, bent, proclivity, disposition, predisposition. **3** *a scientific habit of mind* DISPOSITION, temperament, character, nature, makeup, constitution, frame of mind, bent. **4** *his cocaine habit* ADDICTION, dependence, dependency, craving, fixation, compulsion, obsession, weakness; *informal* monkey on one's back, jones. **5** *a monk's habit* GARMENTS, dress, garb, clothes, clothing, attire, outfit, costume; *informal* gear; *formal* apparel.
■ **in the habit of** ACCUSTOMED TO, used to, given to, wont to, inclined to.

habitable ▶ adjective FIT TO LIVE IN, inhabitable, fit to occupy, in good repair, livable; *formal* tenantable.

habitat ▶ noun NATURAL ENVIRONMENT, natural surroundings, home, domain, haunt; *formal* habitation.

habitation ▶ noun **1** *a house fit for human habitation* OCCUPANCY, occupation, residence, residency, living in, tenancy. **2** *(formal) his main habitation* RESIDENCE, place of residence, house, home, seat, lodging place, billet, quarters, living quarters, rooms, accommodation; *informal* pad, digs; *formal* dwelling, dwelling place, abode, domicile.

habitual ▶ adjective **1** *her father's habitual complaints* CONSTANT, persistent, continual, continuous, perpetual, non-stop, recurrent, repeated, frequent; interminable, incessant, ceaseless, endless, never-ending; *informal* eternal. **2** *habitual drinkers* INVETERATE, confirmed, compulsive, obsessive, incorrigible, hardened, ingrained, dyed-in-the-wool, chronic, regular; addicted; *informal* pathological. **3** *his habitual secretiveness* CUSTOMARY, accustomed, regular, usual, normal, set, fixed, established, routine, common, ordinary, familiar, traditional, typical, general, characteristic, standard, time-honoured; *literary* wonted.
— OPPOSITES: occasional, unaccustomed.

habituate ▶ verb ACCUSTOM, make used, familiarize, adapt, adjust, attune, acclimatize, acculturate, condition; inure, harden; acclimate.

habitué ▶ noun FREQUENT VISITOR, regular visitor/customer/client, familiar face, regular, patron, frequenter, haunter.

hack¹ ▶ verb *the barbarian hacked off the soldier's arm* CUT, chop, hew, lop, saw; slash.
■ **hack it** *(informal)* COPE, manage, get on/by, carry on, come through, muddle along/through; stand it, tolerate it, bear it, endure it, put up with it; *informal* handle it, abide it, stick it out.

hack² ▶ noun **1** *a tabloid hack* JOURNALIST, reporter, newspaperman, newspaperwoman, writer; *informal* journo, scribbler, hackette; *archaic* penny-a-liner. **2** *office hacks* DRUDGE, menial, menial worker, joe-boy, factotum; *informal* gofer, bottle-washer.

hacker ▶ noun CRACKER, cyberpunk, black-hat, pirate, computer criminal, hacktivist.

hackle
■ **make someone's hackles rise** ANNOY, irritate, exasperate, anger, incense, infuriate, irk, nettle, vex, put out, provoke, gall, antagonize, get on someone's nerves, ruffle someone's feathers, rankle with; rub the wrong way; *informal* aggravate, peeve, needle, rile, make someone see red, make someone's blood boil, hack off, get someone's back up, get someone's goat, get someone's dander up, bug, wind up, tee off, tick off, burn up.

hackneyed ▶ adjective OVERUSED, overdone, overworked, worn out, time-worn, platitudinous, vapid, stale, tired, threadbare; trite, banal, hack, clichéd, hoary, commonplace, common, ordinary, stock, conventional, stereotyped, predictable; unimaginative, unoriginal, uninspired, prosaic, dull, boring, pedestrian, run-of-the-mill, boilerplate, routine; *informal* old hat, corny, played out.
— OPPOSITES: original.

Hades ▶ noun. *See* HELL *sense 1.*

haft ▶ noun HANDLE, shaft, hilt, butt, stock, grip, handgrip, helve, shank.

hag ▶ noun CRONE, old woman, gorgon; *informal* witch, crow, cow, old bag.

haggard ▶ adjective DRAWN, tired, exhausted, drained, careworn, unwell, unhealthy, spent, washed out, run-down; gaunt, pinched, peaked, peaky, hollow-cheeked, hollow-eyed, thin, emaciated, wasted, cadaverous; pale, wan, grey, ashen.
— OPPOSITES: healthy.

haggle ▶ verb BARTER, bargain, negotiate, dicker, quibble, wrangle; beat someone down, drive a hard bargain.

ha ha ▶ exclamation HEE HEE, har har, ho ho, tee-hee, hardy har har, yuk yuk.

hail¹ ▶ verb **1** *a friend hailed him from the upper deck* CALL OUT TO, shout to, halloo, address; greet, say hello to, salute. **2** *he hailed a cab* FLAG DOWN, wave down, signal to. **3** *critics hailed the film as a masterpiece* ACCLAIM, praise, applaud, rave about, extol, eulogize, hymn, lionize, sing the praises of, make much of, glorify, cheer, salute, toast, ballyhoo; *formal* laud. **4** *Rick hails from Australia* COME FROM, be from, be a native of, have one's roots in.

hail² ▶ noun *a hail of bullets* BARRAGE, volley, shower, rain, torrent, burst, stream, storm, avalanche, onslaught; bombardment, cannonade, battery, blast, salvo; *historical* broadside.
▶ verb *tons of dust hailed down on us* BEAT, shower, rain, fall, pour; pelt, pepper, batter, bombard, assail.

hair ▶ noun **1** *her thick black hair* LOCKS, curls, ringlets, mane, mop; shock of hair, head of hair; tresses. **2** *I like your hair* HAIRSTYLE, haircut, cut, coiffure; *informal* hairdo, do, coif. **3** *a dog with short, blue-grey hair* FUR, wool; coat, fleece, pelt; mane.
— RELATED TERMS: tricho-.
■ **a hair's breadth** THE NARROWEST OF MARGINS, a

narrow margin, the skin of one's teeth, a split second, a nose, a whisker.

■ **let one's hair down** (*informal*) ENJOY ONESELF, have a good time, have fun, make merry, let oneself go; *informal* have a ball, whoop it up, paint the town red, live it up, have a whale of a time, let it all hang out.

■ **make someone's hair stand on end** HORRIFY, shock, appall, scandalize, stun; make someone's blood run cold; *informal* make someone's hair curl.

■ **split hairs** QUIBBLE, cavil, carp, niggle, chop logic; *informal* nitpick; *archaic* pettifog.

hairdo ▸ noun (*informal*). See HAIRSTYLE.

hairdresser ▸ noun HAIRSTYLIST, stylist, coiffeur, coiffeuse; barber.

hairless ▸ adjective BALD, bald-headed; shaven, shaved, shorn, clean-shaven, beardless, smooth, smooth-faced, depilated; tonsured; *technical* glabrous; *archaic* bald-pated.
— OPPOSITES: hairy.

hairpiece ▸ noun WIG, toupée, periwig; *informal* rug.

hair-raising ▸ adjective TERRIFYING, frightening, petrifying, alarming, chilling, horrifying, shocking, spine-chilling, blood-curdling, bone-chilling, white-knuckle, fearsome, nightmarish; eerie, sinister, weird, ghostly, unearthly; eldritch; *informal* hairy, spooky, scary, creepy.

hair-splitting ▸ adjective PEDANTIC, pettifogging, quibbling, niggling, cavilling, carping, critical, overcritical, hypercritical; *informal* nitpicking, pernickety, persnickety, picky.

hairstyle ▸ noun HAIRCUT, cut, style, hair, coiffure; *informal* hairdo, do, coif. See table.

Hairstyles

Afro	hockey hair
beehive	marcel
big hair	Mohawk
blunt	mullet
bob	mushroom
body wave	pageboy
bouffant	perm
bowl cut	permanent wave
braids	pigtails
brush cut	pixie cut
bun	pompadour
buzz	ponytail
chignon	rat-tail
cornrows	razor cut
crewcut	ringlets
dreadlocks	shag
ducktail	shingle
feathered	tonsure
flat-top	updo
French braid	wet look
French twist	

hairy ▸ adjective **1** *animals with hairy coats* SHAGGY, bushy, long-haired; woolly, furry, fleecy, fuzzy; *Botany & Zoology* pilose. **2** *his hairy face* BEARDED, bewhiskered, moustachioed; unshaven, stubbly, bristly; *formal* hirsute. **3** (*informal*) *a hairy situation* RISKY, dangerous, perilous, hazardous, touch-and-go; tricky, ticklish, difficult, awkward; *informal* dicey, sticky.

halcyon ▸ adjective HAPPY, golden, idyllic, palmy, carefree, blissful, joyful, joyous, contented; flourishing, thriving, prosperous, successful; serene, calm, tranquil, peaceful.

hale ▸ adjective HEALTHY, fit, fighting fit, well, in good

health, bursting with health, in fine fettle, strong, robust, vigorous, hardy, sturdy, hearty, lusty, able-bodied; *informal* in the pink, as right as rain.
— OPPOSITES: unwell.

half ▸ adjective *a half grapefruit* HALVED, bisected, divided in two.
— OPPOSITES: whole.
▸ adverb **1** *half-cooked chicken* PARTIALLY, partly, incompletely, inadequately, insufficiently; in part, part, slightly. **2** *I'm half inclined to believe you* TO A CERTAIN EXTENT/DEGREE, to some extent/degree, (up) to a point, in part, partly, in some measure.
— OPPOSITES: fully.
▸ noun *the first half of the show* PORTION, section, part, period; 50 per cent.

half-baked ▸ adjective **1** *half-baked theories* ILL-CONCEIVED, hare-brained, cockamamie, ill-judged, impractical, unrealistic, unworkable, ridiculous, absurd; *informal* crazy, crackpot, cockeyed. **2** *her half-baked young nephew* FOOLISH, stupid, silly, idiotic, simple-minded, feeble-minded, empty-headed, feather-brained, feather-headed, brainless, witless, unintelligent, ignorant; *informal* dim, dopey, dumb, thick, halfwitted, dim-witted, birdbrained, dozy.
— OPPOSITES: sensible.

half-hearted ▸ adjective UNENTHUSIASTIC, cool, lukewarm, tepid, apathetic, indifferent, uninterested, unconcerned, languid, listless; perfunctory, cursory, superficial, desultory, feeble, lacklustre.
— OPPOSITES: enthusiastic.

halfway ▸ adjective *the halfway point* MIDWAY, middle, mid, central, centre, intermediate; *Anatomy* medial, mesial.
▸ adverb **1** *he stopped halfway down the passage* MIDWAY, in the middle, in the centre; part of the way, part-way. **2** *she seemed halfway friendly* TO SOME EXTENT/DEGREE, in some measure, relatively, comparatively, moderately, somewhat, (up) to a point; just about, almost, nearly.

■ **meet someone halfway** COMPROMISE, come to terms, reach an agreement, make a deal, make concessions, find the middle ground, strike a balance; give and take.

halfwit ▸ noun (*informal*). See FOOL noun sense 1.

halfwitted ▸ adjective (*informal*). See STUPID sense 1.

hall ▸ noun **1** *hang your coat in the hall* ENTRANCE HALL, hallway, entry, entrance, lobby, foyer, vestibule; atrium, concourse; passageway, passage, corridor, entryway. **2** *we booked a hall for the wedding* BANQUET HALL, community centre, assembly hall, community hall ✦, meeting room, chamber; auditorium, concert hall, theatre.

hallmark ▸ noun **1** *the hallmark on silver* ASSAY MARK, official mark, stamp of authenticity. **2** *the tiny bubbles are the hallmark of fine champagnes* MARK, distinctive feature, characteristic, sign, sure sign, telltale sign, badge, stamp, trademark, indication, indicator, calling card.

halloo ▸ verb CALL OUT, shout, cry out, yell, bawl, bellow, roar, whoop; hail, greet; *informal* holler, yoo-hoo.

hallowed ▸ adjective HOLY, sacred, consecrated, sanctified, blessed; revered, venerated, honoured, sacrosanct, worshipped, divine, inviolable.

hallucinate ▸ verb HAVE HALLUCINATIONS, see things, be delirious, fantasize; *informal* trip, see pink elephants.

hallucination ▶ noun DELUSION, illusion, figment of the imagination, vision, apparition, mirage, chimera, fantasy; (**hallucinations**) delirium, phantasmagoria; *informal* trip, pink elephants.

halo ▶ noun RING OF LIGHT, nimbus, aureole, glory, crown of light, corona; *technical* halation; *rare* gloriole.

halt ▶ verb **1** *Jen halted and turned around* STOP, come to a halt, come to a stop, come to a standstill; pull up, draw up. **2** *a further strike has halted production* STOP, bring to a stop, put a stop to, bring to an end, put an end to, terminate, wind up; suspend, break off, arrest; impede, check, curb, stem, staunch, block, stall, hold back; *informal* pull the plug on, put the kibosh on.
— OPPOSITES: start, continue.
▶ noun **1** *the car drew to a halt* STOP, standstill. **2** *a halt in production* STOPPAGE, stopping, discontinuation, break, suspension, pause, interval, interruption, hiatus; cessation, termination, close, end.

halter ▶ noun HARNESS, bridle, headstall.

halting ▶ adjective **1** *a halting conversation* | *halting English* HESITANT, faltering, hesitating, stumbling, stammering, stuttering; broken, imperfect. **2** *his halting gait* UNSTEADY, awkward, faltering, stumbling, limping, hobbling.
— OPPOSITES: fluent.

hamburger ▶ noun BURGER, beefburger, cheeseburger, chicken burger, banquet burger ✦, fishburger, hamburg, (Man. & NW Ont.) nip ✦, veggie burger, soya burger, tofu burger; patty.

ham-handed ▶ adjective CLUMSY, bungling, incompetent, amateurish, inept, unskilful, inexpert, maladroit, gauche, awkward, inefficient, bumbling, useless; *informal* ham-fisted, klutzy; all thumbs.
— OPPOSITES: expert.

hammer ▶ noun *a hammer and chisel* mallet, beetle, gavel, sledgehammer, jackhammer.
▶ verb **1** *the alloy is hammered into a circular shape* BEAT, forge, shape, form, mould, fashion, make. **2** *Sally hammered at the door* BATTER, pummel, beat, bang, pound; strike, hit, knock on, thump on; cudgel, bludgeon, club; *informal* bash, wallop, clobber, whack, thwack. **3** *they hammered away at their non-smoking campaign* WORK HARD, labour, slog away, plod away, grind away, slave away, work like a dog, put one's nose to the grindstone; persist with, persevere with, press on with; *informal* stick at, beaver away, plug away, work one's tail off, soldier on. **4** *anti-racism had been hammered into her* DRUM, instill, inculcate, knock, drive, din; drive home to, impress upon; ingrain. **5** (*informal*) *we've hammered them twice this season. See* TROUNCE.
■ **hammer something out** THRASH OUT, work out, agree on, sort out, decide on, bring about, effect, produce, broker, negotiate, reach an agreement on.

hamper[1] ▶ noun *a picnic hamper* BASKET, pannier, wickerwork basket; box, container, holder.

hamper[2] ▶ verb *the search was hampered by fog* HINDER, obstruct, impede, inhibit, retard, balk, thwart, foil, curb, delay, set back, slow down, hobble, hold up, interfere with; restrict, constrain, trammel, block, check, curtail, frustrate, cramp, bridle, handicap, cripple, hamstring, shackle, fetter; *informal* stymie, hog-tie, throw a wrench in the works of.
— OPPOSITES: help.

hamstring ▶ verb **1** *cattle were killed or hamstrung* CRIPPLE, lame, disable, incapacitate. **2** *he felt hamstrung by the regulations. See* HAMPER[2].

hand ▶ noun **1** *big, strong hands* palm, fist; *informal* paw, mitt, duke, hook, meathook. **2** *the clock's second hand* POINTER, indicator, needle, arrow, marker. **3** *the frontier posts remained in government hands* CONTROL, power, charge, authority; command, responsibility, guardianship, management, care, supervision, jurisdiction; possession, keeping, custody; clutches, grasp, thrall; disposal; *informal* say-so. **4** *let me give you a hand* HELP, a helping hand, assistance, aid, support, succour, relief; a good turn, a favour. **5** (*informal*) *her fans gave her a big hand* ROUND OF APPLAUSE, clap, handclap, ovation, standing ovation; applause, handclapping. **6** *a document written in his own hand* HANDWRITING, writing, script, calligraphy. **7** *a ranch hand* WORKER, workman, labourer, operative, hired hand, roustabout, peon; cowboy.
— RELATED TERMS: manual.
▶ verb PASS, give, reach, let someone have, throw, toss; present to; *informal* chuck.
■ **at hand 1** *keep the manual close at hand* READILY AVAILABLE, available, handy, to hand, within reach, accessible, close (by), near, nearby, at the ready, at one's fingertips, at one's disposal, convenient; *informal* get-at-able. **2** *the time for courage is at hand* IMMINENT, approaching, coming, about to happen, on the horizon; impending.
■ **hand something down** PASS ON, pass down; bequeath, will, leave, make over, give, gift, transfer; *Law* demise, devise.
■ **hand in glove** IN CLOSE COLLABORATION, in close association, in close co-operation, very closely, in partnership, in league, in collusion; *informal* in cahoots, in bed.
■ **hand something on** GIVE, pass, transfer, grant, cede, surrender, relinquish, yield; part with, let go of; bequeath, will, leave.
■ **hand something out** DISTRIBUTE, hand round, give out/round, pass out/round, share out, dole out, dish out, deal out, mete out, issue, dispense; allocate, allot, apportion, disburse; circulate, disseminate.
■ **hand something over** YIELD, give, give up, pass, grant, entrust, surrender, relinquish, cede, turn over, deliver up, forfeit, sacrifice.
■ **hands down** EASILY, effortlessly, with ease, with no trouble, without effort; *informal* by a mile, no sweat.
■ **to hand** *See* AT HAND sense 1.
■ **try one's hand** HAVE A GO, make an attempt, have a shot; attempt, try, try out, give something a try; *informal* have a stab, have a bash, give something a whirl; *formal* essay.

handbag ▶ noun PURSE, bag, shoulder bag, clutch purse, evening bag; pocketbook; *historical* reticule.

handbill ▶ noun NOTICE, advertisement, flyer, leaflet, circular, handout, pamphlet, brochure, fact sheet; *informal* ad.

handbook ▶ noun MANUAL, instructions, instruction manual, ABC, how-to guide; almanac, companion, directory, compendium; guide, guidebook, vade mecum.

handcuff ▶ verb MANACLE, shackle, fetter; restrain, clap/put someone in irons; *informal* cuff.

handcuffs ▶ plural noun MANACLES, shackles, irons, fetters, bonds, restraints; *informal* cuffs, bracelets.

handful ▶ noun **1** *a handful of bad apples* A FEW, a small number, a small amount, a small quantity, one or two, some, not many, a scattering, a trickle. **2** (*informal*) *the child is a real handful* NUISANCE, problem, bother, irritant, thorn in someone's flesh/side;

informal pest, headache, pain, pain in the neck/ backside, pain in the butt.

handgun ▸ noun PISTOL, revolver, gun, side arm, six-shooter, .38 special, derringer; *informal* piece, Saturday night special, rod; *proprietary* Colt.

handicap ▸ noun 1 *a visual handicap* DISABILITY, physical/mental abnormality, defect, impairment, affliction, deficiency, dysfunction. 2 *a handicap to the competitiveness of the industry* IMPEDIMENT, hindrance, obstacle, barrier, bar, obstruction, encumbrance, constraint, restriction, check, block, curb; disadvantage, drawback, stumbling block, difficulty, shortcoming, limitation; ball and chain, albatross, millstone round someone's neck, burden, liability; *literary* trammel.
— OPPOSITES: benefit, advantage.
▸ verb *lack of funding handicapped the research* HAMPER, impede, hinder, impair, hamstring; restrict, check, obstruct, block, curb, bridle, hold back, constrain, trammel, limit, encumber; *informal* stymie.
— OPPOSITES: help.

handicapped ▸ adjective DISABLED, incapacitated, disadvantaged, crippled; infirm, invalid; *euphemistic* physically challenged, differently abled.

handicraft ▸ noun CRAFT, handiwork, craftwork; craftsmanship, workmanship, artisanship, art, skill.

handiwork ▸ noun *jewellery which is the handiwork of Chinese smiths* CREATION, product, work, achievement; handicraft, craft, craftwork.

handkerchief ▸ noun HANKY, tissue; *proprietary* Kleenex; kerchief, bandanna.

handle ▸ verb 1 *the equipment must be handled with care* HOLD, pick up, grasp, grip, lift; feel, touch, finger; *informal* paw. 2 *a car which is easy to handle* CONTROL, drive, steer, operate, manoeuvre, manipulate. 3 *she handled the problems well* DEAL WITH, manage, tackle, take care of, take charge of, attend to, see to, sort out, apply oneself to, take in hand; respond to, field. 4 *the advertising company that is handling the account* ADMINISTER, manage, control, conduct, direct, guide, supervise, oversee, be in charge of, take care of, look after. 5 *the traders handled goods manufactured in the Rhineland* TRADE IN, deal in, buy, sell, supply, peddle, traffic in; purvey, hawk, tout, market.
▸ noun *the knife's handle* HAFT, shank, stock, shaft, grip, handgrip, hilt, helve, butt; knob.

hand-me-down ▸ adjective SECOND-HAND, used, nearly new, handed-down, passed-on, cast-off, worn, old, pre-owned, thrift-store.
— OPPOSITES: new.

handout ▸ noun 1 *she existed on handouts* CHARITY, aid, benefit, financial support, donations, subsidies, welfare, EI ✦, pogey ✦; *historical* alms. 2 *a photocopied handout* LEAFLET, pamphlet, brochure, fact sheet; handbill, flyer, notice, circular.

hand-picked ▸ adjective SPECIALLY CHOSEN, selected, invited; select, elite; choice.

handsome ▸ adjective 1 *a handsome man* GOOD-LOOKING, attractive, striking, gorgeous; *informal* hunky, drop-dead gorgeous, hot, cute. 2 *a handsome woman of 30* STRIKING, imposing, prepossessing, elegant, stately, dignified, statuesque, good-looking, attractive, personable. 3 *a handsome profit* SUBSTANTIAL, considerable, sizeable, princely, large, big, ample, bumper; *informal* tidy, whopping, not to be sneezed at, ginormous.
— OPPOSITES: ugly, meagre.

handwriting ▸ noun WRITING, script, hand, pen;

penmanship, calligraphy, chirography; *informal* scrawl, scribble, chicken scratch.

handy ▸ adjective 1 *a handy reference tool* USEFUL, convenient, practical, easy-to-use, well-designed, user-friendly, user-oriented, helpful, functional, serviceable. 2 *keep your credit card handy* READILY AVAILABLE, available, at hand, to hand, near at hand, within reach, accessible, ready, close (by), near, nearby, at the ready, at one's fingertips; *informal* get-at-able. 3 *he's handy with a needle* SKILFUL, skilled, dexterous, deft, nimble-fingered, adroit, able, adept, proficient, capable; good with one's hands; *informal* nifty.
— OPPOSITES: inconvenient, inept.

handyman ▸ noun BUILDER, odd-job man, odd-jobber, factotum, jack of all trades, do-it-yourselfer, Mr. Fix-it.

hang ▸ verb 1 *lights hung from the trees* BE SUSPENDED, dangle, hang down, be pendent, swing, sway. 2 *hang your pictures at eye level* PUT UP, fix, attach, affix, fasten, post, display, suspend, pin up, nail up. 3 *the room was hung with streamers* DECORATE, adorn, drape, festoon, deck out, trick out, bedeck, array, garland, swathe, cover, ornament; *literary* bedizen. 4 *he was hanged for murder* STRING UP, send to the gallows. 5 *a pall of smoke hung over the city* HOVER, float, drift, be suspended. 6 *the threat of budget cuts is hanging over us* BE IMMINENT, threaten, be close, be impending, impend, loom, be on the horizon.
■ **hang around/round** (*informal*) 1 *they spent their time hanging around in bars* LOITER, linger, wait around, waste time, kill time, mark time, while away the/ one's time, kick/cool one's heels, twiddle one's thumbs; frequent, be a regular visitor to, haunt; *informal* hang out in. 2 *she's hanging around with a gang of marketing types* ASSOCIATE, mix, keep company, socialize, fraternize, consort, rub elbows; *informal* hang out, run around, knock about/around, be thick, hobnob.
■ **hang on** 1 *he hung on to her coat* HOLD ON, hold fast, grip, clutch, grasp, hold tightly, cling, glom on. 2 *her future hung on their decision* DEPEND ON, be dependent on, turn on, hinge on, rest on, be contingent on, be determined by, be decided by. 3 *I'll hang on as long as I can* PERSEVERE, hold out, hold on, go on, carry on, keep on, keep going, keep at it, continue, persist, stay with it, struggle on, plod on; *informal* soldier on, stick at it, stick it out, hang in there. 4 (*informal*) *hang on, let me think* WAIT, wait a minute, hold on, stop; hold the line; *informal* hold your horses, sit tight.

hangdog ▸ adjective SHAMEFACED, sheepish, abashed, ashamed, guilty-looking, abject, cowed, dejected, downcast, crestfallen, woebegone, disconsolate.
— OPPOSITES: unabashed.

hanger-on ▸ noun FOLLOWER, flunky, toady, camp follower, sycophant, parasite, leech, bottom-feeder; henchman, minion, lackey, vassal, dependant, retainer; acolyte; cohort; *informal* groupie, sponger, freeloader, passenger, sidekick.

hanging ▸ noun *silk wall hangings* DRAPE, curtain; drapery; tapestry; textile art.
▸ adjective *hanging fronds of honeysuckle* PENDENT, dangling, trailing, tumbling; suspended.

hangout ▸ noun HAUNT, favourite spot, meeting place, territory; den, refuge, retreat, stomping ground, home away from home.

hang-up ▸ noun NEUROSIS, phobia, preoccupation, fixation, obsession, idée fixe; inhibition, mental block, psychological block, block, difficulty; *informal* complex, thing, bee in one's bonnet.

hank ▶ noun COIL, skein, length, roll, loop, twist, piece; lock, ringlet, curl.

hanker ▶ verb YEARN, long, crave, desire, wish, want, hunger, thirst, lust, ache, pant, be eager, be desperate, be eating one's heart out; fancy, pine for, have one's heart set on; *informal* be dying, have a yen, (have a) jones for, itch.

hankering ▶ noun LONGING, yearning, craving, desire, wish, hunger, thirst, urge, ache, lust, appetite, fancy; *informal* yen, itch; *archaic* appetency.
– OPPOSITES: aversion.

hanky-panky ▶ noun (*informal*) MISBEHAVIOUR, naughtiness, infidelity, unfaithfulness, adultery, philandering, fooling around; funny business, mischief, goings-on, misconduct, chicanery, dishonesty, deception, deceit, trickery, intrigue, skulduggery, subterfuge, machinations, monkey business, shenanigans, carryings-on.

haphazard ▶ adjective RANDOM, unplanned, unsystematic, unmethodical, disorganized, disorderly, irregular, indiscriminate, chaotic, hit-and-miss, arbitrary, aimless, careless, casual, slapdash, slipshod; chance, accidental; *informal* higgledy-piggledy.
– OPPOSITES: methodical.

hapless ▶ adjective UNFORTUNATE, unlucky, luckless, out of luck, ill-starred, ill-fated, jinxed, cursed, doomed; unhappy, forlorn, wretched, miserable, woebegone; *informal* down on one's luck; *literary* star-crossed.
– OPPOSITES: lucky.

happen ▶ verb **1** *remember what happened last time he was here* OCCUR, take place, come about; ensue, result, transpire, materialize, arise, crop up, come up, present itself, supervene; *informal* go down; *formal* eventuate; *literary* come to pass, betide. **2** *I wonder what happened to Joe?* BECOME OF; *literary* befall, betide. **3** *they happened to be in* CHANCE, have the good/bad luck. **4** *she happened on a blue jay's nest* DISCOVER, find, find by chance, come across, chance on, stumble on, hit on.

happening ▶ noun *bizarre happenings* OCCURRENCE, event, incident, proceeding, affair, doing, circumstance, phenomenon, episode, experience, occasion, development, eventuality.
▶ adjective (*informal*) *a happening nightspot* FASHIONABLE, modern, popular, new, latest, up-to-date, up-to-the-minute, in fashion, in vogue, le dernier cri; *informal* trendy, funky, hot, cool, with it, hip, in, big, now, groovy, kicky, tony.
– OPPOSITES: old-fashioned.

happily ▶ adverb **1** *he smiled happily* CONTENTEDLY, cheerfully, cheerily, merrily, delightedly, joyfully, joyously, gaily, gleefully. **2** *I will happily do as you ask* GLADLY, willingly, readily, freely, cheerfully, ungrudgingly, with pleasure; *archaic* fain. **3** *happily, we are living in enlightened times* FORTUNATELY, luckily, thankfully, mercifully, by good luck, by good fortune, as luck would have it; thank goodness, thank God, thank heavens, thank the Lord, thank the stars.

happiness ▶ noun PLEASURE, contentment, satisfaction, cheerfulness, merriment, gaiety, joy, joyfulness, joviality, jollity, glee, delight, good spirits, light-heartedness, well-being, enjoyment; exuberance, exhilaration, elation, ecstasy,

jubilation, rapture, bliss, blissfulness, euphoria, transports of delight.

happy ▶ adjective **1** *Melissa looked happy and excited* CHEERFUL, cheery, merry, joyful, jovial, jolly, jocular, gleeful, carefree, untroubled, delighted, smiling, beaming, grinning, in good spirits, in a good mood, light-hearted, pleased, contented, content, satisfied, gratified, buoyant, radiant, sunny, blithe, joyous, beatific; thrilled, elated, exhilarated, ecstatic, blissful, euphoric, overjoyed, exultant, rapturous, in seventh heaven, on cloud nine, walking on air, jumping for joy, jubilant; *informal* chirpy, over the moon, on top of the world, tickled pink, on a high, as happy as a clam; *formal* jocund. **2** *we will be happy to advise you* GLAD, pleased, delighted; willing, ready, disposed. **3** *a happy coincidence* FORTUNATE, lucky, favourable, advantageous, opportune, timely, well-timed, convenient.
– OPPOSITES: sad, unwilling, unfortunate.

happy-go-lucky ▶ adjective EASYGOING, carefree, casual, free and easy, devil-may-care, blithe, nonchalant, insouciant, blasé, unconcerned, untroubled, unworried, light-hearted, laid-back.
– OPPOSITES: anxious.

harangue ▶ noun *a ten-minute harangue* TIRADE, diatribe, lecture, polemic, rant, fulmination, broadside, attack, onslaught; criticism, condemnation, censure, admonition, sermon; declamation, speech; *informal* blast; *literary* philippic.
▶ verb *he harangued his erstwhile colleagues* RANT AT, hold forth to, lecture, shout at; berate, criticize, attack; *informal* sound off at, mouth off to.

harass ▶ verb **1** *tenants who harass their neighbours* PERSECUTE, intimidate, hound, harry, plague, torment, bully, bullyrag, bedevil; pester, bother, worry, disturb, trouble, provoke, stress; *informal* hassle, bug, devil, ride, give someone a hard time, get on someone's case. **2** *they were sent to harass the enemy flanks* HARRY, attack, beleaguer, set upon, assail.

harassed ▶ adjective STRESSED (OUT), strained, worn out, hard-pressed, careworn, worried, troubled, beleaguered, under pressure, at the end of one's tether, at the end of one's rope; *informal* hassled.
– OPPOSITES: carefree.

harassment ▶ noun PERSECUTION, intimidation, pressure, force, coercion; *informal* hassle.

harbinger ▶ noun HERALD, sign, indication, signal, portent, omen, augury, forewarning, presage; forerunner, precursor, messenger; *literary* foretoken.

harbour ▶ noun **1** *a picturesque harbour* PORT, dock, haven, marina; mooring, moorage, anchorage; waterfront. **2** *a safe harbour for me* REFUGE, haven, safe haven, shelter, sanctuary, retreat, place of safety, port in a storm.
▶ verb **1** *he is harbouring a dangerous criminal* SHELTER, conceal, hide, shield, protect, give sanctuary to; take in, put up, accommodate, house. **2** *Rose had harboured a grudge against him* BEAR, nurse, nurture, cherish, entertain, foster, hold on to, cling to.

hard ▶ adjective **1** *hard ground* FIRM, solid, rigid, stiff, resistant, unbreakable, inflexible, impenetrable, unyielding, solidified, hardened, compact, compacted, dense, close-packed, compressed; steely, tough, strong, stony, rock-like, flinty, as hard as stone; frozen; *literary* adamantine. **2** *hard physical work* ARDUOUS, strenuous, tiring, fatiguing, exhausting, wearying, back-breaking, gruelling, heavy, laborious; difficult, taxing, exacting, testing, challenging, demanding, punishing, tough, formidable, onerous,

rigorous, uphill, Herculean; *informal* murderous, killing, hellish; *formal* exigent; *archaic* toilsome. **3** *hard workers* DILIGENT, hard-working, industrious, sedulous, assiduous, conscientious, energetic, keen, enthusiastic, zealous, earnest, persevering, persistent, unflagging, untiring, indefatigable; studious. **4** *a hard problem* DIFFICULT, puzzling, perplexing, baffling, bewildering, mystifying, knotty, thorny, problematic, complicated, complex, intricate, involved; insoluble, unfathomable, impenetrable, incomprehensible, unanswerable. **5** *times are hard* HARSH, grim, difficult, bad, bleak, dire, tough, austere, unpleasant, uncomfortable, straitened, Spartan; dark, distressing, painful, awful. **6** *a hard taskmaster* STRICT, harsh, firm, severe, stern, tough, rigorous, demanding, exacting; callous, unkind, unsympathetic, cold, heartless, hard-hearted, unfeeling; intransigent, unbending, uncompromising, inflexible, implacable, stubborn, obdurate, unyielding, unrelenting, unsparing, grim, ruthless, merciless, pitiless, cruel; standing no nonsense, ruling with a rod of iron. **7** *a hard winter* BITTERLY COLD, cold, bitter, harsh, severe, bleak, freezing, icy, icy-cold, arctic. **8** *a hard blow* FORCEFUL, heavy, strong, sharp, smart, violent, powerful, vigorous, mighty, hefty, tremendous. **9** *hard facts* RELIABLE, definite, true, confirmed, substantiated, undeniable, indisputable, unquestionable, verifiable. **10** *hard liquor* ALCOHOLIC, strong, intoxicating, potent; *formal* spirituous. **11** *hard drugs* ADDICTIVE, habit-forming; strong, harmful.
— OPPOSITES: soft, easy lazy, gentle.
▶ **adverb 1** *George pushed the door hard* FORCEFULLY, forcibly, roughly, powerfully, strongly, heavily, sharply, vigorously, energetically, with all one's might, with might and main. **2** *they worked hard* DILIGENTLY, industriously, assiduously, conscientiously, sedulously, busily, enthusiastically, energetically, doggedly, steadily; *informal* like mad, like crazy. **3** *this prosperity has been hard won* WITH DIFFICULTY, with effort, after a struggle, painfully, laboriously. **4** *her death hit him hard* SEVERELY, badly, acutely, deeply, keenly, seriously, profoundly, gravely; *formal* grievously. **5** *it was raining hard* HEAVILY, strongly, in torrents, in sheets, cats and dogs, buckets; steadily. **6** *my mother looked hard at me* CLOSELY, attentively, intently, critically, carefully, keenly, searchingly, earnestly, sharply.
■ **hard and fast** DEFINITE, fixed, set, strict, rigid, binding, clear-cut, cast-iron, ironclad; inflexible, immutable, unchangeable, incontestable.
■ **hard by** CLOSE TO, right by, beside, near (to), nearby, not far from, a stone's throw from, on the doorstep of; *informal* within spitting distance of, {a hop, skip, and jump away from}.
■ **hard feelings** RESENTMENT, animosity, ill feeling, ill will, bitterness, bad blood, resentfulness, rancour, malice, acrimony, antagonism, antipathy, animus, friction, anger, hostility, hate, hatred.
■ **hard up** (*informal*) POOR, short of money, badly off, impoverished, impecunious, in reduced circumstances, unable to make ends meet; penniless, destitute, poverty-stricken; *informal* broke, strapped (for cash).

hardbitten ▶ **adjective** HARDENED, tough, cynical, unsentimental, hard-headed, case-hardened, as tough as nails; *informal* hard-nosed, hard-edged, hard-boiled.
— OPPOSITES: sentimental.

hard-boiled ▶ **adjective** (*informal*) *a hard-boiled undercover agent.* See HARDBITTEN.

hard-core ▶ **adjective** *hard-core socialists* DIEHARD, staunch, dedicated, committed, steadfast, dyed-in-the-wool, long-standing; hardline, extreme, entrenched, radical, intransigent, uncompromising, rigid.

harden ▶ **verb 1** *this glue will harden in four hours* SOLIDIFY, set, congeal, clot, coagulate, stiffen, thicken, cake, cure, inspissate; freeze, crystallize; ossify, calcify, petrify. **2** *their suffering had hardened them* TOUGHEN, desensitize, inure, case-harden, harden someone's heart; deaden, numb, benumb, anaesthetize; brutalize.
— OPPOSITES: liquefy, soften.

hardened ▶ **adjective 1** *he was hardened to the violence he had seen* INURED, desensitized, deadened; accustomed, habituated, acclimatized, used. **2** *a hardened criminal* INVETERATE, seasoned, habitual, chronic, compulsive, confirmed, dyed-in-the-wool; incorrigible, incurable, irredeemable, unregenerate.

hard-headed ▶ **adjective** UNSENTIMENTAL, practical, pragmatic, businesslike, realistic, sensible, rational, clear-thinking, cool-headed, down-to-earth, matter-of-fact, no-nonsense, with one's/both feet on the ground; tough, hardbitten; shrewd, astute, sharp, sharp-witted; *informal* hard-nosed, hard-edged, hard-boiled.
— OPPOSITES: idealistic.

hard-hearted ▶ **adjective** UNFEELING, heartless, cold, hard, callous, unsympathetic, uncaring, unloving, unconcerned, indifferent, unmoved, unkind, uncharitable, unemotional, cold-hearted, cold-blooded, mean-spirited, stony-hearted, having a heart of stone, as hard as nails, cruel.
— OPPOSITES: compassionate.

hard-hitting ▶ **adjective** UNCOMPROMISING, blunt, forthright, frank, honest, direct, tough; critical, unsparing, strongly worded, straight-talking, pulling no punches, not mincing one's words, not beating about the bush.

hardiness ▶ **noun** ROBUSTNESS, strength, toughness, ruggedness, sturdiness, resilience, stamina, vigour; healthiness, good health.
— OPPOSITES: frailty.

hardline ▶ **adjective** UNCOMPROMISING, strict, extreme, tough, diehard, inflexible, intransigent, firm, intractable, unyielding, single-minded, not giving an inch.
— OPPOSITES: moderate.

hardly ▶ **adverb** *we hardly know each other* SCARCELY, barely, only just, slightly.

hard-nosed ▶ **adjective** (*informal*) TOUGH-MINDED, unsentimental, no-nonsense, hard-headed, hardbitten, pragmatic, realistic, down-to-earth, practical, rational, shrewd, astute, businesslike; *informal* hard-boiled, hard-edged.
— OPPOSITES: sentimental.

hard-pressed ▶ **adjective 1** *the hard-pressed infantry* UNDER ATTACK, hotly pursued, harried. **2** *the hard-pressed construction industry* IN DIFFICULTIES, under pressure, troubled, beleaguered, harassed, with one's back to/against the wall, in a tight corner, in a tight spot, between a rock and a hard place; overburdened, overworked, overloaded, stressed-out, rushed off one's feet; *informal* pushed, up against it.

hardship ▶ **noun** PRIVATION, deprivation, destitution, poverty, austerity, penury, want, need, neediness,

impecuniousness; misfortune, distress, suffering, affliction, trouble, pain, misery, wretchedness, tribulation, adversity, trials, trials and tribulations, dire straits; *literary* travails.
— OPPOSITES: prosperity, ease.

hardware ▶ noun EQUIPMENT, apparatus, gear, paraphernalia, tackle, kit, machinery; tools, articles, implements, instruments, appliances.

hard-working ▶ adjective DILIGENT, industrious, conscientious, assiduous, sedulous, painstaking, persevering, unflagging, untiring, tireless, indefatigable, studious; keen, enthusiastic, zealous, busy, with one's shoulder to the wheel, with one's nose to the grindstone.
— OPPOSITES: lazy.

hardy ▶ adjective ROBUST, healthy, fit, strong, sturdy, tough, rugged, hearty, lusty, vigorous, hale and hearty, fit as a fiddle, fighting fit, in fine fettle, in good health, in good condition; *dated* stalwart.
— OPPOSITES: delicate.

hare-brained ▶ adjective 1 *a hare-brained scheme* ILL-JUDGED, rash, foolish, foolhardy, reckless, madcap, wild, silly, stupid, ridiculous, absurd, idiotic, asinine, imprudent, impracticable, unworkable, unrealistic, unconsidered, half-baked, ill-thought-out, ill-advised, ill-conceived; *informal* crackpot, crack-brained, cockeyed, crazy, daft. 2 *a hare-brained young girl* FOOLISH, silly, idiotic, unintelligent, empty-headed, scatterbrained, feather-brained, birdbrained, pea-brained, brainless, giddy; *informal* dippy, dizzy, flaky, dopey, dotty, airheaded.
— OPPOSITES: sensible, intelligent.

harem ▶ noun SERAGLIO; zenana.

hark ▶ verb (*literary*) *hark, I hear a warning note* LISTEN, lend an ear, pay attention, attend, mark; *archaic* hearken, give ear.
■ **hark back to** RECALL, call/bring to mind, evoke, put one in mind of.

harlequin ▶ noun JESTER, joker.
▶ adjective *a harlequin pattern* MULTICOLOURED, many-coloured, colourful, parti-coloured, varicoloured, many-hued, rainbow, variegated, jazzy, kaleidoscopic, psychedelic, polychromatic, checkered; *archaic* motley.

harlot ▶ noun (*archaic*) PROSTITUTE, whore, fille de joie, call girl; promiscuous woman; *informal* hooker, hustler, tramp; *dated* streetwalker, hussy, woman of the streets, woman of the night, tart, pro, member of the oldest profession, scarlet woman, loose woman, fallen woman, cocotte, wanton; *archaic* strumpet, courtesan, trollop, doxy, trull.

harm ▶ noun 1 *the voltage is not sufficient to cause harm* INJURY, hurt, pain, trauma; damage, impairment, mischief. 2 *I can't see any harm in it* EVIL, wrong, ill, wickedness, iniquity, sin.
— OPPOSITES: benefit.
▶ verb 1 *he's never harmed anybody in his life* INJURE, hurt, wound, lay a finger on, maltreat, mistreat, misuse, ill-treat, ill-use, abuse, molest. 2 *this could harm her Olympic prospects* DAMAGE, hurt, spoil, mar, do mischief to, impair.

harmful ▶ adjective DAMAGING, injurious, detrimental, dangerous, deleterious, unfavourable, negative, disadvantageous, unhealthy, unwholesome, hurtful, baleful, destructive; noxious, hazardous, poisonous, toxic, deadly, lethal; bad, evil, malign, malignant, malevolent, corrupting,

subversive, pernicious.
— OPPOSITES: beneficial.

harmless ▶ adjective 1 *a harmless substance* SAFE, innocuous, benign, gentle, mild, wholesome, non-toxic, non-poisonous, non-irritant, hypoallergenic; non-addictive. 2 *he seems harmless enough* INOFFENSIVE, innocuous, unobjectionable, unexceptionable.
— OPPOSITES: dangerous.

harmonious ▶ adjective 1 *harmonious music* TUNEFUL, melodious, melodic, sweet-sounding, mellifluous, dulcet, lyrical; euphonious, euphonic, harmonic, polyphonic; *informal* easy on the ear. 2 *their harmonious relationship* FRIENDLY, amicable, cordial, amiable, congenial, easy, peaceful, peaceable, co-operative; compatible, sympathetic, united, attuned, in harmony, in rapport, in tune, in accord, of one mind, seeing eye to eye. 3 *a harmonious blend of traditional and modern* CONGRUOUS, coordinated, balanced, in proportion, compatible, well-matched, well-balanced.
— OPPOSITES: discordant, hostile, incongruous.

harmonize ▶ verb 1 *colours which harmonize in a pleasing way* COORDINATE, go together, match, blend, mix, balance; be compatible, be harmonious, suit each other. 2 *a plan to harmonize tax laws across the country* COORDINATE, systematize, correlate, integrate, synchronize, make consistent, homogenize, bring in line, bring in tune.
— OPPOSITES: clash.

harmony ▶ noun 1 *musical harmony* EUPHONY, polyphony; tunefulness, melodiousness, mellifluousness. 2 *the harmony of the whole structure* BALANCE, symmetry, congruity, consonance, coordination, compatibility. 3 *the villagers live together in harmony* ACCORD, agreement, peace, peacefulness, amity, amicability, friendship, fellowship, co-operation, understanding, consensus, unity, sympathy, rapport, like-mindedness; unison, union, concert, oneness, synthesis; *formal* concord.
— OPPOSITES: dissonance, disagreement.

harness ▶ noun *a horse's harness* TACK, tackle, equipment; trappings; yoke; *archaic* equipage.
▶ verb 1 *he harnessed his horse* HITCH UP, put in harness, yoke, couple. 2 *attempts to harness solar energy* CONTROL, exploit, utilize, use, employ, make use of, put to use; channel, mobilize, apply, capitalize on.

harp ▶ noun 1 *the strings of a harp* lyre, aeolian harp, wind harp, Celtic harp, triple harp, Welsh harp; *historical* trigon. 2 *a blues harp* HARMONICA, mouth organ, mouth harp.
■ **harp on about** KEEP ON ABOUT, go on about, keep talking about, dwell on, make an issue of; labour the point.

harpoon ▶ noun SPEAR, trident, dart, barb, gaff, leister.

harridan ▶ noun SHREW, termagant, virago, harpy, vixen, nag, hag, crone, dragon, ogress; fishwife, hellcat, she-devil, gorgon; martinet, tartar; *informal* old bag, old bat, battleaxe, witch; *archaic* scold.

harried ▶ adjective HARASSED, beleaguered, flustered, agitated, bothered, vexed, stressed, beset, plagued; *informal* hassled, up against it.

harrow ▶ verb DISTRESS, trouble, bother, afflict, grieve, torment, disturb, pain, hurt, mortify.
— OPPOSITES: comfort.

harrowing ▶ adjective DISTRESSING, distressful,

harry ▶ verb **1** *they harried the retreating enemy* ATTACK, assail, assault; charge, rush, strike, set upon; bombard, shell, strafe. **2** *the government was harried by a new lobby* HARASS, hound, bedevil, torment, pester, bother, worry, badger, nag, plague; *informal* hassle, bug, lean on, give someone a hard time.

harsh ▶ adjective **1** *a harsh voice* GRATING, jarring, rasping, strident, raucous, brassy, discordant, unharmonious, unmelodious; rough, coarse, hoarse, gruff, croaky. **2** *harsh colours* GLARING, bright, dazzling; loud, garish, gaudy, lurid, bold. **3** *his harsh rule over them* CRUEL, savage, barbarous, despotic, dictatorial, tyrannical, tyrannous; ruthless, merciless, pitiless, relentless, unmerciful; severe, strict, intolerant, illiberal, iron-fisted; hard-hearted, heartless, unkind, inhuman, inhumane. **4** *they took harsh measures to end the crisis* SEVERE, stringent, draconian, firm, stiff, hard, stern, rigorous, grim, uncompromising; punitive, cruel, brutal. **5** *harsh words* RUDE, discourteous, uncivil, impolite; unfriendly, sharp, bitter, abusive, unkind, disparaging; abrupt, brusque, curt, gruff, short, surly, offhand. **6** *harsh conditions* AUSTERE, grim, Spartan, hard, comfortless, inhospitable, stark, bleak, desolate. **7** *a harsh winter* HARD, severe, cold, bitter, bleak, freezing, icy; arctic, polar, Siberian. **8** *harsh detergents* ABRASIVE, strong, caustic; coarse, rough.
— OPPOSITES: soft, subdued, kind, friendly, comfortable, balmy, mild.

harum-scarum ▶ adjective RECKLESS, impetuous, impulsive, imprudent, rash, wild; daredevil, madcap, hot-headed, hare-brained, foolhardy, incautious, careless, heedless; *informal* devil-may-care; *literary* temerarious.
— OPPOSITES: cautious.

harvest ▶ noun **1** *we all helped with the harvest* HARVESTING, reaping, picking, collecting. **2** *a poor harvest* YIELD, crop, vintage; fruits, produce. **3** *the experiment yielded a meagre harvest* RETURN, result, fruits; product, output, effect; consequence.
▶ verb **1** *he harvested the wheat* GATHER (IN), bring in, reap, pick, collect. **2** *she harvested many honours* ACQUIRE, obtain, gain, get, earn; accumulate, amass, gather, collect; *informal* land, net, bag, scoop.

hash ▶ noun *a whole hash of excuses* MIXTURE, assortment, variety, array, mix, miscellany, selection, medley, mishmash, ragbag, gallimaufry, potpourri, hodgepodge.
■ **make a hash of** (*informal*) BUNGLE, fluff, flub, mess up, make a mess of; mismanage, mishandle, ruin, wreck; botch, muff, muck up, foul up, screw up, blow.

hassle (*informal*) ▶ noun **1** *parking is such a hassle* INCONVENIENCE, bother, nuisance, problem, trouble, struggle, difficulty, annoyance, irritation, thorn in one's side/flesh, fuss; *informal* aggravation, stress, headache, pain (in the neck). **2** *she got into a hassle with that guy. See* QUARREL *noun*.
▶ verb *they were hassling him to pay up* HARASS, pester, nag, keep on at, badger, hound, harry, chivvy, bother, torment, plague; *informal* bug, give someone a hard time, get on someone's case, give someone the gears ♣, breathe down someone's neck.

hassled ▶ adjective (*informal*) HARASSED, agitated, stressed (out), harried, frayed, flustered; beleaguered, hounded, plagued, bothered, beset, tormented; under pressure, hot and bothered; *informal* up against it.
— OPPOSITES: calm.

haste ▶ noun *working with feverish haste* SPEED, hastiness, hurriedness, swiftness, rapidity, quickness, briskness; *formal* expedition.
— OPPOSITES: delay.
■ **in haste** QUICKLY, rapidly, fast, speedily, with urgency, in a rush, in a hurry.

hasten ▶ verb **1** *we hastened back home* HURRY, rush, dash, race, fly, shoot; scurry, scramble, dart, bolt, sprint, run, gallop; go fast, go quickly, go like lightning, go hell for leather; *informal* tear, hare, pelt, scoot, zip, zoom, belt, hotfoot it, bomb, hightail, barrel; *dated* make haste. **2** *chemicals can hasten aging* SPEED UP, accelerate, quicken, precipitate, advance, hurry on, step up, spur on, catalyse; facilitate, aid, assist, boost.
— OPPOSITES: dawdle, delay.

hastily ▶ adverb **1** *Meg retreated hastily* QUICKLY, hurriedly, fast, swiftly, rapidly, speedily, briskly, without delay, post-haste; with all speed, as fast as possible, at breakneck speed, at a run, hotfoot, on the double; *informal* PDQ (pretty damn quick), nippily, like (greased) lightning, like the wind, like a bat out of hell, lickety-split. **2** *an agreement was hastily drawn up* HURRIEDLY, speedily, quickly; on the spur of the moment, prematurely.

hasty ▶ adjective **1** *hasty steps* QUICK, hurried, fast, swift, rapid, speedy, brisk; *literary* fleet. **2** *hasty decisions* RASH, impetuous, impulsive, reckless, precipitate, spur-of-the-moment, premature, unconsidered, unthinking; *literary* temerarious.
— OPPOSITES: slow, considered.

hat ▶ noun CAP, beret, bonnet; lid, toque ♣. *See table.*

hatch ▶ verb **1** *the duck hatched her eggs* INCUBATE, brood. **2** *the plot that you hatched up last night* DEVISE, conceive, concoct, brew, invent, plan, design, formulate; think up, dream up; *informal* cook up.

hatchet ▶ noun AXE, cleaver, mattock, tomahawk.

hate ▶ verb **1** *they hate each other* LOATHE, detest, despise, dislike, abhor, execrate; be repelled by, be unable to bear/stand, find intolerable, recoil from, shrink from; *formal* abominate. **2** *I hate to bother you* BE SORRY, be reluctant, be loath, be unwilling, be disinclined; regret, dislike.
— OPPOSITES: love.
▶ noun **1** *feelings of hate* HATRED, loathing, detestation, dislike, distaste, abhorrence, abomination, execration, aversion; hostility, enmity, animosity, antipathy, revulsion, disgust, contempt, odium. **2** *his pet hate is filling in forms* PEEVE, bugbear, bane, bête noire, bogey, aversion, thorn in one's flesh/side, bugaboo.
— OPPOSITES: love.

hateful ▶ adjective DETESTABLE, horrible, horrid, unpleasant, awful, nasty, disagreeable, despicable, objectionable, insufferable, revolting, loathsome, abhorrent, abominable, execrable, odious, disgusting, distasteful, obnoxious, offensive, vile, heinous, ghastly, beastly, godawful.
— OPPOSITES: delightful.

hatred ▶ noun LOATHING, hate, detestation, dislike, distaste, abhorrence, abomination, execration; aversion, hostility, ill will, ill feeling, enmity, animosity, antipathy; revulsion, disgust, contempt, odium.

haughtiness ▶ noun ARROGANCE, conceit, pride

Hats and Head Coverings

balaclava	Mountie hat ✦
balmoral	nor'wester
baseball cap	opera hat
beanie	panama hat
bearskin	Pangnirtung
beaver hat	hat ✦(North)
beret	petasus *Ancient Greece*
biretta	picture hat
boater	pillbox
bonnet	pith helmet
bowler	porkpie hat
busby	sailor hat
cap	sallet
chapeau	shako
Christie stiff ✦*hist.*	shovel hat
cloche	silk hat
cocked hat	skimmer
coif	skullcap
coolie hat	snap-brim
coonskin	sombrero
cowboy hat	sou'wester
deerstalker	Stetson
derby	stovepipe
Dolly Varden	sun hat
fedora	sun helmet
fez	tam(-o'-shanter)
forage cap	tarboosh
glengarry	tarpaulin
hard hat	10-gallon hat
helmet	topi
high hat	toque
homburg	tricorne
Juliet cap	trilby
kaffiyeh	turban
kepi	watch cap
leghorn	wideawake
mobcap *hist.*	yarmulke
mortarboard	zucchetto

hubris, hauteur, vanity, self-importance, pomposity, condescension, disdain, contempt; snobbishness, snobbery, superciliousness; *informal* snootiness.
— OPPOSITES: modesty.

haughty ▶ adjective PROUD, arrogant, vain, conceited, snobbish, superior, self-important, pompous, supercilious, condescending, patronizing; scornful, contemptuous, disdainful; full of oneself, above oneself; *informal* stuck-up, snooty, hoity-toity, uppity, uppish, big-headed, high and mighty, la-di-da, chesty.
— OPPOSITES: humble.

haul ▶ verb 1 *she hauled the basket along* DRAG, pull, tug, heave, lug, hump, draw, tow; *informal* yank. 2 *a contract to haul coal* TRANSPORT, convey, carry, ship, ferry, move, shift.
▶ noun *the thieves abandoned their haul* BOOTY, loot, plunder; spoils, stolen goods, ill-gotten gains; *informal* swag, boodle.

haunches ▶ plural noun RUMP, hindquarters, rear (end), seat; buttocks, thighs, derrière, bottom; behind, backside; *Anatomy* nates; *informal* bum, butt, fanny, tush, heinie; *humorous* fundament, posterior, gluteus maximus.

haunt ▶ verb 1 *a ghost haunts this house* APPEAR IN, materialize in; visit. 2 *he haunts street markets* FREQUENT, patronize, visit regularly; loiter in, linger in; *informal* hang out in. 3 *the sight haunted me for years*

TORMENT, disturb, trouble, worry, plague, burden, beset, beleaguer; prey on, weigh on, gnaw at, nag at, weigh heavily on, obsess; *informal* bug.
▶ noun *a favourite haunt of artists* HANGOUT, stomping ground, meeting place; territory, domain, resort, retreat, spot.

haunted ▶ adjective 1 *a haunted house* POSSESSED, cursed; ghostly, eerie; *informal* spooky, scary. 2 *her haunted eyes* TORMENTED, anguished, troubled, tortured, worried, disturbed.

haunting ▶ adjective EVOCATIVE, emotive, affecting, moving, touching, stirring, powerful; poignant, nostalgic, wistful, elegiac; memorable, indelible, unforgettable.

hauteur ▶ noun HAUGHTINESS, superciliousness, arrogance, pride, conceit, snobbery, snobbishness, superiority, self-importance; disdain, condescension; airs and graces; *informal* snootiness, uppishness.

have ▶ verb 1 *he had a new car* POSSESS, own, be in possession of, be the owner of; be blessed with, boast, enjoy; keep, retain, hold, occupy. 2 *the apartment has five rooms* COMPRISE, consist of, contain, include, incorporate, be composed of, be made up of; encompass; *formal* comprehend. 3 *they had dinner together* EAT, consume, devour, partake of; drink, imbibe, quaff; *informal* demolish, dispose of, put away, scoff (down); sink, knock back, scarf (down/up). 4 *she had a letter from Mark* RECEIVE, get, be given, be sent, obtain, acquire, come by, take receipt of. 5 *we've decided to have a party* ORGANIZE, arrange, hold, give, host, throw, put on, lay on, set up, fix up. 6 *she's going to have a baby* GIVE BIRTH TO, bear, be delivered of, bring into the world, produce; *informal* drop; *archaic* beget. 7 *we are having guests for dinner* ENTERTAIN, be host to, cater for, receive; invite round/over, ask round/over, wine and dine; accommodate, put up. 8 *he had trouble finding the restaurant* EXPERIENCE, encounter, face, meet, find, run into, go through, undergo. 9 *I have a headache* BE SUFFERING FROM, be afflicted by, be affected by, be troubled with. 10 *I had a good time* EXPERIENCE; enjoy. 11 *many of them have doubts* HARBOUR, entertain, feel, nurse, nurture, sustain, maintain. 12 *he had little patience* MANIFEST, show, display, exhibit, demonstrate. 13 *she had them line up according to height* MAKE, ask to, request to, get to, tell to, require to, induce to, prevail upon someone to; order to, command to, direct to, force to. 14 *I can't have you insulting me* TOLERATE, endure, bear, support, accept, put up with, go along with, take, countenance; permit to, allow to; *informal* stand, abide, stomach; *formal* brook. 15 *I have to get up at six* MUST, be obliged to, be required to, be compelled to, be forced to, be bound to. 16 *(informal) I'd been had* TRICK, fool, deceive, cheat, dupe, take in, hoodwink, swindle; *informal* con, diddle, rip off, shaft, hose, sucker, snooker.
— OPPOSITES: send, give, visit.
■ **have done with** HAVE FINISHED WITH, be done with, be through with, want no more to do with; have given up, have turned one's back on, have washed one's hands of.
■ **have had it** *(informal)* 1 *they admit that they've had it* HAVE NO CHANCE, have no hope, have failed, be finished, have had the biscuit ✦, be done like dinner ✦, be defeated, have lost; *informal* have flopped, have come a cropper, have bought the farm. 2 *if you tell anyone, you've had it* BE IN TROUBLE, be in for a scolding, be in hot water, be in deep doo-doo, be toast, be dead meat.

■ **have something on** *she had a blue dress on* BE WEARING, be dressed in, be clothed in, be attired in, be decked out in, be robed in.

haven ▶ noun **1** *they stopped in a small haven* ANCHORAGE, harbour, harbourage, port, moorage, mooring; road, roadstead; cove, inlet, bay. **2** *a safe haven* REFUGE, retreat, shelter, sanctuary, asylum; port in a storm, oasis, sanctum.

haversack ▶ noun KNAPSACK, backpack, rucksack, pack.

havoc ▶ noun **1** *the hurricane caused havoc* DEVASTATION, destruction, damage, desolation, ruination, ruin; disaster, catastrophe. **2** *hyperactive children create havoc* DISORDER, chaos, disruption, mayhem, bedlam, pandemonium, turmoil, tumult, uproar; commotion, furor, a three-ring circus; *informal* hullabaloo.

hawk ▶ noun See table at RAPTOR.
▶ **verb** PEDDLE, sell, tout, vend, trade in, traffic in, push, flog.

hawker ▶ noun PEDDLER, trader, seller, dealer, purveyor, vendor, huckster, travelling salesman; scalper; *informal* pusher.

hawk-eyed ▶ adjective VIGILANT, observant, alert, sharp-eyed, eagle-eyed; on the alert, on the lookout, with one's eyes peeled; *informal* beady-eyed, not missing a trick, on the ball.
— OPPOSITES: inattentive.

hay ▶ noun FORAGE, dried grass, herbage, silage, fodder, straw.
■ **make hay while the sun shines** make the most of an opportunity, take advantage of something, strike while the iron is hot, seize the day, carpe diem.

haystack ▶ noun haycock, hay rick, stook, stack, coil ✚, mow, shock, cock.

haywire ▶ adjective *(informal)* OUT OF CONTROL, erratic, faulty, malfunctioning, out of order; chaotic, confused, disorganized, disordered, topsy-turvy; *informal* on the blink, on the fritz, shambolic.

hazard ▶ noun **1** *the hazards of radiation* DANGER, risk, peril, threat, menace; problem, pitfall. **2** *(literary) the laws of hazard* CHANCE, probability, fortuity, luck, fate, destiny, fortune, providence.
▶ **verb 1** *he hazarded a guess* VENTURE, advance, put forward, volunteer, float; conjecture, speculate, surmise; *formal* opine. **2** *it's too risky to hazard money on* RISK, jeopardize, gamble, stake, bet, chance; endanger, imperil.

hazardous ▶ adjective RISKY, dangerous, unsafe, perilous, precarious, fraught with danger; unpredictable, uncertain, chancy, high-risk, insecure, touch-and-go; *informal* dicey, hairy.
— OPPOSITES: safe, certain.

haze ▶ noun **1** *a thick haze on the sea* MIST, fog, cloud; smoke, vapour, steam. **2** *a haze of euphoria* BLUR, daze, confusion, muddle, befuddlement.

hazy ▶ adjective **1** *a hazy day* MISTY, foggy, cloudy, overcast; smoggy, murky. **2** *hazy memories* VAGUE, indistinct, unclear, faint, dim, nebulous, shadowy, blurred, fuzzy, confused.

head ▶ noun **1** *she scratched her head thoughtfully* skull, cranium, crown; *informal* nut, noodle, noggin, dome. **2** *he had to use his head* BRAIN(S), brainpower, intellect, intelligence; wit(s), wisdom, mind, sense, reasoning, common sense; *informal* savvy, grey matter, smarts. **3** *she had a good head for business* APTITUDE, faculty, talent, gift, capacity, ability; mind, brain. **4** *the head of the church* LEADER, chief, controller, governor,

superintendent, commander, captain; director, manager; principal, president, premier; chieftain, headman, sachem; CEO; *informal* boss, boss man, kingpin, top dog, Mr. Big, skipper, ringleader, numero uno, head honcho, big kahuna. **5** *the head of the line* FRONT, beginning, start, fore, forefront; top. **6** *the head of the river* SOURCE, origin, headspring, headwater; *literary* wellspring. **7** *beer with a head* FROTH, foam, bubbles, spume, fizz, effervescence; suds.
▶ **adjective** *the head waiter* CHIEF, principal, leading, main, first, foremost, prime, premier, senior, top, highest, supreme, superior, top-ranking, ranking.
— OPPOSITES: subordinate.
▶ **verb 1** *the procession was headed by the mayor* LEAD, be at the front of; be first, lead the way. **2** *Dr. Jones headed a research team* COMMAND, control, lead, run, manage, direct, supervise, superintend, oversee, preside over, rule, govern, captain; *informal* be the boss of. **3** *she was heading for the exit* MOVE TOWARDS, make for, aim for, go in the direction of, be bound for, make a beeline for; set out for, start out for.
■ **at the head of** IN CHARGE OF, controlling, commanding, leading, managing, running, directing, supervising, overseeing; at the wheel of, at the helm of.
■ **come to a head** REACH A CRISIS, come to a climax, reach a critical point, reach a crossroads; *informal* come to the crunch.
■ **go to someone's head 1** *the wine has gone to my head* INTOXICATE, befuddle, make drunk; *informal* make woozy; *formal* inebriate. **2** *her victory went to her head* MAKE CONCEITED, make someone full of themselves, turn someone's head, puff someone up.
■ **head someone/something off 1** *he went to head off the cars* INTERCEPT, divert, deflect, redirect, re-route, draw away, turn away. **2** *they headed off a confrontation* FORESTALL, avert, ward off, fend off, stave off, hold off, nip in the bud, keep at bay; prevent, avoid, stop.
■ **keep one's head** KEEP/STAY CALM, keep one's self-control, maintain one's composure; *informal* keep one's cool, keep one's shirt on, keep it together, cool one's jets.
■ **head start** ADVANTAGE, upper hand, inside track, lead.
■ **lose one's head** LOSE CONTROL, lose one's composure, lose one's equilibrium, go to pieces; panic, get flustered, get confused, get hysterical; *informal* lose one's cool, freak out, crack up.

headache ▶ noun **1** *I've got a headache* PAIN IN THE HEAD, sore head, migraine; neuralgia; *informal* head. **2** *(informal) their behaviour was a headache for the teacher* NUISANCE, trouble, problem, bother, bugbear, pest, worry, inconvenience, vexation, irritant, thorn in one's side; *informal* aggravation, hassle, pain (in the neck), bind.

head case ▶ noun *(informal)* MANIAC, lunatic, madman, madwoman; *informal* loony, nut, nutbar, nutcase, fruitcake, crank, crackpot, screwball, crazy, kook, wacko, dingbat.

headfirst ▶ adjective & adverb **1** *she dived headfirst into the water* HEADLONG, on one's head. **2** *don't plunge headfirst into a relationship* WITHOUT THINKING, without forethought, precipitously, impetuously, rashly, recklessly, heedlessly, hastily, headlong.
— OPPOSITES: cautiously.

heading ▶ noun **1** *chapter headings* TITLE, caption, legend, subtitle, sub-heading, rubric, headline. **2** *this topic falls under four main headings* CATEGORY, division, classification, class, section, group, grouping, subject, topic.

headland ▶ noun CAPE, promontory, point, head, foreland, peninsula, bluff.

headlong ▶ adverb **1** *he fell headlong into the tent* HEADFIRST, on one's head. **2** *she rushed headlong to join the craze* WITHOUT THINKING, without forethought, precipitously, impetuously, rashly, recklessly, carelessly, heedlessly, hastily.
— OPPOSITES: cautiously.
▶ adjective *a headlong dash* BREAKNECK, whirlwind; reckless, precipitate, precipitous, hasty, careless, heedless.
— OPPOSITES: cautious.

headman ▶ noun CHIEF, chieftain, leader, head, ruler, overlord, master, commander; lord, potentate, sachem.
— OPPOSITES: underling.

head-on ▶ adjective **1** *a head-on collision* DIRECT, full on. **2** *a head-on confrontation* DIRECT, face to face, eyeball to eyeball, personal.

headquarters ▶ plural noun HEAD OFFICE, main office, HQ, base, nerve centre, war room, mission control, command post, detachment ♣.

headstone ▶ noun GRAVESTONE, tombstone, stone, grave marker, monument, memorial.

headstrong ▶ adjective WILFUL, strong-willed, stubborn, obstinate, unyielding, obdurate; contrary, perverse, wayward, unruly; *formal* refractory.
— OPPOSITES: tractable.

heads-up ▶ noun WARNING, forewarning, (advance) notice, tipoff, red flag.

headway
■ **make headway** MAKE PROGRESS, progress, make strides, gain ground, advance, proceed, move, get ahead, come along, take shape.

heady ▶ adjective **1** *heady wine* POTENT, intoxicating, strong; alcoholic, vinous; *formal* spirituous. **2** *the heady days of my youth* EXHILARATING, exciting, thrilling, stimulating, invigorating, electrifying, rousing; *informal* mind-blowing.
— OPPOSITES: boring.

heal ▶ verb **1** *he heals sick people* MAKE BETTER, make well, cure, treat, restore to health. **2** *his knee had healed* GET BETTER, get well, be cured, recover, mend, improve. **3** *time will heal the pain of grief* ALLEVIATE, ease, assuage, palliate, relieve, help, lessen, mitigate, attenuate, allay. **4** *we tried to heal the rift* PUT RIGHT, set right, repair, remedy, resolve, correct, settle; conciliate, reconcile, harmonize; *informal* patch up.
— OPPOSITES: aggravate, worsen.

healing ▶ adjective CURATIVE, therapeutic, medicinal, remedial, corrective, reparative; tonic, restorative, health-giving, healthful, beneficial.
— OPPOSITES: harmful.

health ▶ noun **1** *he was restored to health* WELL-BEING, healthiness, fitness, good condition, good shape, fine fettle; strength, vigour, wellness. **2** *bad health forced him to retire* PHYSICAL STATE, physical shape, condition, constitution.
— OPPOSITES: illness.

healthful ▶ adjective HEALTHY, health-giving, beneficial, good for one, salubrious; wholesome, nourishing, nutritious.
— OPPOSITES: unhealthy.

healthy ▶ adjective **1** *a healthy baby* WELL, in good health, fine, fit, in good trim, in good shape, in fine fettle, in tip-top shape; blooming, thriving, hardy,

robust, strong, vigorous, fighting fit, fit as a fiddle, the picture of health; *informal* OK, in the pink, right as rain. **2** *a healthy diet* HEALTH-GIVING, healthful, good for one; wholesome, nutritious, nourishing; beneficial, salubrious.
— OPPOSITES: ill, unwholesome.

heap ▶ noun **1** *a heap of boxes* PILE, stack, mound, mountain, mass, quantity, load, lot, jumble; collection, accumulation, assemblage, store, hoard. **2** (*informal*) *we have heaps of room* A LOT, a fair amount, much, plenty, a good deal, a great deal, an abundance, a wealth, a profusion; (a great) many, a large number, numerous, scores; *informal* hundreds, thousands, millions, a load, loads, a pile, piles, oodles, stacks, lots, masses, scads, reams, wads, oceans, miles, tons, zillions.
▶ verb *she heaped logs on the fire* PILE (UP), stack (up), make a mound of; assemble, collect.
■ **heap something on/upon** *they heaped praise on her* SHOWER ON, lavish on, load on; bestow on, confer on, give, grant, vouchsafe, favour with.

hear ▶ verb **1** *she can't hear* PERCEIVE SOUND; have hearing. **2** *she could hear men's voices* PERCEIVE, make out, discern, catch, get, apprehend; overhear. **3** *I heard that radio show* LISTEN TO, catch. **4** *they heard that I had moved* BE INFORMED, be told, find out, discover, learn, gather, glean, ascertain, get word, get wind. **5** *a jury heard the case* TRY, judge; adjudicate (on), adjudge, pass judgment on. **6** *I totally hear what you're saying* ACKNOWLEDGE, understand, sympathize with, recognize, get, perceive.

hearing ▶ noun **1** *acute hearing* ABILITY TO HEAR, auditory perception, sense of hearing, aural faculty. **2** *she moved out of hearing* EARSHOT, hearing distance, hearing range, auditory range. **3** *I had a fair hearing* CHANCE TO SPEAK, opportunity to be heard; interview, audience. **4** *he gave evidence at the hearing* TRIAL, court case, inquiry, inquest, tribunal; investigation, inquisition, Royal Commission.
— RELATED TERMS: acoustic, auditory, aural.

hearsay ▶ noun RUMOUR, gossip, tittle-tattle, tattle, idle talk; stories, tales; *informal* the grapevine, (esp. *North*) the moccasin telegraph ♣, scuttlebutt, loose lips.

heart ▶ noun **1** *my heart stopped beating informal* ticker. **2** *he poured out his heart* EMOTIONS, feelings, sentiments; soul, mind, bosom, breast; love, affection, passion. **3** *she has no heart* COMPASSION, sympathy, humanity, feeling(s), fellow feeling, tenderness, softness, empathy, understanding; kindness, goodwill. **4** *they may lose heart* ENTHUSIASM, keenness, eagerness, spirit, determination, resolve, purpose, courage, nerve, willpower, fortitude; *informal* guts, spunk. **5** *the heart of the city* CENTRE, middle, hub, core, nucleus, eye, bosom. **6** *the heart of the matter* ESSENCE, crux, core, nub, root, gist, meat, marrow, pith, substance, kernel; *informal* nitty-gritty.
— RELATED TERMS: cardiac, coronary.
— OPPOSITES: edge.
■ **after one's own heart** LIKE-MINDED, of the same mind, kindred, compatible, congenial, sharing one's tastes; *informal* on the same wavelength.
■ **at heart** DEEP DOWN, basically, fundamentally, essentially, in essence, intrinsically; really, actually, truly, in fact; *informal* when you get right down to it.
■ **by heart** FROM MEMORY, down pat, by rote, word for word, verbatim, word-perfect.
■ **do one's heart good** CHEER (UP), please, gladden, make one happy, delight, hearten, gratify, make one

feel good, give one a lift; *informal* give someone a buzz, tickle someone pink, buck up.

■ **eat one's heart out** PINE, long, ache, brood, mope, fret, sigh, sorrow, yearn, agonize; grieve, mourn, lament.

■ **from the (bottom of one's) heart** SINCERELY, earnestly, fervently, passionately, truly, genuinely, heartily, with all sincerity.

■ **give/lose one's heart to** FALL IN LOVE WITH, fall for, be smitten by; *informal* fall head over heels for, be swept off one's feet by, develop a crush on.

■ **have a change of heart** CHANGE ONE'S MIND, flip-flop, change one's tune, have second thoughts, have a rethink, think again, think twice; *informal* get cold feet, pull a U-ey.

■ **have a heart** BE COMPASSIONATE, be kind, be merciful, be lenient, be sympathetic, be considerate, have mercy.

■ **heart and soul** WHOLEHEARTEDLY, enthusiastically, eagerly, zealously; absolutely, completely, entirely, fully, utterly, to the hilt, one hundred per cent.

■ **take heart** BE ENCOURAGED, be heartened, be comforted; cheer up, brighten up, perk up, liven up, revive; *informal* buck up.

■ **with one's heart in one's mouth** IN ALARM, in fear, fearfully, apprehensively, on edge, with trepidation, in suspense, in a cold sweat, with bated breath, on tenterhooks; *informal* with butterflies in one's stomach, in a state, in a stew, in a sweat.

heartache ▶ noun ANGUISH, grief, suffering, distress, unhappiness, misery, sorrow, sadness, heartbreak, via dolorosa, pain, hurt, agony, angst, despondency, despair, woe, desolation.
– OPPOSITES: happiness.

heartbreak ▶ noun. See HEARTACHE.

heartbreaking ▶ adjective DISTRESSING, upsetting, disturbing, heart-rending, sad, tragic, painful, traumatic, agonizing, harrowing; pitiful, poignant, plaintive, moving, tear-jerking, gut-wrenching.
– OPPOSITES: comforting.

heartbroken ▶ adjective ANGUISHED, devastated, broken-hearted, heavy-hearted, grieving, grief-stricken, inconsolable, crushed, shattered, desolate, despairing; upset, distressed, miserable, sorrowful, sad, downcast, disconsolate, crestfallen, despondent; *informal* down in the dumps, cut up.

heartburn ▶ noun INDIGESTION, dyspepsia, pyrosis, acid reflux.

hearten ▶ verb CHEER (UP), encourage, raise someone's spirits, boost, buoy up, perk up, ginger up, inspirit, uplift, elate; comfort, reassure; *informal* buck up, pep up.

heartfelt ▶ adjective SINCERE, genuine, from the heart; earnest, profound, deep, wholehearted, ardent, fervent, passionate, enthusiastic, eager; honest, bona fide.
– OPPOSITES: insincere.

heartily ▶ adverb **1** *we heartily welcome the changes* WHOLEHEARTEDLY, sincerely, genuinely, warmly, profoundly, with all one's heart; eagerly, enthusiastically, earnestly, ardently. **2** *they were heartily sick of her* VERY, extremely, thoroughly, completely, absolutely, really, exceedingly, immensely, most, downright, quite, seriously; *informal* real, mighty.

heartless ▶ adjective UNFEELING, unsympathetic, unkind, uncaring, unconcerned, insensitive, inconsiderate, hard-hearted, stony-hearted,

cold-hearted, mean-spirited; cold, callous, cruel, merciless, pitiless, inhuman.
– OPPOSITES: compassionate.

heart-rending ▶ adjective DISTRESSING, upsetting, disturbing, heartbreaking, sad, tragic, painful, traumatic, harrowing; pitiful, poignant, plaintive, moving, tear-jerking, gut-wrenching.

heartsick ▶ adjective (*literary*) DESPONDENT, dejected, depressed, desolate, downcast, forlorn, unhappy, sad, upset, miserable, wretched, woebegone, inconsolable, grieving, grief-stricken, heavy-hearted, broken-hearted.
– OPPOSITES: happy.

heartthrob ▶ noun (*informal*) IDOL, pin-up, star, superstar; *informal* dreamboat, Adonis.

heart-to-heart ▶ adjective *a heart-to-heart chat* INTIMATE, personal, man-to-man, woman-to-woman; candid, honest, truthful, sincere.
▶ noun *they had a long heart-to-heart* PRIVATE CONVERSATION, tête-à-tête, one-to-one, chat, talk, word; *informal* confab, chinwag, natter.

heart-warming ▶ adjective TOUCHING, moving, heartening, stirring, uplifting, pleasing, cheering, gladdening, encouraging, gratifying.
– OPPOSITES: distressing.

hearty ▶ adjective **1** *a hearty character* EXUBERANT, jovial, ebullient, cheerful, uninhibited, effusive, lively, loud, animated, vivacious, energetic, spirited, dynamic, enthusiastic, eager; warm, cordial, friendly, affable, amiable, good natured. **2** *hearty congratulations* WHOLEHEARTED, heartfelt, sincere, genuine, real, true; earnest, fervent, ardent, enthusiastic. **3** *a hearty woman of sixty-five* ROBUST, healthy, hardy, fit, flourishing, blooming, fighting fit, fit as a fiddle; vigorous, sturdy, strong; *informal* full of vim. **4** *a hearty meal* SUBSTANTIAL, large, ample, sizeable, filling, generous, square, solid; healthy.
– OPPOSITES: introverted, half-hearted, frail, light.

heat ▶ noun **1** *a plant sensitive to heat* WARMTH, hotness, warmness, high temperature; hot weather, warm weather, sultriness, mugginess, humidity; heat wave, hot spell. **2** *he took the heat out of the dispute* PASSION, intensity, vehemence, warmth, fervour, fervency; enthusiasm, excitement, agitation; anger, fury. **3** *a female bear in heat* ESTRUS, season, sexual receptivity.
– RELATED TERMS: thermal.
– OPPOSITES: cold, apathy.

▶ verb **1** *the food was heated* WARM (UP), heat up, make hot, make warm; reheat, cook, microwave; *informal* nuke, zap. **2** *the pipes expand as they heat up* BECOME HOT, become warm, get hotter, get warmer, increase in temperature. **3** *he calmed down as quickly as he had heated up* BECOME IMPASSIONED, become excited, become animated; get angry, become enraged.
– OPPOSITES: cool.

heated ▶ adjective **1** *a heated swimming pool* WARM, hot; thermal. **2** *a heated argument* VEHEMENT, passionate, impassioned, animated, spirited, lively, intense, fiery; angry, bitter, furious, fierce, stormy, tempestuous. **3** *Robert grew heated as he spoke of the risks* EXCITED, animated, inflamed, worked up, wound up, keyed up; *informal* het up, in a state.

heater ▶ noun RADIATOR, furnace, convector, fire, brazier, warmer, Quebec heater ✦, wood stove, airtight stove, Franklin stove.

heathen ▶ noun **1** *the evangelist preached to the heathens* PAGAN, infidel, idolater, heretic, unbeliever, disbeliever, non-believer, atheist, agnostic, skeptic;

archaic paynim. **2** *heathens who spoil good whisky with ice* PHILISTINE, boor, oaf, ignoramus, lout, yahoo, vulgarian, plebeian; *informal* pleb, peasant.
− OPPOSITES: believer.

▶ **adjective** *a heathen practice* PAGAN, infidel, idolatrous, heathenish; unbelieving, non-believing, atheistic, agnostic, heretical, faithless, godless, irreligious, ungodly, unholy; barbarian, barbarous, uncivilized, uncultured, primitive, ignorant, philistine.

heave ▶ **verb** **1** *she heaved the sofa backwards* HAUL, pull, lug, drag, draw, tug, heft; *informal* hump, yank. **2** (*informal*) *she heaved a brick at him* THROW, fling, cast, toss, huck ✖, hurl, lob, pitch; *informal* chuck, sling. **3** *he heaved a sigh of relief* LET OUT, breathe, give, sigh; emit, utter. **4** *the sea heaved* RISE AND FALL, roll, swell, surge, churn, seethe, swirl. **5** *she heaved into the sink* RETCH, gag; vomit, bring up, cough up, be sick, get sick; *informal* throw up, puke, chuck up, hurl, spew, barf, upchuck, ralph.

heaven ▶ **noun** **1** *the good will have a place in heaven* PARADISE, nirvana, Zion; the hereafter, the next world, the next life, Elysium, the Elysian Fields, Valhalla; *literary* the empyrean. **2** *a good book is my idea of heaven* BLISS, ecstasy, rapture, contentment, happiness, delight, joy, seventh heaven; paradise, Utopia, nirvana. **3** *he observed the heavens* THE SKY, the skies, the upper atmosphere, the stratosphere, space; *literary* the firmament, the vault of heaven, the blue, the (wide) blue yonder, the welkin, the empyrean, the azure, the upper regions, the sphere.
− RELATED TERMS: celestial.
− OPPOSITES: hell, misery.

■ **in seventh heaven** ECSTATIC, euphoric, thrilled, elated, delighted, overjoyed, on cloud nine, walking on air, jubilant, rapturous, jumping for joy, transported, delirious, blissful; *informal* over the moon, on top of the world, on a high, tickled pink, as happy as a clam.

■ **move heaven and earth** TRY ONE'S HARDEST, do one's best, do one's utmost, do all one can, give one's all, spare no effort, put oneself out; strive, exert oneself, work hard; *informal* bend over backwards, do one's damnedest, pull out all the stops, go all out, bust a gut.

heavenly ▶ **adjective** **1** *heavenly choirs* DIVINE, holy, celestial, supernal; angelic, seraphic, cherubic; *literary* empyrean. **2** *heavenly constellations* CELESTIAL, cosmic, stellar, astral; planetary; extraterrestrial, superterrestrial. **3** (*informal*) *a heavenly morning* DELIGHTFUL, wonderful, glorious, perfect, excellent, sublime, idyllic, first-class, first-rate; blissful, pleasurable, enjoyable; exquisite, beautiful, lovely, gorgeous, enchanting; *informal* divine, super, great, fantastic, fabulous, terrific.
− OPPOSITES: mortal, infernal, terrestrial, dreadful.

heaven-sent ▶ **adjective** AUSPICIOUS, providential, propitious, felicitous, opportune, golden, favourable, advantageous, serendipitous, lucky, happy, good, fortunate.
− OPPOSITES: inopportune.

heavily ▶ **adverb** **1** *Dad walked heavily* LABORIOUSLY, slowly, ponderously, woodenly, stiffly; with difficulty, painfully, awkwardly, clumsily. **2** *we were heavily defeated* DECISIVELY, conclusively, roundly, soundly; utterly, completely, thoroughly. **3** *he drank heavily* EXCESSIVELY, to excess, immoderately, copiously, inordinately, intemperately, a great deal, too much, overmuch. **4** *the area is heavily planted with trees* DENSELY, closely, thickly. **5** *I became heavily*

involved DEEPLY, very, extremely, greatly, exceedingly, tremendously, profoundly; *informal* seriously, ever so.
− OPPOSITES: easily, narrowly, moderately.

heavy ▶ **adjective** **1** *a heavy box* WEIGHTY, hefty, substantial, ponderous; solid, dense, leaden; burdensome; *informal* hulking, weighing a ton. **2** *a heavy man* OVERWEIGHT, fat, obese, corpulent, large, bulky, stout, stocky, portly, plump, paunchy, fleshy; *informal* hulking, tubby, beefy, porky, pudgy. **3** *a heavy blow to the head* FORCEFUL, hard, strong, violent, powerful, vigorous, mighty, hefty, sharp, smart, severe. **4** *a gardener did the heavy work for me* ARDUOUS, hard, physical, laborious, difficult, strenuous, demanding, tough, onerous, back-breaking, gruelling; *archaic* toilsome. **5** *a heavy burden of responsibility* ONEROUS, burdensome, demanding, challenging, difficult, formidable, weighty; worrisome, stressful, trying, crushing, oppressive. **6** *heavy fog* DENSE, thick, soupy, murky, impenetrable. **7** *a heavy sky* OVERCAST, cloudy, clouded, grey, dull, gloomy, murky, dark, black, stormy, leaden, lowering. **8** *heavy rain* TORRENTIAL, relentless, copious, teeming, severe. **9** *heavy soil* CLAY, clayey, muddy, sticky, wet. **10** *a heavy fine* SIZEABLE, hefty, substantial, colossal, big, considerable; stiff; *informal* tidy, whopping, steep, astronomical. **11** *heavy seas* TEMPESTUOUS, turbulent, rough, wild, stormy, choppy, squally. **12** *heavy fighting* INTENSE, fierce, vigorous, relentless, all-out, severe, serious. **13** *a heavy drinker* IMMODERATE, excessive, intemperate, overindulgent, unrestrained, uncontrolled. **14** *a heavy meal* SUBSTANTIAL, filling, hearty, large, big, ample, sizeable, generous, square, solid. **15** *their diet is heavy on vegetables* ABOUNDING IN, abundant in, lavish with, profuse with, unstinting with, using a lot of. **16** *he felt heavy and very tired* LETHARGIC, listless, sluggish, torpid, languid, apathetic, logy. **17** *a heavy heart* SAD, sorrowful, melancholy, gloomy, downcast, downhearted, heartbroken, dejected, disconsolate, demoralized, despondent, depressed, crestfallen, desolate, down; *informal* blue; *literary* dolorous. **18** *these poems are rather heavy* TEDIOUS, difficult, dull, dry, serious, heavy going, dreary, boring, turgid, uninteresting. **19** *branches heavy with blossoms* LADEN, loaded, covered, filled, groaning, bursting, teeming, abounding. **20** *a heavy crop* BOUNTIFUL, plentiful, abundant, large, bumper, rich, copious, considerable, sizeable, profuse; *informal* whopping; *literary* plenteous. **21** *he has heavy features* COARSE, rough, rough-hewn, unrefined; rugged, craggy.
− OPPOSITES: light, thin, gentle, easy, bright, friable, small, calm, moderate, energetic, cheerful, meagre, delicate.

heavy-handed ▶ **adjective** **1** *they are heavy-handed with the equipment* CLUMSY, awkward, maladroit, unhandy, inept, unskilful; *informal* ham-handed, ham-fisted, all thumbs. **2** *heavy-handed policing* INSENSITIVE, oppressive, overbearing, high-handed, harsh, stern, tyrannical, despotic, ruthless, merciless; tactless, undiplomatic, inept.
− OPPOSITES: dexterous, sensitive.

heavy-hearted ▶ **adjective** MELANCHOLY, sad, sorrowful, mournful, gloomy, depressed, desolate, despondent, dejected, downhearted, downcast, crestfallen, disconsolate, glum, miserable, wretched, dismal, morose, woeful, woebegone, doleful, unhappy; *informal* down in the dumps, down in the mouth, blue; *literary* dolorous.
− OPPOSITES: cheerful.

heckle ▶ verb JEER, taunt, jibe at, shout down, boo, hiss, harass; *informal* give someone a hard time.
— OPPOSITES: cheer.

hectic ▶ adjective FRANTIC, frenetic, frenzied, feverish, manic, busy, active, fast and furious, fast-paced; lively, brisk, bustling, buzzing, abuzz.
— OPPOSITES: leisurely.

hector ▶ verb BULLY, intimidate, browbeat, harass, torment, plague; coerce, strong-arm; threaten, menace; *informal* bulldoze, bullyrag.

hedge ▶ noun **1** *high hedges* HEDGEROW, bushes; windbreak. **2** *an excellent hedge against a fall in the dollar* SAFEGUARD, protection, shield, screen, guard, buffer, cushion; insurance, security. **3** *his analysis is full of hedges* EQUIVOCATION, evasion, fudge, quibble, qualification; temporizing, uncertainty, prevarication, vagueness.
▶ verb **1** *fields hedged with caragana* SURROUND, enclose, encircle, ring, border, edge, bound. **2** *she was hedged in by her education* CONFINE, restrict, limit, hinder, obstruct, impede, constrain, trap; hem in. **3** *he hedged at every new question* PREVARICATE, equivocate, vacillate, quibble, hesitate, stall, dodge the issue, be noncommittal, be evasive, be vague, beat around the bush, pussyfoot around, mince one's words; hem and haw; *informal* sit on the fence, duck the question. **4** *the company hedged its position on the market* SAFEGUARD, protect, shield, guard, cushion; cover, insure.

hedonism ▶ noun SELF-INDULGENCE, pleasure-seeking, self-gratification, lotus-eating, sybaritism; intemperance, immoderation, extravagance, luxury, high living.
— OPPOSITES: self-restraint.

hedonist ▶ noun SYBARITE, sensualist, voluptuary, pleasure-seeker, bon viveur, bon vivant; epicure, gastronome.
— OPPOSITES: ascetic.

hedonistic ▶ adjective SELF-INDULGENT, pleasure-seeking, sybaritic, lotus-eating, epicurean, good-time; unrestrained, intemperate, immoderate, extravagant, decadent.

heed ▶ verb *heed the warnings* PAY ATTENTION TO, take notice of, take note of, pay heed to, attend to, listen to; bear in mind, be mindful of, mind, mark, consider, take into account, follow, obey, adhere to, abide by, observe, take to heart, be alert to.
— OPPOSITES: disregard.
▶ noun *he paid no heed* ATTENTION, notice, note, regard; consideration, thought, care.

heedful ▶ adjective ATTENTIVE, careful, mindful, cautious, prudent, circumspect; alert, aware, wary, chary, watchful, vigilant, on guard, on the alert.

heedless ▶ adjective UNMINDFUL, taking no notice, paying no heed, unheeding, disregardful, neglectful, oblivious, inattentive, blind, deaf; incautious, imprudent, rash, reckless, foolhardy, improvident, unwary.

heel[1] ▶ noun **1** *shoes with low heels* wedge, stiletto. **2** *the heel of a loaf* TAIL END, end, crust, remnant, remainder, remains. **3** *(informal, dated) you're such a heel* SCOUNDREL, rogue, rascal, reprobate, miscreant; *informal* beast, rat, louse, swine, snake, scumbag, scum-bucket, scuzzball, sleazeball, sleazebag, stinker.
■ **take to one's heels** RUN AWAY, run off, make a run for it, take flight, take off, make a break for it, flee, make one's getaway, escape; *informal* beat it, clear off,

vamoose, skedaddle, split, cut and run, hotfoot it, scram, light out, bug out.

heel[2] ▶ verb *the ship heeled to starboard* LEAN OVER, list, careen, tilt, tip, incline, keel over.

heft ▶ verb LIFT (UP), raise (up), heave, hoist, haul; carry, lug, tote; *informal* cart, hump.
▶ noun WEIGHT, heaviness, bulk.

hefty ▶ adjective **1** *a hefty young man* BURLY, heavy, sturdy, strapping, bulky, brawny, husky, strong, muscular, large, big, solid, well-built; portly, stout; *informal* hulking, hunky, beefy. **2** *a hefty kick* POWERFUL, violent, hard, forceful, heavy, mighty. **3** *hefty loads of timber* HEAVY, weighty, bulky, big, large, substantial, massive, ponderous; unwieldy, cumbersome, burdensome, hulking. **4** *a hefty fine* SUBSTANTIAL, sizeable, considerable, stiff, extortionate, large, excessive; *informal* steep, astronomical, whopping.
— OPPOSITES: slight, feeble, light, small.

hegemony ▶ noun LEADERSHIP, dominance, dominion, sway, rule, sovereignty.

height ▶ noun **1** *the height of the wall* SIZE, tallness, extent upwards, vertical measurement, elevation, stature, altitude. **2** *the mountain heights* SUMMIT, top, peak, crest, crown, tip, cap, pinnacle, apex, brow, ridge. **3** *the height of their fame* HIGHEST POINT, crowning moment, peak, acme, zenith, apogee, pinnacle, climax, high-water mark. **4** *the height of bad manners* EPITOME, acme, zenith, quintessence, very limit; ultimate, utmost. **5** *he is terrified of heights* HIGH PLACES, high ground; precipices, cliffs.
— OPPOSITES: width, nadir.

heighten ▶ verb **1** *the roof had to be heightened* RAISE, make higher, lift (up), elevate. **2** *her pleasure was heightened by guilt* INTENSIFY, increase, enhance, add to, augment, boost, strengthen, deepen, magnify, amplify, aggravate, reinforce.
— OPPOSITES: lower, reduce.

heinous ▶ adjective ODIOUS, wicked, evil, atrocious, monstrous, abominable, detestable, contemptible, reprehensible, despicable, egregious, horrific, terrible, awful, abhorrent, loathsome, hideous, unspeakable, execrable; iniquitous, villainous, beyond the pale.
— OPPOSITES: admirable.

heir, heiress ▶ noun SUCCESSOR, next in line, inheritor, beneficiary, legatee; descendant, scion; *Law* devisee.

heist ▶ noun *See* ROBBERY.

helicopter ▶ noun CHOPPER, copter; *informal* egg beater, helo, whirlybird.

helix ▶ noun SPIRAL, coil, corkscrew, curl, twist, gyre, whorl, convolution.

hell ▶ noun **1** *they feared hell* THE NETHERWORLD, the Inferno, the infernal regions, the abyss; eternal damnation, perdition; hellfire, fire and brimstone; Hades, Acheron, Gehenna, Tophet, Sheol; *literary* the pit. **2** *he made her life hell* A MISERY, torture, agony, a torment, a nightmare, an ordeal; anguish, wretchedness, woe.
— RELATED TERMS: infernal.
— OPPOSITES: heaven, paradise.
■ **give someone hell** *(informal)* **1** *when I found out I gave him hell* REPRIMAND SEVERELY, rebuke, admonish, chastise, castigate, chide, upbraid, reprove, scold, berate, remonstrate with, reprehend, take to task, lambaste; read someone the riot act, give someone a piece of one's mind, haul over the coals; *informal* tell

off, dress down, give someone an earful, give someone a roasting, rap over the knuckles, let someone have it, bawl out, come down hard on, lay into, blast, tear a strip off someone, chew out. **2** *she gave me hell when I was her junior* HARASS, hound, plague, harry, bother, trouble, bully, intimidate, pick on, victimize, terrorize; *informal* hassle, give someone a hard time.

■ **raise hell** (*informal*) **1** *they were hollering and raising hell* CAUSE A DISTURBANCE, cause a commotion, be noisy, run riot, run wild, go on the rampage, be out of control; *informal* raise the roof. **2** *he raised hell with the planners* REMONSTRATE, expostulate, be angry, be furious; argue; *informal* kick up a fuss, raise a stink.

hell-bent ▶ adjective INTENT, bent, determined, (dead) set, insistent, fixed, resolved; single-minded, fixated.
— OPPOSITES: half-hearted.

hellish ▶ adjective **1** *the hellish face of Death* INFERNAL, Hadean, chthonic; diabolical, fiendish, satanic, demonic; evil, wicked. **2** (*informal*) *a hellish week* HORRIBLE, rotten, awful, terrible, dreadful, ghastly, horrid, vile, foul, appalling, atrocious, horrendous, frightful; difficult, unpleasant, nasty, disagreeable; stressful, taxing, tough, hard, frustrating, fraught, traumatic, gruelling; *informal* murderous, lousy; beastly, hellacious.
— OPPOSITES: angelic, wonderful.

hello ▶ exclamation HI, howdy, hey, hiya, ciao, aloha.

helm ▶ noun *he took the helm* TILLER, wheel; steering gear, rudder.
■ **at the helm** IN CHARGE, in command, in control, responsible, in authority, at the wheel, in the driver's seat, in the saddle, holding the reins, running the show, calling the shots.

help ▶ verb **1** *can you help me please?* ASSIST, aid, lend a (helping) hand to, give assistance to, come to the aid of; be of service to, be of use to; do someone a favour, do someone a service, do someone a good turn, bail someone out, come to the rescue, give someone a leg up; rally round, pitch in; *informal* get someone out of a tight spot, save someone's bacon, save someone's skin. **2** *this credit card helps cancer research* SUPPORT, contribute to, give money to, donate to; promote, boost, back; further the interests of, bankroll. **3** *sore throats are helped by lozenges* RELIEVE, soothe, ease, alleviate, make better, improve, assuage, lessen; remedy, cure, heal.
— OPPOSITES: hinder, impede, worsen.
▶ noun **1** *this could be of help to you* ASSISTANCE, aid, helping hand, support, succour, advice, guidance, TLC; benefit, use, advantage, service, comfort; *informal* a shot in the arm. **2** *he sought help for his eczema* RELIEF, alleviation, improvement, assuagement, healing; a remedy, a cure, a restorative. **3** *they treated the help badly* DOMESTIC WORKER, domestic servant, cleaner, cleaning lady, housekeeper, home help, maid, housemaid, houseman, hired help, helper.
▶ exclamation SOS, mayday.
■ **cannot help** *he could not help laughing* BE UNABLE TO STOP, be unable to refrain from, be unable to keep from.
■ **help oneself to** STEAL, take, appropriate, 'borrow', 'liberate', pocket, lift, purloin, commandeer; *informal* swipe, nab, filch, snaffle, walk off with, run off with, pinch, knock off.

helper ▶ noun ASSISTANT, aide, helpmate, helpmeet, deputy, auxiliary, second, right-hand man/woman,

attendant, acolyte; co-worker, workmate, teammate, associate, colleague, partner; *informal* sidekick.

helpful ▶ adjective **1** *the staff are helpful* OBLIGING, eager to please, kind, accommodating, supportive, co-operative; sympathetic, neighbourly, charitable. **2** *we found your comments helpful* USEFUL, of use, beneficial, valuable, profitable, advantageous, fruitful, worthwhile, constructive; informative, instructive. **3** *a helpful new tool* HANDY, useful, convenient, practical, easy-to-use, functional, serviceable; *informal* neat, nifty.
— OPPOSITES: unsympathetic, useless, inconvenient.

helping ▶ noun PORTION, serving, piece, slice, share, ration, allocation; *informal* dollop.

helpless ▶ adjective DEPENDENT, incapable, powerless, impotent, weak; defenceless, vulnerable, exposed, unprotected, open to attack; paralyzed, disabled.
— OPPOSITES: independent.

helpmate, helpmeet ▶ noun HELPER, assistant, attendant; supporter, friend, companion; spouse, (life) partner, mate, husband, wife.

helter-skelter ▶ adverb *they ran helter-skelter down the hill* HEADLONG, pell-mell, hotfoot, post-haste, hastily, hurriedly, at full tilt, hell for leather; recklessly, precipitately, heedlessly, wildly; *informal* like a bat out of hell, like the wind, like greased lightning, like a bomb, lickety-split.
▶ adjective *a helter-skelter collection of houses* DISORDERED, disorderly, chaotic, muddled, jumbled, untidy, haphazard, disorganized, topsy-turvy; *informal* higgledy-piggledy.
— OPPOSITES: orderly.

hem ▶ noun *the hem of her dress* EDGE, edging, border, trim, trimming.
■ **hem someone/something in 1** *a bay hemmed in by pine trees* SURROUND, border, edge, encircle, circle, ring, enclose, skirt, fringe, encompass, corral. **2** *we were hemmed in by the rules* RESTRICT, confine, trap, hedge in, fence in; constrain, restrain, limit, curb, check.
■ **hem and haw** HESITATE, dither, vacillate, be indecisive, equivocate, prevaricate, waver, blow hot and cold; *informal* shilly-shally.

he-man ▶ noun (*informal*) MUSCLEMAN, strongman, macho man, iron man; Hercules, Samson, Tarzan; *informal* hunk, tough guy, alpha male, beefcake, bruiser.
— OPPOSITES: wimp.

hence ▶ adverb CONSEQUENTLY, as a consequence, for this reason, therefore, ergo, thus, so, accordingly, as a result, because of that, that being so.

henceforth, henceforward ▶ adverb FROM NOW ON, as of now, in (the) future, hence, subsequently, from this day on, from this day forth; *formal* hereafter.

henchman ▶ noun RIGHT-HAND MAN, assistant, aide, helper; underling, minion, man Friday, lackey, flunky, stooge; bodyguard, minder; *informal* sidekick, crony, heavy, goon.

henpecked ▶ adjective BROWBEATEN, downtrodden, bullied, dominated, subjugated, oppressed, intimidated; meek, timid, cringing, long-suffering; *informal* under someone's thumb.
— OPPOSITES: domineering.

herald ▶ noun **1** (*historical*) *a herald announced the armistice* MESSENGER, courier; proclaimer, announcer, crier. **2** *the first herald of spring* HARBINGER, sign, indicator, indication, signal, prelude, portent, omen; forerunner, precursor; *literary* foretoken.

▶ **verb 1** *shouts heralded their approach* PROCLAIM, announce, broadcast, publicize, declare, trumpet, blazon, advertise. **2** *the speech heralded a policy change* SIGNAL, indicate, announce, spell, presage, augur, portend, promise, foretell; usher in, pave the way for, be a harbinger of; *literary* foretoken, betoken.

herb ▶ **noun**. See table. See also the table at SPICE.

Herbs

angelica	lovage
anise	marjoram
basil	oregano
bay leaf	parsley
bergamot	purslane
bush basil	rosemary
chervil	sage
chive	salad burnet
cilantro	savory
comfrey	tarragon
dill	thyme
dillweed	bouquet garni
fennel	fines herbes
lemon thyme	

Herculean ▶ **adjective 1** *a Herculean task* ARDUOUS, gruelling, laborious, back-breaking, onerous, strenuous, difficult, formidable, hard, tough, huge, massive, uphill; demanding, exhausting, taxing; *archaic* toilsome. **2** *his Herculean build* STRONG, muscular, muscly, powerful, robust, solid, strapping, brawny, burly; *informal* hunky, beefy, hulking.

— OPPOSITES: easy, puny.

herd ▶ **noun 1** *a herd of cows* drove, flock, pack, fold; group, collection. **2** *a herd of actors* CROWD, group, bunch, horde, mob, host, pack, multitude, throng, swarm, company. **3** *they consider themselves above the herd* THE COMMON PEOPLE, the masses, the rank and file, the crowd, the commonality, the plebeians; the hoi polloi, the mob, the proletariat, the rabble, the riff-raff, the great unwashed; *informal* the proles, the plebs.

▶ **verb 1** *we herded the sheep into the pen* DRIVE, shepherd, guide; round up, gather, collect, corral. **2** *we all herded into the room* CROWD, pack, flock; cluster, huddle. **3** *they herd reindeer* TEND, look after, keep, watch (over), mind, guard.

herdsman, herdswoman ▶ **noun** CATTLEMAN, cowherd, cowhand, cowman, cowboy, rancher, shepherd, ranchero, stockman, herder, drover; *informal* cowpuncher, cowpoke; *archaic* herd.

here ▶ **adverb 1** *they lived here* AT/IN THIS PLACE, at/in this spot, at/in this location. **2** *I am here now* PRESENT, in attendance, attending, at hand; available. **3** *come here tomorrow* TO THIS PLACE, to this spot, to this location, over here, nearer, closer; *literary* hither. **4** *here is your opportunity* NOW, at this moment, at this point (in time), at this juncture, at this stage.

— OPPOSITES: absent.

■ **here and there 1** *clumps of heather here and there* IN VARIOUS PLACES, in different places; at random. **2** *they darted here and there* HITHER AND THITHER, around, about, to and fro, back and forth, in all directions.

hereafter ▶ **adverb** (*formal*) *nothing I say hereafter is intended to offend* FROM NOW ON, after this, as of now, from this moment forth, from this day forth, from this day forward, subsequently, in (the) future, hence, henceforth, henceforward; *formal* hereinafter.

▶ **noun** *our preparation for the hereafter* LIFE AFTER DEATH, the afterlife, the afterworld, the next world; eternity, heaven, paradise.

hereditary ▶ **adjective 1** *a hereditary right* INHERITED; bequeathed, willed, handed-down, passed-down, passed-on, transferred; ancestral, family, familial. **2** *a hereditary disease* GENETIC, congenital, inborn, inherited, inbred, innate; in the family, in the blood, in the genes.

heredity ▶ **noun** CONGENITAL TRAITS, genetic makeup, genes; ancestry, descent, extraction, parentage.

heresy ▶ **noun** DISSENSION, dissent, nonconformity, heterodoxy, unorthodoxy, apostasy, blasphemy, freethinking; agnosticism, atheism, non-belief; idolatry, paganism.

heretic ▶ **noun** DISSENTER, nonconformist, apostate, freethinker, iconoclast; agnostic, atheist, non-believer, unbeliever, idolater, idolatress, pagan, heathen; *archaic* paynim.

— OPPOSITES: conformist, believer.

heritage ▶ **noun 1** *they stole his heritage* INHERITANCE, birthright, patrimony; legacy, bequest. **2** *Canada's cultural heritage* TRADITION, history, past, background; culture, customs. **3** *his Greek heritage* ANCESTRY, lineage, descent, extraction, parentage, roots, background, heredity.

hermaphrodite ▶ **noun** ANDROGYNE, intersex, epicene; *Biology* bisexual, gynandromorph.

▶ **adjective** *hermaphrodite creatures* ANDROGYNOUS, intersex, hermaphroditic, hermaphroditical, epicene; *Biology* bisexual.

hermetic ▶ **adjective** AIRTIGHT, tight, sealed, zip-locked, vacuum packed; watertight, waterproof.

hermit ▶ **noun** RECLUSE, solitary, loner, ascetic, marabout, troglodyte; *historical* anchorite, anchoress; *archaic* eremite.

hero ▶ **noun 1** *a war hero* BRAVE MAN, man of courage, man of the hour, lion-heart, warrior, knight; champion, victor, conqueror. **2** *a football hero* STAR, superstar, megastar, idol, celebrity, luminary; ideal, paragon, shining example, demigod; favourite, darling. **3** *the hero of the film* (MALE) PROTAGONIST, principal (male) character/role, main character, title character, starring role, star part; (male) lead, lead (actor), leading man.

— OPPOSITES: coward, loser, villain.

heroic ▶ **adjective** BRAVE, courageous, valiant, valorous, lion-hearted, superhuman, intrepid, bold, fearless, daring, audacious; unafraid, undaunted, dauntless, doughty, plucky, manly, stout-hearted, mettlesome; gallant, chivalrous, noble; *informal* gutsy, spunky, ballsy.

heroin ▶ **noun** OPIATE; *informal* H, horse, skag, dynamite, junk, sugar, China White, smack.

heroine ▶ **noun 1** *she's a heroine — she saved my baby* BRAVE WOMAN, hero, woman of courage, woman of the hour; victor, winner, conqueror. **2** *the literary heroine of Moscow* STAR, superstar, megastar, idol, celebrity, luminary; ideal, paragon, shining example; favourite, darling, queen; *informal* celeb. **3** *the film's heroine* (FEMALE) PROTAGONIST, principal (female) character/role, main character, title character; (female) lead, lead (actress), leading lady; prima donna, diva.

heroism ▶ **noun** BRAVERY, courage, valour, intrepidity, boldness, daring, audacity, fearlessness, dauntlessness, pluck, stout-heartedness, lion-heartedness; backbone, spine, grit, spirit, mettle; gallantry, chivalry; *informal* guts, spunk, balls, cojones, moxie.

hero-worship ▶ noun IDOLIZATION, adulation, admiration, lionization, idealization, worship, adoration, veneration.

hesitancy ▶ noun. See HESITATION.

hesitant ▶ adjective **1** *she is hesitant about buying* UNCERTAIN, undecided, unsure, doubtful, dubious, skeptical; tentative, nervous, reluctant, gun-shy; indecisive, irresolute, hesitating, dithering, vacillating, wavering, waffling, blowing hot and cold; ambivalent, of two minds, hemming and hawing; *informal* iffy. **2** *a hesitant child* LACKING CONFIDENCE, diffident, timid, shy, bashful, insecure, tentative.
– OPPOSITES: certain, decisive, confident.

hesitate ▶ verb **1** *she hesitated, unsure of what to say* PAUSE, delay, wait, shilly-shally, dilly-dally, dither, stall, temporize; be of two minds, be uncertain, be unsure, be doubtful, be indecisive, hedge, equivocate, fluctuate, vacillate, waver, waffle, blow hot and cold, have second thoughts, get cold feet, think twice, hem and haw. **2** *don't hesitate to contact me* BE RELUCTANT, be unwilling, be disinclined, scruple; have misgivings about, have qualms about, shrink from, demur from, think twice about, balk at; *informal* miss a beat.

hesitation ▶ noun HESITANCY, uncertainty, unsureness, doubt, doubtfulness, dubiousness; irresolution, irresoluteness, indecision, indecisiveness, hesitance; equivocation, vacillation, waffling, wavering, second thoughts; dithering, stalling, dawdling, temporization, delay; reluctance, disinclination, unease, ambivalence; *informal* cold feet; *formal* dubiety.

heterodox ▶ adjective UNORTHODOX, nonconformist, dissenting, dissident, rebellious, renegade; heretical, blasphemous, recusant, apostate, skeptical; freethinking, unconventional.
– OPPOSITES: orthodox.

heterogeneous ▶ adjective DIVERSE, varied, varying, variegated, miscellaneous, assorted, mixed, sundry, disparate, multifarious, different, differing, motley; *informal* hodgepodge, mixed-bag; *literary* divers.
– OPPOSITES: homogeneous.

heterosexual ▶ adjective STRAIGHT; *informal* hetero, het.

hew ▶ verb CHOP, hack, cut, lop, axe, cleave, split; fell; carve, chisel, shape, fashion, sculpt, model.

heyday ▶ noun PRIME, peak, height, pinnacle, summit, apex, acme, zenith, climax, high point; day, time, bloom, flowering; prime of life, salad days, halcyon days, glory days.

hiatus ▶ noun PAUSE, break, gap, lacuna, interval, intermission, interlude, interruption, suspension, lull, respite, time out, time off, recess; *informal* breather, let-up.

hibernate ▶ verb **1** *bears hibernate in winter* LIE DORMANT, lie torpid, sleep; overwinter. **2** *he wanted to hibernate in front of a fire for the night* HOLE UP, escape, withdraw, retreat, cocoon.

hick ▶ noun *a hick from the sticks* (COUNTRY) BUMPKIN, yokel, rustic, hillbilly, country-dweller, peasant, hayseed, provincial, country cousin, rube; (*Nfld*) baywop ✦, (*Nfld*) bayman ✦.
▶ adjective **1** *a hick town* RURAL, rustic, backwater, backwoods, outlying, jerkwater. **2** *hick attitudes* SMALL-TOWN, unsophisticated, rural, narrow-minded, small-minded, parochial, bush-league.

hicksville ▶ noun SMALL TOWN, jerkwater, backwoods, boondocks, the sticks, in the middle of nowhere, the back of beyond, hinterland; (*Nfld*) outport ✦, nowheresville, Podunk.

hidden ▶ adjective **1** *a hidden camera* CONCEALED, secret, undercover, invisible, unseen, out of sight, closeted, covert; secluded, tucked away; camouflaged, disguised, masked, cloaked. **2** *a hidden meaning* OBSCURE, unclear, veiled, clouded, shrouded, concealed; cryptic, mysterious, secret, abstruse, arcane; ulterior, deep, subliminal, coded.
– OPPOSITES: visible, obvious.

hide[1] ▶ verb **1** *he hid the money* CONCEAL, secrete, put out of sight; camouflage; lock up, stow away, tuck away, squirrel away, cache; *informal* stash. **2** *they hid in an air vent* CONCEAL ONESELF, sequester oneself, hide out, take cover, keep out of sight; lie low, go underground; *informal* hole up, lie doggo. **3** *clouds hid the moon* OBSCURE, block out, blot out, obstruct, cloud, shroud, veil, blanket, envelop, eclipse. **4** *he could not hide his dislike* CONCEAL, keep secret, cover up, keep quiet about, hush up, bottle up, suppress, curtain, bury; disguise, dissemble, mask, camouflage; *informal* keep under one's hat, keep a/the lid on.
– OPPOSITES: flaunt, reveal.

hide[2] ▶ noun *the hide should be tanned quickly* SKIN, pelt, coat; leather.

hideaway ▶ noun RETREAT, refuge, hiding place, hideout, den, bolthole, shelter, sanctuary, sanctum; hermitage, secret place; *informal* hidey-hole.

hidebound ▶ adjective CONSERVATIVE, reactionary, conventional, orthodox; fundamentalist, diehard, hardline, dyed-in-the-wool, set in one's ways, unyielding, inflexible; narrow-minded, small-minded, intolerant, uncompromising, rigid; prejudiced, bigoted.
– OPPOSITES: liberal.

hideous ▶ adjective UGLY, repulsive, repellent, unsightly, revolting, gruesome, grotesque, monstrous, ghastly; *informal* as ugly as sin; awful, terrible, appalling, dreadful, frightful, horrible, horrendous, horrific, horrifying, shocking, sickening, unspeakable, abhorrent, heinous, abominable, foul, vile, odious, execrable.
– OPPOSITES: beautiful, pleasant.

hideout ▶ noun HIDING PLACE, hideaway, retreat, refuge, shelter, bolthole, safe house, sanctuary, sanctum; *informal* hidey-hole.

hiding[1] ▶ noun (*informal*) *they gave him a hiding* BEATING, battering, thrashing, thumping, pounding, drubbing, pummelling, flogging, whipping, caning, spanking; *informal* licking, belting, bashing, pasting, walloping, whacking, clobbering, tanning, shellacking, going-over.

hiding[2]
■ **in hiding** *the fugitive is in hiding* HIDDEN, concealed, lying low, underground, in a safe house; *informal* lying doggo.

hiding place ▶ noun See HIDEOUT.

hierarchy ▶ noun PECKING ORDER, order, ranking, chain of command, grading, gradation, ladder, scale, range.

higgledy-piggledy (*informal*) ▶ adjective *a big higgledy-piggledy pile of papers* DISORDERED, disorderly,

disorganized, untidy, messy, chaotic, jumbled, muddled, confused, unsystematic, irregular; out of order, in disarray, in a mess, in a muddle, haphazard; *informal* all over the place, upside-down, topsy-turvy, shambolic.
— OPPOSITES: tidy.

▶ adverb *the cars were parked higgledy-piggledy* IN DISORDER, in a muddle, in a jumble, in disarray, untidily, haphazardly, anyhow; *informal* all over the place, helter-skelter, topsy-turvy, every which way, pell-mell, any old how, all over the lot.

high ▶ adjective **1** *a high mountain* TALL, lofty, towering, soaring, elevated, giant, big; multi-storey, high-rise. **2** *a high position in the government* HIGH-RANKING, high-level, leading, top, top-level, prominent, pre-eminent, foremost, senior; influential, powerful, important, elevated, prime, premier, exalted, ranking; *informal* top-notch, chief. **3** *high principles* HIGH-MINDED, noble, lofty, moral, ethical, honourable, exalted, admirable, upright, honest, virtuous, righteous. **4** *high prices* INFLATED, excessive, unreasonable, expensive, costly, exorbitant, extortionate, prohibitive, dear; *informal* steep, stiff, pricey. **5** *high winds* STRONG, powerful, violent, intense, extreme, forceful; BLUSTERY, gusty, stiff, squally, tempestuous, turbulent, howling, roaring. **6** *the high life* LUXURIOUS, lavish, extravagant, grand, opulent; sybaritic, hedonistic, epicurean, decadent; upmarket, upscale; *informal* fancy, classy, swanky. **7** *I have a high opinion of you* FAVOURABLE, good, positive, approving, admiring, complimentary, commendatory, flattering, glowing, adulatory, rapturous. **8** *a high note* HIGH-PITCHED, high-frequency; soprano, treble, falsetto, shrill, sharp, piercing, penetrating. **9** (*informal*) *they are high on drugs* STONED, intoxicated, inebriated, drugged, impaired ◆, stupefied, befuddled, delirious, hallucinating; *informal* wired, hopped up, high as a kite, tripping, hyped up, doped up, spaced out, wasted, wrecked. **10** *high in fibre* ELEVATED, rich, ample, loaded, plentiful, full; *informal* chock full, chockablock, jam-packed.
— OPPOSITES: short, lowly, amoral, cheap, light, abstemious, unfavourable, deep, sober, low.

▶ noun *prices were at a rare high* HIGH LEVEL, high point, peak, high-water mark; pinnacle, zenith, acme, height.
— OPPOSITES: low.

▶ adverb *a jet flew high overhead* AT GREAT HEIGHT, high up, far up, way up, at altitude; in the air, in the sky, on high, aloft, overhead.
— OPPOSITES: low.

■ **high and dry** DESTITUTE, helpless, in the lurch, in difficulties; abandoned, stranded, marooned.

■ **high and low** EVERYWHERE, all over, all around, far and wide, {here, there, and everywhere}, extensively, thoroughly, widely, in every nook and cranny; *informal* all over the place, all over the map.

■ **high and mighty** (*informal*) SELF-IMPORTANT, condescending, patronizing, pompous, disdainful, supercilious, superior, snobbish, snobby, haughty, conceited, above oneself; *informal* stuck-up, puffed up, snooty, hoity-toity, la-di-da, uppity, full of oneself, too big for one's britches/boots.

■ **on a high** (*informal*) ECSTATIC, euphoric, exhilarated, delirious, elated, ebullient, thrilled, overjoyed, beside oneself, walking on air, on cloud nine, in seventh heaven, jumping for joy, in raptures, in high spirits, exultant, jubilant; excited, overexcited;

informal blissed out, over the moon, on top of the world.

high achiever ▶ noun *See* GO-GETTER.

high-born ▶ adjective NOBLE, aristocratic, well-born, titled, patrician, blue-blooded, upper-class, genteel; *informal* upper-crust, top-drawer; *archaic* gentle.
— OPPOSITES: lowly.

highbrow ▶ adjective *his work has a highbrow following* INTELLECTUAL, scholarly, bookish, well-read, literary, cultured, academic, educated, lettered, sophisticated, erudite, learned, cerebral; *informal* brainy, egghead, inkhorn.
— OPPOSITES: lowbrow.

▶ noun *highbrows who hate pop music* INTELLECTUAL, scholar, academic, bluestocking, bookish person, thinker; *informal* egghead, brain, bookworm, brainiac.

high-class ▶ adjective SUPERIOR, upper-class, first-rate; excellent, select, elite, choice, premier, top, top-flight; luxurious, deluxe, upscale, high-quality, top-quality, upmarket; *informal* top-notch, blue-ribbon, five-star, top-drawer, A1, ritzy, tony, classy, posh.

high-end ▶ adjective TOP-LINE, deluxe, best, top of the line, superior, top-notch, high-grade, upscale, upmarket, choice, first-class, first-rate, fancy; expensive, high-priced, pricey, costly.

highfalutin ▶ adjective (*informal*). *See* PRETENTIOUS.

high-flown ▶ adjective GRAND, extravagant, elaborate, flowery, lofty, ornate, overblown, overdone, overwrought, grandiloquent, magniloquent, grandiose, orotund, inflated, high sounding; affected, pretentious, bombastic, pompous, turgid; *informal* windy, purple, highfalutin, la-di-da.
— OPPOSITES: plain.

high-handed ▶ adjective IMPERIOUS, arbitrary, peremptory, arrogant, haughty, domineering, supercilious, pushy, overbearing, heavy-handed, lordly, magisterial; inflexible, rigid; autocratic, authoritarian, dictatorial, tyrannical; *informal* bossy, high and mighty.
— OPPOSITES: modest.

high-impact ▶ adjective IMPRESSIVE, bold, compelling, effective; punchy, forceful, powerful, high-powered, potent, hard-hitting; intensive, energetic, dynamic; *informal* high-octane.

highland ▶ noun UPLANDS, highlands, mountains, hills, heights, moors; upland, tableland, plateau, coteau.

highlight ▶ noun *the highlight of his career* HIGH POINT, best part, climax, peak, pinnacle, height, acme, zenith, summit, crowning moment, high-water mark, centrepiece.
— OPPOSITES: nadir.

▶ verb *he has highlighted shortcomings in the plan* SPOTLIGHT, call attention to, point out, single out, focus on, underline, feature, play up, show up, bring out, accentuate, accent, give prominence to, zero in on, stress, emphasize.

highly ▶ adverb **1** *a highly dangerous substance* VERY, extremely, exceedingly, particularly, most, really, thoroughly, decidedly, distinctly, exceptionally, immensely, greatly, inordinately, singularly, extraordinarily; *informal* awfully, terribly, majorly, seriously, supremely, desperately, hugely, ultra, oh-so, damn, damned; real, mighty, awful; *dated* frightfully. **2** *he was highly regarded* FAVOURABLY, well, appreciatively, admiringly, approvingly, positively,

glowingly, enthusiastically.
— OPPOSITES: slightly, unfavourably.

high-maintenance ▶ adjective DEMANDING, challenging, exacting, difficult, hard to please, needy.

high-minded ▶ adjective HIGH-PRINCIPLED, principled, honourable, moral, upright, upstanding, right-minded, noble, good, honest, decent, ethical, righteous, virtuous, worthy, idealistic.
— OPPOSITES: unprincipled.

high-octane ▶ adjective See HIGH-POWERED.

high-pitched ▶ adjective HIGH, high-frequency, shrill, sharp, piercing; soprano, treble, falsetto.
— OPPOSITES: deep.

high-powered ▶ adjective DYNAMIC, ambitious, energetic, assertive, enterprising, vigorous; forceful, powerful, potent, aggressive, high-octane; informal go-getting.

high-pressure ▶ adjective 1 high-pressure sales tactics FORCEFUL, insistent, persistent, pushy; intensive, high-powered, aggressive, coercive, compelling, not taking no for an answer. 2 a high-pressure job DEMANDING, stressful, nerve-racking, tense, pressured.

high-priced ▶ adjective EXPENSIVE, costly, dear, big-ticket, high end; overpriced, exorbitant, extortionate; informal pricey, steep, stiff.

high-profile ▶ adjective PROMINENT, well-known, famous, renowned, celebrated, legendary, notable, noteworthy, distinguished, eminent; visible, conspicuous; notorious, infamous.

high-ranking ▶ adjective See HIGH adjective sense 2.

high-risk ▶ adjective See RISKY.

high-sounding ▶ adjective See HIGH-FLOWN.

high-speed ▶ adjective FAST, quick, rapid, speedy, swift, breakneck, lightning, brisk, express; informal zippy, supersonic; literary fleet.
— OPPOSITES: slow.

high-spirited ▶ adjective LIVELY, spirited, full of fun, fun-loving, animated, zestful, bouncy, bubbly, sparkling, vivacious, buoyant, cheerful, joyful, exuberant, ebullient, jaunty, irrepressible; informal chirpy, peppy, full of beans; literary frolicsome.

high spirits ▶ plural noun LIVELINESS, vitality, spirit, zest, energy, bounce, sparkle, vivacity, buoyancy, cheerfulness, good humour, joy, joyfulness, exuberance, ebullience, joie de vivre; informal pep, zing.

high-strung ▶ adjective NERVOUS, excitable, agitated, temperamental, sensitive, unstable; brittle, on edge, edgy, jumpy, jittery, restless, anxious, tense, stressed, overwrought, neurotic; informal worked up, uptight, twitchy, wired, wound up, het up, strung out.
— OPPOSITES: easygoing.

highway ▶ noun MAIN ROAD, main route, direct route; parkway, throughway, freeway, expressway, (Que.) autoroute ✤.

hijack ▶ verb COMMANDEER, seize, take over, take control; skyjack, carjack; appropriate, expropriate, confiscate, co-opt.

hijinks ▶ plural noun ANTICS, pranks, escapades, stunts, practical jokes, tricks; fun (and games), skylarking, mischief, silliness, horseplay, tomfoolery, clowning; informal shenanigans, capers, monkey business.

hike ▶ noun a five-mile hike WALK, trek, tramp, trudge, slog, footslog, march; ramble, walkabout.
▶ verb they hiked across the moors WALK, trek, tramp, tromp, trudge, slog, footslog, march; ramble, rove, traipse; informal hoof it, leg it.
■ **hike something up** 1 Roy hiked up his trousers HITCH UP, pull up, hoist, lift, raise; informal yank up. 2 they hiked up the price INCREASE, raise, up, put up, boost up, mark up, push up, inflate; informal jack up, bump up.

hilarious ▶ adjective VERY FUNNY, hysterically funny, hysterical, uproarious, riotous, rollicking, farcical, rib-tickling; humorous, comic, amusing, entertaining jocular, jovial, laughable; informal side-splitting, gut-busting, knee-slapping, thigh-slapping, priceless, a scream, a hoot.

hilarity ▶ noun AMUSEMENT, mirth, laughter, merriment, light-heartedness, levity, fun, humour, jocularity, jollity, gaiety, delight, glee, exuberance, high spirits; comedy.

hill ▶ noun 1 the top of the hill HIGH GROUND, prominence, hillock, foothill, hillside, rise, mound, (Nfld) tolt ✤, mount, knoll, butte, hummock, mesa, coteau; (Maritimes) cradle-hill ✤; bank, bluff, ridge, slope, incline, gradient; (hills) heights, highland, downs, elevation; Geology drumlin; formal eminence. 2 a hill of garbage HEAP, pile, stack, mound, mountain, mass.

hillbilly ▶ noun See HICK.

hillock ▶ noun MOUND, small hill, prominence, elevation, rise, knoll, hummock, (Nfld) tolt ✤, hump, dune; bank, ridge, knob; formal eminence.

hilt ▶ noun HANDLE, haft, handgrip, grip, shaft, shank, helve.
■ **to the hilt** COMPLETELY, fully, wholly, totally, absolutely, entirely, utterly, unreservedly, unconditionally, in every respect, in all respects, one hundred per cent, every inch, to the full, to the maximum extent, all the way, body and soul, heart and soul.

hind ▶ adjective BACK, rear, hinder, hindmost, posterior; dorsal.
— OPPOSITES: fore, front.

hinder ▶ verb HAMPER, obstruct, impede, inhibit, retard, balk, prevent, thwart, foil, curb, delay, arrest, interfere with, set back, slow down, hobble, hold back, hold up, stop, halt; restrict, restrain, constrain, block, check, curtail, frustrate, cramp, handicap, cripple, hamstring; informal stymie, throw a wrench in the works.
— OPPOSITES: facilitate.

hindrance ▶ noun IMPEDIMENT, obstacle, barrier, bar, obstruction, handicap, block, hurdle, restraint, restriction, limitation, encumbrance, interference; complication, delay, drawback, setback, difficulty, inconvenience, snag, catch, hitch, check, stumbling block; informal fly in the ointment, hiccup, wrench in the works.
— OPPOSITES: help.

hinge ▶ verb our future hinges on the election DEPEND, hang, rest, turn, centre, pivot, be contingent, be dependent, be conditional; be determined by, be decided by, revolve around.

hint ▶ noun 1 a hint that he would leave CLUE, inkling, suggestion, indication, indicator, sign, signal, pointer, intimation, insinuation, innuendo, mention, whisper. 2 handy hints about painting TIP, suggestion, pointer, clue, guideline, recommendation; advice, help; informal how-to. 3 a *hint of mint* TRACE, touch, suspicion, suggestion, dash, soupçon, tinge, modicum, whiff, taste, undertone; *informal* smidgen, tad, speck.

▶ **verb** *what are you hinting at?* IMPLY, insinuate, intimate, suggest, indicate, signal; allude to, refer to, drive at, mean; *informal* get at.

hinterland ▶ **noun** THE BACKWOODS, a backwater, the wilds, the wilderness, the bush, the back of beyond, the backcountry, (*Ont. & Que.*) the back concessions ✤; *informal* the sticks, the middle of nowhere, moose pasture ✤, the boondocks, the boonies; *Austral.* the outback.

hip ▶ **adjective** (*informal*) FASHIONABLE, stylish, popular, all the rage, in fashion, in vogue, up-to-the-minute; *informal* trendy, cool, styling/stylin', with it, in, hot, big, happening, now, groovy, funky, sharp, the in thing, phat, kicky, tony, fly.

■ **hip to your meaning** WISE TO, clued in to, tuned in to, in the know about, in touch with, up to speed with.

hippie ▶ **noun** FLOWER CHILD, bohemian, beatnik, long-hair, dropout, pothead, free spirit, nonconformist.

hips ▶ **plural noun** PELVIS, hindquarters, haunches, thighs.

— RELATED TERMS: sciatic.

hipster ▶ **noun** HIP PERSON; *informal* scenester, hepcat.

hire ▶ **verb** **1** *they hire labour in line with demand* EMPLOY, engage, recruit, appoint, take on, sign up, enrol, commission, enlist, contract. **2** *we hired a car* RENT, lease, charter, let, sublet.

— OPPOSITES: dismiss.

hired gun ▶ **noun** MERCENARY, hit man, assassin, gunman, soldier of fortune, (hired) thug; EXPERT, specialist, master; *informal* hotshot; *historical* condottiere.

hired hand ▶ **noun** LABOURER, worker, employee, help, assistant; peon, menial, drudge.

hirsute ▶ **adjective** (*formal*) HAIRY, shaggy, bushy, hair-covered; woolly, furry, fleecy, fuzzy; bearded, unshaven, bristly.

hiss ▶ **verb** **1** *the escaping gas hissed* FIZZ, fizzle, whistle, wheeze; *rare* sibilate. **2** *the audience hissed* JEER, catcall, boo, heckle, whistle, hoot; scoff, jibe.

▶ **noun** **1** *the hiss of the steam* FIZZ, fizzing, whistle, hissing, sibilance, whoosh, pfft; *rare* sibilation. **2** *the speaker received hisses* JEER, catcall, boo, whistle; abuse, scoffing, taunting, derision.

hissy fit ▶ **noun** TEMPER TANTRUM, tantrum, angry outburst, fit of temper, paroxysm (of rage), histrionics; fit of pique, snit, huff.

historic ▶ **adjective** SIGNIFICANT, notable, important, momentous, consequential, memorable, newsworthy, unforgettable, remarkable; famous, famed, celebrated, renowned, legendary; landmark, sensational, groundbreaking, epoch-making, red-letter, earth-shattering.

— OPPOSITES: insignificant.

historical ▶ **adjective** **1** *historical evidence* DOCUMENTED, recorded, chronicled, archival; authentic, factual, actual, true. **2** *historical figures* PAST, bygone, ancient, old, former; *literary* of yore.

— OPPOSITES: contemporary.

history ▶ **noun** **1** *my interest in history* THE PAST, former times, historical events, the olden days, the old days, bygone days, long ago, yesterday, antiquity; *literary* days of yore, yesteryear. **2** *a history of the Riel Rebellion* CHRONICLE, archive, record, diary, report,

narrative, account, study, tale, story, saga; memoir. **3** *she gave details of her history* BACKGROUND, past, life story, biography, experiences, backstory; antecedents.

histrionic ▶ **adjective** MELODRAMATIC, theatrical, dramatic, exaggerated, stagy, showy, affected, artificial, overacted, overdone; *informal* hammy, ham, campy.

histrionics ▶ **plural noun** DRAMATICS, theatrics, tantrums; affectation, staginess, artificiality.

hit ▶ **verb** **1** *she hit her child* STRIKE, slap, smack, spank, cuff, punch, thump, swat; beat, thrash, batter, pound, pummel, box someone's ears; whip, flog, cane; *informal* whack, schmuck ✤, wallop, bash, bop, lam, clout, clip, clobber, sock, swipe, crown, beat the living daylights out of, knock someone around, give someone a (good) hiding, belt, tan, lay into, let someone have it, deck, floor, slug; *literary* smite. **2** *a car hit the barrier* CRASH INTO, run into, smash into, smack into, knock into, bump into, plow into, collide with, meet head-on, impact. **3** *the tragedy hit her hard* DEVASTATE, affect badly, hurt, harm, leave a mark on; upset, shatter, crush, shock, overwhelm, traumatize. **4** (*informal*) *spending will hit $180 million* REACH, touch, arrive at, rise to, climb to. **5** *it hit me that I had forgotten* OCCUR TO, strike, dawn on, come to; enter one's head, cross one's mind, come to mind, spring to mind.

▶ **noun** **1** *he received a hit from behind* BLOW, thump, punch, knock, bang, box, cuff, slap, smack, spank, tap, crack, stroke, welt, karate chop; impact, collision, bump, crash; *informal* whack, thwack, wallop, bash, belt, clout, sock, swipe, clip, slug. **2** *he directed many big hits* SUCCESS, box-office success, sell-out, winner, triumph, sensation; bestseller; *informal* smash (hit), megahit, knockout, crowd-pleaser, chart-topper, chartbuster, wow, biggie, number one.

— OPPOSITES: compliment, failure.

■ **hit back** RETALIATE, respond, reply, react, counter, defend oneself.

■ **hit home** HAVE THE INTENDED EFFECT, strike home, hit the mark, register, be understood, get through, sink in.

■ **hit it off** (*informal*) GET ON (WELL), get along, be friends, be friendly, be compatible, be well matched, feel a rapport, see eye to eye, take to each other, warm to each other; *informal* click, get on like a house on fire, be on the same wavelength.

■ **hit on/upon 1** *he hit on the truth* DISCOVER, come up with, think of, conceive of, dream up, work out, invent, create, devise, design, pioneer; uncover, stumble on, happen upon, chance on, light on, come upon. **2** *he tried to hit on me* FLIRT WITH, show interest in, make eyes at, come on to, chat up, make advances to(wards).

hit-and-miss, hit-or-miss ▶ **adjective** ERRATIC, haphazard, disorganized, undisciplined, unmethodical, uneven; careless, slapdash, slipshod, casual, cursory, lackadaisical, random, aimless, undirected, indiscriminate; *informal* sloppy.

— OPPOSITES: meticulous.

hitch ▶ **verb** **1** *Tom hitched the pony to his cart* HARNESS, yoke, couple, fasten, connect, attach, tether, tie. **2** *she hitched the blanket around her* PULL, jerk, tug, hike, lift, raise, yank, shift. **3** (*informal*) *they hitched a ride* HITCHHIKE; *informal* thumb a ride/lift.

▶ **noun** *it went without a hitch* PROBLEM, difficulty, snag, catch, setback, hindrance, obstacle, obstruction, complication, impediment, stumbling block, barrier;

holdup, interruption, delay; *informal* headache, glitch, hiccup.

hitchhike ▶ verb *See* HITCH verb sense 3.

hither ▶ adverb (*literary*) *See* HERE sense 3.

hitherto ▶ adverb PREVIOUSLY, formerly, earlier, before, beforehand; so far, thus far, to date, as yet, until now, until then, till now, till then, up to now, up to then; *formal* heretofore.

hit man ▶ noun ASSASSIN, killer, murderer, gunman, hired gun.

hoard ▶ noun *a secret hoard of gold* CACHE, stockpile, stock, store, collection, supply, reserve, reservoir, fund, accumulation; treasury, treasure house, treasure trove; *informal* stash.

▶ verb *they hoarded rations* STOCKPILE, store (up), stock up on, put aside, put by, lay by, lay up, set aside, stow away, buy up; cache, amass, collect, save, gather, garner, accumulate, squirrel away, put aside for a rainy day; *informal* stash away, salt away.
— OPPOSITES: squander.

hoarse ▶ adjective ROUGH, harsh, croaky, croaking, throaty, gruff, husky, growly, gravelly, grating, scratchy, raspy, rasping, raucous, with a frog in one's throat.
— OPPOSITES: mellow, clear.

hoary ▶ adjective **1** *hoary cobwebs* GREYISH-WHITE, grey, white, snowy, silver, silvery; frosty; *literary* rimy. **2** *a hoary old man* GREY-HAIRED, white-haired, silver-haired, grizzled; elderly, aged, old, ancient, venerable *informal* getting on.
— OPPOSITES: young, original.

hoax ▶ noun PRACTICAL JOKE, joke, jest, prank, trick; ruse, deception, fraud, bluff, humbug, confidence trick; *informal* con, spoof, scam, set-up.

hoaxer ▶ noun (PRACTICAL) JOKER, prankster, trickster, jester; fraudster, swindler, snake oil salesman; *informal* spoofer, con man, scam artist.

hobble ▶ verb LIMP, walk with difficulty, walk lamely, move unsteadily, walk haltingly; shamble, totter, dodder, stagger, falter, stumble, lurch.

hobby ▶ noun PASTIME, leisure activity, leisure pursuit; sideline, (side) interest, diversion, avocation; recreation, entertainment, amusement.

hobgoblin ▶ noun GOBLIN, imp, sprite, elf, brownie, pixie, puck, leprechaun, gnome; bogey, bugbear, bogeyman/boogeyman.

hobnob ▶ verb (*informal*) ASSOCIATE, mix, fraternize, socialize, keep company, spend time, go around, mingle, consort, network, rub shoulders, rub elbows; *informal* hang around/out, be thick with, schmooze.

hobo ▶ noun TRAMP, vagrant, vagabond, derelict; *informal* bum, down-and-out; drifter, transient, itinerant.

hock ▶ verb *See* PAWN verb.

hockey ▶ noun. *See table.*

hocus-pocus ▶ noun **1** *a little sleight of hand and hocus-pocus* MAGIC, sleight of hand, conjuring, witchcraft, wizardry, sorcery; deception, sham, devilry, trickery; *informal* scam. **2** *she dismissed it as so much hocus-pocus* NONSENSE, rubbish, garbage, balderdash, malarkey, baloney, bunk, hogwash, bull, hokum.

▶ exclamation *she waved her wand and cried, 'hocus-pocus!'* ABRACADABRA, shazam, alakazam.

hodgepodge ▶ noun MIXTURE, mix, mixed bag, assortment, random collection, conglomeration, welter, jumble, ragbag, grab bag, miscellany, medley,

salmagundi, potpourri, patchwork, pastiche; mélange, mishmash, hash, kludge, confusion, farrago, gallimaufry.

hoedown ▶ noun PARTY, shindig, hootenanny, bash, whoop-up ♣, jamboree, (barn) dance, ceilidh, fete, celebration.

hog ▶ noun PIG, sow, swine, porker, piglet, boar; *informal* piggy.

▶ verb (*informal*) *he hogged the limelight* MONOPOLIZE, dominate, take over, corner, control.
— OPPOSITES: share.

hogwash ▶ noun (*informal*). *See* NONSENSE sense 1.

hoi polloi ▶ noun THE MASSES, the common people, the populace, the public, the multitude, the rank and file, the lower orders, the plebeians, the proletariat; the mob, the herd, the rabble, the riff-raff, the great unwashed; *informal* the plebs, the proles; *historical* the third estate.

hoist ▶ verb *we hoisted the mainsail* RAISE, lift (up), haul up, heave up, jack up, hike up, winch up, pull up, heft up, raise up, upraise, uplift, elevate, erect.

▶ noun *a mechanical hoist* LIFTING GEAR, crane, winch, block and tackle, pulley, windlass, derrick; *Nautical* sheerlegs.

hoity-toity ▶ adjective (*informal*) SNOBBISH, snobby, haughty, disdainful, conceited, proud, pretentious, arrogant, supercilious, superior, imperious, above oneself, self-important; *informal* high and mighty, snooty, stuck-up, puffed-up, uppity, uppish, la-di-da.

hokey ▶ adjective *See* CORNY.

hokum ▶ noun *See* NONSENSE.

hold ▶ verb **1** *she held a suitcase* CLASP, clutch, grasp, grip, clench, cling to, hold on to; carry, bear. **2** *I wanted to hold her* EMBRACE, hug, clasp, cradle, enfold, squeeze, fold in one's arms, cling to. **3** *do you hold a degree?* POSSESS, have, own, bear, carry, have to one's name. **4** *the branch held my weight* SUPPORT, bear, carry, take, keep up, sustain, prop up, shore up. **5** *the police were holding him* DETAIN, hold in custody, imprison, lock up, put behind bars, put in prison, put in jail, incarcerate, keep under lock and key, confine, constrain, intern, impound; *informal* put away. **6** *try to hold the audience's attention* MAINTAIN, keep, occupy, engross, absorb, interest, captivate, fascinate, enthrall, rivet, mesmerize, transfix; engage, catch, capture, arrest. **7** *he held a senior post* OCCUPY, have, fill; *informal* hold down. **8** *the tank held 250 gallons* TAKE, contain, accommodate, fit; have a capacity of, have room for. **9** *the court held that there was no evidence* MAINTAIN, consider, take the view, believe, think, feel, deem, be of the opinion; judge, rule, decide; *informal* reckon; *formal* opine, esteem. **10** *let's hope the weather holds* PERSIST, continue, carry on, go on, hold out, keep up, last, endure, stay, remain. **11** *the offer still holds* BE AVAILABLE, be valid, hold good, stand, apply, remain, exist, be the case, be in force, be in effect. **12** *they held a meeting* CONVENE, call, summon; conduct, have, organize, run; *formal* convoke. **13** *hold your fire* STOP, halt, restrain, check, cease, discontinue; *informal* break off, give up; hold back, suppress, repress, refrain from using, stifle, withhold.
— OPPOSITES: release, lose, end, resume.

▶ noun **1** *she kept a hold on my hand* GRIP, grasp, clasp, clutch. **2** *Tom had a hold over his father* INFLUENCE, power, control, dominance, authority, command, leverage, sway, mastery, dominion. **3** *the*

Hockey Terms

Types of Hockey	Plays and Actions	Penalties and Questionable Play	On-Ice Locations and Markings
air hockey	assist	bench penalty	blue line
ball hockey	backcheck	boarding	boards
field hockey	backhand	butt-ending	cage
floor hockey	bodycheck	charging	centre ice
grass hockey ♣(esp. BC)	breakaway	chippy play	crease
pickup hockey	butterfly save	cross-checking	crossbar
pond hockey	check	delayed penalty	dasher boards
road hockey	clearing pass	double-minor	faceoff circle
roller hockey	cross-ice pass	elbowing	goal line
shinny	deke	game misconduct	goalmouth
sponge hockey	dipsy-doodle	high-sticking	hash marks
street hockey	dump-and-chase	hooking	net
table(-top) hockey	empty-netter	major penalty	neutral zone
ringette	even strength	match penalty	point
	faceoff	minor penalty	red line
Positions and Roles	fire-wagon hockey	misconduct	sin bin
blueliner	five-a-side	roughing	slot
centre(man)	forecheck	slashing	up ice
checker	give-and-go	spearing	five-hole
defenceman	hat trick	stickwork	glove side
digger	head-man	tripping	stick side
enforcer	hip-check	two-hander	top shelf
goalie	icing		
goaltender	ice time	**Equipment**	**Venues**
goon	offside	blocker	arena
left winger	open ice	elbow pad	hockey cushion ♣
mucker	overskate	helmet	home ice ♣
netminder	pass	goalie pads	ice pad ♣
penalty killer	penalty shot	hockey glove	ice palace ♣
pivot	poke check	hockey pants	ice rink
point man	power play	hockey socks	rink
power forward	puck-handling	hockey stick	
puckster	ragging the puck	mask	**Trophies**
rearguard	save	neck guard	Allan Cup
right winger	screen shot	puck	Calder Cup
skater	short-handed goal	rubber	Memorial Cup
special team	slapshot	shin pads	Spengler Cup
winger	snap shot	skates	Stanley Cup
linesman	spinarama	sponge puck	
ref	stick-check	trapper	
referee	stickhandling	visor	
stick boy	tap-in	road apple *hist.*	
	tic-tac-toe		
	tip-in		
	transition game		
	wrist shot		
	goals-against average		
	plus-minus		

military tightened their hold on the capital CONTROL, grip, power, stranglehold, chokehold, dominion, authority.

■ **get hold of** (*informal*) CONTACT, get in touch with, communicate with, make contact with, reach, notify; phone, call, speak to, talk to.

■ **hold back** HESITATE, pause, stop oneself, restrain oneself, desist, forbear.

■ **hold someone back** HINDER, hamper, impede, obstruct, inhibit, hobble, check, curb, block, thwart, balk, hamstring, restrain, frustrate, stand in someone's way.

■ **hold something back 1** *Jane held back the tears* SUPPRESS, fight back, choke back, stifle, smother, subdue, rein in, repress, curb, control, keep a tight rein on; *informal* keep a/the lid on. **2** *don't hold anything back from me* WITHHOLD, hide, conceal, keep secret,

keep hidden, keep quiet about, keep to oneself, hush up; *informal* sit on, keep under one's hat.

■ **hold someone/something dear** CHERISH, treasure, prize, appreciate, adore, value highly, care for/about; *informal* put on a pedestal.

■ **hold someone down** OPPRESS, repress, suppress, subdue, subjugate, keep down, keep under, tyrannize, dominate.

■ **hold something down 1** *they will hold down inflation* KEEP DOWN, keep low, freeze, fix. **2** (*informal*) *she held down two jobs* OCCUPY, have, do, fill.

■ **hold forth** SPEAK AT LENGTH, talk at length, go on, sound off; declaim, spout, pontificate, orate, preach, sermonize; *informal* speechify, drone on.

■ **hold off** *the rain held off* STAY AWAY, keep off, not come, delay.

■ **hold something off** RESIST, repel, repulse, rebuff

parry, deflect, fend off, stave off, ward off, keep at bay.

■ **hold on 1** *hold on a minute* WAIT (A MINUTE), just a moment, just a second; stay here, stay put; hold the line; *informal* hang on, sit tight, hold your horses. **2** *if only they could hold on a while* KEEP GOING, persevere, survive, last, continue, struggle on, carry on, go on, hold out, see it through, stay the course; *informal* soldier on, stick at it, hang in there.

■ **hold on to 1** *he held on to the chair* CLUTCH, hang on to, clasp, grasp, grip, cling to. **2** *they can't hold on to their staff* RETAIN, keep, hang on to.

■ **hold one's own**. See OWN.

■ **hold out** PERSIST, last, remain; persevere, continue; withstand, hold off, keep at bay.

■ **hold something out** EXTEND, proffer, offer, present; outstretch, reach out, stretch out, put out.

■ **hold something over** POSTPONE, put off, put back, delay, defer, suspend, shelve, put over, table, take a rain check on; *informal* put on ice, put on the back burner, put in cold storage, mothball.

■ **hold up** *the argument doesn't hold up* BE CONVINCING, be logical, hold water, bear examination, be sound.

■ **hold something up 1** *they held up the trophy* DISPLAY, hold aloft, exhibit, show (off), flourish, brandish; *informal* flash. **2** *concrete pillars hold up the bridge* SUPPORT, bear, carry, take, keep up, prop up, shore up, buttress. **3** *our flight was held up for hours* DELAY, detain, make late, set back, keep back, retard, slow up. **4** *a lack of cash has held up progress* OBSTRUCT, impede, hinder, hamper, inhibit, arrest, balk, thwart, curb, hamstring, frustrate, foil, interfere with, stop; *informal* stymie, hog-tie, throw a wrench in the works of. **5** *two gunmen held up the bank* ROB; *informal* stick up, mug.

■ **hold water**. See WATER.

■ **with no holds barred** CANDIDLY, honestly, frankly, directly, openly, bluntly; *informal* point-blank, without mincing one's words.

holder ▶ noun **1** *a knife holder* CONTAINER, receptacle, case, casing, cover, covering, housing, sheath; stand, rest, rack. **2** *she became a credit card holder* BEARER, owner, possessor, keeper; custodian.

holding pattern

■ **in a holding pattern** IN LIMBO, up in the air, on hold, undecided, undetermined, unresolved; *informal* on the back burner, treading water.

holdings ▶ plural noun ASSETS, funds, capital, resources, savings, investments, securities, equities, bonds, stocks and shares, reserves; property, possessions.

holdup ▶ noun **1** *I ran into a series of holdups* DELAY, setback, hitch, snag, obstruction, difficulty, problem, trouble, stumbling block; *informal* tie-up, log-jam; traffic jam, gridlock, bottleneck, roadblock; *informal* snarl-up, glitch, hiccup. **2** *a bank holdup* (ARMED) ROBBERY, (armed) raid; theft, burglary, mugging; *informal* stickup, heist.

hole ▶ noun **1** *a hole in the roof* OPENING, aperture, gap, space, orifice, vent, chink, breach, break; crack, leak, rift, rupture; puncture, perforation, cut, split, gash, slit, rent, tear, crevice, fissure. **2** *a hole in the ground* PIT, ditch, trench, cavity, crater, depression, indentation, hollow; well, borehole, excavation; dugout; cave, cavern, pothole. **3** *the badger's hole* BURROW, lair, den, earth, set; retreat, shelter. **4** *there are holes in their argument* FLAW, fault, defect, weakness, shortcoming, inconsistency, discrepancy; loophole; error, mistake. **5** (*informal*) *I was living in a real*

hole HOVEL, slum, shack, mess; *informal* dump, dive, pigsty, hole in the wall, rathole, sty. **6** (*informal*) *she has dug herself into a hole* PREDICAMENT, difficult situation, awkward situation, (tight) corner, quandary, dilemma; crisis, emergency, difficulty, trouble, plight, dire straits, imbroglio; *informal* fix, jam, mess, bind, scrape, (tight) spot, pickle, sticky situation, can of worms, hot water.

■ **hole up 1** *the bears hole up in winter* HIBERNATE, lie dormant. **2** (*informal*) *the snipers holed up in a farmhouse* HIDE (OUT), conceal oneself, secrete oneself, shelter, take cover, lie low, lie doggo.

■ **poke holes in** (*informal*) FIND FAULT WITH, pick apart, deconstruct, query, quibble with; deflate, puncture.

■ **in the hole** IN DEBT, in arrears, in deficit, overdrawn, behind; *informal* in the red.

holiday ▶ noun **1** *Sara and Lou's ten-day holiday* VACATION, break, rest, respite, recess; time off, time out, leave, furlough, sabbatical; trip, tour, journey, voyage; *informal* getaway; *formal* sojourn. **2** *Victoria Day is a holiday* PUBLIC HOLIDAY, statutory holiday ♣, stat holiday ♣, festival, feast day, fete, fiesta, celebration, anniversary, jubilee; saint's day, holy day.

holier-than-thou ▶ adjective SANCTIMONIOUS, self-righteous, smug, self-satisfied; priggish, pious, pietistic, Pharisaic.
– OPPOSITES: humble.

holler (*informal*) ▶ verb *he hollers when he's hungry* SHOUT, yell, cry (out), vociferate, call (out), roar, bellow, bawl, bark, howl; boom, thunder, shriek, screech.
– OPPOSITES: whisper.
▶ noun *a euphoric holler* SHOUT, cry, yell, cheer, roar, bellow, bawl, howl, outcry; *informal* whoop.
– OPPOSITES: whisper.

hollow ▶ adjective **1** *each fibre has a hollow core* EMPTY, void, unfilled, vacant. **2** *hollow cheeks* SUNKEN, gaunt, deep-set, concave, depressed, indented. **3** *a hollow sound* DULL, low, flat, toneless, expressionless; muffled, muted. **4** *a hollow victory* MEANINGLESS, empty, valueless, worthless, useless, pyrrhic, nugatory, futile, fruitless, profitless, pointless. **5** *a hollow promise* INSINCERE, hypocritical, feigned, false, sham, deceitful, cynical, spurious, untrue, two-faced; *informal* phony, pretend.
– OPPOSITES: solid, worthwhile, sincere.
▶ noun **1** *a hollow under the tree* HOLE, pit, cavity, crater, trough, bowl, cave, cavern; depression, indentation, dip, dent; niche, nook, cranny, recess. **2** *the village lay in a hollow* VALLEY, vale, dale, basin, glen. *literary* dell.
▶ verb *a tunnel hollowed out of a mountain* GOUGE, scoop, dig, shovel, cut; excavate, channel.

holocaust ▶ noun CATACLYSM, disaster, catastrophe; destruction, devastation, annihilation; massacre, slaughter, mass murder, extermination, extirpation, carnage, butchery; genocide, ethnic cleansing, pogrom.

holy ▶ adjective **1** *holy men* SAINTLY, godly, saintlike, pious, pietistic, religious, devout, God-fearing, spiritual; righteous, good, virtuous, angelic, sinless, pure, numinous, beatific; canonized, beatified, ordained. **2** *a Jewish holy place* SACRED, consecrated, hallowed, sanctified, sacrosanct, venerated, revered, divine, religious, blessed, dedicated.

■ **holy cow!** holy mackerel! holy moly! holy jumpin'! ♣ holy smokes! holy Moses! egad! caramba! yikes!
– OPPOSITES: sinful, irreligious, cursed.

homage ▶ noun RESPECT, honour, reverence,

worship, obeisance, admiration, esteem, adulation, acclaim; tribute, acknowledgement, recognition; accolade, panegyric, paean, encomium, salute, eulogy.

■ **pay homage to** HONOUR, acclaim, applaud, salute, praise, commend, pay tribute to, take one's hat off to; *formal* laud.

home ▶ noun **1** *they fled their homes* RESIDENCE, place of residence, house, flat, apartment, bungalow, cottage; accommodation, property, quarters, lodgings, rooms; a roof over one's head; address, place; *informal* pad, digs, semi; hearth, nest; *formal* domicile, abode, dwelling (place), habitation. **2** *I am far from my home* HOMELAND, native land, hometown, birthplace, roots, fatherland, motherland, mother country, country of origin, the old country. **3** *a home for the elderly* INSTITUTION, nursing home, retirement home, rest home, lodge ♣; children's home; hospice, shelter, refuge, retreat, asylum, hostel, halfway house. **4** *the home of fine wines* ORIGIN, source, cradle, fount, fountainhead.

▶ adjective **1** *the home market* DOMESTIC, internal, local, national, interior. **2** *home movies* HOMEMADE, home-grown, family.
— OPPOSITES: foreign, international.

■ **at home 1** *I was at home all day* IN, in one's house, present, available, indoors, inside, here. **2** *she felt very much at home* AT EASE, comfortable, relaxed, content; in one's element, on one's own turf. **3** *he is at home with mathematics* CONFIDENT WITH, conversant with, proficient in; used to, familiar with, au fait with, au courant with, skilled in, experienced in, well versed in.

■ **bring something home to someone** MAKE SOMEONE REALIZE, make someone understand, make someone aware, make something clear to someone; drive home, impress upon someone, draw attention to, focus attention on, underline, highlight, spotlight, emphasize, stress; *informal* clue someone in to something.

■ **hit home**. *See* HIT.

■ **home free** SAFE, secure, out of danger, off the hook; assured of success, the winner, the best, victorious; *informal* golden.

■ **home in on** FOCUS ON, concentrate on, zero in on, centre on, fix on; highlight, spotlight, target, underline, pinpoint, track, zoom in on.

■ **nothing to write home about** (*informal*) UNEXCEPTIONAL, mediocre, ordinary, commonplace, indifferent, average, middle-of-the-road, run-of-the-mill, garden variety; boring, mundane, humdrum, ho-hum; tolerable, passable, adequate, fair; *informal* OK, so-so, {comme ci, comme ça}, plain-vanilla, no great shakes, not so hot, not up to much.

homegrown ▶ adjective LOCAL, native, indigenous, domestic; *informal* homebrewed.

homeland ▶ noun NATIVE LAND, country of origin, home, fatherland, motherland, mother country, land of one's fathers, the old country.

homeless ▶ adjective *homeless people* OF NO FIXED ADDRESS, without a roof over one's head, on the streets, vagrant, displaced, dispossessed, destitute, down-and-out.
▶ noun *charities for the homeless* PEOPLE OF NO FIXED ADDRESS, vagrants, down-and-outs, street people, tramps, vagabonds, itinerants, transients, migrants, derelicts, drifters, hoboes, bag ladies, bums.

homely ▶ adjective **1** *she's rather homely* UNATTRACTIVE,

plain, unprepossessing, unlovely, ill-favoured, ugly; *informal* not much to look at. **2** *a homely atmosphere*. *See* HOMEY sense 1. **3** *homely pursuits*. *See* HOMEY sense 2.
— OPPOSITES: attractive, formal, sophisticated.

homemade ▶ adjective **1** *homemade bread and jam* HOMESTYLE, homespun, simple, basic, plain; rustic, folksy; *informal* like mom used to make. **2** *a homemade bomb* HANDMADE, makeshift, jerry-built, rudimentary; crude, rough, unsophisticated.

homeowner ▶ noun HOUSEHOLDER, owner, resident, occupant, proprietor.

homespun ▶ adjective UNSOPHISTICATED, plain, simple, basic, unpolished, unrefined, rustic, folksy; coarse, rough, crude, rudimentary, bush-league.
— OPPOSITES: sophisticated.

homey ▶ adjective **1** *the house is homey yet elegant* COZY, homelike, homely, comfortable, snug, welcoming, informal, relaxed, intimate, warm, pleasant, cheerful, friendly, congenial, hospitable; *informal* comfy. **2** *peasant life was simple and homey* UNSOPHISTICATED, homely, unrefined, unpretentious, plain, simple, modest, domestic; everyday, ordinary.
— OPPOSITES: uncomfortable, formal, sophisticated.

homicidal ▶ adjective MURDEROUS, violent, brutal, savage, ferocious, vicious, bloody, bloodthirsty, barbarous, barbaric; deadly, lethal, mortal; *literary* fell; *archaic* sanguinary.

homicide ▶ noun MURDER, killing, slaughter, butchery, massacre; assassination, execution, extermination; patricide, matricide, infanticide; *literary* slaying.

homily ▶ noun SERMON, lecture, discourse, address, lesson, talk, speech, oration.

homogeneous ▶ adjective UNIFORM, identical, unvaried, consistent, indistinguishable, homologous, homogenized; alike, similar, (much) the same, all of a piece, melting-pot.
— OPPOSITES: different.

homogenize ▶ verb MAKE UNIFORM, make similar, standardize, unite, integrate, fuse, merge, blend, meld, coalesce, amalgamate, combine.
— OPPOSITES: diversify.

homogenous ▶ adjective. *See* HOMOGENEOUS.

homosexual ▶ adjective GAY, lesbian, homoerotic, same-sex; *informal* queer, camp, pink, lavender, homo, dykey.
— OPPOSITES: heterosexual.
▶ noun GAY, lesbian; *informal* queer, queen, dyke, butch, femme.
— OPPOSITES: heterosexual.

hone ▶ verb SHARPEN, whet, strop, grind, file; polish, refine, improve, enhance, fine-tune.
— OPPOSITES: blunt, dull.

honest ▶ adjective **1** *an honest man* UPRIGHT, honourable, moral, ethical, principled, righteous, right-minded, respectable; virtuous, good, decent, fair, law-abiding, high-minded, upstanding, incorruptible, truthful, trustworthy, reliable, conscientious, scrupulous, reputable; *informal* on the level, trusty. **2** *I haven't been honest with you* TRUTHFUL, sincere, candid, frank, open, forthright, ingenuous, straight; straightforward, plain-speaking, matter-of-fact; *informal* upfront, above board, on the level. **3** *an honest mistake* GENUINE, true, bona fide, legitimate; *informal* legit, honest-to-goodness.
— OPPOSITES: unscrupulous, insincere.

honestly ▶ adverb **1** *he earned the money honestly* FAIRLY, lawfully, legally, legitimately, honourably, decently, ethically, in good faith, by the book; openly, on the level, above board. **2** *we honestly believe this is for the best* SINCERELY, genuinely, truthfully, truly, wholeheartedly; really, frankly, actually, seriously, to be honest, to tell you the truth, to be frank, in all honesty, in all sincerity; *informal* Scout's honour.

▶ **exclamation** *Honestly! I don't know what to do with you!* FOR HEAVEN'S SAKE, for goodness' sake, for Pete's sake, really, crikey, sheesh, jeepers.

honesty ▶ **noun 1** *I can attest to his honesty* INTEGRITY, uprightness, honourableness, honour, morality, morals, ethics, (high) principles, righteousness, right-mindedness; virtue, goodness, probity, high-mindedness, fairness, incorruptibility, truthfulness, trustworthiness, reliability, dependability, rectitude. **2** *they spoke with honesty about their fears* SINCERITY, candour, frankness, directness, bluntness, truthfulness, truth, openness, straightforwardness.

honey ▶ **noun** *(informal)* SWEETHEART, darling, dear, dearest, love; *informal* angel, sweetie, sugar, pet.

honeyed ▶ **adjective** SWEET, sugary, pleasant, flattering, adulatory; dulcet, soothing, soft, mellow, mellifluous; saccharine, syrupy, unctuous.
— OPPOSITES: harsh.

honk ▶ **verb** BEEP, blow, blare, blast, sound, hoot.

honorarium ▶ **noun** FEE, payment, consideration, allowance, stipend; remuneration, pay, expenses, compensation, recompense, reward; *formal* emolument.

honorary ▶ **adjective** TITULAR, symbolic, in name only, ceremonial, nominal, unofficial, token.

honour ▶ **noun 1** *a man of honour* INTEGRITY, honesty, uprightness, ethics, morals, morality, (high) principles, righteousness, high-mindedness; virtue, goodness, decency, probity, (good) character, scrupulousness, worth, fairness, justness, trustworthiness, reliability, dependability. **2** *a mark of honour* DISTINCTION, recognition, privilege, glory, kudos, cachet, prestige, merit, credit; importance, illustriousness, notability; respect, esteem, approbation. **3** *our honour is at stake* REPUTATION, (good) name, (good) credit, character, esteem, repute, image, standing, stature, status, popularity. **4** *he was welcomed with honour* ACCLAIM, acclamation, applause, accolades, adoration, tributes, compliments, salutes, bouquets; homage, praise, veneration, glory, reverence, adulation, exaltation; *dated* laud. **5** *she had the honour of meeting the Queen* PRIVILEGE, pleasure, pride, joy; compliment, favour, distinction. **6** *military honours* ACCOLADE, award, reward, prize, decoration, distinction, medal, ribbon, star, laurel. *See also the table at* AWARD. **7** *(dated)* *she died defending her honour* CHASTITY, virginity, maidenhead, purity, innocence, modesty; *archaic* virtue, maidenhood.
— OPPOSITES: unscrupulousness, shame.

▶ **verb 1** *we should honour our parents* ESTEEM, respect, admire, defer to, look up to; appreciate, value, cherish, adore; reverence, revere, venerate, worship; *informal* put on a pedestal. **2** *they were honoured at a special ceremony* APPLAUD, acclaim, praise, salute, recognize, celebrate, commemorate, commend, hail, lionize, exalt, eulogize, pay homage to, pay tribute to, sing the praises of; *formal* laud. **3** *he honoured the contract* FULFILL, observe, keep, obey, heed, follow, carry out, discharge, implement, execute, effect; keep to, abide by, adhere to, comply with, conform to,

be true to, live up to.
— OPPOSITES: disgrace, criticize, disobey.

honourable ▶ **adjective 1** *an honourable man* HONEST, moral, ethical, principled, righteous, right-minded; decent, respectable, estimable, virtuous, good, upstanding, upright, worthy, noble, fair, just, truthful, trustworthy, law-abiding, reliable, reputable, creditable, dependable. **2** *an honourable career* ILLUSTRIOUS, distinguished, eminent, great, glorious, renowned, acclaimed, prestigious, noble, creditable, admirable.
— OPPOSITES: crooked, deplorable.

hood ▶ **noun** HEAD COVERING, cowl, snood, head scarf, amice, *(North)* amautik ✦.

hoodlum ▶ **noun** HOOLIGAN, thug, lout, delinquent, vandal, ruffian, low-life; gangster, crook, mobster, criminal; *informal* tough, bruiser, goon, hood, punk, rowdy.

hoodwink ▶ **verb** DECEIVE, trick, dupe, outwit, fool, delude, inveigle, cheat, take in, hoax, mislead, lead on, defraud, double-cross, swindle, gull, scam; *informal* con, bamboozle, hornswoggle, fleece, do, have, sting, gyp, shaft, rip off, lead up the garden path, pull a fast one on, put one over on, take for a ride, pull the wool over someone's eyes, sucker, snooker; *literary* cozen.

hook ▶ **noun 1** *she hung her jacket on the hook* PEG, coat rack. **2** *the dress has six hooks* FASTENER, fastening, catch, clasp, hasp, clip, pin. **3** *I had a fish on the end of my hook* FISH-HOOK, barb, gaff, snare, snag. **4** *a right hook to the chin* PUNCH, blow, hit, cuff, thump, smack; *informal* belt, bop, sock, clout, whack, wallop, slug; *informal* boff.

▶ **verb 1** *they hooked baskets onto the ladder* ATTACH, hitch, fasten, fix, secure, clasp. **2** *he hooked his thumbs in his belt* CURL, bend, crook, loop, curve. **3** *he hooked a 24 lb pike* CATCH, land, net, take, bag, snare, trap.

■ **by hook or by crook** BY ANY MEANS, somehow (or other), no matter how, in one way or another, by fair means or foul.

■ **hook, line, and sinker** COMPLETELY, totally, utterly, entirely, wholly, absolutely, through and through, one hundred per cent, {lock, stock, and barrel}.

■ **off the hook** *(informal)* OUT OF TROUBLE, in the clear, free, home free; acquitted, cleared, reprieved, exonerated, absolved; *informal* let off.

■ **on the hook** RESPONSIBLE, accountable, liable, answerable, committed; *informal* in the hot seat.

hooked ▶ **adjective 1** *a hooked nose* CURVED, hook-shaped, hook-like, aquiline, angular, bent, crooked. **2** *(informal)* *he is hooked on crosswords* KEEN ON, enthusiastic about, addicted to, obsessed with, infatuated with, fixated on, fanatical about; *informal* mad about, crazy about, wild about, nuts about. **3** *she had the audience hooked* CAPTIVATED, enthralled, entranced, bewitched, charmed.
— OPPOSITES: straight.

hooker ▶ **noun** *See* PROSTITUTE *noun*.

hooligan ▶ **noun** TROUBLEMAKER, (juvenile) delinquent, mischief-maker, vandal; rowdy, ruffian, yahoo.

hoop ▶ **noun** RING, band, circle, circlet, bracelet, (hoop) earring, loop; *technical* annulus.

hooray ▶ **exclamation** HURRAH, hallelujah, bravo, cowabunga, hot dog, wahoo, yahoo, whoopee, yay, yee-haw, yippee.

hoot ▶ **noun 1** *the hoot of an owl* SCREECH, shriek, call, cry; tu-whit tu-whoo. **2** *hoots of derision* SHOUT, yell,

cry, snort, howl, shriek, whoop, whistle; boo, hiss, jeer, catcall. **3** (*informal*) *the party was a hoot* GOOD TIME, scream, laugh, laff riot, blast, riot, giggle, barrel of laughs; *dated* caution.
▸ **verb 1** *an owl hooted* SCREECH, shriek, cry, call; tu-whit tu-whoo. **2** *they hooted in disgust* SHOUT, yell, cry, howl, shriek, whistle; boo, hiss, jeer, heckle, catcall.
■ **give a hoot** (*informal*) CARE, be concerned, mind, be interested, be bothered, trouble oneself about; *informal* give a damn/crap/rat's ass.

hop ▸ **verb 1** *he hopped over the fence* JUMP, bound, spring, bounce, leap, vault. **2** (*informal*) *she hopped over the Atlantic* GO, dash; travel, journey; jet, fly; *informal* pop, whip, nip.
▸ **noun 1** *the rabbit had a hop around* JUMP, bound, bounce, leap, spring. **2** (*informal*) *a short hop by taxi* JOURNEY, distance, ride, drive, run, trip, jaunt; flight; *informal* hop, skip, and a jump.

hope ▸ **noun 1** *I had high hopes* ASPIRATION, desire, wish, expectation, ambition, aim, goal, plan, design; dream, daydream, pipe dream. **2** *a life filled with hope* HOPEFULNESS, optimism, expectation, expectancy; confidence, faith, trust, belief, conviction, assurance; promise, possibility. **3** *have we any hope of winning?* CHANCE, prospect, likelihood, probability, possibility; *informal* shot.
— OPPOSITES: pessimism.
▸ **verb 1** *he's hoping for a medal* EXPECT, anticipate, look for, be hopeful of, pin one's hopes on, want; wish for, long for, dream of. **2** *we're hoping to address the issue* AIM, intend, be looking, have the intention, have in mind, plan, aspire.

hopeful ▸ **adjective 1** *he remained hopeful* OPTIMISTIC, full of hope, confident, positive, buoyant, sanguine, expectant, bullish, cheerful, lighthearted; *informal* upbeat. **2** *hopeful signs* PROMISING, encouraging, heartening, inspiring, reassuring, auspicious, favourable, optimistic, propitious, bright, rosy.
▸ **noun** CANDIDATE, aspirant, prospect, possibility; nominee, competitor, contender; *informal* up-and-comer.

hopefully ▸ **adverb 1** *he rode on hopefully* OPTIMISTICALLY, full of hope, confidently, buoyantly, sanguinely; expectantly. **2** *hopefully it will finish soon* IF ALL GOES WELL, God willing, with luck, with any luck; most likely, probably; conceivably, feasibly; *informal* knock on wood, touch wood, fingers crossed.

hopeless ▸ **adjective 1** *she felt weary and hopeless* DESPAIRING, desperate, wretched, forlorn, pessimistic, defeatist, resigned; dejected, downhearted, despondent, demoralized; *archaic* woebegone. **2** *a hopeless case* IRREMEDIABLE, beyond hope, lost, beyond repair, irreparable, irreversible; helpless, incurable; impossible, no-win, unwinnable, futile, unworkable, impracticable, useless; *archaic* bootless. **3** *Joseph was hopeless at tennis* BAD, awful, terrible, dreadful, horrible, atrocious; inferior, incompetent, inadequate, unskilled; *informal* pathetic, useless, lousy, rotten. **4** *a hopeless romantic* INCURABLE, incorrigible, chronic, compulsive; complete, utter, absolute, total, out-and-out; inveterate, confirmed, established, dyed-in-the-wool.

horde ▸ **noun** CROWD, mob, pack, press, crush, gang, group, troop, army, legion, swarm, mass, herd, rabble; throng, multitude, host, band, flock, drove; *informal* crew, tribe, pile.

horizon ▸ **noun 1** *the sun rose above the horizon* SKYLINE. **2** *she wanted to broaden her horizons* OUTLOOK,

perspective, perception; range of experience, range of interests, scope, prospect, ambit, compass, orbit.
■ **on the horizon** IMMINENT, impending, due, close, near, approaching, coming, forthcoming, at hand, on the way, about to happen, upon us, in the offing, in the pipeline, in the air, in the wings, in the cards, just around the corner, coming down the pike; brewing, looming, threatening, menacing.

horizontal ▸ **adjective 1** *a horizontal surface* level, flat, plane, smooth, even; straight, parallel. **2** *she was stretched horizontal on the bed* FLAT, supine, prone, prostrate, recumbent. **3** *a horizontal move* LATERAL, sideways.
— OPPOSITES: vertical.

horny ▸ **adjective** (*informal*) (SEXUALLY) AROUSED, oversexed, excited, stimulated, titillated, inflamed, passionate; lecherous, lascivious, lustful, salacious, lewd; *informal* turned on, hot, hot to trot, randy, hot and bothered; *formal* concupiscent.

horrendous ▸ **adjective**. See HORRIBLE.

horrible ▸ **adjective 1** *a horrible murder* DREADFUL, awful, terrible, shocking, appalling, horrifying, horrific, horrendous, hideous, grisly, ghastly, gruesome, gory, harrowing, heinous, vile, unspeakable; nightmarish, macabre, spine-chilling; blood-curdling; loathsome, monstrous, abhorrent, hateful, hellish, execrable, abominable, atrocious, sickening, foul. **2** (*informal*) *a horrible little man* NASTY, horrid, disagreeable, unpleasant, detestable, awful, dreadful, terrible, appalling, foul, repulsive, repugnant, repellent, ghastly; obnoxious, hateful, odious, hideous, objectionable, insufferable, vile, loathsome, abhorrent; *informal* frightful, godawful.
— OPPOSITES: pleasant, agreeable.

horrid ▸ **adjective** See horrible.

horrific ▸ **adjective** DREADFUL, horrendous, horrible, frightful, fearful, awful, terrible, atrocious, heinous; horrifying, shocking, appalling, harrowing, gruesome; hideous, grisly, gory, ghastly, unspeakable, monstrous, nightmarish, sickening.

horrify ▸ **verb 1** *she horrified us with ghastly tales* FRIGHTEN, scare, terrify, petrify, paralyze, alarm, panic, terrorize, fill with fear, scare someone out of their wits, frighten the living daylights out of, make someone's hair stand on end, make someone's blood run cold, give someone the creeps; *informal* scare the pants off, spook; *archaic* affright. **2** *he was horrified by her remarks* SHOCK, appall, outrage, scandalize, offend; disgust, revolt, nauseate, sicken.

horror ▸ **noun 1** *children screamed in horror* TERROR, fear, fright, alarm, panic; dread, trepidation. **2** *he had a horror of spiders* HATRED, fear, loathing, abhorrence, dislike; disgust, repugnance, revulsion. **3** *to her horror she found herself alone* DISMAY, consternation, perturbation, alarm, distress; disgust, outrage, shock. **4** *the horror of the tragedy* AWFULNESS, frightfulness, savagery, barbarity, hideousness; atrocity, outrage. **5** *he's a little horror* RASCAL, devil, imp, monkey; *informal* terror, scamp, scalawag, tyke, varmint. **6** *her new dress is a horror* EYESORE, monstrosity, abomination, blot, disgrace, mess, sight.
— OPPOSITES: delight, satisfaction, beauty.

horror-struck, horror-stricken ▸ **adjective** HORRIFIED, terrified, petrified, frightened, afraid, fearful, scared, panic-stricken, scared/frightened to death, scared witless; shocked, appalled, aghast; *informal* scared stiff, freaked out.

hors d'oeuvre ▸ **noun** See APPETIZER.

horse ▸ noun EQUINE, mount, charger, cob, nag, hack; pony, foal, yearling, colt, stallion, gelding, mare, filly, bronco; *archaic* steed. *See table.*

■ **horse around/about** (*informal*) FOOL AROUND/ABOUT, play, have fun, clown about/around, monkey about/around, goof around/about, muck about.

Horses

Appaloosa	mustang
Arabian	Newfoundland pony
Belgian	Percheron
Canadian	quarter horse
cayuse	Shetland pony
Clydesdale	standardbred
Dartmoor pony	Tennessee walking
Lippizaner	horse
Morgan	thoroughbred

horseman, horsewoman ▸ noun RIDER, equestrian, jockey; cavalryman, trooper, RCMP (officer) ✦; *historical* hussar, dragoon; *archaic* cavalier.

horseplay ▸ noun TOMFOOLERY, fooling around, roughhousing, clowning, buffoonery, fun; pranks, antics, hijinks; *informal* shenanigans, monkey business.

horse sense ▸ noun (*informal*). *See* COMMON SENSE.

horticulture ▸ noun GARDENING, landscaping, cultivation; floriculture, arboriculture, agriculture.

hosanna ▸ noun SHOUT OF PRAISE, alleluia, hurrah, hurray, hooray, cheer, paean.

hose ▸ noun *See* PIPE *noun* sense 1.

hoser ▸ noun IDIOT, fool, dolt, goof, simpleton, imbecile; dim-wit, dim-bulb, dork, halfwit, dummy, dumdum, loon, jackass, fathead, blockhead, jughead, bonehead, boob, bozo, numbskull, numbnuts, lummox, dunce, moron, meatball, doofus, ninny, nincompoop, dipstick, lamebrain, chump, pea brain, thickhead, dumb-ass, wooden-head, pinhead, airhead, chowderhead, birdbrain; nitwit, twit, goofball, putz, schmuck, oaf, retard; redneck, bubba, Joe Sixpack; *dated* tomfool, muttonhead.

hosiery ▸ noun STOCKINGS, tights, nylons, hose, pantyhose, leotards; socks.

hospice ▸ noun *See* HOME *noun* sense 3.

hospitable ▸ adjective WELCOMING, friendly, congenial, genial, sociable, convivial, cordial, courteous; gracious, well-disposed, amenable, helpful, obliging, accommodating, neighbourly, warm, kind, generous, bountiful.

hospital ▸ noun INFIRMARY, sanatorium, hospice, medical centre, health centre, clinic, nursing station ✦, (*Nfld*) cottage hospital ✦; *Military* field hospital; *dated* asylum.

hospitality ▸ noun FRIENDLINESS, hospitableness, warm reception, welcome, helpfulness, neighbourliness, warmth, kindness, congeniality, geniality, cordiality, courtesy, amenability, generosity, entertainment, catering, food.

host¹ ▸ noun 1 *the host greeted the guests* PARTY-GIVER, hostess, entertainer. 2 *the host of a TV series* PRESENTER, anchor, anchorman, anchorwoman, announcer, emcee, open-liner ✦, master of ceremonies, ringmaster.

— OPPOSITES: guest.

▸ verb 1 *the Queen hosted a dinner party* GIVE, have, hold, throw, put on, provide, arrange, organize. 2 *Jack*

hosted the show PRESENT, introduce, emcee, front, anchor, announce. 3 *she hosted her colleagues from overseas* ENTERTAIN, play host/hostess to; receive, welcome; take in, house, provide accommodation for, put up.

host² ▸ noun 1 *a host of memories* MULTITUDE, lot, abundance, wealth, profusion; *informal* load, heap, mass, pile, ton, number; *literary* myriad. 2 *a host of film stars* CROWD, throng, group, flock, herd, swarm, horde, mob, army, legion, pack, tribe, troop; assemblage, congregation, gathering.

hostage ▸ noun CAPTIVE, prisoner, inmate, detainee, internee; victim, abductee, prey; human shield, pawn, instrument.

hostel ▸ noun CHEAP HOTEL, YMCA, YWCA, bed and breakfast, B&B, inn, boarding house, guest house, pension, dormitory, residence, lodging, accommodation; shelter, refuge, asylum, interval house ✦.

hostile ▸ adjective 1 *a hostile attack* UNFRIENDLY, unkind, bitter, unsympathetic, malicious, vicious, rancorous, venomous, poisonous, virulent; antagonistic, aggressive, confrontational, belligerent, truculent, vitriolic; bellicose, pugnacious, warlike. 2 *hostile conditions* UNFAVOURABLE, adverse, bad, harsh, grim, hard, tough, brutal, fierce, inhospitable, forbidding, menacing, threatening. 3 *they are hostile to the idea* OPPOSED, averse, antagonistic, ill-disposed, disapproving of, unsympathetic, antipathetic; opposing, against, inimical; *informal* anti, down on.

— OPPOSITES: friendly, favourable.

hostility ▸ noun 1 *he glared at her with hostility* ANTAGONISM, unfriendliness, enmity, malevolence, malice, unkindness, rancour, venom, hatred, loathing; resentment, animosity, antipathy, acrimony, ill will, ill feeling; aggression, belligerence. 2 *their hostility to the present regime* OPPOSITION, antagonism, aversion, resistance, dissidence. 3 *a cessation of hostilities* FIGHTING, (armed) conflict, combat, aggression, warfare, war, bloodshed, violence.

hot ▸ adjective 1 *hot food* HEATED, piping (hot), sizzling, steaming, roasting, boiling (hot), searing, scorching, scalding, burning, red-hot. 2 *a hot day* VERY WARM, balmy, summery, tropical, scorching, broiling, searing, blistering; sweltering, torrid, sultry, humid, muggy, close, boiling, baking, roasting. 3 *she felt very hot* FEVERISH, fevered, febrile; burning, flushed, sweaty. 4 *a hot chili* SPICY, spiced, highly seasoned, peppery, fiery, strong; piquant, pungent, aromatic, zesty. 5 *hot competition* FIERCE, intense, keen, competitive, cutthroat, dog-eat-dog, ruthless, aggressive, strong. 6 (*informal*) *hot news* NEW, fresh, recent, late, up to date, up-to-the-minute; just out, hot off the press, real-time. 7 (*informal*) *this band is hot* POPULAR, in demand, sought-after, in favour; fashionable, in vogue, all the rage; *informal* big in, now, hip, trendy, cool. 8 *she thought Mark was hot* GOOD-LOOKING, sexy, attractive, gorgeous, handsome, beautiful; *archaic* comely, fair. 9 *hot goods* STOLEN, illegally obtained, purloined, pilfered, illegal, illicit, unlawful; smuggled, fenced, bootleg, contraband. 10 *her dancing made him hot* (SEXUALLY) AROUSED, excited, stimulated, titillated, inflamed; *informal* turned on, randy, hot to trot.

— OPPOSITES: cold, chilly, mild, dispassionate, old, ugly, lawful, frigid.

■ **blow hot and cold** VACILLATE, dither, shilly-shally,

waver, be indecisive, change one's mind, be undecided, be uncertain, be unsure, hem and haw.
■ **hot and heavy** intense, ardent, passionate, fervid.
■ **have the hots for** be (sexually) attracted to, desire, lust after; *informal* have a crush on, have a thing for, be crazy about.
■ **hot on the heels/trail of** CLOSE BEHIND, directly after, right after, straight after, hard on the heels of, following closely.
■ **hot under the collar**. *See* ANGRY sense 1.

hot air ▶ noun (*informal*) *See* NONSENSE sense 1.

hotbed ▶ noun *a hotbed of crime* BREEDING GROUND, seedbed, den, cradle, nest, stronghold, flashpoint.

hot-blooded ▶ adjective PASSIONATE, amorous, amatory, ardent, fervid, lustful, libidinous, lecherous, sexy, virile; *informal* horny, randy.
— OPPOSITES: cold.

hot-button ▶ adjective *hot-button issues* SENSITIVE, thorny, ticklish, touchy, delicate, controversial, difficult, tough, troublesome; complicated, complex, involved, intricate; current, contemporary, topical, in the news.

hot dog ▶ noun *See table at* SAUSAGE.

hotel ▶ noun INN, motel, boarding house, guest house, bed and breakfast, B&B, hostel, lodge, accommodation, lodging; pension, auberge.

hotfoot
■ **hotfoot it** (*informal*) HURRY, dash, run, rush, race, sprint, bolt, dart, career, careen, charge, shoot, hurtle, fly, speed, zoom, streak; *informal* tear, belt, pelt, scoot, clip, leg it, go like a bat out of hell, bomb, hightail it; *archaic* hie.

hot-headed ▶ adjective IMPETUOUS, impulsive, headstrong, reckless, rash, irresponsible, foolhardy, madcap, devil-may-care; excitable, volatile, explosive, fiery, hot-tempered, quick-tempered, unruly, harum-scarum.

hothouse ▶ noun **1** *tomatoes grew in the hothouse* GREENHOUSE, glasshouse, conservatory, orangery, vinery. **2** *society was becoming a hothouse of narcissism* BREEDING GROUND, seedbed, hotbed.
▶ adjective *the school has a hothouse atmosphere* INTENSE, oppressive, stifling; overprotected, sheltered, insular, isolated, shielded; sensitive.

hotly ▶ adverb **1** *a hotly contested issue* VEHEMENTLY, vigorously, strenuously, fiercely, passionately, heatedly; angrily, indignantly. **2** *a hotly anticipated new movie* EAGERLY, enthusiastically, extremely, highly, hugely, heartily.
— OPPOSITES: calmly.

hotshot ▶ noun *a young programming hotshot* EXPERT, master, genius, virtuoso, maestro, adept, past master, champion, star; *informal* demon, ace, wizard, pro, whiz; maven, crackerjack.
— OPPOSITES: amateur.
▶ adjective *a hotshot lawyer* EXCELLENT, first-rate, first-class, marvellous, wonderful, magnificent, outstanding, superlative, formidable, virtuoso, masterly, expert, champion, consummate, skilful, adept; prominent, celebrated, renowned, eminent, famous, high-profile, important, prestigious, notable, well-known; great, terrific, tremendous, superb, fantastic, sensational, fabulous, fab, fancy-pants, crack, ace, A1, mean, awesome, top-notch; blue-ribbon, blue-chip, brilliant; *slang* wicked.
— OPPOSITES: mediocre. .

hot spot ▶ noun **1** *a local hot spot* POPULAR DESTINATION, fashionable destination, trendy place, happenin'/happening place; restaurant, eatery, eating place, pub, bar, club. **2** *the Middle East has become the latest hot spot* DANGEROUS PLACE, trouble spot, problem area.

hot-tempered ▶ adjective IRASCIBLE, quick-tempered, short-tempered, irritable, fiery, bad-tempered; touchy, volatile, testy, tetchy, fractious, prickly, peppery, hot-headed, pugnacious; *informal* snappish, snappy, chippy, on a short fuse.
— OPPOSITES: easygoing.

hot tub ▶ noun WHIRLPOOL, spa; *proprietary* Jacuzzi.

hound ▶ noun (HUNTING) DOG, canine, mongrel, cur; *informal* doggy, pooch, mutt, pup.
▶ verb **1** *she was hounded by the press* PURSUE, chase, follow, shadow, be hot on someone's heels, hunt (down), stalk, track, trail, tail, dog; harass, hassle, persecute, harry, pester, bother, badger, torment, bedevil; *informal* bug, give someone a hard time, devil. **2** *they hounded him out of office* FORCE, drive, pressure, pressurize, push, urge, coerce, impel, dragoon, strong-arm; nag, bully, browbeat, chivvy; *informal* bulldoze, railroad, hustle.

Houses

adobe house	quadruplex
A-frame house	raised bungalow ♣
backsplit ♣	ranch house
bi-level	row house
bungalow	semi
Cape Cod	semi-detached
century home ♣	sidesplit ♣
chalet	snow house
colonial	split-level
cottage	teepee
country house	timber-framed
detached	townhouse/townhome
duplex	tract house
floathouse	triplex
Georgian	Tudor
greystone ♣	tupik
igloo	Victorian
log house	wickiup
longhouse	wigwam
mansion	

house ▶ noun **1** *a new suburb with 200 houses* RESIDENCE, home, place of residence; homestead; a roof over one's head; *formal* habitation, dwelling (place), abode, domicile. *See table.* **2** *you'll wake the whole house!* HOUSEHOLD, family, occupants; clan, tribe; *informal* brood. **3** *the house of Windsor* FAMILY, clan, tribe; dynasty, line, bloodline, lineage, ancestry, family tree. **4** *a printing house* FIRM, business, company, corporation, enterprise, establishment, institution, organization, operation; *informal* outfit, set-up. **5** *the country's upper house* LEGISLATIVE ASSEMBLY, legislative body, legislature, chamber, council, parliament, congress, senate, diet. **6** *the house applauded* AUDIENCE, crowd, spectators, viewers, listeners; assembly, congregation. **7** *they filled the house* THEATRE, auditorium, amphitheatre, hall, gallery, stalls.
▶ verb **1** *they can house twelve employees* ACCOMMODATE, provide accommodation for, give someone a roof over their head, lodge, quarter, board, billet, take in, sleep, put up; harbour, shelter. **2** *this panel houses the*

main switch CONTAIN, hold, store; cover, protect, enclose.

■ **on the house** (*informal*) FREE (OF CHARGE), without charge, at no cost, for nothing, gratis; courtesy, complimentary; *informal* for free, comp.

housebroken ▶ adjective HOUSE-TRAINED, domesticated, trained.

household ▶ noun *the household was asleep* FAMILY, house, occupants, residents, ménage; clan, tribe; *informal* brood.
▶ adjective *household goods* DOMESTIC, family; everyday, ordinary, common, commonplace, regular, practical, workaday.

householder ▶ noun HOMEOWNER, owner, occupant, resident; tenant, leaseholder; proprietor, landlady, landlord, freeholder.

housekeeper ▶ noun *See* MAID sense 1.

housewife ▶ noun HOMEMAKER, stay-at-home mom, SAHM, hausfrau.

housework ▶ noun DOMESTIC WORK, housecleaning, housekeeping, homemaking, housewifery; chores, cleaning; household management, home economics.

housing ▶ noun **1** *they invested in housing* HOUSES, homes, residences, (apartment) buildings, condominiums; accommodation, lodging, living quarters, shelter; *formal* dwellings, dwelling places, habitations. **2** *the housing for the antennae* CASING, covering, case, cover, holder, sheath, jacket, shell, carapace, capsule.

hovel ▶ noun SHACK, slum, shanty, hut; *informal* dump, hole, dive, pigsty.

hover ▶ verb **1** *helicopters hovered overhead* BE SUSPENDED, be poised, hang, levitate, float; fly. **2** *she hovered anxiously nearby* LINGER, loiter, wait (around); *informal* hang around/about, stick around.

however ▶ adverb **1** *however, gaining weight is not inevitable* NEVERTHELESS, nonetheless, but, still, yet, though, although, even so, for all that, despite that, in spite of that; anyway, anyhow, be that as it may, all the same, having said that, notwithstanding; *informal* still and all. **2** *however you look at it* IN WHATEVER WAY, regardless of how, no matter how.

howl ▶ noun **1** *the howl of a wolf* BAYING, howling, bay, cry, yowl, bark, yelp. **2** *a howl of anguish* WAIL, cry, yell, yelp, yowl; bellow, roar, clamour, shout, shriek, scream, screech.
▶ verb **1** *dogs howled in the distance* BAY, cry, yowl, bark, yelp. **2** *a baby started to howl* WAIL, cry, yell, yowl, bawl, bellow, shriek, scream, screech, caterwaul, keen; *informal* holler. **3** *we howled with laughter* LAUGH, guffaw, roar; be doubled up, split one's sides; *informal* crack up, be in stitches, be rolling in the aisles, be on the floor.

howler ▶ noun (*informal*) MISTAKE, error, blunder, faux pas, fault, gaffe, slip; *formal* solecism; *informal* slip-up, goof-up, boo-boo, botch, blooper, pratfall.

hub ▶ noun **1** *the hub of the wheel* PIVOT, axis, fulcrum, centre, middle. **2** *the hub of family life* CENTRE, core, heart, middle, focus, focal point, central point, nucleus, kernel, nerve centre, pole star.
— OPPOSITES: periphery.

hubbub ▶ noun **1** *her voice was lost in the hubbub* NOISE, din, racket, commotion, clamour, cacophony, babel, rumpus, ruckus, hullabaloo. **2** *she fought through the hubbub* CONFUSION, chaos, pandemonium, bedlam, mayhem, disorder, disturbance, turmoil, tumult, uproar, fracas, hurly-burly, hustle and bustle.

hubris ▶ noun ARROGANCE, conceit, haughtiness, hauteur, pride, self-importance, egotism, pomposity,

superciliousness, superiority; *informal* big-headedness, cockiness.
— OPPOSITES: humility.

huck ▶ verb THROW, hurl, toss, cast, lob, fling, launch, catapult, project, propel, fire; *informal* heave, pitch, chuck, sling, peg.

huckster ▶ noun TRADER, dealer, seller, purveyor, vendor, salesman, salesperson, peddler, hawker; *informal* pusher.

huddle ▶ verb **1** *they huddled together* CROWD, cluster, gather, bunch, throng, flock, herd, collect, group, congregate, mass; press, pack, squeeze. **2** *he huddled beneath the sheets* CURL UP, snuggle, nestle, hunch up.
— OPPOSITES: disperse.
▶ noun **1** *a huddle of passengers* CROWD, cluster, bunch, knot, group, throng, flock, press, pack; collection, assemblage; *informal* gaggle. **2** *the team went into a huddle* CONSULTATION, discussion, debate, talk, parley, meeting, conference; *informal* confab, powwow.

hue ▶ noun COLOUR, shade, tone, tint, tinge.

hue and cry ▶ noun *See* HULLABALOO.

huff ▶ noun BAD MOOD, sulk, fit of pique, temper, tantrum, rage; *informal* grump, snit, state, hissy fit.

huffy ▶ adjective IRRITABLE, irritated, annoyed, cross, grumpy, grouchy, bad-tempered, crotchety, crabby, cantankerous, moody, petulant, sullen, sulky, surly; touchy, testy, owly, tetchy, snappish; *informal* snappy, cranky, miffed, shirty.

hug ▶ verb **1** *they hugged each other* EMBRACE, cuddle, squeeze, clasp, clutch, cradle, cling to, hold close, hold tight, take/fold someone in one's arms, clasp someone to one's bosom. **2** *our route hugged the coastline* FOLLOW CLOSELY, keep close to, stay near to, follow the course of. **3** *we hugged the comforting thought* CLING TO, hold on to, cherish, hold dear; harbour, nurse, foster, retain, keep in mind.
▶ noun *there were hugs as we left* EMBRACE, cuddle, squeeze, bear hug, clasp, hold, clinch.

huge ▶ adjective ENORMOUS, vast, immense, large, big, great, massive, colossal, prodigious, gigantic, gargantuan, mammoth, monumental; giant, towering, elephantine, mountainous, monstrous, titanic; epic, Herculean, Brobdingnagian; *informal* jumbo, mega, monster, king-sized, economy-size(d), oversized, whopping, humongous, honking, hulking, astronomical, cosmic, ginormous.
— OPPOSITES: tiny.

hugely ▶ adverb VERY, extremely, exceedingly, enormously, most, really, particularly, tremendously, greatly, highly, decidedly, exceptionally, immensely, inordinately, extraordinarily, vastly; very much, to a great extent; *informal* terrifically, awfully, terribly, majorly, seriously, mega, ultra, oh-so, ever so, damn, damned, real, mighty, awful; frightfully; *archaic* exceeding.

hulk ▶ noun **1** *the rusting hulks of ships* WRECK, shipwreck, wreckage, ruin, derelict; shell, skeleton, hull. **2** *a great hulk of a man* GIANT, lump, blob, clod; oaf; *informal* clodhopper, ape, gorilla, lummox, lubber.

hulking ▶ adjective (*informal*) LARGE, big, heavy, sturdy, burly, brawny, hefty, strapping; bulky, weighty, massive, ponderous; clumsy, awkward, ungainly, lumbering, lumpish, oafish; *informal* beefy, clunky, clodhopping.
— OPPOSITES: small.

hull ▶ noun **1** *the ship's hull* FRAMEWORK, body, shell, frame, skeleton, structure; fuselage. **2** *seed hulls*

SHELL, husk, pod, case, covering, integument, calyx, shuck; *Botany* pericarp, legume.

hullabaloo ► noun (*informal*) FUSS, commotion, hue and cry, uproar, outcry, clamour, storm, furor, hubbub, ruckus, brouhaha; pandemonium, mayhem, tumult, turmoil, hurly-burly, rumpus, palaver; *informal* hoo-ha, to-do, kerfuffle, song and dance, stink.

hum ► verb 1 *the engine was humming* PURR, drone, murmur, buzz, thrum, whine, whirr, throb, vibrate, rumble. 2 *she hummed a tune* sing, croon, murmur, drone. 3 *the workshops are humming* BE BUSY, be active, be lively, buzz, bustle, be a hive of activity, throb; *informal* be happening.
► noun *a low hum of conversation* MURMUR, drone, purr, buzz, mumble.
■ **hum and haw** *See* HEM AND HAW *at* HEM.

human ► adjective 1 *they're only human* MORTAL, flesh and blood; fallible, weak, frail, imperfect, vulnerable, susceptible, erring, error-prone; physical, bodily, fleshly. 2 *the human side of politics* COMPASSIONATE, humane, kind, considerate, understanding, sympathetic, tolerant; approachable, accessible. 3 *in human form* ANTHROPOMORPHIC, anthropoid, humanoid, hominid.
► noun *the link between humans and animals* PERSON, human being, personage, mortal, member of the human race; man, woman; individual, (living) soul, being; Homo sapiens; earthling.

humane ► adjective COMPASSIONATE, kind, considerate, understanding, sympathetic, tolerant; lenient, forbearing, forgiving, merciful, mild, gentle, tender, clement, benign, humanitarian, benevolent, charitable; warm-hearted, tender-hearted, soft-hearted.
— OPPOSITES: cruel.

humanitarian ► adjective 1 *a humanitarian act* COMPASSIONATE, humane; unselfish, altruistic, generous, magnanimous, benevolent, merciful, kind, sympathetic. 2 *a humanitarian organization* CHARITABLE, philanthropic, public-spirited, socially concerned, welfare; *rare* eleemosynary.
► noun PHILANTHROPIST, altruist, benefactor, patron, social reformer, good Samaritan; do-gooder; *archaic* philanthrope.

humanities ► plural noun (LIBERAL) ARTS, literature, philosophy; classics, classical studies, classical literature.

humanity ► noun 1 *humanity evolved from the apes* HUMANKIND, mankind, man, people, human beings, humans, the human race, mortals; Homo sapiens. 2 *the humanity of Christ* HUMAN NATURE, humanness, mortality. 3 *he praised them for their humanity* COMPASSION, brotherly love, fraternity, fellow feeling, philanthropy, humaneness, kindness, consideration, understanding, sympathy, tolerance; leniency, mercy, mercifulness, clemency, pity, tenderness; benevolence, charity, goodness, magnanimity, generosity.

humanize ► verb CIVILIZE, improve, better; educate, enlighten, instruct; socialize, refine, polish; *formal* edify.

humankind ► noun *See* HUMANITY sense 1.

humble ► adjective 1 *her bearing was humble* MEEK, deferential, respectful, submissive, diffident, self-effacing, unassertive; unpresuming, modest, unassuming, self-deprecating; subdued, chastened.

2 *a humble background* LOWLY, working-class, lower-class, poor, undistinguished, mean, modest, ignoble, low-born, plebeian, underprivileged; common, ordinary, simple, inferior, unremarkable, insignificant, inconsequential. 3 *my humble abode* MODEST, plain, simple, ordinary, unostentatious, unpretentious.
— OPPOSITES: proud, noble, grand.
► verb HUMILIATE, abase, demean, lower, degrade, debase; mortify, shame, abash; *informal* cut (someone) down to size, deflate, make someone eat humble pie, take someone down a peg or two, settle someone's hash, make someone eat crow.

humbug ► noun *that is sheer humbug* HYPOCRISY, hypocritical talk, posturing, empty talk; insincerity, dishonesty, falseness, deceit, deception, fraud; *informal* sham.

humdinger ► noun AMAZING THING, jim-dandy, dandy, dilly, beaut, lollapalooza, ripsnorter, peach, doozy, lulu, whopper.

humdrum ► adjective MUNDANE, dull, dreary, boring, tedious, monotonous, prosaic; unexciting, uninteresting, uneventful, unvaried, repetitive, unremarkable; routine, ordinary, everyday, day-to-day, workaday, quotidian, run-of-the-mill, commonplace, garden variety, pedestrian; *informal* plain-vanilla, ho-hum.
— OPPOSITES: remarkable, exciting.

humidity ► noun *a climate of warm temperatures and high humidity* MUGGINESS, humidness, closeness, sultriness, stickiness, steaminess, airlessness, stuffiness, clamminess; dampness, damp, dankness, moisture, moistness, wetness, dewiness.
— OPPOSITES: freshness, aridity.
— RELATED TERMS: humidex.

humiliate ► verb EMBARRASS, mortify, humble, shame, put to shame, disgrace, chagrin; discomfit, chasten, abash, deflate, crush, squash; abase, debase, demean, degrade, lower; belittle, cause to feel small, cause to lose face; *informal* show up, put down, cut down to size, take down (a peg or two), settle someone's hash, put someone in their place, make someone eat crow.

humiliation ► noun EMBARRASSMENT, mortification, shame, indignity, ignominy, disgrace, discomfiture, dishonour, degradation, discredit, belittlement, opprobrium; loss of face; *informal* blow to one's pride/ego, slap in the face, kick in the teeth, comedown.
— OPPOSITES: honour.

humility ► noun MODESTY, humbleness, meekness, diffidence, unassertiveness; lack of pride, lack of vanity; servility, submissiveness.
— OPPOSITES: pride.

hummock ► noun *See* HILL sense 1.

humorist ► noun COMIC WRITER, wit, wag; comic, funny man/woman, comedian, comedienne, stand-up comic, joker, jester, clown, wisecracker; *informal* cut-up.

humorous ► adjective AMUSING, funny, comic, comical, entertaining, diverting, witty, jocular, jocose, light-hearted, tongue-in-cheek, wry, facetious, laughable, risible; hilarious, uproarious, riotous, zany, farcical, droll; *informal* priceless, side-splitting, gut-busting, rib-tickling, knee-slapping, thigh-slapping; a scream, a hoot, a barrel of laughs, waggish.
— OPPOSITES: serious.

humour ► noun 1 *the humour of the film* COMEDY,

comical aspect, funny side, fun, amusement, funniness, hilarity, jocularity; absurdity, ludicrousness, drollness; satire, irony, farce. **2** *the stories are spiced up with humour* JOKES, joking, jests, jesting, quips, witticisms, bon mots, funny remarks, puns, sallies, badinage; wit, wittiness, funniness, comedy, drollery; *informal* gags, wisecracks, cracks, kidding, waggishness, one-liners. **3** *his good humour was infectious* MOOD, temper, disposition, temperament, nature, state of mind, frame of mind; spirits.
▶ **verb** *she was always humouring him* INDULGE, accommodate, pander to, cater to, yield to, give way to, give in to, go along with; pamper, spoil, baby, overindulge, mollify, placate, gratify, satisfy.

humourless ▶ **adjective** SERIOUS, solemn, sober, sombre, grave, grim, dour, unsmiling, stony-faced, saturnine; gloomy, glum, sad, melancholy, dismal, joyless, cheerless, lugubrious; boring, tedious, dull, dry.
— OPPOSITES: jovial.

hump ▶ **noun** PROTUBERANCE, prominence, lump, bump, knob, protrusion, projection, bulge, swelling, hunch; growth, outgrowth.

hunch ▶ **verb 1** *he hunched his shoulders* ARCH, curve, hump, bend, bow. **2** *I hunched up as small as I could* CROUCH, huddle, curl; hunker down, bend, stoop, slouch, squat, duck.
— OPPOSITES: straighten.
▶ **noun 1** *the hunch on his back* PROTUBERANCE, hump, lump, bump, knob, protrusion, prominence, bulge, swelling; growth, outgrowth. **2** *my hunch is that he'll be back* FEELING, feeling in one's bones, guess, suspicion, impression, conjecture, inkling, idea, sense, notion, fancy, intuition, premonition, presentiment; *informal* gut feeling, gut instinct.

hundred ▶ **cardinal number** century; *informal* ton.
— RELATED TERMS: centi-, hecto-, centenary, centennial.

hunger ▶ **noun 1** *she was faint with hunger* LACK OF FOOD, hungriness, ravenousness, emptiness; starvation, malnutrition, famine, malnourishment, undernourishment. **2** *a hunger for news* DESIRE, craving, longing, yearning, hankering, appetite, thirst; want, need; *informal* itch, yen.
■ **hunger after/for** DESIRE, crave, covet; long for, yearn for, pine for, ache for, hanker after, thirst for, lust for; want, need; *informal* have a yen for, have a jones for, itch for, be dying for.

hungry ▶ **adjective 1** *I was really hungry* RAVENOUS, empty, in need of food, hollow, faint from/with hunger; starving, starved, famished; malnourished, undernourished, underfed; *informal* peckish, able to eat a horse; *archaic* esurient. **2** *they are hungry for success* EAGER, keen, avid, longing, yearning, aching, pining, greedy, covetous; craving, desirous of, hankering after; *informal* itching, dying, hot.
— OPPOSITES: full.

hunk ▶ **noun 1** *a hunk of bread* CHUNK, piece, wedge, block, slab, lump, square, gobbet. **2** *(informal) he's such a hunk* GOOD-LOOKING MAN, heartthrob, macho man; *informal* babe, stud, studmuffin, dreamboat, (male) specimen, looker, beefcake, chick/babe magnet, he-man, hottie.

hunt ▶ **verb 1** *they hunted deer* CHASE, stalk, pursue, course, run down; track, trail, follow, hound, shadow; *informal* tail. **2** *police are hunting for her* SEARCH, look (high and low), scour/sweep/comb the area; seek, try to find; cast about/around/round, scout around,

rummage (about/around/round), root about/around, fish about/around.
▶ **noun 1** *the thrill of the hunt* CHASE, pursuit. **2** *police have stepped up their hunt* SEARCH, look, quest, manhunt.

hunter ▶ **noun** HUNTSMAN, huntswoman, trapper, stalker, woodsman; nimrod; predator.

hurdle ▶ **noun 1** *his leg hit a hurdle* FENCE, jump, barrier, barricade, bar, railing, rail. **2** *the final hurdle to overcome* OBSTACLE, difficulty, problem, barrier, bar, snag, stumbling block, impediment, obstruction, complication, hindrance, hitch; *informal* headache, hiccup, glitch, fly in the ointment, wrench in the works.

hurl ▶ **verb 1** *he hurled an eraser at her head* THROW, toss, huck ♣, fling, pitch, cast, lob, bowl, launch, catapult; project, propel, let fly, fire; *informal* chuck, heave, sling, buzz, peg. *dated* shy. **2** *she felt like she was going to hurl* VOMIT, be sick, puke, throw up, heave, barf, spew, upchuck, retch, ralph, gag.

hurly-burly ▶ **noun** *See* HULLABALOO.

hurricane ▶ **noun** CYCLONE, typhoon, tornado, storm, tempest, windstorm, whirlwind, gale; *informal* twister.

hurried ▶ **adjective 1** *a hurried greeting* QUICK, fast, swift, rapid, speedy, brisk, hasty, abrupt; cursory, perfunctory, brief, short, fleeting, flying, passing, superficial, slapdash. **2** *a hurried decision* HASTY, rushed, speedy, quick, expeditious; impetuous, impulsive, precipitate, precipitous, rash, incautious, imprudent, spur-of-the-moment.
— OPPOSITES: slow, considered.

hurriedly ▶ **adverb** HASTILY, speedily, quickly, fast, rapidly, swiftly, briskly; without delay, at top speed, at full tilt, full bore, full out, on the double; headlong, hotfoot, post-haste; *informal* like the wind, like greased lightning, double-quick, lickety-split.

hurry ▶ **verb 1** *hurry or you'll be late* BE QUICK, hurry up, make speed, press on, push on; run, dash, rush, race, fly; scurry, scramble, scuttle, sprint; *informal* get a move on, move it, step on it, get cracking, get moving, shake a leg, chop-chop, tear, hare, zip, zoom, hotfoot it, leg it, get the lead out; *dated* make haste; *archaic* hie. **2** *she hurried him out* HUSTLE, hasten, push, urge, drive, spur, goad, prod.
— OPPOSITES: dawdle, delay.
▶ **noun** *in all the hurry, we forgot* RUSH, haste, flurry, hustle and bustle, confusion, commotion, hubbub, turmoil; race, scramble, scurry.

hurt ▶ **verb 1** *my back hurts* BE PAINFUL, be sore, be tender, cause pain, cause discomfort; ache, smart, sting, burn, throb; *informal* be killing. **2** *Dad hurt his leg* INJURE, wound, damage, abuse, disable, incapacitate, maim, mutilate, wrench; bruise, cut, gash, graze, scrape, scratch, lacerate. **3** *his words hurt her* DISTRESS, pain, wound, sting, upset, sadden, devastate, grieve, mortify; cut to the quick. **4** *high interest rates are hurting the economy* HARM, damage, be detrimental to, weaken, blight, impede, jeopardize, undermine, ruin, wreck, sabotage, cripple.
— OPPOSITES: heal, comfort, benefit.
▶ **noun** DISTRESS, pain, suffering, injury, grief, misery, anguish, agony, trauma, woe, upset, sadness, sorrow; harm, damage, trouble.
— OPPOSITES: joy.
▶ **adjective 1** *my hurt hand* INJURED, wounded, bruised, grazed, cut, gashed, battered, sore, painful, aching, smarting, throbbing. **2** *Anne's hurt expression* PAINED,

injured, distressed, anguished, upset, sad, mortified, offended; *informal* miffed, peeved, sore.
– OPPOSITES: pleased.

hurtful ▶ **adjective** UPSETTING, distressing, wounding, painful, injurious; unkind, cruel, nasty, mean, malicious, spiteful, vindictive; cutting, barbed, poisonous; *informal* catty, bitchy.

hurtle ▶ **verb** SPEED, rush, run, race, sprint, bolt, dash, career, charge, careen, shoot, streak, flash, gallop, hare, fly, scurry, go like the wind; *informal* belt, pelt, tear, scoot, whiz, zoom, go like a bat out of hell, hightail it, barrel.

husband ▶ **noun** SPOUSE, (life) partner, mate, consort, man, helpmate, helpmeet; groom, bridegroom; *informal* hubby, old man, one's better half, other half, significant other.

husbandry ▶ **noun 1** *farmers have new methods of husbandry* FARM MANAGEMENT, land management, farming, agriculture, agronomy; cultivation; animal husbandry, ranching. **2** *the careful husbandry of their resources* CONSERVATION, management; economy, thrift, thriftiness, frugality.

hush ▶ **verb** SILENCE, quieten (down), shush; soothe, calm, pacify; gag, muzzle, muffle, mute; *informal* shut up.
▶ **exclamation** *Hush! Someone will hear you* BE QUIET, keep quiet, quieten down, be silent, stop talking, hold your tongue; *informal* shut up, sh, hush up, shut your mouth, shut your face, shut your trap, button your lip, pipe down, put a sock in it, give it a rest, save it, not another word.
▶ **noun** *a hush descended* SILENCE, quiet, quietness; stillness, peace, peacefulness, calm, lull, tranquility.
– OPPOSITES: noise.
■ **hush up** KEEP SECRET, conceal, hide, suppress, cover up, keep quiet about; obscure, veil, sweep under the carpet; *informal* sit on, keep under one's hat.

hush-hush ▶ **adjective** (*informal*). See SECRET *adjective* sense 1.

husk ▶ **noun** SHELL, hull, pod, case, covering, integument, shuck; *Botany* pericarp, legume.

husky ▶ **adjective 1** *a husky voice* THROATY, gruff, gravelly, hoarse, croaky, rough, guttural, harsh, rasping, raspy; deep. **2** *Paddy was a husky guy* STRONG, muscular, muscly, muscle-bound, big, brawny, hefty, burly, hulking, strapping, thickset, solid, powerful, heavy, robust, sturdy, stalwart, blocky, Herculean, well-built; *informal* beefy, hunky.
– OPPOSITES: shrill, puny.

hussy ▶ **noun** MINX, coquette, tease, seductress, Lolita, Jezebel; slut, harlot, loose woman; *informal* floozie, tart, vamp, tramp; *dated* trollop; *archaic* jade, strumpet.

hustle ▶ **verb 1** *I was hustled away* MANHANDLE, push, shove, thrust, frogmarch, whisk, bundle (off). **2** *we'll have to hustle to catch the bus* rush, hurry, be quick, hasten; speed up, press on; *informal* get a move on, step on it, get moving, get cracking, shake a leg. **3** *if you want it, you'll have to hustle for it* WORK (HARD), strive, endeavour, apply oneself, exert oneself; *informal* pull out all the stops.
■ **hustle and bustle** HURLY-BURLY, bustle, tumult, hubbub, activity, action, liveliness, animation, excitement, agitation, commotion, flurry, whirl; *informal* ballyhoo, hoo-ha, hullabaloo.

hut ▶ **noun** SHACK, shanty, (log) cabin, cabana, shelter, shed, lean-to, caboose ✦; hovel; fish hut ✦, ice-fishing hut ✦, ice hut ✦; (*Nfld*) tilt ✦.

hybrid ▶ **noun** *a hybrid between a brown and albino mouse* CROSS, cross-breed, mixed-breed, half-breed, half-blood; mixture, blend, amalgamation, combination, composite, compound, fusion.
▶ **adjective** *a hybrid organization* COMPOSITE, cross-bred, interbred, mongrel; heterogeneous, mixed, blended, compound, amalgamated, hyphenated.

hydro ▶ **noun** See ELECTRICITY.

hygiene ▶ **noun** CLEANLINESS, sanitation, sterility, purity, disinfection; public health, environmental health.

hygienic ▶ **adjective** SANITARY, clean, germ-free, disinfected, sterilized, sterile, antiseptic, aseptic, unpolluted, uncontaminated, salubrious, healthy, wholesome, purified; *informal* squeaky clean.
– OPPOSITES: unsanitary.

hymn ▶ **noun** RELIGIOUS SONG, song of praise, anthem, canticle, chorale, psalm, paean, carol; spiritual.

hype (*informal*) ▶ **noun** *her work relies on hype and headlines* PUBLICITY, advertising, promotion, marketing, exposure; *informal* plugging, ballyhoo, promo.
▶ **verb** *a stunt to hype a new product* PUBLICIZE, advertise, promote, push, boost, merchandise, build up; *informal* plug.

hyper ▶ **adjective** HYPERACTIVE, overactive, active, energetic; busy, fidgety; excited, frantic, frenetic, frenzied, feverish; *informal* keyed-up, fired-up, amped-up, high-energy, caffeinated, pumped (up), turbocharged.

hyperbole ▶ **noun** EXAGGERATION, overstatement, magnification, embroidery, embellishment, excess, overkill, rhetoric; *informal* purple prose, puffery.
– OPPOSITES: understatement.

hypnotic ▶ **adjective** MESMERIZING, mesmeric, spellbinding, entrancing, bewitching, irresistible, magnetic, compelling, enthralling, captivating, charming, soporific, sleep-inducing, sedative, numbing; *Medicine* stupefacient.

hypnotize ▶ **verb 1** *he had been hypnotized* MESMERIZE, put into a trance. **2** *they were hypnotized by the dancers* ENTRANCE, mesmerize, spellbind, enthrall, transfix, captivate, bewitch, charm, enrapture, grip, rivet, absorb, fascinate, magnetize.

hypochondriac ▶ **noun** *a hypochondriac who depends on her pills* VALETUDINARIAN, neurotic.
▶ **adjective** *her hypochondriac husband* VALETUDINARIAN, hypochondriacal, malingering, health-obsessed; neurotic, paranoid, phobic.

hypocrisy ▶ **noun** DISSIMULATION, false virtue, cant, posturing, affectation, speciousness, empty talk, insincerity, falseness, deceit, dishonesty, mendacity, pretense, duplicity; sanctimoniousness, sanctimony, pietism, piousness; *informal* phoniness, fraud, humbug.
– OPPOSITES: sincerity.

hypocrite ▶ **noun** DISSEMBLER, humbug, pretender, deceiver, liar, pietist, sanctimonious person, plaster saint; *informal* phony, fraud, sham.

hypothesis ▶ **noun** THEORY, theorem, thesis, conjecture, supposition, postulation, postulate, proposition, premise, assumption; notion, concept, idea, possibility.

hypothetical ▶ **adjective** THEORETICAL, speculative, conjectured, conjectural, notional, suppositional, supposed, putative, assumed; academic.
– OPPOSITES: actual.

hysteria ▶ **noun** FRENZY, feverishness, hysterics, fit

of madness, derangement, mania, delirium; panic, alarm, distress.
— OPPOSITES: calm.

hysterical ▶ **adjective 1** *Janet became hysterical* OVERWROUGHT, overemotional, out of control, frenzied, frantic, wild, feverish, crazed; beside oneself, driven to distraction, distraught, agitated, berserk, manic, delirious, unhinged, deranged, out of one's mind, raving; *informal* in a state. **2** *(informal) her attempts to dance were hysterical* HILARIOUS, uproarious, very funny, very amusing, comical, farcical; *informal* hysterically funny, priceless, side-splitting, rib-tickling, gut-busting, knee-slapping, thigh-slapping, a scream, a hoot, a barrel of laughs; *dated* killing.

hysterics ▶ **plural noun** *(informal)* **1** *a fit of hysterics* HYSTERIA, wildness, feverishness, irrationality, frenzy, loss of control, delirium, derangement, mania. **2** *the girls collapsed in hysterics* FITS OF LAUGHTER, gales/ paroxysms of laughter, uncontrollable laughter, convulsions, fits; *informal* stitches.

Ii

ice ▶ **noun 1** *a roof covered with ice* FROZEN WATER, icicles, (*Nfld*) ice candles ✤; black ice, frost, rime, glaze. **2** *too many players on the ice* ICE RINK, skating rink, hockey rink, ice pad ✤, ice palace ✤, hockey cushion ✤.
— RELATED TERMS: gelid, glacial.
▶ **verb 1** *the lake has iced over* FREEZE (OVER), turn into ice, harden, solidify. **2** *iced drinks* COOL, chill, refrigerate. **3** *she had iced the cake* COVER WITH ICING, glaze, frost.
— OPPOSITES: thaw, heat.
■ **on ice** (*informal*). *See* PENDING *adjective* sense 1.
■ **on thin ice** IN A RISKY SITUATION, at risk, in peril, imperilled, living dangerously, living on the edge.

ice-cold ▶ **adjective** ICY, freezing, glacial, gelid, sub-zero, frozen, wintry, frigid; arctic, polar, Siberian, hypothermic; bitter, biting, cutting, bone-chilling, raw, chilly, frosty, nippy; *literary* rimy.
— OPPOSITES: hot.

ice cream ▶ **noun** FROZEN DESSERT, ice milk, gelato, frozen yogourt, sorbet, sherbet, kulfi; ice cream cone, sundae.

icing ▶ **noun** GLAZE, frosting, topping, filling, fondant, piping.

icon ▶ **noun 1** *an icon of the Virgin* IMAGE, idol, portrait, picture, representation, likeness, symbol, sign; figure, statue. **2** *he became a teen icon* IDOL, paragon, hero/heroine; celebrity, superstar, star; favourite, darling.

iconoclast ▶ **noun** CRITIC, skeptic; heretic, unbeliever, dissident, dissenter, infidel; rebel, renegade, mutineer.

icy ▶ **adjective 1** *icy roads* FROSTY, frozen (over), iced over, ice-bound, ice-covered, iced up; slippery, (*PEI*) glib ✤; *literary* rimy. **2** *an icy wind* FREEZING, cold, chill, chilly, nippy, frigid, frosty, biting, cutting, bitter, raw, arctic, wintry, glacial, Siberian, hypothermic, polar, gelid. **3** *an icy voice* UNFRIENDLY, hostile, forbidding, unwelcoming; cold, cool, chilly, frigid, frosty, glacial, gelid; haughty, stern, hard.

ID ▶ **noun** IDENTIFICATION, (identification/identity) papers, bona fides, documents, credentials.

idea ▶ **noun 1** *the idea of death scares her* CONCEPT, notion, conception, thought; image, visualization; hypothesis, postulation. **2** *our idea is to open a new shop* PLAN, scheme, design, proposal, proposition, suggestion, brainchild, vision; aim, intention, purpose, objective, object, goal, target. **3** *Liz had other ideas on the subject* THOUGHT, theory, view, opinion, feeling, belief, attitude, conclusion; *informal* take. **4** *I had an idea that it might happen* SENSE, feeling, suspicion, fancy, inkling, hunch, clue, theory, notion, impression. **5** *an idea of the cost* ESTIMATE, estimation, approximation, guess, conjecture, rough calculation; *informal* guesstimate. **6** *I get the idea* MEANING, significance, sense, import, essence, gist, drift; intention, purport, implication.

ideal ▶ **adjective 1** *ideal flying weather* PERFECT, best possible, consummate, supreme, excellent, flawless, faultless, exemplary, classic, model, ultimate,

quintessential. **2** *an ideal concept* ABSTRACT, theoretical, conceptual, notional; hypothetical, speculative, conjectural, suppositional. **3** *an ideal world* UNATTAINABLE, unachievable, impracticable, chimerical; unreal, fictitious, hypothetical, theoretical, ivory-towered, imaginary, illusory, idealized, idyllic, visionary, Utopian, fairy-tale.
— OPPOSITES: bad, concrete, real.
▶ **noun 1** *she tried to be his ideal* PERFECTION, paragon, epitome, shining example, ne plus ultra, nonpareil, dream. **2** *an ideal to aim at* MODEL, pattern, exemplar, standard, example, paradigm, archetype, prototype; yardstick, lodestar. **3** *a liberal ideal* PRINCIPLE, standard, value, belief, conviction, persuasion; (**ideals**) morals, morality, ethics, ideology, creed.

idealist ▶ **noun** UTOPIAN, visionary, fantasist, romantic, dreamer, daydreamer, stargazer; Walter Mitty, Don Quixote, fantast; perfectionist.

idealistic ▶ **adjective** UTOPIAN, visionary, romantic, quixotic, dreamy, unrealistic, impractical, starry-eyed; fanciful, airy-fairy; *informal* with one's head in the clouds.

idealize ▶ **verb** ROMANTICIZE, glorify, be unrealistic about, look at something through rose-coloured glasses, paint a rosy picture of, glamorize; deify, put someone on a pedestal.

ideally ▶ **adverb** IN A PERFECT WORLD; preferably, if possible, by choice, as a matter of choice, (much) rather; all things being equal, theoretically, hypothetically, in theory, in principle, on paper.

idée fixe ▶ **noun** *See* OBSESSION.

identical ▶ **adjective 1** *identical badges* INDISTINGUISHABLE, (exactly) the same, similar, uniform, twin, duplicate, interchangeable, synonymous, undifferentiated, homogeneous, of a piece, cut from the same cloth; alike, like, matching, like (two) peas in a pod. **2** *I used the identical technique* THE (VERY) SAME, the selfsame, the very, one and the same; aforementioned, aforesaid, aforenamed, above, above-stated; foregoing, preceding.
— OPPOSITES: different.

identifiable ▶ **adjective** DISTINGUISHABLE, recognizable, known; noticeable, perceptible, discernible, appreciable, detectable, observable, perceivable, ascertainable, visible; distinct, marked, conspicuous, unmistakable, clear.
— OPPOSITES: unrecognizable.

identification ▶ **noun 1** *the identification of the suspect* RECOGNITION, singling out, pinpointing, naming; discerning, distinguishing; *informal* fingering. **2** *early identification of problems* DETERMINATION, establishment, ascertainment, discovery, diagnosis, divination; verification, confirmation. **3** *may I see your identification?* ID, (identity/identification) papers, bona fides, documents, credentials; ID card, identity card, pass, badge, warrant, licence, permit, passport.

identify ▶ **verb 1** *Gail identified her attacker* RECOGNIZE, single out, pick out, spot, point out, pinpoint, put one's finger on, put a name to, name, know; discern, distinguish; remember, recall, recollect; *informal* finger; *formal* espy. **2** *I identified four problem areas* DETERMINE, establish, ascertain, make out, diagnose, discern, distinguish; verify, confirm; *informal* figure out, get a fix on, peg. **3** *we identify sport with glamour* ASSOCIATE, link, connect, relate, bracket, couple; mention in the same breath as, put side by side with. **4** *Peter identifies with the hero* EMPATHIZE, be in tune, have a rapport, feel at one, sympathize; be on the same wavelength as, speak the same language as; understand, relate to, feel for.

identity ▶ noun **1** *the identity of the owner* NAME, ID; specification. **2** *she was afraid of losing her identity* INDIVIDUALITY, self, selfhood; personality, character, originality, distinctiveness, differentness, singularity, uniqueness. **3** *a case of mistaken identity* IDENTIFICATION, recognition, naming, singling out.

ideology ▶ noun BELIEFS, ideas, ideals, principles, ethics, morals; doctrine, creed, credo, faith, teaching, theory, philosophy; tenets, canon(s); conviction(s), persuasion; *informal* ism.

idiocy ▶ noun STUPIDITY, folly, foolishness, foolhardiness, ignorance; madness, insanity, lunacy, nonsense; silliness, brainlessness, thoughtlessness, senselessness, irresponsibility, imprudence, ineptitude, inanity, absurdity, ludicrousness, fatuousness; *informal* craziness.
— OPPOSITES: sense.

idiom ▶ noun LANGUAGE, mode of expression, turn of phrase, style, speech, locution, diction, usage, phraseology, phrasing, phrase, vocabulary, terminology, parlance, jargon, argot, cant, patter, tongue, vernacular; *informal* lingo.

idiomatic ▶ adjective VERNACULAR, colloquial, everyday, conversational; natural, grammatical, correct.

idiosyncrasy ▶ noun PECULIARITY, oddity, eccentricity, mannerism, trait, singularity, quirk, tic, whim, vagary, caprice, kink; fetish, foible, crotchet, habit, characteristic; individuality; unorthodoxy, unconventionality.

idiosyncratic ▶ adjective DISTINCTIVE, individual, individualistic, characteristic, peculiar, typical, special, specific, unique, one-of-a-kind, personal; eccentric, unconventional, irregular, anomalous, odd, quirky, offbeat, queer, strange, weird, wacky, wingy ✤, bizarre, freakish, abnormal; *informal* freaky, far out, off the wall.

idiot ▶ noun FOOL, ass, halfwit, dunce, dolt, ignoramus, simpleton; *informal* dope, ninny, nincompoop, chump, dim-wit, dim-bulb, dumbo, dummy, dumdum, loon, dork, sap, jackass, blockhead, jughead, bonehead, knucklehead, fathead, numbskull, numbnuts, dumb-ass, doofus, dunderhead, ditz, lummox, dipstick, thickhead, meathead, meatball, woodenhead, airhead, pinhead, lamebrain, cretin, moron, imbecile, pea-brain, birdbrain, jerk, nerd, donkey, nitwit, twit, boob, twerp, schmuck, bozo, hoser ✤, turkey, chowderhead, dingbat.
— OPPOSITES: genius.

idiotic ▶ adjective STUPID, silly, foolish, witless, brainless, mindless, thoughtless, unintelligent; imprudent, unwise, ill-advised, ill-considered, half-baked, foolhardy; absurd, senseless, pointless, nonsensical, inane, fatuous, ridiculous; *informal* dumb, dim, dim-witted, halfwitted, dopey, hare-brained, pea-brained, wooden-headed, thick-headed, dumb-ass.

idle ▶ adjective **1** *an idle person* LAZY, indolent, slothful, work-shy, shiftless, inactive, sluggish, lethargic, listless; slack, lax, lackadaisical, good-for-nothing. **2** *I was bored with being idle* UNEMPLOYED, jobless, out-of-work, redundant, between jobs, workless, unwaged, unoccupied. **3** *they left the machine idle* INACTIVE, unused, unoccupied, unemployed, disused; out of action, inoperative, out of service. **4** *their idle hours* UNOCCUPIED, spare, empty, vacant, unfilled, available. **5** *idle remarks* FRIVOLOUS, trivial, trifling, vain, minor, petty, lightweight, shallow, superficial, insignificant, unimportant, worthless, paltry, niggling, peripheral, inane, fatuous; unnecessary, time-wasting. **6** *idle threats* EMPTY, meaningless, pointless, worthless, vain, hollow, insubstantial, futile, ineffective, ineffectual; groundless, baseless.
— OPPOSITES: industrious, employed, working, busy, serious.

▶ verb **1** *Lily idled on the window seat* DO NOTHING, be inactive, vegetate, take it easy, mark time, twiddle one's thumbs, kill time, languish, laze, lounge, loll, loaf, loiter; *informal* hang around/about, veg out, bum around, lallygag. **2** *he let the engine idle* RUN.

idler ▶ noun LOAFER, layabout, (*Atlantic*) hangashore ✤, good-for-nothing, ne'er-do-well, lounger, shirker, sluggard; *informal* slacker, slob, lazybones, slowpoke; *literary* wastrel.
— OPPOSITES: workaholic.

idol ▶ noun **1** *an idol in a shrine* ICON, effigy, statue, figure, figurine, fetish, totem; graven image, false god, golden calf. **2** *a teen idol* HERO, heroine, star, superstar, icon, celebrity; favourite, darling; *informal* pin-up, heartthrob, dreamboat, golden boy/girl.

idolatry ▶ noun IDOLIZATION, fetishization, fetishism, (idol) worship, adulation, adoration, reverence, veneration, glorification, lionization, hero-worshipping.

idolize ▶ verb HERO-WORSHIP, worship, revere, venerate, deify, lionize; stand in awe of, reverence, look up to, admire, adore, exalt; *informal* put on a pedestal.

idyll ▶ noun *See* UTOPIA.

idyllic ▶ adjective PERFECT, wonderful, blissful, halcyon, happy; ideal, idealized; heavenly, paradisal, Utopian, Elysian; peaceful, picturesque, bucolic, unspoiled; *literary* Arcadian.

if ▶ conjunction **1** *if the weather is fine, we can walk* ON CONDITION THAT, provided (that), providing (that), presuming (that), supposing (that), assuming (that), as long as, given that, in the event that. **2** *if I go out she gets nasty* WHENEVER, every time. **3** *I wonder if he noticed* WHETHER, whether or not. **4** *a useful, if unintended innovation* ALTHOUGH, albeit, but, yet, whilst; even though, despite being.

▶ noun *there is one if in all this* UNCERTAINTY, doubt; condition, stipulation, provision, proviso, constraint, precondition, requirement, specification, restriction.

iffy ▶ adjective (*informal*) **1** *an iffy neighbourhood* DUBIOUS, doubtful, questionable, shaky; substandard, second-rate, inferior; sketchy. **2** *the date was a bit iffy* UNCERTAIN, undecided, unsettled, unsure, unresolved, in doubt, dubious, ambivalent; *informal* up in the air, borderline.

ignite ▶ verb **1** *he escaped moments before the gas ignited* CATCH FIRE, burst into flames, combust; be set off, explode. **2** *his cigarette ignited the blanket* LIGHT, set fire to, set on fire, set alight, kindle, spark, touch off;

informal set/put a match to. **3** *the campaign failed to ignite voter interest* AROUSE, kindle, trigger, spark, instigate, excite, provoke, stimulate, animate, stir up, whip up, rally, jump-start, incite, fuel.
— OPPOSITES: go out, extinguish.

ignoble ▶ adjective DISHONOURABLE, unworthy, base, shameful, contemptible, despicable, dastardly, vile, degenerate, shabby, sordid, mean; improper, unprincipled, discreditable; humble, low, lowly, common, plebeian.

ignominious ▶ adjective HUMILIATING, undignified, embarrassing, mortifying; ignoble, inglorious; disgraceful, shameful.
— OPPOSITES: glorious.

ignominy ▶ noun SHAME, humiliation, embarrassment, mortification; disgrace, dishonour, discredit, degradation, scandal, infamy, indignity, ignobility, loss of face.

ignoramus ▶ noun FOOL, ass, halfwit, blockhead, jughead, dunce, simpleton; *informal* dope, doofus, hoser ♣, ninny, nincompoop, chump, boob, dim-wit, dim-bulb, imbecile, moron, dumbo, dummy, dumb-ass, fathead, bozo, numbskull, numbnuts, thickhead, woodenhead, airhead, birdbrain, lummox, nitwit, twit, putz, schmuck, turkey.

ignorance ▶ noun UNAWARENESS, incomprehension, unconsciousness, unfamiliarity, inexperience, innocence, lack of knowledge, illiteracy; lack of intelligence, stupidity, foolishness, idiocy; *informal* cluelessness.
— OPPOSITES: knowledge, education.

ignorant ▶ adjective **1** *an ignorant country girl* UNEDUCATED, unknowledgeable, untaught, unschooled, untutored, untrained, illiterate, unlettered, unlearned, unread, uninformed, unenlightened, benighted; inexperienced, unworldly, unsophisticated. **2** *they were ignorant of working-class life* WITHOUT KNOWLEDGE, unaware, unconscious, oblivious, incognizant, unfamiliar, unacquainted, uninformed, ill-informed, unenlightened, unconversant, inexperienced, naive, innocent, green; *informal* in the dark, clueless.
— OPPOSITES: educated, knowledgeable.

ignore ▶ verb **1** *he ignored the customers* DISREGARD, take no notice of, pay no attention to, pay no heed to; turn a blind eye to, turn a deaf ear to, tune out. **2** *he was ignored by the journalists* SNUB, slight, spurn, shun, look right through, pass over, cut out; *informal* give someone the brush-off, give someone the cold shoulder. **3** *doctors ignored her husband's instructions* SET ASIDE, pay no attention to, take no account of; break, contravene, fail to comply with, fail to observe, disregard, disobey, breach, defy, flout; *informal* pooh-pooh.
— OPPOSITES: acknowledge, obey.

ilk ▶ noun TYPE, sort, class, category, group, family, set, breed, bracket, genre, make, model, kind, brand, vintage, stamp, style, variety.

ill ▶ adjective **1** *she was feeling rather ill* UNWELL, sick, not (very) well, ailing, poorly, sickly, peaked, peaky, indisposed, infirm; out of sorts, not oneself, bad, off, rotten, in a bad way; bedridden, valetudinarian; queasy, nauseous, nauseated; *informal* under the weather, laid up, rough, lousy, pukey, dizzy, woozy. **2** *the ill effects of smoking* HARMFUL, damaging, detrimental, deleterious, adverse, injurious, hurtful, destructive, pernicious, dangerous; unhealthy, unwholesome, poisonous, noxious; *literary* malefic, maleficent. **3** *ill feeling* HOSTILE, antagonistic,

acrimonious, inimical, antipathetic; unfriendly, unsympathetic, unkind; resentful, spiteful, malicious, vindictive, malevolent, bitter. **4** *an ill omen* UNLUCKY, adverse, unfavourable, unfortunate, unpropitious, inauspicious, unpromising, infelicitous, ominous, sinister; *literary* direful. **5** *ill manners* RUDE, discourteous, impolite, improper; impertinent, insolent, impudent, uncivil, disrespectful; *informal* ignorant.
— OPPOSITES: well, healthy, beneficial, auspicious.

▶ noun **1** *the ills of society* PROBLEMS, troubles, evils, difficulties, misfortunes, trials, tribulations; worries, anxieties, concerns; *informal* headaches, hassles. **2** *he wished them no ill* HARM, hurt, injury, damage, pain, trouble, misfortune, suffering, distress. **3** *the body's ills* ILLNESSES, ailments, disorders, complaints, afflictions, sicknesses, diseases, maladies, infirmities.

▶ adverb **1** *such behaviour ill became the king* POORLY, badly, imperfectly. **2** *the look on her face boded ill* UNFAVOURABLY, adversely, badly, inauspiciously. **3** *he can ill afford the loss of income* BARELY, scarcely, hardly, only just, just possibly. **4** *we are ill prepared* INADEQUATELY, unsatisfactorily, insufficiently, imperfectly, poorly, badly.
— OPPOSITES: well, auspiciously, satisfactorily.

■ **ill at ease** AWKWARD, uneasy, uncomfortable, embarrassed, self-conscious, out of place, inhibited, gauche; restless, restive, fidgety, discomfited, worried, anxious, on edge, edgy, nervous, tense, high strung; *informal* twitchy, jittery, discombobulated, antsy.

■ **speak ill of** DENIGRATE, disparage, criticize, be critical of, speak badly of, be malicious about, blacken the name of, run down, insult, abuse, attack, revile, malign, vilify, slur; *informal* badmouth, dis, bitch about, slag; *formal* derogate; *rare* asperse.

ill-advised ▶ adjective UNWISE, injudicious, misguided, imprudent, ill-considered, ill-judged, impolitic; foolhardy, hare-brained, rash, reckless, irresponsible; *informal* crazy, idiotic, crackpot, madcap.
— OPPOSITES: judicious.

ill-assorted ▶ adjective See MISMATCHED.

ill-bred ▶ adjective See ILL-MANNERED.

ill-conceived ▶ adjective BADLY PLANNED, badly thought out, hare-brained, ill-advised, ill-considered, ill-judged, misjudged, injudicious, imprudent, unwise, hasty, rash.

ill-considered ▶ adjective See ILL-ADVISED.

ill-defined ▶ adjective VAGUE, indistinct, unclear, imprecise, nebulous, shadowy, obscure; blurred, fuzzy, hazy, woolly.

ill-disposed ▶ adjective HOSTILE, antagonistic, unfriendly, unsympathetic, antipathetic, inimical, unfavourable, adverse, averse, at odds; *informal* anti.
— OPPOSITES: friendly.

illegal ▶ adjective UNLAWFUL, illicit, illegitimate, criminal, felonious; unlicensed, unauthorized, unsanctioned; outlawed, banned, forbidden, prohibited, proscribed, taboo; contraband, black-market, bootleg; *Law* malfeasant; *informal* crooked, shady, sketchy.
— OPPOSITES: lawful, legitimate.

illegible ▶ adjective UNREADABLE, indecipherable, unintelligible, incomprehensible, hieroglyphic; scrawled, scribbled, crabbed, cramped.

illegitimate ▶ adjective **1** *illegitimate share trading*

ILLEGAL, unlawful, illicit, criminal, felonious; unlicensed, unauthorized, unsanctioned; prohibited, outlawed, banned, forbidden, proscribed; fraudulent, corrupt, dishonest; *Law* malfeasant; *informal* crooked, shady. **2** *an illegitimate child* BORN OUT OF WEDLOCK, bastard; *archaic* natural, misbegotten.
– OPPOSITES: legal, lawful.

ill-fated ▶ **adjective** DOOMED, blighted, damned, cursed, accursed, ill-starred, unlucky, hapless, jinxed; disastrous, unfortunate; *literary* star-crossed.

ill-favoured ▶ **adjective** UNATTRACTIVE, plain, ugly, homely, unprepossessing, displeasing; *informal* not much to look at.
– OPPOSITES: attractive.

ill humour ▶ **noun** See IRRITABILITY.

ill-humoured ▶ **adjective** BAD-TEMPERED, ill-tempered, short-tempered, in a (bad) mood, cross; irritable, irascible, sullen, tetchy, testy, crotchety, touchy, cantankerous, curmudgeonly, peevish, fractious, waspish, prickly, pettish; grumpy, grouchy, crabbed, crabby, splenetic, dyspeptic, choleric; *informal* snappish, snappy, chippy, on a short fuse, shirty, cranky, ornery.
– OPPOSITES: amiable.

illiberal ▶ **adjective** INTOLERANT, narrow-minded, unenlightened, conservative, reactionary, undemocratic, authoritarian, repressive, totalitarian, despotic, tyrannical, oppressive.

illicit ▶ **adjective 1** *illicit drugs* ILLEGAL, unlawful, illegitimate, criminal, felonious; outlawed, banned, forbidden, prohibited, proscribed; unlicensed, unauthorized, unsanctioned; contraband, black-market, bootleg; *Law* malfeasant. **2** *an illicit love affair* TABOO, forbidden, impermissible, unacceptable, adulterous; secret, clandestine.
– OPPOSITES: lawful, legal.

illimitable ▶ **adjective** See LIMITLESS.

illiteracy ▶ **noun 1** *illiteracy was widespread* INABILITY TO READ OR WRITE. **2** *technological illiteracy* IGNORANCE, unawareness, inexperience, unenlightenment, lack of knowledge/education.

illiterate ▶ **adjective 1** *an illiterate peasant* UNABLE TO READ OR WRITE, unlettered. **2** *politically illiterate* IGNORANT, unknowledgeable, uneducated, unschooled, untutored, untrained, uninstructed, uninformed.

ill-judged ▶ **adjective** See ILL-ADVISED.

ill-mannered ▶ **adjective** BAD-MANNERED, discourteous, rude, impolite, uncivil, abusive; insolent, impertinent, impudent, cheeky, presumptuous, audacious, disrespectful; badly behaved, ill-behaved, boorish, loutish, oafish, uncouth, uncivilized, unmannered, ill-bred, vulgar; *informal* ignorant, crass.
– OPPOSITES: polite.

ill-natured ▶ **adjective** MEAN, nasty, spiteful, malicious, disagreeable; ill-tempered, bad-tempered, moody, irritable, irascible, surly, sullen, peevish, petulant, fractious, crabbed, crabby, tetchy, testy, grouchy, bitchy.

illness ▶ **noun** SICKNESS, disease, ailment, complaint, malady, affliction, infection, indisposition, disorder; ill health, poor health, infirmity; *informal* bug, virus; *dated* contagion.
– RELATED TERMS: -pathy.
– OPPOSITES: good health.

illogical ▶ **adjective** IRRATIONAL, unreasonable, unsound, unreasoned, unjustifiable; incorrect,

erroneous, invalid, spurious, faulty, flawed, fallacious, unscientific; specious, sophistic, casuistic; absurd, preposterous, untenable; *informal* way out, off the wall.

ill-starred ▶ **adjective** See ILL-FATED.

ill-tempered ▶ **adjective** BAD-TEMPERED, short-tempered, ill-humoured, moody; in a (bad) mood, cross, irritable, irascible, tetchy, testy, crotchety, touchy, cantankerous, curmudgeonly, peevish, fractious, waspish, prickly, pettish; grumpy, grouchy, crabbed, crabby, splenetic, dyspeptic, choleric; *informal* snappish, snappy, chippy, on a short fuse, shirty, cranky, ornery, bitchy.

ill-timed ▶ **adjective** UNTIMELY, mistimed, badly timed; premature inconvenient, inappropriate, inopportune, malapropos.
– OPPOSITES: timely.

ill-treated ▶ **adjective** ABUSED, mistreated, beaten, molested, misused, oppressed; harmed, injured, damaged, manhandled; *informal* knocked around/ about, roughed up.

illuminate ▶ **verb 1** *the bundle was illuminated by the torch* LIGHT (UP), lighten, throw light on, brighten, shine on, irradiate; *literary* illumine, illume, enlighten. **2** *the manuscripts were illuminated* DECORATE, illustrate, embellish, adorn, ornament. **3** *documents often illuminate people's thought processes* CLARIFY, elucidate, explain, reveal, shed light on, give insight into, demystify; exemplify, illustrate; *informal* spell out.
– OPPOSITES: darken, conceal.

illuminating ▶ **adjective** INFORMATIVE, enlightening, explanatory, instructive, edifying, helpful, educational, revealing; *informal* tell-all.

illumination ▶ **noun 1** *a floodlight provided illumination* LIGHT, lighting, radiance, gleam, glow, glare; shining, shining, glowing; brilliance, luminescence; *literary* illuming, irradiance, lucency, lambency, effulgence, refulgence. **2** *the illumination of a manuscript* DECORATION, illustration, embellishment, adornment, ornamentation. **3** *these books give illumination on the subject* CLARIFICATION, elucidation, explanation, revelation, explication. **4** *moments of real illumination* ENLIGHTENMENT, insight, understanding, awareness; learning, education, edification.

illusion ▶ **noun 1** *he had destroyed her illusions* DELUSION, misapprehension, misconception, false impression; fantasy, fancy, dream, chimera. **2** *the lighting increases the illusion of depth* APPEARANCE, impression, semblance. **3** *it's just an illusion* MIRAGE, hallucination, apparition, figment of the imagination, trick of the light, trompe l'oeil; deception, trick, smoke and mirrors. **4** *magical illusions* (MAGIC) TRICK, conjuring trick; (**illusions**) magic, conjuring, sleight of hand, legerdemain.

illusory ▶ **adjective** DELUSORY, delusive, illusionary, imagined, imaginary, fanciful, fancied, unreal, chimerical; sham, false, fallacious, fake, bogus, mistaken, erroneous, misguided, untrue; *informal* all in one's mind.
– OPPOSITES: genuine.

illustrate ▶ **verb 1** *the photographs that illustrate the book* DECORATE, adorn, ornament, accompany, embellish; add pictures/drawings to, provide artwork for. **2** *this can be illustrated through a brief example* EXPLAIN, explicate, elucidate, clarify, make plain, demonstrate, show, emphasize; *informal* get across.

3 *his sense of humour was illustrated by his screen saver* EXEMPLIFY, typify, epitomize, show, demonstrate, display, represent.

illustrated ▶ **adjective** WITH ILLUSTRATIONS, with pictures, with drawings, pictorial.

illustration ▶ **noun 1** *the illustrations in children's books* PICTURE, drawing, sketch, figure, image, plate, print, artwork; visual aid. **2** *by way of illustration* EXEMPLIFICATION, demonstration, showing; example, typical case, case in point, object lesson, analogy.

illustrative ▶ **adjective** EXEMPLIFYING, explanatory, elucidative, explicative, expository, exegetical; demonstrative, descriptive, representative, indicative, emblematic, symbolic, typical.

illustrious ▶ **adjective** EMINENT, distinguished, acclaimed, notable, noteworthy, prominent, pre-eminent, foremost, leading, important, influential; renowned, famous, famed, well-known, celebrated, legendary; esteemed, honoured, respected, venerable, august, highly regarded, well-thought-of, of distinction; brilliant, glorious, stellar.
– OPPOSITES: unknown.

ill will ▶ **noun** ANIMOSITY, hostility, enmity, acrimony, animus, hatred, hate, loathing, antipathy; ill feeling, bad feeling, bad blood, antagonism, unfriendliness, dislike; spite, spitefulness, resentment, hard feelings, bitterness, malice, rancour; *informal* grudge, friction.
– OPPOSITES: goodwill.

image ▶ **noun 1** *an image of the Madonna* LIKENESS, resemblance, depiction, portrayal, representation; statue, statuette, sculpture, bust, effigy; painting, picture, portrait, drawing, sketch. **2** *images of the planet Neptune* PICTURE, photograph, snapshot, photo. **3** *he contemplated his image in the mirror* REFLECTION, mirror image, likeness. **4** *the image of this country as democratic* CONCEPTION, impression, idea, perception, notion; mental picture, vision; character, reputation; appearance, semblance. **5** *biblical images* SIMILE, metaphor, metonymy; figure of speech, trope, turn of phrase; imagery. **6** *his heartthrob image* PUBLIC PERCEPTION, persona, profile, reputation, stature, standing; face, front, facade, mask, guise. **7** *I'm the image of my grandfather* DOUBLE, living image, look-alike, clone, copy, twin, duplicate, exact likeness, mirror-image, doppelgänger; *informal* spitting image, dead ringer, carbon copy; *archaic* similitude. **8** *a graven image* IDOL, icon, fetish, totem.
– RELATED TERMS: icono-.
▶ **verb** *she imaged imposing castles* ENVISAGE, envision, imagine, picture, see in one's mind's eye.

imagery ▶ **noun** *See* IMAGE sense 5.

imaginable ▶ **adjective** THINKABLE, conceivable, supposable, believable, credible, creditable; possible, plausible, feasible.

imaginary ▶ **adjective** UNREAL, non-existent, fictional, fictitious, pretend, make-believe, mythical, fabulous, fanciful, illusory, fantastic; made-up, dreamed-up, invented, fancied; *archaic* visionary.
– OPPOSITES: real.

imagination ▶ **noun 1** *a vivid imagination* CREATIVE POWER, fancy, vision; *informal* mind's eye. **2** *you need imagination in dealing with these problems* CREATIVITY, imaginativeness, creativeness; vision, inspiration, inventiveness, invention, resourcefulness, ingenuity; originality, innovation, innovativeness. **3** *the album captured the public's imagination* INTEREST, fascination, attention, passion, curiosity.

imaginative ▶ **adjective** CREATIVE, visionary, inspired, inventive, resourceful, ingenious; original, innovative, innovatory, unorthodox, unconventional; fanciful, whimsical, fantastic; *informal* offbeat, off the wall, zany.

imagine ▶ **verb 1** *she imagined castles and knights* VISUALIZE, envisage, envision, picture, see in the mind's eye; dream up, think up/of, conjure up, conceive, conceptualize; *formal* ideate. **2** *I imagine he was at home* ASSUME, presume, expect, take it, presuppose; suppose, think (it likely), dare say, surmise, believe, be of the view, figure; *informal* guess, reckon; *formal* opine.

imbalance ▶ **noun** DISPARITY, variance, variation, lack of harmony; disproportion, lopsidedness, unevenness, inequality; gulf, breach, gap.

imbecile ▶ **noun** *I'd have to be an imbecile to do such a thing. See* FOOL noun sense 1.

imbed ▶ **verb**. *See* EMBED.

imbibe ▶ **verb** (*formal*) **1** *they'd imbibed too much whisky* DRINK, consume, quaff, guzzle, gulp (down); *informal* knock back, down, swill, chug. **2** *he had imbibed liberally* DRINK (ALCOHOL), take strong drink, tipple; *informal* booze, knock a few back, hit the bottle, bend one's elbow. **3** *imbibing local history* ASSIMILATE, absorb, soak up, take in, drink in, digest, learn, acquire, grasp, pick up, familiarize oneself with.

imbroglio ▶ **noun** COMPLICATED SITUATION, complication, problem, difficulty, predicament, trouble, confusion, quandary, entanglement, muddle, mess, quagmire, morass, sticky situation; *informal* bind, jam, pickle, fix, corner, hole, scrape.

imbue ▶ **verb** PERMEATE, saturate, diffuse, suffuse, pervade, bathe, drench, steep; impregnate, inject, inculcate, ingrain, instill, invest, inspire, breathe; fill.

imitate ▶ **verb 1** *other artists have imitated her style* EMULATE, copy, model oneself on, follow, echo, parrot; *informal* rip off, knock off, pirate. **2** *he imitated Jean Chrétien* MIMIC, do an impression of, impersonate, ape; parody, caricature, travesty; *informal* take off, send up, make like, mock; *formal* personate.

imitation ▶ **noun 1** *an imitation of a sailor's hat* COPY, simulation, reproduction, replica; counterfeit, forgery, rip off. **2** *learning by imitation* EMULATION, copying, echoing, parroting. **3** *a perfect imitation of Elvis* IMPERSONATION, impression, parody, mockery, caricature, burlesque, travesty, lampoon, pastiche; mimicry, mimicking, imitating, aping; *informal* send-up, takeoff, spoof.
▶ **adjective** *imitation ivory* ARTIFICIAL, synthetic, simulated, man-made, manufactured, ersatz, substitute; mock, sham, fake, faux, bogus, knock-off, pseudo, phony.
– OPPOSITES: real, genuine.

imitative ▶ **adjective 1** *imitative crime* SIMILAR, like, mimicking; *informal* copycat. **2** *I found the film empty and imitative* DERIVATIVE, unoriginal, unimaginative, uninspired, uninventive, plagiarized, plagiaristic, slavish; clichéd, hackneyed, stale, trite, banal, rehashed; *informal* cribbed, old hat.

imitator ▶ **noun 1** *she has many imitators* COPIER, emulator, follower, mimic, plagiarist, ape, parrot; *informal* copycat. **2** *an Elvis imitator. See* IMPERSONATOR.

immaculate ▶ **adjective 1** *an immaculate white shirt* CLEAN, spotless, pure, pristine, unsoiled, unstained, unsullied; shining, shiny, gleaming; neat, tidy, spic and span; *informal* squeaky clean. **2** *immaculate*

condition PERFECT, pristine, mint; flawless, faultless, unblemished, unspoiled, undamaged; excellent, impeccable; *informal* tip-top, A1. **3** *his immaculate record* UNBLEMISHED, spotless, impeccable, unsullied, undefiled, untarnished, stainless; above reproach; *informal* squeaky clean.
— OPPOSITES: dirty, damaged.

immanent ▶ **adjective** *See* INHERENT.

immaterial ▶ **adjective** **1** *the difference in our ages was immaterial* IRRELEVANT, unimportant, inconsequential, insignificant, of no matter/ consequence, of little account, beside the point, neither here nor there. **2** *the immaterial soul* INTANGIBLE, incorporeal, bodiless, disembodied, impalpable, ethereal, insubstantial, metaphysical; spiritual, unearthly, supernatural.
— OPPOSITES: significant, physical.

immature ▶ **adjective** **1** *an immature Stilton* UNRIPE, not mature, premature, unmellowed; undeveloped, unformed, unfinished, raw, embryonic. **2** *an extremely immature girl* CHILDISH, babyish, infantile, juvenile, adolescent, puerile, sophomoric, jejune, callow, green, tender, young, inexperienced, unsophisticated, unworldly, naive; *informal* wet behind the ears.
— OPPOSITES: ripe.

immeasurable ▶ **adjective** INCALCULABLE, inestimable, innumerable, untold; limitless, boundless, unbounded, unlimited, illimitable, infinite, countless, never-ending, interminable, endless, inexhaustible; vast, immense, extensive, great, abundant; *informal* no end of; *literary* myriad.

immediate ▶ **adjective** **1** *the UN called for immediate action* INSTANT, instantaneous, swift, prompt, fast, speedy, rapid, brisk, quick, expeditious; sudden, hurried, hasty, precipitate; *informal* snappy. **2** *their immediate concerns* CURRENT, present, existing, actual; urgent, pressing, exigent. **3** *the immediate past* RECENT, not long past, just gone, latest. **4** *our immediate neighbours* NEAREST, near, close, closest, next-door; adjacent, adjoining, contiguous. **5** *the immediate cause of death* DIRECT, primary.
— OPPOSITES: delayed, distant.

immediately ▶ **adverb** **1** *it was necessary to make a decision immediately* STRAIGHT AWAY, at once, right away, instantly, now, directly, promptly, forthwith, this/that (very) minute, this/that instant, there and then, then and there, on the spot, here and now, without delay, without further ado, post-haste; quickly, as fast as possible, speedily, as soon as possible, ASAP; *informal* pronto, double-quick, on the double, pretty damn quick, PDQ, in/like a flash, like a shot, tout de suite; *humorous* toot sweet; *archaic* forthright. **2** *I sat immediately behind him* DIRECTLY, right, exactly, precisely, squarely, just, dead; *informal* smack dab.

immemorial ▶ **adjective** ANCIENT, (very) old, age-old, antediluvian, timeless, archaic, venerable, long-standing, time-worn, time-honoured, tried and true; traditional; *literary* of yore.

immense ▶ **adjective** HUGE, vast, massive, enormous, gigantic, colossal, great, very large/big, monumental, towering, tremendous; giant, elephantine, monstrous, mammoth, titanic, king-sized, economy-size(d); *informal* mega, monster, whopping, humongous, honking, jumbo, astronomical, cosmic, ginormous, Brobdingnagian.
— OPPOSITES: tiny.

immensely ▶ **adverb** EXTREMELY, very, exceedingly,

exceptionally, extraordinarily, tremendously, hugely, singularly, distinctly, outstandingly, uncommonly, unusually, decidedly, particularly, eminently, supremely, highly, remarkably, really, truly, mightily, thoroughly, in the extreme; *informal* terrifically, awfully, fearfully, terribly, devilishly, seriously, mega, damn, damned, ever so, real, mighty, powerful, awful, darned; *informal, dated* devilish, frightfully; *archaic* exceeding.
— OPPOSITES: slightly.

immerse ▶ **verb** **1** *litmus paper turns red on being immersed in acid* SUBMERGE, dip, dunk, duck, sink, plunge; soak, drench, saturate, marinate, wet, douse, souse, steep. **2** *Elliot was immersed in his work* ABSORB, engross, occupy, engage, involve, bury, swamp, lose (oneself in); busy, employ, preoccupy, fixate.

immigrant ▶ **noun** NEWCOMER, settler, migrant, emigrant; non-native, foreigner, alien, landed immigrant ♦.
— OPPOSITES: native.

immigrate ▶ **verb** *See* MIGRATE sense 1.

imminent ▶ **adjective** IMPENDING, close (at hand), near, (fast) approaching, coming, forthcoming, on the way, in the offing, in the pipeline, on the horizon, in the air, just around the corner, coming down the pike, expected, anticipated, brewing, looming, threatening, menacing; *informal* in the cards.

immobile ▶ **adjective** **1** *she sat immobile for a long time* MOTIONLESS, without moving, still, stock-still, static, stationary; rooted to the spot, rigid, frozen, transfixed, like a statue, not moving a muscle. **2** *she dreaded being immobile* UNABLE TO MOVE, immobilized; paralyzed, crippled.
— OPPOSITES: moving.

immobilize ▶ **verb** PUT OUT OF ACTION, disable, make inoperative, inactivate, deactivate, paralyze, freeze, cripple; bring to a standstill, halt, stop; restrain, stabilize; clamp, wheel-clamp.

immoderate ▶ **adjective** EXCESSIVE, heavy, intemperate, unrestrained, unrestricted, uncontrolled, unlimited, unbridled, uncurbed, overindulgent, imprudent, reckless; undue, inordinate, unreasonable, unjustified, unwarranted, uncalled for, outrageous; extravagant, lavish, exorbitant, prodigal, profligate.

immodest ▶ **adjective** INDECOROUS, improper, indecent, indelicate, immoral; forward, bold, brazen, impudent, shameless, loose, wanton; *informal* fresh, cheeky, saucy, brassy.

immoral ▶ **adjective** UNETHICAL, bad, morally wrong, wrongful, wicked, evil, foul, unprincipled, unscrupulous, dishonourable, dishonest, unconscionable, iniquitous, disreputable, corrupt, depraved, vile, villainous, nefarious, base, miscreant; sinful, godless, impure, unchaste, unvirtuous, shameless, degenerate, debased, debauched, dissolute, reprobate, lewd, obscene, perverse, perverted; licentious, wanton, promiscuous, loose; *informal* shady, lowdown, crooked, sleazy.
— OPPOSITES: ethical, chaste.

immorality ▶ **noun** WICKEDNESS, immoral behaviour, badness, evil, vileness, corruption, dishonesty, dishonourableness; sinfulness, ungodliness, unchastity, sin, depravity, villainy, vice, degeneracy, debauchery, dissolution, perversion, lewdness, obscenity, wantonness, promiscuity; *informal* shadiness, crookedness; *formal* turpitude.

immortal ▶ **adjective** **1** *our souls are immortal*

UNDYING, deathless, eternal, everlasting, never-ending, endless, lasting, enduring, ceaseless; imperishable, indestructible, inextinguishable, immutable, perpetual, permanent, unfading. **2** *an immortal children's classic* TIMELESS, perennial, classic, time-honoured, enduring; famous, famed, renowned, legendary, great, eminent, outstanding, acclaimed, celebrated.
▸ noun **1** *Greek temples of the immortals* GOD, GODDESS, deity, divine being, supreme being, divinity. **2** *one of the immortals of literature* GREAT, hero, legend, god, celebrity, star, Olympian.

immortality ▸ noun **1** *the immortality of the gods* ETERNAL LIFE, everlasting life, deathlessness; indestructibility, imperishability. **2** *the book has achieved immortality* TIMELESSNESS, legendary status, lasting fame/renown.

immortalize ▸ verb COMMEMORATE, memorialize, eternalize; celebrate, deify, exalt, glorify; eulogize, pay tribute to, honour, salute.

immovable ▸ adjective **1** *lock your bike to something immovable* FIXED, secure, stable, moored, anchored, rooted, braced, set firm, set fast; stuck, jammed, stiff, unbudgeable, four-square. **2** *he sat immovable* MOTIONLESS, unmoving, immobile, stationary, still, stock-still, not moving a muscle, rooted to the spot; transfixed, paralyzed, frozen. **3** *she was immovable in her loyalties* STEADFAST, unwavering, unswerving, resolute, determined, firm, unshakeable, adamant, unfailing, dogged, tenacious, inflexible, unyielding, unbending, uncompromising, obdurate, obstinate, iron-willed; *informal* rock-ribbed, rock-steady, die-hard.
— OPPOSITES: mobile, moving.

immune ▸ adjective RESISTANT, not subject, not liable, unsusceptible, not vulnerable; protected from, safe from, secure against, not in danger of; impervious, invulnerable, unaffected.
— OPPOSITES: susceptible.

immunity ▸ noun **1** *an immunity to malaria* RESISTANCE, non-susceptibility; ability to fight off, protection against, defences against; immunization against, inoculation against. **2** *immunity from prosecution* EXEMPTION, exception, freedom, release, dispensation, amnesty. **3** *diplomatic immunity* INDEMNITY, privilege, prerogative, right, liberty, licence; legal exemption, impunity, protection.

immunize ▸ verb VACCINATE, inoculate, inject; protect from, safeguard against.

immure ▸ verb CONFINE, intern, shut up, lock up, incarcerate, imprison, jail, cage, put behind bars, put under lock and key, hold captive, hold prisoner; detain, hold.

immutable ▸ adjective FIXED, set, rigid, inflexible, permanent, established, carved in stone; unchanging, unchanged, unvarying, unvaried, static, constant, lasting, enduring, steadfast.
— OPPOSITES: variable.

imp ▸ noun **1** *a cheeky young imp* RASCAL, monkey, devil, troublemaker, wretch, urchin; *informal* scamp, brat, monster, horror, terror, tyke, whippersnapper, hellion, varmint, rapscallion; *archaic* scapegrace. **2** *assorted imps, brownies and bogeys* HOBGOBLIN, goblin, bogey, elf, sprite, pixie, brownie, kobold, fairy, puck; *archaic* bugbear.

impact ▸ noun **1** *the force of the impact* COLLISION, crash, smash, bump, bang, knock. **2** *the job losses will have a major impact* EFFECT, influence, significance,

meaning; consequences, repercussions, ramifications, reverberations.
▸ verb **1** *a comet impacted the earth sixty million years ago* CRASH INTO, smash into, collide with, hit, strike, ram, smack into, bang into, slam into. **2** *high interest rates have impacted retail spending* AFFECT, influence, have an effect on, make an impression on; hit, touch, change, alter, modify, transform, shape.

impair ▸ verb HAVE A NEGATIVE EFFECT ON, damage, harm, diminish, reduce, weaken, lessen, decrease, impede, hinder, hobble; undermine, compromise; *formal* vitiate.
— OPPOSITES: improve, enhance.

impaired ▸ adjective **1** *visually impaired* DISABLED, handicapped, incapacitated; *euphemistic* challenged, differently abled. **2** *(Cdn) arrested for driving while impaired* drunk, intoxicated, under the influence, inebriated; *informal* bombed, high, stoned, wasted, smashed, plastered, soused.

impairment ▸ noun See HANDICAP noun sense 1.

impale ▸ verb STICK, skewer, spear, spike, transfix, harpoon; pierce, stab, run through; *literary* transpierce.

impalpable ▸ adjective INTANGIBLE, insubstantial, incorporeal, immaterial; indefinable, elusive, imperceptible, undescribable.

impart ▸ verb **1** *she had news to impart* COMMUNICATE, pass on, convey, transmit, relay, relate, recount, tell, make known, make public, report, announce, proclaim, herald, spread, disseminate, circulate, promulgate, broadcast; disclose, reveal, divulge; *informal* let on about, blab, blurt. **2** *the picture imparts some colour to the drab office* GIVE, bestow, confer, grant, lend, afford, provide, supply.

impartial ▸ adjective UNBIASED, unprejudiced, neutral, non-partisan, disinterested, detached, dispassionate, objective, open-minded, equitable, even-handed, fair, just.
— OPPOSITES: biased, partisan.

impassable ▸ adjective UNPASSABLE, unnavigable, untraversable, impenetrable; closed, blocked, barricaded; dense, thick, blind.

impasse ▸ noun DEADLOCK, dead end, stalemate, standoff; standstill, halt, (full) stop, Catch-22.

impassioned ▸ adjective EMOTIONAL, heartfelt, wholehearted, earnest, sincere, fervent, ardent, passionate, fervid, intense, burning; vehement, zealous, heated; *literary* perfervid.

impassive ▸ adjective EXPRESSIONLESS, inexpressive, inscrutable, unreadable, blank, deadpan, poker-faced, straight-faced; stony, wooden, unresponsive, cold, unmoved, indifferent; serene, calm, peaceful, unruffled, dispassionate, cool, unemotional.
— OPPOSITES: expressive.

impatience ▸ noun **1** *he was shifting in his seat with impatience* RESTLESSNESS, restiveness, agitation, nervousness, anxiety; eagerness, keenness; *informal* jitteriness. **2** *a burst of impatience* IRRITABILITY, testiness, tetchiness, irascibility, querulousness, peevishness, petulance, frustration, exasperation, annoyance, pique.

impatient ▸ adjective **1** *Elaine grew impatient* RESTLESS, restive, agitated, nervous, anxious, tense, ill at ease, edgy, jumpy, keyed up; *informal* twitchy, jittery, uptight, high-strung. **2** *they are impatient to get back home* ANXIOUS, eager, keen, yearning, longing, aching, agog; *informal* itching, dying, raring, gung-ho,

straining at the leash. **3** *an impatient gesture* IRRITATED, annoyed, angry, testy, tetchy, snappy, cross, querulous, peevish, piqued, short-tempered; abrupt, curt, brusque, terse, short; *informal* peeved.
– OPPOSITES: calm, reluctant.

impeach ▸ **verb 1** *moves to impeach the president* INDICT, charge, accuse, lay charges against, arraign, take to court, put on trial, prosecute. **2** *the headlines impeached their clean image* CHALLENGE, question, disparage, criticize, call into question, raise doubts about.

impeccable ▸ **adjective** FLAWLESS, faultless, unblemished, spotless, immaculate, stainless, perfect, exemplary; sinless, irreproachable, blameless, guiltless; *informal* squeaky clean.
– OPPOSITES: imperfect, sinful.

impecunious ▸ **adjective** PENNILESS, poor, impoverished, indigent, insolvent, hard up, poverty-stricken, needy, destitute; in straitened circumstances, unable to make ends meet; *informal* (flat) broke, strapped (for cash); *formal* penurious.
– OPPOSITES: wealthy.

impede ▸ **verb** HINDER, obstruct, hamper, hold back/ up, delay, interfere with, disrupt, retard, slow (down), hobble; block, check, stop, scupper, scuttle, thwart, frustrate, balk, foil, derail; *informal* stymie, throw a (monkey) wrench in the works; *dated* cumber.
– OPPOSITES: facilitate.

impediment ▸ **noun 1** *an impediment to economic improvement* HINDRANCE, obstruction, obstacle, barrier, bar, block, handicap, check, curb, restriction, limitation; setback, difficulty, snag, hitch, hurdle, stumbling block; *informal* fly in the ointment, hiccup, (monkey) wrench in the works, glitch; *archaic* cumber. **2** *a speech impediment* DEFECT; stammer, stutter, lisp.

impel ▸ **verb 1** *financial difficulties impelled her to seek work* FORCE, compel, constrain, oblige, require, make, urge, exhort, press, pressurize, drive, push, spur, prod, goad, incite, prompt, persuade. **2** *vital energies impel him in unforeseen directions* PROPEL, drive, move, get going, get moving.

impending ▸ **adjective** IMMINENT, close (at hand), near, nearing, approaching, coming, forthcoming, upcoming, to come, on the way, about to happen, in store, in the offing, on the horizon, in the air/wind, brewing, looming, threatening, menacing; *informal* coming down the pike.

impenetrable ▸ **adjective 1** *impenetrable armour* UNBREAKABLE, indestructible, solid, thick, unyielding; impregnable, inviolable, invulnerable, unassailable, unpierceable; *informal* bulletproof. **2** *a dark, impenetrable forest* IMPASSABLE, unpassable, inaccessible, unnavigable, untraversable; dense, thick, overgrown. **3** *an impenetrable clique* EXCLUSIVE, closed, secretive, secret, private; restrictive, restricted, limited. **4** *impenetrable statistics* INCOMPREHENSIBLE, unfathomable, inexplicable, unintelligible, inscrutable, unclear, baffling, bewildering, puzzling, perplexing, enigmatic, confusing, abstruse, opaque; complex, complicated, difficult.

impenitent ▸ **adjective** UNREPENTANT, unrepenting, uncontrite, remorseless, unashamed, unapologetic, unabashed.

imperative ▸ **adjective 1** *it is imperative that you find him* VITALLY IMPORTANT, of vital importance, all-important, vital, crucial, critical, essential,

necessary, indispensable, urgent; compulsory, obligatory, mandatory. **2** *the imperative note in her voice* PEREMPTORY, commanding, imperious, authoritative, masterful, dictatorial, magisterial, assertive, firm, insistent.
– OPPOSITES: unimportant, submissive.

imperceptible ▸ **adjective** UNNOTICEABLE, undetectable, indistinguishable, indiscernible, invisible, inaudible, inappreciable, impalpable, unobtrusive, inconspicuous, unseen; slight, small, tiny, minute, microscopic, infinitesimal, subtle, faint, fine, negligible, inconsequential; indistinct, unclear, obscure, vague, indefinite, hard to make out.
– OPPOSITES: noticeable.

imperfect ▸ **adjective 1** *the goods were returned as imperfect* FAULTY, flawed, defective, shoddy, unsound, inferior, second-rate, below standard, substandard; damaged, blemished, torn, broken, cracked, scratched; *informal* not up to scratch, crummy. **2** *an imperfect form of the manuscript* INCOMPLETE, unfinished, half-done; unpolished, unrefined, rough. **3** *she spoke imperfect Arabic* BROKEN, faltering, hesitant, rudimentary, limited.
– OPPOSITES: flawless.

imperfection ▸ **noun 1** *the glass is free from imperfections* DEFECT, fault, flaw, deformity, discoloration, disfigurement; crack, scratch, chip, dent, blemish, stain, spot, mark, taint. **2** *he was aware of his imperfections* FLAW, fault, failing, deficiency, weakness, vice, weak point, shortcoming, foible, inadequacy, frailty, limitation. **3** *the imperfection of the fossil record* INCOMPLETENESS, patchiness, deficiency; roughness, crudeness.
– OPPOSITES: strength.

imperial ▸ **adjective 1** *imperial banners* ROYAL, regal, monarchical, sovereign, kingly, queenly, princely. **2** *her imperial bearing* MAJESTIC, grand, august, dignified, proud, stately, noble, aristocratic, regal; magnificent, imposing, impressive. **3** *our customers thought we were imperial. See* IMPERIOUS.

imperil ▸ **verb** ENDANGER, jeopardize, risk, put in danger, put in jeopardy, expose to danger, hazard; threaten, pose a threat to; *archaic* peril.

imperious ▸ **adjective** PEREMPTORY, high-handed, commanding, imperial, overbearing, overweening, domineering, authoritarian, dictatorial, autocratic, authoritative, lordly, assertive, bossy, arrogant, haughty, presumptuous; *informal* pushy, high and mighty.

imperishable ▸ **adjective** ENDURING, everlasting, undying, deathless, immortal, perennial, long-lasting, indestructible, inextinguishable, ineradicable, unfading, permanent, never-ending, never dying, durable; *literary* sempiternal, perdurable.

impermanent ▸ **adjective** TEMPORARY, transient, transitory, passing, fleeting, momentary, ephemeral, fugitive; short-lived, brief, here today and gone tomorrow; *literary* evanescent.

impermeable ▸ **adjective** WATERTIGHT, waterproof, damp-proof, airtight, (hermetically) sealed, vacuum packed, zip-locked.

impersonal ▸ **adjective 1** *an impersonal judgment* NEUTRAL, unbiased, non-partisan, unprejudiced, objective, detached, disinterested, dispassionate, without favouritism. **2** *he remained strangely impersonal* ALOOF, distant, remote, reserved, withdrawn, unemotional, unsentimental,

dispassionate, cold, cool, indifferent, unconcerned; formal, stiff, businesslike; *informal* starchy, standoffish, wooden.
- OPPOSITES: biased, warm.

impersonate ▸ **verb** IMITATE, mimic, do an impression of, ape, copy, parrot; parody, caricature, burlesque, travesty, satirize, lampoon; masquerade as, pose as, pass oneself off as; *informal* take off, send up, make like; *formal* personate.

impersonation ▸ **noun** IMPRESSION, imitation; parody, caricature, burlesque, travesty, lampoon, pastiche; *informal* takeoff, send-up; *formal* personation.

impersonator ▸ **noun** IMITATOR, impressionist, mimic; parodist, lampooner.

impertinence ▸ **noun** RUDENESS, insolence, impoliteness, bad manners, discourtesy, disrespect, incivility; impudence, cheek, cheekiness, audacity, presumption, temerity, effrontery, nerve, gall, boldness, cockiness, brazenness; *informal* brass, sauce, sass, sassiness, chutzpah, lip, backtalk, guff; *archaic* assumption.

impertinent ▸ **adjective** RUDE, insolent, impolite, ill-mannered, bad-mannered, uncivil, discourteous, disrespectful; impudent, cheeky, audacious, bold, brazen, brash, presumptuous, forward; tactless, undiplomatic; *informal* saucy, pert, sassy, smart-alecky.
- OPPOSITES: polite, relevant.

imperturbable ▸ **adjective** SELF-POSSESSED, composed, {calm, cool, and collected}, cool-headed, self-controlled, serene, relaxed, unexcitable, even-tempered, placid, phlegmatic; unperturbed, unflustered, unruffled; *informal* unflappable, unfazed, nonplussed, laid-back.
- OPPOSITES: excitable.

impervious ▸ **adjective** 1 *he seemed impervious to the chill wind* UNAFFECTED, untouched, immune, invulnerable, insusceptible, resistant, indifferent, heedless, insensible, unconscious, oblivious; proof against. 2 *an impervious rain jacket* IMPERMEABLE, impenetrable, impregnable, waterproof, watertight, water-resistant, repellent; (hermetically) sealed, zip-locked.
- OPPOSITES: susceptible, permeable.

impetuous ▸ **adjective** 1 *an impetuous decision* IMPULSIVE, rash, hasty, overhasty, reckless, heedless, careless, foolhardy, bullheaded, headstrong, incautious, imprudent, injudicious, ill-considered, unthought-out; spontaneous, impromptu, spur-of-the-moment, precipitate, precipitous, hurried, rushed; *informal* devil-may-care, harum-scarum, hot-headed. 2 *an impetuous flow of water* TORRENTIAL, powerful, forceful, vigorous, violent, raging, relentless, uncontrolled; rapid, fast, fast-flowing, swift.
- OPPOSITES: considered, sluggish.

impetus ▸ **noun** 1 *the flywheel lost all its impetus* MOMENTUM, propulsion, impulsion, motive force, driving force, drive, thrust; energy, force, power, push, strength. 2 *the sales force were given fresh impetus* MOTIVATION, stimulus, incitement, incentive, inducement, inspiration, encouragement, boost, fillip, springboard; *informal* a shot in the arm.

impiety ▸ **noun** 1 *a world of impiety and immorality* GODLESSNESS, ungodliness, unholiness, irreligion, irreverence, sinfulness, sin, vice, transgression, wrongdoing, immorality, unrighteousness, blasphemy, sacrilege; apostasy, atheism, agnosticism, paganism, heathenism, non-belief,

unbelief. 2 *not even motherhood was immune to impiety* IRREVERENCE, disrespect, impertinence, insolence, mockery, derision.
- OPPOSITES: faith, reverence.

impinge ▸ **verb** 1 *these issues impinge on all of us* AFFECT, have an effect, touch, influence, make an impact, leave a mark. 2 *the proposed highway would impinge on parkland* ENCROACH, intrude, infringe, invade, trespass, obtrude, cut through, interfere with; violate; *informal* horn in.

impious ▸ **adjective** GODLESS, ungodly, unholy, irreligious, sinful, wicked, immoral, unrighteous, sacrilegious, heretical, profane, blasphemous, irreverent; apostate, atheistic, agnostic, pagan, heathen, faithless, non-believing, unbelieving.

impish ▸ **adjective** 1 *he takes an impish delight in shocking the press* MISCHIEVOUS, naughty, wicked, devilish, rascally, roguish, playful, sportive; mischief-making, full of mischief. 2 *an impish grin* ELFIN, elflike, pixie-like, puckish; mischievous, roguish, sly.

implacable ▸ **adjective** UNAPPEASABLE, unforgiving; intransigent, inflexible, unyielding, unbending, uncompromising, unrelenting, inexorable, ruthless, remorseless, merciless, heartless, pitiless, cruel, hard, harsh, stern, tough, iron-fisted.

implant ▸ **verb** 1 *the microchip is implanted under the skin* INSERT, embed, bury, lodge, place; graft. 2 *he implanted the idea in my mind* INSTILL, inculcate, insinuate, introduce, inject, plant, sow, root, lodge. ▸ **noun** *a silicone implant* TRANSPLANT, graft, implantation, insert.

implausible ▸ **adjective** UNLIKELY, improbable, questionable, doubtful, debatable; unrealistic, unconvincing, far-fetched, incredible, unbelievable, unimaginable, inconceivable, fantastic, fanciful, ridiculous, absurd, preposterous, outrageous; *informal* cock and bull.
- OPPOSITES: convincing.

implement ▸ **noun** *garden implements* TOOL, utensil, instrument, device, apparatus, gadget, contraption, appliance, machine, contrivance; *informal* gizmo; (**implements**) equipment, kit, tackle, accoutrements, paraphernalia. ▸ **verb** *the cost of implementing the new law* EXECUTE, apply, put into effect/action, put into practice, carry out/through, perform, enact; fulfill, discharge, accomplish, bring about, achieve, realize, actualize, phase in; *formal* effectuate.

implicate ▸ **verb** 1 *he had been implicated in a financial scandal* INCRIMINATE, compromise; involve, connect, link, embroil, enmesh, ensnare, entangle; *archaic* inculpate; *informal* finger. 2 *viruses are implicated in the development of cancer* INVOLVE IN, concern with, associate with, connect to/with.

implication ▸ **noun** 1 *he was smarting at their implication* SUGGESTION, insinuation, innuendo, hint, intimation, imputation. 2 *important political implications* CONSEQUENCE, result, ramification, repercussion, reverberation, effect, significance. 3 *his implication in the murder case* INCRIMINATION, involvement, connection, entanglement, association; *archaic* inculpation.

implicit ▸ **adjective** 1 *implicit assumptions* IMPLIED, hinted at, suggested; unspoken, unexpressed, undeclared, unstated, tacit, unacknowledged, taken for granted; inherent, latent, underlying, inbuilt, incorporated; understood, inferred, deducible. 2 *an*

implicit trust in human nature ABSOLUTE, complete, total, wholehearted, perfect, utter; unqualified, unconditional, categorical; unshakeable, unquestioning, firm, steadfast.
– OPPOSITES: explicit.

implicitly ▶ adverb COMPLETELY, absolutely, totally, wholeheartedly, utterly, unconditionally, unreservedly, without reservation.

implied ▶ adjective IMPLICIT, hinted at, suggested, insinuated; unspoken, unexpressed, undeclared, connoted, unstated, tacit, unacknowledged, taken for granted; inferred, understood, deducible.
– OPPOSITES: explicit.

implore ▶ verb *his mother implored him to continue studying* PLEAD WITH, beg, entreat, beseech, appeal to, ask, request, call on; exhort, urge, enjoin, press, push, petition, bid, importune; supplicate.

imply ▶ verb **1** *are you implying he is mad?* INSINUATE, suggest, hint, intimate, say indirectly, indicate, give someone to understand. **2** *the forecasted traffic increase implies more roads* INVOLVE, entail; mean, point to, signify, indicate, signal, connote, denote; necessitate, require, presuppose.

impolite ▶ adjective RUDE, bad-mannered, ill-mannered, discourteous, uncivil, disrespectful, inconsiderate, boorish, churlish, ill-bred, ungentlemanly, unladylike, ungracious; insolent, impudent, impertinent, cheeky; loutish, rough, crude, vulgar, indelicate, indecorous, tactless, gauche, uncouth; *informal* ignorant, lippy, saucy; *archaic* contumelious.

impolitic ▶ adjective IMPRUDENT, unwise, injudicious, incautious, irresponsible; ill-judged, ill-advised, misguided, rash, reckless, foolhardy, foolish, short-sighted; undiplomatic, tactless, thoughtless.
– OPPOSITES: prudent.

import ▶ verb **1** *Canada imports textiles* BUY FROM ABROAD, bring in, ship in. **2** *practices imported from the business world* DERIVE, obtain, take, extract, glean; steal, crib, filch.
– OPPOSITES: export.

▶ noun **1** *a tax on imports* IMPORTED COMMODITY, foreign commodity; goods, merchandise. **2** *the import of foreign books* IMPORTATION, importing, bringing in, bringing from abroad, shipping in. **3** *a matter of great import* IMPORTANCE, significance, consequence, momentousness, magnitude, substance, weight, note, gravity, seriousness; *formal* moment. **4** *the full import of her words* MEANING, sense, essence, gist, drift, purport, connotation, message, thrust, point, substance, implication.
– OPPOSITES: export, insignificance.

importance ▶ noun **1** *an event of immense importance* SIGNIFICANCE, momentousness, import, consequence, note, noteworthiness, substance; seriousness, gravity, weightiness, urgency. **2** *she had a fine sense of her own importance* POWER, influence, authority, sway, weight, dominance; prominence, eminence, pre-eminence, prestige, notability, worth, stature, dignity.
– OPPOSITES: insignificance.

important ▶ adjective **1** *an important meeting* SIGNIFICANT, consequential, momentous, of great import, major; critical, crucial, vital, pivotal, decisive, urgent, historic; serious, grave, weighty, material; *formal* of great moment. **2** *the important thing is that you do well in your exams* MAIN, chief, principal, key, major, salient, prime, foremost, paramount,

overriding, crucial, vital, critical, essential, significant; central, fundamental; *informal* number-one. **3** *the school was important to the community* OF VALUE, valuable, (highly) prized, beneficial, necessary, essential, indispensable, vital; of concern, of interest, relevant, pertinent. **4** *he was an important man* POWERFUL, influential, of influence, well-connected, high-ranking, high-powered; prominent, eminent, pre-eminent, notable, noteworthy, of note; distinguished, esteemed, respected, prestigious, celebrated, famous, great; *informal* major league.
– OPPOSITES: trivial, insignificant.

importune ▶ verb BEG, beseech, entreat, implore, plead with, appeal to, call on, lobby; harass, pester, press, badger, bother, nag, harry; *informal* hassle.

impose ▶ verb **1** *he imposed his ideas on the art director* FOIST, force, inflict, press, urge; *informal* saddle someone with, land someone with. **2** *new taxes will be imposed* LEVY, charge, apply, enforce; set, establish, institute, introduce, bring into effect. **3** *I didn't want to impose* TAKE ADVANTAGE OF, exploit, take liberties with, treat unfairly; bother, trouble, disturb, inconvenience, put out, put to trouble.

imposing ▶ adjective IMPRESSIVE, striking, arresting, eye-catching, dramatic, spectacular, stunning, awesome, awe-inspiring, formidable, splendid, grand, grandiose, majestic, august.
– OPPOSITES: modest.

imposition ▶ noun **1** *the imposition of an alien culture* IMPOSING, foisting, forcing, inflicting. **2** *the imposition of the GST* LEVYING, charging, application, applying, enforcement, enforcing, enjoining; setting, establishment, introduction, institution. **3** *it would be no imposition* BURDEN, encumbrance, strain, bother, worry; *informal* hassle, drag.

impossible ▶ adjective **1** *gale force winds made fishing impossible* NOT POSSIBLE, out of the question, unfeasible, impractical, impracticable, non-viable, unworkable; unthinkable, unimaginable, inconceivable, absurd. **2** *an impossible dream* UNATTAINABLE, unachievable, unobtainable, unwinnable, hopeless, impractical, implausible, far-fetched, outrageous, preposterous, ridiculous, absurd, impracticable, unworkable, futile. **3** (*informal*) *an impossible woman* UNREASONABLE, objectionable, difficult, awkward; intolerable, unbearable, unendurable; exasperating, maddening, infuriating, irritating; *informal* high maintenance.
– OPPOSITES: attainable, bearable.

imposter ▶ noun IMPERSONATOR, masquerader, pretender, imitator, deceiver, hoaxer, trickster, fraudster, swindler; fake, fraud, sham, phony, scammer.

imposture ▶ noun MISREPRESENTATION, pretense, deceit, deception, trickery, artifice, subterfuge, feint; hoax, trick, ruse, dodge; *informal* con, scam, flim-flam.

impotent ▶ adjective **1** *the legal sanctions are impotent* POWERLESS, ineffective, ineffectual, inadequate, weak, feeble, useless, worthless, futile; *literary* impuissant. **2** *forces which man is impotent to control* UNABLE, incapable, powerless, helpless. **3** *she discovered her husband was impotent* STERILE, infertile, unable to reproduce/procreate; *informal* shooting blanks; *archaic* barren.
– OPPOSITES: powerful, effective.

impound ▶ verb **1** *officials began impounding documents* CONFISCATE, appropriate, take possession of, seize, commandeer, expropriate, requisition, sequester, sequestrate; *Law* distrain. **2** *the cattle were impounded* PEN IN, shut up/in, fence in, enclose, cage, confine, corral. **3** *criminals impounded in prison* LOCK UP, incarcerate, imprison, confine, intern, immure, hold captive, hold prisoner.

impoverish ▶ **verb 1** *the widow had been impoverished* MAKE POOR, make penniless, reduce to penury, bankrupt, beggar, ruin, make insolvent, pauperize. **2** *the trees were impoverishing the soil* WEAKEN, sap, exhaust, deplete.

impoverished ▶ **adjective 1** *an impoverished peasant farmer* POOR, poverty-stricken, penniless, destitute, indigent, impecunious, needy, beggared, beggarly, pauperized, down-and-out, bankrupt, ruined, insolvent; *informal* (flat) broke, hard up, dirt poor, on skid row; *formal* penurious. **2** *the soil is impoverished* WEAKENED, exhausted, drained, sapped, depleted, spent; barren, unproductive, unfertile, unfruitful.
– OPPOSITES: rich.

impracticable ▶ **adjective** UNWORKABLE, unfeasible, non-viable, unachievable, unattainable, unrealizable; impractical, impossible.
– OPPOSITES: workable, feasible.

impractical ▶ **adjective 1** *an impractical suggestion* UNREALISTIC, unworkable, unfeasible, non-viable, impracticable; ill-thought-out, impossible, absurd, wild; *informal* cockeyed, crackpot, crazy. **2** *impractical white ankle boots* UNSUITABLE, not sensible, inappropriate, unserviceable. **3** *an impractical scholar* IDEALISTIC, unrealistic, romantic, dreamy, fanciful, quixotic; *informal* ivory-tower, airy-fairy, blue-sky, starry-eyed.
– OPPOSITES: practical, sensible.

imprecation ▶ **noun** *See* CURSE *noun* senses 1,4.

imprecise ▶ **adjective 1** *a rather imprecise definition* VAGUE, loose, indefinite, inexplicit, indistinct, non-specific, unspecific, sweeping, broad, general; hazy, fuzzy, loosey-goosey, woolly, sketchy, nebulous, ambiguous, equivocal, uncertain. **2** *an imprecise estimate* INEXACT, approximate, estimated, rough, ballpark.
– OPPOSITES: exact.

impregnable ▶ **adjective 1** *an impregnable castle* INVULNERABLE, impenetrable, unassailable, inviolable, secure, strong, well fortified, well-defended; invincible, unconquerable, unbeatable, indestructible. **2** *he displayed a calm, impregnable certainty* UNASSAILABLE, unbeatable, undefeatable, unshakeable, invincible, unconquerable, invulnerable.
– OPPOSITES: vulnerable.

impregnate ▶ **verb 1** *a pad impregnated with natural oils* INFUSE, soak, steep, saturate, drench; permeate, pervade, suffuse, imbue. **2** *the woman he had impregnated* MAKE PREGNANT, inseminate, fertilize; *informal* get/put in the family way, knock up, get into trouble; *archaic* get with child.

impresario ▶ **noun** ORGANIZER, (stage) manager, producer; promoter, publicist, showman; director, conductor, maestro.

impress ▶ **verb 1** *Hazel had impressed him* MAKE AN IMPRESSION ON, have an impact on, influence, affect, move, stir, rouse, excite, inspire; dazzle, awe, overawe, take someone's breath away, amaze, astonish; *informal* grab, blow someone away, stick in someone's mind. **2** *goldsmiths impressed his likeness on medallions* IMPRINT, print, stamp, mark, emboss, punch. **3** *you must impress upon her the need to save*

EMPHASIZE TO, stress to, bring home to, instill in, inculcate into, drum into, knock into.
– OPPOSITES: disappoint.

impression ▶ **noun 1** *he got the impression that she was hiding something* FEELING, feeling in one's bones, sense, fancy, (sneaking) suspicion, inkling, premonition, intuition, presentiment, hunch; notion, idea, funny feeling, gut feeling. **2** *a favourable impression* OPINION, view, image, picture, perception, judgment, verdict, estimation. **3** *school made a profound impression on me* IMPACT, effect, influence. **4** *the cap had left a circular impression* INDENTATION, dent, mark, outline, imprint. **5** *he did a good impression of their science teacher* IMPERSONATION, imitation; parody, caricature, burlesque, travesty, lampoon; *informal* takeoff, send-up, spoof; *formal* personation. **6** *an artist's impression of the gardens* REPRESENTATION, portrayal, depiction, rendition, interpretation, picture, drawing.

impressionable ▶ **adjective** EASILY INFLUENCED, suggestible, susceptible, persuadable, pliable, malleable, pliant, trusting, naive, innocent, wide-eyed, credulous, gullible.

impressive ▶ **adjective 1** *an impressive building* MAGNIFICENT, majestic, imposing, splendid, spectacular, grand, awe-inspiring, striking, stunning, breathtaking; *informal* mind-blowing, jaw-dropping. **2** *it was an impressive performance* ADMIRABLE, masterly, accomplished, expert, skilled, skilful, consummate; excellent, outstanding, first-class, first-rate, fine, superb; *informal* great, mean, nifty, ace, crackerjack, bang-up, skookum.
– OPPOSITES: ordinary, mediocre.

imprint ▶ **verb 1** *patterns can be imprinted in the clay* STAMP, print, impress, mark, emboss, brand, inscribe, etch. **2** *the image was imprinted on his mind* FIX, establish, stick, lodge, implant, plant, embed, instill, impress, inculcate.
▶ **noun 1** *her feet left imprints on the floor* IMPRESSION, print, mark, indentation. **2** *colonialism has left its imprint* IMPACT, lasting effect, influence, impression, mark, trace.

imprison ▶ **verb** INCARCERATE, send to prison, jail, lock up, put away, intern, detain, hold prisoner, hold captive; confine, shut up, cage; *informal* put behind bars.
– OPPOSITES: free, release.

imprisoned ▶ **adjective** INCARCERATED, in prison, in jail, jailed, locked up, interned, detained, held prisoner, held captive; *informal* behind bars, doing time, under lock and key, inside.

improbability ▶ **noun** UNLIKELIHOOD, implausibility; doubtfulness, uncertainty, dubiousness; *informal* fat chance, long shot.

improbable ▶ **adjective 1** *it seemed improbable that the hot weather would continue* UNLIKELY, doubtful, dubious, debatable, questionable, uncertain; unthinkable, inconceivable, unimaginable, incredible; *informal* iffy. **2** *an improbable exaggeration* UNCONVINCING, unbelievable, incredible, ridiculous, absurd, preposterous, outrageous; far-fetched, fantastic, fanciful.
– OPPOSITES: certain, believable.

impromptu ▶ **adjective** *an impromptu lecture* UNREHEARSED, unprepared, unscripted, extempore, extemporized, extemporaneous, improvised, spontaneous, unplanned; *informal* off-the-cuff, offhand, spur-of-the-moment, ad-lib.
– OPPOSITES: prepared, rehearsed.

▶ **adverb** *they played the song impromptu* EXTEMPORE, spontaneously, extemporaneously, without preparation, without rehearsal; *informal* off the cuff, off the top of one's head, on the spur of the moment, ad lib.

improper ▶ **adjective 1** *it is improper for policemen to accept gifts* INAPPROPRIATE, unacceptable, unsuitable, unprofessional, irregular; unethical, corrupt, immoral, dishonest, dishonourable. **2** *it was improper for young ladies to drive a young man home* UNSEEMLY, indecorous, unfitting, unladylike, ungentlemanly, indelicate, impolite; indecent, immodest, immoral. **3** *improper installation will affect performance* INCORRECT, wrong, inaccurate, erroneous, mistaken.
— OPPOSITES: acceptable, decent.

impropriety ▶ **noun 1** *a suggestion of impropriety* WRONGDOING, misconduct, dishonesty, corruption, unscrupulousness, unprofessionalism, irregularity; unseemliness, indecorousness, indelicacy, indecency, immorality. **2** *fiscal improprieties* TRANSGRESSION, misdemeanour, offence, misdeed, misconduct, crime; indiscretion, mistake, peccadillo, solecism; *archaic* trespass.

improve ▶ **verb 1** *ways to improve the service* MAKE BETTER, better, ameliorate, upgrade, update, refine, enhance, boost, build on, raise, polish, fix (up), amend; *informal* tweak; *formal* meliorate. **2** *communications improved during the 18th century* GET BETTER, advance, progress, develop; make headway, make progress, pick up, look up. **3** *the dose is not repeated if patient improves* RECOVER, get better, recuperate, gain strength, rally, revive, get back on one's feet, get over something; be on the road to recovery, be on the mend; *informal* turn the corner, take a turn for the better, bounce back. **4** *resources are needed to improve the offer* INCREASE, make larger, raise, augment, enhance, boost, supplement, top up; *informal* up, hike up, bump up, soup up, beef up.
— OPPOSITES: worsen, deteriorate.
■ **improve on** SURPASS, better, do better than, outdo, exceed, beat, top, cap.

improvement ▶ **noun** ADVANCE, development, upgrade, refinement, renovation, enhancement, advancement, upgrading, amelioration, betterment; boost, lift, rise, augmentation, raising, step up; rally, recovery, upswing, upturn.

improvident ▶ **adjective** SPENDTHRIFT, thriftless, wasteful, prodigal, profligate, extravagant, lavish, free-spending, immoderate, excessive; imprudent, irresponsible, careless, reckless, heedless.
— OPPOSITES: thrifty.

improvise ▶ **verb 1** *she was improvising in front of the cameras* EXTEMPORIZE, ad lib, speak impromptu; *informal* speak off the cuff, speak off the top of one's head, wing it; jam, scat. **2** *she improvised a sandpit* CONTRIVE, devise, throw together, cobble together, rig up; *informal* whip up, rustle up.

improvised ▶ **adjective 1** *an improvised speech* IMPROMPTU, unrehearsed, unprepared, unscripted, extempore, extemporized, spontaneous, unplanned; *informal* off-the-cuff, ad-libbed, spur-of-the-moment. **2** *an improvised shelter* MAKESHIFT, thrown together, cobbled together, rough and ready, crude, make-do, temporary, jerry-built, jury-rigged, slapdash.
— OPPOSITES: prepared, rehearsed.

imprudent ▶ **adjective** UNWISE, injudicious, incautious, indiscreet, misguided, ill-advised, ill-judged; thoughtless, unthinking, improvident,

irresponsible, short-sighted, foolish; rash, reckless, heedless.
— OPPOSITES: sensible.

impudence ▶ **noun** IMPERTINENCE, insolence, effrontery, audacity, cheek, cheekiness, cockiness, brazenness, brass, boldness; presumption, presumptuousness, disrespect, flippancy, bumptiousness, brashness; rudeness, impoliteness, ill manners, gall; *informal* chutzpah, nerve, sauce, sass, sassiness.

impudent ▶ **adjective** IMPERTINENT, insolent, cheeky, cocky, brazen, bold, audacious; presumptuous, forward, disrespectful, insubordinate, bumptious, brash; rude, impolite, ill-mannered, discourteous, ill-bred; *informal* saucy, lippy, sassy, brassy, smart-alecky; *archaic* contumelious.
— OPPOSITES: polite.

impugn ▶ **verb** CALL INTO QUESTION, challenge, question, dispute, query, take issue with.

impulse ▶ **noun 1** *she had an impulse to run and hide* URGE, instinct, drive, compulsion, itch; whim, desire, fancy, notion, inclination, temptation. **2** *passions provide the main impulse of poetry* INSPIRATION, stimulation, stimulus, incitement, motivation, encouragement, incentive, spur, catalyst, impetus, thrust. **3** *impulses from the spinal cord to the muscles* PULSE, current, wave, signal.
■ **on (an) impulse** IMPULSIVELY, spontaneously, on the spur of the moment, without forethought, without premeditation.

impulsive ▶ **adjective 1** *he had an impulsive nature* IMPETUOUS, spontaneous, hasty, passionate, emotional, uninhibited; rash, reckless, careless, imprudent, foolhardy, unwise, madcap, devil-may-care, daredevil. **2** *an impulsive decision* IMPROMPTU, snap, spontaneous, unpremeditated, spur-of-the-moment, extemporaneous; impetuous, precipitate, hasty, rash; sudden, ill-considered, ill-thought-out, whimsical.
— OPPOSITES: cautious, premeditated.

impunity ▶ **noun** IMMUNITY, indemnity, exemption (from punishment), amnesty, non-liability, licence.
— OPPOSITES: liability.
■ **with impunity** WITHOUT PUNISHMENT, scot-free, unpunished.

impure ▶ **adjective 1** *impure gold* ADULTERATED, mixed, combined, blended, alloyed; *technical* admixed. **2** *the water was impure* CONTAMINATED, polluted, tainted, unwholesome, poisoned; dirty, filthy, foul, unclean, defiled; unhygienic, unsanitary; *literary* befouled. **3** *impure thoughts* IMMORAL, sinful, wrongful, wicked; unchaste, lustful, lecherous, lewd, lascivious, prurient, obscene, indecent, ribald, risqué, improper, crude, coarse, debased, degenerate; *formal* concupiscent.
— OPPOSITES: clean, chaste.

impurity ▶ **noun 1** *the impurity of the cast iron* ADULTERATION, debasement, degradation, corruption; contamination, pollution. **2** *the impurities in beer* CONTAMINANT, pollutant, foreign body, foreign matter; dross, dirt, filth. **3** *sin and impurity* IMMORALITY, sin, sinfulness, wickedness; unchastity, lustfulness, lechery, lecherousness, lewdness, lasciviousness, prurience, obscenity, dirtiness, crudeness, indecency, ribaldry, impropriety, vulgarity, depravity, coarseness; *formal* concupiscence.

impute ▶ **verb** ATTRIBUTE, ascribe, assign, credit; connect with, associate with.

in ▶ **preposition 1** *she was hiding in the closet* INSIDE, within, in the middle of; surrounded by, enclosed by. **2** *he was covered in mud* WITH, by. **3** *he put a candy in his mouth* INTO, inside. **4** *they met in 1921* DURING, in the course of, over. **5** *I'll see you in half an hour* AFTER, at the end of, following; within, in less than, in under. **6** *one in every five is a winner* TO, per, every, each.
– OPPOSITES: outside.
▶ **adverb 1** *his mum walked in* INSIDE, indoors, into the room, into the house/building. **2** *the tide's in* HIGH, at its highest level, rising.
– OPPOSITES: out.
▶ **adjective 1** *no one is in* PRESENT, (at) home; inside, indoors, in the house/room. **2** (*informal*) *beards are in* FASHIONABLE, in fashion, in vogue, popular, stylish, modern, modish, chic, à la mode, de rigueur, trendy, cool, all the rage, du jour, with it, styling/stylin', the in thing, hip, hot.
– OPPOSITES: out, unfashionable, unpopular.
■ **in for** DUE FOR, in line for; expecting, about to undergo/receive.
■ **in for it** IN TROUBLE, about to be punished; *informal* in hot/deep water.
■ **in on** PRIVY TO, aware of, acquainted with, informed about/of, apprised of; *informal* wise to, in the know about, hip to.
■ **ins and outs** (*informal*) DETAILS, particulars, facts, features, characteristics, nuts and bolts; *informal* nitty gritty.
■ **in with** IN FAVOUR WITH, popular with, friendly with, friends with, on good terms with; liked by, admired by, accepted by.

inability ▶ **noun** LACK OF ABILITY, incapability, incapacity, powerlessness, impotence, helplessness; incompetence, ineptitude, unfitness.

inaccessible ▶ **adjective 1** *an inaccessible woodland site* UNREACHABLE, out of reach, unapproachable; cut-off, isolated, remote, insular, in the back of beyond, out of the way, lonely, solitary, godforsaken. **2** *the book was elitist and inaccessible* INCOMPREHENSIBLE, impenetrable, inscrutable, baffling; obscure, esoteric, abstruse, recondite, arcane; elitist, exclusive, pretentious. **3** *the lecturer was inaccessible to students* UNAPPROACHABLE, aloof, distant, unfriendly, standoffish.

inaccuracy ▶ **noun 1** *the inaccuracy of recent opinion polls* INCORRECTNESS, inexactness, imprecision, erroneousness, mistakenness, fallaciousness, faultiness. **2** *the article contained a number of inaccuracies* ERROR, mistake, fallacy, slip, slip-up, oversight, fault, blunder, gaffe; erratum, solecism; *informal* howler, typo, blooper, goof.
– OPPOSITES: correctness.

inaccurate ▶ **adjective** INEXACT, imprecise, incorrect, wrong, erroneous, careless, faulty, imperfect, flawed, defective, unsound, unreliable; fallacious, false, mistaken, untrue; *informal* wide of the mark.

inaction ▶ **noun** INACTIVITY, non-intervention; neglect, negligence, apathy, inertia, indolence, sluggishness, lethargy, idleness.

inactive ▶ **adjective 1** *I was being horribly inactive* IDLE, indolent, lazy, lifeless, slothful, lethargic, inert, sluggish, unenergetic, listless, torpid, sedentary. **2** *the computer is currently inactive* INOPERATIVE, non-functioning, idle; not working, out of service, unused, not in use; dormant.

inactivity ▶ **noun 1** *long periods of inactivity* IDLENESS, indolence, laziness, lifelessness, slothfulness, lethargy, inertia, sluggishness, listlessness, inaction, torpor. **2** *government inactivity* INACTION, non-intervention; neglect, negligence, apathy, passivity.
– OPPOSITES: action.

inadequacy ▶ **noun 1** *the inadequacy of available resources* INSUFFICIENCY, deficiency, deficit, scarcity, sparseness, dearth, paucity, shortage, want, lack, undersupply; paltriness, meagreness. **2** *her feelings of personal inadequacy* INCOMPETENCE, incapability, unfitness, ineffectiveness, inefficiency, inefficacy, inexpertness, ineptness, uselessness, impotence, powerlessness; inferiority, mediocrity. **3** *the inadequacies of the present system* SHORTCOMING, defect, fault, failing, weakness, weak point, limitation, flaw, imperfection.
– OPPOSITES: abundance, competence.

inadequate ▶ **adjective 1** *inadequate water supplies* INSUFFICIENT, deficient, poor, scant, scanty, scarce, sparse, in short supply; paltry, meagre, niggardly, beggarly, limited; *informal* measly, pathetic; *formal* exiguous. **2** *an inadequate typist* INCOMPETENT, incapable, unsatisfactory, not up to scratch, unfit, unacceptable, ineffective, ineffectual, inefficient, unskilful, inexpert, inept, amateurish, substandard, poor, useless, inferior; *informal* not up to snuff, no great shakes, lame, shabby.
– OPPOSITES: sufficient, competent.

inadmissible ▶ **adjective** UNALLOWABLE, not allowed, invalid, unacceptable, impermissible, disallowed, forbidden, prohibited, precluded.

inadvertent ▶ **adjective** UNINTENTIONAL, unintended, accidental, unpremeditated, unplanned, innocent, uncalculated, unconscious, unthinking, unwitting, involuntary; careless, negligent.
– OPPOSITES: deliberate.

inadvisable ▶ **adjective** UNWISE, ill-advised, imprudent, ill-judged, ill-considered, injudicious, impolitic, foolish, misguided; *medical* contraindicated.
– OPPOSITES: shrewd.

inalienable ▶ **adjective** INVIOLABLE, absolute, sacrosanct; untransferable, non-transferable, non-negotiable; *Law* indefeasible.

inane ▶ **adjective** SILLY, foolish, stupid, fatuous, idiotic, ridiculous, ludicrous, absurd, senseless, asinine, frivolous, vapid; childish, puerile; *informal* dumb, moronic, ditzy, daft.
– OPPOSITES: sensible.

inanimate ▶ **adjective** LIFELESS, insentient, without life, inorganic; dead, defunct.
– OPPOSITES: living.

inapplicable ▶ **adjective** IRRELEVANT, immaterial, not germane, not pertinent, unrelated, unconnected, extraneous, beside the point; unsuitable, inapposite; *formal* impertinent.
– OPPOSITES: relevant.

inappropriate ▶ **adjective** UNSUITABLE, unfitting, unseemly, unbecoming, unbefitting, improper, impolite; incongruous, out of place/keeping, inapposite, inapt, infelicitous, ill-suited; ill-judged, ill-advised; *informal* out of order/line; *formal* malapropos.
– OPPOSITES: suitable.

inapt ▶ **adjective.** *See* INAPPROPRIATE.

inarticulate ▶ **adjective 1** *an inarticulate young man* TONGUE-TIED, lost for words, unable to express oneself. **2** *an inarticulate reply* UNINTELLIGIBLE,

incomprehensible, incoherent, unclear, indistinct, mumbled, muffled. **3** *inarticulate rage* UNSPOKEN, silent, unexpressed, wordless, speechless, unvoiced.
— OPPOSITES: silver-tongued, fluent.

inattentive ▶ adjective **1** *an inattentive pupil* DISTRACTED, lacking concentration, preoccupied, absent-minded, daydreaming, dreamy, abstracted, distrait; *informal* miles away, spaced out. **2** *inattentive service.* See NEGLIGENT.
— OPPOSITES: alert.

inaudible ▶ adjective UNHEARD, out of earshot; indistinct, imperceptible, faint, muted, soft, low, muffled, whispered, muttered, murmured, mumbled; silent, soundless, noiseless, hushed; ultrasonic.

inaugural ▶ adjective FIRST, opening, initial, introductory, initiatory.
— OPPOSITES: final.

inaugurate ▶ verb **1** *he inaugurated a new policy* INITIATE, begin, start, commence, institute, launch, start off, get going, get underway, establish, found, lay the foundations of; bring in, usher in, introduce; *informal* kick off. **2** *the new President will be inaugurated* ADMIT TO OFFICE, install, instate, swear in; invest, ordain, crown. **3** *the museum was inaugurated in September* OPEN, declare open, unveil; dedicate, consecrate.

inauspicious ▶ adjective UNPROMISING, unpropitious, unfavourable, unfortunate, infelicitous, unlucky, ill-omened, ominous; discouraging, disheartening, bleak.
— OPPOSITES: promising.

inborn ▶ adjective INNATE, congenital, connate, instinctive, inherent, natural, inbred, inherited, hereditary, in one's genes.

incalculable ▶ adjective INESTIMABLE, untold, indeterminable, immeasurable, incomputable; infinite, endless, limitless, boundless, measureless; enormous, immense, huge, vast, innumerable, countless.

incandescent ▶ adjective **1** *incandescent fragments of lava* WHITE-HOT, red-hot, burning, fiery, blazing, ablaze, aflame; glowing, aglow, radiant, bright, brilliant, luminous, sparkling; *literary* fervid, lucent; *rare* igneous. **2** *an incandescent speech* PASSIONATE, ardent, fervent, fervid, intense, impassioned, spirited, fiery.

incantation ▶ noun CHANT, invocation, conjuration, magic spell/formula, charm, hex, enchantment, mojo; intonation, recitation.

incapable ▶ adjective INCOMPETENT, inept, inadequate, not good enough, leaving much to be desired, inexpert, unskilful, ineffective, ineffectual, inefficacious, feeble, unfit, unqualified, unequal to the task; unable, incapacitated, helpless, powerless, impotent; *informal* not up to it, not up to snuff, useless, hopeless, pathetic, a dead loss.
— OPPOSITES: competent.

incapacitated ▶ adjective DISABLED, debilitated, indisposed, unfit, impaired; immobilized, paralyzed, out of action, out of commission, hors de combat; *informal* laid up.
— OPPOSITES: fit.

incapacity ▶ noun DISABILITY, incapability, inability, debility, impairment, indisposition; impotence, powerlessness, helplessness; incompetence, inadequacy, ineffectiveness.
— OPPOSITES: capability.

incarcerate ▶ verb IMPRISON, put in prison, send to prison, jail, lock up, put under lock and key, put away, intern, confine, detain, hold, immure, put in chains, hold prisoner, hold captive; *informal* put behind bars.
— OPPOSITES: release.

incarceration ▶ noun IMPRISONMENT, internment, confinement, detention, custody, captivity, restraint; *informal* time; *archaic* durance, duress.

incarnate ▶ adjective IN HUMAN FORM, in the flesh, in physical form, in bodily form, made flesh; corporeal, physical, fleshly, embodied, personified.

incarnation ▶ noun **1** *the incarnation of artistic genius* EMBODIMENT, personification, exemplification, type, epitome; manifestation, bodily form, avatar. **2** *a previous incarnation* LIFETIME, life, existence.

incautious ▶ adjective RASH, unwise, careless, heedless, thoughtless, reckless, unthinking, imprudent, misguided, ill-advised, ill-judged, injudicious, impolitic, unguarded, foolhardy, foolish.
— OPPOSITES: circumspect.

incendiary ▶ adjective **1** *an incendiary bomb* COMBUSTIBLE, flammable, inflammable. **2** *an incendiary speech* INFLAMMATORY, rabble-rousing, provocative, seditious, subversive; contentious, controversial.
▶ noun *a political incendiary* AGITATOR, demagogue, rabble-rouser, firebrand, troublemaker, agent provocateur, revolutionary, insurgent, subversive.

incense ▶ noun *a whiff of incense* PERFUME, fragrance, scent, spice; joss stick.
▶ verb *his taunts used to incense me.* See ENRAGE.

incensed ▶ adjective ENRAGED, very angry, furious, infuriated, irate, mad, in a temper, raging, fuming, seething, beside oneself, outraged; *informal* hopping mad, wild, livid, apoplectic, hot under the collar, foaming at the mouth, steamed up, fit to be tied; *literary* wrathful; *archaic* wroth.

incentive ▶ noun INDUCEMENT, motivation, motive, reason, stimulus, stimulant, spur, impetus, encouragement, impulse; incitement, goad, provocation; attraction, lure, bait; *informal* carrot, sweetener, come-on.
— OPPOSITES: deterrent.

inception ▶ noun BEGINNING, commencement, start, birth, dawn, genesis, origin, outset; establishment, institution, foundation, founding, formation, initiation, setting up, origination, constitution, inauguration, opening, debut, day one; *informal* kickoff.
— OPPOSITES: end.

incessant ▶ adjective CEASELESS, unceasing, constant, continual, unabating, interminable, endless, unending, never-ending, everlasting, eternal, perpetual, continuous, non-stop, round-the-clock, uninterrupted, unbroken, unremitting, persistent, relentless, unrelenting, unrelieved, sustained.
— OPPOSITES: intermittent.

incessantly ▶ adverb CONSTANTLY, continually, all the time, non-stop, without stopping, without a break, round the clock, {morning, noon, and night}, interminably, unremittingly, ceaselessly, endlessly; *informal* 24-7.
— OPPOSITES: occasionally.

inchoate ▶ adjective RUDIMENTARY, undeveloped,

unformed, immature, incipient, embryonic; beginning, fledgling, developing.

incidence ▶ noun OCCURRENCE, prevalence; rate, frequency; amount, degree, extent.

incident ▶ noun **1** *incidents in his youth* EVENT, occurrence, episode, experience, happening, occasion, proceeding, eventuality, affair, business; adventure, exploit, escapade; matter, circumstance, fact, development. **2** *police were investigating the incident* DISTURBANCE, fracas, melee, commotion, rumpus, scene; fight, skirmish, clash, brawl, free-for-all, encounter, conflict, ruckus, confrontation, altercation, contretemps; *informal* ruction. **3** *the journey was not without incident* EXCITEMENT, adventure, drama; danger, peril.

incidental ▶ adjective **1** *incidental details* LESS IMPORTANT, secondary, subsidiary; minor, peripheral, background, non-essential, inessential, unimportant, insignificant, inconsequential, tangential, extrinsic, extraneous, superfluous. **2** *an incidental discovery* CHANCE, accidental, random; fluky, fortuitous, serendipitous, adventitious, coincidental, unlooked-for, unexpected. **3** *the risks incidental to the job* CONNECTED WITH, related to, associated with, accompanying, attending, attendant on, concomitant with.
— OPPOSITES: essential, deliberate.

incidentally ▶ adverb **1** *incidentally, I haven't had a reply yet* BY THE WAY, by the by(e), in passing, en passant, speaking of which; parenthetically; *informal* BTW, as it happens. **2** *the infection was discovered incidentally* BY CHANCE, by accident, accidentally, fortuitously, by a fluke, by happenstance; coincidentally, by coincidence.

incinerate ▶ verb BURN, reduce to ashes, consume by fire, carbonize; cremate.

incipient ▶ adjective DEVELOPING, growing, emerging, emergent, dawning, just beginning, inceptive, initial, inchoate; nascent, embryonic, fledgling, in its infancy, germinal.
— OPPOSITES: full-blown.

incision ▶ noun **1** *a surgical incision* CUT, opening, slit. **2** *incisions on the marble* NOTCH, carving, etching, engraving, inscription, score; nick, scratch, scarification.

incisive ▶ adjective PENETRATING, acute, sharp, sharp-witted, razor-sharp, keen, astute, trenchant, shrewd, piercing, cutting, perceptive, insightful, percipient, perspicacious, discerning, analytical, clever, smart, quick; concise, succinct, pithy, to the point, brief, crisp, clear, effective; *informal* punchy.
— OPPOSITES: rambling, vague.

incite ▶ verb **1** *he was arrested for inciting racial hatred* STIR UP, whip up, encourage, fan the flames of, stoke up, fuel, kindle, ignite, inflame, stimulate, instigate, provoke, excite, arouse, awaken, inspire, engender, trigger, spark off, ferment, foment; *literary* enkindle. **2** *she incited him to commit murder* EGG ON, encourage, urge, goad, provoke, spur on, drive, stimulate, push, prod, prompt, induce, impel; arouse, rouse, excite, inflame, sting, prick; *informal* put up to.
— OPPOSITES: discourage, deter.

incivility ▶ noun RUDENESS, discourtesy, impoliteness, bad manners, disrespect, boorishness, ungraciousness; insolence, impertinence, impudence.
— OPPOSITES: politeness.

inclement ▶ adjective COLD, chilly, bleak, wintry,

freezing, snowy, icy; wet, rainy, drizzly, damp; stormy, blustery, wild, rough, squally, windy; unpleasant, bad, foul, nasty, brutal, severe, extreme, harsh.
— OPPOSITES: fine.

inclination ▶ noun **1** *his political inclinations* TENDENCY, propensity, proclivity, leaning, predisposition, disposition, predilection, desire, wish, impulse, bent, bias; liking, affection, penchant, partiality, preference, appetite, fancy, interest, affinity; stomach, taste; *informal* yen. **2** *an inclination of his head* BOWING, bow, bending, nod, nodding, lowering.
— OPPOSITES: aversion.

incline ▶ verb **1** *his prejudice inclines him to overlook obvious facts* PREDISPOSE, lead, make, make of a mind to, dispose, prejudice, bias; prompt, induce, influence, sway; persuade, convince. **2** *I incline to the opposite view* PREFER, favour, go for; tend, lean, swing, veer, gravitate, be drawn. **3** *he inclined his head* BEND, bow, nod, bob, lower, dip.
▶ noun *a steep incline* SLOPE, gradient, pitch, ramp, bank, ascent, rise, upslope, dip, descent, declivity, downslope; hill, grade, downgrade.

inclined ▶ adjective **1** *if you feel so inclined* DISPOSED, of a mind, willing, ready, prepared; predisposed. **2** *she's inclined to gossip* PRONE, given, in the habit of, liable, likely, apt, wont. **3** *an inclined floor* SLOPING, sloped, slanted, leaning, angled, oblique, at/on a slant, at an angle.

include ▶ verb **1** *activities include sports and drama* INCORPORATE, comprise, encompass, cover, embrace, involve, take in, number, contain; consist of, be made up of, be composed of; *formal* comprehend. **2** *don't forget to include the cost of repairs* ALLOW FOR, count, take into account, take into consideration.
— OPPOSITES: exclude.

inclusive ▶ adjective ALL-IN, all-inclusive, comprehensive, in toto, overall, full, all-round, umbrella, blanket, across-the-board, catch-all, all-encompassing.

incognito ▶ adverb & adjective UNDER AN ASSUMED NAME, under a false name, in disguise, disguised, under cover, in plain clothes, camouflaged, unidentified; secretly, anonymously.

incoherent ▶ adjective **1** *a long, incoherent speech* UNCLEAR, confused, unintelligible, incomprehensible, hard to follow, disjointed, disconnected, disordered, mixed up, garbled, jumbled, scrambled, muddled; rambling, wandering, disorganized, illogical; inarticulate, mumbling, slurred. **2** *she was incoherent and shivering* DELIRIOUS, raving, babbling, hysterical, irrational.
— OPPOSITES: lucid.

income ▶ noun EARNINGS, salary, pay, remuneration, wages, stipend; revenue, receipts, takings, profits, gains, proceeds, turnover, yield, dividend, means, take; *formal* emolument.
— OPPOSITES: expenditure.

incoming ▶ adjective **1** *the incoming train* ARRIVING, entering; approaching, coming (in), inbound. **2** *the incoming president* NEWLY ELECTED, newly appointed, succeeding, new, next, future; elect, to-be, designate. **3** *incoming students* STARTING, beginning, commencing.
— OPPOSITES: outgoing.

incommensurate ▶ adjective *See* DISPROPORTIONATE.

incommodious ▶ adjective UNCOMFORTABLE, small, cramped, tiny.

incommunicado ▶ adjective ISOLATED, out of reach/touch, sequestered, unreachable, secluded.

incomparable ▶ adjective WITHOUT EQUAL, beyond compare, unparalleled, matchless, peerless, unmatched, without parallel, beyond comparison, second to none, in a class of its own, unequalled, unrivalled, inimitable, nonpareil, par excellence; transcendent, superlative, surpassing, unsurpassed, unsurpassable, supreme, top, best, outstanding, consummate, singular, unique, rare, perfect; *informal* one-in-a-million; *formal* unexampled.

incompatible ▶ adjective **1** *she and McBride are totally incompatible* UNSUITED, mismatched, ill-matched. **2** *incompatible economic objectives* IRRECONCILABLE, conflicting, opposed, opposite, contradictory, antagonistic, antipathetic; clashing, inharmonious, discordant; mutually exclusive; poles apart, worlds apart, night and day. **3** *a theory incompatible with that of his predecessor* INCONSISTENT WITH, at odds with, out of keeping with, at variance with, inconsonant with, different to, divergent from, contrary to, in conflict with, in opposition to, antithetical to, (diametrically) opposed to, counter to, irreconcilable with.
– OPPOSITES: well-matched, harmonious, consistent.

incompetent ▶ adjective INEPT, unskilful, unskilled, inexpert, amateurish, unprofessional, bungling, blundering, clumsy, inadequate, substandard, inferior, ineffective, deficient, inefficient, ineffectual, wanting, lacking, leaving much to be desired; incapable, unfit, unqualified; *informal* useless, pathetic, ham-fisted, not up to it, not up to scratch, bush league.

incomplete ▶ adjective **1** *the project is still incomplete* UNFINISHED, uncompleted, partial, half-finished, half-done, half-completed. **2** *inaccurate or incomplete information* DEFICIENT, insufficient, imperfect, defective, partial, patchy, sketchy, fragmentary, fragmented.

incomprehensible ▶ adjective UNINTELLIGIBLE, impossible to understand, impenetrable, unclear, indecipherable, inscrutable, beyond one's comprehension, beyond one, beyond one's grasp, complicated, complex, involved, baffling, bewildering, mystifying, unfathomable, puzzling, cryptic, confusing, perplexing; abstruse, esoteric, recondite, arcane, mysterious, Delphic; *informal* over one's head, all Greek to someone.
– OPPOSITES: intelligible, clear.

inconceivable ▶ adjective UNBELIEVABLE, beyond belief, incredible, unthinkable, unimaginable, extremely unlikely; impossible, beyond the bounds of possibility, out of the question, preposterous, ridiculous, ludicrous, absurd, incomprehensible; *informal* hard to swallow.
– OPPOSITES: likely.

inconclusive ▶ adjective INDECISIVE, proving nothing; indefinite, indeterminate, unresolved, unproved, unsettled, still open to question/doubt, debatable, unconfirmed; moot; vague, ambiguous; *informal* up in the air, left hanging.

incongruous ▶ adjective **1** *the women looked incongruous in their smart hats and fur coats* OUT OF PLACE, out of keeping, inappropriate, unsuitable, unsuited; wrong, strange, odd, curious, queer, absurd, bizarre. **2** *an incongruous collection of objects* ILL-MATCHED, ill-assorted, mismatched,

unharmonious, discordant, dissonant, conflicting, clashing, jarring, incompatible, different, dissimilar, contrasting, disparate.
– OPPOSITES: appropriate, harmonious.

inconsequential ▶ adjective INSIGNIFICANT, unimportant, of little/no consequence, neither here nor there, incidental, inessential, non-essential, immaterial, irrelevant; negligible, inappreciable, inconsiderable, slight, minor, trivial, trifling, petty, paltry, measly; *informal* piddling, piffling.
– OPPOSITES: important.

inconsiderate ▶ adjective THOUGHTLESS, unthinking, insensitive, selfish, self-centred, unsympathetic, uncaring, heedless, unmindful, unkind, uncharitable, ungracious, impolite, discourteous, rude, disrespectful; tactless, undiplomatic, indiscreet, indelicate; *informal* ignorant.
– OPPOSITES: thoughtful.

inconsistent ▶ adjective **1** *his inconsistent behaviour* ERRATIC, changeable, unpredictable, variable, varying, changing, inconstant, unstable, irregular, fluctuating, unsteady, unsettled, uneven; self-contradictory, contradictory, paradoxical; capricious, fickle, flighty, whimsical, unreliable, mercurial, volatile, blowing hot and cold, ever-changing, chameleon-like; *technical* labile. **2** *he had done nothing inconsistent with his morality* INCOMPATIBLE WITH, conflicting with, in conflict with, at odds with, at variance with, differing from, contrary to, in opposition to, (diametrically) opposed to, irreconcilable with, out of keeping with, out of step with; antithetical to.

inconsolable ▶ adjective HEARTBROKEN, broken-hearted, grief-stricken, beside oneself with grief, devastated, wretched, sick at heart, desolate, despairing, distraught, comfortless; miserable, unhappy, sad; *literary* heartsick.

inconspicuous ▶ adjective UNOBTRUSIVE, unnoticeable, unremarkable, unspectacular, unostentatious, undistinguished, unexceptional, modest, unassuming, discreet, hidden, concealed; unseen, in the background, low-profile.
– OPPOSITES: noticeable.

inconstant ▶ adjective FICKLE, faithless, unfaithful, false, wayward, unreliable, untrustworthy, capricious, volatile, flighty, unpredictable, erratic, blowing hot and cold; changeable, mutable, mercurial, variable, irregular; *informal* cheating, two-timing.
– OPPOSITES: faithful.

incontestable ▶ adjective *See* INCONTROVERTIBLE.

incontinent ▶ adjective UNRESTRAINED, lacking self-restraint, uncontrolled, unbridled, unchecked; uncontrollable, ungovernable.

incontrovertible ▶ adjective INDISPUTABLE, incontestable, undeniable, irrefutable, unassailable, beyond dispute, unquestionable, beyond question, indubitable, beyond doubt, unarguable, undebatable; certain, sure, definite, definitive, proven, decisive, conclusive, demonstrable, emphatic, categorical, airtight, watertight.
– OPPOSITES: questionable.

inconvenience ▶ noun **1** *we apologize for any inconvenience caused* TROUBLE, bother, problems, disruption, difficulty, disturbance; vexation, irritation, annoyance; *informal* aggravation, hassle. **2** *his early arrival was clearly an inconvenience* NUISANCE, trouble, bother, problem, vexation, worry, trial, bind, bore, irritant, thorn in someone's side; *informal* headache, pain, pain in the neck, pain in the butt, drag, aggravation, hassle.

▶ verb *I don't want to inconvenience you* TROUBLE, bother, put out, put to any trouble, disturb, impose on, burden, incommode; *informal* hassle, plague; *formal* discommode.

inconvenient ▶ adjective AWKWARD, difficult, inopportune, untimely, ill-timed, unsuitable, inappropriate, unfortunate; tiresome, troublesome, irritating, annoying, vexing, bothersome; *informal* aggravating.

incorporate ▶ verb 1 *the region was incorporated into Moldavian territory* ABSORB, include, subsume, assimilate, integrate, take in, swallow up. 2 *the model incorporates some advanced features* INCLUDE, contain, comprise, embody, embrace, build in, encompass. 3 *literary references were incorporated with photographs* BLEND, mix, mingle, meld; combine, unite, join.

incorporeal ▶ adjective INTANGIBLE, impalpable, non-physical; bodiless, disembodied, discarnate, immaterial; spiritual, ethereal, unsubstantial, insubstantial, transcendental; ghostly, spectral, supernatural.
— OPPOSITES: tangible.

incorrect ▶ adjective 1 *an incorrect answer* WRONG, erroneous, in error, mistaken, inaccurate, wide of the mark, off target; untrue, false, fallacious; *informal* out, way out. 2 *incorrect behaviour* INAPPROPRIATE, wrong, unsuitable, inapt, inapposite; ill-advised, ill-considered, ill-judged, injudicious, unacceptable, unfitting, out of keeping, improper, unseemly, unbecoming, indecorous; *informal* out of line/order.

incorrigible ▶ adjective INVETERATE, habitual, confirmed, hardened, dyed-in-the-wool, incurable, chronic, irredeemable, hopeless, beyond hope; impenitent, unrepentant, unapologetic, unashamed; bad, naughty, terrible.

incorruptible ▶ adjective 1 *an incorruptible man* HONEST, honourable, trustworthy, principled, high-principled, unbribable, moral, ethical, good, virtuous. 2 *an incorruptible substance* IMPERISHABLE, indestructible, indissoluble, enduring, everlasting.
— OPPOSITES: venal.

increase ▶ verb 1 *demand is likely to increase* GROW, get bigger, get larger, enlarge, expand, swell; rise, climb, escalate, soar, surge, rocket, shoot up, spiral; intensify, strengthen, extend, heighten, stretch, spread, widen; multiply, snowball, mushroom, proliferate, balloon, build up, mount up, pile up, accrue, accumulate; *literary* wax. 2 *higher expectations will increase user demand* ADD TO, make larger, make bigger, augment, supplement, top up, build up, extend, raise, swell, inflate; magnify, maximize, intensify, strengthen, heighten, amplify; *informal* up, jack up, hike up, bump up, torque up, crank up.
— OPPOSITES: decrease, reduce.

▶ noun *the increase in size | an increase in demand* GROWTH, rise, enlargement, expansion, extension, multiplication, elevation, inflation; increment, addition, augmentation; magnification, intensification, amplification, climb, escalation, surge, upsurge, upswing, spiral, spurt; *informal* hike.

increasingly ▶ adverb MORE AND MORE, progressively, to an increasing extent, ever more.

incredible ▶ adjective 1 *I find his story incredible* UNBELIEVABLE, beyond belief, hard to believe, unconvincing, far-fetched, implausible, improbable,

highly unlikely, dubious, doubtful; inconceivable, unthinkable, unimaginable, impossible. *informal* hard to swallow/take, cock-and-bull. 2 *an incredible feat of engineering* MAGNIFICENT, wonderful, marvellous, spectacular, remarkable, phenomenal, prodigious, breathtaking, extraordinary, unbelievable, amazing, stunning, astounding, astonishing, awe-inspiring, staggering, formidable, impressive, supreme, great, awesome, superhuman; *informal* fantastic, terrific, tremendous, stupendous, mind-boggling, mind-blowing, jaw-dropping, out of this world, far-out; *literary* wondrous.

incredulous ▶ adjective DISBELIEVING, skeptical, unbelieving, distrustful, mistrustful, suspicious, doubtful, dubious, unconvinced; cynical.

increment ▶ noun INCREASE, addition, supplement, gain, augmentation, enhancement, boost; *informal* hike.
— OPPOSITES: reduction.

incremental ▶ adjective GRADUAL, progressive, steady, step-by-step; increasing, growing.

incriminate ▶ verb IMPLICATE, involve, enmesh; blame, accuse, denounce, inform against, point the finger at; *informal* frame, set up, stick/pin the blame on, rat on; *archaic* inculpate.

inculcate ▶ verb *the beliefs inculcated in him by his father* INSTILL, implant, fix, impress, imprint; hammer into, drum into, drive into, drill into.

incumbent ▶ adjective 1 *it is incumbent on you to tell them* NECESSARY, essential, required, imperative; compulsory, binding, obligatory, mandatory. 2 *the incumbent president* CURRENT, present, in office, in power; reigning.
▶ noun *the first incumbent of the post* HOLDER, bearer, occupant.

incur ▶ verb BRING UPON ONESELF, expose oneself to, lay oneself open to; run up; attract, invite, earn, arouse, cause, give rise to, be liable/subject to, meet with, sustain, experience, contract.

incurable ▶ adjective 1 *an incurable illness* UNTREATABLE, inoperable, irremediable; terminal, fatal, mortal; chronic. 2 *an incurable romantic* INVETERATE, dyed-in-the-wool, confirmed, established, long-established, long-standing, absolute, complete, utter, thorough, out-and-out, through and through; unashamed, unapologetic, unrepentant, incorrigible, hopeless.

incursion ▶ noun ATTACK, assault, raid, invasion, storming, foray, blitz, sortie, sally, advance, push, thrust.
— OPPOSITES: retreat.

indebted ▶ adjective BEHOLDEN, under an obligation, obliged, obligated, grateful, thankful, in someone's debt, owing a debt of gratitude.

indecent ▶ adjective 1 *indecent photographs* OBSCENE, dirty, filthy, rude, coarse, naughty, vulgar, gross, crude, lewd, salacious, improper, smutty, off-colour; pornographic, offensive, prurient, sordid, scatological; ribald, risqué, racy; *informal* porn, porno, X-rated, XXX, raunchy, skin, blue; *euphemistic* adult. 2 *indecent haste* UNSEEMLY, improper, indecorous, unceremonious, indelicate, unbecoming, ungentlemanly, unladylike, unfitting, unbefitting; untoward, unsuitable, inappropriate; in bad taste, tasteless, unacceptable, offensive, crass.

indecipherable ▶ adjective ILLEGIBLE, unreadable, hard to read, unintelligible, unclear; scribbled, scrawled, hieroglyphic, cramped, crabbed.

indecision ▶ noun INDECISIVENESS, irresolution, hesitancy, hesitation, tentativeness; ambivalence, doubt, doubtfulness, uncertainty, incertitude; vacillation, wavering, equivocation, second thoughts; shilly-shallying, dithering, temporizing, hemming and hawing, dilly-dallying, sitting on the fence; *formal* dubiety.

indecisive ▶ adjective **1** *an indecisive result* INCONCLUSIVE, proving nothing, settling nothing, open, indeterminate, undecided, unsettled, borderline, indefinite, unclear, ambiguous, vague; *informal* up in the air. **2** *an indecisive leader* IRRESOLUTE, hesitant, tentative, weak; vacillating, equivocating, dithering, wavering, faltering; ambivalent, divided, blowing hot and cold, of two minds, in a dilemma, in a quandary, torn; doubtful, unsure, uncertain; undecided, uncommitted; *informal* iffy, sitting on the fence, wishy-washy, shilly-shallying, waffly.

indecorous ▶ adjective IMPROPER, unseemly, unbecoming, undignified, immodest, indelicate, indecent, unladylike, ungentlemanly; inappropriate, incorrect, unsuitable, undesirable, unfitting, in bad taste, ill-bred, vulgar.

indeed ▶ adverb **1** *there was, indeed, quite a furor* AS EXPECTED, to be sure; in fact, in point of fact, as a matter of fact, in truth, actually, as it happens/happened, if truth be told, admittedly; *archaic* in sooth. **2** *'May I join you?' 'Yes indeed you may.'* CERTAINLY, assuredly, of course, naturally, without (a) doubt, without question, by all means, yes; *informal* you bet, I'll say; *informal* indeedy. **3** *Ian's future with us looked rosy indeed* VERY, extremely, exceedingly, tremendously, immensely, singularly, decidedly, particularly, remarkably, really.

indefatigable ▶ adjective TIRELESS, untiring, unflagging, unwearied; determined, tenacious, dogged, single-minded, assiduous, industrious, hard-working, unswerving, unfaltering, unwavering, unshakeable, resolute, indomitable; persistent, relentless, unremitting.

indefensible ▶ adjective INEXCUSABLE, unjustifiable, unjustified, unpardonable, unforgivable; uncalled for, unprovoked, gratuitous, unreasonable, unnecessary; insupportable, unacceptable, unwarranted, unwarrantable; flawed, wrong, untenable, unsustainable.

indefinable ▶ adjective HARD TO DEFINE, hard to describe, indescribable, inexpressible, nameless; vague, obscure, nebulous, impalpable, intangible, elusive.

indefinite ▶ adjective **1** *an indefinite period* INDETERMINATE, unspecified, unlimited, unrestricted, undecided, undetermined, undefined, unfixed, unsettled, unknown, uncertain; limitless, infinite, endless, immeasurable. **2** *an indefinite idea* VAGUE, ill-defined, unclear, imprecise, inexact, loose, general, nebulous, fuzzy, hazy, obscure, ambiguous, equivocal.
— OPPOSITES: fixed, clear.

indelible ▶ adjective INERADICABLE, permanent, lasting, ingrained, persisting, enduring, unfading, unforgettable, haunting, never to be forgotten.

indelicate ▶ adjective **1** *an indelicate question* INSENSITIVE, tactless, inconsiderate, undiplomatic, impolitic. **2** *an indelicate sense of humour* VULGAR, rude, crude, tasteless, bawdy, racy, risqué, ribald, earthy, indecent, improper, naughty, indecorous, off-colour, dirty, smutty, raunchy.

indemnity ▶ noun **1** *indemnity against loss* INSURANCE, assurance, protection, security, indemnification, surety, guarantee, warranty, safeguard. **2** *the company was paid $100,000 in indemnity* COMPENSATION, reimbursement, recompense, repayment, restitution, payment, redress, reparation(s), damages. **3** *legislative indemnity* SALARY, wages, pay, remuneration, earnings.

indent ▶ verb NOTCH, make an indentation in, nick; depress, impress, mark, imprint; scallop, groove, furrow.

indentation ▶ noun HOLLOW, depression, dip, dent, cavity, concavity, pit, trough; dimple, cleft; nick, notch, groove; impression, imprint, mark; recess, bay, inlet, cove.

indenture ▶ noun CONTRACT, agreement, compact, deal, covenant, bond.
▶ verb BIND, contract, employ, apprentice, article.

indépendantiste ▶ noun *See* SEPARATIST.

independence ▶ noun **1** *the struggle for Quebec independence* SELF-GOVERNMENT, self-rule, home rule, separation, self-determination, sovereignty, autonomy, freedom, liberty. **2** *he valued his independence* SELF-SUFFICIENCY, self-reliance, autonomy, freedom, liberty. **3** *financial independence* SUCCESS, prosperity, wealth; freedom, comfort, ease.

independent ▶ adjective **1** *an independent country* SELF-GOVERNING, self-ruling, self-determining, sovereign, autonomous, free, non-aligned. **2** *two independent groups of biologists verified the results* SEPARATE, different, unconnected, unrelated, dissociated, discrete. **3** *independent schools* PRIVATE, non-state-run, fee-paying. **4** *her grown-up, independent children* SELF-SUFFICIENT, self-supporting, self-reliant, standing on one's own two feet. **5** *independent advice* IMPARTIAL, unbiased, unprejudiced, neutral, disinterested, uninvolved, uncommitted, detached, dispassionate, objective, non-partisan, non-discriminatory. **6** *an independent spirit* FREETHINKING, free, individualistic, indie, unconventional, maverick, bold, unconstrained, unfettered, untrammelled.
— OPPOSITES: subservient, related, public, biased.

independently ▶ adverb ALONE, on one's own, separately, unaccompanied, solo; unaided, unassisted, without help, by one's own efforts, under one's own steam, single-handed(ly), on one's own initiative.

indescribable ▶ adjective INEXPRESSIBLE, indefinable, beyond words/description, ineffable, incommunicable; unutterable, unspeakable.

indestructible ▶ adjective UNBREAKABLE, shatterproof, durable; lasting, enduring, everlasting, perennial, deathless, undying, immortal, inextinguishable, imperishable; *informal* heavy-duty, industrial-strength; *literary* adamantine.
— OPPOSITES: fragile.

indeterminate ▶ adjective **1** *an indeterminate period of time* UNDETERMINED, uncertain, unknown, unspecified, unstipulated, indefinite, unfixed. **2** *some indeterminate figures* VAGUE, indefinite, unspecific, unclear, nebulous, indistinct; amorphous, shapeless, formless; hazy, faint, fuzzy, shadowy, dim.

index ▶ noun **1** *the library's subject index* LIST, listing, inventory, catalogue, register, directory. **2** *literature is an index to its time* GUIDE, sign, indication, indicator, gauge, measure, signal, mark, evidence, symptom, token; clue, hint.

▶ **verb** *he indexed his sources* LIST, catalogue, make an inventory of, itemize, inventory, record.

indicate ▶ **verb 1** *sales indicate a growing market* POINT TO, be a sign of, be evidence of, evidence, demonstrate, show, testify to, bespeak, be a symptom of, be symptomatic of, denote, connote, mark, signal, signify, suggest, imply; manifest, reveal, betray, display, reflect, represent; *formal* evince; *literary* betoken. **2** *the president indicated his willingness to use force* STATE, declare, make known, communicate, announce, mention, express, reveal, divulge, disclose; put it on record; admit. **3** *please indicate your sex on the form* SPECIFY, designate, mark, stipulate; show. **4** *he indicated the direction we needed to go* POINT TO, point out, gesture towards.

indicated ▶ **adjective** *in such cases surgery is indicated* ADVISABLE, recommended, suggested, desirable, preferable, best, sensible, wise, prudent, in someone's (best) interests; necessary, needed, required, called for.

indication ▶ **noun** SIGN, signal, indicator, symptom, mark, manifestation, demonstration, show, evidence; pointer, guide, hint, clue, intimation, omen, augury, portent, warning, forewarning.

indicative ▶ **adjective** SYMPTOMATIC, expressive, suggestive, representative, emblematic, symbolic; typical, characteristic.

indicator ▶ **noun** MEASURE, gauge, barometer, guide, index, mark, sign, signal, symptom; bellwether, herald, hint; standard, touchstone, yardstick, benchmark, criterion, point of reference, guideline, test, litmus test.

indict ▶ **verb** CHARGE, accuse, arraign, take to court, put on trial, prosecute; summons, cite, impeach.
— OPPOSITES: acquit.

indifference ▶ **noun 1** *his apparent indifference infuriated her* LACK OF CONCERN, unconcern, disinterest, lack of interest, lack of enthusiasm, apathy, nonchalance, insouciance; boredom, unresponsiveness, impassivity, dispassion, detachment, coolness. **2** *a matter of indifference* UNIMPORTANCE, insignificance, irrelevance, inconsequentiality.

indifferent ▶ **adjective 1** *an indifferent shrug* UNCONCERNED, uninterested, uncaring, casual, nonchalant, offhand, uninvolved, unenthusiastic, apathetic, lukewarm, phlegmatic, blasé, insouciant; unimpressed, bored, unmoved, unresponsive, impassive, dispassionate, detached, cool. **2** *an indifferent performance* MEDIOCRE, ordinary, average, middling, middle-of-the-road, uninspired, undistinguished, unexceptional, unexciting, unremarkable, run-of-the-mill, pedestrian, prosaic, lacklustre, forgettable, amateur, amateurish; *informal* OK, so-so, {comme ci, comme ça}, fair-to-middling, no great shakes, bush-league.
— OPPOSITES: enthusiastic, brilliant.

indigenous ▶ **adjective** NATIVE, original, aboriginal, autochthonous; local, domestic, home-grown; earliest, first.

indigent ▶ **adjective** POOR, impecunious, destitute, penniless, impoverished, insolvent, poverty-stricken; needy, in need, hard up, disadvantaged, badly off; *informal* (flat) broke, strapped (for cash), on skid row, down-and-out; *formal* penurious.
— OPPOSITES: rich.

▶ **noun** VAGRANT, homeless person, down-and-out, beggar, pauper, derelict, have-not; *informal* bum.

indigestion ▶ **noun** DYSPEPSIA, heartburn, pyrosis, stomach ache; (an) upset stomach; *informal* bellyache, tummy ache, collywobbles.

indignant ▶ **adjective** AGGRIEVED, resentful, affronted, disgruntled, displeased, cross, angry, mad, annoyed, offended, exasperated, irritated, piqued, nettled, in high dudgeon, chagrined; *informal* peeved, vexed, irked, put out, miffed, aggravated, riled, in a huff, huffy, ticked off, sore.

indignation ▶ **noun** RESENTMENT, umbrage, affront, disgruntlement, displeasure, anger, outrage, annoyance, irritation, exasperation, vexation, offence, pique; *informal* aggravation; *literary* ire.

indignity ▶ **noun** SHAME, humiliation, loss of self-respect, loss of pride, loss of face, embarrassment, mortification, ignominy; disgrace, dishonour, stigma, discredit; affront, insult, abuse, mistreatment, injury, offence, injustice, slight, snub, discourtesy, disrespect; *informal* slap in the face, kick in the teeth.

indirect ▶ **adjective 1** *an indirect effect* INCIDENTAL, accidental, unintended, unintentional, secondary, subordinate, ancillary, concomitant. **2** *the indirect route* ROUNDABOUT, circuitous, wandering, meandering, serpentine, winding, tortuous, zigzag. **3** *an indirect answer* OBLIQUE, inexplicit, implicit, implied, allusive, mealy-mouthed; backhanded.

indirectly ▶ **adverb 1** *I heard about it indirectly* SECOND-HAND, at second hand, from others; *informal* through the grapevine, (esp. *North*) on the moccasin telegraph ♣. **2** *he referred to the subject indirectly* OBLIQUELY, by implication, allusively.

indiscernible ▶ **adjective** See IMPERCEPTIBLE.
— OPPOSITES: distinct.

indiscreet ▶ **adjective** IMPRUDENT, unwise, impolitic, injudicious, incautious, irresponsible, ill-judged, ill-advised, misguided, ill-considered, careless, thoughtless, rash, unwary, hasty, reckless, precipitate, impulsive, foolhardy, foolish, short-sighted; undiplomatic, indelicate, tactless, insensitive; untimely, infelicitous; immodest, indecorous, unseemly, improper.

indiscretion ▶ **noun 1** *he was prone to indiscretion* IMPRUDENCE, injudiciousness, incaution, irresponsibility; carelessness, rashness, recklessness, impulsiveness, foolhardiness, foolishness, folly; tactlessness, thoughtlessness, insensitivity; *humorous* foot-in-mouth disease. **2** *his past indiscretions* BLUNDER, lapse, gaffe, mistake, faux pas, error, slip, impropriety; misdemeanour, transgression, peccadillo, solecism, misdeed; *informal* slip-up.

indiscriminate ▶ **adjective** NON-SELECTIVE, unselective, undiscriminating, uncritical, aimless, hit-or-miss, haphazard, random, arbitrary, unsystematic, undirected; wholesale, general, sweeping, blanket; thoughtless, unthinking, inconsiderate, casual, careless.
— OPPOSITES: selective.

indispensable ▶ **adjective** ESSENTIAL, necessary, all-important, of the utmost importance, of the essence, vital, crucial, key, needed, required, requisite, imperative; invaluable.
— OPPOSITES: superfluous.

indisposed ▶ **adjective 1** *my wife is indisposed* ILL, unwell, sick, on the sick list, poorly, ailing, not (very) well, out of sorts, out of action, hors de combat;

informal under the weather, laid up. **2** *she was indisposed to help him* RELUCTANT, unwilling, disinclined, loath, unprepared, not disposed, averse, opposed.
— OPPOSITES: well, willing.

indisposition ▶ noun *See* ILLNESS.

indisputable ▶ adjective INCONTROVERTIBLE, incontestable, undeniable, irrefutable, beyond dispute, unassailable, unquestionable, beyond question, indubitable, not in doubt, beyond doubt, beyond a shadow of a doubt, unarguable, airtight, watertight; unequivocal, unmistakable, certain, sure, definite, definitive, proven, decisive, conclusive, demonstrable, self-evident, clear, clear-cut, plain, obvious, manifest, patent, palpable.
— OPPOSITES: questionable.

indistinct ▶ adjective **1** *the distant shoreline was indistinct* BLURRED, out of focus, fuzzy, hazy, misty, foggy, cloudy, shadowy, dim, nebulous; unclear, obscure, vague, faint, indistinguishable, indiscernible, barely perceptible, hard to see, hard to make out. **2** *the last two digits are indistinct* INDECIPHERABLE, illegible, unreadable, hard to read. **3** *indistinct sounds* MUFFLED, muted, low, quiet, soft, faint, inaudible, hard to hear; muttered, mumbled.
— OPPOSITES: clear.

indistinguishable ▶ adjective **1** *the two girls were indistinguishable* IDENTICAL, difficult to tell apart, like (two) peas in a pod, like Tweedledum and Tweedledee, very similar, two of a kind. **2** *the image had become indistinguishable* UNINTELLIGIBLE, incomprehensible, hard to make out, indistinct, unclear; inaudible.
— OPPOSITES: unalike, clear.

individual ▶ adjective **1** *exhibitions devoted to individual artists* SINGLE, separate, discrete, independent, solo; sole, lone, solitary, isolated. **2** *he had his own individual style* CHARACTERISTIC, distinctive, distinct, typical, particular, peculiar, personal, personalized, special; original, unique, exclusive, singular, idiosyncratic, different, unusual, novel, unorthodox, atypical, out of the ordinary, one of a kind.
▶ noun **1** *Peter was a rather stuffy individual* PERSON, human being, mortal, soul, creature; man, boy, woman, girl; character, personage; *informal* type, sort, beggar, cookie, customer, guy, geezer, gent, devil, bastard. **2** *she was a real individual* INDIVIDUALIST, free spirit, nonconformist, original, eccentric, character, maverick, rare bird, something else.

individualistic ▶ adjective UNCONVENTIONAL, unorthodox, atypical, singular, unique, original, nonconformist, independent, individual, freethinking; eccentric, maverick, strange, odd, peculiar, quirky, queer, idiosyncratic; *informal* off-the-wall.

individuality ▶ noun DISTINCTIVENESS, distinction, uniqueness, originality, singularity, particularity, peculiarity, differentness, separateness; personality, character, identity, self, ego.

individually ▶ adverb ONE AT A TIME, one by one, singly, separately, severally, independently, apart.
— OPPOSITES: together.

indoctrinate ▶ verb BRAINWASH, propagandize, proselytize, inculcate, instill, re-educate, persuade, convince, condition, program, mould, discipline; instruct, teach, train, school, drill.

indolence ▶ noun LAZINESS, idleness, slothfulness, sloth, shiftlessness, inactivity, inaction, inertia,

sluggishness, lethargy, languor, languidness, torpor; *literary* hebetude.

indolent ▶ adjective LAZY, idle, slothful, loafing, do-nothing, sluggardly, shiftless, lackadaisical, languid, inactive, inert, sluggish, lethargic, torpid; slack, good-for-nothing, feckless.
— OPPOSITES: industrious, energetic.

indomitable ▶ adjective INVINCIBLE, unconquerable, unbeatable, unassailable, invulnerable, unshakeable, unsinkable; indefatigable, unyielding, unbending, stalwart, stout-hearted, lion-hearted, strong-willed, strong-minded, steadfast, staunch, resolute, firm, determined, intransigent, inflexible, adamant; unflinching, courageous, brave, valiant, heroic, intrepid, fearless, plucky, gritty.
— OPPOSITES: submissive.

indoors ▶ adverb INSIDE, in, within; in one's home, at home, under the roof.

indubitable ▶ adjective UNQUESTIONABLE, undoubtable, indisputable, unarguable, undebatable, incontestable, undeniable, irrefutable, incontrovertible, unmistakable, unequivocal, certain, sure, positive, definite, absolute, conclusive, watertight; beyond doubt, beyond the shadow of a doubt, beyond dispute, beyond question, not in question, not in doubt; *informal* sure as shootin'.
— OPPOSITES: doubtful.

induce ▶ verb **1** *the pickets induced many workers to stay away* PERSUADE, convince, prevail upon, get, make, prompt, move, inspire, influence, encourage, motivate; coax into, wheedle into, cajole into, talk into, prod into; *informal* twist someone's arm. **2** *how to induce hypnosis* BRING ABOUT, cause, produce, effect, create, give rise to, generate, instigate, engender, occasion, set in motion, lead to, result in, trigger (off), whip up, stir up, kindle, arouse, rouse, foster, promote, encourage; *literary* beget, enkindle.
— OPPOSITES: dissuade, prevent.

inducement ▶ noun INCENTIVE, encouragement, attraction, temptation, stimulus, bait, lure, pull, draw, spur, goad, impetus, motive, motivation, provocation; bribe, reward; *informal* carrot, come-on, sweetener.
— OPPOSITES: deterrent.

induct ▶ verb **1** *the new ministers were inducted into the cabinet* ADMIT TO, allow into, introduce to, initiate into, install in, instate in, swear into; appoint to. **2** *he inducted me into the skills of magic* INTRODUCE TO, acquaint with, familiarize with, make conversant with; ground in, instruct in, teach in, educate in, school in.

indulge ▶ verb **1** *Sally indulged her passion for long walks* SATISFY, gratify, fulfill, feed, accommodate; yield to, give in to, give way to. **2** *she seldom indulged in sentimentality* WALLOW IN, give oneself up to, give way to, yield to, abandon oneself to, give free rein to; luxuriate in, revel in, lose oneself in. **3** *she did not indulge her children* PAMPER, spoil, overindulge, coddle, mollycoddle, cosset, baby, spoon-feed, pander to, wait on hand and foot, cater to someone's every whim, kill with kindness.
— OPPOSITES: frustrate.
■ **indulge oneself** TREAT ONESELF, give oneself a treat; go on a spree. *informal* go to town, splurge.

indulgence ▶ noun **1** *the indulgence of all his desires* SATISFACTION, gratification, fulfillment. **2** *excessive indulgence contributed to his ill-health* SELF-GRATIFICATION, self-indulgence, overindulgence, intemperance, immoderation, excess, excessiveness, lack of restraint, extravagance, decadence, sybaritism. **3** *they viewed vacations as an indulgence* EXTRAVAGANCE, luxury, treat, non-essential, extra, frill. **4** *his mother's indulgence made him ungovernable* PAMPERING, coddling, mollycoddling, cosseting, babying. **5** *I ask for your indulgence* TOLERANCE, forbearance, understanding, kindness, compassion, sympathy, forgiveness, leniency.

indulgent ▶ adjective PERMISSIVE, easygoing, liberal, tolerant, forgiving, forbearing, lenient, kind, kindly, generous, soft-hearted, compassionate, understanding, sympathetic; fond, doting, soft; compliant, obliging, accommodating.
— OPPOSITES: strict.

industrial ▶ adjective **1** *industrial areas of the city* MANUFACTURING, factory; commercial, business, trade. **2** *industrial plastic* HEAVY-DUTY, durable, strong, tough, rugged.

industrialist ▶ noun MANUFACTURER, factory owner; captain of industry, big businessman, magnate, tycoon, capitalist, financier.

industrious ▶ adjective HARD-WORKING, diligent, assiduous, conscientious, steady, painstaking, sedulous, persevering, unflagging, untiring, tireless, indefatigable, studious; busy, as busy as a bee, active, bustling, energetic, on the go, vigorous, determined, dynamic, zealous, productive; with one's shoulder to the wheel, with one's nose to the grindstone.
— OPPOSITES: indolent.

industry ▶ noun **1** *Canadian industry* MANUFACTURING, production; construction. **2** *the publishing industry* BUSINESS, trade, field, line (of business); *informal* racket. **3** *the kitchen was a hive of industry* ACTIVITY, busyness, energy, vigour, productiveness; hard work, industriousness, diligence, application, dedication.

inebriated ▶ adjective DRUNK, intoxicated, inebriate, impaired ♣, drunken, tipsy, under the influence; *informal* plastered, smashed, bombed, sloshed, sozzled, sauced, lubricated, well-oiled, wrecked, juiced, blasted, stinko, blitzed, half-cut, fried, gassed, polluted, pissed, tanked (up), soaked, out of one's head/skull, loaded, trashed, buzzed, befuddled, besotted, pickled, pixilated, canned, cockeyed, blotto, blind drunk, roaring drunk, dead drunk, punch-drunk, ripped, stewed, tight, merry, the worse for wear, far gone, pie-eyed, in one's cups, three sheets to the wind; *literary* crapulous.
— OPPOSITES: sober.

inedible ▶ adjective UNEATABLE, indigestible, unsavoury, unpalatable, unappetizing, unwholesome; stale, rotten, off, bad.

ineffable ▶ adjective INDESCRIBABLE, inexpressible, beyond words; undefinable, unutterable, untold, unimaginable; overwhelming, breathtaking, awesome, staggering, amazing; unmentionable, taboo, forbidden.

ineffective ▶ adjective **1** *an ineffective scheme* UNSUCCESSFUL, unproductive, fruitless, unprofitable, abortive, futile, purposeless, useless, worthless, ineffectual, inefficient, inefficacious, inadequate; feeble, inept, lame; *archaic* bootless. **2** *an ineffective president* INEFFECTUAL, inefficient, inefficacious, unsuccessful, powerless, impotent, lame-duck; inadequate, incompetent, incapable, unfit, inept, bungling, weak, poor; *informal* useless, hopeless.

ineffectual ▶ adjective. See INEFFECTIVE senses 1, 2.

inefficient ▶ adjective **1** *an inefficient worker* INEFFECTIVE, ineffectual, unproductive, incompetent,

inept, incapable, unfit, unskilful, inexpert, amateurish, unprofessional; disorganized, unprepared; negligent, lax, sloppy, slack, careless; *informal* lousy, useless, good-for-nothing. **2** *inefficient processes* UNECONOMICAL, wasteful, unproductive, time-wasting, slow; deficient, disorganized, unsystematic.

inelegant ▶ adjective **1** *an inelegant laugh* UNREFINED, uncouth, unsophisticated, unpolished, uncultivated; ill-bred, coarse, vulgar, rude, impolite, unmannerly, tasteless. **2** *an inelegant manoeuvre* GRACELESS, ungraceful, ungainly, uncoordinated, awkward, clumsy, lumbering; inept, unskilful, inexpert; *informal* having two left feet, clunky.
— OPPOSITES: refined, graceful.

ineligible ▶ adjective UNQUALIFIED, unsuitable, unacceptable, undesirable, inappropriate, unworthy; ruled out, disqualified, disentitled; *Law* incompetent.
— OPPOSITES: suitable.

inept ▶ adjective INCOMPETENT, unskilful, unskilled, inexpert, amateurish; clumsy, awkward, maladroit, bungling, blundering; unproductive, unsuccessful, ineffectual, not up to scratch; *informal* ham-fisted, butterfingered, klutzy, all thumbs.
— OPPOSITES: competent.

inequality ▶ noun IMBALANCE, inequity, inconsistency, variation, variability; divergence, polarity, disparity, discrepancy, dissimilarity, difference; bias, prejudice, discrimination, unfairness.

inequitable ▶ adjective UNFAIR, unjust, unequal, uneven, unbalanced, one-sided, discriminatory, preferential, biased, partisan, partial, prejudiced.
— OPPOSITES: fair.

inequity ▶ noun UNFAIRNESS, injustice, unjustness, discrimination, partisanship, partiality, favouritism, bias, prejudice.

inert ▶ adjective UNMOVING, motionless, immobile, inanimate, still, stationary, static; dormant, sleeping; unconscious, comatose, lifeless, insensible, insensate, insentient; idle, inactive, sluggish, lethargic, indolent, stagnant, listless, torpid.
— OPPOSITES: active.

inertia ▶ noun INACTIVITY, inaction, inertness; apathy, acedia, malaise, stagnation, enervation, lethargy, listlessness, torpor, idleness, sloth; motionlessness, immobility, lifelessness, stasis.

inescapable ▶ adjective UNAVOIDABLE, inevitable, ineluctable, inexorable; assured, sure, certain, guaranteed; necessary, required, compulsory, mandatory; *rare* ineludible.
— OPPOSITES: avoidable.

inessential ▶ adjective See NON-ESSENTIAL.

inestimable ▶ adjective IMMEASURABLE, incalculable, innumerable, unfathomable, indeterminate, measureless, countless, untold; limitless, boundless, unlimited, infinite, endless, inexhaustible; *informal* no end of; *literary* myriad.
— OPPOSITES: few.

inevitable ▶ adjective UNAVOIDABLE, inescapable, inexorable, ineluctable; assured, certain, sure, fixed; fated, destined, predestined, predetermined; *rare* ineludible.
— OPPOSITES: uncertain.

inevitably ▶ adverb NATURALLY, necessarily, automatically, as a matter of course, of necessity, inescapably, unavoidably, certainly, surely, definitely, undoubtedly; *informal* like it or not; *formal* perforce.

inexact ▶ adjective IMPRECISE, inaccurate, approximate, rough, crude, general, vague, fuzzy, ill-defined; *informal* off-base, ballpark.

inexcusable ▶ adjective INDEFENSIBLE, unjustifiable, unwarranted, unpardonable, unforgivable; blameworthy, censurable, reprehensible, deplorable, unconscionable, unacceptable, unreasonable.

inexhaustible ▶ adjective **1** *her patience is inexhaustible* UNLIMITED, limitless, illimitable, infinite, boundless, endless, never-ending, unfailing, everlasting; immeasurable, incalculable, inestimable, untold; copious, abundant, plentiful, bottomless. **2** *the dancers were inexhaustible* TIRELESS, indefatigable, untiring, unwearied, unwearying, unfaltering, unflagging, unremitting, persevering, persistent, dogged.
– OPPOSITES: limited, weary.

inexorable ▶ adjective **1** *the inexorable advance of science* RELENTLESS, unstoppable, inescapable, inevitable, unavoidable, irrevocable, unalterable; persistent, continuous, non-stop, steady, interminable, incessant, unceasing, unremitting, unrelenting. **2** *inexorable creditors* INTRANSIGENT, unbending, unyielding, inflexible, adamant, obdurate, immovable, unshakeable; implacable, unappeasable, severe, hard, unforgiving, unsparing, uncompromising, ruthless, relentless, pitiless, merciless.

inexpensive ▶ adjective CHEAP, low-priced, low-cost, modest, economical, competitive, affordable, reasonable, budget, bargain, cut-rate, reduced, discounted, discount, rock-bottom, giveaway, bargain-basement, down-market, low-end; *informal* dirt cheap, cheap like borscht ✦.

inexperienced ▶ adjective INEXPERT, unpractised, untrained, unschooled, unqualified, unskilled, amateur, rookie; ignorant, unversed, unseasoned; ill-equipped, ill-prepared; naive, unsophisticated, callow, immature, green, unworldly; *informal* wet behind the ears, raggedy-ass, wide-eyed.

inexpert ▶ adjective UNSKILLED, unskilful, amateur, amateurish, unprofessional, inexperienced; inept, incompetent, maladroit, uncoordinated, clumsy, bungling, blundering; *informal* ham-fisted, butterfingered.

inexplicable ▶ adjective UNACCOUNTABLE, unexplainable, incomprehensible, unfathomable, impenetrable, insoluble; baffling, puzzling, perplexing, mystifying, bewildering, confusing; mysterious, strange.
– OPPOSITES: understandable.

inexpressible ▶ adjective INDESCRIBABLE, undefinable, unutterable, unspeakable, ineffable, beyond words, nameless; unimaginable, inconceivable, unthinkable, untold.

inexpressive ▶ adjective EXPRESSIONLESS, impassive, emotionless; inscrutable, unreadable, blank, vacant, glazed, glassy, lifeless, deadpan, wooden, stony; poker-faced, straight-faced.

inextinguishable ▶ adjective IRREPRESSIBLE, unquenchable, indestructible, undying, immortal, imperishable, unfailing, unceasing, ceaseless, enduring, everlasting, eternal, persistent.

inextricable ▶ adjective **1** *our lives are inextricable* INSEPARABLE, indivisible, entangled, tangled, mixed

up. **2** *an inextricable situation* INESCAPABLE, unavoidable, ineluctable.

infallible ▶ adjective **1** *an infallible sense of timing* UNERRING, unfailing, faultless, flawless, impeccable, perfect, precise, accurate, meticulous, scrupulous. **2** *an infallible remedy* UNFAILING, unerring, guaranteed, dependable, trustworthy, reliable, sure, certain, safe, foolproof, effective; *informal* sure-fire; *formal* efficacious.

infamous ▶ adjective **1** *an infamous serial killer* NOTORIOUS, disreputable; legendary, fabled, famed. **2** *infamous misconduct* ABOMINABLE, outrageous, shocking, shameful, disgraceful, dishonourable, discreditable, contemptible, unworthy; monstrous, atrocious, nefarious, appalling, dreadful, terrible, heinous, egregious, detestable, despicable, loathsome, hateful, vile, unspeakable, unforgivable, iniquitous, scandalous; *informal* dirty, filthy, lowdown.
– OPPOSITES: reputable, honourable.

infamy ▶ noun **1** *public infamy* NOTORIETY, disrepute, ill fame, disgrace, discredit, shame, dishonour, ignominy, scandal, censure, blame, disapprobation, condemnation. **2** *she was punished for her infamy* WICKEDNESS, evil, vileness, iniquity, depravity, degeneracy, immorality; sin, wrongdoing, offence, abuse; *formal* turpitude.

infancy ▶ noun **1** *she died in infancy* BABYHOOD, early childhood. **2** *music video was in its infancy* BEGINNINGS, early days, early stages; seeds, roots; start, commencement, rise, emergence, genesis, dawn, birth, inception.
– OPPOSITES: end.

infant ▶ noun *a fretful infant* BABY, newborn, young child, (tiny) tot, little one, papoose; *Medicine* neonate; *informal* tiny; *literary* babe, babe in arms, suckling.
▶ adjective *an infant stage* DEVELOPING, emergent, emerging, embryonic, nascent, incipient, new, fledgling, budding, up-and-coming.

infantile ▶ adjective CHILDISH, babyish, immature, puerile, juvenile, adolescent, jejune; silly, inane, fatuous.

infantry ▶ noun INFANTRYMEN, foot soldiers, foot guards; the ranks; cannon fodder; *US* GIs; *Military slang* grunts; *historical* footmen.

infatuated ▶ adjective BESOTTED, in love, head over heels, obsessed, taken, lovesick, moonstruck; enamoured of, attracted to, devoted to, captivated by, enthralled by, enchanted by, bewitched by, under the spell of; *informal* smitten with, sweet on, keen on, hot on/for, gone on, hung up on, mad about, crazy about, nuts about, stuck on, carrying a torch for.

infect ▶ verb **1** *he didn't want to infect others with his chicken pox* PASS INFECTION TO, spread disease to, contaminate. **2** *nitrates were infecting rivers* CONTAMINATE, pollute, taint, foul, dirty, blight, damage, ruin; poison. **3** *his high spirits infected everyone* AFFECT, influence, impact on, touch; excite, inspire, stimulate, animate.

infection ▶ noun DISEASE, virus; disorder, condition, affliction, complaint, illness, ailment, sickness, infirmity; germs, bacteria; contamination, poison, septicemia, suppuration; *informal* bug; *dated* contagion; *Medicine* sepsis.

infectious ▶ adjective **1** *infectious disease* CONTAGIOUS, communicable, transmittable, transferable, spreadable; epidemic; *informal* catching; *dated* infective. **2** *her laughter is infectious* IRRESISTIBLE, compelling, persuasive, contagious, catching.

infer ▶ verb DEDUCE, conclude, conjecture, surmise, reason, interpret; gather, understand, presume, assume, take it, extrapolate; read between the lines, figure (out); *informal* suss out, reckon.

inference ▶ noun DEDUCTION, conclusion, reasoning, conjecture, speculation, guess, presumption, assumption, supposition, reckoning, extrapolation.

inferior ▶ adjective **1** *poorer people were thought to be innately inferior* SECOND-CLASS, lower-ranking, subordinate, second-fiddle, junior, minor; lowly, humble, menial, beneath one. **2** *inferior accommodation* SECOND-RATE, substandard, low-quality, low-grade, bush-league, unsatisfactory, shoddy, deficient; poor, bad, awful, dreadful, wretched; *informal* crummy, scuzzy, rotten, lousy, third-rate, tinpot.
– OPPOSITES: superior, luxury.
▶ noun *how dare she treat him as an inferior?* SUBORDINATE, junior, underling, minion, peon.

infernal ▶ adjective **1** *the infernal regions* HELLISH, nether, subterranean, underworld, chthonic, Tartarean; satanic, devilish, diabolical, fiendish, demonic. **2** *(informal) an infernal nuisance* DAMNABLE, wretched, cursed, confounded; annoying, irritating, infuriating, irksome, detestable, exasperating; *informal* damned, damn, blasted, blessed, pesky, aggravating.

infertile ▶ adjective **1** *infertile soil* BARREN, unfruitful, unproductive; sterile, impoverished, arid. **2** *she was infertile* STERILE, barren; childless, unable to procreate/reproduce, impotent; *Medicine* infecund.

infest ▶ verb OVERRUN, spread through, invade, infiltrate, pervade, permeate, inundate, overwhelm; beset, plague, swarm.

infested ▶ adjective OVERRUN, swarming, teeming, crawling, alive, ridden, lousy; plagued, beset.

infidel ▶ noun UNBELIEVER, disbeliever, non-believer, agnostic, atheist; heathen, pagan, idolater, heretic, freethinker, dissenter, nonconformist.

infidelity ▶ noun UNFAITHFULNESS, adultery, cuckoldry, disloyalty, extramarital sex; deceit, falseness; affair, liaison, fling, amour; *informal* fooling/playing around, cheating, two-timing, hanky-panky, a bit on the side; *formal* fornication.

infiltrate ▶ verb INSINUATE ONESELF INTO, worm one's way into, sneak into, slip into, get into, invade, penetrate, enter; permeate, pervade, seep into/through, soak into.

infiltrator ▶ noun SPY, secret agent, undercover agent, operative, informant, informer, mole, plant, spook; intruder, interloper, subversive.

infinite ▶ adjective **1** *the universe is infinite* BOUNDLESS, unbounded, unlimited, limitless, never-ending, interminable; immeasurable, fathomless, imponderable; extensive, vast; immense, great, huge, enormous. **2** *infinite resources* COUNTLESS, uncountable, inestimable, innumerable, numberless, immeasurable, incalculable, untold, myriad.
– OPPOSITES: limited, small.

infinitesimal ▶ adjective MINUTE, tiny, minuscule, very small; microscopic, imperceptible, indiscernible; *informal* teeny, wee, teeny-weeny, itsy-bitsy, little-bitty.
– OPPOSITES: huge.

infinity ▶ noun **1** *the infinity of space* ENDLESSNESS, infinitude, infiniteness, boundlessness, limitlessness; vastness, immensity. **2** *an infinity of accessories* INFINITE NUMBER, great number; abundance, profusion, host, multitude, mass, wealth; *informal* heap, stack.

infirm ▶ adjective FRAIL, weak, feeble, debilitated, decrepit, disabled; ill, unwell, sick, sickly, indisposed, ailing.
– OPPOSITES: healthy.

infirmity ▶ noun ILLNESS, malady, ailment, disease, disorder, sickness, affliction, complaint, indisposition, frailty, weakness; disability, impairment.

inflame ▶ verb **1** *his opinions inflamed his rival* ENRAGE, incense, anger, madden, infuriate, exasperate, provoke, antagonize, rile; *informal* make someone see red, make someone's blood boil. **2** *the case inflamed passions against the pit bull* INCITE, arouse, rouse, provoke, stir up, whip up, kindle, ignite, touch off, foment, inspire, stimulate, agitate. **3** *he inflamed an already tense situation* AGGRAVATE, exacerbate, intensify, worsen, compound.
– OPPOSITES: placate, calm, soothe.

inflamed ▶ adjective **1** *the cut became inflamed* SWOLLEN, puffed up; red, hot, burning; raw, sore, painful, tender, angry; infected, septic. **2** *inflamed feelings* ANGRY, infuriated, furious, enraged; excited, aroused, stimulated, titillated.

inflammable ▶ adjective FLAMMABLE, combustible, incendiary, ignitable; volatile, unstable.
– OPPOSITES: fireproof.

inflammation ▶ noun SWELLING, puffiness; redness, heat, burning; rawness, soreness, tenderness; infection, festering, septicity.

inflammatory ▶ adjective PROVOCATIVE, incendiary, stirring, rousing, rabble-rousing, seditious, subversive, mutinous; fiery, passionate; controversial, contentious.

inflate ▶ verb **1** *she inflated the mattress* BLOW UP, fill up, fill with air, aerate, pump up; dilate, distend, swell. **2** *the demand inflated prices* INCREASE, raise, boost, escalate, put up; *informal* hike up, jack up, bump up, boost up. **3** *the figures were inflated by the press* EXAGGERATE, magnify, overplay, overstate, enhance, embellish, increase, amplify, augment.
– OPPOSITES: decrease, understate.

inflated ▶ adjective **1** *an inflated balloon* BLOWN UP, aerated, filled, puffed up/out, pumped up; distended, expanded, engorged, swollen. **2** *inflated prices* HIGH, sky-high, excessive, unreasonable, prohibitive, outrageous, exorbitant, extortionate; *informal* steep, stiff, pricey. **3** *an inflated opinion of himself* EXAGGERATED, magnified, aggrandized, immoderate, overblown, overstated. **4** *inflated language* HIGH-FLOWN, extravagant, exaggerated, elaborate, flowery, ornate, overblown, overwrought, grandiloquent, magniloquent, lofty, grandiose; affected, pretentious, bombastic, tumid; *informal* windy, highfalutin.

inflection ▶ noun STRESS, cadence, rhythm, accent, intonation, pitch, emphasis, modulation, lilt, tone.

inflexible ▶ adjective **1** *his inflexible attitude* STUBBORN, obstinate, obdurate, intractable, intransigent, unbending, immovable, unaccommodating; hidebound, single-minded, pigheaded, mulish, uncompromising, adamant, firm, resolute, diehard, dyed-in-the-wool; *formal* refractory. **2** *inflexible rules* UNALTERABLE, unchangeable, immutable, unvarying; firm, fixed, set, established, entrenched, hard and fast, carved in

stone; stringent, strict, hardline, ironclad. **3** *inflexible plastic* RIGID, stiff, unyielding, unbending, unbendable; hard, firm, inelastic.
— OPPOSITES: accommodating, pliable.

inflict ▶ verb **1** *he inflicted an injury on James* ADMINISTER TO, deliver to, deal out to, dispense to, mete out to; impose, exact, wreak; cause to, give to; *informal* dish out to. **2** *I won't inflict myself on you any longer* IMPOSE, force, thrust, foist; saddle someone with, burden someone with.

influence ▶ noun **1** *the influence of parents on their children* EFFECT, impact; control, sway, hold, power, authority, mastery, domination, supremacy; guidance, direction; pressure. **2** *a bad influence on young girls* EXAMPLE TO, (role) model for, guide for, inspiration to. **3** *political influence* POWER, authority, sway, leverage, weight, pull, standing, prestige, stature, rank; *informal* clout, muscle, teeth.
▶ verb **1** *bosses can influence our careers* AFFECT, have an impact on, impact, determine, guide, control, shape, govern, decide; change, alter, transform. **2** *an attempt to influence the jury* SWAY, bias, prejudice, suborn; pressure, coerce; dragoon, intimidate, browbeat, brainwash; *informal* twist someone's arm, lean on, put ideas into one's head.

influential ▶ adjective **1** *an influential leader* POWERFUL, dominant, controlling, strong, authoritative, persuasive; important, prominent, distinguished, eminent. **2** *she was influential in shaping his career* INSTRUMENTAL, significant, important, crucial, pivotal.

influx ▶ noun **1** *an influx of tourists* INUNDATION, rush, stream, flood, incursion; invasion, intrusion. **2** *influxes of river water* INFLOW, inrush, flood, inundation.

inform ▶ verb **1** *she informed him that she was ill* TELL, notify, apprise, advise, impart to, communicate to, let someone know; brief, prime, enlighten, send word to, give/supply information to; *informal* fill someone in, clue someone in. **2** *he informed on two villains* DENOUNCE, give away, betray, incriminate, inculpate, report, finger; sell out, stab in the back; *informal* rat on/out, squeal, tell, blab, tattle, blow the whistle, sell down the river, snitch, peach. **3** *the articles were informed by feminism* SUFFUSE, pervade, permeate, infuse, imbue, inspire; characterize.

informal ▶ adjective **1** *an informal chat* UNOFFICIAL, casual, relaxed, easygoing, unceremonious; open, friendly, intimate, simple, unpretentious, easy; *informal* unstuffy, laid-back, chummy. **2** *informal language* COLLOQUIAL, vernacular, idiomatic, demotic, popular; familiar, everyday, unofficial; simple, natural, unpretentious; *informal* slangy, chatty, folksy. **3** *informal clothes* CASUAL, relaxed, comfortable, everyday, sloppy, leisure; *informal* comfy, cazh.
— OPPOSITES: official, literary, formal.

informant ▶ noun *See* INFORMER.

information ▶ noun DETAILS, particulars, facts, figures, statistics, data; knowledge, intelligence; instruction, advice, guidance, direction, counsel, enlightenment; news; *informal* info, the lowdown, the dope, the dirt, the inside story, the scoop, the poop.

informative ▶ adjective INSTRUCTIVE, instructional, illuminating, enlightening, revealing, explanatory; factual, educational, educative, edifying, didactic; *informal* newsy.

informed ▶ adjective KNOWLEDGEABLE, enlightened, literate, educated; sophisticated, cultured; briefed,

versed, up to date, up to speed, in the know, in the loop, au courant, au fait, switched-on, wise, hip.
— OPPOSITES: ignorant.

informer ▶ noun INFORMANT, betrayer, traitor, Judas, collaborator, stool pigeon, spy, double agent, infiltrator, plant, tattletale; *informal* rat, squealer, whistle-blower, snake in the grass, snitch, fink, stoolie.

infraction ▶ noun VIOLATION, contravention, breach, transgression, infringement, offence; neglect, dereliction, non-compliance; *Law* contumacy.

infrequent ▶ adjective RARE, uncommon, unusual, exceptional, few (and far between), as rare/scarce as hen's teeth; unaccustomed, unwonted; isolated, scarce, scattered; sporadic, irregular, intermittent, seldom; *informal* once in a blue moon.
— OPPOSITES: common.

infringe ▶ verb **1** *the statute infringed constitutionally guaranteed rights* CONTRAVENE, violate, transgress, break, breach; disobey, defy, flout, fly in the face of; disregard, ignore, neglect; go beyond, overstep, exceed; *Law* infract. **2** *the new bylaw infringed on his rights* RESTRICT, limit, curb, check, encroach on; undermine, erode, diminish, weaken, impair, damage, compromise.
— OPPOSITES: obey, preserve.

infuriate ▶ verb ENRAGE, incense, anger, inflame; exasperate, antagonize, provoke, rile, annoy, irritate, aggravate, madden, nettle, gall, irk, vex, get on someone's nerves, try someone's patience, rankle; *informal* make someone see red, get someone's back up, make someone's blood boil, needle, hack off, cheese off, tick off, tee off, piss off, PO, wind up, get to, bug.
— OPPOSITES: please.

infuriating ▶ adjective EXASPERATING, maddening, annoying, irritating, irksome, vexatious, trying, tiresome; *informal* aggravating, pesky, infernal.

infuse ▶ verb **1** *she was infused with pride* FILL, suffuse, imbue, inspire, charge, pervade, permeate. **2** *he infused new life into the group* INSTILL, breathe, inject, impart, inculcate, introduce, add. **3** *the oil was infused with spices* STEEP, brew, stew, soak, immerse.

ingenious ▶ adjective INVENTIVE, creative, imaginative, original, innovative, pioneering, resourceful, enterprising, inspired; clever, intelligent, smart, brilliant, masterly, talented, gifted, skilful, astute, sharp-witted, quick-witted, shrewd; elaborate, sophisticated.

ingenuous ▶ adjective NAIVE, innocent, simple, childlike, trusting, over-trusting, unwary; unsuspicious, unworldly, wide-eyed, inexperienced, green; open, sincere, honest, frank, candid, forthright, artless, guileless, genuine, up-front.
— OPPOSITES: artful.

ingest ▶ verb CONSUME, swallow, take in, eat, devour, imbibe, drink; *informal* gobble up, wolf down, put away, down, inhale, scarf (down).

inglorious ▶ adjective SHAMEFUL, dishonourable, ignominious, discreditable, disgraceful, scandalous; humiliating, mortifying, demeaning, ignoble, undignified, wretched.

ingrained ▶ adjective **1** *ingrained attitudes* ENTRENCHED, established, deep-rooted, deep-seated, fixed, firm, unshakeable, ineradicable; inveterate, dyed-in-the-wool, abiding, enduring, stubborn. **2** *ingrained dirt* GROUND-IN, fixed, implanted,

embedded; permanent, indelible, ineradicable.
— OPPOSITES: transient, superficial.

ingratiate
■ **ingratiate oneself** CURRY FAVOUR WITH, cultivate, win over, get in someone's good books; toady to, grovel to, fawn over, kowtow to, play up to, pander to, flatter, court, wheedle, schmooze; *informal* suck up to, lick someone's boots, butter someone up, brown-nose.

ingratiating ▶ **adjective** SYCOPHANTIC, toadying, fawning, unctuous, obsequious; flattering, insincere; smooth-tongued, slick; greasy, oily, saccharine; *informal* smarmy, slimy, sucky.

ingratitude ▶ **noun** UNGRATEFULNESS, thanklessness.

ingredient ▶ **adjective** CONSTITUENT, component, element; part, piece, bit, strand, portion, unit, feature, aspect, attribute; (**ingredients**) contents, makings.

ingress ▶ **noun** ENTRY, entrance, entryway, entree, access, admittance, admission; way in, approach, passage.
— OPPOSITES: exit.

in-group ▶ **noun** INNER CIRCLE, in-crowd, popular crowd, clique, set, circle, coterie; *informal* gang, bunch, crew.

inhabit ▶ **verb** LIVE IN, occupy; settle (in), people, populate, colonize; dwell in, reside in, tenant, lodge in, have one's home in; *formal* be domiciled in, abide in.

inhabitant ▶ **noun** RESIDENT, occupant, occupier, dweller, squatter, settler; local, native, (Que.) habitant ♣, burgher; (**inhabitants**) population, populace, people, public, community, citizenry, townsfolk, townspeople; *formal* denizen.

inhale ▶ **verb** BREATHE IN, inspire, draw in, suck in, take in, sniff in, drink in.

inharmonious ▶ **adjective** See DISSONANT sense 1, 2.
— OPPOSITES: musical, fitting, congenial.

inherent ▶ **adjective** INTRINSIC, innate, immanent, built-in, indwelling, inborn, ingrained, deep-rooted; essential, fundamental, basic, structural, organic; natural, instinctive, instinctual, congenital, native.
— OPPOSITES: acquired.

inherit ▶ **verb** **1** *she inherited his farm* BECOME HEIR TO, come into/by, be bequeathed, be left, be willed, receive; *Law* be devised. **2** *Richard inherited the title* SUCCEED TO, assume, take over, come into; *formal* accede to.

inheritance ▶ **noun** **1** *a comfortable inheritance* LEGACY, bequest, endowment, bestowal, provision; birthright, heritage, patrimony; *Law* devise. **2** *his inheritance of the title* SUCCESSION TO, accession to, assumption of, elevation to.

inhibit ▶ **verb** **1** *the obstacles which inhibit change* IMPEDE, hinder, hamper, hold back, discourage, interfere with, obstruct, slow down, retard; curb, check, suppress, restrict, fetter, cramp, frustrate, stifle, prevent, hinder, thwart, foil, stop, halt. **2** *she feels inhibited from taking part* PREVENT, disallow, exclude, forbid, prohibit, preclude, ban, bar, interdict.
— OPPOSITES: assist, encourage, allow.

inhibited ▶ **adjective** SHY, reticent, reserved, self-conscious, diffident, bashful, coy; wary, reluctant, hesitant, insecure, unconfident, unassertive, timid; withdrawn, repressed, constrained, undemonstrative; *informal* uptight, anal-retentive.

inhibition ▶ **noun** **1** *they overcame their inhibitions*

SHYNESS, reticence, self-consciousness, reserve, diffidence; wariness, hesitancy, hesitation, insecurity; timidity; repression, reservation; psychological block; *informal* hang-up. **2** *writing without inhibition* HINDRANCE, hampering, discouragement, obstruction, impediment, suppression, repression, restriction, restraint, constraint, cramping, stifling, prevention; curb, check, bar, barrier.

inhospitable ▶ **adjective** **1** *the inhospitable landscape* UNINVITING, unwelcoming; bleak, forbidding, cheerless, hostile, savage, wild, harsh, inimical; uninhabitable, barren, bare, austere, desolate, stark, Spartan. **2** *forgive me if I seem inhospitable* UNWELCOMING, unfriendly, unsociable, anti-social, unneighbourly, uncongenial; aloof, cool, cold, frosty, distant, remote, indifferent, uncivil, discourteous, ungracious; ungenerous, unkind, unsympathetic; *informal* standoffish.
— OPPOSITES: welcoming.

inhuman ▶ **adjective** **1** *inhuman treatment* CRUEL, harsh, inhumane, brutal, callous, sadistic, severe, savage, vicious, barbaric; monstrous, heinous, egregious; merciless, ruthless, pitiless, remorseless, cold-blooded, heartless, hard-hearted, dastardly; unkind, inconsiderate, unfeeling, uncaring; *informal* beastly. **2** *he ran at an inhuman pace* SUPERHUMAN, extraordinary, phenomenal, exceptional, incredible, unbelievable.
— OPPOSITES: humane.

inhumane ▶ **adjective.** *See* INHUMAN sense 1.

inimical ▶ **adjective** HARMFUL, injurious, detrimental, deleterious, prejudicial, damaging, hurtful, destructive, ruinous, pernicious; antagonistic, contrary, antipathetic, unfavourable, adverse, opposed, hostile, unkind, unsympathetic, unfriendly, ill-disposed, malevolent; unwelcoming, cold, frosty; *literary* malefic.
— OPPOSITES: friendly.

inimitable ▶ **adjective** INCOMPARABLE, unparalleled, unrivalled, peerless, matchless, unequalled, unsurpassable, superlative, supreme, perfect, beyond compare, second to none, in a class of one's own; unique, distinctive, individual, sui generis; *formal* unexampled.

iniquity ▶ **noun** **1** *a den of sin and iniquity* WICKEDNESS, sinfulness, immorality, impropriety; vice, evil, sin; villainy, criminality; odiousness, atrocity, egregiousness; outrage, monstrosity, obscenity, reprehensibility; *formal* turpitude. **2** *I will forgive their iniquity* SIN, crime, transgression, wrongdoing, wrong, violation, offence, vice.
— OPPOSITES: goodness, virtue.

initial ▶ **adjective** *the initial stages* BEGINNING, opening, commencing, starting, inceptive, embryonic, fledgling; first, early, primary, preliminary, elementary, foundational, preparatory; introductory, inaugural.
— OPPOSITES: final.

▶ **verb** *he initialled the warrant* PUT ONE'S INITIALS ON, initialize, sign, ink, countersign, autograph, endorse, inscribe, witness, verify.

initially ▶ **adverb** AT FIRST, at the start, at the outset, in/at the beginning, to begin with, to start with, originally.

initiate ▶ **verb** **1** *the government initiated the scheme* BEGIN, start (off), commence; institute, inaugurate, launch, instigate, establish, set up, start the ball rolling; originate, pioneer; *informal* kick off, spark. **2** *he was initiated into a cult* ADMIT, induct, install,

incorporate, enlist, enrol, recruit, sign up, swear in; ordain, invest. **3** *she was initiated into the business of publishing* TEACH ABOUT, instruct in, tutor in, school in, prime in, ground in; familiarize with, acquaint with; indoctrinate, inculcate; *informal* show someone the ropes.
– OPPOSITES: finish, expel.

initiation ▶ **noun 1** *the initiation of the program* BEGINNING, starting, commencement; institution, inauguration, launch, opening, instigation, actuation, origination, devising, inception; establishment, setting up; *informal* kickoff. **2** *a rite of initiation into the tribe* INDUCTION, introduction, admission, admittance, installation, incorporation, ordination, investiture, enlistment, enrolment, recruitment; baptism; screech-in ♣.
– OPPOSITES: expulsion; completion, finish.

initiative ▶ **noun 1** *employers are looking for people with initiative* SELF-MOTIVATION, resourcefulness, inventiveness, imagination, ingenuity, originality, creativity, enterprise; drive, dynamism, ambition, motivation, spirit, energy, vision; *informal* get-up-and-go, pep, moxie, spunk, gumption. **2** *a recent initiative on recycling* PLAN, scheme, strategy, stratagem, measure, proposal, step, action, approach.

inject ▶ **verb 1** *he injected a painkiller* ADMINISTER, introduce; inoculate, vaccinate, immunize; *informal* shoot (up), mainline. **2** *a pump injects air into the valve* INSERT, introduce, feed, push, force, shoot. **3** *he injected new life into the team* INTRODUCE, instill, infuse, imbue, breathe. **4** *she injected a note of realism into the debate* INTERJECT, interpose, throw in, add, contribute.

injection ▶ **noun** INOCULATION, vaccination, immunization, booster (shot); *informal* jab, shot, needle, hypo, fix.

injudicious ▶ **adjective** IMPRUDENT, unwise, inadvisable, ill-advised, misguided; ill-considered, ill-judged, incautious, hasty, rash, foolish, foolhardy, hare-brained; inappropriate, impolitic, inexpedient.
– OPPOSITES: prudent.

injunction ▶ **noun** ORDER, ruling, directive, command, instruction; decree, edict, dictum, dictate, fiat, mandate, writ, fatwa; warning, caution, admonition.

injure ▶ **verb 1** *he injured his foot* HURT, wound, damage, harm; cripple, lame, disable; maim, mutilate, deform, mangle, break. **2** *his comments injured her reputation* DAMAGE, mar, impair, spoil, ruin, blight, blemish, tarnish, blacken. **3** *(archaic) my actions have injured no one* WRONG, abuse, do an injustice to, offend against, maltreat, mistreat, ill-use.

injured ▶ **adjective 1** *his injured arm* HURT, wounded, damaged, sore, bruised; crippled, lame, disabled; maimed, mutilated, deformed, mangled, broken, fractured. **2** *the injured party* WRONGED, offended, maltreated, mistreated, ill-used, harmed; defamed, maligned, insulted, dishonoured. **3** *an injured tone* UPSET, hurt, wounded, offended, pained, aggrieved, unhappy, put out.
– OPPOSITES: healthy, offending.

injurious ▶ **adjective** HARMFUL, damaging, deleterious, detrimental, hurtful, baleful; disadvantageous, unfavourable, undesirable, adverse, inimical, unhealthy, pernicious; insulting, libellous, wrongful; *literary* malefic.

injury ▶ **noun 1** *minor injuries* WOUND, bruise, cut, gash, scratch, graze, abrasion, contusion, lesion; *Medicine* trauma. **2** *they escaped without injury* HARM,

hurt, damage, pain, suffering, impairment, affliction. **3** *the injury to her feelings* OFFENCE, abuse; affront, insult, slight, snub; wrong, wrongdoing, injustice.

injustice ▶ **noun 1** *the injustice of the world* UNFAIRNESS, unjustness, inequity; cruelty, tyranny, repression, exploitation, corruption; bias, prejudice, discrimination, intolerance. **2** *his sacking was an injustice* WRONG, offence, crime, sin, misdeed, outrage, atrocity, scandal, disgrace, affront; *informal* raw deal.

inkling ▶ **noun** IDEA, notion, sense, impression, conception, suggestion, indication, whisper, glimmer, (sneaking) suspicion, fancy, hunch, feeling; hint, clue, intimation, sign; *informal* the foggiest (idea), the faintest (idea).

inky ▶ **adjective 1** *the inky darkness* BLACK, jet-black, pitch-black; sable, ebony, dark, raven; *literary* Stygian. **2** *inky fingers* INK-STAINED, stained, blotchy, smudged.

inlaid ▶ **adjective** INSET, set, studded, lined, panelled, laid; ornamented, decorated; mosaic, intarsia, marquetry.

inland ▶ **adjective 1** *inland areas* INTERIOR, inshore, central, internal, upcountry, upriver; landlocked. **2** *inland trade* DOMESTIC, internal, home, local; national, provincial.
– OPPOSITES: coastal, international.
▶ **adverb** *the goods were carried inland* UPCOUNTRY, upriver, inshore, to the interior.

inlet ▶ **noun 1** COVE, bay, *(Nfld)* angle ♣, bight, estuary, fjord, sound, armlet, saltchuck. **2** *a fresh air inlet* VENT, flue, shaft, duct, channel, passage, pipe, pipeline, opening.

inmate ▶ **noun 1** *the inmates of the hospital* PATIENT, in-patient; convalescent; resident, inhabitant, occupant. **2** *the prison's inmates* PRISONER, convict, captive, detainee, internee; *informal* jailbird, con, yardbird, lifer.

inn ▶ **noun** HOTEL, auberge, guest house, lodge, bed and breakfast, B&B, hostel; tavern, bar, hostelry, taproom, pub, public house, beer parlour, watering hole; *dated* alehouse.

innards ▶ **plural noun 1** *the pig's innards* ENTRAILS, internal organs, viscera, intestines, bowels, guts; *informal* insides. **2** *the innards of the engine* (INNER) WORKINGS, mechanism, machinery, components, parts.

innate ▶ **adjective** INBORN, inbred, congenital, inherent, indwelling, natural, intrinsic, instinctive, intuitive, unlearned; hereditary, inherited, in the blood, in the family; inbuilt, deep-rooted, deep-seated, hard-wired, connate.
– OPPOSITES: acquired.

inner ▶ **adjective 1** *the inner gates* INTERNAL, interior, inside, inmost, innermost. **2** *the Premier's inner circle* PRIVILEGED, restricted, exclusive, private, confidential, intimate. **3** *inner feelings* HIDDEN, secret, deep, underlying, unapparent; veiled, unrevealed. **4** *one's inner life* MENTAL, intellectual, psychological, spiritual, emotional.
– OPPOSITES: external, apparent.

innermost ▶ **adjective 1** *the innermost shrine* CENTRAL, middle, internal, interior. **2** *her innermost feelings* DEEPEST, deep-seated, inward, underlying, intimate, private, personal, secret, hidden, concealed, unexpressed, unrevealed, unapparent; true, real, honest.

innkeeper ▶ **noun** LANDLORD, landlady, hotelier,

hotel owner, proprietor, manager, host, hostess, publican.

innocence ▶ noun **1** *he protested his innocence* GUILTLESSNESS, blamelessness, irreproachability. **2** *the innocence of his bride* VIRGINITY, chastity, chasteness, purity; integrity, morality, decency; *dated* honour; *archaic* virtue. **3** *she took advantage of his innocence* NAÏVETÉ, ingenuousness, credulity, inexperience, gullibility, simplicity, unworldliness, guilelessness, greenness.

innocent ▶ adjective **1** *he was entirely innocent* GUILTLESS, blameless, in the clear, unimpeachable, irreproachable, above suspicion, faultless; honourable, honest, upright, law-abiding; *informal* squeaky clean. **2** *innocent fun* HARMLESS, benign, innocuous, safe, inoffensive. **3** *nice innocent girls* VIRTUOUS, pure, moral, decent, righteous, upright, wholesome; demure, modest, chaste, virginal; impeccable, spotless, sinless, unsullied, incorrupt, undefiled; *informal* squeaky clean, lily-white, pure as the driven snow. **4** *she is innocent of guile* FREE FROM, without, lacking (in), clear of, ignorant of, unaware of, untouched by. **5** *at the innocent age of twelve* NAIVE, ingenuous, trusting, credulous, unsuspicious, unwary, unguarded; impressionable, gullible, easily led; inexperienced, unworldly, unsophisticated, green; simple, artless, guileless, wide-eyed; *informal* wet behind the ears, born yesterday.
— OPPOSITES: guilty, sinful, worldly, seasoned.
▶ noun *an innocent in a strange land* INGÉNUE, unworldly person; child, baby; novice; *informal* greenhorn; *literary* babe in arms.

innocuous ▶ adjective **1** *an innocuous fungus* HARMLESS, safe, non-toxic, innocent; edible, eatable. **2** *an innocuous comment* INOFFENSIVE, unobjectionable, unexceptionable, harmless, mild, tame, anodyne.
— OPPOSITES: harmful, offensive.

innovation ▶ noun CHANGE, alteration, revolution, upheaval, transformation, metamorphosis, breakthrough; new measures, new methods, modernization, novelty, newness; creativity, originality, ingenuity, inspiration, inventiveness; *informal* a shake up.

innovative ▶ adjective ORIGINAL, new, novel, fresh, unusual, unprecedented, avant-garde, experimental, inventive, ingenious, creative; advanced, modern, state-of-the-art, pioneering, groundbreaking, revolutionary, radical, newfangled.

innuendo ▶ noun INSINUATION, suggestion, intimation, implication, hint, overtone, undertone, allusion, reference; aspersion, slur.

innumerable ▶ adjective COUNTLESS, numerous, untold, legion, without number, numberless, unnumbered, multitudinous, incalculable, limitless; *informal* umpteen, a slew of, no end of, loads of, stacks of, heaps of, masses of, oodles of, zillions of, gazillions of; *literary* myriad.
— OPPOSITES: few.

inoculation ▶ noun IMMUNIZATION, vaccination, vaccine; injection, booster; *informal* jab, shot, hypo, needle.

inoffensive ▶ adjective HARMLESS, innocuous, unobjectionable, unexceptionable; non-violent, non-aggressive, mild, peaceful, peaceable, gentle; tame, innocent.

inoperable ▶ adjective **1** *an inoperable tumour* UNTREATABLE, incurable, irremediable; malignant; terminal, fatal, deadly, lethal; *archaic* immedicable. **2** *the machine was left inoperable. See* INOPERATIVE *sense 1.* **3** *the agreement is now inoperable* IMPRACTICAL, unworkable, unfeasible, unrealistic, non-viable, impracticable, unsuitable.
— OPPOSITES: curable, workable.

inoperative ▶ adjective **1** *the fan is inoperative* DEFECTIVE, out of order, out of service, down, unserviceable, unusable, inoperable, bust/busted, out of action, shot, broken, faulty, on the blink, on the fritz, out of commission, acting up, kaput. **2** *the contract is inoperative* VOID, null and void, invalid, ineffective, non-viable; cancelled, revoked, terminated; worthless, valueless, unproductive, abortive.
— OPPOSITES: working, valid.

inopportune ▶ adjective INCONVENIENT, unsuitable, inappropriate, malapropos, unfavourable, unfortunate, infelicitous, inexpedient; untimely, ill-timed, unseasonable; awkward, difficult.
— OPPOSITES: convenient.

inordinate ▶ adjective EXCESSIVE, undue, unreasonable, unjustifiable, unwarrantable, disproportionate, unwarranted, unnecessary, needless, uncalled for, gratuitous, exorbitant, extreme; immoderate, extravagant, intemperate; *informal* over the top.
— OPPOSITES: moderate.

input ▶ noun **1** *an error resulted from invalid input* DATA, details, information, material; facts, figures, statistics, particulars, specifics; *informal* info. **2** *I value your input* CONTRIBUTION, offering, idea, opinion.
▶ verb *she input data into the file* FEED IN, put in, load, insert; key in, type in, enter; code, store.

inquest ▶ noun *See* INQUIRY *sense 2.*

inquire ▶ verb **1** *I inquired about part-time training courses* ASK, make inquiries, question someone, request/solicit information. **2** *the commission will inquire into the state of health care* INVESTIGATE, conduct an inquiry, probe, look into; research, examine, explore, delve into, study; *informal* check out.

inquiring *See* INQUISITIVE.

inquiry ▶ noun **1** *an inquiry about our location* QUESTION, query. **2** *an inquiry into alleged security leaks* INVESTIGATION, probe, examination, review, analysis, exploration; inquest, hearing.

inquisition ▶ noun INTERROGATION, questioning, quizzing, cross-examination; investigation, inquiry, inquest, hearing; *informal* grilling; *Law* examination.

inquisitive ▶ adjective CURIOUS, interested, intrigued, prying, spying, eavesdropping, intrusive, busybody, meddlesome, snooping; inquiring, questioning, probing, searching; *informal* nosy, Nosy Parker, snoopy.
— OPPOSITES: uninterested.

inroads ▶ plural noun ADVANCE, progress, forward movement, headway.

insane ▶ adjective **1** *she was declared insane* MENTALLY ILL, mentally disordered, of unsound mind, certifiable; psychotic, schizophrenic; mad, deranged, demented, out of one's mind, non compos mentis, unhinged, unbalanced, unstable, disturbed, crazed; *informal* crazy, (stark) raving mad, not all there, bushed ♣, bonkers, cracked, psycho, batty, cuckoo, loony, loopy, loco, nuts, screwy, bananas, crackers, wacko, off one's rocker, out of one's tree, round the bend, mad as a hatter, buggy, nutso. **2** *insane laughter* MANIACAL, psychotic, crazed, hysterical. **3** *an insane suggestion* FOOLISH, idiotic, stupid, silly, senseless,

Insects

ant	crane fly	horsefly	sandfly
alderfly	cricket	housefly	sawfly
ant-lion	cuckoo bee	hoverfly	sawyer
army ant	cucumber beetle	Japanese beetle	scorpion fly
assassin bug	damselfly	June bug	shadfly
bee	death-watch beetle	katydid	snout beetle
bedbug	deer fly	ladybug	snowflea
beetle	diving beetle	lamellicorn	springtail
blackfly	dragonfly	leafcutter	squash bug
blowfly	dung beetle	lightning bug	stag beetle
bluebottle	elater	locust	stinkbug
botfly	emmet	longicorn	stonefly
bumblebee	firefly	mayfly	syrphid
butterfly	flea	mealy bug	termite
caddis fly	fruit fly	mole cricket	tiger beetle
carpenter ant	furniture beetle	mosquito	tsetse fly
carpenter bee	gall wasp	moth	water beetle
carpet beetle	glow-worm	no-see-um	warble fly
chafer	gnat	paper wasp	wasp
cicada	Goliath beetle	pismire	weevil
click beetle	grasshopper	praying mantis	white ant
cluster fly	Hessian fly	roach	whitefly
cockroach	honeybee	rose chafer	yellow jacket
Colorado beetle	hornet	rove beetle	*See also* BUTTERFLIES & MOTHS.

nonsensical, absurd, ridiculous, ludicrous, lunatic, preposterous, fatuous, inane, asinine, hare-brained, half-baked; impracticable, implausible, irrational, illogical; *informal* crazy, mad, cockeyed, daft.
— OPPOSITES: sensible, calm.

insanity ▶ noun **1** *insanity runs in her family* MENTAL ILLNESS, madness, dementia; lunacy, instability; mania, psychosis; *informal* craziness. **2** *it would be insanity to take this loan* FOLLY, foolishness, madness, idiocy, stupidity, lunacy, silliness; *informal* craziness.

insatiable ▶ adjective UNQUENCHABLE, unappeasable, uncontrollable; voracious, gluttonous, greedy, hungry, ravenous, wolfish; avid, eager, keen; *informal* piggy; *literary* insatiate.

inscribe ▶ verb **1** *his name was inscribed above the door* CARVE, write, engrave, etch, cut, incise; imprint, stamp, impress, mark. **2** *a book inscribed to him by the author* DEDICATE, address, name, sign.

inscription ▶ noun **1** *the inscription on the sarcophagus* ENGRAVING, etching; wording, writing, lettering, legend, epitaph, epigraph. **2** *the book had an inscription* DEDICATION, message; signature, autograph.

inscrutable ▶ adjective MYSTERIOUS, enigmatic, unreadable, inexplicable, unexplainable, incomprehensible, impenetrable, unfathomable, unknowable; opaque, abstruse, arcane, obscure, cryptic.
— OPPOSITES: transparent.

insect ▶ noun. *See table.*

insecure ▶ adjective **1** *an insecure young man* UNCONFIDENT, uncertain, unsure, doubtful, hesitant, self-conscious, unassertive, diffident, unforthcoming, shy, timid, retiring, timorous, inhibited, introverted; anxious, fearful, worried; *informal* mousy. **2** *an insecure railing* UNSTABLE, rickety, rocky, wobbly, shaky, unsteady, precarious; weak, flimsy, unsound, unsafe; *informal* jerry-built.
— OPPOSITES: confident, stable.

insecurity ▶ noun **1** *he hid his insecurity* LACK OF CONFIDENCE, self-doubt, diffidence, unassertiveness,

timidity, uncertainty, nervousness, inhibition; anxiety, worry, unease. **2** *the insecurity of our situation* VULNERABILITY, defencelessness, peril, danger; instability, fragility, frailty, shakiness, unreliability.

insensible ▶ adjective **1** *she was insensible on the floor* UNCONSCIOUS, insensate, senseless, insentient, inert, comatose, knocked out, passed out, blacked out; stunned, numb, numbed; *informal* out (cold), down for the count, out of it, zonked out, dead to the world. **2** *he was insensible to the risks* UNAWARE OF, ignorant of, unconscious of, unmindful of, oblivious to, incognizant of; indifferent to, impervious to, deaf to, blind to, unaffected by; *informal* in the dark about. **3** *he showed insensible disregard* INSENSITIVE, dispassionate, cool, emotionless, unfeeling, unconcerned, detached, indifferent, hardened, tough, callous; *informal* hard-boiled.
— OPPOSITES: conscious, aware, sensitive.

insensitive ▶ adjective **1** *an insensitive bully* HEARTLESS, unfeeling, inconsiderate, thoughtless, thick-skinned; hard-hearted, cold-blooded, uncaring, unconcerned, unsympathetic, unkind, callous, cruel, merciless, pitiless. **2** *he was insensitive to her feelings* IMPERVIOUS TO, oblivious to, unaware of, unresponsive to, indifferent to, unaffected by, unmoved by, untouched by; *informal* in the dark about.
— OPPOSITES: compassionate.

inseparable ▶ adjective **1** *inseparable friends* DEVOTED, bosom, close, fast, firm, good, best, intimate, faithful; *informal* as thick as thieves, joined at the hip. **2** *the laws are inseparable* INDIVISIBLE, indissoluble, inextricable, entangled; (one and) the same.

insert ▶ verb **1** *he inserted a tape in the machine* PUT, place, push, thrust, slide, slip, load, fit, slot, lodge, install; *informal* pop, stick. **2** *she inserted a clause* ENTER, introduce, add, incorporate, interpolate, interpose, interject.
— OPPOSITES: extract, remove.
▶ noun *the newspaper carried an insert* ENCLOSURE,

insertion, supplement; circular, advertisement, pamphlet, leaflet; *informal* ad.

inside ▶ **noun 1** *the inside of a volcano* INTERIOR, inner part; centre, core, middle, heart. **2** (*informal*) *my insides are aching* STOMACH, gut, internal organs, bowels, intestines; *informal* belly, tummy, guts, innards, viscera.
— OPPOSITES: exterior.

▶ **adjective 1** *his inside pocket* INNER, interior, internal, innermost. **2** *inside information* CONFIDENTIAL, classified, restricted, privileged, private, secret, exclusive; *informal* hush-hush.
— OPPOSITES: outer, public.

▶ **adverb 1** *she ushered me inside* INDOORS, within, in. **2** *how do you feel inside?* INWARDLY, within, secretly, privately, deep down, at heart, emotionally, intuitively, instinctively. **3** (*informal*) *if I get caught again I'll be back inside* IN PRISON, in jail, in custody; locked up, imprisoned, incarcerated; *informal* behind bars, doing time.

insidious ▶ **adjective** STEALTHY, subtle, surreptitious, cunning, crafty, treacherous, artful, sly, wily, shifty, underhanded, indirect; *informal* sneaky.

insight ▶ **noun 1** *your insight has been invaluable* INTUITION, discernment, perception, awareness, understanding, comprehension, apprehension, appreciation, penetration, acumen, perspicacity, judgment, acuity; vision, wisdom, prescience; *informal* savvy. **2** *an insight into the government* UNDERSTANDING OF, appreciation of, revelation about; introduction to; *informal* eye-opener.

insightful ▶ **adjective** *he gives an insightful analysis of the text* INTUITIVE, perceptive, discerning, penetrating, penetrative, astute, percipient, perspicacious, sagacious, wise, judicious, shrewd, sharp, sharp-witted, razor-sharp, keen, incisive, acute, imaginative, appreciative, intelligent, thoughtful, sensitive, deep, profound; visionary, far-sighted, prescient; *informal* savvy.

insignia ▶ **noun** BADGE, crest, emblem, symbol, sign, device, mark, seal, logo, colours.

insignificant ▶ **adjective** UNIMPORTANT, trivial, trifling, negligible, inconsequential, of no account, inconsiderable; nugatory, paltry, petty, insubstantial, frivolous, pointless, worthless, meaningless, irrelevant, immaterial, peripheral; *informal* piddling.

insincere ▶ **adjective** FALSE, fake, hollow, artificial, feigned, pretended, put-on, inauthentic; disingenuous, hypocritical, cynical, deceitful, deceptive, duplicitous, double-dealing, two-faced, lying, untruthful, mendacious; *informal* phony, pretend.

insinuate ▶ **verb** *he insinuated that she lied* IMPLY, suggest, hint, intimate, indicate, let it be known, give someone to understand; *informal* make out.
■ **insinuate oneself into** WORM ONE'S WAY INTO, ingratiate oneself with, curry favour with; foist oneself on, introduce oneself into, edge one's way into, insert oneself into; infiltrate, invade, sneak into, manoeuvre oneself into, intrude on, impinge on; *informal* muscle in on.

insinuation ▶ **noun** IMPLICATION, inference, suggestion, hint, intimation, connotation, innuendo, reference, allusion, indication, undertone, overtone; aspersion, slur, allegation.

insipid ▶ **adjective 1** *insipid coffee* TASTELESS,

flavourless, bland, weak, wishy-washy; unappetizing, unpalatable. **2** *insipid pictures* UNIMAGINATIVE, uninspired, uninspiring, characterless, flat, uninteresting, lacklustre, dull, drab, boring, dry, humdrum, ho-hum, tedious, run-of-the-mill, commonplace, pedestrian, trite, tired, hackneyed, stale, lame, wishy-washy, colourless, anemic, lifeless.
— OPPOSITES: tasty, interesting.

insist ▶ **verb 1** *she insisted that they pay up* DEMAND, command, require, dictate; urge, exhort. **2** *he insisted that he knew nothing* MAINTAIN, assert, hold, contend, argue, protest, claim, vow, swear, declare, stress, repeat, reiterate; *formal* aver.
■ **insist on** PERSIST IN, be intent on, be set on, be determined to, stand firm about, stand one's ground about, be resolute about, be emphatic about, be adamant about, not take no for an answer about; *informal* stick to one's guns about.

insistent ▶ **adjective 1** *Tony's insistent questioning* PERSISTENT, determined, adamant, importunate, tenacious, unyielding, dogged, unrelenting, tireless, inexorable; demanding, pushy, forceful, urgent; clamorous, vociferous; emphatic, firm, assertive. **2** *the insistent rattle of the fan* INCESSANT, constant, unremitting, repetitive; obtrusive, intrusive, loud.

insolent ▶ **adjective** IMPERTINENT, impudent, cheeky, ill-mannered, bad mannered, unmannerly, rude, impolite, uncivil, discourteous, disrespectful, insubordinate, contemptuous; audacious, bold, cocky, brazen; insulting, abusive; *informal* fresh, lippy, saucy, pert, sassy, smart-alecky; *archaic* contumelious.
— OPPOSITES: polite.

insoluble ▶ **adjective 1** *some problems are insoluble* UNSOLVABLE, unanswerable, unresolvable; unfathomable, impenetrable, unexplainable, inscrutable, inexplicable. **2** *these minerals are insoluble in water* INDISSOLUBLE.

insolvency ▶ **noun** *See* BANKRUPTCY.

insolvent ▶ **adjective** BANKRUPT, ruined, wiped out, in receivership; penniless, poor, impoverished, impecunious, destitute, without a penny (to one's name), in debt, in arrears; *informal* bust, (flat) broke, belly up, in the red, hard up, strapped (for cash), cleaned out; *formal* penurious.

insomnia ▶ **noun** SLEEPLESSNESS, wakefulness, restlessness.

insouciance ▶ **noun** NONCHALANCE, unconcern, indifference, heedlessness, calm, equanimity, composure, ease, airiness; *informal* cool.
— OPPOSITES: anxiety.

insouciant ▶ **adjective** NONCHALANT, untroubled, unworried, unruffled, unconcerned, indifferent, blasé, heedless, careless; relaxed, calm, equable, serene, composed, easy, easygoing, carefree, free and easy, happy-go-lucky, light-hearted, airy, blithe, mellow; *informal* cool, laid-back, slap-happy.

inspect ▶ **verb** EXAMINE, check, scrutinize, investigate, vet, test, monitor, survey, study, look over, peruse, scan, explore, probe; assess, appraise, review, audit; *informal* check out, give something a/the once-over.

inspection ▶ **noun** EXAMINATION, checkup, survey, scrutiny, probe, exploration, observation, investigation; assessment, appraisal, review, evaluation; *informal* once-over, going-over, look-see.

inspector ▶ **noun** EXAMINER, checker, scrutineer, investigator, surveyor, assessor, appraiser, reviewer, analyst; observer; overseer, supervisor, monitor, watchdog, ombudsman; auditor.

inspiration ▶ noun **1** *her work is a real inspiration to others* GUIDING LIGHT, example, model, muse, motivation, encouragement, influence, spur, stimulus, lift, boost, incentive, impulse, catalyst. **2** *his work lacks inspiration* CREATIVITY, inventiveness, innovation, ingenuity, genius, imagination, originality; artistry, insight, vision; finesse, flair. **3** *she had a sudden inspiration* BRIGHT IDEA, revelation, flash; *informal* brainwave, brainstorm, eureka moment.

inspire ▶ verb **1** *the landscape inspired him to write* STIMULATE, motivate, encourage, influence, rouse, move, stir, energize, galvanize, incite; animate, fire, excite, spark, inspirit, incentivize, affect. **2** *the film inspired a musical* GIVE RISE TO, lead to, bring about, cause, prompt, spawn, engender; *literary* beget. **3** *Charles inspired awe in her* AROUSE, awaken, prompt, induce, ignite, trigger, kindle, produce, bring out; *literary* enkindle.

inspired ▶ adjective OUTSTANDING, wonderful, marvellous, excellent, magnificent, fine, exceptional, first-class, first-rate, virtuoso, supreme, superlative, brilliant; innovative, ingenious, imaginative, original; *informal* tremendous, superb, super, ace, wicked, awesome, out of this world.
− OPPOSITES: poor.

inspiring ▶ adjective INSPIRATIONAL, encouraging, heartening, uplifting, stirring, rousing, stimulating, electrifying; moving, affecting, impassioned, influential.

instability ▶ noun **1** *the instability of political life* UNRELIABILITY, uncertainty, unpredictability, insecurity, riskiness; impermanence, inconstancy, changeability, variability, fluctuation, mutability, transience. **2** *emotional instability* VOLATILITY, unpredictability, variability, capriciousness, flightiness, fickleness, changeability, vacillation. **3** *the instability of the foundations* UNSTEADINESS, unsoundness, shakiness, frailty, fragility, weakness.
− OPPOSITES: steadiness.

install ▶ verb **1** *a photocopier was installed in the office* PUT, position, place, locate, situate, station, site, lodge; insert. **2** *she was installed in the office of chancellor* SWEAR IN, induct, instate, inaugurate, invest; appoint; ordain, consecrate, anoint; enthrone, crown. **3** *she installed herself behind the table* ENSCONCE, establish, position, settle, seat, lodge, plant; sit (down); *informal* plonk, park, take a seat. **4** *she installed new software* LOAD, store.
− OPPOSITES: remove.

instalment ▶ noun **1** *I pay by monthly instalments* PART PAYMENT; deferred payment, premium; *informal* on layaway. **2** *a story published in instalments* PART, portion, section, segment, bit; chapter, episode, volume, issue.

instance ▶ noun *an instance of racism* EXAMPLE, exemplar, illustration, occurrence, case; illustration.
▶ verb *they instanced the previous case as an example* CITE, quote, refer to, mention, allude to, give; specify, name, identify, draw attention to, put forward, offer, advance.
■ **in the first instance** *See* IN THE FIRST PLACE *at* PLACE.

instant ▶ adjective **1** *instant access to your money* IMMEDIATE, instantaneous, on-the-spot, prompt, swift, speedy, rapid, quick, express, lightning; sudden, precipitate, abrupt; *informal* snappy, PDQ (pretty damn quick). **2** *instant meals* PRE-PREPARED, pre-cooked,

ready-made, ready-mixed, heat-and-serve, fast; microwaveable.
− OPPOSITES: delayed.
▶ noun **1** *come here this instant!* MOMENT, time, minute, second; juncture, point. **2** *it all happened in an instant* MOMENT, minute, trice, (split) second, wink/blink/ twinkling of an eye, eyeblink, flash, no time (at all), heartbeat; *informal* sec, jiffy, snap.

instantaneous ▶ adjective IMMEDIATE, instant, on-the-spot, prompt, swift, speedy, rapid, quick, express, lightning; sudden, hurried, precipitate; *informal* snappy, PDQ (pretty damn quick).
− OPPOSITES: delayed.

instantly ▶ adverb IMMEDIATELY, at once, straight away, right away, instantaneously; suddenly, abruptly, all of a sudden; forthwith, then and there, here and now, this/that minute, this/that instant; quickly, rapidly, speedily, promptly; in an instant, in a moment, in a (split) second, in a trice, in/like a flash, like a shot, in the twinkling of an eye, in no time (at all), before you know it; *informal* in a jiffy, pronto, like (greased) lightning, stat, on the double, tout de suite.

instead ▶ adverb *let's travel by bus instead* AS AN ALTERNATIVE, in lieu, alternatively, alternately; rather, by contrast, by choice; on second thoughts, all things being equal, ideally, preferably.
■ **instead of** AS AN ALTERNATIVE TO, as a substitute for, as a replacement for, in place of, in lieu of, in preference to; rather than, as opposed to, as against, as contrasted with, before.

instigate ▶ verb SET IN MOTION, get underway, get off the ground, start, commence, begin, initiate, launch, institute, set up, inaugurate, establish, organize; actuate, generate, bring about; start the ball rolling, kick off; incite, encourage, urge.
− OPPOSITES: halt, dissuade.

instigation ▶ noun PROMPTING, suggestion, recommendation; request, entreaty, demand, insistence; wish, desire, persuasion; *formal* instance.

instigator ▶ noun INITIATOR, prime mover, motivator, architect, designer, planner, inventor, mastermind, originator, author, creator, agent; founder, pioneer, founding father; agitator, fomenter, troublemaker, ringleader, rabble-rouser.

instill ▶ verb **1** *we instill vigilance in our children* INCULCATE, implant, ingrain, impress, imprint, introduce; engender, produce, generate, induce, inspire, promote, foster; drum into, drill into. **2** *he instilled Monet with a love of nature* IMBUE, inspire, infuse, inculcate, inject; indoctrinate; teach.

instinct ▶ noun **1** *some instinct told me to be careful* NATURAL TENDENCY, inherent tendency, inclination, urge, drive, compulsion, need; intuition, feeling, hunch, sixth sense, insight; nose. **2** *his instinct for music* TALENT, gift, ability, aptitude, faculty, skill, flair, feel, genius, knack, bent.

instinctive ▶ adjective INTUITIVE, natural, instinctual, innate, inborn, inherent; unconscious, subconscious, intuitional; automatic, reflex, knee-jerk, mechanical, spontaneous, involuntary, impulsive; *informal* gut, second nature.
− OPPOSITES: learned, voluntary.

institute ▶ noun *See* INSTITUTION sense 1.
▶ verb INITIATE, set in motion, get underway, get off the ground, get going, start, commence, begin, launch; set up, inaugurate, found, establish, organize,

Musical Instruments

Stringed

acoustic guitar
aeolian harp
balalaika
bandura
banjo
bass guitar
bass viol
bouzouki
cello
Celtic harp
cimbalom
cittern
classical guitar
contrabass
dobro*
double bass
dulcimer
fiddle
gittern
guitar
harp
Hawaiian guitar
hurdy-gurdy
kora
koto
electric guitar
lute
lyre

mandolin
pedal steel guitar
rebec
samisen
sarangi
sarod
sitar
steel-string guitar
string bass
tamboura
theorbo
trigon
twelve-string guitar
ukulele
veena
viol
viola
viola d'amore
viola da braccio
viola da gamba
violin
violoncello
Welsh harp
zither

Wind

alto saxophone
bass clarinet
basset horn

bassoon
clarinet
cor anglais
didgeridoo
fife
flute
harmonica
kazoo
oboe
ocarina
pan pipes
pennywhistle
piccolo
recorder
soprano saxophone
tenor saxophone
tin whistle

Keyboard

baby grand
calliope
carillon
celesta
clavichord
clavier
grand piano
harmonium
harpsichord
melodeon

organ
piano
pianola
pipe organ
player piano
spinet
synthesizer
virginals

Brass

althorn
baritone
bugle
cornet
euphonium
flugelhorn
French horn
helicon
horn
sackbut
saxhorn
slide trombone
sousaphone
trombone
trumpet
tuba

See also the table at
ORCHESTRA

*Proprietary term.

---

generate, bring about; start the ball rolling; *informal* kick off.
– OPPOSITES: end, dismiss.

institution ▶ noun **1** *an academic institution* ESTABLISHMENT, organization, institute, foundation, centre; academy, school, college, university; society, association, body, guild, federation, consortium. **2** *they spent their lives in institutions* (RESIDENTIAL) HOME, hospital, asylum, sanatorium; old folks' home, old age home, retirement home, nursing home, lodge ✤. **3** *the institution of marriage* PRACTICE, custom, convention, tradition, habit; phenomenon; fact; system, policy; idea, notion, concept, principle. **4** *the institution of legal proceedings* INITIATION, instigation, launch, start, commencement, beginning, inauguration, generation, origination.

institutional ▶ adjective **1** *an institutional framework for discussions* ORGANIZED, established, bureaucratic, conventional, procedural, prescribed, set, routine, formal, systematic, systematized, methodical, businesslike, orderly, coherent, structured, regulated. **2** *the rooms are rather institutional* IMPERSONAL, formal, regimented, uniform, unvaried, monotonous; insipid, bland, uninteresting, dull; unappealing, uninviting, unattractive, unwelcoming, dreary, drab, colourless; stark, Spartan, bare, clinical, sterile, austere.

instruct ▶ verb **1** *the union instructed them to strike* ORDER, direct, command, tell, enjoin, require, call on, mandate, charge; *literary* bid. **2** *nobody instructed him in how to operate it* TEACH, school, coach, train, enlighten, inform, educate, tutor, guide, prepare, prime. **3** *the judge instructed the jury to consider all of the facts* INFORM, tell, notify, apprise, advise, brief, prime; *informal* fill someone in, clue someone in.

instruction ▶ noun **1** *do not disobey my instructions* ORDER, command, directive, direction, decree, edict,

injunction, mandate, dictate, commandment, bidding; requirement, stipulation; *informal* marching orders; *literary* behest. **2** *read the instructions* DIRECTIONS, key, rubric, specification, how-tos; handbook, manual, guide, tutorial. **3** *he gave instruction in demolition work* TUITION, teaching, coaching, schooling, education, tutelage; lessons, classes, lectures; training, preparation, grounding, guidance.

instructive ▶ adjective INFORMATIVE, instructional, informational, illuminating, enlightening, explanatory; educational, educative, edifying, didactic, pedagogic, heuristic; improving, moralistic, homiletic; useful, helpful.

instructor ▶ noun TRAINER, coach, teacher, tutor; adviser, counsellor, guide; educator, mentor; *formal* pedagogue.

instrument ▶ noun **1** *a wound made with a sharp instrument* IMPLEMENT, tool, utensil; device, apparatus, contrivance, gadget. **2** *check all the cockpit instruments* MEASURING DEVICE, gauge, meter; indicator, dial, display; avionics. **3** *Tony tuned his instruments* MUSICAL INSTRUMENT. *See table.* **4** *drama can be an instrument of learning* AGENT, agency, cause, channel, medium; means, mechanism, vehicle, organ. **5** *he is a mere instrument* PAWN, puppet, creature, dupe, cog; tool, cat's paw; *informal* stooge.

instrumental ▶ adjective INVOLVED, active, influential, contributory; helpful, useful, of service; significant, important, crucial, critical, essential, pivotal, key; (**be instrumental in**) play a part in, contribute to, be a factor in, have a hand in; add to, help, promote, advance, further; be conducive to, make for, lead to, cause.

insubordinate ▶ adjective DISOBEDIENT, unruly, wayward, errant, badly behaved, disorderly, undisciplined, delinquent, troublesome, rebellious,

defiant, recalcitrant, uncooperative, wilful, intractable, unmanageable, uncontrollable; awkward, difficult, perverse, contrary; disrespectful, cheeky.
– OPPOSITES: obedient.

insubordination ▶ noun DISOBEDIENCE, unruliness, indiscipline, bad behaviour, misbehaviour, misconduct, delinquency, insolence; rebellion, defiance, mutiny, revolt; recalcitrance, wilfulness, awkwardness, perversity; informal acting-up; Law contumacy.

insubstantial ▶ adjective **1** an insubstantial structure FLIMSY, fragile, breakable, weak, frail, slight, unstable, shaky, wobbly, rickety, ramshackle, jerry-built. **2** insubstantial evidence WEAK, flimsy, feeble, poor, inadequate, insufficient, tenuous, insignificant, unconvincing, implausible, unsatisfactory, paltry. **3** insubstantial visions INTANGIBLE, impalpable, untouchable, discarnate, unsubstantial, incorporeal; imaginary, unreal, illusory, spectral, ghostlike, vaporous, immaterial. **4** an insubstantial amount SMALL, negligible, inconsequential, inconsiderable, trifling, measly; informal piddling.
– OPPOSITES: sturdy, sound, tangible.

insufferable ▶ adjective **1** the heat was insufferable INTOLERABLE, unbearable, unendurable, insupportable, unacceptable, oppressive, overwhelming, overpowering; informal too much. **2** his win made him insufferable CONCEITED, arrogant, boastful, cocky, cocksure, full of oneself, self-important, swaggering; vain, puffed up, self-satisfied, self-congratulatory, smug; informal big-headed, too big for one's britches/boots, blowhard; literary vainglorious.
– OPPOSITES: bearable, modest.

insufficient ▶ adjective INADEQUATE, deficient, poor, scant, scanty; not enough, too little, too few, too small; scarce, sparse, in short supply, lacking, wanting; paltry, meagre, niggardly; incomplete, restricted, limited; informal measly, pathetic, piddling.

insular ▶ adjective **1** insular attitudes NARROW-MINDED, small-minded, blinkered, inward-looking, parochial, provincial, small-town, short-sighted, hidebound, set in one's ways, inflexible, rigid, entrenched; illiberal, intolerant, prejudiced, bigoted, biased, partisan, xenophobic; informal redneck. **2** an insular existence ISOLATED, inaccessible, cut-off, segregated, detached, solitary, lonely, hermitic.
– OPPOSITES: broad-minded, cosmopolitan.

insulate ▶ verb **1** pipes must be insulated WRAP, sheathe, cover, coat, encase, enclose, envelop; heatproof, soundproof; pad, cushion. **2** they were insulated from the impact of the war PROTECT, save, shield, shelter, screen, cushion, buffer, cocoon; isolate, segregate, sequester, detach, cut off.

insult ▶ verb he insulted my wife ABUSE, be rude to, slight, disparage, discredit, libel, slander, malign, defame, denigrate, cast aspersions on, call someone names, put someone down; offend, affront, hurt, humiliate, wound; informal badmouth, dis; formal derogate, calumniate; rare asperse.
– OPPOSITES: compliment.
▶ noun he hurled insults at us ABUSIVE REMARK, jibe, affront, slight, barb, slur, indignity; injury, libel, slander, defamation; abuse, disparagement, aspersions; informal dig, crack, put-down, slap in the face, kick in the teeth, cheap shot, low blow.

insulting ▶ adjective ABUSIVE, rude, offensive,

disparaging, belittling, derogatory, deprecatory, disrespectful, uncomplimentary, pejorative; disdainful, derisive, scornful, contemptuous; defamatory, slanderous, libellous, scurrilous, blasphemous; informal bitchy, catty, snide.

insupportable ▶ adjective **1** his arrogance was insupportable INTOLERABLE, insufferable, unbearable, unendurable; oppressive, overwhelming, overpowering; informal too much. **2** this view is insupportable UNJUSTIFIABLE, indefensible, inexcusable, unwarrantable, unreasonable; baseless, groundless, unfounded, unsupported, unsubstantiated, unconfirmed, uncorroborated, invalid, untenable, implausible, weak, flawed, specious, defective.
– OPPOSITES: justified, bearable.

insurance ▶ noun **1** insurance for his new car INDEMNITY, indemnification, assurance, (financial) protection, security, coverage. **2** insurance against a third World War PROTECTION, defence, safeguard, security, hedge, precaution, provision, surety; immunity; guarantee, warranty; informal backstop.

insure ▶ verb PROVIDE INSURANCE FOR, indemnify, cover, assure, protect, underwrite; guarantee, warrant.

insurgent ▶ adjective insurgent forces REBELLIOUS, rebel, revolutionary, mutinous, insurrectionist; renegade, seditious, subversive.
– OPPOSITES: loyal.
▶ noun the troops are fighting insurgents REBEL, revolutionary, revolutionist, mutineer, insurrectionist, agitator, subversive, renegade, incendiary; guerrilla, freedom fighter, anarchist, terrorist.
– OPPOSITES: loyalist.

insurmountable ▶ adjective INSUPERABLE, unconquerable, invincible, unassailable; overwhelming, hopeless, impossible.

insurrection ▶ noun REBELLION, revolt, uprising, mutiny, revolution, insurgence, riot, sedition, subversion; civil disorder, unrest, anarchy; coup (d'état).

intact ▶ adjective WHOLE, entire, complete, unbroken, undamaged, unimpaired, faultless, flawless, unscathed, untouched, unspoiled, unblemished, unmarked, perfect, pristine, inviolate, undefiled, unsullied, virgin, in one piece; sound, solid.
– OPPOSITES: damaged.

intangible ▶ adjective **1** an intangible object IMPALPABLE, untouchable, incorporeal, discarnate, abstract; ethereal, insubstantial, immaterial, airy; ghostly, spectral, unearthly, supernatural. **2** an intangible concept INDEFINABLE, indescribable, inexpressible, nameless; vague, obscure, abstract, unclear, indefinite, undefined, subtle, elusive.

integral ▶ adjective **1** an integral part of human behaviour ESSENTIAL, fundamental, basic, intrinsic, inherent, constitutive, innate, structural; vital, necessary, requisite. **2** the dryer has integral cord storage BUILT-IN, integrated, incorporated, included. **3** an integral approach to learning UNIFIED, integrated, comprehensive, composite, combined, aggregate; complete, whole.
– OPPOSITES: peripheral, fragmented.

integrate ▶ verb COMBINE, amalgamate, merge, unite, fuse, blend, mingle, coalesce, consolidate,

meld, intermingle, mix; incorporate, unify, assimilate, homogenize; desegregate.
– OPPOSITES: separate.

integrated ▶ adjective **1** *an integrated package of services* UNIFIED, united, consolidated, amalgamated, combined, merged, fused, homogeneous, assimilated, cohesive, complete. **2** *an integrated school* DESEGREGATED, non-segregated, unsegregated, mixed, multicultural.

integrity ▶ noun **1** *I never doubted his integrity* HONESTY, probity, rectitude, honour, good character, principle(s), ethics, morals, righteousness, morality, virtue, decency, fairness, scrupulousness, sincerity, truthfulness, trustworthiness. **2** *the integrity of the federation* UNITY, unification, coherence, cohesion, togetherness, solidarity. **3** *the structural integrity of the aircraft* SOUNDNESS, strength, sturdiness, solidity, durability, stability, stoutness, toughness.
– OPPOSITES: dishonesty, division, fragility.

intellect ▶ noun **1** *a film that appeals to the intellect* MIND, brain(s), intelligence, reason, understanding, thought, brainpower, sense, judgment, wisdom, wits; *informal* grey matter, IQ, brain cells, smarts. **2** *one of the finest intellects* THINKER, intellectual, sage; mind, brain.

intellectual ▶ adjective **1** *her intellectual capacity* MENTAL, cerebral, cognitive, psychological; rational, abstract, conceptual, theoretical, analytical, logical; academic. **2** *an intellectual man* INTELLIGENT, clever, academic, educated, well-read, lettered, erudite, cerebral, learned, knowledgeable, literary, bookish, donnish, highbrow, scholarly, studious, enlightened, sophisticated, cultured; *informal* brainy.
– OPPOSITES: physical, stupid.
▶ noun *intellectuals are appalled by television* HIGHBROW, learned person, academic, bookworm, man/woman of letters, bluestocking; thinker, brain, scholar, genius, Einstein, polymath, mastermind; *informal* egghead, brains, brainiac, rocket scientist.
– OPPOSITES: dunce.

intelligence ▶ noun **1** *a man of great intelligence* INTELLECTUAL CAPACITY, mental capacity, intellect, mind, brain(s), IQ, brainpower, judgment, reasoning, understanding, comprehension; acumen, wit, sense, insight, perception, penetration, discernment, smartness, canniness, astuteness, intuition, acuity, cleverness, brilliance, ability; *informal* braininess. **2** *intelligence from our operatives* INFORMATION, facts, details, particulars, data, knowledge, reports, inside story; *informal* info, dope, skinny, lowdown. **3** *intelligence operation* INFORMATION GATHERING, surveillance, observation, reconnaissance, spying, espionage, infiltration, ELINT, Humint; *informal* recon.

intelligent ▶ adjective **1** *an intelligent writer* CLEVER, bright, brilliant, quick-witted, quick on the uptake, smart, canny, astute, intuitive, insightful, perceptive, perspicacious, discerning; knowledgeable; able, gifted, talented; *informal* brainy. **2** *an intelligent being* RATIONAL, higher-order, capable of thought.

intelligentsia ▶ plural noun INTELLECTUALS, intelligent people, academics, scholars, literati, cognoscenti, illuminati, highbrows, thinkers, brains; the intelligent; *informal* eggheads.

intelligible ▶ adjective COMPREHENSIBLE, understandable, accessible, digestible, user-friendly, penetrable, fathomable; lucid, clear, coherent, plain, simple, explicit, precise, unambiguous, self-explanatory; *formal* exoteric.

intemperate ▶ adjective IMMODERATE, excessive, undue, inordinate, extreme, unrestrained, uncontrolled; self-indulgent, overindulgent, extravagant, lavish, prodigal, profligate; imprudent, reckless, wild; dissolute, debauched, wanton, dissipated.
– OPPOSITES: moderate.

intend ▶ verb PLAN, mean, have in mind, have the intention, aim, propose; aspire, hope, expect, be resolved, be determined; want, wish; contemplate, think of, envisage, envision; design, earmark, designate, set aside; *formal* purpose.

intended ▶ adjective *the hit was not intended* DELIBERATE, intentional, calculated, conscious, planned, studied, knowing, wilful, purposeful, done on purpose, premeditated, pre-planned, preconceived.
– OPPOSITES: accidental.
▶ noun *(informal)* *when will we meet your intended?* FIANCÉ(E), betrothed, bride-to-be, wife-to-be, husband-to-be, future wife, future husband, prospective spouse.

intense ▶ adjective **1** *intense heat* EXTREME, great, acute, fierce, severe, high; exceptional, extraordinary; harsh, strong, powerful, potent, overpowering, vigorous; *informal* serious. **2** *a very intense young man* PASSIONATE, impassioned, ardent, fervent, zealous, vehement, fiery, emotional; earnest, eager, animated, spirited, vigorous, energetic, fanatical, committed.
– OPPOSITES: mild, apathetic.

intensify ▶ verb ESCALATE, increase, step up, boost, raise, strengthen, augment, reinforce; pick up, build up, heighten, deepen, extend, expand, amplify, magnify; aggravate, exacerbate, worsen, inflame, compound.
– OPPOSITES: abate.

intensity ▶ noun **1** *the intensity of the sun* STRENGTH, power, potency, force; severity, ferocity, vehemence, fierceness, harshness; magnitude, greatness, acuteness, extremity. **2** *a life full of intensity* PASSION, ardour, fervour, zeal, vehemence, fire, heat, emotion; eagerness, animation, spirit, vigour, strength, energy; fanaticism.

intensive ▶ adjective THOROUGH, thoroughgoing, in-depth, rigorous, exhaustive; all-inclusive, comprehensive, complete, full; vigorous, strenuous; concentrated, condensed, accelerated; detailed, minute, close, meticulous, scrupulous, painstaking, methodical, careful.
– OPPOSITES: cursory.

intent ▶ noun *he tried to figure out his father's intent* AIM, intention, purpose, objective, object, goal, target; design, plan, scheme; wish, desire, ambition, idea, aspiration.
▶ adjective **1** *he was intent on proving his point* BENT, set, determined, insistent, resolved, hell-bent; committed to, obsessive about, fanatical about; determined to, anxious to, impatient to. **2** *an intent expression* ATTENTIVE, absorbed, engrossed, fascinated, enthralled, rapt, riveted; focused, earnest, concentrating, intense, studious, preoccupied; alert, watchful.
■ **to all intents and purposes** IN EFFECT, effectively, in essence, essentially, virtually, practically; more or less, just about, all but, as good as, in all but name, almost, nearly; *informal* pretty much, pretty well; *literary* nigh on.

intention ▶ noun **1** *it is his intention to be leader. See*

INTENT *noun* sense 1. **2** *he managed, without intention, to upset me* INTENT, intentionality, deliberateness, design, calculation, meaning; premeditation, forethought, pre-planning; *Law* malice aforethought.

intentional ▶ adjective DELIBERATE, calculated, conscious, intended, planned, meant, studied, knowing, wilful, purposeful, purposive, done on purpose, premeditated, pre-planned, preconceived; *rare* witting.

intentionally ▶ adverb *she would never intentionally hurt anyone* DELIBERATELY, on purpose, purposely, purposefully, by design, knowingly, wittingly, consciously; premeditatedly, calculatedly, in cold blood, wilfully, wantonly; *Law* with malice aforethought.
– OPPOSITES: accidentally.

intently ▶ adverb ATTENTIVELY, closely, keenly, earnestly, hard, carefully, fixedly, raptly, sharply, steadily.

inter ▶ verb *See* BURY sense 1.

interact ▶ verb COMMUNICATE, interface, connect, co-operate; meet, socialize, mix, be in contact, have dealings, work together.

interactive ▶ adjective TWO-WAY, responsive, able to react/respond; hands-on, direct.

intercede ▶ verb MEDIATE, intermediate, arbitrate, conciliate, negotiate, moderate; intervene, interpose, step in, act; plead, petition, advocate.

intercept ▶ verb STOP, head off, cut off; catch, seize, grab, snatch; obstruct, impede, interrupt, block, check, detain; ambush, challenge, waylay.

intercession ▶ noun MEDIATION, intermediation, arbitration, conciliation, negotiation; intervention, involvement; pleading, petition, entreaty, agency; diplomacy.

interchange ▶ verb SUBSTITUTE, transpose, switch, alternate; exchange, swap, trade; reverse, invert, replace.
▶ noun **1** *the interchange of ideas* EXCHANGE, trade, swap, barter, give and take, traffic, reciprocation, reciprocity; *archaic* truck. **2** *a highway interchange* JUNCTION, intersection, crossing; overpass, exit (ramp), cloverleaf.

interchangeable ▶ adjective SIMILAR, identical, indistinguishable, alike, the same, uniform, twin, undifferentiated; corresponding, commensurate, equivalent, synonymous, comparable, equal; transposable; *informal* much of a muchness.

intercom ▶ noun public address system, PA system, paging system; loudspeaker, squawk box; *proprietary* Enterphone ♣, baby monitor.

interconnected ▶ adjective CONNECTING, connected, interconnecting; joined, linked, fused, intertwined.

intercourse ▶ noun **1** *social intercourse* DEALINGS, relations, relationships, association, connections, contact; interchange, communication, communion, correspondence; negotiations, bargaining, transactions; trade, traffic, commerce; *informal* doings, truck. **2** *she did not consent to intercourse* SEXUAL INTERCOURSE, sex, lovemaking, sexual relations, intimacy, coupling, mating, copulation, penetration; *informal* nookie, whoopee, bonking, horizontal mambo; *technical* coitus, coition; *formal* fornication; *dated* carnal knowledge.

interdict ▶ noun *they breached an interdict* PROHIBITION, ban, bar, veto, proscription, interdiction, embargo, moratorium, injunction.
– OPPOSITES: permission.
▶ verb **1** *they interdicted foreign commerce* PROHIBIT, forbid, ban, bar, veto, proscribe, embargo, disallow, debar, outlaw; stop, suppress; *Law* enjoin. **2** *efforts to interdict the flow of heroin* INTERCEPT, stop, head off, cut off; obstruct, impede, block; detain.
– OPPOSITES: permit.

interest ▶ noun **1** *we listened with interest* ATTENTIVENESS, attention, absorption; heed, regard, notice; curiosity, inquisitiveness; enjoyment, delight, enthusiasm. **2** *places of interest* ATTRACTION, appeal, fascination, charm, beauty, allure. **3** *this will be of interest to those involved* CONCERN, consequence, importance, import, significance, note, relevance, value, weight; *formal* moment. **4** *her interests include reading* HOBBY, pastime, leisure pursuit, recreation, diversion, amusement; passion, enthusiasm; *informal* thing, bag, cup of tea. **5** *a financial interest in the firm* STAKE, share, claim, investment, stock, equity; involvement, concern. **6** *what is your interest in the case?* INVOLVEMENT, partiality, partisanship, preference, loyalty; bias, prejudice. **7** *his attorney guarded his interests* CONCERN, business, affair. **8** *her savings earned interest* DIVIDENDS, profits, returns; a percentage.
– OPPOSITES: boredom.
▶ verb **1** *a topic that interests you* APPEAL TO, be of interest to, attract, intrigue, fascinate; absorb, engross, rivet, grip, captivate; amuse, divert, entertain; arouse one's curiosity, whet one's appetite; *informal* float someone's boat, tickle someone's fancy. **2** *can I interest you in a drink?* persuade to have, tempt to have; sell.
– OPPOSITES: bore.
■ **in someone's best interests** OF BENEFIT TO, to the advantage of; for the sake of, for the benefit of.

interested ▶ adjective **1** *an interested crowd* ATTENTIVE, intent, absorbed, engrossed, fascinated, riveted, gripped, captivated, rapt, agog; intrigued, inquisitive, curious; keen, eager; *informal* all ears, nosy, snoopy. **2** *the government consulted with interested groups* CONCERNED, involved, affected, connected, related. **3** *no interested party can judge the contest* PARTISAN, partial, biased, prejudiced, preferential.

interesting ▶ adjective ABSORBING, engrossing, fascinating, riveting, gripping, compelling, compulsive, captivating, engaging, enthralling; appealing, attractive; amusing, entertaining, stimulating, thought-provoking, diverting, intriguing; *informal* unputdownable.

interfere ▶ verb **1** *don't let emotion interfere with duty* IMPEDE, obstruct, stand in the way of, hinder, inhibit, restrict, constrain, hamper, handicap, cramp, check, block; disturb, disrupt, influence, impinge, affect, confuse. **2** *she tried not to interfere in his life* BUTT INTO, barge into, pry into, intrude into, intervene in, get involved in, encroach on, impinge on; meddle in, tamper with; *informal* poke one's nose into, horn in on, muscle in on, stick one's oar in. **3** *he was accused of interfering with children* (SEXUALLY) ABUSE, sexually assault, indecently assault, molest.

interference ▶ noun **1** *they resent state interference* INTRUSION, intervention, intercession, involvement, trespass, meddling, prying; *informal* butting in. **2** *radio interference* DISRUPTION, disturbance, distortion, static.

interim ▶ noun *in the interim they did more research* MEANTIME, meanwhile, intervening time; interlude, interval.

▶ **adjective** *an interim advisory body* PROVISIONAL, temporary, pro tem, stop-gap, short-term, fill-in, caretaker, acting, transitional, makeshift, improvised, impromptu.
— OPPOSITES: permanent.

interior ▶ **adjective** 1 *the house has interior panelling* INSIDE, inner, internal, intramural. 2 *the interior waterways of B.C.* INLAND, inshore, upcountry, inner, innermost, central. 3 *an interior monologue* INNER, mental, spiritual, psychological; private, personal, intimate, secret.
— OPPOSITES: exterior, outer, foreign.
▶ **noun** 1 *the yacht's interior* INSIDE, inner part/space, depths, recesses, bowels, belly; centre, core, heart. 2 *the interior of the province* CENTRE, heartland, hinterland, backcountry, the bush.
— OPPOSITES: exterior, outside.

interject ▶ **verb** INTERPOSE, introduce, throw in, interpolate, add; interrupt, intervene, cut in, break in, butt in, chime in; *informal* put one's oar in, put in one's two cents.

interlace ▶ **verb** INTERWEAVE, mingle, mesh, entwine, intertwine, twine; intersperse, sprinkle, punctuate.

interlock ▶ **verb** INTERCONNECT, interlink, engage, mesh, intermesh, join, unite, connect, couple.

interloper ▶ **noun** INTRUDER, encroacher, trespasser, invader, infiltrator; uninvited guest; outsider, stranger, alien; *informal* gatecrasher, buttinsky.

interlude ▶ **noun** INTERVAL, intermission, break, recess, pause, respite, rest, breathing space, halt, gap, stop, stoppage, hiatus, lull; *informal* breather, time out.

intermediary ▶ **noun** MEDIATOR, go-between, negotiator, intervenor, intercessor, arbitrator, arbiter, conciliator, peacemaker; middleman, broker.

intermediate ▶ **adjective** IN-BETWEEN, middle, mid, midway, halfway, median, medial, intermediary, intervening, transitional.

interminable ▶ **adjective** (SEEMINGLY) ENDLESS, never-ending, unending, non-stop, everlasting, ceaseless, unceasing, incessant, constant, continual, uninterrupted, sustained; monotonous, tedious, long-winded, overlong, rambling.

intermingle ▶ **verb** MIX, intermix, mingle, blend, fuse, merge, combine, amalgamate, integrate, unite; *literary* commingle.

intermission ▶ **noun** INTERVAL, interlude, halftime, entr'acte, break, recess, pause, rest, respite, breathing space, lull, gap, stop, stoppage, halt, hiatus; cessation, suspension; *informal* breather, time out.

intermittent ▶ **adjective** SPORADIC, irregular, fitful, spasmodic, broken, fragmentary, discontinuous, isolated, random, patchy, scattered; occasional, infrequent, periodic, episodic, on and off; *informal* herky-jerky.
— OPPOSITES: continuous.

intern ▶ **verb** 1 *the refugees were interned in camps* CONFINE, detain, hold (captive), lock up, imprison, incarcerate, impound, jail; *informal* put away. 2 *she began interning with an accounting firm* APPRENTICE, *Law* article ♣.
▶ **noun** *an intern at a local firm* TRAINEE, apprentice, co-op student ♣, probationer, (summer) student, novice, beginner.

internal ▶ **adjective** 1 *the internal structure of the building* INNER, interior, inside, intramural; central.

2 *Canada's internal affairs* DOMESTIC, home, interior, civil, local; national, federal, provincial, state. 3 *an internal battle with herself* MENTAL, psychological, emotional; personal, private, secret, hidden.
— OPPOSITES: external, foreign.

international ▶ **adjective** GLOBAL, worldwide, intercontinental, universal; multinational.
— OPPOSITES: national, local.

Internet ▶ **noun** *available on the Internet* WORLD WIDE WEB, web, WWW, cyberspace, Net, information superhighway, Infobahn.
▶ **adjective** *Internet cafés* CYBER, wired, online, virtual, digital, web, web-based, e-, Net.

interplay ▶ **noun** INTERACTION, interchange, exchange; teamwork, co-operation, reciprocation, reciprocity, give and take.

interpolate ▶ **verb** INSERT, interpose, interject, enter, add, incorporate, inset, put, introduce.

interpose ▶ **verb** 1 *he interposed himself between the girls* INSINUATE, insert, place, put. 2 *I must interpose a note of caution* INTRODUCE, insert, interject, add, put in; *informal* slip in. 3 *they interposed to uphold the truce* INTERVENE, intercede, step in, involve oneself; interfere, intrude, butt in, cut in, meddle; *informal* barge in, horn in, muscle in.

interpret ▶ **verb** 1 *the rabbis interpreted the Jewish laws* EXPLAIN, elucidate, expound, explicate, clarify, illuminate, shed light on. 2 *the remark was interpreted as an invitation* UNDERSTAND, construe, take (to mean), see, regard. 3 *the symbols are difficult to interpret* DECIPHER, decode, unscramble, make intelligible; understand, comprehend, make sense of, figure out; *informal* crack. 4 *he interpreted the role of Hamlet* PERFORM, act, play, render, depict, portray.

interpretation ▶ **noun** 1 *the interpretation of the Bible's teachings* EXPLANATION, elucidation, expounding, exposition, explication, exegesis, clarification. 2 *they argued over interpretation* MEANING, understanding, construal, connotation, explanation, inference. 3 *the interpretation of experimental findings* ANALYSIS, evaluation, review, study, examination. 4 *his interpretation of the sonata* RENDITION, rendering, execution, presentation, performance, portrayal.

interpreter ▶ **noun** 1 *he spoke through an interpreter* TRANSLATOR. 2 *a fine interpreter of this role* PERFORMER, presenter, exponent; singer, player, actor, dancer. 3 *interpreters of Soviet history* ANALYST, evaluator, reviewer, critic. 4 *she worked as an interpreter at the Fort* (TOUR) GUIDE, commentator, tour director, docent, spokesperson.

interrogate ▶ **verb** QUESTION, cross-question, cross-examine, quiz, catechize; interview, examine, debrief, give someone the third degree; *informal* pump, grill.

interrogation ▶ **noun** QUESTIONING, cross-questioning, cross-examination, quizzing; interview, debriefing, inquiry, the third degree; *informal* grilling; *Law* examination.

interrupt ▶ **verb** 1 *she opened her mouth to interrupt* CUT IN (ON), break in (on), barge in (on), intervene (in), put one's oar in, put one's two cents in, interject; *informal* butt in (on), chime in (with). 2 *the band had to interrupt their tour* SUSPEND, adjourn, discontinue, break off, put on hold; stop, halt, cease, end, bring to an end/close; *informal* put on ice, put on the back burner. 3 *the coastal plain is interrupted by large lagoons* BREAK (UP), punctuate; pepper, strew, dot, scatter, sprinkle. **4** *their view was interrupted by houses* OBSTRUCT, impede, block, restrict, hamper.

interruption ▶ **noun 1** *he was not pleased at her interruption* CUTTING IN, barging in, intervention, intrusion; *informal* butting in. **2** *an interruption of the power supply* DISCONTINUATION, breaking off, suspension, disruption, stopping, stoppage, halting, cessation. **3** *an interruption in her career* INTERVAL, interlude, break, pause, gap, hiatus.

intersect ▶ **verb 1** *the lines intersect at right angles* CROSS, criss-cross; *technical* decussate. **2** *the cornfield is intersected by a track* BISECT, divide, cut in two/half, cut across/through, crosscut; cross, traverse.

intersection ▶ **noun 1** *the intersection of two lines* CROSSING, criss-crossing; meeting. **2** *the driver stopped at an intersection* (ROAD) JUNCTION, T-intersection, interchange, crossroads, corner, cloverleaf.

intersperse ▶ **verb 1** *giant poppies were interspersed among the rocks* SCATTER, disperse, spread, strew, dot, sprinkle, pepper. **2** *the beech trees are interspersed with pines* INTERMIX, mix, mingle, diversified, punctuate.

intertwine ▶ **verb** ENTWINE, interweave, interlace, twist, braid, plait, splice, knit, weave, mesh.

interval ▶ **noun 1** *Baldwin made two speeches in the interval* INTERIM, interlude, intervening time/period, meantime, meanwhile. **2** *short intervals between contractions* STRETCH, period, time, spell; break, pause, gap. **3** *intervals of still waters* OPENING, distance, span, space, area.

intervene ▶ **verb 1** *had the war not intervened, they might have married* OCCUR, happen, take place, arise, crop up, come about; *literary* come to pass, befall, betide. **2** *she intervened in the dispute* INTERCEDE, involve oneself, get involved, interpose oneself, step in; mediate, referee; interfere, intrude, meddle, interrupt.

interview ▶ **noun** *all applicants will be called for an interview* MEETING, discussion, conference, examination, interrogation; audience, talk, dialogue, exchange, conversation.
▶ **verb** *we interviewed seventy subjects for the survey* TALK TO, have a discussion/dialogue with; question, interrogate, cross-examine, meet with; poll, canvass, survey, sound out; *informal* grill, pump; *Law* examine.

interviewer ▶ **noun** QUESTIONER, interrogator, examiner, assessor, appraiser; journalist, reporter.

interweave ▶ **verb 1** *the threads are interwoven* INTERTWINE, entwine, interlace, splice, braid, plait; twist together, weave together, wind together; *Nautical* marry. **2** *their fates were interwoven* INTERLINK, link, connect; intermix, mix, merge, blend, interlock, knit/bind together, fuse.

intestinal ▶ **adjective** ENTERIC, gastro-enteric, duodenal, celiac, gastric, ventral, stomach, abdominal.

intestines ▶ **plural noun** GUT, guts, entrails, viscera; *informal* insides, innards.
— RELATED TERMS: enteric.

intimacy ▶ **noun 1** *the sisters re-established their old intimacy* CLOSENESS, togetherness, affinity, rapport, attachment, familiarity, friendliness, friendship, amity, affection, warmth, confidence; *informal* chumminess. **2** *the memory of their intimacy* SEXUAL RELATIONS, (sexual) intercourse, sex, lovemaking, copulation; *technical* coitus.

intimate[1] ▶ **adjective 1** *an intimate friend* CLOSE, bosom, dear, cherished, faithful, fast, firm, familiar; *informal* chummy. **2** *an intimate atmosphere* FRIENDLY,

warm, welcoming, hospitable, relaxed, informal; cozy, comfortable, snug; *informal* comfy. **3** *intimate thoughts* PERSONAL, private, confidential, secret; innermost, inner, inward, unspoken, undisclosed. **4** *an intimate knowledge of her history* DETAILED, thorough, exhaustive, deep, in-depth, profound; direct, immediate, first-hand; *informal* up-close-and-personal. **5** *intimate relations* SEXUAL, carnal, amorous.
— OPPOSITES: distant, formal.
▶ **noun** *his circle of intimates* CLOSE FRIEND, best friend, bosom friend, bosom buddy, confidant, confidante; *informal* chum, pal, crony, mate, buddy.

intimate[2] ▶ **verb 1** *he intimated his decision* ANNOUNCE, state, proclaim, declare, make known, make public, publicize, disclose, reveal, divulge. **2** *her feelings were subtly intimated* IMPLY, suggest, hint at, insinuate, indicate, signal, allude to, refer to, convey.

intimation ▶ **noun** SUGGESTION, hint, indication, sign, signal, inkling, suspicion, impression; clue to, undertone of, whisper of, wind of; communication, notification, notice, warning.

intimidate ▶ **verb** FRIGHTEN, menace, terrify, scare, terrorize, cow, dragoon, subdue; threaten, browbeat, bully, pressure, harass, harry, hassle, hound; *informal* lean on, bulldoze, railroad, bullyrag, strong-arm.

intolerable ▶ **adjective** UNBEARABLE, insufferable, unsupportable, insupportable, unendurable, beyond endurance, too much to bear.
— OPPOSITES: bearable.

intolerant ▶ **adjective 1** *intolerant in religious matters* BIGOTED, narrow-minded, small-minded, parochial, provincial, illiberal, uncompromising; prejudiced, biased, partial, partisan, discriminatory. **2** *foods to which you are intolerant* ALLERGIC, sensitive, hypersensitive.

intonation ▶ **noun 1** *she read with the wrong intonation* INFLECTION, pitch, tone, timbre, cadence, lilt, accent, modulation, speech pattern. **2** *the intonation of hymns* CHANTING, intoning, incantation, recitation, singing.

intoxicate ▶ **verb 1** *one glass of wine intoxicated him* INEBRIATE, make drunk, make intoxicated, befuddle, go to someone's head. **2** *he was intoxicated by cinema* EXHILARATE, thrill, elate, delight, captivate, enthrall, entrance, enrapture, excite, stir, rouse, inspire, fire with enthusiasm, transport; *informal* give someone a buzz, give someone a kick, give someone a thrill, make someone high.

intoxicated ▶ **adjective** DRUNK, inebriated, inebriate, impaired ✦, drunken, tipsy, under the influence; *informal* plastered, smashed, bombed, sloshed, sozzled, hammered, sauced, lubricated, well-oiled, wrecked, juiced, blasted, stinko, blitzed, half-cut, fried, gassed, polluted, pissed, tanked (up), soaked, out of one's head/skull, loaded, trashed, buzzed, befuddled, hopped up, besotted, pickled, pixilated, canned, cockeyed, wasted, blotto, blind drunk, roaring drunk, dead drunk, punch-drunk, ripped, stewed, tight, high, merry, the worse for wear, far gone, pie-eyed, in one's cups, three sheets to the wind; *literary* crapulous.
— OPPOSITES: sober.

intoxicating ▶ **adjective 1** *intoxicating drink* ALCOHOLIC, strong, hard, fortified, potent, stiff, intoxicant; *formal* spirituous. **2** *an intoxicating sense of freedom* HEADY, exhilarating, thrilling, exciting, rousing, stirring, stimulating, invigorating,

electrifying; strong, powerful, potent; *informal* mind-blowing.
— OPPOSITES: non-alcoholic.

intractable ▶ adjective **1** *intractable problems* UNMANAGEABLE, uncontrollable, difficult, awkward, troublesome, demanding, burdensome. **2** *an intractable man* STUBBORN, obstinate, obdurate, inflexible, headstrong, wilful, unbending, unyielding, uncompromising, unaccommodating, uncooperative, difficult, awkward, perverse, contrary, pigheaded, stiff-necked.
— OPPOSITES: manageable, compliant.

intransigent ▶ adjective UNCOMPROMISING, inflexible, unbending, unyielding, diehard, unshakeable, unwavering, resolute, rigid, unaccommodating, uncooperative, stubborn, obstinate, obdurate, pigheaded, single-minded, iron-willed, stiff-necked.
— OPPOSITES: compliant.

intrepid ▶ adjective FEARLESS, unafraid, undaunted, unflinching, unshrinking, bold, daring, gallant, audacious, adventurous, heroic, dynamic, spirited, indomitable; brave, courageous, valiant, valorous, stout-hearted, stalwart, plucky, doughty, manly; *informal* gutsy, spunky, ballsy.
— OPPOSITES: fearful.

intricate ▶ adjective COMPLEX, complicated, convoluted, tangled, entangled, twisted; elaborate, ornate, detailed, baroque, delicate; involuted; bewildering, confusing, perplexing, labyrinthine, Byzantine; *informal* fiddly.

intrigue ▶ verb *her answer intrigued him* INTEREST, be of interest to, fascinate, arouse/pique someone's curiosity/interest, attract.
▶ noun **1** *political intrigues* SECRET PLAN, plotting, plot, conspiracy, collusion, conniving, scheme, scheming, stratagem, machination, trickery, sharp practice, double-dealing, underhandedness, subterfuge; *informal* dirty tricks. **2** *the king's intrigues with his nobles' wives* (LOVE) AFFAIR, affair of the heart, liaison, amour, fling, flirtation, dalliance, tryst; adultery, infidelity, unfaithfulness, indiscretion; *informal* fooling around, playing around, hanky-panky.

intriguing ▶ adjective INTERESTING, fascinating, absorbing, compelling, gripping, riveting, captivating, engaging, enthralling, enchanting, attractive, appealing.

intrinsic ▶ adjective INHERENT, innate, inborn, inbred, congenital, connate, natural; deep-rooted, deep-seated, indelible, ineradicable, ingrained; integral, basic, fundamental, essential; built-in.

introduce ▶ verb **1** *she has introduced a new system* INSTITUTE, initiate, launch, inaugurate, establish, found; bring in, usher in, set in motion, start, begin, commence, get going, get underway, originate, pioneer, kick off. **2** *she introduced new legislation* PROPOSE, put forward, suggest, table, submit, bring down; raise, broach, bring up, mention, air, float. **3** *she introduced Lindsey to the young man* PRESENT (FORMALLY), make known, acquaint with. **4** *introducing nitrogen into canned beer* INSERT, inject, put, force, shoot, feed. **5** *she introduced a note of severity into her voice* INSTILL, infuse, inject, add, insert. **6** *the same presenter introduces the program each week* ANNOUNCE, present, give an introduction to; start off, begin, open.

introduction ▶ noun **1** *the introduction of democratic reforms* INSTITUTION, establishment, initiation, launch, inauguration, foundation; start, commencement,

debut, inception, origination. **2** *an introduction to the king* (FORMAL) PRESENTATION; meeting, audience. **3** *the book's introduction* FOREWORD, preface, preamble, prologue, prelude; opening (statement), beginning; *informal* intro, lead-in, prelims; *formal* proem, prolegomenon. **4** *an introduction to the history of the period* PRIMER, basic explanation/account of; the basics, the rudiments, the fundamentals. **5** *a gentle introduction to the life of the school* INITIATION, induction, inauguration, baptism.
— OPPOSITES: afterword.

introductory ▶ adjective **1** *the introductory chapter* OPENING, initial, starting, initiatory, first; prefatory, preliminary, leadoff. **2** *an introductory course* ELEMENTARY, basic, rudimentary, primary; initiatory, preparatory, entry-level, survey; *informal* 101.
— OPPOSITES: final, advanced.

introspection ▶ noun SELF-ANALYSIS, self-examination, soul-searching, introversion; contemplation, meditation, thoughtfulness, pensiveness, reflection; *informal* navel-gazing; *formal* cogitation.

introspective ▶ adjective INWARD-LOOKING, self-analyzing, introverted, introvert, brooding; contemplative, thoughtful, pensive, meditative, reflective; *informal* navel-gazing.

introverted ▶ adjective SHY, reserved, withdrawn, reticent, diffident, retiring, quiet; introspective, introvert, inward-looking, self-absorbed; pensive, contemplative, thoughtful, meditative, reflective.
— OPPOSITES: extroverted.

intrude ▶ verb ENCROACH, impinge, interfere, trespass, infringe, obtrude, invade, violate, disturb, disrupt, interrupt; meddle, barge (in); *informal* horn in, muscle in, poke one's nose into.

intruder ▶ noun TRESPASSER, interloper, invader, infiltrator; burglar, housebreaker, thief, prowler.

intrusion ▶ noun ENCROACHMENT, invasion, incursion, intervention, infringement, impingement; disturbance, disruption, interruption.

intrusive ▶ adjective INTRUDING, invasive, obtrusive, unwelcome, pushy; meddlesome, prying, impertinent, interfering; *informal* nosy, snoopy.

intuition ▶ noun **1** *he works according to intuition* INSTINCT, intuitiveness; sixth sense, clairvoyance, second sight. **2** *this confirms an intuition I had* HUNCH, feeling (in one's bones), inkling, (sneaking) suspicion, idea, sense, notion, premonition, presentiment; *informal* gut feeling, gut instinct.

intuitive ▶ adjective INSTINCTIVE, instinctual; innate, inborn, inherent, natural, congenital; unconscious, subconscious, involuntary, visceral; *informal* gut.

inundate ▶ verb **1** *a flood inundated the temple* FLOOD, deluge, overrun, swamp, drown, submerge, engulf. **2** *we have been inundated with complaints* OVERWHELM, overrun, overload, bog down, swamp, besiege, snow under, bombard, glut.

inure ▶ verb HARDEN, toughen, season, temper, condition; accustom, habituate, familiarize, acclimatize, adjust, adapt, desensitize.
— OPPOSITES: sensitize.

invade ▶ verb **1** *the army invaded the town* OCCUPY, conquer, capture, seize, take (over), annex, win, gain, secure; march into, storm. **2** *someone had invaded our privacy* INTRUDE ON, violate, encroach on, infringe on, trespass on, obtrude on, disturb, disrupt; *informal* horn in on, muscle in on, barge in on. **3** *every summer,*

tourists invaded the beach OVERRUN, swarm, overwhelm, inundate.
– OPPOSITES: withdraw.

invader ▶ noun ATTACKER, aggressor, raider, marauder; occupier, conqueror; intruder, interloper.

invalid[1] ▶ noun a home for invalids ILL PERSON, sick person, valetudinarian; patient, convalescent, shut-in.
▶ adjective her invalid husband ILL, sick, sickly, ailing, unwell, infirm, in poor health, indisposed; incapacitated, bedridden, housebound, frail, feeble, weak, debilitated.
– OPPOSITES: healthy.

invalid[2] ▶ adjective 1 the law was invalid (LEGALLY) VOID, null and void, unenforceable, not binding, illegitimate, inapplicable. 2 the theory is invalid FALSE, untrue, inaccurate, faulty, fallacious, spurious, unconvincing, unsound, weak, wrong, wide of the mark, off target; untenable, baseless, ill-founded, groundless; informal full of holes.
– OPPOSITES: binding, true.

invalidate ▶ verb 1 the court invalidated the statute RENDER INVALID, void, nullify, annul, negate, cancel, disallow, overturn, overrule; informal nix. 2 this case invalidates the general argument DISPROVE, refute, contradict, rebut, negate, belie, discredit, debunk; weaken, undermine, explode; informal poke holes in; formal confute.

invaluable ▶ adjective INDISPENSABLE, crucial, critical, key, vital, necessary, irreplaceable, all-important; immeasurable, incalculable, inestimable, priceless.
– OPPOSITES: dispensable.

invariably ▶ adverb ALWAYS, on every occasion, at all times, without fail, without exception; everywhere, in all places, in all cases/instances; regularly, consistently, repeatedly, habitually, unfailingly, religiously; constantly, steadily.
– OPPOSITES: sometimes, never.

invasion ▶ noun 1 the invasion of the island OCCUPATION, capture, seizure, annexation, annexing, takeover; storming, incursion, attack, assault. 2 an invasion of tourists INFLUX, inundation, flood, rush, torrent, deluge, avalanche, juggernaut. 3 an invasion of my privacy VIOLATION, infringement, interruption, intrusion, encroachment, disturbance, disruption, breach.
– OPPOSITES: withdrawal.

invective ▶ noun ABUSE, insults, expletives, swear words, swearing, curses, bad/foul language, vituperation; informal trash talk; formal obloquy, contumely.
– OPPOSITES: praise.

inveigh ▶ verb FULMINATE, declaim, protest, rail, rage, remonstrate; denounce, censure, condemn, decry, criticize; disparage, denigrate, run down, abuse, vituperate, vilify, impugn; informal sound off about, blast, dis, slam.
– OPPOSITES: support.

inveigle ▶ verb ENTICE, tempt, lure, seduce, beguile; wheedle, cajole, coax, persuade, talk into; informal sweet-talk, butter up, lead on, soft-soap, con, sucker, snow.

invent ▶ verb 1 Louis Braille invented an alphabet for the blind ORIGINATE, create, design, devise, contrive, develop, innovate; conceive, think up, dream up, come up with, pioneer; coin. 2 they invented the story

for a laugh MAKE UP, fabricate, concoct, hatch, dream up, conjure up; informal cook up.

invention ▶ noun 1 the invention of the telescope ORIGINATION, creation, innovation, devising, development, design. 2 medieval inventions INNOVATION, creation, design, contraption, contrivance, construction, device, gadget; informal brainchild. 3 she played with taste and invention INVENTIVENESS, originality, creativity, imagination, inspiration. 4 the story was a total invention FABRICATION, concoction, (piece of) fiction, story, tale; lie, untruth, falsehood, fib, myth, fantasy, make-believe; informal tall tale, cock-and-bull story.

inventive ▶ adjective CREATIVE, original, innovative, imaginative, ingenious, resourceful; unusual, fresh, novel, new, newfangled; experimental, avant-garde, groundbreaking, revolutionary, unorthodox, unconventional.
– OPPOSITES: unimaginative, hackneyed.

inventor ▶ noun ORIGINATOR, creator, innovator; designer, deviser, developer, maker, producer; author, architect; pioneer, mastermind, father, progenitor.

inventory ▶ noun LIST, listing, catalogue, record, register, checklist, log, archive; stock, supply, store.
▶ verb LIST, catalogue, record, register, log, document.

inverse ▶ adjective inverse snobbery. See REVERSE adjective sense 2.
▶ noun alkalinity is the inverse of acidity. See OPPOSITE noun.

invert ▶ verb TURN UPSIDE DOWN, upend, upturn, turn around/about, turn inside out, turn back to front, transpose, reverse, flip (over).

invest ▶ verb 1 he invested in a soap company PUT MONEY INTO, provide capital for, fund, back, finance, subsidize, bankroll, underwrite; buy into, buy shares in; informal grubstake. 2 they invested $18 million SPEND, expend, put in, venture, speculate, risk; informal lay out. 3 they invested in a new car PURCHASE, buy, procure. 4 the scene was invested with magic IMBUE, infuse, charge, steep, suffuse, permeate, pervade. 5 the powers invested in the bishop VEST IN, confer on, bestow on, grant to, entrust to, put in the hands of.

investigate ▶ verb INQUIRE INTO, look into, go into, probe, explore, scrutinize, conduct an investigation into, make inquiries about; inspect, analyze, study, examine, consider, research; informal check out, suss out, scope out, dig, get to the bottom of.

investigation ▶ noun EXAMINATION, inquiry, Royal Commission, study, inspection, exploration, consideration, analysis, appraisal; research, scrutiny, perusal; probe, review, (background) check, survey.

investigator ▶ noun INSPECTOR, examiner, inquirer, inquisitor, explorer, analyzer; researcher, fact-finder, scrutineer, prober, searcher, auditor; detective.

investiture ▶ noun INAUGURATION, appointment, installation, initiation, swearing in; ordination, consecration, crowning, enthronement.

investment ▶ noun 1 investment in a small publishing house INVESTING, speculation; funding, backing, financing, underwriting; buying shares. 2 it's a good investment VENTURE, speculation, risk, gamble; asset, acquisition, holding, possession; informal grubstake. 3 an investment of $305,000 STAKE, share, money/capital invested. 4 a substantial investment of time CONTRIBUTION, surrender, loss, forfeiture, sacrifice.

investor ▶ noun SHAREHOLDER, unitholder, buyer; backer, financier, venture capitalist.

inveterate ▶ adjective **1** *an inveterate gambler* CONFIRMED, hardened, incorrigible, addicted, habitual, compulsive, obsessive; *informal* pathological, chronic. **2** *an inveterate Liberal* STAUNCH, steadfast, committed, devoted, dedicated, dyed-in-the-wool, out and out, diehard, hard-core. **3** *inveterate corruption* INGRAINED, deep-seated, deep-rooted, entrenched, congenital, ineradicable, incurable.

invidious ▶ adjective **1** *that put her in an invidious position* UNPLEASANT, awkward, difficult; undesirable, unenviable; odious, hateful, detestable. **2** *an invidious comparison* UNFAIR, unjust, iniquitous, unwarranted; deleterious, detrimental, discriminatory.
— OPPOSITES: pleasant, fair.

invigorate ▶ verb REVITALIZE, energize, refresh, revive, vivify, brace, rejuvenate, enliven, liven up, perk up, wake up, animate, galvanize, fortify, stimulate, rouse, exhilarate; *informal* buck up, pep up, breathe new life into.
— OPPOSITES: tire.

invincible ▶ adjective INVULNERABLE, indestructible, unconquerable, unbeatable, indomitable, unassailable; impregnable, inviolable; *informal* bulletproof.
— OPPOSITES: vulnerable.

inviolable ▶ adjective *See* INALIENABLE.

inviolate ▶ adjective UNTOUCHED, undamaged, unhurt, unharmed, unscathed; unspoiled, unflawed, unsullied, unstained, undefiled, unprofaned, perfect, pristine, pure; intact, unbroken, whole, entire, complete.

invisible ▶ adjective UNABLE TO BE SEEN, not visible; undetectable, indiscernible, inconspicuous, imperceptible; unseen, unnoticed, unobserved, hidden, veiled, obscured, out of sight.

invitation ▶ noun **1** *an invitation to dinner* request to attend, call, summons; offer; card, note; *informal* invite. **2** *an open door is an invitation to a thief* ENCOURAGEMENT, provocation, temptation, lure, magnet, bait, enticement, attraction, allure; *informal* come-on.

invite ▶ verb **1** *they invited us to Sunday brunch* ASK, summon, have someone over, request (the pleasure of) someone's company. **2** *we invite your comments* ASK FOR, request, call for, appeal for, solicit, seek, summon. **3** *airing such views invites trouble* CAUSE, induce, provoke, create, generate, engender, foster, encourage, lead to; incite, elicit, bring on oneself, arouse, call forth.

inviting ▶ adjective TEMPTING, enticing, alluring, beguiling; attractive, appealing, pleasant, agreeable, delightful; appetizing, mouth-watering; fascinating, enchanting, entrancing, captivating, intriguing, irresistible, seductive.
— OPPOSITES: repellent.

invoice ▶ noun *an invoice for the goods* BILL, account, statement (of charges), check; *informal* tab; *archaic* reckoning.
▶ verb *we'll invoice you for the damage* BILL, charge, send an invoice/bill to.

invoke ▶ verb **1** *he invoked his statutory rights* CITE, refer to, adduce, instance; resort to, have recourse to, turn to. **2** *I invoked the Madonna* APPEAL TO, pray to, call on, supplicate, entreat, solicit, beg, implore; *literary* beseech. **3** *invoking spirits* SUMMON, call (up), conjure (up).

involuntary ▶ adjective *an involuntary urge* SPONTANEOUS, instinctive, unconscious,

unintentional, uncontrollable; reflex, automatic; *informal* knee-jerk.
— OPPOSITES: deliberate.

involve ▶ verb **1** *the inspection involved a lot of work* REQUIRE, necessitate, demand, call for; entail, mean, imply, presuppose. **2** *I try to involve everyone in key decisions* INCLUDE, count in, bring in, take into account, take note of; incorporate, encompass, touch on, embrace, comprehend, cover.
— OPPOSITES: preclude, exclude.

involved ▶ adjective **1** *social workers involved in the case* ASSOCIATED WITH, connected with, concerned in/with. **2** *he had been involved in drug dealing* IMPLICATED, incriminated, inculpated, embroiled, entangled, caught up, mixed up. **3** *a long and involved story* COMPLICATED, intricate, complex, elaborate, convoluted, impenetrable, unfathomable. **4** *very involved with the organization* ENGROSSED, absorbed, immersed, caught up, preoccupied, busy, engaged, intent.
— OPPOSITES: unconnected, straightforward.

involvement ▶ noun **1** *his involvement in a plot to overthrow the government* PARTICIPATION, action, hand; collaboration, collusion, complicity, implication, incrimination, inculpation; association, connection, attachment, entanglement. **2** *emotional involvement* ATTACHMENT, friendship, intimacy; relationship, relations, bond.

invulnerable ▶ adjective IMPERVIOUS, insusceptible, immune; indestructible, impenetrable, impregnable, unassailable, inviolable, invincible, secure; proof (against); *informal* bulletproof.

inward ▶ adjective **1** *an inward curve* TOWARDS THE INSIDE, going in; concave. **2** *an inward smile* INTERNAL, inner, interior, innermost; private, personal, hidden, secret, veiled, masked, concealed, unexpressed.
— OPPOSITES: outward.
▶ adverb *the door opened inward. See* INWARDS.

inwardly ▶ adverb INSIDE, internally, within, deep down (inside), in one's heart (of hearts); privately, secretly, confidentially; *literary* inly.

inwards ▶ adverb INSIDE, into the interior, inward, within.

iota ▶ noun (THE SLIGHTEST) BIT, speck, scrap, shred, ounce, scintilla, atom, jot, grain, whit, trace, mite; *informal* smidgen, titch; *archaic* scruple.

irascible ▶ adjective IRRITABLE, quick-tempered, short-tempered, hot-tempered, snappish, testy, touchy, tetchy, edgy, crabby, chippy, petulant, waspish, dyspeptic; crusty, grouchy, grumpy, cranky, cantankerous, curmudgeonly, ill-natured, peevish, querulous, fractious; *informal* prickly, snappy.

irate ▶ adjective ANGRY, furious, infuriated, incensed, enraged, fuming, seething, cross, mad, livid; raging, ranting, raving, in a frenzy, beside oneself, outraged, up in arms; indignant, annoyed, irritated, irked, piqued, choleric; *informal* foaming at the mouth, hot under the collar, seeing red, cheesed off, hopping mad, PO'd, fit to be tied; *literary* wrathful; *archaic* wroth.

ire ▶ noun (*literary*) ANGER, rage, fury, wrath, outrage, temper, crossness, spleen; annoyance, exasperation, irritation, displeasure, indignation; *literary* choler.

iridescent ▶ adjective OPALESCENT, nacreous; shimmering, luminous, glittering, sparkling, dazzling, shining, gleaming, glowing, lustrous, scintillating; kaleidoscopic, rainbow, multi-coloured; *literary* glistering, coruscating, effulgent.

irk ▶ **verb** IRRITATE, annoy, gall, pique, nettle, exasperate, try someone's patience; anger, infuriate, madden, incense, get on someone's nerves; antagonize, provoke, ruffle someone's feathers, make someone's hackles rise; rub the wrong way, get someone's goat, get/put someone's back up, make someone's blood boil, peeve, miff, frost, rile, aggravate, needle, get (to), bug, drive mad/crazy, cheese off, tee off, tick off, piss off, PO, rankle, ride, drive up the wall, make someone see red.
– OPPOSITES: please.

irksome ▶ **adjective** IRRITATING, annoying, vexing, vexatious, galling, exasperating, disagreeable; tiresome, wearisome, tedious, trying, troublesome, bothersome, nettlesome, obnoxious, awkward, difficult, boring, uninteresting; infuriating, maddening; *informal* infernal.

iron ▶ **noun** 1 *a ship built of iron* metal, pig iron, cast iron, wrought iron. 2 *they were clapped in irons* MANACLES, shackles, fetters, chains, handcuffs, cuffs.
▶ **adjective** 1 *an iron law of politics* INFLEXIBLE, unbreakable, absolute, unconditional, categorical, incontrovertible, infallible. 2 *an iron will* UNCOMPROMISING, unrelenting, unyielding, unbending, resolute, resolved, determined, firm, rigid, steadfast, unwavering, adamantine, steely.
– OPPOSITES: flexible.
■ **iron out** RESOLVE, straighten out, sort out, smooth out, clear up, settle, put right, solve, remedy, rectify, fix, mend, eliminate, eradicate, erase, get rid of; harmonize, reconcile.

ironic ▶ **adjective** 1 *Edward's tone was ironic* SARCASTIC, sardonic, cynical, mocking, satirical, caustic, wry. 2 *it's ironic that I've ended up writing* PARADOXICAL, incongruous.
– OPPOSITES: sincere.

irony ▶ **noun** 1 *that note of irony in her voice* SARCASM, causticity, cynicism, mockery, satire, sardonicism. 2 *the irony of the situation* PARADOX, incongruity, incongruousness.
– OPPOSITES: sincerity.

irradiate ▶ **verb** 1 *her smile irradiated the room* ILLUMINATE, light (up), cast light upon, brighten, shine on; *literary* illumine, illume. 2 *irradiated with gamma rays* RADIATE, charge, blast, shoot; infuse, permeate, saturate, flood; *informal* zap, nuke.

irrational ▶ **adjective** UNREASONABLE, illogical, groundless, baseless, unfounded, unjustifiable; absurd, ridiculous, ludicrous, preposterous, silly, foolish, senseless.
– OPPOSITES: logical.

irreconcilable ▶ **adjective** 1 *irreconcilable differences* INCOMPATIBLE, at odds, at variance, conflicting, clashing, antagonistic, mutually exclusive, diametrically opposed; disparate, poles apart. 2 *irreconcilable enemies* IMPLACABLE, unappeasable, uncompromising, inflexible; mortal, bitter, deadly, sworn, out-and-out.
– OPPOSITES: compatible.

irrefutable ▶ **adjective** INDISPUTABLE, undeniable, unquestionable, incontrovertible, incontestable, beyond question, beyond doubt, conclusive, definite, definitive, decisive, certain, positive, sure; *informal* sure as shootin'.

irregular ▶ **adjective** 1 *irregular features | an irregular coastline* ASYMMETRICAL, non-uniform, uneven, crooked, misshapen, lopsided, twisted; unusual, peculiar, strange, bizarre; jagged, ragged, serrated, indented. 2 *irregular surfaces* ROUGH, bumpy, uneven, pitted, rutted; lumpy, knobbly, gnarled. 3 *an irregular heartbeat* INCONSISTENT, unsteady, uneven, fitful, patchy, variable, varying, changeable, changing, inconstant, erratic, unstable, unsettled, spasmodic, intermittent, fluctuating; *informal* herky-jerky. 4 *irregular financial dealings* AGAINST THE RULES, out of order, improper, illegitimate, unscrupulous, unethical, unprofessional, unacceptable; *informal* shady. 5 *irregular clothing* FLAWED, damaged, imperfect, discard, reject, throwaway.
– OPPOSITES: straight, smooth.

irregularity ▶ **noun** 1 *the irregularity of the coastline* ASYMMETRY, non-uniformity, unevenness, crookedness, lopsidedness; jaggedness, raggedness, indentation. 2 *the irregularity of the surface* ROUGHNESS, bumpiness, unevenness; lumpiness. 3 *irregularity in the fabric* FLAW, damage, imperfection; blemish, mark, spot, stain. 4 *the irregularity of the bus service* INCONSISTENCY, unsteadiness, unevenness, fitfulness, patchiness, instability, variability, changeableness, fluctuation, unpredictability, unreliability. 5 *financial irregularities* IMPROPRIETY, wrongdoing, misconduct, dishonesty, corruption, immorality; *informal* shadiness, crookedness, dodginess. 6 *staff noted any irregularity in operation* ABNORMALITY, unusualness, strangeness, oddness, singularity, anomaly, deviation, aberration, peculiarity, idiosyncrasy.

irrelevant ▶ **adjective** BESIDE THE POINT, immaterial, not pertinent, not germane, off the subject, unconnected, unrelated, peripheral, extraneous, inapposite, inapplicable; unimportant, inconsequential, insignificant, trivial; *formal* impertinent.

irreligious ▶ **adjective** ATHEISTIC, unbelieving, non-believing, agnostic, heretical, faithless, godless, ungodly, impious, profane, infidel, barbarian, heathen, pagan; secular, humanist.
– OPPOSITES: pious.

irreparable ▶ **adjective** IRREVERSIBLE, irrevocable, irrecoverable, unrepairable, beyond repair, unrectifiable; hopeless.
– OPPOSITES: repairable.

irreplaceable ▶ **adjective** UNIQUE, invaluable, priceless, unrepeatable, one-of-a-kind, incomparable, unparalleled; treasured, prized, cherished.

irrepressible ▶ **adjective** 1 *the desire for freedom is irrepressible* INEXTINGUISHABLE, unquenchable, uncontainable, uncontrollable, indestructible, undying, everlasting. 2 *his irrepressible personality* EBULLIENT, exuberant, buoyant, sunny, breezy, jaunty, light-hearted, high-spirited, vivacious, animated, full of life, lively; *informal* bubbly, bouncy, peppy, chipper, chirpy, full of beans.

irreproachable ▶ **adjective** IMPECCABLE, above/beyond reproach, blameless, faultless, flawless, unblemished, untarnished, spotless, immaculate, exemplary, model, outstanding, exceptional, admirable, perfect; *informal* squeaky clean.
– OPPOSITES: reprehensible.

irresistible ▶ **adjective** 1 *her irresistible smile* TEMPTING, enticing, alluring, inviting, seductive; attractive, desirable, fetching, appealing, delightful, captivating, beguiling, enchanting, charming, magnetic. 2 *an irresistible impulse* UNCONTROLLABLE, overwhelming, overpowering, compelling, compulsive, irrepressible, ungovernable.

irresolute ▸ **adjective** INDECISIVE, hesitant, vacillating, equivocating, dithering, wavering, shilly-shallying; ambivalent, blowing hot and cold, of two minds, hemming and hawing, in a dilemma, in a quandary, torn; doubtful, in doubt, unsure, uncertain, undecided, wishy-washy; *informal* sitting on the fence.
— OPPOSITES: decisive.

irrespective ▸ **adjective** REGARDLESS OF, without regard to/for, notwithstanding, whatever, no matter what, without consideration of.

irresponsible ▸ **adjective** RECKLESS, rash, careless, thoughtless, foolhardy, foolish, impetuous, impulsive, devil-may-care, delinquent, derelict, negligent, hare-brained; unreliable, undependable, untrustworthy, flighty, immature.
— OPPOSITES: sensible.

irreverent ▸ **adjective** DISRESPECTFUL, disdainful, scornful, contemptuous, derisive, disparaging; impertinent, impudent, cheeky, saucy, flippant, rude, discourteous.
— OPPOSITES: respectful.

irreversible ▸ **adjective** IRREPARABLE, beyond repair, irremediable, irrevocable, permanent; unalterable, unchangeable, immutable, carved in stone; *Law* peremptory.

irrevocable ▸ **adjective** IRREVERSIBLE, unalterable, unchangeable, immutable, final, binding, permanent, carved in stone; *Law* peremptory.

irrigate ▸ **verb** WATER, bring water to, soak, flood, inundate.

irritability ▸ **noun** IRASCIBILITY, testiness, touchiness, grumpiness, moodiness, grouchiness, (bad) mood, cantankerousness, curmudgeonliness, bad temper, short temper, ill humour, peevishness, crossness, fractiousness, pettishness, crabbiness, tetchiness, waspishness, prickliness, crankiness, orneriness; *literary* choler.

irritable ▸ **adjective** BAD-TEMPERED, short-tempered, irascible, tetchy, testy, touchy, grumpy, grouchy, moody, cranky, ornery, crotchety, shirty, in a (bad) mood, cantankerous, curmudgeonly, ill-tempered, ill-humoured, peevish, cross, fractious, owly, pettish, crabby, bitchy, chippy, waspish, prickly, splenetic, dyspeptic, choleric, on a short fuse.
— OPPOSITES: good-humoured.

irritant ▸ **noun** See IRRITATION sense 2.

irritate ▸ **verb** ANNOY, vex, make angry, make cross, anger, exasperate, irk, gall, pique, nettle, put out, antagonize, get on someone's nerves, try someone's patience, ruffle someone's feathers, make someone's hackles rise, get in someone's hair; infuriate, madden, provoke, pester, rub the wrong way, aggravate, miff, rile, needle, get to, bug, give someone the gears ✤, frost, get under someone's skin, rattle someone's cage, get/put someone's back up, drive mad/crazy, drive someone around the bend, drive up the wall, tee off, tick off, cheese off, rankle, ride.
— OPPOSITES: soothe.

irritated ▸ **adjective** ANNOYED, cross, angry, vexed, exasperated, irked, piqued, nettled, shirty, put out, fed up, disgruntled, in a bad mood, in a temper, testy, in a huff, huffy, aggrieved; irate, infuriated, incensed; *informal* aggravated, peeved, miffed, mad,

riled, frosted, hot under the collar, cheesed off, teed off, ticked off, PO'd, sore; *archaic* wroth.
— OPPOSITES: good-humoured.

irritating ▸ **adjective** ANNOYING, infuriating, exasperating, maddening, trying, tiresome, vexing, vexatious, obnoxious, irksome, nagging, niggling, galling, grating, aggravating, pestilential.

irritation ▸ **noun 1** *she tried not to show her irritation* ANNOYANCE, exasperation, vexation, indignation, impatience, crossness, displeasure, chagrin, pique; anger, rage, fury, wrath, aggravation; *literary* ire. **2** *I realize my presence is an irritation for you* IRRITANT, annoyance, thorn in someone's side/flesh, bother, trial, torment, plague, inconvenience, nuisance, aggravation, pain (in the neck), headache, nudnik, burr under someone's saddle.
— OPPOSITES: delight.

island ▸ **noun** *she lived on an island* ISLE, islet; atoll; (**islands**) archipelago.
— RELATED TERMS: insular.
▸ **verb** *he was islanded from the problems of real life* ISOLATE, cloister, seclude; separate, detach, cut off.

isolate ▸ **verb 1** *the police isolated the area* CORDON OFF, seal off, close off, fence off. **2** *doctors isolated the patients* separate, set/keep apart, segregate, detach, cut off, shut away, keep in solitude, quarantine, cloister, seclude, sequester. **3** *I have isolated the problem* IDENTIFY, single out, pick out, point out, spot, recognize, distinguish, pinpoint, locate.
— OPPOSITES: integrate.

isolated ▸ **adjective 1** *isolated communities* REMOTE, out of the way, outlying, off the beaten track, secluded, lonely, godforsaken, far-flung, inaccessible, cut-off, incommunicado, in the backwoods, in the back of beyond, in the back concessions ✤, in the boonies/boondocks, in the middle of nowhere, in the sticks, hinterland, (Nfld) outport ✤, jerkwater. **2** *he lived a very isolated existence* SOLITARY, lonely, companionless, friendless; secluded, cloistered, segregated, unsociable, reclusive, hermitic, lonesome. **3** *an isolated incident* UNIQUE, lone, solitary; unusual, uncommon, exceptional, anomalous, abnormal, untypical, atypical, freak; *informal* one-off.
— OPPOSITES: accessible, sociable, common.

issue ▸ **noun 1** *the committee discussed the issue* MATTER (IN QUESTION), question, point (at issue), affair, case, subject, topic; problem, bone of contention, hot potato. **2** *the issue of a special stamp* ISSUING, publication, publishing, printing; circulation, distribution. **3** *the latest issue of our magazine* EDITION, number, copy, instalment, volume, publication. **4** *(Law) she died without issue* OFFSPRING, descendants, heirs, successors, children, progeny, family; *archaic* seed, fruit (of one's loins). **5** *an issue of water* DISCHARGE, emission, release, outflow, outflowing, secretion, emanation, exudation, effluence; *technical* efflux.
▸ **verb 1** *the minister issued a statement* SEND OUT, put out, release, deliver, publish, announce, pronounce, broadcast, communicate, circulate, distribute, disseminate, transmit. **2** *the students were issued with new uniforms* SUPPLY, provide, furnish, arm, equip, fit out, rig out, kit out; *informal* fix up. **3** *a smell of onion issued from the kitchen* EMANATE, emerge, exude, flow (out/forth), pour (out/forth); be emitted. **4** *large profits might issue from the deal* RESULT, follow, ensue, stem, spring, arise, proceed, come forth; be the result of, be

brought on/about by, be produced by.
— OPPOSITES: withdraw.

■ **at issue** IN QUESTION, in dispute, under discussion, under consideration, for debate.

■ **take issue** DISAGREE, be in dispute, be in contention, be at variance, be at odds, argue, quarrel; challenge, dispute, (call into) question.

isthmus ▶ noun LAND BRIDGE, bridge, neck.

itch ▶ noun **1** *I have an itch on my back* tingling, irritation, prickle, prickling, tickle, tickling, itchiness. **2** (*informal*) *the itch to travel* LONGING, yearning, craving, ache, hunger, thirst, keenness, urge, hankering; wish, fancy, desire; *informal* yen.
▶ verb **1** *my scar really itches* tingle, prickle, tickle, be irritated, be itchy. **2** (*informal*) *he itched to help her* LONG, yearn, ache, burn, crave, hanker for/after, hunger, thirst, be eager, be desperate; want, wish, desire, pine, fancy, set one's sights on; *informal* have a yen, be dying.

item ▶ noun **1** *an item of farm equipment* | *the main item in a moose's diet* THING, article, object, artifact, piece, product; element, constituent, component, ingredient. **2** *a news item* REPORT, story, account, article, piece, write-up, bulletin, feature. **3** *I hear they are an item* COUPLE, twosome, partners, lovers; thing.

itemize ▶ verb LIST, catalogue, inventory, record, document, register, detail, specify, identify; enumerate, number.

itinerant ▶ adjective *itinerant traders* TRAVELLING, peripatetic, wandering, roving, roaming, touring, saddlebag ✦, nomadic, gypsy, migrant, vagrant, vagabond, of no fixed address.
▶ noun *an encampment of itinerants* TRAVELLER, wanderer, roamer, rover, nomad, gypsy, migrant, transient, drifter, vagabond, hobo, vagrant, tramp.

itinerary ▶ noun TRAVEL PLAN, schedule, timetable, agenda, program, tour; (planned) route.

Jj

jab ► verb *he jabbed the officer with his finger* POKE, prod, dig, nudge, butt, ram; thrust, stab, push.
► noun **1** *a jab in the ribs* POKE, prod, dig, nudge, butt; thrust, stab, push. **2** *felled by a left jab* PUNCH, blow, hit, whack, smack, cuff. **3** *exchanging verbal jabs* INSULT, cutting remark, barb; *informal* dig, put-down.

jabber ► verb *they jabbered away non-stop* PRATTLE, babble, chatter, twitter, prate, gabble, rattle on/away, blather; *informal* yak, yammer, yap, yabber, yatter, blab, blabber, natter.
► noun *stop your jabber!* PRATTLE, babble, chatter, chattering, twitter, twittering, gabble, blather; *informal* yabbering, yatter, blabber, nattering.

jack ► noun *a phone jack* SOCKET, outlet, plug, connection.
■ **jack something up 1** *they jacked up the car* RAISE, hoist, lift (up), winch up, lever up, hitch up, elevate. **2** (*informal*) *they may need to jack up interest rates* INCREASE, raise, up, mark up; *informal* hike (up), bump up, boost.

Jack and Jill ► noun *we threw a Jack and Jill for them at the Legion* (Ont.) stag and doe ♣ (buck and doe ♣), (West) social ♣; shower, bachelor party, stag.

jacket ► noun See table at COATS.

jackpot ► noun *this week's lottery jackpot* TOP PRIZE, first prize; pool, kitty, pot, gold mine, bonanza.
■ **hit the jackpot** (*informal*) STRIKE IT RICH, strike gold, succeed; *informal* clean up, hit the big time, score.

jaded ► adjective SURFEITED, sated, satiated, glutted; dulled, blunted, deadened, inured; unmoved, blasé, apathetic; weary, wearied.
— OPPOSITES: fresh.

jag ► noun **1** *caught his pants on a jag in the rock* SHARP PROJECTION, point, protrusion, barb, thorn, spur, snag, tooth. **2** *a crying jag* BINGE, spree, bout, indulgence, overindulgence.

jagged ► adjective SPIKY, barbed, ragged, rough, uneven, irregular, broken; jaggy, snaggy; serrated, sawtooth, indented.
— OPPOSITES: smooth.

jail ► noun *he was thrown into jail* PRISON, penitentiary, penal institution, lock-up, detention centre, jailhouse, stockade, correctional facility, reformatory, reform school, remand centre; *informal* clink, slammer, inside, big house, jug, brig, can, pen, hoosegow, cooler, cage, slam, pokey.
► verb *she was jailed for killing her husband* IMPRISON, put in prison, send to prison, incarcerate, lock up, put away, intern, detain, hold (prisoner/captive), put into detention, put behind bars, put inside.
— OPPOSITES: acquit, release.

jailer ► noun PRISON OFFICER, warder, warden, guard, captor; *informal* screw.

jalopy ► noun CLUNKER, beater, lemon, bucket of bolts, wreck, junker, tin Lizzie, rustbucket, flivver.

jam¹ ► verb **1** *he jammed a finger in each ear* STUFF, shove, force, ram, thrust, press, push, stick, squeeze, cram. **2** *hundreds of people jammed into the hall* CROWD, pack, pile, press, squeeze, squish, cram, wedge;

throng, mob, occupy, fill, overcrowd, obstruct, block, congest. **3** *the rudder had jammed* STICK, become stuck, catch, seize (up), become trapped. **4** *dust can jam the mechanism* IMMOBILIZE, paralyze, disable, cripple, put out of action, bring to a standstill; clog. **5** *we were just jamming and his amp blew* IMPROVISE, play (music), extemporize, ad lib.
► noun **1** *a traffic jam* CONGESTION, holdup, bottleneck, gridlock, backup, tie-up, snarl-up, traffic. **2** (*informal*) *we are in a real jam* PREDICAMENT, plight, tricky situation, difficulty, problem, quandary, dilemma, muddle, mess, imbroglio, mare's nest, dire straits; *informal* pickle, stew, fix, hole, scrape, bind, tangle, (tight) spot, (tight) corner, hot/deep water, can of worms.

jam² ► noun *raspberry jam* PRESERVE, conserve, jelly, marmalade, fruit spread, compote, (fruit) butter.

jamboree ► noun RALLY, gathering, convention, conference; festival, fete, fiesta, gala, carnival, celebration; *informal* bash, whoop-up ♣, shindig, shindy, hoedown.

jangle ► verb *keys jangled at his waist* CLANK, clink, jingle, tinkle.
► noun *the jangle of his chains* CLANK, clanking, clink, clinking, jangling, jingle, jingling, tintinnabulation.

janitor ► noun CARETAKER, custodian, cleaner, maintenance man, superintendent.

jar¹ ► noun *a jar of honey* (GLASS) CONTAINER, pot, crock, receptacle, cookie jar, Mason jar, (West) sealer (jar) ♣, gem jar ♣, ginger jar.

jar² ► verb **1** *each step jarred my whole body* JOLT, jerk, shake, shock, concuss, rattle, vibrate. **2** *the play's symbolism jarred with the realism of its setting* CLASH, conflict, contrast, be incompatible, be at variance, be at odds, be inconsistent, be discordant.

jargon ► noun SPECIALIZED LANGUAGE, slang, cant, idiom, argot, patter; *informal* -speak, -ese, -babble, Newspeak, journalese, bureaucratese, technobabble, psychobabble; double-talk, doublespeak; gibberish, gobbledegook, blather.

jarring ► adjective CLASHING, conflicting, contrasting, incompatible, incongruous; discordant, dissonant, inharmonious, harsh, grating, strident, shrill, cacophonous; irritating, disturbing.
— OPPOSITES: harmonious.

jaundiced ► adjective BITTER, resentful, envious, jealous, cynical, soured, disenchanted, disillusioned, disappointed, pessimistic, skeptical, distrustful, suspicious, misanthropic.

jaunt ► noun (PLEASURE) TRIP, outing, excursion, day trip, day out, mini holiday, short break; tour, drive, ride, run; *informal* spin.

jaunty ► adjective CHEERFUL, cheery, happy, merry, jolly, joyful; lively, perky, bright, buoyant, bubbly, bouncy, breezy, in good spirits, exuberant, ebullient; carefree, blithe, airy, light-hearted, nonchalant, insouciant, happy-go-lucky; *informal* bright-eyed and bushy-tailed, chirpy.
— OPPOSITES: depressed, serious.

jaw ▶ noun **1** *a broken jaw* JAWBONE, lower/upper jaw, jowl; *Anatomy* mandible, maxilla. **2** *the whale seized a seal pup in its jaws* MOUTH, maw, muzzle; teeth, fangs; *informal* chops.
— RELATED TERMS: mandibular, maxillary.

jazz ▶ noun *See table.*
■ **jazz something up** (*informal*) ENLIVEN, liven up, brighten up, make more interesting/exciting, add (some) colour to, ginger up, spice up; *informal* perk up, pep up.

Types of Jazz

acid	fusion
Afro-Cuban	gutbucket
avant-garde	harmolodics
barrelhouse	hot
bebop	jive
big-band	mainstream
boogie-woogie	modern
bop	New Orleans
cool	progressive
Dixieland	ragtime
free	swing

jazzy ▶ adjective FUNKY, hip, vibrant, lively, spirited, bold, exciting, flamboyant, showy, gaudy, flashy; bright, colourful, brightly coloured, striking, eye-catching, vivid.
— OPPOSITES: dull.

jealous ▶ adjective **1** *he was jealous of his sister's popularity* ENVIOUS, covetous, desirous; resentful, grudging, begrudging, green (with envy). **2** *a jealous lover* SUSPICIOUS, distrustful, mistrustful, doubting, insecure, anxious; possessive, overprotective. **3** *they are very jealous of their rights* PROTECTIVE, vigilant, watchful, heedful, mindful, careful, solicitous.
— OPPOSITES: proud, trusting.

jealousy ▶ noun **1** *he was consumed with jealousy* ENVY, covetousness; resentment, resentfulness, bitterness, spite; *informal* the green-eyed monster. **2** *the jealousy of his long-suffering wife* SUSPICION, suspiciousness, distrust, mistrust, insecurity, anxiety; possessiveness, overprotectiveness.

jeer ▶ verb *the demonstrators jeered at the police* TAUNT, mock, scoff at, ridicule, sneer at, deride, insult, abuse, heckle, catcall at, boo, whistle at, jibe at, hiss at.
— OPPOSITES: cheer.
▶ noun *the jeers of the crowd* TAUNT, sneer, insult, shout, jibe, boo, hiss, catcall, raspberry, Bronx cheer; derision, teasing, scoffing, abuse, scorn, heckling, catcalling.
— OPPOSITES: applause.

jell ▶ verb **1** *leave the mixture to jell* SET, stiffen, solidify, thicken, harden; cake, congeal, jellify, coagulate, clot. **2** *things started to jell very quickly* TAKE SHAPE, fall into place, come together, take form, work out; crystallize.

jelly ▶ noun PRESERVE, marmalade, jam; aspic, gelatin; *proprietary* Jell-O.

jeopardize ▶ verb THREATEN, endanger, imperil, risk, put at risk, put in danger/jeopardy; hazard, stake; leave vulnerable; compromise, be a danger to, pose a threat to.
— OPPOSITES: safeguard.

jeopardy ▶ noun DANGER, peril; at risk.

jerk ▶ noun **1** *she gave the reins a jerk* YANK, tug, pull, wrench, tweak, twitch. **2** *the elevator stopped with a jerk* JOLT, lurch, bump, start, jar, bang, bounce, shake, shock. **3** (*informal*) *I felt like a complete jerk* BASTARD, scoundrel, slimeball, son of a bitch, SOB, scumbag, scum-bucket, scuzzball, dirtbag, sleazeball, sleazebag; rascal, rogue, scamp, scalawag, ingrate, miscreant, good-for-nothing, nogoodnik, reprobate, cur, villain, beast, rat (fink), louse, swine, dog, skunk, heel, snake (in the grass); sleeveen; *dated* hound, cad; *archaic* blackguard, knave, varlet, whoreson.
▶ verb **1** *she jerked her arm free* YANK, tug, pull, wrench, wrest, drag, pluck, snatch, seize, rip, tear. **2** *the car jerked along* JOLT, lurch, bump, rattle, bounce, shake, jounce.

jerky ▶ adjective CONVULSIVE, spasmodic, fitful, twitchy, shaky; JOLTING, lurching, bumpy, bouncy, jarring.
— OPPOSITES: smooth.

jerry-built ▶ adjective SHODDY, makeshift, badly built, gimcrack, flimsy, insubstantial, rickety, ramshackle, crude, chintzy; inferior, poor-quality, second-rate, third-rate, tinpot, low-grade.
— OPPOSITES: sturdy.

jersey ▶ noun PULLOVER, sweater; *informal* woolly.

jest ▶ verb fool around, fool about, play a practical joke, tease, kid, pull someone's leg, pull/jerk/yank someone's chain, have someone on; fun; joke, quip, gag, tell jokes, crack jokes; *informal* wisecrack.
▶ noun *jests were bandied about freely* JOKE, witticism, funny remark, gag, quip, sally, pun; crack, wisecrack, one-liner.
■ **in jest** IN FUN, as a joke, tongue in cheek, playfully, jokingly, facetiously, frivolously, for a laugh.

jester ▶ noun **1** (*historical*) *a court jester* (COURT) FOOL, court jester, clown. **2** *the class jester* JOKER, clown, comedian, comic, humorist, wag, wit, prankster, jokester, trickster, buffoon; *informal* card, hoot, scream, laugh, wisecracker, barrel of laughs, smartass, smart aleck.

jet¹ ▶ noun **1** *a jet of water* STREAM, spurt, squirt, spray, spout; gush, rush, surge, burst. **2** *an executive jet* JET PLANE, jetliner; aircraft, plane, jumbo jet, jump jet.

jet² ▶ adjective *her glossy jet hair* BLACK, jet-black, pitch-black, ink-black, ebony, raven, sable, sooty.

jettison ▶ verb **1** *six aircraft jettisoned their loads* DUMP, drop, ditch, discharge, throw out, unload, throw overboard. **2** *he jettisoned his unwanted papers* | *the scheme was jettisoned* DISCARD, dispose of, throw away/out, get rid of; reject, scrap, axe, abandon, drop; chuck (out), dump, ditch, trash, junk, deep-six.
— OPPOSITES: retain.

jetty ▶ noun PIER, landing (stage), quay, wharf, dock; breakwater, (*Great Lakes*) breakwall ♣, mole, groyne, dike, dockominium, levee.

jewel ▶ noun **1** *priceless jewels* GEM, gemstone, (precious) stone, brilliant; baguette; *informal* sparkler, rock; *archaic* bijou. *See table at* GEM. **2** *the jewel of his collection* FINEST EXAMPLE/SPECIMEN, showpiece, pride (and joy), cream, crème de la crème, jewel in the crown, masterpiece, nonpareil, glory, prize, boast, pick, ne plus ultra.

jewellery ▶ noun JEWELS, gems, gemstones, precious stones, costume jewellery; *informal* bling. *See table.*

jibe ▶ noun *cruel jibes* SNIDE REMARK, cutting remark, taunt, sneer, jeer, insult, barb; *informal* dig, put-down.
▶ verb **1** *Simon jibed in a sarcastic way* JEER, taunt, mock, scoff, sneer. **2** *their story doesn't quite jibe with the*

Jewellery

armlet	locket
bangle	necklace
beads	necklet
bracelet	nose ring
brooch	pendant
cameo	pin
charm bracelet	ring
choker	signet ring
clip	solitaire
cufflinks	studs
eardrops	tiara
earrings	tie pin
eternity ring	torc
fibula	wristlet
girandole	

evidence AGREE, be in accord, jive, be consistent, square, fit.

jiffy
■ **in a jiffy** (*informal*) (VERY) SOON, in a second, in a minute, in a moment, in a trice, in a flash; in a sec, in a snap, in a jiff, in two shakes (of a lamb's tail), in a wink, in a twinkle, in jig time; shortly, any second, any minute (now), in no time (at all), momentarily; *dated* directly.

jig ▶ verb BOB, jump, spring, skip, hop, prance, bounce, jounce.

jiggle ▶ verb SHAKE, joggle, waggle, wiggle; fidget, wriggle, squirm, quiver, tremble.

jilt ▶ verb LEAVE, walk out on, throw over, finish with, break up with, spurn, chuck, ditch, dump, drop, run out on, give someone the old heave-ho; *literary* forsake.

jingle ▶ noun 1 *the jingle of money in the till* CLINK, chink, tinkle, jangle, ding-a-ling, ring, ding, ping, chime, tintinnabulation. **2** *advertising jingles* SLOGAN, catchphrase; ditty, song, rhyme, tune.
▶ verb CLINK, chink, tinkle, jangle, ring, ding, ping, chime.

jingoism ▶ noun EXTREME PATRIOTISM, chauvinism, extreme nationalism, xenophobia, flag-waving; hawkishness, militarism, belligerence, bellicosity.

jinx ▶ noun *after years of bad luck they finally broke the jinx* CURSE, spell, malediction; the evil eye; black magic, voodoo, bad luck, hex; jinker.
▶ verb *the family is jinxed* CURSE, cast a spell on, put the evil eye on, hex.

jitters ▶ plural noun (*informal*) NERVOUSNESS, nerves, edginess, uneasiness, anxiety, nervousness, tension, agitation, restlessness; stage fright; *informal* butterflies (in one's stomach), the willies, the creeps, collywobbles, the heebie-jeebies, jitteriness, the jim-jams.

jittery ▶ adjective (*informal*) NERVOUS, on edge, edgy, tense, anxious, agitated, ill at ease, uneasy, keyed up, overwrought, jumpy, on tenterhooks, worried, apprehensive, with butterflies in one's stomach, twitchy, uptight, het up, in a tizzy, spooky, squirrelly, antsy.
— OPPOSITES: calm.

job ▶ noun 1 *my job involves a lot of travelling* OCCUPATION, profession, trade, position, career, (line of) work, livelihood, post, situation, appointment, métier, craft; vocation, calling; vacancy, opening; *humorous* McJob, joe job ♣. **2** *this job will take three months* TASK, piece of work, assignment, project; chore, errand; undertaking, venture, operation,

enterprise, business. **3** *it's your job to protect her* RESPONSIBILITY, duty, charge, task; role, function, mission; *informal* department. **4** (*informal*) *a bank job* ROBBERY, theft, holdup, burglary, break-in; *informal* stickup, heist.
— RELATED TERMS: vocational.

jobless ▶ adjective UNEMPLOYED, out-of-work, out of a job, between jobs, redundant, laid off, on the dole, unwaged.
— OPPOSITES: employed.

jock ▶ noun JOCKSTRAP, athletic supporter, cup.

jockey ▶ noun RIDER, horseman, horsewoman, equestrian.
▶ verb MANOEUVRE, ease, edge, work, steer; compete, contend, vie; struggle, fight, scramble, jostle.

jocular ▶ adjective HUMOROUS, funny, witty, comic, comical, amusing, droll, waggish, jokey, hilarious, facetious, tongue-in-cheek, teasing, playful; light-hearted, jovial, cheerful, cheery, merry; *formal* jocose, ludic.
— OPPOSITES: solemn.

jocund ▶ adjective (*formal*). See CHEERFUL sense 1.

jog ▶ verb 1 *he jogged along the road* RUN SLOWLY, jogtrot, dogtrot, trot, lope. **2** *something jogged her memory* STIMULATE, prompt, stir, activate, refresh; prod, jar, nudge.
▶ noun 1 *he set off at a jog* RUN, jogtrot, dogtrot, trot, lope. **2** *a jog in the road* BEND, turn, curve, corner, zigzag, kink, dogleg.

joggle ▶ verb SHAKE, jiggle, jerk, jolt, bounce, bob.

joie de vivre ▶ noun JOYFULNESS, cheerfulness, cheeriness, light-heartedness, happiness, joy, gaiety, high spirits, élan, jollity, joviality, exuberance, ebullience, liveliness, vivacity, verve, effervescence, buoyancy, zest, zestfulness; *informal* pep, zing; *literary* blitheness.
— OPPOSITES: sobriety.

join ▶ verb 1 *we joined a bunch of sticks together* FASTEN, attach, tie, bind, couple, connect, unite, link, yoke, weld, fuse, glue. **2** *the two clubs have joined together* COMBINE, amalgamate, merge, join forces, unify, unite. **3** *we joined them in their venture* TEAM UP WITH, band together with, co-operate with, collaborate with. **4** *she joined the volleyball team* SIGN UP WITH, enlist in, enrol in, enter, become a member of, be part of. **5** *where the Ottawa River joins the St. Lawrence* MEET, reach, abut, touch, adjoin, border on, connect with.

joint ▶ noun 1 *cracks in the joint* JUNCTURE, junction, join, intersection, confluence, nexus, link, linkage, connection; weld, seam; *Anatomy* commissure. **2** *the hip joint* ball-and-socket joint, hinge joint, articulation. **3** (*informal*) *a classy joint* ESTABLISHMENT, restaurant, bar, club, nightclub, place; hole, dump, dive. See also BAR sense 4. **4** (*informal*) *he rolled a joint* REEFER, doob, doobie, roach, jay, blunt, spliff; marijuana cigarette, cannabis cigarette.
▶ adjective *matters of joint interest | a joint effort* COMMON, shared, communal, collective; mutual, co-operative, collaborative, concerted, combined, united, bilateral, multilateral.
— OPPOSITES: separate.

jointly ▶ adverb TOGETHER, in partnership, in co-operation, co-operatively, in conjunction, in combination, mutually.

joke ▶ noun 1 *they were telling jokes* FUNNY STORY, jest, witticism, quip; pun, play on words, gag, wisecrack, crack, one-liner, rib-tickler, knee-slapper, thigh-slapper, punchline, groaner. **2** *playing stupid*

jokes TRICK, practical joke, prank, lark, stunt, hoax, jape; *informal* spoof. **3** (*informal*) *he soon became a joke to us* LAUGHINGSTOCK, object of ridicule, stooge, butt, figure of fun. **4** (*informal*) *the present system is a joke* FARCE, travesty, waste of time.
▸ **verb** TELL JOKES, jest, banter, quip, wisecrack, josh, fool (around), play a trick, play a (practical) joke, tease, hoax, pull someone's leg, skylark, kid, chaff, have someone on, pull someone's chain.

joker ▸ **noun** HUMORIST, comedian, comedienne, comic, wit, clown, card, jokester, jester, wisecracker, wag; prankster, practical joker, hoaxer, trickster.

jolly ▸ **adjective** CHEERFUL, happy, cheery, good-humoured, jovial, merry, sunny, joyful, joyous, light-hearted, in high spirits, bubbly, exuberant, ebullient, gleeful, mirthful, genial, affable, fun-loving; *informal* chipper, chirpy, perky, bright-eyed and bushy-tailed, hail-fellow-well-met; *formal* jocund, jocose; *dated* gay; *literary* blithe.
— OPPOSITES: miserable.
▸ **noun** (**jollies**) *people who get their jollies reading the tabloids* PLEASURE, thrill, enjoyment, excitement, titillation.

jolt ▸ **verb** **1** *the train jolted the passengers to one side* PUSH, thrust, jar, bump, knock, bang; shake, joggle, jog. **2** *the car jolted along* BUMP, bounce, jerk, rattle, lurch, shudder, judder, jounce. **3** *she was jolted out of her reverie* STARTLE, surprise, shock, stun, shake, take aback; astonish, astound, amaze, stagger, stop someone in their tracks; *informal* rock, floor.
▸ **noun** **1** *a series of sickening jolts* BUMP, bounce, shake, jerk, lurch. **2** *he woke up with a jolt* START, jerk, jump. **3** *the sight of the dagger gave him a jolt* FRIGHT, the fright of one's life, shock, scare, surprise, wake-up call.

jostle ▸ **verb** BUMP INTO/AGAINST, knock into/against, bang into, cannon into, plow into, jolt; push, shove, elbow, mob, thrust, barge, force, shoulder, bulldoze; STRUGGLE, vie, jockey, scramble.

jot ▸ **verb** *I've jotted down a few details* WRITE, note, make a note of, take down, put on paper; scribble, scrawl.
▸ **noun** *not a jot of evidence* IOTA, scrap, shred, whit, grain, crumb, ounce, (little) bit, jot or tittle, speck, atom, particle, scintilla, trace, hint; *informal* smidgen, tad.

journal ▸ **noun** **1** *a medical journal* PERIODICAL, magazine, gazette, digest, review, newsletter, bulletin; newspaper, paper, tabloid, broadsheet; daily, weekly, monthly, quarterly. **2** *he keeps a journal* DIARY, daily record, daybook, log, logbook, chronicle.

journalism ▸ **noun** THE PRESS, the fourth estate, REPORTING, news writing, news broadcasting, news coverage, reportage, feature writing, photojournalism, sensationalism, the newspaper business; articles, reports, features, pieces, stories.

journalist ▸ **noun** REPORTER, correspondent, columnist, writer, commentator, reviewer; investigative journalist, photojournalist, newspaperman, newspaperwoman, newsman, newswoman, newshound, newshawk, hack, hackette, stringer, journo.

journey ▸ **noun** *their journey around the world* TRIP, expedition, excursion, tour, trek, voyage, junket, cruise, ride, drive, jaunt; crossing, passage, flight; travels, wandering, globe-trotting; odyssey, pilgrimage; peregrination.
▸ **verb** *they journeyed south* TRAVEL, go, voyage, sail, cruise, fly, hike, trek, ride, drive, make one's way; go on a trip/expedition, tour, rove, roam.

joust ▸ **verb** *knights jousted with lances* TOURNEY; fight, spar, clash; *historical* tilt.
▸ **noun** *a medieval joust* TOURNAMENT, tourney; combat, contest, fight, battle, clash; *historical* tilt.

jovial ▸ **adjective** CHEERFUL, jolly, happy, cheery, good-humoured, convivial, genial, good-natured, friendly, amiable, affable, sociable, outgoing; smiling, merry, sunny, joyful, joyous, high-spirited, exuberant; chipper, chirpy, perky, bright-eyed and bushy-tailed, hail-fellow-well-met; *formal* jocund, jocose; *dated* gay; *literary* blithe.
— OPPOSITES: miserable.

joy ▸ **noun** **1** *whoops of joy* DELIGHT, great pleasure, joyfulness, jubilation, triumph, exultation, rejoicing, happiness, gladness, glee, exhilaration, exuberance, elation, euphoria, bliss, ecstasy, rapture; enjoyment, felicity, joie de vivre, jouissance; *literary* jocundity. **2** *it was a joy to be with her* (SOURCE OF) PLEASURE, delight, treat, thrill.
— OPPOSITES: misery, trial.

joyful ▸ **adjective** **1** *his joyful mood* CHEERFUL, happy, jolly, merry, sunny, joyous, light-hearted, in good spirits, bubbly, exuberant, ebullient, cheery, smiling, mirthful, radiant; jubilant, overjoyed, thrilled, ecstatic, euphoric, blissful, on cloud nine, elated, delighted, gleeful; jovial, genial, good-humoured; *informal* chipper, chirpy, peppy, over the moon, on top of the world, upbeat, gay; *formal* jocund; *literary* blithe. **2** *joyful news* PLEASING, happy, good, cheering, gladdening, welcome, heart-warming. **3** *a joyful occasion* HAPPY, cheerful, merry, jolly, festive, joyous.
— OPPOSITES: sad, distressing.

joyless ▸ **adjective** **1** *a joyless man* GLOOMY, melancholy, morose, lugubrious, glum, sombre, saturnine, sullen, dour, humourless. **2** *a joyless room* DEPRESSING, cheerless, gloomy, dreary, bleak, dispiriting, drab, dismal, desolate, austere, sombre; unwelcoming, uninviting, inhospitable; *literary* drear.
— OPPOSITES: cheerful, welcoming.

joyous ▸ **adjective**. See JOYFUL senses 1, 3.

jubilant ▸ **adjective** OVERJOYED, exultant, triumphant, joyful, rejoicing, exuberant, elated, thrilled, gleeful, euphoric, ecstatic, enraptured, in raptures, walking on air, in seventh heaven, on cloud nine, over the moon, on top of the world, on a high.
— OPPOSITES: despondent.

jubilation ▸ **noun** EXULTATION, joy, joyousness, elation, euphoria, rejoicing, ecstasy, rapture, glee, gleefulness, exuberance.

jubilee ▸ **noun** ANNIVERSARY, commemoration; celebration, festival, jamboree; festivities, revelry.

judge ▸ **noun** **1** *the judge sentenced him to five years* JUSTICE, magistrate, sheriff, jurist. **2** *a panel of judges will select the winner* ADJUDICATOR, arbiter, arbitrator, assessor, evaluator, referee, ombudsman, ombudsperson, appraiser, examiner, moderator, mediator.
▸ **verb** **1** *we judged that it was too late to proceed* FORM THE OPINION, conclude, decide; consider, believe, think, deem, view; deduce, gather, infer, gauge, estimate, guess, surmise, conjecture; regard as, look on as, take to be, rate as, class as; *informal* reckon, figure. **2** *the case was judged by a tribunal* TRY, hear; adjudicate, decide, give a ruling/verdict on. **3** *she was judged innocent of murder* ADJUDGE, pronounce, decree, rule, find. **4** *the competition will be judged by last year's winner* ADJUDICATE, arbitrate, mediate, moderate. **5** *entries were judged by a panel of experts* ASSESS, appraise, evaluate; examine, review.

judgment ▶ noun 1 *his temper could affect his judgment* DISCERNMENT, acumen, shrewdness, astuteness, (common) sense, perception, perspicacity, percipience, acuity, discrimination, reckoning, wisdom, wit, judiciousness, prudence, canniness, sharpness, sharp-wittedness, powers of reasoning, reason, logic; savvy, horse sense, street smarts, gumption. 2 *a court judgment* VERDICT, decision, adjudication, ruling, pronouncement, decree, finding; sentence. 3 *critical judgment* ASSESSMENT, evaluation, appraisal; review, analysis, criticism, critique.
■ **against one's better judgment** RELUCTANTLY, unwillingly, grudgingly.

judgmental ▶ adjective CRITICAL, censorious, condemnatory, disapproving, disparaging, deprecating, negative, overcritical, hypercritical.

judicial ▶ adjective LEGAL, juridical, judicatory; official.

judicious ▶ adjective WISE, sensible, prudent, politic, shrewd, astute, canny, sagacious, commonsensical, sound, well-advised, well judged, discerning, percipient, intelligent, smart; *informal* heads-up.
— OPPOSITES: ill-advised.

jug ▶ noun PITCHER, carafe, flask, flagon, bottle, decanter, ewer, crock, jar, urn; *historical* amphora.

juggle ▶ verb *juggling three part-time jobs* HANDLE, manage, deal with, multi-task.

juice ▶ noun 1 *the juice from two lemons* LIQUID, fluid, sap; extract; nectar. 2 *(informal) he ran out of juice on the last lap* ENERGY, power, stamina, steam.

juicy ▶ adjective 1 *a juicy peach* SUCCULENT, tender, moist; ripe; *archaic* mellow. 2 *(informal) juicy gossip* SENSATIONAL, very interesting, fascinating, lurid; scandalous, racy, risqué, spicy; *informal* hot. 3 *(informal) juicy profits | a juicy role* DESIRABLE, appealing, attractive; *informal* to die for.
— OPPOSITES: dry, dull.

jumble ▶ noun *a jumble of books and toys* UNTIDY HEAP, clutter, muddle, mess, confusion, disarray, tangle, imbroglio; hodgepodge, mishmash, miscellany, motley collection, mixed bag, medley, jambalaya, farrago, gallimaufry.
▶ verb *the photographs are all jumbled up* MIX UP, muddle up, disarrange, disorganize, disorder, put in disarray.

jumbo ▶ adjective *(informal).* See HUGE.

jump ▶ verb 1 *the cat jumped off his lap | Flora began to jump around* LEAP, spring, bound, hop; skip, caper, dance, prance, frolic, cavort. 2 *he jumped the fence* VAULT (OVER), leap over, clear, sail over, hop over, hurdle. 3 *pre-tax profits jumped* RISE, go up, shoot up, soar, surge, climb, increase; *informal* skyrocket. 4 *the noise made her jump* START, jerk, jolt, flinch, recoil; *informal* jump out of one's skin. 5 *Polly jumped at the chance* ACCEPT EAGERLY, leap at, welcome with open arms, seize on, snap up, grab, pounce on. 6 *the place was jumping* ROCK, hop, buzz, be lively, be wild. 7 *two attackers jumped him in the alley* ASSAULT, assail, set upon, mug, attack, pounce on.
▶ noun 1 *a short jump across the ditch* LEAP, spring, vault, bound, hop. 2 *a jump in profits* RISE, leap, increase, upsurge, upswing, upturn; *informal* hike. 3 *I woke up with a jump* START, jerk, involuntary movement, spasm.
■ **jump the gun** *(informal)* ACT PREMATURELY, act too soon, be over-hasty, be precipitate, be rash; *informal* be ahead of oneself.

■ **jump to it** *(informal)* HURRY UP, get a move on, be quick; *informal* get cracking, shake a leg, look lively, look sharp, get the lead out; *dated* make haste.

jump-start ▶ verb *efforts to jump-start the stalled economy* REVITALIZE, stimulate, energize, boost, spark, ignite, fire up.

jumpy ▶ adjective 1 *(informal) he was tired and jumpy* NERVOUS, on edge, edgy, tense, anxious, ill at ease, uneasy, restless, fidgety, keyed up, overwrought, on tenterhooks; *informal* a bundle of nerves, jittery, uptight, het up, in a tizz/tizzy; strung out; spooky, squirrelly, antsy. 2 *jumpy black-and-white footage* JERKY, jolting, lurching, bumpy, jarring; fitful, convulsive.
— OPPOSITES: calm.

junction ▶ noun 1 *the junction between the roof and the wall* JOINT, intersection, join, bond, seam, connection, juncture; *Anatomy* commissure. 2 *the junction of the two rivers* CONFLUENCE, convergence, meeting point, juncture. 3 *turn right at the next junction* INTERSECTION, crossroads, crossing, interchange, T-intersection; turn, turnoff, exit; traffic circle, cloverleaf.

juncture ▶ noun 1 *at this juncture, I am unable to tell you* POINT (IN TIME), time, moment (in time); period, occasion, phase. 2 *the juncture of the pipes.* See JUNCTION sense 1. 3 *the juncture of the rivers.* See JUNCTION sense 2.

jungle ▶ noun 1 *the Amazon jungle* TROPICAL FOREST, (tropical) rainforest. 2 *the jungle of city bureaucracy* COMPLEXITY, confusion, complication, chaos, mess; labyrinth, maze, tangle, web.

junior ▶ adjective 1 *the junior members of the family* YOUNGER, youngest. 2 *a junior position in the firm* LOW-RANKING, lower-ranking, entry-level, subordinate, lesser, lower, minor, secondary.
— OPPOSITES: senior, older.

junk *(informal)* ▶ noun *an attic full of junk* RUBBISH, clutter, odds and ends, bric-a-brac, bits and pieces; garbage, trash, refuse, litter, scrap, waste, debris, detritus, dross; *informal* crap.
▶ verb *time to junk the old pickup* THROW AWAY/OUT, discard, get rid of, dispose of, scrap, toss out, jettison; *informal* chuck, dump, ditch, deep-six, bin, get shut of.

junket ▶ noun *(informal)* excursion, outing, spree, trip, jaunt; celebration, party, jamboree, feast, festivity; *informal* bash, shindy, shindig, bunfight.

junkie ▶ noun 1 *a heroin junkie* ADDICT, abuser; *informal* druggy, stoner, -freak, -head. 2 *a figure skating junkie* FAN, enthusiast, devotee, lover, fanatic, aficionado; freak, nut, buff, bum.

junta ▶ noun FACTION, cabal, clique, camarilla, party, set, ring, gang, league, confederacy.

jurisdiction ▶ noun 1 *an area under French jurisdiction* AUTHORITY, control, power, dominion, rule, administration, command, sway, leadership, sovereignty, hegemony. 2 *foreign jurisdictions* TERRITORY, region, province, district, area, domain, realm.

just ▶ adjective 1 *a just and democratic society* FAIR, fair-minded, equitable, even-handed, impartial, unbiased, objective, neutral, disinterested, unprejudiced, open-minded, non-partisan; honourable, upright, decent, honest, righteous, moral, virtuous, principled. 2 *a just reward* (WELL) DESERVED, (well) earned, merited; rightful, due, fitting, appropriate, suitable; *formal* condign; *archaic* meet. 3 *just criticism* VALID, sound, well-founded, justified, justifiable, warranted, legitimate.
— OPPOSITES: unfair, undeserved.
▶ adverb 1 *I just saw him* A MOMENT/SECOND AGO, a short

time ago, very recently, not long ago. **2** *she's just right for him* EXACTLY, precisely, absolutely, completely, totally, entirely, perfectly, utterly, wholly, thoroughly, in all respects; *informal* to a T, dead. **3** *we just made it* NARROWLY, only just, by a hair's breadth; barely, scarcely, hardly; *informal* by the skin of one's teeth, by a whisker. **4** *she's just a child* ONLY, merely, simply, (nothing) but, no more than. **5** *the colour's just fantastic* REALLY, absolutely, completely, positively, entirely, totally, quite; indeed, truly.

■ **just about** (*informal*) NEARLY, almost, practically, all but, virtually, as good as, more or less, to all intents and purposes; *informal* pretty much; *literary* well-nigh, nigh on.

justice ▶ noun **1** *I appealed to his sense of justice* FAIRNESS, justness, fair play, fair-mindedness, equity, even-handedness, impartiality, objectivity, neutrality, disinterestedness, honesty, righteousness, morals, morality. **2** *they were determined to exact justice* PUNISHMENT, judgment, retribution, compensation, just deserts. **3** *an order made by the justices* JUDGE, magistrate, jurist.

■ **do justice to** consider fairly, be worthy of.

justifiable ▶ adjective VALID, legitimate, warranted, well-founded, justified, just, reasonable; defensible, tenable, supportable, acceptable.
— OPPOSITES: indefensible.

justification ▶ noun GROUNDS, reason, basis, rationale, premise, rationalization, vindication, explanation; defence, argument, apologia, apology, case.

justify ▶ verb **1** *directors must justify the expenditure* GIVE GROUNDS FOR, give reasons for, give a justification for, explain, give an explanation for, account for; defend, answer for, vindicate. **2** *the situation justified further investigation* WARRANT, be good reason for, be a justification for.

justly ▶ adverb **1** *he is justly proud of his achievement* JUSTIFIABLY, with (good) reason, legitimately, rightly, rightfully, deservedly. **2** *they were treated justly* FAIRLY, with fairness, equitably, even-handedly, impartially, without bias, objectively, without prejudice, fairly and squarely.
— OPPOSITES: unjustifiably.

jut ▶ verb STICK OUT, project, protrude, bulge out, overhang.

juvenile ▶ adjective **1** *juvenile offenders* YOUNG, teenage, adolescent, boyish, girlish, junior, pubescent, pre-pubescent, youthful. **2** *juvenile behaviour* CHILDISH, immature, puerile, infantile, babyish; jejune, inexperienced, callow, green, unsophisticated, sophomoric, naive, foolish, silly.
— OPPOSITES: adult, mature.
▶ noun *two juveniles were being sought by police* YOUNG PERSON, youngster, child, teenager, adolescent, youth, boy, girl, minor, junior; *informal* kid, punk.
— OPPOSITES: adult.

juxtapose ▶ verb PLACE SIDE BY SIDE, set side by side, collocate, mix; compare, contrast.

Kk

kaleidoscopic ▶ adjective 1 *kaleidoscopic shapes* MULTICOLOURED, many-coloured, multicolour, many-hued, variegated, parti-coloured, varicoloured, psychedelic, rainbow, polychromatic. 2 *the kaleidoscopic political landscape* EVER-CHANGING, changeable, shifting, fluid, protean, variable, inconstant, fluctuating, unpredictable, impermanent.
— OPPOSITES: monochrome, constant.

kaput (*informal*) ▶ adjective *the TV's kaput* BROKEN, malfunctioning, broken-down, inoperative; *informal* conked out, had the biscuit ✦.
■ **go kaput** BREAK DOWN, go wrong, stop working; *informal* conk out, go belly up.

keel
■ **on an even keel** steady, on track, on course, untroubled.
■ **keel over 1** *the boat keeled over* CAPSIZE, turn turtle, turn upside down, founder; overturn, turn over, flip (over), tip over. **2** *the slightest activity made him keel over* COLLAPSE, faint, pass out, black out, lose consciousness, swoon.

keen ▶ adjective 1 *his publishers were keen to capitalize on his success* EAGER, anxious, intent, impatient, determined, ambitious; *informal* raring, itching, dying. **2** *a keen birdwatcher* ENTHUSIASTIC, avid, eager, ardent, passionate, fervent, impassioned; conscientious, committed, dedicated, zealous. **3** *they are keen on horses | a girl he was keen on* ENTHUSIASTIC, interested, passionate; attracted to, fond of, taken with, smitten with, enamoured of, infatuated with; *informal* struck on, hot on/for, mad about, crazy about, nuts about. **4** *a keen cutting edge* SHARP, sharpened, honed, razor-sharp. **5** *keen eyesight* ACUTE, sharp, discerning, sensitive, perceptive, clear. **6** *a keen mind* ACUTE, penetrating, astute, incisive, sharp, perceptive, piercing, razor-sharp, perspicacious, shrewd, discerning, clever, intelligent, brilliant, bright, smart, wise, canny, percipient, insightful. **7** *a keen wind* COLD, icy, freezing, harsh, raw, bitter; penetrating, piercing, biting. **8** *a keen sense of duty* INTENSE, acute, fierce, passionate, burning, fervent, ardent, strong, powerful.
— OPPOSITES: reluctant, unenthusiastic.

keener (*Cdn*) ▶ noun eager beaver, geek, zealot, a keen/enthusiastic/eager person, joiner.

keep ▶ verb 1 *you should keep all the old forms* RETAIN (POSSESSION OF), hold on to, keep hold of, not part with; save, store, conserve, put aside, set aside; *informal* hang on to, stash away. **2** *I tried to keep calm* REMAIN, continue to be, stay, carry on being, persist in being. **3** *he keeps talking about the murder* PERSIST IN, keep on, carry on, continue, do something constantly. **4** *I won't keep you long* DETAIN, keep waiting, delay, hold up, retard, slow down. **5** *most people kept the rules | he had to keep his promise* COMPLY WITH, obey, observe, conform to, abide by, adhere to, stick to, hew to, heed, follow; fulfill, carry out, act on, make good, honour, keep to, stand by. **6** *keeping the old traditions* PRESERVE, keep alive/up, keep going, carry on, perpetuate, maintain, uphold, sustain. **7** *that's where we keep the linen* STORE, house, stow, put (away), place, deposit. **8** *she keeps rabbits* BREED, rear, raise, farm; own, have as a pet. **9** *God keep you* LOOK AFTER, care for, take care of, mind, watch over; protect, keep safe, preserve, defend, guard.
— OPPOSITES: throw away, break, abandon.
▶ noun *money to pay for his keep* MAINTENANCE, upkeep, sustenance, board (and lodging), food, livelihood.
■ **keep at** PERSEVERE WITH/IN/AT, persist in/with, keep going with, carry on with, press on with, work away at, continue with; *informal* stick at, plug away at, hammer away at.
■ **keep something back 1** *she kept back some of the money* (KEEP IN) RESERVE, put by/aside, set aside; retain, hold back, hold on to, not part with; *informal* stash away. **2** *she kept back the details* WITHHOLD, keep secret, keep hidden, conceal, suppress, keep quiet about. **3** *she could hardly keep back her tears* SUPPRESS, stifle, choke back, fight back, hold back/in, repress, keep in check, contain, smother, swallow, bite back.
■ **keep from** REFRAIN FROM, stop oneself from, restrain oneself from, prevent oneself from, forbear from, avoid.
■ **keep someone from something 1** *he could hardly keep himself from laughing* PREVENT, stop, restrain, hold back. **2** *keep them from harm* PRESERVE, protect, keep safe, guard, shield, shelter, safeguard, defend.
■ **keep something from someone** KEEP SECRET, keep hidden, hide, conceal, withhold.
■ **keep off 1** *keep off private land* STAY OFF, not enter, keep/stay away from, not trespass on. **2** *Maud tried to keep off political subjects* AVOID, steer clear of, stay away from, evade, sidestep; *informal* duck. **3** *you should keep off alcohol* ABSTAIN FROM, do without, refrain from, give up, forgo, not touch; *informal* swear off; *formal* forswear.
■ **keep on 1** *they kept on working* CONTINUE, go on, carry on, persist in, persevere in; soldier on, struggle on, keep going. **2** *the commander kept on about vigilance* TALK CONSTANTLY, talk endlessly, keep talking, go on (and on), rant on; *informal* harp on.
■ **keep something up** CONTINUE (WITH), keep on with, keep going, carry on with, persist with, persevere with.
■ **keep up with** *she walked fast to keep up with them* KEEP PACE WITH, keep abreast of; match, equal.

keeper ▶ noun GUARDIAN, custodian, curator, administrator, overseer, steward, caretaker.

keeping
■ **in keeping with** CONSISTENT WITH, in harmony with, in accord with, in agreement with, in line with, in character with, compatible with; appropriate to, befitting, suitable for.

keepsake ▶ noun MEMENTO, souvenir, reminder, remembrance, token; party favour, bomboniere.

keg ▶ noun BARREL, cask, vat, butt, tun, hogshead; *historical* firkin.

ken ▶ noun KNOWLEDGE, awareness, perception,

vision, understanding, grasp, comprehension, realization, appreciation, consciousness.

kerchief ► noun HEAD SCARF, bandana, babushka.

kerfuffle ► noun COMMOTION, uproar, brouhaha, hullabaloo, ballyhoo, ruckus, to-do, hue and cry, fuss, foofaraw, furor; *informal* song and dance, stink.

kernel ► noun **1** *the kernel of a nut* seed, grain, core; nut. **2** *the kernel of the argument* ESSENCE, core, heart, essentials, quintessence, fundamentals, basics, nub, gist, substance; *informal* nitty-gritty. **3** *a kernel of truth* NUCLEUS, germ, grain, nugget.

key ► noun **1** *I put my key in the lock* door key, latchkey, pass key, master key. **2** *the key to the mystery* | *the key to success* ANSWER, clue, solution, explanation; basis, foundation, requisite, precondition, means, way, route, path, passport, secret, formula.
► adjective *a key figure* CRUCIAL, central, essential, indispensable, pivotal, critical, dominant, vital, principal, prime, primary, chief, major, leading, main, important, significant.
— OPPOSITES: peripheral.

keyboard ► noun. *See table at* INSTRUMENT.

keynote ► noun THEME, salient point, gist, substance, burden, tenor, pith, marrow, essence, heart, core, basis, essential feature/element, crux.

keystone ► noun *the keystone of the government's policy* FOUNDATION, basis, linchpin, cornerstone, base, (guiding) principle, core, heart, centre, crux, fundament.

kibosh
■ **put the kibosh on** *(informal)* PUT A STOP TO, stop, halt, put an end to, quash, block, cancel, scotch, thwart, prevent, suppress; *informal* put paid to, stymie; scupper, scuttle.

kick ► verb **1** *she kicked the ball over the fence* BOOT, punt, drop-kick, hoof, strike with the foot. **2** *(informal) he was struggling to kick his drug habit* GIVE UP, break, abandon, end, stop, cease, desist from, renounce; *informal* shake, pack in, leave off, quit.
► noun **1** *a kick on the knee* BLOW WITH THE FOOT; *informal* boot. **2** *(informal) I get a kick out of driving a racing car* THRILL, excitement, stimulation, tingle; fun, enjoyment, amusement, pleasure, gratification; *informal* buzz, high, rush, charge. **3** *(informal) a drink with a powerful kick* POTENCY, stimulant effect, strength, power; tang, zest, bite, piquancy, edge, pungency; *informal* punch. **4** *(informal) a health kick* CRAZE, enthusiasm, obsession, mania, passion; fashion, vogue, trend; *informal* fad.
■ **kick someone/something around** *(informal)* **1** *I'm tired of getting kicked around* ABUSE, mistreat, maltreat, push around, trample on, take for granted; *informal* boss around, walk all over. **2** *they began to kick around some ideas* DISCUSS, talk over, debate, thrash out, consider, toy with, play with.
■ **kick back** *(informal)* RELAX, unwind, take it easy, rest, slow down, let up, ease up/off, sit back, chill (out), hang loose.
■ **kick off** *(informal)* START, commence, begin, get going, get off the ground, get underway; open, start off, set in motion, launch, initiate, introduce, inaugurate, usher in.
■ **kick someone out** *(informal)* EXPEL, eject, banish, exile, throw out, oust, evict, get rid of, axe; dismiss, discharge; *informal* chuck (out), send packing, boot out, give someone their marching orders, give someone their walking papers, give someone the gate, give someone the (old) heave-ho, sack, bounce, fire, turf (out), give someone the bum's rush.

kickback ► noun **1** *the kickback from the gun* RECOIL, kick, rebound. **2** *(informal) they paid kickbacks to politicians* BRIBE, payment, inducement, payola, payoff, boodle, sop, sweetener.

kickoff ► noun *(informal)* BEGINNING, start, commencement, launch, outset, opening.

kick start ► verb START UP, fire up, turn on, get something moving, get something off the ground, energize.

kid ► noun *(informal) they have three kids* CHILD, youngster, little one, baby, toddler, tot, infant, boy/ girl, young person, minor, juvenile, adolescent, teenager, youth, stripling; offspring, son/daughter; *informal* kiddie, shaver, young 'un, rug rat, ankle-biter, munchkin, whippersnapper; *derogatory* brat; *literary* babe.
► verb *(informal)* **1** *I'm not kidding* JOKE, tease, jest, chaff, be facetious, fool around, pull someone's leg, pull someone's chain, have on, rib. **2** *don't kid yourself* DELUDE, deceive, fool, trick, hoodwink, hoax, beguile, dupe, gull; *informal* con, pull the wool over someone's eyes.
■ **no kidding!** no guff! ↓

kidnap ► verb ABDUCT, carry off, capture, seize, snatch, take hostage.

kill ► verb **1** *gangs killed twenty-seven people* MURDER, take/end the life of, assassinate, eliminate, terminate, dispatch, finish off, put to death, execute; slaughter, butcher, massacre, wipe out, annihilate, exterminate, liquidate, mow down, shoot down, cut down, cut to pieces; *informal* bump off, polish off, do away with, do in, knock off, take out, croak, stiff, blow away, dispose of, ice, snuff, rub out, waste, whack, scrag, smoke; *euphemistic* neutralize; *literary* slay. **2** *this would kill all hopes of progress* DESTROY, put an end to, end, extinguish, dash, quash, ruin, wreck, shatter, smash, crush, scotch, thwart; *informal* put paid to, put the kibosh on, stymie, scupper, scuttle. **3** *we had to kill several hours at the airport* WHILE AWAY, fill (up), occupy, pass, spend, waste. **4** *(informal) you must rest or you'll kill yourself* EXHAUST, wear out, tire out, overtax, overtire, fatigue, weary, sap, drain, enervate, knock out. **5** *(informal) my feet were killing me* HURT, cause pain to, torture, torment, cause discomfort to; be painful, be sore, be uncomfortable. **6** *a shot to kill the pain* ALLEVIATE, assuage, soothe, allay, dull, blunt, deaden, stifle, suppress, subdue. **7** *(informal) an opposition attempt to kill the bill* VETO, defeat, vote down, rule against, reject, throw out, overrule, overturn, put a stop to, quash, squash. **8** *(informal) Noel killed the engine* TURN OFF, switch off, stop, shut off/ down, cut.
— RELATED TERMS: -cide.
► noun **1** *the hunter's kill* PREY, quarry, victim, bag. **2** *the wolf was moving in for the kill* DEATH BLOW, killing, dispatch, finish, end, coup de grâce.

killer ► noun **1** *police are searching for the killer* MURDERER, assassin, slaughterer, butcher, serial killer, gunman; executioner, hit man, cutthroat; *literary* slayer; *dated* homicide. **2** *a major killer* CAUSE OF DEATH, fatal/deadly illness.

killing ► noun *a brutal killing* MURDER, assassination, homicide, manslaughter, elimination, putting to death, execution; slaughter, massacre, butchery, carnage, bloodshed, extermination, annihilation; *literary* slaying.
► adjective **1** *a killing blow* DEADLY, lethal, fatal, mortal, death-dealing; murderous, homicidal; *literary* deathly. **2** *(informal) a killing schedule* EXHAUSTING, gruelling,

punishing, taxing, draining, wearing, prostrating, crushing, tiring, fatiguing, debilitating, enervating, arduous, tough, demanding, onerous, strenuous, rigorous; *informal* murderous.

■ **make a killing** (*informal*) MAKE A LARGE PROFIT, make a/one's fortune, make money, rake it in, clean up, cash in, make a pretty penny, make big bucks.

killjoy ▶ **noun** SPOILSPORT, wet blanket, damper, party-pooper, prophet of doom.

kilter

■ **off kilter, out of kilter** AWRY, off balance, unbalanced, out of order, disordered, confused, muddled, out of tune, out of whack, out of step.

kin ▶ **noun** *their own kin* RELATIVES, relations, family (members), kindred, kith and kin; kinsfolk, kinsmen, kinswomen, people; *informal* folks.

kind ▶ **adjective** *she is such a kind and caring person* KINDLY, good-natured, kind-hearted, warm-hearted, caring, affectionate, loving, warm; considerate, helpful, thoughtful, obliging, unselfish, selfless, altruistic, good, attentive; compassionate, sympathetic, understanding, big-hearted, benevolent, benign, friendly, neighbourly, hospitable, well-meaning, public-spirited.
– OPPOSITES: inconsiderate, mean.
▶ **noun 1** *all kinds of gifts* | *the kinds of bird that could be seen* SORT, type, variety, style, form, class, category, genre; genus, species, race, breed; flavour. **2** *they were different in kind* | *the first of its kind* CHARACTER, nature, essence, quality, disposition, makeup; type, style, stamp, manner, description, mould, cast, temperament, ilk, stripe.
■ **kind of** (*informal*) RATHER, quite, fairly, somewhat, a little, slightly, a shade; *informal* sort of, a bit, kinda, pretty, a touch, a tad.

kindle ▶ **verb 1** *he kindled a fire* LIGHT, ignite, set alight, set light to, set fire to, put a match to. **2** *the Beatles kindled my interest in music* ROUSE, arouse, wake, awake, awaken; stimulate, inspire, stir (up), excite, evoke, provoke, fire, inflame, trigger, activate, spark off; *literary* waken, enkindle.
– OPPOSITES: extinguish.

kindliness ▶ **noun** KINDNESS, benevolence, warmth, gentleness, tenderness, care, humanity, sympathy, compassion, understanding; generosity, charity, kind-heartedness, warm-heartedness, solicitousness, thoughtfulness.

kindling ▶ **noun** TINDER, fire starter, (*Nfld*) splits ✦, feathersticks ✦, brush, splints.

kindly ▶ **adjective** *a kindly old lady* BENEVOLENT, kind, kind-hearted, warm-hearted, generous, gentle, warm, good-natured, compassionate, caring, loving, benign, well meaning; helpful, thoughtful, considerate, good-hearted, nice, friendly, neighbourly.
– OPPOSITES: unkind, cruel.
▶ **adverb 1** *she spoke kindly* BENEVOLENTLY, good-naturedly, warmly, affectionately, tenderly, lovingly, compassionately; considerately, thoughtfully, helpfully, obligingly, generously, selflessly, unselfishly, sympathetically. **2** *kindly explain what you mean* PLEASE, if you please, if you wouldn't mind; *archaic* prithee, pray.
– OPPOSITES: unkindly, harshly.

kindness ▶ **noun** *he thanked her for her kindness* KINDLINESS, kind-heartedness, warm-heartedness, affection, warmth, concern, care; consideration, helpfulness, thoughtfulness, unselfishness, selflessness, altruism, compassion,

sympathy, understanding, big-heartedness, benevolence, benignity, friendliness, hospitality, neighbourliness; generosity, magnanimity, charitableness.

kindred ▶ **noun** *his mother's kindred* FAMILY, relatives, relations, kin, kith and kin, one's own flesh and blood; kinsfolk, kinsmen/kinswomen, people; *informal* folks.
▶ **adjective 1** *industrial relations and kindred subjects* RELATED, allied, connected, comparable, similar, like, parallel, associated, analogous. **2** *a kindred spirit* LIKE-MINDED, in sympathy, in harmony, in tune, of one mind, akin, similar, like, compatible; *informal* on the same wavelength.
– OPPOSITES: unrelated, alien.

king ▶ **noun 1** *the king of France* RULER, sovereign, monarch, crowned head, Crown, emperor, prince, potentate, lord. *See also the table at* RULER. **2** (*informal*) *the king of fingerpicking guitar* STAR, leading light, luminary, superstar, giant, master; *informal* supremo, megastar.

kingdom ▶ **noun 1** *his kingdom stretched to the sea* REALM, domain, dominion, country, empire, principality, duchy, land, nation, (sovereign) state, province, territory. **2** *Henry's little kingdom* DOMAIN, province, realm, sphere, dominion, territory, arena, zone. **3** *the plant kingdom* DIVISION, category, classification, grouping, group.

kingly ▶ **adjective 1** *kingly power* ROYAL, regal, monarchical, sovereign, imperial, princely. **2** *kingly robes* REGAL, majestic, stately, noble, lordly, dignified, distinguished, courtly; splendid, magnificent, grand, glorious, rich, gorgeous, resplendent, princely, superb, sumptuous; *informal* splendiferous.

kingpin ▶ **noun** BOSS, head, number one, big cheese, bigwig, top dog.

kink ▶ **noun 1** *your fishing line should have no kinks in it* CURL, twist, twirl, loop, crinkle; knot, tangle, entanglement. **2** *there are still some kinks to iron out* FLAW, defect, imperfection, problem, complication, hitch, snag, shortcoming, weakness; *informal* hiccup, glitch. **3** *a kink in my neck* CRICK, stiffness, pinch, knot.

kinky ▶ **adjective 1** (*informal*) *kinky underwear* PROVOCATIVE, sexy, erotic, titillating, naughty, indecent, immodest. **2** (*informal*) *a kinky relationship* PERVERSE, abnormal, deviant, unconventional, unnatural, degenerate, depraved, perverted; *informal* pervy. **3** *Catriona's long kinky hair* CURLY, crimped, curled, curling, frizzy, frizzed, wavy.

kinship ▶ **noun 1** *the value of kinship in society* family ties, blood ties, common ancestry, consanguinity. **2** *she felt kinship with the others* AFFINITY, sympathy, rapport, harmony, understanding, empathy, closeness, fellow feeling, bond, compatibility; similarity, likeness, correspondence, concordance.

kinsman, kinswoman ▶ **noun** RELATIVE, relation, family member; cousin, aunt, uncle, nephew, niece.

kiosk ▶ **noun** BOOTH, stand, stall, concession, counter, newsstand; info centre.

kiss ▶ **verb 1** *he kissed her on the lips* give a kiss to, brush one's lips against, blow a kiss to, air-kiss; *informal* peck, give a smacker to, smooch, canoodle, neck, buss, make out; *formal/humorous* osculate. **2** *allow your foot just to kiss the floor* BRUSH (AGAINST), caress, touch (gently), stroke, skim over.
▶ **noun 1** *a kiss on the cheek* peck, smack, smacker, smooch, buss, air kiss, French kiss; X; *formal/humorous*

Knives and Daggers

bolo	machete
bowie knife	palette knife
breadknife	parang
buck knife	paring knife
butcher knife	penknife
butter knife	pigsticker
carver	pocket knife
carving knife	poniard
chef's knife	putty knife
clasp knife	scalpel
cleaver	sheath knife
dagger	shiv
dirk	skean
exacto knife	skean-dhu
fish knife	snow knife ✦
flick knife	steak knife
hunting knife	stiletto
jackknife	Swiss Army knife
kirpan	switchblade
kris	table knife
kukri	ulu ✦(North)
lancet	utility knife

osculation. **2** the kiss of the flowers against her cheeks GENTLE TOUCH, caress, brush, stroke.

kit ▶ noun **1** his tool kit EQUIPMENT, tools, implements, instruments, gadgets, utensils, appliances, tools of the trade, gear, (Nfld) fit-out ✦, tackle, hardware, paraphernalia; informal things, stuff, the necessaries; Military accoutrements. **2** a model aircraft kit SET (OF PARTS), DIY kit, do-it-yourself kit.

kitchen ▶ noun kitchenette, cooking area, eat-in kitchen, galley kitchen, country kitchen, scullery, back kitchen, summer kitchen, cookhouse, galley, caboose. See also the table at APPLIANCE.

kitschy ▶ adjective TACKY, tawdry, (Que.) kétaine ✦, showy, gimcrack, gaudy, cheap, catchpenny, Brummagem, tasteless, vulgar.

klutz ▶ noun SCHLUB, butterfingers, stumblebum, oaf, galoot, lubber, lug, lummox, hobbledehoy, boor, ape.

knack ▶ noun **1** a knack for making money GIFT, talent, flair, genius, instinct, faculty, ability, capability, capacity, aptitude, aptness, bent, forte, facility; TECHNIQUE, method, trick, skill, adroitness, art, expertise; informal the hang of something. **2** he has a knack of getting injured at the wrong time TENDENCY, propensity, habit, proneness, liability, predisposition.

knapsack ▶ noun RUCKSACK, backpack, haversack, pack, kit bag, (Nfld) nunny-bag ✦.

knave ▶ noun (archaic). See JERK noun sense 3.

knead ▶ verb kneading the dough PUMMEL, work, pound, squeeze, shape, mould.

knee-jerk ▶ adjective IMPULSIVE, automatic, spontaneous, instinctive, mechanical, unthinking, hasty, rash, reckless, impetuous, precipitate.

kneel ▶ verb FALL TO ONE'S KNEES, get down on one's knees, genuflect; historical kowtow.

knell ▶ noun (literary) **1** the knell of the ship's bell TOLL, tolling, dong, resounding, reverberation; death knell; archaic tocsin. **2** this sounded the knell for the project (BEGINNING OF THE) END, death knell, death warrant.

knick-knack ▶ noun TRINKET, novelty, gewgaw, bibelot, ornament, trifle, bauble, gimcrack, curio;

memento, souvenir, kickshaw, tchotchke; archaic gaud.

knife ▶ noun a sharp knife CUTTING TOOL, blade, cutter. See table.
▶ verb the victims had been knifed STAB, hack, gash, run through, slash, lacerate, cut, pierce, jab, stick, spike, impale, transfix, bayonet, spear.

knight ▶ noun knights in armour CAVALIER, cavalryman, horseman; lord, noble, nobleman; historical chevalier, paladin, banneret.
■ **knight in shining armour** rescuer, saviour, champion, hero, defender, protector, guardian (angel).

knightly ▶ adjective tales of knightly deeds GALLANT, noble, valiant, heroic, courageous, brave, bold, valorous; chivalrous, courteous, honourable.
− OPPOSITES: ignoble.

knit ▶ verb **1** disparate regions began to knit together UNITE, unify, come together, draw together, become closer, bond, fuse, coalesce, merge, meld, blend. **2** Marcus knitted his brows FURROW, tighten, contract, gather, wrinkle.
▶ noun silky knits in pretty shades KNITTED GARMENT, knitwear, woollen; sweater, pullover, jersey, cardigan.

Knitting Terms

Styles	Stitching
argyle pattern	cable stitch
Fair Isle	garter stitch
fisherman's knit	moss stitch
shaker knit	plain stitch
double knit	purl stitch
intarsia	ribbing
	slipstitch
Actions	stocking stitch
casting on	
casting off	
dropping a stitch	

knob ▶ noun **1** a black bill with a knob at the base LUMP, bump, protuberance, protrusion, bulge, swelling, knot, node, nodule, ball, boss. **2** the knobs on the radio DIAL, button. **3** she turned the knob on the door DOORKNOB, (door) handle.

knock ▶ verb **1** he knocked on the door BANG, tap, rap, thump, pound, hammer; strike, hit, beat. **2** she knocked her knee on the table BUMP, bang, hit, strike, crack; injure, hurt, bruise; informal bash, thwack. **3** he knocked into an elderly man COLLIDE WITH, bump into, bang into, be in collision with, run into, crash into, smash into, plow into, impact, bash into. **4** (informal) I'm not knocking the company. See CRITICIZE.
▶ noun **1** a sharp knock at the door TAP, rap, rat-tat-tat, knocking, bang, banging, pounding, hammering, drumming, thump, thud. **2** the casing is tough enough to withstand knocks BUMP, blow, bang, jolt, jar, shock; collision, crash, smash, impact. **3** (informal) this isn't a knock on Dave. See CRITICISM sense 1. **4** life's hard knocks SETBACK, reversal, defeat, failure, difficulty, misfortune, bad luck, mishap, (body) blow, disaster, calamity, disappointment, sorrow, trouble, hardship; informal kick in the teeth.
■ **knock something back** (informal) SWALLOW, gulp down, drink (up), quaff, guzzle, slug, down, swig, drain, swill (down), toss off, scarf (down), snarf.
■ **knock someone/something down** FELL, floor, flatten, bring down, knock to the ground; knock

over, run over/down; DEMOLISH, pull down, tear down, destroy; raze (to the ground), level, bulldoze.

■ **knock it off!** (*informal*) STOP IT; *informal* cut it out, give it a rest, pack it in, that's enough, lay off.

■ **knock someone out 1** *I hit him and knocked him out* KNOCK UNCONSCIOUS, knock senseless; floor, prostrate, put out cold, KO, kayo. **2** *Canada was knocked out* ELIMINATE, beat, defeat, vanquish, overwhelm, trounce. **3** (*informal*) *walking that far knocked her out* EXHAUST, wear out, tire (out), overtire, fatigue, weary, drain; *informal* do in, take it out of, poop, fag out. **4** (*informal*) *the view knocked me out* OVERWHELM, stun, stupefy, amaze, astound, astonish, stagger, take someone's breath away; impress, dazzle, enchant, awe, entrance; *informal* bowl over, flabbergast, blow away.

■ **knock someone up** (*informal*) GET/MAKE PREGNANT, impregnate; *informal* put in the family way.

knockout ▶ noun **1** *the match was won by a knockout* KO, finishing blow, coup de grâce, stunning blow, kayo. **2** (*informal*) *she's a knockout!* BEAUTY, babe, bombshell, vision, dream, hottie, dish, looker, eye-catcher, peach, heartthrob, fox. **3** (*informal*) *the performance was a knockout* MASTERPIECE, sensation, marvel, wonder, triumph, success, feat, coup, master stroke, tour de force; *informal* humdinger, doozy, stunner.

knoll ▶ noun *she walked up the grassy knoll* MOUND, hillock, rise, hummock, hill, drumlin, hump, bank, ridge, elevation, (Nfld) tolt ♣.

knot ▶ noun **1** *tie a small knot* TIE, twist, loop, bow, hitch, half hitch, clove hitch, join, fastening; square knot, reef knot, slip knot, overhand knot, granny knot; tangle, entanglement. **2** *a knot in the wood* NODULE, gnarl, node; lump, knob, swelling, gall, protuberance, bump, burl.
▶ verb *their scarves were knotted round their throats* TIE (UP), fasten, secure, bind, do up.

knotted ▶ adjective TANGLED, tangly, knotty, entangled, matted, snarled, unkempt, uncombed, tousled; *informal* mussed up.

knotty ▶ adjective **1** *a knotty legal problem* COMPLEX, complicated, involved, intricate, convoluted, involuted; difficult, hard, thorny, taxing, awkward, tricky, problematic, troublesome. **2** *knotty roots* GNARLED, knotted, knurled, nodular, knobbly, lumpy, bumpy. **3** *a knotty piece of thread* KNOTTED, tangled, tangly, twisted, entangled, snarled, matted.
— OPPOSITES: straightforward.

know ▶ verb **1** *she doesn't know I'm here* BE AWARE, realize, be conscious, be informed; notice, perceive, see, sense, recognize; *informal* be clued in, savvy. **2** *I don't know his address* HAVE KNOWLEDGE OF, be informed of, be apprised of; *formal* be cognizant of. **3** *do you know the rules* BE FAMILIAR WITH, be conversant with, be acquainted with, have knowledge of, be versed in, have mastered, have a grasp of, understand, comprehend; have learned, have memorized, be up to speed on. **4** *I don't know many people here* BE ACQUAINTED WITH, have met, be familiar with; be friends with, be friendly with, be on good terms with, be close to, be intimate with. **5** *he had known better times* EXPERIENCE, go through, live through, undergo, taste. **6** *my brothers don't know a saucepan from a frying pan* DISTINGUISH, tell (apart), differentiate, discriminate; recognize, pick out, identify.

know-how ▶ noun (*informal*) KNOWLEDGE, expertise, skill, skilfulness, expertness, proficiency, understanding, mastery, technique; ability,

capability, competence, capacity, adeptness, dexterity, deftness, aptitude, adroitness, ingenuity, faculty; *informal* savvy.

knowing ▶ adjective **1** *a knowing smile* SIGNIFICANT, meaningful, eloquent, expressive, suggestive; ARCH, sly, mischievous, impish, teasing, playful. **2** *she's a very knowing child* SOPHISTICATED, worldly, worldly-wise, urbane, experienced; knowledgeable, well-informed, enlightened; shrewd, astute, canny, sharp, wily, perceptive. **3** *a knowing infringement of the rules* DELIBERATE, intentional, conscious, calculated, wilful, done on purpose, premeditated, planned, preconceived.

knowingly ▶ adverb DELIBERATELY, intentionally, consciously, wittingly, on purpose, by design, premeditatedly, wilfully.

know-it-all ▶ noun (*informal*) SMARTY-PANTS; smart alec, wise guy, smarty, wiseacre.

knowledge ▶ noun **1** *his knowledge of history* | *technical knowledge* UNDERSTANDING, comprehension, grasp, command, mastery; expertise, skill, proficiency, expertness, accomplishment, adeptness, capacity, capability; *informal* know-how. **2** *people anxious to display their knowledge* LEARNING, erudition, education, scholarship, schooling, wisdom. **3** *he slipped away without my knowledge* AWARENESS, consciousness, realization, cognition, apprehension, perception, appreciation; *formal* cognizance. **4** *an intimate knowledge of the countryside* FAMILIARITY, acquaintance, intimacy. **5** *inform the police of your knowledge* INFORMATION, facts, intelligence, news, reports; *informal* info.
— OPPOSITES: ignorance.

knowledgeable ▶ adjective **1** *Beryl was a knowledgeable woman* WELL-INFORMED, learned, well-read, (well) educated, erudite, scholarly, cultured, cultivated, enlightened. **2** *he is knowledgeable about modern art* ACQUAINTED, familiar, conversant, au courant, au fait; having a knowledge of, up on, up to date with, up to speed on, abreast of, plugged in, well-grounded.
— OPPOSITES: ill-informed.

known ▶ adjective **1** *a known criminal* RECOGNIZED, well-known, widely known, noted, celebrated, notable, notorious; acknowledged, self-confessed, declared, overt. **2** *the known world* FAMILIAR, known about, well-known; studied, investigated.

knuckle
■ **knuckle under** SURRENDER, submit, capitulate, give in/up, yield, give way, succumb, back down, admit defeat, lay down one's arms, throw in the towel, climb down, quit, raise the white flag.

kosher (*informal*) ▶ adjective PROPER, above board, genuine, correct, legitimate, legit, fine, admissible, acceptable, orthodox.

kowtow ▶ verb **1** *they kowtowed to the Emperor* PROSTRATE ONESELF, bow (down before), genuflect, do/make obeisance, fall on one's knees before, kneel before. **2** *she didn't have to kowtow to a boss* GROVEL, be obsequious, be servile, be sycophantic, fawn over/on, cringe to, bow and scrape, toady, smarm, truckle, abase oneself, humble oneself; curry favour with, dance attendance on, ingratiate oneself with, suck up, kiss up (to), brown-nose, lick someone's boots.

kudos ▶ noun PRAISE, glory, honour, status, standing, distinction, fame, celebrity; admiration, respect, esteem, acclaim, prestige, cachet, credit, full marks, props.

LI

label ▶ noun **1** *the price is clearly stated on the label* TAG, ticket, tab, sticker, marker. **2** *a designer label* BRAND (NAME), trade name, trademark, make, logo. **3** *the label the media came up with for me* DESIGNATION, description, tag; name, epithet, nickname, title, sobriquet, pet name, cognomen; *formal* denomination, appellation.
▶ verb **1** *label each jar with the date* TAG, put labels on, tab, ticket, mark. **2** *tests labelled him an underachiever* CATEGORIZE, classify, class, describe, designate, identify; mark, stamp, brand, condemn, pigeonhole, stereotype, typecast; call, name, term, dub, nickname.

laborious ▶ adjective **1** *a laborious job* ARDUOUS, hard, heavy, difficult, strenuous, gruelling, punishing, exacting, tough, onerous, burdensome, back-breaking, labour-intensive, trying, challenging; tiring, fatiguing, exhausting, wearying, wearing, taxing, demanding, wearisome, tedious, boring, time-consuming; *archaic* toilsome. **2** *Doug's laborious writing style* LABOURED, strained, forced, contrived, affected, stiff, stilted, unnatural, artificial, overwrought, heavy, ponderous, convoluted.
– OPPOSITES: easy, effortless.

labour ▶ noun **1** *manual labour* (HARD) WORK, toil, exertion, industry, drudgery, effort, donkey work, menial work; *informal* slog, grind, sweat, elbow grease, scutwork; *literary* travail, moil. **2** *management and labour need to co-operate* WORKERS, employees, workmen, workforce, staff, working people, blue-collar workers, labourers, labour force, proletariat. **3** *the labours of Hercules* TASK, job, chore, mission, assignment. **4** *a difficult labour* CHILDBIRTH, birth, delivery, nativity; contractions, labour pains; *formal* parturition; *literary* travail; *dated* confinement; *archaic* lying-in, accouchement, childbed.
– OPPOSITES: rest, management.
▶ verb **1** *a project on which he had laboured for many years* WORK (HARD), toil, slave (away), grind away, struggle, strive, exert oneself, work one's fingers to the bone, work like a dog/slave; *informal* slog away, plug away; *literary* travail, moil. **2** *she laboured to unite the party* STRIVE, struggle, endeavour, work (hard), try (hard), make every effort, do one's best, do one's utmost, do all one can, give one's all, go all out, fight, put oneself out, apply oneself, exert oneself; *informal* bend/lean over backwards, pull out all the stops, bust a gut, bust one's chops. **3** *there is no need to labour the point* OVEREMPHASIZE, belabour, overstress, overdo, strain, overplay, make too much of, exaggerate, dwell on, harp on (about). **4** *Rex was labouring under a misapprehension* SUFFER FROM, be a victim of, be deceived by, be misled by.

laboured ▶ adjective **1** *laboured breathing* STRAINED, difficult, forced, laborious. **2** *a rather laboured joke* CONTRIVED, strained, stilted, forced, stiff, unnatural, artificial, overdone, ponderous, over-elaborate, laborious, unconvincing, overwrought.

labourer ▶ noun WORKMAN, worker, working man/woman, labouring man/woman, manual worker, unskilled worker, day labourer, blue-collar worker,

(hired) hand, grunt, peon, roustabout, drudge, menial, joe-boy, coolie.

labyrinth ▶ noun **1** *a labyrinth of little streets* MAZE, warren, network, complex, web, entanglement. **2** *the labyrinth of conflicting regulations* TANGLE, web, morass, jungle, confusion, entanglement, convolution; jumble, mishmash.

labyrinthine ▶ adjective **1** *labyrinthine corridors* MAZE-LIKE, winding, twisting, serpentine, meandering, wandering, rambling. **2** *a labyrinthine system* COMPLICATED, intricate, complex, involved, tortuous, convoluted, involuted, tangled, elaborate; confusing, puzzling, mystifying, bewildering, baffling.

lace ▶ noun **1** *a dress trimmed with white lace* openwork, lacework, tatting; passementerie, needlepoint (lace), filet, bobbin lace, pillow lace, torchon lace, needle lace, point lace, Battenberg lace, Chantilly lace, Mechlin lace, Valenciennes. **2** *brown shoes with laces* SHOELACE, bootlace, skate lace, shoestring, lacing, thong, tie.
▶ verb **1** *he laced up his running shoes* FASTEN, do up, tie up, secure, knot. **2** *he laced his fingers into mine* ENTWINE, intertwine, twine, entangle, interweave, link; braid, plait. **3** *tea laced with rum* FLAVOUR, mix (in), blend, fortify, strengthen, stiffen, season, spice (up), enrich, liven up; doctor, adulterate; *informal* spike. **4** *her brown hair was laced with grey* STREAK, stripe, striate, line.
– OPPOSITES: untie.
■ **lace into** (*informal*) **1** *Danny laced into him*. See BEAT SOMEONE UP at BEAT. **2** *the newspaper laced into the prime minister*. See CRITICIZE.

lacerate ▶ verb CUT (OPEN), gash, slash, tear, rip, rend, shred, score, scratch, scrape, graze; wound, injure, hurt.

laceration ▶ noun *a bleeding laceration* GASH, cut, wound, injury, tear, slash, scratch, scrape, abrasion, graze.

lachrymose ▶ adjective See TEARFUL.
– OPPOSITES: cheerful, comic.

lack ▶ noun *a lack of cash* ABSENCE, want, need, deficiency, dearth, insufficiency, shortage, shortfall, scarcity, paucity, unavailability, deficit.
– OPPOSITES: abundance.
▶ verb *they lack sufficient resources* BE WITHOUT, be in need of, need, be lacking, require, want, be short of, be deficient in, be bereft of, be low on, be pressed for, have insufficient; *informal* be strapped for.
– OPPOSITES: have, possess.

lackadaisical ▶ adjective LETHARGIC, apathetic, listless, sluggish, spiritless, passionless; careless, lazy, lax, unenthusiastic, half-hearted, lukewarm, indifferent, unconcerned, casual, offhand, blasé, insouciant, relaxed; *informal* laid-back, easygoing, couldn't-care-less.
– OPPOSITES: enthusiastic.

lackey ▶ noun **1** *lackeys helped them from their carriage* SERVANT, flunky, footman, manservant, valet, steward, butler, attendant, houseboy, domestic;

archaic scullion. **2** *one of the manager's lackeys* TOADY, flunky, sycophant, flatterer, minion, hanger-on, lickspittle, brown-noser, spaniel, yes-man, running dog, trained seal, bootlicker; doormat, pawn, underling, stooge, drudge, peon.

lacking ▶ adjective **1** *proof was lacking* ABSENT, missing, non-existent, unavailable. **2** *he seemed to be lacking in common sense* DEFICIENT, defective, inadequate, wanting, flawed, faulty, insufficient, unacceptable, imperfect, inferior; without, devoid of, bereft of; deficient in, low on, short on, in need of.
— OPPOSITES: present, plentiful.

lacklustre ▶ adjective UNINSPIRED, uninspiring, unimaginative, dull, humdrum, colourless, characterless, bland, dead, insipid, vapid, flat, dry, lifeless, tame, prosaic, spiritless, lustreless; boring, monotonous, dreary, tedious; *informal* blah.
— OPPOSITES: inspired.

laconic ▶ adjective **1** *his laconic comment* BRIEF, concise, terse, succinct, short, pithy. **2** *their laconic press officer* TACITURN, uncommunicative, reticent, quiet, reserved, silent, unforthcoming, brief.
— OPPOSITES: verbose, loquacious.

lacquer ▶ noun VARNISH, shellac, gloss, glaze, enamel, finish, polish.

lacrosse ▶ noun field lacrosse, box lacrosse ✚ (boxla ✚), inter-lacrosse; *historical* baggataway.

lad ▶ noun *(informal)* *a young lad of eight* BOY, schoolboy, youth, youngster, juvenile, stripling; *informal* kid, whippersnapper, laddie; *derogatory* brat. See also CHILD.

ladder ▶ noun **1** *she climbed down the ladder* steps, set of steps; rope ladder, stepladder, extension ladder. **2** *the academic ladder* HIERARCHY, scale, grading, ranking, pecking order.

laden ▶ adjective LOADED, burdened, weighed down, encumbered, overloaded, piled high, fully charged; full, filled, packed, stuffed, crammed; *informal* chock full, chockablock.

la-di-da ▶ adjective *(informal)* SNOBBISH, pretentious, affected, mannered, pompous, conceited, haughty; *informal* snooty, stuck-up, high and mighty, hoity-toity, uppity, snotty.
— OPPOSITES: common.

ladle ▶ verb *he was ladling out the contents of the pot* SPOON OUT, scoop out, dish up/out, serve.
▶ noun *a soup ladle* SPOON, scoop, dipper, bailer; (*Nfld*) spudgel ✚.

lady ▶ noun **1** *several ladies were present* WOMAN, female; *informal* dame, broad; *literary* maid, damsel; *archaic* wench. **2** *lords and ladies* NOBLEWOMAN, duchess, countess, peeress, viscountess, baroness; *archaic* gentlewoman.

ladylike ▶ adjective GENTEEL, polite, refined, well-bred, cultivated, polished, decorous, proper, respectable, seemly, well-mannered, cultured, sophisticated, elegant, modest, feminine, womanly.
— OPPOSITES: coarse.

lag ▶ verb FALL BEHIND, straggle, fall back, trail (behind), hang back, not keep pace, bring up the rear, dawdle, dilly-dally.
— OPPOSITES: keep up.

laggard ▶ noun STRAGGLER, loiterer, lingerer, dawdler, sluggard, snail, idler, loafer; *informal* lazybones, slacker, slowpoke, foot-dragger.

lagoon ▶ noun BAY, (*Atlantic*) barachois ✚, inland sea, lake, bight, pool.

laid-back ▶ adjective *(informal)* RELAXED, easygoing, free and easy, loosey-goosey, casual, nonchalant,

unexcitable, imperturbable, unruffled, blasé, cool, equable, even-tempered, insouciant, calm, unperturbed, unflustered, unflappable, unworried, unconcerned, unbothered; leisurely, unhurried, Type-B; stoical, phlegmatic, tolerant.
— OPPOSITES: uptight.

lair ▶ noun **1** *the lair of a large python* DEN, burrow, hole, tunnel, cave. **2** *a villain's lair* HIDEOUT, hiding place, hideaway, refuge, sanctuary, haven, shelter, retreat; *informal* hidey-hole.

laissez-faire ▶ noun FREE ENTERPRISE, free trade, non-intervention, free-market capitalism, market forces.

lake ▶ noun POND, pool, tarn, reservoir, slough, lagoon, water, water hole, inland sea, loch; oxbow (lake), pothole (lake), glacial lake; *literary* mere.
— RELATED TERMS: lacustrine.

Fifteen Largest Freshwater Lakes

Lake	Location
Superior	Canada/US
Victoria	Uganda/Tanzania/Kenya
Huron (with Georgian Bay)	Canada/US
Michigan	US
Tanganyika	Tanzania/Zambia/Burundi/ Congo (Dem.Rep.)
Baikal	Russia
Great Bear	Canada
Malawi/Nyasa	Malawi/Mozambique/ Tanzania
Great Slave	Canada
Chad	Chad/Niger/Nigeria
Erie	Canada/US
Winnipeg	Canada
Ontario	Canada/US
Balkhash	Kazakhstan
Ladoga	Russia

lallygag ▶ verb See LOITER sense 1.

lam
■ **on the lam** ON THE LOOSE, at large, on the run, escaped, fugitive, in flight.

lambaste ▶ verb *the coach was lambasted in the media* CRITICIZE, chastise, censure, take to task, harangue, rail at, rant at, fulminate against; upbraid, scold, reprimand, rebuke, castigate, chide, reprove, admonish, berate; *informal* lay into, tear into, tear a strip off, give someone a dressing-down, dress down, give someone what for, give someone a tongue-lashing, tell off, bawl out, chew out; *formal* excoriate.

lambent ▶ adjective FLICKERING, fluttering, incandescent, twinkling, dancing, radiant, brilliant.

lame ▶ adjective **1** *the mare was lame* LIMPING, hobbling; crippled, disabled, incapacitated; *dated* game. **2** *a lame excuse* FEEBLE, weak, thin, flimsy, poor, sorry; unconvincing, implausible, unlikely.
— OPPOSITES: convincing.

lamebrain ▶ adjective See IDIOT.

lament ▶ noun **1** *the widow's laments* WAIL, wailing, lamentation, moan, moaning, weeping, crying, sob, sobbing, keening; jeremiad, Kaddish; complaint. **2** *a lament for the dead* DIRGE, requiem, elegy, threnody, monody; keen.
▶ verb **1** *the mourners lamented* MOURN, grieve, sorrow,

wail, weep, cry, sob, keen, beat one's breast. **2** *he lamented the modernization of the buildings* BEMOAN, bewail, complain about, deplore, rue; protest against, object to, oppose, fulminate against, inveigh against, denounce.
– OPPOSITES: celebrate.

lamentable ▶ adjective DEPLORABLE, regrettable, sad, terrible, awful, wretched, woeful, dire, disastrous, grave, appalling, dreadful, pitiful, shameful, sorrowful, unfortunate.
– OPPOSITES: wonderful.

lamentation ▶ noun WEEPING, wailing, crying, sobbing, moaning, lament, keening, grieving, mourning.

laminate ▶ verb COVER, overlay, coat, surface, face; veneer, glaze, plasticize.
▶ noun VENEER; *proprietary* Arborite ♣; *proprietary* Formica.

lamp ▶ noun LIGHT, lantern; floor lamp, table lamp, chandelier, bedside lamp, flashlight, floodlight, spotlight, arc lamp, lava lamp, banker's lamp, candelabra; *proprietary* Coleman lamp, fluorescent lamp, tiffany lamp, track lights, trilight lamp ♣, storm lantern, street light/lamp, strobe light, sun lamp, torch, Chinese lantern, Japanese Lantern, hurricane lamp; oil lamp, seal-oil lamp, (*North*) kudlik/qullik ♣.

lampoon ▶ verb *he was mercilessly lampooned* SATIRIZE, mock, ridicule, make fun of, caricature, burlesque, parody, take off, tease; *informal* roast, send up.
▶ noun *a lampoon of student life* SATIRE, burlesque, parody, skit, caricature, impersonation, travesty, mockery, squib; *informal* send-up, takeoff, spoof.

lance ▶ noun *a knight with a lance* SPEAR, pike, javelin; harpoon.

land ▶ noun **1** *publicly owned land* GROUNDS, fields, terrain, territory, open space; property, landholding, acres, acreage, estate, lands, real estate, realty; *historical* demesne. **2** *fertile land* SOIL, earth, loam, topsoil, humus; tillage. **3** *many people are leaving the land* THE COUNTRYSIDE, the country, rural areas, (*Ont. & Que.*) the (back) concessions ♣. **4** *Tunisia is a land of variety* COUNTRY, nation, (nation) state, realm, kingdom, province; region, area, domain. **5** *the lookout sighted land to the east* TERRA FIRMA, dry land; coast, coastline, shore.
– RELATED TERMS: terrestrial.
▶ verb **1** *Canadian troops landed at Juno Beach* DISEMBARK, go ashore, debark, alight, get off. **2** *their plane landed at Chicago* TOUCH DOWN, make a landing, come in to land, come down. **3** *a bird landed on the branch* PERCH, settle, come to rest, alight. **4** (*informal*) *Nick landed the job of editor* OBTAIN, get, acquire, secure, be appointed to, gain, net, win, achieve, attain, carry off; *informal* swing, bag. **5** (*informal*) *that habit landed her in trouble* BRING, lead, cause to be in. **6** (*informal*) *he landed a left hook that staggered Curry* INFLICT, deal, deliver, administer, dispense, score, mete out; *informal* fetch.
– OPPOSITES: sail, take off.

landing ▶ noun **1** *a forced landing* ALIGHTING, touchdown, landfall; *informal* greaser. **2** *the ferry landing* HARBOUR, berth, dock, jetty, landing stage, pier, quay, slip, wharf, slipway.
– OPPOSITES: takeoff.

landlord, landlady ▶ noun *the landlady had objected to the noise* PROPERTY OWNER, proprietor, proprietress, lessor, householder, landowner; slumlord.
– OPPOSITES: tenant.

landmark ▶ noun **1** *the cliff is a landmark for hikers* MARKER, mark, indicator, beacon, Inukshuk, cairn, lobstick ♣. **2** *one of Quebec's most famous landmarks* MONUMENT, distinctive feature, prominent feature. **3** *the ruling was hailed as a landmark* TURNING POINT, milestone, watershed, critical point, way station, benchmark.
▶ adjective *a landmark decision* PRECEDENT-SETTING, normative, consequential, historic.

landscape ▶ noun SCENERY, countryside, topography, country, terrain; outlook, view, vista, prospect, aspect, panorama, perspective, sweep.

landslide ▶ noun **1** *floods and landslides* rock slide, mudslide; avalanche. **2** *a Tory landslide* DECISIVE VICTORY, overwhelming majority, triumph, sweep.

lane ▶ noun **1** *country lanes* alley, alleyway, laneway ♣, back alley, back lane, byroad, byway, track, road, street. **2** *cycle lanes* | *a three-lane highway* TRACK, way, course; road division; express lane, collector ♣.

language ▶ noun **1** *the structure of language* SPEECH, writing, communication, conversation, speaking, talking, talk, discourse; words, vocabulary. **2** *the English language* TONGUE, mother tongue, native tongue, heritage language ♣; dialect, patois, slang, idiom, jargon, argot, cant; *informal* lingo. **3** *the booklet is written in simple, everyday language* WORDING, phrasing, phraseology, style, vocabulary, terminology, expressions, turns of phrase, parlance, form/mode of expression, usages, locutions, choice of words, idiolect; *informal* lingo.
– RELATED TERMS: linguistic.

Canadian Population by Mother Tongue (2001 Census)

Mother Tongue	Population
English	17,694,835
French	6,864,615
Chinese	872,395
Italian	493,990
German	455,540
Punjabi	284,750
Spanish	260,785
Portuguese	222,850
Arabic	220,535
Polish	215,015
Tagalog (Pilipino)	199,770
Ukrainian	157,385
Dutch	133,035
Vietnamese	126,760
Greek	126,375

Adapted (2003/01/13) from http://www.statcan.ca/english/IPS/Data/97F0007XIE2001002.htm

languid ▶ adjective **1** *a languid wave of the hand* RELAXED, unhurried, languorous, slow; listless, lethargic, sluggish, lazy, idle, indolent, apathetic; *informal* laid-back. **2** *languid days in the sun* LEISURELY, languorous, relaxed, restful, lazy. **3** *she was pale and languid* SICKLY, weak, faint, feeble, frail, delicate; tired, weary, fatigued.
– OPPOSITES: energetic.

languish ▶ verb **1** *the plants languished and died* WEAKEN, deteriorate, decline; wither, droop, wilt, fade, waste away; *informal* go downhill. **2** *the general is*

now languishing in prison WASTE AWAY, rot, be abandoned, be neglected, be forgotten, suffer, experience hardship.
— OPPOSITES: thrive.

languor ▶ noun **1** *the sultry languor that was stealing over her* LASSITUDE, lethargy, listlessness, torpor, fatigue, weariness, sleepiness, drowsiness; laziness, idleness, indolence, inertia, sluggishness, apathy. **2** *the languor of a hot day* STILLNESS, tranquility, calm, calmness; oppressiveness, heaviness.
— OPPOSITES: vigour.

lanky ▶ adjective TALL, THIN, slender, slim, lean, lank, skinny, spindly, scrawny, spare, bony, gangling, gangly, gawky, rangy.
— OPPOSITES: stocky.

lantern ▶ noun *See* LAMP.

lap¹ ▶ noun *Liam sat on Santa's lap* KNEE, knees, thighs.

lap² ▶ noun *a race of eight laps* CIRCUIT, leg, circle, revolution, round; length.
▶ verb **1** *she lapped the other runners* OVERTAKE, outstrip, leave behind, pass, go past; catch up with; *informal* leapfrog. **2** *(literary) he was lapped in blankets* WRAP, swathe, envelop, enfold, swaddle.

lap³ ▶ verb **1** *waves lapped against the seawall* SPLASH, wash, swish, slosh, break, beat, strike, dash, roll; *literary* plash. **2** *the dog lapped water out of a puddle* DRINK, lick up, swallow, slurp, gulp.
■ **lap something up** RELISH, revel in, savour, delight in, glory in, enjoy.

lapse ▶ noun **1** *a lapse of concentration* FAILURE, failing, slip, error, mistake, blunder, fault, omission, hiccup; *informal* slip-up. **2** *his lapse into petty crime* DECLINE, fall, falling, slipping, drop, deterioration, degeneration, backsliding, regression, retrogression, descent, sinking, slide. **3** *a lapse of time* INTERVAL, gap, pause, interlude, lull, hiatus, break.
▶ verb **1** *our membership has lapsed* EXPIRE, become void, become invalid, run out. **2** *she lapsed into self-pity* REVERT, relapse; drift, slide, slip, sink; deteriorate, decline, fall, degenerate, backslide, regress, retrogress.

lapsed ▶ adjective **1** *a lapsed Catholic* NON-PRACTISING, backsliding, apostate; former. **2** *a lapsed membership* EXPIRED, void, invalid, out of date.
— OPPOSITES: practising, valid.

larceny ▶ noun THEFT, stealing, robbery, pilfering, thieving; burglary, housebreaking, breaking and entering; *informal* filching, swiping, pinching; *formal* peculation.

larder ▶ noun PANTRY, cupboard, (food) store.

large ▶ adjective **1** *a large house | large numbers of people* BIG, great, huge, sizeable, substantial, immense, enormous, colossal, massive, mammoth, vast, prodigious, tremendous, gigantic, giant, monumental, stupendous, gargantuan, elephantine, titanic, mountainous, monstrous; towering, tall, high; mighty, voluminous; king-size(d), economy-size(d), family-size(d), man-size(d), giant-size(d); *informal* jumbo, whopping, mega, humongous, monster, astronomical, ginormous. **2** *a large red-faced man* BIG, burly, heavy, tall, bulky, thickset, chunky, strapping, hulking, hefty, muscular, brawny, solid, powerful, sturdy, strong, rugged; fat, plump, overweight, chubby, stout, meaty, fleshy, portly, rotund, flabby, paunchy, obese, corpulent; hunky, roly-poly, beefy, tubby, well-upholstered, pudgy, well-fed, big-boned, zaftig, full-figured, buxom, corn-fed. **3** *a large supply of wool*

ABUNDANT, copious, plentiful, ample, liberal, generous, lavish, bountiful, bumper, boundless, good, considerable, superabundant; *literary* plenteous. **4** *the measure has large economic implications* WIDE-REACHING, far-reaching, wide, sweeping, large-scale, broad, extensive, comprehensive, exhaustive.
— RELATED TERMS: macro-, mega-.
— OPPOSITES: small, meagre.
■ **at large** **1** *fourteen criminals are still at large* AT LIBERTY, free, (on the) loose, on the run, fugitive, on the lam. **2** *society at large* AS A WHOLE, generally, in general.
■ **by and large** ON THE WHOLE, generally, in general, all things considered, all in all, for the most part, in the main, as a rule, overall, almost always, mainly, mostly; on average, on balance.

largely ▶ adverb MOSTLY, mainly, to a large/great extent, chiefly, predominantly, primarily, principally, for the most part, in the main; usually, typically, commonly.

large-scale ▶ adjective *a large-scale program* EXTENSIVE, wide-ranging, far-reaching, exhaustive, comprehensive; mass, nationwide, global.

largesse ▶ noun **1** *Bob took advantage of his friend's largesse* GENEROSITY, liberality, munificence, bounty, bountifulness, beneficence, altruism, charity, philanthropy, magnanimity, benevolence, charitableness, open-handedness, kindness, big-heartedness; *formal* benefaction. **2** *distributing largesse to the locals* GIFTS, presents, handouts, grants, aid; patronage, sponsorship, backing, help; alms.
— OPPOSITES: meanness.

lark *(informal)* ▶ noun *we were just having a bit of a lark* FUN, amusement, laugh, giggle, joke; escapade, prank, trick, jape, practical joke.

lascivious ▶ adjective LECHEROUS, lewd, lustful, licentious, libidinous, salacious, lubricious, prurient, dirty, smutty, naughty, indecent, ribald; *informal* horny, randy; *formal* concupiscent.

lash ▶ verb **1** *he lashed the beast repeatedly* WHIP, flog, flagellate, beat, thrash, horsewhip, scourge, birch, belt, strap, cane, switch; strike, hit; *informal* wallop, whack, lam, larrup, give someone a hiding, whale. **2** *rain lashed the window panes* BEAT AGAINST, dash against, pound, batter, strike, hit, knock. **3** *the tiger began to lash his tail* SWISH, flick, twitch, whip. **4** *two boats were lashed together* FASTEN, bind, tie (up), tether, hitch, knot, rope, make fast.
▶ noun **1** *he brought the lash down upon the prisoner's back* WHIP, horsewhip, scourge, thong, flail, strap, birch, cane, switch; *historical* cat-o'-nine-tails, cat, knout. **2** *twenty lashes* STROKE, blow, hit, welt, thwack; *archaic* stripe.
■ **lash out** *the president lashed out at the opposition* CRITICIZE, chastise, censure, attack, condemn, denounce, lambaste, rail at/against, harangue, pillory; berate, upbraid, rebuke, reproach, tear a strip off; *informal* lay into, tear into, blast; *formal* castigate.

lassitude ▶ noun LETHARGY, listlessness, weariness, languor, sluggishness, tiredness, fatigue, torpor, lifelessness, apathy.
— OPPOSITES: vigour.

lasso ▶ noun LARIAT.

last ▶ verb **1** *the hearing lasted for six days* CONTINUE, go on, carry on, keep on/going, proceed, take; stay, remain, persist. **2** *how long will he last as manager?* SURVIVE, endure, hold on/out, keep going, persevere; *informal* stick it out, hang on. **3** *the car is built to last*

ENDURE, wear well, stand up, bear up; *informal* go the distance.
▶ **adjective 1** *the last woman in line* REARMOST, hindmost, endmost, at the end, at the back, furthest (back), final, ultimate. **2** *Rembrandt spent his last years in Amsterdam* CLOSING, concluding, final, ending, end, terminal; later, latter. **3** *I'd be the last person to say anything against him* LEAST LIKELY, most unlikely, most improbable; least suitable, most unsuitable, most inappropriate, least appropriate. **4** *we met last year* PREVIOUS, preceding; prior, former. **5** *this was his last chance* FINAL, only remaining.
— OPPOSITES: first, early, next.
▶ **adverb** *the candidate coming last is eliminated* AT THE END, at/in the rear.
▶ **noun** *the most important business was left to the last* END, ending, finish, close, conclusion, finale, termination.
— OPPOSITES: beginning.
■ **at last** FINALLY, at long last, after a long time, in the end, eventually, ultimately, in (the fullness of) time.
■ **the last word 1** *that's my last word* FINAL DECISION, definitive statement, conclusive comment. **2** *she was determined to have the last word* CONCLUDING REMARK, final say, closing statement. **3** *the last word in luxury and efficiency* THE BEST, the peak, the acme, the epitome, the latest; the pinnacle, the apex, the apogee, the ultimate, the height, the zenith, the nonpareil, the crème de la crème; *archaic* the nonsuch.
■ **last hurrah** SWAN SONG, grand finale, (grand) finale, curtain call.

last-ditch ▶ **adjective** LAST-MINUTE, last-chance, eleventh-hour, last-resort, desperate, do-or-die, last-gasp, final.

lasting ▶ **adjective** ENDURING, long-lasting, long-lived, abiding, continuing, long-term, surviving, persisting, permanent, durable, constant, stable, established, secure, long-standing; unchanging, irreversible, immutable, eternal, undying, everlasting, unending, never-ending, unfading, changeless, indestructible, unceasing, unwavering, unfaltering.
— OPPOSITES: ephemeral.

lastly ▶ **adverb** FINALLY, in conclusion, to conclude, to sum up, to end, last, ultimately.
— OPPOSITES: firstly.

latch ▶ **noun** *he lifted the latch* FASTENING, catch, fastener, clasp, lock.
▶ **verb** *Jess latched the back door* FASTEN, secure, make fast, lock.

late ▶ **adjective 1** *the train was late* BEHIND SCHEDULE, behind time, behindhand; tardy, running late, overdue, belated, delayed. **2** *her late husband* DEAD, departed, lamented, passed on/away, deceased.
— OPPOSITES: punctual, early.
▶ **adverb 1** *she had arrived late* BEHIND SCHEDULE, behind time, behindhand, belatedly, tardily, at the last minute, at the buzzer. **2** *I was working late* AFTER (OFFICE) HOURS, overtime. **3** *don't stay out late* LATE AT NIGHT; *informal* till all hours.
■ **of late** RECENTLY, lately, latterly.

lately ▶ **adverb** RECENTLY, of late, latterly, in recent times.

lateness ▶ **noun** UNPUNCTUALITY, tardiness, delay.

latent ▶ **adjective** DORMANT, untapped, unused, undiscovered, hidden, concealed, underlying, invisible, unseen, undeveloped, unrealized, unfulfilled, potential.

later ▶ **adjective** *a later chapter* SUBSEQUENT, following,

succeeding, future, upcoming, to come, ensuing, next; *formal* posterior; *archaic* after.
— OPPOSITES: earlier.
▶ **adverb 1** *later, the film rights were sold* SUBSEQUENTLY, eventually, then, next, later on, after this/that, afterwards, at a later date, in the future, in due course, by and by, in a while, in time. **2** *two days later a letter arrived* AFTERWARDS, later on, after (that), subsequently, following; *formal* thereafter.

lateral ▶ **adjective 1** *lateral movements* SIDEWAYS, sidewise, sideward, edgewise, edgeways, oblique, horizontal. **2** *lateral thinking* UNORTHODOX, inventive, creative, imaginative, original, innovative, non-linear.

latest ▶ **adjective** MOST RECENT, newest, just out, just released, fresh, up to date, up-to-the-minute, state-of-the-art, au courant, dernier cri, current, modern, contemporary, fashionable, in fashion, in vogue; newfangled; *informal* in, with it, trendy, hip, hot, big, funky, happening, cool.
— OPPOSITES: old.

lather ▶ **noun** *a rich, soapy lather* FOAM, froth, suds, soapsuds, bubbles; *literary* spume.
■ **in a lather** AGITATED, flustered, distressed, worked up, strung out, keyed up, in a state, in a tizzy, in a dither, in a twitter, upset.

latitude ▶ **noun 1** *Toronto and Nice are on the same latitude* parallel. **2** *he gave them a lot of latitude* FREEDOM, scope, leeway, (breathing) space, flexibility, liberty, independence, free rein, licence, room to manoeuvre, wiggle room, freedom of action.
— OPPOSITES: longitude, restriction.

latter ▶ **adjective 1** *the latter stages of development* LATER, closing, end, concluding, final; latest, most recent. **2** *Russia chose the latter option* LAST-MENTIONED, second, last, later.
— OPPOSITES: former.

latter-day ▶ **adjective** MODERN, present-day, current, contemporary.

lattice ▶ **noun** GRID, latticework, fretwork, open framework, openwork, trellis, trelliswork, espalier, grille, network, mesh.

laud ▶ **verb** PRAISE, extol, hail, applaud, acclaim, commend, sing the praises of, speak highly of, pay tribute to, lionize, eulogize, rhapsodize over/about; *informal* rave about; *archaic* magnify, panegyrize.
— OPPOSITES: criticize.

laudable ▶ **adjective** PRAISEWORTHY, commendable, admirable, meritorious, worthy, deserving, creditable, estimable.
— OPPOSITES: shameful.

laudatory ▶ **adjective** COMPLIMENTARY, praising, congratulatory, extolling, adulatory, commendatory, approbatory, flattering, celebratory, eulogizing, panegyrical; *informal* glowing; *formal* encomiastic.
— OPPOSITES: disparaging.

laugh ▶ **verb 1** *Norma started to laugh excitedly* CHUCKLE, chortle, guffaw, cackle, giggle, titter, twitter, snigger, snicker, yuk, tee-hee, burst out laughing, roar/hoot/howl/shriek with laughter, crack up, dissolve into laughter, split one's sides, be (rolling) on the floor, be doubled up, be killing oneself (laughing); *informal* be in stitches, be rolling in the aisles. **2** *people laughed at his theories* RIDICULE, mock, deride, scoff at, jeer at, sneer at, jibe at, make fun of, poke fun at, scorn; lampoon, satirize, parody; *informal* send up, pooh-pooh.

▶ **noun 1** *he gave a short laugh* CHUCKLE, chortle, guffaw, giggle, titter, twitter, tee-hee, snigger, snicker, yuk, roar/hoot/howl of laughter, shriek of laughter, belly laugh, horse laugh. **2** *he was a laugh* JOKER, card, jokester, hoot, scream, riot, laff riot, gas, barrel of laughs, wag, wit, clown, jester, prankster, character. **3** *I entered the contest for a laugh* JOKE, prank, jest, escapade, caper, practical joke, lark.
■ **laugh something off** DISMISS, make a joke of, make light of, shrug off, brush aside, scoff at; *informal* pooh-pooh.

laughable ▶ **adjective 1** *the government's new education policy is laughable* RIDICULOUS, ludicrous, absurd, risible, preposterous; foolish, silly, idiotic, stupid, asinine, nonsensical, crazy, insane, outrageous, hare-brained, cockamamie, cockeyed, daffy. **2** *if it wasn't so tragic, it'd be laughable* AMUSING, funny, humorous, hilarious, uproarious, comical, comic, farcical.

laughingstock ▶ **noun** BUTT, dupe, spectacle, figure of fun, stooge, fall guy.

laughter ▶ **noun** *the sound of laughter* LAUGHING, chuckling, chortling, guffawing, giggling, tittering, twittering, cackling, sniggering; *informal* hysterics.

launch ▶ **verb 1** *they've launched the shuttle* SEND INTO ORBIT, blast off, take off, lift off. **2** *he launched the boat* SET AFLOAT, put to sea, put into the water. **3** *a chair was launched at him* THROW, hurl, fling, pitch, lob, let fly; fire, shoot; *informal* chuck, heave, sling. **4** *the government launched a new campaign* SET IN MOTION, get going, get underway, start, commence, begin, embark on, initiate, inaugurate, set up, organize, introduce, bring into being; *informal* kick off, roll out. **5** *he launched into a tirade* START, commence, burst into.

launder ▶ **verb** WASH (AND IRON), clean; dry-clean.

laundry ▶ **noun 1** *a big pile of laundry* (DIRTY) WASHING, dirty clothes. **2** *the facilities include a laundry* LAUNDRY ROOM, launderette, laundromat, cleaners.

laurels ▶ **plural noun** HONOURS, tributes, praise, plaudits, accolades, kudos, acclaim, acclamation, credit, glory, honour, distinction, fame, renown, prestige, recognition; *informal* brownie points.

lavatory ▶ **noun** WASHROOM, bathroom, restroom, toilet, latrine, men's/ladies' room, little girls'/boys' room, WC, water closet, privy, outhouse, powder room, commode, comfort station, facilities; throne room, can, john, lav, loo; *Nautical* head.

lavish ▶ **adjective 1** *lavish parties* SUMPTUOUS, luxurious, costly, expensive, opulent, grand, splendid, rich, fancy, posh; *informal* fancy-dancy, fancy-schmancy. **2** *lavish hospitality* GENEROUS, liberal, bountiful, open-handed, unstinting, unsparing, free, munificent, extravagant, prodigal. **3** *lavish amounts of champagne* ABUNDANT, copious, plentiful, liberal, prolific, generous; *literary* plenteous.
— OPPOSITES: meagre, frugal.
▶ **verb** *she lavished money on her children* GIVE FREELY, spend generously, bestow, heap, shower.

law ▶ **noun 1** *a new law was passed* REGULATION, statute, enactment, act, bill, decree, edict, bylaw, rule, ruling, ordinance, dictum, command, order, directive, pronouncement, proclamation, dictate, diktat, fiat. **2** *a career in law* THE LEGAL PROFESSION, the bar. **3** *I'll take you to law!* LITIGATION, legal action, lawsuit, justice. **4** *(informal) on the run from the law. See* POLICE *noun.* **5** *the laws of the game* RULE, regulation, principle, convention, instruction, guideline. **6** *a*

moral law PRINCIPLE, rule, precept, directive, injunction, commandment, belief, creed, credo, maxim, tenet, doctrine, canon.
— RELATED TERMS: legal, jurisprudence.

law-abiding ▶ **adjective** HONEST, righteous, honourable, upright, upstanding, good, decent, virtuous, moral, dutiful, obedient, compliant.
— OPPOSITES: criminal.

lawbreaker ▶ **noun** CRIMINAL, offender, wrongdoer, malefactor, evildoer, transgressor, miscreant; villain, rogue, ruffian, felon; *Law* malfeasant; *informal* crook, con, jailbird, hood.

lawful ▶ **adjective** LEGITIMATE, legal, licit, just, permissible, permitted, allowable, allowed, rightful, sanctioned, authorized, warranted, within the law; *informal* legit.
— OPPOSITES: illegal, criminal.

lawless ▶ **adjective** *a lawless country* UNGOVERNABLE, unruly, disruptive, anarchic, disorderly, rebellious, insubordinate, riotous, mutinous; uncivilized, wild.
— OPPOSITES: orderly, legal.

lawlessness ▶ **noun** ANARCHY, disorder, chaos, unruliness, criminality, crime.

lawn ▶ **noun** GRASS, yard, front yard, backyard, dooryard.

lawn sale ▶ **noun** YARD SALE, garage sale, street sale.

lawsuit ▶ **noun** (LEGAL) ACTION, suit, case, (legal/judicial) proceedings, litigation, trial, assize ♣.

lawyer ▶ **noun** counsel, Crown attorney/counsel/prosecutor ♣, Queen's Counsel, QC, legal practitioner, legal professional, legal adviser, member of the bar, barrister and solicitor ♣, barrister, solicitor, litigator, advocate, attorney; *informal* ambulance chaser, mouthpiece, legal eagle/beagle.

lax ▶ **adjective** SLACK, slipshod, negligent, remiss, careless, heedless, unmindful, slapdash, offhand, casual; easygoing, lenient, permissive, liberal, indulgent, overindulgent; *informal* sloppy.
— OPPOSITES: strict.

laxative ▶ **noun** PURGATIVE, enema; *Medicine* cathartic.

lay¹ ▶ **verb 1** *Curtis laid the newspaper on the table* PUT (DOWN), place, set (down), deposit, rest, situate, locate, position; *informal* stick, dump, park, plonk. **2** *the act laid the foundation for the new system* SET IN PLACE, set out/up, establish. **3** *I'll lay money that Michelle will be there* BET, wager, gamble, stake, risk, hazard, venture; give odds, speculate. **4** *they are going to lay charges* BRING (FORWARD), press, lodge, register, place, file. **5** *she laid the blame at the Prime Minister's door* ASSIGN, attribute, ascribe, allot, attach; hold someone responsible/accountable, find guilty, pin the blame on. **6** *we laid out plans for the next voyage* DEVISE, arrange, make (ready), prepare, work out, hatch, design, plan, scheme, plot, conceive, put together, draw up, produce, develop, concoct, formulate, cook up. **7** *this will lay responsibility on the court* IMPOSE, apply, entrust, vest, place, put; inflict, encumber, saddle, charge, burden. **8** *we laid the trap and waited* SET, prepare, devise, bait.
■ **lay something aside 1** *farmers laying aside areas for conservation* PUT ASIDE, put to one side, keep, save. **2** *producers must lay aside their conservatism* ABANDON, cast/set aside, reject, renounce, repudiate, disregard, forget, discard; *literary* forsake.
■ **lay something bare** REVEAL, disclose, divulge,

show, expose, exhibit, uncover, unveil, unmask, make a clean breast of, make known, make public.

■ **lay something down 1** *he laid down his glass* PUT DOWN, set down, place down, deposit, rest; *informal* dump, plonk down. **2** *they were forced to lay down their weapons* RELINQUISH, surrender, give up, yield, cede. **3** *the ground rules have been laid down* FORMULATE, stipulate, set down, draw up, frame; prescribe, ordain, dictate, decree; enact, pass, decide, determine, impose, codify.

■ **lay down the law** DOGMATIZE, be dogmatic, be domineering, call the shots.

■ **lay eyes on** (*informal*) SEE, spot, observe, regard, view, catch sight of, set eyes on; *literary* behold, espy, descry.

■ **lay hands on** *wait till I lay my hands on you!* CATCH, lay/get hold of, get one's hands on, seize, grab, grasp, capture.

■ **lay into** (*informal*) **1** *a policeman laying into a protester.* See ASSAULT *verb* sense 1. **2** *he laid into her with a string of insults.* See CRITICIZE.

■ **lay it on thick** (*informal*) EXAGGERATE, overdo it, embellish the truth; flatter, praise, soft-soap, pile it on, sweet-talk.

■ **lay off** (*informal*) **1** *I have to lay off beer* GIVE UP, abstain from, desist from, cut out. **2** *I lay off work at 5* QUIT pack in, leave off, stop. **3** *lay off, will you!* BACK OFF, give it a rest, enough already, shut up, stop it.

■ **lay someone off** MAKE REDUNDANT, dismiss, let go, discharge, give notice to, sack, fire, give someone their marching orders, give someone the boot, give someone the (old) heave-ho.

■ **lay something out 1** *Robyn laid the plans out on the desk* SPREAD OUT, set out, display, exhibit. **2** *a paper laying out our priorities* OUTLINE, sketch out, rough out, detail, draw up, formulate, work out, frame, draft. **3** (*informal*) *he had to lay out $70.* See PAY *verb* sense 2.

■ **lay waste** DEVASTATE, wipe out, destroy, demolish, annihilate, raze, ruin, wreck, level, flatten, ravage, pillage, sack, despoil.

lay² ▶ **adjective 1** *a lay preacher* NON-CLERICAL, non-ordained, secular, temporal. **2** *a lay audience* NON-PROFESSIONAL, amateur, non-specialist, non-technical, untrained, unqualified.

layabout ▶ **noun** IDLER, loafer, slacker, lazybones, lounger, flâneur, shirker, (*Atlantic*) hangashore ♣, sluggard, laggard, slugabed, malingerer, good-for-nothing; *literary* wastrel.

layer ▶ **noun** COATING, sheet, coat, film, covering, blanket, skin, thickness; stratum, band.

layman ▶ **noun**. See LAYPERSON.

layoff ▶ **noun** REDUNDANCY, dismissal, discharge; *informal* sacking, firing, the sack, the boot, the axe, downsizing, rationalizing, rightsizing.
— OPPOSITES: recruitment.

layout ▶ **noun 1** *the layout of the house* ARRANGEMENT, geography, design, organization; plan, map. **2** *the magazine's layout* DESIGN, arrangement, presentation, style, format; structure, organization, composition, configuration.

layperson ▶ **noun 1** *a prayer book for laypeople* UNORDAINED PERSON, member of the congregation, layman, laywoman, member of the laity. **2** *engineering sounds highly specialized to the layperson* NON-EXPERT, layman, non-professional, amateur, non-specialist, dilettante.

laze ▶ **verb** RELAX, unwind, idle, do nothing, loaf (around/about), lounge (around/about), loll (around/

about), lie (around/about), take it easy; *informal* hang around/round, veg (out), bum (around).

lazy ▶ **adjective** IDLE, indolent, slothful, work-shy, shiftless, inactive, sluggish, lethargic; remiss, negligent, slack, lax, lackadaisical.
— OPPOSITES: industrious.

lazybones ▶ **noun** (*informal*) IDLER, loafer, layabout, lounger, good-for-nothing, do-nothing, shirker, sluggard, laggard, slugabed, slacker, flâneur, (*Atlantic*) hangashore ♣; *literary* wastrel.

leach ▶ **verb** DRAIN, filter, percolate, seep, filtrate, strain.

lead¹ ▶ **verb 1** *Michelle led them into the house* GUIDE, conduct, show (the way), lead the way, usher, escort, steer, pilot, shepherd; accompany, see, take. **2** *he led us to believe they were lying* CAUSE, induce, prompt, move, persuade, influence, drive, condition, make; incline, dispose, predispose. **3** *this might lead to job losses* RESULT IN, cause, bring on/about, give rise to, be the cause of, make happen, create, produce, occasion, effect, generate, contribute to, promote; provoke, stir up, spark off, arouse, foment, instigate; involve, necessitate, entail; *formal* effectuate. **4** *he led a march to the city centre* BE AT THE HEAD/FRONT OF, head, spearhead; precede. **5** *she led a coalition of radicals* BE THE LEADER OF, be the head of, preside over, head, command, govern, rule, be in charge of, be in command of, be in control of, run, control, direct, be at the helm of; administer, organize, manage; reign over, be in power over; *informal* head up. **6** *the Stampeders were leading at halftime* BE AHEAD, be winning, be (out) in front, be in the lead, be first, be on top. **7** *the champion was leading the field* BE AT THE FRONT OF, be first in, be ahead of, head; outrun, outstrip, outpace, leave behind, draw away from; outdo, outclass, beat; *informal* leave standing. **8** *I just want to lead a normal life* EXPERIENCE, have, live, spend.
— OPPOSITES: follow.

▶ **noun 1** *I was in the lead early on* LEADING POSITION, first place, van, vanguard; ahead, in front, winning. **2** *they took the lead in the personal computer market* FIRST POSITION, forefront, primacy, dominance, superiority, ascendancy; pre-eminence, supremacy, advantage, upper hand, whip hand. **3** *playing the lead* LEADING ROLE, star/starring role, title role, principal part; principal character, male lead, female lead, leading man, leading lady. **4** *a Labrador on a lead* LEASH, tether, cord, rope, chain. **5** *detectives were following up a new lead* CLUE, pointer, hint, tip, tipoff, suggestion, indication, sign.

▶ **adjective** *the lead position* LEADING, first, top, foremost, front, head; chief, principal, main, premier.

■ **lead something off** BEGIN, start (off), commence, open; *informal* kick off.

■ **lead someone on** DECEIVE, mislead, delude, hoodwink, dupe, trick, fool, pull the wool over someone's eyes; *informal* string along, lead up the garden path, take for a ride, fleece, inveigle, hornswoggle, scam.

■ **lead the way 1** *he led the way to the kitchen* GUIDE, conduct, show the way. **2** *Alberta is leading the way in new technologies* TAKE THE INITIATIVE, break (new) ground, blaze a trail, prepare the way, be at the forefront.

■ **lead up to** PREPARE THE WAY FOR, pave the way for, lay the groundwork for, set the scene for, work round/up to.

lead² ▶ **noun** *a lead-lined box.*
— RELATED TERMS: plumbic, plumbous, plumb-.

■ **get the lead out** HURRY UP, get a move on, be quick; *informal* get cracking, shake a leg, look lively, look sharp; *dated* make haste.

leaden ► adjective **1** *he moved on leaden feet* SLUGGISH, heavy, lumbering, slow, burdensome, cumbersome. **2** *leaden prose* BORING, dull, unimaginative, uninspired, monotonous, heavy, laboured, wooden, lifeless, plodding; depressing. **3** *a leaden sky* GREY, greyish, black, dark; cloudy, gloomy, overcast, dull, sunless, oppressive, threatening; *literary* tenebrous.

leader ► noun **1** *the leader of the Democratic Party* CHIEF, head, principal; commander, captain; superior, headman; chairman, chairwoman, chairperson, chair; (managing) director, CEO, manager, superintendent, supervisor, overseer, administrator, employer, master, mistress; president, premier, governor; ruler, monarch, king, queen, sovereign, emperor; *informal* boss, skipper, number one, numero uno, honcho, sachem, padrone. **2** *a world leader in the use of video conferencing* PIONEER, front-runner, world-beater, innovator, trailblazer, ground-breaker, trend-setter, torch-bearer, rainmaker.
— OPPOSITES: follower, supporter.

leadership ► noun **1** *firm leadership* GUIDANCE, direction, control, management, superintendence, supervision; organization, government. **2** *the leadership of the Conservative Party* DIRECTORSHIP, governorship, governance, administration, captaincy, control, ascendancy, supremacy, rule, command, power, dominion, influence, headship.

leading ► adjective **1** *he played the leading role* MAIN, chief, major, prime, most significant, most important, principal, foremost, key, central, focal, pre-eminent, paramount, dominant, essential. **2** *last season's leading scorer* TOP, highest, best, first; front, lead; unparalleled, matchless, star.
— OPPOSITES: subordinate, minor.

leaf ► noun **1** *sycamore leaves* FROND, leaflet, flag; *Botany* cotyledon, blade, bract. **2** *a leaf in a book* PAGE, sheet, folio.
► verb *he leafed through the documents* FLICK, flip, thumb, skim, browse, glance, riffle, rifle; scan, run one's eye over, peruse.
■ **turn over a new leaf** REFORM, improve, mend one's ways, make a fresh start, change for the better; *informal* go straight.

leaflet ► noun PAMPHLET, booklet, brochure, handbill, circular, flyer, fact sheet, handout, bulletin.

league ► noun **1** *a league of nations* ALLIANCE, confederation, confederacy, federation, union, association, coalition, consortium, affiliation, guild, co-operative, partnership, fellowship, syndicate. **2** *the best team in the league* beer league, big league, bush league, house league, rep league ♣, industrial league ♣, intramural league, Little League, major league, minor league, rec league. **3** *the store is not in the same league* CLASS, group, circle, category, level.
► verb *they leagued together with other companies* ALLY, join forces, join together, unite, band together, affiliate, combine, amalgamate, confederate, team up, join up.
■ **in league with** COLLABORATING WITH, cooperating with, in alliance with, allied with, conspiring with, hand in glove with; *informal* in cahoots with, in bed with.

leak ► verb **1** *oil leaking from the tanker* SEEP (OUT), escape, ooze (out), secrete, bleed, emanate, issue, drip, dribble, drain; discharge, exude. **2** *civil servants leaked information to the press* DISCLOSE, divulge, reveal, make public, tell, impart, pass on, relate, communicate, expose, broadcast, publish, release, let slip, bring into the open; *informal* blab, let the cat out of the bag, spill the beans.
► noun **1** *check that there are no leaks in the pipe* HOLE, opening, aperture, puncture, perforation, gash, slit, nick, rent, break, crack, fissure, rupture. **2** *a gas leak* DISCHARGE, leakage, seepage, drip, escape. **3** *leaks to the media* DISCLOSURE, revelation, exposé, leakage, tipoff.

lean¹ ► verb **1** *Polly leaned against the door* REST, recline, be supported by. **2** *trees leaning in the wind* SLANT, incline, bend, tilt, be at an angle, slope, tip, list. **3** *he leans towards existentialist philosophy* TEND, incline, gravitate; have a preference for, have a penchant for, be partial to, have a liking for, have an affinity with. **4** *a strong shoulder to lean on* DEPEND, be dependent, rely, count, bank, have faith in, trust. **5** (*informal*) *he leaned on me to change my mind* INTIMIDATE, coerce, browbeat, bully, threaten, put pressure on, harass, hassle; *informal* twist someone's arm, put the screws on, hold a gun to someone's head.

lean² ► adjective **1** *a tall, lean man* SLIM, thin, slender, spare, wiry, lanky, skinny. **2** *a lean harvest* MEAGRE, sparse, poor, mean, inadequate, insufficient, paltry, scanty, deficient, insubstantial. **3** *lean times* HARD, bad, difficult, tough, impoverished, poverty-stricken.
— OPPOSITES: fat, abundant, prosperous.

leaning ► noun INCLINATION, tendency, bent, proclivity, propensity, penchant, predisposition, predilection, partiality, preference, bias, attraction, liking, fondness, taste; *informal* yen.

leap ► verb **1** *he leapt over the gate* JUMP (OVER), vault (over), spring over, bound over, hop (over), hurdle, clear. **2** *Claudia leapt to her feet* SPRING, jump (up), hop, bound. **3** *we leapt into the car* RUSH, hurry, hasten. **4** *she leapt at the chance* ACCEPT EAGERLY, grasp (with both hands), grab, take advantage of, seize (on), jump at. **5** *don't leap to conclusions* FORM HASTILY, reach hurriedly; hurry, hasten, jump, rush. **6** *profits leapt by 55%* INCREASE RAPIDLY, soar, rocket, skyrocket, shoot up, escalate.
► noun **1** *an easy leap* JUMP, vault, spring, bound, hop, skip. **2** *a leap of 33%* SUDDEN RISE, surge, upsurge, upswing, upturn.
■ **in/by leaps and bounds** RAPIDLY, swiftly, quickly, speedily.

learn ► verb **1** *learning a foreign language* ACQUIRE A KNOWLEDGE OF, acquire skill in, become competent in, become proficient in, grasp, master, take in, absorb, assimilate, digest, familiarize oneself with; study, read up on, be taught, have lessons in; *informal* get the hang of, bone up on. **2** *she learned the poem by heart* MEMORIZE, learn by heart, commit to memory, get down pat; *archaic* con. **3** *he learned that the school would shortly be closing* DISCOVER, find out, become aware, be informed, hear (tell); gather, understand, ascertain, establish; *informal* get wind of the fact, suss out, get a line on.

learned ► adjective SCHOLARLY, erudite, well-educated, knowledgeable, well-read, well-informed, lettered, cultured, intellectual, academic, literary, bookish, highbrow, studious; *informal* brainy, egghead.
— OPPOSITES: ignorant.

learner ► noun See NOVICE sense 1.

learning ► noun **1** *a centre of learning* STUDY, studying, education, schooling, tuition, teaching,

academic work; research. **2** *the astonishing range of his learning* SCHOLARSHIP, knowledge, education, erudition, intellect, enlightenment, illumination, edification, book learning, information, understanding, wisdom.
— OPPOSITES: ignorance.

lease ▶ **noun** *a 15-year lease* LEASEHOLD, rental agreement, charter; rental, tenancy, tenure, period of occupancy.
— RELATED TERMS: lessor, lessee.
— OPPOSITES: freehold.
▶ **verb 1** *the film crew leased a large hangar* RENT, charter. **2** *they leased the mill to a reputable family* RENT (OUT), let (out), sublet, sublease.

leash ▶ **noun** *keep your dog on a leash* LEAD, tether, rope, chain, restraint.
▶ **verb 1** *she leashed the dog* PUT THE LEASH ON, put the lead on, tether, tie up, secure, restrain. **2** *the fury in her face was barely leashed* CURB, control, keep under control, check, restrain, hold back, suppress, rein in.
■ **straining at the leash** EAGER, impatient, anxious, enthusiastic; *informal* itching, dying.

least ▶ **adjective** *I have not the least idea what this means* SLIGHTEST, smallest, minutest, tiniest, littlest.
■ **at least** AT THE MINIMUM, no/not less than, more than; anyway, at all events, leastways/leastwise.

leather ▶ **noun** *a leather jacket* SKIN, hide. *See table.*

Types of Leather

alligator	mocha
buckskin	morocco
buff	napa
calfskin	nubuck
capeskin	oxhide
chamois	patent leather
cordovan	pigskin
cowhide	rawhide
crocodile	roan
deerskin	Russia leather
doeskin	sealskin
dogskin	shagreen
goatskin	shammy
grain	sheepskin
kid	snakeskin
kidskin	suede
lambskin	

leathery ▶ **adjective 1** *leathery skin* ROUGH, rugged, leathered, hard, hardened, wrinkled, furrowed, lined, weather-beaten, callous, gnarled. **2** *leathery sides of beef* TOUGH, hard, gristly, chewy, stringy, rubbery.

leave¹ ▶ **verb 1** *I left the hotel* DEPART FROM, go (away) from, withdraw from, retire from, take oneself off from, exit from, take one's leave of, pull out of, quit, be gone from, decamp from, disappear from, vacate, absent oneself from; say one's farewells/goodbyes, make oneself scarce; *informal* push off, shove off, clear out/off, cut and run, split, vamoose, scoot, make tracks. **2** *the next morning we left for Victoria* SET OFF, head, make; set sail. **3** *he's left his wife* ABANDON, desert, cast aside, jilt, throw over; *informal* dump, ditch, drop, walk/run out on; *literary* forsake. **4** *he left his job in November* RESIGN FROM, retire from, step down from, withdraw from, pull out of, give up; pack it in, call it quits, hang up one's skates ✦; *informal* quit. **5** *she left her purse on a bus* LEAVE BEHIND, forget, lose, mislay. **6** *I thought I'd leave it to the experts* ENTRUST, hand over,

pass on, refer; delegate. **7** *he left her $100,000* BEQUEATH, will, endow, hand down, make over. **8** *the speech left some feelings of disappointment* CAUSE, produce, generate, give rise to.
— OPPOSITES: arrive.
■ **leave off** (*informal*) STOP, cease, finish, desist from, keep from, break off, lay off, give up, discontinue, refrain from, eschew; *informal* quit, knock off, swear off; *formal* forswear.
■ **leave someone/something out 1** *Adam left out the address* MISS OUT, omit, fail to include, overlook, forget; skip, miss. **2** *he was left out of the game* EXCLUDE, omit, pass over.

leave² ▶ **noun 1** *the judge granted leave to appeal* PERMISSION, consent, authorization, sanction, warrant, dispensation, approval, clearance, blessing, assent, licence; *informal* the go-ahead, the green light, the OK, the rubber stamp, the nod. **2** *he was on leave* HOLIDAY, vacation, break, time off, furlough, sabbatical, leave of absence.
■ **take one's leave** *he took his leave of us* BID FAREWELL TO, say goodbye to.

leaven ▶ **verb 1** *yeast leavens the bread* RAISE, make rise, puff up, expand. **2** *formal proceedings leavened by humour* PERMEATE, infuse, pervade, imbue, suffuse, transform; enliven, liven up, invigorate, energize, electrify, ginger up, season, spice (up), perk up, brighten up, lighten, lift; *informal* buck up, pep up.

lecher ▶ **noun** LECHEROUS MAN, libertine, womanizer, debauchee, rake, roué, profligate, wanton, Don Juan, Casanova, Lothario, Romeo; *informal* lech, dirty old man, goat, wolf, skirt chaser; *formal* fornicator.

lecherous ▶ **adjective** LUSTFUL, licentious, lascivious, libidinous, prurient, lewd, salacious, lubricious, debauched, dissolute, wanton, dissipated, degenerate, depraved, dirty, filthy; *informal* randy, horny, goatish; *formal* concupiscent.
— OPPOSITES: chaste.

lecture ▶ **noun 1** *a lecture on children's literature* SPEECH, talk, address, discourse, disquisition, presentation, oration, lesson; *informal* chalk talk. **2** *Dave got a lecture about his daydreaming* SCOLDING, chiding, reprimand, rebuke, reproof, reproach, upbraiding, berating, admonishment, sermon; *informal* dressing-down, talking-to, tongue-lashing, roasting; *formal* castigation.
▶ **verb 1** *lecturing on the dangers of drugs* GIVE A LECTURE/TALK, talk, make a speech, speak, give an address, discourse, hold forth, declaim, expatiate; *informal* spout, sound off. **2** *she lectures at Memorial University* TEACH, give instruction, give lessons. **3** *she was lectured for her gossiping* SCOLD, chide, reprimand, rebuke, reprove, reproach, upbraid, berate, chastise, admonish, lambaste, rake/haul over the coals, take to task; *informal* give someone a dressing-down, give someone a talking-to, tell off, bawl out; *formal* castigate.

lecturer ▶ **noun** UNIVERSITY/COLLEGE TEACHER, professor, tutor, educator; academic, academician, preceptor; *formal* pedagogue.

ledge ▶ **noun** SHELF, sill, mantel, mantelpiece, shelving; projection, protrusion, overhang, ridge, prominence.

ledger ▶ **noun** (ACCOUNT) BOOK, record book, register, log, accounts; records, books; balance sheet, financial statement.

lee ▶ **noun** SHELTER, protection, cover, refuge, safety, security, *Nfld* lun ✦.

leech ▶ **noun** PARASITE, bloodsucker; *informal* scrounger, sponger, bottom-feeder, freeloader.

leer ▶ **verb** *Henry leered at her* OGLE, look lasciviously, look suggestively, eye, check out; *informal* give someone a/the once-over, lust after/over.
▶ **noun** *a sly leer* LECHEROUS LOOK, lascivious look, ogle; *informal* the once-over, the eye.

leery ▶ **adjective** WARY, cautious, careful, guarded, chary, suspicious, distrustful; worried, anxious, apprehensive, hesitant, uncertain.

leeway ▶ **noun** FREEDOM, scope, latitude, space, room, liberty, flexibility, licence, free hand, free rein.

left ▶ **adjective** LEFT-HAND, sinistral; *Nautical* port, larboard; *Heraldry* sinister.
— RELATED TERMS: laevo-, sinistro-.
— OPPOSITES: right, starboard.

left-handed ▶ **adjective** 1 *a left-handed golfer* sinistral; *informal* southpaw. 2 *a left-handed compliment* BACKHANDED, ambiguous, equivocal, double-edged; dubious, ironic, sardonic, insincere, hypocritical.
— OPPOSITES: right-handed.

leftover ▶ **noun** 1 *a leftover from the 60s* RESIDUE, survivor, vestige, legacy, throwback. 2 *put the leftovers in the fridge* LEAVINGS, uneaten food, remainder, scraps, remnants, remains; excess, surplus.
▶ **adjective** *leftover food* REMAINING, left, uneaten, unconsumed; excess, surplus, superfluous, unused, unwanted, spare.

left-wing ▶ **adjective** SOCIALIST, communist, leftist, left-of-centre, left-leaning, NDP ✦; Labour, Marxist, Bolshevik; *informal* commie, lefty, red, pink.
— OPPOSITES: right-wing, conservative.

leg ▶ **noun** 1 *Lee broke his leg* (LOWER) LIMB, shank; *informal* pin. 2 *the first leg of a European tour* PART, stage, portion, segment, section, phase, stretch, lap.
■ **give someone a leg up** HELP/ASSIST SOMEONE, give someone assistance, lend someone a helping hand, give someone a boost.
■ **leg it** (*informal*) See RUN verb sense 1.
■ **on its/one's last legs** DILAPIDATED, worn out, rickety, about to fall apart, about to become obsolete; failing, dying, terminal, on one's deathbed.
■ **pull someone's leg** TEASE, make fun of, chaff, jest, joke with, play a (practical) joke on, play a trick on, make a monkey out of; hoax, fool, deceive, lead on, hoodwink, dupe, beguile, gull; *informal* kid, have on, rib, take for a ride, put on.
■ **stretch one's legs** GO FOR A WALK, take a stroll, walk, stroll, move about, get some exercise.

legacy ▶ **noun** 1 *a legacy from a great aunt* BEQUEST, inheritance, heritage, endowment, gift, patrimony, settlement, birthright; *formal* benefaction. 2 *a legacy of the residential schools* CONSEQUENCE, effect, upshot, spinoff, repercussion, aftermath, by-product, result.

legal ▶ **adjective** LAWFUL, legitimate, licit, within the law, legalized, valid; permissible, permitted, allowable, allowed, above board, admissible, acceptable; authorized, sanctioned, licensed, constitutional; *informal* legit.
— OPPOSITES: criminal.

legalize ▶ **verb** MAKE LEGAL, decriminalize, legitimize, legitimate, permit, allow, authorize, sanction, license, validate; regularize, normalize; *informal* OK.
— OPPOSITES: prohibit.

legatee ▶ **noun** See BENEFICIARY.

legend ▶ **noun** 1 *Arthurian legends* MYTH, saga, epic, (folk) tale, (folk) story, fairy tale, fable, mythos,

folklore, lore, mythology, fantasy, oral history, folk tradition; urban myth. 2 *film legends* CELEBRITY, star, superstar, icon, phenomenon, luminary, leading light, giant; *informal* celeb, megastar.

legendary ▶ **adjective** 1 *legendary knights* FABLED, heroic, traditional, fairy-tale, storybook, mythical, mythological. 2 *a legendary figure in sports* FAMOUS, celebrated, famed, renowned, acclaimed, illustrious, esteemed, honoured, exalted, venerable, well-known, popular, prominent, distinguished, great, eminent, pre-eminent, high-profile; *formal* lauded.
— OPPOSITES: historical.

legerdemain ▶ **noun** 1 *stage magicians practising legerdemain* SLEIGHT OF HAND, conjuring, magic, wizardry; *formal* prestidigitation; *rare* thaumaturgy. 2 *a piece of management legerdemain* TRICKERY, cunning, artfulness, craftiness, chicanery, skulduggery, deceit, deception, artifice.

legible ▶ **adjective** READABLE, easy to read, easily deciphered, clear, plain, neat, intelligible.

legion ▶ **noun** 1 *a military legion* BRIGADE, regiment, battalion, company, troop, division, squadron, squad, platoon, phalanx, unit, force. 2 *the legions of TV cameras* HORDE, throng, multitude, host, crowd, mass, mob, gang, swarm, flock, herd, score, army, pack.
▶ **adjective** *her fans are legion* NUMEROUS, countless, innumerable, incalculable, many, abundant, plentiful; *literary* myriad.

legislate ▶ **verb** MAKE LAWS, pass laws, enact laws, formulate laws; authorize, decree, order, sanction.

legislation ▶ **noun** LAW, body of laws, rules, rulings, regulations, acts, bills, statutes, enactments, ordinances.

legislative ▶ **adjective** LAW-MAKING, judicial, juridical, parliamentary, governmental, policy-making.

legislator ▶ **noun** LAWMAKER, lawgiver, parliamentarian, Member of Parliament, MP; MPP, MNA, MHA, MLA; *congressman, congresswoman, senator.

legislature ▶ **noun** 1 LEGISLATIVE BODY, parliament, congress, legislative assembly, senate, council, diet. 2 *Cdn* LEGISLATIVE BUILDING, house, leg, chamber.

legitimate ▶ **adjective** 1 *the only form of legitimate gambling* LEGAL, lawful, licit, legalized, authorized, permitted, permissible, allowable, allowed, admissible, sanctioned, approved, licensed, statutory, constitutional; *informal* legit, street legal. 2 *the legitimate heir* RIGHTFUL, lawful, genuine, authentic, real, true, proper, authorized, sanctioned, acknowledged, recognized. 3 *legitimate grounds for unease* VALID, sound, well-founded, justifiable, reasonable, sensible, just, fair, bona fide.
— OPPOSITES: illegal, invalid.

legitimize ▶ **verb** VALIDATE, legitimate, permit, authorize, sanction, license, condone, justify, endorse, support; legalize.
— OPPOSITES: outlaw.

leisure ▶ **noun** *the balance between leisure and work* FREE TIME, spare time, time off; recreation, relaxation, inactivity, pleasure; *informal* R and R, downtime.
— OPPOSITES: work.
■ **at your leisure** AT YOUR CONVENIENCE, when it suits you, in your own (good/sweet) time, without haste, unhurriedly.

leisurely ▶ **adjective** UNHURRIED, relaxed, easy, gentle, sedate, comfortable, restful, undemanding,

slow, lazy.
— OPPOSITES: hurried.

lemon ▶ noun **1** *lemons are sour* CITRUS FRUIT. **2** *the car was a real lemon* DEFECTIVE CAR, clunker, beater, junker, jalopy, tin Lizzie, bucket of bolts, flivver, rustbucket; disappointment, letdown.

lend ▶ verb **1** *I'll lend you my towel* LOAN, let someone use; advance. **2** *these examples lend weight to his assertions* ADD, impart, give, bestow, confer, provide, supply, furnish, contribute.
— OPPOSITES: borrow.

■ **lend an ear** LISTEN, pay attention, take notice, be attentive, concentrate, (pay) heed; *informal* be all ears; *archaic* hearken.

■ **lend a hand** HELP (OUT), give a helping hand, assist, give assistance, make a contribution, do one's bit; *informal* pitch in.

■ **lend itself to** BE SUITABLE FOR, be suited to, be appropriate for, be applicable for.

length ▶ noun **1** *a length of three or four metres* | *the whole length of the valley* EXTENT, distance, linear measure, span, reach; area, expanse, stretch, range, scope. **2** *a considerable length of time* PERIOD, duration, stretch, span. **3** *a length of blue silk* PIECE, swatch, measure. **4** *MPs criticized the length of the speech* LENGTHINESS, extent, prolixity, wordiness, verbosity, long-windedness.

■ **at length 1** *he spoke at length* FOR A LONG TIME, for ages, for hours, interminably, endlessly, ceaselessly, unendingly. **2** *he was questioned at length* THOROUGHLY, fully, in detail, in depth, comprehensively, exhaustively, extensively. **3** *his search led him, at length, to Seattle* AFTER A LONG TIME, eventually, in time, finally, at (long) last, in the end, ultimately.

lengthen ▶ verb ELONGATE, make longer, extend, prolong, protract, stretch out, drag out; expand, widen, broaden, enlarge; grow/get longer, draw out.
— OPPOSITES: shorten.

lengthy ▶ adjective **1** *a lengthy civil war* (VERY) LONG, long-lasting, prolonged, extended; *informal* marathon. **2** *lengthy discussions* PROTRACTED, overlong, long-drawn-out; verbose, wordy, prolix, long-winded; tedious, boring, interminable.
— OPPOSITES: short.

lenient ▶ adjective MERCIFUL, clement, forgiving, forbearing, tolerant, charitable, humane, indulgent, easygoing, magnanimous, sympathetic, compassionate, mild.
— OPPOSITES: severe.

lesbian ▶ noun HOMOSEXUAL WOMAN, gay woman; *informal* butch, femme, dyke, bull-dyke, queer.
— OPPOSITES: heterosexual.
▶ adjective HOMOSEXUAL, gay, same-sex; Sapphic, homoerotic; *informal* butch, dykey, queer.
— OPPOSITES: straight.

lesion ▶ noun WOUND, injury, bruise, abrasion, contusion; ulcer, ulceration, (running) sore, abscess; *Medicine* trauma.

less ▶ pronoun *the fare is less than $1* A SMALLER AMOUNT, not so/as much as, under, below.
— OPPOSITES: more.
▶ adjective *there was less noise now* NOT SO MUCH, smaller, slighter, shorter, reduced; fewer.
▶ adverb *we must use the car less* TO A LESSER DEGREE, to a smaller extent, not so/as much.
▶ preposition *list price less 10 per cent* MINUS, subtracting, excepting, without.
— OPPOSITES: plus.

lessen ▶ verb **1** *the new law did little to lessen the stigma* REDUCE, make less/smaller, minimize, decrease; allay, assuage, alleviate, attenuate, palliate, ease, dull, deaden, blunt, moderate, mitigate, dampen, soften, tone down, dilute, weaken. **2** *the pain began to lessen* GROW LESS, grow smaller, decrease, diminish, decline, subside, abate; fade, die down/off, let up, ease off, tail off, drop (off/away), fall, dwindle, ebb, wane, recede. **3** *his behaviour lessened him in their eyes* DIMINISH, degrade, discredit, devalue, belittle.
— OPPOSITES: increase.

lesser ▶ adjective **1** *a lesser offence* LESS IMPORTANT, minor, secondary, subsidiary, marginal, ancillary, auxiliary, supplementary, peripheral; inferior, insignificant, unimportant, petty. **2** *you look down at us lesser mortals* SUBORDINATE, minor, inferior, second-class, subservient, lowly, humble.
— OPPOSITES: greater, superior.

lesson ▶ noun **1** *a math lesson* CLASS, session, seminar, tutorial, lecture, period (of instruction/ teaching); chalk talk. **2** *they should be industrious at their lessons* EXERCISES, assignments, school work, homework, study. **3** *reading the lesson in church* BIBLE READING, scripture, text, reading, passage. **4** *Stuart's accident should be a lesson to all parents* WARNING, deterrent, caution; example, exemplar, message, moral.

let ▶ verb **1** *let him sleep for now* ALLOW, permit, give permission to, give leave to, authorize, sanction, grant the right to, license, empower, enable, entitle; assent to, consent to, agree to, acquiesce in, tolerate, countenance, give one's blessing to, give assent to, give someone/something the nod; *informal* give the green light to, give the go-ahead to, give the thumbs up to, OK; *formal* accede to; *archaic* suffer. **2** *Wilcox opened the door to let her through* ALLOW TO GO, permit to pass; make way for.
— OPPOSITES: prevent, prohibit.

■ **let someone down** FAIL (TO SUPPORT), disappoint, disillusion; abandon, desert, leave stranded, leave in the lurch.

■ **let something down** LENGTHEN, make longer.

■ **let fly 1** *he let fly with a brick* HURL, fling, throw, propel, pitch, lob, toss, launch; shoot, fire, blast; *informal* chuck, sling, heave, (West) huck ♣. **2** *she let fly at Geoffrey* LOSE ONE'S TEMPER WITH, lash out at, scold, chastise, chide, rant at, inveigh against, rail against; explode, burst out, let someone have it; *informal* tear a strip off someone; *formal* excoriate.

■ **let go** RELEASE (ONE'S HOLD ON), loose/loosen one's hold on, relinquish; *archaic* unhand.

■ **let someone go** MAKE REDUNDANT, dismiss, discharge, lay off, give notice to, axe; *informal* sack, fire, give someone their marching orders, send packing, give someone the boot, give someone the (old) heave-ho, can.

■ **let someone in** ALLOW TO ENTER, allow in, admit, open the door to; receive, welcome, greet.

■ **let someone in on something** INCLUDE, count in, admit, allow to share in, let participate in, inform about, tell about.

■ **let something off** DETONATE, discharge, explode, set off, fire off.

■ **let someone off 1** (*informal*) *I'll let you off this time* PARDON, forgive, grant an amnesty to; deal leniently with, be merciful to, have mercy on; acquit, absolve, exonerate, clear, vindicate; *informal* let someone off the hook; *formal* exculpate. **2** *he let me off work* EXCUSE FROM, exempt from, spare from.

■ **let on** (*informal*) **1** *I never let on that I felt anxious* REVEAL, make known, tell, disclose, mention, divulge, let slip, give away, make public; blab; *informal* let the cat out of the bag, give the game away. **2** *he let on that he'd won* PRETEND, feign, affect, make out, make believe, simulate.

■ **let something out 1** *I let out a cry of triumph* UTTER, emit, give (vent to), produce, issue, express, voice, release. **2** *she let out that he'd given her a lift home* REVEAL, make known, tell, disclose, mention, divulge, let slip, give away, let it be known, blurt out.

■ **let someone out** RELEASE, liberate, (set) free, let go, discharge; set/turn loose, allow to leave.

■ **let up** (*informal*) **1** *the rain has let up* ABATE, lessen, decrease, diminish, subside, relent, slacken, die down/off, ease (off), tail off; ebb, wane, dwindle, fade; stop, cease, finish. **2** *you never let up, do you?* RELAX, ease up/off, slow down; pause, break (off), take a break, rest, stop; *informal* take a breather. **3** *I promise I'll let up on him* TREAT LESS SEVERELY, be more lenient with, be kinder to; *informal* go easy on.

letdown ▶ **noun** DISAPPOINTMENT, anticlimax, comedown, non-event, fiasco, setback, blow, disadvantage; *informal* washout.

lethal ▶ **adjective** FATAL, deadly, mortal, death-dealing, life-threatening, murderous, killing; poisonous, toxic, noxious, venomous; dangerous, destructive, harmful, pernicious; *literary* deathly, nocuous.
— OPPOSITES: harmless, safe.

lethargic ▶ **adjective** SLUGGISH, inert, inactive, slow, torpid, lifeless; languid, listless, lazy, idle, indolent, shiftless, slothful, apathetic, weary, tired, fatigued.

lethargy ▶ **noun** SLUGGISHNESS, inertia, inactivity, inaction, slowness, torpor, torpidity, lifelessness, listlessness, languor, laziness, idleness, indolence, shiftlessness, sloth, apathy, passivity, weariness, tiredness, lassitude, fatigue, inanition; *literary* hebetude.
— OPPOSITES: vigour, energy.

Types of Letter

acknowledgement letter	form letter
air letter	letter of intent
billet-doux	letter of introduction
bread-and-butter letter	letter of
business letter	recommendation
chain letter	letter of thanks
circular	love letter
cover letter	mash letter
dead letter	memo
Dear John letter	memorandum
dunning letter	newsletter
email	open letter
fan letter	poison-pen letter
	thank-you letter

---

letter ▶ **noun 1** *capital letters* (ALPHABETICAL) CHARACTER, sign, symbol, mark, figure, rune; *Linguistics* grapheme. **2** *he wrote Len a letter* (WRITTEN) MESSAGE, (written) communication, note, line, missive, dispatch; correspondence, news, information, intelligence, word; post, mail; *formal* epistle. *See table.* **3** *a man of letters* (BOOK) LEARNING, scholarship, erudition, education, knowledge; intellect, intelligence, enlightenment, wisdom, sagacity, culture.
— RELATED TERMS: epistolary.

■ **to the letter** STRICTLY, precisely, exactly, accurately, closely, faithfully, religiously, punctiliously, literally, verbatim, in every detail.

letter carrier ▶ **noun** POSTAL WORKER; postman, postwoman, mailman; *informal* postie.

lettered ▶ **adjective** LEARNED, erudite, academic, (well) educated, well-read, widely read, knowledgeable, intellectual, well schooled, enlightened, cultured, cultivated, scholarly, bookish, highbrow, studious, cerebral.
— OPPOSITES: ill-educated.

let-up ▶ **noun** (*informal*) ABATEMENT, lessening, decrease, diminishing, diminution, decline, relenting, remission, slackening, weakening, relaxation, dying down, easing off, tailing off, dropping away/off; respite, break, breather, interval, hiatus, suspension, cessation, stop, pause.

level ▶ **adjective 1** *a smooth and level surface* FLAT, smooth, even, uniform, plane, flush, plumb. **2** *he kept his voice level* UNCHANGING, steady, unvarying, even, uniform, regular, constant, invariable, unaltering; calm, unemotional, composed, equable, unruffled, serene, tranquil. **3** *his eyes were level with hers* ALIGNED, on the same level as, on a level, at the same height as, in line.
— OPPOSITES: uneven, unsteady.

▶ **noun 1** *she is at a managerial level* RANK, standing, status, position; echelon, degree, grade, gradation, stage, standard, rung; class, stratum, group, grouping, set, classification. **2** *a high level of unemployment* QUANTITY, amount, extent, measure, degree, volume, size, magnitude, intensity, proportion. **3** *the level of water is rising* HEIGHT, altitude, elevation. **4** *the sixth level* FLOOR, storey, deck.

▶ **verb 1** *tilt the pan to level the mixture* MAKE LEVEL, level out/off, make even, even out, make flat, flatten, smooth (out), make uniform. **2** *bulldozers levelled the building* RAZE, demolish, flatten, topple, destroy; tear down, knock down, pull down, bulldoze. **3** *he levelled his opponent with a single blow* KNOCK DOWN/OUT, lay out, flatten, floor, fell; *informal* KO, kayo. **4** *Carl levelled the playing field* EQUALIZE, make equal, equal, even (up), make level. **5** *he levelled his pistol at me* AIM, point, direct, train, focus, turn, sight, draw a bead on. **6** (*informal*) *I knew you'd level with me* BE FRANK, be open, be honest, be above board, tell the truth, tell all, hide nothing, be straightforward, be upfront; *informal* come clean, set the record straight.

■ **on the level** (*informal*) GENUINE, straight, honest, above board, fair, true, sincere, straightforward, trustworthy; *informal* upfront, on the up and up.

level-headed ▶ **adjective** SENSIBLE, practical, realistic, prudent, pragmatic, wise, reasonable, rational, mature, judicious, sound, sober, businesslike, no-nonsense, composed, calm, {calm, cool, and collected}, confident, well-balanced, equable, cool-headed, self-possessed, having one's feet on the ground; *informal* unflappable, together, grounded.
— OPPOSITES: excitable.

lever ▶ **noun 1** *you can insert a lever and pry the rail off* CROWBAR, bar, jimmy. **2** *he pulled the lever* HANDLE, grip, pull, switch.

▶ **verb** *he levered the door open* PRY, force, wrench, pull, wrest, heave; prise.

leverage ▶ **noun 1** *the long handles provide increased leverage* GRIP, purchase, hold; support, anchorage, force, strength. **2** *the union's bargaining leverage* INFLUENCE, power, authority, weight, sway, pull, control, say, dominance, advantage, pressure; *informal* clout, muscle, teeth, bargaining chip.

levitate ▶ noun FLOAT, rise (into the air), hover, be suspended, glide, hang, fly, soar up.

levity ▶ noun LIGHT-HEARTEDNESS, high spirits, vivacity, liveliness, cheerfulness, cheeriness, humour, gaiety, fun, jocularity, hilarity, frivolity, amusement, mirth, laughter, merriment, glee, comedy, wit, wittiness, jollity, joviality.
— OPPOSITES: seriousness.

levy ▶ verb *the government's right to levy taxes* IMPOSE, charge, exact, raise, collect; tax.
▶ noun **1** *the levy of taxes* IMPOSITION, raising, collection; *formal* exaction. **2** *the levy on alcohol* TAX, tariff, toll, excise, duty, imposition, impost.

lewd ▶ adjective **1** *a lewd old man* LECHEROUS, lustful, licentious, lascivious, dirty, prurient, salacious, lubricious, libidinous; debauched, depraved, degenerate, decadent, dissipated, dissolute, perverted, wanton; *informal* horny, randy; *formal* concupiscent; *archaic* lickerish. **2** *a lewd song* VULGAR, crude, smutty, dirty, filthy, obscene, pornographic, coarse, off-colour, unseemly, indecent, salacious; rude, racy, risqué, naughty, bawdy, ribald; *informal* blue, raunchy, X-rated, XXX, porno; *euphemistic* adult.
— OPPOSITES: chaste, clean.

lexicon ▶ noun DICTIONARY, wordbook, vocabulary list, glossary, thesaurus.

liability ▶ noun **1** *journalists' liability for defamation* ACCOUNTABILITY, (legal) responsibility, answerability; blame, culpability, guilt, fault. **2** *they have big liabilities* FINANCIAL OBLIGATIONS, debts, arrears, dues. **3** *she was proving to be a liability* HINDRANCE, encumbrance, burden, handicap, nuisance, inconvenience; obstacle, impediment, disadvantage, weakness, weak link, shortcoming; millstone round one's neck, albatross, Achilles heel.
— OPPOSITES: immunity, asset.

liable ▶ adjective **1** *they are liable for negligence* (LEGALLY) RESPONSIBLE, accountable, answerable, chargeable, blameworthy, at fault, culpable, guilty. **2** *my income is liable to fluctuate wildly* LIKELY, inclined, tending, disposed, apt, predisposed, prone, given. **3** *areas liable to flooding* EXPOSED, prone, subject, susceptible, vulnerable, in danger of, at risk of.

liaise ▶ verb CO-OPERATE, work together, collaborate; communicate, network, interface, interact, link up.

liaison ▶ noun **1** *Dave was my liaison with the Prime Minister* INTERMEDIARY, mediator, middleman, contact, link, connection, go-between, representative, agent. **2** *a secret liaison* (LOVE) AFFAIR, relationship, romance, attachment, fling, amour, (romantic) entanglement, tryst; *informal* hanky-panky.

liar ▶ noun DECEIVER, fibber, perjurer, false witness, fabricator, equivocator; fabulist; *informal* storyteller.

libation ▶ noun **1** *they pour libations into the holy well* (LIQUID) OFFERING, tribute, oblation. **2** *(humorous) would you like a libation?* (ALCOHOLIC) DRINK, beverage, liquid refreshment; dram, draft, nip, tot, shot; *informal* tipple, nightcap, pick-me-up; *archaic* potation.

libel ▶ noun *she sued two newspapers for libel* DEFAMATION (OF CHARACTER), character assassination, calumny, misrepresentation, scandalmongering; aspersions, denigration, vilification, disparagement, derogation, insult, slander, malicious gossip; lie, slur, smear, untruth, false report; *informal* mud-slinging, badmouthing.
▶ verb *she alleged the magazine had libelled her* DEFAME,

malign, slander, blacken someone's name, sully someone's reputation, speak ill/evil of, traduce, smear, cast aspersions on, drag someone's name through the mud, besmirch, tarnish, taint, tell lies about, stain, impugn someone's character/integrity, vilify, denigrate, disparage, run down, stigmatize, discredit, slur; *informal* dis, badmouth; *formal* derogate, calumniate.

liberal ▶ adjective **1** *the values of a liberal society* TOLERANT, unprejudiced, unbigoted, broad-minded, open-minded, enlightened; permissive, free (and easy), easygoing, libertarian, indulgent, lenient. **2** *a liberal social agenda* PROGRESSIVE, advanced, modern, forward-looking, forward-thinking, progressivist, enlightened, reformist, radical. **3** *a liberal education* WIDE-RANGING, broad-based, general. **4** *a liberal interpretation of divorce laws* FLEXIBLE, broad, loose, rough, free, general, non-literal, non-specific, imprecise, vague, indefinite. **5** *a liberal coating of paint* ABUNDANT, copious, ample, plentiful, generous, lavish, luxuriant, profuse, considerable, prolific, rich; *literary* plenteous. **6** *they were liberal with their cash* GENEROUS, open-handed, unsparing, unstinting, ungrudging, lavish, free, munificent, bountiful, beneficent, benevolent, big-hearted, philanthropic, charitable, altruistic, unselfish; *literary* bounteous.
— OPPOSITES: reactionary, strict, miserly.
▶ noun *liberals and conservatives have found common ground* Grit ✦, (Que.) *hist.* rouge ✦, Red.

liberate ▶ verb **1** *they liberated the prisoners* (SET) FREE, release, let out/go, set/let loose, save, rescue; emancipate, enfranchise. **2** *he liberated a trinket from her jewelry box* STEAL, take; *informal* swipe, nab, (Nfld) buck ✦, pinch, 'borrow'.
— OPPOSITES: imprison, enslave.

libertine ▶ noun *an unrepentant libertine* PHILANDERER, playboy, rake, roué, Don Juan, Lothario, Casanova, Romeo; lecher, seducer, womanizer, adulterer, debauchee, profligate, wanton; *informal* skirt chaser, lady-killer, lech, wolf; *formal* fornicator.

liberty ▶ noun **1** *personal liberty* FREEDOM, independence, free rein, licence, self-determination, free will, latitude. **2** *the fight for liberty* INDEPENDENCE, freedom, autonomy, sovereignty, self government, self rule, self determination; civil liberties, human rights. **3** *the liberty to go where you please* RIGHT, birthright, prerogative, entitlement, privilege, permission, sanction, authorization, authority, licence, power.
— OPPOSITES: constraint, slavery.
■ **at liberty 1** *he was at liberty for three months* FREE, (on the) loose, at large, unconfined; escaped, out, on the lam. **2** *you are at liberty to leave* FREE, permitted, allowed, authorized, able, entitled, eligible.
■ **take liberties** ACT WITH FAMILIARITY, show disrespect, act with impropriety, act indecorously, be impudent, act with impertinence; take advantage, exploit.
■ **take the liberty** PRESUME, venture, make so bold as.

libidinous ▶ adjective LUSTFUL, lecherous, lascivious, lewd, carnal, salacious, prurient, licentious, libertine, lubricious, dissolute, debauched, depraved, degenerate, decadent, dissipated, wanton, promiscuous, lickerish; *informal* horny, goatish, wolfish, randy; *formal* concupiscent.

libido ▶ noun SEX DRIVE, sexual appetite; (sexual) desire, passion, sensuality, sexuality, lust, lustfulness; *informal* horniness, randiness; *formal* concupiscence.

licence ▶ **noun 1** *a driver's licence* PERMIT, certificate, document, documentation, authorization, warrant; certification, credentials; pass, papers. **2** *you have licence to make changes* PERMISSION, authority, right, a free hand, leave, authorization, entitlement, privilege, prerogative; liberty, freedom, power, latitude, scope, free rein, carte blanche, a blank cheque, the go-ahead. **3** *poetic licence* DISREGARD FOR THE FACTS, inventiveness, invention, creativity, imagination, fancy, freedom, looseness.

license ▶ **verb** PERMIT, allow, authorize, grant/give authority to, grant/give permission to, grant/give a licence to; certify, empower, entitle, enable, give approval to, let, qualify, sanction; *informal* rubber stamp.
— OPPOSITES: ban.

licentious ▶ **adjective** DISSOLUTE, dissipated, debauched, degenerate, immoral, naughty, wanton, decadent, depraved, sinful, corrupt; lustful, lecherous, lascivious, libidinous, prurient, lubricious, lewd, promiscuous, lickerish; *formal* concupiscent.
— OPPOSITES: moral.

licit ▶ **adjective** *See* LEGITIMATE sense 1.

lick ▶ **verb 1** *the spaniel licked his face* pass one's tongue over, touch with one's tongue; tongue; lap. **2** *flames licking round the coal* FLICKER, play, flit, dance. **3** (*informal*) *they licked the home side 3-0. See* DEFEAT *verb* sense 1. **4** (*informal*) *we've got that problem licked* OVERCOME, get the better of, find an answer/solution to, conquer, beat, control, master, curb, check.
▶ **noun** (*informal*) **1** *a lick of paint* DAB, bit, drop, dash, spot, touch, splash; *informal* smidgen. **2** *a guitar lick* SHORT SOLO, riff, line, theme.
■ **lick someone's boots/shoes** SUCK UP TO, toady to, be servile to, be obsequious to, fawn over, flatter, butter up, ingratiate oneself with, brown-nose with/to.

lickety-split ▶ **adverb** AT FULL SPEED, very quickly, on the double, as fast as one's legs can carry one, at a gallop, headlong, pell-mell, hell-bent for leather, like the wind, like a bat out of hell, at full tilt.

licking ▶ **noun** (*informal*) **1** *the Canucks took a licking* DEFEAT, beating, trouncing, thrashing; *informal* hiding, pasting, hammering, drubbing, shellacking. **2** *Ray got the worst licking of his life* THRASHING, beating, flogging, whipping; *informal* walloping, hiding, pasting, whaling.

lid ▶ **noun** *the lid of a saucepan* COVER, top, cap, covering.
■ **put a lid on it** stop talking, be quiet, hold your tongue; *informal* shut up, hush up, shut your mouth, shut your face, shut your trap, button your lip, pipe down, put a sock in it, give it a rest, save it, not another word.
■ **blow the lid off** (*informal*) EXPOSE, reveal, make known, make public, bring into the open, disclose, divulge; *informal* spill the beans, blab.

lie¹ ▶ **noun** *loyalty had made him tell lies* UNTRUTH, falsehood, fib, fabrication, deception, invention, (piece of) fiction, falsification; (little) white lie, half-truth, exaggeration; *informal* tall tale, whopper, taradiddle.
— RELATED TERMS: mendacious, mendacity.
— OPPOSITES: truth.
▶ **verb** *he lied to the police* TELL AN UNTRUTH/LIE, fib, dissemble, dissimulate, misinform, mislead, tell a

white lie, perjure oneself, commit perjury, prevaricate; *informal* lie through one's teeth, stretch the truth; *formal* forswear oneself.
■ **give the lie to** DISPROVE, contradict, negate, deny, refute, rebut, controvert, belie, invalidate, discredit, debunk; challenge, call into question; *informal* shoot/poke full of holes, shoot down (in flames); *formal* confute, gainsay.

lie² ▶ **verb 1** *he was lying on a bed* RECLINE, lie down/back, be recumbent, be prostrate, be supine, be prone, be stretched out, sprawl, rest, repose, lounge, loll. **2** *her handbag lay on a chair* BE PLACED, be situated, be positioned, rest. **3** *lying on the border of Switzerland and Austria* BE SITUATED, be located, be placed, be found, be sited. **4** *the difficulty lies in building real quality into the products* CONSIST, be inherent, be present, be contained, exist, reside.
— OPPOSITES: stand.
■ **lie heavy on** TROUBLE, worry, bother, torment, oppress, nag, prey on one's mind, plague, niggle at, gnaw at, haunt; *informal* bug.
■ **lie low** HIDE (OUT), go into hiding, conceal oneself, keep out of sight, go underground; *informal* hole up, lie doggo.

life ▶ **noun 1** *the joy of giving life to a child* EXISTENCE, being, living, animation; sentience, creation, viability. **2** *threats to life on the planet* LIVING BEINGS/CREATURES, the living; human/animal/plant life, fauna, flora, ecosystem; human beings, humanity, humankind, mankind, man. **3** *an easy life* WAY OF LIFE/LIVING, lifestyle, situation, fate, lot. **4** *the last nine months of his life* LIFETIME, life span, days, time on earth, existence. **5** *he is full of life* VIVACITY, animation, liveliness, vitality, verve, high spirits, exuberance, zest, buoyancy, enthusiasm, energy, vigour, dynamism, élan, gusto, brio, bounce, spirit, fire; (hustle and) bustle, movement; *informal* oomph, pizzazz, pep, zing, zip, vim. **6** *the life of the party* MOVING SPIRIT, (vital) spirit, life force, lifeblood, heart, soul. **7** *more than 1,500 lives were lost in the accident* PERSON, human being, individual, soul. **8** *a life of Chopin* BIOGRAPHY, autobiography, life story/history, profile, chronicle, account, portrait; *informal* bio. **9** *I'll miss you, but that's life* THE WAY OF THE WORLD, the way things go, the human condition; fate, destiny, providence, kismet, karma, fortune, luck, chance; *informal* the way the cookie crumbles, the breaks.
— RELATED TERMS: animate, bio-.
— OPPOSITES: death.
■ **come to life 1** *the kids are finally coming to life* BECOME ACTIVE, come alive, wake up, awaken, arouse, rouse, stir; *literary* waken. **2** *the carved angel suddenly came to life* BECOME ANIMATE, come alive.
■ **for dear life** DESPERATELY, with all one's might, for all one is worth, as fast/hard as possible, like the devil.
■ **give one's life 1** *he would give his life for her* DIE (TO SAVE), lay down one's life, sacrifice oneself, offer one's life. **2** *he gave his life to the company* DEDICATE ONESELF, devote oneself, give oneself, surrender oneself.

life-and-death ▶ **adjective** VITAL, of vital importance, crucial, critical, urgent, pressing, pivotal, momentous, important, all-important, key, serious, grave, significant; *informal* earth-shattering; *formal* of great moment.
— OPPOSITES: trivial.

lifeblood ▶ **noun** LIFE (FORCE), essential constituent, driving force, vital spark, inspiration, stimulus, essence, crux, heart, soul, core.

lifeless ▶ adjective **1** *a lifeless body* DEAD, departed, perished, gone, no more, passed on/away, stiff, cold, (as) dead as a doornail; *formal* deceased. **2** *a lifeless rag doll* INANIMATE, without life, inert, insentient. **3** *a lifeless landscape* BARREN, sterile, bare, desolate, stark, arid, infertile, uncultivated, uninhabited; bleak, colourless, characterless, soulless. **4** *a lifeless performance* LACKLUSTRE, spiritless, apathetic, torpid, lethargic; dull, monotonous, boring, tedious, dreary, unexciting, expressionless, emotionless, colourless, characterless.
— OPPOSITES: alive, animate, lively.

lifelike ▶ adjective REALISTIC, true to life, representational, faithful, exact, precise, detailed, vivid, graphic, natural, naturalistic; *Art* kitchen-sink.
— OPPOSITES: unrealistic.

lifelong ▶ adjective LASTING, long-lasting, long-term, constant, stable, established, steady, enduring, permanent.
— OPPOSITES: ephemeral.

lifestyle ▶ noun WAY OF LIFE/LIVING, life, situation, fate, lot; conduct, behaviour, customs, culture, habits, ways, mores; *Anthropology* lifeway.

lifetime ▶ noun **1** *he did a lot in his lifetime* LIFESPAN, life, days, duration of life, one's time (on earth), existence, one's career. **2** *it would take a lifetime* ALL ONE'S LIFE, a very long time, an eternity, years (on end), eons; *informal* ages (and ages), an age.

lift ▶ verb **1** *lift the pack onto your back* RAISE, hoist, heave, haul up, heft, raise up/aloft, elevate, hold high; pick up, grab, take up, scoop up, snatch up; winch up, jack up, lever up; *informal* hump; *literary* upheave. **2** *the news lifted his spirits* BOOST, raise, buoy up, elevate, cheer up, perk up, uplift, brighten up, gladden, encourage, stimulate, revive; *informal* buck up. **3** *the fog had lifted* CLEAR, rise, disperse, dissipate, disappear, vanish, dissolve. **4** *the ban has been lifted* CANCEL, remove, withdraw, revoke, rescind, annul, void, discontinue, end, stop, terminate. **5** *he lifted his voice* AMPLIFY, raise, make louder, increase. **6** (*informal*) *he lifted sections from a 1986 article* PLAGIARIZE, pirate, copy, reproduce, poach, steal; *informal* crib, rip off. **7** (*informal*) *she lifted a wallet. See* STEAL *verb sense 1.*
— OPPOSITES: drop, put down.
▶ noun **1** *give me a lift up* PUSH, boost, hoist, heave, thrust, shove. **2** *he gave me a lift to the airport* (CAR) RIDE, drive. **3** *that goal will give his confidence a real lift* BOOST, fillip, stimulus, impetus, encouragement, spur, push; improvement, enhancement; *informal* shot in the arm, pick-me-up.
■ **lift off** TAKE OFF, become airborne, take to the air, take wing; be launched, blast off, rise.

light¹ ▶ noun **1** *the light of candles* ILLUMINATION, brightness, luminescence, luminosity, shining, gleaming, gleam, brilliance, radiance, lustre, glowing, glow, blaze, glare, dazzle; sunlight, moonlight, starlight, lamplight, firelight; ray of light, beam of light; *literary* effulgence, refulgence, lambency. **2** *there was a light on in the hall* LAMP, wall light; headlight, headlamp, sidelight; street light, floodlight; lantern; torch, flashlight. **3** *have you got a light?* MATCH, (cigarette) lighter. **4** *we'll wait for the light* DAYLIGHT (HOURS), daytime, day; dawn, morning, daybreak, sunrise; natural light, sunlight. **5** *he saw the problem in a different light* ASPECT, angle, slant, approach, interpretation, viewpoint, standpoint, context, hue, complexion. **6** *light dawned on Loretta* UNDERSTANDING, enlightenment, illumination, comprehension, insight, awareness, knowledge. **7** *an*

eminent legal light EXPERT, authority, master, leader, guru, leading light, luminary.
— RELATED TERMS: photo-, lumin-.
— OPPOSITES: darkness.
▶ verb *Alan lit a fire* SET ALIGHT, set light to, set burning, set on fire, set fire to, put/set a match to, ignite, kindle, spark (off).
— OPPOSITES: extinguish.
▶ adjective **1** *a light sunny room* BRIGHT, full of light, well-lit, well illuminated, sunny. **2** *light pastel shades* LIGHT-COLOURED, light-toned, pale, pale-coloured, pastel. **3** *light hair* FAIR, light-coloured, blond(e), golden, flaxen.
— OPPOSITES: dark, gloomy.
■ **bring something to light** REVEAL, disclose, expose, uncover, unearth, dig up/out, bring to notice, identify.
■ **come to light** BE DISCOVERED, be uncovered, be unearthed, come out, become known, become apparent, appear, materialize, emerge.
■ **in (the) light of** TAKING INTO CONSIDERATION/ACCOUNT, considering, bearing in mind, taking note of, in view of.
■ **light into** (*informal*) **1** *we started lighting into our attackers. See* SET ON/UPON *at* SET¹. **2** *my father lit into me for being late. See* SCOLD *verb.*
■ **light on/upon** COME ACROSS, chance on, hit on, happen on, stumble on/across, blunder on, find, discover, uncover, come up with.
■ **light up** **1** *the dashboard lit up* BECOME BRIGHT, brighten, lighten, shine, gleam, flare, blaze, glint, sparkle, shimmer, glisten, scintillate. **2** *he lit up outside the bar* START SMOKING, light a cigarette.
■ **light something up** **1** *a flare lit up the night sky* MAKE BRIGHT, brighten, illuminate, lighten, throw/cast light on, shine on, irradiate; *literary* illumine, illume. **2** *her enthusiasm lit up her face* ANIMATE, irradiate, brighten, cheer up, enliven.
■ **throw/cast/shed light on** EXPLAIN, elucidate, clarify, clear up, interpret.
■ **out like a light** ASLEEP, unconscious, comatose; *informal* out cold, dead to the world.

light² ▶ adjective **1** *it's light enough to carry* EASY TO LIFT, not heavy, lightweight; easy to carry, portable. **2** *a light cotton robe* FLIMSY, lightweight, insubstantial, thin; delicate, floaty, gauzy, gossamer, diaphanous. **3** *she is light on her feet* NIMBLE, agile, lithe, limber, lissome, graceful; light-footed, fleet-footed, quick, quick-moving, spry, sprightly; *informal* twinkle-toed; *literary* fleet, lightsome. **4** *a light soil* FRIABLE, sandy, easily dug, workable, crumbly, loose. **5** *a light dinner* SMALL, modest, simple, easily digested; *informal* low-cal. **6** *light duties* EASY, simple, undemanding, untaxing; *informal* cushy. **7** *his eyes gleamed with light mockery* GENTLE, mild, moderate, slight; playful, light-hearted. **8** *light reading* ENTERTAINING, lightweight, diverting, undemanding, frivolous, superficial, trivial. **9** *a light heart* CAREFREE, light-hearted, cheerful, cheery, happy, merry, jolly, blithe, bright, sunny; buoyant, bubbly, jaunty, bouncy, breezy, optimistic, positive, upbeat, ebullient; *dated* gay. **10** *this is no light matter* UNIMPORTANT, insignificant, trivial, trifling, petty, inconsequential, superficial. **11** *light footsteps* GENTLE, delicate, soft, dainty; faint, indistinct. **12** *her head felt light* DIZZY, giddy, light-headed, faint, vertiginous; *informal* woozy.
— OPPOSITES: heavy.

lighten¹ ▶ verb **1** *the first touch of dawn lightened the sky* MAKE LIGHTER, make brighter, brighten, light up, illuminate, throw/cast light on, shine on, irradiate;

literary illumine, illume. **2** *he used lemon juice to lighten his hair* WHITEN, make whiter, bleach, blanch, make paler.
— OPPOSITES: darken.

lighten² ▶ verb **1** *lightening the burden of taxation* MAKE LIGHTER, lessen, reduce, decrease, diminish, ease; alleviate, mitigate, allay, relieve, palliate, assuage. **2** *his smile lightened her spirits* CHEER (UP), brighten, gladden, hearten, perk up, lift, enliven, boost, buoy (up), uplift, revive, restore, revitalize.
— OPPOSITES: increase, depress.

light-fingered ▶ adjective THIEVING, stealing, pilfering, shoplifting, dishonest; *informal* sticky-fingered, crooked.
— OPPOSITES: honest.

light-headed ▶ adjective DIZZY, giddy, faint, light in the head, vertiginous, reeling; *informal* woozy.

light-hearted ▶ adjective CAREFREE, cheerful, cheery, happy, merry, glad, playful, jolly, jovial, joyful, gleeful, ebullient, high-spirited, lively, blithe, bright, sunny, buoyant, vivacious, bubbly, jaunty, bouncy, breezy; entertaining, amusing, diverting; *informal* chirpy, upbeat; *dated* gay.
— OPPOSITES: miserable.

lightly ▶ adverb **1** *Hermione kissed him lightly on the cheek* SOFTLY, gently, faintly, delicately. **2** *season very lightly* SPARINGLY, slightly, sparsely, moderately, delicately. **3** *he has got off lightly* WITHOUT SEVERE PUNISHMENT, easily, leniently, mildly. **4** *her views are not to be dismissed lightly* CARELESSLY, airily, heedlessly, without consideration, indifferently, unthinkingly, thoughtlessly, uncaringly, flippantly, breezily, frivolously.
— OPPOSITES: hard, heavily.

lightweight ▶ adjective **1** *a lightweight jacket* THIN, light, flimsy, insubstantial; summery. **2** *lightweight entertainment* TRIVIAL, insubstantial, superficial, shallow, unintellectual, undemanding, frivolous; *of little merit/value; informal* Mickey Mouse.
— OPPOSITES: heavy.
▶ noun *he's no lightweight* AMATEUR, second-rater, unimportant person, insignificant person, nobody, nonentity, no-name, cipher, small fry.

like¹ ▶ verb **1** *I like Tony* BE FOND OF, be attached to, have a soft spot for, have a liking for, have regard for, think well of, admire, respect, esteem; be attracted to, fancy, find attractive, be keen on, be taken with; be infatuated with, carry a torch for, be crazy about, have a crush on, have a thing for, have the hots for, take a shine to. **2** *she likes gardening* ENJOY, have a taste for, have a preference for, have a liking for, be partial to, find/take pleasure in, be keen on, find agreeable, have a penchant/passion for, find enjoyable; appreciate, love, adore, relish; *informal* have a thing about, be into, be mad about, be hooked on, get a kick out of. **3** *feel free to say what you like* CHOOSE, please, wish, want, see/think fit, care to, will. **4** *how would she like it if someone did that to her?* FEEL ABOUT, regard, think about, consider.
— OPPOSITES: hate.

like² ▶ preposition **1** *you're just like a teacher* SIMILAR TO, the same as, identical to. **2** *the figure landed like a cat* IN THE SAME WAY/MANNER AS, in the manner of, in a similar way to. **3** *cities like Medicine Hat* SUCH AS, for example, for instance; in particular, namely. **4** *he sounded mean, which isn't like him* CHARACTERISTIC OF, typical of, in character with.
— RELATED TERMS: -esque, -ish.
▶ noun *we shan't see his like again* EQUAL, match,

equivalent, counterpart, twin, parallel; *rare* compeer.
▶ adjective *a like situation* SIMILAR, much the same, comparable, corresponding, resembling, alike, analogous, parallel, equivalent, cognate, related, kindred; identical, same, matching.
— OPPOSITES: dissimilar.

likeable ▶ adjective PLEASANT, nice, friendly, agreeable, affable, amiable, genial, personable, charming, popular, good-natured, engaging, appealing, endearing, convivial, congenial, simpatico, winning, delightful, enchanting, lovable, adorable, sweet; *informal* darling, lovely.
— OPPOSITES: unpleasant.

likelihood ▶ noun PROBABILITY, chance, prospect, possibility, likeliness, odds, feasibility; risk, threat, danger; hope, promise.

likely ▶ adjective **1** *it seemed likely that a scandal would break* PROBABLE, (distinctly) possible, to be expected, odds-on, plausible, imaginable; expected, anticipated, predictable, predicted, foreseeable; *informal* in the cards. **2** *a likely explanation* PLAUSIBLE, reasonable, feasible, acceptable, believable, credible, tenable, conceivable. **3** *a likely story!* UNLIKELY, implausible, unbelievable, incredible, untenable, unacceptable, inconceivable. **4** *a likely-looking place* SUITABLE, appropriate, apposite, fit, fitting, acceptable, right; promising, hopeful.
— OPPOSITES: improbable, unbelievable.
▶ adverb *he was most likely dead* PROBABLY, in all probability, presumably, no doubt, doubtlessly; *informal* (as) like as not, chances are.

likeness ▶ noun **1** *her likeness to Anne is quite uncanny* RESEMBLANCE, similarity, similitude, correspondence. **2** *she appeared in the likeness of a ghost* SEMBLANCE, guise, appearance, (outward) form, shape, image. **3** *a likeness of the last president* REPRESENTATION, image, depiction, portrayal; picture, drawing, sketch, painting, portrait, photograph, study, statue, sculpture.
— OPPOSITES: dissimilarity.

likewise ▶ adverb **1** *an ambush was out of the question, likewise poison* ALSO, in addition, too, as well, to boot; besides, moreover, furthermore. **2** *encourage your family and friends to do likewise* THE SAME, similarly, correspondingly, in the same way, in similar fashion.

liking ▶ noun FONDNESS, love, affection, penchant, attachment; enjoyment, appreciation, taste, passion; preference, partiality, predilection; desire, fancy, inclination.

lilt ▶ noun CADENCE, rise and fall, inflection, intonation, rhythm, swing, beat, pulse, tempo.

limb ▶ noun **1** *his sore limbs* ARM, LEG, appendage; *archaic* member. **2** *the limbs of the tree* BRANCH, bough, offshoot, shoot.
■ **out on a limb** *the government would not go out on a limb* IN A PRECARIOUS POSITION, vulnerable, in a risky situation; *informal* sticking one's neck out.

limber ▶ adjective *I have to practise to keep myself limber* LITHE, supple, nimble, lissome, flexible, fit, agile, acrobatic, loose-jointed, loose-limbed.
— OPPOSITES: stiff.
■ **limber up** WARM UP, loosen up, get into condition, get into shape, practise, train, stretch.

limbo
■ **in limbo** IN ABEYANCE, unattended to, unfinished; suspended, deferred, postponed, put off, pending, on ice, in cold storage; unresolved, undetermined, up in

the air, uncertain; *informal* on the back burner, on hold, treading water, in the balance.

limelight ▶ noun THE FOCUS OF ATTENTION, public attention/interest, media attention, the public eye, the glare of publicity, prominence, the spotlight, face time; centre stage.
− OPPOSITES: obscurity.

limit ▶ noun **1** *the city limits* BOUNDARY (LINE), border, bound, frontier, edge, demarcation line; perimeter, outside, confine, periphery, margin, rim. **2** *a limit of 4,500 people* MAXIMUM, ceiling, limitation, upper limit; restriction, check, control, restraint. **3** *resources are stretched to the limit* UTMOST, breaking point, greatest extent. **4** (*informal*) *I've reached my limit!* BREAKING POINT, last straw; *informal* the end, it, wits' end, max.
▶ verb *the pressure to limit costs* RESTRICT, curb, cap, (hold in) check, restrain, put a brake on, freeze, regulate, control, govern, delimit.
■ **off limits** OUT OF BOUNDS, forbidden, banned, restricted, unacceptable, taboo.

limitation ▶ noun **1** *a limitation on the number of guests* RESTRICTION, curb, restraint, control, check; bar, barrier, block, deterrent. **2** *he is aware of his own limitations* IMPERFECTION, flaw, defect, failing, shortcoming, weak point, deficiency, failure, frailty, weakness, foible.
− OPPOSITES: increase, strength.

limited ▶ adjective **1** *limited resources* RESTRICTED, finite, little, tight, slight, in short supply; short; meagre, scanty, sparse, few, insubstantial, deficient, inadequate, insufficient, paltry, poor, minimal. **2** *the limited powers of the council* RESTRICTED, curbed, checked, controlled, restrained, delimited, qualified.
− OPPOSITES: ample, boundless.

limitless ▶ adjective BOUNDLESS, unbounded, unlimited, illimitable; infinite, endless, never-ending, unending, everlasting, untold, immeasurable, bottomless, fathomless; unceasing, interminable, inexhaustible, constant, perpetual.

limp¹ ▶ verb *she limped out of the house* HOBBLE, walk with a limp, walk lamely/unevenly, walk haltingly, hitch, falter, stumble, lurch.
▶ noun *walking with a limp* LAMENESS, hobble, uneven gait; *Medicine* claudication.

limp² ▶ adjective **1** *a limp handshake* SOFT, flaccid, loose, slack, lax; floppy, drooping, droopy, sagging. **2** *we were all limp with exhaustion* TIRED, fatigued, weary, exhausted, worn out; lethargic, listless, spiritless, weak.
− OPPOSITES: firm, energetic.

limpid ▶ adjective **1** *a limpid pool* CLEAR, transparent, glassy, crystal clear, crystalline, translucent, pellucid, unclouded. **2** *his limpid prose* LUCID, clear, plain, understandable, intelligible, comprehensible, coherent, explicit, unambiguous, simple, vivid, sharp, crystal clear; *formal* perspicuous.
− OPPOSITES: opaque.

line¹ ▶ noun **1** *he drew a line through the name* dash, rule, bar, score; underline, underscore, stroke, slash; *technical* stria, striation. **2** *there were lines around her eyes* WRINKLE, furrow, crease, groove, crinkle, crow's foot, laugh line. **3** *the classic lines of the exterior* CONTOUR, outline, configuration, shape, figure, delineation, profile. **4** *the line between Canada and the U.S.* BOUNDARY (LINE), limit, border, borderline, bounding line, frontier, demarcation line, dividing line, edge, margin, perimeter. **5** *behind enemy lines* POSITION, formation, defence, fieldwork, front (line); trenches. **6** *he put the washing on the line* CORD, rope, string,

cable, wire, thread, twine, strand. **7** *they waited in a line* LINEUP, file, row, queue. **8** *a line of figures* COLUMN, row. **9** *a long line of bad decisions* SERIES, sequence, succession, chain, string, set, cycle. **10** *a line of flight* COURSE, route, track, path, way, run. **11** *they took a very tough line with the industry* | *the party line* COURSE (OF ACTION), procedure, technique, tactic, tack; policy, practice, approach, plan, program, position, stance, philosophy. **12** *her own line of thought* COURSE, direction, drift, tack, tendency, trend. **13** (*informal*) *he fed me a line* STORY, piece of fiction, fabrication; *informal* spiel. **14** *he couldn't remember his lines* WORDS, part, script, speech. **15** *their line of work* (LINE OF) BUSINESS, (line of) work, field, trade, occupation, employment, profession, job, career, specialty, forte, province, department, sphere, area (of expertise). **16** *a new line of cologne* BRAND, kind, sort, type, variety, make. **17** *a noble line* ANCESTRY, family, parentage, birth, descent, lineage, extraction, genealogy, roots, origin, background; stock, bloodline, pedigree. **18** *the opening line of the poem* SENTENCE, phrase, clause, utterance; passage, extract, quotation, quote, citation. **19** *I should drop Ralph a line* NOTE, letter, card, postcard, email, message, communication, missive, memorandum; correspondence, word; *informal* memo; *formal* epistle.
− RELATED TERMS: linear.
▶ verb **1** *her face was lined with age* FURROW, wrinkle, crease, pucker, mark with lines. **2** *the driveway was lined by poplars* BORDER, edge, fringe, bound, rim.
■ **draw the line at** STOP SHORT OF, refuse to accept, balk at; object to, take issue with, take exception to.
■ **in line 1** *the poor stood in line for food* IN A LINEUP, in a row, in a file, in a queue. **2** *the advertisements are in line with the editorial style* IN AGREEMENT, in accord, in accordance, in harmony, in step, in compliance. **3** *he stood in line with the target* IN ALIGNMENT, aligned, level, at the same height; abreast, side by side. **4** *the referee kept him in line* UNDER CONTROL, in order, in check.
■ **in line for** A CANDIDATE FOR, in the running for, on the shortlist for, being considered for.
■ **get a line on** learn something about, find out about, be informed about, hear (tell) about.
■ **lay it on the line** SPEAK FRANKLY/HONESTLY, pull no punches, be blunt, not mince one's words, call a spade a spade; *informal* give it to someone straight.
■ **line up** FORM A LINE/LINEUP, get into rows/columns, queue up, fall in; *Military* dress.
■ **line someone/something up 1** *they lined them up against the wall* ARRANGE IN LINES, put in rows, arrange in columns, align, range; *Military* dress. **2** *we've lined up an all-star cast* ASSEMBLE, put together, organize, prepare, arrange, pre-arrange, fix up; book, schedule, timetable.
■ **on the line** AT RISK, in danger, in jeopardy, endangered, imperilled.
■ **toe the line** CONFORM, obey/observe the rules, comply with the rules, abide by the rules.

line² ▶ verb *a jacket lined with silk* COVER, put a lining in, interline, face, back, pad.
■ **line one's pockets** (*informal*) MAKE MONEY, accept bribes, embezzle money; *informal* feather one's nest, graft, grift, be on the make.

lineage ▶ noun ANCESTRY, family, parentage, birth, descent, line, extraction, derivation, genealogy, roots, origin, background; stock, bloodline, breeding, pedigree.

linear ▶ adjective STRAIGHT, direct, undeviating, as straight as an arrow; sequential.

lineup ▶ noun 1 *a star-studded lineup* LIST OF PERFORMERS, cast, company, bill, program, schedule. 2 *the Oilers' lineup* LIST OF PLAYERS, roster, team, squad, side. 3 *a long lineup of customers* LINE, row, column, file, queue.

linger ▶ verb 1 *the crowd lingered for a long time* WAIT (AROUND), stay (put), remain; loiter, dawdle, dally, take one's time; *informal* stick around, hang around, hang on; *archaic* tarry. 2 *the infection can linger for many years* PERSIST, continue, remain, stay, endure, carry on, last, keep on/up.
— OPPOSITES: vanish.

lingerie ▶ noun WOMEN'S UNDERWEAR, underclothes, underclothing, undergarments, foundation garments; nightwear, nightclothes; *informal* undies, gotchies ✦, underthings. *See also the table at* UNDERWEAR.

lingering ▶ adjective 1 *lingering doubts* REMAINING, surviving, persisting, abiding, nagging, niggling. 2 *a slow, lingering death* PROTRACTED, prolonged, long-drawn-out, long-lasting.

lingo ▶ noun (*informal*) LANGUAGE, tongue, dialect; jargon, terminology, slang, argot, cant, patter, mumbo-jumbo, bafflegab; *informal* -ese, -speak.

link ▶ noun 1 *a chain of steel links* LOOP, ring, connection, connector, coupling, joint. 2 *the links between transport and the environment* CONNECTION, relationship, association, linkage, tie-up. 3 *their links with the labour movement* BOND, tie, attachment, connection, relationship, association, affiliation. 4 *he was an important link in the chain* COMPONENT, constituent, element, part, piece.
▶ verb 1 *four boxes were linked together* JOIN, connect, fasten, attach, bind, unite, combine, amalgamate; clamp, secure, fix, tie, couple, yoke, hitch. 2 *the evidence linking him with the murder* ASSOCIATE, connect, relate, join, bracket.

lion-hearted ▶ adjective BRAVE, courageous, valiant, gallant, intrepid, valorous, fearless, bold, daring; stout-hearted, stalwart, heroic, doughty, plucky, manly; *informal* gutsy, spunky, ballsy.
— OPPOSITES: cowardly.

lionize ▶ verb CELEBRATE, fete, glorify, honour, exalt, acclaim, admire, praise, extol, applaud, hail, venerate, eulogize; *formal* laud.
— OPPOSITES: vilify.

lip ▶ noun 1 *the lip of the crater* EDGE, rim, brim, border, verge, brink. 2 (*informal*) *don't give me any lip!* INSOLENCE, impertinence, impudence, cheek, cheekiness, rudeness, audacity, effrontery, disrespect; *informal* mouth, backtalk, guff, sauce.
— RELATED TERMS: labial, labio-.
■ **bite one's lip** KEEP QUIET, keep one's mouth shut, say nothing, bite one's tongue.
■ **keep a stiff upper lip** KEEP CONTROL OF ONESELF, not show emotion, appear unaffected; *informal* keep one's cool.

liquefy ▶ verb MAKE/BECOME LIQUID, condense, liquidize, melt; deliquesce.

liqueur ▶ noun. *See table at* ALCOHOL.

liquid ▶ adjective 1 *liquid fuels* FLUID, liquefied; melted, molten, thawed, dissolved; *Chemistry* hydrous. 2 *her liquid eyes* CLEAR, limpid, crystal clear, crystalline, pellucid, unclouded, bright. 3 *liquid sounds* PURE, clear, mellifluous, dulcet, mellow, sweet, sweet-sounding, soft, melodious, harmonious. 4 *liquid assets* CONVERTIBLE, disposable, usable, spendable.
— OPPOSITES: solid.

▶ noun *a vat of liquid* FLUID, moisture; liquor, solution, juice.

liquidate ▶ verb 1 *the company was liquidated* CLOSE DOWN, wind up, put into liquidation, dissolve, disband. 2 *he liquidated his share portfolio* CONVERT (TO CASH), cash in, sell off/up. 3 *liquidating the public debt* PAY (OFF), pay in full, settle, clear, discharge, square, honour. 4 (*informal*) *they were liquidated in bloody purges. See* KILL *verb* sense 1.

liquor ▶ noun 1 *he liked his liquor* ALCOHOL, spirits, (alcoholic) drink, intoxicating liquor, intoxicant; *informal* grog, firewater, rotgut, the hard stuff, the bottle, hooch, moonshine, moose milk ✦; juice, the sauce. *See table at* ALCOHOL. 2 *strain the liquor into the sauce* STOCK, broth, bouillon, juice, liquid.

lissome ▶ adjective *See* LITHE.

list[1] ▶ noun *a list of the world's wealthiest people* CATALOGUE, inventory, record, register, roll, file, index, directory, listing, checklist, enumeration.
▶ verb *the accounts are listed alphabetically* RECORD, register, make a list of, enter; itemize, enumerate, catalogue, file, log, categorize, inventory; classify, group, sort, rank, alphabetize, index.

list[2] ▶ verb *the boat listed to one side* LEAN (OVER), tilt, tip, heel (over), keel over, careen, cant, pitch, incline, slant, slope, bank.

listen ▶ verb 1 *are you listening carefully?* HEAR, pay attention, be attentive, attend, concentrate; keep one's ears open, prick up one's ears; *informal* be all ears, lend an ear; *literary* hark; *archaic* hearken. 2 *policy-makers should listen to popular opinion* PAY ATTENTION, take heed, heed, take notice, take note, mind, mark, bear in mind, take into consideration/account, tune in.
■ **listen in** EAVESDROP, spy, overhear, tap, wiretap, bug, monitor.

listless ▶ adjective LETHARGIC, enervated, spiritless, lifeless, languid, languorous, inactive, inert, sluggish, torpid.
— OPPOSITES: energetic.

litany ▶ noun 1 *reciting the litany* PRAYER, invocation, supplication, devotion; *archaic* orison. 2 *a litany of complaints* RECITAL, recitation, repetition, enumeration; list, listing, catalogue, inventory.

literacy ▶ noun ABILITY TO READ AND WRITE, reading/writing proficiency; (book) learning, education, scholarship, schooling.

literal ▶ adjective 1 *the literal sense of the word 'dreadful'* STRICT, factual, plain, simple, exact, straightforward; unembellished, undistorted; objective, correct, true, accurate, genuine, authentic. 2 *a literal translation* WORD-FOR-WORD, verbatim, letter-for-letter; exact, precise, faithful, close, strict, accurate.
— OPPOSITES: figurative, loose.

literary ▶ adjective 1 *literary works* WRITTEN, poetic, artistic, dramatic. 2 *her literary friends* SCHOLARLY, learned, intellectual, cultured, erudite, bookish, highbrow, bluestocking, lettered, academic, cultivated; well-read, widely read, (well) educated. 3 *literary language* FORMAL, written, poetic, dramatic; elaborate, ornate, flowery; *informal* inkhorn.

literary device ▶ noun. *See table at* RHETORICAL.

literate ▶ adjective 1 *many of the workers were not literate* ABLE TO READ/WRITE, educated, schooled. 2 *her literate friends* (WELL) EDUCATED, well-read, widely read, scholarly, learned, knowledgeable, lettered, cultured, cultivated, sophisticated, well-informed.

Nobel Prize Winners for Literature (from 1950)

1950	Bertrand Russell	1968	Kawabata Yasunari	1986	Wole Soyinka
1951	Pär Lagerkvist	1969	Samuel Beckett	1987	Joseph Brodsky
1952	François Mauriac	1970	Alexander Solzhenitsyn	1988	Naguib Mahfouz
1953	Winston Churchill	1971	Pablo Neruda	1989	Camilo José Cela
1954	Ernest Hemingway	1972	Heinrich Böll	1990	Octavio Paz
1955	Halldór Laxness	1973	Patrick White	1991	Nadine Gordimer
1956	Juan Ramón Jiménez	1974	Eyvind Johnson	1992	Derek Walcott
1957	Albert Camus		Harry Martinson	1993	Toni Morrison
1958	Boris Pasternak	1975	Eugenio Montale	1994	Kenzaburo Oë
1959	Salvatore Quasimodo	1976	Saul Bellow	1995	Seamus Heaney
1960	Saint-John Perse	1977	Vicente Aleixandre	1996	Wisława Szymborska
1961	Ivo Andrić	1978	Isaac Bashevis Singer	1997	Dario Fo
1962	John Steinbeck	1979	Odysseus Elytis	1998	José Saramago
1963	George Seferis	1980	Czeslaw Milosz	1999	Günter Grass
1964	Jean-Paul Sartre (declined)	1981	Elias Canetti	2000	Gao Xingjian
1965	Mikhail Sholokhov	1982	Gabriel García Márquez	2001	V.S. Naipaul
1966	Shmuel Yosef Agnon	1983	William Golding	2002	Imre Kertész
	Nelly Sachs	1984	Jaroslav Seifert		
1967	Miguel Angel Asturias	1985	Claude Simon		

3 *he was computer literate* KNOWLEDGEABLE, well-versed, savvy, smart, conversant, competent; *informal* up on, up to speed on, plugged in.
– OPPOSITES: ignorant.

literature ▸ noun **1** *English literature* WRITTEN WORKS, writings, (creative) writing, literary texts, compositions. **2** *the literature on prototype theory* PUBLICATIONS, published writings, texts, reports, studies. **3** *election literature* PRINTED MATTER, brochures, leaflets, pamphlets, circulars, flyers, handouts, handbills, bulletins, fact sheets, publicity, propaganda, notices; *informal* bumph.

lithe ▸ adjective AGILE, graceful, supple, limber, lithesome, loose-limbed, nimble, deft, flexible, lissome, slender, slim, willowy.
– OPPOSITES: clumsy.

litigation ▸ noun (LEGAL/JUDICIAL) PROCEEDINGS, (legal) action, lawsuit, legal dispute, (legal) case, suit, prosecution, indictment.

litter ▸ noun **1** *never drop litter* GARBAGE, refuse, junk, waste, debris, scraps, leavings, fragments, detritus, trash, rubbish. **2** *the litter of papers around her* CLUTTER, jumble, muddle, mess, heap, disorder, untidiness, confusion, disarray; *informal* shambles. **3** *a litter of kittens* BROOD, family. **4** *she was carried on a litter* SEDAN CHAIR, palanquin; stretcher.
▸ verb **1** *clothes littered the floor* MAKE UNTIDY, mess up, make a mess of, clutter up, be strewn about, be scattered about; *informal* make a shambles of. **2** *a paper littered with quotes* FILL, pack, load, clutter.

little ▸ adjective **1** *a little writing desk* SMALL, small-scale, compact; mini, miniature, tiny, minute, minuscule; toy, baby, pocket, undersized, dwarf, midget, wee; *informal* teeny-weeny, teensy-weensy, itsy-bitsy, itty-bitty, little-bitty, half-pint, vest-pocket, li'l, micro. **2** *a little man* SHORT, small, slight, petite, diminutive, tiny; elfin, dwarfish, midget, pygmy, Lilliputian; *informal* teeny-weeny, pint-sized, peewee. **3** *my little sister* YOUNG, younger, junior, small, baby, infant. **4** *I was a bodyguard for a little while* BRIEF, short, short-lived; fleeting, momentary, transitory, transient; fast, quick, hasty, cursory. **5** *a few little problems* MINOR, unimportant, insignificant, trivial, trifling, petty, paltry, inconsequential, nugatory; *informal* dinky, piddling. **6** *they have little political influence* HARDLY ANY, not much, slight, scant, limited, restricted, modest, little or no, minimal, negligible.

7 *you little sneak* CONTEMPTIBLE, mean, spiteful, petty, small-minded.
– OPPOSITES: big, large, elder, important, considerable.
▸ adverb **1** *he is little known as a singer* | *they little thought* HARDLY, barely, scarcely, not much, not at all, (only) slightly. **2** *his art has been little seen in Canada* RARELY, seldom, infrequently, hardly (ever), scarcely (ever), not much.
– OPPOSITES: well, often.
■ **a little** *add a little water* SOME, a small amount of, a bit of, a touch of, a soupçon of, a dash of, a taste of, a spot of; a shade of, a suggestion of, a trace of, a hint of, a suspicion of; a dribble of, a splash of, a pinch of, a sprinkling of, a speck of; *informal* a smidgen of, a tad of. **2** *after a little, Oliver came in* A SHORT TIME, a little while, a bit, an interval, a short period; a minute, a moment, a second, an instant; *informal* a sec, a mo, a jiffy. **3** *this reminds me a little of the Adriatic* SLIGHTLY, faintly, remotely, vaguely; somewhat, a little bit, to some degree.
■ **little by little** GRADUALLY, slowly, by degrees, by stages, step by step, bit by bit, progressively; subtly, imperceptibly.

liturgy ▸ noun RITUAL, worship, service, ceremony, rite, observance, celebration, sacrament; tradition, custom, practice, rubric; *formal* ordinance.

livable ▸ adjective **1** *renovations made the house livable* HABITABLE, inhabitable, fit to live in, in good repair; suitable, acceptable, passable; comfortable, cozy. **2** *life has become livable again* BEARABLE, endurable, tolerable, supportable, sufferable.

live¹ ▸ verb **1** *the greatest mathematician who ever lived* EXIST, be alive, be, have life; breathe, draw breath, walk the earth. **2** *I live in Moose Jaw* RESIDE, have one's home, have one's residence, be settled; be housed, lodge, inhabit, occupy, populate; *formal* dwell, be domiciled. **3** *they lived quietly* PASS/SPEND ONE'S LIFE, have a lifestyle; behave, conduct oneself; *formal* comport oneself. **4** *she had lived a difficult life* EXPERIENCE, spend, pass, lead, have, go through, undergo. **5** *Fred lived by his wits* SURVIVE, make a living, earn one's living, eke out a living; subsist, support oneself, sustain oneself, make ends meet, keep body and soul together. **6** *you should live a little* ENJOY ONESELF, enjoy life, have fun, live life to the full/

fullest.
— OPPOSITES: die, be dead.
■ **live it up** (*informal*) LIVE EXTRAVAGANTLY, live in the lap
of luxury, live in clover; carouse, revel, enjoy oneself,
have a good time, go on a spree; *informal* party, paint
the town red, have a ball, make whoopee, live high
on/off the hog; *archaic* wassail.
■ **live off/on** SUBSIST ON, feed on/off, eat, consume.

live² ▶ adjective **1** *live bait* LIVING, alive, having life,
breathing, animate, sentient. **2** *a live performance* IN
THE FLESH, personal, in person, not recorded. **3** *a live
wire* ELECTRIFIED, charged, powered, active; *informal*
hot. **4** *live coals* (RED) HOT, glowing, aglow; burning,
alight, flaming, aflame, blazing, ignited, on fire;
literary afire. **5** *a live grenade* UNEXPLODED, explosive,
active; unstable, volatile.
— OPPOSITES: dead, inanimate, recorded.
■ **live wire** (*informal*) ENERGETIC PERSON; *informal*
fireball, human dynamo, powerhouse, life of the
party.

livelihood ▶ noun (SOURCE OF) INCOME, means of
support, living, subsistence, keep, maintenance,
sustenance, nourishment, daily bread, bread and
butter; job, work, employment, occupation, vocation.

lively ▶ adjective **1** *a lively young woman* ENERGETIC,
active, animated, dynamic, full of life, outgoing,
spirited, high-spirited, vivacious, enthusiastic,
vibrant, buoyant, exuberant, effervescent, cheerful;
bouncy, bubbly, perky, sparkling, zestful; *informal* full
of beans, chirpy, chipper, peppy. **2** *a lively bar* BUSY,
crowded, bustling, buzzing; vibrant, boisterous, jolly,
festive; *informal* hopping. **3** *a lively debate* HEATED,
vigorous, animated, spirited, enthusiastic, forceful;
exciting, interesting, memorable. **4** *a lively portrait of
the local community* VIVID, colourful, striking, graphic,
bold, strong.
— OPPOSITES: quiet, dull.

liven
■ **liven up** BRIGHTEN UP, cheer up, perk up, revive,
rally, pick up, bounce back; *informal* buck up.
■ **liven someone/something up** BRIGHTEN UP,
cheer up, enliven, animate, raise someone's spirits,
perk up, spice up, make lively, wake up, invigorate,
revive, refresh, vivify, galvanize, stimulate, stir up,
get going; *informal* buck up, pep up.

liver
— RELATED TERMS: hepatic.

livid ▶ adjective **1** (*informal*) *Mum was absolutely livid. See
FURIOUS sense 1.* **2** *a livid bruise* PURPLISH, bluish, dark,
discoloured, purple, greyish-blue; bruised; angry,
black and blue.

living ▶ noun **1** *she cleaned floors for a living* LIVELIHOOD,
(source of) income, means of support, subsistence,
keep, maintenance, sustenance, nourishment, daily
bread, bread and butter; job, work, employment,
occupation, vocation. **2** *healthy living* WAY OF LIFE,
lifestyle, way of living, life; conduct, behaviour,
activities, habits.
▶ adjective **1** *living organisms* ALIVE, live, having life,
animate, sentient; breathing, existing, existent;
informal alive and kicking. **2** *a living language* CURRENT,
contemporary, present; in use, active, surviving,
extant, persisting, remaining, existing, in existence.
3 *a living hell* COMPLETE, total, utter, absolute, real,
veritable, perfect, out-and-out, downright.
— OPPOSITES: dead, extinct.

living room ▶ noun SITTING ROOM, lounge, front
room, family room, living area, great room, den.

lizard ▶ noun. *See table at* REPTILE.
— RELATED TERMS: saurian.

load ▶ noun **1** *he has a load to deliver* CARGO, freight,
consignment, delivery, shipment, goods,
merchandise; pack, bundle, parcel; truckload,
shipload, boatload, vanload. **2** (*informal*) *I bought a load
of clothes* A LOT, a great deal, a large amount/quantity,
an abundance, a wealth, a mountain; many, plenty;
informal a heap, a mass, a pile, a whack, a stack, a ton,
lots, heaps, masses, piles, stacks, tons. **3** *a heavy
teaching load* COMMITMENT, responsibility, duty,
obligation, charge, burden; trouble, worry, strain,
pressure.
▶ verb **1** *we quickly loaded the van* FILL (UP), pack, charge,
stock, stack, lade. **2** *Larry loaded boxes into the jeep*
PACK, stow, store, stack, bundle; place, deposit, put
away. **3** *loading the committee with responsibilities*
BURDEN, weigh down, saddle, charge; overburden,
overwhelm, encumber, tax, strain, trouble, worry.
4 *Richard loaded Marshal with honours* REWARD, ply,
regale, shower. **5** *he loaded a gun* PRIME, charge,
prepare to fire/use. **6** *load the cassette into the camcorder*
INSERT, put, place, slot. **7** *the dice are loaded against him*
BIAS, rig, fix; weight.

loaded ▶ adjective **1** *a loaded freight train* FULL, filled,
laden, packed, stuffed, crammed, brimming, stacked;
informal chock full, chockablock. **2** *a loaded gun* PRIMED,
charged, armed, ready to fire. **3** (*informal*) *they have no
money worries, they're loaded. See* RICH *sense 1.* **4** *he came
home from the party loaded. See* INTOXICATED. **5** *loaded dice*
BIASED, rigged, fixed; juiced; weighted. **6** *a loaded
question* CHARGED, sensitive, delicate.

loaf ▶ verb *he was just loafing around* LAZE, lounge, loll,
idle, waste time; *informal* hang around, bum around,
futz around.

loafer ▶ noun IDLER, (*Atlantic*) hangashore ✦, layabout,
good-for-nothing, lounger, shirker, sluggard,
laggard, slugabed; *informal* slacker, slob, lazybones,
bum.

loan ▶ noun *a loan of $7,000* CREDIT, advance, bridge
financing; mortgage, overdraft; lending,
moneylending.
▶ verb **1** *he loaned me his car* LEND, advance, give credit;
give on loan, lease, charter. **2** *the majority of exhibits
have been loaned* BORROW, receive/take on loan.

loath ▶ adjective RELUCTANT, unwilling, disinclined,
ill-disposed; against, averse, opposed, resistant.
— OPPOSITES: willing.

loathe ▶ verb HATE, detest, abhor, execrate, have a
strong aversion to, feel repugnance towards, not be
able to bear/stand, be repelled by.
— OPPOSITES: love.

loathing ▶ noun HATRED, hate, detestation,
abhorrence, abomination, execration, odium;
antipathy, dislike, hostility, animosity, ill feeling,
bad feeling, malice, animus, enmity, aversion;
repugnance.

loathsome ▶ adjective HATEFUL, detestable,
abhorrent, repulsive, odious, repugnant, repellent,
disgusting, revolting, sickening, abominable,
despicable, contemptible, reprehensible, execrable,
damnable; vile, horrible, hideous, nasty, obnoxious,
gross, foul, horrid; *informal* yucky.

lob ▶ verb THROW, toss, huck ✦, fling, pitch, hurl,
pelt, sling, launch, propel; *informal* chuck, heave.

lobby ▶ noun **1** *the hotel lobby* ENTRANCE (HALL),
hallway, hall, vestibule, foyer, reception area. **2** *the
anti-gun lobby* PRESSURE GROUP, (special) interest

group, movement, campaign, crusade, lobbyists, supporters; faction, camp.

▶ **verb 1** *readers are urged to lobby their MPs* SEEK TO INFLUENCE, try to persuade, bring pressure to bear on, importune, sway; petition, solicit, appeal to, pressurize. **2** *a group lobbying for better rail services* CAMPAIGN, crusade, press, push, ask, call, demand; promote, advocate, champion.

local ▶ **adjective 1** *local government* COMMUNITY, district, neighbourhood, regional, city, town, municipal, county. **2** *a local restaurant* NEIGHBOURHOOD, nearby, near, at hand, close by; accessible, handy, convenient. **3** *a local infection* CONFINED, restricted, contained, localized.

− OPPOSITES: national.

▶ **noun** *complaints from the locals* LOCAL PERSON, native, inhabitant, resident.

− OPPOSITES: outsider.

locale ▶ **noun** PLACE, site, spot, area; position, location, setting, scene, venue, background, backdrop, environment; neighbourhood, district, region, locality.

localize ▶ **verb** LIMIT, restrict, confine, contain, circumscribe, concentrate, delimit.

− OPPOSITES: generalize.

locate ▶ **verb 1** *help me locate this photograph* FIND, discover, pinpoint, detect, track down, unearth, sniff out, smoke out, search out, ferret out, uncover. **2** *a company located near Pittsburgh* SITUATE, site, position, place, base; put, build, establish, found, station, install, settle.

location ▶ **noun** POSITION, place, situation, site, locality, locale, spot, whereabouts, point; scene, setting, area, environment; bearings, orientation; venue, address; *technical* locus.

lock ▶ **noun** *the lock on the door* BOLT, catch, fastener, clasp, bar, hasp, latch.

▶ **verb 1** *he locked the door* BOLT, fasten, bar, secure, seal; padlock, latch, chain. **2** *they locked arms* JOIN, interlock, intertwine, link, mesh, engage, unite, connect, yoke, mate; couple. **3** *the wheels locked* BECOME STUCK, stick, jam, become/make immovable, become/make rigid. **4** *he locked her in an embrace* CLASP, grasp, embrace, hug, squeeze, clench.

− OPPOSITES: unlock, open, separate, divide.

■ **lock horns** ARGUE, quarrel, fight, disagree, squabble, bicker.

■ **lock lips** KISS, smooch, peck, neck, canoodle, make out.

■ **lock someone out** KEEP OUT, shut out, refuse entrance to, deny admittance to; exclude, bar, debar, ban.

■ **lock someone up** IMPRISON, jail, incarcerate, send to prison, put behind bars, put under lock and key, put in chains, clap in irons, cage, pen, coop up; *informal* put away, put inside.

locker ▶ **noun** CUPBOARD, cabinet, chest, safe, box, case, coffer; compartment, storeroom.

lock-up ▶ **noun** JAIL, prison, cell, detention centre, jailhouse, penitentiary, remand centre; *informal* slammer, jug, can, brig, clink, big house, cooler, hoosegow, cage, pen, slam, pokey.

locomotion ▶ **noun** MOVEMENT, motion, moving; travel, travelling; mobility, motility; walking, running; progress, progression, passage; *formal* perambulation.

lodge ▶ **noun 1** *a hunting lodge* HOUSE, cottage, cabin, outpost camp ♣, bush camp ♣, chalet, *historical*

camboose ♣. **2** *we'll eat up at the lodge* MAIN HALL, main building, dining hall. **3** *a beaver's lodge* DEN, lair, hole, set; retreat, haunt, shelter. **4** *a Masonic lodge* HALL, clubhouse, meeting room. **5** *the porter's lodge* GATEHOUSE, cottage.

▶ **verb 1** *William lodged at our house* RESIDE, board, stay, live, have lodgings, have rooms, be put up, be quartered, stop, room; *formal* dwell, be domiciled, sojourn; *archaic* abide. **2** *they were lodged at an inn* ACCOMMODATE, put up, take in, house, board, billet, quarter, shelter. **3** *we lodged a complaint* SUBMIT, register, enter, put forward, advance, lay, present, tender, proffer, put on record, record, table, file. **4** *the money was lodged in a bank* DEPOSIT, put, bank; stash, store, stow, put away, squirrel away. **5** *the bullet lodged in his back* BECOME FIXED, embed itself, become embedded, become implanted, get/become stuck, stick, catch, become caught, wedge.

lodging ▶ **noun** ACCOMMODATION, rooms, chambers, living quarters, place to stay, a roof over one's head, housing, shelter; *informal* digs, pad, nest; *formal* abode, residence, dwelling, dwelling place, habitation.

lofty ▶ **adjective 1** *a lofty tower* TALL, high, giant, towering, soaring, sky-scraping. **2** *lofty ideals* NOBLE, exalted, high, high-minded, worthy, grand, fine, elevated, sublime. **3** *lofty disdain* HAUGHTY, arrogant, disdainful, supercilious, condescending, scornful, patronizing, contemptuous, self-important, conceited, snobbish; aloof, standoffish; *informal* stuck-up, snooty, snotty, hoity-toity.

− OPPOSITES: low, short, base, lowly, modest.

log ▶ **noun 1** *a fallen log* BRANCH, trunk; piece of wood, deadhead, (*Nfld*) nug ♣; (**logs**) timber, firewood, (*Atlantic*) junk ♣. **2** *a log of phone calls* RECORD, register, logbook, journal, diary, minutes, chronicle, daybook, record book, ledger, account, tally.

▶ **verb 1** *all complaints are logged* REGISTER, record, make a note of, note down, write down, jot down, put in writing, enter, file. **2** *the pilot had logged 95 hours* ATTAIN, achieve, chalk up, make, do, go. **3** *he was injured while logging on the west coast* CUT DOWN TREES, chop down trees, fell trees, clear cut, harvest trees.

■ **log in** SIGN IN, register, enter, log-on.

log drive ▶ **noun** river drive ♣, drive ♣.

logger ▶ **noun** LUMBERJACK, lumberman, woodcutter, woodsman, bushman, bushworker ♣; *informal* jack; (*BC*) *historical* whistlepunk ♣, woodman; powderman, pulp cutter, chaser, faller, high rigger, skidder, handlogger, hooktender, bull of the woods.

loggerhead

■ **at loggerheads** IN DISAGREEMENT, at odds, at variance, wrangling, quarrelling, disagreeing, disputing, locking horns, at daggers drawn, in conflict, fighting, at war; *informal* at each other's throats.

logic ▶ **noun 1** *this case appears to defy all logic* REASON, judgment, logical thought, rationality, wisdom, sense, good sense, common sense, sanity; *informal* horse sense. **2** *the logic of their argument* REASONING, line of reasoning, rationale, argument, argumentation.

logical ▶ **adjective 1** *information displayed in a logical fashion* REASONED, well reasoned, reasonable, rational, sound, cogent, well-thought-out, valid; coherent, clear, well-organized, systematic, orderly, methodical, analytical, consistent, objective. **2** *the logical outcome* NATURAL, reasonable, sensible, understandable; predictable, unsurprising, only to be expected, most likely, likeliest, obvious.

— OPPOSITES: illogical, irrational, unlikely, surprising.

logistics ► plural noun ORGANIZATION, planning, plans, management, arrangement, administration, orchestration, coordination, execution, handling, running.

log-jam ► noun DEADLOCK, stalemate, saw-off ✦, tie; impasse, bottleneck, barrier, block.

logo ► noun EMBLEM, trademark, brand, device, figure, symbol, design, sign, mark; insignia, crest, seal.

loiter ► verb **1** *he loitered at bus stops* LINGER, wait, skulk; loaf, lounge, idle, laze, waste time, lallygag; *informal* hang around; *archaic* tarry. **2** *they loitered along the river bank* DAWDLE, dally, stroll, amble, saunter, meander, drift, putter, take one's time; *informal* dilly-dally, mosey, tootle.

loll ► verb **1** *he lolled in an armchair* LOUNGE, sprawl, drape oneself, stretch oneself; slouch, slump; laze, luxuriate, put one's feet up, lean back, sit back, recline, relax, take it easy, take a load off. **2** *her head lolled to one side* HANG (LOOSELY), droop, dangle, sag, drop, flop.

lone ► adjective SOLITARY, single, solo, unaccompanied, unescorted, alone, by oneself/itself, sole, companionless; detached, isolated.

lonely ► adjective **1** *I felt very lonely* ISOLATED, alone, lonesome, friendless, with no one to turn to, forsaken, abandoned, rejected, unloved, unwanted, outcast; gloomy, sad, depressed, desolate, forlorn, cheerless, down, blue. **2** *the lonely life of a writer* SOLITARY, unaccompanied, lone, by oneself/itself, companionless. **3** *a lonely road* DESERTED, uninhabited, unfrequented, unpopulated, desolate, isolated, remote, out of the way, secluded, off the beaten track, in the back of beyond, godforsaken; *informal* in the middle of nowhere.

— OPPOSITES: popular, sociable, crowded.

loner ► noun RECLUSE, introvert, lone wolf, hermit, solitary, misanthrope, outsider; *historical* anchorite.

long¹ ► adjective *a long silence* LENGTHY, extended, prolonged, extensive, protracted, long-lasting, long-drawn(-out), spun out, dragged out, seemingly endless, lingering, interminable.

— OPPOSITES: short, brief.

■ **before long** SOON, shortly, presently, in the near future, in a little while, by and by, in a minute, in a moment, in a second; *informal* anon, in a jiffy; *dated* directly; *literary* ere long.

long² ► verb *I longed for the holidays* YEARN, pine, ache, hanker for/after, hunger, thirst, itch, be eager, be desperate; crave, dream of, set one's heart on; *informal* have a yen, (have a) jones, be dying.

longevity ► noun LENGTH OF LIFE, lifespan, lifetime, shelf life; durability, endurance, resilience, strength, robustness.

longing ► noun *a longing for the countryside* YEARNING, pining, craving, ache, burning, hunger, thirst, hankering; *informal* yen, itch, jones.
► adjective *a longing look* YEARNING, pining, craving, hungry, thirsty, hankering, wistful, covetous.

long-lasting ► adjective ENDURING, lasting, abiding, long-lived, long-running, long-established, long-standing, lifelong, deep-rooted, time-honoured, traditional, permanent.

— OPPOSITES: short-lived, ephemeral.

long shot ► noun **1** *it's a long shot, but you could win big* GAMBLE, venture, speculation, risk, (outside) chance. **2** *he was a long shot in the sprint* UNDERDOG, dark horse, weaker one, little guy, David.

■ **not by a long shot** See NOT BY A LONG SHOT *at* SHOT.

long-standing ► adjective WELL-ESTABLISHED, long-established; time-honoured, traditional, age-old; abiding, enduring, long-lived, surviving, persistent, prevailing, perennial, deep-rooted, long-term, confirmed.

— OPPOSITES: new, recent.

long-suffering ► adjective PATIENT, forbearing, tolerant, uncomplaining, stoic, stoical, resigned; easygoing, indulgent, charitable, accommodating, forgiving, understanding.

— OPPOSITES: impatient, complaining.

long-winded ► adjective VERBOSE, wordy, lengthy, long, overlong, prolix, prolonged, protracted, long-drawn-out, interminable; discursive, diffuse, rambling, tortuous, meandering, repetitious, maundering; *informal* windy.

— OPPOSITES: concise, succinct, laconic.

look ► verb **1** *Mrs. Wright looked at him* GLANCE, gaze, stare, gape, peer; peep, peek, take a look; watch, observe, view, regard, examine, inspect, eye, scan, scrutinize, survey, study, contemplate, consider, take in, ogle; *informal* take a gander, rubberneck, goggle, give someone/something a/the once-over, get a load of, eyeball; *literary* behold. **2** *her room looked out on Broadway* COMMAND A VIEW OF, face, overlook, front. **3** *they looked shocked* SEEM (TO BE), appear (to be), have the appearance/air of being, give the impression of being, give every appearance/indication of being, strike someone as being.

— OPPOSITES: ignore.

► noun **1** *have a look at this report* GLANCE, view, examination, study, inspection, observation, scan, survey, peep, peek, glimpse, gaze, stare; *informal* eyeful, gander, look-see, once-over, squint. **2** *the look on her face* EXPRESSION, mien. **3** *that rustic look* APPEARANCE, air, aspect, bearing, cast, manner, mien, demeanour, facade, impression, effect. **4** *this year's look* FASHION, style, vogue, mode.

■ **look after** TAKE CARE OF, care for, attend to, minister to, tend, mind, keep an eye on, keep safe, be responsible for, protect; nurse, babysit, house-sit.

■ **look back on** REFLECT ON, think back to, remember, recall, reminisce about.

■ **look down on** DISDAIN, scorn, regard with contempt, look down one's nose at, sneer at, despise.

■ **look for** SEARCH FOR, hunt for, try to find, seek, cast about/around for, try to track down, forage for, scout out, quest for/after.

■ **look forward to** *I look forward to Rebecca's call* AWAIT WITH PLEASURE, eagerly anticipate, lick one's lips over, be unable to wait for, count the days until.

■ **look into** INVESTIGATE, inquire into, ask questions about, go into, probe, explore, follow up, research, study, examine; *informal* check out, give something a/the once-over, scope out.

■ **look like** RESEMBLE, bear a resemblance to, look similar to, take after, have the look of, have the appearance of, remind one of, make one think of; *informal* be the spitting image of, be a dead ringer for.

■ **look on/upon** REGARD, consider, think of, deem, judge, see, view, count, reckon.

■ **look out** BEWARE, watch out, be on (one's) guard, be alert, be wary, be vigilant, be careful, take care, be cautious, pay attention, take heed, keep one's eyes open/peeled, keep an eye out; watch your step.

■ **look something over** INSPECT, examine, scan, cast

an eye over, take stock of, vet, view, look through, peruse, read through, check out; *informal* give something a/the once-over, eyeball.

■ **look to 1** *we must look to the future* CONSIDER, think about, turn one's thoughts to, focus on, take heed of, pay attention to, attend to, address, mind, heed. **2** *they look to the government for help* TURN TO, resort to, have recourse to, fall back on, rely on.

■ **look up 1** *things are looking up* IMPROVE, get better, pick up, come along/on, progress, make progress, make headway, perk up, rally, take a turn for the better. **2** *she looked up his number* SEARCH FOR, look for, try to find.

■ **look someone up** (*informal*) GO TO VISIT, pay a visit to, call on, go to see, look in on, visit with, go see; *informal* drop in on, drop by, pop by.

■ **look up to** ADMIRE, have a high opinion of, think highly of, hold in high regard, regard highly, rate highly, respect, esteem, value, venerate.

look-alike ▶ noun DOUBLE, twin, clone, duplicate, exact likeness, replica, copy, facsimile, Doppelgänger; *informal* spitting image, dead ringer.

lookout ▶ noun **1** *he saw the smoke from the lookout* OBSERVATION POST, lookout point, lookout station, lookout tower, watchtower. **2** *a scenic lookout* VIEW, vista, prospect, panorama, scene, aspect, outlook. **3** *he agreed to act as lookout* WATCHMAN, watch, guard, sentry, sentinel.

■ **be on the lookout/keep a lookout** KEEP WATCH, keep an eye out, keep one's eyes peeled, keep a vigil, be alert, be vigilant, be on the qui vive.

loom ▶ verb **1** *ghostly shapes loomed out of the fog* EMERGE, appear, come into view, take shape, materialize, reveal itself. **2** *the church loomed above him* SOAR, tower, rise, rear up; overhang, overshadow, dominate. **3** *without reforms, disaster looms* BE IMMINENT, be on the horizon, impend, threaten, brew, be just around the corner, be in the wind.

■ **loom large** DOMINATE, be important, be significant, be of consequence; count, matter, signify.

loop ▶ noun *a loop of rope* COIL, hoop, ring, circle, noose, oval, spiral, curl, bend, curve, arc, twirl, whorl, twist, hook, helix, convolution.

▶ verb **1** *Dave looped rope around their hands* COIL, wind, twist, snake, wreathe, spiral, curve, bend, turn. **2** *he looped the cables together* FASTEN, tie, join, connect, knot, bind.

loophole ▶ noun MEANS OF EVASION, means of avoidance; window, gap, opening.

loose ▶ adjective **1** *a loose floorboard* NOT FIXED IN PLACE, not secure, unsecured, unattached; detached, unfastened, untied; wobbly, unsteady, movable. **2** *she wore her hair loose* UNTIED, unpinned, unbound, hanging free, down, flowing. **3** *there's a wolf loose* FREE, at large, at liberty, on the loose, escaped; unconfined, untied, unchained, untethered, stray. **4** *a loose interpretation* VAGUE, indefinite, inexact, imprecise, approximate; broad, general, rough; liberal; *informal* ballpark. **5** *a loose jacket* BAGGY, generously cut, slack, roomy; oversized, shapeless, sagging, saggy, sloppy. **6** (*dated*) *a loose woman* PROMISCUOUS, of easy virtue, fast, wanton, unchaste, immoral; licentious, dissolute; *dated* fallen. **7** *loose talk* INDISCREET, unguarded, free, gossipy, gossiping.
— OPPOSITES: secure, literal, narrow, tight, chaste, guarded.

▶ verb **1** *loose the dogs* FREE, set free, unloose, turn loose, set loose, let loose, let go, release; untie, unchain, unfasten, unleash. **2** *the fingers loosed their*

hold RELAX, slacken, loosen; weaken, lessen, reduce, diminish, moderate.
— OPPOSITES: confine, tighten.

■ **at loose ends** WITH NOTHING TO DO, unoccupied, unemployed, at leisure, idle, adrift, with time to kill; bored, twiddling one's thumbs, hanging/kicking around.

■ **let loose.** *See* LOOSE *verb* sense 1.

■ **on the loose** FREE, at liberty, at large, escaped; on the run, fugitive, wanted; *informal* on the lam.

loose-limbed ▶ adjective SUPPLE, limber, lithe, lissome, willowy; agile, nimble, flexible.

loosen ▶ verb **1** *you simply loosen two screws* MAKE SLACK, slacken, unstick; unfasten, detach, release, disconnect, undo, unclasp, unlatch, unbolt. **2** *her fingers loosened* BECOME SLACK, slacken, become loose, let go, ease; work loose, work free. **3** *Philip loosened his grip* WEAKEN, relax, slacken, loose, lessen, reduce, moderate, diminish.
— OPPOSITES: tighten.

■ **loosen up** *you need to loosen up* RELAX, unwind, ease up, calm down; *informal* lighten up, go easy, chill out, kick back.

loot ▶ noun *a bag full of loot* BOOTY, spoils, plunder, stolen goods, contraband, pillage; *informal* swag, hot goods, ill-gotten gains, take.

▶ verb *troops looted the cathedral* PLUNDER, pillage, despoil, ransack, sack, raid, rifle, rob, burgle, burglarize.

lop ▶ verb CUT, chop, hack, saw, hew, slash, axe; prune, sever, clip, trim, snip, dock, crop.

lopsided ▶ adjective CROOKED, askew, awry, off-centre, uneven, out of line, asymmetrical, tilted, at an angle, aslant, slanting; off-balance, off-kilter; *informal* cockeyed, wonky.
— OPPOSITES: even, level, balanced.

loquacious ▶ adjective TALKATIVE, voluble, communicative, expansive, garrulous, unreserved, chatty, gossipy, gossiping; *informal* having the gift of the gab, gabby, gassy, able to talk the hind leg off a donkey, motor-mouthed, talky, windy.
— OPPOSITES: reticent, taciturn.

lord ▶ noun **1** *Jeremy is my lord and master* MASTER, ruler, leader, chief, superior, monarch, sovereign, king, emperor, prince, governor, commander, suzerain, liege, liege lord. **2** *let us pray to our Lord* GOD, the Father, the Almighty, the Creator; Jehovah, Adonai, Yahweh, Elohim, Allah; Jesus Christ, the Messiah, the Saviour, the Son of God, the Redeemer, the Lamb of God, the Prince of Peace, the King of Kings; *informal* the Man Upstairs. **3** *a press lord* MAGNATE, tycoon, mogul, captain, baron, king; industrialist, proprietor; *informal* big shot, (head) honcho; *derogatory* fat cat.
— OPPOSITES: commoner, servant, inferior.

■ **lord it over someone** ORDER ABOUT/AROUND, dictate to, domineer, ride roughshod over, pull rank on, tyrannize, have under one's thumb; be overbearing, put on airs, swagger; *informal* boss around, walk all over, push around, throw one's weight around.

lore ▶ noun **1** *Arthurian legend and lore* MYTHOLOGY, myths, legends, stories, traditions, folklore, fables, oral tradition, mythos. **2** *bush lore* KNOWLEDGE, learning, wisdom; *informal* know-how.

lose ▶ verb **1** *I've lost my watch* MISLAY, misplace, be unable to find, lose track of, lose (behind), fail to keep/retain, fail to keep sight of. **2** *he's lost a lot of blood* BE DEPRIVED OF, suffer the loss of; no longer have. **3** *he*

lost his pursuers ESCAPE FROM, evade, elude, dodge, avoid, give someone the slip, shake off, throw off, throw off the scent; leave behind, outdistance, outstrip, outrun. **4** *they lost their way* STRAY FROM, wander from, depart from, go astray from, fail to keep to. **5** *you've lost your chance* MISS, waste, squander, fail to grasp, fail to take advantage of, let pass, neglect, forfeit; *informal* pass up, lose out on. **6** *they always lose at lacrosse* BE DEFEATED, be beaten, suffer defeat, be the loser, be conquered, be vanquished, be trounced; *informal* come a cropper, go down, take a licking, be bested. **7** *you can lose the phony accent* DISCARD, get rid of, dispose of, dump, jettison, throw out.
— OPPOSITES: find, regain, seize, win, keep.
■ **lose out** BE DEPRIVED OF AN OPPORTUNITY, fail to benefit, be disadvantaged, be the loser.
■ **lose out on** BE UNABLE TO TAKE ADVANTAGE OF, fail to benefit from; *informal* miss out on.
■ **lose out to** BE DEFEATED BY, be beaten by, suffer defeat at the hands of, lose to, be conquered by, be vanquished by, be trounced by; *informal* go down to, be bested by.

loser ▸ noun **1** *the loser still gets the silver medal* DEFEATED PERSON, also-ran, runner-up. **2** *(informal) he's a complete loser* FAILURE, underachiever, ne'er-do-well, write-off, has-been; MISFIT, freak, unpopular person; *informal* geek, dweeb, nerd, hoser ✦; flop, no-hoper, washout, lemon.
— OPPOSITES: winner, success.

loss ▸ noun **1** *the loss of the documents* MISLAYING, misplacement, forgetting. **2** *loss of earnings* DEPRIVATION, disappearance, privation, forfeiture, diminution, erosion, reduction, depletion. **3** *the loss of her husband* DEATH, dying, demise, passing (away/on), end; *formal* decease; *archaic* expiry. **4** *Canadian losses in the war* CASUALTY, fatality, victim; dead; missing; death toll, number killed/dead. **5** *a loss of $15,000* DEFICIT, debit, debt, indebtedness, deficiency.
— OPPOSITES: recovery, profit.
■ **at a loss** BAFFLED, nonplussed, mystified, puzzled, perplexed, bewildered, bemused, at sixes and sevens, confused, dumbfounded, stumped, stuck, blank; *informal* clueless, flummoxed, bamboozled, fazed, floored, beaten, discombobulated.

lost ▸ adjective **1** *her lost keys* MISSING, mislaid, misplaced, vanished, disappeared, gone missing/astray, forgotten, nowhere to be found; absent, not present, strayed; irretrievable, unrecoverable. **2** *I think we're lost* OFF COURSE, off track, disorientated, having lost one's bearings, going around in circles, adrift, at sea, astray. **3** *a lost opportunity* MISSED, forfeited, neglected, wasted, squandered, gone by the board; *informal* down the drain. **4** *lost traditions* BYGONE, past, former, one-time, previous, old, olden, departed, vanished, forgotten, consigned to oblivion, extinct, dead, gone. **5** *lost species and habitats* EXTINCT, died out, defunct, vanished, gone; DESTROYED, wiped out, ruined, wrecked, exterminated, eradicated. **6** *a lost cause* HOPELESS, beyond hope, futile, forlorn, failed, beyond remedy, beyond recovery. **7** *lost souls* DAMNED, fallen, irredeemable, irreclaimable, irretrievable, past hope, past praying for, condemned, cursed, doomed; *literary* accursed. **8** *lost in thought* ENGROSSED, absorbed, rapt, immersed, deep, intent, engaged, wrapped up.
— OPPOSITES: current, saved.

lot ▸ noun **1** *a lot of money | lots of friends* A LARGE AMOUNT, a fair amount, a good/great deal, a great quantity, quantities, an abundance, a wealth, a profusion, plenty, a mass; many, a great many, a large number, a considerable number, numerous; scores; *informal* hundreds, thousands, millions, billions, gazillions, loads, masses, heaps, a pile, a stack, piles, oodles, stacks, scads, reams, wads, pots, oceans, a mountain, mountains, miles, tons, zillions, more —— than one can shake a stick at, gobs, a bunch. **2** *the books were auctioned in lots* ITEM, article; batch, set, collection, group, bundle, quantity, assortment, parcel. **3** *his lot in life* FATE, destiny, fortune, doom; situation, circumstances, state, condition, position, plight, predicament. **4** *some youngsters playing ball in a vacant lot* PATCH OF GROUND, piece of ground, plot, area, tract, parcel, plat.
— OPPOSITES: a little, not much, a few, not many.
▸ adverb *I work in pastels a lot* A GREAT DEAL, a good deal, to a great extent, much; often, frequently, regularly.
— OPPOSITES: a little.
■ **draw/cast lots** DECIDE RANDOMLY, toss/flip a coin, draw straws.
■ **throw in one's lot with** JOIN FORCES WITH, join up with, form an alliance with, ally with, align oneself with, link up with, make common cause with.

lotion ▸ noun OINTMENT, cream, salve, balm, rub, emollient, moisturizer, lubricant, gel, unguent, liniment, embrocation.

lottery ▸ noun **1** *play the lottery* RAFFLE, (prize) draw, sweepstake, lotto, (Que.) loto ✦. **2** *life is a lottery* GAMBLE, speculation, venture, risk, game of chance, matter of luck; *informal* crapshoot.

loud ▸ adjective **1** *loud music* NOISY, blaring, booming, deafening, roaring, thunderous, thundering, ear-splitting, ear-piercing, piercing; carrying, clearly audible; lusty, powerful, forceful, stentorian; *Music* forte, fortissimo. **2** *loud complaints* VOCIFEROUS, clamorous, insistent, vehement, emphatic, urgent. **3** *a loud T-shirt* GARISH, gaudy, flamboyant, lurid, glaring, showy, ostentatious; vulgar, tasteless; *informal* flash, flashy, kitsch, tacky.
— OPPOSITES: quiet, soft, gentle, sober, tasteful.

loudmouth ▸ noun *(informal)* BRAGGART, boaster, bragger, blusterer, swaggerer; *informal* blabbermouth, big mouth, blowhard, show-off.

loudspeaker ▸ noun SPEAKER, monitor, woofer, tweeter; megaphone; public address system, PA (system), intercom, loud-hailer; *informal* squawk box.

lounge ▸ verb *he just lounges in his room* LAZE, lie, loll, lie back, lean back, recline, stretch oneself, drape oneself, relax, rest, repose, take it easy, put one's feet up, unwind, luxuriate; sprawl, slump, slouch, flop; loaf, idle, do nothing; *informal* take a load off, kick back.
▸ noun **1** *a hotel lounge* BAR, pub, club, barroom, beer parlour ✦, taproom. **2** *an airport lounge* WAITING AREA, reception room. **3** *she sat in the lounge* LIVING ROOM, sitting room, front room, drawing room, morning room, salon, family room; *dated* parlour.

lousy *(informal)* ▸ adjective **1** *a lousy film.* See AWFUL sense 2. **2** *the lousy, double-crossing snake!* See DESPICABLE. **3** *I felt lousy.* See ILL adjective sense 1.
■ **be lousy with.** See CRAWL sense 3.

lout ▸ noun RUFFIAN, hooligan, thug, boor, barbarian, oaf, hoodlum, rowdy, lubber; *informal* tough, roughneck, bruiser, yahoo, lug.
— OPPOSITES: gentleman.

lovable ▸ adjective ADORABLE, dear, sweet, cute, charming, darling, lovely, likeable, delightful, captivating, enchanting, engaging, bewitching,

pleasing, appealing, winsome, winning, fetching, endearing.
– OPPOSITES: hateful, loathsome.

love ▶ noun **1** *his friendship with Helen grew into love* DEEP AFFECTION, fondness, tenderness, warmth, intimacy, attachment, endearment; devotion, adoration, doting, idolization, worship; passion, ardour, desire, lust, yearning, infatuation, besottedness. **2** *her love of fashion* LIKING, enjoyment, appreciation, taste, delight, relish, passion, zeal, appetite, zest, enthusiasm, keenness, fondness, soft spot, weakness, bent, leaning, proclivity, inclination, disposition, partiality, predilection, penchant. **3** *their love for their fellow human beings* COMPASSION, care, caring, regard, solicitude, concern, friendliness, friendship, kindness, charity, goodwill, sympathy, kindliness, altruism, unselfishness, philanthropy, benevolence, fellow feeling, humanity. **4** *he was her one true love* BELOVED, loved one, love of one's life, dear, dearest, dear one, darling, sweetheart, sweet, angel, honey; lover, inamorato, inamorata, amour; *archaic* paramour. **5** *their love will survive* RELATIONSHIP, love affair, romance, liaison, affair of the heart, amour. **6** *my mother sends her love* BEST WISHES, regards, good wishes, greetings, kind/kindest regards.
– RELATED TERMS: amatory, phil-.
– OPPOSITES: hatred.

▶ verb **1** *she loves him dearly* CARE VERY MUCH FOR, feel deep affection for, hold very dear, adore, think the world of, be devoted to, dote on, idolize, worship; be in love with, be infatuated with, be smitten with, be besotted with; *informal* be mad/crazy/nuts/wild about, have a crush on, carry a torch for. **2** *Laura loved painting* LIKE VERY MUCH, delight in, enjoy greatly, have a passion for, take great pleasure in, derive great pleasure from, relish, savour; have a weakness for, be partial to, have a soft spot for, have a taste for, be taken with; *informal* get a kick out of, have a thing about, be mad/crazy/nuts/wild about, be hooked on, get off on.
– OPPOSITES: hate.

■ **fall in love with** BECOME INFATUATED WITH, give/lose one's heart to; *informal* fall for, be bowled over by, be swept off one's feet by, develop a crush on.

■ **in love with** INFATUATED WITH, besotted with, enamoured of, smitten with, consumed with desire for; captivated by, bewitched by, enthralled by, entranced by, moonstruck by; devoted to, doting on; *informal* mad/crazy/nuts/wild about.

love affair ▶ noun **1** *he had a love affair with a teacher* RELATIONSHIP, affair, romance, liaison, affair of the heart, affaire de cœur, intrigue, fling, amour, involvement, romantic entanglement; flirtation, dalliance. **2** *a love affair with sports* ENTHUSIASM, mania, devotion, passion.

loveless ▶ adjective PASSIONLESS, unloving, unfeeling, heartless, cold, icy, frigid, undersexed.
– OPPOSITES: loving, passionate.

lovely ▶ adjective **1** *a lovely young woman* BEAUTIFUL, pretty, attractive, good-looking, appealing, handsome, adorable, exquisite, sweet, personable, charming; enchanting, engaging, winsome, seductive, sexy, gorgeous, alluring, ravishing, glamorous; *informal* tasty, knockout, stunning, drop-dead gorgeous; killer, cute, foxy, hot; *formal* beauteous; *archaic* comely, fair. **2** *a lovely view* SCENIC, picturesque, pleasing, easy on the eye; magnificent, stunning, splendid. **3** (*informal*) *we had a lovely day* DELIGHTFUL, very pleasant, very nice, very agreeable,

marvellous, wonderful, sublime, superb, magical; *informal* terrific, fabulous, heavenly, divine, amazing, glorious.
– OPPOSITES: ugly, horrible.

lover ▶ noun **1** *she had a secret lover* BOYFRIEND, GIRLFRIEND, lady-love, beloved, love, darling, sweetheart, inamorata, inamorato; mistress; partner, significant other, main squeeze; *informal* bit on the side, toy boy, boy toy; *dated* beau; *archaic* swain, concubine, paramour. **2** *a dog lover* DEVOTEE, admirer, fan, enthusiast, aficionado; *informal* buff, freak, nut, junkie.
– RELATED TERMS: -phile.

lovesick ▶ adjective LOVELORN, pining, languishing, longing, yearning, infatuated; frustrated.

loving ▶ adjective AFFECTIONATE, fond, devoted, adoring, doting, solicitous, demonstrative; caring, tender, warm, warm-hearted, close; amorous, ardent, passionate, amatory.
– OPPOSITES: cold, cruel.

low ▶ adjective **1** *a low fence* SHORT, small, little; squat, stubby, stunted, dwarf; shallow. **2** *low prices* CHEAP, economical, moderate, reasonable, modest, bargain, budget, bargain-basement, rock-bottom, cut-rate. **3** *supplies were low* SCARCE, scanty, scant, skimpy, meagre, sparse, few, little, paltry; reduced, depleted, diminished. **4** *low quality* INFERIOR, substandard, poor, bad, low-grade, low-end, below par, second-rate, unsatisfactory, deficient, defective, shoddy. **5** *of low birth* HUMBLE, lowly, low-ranking, plebeian, proletarian, peasant, poor; common, ordinary. **6** *low expectations* UNAMBITIOUS, unaspiring, modest. **7** *a low opinion* UNFAVOURABLE, poor, bad, adverse, negative. **8** *a low blow.* See LOWDOWN *adjective*. **9** *low humour* UNCOUTH, uncultured, unsophisticated, rough, rough-hewn, unrefined, tasteless, crass, common, vulgar, coarse, crude. **10** *a low voice* QUIET, soft, faint, gentle, muted, subdued, muffled, hushed, quietened, whispered, stifled. **11** *a low note* BASS, baritone, low-pitched, deep, rumbling, booming, sonorous. **12** *she was feeling low* DEPRESSED, dejected, despondent, downhearted, downcast, low-spirited, down, morose, miserable, dismal, heavy-hearted, mournful, forlorn, woebegone, gloomy, glum, crestfallen, dispirited; without energy, enervated, flat, sapped, weary; *informal* down in the mouth, down in the dumps, blue.
– OPPOSITES: high, expensive, plentiful, superior, noble, favourable, admirable, decent, exalted, loud, cheerful, lively.

▶ noun *the dollar fell to an all-time low* NADIR, low point, lowest point, lowest level, minimum, depth, rock bottom.
– OPPOSITES: high.

lowbrow ▶ adjective MASS-MARKET, tabloid, popular, intellectually undemanding, lightweight, accessible, unpretentious; uncultured, unsophisticated, trashy, philistine, simplistic, down-market; *informal* dumbed-down, rubbishy.
– OPPOSITES: highbrow, intellectual.

lowdown (*informal*) ▶ adjective *a lowdown trick* UNFAIR, mean, despicable, reprehensible, contemptible, lamentable, disgusting, shameful, low, cheap, underhanded, foul, unworthy, shabby, base, dishonourable, unprincipled, sordid; *informal* rotten, dirty; beastly; *dated* dastardly.
– OPPOSITES: kind, honourable.

▶ noun *he gave us the lowdown* FACTS, information, story, intelligence, news, inside story; *informal* info, rundown, the score, the scoop, the word, the dope, the dirt, the skinny.

lower ▶ adjective **1** *the lower house of parliament* SUBORDINATE, inferior, lesser, junior, minor, secondary, lower-level, subsidiary, subservient. **2** *her lower lip* BOTTOM, bottommost, nether, under; underneath, further down, beneath. **3** *a lower price* CHEAPER, reduced, cut, slashed.
— OPPOSITES: upper, higher, increased.
▶ verb **1** *she lowered the mask* MOVE DOWN, let down, take down, haul down, drop, let fall. **2** *lower your voice* SOFTEN, modulate, quieten, hush, tone down, muffle, turn down, mute. **3** *they are lowering their prices* REDUCE, decrease, lessen, bring down, mark down, cut, slash, axe, diminish, curtail, prune, pare (down). **4** *the water level lowered* SUBSIDE, fall (off), recede, ebb, wane; abate, die down, let up, moderate, diminish, lessen. **5** *don't lower yourself to their level* DEGRADE, debase, demean, abase, humiliate, downgrade, discredit, shame, dishonour, disgrace; belittle, cheapen, devalue; (**lower oneself**) stoop, sink, descend.
— OPPOSITES: raise, increase.

lowering ▶ adjective OVERCAST, dark, leaden, grey, cloudy, clouded, gloomy, threatening, menacing, promising rain.

low-grade ▶ adjective POOR-QUALITY, inferior, substandard, second-rate; shoddy, cheap, reject, trashy, gimcrack, chintzy, rubbishy; *informal* two-bit, schlocky, bum, cheapjack.
— OPPOSITES: top-quality, first-class.

low-key ▶ adjective RESTRAINED, modest, understated, muted, subtle, quiet, low-profile, inconspicuous, unostentatious, unobtrusive, discreet, toned-down; casual, informal, mellow, laid-back.
— OPPOSITES: ostentatious, obtrusive.

lowly ▶ adjective HUMBLE, low, low-born, low-ranking, plebeian, proletarian; common, ordinary, plain, average, modest, simple; inferior, ignoble, subordinate, obscure.
— OPPOSITES: aristocratic, exalted.

low-rent ▶ adjective CHEAP, inferior, second-rate, low-end; shoddy, run-down, slummy, seedy, divey.

loyal ▶ adjective FAITHFUL, true, devoted; constant, steadfast, staunch, dependable, reliable, trusted, trustworthy, trusty, dutiful, dedicated, unchanging, unwavering, unswerving; patriotic.
— OPPOSITES: treacherous.

loyalty ▶ noun ALLEGIANCE, faithfulness, obedience, adherence, homage, devotion; steadfastness, staunchness, true-heartedness, dependability, reliability, trustworthiness, duty, dedication, commitment; patriotism; *historical* fealty.
— OPPOSITES: treachery.

lubricant ▶ noun GREASE, oil, lubrication, emollient, lotion, unguent; *informal* lube.

lubricate ▶ verb OIL, GREASE, butter, wax, polish; facilitate, smooth, ease; *informal* lube.

lucid ▶ adjective **1** *a lucid description* INTELLIGIBLE, comprehensible, understandable, cogent, coherent, articulate; clear, transparent; plain, simple, vivid, sharp, straightforward, unambiguous; *formal* perspicuous. **2** *he was not lucid enough to explain* RATIONAL, sane, in one's right mind, in possession of one's faculties, compos mentis, able to think clearly, balanced, clear-headed, sober, sensible; *informal* all

there.
— OPPOSITES: confusing, confused.

luck ▶ noun **1** *with luck you'll make it* GOOD FORTUNE, good luck; fluke, stroke of luck; *informal* lucky break. **2** *I wish you luck* SUCCESS, prosperity, good fortune, good luck. **3** *it is a matter of luck whether it hits or misses* FORTUNE, fate, destiny, Lady Luck, lot, stars, karma, kismet; fortuity, serendipity; chance, accident, a twist of fate.
— OPPOSITES: bad luck, misfortune.
■ **in luck** FORTUNATE, lucky, blessed with good luck, born under a lucky star; successful, having a charmed life.
■ **out of luck** UNFORTUNATE, unlucky, luckless, hapless, unsuccessful, cursed, jinxed, ill-fated; *informal* down on one's luck; *literary* star-crossed.

luckily ▶ adverb FORTUNATELY, happily, providentially, opportunely, by good fortune, as luck would have it, propitiously; mercifully, thankfully.
— OPPOSITES: unfortunately.

luckless ▶ adjective UNLUCKY, unfortunate, unsuccessful, hapless, out of luck, cursed, jinxed, doomed, ill-fated; *informal* down on one's luck; *literary* star-crossed.
— OPPOSITES: lucky.

lucky ▶ adjective **1** *the lucky winner* FORTUNATE, in luck, blessed, favoured, born under a lucky star, charmed; successful, prosperous. **2** *a lucky escape* PROVIDENTIAL, fortunate, advantageous, timely, opportune, serendipitous, expedient, heaven-sent, auspicious; chance, fortuitous, fluky, accidental.
— OPPOSITES: unfortunate.

lucrative ▶ adjective PROFITABLE, profit-making, gainful, remunerative, money-making, paying, high-income, well-paid, bankable; rewarding, worthwhile; thriving, flourishing, successful, booming.
— OPPOSITES: unprofitable.

ludicrous ▶ adjective ABSURD, ridiculous, farcical, laughable, risible, preposterous, foolish, mad, insane, idiotic, stupid, inane, silly, asinine, nonsensical; *informal* crazy.
— OPPOSITES: sensible.

lug ▶ verb *she lugged her groceries to the door* CARRY, lift, bear, tote, heave, hoist, shoulder, manhandle; haul, drag, tug, tow, transport, move, convey, shift; *informal* hump, schlep.
▶ noun *you big lug!* OAF, dolt, idiot, fool, ass, lummox, lout, lubber; galoot, dope, ninny, doofus, twit, nitwit, hoser ✦, dork.

luggage ▶ noun BAGGAGE; bags, suitcases, cases, trunks, weekend bag. *See also* BAG noun sense 2.

lugubrious ▶ adjective MOURNFUL, gloomy, sad, unhappy, doleful, glum, melancholy, woeful, miserable, woebegone, forlorn, sombre, solemn, serious, sorrowful, morose, dour, cheerless, joyless, dismal; funereal, sepulchral; *informal* down in the mouth; *literary* dolorous.
— OPPOSITES: cheerful.

lukewarm ▶ adjective **1** *lukewarm coffee* TEPID, slightly warm, warmish, at room temperature, chambré. **2** *a lukewarm response* INDIFFERENT, cool, half-hearted, apathetic, unenthusiastic, tepid, perfunctory, noncommittal, lackadaisical; *informal* laid-back, unenthused, couldn't-care-less.
— OPPOSITES: hot, cold, enthusiastic.

lull ▶ verb **1** *the sound of the bells lulled us to sleep* SOOTHE, calm, hush; rock to sleep. **2** *his honeyed words*

lulled their suspicions ASSUAGE, allay, ease, alleviate, soothe, quiet, quieten; reduce, diminish; quell, banish, dispel. **3** *they lulled us into a false sense of security* DECEIVE, dupe, trick, fool, hoodwink.
– OPPOSITES: waken, agitate, arouse, intensify.
▶ noun **1** *a lull in the fighting* PAUSE, respite, interval, break, hiatus, suspension, interlude, intermission, breathing space; *informal* let-up, breather. **2** *the lull before the storm* CALM, stillness, quiet, tranquility, peace, silence, hush.
– OPPOSITES: agitation, activity.

lullaby ▶ noun CRADLE SONG, berceuse.

lumber ▶ verb *elephants lumbered past* LURCH, stumble, trundle, shamble, shuffle, waddle; trudge, clump, stump, plod, tramp, tromp; *informal* galumph.
▶ noun *he built with lumber* TIMBER, wood, boards, planks.

lumbering ▶ adjective CLUMSY, awkward, heavy-footed, slow, blundering, bumbling, inept, maladroit, uncoordinated, ungainly, ungraceful, gauche, lumpish, hulking, ponderous; *informal* clodhopping.
– OPPOSITES: nimble, agile.

lumberjack ▶ noun. *See* LOGGER.

luminary ▶ noun LEADING LIGHT, guiding light, inspiration, role model, hero, heroine, leader, expert, master; lion, legend, celebrity, personality, great, giant; *informal* bigwig, rainmaker, VIP.
– OPPOSITES: nobody.

luminous ▶ adjective SHINING, bright, brilliant, radiant, dazzling, glowing, gleaming, scintillating, lustrous; luminescent, phosphorescent, fluorescent, incandescent.
– OPPOSITES: dark.

lummox ▶ noun *See* OAF.

lump¹ ▶ noun **1** *a lump of coal* CHUNK, hunk, piece, mass, block, wedge, slab, cake, nugget, ball, brick, cube, pat, knob, clod, gobbet, dollop, wad; *informal* glob, gob. **2** *a lump on his head* SWELLING, bump, bulge, protuberance, protrusion, growth, outgrowth, nodule, hump; goose egg. **3** *he's such a lump. See* OAF. **4** (**lumps**) *take your lumps* HARD KNOCKS, defeats, losses.
▶ verb *it is convenient to lump them together* COMBINE, put, group, bunch, aggregate, unite, pool, merge, collect, throw, consider together.

lump² ▶ verb (*informal*) *like it or lump it* PUT UP WITH, bear, endure, suffer, take, tolerate, accept.

lunacy ▶ noun **1** *originality demands a degree of lunacy* INSANITY, madness, mental illness, dementia, mania, psychosis; *informal* craziness. **2** *the lunacy of gambling* FOLLY, foolishness, stupidity, silliness, idiocy, madness, recklessness, foolhardiness, imprudence, irresponsibility; *informal* craziness.
– OPPOSITES: sanity, sense, prudence.

lunatic ▶ noun *he drives like a lunatic* MANIAC, madman, madwoman, imbecile, psychopath, psychotic; fool, idiot; eccentric; *informal* loony, nut, nutcase, head case, psycho, moron, screwball, crackpot, fruitcake.
▶ adjective **1** *a lunatic prisoner. See* MAD sense 1. **2** *a lunatic idea. See* MAD sense 3.

lunch ▶ noun MIDDAY MEAL, luncheon, brunch, light meal, snack.
■ **out to lunch** CRAZY, out of one's mind, mad; out of touch, out of it, unaware, absent-minded; cuckoo, batty, flaky, spacey, nutty, wingy ♣, off one's rocker.

lunch box ▶ noun LUNCH PAIL, lunch kit, lunch bucket.

lung
– RELATED TERMS: pulmonary, pneumo-.

lunge ▶ noun *Darren made a lunge at his attacker* THRUST, jab, stab, dive, rush, charge.
▶ verb *he lunged at Finn with a knife* THRUST, dive, spring, launch oneself, rush, make a grab.

lurch ▶ verb **1** *he lurched into the kitchen* STAGGER, stumble, wobble, sway, reel, roll, weave, pitch, totter, blunder. **2** *the ship lurched* SWAY, reel, list, heel, rock, roll, pitch, toss, jerk, shake, judder, flounder, swerve, teeter.
■ **leave someone in the lurch** LEAVE IN TROUBLE, let down, leave stranded, leave high and dry, abandon, desert.

lure ▶ verb *consumers are frequently lured into debt* TEMPT, entice, attract, induce, coax, persuade, inveigle, allure, seduce, win over, cajole, beguile, bewitch, ensnare.
– OPPOSITES: deter, put off.
▶ noun *the lure of the stage* TEMPTATION, enticement, attraction, pull, draw, appeal; inducement, allurement, fascination, interest, magnet; *informal* come-on.

lurid ▶ adjective **1** *lurid colours* BRIGHT, brilliant, vivid, glaring, shocking, fluorescent, flaming, dazzling, intense; gaudy, loud, showy, bold, garish, tacky. **2** *the lurid details* SENSATIONAL, sensationalist, exaggerated, over-dramatized, colourful; salacious, graphic, explicit, unrestrained, prurient, shocking; gruesome, gory, grisly; *informal* juicy, full-frontal.
– OPPOSITES: muted, restrained.

lurk ▶ verb SKULK, loiter, lie in wait, lie low, hide, conceal oneself, take cover, keep out of sight.

luscious ▶ adjective **1** *luscious fruit* DELICIOUS, succulent, lush, juicy, mouth-watering, lip-smacking, sweet, tasty, appetizing; *informal* scrumptious, yummy, nummy; *literary* ambrosial. **2** *a luscious well-tanned beauty* SEXY, sexually attractive, nubile, ravishing, gorgeous, seductive, alluring, sultry, beautiful, stunning; *informal* drop-dead gorgeous, hot, curvy, foxy, cute.
– OPPOSITES: unappetizing, plain, scrawny.

lush ▶ adjective **1** *lush vegetation* LUXURIANT, rich, abundant, profuse, exuberant, riotous, prolific, vigorous; dense, thick, rank, rampant; *informal* jungly. **2** *a lush, ripe peach* SUCCULENT, luscious, juicy, soft, tender, ripe. **3** *a lush apartment* LUXURIOUS, deluxe, sumptuous, palatial, opulent, lavish, elaborate, extravagant, fancy; *informal* plush, ritzy, posh, swanky, swank.
– OPPOSITES: barren, sparse, shrivelled, austere.

lust ▶ noun **1** *his lust for her* SEXUAL DESIRE, sexual appetite, sexual longing, ardour, desire, passion, libido, sex drive, sexuality, biological urge; lechery, lasciviousness, concupiscence; *informal* horniness, the hots, randiness. **2** *a lust for power* GREED, desire, craving, covetousness, eagerness, avidity, cupidity, longing, yearning, hunger, thirst, appetite, hankering.
– OPPOSITES: dread, aversion.
▶ verb **1** *he lusted after his employer's wife* DESIRE, be consumed with desire for, find sexually attractive, crave, covet, ache for, burn for; *informal* have the hots for, fancy, have a thing about/for, drool over. **2** *she lusted after adventure* CRAVE, desire, covet, want, wish for, long for, yearn for, dream of, hanker for, hanker

after, hunger for, thirst for, ache for; *informal* jones for.
— OPPOSITES: dread, avoid.

lustful ▶ adjective LECHEROUS, lascivious, libidinous, licentious, salacious, goatish; wanton, unchaste, impure, naughty, immodest, indecent, dirty, prurient; passionate, sensual, sexy, erotic; *informal* horny, randy, raunchy, lusty; *formal* concupiscent.
— OPPOSITES: chaste, pure.

lustre ▶ noun **1** *her hair lost its lustre* SHEEN, gloss, shine, glow, gleam, shimmer, burnish, polish, patina. **2** *the lustre of the Milky Way* BRILLIANCE, brightness, radiance, sparkle, dazzle, flash, glitter, glint, gleam, luminosity, luminescence.
— OPPOSITES: dullness, dark.

lustreless ▶ adjective DULL, lacklustre, matte, unpolished, tarnished, dingy, dim, dark.
— OPPOSITES: lustrous, bright.

lustrous ▶ adjective SHINY, shining, satiny, glossy, gleaming, shimmering, burnished, polished; radiant, bright, brilliant, luminous; dazzling, sparkling, glistening, twinkling.
— OPPOSITES: dull, dark.

lusty ▶ adjective **1** *a lusty baby* HEALTHY, strong, fit, vigorous, robust, hale and hearty, energetic; rugged, sturdy, muscular, muscly, strapping, hefty, husky, burly, powerful; *informal* beefy; *dated* stalwart. **2** *lusty singing* LOUD, vigorous, hearty, strong, powerful, forceful. **3** *lusty young men. See* LUSTFUL.
— OPPOSITES: feeble, quiet, chaste.

luxuriant ▶ adjective LUSH, rich, abundant, profuse, exuberant, riotous, prolific, vigorous; dense, thick, rank, rampant; *informal* jungly.
— OPPOSITES: barren, sparse.

luxuriate ▶ verb REVEL, bask, delight, take pleasure, wallow; (**luxuriate in**) enjoy, relish, savour, appreciate; *informal* get a kick out of, get a thrill out of.
— OPPOSITES: dislike.

luxurious ▶ adjective **1** *a luxurious hotel* OPULENT, sumptuous, deluxe, rich, grand, palatial, splendid, magnificent, well appointed, extravagant, fancy, upscale, upmarket, five-star; *informal* plush, posh, classy, ritzy, swanky, swank. **2** *a luxurious lifestyle* SELF-INDULGENT, sensual, pleasure-loving, pleasure-seeking, epicurean, hedonistic, sybaritic.
— OPPOSITES: plain, basic, abstemious.

luxury ▶ noun **1** *we'll live in luxury* OPULENCE, luxuriousness, sumptuousness, grandeur, magnificence, splendour, lavishness, the lap of luxury, a bed of roses, (the land of) milk and honey; *informal* the life of Riley. **2** *a TV is his only luxury* INDULGENCE, extravagance, self-indulgence, non-essential, treat, extra, frill.
— OPPOSITES: simplicity, necessity.

lying ▶ noun *she was no good at lying* UNTRUTHFULNESS, fabrication, fibbing, perjury, white lies; falseness, falsity, dishonesty, mendacity, telling stories, invention, misrepresentation, deceit, duplicity; *literary* perfidy.
— OPPOSITES: honesty.
▶ adjective *he was a lying womanizer* UNTRUTHFUL, false, dishonest, mendacious, deceitful, deceiving, duplicitous, double-dealing, two-faced; *literary* perfidious.
— OPPOSITES: truthful.

lynch ▶ verb EXECUTE ILLEGALLY, hang, kill; *informal* string up.

lyrical ▶ adjective **1** *lyrical love poetry* EXPRESSIVE, emotional, deeply felt, personal, subjective, passionate, lyric. **2** *she was lyrical about her success* ENTHUSIASTIC, rhapsodic, effusive, rapturous, ecstatic, euphoric, carried away.
— OPPOSITES: unenthusiastic.

lyrics ▶ plural noun WORDS, libretto, book, text, lines.

Mm

macabre ▶ adjective **1** *a macabre ritual* GRUESOME, grisly, grim, gory, morbid, ghastly, unearthly, grotesque, hideous, horrific, shocking, dreadful, loathsome, repugnant, repulsive, sickening. **2** *a macabre joke* BLACK, weird, unhealthy; *informal* sick.

mace ▶ noun CLUB, cudgel, stick, staff, shillelagh, bludgeon, truncheon, nightstick, billy club, blackjack.

Machiavellian ▶ adjective DEVIOUS, cunning, crafty, artful, wily, sly, scheming, treacherous, two-faced, tricky, double-dealing, unscrupulous, deceitful, dishonest; *literary* perfidious; *informal* foxy.
— OPPOSITES: straightforward, ingenuous.

machinations ▶ plural noun SCHEMING, schemes, plotting, plots, intrigues, conspiracies, ruses, tricks, wiles, stratagems, tactics, manoeuvring.

machine ▶ noun **1** *a threshing machine* APPARATUS, appliance, device, contraption, contrivance, mechanism, engine, gadget, tool. **2** *an efficient publicity machine* ORGANIZATION, system, structure, arrangement, machinery; *informal* set-up. **3** *he's an eating machine* POWERHOUSE, human dynamo; wonder, phenomenon, sensation; automaton.
— RELATED TERMS: mechanical.

machinery ▶ noun **1** *printing machinery* EQUIPMENT, apparatus, hardware, gear, tackle, plant; mechanism; instruments, tools; gadgetry, technology. **2** *the machinery of government* WORKINGS, organization, system, structure, administration, institution; *informal* set-up.

machismo ▶ noun (AGGRESSIVE) MASCULINITY, toughness, male chauvinism, sexism, virility, manliness; bravado; *informal* testosterone, macho.

macho ▶ adjective *a macho man* (AGGRESSIVELY) MALE, (unpleasantly) masculine; manly, virile, red-blooded; *informal* butch.
— OPPOSITES: wimpish.
▶ noun *macho is out.* See MACHISMO.
— OPPOSITES: wimp.

mad ▶ adjective **1** *he felt he was going mad* INSANE, mentally ill, certifiable, deranged, demented, of unsound mind, out of one's mind, not in one's right mind, sick in the head, crazy, crazed, lunatic, non compos mentis, unhinged, bushed ✤, disturbed, raving, psychotic, psychopathic, mad as a hatter, mad as a March hare; *informal* mental, off one's nut, nuts, nutty, nutso, off one's rocker, not right in the head, round the bend, stark raving mad, bats, batty, buggy, bonkers, dotty, cuckoo, cracked, loopy, loony, bananas, loco, screwy, schizoid, psycho, touched, gaga, not all there, not right upstairs, crackers, out of one's tree, meshuga, wacko, gonzo; (**be mad**) have a screw loose, have bats in the/one's belfry; (**go mad**) lose one's reason, lose one's mind, take leave of one's senses, lose one's marbles, crack up. **2** *I'm still mad at him* ANGRY, furious, infuriated, irate, raging, enraged, fuming, incensed, seeing red, beside oneself; *informal* livid, sore; *literary* wrathful; (**get mad**) lose one's temper, get in a rage, rant and rave; *informal* explode, go off the deep end, go ape, flip, flip out, flip one's wig. **3** *some mad scheme* FOOLISH, insane, stupid, lunatic, foolhardy, idiotic, senseless, absurd, impractical, silly, inane, asinine, wild, unwise, imprudent; *informal* crazy, crackpot, crack-brained, daft. **4** *(informal) he's mad about jazz* ENTHUSIASTIC, passionate; ardent, fervent, avid, fanatical; devoted to, infatuated with, in love with, hot for; *informal* crazy, nuts, wild, hooked on, gone on, nutso. **5** *it was a mad dash to get ready* FRENZIED, frantic, frenetic, feverish, wild, hectic, manic.
— OPPOSITES: sane, pleased, sensible, indifferent, calm.
■ **like mad** *(informal)* **1** *I ran like mad* FAST, quickly, rapidly, speedily, hastily, hurriedly. **2** *he had to fight like mad* ENERGETICALLY, enthusiastically, madly, furiously, with a will, for all one is worth, passionately, intensely, ardently, fervently; *informal* like crazy, hammer and tongs.

madcap ▶ adjective **1** *a madcap scheme* RECKLESS, rash, foolhardy, foolish, hare-brained, wild, hasty, imprudent, ill-advised; *informal* crazy, crackpot, crack-brained. **2** *a madcap comedy* ZANY, eccentric, unconventional.
▶ noun *she was a boisterous madcap* ECCENTRIC, crank, madman/madwoman, maniac, lunatic; oddity, character; *informal* crackpot, oddball, weirdo, loony, nut, screwball.

madden ▶ verb **1** *what maddens people most is his vagueness* INFURIATE, exasperate, irritate; incense, anger, enrage, provoke, upset, agitate, vex, irk, make someone's hackles rise, make someone see red; *informal* aggravate, make someone's blood boil, make livid, get someone's goat, get someone's back up, tee off, tick off, steam someone up. **2** *they were maddened with pain* DRIVE MAD, drive insane, derange, unhinge, unbalance; *informal* drive round the bend.

made-up ▶ adjective **1** *a made-up story* INVENTED, fabricated, trumped up, concocted, fictitious, fictional, false, untrue, specious, spurious, bogus, apocryphal, imaginary, mythical. **2** *she was made up for the evening* WEARING MAKEUP; *informal* dolled up, decked out.

madhouse ▶ noun *informal* **1** *his father is shut up in a madhouse* MENTAL HOSPITAL, mental institution, psychiatric hospital, asylum; *informal* nuthouse, funny farm, loony bin; *dated* lunatic asylum. **2** *the place was a total madhouse* BEDLAM, mayhem, chaos, pandemonium, uproar, turmoil, disorder, madness, all hell broken loose, (three-ring) circus, zoo.

madly ▶ adverb **1** *she was smiling madly* INSANELY, deliriously, wildly, like a lunatic; *informal* crazily. **2** *madly snapping pictures* FAST, furiously, hurriedly, quickly, speedily, hastily, energetically; *informal* like mad, like crazy. **3** *(informal) she was madly in love with him* INTENSELY, fervently, wildly, unrestrainedly, to distraction. **4** *(informal) a madly eccentric pair* VERY, extremely, really, exceedingly, exceptionally, remarkably, extraordinarily, immensely, tremendously, wildly, hugely; *informal* awfully,

terribly, terrifically, fantastically.
— OPPOSITES: sanely, slowly, slightly.

madman, madwoman ▶ noun LUNATIC, maniac, psychotic, psychopath, sociopath; *informal* loony, nut, nutcase, head case, psycho, screwball.

madness ▶ noun **1** *today madness is called mental illness* INSANITY, mental illness, dementia, derangement; lunacy, instability; mania, psychosis; *informal* craziness. **2** *it would be madness to do otherwise* FOLLY, foolishness, idiocy, stupidity, insanity, lunacy, silliness; *informal* craziness. **3** *it's absolute madness in here* BEDLAM, mayhem, chaos, pandemonium, craziness, uproar, turmoil, disorder, all hell broken loose, (three-ring) circus.
— OPPOSITES: sanity, common sense, good sense, calm.

maelstrom ▶ noun **1** *a maelstrom in the sea* WHIRLPOOL, vortex, eddy, swirl; *literary* Charybdis. **2** *the maelstrom of war* TURBULENCE, tumult, turmoil, disorder, disarray, chaos, confusion, upheaval, pandemonium, bedlam, whirlwind.

maestro ▶ noun VIRTUOSO, master, expert, genius, wizard, prodigy; *informal* ace, whiz, pro, hotshot.
— OPPOSITES: novice, beginner.

magazine ▶ noun JOURNAL, periodical, serial, supplement, quarterly, monthly, weekly, newsmagazine; *informal* glossy, mag, 'zine, fanzine.

magenta ▶ adjective REDDISH-PURPLE, purplish-red, crimson, plum, carmine red, fuchsia; *literary* incarnadine.

magic ▶ noun **1** *do you believe in magic?* SORCERY, witchcraft, wizardry, necromancy, enchantment, the supernatural, occultism, the occult, black magic, the black arts, voodoo, hoodoo, mojo, shamanism; charm, hex, spell, jinx. **2** *he does magic at children's parties* CONJURING TRICKS, sleight of hand, legerdemain, illusion, prestidigitation. **3** *the magic of the stage* ALLURE, attraction, excitement, fascination, charm, glamour. **4** *her dancing is pure magic* SKILL, brilliance, ability, accomplishment, adeptness, adroitness, deftness, dexterity, aptitude, expertise, art, finesse, talent.
▶ adjective **1** *a magic spell* SUPERNATURAL, enchanted, occult. **2** *a magic place* FASCINATING, captivating, charming, glamorous, magical, enchanting, entrancing, spellbinding, magnetic, irresistible, hypnotic. **3** *(informal) we were magic together* MARVELLOUS, wonderful, excellent, admirable; *informal* terrific, fabulous, brilliant.

magical ▶ adjective **1** *magical incantations* SUPERNATURAL, magic, occult, shamanistic, mystical, paranormal, preternatural, otherworldly. **2** *the news had a magical effect* EXTRAORDINARY, remarkable, exceptional, outstanding, incredible, phenomenal, unbelievable, amazing, astonishing, astounding, stunning, staggering, marvellous, magnificent, wonderful, sensational, breathtaking, miraculous; *informal* fantastic, fabulous, stupendous, out of this world, terrific, tremendous, brilliant; *literary* wondrous. **3** *this magical place* ENCHANTING, entrancing, spellbinding, bewitching, beguiling, fascinating, captivating, alluring, enthralling, charming, attractive, lovely, delightful, beautiful; *informal* dreamy, heavenly, divine, gorgeous.
— OPPOSITES: predictable, boring.

magician ▶ noun **1** *she imagined she was a magician* SORCERER, sorceress, witch, wizard, warlock, enchanter, enchantress, necromancer, shaman.

2 *Houdini was a great magician* CONJUROR, illusionist, prestidigitator. **3** *he is a magician on the ice* GENIUS, marvel, wizard.

magisterial ▶ adjective **1** *a magisterial pronouncement* AUTHORITATIVE, masterful, assured, lordly, commanding, assertive. **2** *his magisterial style of questioning* DOMINEERING, dictatorial, autocratic, imperious, overbearing, peremptory, high-handed, arrogant, supercilious, patronizing; *informal* bossy.
— OPPOSITES: untrustworthy, humble, hesitant, tentative.

magnanimous ▶ adjective GENEROUS, charitable, benevolent, beneficent, big-hearted, handsome, princely, altruistic, philanthropic, unselfish, chivalrous, noble; forgiving, merciful, lenient, indulgent, clement.
— OPPOSITES: mean-spirited, selfish.

magnate ▶ noun TYCOON, mogul, captain of industry, baron, lord, king, magnifico; industrialist, proprietor; *informal* big shot, big cheese, (head) honcho; *derogatory* fat cat.

magnet ▶ noun **1** *you can tell steel by using a magnet* LODESTONE; electromagnet, solenoid. **2** *a magnet for tourists* ATTRACTION, focus, draw, lure, mecca.

magnetic ▶ adjective *a magnetic personality* ALLURING, attractive, fascinating, captivating, enchanting, enthralling, appealing, charming, prepossessing, engaging, entrancing, seductive, inviting, irresistible, charismatic.

magnetism ▶ noun ALLURE, attraction, fascination, appeal, draw, drawing power, pull, charm, enchantment, seductiveness, magic, spell, charisma.

magnification ▶ noun ENLARGEMENT, enhancement, increase, augmentation, extension, expansion, amplification, intensification, inflation.
— OPPOSITES: reduction.

magnificence ▶ noun SPLENDOUR, grandeur, impressiveness, glory, majesty, nobility, pomp, stateliness, elegance, sumptuousness, opulence, luxury, lavishness, richness, brilliance, dazzle, skill, virtuosity.
— OPPOSITES: modesty, tawdriness, weakness.

magnificent ▶ adjective **1** *a magnificent view of the mountains* SPLENDID, spectacular, impressive, striking, glorious, superb, majestic, awesome, awe-inspiring, breathtaking. **2** *a magnificent apartment overlooking the lake* SUMPTUOUS, resplendent, grand, impressive, imposing, monumental, palatial, stately, opulent, luxurious, lavish, rich, dazzling, beautiful, elegant; *informal* splendiferous, ritzy, posh, swanky. **3** *a magnificent performance* MASTERLY, skilful, virtuoso, brilliant.
— OPPOSITES: uninspiring, modest, tawdry, poor, weak.

magnify ▶ verb **1** *the lens magnifies the image* ENLARGE, boost, enhance, maximize, increase, augment, extend, expand, amplify, intensify; *informal* blow up. **2** *they magnified the problem* EXAGGERATE, overstate, overemphasize, overplay, dramatize, colour, embroider, embellish, inflate, make a mountain out of (a molehill); *informal* blow up (out of all proportion), make a big thing out of.
— OPPOSITES: reduce, minimize, understate.

magnitude ▶ noun **1** *the magnitude of the task* IMMENSITY, vastness, hugeness, enormity; size, extent, expanse, greatness, largeness, bigness. **2** *events of tragic magnitude* IMPORTANCE, import, significance,

weight, consequence, mark, notability, note; *formal* moment.
− OPPOSITES: smallness, triviality.
■ **of the first magnitude** OF THE UTMOST IMPORTANCE, of the greatest significance, very important, of great consequence; *formal* of great moment.

maid ▶ noun **1** *the maid cleared the table* FEMALE SERVANT, maidservant, housemaid, parlourmaid, lady's maid, chambermaid, domestic, housekeeper; help, cleaner, cleaning woman/lady. **2** *(literary) a village maid and her swain* GIRL, young woman, young lady, lass, miss, ingenue; *literary* maiden, damsel, nymph; *archaic* wench.

maiden ▶ noun *(literary) a pretty young maiden. See* MAID sense 2.
▶ adjective **1** *a maiden aunt* UNMARRIED, spinster, unwed, unwedded, single, husbandless, celibate. **2** *a maiden voyage* FIRST, initial, inaugural, introductory, initiatory, virgin.

mail ▶ noun *the mail arrived* POST, letters, correspondence; postal system, postal service, post office; delivery, collection; email; *informal* snail mail.
▶ verb *we mailed the card* SEND, post, dispatch, direct, forward, redirect, ship, express, courier; email.

mailman ▶ noun POSTAL WORKER; postman, letter carrier; *informal* postie.

maim ▶ verb INJURE, wound, cripple, disable, incapacitate, impair, mar, mutilate, lacerate, disfigure, deform, mangle.

main ▶ adjective *the main item* PRINCIPAL, chief, head, leading, foremost, most important, major, ruling, dominant, central, focal, key, prime, master, premier, primary, first, fundamental, supreme, predominant, (most) prominent, pre-eminent, paramount, overriding, cardinal, crucial, critical, pivotal, salient, elemental, essential, staple.
− OPPOSITES: subsidiary, minor.
▶ noun *a burst water main* PIPE, channel, duct, conduit.
■ **in the main.** *See* MAINLY.

mainly ▶ adverb MOSTLY, for the most part, in the main, on the whole, largely, by and large, to a large extent, predominantly, chiefly, principally, primarily; generally, usually, typically, commonly, on average, as a rule, almost always.

mainspring ▶ noun MOTIVE, motivation, impetus, driving force, incentive, impulse, prime mover, reason, fountain, fount, wellspring, root, generator.

mainstay ▶ noun CENTRAL COMPONENT, central figure, centrepiece, prop, linchpin, cornerstone, pillar, bulwark, buttress, chief support, backbone, anchor, foundation, base, staple.

mainstream ▶ adjective NORMAL, conventional, ordinary, orthodox, conformist, accepted, established, recognized, common, usual, prevailing, popular.
− OPPOSITES: fringe.

maintain ▶ verb **1** *they wanted to maintain peace* PRESERVE, conserve, keep, retain, keep going, keep alive, keep up, prolong, perpetuate, sustain, carry on, continue. **2** *the province maintains the roads* KEEP IN GOOD CONDITION, keep in (good) repair, keep up, service, care for, take good care of, look after. **3** *the cost of maintaining a dog* SUPPORT, provide for, keep, sustain; nurture, feed, nourish. **4** *he always maintained his innocence | he maintains that he is innocent* INSIST (ON), declare, assert, protest, affirm, avow, profess, claim, allege, contend, argue, swear (to), hold to; *formal* aver.
− OPPOSITES: break, discontinue, neglect, deny.

maintenance ▶ noun **1** *the maintenance of peace* PRESERVATION, conservation, keeping, prolongation, perpetuation, carrying on, continuation, continuance. **2** *car maintenance* UPKEEP, service, servicing, repair(s), care. **3** *the maintenance of his children* SUPPORT, keeping, upkeep, sustenance; nurture, feeding, nourishment. **4** *absent fathers are forced to pay maintenance* FINANCIAL SUPPORT, child support, alimony, provision; keep, subsistence, living expenses.
− OPPOSITES: breakdown, discontinuation, neglect.

majestic ▶ adjective STATELY, dignified, distinguished, solemn, magnificent, grand, splendid, resplendent, glorious, sumptuous, impressive, august, noble, awe-inspiring, monumental, palatial, statuesque, Olympian, imposing, marvellous, sonorous, resounding, heroic.
− OPPOSITES: modest, wretched.

major ▶ adjective **1** *the major Canadian writers* GREATEST, best, finest, most important, chief, main, prime, principal, capital, cardinal, leading, star, foremost, outstanding, first-rate, pre-eminent, arch-; *informal* major league, big league. **2** *an issue of major importance* CRUCIAL, vital, great, considerable, paramount, utmost, prime; *informal* serious. **3** *a major factor* IMPORTANT, big, significant, weighty, crucial, key, sweeping, substantial. **4** *major surgery* SERIOUS, radical, complicated, difficult.
− OPPOSITES: minor, little, trivial.

majority ▶ noun **1** *the majority of cases* LARGER PART/NUMBER, greater part/number, best/better part, most, more than half; plurality, bulk, mass, weight, (main) body, preponderance, predominance, generality, lion's share. **2** *a majority in the election* (WINNING) MARGIN, superiority of numbers/votes; landslide. **3** *my son has reached majority* COMING OF AGE, legal age, adulthood, manhood/womanhood, maturity; age of consent.
− OPPOSITES: minority.

make ▶ verb **1** *he makes models* CONSTRUCT, build, assemble, put together, manufacture, produce, fabricate, create, form, fashion, model. **2** *she made me do it* FORCE, compel, coerce, press, drive, pressure, oblige, require; have someone do something, prevail on, dragoon, bludgeon, strong-arm, impel, constrain; *informal* railroad. **3** *don't make such a noise* CAUSE, create, give rise to, produce, bring about, generate, engender, occasion, effect, set up, establish, institute, found, develop, originate; *literary* beget. **4** *she made a little bow* PERFORM, execute, give, do, accomplish, achieve, bring off, carry out, effect. **5** *they made him chairman* APPOINT, designate, name, nominate, select, elect, vote in, install; induct, institute, invest, ordain. **6** *he had made a will* FORMULATE, frame, draw up, devise, make out, prepare, compile, compose, put together; draft, write, pen. **7** *I've made a mistake* PERPETRATE, commit, be responsible for, be guilty of, be to blame for. **8** *he's made a lot of money* ACQUIRE, obtain, gain, get, realize, secure, win, earn; gross, net, clear; bring in, take (in), rake in. **9** *he made dinner* PREPARE, get ready, put together, concoct, cook, dish up, throw together, whip up, brew; *informal* fix. **10** *we've got to make a decision* REACH, come to, settle on, determine on, conclude. **11** *she made a short announcement* UTTER, give, deliver, give voice to, enunciate, voice, pronounce. **12** *the sofa makes a good bed* BE, act as, serve as, function as, constitute, do duty for. **13** *he'll make the team* GAIN A PLACE IN, get into, gain access to,

enter; achieve, attain. **14** *he just made his train* CATCH, get, arrive/be in time for, arrive at, reach; get to.
— OPPOSITES: destroy, lose, miss.

▶ noun **1** *what make is the car?* BRAND, marque, label. **2** *a man of a different make from his brother* CHARACTER, nature, temperament, temper, disposition, kidney, mould, stamp.

■ **make as if/though** FEIGN, pretend, make a show/ pretense of, affect, feint, make out.

■ **make believe** PRETEND, fantasize, daydream, build castles in the air, dream, imagine, play-act, play.

■ **make do** SCRAPE BY, get by, manage, cope, survive, muddle through, improvise, make ends meet, keep the wolf from the door, keep one's head above water; *informal* make out; (**make do with**) make the best of, get by on, put up with.

■ **make for 1** *she made for the door* GO FOR/TOWARDS, head for/towards, aim for, make one's way towards, move towards, direct one's steps towards, steer a course towards, be bound for, make a beeline for. **2** *constant arguing doesn't make for a happy marriage* CONTRIBUTE TO, be conducive to, produce, promote, facilitate, foster.

■ **make it 1** *he'll never make it as a singer* SUCCEED, be a success, distinguish oneself, get ahead, make good; *informal* make the grade, arrive. **2** *she's very ill — is she going to make it?* SURVIVE, come through, pull through, get better, recover.

■ **make love.** *See* HAVE SEX *at* SEX.

■ **make off with** TAKE, steal, purloin, pilfer, abscond with, run away/off with, carry off, snatch; kidnap, abduct; *informal* walk away/off with, swipe, filch, snaffle, nab, lift, 'liberate', 'borrow', snitch, pinch; heist.

■ **make out** (*informal*) **1** *how did you make out?* GET ON/ ALONG, fare, do, proceed, go, progress, manage, survive, cope, get by. **2** *they made out in the back seat* KISS, neck, caress, pet; *informal* smooch, canoodle, buss, fool around.

■ **make something out 1** *I could just make out a figure in the distance* SEE, discern, distinguish, perceive, pick out, detect, observe, recognize; *literary* descry, espy. **2** *he couldn't make out what he was saying* UNDERSTAND, comprehend, follow, grasp, fathom, work out, make sense of, interpret, decipher, make head or tail of, get, get the drift of, catch. **3** *she made out that he was violent* ALLEGE, claim, assert, declare, maintain, affirm, suggest, imply, hint, insinuate, indicate, intimate, impute; *formal* aver. **4** *he made out a receipt for $20* WRITE OUT, fill out, fill in, complete, draw up.

■ **make something over to someone** TRANSFER, sign over, turn over, hand over/on/down, give, leave, bequeath, bestow, pass on, assign, consign, entrust; *Law* devolve.

■ **make up** *let's kiss and make up* BE FRIENDS AGAIN, bury the hatchet, declare a truce, make peace, forgive and forget, shake hands, become reconciled, settle one's differences, mend fences, call it quits.

■ **make something up 1** *exports make up 42% of earnings* CONSTITUTE, form, compose, account for. **2** *Gina brought a friend to make up a foursome* COMPLETE, round off/out, finish. **3** *the pharmacist made up the prescription* PREPARE, mix, concoct, put together. **4** *he made up an excuse* INVENT, fabricate, concoct, dream up, think up, hatch, trump up; devise, manufacture, formulate, coin; *informal* cook up. **5** *she made up her face* APPLY MAKEUP/COSMETICS TO, powder; (**make oneself**

up) *informal* put on one's face, do/paint one's face, apply one's war paint, doll oneself up.

■ **make up for 1** *she tried to make up for what she'd said* ATONE FOR, make amends for, compensate for, make recompense for, make reparation for, make redress for, make restitution for, expiate. **2** *job satisfaction can make up for low pay* OFFSET, counterbalance, counteract, compensate for; balance, neutralize, cancel out, even up, redeem.

■ **make up one's mind** DECIDE, come to a decision, make/reach a decision; settle on a plan of action, come to a conclusion, reach a conclusion; determine, resolve.

■ **make way** MOVE ASIDE, clear the way, make a space, make room, stand back.

make-believe ▶ noun *that was sheer make-believe* FANTASY, pretense, daydreaming, imagination, invention, fancy, dream, fabrication, play-acting, dreaming in technicolour, charade, masquerade, dress-up.
— OPPOSITES: reality.

▶ adjective *make-believe adventures* IMAGINARY, imagined, made-up, fantasy, dreamed-up, fanciful, fictitious, fictive, feigned, fake, mock, sham, simulated; *informal* pretend, phony.
— OPPOSITES: real, actual.

makeover ▶ noun TRANSFORMATION, renovation, overhaul, new look, remodelling, refurbishment, reconditioning, whitepainting ♣, improvement; *informal* reno, facelift.

maker ▶ noun CREATOR, manufacturer, constructor, builder, producer, fabricator, inventor, architect, designer.

makeshift ▶ adjective TEMPORARY, provisional, interim, stop-gap, make-do, standby, rough and ready, improvised, ad hoc, extempore, jury-rigged, jerry-built, thrown together, cobbled together.
— OPPOSITES: permanent.

makeup ▶ noun **1** *she used excessive makeup* COSMETICS, maquillage; greasepaint, face paint; *informal* war paint. **2** *the cellular makeup of plants* COMPOSITION, constitution, structure, configuration, arrangement, organization, formation. **3** *jealousy isn't part of his makeup* CHARACTER, nature, temperament, personality, disposition, mentality, persona, psyche; *informal* what makes someone tick.

making ▶ noun **1** *the making of cars* MANUFACTURE, mass-production, building, construction, assembly, production, creation, putting together, fabrication, forming, moulding, forging. **2** *she has the makings of a champion* QUALITIES, characteristics, ingredients; potential, promise, capacity, capability; essentials, essence, beginnings, rudiments, basics, stuff.
— OPPOSITES: destruction.

■ **in the making** *a hero in the making* BUDDING, up and coming, emergent, developing, nascent, potential, promising, incipient.

maladjusted ▶ adjective DISTURBED, unstable, neurotic, unbalanced, unhinged, dysfunctional; *informal* mixed up, screwed up, messed up.
— OPPOSITES: normal, stable.

maladroit ▶ adjective BUNGLING, awkward, inept, clumsy, bumbling, incompetent, unskilful, heavy-handed, gauche, tactless, inconsiderate, undiplomatic, impolitic; *informal* ham-fisted, all thumbs, klutzy.
— OPPOSITES: adroit, skilful.

malady ▶ noun ILLNESS, sickness, disease, infection,

ailment, disorder, complaint, indisposition, affliction, infirmity, syndrome; *informal* bug, virus.

malaise ▶ **noun** UNHAPPINESS, uneasiness, unease, discomfort, melancholy, depression, despondency, dejection, angst, Weltschmerz, ennui; lassitude, listlessness, languor, weariness; indisposition, ailment, infirmity, illness, sickness, disease.
– OPPOSITES: comfort, well-being.

malapropism ▶ **noun** WRONG WORD, solecism, misuse, misapplication, infelicity, slip of the tongue, Freudian slip, blunder.

malcontent ▶ **noun** *a group of malcontents* TROUBLEMAKER, mischief-maker, agitator, dissident, rebel, rabble-rouser; discontent, complainer, grumbler, moaner, whiner; *informal* grouch, grump, bellyacher, kvetch, squeaky wheel.
▶ **adjective** *a malcontent employee. See* DISCONTENTED.
– OPPOSITES: happy.

male ▶ **adjective** *male sexual jealousy* MASCULINE, virile, manly, macho, red-blooded.
– OPPOSITES: female.
▶ **noun** *two males walked past. See* MAN *noun* sense 1.
– RELATED TERMS: andro-.

malediction ▶ **noun** CURSE, damnation, oath; spell, hex, jinx; *formal* imprecation; *literary* anathema; *archaic* execration.
– OPPOSITES: blessing.

malefactor ▶ **noun** WRONGDOER, miscreant, offender, criminal, culprit, villain, lawbreaker, felon, evildoer, delinquent, hooligan, hoodlum, sinner, transgressor; *informal* crook, thug; *archaic* trespasser.

malevolent ▶ **adjective** MALICIOUS, hostile, evil-minded, baleful, evil-intentioned, venomous, evil, malign, malignant, rancorous, vicious, vindictive, vengeful; *literary* malefic, maleficent.
– OPPOSITES: benevolent.

malformed ▶ **adjective** DEFORMED, misshapen, misproportioned, ill-proportioned, disfigured, distorted, crooked, contorted, twisted, warped; abnormal, grotesque, monstrous.
– OPPOSITES: perfect, normal, healthy.

malfunction ▶ **verb** *the computer has malfunctioned* CRASH, go wrong, break down, fail, stop working, go down, hang up; *informal* conk out, go kaput, blow up, act up.
▶ **noun** *a computer malfunction* CRASH, breakdown, fault, failure, bug; *informal* glitch.

malice ▶ **noun** SPITE, malevolence, ill will, vindictiveness, vengefulness, revenge, malignity, evil intentions, animus, enmity, rancour; *informal* bitchiness, cattiness; *literary* maleficence.
– OPPOSITES: benevolence.

malicious ▶ **adjective** SPITEFUL, malevolent, evil-intentioned, vindictive, vengeful, malign, mean, nasty, hurtful, mischievous, wounding, cruel, unkind; *informal* bitchy, catty; *literary* malefic, maleficent.
– OPPOSITES: benevolent.

malign ▶ **adjective** *a malign influence* HARMFUL, evil, bad, baleful, hostile, inimical, destructive, malignant, injurious; *literary* malefic, maleficent.
– OPPOSITES: beneficial.
▶ **verb** *he maligned an innocent man* DEFAME, slander, libel, blacken someone's name/character, smear, vilify, speak ill of, cast aspersions on, run down, traduce, denigrate, disparage, slur, abuse, revile; *informal* badmouth, dis, knock; *formal* derogate,

calumniate.
– OPPOSITES: praise.

malignant ▶ **noun** **1** *a malignant disease* VIRULENT, very infectious, invasive, uncontrollable, dangerous, deadly, fatal, life-threatening. **2** *a malignant growth* CANCEROUS; *technical* metastatic. **3** *a malignant thought* SPITEFUL, malicious, malevolent, evil-intentioned, vindictive, vengeful, malign, mean, nasty, hurtful, mischievous, wounding, cruel, unkind; *informal* bitchy, catty; *literary* malefic, maleficent.
– OPPOSITES: benign, benevolent.

malinger ▶ **verb** PRETEND TO BE ILL, feign/fake illness, sham; shirk; *informal* put it on, swing the lead.

malingerer ▶ **noun** SHIRKER, idler, layabout, loafer; *informal* slacker, goof-off, goldbrick.

mall ▶ **noun** SHOPPING CENTRE, plaza, shopping complex, galleria, marketplace, strip mall, megamall, power centre, mini-mall.

malleable ▶ **adjective** **1** *a malleable substance* PLIABLE, ductile, plastic, pliant, soft, workable. **2** *a malleable young woman* EASILY INFLUENCED, suggestible, susceptible, impressionable, pliable, amenable, compliant, tractable; biddable, complaisant, manipulable, persuadable, like putty in someone's hands.
– OPPOSITES: hard, intractable.

malnutrition ▶ **noun** UNDERNOURISHMENT, malnourishment, poor diet, inadequate diet, unhealthy diet, lack of food; hunger, starvation.

malodorous ▶ **adjective** FOUL-SMELLING, evil-smelling, fetid, smelly, stinking (to high heaven), reeking, rank, high, putrid, noxious; *informal* stinky, humming, funky; *literary* noisome, mephitic.
– OPPOSITES: fragrant.

malpractice ▶ **noun** WRONGDOING, (professional) misconduct, breach of ethics, unprofessionalism, unethical behaviour; negligence, carelessness, incompetence.

maltreat ▶ **verb** *See* MISTREAT.

mama's boy ▶ **noun** MILKSOP, namby-pamby, coward, weakling, mollycoddle; *informal* sissy, baby, suck, wuss, sook, wimp, milquetoast, drip, pantywaist, *Atlantic* sooky baby ✤; *archaic* poltroon.

mammoth ▶ **adjective** HUGE, enormous, gigantic, giant, colossal, massive, vast, immense, mighty, stupendous, monumental, Herculean, epic, prodigious, mountainous, monstrous, titanic, towering, elephantine, king-size(d), economy-size(d), gargantuan, Brobdingnagian; *informal* mega, monster, whopping, honking, humongous, bumper, jumbo, astronomical, ginormous.
– OPPOSITES: tiny.

man ▶ **noun** **1** *a handsome man* MALE, adult male, gentleman; *informal* guy, fellow, fella, (esp. *Atlantic*) buddy ✤, joe, geezer, gent, bloke, chap, dude, hombre; (**men**) menfolk. **2** *all men are mortal* HUMAN BEING, human, person, mortal, individual, personage, soul. **3** *the evolution of man* THE HUMAN RACE, the human species, Homo sapiens, humankind, humanity, human beings, humans, people, mankind. **4** *the men voted to go on strike* WORKER, workman, labourer, hand, blue-collar worker. *See also* STAFF *noun* sense 1. **5** *have you met her new man?* BOYFRIEND, partner, husband, spouse, lover, admirer, fiancé; common-law husband, live-in lover, significant other, main squeeze; *informal* fancy man, toy boy, sugar daddy, intended; *dated* beau, steady, young man. **6** *his man*

brought him a cocktail. See MANSERVANT.
— RELATED TERMS: male, masculine, virile.
▶ **verb 1** *the office is manned from 9 a.m. to 5 p.m.* STAFF, crew, occupy, people. **2** *firemen manned the pumps* OPERATE, work, use, utilize.
■ **man to man** FRANKLY, openly, honestly, directly, candidly, plainly, forthrightly, without beating about the bush; woman to woman.
■ **to a man** WITHOUT EXCEPTION, with no exceptions, bar none, one and all, everyone, each and every one, unanimously, as one.
manacle ▶ **verb** SHACKLE, fetter, chain, put/clap in irons, handcuff, restrain; secure; *informal* cuff.
manacles ▶ **plural noun** HANDCUFFS, shackles, chains, irons, fetters, restraints, bonds; *informal* cuffs, bracelets.
manage ▶ **verb 1** *she manages a staff of 80 people* BE IN CHARGE OF, run, be head of, head, direct, control, preside over, lead, govern, rule, command, superintend, supervise, oversee, administer, organize, conduct, handle, guide, be at the helm of; *informal* head up. **2** *he managed a smile* ACCOMPLISH, achieve, do, carry out, perform, undertake, bring about/off, effect, finish; succeed in, contrive, engineer. **3** *will you be able to manage without him?* COPE, get along/on, make do, be/fare/do all right, carry on, survive, get by, muddle through/along, fend for oneself, shift for oneself, make ends meet, weather the storm; *informal* make out, hack it. **4** *she can't manage that horse* CONTROL, handle, master; cope with, deal with.
manageable ▶ **adjective 1** *a manageable amount of work* ACHIEVABLE, doable, practicable, possible, feasible, reasonable, attainable, viable. **2** *a manageable child* COMPLIANT, tractable, pliant, pliable, malleable, biddable, docile, amenable, governable, controllable, accommodating, acquiescent, complaisant, yielding. **3** *a manageable program* USER-FRIENDLY, easy to use, handy.
— OPPOSITES: difficult, impossible.
management ▶ **noun 1** *he's responsible for the management of the firm* ADMINISTRATION, running, managing, organization; charge, care, direction, leadership, control, governing, governance, ruling, command, superintendence, supervision, overseeing, conduct, handling, guidance, operation. **2** *workers are disputing with management* MANAGERS, employers, directors, board of directors, board, directorate, executives, administrators, administration; owners, proprietors; *informal* bosses, top brass.
manager ▶ **noun 1** *the works manager* EXECUTIVE, head of department, supervisor, principal, administrator, head, director, managing director, CEO, employer, superintendent, foreman, forewoman, overseer; proprietor; *informal* boss, chief, head honcho. **2** *the band's manager* ORGANIZER, controller, comptroller; impresario.
mandate ▶ **noun 1** *they won a mandate to form the government* AUTHORITY, approval, acceptance, ratification, endorsement, sanction, authorization. **2** *(Cdn) the Prime Minister promised to finish out his mandate* TERM, time, period (of office), incumbency; *informal* stint. **3** *a mandate from the UN* INSTRUCTION, directive, decree, command, order, injunction, edict, charge, commission, bidding, ruling, fiat; *formal* ordinance.
▶ **verb 1** *catalytic converters were mandated in 1975* MAKE MANDATORY, legislate, authorize, require by law; designate. **2** *they were mandated to strike* INSTRUCT, order, direct, command, tell, require, charge, call on.

mandatory ▶ **adjective** OBLIGATORY, compulsory, binding, required, requisite, necessary, essential, imperative.
— OPPOSITES: optional.
manfully ▶ **adverb** BRAVELY, courageously, boldly, gallantly, pluckily, heroically, intrepidly, fearlessly, valiantly, dauntlessly; resolutely, determinedly, hard, strongly, vigorously, with might and main, like a Trojan; with all one's strength, to the best of one's abilities, as best one can, desperately.
manger ▶ **noun** TROUGH, feeding trough, feeder, crib.
mangle ▶ **verb 1** *the bodies were mangled beyond recognition* MUTILATE, maim, disfigure, damage, injure, crush; hack, cut up, lacerate, tear apart, butcher, maul. **2** *he's mangling the English language* SPOIL, ruin, mar, mutilate, make a mess of, wreck; *informal* murder, make a hash of, butcher.
mangy ▶ **adjective 1** *a mangy cat* SCABBY, scaly, scabious, diseased. **2** *a mangy old armchair* SCRUFFY, moth-eaten, shabby, worn; dirty, squalid, sleazy, seedy, flea-bitten; *informal* tatty, the worse for wear, scuzzy; grotty.
manhandle ▶ **verb 1** *tourists were manhandled by skinheads* PUSH, shove, jostle, hustle; maltreat, ill-treat, mistreat, maul, molest; *informal* paw, rough up, roust. **2** *we manhandled the piano down the stairs* HEAVE, haul, push, shove; pull, tug, drag, lug, carry, lift, manoeuvre; *informal* hump.
manhood ▶ **noun 1** *the transition from boyhood to manhood* MATURITY, sexual maturity, adulthood. **2** *an insult to his manhood* VIRILITY, manliness, machismo, masculinity, maleness; mettle, spirit, strength, fortitude, determination, bravery, courage, intrepidity, valour, heroism, boldness.
mania ▶ **noun 1** *fits of mania* MADNESS, derangement, dementia, insanity, lunacy, psychosis, mental illness; delirium, frenzy, hysteria, raving, wildness. **2** *his mania for gadgets* OBSESSION, compulsion, fixation, fetish, fascination, preoccupation, infatuation, passion, enthusiasm, desire, urge, craving; craze, fad, rage; *informal* thing, yen.
maniac ▶ **noun 1** *a homicidal maniac* LUNATIC, madman, madwoman, psychopath; *informal* loony, fruitcake, nutcase, nut, psycho, head case, sicko, screwball, crazy. **2** *(informal) a techno maniac* ENTHUSIAST, fan, devotee, aficionado; *informal* freak, fiend, fanatic, nut, buff, bum, addict.
manic ▶ **adjective 1** *a manic grin* MAD, insane, deranged, demented, maniacal, lunatic, wild, crazed, demonic, hysterical, raving, unhinged, unbalanced; *informal* crazy. **2** *manic activity* FRENZIED, feverish, frenetic, hectic, intense; *informal* hyper, mad.
— OPPOSITES: sane, calm.
manifest ▶ **verb 1** *she manifested signs of depression* DISPLAY, show, exhibit, demonstrate, betray, present, reveal; *formal* evince. **2** *his positive potential is manifested by his art* BE EVIDENCE OF, be a sign of, indicate, show, attest, reflect, bespeak, prove, establish, evidence, substantiate, corroborate, confirm; *literary* betoken.
— OPPOSITES: hide, mask.
▶ **adjective** *his manifest lack of interest* OBVIOUS, clear, plain, apparent, evident, patent, palpable, distinct, definite, blatant, overt, glaring, barefaced, explicit, transparent, conspicuous, undisguised, unmistakable, noticeable, perceptible, visible, recognizable.
— OPPOSITES: secret.
manifestation ▶ **noun 1** *the manifestation of anxiety*

DISPLAY, demonstration, show, exhibition, presentation. **2** *manifestations of global warming* SIGN, indication, evidence, token, symptom, testimony, proof, substantiation, mark, reflection, example, instance. **3** *a supernatural manifestation* APPARITION, appearance, materialization, visitation.

manifesto ▶ noun POLICY STATEMENT, mission statement, platform, (little) red book, program, declaration, proclamation, pronouncement, announcement.

manifold ▶ adjective MANY, numerous, multiple, multifarious, legion, diverse, various, several, varied, different, miscellaneous, assorted, sundry; *literary* myriad, divers.

manipulate ▶ verb **1** *he manipulated some knobs and levers* OPERATE, work; turn, pull. **2** *she manipulated the muscles of his back* MASSAGE, rub, knead, feel, palpate. **3** *the government tried to manipulate the situation* CONTROL, influence, use/turn to one's advantage, exploit, manoeuvre, engineer, steer, direct, gerrymander; twist someone round one's little finger. **4** *they accused him of manipulating the data* FALSIFY, rig, distort, alter, change, doctor, massage, juggle, tamper with, tinker with, interfere with, misrepresent; *informal* cook, fiddle.

manipulative ▶ adjective SCHEMING, calculating, cunning, crafty, wily, shrewd, devious, designing, conniving, Machiavellian, artful, guileful, slippery, slick, sly, unscrupulous, disingenuous; *informal* foxy.

manipulator ▶ noun EXPLOITER, user, manoeuvrer, conniver, puppet master, wheeler-dealer; *informal* operator, thimblerigger.

mankind ▶ noun THE HUMAN RACE, man, humanity, human beings, humans, Homo sapiens, humankind, people, men and women.

manly ▶ adjective **1** *his manly physique* VIRILE, masculine, strong, muscular, muscly, strapping, well-built, sturdy, robust, rugged, tough, powerful, brawny, red-blooded, vigorous; *informal* hunky. **2** *their manly deeds* BRAVE, courageous, bold, valiant, valorous, fearless, plucky, macho, manful, intrepid, daring, heroic, lion-hearted, gallant, chivalrous, swashbuckling, adventurous, stout-hearted, dauntless, doughty, resolute, determined, stalwart; *informal* gutsy, spunky, ballsy.
– OPPOSITES: effeminate, cowardly.

man-made ▶ adjective ARTIFICIAL, synthetic, manufactured, fabricated; imitation, ersatz, simulated, mock, fake, phony, counterfeit, plastic.
– OPPOSITES: natural, real.

mannequin ▶ noun **1** *mannequins in a shop window* DUMMY, model, figure. **2** *mannequins on the catwalk* MODEL, fashion model, supermodel.

manner ▶ noun **1** *it was dealt with in a very efficient manner* WAY, fashion, mode, means, method, system, style, approach, technique, procedure, process, methodology, modus operandi, form. **2** *what manner of creature is it?* KIND, sort, type, variety, nature, breed, brand, stamp, class, category, genre, order. **3** *her rather unfriendly manner* DEMEANOUR, air, aspect, attitude, bearing, cast, behaviour, conduct; mien; *formal* comportment. **4** *aristocratic manners* CUSTOMS, habits, ways, practices, conventions, usages. **5** *it's bad manners to stare* BEHAVIOUR, conduct, way of behaving; form. **6** *you ought to teach him some manners* CORRECT BEHAVIOUR, etiquette, social graces, good form, protocol, politeness, decorum, propriety, gentility, civility, Ps and Qs.

mannered ▶ adjective AFFECTED, pretentious, unnatural, artificial, contrived, stilted, stiff, forced, put-on, theatrical, precious, stagy, camp; *informal* pseudo.
– OPPOSITES: natural.

mannerism ▶ noun IDIOSYNCRASY, quirk, oddity, foible, trait, peculiarity, habit, characteristic, tic.

mannish ▶ adjective UNFEMININE, unwomanly, masculine, unladylike, Amazonian; *informal* butch.
– OPPOSITES: feminine, girlish.

manoeuvre ▶ verb **1** *I manoeuvred the car into the space* STEER, guide, drive, negotiate, navigate, pilot, direct, manipulate, move, work, jockey. **2** *he manoeuvred things to suit himself* MANIPULATE, contrive, manage, engineer, devise, plan, fix, organize, arrange, set up, orchestrate, choreograph, stage-manage; *informal* wangle. **3** *he began manoeuvring for the party leadership* INTRIGUE, plot, scheme, plan, lay plans, conspire, pull strings.
▶ noun **1** *a tricky parking manoeuvre* OPERATION, exercise, activity, move, movement, action. **2** *diplomatic manoeuvres* STRATAGEM, tactic, gambit, ploy, trick, dodge, ruse, plan, scheme, operation, device, plot, machination, artifice, subterfuge, intrigue. **3** *military manoeuvres* TRAINING EXERCISES, exercises, war games, operations.

manservant ▶ noun VALET, attendant, retainer, equerry, man, steward, butler, houseman, footman, flunky, page, houseboy, lackey.

mansion ▶ noun STATELY HOME, hall, manor, manor house, country house; *informal* palace; *formal* residence.
– OPPOSITES: hovel.

manslaughter ▶ noun KILLING, murder, homicide, assassination; *literary* slaying.

mantle ▶ noun **1** *a dark green velvet mantle* CLOAK, cape, shawl, wrap, stole; *historical* pelisse. **2** *a thick mantle of snow* COVERING, layer, blanket, sheet, veil, curtain, canopy, cover, cloak, pall, shroud. **3** *the mantle of leadership* ROLE, burden, onus, duty, responsibility.
▶ verb *heavy mists mantled the forest* COVER, envelop, veil, cloak, curtain, shroud, swathe, wrap, blanket, conceal, hide, disguise, mask, obscure, surround, clothe; *literary* enshroud.

mantra ▶ noun SLOGAN, motto, maxim, catchphrase, catchword, watchword, byword, buzzword, tag (line).

manual ▶ adjective **1** *manual work* DONE WITH ONE'S HANDS, by hand, labouring, physical, blue-collar. **2** *a manual drill* HAND-OPERATED, hand, non-automatic.
▶ noun *a training manual* HANDBOOK, instruction book, instructions, guide, how-to book, companion, ABC, primer, guidebook, A to Z; *informal* bible.

manufacture ▶ verb **1** *the company manufactures laser printers* MAKE, produce, mass-produce, build, construct, assemble, put together, create, fabricate, turn out, process, engineer. **2** *a story manufactured by the press* MAKE UP, invent, fabricate, concoct, hatch, dream up, think up, trump up, devise, formulate, frame, contrive; *informal* cook up.
▶ noun *the manufacture of aircraft engines* PRODUCTION, making, manufacturing, mass-production, construction, building, assembly, creation, fabrication, prefabrication, processing.

manufacturer ▶ noun MAKER, producer, builder, constructor, creator; factory owner, industrialist, captain of industry.

manure ▶ noun DUNG, muck, excrement, droppings, ordure, guano, cow pats; fertilizer; *informal* cow chips, road apples, horse apples, horse buns ✦, buffalo chips, cow-pies, cow patties, cow flops; turds, scat.

manuscript ▶ noun DOCUMENT, text, script, paper, typescript, draft; codex, palimpsest, scroll; autograph, holograph.

many ▶ adjective **1** *many animals were killed* NUMEROUS, a great/good deal of, a lot of, plenty of, countless, innumerable, scores of, crowds of, droves of, an army of, a horde of, a multitude of, a multiplicity of, multitudinous, multiple, untold; several, various, sundry, diverse, assorted, multifarious; copious, abundant, profuse, an abundance of, a profusion of; frequent; *informal* lots of, umpteen, loads of, masses of, stacks of, scads of, heaps of, piles of, bags of, tons of, oodles of, dozens of, hundreds of, thousands of, millions of, billions of, zillions of, gazillions of, a slew of, a boatload of, more —— than one can shake a stick at; *literary* myriad, divers. **2** *sacrificing the individual for the sake of the many* THE PEOPLE, the common people, the masses, the multitude, the populace, the public, the rank and file; *derogatory* the hoi polloi, the common herd, the mob, the proletariat, the riff-raff, the great unwashed, the proles.
– RELATED TERMS: multi-, poly-.
– OPPOSITES: few.

map ▶ noun PLAN, chart, cartogram, survey, plat, plot; road map, street map, guide; atlas, globe; sketch map, relief map, contour map; Mercator projection, Peters projection.
– RELATED TERMS: cartography.
▶ verb *the region was mapped from the air* CHART, plot, delineate, draw, depict, portray.
■ **map something out** OUTLINE, set out, lay out, sketch out, trace out, rough out, block out, delineate, detail, draw up, formulate, work out, frame, draft, plan, plot out, arrange, design, program.

maple ▶ noun silver maple, Norway maple, red maple (swamp maple), sugar maple (hard maple, rock maple), Manitoba maple, (ash-leaved maple, bastard maple ✦), Japanese maple, bigleaf maple, black maple, Douglas maple, Amur maple, vine maple, snakebark maple, striped maple, mountain maple, paperbark maple.

mar ▶ verb **1** *an ugly scar marred his features* SPOIL, impair, disfigure, detract from, blemish; scar; mutilate, deface, deform. **2** *the celebrations were marred by violence* SPOIL, ruin, impair, damage, wreck; harm, hurt, blight, taint, tarnish, sully, stain, pollute; *informal* foul up; *formal* vitiate.
– OPPOSITES: enhance.

marauder ▶ noun RAIDER, plunderer, pillager, looter, robber, pirate, freebooter, bandit, highwayman, rustler; *literary* brigand; *archaic* buccaneer, corsair, reaver.

marauding ▶ adjective PREDATORY, rapacious, thieving, plundering, pillaging, looting, freebooting, piratical.

march ▶ verb **1** *the men marched past* STRIDE, walk, troop, step, pace, tread; footslog, slog, tramp, tromp, hike, trudge; parade, file, process. **2** *she marched in without even knocking* STALK, stride, strut, flounce, storm, stomp, sweep. **3** *time marches on* ADVANCE, progress, move on, roll on.
▶ noun **1** *a long march* HIKE, trek, tramp, slog, footslog, walk; route march, forced march. **2** *police in riot gear charged the march* PARADE, procession, cortège; demonstration, protest. **3** *the march of technology*

PROGRESS, advance, progression, development, evolution; passage.

margin ▶ noun **1** *the margin of the lake* EDGE, side, verge, border, perimeter, brink, brim, rim, fringe, boundary, limits, periphery, bound, extremity; *literary* bourn, skirt. **2** *there's no margin for error* LEEWAY, latitude, scope, room, room to manoeuvre, space, allowance, extra, surplus. **3** *they won by a narrow margin* GAP, majority, amount, difference.

marginal ▶ adjective **1** *the difference is marginal* SLIGHT, small, tiny, minute, insignificant, minimal, negligible. **2** *a marginal case* BORDERLINE, disputable, questionable, doubtful.

marginalize ▶ verb SIDELINE, trivialize; isolate, cut off, shut out; disenfranchise, alienate, estrange, ghettoize, discriminate against.

marijuana ▶ noun CANNABIS, pot, hashish, hash, dope, grass, weed, Mary Jane, bud, BC Bud ✦, bhang, hemp, kef, ganja, green, sinsemilla, skunkweed, locoweed; joint, reefer, doob, spliff, toke, roach.

marinate ▶ verb STEEP, soak, souse, immerse, marinade, bathe.

marine ▶ adjective **1** *marine plants* SEAWATER, sea, saltwater, oceanic; aquatic; *technical* pelagic. **2** *a marine vessel* MARITIME, nautical, naval; seafaring, seagoing, ocean-going.

mariner ▶ noun SAILOR, seaman, seafarer; *informal* sea dog, salt, rating, bluejacket, fish head, matelot, shellback.

marital ▶ adjective MATRIMONIAL, married, wedded, conjugal, nuptial, marriage, wedding; spousal; *literary* connubial.

maritime ▶ adjective **1** *maritime law* NAVAL, marine, nautical; seafaring, seagoing, sea, ocean-going. **2** *maritime regions* COASTAL, seaside, littoral.
■ *(Cdn)* **the Maritimes** New Brunswick, Prince Edward Island, Nova Scotia; *informal* the East coast, Atlantic provinces.

mark ▶ noun **1** *a dirty mark* BLEMISH, streak, spot, fleck, dot, blot, stain, smear, speck, speckle, blotch, smudge, smut, fingermark, fingerprint; bruise, discoloration; birthmark; *informal* splotch; *technical* stigma. **2** *a punctuation mark* SYMBOL, sign, character; diacritic. **3** *books bearing the mark of a well-known bookseller* LOGO, seal, stamp, imprint, symbol, emblem, device, insignia, badge, brand, trademark, monogram, hallmark, logotype, watermark. **4** *unemployment passed the three million mark* POINT, level, stage, degree. **5** *a mark of respect* SIGN, token, symbol, indication, badge, emblem; symptom, evidence, proof. **6** *the war left its mark on him* IMPRESSION, imprint, traces; effect, impact, influence. **7** *the mark of a civilized society* CHARACTERISTIC, feature, trait, attribute, quality, hallmark, calling card, badge, stamp, property, indicator. **8** *he got good marks for math* GRADE, grading, rating, score, percentage. **9** *the bullet missed its mark* TARGET, goal, aim, bull's eye; objective, object, end.
▶ verb **1** *be careful not to mark the paintwork* DISCOLOUR, stain, smear, smudge, streak, blotch, blemish; dirty, pockmark, bruise; *informal* splotch; *literary* smirch. **2** *her possessions were clearly marked* PUT ONE'S NAME ON, name, initial, label, identify; hallmark, watermark, brand. **3** *I've marked the relevant passages* INDICATE, label, flag, tick, check off, highlight; show, identify, designate, delineate, denote, specify. **4** *a festival to mark the town's 200th anniversary* CELEBRATE, observe, recognize, acknowledge, keep, honour, solemnize,

pay tribute to, salute, commemorate, remember, memorialize. **5** *the incidents marked a new phase in their campaign* REPRESENT, signify, be a sign of, indicate, herald. **6** *his style is marked by simplicity and concision* CHARACTERIZE, distinguish, identify, typify, brand, signalize, stamp. **7** *I have a pile of essays to mark* ASSESS, evaluate, grade, appraise, correct. **8** *it'll cause trouble, you mark my words!* TAKE HEED OF, heed, listen to, take note of, pay attention to, attend to, note, mind, bear in mind, take into consideration.

■ **make one's mark** BE SUCCESSFUL, distinguish oneself, succeed, be a success, prosper, get ahead, make good; *informal* make it, make the grade.

■ **mark something down** REDUCE, decrease, lower, cut, put down, discount; *informal* slash.

■ **mark something up** INCREASE, raise, up, put up, hike (up), escalate; *informal* jack up.

■ **quick off the mark** ALERT, quick, quick-witted, bright, clever, perceptive, sharp, sharp-witted, observant, wide awake, on one's toes; *informal* on the ball, quick on the uptake.

■ **wide of the mark** INACCURATE, incorrect, wrong, erroneous, off target, out, mistaken, misguided, misinformed.

marked ▶ **adjective** NOTICEABLE, pronounced, decided, distinct, striking, clear, glaring, blatant, unmistakable, obvious, plain, manifest, patent, palpable, prominent, signal, significant, conspicuous, notable, recognizable, identifiable, distinguishable, discernible, apparent, evident; written all over one.

— OPPOSITES: imperceptible.

market ▶ **noun 1** MARKETPLACE, mart, flea market, bazaar, souk, fair; *archaic* emporium. **2** *there's no market for such goods* DEMAND, call, want, desire, need, requirement. **3** *the market is sluggish* STOCK MARKET, trading, trade, business, commerce, buying and selling, dealing.

▶ **verb** *the product was marketed worldwide* SELL, retail, vend, merchandise, trade, peddle, hawk; advertise, promote.

■ **on the market** ON SALE, (up) for sale, available, obtainable, on the block.

marksman, markswoman ▶ **noun** SNIPER, sharpshooter, good shot; *informal* crack shot, deadeye, shootist.

maroon ▶ **verb** STRAND, cast away, cast ashore, shipwreck; abandon, leave behind, leave, leave in the lurch, desert, forsake; *informal* leave high and dry.

marriage ▶ **noun 1** *a proposal of marriage* (HOLY) MATRIMONY, wedlock. **2** *the marriage took place at St. Margaret's* WEDDING, wedding ceremony, marriage ceremony, nuptials, union. **3** *a marriage of jazz, pop, and gospel* UNION, alliance, fusion, mixture, mix, blend, amalgamation, combination, merger.

— RELATED TERMS: conjugal, marital, matrimonial.

— OPPOSITES: divorce, separation.

married ▶ **adjective 1** *a married couple* WEDDED, wed; *informal* spliced, hitched, coupled. **2** *married bliss* MARITAL, matrimonial, conjugal, nuptial; *Law* spousal; *literary* connubial.

— OPPOSITES: single.

marry ▶ **verb 1** *the couple married last year* GET/BE MARRIED, wed, be wed, become man and wife, plight/pledge one's troth; *informal* tie the knot, walk down the aisle, take the plunge, get spliced, get hitched, say 'I do'. **2** *John wanted to marry her* WED; *informal* make an honest woman of; *archaic* espouse. **3** *the show marries poetry with art* JOIN, unite, combine, fuse, mix, blend,

merge, amalgamate, link, connect, couple, knit, yoke.

— OPPOSITES: divorce, separate.

marsh ▶ **noun** SWAMP, marshland, bog, peat bog, muskeg, swampland, morass, (*NB & NS*) barren ♣, mire, moor, quagmire, slough, fen, fenland, wetland, bayou.

marshal ▶ **verb 1** *they marshalled an army* ASSEMBLE, gather (together), collect, muster, call together, draw up, line up, align, array, organize, group, arrange, deploy, position, order, dispose; mobilize, rally, round up. **2** *guests were marshalled to their seats* USHER, guide, escort, conduct, lead, shepherd, steer, take.

marsupial ▶ **noun**. *See table.*

Marsupials

bandicoot	pademelon
cuscus	phalanger
dasyure	rat kangaroo
flying phalanger	ringtail
kangaroo	Tasmanian devil
koala	wallaby
numbat	wombat
opossum	

---

martial ▶ **adjective** MILITARY, soldierly, soldier-like, army, naval; warlike, fighting, combative, bellicose, hawkish, pugnacious, militaristic.

martial art ▶ **noun** aikido, jiu-jitsu, judo, karate, kung fu, tae kwon do, Tai chi, Wen-Do ♣, kendo.

martyrdom ▶ **noun** DEATH, suffering, torture, torment, persecution, agony, ordeal; killing, sacrifice, self-sacrifice, crucifixion, immolation, burning, auto-da-fé; *Christianity* Passion.

marvel ▶ **verb** *she marvelled at their courage* BE AMAZED, be astonished, be surprised, be awed, stand in awe, wonder; stare, gape, goggle, not believe one's eyes/ears, be dumbfounded; *informal* be flabbergasted.

▶ **noun** *he's a marvel* WONDER, miracle, sensation, spectacle, phenomenon; *informal* something else, something to shout about.

marvellous ▶ **adjective 1** *his solo climb was marvellous* AMAZING, astounding, astonishing, awesome, breathtaking, sensational, remarkable, spectacular, stupendous, staggering, stunning; phenomenal, prodigious, miraculous, extraordinary, incredible, unbelievable; *literary* wondrous. **2** *marvellous weather* EXCELLENT, splendid, wonderful, magnificent, superb, glorious, sublime, lovely, delightful, too good to be true; *informal* super, great, amazing, fantastic, terrific, tremendous, sensational, heavenly, divine, gorgeous, grand, fabulous, fab, marvy, awesome, to die for, magic, ace, killer, wicked, mind-blowing, jaw-dropping, far out, out of this world; smashing, brilliant, boss; *informal, dated* swell, dreamy.

— OPPOSITES: commonplace, awful.

masculine ▶ **adjective 1** *a masculine trait* MALE, man's, men's; male-oriented. **2** *a powerfully masculine man* VIRILE, macho, manly, muscular, muscly, strong, strapping, well built, rugged, robust, brawny, powerful, red-blooded, vigorous; *informal* hunky. **3** *a rather masculine woman* MANNISH, boyish, unfeminine, unwomanly, unladylike, Amazonian; *informal* butch.

— OPPOSITES: feminine, effeminate.

masculinity ▶ **noun** VIRILITY, manliness, maleness, machismo, vigour, strength, muscularity, ruggedness, robustness; *informal* testosterone.

mash ▶ verb *mash the potatoes* PULP, crush, purée, cream, smash, squash, pound, beat, rice.
▶ noun *first pound the garlic to a mash* PULP, purée, mush, paste.

mask ▶ noun **1** *she wore a mask to conceal her face* DISGUISE, false face; *historical* domino, visor. **2** *he dropped his mask of good humour* PRETENSE, semblance, veil, screen, front, false front, facade, veneer, blind, disguise, guise, concealment, cover, cover-up, cloak, camouflage.
▶ verb *poplar trees masked the factory* HIDE, conceal, disguise, cover up, obscure, screen, cloak, camouflage, veil.

Mason jar ▶ noun *See* JAR.

masquerade ▶ noun **1** *a grand masquerade* MASKED BALL, masque, fancy-dress party, costume party. **2** *he couldn't keep up the masquerade much longer* PRETENSE, deception, pose, act, front, facade, disguise, dissimulation, bluff, play-acting, make-believe; *informal* put-on.
▶ verb *a woman masquerading as a man* PRETEND TO BE, pose as, pass oneself off as, impersonate, disguise oneself as.

Mass ▶ noun EUCHARIST, Holy Communion, Communion, the Lord's Supper, service, liturgy.

mass ▶ noun **1** *a soggy mass of fallen leaves* PILE, heap, accumulation, aggregation, accretion, concretion, buildup; *informal* batch, wad. **2** *a mass of cyclists* CROWD, horde, large group, throng, host, troop, army, herd, flock, drove, swarm, mob, pack, press, crush, flood, multitude. **3** *the mass of Canadian youths* MAJORITY, greater part/number, best/better part, major part, most, bulk, main body, lion's share. **4** (**masses**) THE COMMON PEOPLE, the populace, the public, the people, the rank and file, the crowd, the third estate; *derogatory* the hoi polloi, the mob, the proletariat, the common herd, the great unwashed. **5** (*informal*) *a mass of food*. *See* LOT *noun* sense 1.
▶ adjective *mass hysteria* WIDESPREAD, general, wholesale, universal, large-scale, extensive, pandemic.
▶ verb *they began massing troops in the region* ASSEMBLE, marshal, gather together, muster, round up, mobilize, rally.

massacre ▶ noun **1** *a cold-blooded massacre of innocent civilians* SLAUGHTER, wholesale/mass slaughter, indiscriminate killing, mass murder, mass execution, annihilation, liquidation, decimation, extermination; carnage, butchery, bloodbath, bloodletting, pogrom, genocide, ethnic cleansing, holocaust, night of the long knives; *literary* slaying. **2** (*informal*) *the game was an 8−0 massacre*. *See* ROUT *noun* sense 2.
▶ verb **1** *thousands were brutally massacred* SLAUGHTER, butcher, murder, kill, annihilate, exterminate, execute, liquidate, eliminate, decimate, wipe out, mow down, cut down, put to the sword, put to death; *literary* slay. **2** (*informal*) *they were massacred in the final*. *See* TROUNCE.

massage ▶ noun RUB, rub-down, rubbing, kneading, palpation, manipulation, pummelling; body rub, back rub; shiatsu, reflexology, acupressure, hydromassage, Swedish massage, osteopathy; effleurage, tapotement, Rolfing.
▶ verb **1** *he massaged her tired muscles* RUB, knead, palpate, manipulate, pummel, work. **2** *the statistics have been massaged* ALTER, tamper with, manipulate, doctor, falsify, juggle, fiddle with, tinker with,

distort, change, rig, interfere with, misrepresent; *informal* fix, cook, fiddle.

massive ▶ adjective HUGE, enormous, vast, immense, large, big, mighty, great, colossal, tremendous, prodigious, gigantic, gargantuan, mammoth, monstrous, monumental, giant, towering, elephantine, mountainous, titanic; epic, Herculean, Brobdingnagian; *informal* monster, jumbo, mega, whopping, humongous, hulking, honking, bumper, astronomical, ginormous.
− OPPOSITES: tiny.

mast ▶ noun **1** *a ship's mast* spar, boom, yard, gaff, foremast, mainmast, topmast, mizzen-mast, mizzen, royal mast. **2** *the mast on top of the building* FLAGPOLE, flagstaff, pole, post, rod, upright; aerial, transmitter, pylon.

master ▶ noun **1** (*historical*) *he acceded to his master's wishes* LORD, overlord, lord and master, ruler, sovereign, monarch, liege (lord), suzerain. **2** *the dog's master* OWNER, keeper. **3** *a chess master* EXPERT, adept, genius, past master, maestro, virtuoso, professional, doyen, authority, champion; *informal* ace, pro, wizard, whiz, hotshot, maven, crackerjack. **4** *the master of the ship* CAPTAIN, commander; *informal* skipper. **5** *their spiritual master* GURU, teacher, leader, guide, mentor; swami, Maharishi, rabbi; Roshi.
− OPPOSITES: servant, amateur.
▶ verb **1** *I managed to master my fears* OVERCOME, conquer, beat, quell, quash, suppress, control, overpower, triumph over, subdue, vanquish, subjugate, prevail over, govern, curb, check, bridle, tame, defeat, get the better of, get a grip on, get over; *informal* lick. **2** *it took ages to master the technique* LEARN, become proficient in, know inside out, know backwards; pick up, grasp, understand; *informal* get the hang of.
▶ adjective **1** *a master craftsman* EXPERT, adept, proficient, skilled, skilful, deft, dexterous, adroit, practised, experienced, masterly, accomplished, complete, demon, brilliant; *informal* crack, ace, mean, crackerjack. **2** *the master bedroom* PRINCIPAL, main, chief; biggest.

masterful ▶ adjective **1** *a masterful man* COMMANDING, powerful, imposing, magisterial, lordly, authoritative; dominating, domineering, overbearing, overweening, imperious. **2** *their masterful handling of the situation* EXPERT, adept, clever, masterly, skilful, skilled, adroit, proficient, deft, dexterous, accomplished, polished, consummate; *informal* crack, ace.
− OPPOSITES: weak, inept.

mastermind ▶ verb *he masterminded the whole campaign* PLAN, control, direct, be in charge of, run, conduct, organize, arrange, preside over, orchestrate, stage-manage, engineer, manage, coordinate, conceive, devise, originate, initiate, think up, frame, hatch, come up with; *informal* be the brains behind.
▶ noun *the mastermind behind the project* GENIUS, mind, intellect, author, architect, organizer, originator, prime mover, initiator, inventor; *informal* brain, brains, idea man, bright spark.

masterpiece ▶ noun PIÈCE DE RÉSISTANCE, chef-d'œuvre, masterwork, magnum opus, finest/best work, tour de force.

mastery ▶ noun **1** *her mastery of the language* PROFICIENCY, ability, capability; knowledge, understanding, comprehension, familiarity, command, grasp, grip. **2** *they played with tactical mastery* SKILL, skilfulness, expertise, dexterity, finesse, adroitness, virtuosity, prowess, deftness, proficiency; *informal* know-how. **3** *man's mastery over nature* CONTROL, domination, command, ascendancy, supremacy, pre-eminence, superiority; triumph, victory, the upper hand, the whip hand, rule, government, power, sway, authority, jurisdiction, dominion, sovereignty.

masticate ▶ verb CHEW, munch, champ, chomp, crunch, eat; *formal* manducate.

mat ▶ noun **1** *the cat sat on the mat* RUG, runner, carpet, doormat, welcome mat, bath mat, hearth rug, floor cloth; dhurrie, numdah; kilim, flokati, (Que.) catalogne ✦, tatami. **2** *he placed his glass on the mat* COASTER, table mat, placemat, beer mat. **3** *a thick mat of hair* MASS, tangle, knot, mop, thatch, shock, mane.
▶ verb *his hair was matted with blood* TANGLE, entangle, knot, snarl up.

match ▶ noun **1** *we won the match* CONTEST, competition, game, tournament, event, trial, test, meet, matchup; bout, fight; derby; play-off, replay, rematch, engagement, bonspiel. **2** *he was no match for the champion* EQUAL, rival, equivalent, peer, counterpart; *formal* compeer. **3** *the vase was an exact match of the one she already owned* LOOK-ALIKE, double, twin, duplicate, mate, fellow, companion, counterpart, pair; replica, copy; *informal* spitting image, dead ringer. **4** *a love match* MARRIAGE, betrothal, relationship, partnership, union.
▶ verb **1** *the curtains matched the duvet cover* GO WITH, coordinate with, complement, suit; be the same as, be similar to. **2** *did their statements match?* CORRESPOND, be in agreement, tally, agree, match up, coincide, accord, conform, square. **3** *no one can match him at chess* EQUAL, be a match for, measure up to, compare with, parallel, be in the same league as, be on a par with, touch, keep pace with, keep up with, emulate, rival, vie with, compete with, contend with; *informal* hold a candle to.

matching ▶ adjective CORRESPONDING, equivalent, parallel, analogous; coordinating, complementary; paired, twin, identical, like, like (two) peas in a pod, alike.
– OPPOSITES: different, clashing.

matchless ▶ adjective INCOMPARABLE, unrivalled, inimitable, beyond compare/comparison, unparalleled, unequalled, without equal, peerless, second to none, unsurpassed, unsurpassable, nonpareil, unique, consummate, perfect, rare, transcendent, surpassing; *formal* unexampled.

mate ▶ noun **1** *she's finally found her ideal mate* (LIFE) PARTNER, husband, wife, spouse, lover, live-in lover, significant other, companion, helpmate, helpmeet, consort; *informal* better half, other half, main squeeze, hubby, missus, missis, old lady, old man. **2** *this sock has lost its mate* MATCH, fellow, twin, companion, pair, other half, equivalent. **3** (*informal*) *he's gone out with his mates. See* CHUM.
▶ verb *pandas rarely mate in captivity* BREED, couple, copulate.

material ▶ noun **1** *the decomposition of organic material* MATTER, substance, stuff, medium. **2** *the materials for a new building* CONSTITUENT, raw material, element, component. **3** *cleaning materials* THINGS, items, articles, stuff, necessaries. **4** *curtain material* FABRIC, cloth, textiles. **5** *material for a magazine article* INFORMATION, data, facts, facts and figures, statistics, evidence, details, particulars, background, notes; *informal* info, dope, lowdown.
▶ adjective **1** *the material world* PHYSICAL, corporeal,

tangible, non-spiritual, mundane, worldly, earthly, secular, temporal, concrete, real, solid, substantial. **2** *she was too fond of material comforts* SENSUAL, physical, carnal, corporal, fleshly, bodily, creature. **3** *information that could be material to the inquiry* RELEVANT, pertinent, important, applicable, germane; apropos, to the point; vital, essential, key. **4** *the storms caused material damage* SIGNIFICANT, major, important.
– OPPOSITES: spiritual, aesthetic, irrelevant.

materialistic ▶ adjective CONSUMERIST, acquisitive, greedy; worldly, capitalistic, bourgeois.

materialize ▶ verb **1** *the forecasted rain did not materialize* HAPPEN, occur, come about, take place, come into being, transpire; *informal* come off; *formal* eventuate; *literary* come to pass. **2** *Harry materialized at the door* APPEAR, turn up, arrive, make/put in an appearance, present oneself/itself, emerge, surface, reveal oneself/itself, show one's face, pop up; *informal* show up, fetch up, pitch up.

maternal ▶ adjective **1** *her maternal instincts* MOTHERLY, protective, caring, nurturing, loving, devoted, affectionate, fond, warm, tender, gentle, kind, kindly, comforting. **2** *his maternal grandparents* ON ONE'S MOTHER'S SIDE.

mathematical ▶ adjective **1** *mathematical symbols* ARITHMETICAL, numerical; statistical, algebraic, geometric, trigonometric. **2** *mathematical precision* RIGOROUS, meticulous, scrupulous, punctilious, scientific, strict, precise, exact, accurate, pinpoint, correct, careful, unerring.

Branches of Mathematics

algebra	integral calculus
applied mathematics	mechanics
arithmetic	number theory
calculus	quadratics
conics	set theory
differential calculus	statistics
game theory	topology
geodesy	trigonometry
geometry	

matrimonial ▶ adjective *See* MARITAL.

matrimony ▶ noun MARRIAGE, wedlock, union; nuptials.
– OPPOSITES: divorce.

matted ▶ adjective TANGLED, tangly, knotted, knotty, tousled, dishevelled, uncombed, unkempt; *informal* ratty, mussy.

matter ▶ noun **1** *decaying vegetable matter* MATERIAL, substance, stuff. **2** *the heart of the matter* AFFAIR, business, proceeding, situation, circumstance, event, happening, occurrence, incident, episode, experience; subject, topic, issue, question, point, point at issue, case, concern. **3** *it is of little matter now* IMPORTANCE, consequence, significance, note, import, weight; *formal* moment. **4** *what's the matter?* PROBLEM, trouble, difficulty, complication; upset, worry. **5** *the matter of the book* CONTENT, subject matter, text, argument, substance.
▶ verb *it doesn't matter what you wear* BE IMPORTANT, make any/a difference, be of importance, be of consequence, signify, be relevant, count; *informal* cut any ice.
■ **as a matter of fact** ACTUALLY, in (actual) fact, in point of fact, as it happens, really, believe it or not, in reality, in truth, to tell the truth.
■ **no matter** IT DOESN'T MATTER, it makes no

difference/odds, it's not important, never mind, don't worry about it.

matter-of-fact ▶ adjective UNEMOTIONAL, practical, down-to-earth, sensible, realistic, rational, sober, unsentimental, pragmatic, businesslike, commonsensical, level-headed, hard-headed, no-nonsense, factual, literal, straightforward, straight-out, plain, unembellished, unvarnished, unadorned; unimaginative, prosaic.

mature ▶ adjective **1** *a mature woman* ADULT, grown-up, grown, fully grown, full-grown, of age, fully developed, in one's prime, middle-aged. **2** *he's very mature for his age* SENSIBLE, responsible, adult, level-headed, reliable, dependable; wise, discriminating, shrewd, sophisticated. **3** *mature cheese* RIPE, ripened, mellow; ready to eat/drink. **4** *on mature reflection, he decided not to go* CAREFUL, thorough, deep, considered.
– OPPOSITES: adolescent, childish.
▶ verb **1** *kittens mature when they are about a year old* BE FULLY GROWN, be full-grown; come of age, reach adulthood, reach maturity. **2** *he's matured since he left home* GROW UP, become more sensible/adult; blossom. **3** *leave the cheese to mature* RIPEN, mellow; age. **4** *their friendship didn't have time to mature* DEVELOP, grow, evolve, bloom, blossom, flourish, thrive.

maturity ▶ noun **1** *her progress from childhood to maturity* ADULTHOOD, majority, coming-of-age, manhood/womanhood. **2** *he displayed a maturity beyond his years* RESPONSIBILITY, sense, level-headedness; wisdom, discrimination, shrewdness, sophistication.

maudlin ▶ adjective **1** *maudlin self-pity* SENTIMENTAL, over-sentimental, emotional, over-emotional, tearful, lachrymose; *informal* weepy, misty-eyed. **2** *a maudlin ballad* MAWKISH, sentimental, over-sentimental, twee; *informal* mushy, slushy, sloppy, schmaltzy, cheesy, corny, soppy, cornball, three-hankie.

maul ▶ verb **1** *he had been mauled by a lion* SAVAGE, attack, tear to pieces, lacerate, claw, scratch. **2** *she hated being mauled by men* MOLEST, feel, fondle, manhandle; *informal* grope, paw, touch up. **3** *his book was mauled by the critics. See* CRITICIZE.

maunder ▶ verb **1** *he maundered on about his problems* RAMBLE, prattle, blather, rattle, chatter, jabber, babble; *informal* yak, yatter, waffle, natter. **2** *she maundered across the road* WANDER, drift, meander, amble, putter.

mausoleum ▶ noun TOMB, sepulchre, crypt, vault, charnel house, burial chamber, catacomb.

maverick ▶ noun INDIVIDUALIST, nonconformist, free spirit, unorthodox person, original, eccentric; rebel, dissenter, dissident, enfant terrible; *informal* cowboy, loose cannon.
– OPPOSITES: conformist.

maw ▶ noun **1** *cats scrub their maws with their forelegs* MOUTH, jaws, muzzle; throat, gullet; *informal* trap, chops, kisser. **2** *he walked forward into the gaping maw of the tunnel* ENTRANCE, opening, gap, hole, chasm, black hole, abyss.

mawkish ▶ adjective SENTIMENTAL, over-sentimental, maudlin, cloying, sickly, saccharine, sugary, syrupy, nauseating, twee; *informal* mushy, slushy, sloppy, schmaltzy, weepy, cutesy, lovey-dovey, cheesy, corny, soppy, cornball, hokey, three-hankie.

maxim ▶ noun SAYING, adage, aphorism, proverb, motto, saw, axiom, dictum, precept, epigram; truism, cliché.

maximum ▶ adjective *the maximum amount* GREATEST, highest, biggest, largest, top, topmost, most, utmost, maximal.
– OPPOSITES: minimum.
▶ noun *production levels are near their maximum* UPPER LIMIT, limit, utmost, uttermost, greatest, most, extremity, peak, height, ceiling, top, apex; *informal* max.
– OPPOSITES: minimum.

maybe ▶ adverb PERHAPS, possibly, conceivably, it could be, it is possible, for all one knows; *literary* peradventure, perchance.

mayhem ▶ noun CHAOS, disorder, havoc, bedlam, pandemonium, tumult, uproar, turmoil, commotion, all hell broken loose, maelstrom, trouble, disturbance, confusion, riot, anarchy, violence, insanity, madness; *informal* madhouse.

maze ▶ noun LABYRINTH, complex network, warren; web, tangle, jungle, snarl; puzzle.

meadow ▶ noun FIELD, paddock; pasture, pasture land, prairie; *literary* lea, mead.

meagre ▶ adjective **1** *their meagre earnings* INADEQUATE, scanty, scant, paltry, limited, restricted, modest, insufficient, sparse, deficient, negligible, skimpy, slender, poor, miserable, pitiful, puny, miserly, niggardly, beggarly; *informal* measly, stingy, pathetic, piddling; *formal* exiguous. **2** *a tall, meagre man* THIN, lean, skinny, spare, scrawny, gangling, gangly, spindly, stringy, bony, raw-boned, gaunt, underweight, underfed, undernourished, emaciated, skeletal.
– OPPOSITES: abundant, fat.

meal ▶ noun snack; feast, banquet; *informal* bite (to eat), spread, blowout, feed, scoff; *formal* repast, collation; *literary* refection. *See table.*
– RELATED TERMS: prandial.

Types of Meal

afternoon tea	lunch
à la carte	luncheon
bag lunch	mechoui ✦(Que.)
balti	picnic
barbecue	potluck
bite	power lunch
blue plate special	prix fixe
box lunch	réveillon
breakfast	rijsttafel
brunch	shore lunch ✦
buffet	sit-down meal
chuckwagon dinner	smorgasbord
clambake	supper
collation	surf and turf
cookout	table d'hôte
dinner	takeout
feast	thali
full-course meal	TV dinner
high tea	wiener roast
lobster supper	

mean¹ ▶ verb **1** *flashing lights mean the road is blocked* SIGNIFY, convey, denote, designate, indicate, connote, show, express, spell out; stand for, represent, symbolize; imply, suggest, intimate, hint at, insinuate, drive at, refer to, allude to, point to; *literary* betoken. **2** *she didn't mean to break it* INTEND, aim, plan, design, have in mind, contemplate, purpose, propose, set out, aspire, desire, want, wish, expect. **3** *he was hit by a bullet meant for a soldier* INTEND, design; destine, predestine. **4** *the closures will mean a rise in unemployment* ENTAIL, involve, necessitate, lead to, result in, give rise to, bring about, cause, engender, produce. **5** *this means a lot to me* MATTER, be important, be significant. **6** *a red sky in the morning usually means rain* PRESAGE, portend, foretell, augur, promise, foreshadow, herald, signal, bode; *literary* betoken.

mean² ▶ adjective **1** *a mean trick* UNKIND, nasty, unpleasant, spiteful, malicious, unfair, cruel, shabby, foul, despicable, contemptible, obnoxious, vile, odious, loathsome, base, low; *informal* horrible, horrid, hateful, rotten, lowdown; beastly. **2** *he's too mean to leave a tip* MISERLY, niggardly, close-fisted, parsimonious, penny-pinching, cheese-paring, Scrooge-like; *informal* tight-fisted, stingy, tight, mingy, money-grubbing, cheap; *formal* penurious. **3** *the truth was obvious to even the meanest intelligence* INFERIOR, poor, limited, restricted. **4** *their mean origins* LOWLY, humble, ordinary, low, low-born, modest, common, base, proletarian, plebeian, obscure, ignoble, undistinguished; *archaic* baseborn. **5** (*informal*) *he's a mean cook. See* EXCELLENT.
– OPPOSITES: generous, kind, luxurious.

mean³ ▶ noun *a mean between frugality and miserliness* MIDDLE COURSE, middle way, midpoint, happy medium, golden mean, compromise, balance; median, norm, average.
▶ adjective *the mean temperature* AVERAGE, median, middle, medial, medium, normal, standard.

meander ▶ verb **1** *the river meandered gently* ZIGZAG, wind, twist, turn, curve, curl, bend, snake. **2** *we meandered along the path* STROLL, saunter, amble, wander, ramble, drift, maunder; *informal* mosey, tootle, toodle.

meandering ▶ adjective **1** *a meandering stream* WINDING, windy, zigzag, twisting, turning, curving, serpentine, sinuous, twisty. **2** *meandering reminiscences* RAMBLING, maundering, circuitous, roundabout, digressive, discursive, indirect, tortuous, convoluted.
– OPPOSITES: straight, succinct.

meaning ▶ noun **1** *the meaning of his remark* SIGNIFICANCE, sense, signification, import, gist, thrust, drift, implication, tenor, message, essence, substance, purport, intention. **2** *the word has several different meanings* DEFINITION, sense, explanation, denotation, connotation, interpretation, nuance. **3** *my life has no meaning* VALUE, validity, worth, consequence, account, use, usefulness, significance, point. **4** *his smile was full of meaning* EXPRESSIVENESS, significance, eloquence, implications, insinuations.
– RELATED TERMS: semantic.
▶ adjective *a meaning look. See* MEANINGFUL sense 3.

meaningful ▶ adjective **1** *a meaningful remark* SIGNIFICANT, relevant, important, consequential, telling, material, valid, worthwhile. **2** *a meaningful relationship* SINCERE, deep, serious, in earnest, significant, important. **3** *a meaningful glance* EXPRESSIVE, eloquent, pointed, significant, meaning; pregnant, speaking, telltale, revealing, suggestive, charged, loaded.
– OPPOSITES: inconsequential.

meaningless ▶ adjective **1** *a jumble of meaningless words* UNINTELLIGIBLE, incomprehensible, incoherent. **2** *she felt her life was meaningless* FUTILE, pointless, aimless, empty, hollow, blank, vain, purposeless, valueless, useless, of no use, worthless, senseless,

trivial, trifling, unimportant, insignificant, inconsequential.
– OPPOSITES: worthwhile.

means ▶ plural noun **1** *the best means to achieve your goal* METHOD, way, manner, mode, measure, technique, expedient, agency, medium, instrument, channel, vehicle, avenue, course, process, procedure. **2** *she doesn't have the means to support herself* MONEY, resources, capital, income, finance, funds, cash, the wherewithal, assets; *informal* dough, bread, moolah. **3** *a man of means* WEALTH, riches, affluence, substance, fortune, property, money, capital.
■ **by all means** OF COURSE, certainly, definitely, surely, absolutely, with pleasure; *informal* sure thing.
■ **by means of** USING, utilizing, employing, through, with the help of; as a result of, by dint of, by way of, by virtue of.
■ **by no means** NOT AT ALL, in no way, not in the least, not in the slightest, not the least bit, not by a long shot, certainly not, absolutely not, definitely not, on no account, under no circumstances; *informal* no way.

meantime
■ **in the meantime** *See* MEANWHILE.

meanwhile ▶ adverb **1** *meanwhile, I'll stay here* FOR NOW, for the moment, for the present, for the time being, meantime, in the meantime, in the interim, in the interval. **2** *cook for a further half hour; meanwhile, make the stuffing* AT THE SAME TIME, simultaneously, concurrently, the while.

measly ▶ adjective **1** *her measly salary* PALTRY, meagre, scanty, niggardly, miserable, inadequate, insufficient; *informal* pathetic, stingy. **2** *you measly little twerp* CONTEMPTIBLE, worthless, wretched, inconsequential, inferior.

measurable ▶ adjective **1** *a measurable amount* QUANTIFIABLE, computable. **2** *a measurable improvement* APPRECIABLE, noticeable, significant, visible, perceptible, definite, obvious.

measure ▶ verb **1** *they measured the length of the room* CALCULATE, compute, count, meter, quantify, weigh, size, evaluate, assess, gauge, plumb, determine. **2** *she did not need to measure herself against some ideal* COMPARE WITH, pit against, set against, test against, judge by.
▶ noun **1** *cost-cutting measures* ACTION, act, course (of action), deed, proceeding, procedure, step, means, expedient; manoeuvre, initiative, program, operation. **2** *the House passed the measure* STATUTE, act, bill, law, legislation. **3** *the original dimensions were in imperial measure* SYSTEM, standard, units, scale. **4** *a measure of egg white* QUANTITY, amount, portion. **5** *the students retain a measure of independence* CERTAIN AMOUNT, degree; some. **6** *sales are the measure of the company's success* YARDSTICK, test, standard, barometer, touchstone, litmus test, criterion, benchmark.
■ **beyond measure** IMMENSELY, extremely, vastly, greatly, excessively, immeasurably, incalculably, infinitely.
■ **for good measure** AS A BONUS, as an extra, into the bargain, to boot, in addition, besides, as well.
■ **get/have the measure of** EVALUATE, assess, gauge, judge, understand, fathom, read, be wise to, see through; *informal* have someone's number.
■ **measure up** PASS MUSTER, match up, come up to standard, fit/fill the bill, be acceptable; *informal* come up to scratch, make the grade, cut the mustard, be up to snuff.
■ **measure up to** MEET, come up to, equal, match,

bear comparison with, be on a level with; achieve, satisfy, fulfill.

measured ▶ adjective **1** *his measured steps* REGULAR, steady, even, rhythmic, rhythmical, unfaltering; slow, dignified, stately, sedate, leisurely, unhurried. **2** *his measured tones* THOUGHTFUL, careful, carefully chosen, studied, calculated, planned, considered, deliberate, restrained.

measureless ▶ adjective BOUNDLESS, limitless, unlimited, unbounded, untold, immense, vast, endless, inexhaustible, infinite, illimitable, immeasurable, incalculable.
– OPPOSITES: limited.

measurement ▶ noun **1** *measurement of the effect is difficult* QUANTIFICATION, computation, calculation, mensuration; evaluation, assessment, gauging. **2** *all measurements are given in metric form* SIZE, dimension, proportions, magnitude, amplitude; mass, bulk, volume, capacity, extent; value, amount, quantity, area, length, height, depth, weight, width, range.

Meat

Types	hock
beef	kidney
chicken	knuckle
duck	knucklebone
game	leg
lamb	liver
mutton	loin
pork	medallion
poultry	neck
rabbit	noisette
turkey	oxtail
veal	picnic shoulder
venison	porterhouse steak
Cuts	pot roast
back ribs	prime rib
backstrap	rack
bacon	rib
baron of beef	riblets
blade	round
bottom round	round steak
breast	roast
brisket	rump
butt	saddle
chateaubriand	scaloppine
chine	scrag
chop	shank
chuck	short loin
chump	short rib
cold cuts	shoulder
cross rib	shin
cutlet	side
entrecôte	side ribs ✤
escalope	sirloin
eye of round	sirloin tip
fillet	spareribs
flank	steak
gammon	tongue
gigot	T-bone
ground	tenderloin
ham	thighs
hamburger	tournedos
hand	tripe
	trotters
	wing

meat ▶ noun **1** FLESH, animal flesh. *See table.*

2 (*archaic*) *meat and drink* FOOD, nourishment, sustenance, provisions, rations, fare, foodstuff(s), provender, daily bread; *informal* grub, eats, chow, nosh; *informal* scoff; *formal* comestibles; *dated* victuals; *literary* viands. **3** *the meat of the matter* SUBSTANCE, pith, marrow, heart, kernel, core, nucleus, nub, essence, essentials, gist, fundamentals, basics; *informal* nitty-gritty.

meaty ▶ adjective **1** *a tall, meaty man* BEEFY, brawny, burly, muscular, muscly, powerful, sturdy, strapping, well-built, solidly built, thickset; fleshy, stout. **2** *a good, meaty story* INTERESTING, thought-provoking, three-dimensional, stimulating; substantial, satisfying, meaningful, deep, profound.

mechanic ▶ noun TECHNICIAN, ENGINEER, repairman, serviceman; *informal* grease monkey.

mechanical ▶ adjective **1** *a mechanical device* MECHANIZED, machine-driven, automated, automatic, power-driven, robotic. **2** *a mechanical response* AUTOMATIC, unthinking, robotic, involuntary, reflex, knee-jerk, gut, habitual, routine, unemotional, unfeeling, lifeless; perfunctory, cursory, careless, casual.
– OPPOSITES: manual, conscious.

mechanism ▶ noun **1** *an electrical mechanism* MACHINE, piece of machinery, appliance, apparatus, device, instrument, contraption, gadget; *informal* gizmo. **2** *the train's safety mechanism* MACHINERY, workings, works, movement, action, gears, components. **3** *a formal mechanism for citizens to lodge complaints* PROCEDURE, process, system, operation, method, technique, means, medium, agency, channel.

medal ▶ noun DECORATION, ribbon, star, badge, laurel, palm, award; honour.

meddle ▶ verb **1** *don't meddle in my affairs* INTERFERE, butt in, intrude, intervene, pry; *informal* poke one's nose in, horn in on, muscle in on, snoop, stick one's oar in, kibitz. **2** *someone had been meddling with her things* FIDDLE, interfere, tamper, tinker, fool around, muck around.

meddlesome ▶ adjective INTERFERING, meddling, intrusive, prying, busybody; *informal* nosy, Nosy Parker.

media ▶ noun THE PRESS, the fourth estate, the news, the papers; broadcasting, publishing.

median ▶ adjective medial, mean, middle, average, mid, central, intermediate.
▶ noun MEDIAN STRIP, guardrail, divider, boulevard, barrier; curb.

mediate ▶ verb **1** *the UN tried to mediate between the two countries* ARBITRATE, conciliate, moderate, act as peacemaker, make peace; intervene, step in, intercede, act as an intermediary, liaise. **2** *a tribunal was set up to mediate disputes* RESOLVE, settle, arbitrate in, umpire, reconcile, referee; mend, clear up; *informal* patch up. **3** *he attempted to mediate a solution to the conflict* NEGOTIATE, bring about, effect; *formal* effectuate.

mediation ▶ noun ARBITRATION, conciliation, reconciliation, intervention, intercession, good offices; negotiation, shuttle diplomacy.

mediator ▶ noun ARBITRATOR, arbiter, negotiator, conciliator, peacemaker, go-between, middleman, intermediary, moderator, intervenor, intercessor, broker, honest broker, liaison officer; umpire, referee, adjudicator, judge.

medicinal ▶ adjective CURATIVE, healing, remedial,

Branches of Medicine

Branch	Concern	Branch	Concern
anesthesiology	anaesthetics	nuclear medicine	radioactivity
allopathy	conventional drugs	obstetrics	pregnancy & childbirth
audiology	hearing	odontology	teeth
cardiology	heart	oncology	cancer
chiropody	feet	ophthalmology	eye
cytology	cells	orthopaedics	skeletal system
dentistry	teeth	otology	ear
dermatology	skin	otorhinolaryngology	ear, nose, throat
embryology	embryos	pediatrics	children
endocrinology	glands & hormones	pathology	diseases
epidemiology	disease control	periodontics	gums
etiology	disease causes	pharmacology	drugs
family practice	general medicine	physiotherapy	manipulation, exercise
gastroenterology	stomach/intestines	podiatry	feet
general practice	general medicine	proctology	rectum
geriatrics	the elderly	prosthetics	artificial body parts
gerontology	old age	psychiatry	mental disease
gynecology	women	radiology	radiation
hematology	blood	serology	blood sera
histology	tissues	surgery	incisions
immunology	immune system	symptomatology	symptoms
internal medicine	internal organs	therapeutics	disease treatment
myology	muscles	toxicology	poisons
neurology	nervous system	urology	kidney & urinary tract
nosology	disease classification	veterinary medicine	animals

Forms of Medication

balsam	lotion
cachet	lozenge
caplet	nasal spray
capsule	nebulizer
cream	ointment
drip	pastille
drops	pill
enema	poultice
gargle	powder
hypodermic	rub
inhalant	salve
injectable	suppository
intravenous	tablet
IV	

therapeutic, restorative, corrective, health-giving; medical.

medicine ▶ noun **1** *the practice of medicine. See table.* **2** *take your medicine* MEDICATION, medicament, drug, prescription, pharmaceutical, dose, treatment, remedy, cure; nostrum, panacea, cure-all; *informal* meds; *archaic* physic. *See table.*
− RELATED TERMS: pharmaceutical.

medicine man ▶ noun SHAMAN, healer, (*North*) angakok ♣.

medieval ▶ adjective **1** *medieval times* OF THE MIDDLE AGES, of the Dark Ages, Dark-Age; Gothic. **2** (*informal*) *his attitudes are positively medieval* PRIMITIVE, antiquated, archaic, antique, antediluvian, old-fashioned, out of date, outdated, outmoded, anachronistic, passé, obsolete; *informal* horse-and-buggy.
− OPPOSITES: modern.

mediocre ▶ adjective ORDINARY, average, middling, middle-of-the-road, uninspired, undistinguished, indifferent, unexceptional, unexciting, unremarkable, run-of-the-mill, pedestrian, prosaic, lacklustre, forgettable, amateur, amateurish; *informal* OK, so-so, {comme ci, comme ça}, plain-vanilla, fair-to-middling, no great shakes, not up to much, bush-league.
− OPPOSITES: excellent.

meditate ▶ verb CONTEMPLATE, think, consider, ponder, muse, reflect, deliberate, ruminate, chew the cud, brood, mull over; be in a brown study, be deep/lost in thought, debate with oneself; pray; *informal* put on one's thinking cap; *formal* cogitate.

meditation ▶ noun CONTEMPLATION, thought, thinking, musing, pondering, consideration, reflection, deliberation, rumination, brooding, reverie, brown study, concentration; prayer; *formal* cogitation.

medium ▶ noun **1** *using technology as a medium for job creation* MEANS, method, way, form, agency, avenue, channel, vehicle, organ, instrument, mechanism. **2** *organisms growing in their natural medium* HABITAT, element, environment, surroundings, milieu, setting, conditions. **3** *she consulted a medium* SPIRITUALIST, spiritist, necromancer, channeller; fortune teller, clairvoyant, psychic. **4** *a happy medium* MIDDLE WAY, middle course, middle ground, middle, mean, median, midpoint; compromise, golden mean.
▶ adjective *medium height* AVERAGE, middling, medium-sized, middle-sized, moderate, normal, standard.

medley ▶ noun ASSORTMENT, miscellany, mixture, mélange, variety, mixed bag, grab bag, mix, collection, selection, potpourri, patchwork, bricolage; motley collection, ragbag, gallimaufry, mishmash, jumble, hodgepodge, salmagundi.

meek ▶ adjective SUBMISSIVE, yielding, obedient, compliant, tame, biddable, tractable, acquiescent, deferential, timid, unprotesting, unresisting, like a lamb to the slaughter; quiet, mild, gentle, docile, lamblike, shy, diffident, unassuming, self-effacing.
− OPPOSITES: assertive.

meet ▶ verb **1** *I met an old friend on the train* ENCOUNTER, meet up with, come face to face with, run into, run across, come across/upon, chance on, happen on, stumble across/on; *informal* bump into. **2** *she first met Paul at a party* GET TO KNOW, be introduced to, make the acquaintance of. **3** *the committee met on Saturday* ASSEMBLE, gather, come together, get together, congregate, convene. **4** *the place where three roads meet* CONVERGE, connect, touch, link up, intersect, cross, join. **5** *she met death bravely* FACE, encounter, undergo, experience, go through, suffer, endure, bear; cope with, handle. **6** *the announcement was met with widespread hostility* GREET, receive, answer, treat. **7** *he does not meet the job's requirements* FULFILL, satisfy, fill, measure up to, match (up to), conform to, come up to, comply with, answer. **8** *shipowners would meet the cost of oil spills* PAY, settle, clear, honour, discharge, pay off, square.
▶ noun *a track meet* EVENT, tournament, game, match, contest, competition.
■ **meet someone halfway.** See HALFWAY.

meeting ▶ noun **1** *he stood up to address the meeting* GATHERING, assembly, conference, congregation, convention, summit, forum, convocation, conclave, council, rally, caucus; *informal* get-together. **2** *she demanded a meeting with the minister* CONSULTATION, audience, interview. **3** *he intrigued her on their first meeting* ENCOUNTER, contact; appointment, assignation, rendezvous; *literary* tryst. **4** *the meeting of land and sea* CONVERGENCE, coming together, confluence, conjunction, union, junction, abutment; intersection, T-junction, crossing.

mega ▶ adjective *she signed a mega contract.* See HUGE.

megalomania ▶ noun DELUSIONS OF GRANDEUR, folie de grandeur, thirst/lust for power; self-importance, egotism, conceit, conceitedness.

melancholy ▶ adjective *a melancholy expression* SAD, sorrowful, unhappy, desolate, mournful, lugubrious, gloomy, despondent, dejected, depressed, downhearted, downcast, disconsolate, glum, miserable, wretched, dismal, morose, woeful, woebegone, doleful, joyless, heavy-hearted; *informal* down in the dumps, down in the mouth, blue; *formal* atrabilious.
— OPPOSITES: cheerful.
▶ noun *a feeling of melancholy* SADNESS, sorrow, unhappiness, woe, desolation, melancholia, dejection, depression, despondency, cafard, gloom, gloominess, misery; *informal* the dumps, the blues.

mélange ▶ noun MIXTURE, medley, assortment, blend, variety, mixed bag, grab bag, mix, miscellany, selection, potpourri, patchwork, bricolage; motley collection, ragbag, gallimaufry, hash, mishmash, jumble, hodgepodge.

meld ▶ verb BLEND, merge, combine, fuse, mesh, alloy.

melee ▶ noun FRACAS, disturbance, rumpus, tumult, commotion, ruckus, disorder, fray; brawl, fight, scuffle, struggle, skirmish, scrimmage, free-for-all, tussle; *informal* scrap, set-to, ruction, slugfest.

mellifluous ▶ adjective SWEET-SOUNDING, dulcet, honeyed, mellow, soft, liquid, silvery, soothing, rich, smooth, euphonious, harmonious, tuneful, musical.
— OPPOSITES: cacophonous.

mellow ▶ adjective **1** *a mellow mood* GENIAL, affable, amiable, good-humoured, good-natured, amicable, pleasant, relaxed, easygoing, placid; jovial, jolly, cheerful, happy, merry. **2** *the mellow tone of his voice* DULCET, sweet-sounding, tuneful, melodious,

mellifluous; soft, smooth, warm, full, rich. **3** *a mellow wine* FULL-BODIED, mature, well matured, full-flavoured, rich, smooth.
■ **mellow out** *you need to mellow out* RELAX, unwind, loosen up, de-stress, slow down, take it easy; *informal* chill (out), take a (chill) pill.

melodious ▶ adjective TUNEFUL, melodic, musical, mellifluous, dulcet, sweet-sounding, silvery, harmonious, euphonious, lyrical; *informal* easy on the ear.
— OPPOSITES: discordant.

melodramatic ▶ adjective EXAGGERATED, histrionic, over-dramatic, overdone, operatic, sensationalized, over-emotional, overwrought, sentimental, extravagant; theatrical, stagy, actressy; *informal* hammy.

melody ▶ noun *familiar melodies* TUNE, air, strain, theme, song, refrain, piece of music; *informal* ditty.

melt ▶ verb **1** *the snow was beginning to melt* LIQUEFY, thaw, defrost, soften, dissolve, deliquesce. **2** *his smile melted her heart* SOFTEN, disarm, touch, affect, move. **3** *his anger melted away* VANISH, disappear, fade away, dissolve, evaporate; *literary* evanesce.
▶ noun *spring melt* THAW, breakup ✤, spring breakup ✤.

meltdown ▶ noun (NERVOUS) BREAKDOWN, mental collapse; *informal* freak-out, crack-up, fit, tantrum; disintegration, collapse.

member ▶ noun **1** *a member of the club* SUBSCRIBER, associate, affiliate, life member, card-carrying member. **2** *a member of a mathematical set* CONSTITUENT, element, component, part, portion, piece, unit. **3** (*archaic*) *many victims had injured members* LIMB, organ; arm, leg, appendage.

membrane ▶ noun LAYER, sheet, skin, film, tissue, integument, overlay; *technical* pellicle.

memento ▶ noun SOUVENIR, keepsake, reminder, remembrance, token, memorial bomboniere; trophy, relic.

memo ▶ noun See MEMORANDUM.

memoir ▶ noun **1** *a touching memoir of her childhood* ACCOUNT, history, record, chronicle, narrative, story, portrayal, depiction, sketch, portrait, profile, biography, monograph. **2** *he published his memoirs in 1955* AUTOBIOGRAPHY, life story, memories, recollections, reminiscences; journal, diary.

memorable ▶ adjective UNFORGETTABLE, indelible, catchy, haunting; momentous, significant, historic, notable, noteworthy, important, consequential, remarkable, special, signal, outstanding, extraordinary, striking, vivid, arresting, impressive, distinctive, distinguished, famous, celebrated, renowned, illustrious, glorious.

memorandum ▶ noun MESSAGE, communication, note, email, letter, missive, directive; reminder, aide-mémoire; *informal* memo.

memorial ▶ noun **1** *the war memorial* MONUMENT, cenotaph, mausoleum; statue, plaque, cairn; shrine; tombstone, gravestone, headstone. **2** *the Festschrift is a memorial to his life's work* TRIBUTE, testimonial; remembrance, memento.
▶ adjective *a memorial service* COMMEMORATIVE, remembrance, commemorating.

memorize ▶ verb COMMIT TO MEMORY, remember, learn by heart, get off by heart, learn, learn by rote, become word-perfect in, get something down pat; *archaic* con.

memory ▶ noun **1** *she is losing her memory* ABILITY TO

REMEMBER, powers of recall. **2** *happy memories of her young days* RECOLLECTION, remembrance, reminiscence; impression. **3** *the town built a statue in memory of him* COMMEMORATION, remembrance; honour, tribute, recognition, respect. **4** *a computer's memory* MEMORY BANK, store, cache, disk, RAM, ROM, hard drive.
– RELATED TERMS: mnemonic.

menace ▸ noun **1** *an atmosphere full of menace* THREAT, ominousness, intimidation, warning, ill omen. **2** *a menace to Canadian society* DANGER, peril, risk, hazard, threat; jeopardy. **3** *that dog is a menace* NUISANCE, pest, annoyance, plague, torment, terror, troublemaker, mischief-maker, thorn in someone's side/flesh.
▸ verb **1** *gorillas are still menaced by poaching* THREATEN, be a danger to, put at risk, jeopardize, imperil. **2** *a gang of skinheads menaced local residents* INTIMIDATE, threaten, terrorize, frighten, scare, terrify.

menacing ▸ adjective THREATENING, ominous, intimidating, frightening, terrifying, alarming, forbidding, black, thunderous, glowering, unfriendly, hostile, sinister, baleful, warning; *formal* minatory.
– OPPOSITES: friendly.

mend ▸ verb **1** *workmen were mending faulty cabling* REPAIR, fix, put back together, piece together, restore; sew (up), stitch, darn, patch, cobble; rehabilitate, renew, renovate; *informal* patch up. **2** *they mended their quarrel* PUT/SET RIGHT, set straight, straighten out, sort out, rectify, remedy, cure, right, resolve, square, settle, put to rights, correct, retrieve, improve, make better.
– OPPOSITES: break, worsen.

mendacious ▸ adjective LYING, untruthful, dishonest, deceitful, false, dissembling, insincere, disingenuous, hypocritical, fraudulent, double-dealing, two-faced, two-timing, duplicitous, perjured; untrue, fictitious, falsified, fabricated, fallacious, invented, made up; *informal* full of crap; *literary* perfidious.
– OPPOSITES: truthful.

mendicant ▸ noun See BEGGAR noun sense 1.

menial ▸ adjective *a menial job* UNSKILLED, lowly, humble, low-status, inferior, degrading; routine, humdrum, boring, dull.
▸ noun *they were treated like menials* SERVANT, drudge, minion, joe-boy, factotum, lackey, hired hand; *informal* wage slave, gofer, peon, grunt; *archaic* scullion.

menstruation ▸ noun PERIOD, menses, menorrhoea, menstrual cycle; menarche; *informal* the curse, monthlies, one's/the time of the month.

mental ▸ adjective **1** *mental faculties* INTELLECTUAL, cerebral, brain, rational, cognitive. **2** *a mental disorder* PSYCHIATRIC, psychological, psychogenic. **3** (*informal*) *he's completely mental. See* MAD sense 1.
– OPPOSITES: physical.

mentality ▸ noun **1** *I can't understand the mentality of these people* WAY OF THINKING, mind set, cast of mind, frame of mind, turn of mind, mind, psychology, mental attitude, outlook, disposition, makeup. **2** *a person of limited mentality* INTELLECT, intellectual capabilities, intelligence, IQ, (powers of) reasoning, rationality; *informal* brains, smarts.

mentally ▸ adverb IN ONE'S MIND, in one's head, inwardly, intellectually, cognitively.

mention ▸ verb **1** *don't mention the war* ALLUDE TO, refer to, touch on/upon; bring up, raise, broach, introduce, moot. **2** *Jim mentioned that he'd met them*

before STATE, say, indicate, let someone know, disclose, divulge, reveal. **3** *I'll gladly mention your work to my friends* RECOMMEND, commend, put in a good word for, speak well of.
▸ noun **1** *he made no mention of your request* REFERENCE, allusion, remark, statement, announcement, indication. **2** *my book got a mention on the show* RECOMMENDATION, commendation, a good word.
■ **don't mention it** DON'T APOLOGIZE, it doesn't matter, it makes no difference, it's not important, never mind, don't worry.
■ **not to mention** IN ADDITION TO, as well as; not counting, not including, to say nothing of, aside from, besides.

mentor ▸ noun **1** *his political mentors* ADVISER, guide, guru, counsellor, consultant; confidant(e). **2** *regular meetings between mentor and trainee* TRAINER, teacher, tutor, instructor.

menu ▸ noun **1** *she studied the menu before ordering* BILL OF FARE, set menu, table d'hôte. **2** *a drop-down menu* LIST OF COMMANDS, options, toolbar.

meow ▸ verb MEW, mewl, cry.

mephitic ▸ adjective (*literary*). See MALODOROUS.

mercantile ▸ adjective COMMERCIAL, trade, trading, business, merchant, sales.

mercenary ▸ adjective **1** *mercenary self-interest* MONEY-ORIENTED, grasping, greedy, acquisitive, avaricious, covetous, bribable, venal, materialistic; *informal* money-grubbing. **2** *mercenary soldiers* HIRED, paid, bought, professional.
▸ noun *a group of mercenaries* SOLDIER OF FORTUNE, professional soldier, hired soldier, gunman; *informal* hired gun; *historical* condottiere.

merchandise ▸ noun *a wide range of merchandise* GOODS, wares, stock, commodities, lines, produce, products.
▸ verb *a new product that can be easily merchandised* PROMOTE, market, sell, retail; advertise, publicize, push; *informal* plug.

merchant ▸ noun TRADER, dealer, wholesaler, broker, agent, seller, buyer, buyer and seller, vendor, distributor, peddler, retailer, shopkeeper, storekeeper.

merciful ▸ adjective **1** *God is merciful* FORGIVING, compassionate, clement, pitying, forbearing, lenient, humane, mild, kind, soft-hearted, tender-hearted, gracious, sympathetic, humanitarian, liberal, tolerant, indulgent, generous, magnanimous, benign, benevolent. **2** *a merciful silence fell* WELCOME, blessed.
– OPPOSITES: cruel.
■ **be merciful to** HAVE MERCY ON, have pity on, show mercy to, spare, pardon, forgive, be lenient to; *informal* go/be easy on, let off.

mercifully ▸ adverb LUCKILY, fortunately, happily, thank goodness/God/heavens.

merciless ▸ adjective RUTHLESS, remorseless, pitiless, unforgiving, unsparing, implacable, inexorable, relentless, unremitting, inflexible, inhumane, inhuman, unsympathetic, unfeeling, intolerant, rigid, severe, cold-blooded, hard-hearted, stony-hearted, heartless, harsh, callous, cruel, brutal, barbarous, cutthroat.
– OPPOSITES: compassionate.

mercurial ▸ adjective VOLATILE, capricious, temperamental, excitable, fickle, changeable, unpredictable, variable, protean, mutable, erratic, quicksilver, inconstant, inconsistent, unstable,

unsteady, fluctuating, ever-changing, moody, flighty, wayward, whimsical, impulsive; *technical* labile.
− OPPOSITES: stable.

mercy ► noun **1** *he showed no mercy to the others* LENIENCY, clemency, compassion, grace, pity, charity, forgiveness, forbearance, quarter, humanity; soft-heartedness, tender-heartedness, kindness, sympathy, liberality, indulgence, tolerance, generosity, magnanimity, beneficence. **2** *we must be thankful for small mercies* BLESSING, godsend, boon, favour, piece/stroke of luck, windfall.
− OPPOSITES: ruthlessness, cruelty.
■ **at the mercy of 1** *they found themselves at the mercy of the tyrant* IN THE POWER OF, under/in the control of, in the clutches of, subject to. **2** *he was at the mercy of the elements* DEFENCELESS AGAINST, vulnerable to, exposed to, susceptible to, prey to, (wide) open to.

mere ► adjective NO MORE THAN, just, only, merely; no better than; paltry, measly, insignificant, ordinary, minor, little, piddling, piffling.

merely ► adverb ONLY, purely, solely, simply, just, but.

meretricious ► adjective WORTHLESS, valueless, cheap, tawdry, trashy, Brummagem, tasteless, kitsch, (Que.) kétaine ♣; false, artificial, fake, imitation; *informal* tacky, chintzy.

merge ► verb **1** *the company merged with a U.S. firm* JOIN (TOGETHER), join forces, amalgamate, unite, affiliate, team up, link (up). **2** *the two organizations were merged* AMALGAMATE, bring together, join, consolidate, conflate, unite, unify, combine, incorporate, integrate, link (up), knit, yoke. **3** *the two colours merged* MINGLE, blend, fuse, mix, intermix, intermingle, coalesce; *literary* commingle.
− OPPOSITES: separate.

merger ► noun AMALGAMATION, combination, union, fusion, coalition, affiliation, unification, incorporation, consolidation, link-up, alliance.
− OPPOSITES: split.

merit ► noun **1** *composers of outstanding merit* EXCELLENCE, quality, calibre, worth, worthiness, credit, value, distinction, eminence. **2** *the merits of the scheme* GOOD POINT, strong point, advantage, benefit, value, asset, plus.
− OPPOSITES: inferiority, fault, disadvantage.
► verb *the accusation did not merit a response* DESERVE, earn, be deserving of, warrant, rate, justify, be worthy of, be worth, be entitled to, have a right to, have a claim to/on.

meritorious ► adjective PRAISEWORTHY, laudable, commendable, admirable, estimable, creditable, worthy, deserving, excellent, exemplary, good.
− OPPOSITES: discreditable.

merriment ► noun HIGH SPIRITS, high-spiritedness, exuberance, cheerfulness, gaiety, fun, effervescence, verve, buoyancy, levity, zest, liveliness, cheer, joy, joyfulness, joyousness, jolliness, jollity, happiness, gladness, jocularity, conviviality, festivity, merrymaking, revelry, mirth, glee, gleefulness, laughter, hilarity, light-heartedness, amusement, pleasure.
− OPPOSITES: misery.

merry ► adjective *merry throngs of students* CHEERFUL, cheery, in high spirits, high-spirited, bright, sunny, smiling, light-hearted, buoyant, lively, carefree, without a care in the world, joyful, joyous, jolly, convivial, festive, mirthful, gleeful, happy, glad, laughing; *informal* chirpy; *formal* jocund; *dated* gay; *literary* blithe.
− OPPOSITES: miserable.
■ **make merry** HAVE FUN, have a good time, enjoy oneself, have a party, celebrate, carouse, feast, {eat, drink, and be merry}, revel, roister; *informal* party, have a ball.

mesh ► noun *wire mesh* NETTING, net, network; web, webbing, lattice, latticework.
► verb **1** *the gear meshes with the other* ENGAGE, connect, lock, interlock. **2** *our ideas just do not mesh* HARMONIZE, fit together, match, dovetail.

mesmerize ► verb ENTHRALL, hold spellbound, entrance, dazzle, clutter, shambles, jumble, captivate, enchant, fascinate, transfix, grip, hypnotize.

mess ► noun **1** *please clear up the mess* UNTIDINESS, disorder, disarray, clutter, shambles, jumble, muddle, chaos. **2** *don't step in the dog mess* EXCREMENT, muck, feces, excreta. **3** *I've got to get out of this mess* PLIGHT, predicament, tight spot/corner, difficulty, trouble, quandary, dilemma, problem, muddle, mix-up, imbroglio; *informal* jam, fix, pickle, stew, scrape. **4** *he made a mess of the project* MUDDLE, bungle; *informal* botch, hash, foul-up, snafu.
■ **make a mess of** MISMANAGE, mishandle, bungle, fluff, spoil, ruin, wreck; *informal* mess up, botch, make a hash of, muck up, foul up.
■ **mess about/around** PUTTER ABOUT, pass the time, fiddle about/around, play about/around, fool about/around; fidget, toy, trifle, tamper, tinker, interfere, meddle, monkey (about/around); *informal* piddle about/around, muck about/around.
■ **mess something up 1** *he messed up my kitchen* DIRTY; clutter up, disarrange, jumble, dishevel, rumple; *informal* muss up; *literary* befoul. **2** (*informal*) *Eddie messed things up. See* MAKE A MESS OF.

message ► noun **1** *are there any messages for me?* COMMUNICATION, piece of information, news, note, memorandum, memo, email, letter, missive, report, bulletin, communiqué, dispatch. **2** *the message of his teaching* MEANING, sense, import, idea; point, thrust, gist, essence, content, subject (matter), substance, implication, drift, lesson.
■ **get the message** (*informal*) UNDERSTAND, get the point, comprehend; *informal* catch on, get the picture.

messenger ► noun MESSAGE-BEARER, courier, runner, envoy, emissary, agent, go-between; postman, letter carrier, mailman, postie; *historical* herald; *archaic* legate.

messy ► adjective **1** *messy oil spills* | *messy hair* DIRTY, filthy, grubby, soiled, grimy; mucky, muddy, slimy, sticky, sullied, spotted, stained, smeared, smudged; dishevelled, scruffy, unkempt, rumpled, matted, tousled, bedraggled, tangled; *informal* yucky, grungy. **2** *a messy kitchen* DISORDERLY, disordered, in a muddle, chaotic, confused, disorganized, in disarray, disarranged; untidy, cluttered, in a jumble; *informal* like a bomb's hit it, shambolic. **3** *a messy legal battle* COMPLEX, intricate, tangled, confused, convoluted; unpleasant, nasty, bitter, acrimonious.
− OPPOSITES: clean, tidy.

metal ► noun. *See table.*

metallic ► adjective **1** *a metallic sound* TINNY, jangling, jingling; grating, harsh, jarring, dissonant. **2** *metallic paint* METALLIZED, burnished; shiny, glossy, lustrous.

metamorphosis ► noun TRANSFORMATION, mutation, transmutation, change, alteration,

Metals

Elements	Alloys
aluminum	brass
chromium	bronze
copper	cast iron
gold	chrome steel
iron	pewter
lead	stainless steel
mercury	steel
nickel	white gold
platinum	
silver	
tin	
titanium	
tungsten	
uranium	
zinc	

conversion, modification, remodelling, reconstruction; *humorous* transmogrification; *formal* transubstantiation.

metaphor ▶ noun FIGURE OF SPEECH, image, trope, analogy, comparison, symbol, word painting/picture.

metaphorical ▶ adjective FIGURATIVE, allegorical, symbolic; imaginative, extended.
— OPPOSITES: literal.

metaphysical ▶ adjective **1** *metaphysical questions* ABSTRACT, theoretical, conceptual, notional, philosophical, speculative, intellectual, academic. **2** *Good and Evil are inextricably linked in a metaphysical battle* TRANSCENDENTAL, spiritual, supernatural, paranormal.

mete
■ **mete something out** DISPENSE, hand out, allocate, allot, apportion, issue, deal out, dole out, dish out, assign, administer.

meteor ▶ noun FALLING STAR, shooting star, meteorite, meteoroid, bolide. *See table.*

Meteor Showers

Approx. peak date	Meteor Shower
January 3	Quadrantids
April 22	April Lyrids
May 5	Eta Aquariids
June 16	June Lyrids
July 29	Delta Aquariids
August 12	Perseids
October 22	Orionids
November 4	Taurids
November 17	Leonids
December 14	Geminids
December 23	Ursids

meteoric ▶ adjective RAPID, lightning, swift, fast, quick, speedy, accelerated, instant, sudden, spectacular, dazzling, brilliant.
— OPPOSITES: gradual.

meteorologist ▶ noun WEATHER FORECASTER, weatherman, weatherwoman.

method ▶ noun **1** *they use very old-fashioned methods* PROCEDURE, technique, system, practice, routine, modus operandi, process; strategy, tactic, plan. **2** *there's a method to his madness* ORDER, orderliness, organization, structure, form, system, logic, planning, design, sense.
— OPPOSITES: disorder.

methodical ▶ adjective ORDERLY, well-ordered, well-organized, (well) planned, efficient, businesslike, systematic, structured, logical, analytic, disciplined; meticulous, punctilious.

meticulous ▶ adjective CAREFUL, conscientious, diligent, scrupulous, punctilious, painstaking, accurate; thorough, studious, rigorous, detailed, perfectionist, fastidious, methodical, particular.
— OPPOSITES: careless.

métier ▶ noun **1** *he had another métier besides teaching* OCCUPATION, job, work, profession, business, employment, career, vocation, trade, craft, line (of work), specialty. **2** *improvisation is more my métier* FORTE, strong point, strength, specialty, talent, bent; *informal* thing, cup of tea.

metropolis ▶ noun CAPITAL (CITY), chief town, county town; big city, conurbation, megalopolis, megacity; *informal* big smoke.

mettle ▶ noun **1** *a man of mettle* SPIRIT, fortitude, strength of character, moral fibre, steel, determination, resolve, resolution, backbone, grit, true grit, courage, courageousness, bravery, valour, fearlessness, daring; *informal* guts, spunk, balls. **2** *Frazer was of a very different mettle* CALIBRE, character, disposition, nature, temperament, personality, makeup, stamp.

mew ▶ verb *the cat mewed plaintively* MEOW, mewl, cry.

mewl ▶ verb WHIMPER, cry, whine; *literary* pule.

miasma ▶ noun (*literary*) STINK, reek, stench, fetor, smell, fume, odour, whiff; gas, cloud, smog, vapour.

miasmic, miasmal ▶ adjective (*literary*) FOUL-SMELLING, fetid, smelly, stinking (to high heaven), reeking, rank, putrid, noxious, malodorous; *literary* noisome, mephitic.

microbe ▶ noun MICRO-ORGANISM, bacillus, bacterium, virus, germ; *informal* bug.

microscopic ▶ adjective TINY, very small, minute, infinitesimal, minuscule; little, micro, diminutive; *informal* teeny, weeny, teeny-weeny, teensy-weensy, itsy-bitsy, little-bitty; *Scottish* wee.
— OPPOSITES: huge.

midday ▶ noun NOON, twelve noon, high noon, noontide, noonday.
— OPPOSITES: midnight.

middle ▶ noun **1** *a shallow dish with a spike in the middle* CENTRE, midpoint, halfway point, dead centre, focus, hub; eye, heart, core, kernel. **2** *he had a towel round his middle* MIDRIFF, waist, belly, stomach, abdomen; *informal* tummy, tum, gut.
— OPPOSITES: outside.
▶ adjective **1** *the middle point* CENTRAL, mid, mean, medium, medial, median, midway, halfway. **2** *the middle level* INTERMEDIATE, intermediary.
— RELATED TERMS: meso-.

middle-class ▶ adjective BOURGEOIS, conventional, mainstream, plain-vanilla; suburban, white-picket-fence, Waspish, WASP, yuppie.

middleman ▶ noun INTERMEDIARY, intercessor, go-between, liaison, mediator; dealer, broker, agent, factor, wholesaler, distributor.

middling ▶ adjective AVERAGE, standard, normal, middle-of-the-road; moderate, ordinary, commonplace, everyday, workaday, tolerable, passable; run-of-the-mill, fair, mediocre, undistinguished, unexceptional, unremarkable; *informal* OK, so-so, {comme ci, comme ça}, fair-to-middling, plain-vanilla.

midget ▶ noun *the inhabitants must have been midgets*

SMALL PERSON, dwarf, homunculus, Lilliputian, gnome, pygmy; *informal* shrimp.
▶ **adjective 1** *a story about midget matadors* DIMINUTIVE, dwarfish, petite, very small, pygmy, baby; *informal* pint-sized, peewee. **2** *a midget camera* MINIATURE, pocket, dwarf, baby, mini.
– OPPOSITES: giant.

midnight ▶ **noun** TWELVE MIDNIGHT, the middle of the night, the witching hour.
– OPPOSITES: midday.

midpoint ▶ **noun** CENTRE (POINT), middle, halfway point, midway point.

midriff ▶ **noun** STOMACH, belly, midsection, waist, middle, abdomen, tummy.

midst (*literary*) ▶ **noun** MIDDLE, centre, heart, core, midpoint, kernel, nub; depth(s), thick; (**in the midst of**) in the course of, halfway through, at the heart/core of.
■ **in our midst** AMONG US, in our group, with us.

midway ▶ **adverb** HALFWAY, in the middle, at the midpoint, in the centre; part-way, at some point.
▶ **noun** *we rode all the rides at the midway* FAIR, carnival, fun fair, exhibition.

mien ▶ **noun** APPEARANCE, look, expression, countenance, aura, demeanour, attitude, air, manner, bearing; *formal* comportment.

miffed ▶ **adjective** (*informal*). *See* ANNOYED.

might ▶ **noun** STRENGTH, force, power, vigour, energy, brawn, powerfulness, forcefulness.

mightily ▶ **adverb 1** *she is mightily pleased with herself* EXTREMELY, exceedingly, enormously, immensely, tremendously, hugely, dreadfully, very (much); *informal* awfully, majorly, mega, mighty, plumb. **2** *Ann and I laboured mightily* STRENUOUSLY, energetically, powerfully, hard, with all one's might, with might and main, all out, heartily, vigorously, diligently, assiduously, persistently, indefatigably; *informal* like mad, like crazy.

mighty ▶ **adjective 1** *a mighty blow* POWERFUL, forceful, violent, vigorous, hefty, thunderous. **2** *a mighty warrior* FEARSOME, ferocious; big, tough, robust, muscular, strapping. **3** *mighty industrial countries* DOMINANT, influential, strong, powerful, important, predominant. **4** *mighty oak trees* HUGE, enormous, massive, gigantic, big, large, giant, colossal, mammoth, immense; *informal* monster, whopping (great), humongous, jumbo(-sized), ginormous.
– OPPOSITES: feeble, puny, tiny.
▶ **adverb** (*informal*) *I'm mighty pleased to see you* EXTREMELY, exceedingly, enormously, immensely, tremendously, hugely, mightily, very (much); *informal* awfully, dreadfully, majorly, mega, plumb, right; *informal, dated* frightfully.

migrant ▶ **noun** *economic migrants* IMMIGRANT, EMIGRANT; nomad, itinerant, traveller, vagrant, transient, rover, wanderer, drifter.
▶ **adjective** *migrant workers* TRAVELLING, wandering, drifting, nomadic, roving, roaming, itinerant, vagrant, transient.

migrate ▶ **verb 1** *rural populations migrated to urban areas* RELOCATE, resettle, move (house), go down the road ✦; immigrate; emigrate, go abroad, go overseas, pull up stakes; *dated* remove. **2** *wildebeest migrate across the Serengeti* ROAM, wander, drift, rove, travel (around).

migratory ▶ **adjective** MIGRANT, migrating, moving, travelling.

mild ▶ **adjective 1** *a mild tone of voice* GENTLE, tender,

soft-hearted, tender-hearted, sensitive, sympathetic, warm, placid, calm, tranquil, serene, peaceable, good-natured, mild-mannered, amiable, affable, genial, easygoing. **2** *a mild punishment* LENIENT, light; compassionate, merciful, humane. **3** *he was eyeing her with mild interest* SLIGHT, faint, vague, minimal, nominal, moderate, token, feeble. **4** *mild weather* WARM, balmy, temperate, clement. **5** *a mild curry* BLAND, insipid, tame.
– OPPOSITES: harsh, strong, severe.

mildew ▶ **noun** *See* MOULD[2].

milestone ▶ **noun** LANDMARK, significant event, achievement, highlight, watershed, benchmark, touchstone.

milieu ▶ **noun** ENVIRONMENT, sphere, background, backdrop, setting, context, atmosphere; location, conditions, surroundings, environs; *informal* stomping grounds, turf.

militant ▶ **adjective** *militant supporters* AGGRESSIVE, violent, belligerent, bellicose, vigorous, forceful, active, fierce, combative, pugnacious; radical, extremist, extreme, zealous, fanatical.
▶ **noun** *the demands of the militants* ACTIVIST, extremist, radical, young turk, zealot.

militaristic ▶ **adjective** WARMONGERING, warlike, martial, hawkish, pugnacious, combative, aggressive, belligerent, bellicose.
– OPPOSITES: peaceable.

military ▶ **adjective** *military activity* FIGHTING, service, army, armed, defence, martial.
– OPPOSITES: civilian.
▶ **noun** *the military took power* (ARMED) FORCES, services, militia; army, navy, air force, marines. *For Canadian military ranks see table at* RANK.

militate ▶ **verb** TEND TO PREVENT, work against, hinder, discourage, prejudice, be detrimental to.

milk ▶ **verb 1** *Pam was milking the cows* DRAW MILK FROM, express milk from. **2** *milk a little of the liquid* DRAW OFF, siphon (off), pump off, tap, drain, extract. **3** *milking rich clients* EXPLOIT, take advantage of, cash in on, suck dry; *informal* bleed, squeeze, fleece.
– RELATED TERMS: dairy, lactic.
▶ **noun** MOO JUICE; skim, two per cent, homo.

milksop ▶ **noun** *See* MAMA'S BOY.

milky ▶ **adjective** PALE, white, milk-white, whitish, off-white, cream, creamy, chalky, pearly, nacreous, ivory, alabaster; cloudy, frosted, opaque.
– OPPOSITES: swarthy.

mill ▶ **noun 1** *a steel mill* FACTORY, (processing) plant, works, workshop, shop, foundry. **2** *a pepper mill* GRINDER, quern, crusher.
▶ **verb** *the wheat is milled into flour* GRIND, pulverize, powder, granulate, pound, crush, press; *technical* comminute, triturate.
■ **mill around/about** THRONG, swarm, crowd.

millstone ▶ **noun** BURDEN, encumbrance, dead weight, cross to bear, albatross, load; duty, responsibility, obligation, liability, misfortune.

mime ▶ **noun** *a mime of someone fencing* PANTOMIME, charade, dumb show.
▶ **verb** *she mimed picking up a phone* ACT OUT, pantomime, gesture, simulate, represent, indicate by dumb show.

mimic ▶ **verb 1** *she mimicked his accent* IMITATE, copy, impersonate, do an impression of, ape, caricature, parody, lampoon, burlesque, parrot; *informal* send up, take off, spoof. **2** *most hoverflies mimic wasps* RESEMBLE, look like, have the appearance of, simulate; *informal* make like.

▶ **noun** *he was a superb mimic* IMPERSONATOR, impressionist, imitator, parodist, caricaturist, lampooner, lampoonist; *informal* copycat; *archaic* ape.

mimicry ▶ **noun** IMITATION, imitating, impersonation, copying, aping.

mince ▶ **verb 1** *mince the meat and onions* GRIND, chop up, cut up, dice, hash, chop fine. **2** *she minced out of the room* WALK AFFECTEDLY; *informal* sashay, flounce, strut.

■ **not mince (one's) words** TALK STRAIGHT, not beat around the bush, call a spade a spade, speak straight from the heart, pull no punches, not put too fine a point on it, tell it like it is, talk turkey.

mincing ▶ **adjective** AFFECTED, dainty, effeminate, pretentious, dandified, foppish; *informal* camp.

mind ▶ **noun 1** *expand your mind* BRAIN, intelligence, intellect, intellectual capabilities, brains, brainpower, wits, understanding, reasoning, judgment, sense, head; *informal* grey matter, brain cells, smarts. **2** *he kept his mind on the job* ATTENTION, thoughts, concentration, attentiveness. **3** *the tragedy affected her mind* SANITY, mental faculties, senses, wits, reason, reasoning, judgment; *informal* marbles. **4** *Justin's words stuck in her mind* MEMORY, recollection. **5** *the country's great minds* INTELLECT, thinker, brain, scholar, academic. **6** *I've a mind to complain* INCLINATION, desire, wish, urge, notion, fancy, intention, will. **7** *we're of the same mind* OPINION, way of thinking, outlook, attitude, view, viewpoint, point of view.

– RELATED TERMS: mental.

▶ **verb 1** *do you mind if I smoke?* CARE, object, be bothered, be annoyed, be upset, take offence, disapprove, dislike it, look askance; *informal* give a damn, give/care a hoot. **2** *mind the step!* BE CAREFUL OF, watch out for, look out for, beware of, be on one's guard for, be wary of. **3** *mind you wipe your feet* BE/MAKE SURE (THAT), see (that); remember to, don't forget to. **4** *her husband was minding the baby* LOOK AFTER, take care of, keep an eye on, attend to, care for, tend, babysit. **5** *mind what your mother says* PAY ATTENTION TO, heed, pay heed to, attend to, take note/notice of, note, mark, listen to, be mindful of; obey, follow, comply with.

■ **be of two minds** BE UNDECIDED, be uncertain, be unsure, hesitate, waver, vacillate, hem and haw, hum and haw; *informal* dilly-dally, shilly-shally.

■ **bear/keep in mind** REMEMBER, note, be mindful of, take note of; *formal* take cognizance of.

■ **cross one's mind** OCCUR TO ONE, enter one's mind/head, strike one, hit one, dawn on one.

■ **give someone a piece of one's mind**. *See* REPRIMAND *verb.*

■ **have something in mind** THINK OF, contemplate; intend, plan, propose, desire, want, wish.

■ **never mind 1** *never mind the cost* DON'T BOTHER ABOUT, don't worry about, disregard, forget. **2** *never mind, it's all right now* DON'T APOLOGIZE, forget it, don't worry about it, it doesn't matter.

■ **out of one's mind 1** *you must be out of your mind! See* MAD sense 1. **2** *I've been out of my mind with worry* FRANTIC, beside oneself, distraught, in a frenzy.

■ **put someone in mind of** REMIND OF, recall, conjure up, suggest; RESEMBLE, look like.

■ **to my mind** IN MY OPINION, in my view, as I see it, personally, in my estimation, in my book, if you ask me.

mindful ▶ **adjective** AWARE, conscious, sensible, alive, alert, acquainted, heedful, wary, chary; *informal* wise, hip; *formal* cognizant, regardful.

– OPPOSITES: heedless.

mindless ▶ **adjective 1** *a mindless idiot* STUPID, idiotic, brainless, imbecilic, imbecile, asinine, witless, foolish, empty-headed, slow-witted, stunned ♣, obtuse, feather-brained, doltish; *informal* dumb, pig-ignorant, brain-dead, cretinous, moronic, thick, birdbrained, pea-brained, dopey, dim, halfwitted, dippy, fat-headed, boneheaded, chowderheaded. **2** *mindless acts of vandalism* UNTHINKING, thoughtless, senseless, gratuitous, wanton, indiscriminate, unreasoning. **3** *a mindless task* MECHANICAL, automatic, routine; tedious, boring, monotonous, brainless, mind-numbing.

■ **mindless of** INDIFFERENT TO, heedless of, unaware of, unmindful of, careless of, blind to.

mine ▶ **noun 1** *a coal mine* PIT, excavation, quarry, workings, diggings; strip mine, open-pit mine, placer (mine), hardrock mine. **2** *a mine of information* RICH SOURCE, repository, store, storehouse, reservoir, gold mine, treasure house, treasury, reserve, fund, wealth, stock. **3** *he was killed by a mine* EXPLOSIVE, land mine, limpet mine, magnetic mine, depth charge.

▶ **verb 1** *the iron ore was mined from shallow pits* QUARRY, excavate, dig (up), extract, remove; strip-mine, pan. **2** *medical data was mined for relevant statistics* SEARCH, delve into, scour, scan, read through, survey. **3** *the entrance to the harbour had been mined* DEFEND WITH MINES, lay with mines.

miner ▶ **noun** DIGGER, collier, gold panner; *dated* sourdough.

mingle ▶ **verb 1** *fact and fiction are skilfully mingled in his novels* MIX, blend, intermingle, intermix, interweave, interlace, combine, merge, fuse, unite, join, amalgamate, meld, mesh; *literary* commingle. **2** *wedding guests mingled in the marquee* SOCIALIZE, circulate, fraternize, get together, associate with others; *informal* hobnob, rub elbows.

– OPPOSITES: separate.

miniature ▶ **adjective** *a miniature railway* SMALL-SCALE, mini; tiny, little, small, minute, baby, toy, pocket, dwarf, pygmy, minuscule, diminutive, vest-pocket; *informal* teeny, teeny-weeny, teensy, teensy-weensy, itsy-bitsy, eensy, eensy-weensy; *Scottish* wee.

– OPPOSITES: giant.

minimal ▶ **adjective** VERY LITTLE, minimum, the least (possible); nominal, token, negligible.

– OPPOSITES: maximum.

minimize ▶ **verb 1** *the aim is to minimize costs* KEEP DOWN, keep at/to a minimum, reduce, decrease, cut down, lessen, curtail, diminish, prune; *informal* slash. **2** *we should not minimize his contribution* BELITTLE, make light of, play down, underestimate, underrate, downplay, undervalue, understate; *informal* pooh-pooh; *archaic* hold cheap.

– OPPOSITES: maximize, exaggerate.

minimum ▶ **noun** *costs will be kept to the minimum* LOWEST LEVEL, lower limit, bottom level, rock bottom, nadir; least, lowest, slightest.

– OPPOSITES: maximum.

▶ **adjective** *the minimum amount of effort* MINIMAL, least, smallest, least possible, slightest, lowest, minutest.

minion ▶ **noun** UNDERLING, henchman, flunky, lackey, hanger-on, follower, servant, hireling, vassal, stooge, toady, sycophant; *informal* yes-man, trained seal, bootlicker, brown-noser, browner ♣, suck-up.

minister ▶ noun **1** *a government minister* MEMBER OF THE GOVERNMENT, cabinet minister, secretary of state, undersecretary. **2** *a minister of religion* CLERGYMAN, clergywoman, cleric, ecclesiastic, pastor, vicar, rector, priest, parson, deacon, father, man/woman of the cloth, man/woman of God, churchman, churchwoman; curate, chaplain; *informal* reverend, padre, Holy Joe, sky pilot. **3** *the Canadian minister in Egypt* AMBASSADOR, chargé d'affaires, plenipotentiary, envoy, emissary, diplomat, consul, representative; *archaic* legate.
▶ verb *doctors were ministering to the injured* TEND, care for, take care of, look after, nurse, treat, attend to, see to, administer to, help, assist.

ministrations ▶ plural noun ATTENTION, treatment, help, assistance, aid, care, services; *informal* TLC.

ministry ▶ noun **1** *the ministry for foreign affairs* (GOVERNMENT) DEPARTMENT, bureau, agency, office. **2** *he's training for the ministry* HOLY ORDERS, the priesthood, the cloth, the church. **3** *the ministry of Jesus* TEACHING, preaching, evangelism.

minor ▶ adjective **1** *a minor problem* SLIGHT, small; unimportant, insignificant, inconsequential, inconsiderable, subsidiary, negligible, trivial, trifling, paltry, petty, nickel-and-dime; *informal* piffling, piddling. **2** *a minor poet* LITTLE KNOWN, unknown, lesser, unimportant, insignificant, obscure, minor-league; *informal* small-time, two-bit.
— OPPOSITES: major, important.
▶ noun *the heir to the throne was a minor* CHILD, infant, youth, adolescent, teenager, boy, girl; *informal* kid, kiddie.
— OPPOSITES: adult.

minstrel ▶ noun *(historical)* MUSICIAN, singer, balladeer, poet; *historical* troubadour, jongleur; *literary* bard.

mint ▶ noun *(informal) the bank made a mint out of the deal* A VAST SUM OF MONEY, a king's ransom, millions, billions; *informal* a (small) fortune, a tidy sum, a bundle, a pile, big money, big bucks, megabucks.
▶ adjective *in mint condition* BRAND NEW, pristine, perfect, immaculate, unblemished, undamaged, unmarked, unused, first-class, excellent.
▶ verb **1** *the shilling was minted in 1742* COIN, stamp, strike, cast, forge, manufacture. **2** *the slogan had been freshly minted* CREATE, invent, make up, think up, dream up, coin.

minuscule ▶ adjective TINY, minute, microscopic, very small, little, micro, diminutive, miniature, baby, dwarf, Lilliputian; *informal* teeny, teeny-weeny, teensy, teensy-weensy, itsy-bitsy, eensy, eensy-weensy; *Scottish* wee.
— OPPOSITES: huge.

minute[1] ▶ noun **1** *it'll only take a minute* MOMENT, short time, little while, second, instant; *informal* sec, jiffy, flash. **2** *at that minute, Tony walked in* POINT (IN TIME), moment, instant, juncture. **3** *their objection was noted in the minutes* RECORD(S), proceedings, log, notes; transcript, summary, resumé.
■ **in a minute** VERY SOON, in a moment/second/instant, in a trice, shortly, any minute (now), in a short time, in (less than) no time, before long, momentarily; *informal* anon, in a jiffy, in two shakes, in a snap; *literary* ere long.
■ **this minute** AT ONCE, immediately, directly, this second, instantly, straight away, right away/now, forthwith; *informal* pronto, straight off, right off, tout de suite.
■ **up-to-the-minute** LATEST, newest, up-to-date, modern, fashionable, smart, chic, stylish, all the

rage, in vogue, hip; *informal* trendy, with it, in, styling, phat.
■ **wait a minute** BE PATIENT, wait a moment/second, just a moment/minute/second, hold on; *informal* hang on, hold your horses.

minute[2] ▶ adjective **1** *minute particles. See* MINUSCULE. **2** *a minute chance of success* NEGLIGIBLE, slight, infinitesimal, minimal, insignificant, inappreciable. **3** *minute detail* EXHAUSTIVE, painstaking, meticulous, rigorous, scrupulous, punctilious, detailed, precise, accurate.
— OPPOSITES: huge.

minutiae ▶ plural noun DETAILS, niceties, finer points, particulars, trivia, trivialities.

miracle ▶ noun WONDER, marvel, sensation, (supernatural) phenomenon, mystery.

miraculous ▶ adjective **1** *the miraculous help of St. Blaise* SUPERNATURAL, preternatural, inexplicable, unaccountable, magical. **2** *a miraculous escape* AMAZING, astounding, remarkable, extraordinary, incredible, unbelievable, sensational, marvellous, phenomenal; *informal* mind-boggling, mind-blowing, out of this world.

mirage ▶ noun OPTICAL ILLUSION, hallucination, phantasmagoria, apparition, fantasy, chimera, vision, figment of the imagination; *literary* phantasm.

mire ▶ noun **1** *it's a mire out there* SWAMP, bog, morass, quagmire, slough; swampland, wetland, marshland. **2** *they were stuck in the mire* MUD, slime, dirt, filth, muck. **3** *struggling to pull Russia out of the mire* MESS, difficulty, plight, predicament, tight spot, trouble, quandary, muddle; *informal* jam, fix, pickle, hot water.
▶ verb **1** *Frank's horse got mired in a bog* BOG DOWN, sink (down). **2** *he has become mired in lawsuits* ENTANGLE, tangle up, embroil, catch up, mix up, involve.

mirror ▶ noun **1** *a quick look in the mirror* LOOKING GLASS, glass, reflecting surface; full-length mirror, hand mirror, side mirror, rear-view mirror. **2** *his life was a mirror of her own* REFLECTION, twin, replica, copy, match, parallel.
— RELATED TERMS: catoptric, specular.
▶ verb *pop music mirrored the mood of desperation* REFLECT, match, reproduce, imitate, simulate, copy, mimic, echo, parallel, correspond to.

mirth ▶ noun MERRIMENT, high spirits, cheerfulness, cheeriness, hilarity, glee, laughter, gaiety, buoyancy, blitheness, euphoria, exhilaration, light-heartedness, joviality, joy, joyfulness, joyousness.
— OPPOSITES: misery.

misadventure ▶ noun ACCIDENT, problem, difficulty, misfortune, mishap; setback, reversal (of fortune), stroke of bad luck, blow, contretemps; failure, disaster, tragedy, calamity, woe, trial, tribulation, catastrophe.

misanthrope ▶ noun HATER OF MANKIND, cynic; recluse, hermit; *informal* grouch, grump.

misanthropic ▶ adjective ANTI-SOCIAL, unsociable, unfriendly, reclusive, uncongenial, cynical, jaundiced.

misapprehend ▶ verb MISUNDERSTAND, misinterpret, misconstrue, misconceive, mistake, misread, get the wrong idea about, take something the wrong way.

misappropriate ▶ verb EMBEZZLE, expropriate, steal, thieve, pilfer, pocket, help oneself to, make off with; *informal* swipe, filch, rip off, snitch, pinch.

misbegotten ▶ adjective **1** *a misbegotten scheme*

ILL-CONCEIVED, ill-advised, badly planned, badly thought-out, hare-brained. **2** *you misbegotten hound!* CONTEMPTIBLE, despicable, wretched, miserable, confounded; *informal* infernal, damned; *dated* cursed, accursed. **3** *(archaic) misbegotten children.* See ILLEGITIMATE sense 2.

misbehave ▶ verb BEHAVE BADLY, be misbehaved, be naughty, be disobedient, disobey, get up to mischief, get up to no good; be bad-mannered, be rude; *informal* carry on, act up.

miscalculate ▶ verb MISJUDGE, make a mistake (about), calculate wrongly, estimate wrongly, overestimate, underestimate, overvalue, undervalue; misconstrue, misinterpret, misunderstand; go wrong, err, be wide of the mark.

miscalculation ▶ noun ERROR OF JUDGMENT, misjudgment, mistake, overestimate, underestimate.

miscarriage ▶ noun **1** *she's had a miscarriage* STILLBIRTH, spontaneous abortion. **2** *the miscarriage of the project* FAILURE, foundering, ruin, ruination, collapse, breakdown, thwarting, frustration, undoing, non-fulfillment, mismanagement.

miscarry ▶ verb **1** *the shock caused her to miscarry* LOSE ONE'S BABY, have a miscarriage, abort, have a spontaneous abortion. **2** *our plan miscarried* GO WRONG, go awry, go amiss, be unsuccessful, be ruined, fail, misfire, abort, founder, come to nothing, fall through, fall flat; *informal* flop, go up in smoke.
– OPPOSITES: succeed.

miscellaneous ▶ adjective VARIOUS, varied, different, assorted, mixed, sundry, diverse, disparate; diversified, motley, multifarious, ragtag, raggle-taggle, heterogeneous, eclectic, odd; *literary* divers.

miscellany ▶ noun ASSORTMENT, mixture, mélange, blend, variety, mixed bag, grab bag, mix, medley, diversity, assemblage, potpourri, pastiche, mishmash, ragbag, salmagundi, gallimaufry, hodgepodge, hash; selection, collection, anthology, treasury.

mischief ▶ noun **1** *the boys are always getting into mischief* NAUGHTINESS, bad behaviour, misbehaviour, mischievousness, misconduct, disobedience; pranks, tricks, capers, nonsense, devilry, funny business; *informal* monkey business, shenanigans, carryings-on. **2** *the mischief in her eyes* IMPISHNESS, roguishness, devilment.

mischievous ▶ adjective **1** *a mischievous child* NAUGHTY, badly behaved, misbehaving, disobedient, troublesome, full of mischief; rascally, roguish. **2** *a mischievous smile* PLAYFUL, teasing, wicked, impish, roguish, arch.
– OPPOSITES: well-behaved.

misconception ▶ noun MISAPPREHENSION, misunderstanding, mistake, error, misinterpretation, misconstruction, misreading, misjudgment, misbelief, miscalculation, false impression, illusion, fallacy, delusion.

misconduct ▶ noun **1** *allegations of misconduct* WRONGDOING, unlawfulness, lawlessness, crime, felony, criminality, sin, sinfulness; unethical behaviour, unprofessionalism, malpractice, negligence, impropriety. **2** *he was reprimanded for his misconduct* MISBEHAVIOUR, bad behaviour, misdeeds, misdemeanours, disorderly conduct, mischief, naughtiness, rudeness.

misconstrue ▶ verb MISUNDERSTAND, misinterpret,

misconceive, misapprehend, mistake, misread; be mistaken about, get the wrong idea about, get it/ someone wrong.

miscreant ▶ noun CRIMINAL, culprit, wrongdoer, malefactor, offender, villain, lawbreaker, evildoer, delinquent, hoodlum, reprobate; *Law* malfeasant.

misdeed ▶ noun See MISDEMEANOUR.

misdemeanour ▶ noun WRONGDOING, evil deed, crime, felony; misdeed, misconduct, offence, error, peccadillo, transgression, sin; *informal* no-no; *archaic* trespass, misdoing.

miser ▶ noun PENNY-PINCHER, Scrooge, pinchpenny; *informal* skinflint, money-grubber, cheapskate, tightwad, piker, greedhead.
– OPPOSITES: spendthrift.

miserable ▶ adjective **1** *I'm too miserable to eat* UNHAPPY, sad, sorrowful, dejected, depressed, downcast, downhearted, down, despondent, disconsolate, wretched, glum, gloomy, dismal, melancholy, woebegone, doleful, forlorn, heartbroken; *informal* blue, down in the mouth/ dumps. **2** *their miserable surroundings* DREARY, dismal, gloomy, drab, wretched, depressing, grim, cheerless, bleak, desolate; poor, shabby, squalid, seedy, dilapidated; *informal* flea-bitten. **3** *miserable weather* UNPLEASANT, disagreeable, depressing; wet, rainy, stormy; *informal* rotten. **4** *a miserable old grouch* GRUMPY, sullen, gloomy, bad-tempered, ill-tempered, ill-natured, dour, surly, sour, glum, moody, unsociable, saturnine, lugubrious, irritable, churlish, cantankerous, crotchety, cross, crabby, cranky, grouchy, testy, peevish, crusty, waspish. **5** *miserable wages* INADEQUATE, meagre, scanty, paltry, small, poor, pitiful, niggardly; *informal* measly, stingy, pathetic; *formal* exiguous. **6** *all that fuss about a few miserable dollars* WRETCHED, confounded; *informal* blithering, blessed, damned, blasted; *dated* accursed.
– OPPOSITES: cheerful, lovely.

miserly ▶ adjective **1** *his miserly great-uncle* MEAN, niggardly, parsimonious, close, close-fisted, penny-pinching, cheese-paring, grasping, Scrooge-like, stingy, tight, tight-fisted, cheap, el cheapo; *archaic* near. **2** *the prize is a miserly $300.* See MEAGRE sense 1.
– OPPOSITES: generous.

misery ▶ noun **1** *periods of intense misery* UNHAPPINESS, distress, wretchedness, suffering, anguish, anxiety, angst, torment, pain, grief, heartache, heartbreak, despair, despondency, dejection, depression, desolation, gloom, melancholy, melancholia, woe, sadness, sorrow; *informal* the dumps, the blues; *literary* dolour. **2** *the miseries of war* AFFLICTION, misfortune, difficulty, problem, ordeal, trouble, hardship, deprivation; pain, sorrow, trial, tribulation, woe.
– OPPOSITES: contentment, pleasure.

misfire ▶ verb GO WRONG, go awry, be unsuccessful, fail, founder, fall through/flat; backfire; *informal* flop, go up in smoke.

misfit ▶ noun NONCONFORMIST, eccentric, maverick, individualist, square peg in a round hole; *informal* oddball, odd duck, weirdo, freak, screwball.

misfortune ▶ noun PROBLEM, difficulty, setback, trouble, adversity, stroke of bad luck, reversal (of fortune), misadventure, mishap, blow, failure, accident, disaster, catastrophe; sorrow, misery, woe, trial, tribulation, tragedy.

misgiving ▶ noun QUALM, doubt, reservation; suspicion, distrust, mistrust, lack of confidence, second thoughts; trepidation, skepticism, unease, uneasiness, anxiety, apprehension, disquiet.

misguided ▶ adjective **1** *the policy is misguided* ERRONEOUS, fallacious, unsound, misplaced, misconceived, ill-advised, ill-considered, ill-judged, ill-founded, inappropriate, unwise, injudicious, imprudent. **2** *you are quite misguided* MISINFORMED, misled, wrong, mistaken, deluded, confused; *informal* off base.

mishandle ▶ verb **1** *the officer mishandled the situation* BUNGLE, fumble, make a mess of, mismanage, spoil, ruin, wreck; *informal* botch, make a hash of, mess up, muck up, screw up, fluff. **2** *he mishandled his dog* BULLY, persecute, ill-treat, mistreat, maltreat, manhandle, abuse, knock about/around, hit, beat; *informal* beat up. **3** *the equipment could be dangerous if mishandled* MISUSE, abuse, handle/treat roughly.

mishap ▶ noun ACCIDENT, trouble, problem, difficulty, setback, adversity, reversal (of fortune), misfortune, blow; failure, disaster, tragedy, catastrophe, calamity, mischance, misadventure.

mishmash ▶ noun JUMBLE, confusion, ragbag, patchwork, bricolage, farrago, assortment, medley, miscellany, mixture, mélange, blend, mix, potpourri, conglomeration, kludge, gallimaufry, salmagundi, hodgepodge, hash.

misinform ▶ verb MISLEAD, misguide, give wrong information, delude, take in, deceive, lie to, hoodwink; *informal* lead up the garden path, take for a ride, give someone a bum steer.

misinterpret ▶ verb MISUNDERSTAND, misconceive, misconstrue, misapprehend, mistake, misread; confuse, be mistaken, get the wrong idea, take amiss.

misjudge ▶ verb GET THE WRONG IDEA ABOUT, get wrong, judge incorrectly, estimate wrongly, be wrong about, miscalculate, misread; overestimate, underestimate, overvalue, undervalue, underrate.

mislay ▶ verb LOSE, misplace, put in the wrong place, be unable to find, forget the whereabouts of.
— OPPOSITES: find.

mislead ▶ verb DECEIVE, delude, take in, lie to, fool, hoodwink, throw off the scent, pull the wool over someone's eyes, misguide, misinform, give wrong information to; *informal* lead up the garden path, take for a ride, give someone a bum steer.

misleading ▶ adjective DECEPTIVE, confusing, deceiving, equivocal, ambiguous, fallacious, specious, spurious, false.

mismanage ▶ verb BUNGLE, make a mess of, mishandle, spoil, ruin, wreck; *informal* botch, make a hash of, mess up, muck up, screw up, fluff.

mismatched ▶ adjective ILL-ASSORTED, ill-matched, incongruous, unsuited, incompatible, inconsistent, at odds; out of keeping, clashing, dissimilar, unalike, different, at variance, disparate, unrelated, divergent, contrasting.
— OPPOSITES: matching.

misogynist ▶ noun WOMAN-HATER; anti-feminist, (male) chauvinist, sexist; *informal* male chauvinist pig.

misplace ▶ verb LOSE, mislay, put in the wrong place, be unable to find, forget the whereabouts of.
— OPPOSITES: find.

misplaced ▶ adjective **1** *his affections were misplaced* MISGUIDED, unwise, ill-advised, ill-considered, ill-judged, inappropriate. **2** *misplaced keys* LOST, mislaid, missing.

misprint ▶ noun MISTAKE, error, typographical

mistake/error, typing mistake/error, erratum; *informal* typo.

misquote ▶ verb MISREPORT, misrepresent, misstate, take/quote out of context, distort, twist, slant, bias, put a spin on, falsify.

misrepresent ▶ verb GIVE A FALSE ACCOUNT/IDEA OF, misreport, misquote, quote/take out of context, misinterpret, put a spin on, skew, warp, falsify, distort, misstate, exaggerate.

miss¹ ▶ verb **1** *the shot missed her by inches* FAIL TO HIT, be/go wide of, fall short of. **2** *Mandy missed the catch* FAIL TO CATCH, drop, fumble, bobble, fluff, flub, mishandle, screw up. **3** *I've missed my bus* BE TOO LATE FOR, fail to catch/get. **4** *I missed what you said* FAIL TO HEAR, mishear. **5** *you can't miss the station* FAIL TO SEE/NOTICE, overlook. **6** *she never missed a class* FAIL TO ATTEND, be absent from, play truant from, cut, skip. **7** *don't miss this exciting opportunity!* LET SLIP, fail to take advantage of, let go/pass, pass up. **8** *I left early to miss rush hour* AVOID, beat, evade, escape, dodge, sidestep, elude, circumvent, steer clear of, find a way round, bypass. **9** *she missed him when he was away* PINE FOR, yearn for, ache for, long for, long to see.
— OPPOSITES: hit, catch.

▶ noun *one hit and three misses* FAILURE, omission, slip, blunder, error, mistake.

miss² ▶ noun *a silly young miss* YOUNG WOMAN, young lady, girl, schoolgirl, missy; *Scottish* lass, lassie; *French* mademoiselle; *informal* girlie, chick, doll, gal; *literary* maiden, maid, damsel; *archaic* wench.

misshapen ▶ adjective DEFORMED, malformed, distorted, crooked, twisted, warped, out of shape, bent, asymmetrical, irregular, misproportioned, ill-proportioned, disfigured, grotesque.

missing ▶ adjective **1** *his wallet is missing* LOST, mislaid, misplaced, absent, gone (astray), gone AWOL, unaccounted for; disappeared, vanished. **2** *passion was missing from her life* ABSENT, not present, lacking, wanting.
— OPPOSITES: present.

mission ▶ noun **1** *a mercy mission to Africa* ASSIGNMENT, commission, expedition, journey, trip, undertaking, operation; task, job, labour, work, duty, charge, trust. **2** *her mission in life* VOCATION, calling, goal, aim, quest, purpose, function, life's work. **3** *a trade mission* DELEGATION, deputation, commission, legation. **4** *a teacher in a mission* missionary post, missionary station, missionary school. **5** *a bombing mission* SORTIE, operation, raid.

missionary ▶ noun EVANGELIST, apostle, proselytizer, preacher, minister, priest; *historical* black robe ♣.

missive ▶ noun MESSAGE, communication, letter, word, note, email, memorandum, line, communiqué, dispatch, news; *informal* memo; *formal* epistle; *literary* tidings.

misspent ▶ adjective WASTED, dissipated, squandered, thrown away, frittered away, misused, misapplied.

misstep ▶ noun MISTAKE, error, blunder, slip, faux pas, infelicity; *informal* blooper, boner, flub, slip-up.

mist ▶ noun *the mist was clearing* HAZE, fog, smog, murk, cloud, Scotch mist, drizzle.

mistake ▶ noun *I assumed it had been a mistake* ERROR, fault, inaccuracy, omission, slip, blunder, miscalculation, misunderstanding, oversight, misinterpretation, gaffe, faux pas, solecism; *informal* slip-up, boo-boo, blooper, boner, goof, flub.

▶ verb **1** *did I mistake your meaning?* MISUNDERSTAND, misinterpret, get wrong, misconstrue, misread. **2** *children often mistake vitamin pills for candies* CONFUSE WITH, mix up with, take for, misinterpret as.

■ **be mistaken** BE WRONG, be in error, be under a misapprehension, be misinformed, be misguided; *informal* be barking up the wrong tree.

■ **make a mistake** GO WRONG, err, make an error, blunder, miscalculate; *informal* slip up, make a boo-boo, drop the ball, goof (up).

mistaken ▶ adjective WRONG, erroneous, inaccurate, incorrect, false, fallacious, unfounded, misguided, misinformed.
– OPPOSITES: correct.

mistakenly ▶ adverb **1** *she mistakenly assumed that she knew him* WRONGLY, in error, erroneously, incorrectly, falsely, fallaciously, inaccurately. **2** *Matt mistakenly opened the letter* BY ACCIDENT, accidentally, inadvertently, unintentionally, unwittingly, unconsciously, by mistake.
– OPPOSITES: correctly, intentionally.

mistimed ▶ adjective ILL-TIMED, badly timed, inopportune, inappropriate, inconvenient, malapropos, untimely, unseasonable.
– OPPOSITES: opportune.

mistreat ▶ verb ILL-TREAT, maltreat, abuse, knock about/around, hit, beat, strike, molest, injure, harm, hurt; misuse, mishandle; *informal* beat up, rough up, mess up, kick around.

mistress ▶ noun LOVER, girlfriend, kept woman; courtesan, concubine, hetaera; *informal* bit on the side, the other woman; *archaic* paramour.

mistrust ▶ verb **1** *I mistrust his motives* BE SUSPICIOUS OF, be mistrustful of, be distrustful of, be skeptical of, be wary of, be chary of, distrust, have doubts about, have misgivings about, have reservations about, suspect. **2** *don't mistrust your impulses* QUESTION, challenge, doubt, have no confidence/faith in.
▶ noun **1** *mistrust of Russia was widespread* SUSPICION, distrust, doubt, misgivings, wariness. **2** *their mistrust of David's competence* QUESTIONING, lack of confidence/faith in, doubt about.

mistrustful ▶ adjective SUSPICIOUS, chary, wary, distrustful, doubtful, dubious, uneasy, skeptical, leery.

misty ▶ adjective **1** *misty weather* HAZY, foggy, (*Nfld*) mauzy ♣, cloudy; smoggy. **2** *a misty outline* BLURRY, fuzzy, blurred, clouded, dim, indistinct, unclear, vague. **3** *misty memories* VAGUE, unclear, indefinite, hazy, nebulous.
– OPPOSITES: clear.

misunderstand ▶ verb MISAPPREHEND, misinterpret, misconstrue, misconceive, mistake, misread; be mistaken, get the wrong idea, receive a false impression; *informal* be barking up the wrong tree, miss the boat.

misunderstanding ▶ noun **1** *a fundamental misunderstanding of juvenile crime* MISINTERPRETATION, misconstruction, misreading, misapprehension, misconception, the wrong idea, false impression. **2** *we have had some misunderstandings* DISAGREEMENT, difference (of opinion), dispute, falling-out, quarrel, argument, altercation, squabble, wrangle, row, clash; *informal* spat, scrap, tiff, rhubarb.

misuse ▶ verb **1** *misusing public funds* PUT TO WRONG USE, misemploy, embezzle, use fraudulently; abuse, squander, waste. **2** *she had been misused by her husband.* See MISTREAT.

▶ noun **1** *a misuse of company assets* WRONG USE, embezzlement, fraud; squandering, waste. **2** *the misuse of drugs* ILLEGAL USE, abuse.

mitigate ▶ verb ALLEVIATE, reduce, diminish, lessen, weaken, lighten, attenuate, take the edge off, allay, ease, assuage, palliate, relieve, tone down.
– OPPOSITES: aggravate.

mitigating ▶ adjective EXTENUATING, justificatory, justifying, vindicating, qualifying; face-saving; *formal* exculpatory.

mitt ▶ noun. *See table at* GLOVE.

mix ▶ verb **1** *mix all the ingredients together* BLEND, mix up, mingle, combine, put together, jumble; fuse, unite, unify, join, amalgamate, incorporate, meld, marry, coalesce, homogenize, intermingle, intermix; *technical* admix; *literary* commingle. **2** *she mixes with all sorts* ASSOCIATE, socialize, fraternize, keep company, consort; mingle, circulate, rub elbows; *informal* hang out/around, knock about/around, hobnob, network. **3** *we just don't mix* BE COMPATIBLE, get along/on, be in harmony, see eye to eye, agree; *informal* hit it off, click, be on the same wavelength.
– OPPOSITES: separate.
▶ noun *a mix of ancient and modern* MIXTURE, blend, mingling, combination, compound, fusion, alloy, union, amalgamation; medley, mélange, collection, selection, assortment, variety, mixed bag, grab bag, miscellany, potpourri, jumble, ragbag, patchwork, bricolage, farrago, gallimaufry, salmagundi, hodgepodge.

■ **mix something up 1** *mix up the ingredients. See* MIX verb sense 1. **2** *I mixed up the dates* CONFUSE, get confused, muddle (up), get muddled up, mistake.

■ **mixed up in** INVOLVED IN, embroiled in, caught up in.

mixed ▶ adjective **1** *a mixed collection* ASSORTED, varied, variegated, miscellaneous, disparate, diverse, diversified, motley, sundry, jumbled, heterogeneous. **2** *mixed breeds* HYBRID, half-caste, cross-bred, interbred, mongrel. **3** *mixed reactions* AMBIVALENT, equivocal, contradictory, conflicting, confused, muddled.
– OPPOSITES: homogeneous.

mixed up ▶ adjective (*informal*) CONFUSED, befuddled, bemused, bewildered, muddled; disturbed, neurotic, unbalanced; *informal* hung up, messed up, at sea.

mixer ▶ noun **1** *a kitchen mixer* BLENDER, food processor, beater, churn. **2** *he attended a mixer* GATHERING, social, function, get-together, meet-and-greet.

mixture ▶ noun **1** *the pudding mixture* BLEND, mix, brew, combination, concoction; composition, compound, alloy, amalgam. **2** *a strange mixture of people* ASSORTMENT, miscellany, medley, mélange, blend, variety, mixed bag, grab bag, mix, diversity, collection, selection, potpourri, mishmash, ragbag, patchwork, bricolage, farrago, gallimaufry, salmagundi, hodgepodge, hash. **3** *the animals were a mixture of genetic strands* CROSS, cross-breed, mongrel, hybrid, half-breed, half-caste.

mix-up ▶ noun CONFUSION, muddle, misunderstanding, mistake, error; *informal* screw-up.

moan ▶ noun **1** *moans of pain* GROAN, wail, whimper, sob, cry. **2** *the moan of the wind* SOUGH, sigh, murmur. **3** (*informal*) *there were moans about the delay* COMPLAINT, complaining, grouse, grousing, grumble, grumbling, whine, whining, carping; *informal* gripe, griping, grouching, bellyaching, bitching, whingeing, beef, beefing.

▶ **verb 1** *he moaned in agony* GROAN, wail, whimper, sob, cry. **2** *the wind moaned in the trees* SOUGH, sigh, murmur. **3** (*informal*) *you're always moaning about the weather* COMPLAIN, grouse, grumble, whine, carp; *informal* gripe, grouch, bellyache, bitch, beef, whinge, kvetch.

mob ▶ **noun 1** *troops dispersed the mob* CROWD, horde, multitude, rabble, mass, throng, group, gang, gathering, assemblage. **2** *he was hiding from the Mob* MAFIA, Cosa Nostra, Camorra. **3** *the mob was excluded from political life* THE COMMON PEOPLE, the masses, the rank and file, the commonality, the third estate, the plebeians, the proletariat; the hoi polloi, the lower classes, the rabble, the riff-raff, the great unwashed; *informal* the proles, the plebs.

▶ **verb 1** *the Prime Minister was mobbed when he visited Vancouver* SURROUND, swarm, besiege, jostle. **2** *reporters mobbed her hotel* CROWD (INTO), fill, pack, throng, press into, squeeze into.

mobile ▶ **adjective 1** *both patients are mobile* ABLE TO MOVE (AROUND), moving, walking; *Zoology* motile; *Medicine* ambulant. **2** *a mobile library* TRAVELLING, transportable, portable, movable; itinerant, peripatetic. **3** *highly mobile young people* ADAPTABLE, flexible, versatile, adjustable.
— OPPOSITES: motionless, static.

mobility ▶ **noun 1** *restricted mobility* ABILITY TO MOVE, movability. **2** *the mobility of Billy's face* EXPRESSIVENESS, eloquence, animation. **3** *mobility in the workforce* ADAPTABILITY, flexibility, versatility, adjustability.

mobilize ▶ **verb 1** *the government mobilized the troops* MARSHAL, deploy, muster, rally, call up, assemble, mass, organize, prepare. **2** *mobilizing support for the party* GENERATE, arouse, awaken, excite, incite, provoke, foment, prompt, stimulate, stir up, galvanize, encourage, inspire, whip up; *literary* enkindle.

mobster ▶ **noun** GANGSTER, hoodlum, criminal, crook, gang member; Mafioso, goodfella, soldier, capo, godfather, don; *informal* goon, hood.

mock ▶ **verb 1** *they mocked her accent* RIDICULE, jeer at, sneer at, deride, scorn, make fun of, laugh at, scoff at, tease, taunt; *informal* josh, rag on, pull someone's chain. **2** *they mocked the way he speaks* PARODY, ape, take off, satirize, lampoon, imitate, impersonate, mimic; *informal* send up.

▶ **adjective** *mock leather* IMITATION, artificial, man-made, simulated, synthetic, ersatz, fake, reproduction, dummy, sham, false, faux, spurious, bogus, counterfeit, inauthentic, pseudo; *informal* pretend, phony.
— OPPOSITES: genuine.

mockery ▶ **noun 1** *the mockery in his voice* RIDICULE, derision, jeering, sneering, contempt, scorn, scoffing, teasing, taunting, sarcasm. **2** *the trial was a mockery* TRAVESTY, charade, farce, parody.

mode ▶ **noun 1** *an informal mode of policing* MANNER, way, fashion, means, method, system, style, approach, technique, procedure, process, practice. **2** *the camera is in manual mode* FUNCTION, position, operation. **3** *the mode for activewear* FASHION, vogue, style, look, trend; craze, rage, fad.

model ▶ **noun 1** *a working model* REPLICA, copy, representation, mock-up, dummy, imitation, duplicate, reproduction, facsimile. **2** *the Canadian model of health care* PROTOTYPE, stereotype, archetype, type, version; mould, template, framework, pattern,

design, blueprint. **3** *she was a model of patience* IDEAL, paragon, perfect example/specimen; perfection, acme, epitome, nonpareil, crème de la crème. **4** *a runway model* FASHION MODEL, supermodel, mannequin. **5** *an artist's model* SITTER, poser, subject. **6** *the latest model of car* VERSION, type, design, variety, kind, sort.

▶ **adjective 1** *model trains* REPLICA, TOY, miniature, dummy, imitation, duplicate, reproduction, facsimile. **2** *model farms* PROTOTYPICAL, prototypal, archetypal. **3** *a model teacher* IDEAL, perfect, exemplary, classic, flawless, faultless.

moderate ▶ **adjective 1** *moderate success* AVERAGE, modest, medium, middling, ordinary, common, commonplace, everyday, workaday; tolerable, passable, adequate, fair; mediocre, indifferent, unexceptional, unremarkable, run-of-the-mill; *informal* OK, so-so, {comme ci, comme ça}, fair-to-middling, plain-vanilla, no great shakes, not up to much. **2** *moderate prices* REASONABLE, acceptable, inexpensive, low, fair, modest. **3** *moderate views* MIDDLE-OF-THE-ROAD, non-extreme, non-radical, centrist. **4** *moderate behaviour* RESTRAINED, controlled, sober; tolerant, lenient.
— OPPOSITES: great, unreasonable, extreme.

▶ **verb 1** *the wind has moderated somewhat* DIE DOWN, abate, let up, calm down, lessen, decrease, diminish; recede, weaken, subside. **2** *you can help to moderate her anger* CURB, control, check, temper, restrain, subdue; repress, tame, lessen, decrease, lower, reduce, diminish, alleviate, allay, appease, assuage, ease, soothe, calm, tone down. **3** *the panel was moderated by one of the writers* CHAIR, take the chair of, preside over.
— OPPOSITES: increase.

moderately ▶ **adverb** SOMEWHAT, quite, rather, fairly, reasonably, comparatively, relatively, to some extent; tolerably, passably, adequately; *informal* pretty.

moderation ▶ **noun 1** *he urged them to show moderation* SELF-RESTRAINT, restraint, self-control, self-discipline; temperance, leniency, fairness. **2** *a moderation of their confrontational style* RELAXATION, easing (off), reduction, abatement, weakening, slackening, tempering, softening, diminution, diminishing, lessening, decline, modulation, modification, mitigation, allaying; *informal* let-up.
■ **in moderation** IN MODERATE QUANTITIES/AMOUNTS, within (sensible) limits; moderately.

modern ▶ **adjective 1** *modern times* PRESENT-DAY, contemporary, present, current, 21st-century, latter-day, modern-day, recent. **2** *her clothes are very modern* FASHIONABLE, in fashion, in style, in vogue, up to date, all the rage, trend-setting, stylish, styling/ stylin', voguish, modish, chic, à la mode; the latest, new, newest, newfangled, modernistic, advanced; *informal* trendy, cool, in, with it, now, hip, phat, happening, kicky, tony, fly.
— OPPOSITES: past, old-fashioned.

modernize ▶ **verb 1** *they are modernizing their manufacturing facilities* UPDATE, bring up to date, streamline, overhaul; renovate, remodel, refashion, revamp. **2** *we must modernize to survive* GET UP TO DATE, move with the times, innovate; *informal* get in the swim, get with it, go with the flow.

modest ▶ **adjective 1** *she was modest about her poetry* SELF-EFFACING, self-deprecating, humble, unpretentious, unassuming, unostentatious; shy, bashful, self-conscious, diffident, reserved, reticent, coy. **2** *modest success* MODERATE, fair, limited, tolerable, passable, adequate, satisfactory, acceptable,

unexceptional. **3** *a modest house* SMALL, ordinary, simple, plain, humble, inexpensive, unostentatious, unpretentious. **4** *her modest dress* DECOROUS, decent, seemly, demure, proper.
– OPPOSITES: conceited, great, grand.

modesty ▸ noun **1** *Hannah's modesty cloaks many talents* SELF-EFFACEMENT, humility, unpretentiousness; shyness, bashfulness, self-consciousness, reserve, reticence, timidity. **2** *the modesty of his aspirations* LIMITED SCOPE, moderation. **3** *the modesty of his home* UNPRETENTIOUSNESS, simplicity, plainness.

modicum ▸ noun SMALL AMOUNT, particle, speck, fragment, scrap, crumb, grain, morsel, shred, dash, drop, pinch, soupçon, jot, iota, whit, atom, smattering, scintilla, hint, suggestion, tinge; *informal* smidgen, tad, titch.

modification ▸ noun **1** *the design is undergoing modification* ALTERATION, adjustment, change, adaptation, refinement, revision. **2** *some minor modifications were made* REVISION, refinement, improvement, amendment, adaptation, adjustment, change, alteration. **3** *the modification of his views* SOFTENING, moderation, tempering, qualification.

modify ▸ verb **1** *their economic policy has been modified* ALTER, change, adjust, adapt, amend, revise, reshape, refashion, restyle, revamp, rework, remodel, refine; *informal* tweak, doctor. **2** *he modified his more extreme views* MODERATE, revise, temper, soften, tone down, qualify.

modish ▸ adjective FASHIONABLE, stylish, chic, modern, contemporary, all the rage, in vogue, voguish, up-to-the-minute, à la mode, du jour; *informal* trendy, cool, with it, in, now, hip, styling/stylin', happening, phat, funky, kicky, tony, fly.

modulate ▸ verb **1** *the cells modulate the body's response* REGULATE, adjust, set, modify, moderate. **2** *she modulated her voice* ADJUST, change the tone of, temper, soften.

modus operandi ▸ noun METHOD (OF WORKING), way, MO, manner, technique, style, procedure, approach, methodology, strategy, plan, formula; *formal* praxis.

mogul ▸ noun MAGNATE, tycoon, VIP, notable, personage, baron, captain, king, lord, grandee, nabob; *informal* bigwig, big shot, big cheese, top dog, top banana, big kahuna, big enchilada.

moist ▸ adjective **1** *the air was moist* DAMP, dampish, steamy, humid, muggy, clammy, dank, wet, wettish, soggy, sweaty, sticky. **2** *a moist fruitcake* SUCCULENT, juicy, soft. **3** *her eyes grew moist* TEARFUL, watery, misty, dewy.
– OPPOSITES: dry.

moisten ▸ verb DAMPEN, wet, damp, water, humidify; *literary* bedew.

moisture ▸ noun WETNESS, wet, water, liquid, condensation, dew, steam, vapour, dampness, damp, humidity, clamminess, mugginess, dankness, wateriness.

moisturizer ▸ noun LOTION, cream, balm, emollient, salve, unguent, lubricant; *technical* humectant.

mojo ▸ noun **1** *get your mojo working* MAGIC, voodoo, hoodoo, wizardry, sorcery; charm, lucky charm, amulet, talisman, churinga. **2** *he's lost his mojo* ENERGY, vitality, spirit, zest, verve; power, dynamism, drive; fire, passion, ardour, zeal; *informal* zip, zing, pep, pizzazz, punch, bounce, oomph, moxie, go, get-up-and-go, vim and vigour, feistiness.

molasses ▸ noun treacle, syrup, blackstrap, *(Nfld)* lassie ♣.

mold ▸ noun *See* MOULD 2.

mole ▸ noun **1** *the mole on his left cheek* MARK, freckle, blotch, spot, blemish, beauty spot, beauty mark. **2** *an undercover mole* SPY, (secret) agent, undercover agent, operative, plant, infiltrator, sleeper, informant, informer; *informal* spook; *archaic* intelligencer.

molest ▸ verb **1** *the crowd molested the police* HARASS, harry, hassle, pester, bother, annoy, beset, persecute, torment; *informal* roust. **2** *he molested a ten-year-old boy* (SEXUALLY) ABUSE, (sexually) assault, interfere with, rape, violate; *informal* grope, paw, fondle; *literary* ravish.

mollify ▸ verb **1** *they tried to mollify the protesters* APPEASE, placate, pacify, conciliate, soothe, calm (down). **2** *mollifying the fears of the public* ALLAY, assuage, alleviate, mitigate, ease, reduce, moderate, temper, tone down, soften; *informal* blunt.
– OPPOSITES: enrage.

mollusc ▸ noun. *See table.*
– RELATED TERMS: malacology.

Molluscs

bivalves	gastropods
bar clam	abalone
bay scallop	conch
Caraquet ♣	cowrie
cherrystone clam	haliotis
clam	limpet
cockle	murex
gaper	nudibranch
geoduck	paua
littleneck	ram's-horn-snail
Malpeque oyster ♣	sea slug
mussel	sea snail
oyster	slug
pearl oyster	snail
pecten	volute
piddock	wentletrap
quahog	whelk
razor clam	winkle
scallop	
sea scallop	**cephalopods**
shipworm	cuttlefish
steamer clam	nautilus
zebra mussel	octopus
	squid

mollycoddle ▸ verb *his parents mollycoddle him* PAMPER, cosset, coddle, spoil, indulge, overindulge, pet, baby, nanny, wait on hand and foot.
▸ noun *(informal) the boy's a mollycoddle! See* MAMA'S BOY.

molten ▸ adjective LIQUEFIED, liquid, fluid, melted, flowing.

moment ▸ noun **1** *he thought for a moment* LITTLE WHILE, short time, bit, minute, instant, (split) second; *informal* sec, jiffy. **2** *the moment they met* POINT (IN TIME), time, hour. **3** *(formal) issues of little moment* IMPORTANCE, import, significance, consequence, note, weight, concern, interest.
■ **in a moment** VERY SOON, in a minute, in a second, in a trice, shortly, any minute (now), in the twinkling of an eye, in (less than) no time, in no time at all, momentarily; *informal* in a jiffy, in two shakes (of a lamb's tail), in the blink of an eye, in a snap, in a heartbeat, in a flash; *literary* ere long.

momentarily ▸ adverb **1** *he paused momentarily* BRIEFLY, fleetingly, for a moment, for a second, for an instant. **2** *my husband will be here momentarily. See* IN A MOMENT at MOMENT.

momentary ▶ **adjective** BRIEF, short, short-lived, fleeting, passing, transient, transitory, ephemeral; *literary* evanescent.
— OPPOSITES: lengthy.

momentous ▶ **adjective** IMPORTANT, significant, historic, portentous, critical, crucial, life-and-death, decisive, pivotal, consequential, of consequence, far-reaching, earth-shattering, earth-shaking; *formal* of moment.
— OPPOSITES: insignificant.

momentum ▶ **noun** IMPETUS, energy, force, power, strength, thrust, speed, velocity.

monarch ▶ **noun** SOVEREIGN, ruler, the Crown, crowned head, potentate; king, queen, emperor, empress, prince, princess.

monastery ▶ **noun** RELIGIOUS COMMUNITY; friary, abbey, priory, nunnery, cloister, convent.

monastic ▶ **adjective 1** *a monastic community* CLOISTERED, cloistral, claustral. **2** *a monastic existence* AUSTERE, ascetic, simple, solitary, monkish, celibate, quiet, cloistered, sequestered, secluded, reclusive, hermit-like, hermitic, incommunicado.

monetary ▶ **adjective** FINANCIAL, fiscal, pecuniary, money, cash, economic, budgetary.

money ▶ **noun 1** *I haven't got enough money* (HARD) CASH, ready money; the means, the wherewithal, funds, capital, finances, (filthy) lucre; coins, change, specie, silver, currency, bills, (bank) notes; *informal* dough, bread, loot, shekels, moolah, dinero, bucks, mazuma; *US informal* greenbacks; *archaic* pelf. **2** *she married him for his money* WEALTH, riches, fortune, affluence, (liquid) assets, resources, means. **3** *the money here is better* PAY, salary, wages, remuneration; *formal* emolument.
— RELATED TERMS: pecuniary, monetary, numismatic.
■ **for my money** IN MY OPINION, to my mind, in my view, as I see it, personally, in my estimation, in my judgment, if you ask me.
■ **in the money** (*informal*) *See* MONEYED.

moneyed ▶ **adjective** RICH, wealthy, affluent, well-to-do, well off, prosperous, in clover, opulent, of means, of substance; *informal* in the money, rolling in it, loaded, stinking/filthy rich, well-heeled, made of money.
— OPPOSITES: poor.

money-grubbing ▶ **adjective** (*informal*) ACQUISITIVE, avaricious, grasping, money-grabbing, gold-digging, rapacious, mercenary, materialistic, grabby.

money-making ▶ **adjective** PROFITABLE, profit-making, remunerative, lucrative, successful, financially rewarding.
— OPPOSITES: loss-making.

mongrel ▶ **noun** *a rough-haired mongrel* CROSS-BREED, cross, mixed breed, half-breed; tyke, cur, mutt, (*Nfld*) crackie ✚; *informal* Heinz 57.
▶ **adjective** *a mongrel bitch* CROSS-BRED, of mixed breed, half-breed, inter-bred, mixed.
— OPPOSITES: pedigree.

monitor ▶ **noun 1** *a fetal monitor* DETECTOR, scanner, recorder; listening device; security camera. **2** *UN monitors* OBSERVER, watchdog, overseer, supervisor. **3** *a computer monitor* SCREEN, video display terminal, VDT.
▶ **verb** *his movements were closely monitored* OBSERVE, watch, track, keep an eye on, keep under observation,

keep watch on, keep under surveillance, record, note, oversee; *informal* keep tabs on.

monk ▶ **noun** brother, religious, cenobite, contemplative, mendicant; friar; abbot, prior; novice, oblate, postulant; lama, marabout.
— RELATED TERMS: monastic, monastery.

monkey ▶ **noun 1** SIMIAN, primate, ape. *See table at* PRIMATE. **2** *you little monkey! See* RASCAL.
■ **make a monkey (out) of** MAKE SOMEONE LOOK FOOLISH, make a fool of, make a laughingstock of, ridicule, make fun of, poke fun at.
■ **monkey with** TAMPER WITH, fiddle with, interfere with, meddle with, tinker with, play with; *informal* mess with, muck about/around with.

monkey business ▶ **noun** (*informal*) MISCHIEF, misbehaviour, mischievousness, devilry, devilment, tomfoolery; dishonesty, trickery, chicanery, skulduggery; *informal* shenanigans, funny business, hanky-panky, monkeyshines.

monolith ▶ **noun** STANDING STONE, menhir, sarsen (stone), megalith.

monolithic ▶ **adjective 1** *a monolithic building* MASSIVE, huge, vast, colossal, gigantic, immense, giant, enormous; featureless, characterless. **2** *the old monolithic Communist party* INFLEXIBLE, rigid, unbending, unchanging, fossilized.

monologue ▶ **noun** SOLILOQUY, speech, address, lecture, sermon, homily; *formal* oration.

monomania ▶ **noun** OBSESSION, fixation, consuming passion, mania, compulsion.

monopolize ▶ **verb 1** *the company has monopolized the market* CORNER, control, take over, gain control/dominance over; *archaic* engross. **2** *he monopolized the conversation* DOMINATE, take over; *informal* hog. **3** *she monopolized the guest of honour* TAKE UP ALL THE ATTENTION OF, keep to oneself; *informal* tie up.

monotonous ▶ **adjective 1** *a monotonous job* TEDIOUS, boring, dull, uninteresting, unexciting, wearisome, tiresome, repetitive, repetitious, unvarying, unchanging, unvaried, humdrum, ho-hum, routine, mechanical, mind-numbing, soul-destroying; colourless, featureless, dreary; *informal* deadly, samey, dullsville. **2** *a monotonous voice* TONELESS, flat, uninflected, soporific.
— OPPOSITES: interesting.

monotony ▶ **noun 1** *the monotony of everyday life* TEDIUM, tediousness, lack of variety, dullness, boredom, repetitiveness, uniformity, routineness, wearisomeness, tiresomeness; lack of excitement, uneventfulness, dreariness, colourlessness, featurelessness; *informal* deadliness. **2** *the monotony of her voice* TONELESSNESS, flatness.

monster ▶ **noun 1** *legendary sea monsters* FABULOUS CREATURE, mythical creature. *See table.* **2** *her husband is a monster* BRUTE, fiend, beast, devil, demon, barbarian, savage, animal; *informal* swine, pig. **3** *the boy's a little monster* RASCAL, imp, monkey, wretch, devil; *informal* horror, scamp, scalawag, tyke, varmint, hellion; *archaic* scapegrace, rapscallion. **4** *he's a monster of a man* GIANT, mammoth, colossus, leviathan, titan; *informal* jumbo.
▶ **adjective** (*informal*) *a monster truck. See* HUGE.

monstrosity ▶ **noun 1** *a concrete monstrosity* EYESORE, blot on the landscape, excrescence, horror. **2** *a biological monstrosity* MUTANT, mutation, freak (of nature), monster, abortion.

monstrous ▶ **adjective 1** *a monstrous creature* GROTESQUE, hideous, ugly, ghastly, gruesome,

Months of the Year

Gregorian Calendar	Islamic Calendar	Chinese Agricultural Calendar
January	Muharram	Li Chun
February	Safar	Yu Shui
March	Rabi I	Jing Zhe
April	Rabi II	Chun Fen
May	Jumada I	Qing Ming
June	Jumada II	Gu Yu
July	Rajab	Li Xia
August	Shaban	Xiao Man
September	Ramadan	Mang Zhong
October	Shawwal	Xia Zhi
November	Dhu al-Qadah	Xiao Shu
December	Dhu al-Hijjah	Da Shu
		Li Qui
Jewish Calendar	**Hindu Calendar**	Chu Shu
Nisan	Chaitra	Bai Lu
Iyar	Vaisakha	Qui Fen
Sivan	Jyaistha	Han Lu
Tammuz	Asadha	Shuang Jiang
Ab	Sravana	Li Dong
Elul	Bhadra	Xiao Xue
Tishri	Asvina	Da Xue
Cheshvan	Kartika	Dong Zhi
Kislev	Agrahayana/Margasirsa	Xiao Han
Tebet	Pausa	Da Han
Shebat	Magha	
Adar	Phalguna	*(Months do not necessarily correspond from one calendar to another.)*

Monsters and Creatures

abominable snowman	loup-garou
Argus	lycanthrope
basilisk	manticore
Bigfoot	mermaid
Cadborosaurus	merman
(Caddy) ♣	Minotaur
centaur	Ogopogo ♣
Chimera	phoenix
cockatrice	sasquatch
Cyclops	satyr
dragon	Scylla
erl-king	sea serpent
fairy	sea snake
Frankenstein	shape-shifter
gnome	siren
goblin	Sphinx
Gorgon	Tiamat
Grendel	troll
griffin	Typhon
harpy	urchin
hippogriff	vampire
hobbit	werewolf
Hydra	windigo
kraken	witch
leviathan	yeti.
Lilith	*See also* SPIRITS.
Loch Ness Monster	

horrible, horrific, horrifying, grisly, disgusting, repulsive, repellent, dreadful, frightening, terrifying, malformed, misshapen. **2** *a monstrous tidal wave. See* HUGE. **3** *monstrous acts of violence* APPALLING, heinous, egregious, evil, wicked, abominable, terrible, horrible, dreadful, vile, outrageous, shocking, disgraceful; unspeakable, despicable, vicious, savage, barbaric, barbarous, inhuman, beastly.
— OPPOSITES: lovely, small.

month ▶ noun. *See table.*

monument ▶ noun **1** *a stone monument* MEMORIAL, statue, pillar, column, obelisk, cross; cenotaph, tomb, mausoleum, shrine. **2** *a monument was placed over the grave* GRAVESTONE, headstone, tombstone, grave marker, plaque. **3** *a monument to a past era of aviation* TESTAMENT, record, reminder, remembrance, memorial, commemoration.

monumental ▶ adjective **1** *a monumental task* HUGE, great, enormous, gigantic, massive, colossal, mammoth, immense, tremendous, mighty, stupendous. **2** *a monumental error of judgment* TERRIBLE, dreadful, awful, colossal, staggering, huge, enormous, unforgivable, egregious. **3** *her monumental achievement* IMPRESSIVE, striking, outstanding, remarkable, magnificent, majestic, stupendous, ambitious, large-scale, grand, awe-inspiring, important, significant, distinguished, memorable, immortal.

mooch ▶ verb **1** *he was always mooching money from us* BEG, ask for money, borrow; *informal* scrounge, bum, sponge, cadge. **2** *we were just mooching around* LOITER, saunter, stroll, amble, wander, ramble, meander, dawdle, dally; *informal* traipse, mosey, putter.
▶ noun *she is such a mooch* BEGGAR *informal* bum, scrounger, sponger, cadger, freeloader, moocher, schnorrer.

mood ▶ noun **1** *she's in a good mood* FRAME/STATE OF MIND, humour, temper; disposition, spirit, tenor. **2** *he's obviously in a mood* BAD MOOD, (bad) temper, sulk, fit of pique; low spirits, the doldrums, the blues, blue funk; *informal* the dumps, grumps. **3** *the mood of the film*

ATMOSPHERE, feeling, spirit, ambience, aura, character, tenor, flavour, feel, tone.

■ **in the mood** IN THE RIGHT FRAME OF MIND, feeling like, wanting to, inclined to, disposed to, minded to, eager to, willing to.

moody ▶ adjective TEMPERAMENTAL, emotional, volatile, capricious, changeable, mercurial; sullen, sulky, morose, glum, depressed, dejected, despondent, doleful, dour, sour, saturnine, manic-depressive; *informal* blue, down in the dumps/ mouth.
— OPPOSITES: cheerful.

moon ▶ noun SATELLITE.
— RELATED TERMS: lunar.
▶ verb **1** *stop mooning about* WASTE TIME, loaf, idle, mope; *informal* lallygag. **2** *he's mooning over her photograph* MOPE, pine, brood, daydream, fantasize, be in a reverie.
■ **many moons ago** (*informal*) A LONG TIME AGO, ages ago, years ago; *informal* donkey's years ago.
■ **once in a blue moon** (*informal*) HARDLY EVER, scarcely ever, rarely, very seldom.
■ **over the moon** (*informal*) *See* ECSTATIC.

moonshine ▶ noun **1** *See* NONSENSE sense 1. **2** *they brewed up a batch of moonshine* ALCOHOL, bootleg liquor, drink; *informal* booze, shine, hooch, (*Atlantic*) swish ♣, moose milk ♣, white lightning, homebrew; rotgut, firewater, *Nfld* screech ♣.

moor[1] ▶ verb *a boat was moored to the quay* TIE UP, secure, make fast, fix firmly, anchor, berth, dock.

moor[2] ▶ noun *a walk on the moor* UPLAND, moorland; heath.

moot ▶ adjective *a moot point* DEBATABLE, open to discussion/question, arguable, questionable, at issue, open to doubt, disputable, controversial, contentious, disputed, unresolved, unsettled, up in the air.
▶ verb *the idea was first mooted in the 1930s* RAISE, bring up, broach, mention, put forward, introduce, advance, propose, suggest.

mop ▶ noun *her tousled mop of hair* SHOCK, mane, tangle, mass.
▶ verb *a man was mopping the floor* WASH, clean, wipe, swab.
■ **mop something up 1** *I mopped up the spilt coffee* WIPE UP, clean up, sponge up. **2** *troops mopped up the last pockets of resistance* FINISH OFF, deal with, dispose of, take care of, clear up, eliminate.

mope ▶ verb **1** *it's no use moping* BROOD, sulk, be miserable, be despondent, pine, eat one's heart out, fret, grieve; *informal* be down in the dumps/mouth; *literary* repine. **2** *she was moping about the house* LANGUISH, moon, idle, loaf; *informal* lallygag.

moral ▶ adjective **1** *moral issues* ETHICAL, social, having to do with right and wrong. **2** *a very moral man* VIRTUOUS, good, righteous, upright, upstanding, high-minded, principled, honourable, honest, just, noble, incorruptible, scrupulous, respectable, decent, clean-living, law-abiding. **3** *moral support* PSYCHOLOGICAL, emotional, mental.
— OPPOSITES: dishonourable.
▶ noun **1** *the moral of the story* LESSON, message, meaning, significance, signification, import, point, teaching. **2** *he has no morals* MORAL CODE, code of ethics, moral standards/values, principles, standards, (sense of) morality, scruples.

morale ▶ noun CONFIDENCE, self-confidence, self-esteem, spirit(s), team spirit, enthusiasm.

morality ▶ noun **1** *the morality of nuclear weapons* ETHICS, rights and wrongs, ethicality. **2** *a sharp decline in morality* VIRTUE, goodness, good behaviour, righteousness, rectitude, uprightness; morals, principles, honesty, integrity, propriety, honour, justice, decency; ethics, standards/principles of behaviour, mores, standards.

moralize ▶ verb PONTIFICATE, sermonize, lecture, preach.

morass ▶ noun **1** *the muddy morass* QUAGMIRE, swamp, bog, marsh, muskeg, mire, marshland, wetland, slough, moor. **2** *a morass of paperwork* CONFUSION, chaos, muddle, tangle, entanglement, imbroglio, jumble, clutter; *informal* log-jam.

moratorium ▶ noun EMBARGO, ban, prohibition, suspension, postponement, stay, stoppage, halt, freeze, standstill, respite.

morbid ▶ adjective **1** *a morbid fascination with contemporary warfare* GHOULISH, macabre, unhealthy, gruesome, unwholesome; abnormal, aberrant, disturbing, worrisome; *informal* sick, weird. **2** *I felt decidedly morbid* GLOOMY, glum, melancholy, morose, dismal, sombre, doleful, despondent, dejected, sad, depressed, downcast, down, disconsolate, miserable, unhappy, downhearted, dispirited, low; *informal* blue, down in the dumps/mouth.
— OPPOSITES: wholesome, cheerful.

mordant ▶ adjective CAUSTIC, trenchant, biting, cutting, acerbic, sardonic, sarcastic, scathing, acid, sharp, keen; critical, bitter, virulent, vitriolic.

more ▶ adjective *I could do with some more clothes* ADDITIONAL, further, added, extra, increased, new, other, supplementary.
— OPPOSITES: less, fewer.
▶ adverb **1** *he was able to concentrate more on his writing* TO A GREATER EXTENT, further, some more, better. **2** *he was rich, and more, he was handsome*. *See* MOREOVER.
▶ pronoun *we're going to need more* EXTRA, an additional amount/number, an addition, an increase.
— OPPOSITES: less, fewer.
■ **more or less** APPROXIMATELY, roughly, nearly, almost, close to, about, in/of the order of, in the region of.

moreover ▶ adverb BESIDES, furthermore, what's more, in addition, also, as well, too, to boot, additionally, on top of that, into the bargain, more, likewise; *archaic* withal.

mores ▶ plural noun CUSTOMS, conventions, ways, way of life, traditions, practices, habits, lifeways; *formal* praxis.

morgue ▶ noun MORTUARY, funeral parlour, funeral home.

moribund ▶ adjective **1** *the patient was moribund* DYING, expiring, terminal, on one's deathbed, near death, at death's door, not long for this world. **2** *the moribund shipbuilding industry* DECLINING, in decline, waning, dying, stagnating, stagnant, crumbling, on its last legs.
— OPPOSITES: thriving.

morning ▶ noun **1** *I've got a meeting this morning* BEFORE NOON, before lunch(time), a.m., forenoon; *literary* morn. **2** *morning is on its way* DAWN, daybreak, sunrise, first light, cock crow, sun-up; *literary* dayspring, dawning, aurora.
— RELATED TERMS: matutinal.
■ **morning, noon, and night** ALL THE TIME, without a break, constantly, continually, incessantly, ceaselessly, perpetually, unceasingly; *informal* 24-7.

moron ▶ **noun** FOOL, ass, idiot, halfwit, dunce, dolt, ignoramus, simpleton; *informal* dope, ninny, nincompoop, chump, dim-wit, dim-bulb, dumbo, dummy, dumdum, loon, dork, jackass, blockhead, jughead, bonehead, knucklehead, fathead, numbskull, numbnuts, dumb-ass, doofus, dunderhead, ditz, lummox, galoot, dipstick, thickhead, meathead, meatball, airhead, pinhead, lamebrain, cretin, imbecile, goof, pea-brain, birdbrain, jerk, nerd, donkey, nitwit, twit, boob, twerp, schmuck, bozo, hoser ♣, turkey, chowderhead, dingbat.
– OPPOSITES: genius.

moronic ▶ **adjective** STUPID, FOOLISH, senseless, brainless, mindless, idiotic, imbecile, insane, lunatic, asinine, ridiculous, ludicrous, absurd, preposterous, silly, inane, witless, half-baked, empty-headed, unintelligent, slow-witted, weak-minded; *informal* crazy, dumb, brain-dead, cretinous, imbecilic, doltish, thick, thick-headed, birdbrained, pea-brained, pinheaded, dopey, dim, dim-witted, halfwitted, dippy, fat-headed, blockheaded, boneheaded, lamebrained, chuckleheaded, dunderheaded, muttonheaded; daft, dumb-ass, chowderheaded.

morose ▶ **adjective** SULLEN, sulky, gloomy, bad-tempered, ill-tempered, dour, surly, sour, glum, moody, ill-humoured, melancholy, melancholic, brooding, broody, doleful, miserable, depressed, dejected, despondent, downcast, unhappy, low, down, grumpy, irritable, churlish, cantankerous, crotchety, cross, crabby, cranky, grouchy, testy, snappish, peevish, crusty; *informal* blue, down in the dumps/mouth.
– OPPOSITES: cheerful.

morsel ▶ **noun** MOUTHFUL, bite, nibble, bit, soupçon, taste, spoonful, forkful, sliver, drop, dollop, spot, gobbet, tidbit.

mortal ▶ **adjective** **1** *mortal remains | all men are mortal* PERISHABLE, physical, bodily, corporeal, fleshly, earthly; human, impermanent, transient, ephemeral. **2** *a mortal blow* DEADLY, fatal, lethal, death-dealing, murderous, terminal. **3** *mortal enemies* IRRECONCILABLE, deadly, sworn, bitter, out-and-out, implacable. **4** *a mortal sin* UNPARDONABLE, unforgivable. **5** *living in mortal fear* EXTREME, (very) great, terrible, awful, dreadful, intense, severe, grave, dire, unbearable.
– OPPOSITES: venial.
▶ **noun** *we are mere mortals* HUMAN (BEING), person, man/ woman; earthling.

mortality ▶ **noun** **1** *a sense of his own mortality* IMPERMANENCE, transience, ephemerality, perishability; humanity; corporeality. **2** *the causes of mortality* DEATH, loss of life, dying.

mortify ▶ **verb** **1** *I'd be mortified if my friends found out* EMBARRASS, humiliate, chagrin, discomfit, shame, abash, horrify, appall. **2** *he was mortified at being excluded* HURT, wound, affront, offend, put out, pique, irk, annoy, vex; *informal* rile. **3** *mortifying the flesh* SUBDUE, suppress, subjugate, control; discipline, chasten, punish.

mortuary ▶ **noun** See MORGUE.

mosaic ▶ **noun** PATTERN, design, arrangement, collection, collage, picture, pastiche.

mosquito ▶ **noun** skeeter, (Nfld) nipper ♣, bloodsucker.

most ▶ **pronoun** *most of the guests brought flowers*

NEARLY ALL, almost all, the greatest part/number, the majority, the bulk, the preponderance.
– OPPOSITES: little, few.
■ **for the most part** *See* MOSTLY senses 1, 2.

mostly ▶ **adverb** **1** *the other passengers were mostly businessmen* MAINLY, for the most part, on the whole, in the main, largely, chiefly, predominantly, principally, primarily. **2** *I mostly wear jeans* USUALLY, generally, in general, as a rule, ordinarily, normally, customarily, typically, most of the time, almost always, on average, on balance.

mote ▶ **noun** SPECK, particle, grain, spot, fleck, atom, scintilla.

motel ▶ **noun** HOTEL, inn, motor inn, motor court, lodge; accommodation, lodging, rooms.

moth ▶ **noun.** *See table at* BUTTERFLY.

moth-eaten ▶ **adjective** THREADBARE, worn (out), well-worn, old, shabby, scruffy, tattered, ragged; *informal* tatty, the worse for wear, raggedy.

mother ▶ **noun** **1** *I will ask my mother* FEMALE PARENT, materfamilias, matriarch; *informal* ma, mama, old lady, old woman; mum, mummy, mom, mommy, mammy. **2** *the foal's mother* DAM. **3** *necessity is the mother of invention* SOURCE, origin, genesis, fountainhead, inspiration, stimulus; *literary* wellspring. **4** *(informal) a mother of a storm* HUMDINGER, dilly, doozy, lulu, whopper.
– RELATED TERMS: maternal, matri-.
– OPPOSITES: child, father.
▶ **verb** **1** *she mothered her husband* LOOK AFTER, care for, take care of, nurse, protect, tend, raise, rear; pamper, coddle, cosset, fuss over. **2** *she mothered an illegitimate daughter* GIVE BIRTH TO, have, bear, produce, birth; *archaic* be brought to bed of.
– OPPOSITES: neglect.
▶ **adjective** *my mother tongue* NATIVE, first, original; ancestral.

motherly ▶ **adjective** MATERNAL, maternalistic, protective, caring, loving, devoted, affectionate, fond, warm, tender, gentle, kind, kindly, understanding, compassionate.

motif ▶ **noun** **1** *a colourful tulip motif* DESIGN, pattern, decoration, figure, shape, device, emblem, ornament. **2** *a recurring motif in her work* THEME, idea, concept, subject, topic, leitmotif, element.

motion ▶ **noun** **1** *the rocking motion of the boat | a planet's motion around the sun* MOVEMENT, moving, locomotion, rise and fall, shifting; progress, passage, passing, transit, course, travel, travelling. **2** *a motion of the hand* GESTURE, movement, signal, sign, indication; wave, nod, gesticulation. **3** *the motion failed to obtain a majority* PROPOSAL, proposition, recommendation, suggestion.
– RELATED TERMS: kinetic.
▶ **verb** *he motioned her to sit down* GESTURE, signal, direct, indicate; wave, beckon, nod, gesticulate.
■ **in motion** MOVING, on the move, going, travelling, running, functioning, operational.
■ **set in motion** START, commence, begin, activate, initiate, launch, get underway, get going, get off the ground; trigger off, set off, spark off, generate, cause.

motionless ▶ **adjective** UNMOVING, still, stationary, stock-still, immobile, static, not moving a muscle, rooted to the spot, transfixed, paralyzed, frozen.
– OPPOSITES: moving.

motivate ▶ **verb** **1** *she was primarily motivated by the desire for profit* PROMPT, drive, move, inspire, stimulate, influence, activate, impel, push, propel,

Mountain Ranges in Canada

Range	Location	Highest Peak	Height (m)
St. Elias	Yukon / BC	Mount Logan	5 959
Coast	W BC	Mount Waddington	4 016
Rocky	BC / Alta	Mount Robson	3 954
Selkirk	SE BC	Mount Sir Sandford	3 522
Cariboo	E-Central BC	Mount Sir Wilfrid Laurier	3 520
Purcell	SE BC	Mount Farnham	3 481
Monashee	SE BC	Torii Mountain	3 429
Mackenzie	Yukon / NWT	Keele Peak	2 952
Ogilvie	W-Central Yukon	Mount MacDonald	2 758
Cassiar	S Yukon / N BC	Thudaka Peak	2 751
Ellesmere Island	Nunavut	Barbeau Peak	2 616
Vancouver Island	BC	Elkhorn Mountain	2 210
Baffin Island	Nunavut	Unnamed peak	2 140
Torngat	Quebec / Labrador	Mount Caubvick/Mont D'Iberville	1 650
Franklin	W NWT	Cap Mountain	1 577
Cypress Hills	S Alta / Sask.	Highest Point of Cypress Hills	1 468
Chic-Chocs	E Quebec	Mont Jacques-Cartier	1 268
Laurentian	S-Central Quebec	Mont Raoul-Blanchard	1 181
Long Range	Nfld	Highest point of Lewis Hills	814
Cape Breton Highlands	NS	White Hill	532
Cobequid	NS	Nuttby Mountain	360

spur (on). **2** *it's the teacher's job to motivate the child* INSPIRE, stimulate, encourage, spur (on), excite, inspirit, incentivize, fire with enthusiasm.

motivation ▶ noun **1** *his motivation was financial* MOTIVE, motivating force, incentive, stimulus, stimulation, inspiration, inducement, incitement, spur, reason; *informal* carrot. **2** *keep up the staff's motivation* ENTHUSIASM, drive, ambition, initiative, determination, enterprise; *informal* get-up-and-go.

motive ▶ noun **1** *the motive for the attack* REASON, motivation, motivating force, rationale, grounds, cause, basis, object, purpose, intention; incentive, inducement, incitement, lure, inspiration, stimulus, stimulation, spur. **2** *religious motives in art* MOTIF, theme, idea, concept, subject, topic, leitmotif.
▶ adjective *motive power* KINETIC, driving, impelling, propelling, propulsive, motor.

motley ▶ adjective MISCELLANEOUS, disparate, diverse, assorted, varied, diversified, heterogeneous; *informal* ragtag, raggle-taggle.
− OPPOSITES: homogeneous.

motorhome ▶ noun See CAMPER.

mottled ▶ adjective BLOTCHY, blotched, spotted, spotty, speckled, streaked, streaky, marbled, flecked, freckled, dappled, stippled; piebald, skewbald, brindled, brindle, pinto, calico; *informal* splotchy.

motto ▶ noun MAXIM, saying, proverb, aphorism, adage, saw, axiom, apophthegm, formula, expression, phrase, dictum, precept; slogan, catchphrase, mantra; truism, cliché, platitude.

mould¹ ▶ noun **1** *the molten metal is poured into a mould* CAST, die, form, matrix, shape, template, pattern, frame. **2** *an actress in the traditional Hollywood mould* PATTERN, form, shape, format, model, kind, type, style; archetype, prototype. **3** *he is a figure of heroic mould* CHARACTER, nature, temperament, disposition; calibre, kind, sort, variety, stamp, type.
▶ verb **1** *a figure moulded from clay* SHAPE, form, fashion, model, work, construct, make, create, manufacture, sculpt, sculpture; forge, cast. **2** *moulding foreign policy* DETERMINE, direct, control, guide, lead, influence, shape, form, fashion, make.

mould² ▶ noun *walls stained with mould* MILDEW, fungus, dry rot, must, mouldiness, mustiness.

moulder ▶ verb DECAY, decompose, rot (away), go mouldy, go off, go bad, spoil, putrefy.

mouldy ▶ adjective MILDEWED, mildewy, musty, mouldering, fusty, (*Nfld*) fousty ✦; decaying, decayed, rotting, rotten, bad, spoiled, decomposing.

mound ▶ noun **1** *a mound of leaves* HEAP, pile, stack, mountain; mass, accumulation, assemblage. **2** *high on the mound* HILLOCK, hill, knoll, (*Nfld*) tolt ✦, rise, hummock, hump, embankment, bank, ridge, elevation; *Geology* drumlin.
▶ verb *mound up the rice on a serving plate* PILE (UP), heap (up).

mount ▶ verb **1** *he mounted the stairs* GO UP, ascend, climb (up), scale. **2** *the committee mounted the platform* CLIMB ON TO, jump on to, clamber on to, get on to. **3** *they mounted their horses* GET ASTRIDE, bestride, get on to, hop on to. **4** *the museum is mounting an exhibition* (PUT ON) DISPLAY, exhibit, present, install; organize, put on, stage. **5** *the company mounted a takeover bid* ORGANIZE, stage, prepare, arrange, set up; launch, set in motion, initiate. **6** *their losses mounted rapidly* INCREASE, grow, rise, escalate, soar, spiral, shoot up, rocket, climb, accumulate, build up, multiply. **7** *cameras were mounted above the door* INSTALL, place, fix, set, put up, put in position.
− OPPOSITES: descend.

mountain ▶ noun **1** *a range of mountains* PEAK, height, mount, prominence, summit, pinnacle, alp; (**mountains**) range, massif, sierra, cordillera. *See table.* **2** *a mountain of work* A GREAT DEAL, a lot; profusion, abundance, quantity, backlog; *informal* heap, pile, stack, slew, lots, loads, heaps, piles, tons, masses; gobs.
■ **move mountains 1** *faith can move mountains* PERFORM MIRACLES, work/do wonders. **2** *his fans move mountains to attend his performances* MAKE EVERY EFFORT, pull out all the stops, do one's utmost/best; *informal* bend/lean over backwards.

mountainous ▶ adjective **1** *a mountainous region* HILLY, craggy, rocky, alpine; upland, highland. **2** *mountainous waves* HUGE, enormous, gigantic,

massive, giant, colossal, immense, tremendous, mighty; *informal* whopping, humongous, ginormous.
— OPPOSITES: flat, tiny.

mountebank ▶ noun SWINDLER, charlatan, confidence trickster, fraud, fraudster, imposter, trickster, hoaxer; *informal* con man, flim-flammer, snake oil salesman, sharp, grifter, bunco artist.

mourn ▶ verb **1** *Isobel mourned her husband* GRIEVE FOR, sorrow over, lament for, weep for, wail/keen over. **2** *he mourned the loss of the beautiful buildings* DEPLORE, bewail, bemoan, rue, regret.

mournful ▶ adjective SAD, sorrowful, doleful, melancholy, melancholic, woeful, grief-stricken, miserable, unhappy, heartbroken, broken-hearted, gloomy, dismal, desolate, dejected, despondent, depressed, downcast, disconsolate, woebegone, forlorn, rueful, lugubrious, joyless, cheerless; *literary* dolorous.
— OPPOSITES: cheerful.

mourning ▶ noun **1** *a period of mourning* GRIEF, grieving, sorrowing, lamentation, lament, keening, wailing, weeping. **2** *she was dressed in mourning* BLACK (CLOTHES), (widow's) weeds; *archaic* sables.

mouse ▶ noun. See table at RODENT.
— RELATED TERMS: murine.

mousy ▶ adjective **1** *mousy hair* LIGHTISH BROWN, brownish, brownish-grey, dun-coloured; dull, lacklustre. **2** *a small, mousy woman* TIMID, quiet, fearful, timorous, shy, self-effacing, diffident, unassertive, unforthcoming, withdrawn, introverted, introvert.

mouth ▶ noun **1** *open your mouth* lips, jaws; maw, muzzle; *informal* trap, chops, kisser, puss. **2** *the mouth of the cave* ENTRANCE, opening, entry, way in, access, ingress. **3** *the mouth of the bottle* OPENING, rim, lip. **4** *the mouth of the river* OUTFALL, outlet, debouchment; estuary. **5** (*informal*) *don't give me any mouth* IMPUDENCE, cheek, cheekiness, insolence, impertinence, effrontery, presumption, presumptuousness, rudeness, disrespect; *informal* lip, sauce, sass, sassiness, back talk.
▶ verb **1** *he mouthed platitudes* UTTER, speak, say; pronounce, enunciate, articulate, voice, express; say insincerely, say for form's sake, pay lip service to. **2** *he mouthed the words to the song* LIP-SYNCH.
■ **down in the mouth** (*informal*). See UNHAPPY sense 1.
■ **keep one's mouth shut** (*informal*) SAY NOTHING, keep quiet, not breathe a word, not tell a soul; *informal* keep mum, not let the cat out of the bag.
■ **mouth off** (*informal*) **1** *he was mouthing off about politics again* RANT, spout, declaim, sound off. **2** *the students mouthed off to their teacher* TALK INSOLENTLY TO, be disrespectful to; *informal* lip off.

mouthful ▶ noun **1** *a mouthful of pizza* BITE, nibble, taste, bit, piece; spoonful, forkful. **2** *a mouthful of beer* SIP, swallow, drop, gulp, slug; *informal* swig. **3** *'sesquipedalian' is a bit of a mouthful* TONGUE-TWISTER, long word, difficult word.

mouthpiece ▶ noun **1** *the flute's mouthpiece* EMBOUCHURE. **2** *a mouthpiece for the government* SPOKESPERSON, spokesman, spokeswoman, speaker, agent, representative, propagandist, voice; organ, channel, vehicle, instrument.

movable ▶ adjective **1** *movable objects* PORTABLE, transportable, transferable; mobile. **2** *movable dates* VARIABLE, changeable, alterable.
— OPPOSITES: fixed.

move ▶ verb **1** *she moved to the door | don't move!* GO, walk, proceed, progress, advance; budge, stir, shift, change position. **2** *he moved the chair closer to the fire* CARRY, transport, transfer, shift. **3** *things were moving too fast* (MAKE) PROGRESS, make headway, advance, develop. **4** *he urged the council to move quickly* TAKE ACTION, act, take steps, do something, take measures; *informal* get moving. **5** *she's moved to Whitehorse* RELOCATE, move house, move away, change address/house, leave, go away, go down the road ♣, decamp, pull up stakes. **6** *I was deeply moved by the story* AFFECT, touch, impress, shake, upset, disturb, make an impression on. **7** *she was moved to act* INSPIRE, prompt, stimulate, motivate, provoke, influence, rouse, induce, incite. **8** *they are not prepared to move on this issue* CHANGE, budge, shift one's ground, change one's tune, change one's mind, have second thoughts; make a U-turn, do an about-face. **9** *she moves in the art world* CIRCULATE, mix, socialize, keep company, associate; *informal* hang out/around. **10** *I move that we adjourn* PROPOSE, submit, suggest, advocate, recommend, urge.
▶ noun **1** *his eyes followed her every move* MOVEMENT, motion, action; gesture, gesticulation. **2** *his recent move to Toronto* RELOCATION, change of house/address, transfer, posting. **3** *the latest move in the war against drugs* INITIATIVE, step, action, act, measure, manoeuvre, tactic, stratagem. **4** *it's your move* TURN, go; opportunity, chance.
■ **get a move on** (*informal*) HURRY UP, speed up, move faster; *informal* get cracking, get moving, step on it, shake a leg, hop to it; *dated* make haste.
■ **make a move** *waiting for the other side to make a move* DO SOMETHING, take action, act, take the initiative; *informal* get moving.
■ **on the move 1** *she's always on the move* TRAVELLING, in transit, moving, journeying, on the road; *informal* on the go. **2** *the economy is on the move* PROGRESSING, making progress, advancing, developing.

movement ▶ noun **1** *Rachel made a sudden movement | there was almost no movement* MOTION, move; gesture, gesticulation, sign, signal; action, activity. **2** *the movement of supplies* TRANSPORTATION, shift, shifting, conveyance, moving, transfer. **3** *the labour movement* POLITICAL GROUP, party, faction, wing, lobby, camp. **4** *a movement to declare war on poverty* CAMPAIGN, crusade, drive, push. **5** *there have been movements in the financial markets* DEVELOPMENT, change, fluctuation, variation. **6** *the movement towards equality* TREND, tendency, drift, swing. **7** *some movement will be made by the end of the month* PROGRESS, progression, advance. **8** *a symphony in three movements* PART, section, division.

movie ▶ noun **1** *a horror movie | they rented a movie* FILM, (motion) picture, feature (film); video, DVD; *informal* flick, pic; *dated* moving picture. **2** *he adored going to the movies* THE CINEMA, the pictures, the silver screen, multiplex, the movie theatre, movie house, cinematheque; *informal* the big screen. **3** *she works in the movies* FILM INDUSTRY, Hollywood, Bollywood; *informal* tinsel town.

movie star ▶ noun (FILM) ACTOR/ACTRESS, film star, leading man/woman, leading lady, lead; celebrity, star, starlet, matinee idol, superstar; *informal* celeb.

moving ▶ adjective **1** *moving parts | a moving train* IN MOTION, operating, operational, working, going, on the move, active; movable, mobile. **2** *a moving book* AFFECTING, touching, poignant, heart-warming, heart-rending, emotional, disturbing; inspiring, inspirational, stimulating, stirring.
— OPPOSITES: fixed, stationary.

mow ▶ verb *she had mown the lawn* CUT (DOWN), trim; crop, clip, prune, manicure.

■ **mow someone/something down** KILL, run down, gun down, shoot down, cut down, cut to pieces, butcher, slaughter, massacre, annihilate, wipe out; *informal* blow away.

much ▶ adjective *did you get much help?* A LOT OF, a great/good deal of, a great/large amount of, plenty of, ample, copious, abundant, plentiful, considerable; *informal* lots of, loads of, heaps of, masses of, tons of, piles of, mucho.
— OPPOSITES: little.
▶ adverb **1** *it didn't hurt much* GREATLY, to a great extent/degree, a great deal, a lot, considerably, appreciably. **2** *does he come here much?* OFTEN, frequently, many times, repeatedly, regularly, habitually, routinely, usually, normally, commonly; *informal* a lot.
▶ pronoun *he did so much for our team* A LOT, a great/good deal, plenty; *informal* lots, loads, heaps, masses.

muck ▶ noun **1** *I'll just clean off the muck* DIRT, grime, filth, mud, slime, mess; *informal* crud, gunk, grunge, gunge, guck, glop. **2** *spreading muck on the fields* DUNG, manure, ordure, excrement, excreta, droppings, feces, sewage, sludge, biosolids; *informal* cow chips, horse apples, horse buns ♣.
■ **muck something up** (*informal*) MAKE A MESS OF, mess up, bungle, spoil, ruin, wreck; *informal* botch, make a hash of, muff, fluff, foul up, louse up, goof up.
■ **muck about/around** (*informal*) **1** *he was mucking around with his friends* FOOL ABOUT/AROUND, play about/around, clown about/around; *informal* mess about/around, horse about/around. **2** *someone's been mucking about with the VCR* INTERFERE, fiddle (about/around), play about/around, tamper, meddle, tinker; *informal* mess (about/around).

mucky ▶ adjective DIRTY, filthy, grimy, muddy, grubby, messy, soiled, stained, smeared, slimy, sticky, bespattered; *informal* cruddy, grungy, grotty, yucky; *literary* besmirched, begrimed, befouled.
— OPPOSITES: clean.

mud ▶ noun MIRE, sludge, ooze, silt, clay, dirt, soil, gumbo.
■ **as clear as mud** UNCLEAR, unintelligible, opaque, unfathomable, incomprehensible, baffling, perplexing, inscrutable.

muddle ▶ verb **1** *you've muddled things up* CONFUSE, mix up, jumble (up), disarrange, disorganize, disorder, disturb, mess up. **2** *she became muddled* BEWILDER, confuse, bemuse, perplex, puzzle, baffle, mystify.
▶ noun **1** *the files are in a muddle* MESS, confusion, jumble, tangle, mishmash, chaos, disorder, disarray, disorganization, imbroglio, hodgepodge. **2** *a bureaucratic muddle* MIX-UP, misunderstanding; *informal* foul-up, snafu.
■ **muddle along/through** COPE, manage, get by/along, scrape by/along, make do.

muddy ▶ adjective **1** *muddy ground* WATERLOGGED, boggy, marshy, swampy, squelchy, squishy, mucky, slimy, spongy, wet, soft, heavy; *archaic* quaggy. **2** *muddy boots* MUD-CAKED, muddied, dirty, filthy, mucky, grimy, soiled; *literary* begrimed. **3** *muddy water* MURKY, cloudy, muddied, turbid, riled. **4** *a muddy pink* DINGY, dirty, drab, dull, sludgy.
— OPPOSITES: clean, clear.
▶ verb **1** *don't muddy your boots* MAKE MUDDY, dirty, soil, spatter, bespatter; *literary* besmirch, begrime. **2** *these results muddy the situation* MAKE UNCLEAR, obscure,

confuse, obfuscate, blur, cloud, befog.
— OPPOSITES: clarify.

muffle ▶ verb **1** *everyone was muffled up in coats* WRAP (UP), swathe, enfold, envelop, cloak. **2** *the sound of their footsteps was muffled* DEADEN, dull, dampen, mute, soften, quieten, tone down, mask, stifle, smother.

muffled ▶ adjective INDISTINCT, faint, muted, dull, soft, stifled, smothered.
— OPPOSITES: loud.

mug ▶ noun **1** *a china mug* CUP, glass; stein, flagon, tankard; *archaic* stoup. **2** (*informal*) *her ugly mug. See* FACE *noun sense 1.*
▶ verb (*informal*) *he was mugged by three youths* ASSAULT, attack, set upon, beat up, rob; *informal* jump, rough up, lay into, do over.

mugger ▶ noun See ROBBER.

muggy ▶ adjective HUMID, close, sultry, sticky, oppressive, airless, stifling, suffocating, stuffy, clammy, damp, heavy.
— OPPOSITES: fresh.

mulish ▶ adjective OBSTINATE, stubborn, pigheaded, recalcitrant, intransigent, unyielding, inflexible, bullheaded, stiff-necked.

mull
■ **mull something over** PONDER, consider, think over/about, reflect on, contemplate, turn over in one's mind, chew over, cogitate on, give some thought to.

multicoloured ▶ adjective KALEIDOSCOPIC, psychedelic, colourful, multicolour, many-coloured, many-hued, rainbow, variegated, polychromatic.
— OPPOSITES: monochrome.

multifarious ▶ adjective DIVERSE, many, numerous, various, varied, diversified, multiple, multitudinous, multiplex, manifold, multi-faceted, different, heterogeneous, miscellaneous, assorted; *literary* myriad, divers.
— OPPOSITES: homogeneous.

multiple ▶ adjective NUMEROUS, many, various, different, diverse, several, manifold, multifarious, multitudinous; *literary* myriad, divers.
— OPPOSITES: single.

multiplicity ▶ noun ABUNDANCE, scores, mass, host, array, variety; range, diversity, heterogeneity, plurality, profusion; *informal* loads, stacks, heaps, masses, tons; *literary* myriad.

multiply ▶ verb **1** *their difficulties seem to be multiplying* INCREASE, grow, become more numerous, accumulate, proliferate, mount up, mushroom, snowball. **2** *the rabbits have multiplied* BREED, reproduce, procreate.
— OPPOSITES: decrease.

multitude ▶ noun **1** *a multitude of birds* A LOT, a great/large number, a great/large quantity, host, horde, mass, swarm, abundance, profusion; scores, quantities, droves; *informal* slew, lots, loads, masses, stacks, heaps, piles, tons, dozens, hundreds, thousands, millions, gazillions. **2** *Father Peter addressed the multitude* CROWD, gathering, assembly, congregation, flock, throng, horde, mob; *formal* concourse. **3** *political power in the hands of the multitude* THE (COMMON) PEOPLE, the populace, the masses, the rank and file, the commonality, the plebeians; the hoi polloi, the mob, the proletariat, the (common) herd; *informal* the rabble, the proles, the plebs.

multitudinous ▶ adjective NUMEROUS, many, abundant, profuse, prolific, copious, multifarious, innumerable, countless, numberless, infinite; *literary* divers, myriad.

mum¹ ▶ noun (*informal*) *my mum looks after me. See* MOTHER noun sense 1.

mum² (*informal*) ▶ adjective *he was keeping mum* SILENT, quiet, mute, dumb, tight-lipped, unforthcoming, reticent.

■ **mum's the word** (*informal*) SAY NOTHING, keep quiet, don't breathe a word, don't tell a soul, keep it secret, keep it to yourself, keep it under your hat; *informal* don't let on, don't let the cat out of the bag.

mumble ▶ verb MUTTER, murmur, speak indistinctly, talk under one's breath.

mumbo-jumbo ▶ noun **1** *they think hypnosis is mumbo-jumbo* MAGIC, witchcraft, wizardry, sorcery, hocus-pocus. **2** *just so much mumbo-jumbo* NONSENSE, gibberish, claptrap, rubbish, balderdash, blather, hocus-pocus; *informal* gobbledegook, bafflegab.

mummer ▶ noun MIME, actor; (*Nfld*) janny ✦, belsnickle.

munch ▶ verb CHEW, champ, chomp, masticate, crunch, eat, gnaw, nibble, snack, chow down on.

mundane ▶ adjective **1** *her mundane life* HUMDRUM, dull, boring, tedious, monotonous, tiresome, wearisome, unexciting, uninteresting, uneventful, unvarying, unremarkable, repetitive, repetitious, routine, ordinary, everyday, day-to-day, run-of-the-mill, commonplace, workaday; *informal* plain-vanilla, ho-hum. **2** *the mundane world* EARTHLY, worldly, terrestrial, material, temporal, secular; *literary* sublunary.
– OPPOSITES: extraordinary, spiritual.

municipal ▶ adjective CIVIC, civil, metropolitan, urban, city, town, borough.
– OPPOSITES: rural.

municipality ▶ noun BOROUGH, town, city, district, precinct, township.

munificent ▶ adjective GENEROUS, bountiful, open-handed, magnanimous, philanthropic, princely, handsome, lavish, liberal, charitable, big-hearted, beneficent; *literary* bounteous.
– OPPOSITES: mean.

mural ▶ noun See PICTURE noun sense 1.

murder ▶ noun **1** *a brutal murder* KILLING, homicide, assassination, liquidation, extermination, execution, slaughter, butchery, massacre; manslaughter; *literary* slaying. **2** (*informal*) *driving there was murder* HELL (ON EARTH), a nightmare, an ordeal, a trial, misery, torture, agony.
▶ verb **1** *someone tried to murder him* KILL, put/do to death, assassinate, execute, liquidate, eliminate, dispatch, butcher, slaughter, massacre, wipe out; *informal* bump off, do in, do away with, knock off, blow away, blow someone's brains out, take out, dispose of, ice, rub out, smoke, waste; *literary* slay. **2** (*informal*) *Anna was murdering a Mozart sonata. See* MANGLE sense 2. **3** (*informal*) *he murdered his opponent. See* TROUNCE.

murderer, murderess ▶ noun KILLER, assassin, serial killer, butcher, slaughterer; *informal* hit man, gunman, hired gun; *literary* slayer.

murderous ▶ adjective **1** *a murderous attack* HOMICIDAL, brutal, violent, savage, ferocious, fierce, vicious, bloodthirsty, barbarous, barbaric; fatal, lethal, deadly, mortal, death-dealing; *archaic* sanguinary. **2** (*informal*) *a murderous schedule* ARDUOUS, gruelling, strenuous, punishing, onerous, exhausting, taxing, difficult, rigorous; *informal* killing, hellish.

murky ▶ adjective **1** *a murky winter afternoon* DARK, gloomy, grey, leaden, dull, dim, overcast, cloudy, clouded, sunless, dismal, dreary, bleak; *literary* tenebrous. **2** *murky water* DIRTY, muddy, cloudy, turbid, riled, roily. **3** *her murky past* QUESTIONABLE, suspicious, suspect, dubious, dark, mysterious, secret; *informal* shady, sketchy.
– OPPOSITES: bright, clear.

murmur ▶ noun **1** *his voice was a murmur* WHISPER, undertone, mutter, mumble. **2** *they left without a murmur* COMPLAINT, grumble, grouse; *informal* gripe, moan. **3** *the murmur of bees* HUM, humming, buzz, buzzing, thrum, thrumming, drone; sigh, rustle; *literary* susurration, murmuration.
▶ verb **1** *he heard them murmuring in the hall* MUTTER, mumble, whisper, talk under one's breath, speak softly. **2** *no one murmured at the delay* COMPLAIN, mutter, grumble, grouse; *informal* gripe, moan. **3** *the wind was murmuring through the trees* RUSTLE, sigh; burble, purl; *literary* whisper.

muscle ▶ noun **1** *he had muscle but no brains* STRENGTH, power, muscularity, brawn, burliness; *informal* beef, beefiness; *literary* thew. **2** *financial muscle* INFLUENCE, power, strength, might, force, forcefulness, weight; *informal* clout.
■ **muscle in** (*informal*) INTERFERE WITH, force one's way into, impose oneself on, encroach on; *informal* horn in on, barge in on.

muscular ▶ adjective **1** *muscular tissue* FIBROUS, sinewy. **2** *he's very muscular* STRONG, brawny, muscly, sinewy, powerfully built, well muscled, burly, strapping, sturdy, powerful, athletic; *Physiology* mesomorphic; *informal* hunky, beefy, muscle-bound; *literary* thewy. **3** *a muscular economy* VIGOROUS, robust, strong, powerful, dynamic, potent, active.

muse¹ ▶ noun *the poet's muse* INSPIRATION, creative influence, stimulus; *formal* afflatus. *See table.*

The Nine Muses

Calliope	epic poetry
Clio	history
Erato	lyric poetry and hymns
Euterpe	flute playing
Melpomene	tragedy
Polyhymnia	mime
Terpsichore	lyric poetry and dance
Thalia	comedy
Urania	astronomy

muse² ▶ verb *I mused on Toby's story* PONDER, consider, think over/about, mull over, reflect on, contemplate, turn over in one's mind, chew over, give some thought to, cogitate on; think, be lost in contemplation/thought, daydream.

mush ▶ noun **1** *some sort of greyish mush* PAP, pulp, slop, paste, purée, mash, porridge; *informal* gloop, goo, gook, glop, sludge, guck. **2** *romantic mush* SENTIMENTALITY, mawkishness; *informal* schmaltz, corn, slush, slop.

mushroom ▶ noun FUNGUS, blewits, button mushroom, cep, chanterelle, cremini, enoki, field mushroom, honey mushroom, horse mushroom, matsutake, morel, oyster mushroom, pine mushroom, porcini, portobello, shiitake, death cap, magic mushroom, shaggymane, boletus.
▶ verb *ecotourism mushroomed in the 1980s* PROLIFERATE, grow/develop rapidly, burgeon, spread, increase,

expand, boom, explode, snowball, rocket, skyrocket; thrive, flourish, prosper.
— OPPOSITES: contract.

mushy ▶ adjective **1** *cook until the fruit is mushy* SOFT, semi-liquid, pulpy, sloppy, spongy, squashy, squelchy, squishy; *informal* gooey. **2** (*informal*) *a mushy film* SENTIMENTAL, mawkish, emotional, saccharine; *informal* slushy, schmaltzy, weepy, corny, soppy, cornball, sappy, hokey, three-hankie, cheesy.
— OPPOSITES: firm.

music ▶ noun. *See tables.*

Types of Music

a cappella	industrial
acid house	jazz
acid rock	jungle
alternative	klezmer
barbershop	Latin
barrelhouse	mariachi
bebop	merengue
bluegrass	Motown
blues	New Age
boogie-woogie	new country
bubblegum	new wave
calypso	opera
chant	plainchant
choral	pop
country	progressive rock
country and western	psychedelic
cowpunk	punk
dancehall	rap
death metal	reggae
disco	rhythm and blues
Dixieland	rock
easy listening	rockabilly
elevator	rock and roll
flamenco	sacred
folk	salsa
funk	ska
gangsta	soul
glam rock	swing
gospel	technofunk
Goth	thrash metal
grunge	trance
hard rock	trip hop
heavy metal	world music
hip hop	zydeco

musical ▶ adjective TUNEFUL, melodic, melodious, harmonious, sweet-sounding, sweet, mellifluous, euphonious, euphonic.
— OPPOSITES: discordant.

musical instrument ▶ noun. *See table at* INSTRUMENT.

musician ▶ noun PLAYER, performer, instrumentalist, accompanist, soloist, virtuoso, maestro; *historical* minstrel.

musing ▶ noun MEDITATION, thinking, contemplation, deliberation, pondering, reflection, rumination, introspection, daydreaming, reverie, dreaming, preoccupation, brooding; *formal* cogitation.

muskeg ▶ noun marsh, bog, marshland, mire, peatland, peat bog, (*NB & NS*) barren ✦, swamp.

muss ▶ verb (*informal*) RUFFLE, tousle, dishevel, rumple, mess up, make a mess of, disarrange, make untidy.

must[1] ▶ verb *I must go* OUGHT TO, should, have (got) to, need to, be obliged to, be required to, be compelled to.

▶ noun (*informal*) *this video is a must* NOT TO BE MISSED, very good; necessity, essential, requirement, requisite.

must[2] ▶ noun *a smell of must* MOULD, mustiness, mouldiness, mildew, fustiness, decay, rot.

muster ▶ verb **1** *they mustered 50,000 troops* ASSEMBLE, mobilize, rally, raise, summon, gather (together), mass, collect, convene, call up, call to arms, recruit, conscript, draft; *archaic* levy. **2** *reporters mustered outside her house* CONGREGATE, assemble, gather together, come together, collect together, convene, mass, rally. **3** *she mustered her courage* SUMMON (UP), screw up, call up, rally.
▶ noun *the colonel called a muster* ROLL-CALL, assembly, rally, meeting, gathering, assemblage, congregation, convention; parade, review.
■ **pass muster** BE GOOD ENOUGH, come up to standard, come up to scratch, measure up, be acceptable/adequate, fill/fit the bill; *informal* make the grade, come/be up to snuff.

musty ▶ adjective **1** *the room smelled musty* MOULDY, stale, fusty, damp, dank, mildewy, (*Nfld*) fousty ✦, smelly, stuffy, airless, unventilated; *informal* funky. **2** *the play seemed musty* UNORIGINAL, uninspired, unimaginative, hackneyed, stale, flat, tired, banal, trite, clichéd, old-fashioned, outdated; *informal* old hat.
— OPPOSITES: fresh.

mutable ▶ adjective *the mutable nature of fashion* CHANGEABLE, variable, varying, fluctuating, shifting, inconsistent, unpredictable, inconstant, fickle, uneven, unstable, protean; *literary* fluctuant.
— OPPOSITES: invariable.

mutant ▶ noun FREAK (OF NATURE), deviant, monstrosity, monster, mutation.

mutate ▶ verb CHANGE, metamorphose, evolve; transmute, transform, convert; *humorous* transmogrify.

mutation ▶ noun **1** ALTERATION, change, variation, modification, transformation, metamorphosis, transmutation; *humorous* transmogrification. **2** *a genetic mutation* MUTANT, freak (of nature), deviant, monstrosity, monster, anomaly.

mute ▶ adjective **1** *she remained mute* SILENT, speechless, dumb, unspeaking, tight-lipped, taciturn; *informal* mum, tongue-tied. **2** *a mute appeal* WORDLESS, silent, dumb, unspoken, unvoiced, unexpressed. **3** *the forest was mute* QUIET, silent, hushed. **4** *he was deaf and mute* DUMB, unable to speak; *Medicine* aphasic.
— OPPOSITES: voluble, spoken.
▶ verb **1** *the noise was muted by the heavy curtains* DEADEN, muffle, dampen, soften, quieten, hush; stifle, smother, suppress. **2** *Bruce muted his criticisms* RESTRAIN, soften, tone down, moderate, temper.
— OPPOSITES: intensify.

muted ▶ adjective **1** *the muted hum of traffic* MUFFLED, faint, indistinct, quiet, soft, low. **2** *muted colours* SUBDUED, pastel, delicate, subtle, understated, restrained.

mutilate ▶ verb **1** *the bodies had been mutilated* MANGLE, maim, disfigure, butcher, dismember, cripple. **2** *the painting had been mutilated* VANDALIZE, damage, deface, ruin, spoil, destroy, wreck, violate, desecrate; *informal* trash.

mutinous ▶ adjective REBELLIOUS, insubordinate, subversive, seditious, insurgent, insurrectionary, rebel, riotous.

mutiny ▶ noun *there was a mutiny over wages*

Musical Directions

Term	Translation	Term	Translation
a cappella	unaccompanied	meno	less
accel(erando)	accelerating	meno mosso	less quickly
adagio	slowly	mezzo	half
ad lib(itum)	at will	mezzo forte *or* mf	fairly loudly
al fine	to the end	mezzo piano *or* mp	fairly softly
allargando	broadening	moderato	at a moderate pace
allegretto	fairly lively	molto	very
allegro	lively	mosso	fast and with animation
al segno	as far as the sign	moto	motion
andante	moderately slow	non troppo	not too much
andantino	slightly faster than andante	obbligato	not to be omitted
arco	with the bow	ped.	pedal
assai	very	pianissimo *or* pp	very softly
a tempo	in the original tempo	p(iano)	softly
bis	repeat	più	more
con brio	with vigour	pizz(icato)	plucked
con moto	with movement	poco	a little
cresc(endo)	becoming louder	rall(entando)	slowing down
da capo *or* DC	from the beginning	rit(ardando)	slowing down
dal segno *or* DS	from the sign	ritenuto	suddenly more slowly
decresc(endo)	becoming quieter	scherzando	playfully
dim(inuendo)	becoming quieter	segno	sign
dolce	sweetly	sempre	always/throughout
fine	end	sf(orzando) *or* sfz	strongly accented
f(orte)	loudly	smorzando	dying away
forte piano	loudly then immediately softly	sordino	with a mute
fortissimo *or* ff	very loudly	sost(enuto)	sustained
glissando	sliding	sotto voce	in an undertone
larghetto	fairly slowly	stacc(ato)	detached
largo	very slowly	tacet	voice/instrument remains silent
legato	tied/smoothly	ten(uto)	held
lento	slowly	troppo	too much
maestoso	majestically	tutti	all players/singers
marcato	accented	vivace	lively

INSURRECTION, rebellion, revolt, riot, uprising, insurgence, insubordination.
▶ **verb** *thousands of soldiers mutinied* RISE UP, rebel, revolt, riot, disobey/defy authority, be insubordinate.

mutt ▶ **noun** (*informal*) See MONGREL *noun*.

mutter ▶ **verb 1** *a group of men stood muttering* TALK UNDER ONE'S BREATH, murmur, mumble, whisper, speak in an undertone. **2** *backbenchers muttered about the reshuffle* GRUMBLE, complain, grouse, carp, whine; *informal* moan, gripe, beef, whinge, kvetch.

mutual ▶ **adjective** RECIPROCAL, reciprocated, returned; common, joint, shared.

muzzle ▶ **noun 1** *the dog's velvety muzzle* SNOUT, nose, mouth, maw. **2** *the muzzle of a gun* BARREL, end.
▶ **verb** *attempts to muzzle the media* GAG, silence, censor, stifle, restrain, check, curb, fetter.

muzzy ▶ **adjective 1** *she felt muzzy* GROGGY, light-headed, faint, dizzy, befuddled, befogged, dazed, fuddled; *informal* dopey, woozy. **2** *a muzzy image* BLURRED, blurry, fuzzy, unfocused, unclear, ill-defined, foggy, hazy.
— OPPOSITES: clear.

myopic ▶ **adjective 1** *a myopic patient* SHORT-SIGHTED, near-sighted. **2** *the government's myopic attitude* UNIMAGINATIVE, uncreative, unadventurous, narrow-minded, small-minded, short-term.
— OPPOSITES: far-sighted.

myriad (*literary*) ▶ **noun** *myriads of insects* MULTITUDE, a large/great number, a large/great quantity, scores, quantities, mass, host, droves, horde; *informal* lots, loads, masses, stacks, scads, tons, hundreds, thousands, millions, gazillions.
▶ **adjective** *the myriad lights of the city* INNUMERABLE, countless, infinite, numberless, untold, unnumbered, immeasurable, multitudinous, numerous; *literary* numerous.

mysterious ▶ **adjective 1** *he vanished in mysterious circumstances* PUZZLING, strange, peculiar, curious, funny, queer, odd, weird, bizarre, mystifying, inexplicable, baffling, perplexing, incomprehensible, unexplainable, unfathomable. **2** *he was being very mysterious* ENIGMATIC, inscrutable, secretive, reticent, evasive, furtive, surreptitious.
— OPPOSITES: straightforward.

mystery ▶ **noun 1** *his death remains a mystery* PUZZLE, enigma, conundrum, riddle, secret, (unsolved) problem. **2** *her past is shrouded in mystery* SECRECY, obscurity, uncertainty, mystique. **3** *a murder mystery* THRILLER, detective story/novel, murder story, crime novel; *informal* whodunit.

mystic, mystical ▶ **adjective 1** *a mystic experience* SPIRITUAL, religious, transcendental, paranormal, otherworldly, supernatural, occult, metaphysical. **2** *mystic rites* SYMBOLIC, symbolical, allegorical, representational, metaphorical. **3** *a figure of mystical significance* CRYPTIC, concealed, hidden, abstruse, arcane, esoteric, inscrutable, inexplicable, unfathomable, mysterious, secret, enigmatic.

mystify ▶ **verb** BEWILDER, puzzle, perplex, baffle,

confuse, confound, bemuse, bedazzle, throw; *informal* flummox, stump, bamboozle, fox.

mystique ▶ noun CHARISMA, glamour, romance, mystery, magic, charm, appeal, allure.

myth ▶ noun 1 *ancient Greek myths* (FOLK) TALE, (folk) story, legend, fable, saga, mythos, lore, folklore, mythology. 2 *the myths surrounding childbirth* MISCONCEPTION, fallacy, false notion, old wives' tale, fairy story/tale, fiction; *informal* (tall) story/tale, cock-and-bull story, urban myth/legend.

mythical ▶ adjective 1 *mythical beasts* LEGENDARY, mythological, fabled, fabulous, folkloric, fairy-tale, storybook; fantastical, imaginary, imagined, fictitious. 2 *her mythical child* IMAGINARY, fictitious, make-believe, fantasy, invented, made-up, non-existent; *informal* pretend.

mythological ▶ adjective FABLED, fabulous, folkloric, fairy-tale, legendary, mythical, mythic, traditional; fictitious, imaginary.

mythology ▶ noun MYTH(S), legend(s), folklore, folk tales/stories, lore, tradition.

Nn

nab ▶ verb (*informal*) CATCH, capture, apprehend, arrest, seize, grab; *informal* nail, pull in, pick up.

nabob ▶ noun VERY RICH PERSON, tycoon, magnate, millionaire, billionaire, multi-millionaire; *informal* fat cat.

nadir ▶ noun THE LOWEST POINT/LEVEL, the all-time low, the bottom, rock-bottom; *informal* the pits.
– OPPOSITES: zenith.

nag¹ ▶ verb **1** *she's constantly nagging me* HARASS, badger, give someone a hard time, chivvy, hound, harry, criticize, carp, find fault with, keep on at, grumble at, go on at, henpeck; *informal* hassle, get on someone's case, ride. **2** *this has been nagging me for weeks* TROUBLE, worry, bother, plague, torment, niggle, prey on one's mind; annoy, irritate; *informal* bug, aggravate.
▶ noun *don't be such a nag* SHREW, harpy, termagant, harridan; *archaic* scold.

nag² ▶ noun *she rode the old nag* WORN-OUT HORSE, old horse, hack; *informal* plug, crowbait; *archaic* jade.

nagging ▶ adjective **1** *his nagging wife* SHREWISH, complaining, grumbling, fault-finding, scolding, carping, criticizing. **2** *a nagging pain* PERSISTENT, continuous, niggling, unrelenting, unremitting, unabating.

nail ▶ noun **1** *fastened with nails* TACK, spike, pin, rivet; hobnail, finishing nail, roofing nail, ardox nail ♣, brad. **2** *biting her nails* FINGERNAIL, thumbnail, toenail.
– RELATED TERMS: ungual.
▶ verb **1** *a board was nailed to the wall* FASTEN, attach, fix, affix, secure, tack, hammer, pin. **2** (*informal*) *he nailed the suspect* CATCH, capture, apprehend, arrest, seize; *informal* collar, nab, pull in, pick up. **3** *she nailed that somersault* PERFORM WELL, succeed in, execute, complete, bring about/off; *informal* land, pull off, score.
■ **hard as nails** CALLOUS, hard-hearted, heartless, unfeeling, unsympathetic, uncaring, insensitive, unsentimental, hardbitten, tough, lacking compassion.
■ **hit the nail on the head** GET IT (RIGHT), guess correctly, speak (the) truth.

naive ▶ adjective INNOCENT, unsophisticated, artless, ingenuous, inexperienced, guileless, unworldly, trusting; gullible, credulous, immature, callow, raw, green, wide-eyed; *informal* wet behind the ears, born yesterday.
– OPPOSITES: worldly.

naiveté, naivety ▶ noun INNOCENCE, ingenuousness, guilelessness, artlessness, unworldliness, trustfulness; gullibility, credulity, immaturity, callowness.

naked ▶ adjective **1** *naked bathers* NUDE, bare, in the nude, stark naked, having nothing on, stripped, unclothed, undressed; *informal* without a stitch on, in one's birthday suit, in the buff, in the raw, in the altogether, starkers, buck-naked, butt-naked, mother-naked. **2** *a naked flame* UNPROTECTED, uncovered, exposed, unguarded. **3** *the naked branches of the trees* BARE, barren, denuded, stripped,

uncovered. **4** *I felt naked and exposed* VULNERABLE, helpless, weak, powerless, defenceless, exposed, open to attack. **5** *the naked truth | naked hostility* UNDISGUISED, plain, unadorned, unvarnished, unqualified, stark, bald; overt, obvious, open, patent, evident, apparent, manifest, unmistakable, blatant.
– OPPOSITES: clothed, covered.

namby-pamby ▶ adjective WEAK, feeble, spineless, effeminate, effete; ineffectual; *informal* weedy, wimpy, sissy.

name ▶ noun **1** *her name's Emma* designation, honorific, title, tag, epithet, label; *informal* moniker, handle; *formal* denomination, appellation. **2** *the top names in the fashion industry* CELEBRITY, star, superstar, VIP, leading light, big name, luminary; expert, authority; *informal* celeb, somebody, megastar, big shot, bigwig, big gun, great, giant. **3** *the good name of the firm* REPUTATION, character, repute, standing, stature, esteem, prestige, cachet, kudos; renown, popularity, notability, distinction.
– RELATED TERMS: nominal, onomastic.
▶ verb **1** *they named the child Phoebe* CALL, give a name to, dub; label, style, term, title, entitle; baptize, christen; *formal* denominate. **2** *he named the child in the photograph* IDENTIFY, specify. **3** *he has named his successor* CHOOSE, select, pick, decide on, nominate, designate.

nameless ▶ adjective **1** *a nameless photographer* UNNAMED, unidentified, anonymous, incognito, unspecified, unacknowledged, uncredited; unknown, unsung, uncelebrated. **2** *nameless fears* UNSPEAKABLE, unutterable, inexpressible, indescribable; indefinable, vague, unspecified.

namely ▶ adverb THAT IS (TO SAY), in other words, to be specific, specifically, viz, to wit.

nanny ▶ noun *the children's nanny* NURSEMAID, caregiver, caretaker, babysitter, au pair, governess; *dated* nurse.
▶ verb *stop nannying me* MOLLYCODDLE, cosset, coddle, baby, spoil, pamper, indulge, overindulge.

nap¹ ▶ verb *they were napping on the sofa* DOZE, sleep (lightly), take a nap, catnap, rest, take a siesta; *informal* snooze, catch forty winks, get some shut-eye, catch some zees, catch a few zees.
▶ noun *she is taking a nap* (LIGHT) SLEEP, catnap, siesta, doze, lie-down, rest; *informal* snooze, forty winks, shut-eye, beauty sleep, power nap.
■ **catch someone napping** CATCH OFF GUARD, catch unawares, (take by) surprise, catch out, find unprepared; *informal* catch someone with their pants down.

nap² ▶ noun *the nap of the velvet* PILE, fibres, threads, weave, surface, grain.

napkin ▶ noun table napkin, cocktail napkin, serviette, paper towel.

narcissism ▶ noun VANITY, self-love, self-admiration, self-absorption, self-obsession, conceit, self-centredness, self-regard, egotism, egoism.
– OPPOSITES: modesty.

narcissistic ▶ adjective VAIN, self-loving, self-admiring, self-absorbed, self-obsessed, conceited, self-centred, self-regarding, egotistic, egotistical, egoistic; *informal* full of oneself.

narcotic ▶ noun SOPORIFIC (DRUG), opiate, sleeping pill; painkiller, pain reliever, analgesic, anodyne, palliative, anaesthetic; tranquilizer, sedative; *informal* downer, dope; *Medicine* stupefacient.
▶ adjective SOPORIFIC, sleep-inducing, opiate; painkilling, pain-relieving, analgesic, anodyne, anaesthetic, tranquilizing, sedative; *Medicine* stupefacient.

narrate ▶ verb TELL, relate, recount, describe, chronicle, give a report of, report; voice-over.

narrative ▶ noun ACCOUNT, chronicle, history, description, record, report, story.

narrator ▶ noun **1** *the narrator of 'the Arabian Nights'* STORYTELLER, teller of tales, relater, chronicler, raconteur, anecdotalist. **2** *the film's narrator* VOICE-OVER, commentator, speaker.
— OPPOSITES: listener, audience.

narrow ▶ adjective **1** *the path became narrow* SMALL, tapered, tapering, narrowing; *archaic* strait. **2** *her narrow waist* SLENDER, slim, slight, spare, attenuated, thin. **3** *a narrow space* CONFINED, cramped, tight, restricted, limited, constricted. **4** *a narrow range of products* LIMITED, restricted, circumscribed, small, inadequate, insufficient, deficient. **5** *a narrow view of the world. See* NARROW-MINDED. **6** *nationalism in the narrowest sense of the word* STRICT, literal, exact, precise. **7** *a narrow escape* BY A VERY SMALL MARGIN, close, near, by a hair's breadth; *informal* by a whisker.
— OPPOSITES: wide, broad.
▶ verb *the path narrowed* | *narrowing the gap between rich and poor* GET/BECOME/MAKE NARROWER, get/become/ make smaller, taper, diminish, decrease, reduce, contract, shrink, constrict; *archaic* straiten.

narrowly ▶ adverb **1** *one bullet narrowly missed him* (ONLY) JUST, barely, scarcely, hardly, by a hair's breadth; *informal* by a whisker. **2** *she looked at me narrowly* CLOSELY, carefully, searchingly, attentively.

narrow-minded ▶ adjective INTOLERANT, illiberal, reactionary, conservative, parochial, provincial, insular, small-minded, petty, blinkered, inward-looking, narrow, parish-pump, hidebound, prejudiced, bigoted; *informal* redneck.
— OPPOSITES: tolerant.

narrows ▶ plural noun STRAIT(S), sound, channel, (*Atlantic*) run ♣, waterway, (sea) passage, (*Atlantic*) tickle ♣.

nascent ▶ adjective JUST BEGINNING, budding, developing, growing, embryonic, incipient, young, fledgling, evolving, emergent, dawning, burgeoning.

nastiness ▶ noun **1** *my mother tried to shut herself off from nastiness* UNPLEASANTNESS, disagreeableness, offensiveness, vileness, foulness. **2** *her uncharacteristic nastiness* UNKINDNESS, unpleasantness, unfriendliness, disagreeableness, rudeness, churlishness, spitefulness, maliciousness, meanness, ill temper, ill nature, viciousness, malevolence; *informal* bitchiness, cattiness.

nasty ▶ adjective **1** *a nasty smell* UNPLEASANT, disagreeable, disgusting, distasteful, awful, dreadful, horrible, terrible, vile, foul, abominable, frightful, loathsome, revolting, repulsive, odious, sickening, nauseating, repellent, repugnant, horrendous, appalling, atrocious, offensive, objectionable, obnoxious, unsavoury, unappetizing, off-putting;

noxious, foul-smelling, smelly, stinking, rank, fetid, malodorous, mephitic; *informal* ghastly, horrid, gruesome, diabolical, yucky, skanky, godawful, gross, beastly, grotty, lousy, funky; *literary* miasmal, noisome. **2** *the weather turned nasty* UNPLEASANT, disagreeable, foul, filthy, inclement; wet, stormy, cold, blustery, blizzardy. **3** *she can be really nasty* UNKIND, unpleasant, unfriendly, disagreeable, rude, churlish, spiteful, malicious, mean, ill-tempered, ill-natured, vicious, malevolent, obnoxious, hateful, hurtful; *informal* bitchy, catty. **4** *a nasty accident* | *a nasty cut* SERIOUS, dangerous, bad, awful, dreadful, terrible, severe; painful, ugly. **5** *she had the nasty habit of appearing unannounced* ANNOYING, irritating, infuriating, disagreeable, unpleasant, maddening, exasperating. **6** *they wrote nasty things on the wall* OBSCENE, indecent, offensive, crude, rude, dirty, filthy, vulgar, foul, gross, disgusting, pornographic, smutty, lewd; *informal* sick, X-rated.
— OPPOSITES: nice.

nation ▶ noun COUNTRY, (sovereign/nation) state, land, realm, kingdom, republic; fatherland, motherland; people, race. *See table at* COUNTRY.

national ▶ adjective **1** *national politics* STATE, public, federal, governmental, civic, civil, domestic, internal. **2** *a national strike. See* NATIONWIDE.
— OPPOSITES: local, international.
▶ noun *a Canadian national* CITIZEN, subject, native; voter.

nationalism ▶ noun PATRIOTISM, patriotic sentiment, flag-waving, xenophobia, chauvinism, jingoism.

nationality ▶ noun **1** *what is your nationality?* CITIZENSHIP. **2** *all the main nationalities of Ethiopia* ETHNIC GROUP, ethnic minority, tribe, clan, race, nation.

nationwide ▶ adjective NATIONAL, countrywide, state, general, widespread, extensive.
— OPPOSITES: local.

native ▶ noun *a native of Lethbridge* INHABITANT, resident, local; citizen, national; aborigine, autochthon; *formal* dweller.
— OPPOSITES: foreigner.
▶ adjective **1** *the native peoples* INDIGENOUS, original, first, earliest, aboriginal, autochthonous, First Nations ♣. **2** *native produce* | *native plants* DOMESTIC, home-grown, homemade, local; indigenous. **3** *a native instinct for politics* INNATE, inherent, inborn, instinctive, intuitive, natural; hereditary, inherited, congenital, inbred, connate. **4** *her native tongue* MOTHER, vernacular, first.
— OPPOSITES: immigrant.

Native Peoples ▶ plural noun FIRST PEOPLES, Native Canadians, Native Americans, Aboriginal Peoples, Indigenous Peoples; First Nations, Indians, Inuit, Metis. *See table at* FIRST PEOPLES.

natter (*informal*) ▶ verb *they nattered away.* SEE CHAT *verb.*

natty ▶ adjective (*informal*) SMART, stylish, fashionable, dapper, debonair, dashing, spruced up, well-dressed, chic, elegant, trim; *informal* snazzy, trendy, snappy, nifty, sassy, spiffy, fly, kicky, styling/stylin', sharp.
— OPPOSITES: scruffy.

natural ▶ adjective **1** *a natural occurrence* NORMAL, ordinary, everyday, usual, regular, common, commonplace, typical, routine, standard, established, customary, accustomed, habitual. **2** *natural produce* UNPROCESSED, organic, pure, wholesome, unrefined, pesticide-free, additive-free. **3** *Alex is a natural leader* BORN, naturally gifted,

untaught. **4** *his natural instincts* INNATE, inborn, inherent, native, instinctive, intuitive; hereditary, inherited, inbred, congenital, connate. **5** *she seemed very natural* UNAFFECTED, spontaneous, uninhibited, relaxed, unselfconscious, genuine, open, artless, guileless, ingenuous, unpretentious, without airs. **6** *it was quite natural to think that* REASONABLE, logical, understandable, (only) to be expected, predictable.
— OPPOSITES: abnormal, artificial, affected.

naturalist ▶ noun NATURAL HISTORIAN, life scientist, wildlife expert; biologist, botanist, zoologist, ornithologist, entomologist, ecologist.

naturalistic ▶ adjective REALISTIC, real-life, true-to-life, lifelike, graphic, representational, faithful, photographic.
— OPPOSITES: abstract.

naturalize ▶ verb **1** *he was naturalized in 1950* GRANT CITIZENSHIP TO, make a citizen, give a passport to, enfranchise. **2** *they naturalized new species of grass and wildflowers* ESTABLISH, introduce, acclimatize, domesticate; acclimate.

naturally ▶ adverb **1** *he's naturally shy* BY NATURE, by character, inherently, innately, congenitally. **2** *try to act naturally* NORMALLY, in a natural manner/way, unaffectedly, spontaneously, genuinely, unpretentiously; *informal* natural. **3** *naturally, they wanted everything kept quiet* OF COURSE, as might be expected, needless to say; obviously, clearly, it goes without saying.
— OPPOSITES: self-consciously.

nature ▶ noun **1** *the beauty of nature* THE NATURAL WORLD, Mother Nature, Mother Earth, the environment; the universe, the cosmos; wildlife, flora and fauna, the countryside. **2** *such crimes are, by their very nature, difficult to hide* ESSENCE, inherent/basic/essential qualities, inherent/basic/essential features, character, complexion. **3** *it was not in her nature to argue* CHARACTER, personality, disposition, temperament, makeup, psyche, constitution. **4** *experiments of a similar nature* KIND, sort, type, variety, category, ilk, class, species, genre, style, cast, order, kidney, mould, stamp, stripe.

naught ▶ noun (*archaic*) NOTHING (AT ALL), nil, zero, nought; *informal* zilch, zip, nada, diddly-squat.

naughty ▶ adjective **1** *a naughty boy* BADLY BEHAVED, disobedient, bad, misbehaved, misbehaving, wayward, defiant, unruly, insubordinate, wilful, delinquent, undisciplined, uncontrollable, ill-mannered, ungovernable, unbiddable, disorderly, disruptive, fractious, recalcitrant, wild, wicked, obstreperous, difficult, troublesome, awkward, contrary, perverse, incorrigible; mischievous, playful, impish, roguish, rascally; *informal* bratty; *formal* refractory. **2** *naughty jokes* INDECENT, risqué, rude, racy, ribald, bawdy, suggestive, improper, indelicate, indecorous; vulgar, dirty, filthy, smutty, crude, coarse, obscene, lewd, pornographic; *informal* raunchy, saucy; *euphemistic* adult.
— OPPOSITES: well-behaved, decent.

nausea ▶ noun **1** *symptoms include nausea and headaches* SICKNESS, biliousness, queasiness; vomiting, retching, gagging; upset stomach; travel-sickness, seasickness, carsickness, airsickness. **2** *it induces a feeling of nausea* DISGUST, revulsion, repugnance, repulsion, distaste, aversion, loathing, abhorrence.

nauseating ▶ adjective SICKENING, nauseous, stomach-churning, emetic, sickly; disgusting,

revolting, offensive, loathsome, obnoxious, foul, vomitous; *informal* gross, gut-churning.

nauseous ▶ adjective **1** *the food made her feel nauseous* SICK, nauseated, queasy, bilious, green around/at the gills, ill, unwell; seasick, carsick, airsick, travel-sick, barfy. **2** *a nauseous stench. See* NAUSEATING.

nautical ▶ adjective MARITIME, marine, naval, seafaring; boating, sailing.

navel ▶ noun **1** *informal* belly button; *Anatomy* umbilicus. **2** *the navel of Byzantine culture* CENTRE, central point, hub, focal point, focus, nucleus, heart, core; *literary* omphalos.
— RELATED TERMS: umbilical, omphalo-.

navigable ▶ adjective PASSABLE, negotiable, traversable; clear, open, unobstructed, unblocked.

navigate ▶ verb **1** *he navigated the yacht across the Atlantic* STEER, pilot, guide, direct, helm, captain; *Nautical* con; *informal* skipper. **2** *the upper reaches are dangerous to navigate* SAIL/GET (ACROSS/OVER), cross, traverse, negotiate, pass. **3** *I'll drive — you can navigate* MAP-READ, give directions.

navigator ▶ noun HELMSMAN, steersman, pilot, guide, wheelman.

navy ▶ noun **1** *a 600-ship navy* FLEET, flotilla, armada; Maritime Command ✿. **2** *a navy blazer* NAVY BLUE, dark blue, midnight blue, indigo.

near ▶ adverb **1** *her children live near. See* NEARBY *adverb*. **2** *near perfect conditions* ALMOST, just about, nearly, practically, virtually; *literary* well-nigh.
▶ preposition *a hotel near the seafront* CLOSE TO, close by, a short distance from, in the vicinity of, in the neighbourhood of, within reach of, a stone's throw away from; *informal* within spitting distance of.
▶ adjective **1** *the nearest house* CLOSE, nearby, close/near at hand, at hand, a stone's throw away, within reach, accessible, handy, convenient; *informal* within spitting distance. **2** *the final judgment is near* IMMINENT, in the offing, close/near at hand, at hand, (just) around the corner, impending, looming. **3** *a near relation* CLOSELY RELATED, close, related. **4** *a near escape* NARROW, close, by a hair's breadth; *informal* by a whisker.
— OPPOSITES: far, distant.
▶ verb **1** *by dawn we were nearing Moscow* APPROACH, draw near/nearer to, get close/closer to, advance towards, close in on. **2** *the death toll is nearing 3,000* VERGE ON, border on, approach.

nearby ▶ adjective *one of the nearby villages* NOT FAR AWAY/OFF, close/near at hand, close (by), near, within reach, at hand, neighbouring; accessible, handy, convenient.
— OPPOSITES: faraway.
▶ adverb *her mother lives nearby* CLOSE (BY), close/near at hand, near, a short distance away, in the neighbourhood, in the vicinity, at hand, within reach, on the doorstep, (just) round the corner.

nearly ▶ adverb ALMOST, (just) about, more or less, practically, virtually, all but, as good as, not far off, to all intents and purposes; not quite; *informal* pretty much, pretty well; *literary* well-nigh.

near miss ▶ noun CLOSE THING, near thing, narrow escape; *informal* close shave.

near-sighted ▶ adjective *See* SHORT-SIGHTED *senses* 1, 2.

neat ▶ adjective **1** *the bedroom was neat and clean* TIDY, orderly, well-ordered, in (good) order, shipshape, in apple-pie order, spic and span, uncluttered, straight, trim. **2** *he's very neat* SMART, dapper, trim, well-groomed, well-turned-out, spruce; *informal* natty. **3** *her neat script* WELL-FORMED, regular, precise,

elegant, well-proportioned. **4** *this neat little gadget* COMPACT, well designed, handy. **5** *his neat footwork* SKILFUL, deft, dexterous, adroit, adept, expert; *informal* nifty. **6** *a neat solution* CLEVER, ingenious, inventive. **7** *neat gin* UNDILUTED, straight, unmixed; *informal* straight up. **8** (*informal*) *we had a really neat time.* See WONDERFUL.
– OPPOSITES: untidy.
▶ **exclamation** COOL, excellent, awesome, neat-o, groovy, far-out, funky, right on, wicked, brilliant; *dated* keen.

neat freak ▶ **noun** NEAT PERSON, neatnik.

neatly ▶ **adverb** **1** *neatly arranged papers* TIDILY, methodically, systematically; smartly, sprucely. **2** *the point was neatly put* CLEVERLY, aptly, elegantly. **3** *a neatly executed turn* SKILFULLY, deftly, adroitly, adeptly, expertly.

nebulous ▶ **adjective** **1** *the figure was nebulous* INDISTINCT, indefinite, unclear, vague, hazy, cloudy, fuzzy, misty, blurred, blurry, foggy; faint, shadowy, obscure, formless, amorphous. **2** *nebulous ideas* VAGUE, ill-defined, unclear, hazy, uncertain, indefinite, indeterminate, imprecise, unformed, muddled, confused, ambiguous.
– OPPOSITES: clear.

necessarily ▶ **adverb** AS A CONSEQUENCE, as a result, automatically, as a matter of course, certainly, surely, definitely, incontrovertibly, undoubtedly, inevitably, unavoidably, inescapably, ineluctably, of necessity; *formal* perforce.

necessary ▶ **adjective** **1** *parental permission is necessary* OBLIGATORY, requisite, required, compulsory, mandatory, imperative, needed, de rigueur; essential, indispensable, vital. **2** *a necessary consequence* INEVITABLE, unavoidable, inescapable, inexorable, ineluctable; predetermined, preordained.

necessitate ▶ **verb** MAKE NECESSARY, entail, involve, mean, require, demand, call for, be grounds for, warrant, constrain, force.

necessitous ▶ **adjective** NEEDY, poor, short of money, disadvantaged, underprivileged, in straitened circumstances, impoverished, poverty-stricken, penniless, impecunious, destitute, pauperized, indigent, without a cent to one's name; *informal* hard up, without two coins/cents to rub together; *formal* penurious.
– OPPOSITES: wealthy.

necessity ▶ **noun** **1** *the microwave is now regarded as a necessity* ESSENTIAL, indispensable item, requisite, prerequisite, necessary, basic, sine qua non, desideratum; *informal* must-have. **2** *political necessity forced him to resign* FORCE OF CIRCUMSTANCE, obligation, need, call, exigency; force majeure. **3** *the necessity of growing old* INEVITABILITY, certainty, inescapability, inexorability, ineluctability. **4** *necessity made them steal* POVERTY, need, neediness, want, deprivation, privation, penury, destitution, indigence.
■ **of necessity** NECESSARILY, inevitably, unavoidably, inescapably, ineluctably; as a matter of course, naturally, automatically, certainly, surely, definitely, incontrovertibly, undoubtedly; *formal* perforce.

neck ▶ **noun** nape, scruff; *technical* cervix.
– RELATED TERMS: cervical, jugular.
▶ **verb** (*informal*) KISS, caress, pet; *informal* smooch, canoodle, make out; *informal, dated* spoon.
■ **neck and neck** LEVEL, equal, tied, side by side, close; *informal* even-steven(s).

necklace ▶ **noun** CHAIN, choker, necklet; beads, pearls; pendant, locket; *historical* torc.

necromancer ▶ **noun** SORCERER, sorceress, (black) magician, wizard, warlock, witch, enchantress, occultist, diviner; spiritualist, medium.

necromancy ▶ **noun** SORCERY, (black) magic, witchcraft, witchery, wizardry, the occult, occultism, voodoo, hoodoo; divination; spiritualism.

necropolis ▶ **noun** CEMETERY, graveyard, churchyard, burial ground; *informal* boneyard; *historical* potter's field.

need ▶ **verb** **1** *do you need money?* REQUIRE, be in need of, have need of, want; be crying out for, be desperate for; demand, call for, necessitate, entail, involve; lack, be without, be short of. **2** *you needn't come* HAVE TO, be obliged to, be compelled to. **3** *she needed him so much* YEARN FOR, pine for, long for, desire, miss.
▶ **noun** **1** *there's no need to apologize* NECESSITY, obligation, requirement, call, demand. **2** *basic human needs* REQUIREMENT, essential, necessity, want, requisite, prerequisite, demand, desideratum. **3** *their need was particularly pressing* NEEDINESS, want, poverty, deprivation, privation, hardship, destitution, indigence. **4** *my hour of need* DIFFICULTY, trouble, distress; crisis, emergency, urgency, extremity.
■ **in need** NEEDY, necessitous, deprived, disadvantaged, underprivileged, poor, impoverished, poverty-stricken, destitute, impecunious, indigent; *formal* penurious.

needful ▶ **adjective** (*formal*) NECESSARY, needed, required, requisite; essential, imperative, vital, indispensable.

needle ▶ **noun** **1** *a needle and thread* bodkin. **2** *the virus is transmitted via needles* hypodermic needle, syringe; *informal* hypo, spike. **3** *the needle on the meter* INDICATOR, pointer, marker, arrow, hand. **4** *put the needle on the record* STYLUS.
▶ **verb** (*informal*) *he needled her too much* GOAD, provoke, bait, taunt, pester, harass, prick, prod, sting, tease; IRRITATE, annoy, anger, vex, irk, nettle, pique, exasperate, infuriate, get on someone's nerves, rub the wrong way, ruffle someone's feathers, try someone's patience; *informal* aggravate, rile, niggle, get in someone's hair, hassle, get to, bug, miff, peeve, get/put someone's back up, get under someone's skin, get at, ride.

needless ▶ **adjective** UNNECESSARY, inessential, non-essential, unneeded, undesired, unwanted, uncalled for; gratuitous, pointless; dispensable, expendable, superfluous, redundant, excessive, supererogatory.
– OPPOSITES: necessary.
■ **needless to say** OF COURSE, as one would expect, not unexpectedly, it goes without saying, obviously, naturally; *informal* natch.

needlework ▶ **noun** SEWING, stitching, embroidery, needlepoint, needlecraft, tapestry, crewel work.

needy ▶ **adjective** POOR, deprived, disadvantaged, underprivileged, necessitous, in need, needful, hard up, in straitened circumstances, poverty-stricken, indigent, impoverished, pauperized, destitute, impecunious, penniless, moneyless; *informal* broke, strapped (for cash), without two coins/cents to rub together, busted; *formal* penurious.
– OPPOSITES: wealthy.

ne'er-do-well ▶ **noun** GOOD-FOR-NOTHING, layabout, loafer, idler, shirker, sluggard, slugabed, drone; *informal* lazybones, bum, *Atlantic* hangashore ✤; *archaic* wastrel.

nefarious ▶ adjective WICKED, evil, sinful, iniquitous, egregious, heinous, atrocious, vile, foul, abominable, odious, depraved, monstrous, fiendish, diabolical, unspeakable, despicable; villainous, criminal, corrupt, illegal, unlawful; *dated* dastardly.
— OPPOSITES: good.

negate ▶ verb **1** *they negated the court's ruling* INVALIDATE, nullify, neutralize, cancel; undo, reverse, annul, void, revoke, rescind, repeal, retract, countermand, overrule, overturn; *informal* nix; *formal* abrogate. **2** *he negates the political nature of education* DENY, dispute, contradict, controvert, refute, rebut, reject, repudiate; *formal* gainsay.
— OPPOSITES: validate, confirm.

negation ▶ noun **1** *negation of the findings* DENIAL, contradiction, repudiation, refutation, rebuttal; nullification, cancellation, revocation, repeal, retraction; *formal* abrogation. **2** *evil is not just the negation of goodness* OPPOSITE, reverse, antithesis, contrary, inverse, converse; absence, want.

negative ▶ adjective **1** *a negative reply* OPPOSING, opposed, contrary, anti-, dissenting, saying 'no', in the negative. **2** *stop being so negative* PESSIMISTIC, defeatist, gloomy, cynical, fatalistic, dismissive, antipathetic, critical; unenthusiastic, uninterested, unresponsive. **3** *a negative effect on the economy* HARMFUL, bad, adverse, damaging, detrimental, unfavourable, disadvantageous.
— OPPOSITES: positive, optimistic, favourable.
▶ noun *he murmured a negative* 'NO', refusal, rejection, veto; dissension, contradiction; denial; *informal* thumbs-down.

neglect ▶ verb **1** *she neglected the children* FAIL TO LOOK AFTER, leave alone, abandon, desert; *literary* forsake. **2** *he's neglecting his work* PAY NO ATTENTION TO, let slide, not attend to, be remiss about, be lax about, leave undone, shirk. **3** *don't neglect our advice* DISREGARD, ignore, pay no attention to, take no notice of, pay no heed to, overlook; disdain, scorn, spurn. **4** *I neglected to inform her* FAIL, omit, forget.
— OPPOSITES: cherish, heed, remember.
▶ noun **1** *the place had an air of neglect* DISREPAIR, dilapidation, deterioration, shabbiness, disuse, abandonment. **2** *her doctor was guilty of neglect* NEGLIGENCE, dereliction of duty, carelessness, heedlessness, unconcern, laxity, slackness, irresponsibility; *formal* delinquency. **3** *the neglect of women's concerns* DISREGARD, ignoring, overlooking; inattention to, indifference to, heedlessness to.
— OPPOSITES: care, attention.

neglected ▶ adjective **1** *neglected animals* UNCARED FOR, abandoned; mistreated, maltreated; *literary* forsaken. **2** *a neglected cottage* DERELICT, dilapidated, tumbledown, ramshackle, untended. **3** *a neglected masterpiece of prose* DISREGARDED, forgotten, overlooked, ignored, unrecognized, unnoticed, unsung, underestimated, undervalued, unappreciated.

neglectful ▶ adjective. See NEGLIGENT.

negligent ▶ adjective NEGLECTFUL, remiss, careless, lax, irresponsible, inattentive, heedless, thoughtless, unmindful, forgetful; slack, sloppy, derelict; *formal* delinquent.
— OPPOSITES: dutiful.

negligible ▶ adjective TRIVIAL, trifling, insignificant, unimportant, minor, inconsequential; minimal, small, slight, inappreciable, infinitesimal, nugatory, petty; paltry, inadequate, insufficient,

meagre, pitiful; *informal* minuscule, piddling, measly; *formal* exiguous.
— OPPOSITES: significant.

negotiable ▶ adjective **1** *salary is negotiable* OPEN TO DISCUSSION, discussable, flexible, open to modification; unsettled, undecided. **2** *the pathway was negotiable* PASSABLE, navigable, crossable, traversable; clear, unblocked, unobstructed. **3** *negotiable cheques* transferable; valid.

negotiate ▶ verb **1** *she refused to negotiate* DISCUSS TERMS, talk, consult, parley, confer, debate; compromise; mediate, intercede, arbitrate, moderate, conciliate; bargain, haggle. **2** *he negotiated a new contract* ARRANGE, broker, work out, thrash out, agree on; settle, clinch, conclude, pull off, bring off, transact; *informal* sort out, swing. **3** *I negotiated the obstacles* GET ROUND, get past, get over, clear, cross; surmount, overcome, deal with, cope with.

negotiation ▶ noun **1** *the negotiations resume next week* DISCUSSION(S), talks, deliberations; conference, debate, dialogue, consultation; mediation, arbitration, conciliation. **2** *the negotiation of the deal* ARRANGEMENT, brokering; settlement, conclusion, completion, transaction.

negotiator ▶ noun MEDIATOR, arbitrator, arbiter, moderator, go-between, middleman, intermediary, intercessor, intervener, conciliator; representative, spokesperson, broker, bargainer.

neigh ▶ verb WHINNY, bray, nicker, snicker, whicker.

neighbourhood ▶ noun **1** *a quiet neighbourhood* DISTRICT, area, locality, locale, quarter, community; part, region, zone; *informal* neck of the woods, hood, nabe, stomping ground. **2** *in the neighbourhood of Vancouver* VICINITY, environs, purlieus, precincts, vicinage.
■ **in the neighbourhood of** APPROXIMATELY, about, around, roughly, in the region of, of the order of, nearly, almost, close to, just about, practically, there or thereabouts, circa.

neighbouring ▶ adjective ADJACENT, adjoining, bordering, connecting, abutting; proximate, near, close (at hand), next-door, nearby, in the vicinity.
— OPPOSITES: remote.

neighbourly ▶ adjective OBLIGING, helpful, friendly, kind, amiable, amicable, affable, genial, agreeable, hospitable, companionable, well disposed, civil, cordial, good-natured, nice, pleasant, generous, considerate, thoughtful, unselfish, decent.
— OPPOSITES: unfriendly.

nemesis ▶ noun **1** *they were beaten in the final by their nemesis* ARCH RIVAL, adversary, foe, opponent, arch enemy. **2** *this could be the bank's nemesis* DOWNFALL, undoing, ruin, ruination, destruction, Waterloo. **3** *the nemesis that his crime deserved* RETRIBUTION, vengeance, punishment, just deserts; fate, destiny.

neologism ▶ noun NEW WORD, new expression, new term, new phrase, coinage; made-up word, nonce-word.

neophyte ▶ noun **1** *a neophyte of the monastery* NOVICE, novitiate; postulant, catechumen. **2** *cooking classes are offered to neophytes* BEGINNER, learner, novice, newcomer; initiate, tyro, fledgling; trainee, apprentice, probationer, tenderfoot; *informal* rookie, newbie, greenhorn.

ne plus ultra ▶ noun THE LAST WORD, the ultimate, the perfect example, the height, the acme, the zenith, the epitome, the quintessence.

nepotism ▶ noun FAVOURITISM, preferential

treatment, the old boy network, looking after one's own, bias, partiality, partisanship.

— OPPOSITES: impartiality.

nerd ▶ noun (informal) BORE; informal dork, dweeb, geek, loser; techie.

nerve ▶ noun 1 *the nerves that transmit pain* nerve fibre, neuron, axon, dendrite. 2 *the match will be a test of nerve* CONFIDENCE, assurance, cool-headedness, self-possession; courage, bravery, pluck, boldness, intrepidity, fearlessness, daring; determination, willpower, spirit, backbone, fortitude, intestinal fortitude, mettle, grit, true grit, stout-heartedness; informal guts, spunk, moxie. 3 *he had the nerve to ask her out again* AUDACITY, cheek, effrontery, gall, temerity, presumption, boldness, brazenness, impudence, impertinence, arrogance, cockiness; informal face, front, chutzpah, sauce. 4 *pre-wedding nerves* ANXIETY, tension, nervousness, stress, worry, cold feet, apprehension; informal butterflies (in one's stomach), collywobbles, the jitters, the shakes, jim-jams, the heebie-jeebies.

— RELATED TERMS: neural, neuro-.

■ **get on someone's nerves** IRRITATE, annoy, irk, anger, bother, vex, provoke, displease, exasperate, infuriate, gall, pique, needle, ruffle someone's feathers, try someone's patience; jar on, grate on, rankle; rub the wrong way; informal aggravate, get to, bug, miff, peeve, rile, nettle, get someone's goat, cheese off, tick off, wind up.

■ **nerve oneself** BRACE ONESELF, steel oneself, summon one's courage, gear oneself up, prepare oneself; fortify oneself; informal psych oneself up; literary gird one's loins.

nerve-racking ▶ adjective STRESSFUL, anxious, worrying, fraught, nail-biting, tense, difficult, trying, worrisome, daunting, frightening; informal scary, hairy.

nervous ▶ adjective 1 *a nervous woman* HIGH-STRUNG, anxious, edgy, tense, excitable, jumpy, skittish, brittle, neurotic; timid, mousy, shy, fearful. 2 *he was so nervous he couldn't eat* ANXIOUS, worried, apprehensive, on edge, edgy, tense, stressed, agitated, uneasy, restless, worked up, keyed up, overwrought, jumpy; fearful, frightened, scared, shaky, in a cold sweat, gun-shy; informal with butterflies in one's stomach, jittery, twitchy, in a state, uptight, wired, in a flap, het up, strung out, having kittens, squirrely. 3 *a nervous disorder* NEUROLOGICAL, neural.

— OPPOSITES: relaxed, calm.

nervous breakdown ▶ noun (MENTAL) COLLAPSE, breakdown, crisis, trauma; nervous exhaustion, mental illness.

nervousness ▶ noun ANXIETY, edginess, tension, agitation, stress, worry, apprehension, uneasiness, disquiet, fear, trepidation, perturbation, alarm; informal butterflies (in one's stomach), collywobbles, the jitters, the willies, the heebie-jeebies, the shakes.

nervy ▶ adjective *it was a nervy move* AUDACIOUS, impudent, brazen, cheeky, saucy, spunky, plucky, gutsy, ballsy, bold.

nest ▶ noun 1 *the birds built a nest* ROOST, eyrie. 2 *the animals disperse rapidly from the nest* LAIR, den, burrow. 3 *a cozy love nest* HIDEAWAY, hideout, retreat, shelter, refuge, den; informal hidey-hole. 4 *a nest of intrigue* HOTBED, den, breeding ground, cradle.

nest egg ▶ noun (LIFE) SAVINGS, cache, funds, reserve.

nestle ▶ verb SNUGGLE, cuddle, huddle, nuzzle, settle, burrow.

Net ▶ noun INTERNET, World Wide Web, web, cyberspace, information superhighway, Infobahn.

net¹ ▶ noun 1 *fishermen mending their nets* FISHING NET, dragnet, drift net, trawl net, landing net, gill net, cast net, seine, (Nfld) linnet ♣. 2 *a dress of green net* NETTING, meshwork, webbing, tulle, fishnet, openwork, lace, latticework. 3 *he managed to escape the net* TRAP, snare.
▶ verb *they netted big criminals* CATCH, capture, trap, entrap, snare, ensnare, bag, hook, land; informal nab, collar.

net² ▶ adjective 1 *net earnings* AFTER TAX, after deductions, take-home, final; informal bottom line. 2 *the net result* FINAL, end, ultimate, closing; overall, actual, effective.

— OPPOSITES: gross.

▶ verb *she netted $50,000* EARN, make, get, gain, obtain, acquire, accumulate, take home, bring in, pocket, realize, be paid, rake in.

nether ▶ adjective LOWER, low, bottom, bottommost, under, basal; underground.

— OPPOSITES: upper.

netherworld ▶ noun HELL, the underworld, the infernal regions, the abyss; eternal damnation, perdition; Hades, Acheron, Gehenna, Tophet, Sheol; literary the pit.

— OPPOSITES: heaven.

netminder ▶ noun GOALIE, goaltender, goalkeeper, backstop.

nettle ▶ verb IRRITATE, annoy, irk, gall, vex, anger, exasperate, infuriate, provoke; upset, displease, offend, affront, pique, get on someone's nerves, try someone's patience, ruffle someone's feathers; rub the wrong way, rankle; informal peeve, aggravate, miff, rile, needle, get to, bug, get someone's goat, wind up, tick off.

network ▶ noun 1 *a network of arteries* WEB, lattice, net, matrix, mesh, criss-cross, grid, reticulum, reticulation; Anatomy plexus. 2 *a network of lanes* MAZE, labyrinth, warren, tangle. 3 *a network of friends* SYSTEM, complex, nexus, web, webwork.

neurosis ▶ noun MENTAL ILLNESS, mental disorder, psychological disorder; psychoneurosis, psychopathy; obsession, phobia, fixation; Medicine neuroticism.

neurotic ▶ adjective 1 *(Medicine) neurotic patients* MENTALLY ILL, mentally disturbed, unstable, unbalanced, maladjusted; psychopathic, phobic, obsessive-compulsive. 2 *a neurotic, self-obsessed woman* OVER-ANXIOUS, over-sensitive, nervous, tense, high-strung, strung-out, paranoid; obsessive, fixated, hysterical, overwrought, worked-up, irrational, twitchy.

— OPPOSITES: stable, calm.

neuter ▶ adjective ASEXUAL, sexless, unsexed; androgynous, epicene.

▶ verb *have your pets neutered* STERILIZE, castrate, spay, geld, fix, desex, alter, doctor; archaic emasculate.

neutral ▶ adjective 1 *a neutral judge* IMPARTIAL, unbiased, unprejudiced, objective, open-minded, non-partisan, disinterested, dispassionate, detached, impersonal, unemotional, indifferent, uncommitted. 2 *Switzerland remained neutral* UNALIGNED, non-aligned, unaffiliated, unallied, uninvolved; non-combatant. 3 *a neutral topic of conversation* INOFFENSIVE, bland, unobjectionable, unexceptionable, anodyne, unremarkable, ordinary,

commonplace; safe, harmless, innocuous. **4** *a neutral background* PALE, light; beige, cream, taupe, oatmeal, ecru, buff, fawn, grey; colourless, uncoloured, achromatic; indeterminate, insipid, nondescript, dull, drab.
– OPPOSITES: biased, partisan, provocative, colourful.

neutralize ▶ verb COUNTERACT, offset, counterbalance, balance, counterpoise, countervail, compensate for, make up for; cancel out, nullify, negate, negative; equalize.

never ▶ adverb **1** *his room is never tidy* NOT EVER, at no time, not at any time, not once; *literary* ne'er. **2** *she will never agree to it* NOT AT ALL, certainly not, not for a moment, under no circumstances, on no account, nevermore; *informal* no way, not on your life, not in a million years, when pigs fly, when hell freezes over.
– OPPOSITES: always, definitely.

never-ending ▶ adjective *never-ending noise* INCESSANT, continuous, unceasing, ceaseless, constant, continual, perpetual, uninterrupted, unbroken, steady, unremitting, relentless, persistent, interminable, non-stop, endless, unending, everlasting, eternal.

nevertheless ▶ adverb NONETHELESS, even so, however, but, still, yet, though; in spite of that, despite that, be that as it may, for all that, that said, just the same, all the same; notwithstanding, regardless, anyway, anyhow, still and all.

new ▶ adjective **1** *new technology* RECENTLY DEVELOPED, up to date, latest, current, state-of-the-art, contemporary, advanced, recent, modern, cutting-edge, leading-edge. **2** *new ideas* NOVEL, original, fresh, imaginative, creative, experimental; contemporary, modernist, up to date; newfangled, ultra-modern, avant-garde, futuristic; *informal* way out, far out. **3** *is your boat new?* UNUSED, brand new, pristine, fresh, in mint condition. **4** *we have to find a new approach* DIFFERENT, another, alternative; unfamiliar, unknown, strange; unaccustomed, untried. **5** *they had a new classroom built* ADDITIONAL, extra, supplementary, further, another, fresh. **6** *I came back a new woman* REINVIGORATED, restored, revived, improved, refreshed, regenerated, reborn.
– RELATED TERMS: neo-.
– OPPOSITES: old, hackneyed, second-hand, present.

newbie ▶ noun NOVICE, neophyte, newcomer, rookie.

newborn ▶ adjective *newborn babies* JUST BORN, recently born.
▶ noun *the bacteria are dangerous to newborns* YOUNG BABY, tiny baby, infant; *Medicine* neonate.

newcomer ▶ noun **1** *a newcomer to the village* (NEW) ARRIVAL, immigrant, settler; stranger, outsider, (*Atlantic*) come from away ✦, foreigner, alien; *informal* johnny-come-lately, new kid on the block. **2** *photography tips for the newcomer* BEGINNER, novice, learner; trainee, apprentice, tyro, initiate, neophyte, tenderfoot; *informal* rookie, newbie, greenhorn.

newfangled ▶ adjective NEW, the latest, modern, ultra-modern, up-to-the-minute, state-of-the-art, advanced, contemporary, new-generation; *informal* trendy, flash.
– OPPOSITES: dated.

newly ▶ adverb RECENTLY, (only) just, lately, freshly; not long ago, a short time ago, only now, of late; new-.

news ▶ noun REPORT, announcement, story, account; article, news flash, newscast, headlines, press release, communication, communiqué, bulletin;

message, dispatch, statement, intelligence; disclosure, revelation, word, talk, gossip; *informal* scoop; *literary* tidings.

news conference ▶ noun PRESS CONFERENCE, scrum ✦, lock-up ✦, bear-pit session ✦.

newsgroup ▶ noun DISCUSSION GROUP, bulletin board, listserv, chat group.

newspaper ▶ noun PAPER, journal, gazette, tabloid, broadsheet, local (paper), daily (paper), weekly (paper); scandal sheet; *informal* rag, tab.

newsworthy ▶ adjective INTERESTING, topical, notable, noteworthy, important, significant, momentous, historic, remarkable, sensational.
– OPPOSITES: unremarkable.

next ▶ adjective **1** *the next chapter* FOLLOWING, succeeding, upcoming, to come. **2** *the next house in the street* NEIGHBOURING, adjacent, adjoining, next-door, bordering, connected, attached; closest, nearest.
– OPPOSITES: previous.
▶ adverb *where shall we go next?* THEN, after, afterwards, after this/that, following that/this, later, subsequently; *formal* thereafter, thereupon.
– OPPOSITES: before.
■ **next to** BESIDE, by, alongside, by the side of, next door to, adjacent to, side by side with; close to, near, neighbouring, adjoining.

nibble ▶ verb **1** *they nibbled at mangoes* TAKE SMALL BITES (FROM), pick, gnaw, peck, snack on; toy with; taste, sample; *informal* graze (on). **2** *the mouse nibbled his finger* PECK, nip, bite.
▶ noun **1** *the fish enjoyed a nibble on the lettuce* BITE, gnaw, chew; taste. **2** *nuts and nibbles* MORSEL, mouthful, bite; snack, tidbit, canapé, hors d'oeuvre, munchies.

nice ▶ adjective **1** *have a nice time* ENJOYABLE, pleasant, agreeable, good, satisfying, gratifying, delightful, marvellous; entertaining, amusing, diverting, lovely, great. **2** *a nice landlord* PLEASANT, likeable, agreeable, personable, congenial, amiable, affable, genial, friendly, charming, delightful, engaging; sympathetic, simpatico, compassionate, good. **3** *nice manners* POLITE, courteous, civil, refined, polished, genteel, elegant. **4** *that's a rather nice distinction* SUBTLE, fine, delicate, minute, precise, strict, close; careful, meticulous, scrupulous. **5** *it's a nice day* FINE, pleasant, agreeable; dry, sunny, warm, mild.
– OPPOSITES: unpleasant, nasty, rough.

nicety ▶ noun **1** *legal niceties* SUBTLETY, fine point, nuance, refinement, detail. **2** *great nicety of control* PRECISION, accuracy, exactness, meticulousness.

niche ▶ noun **1** *a niche in the wall* RECESS, alcove, nook, cranny, hollow, bay, cavity, cubbyhole, pigeonhole. **2** *he found his niche in life* IDEAL POSITION, place, function, vocation, calling, métier, job.

nick ▶ verb **1** *I nicked my toe* CUT, scratch, incise, gouge, gash, score. **2** (*informal*) *she nicked his wallet.* See STEAL verb sense 1, 2.
▶ noun *a slight nick in the surface* CUT, scratch, incision, notch, chip, gouge, gash; dent, indentation.
■ **in the nick of time** JUST IN TIME, not a moment too soon, at the critical moment, at the last second, at the buzzer, just under the wire.

nickname ▶ noun SOBRIQUET, byname, tag, label, epithet, cognomen; pet name, diminutive, endearment; *informal* moniker; *formal* appellation.

nifty ▶ adjective (*informal*) **1** *nifty camerawork* SKILFUL, deft, agile, capable. **2** *a nifty little gadget* USEFUL, handy, practical. **3** *a nifty suit* FASHIONABLE, stylish,

smart.
— OPPOSITES: clumsy.

niggardly ▶ adjective **1** *a niggardly person* CHEAP, mean, miserly, parsimonious, close-fisted, penny-pinching, cheese-paring, grasping, ungenerous, illiberal; *informal* stingy, tight, tight-fisted. **2** *niggardly rations* MEAGRE, inadequate, scanty, scant, skimpy, paltry, sparse, insufficient, deficient, short, lean, small, slender, poor, miserable, pitiful, puny; *informal* measly, stingy, pathetic, piddling.
— OPPOSITES: generous.

niggle ▶ verb **1** *his behaviour does niggle me* IRRITATE, annoy, bother, provoke, exasperate, upset, gall, irk, rankle with; *informal* rile, get to, bug. **2** *he niggles on about the prices* COMPLAIN, quibble, nitpick, fuss, carp, cavil, grumble, gripe, grouse, moan.
▶ noun *niggles about the lack of equipment* QUIBBLE, trivial complaint, criticism, grumble, grouse, cavil; *informal* gripe, moan, beef.

night ▶ noun nighttime; (hours of) darkness, dark; nightfall, sunset.
— RELATED TERMS: nocturnal.
— OPPOSITES: day.
■ **night and day** ALL THE TIME, around the clock, {morning, noon, and night}, {day in, day out}, ceaselessly, endlessly, incessantly, unceasingly, interminably, constantly, perpetually, continually, relentlessly; *informal* 24-7.

nightclub ▶ noun DISCO, discotheque, nightspot, club, bar, lounge, café. *See also* BAR sense 4.

nightfall ▶ noun SUNSET, sundown, dusk, twilight, evening, close of day, dark; *literary* eventide.
— OPPOSITES: dawn.

nightly ▶ adjective **1** *nightly raids* EVERY NIGHT, each night, night after night. **2** *his nightly wanderings* NOCTURNAL, nighttime.
▶ adverb *a band plays there nightly* EVERY NIGHT, each night, night after night.

nightmare ▶ noun **1** *she woke from a nightmare* BAD DREAM, night terrors; *archaic* incubus. **2** *the journey was a nightmare* ORDEAL, trial, torment, horror, hell, misery, agony, torture, murder; curse, bane.

nightmarish ▶ adjective UNEARTHLY, spine-chilling, hair-raising, horrific, macabre, hideous, unspeakable, gruesome, grisly, ghastly, harrowing, disturbing, Kafkaesque; *informal* scary, creepy.

nightstick ▶ noun BLUDGEON, truncheon, club, billy club, stick.

nihilism ▶ noun SKEPTICISM, negativity, cynicism, pessimism; disbelief, unbelief, agnosticism, atheism.

nihilist ▶ noun SKEPTIC, negativist, cynic, pessimist; disbeliever, unbeliever, agnostic, atheist.

nil ▶ noun NOTHING, none; nought, zero, 0; *Tennis* love; *informal* zilch, zip, nada, a goose egg, nix; *dated* cipher; *archaic* naught.

nimble ▶ adjective **1** *he was nimble on his feet* AGILE, sprightly, light, spry, lively, quick, graceful, lithe, limber; skilful, deft, dextrous, adroit; *informal* nippy, twinkle-toed; *literary* lightsome. **2** *a nimble mind* QUICK-WITTED, quick, alert, lively, wide awake, observant, astute, astute, adroit, perceptive, penetrating, discerning, shrewd, sharp; intelligent, bright, smart, clever, brilliant; *informal* brainy, quick on the uptake.
— OPPOSITES: clumsy, dull.

nincompoop ▶ noun (*informal*). See IDIOT.

nine ▶ cardinal number NONET.
— RELATED TERMS: nona-.

nip ▶ verb *the child nipped her* BITE, nibble, peck; pinch, tweak, squeeze, grip.
▶ noun *a nip in the air* CHILL, biting cold, iciness.
■ **nip something in the bud** CUT SHORT, curtail, check, curb, thwart, frustrate, stop, halt, arrest, stifle, obstruct, block, squash, quash, subdue, crack down on, stamp out; *informal* put the kibosh on.

nipple ▶ noun TEAT, dug; *Anatomy* mamilla.

nippy ▶ adjective *it's a bit nippy in here* COLD, chilly, icy, bitter, raw.
— OPPOSITES: warm.

nirvana ▶ noun PARADISE, heaven; bliss, ecstasy, joy, peace, serenity, tranquility; enlightenment.
— OPPOSITES: hell.

nitpicking ▶ adjective (*informal*). See PEDANTIC.

nitty-gritty ▶ noun (*informal*) BASICS, essentials, fundamentals, substance, quintessence, heart of the matter; nub, crux, gist, meat, kernel, marrow; *informal* brass tacks, bottom line; nuts and bolts.

nitwit ▶ noun (*informal*). See IDIOT.

nix ▶ verb REJECT, veto, turn down, scrap, scrub, ditch, scuttle, stymie, call off, put the kibosh on.

no ▶ adverb absolutely not, most certainly not, of course not, under no circumstances, by no means, not at all, negative, never, not really; *informal* nope, uh-uh, nah, not on your life, no way, no way José, ixnay; *archaic* nay.
— OPPOSITES: yes.

Nobel Prize ▶ See tables at LITERATURE *and* PEACE.

nobility ▶ noun **1** *a member of the nobility* ARISTOCRACY, aristocrats, peerage, peers (of the realm), lords, nobles, noblemen, noblewomen, patricians; *informal* aristos. **2** *the nobility of his deed* VIRTUE, goodness, honour, decency, integrity; magnanimity, generosity, selflessness.

noble ▶ adjective **1** *a noble family* ARISTOCRATIC, patrician, blue-blooded, high-born, titled. **2** *a noble cause* RIGHTEOUS, virtuous, good, honourable, upright, decent, worthy, moral, ethical, reputable; magnanimous, unselfish, generous. **3** *a noble pine forest* MAGNIFICENT, splendid, grand, stately, imposing, dignified, proud, striking, impressive, majestic, glorious, awesome, monumental, statuesque, regal, imperial.
— OPPOSITES: humble, dishonourable, base.
▶ noun *Scottish nobles* ARISTOCRAT, nobleman, noblewoman, lord, lady, peer (of the realm), peeress, patrician; *informal* aristo.

nobody ▶ pronoun NO ONE, none, not a soul, nary a soul.
▶ noun NONENTITY, no-name, zero, cipher, non-person, no-hoper, nothing, picayune; *informal* nobody.

no-brainer ▶ noun EASY TASK/DECISION; foregone conclusion, sure thing, certainty; *informal* cert, dead cert.

nocturnal ▶ adjective NIGHTTIME, nightly, evening, late-night, crepuscular, vespertine.

nod ▶ verb **1** *she nodded her head* INCLINE, bob, bow, dip. **2** *he nodded to me to start* SIGNAL, gesture, gesticulate, motion, sign, indicate.
▶ noun **1** *she gave a nod to the manager* SIGNAL, indication, sign, cue; gesture. **2** *a quick nod of his head* INCLINATION, bob, bow, dip. **3** *Halifax will get the nod as host city* APPROVAL, selection, sanction, endorsement; *informal* the OK, the A-OK, the green light, the thumbs up.
■ **nod off** FALL ASLEEP, go to sleep, doze off, drop off;

informal drift off, flake out, go out like a light, sack out, drift into the arms of Morpheus.

node ▸ **noun** JUNCTION, intersection, interchange, fork, confluence, convergence, crossing.

noise ▸ **noun** SOUND, din, hubbub, clamour, racket, uproar, tumult, commotion, pandemonium, babel; *informal* hullabaloo.
− OPPOSITES: silence.

noiseless ▸ **adjective** SILENT, quiet, hushed, soundless.

noisome ▸ **adjective** (*literary*). See ODIOUS.

noisy ▸ **adjective 1** *a noisy crowd* ROWDY, clamorous, boisterous, turbulent, uproarious, riotous, rambunctious, rackety; chattering, talkative, vociferous, shouting, screaming. **2** *noisy music* LOUD, fortissimo, blaring, booming, deafening, thunderous, tumultuous, clamorous, ear-splitting, piercing, strident, cacophonous, raucous.
− OPPOSITES: quiet, soft.

nomad ▸ **noun** ITINERANT, traveller, migrant, wanderer, roamer, rover; gypsy, Bedouin; transient, drifter, vagabond, vagrant, tramp.

nominal ▸ **adjective 1** *the nominal head of the campaign* IN NAME ONLY, titular, formal, official; theoretical, supposed, ostensible, so-called. **2** *a nominal rent* TOKEN, symbolic; tiny, minute, minimal, small, insignificant, trifling; *informal* minuscule, piddling, piffling.
− OPPOSITES: real, considerable.

nominate ▸ **verb 1** *you may nominate a candidate* PROPOSE, recommend, suggest, name, put forward, present, submit. **2** *he nominated his assistant* APPOINT, select, choose, elect, commission, designate, name, delegate.

nominee ▸ **noun** CANDIDATE, contender, contestant, prospect, runner, choice, possibility.

no-name ▸ **noun** *on that team I was just a no-name* NOBODY, nonentity, zero, cipher, non-person, insignificant person.
▸ **adjective** *a no-name product* UNBRANDED, generic, non-proprietary.

non-believer ▸ **noun** UNBELIEVER, disbeliever, skeptic, doubter, doubting Thomas, cynic, nihilist; atheist, agnostic, freethinker; infidel, pagan, heathen.

nonce
■ **for the nonce** FOR THE TIME BEING, temporarily, pro tem, for now, for the moment, for the interim, for a while, for the present, in the meantime; provisionally.

nonchalant ▸ **adjective** CALM, composed, unconcerned, cool, {calm, cool, and collected}, cool as a cucumber; indifferent, blasé, dispassionate, apathetic, casual, insouciant; *informal* laid-back.
− OPPOSITES: anxious.

noncommittal ▸ **adjective** EVASIVE, equivocal, guarded, circumspect, reserved; discreet, uncommunicative, tactful, diplomatic, vague; *informal* cagey.
■ **be noncommittal** PREVARICATE, give nothing away, dodge the issue, sidestep the issue, hedge, pussyfoot around, beat around the bush, equivocate, temporize, shilly-shally, vacillate, waver; hem and haw, sit on the fence.

non compos mentis ▸ **adjective**. See INSANE sense 1.

nonconformist ▸ **noun** DISSENTER, dissentient, protester, rebel, renegade, schismatic; freethinker, apostate, heretic; individualist, free spirit, maverick, eccentric, original, deviant, misfit, dropout, outsider, bohemian.

nondescript ▸ **adjective** UNDISTINGUISHED, unremarkable, unexceptional, featureless, characterless, faceless, unmemorable, lacklustre; ordinary, commonplace, average, run-of-the-mill, mundane, garden-variety; uninteresting, uninspiring, colourless, bland, dull.
− OPPOSITES: distinctive.

non-drinker ▸ **noun** TEETOTALLER, abstainer.

none ▸ **pronoun 1** *none of the fish are unusual* NOT ONE, not a (single) one. **2** *none of this concerns me* NO PART, not a bit, not any. **3** *none can know better than you* NOT ONE, no one, nobody, not a soul, not a single person, no man.
− OPPOSITES: all.
■ **none the** ——— *we were left none the wiser* NOT AT ALL, not a bit, not the slightest bit, in no way, by no means any.

nonentity ▸ **noun** NOBODY, unimportant person, cipher, non-person, no-name, nothing, small fry, lightweight, mediocrity; *informal* no-hoper, non-starter.
− OPPOSITES: celebrity.

non-essential ▸ **adjective** UNNECESSARY, inessential, unessential, needless, unneeded, superfluous, uncalled for, redundant, dispensable, expendable, unimportant, extraneous.

nonetheless ▸ **adverb** NEVERTHELESS, even so, however, but, still, yet, though; in spite of that, despite that, be that as it may, for all that, that said, just the same, all the same; notwithstanding, regardless, anyway, anyhow, still and all.

non-existent ▸ **adjective** IMAGINARY, imagined, unreal, fictional, fictitious, made up, invented, fanciful; fantastic, mythical; illusory, hallucinatory, chimerical, notional, shadowy, insubstantial; missing, absent; *literary* illusive.
− OPPOSITES: real.

non-intervention ▸ **noun** LAISSEZ-FAIRE, non-participation, non-interference, inaction, passivity, neutrality; live and let live.

non-observance ▸ **noun** INFRINGEMENT, breach, violation, contravention, transgression, non-compliance, infraction; dereliction, neglect.

no-nonsense ▸ **adjective** STRAIGHTFORWARD, forthright, upfront, pragmatic, down-to-earth, down-to-business, matter-of-fact.

nonpareil ▸ **adjective** *a nonpareil storyteller* INCOMPARABLE, matchless, unrivalled, unparalleled, unequalled, peerless, beyond compare, second to none, unsurpassed, unbeatable, inimitable; unique, consummate, superlative, supreme; *formal* unexampled.
− OPPOSITES: mediocre.
▸ **noun** *without a doubt, theirs is the nonpareil* BEST, finest, crème de la crème, peak of perfection, elite, jewel in the crown, ne plus ultra, paragon; *archaic* nonsuch.

non-partisan ▸ **noun** UNBIASED, impartial, neutral, objective.

nonplussed ▸ **verb 1** *Nigel was nonplussed by the suggestion that he'd acted unkindly* SURPRISED, stunned, dumbfounded, confounded, taken aback, disconcerted, thrown (off balance); puzzled, perplexed, mystified, baffled, bemused, bewildered; *informal* fazed, flummoxed, stumped, bamboozled, discombobulated. **2** *Tex remained nonplussed* *throughout the scandal* UNPERTURBED, unruffled, unfazed, composed.

nonsense ▶ noun **1** *he was talking nonsense* RUBBISH, balderdash, gibberish, claptrap, blarney, moonshine, garbage, hogwash, baloney, jive, guff, tripe, drivel, bilge, bull, bunk, BS, bafflegab, piffle, poppycock, hooey, twaddle, gobbledegook, codswallop, flapdoodle, hot air; *dated* bunkum, tommyrot. **2** *she stands no nonsense* MISCHIEF, naughtiness, bad behaviour, misbehaviour, misconduct, misdemeanour; pranks, tricks, clowning, buffoonery, funny business; *informal* tomfoolery, monkey business, shenanigans, hanky-panky. **3** *they dismissed the concept as a nonsense* ABSURDITY, folly, stupidity, ludicrousness, inanity, foolishness, idiocy, insanity, madness.
— OPPOSITES: sense, wisdom.
▶ exclamation *'Nonsense!' she retorted* BALDERDASH, pshaw, no way, get out of here, phooey, puh-leeze, hooey, poppycock, come off it, like hell.

nonsensical ▶ adjective **1** *her nonsensical way of talking* MEANINGLESS, senseless, illogical. **2** *a nonsensical generalization* FOOLISH, insane, stupid, idiotic, illogical, irrational, senseless, absurd, silly, inane, hare-brained, ridiculous, ludicrous, preposterous; *informal* crazy, crackpot, nutty; daft.
— OPPOSITES: logical, sensible.

non-stop ▶ adjective *non-stop entertainment* CONTINUOUS, constant, continual, perpetual, incessant, unceasing, ceaseless, endless, uninterrupted, round-the-clock; unremitting, relentless, persistent, never-ending.
— OPPOSITES: occasional.
▶ adverb *we worked non-stop* CONTINUOUSLY, continually, incessantly, unceasingly, ceaselessly, all the time, constantly, perpetually, round the clock, day and night, steadily, relentlessly, persistently; *informal* 24-7.
— OPPOSITES: occasionally.

non-violent ▶ adjective PEACEFUL, peaceable, orderly, well-behaved.

noodle ▶ noun *overcooked noodles. See box at* PASTA.

nook ▶ noun RECESS, corner, alcove, niche, cranny, bay, inglenook, cavity, cubbyhole, pigeonhole; opening, gap, aperture; hideaway, hiding place, hideout, shelter; *informal* hidey-hole.

noon ▶ noun MIDDAY, twelve o'clock, twelve hundred hours, twelve noon, high noon, noon hour, noonday; *literary* noontime, noontide.
— RELATED TERMS: meridian.

no one ▶ pronoun NOBODY, not a soul, not anyone, not a single person, never a one, none.

norm ▶ noun **1** *norms of diplomatic behaviour* CONVENTION, standard; criterion, yardstick, benchmark, touchstone, rule, formula, pattern, guide, guideline, model, exemplar. **2** *such teams are now the norm* STANDARD, usual, the rule; normal, typical, average, unexceptional, par for the course, expected.

normal ▶ adjective **1** *they issue books in the normal way* USUAL, standard, ordinary, customary, conventional, habitual, accustomed, expected, wonted; typical, stock, common, everyday, regular, routine, established, set, fixed, traditional, time-honoured. **2** *a normal couple* ORDINARY, average, typical, run-of-the-mill, middle-of-the-road, common, conventional, mainstream, unremarkable, unexceptional, garden-variety, a dime a dozen.
— OPPOSITES: unusual, insane.

normality ▶ noun NORMALCY, business as usual, the daily round; routine, order, regularity.

normally ▶ adverb **1** *she wanted to walk normally* NATURALLY, conventionally, ordinarily; as usual, as normal. **2** *normally we'd keep quiet about this* USUALLY, ordinarily, as a rule, generally, in general, mostly, for the most part, by and large, mainly, most of the time, on the whole; typically, customarily, traditionally.

north ▶ adjective NORTHERN, northerly, polar, Arctic, boreal.
▶ noun ARCTIC, northland, land of the midnight sun, north of sixty, the Barrens.

nose ▶ noun **1** *a punch on the nose* SNOUT, muzzle, proboscis, trunk; *informal* beak, snoot, schnozz, schnozzola, sniffer. **2** *a nose for scandal* INSTINCT, feeling, sixth sense, intuition, insight, perception. **3** *wine with a fruity nose* SMELL, bouquet, aroma, fragrance, perfume, scent, odour. **4** *the plane's nose* dipped nose-cone, bow, prow, front end.
— RELATED TERMS: nasal, rhinal.
▶ verb **1** *the dog nosed the ball* NUZZLE, nudge, push. **2** *she's nosing into my business* PRY, inquire, poke about/around, interfere (in), meddle (in); be a busybody, stick/poke one's nose in; *informal* be nosy (about), snoop. **3** *he nosed the car into the traffic* EASE, inch, edge, move, manoeuvre, steer, guide.
■ **by a nose** (ONLY) JUST, barely, narrowly, by a hair's breadth, by the skin of one's teeth, by a whisker.
■ **nose around/about** INVESTIGATE, explore, ferret (around), rummage, search; delve into, peer into; prowl around; *informal* snoop about/around.
■ **nose something out** DETECT, find, discover, bring to light, track down, dig up, ferret out, root out, uncover, unearth, sniff out.
■ **on the nose** (*informal*) EXACTLY, precisely, sharp, on the dot, on the button, promptly, prompt, dead on, bang on.

nosedive ▶ noun **1** *the plane went into a nosedive* DIVE, descent, drop, plunge, plummet, fall. **2** (*informal*) *the dollar took a nosedive* FALL, drop, plunge, plummet, tumble, decline, slump; *informal* crash, toboggan slide ♣.
— OPPOSITES: climb, rise.
▶ verb **1** *the device nosedived to earth* DIVE, plunge, pitch, drop, plummet. **2** (*informal*) *costs have nosedived* FALL, take a header, drop, sink, plunge, plummet, tumble, slump, go down, decline; *informal* crash.
— OPPOSITES: soar, rise.

nosh (*informal*) ▶ noun *all kinds of nosh. See* FOOD sense 1.
▶ verb *they noshed on smoked salmon. See* EAT sense 1.

nostalgia ▶ noun REMINISCENCE, remembrance, recollection; wistfulness, regret, sentimentality; homesickness.

nostalgic ▶ adjective WISTFUL, evocative, romantic, sentimental; regretful, dewy-eyed, misty-eyed, maudlin; homesick.

nostrum ▶ noun **1** *they have to prove their nostrums work* MEDICINE, quack remedy, potion, elixir, panacea, cure-all, wonder drug; *informal* magic bullet. **2** *right-wing nostrums* MAGIC FORMULA, recipe for success, remedy, cure, prescription, answer.

nosy ▶ adjective (*informal*) PRYING, inquisitive, curious, busybody, spying, eavesdropping, intrusive; *informal* snooping, snoopy.

notable ▶ adjective **1** *notable examples of workmanship* NOTEWORTHY, remarkable, outstanding, important, significant, momentous, memorable; marked, striking, impressive; uncommon, unusual, special,

exceptional, signal. **2** *a notable author* PROMINENT, important, well-known, famous, famed, noted, distinguished, great, eminent, illustrious, respected, esteemed, renowned, celebrated, acclaimed, influential, prestigious, of note.
– OPPOSITES: unremarkable, unknown.
▶ **noun** *movie stars and other notables* CELEBRITY, public figure, VIP, personage, notability, dignitary, worthy, luminary; star, superstar, icon, (big) name; *informal* celeb, somebody, bigwig, big shot, big cheese, big fish, megastar, big kahuna, high muckamuck.
– OPPOSITES: nonentity, no-name.

notably ▶ **adverb** *these are notably short-lived birds* REMARKABLY, especially, specially, very, extremely, exceptionally, singularly, particularly, peculiarly, distinctly, significantly, unusually, extraordinarily, strikingly, uncommonly, incredibly, really, decidedly, surprisingly, conspicuously; in particular, primarily, principally.

notation ▶ **noun** **1** *algebraic notation* SYMBOLS, alphabet, syllabary, script; code, cipher, hieroglyphics. **2** *notations in the margin* ANNOTATION, jotting, comment, footnote, entry, memo, gloss, explanation.

notch ▶ **noun** **1** *a notch in the end of the arrow* NICK, cut, incision, score, scratch, slit, slot, groove, cleft, indentation. **2** *her opinion of Nick dropped a notch* DEGREE, level, rung, point, mark, measure, grade.
▶ **verb** *notch the plank* NICK, cut, score, incise, carve, scratch, slit, gouge, groove, furrow.
■ **notch something up** SCORE, achieve, attain, gain, earn, make; rack up, chalk up; register, record.

note ▶ **noun** **1** *a note in her diary* RECORD, entry, item, notation, jotting, memorandum, reminder, aide-mémoire; *informal* memo. **2** *he will take notes of the meeting* MINUTES, records, details; report, account, commentary, transcript, proceedings, transactions; synopsis, summary, outline. **3** *notes in the margins* ANNOTATION, footnote, commentary, comment; marginalia, exegesis. **4** *he dropped me a note* MESSAGE, communication, letter, line; *formal* epistle, missive. **5** *this note is legal tender* BILL; banknote; (**notes**) paper money. **6** *this is worthy of* (*note* ATTENTION, consideration, notice, heed, observation, regard. **7** *a composer of note* DISTINCTION, importance, eminence, prestige, fame, celebrity, acclaim, renown, repute, stature, standing, consequence, account. **8** *a note of hopelessness in her voice* TONE, intonation, inflection, sound; hint, indication, sign, element, suggestion.
▶ **verb** **1** *we will note your suggestion* BEAR IN MIND, be mindful of, consider, observe, heed, take notice of, pay attention to, take in. **2** *the letter noted the ministers' concern* MENTION, refer to, touch on, indicate, point out, make known, state. **3** *note the date in your diary* WRITE DOWN, put down, jot down, take down, inscribe, enter, mark, record, register, pencil.

notebook ▶ **noun** NOTEPAD, scratch pad, exercise book, workbook, scribbler ♣, memo pad; register, logbook, log, diary, daybook, journal, record, tablet.

noted ▶ **adjective** RENOWNED, well-known, famous, famed, prominent, celebrated; notable, of note, important, eminent, distinguished, illustrious, acclaimed, esteemed; of distinction, of repute.
– OPPOSITES: unknown.

noteworthy ▶ **adjective** NOTABLE, interesting, significant, important; remarkable, impressive, striking, outstanding, memorable, unique, special; unusual, extraordinary, singular, rare.
– OPPOSITES: unexceptional.

nothing ▶ **noun** **1** *there's nothing I can do* NOT A THING, not anything, nil, zero; *informal* zilch, zip, nada, diddly-squat, squat; *archaic* naught. **2** *forget it – it's nothing* A TRIFLING MATTER, a trifle; neither here nor there; *informal* no big deal. **3** *he treats her as nothing* A NOBODY, an unimportant person, a nonentity, a cipher, a no-name, a non-person, small beer. **4** *the share value fell to nothing* ZERO, nought, 0; *Tennis* love.
– OPPOSITES: something.
■ **be/have nothing to do with 1** *it has nothing to do with you* BE UNCONNECTED WITH, be unrelated to, not concern; be irrelevant to, be inapplicable to, be inapposite to. **2** *I'll have nothing to do with him* AVOID, shun, ignore, have no truck with, have no contact with, steer clear of, give a wide berth to.
■ **for nothing 1** *she hosted the show for nothing* FREE (OF CHARGE), gratis, without charge, at no cost; *informal* for free, on the house. **2** *all this trouble for nothing* IN VAIN, to no avail, to no purpose, with no result, needlessly, pointlessly.
■ **nothing but** *he's nothing but a nuisance* MERELY, only, just, solely, simply, purely, no more than.

nothingness ▶ **noun** **1** *the nothingness of death* OBLIVION, nullity, blankness; void, vacuum; *rare* nihility. **2** *the nothingness of it all overwhelmed him* UNIMPORTANCE, insignificance, triviality, pointlessness, uselessness, worthlessness.

notice ▶ **noun** **1** *nothing escaped his notice* ATTENTION, observation, awareness, consciousness, perception; regard, consideration, scrutiny; watchfulness, vigilance, attentiveness. **2** *a notice on the wall* POSTER, bill, handbill, advertisement, announcement, bulletin; flyer, leaflet, pamphlet; sign, card; *informal* ad. **3** *show times may change without notice* NOTIFICATION, (advance) warning, announcement; information, news, communication, word. **4** *I handed in my notice* RESIGNATION. **5** *the film got bad notices* REVIEW, write-up, critique, criticism.
▶ **verb** *I noticed that the door was open* OBSERVE, perceive, note, see, discern, detect, spot, distinguish, mark, remark, descry; *literary* behold.
– OPPOSITES: overlook.
■ **take no notice (of)** IGNORE, pay no attention (to), disregard, pay no heed (to), take no account (of), brush aside, shrug off, turn a blind eye (to), pass over, let go, overlook, look the other way.

noticeable ▶ **adjective** DISTINCT, evident, obvious, apparent, manifest, patent, plain, clear, marked, conspicuous, unmistakable, undeniable, pronounced, prominent, striking, arresting; perceptible, discernible, detectable, observable, visible, appreciable.

notice board ▶ **noun** cork board, bulletin board, call board, message board; hoarding.

notification ▶ **noun** **1** *the notification of the victim's wife* INFORMING, telling, alerting, filling in. **2** *she received notification that he was on the way* INFORMATION, word, advice, news, intelligence; communication, message; *literary* tidings.

notify ▶ **verb** *we will notify you as soon as possible* INFORM, tell, advise, brief, apprise, let someone know, put in the picture, fill in; alert, warn.

notion ▶ **noun** **1** *he had a notion that something was wrong* IDEA, belief, conviction, opinion, view, thought, impression, perception; hypothesis, theory; (funny) feeling, (sneaking) suspicion, hunch. **2** *Claire had no notion of what he meant* UNDERSTANDING, idea, awareness, knowledge, clue, inkling. **3** *he got a notion* *to return* IMPULSE, inclination, whim, desire, wish, fancy.

notional ▶ adjective HYPOTHETICAL, theoretical, speculative, conjectural, suppositional, putative, conceptual; imaginary, fanciful, unreal, illusory.
— OPPOSITES: actual.

notoriety ▶ noun INFAMY, disrepute, ill repute, bad name, dishonour, discredit; *dated* ill fame.

notorious ▶ adjective INFAMOUS, scandalous; well known, famous, famed, legendary.

notwithstanding ▶ preposition *notwithstanding his workload, he is a dedicated father* DESPITE, in spite of, regardless of, for all.
▶ adverb *she is bright — notwithstanding, she is now jobless* NEVERTHELESS, nonetheless, even so, all the same, in spite of this, despite this, however, still, yet, that said, just the same, anyway, in any event, at any rate.
▶ conjunction *notwithstanding that there was no space, they played on* ALTHOUGH, even though, though, in spite of the fact that, despite the fact that.

nought ▶ noun *(archaic) my work has all been for nought* NOTHING, naught; no point, no purpose, no effect; *informal* zilch, zip, nada.

nourish ▶ verb 1 *patients must be well nourished* FEED, provide for, sustain, maintain. 2 *we nourish the talents of children* ENCOURAGE, promote, foster, nurture, cultivate, stimulate, boost, advance, assist, help, aid, strengthen, enrich. 3 *the hopes Emma nourished* CHERISH, nurture, foster, harbour, nurse, entertain, maintain, hold, have.

nourishing ▶ adjective NUTRITIOUS, nutritive, wholesome, good for one, healthy, health-giving, healthful, beneficial, sustaining.
— OPPOSITES: unhealthy.

nourishment ▶ noun FOOD, sustenance, nutriment, nutrition, subsistence, provisions, provender, fare; *informal* grub, nosh, chow, eats, vittles, scoff, chuck; *formal* comestibles; *dated* victuals.

nouveau riche ▶ plural noun the new rich, parvenus, arrivistes, upstarts, social climbers, vulgarians.

Nova Scotian ▶ noun Bluenose ♣, Bluenoser ♣.

novel[1] ▶ noun *curl up with a good novel* BOOK, paperback, hardcover; STORY, tale, narrative, romance, roman à clef; bestseller, blockbuster; potboiler, pulp (fiction).

novel[2] ▶ adjective *a novel way of making money* NEW, original, unusual, unfamiliar, unconventional, unorthodox; different, fresh, imaginative, innovative, innovatory, inventive, modern, neoteric, avant-garde, pioneering, groundbreaking, revolutionary; rare, unique, singular, unprecedented; experimental, untested, untried; strange, exotic, newfangled.
— OPPOSITES: traditional.

novelist ▶ noun WRITER, author, fictionist, man/woman of letters, scribe; *informal* penman, scribbler.

novelty ▶ noun 1 *the novelty of our approach* ORIGINALITY, newness, freshness, unconventionality, unfamiliarity; difference, imaginativeness, creativity, innovation, modernity. 2 *we sell seasonal novelties* KNICK-KNACK, trinket, bauble, toy, trifle, gewgaw, gimcrack, ornament, kickshaw.

novice ▶ noun 1 *a five-day course for novices* BEGINNER, learner, neophyte, newcomer, initiate, tyro, fledgling; apprentice, trainee, probationer, student, pupil, tenderfoot; *informal* rookie, newbie, greenhorn.

2 *a novice who was never ordained* NEOPHYTE, novitiate; postulant, proselyte, catechumen.
— OPPOSITES: expert, veteran.

novitiate ▶ noun 1 *his novitiate lasts a year* PROBATIONARY PERIOD, probation, trial period, test period, apprenticeship, training period, traineeship, training, initiation. 2 *two young novitiates* NOVICE, neophyte; postulant, proselyte, catechumen.

now ▶ adverb 1 *I'm extremely busy now* AT THE MOMENT, at present, at the present (time/moment), at this moment in time, currently, presently. 2 *television is now the main source of news* NOWADAYS, today, these days, in this day and age; in the present climate. 3 *you must leave now* AT ONCE, straight away, right away, right now, this minute, this instant, immediately, instantly, directly, without further ado, promptly, without delay, as soon as possible; *informal* pronto, straight off, ASAP.
■ **as of now** FROM THIS TIME ON, from now on, henceforth, from this day forward, in future; *formal* hereafter.
■ **for now** FOR THE TIME BEING, for the moment, for the present, for the meantime, for the nonce.
■ **not now** LATER (ON), sometime, one day, some day, one of these days, sooner or later, in due course, by and by, eventually, ultimately.
■ **now and again** OCCASIONALLY, now and then, from time to time, sometimes, every so often, (every) now and again, at times, on occasion(s), (every) once in a while; periodically, once in a blue moon.

nowadays ▶ adverb THESE DAYS, today, at the present time, in these times, in this day and age, now, currently, at the moment, at present, at this moment in time; in the present climate, presently.

nowhere
■ **in the middle of nowhere** BACK OF BEYOND, rural areas, (Ont. & Que.) the back concessions ♣, backwoods, hinterland, bush, backcountry; *informal* sticks, boondocks, boonies; *Austral.* outback.

noxious ▶ adjective POISONOUS, toxic, deadly, harmful, dangerous, pernicious, damaging, destructive; unpleasant, nasty, disgusting, awful, dreadful, horrible, terrible; vile, revolting, foul, nauseating, appalling, offensive; malodorous, fetid, putrid; *informal* ghastly, horrid; *literary* noisome.
— OPPOSITES: innocuous.

nuance ▶ noun FINE DISTINCTION, subtle difference; shade, shading, gradation, variation, degree; subtlety, nicety, overtone.

nub ▶ noun CRUX, central point, main point, core, heart (of the matter), nucleus, essence, quintessence, kernel, marrow, meat, pith; gist, substance; *informal* nitty-gritty.

nubile ▶ adjective SEXUALLY MATURE, marriageable; sexually attractive, desirable, sexy, luscious; *informal* beddable.

nucleus ▶ noun CORE, centre, central part, heart, nub, hub, middle, eye, focus, focal point, pivot, crux.

nude ▶ adjective (STARK) NAKED, bare, unclothed, undressed, disrobed, stripped, unclad, au naturel, without a stitch on, in one's birthday suit, in the raw, in the altogether, in the buff, starkers; *informal* buck-naked, butt-naked, mother-naked, buck.
— OPPOSITES: clothed.

nudge ▶ verb 1 *he nudged Ben* POKE, elbow, dig, prod, jog, jab. 2 *the canoe nudged a bank* TOUCH, bump (against), push (against), run into. 3 *we nudged them into action* PROMPT, encourage, stimulate, prod, galvanize. **4** *unemployment was nudging 3,000,000* APPROACH, near, come close to, be verging on, border on.

▶ **noun 1** *Maggie gave him a nudge* POKE, dig (in the ribs), prod, jog, jab, push. **2** *after a nudge, she remembered Lilian* REMINDER, prompt, prompting, prod, encouragement.

nudity ▶ **noun** NAKEDNESS, bareness, state of undress, undress; *informal* one's birthday suit.

nugatory ▶ **adjective 1** *a nugatory observation* WORTHLESS, unimportant, inconsequential, valueless, trifling, trivial, insignificant, meaningless. **2** *the shortages will render our hopes nugatory* FUTILE, useless, vain, unavailing, null, invalid.

nugget ▶ **noun** LUMP, nub, chunk, piece, hunk, wad, gobbet, (Nfld) nug ♣; *informal* gob.

nuisance ▶ **noun** ANNOYANCE, inconvenience, bore, bother, irritation, problem, trouble, trial, burden; pest, plague, thorn in one's side/flesh; *informal* pain (in the neck), hassle, bind, drag, chore, aggravation, headache, nudnik.
— OPPOSITES: blessing.

nuke ▶ **verb 1** *they nuked the enemy* BOMB, bombard, attack, destroy, demolish, flatten; shell, torpedo, blow up. **2** *she nuked the leftovers for five minutes* MICROWAVE, reheat, warm, cook; irradiate; zap.

null ▶ **adjective** *their marriage was declared null* INVALID, null and void, void; annulled, nullified, cancelled, revoked.
— OPPOSITES: valid.

nullify ▶ **verb 1** *they nullified the legislation* ANNUL, render null and void, void, invalidate; repeal, reverse, rescind, revoke, disallow ♣, cancel, abolish; countermand, do away with, terminate, quash; *Law* vacate; *formal* abrogate. **2** *the costs would nullify any tax relief* CANCEL OUT, neutralize, negate, negative.
— OPPOSITES: ratify.

numb ▶ **adjective** *his fingers were numb* WITHOUT SENSATION, without feeling, numbed, benumbed, desensitized, insensible, senseless, unfeeling; anaesthetized; dazed, stunned, stupefied, paralyzed, immobilized, frozen.
— OPPOSITES: sensitive.
▶ **verb** *the cold numbed her senses* DEADEN, benumb, desensitize, dull; anaesthetize; daze, stupefy, paralyze, immobilize, freeze.
— OPPOSITES: sensitize.

number ▶ **noun 1** *a whole number* NUMERAL, integer, figure, digit; character, symbol; decimal, unit; cardinal number, ordinal number. **2** *a large number of complaints* AMOUNT, quantity; total, aggregate, tally; quota. **3** *the wedding of one of their number* GROUP, company, crowd, circle, party, band, crew, set, gang. **4** *the band performed another number* SONG, piece (of music), tune, track; routine, sketch, dance, act.
— RELATED TERMS: numerical.
▶ **verb 1** *visitors numbered more than two million* ADD UP TO, amount to, total, come to. **2** *he numbers the fleet at a thousand* CALCULATE, count, total, compute, reckon, tally; assess, tot up; *formal* enumerate. **3** *each paragraph is numbered* assign a number to, mark with a number; itemize, enumerate. **4** *he numbers her among his friends* INCLUDE, count, reckon, deem. **5** *his days are numbered* LIMIT, restrict, fix.
■ **a number of** SEVERAL, various, quite a few, sundry.
■ **without number** COUNTLESS, innumerable, unlimited, endless, limitless, untold, numberless, uncountable, uncounted; numerous, many, multiple, manifold, legion.

numberless ▶ **adjective** INNUMERABLE, countless, unlimited, endless, limitless, untold, uncountable, uncounted; numerous, many, multiple, manifold, legion; *informal* more —— than one can shake a stick at; *literary* myriad.

numbing ▶ **adjective 1** *menthol has a numbing effect* DESENSITIZING, deadening, benumbing, anaesthetic, anaesthetizing; paralysing. **2** *numbing cold* FREEZING, raw, bitter, biting, arctic, icy. **3** *numbing boredom* STUPEFYING, mind-numbing, boring, stultifying, soul-destroying; soporific.

numbskull ▶ **noun** (*informal*). See IDIOT.

numeral ▶ **noun** NUMBER, integer, figure, digit; character, symbol, unit. *See table.*

Roman Numerals

Roman	Arabic	Roman	Arabic
I	1	XVI	16
II	2	XVII	17
III	3	XVIII	18
IV	4	XIX	19
V	5	XX	20
VI	6	L	50
VII	7	C	100
VIII	8	D	500
IX	9	M	1000
X	10	$\overline{\text{V}}$	5000
XI	11	$\overline{\text{X}}$	10 000
XII	12	$\overline{\text{L}}$	50 000
XIII	13	$\overline{\text{C}}$	100 000
XIV	14	$\overline{\text{D}}$	500 000
XV	15	$\overline{\text{M}}$	1 000 000

numerous ▶ **adjective** (VERY) MANY, a lot of, scores of, countless, numberless, innumerable; several, quite a few, various; plenty of, copious, a quantity of, an abundance of, a profusion of, a multitude of; frequent; *informal* umpteen, lots of, loads of, masses of, stacks of, heaps of, bags of, tons of, oodles of, hundreds of, thousands of, millions of, gazillions of, more —— than one can shake a stick at; *literary* myriad.
— OPPOSITES: few.

numinous ▶ **adjective** SPIRITUAL, religious, divine, holy, sacred; mysterious, otherworldly, unearthly, transcendent.

nun ▶ **noun** sister, abbess, prioress, Mother Superior, Reverend Mother; novice; bride of Christ, religious, conventual, contemplative, canoness; *literary* vestal; *historical* anchoress.

nuncio ▶ **noun** (PAPAL) AMBASSADOR, legate, envoy, messenger.

nunnery ▶ **noun** CONVENT, priory, abbey, cloister, religious community.

nuptial ▶ **adjective** MATRIMONIAL, marital, marriage, wedding, conjugal, bridal; married, wedded; *literary* connubial; *Law* spousal.

nuptials ▶ **plural noun** WEDDING (CEREMONY), marriage, union; *archaic* espousal.

nurse ▶ **noun 1** *skilled nurses* CAREGIVER, RN, nurse practitioner, nursing assistant, LPN, health care worker; *informal* Florence Nightingale; VON. **2** (*archaic*) *she had been his nurse in childhood* NANNY, nursemaid, wet nurse, governess, au pair, babysitter, ayah.
▶ **verb 1** *they nursed smallpox patients* CARE FOR, take care of, look after, tend, minister to. **2** *I nursed my sore finger* TREAT, medicate, tend; dress, bandage, soothe, doctor. **3** *Rosa was nursing her baby* BREASTFEED, suckle,

Nuts

acorn	cola nut
almond	filbert
areca nut	hazelnut
beechnut	hickory nut
betel nut	horse chestnut
bitternut	ivory nut
black walnut	litchi nut
Brazil nut	macadamia nut
butternut	peanut
cashew	pecan
chestnut	pine nut
cobnut	piñon
coco-de-mer	pistachio
coconut	sweet chestnut
coffee nut	walnut

feed; wet-nurse. **4** *they nursed old grievances* HARBOUR, foster, entertain, bear, have, hold (on to), cherish, cling to, retain.

nursemaid ▶ **noun**. See NURSE *noun* sense 2.

nursery ▶ **noun** CHILD CARE CENTRE, daycare (centre); playroom, rumpus room.

nurture ▶ **verb 1** *she nurtured her children into adulthood* BRING UP, care for, take care of, look after, tend, rear, raise, support, foster; parent, mother. **2** *we nurtured these plants* CULTIVATE, grow, keep, tend. **3** *he nurtured my love of art* ENCOURAGE, promote, stimulate, develop, foster, cultivate, boost, contribute to, assist, help, abet, strengthen, fuel.
— OPPOSITES: neglect, hinder.
▶ **noun 1** *we are what nature and nurture have made us* UPBRINGING, rearing, raising, child care; training, education. **2** *the nurture of ideas* ENCOURAGEMENT, promotion, fostering, development, cultivation.
— OPPOSITES: nature.

nut ▶ **noun 1** *nuts in their shells* kernel, nutmeat. *See table.* **2** *(informal) some nut arrived at the office* MANIAC, lunatic, madman, madwoman; eccentric; *informal* loony, nutcase, nutbar, fruitcake, head case, crank, crackpot, weirdo, screwball, crazy, dingbat. **3** *(informal) a health nut* ENTHUSIAST, fan, devotee, aficionado; *informal* freak, fiend, fanatic, addict, buff, bum.
■ **off one's nut** *(informal). See* MAD sense 1.

nutrition ▶ **noun** NOURISHMENT, nutriment, nutrients, sustenance, food; *informal* grub, chow, nosh, vittles; *literary* viands; *dated* victuals.
— RELATED TERMS: trophic.

nutritious ▶ **adjective** NOURISHING, good for one, full of nutrients, nutritive, nutritional, wholesome, healthy, healthful, beneficial, sustaining.

nuts ▶ **adjective** *(informal)* **1** *they thought we were nuts. See* MAD sense 1. **2** *he's nuts about her* INFATUATED WITH, keen on, devoted to, in love with, smitten with, enamoured of, hot for; *informal* mad, crazy, nutty, wild, hooked on, gone on.

nuts and bolts ▶ **plural noun** PRACTICAL DETAILS, fundamentals, basics, practicalities, essentials, mechanics, rudiments, ABC's; *informal* nitty-gritty, ins and outs, brass tacks, meat and potatoes.

nutty ▶ **adjective** *(informal)* **1** *they're all nutty. See* MAD sense 1. **2** *she's nutty about Elvis. See* NUTS sense 2.

nuzzle ▶ **verb 1** *the horse nuzzled at her pocket* NUDGE, nose, prod, push, root. **2** *she nuzzled up to her boyfriend* SNUGGLE, cuddle, nestle, burrow, embrace, hug.

nymph ▶ **noun 1** *a nymph with winged sandals* SPRITE, sylph, spirit. **2** *(literary) a skinny nymph with brown eyes* GIRL, belle, nymphet, sylph, ingenue; young woman, young lady; *Scottish* lass; *literary* maid, maiden, damsel.

Oo

oaf ▶ noun LOUT, boor, barbarian, Neanderthal, churl, bumpkin, hoser ♣, yokel; fool, idiot, imbecile, moron; *informal* cretin, ass, goon, yahoo, ape, lump, clod, meathead, meatball, bonehead, knucklehead, lamebrain, palooka, bozo, dumbhead, lummox, klutz, goofus, doofus, turkey, dingbat; *archaic* lubber.

oafish ▶ adjective STUPID, foolish, idiotic; loutish, awkward, clumsy, lumbering, ape-like, cloddish, Neanderthal, uncouth, uncultured, boorish, rough, coarse, brutish, ill-mannered, unrefined; *informal* clodhopping, blockheaded, boneheaded, thick-headed; *archaic* lubberly.

oar ▶ noun PADDLE, scull, blade.
■ **put/stick one's oar in** MEDDLE, interfere, butt in, intrude, intervene, pry; *informal* poke one's nose in, horn in on, muscle in on, snoop, kibitz.

oasis ▶ noun **1** *an oasis near Cairo* WATERING HOLE, watering place, water hole, spring. **2** *a cool oasis in a hot summer* REFUGE, haven, retreat, sanctuary, sanctum, harbour, asylum.

oath ▶ noun **1** *an oath of allegiance* VOW, pledge, promise, avowal, affirmation, word (of honour), bond, guarantee; *formal* troth. **2** *he uttered a stream of oaths* SWEAR WORD, profanity, expletive, four-letter word, dirty word, obscenity, vulgarity, curse, malediction; *informal* cuss (word); *formal* imprecation.

obdurate ▶ adjective STUBBORN, obstinate, intransigent, inflexible, unyielding, unbending, pigheaded, mulish, stiff-necked; headstrong, unshakeable, intractable, unpersuadable, immovable, inexorable, uncompromising, iron-willed, adamant, firm, determined; *informal* bloody-minded.
— OPPOSITES: malleable.

obedient ▶ adjective COMPLIANT, biddable, acquiescent, tractable, amenable, malleable, pliable, pliant; dutiful, good, law-abiding, deferential, respectful, duteous, well trained, well-disciplined, manageable, governable, docile, tame, meek, passive, submissive, unresisting, yielding.
— OPPOSITES: rebellious.

obeisance ▶ noun **1** *a gesture of obeisance* RESPECT, homage, worship, adoration, reverence, veneration, honour, submission, deference. **2** *she made a deep obeisance* BOW, curtsy, bob, genuflection, salaam; *historical* kowtow.

obelisk ▶ noun COLUMN, pillar, needle, shaft, monolith, monument.

obese ▶ adjective FAT, overweight, corpulent, gross, stout, fleshy, heavy, portly, paunchy, pot-bellied, beer-bellied, well-upholstered, well padded, broad in the beam, bulky, bloated, flabby; *informal* porky, roly-poly, blubbery, pudgy.
— OPPOSITES: thin.

obey ▶ verb **1** *I obeyed him without question* DO WHAT SOMEONE SAYS, carry out someone's orders; submit to, defer to, bow to, yield to. **2** *he refused to obey the order* CARRY OUT, perform, act on, execute, discharge, implement, fulfill. **3** *health and safety regulations have*

to be obeyed COMPLY WITH, adhere to, observe, abide by, act in accordance with, conform to, respect, follow, keep to, stick to; play it by the book, toe the line.
— OPPOSITES: defy, ignore.

obfuscate ▶ verb OBSCURE, confuse, blur, muddle, complicate, muddy, cloud, befog; muddy the waters.
— OPPOSITES: clarify.

obituary ▶ noun DEATH NOTICE, in memoriam, eulogy; *informal* obit.

object ▶ noun **1** *wooden objects* THING, article, item, device, gadget; *informal* doodad, thingamajig, thingamabob, thingummy, whatsit, whatchamacallit, thingy, doohickey, dingus. **2** *he became the object of criticism* TARGET, butt, focus, recipient, victim. **3** *his object was to resolve the crisis* OBJECTIVE, aim, goal, target, purpose, end, plan, object of the exercise, point; ambition, design, intent, intention, idea.
▶ verb *teachers objected to the scheme* PROTEST ABOUT, oppose, raise objections to, express disapproval of, take exception to, take issue with, take a stand against, argue against, quarrel with, condemn, draw the line at, demur at, mind, complain about, cavil at, quibble about; beg to differ; *informal* kick up a fuss/stink about.
— OPPOSITES: approve, accept.

objection ▶ noun PROTEST, protestation, demur, demurral, complaint, expostulation, grievance, cavil, quibble, opposition, argument, counter-argument, disagreement, disapproval, dissent; *informal* niggle.

objectionable ▶ adjective UNPLEASANT, disagreeable, distasteful, displeasing, off-putting, undesirable, obnoxious, offensive, nasty, horrible, horrid, disgusting, awful, terrible, dreadful, frightful, appalling, insufferable, odious, vile, foul, unsavoury, repulsive, repellent, repugnant, revolting, abhorrent, loathsome, hateful, detestable, reprehensible, deplorable, ghastly; beastly; *formal* exceptionable, rebarbative.
— OPPOSITES: pleasant.

objective ▶ adjective **1** *an interviewer must try to be objective* IMPARTIAL, unbiased, unprejudiced, non-partisan, disinterested, neutral, uninvolved, even-handed, equitable, fair, fair-minded, just, open-minded, dispassionate, detached. **2** *the world of objective knowledge* FACTUAL, actual, real, empirical, verifiable.
— OPPOSITES: biased, subjective.
▶ noun *our objective is to build a profitable business* AIM, intention, purpose, target, goal, intent, object, object of the exercise, point, end; idea, design, plan, ambition, aspiration, desire, hope.

objectively ▶ adverb IMPARTIALLY, without bias, without prejudice, even-handedly, dispassionately, detachedly, equitably, fairly, justly, with an open mind.

objectivity ▶ noun IMPARTIALITY, lack of bias/prejudice, fairness, fair-mindedness, neutrality, even-handedness, justice, open-mindedness, disinterest, detachment, dispassion.

oblation ▸ noun RELIGIOUS OFFERING, offering, sacrifice, peace offering, burnt offering, libation.

obligate ▸ verb OBLIGE, compel, commit, bind, require, constrain, force, impel, make.

obligation ▸ noun **1** *his professional obligations* DUTY, commitment, responsibility; function, task, job, assignment, commission, burden, charge, onus, liability, accountability, requirement, debt. **2** *a sense of obligation* DUTY, compulsion, indebtedness; duress, necessity, pressure, constraint.
■ **under an obligation** BEHOLDEN, obliged, in someone's debt, indebted, obligated, owing someone a debt of gratitude, duty-bound, honour-bound.

obligatory ▸ adjective COMPULSORY, mandatory, prescribed, required, demanded, statutory, enforced, binding, incumbent; requisite, necessary, imperative, unavoidable, inescapable, essential.
– OPPOSITES: optional.

oblige ▸ verb **1** *both parties are obliged to accept the decision* REQUIRE, compel, bind, constrain, obligate, leave someone no option, force. **2** *I'll be happy to oblige you* DO SOMEONE A FAVOUR, accommodate, help, assist, serve; gratify someone's wishes, indulge, humour.

obliged ▸ adjective THANKFUL, grateful, appreciative, much obliged; beholden, indebted, in someone's debt.

obliging ▸ adjective HELPFUL, accommodating, willing, co-operative, considerate, complaisant, agreeable, amenable, generous, kind, neighbourly, hospitable, pleasant, good-natured, amiable, gracious, unselfish, civil, courteous, polite, decent.
– OPPOSITES: unhelpful.

oblique ▸ adjective **1** *an oblique line* SLANTING, slanted, sloping, at an angle, angled, diagonal, aslant, slant, slantwise, skew, askew, cater-cornered. **2** *an oblique reference* INDIRECT, inexplicit, roundabout, circuitous, circumlocutory, implicit, implied, elliptical, evasive, mealy-mouthed, backhanded. **3** *an oblique glance* SIDELONG, sideways, furtive, covert, sly, surreptitious.
– OPPOSITES: straight, direct.
▸ noun SLASH, solidus, backslash, diagonal, virgule.

obliquely ▸ adverb **1** *the sun shone obliquely across the tower* DIAGONALLY, at an angle, slantwise, sideways, sidelong, aslant. **2** *he referred obliquely to the war* INDIRECTLY, in a roundabout way, not in so many words, circuitously, evasively.

obliterate ▸ verb **1** *he tried to obliterate the memory* ERASE, eradicate, expunge, efface, wipe out, blot out, rub out, remove all traces of. **2** *a nuclear explosion that would obliterate a city* DESTROY, wipe out, annihilate, demolish, liquidate, wipe off the face of the earth, wipe off the map; *informal* zap, nuke. **3** *clouds were darkening, obliterating the sun* HIDE, obscure, blot out, block, cover, screen.

oblivion ▸ noun **1** *they drank themselves into oblivion* UNCONSCIOUSNESS, insensibility, stupor, stupefaction; coma, blackout. **2** *they rescued him from artistic oblivion* OBSCURITY, limbo, anonymity, neglect, disregard.
– OPPOSITES: consciousness, fame.

oblivious ▸ adjective UNAWARE, unconscious, heedless, unmindful, insensible, unheeding, ignorant, incognizant, blind, deaf, unsuspecting, unobservant; unconcerned, impervious, unaffected.
– OPPOSITES: conscious.

obloquy ▸ noun **1** *he endured years of contempt and obloquy* VILIFICATION, opprobrium, vituperation, condemnation, denunciation, abuse, criticism,

censure, defamation, denigration, calumny, insults; *informal* flak; *formal* castigation, excoriation; *archaic* contumely. **2** *conduct to which no moral obloquy could reasonably attach* DISGRACE, dishonour, shame, discredit, stigma, humiliation, loss of face, ignominy, odium, opprobrium, disfavour, disrepute, ill repute, infamy, stain, notoriety, scandal.
– OPPOSITES: praise, honour.

obnoxious ▸ adjective UNPLEASANT, disagreeable, nasty, distasteful, offensive, objectionable, unsavoury, unpalatable, awful, terrible, dreadful, frightful, revolting, repulsive, repellent, repugnant, disgusting, odious, vile, foul, abhorrent, loathsome, nauseating, sickening, hateful, insufferable, intolerable; *informal* horrible, horrid, ghastly, gross, putrid, yucky, godawful; beastly.
– OPPOSITES: delightful.

obscene ▸ adjective **1** *obscene literature* PORNOGRAPHIC, indecent, smutty, dirty, filthy, X-rated, 'adult', explicit, lewd, rude, vulgar, coarse, crude, immoral, improper, off-colour; scatological, profane; *informal* blue, porn, porno, skin. **2** *an obscene waste of money* SHOCKING, scandalous, vile, foul, atrocious, outrageous, heinous, odious, abhorrent, abominable, disgusting, hideous, repugnant, offensive, repulsive, revolting, repellent, loathsome, nauseating, sickening, awful, dreadful, terrible, frightful.

obscenity ▸ noun **1** *the book was banned on the grounds of obscenity* INDECENCY, immorality, impropriety, smuttiness, smut, lewdness, rudeness, vulgarity, dirt, filth, coarseness, crudity; profanity. **2** *the men scowled and muttered obscenities* EXPLETIVE, swear word, oath, profanity, curse, four-letter word, dirty word, blasphemy; *informal* cuss, cuss word; *formal* imprecation.

obscure ▸ adjective **1** *his origins and parentage remain obscure* UNCLEAR, uncertain, unknown, in doubt, doubtful, dubious, mysterious, hazy, vague, indeterminate, concealed, hidden. **2** *obscure references to Proust* MYSTIFYING, puzzling, perplexing, baffling, ambiguous, cryptic, enigmatic, Delphic, oracular, oblique, opaque, elliptical, unintelligible, incomprehensible, impenetrable, unfathomable, abstruse, recondite, arcane, esoteric; *informal* as clear as mud, inkhorn. **3** *an obscure Peruvian painter* LITTLE KNOWN, unknown, unheard of, undistinguished, unimportant, nameless, minor; unsung, unrecognized, forgotten. **4** *an obscure shape* INDISTINCT, faint, vague, nebulous, ill-defined, unclear, blurred, blurry, misty, hazy.
– OPPOSITES: clear, plain, famous, distinct.
▸ verb **1** *grey clouds obscured the sun* HIDE, conceal, cover, veil, shroud, screen, mask, cloak, cast a shadow over, shadow, block, obliterate, eclipse, darken. **2** *recent events have obscured the issue* CONFUSE, complicate, obfuscate, cloud, blur, muddy; muddy the waters; *literary* befog.
– OPPOSITES: reveal, clarify.

obscurity ▸ noun **1** *the discovery rescued him from relative obscurity* INSIGNIFICANCE, inconspicuousness, unimportance, anonymity; limbo, twilight, oblivion. **2** *poems of impenetrable obscurity* INCOMPREHENSIBILITY, impenetrability, unintelligibility, opacity.
– OPPOSITES: fame, simplicity.

obsequies ▸ plural noun FUNERAL RITES, funeral service, funeral, burial, interment, entombment, inhumation, last offices; *archaic* sepulture.

obsequious ▸ adjective SERVILE, ingratiating,

sycophantic, fawning, unctuous, oily, oleaginous, grovelling, cringing, subservient, submissive, slavish; *informal* slimy, bootlicking, smarmy.

observable ▶ **adjective** NOTICEABLE, visible, perceptible, perceivable, detectable, distinguishable, discernible, recognizable, evident, apparent, manifest, obvious, patent, clear, distinct, plain, unmistakable.

observance ▶ **noun** 1 *strict observance of the rules* COMPLIANCE, adherence, accordance, respect, observation, fulfillment, obedience; keeping, obeying. 2 *religious observances* RITE, ritual, ceremony, ceremonial, celebration, practice, service, office, festival, tradition, custom, usage, formality, form.

observant ▶ **adjective** ALERT, sharp-eyed, sharp, eagle-eyed, hawk-eyed, having eyes like a hawk, watchful, heedful, aware; on the lookout, on the qui vive, on guard, attentive, vigilant, having one's eyes open/peeled; *informal* beady-eyed, not missing a trick, on the ball.
– OPPOSITES: inattentive.

observation ▶ **noun** 1 *detailed observation of the animal's behaviour* MONITORING, watching, scrutiny, examination, inspection, survey, surveillance, attention, consideration, study. 2 *his observations were concise and to the point* REMARK, comment, statement, utterance, pronouncement, declaration; opinion, impression, thought, reflection. 3 *the observation of the law* OBSERVANCE, compliance, adherence, respect, obedience; keeping, obeying.

observe ▶ **verb** 1 *she observed that all the chairs were occupied* NOTICE, see, note, perceive, discern, spot; *literary* espy, descry. 2 *she was alarmed to discover he had been observing her* WATCH, look at, eye, contemplate, view, survey, regard, keep an eye on, scrutinize, keep under observation, keep watch on, keep under surveillance, monitor, keep a weather eye on, keep tabs on; *literary* behold. 3 *'You look tired,' she observed* REMARK, comment, say, mention, declare, announce, state, pronounce; *formal* opine. 4 *both countries agreed to observe the ceasefire* COMPLY WITH, abide by, keep, obey, adhere to, heed, honour, fulfill, respect, follow, consent to, acquiesce in, accept. 5 *townspeople observed the one-year anniversary of the flood* COMMEMORATE, mark, keep, memorialize, remember, celebrate.

observer ▶ **noun** 1 *a casual observer might not have noticed* SPECTATOR, onlooker, watcher, looker-on, fly on the wall, viewer, witness; *informal* rubberneck; *literary* beholder. 2 *industry observers expect the deal to be finalized today* COMMENTATOR, reporter; monitor.

obsess ▶ **verb** PREOCCUPY, be uppermost in someone's mind, prey on someone's mind, prey on, possess, haunt, consume, plague, torment, hound, bedevil, beset, take control of, take over, have a hold on, eat up, grip.

obsessed ▶ **adjective** FIXATED, possessed, consumed; infatuated, besotted; *informal* smitten, hung up.

obsession ▶ **noun** FIXATION, ruling/consuming passion, passion, mania, idée fixe, compulsion, preoccupation, infatuation, addiction, fetish, craze; hobby horse; phobia, complex, neurosis; *informal* bee in one's bonnet, hang-up, thing.

obsessive ▶ **adjective** ALL-CONSUMING, consuming, compulsive, controlling, obsessional, fanatical, neurotic, excessive, besetting, tormenting, inescapable, pathological.

obsolescent ▶ **adjective** DYING OUT, on the decline, declining, waning, on the wane, disappearing, past its prime, aging, moribund, on its last legs, out of date, outdated, old-fashioned, outmoded, on the way out, past it.

obsolete ▶ **adjective** OUT OF DATE, outdated, outmoded, old-fashioned, démodé, passé; no longer in use, disused, fallen into disuse, superannuated, outworn, antiquated, antediluvian, anachronistic, discontinued, old, dated, archaic, ancient, fossilized, extinct, defunct, dead, bygone; *informal* prehistoric.
– OPPOSITES: current, modern.

obstacle ▶ **noun** BARRIER, hurdle, stumbling block, obstruction, bar, block, impediment, hindrance, snag, catch, drawback, hitch, handicap, deterrent, complication, difficulty, problem, disadvantage, curb, check; *informal* fly in the ointment; wrench in the works.
– OPPOSITES: advantage, aid.

obstinacy ▶ **noun** STUBBORNNESS, inflexibility, intransigence, intractability, obduracy, mulishness, pigheadedness, wilfulness, contrariness, perversity, recalcitrance, implacability; persistence, tenacity, tenaciousness, doggedness, single-mindedness, determination; *informal* bloody-mindedness; *formal* pertinacity, refractoriness.

obstinate ▶ **adjective** STUBBORN, unyielding, inflexible, unbending, intransigent, intractable, obdurate, mulish, bullheaded, stubborn as a mule, pigheaded, self-willed, strong-willed, headstrong, wilful, contrary, perverse, recalcitrant, uncooperative, unmanageable, stiff-necked, uncompromising, implacable, unrelenting, immovable, unshakeable; persistent, tenacious, dogged, single-minded, adamant, determined, bloody-minded, balky; *formal* refractory, pertinacious.
– OPPOSITES: compliant.

obstreperous ▶ **adjective** UNRULY, unmanageable, disorderly, undisciplined, uncontrollable, rowdy, disruptive, truculent, difficult, rebellious, mutinous, riotous, out of control, wild, turbulent, uproarious, boisterous; noisy, loud, clamorous, raucous, vociferous, rambunctious; *formal* refractory.
– OPPOSITES: quiet, restrained.

obstruct ▶ **verb** 1 *ensure that the air vents are not obstructed* BLOCK (UP), clog (up), get in the way of, occlude, cut off, shut off, bung up, choke, dam up; barricade, bar, gunge up. 2 *he was charged with obstructing the traffic* HOLD UP, bring to a standstill, stop, halt, block. 3 *fears that the regime would obstruct the distribution of food* IMPEDE, hinder, interfere with, hamper, hobble, block, interrupt, hold up, stand in the way of, frustrate, thwart, balk, inhibit, hamstring, sabotage; slow down, retard, delay, stonewall, stop, halt, restrict, limit, curb, put a brake on, bridle.
– OPPOSITES: clear, facilitate.

obstruction ▶ **noun** OBSTACLE, barrier, stumbling block, hurdle, bar, block, impediment, hindrance, snag, difficulty, catch, drawback, hitch, handicap, deterrent, curb, check, restriction; blockage, stoppage, congestion, bottleneck, holdup, jam; *Medicine* occlusion; *informal* fly in the ointment, wrench in the works.

obstructive ▶ **adjective** UNHELPFUL, uncooperative, awkward, difficult, unaccommodating, disobliging, perverse, contrary; bloody-minded, balky.
– OPPOSITES: helpful.

obtain ▶ **verb** 1 *the newspaper obtained a copy of the letter* GET, acquire, come by, secure, procure, come into the possession of, pick up, be given; gain, earn,

achieve, attain; *informal* get hold of, get/lay one's hands on, get one's mitts on, land. **2** *(formal) rules obtaining in other jurisdictions* PREVAIL, be in force, apply, exist, be in use, be in effect, stand, hold, be the case.
— OPPOSITES: lose.

obtainable ▶ **adjective** AVAILABLE, to be had, in circulation, on the market, in season, at one's disposal, at hand, attainable, procurable, accessible; *informal* up for grabs, on tap, get-at-able.

obtrusive ▶ **adjective** CONSPICUOUS, prominent, noticeable, obvious, unmistakable, intrusive, out of place; *informal* sticking out like a sore thumb.
— OPPOSITES: inconspicuous.

obtuse ▶ **adjective** STUPID, foolish, slow-witted, stunned ♣, slow, dull-witted, unintelligent, ignorant, simple-minded; insensitive, imperceptive, uncomprehending; *informal* dim, dim-witted, dense, dumb, slow on the uptake, halfwitted, brain-dead, moronic, cretinous, thick, dopey, dozy, dumb-ass, wooden-headed, boneheaded, chowderheaded.
— OPPOSITES: clever.

obviate ▶ **verb** PRECLUDE, prevent, remove, get rid of, do away with, get round, rule out, eliminate, make unnecessary.

obvious ▶ **adjective** CLEAR, crystal clear, plain, evident, apparent, manifest, patent, conspicuous, pronounced, transparent, palpable, prominent, marked, decided, distinct, noticeable, unmissable, perceptible, visible, discernible; unmistakable, indisputable, self-evident, incontrovertible, incontestable, undeniable, as clear as day, staring someone in the face; overt, open, undisguised, unconcealed, frank, glaring, blatant, written all over someone; *informal* as plain as the nose on your face, sticking out like a sore thumb,
— OPPOSITES: imperceptible.

obviously ▶ **adverb** CLEARLY, evidently, plainly, patently, visibly, discernibly, manifestly, noticeably; unmistakably, undeniably, incontrovertibly, demonstrably, unquestionably, undoubtedly, without doubt, doubtless; of course, naturally, needless to say, it goes without saying.
— OPPOSITES: perhaps.

occasion ▶ **noun 1** *a previous occasion* TIME, instance, juncture, point; event, occurrence, affair, incident, episode, experience; situation, case, circumstance. **2** *a family occasion* SOCIAL EVENT, event, affair, function, celebration, party, get-together, gathering; *informal* do, bash. **3** *I doubt if the occasion will arise* OPPORTUNITY, right moment, chance, opening, window. **4** *it's the first time I've had occasion to complain* REASON, cause, call, grounds, justification, need, motive.
▶ **verb** *her situation occasioned a good deal of sympathy* CAUSE, give rise to, bring about, result in, lead to, prompt, elicit, call forth, produce, create, arouse, generate, engender, precipitate, provoke, stir up, inspire, spark off, trigger; *literary* beget.
■ **on occasion**. *See* OCCASIONALLY.

occasional ▶ **adjective** INFREQUENT, intermittent, irregular, periodic, sporadic, odd, random, uncommon, few and far between, isolated, rare, sometime.
— OPPOSITES: regular, frequent.

occasionally ▶ **adverb** SOMETIMES, from time to time, (every) now and then, (every) now and again, at times, every so often, (every) once in a while, on occasion, periodically, at intervals, irregularly,

sporadically, infrequently, intermittently, on and off, off and on.
— OPPOSITES: often.

occlude ▶ **verb** BLOCK (UP), stop (up), obstruct, clog (up), close, shut, bung up, choke.

occult ▶ **noun** *his interest in the occult* THE SUPERNATURAL, supernaturalism, magic, black magic, witchcraft, sorcery, necromancy, wizardry, the black arts, occultism, diabolism, devil worship, devilry, voodoo, hoodoo, white magic, mysticism.
▶ **adjective 1** *occult powers* SUPERNATURAL, magic, magical, mystical, mystic, psychic, preternatural, transcendental; cabbalistic, hermetic. **2** *the typically occult language of the time* ESOTERIC, arcane, recondite, abstruse, secret; obscure, incomprehensible, impenetrable, puzzling, perplexing, mystifying, mysterious, enigmatic.

occupancy ▶ **noun** OCCUPATION, tenancy, tenure, residence, residency, inhabitation, habitation, living, lease, holding; *formal* dwelling.

occupant ▶ **noun 1** *the occupants of the houses* RESIDENT, inhabitant, owner, householder, tenant, renter, leaseholder, lessee; addressee, occupier; *formal* dweller. **2** *the first occupant of the post* INCUMBENT, holder.

occupation ▶ **noun 1** *his father's occupation* JOB, profession, (line) of work, trade, employment, position, post, situation, business, career, métier, vocation, calling, craft. **2** *her leisure occupations* PASTIME, activity, hobby, pursuit, interest, entertainment, recreation, amusement, divertissement. **3** *a property suitable for occupation by seniors* RESIDENCE, residency, habitation, inhabitation, occupancy, tenancy, tenure, lease, living in; *formal* dwelling. **4** *the Roman occupation of Britain* CONQUEST, capture, invasion, seizure, takeover, annexation, overrunning, subjugation, subjection, appropriation; colonization, rule, control, suzerainty.

occupational ▶ **adjective** JOB-RELATED, work, professional, vocational, employment, business, career.

occupied ▶ **adjective 1** *tasks which kept her occupied all day* BUSY, engaged, working, at work, active; *informal* tied up, hard at it, on the go. **2** *all the tables were occupied* IN USE, full, engaged, taken. **3** *only two of the apartments are occupied* INHABITED, lived-in, tenanted, settled.
— OPPOSITES: free, vacant.

occupy ▶ **verb 1** *Carol occupied the basement apartment* LIVE IN, inhabit, be the tenant of, lodge in; move into, take up residence in; people, populate, settle; *formal* reside in, dwell in. **2** *two windows occupied almost the whole of the end wall* TAKE UP, fill, fill up, cover, use up. **3** *he occupies a senior post at the firm* HOLD, fill, have, hold down. **4** *I need something to occupy my mind* ENGAGE, busy, employ, distract, absorb, engross, preoccupy, hold, interest, involve, entertain, amuse, divert. **5** *the region was occupied by Soviet troops* CAPTURE, seize, take possession of, conquer, invade, overrun, take over, colonize, garrison, annex, subjugate.

occur ▶ **verb 1** *the accident occurred at about 3:30* HAPPEN, take place, come about, transpire, materialize, arise, crop up; *informal* go down; *literary* come to pass, befall, betide; *formal* eventuate. **2** *the disease occurs chiefly in tropical climates* BE FOUND, be present, exist, appear, prevail, present itself, manifest itself, turn up. **3** *an idea occurred to her* ENTER

ONE'S HEAD/MIND, cross one's mind, come to mind, spring to mind, strike one, hit one, dawn on one, suggest itself.

occurrence ▸ noun **1** *vandalism used to be a rare occurrence* EVENT, incident, happening, phenomenon, affair, matter, circumstance. **2** *the occurrence of cancer increases with age* EXISTENCE, instance, appearance, manifestation, materialization, development; frequency, incidence, rate, prevalence; *Statistics* distribution.

ocean ▸ noun **1** *the ocean was calm* THE SEA; *informal* the drink, the briny; *West* the chuck, saltchuck; *literary* the deep, the waves, the main. *See table at* SEA. **2** (*informal*) *she had oceans of energy. See* LOT *noun sense 1.*

odd ▸ adjective **1** *an odd man* STRANGE, peculiar, weird, queer, funny, eccentric, unusual, unconventional, outlandish, quirky, zany; *informal* wacky, kooky, screwy, freaky, oddball, offbeat, off the wall. **2** *quite a few odd things had happened* STRANGE, unusual, peculiar, funny, curious, bizarre, weird, uncanny, queer, outré, unexpected, unfamiliar, abnormal, atypical, anomalous, different, out of the ordinary, out of the way, exceptional, rare, extraordinary, remarkable, puzzling, mystifying, mysterious, perplexing, baffling, freaky, unaccountable, uncommon, irregular, singular, deviant, aberrant, freak, freakish. **3** *he does odd jobs for friends* OCCASIONAL, casual, irregular, isolated, random, sporadic, periodic; miscellaneous, various, varied, sundry. **4** *odd socks* MISMATCHED, unmatched, unpaired; single, lone, solitary, extra, surplus, leftover, remaining.
– OPPOSITES: normal, ordinary, regular.
■ **odd man out** OUTSIDER, exception, oddity, nonconformist, maverick, individualist, misfit, fish out of water, square peg in a round hole.

oddity ▸ noun **1** *she was regarded as a bit of an oddity* ECCENTRIC, crank, misfit, maverick, nonconformist, rare bird; *informal* character, oddball, weirdo, crackpot, nut, freak, screwball, kook; *informal, dated* case. **2** *his work remains an oddity in some respects* ANOMALY, aberration, curiosity, rarity. **3** *the oddities of human nature* PECULIARITY, idiosyncrasy, eccentricity, quirk, irregularity, twist.

oddments ▸ plural noun **1** *oddments of material* SCRAPS, remnants, odds and ends, bits, pieces, bits and pieces, leftovers, fragments, snippets, offcuts, ends, shreds, tail ends. **2** *a cellar full of oddments. See* ODDS AND ENDS at ODDS.

odds ▸ plural noun **1** *odds are that he is no longer alive* LIKELIHOOD, probability, chances, chance, balance. **2** *the odds are in our favour* ADVANTAGE, edge; superiority, supremacy, ascendancy.
■ **at odds 1** *he was at odds with his colleagues* IN CONFLICT, in disagreement, on bad terms, at cross purposes, at loggerheads, quarrelling, arguing, at daggers drawn, at each other's throats, on the outs. **2** *behaviour at odds with the interests of the company* AT VARIANCE, out of keeping, out of line, in opposition, conflicting, contrary, incompatible, inconsistent, irreconcilable.
■ **odds and ends** BITS AND PIECES, bits, pieces, stuff, paraphernalia, things, sundries, miscellanea, bric-a-brac, knick-knacks, oddments, junk.

odious ▸ adjective REVOLTING, repulsive, repellent, repugnant, disgusting, offensive, objectionable, vile, foul, abhorrent, loathsome, nauseating, sickening, hateful, detestable, execrable, abominable, monstrous, appalling, reprehensible, deplorable,

insufferable, intolerable, despicable, contemptible, unspeakable, atrocious, awful, terrible, dreadful, frightful, obnoxious, unsavoury, unpalatable, unpleasant, disagreeable, nasty, noisome, distasteful; *informal* ghastly, horrible, horrid, gross, godawful; beastly.
– OPPOSITES: delightful.

odium ▸ noun DISGUST, abhorrence, repugnance, revulsion, loathing, detestation, hatred, hate, obloquy, dislike, distaste, disfavour, antipathy, animosity, animus, enmity, hostility, contempt; disgrace, shame, opprobrium, discredit, dishonour.
– OPPOSITES: approval.

odorous ▸ adjective SMELLY, malodorous, pungent, acrid, foul-smelling, evil-smelling, stinking, reeking, fetid, rank, stinky; *literary* miasmic, noisome, mephitic.

odour ▸ noun **1** *an odour of sweat* SMELL, stench, stink, reek, whiff, fetor; *informal* funk; *literary* miasma. **2** *an odour of suspicion* ATMOSPHERE, air, aura, quality, flavour, savour, hint, suggestion, impression, whiff.

odyssey ▸ noun JOURNEY, voyage, trek, travels, quest, crusade, pilgrimage, wandering, journeying; *archaic* peregrination.

off ▸ adjective **1** *Kate's off work today* AWAY, absent, unavailable, not at work, off duty, on holiday, on leave, on vacation; free, at leisure. **2** *the game's off* CANCELLED, postponed, called off. **3** *the fish was a bit off* ROTTEN, bad, stale, mouldy, high, sour, (of beer) skunky ♣, rancid, turned, spoiled, putrid, putrescent. **4** (*informal*) *I felt decidedly off. See* ILL.
■ **off and on** PERIODICALLY, at intervals, on and off, (every) once in a while, every so often, (every) now and then/again, from time to time, occasionally, sometimes, intermittently, irregularly.

offbeat ▸ adjective (*informal*) UNCONVENTIONAL, unorthodox, unusual, eccentric, idiosyncratic, outré, strange, bizarre, weird, peculiar, odd, freakish, outlandish, out of the ordinary, bohemian, alternative, zany, quirky, wacky, freaky, way-out, off the wall, kooky, oddball.
– OPPOSITES: conventional.

off-colour ▸ adjective *off-colour jokes* SMUTTY, dirty, rude, crude, suggestive, indecent, indelicate, risqué, racy, bawdy, naughty, blue, vulgar, ribald, broad, salacious, coarse, raunchy; *euphemistic* adult.

offence ▸ noun **1** *he denied having committed any offence* CRIME, illegal/unlawful act, misdemeanour, breach of the law, felony, wrongdoing, wrong, misdeed, peccadillo, sin, transgression, infringement; *Law* malfeasance; *informal* no-no; *archaic* trespass. **2** *an offence to basic justice* AFFRONT, slap in the face, insult, outrage, violation. **3** *I do not want to cause offence* ANNOYANCE, anger, resentment, indignation, irritation, exasperation, wrath, displeasure, hard/bad/ill feelings, disgruntlement, pique, vexation, animosity.
■ **take offence** BE OFFENDED, take exception, take something personally, feel affronted, feel resentful, take something amiss, take umbrage, get upset, get annoyed, get angry, get into a huff.

offend ▸ verb **1** *I'm sorry if I offended him* HURT SOMEONE'S FEELINGS, give offence to, affront, displease, upset, distress, hurt, wound, annoy, anger, exasperate, irritate, vex, pique, gall, irk, nettle, tread on someone's toes; rub the wrong way; *informal* rile, rattle, peeve, needle, put someone's nose out of joint, put someone's back up. **2** *the smell of cigarette smoke offended him* DISPLEASE, be distasteful to, be disagreeable to, be offensive to, disgust, repel, revolt, sicken, nauseate; *informal* turn off, gross out. **3** *criminals who offend again and again* BREAK THE LAW, commit a crime, do wrong, sin, transgress; *archaic* trespass.

offended ▶ adjective AFFRONTED, insulted, aggrieved, displeased, upset, hurt, wounded, disgruntled, put out, annoyed, angry, cross, exasperated, indignant, irritated, piqued, vexed, irked, stung, galled, nettled, resentful, in a huff, huffy, in high dudgeon; *informal* riled, miffed, peeved, aggravated, sore.
– OPPOSITES: pleased.

offender ▶ noun WRONGDOER, criminal, lawbreaker, miscreant, malefactor, felon, delinquent, culprit, guilty party, sinner, transgressor; *Law* malefeasant.

offensive ▶ adjective **1** *offensive remarks* INSULTING, rude, impertinent, insolent, derogatory, disrespectful, hurtful, wounding, abusive; annoying, exasperating, irritating, galling, provocative, outrageous; discourteous, uncivil, impolite; *formal* exceptionable. **2** *an offensive smell* UNPLEASANT, disagreeable, nasty, distasteful, displeasing, objectionable, off-putting, awful, terrible, dreadful, frightful, obnoxious, abominable, disgusting, repulsive, repellent, repugnant, revolting, abhorrent, loathsome, odious, vile, foul, sickening, nauseating; *informal* ghastly, horrible, horrid, gross, godawful; *beastly*. **3** *an offensive air strike* HOSTILE, attacking, aggressive, invading, combative, belligerent, on the attack.
– OPPOSITES: complimentary, pleasant, defensive.
▶ noun *a military offensive* ATTACK, assault, onslaught, drive, invasion, push, thrust, charge, sortie, sally, foray, raid, incursion, blitz, campaign.

offer ▶ verb **1** *Frank offered another suggestion* PUT FORWARD, proffer, give, present, come up with, suggest, recommend, propose, advance, submit, tender, render. **2** *she offered to help* VOLUNTEER (ONE'S SERVICES), be at someone's disposal, be at someone's service, step/come forward. **3** *the product is offered at a competitive price* PUT UP FOR SALE, put on the market, sell, market, put under the hammer; *Law* vend. **4** *he offered $200* BID, tender, put in a bid of, put in an offer of. **5** *a job offering good career prospects* PROVIDE, afford, supply, give, furnish, present, hold out. **6** *she offered no resistance* ATTEMPT, try, give, show, express; *formal* essay. **7** *birds were offered to the gods* SACRIFICE, offer up, immolate.
– OPPOSITES: withdraw, refuse.
▶ noun **1** *offers of help* PROPOSAL, proposition, suggestion, submission, approach, overture. **2** *the highest offer* BID, tender, bidding price.

offering ▶ noun **1** *you may place offerings in the charity box* CONTRIBUTION, donation, gift, present, handout, charity; *formal* benefaction; *historical* alms. **2** *many offerings were made to the goddess* SACRIFICE, oblation, burnt offering, immolation, libation.

offhand ▶ adjective *an offhand manner* CASUAL, careless, uninterested, unconcerned, indifferent, cool, nonchalant, blasé, insouciant, cavalier, glib, perfunctory, cursory, unceremonious, ungracious, dismissive, discourteous, uncivil, impolite, terse, abrupt, curt; couldn't-care-less, take-it-or-leave-it.
▶ adverb *I can't think of a better answer offhand* ON THE SPUR OF THE MOMENT, without consideration, extempore, impromptu, ad lib; extemporaneously, spontaneously; *informal* off the cuff, off the top of one's head, just like that.

office ▶ noun **1** *her office on Bay Street* PLACE OF WORK, place of business, workplace, workroom, workspace, cubicle, cube. **2** *the newspaper's Paris office* BRANCH, division, section, bureau, department; agency. **3** *he assumed the office of Premier* POST, position, appointment, job, occupation, role, situation, function, capacity. **4** *he was saved by the good offices of his uncle* ASSISTANCE, help, aid, services, intervention, intercession, mediation, agency. **5** *the offices of a nurse* DUTY, job, task, chore, obligation, assignment, responsibility, charge, commission.

officer ▶ noun **1** *an officer in the army* military officer, commissioned officer, non-commissioned officer, NCO, commanding officer, CO. **2** *all officers carry guns. See* POLICE OFFICER. **3** *the officers of the society* OFFICIAL, office-holder, committee member, board member; public servant, administrator, executive, functionary, bureaucrat.

official ▶ adjective **1** *an official inquiry* AUTHORIZED, approved, validated, authenticated, certified, accredited, endorsed, sanctioned, licensed, recognized, accepted, legitimate, legal, lawful, valid, bona fide, proper, ex cathedra, kosher. **2** *an official function* CEREMONIAL, formal, solemn, ceremonious; bureaucratic; *informal* stuffed-shirt.
– OPPOSITES: unauthorized, informal.
▶ noun *a union official* OFFICER, office-holder, administrator, executive, appointee, functionary; bureaucrat, mandarin; representative, agent.

officiate ▶ verb **1** *he officiated the game* BE IN CHARGE OF, referee, take charge of, preside over; oversee, superintend, supervise, conduct, run. **2** *Father Buckley officiated at the wedding service* CONDUCT, perform, celebrate, solemnize.

officious ▶ adjective SELF-IMPORTANT, bumptious, self-assertive, pushy, overbearing, overzealous, domineering, opinionated, interfering, intrusive, meddlesome, meddling, bossy.
– OPPOSITES: self-effacing.

offing
■ **in the offing** ON THE WAY, coming, (close) at hand, near, imminent, in prospect, on the horizon, in the wings, just around the corner, in the air, in the wind, brewing, upcoming, forthcoming, in the cards, coming down the pike.

off-key ▶ adjective **1** *an off-key rendition of 'Amazing Grace'* OUT OF TUNE, flat, tuneless, discordant, unharmonious. **2** *the cinematic effects are distractingly off-key* INCONGRUOUS, inappropriate, unsuitable, out of place, out of keeping, jarring, dissonant, inharmonious.
– OPPOSITES: harmonious.

off-kilter ▶ adjective **1** *positioned at off-kilter angles* OUT OF ALIGNMENT, off-centre, crooked, askew, awry, out of line, at an angle, off-balance, lopsided, skewed, cockeyed, wonky. **2** *her sense of humour is a bit off-kilter* OFFBEAT, eccentric, zany, unconventional, unorthodox, bizarre, weird, funny, wacky, kooky, off the wall.

off-load ▶ verb **1** *the cargo was being off-loaded* UNLOAD, remove, empty (out), tip (out); *archaic* unlade. **2** *he off-loaded 5,000 shares* DISPOSE OF, dump, jettison, get rid of, transfer, shift; palm off, foist, fob off.

off-putting ▶ adjective **1** *an off-putting aroma* UNPLEASANT, unappealing, uninviting, unattractive, disagreeable, repellent, offensive, distasteful, unsavoury, unpalatable, unappetizing, objectionable, nasty, disgusting, horrid, horrible. **2** *her manner was off-putting* DISCOURAGING, disheartening, demoralizing, dispiriting, daunting, disconcerting, unnerving, unsettling; *formal* rebarbative.

offset ▶ **verb** COUNTERBALANCE, balance (out), cancel (out), even out/up, counteract, countervail, neutralize, compensate for, make up for, make good, redeem.

offshoot ▶ **noun** 1 *the plant's offshoots* SIDE SHOOT, shoot, sucker, tendril, runner, scion, slip, offset, stolon; twig, branch, bough, limb. 2 *an offshoot of Cromwell's line* DESCENDANT, scion. 3 *rap music began as an underground offshoot of disco* OUTCOME, result, (side) effect, corollary, consequence, upshot, product, by-product, spinoff, development, ramification, fallout.

offspring ▶ **noun** CHILDREN, sons and daughters, progeny, family, youngsters, babies, infants, brood; descendants, heirs, successors; *Law* issue; *informal* kids; *derogatory* spawn; *archaic* fruit of one's loins.

often ▶ **adverb** FREQUENTLY, many times, many a time, on many/numerous occasions, a lot, as often as not, repeatedly, again and again; regularly, routinely, usually, habitually, commonly, generally, in many cases/instances, ordinarily, oftentimes; *literary* oft.
– OPPOSITES: seldom.

ogle ▶ **verb** LEER AT, stare at, eye (up), make eyes at, admire, check out, lech after, mentally undress.

ogre ▶ **noun** 1 *an ogre with two heads* MONSTER, giant, troll. 2 *he is not the ogre he sometimes seems to be* BRUTE, fiend, monster, beast, barbarian, savage, animal, tyrant; *informal* bastard, swine, pig.

ogress ▶ **noun** 1 *a one-eyed ogress* MONSTER, giantess. 2 *the French teacher was a real ogress* HARRIDAN, tartar, termagant, gorgon, virago; *informal* battleaxe.

oil ▶ **noun** *make sure the car has enough oil* LUBRICANT, lubrication, grease; crude; *informal* black gold.
▶ **verb** *I'll oil that gate for you tomorrow* LUBRICATE, grease, smear/cover/rub with oil; *informal* lube.

oily ▶ **adjective** 1 *oily substances* GREASY, oleaginous; *technical* sebaceous; *formal* pinguid. 2 *oily food* GREASY, fatty, buttery, swimming in oil/fat. 3 *an oily man* UNCTUOUS, ingratiating, smooth-talking, fulsome, flattering, obsequious, sycophantic, oleaginous; *informal* smarmy, slimy.

ointment ▶ **noun** LOTION, cream, salve, liniment, embrocation, rub, gel, balm, emollient, unguent; *technical* humectant.

OK, okay (*informal*) ▶ **exclamation** *OK, I'll go with him* ALL RIGHT, right, very well, very good, fine, fair enough; *informal* okey-doke(y).
▶ **adjective** 1 *the film was OK* SATISFACTORY, all right, acceptable, competent; adequate, tolerable, passable, reasonable, fair, decent, not bad, average, middling, moderate, unremarkable, unexceptional; *informal* so-so, {comme ci, comme ça}, fair-to-middling. 2 *Jo's feeling OK now* FINE, all right, well, hunky-dory, in good shape, in good health, fit, healthy, as fit as a fiddle. 3 *is it OK for me to come?* PERMISSIBLE, allowable, acceptable, all right, in order, permitted, fitting, suitable, appropriate; *informal* kosher.
– OPPOSITES: unsatisfactory, ill.
▶ **noun** *he's just given me the OK* AUTHORIZATION, approval, seal of approval, agreement, consent, assent, permission, endorsement, ratification, sanction, approbation, confirmation, blessing, leave; *informal* the go-ahead, the green light, the thumbs up, say-so.
– OPPOSITES: refusal.

▶ **verb** *the move must be okayed by the president* AUTHORIZE, approve, agree to, consent to, sanction, pass, ratify, endorse, allow, give something the nod, rubber-stamp; *informal* give the go-ahead, give the green light, give the thumbs up; *formal* accede to.
– OPPOSITES: refuse, veto.

old ▶ **adjective** 1 *old people* ELDERLY, aged, older, senior, advanced in years, venerable; in one's dotage, long in the tooth, grey-haired, grizzled, hoary, past one's prime, not as young as one was, ancient, decrepit, doddering, doddery, not long for this world, senescent, senile, superannuated; *informal* getting on, past it, over the hill, no spring chicken. 2 *old farm buildings* DILAPIDATED, broken-down, beat-up, run-down, tumbledown, ramshackle, decaying, crumbling, disintegrating. 3 *old clothes* WORN, worn out, shabby, threadbare, holey, torn, frayed, patched, tattered, moth-eaten, ragged; old-fashioned, out of date, outmoded; cast-off, hand-me-down; *informal* tatty. 4 *old cars* ANTIQUE, veteran, vintage, classic. 5 *she's old for her years* MATURE, wise, sensible, experienced, worldly-wise, knowledgeable. 6 *in the old days* BYGONE, past, former, olden, of old, previous, early, earlier, earliest; medieval, ancient, classical, primeval, primordial, prehistoric. 7 *the same old phrases* HACKNEYED, hack, banal, trite, overused, overworked, tired, worn out, stale, clichéd, platitudinous, unimaginative, stock, conventional; out of date, outdated, old-fashioned, outmoded, hoary; *informal* old hat, corny, played out. 8 *an old girlfriend* FORMER, previous, ex-, one-time, sometime, erstwhile; *formal* quondam.
– OPPOSITES: young, new, modern.

■ **old age** DECLINING YEARS, advanced years, age, oldness, winter/autumn of one's life, senescence, senility, dotage.

■ **old person** SENIOR CITIZEN, senior, (old-age) pensioner, elder, geriatric, dotard, golden ager; crone; Methuselah; *informal* old-timer, oldie, oldster, crock, codger.

old-fashioned ▶ **adjective** OUT OF DATE, outdated, dated, out of fashion, outmoded, unfashionable, passé, démodé, frumpy; outworn, old, old-time, behind the times, archaic, obsolescent, obsolete, ancient, antiquated, superannuated, defunct; medieval, prehistoric, antediluvian, old-fogeyish, conservative, backward-looking, quaint, anachronistic, fusty, moth-eaten, olde worlde; *informal* old hat, square, not with it; horse-and-buggy, clunky, rinky-dink.
– OPPOSITES: modern.

old-time ▶ **adjective** FORMER, past, bygone, old-fashioned; traditional, folk, old-world, quaint.
– OPPOSITES: modern.

Olympic Games *See table.*

omen ▶ **noun** PORTENT, sign, signal, token, forewarning, warning, foreshadowing, prediction, forecast, prophecy, harbinger, augury, auspice, presage; writing on the wall, indication, hint; *literary* foretoken.

ominous ▶ **adjective** THREATENING, menacing, baleful, forbidding, sinister, inauspicious, unpropitious, portentous, unfavourable, unpromising; black, dark, gloomy; *formal* minatory; *literary* direful.
– OPPOSITES: promising.

omission ▶ **noun** 1 *the omission of recent publications from her biography* EXCLUSION, leaving out; deletion, cut, excision, elimination. 2 *the damage was not caused*

Host Cities of the Olympic Games

Summer Olympic Games			Winter Olympic Games		
Year	**City**	**Country**	**Year**	**City**	**Country**
1896	Athens	Greece	1924	Chamonix	France
1900	Paris	France	1928	St. Moritz	Switzerland
1904	St. Louis	USA	1932	Lake Placid	USA
1908	London	UK	1936	Garmisch-Partenkirchen	Germany
1912	Stockholm	Sweden	1948	St. Moritz	Switzerland
1920	Antwerp	Belgium	1952	Oslo	Norway
1924	Paris	France	1956	Cortina d'Ampezzo	Italy
1928	Amsterdam	Netherlands	1960	Squaw Valley	USA
1932	Los Angeles	USA	1964	Innsbruck	Austria
1936	Berlin	Germany	1968	Grenoble	France
1948	London	UK	1972	Sapporo	Japan
1952	Helsinki	Finland	1976	Innsbruck	Austria
1956	Melbourne	Australia	1980	Lake Placid	USA
1960	Rome	Italy	1984	Sarajevo	Yugoslavia
1964	Tokyo	Japan	1988	Calgary	Canada
1968	Mexico City	Mexico	1992	Albertville	France
1972	Munich	West Germany	1994	Lillehammer	Norway
1976	Montreal	Canada	1998	Nagano	Japan
1980	Moscow	USSR	2002	Salt Lake City	USA
1984	Los Angeles	USA	2006	Turin	Italy
1988	Seoul	South Korea			
1992	Barcelona	Spain			
1996	Atlanta	USA			
2000	Sydney	Australia			
2004	Athens	Greece			
2008	Beijing	China			

by any omission on behalf of the carrier NEGLIGENCE, neglect, neglectfulness, dereliction, forgetfulness, oversight, default, lapse, failure.

omit ▶ **verb 1** *they omitted his name from the list* LEAVE OUT, exclude, leave off, take out, miss out, miss, drop, cut; delete, eliminate, rub out, cross out, strike out. **2** *I omitted to mention our guest lecturer* FORGET, neglect, fail; leave undone, overlook, skip.
— OPPOSITES: add, include, remember.

omnipotence ▶ **noun** ALL-POWERFULNESS, supremacy, pre-eminence, supreme power, unlimited power; invincibility.

omnipotent ▶ **adjective** ALL-POWERFUL, almighty, supreme, pre-eminent; invincible, unconquerable.

omnipresent ▶ **adjective** UBIQUITOUS, all-pervasive, everywhere; rife, pervasive, prevalent.

omniscient ▶ **adjective** ALL-KNOWING, all-wise, all-seeing.

omnivorous ▶ **adjective 1** *most duck species are omnivorous* ABLE TO EAT ANYTHING; *rare* omnivorant. **2** *an omnivorous reader* VORACIOUS; undiscriminating, indiscriminate, unselective.

on ▶ **adjective** *the computer's on* FUNCTIONING, in operation, working, in use, operating.
— OPPOSITES: off.
▶ **adverb** *she droned on* INTERMINABLY, at length, for a long time, continuously, endlessly, ceaselessly, without a pause/break.
■ **on and off.** *See* OFF AND ON *at* OFF.
■ **on and on** FOR A LONG TIME, for ages, for hours, at (great) length, incessantly, ceaselessly, constantly, continuously, continually, endlessly, unendingly, eternally, forever, interminably, unremittingly, relentlessly, indefatigably, without let-up, without a pause/break, without cease.

once ▶ **adverb 1** *I only met him once* ON ONE OCCASION, one time, one single time. **2** *he did not once help* EVER, at any time, on any occasion, at all. **3** *they were friends once* FORMERLY, previously, in the past, at one time, at one point, once upon a time, time was when, in days/times gone by, in times past, in the (good) old days, long ago; *archaic* sometime, erstwhile, whilom; *literary* in days/times of yore.
— OPPOSITES: often, now.
▶ **conjunction** *he'll be all right once she's gone* AS SOON AS, when, after.
■ **at once 1** *you must leave at once* IMMEDIATELY, right away, right now, this moment/instant/second/minute, now, straight away, instantly, directly, forthwith, promptly, without delay/hesitation, without further ado; quickly, as fast as possible, as soon as possible, ASAP, speedily; *informal* like a shot, in/like a flash, pronto. **2** *all the guests arrived at once* AT THE SAME TIME, at one and the same time, (all) together, simultaneously; as a group, in unison, in concert, in chorus.
■ **once and for all** CONCLUSIVELY, decisively, finally, positively, definitely, definitively, irrevocably; for good, for always, forever, permanently.
■ **once in a while** OCCASIONALLY, from time to time, (every) now and then/again, every so often, on occasion, at times, sometimes, off and on, at intervals, periodically, sporadically, intermittently.

oncoming ▶ **adjective** APPROACHING, advancing, nearing, forthcoming, on the way, imminent, impending, looming, gathering, (close) at hand, about to happen, to come.

one ▶ **cardinal number 1** UNIT, item; *technical* monad. **2** *only one person came* A SINGLE, a solitary, a sole, a lone. **3** *her one concern was her daughter* ONLY, single, solitary, sole, exclusive. **4** *they have now become one* UNITED, a unit, unitary, amalgamated, consolidated, integrated, combined, incorporated, allied,

affiliated, linked, joined, unified, in league, in partnership; wedded, married.
— RELATED TERMS: mono-, uni-.

onerous ▶ adjective BURDENSOME, arduous, strenuous, difficult, hard, severe, heavy, back-breaking, oppressive, weighty, uphill, effortful, formidable, laborious, Herculean, exhausting, tiring, taxing, demanding, punishing, gruelling, exacting, wearing, wearisome, fatiguing; archaic toilsome.
— OPPOSITES: easy.

oneself
■ **by oneself**. See BY.

one-sided ▶ adjective **1** a one-sided account BIASED, prejudiced, partisan, partial, preferential, discriminatory, slanted, inequitable, unfair, unjust. **2** a one-sided game UNEQUAL, uneven, unbalanced.
— OPPOSITES: impartial.

one-time ▶ adjective FORMER, ex-, old, previous, sometime, erstwhile; lapsed; formal quondam.

ongoing ▶ adjective **1** negotiations are ongoing IN PROGRESS, underway, going on, continuing, taking place, proceeding, progressing, advancing; unfinished. **2** an ongoing struggle CONTINUOUS, continuing, uninterrupted, unbroken, non-stop, constant, ceaseless, unceasing, unending, endless, never-ending, unremitting, relentless, unfaltering.

online ▶ adjective **1** online shopping environments INTERNET, virtual, digital, cyber-, e-. **2** our computers are now online WEB-ENABLED, wired, hooked up.

onlooker ▶ noun EYEWITNESS, witness, observer, looker-on, fly on the wall, spectator, watcher, viewer, bystander; sightseer; informal rubberneck; literary beholder.

only ▶ adverb **1** there was only enough for two AT MOST, at best, (only) just, no/not more than; barely, scarcely, hardly. **2** she only works on one painting at a time EXCLUSIVELY, solely, to the exclusion of everything else. **3** you're only saying that MERELY, simply, just.
▶ adjective their only son SOLE, single, one (and only), solitary, lone, unique; exclusive.

onomatopoeic ▶ adjective IMITATIVE, echoic.

onset ▶ noun START, beginning, commencement, arrival, (first) appearance, inception, day one; outbreak.
— OPPOSITES: end.

onslaught ▶ noun ASSAULT, attack, offensive, advance, charge, onrush, rush, storming, sortie, sally, raid, descent, incursion, invasion, foray, push, thrust, drive, blitz, bombardment, barrage, salvo; historical broadside.

onus ▶ noun BURDEN, responsibility, liability, obligation, duty, weight, load, charge, encumbrance; cross to bear, millstone round one's neck, albatross.

oops ▶ exclamation See WHOOPS.

ooze ▶ verb **1** blood oozed from the wound SEEP, discharge, flow, exude, trickle, drip, dribble, issue, filter, percolate, escape, leak, drain, empty, bleed, sweat, well; Medicine extravasate. **2** she was positively oozing charm EXUDE, gush, drip, pour forth, emanate, radiate.
▶ noun **1** the ooze of blood SEEPAGE, seeping, discharge, flow, exudation, trickle, drip, dribble, percolation, escape, leak, leakage, drainage; secretion; Medicine extravasation. **2** the ooze on the ocean floor MUD, slime, alluvium, silt, mire, sludge, muck, dirt, deposit.

opalescent ▶ adjective IRIDESCENT, prismatic, rainbow-like, kaleidoscopic, multicoloured, many-hued, lustrous, shimmering, glittering,

sparkling, variegated, shot, moiré, opaline, milky, pearly, nacreous.

opaque ▶ adjective **1** opaque glass NON-TRANSPARENT, cloudy, filmy, blurred, smeared, smeary, misty, dirty, muddy, muddied, grimy. **2** the technical jargon was opaque to him OBSCURE, unclear, mysterious, puzzling, perplexing, baffling, mystifying, confusing, unfathomable, incomprehensible, unintelligible, impenetrable, hazy, foggy; informal as clear as mud.
— OPPOSITES: transparent, clear.

open ▶ adjective **1** the door's open NOT SHUT, not closed, unlocked, unbolted, unlatched, off the latch, unfastened, unsecured; ajar, gaping, yawning. **2** a blue silk shirt, open at the neck UNFASTENED, not done up, undone, unbuttoned, unzipped, loose. **3** the main roads are open CLEAR, passable, navigable, unblocked, unobstructed. **4** open countryside | open spaces UNENCLOSED, rolling, sweeping, extensive, wide (open), unfenced, exposed, unsheltered; spacious, airy, uncrowded, uncluttered; undeveloped, unbuilt-up. **5** a map was open beside him SPREAD OUT, unfolded, unfurled, unrolled, extended, stretched out. **6** the bank wasn't open OPEN FOR BUSINESS, open to the public. **7** the position is still open AVAILABLE, vacant, free, unfilled; informal up for grabs. **8** the system is open to abuse VULNERABLE, subject, susceptible, liable, exposed, an easy target for, at risk of. **9** she was open about her feelings FRANK, candid, honest, forthcoming, communicative, forthright, direct, unreserved, plain-spoken, outspoken, free-spoken, not afraid to call a spade a spade; informal upfront. **10** open hostility OVERT, obvious, patent, manifest, palpable, conspicuous, plain, undisguised, unconcealed, clear, apparent, evident; blatant, flagrant, barefaced, brazen. **11** the case is still open UNRESOLVED, undecided, unsettled, up in the air; open to debate, open for discussion, arguable, debatable, moot. **12** an open mind IMPARTIAL, unbiased, unprejudiced, objective, disinterested, non-partisan, non-discriminatory, neutral, dispassionate, detached. **13** I'm open to suggestions RECEPTIVE, amenable, willing/ready to listen, responsive. **14** what other options are open to us? AVAILABLE, accessible, on hand, obtainable. **15** an open meeting PUBLIC, general, unrestricted, non-exclusive, non-restrictive.
— OPPOSITES: shut.
▶ verb **1** she opened the front door UNFASTEN, unlatch, unlock, unbolt, unbar; throw wide. **2** Katherine opened the parcel UNWRAP, undo, untie, unseal. **3** shall I open another bottle? UNCORK, broach, crack (open). **4** Adam opened the map SPREAD OUT, unfold, unfurl, unroll, straighten out. **5** he opened his heart to her REVEAL, uncover, expose, lay bare, bare, pour out, disclose, divulge. **6** we're hoping to open next month OPEN FOR BUSINESS, start trading, set up shop; informal hang out one's shingle. **7** Valerie opened the meeting BEGIN, start, commence, initiate, set in motion, launch, get going, get underway, set the ball rolling, get off the ground; inaugurate; informal kick off, get the show on the road. **8** the lounge opens on to a balcony GIVE ACCESS, lead, be connected, communicate with.
— OPPOSITES: close, shut, end.

open-air ▶ adjective OUTDOOR, outdoors, out-of-doors, outside, alfresco.
— OPPOSITES: indoor.

open-handed ▶ adjective GENEROUS, magnanimous, charitable, benevolent, beneficent, munificent, bountiful, liberal, altruistic,

philanthropic; *literary* bounteous.
— OPPOSITES: tight-fisted.

opening ▶ noun 1 *an opening in the centre of the roof* HOLE, gap, aperture, orifice, vent, crack, slit, chink; peephole; *Anatomy* foramen. 2 *the opening in the wall* DOORWAY, gateway, entrance, (means of) entry, way in/out, exit. 3 *their defensive lapse gave Eriq the opening he needed* OPPORTUNITY, chance, window (of opportunity), possibility. 4 *an opening at the publishing house* VACANCY, position, job. 5 *the opening of the session* BEGINNING, start, commencement, outset; introduction, prefatory remarks, opening statement; *informal* kickoff; *formal* proem. 6 *a gallery opening* OPENING CEREMONY, official opening, launch, inauguration; opening/first night, premiere; vernissage.

openly ▶ adverb 1 *drugs were openly on sale* PUBLICLY, blatantly, flagrantly, overtly, in full view. 2 *the premier spoke openly of his drinking problems* FRANKLY, candidly, explicitly, honestly, sincerely, forthrightly, bluntly, without constraint, without holding back, straight from the hip.
— OPPOSITES: secretly.

open-minded ▶ adjective 1 *open-minded attitudes* UNBIASED, unprejudiced, neutral, non-judgmental, non-discriminatory, objective, disinterested; tolerant, liberal, permissive, broad-minded. 2 *musicians need to be open-minded* RECEPTIVE, open (to suggestions), amenable, flexible, willing to change.
— OPPOSITES: prejudiced, narrow-minded.

open-mouthed ▶ adjective ASTOUNDED, amazed, in amazement, surprised, stunned, bowled over, staggered, thunderstruck, aghast, stupefied, taken aback, shocked, speechless, dumbfounded, dumbstruck; *informal* flabbergasted.

operate ▶ verb 1 *he can operate the machine* WORK, make go, run, use, utilize, handle, control, manage; drive, steer, manoeuvre. 2 *the machine ceased to operate* FUNCTION, work, go, run, be in working/running order, be operative. 3 *the way the law operates in practice* TAKE EFFECT, act, apply, be applied, function. 4 *he operated the mine until 1931* DIRECT, control, manage, run, govern, administer, superintend, head (up), supervise, oversee, be in control/charge of. 5 *doctors decided to operate* do an operation, perform surgery.

operation ▶ noun 1 *the slide bars ensure smooth operation* FUNCTIONING, working, running, performance, action. 2 *the operation of the factory* MANAGEMENT, running, governing, administration, supervision. 3 *a heart bypass operation* SURGERY, surgical operation. 4 *a military operation* ACTION, activity, exercise, undertaking, enterprise, manoeuvre, campaign. 5 *their mining operations* BUSINESS, enterprise, company, firm; *informal* outfit.
■ **in operation.** See OPERATIONAL.

operational ▶ adjective (UP AND) RUNNING, working, functioning, operative, in operation, in use, in action; in working order, workable, serviceable, functional, usable.

operative ▶ adjective 1 *the act is not operative at the moment* IN FORCE, in operation, in effect, valid. 2 *the steam railway is operative.* See OPERATIONAL. 3 *the operative word* KEY, significant, relevant, applicable, pertinent, apposite, germane, crucial, critical, pivotal.
— OPPOSITES: invalid.
▶ noun 1 *the operatives clean the machines* MACHINIST, (machine) operator, mechanic, engineer, worker, workman, (factory) hand, blue-collar worker. 2 *an operative of CSIS* (SECRET) AGENT, undercover agent,

spy, mole, plant, double agent; *informal* spook; *archaic* intelligencer. 3 *a private operative* (PRIVATE) DETECTIVE, (private) investigator, sleuth; *informal* private eye, gumshoe.

operator ▶ noun 1 *a machine operator* MACHINIST, mechanic, operative, engineer, worker. 2 *a tour operator* CONTRACTOR, entrepreneur, promoter, arranger, fixer, outfitter, expediter. 3 (*informal*) *a ruthless operator* MANIPULATOR, manoeuvrer, mover and shaker, wheeler-dealer, hustler, wire-puller.

opiate ▶ noun DRUG, narcotic, sedative, tranquilizer, depressant, soporific, anaesthetic, painkiller, analgesic, anodyne; morphine, opium, codeine; *informal* dope; *Medicine* stupefacient.

opine ▶ verb (*formal*) SUGGEST, say, declare, observe, comment, remark; think, believe, consider, maintain, imagine, reckon, guess, assume, presume, take it, suppose; *informal* allow.

opinion ▶ noun *she did not share her husband's opinion* BELIEF, judgment, thought(s), (way of) thinking, mind, (point of) view, viewpoint, attitude, stance, position, standpoint.
■ **a matter of opinion** OPEN TO QUESTION, debatable, open to debate, a moot point.
■ **be of the opinion** BELIEVE, think, consider, maintain, reckon, estimate, feel, be convinced; *informal* allow; *formal* opine.
■ **in my opinion** AS I SEE IT, to my mind, (according) to my way of thinking, personally, in my estimation, if you ask me.

opinionated ▶ adjective DOGMATIC, of fixed views; inflexible, uncompromising, prejudiced, bigoted.

opponent ▶ noun 1 *his capitalist opponent* RIVAL, adversary, opposer, the opposition, fellow contestant, (fellow) competitor, enemy, antagonist, combatant, contender, challenger; *literary* foe. 2 *an opponent of the reforms* OPPOSER, objector, dissenter.
— OPPOSITES: ally, supporter.

opportune ▶ adjective AUSPICIOUS, propitious, favourable, advantageous, golden, felicitous; timely, convenient, suitable, appropriate, apt, fitting.
— OPPOSITES: disadvantageous.

opportunism ▶ noun EXPEDIENCY, pragmatism, Machiavellianism; striking while the iron is hot, making hay while the sun shines.

opportunity ▶ noun (LUCKY) CHANCE, favourable time/occasion/moment, time, occasion, moment, opening, option, window (of opportunity), possibility, scope, room, freedom, liberty; *informal* shot, kick at the can/cat ♣, break, new lease on life.

oppose ▶ verb BE AGAINST, object to, be hostile to, be in opposition to, disagree with, dislike, disapprove of; resist, take a stand against, put up a fight against, stand up to, fight, challenge; take issue with, dispute, argue with/against, quarrel with; *informal* be anti-; *formal* gainsay.
— OPPOSITES: support.

opposed ▶ adjective 1 *the population is opposed to the nuclear power plants* AGAINST, (dead) set against; in opposition, averse, hostile, antagonistic, antipathetic, resistant; *informal* anti. 2 *their interests were opposed* CONFLICTING, contrasting, incompatible, irreconcilable, antithetical, contradictory, clashing, at variance, at odds, divergent, poles apart.
— OPPOSITES: in favour of.
■ **as opposed to** IN CONTRAST WITH, as against, as contrasted with, rather than, instead of.

opposing ▶ adjective 1 *the two opposing points of view*

CONFLICTING, contrasting, opposite, incompatible, irreconcilable, contradictory, antithetical, clashing, at variance, at odds, divergent, opposed, poles apart. **2** *opposing sides in the war* RIVAL, opposite, enemy. **3** *the opposing page* OPPOSITE, facing.

opposite ▶ **adjective 1** *they sat opposite each other* FACING, face to face with, across from; *informal* eyeball to eyeball with. **2** *the opposite page* FACING, opposing. **3** *opposite views* CONFLICTING, contrasting, incompatible, irreconcilable, antithetical, contradictory, clashing, at variance, at odds, different, differing, divergent, dissimilar, unalike, disagreeing, opposed, opposing, poles apart. **4** *opposite sides in a war* RIVAL, opposing, enemy.
— OPPOSITES: same.
▶ **noun** *the opposite was also true* REVERSE, converse, antithesis, contrary, inverse, obverse, antipode; the other side of the coin; *informal* flip side.

opposition ▶ **noun 1** *the proposal met with opposition* RESISTANCE, hostility, antagonism, antipathy, objection, dissent, disapproval; defiance, non-compliance, obstruction. **2** *they beat the opposition* OPPONENTS, opposing side, other side/team, competition, opposers, rivals, adversaries. **3** *the opposition between the public and the private domains* CONFLICT, clash, disparity, antithesis, polarity.

oppress ▶ **verb 1** *the invaders oppressed the people* PERSECUTE, abuse, maltreat, ill-treat, tyrannize, crush, repress, suppress, subjugate, subdue, keep down, grind down, ride roughshod over. **2** *the gloom oppressed her* DEPRESS, make gloomy/despondent, weigh down, weigh heavily on, cast down, dampen someone's spirits, dispirit, dishearten, discourage, sadden, get down; *archaic* deject.

oppressed ▶ **adjective** PERSECUTED, downtrodden, abused, maltreated, ill-treated, subjugated, tyrannized, repressed, subdued, crushed; disadvantaged, underprivileged.

oppression ▶ **noun** PERSECUTION, abuse, maltreatment, ill-treatment, tyranny, repression, suppression, subjection, subjugation; cruelty, brutality, injustice, hardship, suffering, misery.

oppressive ▶ **adjective 1** *an oppressive dictatorship* HARSH, cruel, brutal, repressive, tyrannical, autocratic, dictatorial, despotic, undemocratic, ruthless, merciless, pitiless. **2** *an oppressive sense of despair* OVERWHELMING, overpowering, unbearable, unendurable, intolerable. **3** *it was grey and oppressive* MUGGY, close, heavy, hot, humid, sticky, steamy, airless, stuffy, stifling, sultry.
— OPPOSITES: lenient.

oppressor ▶ **noun** PERSECUTOR, tyrant, despot, autocrat, dictator, subjugator, tormentor.

opprobrious ▶ **adjective** ABUSIVE, vituperative, derogatory, disparaging, denigratory, pejorative, deprecatory, insulting, offensive; scornful, contemptuous, derisive; *informal* bitchy.

opprobrium ▶ **noun 1** *the government endured months of opprobrium* VILIFICATION, abuse, vituperation, condemnation, criticism, censure; denunciation, defamation, denigration, disparagement, obloquy, derogation, slander, calumny, execration, bad press, invective; *informal* flak, mud-slinging, badmouthing; *formal* castigation, excoriation. **2** *the opprobrium of being associated with thugs* DISGRACE, shame, dishonour, stigma, humiliation, loss of face, ignominy, disrepute, infamy, notoriety, scandal.
— OPPOSITES: praise, honour.

opt ▶ **verb** CHOOSE, select, pick (out), decide on, go for, settle on.

optimism ▶ **noun** HOPEFULNESS, hope, confidence, buoyancy, sanguineness, positiveness, positive attitude.

optimistic ▶ **adjective 1** *she felt optimistic about the future* POSITIVE, confident, hopeful, sanguine, bullish, buoyant; *informal* upbeat, Pollyannaish. **2** *the forecast is optimistic* ENCOURAGING, promising, hopeful, reassuring, favourable, auspicious, propitious.
— OPPOSITES: pessimistic.

optimum ▶ **adjective** BEST, most favourable, most advantageous, ideal, perfect, prime, optimal.

option ▶ **noun** CHOICE, alternative, possibility, course of action.

optional ▶ **adjective** VOLUNTARY, discretionary, non-compulsory, non-mandatory; *Law* permissive.
— OPPOSITES: compulsory.

opulence ▶ **noun 1** *the opulence of the room* LUXURIOUSNESS, sumptuousness, lavishness, richness, luxury, luxuriance, splendour, magnificence, grandeur, splendidness; *informal* plushness. **2** *a display of opulence* WEALTH, affluence, wealthiness, richness, riches, prosperity, money.
— OPPOSITES: poverty.

opulent ▶ **adjective 1** *his opulent home* LUXURIOUS, sumptuous, palatial, lavishly appointed, rich, splendid, magnificent, grand, grandiose, fancy; *informal* plush, swank, swanky. **2** *an opulent family* WEALTHY, rich, affluent, well off, well-to-do, moneyed, prosperous, of substance; *informal* well-heeled, rolling in money, loaded, stinking/filthy rich, made of money. **3** *her opulent red hair* COPIOUS, abundant, profuse, prolific, plentiful, luxuriant.
— OPPOSITES: Spartan, poor.

opus ▶ **noun** COMPOSITION, work (of art), oeuvre.

oracle ▶ **noun 1** *the oracle of Apollo* PROPHET, PROPHETESS, sibyl, seer, augur, prognosticator, diviner, soothsayer, fortune teller. **2** *our oracle on Africa* AUTHORITY, expert, specialist, pundit, mentor, adviser.

oracular ▶ **adjective 1** *his every utterance was given oracular significance* PROPHETIC, prophetical, sibylline, predictive, prescient, prognostic, divinatory, augural. **2** *oracular responses* ENIGMATIC, cryptic, abstruse, unclear, obscure, confusing, mystifying, puzzling, mysterious, arcane; ambiguous, equivocal.

oral ▶ **adjective** *an oral agreement* SPOKEN, verbal, unwritten, vocal, uttered, said.
— OPPOSITES: written.
▶ **noun** *studying for French orals* ORAL EXAMINATION, viva voce.

orate ▶ **verb** DECLAIM, make a speech, hold forth, speak, discourse, pontificate, preach, sermonize, sound off, spout off; *informal* spiel; *formal* perorate.

oration ▶ **noun** SPEECH, address, lecture, talk, homily, sermon, discourse, declamation; *informal* spiel.

orator ▶ **noun** (PUBLIC) SPEAKER, speech-maker, lecturer, declaimer, rhetorician, rhetor.

oratorical ▶ **adjective** RHETORICAL, grandiloquent, magniloquent, high-flown, orotund, bombastic, grandiose, pompous, pretentious, overblown, turgid, flowery, florid.

oratory ▶ **noun** RHETORIC, eloquence, grandiloquence, magniloquence, public speaking, speech-making, declamation.

orb ▶ **noun** SPHERE, globe, ball, circle.

orbit ▶ noun **1** *the earth's orbit around the sun* COURSE, path, circuit, track, trajectory, rotation, revolution, circle. **2** *the problem comes outside our orbit* SPHERE (OF INFLUENCE), area of activity, range, scope, ambit, compass, jurisdiction, authority, domain, realm, province, territory; *informal* bailiwick.
▶ verb *Mercury orbits the sun* REVOLVE AROUND, circle around, go around, travel around.

orchestra ▶ noun ENSEMBLE; *informal* band. *See table.*

Instruments in a Symphony Orchestra

bass clarinet	glockenspiel
bass drum	harp
bassoon	oboe
celsta	piccolo
cello	snare drum
clarinet	timpani
contrabassoon	triangle
cor anglais	trombone
cymbals	trumpet
double bass	tuba
flute	viola
French horn	violin

orchestrate ▶ verb **1** *the piece was orchestrated by Mozart* ARRANGE, adapt, score. **2** *orchestrating a campaign of civil disobedience* ORGANIZE, arrange, plan, set up, bring about, mobilize, mount, stage, stage-manage, mastermind, coordinate, direct, engineer.

ordain ▶ verb **1** *the Church voted to ordain women* CONFER HOLY ORDERS ON, appoint, anoint, consecrate. **2** *the path ordained by fate* PREDETERMINE, predestine, preordain, determine, prescribe, designate. **3** *she ordained that anyone found hunting in the forest must pay a fine* DECREE, rule, order, command, lay down, legislate, prescribe, pronounce.

ordeal ▶ noun UNPLEASANT EXPERIENCE, painful experience, trial, tribulation, nightmare, trauma, hell (on earth), trouble, difficulty, torture, torment, agony.

order ▶ noun **1** *alphabetical order* SEQUENCE, arrangement, organization, disposition, system, series, succession; grouping, classification, categorization, codification, systematization. **2** *his tidy desk demonstrates his sense of order* TIDINESS, neatness, orderliness, organization, method, system; symmetry, uniformity, regularity; routine. **3** *the police were needed to keep order* PEACE, control, law (and order), lawfulness, discipline, calm, (peace and) quiet, peacefulness, peaceableness. **4** *the equipment was in good order* CONDITION, state, repair, shape. **5** *I had to obey her orders* COMMAND, instruction, directive, direction, decree, edict, injunction, mandate, dictate, commandment, rescript; law, rule, regulation, diktat; demand, bidding, requirement, stipulation; *informal* say-so; *formal* ordinance; *literary* behest. **6** *the company has won the order* COMMISSION, contract, purchase order, request, requisition; booking, reservation. **7** *the lower orders of society* CLASS, level, rank, grade, degree, position, category; *dated* station. **8** *the established social order* (CLASS) SYSTEM, hierarchy, pecking order, grading, ranking, scale. **9** *the higher orders of insects* TAXONOMIC GROUP, class, family, species, breed; taxon. **10** *a religious order* COMMUNITY, brotherhood, sisterhood, organization, association, society, fellowship, fraternity, confraternity, congregation, sodality, lodge, guild, league, union, club; sect. **11** *skills of a very high order* TYPE, kind, sort, nature, variety; quality, calibre, standard.
– OPPOSITES: chaos.
▶ verb **1** *he ordered me to return* INSTRUCT, command, direct, enjoin, tell, require, charge; *formal* adjure; *literary* bid. **2** *the judge ordered that their assets be confiscated* DECREE, ordain, rule, legislate, dictate, prescribe. **3** *you can order your tickets by phone* REQUEST, apply for, place an order for; book, reserve; *formal* bespeak. **4** *the messages are ordered chronologically* ORGANIZE, put in order, arrange, sort out, marshal, dispose, lay out; group, classify, categorize, catalogue, codify, systematize, systemize.
■ **in order 1** *list the dates in order* IN SEQUENCE, in series. **2** *he found everything in order* TIDY, neat, orderly, straight, trim, shipshape, in apple-pie order; in position, in place. **3** *I think it's in order for me to take the credit* APPROPRIATE, fitting, suitable, acceptable, (all) right, permissible, permitted, allowable; *informal* okay.
■ **order someone about/around** TELL SOMEONE WHAT TO DO, give orders to, dictate to; lay down the law; *informal* boss about/around, push about/around.
■ **out of order** *the elevator's out of order* NOT WORKING, not in working order, not functioning, broken, broken-down, out of service, out of commission, faulty, defective, inoperative; down; *informal* conked out, bust, (gone) kaput, on the fritz, on the blink, out of whack.

orderly ▶ adjective **1** *an orderly room* NEAT, tidy, well-ordered, in order, trim, in apple-pie order, spic and span, shipshape. **2** *the orderly presentation of information* (WELL) ORGANIZED, efficient, methodical, systematic, meticulous, punctilious; coherent, structured, logical, well-planned, well regulated, systematized. **3** *the crowd was orderly* WELL-BEHAVED, law-abiding, disciplined, peaceful, peaceable, non-violent.
– OPPOSITES: untidy, disorganized.

ordinance ▶ noun (*formal*) **1** *the president issued an ordinance* EDICT, decree, law, injunction, fiat, command, order, rule, ruling, dictum, dictate, directive, mandate. **2** *religious ordinances* RITE, ritual, ceremony, sacrament, observance, service.

ordinarily ▶ adverb USUALLY, normally, as a (general) rule, generally, in general, for the most part, mainly, mostly, most of the time, typically, habitually, commonly, routinely.

ordinary ▶ adjective **1** *the ordinary course of events* USUAL, normal, standard, typical, common, customary, habitual, everyday, regular, routine, day-to-day. **2** *my life seemed very ordinary* AVERAGE, normal, run-of-the-mill, standard, typical, middle-of-the-road, conventional, unremarkable, unexceptional, workaday, undistinguished, nondescript, colourless, commonplace, humdrum, mundane, unmemorable, pedestrian, prosaic, quotidian, uninteresting, uneventful, dull, boring, bland, suburban, hackneyed, garden-variety; *informal* plain-vanilla, nothing to write home about, no great shakes.
– OPPOSITES: unusual.
■ **out of the ordinary** UNUSUAL, exceptional, remarkable, extraordinary, unexpected, surprising, unaccustomed, unfamiliar, abnormal, atypical, different, special, exciting, memorable, noteworthy, unique, singular, outstanding; unconventional,

unorthodox, strange, peculiar, odd, queer, curious, bizarre, outlandish; *informal* offbeat.

ordnance ▸ noun GUNS, cannon, artillery, weapons, arms; munitions.

ordure ▸ noun EXCREMENT, excreta, dung, manure, muck, droppings, feces, stools, night soil, sewage; *informal* poo, poop.

organ ▸ noun 1 *the internal organs* BODY PART, biological structure. 2 *the official organ of the Communist Party* NEWSPAPER, paper, journal, periodical, magazine, newsletter, gazette, publication, mouthpiece; *informal* rag.

organic ▸ adjective 1 *organic matter* LIVING, live, animate, biological, biotic. 2 *organic vegetables* PESTICIDE-FREE, additive-free, natural. 3 *the love scenes were an organic part of the drama* ESSENTIAL, fundamental, integral, intrinsic, vital, indispensable, inherent. 4 *a society is an organic whole* STRUCTURED, organized, coherent, integrated, coordinated, ordered, harmonious.

organism ▸ noun 1 *fish and other organisms* LIVING THING, being, creature, animal, plant, life form. 2 *a complex political organism* STRUCTURE, system, organization, entity.

organization ▸ noun 1 *the organization of conferences* PLANNING, arrangement, coordination, administration, organizing, running, management. 2 *the overall organization of the book* STRUCTURE, arrangement, plan, pattern, order, form, format, framework, composition, constitution. 3 *his lack of organization* EFFICIENCY, order, orderliness, planning. 4 *a large international organization* COMPANY, firm, corporation, institution, group, consortium, conglomerate, agency, association, society; *informal* outfit.

organize ▸ verb 1 *organizing and disseminating information* (PUT IN) ORDER, arrange, sort (out), assemble, marshal, put straight, group, classify, collocate, categorize, catalogue, codify, systematize, systemize; *rare* methodize. 2 *they organized a search party* MAKE ARRANGEMENTS FOR, arrange, coordinate, sort out, put together, fix up, set up, orchestrate, take care of, see to/about, deal with, manage, conduct, administrate, mobilize; schedule, timetable, program; *formal* concert.

organized ▸ adjective (WELL) ORDERED, well run, well regulated, structured; orderly, efficient, neat, tidy, methodical; *informal* together.
— OPPOSITES: inefficient.

orgiastic ▸ adjective DEBAUCHED, wild, riotous, wanton, dissolute, depraved.

orgy ▸ noun 1 *a drunken orgy* WILD PARTY, debauch, carousal, carouse, revel, revelry; *informal* binge, booze-up, jag, bender, love-in, toot; *literary* bacchanal; *archaic* wassail. 2 *an orgy of violence* BOUT, excess, spree, surfeit; *informal* binge.

orient, orientate ▸ verb 1 *there were no street names to enable her to orient herself* GET/FIND ONE'S BEARINGS, establish one's location. 2 *you need to orientate yourself to your new way of life* ADAPT, adjust, familiarize, acclimatize, accustom, attune; acclimate. 3 *magazines oriented to the business community* AIM, direct, pitch, design, intend. 4 *the fires are oriented in line with the sunset* ALIGN, place, position, dispose.

oriental ▸ adjective EASTERN, Far Eastern, Asian; *literary* orient.

orientation ▸ noun 1 *the orientation of the radar station* POSITIONING, location, position, situation,

placement, alignment. 2 *his orientation to his new way of life* ADAPTATION, adjustment, acclimatization. 3 *broadly Marxist in orientation* ATTITUDE, inclination. 4 *orientation courses* INDUCTION, training, initiation, briefing.

orifice ▸ noun OPENING, hole, aperture, slot, slit, cleft.

origin ▸ noun 1 *the origins of life* BEGINNING, start, commencement, origination, genesis, birth, dawning, dawn, emergence, creation, birthplace, cradle; source, basis, cause, root(s); *formal* radix. 2 *the Latin origin of the word* SOURCE, derivation, root(s), provenance, etymology. 3 *her Scottish origins* DESCENT, ancestry, parentage, pedigree, lineage, line (of descent), heritage, birth, extraction, family, stock, blood, bloodline.

original ▸ adjective 1 *the original inhabitants* INDIGENOUS, native, aboriginal, autochthonous; first, earliest, early. 2 *original Rembrandts* AUTHENTIC, genuine, actual, true, bona fide; *informal* kosher. 3 *the film is highly original* INNOVATIVE, creative, imaginative, inventive; new, novel, fresh, refreshing; unusual, unconventional, unorthodox, groundbreaking, pioneering, avant-garde, cutting-edge, unique, distinctive.
▸ noun 1 *a copy of the original* ARCHETYPE, prototype, source, master. 2 *he really is an original* INDIVIDUALIST, individual, eccentric, nonconformist, free spirit, maverick; *informal* character, oddball, screwball, kook.

originality ▸ noun INVENTIVENESS, ingenuity, creativeness, creativity, innovation, novelty, freshness, imagination, imaginativeness, individuality, unconventionality, uniqueness, distinctiveness.

originally ▸ adverb (AT) FIRST, in/at the beginning, to begin with, initially, in the first place, at the outset.

originate ▸ verb 1 *the disease originates in Africa* ARISE, have its origin, begin, start, stem, spring, emerge, emanate. 2 *Tom originated the idea* INVENT, create, initiate, devise, think up, dream up, conceive, formulate, form, develop, generate, engender, produce, mastermind, pioneer; *literary* beget.

originator ▸ noun INVENTOR, creator, architect, author, father, mother, initiator, innovator, founder, pioneer, mastermind; *literary* begetter.

ornament ▸ noun 1 *small tables covered with ornaments* KNICK-KNACK, trinket, bauble, bibelot, gewgaw, gimcrack, furbelow; *informal* whatnot, doodad, tchotchke. 2 *the dress had no ornament at all* DECORATION, adornment, embellishment, ornamentation, trimming, accessories.
▸ verb *the room was highly ornamented* DECORATE, adorn, embellish, trim, bedeck, deck (out), festoon; *literary* bedizen.

ornamental ▸ adjective DECORATIVE, fancy, ornate, ornamented.

ornamentation ▸ noun DECORATION, adornment, embellishment, ornament, trimming, accessories.

ornate ▸ adjective 1 *an ornate mirror* ELABORATE, decorated, embellished, adorned, ornamented, fancy, fussy, ostentatious, showy; *informal* flash, flashy. 2 *ornate language* ELABORATE, flowery, florid, grandiose, pompous, pretentious, high-flown, orotund, magniloquent, grandiloquent, rhetorical, oratorical, bombastic, overwrought, overblown; *informal* highfalutin, purple.
— OPPOSITES: plain.

ornery ▸ adjective GROUCHY, grumpy, cranky,

crotchety, cantankerous, bad-tempered, ill-tempered, dyspeptic, irascible, waspish; truculent, cussed, stubborn.

orotund ▶ adjective **1** *an orotund singing voice* DEEP, sonorous, strong, powerful, full, rich, resonant, loud, booming. **2** *the orotund rhetoric of his prose* POMPOUS, pretentious, affected, fulsome, grandiose, ornate, overblown, flowery, florid, high-flown, magniloquent, grandiloquent, rhetorical, oratorical; *informal* highfalutin, purple.

orthodox ▶ adjective **1** *orthodox views* CONVENTIONAL, mainstream, conformist, (well) established, traditional, traditionalist, prevalent, popular, conservative, unoriginal. **2** *an orthodox Hindu* CONSERVATIVE, traditional, observant, devout, strict.
— OPPOSITES: unconventional.

orthodoxy ▶ noun **1** *a pillar of orthodoxy* CONVENTIONALITY, conventionalism, conformism, conservatism, traditionalism, conformity. **2** *Christian orthodoxies* DOCTRINE, belief, conviction, creed, dogma, credo, theory, tenet, teaching.

oscillate ▶ verb **1** *the pendulum started to oscillate* SWING (TO AND FRO), swing back and forth, sway; *informal* wigwag. **2** *oscillating between fear and bravery* WAVER, swing, fluctuate, alternate, see-saw, yo-yo, sway, vacillate, waffle, hover; *informal* wobble.

oscillation ▶ noun **1** *the oscillation of the pendulum* SWINGING (TO AND FRO), swing, swaying. **2** *his oscillation between commerce and art* WAVERING, swinging, fluctuation, see-sawing, yo-yoing, vacillation.

ossify ▶ verb **1** *the cartilage may ossify* TURN INTO BONE, become bony, harden, solidify, rigidify, petrify. **2** *ossified political institutions* BECOME INFLEXIBLE, become rigid, fossilize, calcify, rigidify, stagnate.

ostensible ▶ adjective APPARENT, outward, superficial, professed, supposed, alleged, purported.
— OPPOSITES: genuine.

ostensibly ▶ adverb APPARENTLY, seemingly, on the face of it, to all intents and purposes, outwardly, superficially, allegedly, supposedly, purportedly.

ostentation ▶ noun SHOWINESS, show, pretentiousness, vulgarity, conspicuousness, display, flamboyance, gaudiness, brashness, extravagance, ornateness, exhibitionism; *informal* flashiness, glitz, glitziness, ritziness.

ostentatious ▶ adjective SHOWY, pretentious, conspicuous, flamboyant, gaudy, brash, vulgar, loud, extravagant, fancy, ornate, over-elaborate; *informal* flash, flashy, splashy, over the top, glitzy, ritzy, superfly.
— OPPOSITES: restrained.

ostracize ▶ verb EXCLUDE, shun, spurn, cold-shoulder, reject, shut out, avoid, ignore, snub, cut dead, keep at arm's length, leave out in the cold; blackball, blacklist; *informal* freeze out.
— OPPOSITES: welcome.

other ▶ adjective **1** *these homes use other fuels* ALTERNATIVE, different, dissimilar, disparate, distinct, separate, contrasting. **2** *are there any other questions?* MORE, further, additional, extra, added, supplementary.

otherwise ▶ adverb **1** *hurry up, otherwise we'll be late* OR (ELSE), if not. **2** *she's exhausted, but otherwise she's fine* IN OTHER RESPECTS, apart from that. **3** *he could not have acted otherwise* IN ANY OTHER WAY, differently.

otherworldly ▶ adjective ETHEREAL, dreamy, spiritual, mystic, mystical; unearthly, unworldly,

supernatural.
— OPPOSITES: realistic.

ounce ▶ noun PARTICLE, scrap, bit, speck, iota, whit, jot, trace, atom, shred, crumb, fragment, grain, drop, soupçon, spot; *informal* smidgen.

oust ▶ verb DRIVE OUT, expel, force out, throw out, remove (from office/power), eject, get rid of, depose, dethrone, topple, unseat, overthrow, bring down, overturn, dismiss, dislodge, displace; *informal* boot out, kick out, turf out.

out ▶ adjective & adverb **1** *she's out at the moment* NOT HERE, not at home, not in, (gone) away, elsewhere, absent. **2** *the secret was out* REVEALED, (out) in the open, common/public knowledge, known, disclosed, divulged. **3** *the roses are out* IN FLOWER, flowering, in (full) bloom, blooming, in blossom, blossoming, open. **4** *the book should be out soon* AVAILABLE, for sale, obtainable, in stores, published, in print. **5** *the fire was nearly out* EXTINGUISHED, no longer alight. **6** *(informal) grunge is out* UNFASHIONABLE, out of fashion, dated, outdated, passé; *informal* old hat, old school, not with it, not in. **7** *he was slightly out in his calculations* MISTAKEN, inaccurate, incorrect, off track, wrong, in error.
— OPPOSITES: in.
▶ verb *(informal) it was not our intention to out him* EXPOSE, unmask.
■ **out cold** UNCONSCIOUS, knocked out, out for the count; *informal* KO'd, kayoed.

outage ▶ noun POWER FAILURE, brownout, blackout.

out-and-out ▶ adjective UTTER, downright, thoroughgoing, absolute, complete, thorough, total, unmitigated, outright, full-bore, real, perfect, consummate.
— OPPOSITES: partial.

outbreak ▶ noun **1** *the latest outbreak of hostility* ERUPTION, flare-up, upsurge, groundswell, outburst, rash, wave, spate, flood, explosion, burst, flurry. **2** *on the outbreak of war* START, beginning, commencement, onset, outset.

outburst ▶ noun ERUPTION, explosion, burst, outbreak, flare-up, access, rush, flood, storm, outpouring, surge, upsurge, outflowing.

outcast ▶ noun PARIAH, persona non grata, reject, black sheep, outsider, leper.

outclass ▶ verb SURPASS, be superior to, be better than, outshine, overshadow, eclipse, outdo, outplay, outmanoeuvre, outstrip, get the better of, upstage; top, cap, beat, defeat, exceed; *informal* be a cut above, be head and shoulders above, run rings round.

outcome ▶ noun (END) RESULT, consequence, net result, upshot, after-effect, aftermath, conclusion, issue, end (product).

outcry ▶ noun **1** *an outcry of passion* SHOUT, exclamation, cry, yell, howl, roar, scream; *informal* holler. **2** *public outcry* PROTEST(S), protestation(s), complaints, objections, furor, fuss, commotion, uproar, outbursts, opposition, dissent; *informal* hullabaloo, ballyhoo, ructions, stink.

outdated ▶ adjective OLD-FASHIONED, out of date, outmoded, out of fashion, unfashionable, dated, passé, old, behind the times, behindhand, obsolete, antiquated; *informal* out, old hat, square, not with it, horse-and-buggy, clunky.
— OPPOSITES: modern.

outdistance ▶ verb **1** *the hare outdistanced the fox* OUTRUN, outstrip, outpace, leave behind, get (further) ahead of; overtake, pass. **2** *the mill outdistanced all its* rivals SURPASS, outshine, outclass, outdo, exceed, transcend, top, cap, beat, better, leave behind; *informal* leave standing.

outdo ▸ verb SURPASS, outshine, overshadow, eclipse, outclass, outmanoeuvre, get the better of, put in the shade, upstage; exceed, transcend, top, cap, beat, better, leave behind, get ahead of; *informal* be a cut above, be head and shoulders above, run rings round.

outdoor ▸ adjective OPEN-AIR, outdoors, outside, alfresco, field.
– OPPOSITES: indoor.

outer ▸ adjective **1** *the outer layer* OUTSIDE, outermost, outward, exterior, external, surface. **2** *outer areas of the city* OUTLYING, distant, remote, faraway, furthest, peripheral; suburban.
– OPPOSITES: inner.

outfit ▸ noun **1** *a new outfit* COSTUME, suit, uniform, ensemble, attire, clothes, clothing, dress, garb; *informal* getup, gear, togs, threads; *formal* apparel; *archaic* habit, raiment. **2** *a studio lighting outfit* KIT, equipment, tools, implements, tackle, apparatus, paraphernalia, things, stuff. **3** *a local manufacturing outfit* ORGANIZATION, set-up, enterprise, company, firm, business; group, band, body, team.
▸ verb *enough swords to outfit an army* EQUIP, kit out, fit out/up, rig out, supply, arm; dress, attire, clothe, deck out; *archaic* apparel, invest, habit.

outfitter ▸ noun **1** *our outfitters planned the canoe route* supplier, expediter ♣, grubstaker; guide. **2** CLOTHIER, tailor, couturier, costumier, dressmaker, seamstress; *dated* modiste.

outflow ▸ noun DISCHARGE, outflowing, outpouring, rush, flood, deluge, issue, spurt, jet, cascade, stream, torrent, gush, outburst; flow, flux; *technical* efflux.

outgoing ▸ adjective **1** *outgoing children* EXTROVERT, uninhibited, unreserved, demonstrative, affectionate, warm, friendly, genial, cordial, affable, easygoing, sociable, convivial, lively, gregarious; communicative, responsive, open, forthcoming, frank. **2** *the outgoing president* DEPARTING, retiring, leaving.
– OPPOSITES: introverted, incoming.

outgrowth ▸ noun PROTUBERANCE, swelling, excrescence, growth, lump, bump, bulge; tumour, cancer, boil, carbuncle, pustule.

outhouse ▸ noun PRIVY, biffy, latrine, outdoor toilet, backhouse.

outing ▸ noun **1** *family outings* (PLEASURE) TRIP, excursion, jaunt, expedition, day out, (mystery) tour, drive, ride, run; *informal* junket, spin. **2** (*informal*) *the outing of public figures* EXPOSURE, unmasking, revelation.

outlandish ▸ adjective WEIRD, queer, far out, quirky, zany, eccentric, idiosyncratic, unconventional, unorthodox, funny, bizarre, unusual, singular, extraordinary, strange, unfamiliar, peculiar, odd, curious; *informal* offbeat, off the wall, way-out, wacky, freaky, kooky, kinky, oddball, in left field.
– OPPOSITES: ordinary.

outlast ▸ verb OUTLIVE, survive, live/last longer than; ride out, weather, withstand.

outlaw ▸ noun *bands of outlaws* FUGITIVE, (wanted) criminal, public enemy, outcast, exile, pariah; bandit, robber; *dated* desperado.
▸ verb **1** *they voted to outlaw the grizzly hunt* BAN, bar, prohibit, forbid, veto, make illegal, proscribe, interdict. **2** *she feared she would be outlawed* BANISH,

exile, expel.
– OPPOSITES: permit.

outlay ▸ noun EXPENDITURE, expenses, spending, cost, price, payment, investment.
– OPPOSITES: profit.

outlet ▸ noun **1** *a power outlet* SOCKET, receptacle, power bar, power source. **2** *the outlet of the drain* VENT (HOLE), way out, egress; outfall, opening, channel, conduit, duct. **3** *an outlet for farm produce* STORE, market, marketplace, shop, source. **4** *an outlet for their creative energies* MEANS OF EXPRESSION, (means of) release, vent, avenue, channel.

outline ▸ noun **1** *the outline of the building* SILHOUETTE, profile, shape, contours, form, line, delineation; diagram, sketch; *literary* lineaments. **2** *an outline of expenditure for each department* ROUGH IDEA, thumbnail sketch, (quick) rundown, summary, synopsis, resumé, précis; essence, main/key points, gist, (bare) bones, draft, sketch.
▸ verb **1** *the plane was outlined against the sky* SILHOUETTE, define, demarcate; sketch, delineate, trace. **2** *she outlined the plan briefly* ROUGH OUT, sketch out, draft, give a rough idea of, summarize, précis.

outlive ▸ verb LIVE ON AFTER, live longer than, outlast, survive.

outlook ▸ noun **1** *the two men were wholly different in outlook* POINT OF VIEW, viewpoint, views, opinion, (way of) thinking, perspective, attitude, standpoint, stance, frame of mind. **2** *a lovely open outlook* VIEW, vista, prospect, panorama, scene, aspect. **3** *the outlook for the economy* PROSPECTS, expectations, hopes, future, lookout.

outlying ▸ adjective DISTANT, remote, outer, out of the way, faraway, far-flung, inaccessible, off the beaten track.

outmanoeuvre ▸ verb **1** *the army was outmanoeuvred* OUTFLANK, circumvent, bypass. **2** *he outmanoeuvred his critics* OUTWIT, outsmart, out-think, outplay, steal a march on, trick, get the better of; *informal* outfox, put one over on, euchre.

outmoded ▸ adjective OUT OF DATE, old-fashioned, out of fashion, outdated, dated, behind the times, antiquated, obsolete, passé, unstylish, untrendy, uncool; *informal* old hat, old school.

out of date ▸ adjective **1** *this design is out of date* OLD-FASHIONED, outmoded, out of fashion, unfashionable, frumpish, frumpy, outdated, dated, old, passé, behind the times, behindhand, obsolete, antiquated; *informal* out, old hat, square, not with it, horse-and-buggy, clunky. **2** *many of the facts are out of date* SUPERSEDED, obsolete, expired, lapsed, invalid, (null and) void.
– OPPOSITES: fashionable, current.

out-of-the-way ▸ adjective OUTLYING, distant, remote, faraway, far-flung, isolated, lonely, godforsaken, inaccessible, off the beaten track.
– OPPOSITES: accessible.

out of work ▸ adjective UNEMPLOYED, jobless, out of a job; redundant, laid off, on welfare, on the dole, on pogey ♣, on EI; *euphemistic* between jobs.

outpouring ▸ noun OUTFLOW, outflowing, rush, flood, deluge, discharge, issue, spurt, jet, cascade, stream, torrent, gush, outburst, niagara, flow, flux; *technical* efflux.

output ▸ noun PRODUCTION, amount/quantity produced, yield, gross domestic product, works, writings.

outrage ▸ noun **1** *widespread public outrage*

INDIGNATION, fury, anger, rage, disapproval, wrath, resentment. **2** *it is an outrage* SCANDAL, offence, insult, injustice, disgrace. **3** *the bomb outrage* ATROCITY, act of violence/wickedness, crime, wrong, barbarism, inhumane act.
▶ **verb** *his remarks outraged his parishioners* ENRAGE, infuriate, incense, anger, scandalize, offend, give offence to, affront, shock, horrify, disgust, appall.

outrageous ▶ **adjective 1** *outrageous acts of cruelty* SHOCKING, disgraceful, scandalous, atrocious, appalling, monstrous, heinous; evil, wicked, abominable, terrible, horrendous, dreadful, foul, nauseating, sickening, vile, nasty, odious, loathsome, unspeakable; beastly. **2** *the politician's outrageous promises* FAR-FETCHED, (highly) unlikely, doubtful, dubious, questionable, implausible, unconvincing, unbelievable, incredible, preposterous, extravagant, excessive. **3** *outrageous clothes* EYE-CATCHING, flamboyant, showy, gaudy, ostentatious; shameless, brazen, shocking; *informal* saucy, flashy.

outré ▶ **adjective** WEIRD, queer, outlandish, far out, freakish, quirky, zany, eccentric, off-centre, unconventional, unorthodox, funny, bizarre, fantastic, unusual, singular, extraordinary, strange, unfamiliar, peculiar, odd, out of the way; *informal* way-out, wacky, freaky, kooky, oddball, off the wall, offbeat, in left field.

outright ▶ **adverb 1** *he rejected the proposal outright* COMPLETELY, entirely, wholly, fully, totally, categorically, absolutely, utterly, flatly, unreservedly, in every respect. **2** *I told her outright* EXPLICITLY, directly, forthrightly, openly, frankly, candidly, honestly, sincerely, bluntly, plainly, in plain language, truthfully, to someone's face, straight from the shoulder, straight up, in no uncertain terms. **3** *they were killed outright* INSTANTLY, instantaneously, immediately, at once, straight away, then and there, on the spot. **4** *paintings have to be bought outright* ALL AT ONCE, in one go.
▶ **adjective 1** *an outright lie* OUT-AND-OUT, absolute, complete, downright, utter, sheer, categorical, unqualified, unmitigated, unconditional. **2** *the outright winner* DEFINITE, unequivocal, clear, unqualified, incontestable, unmistakable.

outrun ▶ **verb** RUN FASTER THAN, outstrip, outdistance, outpace, leave behind, lose; *informal* leave standing.

outset ▶ **noun** START, starting point, beginning, commencement, dawn, birth, origin, inception, opening, launch, inauguration; *informal* the word go.
— OPPOSITES: end.

outshine ▶ **verb** SURPASS, overshadow, eclipse, outclass, put in the shade, upstage, exceed, transcend, top, cap, beat, better; *informal* be a cut above, be head and shoulders above, run rings round.

outside ▶ **noun** *the outside of the building* OUTER/ EXTERNAL SURFACE, exterior, outer side/layer, case, skin, shell, covering, facade.
— RELATED TERMS: ecto-, exo-, extra-.
▶ **adjective 1** *outside lights* EXTERIOR, external, outer, outdoor, out-of-doors. **2** *outside contractors* INDEPENDENT, hired, temporary, freelance, casual, external, extramural. **3** *an outside chance* SLIGHT, slender, slim, small, tiny, faint, negligible, remote, vague.
▶ **adverb** *they went outside* | *shall we eat outside?* OUTDOORS, out of doors, alfresco.
— OPPOSITES: inside.

outsider ▶ **noun** STRANGER, visitor, non-member;

foreigner, (*Atlantic*) come from away ♣, alien, immigrant, emigrant, émigré; newcomer, parvenu.

outsize ▶ **adjective 1** *her outsize handbag* HUGE, oversized, enormous, gigantic, very big/large, great, giant, colossal, massive, mammoth, vast, immense, tremendous, monumental, prodigious, mountainous, king-sized, economy-size(d); *informal* mega, monster, humongous, jumbo, bumper, ginormous. **2** *an outsize actor* VERY LARGE, big, massive, fat, corpulent, stout, heavy, plump, portly, ample, bulky; *informal* pudgy, tubby, zaftig.

outskirts ▶ **plural noun** OUTLYING DISTRICTS, edges, fringes, suburbs, suburbia, bedroom community, commutershed; purlieus, borders, environs.

outsmart ▶ **verb** OUTWIT, outmanoeuvre, outplay, steal a march on, trick, get the better of; *informal* outfox, pull a fast one on, put one over on.

outsource ▶ **verb** CONTRACT OUT, farm out, subcontract, delegate.

outspoken ▶ **adjective** FORTHRIGHT, direct, candid, frank, straightforward, honest, open, round, plain-spoken; blunt, abrupt, bluff, brusque.

outspread ▶ **adjective** FULLY EXTENDED, outstretched, spread-eagled, spread out, fanned out, unfolded, unfurled, (wide) open, opened out.

outstanding ▶ **adjective 1** *an outstanding painter* EXCELLENT, marvellous, magnificent, superb, fine, wonderful, superlative, exceptional, first-class, first-rate; *informal* great, terrific, tremendous, super, amazing, fantastic, sensational, fabulous, ace, neat, killer, crack, A1, mean, awesome, bang-up, skookum, out of this world; smashing, brilliant. **2** *the outstanding decorative element in this presentation* REMARKABLE, extraordinary, exceptional, striking, eye-catching, arresting, impressive, distinctive, unforgettable, memorable, special, momentous, significant, notable, noteworthy; *informal* out of this world. **3** *how much work is still outstanding?* TO BE DONE, undone, unattended to, unfinished, incomplete, remaining, pending, ongoing. **4** *outstanding debts* UNPAID, unsettled, owing, past due, owed, to be paid, payable, due, overdue, undischarged, delinquent.
— OPPOSITES: unexceptional.

outstrip ▶ **verb 1** *he outstripped the police cars* GO FASTER THAN, outrun, outdistance, outpace, leave behind, get (further) ahead of, lose; *informal* leave standing. **2** *demand far outstrips supply* SURPASS, exceed, be more than, top, eclipse.

outward ▶ **adjective** EXTERNAL, outer, outside, exterior; surface, superficial, seeming, apparent, ostensible.
— OPPOSITES: inward.

outwardly ▶ **adverb** EXTERNALLY, on the surface, superficially, on the face of it, to all intents and purposes, apparently, ostensibly, seemingly.

outweigh ▶ **verb** BE GREATER THAN, exceed, be superior to, prevail over, have the edge on/over, override, supersede, offset, cancel out, (more than) make up for, outbalance, compensate for.

outwit ▶ **verb** OUTSMART, outmanoeuvre, outplay, steal a march on, trick, gull, get the better of, euchre; *informal* outfox, pull a fast one on, put one over on.

oval ▶ **adjective** EGG-SHAPED, ovoid, ovate, oviform, elliptical.

ovation ▶ **noun** (ROUND OF) APPLAUSE, hand-clapping, clapping, cheering, cheers, bravos, acclaim, acclamation, tribute, standing ovation; *informal* (big) hand.

oven ▶ noun (KITCHEN) STOVE, microwave (oven), (kitchen) range; roaster; kiln.

over ▶ preposition **1** *there will be cloud over most of the province* ABOVE, on top of, higher (up) than, atop, covering. **2** *he walked over the grass* ACROSS, around, throughout. **3** *over 200,000 people live in the area* MORE THAN, above, in excess of, upwards of. **4** *lengthy discussions over what to do next* ON THE SUBJECT OF, about, concerning, apropos of, with reference to, regarding, relating to, in connection with, vis-à-vis.
— OPPOSITES: under.
▶ adverb **1** *a flock of geese flew over* OVERHEAD, on high, above, past, by. **2** *the relationship is over* AT AN END, finished, concluded, terminated, ended, no more, a thing of the past; *informal* kaput. **3** *he had some money left over* REMAINING, unused, surplus, in excess, in addition.
■ **over and above** IN ADDITION TO, on top of, plus, as well as, besides, along with.
■ **over and over** REPEATEDLY, again and again, over and over again, time and (time) again, many times over, frequently, constantly, continually, persistently, ad nauseam.

overact ▶ verb EXAGGERATE, overdo it, overplay it; *informal* ham it up, camp it up.

overall ▶ adjective *the overall cost* ALL-INCLUSIVE, general, comprehensive, universal, all-embracing, gross, net, final, inclusive, total; wholesale, complete, across the board, global, worldwide.
▶ adverb *overall, things have improved* GENERALLY (SPEAKING), broadly, in general, altogether, all in all, on balance, on average, for the most part, in the main, on the whole, by and large, to a large extent.

overawe ▶ verb INTIMIDATE, daunt, cow, disconcert, unnerve, subdue, dismay, frighten, alarm, scare, terrify; *informal* psych out.

overbalance ▶ verb FALL OVER, topple over, lose one's balance, tip over, keel over; push over, upend, upset.

overbearing ▶ adjective DOMINEERING, dominating, autocratic, tyrannical, despotic, oppressive, high-handed, bullying; *informal* bossy.

overblown ▶ adjective OVERWRITTEN, florid, grandiose, pompous, over-elaborate, flowery, overwrought, pretentious, high-flown, turgid, grandiloquent, magniloquent, orotund; *informal* highfalutin.

overcast ▶ adjective CLOUDY, clouded (over), sunless, darkened, dark, grey, black, leaden, heavy, dull, murky, dismal, dreary.
— OPPOSITES: bright.

overcharge ▶ verb **1** *clients are being overcharged* SWINDLE, charge too much, cheat, defraud, fleece, short-change; *informal* rip off, sting, screw, rob, diddle, have, rook, gouge. **2** *the decoration is overcharged* OVERSTATE, overdo, exaggerate, over-embroider, over-embellish; overwrite, overdraw.

overcome ▶ verb **1** *we overcame the home team* DEFEAT, beat, conquer, trounce, thrash, rout, vanquish, overwhelm, overpower, get the better of, triumph over, prevail over, win over/against, outdo, outclass, worst, crush; *informal* drub, slaughter, clobber, hammer, lick, best, crucify, demolish, wipe the floor with, make mincemeat of, blow out of the water, take to the cleaners, shellac, skunk. **2** *they overcame their fear of flying* GET THE BETTER OF, prevail over, control, get/bring under control, master,

conquer, defeat, beat; get over, get a grip on, curb, subdue; *informal* lick, best.
▶ adjective *I was overcome* OVERWHELMED, emotional, moved, affected, speechless.

overconfident ▶ adjective COCKSURE, cocky, smug, conceited, self-assured, brash, blustering, overbearing, presumptuous, heading for a fall, riding for a fall; *informal* too big for one's britches/boots.

overcritical ▶ adjective FAULT-FINDING, hypercritical, captious, carping, cavilling, quibbling, hair-splitting, over-particular; fussy, finicky, fastidious, pedantic, over-scrupulous, punctilious; *informal* nitpicking, persnickety.

overcrowded ▶ adjective OVERFULL, overflowing, full to overflowing/bursting, crammed full, congested, overpopulated, overpeopled, crowded, swarming, teeming; *informal* bursting/bulging at the seams, full to the gunwales, jam-packed.
— OPPOSITES: empty.

overdo ▶ verb **1** *she overdoes the love scenes* EXAGGERATE, overstate, overemphasize, overplay, go overboard with, over-dramatize; *informal* ham up, camp up. **2** *don't overdo the drink* OVERINDULGE IN, have/use/eat/drink too much of, have/use/eat/drink to excess. **3** *they overdid the beef* OVERCOOK, burn.
— OPPOSITES: understate.
■ **overdo it** WORK TOO HARD, overwork, do too much, burn the candle at both ends, overtax oneself, drive/push oneself too hard, work/run oneself into the ground, wear oneself out, bite off more than one can chew, strain oneself; *informal* kill oneself, knock oneself out.

overdone ▶ adjective **1** *the flattery was overdone* EXCESSIVE, too much, undue, immoderate, inordinate, disproportionate, inflated, overstated, overworked, exaggerated, overemphasized, over-enthusiastic, over-effusive; *informal* a bit much, over the top. **2** *overdone food* OVERCOOKED, dried out, burnt.
— OPPOSITES: understated, underdone.

overdue ▶ adjective **1** *the ship is overdue* LATE, behind schedule, behind time, delayed, unpunctual. **2** *overdue payments* UNPAID, unsettled, owing, owed, payable, due, outstanding, undischarged, delinquent.
— OPPOSITES: early, punctual.

overeat ▶ verb EAT TOO MUCH, be greedy, gorge (oneself), overindulge (oneself), feast, gourmandize, gluttonize; *informal* binge, make a pig of oneself, pig out, have eyes bigger than one's stomach.
— OPPOSITES: starve.

overemphasize ▶ verb PLACE/LAY TOO MUCH EMPHASIS ON, overstress, place/lay too much stress on, exaggerate, make too much of, overplay, overdo, over-dramatize; *informal* make a big thing about/of, blow up out of all proportion.
— OPPOSITES: understate, play down.

overflow ▶ verb *a lot of cream had overflowed the edges of the shallow dish* SPILL OVER, flow over, brim over, well over, pour forth, stream forth, flood.
▶ noun **1** *an overflow from the tank* OVERSPILL, spill, spillage, flood. **2** *to accommodate the overflow, five more offices were built* SURPLUS, excess, additional people/things, extra people/things, remainder, overspill.

overflowing ▶ adjective OVERFULL, full to overflowing/bursting, spilling over, running over, crammed full, overcrowded, overloaded; *informal*

bursting/bulging at the seams, jam-packed.
— OPPOSITES: empty.

overhang ▶ verb STICK OUT (OVER), stand out (over), extend (over), project (over), protrude (over), jut out (over), bulge out (over), hang over.

overhaul ▶ verb *I've been overhauling the engine* SERVICE, maintain, repair, mend, fix up, rebuild, renovate, recondition, refit, refurbish; *informal* do up, patch up.

overhead ▶ adverb *a burst of thunder erupted overhead* (UP) ABOVE, high up, (up) in the sky, on high, above/over one's head.
— OPPOSITES: below.
▶ adjective *overhead lines* AERIAL, elevated, raised, suspended.
— OPPOSITES: underground.
▶ noun (RUNNING) COSTS, operating costs, fixed costs, expenses.

overindulge ▶ verb **1** *we overindulged at Christmas* DRINK/EAT TOO MUCH, overeat, overdrink, be greedy, be intemperate, overdo it, drink/eat to excess, gorge (oneself), feast, gourmandize, gluttonize; *informal* binge, stuff oneself, go overboard, make a pig of oneself, pig out. **2** *his mother had overindulged him* SPOIL, give in to, indulge, humour, pander to, pamper, mollycoddle, baby.
— OPPOSITES: abstain.

overindulgence ▶ noun INTEMPERANCE, immoderation, excess, overeating, overdrinking, gorging; *informal* binge.
— OPPOSITES: abstention.

overjoyed ▶ adjective ECSTATIC, euphoric, thrilled, elated, delighted, on cloud nine, in seventh heaven, jubilant, rapturous, jumping for joy, delirious, blissful, in raptures, as pleased as punch; *informal* over the moon, on top of the world, tickled pink, as happy as a clam.
— OPPOSITES: unhappy.

overkill ▶ noun EXCESS, embroidery, embellishment, hyperbole, gilding the lily.

overlap ▶ verb IMBRICATE, lap over, fold over; coincide.

overlay ▶ verb *the area was overlaid with marble* COVER, face, surface, veneer, inlay, laminate, plaster; coat, varnish, glaze.
▶ noun *an overlay of glass-fibre insulation* COVERING, cover, layer, face, surface, veneer, lamination; coat, varnish, glaze, wash.

overload ▶ verb **1** *avoid overloading the ship* OVERBURDEN, put too much in, overcharge, weigh down. **2** *don't overload the wiring* STRAIN, overtax, overwork, overuse, swamp, oversupply, overwhelm.
▶ noun *there was an overload of demands* EXCESS, overabundance, superabundance, profusion, glut, surfeit, surplus, superfluity; avalanche, deluge, flood.

overlook ▶ verb **1** *he overlooked the mistake* FAIL TO NOTICE, fail to spot, miss. **2** *his work has been overlooked* DISREGARD, neglect, ignore, pay no attention/heed to, pass over, forget. **3** *she was almost willing to overlook his faults* DELIBERATELY IGNORE, not take into consideration, disregard, take no notice of, make allowances for, turn a blind eye to, excuse, pardon, forgive. **4** *the breakfast room overlooks the garden* HAVE A VIEW OF, look over/across, look on to, look out on/over, give on to, command a view of.

overly ▶ adverb UNDULY, excessively, inordinately,

too; wildly, absurdly, ridiculously, outrageously, unreasonably, exorbitantly, impossibly.

overpower ▶ verb **1** *the prisoners might overpower the crew* GAIN CONTROL OVER, overwhelm, prevail over, get the better of, outdo, gain mastery over, overthrow, overturn, subdue, suppress, subjugate, repress, bring someone to their knees, conquer, defeat, triumph over, worst, trounce; *informal* thrash, lick, best, clobber, wipe the floor with. **2** *he was overpowered by grief* OVERCOME, overwhelm, move, stir, affect, touch, stun, shake, devastate, take aback, leave speechless; *informal* bowl over.

overpowering ▶ adjective **1** *overpowering grief* OVERWHELMING, oppressive, unbearable, unendurable, intolerable, shattering. **2** *an overpowering smell* STIFLING, suffocating, strong, pungent, powerful; nauseating, offensive, acrid, fetid, mephitic. **3** *overpowering evidence* IRREFUTABLE, undeniable, indisputable, incontestable, incontrovertible, compelling, conclusive.

overrate ▶ verb OVERESTIMATE, overvalue, think too much of, attach too much importance to, praise too highly.
— OPPOSITES: underestimate.

overreach
■ **overreach oneself** TRY TO DO TOO MUCH, overestimate one's ability, overdo it, overstretch oneself, wear/burn oneself out, bite off more than one can chew.

overreact ▶ verb REACT DISPROPORTIONATELY, act irrationally, lose one's sense of proportion, blow something up out of all proportion, make a mountain out of a molehill.

override ▶ verb **1** *the court could not override her decision* DISALLOW, overrule, countermand, veto, quash, overturn, overthrow; cancel, reverse, rescind, revoke, repeal, annul, nullify, invalidate, negate, void; *Law* vacate; *formal* abrogate. **2** *the government can override all opposition* DISREGARD, pay no heed to, take no account of, turn a deaf ear to, ignore, ride roughshod over. **3** *a positive attitude will override any negative thoughts* OUTWEIGH, supersede, take priority over, take precedence over, offset, cancel out, (more than) make up for, outbalance, compensate for.

overriding ▶ adjective DECIDING, decisive, most important, of greatest importance, of greatest significance, uppermost, top, first (and foremost), highest, pre-eminent, predominant, principal, primary, paramount, chief, main, major, foremost, central, key, focal, pivotal; *informal* number-one.

overrule ▶ verb COUNTERMAND, cancel, reverse, rescind, repeal, revoke, retract, disallow, override, veto, quash, overturn, overthrow, annul, nullify, invalidate, negate, void; *Law* vacate; *formal* abrogate; *archaic* recall.

overrun ▶ verb **1** *guerrillas overran the barracks* INVADE, storm, occupy, swarm into, surge into, inundate, overwhelm. **2** *the talks overran the deadline* EXCEED, go beyond/over, run over.

oversee ▶ verb SUPERVISE, superintend, be in charge/control of, be responsible for, look after, keep an eye on, inspect, administer, organize, manage, micromanage, direct, preside over.

overseer ▶ noun SUPERVISOR, foreman, forewoman, team leader, controller, (line) manager, manageress, head (of department), superintendent, captain; *informal* boss, chief, straw boss.

overshadow ▶ verb **1** *a massive hill overshadows the* *town* CAST A SHADOW OVER, shade, darken, conceal, obscure, screen; dominate, overlook. **2** *this feeling of tragedy overshadowed his story* CAST GLOOM OVER, blight, take the edge off, mar, spoil, ruin. **3** *he was overshadowed by his brilliant elder brother* OUTSHINE, eclipse, surpass, exceed, be superior to, outclass, outstrip, outdo, upstage; *informal* be head and shoulders above.

overshoes ▶ **plural noun** GALOSHES, rubbers, gumshoes, toe rubbers ♣.

oversight ▶ **noun 1** *a stupid oversight* MISTAKE, error, omission, lapse, slip, blunder; *informal* slip-up, boo-boo, goof, flub. **2** *the omission was due to oversight* CARELESSNESS, inattention, negligence, forgetfulness, laxity.

overstate ▶ **verb** EXAGGERATE, overdo, overemphasize, overplay, dramatize, embroider, embellish; *informal* blow up out of all proportion.
— OPPOSITES: understate.

overstatement ▶ **noun** EXAGGERATION, overemphasis, dramatization, embroidery, embellishment, enhancement, hyperbole.

overt ▶ **adjective** UNDISGUISED, unconcealed, plain (to see), clear, apparent, conspicuous, obvious, noticeable, manifest, patent, open, blatant.
— OPPOSITES: covert.

overtake ▶ **verb 1** *a green car overtook the taxi* PASS, go past/by, get/pull ahead of, leave behind, outdistance, outstrip. **2** *tourism overtook lumber as the main revenue source* OUTSTRIP, surpass, overshadow, eclipse, outshine, outclass; dwarf, put in the shade, exceed, top, cap. **3** *the calamity which overtook us* BEFALL, happen to, come upon, hit, strike, overwhelm, overcome, be visited on; *literary* betide.

overthrow ▶ **verb 1** *the President was overthrown* REMOVE (FROM OFFICE/POWER), bring down, topple, depose, oust, displace, unseat, dethrone. **2** *an attempt to overthrow military rule* PUT AN END TO, defeat, conquer.
▶ **noun 1** *the overthrow of the General* REMOVAL (FROM OFFICE/POWER), downfall, fall, toppling, deposition, ousting, displacement, supplanting, unseating. **2** *the overthrow of capitalism* ENDING, defeat, displacement, fall, collapse, downfall, demise.

overtone ▶ **noun** CONNOTATION, hidden meaning, implication, association, undercurrent, undertone, echo, vibrations, hint, suggestion, insinuation, intimation, suspicion, feeling, nuance.

overture ▶ **noun 1** *the overture to Don Giovanni* PRELUDE, introduction, opening, introductory movement. **2** *the overture to a long debate* PRELIMINARY, prelude, introduction, lead-in, precursor, start, beginning. **3** *peace overtures* (OPENING) MOVE, approach, advances, feeler, signal, proposal, proposition.

overturn ▶ **verb 1** *the boat overturned* CAPSIZE, turn turtle, keel over, tip over, topple over, turn over, flip; *Nautical* pitchpole. **2** *I overturned the stool* UPSET, tip over, topple over, turn over, knock over, upend. **3** *the Supreme Court may overturn this ruling* CANCEL, reverse, rescind, repeal, revoke, retract, countermand, disallow, override, overrule, veto, quash, overthrow, annul, nullify, invalidate, negate, void; *Law* vacate; *formal* abrogate; *archaic* recall.

overused ▶ **adjective** HACKNEYED, overworked, worn out, time-worn, tired, played out, clichéd, stale, trite, banal, stock, unoriginal.

overweening ▶ **adjective** OVERCONFIDENT,

conceited, cocksure, cocky, smug, haughty, supercilious, lofty, patronizing, arrogant, proud, vain, self-important, imperious, overbearing; *informal* high and mighty, uppish.
— OPPOSITES: unassuming.

overweight ▶ **adjective** FAT, obese, stout, corpulent, gross, fleshy, plump, portly, chubby, rotund, paunchy, pot-bellied, flabby, well-upholstered, broad in the beam; *informal* porky, tubby, blubbery, pudgy.
— OPPOSITES: skinny.

overwhelm ▶ **verb 1** *advancing sand dunes could overwhelm the village* SWAMP, submerge, engulf, bury, deluge, flood, inundate. **2** *Canada overwhelmed the U.S. in the hockey final* DEFEAT (UTTERLY/HEAVILY), trounce, rout, beat (hollow), conquer, vanquish, be victorious over, triumph over, worst, overcome, overthrow, crush; *informal* thrash, steamroller, lick, best, massacre, clobber, wipe the floor with. **3** *she was overwhelmed by a sense of tragedy* OVERCOME, move, stir, affect, touch, strike, dumbfound, shake, devastate, floor, leave speechless; *informal* bowl over, snow under.

overwhelming ▶ **adjective 1** *an overwhelming number of players were unavailable* VERY LARGE, enormous, immense, inordinate, massive, huge. **2** *overwhelming desire to laugh* VERY STRONG, forceful, uncontrollable, irrepressible, irresistible, overpowering, compelling.

overwork ▶ **verb 1** *we should not overwork* WORK TOO HARD, work/run oneself into the ground, wear oneself to a shadow, work one's fingers to the bone, burn the candle at both ends, overtax oneself, burn oneself out, do too much, overdo it, strain oneself, overload oneself, drive/push oneself too hard; *informal* kill oneself, knock oneself out. **2** *my colleagues did not overwork me* DRIVE (TOO HARD), exploit, drive into the ground, tax, overtax, overburden, put upon, impose on.

overworked ▶ **adjective 1** *overworked staff* STRESSED (OUT), stress-ridden, overtaxed, overburdened, overloaded, exhausted, worn out, burned out. **2** *an overworked phrase* HACKNEYED, overused, worn out, tired, played out, clichéd, threadbare, stale, trite, banal, stock, unoriginal.
— OPPOSITES: relaxed, original.

overwrought ▶ **adjective 1** *she was too overwrought to listen* TENSE, agitated, nervous, on edge, edgy, keyed up, worked up, high-strung, neurotic, overexcited, beside oneself, distracted, distraught, frantic, hysterical; *informal* in a state, in a tizzy, uptight, wound up, het up, strung out. **2** *the painting is overwrought* OVER-ELABORATE, over-ornate, overblown, overdone, contrived, overworked, strained.
— OPPOSITES: calm, understated.

owe ▶ **verb** BE IN DEBT (TO), be indebted (to), be in arrears (to), be under an obligation (to).

owing ▶ **adjective** *the rent was owing* UNPAID, to be paid, payable, due, past due, overdue, undischarged, owed, outstanding, in arrears, delinquent.
— OPPOSITES: paid.
■ **owing to** BECAUSE OF, as a result of, on account of, due to, as a consequence of, thanks to, in view of, by dint of; *formal* by reason of.

owl ▶ **noun**. *See table at* RAPTOR.

own ▶ **adjective** *he has his own reasons* PERSONAL, individual, particular, private, personalized, unique.
▶ **verb 1** *I own this house* BE THE OWNER OF, possess, be the possessor of, have in one's possession, have (to

one's name). **2** *she had to own that she agreed* ADMIT, concede, grant, accept, acknowledge, agree, confess.

■ **get one's own back** (*informal*) HAVE/GET/TAKE ONE'S REVENGE (ON), be revenged (on), hit back, get (back at), get even (with), settle accounts (with), repay, pay someone back, give someone their just deserts, retaliate (against/on), take reprisals (against), exact retribution (on), give someone a taste of their own medicine.

■ **hold one's own** STAND FIRM, stand one's ground, keep one's end up, keep one's head above water, compete, survive, cope, get on/along.

■ **on one's own 1** *I am all on my own* (ALL) ALONE, (all) by oneself, solitary, unaccompanied, companionless; *informal* by one's lonesome. **2** *she works well on her own* UNAIDED, unassisted, without help, without assistance, (all) by oneself, independently.

■ **own up** CONFESS (TO), admit to, admit guilt, plead guilty, accept blame/responsibility, tell the truth (about), make a clean breast of it, tell all; *informal* come clean (about).

owner ▶ noun POSSESSOR, holder, proprietor/proprietress, homeowner, freeholder, landlord, landlady.
— RELATED TERMS: proprietary.

ownership ▶ noun (RIGHT OF) POSSESSION, freehold, proprietorship, proprietary rights, title.

ox ▶ noun bull, bullock, steer; *Farming* beef.

Pp

pace ▶ noun **1** *he stepped back a pace* STEP, stride. **2** *a slow, steady pace* GAIT, stride, walk, march. **3** *he drove home at a furious pace* SPEED, rate, velocity; *informal* clip, lick.
▶ verb *she paced up and down* WALK, stride, tread, march, pound, patrol.

pacific ▶ adjective **1** *a pacific community* PEACE-LOVING, peaceable, pacifist, non-violent, non-aggressive, non-belligerent, unwarlike. **2** *their pacific intentions* CONCILIATORY, peacemaking, placatory, propitiatory, appeasing, mollifying, mediatory, dovish; *formal* irenic. **3** *pacific waters* CALM, still, smooth, tranquil, placid, waveless, unruffled, like a millpond.
— OPPOSITES: aggressive, stormy.

pacifier ▶ noun *babies sucking on pacifiers* SOOTHER, dummy, plug.

pacifism ▶ noun PEACEMAKING, conscientious objection(s), passive resistance, peace-mongering, non-violence.

pacifist ▶ noun PEACE-LOVER, conscientious objector, passive resister, peacemaker, peace-monger, dove.
— OPPOSITES: warmonger.

pacify ▶ verb PLACATE, appease, calm (down), conciliate, propitiate, assuage, mollify, soothe.
— OPPOSITES: enrage.

pack ▶ noun **1** *a pack of cigarettes* PACKET, container, package, box, carton, parcel. **2** *a 45kg pack* BACKPACK, rucksack, knapsack, day pack, kit bag, (Nfld) nunny-bag ♣, bag, load. **3** *a pack of youngsters* CROWD, mob, group, band, troupe, troop, party, set, clique, gang, rabble, horde, herd, throng, huddle, mass, assembly, gathering, host; *informal* crew, bunch.
▶ verb **1** *she helped pack the hamper* FILL (UP), put things in, load. **2** *they packed their belongings* STOW, put away, store, box up. **3** *the glasses were packed in straw* WRAP (UP), package, parcel, swathe, swaddle, encase, enfold, envelop, bundle. **4** *Christmas shoppers packed the store* THRONG, crowd (into), fill (to overflowing), cram, jam, squash into, squeeze into. **5** *pack the cloth against the wall* COMPRESS, press, squash, squeeze, jam, tamp.
■ **pack someone off** (*informal*) SEND OFF, dispatch, bundle off.
■ **pack up** (*informal*) *it's time to pack up* STOP, call it a day, finish, cease; *informal* knock off, quit, pack it in.
■ **pack something up** PUT AWAY, tidy up/away, clear up/away.

package ▶ noun **1** *the delivery of a package* PARCEL, packet, container, box. **2** *a complete package of services* COLLECTION, bundle, combination.
▶ verb *goods packaged in recyclable materials* WRAP (UP), gift-wrap; pack (up), parcel (up), box, encase.

packaging ▶ noun WRAPPING, wrappers, packing, covering.

packed ▶ adjective CROWDED, full, filled (to capacity), crammed, jammed, solid, overcrowded, overfull, teeming, seething, swarming; *informal* jam-packed, chock full, standing room only, chockablock, full to the gunwales, bursting/bulging at the seams.

packet ▶ noun PACK, carton, (cardboard) box, container, case, package.

pact ▶ noun AGREEMENT, treaty, entente, protocol, deal, settlement, concordat, accord; armistice, truce; *formal* concord.

pad¹ ▶ noun **1** *a pad over the eye* PIECE OF COTTON, dressing, pack, padding, wadding, wad. **2** *a seat pad* CUSHION, squab. **3** *making notes on a pad* NOTEBOOK, notepad, writing pad, memo pad, scribbler ♣, block, sketch pad, steno pad, sketchbook, scratch pad.
▶ verb *a quilted jacket padded with goose down* STUFF, fill, pack, wad.
■ **pad something out** EXPAND UNNECESSARILY, fill out, amplify, increase, flesh out, lengthen, spin out, overdo, elaborate.

pad² ▶ verb *he padded along towards the bedroom* WALK QUIETLY, tread warily, creep, tiptoe, steal, pussyfoot.

padding ▶ noun **1** *padding around the ankle* WADDING, cushioning, stuffing, packing, filling, lining. **2** *a concise style with no padding* VERBIAGE, verbosity, wordiness, prolixity, filler.

paddle¹ ▶ noun *use the paddles to row ashore* OAR, scull, blade.
▶ verb *we paddled around the bay* row gently, pull, scull, canoe, kayak.

paddle² ▶ verb *children were paddling in the water* SPLASH ABOUT, wade; dabble.

paddock ▶ noun FIELD, meadow, pasture; pen, pound, corral.

padlock ▶ verb LOCK (UP), fasten, secure.

padre ▶ noun PRIEST, chaplain, minister (of religion), pastor, father, parson, clergyman, cleric, ecclesiastic, man of the cloth, churchman, vicar, rector, curate, preacher; *informal* reverend, Holy Joe, sky pilot.

paean ▶ noun SONG OF PRAISE, hymn, alleluia, plaudit, glorification, eulogy, tribute, panegyric, accolade, acclamation; *formal* encomium.

pagan ▶ noun *pagans worshipped the sun* HEATHEN, infidel, idolater, idolatress; *archaic* paynim.
▶ adjective *the pagan festival* HEATHEN, ungodly, irreligious, infidel, idolatrous.

page¹ ▶ noun **1** *a book of 672 pages* FOLIO, sheet, side, leaf. **2** *a glorious page in her life* PERIOD, time, stage, phase, epoch, era, chapter; episode, event.

page² ▶ noun MESSENGER, errand boy.
▶ verb *could you please page Mr. Johnson?* CALL (FOR), summon, send for, buzz.

pageant ▶ noun PARADE, procession, cavalcade, tableau (vivant); spectacle, extravaganza, show.

pageantry ▶ noun SPECTACLE, display, ceremony, magnificence, pomp, splendour, grandeur, show; *informal* razzle-dazzle, razzmatazz.

pain ▶ noun **1** *she endured great pain* SUFFERING, agony, torture, torment, discomfort. **2** *a pain in the stomach* ACHE, aching, soreness, throb, throbbing, sting, stinging, twinge, shooting pain, stab, pang, cramps;

discomfort, irritation, tenderness. **3** *the pain of losing a loved one* SORROW, grief, heartache, heartbreak, sadness, unhappiness, distress, desolation, misery, wretchedness, despair; agony, torment, torture, via dolorosa. **4** (*informal*) *that child is a pain. See* NUISANCE. **5** *he took great pains to hide his feelings* CARE, effort, bother, trouble.

▶ **verb 1** *her foot is still paining her* HURT, cause pain, be painful, be sore, be tender, ache, throb, sting, twinge, cause discomfort; *informal* kill. **2** *the memory pains her* SADDEN, grieve, distress, trouble, perturb, oppress, cause anguish to.

■ **be at pains** TRY HARD, make a great effort, take (great) pains, put oneself out; strive, endeavour, try, do one's best, do one's utmost, go all out; *informal* bend/fall/lean over backwards.

pained ▶ **adjective** UPSET, hurt, wounded, injured, insulted, offended, aggrieved, displeased, disgruntled, annoyed, angered, angry, cross, indignant, irritated, resentful; *informal* riled, miffed, aggravated, peeved, hacked off, cheesed off, teed off, ticked off, sore.

painful ▶ **adjective 1** *a painful arm* SORE, hurting, tender, aching, throbbing, angry. **2** *a painful experience* DISAGREEABLE, unpleasant, nasty, bitter, distressing, upsetting, traumatic, miserable, sad, heartbreaking, agonizing, harrowing.

painkiller ▶ **noun** ANALGESIC, pain reliever, anodyne, anaesthetic, narcotic; palliative.

painless ▶ **adjective 1** *any killing of animals should be painless* WITHOUT PAIN, pain-free. **2** *getting rid of him proved painless* EASY, trouble-free, effortless, simple, plain sailing; *informal* as easy as pie, a piece of cake, child's play, a cinch.
— OPPOSITES: painful, difficult.

painstaking ▶ **adjective** CAREFUL, meticulous, thorough, assiduous, sedulous, attentive, diligent, industrious, conscientious, punctilious, scrupulous, rigorous, particular; pedantic, fussy.
— OPPOSITES: slapdash.

paint ▶ **noun** COLOURING, colourant, tint, dye, stain, pigment, colour. *See table.*

▶ **verb 1** *simply paint the ceiling* COLOUR, apply paint to, decorate, whitewash, emulsion, gloss, spray-paint, airbrush. **2** *painting slogans on a wall* DAUB, smear, spray-paint, airbrush. **3** *Rembrandt painted his mother* PORTRAY, picture, paint a picture of, depict, represent. **4** *you paint a very stark picture of the suffering* TELL, recount, outline, sketch, describe, depict, evoke, conjure up.

■ **paint the town red** (*informal*) CELEBRATE, carouse, enjoy oneself, have a good/wild time, have a party; *informal* go out on the town, whoop it up, make whoopee, live it up, party, have a ball.

Types of Paint

acrylic	matte
colour wash	oil
distemper	poster paint
eggshell	primer
emulsion	tempera
enamel	undercoat
gloss	watercolour
gouache	whitewash

painting ▶ **noun** PICTURE, illustration, portrayal, depiction, representation, image, artwork; oil (painting), watercolour, canvas.

pair ▶ **noun 1** *a pair of gloves* SET (OF TWO), matching set, two of a kind. **2** *the pair were arrested* TWO, couple, duo, brace, twosome, duplet; twins. **3** *a pair of lines* COUPLET; *Prosody* distich. **4** *the happy pair* COUPLE, man/husband and wife.

▶ **verb** *a cardigan paired with a matching skirt* MATCH, put together, couple, twin.

■ **pair off/up** GET TOGETHER, team up, form a couple, make a twosome, hook up, marry.

pal (*informal*) ▶ **noun** *my best pal. See* FRIEND sense 1.

palace ▶ **noun** ROYAL/OFFICIAL RESIDENCE, castle, château, schloss, mansion, stately home.
— RELATED TERMS: palatial.

palatable ▶ **adjective 1** *palatable meals* EDIBLE, eatable, digestible, tasty, appetizing, flavourful; *formal* comestible. **2** *the truth is not always palatable* PLEASANT, acceptable, pleasing, agreeable, to one's liking.
— OPPOSITES: disagreeable.

palate ▶ **noun 1** *the tea burned her palate* ROOF OF THE MOUTH, hard/soft palate. **2** *menus to suit the tourist palate* (SENSE OF) TASTE, appetite, stomach. **3** *wine with a peachy palate* FLAVOUR, savour, taste.

palatial ▶ **adjective** LUXURIOUS, deluxe, magnificent, sumptuous, splendid, grand, opulent, lavish, stately, regal; fancy, upscale, upmarket; *informal* plush, swanky, posh, ritzy, swish.
— OPPOSITES: modest.

palaver (*informal*) ▶ **noun** FUSS, commotion, trouble, rigmarole, folderol; *informal* song and dance, performance, to-do, carrying-on, kerfuffle, hoo-ha, hullabaloo, ballyhoo.

pale¹ ▶ **noun 1** *the pales of a fence* STAKE, post, pole, picket, upright. **2** *outside the pale of decency* BOUNDARY, confines, bounds, limits.

■ **beyond the pale** UNACCEPTABLE, unseemly, improper, unsuitable, unreasonable, unforgivable, intolerable, disgraceful, deplorable, outrageous, scandalous, shocking; *informal* not on, out of line; *formal* exceptionable.

pale² ▶ **adjective 1** *she looked pale and drawn* WHITE, pallid, pasty, wan, colourless, anemic, bloodless, washed out, peaky, peaked, ashen, grey, whitish, white-faced, whey-faced, drained, sickly, sallow, as white as a sheet, deathly pale; milky, creamy, cream, ivory, milk-white, alabaster; *informal* like death warmed over. **2** *pale colours* LIGHT, light-coloured, pastel, muted, subtle, soft; faded, bleached, washed out. **3** *the pale light of morning* DIM, faint, weak, feeble. **4** *a pale imitation* FEEBLE, weak, insipid, bland, poor, inadequate; uninspired, unimaginative, lacklustre, spiritless, lifeless; *informal* pathetic.
— OPPOSITES: dark.

▶ **verb 1** *his face paled* GO/TURN WHITE, grow/turn pale, blanch, lose colour. **2** *everything else pales by comparison* DECREASE IN IMPORTANCE, lose significance, pale into insignificance, fade into the background.

palisade ▶ **noun** FENCE, paling, barricade, stockade.

pall¹ ▶ **noun 1** *a rich velvet pall* FUNERAL CLOTH, coffin covering. **2** *a pall of black smoke* CLOUD, covering, cloak, veil, shroud, layer, blanket.

■ **cast a pall over** SPOIL, cast a shadow over, overshadow, cloud, put a damper on.

pall² ▶ **verb** *the high life was beginning to pall* BECOME/GROW TEDIOUS, become/grow boring, lose its/their interest, lose attraction, wear off; weary, sicken, nauseate; irritate, irk.

palliate ▶ **verb 1** *the treatment works by palliating* *symptoms* ALLEVIATE, ease, relieve, soothe, take the edge off, assuage, moderate, temper, diminish, decrease, blunt, deaden. **2** *there is no way to palliate his dirty deed* DISGUISE, hide, gloss over, conceal, cover (up), camouflage, mask; excuse, justify, extenuate, mitigate.

palliative ▶ adjective *palliative medicine* SOOTHING, alleviating, sedative, calmative; for the terminally ill.
▶ noun *antibiotics and palliatives* PAINKILLER, analgesic, pain reliever, sedative, tranquilizer, anodyne, calmative, opiate, bromide.

pallid ▶ adjective **1** *a pallid child* PALE, white, pasty, wan, colourless, anemic, washed out, peaky, peaked, whey-faced, ashen, grey, whitish, drained, sickly, sallow; *informal* like death warmed over. **2** *pallid watercolours* INSIPID, uninspired, colourless, uninteresting, unexciting, unimaginative, lifeless, spiritless, sterile, bland.

pallor ▶ noun PALENESS, pallidness, lack of colour, wanness, ashen hue, pastiness, peakiness, greyness, sickliness, sallowness.

palm¹
■ **grease someone's palm** (*informal*) BRIBE, buy (off), corrupt, suborn, give an inducement to; *informal* give a sweetener to.
■ **have someone in the palm of one's hand** HAVE CONTROL OVER, have influence over, have someone eating out of one's hand, have someone on a string, have someone in one's hip pocket, have someone wrapped around one's finger.
■ **palm something off** FOIST, fob off, get rid of, dispose of, unload.

palm² ▶ noun *the palm of victory* PRIZE, trophy, award, crown, laurel wreath, laurels, bays.

palmistry ▶ noun FORTUNE TELLING, palm-reading, clairvoyance, chiromancy.

palmy ▶ adjective HAPPY, fortunate, glorious, triumphant, prosperous, halcyon, golden, rosy.

palpable ▶ adjective **1** *a palpable bump* TANGIBLE, touchable, noticeable, detectable. **2** *his reluctance was palpable* PERCEPTIBLE, perceivable, visible, noticeable, discernible, detectable, observable, tangible, unmistakable, transparent, self-evident; obvious, clear, plain (to see), evident, apparent, manifest, staring one in the face, written all over someone.
– OPPOSITES: imperceptible.

palpitate ▶ verb **1** *her heart began to palpitate* BEAT RAPIDLY, pound, throb, pulsate, pulse, thud, thump, hammer, race. **2** *palpitating with terror* TREMBLE, quiver, quake, shake (like a leaf).

paltry ▶ adjective **1** *a paltry sum of money* SMALL, meagre, trifling, insignificant, negligible, inadequate, insufficient, derisory, pitiful, pathetic, miserable, niggardly, beggarly; *informal* measly, piddling; *formal* exiguous. **2** *naval glory struck him as paltry* WORTHLESS, petty, trivial, unimportant, insignificant, inconsequential, of little account.
– OPPOSITES: considerable.

pamper ▶ verb SPOIL, indulge, overindulge, cosset, mollycoddle, coddle, baby, wait on someone hand and foot.

pamphlet ▶ noun BROCHURE, leaflet, booklet, chapbook, circular, flyer, fact sheet, handbill, mailer, folder.

pan¹ ▶ noun **1** *a heavy pan* SAUCEPAN, frying pan, pot, wok, skillet. **2** *salt pans* HOLLOW, pit, depression, dip, crater, concavity.
▶ verb **1** (*informal*) *the movie was panned by the critics. See*

CRITICIZE. **2** *prospectors panned for gold* SIFT, search for, look for.
– OPPOSITES: praise.
■ **pan out 1** *Bob's idea hadn't panned out* SUCCEED, be successful, work (out), turn out well, come to fruition. **2** *the deal panned out badly* TURN OUT, work out, end (up), come out, fall out, evolve; *formal* eventuate.

pan² ▶ verb *the camera panned to the building* SWING (ROUND), sweep, move, turn, circle.

panacea ▶ noun UNIVERSAL CURE, cure-all, cure for all ills, universal remedy, elixir, wonder drug; *informal* magic bullet.

panache ▶ noun FLAMBOYANCE, confidence, self-assurance, style, flair, élan, dash, verve, zest, spirit, brio, éclat, vivacity, gusto, liveliness, vitality, energy; *informal* pizzazz, oomph, zip, zing.

pancake ▶ noun crepe, flapjack, blini, blintz, galette, griddle cake; *US* hotcake, (*Nfld*) touton ✦, dosa, palacsinta, latke, ploye ✦, potato pancake.

pandemic ▶ adjective WIDESPREAD, prevalent, pervasive, rife, rampant.

pandemonium ▶ noun BEDLAM, chaos, mayhem, uproar, turmoil, tumult, commotion, confusion, anarchy, furor, hubbub, rumpus; *informal* hullabaloo, hoopla.
– OPPOSITES: peace.

pander
■ **pander to** INDULGE, gratify, satisfy, cater to, give in to, accommodate, comply with.

pane ▶ noun SHEET OF GLASS, windowpane.

panegyric ▶ noun EULOGY, speech of praise, paean, accolade, tribute.

panel ▶ noun **1** *a control panel* CONSOLE, instrument panel, dashboard; instruments, controls, dials. **2** *a panel of judges* GROUP, team, body, committee, board, jury.

pang ▶ noun **1** *hunger pangs* (SHARP) PAIN, shooting pain, twinge, stab, spasm. **2** *a pang of remorse* QUALM, twinge, prick.

panic ▶ noun *a wave of panic* ALARM, anxiety, nervousness, fear, fright, trepidation, dread, terror, agitation, hysteria, consternation, perturbation, dismay, apprehension; *informal* flap, fluster, cold sweat, funk, tizzy, swivet.
– OPPOSITES: calm.
▶ verb **1** *there's no need to panic* BE ALARMED, be scared, be nervous, be afraid, take fright, be agitated, be hysterical, lose one's nerve, get overwrought, get worked up; *informal* flap, get in a flap, lose one's cool, get into a tizzy, freak out, get in a stew, have kittens. **2** *talk of love panicked her* FRIGHTEN, alarm, scare, unnerve; *informal* throw into a tizzy, freak out.

panic-stricken ▶ adjective ALARMED, frightened, scared (stiff), terrified, terror-stricken, petrified, horrified, horror-stricken, fearful, afraid, panicky, frantic, in a frenzy, nervous, agitated, hysterical, beside oneself, worked up, overwrought; *informal* in a cold sweat, in a flap, in a fluster, in a tizzy.

panoply ▶ noun **1** *the full panoply of US military might* ARRAY, range, collection. **2** *all the panoply of religious liturgy* TRAPPINGS, regalia; splendour, spectacle, ceremony, ritual.

panorama ▶ noun **1** *he surveyed the panorama* (SCENIC) VIEW, vista, prospect, scene, scenery, landscape, seascape. **2** *a panorama of the art scene* OVERVIEW, survey, review, presentation, appraisal.

panoramic ▶ adjective **1** *a panoramic view* SWEEPING, wide, extensive, scenic, commanding. **2** *a panoramic look at the 20th century* WIDE-RANGING, extensive, broad, far-reaching, comprehensive, all-embracing.

pant ▶ **verb 1** *he was panting as they reached the top* BREATHE HEAVILY, breathe hard, puff, huff and puff, gasp, wheeze. **2** *it makes you pant for more* YEARN FOR, long for, crave, hanker after/for, ache for, hunger for, thirst for, be hungry for, be thirsty for, wish for, desire, want; *informal* itch for, be dying for.

panting ▶ **adjective** OUT OF BREATH, breathless, short of breath, puffing, huffing and puffing, gasping (for breath), wheezing, wheezy, hyperventilating.

pantry ▶ **noun** LARDER, store, storeroom; *archaic* spence.

pants ▶ **plural noun** TROUSERS, slacks, britches. *See table.*

Pants

baggies	hiphuggers
bell-bottoms	hot pants
Bermuda shorts	jeans
bicycle shorts	jodhpurs
bloomers	knee breeches
blue jeans	knee pants
breeches	knickerbockers
britches	knickers
capri pants	overalls
cargo pants	palazzo pants
chinos	pantaloons
clamdiggers	pedal-pushers
cords	rugby pants
corduroys	salopettes
culottes	shorts
cut-offs	slacks
dress pants	splash pants
dungarees	stirrup pants
flannels	sweatpants
flares	toreadors
galligaskins	track pants
gauchos	walking shorts
harem pants	

pap ▶ **noun 1** *a plateful of tasteless pap* SOFT FOOD, mush, slop, pulp, purée, mash, *proprietary* Pablum; *informal* goo, gloop, glop, gook. **2** *commercial pap* TRIVIA, pulp (fiction), garbage, rubbish, nonsense; *informal* dreck, drivel, trash, twaddle, pablum.

paper ▶ **noun 1** *a sheet of paper* writing paper, notepaper, foolscap, vellum. **2** *the local paper* NEWSPAPER, journal, gazette, periodical; tabloid, broadsheet, daily, weekly, evening paper; *informal* rag, tab. **3** *the paper was peeling off the walls* WALLPAPER, wallcovering. **4** *a three-hour paper* EXAM, examination, test, quiz. **5** *she has just published a paper* ESSAY, article, monograph, thesis, work, dissertation, treatise, study, report, analysis, tract, critique, exegesis, review, term paper, theme. **6** *personal papers* DOCUMENTS, certificates, letters, files, deeds, records, archives, paperwork, documentation; *Law* muniments. **7** *they asked us for our papers* IDENTIFICATION PAPERS/DOCUMENTS, identity card, ID, credentials.
▶ **verb** *we papered the walls* WALLPAPER, hang wallpaper on.
■ **paper something over** COVER UP, hide, conceal, disguise, camouflage, gloss over.
■ **on paper 1** *he put his thoughts down on paper* IN WRITING, in black and white, in print. **2** *the combatants*

were evenly matched on paper IN THEORY, theoretically, supposedly.

papery ▶ **adjective** THIN, paper-thin, flimsy, delicate, insubstantial, light, lightweight.

par
■ **below par 1** *their performances have been below par* SUBSTANDARD, inferior, not up to scratch, subpar, under par, below average, second-rate, mediocre, poor, undistinguished; *informal* not up to snuff, bush-league. **2** *I'm feeling below par* SLIGHTLY UNWELL, not (very) well, not oneself, out of sorts; ill, unwell, poorly, washed out, run-down, peaky, peaked, off; *informal* under the weather, not up to snuff, lousy, rough.
■ **on a par with** AS GOOD AS, comparable with, in the same class/league as, equivalent to, equal to, on a level with, of the same standard as.
■ **par for the course** NORMAL, typical, standard, usual, what one would expect.
■ **up to par** GOOD ENOUGH, up to the mark, satisfactory, acceptable, adequate, up to scratch; *informal* up to snuff.

parable ▶ **noun** ALLEGORY, moral story/tale, fable, exemplum.

parade ▶ **noun 1** *a Canada Day parade* PROCESSION, march, cavalcade, motorcade, spectacle, display, pageant; review, dress parade, tattoo; march past. **2** *she made a great parade of doing the housework* EXHIBITION, show, display, performance, spectacle, fuss; *informal* hoo-ha, to-do.
▶ **verb 1** *the teams paraded through the city* MARCH, process, file, troop. **2** *she paraded up and down* STRUT, swagger, stride. **3** *he was keen to parade his knowledge* DISPLAY, exhibit, make a show of, flaunt, show (off), demonstrate.

paradigm ▶ **noun** MODEL, pattern, example, exemplar, template, standard, prototype, archetype.

paradisal ▶ **adjective** HEAVENLY, idyllic, blissful, divine, sublime, perfect.

paradise ▶ **noun 1** *the souls in paradise* (THE KINGDOM OF) HEAVEN, the heavenly kingdom, Elysium, the Elysian Fields, Valhalla, Avalon. **2** *Adam and Eve's expulsion from Paradise* THE GARDEN OF EDEN, Eden. **3** *a tropical paradise* UTOPIA, Shangri-La, heaven, idyll, nirvana. **4** *this is sheer paradise!* BLISS, heaven, ecstasy, delight, joy, happiness, nirvana, heaven on earth.
— OPPOSITES: hell.

paradox ▶ **noun** CONTRADICTION (IN TERMS), self-contradiction, inconsistency, incongruity; oxymoron; conflict, anomaly; enigma, puzzle, mystery, conundrum.

paradoxical ▶ **adjective** CONTRADICTORY, self-contradictory, inconsistent, incongruous, anomalous; illogical, puzzling, baffling, incomprehensible, inexplicable.

paragon ▶ **noun** PERFECT EXAMPLE, shining example, model, epitome, archetype, ideal, exemplar, nonpareil, embodiment, personification, quintessence, apotheosis, acme; jewel, gem, angel, treasure; *informal* one in a million, the tops; *archaic* nonsuch.

paragraph ▶ **noun 1** *the concluding paragraph* SECTION, subdivision, part, subsection, division, portion, segment, passage. **2** *a paragraph in the newspaper* REPORT, article, item, sidebar, piece, write-up, mention.

parallel ▶ **adjective 1** *parallel lines* SIDE BY SIDE, aligned, collateral, equidistant. **2** *parallel careers*

SIMILAR, analogous, comparable, corresponding, like, of a kind, akin, related, equivalent, matching, homologous. **3** *a parallel universe* COEXISTING, coexistent, concurrent; contemporaneous, simultaneous, synchronous.
− OPPOSITES: divergent.
▶ **noun 1** *an exact parallel* COUNTERPART, analogue, equivalent, likeness, match, twin, duplicate, mirror. **2** *there is an interesting parallel between these figures* SIMILARITY, likeness, resemblance, analogy, correspondence, equivalence, correlation, relation, symmetry, parity.
▶ **verb 1** *his experiences parallel mine* RESEMBLE, be similar to, be like, bear a resemblance to; correspond to, be analogous to, be comparable/equivalent to, equate with/to, correlate with, imitate, echo, remind one of, duplicate, mirror, follow, match. **2** *her performance has never been paralleled* EQUAL, match, rival, emulate.

paralysis ▶ **noun 1** *the disease can cause paralysis* IMMOBILITY, powerlessness, incapacity, debilitation; *Medicine* paraplegia, quadriplegia, tetraplegia, monoplegia, hemiplegia, diplegia, paresis, paraparesis. **2** *complete paralysis of the ports* SHUTDOWN, immobilization, stoppage.

paralytic ▶ **adjective** PARALYZED, crippled, disabled, incapacitated, powerless, immobilized, useless.

paralyze ▶ **verb 1** *both of his legs were paralyzed* DISABLE, cripple, immobilize, incapacitate, debilitate; *formal* torpefy. **2** *Sally was paralyzed by the sight of him* IMMOBILIZE, transfix, become rooted to the spot, freeze, stun, render motionless. **3** *the capital was paralyzed by a general strike* BRING TO A STANDSTILL, immobilize, bring to a (grinding) halt, freeze, cripple, disable.

paralyzed ▶ **adjective** DISABLED, crippled, handicapped, incapacitated, paralytic, powerless, immobilized, useless; *Medicine* paraplegic, quadriplegic, tetraplegic, monoplegic, hemiplegic, paretic, paraparetic.

parameter ▶ **noun** FRAMEWORK, variable, limit, boundary, limitation, restriction, criterion, guideline.

paramount ▶ **adjective** MOST IMPORTANT, of greatest/prime importance; uppermost, supreme, chief, overriding, predominant, foremost, prime, primary, principal, highest, main, key, central, leading, major, top; *informal* number-one.

paramour ▶ **noun** (*archaic*) LOVER, significant other, inamorata; mistress, girlfriend, kept woman, other woman; boyfriend, main squeeze, other man, inamorato; *informal* toy boy, sugar daddy, bit on the side; *archaic* concubine, courtesan.

paranoia ▶ **noun** PERSECUTION COMPLEX, delusions, obsession, psychosis.

paranoid ▶ **adjective** OVER-SUSPICIOUS, paranoiac, suspicious, mistrustful, fearful, insecure.

parapet ▶ **noun 1** *Marian leaned over the parapet* BALUSTRADE, barrier, wall. **2** *the sandbags making up the parapet* BARRICADE, rampart, bulwark, bank, embankment, fortification, defence, earthwork, breastwork, bastion.

paraphernalia ▶ **plural noun** EQUIPMENT, stuff, things, apparatus, kit, implements, tools, utensils, material(s), appliances, accoutrements, appurtenances, odds and ends, bits and pieces; *informal* gear.

paraphrase ▶ **verb** *paraphrasing literary texts* REWORD, rephrase, put/express in other words, rewrite, gloss.
▶ **noun** *this paraphrase of Frye's words* REWORDING, rephrasing, rewriting, rewrite, rendition, rendering, gloss.

parasite ▶ **noun** HANGER-ON, cadger, leech, passenger; *informal* bloodsucker, sponger, bottom-feeder, scrounger, freeloader, mooch.

parcel ▶ **noun 1** *a parcel of clothes* PACKAGE, packet; pack, bundle, box, case, bale. **2** *a parcel of land* PLOT, piece, patch, tract, allotment, lot, plat.
▶ **verb 1** *she parcelled up the papers* PACK (UP), package, wrap (up), gift-wrap, tie up, bundle up. **2** *parcelling out commercial farmland* DIVIDE UP, portion out, distribute, share out, allocate, allot, apportion, hand out, dole out, dish out; *informal* divvy up.

parched ▶ **adjective 1** *the parched earth* (BONE) DRY, dried up/out, arid, desiccated, dehydrated, baked, burned, scorched; withered, shrivelled. **2** (*informal*) *I'm parched.* See THIRSTY sense 1.
− OPPOSITES: soaking.

pardon ▶ **noun 1** *pardon for your sins* FORGIVENESS, absolution, clemency, mercy, leniency, remission. **2** *he offered them a full pardon* REPRIEVE, free pardon, amnesty, exoneration, release, acquittal, discharge; *formal* exculpation.
▶ **verb 1** *I know she will pardon me* FORGIVE, absolve, have mercy on; excuse, condone, overlook. **2** *they were subsequently pardoned* EXONERATE, acquit, amnesty; reprieve, release, free; *informal* let off; *formal* exculpate.
− OPPOSITES: blame, punish.
▶ **exclamation** *Pardon?* WHAT (DID YOU SAY), what's that, pardon me, I beg your pardon, sorry, excuse me; *informal* come again, say what.

pardonable ▶ **adjective** EXCUSABLE, forgivable, condonable, understandable, minor, venial, slight.
− OPPOSITES: inexcusable.

pare ▶ **verb 1** *pare the peel from the lemon* CUT (OFF), trim (off), peel (off), strip (off), skin; *technical* decorticate. **2** *domestic operations have been pared down* REDUCE, diminish, decrease, cut (back/down), trim, slim down, prune, curtail.

parent ▶ **noun** MOTHER, FATHER, birth/biological parent, progenitor; adoptive parent, foster-parent, step-parent, guardian; *literary* begetter.
▶ **verb** *those who parent young children* RAISE, bring up, look after, take care of, rear.

parentage ▶ **noun** ORIGINS, extraction, birth, family, ancestry, lineage, heritage, pedigree, descent, blood, stock, roots.

parenthetical ▶ **adjective** INCIDENTAL, supplementary, in brackets, in parentheses, parenthetic; explanatory, qualifying.

parenthetically ▶ **adverb** INCIDENTALLY, by the way, by the by(e), in passing, in parenthesis.

parenthood ▶ **noun** CHILD CARE, child-rearing, motherhood, fatherhood, parenting.

pariah ▶ **noun** OUTCAST, persona non grata, black sheep, leper, undesirable, unperson, non-person.

parings ▶ **plural noun** PEELINGS, clippings, peel, rind, cuttings, trimmings, shavings.

parish ▶ **noun 1** *the municipal council of the parish of Oka* DISTRICT, community. **2** *the story scandalized the parish* PARISHIONERS, churchgoers, congregation, fold, flock, community.
− RELATED TERMS: parochial.

parity ▶ **noun** EQUALITY, equivalence, uniformity,

consistency, correspondence, congruity, levelness, unity, coequality.

park ▶ noun **1** *we were playing in the park* PUBLIC GARDEN, garden(s), recreation ground, parkette ✦, playground, play area, green space, green. **2** *a new national park* PARKLAND, wilderness area, protected area, nature reserve, game reserve.
▶ verb **1** *she parked her car* LEAVE, position; stop, pull up, pull over. **2** (*informal*) *park your bag by the door* PUT (DOWN), place, deposit, leave, stick, shove, dump; *informal* plonk.
■ **park oneself** (*informal*) SIT DOWN, seat oneself, settle (oneself), install oneself; *informal* plonk oneself.

parka ▶ noun (*North*) amautik ✦, atigi ✦, packing parka ✦, Mother Hubbard ✦, sunburst ✦; winter coat, duffle coat.

parking lot ▶ noun parking garage, car park, parkade ✦, park-and-ride.

parlance ▶ noun JARGON, language, phraseology, talk, speech, argot, patois, cant; *informal* lingo, -ese, -speak.

parley ▶ noun *a peace parley* NEGOTIATION, talk(s), conference, summit, discussion, powwow; *informal* confab; *formal* colloquy, confabulation.
▶ verb *the two parties were willing to parley* DISCUSS TERMS, talk, hold talks, negotiate, deliberate; *informal* powwow.

parliament ▶ noun **1** *the Governor General's speech to Parliament* THE HOUSES OF PARLIAMENT, the (House of) Commons, the House, Ottawa, the Senate, Parliament Hill; *informal* the Hill ✦. **2** *the Russian parliament* LEGISLATURE, legislative assembly, congress, senate, (upper/lower) house, (upper/lower) chamber, diet, assembly.

parliamentary ▶ adjective LEGISLATIVE, law-making, governmental, congressional, senatorial, democratic, elected, representative.

parlous ▶ adjective BAD, dire, dreadful, awful, terrible, grave, serious, desperate, precarious; sorry, poor, lamentable, hopeless; unsafe, perilous, dangerous, risky; *informal* dicey, hairy, woeful.

parochial ▶ adjective NARROW-MINDED, small-minded, provincial, narrow, small-town, conservative, illiberal, intolerant; *informal* jerkwater.
— OPPOSITES: broad-minded.

parochialism ▶ noun NARROW-MINDEDNESS, provincialism, small-mindedness.

parody ▶ noun **1** *a parody of the Gothic novel* SATIRE, burlesque, lampoon, pastiche, caricature, imitation, mockery; *informal* spoof, takeoff, send-up. **2** *a parody of the truth* DISTORTION, travesty, caricature, misrepresentation, perversion, corruption, debasement.
▶ verb *parodying schoolgirl fiction* SATIRIZE, burlesque, lampoon, caricature, mimic, imitate, ape, copy, make fun of, travesty, take off; *informal* send up.

paroxysm ▶ noun SPASM, attack, fit, burst, bout, convulsion, seizure, outburst, eruption, explosion, access.

parrot ▶ noun PSITTACINE. *See table.*
▶ verb *they parroted slogans without appreciating their significance* REPEAT (MINDLESSLY), repeat mechanically, echo.

parry ▶ verb **1** *Alfonso parried the blow* WARD OFF, fend off; deflect, hold off, block, counter, repel, repulse. **2** *I parried her constant questions* EVADE, sidestep, avoid, dodge, answer evasively, field, fend off.

parsimonious ▶ adjective CHEAP, miserly, mean,

Parrots

Amazon parrot	kea
budgerigar	lorikeet
cockatiel	lory
cockatoo	lovebird
conure	macaw
corella	parakeet
kaka	parrot
kakapo	rainbow lorikeet

niggardly, close-fisted, close, penny-pinching, ungenerous, Scrooge-like; *informal* tight-fisted, cheese-paring, tight, stingy, mingy; *formal* penurious.
— OPPOSITES: generous.

parsimony ▶ noun CHEAPNESS, miserliness, meanness, parsimoniousness, niggardliness, close-fistedness, closeness, penny-pinching; *informal* stinginess, minginess, tightness, tight-fistedness, cheese-paring; *formal* penuriousness.

parson ▶ noun VICAR, rector, clergyman, cleric, chaplain, pastor, curate, man of the cloth, ecclesiastic, minister, priest, preacher; *informal* reverend, padre.

part ▶ noun **1** *the last part of the cake* | *a large part of their life* BIT, slice, chunk, lump, hunk, wedge, fragment, scrap, piece; portion, proportion, percentage, fraction. **2** *car parts* COMPONENT, bit, constituent, element, module. **3** *body parts* PART OF THE BODY, organ, limb, member. **4** *the third part of the book* SECTION, division, volume, chapter, act, scene, instalment. **5** *another part of the country* DISTRICT, neighbourhood, quarter, section, area, region. **6** *the part of Juliet* (THEATRICAL) ROLE, character, persona. **7** *she's learning her part* LINES, words, script, speech; libretto, lyrics, score. **8** *he was jailed for his part in the affair* INVOLVEMENT, role, function, hand, work, responsibility, capacity, position, participation, contribution; *informal* bit.
— OPPOSITES: whole.
▶ verb **1** *the curtains parted* SEPARATE, divide (in two), split (in two), move apart. **2** *we parted on bad terms* LEAVE, take one's leave, say goodbye/farewell, say one's goodbyes/farewells, go one's (separate) ways, split, go away, depart.
— OPPOSITES: join, meet.
▶ adjective *a part payment* INCOMPLETE, partial, half, semi-, limited, inadequate, insufficient, unfinished.
— OPPOSITES: complete.
▶ adverb *it is part finished* TO A CERTAIN EXTENT/DEGREE, to some extent/degree, partly, partially, in part, half, relatively, comparatively, (up) to a point, somewhat; not totally, not entirely, (very) nearly, almost, just about, all but.
— OPPOSITES: completely.
■ **for the most part**. *See* MOSTLY.
■ **in part** TO A CERTAIN EXTENT/DEGREE, to some extent/degree, partly, partially, slightly, in some measure, (up) to a point.
■ **on the part of** (MADE/DONE) BY, carried out by, caused by, from.
■ **part with** GIVE UP/AWAY, relinquish, forgo, surrender, hand over, deliver up, dispose of.
■ **take part** PARTICIPATE, join in, get involved, enter, play a part/role, be a participant, contribute, have a hand, help, assist, lend a hand; *informal* get in on the act.
■ **take part in** PARTICIPATE IN, engage in, join in, get involved in, share in, play a part/role in, be a

participant in, contribute to, be associated with, have a hand in.

■ **take someone's part** SUPPORT, give one's support to, take the side of, side with, stand by, stick up for, be supportive of, back (up), give one's backing to, be loyal to, defend, come to the defence of, champion.

partake ▶ verb **1** (formal) visitors can partake in golf PARTICIPATE IN, take part in, engage in, join in, get involved in. **2** she had partaken of lunch CONSUME, have, eat, drink, devour; informal wolf down, polish off. **3** Bohemia partakes of both East and West HAVE THE QUALITIES/ATTRIBUTES OF, suggest, evoke, be characterized by.

partial ▶ adjective **1** a partial recovery INCOMPLETE, limited, qualified, imperfect, fragmentary, unfinished. **2** a very partial view of the situation BIASED, prejudiced, partisan, one-sided, slanted, skewed, coloured, unbalanced.
— OPPOSITES: complete, unbiased.
■ **be partial to** LIKE, love, enjoy, have a liking for, be fond of, be keen on, have a soft spot for, have a taste for, have a penchant for; informal adore, be mad about/for, have a thing about, be crazy about, be nutty about, cotton to.

partiality ▶ noun **1** his partiality towards their cause BIAS, prejudice, favouritism, favour, partisanship. **2** her partiality for brandy LIKING, love, fondness, taste, soft spot, predilection, penchant, passion.

partially ▶ adverb TO A LIMITED EXTENT/DEGREE, to a certain extent/degree, partly, in part, not totally, not entirely, relatively, moderately, (up) to a point, somewhat, comparatively, slightly.

participant ▶ noun PARTICIPATOR, contributor, party, member; entrant, competitor, player, contestant, candidate.

participate ▶ verb TAKE PART, engage, join, get involved, share, play a part/role, be a participant, partake, have a hand in, be associated with; co-operate, help, assist, lend a hand.

participation ▶ noun INVOLVEMENT, part, contribution, association.

particle ▶ noun **1** minute particles of rock (TINY) BIT, (tiny) piece, speck, spot, fleck; fragment, sliver, splinter. **2** he never showed a particle of sympathy IOTA, jot, whit, bit, scrap, shred, crumb, drop, hint, touch, trace, suggestion, whisper, suspicion, scintilla; informal smidgen.

particular ▶ adjective **1** a particular group of companies SPECIFIC, certain, distinct, separate, discrete, definite, precise; single, individual. **2** an issue of particular importance (EXTRA) SPECIAL, especial, exceptional, unusual, singular, uncommon, notable, noteworthy, remarkable, unique; formal peculiar. **3** he was particular about what he ate FUSSY, fastidious, finicky, meticulous, punctilious, discriminating, selective, painstaking, exacting, demanding; informal persnickety, choosy, picky.
— OPPOSITES: general, careless.
▶ noun the same in every particular DETAIL, item, point, specific, element, aspect, respect, regard, particularity, fact, feature.
■ **in particular 1** nothing in particular SPECIFIC, special. **2** the poor, in particular, were hit by rising prices PARTICULARLY, specifically, especially, specially.

particularity ▶ noun **1** the particularity of each human being INDIVIDUALITY, distinctiveness, uniqueness, singularity, originality. **2** a great degree of particularity DETAIL, precision, accuracy, thoroughness, scrupulousness, meticulousness.

particularize ▶ verb SPECIFY, detail, itemize, list, enumerate, spell out, cite, stipulate, instance.

particularly ▶ adverb **1** the acoustics are particularly good ESPECIALLY, specially, very, extremely, exceptionally, singularly, peculiarly, unusually, extraordinarily, remarkably, outstandingly, amazingly, incredibly, really, seriously. **2** he particularly asked that I should help you SPECIFICALLY, explicitly, expressly, in particular, especially, specially.

parting ▶ noun **1** an emotional parting FAREWELL, leave-taking, goodbye, adieu, departure; valediction. **2** they kept their parting quiet SEPARATION, breakup, split, divorce, rift, estrangement. **3** the parting of the Red Sea DIVISION, dividing, separation, separating, splitting, breaking up/apart, partition, partitioning.
▶ adjective a parting kiss FAREWELL, goodbye, last, final, valedictory.

partisan ▶ noun **1** Conservative partisans SUPPORTER, follower, adherent, devotee, champion; fanatic, fan, enthusiast, stalwart, zealot, booster. **2** the partisans opened fire from the woods GUERRILLA, freedom fighter, resistance fighter, underground fighter, irregular (soldier).
▶ adjective partisan attitudes BIASED, prejudiced, one-sided, discriminatory, coloured, partial, interested, sectarian, factional.
— OPPOSITES: unbiased.

partisanship ▶ noun BIAS, prejudice, one-sidedness, discrimination, favour, favouritism, partiality, sectarianism, factionalism.

partition ▶ noun **1** the partition of Palestine DIVIDING UP, partitioning, separation, division, dividing, subdivision, splitting (up), breaking up, breakup. **2** room partitions SCREEN, (room) divider, (dividing) wall, barrier, panel.
▶ verb **1** the resolution partitioned Poland DIVIDE (UP), subdivide, separate, split (up), break up; share (out), parcel out. **2** the huge hall was partitioned SUBDIVIDE, divide (up); separate (off), section off, screen off.

partly ▶ adverb TO A CERTAIN EXTENT/DEGREE, to some extent/degree, in part, partially, a little, somewhat, not totally, not entirely, relatively, moderately, (up) to a point, in some measure, slightly.
— OPPOSITES: completely.

partner ▶ noun **1** business partners COLLEAGUE, associate, co-worker, fellow worker, collaborator, comrade, teammate; archaic compeer. **2** his partner in crime ACCOMPLICE, confederate, accessory, collaborator, fellow conspirator, helper; informal sidekick. **3** your relationship with your partner SPOUSE, husband, wife, consort, life partner; lover, girlfriend, boyfriend, fiancé, fiancée, significant other, main squeeze, live-in lover, common-law husband/wife, man, woman, mate; informal hubby, missus, old man, old lady/woman, better half, intended, other half.

partnership ▶ noun **1** close partnership CO-OPERATION, association, collaboration, coalition, alliance, union, affiliation, relationship, connection. **2** thriving partnerships COMPANY, firm, business, corporation, organization, association, consortium, syndicate.

parturition ▶ noun (formal) CHILDBIRTH, birth, delivery, labour.

party ▶ noun **1** 150 people attended the party (SOCIAL) GATHERING, (social) function, get-together,

celebration, reunion, festivity, jamboree, reception, at-home, social; dance, ball, ceilidh, frolic, soiree, carousal, carouse, fete, hoedown, field party ♣, shower, bake, cookout, levee; *informal* bash, whoop-up ♣, shindig, rave, do, shebang, bop, hop, bunfight, blast, wingding, (*Atlantic*) time ♣. **2** *a party of German tourists* GROUP, company, body, gang, band, crowd, pack, contingent; *informal* bunch, crew, load. **3** *the left-wing parties* FACTION, political party, group, grouping, cabal, junta, bloc, camp, caucus. **4** *don't mention a certain party* PERSON, individual, somebody, someone.
▶ **verb** (*informal*) *let's party!* CELEBRATE, have fun, enjoy oneself, have a party, have a good/wild time, go on a spree, rave it up, carouse, make merry; *informal* go out on the town, paint the town red, whoop it up, let one's hair down, make whoopee, live it up, have a ball.
■ **be a party to** GET INVOLVED IN/WITH, be associated with, be a participant in.

Parties

bachelorette party	lawn party
bachelor party	mechoui ♣(*Que.*)
birthday party	milling frolic ♣(*NS*)
block party	pyjama party
bush party ♣	rehearsal party
cocktail party	slumber party
dinner party	stag party
field party ♣	sugaring-off party
garden party	tailgate party
house party	tea party
housewarming party	warehouse party
keg party	wrap party
kitchen	
party/racket ♣(*Maritimes*)	

party-pooper ▶ **noun** KILLJOY, sourpuss, spoilsport, wet blanket, damper.

parvenu ▶ **noun** UPSTART, social climber, arriviste, a jumped-up ——.

pass¹ ▶ **verb 1** *the traffic passing through the village* GO, proceed, move, progress, make one's way, travel. **2** *a car passed him* OVERTAKE, go past/by, pull ahead of, overhaul, leave behind; *informal* leapfrog. **3** *time passed* ELAPSE, go by/past, advance, wear on, roll by, tick by. **4** *he passed the time writing letters* OCCUPY, spend, fill, use (up), employ, while away. **5** *pass me the salt* HAND (OVER), let someone have, give, reach. **6** *Max passed the ball back* KICK, hit, throw, lob. **7** *her estate passed to her grandson* BE TRANSFERRED, go, be left, be bequeathed, be handed down/on, be passed on; *Law* devolve. **8** *his death passed almost unnoticed* HAPPEN, occur, take place, come about, transpire, come and go; *literary* befall. **9** *the storm passed* ABATE, fade (away), come to an end, blow over, run its course, die out, finish, end, cease, subside. **10** *Nature's complexity passes all human understanding* SURPASS, exceed, transcend. **11** *he passed the exam* BE SUCCESSFUL IN, succeed in, gain a pass in, get through; *informal* sail through, scrape through. **12** *the Senate passed the bill* APPROVE, vote for, accept, ratify, adopt, agree to, authorize, endorse, legalize, enact; *informal* OK. **13** *she could not let that comment pass* GO (UNNOTICED), stand, go unremarked, go undisputed. **14** *we should not pass judgment* DECLARE, pronounce, utter, express, deliver, issue. **15** *passing urine* DISCHARGE, excrete, evacuate, expel,

emit, release.
– OPPOSITES: stop, fail, reject.
▶ **noun 1** *you must show your pass* PERMIT, warrant, authorization, licence. **2** *a cross-field pass* KICK, hit, throw, set-up, cross, lateral.
■ **come to pass** (*literary*) HAPPEN, come about, occur, transpire, arise; *literary* befall.
■ **make a pass at** MAKE (SEXUAL) ADVANCES TO, proposition; *informal* come on to, make a play for, hit on, make time with, put the make on.
■ **pass away/on.** See DIE sense 1.
■ **pass as/for** BE MISTAKEN FOR, be taken for, be accepted as.
■ **pass off** *the rally passed off peacefully* TAKE PLACE, go off, happen, occur, be completed, turn out.
■ **pass someone off** MISREPRESENT, falsely represent; disguise.
■ **pass out** FAINT, lose consciousness, black out.
■ **pass something over** DISREGARD, overlook, ignore, pay no attention to, let pass, gloss over, take no notice of, pay no heed to, turn a blind eye to.
■ **pass something up** TURN DOWN, reject, refuse, decline, give up, forgo, let pass, miss (out on); *informal* give something a miss.

pass² ▶ **noun** *a pass through the mountains* ROUTE, way, road, passage, cut, gap, notch.

passable ▶ **adjective 1** *the beer was passable* ADEQUATE, all right, fairly good, acceptable, satisfactory, moderately good, not (too) bad, average, tolerable, fair; mediocre, middling, ordinary, indifferent, unremarkable, unexceptional; *informal* OK, so-so, {comme ci, comme ça}, nothing to write home about. **2** *the road is still passable* NAVIGABLE, traversable, negotiable, unblocked, unobstructed, open, clear.

passably ▶ **adverb** QUITE, rather, somewhat, fairly, reasonably, moderately, comparatively, relatively, tolerably; *informal* pretty.

passage ▶ **noun 1** *their passage through the country* TRANSIT, progress, passing, movement, motion, travelling. **2** *the passage of time* PASSING, advance, course, march. **3** *a passage from the embassy* SAFE CONDUCT, warrant, visa; admission, access. **4** *the overnight passage* VOYAGE, crossing, trip, journey. **5** *clearing a passage to the front door* WAY (THROUGH), route, path. **6** *a passage to the kitchen* See PASSAGEWAY sense 1. **7** *a passage between the buildings.* See PASSAGEWAY sense 2. **8** *the nasal passages* DUCT, orifice, opening, channel; inlet, outlet. **9** *the passage to democracy* TRANSITION, development, progress, move, change, shift. **10** *the passage of the bill* ENACTMENT, passing, ratification, royal assent, approval, adoption, authorization, legalization. **11** *a passage from 'Macbeth'* EXTRACT, excerpt, quotation, quote, citation, reading, piece, selection.

passageway ▶ **noun 1** *secret passageways* CORRIDOR, hall, passage, hallway, walkway, aisle. **2** *a narrow passageway off the main street* ALLEY, alleyway, passage, lane, path, pathway, footpath, track, thoroughfare, areaway.

passé ▶ **adjective.** See OLD-FASHIONED.

passenger ▶ **noun** *rail passengers* TRAVELLER, commuter, fare, rider, fare payer.

passerby ▶ **noun** BYSTANDER, eyewitness, witness.

passing ▶ **adjective 1** *of passing interest* FLEETING, transient, transitory, ephemeral, brief, short-lived, temporary, momentary; *literary* evanescent. **2** *a passing glance* HASTY, rapid, hurried, brief, quick; cursory, superficial, casual, perfunctory.

▶ **noun 1** *the passing of time* PASSAGE, course, progress, advance. **2** *Jack's passing* DEATH, demise, passing away/on, end, loss, quietus; *formal* decease. **3** *the passing of the new bill* ENACTMENT, ratification, approval, adoption, authorization, legalization, endorsement.
■ **in passing** INCIDENTALLY, by the by/way, en passant.

passion ▶ **noun 1** *the passion of activists* FERVOUR, ardour, enthusiasm, eagerness, zeal, zealousness, vigour, fire, fieriness, energy, fervency, animation, spirit, spiritedness, fanaticism. **2** *he worked himself up into a passion* (BLIND) RAGE, fit of anger/temper, temper, towering rage, tantrum, fury, frenzy. **3** *hot with passion* LOVE, (sexual) desire, lust, ardour, infatuation, lasciviousness, lustfulness. **4** *his passion for football* ENTHUSIASM, love, mania, fascination, obsession, fanaticism, fixation, compulsion, appetite, addiction; *informal* thing. **5** *Canadian literature is my passion* OBSESSION, preoccupation, craze, mania, hobby horse. **6** *the Passion of Christ* CRUCIFIXION, suffering, agony, martyrdom.
— OPPOSITES: apathy.

passionate ▶ **adjective 1** *a passionate entreaty* INTENSE, impassioned, ardent, fervent, vehement, heated, emotional, heartfelt, eager, excited, animated, spirited, energetic, fervid, frenzied, fiery, wild, consuming, violent; *literary* perfervid. **2** *Elizabeth is passionate about sports* VERY KEEN, very enthusiastic, addicted; *informal* mad, crazy, hooked, nuts, nutso. **3** *a passionate kiss* AMOROUS, ardent, hot-blooded, aroused, loving, sexy, sensual, erotic, lustful; *informal* steamy, hot, red-hot, turned on. **4** *a passionate woman* EXCITABLE, emotional, fiery, volatile, mercurial, quick-tempered, high-strung, impulsive, temperamental.
— OPPOSITES: apathetic.

passionless ▶ **adjective** UNEMOTIONAL, cold, cold-blooded, emotionless, frigid, cool, unfeeling, unloving, unresponsive, undemonstrative, impassive.

passive ▶ **adjective 1** *a passive role* INACTIVE, non-active, non-participative, uninvolved. **2** *passive victims* SUBMISSIVE, acquiescent, unresisting, unassertive, compliant, pliant, obedient, docile, tractable, malleable, pliable. **3** *the woman's face was passive* EMOTIONLESS, impassive, unemotional, unmoved, dispassionate, passionless, detached, unresponsive, undemonstrative, apathetic, phlegmatic.
— OPPOSITES: active.

passport ▶ **noun 1** TRAVEL PERMIT, (travel) papers, visa, laissez-passer. **2** *qualifications are the passport to success* KEY, path, way, route, avenue, door, doorway.

past ▶ **adjective 1** *memories of times past* GONE (BY), over (and done with), no more, done, bygone, former, (of) old, olden, long-ago; *literary* of yore. **2** *the past few months* LAST, recent, preceding. **3** *a past chairman* PREVIOUS, former, foregoing, erstwhile, one-time, sometime, ex-; *formal* quondam.
— OPPOSITES: present, future.
▶ **noun** *details about her past* HISTORY, background, life (story).
▶ **preposition 1** *she walked past the café* IN FRONT OF, by. **2** *he's past retirement age* BEYOND, in excess of.
▶ **adverb** *they hurried past* ALONG, by, on.
■ **in the past** FORMERLY, previously, in days/years/times gone by, in former times, in the (good) old days, in days of old, in olden times, once (upon a time); *literary* in days of yore, in yesteryear.

pasta ▶ **noun.** *See table.*

Types of Pasta

agnolotti	ravioli
angel hair	rigatoni
bow tie	shell pasta
bucatini	spaghetti
cannelloni	spaghettini
capellini	tagliatelle
cappelletti	tortellini
farfalle	vermicelli
fettuccine	ziti
fusilli	
lasagna	**Sauces**
linguine	alfredo
macaroni	arrabbiata
manicotti	bolognese
orecchiette	carbonara
orzo	marinara
pappardelle	primavera
penne	puttanesca

paste ▶ **noun 1** *blend the ingredients to a paste* PURÉE, pulp, mush, mash, blend. **2** *wallpaper paste* ADHESIVE, glue, gum, fixative, mucilage.
▶ **verb** *a notice was pasted on the door* GLUE, stick, gum, fix, affix.

pastel ▶ **adjective** PALE, soft, light, light-coloured, muted, subtle, subdued, soft-hued.
— OPPOSITES: dark, bright.

pastiche ▶ **noun 1** *a pastiche of literary models* MIXTURE, blend, medley, mélange, miscellany, mixed bag, potpourri, mix, compound, composite, collection, assortment, conglomeration, jumble, ragbag, hodgepodge. **2** *a pastiche of 18th-century style* IMITATION, parody; *informal* takeoff.

pastime ▶ **noun** HOBBY, leisure activity/pursuit, sport, game, recreation, amusement, diversion, avocation, entertainment, interest, sideline.

past master ▶ **noun** EXPERT, master, wizard, genius, old hand, old sweat, veteran, maestro, connoisseur, authority, grandmaster; *informal* ace, pro, star, hotshot, maven, crackerjack.

pastor ▶ **noun** PRIEST, minister (of religion), parson, clergyman, cleric, chaplain, padre, ecclesiastic, man of the cloth, churchman, vicar, rector, curate, preacher, imam; *informal* reverend.

pastoral ▶ **adjective 1** *a pastoral scene* RURAL, country, countryside, rustic, agricultural, bucolic; *literary* sylvan, Arcadian. **2** *his pastoral duties* PRIESTLY, clerical, ecclesiastical, ministerial.
— OPPOSITES: urban.

pastry ▶ **noun 1** *sweet pastries on the breakfast buffet* TART, tartlet, pie, pasty, patty, sweet bread, cake. **2** *two layers of pastry* CRUST, piecrust, croûte.

pasture ▶ **noun** GRAZING (LAND), grassland, grass, pasture land, pasturage, ley; meadow, field; *literary* lea, mead, greensward.

pasty ▶ **adjective** PALE, pallid, wan, colourless, anemic, ashen, white, grey, pasty-faced, washed out, sallow.

pat¹ ▶ **verb** *Brian patted her on the shoulder* TAP, slap lightly, clap, touch.
▶ **noun 1** *a pat on the cheek* TAP, light blow, clap, touch. **2** *a pat of butter* PIECE, dab, lump, portion, knob, mass, gobbet, ball, curl.
■ **pat someone on the back** CONGRATULATE, praise,

take one's hat off to; commend, compliment, applaud, acclaim.

pat² ▶ adjective *pat answers* GLIB, simplistic, facile, unconvincing.

▶ adverb *his reply came rather pat* OPPORTUNELY, conveniently, at just/exactly the right moment, expediently, favourably, appropriately, fittingly, auspiciously, providentially, felicitously, propitiously.

■ **down pat** WORD-PERFECT, by heart, by rote, by memory.

■ **get something down pat** MEMORIZE, commit to memory, remember, learn by heart, learn (by rote).

patch ▶ noun **1** *a patch over one eye* COVER, eye patch, covering, pad. **2** *a reddish patch on her wrist* BLOTCH, mark, spot, smudge, speckle, smear, stain, streak, blemish; *informal* splotch. **3** *a patch of ground* PLOT, area, piece, strip, tract, parcel; bed, allotment, lot, plat. **4** *(informal) they are going through a difficult patch* PERIOD, time, spell, phase, stretch.

▶ verb *her jeans were neatly patched* MEND, repair, put a patch on, sew (up), stitch (up).

■ **patch something up** *(informal)* **1** *the houses were being patched up* REPAIR, mend, fix hastily, do a makeshift repair on. **2** *he's trying to patch things up with his wife* RECONCILE, make up, settle, remedy, put to rights, rectify, clear up, set right, make good, resolve, square.

patchwork ▶ noun ASSORTMENT, miscellany, mixture, mélange, medley, blend, mixed bag, mix, collection, selection, assemblage, combination, potpourri, jumble, mishmash, bricolage, ragbag, hodgepodge.

patchy ▶ adjective **1** *their education has been patchy* UNEVEN, varying, variable, intermittent, fitful, sporadic, erratic, irregular, haphazard, hit-and-miss. **2** *patchy evidence* FRAGMENTARY, inadequate, insufficient, rudimentary, limited, sketchy.
— OPPOSITES: uniform, comprehensive.

patent ▶ noun *there is a patent on the chemical* COPYRIGHT, licence, legal protection, registered trademark.

▶ adjective **1** *patent nonsense* OBVIOUS, clear, plain, evident, manifest, self-evident, transparent, overt, conspicuous, blatant, downright, barefaced, flagrant, undisguised, unconcealed, unmistakable. **2** *patent medicines* PROPRIETARY, patented, licensed, branded.

paternal ▶ adjective **1** *his face showed paternal concern* FATHERLY, fatherlike, patriarchal; protective, solicitous, compassionate, sympathetic. **2** *his paternal grandfather* ON ONE'S FATHER'S SIDE, patrilineal.
— OPPOSITES: maternal.

paternity ▶ noun FATHERHOOD.

path ▶ noun **1** *a path down to the beach* TRAIL, pathway, walkway, track, footpath, trackway, bridleway, bridle path, *(West)* monkey trail ✦, portage trail, lane, alley, alleyway, passage, passageway; sidewalk, bikeway, pedway. **2** *journalists blocked his path* ROUTE, way, course; direction, bearing, line; orbit, trajectory. **3** *the best path towards a settlement* COURSE OF ACTION, route, road, avenue, line, approach, tack, strategy, tactic.

pathetic ▶ adjective **1** *a pathetic groan* PITIFUL, pitiable, piteous, moving, touching, poignant, plaintive, distressing, upsetting, heartbreaking, heart-rending, harrowing, wretched, forlorn. **2** *(informal) a pathetic excuse* FEEBLE, woeful, sorry, poor, pitiful, lamentable, deplorable, contemptible,

inadequate, paltry, insufficient, insubstantial, unsatisfactory.

pathfinder ▶ noun PIONEER, ground-breaker, trailblazer, trend-setter, leader, torch-bearer, pacemaker.

pathological ▶ adjective **1** *a pathological condition* MORBID, diseased. **2** *(informal) a pathological liar* COMPULSIVE, obsessive, inveterate, habitual, persistent, chronic, hardened, confirmed.

pathos ▶ noun POIGNANCY, tragedy, sadness, pitifulness, piteousness, pitiableness.

patience ▶ noun **1** *she tried everyone's patience* FORBEARANCE, tolerance, restraint, self-restraint, stoicism; calmness, composure, equanimity, serenity, tranquility, imperturbability, phlegm, understanding, indulgence. **2** *a task requiring patience* PERSEVERANCE, persistence, endurance, tenacity, assiduity, application, staying power, doggedness, determination, resolve, resolution, resoluteness.

patient ▶ adjective **1** *I must ask you to be patient* FORBEARING, uncomplaining, tolerant, resigned, stoical; calm, composed, even-tempered, imperturbable, unexcitable, accommodating, understanding, indulgent; *informal* unflappable, cool. **2** *a good deal of patient work* PERSEVERING, persistent, tenacious, indefatigable, dogged, determined, resolved, resolute, single-minded; *formal* pertinacious.

▶ noun *a doctor's patient* SICK PERSON, case; invalid, convalescent, outpatient, in-patient.

patio ▶ noun TERRACE, sundeck, deck; courtyard.

patois ▶ noun VERNACULAR, (local) dialect, regional language; jargon, argot, cant; *informal* (local) lingo.

patriarch ▶ noun SENIOR FIGURE, father, paterfamilias, leader, elder.

patrician ▶ noun *the great patricians* ARISTOCRAT, grandee, noble, nobleman, noblewoman, lord, lady, peer, peeress; blueblood.

▶ adjective *patrician families* ARISTOCRATIC, noble, titled, blue-blooded, high-born, upper-class, landowning; *informal* upper-crust; *archaic* gentle.

patrimony ▶ noun HERITAGE, inheritance, birthright; legacy, bequest, endowment.

patriot ▶ noun NATIONALIST, loyalist; chauvinist, jingoist, flag-waver.

patriotic ▶ adjective NATIONALIST, nationalistic, loyalist, loyal; chauvinistic, jingoistic, flag-waving.
— OPPOSITES: traitorous.

patrol ▶ noun **1** *an all-night patrol to protect the witness* VIGIL, guard, watch, monitoring, policing, patrolling. **2** *the patrol stopped a suspect* SECURITY GUARD, sentry, sentinel, patrolman; scout, scouting party.

▶ verb *a security guard was patrolling the neighbourhood* KEEP GUARD (ON), guard, keep watch (on); police, make the rounds (of); stand guard (over), keep a vigil (on), defend, safeguard.

patron ▶ noun **1** *a patron of the arts* SPONSOR, backer, financier, benefactor, benefactress, contributor, subscriber, donor; philanthropist, promoter, friend, supporter; *informal* angel. **2** *club patrons* CUSTOMER, client, frequenter, consumer, user, visitor, guest; *informal* regular, habitué.

patronage ▶ noun **1** *art patronage* SPONSORSHIP, backing, funding, financing, promotion, assistance, support. **2** *political patronage* POWER OF APPOINTMENT, favouritism, nepotism, preferential treatment, cronyism, pork-barrelling. **3** *thank you for your patronage* CUSTOM, trade, business.

patronize ▶ verb **1** *don't patronize me!* TREAT

CONDESCENDINGLY, condescend to, look down on, talk down to, put down, treat like a child, treat with disdain. **2** *they patronized local tradesmen* DO BUSINESS WITH, buy from, shop at, be a customer of, be a client of, deal with, trade with, frequent, support. **3** *he patronized a national museum* SPONSOR, back, fund, finance, be a patron of, support, champion.

patronizing ▶ adjective CONDESCENDING, disdainful, supercilious, superior, imperious, scornful, contemptuous; *informal* uppity, high and mighty.

patter[1] ▶ verb **1** *raindrops pattered against the window* GO PITTER-PATTER, tap, drum, beat, pound, rat-a-tat, go pit-a-pat, thrum. **2** *she pattered across the floor* SCURRY, scuttle, skip, trip.
▶ noun *the patter of rain* PITTER-PATTER, tapping, pattering, drumming, beat, beating, pounding, rat-a-tat, pit-a-pat, clack, thrum, thrumming.

patter[2] ▶ noun **1** *this witty patter* PRATTLE, prating, blather, blither, drivel, chatter, jabber, babble; *informal* yabbering, yatter; *archaic* twaddle. **2** *the salesmen's patter* (SALES) PITCH, sales talk; *informal* line, spiel. **3** *the local patter* SPEECH, language, parlance, dialect; *informal* lingo.
▶ verb *she pattered on incessantly* PRATTLE, prate, blather, blither, drivel, chatter, jabber, babble; *informal* yabber, yatter.

pattern ▶ noun **1** *the pattern on the wallpaper* DESIGN, decoration, motif, marking, ornament, ornamentation. *See table.* **2** *the patterns of ant behaviour* SYSTEM, order, arrangement, form, method, structure, scheme, plan, format, framework. **3** *this would set the pattern for a generation* MODEL, example, criterion, standard, basis, point of reference, gauge, norm, yardstick, touchstone, benchmark; blueprint, archetype, prototype. **4** *textile patterns* SAMPLE, specimen, swatch.
▶ verb *someone else is patterning my life* SHAPE, influence, model, fashion, mould, style, determine, control.

Patterns

argyle	paisley
checkered	plaid
dog-tooth	polka dot
houndstooth	tartan
herringbone	

patterned ▶ adjective DECORATED, ornamented, fancy, adorned, embellished.
— OPPOSITES: plain.

paucity ▶ noun SCARCITY, sparseness, sparsity, dearth, shortage, poverty, insufficiency, deficiency, lack, want.
— OPPOSITES: abundance.

paunch ▶ noun POT-BELLY, beer belly, beer gut, spare tire, Molson muscle ♣, pot.

pauper ▶ noun POOR PERSON, indigent, down-and-out; *informal* have-not.

pause ▶ noun *a pause in the conversation* STOP, cessation, break, halt, interruption, check, lull, respite, breathing space, discontinuation, hiatus, gap, interlude; adjournment, suspension, rest, wait, hesitation; *informal* let-up, breather.
▶ verb *Hannah paused for a moment* STOP, cease, halt, discontinue, break off, take a break; adjourn, rest, wait, hesitate, falter, waver; *informal* take a breather, take five.

pave ▶ verb *the yard was paved* TILE, surface, flag.
■ **pave the way for** PREPARE (THE WAY) FOR, make

preparations for, get ready for, lay the foundations for, herald, precede.

paw ▶ noun FOOT, forepaw, hind paw.
▶ verb **1** *their offspring were pawing each other* HANDLE ROUGHLY, pull, grab, maul, manhandle. **2** *some Casanova tried to paw her* FONDLE, feel, maul, molest; *informal* grope, feel up, goose.

pawn ▶ verb *he pawned his watch* PLEDGE, put in pawn, give as security, use as collateral; *informal* hock, put in hock.
▶ noun *a pawn in the battle for the throne* PUPPET, dupe, hostage, tool, cat's paw, instrument.

pay ▶ verb **1** *I must pay him for his work* REWARD, reimburse, recompense, give payment to, remunerate. **2** *Tom must pay a few more dollars* SPEND, expend, pay out, dish out, disburse; *informal* lay out, shell out, fork out, cough up; ante up, pony up. **3** *he paid his debts* DISCHARGE, settle, pay off, clear, liquidate. **4** *hard work will pay dividends* YIELD, return, produce. **5** *he made the buses pay* BE PROFITABLE, make money, make a profit. **6** *it doesn't pay to get involved* BE ADVANTAGEOUS, be of advantage, be beneficial, benefit. **7** *paying compliments* BESTOW, grant, give, offer. **8** *he will pay for his mistakes* SUFFER (THE CONSEQUENCES), be punished, atone, pay the penalty/price.
▶ noun *equal pay for women* SALARY, wages, payment; earnings, remuneration, reimbursement, income, revenue; *formal* emolument(s); *Parliament* indemnity ♣.
■ **pay someone back** GET ONE'S REVENGE ON, be revenged on, avenge oneself on, get back at, get even with, settle accounts with, exact retribution on.
■ **pay something back** REPAY, pay off, give back, return, reimburse, refund.
■ **pay for** FUND, finance, defray the cost of, settle up for, treat someone to; *informal* foot the bill for, shell out for, fork out for, cough up for, ante up for, pony up for.
■ **pay someone off** BRIBE, suborn, buy (off); *informal* grease someone's palm.
■ **pay something off** PAY (IN FULL), settle, discharge, clear, liquidate.
■ **pay off** (*informal*) MEET WITH SUCCESS, be successful, be effective, get results.
■ **pay something out** SPEND, expend, dish out, put up, part with, hand over; *informal* shell out, fork out/up, lay out, cough up.
■ **pay up** MAKE PAYMENT, settle up, pay (in full); *informal* cough up.

payable ▶ adjective DUE, owed, owing, outstanding, unpaid, overdue, in arrears, delinquent.

payment ▶ noun **1** *discounts for early payment* REMITTANCE, settlement, discharge, clearance, liquidation. **2** *monthly payments* INSTALMENT, premium. **3** *extra payment for good performance* SALARY, wages, pay, earnings, fee(s), remuneration, reimbursement, income; *formal* emolument(s).

payoff ▶ noun (*informal*) **1** *the lure of enormous payoffs* PAYMENT, payout, reward; bribe, inducement, incentive, payola; *informal* kickback, sweetener. **2** *a payoff of $160,000* RETURN (ON INVESTMENT), yield, payback, profit, gain, dividend. **3** *a dramatic payoff* OUTCOME, denouement, culmination, conclusion, development, result.

peace ▶ noun **1** *can't a man get any peace around here?* TRANQUILITY, calm, restfulness, peace and quiet, peacefulness, quiet, quietness; privacy, solitude. **2** *peace of mind* SERENITY, peacefulness, tranquility, equanimity, calm, calmness, composure, ease, contentment, contentedness. **3** *we pray for peace* LAW

Nobel Prize Winners for Peace (from 1950)

1950 Ralph Bunche
1951 Léon Jouhaux
1952 Albert Schweitzer
1953 George Catlett Marshall
1954 Office of the United Nations High
Commissioner for Refugees (UNHCR)
1955 no award
1956 no award
1957 Lester Bowles Pearson
1958 Georges Pire
1959 Philip J. Noel-Baker
1960 Albert John Lutuli
1961 Dag Hjalmar Agne Carl Hammarskjöld
1962 Linus Carl Pauling
1963 International Committee of the Red Cross
League of Red Cross Societies
1964 Martin Luther King Jr.
1965 United Nations Children's Fund (UNICEF)
1966 no award
1967 no award
1968 René Cassin
1969 International Labour Organization (I.L.O.)
1970 Norman E. Borlaug
1971 Willy Brandt
1972 no award
1973 Henry A. Kissinger
Le Duc Tho
1974 Seán MacBride
Eisaku Sato
1975 Andrei Dmitrievich Sakharov
1976 Betty Williams
Mairead Corrigan
1977 Amnesty International
1978 Mohamed Anwar al-Sadat
Menachem Begin
1979 Mother Teresa

1980 Adolfo Pérez Esquivel
1981 Office of the United Nations High
Commissioner for Refugees (UNHCR)
1982 Alva Myrdal
Alfonso García Robles
1983 Lech Walesa
1984 Desmond Mpilo Tutu
1985 International Physicians for the Prevention of
Nuclear War Inc.
1986 Elie Wiesel
1987 Oscar Arias Sanchez
1988 United Nations Peace-keeping Forces
1989 The 14th Dalai Lama (Tenzin Gyatso)
1990 Mikhail Sergeyevich Gorbachev
1991 Aung San Suu Kyi
1992 Rigoberta Menchú Tum
1993 Nelson Mandela
Frederik Willem de Klerk
1994 Yasser Arafat
Shimon Peres
Yitzhak Rabin
1995 Joseph Rotblat
Pugwash Conferences on Science and World
Affairs
1996 Carlos Filipe Ximenes Belo
José Ramos-Horta
1997 International Campaign to Ban Landmines
Jody Williams
1998 John Hume
David Trimble
1999 Médecins Sans Frontières
2000 Kim Dae Jung
2001 United Nations (U.N.)
Kofi Annan
2002 James Earl (Jimmy) Carter Jr.

AND ORDER, lawfulness, order, peacefulness, peaceableness, harmony, non-violence; *formal* concord. **4** *a lasting peace* TREATY, truce, ceasefire, armistice, cessation/suspension of hostilities.
— OPPOSITES: noise, war.

peaceable ▶ **adjective 1** *a peaceable man* PEACE-LOVING, non-violent, non-aggressive, easygoing, placid, gentle, inoffensive, good-natured, even-tempered, amiable, amicable, friendly, affable, genial, pacific, dovelike, dovish, unwarlike, pacifist; *formal* irenic. **2** *a peaceable society* PEACEFUL, strife-free, harmonious; law-abiding, disciplined, orderly, civilized.
— OPPOSITES: aggressive.

peaceful ▶ **adjective 1** *everything was quiet and peaceful* TRANQUIL, calm, restful, quiet, still, relaxing, soothing, undisturbed, untroubled, private, secluded. **2** *his peaceful mood* SERENE, calm, tranquil, composed, placid, at ease, untroubled, unworried, content. **3** *peaceful relations* HARMONIOUS, at peace, peaceable, on good terms, amicable, friendly, cordial, non-violent.
— OPPOSITES: noisy, agitated, hostile.

peacemaker ▶ **noun** ARBITRATOR, arbiter, mediator, negotiator, conciliator, go-between, intermediary, pacifier, appeaser, peace-monger, pacifist, peace-lover, dove; *informal* peacenik.

peak ▶ **noun 1** *the peaks of the mountains* SUMMIT, top, crest, pinnacle, apex, crown, cap. **2** *the highest peak* MOUNTAIN, hill, height, mount, alp. **3** *the peak of a cap*

BRIM, visor. **4** *the peak of his career* HEIGHT, high point/spot, pinnacle, summit, top, climax, culmination, apex, zenith, crowning point, acme, capstone, apogee, prime, heyday.
▶ **verb** *Conservative support has peaked* REACH ITS HEIGHT, climax, reach a climax, come to a head.
▶ **adjective** *peak loads* MAXIMUM, top, greatest, highest; ultimate, best, optimum.

peaky ▶ **adjective** PALE, pasty, wan, drained, washed out, drawn, pallid, anemic, ashen, grey, pinched, sickly, sallow, ill, unwell, poorly, indisposed, run down, off; *informal* under the weather, rough, lousy.

peal ▶ **noun 1** *a peal of bells* CHIME, carillon, ring, ringing, tintinnabulation. **2** *peals of laughter* SHRIEK, shout, scream, howl, gale, fit, roar, hoot. **3** *a peal of thunder* RUMBLE, roar, boom, crash, clap, crack.
▶ **verb 1** *the bell pealed* RING (OUT), chime (out), clang, sound, ding, jingle. **2** *the thunder pealed* RUMBLE, roar, boom, crash, resound.

peasant ▶ **noun 1** *peasants working the land* AGRICULTURAL WORKER, small farmer, rustic, swain, villein, serf, campesino; *historical* habitant ✦. **2** (*informal*) *you peasants! See* BOOR.

peccadillo ▶ **noun** MISDEMEANOUR, petty offence, indiscretion, lapse, misdeed.

peck ▶ **verb 1** *the cockerel pecked my heel* BITE, nip, strike, hit, tap, rap, jab. **2** *he pecked her on the cheek* KISS, give someone a peck. **3** (*informal*) *the old lady pecked at her food* NIBBLE, pick at, take very small bites from, toy with, play with.

peculiar ▶ adjective **1** *something peculiar began to happen* STRANGE, unusual, odd, funny, curious, bizarre, weird, queer, unexpected, unfamiliar, abnormal, atypical, anomalous, out of the ordinary; exceptional, extraordinary, remarkable; puzzling, mystifying, mysterious, perplexing, baffling; suspicious, eerie, uncanny, unnatural; *informal* freaky, fishy, creepy, spooky. **2** *peculiar behaviour* BIZARRE, eccentric, strange, odd, weird, queer, funny, unusual, abnormal, idiosyncratic, unconventional, outlandish, quirky; *informal* wacky, freakish, oddball, offbeat, off the wall, wacko. **3** *mannerisms peculiar to the islanders* CHARACTERISTIC OF, typical of, representative of, indicative of, suggestive of, exclusive to, unique to. **4** *their own peculiar contribution* DISTINCTIVE, characteristic, distinct, individual, special, idiosyncratic, unique, personal.
— OPPOSITES: ordinary.

peculiarity ▶ noun **1** *a legal peculiarity* ODDITY, anomaly, abnormality. **2** *a physical peculiarity* IDIOSYNCRASY, mannerism, quirk, foible. **3** *one of the peculiarities of the city* CHARACTERISTIC, feature, (essential) quality, property, trait, attribute, hallmark, trademark. **4** *the peculiarity of this notion* STRANGENESS, oddness, bizarreness, weirdness, queerness, unexpectedness, unfamiliarity, incongruity. **5** *there is a certain peculiarity about her appearance* OUTLANDISHNESS, bizarreness, unconventionality, idiosyncrasy, weirdness, oddness, eccentricity, unusualness, abnormality, queerness, strangeness, quirkiness; *informal* wackiness, freakiness.

pecuniary ▶ adjective FINANCIAL, monetary, money, fiscal, economic.

pedagogic ▶ adjective EDUCATIONAL, educative, pedagogical, teaching, instructional, instructive, didactic; academic, scholastic.

pedagogue (*formal*) ▶ noun TEACHER, schoolteacher, schoolmaster, schoolmistress, master, mistress, tutor; lecturer, academic, don, professor, instructor, educator, educationist, educationalist.

pedant ▶ noun DOGMATIST, purist, literalist, formalist, doctrinaire, perfectionist; quibbler, hair-splitter, casuist, sophist; *informal* nitpicker.

pedantic ▶ adjective OVER-SCRUPULOUS, scrupulous, precise, exact, perfectionist, punctilious, meticulous, fussy, fastidious, finicky; dogmatic, purist, literalist, literalistic, formalist; casuistic, casuistical, sophistic, sophistical; captious, hair-splitting, quibbling; *informal* nitpicking, persnickety.

pedantry ▶ noun DOGMATISM, purism, literalism, formalism; over-scrupulousness, scrupulousness, perfectionism, fastidiousness, punctiliousness, meticulousness; captiousness, quibbling, hair-splitting, casuistry, sophistry; *informal* nitpicking.

peddle ▶ verb **1** *they are peddling water filters* SELL (FROM DOOR TO DOOR), hawk, tout, vend; trade (in), deal in, traffic in. **2** *peddling unorthodox views* ADVOCATE, champion, preach, put forward, proclaim, propound, promote, promulgate.

peddler ▶ noun **1** *a poor and lonesome peddler* TRAVELLING SALESPERSON, door-to-door salesperson, huckster; street trader, hawker; *archaic* chapman. **2** *a drug peddler* TRAFFICKER, dealer; *informal* pusher.

pedestal ▶ noun *a bust on a pedestal* PLINTH, base, support, mounting, stand, foundation, pillar, column, pier; *Architecture* socle.
■ **put someone on a pedestal** IDEALIZE, lionize,

look up to, respect, hold in high regard, think highly of, admire, esteem, revere, worship.

pedestrian ▶ noun *accidents involving pedestrians* WALKER, person on foot; (**pedestrians**) foot traffic.
— OPPOSITES: driver.
▶ adjective *pedestrian lives* DULL, boring, tedious, monotonous, uneventful, unremarkable, tiresome, wearisome, uninspired, unimaginative, unexciting, uninteresting; unvarying, unvaried, repetitive, routine, commonplace, workaday; ordinary, everyday, run-of-the-mill, mundane, humdrum; *informal* plain-vanilla.
— OPPOSITES: exciting.

pedigree ▶ noun *a long pedigree* ANCESTRY, descent, lineage, line (of descent); genealogy, family tree, extraction, derivation, origin(s), heritage, parentage, bloodline, background, roots.
▶ adjective *a pedigree cat* PURE-BRED, thoroughbred, pure-blooded.

pedlar ▶ noun See PEDDLER.

pee ▶ verb URINATE, relieve oneself, pass water, make water, have/take a leak, piddle, have a tinkle, take a whiz; *informal* piss; *formal* micturate.

peek ▶ verb **1** *Hermione peeked from behind the curtains* (HAVE A) PEEP, have a peek, spy, take a sly/stealthy look, sneak a look; *informal* take a gander. **2** *the deer's antlers peeked out from the trees* APPEAR (SLOWLY/PARTLY), show, come into view/sight, become visible, emerge, peep (out).
▶ noun *a peek at the map* SECRET LOOK, sly look, stealthy look, sneaky look, peep, glance, glimpse, hurried/quick look; *informal* gander, squint.

peel ▶ verb **1** *peel and core the fruit* PARE, skin, take the skin/rind off; hull, shell, husk, shuck; *technical* decorticate. **2** *use a long knife to peel the veneer* TRIM (OFF), peel off, pare, strip (off), shave (off), remove. **3** *the wallpaper was peeling* FLAKE (OFF), peel off, come off in layers/strips.
▶ noun *orange peel* RIND, skin, covering, zest; hull, pod, integument, shuck.
■ **keep one's eyes peeled** KEEP A (SHARP) LOOKOUT, look out, keep one's eyes open, keep watch, be watchful, be alert, be on the alert, be on the qui vive, be on guard.

peep¹ ▶ verb **1** *I peeped through the keyhole* LOOK QUICKLY, cast a brief look, take a secret look, sneak a look, (have a) peek, glance; *informal* take a gander. **2** *the moon peeped through the clouds* APPEAR (SLOWLY/PARTLY), show, come into view/sight, become visible, emerge, peek, peer out.
▶ noun *I'll just take a peep at it* QUICK LOOK, brief look, (sneak) peek, glance; *informal* gander, squint.

peep² ▶ noun **1** *I heard a quiet peep* CHEEP, chirp, chirrup, tweet, twitter, chirr, warble. **2** *there's been not a peep out of the children* SOUND, noise, cry, word. **3** *the painting was sold without a peep* COMPLAINT, grumble, mutter, murmur, grouse, objection, protest, protestation; *informal* moan, gripe, grouch.

peephole ▶ noun OPENING, gap, cleft, slit, crack, chink, keyhole, squint, judas (hole).

peer¹ ▶ verb *he peered at the manuscript* LOOK CLOSELY, try to see, narrow one's eyes, screw up one's eyes, squint.

peer² ▶ noun **1** *hereditary peers* ARISTOCRAT, lord, lady, peer of the realm, peeress, noble, nobleman, noblewoman, titled man/woman, patrician; duke/duchess, marquess/marchioness, earl/countess, viscount/viscountess, baron/baroness, marquis/

marquise, count. **2** *his academic peers* EQUAL, coequal, fellow, confrere; contemporary; *formal* compeer.

peerage ▶ noun ARISTOCRACY, nobility, peers and peeresses, lords and ladies, patriciate; the House of Lords, the Lords.

peerless ▶ adjective INCOMPARABLE, matchless, unrivalled, inimitable, beyond compare/comparison, unparalleled, unequalled, without equal, second to none, unsurpassed, unsurpassable, nonpareil; unique, consummate, perfect, rare, transcendent, surpassing; *formal* unexampled.

peeve ▶ verb (*informal*) IRRITATE, annoy, vex, anger, exasperate, irk, gall, pique, nettle, put out, get on someone's nerves, try someone's patience, ruffle someone's feathers; rub the wrong way; *informal* aggravate, rile, needle, get to, bug, hack off, get someone's goat, get/put someone's back up, wind up, tee off, tick off.

peeved ▶ adjective (*informal*) IRRITATED, annoyed, cross, angry, vexed, displeased, disgruntled, indignant, exasperated, galled, irked, put out, aggrieved, offended, affronted, piqued, nettled, in high dudgeon; *informal* aggravated, miffed, riled, hacked off, cheesed off, teed off, ticked off, sore.

peevish ▶ adjective IRRITABLE, fractious, fretful, cross, petulant, querulous, pettish, crabby, crotchety, cantankerous, curmudgeonly, sullen, grumpy, bad-tempered, short-tempered, touchy, testy, tetchy, snappish, irascible, waspish, prickly, crusty, dyspeptic, splenetic, choleric; *informal* cranky, ornery.
— OPPOSITES: good-humoured.

peewee ▶ adjective TINY, very small, baby, pint-sized, diminutive, miniature.

peg ▶ noun PIN, nail, dowel, skewer, spike, rivet, brad, screw, bolt, hook, spigot; *Mountaineering* piton; *Golf* tee.
▶ verb **1** *the flysheet is pegged to the ground* FIX, pin, attach, fasten, secure, make fast. **2** *we decided to peg our prices* HOLD DOWN, keep down, fix, set, hold, freeze.
■ **take someone down a peg or two** HUMBLE, humiliate, mortify, bring down, shame, embarrass, abash, put someone in their place, chasten, subdue, squash, deflate, make someone eat humble pie; *informal* show up, settle someone's hash, cut down to size, make someone eat crow.

pejorative ▶ adjective DISPARAGING, derogatory, denigratory, deprecatory, defamatory, slanderous, libellous, abusive, insulting, slighting; *informal* bitchy.
— OPPOSITES: complimentary.

pellet ▶ noun **1** *a pellet of mud* LITTLE BALL, little piece. **2** *pellet wounds* BULLET, shot, lead shot, buckshot, slug. **3** *rabbit pellets* EXCREMENT, excreta, droppings, feces, dung, turd.

pell-mell ▶ adverb **1** *men streamed pell-mell from the building* HELTER-SKELTER, headlong, (at) full tilt, hotfoot, post-haste, hurriedly, hastily, recklessly, precipitately. **2** *the sacks' contents were thrown pell-mell to the ground* UNTIDILY, in disarray, in a mess, in a muddle; *informal* all over the place, every which way, any old how, all over the map, all over the lot.

pellucid ▶ adjective **1** *the pellucid waters* TRANSLUCENT, transparent, clear, crystal clear, crystalline, glassy, limpid, unclouded, gin-clear. **2** *pellucid prose* LUCID, limpid, clear, crystal clear, articulate; coherent, comprehensible, understandable, intelligible, straightforward, simple, clean, well-constructed; *formal* perspicuous.

pelt¹ ▶ verb **1** *they pelted him with snowballs* BOMBARD, shower, attack, assail, pepper. **2** *rain was pelting down* POUR DOWN, teem down, stream down, rain cats and dogs, rain hard, bucket down. **3** (*informal*) *they pelted into the factory* DASH, run, race, rush, sprint, bolt, dart, career, charge, shoot, hurtle, careen, hare, fly, speed, zoom, streak; hasten, hurry; *informal* tear, belt, hotfoot it, scoot, leg it, go like a bat out of hell, bomb, hightail it.

pelt² ▶ noun *an animal's pelt* SKIN, hide, fleece, coat, fur.

pen¹ ▶ noun *you'll need a pen and paper* fountain pen, ballpoint (pen), rollerball; fibre tip (pen), felt tip (pen), highlighter, marker (pen).
▶ verb *she penned a number of articles* WRITE, compose, draft, dash off; write down, jot down, set down, take down, scribble.

pen² ▶ noun *a sheep pen* ENCLOSURE, fold, sheepfold, pound, compound, stockade; sty, coop, corral.
▶ verb *the hostages had been penned up in a basement* CONFINE, coop (up), cage, shut in, box up/in, lock up/in, trap, imprison, incarcerate, immure.

penal ▶ adjective **1** *a penal institution* DISCIPLINARY, punitive, corrective, correctional. **2** *penal rates of interest* EXORBITANT, extortionate, excessive, outrageous, preposterous, unreasonable, inflated, sky-high.

penalize ▶ verb **1** *if you break the rules you will be penalized* PUNISH, discipline, inflict a penalty on. **2** *people with certain medical conditions would be penalized* HANDICAP, disadvantage, put at a disadvantage, cause to suffer.
— OPPOSITES: reward.

penalty ▶ noun **1** *increased penalties for dumping oil at sea* PUNISHMENT, sanction, punitive action, retribution; fine, forfeit, sentence; penance; *formal* mulct. **2** *a game full of penalties* FOUL, infraction. **3** *the penalties of old age* DISADVANTAGE, difficulty, drawback, handicap, downside, minus; trial, tribulation, bane, affliction, burden, trouble.
— OPPOSITES: reward.

penance ▶ noun ATONEMENT, expiation, self-punishment, self-mortification, self-abasement, amends; punishment, penalty.

penchant ▶ noun LIKING, fondness, preference, taste, relish, appetite, partiality, soft spot, love, passion, desire, fancy, whim, weakness, inclination, bent, bias, proclivity, predilection, predisposition.

pencil ▶ noun **1** *a sharpened pencil* lead pencil, mechanical pencil, pencil crayon ♣, coloured pencil; grease pencil; eyebrow pencil, lip pencil. **2** *a pencil of light* BEAM, ray, shaft, finger, gleam.
▶ verb **1** *he pencilled his name inside the cover* WRITE, write down, jot down, scribble, note, take down. **2** *pencil a line along the top of the moulding* DRAW, trace, sketch.

pendant ▶ noun NECKLACE, locket, medallion.

pendent ▶ adjective HANGING, suspended, dangling, pendulous, pensile, pendant, drooping, droopy, trailing.

pending ▶ adjective **1** *nine cases were still pending* UNRESOLVED, undecided, unsettled, awaiting decision/action, undetermined, open, hanging fire, (up) in the air, on ice, ongoing, outstanding, not done, unfinished, incomplete; *informal* on the back burner. **2** *with a general election pending* IMMINENT, impending, about to happen, forthcoming, upcoming, on the way, coming, approaching, looming, gathering, near, nearing, close, close at hand, in the offing, to come.

▶ **preposition** *they were released on bail pending an appeal* AWAITING, until, till, until there is/are.

pendulous ▶ **adjective** DROOPING, dangling, trailing, droopy, sagging, saggy, floppy; hanging, pendent, pensile.

penetrable ▶ **adjective** 1 *a penetrable subsoil* PERMEABLE, pervious, porous. 2 *books which are barely penetrable to anyone under 50* UNDERSTANDABLE, fathomable, comprehensible, intelligible.

penetrate ▶ **verb** 1 *the knife penetrated his lungs* PIERCE, puncture, make a hole in, perforate, stab, prick, gore, spike. 2 *they penetrated the enemy territory* INFILTRATE, slip into, sneak into, insinuate oneself into. 3 *fear penetrated her bones* PERMEATE, pervade, fill, spread throughout, suffuse, seep through. 4 *he seemed to have penetrated the mysteries of nature* UNDERSTAND, comprehend, apprehend, fathom, grasp, perceive, discern, get to the bottom of, solve, resolve, make sense of, interpret, puzzle out, work out, unravel, decipher, make heads or tails of; *informal* crack, get, figure out, suss out. 5 *her words finally penetrated* REGISTER, sink in, be understood, be comprehended, become clear, fall into place; *informal* click.

penetrating ▶ **adjective** 1 *a penetrating wind* PIERCING, cutting, biting, stinging, keen, sharp, harsh, raw, freezing, chill, wintry, cold. 2 *a penetrating voice* SHRILL, strident, piercing, carrying, loud, high, high-pitched, piping, ear-splitting, screechy, intrusive. 3 *a penetrating smell* PUNGENT, pervasive, strong, powerful, sharp, acrid; heady, aromatic. 4 *her penetrating gaze* OBSERVANT, searching, intent, alert, shrewd, perceptive, probing, piercing, sharp, keen. 5 *a penetrating analysis* PERCEPTIVE, insightful, keen, sharp, sharp-witted, intelligent, clever, smart, incisive, piercing, razor-edged, trenchant, astute, shrewd, clear, acute, percipient, perspicacious, discerning, sensitive, thoughtful, deep, profound.
— OPPOSITES: mild, soft.

penetration ▶ **noun** 1 *skin penetration by infective larvae* PERFORATION, piercing, puncturing, puncture, stabbing, pricking. 2 *remarks of great penetration* INSIGHT, discernment, perception, perceptiveness, intelligence, sharp-wittedness, cleverness, incisiveness, keenness, sharpness, trenchancy, astuteness, shrewdness, acuteness, clarity, acuity, percipience, perspicacity, discrimination, sensitivity, thoughtfulness, profundity; *formal* perspicuity.

peninsula ▶ **noun** CAPE, promontory, point, head, headland, foreland, ness, horn, bill, bluff.

penitence ▶ **noun** REPENTANCE, contrition, regret, remorse, remorsefulness, ruefulness, sorrow, sorrowfulness, pangs of conscience, self-reproach, shame, guilt, compunction; *archaic* rue.

penitent ▶ **adjective** REPENTANT, contrite, remorseful, sorry, apologetic, regretful, conscience-stricken, rueful, ashamed, shamefaced, abject, in sackcloth and ashes.
— OPPOSITES: unrepentant.

pen name ▶ **noun** PSEUDONYM, nom de plume, assumed name, alias, professional name.

pennant ▶ **noun** FLAG, standard, ensign, colour(s), banner, banderole, guidon; *Nautical* burgee.

penniless ▶ **adjective** DESTITUTE, poverty-stricken, impoverished, poor, indigent, impecunious, in penury, moneyless, without a sou, necessitous, needy, bankrupt, insolvent, without a cent (to one's

name); *informal* (flat) broke, cleaned out, strapped for cash, bust; *formal* penurious.
— OPPOSITES: wealthy.

penny
■ **a pretty penny** (*informal*) A LOT OF MONEY, millions, billions, a king's ransom; *informal* a (small) fortune, lots/pots/heaps of money, a mint, a killing, a bundle, a packet, a tidy sum, big money, big bucks, an arm and a leg.

penny-pincher ▶ **noun** MISER, Scrooge; *informal* skinflint, money-grubber, cheapskate, tightwad.
— OPPOSITES: spendthrift.

penny-pinching ▶ **adjective** MEAN, miserly, niggardly, parsimonious, close-fisted, cheese-paring, grasping, Scrooge-like; *informal* stingy, mingy, tight, tight-fisted, money-grubbing; *formal* penurious; *archaic* near.
— OPPOSITES: generous.

pension ▶ **noun** OLD-AGE PENSION, old age security ✦, retirement pension, CPP ✦, OAP ✦, RRSP, RRIF, LIRA, QPP, regular payment, superannuation; allowance, benefit, support, welfare.

pensioner ▶ **noun** SENIOR, senior citizen, old-age pensioner, retired person, retiree, golden ager.

pensive ▶ **adjective** THOUGHTFUL, reflective, contemplative, musing, meditative, introspective, ruminative, absorbed, preoccupied, deep/lost in thought, in a brown study, brooding; *formal* cogitative.

pent-up ▶ **adjective** REPRESSED, suppressed, stifled, smothered, restrained, confined, bottled up, held in/back, kept in check, curbed, bridled.

penurious ▶ **adjective** (*formal*) 1 *a penurious student* POOR, as poor as a church mouse, poverty-stricken, destitute, necessitous, impecunious, impoverished, indigent, needy, in need/want, badly off, in reduced/straitened circumstances, hard up, unable to make ends meet, penniless, without a sou, without a cent (to one's name); *informal* (flat) broke, strapped for cash. 2 *a penurious old skinflint* MEAN, miserly, niggardly, parsimonious, penny-pinching, close-fisted, cheese-paring, Scrooge-like; *informal* stingy, mingy, tight, tight-fisted, money-grubbing; *archaic* near.
— OPPOSITES: wealthy, generous.

penury ▶ **noun** EXTREME POVERTY, destitution, pennilessness, impecuniousness, impoverishment, indigence, pauperism, privation, beggary.

people ▶ **noun** 1 *crowds of people* HUMAN BEINGS, persons, individuals, humans, mortals, (living) souls, personages, {men, women, and children}; *informal* folks. 2 *the Canadian people* CITIZENS, subjects, electors, voters, taxpayers, residents, inhabitants, (general) public, citizenry, nation, population, populace. 3 *a man of the people* THE COMMON PEOPLE, the proletariat, the masses, the populace, the rank and file, commonality, the third estate, the plebeians; *derogatory* the hoi polloi, the common herd, the great unwashed, the proles, the plebs. 4 *her people don't live far away* FAMILY, parents, relatives, relations, folks, kinsmen, kin, kith and kin, kinsfolk, flesh and blood, nearest and dearest. 5 *the peoples of Africa* RACE, (ethnic) group, tribe, clan.
▶ **verb** *the Beothuk who once peopled Newfoundland* POPULATE, settle (in), colonize, inhabit, live in, occupy; *formal* reside in, be domiciled in, dwell in.

pep (*informal*) ▶ **noun** *a performance full of pep* DYNAMISM, life, energy, spirit, liveliness, animation, bounce, sparkle, effervescence, verve, spiritedness,

ebullience, high spirits, enthusiasm, vitality, vivacity, fire, dash, panache, élan, zest, exuberance, vigour, gusto, brio; *informal* feistiness, get-up-and-go, oomph, pizzazz, vim.
■ **pep something up** ENLIVEN, animate, liven up, put some/new life into, invigorate, vitalize, revitalize, vivify, ginger up, energize, galvanize, put some spark into, stimulate, get something going, perk up; brighten up, cheer up; *informal* buck up.

pepper ▶ verb **1** *salt and pepper the potatoes* ADD PEPPER TO, season, flavour. **2** *stars peppered the desert skies* SPRINKLE, fleck, dot, spot, stipple; cover, fill. **3** *another burst of bullets peppered the tank* BOMBARD, pelt, shower, rain down on, attack, assail, batter, strafe, rake, blitz, hit.

peppery ▶ adjective **1** *a peppery sauce* SPICY, spiced, peppered, hot, highly seasoned, piquant, pungent, sharp. **2** *a peppery old man* IRRITABLE, cantankerous, irascible, bad-tempered, ill-tempered, grumpy, grouchy, crotchety, short-tempered, tetchy, testy, crusty, crabby, curmudgeonly, peevish, cross, fractious, pettish, prickly, waspish; *informal* ornery, snappish, snappy, chippy, cranky.
— OPPOSITES: mild, bland, affable.

perceive ▶ verb **1** *I immediately perceived the flaws in her story* DISCERN, recognize, become aware of, see, distinguish, realize, grasp, understand, take in, make out, find, identify, hit on, comprehend, apprehend, appreciate, sense, divine; *informal* figure out, twig; *formal* become cognizant of. **2** *she perceived a twitch in his nose whenever he lied* SEE, discern, detect, catch sight of, spot, observe, notice. **3** *she was perceived as too negative* REGARD, look on, view, consider, think of, judge, deem, adjudge.

perceptible ▶ adjective NOTICEABLE, perceivable, detectable, discernible, visible, observable, recognizable, appreciable; obvious, apparent, evident, manifest, patent, clear, distinct, plain, conspicuous.

perception ▶ noun **1** *our perception of our own limitations* RECOGNITION, awareness, consciousness, appreciation, realization, knowledge, grasp, understanding, comprehension, apprehension; *formal* cognizance. **2** *popular perceptions of old age* IMPRESSION, idea, conception, notion, thought, belief, judgment, estimation. **3** *he talks with great perception* INSIGHT, perceptiveness, percipience, perspicacity, understanding, sharpness, sharp-wittedness, intelligence, intuition, cleverness, incisiveness, trenchancy, astuteness, shrewdness, acuteness, acuity, discernment, sensitivity, penetration, thoughtfulness, profundity; *formal* perspicuity.

perceptive ▶ adjective INSIGHTFUL, discerning, sensitive, intuitive, observant; piercing, penetrating, percipient, perspicacious, penetrative, clear-sighted, far-sighted, intelligent, clever, canny, keen, sharp, sharp-witted, astute, shrewd, quick, smart, acute, discriminating; *informal* on the ball, heads-up, with it.
— OPPOSITES: obtuse.

perch ▶ noun *the chicken's perch* POLE, rod, branch, roost, rest, resting place.
▶ verb **1** *three swallows perched on the telegraph wire* ROOST, sit, rest; alight, settle, land, come to rest. **2** *she perched her glasses on her nose* PUT, place, set, rest, balance. **3** *the church is perched on a hill* BE LOCATED, be situated, be positioned, be sited, stand.

perchance ▶ adverb (*literary*) MAYBE, perhaps, possibly, for all one knows, it could be, it's possible, conceivably; *literary* peradventure.

percipient ▶ adjective. See PERCEPTIVE.

percolate ▶ verb **1** *water percolated through the soil* FILTER, drain, drip, ooze, seep, trickle, dribble, leak, leach. **2** *these views began to percolate through society as a whole* SPREAD, be disseminated, filter, pass; permeate, pervade. **3** *he put some coffee on to percolate* BREW; *informal* perk.

perdition ▶ noun DAMNATION, eternal punishment; hell, hellfire, doom.

peregrinations ▶ plural noun (*archaic*) TRAVELS, wanderings, journeys, globe-trotting, voyages, expeditions, odysseys, trips, treks, excursions; *formal* perambulations.

peremptory ▶ adjective **1** *a peremptory reply* BRUSQUE, imperious, high-handed, brisk, abrupt, summary, commanding, dictatorial, autocratic, overbearing, dogmatic, arrogant, overweening, lordly, magisterial, authoritarian; emphatic, firm, insistent; *informal* bossy. **2** *a peremptory order of the court* IRREVERSIBLE, binding, absolute, final, conclusive, decisive, definitive, categorical, irrefutable, incontrovertible; *Law* unappealable.

perennial ▶ adjective ABIDING, enduring, lasting, everlasting, perpetual, eternal, continuing, unending, unceasing, never-ending, endless, undying, ceaseless, persisting, permanent, constant, continual, unfailing, unchanging, never-changing.

perfect ▶ adjective **1** *she strove to be the perfect wife* IDEAL, model, without fault, faultless, flawless, consummate, quintessential, exemplary, best, ultimate, copybook; unrivalled, unequalled, matchless, unparalleled, beyond compare, without equal, second to none, too good to be true, Utopian, incomparable, nonpareil, peerless, inimitable, unexcelled, unsurpassed, unsurpassable. **2** *a classic Les Paul guitar in perfect condition* FLAWLESS, mint, as good as new, pristine, impeccable, immaculate, superb, superlative, optimum, prime, optimal, peak, excellent, faultless, as sound as a bell, unspoiled, unblemished, undamaged, spotless, unmarred; *informal* tip-top, A1. **3** *a perfect copy* EXACT, precise, accurate, faithful, correct, unerring, inerrant, right, true, strict; *informal* on the money. **4** *the perfect Christmas present for golfers everywhere* IDEAL, just right, right, appropriate, fitting, fit, suitable, apt, made to order, tailor-made; very. **5** *she felt like a perfect idiot* ABSOLUTE, complete, total, real, out-and-out, thorough, thoroughgoing, downright, utter, sheer, arrant, unmitigated, unqualified, veritable, in every respect, unalloyed.
▶ verb *he's busy perfecting his bowling technique* IMPROVE, better, polish (up), hone, refine, put the finishing/final touches to, brush up, fine-tune.

perfection ▶ noun **1** *the perfection of her technique* IMPROVEMENT, betterment, refinement, refining, honing. **2** *for him, she was still perfection* THE IDEAL, a paragon, the ne plus ultra, a nonpareil, the crème de la crème, the last word, the ultimate, the best; *informal* one in a million, the tops, the bee's knees, the cat's meow/pyjamas/whiskers/ass, da bomb.

perfectionist ▶ noun PURIST, stickler for perfection, idealist; pedant.

perfectly ▶ adverb **1** *a perfectly cooked meal* FAULTLESSLY, superbly, superlatively, excellently, flawlessly, to perfection, without fault, ideally, inimitably, incomparably, impeccably, immaculately, consummately; *informal* like a dream, to a T. **2** *I think we understand each other perfectly* ABSOLUTELY, utterly, completely, altogether, entirely, wholly, totally, thoroughly, fully, in every respect. **3** *you know perfectly well that is not what I meant* VERY, quite, full; *informal* damn, damned, bloody, darned.

perfidious ▶ adjective (*literary*) TREACHEROUS, duplicitous, deceitful, disloyal, faithless, unfaithful, traitorous, treasonous, false, false-hearted, double-dealing, two-faced, untrustworthy.
— OPPOSITES: faithful.

perfidy ▶ noun (*literary*) TREACHERY, duplicity, deceit, deceitfulness, disloyalty, infidelity, faithlessness, unfaithfulness, betrayal, treason, double-dealing, untrustworthiness, breach of trust; *literary* perfidiousness.

perforate ▶ verb PIERCE, penetrate, enter, puncture, prick, bore through, riddle.

perforce ▶ adverb (*formal*) NECESSARILY, of necessity, inevitably, unavoidably, by force of circumstances, needs must; *informal* like it or not; *formal* nolens volens.

perform ▶ verb **1** *I have my duties to perform* CARRY OUT, do, execute, discharge, bring about, bring off, accomplish, achieve, fulfill, complete, conduct, effect, dispatch, work, implement; *informal* pull off; *formal* effectuate; *archaic* acquit oneself of. **2** *a car which performs well at low speeds* FUNCTION, work, operate, run, go, respond, behave, act, acquit oneself/itself. **3** *the play has been performed in Stratford* STAGE, put on, present, mount, enact, act, produce. **4** *the band performed live in High Park* APPEAR, play, be on stage, sing, dance, act; busk.
— OPPOSITES: neglect.

performance ▶ noun **1** *the evening performance* SHOW, production, showing, presentation, staging; concert, recital; *informal* gig. **2** *their performance of Mozart's concerto in E flat* RENDITION, rendering, interpretation, reading, playing, acting, representation. **3** *the continual performance of a single task* CARRYING OUT, execution, discharge, accomplishment, completion, fulfillment, dispatch, implementation; *formal* effectuation. **4** *the performance of the processor* FUNCTIONING, working, operation, running, behaviour, capabilities, capability, capacity, power, potential. **5** (*informal*) *he made a great performance of telling her about it* FUSS, production, palaver, scene, business, pantomime; *informal* song and dance, big deal, to-do, hoo-ha.

performer ▶ noun ACTOR, ACTRESS, thespian, artiste, artist, entertainer, trouper, player, musician, singer, dancer, comic, comedian, comedienne.

perfume ▶ noun **1** *a bottle of perfume* FRAGRANCE, scent, eau de toilette, toilet water, eau de cologne, cologne, aftershave. **2** *the heady perfume of lilacs* SMELL, scent, fragrance, aroma, bouquet, redolence.

perfumed ▶ adjective SWEET-SMELLING, scented, fragrant, fragranced, perfumy, aromatic.

perfunctory ▶ adjective CURSORY, desultory, quick, brief, hasty, hurried, rapid, fleeting, token, casual, superficial, careless, half-hearted, sketchy, mechanical, automatic, routine, offhand, inattentive.
— OPPOSITES: careful, thorough.

perhaps ▶ adverb MAYBE, for all one knows, it could be, it may be, it's possible, possibly, conceivably; *literary* peradventure, perchance.

peril ▶ noun DANGER, jeopardy, risk, hazard, insecurity, uncertainty, menace, threat, perilousness; pitfall, problem.

perilous ▶ adjective DANGEROUS, fraught with

danger, hazardous, risky, unsafe, treacherous; precarious, vulnerable, uncertain, insecure, exposed, at risk, in jeopardy, in danger, touch-and-go; *informal* dicey.
— OPPOSITES: safe.

perimeter ▶ noun **1** *the perimeter of a circle* CIRCUMFERENCE, outside, outer edge. **2** *the perimeter of the vast estate* BOUNDARY, border, limits, bounds, confines, edge, margin, fringe(s), periphery, borderline, verge; *literary* bourn, marge.

period ▶ noun **1** *a six-week period* TIME, spell, interval, stretch, term, span, phase, bout, run, duration, chapter, stage; while, patch. **2** *the post-war period* ERA, age, epoch, time, days, years; *Geology* eon. **3** *a double math period* LESSON, class, session. **4** *women who suffer from painful periods* MENSTRUATION, menstrual flow, menses; *informal* the curse, monthlies, time of the month. **5** *a comma instead of a period* POINT, full stop.

periodic ▶ adjective REGULAR, periodical, at fixed intervals, recurrent, recurring, repeated, cyclical, cyclic, seasonal; occasional, infrequent, intermittent, sporadic, spasmodic, odd.

periodical ▶ noun *he wrote for two periodicals* JOURNAL, publication, magazine, newspaper, paper, review, digest, gazette, newsletter, organ, quarterly, annual, weekly; *informal* mag, glossy.

peripatetic ▶ adjective NOMADIC, itinerant, travelling, wandering, roving, roaming, migrant, migratory, unsettled.

peripheral ▶ adjective **1** *the city's peripheral subdivisions* OUTLYING, outer, on the edge/outskirts, surrounding. **2** *peripheral issues* SECONDARY, subsidiary, incidental, tangential, marginal, minor, unimportant, lesser, inessential, non-essential, immaterial, ancillary.
— OPPOSITES: central.

periphery ▶ noun EDGE, outer edge, margin, fringe, boundary, border, perimeter, rim, verge, borderline; outskirts, outer limits/reaches, bounds; *literary* bourn, marge.
— OPPOSITES: centre.

periphrastic ▶ adjective CIRCUMLOCUTORY, circuitous, roundabout, indirect, tautological, pleonastic, prolix, verbose, wordy, long-winded, rambling, wandering, tortuous, diffuse.

perish ▶ verb **1** *millions of soldiers perished* DIE, lose one's life, be killed, fall, expire, meet one's death, be lost, lay down one's life, breathe one's last, pass away, go the way of all flesh, give up the ghost, go to glory, meet one's maker, cross the great divide; *informal* kick the bucket, turn up one's toes, shuffle off this mortal coil, buy it, croak, bite the big one, buy the farm; *archaic* decease, depart this life. **2** *must these hopes perish so soon?* COME TO AN END, die (away), disappear, vanish, fade, dissolve, evaporate, melt away, wither. **3** *the wood had perished* GO BAD, go off, spoil, rot, go mouldy, moulder, putrefy, decay, decompose.

perjure
■ **perjure oneself** LIE UNDER OATH, lie, commit perjury, give false evidence/testimony; *formal* forswear oneself, be forsworn.

perjury ▶ noun LYING UNDER OATH, giving false evidence/testimony, making false statements, wilful falsehood.

perk¹
■ **perk up 1** *you seem to have perked up* CHEER UP, brighten up, liven up, take heart; *informal* buck up. **2** *the economy has been slow to perk up* RECOVER, rally,

improve, revive, take a turn for the better, look up, pick up, bounce back.

■ **perk someone/something up** *you could do with something to perk you up* CHEER UP, liven up, brighten up, raise someone's spirits, give someone a boost/lift, revitalize, invigorate, energize, enliven, ginger up, put new life/heart into, put some spark into, rejuvenate, refresh, vitalize; *informal* buck up, pep up.

perk² ▶ noun *a job with a lot of perks* FRINGE BENEFIT, additional benefit, benefit, advantage, bonus, extra, plus; *informal* freebie; *formal* perquisite.

perky ▶ adjective CHEERFUL, lively, vivacious, animated, bubbly, effervescent, bouncy, spirited, high-spirited, in high spirits, cheery, merry, buoyant, ebullient, exuberant, jaunty, frisky, sprightly, spry, bright, sunny, jolly, sparkly, pert; *informal* full of beans, bright-eyed and bushy-tailed, chirpy, chipper, peppy.

permanence ▶ noun STABILITY, durability, permanency, fixity, fixedness, changelessness, immutability, endurance, constancy, continuity, immortality, indestructibility, perpetuity, endlessness.

permanent ▶ adjective **1** *permanent brain damage* LASTING, enduring, indefinite, continuing, perpetual, everlasting, eternal, abiding, constant, irreparable, irreversible, lifelong, indissoluble, indelible, standing, perennial, unending, endless, never-ending, immutable, undying, imperishable, indestructible, ineradicable; *literary* sempiternal, perdurable. **2** *a permanent job* LONG-TERM, stable, secure, durable.
— OPPOSITES: temporary.

permanently ▶ adverb **1** *the attack left her permanently disabled* FOR ALL TIME, forever, forevermore, for good, for always, for ever and ever, (for) evermore, until hell freezes over, in perpetuity, indelibly, immutably, until the end of time; *informal* for keeps, until the cows come home, until kingdom come; *archaic* for aye. **2** *I was permanently hungry* CONTINUALLY, constantly, perpetually, always.

permeable ▶ adjective POROUS, pervious, penetrable, absorbent, absorptive.

permeate ▶ verb **1** *the delicious smell permeated the entire apartment* PERVADE, spread through, fill, filter through, diffuse through, imbue, penetrate, pass through, percolate through, perfuse, charge, suffuse, steep, impregnate, inform. **2** *these resins are able to permeate the timber* SOAK THROUGH, penetrate, seep through, saturate, transfuse, percolate through, leach through.

permissible ▶ adjective PERMITTED, allowable, allowed, acceptable, legal, lawful, legitimate, admissible, licit, authorized, sanctioned, tolerated; *informal* legit, OK.
— OPPOSITES: forbidden.

permission ▶ noun AUTHORIZATION, consent, leave, authority, sanction, licence, dispensation, assent, acquiescence, agreement, approval, seal/stamp of approval, approbation, endorsement, blessing, imprimatur, clearance, allowance, tolerance, sufferance, empowerment; *informal* the go-ahead, the thumbs up, the OK, the green light, say-so.

permissive ▶ adjective LIBERAL, broad-minded, open-minded, free, free and easy, easygoing, live-and-let-live, latitudinarian, laissez-faire, libertarian, tolerant, forbearing, indulgent, lenient;

overindulgent, lax, soft.
— OPPOSITES: intolerant, strict.

permit ▶ verb *I cannot permit you to leave* ALLOW, let, authorize, give someone permission, sanction, grant, give someone the right, license, empower, enable, entitle, qualify; consent to, assent to, give one's blessing to, give the nod to, acquiesce in, agree to, tolerate, countenance, admit of; legalize, legitimate; *informal* give the go-ahead to, give the thumbs up to, OK, give the OK to, give the green light to, say the word; *formal* accede to; *archaic* suffer.
— OPPOSITES: ban, forbid.
▶ noun *I need to see your permit* AUTHORIZATION, licence, pass, ticket, warrant, document, certification; passport, visa.

permutation ▶ noun ARRANGEMENT, form, version, configuration, incarnation, order, organization, selection.

pernicious ▶ adjective HARMFUL, damaging, destructive, injurious, hurtful, detrimental, deleterious, dangerous, adverse, inimical, unhealthy, unfavourable, bad, evil, baleful, wicked, malign, malevolent, malignant, noxious, poisonous, corrupting; *literary* maleficent.
— OPPOSITES: beneficial.

perpendicular ▶ adjective **1** *the perpendicular stones* UPRIGHT, vertical, erect, plumb, straight (up and down), on end, standing, upended. **2** *lines perpendicular to each other* AT RIGHT ANGLES, at 90 degrees. **3** *the perpendicular hillside* STEEP, sheer, precipitous, abrupt, bluff, vertiginous.
— OPPOSITES: horizontal.

perpetrate ▶ verb COMMIT, carry out, perform, execute, do, effect, bring about, accomplish; be guilty of, be to blame for, be responsible for, inflict, wreak; *informal* pull off; *formal* effectuate.

perpetual ▶ adjective **1** *deep caves in perpetual darkness* EVERLASTING, never-ending, eternal, permanent, unending, endless, without end, lasting, long-lasting, constant, abiding, enduring, perennial, timeless, ageless, deathless, undying, immortal; unfailing, unchanging, never-changing, changeless, unfading; *literary* sempiternal, perdurable. **2** *a perpetual state of fear* CONSTANT, permanent, uninterrupted, continuous, unremitting, unending, unceasing, persistent, unbroken. **3** *her mother's perpetual nagging* INTERMINABLE, incessant, ceaseless, endless, without respite, relentless, unrelenting, persistent, continual, continuous, non-stop, never-ending, recurrent, repeated, unremitting, sustained, round-the-clock, unabating; *informal* eternal.
— OPPOSITES: temporary, intermittent.

perpetuate ▶ verb KEEP ALIVE, keep going, preserve, conserve, sustain, maintain, continue, extend, carry on, keep up, prolong; immortalize, commemorate, memorialize, eternalize.

perpetuity
■ **in perpetuity** FOREVER, forevermore, permanently, for always, for good, perpetually, for ever and ever, for all time, until the end of time, until hell freezes over, eternally, for eternity, everlastingly; *informal* for keeps; *archaic* for aye.

perplex ▶ verb PUZZLE, baffle, mystify, bemuse, bewilder, confound, confuse, disconcert, dumbfound, throw, throw/catch off balance, exercise, worry; *informal* flummox, be all Greek to, stump, bamboozle, floor, beat, faze, fox; *informal* discombobulate.

perplexing ▶ adjective PUZZLING, baffling, mystifying, mysterious, bewildering, confusing, disconcerting, worrying, unaccountable, difficult to understand, beyond one, paradoxical, peculiar, funny, strange, weird, odd.

perplexity ▶ noun **1** *he scratched his head in perplexity* CONFUSION, bewilderment, puzzlement, bafflement, incomprehension, mystification, bemusement; *informal* bamboozlement, discombobulation. **2** *the perplexities of international relations* COMPLEXITY, complication, intricacy, problem, difficulty, mystery, puzzle, enigma, paradox.

perquisite ▶ noun *(formal)*. See PERK[2].

per se ▶ adverb IN ITSELF, of itself, by itself, as such, intrinsically; by its very nature, in essence, by definition, essentially.

persecute ▶ verb **1** *they were persecuted for their religious beliefs* OPPRESS, abuse, victimize, ill-treat, mistreat, maltreat, tyrannize, torment, torture; martyr. **2** *she was persecuted by the press* HARASS, hound, plague, badger, harry, intimidate, pick on, pester, bother, devil, bully, victimize, terrorize; *informal* hassle, give someone a hard time, get on someone's case.

persecution ▶ noun **1** *victims of religious persecution* OPPRESSION, victimization, maltreatment, ill-treatment, mistreatment, abuse, ill-usage, discrimination, tyranny; *informal* witch hunt. **2** *the persecution she endured at school* HARASSMENT, hounding, intimidation, bullying.

perseverance ▶ noun PERSISTENCE, tenacity, determination, staying power, indefatigability, steadfastness, purposefulness; patience, endurance, application, diligence, dedication, commitment, doggedness, assiduity, tirelessness, stamina; intransigence, obstinacy; *informal* stick-to-it-iveness; *formal* pertinacity.

persevere ▶ verb PERSIST, continue, carry on, go on, keep on, keep going, struggle on, hammer away, be persistent, be determined, see/follow something through, keep at it, press on/ahead, not take no for an answer, be tenacious, stand one's ground, stand fast/firm, hold on, go the distance, stay the course, plod on, stop at nothing, leave no stone unturned; *informal* soldier on, hang on, plug away, stick to one's guns, stick it out, hang in there. — OPPOSITES: give up.

persist ▶ verb **1** *Corbett persisted with his questioning.* See PERSEVERE. **2** *if dry weather persists, water the lawn thoroughly* CONTINUE, hold, carry on, last, keep on, keep up, remain, linger, stay, endure.

persistence ▶ noun. See PERSEVERANCE.

persistent ▶ adjective **1** *a very persistent man* TENACIOUS, persevering, determined, resolute, purposeful, dogged, single-minded, tireless, indefatigable, patient, unflagging, untiring, insistent, importunate, relentless, unrelenting; stubborn, intransigent, obstinate, obdurate; *formal* pertinacious. **2** *persistent rain* CONSTANT, continuous, continuing, continual, non-stop, never-ending, steady, uninterrupted, unbroken, interminable, incessant, unceasing, endless, unending, perpetual, unremitting, unrelenting, relentless, unrelieved, sustained. **3** *a persistent cough* CHRONIC, permanent, nagging, frequent; repeated, habitual. — OPPOSITES: irresolute, intermittent.

persnickety ▶ adjective *(informal)* FUSSY, difficult to please, difficult, finicky, over-fastidious, fastidious, over-particular, particular, faddish, punctilious, hair-splitting, critical, overcritical; *informal* nitpicking, choosy, picky, pernickety. — OPPOSITES: easygoing.

person ▶ noun HUMAN BEING, individual, man/woman, child, human, being, (living) soul, mortal, creature; personage, character, customer; *informal* type, sort, cookie; *informal, dated* body, dog; *archaic* wight. ■ **in person** PHYSICALLY, in the flesh, in propria persona, personally; oneself; *informal* as large as life.

persona ▶ noun IMAGE, face, public face, character, personality, identity, self; front, facade, guise, exterior, role, part.

personable ▶ adjective PLEASANT, agreeable, likeable, nice, amiable, affable, charming, congenial, genial, simpatico, engaging, pleasing; attractive, presentable, good-looking, nice-looking, pretty, appealing; *Scottish* bonny. — OPPOSITES: disagreeable, unattractive.

personage ▶ noun IMPORTANT PERSON, VIP, luminary, celebrity, personality, name, famous name, household name, public figure, star, leading light, dignitary, notable, notability, worthy, panjandrum; person; *informal* celeb, somebody, big shot, big wheel, big kahuna, big cheese.

personal ▶ adjective **1** *a highly personal style* DISTINCTIVE, characteristic, unique, individual, one's own, particular, peculiar, idiosyncratic, individualized, personalized. **2** *a personal appearance* IN PERSON, in the flesh, actual, live, physical. **3** *his personal life* PRIVATE, intimate; confidential, secret. **4** *a personal friend* INTIMATE, close, dear, great, bosom. **5** *I have personal knowledge of the family* DIRECT, empirical, first-hand, immediate, experiential. **6** *personal remarks* DEROGATORY, ad hominem; disparaging, belittling, insulting, critical, rude, slighting, disrespectful, offensive, pejorative. — OPPOSITES: public, general.

personality ▶ noun **1** *her cheerful personality* CHARACTER, nature, disposition, temperament, makeup, persona, psyche. **2** *she had loads of personality* CHARISMA, magnetism, strength/force of personality, character, charm, presence. **3** *a famous personality* CELEBRITY, VIP, star, superstar, name, famous name, household name, big name, somebody, leading light, luminary, notable, personage, notability; *informal* celeb.

personalize ▶ verb **1** *products which can be personalized to your requirements* CUSTOMIZE, individualize. **2** *attempts to personalize God* PERSONIFY, humanize, anthropomorphize.

personally ▶ adverb **1** *I'd like to thank you personally* IN PERSON, oneself. **2** *personally, I think it's a good idea* FOR MY PART, for myself, to my way of thinking, to my mind, in my estimation, as far as I am concerned, in my view/opinion, from my point of view, from where I stand, as I see it, if you ask me, my sense is, for my money, in my book; privately; *informal* IMHO (in my humble opinion). ■ **take something personally** TAKE OFFENCE, take something amiss, be offended, be upset, be affronted, take umbrage, take exception, feel insulted, feel hurt.

personification ▶ noun EMBODIMENT, incarnation, epitome, quintessence, essence, type, symbol, soul, model, exemplification, exemplar, image, representation.

personify ▶ verb EPITOMIZE, embody, hypostatize, typify, exemplify, represent, symbolize, stand for, be the incarnation of, body forth, put a face on.

personnel ▶ noun STAFF, employees, workforce, workers, labour force, human resources, manpower, wage labour; *informal* liveware.

perspective ▶ noun 1 *her perspective on things had changed* OUTLOOK, view, viewpoint, point of view, POV, standpoint, position, stand, stance, angle, slant, attitude, frame of mind, frame of reference, approach, way of looking, interpretation. 2 *a perspective of the whole valley* VIEW, vista, panorama, prospect, bird's-eye view, outlook, aspect.

perspicacious ▶ adjective DISCERNING, shrewd, perceptive, astute, penetrating, observant, percipient, sharp-witted, sharp, smart, alert, clear-sighted, far-sighted, acute, clever, canny, intelligent, insightful, wise, sage, sensitive, intuitive, understanding, aware, discriminating; *informal* on the ball, heads-up, with it.
– OPPOSITES: stupid.

perspiration ▶ noun SWEAT, moisture; *Medicine* diaphoresis.

perspire ▶ verb SWEAT, be dripping/pouring with sweat, glow.

persuadable ▶ adjective MALLEABLE, tractable, pliable, compliant, amenable, adaptable, accommodating, co-operative, flexible, acquiescent, yielding, biddable, complaisant, like putty in one's hands, suggestible.

persuade ▶ verb 1 *he tried to persuade her to come with him* PREVAIL ON, talk into, coax, convince, make, get, induce, win over, bring round, coerce, influence, sway, inveigle, entice, tempt, lure, cajole, wheedle; *Law* procure; *informal* sweet-talk, twist someone's arm. 2 *a shortage of money persuaded them to abandon the scheme* CAUSE, lead, move, dispose, incline.
– OPPOSITES: dissuade, deter.

persuasion ▶ noun 1 *Monica needed plenty of persuasion* COAXING, persuading, coercion, inducement, convincing, blandishment, encouragement, urging, inveiglement, cajolery, enticement, wheedling; *informal* sweet-talking, arm-twisting; *formal* suasion. 2 *various political and religious persuasions* GROUP, grouping, sect, denomination, party, camp, side, faction, affiliation, school of thought, belief, creed, credo, faith, philosophy.

persuasive ▶ adjective CONVINCING, cogent, compelling, potent, forceful, powerful, eloquent, impressive, influential, sound, valid, strong, effective, winning, telling; plausible, credible.
– OPPOSITES: unconvincing.

pert ▶ adjective 1 *a pert little hat* JAUNTY, neat, chic, trim, stylish, smart, perky, rakish; *informal* natty, sassy. 2 *a young girl with a pert manner* IMPUDENT, impertinent, cheeky, irreverent, forward, insolent, disrespectful, flippant, familiar, presumptuous, bold, as bold as brass, brazen; *informal* fresh, lippy, saucy, sassy.

pertain ▶ verb 1 *developments pertaining to the economy* CONCERN, relate to, be related to, be connected with, be relevant to, regard, apply to, be pertinent to, refer to, have a bearing on, appertain to, bear on, affect, involve, touch. 2 *the stock and assets pertaining to the business* BELONG TO, be a part of, be included in. 3 *the economic situation which pertained at*

that time EXIST, be the order of the day, be the case, prevail; *formal* obtain.

pertinacious ▶ adjective *(formal)* DETERMINED, tenacious, persistent, persevering, purposeful, resolute, dogged, indefatigable, insistent, single-minded, unrelenting, relentless, tireless, unshakeable; stubborn, obstinate, inflexible, unbending.
– OPPOSITES: irresolute, tentative.

pertinent ▶ adjective RELEVANT, to the point, apposite, appropriate, suitable, fitting, fit, apt, applicable, material, germane, to the purpose, apropos; *formal* ad rem.
– OPPOSITES: irrelevant.

perturb ▶ verb WORRY, upset, unsettle, disturb, concern, trouble, disquiet; disconcert, discomfit, unnerve, alarm, bother, distress, dismay, gnaw at, agitate, fluster, ruffle, discountenance, exercise; *informal* rattle, throw.
– OPPOSITES: reassure.

perturbed ▶ adjective UPSET, worried, unsettled, disturbed, concerned, troubled, anxious, ill at ease, uneasy, disquieted, fretful; disconcerted, discomposed, distressed, unnerved, alarmed, bothered, dismayed, agitated, flustered, ruffled, shaken, discountenanced; *informal* twitchy, rattled, fazed, unstrung; discombobulated.
– OPPOSITES: calm.

peruse ▶ verb READ, study, scrutinize, inspect, examine, wade through, look through; browse through, leaf through, scan, run one's eye over, glance through, flick through, skim through, thumb through, dip into.

pervade ▶ verb PERMEATE, spread through, fill, suffuse, be diffused through, imbue, penetrate, filter through, percolate through, infuse, perfuse, flow through; charge, steep, saturate, impregnate, inform.

pervasive ▶ adjective PREVALENT, pervading, permeating, extensive, ubiquitous, omnipresent, universal, rife, widespread, general.

perverse ▶ adjective 1 *he is being deliberately perverse* AWKWARD, contrary, difficult, unreasonable, uncooperative, unhelpful, obstructive, disobliging, recalcitrant, stubborn, obstinate, obdurate, mulish, pigheaded, bullheaded; *informal* cussed, bloody-minded, balky; *formal* refractory. 2 *a verdict that is manifestly perverse* ILLOGICAL, irrational, unreasonable, wrong, wrong-headed. 3 *an evil life dedicated to perverse pleasure* PERVERTED, depraved, unnatural, abnormal, deviant, degenerate, immoral, warped, twisted, corrupt; wicked, base, evil; *informal* kinky, sick, pervy.
– OPPOSITES: accommodating, reasonable.

perversion ▶ noun 1 *a twisted perversion of the truth* DISTORTION, misrepresentation, falsification, travesty, misinterpretation, misconstruction, twisting, corruption, subversion, misuse, misapplication, debasement. 2 *sexual perversion* DEVIANCE, abnormality; depravity, degeneracy, debauchery, corruption, vice, wickedness, immorality.

perversity ▶ noun 1 *out of sheer perversity, he refused* CONTRARINESS, awkwardness, recalcitrance, stubbornness, obstinacy, obduracy, mulishness, pigheadedness; cussedness, bloody-mindedness; *formal* refractoriness. 2 *the perversity of the decision* UNREASONABLENESS, irrationality, illogicality, wrong-headedness.

pervert ▶ verb 1 *people who attempt to pervert the rules*

DISTORT, corrupt, subvert, twist, bend, abuse, misapply, misuse, misrepresent, misinterpret, falsify. **2** *men can be perverted by power* CORRUPT, lead astray, debase, warp, pollute, poison, deprave, debauch.
▶ **noun** *a sexual pervert* DEVIANT, degenerate; *informal* perv, dirty old man, sicko.

perverted ▶ **adjective** UNNATURAL, deviant, warped, corrupt, twisted, abnormal, unhealthy, depraved, perverse, aberrant, immoral, debauched, debased, degenerate, evil, wicked, vile, amoral, wrong, bad; *informal* sick, sicko, kinky, pervy.

pessimism ▶ **noun** DEFEATISM, negativity, doom and gloom, gloominess, cynicism, fatalism; hopelessness, depression, despair, despondency, angst.

pessimist ▶ **noun** DEFEATIST, fatalist, prophet of doom, cynic, doomsayer, doomster, Cassandra; skeptic, doubter, doubting Thomas; misery, killjoy, Job's comforter; *informal* doom (and gloom) merchant, wet blanket, Chicken Little, gloomy Gus.
— OPPOSITES: optimist, Pollyanna.

pessimistic ▶ **adjective** GLOOMY, negative, defeatist, downbeat, cynical, bleak, fatalistic, dark, black, despairing, despondent, depressed, hopeless; suspicious, distrustful, doubting.
— OPPOSITES: optimistic.

pest ▶ **noun** NUISANCE, annoyance, irritation, irritant, thorn in one's flesh/side, vexation, trial, the bane of one's life, menace, trouble, problem, worry, bother; *informal* pain (in the neck), aggravation, headache, nudnik.

pester ▶ **verb** BADGER, hound, harass, plague, annoy, bother, give someone the gears ✦, trouble, keep after, persecute, torment, bedevil, harry, worry, beleaguer, chivvy, nag, hassle, bug, devil, get on someone's case.

pestilence ▶ **noun** (*archaic*). See PLAGUE noun sense 1.

pestilential ▶ **adjective** **1** *pestilential fever* PLAGUE-LIKE, infectious, contagious, communicable, epidemic, virulent; *informal* catching. **2** (*informal*) *a pestilential man!* ANNOYING, irritating, infuriating, exasperating, maddening, tiresome, troublesome, irksome, vexing, vexatious; *informal* aggravating, pesky, infernal.

pet ▶ **noun** *the teacher's pet* FAVOURITE, darling, the apple of one's eye; *informal* fair-haired boy/girl.
▶ **adjective 1** *a pet lamb* TAME, domesticated, domestic, housebroken, house-trained. **2** *his pet theory* FAVOURITE, favoured, cherished, dear to one's heart; particular, special, personal.
▶ **verb 1** *the cats came to be petted* STROKE, caress, fondle, pat. **2** *she had always been petted by her parents* PAMPER, spoil, mollycoddle, coddle, cosset, baby, indulge, overindulge. **3** *couples were petting in their cars* KISS AND CUDDLE, kiss, cuddle, embrace, caress; *informal* make out, canoodle, neck, smooch, get it on.
■ **pet name** AFFECTIONATE NAME, term of endearment, endearment, nickname, diminutive; *rare* hypocoristic.

peter
■ **peter out** FIZZLE OUT, fade (away), die away/out, dwindle, diminish, taper off, tail off, trail away/off, wane, ebb, melt away, evaporate, disappear, come to an end, subside.

petite ▶ **adjective** SMALL, dainty, diminutive, slight, little, tiny, elfin, delicate, small-boned; *Scottish* wee; *informal* pint-sized.

petition ▶ **noun 1** *over 1,000 people signed the petition*

APPEAL, round robin. **2** *petitions to Allah* ENTREATY, supplication, plea, prayer, appeal, request, invocation, suit; *archaic* orison.
▶ **verb** *they petitioned the king to revoke the decision* APPEAL TO, request, ask, call on, entreat, beg, implore, plead with, apply to, press, urge; *formal* adjure; *literary* beseech.

petrified ▶ **adjective 1** *she looked petrified* TERRIFIED, terror-stricken, horrified, scared/frightened out of one's wits, scared/frightened to death. **2** *petrified remains of prehistoric animals* OSSIFIED, fossilized, calcified.

petrify ▶ **verb** TERRIFY, horrify, frighten, scare, scare/frighten to death, scare/frighten the living daylights out of, scare/frighten the life out of, strike terror into, put the fear of God into; paralyze, transfix; *informal* scare the pants off, scare the bejesus out of.

petticoat ▶ **noun** SLIP, underskirt, half-slip, undergarment; *archaic* kirtle; *historical* crinoline.

petty ▶ **adjective 1** *petty regulations* TRIVIAL, trifling, minor, small, unimportant, insignificant, inconsequential, inconsiderable, negligible, paltry, footling, pettifogging; *informal* piffling, piddling, fiddling. **2** *a petty form of revenge* SMALL-MINDED, mean, ungenerous, shabby, spiteful.
— OPPOSITES: important, magnanimous.

petulant ▶ **adjective** PEEVISH, bad-tempered, querulous, pettish, fretful, cross, irritable, sulky, snappish, crotchety, touchy, tetchy, testy, fractious, grumpy, disgruntled, crabbed, crabby; *informal* grouchy, cranky.
— OPPOSITES: good-humoured.

phantasmagorical ▶ **adjective** DREAMLIKE, psychedelic, kaleidoscopic, surreal, unreal, hallucinatory, fantastic, fantastical, chimerical.

phantom ▶ **noun 1** *a phantom who haunts lonely roads* GHOST, apparition, spirit, spectre, wraith; *informal* spook; *literary* phantasm, shade. **2** *the phantoms of an overactive imagination* DELUSION, figment of the imagination, hallucination, illusion, chimera, vision, mirage.

phase ▶ **noun 1** *the final phase of the campaign* STAGE, period, chapter, episode, part, step, point, time, juncture. **2** *he's going through a difficult phase* PERIOD, stage, time, spell, patch. **3** *the phases of the moon* ASPECT, shape, form, appearance, state, condition.
■ **phase something in** INTRODUCE GRADUALLY, begin to use, ease in.
■ **phase something out** WITHDRAW GRADUALLY, discontinue, stop using, run down, wind down.

phenomenal ▶ **adjective** REMARKABLE, exceptional, extraordinary, amazing, astonishing, astounding, sensational, stunning, incredible, unbelievable; marvellous, magnificent, wonderful, outstanding, singular, out of the ordinary, unusual, unprecedented; *informal* fantastic, terrific, tremendous, stupendous, awesome, out of this world; *literary* wondrous.
— OPPOSITES: ordinary.

phenomenon ▶ **noun 1** *a rare phenomenon* OCCURRENCE, event, happening, fact, situation, circumstance, experience, case, incident, episode. **2** *the band was a pop phenomenon* MARVEL, sensation, wonder, prodigy, miracle, rarity, nonpareil; *informal* humdinger, phenom, stunner, doozy, ripsnorter.

philander ▶ **verb** WOMANIZE, have affairs, flirt; *informal* play around, carry on, play the field, sleep around, fool around.

philanderer ▶ noun WOMANIZER, Casanova, Don Juan, Lothario, flirt, ladies' man, playboy, rake, roué; *informal* stud, skirt chaser, lady-killer, wolf.

philanthropic ▶ adjective CHARITABLE, generous, benevolent, humanitarian, public-spirited, altruistic, magnanimous, munificent, open-handed, bountiful, liberal, generous to a fault, beneficent, caring, compassionate, unselfish, kind, kind-hearted, big-hearted; *formal* eleemosynary.
— OPPOSITES: selfish, mean.

philanthropist ▶ noun BENEFACTOR, benefactress, patron, patroness, donor, contributor, sponsor, backer, helper, good Samaritan; do-gooder, Lady Bountiful; *historical* almsgiver.

philanthropy ▶ noun BENEVOLENCE, generosity, humanitarianism, public-spiritedness, altruism, social conscience, charity, charitableness, brotherly love, fellow feeling, magnanimity, munificence, liberality, largesse, open-handedness, bountifulness, beneficence, unselfishness, humanity, kindness, kind-heartedness, compassion; *historical* almsgiving.

philippic ▶ noun (*literary*) TIRADE, diatribe, harangue, lecture, attack, onslaught, denunciation, rant, polemic, broadside, fulmination, condemnation, criticism, censure; *informal* blast.

philistine ▶ adjective UNCULTURED, lowbrow, anti-intellectual, uncultivated, uncivilized, uneducated, unenlightened, commercial, materialist, bourgeois; ignorant, crass, boorish, barbarian.

philosopher ▶ noun THINKER, theorist, theorizer, theoretician, metaphysicist, metaphysician; scholar, intellectual, sage, wise man.

philosophical ▶ adjective **1** *a philosophical question* THEORETICAL, metaphysical. **2** *a philosophical mood* THOUGHTFUL, reflective, pensive, meditative, contemplative, introspective, ruminative; *formal* cogitative. **3** *he was philosophical about losing the contract* CALM, composed, cool, collected, {calm, cool, and collected}, self-possessed, serene, tranquil, stoical, impassive, dispassionate, phlegmatic, unperturbed, imperturbable, unruffled, patient, forbearing, long-suffering, resigned, rational, realistic.

philosophize ▶ verb THEORIZE, speculate; pontificate, preach, sermonize, moralize.

philosophy ▶ noun **1** *the philosophy of Aristotle* THINKING, thought, reasoning. **2** *her political philosophy* BELIEFS, credo, convictions, ideology, ideas, thinking, notions, theories, doctrine, tenets, principles, views, school of thought; *informal* ism.

phlegm ▶ noun MUCUS, catarrh.

phlegmatic ▶ adjective CALM, cool, composed, {calm, cool, and collected}, controlled, serene, tranquil, placid, impassive, imperturbable, unruffled, dispassionate, philosophical; stolid, dull, bland, unemotional, lifeless; *informal* unflappable.
— OPPOSITES: excitable.

phobia ▶ noun FEAR, irrational fear, obsessive fear, dread, horror, terror, hatred, loathing, detestation, aversion, antipathy, revulsion; complex, neurosis; *informal* thing, hang-up.

phone ▶ noun TELEPHONE, cellphone, cell, car phone, cordless phone, speakerphone; extension; *informal* blower, horn.
▶ verb *I'll phone you later* TELEPHONE, call, give someone a call; *informal* call up, give someone a buzz, get someone on the horn/blower.

phony (*informal*) ▶ adjective *a phony address* BOGUS, false, fake, fraudulent, spurious; counterfeit, forged, feigned; pseudo, imitation, sham, man-made, mock, ersatz, synthetic, artificial; simulated, pretended, contrived, affected, insincere, inauthentic; *informal* pretend, put-on.
— OPPOSITES: authentic.
▶ noun **1** *he's nothing but a phony* IMPOSTER, sham, fake, fraud, charlatan; *informal* con artist. **2** *the diamond's a phony* FAKE, imitation, counterfeit, forgery.

photocopy ▶ noun COPY, facsimile, duplicate, reproduction; *proprietary* Xerox.

photograph ▶ noun *a photograph of her father* PICTURE, photo, snapshot, shot, image, likeness, print, slide, transparency, still, enlargement, snap; *informal* mug shot, head shot.
▶ verb *she was photographed leaving the castle* TAKE SOMEONE'S PICTURE/PHOTO, snap, shoot, film.

photographer ▶ noun SHUTTERBUG, paparazzo, photojournalist; lensman, cameraman.

photographic ▶ adjective **1** *a photographic record* PICTORIAL, in photographs; cinematic, filmic. **2** *a photographic memory* DETAILED, graphic, exact, precise, accurate, vivid, picture-perfect.

phrase ▶ noun *familiar words and phrases* EXPRESSION, group of words, construction, locution, term, turn of phrase; idiom, idiomatic expression; saying, tag.
▶ verb *how could I phrase the question?* EXPRESS, put into words, put, word, style, formulate, couch, frame, articulate, verbalize.

phraseology ▶ noun WORDING, choice of words, phrasing, way of speaking/writing, usage, idiom, diction, parlance, words, language, vocabulary, terminology; jargon; *informal* lingo, -speak, -ese.

physical ▶ adjective **1** *physical pleasure* BODILY, corporeal, corporal, somatic; carnal, fleshly, non-spiritual. **2** *hard physical work* MANUAL, labouring, blue-collar. **3** *the physical universe* MATERIAL, concrete, tangible, palpable, solid, substantial, real, actual, visible.
— OPPOSITES: mental, spiritual.

physician ▶ noun DOCTOR, doctor of medicine, MD, medical practitioner, general practitioner, GP, clinician, family doctor; specialist, consultant; *informal* doc, quack, medic, medico; intern, resident; *informal, dated* sawbones.

physiognomy ▶ noun FACE, features, countenance, expression, look, mien; *informal* mug, phiz, puss; *literary* visage, lineaments.

physique ▶ noun BODY, build, figure, frame, anatomy, shape, form, proportions; muscles, musculature; *informal* vital statistics, bod.

pick ▶ verb **1** *I got a job picking apples* HARVEST, gather (in), collect, pluck; *literary* cull. **2** *pick the time that suits you best* CHOOSE, select, pick out, single out, take, opt for, elect, decide on, settle on, fix on, sift out, sort out; name, nominate. **3** *Beth picked at her food* NIBBLE, toy with, play with, eat like a bird. **4** *people were singing and picking guitars* STRUM, twang, thrum, pluck. **5** *he tried to pick a fight* PROVOKE, start, cause, incite, stir up, whip up, instigate, prompt, bring about.
▶ noun **1** *take your pick* CHOICE, selection, option, decision; preference, favourite. **2** *the pick of the crop* BEST, finest, top, choice, choicest, prime, cream, flower, prize, pearl, gem, jewel, jewel in the crown, crème de la crème, elite.
■ **pick on** BULLY, victimize, tyrannize, torment,

persecute, criticize, harass, hound, taunt, tease; *informal* get at, have it in for, be down on, needle.

■ **pick something out 1** *one painting was picked out for special mention* CHOOSE, select, single out, opt for, decide on, elect, settle on, fix on, sift out, sort out; name, nominate. **2** *she picked out Jessica in the crowd* SEE, make out, distinguish, discern, spot, perceive, detect, notice, recognize, identify, catch sight of, glimpse; *literary* espy, behold, descry.

■ **pick up** IMPROVE, recover, be on the road to recovery, rally, make a comeback, bounce back, perk up, look up, take a turn for the better, turn the/a corner, be on the mend, make headway, make progress.

■ **pick someone/something up** LIFT, take up, raise, hoist, scoop up, gather up, snatch up.

■ **pick someone up 1** *I'll pick you up after lunch* FETCH, collect, call for. **2** *(informal) she was picked up by the police* ARREST, apprehend, detain, take into custody, seize; *informal* nab, run in, bust.

■ **pick something up 1** *we picked it up at a thrift store* FIND, discover, come across, stumble across, happen on, chance on; acquire, obtain, come by, get, procure, purchase, buy; *informal* get hold of, get/lay one's hands on, get one's mitts on, bag, land. **2** *she picked up a virus* CATCH, contract, get, go/come down with. **3** *he told us the bits of gossip he'd picked up* HEAR, hear tell, get wind of, be told, learn; glean, garner. **4** *we're picking up a distress signal* RECEIVE, detect, get, hear.

picket ▶ **noun 1** *forty pickets were arrested* STRIKER, demonstrator, protester, objector, picketer; flying picket. **2** *fences made of cedar pickets* STAKE, post, paling; upright, stanchion, piling.
▶ **verb** *over 200 people picketed the factory* DEMONSTRATE AT, protest at, strike at, form a picket at, man the picket line at; blockade, shut off.

pickle ▶ **noun** *(informal) they got into a real pickle over this one* PLIGHT, predicament, mess, difficulty, trouble, dire/desperate straits, problem, quandary; *informal* tight corner, tight spot, jam, fix, scrape, bind, hole, hot water, fine kettle of fish.
▶ **verb** *fish pickled in brine* PRESERVE, souse, marinate, conserve.

pick-me-up ▶ **noun 1** *a drink that's a very good pick-me-up* TONIC, restorative, energizer, stimulant, refresher, reviver; *informal* bracer; *Medicine* analeptic. **2** *his winning goal was a perfect pick-me-up* BOOST, boost to the spirits, fillip, stimulant, stimulus; *informal* shot in the arm.

pickpocket ▶ **noun** THIEF, petty thief, purse-snatcher, sneak thief; *archaic* cutpurse.

picnic ▶ **noun 1** *a picnic on the beach* OUTDOOR MEAL, alfresco meal, cookout, barbecue. **2** *(informal) working for him was no picnic* EASY TASK/JOB, child's play, five-finger exercise, gift, walkover, laugher; *informal* piece of cake, cinch, breeze, kids' stuff, cakewalk, pushover, duck soup.

pictorial ▶ **adjective** ILLUSTRATED, in pictures, in picture form, in photographs, photographic, graphic.

picture ▶ **noun 1** *pictures in an art gallery* PAINTING, DRAWING, sketch, oil painting, watercolour, print, canvas, portrait, portrayal, illustration, artwork, depiction, likeness, representation, image, icon, miniature, landscape; fresco, mural, wall painting; *informal* oil. **2** *we were told not to take pictures* PHOTOGRAPH, photo, snap, snapshot, shot, print, slide, transparency, exposure, still, enlargement. **3** *do you have a picture of what your ideal home might look like?* CONCEPT, idea, impression, view, (mental) image,

vision, visualization, notion. **4** *the picture of health* PERSONIFICATION, embodiment, epitome, essence, quintessence, perfect example, soul, model. **5** *a picture starring Robert de Niro* MOVIE, film, feature film, motion picture; *informal* flick; *dated* moving picture.
▶ **verb 1** *he was pictured with his guests* PHOTOGRAPH, take a photograph/photo of, snap, shoot, film. **2** *in the drawing they were pictured against a snowy background* PAINT, DRAW, sketch, depict, delineate, portray, show, illustrate. **3** *Anne still pictured Richard as he had been* VISUALIZE, see in one's mind's eye, conjure up a picture/image of, imagine, see, evoke.

■ **put someone in the picture** INFORM, fill in, explain the situation/circumstances to, bring up to date, update, brief, keep posted, clue in, bring up to speed.

picturesque ▶ **adjective 1** *a picturesque village* ATTRACTIVE, pretty, beautiful, lovely, scenic, charming, quaint, pleasing, delightful, picture-perfect. **2** *a picturesque description* VIVID, graphic, colourful, impressive, striking.
— OPPOSITES: ugly, dull.

piddling ▶ **adjective** *(informal)* TRIVIAL, trifling, petty, footling, slight, small, insignificant, unimportant, inconsequential, inconsiderable, negligible; meagre, inadequate, insufficient, paltry, scant, scanty, derisory, pitiful, miserable, puny, niggardly, beggarly, mere; *informal* measly, pathetic, piffling, mingy, nickel-and-dime.

pie ▶ **noun** PASTRY, tart, tartlet, quiche, pasty, patty, turnover, strudel. *See table.*

■ **pie in the sky** *(informal)* FALSE HOPE, illusion, delusion, fantasy, pipe dream, daydream, castle in the air, castle in Spain.

Pies, Tarts, & Turnovers

sweet pies	savoury pies
angel pie	bridie
baklava	calzone
Bakewell tart	cipaille ♣
Banbury tart	Cornish pasty
Boston cream pie	empanada
bumbleberry pie ♣	flipper pie ♣(Nfld)
butter tart ♣	Jamaican patty
Cape Breton pork pie ♣	panzerotto ♣
chiffon pie	patty
cream pie	piroshki
custard pie	pork pie
Dutch apple pie	pot pie
flan	quiche
key lime pie	Scotch pie
lemon meringue pie	sea pie ♣
mince pie	seal flipper pie ♣(Nfld)
mud pie	shepherd's pie
poutine ♣(NB)	spanakopita
shoofly pie	tourtière ♣
strudel	*See also* STEWS AND
sugar pie ♣(esp. Que.)	CASSEROLES.
tart	
turnover	

See also CAKES AND PUDDINGS.

piebald ▶ **adjective**. *See* PIED.

piece ▶ **noun 1** *a piece of cheese | a piece of wood* BIT, slice, chunk, segment, section, lump, hunk, wedge, slab, block, cake, bar, cube, stick, length; offcut, sample, fragment, sliver, splinter, wafer, chip, crumb, scrap, remnant, shred, shard, snippet;

mouthful, morsel. **2** *the pieces of a clock* COMPONENT, part, bit, section, segment, constituent, element; unit, module. **3** *a piece of furniture* ITEM, article, specimen. **4** *a piece of the profit* SHARE, portion, slice, quota, part, bit, percentage, amount, quantity, ration, fraction, division; *informal* cut, rake-off. **5** *pieces from his private collection* WORK (OF ART), creation, production; composition, opus. **6** *the reporter who wrote the piece* ARTICLE, item, story, report, essay, study, review, composition, column. **7** *the pieces on a game board* TOKEN, counter, man, disc, chip, marker.
■ **in one piece 1** *the camera was still in one piece* UNBROKEN, entire, whole, intact, undamaged, unharmed. **2** *I'll bring her back in one piece* UNHURT, uninjured, unscathed, safe, safe and sound.
■ **in pieces** BROKEN, in bits, shattered, smashed, in smithereens; *informal* bust.
■ **go/fall to pieces** HAVE A BREAKDOWN, break down, go out of one's mind, lose control, lose one's head, fall apart; *informal* crack up, lose it, come/fall apart at the seams, freak, freak out.

pièce de résistance ▶ **noun** MASTERPIECE, magnum opus, chef-d'œuvre, masterwork, tour de force, showpiece, prize, jewel in the crown.

piecemeal ▶ **adverb** A LITTLE AT A TIME, piece by piece, bit by bit, gradually, slowly, in stages, in steps, step by step, little by little, by degrees, in/by fits and starts.

pied ▶ **adjective** PARTI-COLOURED, multicoloured, variegated, black and white, brown and white, piebald, skewbald, dappled, brindle, spotted, mottled, speckled, flecked, pinto, calico, tabby.

pier ▶ **noun 1** *a boat was tied to the pier* JETTY, quay, wharf, dock, levee, landing, landing stage. **2** *the piers of the bridge* SUPPORT, cutwater, pile, piling, abutment, buttress, stanchion, prop, stay, upright, pillar, post, column.

pierce ▶ **verb 1** *the metal pierced his flesh* PENETRATE, puncture, perforate, prick, lance; stab, spike, stick, impale, transfix, bore through, drill through. **2** *his anguish pierced her very soul* HURT, wound, pain, sting, sear, grieve, distress, upset, trouble, harrow, afflict; affect, move.

piercing ▶ **adjective 1** *a piercing shriek* SHRILL, ear-splitting, high-pitched, penetrating, strident, loud. **2** *the piercing wind* BITTER, biting, cutting, penetrating, sharp, keen, stinging, raw; freezing, frigid, glacial, arctic, chill. **3** *a piercing pain* INTENSE, excruciating, agonizing, sharp, stabbing, shooting, stinging, severe, extreme, fierce, searing, racking. **4** *his piercing gaze* SEARCHING, probing, penetrating, penetrative, shrewd, sharp, keen. **5** *his piercing intelligence* PERCEPTIVE, percipient, perspicacious, penetrating, discerning, discriminating, intelligent, quick-witted, sharp, sharp-witted, shrewd, insightful, keen, acute, astute, clever, smart, incisive, razor-edged, trenchant.

piety ▶ **noun** DEVOUTNESS, devotion, piousness, religion, holiness, godliness, saintliness; veneration, reverence, faith, religious duty, spirituality, religious zeal, fervour; pietism, religiosity.

piffle ▶ **noun** (*informal*). See NONSENSE sense 1.

pig ▶ **noun 1** *a herd of pigs* HOG, boar, sow, porker, swine, piglet; *children's word* piggy. **2** (*informal*) *he's eaten the lot, the pig* GLUTTON, guzzler; *informal* hog, greedy guts.
— RELATED TERMS: porcine.

pigeonhole ▶ **verb 1** *they were pigeonholed as an indie guitar band* CATEGORIZE, compartmentalize, classify, characterize, label, brand, tag, typecast, ghettoize,

designate. **2** *the plan was pigeonholed last year* POSTPONE, put off, put back, defer, shelve, hold over, put to one side, put on ice, mothball, put in cold storage; *informal* put on the back burner.

pigheaded ▶ **adjective** OBSTINATE, stubborn (as a mule), mulish, bullheaded, obdurate, headstrong, self-willed, wilful, perverse, contrary, recalcitrant, stiff-necked; uncooperative, inflexible, uncompromising, intractable, intransigent, unyielding, bloody-minded; *formal* refractory.

pigment ▶ **noun** COLOURING MATTER, colouring, colourant, colour, tint, dye, dyestuff.

pile¹ ▶ **noun 1** *a pile of stones* HEAP, stack, mound, pyramid, mass, quantity; collection, accumulation, assemblage, store, stockpile, hoard. **2** (*informal*) *I've got a pile of work to do* GREAT DEAL, lot, large quantity/ amount, quantities, reams, mountain; abundance, cornucopia, plethora; *informal* load, heap, mass, slew, ocean, stack, ton. **3** (*informal*) *he'd made his pile in the fur trade* FORTUNE, millions, billions; *informal* small fortune, bomb, bundle, wad.
▶ **verb 1** *she piled up the plates* HEAP (UP), stack (up). **2** *he piled his plate with fried eggs* LOAD, heap, fill (up), lade, stack, charge, stock. **3** *our debts were piling up* INCREASE, grow, mount up, escalate, soar, spiral, leap up, shoot up, rocket, climb, accumulate, accrue, build up, multiply. **4** *we piled into the car* CROWD, climb, pack, squeeze, push, shove.
■ **pile it on** (*informal*) EXAGGERATE, overstate the case, make a mountain out of a molehill, overdo it, overplay it, over-dramatize; *informal* lay it on thick.

pile² ▶ **noun** *a wall supported by timber piles* POST, stake, pillar, column, support, foundation, piling, abutment, pier, cutwater, buttress, stanchion, upright.

pile³ ▶ **noun** *a carpet with a short pile* NAP, fibres, threads.

pileup ▶ **noun** CRASH, multiple crash, collision, multiple collision, smash, accident, road accident, wreck; *informal* smash-up.

pilfer ▶ **verb** STEAL, thieve, take, snatch, purloin, loot; *informal* swipe, rob, nab, rip off, lift, (*Nfld*) buck ✿, 'liberate', 'borrow', filch, snaffle; pinch, heist.

pilgrim ▶ **noun** worshipper, devotee, believer; traveller, crusader; *literary* wayfarer; *historical* palmer.

pilgrimage ▶ **noun** RELIGIOUS JOURNEY, religious expedition, hajj, crusade, mission.

pill ▶ **noun** TABLET, capsule, caplet, cap, gelcap, pellet, lozenge, pastille, horse pill; *Veterinary Medicine* bolus.

pillage ▶ **verb 1** *the abbey was pillaged* RANSACK, rob, plunder, despoil, raid, loot; sack, devastate, lay waste, ravage, rape. **2** *columns pillaged from an ancient town* STEAL, pilfer, thieve, take, snatch, purloin, loot; *informal* swipe, rob, nab, rip off, lift, 'liberate', 'borrow', filch, snaffle, pinch, heist.
▶ **noun** *the rebels were intent on pillage* ROBBERY, robbing, raiding, plunder, looting, sacking, rape, marauding; *literary* rapine.

pillar ▶ **noun 1** *stone pillars* COLUMN, post, support, upright, baluster, pier, pile, pilaster, stanchion, prop, newel; obelisk, monolith. **2** *a pillar of the community* STALWART, mainstay, bastion, rock; leading light, worthy, backbone, support, upholder, champion, tower of strength.

pillory ▶ **noun** *offenders were put in the pillory* STOCKS.
▶ **verb 1** *he was pilloried by the press* ATTACK, criticize, censure, condemn, denigrate, lambaste, savage, stigmatize, denounce; *informal* knock, slam, pan, bash,

crucify, hammer, pummel; *formal* excoriate. **2** *they were pilloried at school* RIDICULE, jeer at, sneer at, deride, mock, scorn, make fun of, poke fun at, laugh at, scoff at, tease, taunt; *informal* rib, josh, razz.

pillow ▸ noun *his head rested on the pillow* CUSHION, bolster, pad; headrest.
▸ verb *she pillowed her head on folded arms* CUSHION, cradle, rest, lay, support.

pilot ▸ noun **1** *a fighter pilot* AIRMAN/AIRWOMAN, flyer; captain, commander, co-pilot, wingman, first officer, bush pilot; *informal* skipper; *dated* aviator, aeronaut. **2** *a harbour pilot* NAVIGATOR, helmsman, steersman, coxswain. **3** *a pilot for a TV series* TRIAL EPISODE; sample, experiment, trial run.
▸ adjective *a pilot project* EXPERIMENTAL, exploratory, trial, test, sample, speculative; preliminary.
▸ verb **1** *he piloted the jet to safety* NAVIGATE, guide, manoeuvre, steer, control, direct, captain, shepherd; fly, drive; sail; *informal* skipper. **2** *the questionnaire has been piloted* TEST, trial, try out; assess, investigate, examine, appraise, evaluate.

pimp ▸ noun PROCURER, procuress; brothel-keeper, fancy man, pander, madam; *archaic* bawd.

pimple ▸ noun ZIT, pustule, bleb, boil, swelling, eruption, blackhead, whitehead, carbuncle, blister, spot; *technical* comedo, papule; (**pimples**) acne, bad skin.

pin ▸ noun **1** *fasten the hem with a pin* TACK, safety pin, nail, staple, fastener. **2** *a broken pin in the machine* BOLT, peg, rivet, dowel, screw. **3** *souvenir pins* BADGE, brooch.
▸ verb **1** *she pinned the brooch to her dress* ATTACH, fasten, affix, fix, tack, clip; join, secure. **2** *they pinned him to the ground* HOLD, press, hold fast, hold down; restrain, pinion, immobilize. **3** *they pinned the crime on him* BLAME FOR, hold responsible for, attribute to, impute to, ascribe to; lay something at someone's door; *informal* stick on.
■ **pin someone/something down 1** *our troops can pin down the enemy* CONFINE, TRAP, hem in, corner, close in, shut in, hedge in, pen in, restrain, entangle, enmesh, immobilize. **2** *she tried to pin him down to a plan* CONSTRAIN, make someone commit themselves, pressure, tie down, nail down. **3** *it evoked a memory but he couldn't pin it down* DEFINE, put one's finger on, put into words, express, name, specify, identify, pinpoint, place.

pinch ▸ verb **1** *he pinched my arm* NIP, tweak, squeeze, grasp. **2** *my new shoes pinch my toes* HURT, pain; squeeze, crush, cramp; be uncomfortable. **3** *I scraped and pinched to afford it* ECONOMIZE, scrimp (and save), be sparing, be frugal, cut back, tighten one's belt, retrench, cut one's coat according to one's cloth; *informal* be stingy, be tight. **4** (*informal*) *you pinched his hockey cards* STEAL, thieve, take, snatch, pilfer, purloin, loot; *informal* swipe, rob, nab, lift, 'liberate', 'borrow', filch, heist.
▸ noun **1** *he gave her arm a pinch* NIP, tweak, squeeze. **2** *a pinch of salt* BIT, touch, dash, spot, trace, soupçon, speck, taste; *informal* smidgen, tad.
■ **feel the pinch** SUFFER HARDSHIP, be short of money, be poor, be impoverished.
■ **in a pinch** IF NECESSARY, if need be, in an emergency, just possibly, with difficulty.

pinched ▸ adjective *their pinched faces* STRAINED, stressed, fraught, tense, taut; tired, worn, drained, sapped; wan, peaky, peaked, pale, grey, blanched; thin, drawn, haggard, gaunt.
— OPPOSITES: healthy.

pine ▸ verb **1** *I am pining away from love* LANGUISH, decline, weaken, waste away, wilt, wither, fade, sicken, droop; brood, mope, moon. **2** *he was pining for his son* YEARN, long, ache, sigh, hunger, languish; miss, mourn, lament, grieve over, shed tears for, bemoan, rue, eat one's heart out over; *informal* itch.

pinion ▸ verb HOLD DOWN, pin down, restrain, hold fast, immobilize; tie, bind, truss (up), shackle, fetter, hobble, manacle, handcuff; *informal* cuff.

pink ▸ adjective ROSE, rosy, rosé, pale red, salmon, coral; flushed, blushing.
▸ noun (*informal*) *she's in the pink of condition* PRIME, perfection, best, finest, height; utmost, greatest, apex, zenith, acme, bloom.
■ **in the pink** (*informal*) IN GOOD HEALTH, very healthy, very well, hale and hearty; blooming, flourishing, thriving, vigorous, strong, lusty, robust, in fine fettle, (as) fit as a fiddle, in excellent shape.

pinnacle ▸ noun **1** *pinnacles of rock* PEAK, needle, aiguille, hoodoo, crag, tor; summit, crest, apex, tip. **2** *the pinnacles of the clock tower* TURRET, minaret, spire, finial, mirador. **3** *the pinnacle of the sport* HIGHEST LEVEL, peak, height, high point, top, capstone, apex, zenith, apogee, acme.
— OPPOSITES: nadir.

pinpoint ▸ noun *a pinpoint of light* POINT, spot, speck, dot, speckle.
▸ adjective *pinpoint accuracy* PRECISE, strict, exact, meticulous, scrupulous, punctilious, accurate, careful.
▸ verb *pinpoint the cause of the trouble* IDENTIFY, determine, distinguish, discover, find, locate, detect, track down, spot, diagnose, recognize, pin down, home in on, put one's finger on.

pioneer ▸ noun **1** *the pioneers of the Wild West* SETTLER, colonist, colonizer, frontiersman/woman, explorer, trailblazer, bushwhacker. **2** *an aviation pioneer* DEVELOPER, innovator, trailblazer, ground-breaker, spearhead; founder, founding father, architect, creator.
▸ verb *he pioneered the sale of insurance* INTRODUCE, develop, evolve, launch, instigate, initiate, spearhead, institute, establish, found, be the father/mother of, originate, set in motion, create; lay the groundwork, prepare the way, blaze a trail, break new ground.

pious ▸ adjective **1** *a pious family* RELIGIOUS, devout, God-fearing, churchgoing, spiritual, prayerful, holy, godly, saintly, dedicated, reverent, dutiful, righteous. **2** *a pious platitude* SANCTIMONIOUS, hypocritical, insincere, self-righteous, holier-than-thou, pietistic, churchy; *informal* goody-goody. **3** *a pious hope* FORLORN, vain, doomed, hopeless, desperate; unlikely, unrealistic.
— OPPOSITES: irreligious, sincere.

pip ▸ noun SEED, stone, pit.

pipe ▸ noun **1** *a water pipe* TUBE, conduit, hose, main, duct, line, channel, pipeline, drain; tubing, piping, siphon. **2** *he smokes a pipe* brier (pipe), meerschaum, chibouk; hookah, narghile, hubble-bubble, bong, churchwarden. **3** *she was playing a pipe* WHISTLE, pennywhistle, tin whistle, flute, recorder, fife; chanter. **4** *regimental pipes and drums* BAGPIPES, uillean pipes; pan pipes.
▸ verb **1** *the beer is piped into barrels* SIPHON, feed, channel, run, convey. **2** *television shows piped in from Toronto* TRANSMIT, feed, patch. **3** *he heard a tune being piped* PLAY ON A PIPE, tootle, whistle; *literary* flute. **4** *a*

curlew piped CHIRP, cheep, chirrup, twitter, warble, trill, peep, sing, shrill.

■ **pipe down** (*informal*) BE QUIET, be silent, hush, stop talking, hold one's tongue, settle down; *informal* shut up, shut one's mouth, zip it, button it, button one's lip, put a sock in it.

pipe dream ▶ noun FANTASY, false hope, illusion, delusion, daydream, chimera; castle in the air, castle in Spain; *informal* pie in the sky.

pipeline ▶ noun *a gas pipeline* PIPE, conduit, main, line, duct, tube, (*North*) utilidor ✦.

■ **in the pipeline** ON THE WAY, coming, forthcoming, upcoming, imminent, about to happen, near, close, brewing, in the offing, in the wind.

pipsqueak ▶ noun (*informal*) NOBODY, nonentity, insignificant person, no-name, non-person, cipher, small fry; upstart, stripling; *informal* squirt, whippersnapper; picayune.

piquant ▶ adjective 1 *a piquant sauce* SPICY, tangy, peppery, hot; tasty, flavourful, appetizing, savoury; pungent, sharp, tart, zesty, strong, salty. 2 *a piquant story* INTRIGUING, stimulating, interesting, fascinating, colourful, exciting, lively; spicy, provocative, racy; *informal* juicy.
— OPPOSITES: bland, dull.

pique ▶ noun *a fit of pique* IRRITATION, annoyance, resentment, anger, displeasure, indignation, petulance, ill humour, vexation, exasperation, disgruntlement, discontent; offence, umbrage.
▶ verb 1 *his curiosity was piqued* STIMULATE, arouse, rouse, provoke, whet, awaken, excite, kindle, stir, galvanize. 2 *she was piqued by his neglect* IRRITATE, annoy, bother, vex, displease, upset, offend, affront, anger, exasperate, infuriate, gall, irk, nettle; *informal* peeve, aggravate, miff, rile, bug, needle, get someone's back up, hack off, get someone's goat, tick off, tee off.

piracy ▶ noun 1 *piracy on the high seas* FREEBOOTING, robbery at sea; *archaic* buccaneering. 2 *software piracy* ILLEGAL COPYING, plagiarism, copyright infringement, bootlegging.

pirate ▶ noun 1 *pirates boarded the ship* FREEBOOTER, marauder, raider; *historical* privateer; *archaic* buccaneer, corsair. 2 *software pirates* COPYRIGHT INFRINGER, plagiarist, plagiarizer.
▶ verb *designers may pirate good ideas* STEAL, plagiarize, poach, copy illegally, reproduce illegally, appropriate, bootleg; *informal* crib, lift, rip off, pinch.

pirouette ▶ noun *she did a little pirouette* SPIN, twirl, whirl, turn, twizzle.
▶ verb *she pirouetted before the mirror* SPIN ROUND, twirl, whirl, turn round, revolve, pivot.

pistol ▶ noun REVOLVER, gun, handgun, side arm; automatic, six-shooter, thirty-eight, derringer; *informal* gat, piece; *proprietary* Colt, Luger.

pit¹ ▶ noun 1 *a pit in the ground* HOLE, ditch, trench, trough, hollow, excavation, cavity, crater, pothole; shaft, mineshaft, sump. 2 *pit closures* COAL MINE, colliery, quarry. 3 *the pits in her skin* POCKMARK, pock, hollow, indentation, depression, dent, dimple.
▶ verb 1 *his skin had been pitted by acne* MARK, pockmark, scar, blemish, disfigure. 2 *raindrops pitted the bare earth* MAKE HOLES IN, make hollows in, dent, indent.
■ **pit someone/something against** SET AGAINST, match against, put in opposition to, put in competition with; compete with, contend with, vie with, wrestle with.
■ **the pits** (*informal*) HELL, the worst, the lowest of the

low, a nightmare; rock-bottom, extremely bad, awful, terrible, dreadful, deplorable; *informal* appalling, lousy, abysmal.

pit² ▶ noun *cherry pits* STONE, pip, seed.

pitch¹ ▶ noun 1 *her voice rose in pitch* TONE, timbre, key, modulation, frequency. 2 *the pitch of the roof* GRADIENT, slope, slant, angle, steepness, tilt, incline, inclination. 3 *her anger reached such a pitch that she screamed* LEVEL, intensity, point, degree, height, extent. 4 *a pitch of the ball* THROW, fling, hurl, toss, lob; delivery; *informal* chuck, heave. 5 *his sales pitch* PATTER, talk; *informal* spiel, line.
▶ verb 1 *she pitched the note into the fire* THROW, toss, huck ✦, fling, hurl, cast, lob, flip, propel, bowl; *informal* chuck, sling, heave, peg. 2 *he pitched overboard* FALL, tumble, topple, plunge, plummet. 3 *they pitched their tents* PUT UP, set up, erect, raise. 4 *the boat pitched* LURCH, toss (about), plunge, roll, reel, sway, rock, keel, list, wallow, labour.
■ **make a pitch for** TRY TO OBTAIN, try to acquire, try to get, bid for, make a bid for.
■ **pitch in** HELP (OUT), assist, lend a hand, join in, participate, contribute, do one's bit, chip in, co-operate, collaborate.

pitch² ▶ noun *cement coated with pitch* BITUMEN, asphalt, tar.

pitch-black ▶ adjective BLACK, dark, pitch-dark, inky, jet-black, coal-black, jet, ebony; starless, moonless; *literary* Stygian.

pitcher ▶ noun *a pitcher of beer* JUG, ewer, jar, creamer.

piteous ▶ adjective SAD, pitiful, pitiable, pathetic, heart-rending, heartbreaking, moving, touching; plaintive, poignant, forlorn; poor, wretched, miserable.

pitfall ▶ noun HAZARD, danger, risk, peril, difficulty, catch, snag, stumbling block, drawback.

pith ▶ noun 1 *the pith of the argument* ESSENCE, main point, fundamentals, heart, substance, nub, core, quintessence, crux, gist, meat, kernel, marrow, burden; *informal* nitty-gritty. 2 *he writes with pith and exactitude* SUCCINCTNESS, conciseness, concision, pithiness, brevity; cogency, weight, depth, force.

pithy ▶ adjective SUCCINCT, terse, concise, compact, short (and sweet), brief, condensed, to the point, epigrammatic, crisp, thumbnail; significant, meaningful, expressive, telling; *formal* compendious.
— OPPOSITES: verbose.

pitiful ▶ adjective 1 *a child in a pitiful state* DISTRESSING, sad, piteous, pitiable, pathetic, heart-rending, heartbreaking, moving, touching, tear-jerking; plaintive, poignant, forlorn; poor, sorry, wretched, abject, miserable. 2 *a pitiful $500 a month* PALTRY, miserable, meagre, insufficient, trifling, negligible, pitiable, derisory; *informal* pathetic, measly, piddling, mingy. 3 *his performance was pitiful* WOEFUL, deplorable, awful, terrible, lamentable, hopeless, poor, bad, feeble, pitiable, dreadful, inadequate, below par, laughable; *informal* pathetic, useless, appalling, lousy, abysmal, dire.

pitiless ▶ adjective MERCILESS, unmerciful, unpitying, ruthless, cruel, heartless, remorseless, hard-hearted, cold-hearted, harsh, callous, severe, unsparing, unforgiving, unfeeling, uncaring, unsympathetic, uncharitable, brutal, inhuman, inhumane, barbaric, sadistic.
— OPPOSITES: merciful.

pittance ▶ noun A TINY AMOUNT, next to nothing, very

little; *informal* peanuts, chicken feed, slave wages, chump change.

pitted ▶ adjective **1** *his skin was pitted* POCKMARKED, pocked, scarred, marked, blemished. **2** *the pitted lane* POTHOLED, rutted, rutty, holey, bumpy, rough, uneven.
− OPPOSITES: smooth.

pity ▶ noun **1** *a voice full of pity* COMPASSION, commiseration, condolence, sympathy, fellow feeling, understanding; sorrow, regret, sadness. **2** *it's a pity he never had children* SHAME, sad thing, bad luck, misfortune; *informal* crime, bummer, sin.
− OPPOSITES: indifference, cruelty.
▶ verb *they pitied me* FEEL SORRY FOR, feel for, sympathize with, empathize with, commiserate with, take pity on, be moved by, grieve for.
■ **take pity on** FEEL SORRY FOR, relent, be compassionate towards, be sympathetic towards, have mercy on, help (out), put someone out of their misery.
■ **what a pity!** HOW SAD, what a shame, too bad, tant pis, oh dear, bummer.

pivot ▶ noun **1** *the machine turns on a pivot* FULCRUM, axis, axle, swivel; pin, shaft, hub, spindle, hinge, kingpin, gudgeon. **2** *the pivot of government policy* CENTRE, focus, hub, heart, nucleus, crux, keystone, cornerstone, linchpin, kingpin.
▶ verb **1** *the panel pivots inwards* ROTATE, turn, swivel, revolve, spin. **2** *it all pivoted on his response* DEPEND, hinge, turn, centre, hang, rely, rest; revolve around.

pivotal ▶ adjective CENTRAL, crucial, vital, critical, focal, essential, key, decisive.

pixie ▶ noun ELF, fairy, sprite, imp, brownie, puck, leprechaun; *literary* faerie, fay.

placard ▶ noun NOTICE, poster, sign, bill, advertisement; banner; *informal* ad.

placate ▶ verb PACIFY, calm, appease, mollify, soothe, win over, conciliate, propitiate, make peace with, humour.
− OPPOSITES: provoke.

place ▶ noun **1** *an ideal place for dinner* LOCATION, site, spot, setting, position, situation, area, region, locale; venue; *technical* locus. **2** *foreign places* COUNTRY, state, area, region, town, city; locality, district; *literary* clime. **3** *a place of her own* HOME, house, flat, apartment; accommodation, property, pied-à-terre; rooms, quarters; *informal* pad, digs; *formal* residence, abode, dwelling (place), domicile, habitation. **4** *if I were in your place, I'd sell now* SITUATION, position, circumstances; *informal* shoes. **5** *a place was reserved for her* SEAT, chair, space. **6** *I offered him a place in the company* JOB, position, post, appointment, situation, office; employment. **7** *I know my place* STATUS, position, standing, rank, niche; *dated* estate, station. **8** *it was not her place to sort it out* RESPONSIBILITY, duty, job, task, role, function, concern, affair, charge; right, privilege, prerogative.
▶ verb **1** *books were placed on the table* PUT (DOWN), set (down), lay, deposit, position, plant, rest, stand, station, situate, leave; *informal* stick, dump, park, plonk, pop, plunk. **2** *the trust you placed in me* PUT, lay, set, invest. **3** *a survey placed the company sixth* RANK, order, grade, class, classify, categorize; put, set, assign. **4** *Joe couldn't quite place her* IDENTIFY, recognize, remember, put a name to, pin down; locate, pinpoint. **5** *we were placed with foster parents* ACCOMMODATE, house, billet; allocate, assign, appoint.
■ **in the first place** INITIALLY, at first, at the start, at

the outset, in/at the beginning, in the first instance, to begin with, to start with, originally.
■ **in place 1** *the veil was held in place by pearls* IN POSITION, in situ. **2** *the plans are in place* READY, set up, all set, established, arranged, in order.
■ **in place of** INSTEAD OF, rather than, as a substitute for, as a replacement for, in exchange for, in lieu of; in someone's stead.
■ **out of place 1** *she never had a hair out of place* OUT OF POSITION, out of order, in disarray, disarranged, in a mess, messy, topsy-turvy, muddled. **2** *he said something out of place* INAPPROPRIATE, unsuitable, unseemly, improper, untoward, out of keeping, unbecoming, wrong. **3** *she seemed out of place at the literary parties* INCONGRUOUS, out of one's element, like a fish out of water; uncomfortable, uneasy.
■ **put someone in their place** HUMILIATE, take down a peg or two, deflate, crush, squash, humble; *informal* cut down to size, settle someone's hash, make someone eat crow.
■ **take place** HAPPEN, occur, come about, transpire, crop up, materialize, arise, go down; *literary* come to pass, befall, betide.
■ **take the place of** REPLACE, stand in for, substitute for, act for, fill in for, cover for, relieve.

placement ▶ noun **1** *the placement of the chairs* POSITIONING, placing, arrangement, position, deployment, location, disposition. **2** *teaching placements* JOB, post, assignment, posting, position, appointment, engagement.

placid ▶ adjective **1** *she's normally very placid* EVEN-TEMPERED, calm, tranquil, equable, unexcitable, serene, mild, {calm, cool, and collected}, composed, self-possessed, poised, easygoing, level-headed, steady, unruffled, unperturbed, phlegmatic; *informal* unflappable. **2** *a placid village* QUIET, calm, tranquil, still, peaceful, undisturbed, restful, sleepy.
− OPPOSITES: excitable, bustling.

plagiarism ▶ noun COPYING, infringement of copyright, piracy, theft, stealing; *informal* cribbing.

plagiarize ▶ verb COPY, infringe the copyright of, pirate, steal, poach, appropriate; *informal* rip off, crib, 'borrow', pinch.

plague ▶ noun **1** *they died of the plague* BUBONIC PLAGUE, pneumonic plague, the Black Death; disease, sickness, epidemic; *dated* contagion; *archaic* pestilence. **2** *a plague of fleas* INFESTATION, epidemic, invasion, swarm, multitude, host. **3** *theft is the plague of restaurants* BANE, curse, scourge, affliction, blight.
▶ verb **1** *he was plagued by poor health* AFFLICT, bedevil, torment, trouble, beset, dog, curse. **2** *he plagued her with questions* PESTER, harass, badger, bother, torment, persecute, bedevil, harry, hound, trouble, irritate, nag, annoy, vex, molest; *informal* hassle, bug, aggravate, devil.

plaid ▶ adjective CHECKERED, checked, tartan.

plain ▶ adjective **1** *it was plain that something was wrong* OBVIOUS, (crystal) clear, evident, apparent, manifest, patent, discernible, perceptible, noticeable, recognizable, unmistakable, transparent; pronounced, marked, striking, conspicuous, self-evident, indisputable; writ large; *informal* standing/sticking out like a sore thumb. **2** *plain English* INTELLIGIBLE, comprehensible, clear, understandable, coherent, uncomplicated, lucid, unambiguous, simple, straightforward, user-friendly; *formal* perspicuous. **3** *plain speaking* CANDID, frank, outspoken, forthright, direct, honest, truthful, blunt, bald, explicit, unequivocal; *informal*

upfront. **4** *a plain dress* SIMPLE, ordinary, unadorned, unembellished, unornamented, unostentatious, unfussy, basic, modest, unsophisticated, without frills, homespun; restrained, muted; everyday, workaday. **5** *a plain girl* HOMELY, unattractive, unprepossessing, ugly, ill-favoured, unlovely, ordinary; *informal* not much to look at. **6** *it was plain bad luck* SHEER, pure, downright, out-and-out, unmitigated.
– OPPOSITES: obscure, fancy, attractive, pretentious.
▶ **adverb** *this is just plain stupid* DOWNRIGHT, utterly, absolutely, completely, totally, really, thoroughly, positively, simply, unquestionably, undeniably; *informal* plumb.
▶ **noun** *the endless grassy plains* GRASSLAND, prairie, flatland, lowland, pasture, meadowland, savannah, steppe; tableland, tundra, pampas, veld.

plain-spoken ▶ **adjective** CANDID, frank, outspoken, forthright, direct, honest, truthful, open, blunt, straightforward, explicit, unequivocal, unambiguous, not afraid to call a spade a spade, tell-it-like-it-is; *informal* upfront.
– OPPOSITES: evasive.

plaintive ▶ **adjective** MOURNFUL, sad, wistful, doleful, pathetic, pitiful, piteous, melancholy, sorrowful, unhappy, wretched, woeful, forlorn, woebegone; *literary* dolorous.

plan ▶ **noun** **1** *a plan for raising money* PROCEDURE, scheme, strategy, idea, proposal, proposition, suggestion; project, program, system, method, stratagem, formula, recipe; way, means, measure, tactic. **2** *her plan was to win a medal* INTENTION, aim, idea, intent, objective, object, goal, target, ambition. **3** *plans for the clubhouse* BLUEPRINT, drawing, diagram, sketch, layout; illustration, representation.
▶ **verb** **1** *plan your route in advance* ORGANIZE, arrange, work out, design, outline, map out, prepare, schedule, formulate, frame, develop, devise, concoct; plot, scheme, hatch, brew, slate. **2** *he plans to buy a house* INTEND, aim, propose, mean, hope, want, wish, desire, envisage; *formal* purpose. **3** *I'm planning a new garden* DESIGN, draw up, sketch out, map out.

plane¹ ▶ **noun** **1** *a horizontal plane* FLAT SURFACE, level surface; horizontal. **2** *a higher plane of achievement* LEVEL, degree, standard, stratum; position, rung, echelon.
▶ **adjective** *a plane surface* FLAT, level, horizontal, even; smooth, regular, uniform; *technical* planar.
▶ **verb** **1** *seagulls planed overhead* SOAR, glide, float, drift, wheel. **2** *boats planed across the water* SKIM, glide.

plane² ▶ **noun** *the plane took off* AIRCRAFT, airplane, airliner, (jumbo) jet, jetliner, bush plane, float plane, seaplane, crop-duster, water bomber; *dated* flying machine.

planet ▶ **noun** CELESTIAL BODY, heavenly body, satellite, moon, earth, asteroid, planetoid; *literary* orb. See table.

plangent ▶ **adjective** (*literary*) MELANCHOLY, mournful, plaintive; sonorous, resonant, loud.

plank ▶ **noun** BOARD, floorboard, timber, stave.

planning ▶ **noun** PREPARATION(S), organization, arrangement, design; forethought, groundwork.

plant ▶ **noun** **1** *garden plants* flower, vegetable, herb, shrub, weed, forb; (**plants**) vegetation, greenery, flora, herbage, verdure. **2** *a CIA plant* SPY, informant, informer, (secret) agent, mole, infiltrator, operative; *informal* spook. **3** *the plant commenced production*

Planet	Satellite(s)
Mercury	
Venus	
Earth	Moon
Mars	Phobos, Deimos
Jupiter	Metis, Adrastea, Amalthea, Thebe, Io, Europa, Ganymede, Callisto, Leda, Himalia, Lysithea, Elara, Ananke, Carme, Pasiphae, Sinope
Saturn	Pan, Atlas, Prometheus, Pandora, Epimethus, Janus, Mimas, Enceladus, Tethys, Telesto, Calypso, Dione, Helene, Rhea, Titan, Hyperion, Iapetus, Phoebe
Uranus	Cordelia, Ophelia, Bianca, Cressida, Desdemona, Juliet, Portia, Rosalind, Belinda, Puck, Miranda, Ariel, Umbriel, Titania, Oberon, Caliban, Sycorax, Prospero, Setebos, Stephano
Neptune	Naiad, Thalassa, Despina, Galatea, Larissa, Proteus, Triton, Nereid
Pluto	Charon

Planets of the Solar System

FACTORY, works, foundry, mill, workshop, shop.
– RELATED TERMS: phyto-, -phyte.
▶ **verb** **1** *plant the seeds this autumn* SOW, scatter, seed; bed out, transplant. **2** *he planted his feet on the ground* PLACE, put, set, position, situate, settle; *informal* plonk. **3** *she planted the idea in his mind* INSTILL, implant, impress, imprint, put, place, introduce, fix, establish, lodge. **4** *letters were planted to embarrass them* HIDE, conceal, secrete.

plaque ▶ **noun** PLATE, tablet, panel, sign, cartouche, brass.

plaster ▶ **noun** **1** *the plaster covering the bricks* PLASTERWORK, stucco, parging. **2** *a statuette made of plaster* PLASTER OF PARIS, gypsum.
▶ **verb** **1** *bread plastered with butter* COVER THICKLY, smother, spread, smear, cake, coat, slather. **2** *his hair was plastered down with sweat* FLATTEN (DOWN), smooth down, slick down.

plastic ▶ **adjective** **1** *at high temperatures the rocks become plastic* MALLEABLE, mouldable, pliable, pliant, ductile, flexible, soft, workable, bendable; *informal* bendy. **2** *the plastic minds of children* IMPRESSIONABLE, malleable, receptive, pliable, pliant, flexible; compliant, tractable, biddable, persuadable, susceptible, manipulable. **3** *a plastic smile* ARTIFICIAL, false, fake, superficial, pseudo, bogus, unnatural, insincere; *informal* phony, pretend.
– OPPOSITES: rigid, intractable, genuine.

plate ▶ **noun** **1** *a dinner plate* DISH, platter, salver, paten; *historical* trencher. **2** *a plate of spaghetti* PLATEFUL, helping, portion, serving. **3** *steel plates* PANEL, sheet, layer, pane, slab. **4** *a brass plate on the door* PLAQUE, sign, tablet, cartouche, brass. **5** *the book has colour plates* PICTURE, print, illustration, photograph, photo.
▶ **verb** *the roof was plated with steel* COVER, coat, overlay, laminate, veneer; electroplate, galvanize, gild.

plateau ▶ **noun** **1** *a windswept plateau* UPLAND, tableland, plain, mesa, highland, coteau. **2** *prices reached a plateau* quiescent period; let-up, respite, lull.

platform ▶ **noun** **1** *he made a speech from the platform* STAGE, dais, rostrum, podium, soapbox. **2** *the New Democratic Party's platform* POLICY, program, party line, manifesto, plan, principles, objectives, aims.

platitude ▶ noun CLICHÉ, truism, commonplace, banality, old chestnut, bromide, inanity, banal/trite/hackneyed/stock phrase.

platitudinous ▶ adjective HACKNEYED, overworked, overused, clichéd, banal, trite, commonplace, well-worn, stale, tired, unoriginal; *informal* corny, old hat.
– OPPOSITES: original.

platonic ▶ adjective NON-SEXUAL, non-physical, chaste; intellectual, friendly.
– OPPOSITES: sexual.

platoon ▶ noun UNIT, patrol, troop, squad, squadron, team, company, corps, outfit, detachment, contingent.

platter ▶ noun PLATE, dish, salver, paten, tray; *historical* trencher.

plaudits ▶ plural noun PRAISE, acclaim, commendation, congratulations, accolades, compliments, cheers, applause, tributes, bouquets; a pat on the back; *informal* a (big) hand.
– OPPOSITES: criticism.

plausible ▶ adjective CREDIBLE, reasonable, believable, likely, feasible, tenable, possible, conceivable, imaginable; convincing, persuasive, cogent, sound, rational, logical, thinkable.
– OPPOSITES: unlikely.

play ▶ verb **1** *Aidan and Robert were playing with their toys* AMUSE ONESELF, entertain oneself, enjoy oneself, have fun; relax, occupy oneself, divert oneself; frolic, frisk, romp, caper; *informal* mess about/around, lark (about/around). **2** *I used to play hockey* TAKE PART IN, participate in, be involved in, compete in, do. **3** *Edmonton plays Calgary on Sunday* COMPETE AGAINST, take on, challenge, vie with, face, go up against. **4** *he was to play Macbeth* ACT (THE PART OF), take the role of, appear as, portray, depict, impersonate, represent, render, perform, enact; *formal* personate. **5** *get your guitar and let's play* PERFORM, make music, jam. **6** *Bryanna played a note on the flute* MAKE, produce, reproduce; blow, toot; plunk, bang out; sound. **7** *the sunlight played on the water* DANCE, flit, ripple, touch; sparkle, glint.
▶ noun **1** *a balance between work and play* AMUSEMENT, entertainment, relaxation, recreation, diversion, distraction, leisure; enjoyment, pleasure, fun, games, fun and games; horseplay, merrymaking, revelry; *informal* living it up. **2** *a Shakespeare play* DRAMA, theatrical work; screenplay, comedy, tragedy; production, performance, show, sketch. **3** *a new tool came into play* ACTION, activity, operation, working, function; interaction, interplay. **4** *there is foul play afoot* BEHAVIOUR, goings-on, activity, action, deed. **5** *there was a little play in the rope* MOVEMENT, slack, give; room to manoeuvre, scope, latitude.
■ **play around** (*informal*) WOMANIZE, philander, have affairs, flirt; *informal* carry on, mess about/around, play the field, sleep around, fool around.
■ **play at** PRETEND TO BE, pass oneself off as, masquerade as, profess to be, pose as, impersonate; fake, feign, simulate, affect; *informal* make like.
■ **play ball** (*informal*) CO-OPERATE, collaborate, play the game, help, lend a hand, assist, contribute; *informal* pitch in.
■ **play something down** MAKE LIGHT OF, make little of, gloss over, de-emphasize, downplay, understate; soft-pedal, tone down, diminish, trivialize, underrate, underestimate, undervalue; disparage, belittle, scoff at, sneer at, shrug off; *informal* pooh-pooh.

■ **play for time** STALL, temporize, delay, hold back, hang fire, procrastinate, drag one's feet.
■ **play it by ear** IMPROVISE, extemporize, ad lib; *informal* wing it.
■ **play on** *they play on our fears* EXPLOIT, take advantage of, use, turn to (one's) account, profit by, capitalize on, trade on, milk, abuse.
■ **play the fool** CLOWN ABOUT/AROUND, fool about/around, mess about/around, lark about/around, monkey about/around, joke; *informal* horse about/around, muck about/around.
■ **play the game** PLAY FAIR, be fair, play by the rules, conform, be a good sport, toe the line.
■ **play something up** EMPHASIZE, accentuate, call attention to, point up, underline, highlight, spotlight, foreground, feature, stress, accent.
■ **play up to** INGRATIATE ONESELF WITH, curry favour with, court, fawn over, make up to, toady to, crawl to, pander to, flatter; *informal* soft-soap, suck up to, butter up, lick someone's boots.

playboy ▶ noun SOCIALITE, pleasure-seeker, sybarite; ladies' man, womanizer, philanderer, wolf, rake, roué; *informal* lady-killer.

player ▶ noun **1** *a tournament for young players* PARTICIPANT, contestant, competitor, contender; sportsman/woman, athlete. **2** *the players in the orchestra* MUSICIAN, performer, instrumentalist, soloist, virtuoso. **3** *the players at the Shaw Festival* ACTOR, actress, performer, thespian, entertainer, artist(e), trouper.

playful ▶ adjective **1** *a playful mood* FRISKY, jolly, lively, full of fun, frolicsome, sportive, high-spirited, exuberant, perky; mischievous, impish, clownish, kittenish, rascally, tricksy; *informal* full of beans; *formal* ludic. **2** *a playful remark* LIGHT-HEARTED, in jest, joking, jokey, teasing, humorous, jocular, good-natured, tongue-in-cheek, facetious, frivolous, flippant, arch; *informal* waggish.
– OPPOSITES: serious.

playground ▶ noun PLAY AREA, park, playing field, recreation ground.

playmate ▶ noun FRIEND, companion.

plaything ▶ noun TOY, game.

playwright ▶ noun DRAMATIST, dramaturge, scriptwriter, screenwriter, writer, scenarist; tragedian.

plea ▶ noun **1** *a plea for aid* APPEAL, entreaty, supplication, petition, request, call, suit, solicitation. **2** *her plea of a headache was unconvincing* CLAIM, explanation, defence, justification; excuse, pretext.

plead ▶ verb **1** *he pleaded with her to stay* BEG, implore, entreat, appeal to, supplicate, importune, petition, request, ask, call on; *literary* beseech. **2** *she pleaded ignorance* CLAIM, use as an excuse, assert, allege, argue, state.

pleasant ▶ adjective **1** *a pleasant evening* ENJOYABLE, pleasurable, nice, agreeable, pleasing, satisfying, gratifying, good; entertaining, amusing, delightful, charming; fine, balmy; *informal* lovely, great. **2** *the staff are pleasant* FRIENDLY, agreeable, amiable, nice, genial, cordial, likeable, amicable, good-humoured, good-natured, personable; hospitable, approachable, gracious, courteous, polite, obliging, helpful, considerate; charming, lovely, delightful, sweet, sympathetic, simpatico.
– OPPOSITES: disagreeable.

pleasantry ▶ noun **1** *we exchanged pleasantries* BANTER, badinage; polite remark, casual remark. **2** *he* laughed at his own pleasantry JOKE, witticism, quip, jest, gag, bon mot; *informal* wisecrack, crack.

please ▶ verb **1** *he'd do anything to please her* MAKE HAPPY, give pleasure to, make someone feel good; delight, charm, amuse, entertain; satisfy, gratify, humour, oblige, content, suit. **2** *do as you please* LIKE, want, wish, desire, see fit, think fit, choose, will, prefer.
— OPPOSITES: annoy.
▶ adverb *please sit down* IF YOU PLEASE, if you wouldn't mind, if you would be so good; kindly, pray; *archaic* prithee.

pleased ▶ adjective HAPPY, glad, delighted, gratified, grateful, thankful, content, contented, satisfied; thrilled, elated, overjoyed; *informal* over the moon, tickled pink, on cloud nine.
— OPPOSITES: unhappy.

pleasing ▶ adjective **1** *a pleasing day* NICE, agreeable, pleasant, pleasurable, satisfying, gratifying, good, enjoyable, entertaining, amusing, delightful; *informal* lovely, great. **2** *her pleasing manner* FRIENDLY, amiable, pleasant, agreeable, affable, nice, genial, likeable, good-humoured, charming, engaging, delightful; *informal* lovely, simpatico.

pleasurable ▶ adjective PLEASANT, enjoyable, delightful, nice, pleasing, agreeable, gratifying; fun, entertaining, amusing, diverting; *informal* lovely, great.

pleasure ▶ noun **1** *she smiled with pleasure* HAPPINESS, delight, joy, gladness, glee, satisfaction, gratification, contentment, enjoyment, amusement. **2** *his greatest pleasures in life* JOY, amusement, diversion, recreation, pastime; treat, thrill. **3** *don't mix business and pleasure* ENJOYMENT, fun, entertainment; recreation, leisure, relaxation; *informal* jollies. **4** *a life of pleasure* HEDONISM, indulgence, self-indulgence, self-gratification, lotus-eating. **5** *what's your pleasure?* WISH, desire, preference, will, inclination, choice.
■ **take pleasure in** ENJOY, delight in, love, like, adore, appreciate, relish, savour, revel in, glory in; *informal* get a kick out of, get a thrill out of.
■ **with pleasure** GLADLY, willingly, happily, readily; by all means, of course; *archaic* fain.

pleat ▶ noun *a curtain pleat* FOLD, crease, gather, tuck, crimp; pucker.
▶ verb *the dress is pleated at the front* FOLD, crease, gather, tuck, crimp; pucker.

plebeian ▶ noun *plebeians and gentry lived together* PROLETARIAN, commoner, working-class person, worker; peasant; *informal* pleb, prole.
— OPPOSITES: aristocrat.
▶ adjective **1** *people of plebeian descent* LOWER-CLASS, working-class, proletarian, common, peasant; mean, humble, lowly. **2** *plebeian tastes* UNCULTURED, uncultivated, unrefined, lowbrow, philistine, uneducated; coarse, uncouth, common, vulgar.
— OPPOSITES: noble, refined.

plebiscite ▶ noun VOTE, referendum, ballot, poll.

pledge ▶ noun **1** *his election pledge* PROMISE, undertaking, vow, word (of honour), commitment, assurance, oath, guarantee. **2** *he gave it as a pledge to a creditor* SURETY, bond, security, collateral, guarantee, deposit. **3** *a pledge of my sincerity* TOKEN, symbol, sign, earnest, mark, testimony, proof, evidence.
▶ verb **1** *he pledged to root out corruption* PROMISE, vow, swear, undertake, engage, commit oneself, declare, affirm, avow. **2** *they pledged $10 million* PROMISE (TO GIVE), donate, contribute, give, put up. **3** *his home is*

pledged as security against the loan MORTGAGE, put up as collateral, guarantee, pawn.

plenary ▶ adjective **1** *the council has plenary powers in this matter* UNCONDITIONAL, unlimited, unrestricted, unqualified, absolute, sweeping, comprehensive; plenipotentiary. **2** *a plenary session of the parliament* FULL, complete, entire.

plenipotentiary ▶ noun *a plenipotentiary in Paris* DIPLOMAT, dignitary, ambassador, minister, emissary, chargé d'affaires, envoy.
▶ adjective *plenipotentiary powers. See* PLENARY *sense 1.*

plenitude ▶ noun *(formal)* ABUNDANCE, lot, wealth, profusion, cornucopia, plethora, superabundance; *informal* load, slew, heap, ton.

plenteous ▶ adjective *(literary). See* PLENTIFUL.

plentiful ▶ adjective ABUNDANT, copious, ample, profuse, rich, lavish, generous, bountiful, large, great, bumper, superabundant, inexhaustible, prolific; *informal* galore; *literary* plenteous.
— OPPOSITES: scarce.

plenty ▶ noun *times of plenty* PROSPERITY, affluence, wealth, opulence, comfort, luxury; plentifulness, abundance; *literary* plenteousness.
▶ pronoun *there are plenty of books* A LOT OF, many, a great deal of, a plethora of, enough (and to spare), no lack of, sufficient, a wealth of; *informal* loads of, lots of, heaps of, stacks of, masses of, tons of, oodles of, scads of, a slew of.

plethora ▶ noun EXCESS, abundance, superabundance, surplus, glut, superfluity, surfeit, profusion, too many, too much, enough and to spare; *informal* more —— than one can shake a stick at.
— OPPOSITES: dearth.

pliable ▶ adjective **1** *leather is pliable* FLEXIBLE, pliant, bendable, elastic, supple, malleable, workable, plastic, springy, ductile; *informal* bendy. **2** *pliable teenage minds* MALLEABLE, impressionable, flexible, adaptable, pliant, compliant, biddable, tractable, yielding, amenable, susceptible, suggestible, persuadable, manipulable, receptive.
— OPPOSITES: rigid, obdurate.

pliant ▶ adjective. *See* PLIABLE *senses 1, 2.*

plight ▶ noun PREDICAMENT, quandary, difficult situation, dire straits, trouble, difficulty, extremity, bind; *informal* dilemma, tight corner, tight spot, hole, pickle, jam, fix.

plod ▶ verb **1** *Mom plodded wearily upstairs* TRUDGE, walk heavily, clump, stomp, tramp, tromp, lumber, slog. **2** *I have to plod through the whole book* WADE, plow, trawl, toil, labour; *informal* slog.

plot ▶ noun **1** *a plot to overthrow him* CONSPIRACY, intrigue, secret plan; machinations. **2** *the plot of her novel* STORYLINE, story, scenario, action, thread; *formal* diegesis. **3** *a three-acre plot* PIECE OF GROUND, patch, area, tract, acreage, allotment, lot, plat, homesite.
▶ verb **1** *he plotted their downfall* PLAN, scheme, arrange, organize, hatch, concoct, devise, dream up; *informal* cook up. **2** *his brother was plotting against him* CONSPIRE, scheme, intrigue, collude, connive, machinate. **3** *the fifty-three sites were plotted* MARK, chart, map, represent, graph.

plotter ▶ noun CONSPIRATOR, schemer, intriguer, machinator; planner.

plow ▶ verb **1** *the fields were plowed* TILL, furrow, harrow, cultivate, work, break up. **2** *the streets haven't been plowed yet* CLEAR (OF SNOW), shovel. **3** *the car plowed into a lamp post* CRASH, smash, career, plunge, bulldoze, hurtle, careen, cannon, run, drive, barrel.

4 *they plowed through deep snow* TRUDGE, plod, toil, wade; *informal* slog.

ploy ▶ noun RUSE, tactic, move, device, stratagem, scheme, trick, gambit, plan, manoeuvre, dodge, subterfuge, wile.

pluck ▶ verb **1** *he plucked a thread from his lapel* REMOVE, pick (off), pull (off/out), extract, take (off). **2** *she plucked at his T-shirt* PULL (AT), tug (at), clutch (at), snatch (at), grab, catch (at), tweak, jerk; *informal* yank. **3** *the turkeys are plucked* DEPLUME, remove the feathers from. **4** *Jen plucked the guitar strings* STRUM, pick, plunk, thrum, twang; play pizzicato.
▶ noun *the task took a lot of pluck* COURAGE, bravery, nerve, backbone, spine, daring, spirit, intrepidity, fearlessness, mettle, grit, true grit, determination, fortitude, resolve, stout-heartedness, dauntlessness, valour, heroism, audacity; *informal* guts, spunk, gumption, moxie.

plucky ▶ adjective BRAVE, courageous, bold, daring, fearless, intrepid, spirited, game, valiant, valorous, stout-hearted, dauntless, resolute, determined, undaunted, unflinching, audacious, unafraid, doughty, mettlesome; *informal* gutsy, spunky.
— OPPOSITES: timid.

plug ▶ noun **1** *she pulled out the plug* STOPPER, bung, cork, seal, spigot, spile. **2** *a plug of tobacco* WAD, quid, twist, chew, cake, stick. **3** *(informal) a plug for her new book* ADVERTISEMENT, promotion, commercial, recommendation, mention, good word; *informal* hype, push, puff piece, ad, boost, ballyhoo.
▶ verb **1** *plug the holes* STOP (UP), seal (up/off), close (up/off), cork, stopper, bung, block (up/off), fill (up). **2** *(informal) she plugged her new film* PUBLICIZE, promote, advertise, mention, bang the drum for, draw attention to; *informal* hype (up), push, puff. **3** *(informal) don't move or I'll plug you* SHOOT, gun down; *informal* blast, pump full of lead.
■ **plug away** *(informal)* TOIL, labour, slave away, soldier on, persevere, persist, keep on; *informal* slog away, beaver away.

plum ▶ adjective *(informal) a plum job* EXCELLENT, very good, wonderful, marvellous, choice, first-class; *informal* great, terrific, cushy.

plumb[1] ▶ verb *an attempt to plumb her psyche* EXPLORE, probe, delve into, search, examine, investigate, fathom, penetrate, understand.
▶ adverb **1** *(informal) it went plumb through the screen* RIGHT, exactly, precisely, directly, dead, straight; *informal* bang. **2** *(informal) I plumb forgot* COMPLETELY, absolutely, downright, totally, quite, thoroughly. **3** *(archaic) the bell hangs plumb* VERTICALLY, perpendicularly, straight down.
▶ adjective *a plumb drop* VERTICAL, perpendicular, straight.
■ **plumb the depths** FIND, experience the extremes, reach the lowest point; reach rock bottom.

plumb[2] ▶ verb *he plumbed in the washing machine* INSTALL, put in, fit.

plume ▶ noun *ostrich plumes* FEATHER, quill; *Ornithology* plumule, covert.

plummet ▶ verb **1** *the plane plummeted to the ground* PLUNGE, nosedive, dive, drop, fall, descend, hurtle. **2** *share prices plummeted* FALL STEEPLY, plunge, tumble, drop rapidly, go down, slump; *informal* crash, nosedive.

plummy ▶ adjective *(informal) a plummy voice* UPPER-CLASS, refined, aristocratic, grand.

plump[1] ▶ adjective *a plump child* CHUBBY, fat, stout, rotund, well padded, ample, round, chunky, portly,

overweight, fleshy, paunchy, bulky, corpulent; *informal* tubby, roly-poly, pudgy, beefy, porky, blubbery, zaftig, corn-fed.
— OPPOSITES: thin.

plump[2] ▶ verb **1** *Jack plumped down on to a chair* FLOP, COLLAPSE, sink, fall, drop, slump; *informal* plonk/plank/plunk oneself. **2** *she plumped her bag on the table* PUT (DOWN), set (down), place, deposit, dump, stick; *informal* plonk, plunk.

plunder ▶ verb **1** *they plundered the countryside* PILLAGE, loot, rob, raid, ransack, despoil, strip, ravage, lay waste, devastate, sack, rape. **2** *money plundered from pension funds* STEAL, purloin, thieve, seize, pillage; embezzle.
▶ noun **1** *the plunder of the villages* LOOTING, pillaging, plundering, raiding, ransacking, devastation, sacking; *literary* rapine. **2** *the army took huge quantities of plunder* BOOTY, loot, stolen goods, spoils, ill-gotten gains; *informal* swag.

plunge ▶ verb **1** *Joy plunged into the sea* DIVE, jump, throw oneself, launch oneself. **2** *the aircraft plunged to the ground* PLUMMET, nosedive, drop, fall, pitch, tumble, descend, dive-bomb. **3** *the car plunged down an alley* CHARGE, hurtle, career, plow, cannon, tear; *informal* barrel. **4** *oil prices plunged* FALL SHARPLY, plummet, drop, go down, tumble, slump; *informal* crash, nosedive. **5** *he plunged the dagger into her back* THRUST, jab, stab, sink, stick, ram, drive, push, shove, force. **6** *plunge the pears into water* IMMERSE, submerge, dip, dunk. **7** *the room was plunged into darkness* THROW, cast, pitch.
▶ noun **1** *a plunge into the deep end* DIVE, jump, nosedive, fall, pitch, drop, plummet, descent. **2** *a plunge in profits* FALL, drop, slump; *informal* nosedive, crash.
■ **take the plunge** COMMIT ONESELF, go for it, do the deed, throw caution to the wind(s), risk it; *informal* jump in at the deep end, go for broke.

plurality ▶ noun **1** *a plurality of theories* WIDE VARIETY, diversity, range, lot, multitude, multiplicity, galaxy, wealth, profusion, abundance, plethora, host; *informal* load, stack, heap, mass. **2** *in the plurality of cases* PREPONDERANCE, bulk, largest number; majority.

plus ▶ preposition **1** *three plus three makes six* AND, added to. **2** *he wrote four novels plus various poems* AS WELL AS, together with, along with, in addition to, and, not to mention, besides.
— OPPOSITES: minus.
▶ noun *one of the pluses of the job* ADVANTAGE, good point, asset, pro, (fringe) benefit, bonus, extra, attraction; *informal* perk; *formal* perquisite.
— OPPOSITES: disadvantage.

plush ▶ adjective *(informal)* LUXURIOUS, luxury, deluxe, sumptuous, palatial, lavish, opulent, magnificent, lush, rich, expensive, fancy, grand, upscale, upmarket; *informal* posh, ritzy, swanky, classy, swank.
— OPPOSITES: austere.

plutocrat ▶ noun RICH PERSON, magnate, millionaire, billionaire, multi-millionaire; nouveau riche; *informal* fat cat, moneybags.

ply[1] ▶ verb **1** *the gondolier plied his oar* USE, wield, work, manipulate, handle, operate, utilize, employ. **2** *he plied a profitable trade* ENGAGE IN, carry on, pursue, conduct, practise; *archaic* prosecute. **3** *ferries ply between all lake resorts* GO REGULARLY, travel, shuttle, go back and forth. **4** *she plied me with scones* PROVIDE, supply, lavish, shower, regale. **5** *he plied her with questions* BOMBARD, assail, beset, pester, plague, harass, importune; *informal* hassle, devil.

ply² ▸ noun *a three-ply tissue* LAYER, thickness, strand, sheet, leaf.

poach ▸ verb **1** *he's been poaching salmon* HUNT ILLEGALLY, catch illegally, jacklight, jack; steal. **2** *workers were poached by other firms* STEAL, appropriate, purloin, take, lure away; *informal* nab, swipe, pinch.

pocket ▸ noun **1** *a bag with two pockets* POUCH, compartment. **2** *these donors have deep pockets* MEANS, budget, resources, finances, funds, money, wherewithal, pocketbook. **3** *pockets of disaffection* (ISOLATED) AREA, patch, region, island, cluster, centre.
▸ adjective *a pocket dictionary* SMALL, little, miniature, mini, compact, concise, abridged, portable, vest-pocket.
▸ verb *he pocketed $900,000 of their money* STEAL, take, appropriate, thieve, purloin, misappropriate, embezzle; *informal* filch, swipe, snaffle, pinch.

pockmark ▸ noun SCAR, pit, pock, mark, blemish.

pod ▸ noun SHELL, husk, hull, case; shuck; *Botany* pericarp, capsule.

podium ▸ noun PLATFORM, stage, dais, rostrum, stand, soapbox.

poem ▸ noun VERSE, rhyme, piece of poetry, song.

poet ▸ noun WRITER OF POETRY, versifier, rhymester, rhymer, sonneteer, lyricist, lyrist; laureate; *literary* bard; *derogatory* poetaster; *historical* troubadour, balladeer.

poetic ▸ adjective **1** *poetic compositions* POETICAL, verse, metrical, lyrical, lyric, elegiac. **2** *poetic language* EXPRESSIVE, figurative, symbolic, flowery, artistic, elegant, fine, beautiful; sensitive, imaginative, creative.

poetry ▸ noun POEMS, verse, versification, metrical composition, rhymes, balladry; *archaic* poesy.

pogrom ▸ noun MASSACRE, slaughter, mass murder, annihilation, extermination, decimation, carnage, bloodbath, bloodletting, butchery, genocide, holocaust, purge, ethnic cleansing.

poignancy ▸ noun PATHOS, pitifulness, piteousness, sadness, sorrow, mournfulness, wretchedness, misery, tragedy.

poignant ▸ adjective TOUCHING, moving, sad, affecting, pitiful, piteous, pathetic, sorrowful, mournful, wretched, miserable, distressing, heart-rending, tear-jerking, plaintive, tragic.

point¹ ▸ noun **1** *the point of a needle* TIP, (sharp) end, extremity; prong, spike, tine, nib, barb. **2** *points of light* PINPOINT, dot, spot, speck, fleck. **3** *a meeting point* PLACE, position, location, site, spot, area. **4** *this point in her life* TIME, stage, juncture, period, phase. **5** *the tension had reached such a high point* LEVEL, degree, stage, pitch, extent. **6** *an important point* DETAIL, item, fact, thing, argument, consideration, factor, element; subject, issue, topic, question, matter. **7** *get to the point* HEART OF THE MATTER, most important part, essence, nub, keynote, core, pith, crux; meaning, significance, gist, substance, thrust, bottom line, burden, relevance; *informal* brass tacks, nitty-gritty. **8** *what's the point of this?* PURPOSE, aim, object, objective, goal, intention; use, sense, value, advantage. **9** *he had his good points* ATTRIBUTE, characteristic, feature, trait, quality, property, aspect, side.
▸ verb **1** *she pointed the gun at him* AIM, direct, level, train. **2** *the evidence pointed to his guilt* INDICATE, suggest, evidence, signal, signify, denote, bespeak, reveal, manifest.

Poetic Forms, Metres, & Feet

alexandrine	iamb
anapest	iambic
aubade	idyll
ballad	lay
ballade	limerick
blank verse	lyric
bucolic	madrigal
choriamb	monody
choriambic	nursery rhyme
dactyl	ode
dactylic	pastoral
decasyllable	pentameter
dimeter	Petrarchan sonnet
dirge	prothalamion
disyllable	rhyme royal
dithyramb	rondeau
dramatic monologue	roundel
eclogue	roundelay
elegy	saga
encomium	sapphics
epic	satire
epigram	sestina
epithalamium	sonnet
epode	spondee
epyllion	tanka
free verse	tetrameter
georgic	threnody
ghazal	trimeter
haiku	triolet
heptameter	trochaics
heroic	trochee
hexameter	virelay

■ **beside the point** IRRELEVANT, immaterial, unimportant, neither here nor there, inconsequential, incidental, out of place, unconnected, peripheral, tangential, extraneous.

■ **in point of fact** IN FACT, as a matter of fact, actually, in actual fact, really, in reality, as it happens, in truth.

■ **make a point of** MAKE AN EFFORT TO, go out of one's way to, put emphasis on.

■ **on the point of** (JUST) ABOUT TO, on the verge of, on the brink of, going to, all set to.

■ **point of view** OPINION, view, belief, attitude, feeling, sentiment, thoughts; position, perspective, viewpoint, standpoint, outlook.

■ **point something out** IDENTIFY, show, designate, draw attention to, indicate, specify, detail, mention.

■ **point something up** EMPHASIZE, highlight, draw attention to, accentuate, underline, spotlight, foreground, put emphasis on, stress, play up, accent, bring to the fore.

■ **to the point** RELEVANT, pertinent, apposite, germane, applicable, apropos, appropriate, apt, fitting, suitable, material; *formal* ad rem.

■ **up to a point** PARTLY, to some extent, to a certain degree, in part, somewhat, partially.

point² ▸ noun *the ship rounded the point* PROMONTORY, headland, foreland, cape, spit, peninsula, bluff, ness, horn.

point-blank ▸ adverb **1** *he fired the pistol point-blank* AT CLOSE RANGE, close up, close to. **2** *she couldn't say it point-blank* BLUNTLY, directly, straight, frankly, candidly, openly, explicitly, unequivocally, unambiguously, plainly, flatly, categorically, outright.

▶ **adjective** *a point-blank refusal* BLUNT, direct, straight, straightforward, frank, candid, forthright, explicit, unequivocal, plain, clear, flat, decisive, unqualified, categorical, outright.

pointed ▶ **adjective 1** *a pointed stick* SHARP, tapering, tapered, conical, jagged, spiky, spiked, barbed; *informal* pointy. **2** *a pointed remark* CUTTING, trenchant, biting, incisive, acerbic, caustic, scathing, venomous, sarcastic; *informal* snarky.

pointer ▶ **noun 1** *the pointer moved to 100rpm* INDICATOR, needle, arrow, hand. **2** *he used a pointer on the chart* STICK, rod, cane; cursor. **3** *a pointer to the outcome of the election* INDICATION, indicator, clue, hint, sign, signal, evidence, intimation, inkling, suggestion. **4** *I can give you a few pointers* TIP, hint, suggestion, guideline, recommendation.

pointless ▶ **adjective** SENSELESS, futile, hopeless, fruitless, useless, needless, in vain, unavailing, aimless, idle, worthless, valueless; absurd, insane, stupid, silly, foolish.
– OPPOSITES: valuable.

poise ▶ **noun 1** *poise and good deportment* GRACE, gracefulness, elegance, balance, control. **2** *in spite of the setback she retained her poise* COMPOSURE, equanimity, self-possession, aplomb, presence of mind, self-assurance, self-control, nerve, calm, sang-froid, dignity; *informal* cool, unflappability.
▶ **verb 1** *she was poised on one foot* BALANCE, hold (oneself) steady, be suspended, remain motionless, hang, hover. **2** *he was poised for action* PREPARE ONESELF, ready oneself, brace oneself, gear oneself up, stand by.

poison ▶ **noun 1** *a deadly poison* TOXIN, toxicant, venom; *archaic* bane. **2** *Marianne would spread her poison* MALICE, ill will, hate, malevolence, bitterness, spite, spitefulness, venom, acrimony, rancour; bad influence, cancer, corruption, pollution.
– RELATED TERMS: toxic.
▶ **verb 1** *her mother poisoned her* GIVE POISON TO; murder. **2** *a blackmailer poisoning pet food* CONTAMINATE, put poison in, envenom, adulterate, spike, lace, doctor. **3** *the Amazon is being poisoned* POLLUTE, contaminate, taint, blight, spoil; *literary* befoul. **4** *they poisoned his mind* PREJUDICE, bias, jaundice, embitter, sour, envenom, warp, corrupt, subvert.

poisonous ▶ **adjective 1** *a poisonous snake* VENOMOUS, deadly. **2** *a poisonous chemical* TOXIC, noxious, deadly, fatal, lethal, mortal, death-dealing. **3** *a poisonous glance* MALICIOUS, malevolent, hostile, vicious, spiteful, bitter, venomous, vindictive, vitriolic, rancorous, malign, pernicious, mean, nasty; *informal* bitchy, catty.
– OPPOSITES: harmless, non-toxic, benevolent.

poke ▶ **verb 1** *she poked him in the ribs* PROD, jab, dig, nudge, butt, shove, jolt, stab, stick. **2** *leave the cable poking out* STICK OUT, jut out, protrude, project, extend.
▶ **noun** PROD, jab, dig, elbow, nudge, shove, stab.
■ **poke about/around** SEARCH, hunt, rummage (around), forage, grub, root about/around, scavenge, nose around, ferret (about/around); sift through, rifle through, scour, comb, probe.
■ **poke fun at** MOCK, make fun of, ridicule, laugh at, jeer at, sneer at, deride, scorn, scoff at, pillory, lampoon, tease, taunt, chaff, jibe at; *informal* send up, kid, rib, goof on.
■ **poke one's nose into** PRY INTO, interfere in,

intrude on, butt into, meddle with; *informal* snoop into.

poker ▶ **noun**. *See table.*

Poker hands

royal flush
straight flush
four of a kind
full house
flush
straight
three of a kind
two pairs
one pair

poky ▶ **adjective** SMALL, little, tiny, cramped, confined, restricted, boxy; *euphemistic* compact, bijou.
– OPPOSITES: spacious.

polar ▶ **adjective 1** *polar regions* ARCTIC, Antarctic, circumpolar, Nearctic. **2** *polar conditions* COLD, freezing, icy, glacial, chilly, gelid, hypothermic. **3** *polar opposites* OPPOSITE, opposed, dichotomous, extreme, contrary, contradictory, antithetical.

polarity ▶ **noun** DIFFERENCE, dichotomy, separation, opposition, contradiction, antithesis, antagonism.

pole¹ ▶ **noun** POST, pillar; telephone pole, utility pole, hydro pole ✦; stanchion, paling, stake, *(Atlantic)* longer ✦, stick, support, prop, batten, bar, rail, rod, beam; staff, stave, cane, baton.

pole² ▶ **noun** *points of view at opposite poles* EXTREMITY, extreme, limit, antipode.
■ **poles apart** COMPLETELY DIFFERENT, directly opposed, antithetical, incompatible, irreconcilable, worlds apart, at opposite extremes.

polemic ▶ **noun 1** *a polemic against injustice* DIATRIBE, invective, rant, tirade, broadside, attack, harangue, condemnation, criticism, stricture, admonition, rebuke; abuse; *informal* blast; *formal* castigation; *literary* philippic. **2** *he is skilled in polemics* ARGUMENTATION, argument, debate, contention, disputation, discussion, altercation; *formal* contestation.
▶ **adjective** *his famous polemic book. See* POLEMICAL.

polemical ▶ **adjective** CRITICAL, hostile, bitter, polemic, virulent, vitriolic, venomous, caustic, trenchant, cutting, acerbic, sardonic, sarcastic, scathing, sharp, incisive, devastating.

police ▶ **noun** the police force, police officers, policemen, policewomen, officers of the law, the forces of law and order, constabulary; the RCMP ✦, the Royal Newfoundland Constabulary ✦, the QPF, the Sûreté du Québec, the OPP; *informal* the cops, the Mounties ✦, the fuzz, (the long arm of) the law, the boys in blue; coppers, the force, the heat, the pigs.
▶ **verb 1** *we must police the area* GUARD, watch over, protect, defend, patrol; control, regulate. **2** *the regulations will be policed by the ministry* ENFORCE, regulate, oversee, supervise, monitor, observe, check.

police officer ▶ **noun** COP, policeman, policewoman, officer (of the law), patrolman, roundsman; constable, sergeant, inspector, corporal, captain, lieutenant, superintendent; *informal* flatfoot, pig.

policy ▶ **noun 1** *government policy* PLANS, strategy, stratagem, approach, code, system, guidelines, theory; line, position, stance, attitude. **2** *it's good policy to listen to your elders* PRACTICE, custom, idea, procedure, conduct, convention.

polish ▶ verb **1** *I polished his shoes* SHINE, wax, buff, rub up/down; gloss, burnish; varnish, oil, glaze, lacquer, japan, shellac. **2** *polish up your essay* PERFECT, refine, improve, hone, enhance; brush up, revise, edit, correct, rewrite, go over, touch up; *informal* clean up.
▶ noun **1** *furniture polish* WAX, glaze, varnish; lacquer, japan, shellac. **2** *a good surface polish* SHINE, gloss, lustre, sheen, sparkle, patina, finish. **3** *his polish made him stand out* SOPHISTICATION, refinement, urbanity, suaveness, elegance, style, grace, finesse, cultivation, civility, gentility, breeding, courtesy, (good) manners; *informal* class.
■ **polish something off** (*informal*) **1** *he polished off an apple pie* EAT, finish, consume, devour, guzzle, wolf down, down, bolt; drink up, drain, quaff, gulp (down), binge on, gorge on; *informal* stuff oneself with, put away, scoff, shovel down, pig out on, swill, knock back, scarf (down/up), snarf (down/up). **2** *the enemy tried to polish him off* DESTROY, finish off, dispatch, do away with, eliminate, kill, liquidate; *informal* bump off, knock off, do in, take out, dispose of; rub out. **3** *I'll polish off the last few pages* COMPLETE, finish, deal with, accomplish, discharge, do; end, conclude, close, finalize, round off, wind up; *informal* wrap up, sew up.

polished ▶ adjective **1** *a polished table* SHINY, glossy, gleaming, lustrous, glassy; waxed, buffed, burnished; varnished, glazed, lacquered, japanned, shellacked. **2** *a polished performance* EXPERT, accomplished, masterly, masterful, skilful, adept, adroit, dexterous; impeccable, flawless, perfect, consummate, exquisite, outstanding, excellent, superb, superlative, first-rate, fine; *informal* ace. **3** *polished manners* REFINED, cultivated, civilized, well-bred, polite, courteous, genteel, decorous, respectable, urbane, suave, sophisticated.
— OPPOSITES: dull, inexpert, gauche.

polite ▶ adjective **1** *a very polite girl* WELL-MANNERED, civil, courteous, mannerly, respectful, deferential, well-behaved, well-bred, gentlemanly, ladylike, genteel, gracious, urbane; tactful, diplomatic. **2** *polite society* CIVILIZED, refined, cultured, sophisticated, genteel, courtly.
— OPPOSITES: rude, uncivilized.

politic ▶ adjective WISE, prudent, sensible, judicious, canny, sagacious, shrewd, astute; recommended, advantageous, beneficial, profitable, desirable, advisable; appropriate, suitable, fitting, apt.
— OPPOSITES: unwise.

political ▶ adjective **1** *the political affairs of the nation* GOVERNMENTAL, government, constitutional, ministerial, parliamentary, diplomatic, legislative, administrative, bureaucratic; public, civic, state. **2** *he's a political man* POLITICALLY ACTIVE, party (political); militant, factional, partisan.

politician ▶ noun LEGISLATOR, elected official, Member of Parliament, MP, minister, statesman, stateswoman, public servant; senator, congressman/woman; *informal* politico, pol.

politics ▶ noun **1** *a career in politics* GOVERNMENT, affairs of state, public affairs; diplomacy. **2** *he studies politics* POLITICAL SCIENCE, civics, statecraft. **3** *what are his politics?* POLITICAL VIEWS, political leanings, party politics. **4** *office politics* POWER STRUGGLE, machinations, manoeuvring, opportunism, realpolitik.

poll ▶ noun **1** *a second-round poll* VOTE, ballot, show of hands, referendum, plebiscite; election. **2** *the poll was*

unduly low VOTING FIGURES, vote, returns, count, tally. **3** *a poll to investigate holiday choices* SURVEY, opinion poll, straw poll, canvass, market research, census.
▶ verb **1** *most of those polled supported him* CANVASS, survey, ask, question, interview, ballot. **2** *she polled 119 votes* GET, gain, register, record, return.

pollute ▶ verb **1** *fish farms will pollute the lake* CONTAMINATE, adulterate, taint, poison, foul, dirty, soil, infect; *literary* befoul. **2** *propaganda polluted this nation* CORRUPT, poison, warp, pervert, deprave, defile, blight, sully; *literary* besmirch.
— OPPOSITES: purify.

pollution ▶ noun **1** *air and water pollution* CONTAMINATION, adulteration, impurity; dirt, filth, toxins, infection; smog. **2** *the pollution of young minds* CORRUPTION, defilement, poisoning, warping, depravation, sullying, violation.

pomp ▶ noun CEREMONY, ceremonial, solemnity, ritual, display, spectacle, pageantry; show, showiness, ostentation, splendour, grandeur, magnificence, majesty, stateliness, glory, opulence, brilliance, drama, resplendence, splendidness; *informal* razzmatazz.

pompous ▶ adjective SELF-IMPORTANT, imperious, overbearing, domineering, magisterial, pontifical, sententious, grandiose, affected, pretentious, puffed up, arrogant, vain, haughty, proud, conceited, egotistic, supercilious, condescending, patronizing; *informal* snooty, uppity, uppish.
— OPPOSITES: modest.

pond ▶ noun POOL, water hole, lake, tarn, reservoir, slough, (*Nfld*) steady ♣, beaver pond, (*Maritimes*) headpond ♣, (*Maritimes*) flowage ♣, (*Atlantic*) barachois ♣, pothole, (*Nfld*) gully ♣, (*Prairies*) dugout ♣, tank.

ponder ▶ verb THINK ABOUT, contemplate, consider, review, reflect on, mull over, meditate on, muse on, deliberate about, cogitate on, dwell on, brood on, ruminate on, chew over, puzzle over, turn over in one's mind.

ponderous ▶ adjective **1** *a ponderous dance* CLUMSY, heavy, awkward, lumbering, slow, cumbersome, ungainly, graceless, uncoordinated, blundering; *informal* clodhopping, clunky. **2** *his ponderous sentences* LABOURED, laborious, awkward, clumsy, forced, stilted, unnatural, artificial; stodgy, lifeless, plodding, pedestrian, boring, dull, tedious, monotonous; over-elaborate, convoluted, windy.
— OPPOSITES: light, lively.

pontifical ▶ adjective POMPOUS, cocksure, self-important, arrogant, superior; opinionated, dogmatic, doctrinaire, authoritarian, domineering; adamant, obstinate, stubborn, single-minded, inflexible.
— OPPOSITES: humble.

pontificate ▶ verb HOLD FORTH, expound, declaim, preach, lay down the law, sound off, dogmatize, sermonize, moralize, lecture; *informal* preachify, mouth off.

pooh-pooh ▶ verb (*informal*) DISMISS, reject, spurn, rebuff, wave aside, disregard, discount; play down, make light of, belittle, deride, mock, scorn, scoff at, sneer at.

pool¹ ▶ noun **1** *pools of water* PUDDLE, pond, slough; *literary* plash. **2** *the hotel has a pool* SWIMMING POOL, baths, lap pool, natatorium.

pool² ▶ noun **1** *a pool of skilled labour* SUPPLY, reserve(s), reservoir, fund; store, stock, accumulation, cache. **2** *a pool of money for emergencies* FUND, reserve, kitty, pot, bank, purse. **3** *the office hockey pool* LOTTERY, bet.

▶ **verb** *they pooled their skills* COMBINE, amalgamate, group, join, unite, merge; fuse, conglomerate, integrate; share.

poor ▶ **adjective 1** *a poor family* POVERTY-STRICKEN, penniless, moneyless, impoverished, low-income, necessitous, impecunious, indigent, needy, destitute, pauperized, unable to make ends meet, without a sou; insolvent, in debt, without a cent (to one's name); *informal* (flat) broke, hard up, cleaned out, strapped, without two coins/cents to rub together; *formal* penurious. **2** *poor workmanship* SUBSTANDARD, below par, bad, deficient, defective, faulty, imperfect, inferior; appalling, abysmal, atrocious, awful, terrible, dreadful, unsatisfactory, second-rate, third-rate, tinpot, shoddy, crude, lamentable, deplorable, inadequate, unacceptable; *informal* crummy, lame, crappy, rubbishy, dismal, bum, rotten. **3** *a poor crop* MEAGRE, scanty, scant, paltry, disappointing, limited, reduced, modest, insufficient, inadequate, sparse, spare, deficient, insubstantial, skimpy, short, small, lean, slender; *informal* measly, stingy, pathetic, piddling; *formal* exiguous. **4** *poor soil* UNPRODUCTIVE, barren, unyielding, unfruitful; arid, sterile. **5** *the waters are poor in nutrients* DEFICIENT, lacking, wanting, weak; short of, low on. **6** *you poor thing!* UNFORTUNATE, unlucky, luckless, unhappy, hapless, ill-fated, ill-starred, pitiable, pitiful, wretched.
— OPPOSITES: rich, superior, good, fertile, lucky.

poorly ▶ **adverb** *the text is poorly written* BADLY, deficiently, defectively, imperfectly, incompetently; appallingly, abysmally, atrociously, awfully, dreadfully; crudely, shoddily, inadequately.

▶ **adjective** *she felt poorly* ILL, unwell, not (very) well, ailing, indisposed, out of sorts, under/below par, peaky, peaked; sick, queasy, nauseous; off; *informal* under the weather, funny, peculiar, lousy, rough.

pop ▶ **verb 1** *champagne corks popped* GO BANG, go off; crack, snap, burst, explode. **2** *I'm just popping home* GO; drop in, stop by, visit; *informal* whip, nip. **3** *pop a bag over the pot* PUT, place, slip, slide, stick, set, lay, install, position, arrange.

▶ **noun 1** *the balloons burst with a pop* BANG, crack, snap; explosion, report. **2** (*informal*) *a bottle of pop* SOFT DRINK, fizzy drink, soda, carbonated drink.

■ **pop up** APPEAR (SUDDENLY), occur (suddenly), arrive, materialize, come along, happen, emerge, arise, crop up, turn up, present itself, come to light; *informal* show up.

pope ▶ **noun** PONTIFF, Bishop of Rome, Holy Father, Vicar of Christ, His Holiness.
— RELATED TERMS: papal, pontifical.

pop music ▶ **noun** POP, popular music, Top 40, bubble gum music, chart music.

poppycock ▶ **noun** (*informal*) NONSENSE, rubbish, claptrap, balderdash, blather, moonshine, garbage; *informal* rot, tripe, jive, hogwash, baloney, drivel, bilge, bunk, eyewash, piffle, phooey, twaddle, codswallop; *informal* bushwa, malarkey, gobbledegook, bafflegab, mumbo-jumbo; *informal, dated* bunkum, tommyrot.

populace ▶ **noun** POPULATION, inhabitants, residents, natives; community, country, (general) public, people, nation; common people, man/woman in the street, masses, multitude, rank and file, commonalty, commonality, third estate, plebeians, proletariat; *informal* proles, plebs; Joe Public, John Q.

Public; *formal* denizens; *derogatory* the hoi polloi, common herd, rabble, riff-raff.

popular ▶ **adjective 1** *the most popular restaurant* WELL-LIKED, favoured, sought-after, in demand, desired, wanted; commercial, marketable, fashionable, trendy, in vogue, all the rage, hot; *informal* in, cool, big. **2** *popular science* NON-SPECIALIST, non-technical, amateur, lay person's, general, middle-of-the-road; accessible, simplified, plain, simple, easy, straightforward, understandable; mass-market, middlebrow, lowbrow, pop. **3** *popular opinion* WIDESPREAD, general, common, current, prevalent, prevailing, standard, stock; ordinary, usual, accepted, established, acknowledged, conventional, orthodox. **4** *a popular movement for independence* MASS, general, communal, collective, social, collaborative, group, civil, public.
— OPPOSITES: highbrow.

popularize ▶ **verb 1** *tobacco was popularized by Sir Walter Raleigh* MAKE POPULAR, make fashionable; market, publicize; *informal* hype. **2** *he popularized the subject* SIMPLIFY, make accessible, give mass-market appeal to, universalize, vulgarize. **3** *the report popularized the unfounded notion* GIVE CURRENCY TO, spread, propagate, give credence to.

popularly ▶ **adverb 1** *old age is popularly associated with illness* WIDELY, generally, universally, commonly, usually, customarily, habitually, conventionally, traditionally, as a rule. **2** *the bar was popularly known as 'the May'* INFORMALLY, unofficially; by lay people. **3** *the President is popularly elected* DEMOCRATICALLY, by the people.

populate ▶ **verb 1** *the state is populated by 40,000 people* INHABIT, occupy, people; live in, reside in. **2** *an attempt to populate the island* SETTLE, colonize, people, occupy, move into, make one's home in.

population ▶ **noun** INHABITANTS, residents, people, citizens, citizenry, public, community, populace, society, body politic, natives, occupants; *formal* denizens.
— RELATED TERMS: demo-.

populous ▶ **adjective** DENSELY POPULATED, heavily populated, congested, crowded, packed, jammed, crammed, teeming, swarming, seething, crawling; *informal* jam-packed.
— OPPOSITES: deserted.

porch ▶ **noun** VESTIBULE, foyer, entrance (hall), entry, portico, lobby; veranda, terrace; (*Nfld*) linny ♣, stoop; *Architecture* lanai, tambour, narthex.

pore[1] ▶ **noun** *pores in the skin* OPENING, orifice, aperture, hole, outlet, inlet, vent; *Biology* stoma, foramen.

pore[2] ▶ **verb** *they pored over the map* STUDY, read intently, peruse, scrutinize, scan, examine, go over.

pornographic ▶ **adjective** OBSCENE, indecent, crude, lewd, dirty, vulgar, smutty, filthy; erotic, titillating, arousing, suggestive, sexy, risqué; off-colour, adult, X-rated, hard-core, soft-core; *informal* porn, porno, blue, skin.
— OPPOSITES: wholesome.

pornography ▶ **noun** erotica, pornographic material, dirty books; smut, filth, vice; *informal* (hard/soft) porn, porno, girlie magazines, skin flicks.

porous ▶ **adjective** PERMEABLE, penetrable, pervious, cellular, holey; absorbent, absorptive, spongy.
— OPPOSITES: impermeable.

porridge ▶ **noun** OATMEAL, mush; *proprietary* Red River Cereal ♣; stirabout, samp.

port¹ ► noun **1** *the German port of Kiel* SEAPORT. **2** *shells exploded down by the port* HARBOUR, dock(s), haven, marina; anchorage, moorage, harbourage, roads.

port² ► noun *push the supply pipes into the ports* APERTURE, opening, outlet, inlet, socket, vent.

portable ► adjective TRANSPORTABLE, movable, mobile, travel; lightweight, compact, handy, convenient.

portage ► noun CARRY, carrying place, portage trail/path.

portal ► noun DOORWAY, gateway, entrance, exit, opening; door, gate, entryway; *formal* egress.

portend ► verb PRESAGE, augur, foreshadow, foretell, prophesy; be a sign, warn, be an omen, indicate, herald, signal, bode, promise, threaten, signify, spell, denote; *literary* betoken, foretoken, forebode.

portent ► noun **1** *a portent of things to come* OMEN, sign, signal, token, forewarning, warning, foreshadowing, prediction, forecast, prophecy, harbinger, augury, auspice, presage; writing on the wall, indication, hint; *literary* foretoken. **2** *the word carries terrifying portent* SIGNIFICANCE, importance, import, consequence, meaning, weight; *formal* moment.

portentous ► adjective **1** *portentous signs* OMINOUS, warning, premonitory, threatening, menacing, ill-omened, foreboding, inauspicious, unfavourable. **2** *portentous dialogue* POMPOUS, bombastic, self-important, pontifical, solemn, sonorous, grandiloquent.

porter¹ ► noun *a porter helped with the bags* CARRIER, bearer, redcap.

porter² ► noun *the college porter* DOORMAN, doorkeeper, commissionaire, gatekeeper.

portfolio ► noun **1** *an artist's portfolio* SAMPLES, examples, selection. **2** *your financial portfolio* INVESTMENTS, holdings, funds. **3** *the minister took on the environment portfolio* OFFICE, department, ministry; position, post, bailiwick, responsibility. **4** *he kept the papers in his portfolio* BRIEFCASE, case, valise, bag, attaché.

portion ► noun **1** *the upper portion of the chimney* PART, piece, bit, section, segment. **2** *her portion of the allowance* SHARE, slice, quota, quantum, part, percentage, amount, quantity, ration, fraction, division, allocation, measure; *informal* cut, rake-off. **3** *a portion of cake* HELPING, serving, amount, quantity; plateful, bowlful; slice, piece, chunk, wedge, slab, hunk. **4** *(archaic) poverty was certain to be his portion. See* DESTINY sense 1.
► verb *she portioned out the food* SHARE OUT, allocate, allot, apportion; distribute, hand out, deal out, dole out, give out, dispense, mete out; *informal* divvy up.

portly ► adjective STOUT, plump, fat, overweight, heavy, corpulent, fleshy, paunchy, pot-bellied, well padded, rotund, stocky, heavy-set, bulky; *informal* tubby, roly-poly, beefy, porky, pudgy; *informal* corn-fed. — OPPOSITES: slim.

portrait ► noun **1** *a portrait of the King* PAINTING, picture, drawing, sketch, likeness, image, study, miniature; *informal* oil; *formal* portraiture. **2** *a vivid portrait of Italy* DESCRIPTION, portrayal, representation, depiction, impression, account; sketch, vignette, profile.

portray ► verb **1** *she portrays the older architecture of her province* PAINT, draw, sketch, picture, depict, represent, illustrate, render. **2** *the Newfoundland*

portrayed by Proulx DESCRIBE, depict, characterize, represent, present, delineate, evoke, tell of. **3** *the actor portrays a spy* PLAY, act the part of, take the role of, represent, appear as; *formal* personate.

portrayal ► noun **1** *a portrayal of a parrot* PAINTING, picture, portrait, drawing, sketch, representation, depiction, study. **2** *her portrayal of adolescence* DESCRIPTION, representation, characterization, depiction, evocation. **3** *Brando's portrayal of Corleone* PERFORMANCE AS, representation, interpretation, rendering, reading; *formal* personation.

pose ► verb **1** *pollution poses a threat to health* CONSTITUTE, present, create, cause, produce, be. **2** *the question posed earlier* RAISE, ask, put, set, submit, advance, propose, suggest, moot. **3** *she posed for the artist* MODEL, sit. **4** *he posed her on the sofa* POSITION, place, put, arrange, dispose, locate, situate. **5** *fashion victims were posing at the bar* BEHAVE AFFECTEDLY, strike a pose, posture, attitudinize, put on airs; *informal* show off.
► noun **1** *a sexy pose* POSTURE, position, stance, attitude, bearing. **2** *her pose of aggrieved innocence* PRETENSE, act, affectation, facade, show, front, display, masquerade, posture.
■ **pose as** PRETEND TO BE, impersonate, pass oneself off as, masquerade as, profess to be, represent oneself as; *formal* personate.

poser¹ ► noun *this situation's a bit of a poser* DIFFICULT QUESTION, vexed question, awkward problem, tough one, puzzle, mystery, conundrum, puzzler, enigma, riddle; *informal* dilemma, toughie, stumper.

poser² ► noun *he's such a poser* EXHIBITIONIST, poseur, posturer, fake; *informal* show-off.

poseur ► noun. *See* POSER².

posh ► adjective *a posh hotel* SMART, stylish, fancy, high-class, fashionable, chic, luxurious, luxury, deluxe, exclusive, opulent, lavish, grand, showy, upscale, upmarket; *informal* classy, swanky, snazzy, plush, ritzy, flash, la-di-da, fancy-dancy, fancy-schmancy, swank, tony.

posit ► verb POSTULATE, put forward, advance, propound, submit, hypothesize, propose, assert.

position ► noun **1** *the aircraft's position* LOCATION, place, situation, spot, site, locality, setting, area; whereabouts, bearings, orientation; *technical* locus. **2** *a standing position* POSTURE, stance, attitude, pose. **3** *our financial position* SITUATION, state, condition, circumstances; predicament, plight, strait(s). **4** *the two parties jockeyed for position* ADVANTAGE, the upper hand, the edge, the whip hand, primacy; *informal* the catbird seat. **5** *their position in society* STATUS, place, level, rank, standing, stature, prestige, influence, reputation, importance, consequence, class; *dated* station. **6** *a secretarial position* JOB, post, situation, appointment, role, occupation, employment; office, capacity, duty, function; opening, vacancy, placement. **7** *the government's position on the matter* VIEWPOINT, opinion, outlook, attitude, stand, standpoint, stance, perspective, approach, slant, thinking, policy, feelings.
► verb *he positioned a chair between them* PUT, place, locate, situate, set, site, stand, station; plant, stick, install; arrange, dispose; *informal* plonk, park.

positive ► adjective **1** *a positive response* AFFIRMATIVE, favourable, good, approving, enthusiastic, supportive, encouraging. **2** *do something positive* CONSTRUCTIVE, practical, useful, productive, helpful, worthwhile, beneficial, effective. **3** *she seems a lot more positive* OPTIMISTIC, hopeful, confident, cheerful,

sanguine, buoyant; *informal* upbeat. **4** *positive economic signs* FAVOURABLE, good, promising, encouraging, heartening, propitious, auspicious. **5** *positive proof* DEFINITE, conclusive, certain, categorical, unequivocal, incontrovertible, indisputable, undeniable, unmistakable, irrefutable, reliable, concrete, tangible, clear-cut, explicit, firm, decisive, real, actual. **6** *I'm positive he's coming back* CERTAIN, sure, convinced, confident, satisfied, assured.
— OPPOSITES: negative, pessimistic, doubtful, unsure.

positively ▶ adverb **1** *I could not positively identify the voice* CONFIDENTLY, definitely, emphatically, categorically, with certainty, conclusively, unquestionably, undoubtedly, indisputably, unmistakably, assuredly. **2** *he was positively livid* ABSOLUTELY, really, downright, thoroughly, completely, utterly, totally, extremely, fairly; *informal* plain.

posse ▶ noun GANG, band, group, crowd, pack, horde, herd, throng, mob, swarm, troop, cluster; company, gathering; *informal* bunch, gaggle, load.

possess ▶ verb **1** *the only hat she possessed* OWN, have (to one's name), hold. **2** *he did not possess a sense of humour* HAVE, be blessed with, be endowed with; enjoy, boast. **3** *a supernatural force possessed him* TAKE CONTROL OF, take over, control, dominate, influence; bewitch, enchant, enthrall. **4** *she was possessed by a need to talk to him* OBSESS, haunt, preoccupy, consume; eat someone up, prey on one's mind.
■ **possess oneself of** ACQUIRE, obtain, get (hold of), procure, get one's hands on; take, seize; *informal* get one's mitts on.

possessed ▶ adjective MAD, demented, insane, crazed, berserk, out of one's mind; bewitched, enchanted, haunted, under a spell.

possession ▶ noun **1** *the estate came into their possession* OWNERSHIP, control, hands, keeping, care, custody, charge, hold, title, guardianship. **2** *her possession of the premises* OCCUPANCY, occupation, tenure, holding, tenancy. **3** *she packed her possessions* BELONGINGS, things, property, (worldly) goods, (personal) effects, assets, chattels, movables, valuables; stuff, bits and pieces; luggage, baggage; *informal* gear, junk. **4** *colonial possessions* COLONY, dependency, territory, holding, protectorate.
■ **take possession of** SEIZE, appropriate, impound, expropriate, sequestrate, sequester, confiscate; take, get, acquire, obtain, procure, possess oneself of, get hold of, get one's hands on; capture, commandeer, requisition; *Law* distrain; *informal* get one's mitts on.

possessive ▶ adjective **1** *he was very possessive* PROPRIETORIAL, overprotective, controlling, dominating, jealous, clingy. **2** *kids are possessive of their own property* COVETOUS, selfish, unwilling to share; grasping, greedy, acquisitive, grabby.

possibility ▶ noun **1** *there is a possibility that he might be alive* CHANCE, likelihood, probability, hope; risk, hazard, danger, fear. **2** *they discussed the possibility of launching a new project* FEASIBILITY, practicability, chances, odds, probability. **3** *buying a smaller house is one possibility* OPTION, alternative, choice, course of action, solution. **4** *the idea has distinct possibilities* POTENTIAL, promise, prospects.

possible ▶ adjective **1** *it's not possible to check the figures* FEASIBLE, practicable, practical, viable, within the bounds/realms of possibility, attainable, achievable, workable; *informal* doable. **2** *a possible reason for his disappearance* CONCEIVABLE, plausible,

imaginable, believable, likely, potential, probable, credible. **3** *a possible future leader* POTENTIAL, prospective, likely, probable.
— OPPOSITES: unlikely.

possibly ▶ adverb **1** *possibly he took the boy with him* PERHAPS, maybe, it is possible, for all one knows, very likely; *literary* peradventure, perchance, mayhap. **2** *you can't possibly refuse* CONCEIVABLY, under any circumstances, by any means. **3** *could you possibly help me?* PLEASE, kindly, be so good as to.

post[1] ▶ noun *wooden posts* POLE, stake, upright, longer ♣, shaft, prop, support, picket, strut, pillar, pale, paling, stanchion; *historical* puncheon.
▶ verb **1** *the notice posted on the wall* AFFIX, attach, fasten, display, pin (up), put up, stick (up), tack (up). **2** *the group posted a net profit* ANNOUNCE, report, make known, publish.

post[2] ▶ noun *Canada Post* MAIL, the postal service; airmail, surface mail, registered mail; *informal* snail mail.
▶ verb **1** *post the order form today* MAIL, send (off), put in the mail. **2** *post the transaction in the second column* RECORD, write in, enter, register.
■ **keep someone posted** KEEP INFORMED, keep up to date, keep in the picture, keep briefed, update, fill in; *informal* keep up to speed.

post[3] ▶ noun **1** *there were seventy candidates for the post* JOB, position, appointment, situation, place; vacancy, opening. **2** *back to your posts!* (ASSIGNED) POSITION, station, observation post.
▶ verb **1** *he'd been posted to Berlin* SEND, assign to a post, dispatch. **2** *armed guards were posted beside the exit* PUT ON DUTY, station, position, situate, locate.

poster ▶ noun NOTICE, placard, bill, sign, advertisement, playbill.

posterior ▶ adjective **1** *the posterior part of the skull* REAR, hind, back, hinder; *technical* dorsal, caudal. **2** *(formal) a date posterior to the Reform Bill* LATER THAN, subsequent to, following, after.
— OPPOSITES: anterior, previous.
▶ noun *(humorous) her plump posterior.* See BUTTOCKS.

posterity ▶ noun FUTURE GENERATIONS, the future.

post-haste ▶ adverb AS QUICKLY AS POSSIBLE, without delay, (very) quickly, speedily, without further/more ado, with all speed, promptly, immediately, at once, straight away, right away; *informal* pronto, straight off.

postman, postwoman ▶ noun POSTAL WORKER, mailman, letter carrier; *informal* postie.

post-mortem ▶ noun **1** *the hospital carried out a post-mortem* AUTOPSY, post-mortem examination, PM, necropsy. **2** *a post-mortem of her failed relationship* ANALYSIS, evaluation, assessment, appraisal, examination, review.

postpone ▶ verb PUT OFF/BACK, delay, defer, reschedule, adjourn, shelve, put over, take a rain check on; *informal* put on ice, put on the back burner; *rare* remit.
— OPPOSITES: bring forward.

postponement ▶ noun DEFERRAL, deferment, delay, putting off/back, rescheduling, adjournment, shelving.

postscript ▶ noun **1** *a handwritten postscript* AFTERTHOUGHT, PS, additional remark. **2** *he added postscripts of his own* ADDENDUM, supplement, appendix, codicil, afterword, addition.

postulate ▶ verb PUT FORWARD, suggest, advance, posit, hypothesize, propose; assume, presuppose, presume, take for granted.

posture ▶ noun **1** *a kneeling posture* POSITION, pose, attitude, stance. **2** *good posture* BEARING, carriage, stance, comportment. **3** *trade unions adopted a militant posture* ATTITUDE, stance, standpoint, point of view, opinion, position, frame of mind.
▶ verb *Keith postured, flexing his biceps* POSE, strike an attitude, strut.

posy ▶ noun BOUQUET, bunch (of flowers), spray, nosegay, corsage; boutonniere.

pot ▶ noun **1** *pots and pans* COOKING UTENSIL, pan, saucepan, casserole, stewpot, stockpot, kettle. **2** *earthenware pots* FLOWERPOT, planter, jardinière. **3** *Jim raked in half the pot* BANK, kitty, pool, purse, jackpot.
■ **go to pot** (*informal*) DETERIORATE, decline, degenerate, go to (rack and) ruin, go downhill, go to seed, become run-down; *informal* go to the dogs, go down the tubes, go haywire.

potable ▶ adjective DRINKABLE, palatable, fit to drink, pure, clean, safe, unpolluted, untainted, uncontaminated.

potato ▶ noun spud, tater, tattie, *Nfld & Irish* pratie ✦.

pot-bellied ▶ adjective PAUNCHY, beer-bellied, portly, rotund; *informal* tubby, roly-poly.

pot-belly ▶ noun PAUNCH, (beer) belly; *informal* beer gut, Molson muscle ✦, pot, tummy.

potency ▶ noun **1** *the potency of his words* FORCEFULNESS, force, effectiveness, persuasiveness, cogency, influence, strength, authoritativeness, authority, power, powerfulness; *literary* puissance. **2** *the potency of the drugs* STRENGTH, powerfulness, power, effectiveness; *formal* efficacy; efficaciousness.

potent ▶ adjective **1** *a potent political force* POWERFUL, strong, mighty, formidable, influential, dominant, forceful; *literary* puissant. **2** *a potent argument* FORCEFUL, convincing, cogent, compelling, persuasive, powerful, strong. **3** *a potent drug* STRONG, powerful, effective; *formal* efficacious.
— OPPOSITES: weak.

potentate ▶ noun RULER, monarch, sovereign, king, queen, emperor, empress, sultan, shah, raja, pharaoh.

potential ▶ adjective *a potential source of conflict* POSSIBLE, likely, prospective, future, probable; latent, inherent, undeveloped.
▶ noun *economic potential* POSSIBILITIES, potentiality, prospects; promise, capability, capacity.

potion ▶ noun CONCOCTION, mixture, brew, elixir, philtre, drink, decoction; medicine, tonic; *literary* draft.

potpourri ▶ noun MIXTURE, assortment, collection, selection, assemblage, medley, miscellany, mix, mélange, variety, mixed bag, patchwork, bricolage; ragbag, mishmash, salmagundi, jumble, farrago, hodgepodge, gallimaufry.

pottery ▶ noun CHINA, crockery, ceramics, earthenware, stoneware.

pouch ▶ noun **1** *a leather pouch* BAG, purse, sack, sac, pocket. **2** *a kangaroo's pouch* Zoology marsupium.

pounce ▶ verb *two men pounced on him* JUMP ON, spring, leap, dive, lunge, fall on, set on, attack suddenly; *informal* jump, mug.
▶ noun *a sudden pounce* LEAP, spring, jump, dive, lunge, bound.

pound¹ ▶ verb **1** *the two men pounded him with their fists* BEAT, strike, hit, batter, thump, pummel, schmuck ✦, punch, rain blows on, belabour, hammer, thrash, set on, tear into; *informal* bash,

clobber, wallop, beat the living daylights out of, whack, thwack, lay into, pitch into, light into, whale. **2** *waves pounded the seafront* BEAT AGAINST, crash against, batter, dash against, lash, buffet. **3** *gunships pounded the capital* BOMBARD, bomb, shell, fire on; *archaic* cannonade. **4** *pound the cloves with salt* CRUSH, grind, pulverize, mill, mash, pulp; *technical* triturate. **5** *I heard him pounding along the gangway* WALK/RUN HEAVILY, stomp, lumber, clomp, clump, tramp, tromp, trudge. **6** *her heart was pounding* THROB, thump, thud, hammer, pulse, race, go pit-a-pat; *literary* pant, thrill.

pound² ▶ noun *a dog pound* ENCLOSURE, compound, pen, yard, corral.

pour ▶ verb **1** *blood was pouring from his nose* STREAM, flow, run, gush, course, jet, spurt, surge, spill. **2** *Amy poured wine into his glass* TIP, let flow, splash, spill, decant; *informal* slosh, slop. **3** *it was pouring when we set out* RAIN HEAVILY/HARD, teem down, pelt down, come down in torrents/sheets, rain cats and dogs, bucket down. **4** *people poured off the train* THRONG, crowd, swarm, stream, flood.

pout ▶ verb *Crystal pouted sullenly* LOOK PETULANT, pull a face, look sulky.
▶ noun *a childish pout* PETULANT EXPRESSION, sulky expression, moue.

poverty ▶ noun **1** *abject poverty* PENURY, destitution, pauperism, pauperdom, beggary, indigence, pennilessness, impoverishment, neediness, need, hardship, impecuniousness. **2** *the poverty of choice* SCARCITY, deficiency, dearth, shortage, paucity, insufficiency, absence, lack. **3** *the poverty of her imagination* INFERIORITY, mediocrity, poorness, sterility.
— OPPOSITES: wealth, abundance.

poverty-stricken ▶ adjective EXTREMELY POOR, impoverished, destitute, penniless, as poor as a church mouse, in penury, impecunious, indigent, needy, in need/want, without a cent (to one's name); *informal* without two coins/cents to rub together; *formal* penurious.

powder ▶ noun DUST, fine particles; talcum powder, talc.
▶ verb **1** *she powdered her face* DUST, sprinkle/cover with powder. **2** *the grains are powdered* CRUSH, grind, pulverize, pound, mill; *technical* comminute. **3** *powdered milk* dry, freeze-dry; *technical* lyophilize.

powdery ▶ adjective FINE, dry, fine-grained, powder-like, dusty, chalky, floury, sandy, crumbly, friable.

power ▶ noun **1** *the power of speech* ABILITY, capacity, capability, potential, faculty, competence. **2** *the unions wield enormous power* CONTROL, authority, influence, dominance, mastery, domination, dominion, sway, weight, leverage; *informal* clout, teeth, drag; *literary* puissance. **3** *police have the power to stop and search* AUTHORITY, right, authorization, warrant, licence. **4** *a major international power* STATE, country, nation. **5** *he hit the ball with as much power as he could* STRENGTH, powerfulness, might, force, forcefulness, vigour, energy; brawn, muscle; *informal* punch; *literary* thew. **6** *the power of his arguments* FORCEFULNESS, powerfulness, potency, strength, force, cogency, persuasiveness. **7** *the new engine has more power* DRIVING FORCE, horsepower, h.p., acceleration; *informal* oomph. **8** *generating power from waste* ENERGY, electrical power. **9** (*informal*) *the holiday did him a power of good* A GREAT DEAL OF, a lot of, much; *informal* lots of, loads of.
— OPPOSITES: inability, weakness.

■ **have someone in/under one's power** HAVE CONTROL OVER, have influence over, have under one's thumb, have at one's mercy, have in one's clutches, have in the palm of one's hand, have someone wrapped around one's little finger, have in one's hip pocket; *informal* have over a barrel.

■ **the powers that be** THE AUTHORITIES, the people in charge, the government.

powerful ▶ adjective **1** *powerful shoulders* STRONG, muscular, muscly, sturdy, strapping, robust, brawny, burly, athletic, manly, well built, solid; *informal* beefy, hunky; *dated* stalwart; *literary* stark, thewy. **2** *a powerful drink* INTOXICATING, hard, strong, stiff, industrial-strength; *formal* spirituous. **3** *a powerful blow* VIOLENT, forceful, hard; mighty. **4** *he felt a powerful desire to kiss her* INTENSE, keen, fierce, passionate, ardent, burning, strong, irresistible, overpowering, overwhelming. **5** *a powerful nation* INFLUENTIAL, strong, important, dominant, commanding, potent, forceful, formidable; *literary* puissant. **6** *a powerful critique* COGENT, compelling, convincing, persuasive, forceful; dramatic, graphic, vivid, moving.
— OPPOSITES: weak, gentle.

powerless ▶ adjective IMPOTENT, helpless, ineffectual, ineffective, useless, defenceless, vulnerable; lame-duck; *literary* impuissant.

practicable ▶ adjective REALISTIC, feasible, possible, within the bounds/realms of possibility, viable, reasonable, sensible, workable, achievable; *informal* doable.

practical ▶ adjective **1** *practical experience* EMPIRICAL, hands-on, actual, active, applied, heuristic, experiential. **2** *there are no practical alternatives* FEASIBLE, practicable, realistic, viable, workable, possible, reasonable, sensible; *informal* doable. **3** *practical clothes* FUNCTIONAL, sensible, utilitarian, workaday. **4** *try to be more practical* REALISTIC, sensible, down-to-earth, businesslike, commonsensical, hard-headed, no-nonsense; *informal* hard-nosed. **5** *a practical certainty* VIRTUAL, effective, near.
— OPPOSITES: theoretical.

practicality ▶ noun **1** *the practicality of the proposal* FEASIBILITY, practicability, viability, workability. **2** *practicality of design* FUNCTIONALISM, functionality, serviceability, utility. **3** *his calm practicality* (COMMON) SENSE, realism, pragmatism. **4** *the practicalities of army life* PRACTICAL DETAILS; *informal* nitty gritty, nuts and bolts.

practical joke ▶ noun TRICK, joke, prank, jape, hoax.

practically ▶ adverb **1** *the cinema was practically empty* ALMOST, (very) nearly, virtually, just about, all but, more or less, as good as, to all intents and purposes, verging on, bordering on; *informal* pretty near, pretty well; *literary* well-nigh. **2** *'You can't afford it,' he pointed out practically* REALISTICALLY, sensibly, reasonably.

practice ▶ noun **1** *the practice of radiotherapy* APPLICATION, exercise, use, operation, implementation, execution. **2** *common practice* CUSTOM, procedure, policy, convention, tradition; *formal* praxis. **3** *it takes lots of practice | the team's final practice* TRAINING, rehearsal, repetition, preparation; practice session, dummy run, run-through; *informal* dry run. **4** *the practice of medicine* PROFESSION, career, business, work. **5** *a small legal practice* BUSINESS, firm, office, company; *informal* outfit.

■ **in practice** IN REALITY, realistically, practically.

■ **out of practice** RUSTY, unpractised.

■ **put something into practice** USE, make use of, put to use, utilize, apply.

practise ▶ verb **1** *he practised the songs every day* REHEARSE, run through, go over/through, work on/at; polish, perfect. **2** *the performers were practising* TRAIN, rehearse, prepare, go through one's paces. **3** *we still practise these rituals today* CARRY OUT, perform, observe. **4** *she practises medicine* WORK AT, pursue a career in.

practised ▶ adjective EXPERT, experienced, seasoned, skilled, skilful, accomplished, proficient, talented, able, adept, consummate, master, masterly; *informal* crack, ace, mean, crackerjack.

pragmatic ▶ adjective PRACTICAL, matter of fact, sensible, down-to-earth, commonsensical, businesslike, having both/one's feet on the ground, hard-headed, no-nonsense; *informal* hard-nosed.
— OPPOSITES: impractical.

prairie ▶ noun PLAINS, grasslands.

■ (*Cdn*) **the Prairies** Alberta, Saskatchewan, and Manitoba; the Prairie Provinces.

praise ▶ verb **1** *the police praised Pauline for her courage* COMMEND, express admiration for, applaud, pay tribute to, speak highly of, eulogize, compliment, congratulate, sing the praises of, rave about, go into raptures about, heap praise on, wax lyrical about, make much of, pat on the back, take one's hat off to, lionize, admire, hail, ballyhoo; *formal* laud. **2** *we praise God* WORSHIP, glorify, honour, exalt, adore, pay tribute to, give thanks to, venerate, reverence; *formal* laud; *archaic* magnify.
— RELATED TERMS: laudatory.
— OPPOSITES: criticize.
▶ noun **1** *James was full of praise for the medical teams* APPROVAL, acclaim, admiration, approbation, acclamation, plaudits, congratulations, commendation; tribute, accolade, compliment, a pat on the back, eulogy, panegyric; *formal* encomium. **2** *give praise to God* HONOUR, thanks, glory, worship, devotion, adoration, reverence.

praiseworthy ▶ adjective COMMENDABLE, admirable, laudable, worthy (of admiration), meritorious, estimable, exemplary.

prance ▶ verb CAVORT, dance, jig, trip, caper, jump, leap, spring, bound, skip, hop, frisk, romp, frolic.

prank ▶ noun (PRACTICAL) JOKE, trick, piece of mischief, escapade, stunt, caper, jape, game, hoax, antic; *informal* lark.

prattle ▶ verb *he prattled on for ages.* See CHAT *verb.*
▶ noun *childish prattle.* See CHATTER *noun.*

pray ▶ verb **1** *let us pray* SAY ONE'S PRAYERS, make one's devotions, offer a prayer/prayers. **2** *she prayed God to forgive her* INVOKE, call on, implore, appeal to, entreat, beg, petition, supplicate; *literary* beseech.

prayer ▶ noun **1** *the priest's murmured prayers* INVOCATION, intercession, devotion; *archaic* orison. **2** *a quick prayer that she wouldn't bump into him* APPEAL, plea, entreaty, petition, supplication, invocation.

■ **not have a prayer** (*informal*) HAVE NO HOPE, have/ stand no chance, not have/stand (the ghost of) a chance; *informal* not have a hope in hell.

preach ▶ verb **1** *he preached to a large congregation* GIVE A SERMON/HOMILY, sermonize, address, speak. **2** *preaching the gospel* PROCLAIM, teach, spread, propagate, expound. **3** *they preach toleration* ADVOCATE, recommend, advise, urge, teach, counsel. **4** *who are*

you to preach at me? MORALIZE, sermonize, pontificate, lecture, harangue; *informal* preachify.
− RELATED TERMS: homiletic.

preacher ▶ **noun** MINISTER (OF RELIGION), parson, clergyman, clergywoman, member of the clergy, priest, imam, rabbi, man/woman of the cloth, man/woman of God, cleric, churchman, churchwoman, evangelist; *informal* reverend, padre, Holy Joe, sky pilot.

preaching ▶ **noun** RELIGIOUS TEACHING, message, sermons, Bible-thumping.

preachy ▶ **adjective** (*informal*) MORALISTIC, moralizing, sanctimonious, self-righteous, holier-than-thou, sententious.

preamble ▶ **noun** INTRODUCTION, preface, prologue; foreword, prelude, front matter; *informal* intro, lead-in; *formal* exordium, proem, prolegomenon.

pre-arranged ▶ **adjective** ARRANGED BEFOREHAND, agreed in advance, predetermined, pre-established, pre-planned.

precarious ▶ **adjective** UNCERTAIN, insecure, unpredictable, risky, parlous, hazardous, dangerous, unsafe; unsettled, unstable, unsteady, shaky; *informal* dicey, chancy, iffy.
− OPPOSITES: safe.

precaution ▶ **noun** SAFEGUARD, preventative/preventive measure, safety measure, contingency (plan), insurance.

precautionary ▶ **adjective** PREVENTATIVE, preventive, safety.

precede ▶ **verb 1** *commercials preceded the movie* GO/COME BEFORE, lead (up) to, pave/prepare the way for, herald, introduce, usher in. **2** *Catherine preceded him into the studio* GO AHEAD OF, go in front of, go before, go first, lead the way. **3** *he preceded the book with a poem* PREFACE, introduce, begin, open.
− OPPOSITES: follow.

precedence ▶ **noun** *quarrels over precedence* PRIORITY, rank, seniority, superiority, primacy, pre-eminence, eminence.
■ **take precedence over** TAKE PRIORITY OVER, outweigh, prevail over, come before.

precedent ▶ **noun** MODEL, exemplar, example, pattern, previous case, prior instance/example; paradigm, criterion, yardstick, standard.

preceding ▶ **adjective** FOREGOING, previous, prior, former, precedent, earlier, above, aforementioned, antecedent; *formal* anterior, prevenient.

precept ▶ **noun 1** *the precepts of Orthodox Judaism* PRINCIPLE, rule, tenet, canon, doctrine, command, order, decree, dictate, dictum, injunction, commandment; *Judaism* mitzvah; *formal* prescript. **2** *precepts that her grandmother used to quote* MAXIM, saying, adage, axiom, aphorism, apophthegm.

precinct ▶ **noun 1** *a pedestrian precinct* AREA, zone, sector. **2** *within the precincts of the City* BOUNDS, boundaries, limits, confines. **3** *the cathedral precinct* ENCLOSURE, close, court. **4** *the friendliest cop of the 20th precinct* division ♣.

precious ▶ **adjective 1** *precious works of art* VALUABLE, costly, expensive; invaluable, priceless, beyond price. **2** *her most precious possession* VALUED, cherished, treasured, prized, favourite, dear, dearest, beloved, darling, adored, loved, special. **3** *his precious manners* AFFECTED, over-refined, pretentious; *informal* la-di-da.

precipice ▶ **noun** CLIFF (FACE), steep cliff, rock face, sheer drop, crag, bluff, escarpment, (*BC, Alta., & North*) rampart ♣, scarp; *literary* steep.

precipitate ▶ **verb 1** *the incident precipitated a crisis*

BRING ABOUT/ON, cause, lead to, give rise to, instigate, trigger, spark, touch off, provoke, hasten, accelerate, expedite. **2** *they were precipitated down the mountain* HURL, catapult, throw, plunge, launch, fling, propel.
▶ **adjective 1** *their actions were precipitate* HASTY, overhasty, rash, hurried, rushed; impetuous, impulsive, spur-of-the-moment, precipitous, incautious, imprudent, injudicious, ill-advised, reckless, harum-scarum; *informal* previous; *literary* temerarious. **2** *a precipitate decline.* See PRECIPITOUS sense 2.

precipitous ▶ **adjective 1** *a precipitous drop* STEEP, sheer, perpendicular, abrupt, sharp, vertical. **2** *his fall from power was precipitous* SUDDEN, rapid, swift, abrupt, headlong, speedy, quick, fast, precipitate. **3** *she was too precipitous.* See PRECIPITATE adjective sense 1.

précis ▶ **noun** *a précis of the report* SUMMARY, synopsis, resumé, abstract, outline, summarization, summation; abridgement, digest, overview, epitome, wrap-up.
▶ **verb** *précising a passage* SUMMARIZE, sum up, give a summary/précis of, give the main points of; abridge, condense, shorten, synopsize, abstract, outline, abbreviate; *archaic* epitomize.

precise ▶ **adjective 1** *precise measurements* EXACT, accurate, correct, specific, detailed, explicit, unambiguous, definite. **2** *at that precise moment the car stopped* EXACT, particular, very, specific. **3** *the attention to detail is very precise* METICULOUS, careful, exact, scrupulous, punctilious, conscientious, particular, methodical, strict, rigorous.
− OPPOSITES: inaccurate.

precisely ▶ **adverb 1** *at 2 o'clock precisely* EXACTLY, sharp, promptly, prompt, dead (on), on the stroke of; *informal* bang (on), on the button/nose/dot. **2** *precisely the kind of man I am looking for* EXACTLY, absolutely, just, in all respects; *informal* to a T. **3** *fertilization can be timed precisely* ACCURATELY, exactly; clearly, distinctly, strictly. **4** *'So it's all done?' 'Precisely.'* YES, exactly, absolutely, (that's) right, quite so, indubitably, definitely; *informal* you bet, I'll say.

precision ▶ **noun** EXACTNESS, exactitude, accuracy, correctness, preciseness; care, carefulness, meticulousness, scrupulousness, punctiliousness, methodicalness, rigour, rigorousness.

preclude ▶ **verb** PREVENT, make it impossible for, rule out, stop, prohibit, debar, bar, hinder, impede, inhibit, exclude.

precocious ▶ **adjective** ADVANCED FOR ONE'S AGE, forward, mature, gifted, talented, clever, intelligent, quick; *informal* smart.
− OPPOSITES: backward.

preconceived ▶ **adjective** PREDETERMINED, prejudged; prejudiced, biased.

preconception ▶ **noun** PRECONCEIVED IDEA/NOTION, presupposition, assumption, presumption, prejudgment; prejudice.

precondition ▶ **noun** PREREQUISITE, (necessary/essential) condition, requirement, necessity, essential, imperative, sine qua non; *informal* must.

precursor ▶ **noun 1** *a three-stringed precursor of the guitar* FORERUNNER, predecessor, forefather, father, antecedent, ancestor, forebear. **2** *a precursor of disasters to come* HARBINGER, herald, sign, indication, portent, omen.

precursory ▶ **adjective** PRELIMINARY, prior, previous, introductory, preparatory, prefatory; *formal* anterior, prevenient.

predatory ► adjective **1** *predatory birds* PREDACIOUS, carnivorous, hunting, raptorial; of prey. **2** *a predatory gleam in his eyes* EXPLOITATIVE, wolfish, rapacious, vulturine, vulturous.

predecessor ► noun **1** *the Prime Minister's predecessor* FORERUNNER, precursor, antecedent. **2** *our Victorian predecessors* ANCESTOR, forefather, forebear, antecedent.
– OPPOSITES: successor, descendant.

predestined ► adjective PREORDAINED, ordained, predetermined, destined, fated.

predetermined ► adjective **1** *a predetermined budget* PRE-ARRANGED, established in advance, preset, set, fixed, agreed. **2** *our predetermined fate* PREDESTINED, preordained.

predicament ► noun DIFFICULT SITUATION, mess, difficulty, plight, quandary, muddle, mare's nest; *informal* hole, fix, jam, pickle, scrape, bind, tight spot/corner, dilemma, can of worms.

predicate ► verb BASE, be dependent, found, establish, rest, ground, premise.

predict ► verb FORECAST, foretell, foresee, prophesy, anticipate, tell in advance, envision, envisage; *literary* previse; *archaic* augur, presage.

predictable ► adjective FORESEEABLE, (only) to be expected, anticipated, foreseen, unsurprising; *informal* inevitable.

prediction ► noun FORECAST, prophecy, prognosis, prognostication, augury; projection, conjecture, guess.

predilection ► noun LIKING, fondness, preference, partiality, taste, penchant, weakness, soft spot, fancy, inclination, leaning, bias, propensity, bent, proclivity, predisposition, appetite.
– OPPOSITES: dislike.

predispose ► verb **1** *lack of exercise may predispose an individual to high blood pressure* MAKE SUSCEPTIBLE, make liable, make prone, make vulnerable, put at risk of. **2** *attitudes which predispose people to behave badly* LEAD, influence, sway, induce, prompt, dispose; bias, prejudice.

predisposed ► adjective INCLINED, prepared, ready, of a mind, disposed, minded, willing.

predisposition ► noun **1** *a predisposition to heart disease* SUSCEPTIBILITY, proneness, tendency, liability, inclination, disposition, vulnerability. **2** *their political predispositions* PREFERENCE, predilection, inclination, leaning.

predominance ► noun **1** *the predominance of women caregivers* PREVALENCE, dominance, preponderance. **2** *the superpower's military predominance* SUPREMACY, mastery, control, power, ascendancy, dominance, pre-eminence, superiority.

predominant ► adjective **1** *our predominant objectives* MAIN, chief, principal, most important, primary, prime, central, leading, foremost, key, paramount; *informal* number-one. **2** *the predominant political forces* CONTROLLING, dominant, predominating, more/most powerful, pre-eminent, ascendant, superior, in the ascendancy.
– OPPOSITES: subsidiary.

predominantly ► adverb MAINLY, mostly, for the most part, chiefly, principally, primarily, predominately, in the main, on the whole, largely, by and large, typically, generally, usually.

predominate ► verb **1** *small-scale producers predominate* BE IN THE MAJORITY, preponderate, be predominant, prevail, be most prominent. **2** *private*

interest predominates over the public good PREVAIL, dominate, be dominant, carry most weight; override, outweigh.

pre-eminence ► noun SUPERIORITY, supremacy, greatness, excellence, distinction, prominence, predominance, eminence, importance, prestige, stature, fame, renown, celebrity.

pre-eminent ► adjective GREATEST, leading, foremost, best, finest, chief, outstanding, excellent, distinguished, prominent, eminent, important, top, famous, renowned, celebrated, illustrious, supreme, marquee.
– OPPOSITES: undistinguished.

pre-eminently ► adverb PRIMARILY, principally, above all, chiefly, mostly, mainly, in particular.

pre-empt ► verb **1** *his action may have pre-empted war* FORESTALL, prevent. **2** *many tables were already pre-empted by family parties* COMMANDEER, occupy, seize, arrogate, appropriate, take over, secure, reserve.

preen ► verb **1** *the robin preened its feathers* CLEAN, tidy, groom, smooth, arrange; *archaic* plume. **2** *she preened before the mirror* ADMIRE ONESELF, primp oneself, groom oneself, spruce oneself up; *informal* titivate oneself, doll oneself up, tart oneself up, gussy oneself up.
■ **preen oneself** CONGRATULATE ONESELF, be pleased with oneself, be proud of oneself, pat oneself on the back, feel self-satisfied.

preface ► noun *the preface to the novel* INTRODUCTION, foreword, preamble, prologue, prelude; front matter; *informal* prelims, intro, lead-in; *formal* exordium, proem, prolegomenon.
► verb *the chapter is prefaced by a poem* PRECEDE, introduce, begin, open, start.

prefatory ► adjective INTRODUCTORY, preliminary, opening, initial, preparatory, initiatory, precursory.
– OPPOSITES: closing.

prefer ► verb **1** *I prefer white wine to red* LIKE BETTER, would rather (have), would sooner (have), favour, be more partial to; choose, select, pick, opt for, go for. **2** *(formal) do you want to prefer charges?* BRING, press, file, lodge, lay. **3** *(archaic) he was preferred to the post* PROMOTE, upgrade, raise, elevate.

preferable ► adjective BETTER, best, more desirable, more suitable, advantageous, superior, preferred, recommended.

preferably ► adverb IDEALLY, if possible, for preference, from choice.

preference ► noun **1** *her preference for boys' games* LIKING, partiality, predilection, proclivity, fondness, taste, inclination, leaning, bias, bent, penchant, predisposition. **2** *my preference is rock music* FAVOURITE, (first) choice, selection; *informal* cup of tea, thing, druthers. **3** *preference will be given to applicants speaking Japanese* PRIORITY, favour, precedence, preferential treatment.
■ **in preference to** RATHER THAN, instead of, in place of, sooner than.

preferential ► adjective SPECIAL, better, privileged, superior, favourable; partial, discriminatory, partisan, biased.

preferment ► noun PROMOTION, advancement, elevation, being upgraded, a step up (the ladder); *informal* a kick upstairs.
– OPPOSITES: demotion.

prefigure ► verb FORESHADOW, presage, be a harbinger of, herald; *literary* foretoken.

pregnancy ► noun gestation.
– RELATED TERMS: antenatal, maternity.

pregnant ► adjective 1 *she is pregnant* EXPECTING A BABY, expectant, carrying a child; *informal* expecting, in the family way, preggers, with a bun in the oven, knocked up; *informal, dated* in trouble; *archaic* with child; *technical* gravid, parturient. 2 *a ceremony pregnant with religious significance* FILLED, charged, heavy; full of. 3 *a pregnant pause* MEANINGFUL, significant, suggestive, expressive, charged.

prehistoric ► adjective 1 *prehistoric times* PRIMITIVE, primeval, primordial, primal, ancient, early, antediluvian. 2 *the special effects look prehistoric* OUT OF DATE, outdated, outmoded, old-fashioned, passé, antiquated, archaic, behind the times, primitive, antediluvian; *informal* horse-and-buggy, clunky.
— RELATED TERMS: archaeo-.
— OPPOSITES: modern.

prejudice ► noun 1 *male prejudices about women* PRECONCEIVED IDEA, preconception, prejudgment. 2 *they are motivated by prejudice* BIGOTRY, bias, partisanship, partiality, intolerance, discrimination, unfairness, inequality. 3 *without prejudice to the interests of others* DETRIMENT, harm, damage, injury, hurt, loss.
► verb 1 *the article could prejudice the jury* BIAS, influence, sway, predispose, make biased, make partial, colour. 2 *this could prejudice his chances of victory* DAMAGE, be detrimental to, be prejudicial to, injure, harm, hurt, spoil, impair, undermine, hinder, compromise.

prejudiced ► adjective BIASED, bigoted, discriminatory, partisan, intolerant, narrow-minded, unfair, unjust, inequitable, coloured.
— OPPOSITES: impartial.

prejudicial ► adjective DETRIMENTAL, damaging, injurious, harmful, disadvantageous, hurtful, deleterious.
— OPPOSITES: beneficial.

preliminary ► adjective *the discussions are still at a preliminary stage* PREPARATORY, introductory, initial, opening, prefatory, precursory; early, exploratory.
— OPPOSITES: final.
► noun 1 *he began without any preliminaries* INTRODUCTION, preamble, opening/prefatory remarks, formalities. 2 *a preliminary to the resumption of war* PRELUDE, preparation, preparatory measure, preliminary action.
■ **preliminary to** IN PREPARATION FOR, before, in advance of, prior to, preparatory to.

prelude ► noun 1 *a ceasefire was a prelude to peace negotiations* PRELIMINARY, overture, opening, preparation, introduction, start, commencement, beginning, lead-in, precursor. 2 *an orchestral prelude* OVERTURE, introductory movement, introduction, opening. 3 *the passage forms a prelude to Part III* INTRODUCTION, preface, prologue, foreword, preamble; *informal* intro, lead-in; *formal* exordium, proem, prolegomenon.

premature ► adjective 1 *his premature death* UNTIMELY, (too) early, unseasonable, before time. 2 *a premature baby* PRETERM. 3 *such a step would be premature* RASH, ill-considered, overhasty, hasty, precipitate, precipitous, impulsive, impetuous, inopportune; *informal* previous.
— OPPOSITES: overdue.

premeditated ► adjective PLANNED, intentional, deliberate, pre-planned, calculated, cold-blooded, conscious, pre-arranged.
— OPPOSITES: spontaneous.

premeditation ► noun (ADVANCE) PLANNING, forethought, pre-planning, (criminal) intent; *Law* malice aforethought.

premier ► adjective *a premier chef* LEADING, foremost, chief, principal, head, top-ranking, top, prime, primary, first, highest, pre-eminent, nonpareil, senior, outstanding, master, ranking; *informal* top-notch, blue-ribbon, blue-chip.
► noun *the Nova Scotian premier* LEADER, head of government, first minister, government leader; president, chancellor, prime minister, PM.

premiere ► noun FIRST PERFORMANCE, first night, opening night.

premise ► noun *the premise that human life consists of a series of choices* PROPOSITION, assumption, hypothesis, thesis, presupposition, postulation, postulate, supposition, presumption, surmise, conjecture, speculation, assertion, belief.
► verb *they premised that the cosmos is indestructible* POSTULATE, hypothesize, conjecture, posit, theorize, suppose, presuppose, surmise, assume.

premises ► plural noun BUILDING(S), property, site, office.

premium ► noun 1 *monthly premiums of $30* (REGULAR) PAYMENT, instalment. 2 *you must pay a premium for organic fruit* SURCHARGE, additional payment, extra amount. 3 *a foreign service premium* BONUS, extra; *informal* perk; *formal* perquisite.
■ **at a premium** SCARCE, in great demand, hard to come by, in short supply, thin on the ground.
■ **put/place a premium on** 1 *I place a high premium on our relationship* VALUE GREATLY, attach great/special importance to, set great store by, put a high value on. 2 *the high price of oil put a premium on the coal industry* MAKE VALUABLE, make invaluable, make important.

premonition ► noun FOREBODING, presentiment, intuition, (funny) feeling, hunch, suspicion, feeling in one's bones; misgiving, apprehension, fear; *archaic* presage.

preoccupation ► noun 1 *an air of preoccupation* PENSIVENESS, concentration, engrossment, absorption, self-absorption, musing, thinking, deep thought, brown study, brooding; abstraction, absent-mindedness, distraction, forgetfulness, inattentiveness, woolgathering, daydreaming. 2 *their main preoccupation was feeding their family* OBSESSION, concern; passion, enthusiasm, hobby horse.

preoccupied ► adjective 1 *officials preoccupied with their careers* OBSESSED, concerned, absorbed, engrossed, intent, involved, wrapped up. 2 *she looked preoccupied* LOST/DEEP IN THOUGHT, in a brown study, pensive, absent-minded, distracted, abstracted.

preoccupy ► verb ENGROSS, concern, absorb, take up someone's attention, distract, obsess, occupy, prey on someone's mind.

preordain ► verb PREDESTINE, destine, foreordain, ordain, fate, predetermine, determine.

preparation ► noun 1 *the preparation of contingency plans* DEVISING, putting together, drawing up, construction, composition, production, getting ready, development. 2 *preparations for the party* ARRANGEMENTS, planning, plans, preparatory measures. 3 *preparation for exams* INSTRUCTION, teaching, coaching, training, tutoring, drilling, priming. 4 *a preparation to kill off mites* MIXTURE, compound, concoction, solution, tincture, medicine, potion, cream, ointment, lotion.

preparatory ► adjective *preparatory work*

PRELIMINARY, initial, introductory, prefatory, opening, preparative, precursory.

■ **preparatory to** IN PREPARATION FOR, before, prior to, preliminary to.

prepare ▶ verb **1** *I want you to prepare a report* MAKE/ GET READY, put together, draw up, produce, arrange, assemble, construct, compose, formulate. **2** *the meal was easy to prepare* COOK, make, get, put together, concoct; *informal* fix, rustle up. **3** *preparing for war* GET READY, make preparations, arrange things, make provision, get everything set. **4** *athletes preparing for the Olympics* TRAIN, get into shape, practise, get ready. **5** *I must prepare for my exams* STUDY, review. **6** *this course prepares students for their exams* INSTRUCT, coach, train, tutor, drill, prime. **7** *prepare yourself for a shock* BRACE, make ready, tense, steel, steady.

prepared ▶ adjective **1** *he needs to be prepared for the worst* READY, (all) set, equipped, primed; waiting, on hand, poised, in position. **2** *I'm not prepared to cut the price* WILLING, ready, disposed, predisposed, (favourably) inclined, of a mind, minded.

preponderance ▶ noun **1** *the preponderance of women among older people* PREVALENCE, predominance, dominance. **2** *the preponderance of the evidence* BULK, majority, larger part, best/better part. **3** *the preponderance of the trade unions* PREDOMINANCE, dominance, ascendancy, supremacy, power.

preponderant ▶ adjective DOMINANT, predominant, pre-eminent, in control, more/most powerful, superior, supreme, ascendant, in the ascendancy.

preponderate ▶ verb BE IN THE MAJORITY, predominate, be predominant; be more/most important, prevail, dominate.

prepossessing ▶ adjective ATTRACTIVE, beautiful, pretty, handsome, good-looking, fetching, charming, delightful, enchanting, captivating; *archaic* fair.
— OPPOSITES: ugly.

preposterous ▶ adjective ABSURD, ridiculous, foolish, stupid, ludicrous, farcical, laughable, comical, risible, nonsensical, senseless, insane; outrageous, monstrous; *informal* crazy.
— OPPOSITES: sensible.

prerequisite ▶ noun *a prerequisite for the course* (NECESSARY) CONDITION, precondition, essential, requirement, requisite, necessity, sine qua non; *informal* must.
▶ adjective *the prerequisite qualifications* NECESSARY, required, called for, essential, requisite, obligatory, compulsory.
— OPPOSITES: unnecessary.

prerogative ▶ noun ENTITLEMENT, right, privilege, advantage, due, birthright.

presage ▶ verb *the owl's hooting presages death* PORTEND, augur, foreshadow, foretell, prophesy, be an omen of, herald, be a sign of, be the harbinger of, warn of, be a presage of, signal, bode, promise, threaten; *literary* betoken, foretoken, forebode.
▶ noun *a sombre presage of his final illness* OMEN, sign, indication, portent, warning, forewarning, harbinger, augury, prophecy, foretoken.

prescience ▶ noun FAR-SIGHTEDNESS, foresight, foreknowledge; psychic powers, clairvoyance; prediction, prognostication, divination, prophecy, augury; insight, intuition, perception, percipience.

prescient ▶ adjective PROPHETIC, predictive, visionary; psychic, clairvoyant; far-sighted, prognostic, divinatory; insightful, intuitive, perceptive, percipient.

prescribe ▶ verb **1** *the doctor prescribed antibiotics* WRITE A PRESCRIPTION FOR, authorize. **2** *traditional values prescribe a life of domesticity* ADVISE, recommend, advocate, suggest, endorse, champion, promote. **3** *rules prescribing your duty* STIPULATE, lay down, dictate, specify, determine, establish, fix.

prescription ▶ noun **1** *the doctor wrote a prescription* INSTRUCTION, authorization; *informal* scrip; *archaic* recipe. **2** *he fetched the prescription from the drug store* MEDICINE, drugs, medication. **3** *a painless prescription for improvement* METHOD, measure; recommendation, suggestion, recipe, formula.

prescriptive ▶ adjective DICTATORIAL, narrow, rigid, authoritarian, arbitrary, repressive, dogmatic.

presence ▶ noun **1** *the presence of a train was indicated electrically* EXISTENCE, being there. **2** *I requested the presence of an adjudicator* ATTENDANCE, appearance; company, companionship. **3** *a woman of great presence* AURA, charisma, (strength/force of) personality; poise, self-assurance, self-confidence. **4** *she felt a presence in the castle* GHOST, spirit, spectre, phantom, apparition, supernatural being; *informal* spook; *literary* shade.
— OPPOSITES: absence.

■ **presence of mind** COMPOSURE, equanimity, self-possession, level-headedness, self-assurance, calmness, sang-froid, imperturbability; alertness, quick-wittedness; *informal* cool, unflappability.

present[1] ▶ adjective **1** *a doctor must be present at the ringside* IN ATTENDANCE, here, there, near, nearby, (close/near) at hand, available. **2** *organic compounds are present in the waste* IN EXISTENCE, existing, existent. **3** *the present economic climate* CURRENT, present-day, existing.
— OPPOSITES: absent.
▶ noun *forget the past and think about the present* NOW, today, the present time/moment, the here and now.
— OPPOSITES: past, future.

■ **at present** AT THE MOMENT, just now, right now, at the present time, currently, at this moment in time.
■ **for the present** FOR THE TIME BEING, for now, for the moment, for a while, temporarily, pro tem.
■ **the present day** MODERN TIMES, nowadays.

present[2] ▶ verb **1** *the president presented a cheque to the winner* HAND OVER/OUT, give (out), confer, bestow, award, grant, accord. **2** *the committee presented its report* SUBMIT, set forth, put forward, proffer, offer, tender, table. **3** *may I present my wife?* INTRODUCE, make known, acquaint someone with. **4** *I called to present my warmest compliments* OFFER, give, express. **5** *they presented their new product last month* DEMONSTRATE, show, put on show/display, exhibit, display, launch, unveil. **6** *presenting good quality opera* STAGE, put on, produce, perform. **7** *she presents a TV show* HOST, introduce, be the presenter of, emcee. **8** *the authorities present him as a common criminal* REPRESENT, describe, portray, depict.

■ **present oneself 1** *he presented himself at ten* BE PRESENT, make an appearance, appear, turn up, arrive. **2** *an opportunity that presented itself* OCCUR, arise, happen, come about/up, appear, crop up, turn up.

present[3] ▶ noun *a birthday present* GIFT, donation, offering, contribution; *informal* freebie; *formal* benefaction.

presentable ▶ adjective **1** *I'm making the place look presentable* TIDY, neat, straight, clean, spic and span, in good order, shipshape. **2** *make yourself presentable* SMARTLY DRESSED, tidily dressed, tidy, well-groomed, trim, spruce; *informal* natty. **3** *presentable videos* FAIRLY

GOOD, passable, all right, satisfactory, moderately good, not (too) bad, average, fair; *informal* OK.

presentation ▸ noun **1** *the presentation of his certificate* AWARDING, presenting, giving, handing over/out, bestowal, granting, award. **2** *the presentation of food* APPEARANCE, arrangement, packaging, disposition, display, layout. **3** *the presentation of new proposals* SUBMISSION, proffering, offering, tendering, advancing, proposal, suggestion, mooting, tabling. **4** *a sales presentation* DEMONSTRATION, talk, lecture, address, speech, show, exhibition, display, introduction, launch, launching, unveiling. **5** *a presentation of his latest play* STAGING, production, performance, mounting, showing.

present-day ▸ adjective CURRENT, present, contemporary, latter-day, present-time, modern, twenty-first-century; up-to-date, up-to-the-minute, fashionable, trend-setting, the latest, new, newest, newfangled; *informal* trendy, now.

presentiment ▸ noun PREMONITION, foreboding, intuition, (funny) feeling, hunch, feeling in one's bones, sixth sense; *archaic* presage.

presently ▸ adverb **1** *I shall see you presently* SOON, shortly, directly, quite soon, in a short time, in a little while, at any moment/minute/second, in next to no time, before long, momentarily; *informal* pretty soon, any moment now, in a jiffy, in two shakes of a lamb's tail; *literary* ere long. **2** *he is presently abroad* CURRENTLY, at present, at the/this moment, at the present moment/time, now, nowadays, these days.

preservation ▸ noun **1** *wood preservation* CONSERVATION, protection, care. **2** *the preservation of the status quo* CONTINUATION, conservation, maintenance, upholding, sustaining, perpetuation. **3** *the preservation of food* CONSERVING, bottling, canning, freezing, drying; curing, smoking, pickling.

preserve ▸ verb **1** *oil helps preserve wood* CONSERVE, protect, maintain, care for, look after. **2** *they wish to preserve the status quo* CONTINUE (WITH), conserve, keep going, maintain, uphold, sustain, perpetuate. **3** *preserving him from harassment* GUARD, protect, keep, defend, safeguard, shelter, shield. **4** *spices enable us to preserve food* CONSERVE, bottle, can, freeze, dry, freeze-dry; cure, smoke, pickle.
▸ noun **1** *strawberry preserve* JAM, jelly, marmalade, conserve, fruit spread. **2** *the preserve of an educated middle-class* DOMAIN, area, field, sphere, orbit, realm, province, territory; *informal* turf, bailiwick. **3** *a game preserve* SANCTUARY, (game) reserve, reservation, protected area.

preside ▸ verb *the chairman presides at the meeting* CHAIR, be chairman/chairwoman/chairperson, officiate (at), conduct, lead.
■ **preside over** BE IN CHARGE OF, be responsible for, be at the head/helm of, head, be head of, manage, administer, be in control of, control, direct, lead, govern, rule, command, supervise, oversee; *informal* head up, be boss of, be in the driving/driver's seat, be in the saddle.

president ▸ noun **1** *terrorists assassinated the president* HEAD OF STATE. **2** *the president of the society* HEAD, chief, director, leader, governor, principal, master; *informal* prez. **3** *the president of the company* CHAIRMAN, chairwoman, chief executive (officer), CEO; owner, managing director.

press ▸ verb **1** *press the paper down firmly* PUSH (DOWN), press down, depress, hold down, force, thrust, squeeze, compress. **2** *his shirt was pressed* SMOOTH (OUT), iron, remove creases from. **3** *we pressed the grapes* CRUSH, squeeze, squash, mash, pulp, pound, pulverize, macerate. **4** *she pressed the child to her bosom* CLASP, hold close, hug, cuddle, squeeze, clutch, grasp, embrace. **5** *Hillary pressed his hand* SQUEEZE, grip, clutch. **6** *the crowd pressed round* CLUSTER, gather, converge, congregate, flock, swarm, throng, crowd. **7** *the government pressed its claim* PLEAD, urge, advance insistently, present, submit, put forward. **8** *they pressed him to agree* URGE, put pressure on, force, push, coerce, dragoon, steamroller, browbeat; *informal* lean on, put the screws on, twist someone's arm, railroad, bulldoze. **9** *they pressed for a ban on the ivory trade* CALL, ask, advocate, clamour, push, campaign, demand, lobby.
▸ noun **1** *a small literary press* PUBLISHING HOUSE, publisher; printing house/company; printing press. **2** *the freedom of the press* THE MEDIA, the newspapers, the papers, the news media, the fourth estate; journalists, reporters, newspapermen/women, newsmen, pressmen; *informal* journos, newshounds, newsies. **3** *the company had some bad press* (PRESS) REPORTS, press coverage, press articles, (press) reviews.
■ **be pressed for** HAVE TOO LITTLE, be short of, have insufficient, lack, be lacking (in), be deficient in, need, be/stand in need of; *informal* be strapped for.
■ **press on** PROCEED, keep going, continue, carry on, make progress, make headway, press ahead, forge on/ahead, soldier on, push on, keep on, struggle on, persevere, keep at it, stay with it, stick with it, plod on, plug away.

press conference ▸ noun NEWS CONFERENCE, scrum ✦, lock-up ✦, bear-pit session ✦.

pressing ▸ adjective **1** *a pressing problem* URGENT, critical, crucial, acute, desperate, serious, grave, life-and-death. **2** *a pressing engagement* IMPORTANT, high-priority, critical, crucial, compelling, inescapable.

pressure ▸ noun **1** *a confined gas exerts a constant pressure* PHYSICAL FORCE, load, stress, thrust; compression, weight. **2** *they put pressure on us to borrow money* COERCION, force, compulsion, constraint, duress; pestering, harassment, nagging, badgering, intimidation, arm-twisting, persuasion. **3** *she had a lot of pressure from work* STRAIN, stress, tension, trouble, difficulty; *informal* hassle.
▸ verb *they pressured him into resigning.* COERCE, pressure, put pressure on, press, push, persuade, force, bulldoze, hound, harass, nag, harry, badger, goad, pester, browbeat, bully, bludgeon, intimidate, dragoon, twist someone's arm, strong-arm; *informal* railroad, lean on, hustle.

prestige ▸ noun STATUS, standing, stature, reputation, repute, regard, fame, note, renown, honour, esteem, celebrity, importance, prominence, influence, eminence; kudos, cachet; *informal* clout.

prestigious ▸ adjective **1** *prestigious journals* REPUTABLE, distinguished, respected, esteemed, eminent, august, highly regarded, well-thought-of, acclaimed, authoritative, celebrated, illustrious, leading, renowned. **2** *a prestigious job* IMPRESSIVE, important, prominent, high-ranking, influential, powerful, glamorous; well paid, expensive, upmarket.
— OPPOSITES: obscure, minor.

presumably ▸ adverb I PRESUME, I expect, I assume, I take it, I suppose, I imagine, I dare say, I guess, in all probability, probably, in all likelihood, as likely as not, doubtless, undoubtedly, no doubt.

presume ▶ verb **1** *I presumed that it had once been an attic* ASSUME, suppose, dare say, imagine, take it, expect, believe, think, surmise, guess, judge, conjecture, speculate, postulate, presuppose. **2** *let me presume to give you some advice* VENTURE, dare, have the audacity/effrontery, be so bold as, take the liberty of.
■ **presume on** TAKE (UNFAIR) ADVANTAGE OF, exploit, take liberties with; count on, bank on, place reliance on.

presumption ▶ noun **1** *this presumption may be easily rebutted* ASSUMPTION, supposition, presupposition, belief, guess, judgment, surmise, conjecture, speculation, hypothesis, postulation, inference, deduction, conclusion. **2** *he apologized for his presumption* BRAZENNESS, audacity, boldness, audaciousness, temerity, arrogance, presumptuousness, forwardness; cockiness, insolence, impudence, bumptiousness, impertinence, effrontery, cheek, cheekiness; rudeness, impoliteness, disrespect, familiarity; *informal* nerve, chutzpah, sass, sassiness; *archaic* assumption.

presumptive ▶ adjective **1** *a presumptive diagnosis* CONJECTURAL, speculative, tentative; theoretical, unproven, unconfirmed. **2** *the heir presumptive* PROBABLE, likely, prospective, assumed, supposed, expected.

presumptuous ▶ adjective BRAZEN, overconfident, arrogant, bold, audacious, forward, familiar, impertinent, insolent, impudent, cocky; cheeky, rude, impolite, uncivil, bumptious; *informal* sassy.

presuppose ▶ verb **1** *this presupposes the existence of a policy-making group* REQUIRE, necessitate, imply, entail, mean, involve, assume. **2** *I had presupposed that theme parks make people happy* PRESUME, assume, take it for granted, take it as read, suppose, surmise, think, accept, consider.

presupposition ▶ noun PRESUMPTION, assumption, preconception, supposition, hypothesis, surmise, thesis, theory, premise, belief, postulation.

pretend ▶ verb **1** *they just pretend to listen* MAKE AS IF, profess, affect; dissimulate, dissemble, put it on, put on a false front, go through the motions, sham, fake it. **2** *I'll pretend to be the dragon* PUT ON AN ACT, make believe, play at, act, play-act, impersonate. **3** *it was useless to pretend innocence* FEIGN, sham, fake, simulate, put on, counterfeit, affect. **4** *he cannot pretend to sophistication* CLAIM, lay claim to, purport to have, profess to have.
▶ adjective *(informal) a pretend conversation* IMAGINARY, imagined, pretended, make-believe, made-up, fantasy, fantasized, dreamed-up, unreal, invented, fictitious, mythical, feigned, fake, mock, sham, simulated, artificial, ersatz, false, pseudo; *informal* phony.

pretended ▶ adjective FAKE, faked, affected, assumed, professed, spurious, mock, imitation, simulated, make-believe, pseudo, sham, false, bogus; *informal* pretend, phony.

pretender ▶ noun CLAIMANT, aspirant.

pretense ▶ noun **1** *cease this pretense* MAKE-BELIEVE, putting on an act, acting, dissembling, shamming, faking, feigning, simulation, dissimulation, play-acting, posturing; deception, deceit, deceitfulness, fraud, fraudulence, duplicity, subterfuge, trickery, dishonesty, hypocrisy, falsity, lying, mendacity. **2** *he made a pretense of being unconcerned* (FALSE) SHOW, semblance, affectation, (false) appearance, outward appearance, impression, (false) front, guise, facade, display. **3** *she had dropped any pretense to faith* CLAIM, profession. **4** *he was absolutely without pretense* PRETENTIOUSNESS, display, ostentation, affectation, showiness, posturing, humbug.
– OPPOSITES: honesty.

pretension ▶ noun **1** *the author has no pretension to exhaustive coverage* ASPIRATION, claim, assertion, pretense, profession. **2** *she spoke without pretension* PRETENTIOUSNESS, affectation, ostentation, artificiality, airs, posing, posturing, show, flashiness; pomposity, pompousness, grandiosity, grandiloquence, magniloquence.

pretentious ▶ adjective AFFECTED, ostentatious, showy; over-ambitious, pompous, artificial, inflated, overblown, high-sounding, flowery, grandiose, elaborate, extravagant, flamboyant, ornate, grandiloquent, magniloquent, sophomoric; *informal* flashy, highfalutin, la-di-da, pseudo.

preternatural ▶ adjective EXTRAORDINARY, exceptional, unusual, uncommon, singular, unprecedented, remarkable, phenomenal, abnormal, inexplicable, unaccountable; strange, mysterious, fantastic.

pretext ▶ noun (FALSE) EXCUSE, ostensible reason, alleged reason; guise, ploy, pretense, ruse.

prettify ▶ verb BEAUTIFY, make attractive, make pretty, titivate, adorn, ornament, decorate, smarten (up); *informal* doll up, do up, give something a facelift, tart up.

pretty ▶ adjective *a pretty child* ATTRACTIVE, lovely, good-looking, nice-looking, personable, fetching, prepossessing, appealing, charming, delightful, cute, as pretty as a picture; *Scottish* bonny; *informal* easy on the eye; *literary* beauteous; *archaic* fair, comely.
– OPPOSITES: plain, ugly.
▶ adverb *a pretty large sum* QUITE, rather, somewhat, fairly, reasonably, comparatively, relatively.
▶ verb *she's prettying herself up* BEAUTIFY, make attractive, make pretty, prettify, titivate, adorn, ornament, smarten; *informal* do oneself up, tart oneself up.

prevail ▶ verb **1** *common sense will prevail* WIN (OUT/THROUGH), triumph, be victorious, carry the day, come out on top, succeed, prove superior, conquer, overcome; rule, reign. **2** *the conditions that prevailed in the 1950s* EXIST, be in existence, be present, be the case, occur, be prevalent, be current, be the order of the day, be customary, be common, be widespread, be in force/effect; *formal* obtain.
■ **prevail on/upon** PERSUADE, induce, talk someone into, coax, convince, make, get, press someone into, argue someone into, urge, pressure someone into, coerce; *informal* sweet-talk, soft-soap.

prevailing ▶ adjective CURRENT, existing, prevalent, usual, common, general, widespread.

prevalence ▶ noun COMMONNESS, currency, widespread presence, generality, popularity, pervasiveness, universality, extensiveness; rampancy, rifeness.

prevalent ▶ adjective WIDESPREAD, prevailing, frequent, usual, common, current, popular, general, universal; endemic, rampant, rife.
– OPPOSITES: rare.

prevaricate ▶ verb BE EVASIVE, beat around the bush, hedge, fence, shilly-shally, dodge (the issue), sidestep (the issue), equivocate, waffle; temporize, stall (for time); hem and haw; *rare* tergiversate.

prevent ▸ verb STOP, put a stop to, avert, nip in the bud, fend off, stave off, ward off; hinder, impede, hamper, obstruct, balk, foil, thwart, forestall, counteract, inhibit, curb, restrain, preclude, pre-empt, save, help; disallow, prohibit, forbid, proscribe, exclude, debar, bar; *literary* stay.
— OPPOSITES: allow.

preventive ▸ adjective **1** *preventive maintenance* PRE-EMPTIVE, deterrent, precautionary, protective. **2** *preventive medicine* PROPHYLACTIC, disease-preventing.
▸ noun **1** *a preventive against crime* PRECAUTIONARY MEASURE, deterrent, safeguard, security, protection, defence. **2** *disease preventives* PROPHYLACTIC (DEVICE), prophylactic medicine, preventive drug.

previous ▸ adjective FOREGOING, preceding, antecedent; old, earlier, prior, former, ex-, past, last, sometime, one-time, erstwhile; *formal* quondam, anterior.
— OPPOSITES: next.
▪ **previous to** BEFORE, prior to, until, (leading) up to, earlier than, preceding; *formal* anterior to.

previously ▸ adverb FORMERLY, earlier (on), before, hitherto, once, at one time, in the past, in days/times gone by, in bygone days, in times past, in former times; in advance, already, beforehand; *formal* heretofore.

prey ▸ noun **1** *the lions killed their prey* QUARRY, kill. **2** *she was easy prey* VICTIM, target, dupe, gull; *informal* sucker, soft touch, pushover, patsy, sap, schlemiel.
— OPPOSITES: predator.
▪ **prey on 1** *hoverfly larvae prey on aphids* HUNT, catch; eat, feed on, live on/off. **2** *they prey on the elderly* EXPLOIT, victimize, pick on, take advantage of; trick, swindle, cheat, hoodwink, fleece; *informal* con. **3** *the problem preyed on his mind* OPPRESS, weigh (heavily) on, lie heavy on, gnaw at; trouble, worry, beset, disturb, distress, haunt, nag, torment, plague, obsess.

price ▸ noun **1** *the purchase price* COST, charge, fee, fare, levy, amount, sum; outlay, expense, expenditure; valuation, quotation, estimate, asking price; *informal, humorous* damage. **2** *spinsterhood was the price of her career* CONSEQUENCE, result, cost, penalty, sacrifice; downside, snag, drawback, disadvantage, minus. **3** *he had a price on his head* REWARD, bounty, premium.
▸ verb *a ticket is priced at $5.00* FIX/SET THE PRICE OF, cost, value, rate; estimate.

priceless ▸ adjective **1** *priceless works of art* INVALUABLE, of incalculable value/worth, of immeasurable value/worth, beyond price; irreplaceable, incomparable, unparalleled. **2** *(informal) that's priceless! See* HILARIOUS *sense 1*.
— OPPOSITES: worthless, cheap.

pricey ▸ adjective *(informal). See* EXPENSIVE.

prick ▸ verb **1** *prick the potatoes with a fork* PIERCE, puncture, make/put a hole in, stab, perforate, nick, jab. **2** *her conscience pricked her* TROUBLE, worry, distress, perturb, disturb, cause someone anguish, afflict, torment, plague, prey on, gnaw at. **3** *ambition pricked him on to greater effort* GOAD, prod, incite, provoke, urge, spur, stimulate, encourage, inspire, motivate, push, propel, impel. **4** *the horse pricked up its ears* RAISE, erect.
▸ noun **1** *it felt like the prick of a pin* JAB, sting, pinprick, prickle, stab. **2** *the prick of tears behind her eyelids* STING, stinging, smart, smarting, burning. **3** *the prick of conscience* PANG, twinge, stab.
▪ **prick up one's ears** LISTEN CAREFULLY, pay

attention, become attentive, begin to take notice, attend; *informal* be all ears.

prickle ▸ noun **1** *the cactus is covered with prickles* THORN, needle, barb, spike, point, spine. **2** *Willie felt a cold prickle of fear* TINGLE, tingling (sensation), prickling sensation, chill, thrill; *Medicine* paresthesia.
▸ verb *its tiny spikes prickled his skin* STING, prick.

prickly ▸ adjective **1** *a prickly hedgehog* SPIKY, spiked, thorny, barbed, spiny; briery, brambly; rough, scratchy; *technical* spiculate, spicular, aculeate, spinose. **2** *my skin feels prickly* TINGLY, tingling, prickling. **3** *a prickly character. See* IRRITABLE. **4** *the prickly question of the refugees* PROBLEMATIC, awkward, ticklish, tricky, delicate, sensitive, difficult, knotty, thorny, irksome, tough, troublesome, bothersome, vexatious.

pride ▸ noun **1** *their triumphs were a source of pride* SELF-ESTEEM, dignity, honour, self-respect, self-worth, self-regard, pride in oneself. **2** *take pride in a good job well done* PLEASURE, joy, delight, gratification, fulfillment, satisfaction, sense of achievement. **3** *he refused her offer out of pride* ARROGANCE, vanity, self-importance, hubris, conceit, conceitedness, self-love, self-adulation, self-admiration, narcissism, egotism, superciliousness, haughtiness, snobbery, snobbishness; *informal* big-headedness; *literary* vainglory. **4** *the bull is the pride of the herd* BEST, finest, top, cream, pick, choice, prize, glory, the jewel in the crown. **5** *the vegetable garden was the pride of the gardener* SOURCE OF SATISFACTION, pride and joy, treasured possession, joy, delight.
— OPPOSITES: shame, humility.
▪ **pride oneself on** BE PROUD OF, be proud of oneself for, take pride in, take satisfaction in, congratulate oneself on, pat oneself on the back for.

priest ▸ noun CLERGYMAN, CLERGYWOMAN, minister (of religion), cleric, ecclesiastic, pastor, vicar, rector, parson, churchman, churchwoman, man/woman of the cloth, man/woman of God, father, curate, chaplain, curé, canon, monsignor, evangelist, preacher, imam; *historical* black robe ✚; *informal* reverend, padre, Holy Joe, sky pilot; *dated* divine.

priestly ▸ adjective CLERICAL, pastoral, priestlike, ecclesiastical, sacerdotal, hieratic, rectorial.

prig ▸ noun PRUDE, puritan, killjoy; *informal* goody-goody, holy Joe.

priggish ▸ adjective SELF-RIGHTEOUS, moralistic, holier-than-thou, sanctimonious, prudish, puritanical, prim, straitlaced, stuffy, prissy, narrow-minded; *informal* goody-goody, starchy.
— OPPOSITES: broad-minded.

prim ▸ adjective DEMURE, (prim and) proper, formal, stuffy, straitlaced, prudish; prissy, priggish, puritanical; *informal* starchy.

primacy ▸ noun GREATER IMPORTANCE, priority, precedence, pre-eminence, superiority, supremacy, ascendancy, dominance, dominion, leadership.

prima donna ▸ noun **1** LEADING SOPRANO, leading lady, diva, (opera) star, principal singer. **2** *a city council filled with prima donnas* EGO, self-important person, his nibs, temperamental person, princess, diva, pooh-bah.

primal ▸ adjective **1** *primal masculine instincts* BASIC, fundamental, essential, elemental, vital, central, intrinsic, inherent. **2** *the primal source of living things* ORIGINAL, initial, earliest, first, primitive, primeval.

primarily ▸ adverb **1** *the bishop was primarily a leader of the local community* FIRST (AND FOREMOST), firstly, essentially, in essence, fundamentally, principally, predominantly, basically. **2** *such work is undertaken primarily for large institutions* MOSTLY, for the most part, chiefly, mainly, in the main, on the whole, largely, to a large extent, especially, generally, usually, typically, commonly, as a rule.

primary ▶ adjective **1** *our primary role* MAIN, chief, key, prime, central, principal, foremost, first, most important, predominant, paramount; *informal* number-one. **2** *the primary cause* ORIGINAL, earliest, initial, first; essential, fundamental, basic.
— OPPOSITES: secondary.

primate ▶ noun. *See table.*

Primates

ape	lemur
aye-aye	loris
baboon	macaque
Barbary ape	mandrill
bonnet monkey	mangabey
bonobo	marmoset
capuchin	monkey
chimpanzee	orangutan
colobus	proboscis monkey
douroucouli	rhesus monkey
drill	silverback
galago	slender loris
gelada	slow loris
gibbon	spider monkey
gorilla	squirrel monkey
guenon	tamarin
hamadryas	tarsier
hanuman	titi
howler	vervet
indri	wanderoo
langur	

prime¹ ▶ adjective **1** *his prime reason for leaving* MAIN, chief, key, primary, central, principal, foremost, first, most important, paramount, major; *informal* number-one. **2** *the prime cause of flooding* FUNDAMENTAL, basic, essential, primary, central. **3** *prime agricultural land* TOP-QUALITY, top, best, first-class, first-rate, grade A, superior, supreme, choice, select, finest; excellent, superb, fine; *informal* tip-top, A1, top-notch, blue-ribbon. **4** *a prime example* ARCHETYPAL, prototypical, typical, classic, excellent, characteristic, quintessential.
— OPPOSITES: secondary, inferior.
▶ noun *he is in his prime* HEYDAY, best days/years, prime of one's life; youth, salad days; peak, pinnacle, high point/spot, zenith.

prime² ▶ verb **1** *he primed the gun* PREPARE, load, get ready. **2** *Lucy had primed him carefully* BRIEF, fill in, prepare, put in the picture, inform, advise, instruct, coach, drill; *informal* clue in, give someone the lowdown.

prime minister ▶ noun first minister, head of the government, PM; ruler, premier, president.

primeval ▶ adjective **1** *primeval forest* ANCIENT, earliest, first, prehistoric, antediluvian, primordial; pristine, original, virgin. **2** *primeval fears* INSTINCTIVE, primitive, basic, primal, primordial, intuitive, inborn, innate, inherent.

primitive ▶ adjective **1** *primitive times* ANCIENT, earliest, first, prehistoric, antediluvian, primordial, primeval, primal. **2** *primitive peoples* UNCIVILIZED, barbarian, barbaric, barbarous, savage, ignorant,

uncultivated. **3** *primitive tools* CRUDE, simple, rough (and ready), basic, rudimentary, unrefined, unsophisticated, rude, makeshift. **4** *primitive art* SIMPLE, natural, unsophisticated, unaffected, undeveloped, unpretentious.
— OPPOSITES: sophisticated, civilized.

primordial ▶ adjective **1** *the primordial oceans* ANCIENT, earliest, first, prehistoric, antediluvian, primeval. **2** *their primordial desires* INSTINCTIVE, primitive, basic, primal, primeval, intuitive, inborn, innate, inherent, visceral.

primp ▶ verb GROOM, tidy, arrange, brush, comb; smarten (up), spruce up; *informal* titivate, doll up, tart up, gussy up.

prince ▶ noun RULER, sovereign, monarch, king, princeling; crown prince; emir, sheikh, sultan, maharaja, raja.

princely ▶ adjective **1** *princely buildings.* See SPLENDID sense 1. **2** *a princely sum.* See HANDSOME sense 3.

principal ▶ adjective *the principal cause of poor air quality* MAIN, chief, primary, leading, foremost, first, most important, predominant, dominant, (most) prominent; key, crucial, vital, essential, basic, prime, central, focal; premier, paramount, major, overriding, cardinal, pre-eminent, uppermost, highest, top, topmost; *informal* number-one.
— OPPOSITES: minor.
▶ noun **1** *the principal of the firm* CHIEF, chief executive (officer), CEO, president, chairman, chairwoman, director, managing director, manager, head; *informal* boss. **2** *the school's principal* HEADMASTER, headmistress; dean, rector, chancellor, vice-chancellor, president, provost. **3** *a principal in a soap opera* LEADING ACTOR/ACTRESS, leading player/ performer/dancer, leading role, lead, star. **4** *repayment of the principal* CAPITAL (SUM), debt, loan.

principally ▶ adverb MAINLY, mostly, chiefly, for the most part, in the main, on the whole, largely, to a large extent, predominantly, basically, primarily.

principle ▶ noun **1** *elementary principles* TRUTH, proposition, concept, idea, theory, assumption, fundamental, essential, ground rule. **2** *the principle of laissez-faire* DOCTRINE, belief, creed, credo, (golden) rule, criterion, tenet, code, ethic, dictum, canon, law. **3** *a woman of principle | sticking to one's principles* MORALS, morality, (code of) ethics, beliefs, ideals, standards; integrity, uprightness, righteousness, virtue, probity, (sense of) honour, decency, conscience, scruples.
■ **in principle 1** *there is no reason, in principle, why we couldn't work together* IN THEORY, theoretically, on paper. **2** *he has accepted the idea in principle* IN GENERAL, in essence, on the whole, in the main.

principled ▶ adjective MORAL, ethical, virtuous, righteous, upright, upstanding, high-minded, honourable, honest, incorruptible.

print ▶ verb **1** *the newspaper is printed just after midnight* SEND TO PRESS, set in print, run off, reprint. **2** *patterns were printed on the cloth* IMPRINT, impress, stamp, mark. **3** *they printed 30,000 copies* PUBLISH, issue, release, circulate. **4** *the incident is printed on her memory* REGISTER, record, impress, imprint, engrave, etch, stamp, mark.
▶ noun **1** *small print* TYPE, printing, letters, lettering, characters, type size, typeface, font. **2** *prints of his left hand* IMPRESSION, fingerprint, footprint. **3** *Group of Seven prints are on sale in the lobby* PICTURE, design, engraving, etching, lithograph, linocut, woodcut. **4** *prints and negatives* PHOTOGRAPH, photo, snap,

snapshot, picture, still. **5** *soft floral prints* PRINTED CLOTH/FABRIC, patterned cloth/fabric, chintz.

■ **in print** PUBLISHED, printed, available in bookstores.

■ **out of print** NO LONGER AVAILABLE, unavailable, unobtainable, discontinued.

prior ▶ **adjective** *by prior arrangement* EARLIER, previous, preceding, foregoing, antecedent, advance; *formal* anterior.
– OPPOSITES: subsequent.

■ **prior to** BEFORE, until, till, up to, previous to, earlier than, preceding, leading up to; *formal* anterior to.

prioritize ▶ **verb 1** *we must prioritize pollution control* EMPHASIZE, concentrate on, put first, focus on, fast-track, expedite, make a priority. **2** *they prioritize patients according to need* RANK, order, hierarchize, triage; grade, class, categorize.

priority ▶ **noun 1** *safety is our priority* PRIME CONCERN, most important consideration, primary issue. **2** *giving priority to elementary schools* PRECEDENCE, greater importance, preference, pre-eminence, predominance, primacy, first place. **3** *traffic in the right lane has priority* RIGHT OF WAY.

priory ▶ **noun** RELIGIOUS HOUSE, abbey, cloister; monastery, friary; convent, nunnery.

prison ▶ **noun** JAIL, lock-up, penal institution, detention centre, jailhouse, penitentiary, correctional facility, remand centre; *informal* clink, slammer, hoosegow, the big house, stir, jug, brig, can, pen, cooler, pokey, slam; (**be in prison**) *informal* be inside, be behind bars, do time.
– RELATED TERMS: custodial.

prisoner ▶ **noun 1** *a prisoner serving a life sentence* CONVICT, detainee, inmate; *informal* jailbird, con, lifer, yardbird. **2** *the army took many prisoners* CAPTIVE, internee, prisoner of war, POW.

prissy ▶ **adjective** PRUDISH, priggish, prim, prim and proper, straitlaced, Victorian, old-maidish, schoolmarmish; *informal* starchy.
– OPPOSITES: broad-minded.

pristine ▶ **adjective** IMMACULATE, perfect, in mint condition, as new, unspoiled, spotless, flawless, clean, fresh, new, virgin, pure, unused.
– OPPOSITES: dirty, spoiled.

privacy ▶ **noun** SECLUSION, solitude, isolation, freedom from disturbance, freedom from interference.

private ▶ **adjective 1** *his private plane* PERSONAL, own, individual, special, exclusive, privately owned. **2** *private talks* CONFIDENTIAL, secret, classified, unofficial, off the record, closet, in camera; backstage, privileged, one-on-one, tête-à-tête, sub-rosa. **3** *private thoughts* INTIMATE, personal, secret; innermost, undisclosed, unspoken, unvoiced. **4** *a very private man* RESERVED, introvert, introverted, self-contained, reticent, discreet, uncommunicative, unforthcoming, retiring, unsociable, withdrawn, solitary, reclusive, hermitic. **5** *they found a private place in which to talk* SECLUDED, solitary, undisturbed, concealed, hidden, remote, isolated, out of the way, sequestered. **6** *we can be private here* UNDISTURBED, uninterrupted; alone, by ourselves. **7** *the premier attended in a private capacity* UNOFFICIAL, personal. **8** *private industry* INDEPENDENT, non-state; privatized, denationalized; commercial, private-enterprise.
– OPPOSITES: public, open, extrovert, busy, crowded, official, state, nationalized.

▶ **noun** *a private in the army* PRIVATE SOLDIER, common

soldier; trooper; sapper, gunner; enlisted personnel; *US* GI.

■ **in private** IN SECRET, secretly, privately, behind closed doors, in camera; in confidence, confidentially, between ourselves, entre nous, off the record; *formal* sub rosa.

private detective ▶ **noun** PRIVATE INVESTIGATOR; *informal* private eye, PI, sleuth, snoop, shamus, gumshoe; *informal, dated* private dick.

privately ▶ **adverb 1** *we must talk privately* IN SECRET, secretly, in private, behind closed doors, in camera; in confidence, confidentially, between ourselves, entre nous, off the record; *formal* sub rosa. **2** *privately, I am glad* SECRETLY, inwardly, deep down, personally, unofficially. **3** *he lived very privately* OUT OF THE PUBLIC EYE, out of public view, in seclusion, in solitude, alone.
– OPPOSITES: publicly.

privation ▶ **noun** DEPRIVATION, hardship, destitution, impoverishment, want, need, neediness, austerity.
– OPPOSITES: plenty, luxury.

privilege ▶ **noun 1** *senior students have certain privileges* ADVANTAGE, benefit; prerogative, entitlement, right; concession, freedom, liberty. **2** *it was a privilege to meet her* HONOUR, pleasure. **3** *parliamentary privilege* IMMUNITY, exemption, dispensation.

privileged ▶ **adjective 1** *a privileged background* WEALTHY, rich, affluent, prosperous; LUCKY, fortunate, elite, favoured; (socially) advantaged. **2** *privileged information* CONFIDENTIAL, private, secret, restricted, classified, not for publication, off the record, inside; *informal* hush-hush. **3** *MPs are privileged* IMMUNE (FROM PROSECUTION), protected, exempt, excepted.
– OPPOSITES: underprivileged, disadvantaged, public, liable.

privy ▶ **adjective** *he was not privy to the discussions* IN THE KNOW ABOUT, acquainted with, in on, informed of, advised of, apprised of; *informal* wise to; *formal* cognizant of.

▶ **noun** *he went out to the privy. See* TOILET *sense 1.*

prize ▶ **noun 1** *an art prize* AWARD, reward, premium, purse; trophy, medal; honour, accolade, crown, laurels, palm. **2** *the prizes of war* SPOILS, booty, plunder, loot, pickings.

▶ **adjective 1** *a prize bull* CHAMPION, award-winning, prize-winning, winning, top, best. **2** *a prize example* OUTSTANDING, excellent, superlative, superb, supreme, very good, prime, fine, magnificent, marvellous, wonderful; *informal* great, terrific, tremendous, fantastic. **3** *a prize idiot* COMPLETE, utter, total, absolute, real, perfect, veritable.
– OPPOSITES: second-rate.

▶ **verb** *many collectors prize his work* VALUE, set great store by, rate highly, attach great importance to, esteem, hold in high regard, think highly of, treasure, cherish.

prized ▶ **adjective** TREASURED, precious, cherished, much loved, beloved, valued, esteemed, highly regarded.

prizewinner ▶ **noun** CHAMPION, winner, gold medallist, victor; *informal* champ, number one.

proactive ▶ **adjective** ENTERPRISING, take-charge, energetic, driven, bold, dynamic, motivated, go-ahead.

probability ▶ **noun 1** *the probability of winning* LIKELIHOOD, prospect, chance, chances, odds. **2** *relegation is a distinct probability* PROBABLE EVENT, prospect, possibility, good/fair/reasonable bet.

probable ▶ adjective LIKELY, most likely, odds-on, expected, anticipated, predictable, foreseeable, ten to one; *informal* in the cards, a good/fair/reasonable bet.
— OPPOSITES: unlikely.

probably ▶ adverb IN ALL LIKELIHOOD, in all probability, as likely as not, (very/most) likely, ten to one, the chances are, doubtless, no doubt; *archaic* like enough.

probation ▶ noun TRIAL PERIOD, test period, experimental period, trial.

probe ▶ noun *a probe into an air crash* INVESTIGATION, inquiry, examination, inquest, exploration, study, analysis.
▶ verb 1 *alien hands probed his body* EXAMINE, feel, feel around, explore, prod, poke, check. 2 *police probed the tragedy* INVESTIGATE, inquire into, look into, study, examine, scrutinize, go into, carry out an inquest into.

probity ▶ noun INTEGRITY, honesty, uprightness, decency, morality, rectitude, goodness, virtue, right-mindedness, trustworthiness, truthfulness, honour.
— OPPOSITES: untrustworthiness.

problem ▶ noun 1 *they ran into a problem* DIFFICULTY, trouble, worry, complication, difficult situation; snag, hitch, drawback, stumbling block, obstacle, hurdle, hiccup, setback, catch; predicament, plight; misfortune, mishap, misadventure; dilemma, quandary; *informal* headache, nightmare. 2 *I don't want to be a problem* NUISANCE, bother, pest, irritant, thorn in one's side/flesh, vexation; *informal* drag, pain, pain in the neck. 3 *arithmetical problems* PUZZLE, question, poser, enigma, riddle, conundrum; *informal* teaser, brainteaser.
▶ adjective *a problem child* TROUBLESOME, difficult, unmanageable, unruly, disobedient, uncontrollable, recalcitrant, delinquent.
— OPPOSITES: well-behaved, manageable.

problematic ▶ adjective DIFFICULT, hard, taxing, troublesome, tricky, awkward, controversial, ticklish, complicated, complex, knotty, thorny, prickly, vexed; *informal* sticky.
— OPPOSITES: easy, simple, straightforward.

procedure ▶ noun COURSE OF ACTION, plan of action, action plan, policy, series of steps, method, system, strategy, way, approach, formula, mechanism, methodology, MO (modus operandi), technique; routine, drill, practice, operation.

proceed ▶ verb 1 *she was uncertain how to proceed* BEGIN, make a start, get going, move, set something in motion; TAKE ACTION, act, go on, go ahead, make progress, make headway. 2 *he proceeded down the road* GO, make one's way, advance, move, progress, carry on, press on, push on. 3 *we should proceed with the talks* GO AHEAD, carry on, go on, continue, keep on, get on, get ahead; pursue, prosecute. 4 *there is not enough evidence to proceed against him* TAKE SOMEONE TO COURT, start/take proceedings against, start an action against, mount a case against, sue. 5 *all power proceeds from God* ORIGINATE, spring, stem, come, derive, arise, issue, flow, emanate.
— OPPOSITES: stop.

proceedings ▶ plural noun 1 *the evening's proceedings are underway* EVENTS, activities, happenings, goings-on, doings. 2 *they published the proceedings of the meeting* REPORT, transactions, minutes, account, record(s); annals, archives. 3 *legal proceedings* LEGAL ACTION, court/judicial proceedings, litigation; lawsuit, case, prosecution.

proceeds ▶ plural noun PROFITS, earnings, receipts, returns, takings, take, avails ♣, income, revenue, royalty; *Sport* gate (money/receipts).

process ▶ noun 1 *investigation is a long process* PROCEDURE, operation, action, activity, exercise, affair, business, job, task, undertaking. 2 *a new canning process* METHOD, system, technique, means, practice, way, approach, methodology.
▶ verb *applications are processed rapidly* DEAL WITH, attend to, see to, sort out, handle, take care of, action.
■ **in the process of** IN THE MIDDLE OF, in the course of, in the midst of, in the throes of, busy with, occupied in/with, taken up with/by, involved in.

procession ▶ noun PARADE, march, march past, cavalcade, motorcade, cortège; column, file, train.

proclaim ▶ verb 1 *messengers proclaimed the good news* DECLARE, announce, pronounce, state, make known, give out, advertise, publish, broadcast, promulgate, trumpet, blazon. 2 *the men proclaimed their innocence* ASSERT, declare, profess, maintain, protest. 3 *she proclaimed herself president* DECLARE, pronounce, announce. 4 *cheap soap soon proclaims its cheapness* DEMONSTRATE, indicate, show, reveal, manifest, betray, testify to, signify.

proclamation ▶ noun DECLARATION, announcement, pronouncement, statement, notification, publication, broadcast, promulgation, blazoning; assertion, profession, protestation; DECREE, order, edict, ruling.

proclivity ▶ noun INCLINATION, tendency, leaning, disposition, proneness, propensity, bent, bias, penchant, predisposition; predilection, partiality, liking, preference, taste, fondness, weakness.

procrastinate ▶ verb DELAY, put off doing something, postpone action, defer action, be dilatory, use delaying tactics, stall, temporize, drag one's feet/heels, take one's time, play for time, play a waiting game.

procreate ▶ verb PRODUCE OFFSPRING, reproduce, multiply, propagate, breed.

procure ▶ verb 1 *he managed to procure a coat* OBTAIN, acquire, get, find, come by, secure, pick up; buy, purchase, engage; *informal* get hold of, get one's hands on. 2 *the police found that he was procuring* PIMP.

prod ▶ verb 1 *Cassie prodded him in the chest* POKE, jab, dig, elbow, butt, stab. 2 *they hoped to prod the government into action* SPUR, stimulate, stir, rouse, prompt, drive, galvanize; persuade, urge, chivvy; incite, goad, egg on, provoke.
▶ noun 1 *a prod in the ribs* POKE, jab, dig, elbow, butt, thrust. 2 *they need a prod to get them to act* STIMULUS, push, prompt, reminder, spur; incitement, goad.

prodigal ▶ adjective 1 *prodigal habits die hard* WASTEFUL, extravagant, spendthrift, profligate, improvident, imprudent. 2 *a composer who is prodigal with his talents* GENEROUS, lavish, liberal, unstinting, unsparing; *literary* bounteous. 3 *a dessert prodigal with whipped cream* ABOUNDING IN, abundant in, rich in, covered in, awash with, slathered with.
— OPPOSITES: thrifty, mean, deficient.

prodigious ▶ adjective ENORMOUS, huge, colossal, immense, vast, great, massive, gigantic, mammoth, tremendous, inordinate, monumental; amazing, astonishing, astounding, staggering, stunning, remarkable, phenomenal, terrific, miraculous, impressive, striking, startling, sensational,

spectacular, extraordinary, exceptional, breathtaking, incredible; *informal* humongous, stupendous, fantastic, fabulous, mega, awesome, ginormous; *literary* wondrous.
— OPPOSITES: small, unexceptional.

prodigy ▶ noun **1** *a seven-year-old prodigy* GENIUS, mastermind, virtuoso, wunderkind, wonder child, boy wonder; *informal* whiz kid, whiz, wizard. **2** *Germany seemed a prodigy of industrial discipline* MODEL, classic example, paragon, paradigm, epitome, exemplar, archetype.

produce ▶ verb **1** *the company produces furniture* MANUFACTURE, make, construct, build, fabricate, put together, assemble, turn out, create; mass-produce; *informal* churn out. **2** *the vineyards produce excellent wines* YIELD, grow, give, supply, provide, furnish, bear, bring forth. **3** *she produced ten puppies* GIVE BIRTH TO, bear, deliver, bring forth, bring into the world. **4** *he produced five novels* CREATE, originate, fashion, turn out; compose, write, pen; paint. **5** *she produced an ID card* PULL OUT, extract, fish out; present, offer, proffer, show. **6** *no evidence was produced* PRESENT, offer, provide, furnish, advance, put forward, bring forward, come up with. **7** *that will produce a reaction* GIVE RISE TO, bring about, cause, occasion, generate, engender, lead to, result in, effect, induce, set off; provoke, precipitate, breed, spark off, trigger; *literary* beget. **8** *James produced the play* STAGE, put on, mount, present.
— RELATED TERMS: -facient, -genic.
▶ noun *fresh produce* FOOD, foodstuff(s), products; harvest, crops, fruit, vegetables, greens.

producer ▶ noun **1** *a car producer* MANUFACTURER, maker, builder, constructor, fabricator. **2** *coffee producers* GROWER, farmer. **3** *the producer of the show* IMPRESARIO, manager, administrator, promoter, regisseur.

product ▶ noun **1** *a household product* ARTIFACT, commodity, manufactured article; creation, invention; (**products**) goods, wares, merchandise, produce. **2** *his skill is a product of experience* RESULT, consequence, outcome, effect, upshot, fruit, by-product, spinoff.

production ▶ noun **1** *the production of cars* MANUFACTURE, making, construction, building, fabrication, assembly, creation; mass-production. **2** *the production of literary works* CREATION, origination, fashioning; composition, writing. **3** *literary productions* WORK, opus, creation; publication, composition, piece; work of art, painting, picture; *Law* intellectual property. **4** *agricultural production* OUTPUT, yield; productivity. **5** *admission only on production of a ticket* PRESENTATION, proffering, showing. **6** *a theatre production* PERFORMANCE, staging, presentation, show, piece, play.

productive ▶ adjective **1** *a productive artist* PROLIFIC, inventive, creative; energetic. **2** *productive talks* USEFUL, constructive, profitable, fruitful, gainful, valuable, effective, worthwhile, helpful. **3** *productive land* FERTILE, fruitful, rich, fecund.
— OPPOSITES: sterile, barren.

productivity ▶ noun **1** *workers have boosted productivity* EFFICIENCY, work rate; output, yield; production. **2** *the productivity of the soil* FRUITFULNESS, fertility, richness, fecundity.
— OPPOSITES: sterility, barrenness.

profane ▶ adjective **1** *subjects both sacred and profane* SECULAR, lay, non-religious, temporal; *formal* laic. **2** *a profane man* IRREVERENT, irreligious, ungodly, godless,

unbelieving, impious, disrespectful, sacrilegious. **3** *profane language* OBSCENE, blasphemous, indecent, foul, vulgar, crude, filthy, dirty, smutty, coarse, rude, offensive, indecorous.
— OPPOSITES: religious, sacred, reverent, decorous.
▶ verb *invaders profaned our sacred temples* DESECRATE, violate, defile, treat sacrilegiously.

profanity ▶ noun **1** *he hissed a profanity | an outburst of profanity* OATH, swear word, expletive, curse, obscenity, four-letter word, dirty word; blasphemy, swearing, foul language, bad language, cursing; *informal* cuss, cuss word; *formal* imprecation; *archaic* execration. **2** *some traditional festivals were tainted with profanity* SACRILEGE, blasphemy, irreligion, ungodliness, impiety, irreverence, disrespect.

profess ▶ verb **1** *he professed his love* DECLARE, announce, proclaim, assert, state, affirm, avow, maintain, protest; *formal* aver. **2** *she professed to loathe publicity* CLAIM, pretend, purport, affect; make out; *informal* let on. **3** *the Emperor professed Christianity* AFFIRM ONE'S FAITH IN, affirm one's allegiance to, avow, confess.

professed ▶ adjective **1** *his professed ambition* CLAIMED, supposed, ostensible, self-styled, apparent, pretended, purported. **2** *a professed libertarian* DECLARED, self-acknowledged, self-confessed, confessed, sworn, avowed, confirmed.

profession ▶ noun **1** *his chosen profession of teaching* CAREER, occupation, calling, vocation, métier, line (of work), walk of life, job, business, trade, craft; *informal* racket. **2** *a profession of allegiance* DECLARATION, affirmation, statement, announcement, proclamation, assertion, avowal, vow, claim, protestation; *formal* averment.

professional ▶ adjective **1** *people in professional occupations* WHITE-COLLAR, non-manual. **2** *a professional rugby player* PAID, salaried. **3** *a thoroughly professional performance* EXPERT, accomplished, skilful, masterly, masterful, fine, polished, skilled, proficient, competent, able, experienced, practised, trained, seasoned, businesslike, deft; *informal* ace, crack, top-notch. **4** *not a professional way to behave* APPROPRIATE, fitting, proper, honourable, ethical, correct, comme il faut.
— OPPOSITES: manual, amateur, amateurish, inappropriate, unethical.
▶ noun **1** *affluent young professionals* WHITE-COLLAR WORKER, office worker. **2** *his first season as a professional* PROFESSIONAL PLAYER, paid player, salaried player; *informal* pro. **3** *she was a real professional on stage* EXPERT, virtuoso, old hand, old sweat, master, maestro, past master; *informal* pro, ace, wizard, whiz, hotshot, maven, crackerjack.
— OPPOSITES: manual worker, amateur.

professor ▶ noun PROF, tenured faculty member, dean, full/assistant/associate professor, instructor, lecturer, doctor, scholar, academic.

proffer ▶ verb OFFER, tender, submit, extend, volunteer, suggest, propose, put forward; hold out.
— OPPOSITES: refuse, withdraw.

proficiency ▶ noun SKILL, expertise, experience, accomplishment, competence, mastery, prowess, professionalism, deftness, adroitness, dexterity, finesse, ability, facility; *informal* know-how.
— OPPOSITES: incompetence.

proficient ▶ adjective SKILLED, skilful, expert, experienced, accomplished, competent, masterly, adept, adroit, deft, dexterous, able, professional,

consummate, complete, master; *informal* crack, ace, mean.
– OPPOSITES: incompetent.

profile ▶ noun **1** *his handsome profile* SIDE VIEW, outline, silhouette, contour, shape, form, figure, lines. **2** *she wrote a profile of the organization* DESCRIPTION, account, study, portrait, portrayal, depiction, rundown, sketch, outline.
▶ verb *he was profiled in the local paper* DESCRIBE, write about, give an account of, portray, depict, sketch, outline.
■ **keep a low profile** LIE LOW, keep quiet, keep out of the public eye, avoid publicity, keep out of sight.

profit ▶ noun **1** *the firm made a profit* (FINANCIAL) GAIN, return(s), yield, earnings, winnings, surplus, excess; *informal* pay dirt, bottom line. **2** *there was little profit in continuing the hike* ADVANTAGE, benefit, value, use, good, avail; *informal* mileage.
– OPPOSITES: loss, disadvantage.
▶ verb **1** *this company must not profit from its wrongdoing* MAKE MONEY, make a profit; *informal* rake it in, clean up, make a killing, make a bundle, make big bucks, make a fast/quick buck. **2** *how will that profit us?* BENEFIT, be beneficial to, be of benefit to, be advantageous to, be of advantage to, be of use to, be of value to, do someone good, help, be of service to, serve, assist, aid.
– OPPOSITES: lose, disadvantage.
■ **profit by/from** BENEFIT FROM, take advantage of, derive benefit from, capitalize on, make the most of, turn to one's advantage, put to good use, do well out of, exploit, gain from; *informal* cash in on.

profitable ▶ adjective **1** *a profitable company* MONEY-MAKING, profit-making, commercial, successful, solvent, in the black, gainful, remunerative, financially rewarding, paying, lucrative, bankable. **2** *profitable study* BENEFICIAL, useful, advantageous, valuable, productive, worthwhile, rewarding, fruitful, illuminating, informative, well-spent.
– OPPOSITES: loss-making, fruitless, useless.

profiteer ▶ verb *a store owner was charged with profiteering* OVERCHARGE, racketeer; cheat someone, fleece someone; *informal* rip someone off, rob someone.
▶ noun *he was a war profiteer* RACKETEER, exploiter, black marketeer; *informal* bloodsucker, vampire.

profligate ▶ adjective **1** *profligate local authorities* WASTEFUL, extravagant, spendthrift, improvident, prodigal. **2** *a profligate lifestyle* DISSOLUTE, degenerate, dissipated, debauched, corrupt, depraved; PROMISCUOUS, loose, wanton, licentious, libertine, decadent, abandoned, fast; SYBARITIC, voluptuary.
– OPPOSITES: thrifty, frugal, moral, upright.
▶ noun *he was an out-and-out profligate* LIBERTINE, debauchee, degenerate, dissolute, roué, rake, sybarite, voluptuary.

profound ▶ adjective **1** *profound relief* HEARTFELT, intense, keen, great, extreme, acute, severe, sincere, earnest, deep, deep-seated, overpowering, overwhelming, fervent, ardent. **2** *profound silence* COMPLETE, utter, total, absolute. **3** *a profound change* FAR-REACHING, radical, extensive, sweeping, exhaustive, thoroughgoing. **4** *a profound analysis* WISE, learned, clever, intelligent, scholarly, sage, erudite, discerning, penetrating, perceptive, astute, thoughtful, insightful, percipient, perspicacious; *rare* sapient. **5** *profound truths* COMPLEX, abstract, deep, weighty, difficult, abstruse, recondite, esoteric.
– OPPOSITES: superficial, mild, slight, simple.

profoundly ▶ adverb **1** *she was profoundly grateful that none of her colleagues could see her* EXTREMELY, very, deeply, exceedingly, greatly, immensely, enormously, tremendously, intensely, heartily, keenly, acutely, painfully, from the bottom of one's heart, downright, thoroughly, sincerely, so; *informal* awfully, terribly, seriously, majorly, oh-so, mighty. **2** *he spoke profoundly on the subject* PENETRATINGLY, discerningly, wisely, sagaciously, thoughtfully, philosophically, weightily, seriously, learnedly, eruditely.

profuse ▶ adjective **1** *profuse apologies* COPIOUS, prolific, abundant, liberal, unstinting, fulsome, effusive, extravagant, lavish, gushing; *informal* over the top, gushy. **2** *profuse blooms* LUXURIANT, plentiful, copious, abundant, lush, rich, exuberant, riotous, teeming, rank, rampant; *informal* jungly.
– OPPOSITES: meagre, sparse.

profusion ▶ noun ABUNDANCE, mass, host, cornucopia, riot, plethora, superabundance; *informal* sea, wealth; *formal* plenitude.

progenitor ▶ noun **1** *the progenitor of an illustrious family* ANCESTOR, forefather, forebear, parent, primogenitor; *Law* stirps; *archaic* begetter. **2** *the progenitor of modern jazz* ORIGINATOR, creator, founder, architect, inventor, pioneer.

progeny ▶ noun OFFSPRING, young, babies, children, sons and daughters, family, brood; DESCENDANTS, heirs, scions; *Law* issue; *archaic* seed, fruit of one's loins.

prognosis ▶ noun FORECAST, prediction, prognostication, prophecy, divination, augury.

prognosticate ▶ verb FORECAST, predict, prophesy, foretell, foresee, forewarn of.

prognostication ▶ noun PREDICTION, forecast, prophecy, prognosis, divination, augury.

program ▶ noun **1** *our program for the day* SCHEDULE, agenda, calendar, timetable; order of events, lineup. **2** *the government's reform program* PLAN of action, series of measures, strategy, scheme. **3** *a television program* BROADCAST, production, show, presentation, transmission, performance, telecast. **4** *a program of study* COURSE, syllabus, curriculum. **5** *a theatre program* GUIDE, list of performers, cast list, playbill.
▶ verb *they programmed the day well* ARRANGE, organize, schedule, plan, map out, timetable, line up, slate.

progress ▶ noun **1** *boulders made progress difficult* FORWARD MOVEMENT, advance, going, progression, headway, passage. **2** *scientific progress* DEVELOPMENT, advance, advancement, headway, step(s) forward; improvement, betterment, growth.
– OPPOSITES: relapse.
▶ verb **1** *they progressed slowly down the road* GO, make one's way, move, move forward, go forward, proceed, advance, go on, continue, make headway, work one's way. **2** *the school has progressed rapidly* DEVELOP, make progress, advance, make headway, take steps forward, move on, get on, gain ground; improve, get better, come on, come along, make strides; thrive, prosper, blossom, flourish; *informal* be getting there.
– OPPOSITES: relapse.
■ **in progress** UNDERWAY, going on, ongoing, happening, occurring, taking place, proceeding, continuing; unfinished, in the works.

progression ▶ noun **1** *progression to the next stage* PROGRESS, advancement, movement, passage, march; development, evolution, growth. **2** *a progression of* *peaks on the graph* SUCCESSION, series, sequence, string, stream, chain, concatenation, train, row, cycle.

progressive ▶ adjective **1** *progressive deterioration* CONTINUING, continuous, increasing, growing, developing, ongoing, accelerating, escalating; gradual, step-by-step, cumulative. **2** *progressive views* MODERN, liberal, advanced, forward-thinking, enlightened, enterprising, innovative, pioneering, dynamic, bold, avant-garde, reforming, reformist, radical; *informal* go-ahead.
— OPPOSITES: conservative, reactionary.
▶ noun *he is very much a progressive* INNOVATOR, reformer, reformist, liberal, libertarian.

prohibit ▶ verb **1** *state law prohibits gambling* FORBID, ban, bar, interdict, proscribe, make illegal, embargo, outlaw, disallow, veto; *Law* enjoin. **2** *a cash shortage prohibited the visit* PREVENT, stop, rule out, preclude, make impossible.
— OPPOSITES: allow.

prohibited ▶ adjective ILLEGAL, illicit, taboo, against the law, verboten; *informal* out, no go; *formal* non licet.
— OPPOSITES: permitted.

prohibition ▶ noun **1** *the prohibition of cannabis* BANNING, forbidding, prohibiting, barring, debarment, vetoing, proscription, interdiction, outlawing. **2** *a prohibition was imposed* BAN, bar, interdict, veto, embargo, injunction, moratorium.

prohibitive ▶ adjective **1** *prohibitive costs* EXORBITANT, excessively high, sky-high, over-inflated; out of the question, beyond one's means; extortionate, unreasonable; *informal* steep, criminal. **2** *prohibitive regulations* PROSCRIPTIVE, prohibitory, restrictive, repressive.

project ▶ noun **1** *an engineering project* PLAN, program, enterprise, undertaking, venture; proposal, idea, concept, scheme. **2** *a history project* ASSIGNMENT, piece of work, piece of research, task.
▶ verb **1** *profits are projected to rise* FORECAST, predict, expect, estimate, calculate, reckon. **2** *his projected book* INTEND, plan, propose, devise, design, outline. **3** *balconies projected over the lake* STICK OUT, jut (out), protrude, extend, stand out, bulge out, poke out, thrust out, cantilever. **4** *seeds are projected from the tree* PROPEL, discharge, launch, throw, cast, fling, hurl, shoot. **5** *the sun projected his shadow on the wall* CAST, throw, send, shed, shine. **6** *she tried to project a calm image* CONVEY, put across, put over, communicate, present, promote.

projectile ▶ noun MISSILE.

projecting ▶ adjective STICKING OUT, protuberant, protruding, prominent, jutting, overhanging, beetling, proud, bulging.
— OPPOSITES: sunken, flush.

projection ▶ noun **1** *a sales projection* FORECAST, prediction, prognosis, outlook, expectation, estimate. **2** *tiny projections on the cliff face* PROTUBERANCE, protrusion, prominence, eminence, outcrop, outgrowth, jut, jag, snag; overhang, ledge, shelf.

proletarian ▶ adjective *a proletarian background* WORKING-CLASS, plebeian, common, blue-collar.
— OPPOSITES: aristocratic.
▶ noun *disaffected proletarians* WORKING-CLASS PERSON, (blue-collar) worker, plebeian, commoner, man/woman/person in the street; *derogatory* prole.
— OPPOSITES: aristocrat.

proletariat ▶ noun THE WORKERS, working-class people, wage earners, the labouring classes, the common people, the lower classes, the masses, the rank and file, the third estate, the plebeians; *derogatory* the hoi polloi, the plebs, the proles, the great unwashed, the mob, the rabble.
— OPPOSITES: aristocracy.

proliferate ▶ verb INCREASE RAPIDLY, grow rapidly, multiply, rocket, mushroom, snowball, burgeon, run riot.
— OPPOSITES: decrease, dwindle.

prolific ▶ adjective **1** *a prolific crop of tomatoes* PLENTIFUL, abundant, bountiful, profuse, copious, luxuriant, rich, lush; fruitful, fecund; *literary* plenteous, bounteous. **2** *a prolific composer* PRODUCTIVE, creative, inventive, fertile.

prolix ▶ adjective LONG-WINDED, verbose, wordy, pleonastic, discursive, rambling, long-drawn-out, overlong, lengthy, protracted, interminable; *informal* windy, waffly.

prologue ▶ noun INTRODUCTION, foreword, preface, preamble, prelude; *informal* intro, lead-in; *formal* exordium, proem, prolegomenon.
— OPPOSITES: epilogue.

prolong ▶ verb LENGTHEN, extend, draw out, drag out, protract, spin out, stretch out, string out, elongate; carry on, continue, keep up, perpetuate.
— OPPOSITES: shorten.

promenade ▶ noun **1** *the tree-lined promenade* ESPLANADE, front, seafront, parade, walk, boulevard, avenue, boardwalk. **2** *our nightly promenade* WALK, stroll, turn, amble, airing; *dated* constitutional.
▶ verb *we promenaded in the park* WALK, stroll, saunter, wander, amble, stretch one's legs, take a turn.

prominence ▶ noun **1** *his rise to prominence* FAME, celebrity, eminence, pre-eminence, importance, distinction, greatness, note, notability, prestige, stature, standing, position, rank. **2** *the press gave prominence to the reports* GOOD COVERAGE, importance, precedence, weight, a high profile, top billing. **3** *a rocky prominence* HILLOCK, hill, hummock, mound; outcrop, crag, spur, rise; ridge, arête; peak, pinnacle; promontory, cliff, headland.

prominent ▶ adjective **1** *a prominent surgeon* IMPORTANT, well-known, leading, eminent, distinguished, notable, noteworthy, noted, illustrious, celebrated, famous, renowned, acclaimed, famed, influential, major-league. **2** *prominent cheekbones* PROTUBERANT, protruding, projecting, jutting (out), standing out, sticking out, proud, bulging, bulbous. **3** *a prominent feature of the landscape* CONSPICUOUS, noticeable, easily seen, obvious, unmistakable, eye-catching, pronounced, salient, striking, dominant; obtrusive.
— OPPOSITES: unimportant, unknown, inconspicuous.

promiscuity ▶ noun LICENTIOUSNESS, wantonness, immorality; *informal* sleeping around, sluttishness, whorishness; *dated* looseness.
— OPPOSITES: chastity, virtue.

promiscuous ▶ adjective **1** *a promiscuous woman* LICENTIOUS, sexually indiscriminate, wanton, immoral, fast; *informal* easy, swinging, sluttish, whorish, bed-hopping; *dated* loose, fallen. **2** *promiscuous reading* INDISCRIMINATE, undiscriminating, unselective, random, haphazard, irresponsible, unthinking, unconsidered.
— OPPOSITES: chaste, virtuous, selective.

promise ▶ noun **1** *you broke your promise* WORD (OF HONOUR), assurance, pledge, vow, guarantee, oath,

bond, undertaking, agreement, commitment, contract, covenant. **2** *he shows promise* POTENTIAL, ability, aptitude, capability, capacity. **3** *a promise of fine weather* INDICATION, hint, suggestion, sign.
▶ **verb 1** *she promised to go* GIVE ONE'S WORD, swear, pledge, vow, undertake, guarantee, contract, engage, give an assurance, commit oneself, bind oneself, swear/take an oath, covenant; *archaic* plight. **2** *the skies promised sunshine* INDICATE, lead one to expect, point to, denote, signify, be a sign of, be evidence of, give hope of, bespeak, presage, augur, herald, bode, portend; *literary* betoken, foretoken, forebode.

promising ▶ **adjective 1** *a promising start* GOOD, encouraging, favourable, hopeful, full of promise, auspicious, propitious, bright, rosy, heartening, reassuring. **2** *a promising actor* WITH POTENTIAL, budding, up-and-coming, rising, coming, in the making.
— OPPOSITES: unfavourable, hopeless.

promontory ▶ **noun** HEADLAND, point, cape, head, foreland, horn, bill, peninsula.

promote ▶ **verb 1** *she's been promoted at work* UPGRADE, give promotion to, elevate, advance, move up; *humorous* kick upstairs; *archaic* prefer. **2** *an organization promoting justice* ENCOURAGE, advocate, further, advance, assist, aid, help, contribute to, foster, nurture, develop, boost, stimulate, forward, work for. **3** *she is promoting her new film* ADVERTISE, publicize, give publicity to, beat/bang the drum for, market, merchandise; *informal* push, plug, hype, puff, boost, ballyhoo, flack.
— OPPOSITES: demote, obstruct, play down.

promoter ▶ **noun** ADVOCATE, champion, supporter, backer, proponent, protagonist, campaigner, booster, flack, publicist; impresario.

promotion ▶ **noun 1** *her promotion at work* UPGRADING, preferment, elevation, advancement, step up (the ladder). **2** *the promotion of justice* ENCOURAGEMENT, advocacy, furtherance, furthering, advancement, assistance, aid, help, contribution to, fostering, boosting, stimulation, boosterism. **3** *the promotion of her new film* ADVERTISING, publicizing, marketing; publicity, campaign, propaganda; *informal* hard sell, blitz, plug, hype, puff, ballyhoo.

prompt ▶ **verb 1** *curiosity prompted him to look* INDUCE, make, move, motivate, lead, dispose, persuade, incline, encourage, stimulate, prod, impel, spur on, inspire. **2** *the statement prompted a hostile reaction* GIVE RISE TO, bring about, cause, occasion, result in, lead to, elicit, produce, bring on, engender, induce, precipitate, trigger, spark off, provoke. **3** *the actors needed prompting* REMIND, cue, feed, help out; jog someone's memory.
— OPPOSITES: deter.
▶ **adjective** *a prompt reply* QUICK, swift, rapid, speedy, fast, direct, immediate, instant, expeditious, early, punctual, in good time, on time, timely.
— OPPOSITES: slow, late.
▶ **noun** *the actor stopped, and Julia supplied a prompt* REMINDER, cue, feed.

promptly ▶ **adverb 1** *William arrived promptly at 7:30* PUNCTUALLY, on time; *informal* bang on, on the button, on the dot, on the nose. **2** *I expect the matter to be dealt with promptly* WITHOUT DELAY, straight away, right away, at once, immediately, now, as soon as possible; QUICKLY, swiftly, rapidly, speedily, fast, expeditiously, momentarily; *informal* pronto, ASAP, PDQ (pretty damn quick).
— OPPOSITES: late, slowly.

promulgate ▶ **verb 1** *they promulgated their own views* MAKE KNOWN, make public, publicize, spread, communicate, propagate, disseminate, broadcast, promote, preach; *literary* bruit abroad. **2** *the law was promulgated in 1942* PUT INTO EFFECT, enact, implement, enforce.

prone ▶ **adjective 1** *softwood is prone to rotting* | *prone to rot* SUSCEPTIBLE, vulnerable, subject, open, liable, given, predisposed, likely, disposed, inclined, apt; at risk of. **2** *his prone body* (LYING) FACE DOWN, face downwards, on one's stomach/front; LYING FLAT/DOWN, horizontal, prostrate.
— OPPOSITES: resistant, immune, upright.

prong ▶ **noun** TINE, spike, point, tip, projection.

pronounce ▶ **verb 1** *his name is difficult to pronounce* SAY, enunciate, articulate, utter, voice, sound, vocalize, get one's tongue around. **2** *the doctor pronounced that I had a virus* ANNOUNCE, proclaim, declare, affirm, assert; judge, rule, decree.

pronounced ▶ **adjective** NOTICEABLE, marked, strong, conspicuous, striking, distinct, prominent, unmistakable, obvious, recognizable, identifiable.
— OPPOSITES: slight.

pronouncement ▶ **noun** ANNOUNCEMENT, proclamation, declaration, assertion; judgment, ruling, decree; *formal* ordinance.

pronunciation ▶ **noun** ACCENT, manner of speaking, speech, diction, delivery, elocution, intonation; articulation, enunciation, voicing, vocalization, sounding.

proof ▶ **noun 1** *proof of ownership* EVIDENCE, verification, corroboration, authentication, confirmation, certification, documentation, validation, attestation, substantiation. **2** *the proofs of a book* PAGE PROOF, galley proof, galley.
▶ **adjective** *no system is proof against theft* RESISTANT, immune, unaffected, invulnerable, impenetrable, impervious, repellent.

prop ▶ **noun 1** *the roof is held up by props* POLE, post, support, upright, brace, buttress, strut, stanchion, shore, pier, pillar, pile, piling, bolster, truss, column. **2** *a prop for the economy* MAINSTAY, pillar, anchor, backbone, support, foundation, cornerstone.
▶ **verb 1** *she propped her bike against the wall* LEAN, rest, stand, balance, steady. **2** *this post is propping the wall up* HOLD UP, shore up, bolster up, buttress, support, brace, underpin. **3** *they prop up failing industries* SUBSIDIZE, underwrite, fund, finance.

propaganda ▶ **noun** INFORMATION, promotion, advertising, publicity, spin; disinformation, counter-information, the big lie; *historical* agitprop; *informal* info, hype, plugging; puff piece.

propagandist ▶ **noun** PROMOTER, champion, supporter, proponent, advocate, campaigner, crusader, publicist, flack, evangelist, apostle.

propagate ▶ **verb 1** *an easy plant to propagate* BREED, grow, cultivate. **2** *these shrubs propagate easily* REPRODUCE, multiply, proliferate, increase, spread, self-seed, self-sow. **3** *they propagated socialist ideas* SPREAD, disseminate, communicate, make known, promulgate, circulate, broadcast, publicize, proclaim, preach, promote; *literary* bruit abroad.

propel ▶ **verb 1** *a boat propelled by oars* MOVE, power, push, drive. **2** *he propelled the ball into the air* THROW, thrust, toss, fling, hurl, launch, pitch, project, send, shoot. **3** *confusion propelled her into action* SPUR, drive, prompt, precipitate, catapult, motivate, force, impel.

propeller ▶ **noun** ROTOR, screw; *informal* prop.

propensity ▶ noun TENDENCY, inclination, predisposition, proneness, proclivity, readiness, liability, disposition, leaning, weakness.

proper ▶ adjective **1** *he's not a proper scientist* REAL, genuine, actual, true, bona fide; *informal* kosher. **2** *the proper channels* RIGHT, correct, accepted, orthodox, conventional, established, official, formal, regular, acceptable, appropriate, de rigueur; *archaic* meet. **3** *they were terribly proper* RESPECTABLE, decorous, seemly, decent, refined, ladylike, gentlemanly, genteel; formal, conventional, correct, comme il faut, orthodox, polite, punctilious.
– OPPOSITES: fake, inappropriate, wrong, unconventional.

property ▶ noun **1** *lost property* POSSESSIONS, belongings, things, effects, stuff, gear, chattels, movables; resources, assets, valuables, fortune, capital, riches, wealth; *Law* personalty, goods and chattels. **2** *private property* BUILDING(S), premises, house(s), land, estates, realty, real estate. **3** *healing properties* QUALITY, attribute, characteristic, feature, power, trait, mark, hallmark.

prophecy ▶ noun **1** *her prophecy is coming true* PREDICTION, forecast, prognostication, prognosis, divination, augury. **2** *the gift of prophecy* DIVINATION, fortune telling, crystal-gazing, prediction, second sight, prognostication, augury, soothsaying.

prophesy ▶ verb PREDICT, foretell, forecast, foresee, forewarn of, prognosticate.

prophet, prophetess ▶ noun SEER, soothsayer, fortune teller, clairvoyant, diviner; oracle, augur, sibyl.
■ **prophet of doom** PESSIMIST, doom-monger, doomsayer, doomster, Cassandra, Jeremiah; *informal* Chicken Little.

prophetic ▶ adjective PRESCIENT, predictive, far-seeing, prognostic, divinatory, sibylline, apocalyptic; *rare* vatic.

prophylactic ▶ adjective *prophylactic measures* PREVENTIVE, preventative, precautionary, protective, inhibitory.
▶ noun **1** *a prophylactic against malaria* PREVENTIVE MEASURE, precaution, safeguard, safety measure; preventive medicine. **2** *prophylactic dispensers in public washrooms. See* CONDOM.

prophylaxis ▶ noun PREVENTIVE TREATMENT, prevention, protection, precaution.

propitiate ▶ verb APPEASE, placate, mollify, pacify, make peace with, conciliate, make amends to, soothe, calm.
– OPPOSITES: provoke.

propitious ▶ adjective FAVOURABLE, auspicious, promising, providential, advantageous, optimistic, bright, rosy, heaven-sent, hopeful; opportune, timely.
– OPPOSITES: inauspicious, unfortunate.

proponent ▶ noun ADVOCATE, champion, supporter, backer, promoter, protagonist, campaigner, booster, cheerleader.

proportion ▶ noun **1** *a small proportion of the land* PART, portion, amount, quantity, bit, piece, percentage, fraction, section, segment, share. **2** *the proportion of water to alcohol* RATIO, distribution, relative amount/number; relationship. **3** *the drawing is out of proportion* BALANCE, symmetry, harmony, correspondence, correlation, agreement. **4** *men of huge proportions* SIZE, dimensions, magnitude,

measurements; mass, volume, bulk; expanse, extent, width, breadth.

proportional ▶ adjective CORRESPONDING, proportionate, comparable, in proportion, pro rata, commensurate, equivalent, consistent, relative, analogous.
– OPPOSITES: disproportionate.

proposal ▶ noun **1** *the proposal was rejected* PLAN, idea, scheme, project, program, manifesto, motion, proposition, suggestion, submission, trial balloon. **2** *the proposal of a new constitution* PUTTING FORWARD, proposing, suggesting, submitting.
– OPPOSITES: withdrawal.

propose ▶ verb **1** *he proposed a solution* PUT FORWARD, suggest, submit, advance, offer, present, move, come up with, lodge, table, nominate. **2** *do you propose to go?* INTEND, mean, plan, have in mind/view, resolve, aim, purpose, think of, aspire, want. **3** *you've proposed to her!* ASK SOMEONE TO MARRY YOU, make an offer of marriage, offer marriage; *informal* pop the question; *dated* ask for someone's hand in marriage.
– OPPOSITES: withdraw.

proposition ▶ noun **1** *the analysis derives from one proposition* THEORY, hypothesis, thesis, argument, premise, principle, theorem, concept, idea, statement. **2** *a business proposition* PROPOSAL, scheme, plan, project, idea, program, bid. **3** *doing it for real is a very different proposition* TASK, job, undertaking, venture, activity, affair, problem.
▶ verb *he never dared proposition her* PROPOSE SEX WITH, make sexual advances to, make an indecent proposal to, make an improper suggestion to; *informal* hit on.

propound ▶ verb PUT FORWARD, advance, offer, proffer, present, set forth, submit, tender, suggest, introduce, postulate, propose, pose, posit; advocate, promote, peddle, spread.

proprietary ▶ adjective COPYRIGHTED, trademarked, owned, private, registered, patented, exclusive.

proprietor, proprietress ▶ noun OWNER, possessor, holder, master/mistress; landowner, landlord/landlady; innkeeper, hotel-keeper, hotelier, storekeeper.

propriety ▶ noun **1** *she behaves with the utmost propriety* DECORUM, respectability, decency, correctness, protocol, appropriateness, suitability, good manners, courtesy, politeness, rectitude, morality, civility, modesty, demureness; sobriety, refinement, discretion. **2** *he was careful to preserve the proprieties in public* ETIQUETTE, convention(s), social grace(s), niceties, one's Ps and Qs, protocol, standards, civilities, formalities, accepted behaviour, good form, the done thing, the thing to do, punctilio.
– OPPOSITES: indecorum.

propulsion ▶ noun THRUST, motive force, impetus, impulse, drive, driving force, actuation, push, pressure, power.

prosaic ▶ adjective ORDINARY, everyday, commonplace, conventional, straightforward, routine, run-of-the-mill, by-the-numbers, workaday; UNIMAGINATIVE, uninspired, uninspiring, matter-of-fact, dull, dry, dreary, tedious, boring, humdrum, mundane, pedestrian, tame, plodding; bland, insipid, banal, trite, literal, factual, unpoetic, unemotional, unsentimental.
– OPPOSITES: interesting, imaginative, inspired.

proscribe ▶ verb **1** *gambling was proscribed* FORBID, prohibit, ban, bar, interdict, make illegal, embargo, outlaw, disallow, veto; *Law* enjoin. **2** *the book was*

proscribed by the Church CONDEMN, denounce, attack, criticize, censure, damn, reject, taboo.
– OPPOSITES: allow, authorize, accept.

proscription ▶ noun 1 *the proscription of alcohol* BANNING, forbidding, prohibition, prohibiting, barring, debarment, vetoing, interdiction, outlawing. 2 *a proscription was imposed* BAN, prohibition, bar, interdict, veto, embargo, moratorium. 3 *the proscription of his literary works* CONDEMNATION, denunciation, attacking, criticism, censuring, damning, rejection.
– OPPOSITES: allowing, authorization, acceptance.

prose ▶ noun TEXT, style, writing; fiction, non-fiction.

prosecute ▶ verb 1 *they prosecute offenders* TAKE TO COURT, bring/institute legal proceedings against, bring an action against, take legal action against, sue, try, impeach, bring to trial, put on trial, put in the dock, bring a suit against, indict, arraign. 2 *they helped him prosecute the war* PURSUE, fight, wage, carry on, conduct, direct, engage in, proceed with, continue (with), keep on with.
– OPPOSITES: defend, let off, give up.

proselyte ▶ noun CONVERT, new believer, catechumen.

proselytize ▶ verb 1 *I'm not here to proselytize* EVANGELIZE, convert, save, redeem, win over, preach (to), recruit, act as a missionary. 2 *he wanted to proselytize his ideas* PROMOTE, advocate, champion, advance, further, spread, proclaim, peddle, preach, endorse, urge, recommend, boost.

prospect ▶ noun 1 *there is little prospect of success* LIKELIHOOD, hope, expectation, anticipation, (good/poor) chance, odds, probability, possibility, promise; fear, danger. 2 *her job prospects* POSSIBILITIES, potential, promise, expectations, outlook. 3 *a daunting prospect* VISION, thought, idea; task, undertaking. 4 *Jack is an exciting prospect* CANDIDATE, possibility; *informal* catch. 5 *there is a pleasant prospect from the lounge* VIEW, vista, outlook, perspective, panorama, aspect, scene; picture, spectacle, sight.
▶ verb *they are prospecting for gold* SEARCH, look, explore, survey, scout, hunt, reconnoitre, examine, inspect.

prospective ▶ adjective POTENTIAL, possible, probable, likely, future, eventual, -to-be, soon-to-be, in the making; intending, aspiring, would-be; forthcoming, approaching, coming, imminent.

prospectus ▶ noun BROCHURE, pamphlet, description, particulars, announcement, advertisement; syllabus, curriculum, catalogue, program, list, fact sheet, scheme, schedule.

prosper ▶ verb FLOURISH, thrive, do well, bloom, blossom, burgeon, progress, do all right for oneself, get ahead, get on (in the world), be successful; *informal* go places.
– OPPOSITES: fail, flounder.

prosperity ▶ noun SUCCESS, profitability, affluence, wealth, opulence, luxury, the good life, milk and honey, (good) fortune, ease, plenty, comfort, security, well-being.
– OPPOSITES: hardship, failure.

prosperous ▶ adjective THRIVING, flourishing, successful, strong, vigorous, profitable, lucrative, expanding, booming, burgeoning; AFFLUENT, wealthy, rich, moneyed, well off, well-to-do, opulent, substantial, in clover; *informal* on a roll, in the money.
– OPPOSITES: ailing, poor.

prostitute ▶ noun CALL GIRL, sex worker, whore;

informal hooker; tart, moll, working girl, courtesan, member of the oldest profession, fille de joie, escort, hustler, chippy; ho, camp follower; *dated* streetwalker, lady/woman of the night, scarlet woman, cocotte, strumpet, harlot, trollop, woman of ill repute, wench.
▶ verb *they prostituted their art* BETRAY, sacrifice, sell, sell out, debase, degrade, demean, devalue, cheapen, lower, shame, misuse, pervert; abandon one's principles, be untrue to oneself.

prostitution ▶ noun THE SEX TRADE, the sex industry, whoring, streetwalking, sex tourism; *informal* the oldest profession, hooking, hustling; *dated* whoredom; *archaic* harlotry.

prostrate ▶ adjective 1 *the prostrate figure on the ground* PRONE, lying flat, lying down, stretched out, spread-eagled, sprawling, horizontal, recumbent; *rare* procumbent. 2 *his wife was prostrate with shock* OVERWHELMED, overcome, overpowered, brought to one's knees, stunned, dazed; speechless, helpless. 3 *the fever left me prostrate* WORN OUT, exhausted, fatigued, tired out, sapped, dog-tired, spent, drained, debilitated, enervated, laid low; *informal* dead, dead beat, dead on one's feet, ready to drop, bushed, frazzled, worn to a frazzle, whacked, pooped.
– OPPOSITES: upright, fresh.
▶ verb *she was prostrated by the tragedy* OVERWHELM, overcome, overpower, bring to one's knees, devastate, debilitate, weaken, enfeeble, enervate, lay low, wear out, exhaust, tire out, drain, sap, wash out, take it out of; *informal* frazzle, do in, poop.
■ **prostrate oneself** THROW ONESELF FLAT/DOWN, lie down, stretch oneself out, throw oneself at someone's feet.

prostration ▶ noun COLLAPSE, weakness, debility, lassitude, exhaustion, fatigue, tiredness, enervation, emotional exhaustion.

protagonist ▶ noun 1 *the protagonist in the plot* CHIEF/CENTRAL/PRINCIPAL/MAIN/LEADING CHARACTER, chief etc. participant/figure/player, principal, hero/heroine, leading man/lady, title role, lead. 2 *a protagonist of deregulation* CHAMPION, advocate, upholder, supporter, backer, promoter, proponent, exponent, campaigner, fighter, crusader; apostle, apologist, booster.
– OPPOSITES: opponent.

protean ▶ adjective 1 *the protean nature of mental disorders* EVER-CHANGING, variable, changeable, mutable, kaleidoscopic, inconstant, inconsistent, unstable, shifting, unsettled, fluctuating, fluid, wavering, vacillating, mercurial, volatile; *technical* labile. 2 *a remarkably protean composer* VERSATILE, adaptable, flexible, all-round, multi-faceted, multitalented, many-sided.
– OPPOSITES: constant, consistent, limited.

protect ▶ verb KEEP SAFE, keep from harm, save, safeguard, preserve, defend, shield, cushion, insulate, hedge, shelter, screen, secure, fortify, guard, watch over, look after, take care of, keep; inoculate.
– OPPOSITES: expose, neglect, attack, harm.

protection ▶ noun 1 *protection against frost* DEFENCE, security, shielding, preservation, conservation, safekeeping, safeguarding, safety, sanctuary, shelter, refuge, lee, immunity, insurance, indemnity. 2 *under the protection of the Church* SAFEKEEPING, care, charge, keeping, protectorship, guidance, aegis, auspices, umbrella, guardianship, support, patronage, championship, providence. 3 *good protection against* *noise* BARRIER, buffer, shield, screen, hedge, cushion, preventative, armour, refuge, bulwark.

protective ▶ adjective **1** *protective clothing* PRESERVATIVE, protecting, safeguarding, shielding, defensive, safety, precautionary, preventive, preventative. **2** *he felt protective towards the dog* SOLICITOUS, caring, warm, paternal/maternal, fatherly/motherly, gallant, chivalrous; overprotective, possessive, jealous.

protector ▶ noun **1** *a protector of the environment* DEFENDER, preserver, guardian, guard, champion, watchdog, ombudsman, knight in shining armour, guardian angel, patron, chaperone, escort, keeper, custodian, bodyguard, minder; *informal* hired gun. **2** *ear protectors* GUARD, shield, buffer, cushion, pad, screen.

protege ▶ noun PUPIL, student, trainee, apprentice; disciple, follower; discovery, find, ward.

protest ▶ noun **1** *he resigned as a protest* OBJECTION, complaint, exception, disapproval, challenge, dissent, demurral, remonstration, fuss, outcry. **2** *women staged a protest* DEMONSTRATION, (protest) march, rally; sit-in, occupation; work-to-rule, industrial action, stoppage, strike, walkout, mutiny, picket, boycott; *informal* demo.
– OPPOSITES: support, approval.
▶ verb **1** *residents protested against the plans* EXPRESS OPPOSITION, object, dissent, take issue, make/take a stand, put up a fight, kick, take exception, complain, express disapproval, disagree, demur, remonstrate, make a fuss; cry out, speak out, rail, inveigh, fulminate; *informal* kick up a fuss/stink. **2** *people protested outside the cathedral* DEMONSTRATE, march, hold a rally, sit in, occupy somewhere; work to rule, take industrial action, stop work, strike, go on strike, walk out, mutiny, picket; boycott something. **3** *he protested his innocence* INSIST ON, maintain, assert, affirm, announce, proclaim, declare, profess, contend, argue, claim, vow, swear (to), stress; *formal* aver.
– OPPOSITES: acquiesce, support, deny.

protestation ▶ noun **1** *her protestations of innocence* DECLARATION, announcement, profession, assertion, insistence, claim, affirmation, assurance, oath, vow. **2** *we helped him despite his protestations* OBJECTION, protest, exception, complaint, disapproval, opposition, challenge, dissent, demurral, remonstration, fuss, outcry; *informal* stink.
– OPPOSITES: denial, acquiescence, support.

protester ▶ noun DEMONSTRATOR, objector, opposer, opponent, complainant, complainer, dissenter, dissident, nonconformist, protest marcher; striker, picket.

protocol ▶ noun **1** *a stickler for protocol* ETIQUETTE, conventions, formalities, customs, rules of conduct, procedure, ritual, accepted behaviour, propriety, proprieties, one's Ps and Qs, decorum, good form, the done thing, the thing to do, punctilio. **2** *the two countries signed a protocol* AGREEMENT, treaty, entente, concordat, convention, deal, pact, contract, compact; *formal* concord.

prototype ▶ noun **1** *a prototype of the weapon* ORIGINAL, first example/model, master, mould, template, framework, mock-up, pattern, sample; DESIGN, guide, blueprint. **2** *the prototype of an ideal wife* PARADIGM, typical example, archetype, exemplar, essence.

protract ▶ verb PROLONG, lengthen, extend, draw out, drag out, spin out, stretch out, string out, elongate; carry on, continue, keep up, perpetuate.
– OPPOSITES: curtail, shorten.

protracted ▶ adjective PROLONGED, long-lasting, extended, long-drawn-out, spun out, dragged out, strung out, lengthy, long; *informal* marathon.
– OPPOSITES: short.

protrude ▶ verb STICK OUT, jut (out), project, extend, stand out, bulge out, poke out, thrust out, cantilever.

protruding ▶ adjective STICKING OUT, protuberant, projecting, prominent, jutting, overhanging, beetling, proud, bulging.
– OPPOSITES: sunken, flush.

protrusion ▶ noun **1** *the neck vertebrae have short vertical protrusions* BUMP, lump, knob; protuberance, projection, prominence, swelling, eminence, outcrop, outgrowth, jut, jag, snag; ledge, shelf, ridge. **2** *protrusion of the lips* STICKING OUT, jutting, projection, obtrusion, prominence; swelling, bulging.

protuberance ▶ noun **1** *a protuberance can cause drag* BUMP, lump, knob, projection, protrusion, prominence, swelling, eminence, outcrop, outgrowth, jut, jag, snag; ledge, shelf, ridge. **2** *the protuberance of the incisors* STICKING OUT, jutting, projection, obtrusion, prominence; swelling, bulging.

protuberant ▶ adjective STICKING OUT, protruding, projecting, prominent, jutting, overhanging, proud, bulging.
– OPPOSITES: sunken, flush.

proud ▶ adjective **1** *the proud parents beamed* PLEASED, glad, happy, delighted, joyful, overjoyed, thrilled, satisfied, gratified, content. **2** *a proud day* PLEASING, gratifying, satisfying, cheering, heart-warming, happy, good, glorious, memorable, notable, red-letter. **3** *they were poor but proud* SELF-RESPECTING, dignified, noble, worthy; independent. **4** *I'm not too proud to admit I'm wrong* ARROGANT, conceited, vain, self-important, full of oneself, puffed up, jumped-up, smug, complacent, disdainful, condescending, scornful, supercilious, snobbish, imperious, pompous, overbearing, bumptious, haughty; *informal* big-headed, too big for one's britches/boots, high and mighty, stuck-up, uppity, snooty, highfalutin; *literary* vainglorious; *rare* hubristic. **5** *the proud ships* MAGNIFICENT, splendid, resplendent, grand, noble, stately, imposing, dignified, striking, impressive, majestic, glorious, awe-inspiring, awesome, monumental.
– OPPOSITES: ashamed, shameful, humble, modest, unimpressive.

prove ▶ verb **1** *that proves I'm right* SHOW (TO BE TRUE), demonstrate (the truth of), show beyond doubt, manifest, produce proof/evidence; witness to, give substance to, determine, substantiate, verify, ratify, validate, authenticate, document, bear out, confirm; *formal* evince. **2** *the rumour proved to be correct* TURN OUT, be found, happen.
– OPPOSITES: disprove.
■ **prove oneself** DEMONSTRATE ONE'S ABILITIES/QUALITIES, show one's (true) mettle, show what one is made of.

provenance ▶ noun ORIGIN, source, place of origin; birthplace, fount, roots, pedigree, derivation, root, etymology; *formal* radix.

proverb ▶ noun SAYING, adage, saw, maxim, axiom,

motto, bon mot, aphorism, apophthegm, epigram, gnome, dictum, precept; words of wisdom.

proverbial ▶ **adjective** WELL-KNOWN, famous, famed, renowned, traditional, time-honoured, legendary; notorious, infamous.

provide ▶ **verb** 1 *the Foundation will provide funds* SUPPLY, give, issue, furnish, come up with, dispense, bestow, impart, produce, yield, bring forth, bear, deliver, donate, contribute, pledge, advance, spare, part with, allocate, distribute, allot, put up; *informal* fork out, lay out, ante up, pony up. 2 *she was provided with enough tools* EQUIP, furnish, issue, supply, outfit; fit out, rig out, arm, provision; *informal* fix up. 3 *he had to provide for his family* FEED, nurture, nourish; SUPPORT, maintain, keep, sustain, provide sustenance for, fend for, finance, endow. 4 *the test may provide the answer* MAKE AVAILABLE, present, offer, afford, give, add, bring, yield, impart. 5 *we have provided for further restructuring* PREPARE, allow, make provision, be prepared, arrange, get ready, plan, cater. 6 *the banks have to provide against bad debts* TAKE PRECAUTIONS, take steps/measures, guard, forearm oneself; make provision for. 7 *the Act provides that factories must be kept clean* STIPULATE, lay down, make it a condition, require, order, ordain, demand, prescribe, state, specify.
— OPPOSITES: refuse, withhold, deprive, neglect.

provided ▶ **conjunction** IF, on condition that, providing (that), provided that, presuming (that), assuming (that), on the assumption that, as long as, given (that), with the provision/proviso that, with/on the understanding that, contingent on.

providence ▶ **noun** 1 *a life mapped out by providence* FATE, destiny, nemesis, kismet, God's will, divine intervention, predestination, predetermination, the stars; one's lot (in life); *archaic* one's portion. 2 *he had a streak of providence* PRUDENCE, foresight, forethought, far-sightedness, judiciousness, shrewdness, circumspection, wisdom, sagacity, common sense; careful budgeting, thrift, economy.

provident ▶ **adjective** PRUDENT, far-sighted, judicious, shrewd, circumspect, forearmed, wise, sagacious, sensible; thrifty, economical.
— OPPOSITES: improvident.

providential ▶ **adjective** OPPORTUNE, advantageous, favourable, auspicious, propitious, heaven-sent, welcome, golden, lucky, happy, fortunate, felicitous, timely, well-timed, seasonable, convenient, expedient.
— OPPOSITES: inopportune.

provider ▶ **noun** 1 *a service provider* SUPPLIER, donor, giver, contributor, source. 2 *the family's provider* BREADWINNER, wage earner.

providing ▶ **conjunction.** See PROVIDED.

province ▶ **noun** 1 *Canada's westernmost province* TERRITORY, region, state, department, canton, area, district, sector, zone, division. *See table at* EMBLEM. 2 *that's outside my province* RESPONSIBILITY, area of activity, area of interest, knowledge, department, sphere, world, realm, field, domain, territory, orbit, preserve; business, affair, concern; specialty, forte; jurisdiction, authority; *informal* bailiwick, turf.
— RELATED TERMS: (*Cdn*) provincehood

provincial ▶ **adjective** 1 *the provincial government* REGIONAL, state, territorial, district; sectoral, zonal, cantonal. 2 *provincial areas* NON-METROPOLITAN, small-town, non-urban, outlying, rural, country, rustic, backwoods, backwater; *informal* one-horse,

hick, jerkwater, freshwater. 3 *provincial attitudes* UNSOPHISTICATED, narrow-minded, parochial, small-town, suburban, insular, bush-league, inward-looking, conservative; small-minded, blinkered, bigoted, prejudiced; *informal* jerkwater, corn-fed.
— OPPOSITES: national, metropolitan, cosmopolitan, sophisticated, broad-minded.
▶ **noun** *they were dismissed as provincials* HILLBILLY, (country) bumpkin, country cousin, rustic, yokel, village idiot, peasant, hayseed, hick, rube, redneck.
— OPPOSITES: sophisticate.

provision ▶ **noun** 1 *the provision of weapons to guerrillas* SUPPLYING, supply, providing, giving, presentation, donation; equipping, furnishing. 2 *there has been limited provision for gifted children* FACILITIES, services, amenities, resource(s), arrangements; means, funds, benefits, assistance, allowance(s). 3 *provisions for the trip* SUPPLIES, food and drink, stores, groceries, foodstuff(s), provender, rations; *informal* grub, eats, nosh, chuck; *formal* comestibles; *literary* viands; *dated* victuals. 4 *he made no provision for the future* PREPARATIONS, plans, arrangements, pre-arrangement, precautions, contingency. 5 *the provisions of the Act* TERM, clause; requirement, specification, stipulation; proviso, condition, qualification, restriction, limitation.

provisional ▶ **adjective** INTERIM, temporary, pro tem; transitional, changeover, stop-gap, short-term, fill-in, acting, caretaker, subject to confirmation; pencilled in, working, tentative, contingent.
— OPPOSITES: permanent, definite.

provisionally ▶ **adverb** TEMPORARILY, short-term, pro tem, for the interim, for the present, for the time being, for now, for the nonce; subject to confirmation, conditionally, tentatively.

proviso ▶ **noun** CONDITION, stipulation, provision, clause, rider, qualification, restriction, caveat.

provocation ▶ **noun** 1 *he remained calm despite severe provocation* GOADING, prodding, egging on, incitement, pressure; ANNOYANCE, irritation, nettling; harassment, plaguing, molestation; teasing, taunting, torment; affront, insults; *informal* hassle, aggravation. 2 *without provocation, Bill punched Mrs. Cartwright* JUSTIFICATION, excuse, pretext, occasion, call, motivation, motive, cause, grounds, reason, need; *formal* casus belli.

provocative ▶ **adjective** 1 *provocative remarks* ANNOYING, irritating, exasperating, infuriating, maddening, vexing, galling; insulting, offensive, inflammatory, incendiary, controversial; *informal* aggravating, in-your-face. 2 *a provocative pose* SEXY, sexually arousing, sexually exciting, alluring, seductive, suggestive, inviting, tantalizing, titillating; indecent, pornographic, indelicate, immodest, shameless; erotic, sensuous, slinky, coquettish, amorous, flirtatious; *informal* tarty, come-hither.
— OPPOSITES: soothing, calming, modest, decorous.

provoke ▶ **verb** 1 *the plan has provoked outrage* AROUSE, produce, evoke, cause, give rise to, occasion, call forth, elicit, induce, excite, spark off, touch off, kindle, generate, engender, instigate, result in, lead to, bring on, precipitate, prompt, trigger; *literary* beget. 2 *she was provoked into replying* GOAD, spur, prick, sting, prod, egg on, incite, rouse, stir, move, stimulate, motivate, excite, inflame, work/fire up, impel. 3 *he wouldn't be provoked* ANNOY, anger, incense, enrage, irritate, infuriate, exasperate, madden,

nettle, get/take a rise out of, ruffle, ruffle someone's feathers, make someone's hackles rise; harass, harry, plague, molest; tease, taunt, torment; rub the wrong way; *informal* peeve, aggravate, hassle, miff, needle, rankle, ride, rile, get, bug, hack off, make someone's blood boil, get under someone's skin, get in someone's hair, get/put someone's back up, get someone's goat, wind up.
— OPPOSITES: allay, deter, pacify, appease.

prow ▶ noun BOW(S), stem, front, nose, head, cutwater.

prowess ▶ noun **1** *his prowess as a winemaker* SKILL, expertise, mastery, facility, ability, capability, capacity, savoir faire, talent, genius, adeptness, aptitude, dexterity, deftness, competence, accomplishment, proficiency, finesse; *informal* know-how. **2** *the knights' prowess in battle* COURAGE, bravery, gallantry, valour, heroism, intrepidity, nerve, pluck, pluckiness, feistiness, boldness, daring, audacity, fearlessness; *informal* guts, spunk, moxie, grit, sand.
— OPPOSITES: inability, ineptitude, cowardice.

prowl ▶ verb MOVE STEALTHILY, slink, skulk, steal, nose, pussyfoot, sneak, stalk, creep; *informal* snoop.

proximity ▶ noun CLOSENESS, nearness, propinquity; accessibility, handiness; *archaic* vicinity.

proxy ▶ noun DEPUTY, representative, substitute, delegate, agent, surrogate, stand-in, attorney, go-between.

prude ▶ noun PURITAN, prig, killjoy, moralist, pietist; *informal* goody-goody.

prudence ▶ noun **1** *you have gone beyond the bounds of prudence* WISDOM, judgment, good judgment, common sense, sense, sagacity, shrewdness, advisability. **2** *financial prudence* CAUTION, care, providence, far-sightedness, foresight, forethought, shrewdness, circumspection; thrift, economy.
— OPPOSITES: folly, recklessness, extravagance.

prudent ▶ adjective **1** *it is prudent to obtain consent* WISE, well judged, sensible, politic, judicious, sagacious, sage, shrewd, advisable, well-advised. **2** *a prudent approach to borrowing* CAUTIOUS, careful, provident, far-sighted, judicious, shrewd, circumspect; thrifty, economical.
— OPPOSITES: unwise, reckless, extravagant.

prudish ▶ adjective PURITANICAL, priggish, prim, prim and proper, moralistic, pietistic, sententious, censorious, straitlaced, Victorian, old-maidish, fussy, stuffy, strict; *informal* goody-goody, starchy.
— OPPOSITES: permissive.

prune ▶ verb **1** *I pruned the roses* CUT BACK, trim, thin, pinch back, clip, shear, pollard, top, dock. **2** *prune lateral shoots of wisteria* CUT OFF, lop (off), chop off, clip, snip (off), nip off, dock. **3** *staff numbers have been pruned* REDUCE, cut (back/down), pare (down), slim down, make reductions in, make cutbacks in, trim, decrease, diminish, downsize, axe, shrink; *informal* slash.
— OPPOSITES: increase.
▶ noun *he ate a bowl of prunes every morning.* (*humorous*) CPR strawberries ✦.

prurient ▶ adjective SALACIOUS, licentious, voyeuristic, lascivious, lecherous, lustful, lewd, libidinous, lubricious; *formal* concupiscent.

pry¹ ▶ verb INQUIRE IMPERTINENTLY, be inquisitive, be curious, poke about/around, ferret (about/around), spy, be a busybody; eavesdrop, listen in, tap

someone's phone, intrude; *informal* stick/poke one's nose in/into, be nosy, nose, snoop.
— OPPOSITES: mind one's own business.

pry² ▶ verb **1** *I pried the lid off* LEVER, jimmy, prise; wrench, wrest, twist. **2** *he had to pry information from them* WRING, wrest, worm out, winkle out, screw, squeeze, extract, prise.

psalm ▶ noun SACRED SONG, religious song, hymn, song of praise; (**psalms**) psalmody, psalter.

pseudo ▶ adjective BOGUS, sham, phony, artificial, mock, ersatz, quasi-, fake, false, spurious, deceptive, misleading, assumed, contrived, affected, insincere; *informal* pretend, put-on.
— OPPOSITES: genuine.
▶ noun POSER, poseur, phony, fake, fraud.

pseudonym ▶ noun PEN NAME, nom de plume, assumed name, false name, alias, professional name, sobriquet, stage name, nom de guerre.

psych (*informal*)
■ **psych someone out** INTIMIDATE, daunt, browbeat, bully, cow, tyrannize, scare, terrorize, frighten, dishearten, unnerve, subdue; *informal* bulldoze.
■ **psych oneself up** NERVE ONESELF, steel oneself, brace oneself, summon one's courage, prepare oneself, gear oneself up, urge oneself on, gird (up) one's loins.

psyche ▶ noun SOUL, spirit, (inner) self, ego, true being, inner man/woman, persona, subconscious, mind, intellect; *technical* anima.
— OPPOSITES: body.

psychedelic ▶ adjective **1** *a psychedelic experience* HALLUCINATORY, trippy, dream-like, mind-bending, mind-altering, mind-expanding, mind-blowing, bizarre, surreal. **2** *psychedelic design* COLOURFUL, chromatic, multicoloured, vivid, abstract.

psychiatrist ▶ noun PSYCHOTHERAPIST, psychoanalyst; *informal* shrink, head doctor.

psychic ▶ adjective **1** *psychic powers* SUPERNATURAL, paranormal, otherworldly, supernormal, preternatural, metaphysical, extrasensory, magic, magical, mystical, mystic, occult. **2** *I'm not psychic* CLAIRVOYANT, telepathic, having second sight, having a sixth sense. **3** *psychic development* EMOTIONAL, spiritual, inner; cognitive, psychological, intellectual, mental, psychiatric, psychogenic.
— OPPOSITES: normal, physical.
▶ noun *she is a psychic* CLAIRVOYANT, fortune teller, crystal-gazer; medium, channeller, spiritualist; telepath, mind-reader, palmist, palm-reader.

psychological ▶ adjective **1** *his psychological state* MENTAL, emotional, intellectual, inner, cerebral, brain, rational, cognitive. **2** *her pain was psychological* (ALL) IN THE MIND, psychosomatic, emotional, irrational, subjective, subconscious, unconscious.
— OPPOSITES: physical.

psychology ▶ noun **1** *a degree in psychology* STUDY OF THE MIND, science of the mind. **2** *the psychology of the motorist* MINDSET, mind, mental processes, thought processes, way of thinking, cast of mind, mentality, persona, psyche, (mental) attitude(s), makeup, character; *informal* what makes someone tick.

psychopath ▶ noun MADMAN, MADWOMAN, maniac, lunatic, psychotic, sociopath; *informal* loony, fruitcake, nutcase, nutbar, nut, psycho, schizo, head case, sicko, screwball, crazy, kook.

psychopathic . ▶ adjective. See MAD sense 1.

psychosomatic ▶ adjective (ALL) IN THE MIND, psychological, irrational, stress-related, stress-induced, subjective, subconscious, unconscious.

psychotic ▶ adjective. See MAD sense 1.

pub ▶ noun BAR, inn, tavern, hostelry, wine bar, taproom, roadhouse, (*Que.*) brasserie ✦; public house, hotel; *informal* watering hole; *dated* alehouse; *historical* saloon. See also BAR sense 4.

puberty ▶ noun ADOLESCENCE, pubescence, sexual maturity, growing up; youth, young adulthood, teenage years, teens, the awkward age; *formal* juvenescence.

public ▶ adjective **1** *public affairs* STATE, national, federal, government; constitutional, civic, civil, official, social, municipal, community, communal, local; nationalized. **2** *by public demand* POPULAR, general, common, communal, joint, universal, widespread. **3** *a public figure* PROMINENT, well-known, important, leading, eminent, distinguished, notable, noteworthy, noted, celebrated, notable, household, famous, famed, influential, major-league. **4** *public places* OPEN (TO THE PUBLIC), communal, accessible to all, available, free, unrestricted, community. **5** *the news became public* KNOWN, published, publicized, in circulation, exposed, overt, plain, obvious.
− OPPOSITES: private, obscure, unknown, restricted, secret.
▶ noun **1** *the Canadian public* PEOPLE, citizens, subjects, general public, electors, electorate, voters, taxpayers, residents, inhabitants, citizenry, population, populace, community, society, country, nation, world; everyone. **2** *his adoring public* AUDIENCE, spectators, followers, following, fans, devotees, aficionados, admirers; patrons, clientele, market, consumers, buyers, customers, readers, viewers, listeners.
■ **in public** PUBLICLY, in full view of people, openly, in the open, for all to see, undisguisedly, blatantly, flagrantly, brazenly, overtly.

publication ▶ noun **1** *the author of this publication* BOOK, volume, title, work, tome, opus; newspaper, paper, magazine, periodical, newsletter, bulletin, journal, report; organ, booklet, chapbook, brochure, catalogue; daily, weekly, monthly, quarterly, annual; *informal* rag, mag, 'zine. **2** *the publication of her new book* ISSUING, announcement, publishing, printing, notification, reporting, declaration, communication, proclamation, broadcasting, publicizing, advertising, distribution, spreading, dissemination, promulgation, issuance, appearance.

publicity ▶ noun **1** *the blaze of publicity* PUBLIC ATTENTION, public interest, public notice, media attention/interest, face time, exposure, glare, limelight. **2** *publicity should boost sales* PROMOTION, advertising, propaganda; boost, push; *informal* hype, ballyhoo, puff, puffery, buildup, razzmatazz; plug.

publicize ▶ verb **1** *I never publicize the fact* MAKE KNOWN, make public, publish, announce, report, post, communicate, broadcast, issue, put out, distribute, spread, promulgate, disseminate, circulate, air; disclose, reveal, divulge, leak. **2** *she just wants to publicize her book* ADVERTISE, promote, build up, talk up, push, beat the drum for; boost; *informal* hype, flack, plug, puff (up).
− OPPOSITES: conceal, suppress.

public-spirited ▶ adjective COMMUNITY-MINDED, socially concerned, philanthropic, charitable; ALTRUISTIC, humanitarian, generous, unselfish.

publish ▶ verb **1** *we publish novels* ISSUE, bring out, produce, print. **2** *he ought to publish his views* MAKE KNOWN, make public, publicize, announce, report, post, communicate, broadcast, issue, put out, distribute, spread, promulgate, disseminate, circulate, air; disclose, reveal, divulge, leak.

pucker ▶ verb *she puckered her forehead* WRINKLE, crinkle, crease, furrow, crumple, rumple, ruck up, scrunch up, corrugate, ruffle, screw up, shrivel; cockle.
▶ noun *a pucker in the sewing* WRINKLE, crinkle, crumple, corrugation, furrow, line, fold.

puckish ▶ adjective MISCHIEVOUS, naughty, impish, roguish, playful, arch, prankish; *informal* waggish.

puddle ▶ noun POOL, spill, splash; *literary* plash.

pudgy ▶ adjective (*informal*) CHUBBY, plump, fat, stout, rotund, well-padded, ample, round, chunky, portly, overweight, fleshy, paunchy, bulky, corpulent; *informal* tubby, roly-poly, beefy, porky, blubbery, zaftig, corn-fed.
− OPPOSITES: thin.

puerile ▶ adjective CHILDISH, immature, infantile, juvenile, babyish; silly, inane, fatuous, jejune, asinine, foolish, petty.
− OPPOSITES: mature, sensible.

puff ▶ noun **1** *a puff of wind* GUST, blast, flurry, rush, draft, waft, breeze, breath. **2** *he took a puff at his cigar* PULL; *informal* drag. **3** (*informal*) *they expected a puff in our review column* FAVOURABLE MENTION, review, recommendation, good word, advertisement, promotion, commercial; *informal* ad. **4** (*informal*) *a salesman's puff* PUBLICITY, advertising, promotion, marketing, propaganda, buildup; patter, line, pitch, sales talk; *informal* spiel.
▶ verb **1** *she walked fast, puffing a little* BREATHE HEAVILY, pant, blow; gasp, fight for breath. **2** *she puffed at her cigarette* SMOKE, draw on, drag on, suck at/on. **3** (*informal*) *new ways to puff our products* ADVERTISE, promote, publicize, push, recommend, endorse, beat the drum for; *informal* hype (up), plug.
■ **puff up** BULGE, swell up, stick out, distend, tumefy, balloon (up/out), expand, inflate, enlarge.

puffed-up ▶ adjective SELF-IMPORTANT, conceited, arrogant, bumptious, pompous, overbearing; affected, stiff, vain, vainglorious, proud; *informal* snooty, uppity, uppish.

puffy ▶ adjective SWOLLEN, puffed up, distended, enlarged, inflated, dilated, bloated, engorged, bulging, tumid, tumescent.

pugilist ▶ noun (*dated*) BOXER, fighter, prizefighter; *informal* bruiser, pug.

pugnacious ▶ adjective COMBATIVE, aggressive, antagonistic, belligerent, bellicose, warlike, quarrelsome, argumentative, contentious, disputatious, hostile, threatening, truculent; fiery, hot-tempered.
− OPPOSITES: peaceable.

puke ▶ verb (*informal*). See VOMIT verb senses 1, 2.

pull ▶ verb **1** *he pulled the box towards him* TUG, haul, drag, draw, tow, heave, lug, jerk, wrench; *informal* yank. **2** *he pulled the bad tooth out* EXTRACT, take out, remove. **3** *she pulled a muscle* STRAIN, sprain, wrench, turn, tear; damage. **4** *race day pulled big crowds* ATTRACT, draw, bring in, pull in, lure, seduce, entice, tempt, beckon, interest, fascinate.
− OPPOSITES: push, repel.
▶ noun **1** *give the chain a pull* TUG, jerk, heave; *informal* yank. **2** *she took a pull on her beer* GULP, draft, drink, swallow, mouthful, slug; *informal* swill, swig. **3** *a pull*

on a cigarette PUFF, drag. **4** *she felt the pull of the sea* ATTRACTION, draw, lure, allurement, enticement, magnetism, temptation, fascination, appeal. **5** *he has a lot of pull in finance* INFLUENCE, sway, power, authority, say, prestige, standing, weight, leverage, muscle, teeth, clout.

■ **pull something apart** DISMANTLE, disassemble, take/pull to pieces, take/pull to bits, take apart, strip down; demolish, destroy, break up.

■ **pull back** WITHDRAW, retreat, fall back, back off; pull out, retire, disengage; flee, turn tail.

■ **pull something down** DEMOLISH, knock down, tear down, dismantle, raze (to the ground), level, flatten, bulldoze, destroy.

■ **pull in** STOP, halt, come to a halt, pull over, pull up, draw up, brake, park.

■ **pull someone's leg** TEASE, fool, play a trick on, rag, pull the wool over someone's eyes; *informal* kid, rib, take for a ride, have on.

■ **pull something off** ACHIEVE, fulfill, succeed in, accomplish, bring off, carry off, perform, discharge, complete, clinch, fix, effect, engineer.

■ **pull out** WITHDRAW, resign, leave, retire, step down, bow out, back out, give up; *informal* quit.

■ **pull through** GET BETTER, get well again, improve, recover, rally, come through, recuperate.

■ **pull oneself together** REGAIN ONE'S COMPOSURE, recover, get a grip on oneself, get over it; *informal* snap out of it, get one's act together, buck up.

■ **pull over.** *See* PULL IN.

pulp ▶ **noun 1** *he kneaded it into a pulp* MUSH, mash, paste, purée, pomace, pap, slop, slush, mulch; *informal* gloop, goo, glop. **2** *the sweet pulp on cocoa seeds* FLESH, marrow, meat.

▶ **verb** *pulp the blueberries* MASH, purée, cream, crush, press, liquidize, liquefy, sieve, squash, pound, macerate, grind, mince.

▶ **adjective** *pulp fiction* TRASHY, cheap, sensational, lurid, tasteless; *informal* tacky, rubbishy.

pulpit ▶ **noun** STAND, lectern, platform, podium, stage, dais, rostrum.

pulpy ▶ **adjective** *cook the rhubarb slowly until it is soft and pulpy* MUSHY, soft, semi-liquid, slushy, sloppy, spongy, squashy, squishy; succulent, juicy, gooey.

pulsate ▶ **verb** PALPITATE, pulse, throb, pump, undulate, surge, heave, rise and fall; beat, thump, drum, thrum; flutter, quiver.

pulse¹ ▶ **noun 1** *the pulse in her neck* HEARTBEAT, pulsation, pulsing, throbbing, pounding. **2** *the pulse of the train wheels* RHYTHM, beat, tempo, cadence, pounding, thudding, drumming. **3** *pulses of ultrasound* BURST, blast, spurt, impulse, surge.

▶ **verb** *music pulsed through the building* THROB, pulsate, vibrate, beat, pound, thud, thump, drum, thrum, reverberate, echo.

pulse² ▶ **noun** *eat plenty of pulses* LEGUME, pea, bean, lentil.

pulverize ▶ **verb 1** *the seeds are pulverized into flour* GRIND, crush, pound, powder, mill, crunch, squash, press, pulp, mash, sieve, mince, macerate; *technical* comminute. **2** *(informal) he pulverized the opposition. See* TROUNCE.

pummel ▶ **verb** BATTER, pound, belabour, drub, beat; punch, strike, hit, thump, thrash, cold-cock; *informal* clobber, wallop, bash, whack, beat the living daylights out of, give someone a (good) hiding, belt, lay into, lam, bust, slug; *literary* smite.

pump ▶ **verb 1** *I pumped air out of the tube* FORCE, drive, push; suck, draw, tap, siphon, withdraw, expel,

extract, bleed, drain. **2** *she pumped up the tire* INFLATE, aerate, blow up, fill up; swell, enlarge, distend, expand, dilate, puff up. **3** *blood was pumping from his leg* SPURT, spout, squirt, jet, surge, spew, gush, stream, flow, pour, spill, well, cascade, run, course. **4** *(informal) I pumped them for information* INTERROGATE, cross-examine, ask, question, quiz, probe, sound out, catechize, give someone the third degree; *informal* grill.

pun ▶ **noun** PLAY ON WORDS, wordplay, double entendre, innuendo, witticism, quip, bon mot.

punch¹ ▶ **verb** *Diana punched him in the face* HIT, strike, thump, jab, smash, welt, cuff, clip; batter, buffet, pound, pummel; *informal* sock, slug, bop, wallop, clobber, bash, whack, thwack, clout, lam, whomp, cold-cock, boff, bust; *literary* smite.

▶ **noun 1** *a punch on the nose* BLOW, hit, knock, thump, box, jab, clip, uppercut, hook; *informal* sock, slug, bop, bust, bop, wallop, bash, whack, clout, belt, knuckle sandwich; *dated* buffet. **2** *the album is full of punch* VIGOUR, liveliness, vitality, drive, strength, zest, verve, enthusiasm; impact, bite, kick; *informal* oomph, zing, pep.

punch² ▶ **verb** *he punched her ticket* MAKE A HOLE IN, perforate, puncture, pierce, prick, hole, spike, skewer; *literary* transpierce.

punch-up ▶ **noun** *(informal). See* FIGHT *noun* sense 1.

punchy ▶ **adjective** *punchy dialogue* FORCEFUL, incisive, strong, powerful, vigorous, dynamic, peppy, effective, impressive, telling, compelling; dramatic, passionate, graphic, vivid, potent, authoritative, aggressive; *informal* in-your-face.
— OPPOSITES: ineffectual.

punctilio ▶ **noun 1** *a stickler for punctilio* CONFORMITY, conscientiousness, punctiliousness; etiquette, protocol, conventions, formalities, propriety, decorum, manners, politesse, good form, the done thing. **2** *the punctilios of court procedure* NICETY, detail, fine point, subtlety, nuance, refinement.
— OPPOSITES: informality.

punctilious ▶ **adjective** METICULOUS, conscientious, diligent, scrupulous, careful, painstaking, rigorous, perfectionist, methodical, particular, strict; fussy, fastidious, finicky, pedantic; *informal* nitpicking, pernickety, persnickety.
— OPPOSITES: careless.

punctual ▶ **adjective** ON TIME, prompt, on schedule, in (good) time; *informal* on the dot.
— OPPOSITES: late.

punctuate ▶ **verb 1** *how to punctuate direct speech* ADD PUNCTUATION TO, put punctuation marks in. **2** *slides punctuated the talk* BREAK UP, interrupt, intersperse, pepper, sprinkle, scatter.

punctuation *See table.*

puncture ▶ **noun 1** *the tire developed a puncture* HOLE, perforation, rupture; cut, slit; leak. **2** *my car has a puncture* FLAT TIRE; *informal* flat.

▶ **verb 1** *he punctured the child's balloon* MAKE A HOLE IN, pierce, rupture, perforate, stab, cut, slit, prick, spike, stick, lance; deflate. **2** *she knows how to puncture his speeches* PUT AN END TO, cut short, deflate, reduce.

pundit ▶ **noun** EXPERT, authority, specialist, doyen(ne), master, guru, sage, savant, maven; *informal* buff, whiz.

pungent ▶ **adjective 1** *a pungent marinade* STRONG, powerful, pervasive, penetrating; sharp, acid, sour, biting, bitter, tart, vinegary, tangy; highly flavoured, aromatic, spicy, piquant, peppery, hot. **2** *pungent*

Punctuation Marks

(round) brackets	( )
angle brackets	< >
braces/curly brackets	{ }
square brackets	[ ]
period/full stop	.
comma	,
semicolon	;
colon	:
underscore	_
ellipsis	...
dash	-
em dash	—
en dash	–
exclamation mark	!
question mark	?
apostrophe	'
single quotation marks/ inverted commas	' '
(double) quotation marks	" "
backslash	\
solidus/forward slash	/

remarks CAUSTIC, biting, trenchant, cutting, acerbic, sardonic, sarcastic, scathing, acrimonious, barbed, sharp, tart, incisive, bitter, venomous, waspish.
— OPPOSITES: bland, mild.

punish ▶ verb **1** *they punished their children* DISCIPLINE, bring someone to book, teach someone a lesson; tan someone's hide; *informal* murder, wallop, come down on (like a ton of bricks), have someone's guts for garters. **2** *higher charges would punish the poor* PENALIZE, unfairly disadvantage, handicap, hurt, wrong, ill-use, maltreat.

punishable ▶ adjective ILLEGAL, unlawful, illegitimate, criminal, felonious, actionable, indictable, penal; blameworthy, dishonest, fraudulent, unauthorized, outlawed, banned, forbidden, prohibited, interdicted, proscribed.

punishing ▶ adjective *a punishing schedule* ARDUOUS, demanding, taxing, onerous, burdensome, strenuous, rigorous, stressful, trying; hard, difficult, tough, exhausting, tiring, gruelling, crippling, relentless; *informal* killing.
— OPPOSITES: easy.

punishment ▶ noun **1** *the punishment of the guilty* PENALIZING, punishing, disciplining; retribution; *dated* chastisement. **2** *the teacher imposed punishments* PENALTY, penance, sanction, sentence, one's just deserts; discipline, correction, vengeance, justice, judgment; *informal* comeuppance. **3** *both boxers took punishment* A BATTERING, a thrashing, a beating, a drubbing; *informal* a hiding. **4** *ovens take continual punishment* MALTREATMENT, mistreatment, abuse, ill-use, manhandling; damage, harm.
— RELATED TERMS: punitive, penal.

punitive ▶ adjective **1** *punitive measures* PENAL, disciplinary, corrective, correctional, retributive. **2** *punitive taxes* HARSH, severe, stiff, stringent, burdensome, demanding, crushing, crippling; high, sky-high, inflated, exorbitant, extortionate, excessive, inordinate, unreasonable.

puny ▶ adjective **1** *he grew up puny* UNDERSIZED, undernourished, underfed, stunted, slight, small, little; weak, feeble, sickly, delicate, frail, fragile; *informal* weedy, pint-sized. **2** *puny efforts to save their homes* PITIFUL, pitiable, inadequate, insufficient, derisory, miserable, sorry, meagre, paltry, trifling,

inconsequential; *informal* pathetic, measly, piddling; *formal* exiguous.
— OPPOSITES: sturdy, substantial.

pupil ▶ noun **1** *former pupils of the school* STUDENT, scholar; schoolchild, schoolboy, schoolgirl. **2** *the guru's pupils* DISCIPLE, follower, student, protege, apprentice, trainee, novice.

puppet ▶ noun **1** *a show with puppets* MARIONETTE; glove puppet, hand puppet, finger puppet. **2** *a puppet of the government* PAWN, tool, instrument, cat's paw, creature, dupe; mouthpiece, minion, stooge.

purchase ▶ verb *we purchased the software* BUY, pay for, acquire, obtain, pick up, snap up, take, procure; invest in; *informal* get hold of, score.
— OPPOSITES: sell.
▶ noun **1** *he's happy with his purchase* ACQUISITION, buy, investment, order, bargain; shopping, goods. **2** *he could get no purchase on the wall* GRIP, grasp, hold, foothold, toehold, anchorage, attachment, support; resistance, friction, leverage.
— OPPOSITES: sale.

purchaser ▶ noun BUYER, shopper, customer, consumer, patron; *Law* vendee.

pure ▶ adjective **1** *pure gold* UNADULTERATED, uncontaminated, unmixed, undiluted, unalloyed, unblended; sterling, solid, refined, one hundred per cent; clarified, clear, filtered; flawless, perfect, genuine, real. **2** *the air is so pure* CLEAN, clear, fresh, sparkling, unpolluted, uncontaminated, untainted; wholesome, natural, healthy; sanitary, uninfected, disinfected, germ-free, sterile, sterilized, aseptic. **3** *pure in body and mind* VIRTUOUS, moral, ethical, good, righteous, saintly, honourable, reputable, wholesome, clean, honest, upright, upstanding, exemplary, irreproachable; chaste, virginal, maidenly; decent, worthy, noble, blameless, guiltless, spotless, unsullied, uncorrupted, undefiled; *informal* squeaky clean. **4** *pure math* THEORETICAL, abstract, conceptual, academic, hypothetical, speculative, conjectural. **5** *three hours of pure magic* SHEER, utter, absolute, out-and-out, complete, total, perfect, unmitigated.
— OPPOSITES: adulterated, polluted, immoral, practical.

pure-bred ▶ adjective PEDIGREE, thoroughbred, full-bred, blooded, pedigreed, pure.
— OPPOSITES: hybrid.

purely ▶ adverb ENTIRELY, completely, absolutely, wholly, exclusively, solely, only, just, merely.

purgative ▶ adjective *purgative medicine* LAXATIVE, evacuant; *Medicine* aperient.
▶ noun *orrisroot is a purgative* LAXATIVE, evacuant; *Medicine* aperient; *dated* purge.

purgatory ▶ noun TORMENT, torture, misery, suffering, affliction, anguish, agony, woe, hell; an ordeal, a nightmare.
— OPPOSITES: paradise.

purge ▶ verb **1** *he purged them of their doubt* CLEANSE, clear, purify, wash, shrive, absolve. **2** *lawbreakers were purged from the army* REMOVE, get rid of, expel, eject, exclude, dismiss, sack, oust, eradicate, clear out, weed out.
▶ noun *the purge of dissidents* REMOVAL, expulsion, ejection, exclusion, eviction, dismissal, sacking, ousting, eradication.

purify ▶ verb **1** *trees help to purify the air* CLEAN, cleanse, refine, decontaminate; filter, clarify, clear, freshen, deodorize; sanitize, disinfect, sterilize.

2 *they purify themselves before the ceremony* PURGE, cleanse, unburden, deliver; redeem, shrive, exorcize, sanctify.

purist ▶ **noun** PEDANT, perfectionist, formalist, literalist, stickler, traditionalist, doctrinaire, quibbler, dogmatist; *informal* nitpicker.

puritanical ▶ **adjective** MORALISTIC, puritan, pietistic, straitlaced, stuffy, prudish, prim, priggish; narrow-minded, sententious, censorious; austere, severe, ascetic, abstemious; *informal* goody-goody, starchy.
– OPPOSITES: permissive.

purity ▶ **noun 1** *the purity of our tap water* CLEANNESS, clearness, clarity, freshness; sterility, healthiness, safety. **2** *they sought purity in a foul world* VIRTUE, morality, goodness, righteousness, saintliness, piety, honour, honesty, integrity, decency, ethicality, impeccability; innocence, chastity.

purloin ▶ **verb** *(formal)* STEAL, thieve, rob, take, snatch, pilfer, loot, appropriate; *informal* swipe, (*Nfld*) buck ♣, nab, rip off, lift, 'liberate', 'borrow', filch, snaffle, pinch, heist.

purport ▶ **verb** *this work purports to be authoritative* CLAIM, profess, pretend; appear, seem; be ostensibly, pose as, impersonate, masquerade as, pass for.
▶ **noun 1** *the purport of his remarks* GIST, substance, drift, implication, intention, meaning, significance, sense, essence, thrust, message. **2** *the purport of the attack* INTENTION, purpose, object, objective, aim, goal, target, end, design, idea.

purpose ▶ **noun 1** *the purpose of his visit* MOTIVE, motivation, grounds, cause, occasion, reason, point, basis, justification. **2** *their purpose was to subvert the economy* INTENTION, aim, object, objective, goal, end, plan, scheme, target; ambition, aspiration. **3** *I cannot see any purpose in it* ADVANTAGE, benefit, good, use, value, merit, worth, profit; *informal* mileage, percentage. **4** *the original purpose of the porch* FUNCTION, role, use. **5** *they started the game with purpose* DETERMINATION, resolution, resolve, steadfastness, backbone, drive, push, enthusiasm, ambition, motivation, commitment, conviction, dedication; *informal* get-up-and-go.
▶ **verb** *(formal)* *they purposed to reach the summit* INTEND, mean, aim, plan, design, have the intention; decide, resolve, determine, propose, aspire, set one's sights on.
■ **on purpose** DELIBERATELY, intentionally, purposely, by design, wilfully, knowingly, consciously, of one's own volition; expressly, specifically, especially, specially.

purposeful ▶ **adjective** DETERMINED, resolute, steadfast, single-minded; enthusiastic, motivated, committed, dedicated, persistent, dogged, tenacious, unfaltering, unshakeable.
– OPPOSITES: aimless.

purposely ▶ **adverb** *See* ON PURPOSE *at* PURPOSE.

purse ▶ **noun 1** *a woman's purse. See* HANDBAG. **2** *the public purse* FUND(S), kitty, coffers, pool, bank, treasury, exchequer; money, finances, wealth, reserves, cash, capital, assets. **3** *the fight will net him a $75,000 purse* PRIZE, reward, award; winnings, stake(s).
▶ **verb** *she pursed her lips* PRESS TOGETHER, compress, tighten, pucker, pout.

pursue ▶ **verb 1** *I pursued him through the garden* FOLLOW, run after, chase; hunt, stalk, track, trail, shadow, hound, course; *informal* tail. **2** *pursue the goal of political union* STRIVE FOR, work towards, seek, search

for, aim at/for, aspire to. **3** *he had been pursuing her for weeks* WOO, chase, run after, go after; *informal* make up to; *dated* court, romance. **4** *she pursued a political career* ENGAGE IN, be occupied in, practise, follow, prosecute, conduct, ply, take up, undertake, carry on. **5** *we will not pursue the matter* INVESTIGATE, research, inquire into, look into, examine, scrutinize, analyze, delve into, probe.
– OPPOSITES: avoid, shun.

pursuit ▶ **noun 1** *the pursuit of profit* STRIVING TOWARDS, quest after/for, search for; aim, goal, objective, dream. **2** *a worthwhile pursuit* ACTIVITY, hobby, pastime, diversion, recreation, relaxation, divertissement, amusement; occupation, trade, vocation, business, work, job, employment.

purvey ▶ **verb** SELL, supply, provide, furnish, cater, retail, deal in, trade, stock, offer; peddle, hawk, traffic in; *informal* flog.

purveyor ▶ **noun** SELLER, vendor, retailer, supplier, trader, peddler, hawker.

pus ▶ **noun** SUPPURATION, matter; discharge, secretion.
– RELATED TERMS: purulent.

push ▶ **verb 1** *she tried to push him away* SHOVE, thrust, propel; send, drive, force, prod, poke, nudge, elbow, shoulder; sweep, bundle, hustle, manhandle. **2** *she pushed her way into the apartment* FORCE, shove, thrust, squeeze, jostle, elbow, shoulder, bundle, hustle; work, inch. **3** *he pushed the panic button* PRESS, depress, bear down on, hold down, squeeze; operate, activate. **4** *don't push her to join in* URGE, press, pressure, force, impel, coerce, nag; prevail on, browbeat into; *informal* lean on, twist someone's arm, bulldoze. **5** *they push their own products* ADVERTISE, publicize, promote, bang the drum for; sell, market, merchandise; *informal* plug, hype (up), puff (up), flog, ballyhoo.
– OPPOSITES: pull.
▶ **noun 1** *I felt a push in the back* SHOVE, thrust, nudge, ram, bump, jolt, butt, prod, poke. **2** *the enemy's eastward push* ADVANCE, drive, thrust, charge, attack, assault, onslaught, onrush, offensive, sortie, sally, incursion.
■ **push someone around** BULLY, domineer, ride roughshod over, trample on, bulldoze, browbeat, tyrannize, intimidate, threaten, victimize, pick on; *informal* lean on, boss around.
■ **push for** DEMAND, call for, request, press for, campaign for, lobby for, speak up for; urge, promote, advocate, champion, espouse.
■ **push off** *(informal)* GO AWAY, depart, leave, get out; go, get moving, be off (with you), shoo; *informal* skedaddle, vamoose, split, scram, run along, beat it, get lost, shove off, buzz off, clear off, bug off, take a powder, take a hike; *literary* begone.
■ **push on** PRESS ON, continue one's journey, carry on, advance, proceed, go on, progress, make headway, forge ahead.

pushcart ▶ **noun** HANDCART, cart, wheelbarrow.

pushover ▶ **noun 1** *the teacher was a pushover* WEAKLING, feeble opponent, straw man, prey; *informal* soft touch. **2** *this course is no pushover* EASY TASK, walkover, laugher, five-finger exercise, gift; child's play, bird course ♣, Mickey Mouse course; *informal* piece of cake, picnic, cinch, breeze, duck soup, snap; *dated* snip.

pushy ▶ **adjective** ASSERTIVE, self-assertive, overbearing, domineering, aggressive, forceful, forward, bold, bumptious, officious; thrusting, ambitious, overconfident, cocky; *informal* bossy.
– OPPOSITES: submissive.

pusillanimous ▶ adjective TIMID, timorous, cowardly, fearful, faint-hearted, lily-livered, spineless, craven, shrinking; informal chicken, gutless, wimpy, wimpish, sissy, yellow, yellow-bellied.
— OPPOSITES: brave.

pussyfoot ▶ verb **1** you can't pussyfoot around with this EQUIVOCATE, tergiversate, be evasive, be noncommittal, sidestep the issue, prevaricate, quibble, hedge, waffle, beat around the bush, hem and haw; informal duck the question, sit on the fence, shilly-shally. **2** I had to pussyfoot over the gravel CREEP, tiptoe, pad, soft-shoe, steal, sneak, slink.

pustule ▶ noun PIMPLE, spot, bleb, boil, swelling, eruption, carbuncle, blister, abscess; informal whitehead, zit, blackhead; technical comedo, papule.

put ▶ verb **1** she put the parcel on a chair PLACE, set (down), lay (down), deposit, position, settle; leave, plant; informal stick, dump, park, plonk, plunk, pop. **2** he didn't want to be put in a category ASSIGN TO, consign to, allocate to, place in. **3** don't put the blame on me LAY, pin, place, fix; attribute to, impute to, assign to, allocate to, ascribe to. **4** the proposals put to the committee SUBMIT, present, tender, offer, proffer, advance, suggest, propose. **5** she put it bluntly EXPRESS, word, phrase, frame, formulate, render, convey, couch; state, say, utter. **6** he put the cost at $8,000 ESTIMATE, calculate, reckon, gauge, assess, evaluate, value, judge, measure, compute, fix, set, peg; informal guesstimate.
■ **put about** the ship put about TURN ROUND, come about, change course.
■ **put something about** the rumour had been put about SPREAD, circulate, make public, disseminate, broadcast, publicize, pass on, propagate, bandy about.
■ **put something across/over** COMMUNICATE, convey, get across/over, explain, make clear, spell out, clarify; get through to someone.
■ **put something aside 1** we've got a bit put aside in the bank SAVE, put by, set aside, deposit, reserve, store, stockpile, hoard, stow, cache; informal salt away, squirrel away, stash away. **2** they put aside their differences DISREGARD, set aside, ignore, forget, discount, bury.
■ **put someone away** (informal) **1** they put him away for life JAIL, imprison, put in prison, put behind bars, lock up, incarcerate; informal cage, jug. **2** you should be put away! CERTIFY, commit, institutionalize, hospitalize, consign to a psychiatric hospital.
■ **put something away 1** I put away some money. See PUT SOMETHING ASIDE sense 1. **2** she never puts her toys away REPLACE, put back, tidy away, tidy up, clear away. **3** (informal) he can put away a lot of pies. See EAT sense 1.
■ **put something back 1** he put the books back REPLACE, return, restore, put away, tidy away. **2** they put back the film's release date. See PUT SOMETHING OFF.
■ **put someone down 1** (informal) she often puts me down CRITICIZE, belittle, disparage, deprecate, denigrate, slight, humiliate, shame, crush, squash, deflate; informal show up, cut down to size. **2** I put him down as shy CONSIDER TO BE, judge to be, reckon to be, take to be; regard, have down, take for.
■ **put something down 1** she put her ideas down on paper WRITE DOWN, note down, jot down, take down, set down; list, record, register, log. **2** they put down the rebellion SUPPRESS, check, crush, quash, squash, quell, overthrow, stamp out, repress, subdue. **3** the horse had to be put down DESTROY, put to sleep, put out of its misery, put to death, kill, euthanize. **4** put it down to

inexperience ATTRIBUTE, ascribe, chalk up, impute; blame on.
■ **put something forward**. See PUT sense 4.
■ **put in for** APPLY FOR, put in an application for, try for; request, seek, ask for.
■ **put someone off** DETER, discourage, dissuade, daunt, unnerve, intimidate, scare off, repel, repulse; distract, disturb, divert, sidetrack; informal turn off.
■ **put something off** POSTPONE, defer, delay, put back, adjourn, hold over, reschedule, shelve, table; informal put on ice, put on the back burner.
■ **put it on** PRETEND, play-act, make believe, fake it, fool, go through the motions.
■ **put something on 1** she put on jeans DRESS IN, don, pull on, throw on, slip into, change into; informal doll oneself up in. **2** I put the light on SWITCH ON, turn on, activate. **3** they put on an extra train PROVIDE, lay on, supply, make available. **4** the museum put on an exhibition ORGANIZE, stage, mount, present, produce. **5** she put on a funny English accent FEIGN, fake, simulate, mimic, affect, assume. **6** she put ten dollars on the nag to win BET, gamble, stake, wager; place, lay; risk, chance, hazard.
■ **put one over on** (informal). See HOODWINK.
■ **put someone out 1** Maria was put out by the slur ANNOY, anger, irritate, offend, affront, displease, irk, vex, pique, nettle, gall, upset; informal rile, miff, peeve. **2** I don't want to put you out INCONVENIENCE, trouble, bother, impose on, disoblige; informal put someone on the spot; formal discommode.
■ **put something out 1** firemen put out the blaze EXTINGUISH, quench, douse, smother; blow out, snuff out, (Nfld) dout ♣. **2** he put out a press release ISSUE, publish, release, bring out, circulate, publicize, post.
■ **put someone up 1** we can put him up for a few days ACCOMMODATE, house, take in, lodge, quarter, billet; give someone a roof over their head. **2** they put up a candidate NOMINATE, propose, put forward, recommend.
■ **put something up 1** the building was put up 100 years ago BUILD, construct, erect, raise. **2** she put up a poster DISPLAY, pin up, stick up, hang up, post. **3** we put up alternative schemes PROPOSE, put forward, present, submit, suggest, tender. **4** the chancellor put up taxes INCREASE, raise; informal jack up, hike, bump up. **5** he put up most of the funding PROVIDE, supply, furnish, give, contribute, donate, pledge, pay; informal fork out, cough up, shell out, ante up, pony up.
■ **put upon** (informal) TAKE ADVANTAGE OF, impose on, exploit, use, misuse; informal walk all over.
■ **put someone up to something** (informal) PERSUADE TO, encourage to, urge to, egg on to, incite to, goad into.
■ **put up with** TOLERATE, take, stand (for), accept, stomach, swallow, endure, bear, support, take something lying down; informal abide, lump it; formal brook.

putative ▶ adjective SUPPOSED, assumed, presumed; accepted, recognized; commonly regarded, presumptive, alleged, reputed, reported, rumoured.

put-down ▶ noun (informal) SNUB, slight, affront, rebuff, sneer, disparagement, humiliation, barb, jibe, criticism; informal dig.

putrefy ▶ verb DECAY, rot, decompose, go bad, go off, spoil, fester, perish, deteriorate; moulder.

putrid ▶ adjective DECOMPOSING, decaying, rotting, rotten, bad, off, putrefied, putrescent, rancid, mouldy; foul, fetid, rank.

putter ▶ noun he likes to putter around in his workshop

DABBLE, fiddle, noodle, doodle, lallygag, mess, futz, occupy oneself.

puzzle ▶ **verb 1** *her decision puzzled me* PERPLEX, confuse, bewilder, bemuse, baffle, mystify, confound; *informal* flummox, faze, stump, beat, discombobulate. **2** *she puzzled over the problem* THINK HARD ABOUT, mull over, muse over, ponder, contemplate, meditate on, consider, deliberate on, chew over, wonder about. **3** *she tried to puzzle out what he meant* WORK OUT, understand, comprehend, sort out, reason out, solve, make sense of, make head or tail of, unravel, decipher; *informal* figure out, suss out.
▶ **noun** *the poem has always been a puzzle* ENIGMA, mystery, paradox, conundrum, poser, riddle, problem, quandary; *informal* stumper.

puzzled ▶ **adjective** PERPLEXED, confused, bewildered, bemused, baffled, mystified, confounded, nonplussed, at a loss, at sea; *informal* flummoxed, stumped, fazed, clueless, discombobulated.

puzzling ▶ **adjective** BAFFLING, perplexing, bewildering, confusing, complicated, unclear, mysterious, enigmatic, ambiguous, obscure, abstruse, unfathomable, incomprehensible, impenetrable, cryptic.
− OPPOSITES: clear.

pygmy ▶ **noun 1** *a Congo pygmy* DWARF, midget, very small person, homunculus, manikin; Lilliputian; *informal* shrimp. **2** *an intellectual pygmy* LIGHTWEIGHT, mediocrity, nonentity, nobody, no-name, cipher; small fry; *informal* pipsqueak, no-hoper, picayune.
− OPPOSITES: giant.

pyjamas ▶ **noun** PJS, jammies, sleepers; nightgown.

pyromaniac ▶ **noun** ARSONIST, incendiary; *informal* firebug, pyro, torch.

Qq

quack ▶ noun *a quack selling fake medicines* SWINDLER, charlatan, mountebank, trickster, fraud, fraudster, imposter, hoaxer, sharper; *informal* con man, snake oil salesman, shark, grifter.

quadrangle ▶ noun COURTYARD, quad, court, cloister, precinct; square, plaza, piazza.

quaff ▶ verb DRINK, swallow, gulp (down), guzzle, slurp, down, drain, empty; imbibe, partake of, consume; *informal* kill, glug, swig, swill, slug, knock back, toss off, chug, chugalug, snarf (down).

quagmire ▶ noun **1** *the field became a quagmire* SWAMP, morass, bog, marsh, muskeg, mire, slough; *archaic* quag. **2** *a judicial quagmire* MUDDLE, mix-up, mess, predicament, mare's nest, can of worms, quandary, tangle, imbroglio; trouble, confusion, difficulty; *informal* sticky situation, pickle, stew, dilemma, fix, bind.

quail ▶ verb COWER, cringe, flinch, shrink, recoil, shy (away), pull back; shiver, tremble, shake, quake, blench, blanch.

quaint ▶ adjective **1** *a quaint town* PICTURESQUE, charming, sweet, attractive, old-fashioned, old-world, twee, cunning; *pseudo-archaic* olde (worlde). **2** *quaint customs* UNUSUAL, different, out of the ordinary, curious, eccentric, quirky, bizarre, whimsical, unconventional; *informal* offbeat.
— OPPOSITES: ugly, ordinary.

quake ▶ verb **1** *the ground quaked* SHAKE, tremble, quiver, shudder, sway, rock, wobble, move, heave, convulse. **2** *we quaked when we saw the soldiers* TREMBLE, shake, quiver, shiver; blench, blanch, flinch, shrink, recoil, cower, cringe.

qualification ▶ noun **1** *a teaching qualification* CERTIFICATE, diploma, degree, licence, document, warrant; eligibility, acceptability, adequacy; proficiency, skill, ability, capability, aptitude. **2** *I can't accept it without qualification* MODIFICATION, limitation, reservation, stipulation; alteration, amendment, revision, moderation, mitigation; condition, proviso, caveat.

qualified ▶ adjective CERTIFIED, certificated, chartered, licensed, professional; trained, fit, competent, accomplished, proficient, skilled, experienced, expert.

qualify ▶ verb **1** *I qualify for free travel* BE ELIGIBLE, meet the requirements; be entitled to, be permitted. **2** *they qualify as refugees* COUNT, be considered, be designated, be eligible. **3** *she qualified as a doctor* BE CERTIFIED, be licensed; pass, graduate, make the grade, succeed, pass muster. **4** *the course qualified them to teach* AUTHORIZE, empower, allow, permit, license; equip, prepare, train, educate, teach. **5** *they qualified their findings* MODIFY, limit, restrict, make conditional; moderate, temper, modulate, mitigate.

quality ▶ noun **1** *a poor quality of signal* STANDARD, grade, class, calibre, condition, character, nature, form, rank, value, level; sort, type, kind, variety. **2** *work of such quality* EXCELLENCE, superiority, merit, worth, value, virtue, calibre, eminence, distinction,

incomparability; talent, skill, virtuosity, craftsmanship. **3** *her good qualities* FEATURE, trait, attribute, characteristic, point, aspect, facet, side, property.

qualm ▶ noun MISGIVING, doubt, reservation, second thought, worry, concern, anxiety; (**qualms**) hesitation, hesitance, hesitancy, demur, reluctance, disinclination, apprehension, trepidation, unease; scruples, remorse, compunction.

quandary ▶ noun PREDICAMENT, plight, difficult situation, awkward situation; trouble, muddle, mess, confusion, difficulty, mare's nest; *informal* dilemma, sticky situation, pickle, hole, stew, fix, bind, jam.

quantity ▶ noun **1** *the quantity of food collected* AMOUNT, total, aggregate, sum, quota, mass, weight, volume, bulk; quantum, proportion, portion, part. **2** *a quantity of ammunition* AMOUNT, lot, great deal, good deal, abundance, wealth, profusion, plenty; *informal* pile, ton, load, heap, mass, stack, whack.

quarrel ▶ noun *they had a quarrel about money* ARGUMENT, disagreement, squabble, fight, dispute, wrangle, clash, altercation, feud, contretemps, disputation, falling-out, war of words, shouting match; *informal* tiff, slanging match, run-in, hassle, blow-up, row, bust-up.
▶ verb *don't quarrel over it* ARGUE, fight, disagree, fall out; differ, be at odds; bicker, squabble, cross swords, lock horns, be at each other's throats.
■ **quarrel with** *you can't quarrel with the verdict* FAULT, criticize, object to, oppose, take exception to; attack, take issue with, impugn, contradict, dispute, controvert; *informal* knock; *formal* gainsay.

quarrelsome ▶ adjective ARGUMENTATIVE, disputatious, confrontational, captious, pugnacious, combative, antagonistic, contentious, bellicose, belligerent, cantankerous, choleric; *informal* scrappy.
— OPPOSITES: peaceable.

quarry ▶ noun PREY, victim; object, goal, target; kill, game.

quarter ▶ noun **1** *the Italian quarter* DISTRICT, area, region, part, side, neighbourhood, precinct, locality, sector, zone; ghetto, community, enclave, Little ——, —— town. **2** *help from an unexpected quarter* SOURCE, direction, place, location; person. **3** *the servants' quarters* ACCOMMODATION, lodgings, rooms, chambers; home; *informal* pad, digs; *formal* abode, residence, domicile. **4** *the riot squads gave no quarter* MERCY, leniency, clemency, lenity, compassion, pity, charity, sympathy, tolerance.
▶ verb **1** *they were quartered in a villa* ACCOMMODATE, house, board, lodge, put up, take in, install, shelter; *Military* billet. **2** *I quartered the streets* PATROL, range over, tour, reconnoitre, traverse, survey, scout.

quash ▶ verb **1** *he may quash the sentence* CANCEL, reverse, rescind, repeal, revoke, retract, countermand, withdraw, overturn, overrule, veto, annul, nullify, invalidate, negate, void; *Law* vacate; *formal* abrogate. **2** *we want to quash these rumours* PUT AN END TO, put a stop to, stamp out, crush, put down, check, curb, nip in the bud, squash, quell, subdue,

suppress, extinguish, stifle; *informal* squelch, put the kibosh on, deep-six.
— OPPOSITES: validate.

quasi- ► **combining form 1** *quasi-scientific* SUPPOSEDLY, seemingly, apparently, allegedly, ostensibly, on the face of it, on the surface, to all intents and purposes, outwardly, superficially, purportedly, nominally; pseudo-. **2** *a quasi-autonomous organization* PARTLY, partially, part, to a certain extent, to some extent, half, relatively, comparatively, (up) to a point; almost, nearly, just about, all but.

quaver ► **verb** TREMBLE, waver, quiver, shake, vibrate, oscillate, fluctuate, falter, warble.

quay ► **noun** WHARF, pier, jetty, landing stage, berth; marina, dock, harbour.

queasy ► **adjective** NAUSEOUS, nauseated, bilious, sick; ill, unwell, poorly, green around/at the gills.

queen ► **noun 1** *the Queen was crowned* MONARCH, sovereign, ruler, head of state; Her Majesty; king's consort, queen consort. *See also the table at* RULER. **2** (*informal*) *the queen of country music* DOYENNE, star, superstar, leading light, big name, queen bee, prima donna, idol, heroine, favourite, darling, goddess.

queer ► **adjective 1** *his diction is archaic and queer* ODD, strange, unusual, funny, peculiar, curious, bizarre, weird, uncanny, freakish, eerie, unnatural; unconventional, unorthodox, unexpected, unfamiliar, abnormal, anomalous, atypical, untypical, out of the ordinary, incongruous, irregular; puzzling, perplexing, baffling, unaccountable; *informal* fishy, spooky, freaky. **2** *queer culture. See* GAY *adjective sense* 1.
— OPPOSITES: normal.

quell ► **verb 1** *troops quelled the unrest* PUT AN END TO, put a stop to, end, crush, put down, check, crack down on, curb, suppress, overcome; *informal* squelch. **2** *he quelled his misgivings* CALM, soothe, pacify, settle, quieten, quiet, silence, allay, assuage, mitigate, moderate; *literary* stay.

quench ► **verb 1** *they quenched their thirst* SATISFY, slake, sate, satiate, gratify, relieve, assuage, take the edge off, indulge; lessen, reduce, diminish, check, suppress, extinguish, overcome. **2** *the flames were quenched* EXTINGUISH, put out, snuff out, smother, douse.

querulous ► **adjective** PETULANT, peevish, pettish, complaining, fractious, fretful, irritable, testy, tetchy, cross, snappish, crabby, crotchety, cantankerous, miserable, moody, grumpy, bad-tempered, sullen, sulky, sour, churlish; *informal* snappy, grouchy, cranky.

query ► **noun 1** *we are happy to answer any queries* QUESTION, inquiry. **2** *there was a query as to who owned the hotel* DOUBT, uncertainty, question (mark), reservation; skepticism.
► **verb 1** *'Why do that?' queried Isobel* ASK, inquire, question. **2** *some folk may query his credentials* QUESTION, call into question, challenge, dispute, cast aspersions on, doubt, have suspicions about, have reservations about.

quest ► **noun 1** *their quest for her killer* SEARCH, hunt; pursuance of. **2** *Sir Galahad's quest* EXPEDITION, journey, voyage, trek, travels, odyssey, adventure, exploration, search; crusade, mission, pilgrimage; *informal* Holy Grail.
■ **in quest of** IN SEARCH OF, in pursuit of, seeking, looking for, on the lookout for, after.

question ► **noun 1** *please answer my question* INQUIRY, query; interrogation. **2** *there is no question that he is ill* DOUBT, dispute, argument, debate, uncertainty, dubiousness, reservation. **3** *the political questions of the day* ISSUE, matter, business, problem, concern, topic, theme, case; debate, argument, dispute, controversy.
— RELATED TERMS: interrogative.
— OPPOSITES: answer, certainty.
► **verb 1** *the magistrate questions the suspect* INTERROGATE, cross-examine, cross-question, quiz, catechize; interview, debrief, examine, give the third degree to; *informal* grill, pump. **2** *she questioned his motives* QUERY, call into question, challenge, dispute, cast aspersions on, doubt, suspect, have suspicions about, have reservations about.
■ **beyond question 1** *her loyalty is beyond question* UNDOUBTED, beyond doubt, certain, indubitable, indisputable, incontrovertible, unquestionable, undeniable, clear, patent, manifest. **2** *the results demonstrated this beyond question* INDISPUTABLY, irrefutably, incontestably, incontrovertibly, unquestionably, undeniably, undoubtedly, beyond doubt, without doubt, clearly, patently, obviously.
■ **in question** AT ISSUE, under discussion, under consideration, on the agenda, to be decided.
■ **out of the question** IMPOSSIBLE, impracticable, unfeasible, unworkable, inconceivable, unimaginable, unrealizable, unsuitable.

questionable ► **adjective 1** *the premise to the argument remains questionable* CONTROVERSIAL, contentious, doubtful, dubious, uncertain, debatable, arguable; unverified, unprovable, unresolved, unconvincing, implausible, improbable; borderline, marginal, moot; *informal* iffy. **2** *questionable financial dealings* SUSPICIOUS, suspect, dubious, irregular, odd, strange, murky, dark, unsavoury, disreputable; *informal* funny, fishy, shady, iffy.
— OPPOSITES: indisputable, honest.

questionnaire ► **noun** QUESTION SHEET, survey (form), opinion poll; test, exam, examination, quiz.

queue ► **noun** LINEUP, line, row, column, file, chain, string; procession, train, cavalcade; waiting list, wait-list.
► **verb** *we queued for ice cream* LINE UP, wait in line, form a line, fall in, form a queue, queue up.

quibble ► **noun** *I have just one quibble* CRITICISM, objection, complaint, protest, argument, exception, grumble, grouse, cavil; *informal* niggle, moan, gripe, beef, grouch.
► **verb** *no one quibbled with the title* OBJECT TO, find fault with, complain about, cavil at; split hairs, chop logic; criticize, query, fault, pick holes in; *informal* nitpick; *archaic* pettifog.

quick ► **adjective 1** *a quick car* FAST, swift, rapid, speedy, high-speed, breakneck, expeditious, brisk, smart; *informal* zippy; *literary* fleet. **2** *she took a quick trip down memory lane* HASTY, hurried, cursory, perfunctory, desultory, superficial, summary; brief, short, fleeting, transient, transitory, short-lived, lightning, momentary, whirlwind, whistle stop. **3** *a quick end to the recession* SUDDEN, instantaneous, immediate, instant, abrupt, precipitate. **4** *she isn't quick enough to go to university* INTELLIGENT, bright, clever, gifted, able, astute, quick-witted, sharp-witted, smart; observant, alert, sharp, perceptive; *informal* brainy, on the ball, quick on the uptake.
— OPPOSITES: slow, long.

quicken ► **verb 1** *she quickened her pace* SPEED UP, accelerate, step up, hasten, hurry (up). **2** *the film* *quickened his interest in nature* STIMULATE, excite, arouse, rouse, stir up, activate, galvanize, whet, inspire, kindle; invigorate, revive, revitalize.

quickly ▶ adverb **1** *he walked quickly* FAST, swiftly, briskly, rapidly, speedily, at the speed of light, at full tilt, as fast as one's legs can carry one, at a gallop, on the double, post-haste, hotfoot; *informal* PDQ (pretty damn quick), like (greased) lightning, hell for leather, like mad, like blazes, like the wind, lickety-split; *literary* apace. **2** *you'd better leave quickly* IMMEDIATELY, directly, at once, now, straight away, right away, instantly, forthwith, without delay, without further ado; soon, promptly, early, momentarily; *informal* like a shot, ASAP (as soon as possible), pronto, straight off. **3** *he quickly inspected it* BRIEFLY, fleetingly, briskly; hastily, hurriedly, cursorily, perfunctorily, superficially, desultorily.

quick-tempered ▶ adjective IRRITABLE, irascible, hot-tempered, short-tempered, snappish, fiery, touchy, volatile; cross, crabby, crotchety, cantankerous, grumpy, ill-tempered, bad-tempered, testy, tetchy, prickly, choleric; *informal* snappy, chippy, grouchy, cranky, on a short fuse.

quick-witted ▶ adjective INTELLIGENT, bright, clever, gifted, able, astute, quick, smart, sharp-witted; observant, alert, sharp, perceptive; *informal* brainy, on the ball, quick on the uptake.
− OPPOSITES: slow.

quid pro quo ▶ noun EXCHANGE, trade, trade-off, swap, switch, barter, substitute, reciprocation, return; amends, compensation, recompense, restitution, reparation.

quiescent ▶ adjective INACTIVE, inert, idle, dormant, at rest, inoperative, deactivated, quiet; still, motionless, immobile, passive.
− OPPOSITES: active.

quiet ▶ adjective **1** *the whole pub went quiet* SILENT, still, hushed, noiseless, soundless; mute, dumb, speechless. **2** *a quiet voice* SOFT, low, muted, muffled, faint, indistinct, inaudible, hushed, whispered, suppressed. **3** *a quiet village* PEACEFUL, sleepy, tranquil, calm, still, restful, undisturbed, untroubled; unfrequented. **4** *can I have a quiet word?* PRIVATE, confidential, secret, discreet, unofficial, off the record, between ourselves. **5** *quiet colours* UNOBTRUSIVE, restrained, muted, understated, subdued, subtle, low-key; soft, pale, pastel. **6** *you can't keep it quiet for long* SECRET, confidential, classified, unrevealed, undisclosed, unknown, under wraps; *informal* hush-hush, mum; *formal* sub rosa. **7** *business is quiet* SLOW, stagnant, slack, sluggish, inactive, idle.
− OPPOSITES: loud, busy, public.
▶ noun *the quiet of the countryside* PEACEFULNESS, peace, restfulness, calm, tranquility, serenity; silence, quietness, stillness, still, quietude, hush, soundlessness.

quieten ▶ verb **1** *quieten the children down* SILENCE, hush, shush, quiet; *informal* shut up. **2** *her companions quietened* FALL SILENT, stop talking, break off, shush, hold one's tongue; *informal* shut up, clam up, shut it, pipe down, shut one's mouth, put a sock in it, button it. **3** *he tried to quieten manic patients* PACIFY, calm (down), soothe, subdue, tranquilize, relax, comfort, compose.

quietly ▶ adverb **1** *she quietly entered the room* SILENTLY, in silence, noiselessly, soundlessly, inaudibly; mutely. **2** *he spoke quietly* SOFTLY, in a low voice, in a whisper, in a murmur, under one's breath, in an

undertone, sotto voce, gently, faintly, weakly, feebly. **3** *some bonds were sold quietly* DISCREETLY, privately, confidentially, secretly, unofficially, off the record. **4** *she is quietly confident* CALMLY, patiently, placidly, serenely.

quilt ▶ noun DUVET, cover(s), eiderdown, comforter.

quintessence ▶ noun **1** *it's the quintessence of the modern home* PERFECT EXAMPLE, exemplar, prototype, stereotype, picture, epitome, embodiment, ideal, apotheosis; best, pick, prime, acme, crème de la crème. **2** *brain scientists are investigating the quintessence of intelligence* ESSENCE, soul, spirit, nature, core, heart, crux, kernel, marrow, substance; *informal* nitty-gritty; *Philosophy* quiddity, esse.

quintessential ▶ adjective TYPICAL, prototypical, stereotypical, archetypal, classic, model, standard, stock, representative, conventional; ideal, consummate, exemplary, definitive, best, ultimate.

quip ▶ noun *the quip provoked a smile* JOKE, witty remark, witticism, jest, pun, sally, pleasantry, bon mot; *informal* one-liner, gag, crack, wisecrack, funny.
▶ verb *'I think he got the point,' quipped Sean* JOKE, jest, pun, sally; *informal* gag, wisecrack.

quirk ▶ noun **1** *they all know his quirks* IDIOSYNCRASY, peculiarity, oddity, eccentricity, foible, whim, vagary, caprice, fancy, crotchet, habit, characteristic, trait, fad; *informal* hang-up. **2** *a quirk of fate* CHANCE, fluke, freak, anomaly, twist.

quirky ▶ adjective ECCENTRIC, idiosyncratic, unconventional, unorthodox, unusual, strange, bizarre, peculiar, odd, outlandish, zany; *informal* wacky, freaky, kinky, way-out, far out, kooky, offbeat.
− OPPOSITES: conventional.

quisling ▶ noun COLLABORATOR, colluder, sympathizer; traitor, turncoat, backstabber, double-crosser, defector, Judas, snake in the grass, fifth columnist.

quit ▶ verb **1** *she quit the office at 12:30* LEAVE, vacate, exit, depart from, withdraw from; abandon, desert. **2** *he's decided to quit his job* RESIGN FROM, leave, give up, hand in one's notice, stand down from, relinquish, vacate, walk out on, retire from; *informal* chuck, pack in; pack it in, call it quits, hang up one's skates ♣. **3** *(informal)* quit living in the past GIVE UP, stop, cease, discontinue, drop, break off, abandon, abstain from, desist from, refrain from, avoid, forgo; *informal* pack (it) in, leave off.

quite ▶ adverb **1** *two quite different types* COMPLETELY, entirely, totally, wholly, absolutely, utterly, thoroughly, altogether. **2** *red hair was quite common* FAIRLY, rather, somewhat, slightly, relatively, comparatively, moderately, reasonably, to a certain extent; *informal* pretty, kind of, kinda, sort of.

quiver ▶ verb **1** *I quivered with terror* TREMBLE, shake, shiver, quaver, quake, shudder. **2** *the bird quivers its wings* FLUTTER, flap, beat, agitate, vibrate.
▶ noun *a quiver in her voice* TREMOR, tremble, shake, quaver, flutter, fluctuation, waver.

quixotic ▶ adjective IDEALISTIC, romantic, visionary, Utopian, extravagant, starry-eyed, unrealistic, unworldly; impractical, impracticable, unworkable, impossible.

quiz ▶ noun **1** *there may be a short quiz next class* EXAM, test, pop quiz. **2** *a music quiz on the radio* COMPETITION, game, game show.
▶ verb *a man was being quizzed by police* QUESTION, interrogate, cross-examine, cross-question,

interview, sound out, give someone the third degree; test, examine; *informal* grill, pump.

quizzical ▶ adjective INQUIRING, questioning, curious; puzzled, perplexed, baffled, mystified; amused, mocking, teasing.

quota ▶ noun ALLOCATION, share, allowance, limit, ration, portion, dispensation, slice (of the cake); percentage, commission; proportion, fraction, bit, amount, quantity; *informal* cut, rake-off.

quotation ▶ noun **1** *a quotation from Mowat* CITATION, quote, excerpt, extract, passage, line, paragraph, verse, phrase; reference, allusion. **2** *a quotation for the building work* ESTIMATE, quote, price, tender, bid, costing, charge, figure.

quote ▶ verb **1** *he quoted a sentence from the book* RECITE, repeat, reproduce, retell, echo, parrot, iterate; take, extract. **2** *she quoted one case in which a girl died* CITE, mention, refer to, name, instance, specify, identify; relate, recount; allude to, point out, present, offer, advance.
▶ noun **1** *a Shakespeare quote.* See QUOTATION sense 1. **2** *ask the contractor for a quote.* See QUOTATION sense 2.

quotidian ▶ adjective **1** *the quotidian routine* DAILY, everyday, day-to-day, diurnal. **2** *her horribly quotidian furniture* ORDINARY, average, run-of-the-mill, everyday, standard, typical, middle-of-the-road, common, conventional, mainstream, unremarkable, unexceptional, workaday, commonplace, mundane, uninteresting; *informal* nothing to write home about, a dime a dozen.
− OPPOSITES: unusual.

Rr

rabbit ▶ noun buck, doe; cony; *informal* bunny.

rabble ▶ noun **1** *a rabble of noisy youths* MOB, crowd, throng, gang, swarm, horde, pack, mass, group. **2** *rule by the rabble* THE COMMON PEOPLE, the masses, the populace, the multitude, the rank and file, the commonality, the plebeians, the proletariat, the peasantry, the hoi polloi, the lower classes, the riff-raff; *informal* the proles, the plebs.
— OPPOSITES: nobility.

rabble-rouser ▶ noun AGITATOR, troublemaker, instigator, firebrand, revolutionary, insurgent, demagogue.

rabid ▶ adjective **1** *a rabid dog* rabies-infected, mad. **2** *a rabid anti-royalist* EXTREME, fanatical, overzealous, extremist, maniacal, passionate, fervent, diehard, uncompromising, illiberal; *informal* gung-ho, foaming at the mouth.
— OPPOSITES: moderate.

race¹ ▶ noun **1** *Sasha won the race* CONTEST, competition, event, heat, trial(s). **2** *the race for naval domination* COMPETITION, rivalry, contention; quest. **3** *the water in the the mill race* CHANNEL, waterway, raceway, conduit, sluice, chute, spillway.
▶ verb *he will race in the final* COMPETE, contend; run. **2** *Claire raced after him* HURRY, dash, rush, run, sprint, bolt, dart, gallop, career, charge, shoot, hurtle, careen, hare, fly, speed, scurry; *informal* tear, take off, belt, pelt, scoot, hotfoot it, leg it, bomb, hightail it. **3** *her heart was racing* POUND, beat rapidly, throb, pulsate, thud, thump, hammer, palpitate, flutter, pitter-patter, go pit-a-pat, quiver, pump.

race² ▶ noun **1** *pupils of many different races* ETHNIC GROUP, racial type, (ethnic) origin, colour. **2** *a bloodthirsty race* PEOPLE, nation.

racial ▶ adjective ETHNIC, ethnological, race-related; cultural, national, tribal.

racism ▶ noun RACIAL DISCRIMINATION, racialism, racial prejudice, xenophobia, chauvinism, bigotry.

racist ▶ noun *he was exposed as a racist* RACIAL BIGOT, racialist, xenophobe, chauvinist, supremacist.
▶ adjective *a racist society* (RACIALLY) DISCRIMINATORY, racialist, prejudiced, bigoted.

rack ▶ noun *put the cake on a wire rack* FRAME, framework, stand, holder, trestle, support, shelf.
▶ verb *she was racked with guilt* TORMENT, afflict, torture, agonize, harrow; plague, bedevil, persecute, trouble, worry.
■ **on the rack** UNDER PRESSURE, under stress, under a strain, in distress; in trouble, in difficulties, having problems.
■ **rack one's brains** THINK HARD, concentrate, cudgel one's brains; *informal* scratch one's head.

racket ▶ noun **1** *the engine makes such a racket* NOISE, din, hubbub, clamour, uproar, tumult, commotion, rumpus, pandemonium, babel; *informal* hullabaloo. **2** (*informal*) *a gold-smuggling racket* SCHEME, fraud, swindle; *informal* rip-off, shakedown.

raconteur ▶ noun STORYTELLER, narrator, anecdotalist.

racy ▶ adjective RISQUÉ, suggestive, naughty, sexy, spicy, ribald; indecorous, indecent, immodest, off-colour, dirty, rude, smutty, crude, salacious; *informal* raunchy, blue; *euphemistic* adult.
— OPPOSITES: prim.

raddled ▶ adjective HAGGARD, untidy, unkempt, drawn, tired, worn out, washed out; unwell, unhealthy; *informal* the worse for wear.

radiance ▶ noun **1** *the radiance of the sun* LIGHT, brightness, brilliance, luminosity, beams, rays, illumination, blaze, glow, gleam, lustre, glare; luminescence, incandescence. **2** *her face flooded with radiance* JOY, elation, jubilation, ecstasy, rapture, euphoria, delirium, happiness, delight, pleasure.

radiant ▶ adjective **1** *the radiant moon* SHINING, bright, illuminated, brilliant, gleaming, glowing, ablaze, luminous, luminescent, lustrous, incandescent, dazzling, shimmering, resplendent; *archaic* splendent. **2** *she looked radiant* JOYFUL, elated, thrilled, overjoyed, jubilant, rapturous, ecstatic, euphoric, in seventh heaven, on cloud nine, delighted, very happy; *informal* on top of the world, over the moon.
— OPPOSITES: dark, gloomy.

radiate ▶ verb **1** *the stars radiate energy* EMIT, give off, give out, discharge, diffuse; shed, cast. **2** *light radiated from the hall* SHINE, beam, emanate. **3** *their faces radiate hope* DISPLAY, show, exhibit; emanate, breathe, be a picture of. **4** *four spokes radiate from the hub* FAN OUT, spread out, branch out/off, extend, issue.

radical ▶ adjective **1** *radical reform* THOROUGHGOING, thorough, complete, total, comprehensive, exhaustive, sweeping, far-reaching, wide-ranging, extensive, across the board, profound, major, stringent, rigorous. **2** *radical differences between the two theories* FUNDAMENTAL, basic, essential, quintessential; structural, deep-seated, intrinsic, organic, constitutive. **3** *a radical political movement* REVOLUTIONARY, progressive, reformist, revisionist, progressivist; extreme, extremist, fanatical, militant, diehard, hard-core.
— OPPOSITES: superficial, minor, conservative.
▶ noun *the arrested man was a radical* REVOLUTIONARY, progressive, reformer, revisionist; militant, zealot, extremist, fanatic, diehard; *informal* ultra.
— OPPOSITES: conservative.

radio ▶ noun *a two-way radio* TRANSCEIVER, CB, walkie-talkie, ship-to-shore, radio phone; receiver, tuner.

raffish ▶ adjective RAKISH, unconventional, bohemian; devil-may-care, casual, careless; louche, disreputable, dissolute, decadent.

raffle ▶ noun LOTTERY, lotto, (prize) draw, sweepstake, sweeps.

raft ▶ noun LIFEBOAT; *proprietary* Zodiac.

rag ▶ noun **1** *an oily rag* CLOTH, scrap of cloth; *informal* shmatte. **2** *a man dressed in rags* TATTERS, torn clothing, old clothes; cast-offs, hand-me-downs.

ragamuffin ▶ noun URCHIN, waif, guttersnipe, street kid; *informal* scarecrow.

ragbag ▶ noun JUMBLE, mishmash, mess, hash; assortment, mixture, miscellany, medley, mixed bag, mélange, variety, diversity, potpourri, hodgepodge.

rage ▶ noun 1 *his rage is due to frustration* FURY, anger, wrath, outrage, indignation, temper, spleen, resentment, pique, annoyance, vexation, displeasure; pet, tantrum, (bad) mood; *literary* ire, choler. 2 *the current rage for home improvement* CRAZE, passion, fashion, taste, trend, vogue, fad, enthusiasm, obsession, compulsion, fixation, fetish, mania, preoccupation; *informal* thing.
▶ verb 1 *she raged silently* BE ANGRY, be furious, be enraged, be incensed, seethe, be beside oneself, rave, storm, fume, spit; *informal* be livid, be wild, foam at the mouth, have a fit, be steamed up. 2 *he raged against the reforms* PROTEST ABOUT, complain about, oppose, denounce; fulminate, storm, rail. 3 *a storm was raging* THUNDER, rampage, be violent, be turbulent, be tempestuous.
■ **(all) the rage** POPULAR, fashionable, in fashion, in vogue, the (latest) thing, in great demand, sought-after, le dernier cri; *informal* in, the in thing, cool, big, trendy, red-hot, hip.

ragged ▶ adjective 1 *ragged jeans* TATTERED, in tatters, torn, ripped, holey, in holes, moth-eaten, frayed, worn (out), falling to pieces, threadbare, scruffy, shabby; *informal* tatty. 2 *a ragged child* SHABBY, scruffy, down-at-the-heel, unkempt, raddled, dressed in rags. 3 *a ragged coastline* JAGGED, craggy, rugged, uneven, rough, irregular; serrated, sawtooth, indented; *technical* crenulate, crenulated.
− OPPOSITES: smart.

raging ▶ adjective 1 *a raging mob* ANGRY, furious, enraged, incensed, infuriated, irate, fuming, seething, ranting; *literary* livid, wild; *literary* wrathful. 2 *raging seas* STORMY, violent, wild, turbulent, tempestuous. 3 *a raging headache* EXCRUCIATING, agonizing, painful, throbbing, acute, bad. 4 *her raging thirst* SEVERE, extreme, great, excessive.

raid ▶ noun 1 *the raid on Dieppe* ATTACK, assault, descent, blitz, incursion, sortie; onslaught, storming, charge, offensive, invasion, blitzkrieg. 2 *a raid on a store* ROBBERY, burglary, holdup, break-in, looting, plunder; *informal* smash-and-grab, stickup, heist. 3 *a police raid on the apartment* SWOOP, search; *informal* bust, takedown.
▶ verb 1 *they raided shipping in the harbour* ATTACK, assault, set upon, descend on, swoop on, blitz, assail, storm, rush. 2 *armed men raided the store* ROB, hold up, break into; plunder, steal from, pillage, loot, ransack, sack; *informal* stick up, heist. 3 *homes were raided by police* SEARCH, swoop on; *informal* bust.

raider ▶ noun ROBBER, burglar, thief, housebreaker, plunderer, pillager, looter, marauder; attacker, assailant, invader.

rail ▶ verb *he rails against injustice* PROTEST, fulminate, inveigh, rage, speak out, make a stand; expostulate about, criticize, denounce, condemn; object to, oppose, complain about, challenge; *informal* kick up a fuss about.
▶ noun *travel by rail* TRAIN, locomotive; *informal* iron horse.

railing ▶ noun FENCE, fencing, rail(s), paling, palisade, balustrade, banister.

raillery ▶ noun TEASING, mockery, chaff, ragging; banter, badinage; *informal* leg-pulling, joshing, ribbing, kidding.

rain ▶ noun 1 *the rain had stopped* RAINFALL, precipitation, raindrops, wet weather; drizzle,

shower, rainstorm, cloudburst, torrent, downpour, deluge, storm. 2 *a rain of hot ash* SHOWER, deluge, flood, torrent, avalanche, flurry; storm, hail.
− RELATED TERMS: pluvial.
▶ verb 1 *it rained heavily* POUR (DOWN), pelt down, tip down, teem down, beat down, lash down, sheet down, rain cats and dogs; fall, drizzle, spit, bucket down. 2 *bombs rained on the city* FALL, hail, drop, shower.

rainy ▶ adjective WET, showery, drizzly, damp, inclement.

raise ▶ verb 1 *he raised a hand in greeting* LIFT (UP), hold aloft, elevate, uplift, upraise, upthrust; hoist, haul up, hitch up, hoick up. 2 *he raised himself in the bed* SET UPRIGHT, set vertical; sit up, stand up. 3 *they raised prices* INCREASE, put up, push up, mark up, escalate, inflate; *informal* hike (up), jack up, bump up. 4 *he raised his voice* AMPLIFY, louden, magnify, intensify, boost, lift, increase, heighten, augment. 5 *the temple was raised in 900 BC* BUILD, construct, erect, assemble, put up. 6 *how will you raise the money?* GET, obtain, acquire; accumulate, amass, collect, fetch, net, make. 7 *the city raised troops to fight for them* RECRUIT, enlist, sign up, conscript, call up, mobilize, rally, assemble, draft. 8 *a tax raised on imports* LEVY, impose, exact, demand, charge. 9 *he raised several objections* BRING UP, air, ventilate; present, table, propose, submit, advance, suggest, moot, put forward. 10 *the disaster raised doubts about safety* GIVE RISE TO, occasion, cause, produce, engender, elicit, create, result in, lead to, prompt, awaken, arouse, induce, kindle, incite, stir up, trigger, spark off, provoke, instigate, foment, whip up; *literary* beget. 11 *most parents raise their children well* BRING UP, rear, nurture, look after, care for, provide for, mother, parent, tend, cherish; educate, train. 12 *she raised cattle* BREED, rear, nurture, keep, tend; grow, farm, cultivate, produce. 13 *he was raised to the peerage* PROMOTE, advance, upgrade, elevate, ennoble; *informal* kick upstairs. 14 *raise them on the radio phone* CONTACT, get hold of, reach, get in touch with, communicate with, call.
− OPPOSITES: lower, reduce, demolish.
▶ noun *the workers wanted a raise* pay increase, increment.
■ **raise hell** (*informal*). See HELL.

raised ▶ adjective EMBOSSED, relief, relievo, die-stamped.

rake¹ ▶ verb 1 *he raked the leaves into a pile* SCRAPE UP, collect, gather. 2 *she raked the gravel* SMOOTH (OUT), level, even out, flatten, comb. 3 *the cat raked his arm with its claws* SCRATCH, lacerate, scrape, rasp, graze, grate; *Medicine* excoriate. 4 *she raked a hand through her hair* DRAG, pull, scrape, tug, comb. 5 *I raked through my pockets* RUMMAGE, search, hunt, sift, rifle. 6 *machine-gun fire raked the streets* SWEEP, enfilade, pepper, strafe.
■ **rake something in** (*informal*) EARN, make, get, gain, garner, obtain, acquire, accumulate, bring in, pull in, pocket, realize, fetch, return, yield, raise, net, gross.
■ **rake something up** REMIND PEOPLE OF, recollect, remember, call to mind; drag up, dredge up.

rake² ▶ noun *he was something of a rake* PLAYBOY, libertine, profligate; degenerate, roué, debauchee; lecher, seducer, womanizer, philanderer, adulterer, Don Juan, Lothario, Casanova; *informal* lady-killer, ladies' man, lech.

rake-off ▶ noun (*informal*). See CUT noun sense 3.

rakish ▶ adjective DASHING, debonair, stylish, jaunty,

devil-may-care; raffish, disreputable, louche; *informal* sharp.

rally ▸ **verb 1** *the troops rallied and held their ground* REGROUP, reassemble, re-form, reunite. **2** *he rallied an army* MUSTER, marshal, mobilize, raise, call up, recruit, enlist, conscript; assemble, gather, round up, draft; *formal* convoke. **3** *ministers rallied to denounce the rumours* GET TOGETHER, band together, assemble, join forces, unite, ally, collaborate, co-operate, pull together. **4** *share prices rallied* RECOVER, improve, get better, pick up, revive, bounce back, perk up, look up, turn a corner.
− OPPOSITES: disperse, disband, slump.
▸ **noun 1** *a rally in support of the strike* (MASS) MEETING, gathering, assembly; demonstration, (protest) march, protest; *informal* demo. **2** *a rally in oil prices* RECOVERY, upturn, improvement, comeback, resurgence.
− OPPOSITES: slump.

ram ▸ **verb 1** *he rammed his sword into its sheath* FORCE, thrust, plunge, stab, push, sink, dig, stick, cram, jam, stuff, pack. **2** *a van rammed the police car* HIT, strike, crash into, collide with, impact, run into, smash into, smack into, bump (into), butt.

ramble ▸ **verb 1** *we rambled around the lanes* WALK, hike, tramp, trek, backpack; wander, stroll, saunter, amble, roam, range, rove, traipse; *informal* mosey, tootle; *formal* perambulate. **2** *she does ramble on* CHATTER, babble, prattle, prate, blather, gabble, jabber, twitter, rattle, maunder; *informal* jaw, gas, gab, yak, yabber; natter, waffle.
▸ **noun** *a ramble in the hills* WALK, hike, trek; wander, stroll, saunter, amble, roam, traipse, jaunt, promenade; *informal* mosey, tootle; *formal* perambulation.

rambler ▸ **noun** WALKER, hiker, backpacker, wanderer, rover; *literary* wayfarer.

rambling ▸ **adjective 1** *a rambling speech* LONG-WINDED, verbose, wordy, prolix; digressive, maundering, roundabout, circuitous, tortuous, circumlocutory; disconnected, disjointed, incoherent. **2** *rambling streets* WINDING, twisting, twisty, tortuous, labyrinthine; sprawling. **3** *a rambling rose* TRAILING, creeping, climbing, vining.
− OPPOSITES: concise.

rambunctious ▸ **adjective** BOISTEROUS, rowdy, obstreperous, wild, turbulent, unruly, disorderly.

ramification ▸ **noun** CONSEQUENCE, result, aftermath, outcome, effect, upshot; development, implication; product, by-product.

ramp ▸ **noun** SLOPE, bank, incline, gradient, tilt; rise, ascent, drop, descent, declivity.

rampage ▸ **verb** *mobs rampaged through the streets* RIOT, run riot, go on the rampage, run amok, go berserk; storm, charge, tear.
■ **go on the rampage** RIOT, go berserk, get out of control, run amok; *informal* go postal.

rampant ▸ **adjective 1** *rampant inflation* UNCONTROLLED, unrestrained, unchecked, unbridled, widespread; out of control, out of hand, rife. **2** *rampant dislike* VEHEMENT, strong, violent, forceful, intense, passionate, fanatical. **3** *rampant vegetation* LUXURIANT, exuberant, lush, rich, riotous, rank, profuse, vigorous; *informal* jungly.
− OPPOSITES: controlled, mild.

rampart ▸ **noun** DEFENSIVE WALL, embankment, earthwork, parapet, breastwork, battlement, bulwark, outwork.

ramshackle ▸ **adjective** TUMBLEDOWN, dilapidated, derelict, decrepit, neglected, run down, gone to rack and ruin, beat-up, crumbling, decaying; rickety, shaky, unsound; *informal* shacky.
− OPPOSITES: sound.

rancid ▸ **adjective** SOUR, stale, turned, rank, putrid, foul, rotten, bad, off; gamy, high, fetid, stinking, malodorous, foul-smelling; *literary* noisome.
− OPPOSITES: fresh.

rancorous ▸ **adjective** BITTER, spiteful, hateful, resentful, acrimonious, malicious, malevolent, hostile, venomous, vindictive, baleful, vitriolic, vengeful, pernicious, mean, nasty; *informal* bitchy, catty.
− OPPOSITES: amicable.

rancour ▸ **noun** BITTERNESS, spite, hate, hatred, resentment, malice, ill will, malevolence, animosity, antipathy, enmity, hostility, acrimony, venom, vitriol.

random ▸ **adjective** *random spot checks* UNSYSTEMATIC, unmethodical, arbitrary, unplanned, undirected, casual, indiscriminate, non-specific, haphazard, stray, erratic; chance, accidental.
− OPPOSITES: systematic.
■ **at random** UNSYSTEMATICALLY, arbitrarily, randomly, unmethodically, haphazardly.

range ▸ **noun 1** *his range of vision* SPAN, scope, compass, sweep, extent, area, field, orbit, ambit, horizon, latitude; limits, bounds, confines, parameters. **2** *a range of mountains* ROW, chain, sierra, ridge, massif; line, string, series. **3** *a range of quality foods* ASSORTMENT, variety, diversity, mixture, collection, array, selection, choice. **4** *she put the dish into the range* STOVE, oven. **5** *cows grazed on the open range* PASTURE, pasturage, pasture land, prairie, grass, grassland, grazing land, bocage, veld; *literary* greensward.
▸ **verb 1** *charges range from 1% to 5%* VARY, fluctuate, differ; extend, stretch, reach, cover, go, run. **2** *on the stalls are ranged fresh foods* ARRANGE, line up, order, position, dispose, set out, array. **3** *they ranged over the dark lands* ROAM, rove, traverse, travel, journey, wander, drift, ramble, meander, stroll, traipse, walk, hike, trek.

rangy ▸ **adjective** LONG-LEGGED, long-limbed, leggy, tall; slender, slim, lean, thin, gangling, gangly, lanky, spindly, skinny, spare.
− OPPOSITES: squat.

rank¹ ▸ **noun 1** *she was elevated to ministerial rank* POSITION, level, grade, echelon; class, status, standing; *dated* station. *See table.* **2** *a family of rank* HIGH STANDING, blue blood, high birth, nobility, aristocracy; eminence, distinction, prestige; prominence, influence, consequence, power. **3** *a rank of riflemen* ROW, line, file, column, string, train, procession.
▸ **verb 1** *the plant is ranked as endangered* CLASSIFY, class, categorize, rate, grade, bracket, group, pigeonhole, designate; catalogue, file, list. **2** *he ranked them in order of prettiness* PRIORITIZE, order, organize, arrange, list; triage. **3** *she ranked below the others* HAVE A RANK, be graded, have a status, be classed, be classified, be categorized; belong. **4** *tulips ranked like guardsmen* LINE UP, align, order, arrange, dispose, set out, array, range.
■ **the rank and file 1** *the officers and the rank and file* OTHER RANKS, soldiers, NCOs, lower ranks, enlisted personnel; men, troops. **2** *a speech appealing to the rank and file* THE (COMMON) PEOPLE, the proletariat, the masses, the populace, the commonality, the third

Canadian Military Ranks

AIR FORCE	ARMY	NAVY
General Officers	**General Officers**	**Flag Officers**
general	general	admiral
lieutenant-general	lieutenant-general	vice-admiral
major-general	major-general	rear-admiral
brigadier-general	brigadier-general	commodore
Senior Officers	**Senior Officers**	**Senior Officers**
colonel	colonel	captain
lieutenant-colonel	lieutenant-colonel	commander
major	major	lieutenant-commander
Junior Officers	**Junior Officers**	**Junior Officers**
captain	captain	lieutenant
lieutenant	lieutenant	sub-lieutenant
second lieutenant	second lieutenant	acting sub-lieutenant
Subordinate Officers	**Subordinate Officers**	**Subordinate Officers**
officer cadet	officer cadet	naval cadet
Non-Commissioned Members	**Non-Commissioned Members**	**Non-Commissioned Members**
chief warrant officer	chief warrant officer	chief petty officer first class
master warrant officer	master warrant officer	chief petty officer second class
warrant officer	warrant officer	petty officer first class
sergeant	sergeant	petty officer second class
master corporal	master corporal	master seaman
corporal	corporal	leading seaman
private	private	able seaman
private recruit	private recruit	ordinary seaman

estate, the plebeians; the hoi polloi, the rabble, the riff-raff, the great unwashed; *informal* the proles, the plebs.

rank² ▶ **adjective 1** *rank vegetation* ABUNDANT, lush, luxuriant, dense, profuse, vigorous, overgrown; *informal* jungly. **2** *a rank smell* OFFENSIVE, unpleasant, nasty, revolting, sickening, obnoxious, noxious; foul, fetid, smelly, stinking, reeking, high, off, rancid, putrid, malodorous; humming; *literary* noisome. **3** *rank stupidity* DOWNRIGHT, utter, outright, out-and-out, absolute, complete, sheer, arrant, thoroughgoing, unqualified, unmitigated, positive, perfect, patent, pure, total.
– OPPOSITES: sparse, pleasant.

rankle ▶ **verb** CAUSE RESENTMENT, annoy, upset, anger, irritate, offend, affront, displease, provoke, irk, vex, pique, nettle, gall; *informal* rile, miff, peeve, aggravate, hack off, tick off.

ransack ▶ **verb** PLUNDER, pillage, raid, rob, loot, sack, strip, despoil; ravage, devastate, turn upside down; scour, rifle, comb, search.

ransom ▶ **noun** *they demanded a huge ransom* PAYOFF, payment, sum, price.
▶ **verb** *the girl was ransomed for $4 million* RELEASE, free, deliver, liberate, rescue; exchange for a ransom, buy the freedom of.

rant ▶ **verb** *she ranted on about the unfairness* HOLD FORTH, go on, fulminate, vociferate, sound off, spout, pontificate, bluster, declaim; shout, yell, bellow; *informal* mouth off.
▶ **noun** *he went into a rant about them* TIRADE, diatribe, broadside; *literary* philippic.

rap ▶ **verb 1** *she rapped his fingers with a ruler* HIT, strike; *informal* whack, thwack, bash, wallop; *literary* smite. **2** *I rapped on the door* KNOCK, tap, bang, hammer, pound. **3** (*informal*) *banks were rapped for high charges. See* REPRIMAND *verb*.
▶ **noun 1** *a rap on the knuckles* BLOW, hit, knock, bang, crack; *informal* whack, thwack, bash, wallop. **2** *a rap at the door* KNOCK, tap, rat-tat, bang, hammering, pounding.
■ **take the rap** (*informal*) BE PUNISHED, take the blame, suffer (the consequences), pay (the price).

rapacious ▶ **adjective** GRASPING, greedy, avaricious, acquisitive, covetous; mercenary, materialistic; insatiable, predatory; *informal* money-grubbing, grabby.
– OPPOSITES: generous.

rape ▶ **noun 1** *he was charged with rape* SEXUAL ASSAULT, sexual abuse, sexual interference; *archaic* ravishment, defilement. **2** *the rape of rainforest* DESTRUCTION, violation, ravaging, pillaging, plundering, desecration, defilement, sacking, sack.
▶ **verb 1** *he raped her at knifepoint* SEXUALLY ASSAULT, sexually abuse, violate, force oneself on; *literary* ravish; *archaic* defile. **2** *they raped our country* RAVAGE, violate, desecrate, defile, plunder, pillage, despoil; lay waste, ransack, sack.

rapid ▶ **adjective** QUICK, fast, swift, speedy, expeditious, express, brisk; lightning, meteoric, whirlwind; sudden, instantaneous, instant, immediate; hurried, hasty, precipitate; *informal* PDQ (pretty damn quick); *literary* fleet.
– OPPOSITES: slow.
▶ **noun** *learning to run rapids in an open canoe* fast water, chute ♣, whitewater, riffle, (*Nfld & NS*) rattle ♣; swift ♣.

rapidly ▶ **adverb** QUICKLY, fast, swiftly, speedily, at the speed of light, post-haste, hotfoot, at full tilt, briskly; hurriedly, hastily, in haste, in a rush, precipitately; *informal* like a shot, PDQ (pretty damn quick), in a flash, hell for leather, at the double, like a bat out of hell, like (greased) lightning, like mad, like the wind, lickety-split; *literary* apace.
– OPPOSITES: slowly.

rapport ▶ noun AFFINITY, close relationship, (mutual) understanding, bond, empathy, sympathy, accord.

rapprochement ▶ noun *growing political and diplomatic rapprochement between the two countries* RECONCILIATION, increased understanding, détente, restoration of harmony, agreement, co-operation, harmonization, softening.

rapt ▶ adjective FASCINATED, enthralled, spellbound, captivated, riveted, gripped, mesmerized, enchanted, entranced, bewitched, moonstruck; transported, enraptured, thrilled, ecstatic.
 − OPPOSITES: inattentive.

raptor ▶ noun *See table.*

Birds of Prey

accipiter	kestrel
American eagle	kite
bald eagle	lammergeier
barn owl	lanner
barred owl	marsh harrier
boreal owl	marsh hawk
brown owl	merlin
burrowing owl	northern harrier
buteo	osprey
buzzard	owl
caracara	peregrine falcon
chicken hawk	pigeon hawk
condor	red-tailed hawk
eagle owl	ringtail
eagle	rough-legged hawk
falcon	saker
falconet	saw-whet owl
fish eagle	screech owl
fish hawk	sea eagle
golden eagle	sharp-shinned hawk
goshawk	sort-eared owl
great grey owl	snowy owl
great horned owl	sparrow hawk
gyrfalcon	spotted owl
harpy eagle	tawny eagle
harrier	tawny owl
hawk owl	tercel
horned owl	turkey vulture

rapture ▶ noun *she gazed at him in rapture* ECSTASY, bliss, exaltation, euphoria, elation, joy, enchantment, delight, happiness, pleasure.
 ■ **go into raptures** ENTHUSE, rhapsodize, rave, gush, wax lyrical; praise something to the skies.

rapturous ▶ adjective ECSTATIC, joyful, elated, euphoric, enraptured, on cloud nine, in seventh heaven, transported, enchanted, blissful, happy; enthusiastic, delighted, thrilled, overjoyed, rapt; *informal* over the moon, on top of the world, blissed out.

rare ▶ adjective **1** *rare moments of privacy* INFREQUENT, scarce, sparse, few and far between, thin on the ground, like gold dust; occasional, limited, odd, isolated, unaccustomed, unwonted. **2** *rare stamps* UNUSUAL, recherché, uncommon, unfamiliar, atypical, singular. **3** *a man of rare talent* EXCEPTIONAL, outstanding, unparalleled, peerless, matchless, unique, unrivalled, inimitable, beyond compare, without equal, second to none, unsurpassed; consummate, superior, superlative, first-class; *informal* A1, top-notch.
 − OPPOSITES: common, commonplace.

rare bird ▶ noun RARITY, rara avis, wonder, marvel, nonpareil, nonsuch, one of a kind; curiosity, oddity, freak.

rarefied ▶ adjective ESOTERIC, exclusive, select; elevated, lofty.

rarely ▶ adverb SELDOM, infrequently, hardly (ever), scarcely, not often; once in a while, now and then, occasionally; *informal* once in a blue moon.
 − OPPOSITES: often.

raring ▶ adjective EAGER, keen, enthusiastic; impatient, longing, desperate; ready; *informal* dying, itching.

rarity ▶ noun **1** *the rarity of earthquakes in the UK* INFREQUENCY, rareness, scarcity, unusualness, uncommonness. **2** *this book is a rarity* COLLECTOR'S ITEM, rare thing, rare bird, rara avis; wonder, nonpareil, one of a kind; curiosity, oddity.

rascal ▶ noun SCALAWAG, imp, monkey, mischief-maker, wretch; *informal* scamp, tyke, horror, monster, varmint; *archaic* rapscallion.

rash¹ ▶ noun **1** *he broke out in a rash* SPOTS, breakout, eruption; hives; *Medicine* erythema, exanthema, urticaria. **2** *a rash of articles in the press* SERIES, succession, spate, wave, flood, deluge, torrent; outbreak, epidemic, flurry.

rash² ▶ adjective *a rash decision* RECKLESS, impulsive, impetuous, hasty, foolhardy, incautious, precipitate; careless, heedless, thoughtless, imprudent, foolish; ill-advised, injudicious, ill-judged, misguided, hare-brained, trigger-happy; *literary* temerarious.
 − OPPOSITES: prudent.

rasp ▶ verb **1** *enamel is rasped off the teeth* SCRAPE, rub, abrade, grate, grind, sand, file, scratch, scour; *Medicine* excoriate. **2** *'Help!' he rasped* CROAK, squawk, caw, say hoarsely.

rasping ▶ adjective HARSH, grating, jarring; raspy, scratchy, hoarse, rough, gravelly, croaky, gruff, husky, throaty, guttural.

rat (*informal*) ▶ noun **1** *rats in the basement. See table at* RODENT. **2** *her husband is a rat* SCOUNDREL, wretch, rogue; *informal* beast, pig, swine, creep, louse, low-life, scumbag, scum-bucket, scuzzball, sleazeball, sleazebag, heel, dog, weasel, rat fink. **3** *the most famous rat in mob history* INFORMER, betrayer, stool pigeon; *informal* snitch, squealer, fink, stoolie.
 ■ **rat on 1** *we don't rat on our friends* INFORM ON, betray, be unfaithful to, stab in the back; *informal* tell on, sell down the river, blow the whistle on, squeal on, peach on, rat out, finger. **2** *he ratted on his pledge* BREAK, renege on, go back on, welsh on.

rate ▶ noun **1** *a fixed rate of interest* PERCENTAGE, ratio, proportion; scale, standard, level. **2** *an hourly rate of $30* CHARGE, price, cost, tariff, fare, levy, toll; fee, remuneration, payment, wage, allowance. **3** *the rate of change* SPEED, pace, tempo, velocity, momentum.
 ▶ verb **1** *they rated their driving ability* ASSESS, evaluate, appraise, judge, estimate, calculate, gauge, measure, adjudge; grade, rank, classify, categorize. **2** *the scheme was rated effective* CONSIDER, judge, reckon, think, hold, deem, find; regard as, look on as, count as. **3** *he rated only a brief mention* MERIT, deserve, warrant, be worthy of, be deserving of.
 ■ **at any rate** IN ANY CASE, anyhow, anyway, in any event, nevertheless; whatever happens, come what may, regardless, notwithstanding.

rather ▶ adverb **1** *I'd rather you went* SOONER, by preference, preferably, by choice. **2** *it's rather complicated* QUITE, a bit, a little, fairly, slightly, somewhat, relatively, to some degree, comparatively;

informal pretty, sort of, kind of, kinda. **3** *her true feelings — or rather, lack of feelings* MORE PRECISELY, to be precise, to be exact, strictly speaking. **4** *she seemed sad rather than angry* MORE; as opposed to, instead of. **5** *it was not impulsive, but rather a considered decision* ON THE CONTRARY, au contraire, instead.

ratify ▶ verb CONFIRM, approve, sanction, endorse, agree to, accept, uphold, authorize, formalize, validate, recognize; sign.
— OPPOSITES: reject.

rating ▶ noun GRADE, grading, classification, ranking, rank, category, designation; assessment, evaluation, appraisal; mark, score.

ratio ▶ noun PROPORTION, comparative number, correlation, relationship, correspondence; percentage, fraction, quotient.

ration ▶ noun **1** *a daily ration of chocolate* ALLOWANCE, allocation, quota, quantum, share, portion, helping; amount, quantity, measure, proportion, percentage. **2** *the garrison ran out of rations* SUPPLIES, provisions, food, foodstuffs, eatables, edibles, provender; stores; *informal* grub, eats, chuck; *formal* comestibles; *dated* victuals.
▶ verb *fuel supplies were rationed* CONTROL, limit, restrict; conserve.

rational ▶ adjective **1** *a rational approach* LOGICAL, reasoned, sensible, reasonable, cogent, intelligent, judicious, shrewd, common-sense, commonsensical, sound, prudent; down-to-earth, practical, pragmatic. **2** *she was not rational at the time of signing* SANE, compos mentis, in one's right mind, of sound mind; normal, balanced, lucid, coherent; *informal* all there. **3** *humans are rational beings* INTELLIGENT, thinking, reasoning; cerebral, logical, analytical; *formal* ratiocinative.
— OPPOSITES: illogical, insane.

rationale ▶ noun REASON(S), reasoning, thinking, logic, grounds, sense; principle, theory, argument, case; motive, motivation, explanation, justification, excuse; the whys and wherefores.

rationalize ▶ verb **1** *he tried to rationalize his behaviour* JUSTIFY, explain (away), account for, defend, vindicate, excuse. **2** *an attempt to rationalize the industry* STREAMLINE, reorganize, modernize, update; trim, hone, simplify, downsize, prune.

rattle ▶ verb **1** *hailstones rattled against the window* CLATTER, patter; clink, clunk. **2** *he rattled some coins* JINGLE, jangle, clink, tinkle. **3** *the bus rattled along* JOLT, bump, bounce, jounce, shake, judder. **4** *the government was rattled by the strike* UNNERVE, disconcert, disturb, fluster, shake, perturb, discompose, discomfit, ruffle, throw; *informal* faze.
▶ noun **1** *the rattle of the bottles* CLATTER, clank, clink, clang; jingle, jangle. **2** *she gave the baby a rattle* NOISEMAKER, shaker, rain stick, maraca.
■ **rattle something off** REEL OFF, recite, list, fire off, run through, enumerate.
■ **rattle on/away** PRATTLE, babble, chatter, gabble, prate, go on, jabber, gibber, blether, ramble; *informal* gab, yak, yap, waffle.

raucous ▶ adjective **1** *raucous laughter* HARSH, strident, screeching, piercing, shrill, grating, discordant, dissonant; noisy, loud, cacophonous. **2** *a raucous party* ROWDY, noisy, boisterous, roisterous, wild.
— OPPOSITES: soft, quiet.

raunchy ▶ adjective (*informal*). See SEXY sense 2.

ravage ▶ verb LAY WASTE, devastate, ruin, destroy,

wreak havoc on, leave desolate; pillage, plunder, despoil, ransack, sack, loot, rape.

ravages ▶ plural noun **1** *the ravages of time* DAMAGING EFFECTS, ill effects. **2** *the ravages carried out by humanity* (ACTS OF) DESTRUCTION, damage, devastation, ruin, havoc, depredation(s).

rave ▶ verb **1** *he was raving about the fires of hell* TALK WILDLY, babble, jabber, talk incoherently. **2** *I raved and swore at them* RANT (AND RAVE), rage, lose one's temper, storm, fulminate, fume; shout, roar, thunder, bellow; *informal* fly off the handle, blow one's top, hit the roof, flip one's wig. **3** *he raved about her talent* PRAISE ENTHUSIASTICALLY, go into raptures about/over, wax lyrical about, sing the praises of, rhapsodize over, enthuse about/over, acclaim, eulogize, extol; *informal* ballyhoo; *formal* laud; *archaic* panegyrize.
— OPPOSITES: criticize.
▶ noun (*informal*) **1** *the food won raves from the critics* ENTHUSIASTIC/LAVISH PRAISE, a rapturous reception, tribute, plaudits, acclaim. **2** *an all-night rave.* See PARTY noun sense 1.
— OPPOSITES: criticism.
▶ adjective (*informal*) *rave reviews* VERY ENTHUSIASTIC, rapturous, glowing, ecstatic, excellent, highly favourable.

raven ▶ noun.
— RELATED TERMS: corvine.
▶ adjective *raven hair* BLACK, jet-black, ebony; *literary* sable.

ravenous ▶ adjective **1** *I'm absolutely ravenous* VERY HUNGRY, starving, famished; *rare* esurient. **2** *her ravenous appetite* VORACIOUS, insatiable; greedy, gluttonous; *literary* insatiate.

ravine ▶ noun GORGE, canyon, gully, defile, (*Atlantic*) droke ✦, couloir; chasm, abyss, gulf, gulch, coulee.

raving ▶ adjective See MAD sense 1.

ravings ▶ plural noun GIBBERISH, rambling, babbling, wild/incoherent talk.

ravish ▶ verb **1** (*literary*) *he tried to ravish her* RAPE, sexually assault/abuse, violate, force oneself on, molest; *archaic* dishonour, defile. **2** (*literary*) *you will be ravished by this wine* ENRAPTURE, enchant, delight, charm, entrance, enthrall, captivate. **3** (*archaic*) *her child was ravished from her breast* SEIZE, snatch, carry off/away, steal, abduct.

ravishing ▶ adjective VERY BEAUTIFUL, gorgeous, stunning, wonderful, lovely, striking, magnificent, dazzling, radiant, delightful, charming, enchanting; *informal* amazing, sensational, fantastic, fabulous, terrific, bodacious, hot, red-hot.
— OPPOSITES: hideous.

raw ▶ adjective **1** *raw carrot* UNCOOKED, fresh. **2** *raw material* UNPROCESSED, untreated, unrefined, crude, natural; unedited, undigested, unprepared. **3** *raw recruits* INEXPERIENCED, new, untrained, untried, untested, unseasoned; callow, immature, green, naive; *informal* wet behind the ears, raggedy-ass. **4** *his skin is raw* SORE, red, painful, tender; abraded, chafed; *Medicine* excoriated. **5** *a raw morning* BLEAK, cold, chilly, bone-chilling, freezing, icy, icy-cold, wintry, bitter, biting; *informal* nippy. **6** *raw emotions* STRONG, intense, passionate, fervent, powerful, violent; undisguised, unconcealed, unrestrained, uninhibited. **7** *raw images of Latin America* REALISTIC, unembellished, unvarnished, brutal, harsh, gritty.
— OPPOSITES: cooked, processed.
■ **in the raw** (*informal*). See NAKED sense 1.

raw-boned ▶ adjective THIN, lean, gaunt, bony, skinny, spare.
— OPPOSITES: plump.

rawhide ▶ noun hide, whip, cord.

ray ▶ noun 1 *rays of light* BEAM, shaft, streak, stream. 2 *a ray of hope* GLIMMER, flicker, spark, hint, suggestion, sign.

raze ▶ verb DESTROY, demolish, raze to the ground, tear down, pull down, knock down, level, flatten, bulldoze, wipe out, lay waste.

re ▶ preposition ABOUT, concerning, regarding, with regard to, relating to, vis-à-vis, apropos (of), on the subject of, with respect to, with reference to, in connection with.

reach ▶ verb 1 *Travis reached out a hand* STRETCH OUT, hold out, extend, outstretch, thrust out, stick out. 2 *reach me that book* PASS, hand, give, let someone have. 3 *soon she reached Helen's house* ARRIVE AT, get to, come to; end up at; *informal* make. 4 *the temperature reached 32 degrees* ATTAIN, get to; rise to, climb to; fall to, sink to, drop to; *informal* hit. 5 *the leaders reached an agreement* ACHIEVE, attain, work out, draw up, put together, negotiate, thrash out, hammer out. 6 *I have been trying to reach you all day* GET IN TOUCH WITH, contact, get through to, get, speak to; *informal* get hold of. 7 *our concern is to reach more people* INFLUENCE, sway, get (through) to, make an impression on, have an impact on.
▶ noun 1 *Bobby moved out of her reach* GRASP, range. 2 *small goals within your reach* CAPABILITIES, capacity. 3 *beyond the reach of the law* JURISDICTION, authority, influence; scope, range, compass, ambit.

react ▶ verb 1 *how would he react if she told him the truth?* BEHAVE, act, take it, conduct oneself; respond, reply, answer. 2 *she reacted against the new regulations* REBEL AGAINST, oppose, rise up against.

reaction ▶ noun 1 *his reaction had bewildered her* RESPONSE, answer, reply, rejoinder, retort, riposte; *informal* comeback. 2 *a reaction against modernism* BACKLASH, counteraction.

reactionary ▶ adjective *a reactionary policy* RIGHT-WING, conservative, rightist, traditionalist, conventional, redneck, unprogressive.
— OPPOSITES: progressive.
▶ noun *an extreme reactionary* RIGHT-WINGER, conservative, rightist, traditionalist, dinosaur.
— OPPOSITES: radical.

read ▶ verb 1 *Nadine and Ian were reading the paper by the fireplace* PERUSE, study, scrutinize, look through; pore over, be absorbed in; run one's eye over, cast an eye over, leaf through, scan, flick through, skim through, thumb through. 2 *he read a passage of the letter* READ OUT/ALOUD, recite, declaim. 3 *I can't read my own writing* DECIPHER, make out, make sense of, interpret, understand. 4 *her remark could be read as a criticism* INTERPRET, take (to mean), construe, see, understand. 5 *the dial read 70 km/h* INDICATE, register, record, display, show.
— RELATED TERMS: legible.
▶ noun *have a read of this* PERUSAL, study, scan; look (at), browse (through), leaf (through), flick (through), skim (through).
■ **read something into something** INFER FROM, interpolate from, assume from, attribute to; read between the lines.
■ **read up on** STUDY, brush up on; *informal* bone up on.

readable ▶ adjective 1 *the inscription is perfectly readable* LEGIBLE, easy to read, decipherable, clear,

intelligible, comprehensible, reader-friendly. 2 *her novels are immensely readable* ENJOYABLE, entertaining, interesting, absorbing, gripping, enthralling, engrossing, stimulating; *informal* unputdownable.
— OPPOSITES: illegible.

readily ▶ adverb 1 *Durkin readily offered to drive him* WILLINGLY, without hesitation, unhesitatingly, ungrudgingly, gladly, happily, eagerly, promptly. 2 *the island is readily accessible* EASILY, with ease, without difficulty.
— OPPOSITES: reluctantly.

readiness ▶ noun 1 *their readiness to accept change* WILLINGNESS, enthusiasm, eagerness, keenness; promptness, quickness, alacrity. 2 *a state of readiness* PREPAREDNESS, preparation. 3 *the readiness of his reply* PROMPTNESS, quickness, rapidity, swiftness, speed, speediness.
■ **in readiness** (AT THE) READY, available, on hand, accessible, handy; prepared, primed, on standby, standing by, on full alert.

reading ▶ noun 1 *a cursory reading of the financial pages* PERUSAL, study, scan, scanning; browse (through), look (through), glance (through), leaf (through), flick (through), skim (through). 2 *a man of wide reading* (BOOK) LEARNING, scholarship, education, erudition. 3 *readings from the Bible* PASSAGE, lesson; section, piece; recital, recitation. 4 *my reading of the situation* INTERPRETATION, construal, understanding, explanation, analysis. 5 *a meter reading* RECORD, figure, indication, measurement.

ready ▶ adjective 1 *are you ready?* PREPARED, (all) set, organized, primed; *informal* fit, psyched up, geared up. 2 *everything is ready* COMPLETED, finished, prepared, organized, done, arranged, fixed, in readiness. 3 *he's always ready to help* WILLING, prepared, pleased, inclined, disposed, predisposed; eager, keen, happy, glad; *informal* game. 4 *she looked ready to collapse* ABOUT TO, on the point of, on the verge of, close to, liable to, likely to. 5 *a ready supply of food* (EASILY) AVAILABLE, accessible, handy, close/near at hand, to/on hand, convenient, within reach, at the ready, near, at one's fingertips. 6 *a ready answer* PROMPT, quick, swift, speedy, fast, immediate, unhesitating; clever, sharp, astute, shrewd, keen, perceptive, discerning.
▶ verb *he needed time to ready himself* PREPARE, get/make ready, organize; gear oneself up; *informal* psych oneself up.
■ **at the ready** IN POSITION, poised, ready for use/action, waiting, on deck.
■ **make ready** PREPARE, make preparations, get everything ready, gear up for.

ready-made ▶ adjective 1 *ready-made clothing* READY-TO-WEAR, off-the-rack, prêt-à-porter. 2 *ready-made meals* PRE-COOKED, oven-ready, convenience, packaged.
— OPPOSITES: tailor-made.

real ▶ adjective 1 *is she a fictional character or a real person?* ACTUAL, non-fictional, factual, real-life; historical; material, physical, tangible, concrete, palpable. 2 *real gold* GENUINE, authentic, bona fide; *informal* kosher, honest-to-goodness/God. 3 *my real name* TRUE, actual. 4 *tears of real grief* SINCERE, genuine, true, unfeigned, heartfelt, unaffected. 5 *a real man* PROPER, true; *informal* regular. 6 *you're a real idiot* COMPLETE, utter, thorough, absolute, total, prize, perfect.
— OPPOSITES: imaginary, imitation.
▶ adverb (*informal*) *that's real good of you. See* VERY *adverb*.

realism ▶ noun 1 *optimism tinged with realism*

PRAGMATISM, practicality, common sense, level-headedness. **2** *a degree of realism* AUTHENTICITY, fidelity, verisimilitude, truthfulness, faithfulness.

realistic ▶ adjective **1** *you've got to be realistic* PRACTICAL, pragmatic, matter-of-fact, down-to-earth, sensible, commonsensical; rational, reasonable, level-headed, clear-sighted, businesslike; *informal* having both/one's feet on the ground, hard-nosed, no-nonsense. **2** *a realistic aim* ACHIEVABLE, attainable, feasible, practicable, viable, reasonable, sensible, workable; *informal* doable. **3** *a realistic portrayal of war* TRUE (TO LIFE), lifelike, truthful, faithful, unidealized, real-life, naturalistic, graphic.
— OPPOSITES: idealistic, impracticable.

reality ▶ noun **1** *distinguishing fantasy from reality* THE REAL WORLD, real life, actuality; truth; physical existence. **2** *the harsh realities of life* FACT, actuality, truth. **3** *the reality of the detail* VERISIMILITUDE, authenticity, realism, fidelity, faithfulness.
— OPPOSITES: fantasy.
■ **in reality** IN (ACTUAL) FACT, in point of fact, as a matter of fact, actually, really, in truth; in practice; *archaic* in sooth.

realization ▶ noun **1** *a growing realization of the danger* AWARENESS, understanding, comprehension, consciousness, appreciation, recognition, discernment; *formal* cognizance. **2** *the realization of our dreams* FULFILLMENT, achievement, accomplishment, attainment; *formal* effectuation.

realize ▶ verb **1** *I suddenly realized what she meant* REGISTER, perceive, discern, be/become aware of (the fact that), be/become conscious of (the fact that); notice; understand, grasp, comprehend, see, recognize, work out, fathom, apprehend; *informal* latch on to, cotton on to, savvy, figure out, get (the message); twig, clue; *formal* be/become cognizant of. **2** *they realized their dream* FULFILL, achieve, accomplish, make a reality, make happen, bring to fruition, bring about/off, carry out/through; *formal* effectuate. **3** *the company realized significant profits* MAKE, clear, gain, earn, return, produce. **4** *the goods realized $3000* BE SOLD FOR, fetch, go for, make, net. **5** *he realized his assets* CASH IN, liquidate, capitalize.

really ▶ adverb **1** *he is really very wealthy* IN (ACTUAL) FACT, actually, in reality, in point of fact, as a matter of fact, in truth, to tell the truth; *archaic* in sooth. **2** *he really likes her* GENUINELY, truly, honestly; undoubtedly, without a doubt, indubitably, certainly, assuredly, unquestionably; *archaic* verily. **3** *they were really kind to me* VERY, extremely, thoroughly, decidedly, exceptionally, exceedingly, immensely, monumentally, tremendously, uncommonly, unbelievably, remarkably, eminently, extraordinarily, incredibly, most, downright, terrifically, awfully, (ever) so; *informal* totally, ultra, too —— for words, seriously, real, mighty, awful, plumb, powerful, way.
▶ exclamation *'They've split up.' 'Really?'* NO KIDDING, for real, is that so, is that a fact, is that right.

realm ▶ noun **1** *peace in the realm* KINGDOM, country, land, dominion, nation. **2** *the realm of academia* DOMAIN, sphere, area, field, world, province, territory.

realty ▶ noun REAL ESTATE, property, land.

ream
■ **ream out** *See* BERATE.

reap ▶ verb **1** *the corn has been reaped* HARVEST, garner, gather in, bring in. **2** *reaping the benefits* RECEIVE, obtain, get, acquire, secure, realize.

rear[1] ▶ verb **1** *I was reared on a farm* BRING UP, raise, care for, look after, nurture, parent; educate. **2** *he reared cattle* BREED, raise, keep, farm, ranch. **3** *laboratory-reared plants* GROW, cultivate. **4** *the bear reared its head* RAISE, lift (up), hold up, uplift. **5** *Mount Logan reared up before them* RISE (UP), tower, soar, loom.

rear[2] ▶ noun **1** *the rear of the building* BACK (PART), hind part, back end; *Nautical* stern. **2** *the rear of the queue* (TAIL) END, rear end, back end, tail, tag end. **3** *he slapped the horse on the rear. See* BUTTOCKS.
— OPPOSITES: front.
▶ adjective *the rear bumper* BACK, end, rearmost; hind, hinder, hindmost; *technical* posterior.

rearrange ▶ verb **1** *the furniture has been rearranged* REPOSITION, move round, change round, arrange differently. **2** *Tony had rearranged his schedule* REORGANIZE, alter, adjust, change (round), reschedule, rejig.

reason ▶ noun **1** *the main reason for his decision* CAUSE, ground(s), basis, rationale; motive, motivation, purpose, point, aim, intention, objective, goal; explanation, justification, argument, defence, vindication, excuse, pretext. **2** *postmodern voices railing against reason* RATIONALITY, logic, logical thought, reasoning, cognition; *formal* ratiocination. **3** *he was losing his reason* SANITY, mind, mental faculties; senses, wits; *informal* marbles. **4** *he continues, against reason, to love her* GOOD SENSE, good judgment, common sense, wisdom, sagacity, reasonableness.
▶ verb **1** *a young child is unable to reason* THINK RATIONALLY, think logically, use one's common sense, use one's head/brain; *formal* cogitate, ratiocinate. **2** *Scott reasoned that Annabel might be ill* CALCULATE, come to the conclusion, conclude, reckon, think, judge, deduce, infer, surmise; *informal* figure. **3** *she tried to reason with her husband* TALK ROUND, bring round, win round, persuade, prevail on, convince, make someone see the light.
■ **by reason of** (*formal*) BECAUSE OF, on account of, as a result of, owing to, due to, by virtue of, thanks to.
■ **reason something out** WORK OUT, think through, make sense of, get to the bottom of, puzzle out; *informal* figure out.
■ **reason with someone** TALK ROUND, bring round, persuade, prevail on, convince; make someone see the light.
■ **with reason** JUSTIFIABLY, justly, legitimately, rightly, reasonably.

reasonable ▶ adjective **1** *a reasonable man | a reasonable explanation* SENSIBLE, rational, logical, fair, fair-minded, just, equitable; intelligent, wise, level-headed, practical, realistic; sound, (well) reasoned, valid, commonsensical; tenable, plausible, credible, believable. **2** *you must take all reasonable precautions* WITHIN REASON, practicable, sensible; appropriate, suitable. **3** *cars in reasonable condition* FAIRLY GOOD, acceptable, satisfactory, average, adequate, fair, all right, tolerable, passable; *informal* OK. **4** *reasonable prices* INEXPENSIVE, moderate, low, cheap, budget, bargain, down-market; competitive.

reasoned ▶ adjective LOGICAL, rational, well-thought-out, clear, lucid, coherent, cogent, well expressed, well-presented, considered, sensible.

reasoning ▶ noun THINKING, reason, (train of) thought, thought process, logic, analysis, interpretation, explanation, rationalization; reasons, rationale, arguments; *formal* ratiocination.

reassure ▶ verb PUT/SET SOMEONE'S MIND AT REST, put

someone at ease, encourage, inspirit, hearten, buoy up, cheer up; comfort, soothe.
— OPPOSITES: alarm.

rebate ▶noun (PARTIAL) REFUND, repayment; discount, deduction, reduction, decrease.

rebel ▶noun **1** *the rebels took control of the capital* REVOLUTIONARY, insurgent, revolutionist, mutineer, insurrectionist, insurrectionary, guerrilla, terrorist, freedom fighter. **2** *the concept of the artist as a rebel* NONCONFORMIST, dissenter, dissident, iconoclast, maverick.
▶verb **1** *the citizens rebelled* REVOLT, mutiny, riot, rise up, take up arms, stage/mount a rebellion, be insubordinate. **2** *his stomach rebelled at the thought of food* RECOIL, show/feel repugnance. **3** *teenagers rebelling against their parents* DEFY, disobey, refuse to obey, kick against, challenge, oppose, resist.
— OPPOSITES: obey.
▶adjective **1** *rebel troops* INSURGENT, revolutionary, mutinous, rebellious, insurrectionary, insurrectionist. **2** *rebel MPs* REBELLIOUS, defiant, disobedient, insubordinate, subversive, resistant, recalcitrant; nonconformist, maverick, iconoclastic; *archaic* contumacious.
— OPPOSITES: compliant.

rebellion ▶noun **1** *troops suppressed the rebellion* UPRISING, revolt, insurrection, mutiny, revolution, insurgence, insurgency; rioting, riot, disorder, unrest. **2** *an act of rebellion* DEFIANCE, disobedience, rebelliousness, insubordination, subversion, subversiveness, resistance.

rebellious ▶adjective **1** *rebellious troops* REBEL, insurgent, mutinous, mutinying, rebelling, rioting, riotous, insurrectionary, insurrectionist, revolutionary. **2** *a rebellious adolescent* DEFIANT, disobedient, insubordinate, unruly, mutinous, wayward, obstreperous, recalcitrant, intractable; *formal* refractory; *archaic* contumacious.

rebirth ▶noun REVIVAL, renaissance, resurrection, reawakening, renewal, regeneration; revitalization, rejuvenation; *formal* renascence.

rebound ▶verb **1** *the ball rebounded off the wall* BOUNCE (BACK), spring back, ricochet, boomerang, carom. **2** *finally the dollar rebounded* RECOVER, rally, pick up, make a recovery. **3** *Thomas's tactics rebounded on him* BACKFIRE, boomerang, have unwelcome repercussions; come back to haunt; *archaic* redound on.

rebuff ▶verb *his offer was rebuffed* REJECT, turn down, spurn, refuse, decline, repudiate; snub, slight, repulse, repel, dismiss, brush off, give someone the cold shoulder; *informal* give someone the brush-off, give someone the bum's rush, freeze out.
— OPPOSITES: accept.
▶noun *the rebuff did little to dampen his ardour* REJECTION, snub, slight, repulse; refusal, spurning, cold-shouldering, discouragement; *informal* brush-off, kick in the teeth, slap in the face.

rebuild ▶verb RECONSTRUCT, renovate, restore, remodel, remake, reassemble.
— OPPOSITES: demolish.

rebuke ▶verb *she never rebuked him in front of others* REPRIMAND, reproach, scold, admonish, reprove, chastise, upbraid, berate, take to task, criticize, censure; *informal* tell off, give someone a talking-to, give someone a dressing-down, give someone an earful, chew out, ream out; *formal* castigate.
— OPPOSITES: praise.
▶noun *Damian was silenced by the rebuke* REPRIMAND,

reproach, reproof, scolding, admonishment, admonition, upbraiding; *informal* dressing-down; *formal* castigation.
— OPPOSITES: compliment.

rebut ▶verb REFUTE, deny, disprove; invalidate, negate, contradict, controvert, counter, discredit, give the lie to, explode; *informal* poke holes in; *formal* confute.
— OPPOSITES: confirm.

rebuttal ▶noun REFUTATION, denial, countering, invalidation, negation, contradiction.

recalcitrant ▶adjective UNCOOPERATIVE, intractable, obstreperous, truculent, insubordinate, defiant, rebellious, wilful, wayward, headstrong, self-willed, contrary, perverse, difficult, awkward, bloody-minded; *formal* refractory; *archaic* froward, contumacious.
— OPPOSITES: amenable.

recall ▶verb **1** *he recalled his student days* REMEMBER, recollect, call to mind; think back on/to, look back on, reminisce about. **2** *their exploits recall the days of chivalry* BRING TO MIND, call to mind, put one in mind of, call up, conjure up, evoke. **3** *the ambassador was recalled* SUMMON BACK, order back, call back.
— OPPOSITES: forget.
▶noun **1** *the recall of the ambassador* SUMMONING BACK, ordering back, calling back. **2** *their recall of dreams* RECOLLECTION, remembrance, memory.

recant ▶verb **1** *he was forced to recant his political beliefs* RENOUNCE, disavow, deny, repudiate, renege on; *formal* forswear, abjure. **2** *he refused to recant* CHANGE ONE'S MIND, be apostate; *rare* tergiversate. **3** *he recanted his testimony* RETRACT, take back, withdraw, unsay.

recantation ▶noun RENUNCIATION, renouncement, disavowal, denial, repudiation, retraction, withdrawal.

recapitulate ▶verb SUMMARIZE, sum up; restate, repeat, reiterate, go over, review; *informal* recap.

recede ▶verb **1** *the flood waters receded* RETREAT, go back/down, move back/away, withdraw, ebb, subside, abate. **2** *the lights receded into the distance* DISAPPEAR FROM VIEW, fade into the distance, be lost to view. **3** *fears of violence have receded* DIMINISH, lessen, decrease, dwindle, fade, abate, subside, ebb, wane.
— OPPOSITES: advance, grow.

receipt ▶noun **1** *the receipt of a letter* RECEIVING, getting, obtaining, gaining; arrival, delivery. **2** *make sure you get a receipt* PROOF OF PURCHASE, bill, bill of sale, invoice, sales ticket. **3** *receipts from house sales* PROCEEDS, takings, money/payment received, income, revenue, earnings; profits, (financial) return(s), take.

receive ▶verb **1** *Tony received an award* | *they received $650 in damages* BE GIVEN, be presented with, be awarded, collect, garner; get, obtain, gain, acquire; win, be paid, earn, gross, net. **2** *she received a letter* BE SENT, be in receipt of, accept (delivery of). **3** *Alec received the news on Monday* BE TOLD, be informed of, be notified of, hear, discover, find out (about), learn; *informal* get wind of. **4** *he received my suggestion with a complete lack of interest* HEAR, listen to; respond to, react to. **5** *she received a serious injury* EXPERIENCE, sustain, undergo, meet with; suffer, bear. **6** *they received their guests* GREET, welcome, say hello to. **7** *she's not receiving visitors* ENTERTAIN, see.
— OPPOSITES: give, send.

receiver ▶noun **1** *the receiver of a gift* RECIPIENT,

beneficiary, donee. **2** *a telephone receiver* HANDSET.
— OPPOSITES: donor.

recent ▶ adjective **1** *recent research* NEW, the latest, current, fresh, modern, contemporary, up-to-date, up-to-the-minute. **2** *his recent visit* NOT LONG PAST, occurring recently, just gone.
— OPPOSITES: old.

recently ▶ adverb NOT LONG AGO, a short time ago, in the past few days/weeks/months, a little while back; lately, latterly, just now.

receptacle ▶ noun CONTAINER, holder, repository; box, tin, bin, can, canister, case, pot, bag.

reception ▶ noun **1** *the reception of the goods* RECEIPT, receiving, getting. **2** *the reception of foreign diplomats* GREETING, welcoming, entertaining. **3** *a chilly reception* RESPONSE, reaction, treatment. **4** *a wedding reception* (FORMAL) PARTY, function, social occasion, soiree, levee, meet-and-greet; *informal* do, bash, bunfight.

receptive ▶ adjective OPEN-MINDED, responsive, amenable, well-disposed, flexible, approachable, accessible; *archaic* susceptive.
— OPPOSITES: unresponsive.

recess ▶ noun **1** *two recesses fitted with bookshelves* ALCOVE, bay, niche, nook, corner, hollow, oriel. **2** *the deepest recesses of the castle* INNERMOST PARTS/REACHES, remote/secret places, heart, depths, bowels. **3** *the Christmas recess* ADJOURNMENT, break, interlude, interval, rest; holiday, vacation; *informal* breather.
▶ verb *let's recess for lunch* ADJOURN, take a recess, stop, pause, (take a) break; *informal* take five, take a time out.

recession ▶ noun ECONOMIC DECLINE, downturn, depression, slump, slowdown.
— OPPOSITES: boom.

recherché ▶ adjective OBSCURE, rare, esoteric, abstruse, arcane, recondite, exotic, strange, unusual, unfamiliar, out of the ordinary.

recipe ▶ noun **1** *a tasty recipe* cooking instructions/directions; *archaic* receipt. **2** *a recipe for success* MEANS/WAY OF ACHIEVING, prescription, formula, blueprint.

recipient ▶ noun RECEIVER, beneficiary, legatee, donee.
— OPPOSITES: donor.

reciprocal ▶ adjective **1** *reciprocal love* GIVEN/FELT IN RETURN, requited, reciprocated. **2** *reciprocal obligations and duties* MUTUAL, common, shared, joint, corresponding, complementary.

reciprocate ▶ verb **1** *I was happy to reciprocate* DO THE SAME (IN RETURN), return the favour. **2** *love that was not reciprocated* REQUITE, return, give back.

recital ▶ noun **1** *a piano recital* CONCERT, (musical) performance, solo (performance); *informal* gig. **2** *her recital of Bob's failures* ENUMERATION, list, litany, catalogue, listing, detailing; account, report, description, recapitulation, recounting. **3** *a recital of the Lord's Prayer. See* RECITATION *sense 1.*

recitation ▶ noun **1** *the recitation of his poem* RECITAL, saying aloud, declamation, rendering, rendition, delivery, performance. **2** *a recitation of her life story* ACCOUNT, description, narration, narrative, story. **3** *songs and recitations* READING, passage; poem, verse, monologue.

recite ▶ verb *he began to recite verses of the Koran* REPEAT FROM MEMORY, say aloud, declaim, quote, deliver, render. **2** *he stood up and started reciting* GIVE A RECITATION, say a poem. **3** *Sir John recited the facts they knew* ENUMERATE, list, detail, reel off; recount, describe, narrate, give an account of, recapitulate, repeat.

reckless ▶ adjective RASH, careless, thoughtless, heedless, unheeding, hasty, overhasty, precipitate, precipitous, impetuous, impulsive, daredevil, devil-may-care; irresponsible, foolhardy, audacious, over-adventurous; ill-advised, injudicious, madcap, imprudent, unwise, ill-considered, kamikaze, wildcat; *literary* temerarious.
— OPPOSITES: careful.

reckon ▶ verb **1** *the cost was reckoned at $6,000* CALCULATE, compute, peg, work out, put a figure on, figure; count (up), add up, total, tot up. **2** *Anselm reckoned Hugh among his friends* INCLUDE, count, consider to be, regard as, look on as. **3** (*informal*) *I reckon I can manage that* BELIEVE, think, be of the opinion/view, be convinced, dare say, imagine, guess, suppose, consider, figure. **4** *it was reckoned a failure* REGARD AS, consider, judge, hold to be, think of as; deem, rate, gauge, count. **5** *I reckon to get good value for money* EXPECT, anticipate, hope to, be looking to; count on, rely on, depend on, bank on, figure on.
■ **to be reckoned with** IMPORTANT, of considerable importance, significant; influential, estimable, powerful, strong, potent, formidable, redoubtable.
■ **reckon with 1** *it's her mother you'll have to reckon with* DEAL WITH, contend with, face (up to). **2** *they hadn't reckoned with her burning ambition* TAKE INTO ACCOUNT, take into consideration, bargain for/on, anticipate, foresee, be prepared for, consider.
■ **reckon without** OVERLOOK, fail to take account of, disregard.

reckoning ▶ noun **1** *by my reckoning, this comes to $2 million* CALCULATION, estimation, count, computation, working out, summation, addition. **2** *by her reckoning, the train was late* OPINION, view, judgment, evaluation, estimate, estimation. **3** *the terrible reckoning that he deserved* RETRIBUTION, fate, doom, nemesis, punishment.
■ **day of reckoning** JUDGMENT DAY, day of retribution, doomsday, D-Day.

reclaim ▶ verb **1** *travelling expenses can be reclaimed* GET BACK, claim back, recover, regain, retrieve, recoup. **2** *Henrietta had reclaimed him from a life of vice* SAVE, rescue, redeem; reform.

recline ▶ verb LIE (DOWN/BACK), lean back; be recumbent; relax, repose, loll, lounge, sprawl, stretch out; *literary* couch.

recluse ▶ noun **1** *a religious recluse* HERMIT, ascetic, eremite, marabout; *historical* anchorite, anchoress. **2** *a natural recluse* LONER, solitary, lone wolf, troglodyte.

reclusive ▶ adjective SOLITARY, secluded, isolated, hermit-like, hermitic, eremitic, eremitical, cloistered.
— OPPOSITES: gregarious.

recognition ▶ noun **1** *there was no sign of recognition on his face* IDENTIFICATION, recollection, remembrance. **2** *his recognition of his lack of experience* ACKNOWLEDGEMENT, acceptance, admission; realization, awareness, consciousness, knowledge, appreciation; *formal* cognizance. **3** *official recognition* OFFICIAL APPROVAL, certification, accreditation, endorsement, validation. **4** *you deserve recognition for the tremendous job you are doing* APPRECIATION, gratitude, thanks, congratulations, credit, commendation, acclaim, acknowledgement; *informal* bouquets.

recognizable ▶ adjective IDENTIFIABLE, noticeable, perceptible, discernible, detectable, distinguishable, observable, perceivable; distinct, unmistakable,

clear.
— OPPOSITES: imperceptible.

recognize ▶ verb **1** *Hannah recognized him at once* IDENTIFY, place, know, put a name to; remember, recall, recollect; know by sight. **2** *they recognized Alan's ability* ACKNOWLEDGE, accept, admit; realize, be aware of, be conscious of, perceive, discern, appreciate; *formal* be cognizant of. **3** *psychotherapists who are recognized* OFFICIALLY APPROVE, certify, accredit, endorse, sanction, validate. **4** *the board recognized their hard work* PAY TRIBUTE TO, show appreciation of, appreciate, be grateful for, acclaim, commend.

recoil ▶ verb **1** *she instinctively recoiled* DRAW BACK, jump back, pull back; flinch, shy away, shrink (back), blench. **2** *he recoiled from the thought* FEEL REVULSION AT, feel disgust at, be unable to stomach, shrink from, balk at. **3** *her rifle recoiled* KICK (BACK), jerk back, spring back. **4** *this will eventually recoil on him* HAVE AN ADVERSE EFFECT ON, rebound on, affect badly, backfire, boomerang, come back to haunt; *archaic* redound on.
▶ noun *the recoil of the gun* KICKBACK, kick.

recollect ▶ verb REMEMBER, recall, call to mind, think of; think back to, look back on, reminisce about.
— OPPOSITES: forget.

recollection ▶ noun MEMORY, remembrance, impression, reminiscence.

recommend ▶ verb **1** *her former employer recommended her for the post* ADVOCATE, endorse, commend, suggest, put forward, propose, nominate, put up; speak favourably of, speak well of, put in a good word for, vouch for; *informal* plug. **2** *the committee recommended a cautious approach* ADVISE, counsel, urge, exhort, enjoin, prescribe, argue for, back, support; suggest, advocate, propose. **3** *there was little to recommend her* HAVE IN ONE'S FAVOUR, give an advantage to; *informal* have going for one.

recommendation ▶ noun **1** *the advisory group's recommendations* ADVICE, counsel, guidance, direction, suggestion, proposal. **2** *a personal recommendation* COMMENDATION, endorsement, good word, favourable mention, testimonial; suggestion, tip; *informal* plug. **3** *a place whose only recommendation is that it has few traffic problems* ADVANTAGE, good point/feature, benefit, asset, boon, attraction, appeal.

recompense ▶ verb **1** *offenders should recompense their victims* COMPENSATE, indemnify, repay, reimburse, make reparation to, make restitution to, make amends to. **2** *she wanted to recompense him* REWARD, pay back. **3** *nothing could recompense her loss* MAKE UP FOR, compensate for, make amends for, make restitution for, make reparation for, restore, redress, make good.
▶ noun *damages were paid in recompense* COMPENSATION, reparation, restitution, indemnification, indemnity; reimbursement, repayment, redress; *archaic* guerdon.

reconcilable ▶ adjective COMPATIBLE, consistent, congruous, congruent.

reconcile ▶ verb **1** *the news reconciled us* REUNITE, bring (back) together (again), restore friendly relations between, make peace between; pacify, appease, placate, mollify; *formal* conciliate. **2** *her divorced parents have reconciled* SETTLE ONE'S DIFFERENCES, make (one's) peace, (kiss and) make up, bury the hatchet, declare a truce. **3** *trying to reconcile his religious beliefs with his career* MAKE COMPATIBLE, harmonize, square, make congruent, balance. **4** *the quarrel was reconciled* SETTLE, resolve, sort out, mend, remedy, heal, rectify; *informal* patch up. **5** *they had to*

reconcile themselves to drastic losses (COME TO) ACCEPT, resign oneself to, come to terms with, learn to live with, get used to.
— OPPOSITES: estrange, quarrel.

reconciliation ▶ noun **1** *the reconciliation of the disputants* REUNITING, reunion, bringing together (again), conciliation, reconcilement, rapprochement, fence-mending; pacification, appeasement, placating, mollification. **2** *a reconciliation of their differences* RESOLUTION, settlement, settling, resolving, mending, remedying. **3** *there was little hope of reconciliation* AGREEMENT, compromise, understanding, peace; *formal* concord. **4** *the reconciliation of theory with practice* HARMONIZING, harmonization, squaring, balancing.

recondite ▶ adjective OBSCURE, abstruse, arcane, esoteric, recherché, profound, difficult, complex, complicated, involved; incomprehensible, unfathomable, impenetrable, cryptic, opaque.

recondition ▶ verb OVERHAUL, rebuild, renovate, restore, repair, reconstruct, remodel, refurbish; *informal* do up, revamp.

reconnaissance ▶ noun (PRELIMINARY) SURVEY, exploration, observation, investigation, examination, inspection; patrol, search; reconnoitring; *informal* recon.

reconnoitre ▶ verb SURVEY, make a reconnaissance of, explore; investigate, examine, scrutinize, inspect, observe, take a look at; patrol; *informal* check out, scope out, recon.

reconsider ▶ verb RETHINK, review, revise, re-examine, re-evaluate, reassess, reappraise; change, alter, modify; have second thoughts, change one's mind.

reconsideration ▶ noun REVIEW, rethink, re-examination, reassessment, re-evaluation, reappraisal.

reconstruct ▶ verb **1** *the building had to be reconstructed* REBUILD, restore, renovate, recreate, remake, reassemble, remodel, refashion, revamp, recondition, refurbish. **2** *reconstructing the events of that day* RECREATE, build up a picture/impression of, piece together, re-enact.

record ▶ noun **1** *written records of the past* ACCOUNT(S), document(s), documentation, data, file(s), dossier(s), evidence, report(s); annal(s), archive(s), chronicle(s); minutes, transactions, proceedings, transcript(s); certificate(s), instrument(s), deed(s); register, log, logbook; *Law* muniment(s). **2** *listening to records* ALBUM, vinyl; *dated* phonograph record, LP, EP, single, forty-five, seventy-eight. **3** *his previous good record* PREVIOUS CONDUCT/PERFORMANCE, track record, (life) history, reputation. **4** *she's got armed robbery on her record* CRIMINAL RECORD, police record; *informal* rap sheet. **5** *a new Canadian record* BEST PERFORMANCE, highest achievement; best time, fastest time; world record. **6** *a lasting record of what they have achieved* REMINDER, memorial, souvenir, memento, remembrance, testament.
▶ adjective *record profits* RECORD-BREAKING, best ever, unsurpassed, unparalleled, unequalled, second to none.
▶ verb **1** *the doctor recorded her blood pressure* WRITE DOWN, put in writing, take down, note, make a note of, jot down, put down on paper; document, put on record, enter, minute, register, log; list, catalogue. **2** *the thermometer recorded a high temperature* INDICATE, register, show, display. **3** *the team recorded their fourth away win* ACHIEVE, accomplish, chalk up, notch up.

4 *the recital was recorded live* MAKE A RECORD/RECORDING OF, tape, tape-record; video-record, videotape, video.
■ **off the record 1** *his comments were off the record* UNOFFICIAL, confidential, in (strict) confidence, not to be made public. **2** *they admitted, off the record, that they had made a mistake* UNOFFICIALLY, privately, in (strict) confidence, confidentially, between ourselves.

recorder ▸ noun **1** *he put a cassette in the recorder* tape recorder, cassette recorder; VCR, videotape recorder. **2** *a recorder of rural life* RECORD KEEPER, archivist, annalist, diarist, chronicler, historian.

recount ▸ verb TELL, relate, narrate, give an account of, describe, report, outline, delineate, relay, convey, communicate, impart.

recoup ▸ verb GET BACK, regain, recover, win back, retrieve, redeem, recuperate.

recourse ▸ noun *surgery may be the only recourse* OPTION, possibility, alternative, resort, way out, hope, remedy, choice, expedient.
■ **have recourse to** RESORT TO, make use of, avail oneself of, turn to, call on, look to, fall back on.

recover ▸ verb **1** *he's recovering from a heart attack* RECUPERATE, get better, convalesce, regain one's strength, get stronger, get back on one's feet; be on the mend, be on the road to recovery, pick up, rally, respond to treatment, improve, heal, pull through, bounce back. **2** *later, shares recovered* RALLY, improve, pick up, make a recovery, rebound, bounce back. **3** *the stolen material has been recovered* RETRIEVE, regain (possession of), get back, recoup, reclaim, repossess, redeem, recuperate, find (again), track down. **4** *gold coins recovered from a wreck* SALVAGE, save, rescue, retrieve.
— OPPOSITES: deteriorate.
■ **recover oneself** PULL ONESELF TOGETHER, regain one's composure, regain one's self-control; *informal* get a grip (on oneself).

recovery ▸ noun **1** *her recovery may be slow* RECUPERATION, convalescence. **2** *the economy was showing signs of recovery* IMPROVEMENT, rallying, picking up, upturn, upswing. **3** *the recovery of the stolen goods* RETRIEVAL, regaining, repossession, getting back, reclamation, recouping, redemption, recuperation.
— OPPOSITES: relapse, deterioration.

recreation ▸ noun **1** *she cycles for recreation* PLEASURE, leisure, relaxation, fun, enjoyment, entertainment, amusement; play, sport; *informal* R and R, rec; *archaic* disport. **2** *his favourite recreations* PASTIME, hobby, leisure activity.
— OPPOSITES: work.

recrimination ▸ noun ACCUSATION(S), counter-accusation(s), countercharge(s), counter-attack(s), retaliation(s).

recruit ▸ verb **1** *more soldiers were recruited* ENLIST, call up, conscript, draft, muster in; *archaic* levy. **2** *the king recruited an army* MUSTER, form, raise, mobilize. **3** *the company is recruiting staff* HIRE, employ, take on; enrol, sign up, engage.
— OPPOSITES: disband, dismiss.
▸ noun **1** *new recruits were enlisted* CONSCRIPT, new soldier; *US* draftee, yardbird. **2** *top-quality recruits* NEW MEMBER, new entrant, newcomer, initiate, beginner, novice, tenderfoot, hire; *informal* rookie, newbie, greenhorn.

rectify ▸ verb CORRECT, (put) right, put to rights, sort out, deal with, amend, remedy, repair, fix, make good, resolve, settle; *informal* patch up.

rectitude ▸ noun RIGHTEOUSNESS, goodness, virtue, morality, honour, honourableness, integrity, principle, probity, honesty, trustworthiness, uprightness, decency, good character.

recumbent ▸ adjective LYING, flat, horizontal, stretched out, sprawled (out), reclining, prone, prostrate, supine; lying down.
— OPPOSITES: upright.

recuperate ▸ verb **1** *she went to Winnipeg to recuperate* GET BETTER, recover, convalesce, get well, regain one's strength/health, get over something. **2** *he recuperated the money* GET BACK, regain, recover, recoup, retrieve, reclaim, repossess, redeem.

recur ▸ verb HAPPEN AGAIN, reoccur, occur again, repeat (itself); come back (again), return, reappear, appear again.

recurrent ▸ adjective REPEATED, recurring, repetitive, periodic, cyclical, seasonal, perennial, regular, frequent; intermittent, sporadic, spasmodic.

recycle ▸ verb REUSE, reprocess, reclaim, recover; salvage, save.

red ▸ adjective **1** *a red dress* scarlet, vermilion, crimson, ruby, cherry, cerise, cardinal, carmine, wine, blood-red; coral, cochineal, rose; brick-red, maroon, rusty, rufous; reddish; *literary* damask, vermeil, sanguine. **2** *he was red in the face* FLUSHED, reddish, crimson, pink, pinkish, florid, rubicund; ruddy, rosy, glowing; burning, feverish; *literary* rubescent; *archaic* sanguine. **3** *his eyes were red* BLOODSHOT, sore. **4** *red hair* reddish, auburn, titian, chestnut, carroty, ginger, sandy.
■ **in the red** OVERDRAWN, in debt, in debit, in deficit, in arrears.
■ **see red** (*informal*) BECOME VERY ANGRY, become enraged, lose one's temper; *informal* go mad, go crazy, go wild, go bananas, hit the roof, fly off the handle, blow one's top, flip out, go ballistic, flip one's wig, blow one's stack.

red-blooded ▸ adjective MANLY, masculine, virile, macho.

redden ▸ verb GO/TURN RED, blush, flush, colour (up), burn.

redeem ▸ verb **1** *one feature redeems the book* SAVE, compensate for the defects of, vindicate. **2** *he fully redeemed himself next time* VINDICATE, free from blame, absolve. **3** *you cannot redeem their sins* ATONE FOR, make amends for, make restitution for. **4** *we are redeeming the sinners* SAVE, deliver from sin, convert. **5** *Billy redeemed his drums from the pawnbrokers* RETRIEVE, regain, recover, get back, reclaim, repossess; buy back. **6** *this voucher can be redeemed at any branch* (GIVE IN) EXCHANGE, cash in, convert, trade in. **7** *they could not redeem their debts* PAY OFF/BACK, clear, discharge, honour. **8** *he made no effort to redeem his promise* FULFILL, carry out, discharge, make good; keep (to), stick to, hold to, adhere to, abide by, honour.

redeeming ▸ adjective COMPENSATING, compensatory, extenuating, redemptive.

redemption ▸ noun **1** *God's redemption of his people* SAVING, freeing from sin, absolution. **2** *the redemption of their possessions* RETRIEVAL, recovery, reclamation, repossession, return. **3** *the redemption of credit vouchers* EXCHANGE, cashing in, conversion. **4** *the redemption of the mortgage* PAYING OFF/BACK, discharge, clearing, honouring. **5** *the redemption of his obligations* FULFILLMENT, carrying out, discharge, performing, honouring, meeting.

red-handed ▸ adjective IN THE ACT, with one's

fingers/hand in the till, with one's hand in the cookie jar, in flagrante delicto; with one's pants down.

redneck ▶ noun bubba, hoser ✦, Joe Sixpack, hard hat.

redolent ▶ adjective EVOCATIVE, suggestive, reminiscent.

redoubtable ▶ adjective FORMIDABLE, awe-inspiring, fearsome, daunting; impressive, commanding, indomitable, invincible, doughty, mighty.

redound ▶ verb (formal) CONTRIBUTE TO, be conducive to, result in, lead to, have an effect; formal conduce to.

redress ▶ verb 1 we redressed the problem RECTIFY, correct, right, put to rights, compensate for, amend, remedy, make good, resolve, settle. 2 we aim to redress the balance EVEN UP, regulate, equalize.
▶ noun your best hope of redress COMPENSATION, reparation, restitution, recompense, repayment, indemnity, indemnification, retribution, satisfaction; justice.

reduce ▶ verb 1 the aim to reduce pollution LESSEN, make smaller, lower, bring down, decrease, diminish, minimize; shrink, narrow, contract, shorten; axe, cut (back/down), make cutbacks in, trim, curtail, slim (down), prune; informal chop. 2 she reduced him to tears BRING TO, bring to the point of, drive to. 3 he was reduced to the ranks DEMOTE, downgrade, lower (in rank). 4 bread has been reduced DISCOUNT, mark down, lower the price of, cut (in price), make cheaper, put on sale; informal slash, knock down.
— OPPOSITES: increase, put up.
■ **in reduced circumstances** IMPOVERISHED, broke, in straitened circumstances, ruined, bankrupted; poor, indigent, impecunious, in penury, poverty-stricken, destitute; needy, badly off, hard up; informal without two coins/cents to rub together, strapped for cash; formal penurious.

reduction ▶ noun 1 a reduction in pollution LESSENING, lowering, decrease, diminution, fade-out. 2 a staff reduction CUTBACK, cut, downsizing, scaling down, trimming, pruning, axing, chopping. 3 a reduction in inflationary pressure EASING, lightening, moderation, alleviation. 4 a reduction in status DEMOTION, downgrading, lowering. 5 substantial reductions DISCOUNT, markdown, deduction, (price) cut.

redundancy ▶ noun 1 redundancy in language SUPERFLUITY, unnecessariness, excess. 2 redundancies are in the offing LAYOFF, dismissal, firing, sacking, discharge; unemployment.

redundant ▶ adjective 1 many churches are now redundant UNNECESSARY, not required, unneeded, uncalled for, surplus (to requirements), superfluous. 2 2,000 workers were made redundant SACKED, dismissed, laid off, discharged; unemployed, jobless, out-of-work.
— OPPOSITES: employed.

reef ▶ noun SHOAL, bar, sandbar, sandbank, spit, (Nfld) sunker ✦; (Nfld & Scottish) skerry.

reek ▶ verb the whole place reeked STINK, smell (bad); stink to high heaven.
▶ noun the reek of cattle dung STINK, bad smell, stench, fetor, whiff; literary miasma.

reel ▶ verb 1 he reeled as the ship began to roll STAGGER, lurch, sway, rock, stumble, totter, wobble, falter. 2 we were reeling from the crisis BE SHAKEN, be stunned, be in shock, be shocked, be taken aback, be staggered, be

aghast, be upset. 3 the room reeled GO ROUND (AND ROUND), whirl, spin, revolve, swirl, twirl, turn, swim.
■ **reel something off** RECITE, rattle off, list rapidly, run through, enumerate, detail, itemize.

refer ▶ verb 1 he referred to errors in the article MENTION, make reference to, allude to, touch on, speak of/about, talk of/about, write about, comment on, deal with, point out, call attention to. 2 the matter has been referred to my insurers PASS, hand on/over, send on, transfer, remit, entrust, assign. 3 these figures refer only to 2001 APPLY TO, be relevant to, concern, relate to, be connected with, pertain to, appertain to, be pertinent to, have a bearing on, cover. 4 the name refers to a native village DENOTE, describe, indicate, mean, signify, designate. 5 the constable referred to his notes CONSULT, turn to, look at, have recourse to.

referee ▶ noun 1 the referee blew his whistle UMPIRE, judge, linesman; informal ref, ump. 2 include the names of two referees SUPPORTER, character witness, advocate.
▶ verb 1 he refereed the game UMPIRE, judge; informal ump. 2 they asked him to referee in the dispute ARBITRATE, mediate.

reference ▶ noun 1 his journal contains many references to railways MENTION OF, allusion to, comment on, remark about. 2 references are given in the bibliography SOURCE, citation, authority, credit; bibliographical data. 3 reference to a higher court REFERRAL, transfer, remission. 4 a glowing reference TESTIMONIAL, character reference, recommendation; credentials.
■ **with reference to** APROPOS, with regard to, regarding, with respect to, on the subject of, re; in relation to, relating to, vis-à-vis, in connection with.

referendum ▶ noun (POPULAR) VOTE, plebiscite, ballot, poll.

refine ▶ verb 1 refining our cereal foods PURIFY, process, treat. 2 helping students to refine their language skills IMPROVE, perfect, polish (up), hone, fine-tune.

refined ▶ adjective 1 refined sugar PURIFIED, processed, treated. 2 a refined lady CULTIVATED, cultured, polished, stylish, elegant, sophisticated, urbane; polite, gracious, well-mannered, well-bred, gentlemanly, ladylike, genteel. 3 a person of refined taste DISCRIMINATING, discerning, fastidious, exquisite, impeccable, fine.
— OPPOSITES: crude, coarse.

refinement ▶ noun 1 the refinement of sugar PURIFICATION, refining, processing, treatment, treating. 2 all writing needs endless refinement IMPROVEMENT, polishing, honing, fine-tuning, touching up, finishing off, revision, editing, reworking. 3 a woman of refinement STYLE, elegance, finesse, polish, sophistication, urbanity; politeness, grace, graciousness, good manners, good breeding, gentility; cultivation, taste, discrimination.

reflect ▶ verb 1 the snow reflects light SEND BACK, throw back, cast back. 2 their expressions reflected their feelings INDICATE, show, display, demonstrate, be evidence of, register, reveal, betray, disclose; express, communicate; formal evince. 3 he reflected on his responsibilities THINK ABOUT, give thought to, consider, give consideration to, review, mull over, contemplate, cogitate about/on, meditate on, muse on, brood on/over, turn over in one's mind; archaic pore on.
■ **reflect badly on** DISCREDIT, disgrace, dishonour, shame, put in a bad light, damage, tarnish the reputation of, give a bad name to, bring into disrepute.

reflection ▸ noun **1** *the reflection of light* SENDING BACK, throwing back, casting back. **2** *her reflection in the mirror* (MIRROR) IMAGE, likeness. **3** *your hands are a reflection of your well-being* INDICATION, display, demonstration, manifestation; expression, evidence. **4** *a sad reflection on society* SLUR, aspersion, imputation, reproach, shame, criticism. **5** *after some reflection, he turned it down* THOUGHT, thinking, consideration, contemplation, deliberation, pondering, meditation, musing, rumination; *formal* cogitation. **6** *write down your reflections* OPINION, thought, view, belief, feeling, idea, impression, conclusion, assessment; comment, observation, remark.

reflex ▸ adjective INSTINCTIVE, automatic, involuntary, reflexive, impulsive, intuitive, spontaneous, unconscious, unconditioned, untaught, unlearned.
– OPPOSITES: conscious.

reform ▸ verb **1** *a plan to reform the system* IMPROVE, (make) better, ameliorate, refine; alter, make alterations to, change, adjust, make adjustments to, adapt, amend, revise, reshape, refashion, redesign, restyle, revamp, rebuild, reconstruct, remodel, reorganize. **2** *after his marriage he reformed* MEND ONE'S WAYS, change for the better, turn over a new leaf, improve.
▸ noun *the reform of the prison system* IMPROVEMENT, amelioration, refinement; alteration, change, adaptation, amendment, revision, reshaping, refashioning, redesigning, restyling, revamp, revamping, renovation, rebuilding, reconstruction, remodelling, reorganizing, reorganization.

refractory ▸ adjective *(formal)* OBSTINATE, stubborn, mulish, pigheaded, obdurate, headstrong, self-willed, wayward, wilful, perverse, contrary, recalcitrant, obstreperous, disobedient, difficult, bloody-minded; *informal* balky; *archaic* contumacious, froward.
– OPPOSITES: obedient.

refrain ▸ verb ABSTAIN, desist, hold back, stop oneself, forbear, avoid, eschew, shun, renounce; *informal* swear off; *formal* forswear, abjure.

refresh ▸ verb **1** *the cool air will refresh me* REINVIGORATE, revitalize, revive, restore, fortify, enliven, perk up, stimulate, freshen, energize, exhilarate, reanimate, wake up, revivify, inspirit; blow away the cobwebs; *informal* buck up, pep up. **2** *let me refresh your memory* JOG, stimulate, prompt, prod. **3** *I refreshed his glass* REFILL, top up, replenish, recharge.
– OPPOSITES: weary.

refreshing ▸ adjective **1** *a refreshing drink* INVIGORATING, revitalizing, reviving, restoring, bracing, fortifying, enlivening, inspiriting, stimulating, energizing, exhilarating. **2** *a refreshing change of direction* WELCOME, stimulating, fresh, imaginative, innovative, innovatory.

refreshment ▸ noun **1** *refreshments were available during the intermission* FOOD AND DRINK, sustenance, provender; snacks, tidbits, eatables; *informal* nibbles, nibblies, eats, grub, nosh; *formal* comestibles; *literary* viands; *dated* victuals; *archaic* aliment. **2** *spiritual refreshment* INVIGORATION, revival, stimulation, reanimation, revivification, rejuvenation, regeneration, renewal.

refrigerate ▸ verb KEEP COLD, cool (down), chill.
– OPPOSITES: heat.

refuge ▸ noun **1** *homeless people seeking refuge in subway stations* SHELTER, protection, safety, security, asylum, sanctuary. **2** *a refuge for mountain gorillas* SANCTUARY, shelter, place of safety, (safe) haven, sanctum; retreat, bolthole, hiding place, hideaway, hideout.

refugee ▸ noun ÉMIGRÉ, fugitive, exile, displaced person, asylum seeker; boat people.

refund ▸ verb **1** *we will refund your money if you're not satisfied* REPAY, give back, return, pay back. **2** *they refunded the subscribers* REIMBURSE, compensate, recompense, remunerate, indemnify.
▸ noun *a full refund* REPAYMENT, reimbursement, rebate.

refurbish ▸ verb RENOVATE, recondition, rehabilitate, revamp, overhaul, restore, renew, redevelop, rebuild, reconstruct; redecorate, spruce up, upgrade, refit, retrofit, bring up to code; *informal* do up, rehab.

refusal ▸ noun **1** *we had one refusal to our invitation* NON-ACCEPTANCE, no, dissent, demurral, negation, turndown; regrets. **2** *you can have first refusal* OPTION, choice, opportunity to purchase. **3** *the refusal of planning permission* WITHHOLDING, denial, turndown.

refuse[1] ▸ verb **1** *he refused their invitation* DECLINE, turn down, say no to; reject, spurn, rebuff, dismiss; send one's regrets; *informal* pass up. **2** *the City refused planning permission* WITHHOLD, not grant, deny.
– OPPOSITES: accept, grant.

refuse[2] ▸ noun *piles of refuse* GARBAGE, trash, waste, debris, litter, detritus, dross; dregs, leftovers; *informal* dreck, junk.

refute ▸ verb **1** *attempts to refute Einstein's theory* DISPROVE, prove wrong/false, controvert, rebut, give the lie to, explode, debunk, discredit, invalidate; *informal* poke holes in; *formal* confute. **2** *she refuted the allegation* DENY, reject, repudiate, rebut; contradict; *formal* gainsay.

regain ▸ verb **1** *government troops regained the capital* RECOVER, get back, win back, recoup, retrieve, reclaim, repossess; take back, retake, recapture, reconquer. **2** *they regained dry land* RETURN TO, get back to, reach again, rejoin.

regal ▸ adjective **1** *a regal feast.* See SPLENDID sense 1. **2** *his regal forebears* ROYAL, kingly, queenly, princely.

regale ▸ verb **1** *they were lavishly regaled* ENTERTAIN, wine and dine, fete, feast, serve, feed. **2** *he regaled her with colourful stories* ENTERTAIN, amuse, divert, delight, fascinate, captivate.

regard ▸ verb **1** *we regard these results as encouraging* CONSIDER, look on, view, see, think of, judge, deem, estimate, assess, reckon, adjudge, rate, gauge. **2** *he regarded her coldly* LOOK AT, contemplate, eye, gaze at, stare at; watch, observe, view, study, scrutinize; *literary* behold.
▸ noun **1** *she has no regard for human life* CONSIDERATION, care, concern, thought, notice, heed, attention. **2** *doctors are held in high regard* ESTEEM, respect, acclaim, admiration, approval, approbation, estimation. **3** *Jamie sends his regards* BEST WISHES, good wishes, greetings, kind/kindest regards, felicitations, salutations, respects, compliments, best, love. **4** *his steady regard* (FIXED) LOOK, gaze, stare; observation, contemplation, study, scrutiny. **5** *in this regard I disagree with you* RESPECT, aspect, point, item, particular, detail, specific; matter, issue, topic, question.
■ **with regard to.** See REGARDING.

regarding ▸ preposition CONCERNING, as regards, with/in regard to, with respect to, with reference to, relating to, respecting, re, about, apropos, on the subject of, in connection with, vis-à-vis.

regardless ▶ adverb *he decided to go, regardless* ANYWAY, anyhow, in any case, nevertheless, nonetheless, despite everything, in spite of everything, even so, all the same, in any event, come what may.

■ **regardless of** IRRESPECTIVE OF, without regard to, without reference to, disregarding, without consideration of, discounting, ignoring, notwithstanding, no matter.

regenerate ▶ verb REVIVE, revitalize, renew, restore, breathe new life into, revivify, rejuvenate, reanimate, resuscitate; *informal* give a shot in the arm to.

regime ▶ noun **1** *the former Communist regime* (SYSTEM OF) GOVERNMENT, authorities, rule, authority, control, command, administration, leadership. **2** *a health regime* SYSTEM, arrangement, order, pattern, method, procedure, routine, course, plan, program.

regiment ▶ noun *the regiment was fighting in Europe* UNIT, outfit, force, corps, division, brigade, battalion, squadron, company, platoon.
▶ verb *their life is strictly regimented* ORGANIZE, order, systematize, control, regulate, manage, discipline.

region ▶ noun *the western region of the country* DISTRICT, province, territory, division, area, section, sector, zone, belt, part, quarter; *informal* parts.
■ **in the region of**. See APPROXIMATELY.

regional ▶ adjective **1** *regional variation* GEOGRAPHICAL, territorial; by region. **2** *a regional parliament* LOCAL, localized, provincial, district, parochial.
— OPPOSITES: national.

register ▶ noun **1** *the register of electors* OFFICIAL LIST, listing, roll, roster, index, directory, catalogue, inventory. **2** *the parish register* RECORD, chronicle, log, logbook, ledger, archive; annals, files. **3** *the lower register of the piano* RANGE, reaches; notes, octaves.
▶ verb **1** *I wish to register a complaint* RECORD, put on record, enter, file, lodge, write down, put in writing, submit, report, note, minute, log. **2** *it is not too late to register* ENROL, put one's name down, enlist, sign on/up, be enumerated ✦, apply. **3** *the dial registered a speed of 100 km/h* INDICATE, read, record, show, display. **4** *her face registered anger* DISPLAY, show, express, exhibit, betray, evidence, reveal, manifest, demonstrate, bespeak; *formal* evince. **5** *the content of her statement did not register* MAKE AN IMPRESSION, get through, sink in, penetrate, have an effect, strike home.

regress ▶ verb REVERT, retrogress, relapse, lapse, backslide, slip back; deteriorate, decline, worsen, degenerate, get worse; *informal* go downhill.
— OPPOSITES: progress.

regret ▶ verb **1** *they came to regret their decision* BE SORRY ABOUT, feel contrite about, feel remorse about/for, be remorseful about, rue, repent (of), feel repentant about, be regretful at/about. **2** *regretting the passing of youth* MOURN, grieve for/over, feel grief at, weep over, sigh over, feel sad about, lament, sorrow for, deplore.
— OPPOSITES: welcome.
▶ noun **1** *both players later expressed regret* REMORSE, sorrow, contrition, contriteness, repentance, penitence, guilt, compunction, remorsefulness, ruefulness. **2** *please give your grandmother my regrets* APOLOGY, apologies; refusal. **3** *they left with genuine*

regret SADNESS, sorrow, disappointment, unhappiness, grief.
— OPPOSITES: satisfaction.

regretful ▶ adjective SORRY, remorseful, contrite, repentant, rueful, penitent, conscience-stricken, apologetic, guilt-ridden, ashamed, shamefaced.
— OPPOSITES: unrepentant.

regrettable ▶ adjective UNDESIRABLE, unfortunate, unwelcome, sorry, woeful, disappointing; deplorable, lamentable, shameful, disgraceful.

regular ▶ adjective **1** *plant them at regular intervals* UNIFORM, even, consistent, constant, unchanging, unvarying, fixed. **2** *a regular beat* RHYTHMIC, steady, even, uniform, constant, unchanging, unvarying. **3** *the subject of regular protests* FREQUENT, repeated, continual, recurrent, periodic, constant, perpetual, numerous. **4** *regular methods of business* ESTABLISHED, conventional, orthodox, proper, official, approved, bona fide, standard, usual, traditional, tried and tested. **5** *a regular procedure* METHODICAL, systematic, structured, well-ordered, well-organized, orderly, efficient. **6** *his regular route to work* USUAL, normal, customary, habitual, routine, typical, accustomed, established.
— OPPOSITES: erratic, occasional.

regulate ▶ verb **1** *the flow of the river has been regulated* CONTROL, adjust, manage. **2** *a new act regulating businesses* SUPERVISE, police, monitor, check (up on), be responsible for; control, manage, direct, guide, govern.

regulation ▶ noun **1** *they obey all the regulations* RULE, ruling, order, directive, act, law, bylaw, statute, edict, canon, pronouncement, dictate, dictum, decree, fiat, command, precept. **2** *the regulation of blood sugar* ADJUSTMENT, control, management, balancing. **3** *the regulation of financial services* SUPERVISION, policing, superintendence, monitoring, inspection; control, management, responsibility for.
▶ adjective *regulation dress* OFFICIAL, prescribed, set, fixed, mandatory, compulsory, obligatory, de rigueur.
— OPPOSITES: unofficial.

regurgitate ▶ verb **1** *a ruminant continually regurgitates food* DISGORGE, bring up. **2** *regurgitating facts* REPEAT, say again, restate, reiterate, recite, parrot; *informal* trot out.

rehabilitate ▶ verb **1** *efforts to rehabilitate patients* RESTORE TO NORMALITY, reintegrate, readapt; *informal* rehab. **2** *former dissidents were rehabilitated* REINSTATE, restore, bring back; pardon, absolve, exonerate, forgive; *formal* exculpate. **3** *rehabilitating vacant housing* RECONDITION, restore, renovate, refurbish, revamp, overhaul, redevelop, rebuild, reconstruct; redecorate, spruce up; upgrade, refit, modernize; *informal* do up, rehab.

rehearsal ▶ noun PRACTICE (SESSION), trial performance, read-through, run-through, walk-through; *informal* dry run.

rehearse ▶ verb **1** *I rehearsed the role* PREPARE, practise, read through, run through/over, go over. **2** *he rehearsed the Vienna Philharmonic* TRAIN, drill, prepare, coach, put someone through their paces. **3** *the document rehearsed all the arguments* ENUMERATE, list, itemize, detail, spell out, catalogue, recite, rattle off; restate, repeat, reiterate, regurgitate, recapitulate, go over, run through; *informal* recap.

reign ▶ verb **1** *Robert II reigned for nineteen years* BE KING/QUEEN, be monarch, be sovereign, sit on the throne, wear the crown, rule. **2** *chaos reigned* PREVAIL, exist, be present, be the case, occur, be prevalent, be current, be rife, be rampant, be the order of the day, be in force, be in effect; *formal* obtain.

▶ **noun 1** *during Henry's reign* RULE, sovereignty, monarchy. **2** *his reign as manager* PERIOD IN OFFICE, incumbency, managership, leadership.

reigning ▶ **adjective 1** *the reigning monarch* RULING, regnant; on the throne. **2** *the reigning world champion* INCUMBENT, current. **3** *the reigning legal conventions* PREVAILING, existing, current; usual, common, recognized, established, accepted, popular, widespread.

reimburse ▶ **verb 1** *they will reimburse your travel costs* REPAY, refund, return, pay back. **2** *we'll reimburse you* COMPENSATE, recompense, repay.

rein ▶ **noun** *there is no rein on his behaviour* RESTRAINT, check, curb, constraint, restriction, limitation, control, brake.

▶ **verb** *they reined back costs* RESTRAIN, check, curb, constrain, hold back/in, keep under control, regulate, restrict, control, curtail, limit.

■ **free rein** FREEDOM, a free hand, leeway, latitude, flexibility, liberty, independence, free play, licence, room to manoeuvre, carte blanche, a blank cheque.

■ **keep a tight rein on** EXERCISE STRICT CONTROL OVER, regulate, discipline, regiment, keep in line.

reincarnation ▶ **noun** REBIRTH, transmigration of the soul, metempsychosis.

reinforce ▶ **verb 1** *troops reinforced the dam* STRENGTHEN, fortify, bolster up, shore up, buttress, prop up, underpin, brace, support. **2** *reinforcing links between colleges and companies* STRENGTHEN, fortify, support; cement, boost, promote, encourage, deepen, enrich, enhance, intensify, improve. **3** *the need to reinforce NATO troops* AUGMENT, increase, add to, supplement, boost, top up.

reinforcement ▶ **noun 1** *the reinforcement of our defences* STRENGTHENING, fortification, bolstering, shoring up, buttressing, bracing. **2** *reinforcement of the bomber force* AUGMENTATION, increase, supplementing, boosting, topping up. **3** *they returned later with reinforcements* ADDITIONAL TROOPS, fresh troops, auxiliaries, reserves; support, backup, help.

reinstate ▶ **verb** RESTORE, return to power, put back, bring back, reinstitute, reinstall.

reiterate ▶ **verb** REPEAT, say again, restate, recapitulate, go over (and over), rehearse.

reject ▶ **verb 1** *the loggers rejected the offer* TURN DOWN, refuse, decline, say no to, spurn; *informal* give the thumbs down to. **2** *Jamie rejected her* REBUFF, spurn, shun, snub, repudiate, cast off/aside, discard, abandon, desert, turn one's back on, have nothing (more) to do with, wash one's hands of; *informal* give someone the brush-off; *literary* forsake.
— OPPOSITES: accept.

▶ **noun 1** *it is only a reject* SUBSTANDARD ARTICLE, discard, second. **2** *what a reject!* FAILURE, loser, incompetent.

rejection ▶ **noun 1** *a rejection of the offer* REFUSAL, declining, turning down, dismissal, spurning. **2** *Madeleine's rejection of him* REPUDIATION, rebuff, spurning, abandonment, desertion; *informal* brush-off; *literary* forsaking.

rejoice ▶ **verb 1** *they rejoiced when she returned* BE JOYFUL, be happy, be pleased, be glad, be delighted, be elated, be ecstatic, be euphoric, be overjoyed, be as pleased as punch, be jubilant, be in raptures, be beside oneself with joy, be delirious, be thrilled, be

on cloud nine, be in seventh heaven; celebrate, make merry; *informal* be over the moon, be on top of the world; *literary* joy; *archaic* jubilate. **2** *he rejoiced in their success* TAKE DELIGHT, find/take pleasure, feel satisfaction, find joy, enjoy, revel in, glory in, delight in, relish, savour.
— OPPOSITES: mourn.

rejoicing ▶ **noun** HAPPINESS, pleasure, joy, gladness, delight, elation, jubilation, exuberance, exultation, celebration, revelry, merrymaking.

rejoin¹ ▶ **verb** *the path rejoins the main road further on* RETURN TO, be reunited with, join again, reach again, regain.

rejoin² ▶ **verb** *Eugene rejoined that you couldn't expect much* ANSWER, reply, respond, return, retort, riposte, counter.

rejoinder ▶ **noun** ANSWER, reply, response, retort, riposte, counter; *informal* comeback.

rejuvenate ▶ **verb** REVIVE, revitalize, regenerate, breathe new life into, revivify, reanimate, resuscitate, refresh, reawaken, put new life into; *informal* give a shot in the arm to, pep up, buck up.

relapse ▶ **verb 1** *a few patients relapse* GET ILL/WORSE AGAIN, have/suffer a relapse, deteriorate, degenerate, take a turn for the worse. **2** *she relapsed into silence* REVERT, lapse; regress, retrogress, slip back, slide back, degenerate.
— OPPOSITES: improve.

▶ **noun 1** *one patient suffered a relapse* DETERIORATION, turn for the worse. **2** *a relapse into alcoholism* DECLINE, lapse, deterioration, degeneration, reversion, regression, retrogression, fall, descent, slide.

relate ▶ **verb 1** *he related many stories* TELL, recount, narrate, report, chronicle, outline, delineate, retail, recite, repeat, communicate, impart. **2** *suicide rates are related to unemployment levels* CONNECT (WITH), associate (with), link (with), correlate (with), ally (with), couple (with). **3** *the charges relate to offences committed in August* APPLY, be relevant, concern, pertain to, be pertinent to, have a bearing on, appertain to, involve. **4** *she cannot relate to her step-father* HAVE A RAPPORT, get on (well), feel sympathy, feel for, identify with, empathize with, understand; *informal* hit it off with.

related ▶ **adjective 1** *related ideas* CONNECTED, interconnected, associated, linked, coupled, allied, affiliated, concomitant, corresponding, analogous, kindred, parallel, comparable, homologous, equivalent. **2** *are you two related?* OF THE SAME FAMILY, kin, akin, kindred; *formal* cognate, consanguineous.
— OPPOSITES: unconnected.

relation ▶ **noun 1** *the relation between church and state* CONNECTION, relationship, association, link, correlation, correspondence, parallel, alliance, bond, interrelation, interconnection. **2** *this had no relation to national security* RELEVANCE, applicability, reference, pertinence, bearing. **3** *are you a relation of his?* RELATIVE, member of the family, kinsman, kinswoman; (**relations**) family, (kith and) kin, kindred. **4** *improving relations with China* DEALINGS, communication, relationship, connections, contact, interaction. **5** *sexual relations. See* SEX *sense 1.*

relationship ▶ **noun 1** *the relationship between diet and diabetes* CONNECTION, relation, association, link, correlation, correspondence, parallel, alliance, bond, interrelation, interconnection. **2** *evidence of their relationship to a common ancestor* FAMILY TIES/ CONNECTIONS, blood ties/relationship, kinship, affinity, consanguinity, common ancestry/lineage. **3** *the end of their relationship* ROMANCE, (love) affair, love, liaison, amour, partnership.

relative ▶ **adjective 1** *the relative importance of each factor* COMPARATIVE, respective, comparable, correlative, parallel, corresponding. **2** *the food required is relative to body weight* PROPORTIONATE, proportional, in proportion, commensurate, corresponding. **3** *relative ease* MODERATE, reasonable, a fair degree of, considerable, comparative.
▶ **noun** *he's a relative of mine* RELATION, member of someone's/the family, kinsman, kinswoman; (**relatives**) family, (kith and) kin, kindred, kinsfolk.

relatively ▶ **adverb** COMPARATIVELY, by comparison; quite, fairly, reasonably, rather, somewhat, to a (certain) degree, tolerably, passably; *informal* pretty, kind of, kinda, sort of.

relax ▶ **verb 1** *yoga is helpful in learning to relax* UNWIND, loosen up, ease up/off, slow down, de-stress, unbend, rest, put one's feet up, take it easy; *informal* unbutton, hang loose, chill (out), take a load off. **2** *a walk will relax you* CALM (DOWN), unwind, loosen up, make less tense/uptight, soothe, pacify, compose. **3** *he relaxed his grip* LOOSEN, loose, slacken, unclench, weaken, lessen. **4** *her muscles relaxed* BECOME LESS TENSE, loosen, slacken, unknot. **5** *they relaxed the restrictions* MODERATE, modify, temper, ease (up on), loosen, lighten, dilute, weaken, reduce, decrease; *informal* let up on.
− OPPOSITES: tense, tighten.

relaxation ▶ **noun 1** *a state of relaxation* (MENTAL) REPOSE, calm, tranquility, peacefulness, loosening up, unwinding. **2** *I just play for relaxation* RECREATION, enjoyment, amusement, entertainment, fun, pleasure, leisure; *informal* R and R, downtime. **3** *muscle relaxation* LOOSENING, slackening. **4** *relaxation of censorship rules* MODERATION, easing, loosening, lightening; alleviation, mitigation, dilution, weakening, reduction; *informal* letting up.

relay ▶ **noun** *a live relay of the performance* BROADCAST, transmission, showing.
▶ **verb** *relaying messages through a third party* PASS ON, hand on, transfer, repeat, communicate, send, transmit, disseminate, spread, circulate.

release ▶ **verb 1** *all prisoners were released* (SET) FREE, let go/out, allow to leave, liberate, set at liberty. **2** *Burke released the animal* UNTIE, undo, loose, let go, unleash, unfetter. **3** *released staff for other duties* MAKE AVAILABLE, free (up), put at someone's disposal, supply, furnish, provide. **4** *she released Stephen from his promise* EXCUSE, exempt, discharge, deliver, absolve; *informal* let off. **5** *police released the news yesterday* MAKE PUBLIC, make known, issue, break, announce, declare, report, reveal, divulge, disclose, publish, broadcast, circulate, communicate, disseminate. **6** *the film has been released on video* LAUNCH, put on the market, put on sale, bring out, make available.
− OPPOSITES: imprison, tie up.
▶ **noun 1** *the release of political prisoners* FREEING, liberation, deliverance, bailout; freedom, liberty. **2** *the release of the news* ISSUING, announcement, declaration, reporting, revealing, divulging, disclosure, publication, communication, dissemination. **3** *a press release* ANNOUNCEMENT, bulletin, news flash, dispatch, proclamation. **4** *the hot new band's latest release* CD, album, single, record; video, film; book.

relegate ▶ **verb** DOWNGRADE, lower (in rank/status),

put down, move down; demote, degrade.
− OPPOSITES: upgrade.

relent ▶ **verb 1** *the government finally relented* CHANGE ONE'S MIND, backpedal, do a U-turn, back down, give way/in, capitulate; become merciful, become lenient, agree to something, allow something, concede something; *formal* accede. **2** *the rain has relented* EASE (OFF/UP), slacken, let up, abate, drop, die down, lessen, decrease, subside, weaken, tail off.

relentless ▶ **adjective 1** *their relentless pursuit of quality* PERSISTENT, continuing, constant, continual, continuous, non-stop, never-ending, unabating, interminable, incessant, unceasing, endless, unending, unremitting, unrelenting, unrelieved; unfaltering, unflagging, untiring, unwavering, dogged, tenacious, single-minded, tireless, indefatigable; *formal* pertinacious. **2** *a relentless taskmaster* HARSH, grim, cruel, severe, strict, remorseless, merciless, pitiless, ruthless, unmerciful, heartless, hard-hearted, unforgiving; inflexible, unbending, uncompromising, obdurate, unyielding.

relevant ▶ **adjective** PERTINENT, applicable, apposite, material, apropos, to the point, germane; connected, related, linked.

reliable ▶ **adjective 1** *reliable evidence* DEPENDABLE, good, well-founded, authentic, valid, genuine, sound, true. **2** *a reliable friend* TRUSTWORTHY, dependable, good, true, faithful, devoted, steadfast, staunch, constant, loyal, trusty, dedicated, unfailing; truthful, honest. **3** *reliable brakes* DEPENDABLE, safe, fail-safe. **4** *a reliable firm* REPUTABLE, dependable, trustworthy, honest, responsible, established, proven.
− OPPOSITES: untrustworthy.

reliance ▶ **noun 1** *reliance on the state* DEPENDENCE, dependency. **2** *reliance on his own judgment* TRUST, confidence, faith, belief, conviction.

relic ▶ **noun 1** *a Viking relic* ARTIFACT, historical object, ancient object, antiquity, antique. **2** *a saint's relics* REMAINS, corpse, bones, *Medicine* cadaver.

relief ▶ **noun 1** *it was such a relief to share my worries* REASSURANCE, consolation, comfort, solace. **2** *the relief of pain* ALLEVIATION, alleviating, relieving, assuagement, assuaging, palliation, allaying, soothing, easing, lessening, reduction. **3** *relief from her burden* FREEDOM, release, liberation, deliverance. **4** *a little light relief* RESPITE, amusement, diversion, entertainment, jollity, jollification, recreation. **5** *bringing relief to the starving* HELP, aid, assistance, succour, sustenance, TLC; charity, gifts, donations. **6** *his relief arrived to take over* REPLACEMENT, substitute, deputy, reserve, cover, stand-in, supply, locum (tenens), understudy.
− OPPOSITES: intensification.
■ **throw something into relief** HIGHLIGHT, spotlight, give prominence to, point up, show up, emphasize, bring out, stress, accent, underline, underscore, accentuate.

relieve ▶ **verb 1** *this helps relieve pain* ALLEVIATE, mitigate, assuage, ease, dull, reduce, lessen, diminish. **2** *relieving the boredom* COUNTERACT, reduce, alleviate, mitigate; interrupt, vary, stop, dispel, prevent. **3** *the helpers relieved us* REPLACE, take over from, stand in for, fill in for, substitute for, deputize for, cover for. **4** *this relieves the teacher of a heavy load* (SET) FREE, release, exempt, excuse, absolve, let off, discharge.
− OPPOSITES: aggravate.

relieved ▸ adjective GLAD, thankful, grateful, pleased, happy, easy/easier in one's mind, reassured. — OPPOSITES: worried.

religion ▸ noun FAITH, belief, worship, creed; sect, cult, church, denomination.

religious ▸ adjective **1** *a religious person* DEVOUT, pious, reverent, godly, God-fearing, churchgoing, practising, faithful, devoted, committed. **2** *religious beliefs* SPIRITUAL, theological, scriptural, doctrinal, ecclesiastical, church, churchly, holy, divine, sacred. **3** *religious attention to detail* SCRUPULOUS, conscientious, meticulous, sedulous, punctilious, strict, rigorous, close. — OPPOSITES: atheistic, secular.

relinquish ▸ verb **1** *he relinquished control of the company* RENOUNCE, give up/away, hand over, let go of. **2** *she relinquished her post* LEAVE, resign from, stand down from, bow out of, give up; *informal* quit, chuck. **3** *he relinquished his pipe-smoking* DISCONTINUE, stop, cease, give up, desist from; *informal* quit, leave off, kick; *formal* forswear. **4** *she relinquished her grip* LET GO, release, loose, loosen, relax. — OPPOSITES: retain, continue.

relish ▸ noun **1** *he dug into his food with relish* ENJOYMENT, gusto, delight, pleasure, glee, rapture, satisfaction, contentment, appreciation, enthusiasm, appetite; *humorous* delectation. **2** *a hot relish* CONDIMENT, sauce, dressing, flavouring, seasoning, dip, chutney, pickle, chili sauce. — OPPOSITES: dislike.
▸ verb **1** *she was relishing her moment of glory* ENJOY, delight in, love, adore, take pleasure in, rejoice in, appreciate, savour, revel in, luxuriate in, glory in. **2** *I don't relish the drive* LOOK FORWARD TO, fancy, anticipate with pleasure.

relocate ▸ verb *the family relocated to Alberta* MOVE, migrate, go down the road ✦; pull up stakes.

reluctance ▸ noun UNWILLINGNESS, disinclination; hesitation, wavering, vacillation; doubts, second thoughts, misgivings.

reluctant ▸ adjective **1** *her parents were reluctant* UNWILLING, disinclined, unenthusiastic, resistant, resisting, opposed; hesitant. **2** *a reluctant smile* SHY, bashful, coy, diffident, reserved, timid, timorous. **3** *he was reluctant to leave* LOATH, unwilling, disinclined, indisposed; not in favour of, against, opposed to. — OPPOSITES: willing, eager.

rely ▸ verb **1** *we can rely on his discretion* DEPEND, count, bank, place reliance, reckon; be confident of, be sure of, believe in, have faith in, trust in; *informal* swear by, figure on. **2** *we rely on government funding* BE DEPENDENT, depend, be unable to manage without.

remain ▸ verb **1** *the problem will remain* CONTINUE TO EXIST, endure, last, abide, carry on, persist, stay (around), prevail, survive, live on. **2** *he remained in hospital* STAY (BEHIND/PUT), wait (around), be left, hang on; *informal* hang around. **3** *union leaders remain skeptical* CONTINUE TO BE, stay, keep, persist in being, carry on being. **4** *the few minutes that remain* BE LEFT (OVER), be still available, be unused; have not yet passed.

remainder ▸ noun RESIDUE, balance, remaining part/number, rest, others, those left, remnant(s), surplus, extra, excess, overflow; *technical* residuum.

remaining ▸ adjective **1** *the remaining workers* RESIDUAL, surviving, left (over); extra, surplus, spare, superfluous, excess. **2** *his remaining jobs* UNSETTLED,

outstanding, unfinished, incomplete, to be done, unattended to. **3** *my only remaining memories* SURVIVING, lasting, enduring, continuing, persisting, abiding, (still) existing.

remains ▸ plural noun **1** *the remains of her drink* REMAINDER, residue, remaining part/number, rest, remnant(s); *technical* residuum. **2** *Roman remains* ANTIQUITIES, relics. **3** *the saint's remains* CORPSE, (dead) body, carcass; bones, skeleton; *Medicine* cadaver.

remark ▸ verb **1** *'You're quiet,' he remarked* COMMENT, say, observe, mention, reflect, state, declare, announce, pronounce, assert; *formal* opine. **2** *many critics remarked on their rapport* COMMENT, mention, refer to, speak of, pass comment on. **3** *she remarked the absence of policemen* NOTE, notice, observe, take note of, perceive, discern.
▸ noun **1** *his remarks have been misinterpreted* COMMENT, statement, utterance, observation, declaration, pronouncement. **2** *worthy of remark* ATTENTION, notice, comment, mention, observation, acknowledgement.

remarkable ▸ adjective EXTRAORDINARY, exceptional, amazing, astonishing, astounding, marvellous, wonderful, sensational, stunning, incredible, unbelievable, phenomenal, outstanding, momentous; out of the ordinary, unusual, uncommon, surprising; *informal* fantastic, terrific, tremendous, stupendous, awesome; *literary* wondrous. — OPPOSITES: ordinary.

remediable ▸ adjective CURABLE, treatable, operable; solvable, reparable, rectifiable, resolvable. — OPPOSITES: incurable.

remedy ▸ noun **1** *herbal remedies* TREATMENT, cure, medicine, medication, medicament, drug; *archaic* physic. **2** *a remedy for all kinds of problems* SOLUTION, answer, cure, antidote, curative, nostrum, panacea, cure-all; *informal* magic bullet.
▸ verb **1** *remedying the situation* PUT/SET RIGHT, put/set to rights, right, rectify, solve, sort out, straighten out, resolve, correct, repair, mend, make good. **2** *anemia can be remedied by iron pills* CURE, treat, heal, make better; relieve, ease, alleviate, palliate.

remember ▸ verb **1** *remembering happy times* RECALL, call to mind, recollect, think of; reminisce about, look back on; *archaic* bethink oneself of. **2** *can you remember all that?* MEMORIZE, commit to memory, retain; learn off by heart. **3** *you must remember she's only five* BEAR/KEEP IN MIND, be mindful of the fact; take into account, take into consideration. **4** *remember to feed the cat* BE SURE, be certain; mind that you, make sure that you. **5** *remember me to Alice* SEND ONE'S BEST WISHES TO, send one's regards to, give one's love to, send one's compliments to, say hello to. **6** *the nation remembered those who gave their lives* COMMEMORATE, pay tribute to, honour, salute, pay homage to. **7** *she remembered them in her will* BEQUEATH SOMETHING TO, leave something to, bestow something on. — OPPOSITES: forget.

remembrance ▸ noun **1** *an expression of remembrance* RECOLLECTION, reminiscence; remembering, recalling, recollecting, reminiscing. **2** *she smiled at the remembrance* MEMORY, recollection, reminiscence, thought. **3** *we sold poppies in remembrance* COMMEMORATION, memory, recognition. **4** *a remembrance of my father* MEMENTO, reminder, keepsake, souvenir, memorial, token.

remind ▸ verb **1** *I left a note to remind him* JOG SOMEONE'S MEMORY, help someone remember, prompt. **2** *the song reminded me of my sister* MAKE ONE

THINK OF, cause one to remember, put one in mind of, bring/call to mind, evoke.

reminder ▶ noun PROMPT, prompting, aide-mémoire, mental note, mnemonic.

reminisce ▶ verb REMEMBER (WITH PLEASURE), cast one's mind back to, look back on, be nostalgic about, recall, recollect, reflect on, call to mind.

reminiscences ▶ plural noun MEMORIES, recollections, reflections, remembrances.

reminiscent ▶ adjective SIMILAR TO, comparable with, evocative of, suggestive of, redolent of.

remiss ▶ adjective NEGLIGENT, neglectful, irresponsible, careless, thoughtless, heedless, lax, slack, slipshod, lackadaisical, derelict; *informal* sloppy; *formal* delinquent.
− OPPOSITES: careful.

remission ▶ noun **1** *the remission of all fees* CANCELLATION, setting aside, suspension, revocation; *formal* abrogation. **2** *the cancer is in remission* RESPITE, abeyance. **3** *the wind howled without remission* RESPITE, lessening, abatement, easing, decrease, reduction, diminution, dying down, slackening, lull; *informal* let-up. **4** *the remission of sins* FORGIVENESS, pardoning, absolution, exoneration; *formal* exculpation.

remit ▶ verb **1** *the fines were remitted* CANCEL, set aside, suspend, revoke; *formal* abrogate. **2** *remitting duties to the authorities* SEND, dispatch, forward, hand over; pay. **3** *the case was remitted to the Supreme Court* PASS (ON), refer, send on, transfer. **4** *(rare) we remitted all further discussion* POSTPONE, defer, put off/back, shelve, delay, suspend, table; *informal* put on the back burner, put on ice. **5** *remitting their sins* PARDON, forgive; excuse.

remittance ▶ noun **1** *send the form with your remittance* PAYMENT, money, fee; cheque; *formal* monies. **2** *a monthly remittance* ALLOWANCE, sum of money.

remnant ▶ noun **1** *the remnants of the picnic* REMAINS, remainder, leftovers, residue, rest; *technical* residuum. **2** *remnants of cloth* SCRAP, piece, bit, fragment, shred, offcut, oddment.

remonstrate ▶ verb **1** *'I'm not a child!' he remonstrated* PROTEST, complain, expostulate; argue with, take issue with. **2** *we remonstrated against this proposal* OBJECT STRONGLY TO, complain vociferously about, protest against, argue against, oppose strongly, make a fuss about, challenge; deplore, condemn, denounce, criticize; *informal* kick up a fuss/stink about.

remorse ▶ noun CONTRITION, deep regret, repentance, penitence, guilt, compunction, remorsefulness, ruefulness, contriteness; pangs of conscience, breast-beating.

remorseful ▶ adjective SORRY, full of regret, regretful, contrite, repentant, penitent, guilt-ridden, conscience-stricken, guilty, chastened.
− OPPOSITES: unrepentant.

remorseless ▶ adjective **1** HEARTLESS, pitiless, merciless, ruthless, callous, cruel, hard-hearted, inhumane, unmerciful, unforgiving, unfeeling. **2** *remorseless cost-cutting* RELENTLESS, unrelenting, unremitting, unabating, inexorable, unstoppable.
− OPPOSITES: compassionate.

remote ▶ adjective **1** *areas remote from hospitals* FARAWAY, distant, far (off), far removed. **2** *a remote mountain village* ISOLATED, out of the way, off the beaten track, secluded, lonely, in the back of beyond, godforsaken, inaccessible, far-flung; *informal* in the sticks, in the middle of nowhere. **3** *events remote from modern times*

IRRELEVANT TO, unrelated to, unconnected to, unconcerned with, not pertinent to, immaterial to, unassociated with; foreign to, alien to. **4** *a remote possibility* UNLIKELY, improbable, implausible, doubtful, dubious; faint, slight, slim, small, slender. **5** *she seems very remote* ALOOF, distant, detached, withdrawn, reserved, uncommunicative, unforthcoming, unapproachable, unresponsive, unfriendly, unsociable, introspective, introverted; *informal* standoffish.
− OPPOSITES: close, central.

removal ▶ noun **1** *the removal of heavy artillery* TAKING AWAY, moving, carrying away. **2** *his removal from office* DISMISSAL, ejection, expulsion, ousting, displacement, deposition, ouster; *informal* firing, sacking. **3** *the removal of customs barriers* WITHDRAWAL, elimination, taking away. **4** *the removal of errors in the copy* DELETION, elimination, erasing, effacing, obliteration. **5** *the removal of weeds* UPROOTING, eradication. **6** *the removal of old branches from the tree* CUTTING OFF, chopping off, hacking off. **7** *her removal to the West Coast* MOVE, transfer, relocation. **8** *the removal of a rival* DISPOSAL, elimination, killing, murder, dispatch; *informal* liquidation.
− OPPOSITES: installation.

remove ▶ verb **1** *remove the plug* DETACH, unfasten; pull out, take out, disconnect. **2** *she removed the lid* TAKE OFF, undo, unfasten. **3** *he removed a note from his wallet* TAKE OUT, produce, bring out, get out, pull out, withdraw. **4** *police removed boxes of documents* TAKE AWAY, carry away, move, transport; confiscate; *informal* cart off. **5** *Sheila removed the mud* CLEAN OFF, wash off, wipe off, rinse off, scrub off, sponge out. **6** *Henry removed his coat* TAKE OFF, pull off, slip out of, peel off. **7** *she was removed from her post* DISMISS, discharge, get rid of, dislodge, displace, expel, oust, depose; *informal* fire, sack, kick out, boot out, turf out. **8** *tax relief was removed* WITHDRAW, abolish, eliminate, get rid of, do away with, stop, cut, axe. **9** *Gabriel removed two words* DELETE, erase, rub out, cross out, strike out, score out, deep-six. **10** *weeds have to be removed* UPROOT, pull out, eradicate. **11** *removing branches* CUT OFF, chop off, lop off, hack off.
− OPPOSITES: attach, insert, replace.
▶ noun *it is impossible, at this remove, to reconstruct the accident* DISTANCE, space of time, interval.

removed ▶ adjective DISTANT, remote, disconnected; unrelated, unconnected, alien, foreign, outside.

remunerate ▶ verb PAY, reward, reimburse, recompense.

remuneration ▶ noun PAYMENT, pay, salary, wages; earnings, fee(s), reward, recompense, reimbursement; *formal* emolument(s).

remunerative ▶ adjective LUCRATIVE, well-paid, financially rewarding; profitable.

renaissance ▶ noun REVIVAL, renewal, resurrection, reawakening, re-emergence, rebirth, reappearance, resurgence, regeneration; *formal* renascence.

rend ▶ verb TEAR/RIP APART, tear/rip in two, split, rupture, sever; *literary* tear/rip asunder, sunder; *rare* dissever.

render ▶ verb **1** *her fury rendered her speechless* MAKE, cause to be/become, leave. **2** *rendering assistance* GIVE, provide, supply, furnish, contribute; offer, proffer. **3** *the invoices rendered by the accountants* SEND IN, present, submit. **4** *the jury rendered its verdict* DELIVER, return, hand down, give, announce. **5** *paintings rendered in vivid colours* PAINT, draw, depict, portray, represent, execute; *literary* limn. **6** *she rendered all three verses* PERFORM, sing. **7** *the characters are vividly rendered* ACT, perform, play, depict, interpret. **8** *the phrase was rendered into English* TRANSLATE, put, express, rephrase, reword. **9** *the fat can be rendered* MELT DOWN, clarify.

rendezvous ▶ noun *Edward was late for their rendezvous* MEETING, appointment, assignation; *informal* date; *literary* tryst.
▶ verb *the bar where they had agreed to rendezvous* MEET, come together, gather, assemble.

rendition ▶ noun **1** *our rendition of Beethoven's Fifth* PERFORMANCE, rendering, interpretation, presentation, execution, delivery. **2** *the artist's rendition of Adam and Eve* DEPICTION, portrayal, representation. **3** *an interpreter's rendition of the message* TRANSLATION, interpretation, version.

renegade ▶ noun **1** *he was denounced as a renegade* TRAITOR, defector, deserter, turncoat, rebel, mutineer. **2** (*archaic*) *a religious renegade* APOSTATE, heretic, dissenter.
▶ adjective **1** *renegade troops* TREACHEROUS, traitorous, disloyal, treasonous, rebel, mutinous. **2** *a renegade monk* APOSTATE, heretic, heretical, dissident.
— OPPOSITES: loyal.

renege ▶ verb DEFAULT ON, fail to honour, go back on, break, back out of, withdraw from, retreat from, welsh on, backtrack on; break one's word/promise.
— OPPOSITES: honour.

renew ▶ verb **1** *I renewed my search* RESUME, return to, take up again, come back to, begin again, start again, restart, recommence; continue (with), carry on (with). **2** *they renewed their vows* REAFFIRM, reassert; repeat, reiterate, restate. **3** *something to renew her interest in life* REVIVE, regenerate, revitalize, reinvigorate, restore, resuscitate, breathe new life into, rekindle. **4** *the hotel was completely renewed* RENOVATE, restore, refurbish, modernize, overhaul, redevelop, rebuild, reconstruct, remodel, bring something up to code; *informal* do up, rehab. **5** *they renewed Jackie's contract* EXTEND, prolong. **6** *I renewed my supply of toilet paper* REPLENISH, restock, resupply, top up, replace.

renewal ▶ noun **1** *the renewal of our friendship* RESUMPTION, recommencement, re-establishment; continuation. **2** *spiritual renewal* REGENERATION, revival, reinvigoration, revitalization. **3** *the renewal of older urban areas* RENOVATION, restoration, modernization, reconditioning, overhauling, redevelopment, rebuilding, reconstruction.

renounce ▶ verb **1** *Edward renounced his claim to the throne* GIVE UP, relinquish, abandon, abdicate, surrender, waive, forego; *Law* disclaim; *formal* abnegate. **2** *Hungary renounced the agreement* REJECT, refuse to abide by, repudiate. **3** *she renounced her family* REPUDIATE, deny, reject, abandon, wash one's hands of, turn one's back on, disown, spurn, shun; *literary* forsake. **4** *he renounced alcohol* ABSTAIN FROM, give up, desist from, refrain from, keep off, eschew; *informal* quit, pack in, lay off; *formal* forswear.
— OPPOSITES: assert, accept.
■ **renounce the world** BECOME A RECLUSE, turn one's back on society, cloister oneself, hide oneself away.

renovate ▶ verb MODERNIZE, restore, refurbish, revamp, recondition, rehabilitate, overhaul, redevelop; update, upgrade, refit, bring something up to code; *informal* do up, rehab.

renovation ▶ noun MODERNIZATION, restoration, redecoration, refurbishment, revamping, makeover, reconditioning, rehabilitation, overhauling,

whitepainting ♣, repair, redevelopment, rebuilding, reconstruction, remodelling, updating, improvement; gentrification, upgrading; refitting; *informal* facelift, reno ♣.

renown ▶ noun FAME, distinction, eminence, pre-eminence, prominence, repute, reputation, prestige, acclaim, celebrity, notability.

renowned ▶ adjective FAMOUS, celebrated, famed, eminent, distinguished, acclaimed, illustrious, pre-eminent, prominent, great, esteemed, of note, of repute, well-known, well-thought-of.
— OPPOSITES: unknown.

rent[1] ▶ noun *I can't afford to pay the rent* RENTAL, fee, lease.
▶ verb **1** *she rented a car* lease, charter. **2** *why don't you rent it out?* LET (OUT), lease (out), hire (out); sublet, sublease.

rent[2] ▶ noun **1** *the rent in his pants* RIP, tear, split, hole, slash, slit. **2** *a vast rent in the mountains* GORGE, chasm, fault, rift, fissure, crevasse.

renunciation ▶ noun **1** *the Queen's renunciation of her throne* RELINQUISHMENT, giving up, abandonment, abdication, surrender, waiving, foregoing; *Law* disclaimer; *rare* abnegation. **2** *his renunciation of luxury* ABSTENTION, refraining, going without, giving up, eschewal; *formal* forswearing. **3** *their renunciation of terrorism* REPUDIATION, rejection, abandonment.

reorganize ▶ verb RESTRUCTURE, change, alter, adjust, transform, shake up, rationalize, rearrange, reshape, overhaul; *informal* clean house.

repair[1] ▶ verb **1** *the car was repaired* MEND, fix (up), put/set right, restore (to working order), overhaul, service; *informal* patch up. **2** *they repaired the costumes* MEND, darn; *informal* patch up. **3** *repairing relations with other countries* PUT/SET RIGHT, mend, fix, straighten out, smooth, improve, warm up; *informal* patch up. **4** *she sought to repair the wrong she had done* RECTIFY, make good, (put) right, correct, make up for, make amends for, make reparation for.
▶ noun **1** *in need of repair* RESTORATION, fixing (up), mending, renovation; *archaic* reparation. **2** *an invisible repair* MEND, darn. **3** *in good repair* CONDITION, working order, state, shape, fettle.
■ **beyond repair** IRREPARABLE, irreversible, irretrievable, irremediable, irrecoverable, past hope.

repair[2] ▶ verb (*formal*) *we repaired to the sitting room* GO TO, head for, adjourn, wend one's way; *formal* remove; *literary* betake oneself.

reparable ▶ adjective RECTIFIABLE, remediable, curable, restorable, recoverable, retrievable, salvageable.

reparation ▶ noun AMENDS, restitution, redress, compensation, recompense, repayment, atonement.

repartee ▶ noun BANTER, badinage, bantering, raillery, witticism(s), ripostes, sallies, quips, joking, jesting, chaff, chaffing; *formal* persiflage.

repast ▶ noun (*formal*) MEAL, feast, banquet; *informal* spread, feed, bite (to eat); *formal* collation.

repay ▶ verb **1** *repaying customers who have been cheated* REIMBURSE, refund, pay back/off, recompense, compensate, indemnify. **2** *the grants have to be repaid* PAY BACK, return, refund, reimburse. **3** *I'd like to repay her generosity* RECIPROCATE, return, requite, recompense, reward. **4** *interesting books that would repay further study* BE WELL WORTH, be worth one's while.

repayment ▶ noun **1** *the repayment of tax* REFUND,

reimbursement, paying back. **2** *repayment for all they have done* RECOMPENSE, reward, compensation.

repeal ▶ verb *the Act was repealed* REVOKE, rescind, cancel, reverse, annul, nullify, declare null and void, quash, abolish; *Law* vacate; *formal* abrogate; *archaic* recall.
— OPPOSITES: enact.
▶ noun *the repeal of the law* REVOCATION, rescinding, cancellation, reversal, annulment, nullification, quashing, abolition; *formal* abrogation; *archaic* recall.

repeat ▶ verb **1** *she repeated her story* SAY AGAIN, restate, reiterate, go/run through again, recapitulate; *informal* recap. **2** *children can repeat large chunks of text* RECITE, quote, parrot, regurgitate; *informal* trot out. **3** *Steele was invited to repeat his work* DO AGAIN, redo, replicate, rehash, duplicate. **4** *the episodes were repeated* REBROADCAST, rerun.
▶ noun **1** *a repeat of the previous year's final* REPETITION, duplication, replication, duplicate, rehash. **2** *repeats of the classic sitcom* RERUN, rebroadcast.
■ **repeat itself** REOCCUR, recur, occur again, happen again.

repeated ▶ adjective RECURRENT, frequent, persistent, continual, incessant, constant; regular, periodic, numerous, (very) many, a great many.
— OPPOSITES: occasional.

repeatedly ▶ adverb FREQUENTLY, often, again and again, over and over (again), time and (time) again, time after time, many times, many a time; persistently, recurrently, constantly, continually, regularly, oftentimes; *informal* 24-7; *literary* oft, oft-times.

repel ▶ verb **1** *the rebels were repelled* FIGHT OFF, repulse, drive back/away, force back, beat back, push back; hold off, ward off, keep at bay; *archaic* rebut. **2** *the coating will repel water* BE IMPERVIOUS TO, be impermeable to, keep out, resist, be —— proof. **3** *the thought of kissing him repelled me* REVOLT, disgust, repulse, sicken, nauseate, turn someone's stomach, be repulsive, be distasteful, be repugnant; *informal* turn off, gross out.

repellent ▶ adjective **1** *a repellent stench* REVOLTING, repulsive, disgusting, repugnant, sickening, nauseating, stomach-turning, nauseous, vile, nasty, foul, horrible, awful, dreadful, terrible, obnoxious, loathsome, offensive, objectionable; abhorrent, despicable, reprehensible, contemptible, odious, hateful, execrable, vomitous; *informal* ghastly, horrid, gross, yucky, icky, funky; *literary* noisome. **2** *a repellent coating* IMPERMEABLE, impervious, resistant; -proof.
— OPPOSITES: delightful.

repent ▶ verb FEEL REMORSE, regret, be sorry, rue, reproach oneself, be ashamed, feel contrite; be penitent, be remorseful, be repentant.

repentance ▶ noun REMORSE, contrition, contriteness, penitence, regret, ruefulness, remorsefulness, shame, guilt.

repentant ▶ adjective PENITENT, contrite, regretful, rueful, remorseful, apologetic, chastened, ashamed, shamefaced.
— OPPOSITES: impenitent.

repercussion ▶ noun CONSEQUENCE, result, effect, outcome; reverberation, backlash, aftermath, fallout, tremor.

repertoire ▶ noun COLLECTION, stock, range, repertory, reserve, store, repository, supply.

repetition ▶ noun **1** *the facts bear repetition* REITERATION, repeating, restatement, retelling. **2** *endless repetition of passages of poetry* REPEATING, echoing, parroting. **3** *a repetition of the scene in the kitchen* RECURRENCE, reoccurrence, rerun, repeat; *informal* déjà vu, instant replay. **4** *the author is guilty of repetition* REPETITIOUSNESS, repetitiveness, redundancy, tautology.

repetitious ▶ adjective *repetitious work. See* REPETITIVE.

repetitive ▶ adjective MONOTONOUS, tedious, boring, humdrum, mundane, dreary, tiresome; unvaried, unchanging, unvarying, recurrent, recurring, repeated, repetitious, routine, mechanical, automatic.

rephrase ▶ verb REWORD, recast, put in other words, express differently, paraphrase.

replace ▶ verb **1** *Eve replaced the receiver* PUT BACK, return, restore. **2** *a new chairman came in to replace him* TAKE THE PLACE OF, succeed, take over from, supersede; stand in for, substitute for, deputize for, cover for, relieve; *informal* step into someone's shoes/boots. **3** *she replaced the spoon with a fork* SUBSTITUTE, exchange, change, swap.
— OPPOSITES: remove.

replacement ▶ noun **1** *we have to find a replacement* SUCCESSOR; SUBSTITUTE, stand-in, locum, relief, cover. **2** *the wiring was in need of replacement* RENEWAL, replacing.

replenish ▶ verb **1** *she replenished their glasses* REFILL, top up, fill up, recharge, freshen. **2** *their supplies were replenished* STOCK UP, restock, restore, replace.
— OPPOSITES: empty, exhaust.

replete ▶ adjective **1** *the guests were replete* WELL-FED, sated, satiated, full (up); glutted, gorged; *informal* stuffed. **2** *a sumptuous environment replete with antiques* FILLED, full, well-stocked, well supplied, crammed, packed, jammed, teeming, overflowing, bursting; *informal* jam-packed, chockablock, chock full.

replica ▶ noun **1** *is it real or a replica?* (CARBON) COPY, model, duplicate, reproduction, replication; dummy, imitation, facsimile. **2** *a replica of her mother* PERFECT LIKENESS, double, look-alike, (living) image, twin, clone; *informal* (dead) ringer.

replicate ▶ verb COPY, reproduce, duplicate, recreate, repeat, perform again; clone.

reply ▶ verb ANSWER, respond, come back, write back, retort, riposte, counter.
▶ noun ANSWER, response, rejoinder, retort, riposte; *informal* comeback.

report ▶ verb **1** *the government reported a fall in inflation* ANNOUNCE, describe, give an account of, detail, outline, communicate, divulge, disclose, reveal, make public, publish, broadcast, proclaim, publicize. **2** *the newspapers reported on the scandal* COVER, write about, describe, give details of, commentate on; investigate, look into, inquire into. **3** *I reported him to the police* INFORM ON, tattle on; *informal* shop, tell on, squeal on, rat on, peach on. **4** *Juliet reported for duty* PRESENT ONESELF, arrive, turn up, clock in, sign in, punch in; *informal* show up.
▶ noun **1** *a full report on the meeting* ACCOUNT, review, record, description, statement; transactions, proceedings, transcripts, minutes. **2** *reports of drug dealing* NEWS, information, word, intelligence; *literary* tidings. **3** *newspaper reports* STORY, account, article, piece, item, column, feature, bulletin, dispatch. **4** *a school report* ASSESSMENT, report card, evaluation, appraisal. **5** *reports of his imminent resignation* RUMOUR, whisper; *informal* buzz; *archaic* bruit. **6** *the report of a gun* BANG, blast, crack, shot, gunshot, explosion, boom.

reporter ▶ noun JOURNALIST, correspondent, newspaperman, newspaperwoman, newsman, newswoman, columnist, pressman; *informal* newshound, hack, stringer, journo, newsy.

repose ▶ noun 1 *a face in repose* REST, relaxation, inactivity; sleep, slumber. 2 *they found true repose* PEACE (AND QUIET), peacefulness, quiet, quietness, calm, tranquility. 3 *he lost his repose* COMPOSURE, serenity, equanimity, poise, self-possession, aplomb.
▶ verb 1 *the diamond reposed on a bed of velvet* LIE, rest, be placed, be situated. 2 *the trust he had reposed in her* PUT, place, invest, entrust. 3 *the beds where we reposed* LIE (DOWN), recline, rest, sleep; *literary* slumber.

repository ▶ noun STORE, storehouse, depository; reservoir, bank, cache, treasury, fund, mine.

reprehensible ▶ adjective DEPLORABLE, disgraceful, discreditable, despicable, blameworthy, culpable, wrong, bad, shameful, dishonourable, objectionable, opprobrious, repugnant, inexcusable, unforgivable, indefensible, unjustifiable; criminal, sinful, scandalous, iniquitous; *formal* exceptionable.
— OPPOSITES: praiseworthy.

represent ▶ verb 1 *a character representing a single quality* SYMBOLIZE, stand for, personify, epitomize, typify, embody, illustrate. 2 *the initials which represent her qualification* STAND FOR, designate, denote; *literary* betoken. 3 *Hathor is represented as a woman with cow's horns* DEPICT, portray, render, picture, delineate, show, illustrate; *literary* limn. 4 *he represented himself as the owner of the factory* DESCRIBE AS, present as, profess to be, claim to be, pass oneself off as, pose as, pretend to be. 5 *aging represents a threat to one's independence* CONSTITUTE, be, amount to, be regarded as. 6 *a panel representing a cross-section of the public* BE A TYPICAL SAMPLE OF, be representative of, typify. 7 *her lawyer represented her in court* APPEAR FOR, act for, speak on behalf of, go to bat for. 8 *the Governor General represented the Royal Family* DEPUTIZE FOR, substitute for, stand in for. 9 *(formal) I represented the case as I saw it* POINT OUT, state, present, put forward.

representation ▶ noun 1 *Rossetti's representation of women* PORTRAYAL, depiction, delineation, presentation, rendition. 2 *representations of the human form* LIKENESS, painting, drawing, picture, illustration, sketch, image, model, figure, figurine, statue, statuette. 3 *(formal) making representations to the council* STATEMENT, deposition, allegation, declaration, exposition, report, protestation.

representative ▶ adjective 1 *a representative sample* TYPICAL, prototypical, characteristic, illustrative, archetypal. 2 *an image representative of Canada* SYMBOLIC, emblematic. 3 *representative government* ELECTED, elective, democratic, popular.
— OPPOSITES: atypical, totalitarian.
▶ noun 1 *a representative of Greenpeace* SPOKESPERSON, spokesman, spokeswoman, agent, official, mouthpiece. 2 *a sales representative* SALESPERSON, salesman, saleswoman, commercial traveller, agent; *informal* rep, drummer. 3 *the Cambodian representative at the UN* DELEGATE, commissioner, ambassador, attaché, envoy, emissary, chargé d'affaires, deputy. 4 *our representatives in parliament* MEMBER (OF PARLIAMENT), MP, MLA, MPP, MNA, MHA; councillor, alderman, senator, legislator, lawmaker; voice. 5 *he acted as his father's representative* DEPUTY, substitute, stand-in, proxy. 6 *fossil representatives of lampreys* EXAMPLE, specimen, exemplar, exemplification.

repress ▶ verb 1 *the rebellion was repressed* SUPPRESS, quell, quash, subdue, put down, crush, extinguish,

stamp out, defeat, conquer, rout, overwhelm, contain. 2 *the peasants were repressed* OPPRESS, subjugate, keep down, rule with a rod of iron, intimidate, tyrannize, crush. 3 *these emotions may well be repressed* RESTRAIN, hold back/in, keep back, suppress, keep in check, control, keep under control, curb, stifle, bottle up; *informal* button up, keep the lid on.

repressed ▶ adjective 1 *a repressed country* OPPRESSED, subjugated, subdued, tyrannized. 2 *repressed feelings* RESTRAINED, suppressed, held back/in, kept in check, stifled, pent up, bottled up. 3 *emotionally repressed* INHIBITED, frustrated, restrained; *informal* uptight, hung up.
— OPPOSITES: democratic, uninhibited.

repression ▶ noun 1 *the repression of the protests* SUPPRESSION, quashing, subduing, crushing, stamping out. 2 *political repression* OPPRESSION, subjugation, suppression, tyranny, despotism, authoritarianism. 3 *the repression of sexual urges* RESTRAINT, restraining, holding back, keeping back, suppression, keeping in check, control, keeping under control, stifling, bottling up.

repressive ▶ adjective OPPRESSIVE, authoritarian, despotic, tyrannical, dictatorial, fascist, autocratic, totalitarian, undemocratic.

reprieve ▶ verb 1 *she was reprieved* GRANT A STAY OF EXECUTION TO, pardon, spare, grant an amnesty to, amnesty; *informal* let off (the hook). 2 *the project has been reprieved* SAVE, rescue; *informal* take off the hit list.
▶ noun *a last-minute reprieve* STAY OF EXECUTION, remission, pardon, amnesty; *US Law* continuance.

reprimand ▶ verb *he was publicly reprimanded* REBUKE, admonish, chastise, chide, upbraid, reprove, reproach, scold, berate, take to task, lambaste, give someone a piece of one's mind, haul over the coals, lecture, criticize, censure; *informal* give someone a talking-to, tell off, dress down, give someone a dressing-down, give someone an earful, give someone a roasting, rap over the knuckles, rap, slap someone's wrist, bawl out, pitch into, lay into, lace into, blast, tear a strip off, give someone what for, chew out, ream out; *formal* castigate.
— OPPOSITES: praise.
▶ noun *they received a severe reprimand* REBUKE, reproof, admonishment, admonition, reproach, scolding, upbraiding, censure; *informal* rap over the knuckles, slap on the wrist, dressing-down, earful, roasting, tongue-lashing; *formal* castigation.
— OPPOSITES: commendation.

reprisal ▶ noun RETALIATION, counter-attack, comeback; revenge, vengeance, retribution, requital; *informal* a taste of one's own medicine.

reproach ▶ verb *Albert reproached him for being late.* See REPRIMAND *verb.*
▶ noun 1 *an expression of reproach.* See REPRIMAND *noun.* 2 *this party is a reproach to Canadian politics* DISGRACE, discredit, source of shame, blemish, stain, blot; *literary* smirch.
■ **beyond/above reproach** PERFECT, blameless, above suspicion, without fault, faultless, flawless, irreproachable, exemplary, impeccable, immaculate, unblemished, spotless, untarnished, stainless, unsullied, whiter than white; *informal* squeaky clean.

reproachful ▶ adjective DISAPPROVING, reproving, critical, censorious, disparaging, withering, accusatory, admonitory.
— OPPOSITES: approving.

reprobate ▶ noun *a hardened reprobate* ROGUE, rascal,

scoundrel, miscreant, good-for-nothing, villain, wretch, rake, degenerate, libertine, debauchee; *informal*, *dated* cad; *archaic* blackguard, knave, rapscallion.

▶ **adjective** *reprobate behaviour* UNPRINCIPLED, bad, roguish, wicked, rakish, shameless, immoral, degenerate, dissipated, debauched, depraved; *archaic* knavish.

reproduce ▶ **verb** 1 *each artwork is reproduced in colour* COPY, duplicate, replicate; photocopy, xerox, print. 2 *this work has not been reproduced in other laboratories* REPEAT, replicate, recreate, redo; simulate, imitate, emulate, mirror, mimic. 3 *some animals reproduce prolifically* BREED, produce offspring, procreate, propagate, multiply.

reproduction ▶ **noun** 1 *colour reproduction* COPYING, duplication, duplicating; photocopying, xeroxing, printing. 2 *a reproduction of the original* PRINT, copy, reprint, duplicate, facsimile, carbon copy, photocopy; *proprietary* Xerox. 3 *the process of reproduction* BREEDING, procreation, multiplying, propagation.

reproductive ▶ **adjective** GENERATIVE, procreative, propagative; sexual, genital.

reproof ▶ **noun** REBUKE, reprimand, reproach, admonishment, admonition; disapproval, censure, criticism, condemnation; *informal* dressing down.

reprove ▶ **verb** REPRIMAND, rebuke, reproach, scold, admonish, chastise, chide, upbraid, berate, take to task, haul over the coals, criticize, censure; *informal* tell off, give someone a talking-to, dress down, give someone a dressing-down, give someone an earful, give someone a roasting, rap over the knuckles, slap someone's wrist, tear a strip off; *formal* castigate.

reptile *See table.*
— RELATED TERMS: saurian.

Reptiles

alligator	green turtle
alligator snapping turtle	hawksbill
	horned toad
basilisk	iguana
blindworm	Komodo dragon
box turtle	leatherback turtle
caiman	lizard
chameleon	loggerhead turtle
chuckwalla	monitor lizard
crocodile	mugger
diamondback	painted turtle
flying dragon	skink
flying lizard	slow-worm
frill lizard	snapping turtle
galliwasp	terrapin
gecko	tortoise
gharial	tuatara
Gila monster	turtle
glass lizard	*See also* SNAKES.
goanna	*See also* AMPHIBIANS.
	See also DINOSAURS.

reptilian ▶ **adjective** 1 *reptilian species* REPTILE, reptile-like, saurian; cold-blooded. 2 *a reptilian smirk* UNPLEASANT, distasteful, nasty, disagreeable, unattractive, off-putting, repulsive, horrible, horrid; unctuous, ingratiating, grovelling, oily, oleaginous; *informal* smarmy, slimy, creepy.

repudiate ▶ **verb** 1 *she repudiated communism* REJECT, renounce, abandon, give up, turn one's back

on, disown, cast off, lay aside; *formal* forswear, abjure; *literary* forsake. 2 *Hansen repudiated the allegations* DENY, refute, contradict, controvert, rebut, dispute, dismiss, brush aside; *formal* gainsay. 3 *Egypt repudiated the treaty* CANCEL, revoke, rescind, reverse, overrule, overturn, invalidate, nullify; disregard, flout, renege on; *Law* disaffirm; *formal* abrogate.
— OPPOSITES: embrace, confirm.

repudiation ▶ **noun** 1 *the repudiation of one's religion* REJECTION, renunciation, abandonment, forswearing, giving up; *rare* abjuration. 2 *his repudiation of the allegations* DENIAL, refutation, rebuttal, rejection. 3 *a repudiation of the contract* CANCELLATION, revocation, reversal, invalidation, nullification. *formal* abrogation.

repugnance ▶ **noun** REVULSION, disgust, abhorrence, repulsion, loathing, hatred, detestation, aversion, distaste, antipathy, contempt.

repugnant ▶ **adjective** 1 *the idea of cannibalism is repugnant* ABHORRENT, revolting, repulsive, repellent, disgusting, offensive, objectionable, vile, foul, nasty, loathsome, sickening, nauseating, hateful, detestable, execrable, abominable, monstrous, appalling, insufferable, intolerable, unacceptable, contemptible, unsavoury, unpalatable; *informal* ghastly, gross, horrible, horrid; *literary* noisome. 2 *(formal) the restriction is repugnant to the tenancy* INCOMPATIBLE WITH, in conflict with, contrary to, at variance with, inconsistent with.
— OPPOSITES: pleasant.

repulse ▶ **verb** 1 *the rebels were repulsed* REPEL, drive back/away, fight back/off, put to flight, force back, beat off/back; ward off, hold off; *archaic* rebut. 2 *her advances were repulsed* REBUFF, reject, spurn, snub, cold-shoulder; *informal* give someone the brush-off, freeze out, give someone the bum's rush. 3 *his bid for the company was repulsed* REJECT, turn down, refuse, decline. 4 *the brutality repulsed her* REVOLT, disgust, repel, sicken, nauseate, turn someone's stomach, be repugnant to; *informal* turn off, gross out.

▶ **noun** 1 *the repulse of the attack* REPELLING, driving back; warding off, holding off. 2 *he was mortified by this repulse* REBUFF, rejection, snub, slight; *informal* brush-off.

repulsion ▶ **noun** DISGUST, revulsion, abhorrence, repugnance, nausea, horror, aversion, abomination, distaste.

repulsive ▶ **adjective** REVOLTING, disgusting, abhorrent, repellent, repugnant, offensive, objectionable, vile, foul, nasty, loathsome, sickening, nauseating, hateful, detestable, execrable, abominable, monstrous, noxious, horrendous, awful, terrible, dreadful, frightful, obnoxious, unsavoury, unpleasant, disagreeable, distasteful; ugly, hideous, grotesque; *informal* ghastly, horrible, horrid, gross; *literary* noisome; *archaic* loathly.
— OPPOSITES: attractive.

reputable ▶ **adjective** WELL-THOUGHT-OF, highly regarded, (well) respected, respectable, of (good) repute, prestigious, established; reliable, dependable, trustworthy.
— OPPOSITES: untrustworthy.

reputation ▶ **noun** (GOOD) NAME, character, repute, standing, stature, status, position, renown, esteem, prestige; *informal* rep, rap.

repute ▶ **noun** 1 *a woman of ill repute* REPUTATION, name, character. 2 *a firm of international repute* FAME, renown, celebrity, distinction, high standing, stature, prestige.

reputed ▶ adjective **1** *they are reputed to be very rich* THOUGHT, said, reported, rumoured, believed, held, considered, regarded, deemed, alleged. **2** *his reputed father* SUPPOSED, putative. **3** *a reputed naturalist* WELL-THOUGHT-OF, (well) respected, highly regarded, of good repute.

reputedly ▶ adverb SUPPOSEDLY, by all accounts, so I'm told, so people say, allegedly.

request ▶ noun **1** *requests for assistance* APPEAL, entreaty, plea, petition, application, demand, call; *formal* adjuration; *literary* behest. **2** *Charlotte spoke, at Ursula's request* BIDDING, entreaty, demand, insistence. **3** *indicate your requests on the form* REQUIREMENT, wish, desire; choice.
▶ verb **1** *the government requested military aid* ASK FOR, appeal for, call for, seek, solicit, plead for, apply for, demand; *formal* adjure. **2** *I requested him to help* CALL ON, beg, entreat, implore; *literary* beseech.

require ▶ verb **1** *the child required hospital treatment* NEED, be in need of. **2** *a situation requiring patience* NECESSITATE, demand, call for, involve, entail. **3** *unquestioning obedience is required* DEMAND, insist on, call for, ask for, expect. **4** *she was required to pay costs* ORDER, instruct, command, enjoin, oblige, compel, force. **5** *do you require anything else?* WANT, wish to have, desire; lack, be short of.

required ▶ adjective **1** *required reading* ESSENTIAL, vital, indispensable, necessary, compulsory, obligatory, mandatory, prescribed. **2** *cut it to the required length* DESIRED, preferred, chosen; correct, proper, right.
– OPPOSITES: optional.

requirement ▶ noun NEED, wish, demand, want, necessity, essential, prerequisite, stipulation.

requisite ▶ adjective *he lacks the requisite skills* NECESSARY, required, prerequisite, essential, indispensable, vital.
– OPPOSITES: optional.
▶ noun *a requisite for a successful career* NECESSITY, essential (requirement), prerequisite, precondition, sine qua non; *informal* must.

requisition ▶ noun **1** *requisitions for staff* ORDER, request, call, application, claim, demand. **2** *the requisition of cultural treasures* APPROPRIATION, commandeering, seizure, confiscation, expropriation.
▶ verb **1** *the house was requisitioned by the army* COMMANDEER, appropriate, take over, take possession of, occupy, seize, confiscate, expropriate. **2** *she requisitioned statements* REQUEST, order, call for, demand.

requital ▶ noun **1** *in requital of your kindness* REPAYMENT, return, payment, recompense. **2** *personal requital* REVENGE, vengeance, retribution, redress.

requite ▶ verb **1** *requiting their hospitality* RETURN, reciprocate, repay. **2** *Drake had requited the wrongs inflicted on them* AVENGE, exact revenge for, revenge, pay someone back for; take reprisals, settle the score, get even. **3** *she did not requite his love* RECIPROCATE, return.

rescind ▶ verb REVOKE, repeal, cancel, reverse, overturn, overrule, annul, nullify, void, invalidate, quash, abolish; *Law* vacate; *formal* abrogate.
– OPPOSITES: enforce.

rescission ▶ noun (*formal*) REVOCATION, repeal, annulment, nullification, invalidation, voiding; *formal* abrogation.

rescue ▶ verb **1** *an attempt to rescue the hostages* SAVE (FROM DANGER), save the life of, come to the aid of; (set) free, release, liberate. **2** *Boyd rescued his papers* RETRIEVE, recover, salvage, get back.
▶ noun *the rescue of 10 crewmen* SAVING, rescuing; release, freeing, liberation, bailout, deliverance, redemption.
■ **come to someone's rescue** HELP, assist, lend a (helping) hand to, bail out; *informal* save someone's bacon, save someone's neck, save someone's skin.

research ▶ noun **1** *medical research* INVESTIGATION, experimentation, testing, analysis, fact-finding, fieldwork, examination, scrutiny. **2** *he continued his researches* EXPERIMENTS, experimentation, tests, inquiries, studies.
▶ verb **1** *the phenomenon has been widely researched* INVESTIGATE, study, inquire into, look into, probe, explore, analyze, examine, scrutinize, review. **2** *I researched all the available material* STUDY, read (up on), sift through, look into; *informal* check out.

resemblance ▶ noun SIMILARITY, likeness, similitude, correspondence, congruity, congruence, coincidence, conformity, agreement, equivalence, comparability, parallelism, uniformity, sameness.

resemble ▶ verb LOOK LIKE, be similar to, be like, bear a resemblance to, remind one of, take after, favour, have the look of; approximate to, smack of, have (all) the hallmarks of, correspond to, echo, mirror, parallel.

resent ▶ verb BEGRUDGE, feel aggrieved at/about, feel bitter about, grudge, be annoyed at/about, be resentful of, dislike, take exception to, object to, take amiss, take offence at, take umbrage at, bear/harbour a grudge about.
– OPPOSITES: welcome.

resentful ▶ adjective AGGRIEVED, indignant, irritated, piqued, put out, in high dudgeon, dissatisfied, disgruntled, discontented, offended, bitter, jaundiced; envious, jealous; brooding; *informal* miffed, peeved, sore.

resentment ▶ noun BITTERNESS, indignation, irritation, pique, dissatisfaction, disgruntlement, discontentment, discontent, resentfulness, bad feelings, hard feelings, ill will, acrimony, rancour, animosity, jaundice; envy, jealousy.

reservation ▶ noun **1** *grave reservations* DOUBT, qualm, scruple; misgivings, skepticism, unease, hesitation, objection. **2** *the reservation of the room* BOOKING, ordering, securing.
■ **without reservation** WHOLEHEARTEDLY, unreservedly, without qualification, fully, completely, totally, entirely, wholly, unconditionally.

reserve ▶ verb **1** *ask the library to reserve you a copy* PUT TO ONE SIDE, put aside, set aside, keep (back), save, hold, put on hold, keep in reserve, earmark. **2** *he reserved a table* BOOK, make a reservation for, order, arrange for, secure; *formal* bespeak; *dated* engage. **3** *the management reserves the right to alter the program* RETAIN, maintain, keep, hold. **4** *reserve your judgment until you know him better* DEFER, postpone, put off, delay, withhold.
▶ noun **1** *reserves of gasoline* STOCK, store, supply, stockpile, pool, hoard, cache. **2** *the army is calling up reserves* REINFORCEMENTS, the militia, extras, auxiliaries. **3** (*Cdn*) *an Indian reserve* territory, nation; *informal* rez; *US* reservation. **4** *a nature reserve* NATIONAL/ PROVINCIAL PARK, sanctuary, preserve, conservation area, protected area, wildlife park. **5** *his natural reserve* RETICENCE, detachment, distance, remoteness, coolness, aloofness, constraint, formality; shyness,

diffidence, timidity, taciturnity, inhibition; *informal* standoffishness. **6** *she trusted him without reserve* RESERVATION, qualification, condition, limitation, hesitation, doubt.

▶ **adjective** *a reserve goaltender* BACKUP, substitute, stand-in, relief, replacement, fallback, spare, extra.

■ **in reserve** AVAILABLE, to/on hand, ready, in readiness, set aside, at one's disposal.

reserved ▶ **adjective 1** *Rodney is rather reserved* RETICENT, quiet, private, uncommunicative, unforthcoming, undemonstrative, unsociable, formal, constrained, cool, aloof, detached, distant, remote, unapproachable, unfriendly, withdrawn, secretive, silent, taciturn; shy, retiring, diffident, timid, self-effacing, inhibited, introverted; *informal* standoffish. **2** *that table is reserved* BOOKED, taken, spoken for, pre-arranged; *dated* engaged; *formal* bespoken.
− OPPOSITES: outgoing.

reservoir ▶ **noun 1** *water pumped from the reservoir* pool, pond, (*Prairies*) dugout ♣; water supply, water tower. **2** *an ink reservoir* RECEPTACLE, container, holder, repository, tank. **3** *the reservoir of managerial talent* STOCK, store, stockpile, reserve(s), supply, bank, pool, fund.

reshuffle ▶ **verb** *the prime minister reshuffled his cabinet* REORGANIZE, restructure, rearrange, change (around), shake up, shuffle.

▶ **noun** *a management reshuffle* REORGANIZATION, restructuring, change, rearrangement; *informal* shake-up, housecleaning, musical chairs.

reside ▶ **verb 1** *most students reside in apartments* LIVE IN, occupy, inhabit, stay in, lodge in; *formal* dwell in, be domiciled in. **2** *the paintings reside in an air-conditioned vault* BE SITUATED, be found, be located, lie. **3** *executive power resides in the president* BE VESTED IN, be bestowed on, be conferred on, be in the hands of. **4** *the qualities that reside within each individual* BE INHERENT, be present, exist.

residence ▶ **noun 1** (*formal*) *her private residence* HOME, house, place of residence, address; quarters, lodgings; *informal* pad; *formal* dwelling (place), domicile, abode. **2** *the university residence* DORMITORY, res ♣, dorm. **3** *his place of residence* OCCUPANCY, habitation, residency; *formal* abode.

resident ▶ **noun** *the residents of Moose Jaw* INHABITANT, local, citizen, native; townsfolk, townspeople; householder, homeowner, occupier, tenant; *formal* denizen.

▶ **adjective 1** *is he currently resident in New Brunswick?* LIVING, residing, in residence; *formal* dwelling. **2** *a resident nurse* LIVE-IN, living in.

residential ▶ **adjective** *residential neighborhoods* SUBURBAN, commuter, dormitory.

residual ▶ **adjective 1** *residual heat* REMAINING, leftover, unused, unconsumed. **2** *residual affection* LINGERING, enduring, abiding, surviving, vestigial.

residue ▶ **noun** REMAINDER, remaining part, rest, remnant(s); surplus, extra, excess; remains, leftovers; *technical* residuum.

resign ▶ **verb 1** *the executive director resigned* LEAVE, hand in one's notice, give notice, stand down, step down; *informal* quit, jump ship, hang up one's skates. **2** *19 MPs resigned their seats* GIVE UP, leave, vacate, stand down from; *informal* quit, pack in. **3** *he resigned his right to the title* RENOUNCE, relinquish, give up, abandon, surrender, forego, cede; *Law* disclaim; *literary* forsake.

4 *we resigned ourselves to a long wait* RECONCILE ONESELF TO, become resigned to, come to terms with, accept.

resignation ▶ **noun 1** *his resignation from his post* DEPARTURE, leaving, standing down, stepping down; *informal* quitting. **2** *she handed in her resignation* NOTICE (TO QUIT), letter of resignation. **3** *he accepted his fate with resignation* PATIENCE, forbearance, stoicism, fortitude, fatalism, acceptance, acquiescence, compliance, passivity.

resigned ▶ **adjective** PATIENT, long-suffering, uncomplaining, forbearing, stoical, philosophical, fatalistic, acquiescent, compliant, passive, submissive.

resilient ▶ **adjective 1** *resilient materials* FLEXIBLE, pliable, supple; durable, hard-wearing, stout, strong, sturdy, tough. **2** *young and resilient* STRONG, tough, hardy; quick to recover, buoyant, irrepressible.

resist ▶ **verb 1** *built to resist cold winters* WITHSTAND, be proof against, combat, weather, endure, be resistant to, keep out. **2** *they resisted his attempts to change things* OPPOSE, fight against, refuse to accept, object to, defy, set one's face against, kick against; obstruct, impede, hinder, block, thwart, frustrate. **3** *I resisted the urge to retort* REFRAIN FROM, abstain from, forbear from, desist from, not give in to, restrain oneself from, stop oneself from. **4** *she tried to resist him* STRUGGLE WITH/ AGAINST, fight (against), stand up to, withstand, hold off; fend off, ward off.
− OPPOSITES: welcome, submit.

■ **cannot resist** LOVE, adore, relish, have a weakness for, be very keen on, like, delight in, enjoy, take great pleasure in; *informal* be mad about, get a kick/thrill out of, cannot help (wanting).

resistance ▶ **noun 1** *resistance to change* OPPOSITION, hostility, refusal to accept. **2** *a spirited resistance* OPPOSITION, fight, stand, struggle. **3** *the body's resistance to disease* ABILITY TO FIGHT OFF, immunity from, defences against. **4** *the French resistance* RESISTANCE MOVEMENT, freedom fighters, underground, partisans.

resistant ▶ **adjective 1** *resistant to water* IMPERVIOUS, unsusceptible, immune, invulnerable, proof against, unaffected by. **2** *resistant to change* OPPOSED, averse, hostile, inimical, against; *informal* anti.

resolute ▶ **adjective** DETERMINED, purposeful, resolved, adamant, single-minded, firm, unswerving, unwavering, steadfast, staunch, stalwart, unfaltering, unhesitating, persistent, indefatigable, tenacious, strong-willed, unshakeable; stubborn, dogged, obstinate, obdurate, inflexible, intransigent, implacable, unyielding, unrelenting; spirited, brave, bold, courageous, plucky, indomitable, rock-ribbed; *informal* gutsy, spunky, feisty; *formal* pertinacious.
− OPPOSITES: half-hearted.

resolution ▶ **noun 1** *her resolution not to smoke* INTENTION, resolve, decision, intent, aim, plan; commitment, pledge, promise. **2** *the committee passed the resolution* MOTION, proposal, proposition, resolve. **3** *she handled the work with resolution* DETERMINATION, purpose, purposefulness, resolve, resoluteness, single-mindedness, firmness (of purpose); steadfastness, staunchness, perseverance, persistence, indefatigability, tenacity, tenaciousness, staying power, dedication, commitment; stubbornness, doggedness, obstinacy, obduracy; boldness, spiritedness, braveness, bravery, courage, pluck, grit, courageousness; *informal* guts, spunk; *formal* pertinacity. **4** *a satisfactory resolution of the* *problem* SOLUTION, answer, end, ending, settlement, conclusion.

resolve ▶ verb **1** *this matter cannot be resolved overnight* SETTLE, sort out, solve, find a solution to, fix, straighten out, deal with, put right, put to rights, rectify; *informal* hammer out, thrash out, figure out. **2** *Bob resolved not to wait any longer* DETERMINE, decide, make up one's mind, make a decision. **3** *the committee resolved that the project should proceed* VOTE, pass a resolution, rule, decide formally, agree. **4** *the compounds were resolved into their active constituents* BREAK DOWN/UP, separate, reduce, divide. **5** *the ability to resolve facts into their legal categories* ANALYZE, dissect, break down, categorize. **6** *the grey smudge resolved into a sandy beach* TURN, change, be transformed, be convert.

▶ noun **1** *their intimidation merely strengthened his resolve.* See RESOLUTION sense 3. **2** *he made a resolve not to go there again* DECISION, resolution, commitment.

resolved ▶ adjective DETERMINED, hell-bent, intent, set.

resonant ▶ adjective **1** *a resonant voice* DEEP, low, sonorous, full, full-bodied, vibrant, rich, clear, ringing; loud, booming, thunderous. **2** *valleys resonant with the sound of church bells* REVERBERATING, reverberant, resounding, echoing, filled. **3** *resonant words* EVOCATIVE, suggestive, expressive, redolent.

resort ▶ noun **1** *a seaside resort* HOLIDAY DESTINATION, (tourist) centre, vacationland. **2** *settle the matter without resort to legal proceedings* RECOURSE TO, turning to, the use of, utilizing. **3** *strike action is our last resort* EXPEDIENT, measure, step, recourse, alternative, option, choice, possibility, hope.

■ **resort to** HAVE RECOURSE TO, fall back on, turn to, make use of, use, employ, avail oneself of; stoop to, descend to, sink to.

resound ▶ verb **1** *the explosion resounded round the silent street* ECHO, re-echo, reverberate, ring out, boom, thunder, rumble. **2** *resounding with the clang of hammers* REVERBERATE, echo, re-echo, resonate, ring. **3** *nothing will resound like their earlier achievements* BE ACCLAIMED, be celebrated, be renowned, be famed, be glorified, be trumpeted.

resounding ▶ adjective **1** *a resounding voice* REVERBERANT, reverberating, resonant, resonating, echoing, ringing, sonorous, deep, full-throated, rich, clear; loud, booming. **2** *a resounding success* ENORMOUS, huge, very great, tremendous, terrific, colossal; emphatic, decisive, conclusive, outstanding, remarkable, phenomenal.

resource ▶ noun **1** *use your resources efficiently* ASSETS, funds, wealth, money, capital; staff; supplies, (raw) materials, store(s), stock(s), reserve(s). **2** *your tutor is there as a resource* FACILITY, amenity, aid, help, support. **3** *tears were her only resource* EXPEDIENT, resort, course, scheme, stratagem; trick, ruse, device. **4** *a person of resource* INITIATIVE, resourcefulness, enterprise, ingenuity, inventiveness; talent, ability, capability; *informal* gumption.

resourceful ▶ adjective INGENIOUS, enterprising, inventive, creative; clever, talented, able, capable.

respect ▶ noun **1** *the respect due to a great artist* ESTEEM, regard, high opinion, admiration, reverence, deference, honour. **2** *he spoke to her with respect* DUE REGARD, politeness, courtesy, civility, deference. **3** *paying one's respects* (KIND) REGARDS, compliments, greetings, best/good wishes, felicitations, salutations; *archaic* remembrances. **4** *the report was*

accurate in every respect ASPECT, regard, facet, feature, way, sense, particular, point, detail.
– OPPOSITES: contempt.

▶ verb **1** *she is highly respected in the book industry* ESTEEM, admire, think highly of, have a high opinion of, hold in high regard, hold in (high) esteem, look up to, revere, reverence, honour. **2** *they respected our privacy* SHOW CONSIDERATION FOR, have regard for, observe, be mindful of, be heedful of; *formal* take cognizance of. **3** *her father respected her wishes* ABIDE BY, comply with, follow, adhere to, conform to, act in accordance with, defer to, obey, observe, keep (to).
– OPPOSITES: despise, disobey.

■ **with respect to/in respect of** CONCERNING, regarding, in/with regard to, with reference to, respecting, re, about, apropos, on the subject of, in connection with, vis-à-vis.

respectable ▶ adjective **1** *a respectable middle-class background* REPUTABLE, of good repute, upright, honest, honourable, trustworthy, decent, good, well-bred, clean-living. **2** *a respectable salary* FAIRLY GOOD, decent, fair, reasonable, moderately good; substantial, considerable, sizable.
– OPPOSITES: disreputable, paltry.

respectful ▶ adjective DEFERENTIAL, reverent, reverential, dutiful; polite, well-mannered, civil, courteous, gracious.
– OPPOSITES: rude.

respective ▶ adjective SEPARATE, personal, own, particular, individual, specific, special, appropriate, different, various.

respite ▶ noun **1** *a brief respite* REST, break, breathing space, interval, intermission, interlude, recess, lull, pause, time out; relief, relaxation, repose; *informal* breather, let-up. **2** *respite from debts* POSTPONEMENT, deferment, delay, reprieve; *US Law* continuance.

resplendent ▶ adjective SPLENDID, magnificent, brilliant, dazzling, glittering, gorgeous, impressive, imposing, striking, stunning, majestic; *informal* splendiferous.

respond ▶ verb **1** *they do not respond to questions* ANSWER, reply, make a response, make a rejoinder. **2** *'No,' she responded* SAY IN RESPONSE, answer, reply, rejoin, retort, riposte, counter. **3** *they were slow to respond* REACT, make a response, reciprocate, retaliate.

response ▶ noun **1** *his response to the question* ANSWER, reply, rejoinder, retort, riposte; *informal* comeback. **2** *an angry response* REACTION, reply, retaliation, feedback; *informal* comeback.
– OPPOSITES: question.

responsibility ▶ noun **1** *it was his responsibility to find witnesses* DUTY, task, function, job, role, business. **2** *they denied responsibility for the bomb attack* BLAME, fault, guilt, culpability, liability. **3** *let's show some social responsibility* (common) sense, trustworthiness, maturity, reliability, dependability. **4** *a job with greater responsibility* AUTHORITY, control, power, leadership.

responsible ▶ adjective **1** *who is responsible for prisons?* IN CHARGE OF, in control of, at the helm of, accountable for, liable for. **2** *I am responsible for the mistake* ACCOUNTABLE, answerable, to blame, guilty, culpable, blameworthy, at fault, in the wrong. **3** *a responsible job* IMPORTANT, powerful, executive. **4** *he is responsible to the president* ANSWERABLE, accountable. **5** *a responsible tenant* TRUSTWORTHY, sensible, mature, reliable, dependable.

responsive ▶ adjective QUICK TO REACT, reactive, receptive, open to suggestions, amenable, flexible, forthcoming.

rest[1] ▶ verb **1** *he needed to rest* RELAX, take a rest, ease up/off, let up, slow down, have/take a break, unbend, unwind, recharge one's batteries, be at leisure, take it easy, put one's feet up; lie down, go to bed, have/take a nap, catnap, doze, sleep; *informal* take five, have/take a breather, snatch forty winks, get some shut-eye, take a load off, chill (out), catch some zees. **2** *his hands rested on the rail* LIE, be laid, repose, be placed, be positioned, be supported by. **3** *she rested her basket on the ground* SUPPORT, prop (up), lean, lay, set, stand, position, place, put. **4** *the film script rests on an improbable premise* BE BASED, depend, be dependent, rely, hinge, turn on, be contingent, revolve around.
▶ noun **1** *get some rest* REPOSE, relaxation, leisure, respite, time off, breathing space, downtime; sleep, nap, doze; *informal* shut-eye, snooze, lie-down, forty winks. **2** *a short rest from work* HOLIDAY, vacation, break, breathing space, interval, interlude, intermission, time off/out; *informal* breather. **3** *she took the poker from its rest* STAND, base, holder, support, rack, frame, shelf. **4** *we came to rest 100 metres lower* A STANDSTILL, a halt, a stop.

rest[2] ▶ noun *the rest of the board members are appointees* REMAINDER, residue, balance, remaining part/number/quantity, others, those left, remains, remnant(s), surplus, excess; *technical* residuum.
▶ verb *you may rest assured that he is there* REMAIN, continue to be, stay, keep, carry on being.

rest area ▶ noun REST STOP, picnic area, stopping place, pit stop.

restaurant ▶ noun See table.

Restaurants

beanery	foodery
bistro	greasy spoon
brasserie	pizzeria
café	ristorante
cafeteria	roadhouse
canteen	rotisserie
chophouse	snack bar
coffee shop	steakhouse
diner	sushi bar
eatery	taverna
fast food	trattoria
fish house	truck stop

restful ▶ adjective RELAXED, relaxing, quiet, calm, calming, tranquil, soothing, peaceful, placid, reposeful, leisurely, undisturbed, untroubled.
— OPPOSITES: exciting.

restitution ▶ noun **1** *restitution of the land seized* RETURN, restoration, handing back, surrender. **2** *restitution for the damage caused* COMPENSATION, recompense, reparation, damages, indemnification, indemnity, reimbursement, repayment, redress, remuneration.

restive ▶ adjective **1** *Edward is getting restive. See* RESTLESS sense 1. **2** *the militants are increasingly restive* UNRULY, disorderly, uncontrollable, unmanageable, wilful, recalcitrant, insubordinate; *formal* refractory; *archaic* contumacious.

restless ▶ adjective **1** *Maria was restless throughout the meeting* UNEASY, ill at ease, restive, fidgety, edgy, on edge, tense, worked up, nervous, agitated, anxious, on tenterhooks, keyed up; *informal* jumpy,

jittery, twitchy, uptight, antsy. **2** *a restless night* SLEEPLESS, wakeful; fitful, broken, disturbed, troubled, unsettled.

restlessness ▶ noun UNEASE, restiveness, edginess, tenseness, nervousness, agitation, anxiety, fretfulness, apprehension, disquiet; *informal* jitteriness.

restoration ▶ noun **1** *the restoration of democracy* REINSTATEMENT, reinstitution, re-establishment, reimposition, return. **2** *the restoration of derelict housing* REPAIR, repairing, fixing, mending, whitepainting ♣, refurbishment, reconditioning, rehabilitation, rebuilding, reconstruction, overhaul, redevelopment, renovation; *informal* rehab.

restore ▶ verb **1** *the aim to restore democracy* REINSTATE, bring back, reinstitute, reimpose, reinstall, re-establish. **2** *he restored it to its rightful owner* RETURN, give back, hand back. **3** *the building has been restored* REPAIR, fix, mend, refurbish, recondition, rehabilitate, rebuild, reconstruct, remodel, overhaul, redevelop, renovate; *informal* do up, rehab. **4** *a good sleep can restore you* REINVIGORATE, revitalize, revive, refresh, energize, fortify, revivify, regenerate, stimulate, freshen.
— OPPOSITES: abolish.

restrain ▶ verb **1** *Charles restrained his anger* CONTROL, keep under control, check, hold/keep in check, curb, suppress, repress, contain, dampen, subdue, smother, choke back, stifle, bottle up, rein back/in; *informal* keep the lid on. **2** *she could barely restrain herself from swearing* PREVENT, stop, keep, hold back. **3** *that beast ought to be restrained* TIE UP, bind, tether, chain (up), fetter, shackle, manacle, put in irons; *informal* hog-tie.

restrained ▶ adjective **1** *Julie was quite restrained* SELF-CONTROLLED, self-restrained, not given to excesses, sober, steady, unemotional, undemonstrative. **2** *restrained elegance* MUTED, soft, discreet, subtle, quiet, unobtrusive, unostentatious, understated, tasteful.

restraint ▶ noun **1** *a restraint on their impulsiveness* CONSTRAINT, check, control, restriction, limitation, curtailment; rein, bridle, brake, damper, impediment, obstacle. **2** *the admirable restraint of the protestors* SELF-CONTROL, self-restraint, self-discipline, control, moderation, prudence, judiciousness, abstemiousness. **3** *the room has been decorated with restraint* SUBTLETY, understatedness, taste, tastefulness, discretion, discrimination. **4** *a child restraint* BELT, harness, strap.

restrict ▶ verb **1** *a busy working life restricted his leisure activities* LIMIT, keep within bounds, regulate, control, moderate, cut down. **2** *the cuff supports the ankle without restricting movement* HINDER, interfere with, impede, hamper, obstruct, block, check, curb, shackle. **3** *he restricted himself to a 15-minute speech* CONFINE, limit.

restricted ▶ adjective **1** *restricted space* CRAMPED, confined, constricted, small, narrow, tight. **2** *a restricted calorie intake* LIMITED, controlled, regulated, reduced. **3** *a restricted zone* OUT OF BOUNDS, off limits, private, exclusive. **4** *restricted information* (TOP) SECRET, classified; *informal* hush-hush.
— OPPOSITES: unlimited.

restriction ▶ noun **1** *there is no restriction on the number of places* LIMITATION, limit, constraint, control, check, curb; condition, proviso, qualification. **2** *the restriction of personal freedom* REDUCTION, limitation, diminution, curtailment. **3** *restriction of movement*

HINDRANCE, impediment, slowing, reduction, limitation.

result ▶ noun **1** *stress is the result of overwork* CONSEQUENCE, outcome, product, upshot, sequel, effect, reaction, repercussion, ramification, conclusion, culmination. **2** *having made the calculation, what is your result?* ANSWER, solution; sum, total, product. **3** *exam results* GRADE, score, mark. **4** *the result of the trial* VERDICT, decision, outcome, conclusion, judgment, findings, ruling.
— OPPOSITES: cause.

▶ verb **1** *differences between species could result from their habitat* FOLLOW, ensue, develop, stem, spring, arise, derive, evolve, proceed; occur, happen, take place, come about; be caused by, be brought about by, be produced by, originate in, be consequent on. **2** *the shooting resulted in five deaths* END IN, culminate in, finish in, terminate in, lead to, prompt, precipitate, trigger; cause, bring about, occasion, effect, give rise to, produce, engender, generate; *literary* beget.

resume ▶ verb **1** *the government resumed negotiations* RESTART, recommence, begin again, start again, reopen; renew, return to, continue with, carry on with. **2** *the priest resumed his kneeling posture* RETURN TO, come back to, take up again, reoccupy.
— OPPOSITES: suspend, abandon.

resumé ▶ noun **1** *give your resumé to the HR department* CV, curriculum vitae. **2** *a resumé of the course material* SUMMARY, précis, synopsis, abstract, outline, summarization, summation, epitome; abridgement, digest, condensation, abbreviation, overview, review.

resumption ▶ noun RESTART, restarting, recommencement, reopening; continuation, carrying on, renewal, return to.

resurgence ▶ noun RENEWAL, revival, recovery, comeback, reawakening, resurrection, reappearance, re-emergence, regeneration; resumption, recommencement, continuation, renaissance.

resurrect ▶ verb **1** *Jesus was resurrected* RAISE FROM THE DEAD, restore to life, revive. **2** *resurrecting his career* REVIVE, restore, regenerate, revitalize, breathe new life into, bring back to life, reinvigorate, resuscitate, rejuvenate, stimulate, re-establish, relaunch.

resuscitate ▶ verb **1** *medics resuscitated him* BRING ROUND, revive, bring back to consciousness; give CPR/ artificial respiration to, give the kiss of life to. **2** *measures to resuscitate the economy* REVIVE, resurrect, restore, regenerate, revitalize, breathe new life into, reinvigorate, rejuvenate, stimulate.

retain ▶ verb **1** *the government retained a share in the industries* KEEP (POSSESSION OF), keep hold of, hold on to, hang on to. **2** *existing footpaths are to be retained* MAINTAIN, keep, preserve, conserve. **3** *some students retain facts easily* REMEMBER, memorize, keep in one's mind/memory, store. **4** *we have decided to retain a company lawyer* EMPLOY, contract, keep on the payroll.
— OPPOSITES: give up.

retainer ▶ noun **1** *they're paid a retainer* (RETAINING) FEE, periodic payment, advance, standing charge. **2** *a faithful retainer. See* SERVANT *sense 1.*

retaliate ▶ verb FIGHT BACK, hit back, respond, react, reply, reciprocate, counter-attack, return like for like, get back at someone, give tit for tat, take reprisals, get even, get one's own back, pay someone back, give someone a taste of their own medicine; have/get/take one's revenge, be revenged, avenge oneself.

retaliation ▶ noun REVENGE, vengeance, reprisal,

retribution, requital, recrimination, repayment; response, reaction, reply, counter-attack.

retard ▶ verb DELAY, slow down/up, hold back/up, set back, postpone, put back, detain, decelerate; hinder, hamper, obstruct, inhibit, impede, check, restrain, restrict, trammel; *literary* stay.
— OPPOSITES: accelerate.

retch ▶ verb **1** *the sour taste made her retch* GAG, heave. **2** *he retched all over the table. See* VOMIT *verb sense 1.*

reticence ▶ noun RESERVE, restraint, inhibition, diffidence, shyness; unresponsiveness, quietness, taciturnity, secretiveness.

reticent ▶ adjective RESERVED, withdrawn, introverted, inhibited, diffident, shy; uncommunicative, unforthcoming, unresponsive, tight-lipped, quiet, taciturn, silent, guarded, secretive.
— OPPOSITES: expansive.

retinue ▶ noun ENTOURAGE, escort, company, court, staff, personnel, household, train, suite, following, bodyguard; aides, attendants, servants, retainers.

retire ▶ verb **1** *he has retired* GIVE UP WORK, stop working, stop work; pack it in, call it quits, hang up one's skates ♣. **2** *we've retired him on full pension* PENSION OFF, force to retire, give someone the golden handshake. **3** *Gillian retired to her office* WITHDRAW, go away, take oneself off, decamp, shut oneself away; *formal* repair; *literary* betake oneself. **4** *their forces retired* RETREAT, withdraw, pull back, fall back, disengage, back off, give ground. **5** *everyone retired early* GO TO BED, call it a day, go to sleep; *informal* turn in, hit the hay/sack.

retired ▶ adjective *a retired schoolteacher* FORMER, ex-, past, in retirement, superannuated.
▶ noun *apartments for the retired* RETIRED PEOPLE, (old-age) pensioners, senior citizens, the elderly, seniors.

retirement ▶ noun **1** *they are nearing retirement* GIVING UP WORK, stopping work, golden age. **2** *retirement in a rural community* SECLUSION, retreat, solitude, privacy, isolation, obscurity.

retiring ▶ adjective **1** *the retiring president* DEPARTING, outgoing. **2** *a retiring sort of man* SHY, diffident, self-effacing, unassuming, unassertive, reserved, reticent, quiet, timid, modest; private, secret, secretive, withdrawn, reclusive, unsociable.
— OPPOSITES: incoming, outgoing.

retort ▶ verb '*Oh, sure,' she retorted* ANSWER, reply, respond, say in response, return, counter, rejoin, riposte, retaliate, snap back.
▶ noun *a sarcastic retort* ANSWER, reply, response, return, counter, rejoinder, riposte, retaliation; *informal* comeback.

retract ▶ verb **1** *the sea otter can retract its claws* PULL IN/BACK, draw in. **2** *she retracted her allegation* TAKE BACK, withdraw, recant, disavow, disclaim, repudiate, renounce, reverse, revoke, rescind, go back on, backtrack on, unsay; *formal* abjure.

retreat ▶ verb **1** *the army retreated* WITHDRAW, retire, draw back, pull back/out, fall back, give way, give ground, beat a retreat. **2** *the tide was retreating* GO OUT, ebb, recede, fall, go down. **3** *the government had to retreat* CHANGE ONE'S MIND, change one's plans; back down, climb down, do a U-turn, backtrack, backpedal, give in, concede defeat; *informal* pull a U-ey, do a one-eighty.
— OPPOSITES: advance.
▶ noun **1** *the retreat of the army* WITHDRAWAL, pulling

back. **2** *the President's retreat* CLIMBDOWN, about-face, U-turn; *informal* one-eighty. **3** *her rural retreat* REFUGE, haven, sanctuary; hideaway, hideout, hiding place, escape; *informal* hidey-hole. **4** *a period of retreat from the world* SECLUSION, withdrawal, retirement, solitude, isolation, sanctuary.

retrench ▶ verb **1** *we have to retrench* ECONOMIZE, cut back, make cutbacks, make savings, make economies, reduce expenditure, be economical, be frugal, tighten one's belt. **2** *services have to be retrenched* REDUCE, cut (back/down), pare (down), slim down, make reductions in, make cutbacks in, trim, prune; shorten, abridge; *informal* slash.

retribution ▶ noun PUNISHMENT, penalty, one's just deserts; revenge, reprisal, requital, retaliation, vengeance, an eye for an eye (and a tooth for a tooth), tit for tat, lex talionis; redress, reparation, restitution, recompense, repayment, atonement, indemnification, amends.

retrieve ▶ verb **1** *I retrieved our balls from their garden* GET BACK, bring back, recover, regain (possession of), recoup, reclaim, repossess, redeem, recuperate. **2** *they were trying to retrieve the situation* PUT/SET RIGHT, rectify, remedy, restore, sort out, straighten out, resolve, save.

retrograde ▶ adjective **1** *a retrograde step* FOR THE WORSE, regressive, negative, downhill, unwelcome. **2** *retrograde motion* BACKWARD(S), reverse, rearward.
— OPPOSITES: positive.

retrospect
■ **in retrospect** LOOKING BACK, on reflection, in/with hindsight.

retrospective ▶ adjective BACKDATED, retroactive, ex post facto.
▶ noun LOOK BACK, reflection, review.

return ▶ verb **1** *he returned to Halifax* GO BACK, come back, arrive back, come home. **2** *the symptoms returned* RECUR, reoccur, occur again, repeat (itself); reappear, appear again. **3** *he returned the money* GIVE BACK, hand back; pay back, repay. **4** *Peter returned the book to the shelf* RESTORE, put back, replace, reinstall. **5** *he returned the volley* HIT BACK, throw back. **6** *she returned his kiss* RECIPROCATE, requite, give in return, respond to, repay, give back. **7** *'Later,' returned Isabel* ANSWER, reply, respond, counter, rejoin, retort. **8** *the jury returned a unanimous verdict* DELIVER, bring in, hand down. **9** *the club returned a profit* YIELD, earn, realize, net, gross, clear. **10** *the NDP candidate was returned* ELECT, vote in, choose, select.
— OPPOSITES: depart, disappear, keep.
▶ noun **1** *his return to Gander* HOMECOMING. **2** *the return of hard times* RECURRENCE, reoccurrence, repeat, repetition, reappearance, revival, resurrection, re-emergence, resurgence, renaissance. **3** *I requested the return of my books* GIVING BACK, handing back, replacement, restoration, reinstatement, restitution. **4** *two returns to Yellowknife* RETURN TICKET/FARE, round-trip ticket/fare. **5** *a quick return on investments* YIELD, profit, gain, revenue, interest, dividend, ROI. **6** *a census return* STATEMENT, report, submission, record, dossier; document, form.
— OPPOSITES: departure, disappearance, single.
■ **in return for** IN EXCHANGE FOR, as a reward for, as compensation for.

revamp ▶ verb RENOVATE, redecorate, refurbish, recondition, rehabilitate, overhaul, make over; upgrade, refit, re-equip; remodel, refashion, redesign, restyle; *informal* do up, give something a facelift, rehab.

reveal ▶ verb **1** *the police can't reveal his whereabouts* DIVULGE, disclose, tell, let slip/drop, give away/out, blurt (out), release, leak; make known, make public, broadcast, publicize, circulate, disseminate; *informal* let on. **2** *the screen moved back to reveal the new car* SHOW, display, exhibit, disclose, uncover, unveil; *literary* uncloak. **3** *the data reveal a good deal of information* BRING TO LIGHT, uncover, lay bare, unearth, expose; *formal* evince; *literary* uncloak.
— OPPOSITES: hide.

revel ▶ verb **1** *they revelled all night* CELEBRATE, make merry, have a party, carouse, roister, go on a spree; *informal* party, live it up, whoop it up, make whoopee, rave, paint the town red. **2** *she revelled in the applause* ENJOY, delight in, love, like, adore, be pleased by, take pleasure in, appreciate, relish, lap up, savour; *informal* get a kick out of.
▶ noun *late-night revels* CELEBRATION, festivity, jollification, merrymaking, carousing, spree; party, jamboree, hedonism; *informal* rave, shindig, bash, wingding, blast.

revelation ▶ noun **1** *revelations about his personal life* DISCLOSURE, surprising fact, announcement, report; admission, confession. **2** *the revelation of a secret* DIVULGING, divulgence, disclosure, disclosing, letting slip/drop, giving away/out, leaking, leak, betrayal, unveiling, making known, making public, broadcasting, publicizing, dissemination, reporting, report, declaring, declaration.

reveller ▶ noun PARTY-GOER, merrymaker, carouser, roisterer; *archaic* wassailer.

revenge ▶ noun **1** *she is seeking revenge* VENGEANCE, retribution, retaliation, reprisal, requital, recrimination, an eye for an eye (and a tooth for a tooth), redress, satisfaction. **2** *they were filled with revenge* VENGEFULNESS, vindictiveness, vitriol, spite, spitefulness, malice, maliciousness, malevolence, ill will, animosity, hate, hatred, rancour, bitterness; *literary* maleficence.
▶ verb AVENGE, take/exact revenge for, exact retribution for, take reprisals for, get redress for, get satisfaction for.

revenue ▶ noun INCOME, takings, receipts, proceeds, earnings, sales, avails ♣; profit(s).
— OPPOSITES: expenditure.

reverberate ▶ verb RESOUND, echo, re-echo, resonate, ring, boom, rumble, vibrate.

reverberation ▶ noun **1** *natural reverberation* RESONANCE, echo, echoing, re-echoing, resounding, ringing, booming, rumbling. **2** *political reverberations* REPERCUSSIONS, ramifications, consequences, shock waves, tremors, vibrations; aftermath, fallout, backlash.

revere ▶ verb RESPECT, admire, think highly of, have a high opinion of, esteem, hold in high esteem/regard, look up to, put on a pedestal, reverence.
— OPPOSITES: despise.

reverence ▶ noun *reverence for the countryside* HIGH ESTEEM, high regard, great respect, acclaim, admiration, appreciation, estimation, favour.
— OPPOSITES: scorn.
▶ verb *they reverence modern jazz. See* REVERE.

reverent ▶ adjective RESPECTFUL, reverential, admiring, devoted, devout, dutiful, awed, deferential.

reverie ▶ noun DAYDREAM, daydreaming, trance, musing;   inattention,   inattentiveness, woolgathering, preoccupation, absorption, abstraction, lack of concentration.

reversal ▶ noun **1** *there was no reversal on this issue* TURNAROUND, turnabout, about-face, volte-face, change of heart, U-turn, one-eighty, backtracking; *rare* tergiversation. **2** *a reversal of roles* SWAP, exchange, change, swapping, interchange. **3** *the reversal of the decision* ALTERATION, changing; countermanding, undoing, overturning, overthrow, disallowing, overriding, overruling, veto, vetoing, revocation, repeal, rescinding, annulment, nullification, voiding, invalidation, abrogation. **4** *they suffered a reversal* SETBACK, reverse, upset, failure, misfortune, mishap, disaster, blow, disappointment, adversity, hardship, affliction, vicissitude, defeat; bad luck.

reverse ▶ verb **1** *the car reversed into a lamp post* BACK, back up, drive back/backwards, move back/ backwards. **2** *reverse the bottle in the ice bucket* TURN UPSIDE DOWN, turn over, upend, upturn, invert. **3** *I reversed my jacket* TURN INSIDE OUT, turn outside in. **4** *reverse your roles* SWAP (ROUND), change (round), exchange, interchange, switch (round). **5** *the umpire reversed the decision* ALTER, change; overturn, overthrow, disallow, override, overrule, veto, revoke, repeal, rescind, annul, nullify, void, invalidate; *formal* abrogate.
▶ adjective **1** *in reverse order* BACKWARD(S), reversed, inverted, transposed. **2** *reverse racism* INVERSE, reversed, opposite, converse, contrary, counter, antithetical.
▶ noun **1** *the reverse is the case* OPPOSITE, contrary, converse, inverse, obverse, antithesis. **2** *successes and reverses. See* REVERSAL *sense 4*. **3** *the reverse of the page* OTHER SIDE, reverse side, back, underside, wrong side, verso.

revert ▶ verb **1** *life will soon revert to normal* RETURN, go back, change back, default; fall back, regress, relapse. **2** *the property reverted to the landlord* BE RETURNED; *historical* escheat.

review ▶ noun **1** *the Council undertook a review* ANALYSIS, evaluation, assessment, appraisal, examination, investigation, inquiry, probe, inspection, study. **2** *the rent is due for review* RECONSIDERATION, reassessment, re-evaluation, reappraisal; change, alteration, modification, revision. **3** *book reviews* CRITICISM, critique, assessment, evaluation, commentary; *informal* take. **4** *a scientific review* JOURNAL, periodical, magazine, publication. **5** *their review of the economy* SURVEY, report, study, account, description, statement, overview, analysis. **6** *a military review* INSPECTION, parade, tattoo, procession, march past.
▶ verb **1** *I reviewed the evidence* SURVEY, study, research, consider, analyze, examine, scrutinize, explore, look into, probe, investigate, inspect, assess, appraise; *informal* size up. **2** *the referee reviewed his decision* RECONSIDER, re-examine, reassess, re-evaluate, reappraise, rethink; change, alter, modify, revise. **3** *he reviewed the day* REMEMBER, recall, reflect on, think through, go over in one's mind, look back on. **4** *reviewing troops* INSPECT, view. **5** *she reviewed the play* COMMENT ON, evaluate, assess, appraise, judge, critique, criticize.

reviewer ▶ noun CRITIC, COMMENTATOR, judge, observer, pundit, analyst.

revile ▶ verb CRITICIZE, censure, condemn, attack, inveigh against, rail against, castigate, lambaste, denounce; slander, libel, malign, vilify, abuse; *informal* knock, slam, pan, crucify, roast, tear into, badmouth, dis, pummel; *formal* excoriate, calumniate.
– OPPOSITES: praise.

revise ▶ verb **1** *she revised her opinion* RECONSIDER, review, re-examine, reassess, re-evaluate, reappraise, rethink; change, alter, modify. **2** *the editor revised the text* AMEND, emend, correct, alter, change, edit, rewrite, redraft, rephrase, rework.

revision ▶ noun **1** *a revision of the Prayer Book* EMENDATION, correction, alteration, adaptation, editing, rewriting, redrafting. **2** *a new revision* VERSION, edition, rewrite. **3** *a major revision of the system* RECONSIDERATION, review, re-examination, reassessment, re-evaluation, reappraisal, rethink; change, alteration, modification.

revitalize ▶ verb REINVIGORATE, re-energize, boost, regenerate, revive, revivify, rejuvenate, reanimate, resuscitate, refresh, stimulate, breathe new life into; *informal* give a shot in the arm to, pep up, jump-start, buck up.

revival ▶ noun **1** *a revival in the economy* IMPROVEMENT, recovery, rallying, picking up, amelioration, turn for the better, upturn, upswing, resurgence. **2** *the revival of traditional crafts* COMEBACK, re-establishment, reintroduction, restoration, reappearance, resurrection, regeneration, renaissance, rejuvenation.
– OPPOSITES: downturn, disappearance.

revive ▶ verb **1** *attempts to revive her failed* RESUSCITATE, bring round, bring back to consciousness. **2** *the man soon revived* REGAIN CONSCIOUSNESS, come round, wake up. **3** *a cup of tea revived her* REINVIGORATE, revitalize, refresh, energize, reanimate, resuscitate, revivify, rejuvenate, regenerate, enliven, stimulate. **4** *reviving old traditions* REINTRODUCE, re-establish, restore, resurrect, bring back, regenerate, resuscitate, rekindle.

revoke ▶ verb CANCEL, repeal, rescind, reverse, annul, nullify, void, invalidate, countermand, retract, withdraw, overrule, override; *Law* vacate; *formal* abrogate.

revolt ▶ verb **1** *the people revolted* REBEL, rise (up), take to the streets, riot, mutiny. **2** *the smell revolted him* DISGUST, sicken, nauseate, make nauseous, make someone sick, make someone's gorge rise, turn someone's stomach, be repugnant to, be repulsive to, put off, be offensive to; *informal* turn off, gross out.
▶ noun *an armed revolt* REBELLION, revolution, insurrection, mutiny, uprising, riot, rioting, insurgence, seizure of power, coup (d'état).

revolting ▶ adjective DISGUSTING, sickening, nauseating, stomach-turning, stomach-churning, repulsive, repellent, repugnant, appalling, abominable, hideous, horrible, awful, dreadful, terrible, obnoxious, vile, nasty, foul, loathsome, offensive, objectionable, off-putting, distasteful, disagreeable, vomitous; *informal* ghastly, putrid, horrid, gross, gut-churning, yucky, icky; *formal* rebarbative; *literary* noisome; *archaic* loathly.
– OPPOSITES: attractive, pleasant.

revolution ▶ noun **1** *the French Revolution* REBELLION, revolt, insurrection, mutiny, uprising, riot, rioting, insurgence, seizure of power, coup (d'état). **2** *a revolution in printing techniques* DRAMATIC CHANGE, radical alteration, sea change, metamorphosis, transformation, innovation, reorganization, restructuring; *informal* shake-up, shakedown. **3** *one revolution of a wheel* (SINGLE) TURN, rotation, circle, spin; circuit, lap. **4** *the revolution of the earth* TURNING, rotation, circling; orbit.

revolutionary ▶ **adjective 1** *revolutionary troops* REBELLIOUS, rebel, insurgent, rioting, mutinous, renegade, insurrectionary, insurrectionist, seditious, subversive, extremist. **2** *revolutionary change* THOROUGHGOING, thorough, complete, total, absolute, utter, comprehensive, sweeping, far-reaching, extensive, profound. **3** *a revolutionary kind of wheelchair* NEW, novel, original, unusual, unconventional, unorthodox, newfangled, innovative, modern, state-of-the-art, cutting-edge, futuristic, pioneering.
▶ **noun** *political revolutionaries* REBEL, insurgent, revolutionist, mutineer, insurrectionist, agitator, subversive.

revolutionize ▶ **verb** TRANSFORM, alter dramatically, shake up, turn upside down, restructure, reorganize, transmute, metamorphose; *humorous* transmogrify.

revolve ▶ **verb 1** *a fan revolved slowly* GO ROUND, turn round, rotate, spin. **2** *the moon revolves around the earth* CIRCLE, travel, orbit. **3** *his life revolves around cars* BE CONCERNED WITH, be preoccupied with, focus on, centre on/around.

revulsion ▶ **noun** DISGUST, repulsion, abhorrence, repugnance, nausea, horror, aversion, abomination, distaste.
− OPPOSITES: delight.

reward ▶ **noun** *a reward for its safe return* RECOMPENSE, prize, award, honour, decoration, bonus, premium, bounty, present, gift, payment; *informal* payoff, perk; *formal* perquisite.
▶ **verb** *they were well rewarded* RECOMPENSE, pay, remunerate, make something worth someone's while; give an award to.
− OPPOSITES: punish.

rewarding ▶ **adjective** SATISFYING, gratifying, pleasing, fulfilling, enriching, edifying, beneficial, illuminating, worthwhile, productive, fruitful.

reword ▶ **verb** REWRITE, rephrase, recast, put in other words, express differently, redraft, revise; paraphrase.

rewrite ▶ **verb** REVISE, recast, reword, rephrase, redraft.

rhetoric ▶ **noun 1** *a form of rhetoric* ORATORY, eloquence, command of language, way with words. **2** *empty rhetoric* BOMBAST, turgidity, grandiloquence, magniloquence, pomposity, extravagant language, purple prose; wordiness, verbosity, prolixity; *informal* hot air; *rare* fustian.

rhetorical ▶ **adjective 1** *rhetorical devices* STYLISTIC, oratorical, linguistic, verbal. *See table*. **2** *rhetorical hyperbole* EXTRAVAGANT, grandiloquent, magniloquent, high-flown, orotund, bombastic, grandiose, pompous, pretentious, overblown, oratorical, turgid, flowery, florid; *informal* highfalutin; *rare* fustian.

rhyme ▶ **noun** POEM, piece of poetry, verse; (**rhymes**) poetry, doggerel.

rhythm ▶ **noun 1** *the rhythm of the music* BEAT, cadence, tempo, time, pulse, throb, swing. **2** *poetic features such as rhythm* METRE, measure, stress, accent, cadence. **3** *the rhythm of daily life* PATTERN, flow, tempo.

rhythmic ▶ **adjective** RHYTHMICAL, with a steady pulse, measured, throbbing, beating, pulsating, regular, steady, even.

Rhetorical Devices

alliteration	metaphor
anacoluthon	oxymoron
anaphora	paralipsis
aporia	prosopopoeia
chiasmus	simile
epistrophe	syllepsis
hendiadys	synecdoche
hyperbole	trope
hysteron proteron	zeugma
litotes	

rib ▶ **noun.**
− RELATED TERMS: costal.

ribald ▶ **adjective.** *See* CRUDE *sense 3.*

ribbon ▶ **noun** STRIP, tape, band, cord.

rice ▶ **noun.** *See the table at* CEREAL.

rich ▶ **adjective 1** *rich people* WEALTHY, affluent, moneyed, well off, well-to-do, prosperous, opulent, silk-stocking; *informal* rolling in money/it, in the money, loaded, flush, stinking rich, filthy rich, well-heeled, made of money. **2** *rich furnishings* SUMPTUOUS, opulent, luxurious, luxury, deluxe, lavish, gorgeous, splendid, magnificent, costly, expensive, fancy; *informal* posh, plush, ritzy, swanky, classy, swank. **3** *a garden rich in flowers* ABOUNDING, well provided, well-stocked, crammed, packed, teeming, bursting; *informal* jam-packed, chockablock, chock full. **4** *a rich supply of restaurants* PLENTIFUL, abundant, copious, ample, profuse, lavish, liberal, generous, bountiful; *literary* plenteous, bounteous. **5** *rich soil* FERTILE, productive, fecund, fruitful. **6** *a rich sauce* CREAMY, fatty, heavy, full-flavoured. **7** *a rich wine* FULL-BODIED, heavy, fruity. **8** *rich colours* STRONG, deep, full, intense, vivid, brilliant. **9** *her rich voice* SONOROUS, full, resonant, deep, clear, mellow, mellifluous, full-throated.
− OPPOSITES: poor, light.

riches ▶ **plural noun 1** *his new-found riches* MONEY, wealth, funds, (hard) cash, (filthy) lucre, wherewithal, means, (liquid) assets, capital, resources, reserves; opulence, affluence, prosperity; *informal* dough, bread, loot, shekels, moolah, the necessary, bucks, mazuma, dinero, jack. **2** *underwater riches* RESOURCES, treasure(s), bounty, jewels, gems.

richly ▶ **adverb 1** *the richly furnished chamber* SUMPTUOUSLY, opulently, luxuriously, lavishly, gorgeously, splendidly, magnificently; *informal* plushly, ritzily, swankily, classily. **2** *the joy she richly deserves* FULLY, thoroughly, in full measure, well, completely, wholly, totally, entirely, absolutely, amply, utterly.
− OPPOSITES: meanly.

rickety ▶ **adjective** SHAKY, unsteady, unsound, unsafe, tumbledown, broken-down, dilapidated, ramshackle; *informal* shacky.

rid ▶ **verb** *ridding the building of asbestos* CLEAR, free, purge, empty, strip.
■ **get rid of 1** *we must get rid of some stuff* DISPOSE OF, throw away/out, clear out, discard, scrap, dump, bin, jettison, divest oneself of; *informal* chuck (away), ditch, junk, get shut of, trash, deep-six. **2** *the cats got rid of the rats* DESTROY, eliminate, annihilate, obliterate, wipe out, kill.

riddle¹ ▶ **noun** *an answer to the riddle* PUZZLE, conundrum, brainteaser, (unsolved) problem, question, poser, enigma, mystery, quandary; *informal* stumper.

riddle² ▶ **verb** 1 *his car was riddled by gunfire* PERFORATE, hole, pierce, puncture, pepper. 2 *he was riddled with cancer* PERMEATE, suffuse, fill, pervade, spread through, imbue, saturate, overrun, beset. 3 *the soil must be riddled* SIEVE, sift, strain, screen, filter.

ride ▶ **verb** 1 *she can ride a horse* SIT ON, mount, bestride; manage, handle, control. 2 *riding through the town on motor bikes* TRAVEL, move, proceed, make one's way; drive, cycle; trot, canter, gallop.
▶ **noun** *a ride in the new car* TRIP, journey, drive, run, excursion, outing, jaunt; lift; *informal* spin.

ridicule ▶ **noun** *she was subjected to ridicule* MOCKERY, derision, laughter, scorn, scoffing, contempt, jeering, sneering, sneers, jibes, jibing, teasing, taunts, taunting, badinage, chaffing, sarcasm, satire; *informal* kidding, ribbing, joshing, goofing, razzing.
— OPPOSITES: respect.
▶ **verb** *his theory was ridiculed* DERIDE, mock, laugh at, heap scorn on, jeer at, jibe at, sneer at, treat with contempt, scorn, make fun of, poke fun at, scoff at, satirize, lampoon, burlesque, caricature, parody, tease, taunt, chaff; *informal* kid, rib, josh, razz, pull someone's chain.

ridiculous ▶ **adjective** 1 *she looked ridiculous in her dad's oversized shorts and striped socks* LAUGHABLE, absurd, comical, funny, hilarious, risible, droll, amusing, farcical, silly, ludicrous; *rare* derisible. 2 *a ridiculous suggestion* SENSELESS, silly, foolish, foolhardy, stupid, inane, fatuous, childish, puerile, half-baked, hare-brained, cockamamie, ill-thought-out, crackpot, idiotic. 3 *a ridiculous exaggeration* ABSURD, preposterous, ludicrous, risible, laughable, nonsensical, senseless, outrageous.
— OPPOSITES: sensible.

riding (*Cdn*) ▶ **noun** *MPs returned to their ridings for the summer* constituency, electoral district.

rife ▶ **adjective** 1 *violence is rife* WIDESPREAD, general, common, universal, extensive, ubiquitous, omnipresent, endemic, inescapable, insidious, prevalent. 2 *the village was rife with gossip* OVERFLOWING, bursting, alive, teeming, abounding.
— OPPOSITES: unknown.

riff-raff ▶ **noun** RABBLE, scum, good-for-nothings, undesirables, low-lifes, hoi polloi, the lowest of the low; *informal* peasants.
— OPPOSITES: elite.

rifle ▶ **verb** 1 *she rifled through her wardrobe* RUMMAGE, search, hunt, forage. 2 *a thief rifled her home* BURGLE, burglarize, rob, steal from, loot, raid, plunder, ransack.
▶ **noun** *he refused to register the rifle* FIREARM, gun, shotgun, 30-30; *proprietary* Winchester.

rift ▶ **noun** 1 *a deep rift in the ice* CRACK, fault, flaw, split, break, breach, fissure, fracture, cleft, crevice, cavity, opening. 2 *the rift between them* BREACH, division, split, quarrel, squabble, disagreement, falling-out, row, argument, dispute, conflict, feud; estrangement; *informal* spat, scrap.

rig¹ ▶ **verb** 1 *the boats were rigged with a single sail* EQUIP, fit out, supply, furnish, provide, arm. 2 *I rigged myself out in black* DRESS, clothe, attire, robe, garb, array, deck out, drape, accoutre, outfit, get up, trick out/up; *informal* doll up; *archaic* apparel. 3 *he will rig up a shelter* SET UP, erect, assemble, build; throw together, cobble together, put together, whip up, improvise, contrive.
▶ **noun** 1 *a CB radio rig* APPARATUS, appliance, machine,

device, instrument, contraption, system; tackle, gear, kit, outfit. 2 *the rig of a Civil War artillery officer* UNIFORM, costume, ensemble, outfit, livery, attire, clothes, clothing, garments, dress, garb, regalia, trappings; *informal* getup, gear, togs, kit; *formal* apparel; *archaic* raiment, vestments.

rig² ▶ **verb** *they rigged the election* MANIPULATE, engineer, distort, misrepresent, pervert, tamper with, doctor; falsify, fake, trump up; *informal* fix, fiddle with.

right ▶ **adjective** 1 *it wouldn't be right to do that* JUST, fair, proper, good, upright, righteous, virtuous, moral, ethical, honourable, honest; lawful, legal. 2 *Mr. Hubert had the right answer* CORRECT, accurate, exact, precise; proper, valid, conventional, established, official, formal. 3 *the right person for the job* SUITABLE, appropriate, fitting, correct, proper, desirable, preferable, ideal; *archaic* meet. 4 *you've come at the right time* OPPORTUNE, advantageous, favourable, propitious, good, lucky, happy, fortunate, providential, felicitous; timely, seasonable, convenient, expedient, suitable, appropriate. 5 *he's not right in the head* SANE, lucid, rational, balanced, together, compos mentis; healthy, well; *informal* all there. 6 *my right hand* DEXTRAL.
— OPPOSITES: wrong, insane.
▶ **adverb** 1 *she was right at the limit of her patience* COMPLETELY, fully, totally, absolutely, utterly, thoroughly, quite. 2 *right in the middle of the village* EXACTLY, precisely, directly, immediately, just, squarely, dead; *informal* bang, smack, plumb, smack dab. 3 *keep going right ahead* STRAIGHT, directly. 4 (*informal*) *he'll be right down* STRAIGHT, immediately, instantly, at once, straight away, now, right now, this minute, directly, forthwith, without further ado, promptly, quickly, as soon as possible, ASAP, in short order; *informal* straight off, PDQ (pretty damn quick), pronto, lickety-split. 5 *I think I heard right* CORRECTLY, accurately, properly, precisely, aright, rightly, perfectly. 6 *make sure you're treated right by the authorities* WELL, properly, justly, fairly, nicely, equitably, impartially, honourably, lawfully, legally, ethically. 7 *things will turn out right* WELL, for the best, favourably, happily, advantageously, profitably, providentially, luckily, conveniently.
— OPPOSITES: wrong, badly.
▶ **noun** 1 *the difference between right and wrong* GOODNESS, righteousness, virtue, integrity, rectitude, propriety, morality, truth, honesty, honour, justice, fairness, equity; lawfulness, legality. 2 *you have the right to say no* ENTITLEMENT, prerogative, privilege, advantage, due, birthright, liberty, authority, power, licence, permission, dispensation, leave, sanction, freedom; *Law, historical* droit.
— OPPOSITES: wrong.
▶ **verb** 1 *the way to right a capsized dinghy* SET UPRIGHT, turn back over. 2 *we must right the situation* REMEDY, put right, rectify, retrieve, fix, resolve, sort out, settle, square; straighten out, correct, repair, mend, redress, make good, ameliorate, better.
■ **by rights** PROPERLY, correctly, technically, in fairness; legally, de jure.
■ **in the right** JUSTIFIED, vindicated.
■ **put something to rights**. *See* RIGHT *verb* sense 2.
■ **right away** AT ONCE, straight away, (right) now, this (very) minute, this instant, immediately, instantly, directly, forthwith, without further ado, promptly, quickly, without delay, as soon as possible, ASAP, in short order; *informal* straight off, PDQ (pretty damn quick), pronto, lickety-split.
■ **within one's rights** ENTITLED, permitted, allowed,

at liberty, empowered, authorized, qualified, licensed, justified.

righteous ▶ adjective **1** *righteous living* GOOD, virtuous, upright, upstanding, decent; ethical, principled, moral, high-minded, law-abiding, honest, honourable, blameless, irreproachable, noble; saintly, angelic, pure. **2** *righteous anger* JUSTIFIABLE, justified, legitimate, defensible, supportable, rightful; admissible, allowable, understandable, excusable, acceptable, reasonable.
− OPPOSITES: sinful, unjustifiable.

rightful ▶ adjective **1** *the car's rightful owner* LEGAL, lawful, real, true, proper, correct, recognized, genuine, authentic, acknowledged, approved, licensed, valid, bona fide, de jure; *informal* legit, kosher. **2** *their rightful place in society* DESERVED, merited, due, just, right, fair, proper, fitting, appropriate, suitable.

right-wing ▶ adjective CONSERVATIVE, rightist, right-of-centre, ultra-conservative, blimpish, diehard; reactionary, traditionalist, conventional, unprogressive; fascist.
− OPPOSITES: left-wing.

rigid ▶ adjective **1** *a rigid container* STIFF, hard, firm, inflexible, unbending, unyielding, inelastic. **2** *a rigid routine* FIXED, set, firm, inflexible, unalterable, unchangeable, immutable, unvarying, invariable, hard and fast, cast-iron, ironclad. **3** *a rigid approach to funding* STRICT, severe, stern, stringent, rigorous, inflexible, uncompromising, intransigent.
− OPPOSITES: flexible, lenient.

rigmarole ▶ noun **1** *the rigmarole of dressing up* FUSS, bother, trouble, palaver, ado, pother, song and dance, performance, to-do, pantomime, hassle, folderol. **2** *that rigmarole about the house being haunted* TALE, saga, yarn, shaggy-dog story; *informal* spiel.

rigorous ▶ adjective **1** *rigorous attention to detail* METICULOUS, conscientious, punctilious, careful, diligent, attentive, scrupulous, painstaking, exact, precise, accurate, thorough, particular, strict, demanding, exacting; *informal* pernickety, persnickety. **2** *the rigorous enforcement of rules* STRICT, severe, stern, stringent, tough, harsh, rigid, relentless, unsparing, inflexible, draconian, intransigent, uncompromising, exacting. **3** *rigorous yachting conditions* HARSH, severe, bad, bleak, extreme, inclement; unpleasant, disagreeable, foul, nasty, filthy; stormy, wild, tempestuous.
− OPPOSITES: slapdash, lax, mild.

rigour ▶ noun **1** *a mine operated under conditions of rigour* STRICTNESS, severity, stringency, toughness, harshness, rigidity, inflexibility, intransigence. **2** *intellectual rigour* METICULOUSNESS, thoroughness, carefulness, diligence, scrupulousness, exactness, exactitude, precision, accuracy, correctness, strictness. **3** *the rigours of the journey* HARDSHIP, harshness, severity, adversity; ordeal, misery, trial; discomfort, inconvenience, privation.

rile ▶ verb (*informal*). See ANNOY.

rim ▶ noun **1** *the rim of her cup* BRIM, edge, lip. **2** *the rim of the crater* EDGE, border, side, margin, brink, fringe, boundary, perimeter, limits, periphery.

rind ▶ noun SKIN, peel, zest, integument; *Botany* pericarp.

ring¹ ▶ noun **1** *the rings around Saturn* CIRCLE, band, loop, hoop, halo, disc. **2** *she wore a ring* WEDDING RING, band. **3** *a circus ring* ARENA, enclosure, field, ground; amphitheatre, stadium. **4** *a ring of onlookers* CIRCLE,

group, knot, cluster, bunch, band, throng, crowd, flock, pack. **5** *a spy ring* GANG, syndicate, cartel, mob, band, circle, organization, association, society, alliance, league, coterie, cabal, cell.
▶ verb *police ringed the building* SURROUND, circle, encircle, encompass, girdle, enclose, hem in, confine, seal off.

ring² ▶ verb **1** *church bells rang all day* TOLL, sound, peal, chime, clang, bong, ding, jingle, tinkle; *literary* knell. **2** *the room rang with laughter* RESOUND, reverberate, resonate, echo.
▶ noun *the ring of a bell* CHIME, toll, peal, clang, clink, ding, jingle, tinkle, tintinnabulation, sound; *literary* knell.
■ **ring something in** HERALD, signal, announce, proclaim, usher in, introduce; mark, signify, indicate; *literary* betoken, knell.

rink ▶ noun skating rink, hockey rink, ice rink, arena, ice pad ✦, ice palace ✦, *dated* hockey cushion ✦.

rinse ▶ verb WASH (OUT), clean, cleanse, bathe; dip, drench, splash, swill, sluice, hose down.

riot ▶ noun **1** *a riot in the capital* UPROAR, commotion, upheaval, disturbance, furor, tumult, melee, scuffle, fracas, fray, brawl, free-for-all; violence, fighting, vandalism, mayhem, turmoil, lawlessness, anarchy, violent protest. **2** *the garden was a riot of colour* MASS, sea, splash, show, exhibition.
▶ verb *the miners rioted* (GO ON THE) RAMPAGE, run riot, fight in the streets, run wild, run amok, go berserk; *informal* raise hell.
■ **run riot 1** *the children ran riot* (GO ON THE) RAMPAGE, riot, run amok, go berserk, go out of control; *informal* raise hell. **2** *the vegetation has run riot* GROW PROFUSELY, spread uncontrolled, grow rapidly, spread like wildfire; burgeon, multiply, rocket.

riotous ▶ adjective **1** *the demonstration turned riotous* UNRULY, rowdy, disorderly, uncontrollable, unmanageable, undisciplined, uproarious, tumultuous; violent, wild, ugly, lawless, anarchic. **2** *a riotous party* BOISTEROUS, lively, loud, noisy, unrestrained, uninhibited, uproarious, unruly, rollicking, knockabout; *informal* rambunctious.
− OPPOSITES: peaceable.

rip ▶ verb **1** *he ripped the posters down* TEAR, wrench, wrest, pull, snatch, tug, pry, heave, drag, peel, pluck; *informal* yank. **2** *she ripped Leo's note into pieces* TEAR, claw, hack, slit, cut; *literary* rend.
▶ noun *a rip in my sleeve* TEAR, slit, split, rent, laceration, cut, gash, slash.

ripe ▶ adjective **1** *a ripe tomato* MATURE, ripened, full grown, ready to eat; luscious, juicy, tender, sweet. **2** *the dock is ripe for development* READY, fit, suitable, right. **3** *the ripe old age of ninety* ADVANCED, hoary, venerable, old. **4** *the time is ripe for his return* OPPORTUNE, advantageous, favourable, auspicious, propitious, promising, good, right, fortunate, benign, providential, felicitous, seasonable; convenient, suitable, appropriate, apt, fitting.
− OPPOSITES: unsuitable, young.

ripen ▶ verb BECOME RIPE, mature, mellow.

rip-off ▶ noun (*informal*) FRAUD, cheat, deception, swindle, confidence trick; *informal* con, scam, flim-flam, gyp, rip, gouge, shakedown, bunco.

riposte ▶ noun *an indignant riposte* RETORT, counter, rejoinder, sally, return, answer, reply, response; *informal* comeback.
▶ verb *'Heaven help you,' riposted Alicia* RETORT, counter,

rejoin, return, retaliate, hurl back, answer, reply, respond, come back.

ripple ▶ noun *he blew ripples in his coffee* WAVELET, wave, undulation, ripplet, ridge, ruffle.
▶ verb *a breeze rippled the lake* FORM RIPPLES ON, ruffle, wrinkle.

rise ▶ verb **1** *the sun rose* MOVE UP/UPWARDS, come up, make one's/its way up, arise, ascend, climb, mount, soar. **2** *the mountains rising above us* LOOM, tower, soar, rise up, rear (up). **3** *prices rose* GO UP, increase, soar, shoot up, surge, leap, jump, rocket, escalate, spiral. **4** *living standards have risen* IMPROVE, get better, advance, go up, soar, shoot up. **5** *her voice rose* GET HIGHER, grow, increase, become louder, swell, intensify. **6** *he rose from his chair* STAND UP, get to one's feet, get up, jump up, leap up; *formal* arise. **7** *she rises at dawn* GET UP, get out of bed, rouse oneself, stir, bestir oneself, be up and about; *informal* rise and shine, surface; *formal* adjourn. **8** *the court rose at midday* ADJOURN, recess, be suspended, pause, take a break; *informal* knock off, take five. **9** *he rose through the ranks* MAKE PROGRESS, climb, advance, get on, work one's way, be promoted. **10** *she wouldn't rise to the bait* REACT, respond; take. **11** *Christ rose again* COME BACK TO LIFE, be resurrected, revive. **12** *the dough started to rise* SWELL, expand, enlarge, puff up. **13** *the nation rose against its oppressors* REBEL, revolt, mutiny, riot, take up arms. **14** *the river rises in the mountains* ORIGINATE, begin, start, emerge; issue from, spring from, flow from, emanate from. **15** *her spirits rose* BRIGHTEN, lift, cheer up, improve, pick up; *informal* buck up. **16** *the ground rose gently* SLOPE UPWARDS, go uphill, incline, climb.
— OPPOSITES: fall, descend, drop, sit, retire, resume, die.
▶ noun **1** *a price rise* INCREASE, hike, leap, upsurge, upswing, climb, escalation. **2** *a rise in standards* IMPROVEMENT, amelioration, upturn, leap. **3** *her rise to power* PROGRESS, climb, promotion, elevation, aggrandizement. **4** *we walked up the rise* SLOPE, incline, hillock, hill; *formal* eminence.

risible ▶ adjective LAUGHABLE, ridiculous, absurd, comical, comic, amusing, funny, hilarious, humorous, droll, farcical, silly, ludicrous, hysterical; *informal* rib-tickling, priceless.

risk ▶ noun **1** *there is a certain amount of risk* CHANCE, uncertainty, unpredictability, precariousness, instability, insecurity, perilousness, riskiness. **2** *the risk of fire* POSSIBILITY, chance, probability, likelihood, danger, peril, threat, menace, fear, prospect.
— OPPOSITES: safety, impossibility.
▶ verb **1** *he risked his life to save them* ENDANGER, imperil, jeopardize, hazard, gamble (with), chance; put on the line, put in jeopardy. **2** *you risk getting cold and wet* CHANCE, stand a chance of.
■ **at risk** IN DANGER, in peril, in jeopardy, under threat.

risky ▶ adjective DANGEROUS, hazardous, perilous, high-risk, fraught with danger, unsafe, insecure, precarious, parlous, touch-and-go, treacherous; uncertain, unpredictable; *informal* chancy, dicey, hairy, gnarly.

risqué ▶ adjective RIBALD, rude, bawdy, racy, earthy, indecent, suggestive, improper, naughty, locker-room; vulgar, dirty, smutty, crude, coarse, obscene, lewd, X-rated; *informal* blue, raunchy, off-colour.

rite ▶ noun CEREMONY, ritual, ceremonial; service, sacrament, liturgy, worship, office; act, practice,

custom, tradition, convention, institution, procedure.

ritual ▶ noun *an elaborate civic ritual* CEREMONY, rite, ceremonial, observance; service, sacrament, liturgy, worship; act, practice, custom, tradition, convention, formality, procedure, protocol.
▶ adjective *a ritual burial* CEREMONIAL, ritualistic, prescribed, set, formal; sacramental, liturgical; traditional, conventional.

ritzy ▶ adjective *(informal).* See POSH sense 1.

rival ▶ noun **1** *his rival for the nomination* OPPONENT, challenger, competitor, contender; adversary, antagonist, enemy; *literary* foe. **2** *the tool has no rival* EQUAL, match, peer, equivalent, counterpart, like.
— OPPOSITES: ally.
▶ verb *few countries can rival ours for modesty* MATCH, compare with, compete with, vie with, equal, measure up to, be in the same league as, be on a par with, touch, challenge; *informal* hold a candle to.
▶ adjective *rival candidates* COMPETING, opposing, contending.

rivalry ▶ noun COMPETITIVENESS, competition, contention, vying; opposition, conflict, feuding, antagonism, friction, enmity; *informal* keeping up with the Joneses.

riven ▶ adjective *a country riven by civil war* TORN APART, split, rent, severed; *literary* cleft, torn asunder.

river ▶ noun **1** WATERCOURSE, waterway, tributary, stream, rivulet, brook, inlet, rill, runnel, freshet; bourn; creek. *See table.* **2** *a river of molten lava* STREAM, torrent, flood, deluge, cascade.
— RELATED TERMS: fluvial, fluvio-.
■ **sell someone down the river** *(informal).* See DOUBLE-CROSS.

Longest River Systems in Canada

Mackenzie/Peace/Finlay	4241 km
St. Lawrence/Great Lakes	3058 km
Nelson/Saskatchewan/ South Saskatchewan/Bow	2575 km
Churchill	1609 km
Fraser	1370 km
North Saskatchewan	1287 km
Ottawa	1271 km
Athabasca	1231 km
Yukon	1149 km in Canada (3185 km total)
Liard	1115 km
Assiniboine	1070 km

riveted ▶ adjective **1** *she stood riveted to the spot* FIXED, rooted, frozen, welded, unable to move; motionless, unmoving, immobile, stock-still. **2** *he was riveted by the newsreels* FASCINATED, engrossed, gripped, captivated, enthralled, spellbound, mesmerized, transfixed. **3** *their eyes were riveted on the teacher* FIXED, fastened, focused, concentrated, locked.
— OPPOSITES: bored.

riveting ▶ adjective FASCINATING, gripping, engrossing, interesting, intriguing, absorbing, captivating, enthralling, compelling, spellbinding, mesmerizing; *informal* unputdownable.
— OPPOSITES: boring.

road ▶ noun **1** *the roads were crowded with traffic* STREET, thoroughfare, roadway, avenue, broadway, bypass, ring road, trunk road, byroad; lane, crescent, drive, parade, row, highway, freeway, parkway,

boulevard, throughway, expressway, autoroute, turnpike, interstate. *See also the table.* **2** *a step on the road to recovery* WAY, path, route, course.
■ **on the road** ON TOUR, touring, travelling.

Roads

access road	lumber road
back road	plank road ✦
bush road	ring road
byroad	section road
concession (line/road) ✦	service road
corduroy road *hist.*	side road
dirt road	tote road
frontage road	town line
grid road ✦	trail
ice road ✦	trunk road ✦
line ✦(*Nfld*)	unassumed road
logging road	winter (ice) road ✦

roadblock ▶ **noun** BARRIER, barricade, obstruction, checkpoint.

road hockey (*Cdn*) ▶ **noun** street hockey ✦, ball hockey ✦.

roam ▶ **verb** WANDER, rove, ramble, drift, walk, traipse; range, travel, tramp, traverse, trek; *informal* cruise, mosey; *formal* perambulate; *archaic* peregrinate.

roar ▶ **noun** **1** *the roars of the crowd* SHOUT, bellow, yell, cry, howl; clamour; *informal* holler. **2** *the roar of the sea* BOOM, crash, rumble, roll, thundering. **3** *roars of laughter* GUFFAW, howl, hoot, shriek, gale, peal.
▶ **verb** **1** '*Get out!*' *roared Angus* BELLOW, yell, shout, bawl, howl; *informal* holler. **2** *thunder roared* BOOM, rumble, crash, roll, thunder. **3** *the movie left them roaring* GUFFAW, laugh, hoot; *informal* split one's sides, be rolling in the aisles, be doubled up, crack up, be in stitches, die laughing. **4** *a motorbike roared past* SPEED, zoom, whiz, flash; belt, tear, zip, bomb.

roaring ▶ **adjective** **1** *a roaring fire* BLAZING, burning, flaming. **2** (*informal*) *a roaring success* ENORMOUS, huge, massive, (very) great, tremendous; complete, out-and-out, thorough; *informal* rip-roaring, whopping, fantastic.

roast ▶ **verb** **1** *potatoes roasted in olive oil* COOK, bake, grill, broil. **2** (*informal*) *they roasted him for wasting time.* See CRITICIZE.

roasting (*informal*) ▶ **noun** *the boss gave him a roasting.* See LECTURE *noun* sense 2.

rob ▶ **verb** **1** *the gang robbed the local bank* BURGLE, burglarize, steal from, hold up, break into; raid, loot, plunder, pillage, burglarize; *informal* knock off, stick up. **2** *he robbed an old woman* STEAL FROM; *informal* mug, jump, clip. **3** *she was robbed of her savings* CHEAT, swindle, defraud; *informal* do out of, con out of, fleece; *informal* stiff. **4** (*informal*) *it cost $70 — I was robbed* OVERCHARGE; *informal* rip off, sting, have, diddle, gouge. **5** *a dubious call robbed him of his title* DEPRIVE, strip, divest; deny.

robber ▶ **noun** BURGLAR, thief, housebreaker, mugger, shoplifter, purse-snatcher; stealer, pilferer, raider, looter, plunderer, pillager; bandit, highwayman; *informal* crook, yegg; *literary* brigand.

robbery ▶ **noun** **1** *they were arrested for the robbery* BURGLARY, theft, thievery, stealing, breaking and entering, home invasion, housebreaking, larceny, shoplifting, purse-snatching; embezzlement, fraud; holdup, break-in, raid; *informal* mugging, smash-and-grab, stickup, heist, B and E. **2** (*informal*) *Six bucks? That's robbery!* A SWINDLE; *informal* a con, a rip-off, a rip.

robe ▶ **noun** **1** *the women wore black robes* CLOAK, kaftan, djellaba, wrap, mantle, cape, kimono, wrapper. **2** *coronation robes* GARB, regalia, costume, finery; garments, clothes; *formal* apparel; *archaic* raiment, habiliments, vestments. **3** *priestly robes* VESTMENT, surplice, cassock, soutane, rochet, alb, dalmatic, chasuble, tunicle, Geneva gown; canonicals. **4** *he pulled on his robe after swimming* DRESSING GOWN, bathrobe, housecoat, wrapper, cover-up.
▶ **verb** *he robed for Mass* DRESS, vest, clothe oneself; *formal* enrobe.

robot ▶ **noun** AUTOMATON, android, golem; *informal* bot, droid.

robust ▶ **adjective** **1** *a large, robust man* STRONG, vigorous, sturdy, tough, powerful, solid, muscular, sinewy, rugged, hardy, strapping, brawny, burly, husky; healthy, (fighting) fit, hale and hearty, lusty, in fine fettle; *informal* beefy, hunky. **2** *these knives are robust* DURABLE, resilient, tough, hard-wearing, long-lasting, sturdy, strong. **3** *her usual robust view of things* DOWN-TO-EARTH, practical, realistic, pragmatic, common-sense, commonsensical, matter-of-fact, businesslike, sensible, unromantic, unsentimental; *informal* no-nonsense. **4** *a robust red wine* STRONG, full-bodied, flavourful, rich.
– OPPOSITES: frail, fragile, romantic, insipid.

rock[1] ▶ **verb** **1** *the ship rocked on the water* MOVE TO AND FRO, move back and forth, sway, see-saw; roll, pitch, plunge, toss, lurch, reel, list; wobble, oscillate. **2** *the building began to rock* SHAKE, vibrate, quake, tremble. **3** *Bay Street was rocked by the news* STUN, shock, stagger, astonish, startle, surprise, shake (up), take aback, throw, unnerve, disconcert. **4** (*informal*) *this game totally rocks* KICK BUTT, blow one away, blow one's mind, rock one's world, be cool, be impressive, be on fire.

rock[2] ▶ **noun** **1** *a gully strewn with rocks* BOULDER, stone, pebble. **2** *a castle built on a rock* CRAG, cliff, outcrop. **3** *Tony was the rock on which they relied* FOUNDATION, cornerstone, support, prop, mainstay; tower of strength, bulwark, anchor. **4** (*informal*) *she wore a massive rock* DIAMOND (RING), jewel, precious stone.
– RELATED TERMS: litho-, petro-.
■ **on the rocks** (*informal*) **1** *her marriage is on the rocks* IN DIFFICULTY, in trouble, breaking up, over; in tatters, in ruins, ruined. **2** *a Scotch on the rocks* WITH ICE, on ice.

rocket ▶ **noun** **1** *guerrillas fired rockets at them* MISSILE, projectile. **2** *they lit some colourful rockets* FIREWORK, firecracker, Roman candle, banger.
▶ **verb** **1** *prices have rocketed* SHOOT UP, soar, increase, rise, escalate, spiral; *informal* go through the roof. **2** *they rocketed into the alley* SPEED, zoom, shoot, whiz, tear, career, bomb; *informal* barrel, hightail it.
– OPPOSITES: plummet.

rocky[1] ▶ **adjective** *a rocky path* STONY, pebbly, shingly; rough, bumpy; craggy, mountainous.

rocky[2] ▶ **adjective** **1** *that table's rocky* UNSTEADY, shaky, unstable, wobbly, tottery, rickety, flimsy. **2** *a rocky marriage* DIFFICULT, problematic, precarious, unstable, unreliable, undependable; *informal* iffy, up and down.
– OPPOSITES: steady, stable.

rococo ▶ **adjective** ORNATE, fancy, elaborate, extravagant, baroque; fussy, busy, ostentatious, showy; flowery, florid, flamboyant, high-flown,

Rocks

Metamorphic	Sedimentary
amphibolite	arenite
blueschist	argillite
eclogite	breccia
epidiorite	chalk
epidosite	chert
gneiss	claystone
granulite	coal
hornfels	conglomerate
lazurite	diatomite
marble	dolomite
mica schist	flint
mylonite	ironstone
phyllite	limestone
psammite	marl
pyroxenite	mudstone
quartzite	oil shale
schist	oolite
serpentinite	pholphorite
slate	pisolite
verdite	radiolarite

rag	lava
rudite	monzonite
sandstone	obsidian
shale	ophiolite
siltstone	pegmatite
tillite	peridotite
	phonolite
Igneous	picrite
andesite	porphyry
anorthosite	pumice
aplite	rhyolite
basalt	syenite
diorite	tephrite
dolerite	tonalite
dunite	trachyte
elvan	trap rock
felsite	tuff
gabbro	variolite
granite	vitrophyre
greenstone	
kimberlite	
lamprophyre	

magniloquent, orotund, bombastic, overwrought, overblown, inflated, turgid; *informal* highfalutin.
— OPPOSITES: plain.

rod ▶ noun **1** *an iron rod* BAR, stick, pole, baton, staff; shaft, strut, rail, spoke. **2** *the ceremonial rod* STAFF, mace, sceptre. **3** *instruction was accompanied by the rod* CORPORAL PUNISHMENT, the cane, the lash, the birch; beating, flogging, caning, birching.

rodent ▶ noun. See table.

Rodents

agouti	jumping mouse
Arctic ground squirrel	kangaroo mouse
bandicoot rat	kangaroo rat
beaver	lemming
black squirrel	marmot
brown rat	mole rat
bushy-tailed woodrat	mouse
capybara	muskrat
cavy	Norway rat
chinchilla	paca
chipmunk	pack rat
collared lemming	pocket gopher
coypu	porcupine
deer mouse	prairie dog
dormouse	rat
field mouse	red squirrel
flying squirrel	Richardson's ground
gerbil	squirrel
golden hamster	sewer rat
gopher	squirrel
grey squirrel	suslik
groundhog	viscacha
ground squirrel	vole
guinea pig	water rat
hamster	water vole
hoary marmot	woodchuck
house mouse	woodmouse
jerboa	woodrat

rodeo ▶ noun. See table.

rogue ▶ noun **1** *a rogue without ethics* SCOUNDREL, villain, miscreant, reprobate, rascal, good-for-nothing, ne'er-do-well, wretch; *informal* rat,

Rodeo Events

bareback riding	mutton busting
barrel racing	saddle bronc riding
bull riding	steer roping
calf roping	steer
chuckwagon racing	wrestling/bulldogging

dog, louse, crook; *informal, dated* cad; *archaic* blackguard, picaroon, knave. **2** *your boy's a little rogue* RASCAL, imp, devil, monkey; *informal* scamp, scalawag, monster, horror, terror, hellion.

roguish ▶ adjective **1** *a roguish character* UNPRINCIPLED, dishonest, deceitful, unscrupulous, untrustworthy, shameless; wicked, villainous; *informal* shady, scoundrelly, rascally; *archaic* knavish. **2** *a roguish grin* MISCHIEVOUS, playful, teasing, cheeky, naughty, wicked, impish, devilish, arch; *informal* waggish.

roister ▶ verb ENJOY ONESELF, celebrate, revel, carouse, frolic, romp, have fun, make merry, rollick; *informal* party, live it up, whoop it up, have a ball, make whoopee.

role ▶ noun **1** *a small role in the film* PART; character, cameo. **2** *his role as class president* CAPACITY, position, job, post, office, duty, responsibility, mantle, place; function, part.

roll ▶ verb **1** *the bottle rolled down the table* BOWL, turn over and over, spin, rotate. **2** *waiters rolled in the trolleys* WHEEL, push, trundle. **3** *we rolled past fields* TRAVEL, go, move, pass, cruise, sweep. **4** *the months rolled by* PASS, go by, slip by, fly by, elapse, wear on, march on. **5** *tears rolled down her cheeks* FLOW, run, course, stream, pour, spill, trickle. **6** *the mist rolled in* BILLOW, undulate, tumble. **7** *he rolled his handkerchief into a ball* WIND, coil, fold, curl; twist. **8** *roll out the pastry* FLATTEN, level; even out. **9** *they rolled about with laughter* STAGGER, lurch, reel, totter, teeter, wobble. **10** *the ship began to roll* LURCH, toss, rock, pitch, plunge, sway, reel, list, keel. **11** *thunder rolled* RUMBLE, reverberate, echo, resound, boom, roar, grumble.
▶ noun **1** *a roll of wrapping paper* CYLINDER, tube, scroll; bolt. **2** *a roll of film* REEL, spool. **3** *a roll of $20 bills* WAD, bundle. **4** *a roll of the dice* THROW, toss, turn, spin.

Rooms

anteroom	cubbyhole	laundry room	rumpus room
assembly room	cutting room	lavatory	salesroom
attic	darkroom	library	salon
backroom	day room	living room	schoolroom
ballroom	den	lobby	scullery
barroom	dining room	locker room	showroom
basement	drawing-room	loft	sitting room
bathroom	dressing room	lounge	solarium
bedchamber	emergency room	lunchroom	staff room
bedroom	engine room	mailroom	stockroom
boardroom	family room	men's room	storeroom
boiler room	fitting room	morning room	strongroom
boudoir	Florida room	mud room	studio
cell	foyer	Muskoka room ♣	study
cellar	front room	newsroom	suite
chamber	games room	nursery	sunroom
change room	garret	office	tack room
chapel	great room	operating room	throne room
checkroom	green room	operations room	utility room
classroom	guardroom	pantry	vestibule
cloakroom	gunroom	parlour	waiting room
coatroom	hall	playroom	wardroom
cold room	homeroom	poolroom	washroom
common room	kitchen	powder room	water closet
conservatory	kitchenette	recovery room	weight room
courtroom	ladies' room	rec room	women's room
crying room	larder	restroom	workroom

5 *crusty rolls* BREAD ROLL, bun, bagel, hoagie, kaiser. *See table at* BREAD. **6** *the electoral roll* LIST, register, directory, record, file, index, catalogue, inventory; census. **7** *a roll of thunder* RUMBLE, reverberation, echo, boom, clap, crack, roar, grumble.

■ **roll in** (*informal*) **1** *money has been rolling in* POUR IN, flood in, flow in. **2** *he rolled in at nine o'clock* ARRIVE, turn up, appear, show one's face; *informal* show up, roll up, blow in.

■ **rolling in it** (*informal*). *See* RICH *sense* 1.

■ **roll something out** UNROLL, spread out, unfurl, unfold, open (out), unwind, uncoil.

■ **roll something up** FOLD (UP), furl, wind up, coil (up), bundle up.

■ **roll up** (*informal*). *See* ROLL IN *sense* 2.

rollicking ▶ adjective *a rollicking party* LIVELY, boisterous, exuberant, spirited; riotous, noisy, wild, rowdy, roisterous, knockabout, rambunctious.

roly-poly ▶ adjective (*informal*) CHUBBY, plump, fat, stout, rotund, round, dumpy, chunky, portly, overweight, fleshy, paunchy, bulky, corpulent; *informal* tubby, pudgy, beefy, porky, blubbery, zaftig, corn-fed.
— OPPOSITES: skinny.

romance ▶ noun **1** *their romance blossomed* LOVE, passion, ardour, adoration, devotion; affection, fondness, attachment. **2** *he's had many romances* LOVE AFFAIR, relationship, liaison, courtship, attachment; flirtation, dalliance. **3** *an author of historical romances* LOVE STORY, novel; romantic fiction; *informal* tearjerker, bodice-ripper. **4** *the romance of the Far East* MYSTERY, glamour, excitement, exoticism, mystique; appeal, allure, charm.
▶ verb **1** (*dated*) *he was romancing Meg* WOO, chase, pursue; go out with, seduce; *informal* see, go steady with, date; *dated* court, make love to. **2** *I am romancing the past* ROMANTICIZE, idealize, paint a rosy picture of.

romantic ▶ adjective **1** *he's so romantic* LOVING, amorous, passionate, tender, affectionate; *informal* lovey-dovey. **2** *a romantic picture* SENTIMENTAL, mawkish, sickly, saccharine, syrupy; *informal* slushy, mushy, schmaltzy, gooey, treacly, cheesy, corny, sappy, soppy, cornball. **3** *a romantic setting* IDYLLIC, picturesque, fairy-tale; beautiful, lovely, charming, pretty. **4** *romantic notions of life in rural communities* IDEALISTIC, idealized, romanticized, unrealistic, fanciful, impractical; head-in-the-clouds, starry-eyed, optimistic, hopeful, visionary, Utopian, fairy-tale.
— OPPOSITES: unsentimental, realistic.
▶ noun *an incurable romantic* IDEALIST, sentimentalist, romanticist; dreamer, visionary, Utopian, Don Quixote, fantasist, fantast.
— OPPOSITES: realist.

Romeo ▶ noun LADIES' MAN, Don Juan, Casanova, Lothario, womanizer, playboy, lover, seducer, philanderer, flirt; gigolo; *informal* lady-killer, stud, chick/babe magnet.

romp ▶ verb **1** *two fox cubs romped playfully* PLAY, frolic, frisk, gambol, skip, prance, caper, cavort, rollick; *dated* sport. **2** *South Africa romped to a win* SAIL, coast, sweep; win hands down, run away with it; *informal* win by a mile, walk it.

roof
■ **hit the roof** (*informal*) BE VERY ANGRY, be furious, lose one's temper; *informal* go mad, go crazy, go wild, go bananas, have a fit, blow one's top, go postal, go ballistic, go up the wall, go off the deep end, go ape, flip.

room ▶ noun **1** *there isn't much room* SPACE; headroom, legroom; area, expanse, extent; *informal* elbow room. **2** *room for improvement* SCOPE, capacity, leeway, latitude; freedom; opportunity, chance. **3** *she wandered around the room* CHAMBER. *See table.* **4** *he had rooms at Chester Court* LODGINGS, quarters; accommodation; a suite, an apartment, an efficiency unit ♣, bachelor (apartment) ♣; *informal* a pad, digs.
▶ verb *she roomed there in September* LODGE, board, live,

stay; be quartered, be housed, be billeted; *formal* dwell, reside, sojourn.

roomy ► adjective SPACIOUS, capacious, sizeable, generous, big, large, extensive; voluminous, ample; *formal* commodious.
– OPPOSITES: cramped.

roost ► noun PERCH, branch, home, accommodation.
► verb PERCH, rest, sleep, overnight.

root ► noun 1 *a plant's roots* rootstock, tuber, rootlet; *Botany* rhizome, radicle. 2 *the root of the problem* SOURCE, origin, germ, beginnings, genesis; cause, reason, basis, foundation, bottom, seat; core, heart, nub, essence; *informal* ground zero. 3 *he rejected his roots* ORIGINS, beginnings, family, ancestors, predecessors, heritage; birthplace, homeland.
– RELATED TERMS: radical, rhizo-.
► verb 1 *has the shoot rooted?* TAKE ROOT, grow roots, establish, strike, take. 2 *root the cuttings* PLANT, bed out, sow. 3 *he rooted around in the cupboard* RUMMAGE, hunt, search, rifle, delve, forage, dig, nose, poke.
■ **put down roots** SETTLE, establish oneself, set up home.
■ **root and branch 1** *the firm should be eradicated, root and branch* COMPLETELY, entirely, wholly, totally, thoroughly. 2 *a root-and-branch reform* COMPLETE, total, thorough, radical.
■ **root for** (*informal*) CHEER (ON), applaud, support, encourage.
■ **root something out 1** *the hedge was rooted out* UPROOT, deracinate, pull up, grub out. 2 *root out corruption* ERADICATE, eliminate, weed out, destroy, wipe out, stamp out, extirpate, abolish, end, put a stop to. 3 *he rooted out a dark secret* UNEARTH, dig up, bring to light, uncover, discover, dredge up, ferret out, expose.
■ **take root 1** *leave the plants to take root* GERMINATE, sprout, establish, strike, take. 2 *Christianity took root in Persia* BECOME ESTABLISHED, take hold; develop, thrive, flourish.

rooted ► adjective 1 *views rooted in Inuit culture* EMBEDDED, fixed, established, entrenched, ingrained. 2 *Neil was rooted to the spot* FROZEN, riveted, paralyzed, glued, fixed; stock-still, motionless, unmoving.

rootless ► adjective ITINERANT, unsettled, drifting, roving, footloose; homeless, of no fixed abode.

rootsy ► adjective TRADITIONAL, folksy, uncommercialized, authentic, real, time-honoured, old-fashioned; bluesy, acoustic; *informal* trad.

rope ► noun CORD, cable, line, hawser; string; lasso, lariat.
– RELATED TERMS: funicular.
► verb *his feet were roped together* TIE, bind, lash, truss; secure, moor, fasten, attach; hitch, tether, lasso.
■ **know the ropes** (*informal*) KNOW WHAT TO DO, know the routine, know one's way around, know one's stuff, know what's what; be experienced; *informal* know the drill, know the score, be streetwise.
■ **rope someone in/into** PERSUADE TO/INTO, talk into, trap into, inveigle into; enlist, engage.

ropy ► adjective *ropy strands of lava* STRINGY, thready, fibrous, filamentous; viscous, sticky, mucilaginous, thick.

roster ► noun SCHEDULE, list, listing, register, agenda, calendar, table.

rostrum ► noun DAIS, platform, podium, stage; soapbox.

rosy ► adjective 1 *a rosy complexion* PINK, pinkish, roseate, reddish, peaches-and-cream; glowing, healthy, fresh, radiant, blooming; blushing, flushed; ruddy, high-coloured, florid, rubicund. 2 *his future looks rosy* PROMISING, optimistic, auspicious, hopeful, encouraging, favourable, bright, golden; *informal* upbeat.
– OPPOSITES: pale, bleak.

rot ► verb 1 *the floorboards rotted* DECAY, decompose, become rotten; disintegrate, crumble, perish. 2 *the meat began to rot* GO BAD, go off, spoil; moulder, putrefy, fester. 3 *poor neighbourhoods have been left to rot* DETERIORATE, degenerate, decline, decay, go to rack and ruin, go to seed, go downhill; *informal* go to pot, go to the dogs.
– RELATED TERMS: sapro-.
– OPPOSITES: improve.
► noun 1 *the leaves turned black with rot* DECAY, decomposition, mould, mildew, blight, canker; putrefaction. 2 *traditionalists said the rot had set in* DETERIORATION, decline; corruption, cancer.

rotary ► adjective ROTATING, rotational, revolving, turning, spinning, gyrating; *formal* rotatory.

rotate ► verb 1 *the wheels rotate continually* REVOLVE, go round, turn (round), spin, gyrate, whirl, twirl, swivel, circle, pivot. 2 *many nurses rotate jobs* ALTERNATE, take turns, change, switch, interchange, exchange, swap; move around.

rotation ► noun 1 *the rotation of the wheels* REVOLVING, turning, spinning, gyration, circling. 2 *a rotation of the Earth* TURN, revolution, orbit, spin. 3 *each member is chair for six months in rotation* SEQUENCE, succession; alternation, cycle.
– RELATED TERMS: gyro-.

rote
■ **by rote** MECHANICALLY, automatically, unthinkingly, mindlessly; from memory, by heart.

rotten ► adjective 1 *rotten meat* DECAYING, rotting, bad, off, decomposing, putrid, putrescent, perished, mouldy, mouldering, mildewy, rancid, festering, fetid; maggoty, wormy. 2 *rotten teeth* DECAYING, decayed, carious, black; disintegrating, crumbling. 3 *he's rotten to the core* CORRUPT, unprincipled, dishonest, dishonourable, unscrupulous, untrustworthy, immoral; villainous, bad, wicked, evil, iniquitous, venal; *informal* crooked. 4 (*informal*) *a rotten thing to do* NASTY, unkind, unpleasant, obnoxious, vile, contemptible, despicable, shabby, loathsome; spiteful, mean, low, malicious, hateful, hurtful; unfair, uncharitable, uncalled for; *informal* dirty, lowdown. 5 (*informal*) *he was a rotten singer* BAD, poor, dreadful, awful, terrible, frightful, atrocious, hopeless, inadequate, inferior, substandard; *informal* crummy, pathetic, useless, lousy, appalling, abysmal. 6 (*informal*) *I feel rotten about it* GUILTY, conscience-stricken, remorseful, ashamed, shamefaced, chastened, contrite, sorry, regretful, repentant, penitent. 7 (*informal*) *I felt rotten with that cold. See* ILL *adjective sense 1.*
– OPPOSITES: fresh, honourable, kind, good, well.

rotund ► adjective 1 *a small, rotund man* PLUMP, chubby, fat, stout, portly, dumpy, round, chunky, overweight, heavy, paunchy, ample; flabby, fleshy, bulky, heavy-set, corpulent, obese; *informal* tubby, roly-poly, pudgy, porky, blubbery, zaftig, corn-fed. 2 *rotund cauldrons* ROUND, bulbous, spherical, spheric.
– OPPOSITES: thin.

roué ► noun LIBERTINE, rake, debauchee, degenerate, profligate; lecher, seducer, womanizer, philanderer, adulterer, Don Juan, Lothario; *informal* lady-killer, skirt chaser, lech, dirty old man, goat.

rough ▶ adjective **1** *rough ground* UNEVEN, irregular, bumpy, lumpy, knobbly, stony, rocky, rugged, rutted, pitted, rutty. **2** *the terrier's rough coat* COARSE, bristly, scratchy, prickly; shaggy, hairy, bushy. **3** *rough skin* DRY, leathery, weather-beaten; chapped, calloused, scaly, scabrous. **4** *his voice was rough* GRUFF, hoarse, harsh, rasping, raspy, croaking, croaky, husky, throaty, gravelly, guttural. **5** *rough red wine* SHARP, sour, acidic, acid, vinegary, acidulous. **6** *he gets rough when he's drunk* VIOLENT, brutal, vicious; AGGRESSIVE, belligerent, pugnacious, thuggish; boisterous, rowdy, disorderly, unruly, riotous. **7** *a machine that can take rough handling* CARELESS, clumsy, inept, unskilful. **8** *rough manners* BOORISH, loutish, oafish, brutish, coarse, crude, uncouth, vulgar, unrefined, unladylike, ungentlemanly, uncultured; unmannerly, impolite, discourteous, uncivil, ungracious, rude. **9** *rough seas* TURBULENT, stormy, tempestuous, violent, heavy, heaving, choppy. **10** *(informal) I've had a rough time* DIFFICULT, hard, tough, bad, unpleasant; demanding, arduous. **11** *(informal) you were a bit rough on her* HARSH, hard, tough, stern, severe, unfair, unjust; insensitive, nasty, cruel, unkind, unsympathetic, brutal, heartless, merciless. **12** *(informal) I'm feeling rough. See* ILL *adjective* sense 1. **13** *a rough draft* PRELIMINARY, hasty, quick, sketchy, cursory, basic, crude, rudimentary, raw, unpolished; incomplete, unfinished. **14** *a rough estimate* APPROXIMATE, inexact, imprecise, vague, estimated, hazy; *informal* ballpark. **15** *the accommodations are rather rough* PLAIN, BASIC, simple, rough and ready, rude, crude, primitive, Spartan.
— OPPOSITES: smooth, sleek, soft, dulcet, sweet, gentle, careful, refined, calm, easy, kind, well, exact, luxurious.
▶ noun *the artist's initial roughs* SKETCH, draft, outline, mock-up.
▶ verb *rough the surface with sandpaper* ROUGHEN.
■ **rough something out** DRAFT, sketch out, outline, block out, mock up.
■ **rough someone up** *(informal)* BEAT UP, attack, assault, knock about/around, batter, manhandle; *informal* do over, beat the living daylights out of.

rough and ready ▶ adjective BASIC, simple, crude, unrefined, unsophisticated; makeshift, provisional, stop-gap, improvised, extempory, ad hoc; hurried, sketchy.

rough-and-tumble ▶ adjective *rough-and-tumble play* DISORDERLY, unruly, boisterous, rough, riotous, rowdy, knockabout, noisy, loud.
▶ noun *a political rough-and-tumble* SCUFFLE, fight, brawl, melee, free-for-all, fracas, rumpus; horseplay; *informal* scrap, dust-up, punch-up, shindy, roughhouse.

roughly ▶ adverb **1** *he shoved her roughly away* VIOLENTLY, forcefully, forcibly, abruptly, unceremoniously. **2** *they treated him roughly* HARSHLY, unkindly, unsympathetically; brutally, savagely, mercilessly, cruelly, heartlessly. **3** *roughly $2.4 million* APPROXIMATELY, (round) about, around, circa, in the region of, something like, in/of the order of, or so, or thereabouts, more or less, give or take; nearly, close to, approaching.

roughneck ▶ noun *(informal). See* RUFFIAN.

round ▶ adjective **1** *a round window* CIRCULAR, disc-shaped, ring-shaped, hoop-shaped; spherical, spheroidal, globular, globe-shaped, orb-shaped; cylindrical; bulbous, rounded, rotund; *technical* annular, discoid. **2** *round cheeks* PLUMP, chubby, fat,

full. **3** *his deep, round voice* SONOROUS, resonant, rich, full, mellow, mellifluous, orotund. **4** *a round dozen* COMPLETE, entire, whole, full. **5** *she berated him in round terms* CANDID, frank, direct, honest, truthful, straightforward, plain, blunt, forthright, bald, explicit, unequivocal, unmistakable, categorical.
— OPPOSITES: thin, reedy.
▶ noun **1** *mould the dough into rounds* BALL, sphere, globe, orb, circle, disc, ring, hoop; *technical* annulus. **2** *a policeman on his rounds* CIRCUIT, beat, route, tour. **3** *the first round of the contest* STAGE, level; heat, game, bout, contest; go-round. **4** *an endless round of parties* SUCCESSION, sequence, series, cycle. **5** *the gun fires thirty rounds per second* BULLET, cartridge, shell, shot.
▶ preposition & adverb *See* AROUND.
▶ verb *the ship rounded the point* GO AROUND, travel around, skirt, circumnavigate, orbit.
■ **round about** *See* AROUND *preposition* sense 3.
■ **round the bend** *See* MAD sense 1.
■ **round the clock 1** *we're working round the clock* DAY AND NIGHT, night and day, all the time, {morning, noon, and night}, continuously, non-stop, steadily, unremittingly; *informal* 24-7. **2** *round-the-clock supervision* CONTINUOUS, constant, non-stop, continual, uninterrupted.
■ **round something off 1** *the square edges were rounded off* SMOOTH OFF, plane off, sand off, level off, blunt. **2** *the party rounded off a successful year* COMPLETE, finish off, crown, cap, top; conclude, close, end.
■ **round on someone** SNAP AT, attack, turn on, let fly at, lash out at, hit out at; *informal* bite someone's head off, jump down someone's throat, lay into, tear into, light into.
■ **round someone/something up** GATHER TOGETHER, herd together, muster, marshal, rally, assemble, collect, group, corral.

roundabout ▶ adjective **1** *a roundabout route* CIRCUITOUS, indirect, meandering, serpentine, tortuous. **2** *I asked in a roundabout sort of way* INDIRECT, oblique, circuitous, circumlocutory, periphrastic, digressive, long-winded; evasive.
— OPPOSITES: direct.

roundly ▶ adverb **1** *he was roundly condemned* VEHEMENTLY, emphatically, fiercely, forcefully, severely; plainly, frankly, candidly. **2** *she was roundly defeated* UTTERLY, completely, thoroughly, decisively, conclusively, heavily, soundly.

round-trip ▶ adjective *a round-trip ticket* RETURN, two-way.

roundup ▶ noun **1** *a cattle roundup* ASSEMBLY, muster, rally, rodeo. **2** *the sports roundup* SUMMARY, synopsis, overview, review, outline, digest, précis, wrap-up; *informal* recap.

rouse ▶ verb **1** *he roused Ralph at dawn* WAKE (UP), awaken, arouse; *formal* waken. **2** *she roused and looked around* WAKE UP, awake, awaken, come to, get up, rise, bestir oneself; *formal* arise. **3** *he roused the crowd* STIR UP, excite, galvanize, electrify, stimulate, inspire, inspirit, move, inflame, agitate, goad, provoke; incite, spur on, light a fire under. **4** *he's got a temper when he's roused* PROVOKE, annoy, anger, infuriate, madden, incense, vex, irk; *informal* aggravate. **5** *her disappearance roused my suspicions* AROUSE, awaken, prompt, provoke, stimulate, pique, trigger, spark off, touch off, kindle, elicit.
— OPPOSITES: calm, pacify, allay.

rousing ▶ adjective STIRRING, inspiring, exciting, stimulating, moving, electrifying, invigorating, energizing, exhilarating; enthusiastic, vigorous, spirited.

rout ▶ noun **1** *the army's ignominious rout* RETREAT, flight. **2** *the game was a rout for Winnipeg* CRUSHING DEFEAT, trouncing, annihilation; debacle, fiasco; *informal* licking, hammering, thrashing, drubbing, massacre.
– OPPOSITES: victory.
▶ verb **1** *his army was routed* PUT TO FLIGHT, drive off, scatter; defeat, beat, conquer, vanquish, crush, overpower. **2** *he routed the defending champion*. See DEFEAT *verb* sense 1.

route ▶ noun *a different route to school* WAY, course, road, path, direction; passage, journey.
▶ verb *inquiries are routed to the relevant desk* DIRECT, send, convey, dispatch, forward.

routine ▶ noun **1** *his morning routine* PROCEDURE, practice, pattern, drill, regimen; program, schedule, plan; formula, method, system; customs, habits; wont. **2** *a stand-up routine* ACT, performance, number, turn, piece; *informal* spiel, patter, shtick.
▶ adjective *a routine health check* STANDARD, regular, customary, normal, usual, ordinary, typical; everyday, common, commonplace, conventional, habitual, wonted.
– OPPOSITES: unusual.

rove ▶ verb WANDER, roam, ramble, drift, meander; range, travel.

rover ▶ noun WANDERER, traveller, globetrotter, drifter, roamer, itinerant, transient; nomad, gypsy, tramp, vagrant, vagabond, hobo.

row¹ ▶ noun **1** *rows of children* LINE, column, file, queue; procession, chain, string, succession. **2** *the middle row of seats* TIER, line, rank, bank.
■ **in a row** *three days in a row* CONSECUTIVELY, in succession; running, straight.

row² (*informal*) ▶ noun *the couple was having a row* ARGUMENT, quarrel, squabble, fight, contretemps, falling-out, disagreement, dispute, clash, altercation, shouting match; *informal* tiff, set-to, run-in, blow-up, spat, bust-up.

rowdy ▶ adjective *rowdy youths* UNRULY, disorderly, obstreperous, riotous, undisciplined, uncontrollable, ungovernable, disruptive, out of control, rough, wild, lawless; boisterous, uproarious, noisy, loud, clamorous; *informal* rambunctious.
– OPPOSITES: peaceful.
▶ noun *the bar was full of rowdies* RUFFIAN, troublemaker, lout, hooligan, thug, hoodlum; *informal* tough, yahoo, punk.

royal ▶ adjective **1** *the royal prerogative* REGAL, kingly, queenly, princely, sovereign, monarchical. **2** *a royal welcome* EXCELLENT, fine, magnificent, splendid, superb, wonderful, first-rate, first-class; *informal* fantastic, great, tremendous.

rub ▶ verb **1** *Sally rubbed her arm* MASSAGE, knead; stroke, pat. **2** *he rubbed sunscreen on her back* APPLY, smear, spread, work in. **3** *my shoes rub painfully* CHAFE, pinch; hurt, be painful.
▶ noun **1** *she gave his back a rub* MASSAGE, rub-down. **2** *I gave my shoes a rub* POLISH, wipe, clean. **3** *it's too complicated—that's the rub* PROBLEM, difficulty, trouble, drawback, hindrance, impediment; snag, hitch, catch.
■ **rub something down** CLEAN, sponge, wash; groom.
■ **rub it in** (*informal*) EMPHASIZE, stress, underline,

highlight; go on, harp on; *informal* rub someone's nose in it.
■ **rub off on** BE TRANSFERRED TO, be passed on to, be transmitted to, be communicated to; affect, influence.
■ **rub something out** ERASE, delete, remove, efface, obliterate, expunge.
■ **rub elbows with** ASSOCIATE WITH, mingle with, fraternize with, socialize with, mix with, keep company with, consort with; *informal* hang around/out with, hobnob with.
■ **rub someone the wrong way** IRRITATE, annoy, irk, vex, provoke, displease, exasperate, infuriate, get on someone's nerves, put out, pique, upset, nettle, ruffle someone's feathers, make someone's hackles rise, try someone's patience, grate on; *informal* aggravate, get, get to, bug, miff, peeve, rile, needle, tick off, tee off, get under someone's skin, get in someone's hair, get/put someone's back up, get someone's goat, wind up, rankle, ride.

rubbish ▶ noun **1** *throw away that rubbish*. See GARBAGE sense 1. **2** *she's talking rubbish* NONSENSE, balderdash, gibberish, claptrap, blarney, moonshine, garbage; *informal* hogwash, baloney, jive, guff, tripe, drivel, bilge, bunk, BS, bafflegab, piffle, poppycock, hooey, twaddle, gobbledegook, codswallop, flapdoodle; *dated* bunkum, tommyrot.

rubble ▶ noun DEBRIS, remains, ruins, wreckage.

rubby ▶ noun See ALCOHOLIC *noun*.

ruckus ▶ noun DISTURBANCE, noise, racket, din, commotion, hubbub, fuss, uproar, furor, hue and cry, rumpus, ruction, fracas; *informal* to-do, hullabaloo, hoo-ha, ballyhoo, stink, kerfuffle, foofaraw.

ruddy ▶ adjective *a ruddy complexion* ROSY, red, pink, roseate, rubicund; healthy, glowing, fresh; flushed, blushing; florid, high-coloured; *literary* rubescent.
– OPPOSITES: pale.

rude ▶ adjective **1** *a rude man* ILL-MANNERED, bad-mannered, impolite, discourteous, uncivil, unmannerly, mannerless; impertinent, insolent, impudent, disrespectful, cheeky; churlish, curt, brusque, brash, offhand, short, sharp; offensive, insulting, derogatory, disparaging, abusive; tactless, undiplomatic, uncomplimentary. **2** *rude jokes* VULGAR, coarse, smutty, dirty, filthy, crude, lewd, obscene, off-colour, offensive, indelicate, tasteless; risqué, naughty, ribald, bawdy, racy; *informal* blue; *euphemistic* adult. **3** *a rude awakening* ABRUPT, sudden, sharp, startling; unpleasant, nasty, harsh. **4** (*dated*) *a rude cabin* PRIMITIVE, crude, rudimentary, rough, simple, basic.
– OPPOSITES: polite, clean, luxurious.

rudimentary ▶ adjective **1** *rudimentary carpentry skills* BASIC, elementary, primary, fundamental, essential. **2** *the equipment was rudimentary* PRIMITIVE, crude, simple, unsophisticated, rough (and ready), makeshift. **3** *a rudimentary thumb* VESTIGIAL, undeveloped, incomplete; *Biology* abortive, primitive.
– OPPOSITES: advanced, sophisticated, developed.

rudiments ▶ plural noun BASICS, fundamentals, essentials, first principles, foundation; *informal* nuts and bolts, ABC's.

rue ▶ verb REGRET, be sorry about, feel remorseful about, repent of, reproach oneself for; deplore, lament, bemoan, bewail.

rueful ▶ adjective REGRETFUL, apologetic, sorry, remorseful, shamefaced, sheepish, abashed, hangdog, contrite, repentant, penitent, conscience-stricken, sorrowful, sad.

ruffian ▶ noun THUG, lout, hooligan, hoodlum, vandal, delinquent, rowdy, scoundrel, villain, rogue, roughneck, bully boy, brute; *informal* tough, bruiser, heavy, yahoo, goon, plug-ugly.

ruffle ▶ verb **1** *he ruffled her hair* DISARRANGE, tousle, dishevel, rumple, disorder, mess up, tangle; *informal* muss up. **2** *the wind ruffled the water* RIPPLE, riffle. **3** *don't let him ruffle you* ANNOY, irritate, vex, nettle, anger, exasperate; disconcert, unnerve, fluster, agitate, harass, upset, disturb, discomfit, put off, perturb, unsettle, bother, worry, trouble; *informal* rattle, faze, throw, get to, rile, needle, aggravate, bug, peeve.
— OPPOSITES: smooth, soothe.
▶ noun *a shirt with ruffles* FRILL, flounce, ruff, ruche, jabot, furbelow.

rug ▶ noun **1** *they sat on the rug* MAT, carpet, runner; hearth rug, floor cloth. See table at CARPET. **2** (*informal*) *who is he trying to fool with that rug* TOUPÉE, wig, hairpiece.

rugged ▶ adjective **1** *a rugged path* ROUGH, uneven, bumpy, rocky, stony, pitted, jagged, craggy. **2** *a rugged vehicle* ROBUST, durable, sturdy, strong, tough, resilient. **3** *rugged manly types* WELL-BUILT, burly, strong, muscular, muscly, brawny, strapping, husky, hulking; tough, hardy, robust, sturdy, lusty, solid; *informal* hunky, beefy. **4** *his rugged features* STRONG, craggy, rough-hewn; manly, masculine; irregular, weathered.
— OPPOSITES: smooth, flimsy, weedy, delicate.

ruin ▶ noun **1** *the buildings were saved from ruin* DISINTEGRATION, decay, disrepair, dilapidation, ruination; destruction, demolition, wreckage. **2** *the ruins of a church* REMAINS, remnants, fragments, relics; rubble, debris, wreckage. **3** *he was careening toward his ruin* DOWNFALL, collapse, defeat, undoing, failure, breakdown, ruination; Waterloo. **4** *shopkeepers are facing ruin* BANKRUPTCY, insolvency, penury, poverty, destitution, impoverishment, indigence; failure.
— OPPOSITES: preservation, triumph, wealth.
▶ verb **1** *don't ruin my plans* WRECK, destroy, spoil, mar, blight, shatter, dash, torpedo, scotch, mess up; sabotage; *informal* screw up, foul up, put the kibosh on, nix, scupper, scuttle. **2** *the bank's collapse ruined them all* BANKRUPT, make insolvent, impoverish, pauperize, wipe out, break, cripple, devastate; bring someone to their knees. **3** *a country ruined by civil war* DESTROY, devastate, lay waste, ravage; raze, demolish, wreck, wipe out, flatten.
— OPPOSITES: save, rebuild.
■ **in ruins 1** *the abbey is in ruins* DERELICT, ruined, in disrepair, falling to pieces, dilapidated, tumbledown, ramshackle, decrepit, decaying, ruinous. **2** *his career is in ruins* DESTROYED, ruined, in pieces, over, finished; *informal* in tatters, on the rocks, has had the biscuit ✚, done for.

ruined ▶ adjective **1** *a ruined building* DERELICT, in ruins, dilapidated, ruinous, tumbledown, ramshackle, decrepit, falling to pieces, crumbling, decaying, disintegrating. **2** *he was financially ruined* DESTITUTE, impoverished, bankrupt, pauperized, wiped out, wrecked, cleaned out.

ruinous ▶ adjective **1** *a ruinous trade war* DISASTROUS, devastating, catastrophic, calamitous, crippling, crushing, damaging, destructive, harmful; costly. **2** *ruinous interest rates* EXTORTIONATE, exorbitant,

excessive, sky-high, outrageous, inflated; *informal* criminal, steep.

rule ▶ noun **1** *health and safety rules* REGULATION, ruling, directive, order, act, law, statute, edict, canon, mandate, command, dictate, decree, fiat, injunction, commandment, stipulation, requirement, guideline, direction; *formal* ordinance. **2** *lateness was the general rule* PROCEDURE, practice, protocol, convention, norm, routine, custom, habit, wont; *formal* praxis. **3** *moderation is the golden rule* PRECEPT, principle, standard, axiom, truth, maxim. **4** *Punjab came under British rule* CONTROL, jurisdiction, command, power, dominion; government, administration, sovereignty, leadership, supremacy, authority; raj.
— RELATED TERMS: hegemonic, -cracy, -archy.
▶ verb **1** *El Salvador was ruled by Spain* GOVERN, preside over, control, lead, dominate, run, head, administer, manage. **2** *Elizabeth has ruled for fifty years* BE IN POWER, be in control, be in command, be in charge, govern; reign, be monarch, be sovereign. **3** *the judge ruled that they be set free* DECREE, order, pronounce, judge, adjudge, ordain; decide, find, determine, resolve, settle. **4** *chaos ruled* PREVAIL, predominate, be the order of the day, reign supreme; *formal* obtain.
■ **as a rule** USUALLY, generally, in general, normally, ordinarily, customarily, for the most part, on the whole, by and large, in the main, mainly, mostly, commonly, typically.
■ **rule something out** EXCLUDE, eliminate, disregard; preclude, prohibit, prevent, disallow.

ruler ▶ noun LEADER, sovereign, monarch, potentate, king, queen, emperor, empress, prince, princess; crowned head, head of state, president, premier, governor; overlord, chief, chieftain, lord; dictator, autocrat, Caesar. See also the table.
— OPPOSITES: subject.

Rulers

aga	prince
caesar	princess
caliph	queen
emir	raja
emperor	rani
empress	regent
kaiser	satrap
king	shah
khan	sheikh
maharajah	shogun
mikado	sovereign
monarch	sultan
negus	czar
pharaoh	viceroy

ruling ▶ noun *the judge's ruling* JUDGMENT, decision, adjudication, finding, verdict; pronouncement, resolution, decree, injunction.
▶ adjective **1** *the ruling class* GOVERNING, controlling, commanding, supreme, leading, dominant, ascendant, reigning. **2** *hockey was their ruling passion* MAIN, chief, principal, major, prime, dominating, foremost; predominant, central, focal; *informal* number-one.

rumble ▶ verb BOOM, thunder, roll, roar, resound, reverberate, echo, grumble.

ruminate ▶ verb THINK ABOUT, contemplate, consider, meditate on, muse on, mull over, ponder on/over, deliberate about/on, chew over, puzzle over; *formal* cogitate about.

rummage ▶ **verb** SEARCH, hunt, root about/around, ferret about/around, fish about/around, poke around in, dig, delve, go through, explore, sift through, rifle through.

rumour ▶ **noun** GOSSIP, hearsay, talk, tittle-tattle, speculation, word; (**rumours**) reports, stories, whispers, canards; *informal* the grapevine, the word on the street, (esp. *North*) the moccasin telegraph ✤, the buzz, the dirt, scuttlebutt, loose lips.

rump ▶ **noun** **1** *a smack on the rump* REAR (END), backside, seat; buttocks, cheeks, bottom; *informal* behind; sit-upon, buns, derrière, bum, butt, fanny, tush, tail, heinie, caboose; *humorous* fundament, posterior, stern; *Anatomy* nates. **2** *the rump of the army* REMAINDER, rest, remnant, remains.

rumple ▶ **verb** **1** *the sheet was rumpled* CRUMPLE, crease, wrinkle, crinkle, scrunch up. **2** *Ian rumpled her hair* RUFFLE, disarrange, tousle, dishevel, mess up; *informal* muss up.
— OPPOSITES: smooth.

rumpus ▶ **noun** See RUCKUS.

run ▶ **verb** **1** *she ran across the road* SPRINT, race, dart, rush, dash, hasten, hurry, scurry, scamper, bolt, fly, gallop, career, charge, shoot, hurtle, speed, zoom, go like lightning, go hell-bent for leather, go like the wind, go like a bat out of hell; jog, trot; *informal* tear, pelt, scoot, hotfoot it, leg it, belt, zip, whip, bomb, hightail it, barrel. **2** *the robbers turned and ran* FLEE, run away, run off, run for it, take flight, make off, take off, take to one's heels, make a break for it, bolt, make one's getaway, escape; *informal* beat it, clear off/out, vamoose, skedaddle, split, leg it, scram, light out, take a powder, make tracks. **3** *he ran in the marathon* COMPETE, take part, participate. **4** *a shiver ran down my spine* GO, pass, slide, move, travel. **5** *he ran his eye down the list* CAST, pass, skim, flick. **6** *the road runs the length of the valley* EXTEND, stretch, reach, continue. **7** *water ran from the eaves* FLOW, pour, stream, gush, flood, cascade, roll, course, spill, trickle, drip, dribble, leak. **8** *a bus runs to Sorrento* TRAVEL, go. **9** *I'll run you home* DRIVE, take, bring, ferry, chauffeur, give someone a ride/lift. **10** *he runs a transport company* BE IN CHARGE OF, manage, direct, control, head, govern, supervise, superintend, oversee; operate, conduct, own. **11** *it's expensive to run a car* MAINTAIN, keep, own, possess, have; drive. **12** *they ran some tests* CARRY OUT, do, perform, execute. **13** *he left the engine running* OPERATE, function, work, go; idle. **14** *the lease runs for twenty years* BE VALID, last, be in effect, be operative, continue, be effective. **15** *the show ran for two years* BE STAGED, be performed, be on, be mounted, be screened. **16** *he ran for president* STAND FOR, be a candidate for, be a contender for; re-offer ✤. **17** *the paper ran the story* PUBLISH, print, feature, carry, put out, release, issue. **18** *they run drugs* SMUGGLE, traffic in, deal in. **19** *they were run out of town* CHASE, drive, hound.
▶ **noun** **1** *his morning run* SPRINT, jog, dash, gallop, trot. **2** *she did the school run* ROUTE, journey; circuit, round, beat. **3** *an unbeaten run of victories* SERIES, succession, sequence, string, chain, streak, spell, stretch, spate. **4** *a run on umbrellas* DEMAND FOR, rush on. **5** *they had the run of the house* FREE USE OF, unrestricted access to. **6** *the usual run of movies* TYPE, kind, sort, variety, class. **7** *a chicken run* ENCLOSURE, pen, coop. **8** *a ski/toboggan run* SLOPE, track, piste, trail, slide. **9** *a run in her pantyhose* RIP, tear, snag, hole, pull.

■ **in the long run** EVENTUALLY, in the end, ultimately, when all is said and done, in the fullness of time, over the long haul, at the end of the day.
■ **on the run** ON THE LOOSE, at large, loose; running away, fleeing, fugitive; *informal* AWOL, on the lam.
■ **run across** MEET (BY CHANCE), come across, run into, chance on, stumble on, happen on; *informal* bump into.
■ **run after** (*informal*) PURSUE, chase; make advances to, flirt with; *informal* make up to, come on to, be all over; *dated* set one's cap at.
■ **run along** (*informal*) GO AWAY, be off with you, shoo; *informal* scram, buzz off, skedaddle, scat, beat it, get lost, shove off, clear off; *literary* begone.
■ **run around** (*informal*) BE UNFAITHFUL, have affairs, philander; *informal* play the field, sleep around, fool around.
■ **run away 1** *her attacker ran away.* See RUN verb sense 2. **2** *she ran away with the championship* WIN EASILY, win hands down; *informal* win by a mile.
■ **run down** DECLINE, degenerate, go downhill, go to seed, decay, go to rack and ruin; *informal* go to pot, go to the dogs.
■ **run someone down 1** *he was run down by joyriders* RUN OVER, knock down/over; hit, strike. **2** *she ran him down in front of other people* CRITICIZE, denigrate, belittle, disparage, deprecate, find fault with; *informal* put down, knock, badmouth, dis; *formal* derogate.
■ **run for it.** See RUN verb sense 2.
■ **run high** *feelings were running high* BE STRONG, be fervent, be passionate, be intense.
■ **run in** *heart disease runs in the family* BE COMMON IN, be inherent in.
■ **run someone in** (*informal*). See ARREST verb sense 1.
■ **run into 1** *a car ran into his van* COLLIDE WITH, hit, strike, crash into, smash into, plow into, ram, impact. **2** *I ran into Hugo the other day* MEET (BY CHANCE), run across, chance on, stumble on, happen on; *informal* bump into. **3** *we ran into a problem* EXPERIENCE, encounter, meet with, be faced with, be confronted with. **4** *his debts run into six figures* REACH, extend to, be as much as.
■ **run low** *supplies were running low* DWINDLE, diminish, become depleted, be used up, be in short supply, be tight.
■ **run off 1** *the youths ran off.* See RUN verb sense 2. **2** *he ran off with her money.* See STEAL verb sense 1.
■ **run something off 1** *would you run off that list for me?* COPY, photocopy, xerox, duplicate, print, reproduce. **2** *run off some of the excess water* DRAIN, bleed, draw off, pump out.
■ **run on 1** *the call ran on for hours* CONTINUE, go on, carry on, last, keep going, stretch. **2** *your mother does run on* TALK INCESSANTLY, talk a lot, go on, chatter on, ramble on; *informal* yak, gab, run off at the mouth.
■ **run out 1** *supplies ran out* BE USED UP, dry up, be exhausted, be finished, peter out. **2** *they ran out of cash* BE OUT OF; use up, consume, eat up; *informal* be fresh out of. **3** *her contract ran out* EXPIRE, end, terminate, finish; lapse.
■ **run out on someone** (*informal*). See ABANDON verb sense 3.
■ **run over 1** *the bathwater ran over* OVERFLOW, spill over, brim over. **2** *the project ran over budget* EXCEED, go over, overshoot, overreach. **3** *he quickly ran over the story* RECAPITULATE, repeat, run through, go over, reiterate, review; look over, read through; *informal* recap.
■ **run someone over.** See RUN SOMEONE DOWN sense 1.
■ **run the show** (*informal*) BE IN CHARGE, be in control,

be at the helm, be in the driver's seat, be at the wheel; *informal* be the boss, call the shots.

■ **run through 1** *they quickly ran through their money* SQUANDER, spend, fritter away, dissipate, waste, go through, consume, use up; *informal* blow. **2** *the attitude that runs through his writing* PERVADE, permeate, suffuse, imbue, inform. **3** *he ran through his notes.* See RUN OVER sense 3. **4** *let's run through scene three* REHEARSE, practise, go over, repeat; *informal* recap.

■ **run someone through** STAB, pierce, transfix, impale.

■ **run to 1** *the bill ran to $22,000* AMOUNT TO, add up to, total, come to, equal, reach, be as much as. **2** *we can't run to champagne* AFFORD, stretch to, manage. **3** *he was running to fat* TEND TO, become, get, grow.

runaway ▶ noun *a teenage runaway* FUGITIVE, escaper, escapee; refugee; truant; absconder, deserter.

▶ adjective **1** *a runaway horse* OUT OF CONTROL, escaped, loose, on the loose. **2** *a runaway victory* EASY, effortless; *informal* as easy as pie. **3** *runaway inflation* RAMPANT, out of control, unchecked, unbridled.

rundown ▶ noun *here's a rundown on the latest digital gear* SUMMARY, synopsis, précis, run-through, summarization, summation, review, overview, briefing, sketch, outline; *informal* lowdown, recap.

run-down ▶ adjective **1** *a run-down area* DILAPIDATED, tumbledown, ramshackle, derelict, ruinous, in ruins, crumbling, beat-up; neglected, uncared-for, depressed, seedy, shabby, slummy, squalid, flea-bitten; *informal* grotty. **2** *she was feeling rather run-down* UNWELL, ill, poorly, unhealthy, peaky, peaked; tired, drained, exhausted, fatigued, worn out, below par, washed out; *informal* under the weather, off; *dated* seedy.

run-in ▶ noun *(informal)* DISAGREEMENT, argument, dispute, altercation, confrontation, contretemps, quarrel; brush, encounter, tangle, blow-up, fight, clash; *informal* spat, scrap, row.

runner ▶ noun **1** *the runners were limbering up* ATHLETE, sprinter, hurdler, racer, jogger. **2** *a strawberry runner* SHOOT, offshoot, sprout, tendril; *Botany* stolon. **3** *he worked as a runner for the mob* MESSENGER, courier, errand boy; *informal* gofer.

running ▶ noun **1** *his running was particularly fast* SPRINTING, sprint, racing, jogging, jog. **2** *the running of the school* ADMINISTRATION, management, organization, coordination, orchestration, handling, direction, control, regulation, supervision. **3** *the smooth running of her department* OPERATION, working, function, performance.

▶ adjective **1** *running water* FLOWING, gushing, rushing, moving. **2** *a running argument* ONGOING, sustained, continuous, incessant, ceaseless, constant, perpetual; recurrent, recurring. **3** *she was late two days running* IN SUCCESSION, in a row, in sequence, consecutively; straight, together.

■ **in the running** *he's in the running for a prize* LIKELY TO GET, a candidate for, in line for, on the shortlist for, up for.

running shoes ▶ plural noun athletic shoes, gym shoes, runners ♣, sneakers, cross-trainers, track shoes, court shoes, joggers, tennis shoes.

runny ▶ adjective LIQUEFIED, liquid, fluid, melted, molten; watery, thin.
— OPPOSITES: solid.

run-of-the-mill ▶ adjective ORDINARY, average, middle-of-the-road, commonplace, humdrum, mundane, standard, nondescript, characterless, conventional; unremarkable, unexceptional,

uninteresting, dull, boring, routine, bland, lacklustre, garden-variety; *informal* nothing to write home about, nothing special, a dime a dozen.
— OPPOSITES: exceptional.

rupture ▶ noun **1** *pipeline ruptures* BREAK, fracture, crack, breach, burst, split, fissure. **2** *a rupture due to personal differences* RIFT, estrangement, falling-out, breakup, breach, split, separation, parting, division, schism; *informal* bust-up. **3** *an abdominal rupture* HERNIA.

▶ verb **1** *the reactor core might rupture* BREAK, fracture, crack, breach, burst, split; *informal* bust. **2** *the problem ruptured their relationships* SEVER, break off, breach, disrupt; *literary* sunder.

rural ▶ adjective COUNTRY, countryside, bucolic, rustic, pastoral; agricultural, agrarian; *literary* sylvan, georgic.
— OPPOSITES: urban.

ruse ▶ noun PLOY, stratagem, tactic, scheme, trick, gambit, cunning plan, dodge, subterfuge, machination, wile.

rush ▶ verb **1** *she rushed home* HURRY, dash, run, race, sprint, bolt, dart, gallop, career, charge, shoot, hurtle, career, hare, fly, speed, zoom, scurry, scuttle, scamper, hasten; *informal* tear, belt, pelt, scoot, zip, whip, hotfoot it, leg it, bomb, hightail it. **2** *water rushed along gutters* FLOW, pour, gush, surge, stream, cascade, run, course. **3** *the tax was rushed through parliament* PUSH, hurry, hasten, speed, hustle, press, force. **4** *the mob rushed the police* ATTACK, charge, run at, assail, storm.

▶ noun **1** *Tim made a rush for the exit* DASH, run, sprint, dart, bolt, charge, scramble, break. **2** *the lunch rush* HUSTLE AND BUSTLE, commotion, hubbub, hurly-burly, stir; busy time. **3** *a last minute rush for flights* DEMAND, clamour, call, request; run on. **4** *he was in no rush to leave* HURRY, haste, urgency. **5** *a rush of adrenalin* SURGE, flow, flood, spurt, stream; thrill, flash; *informal* charge, jolt, kick. **6** *a rush of cold air* GUST, draft. **7** *I made a sudden rush at him* CHARGE, onslaught, attack, assault, onrush. **8** *the defenceman joined the rush* ATTACK, breakout.

▶ adjective *a rush job* URGENT, high-priority, emergency; hurried, hasty, fast, quick, swift; *informal* hurry-up.

rushed ▶ adjective **1** *a rushed divorce* HASTY, fast, speedy, quick, swift, rapid, hurried. **2** *he was too rushed to enjoy his stay* PRESSED FOR TIME, busy, in a hurry, run off one's feet.

rust ▶ verb CORRODE, oxidize, become rusty, tarnish.
— RELATED TERMS: ferruginous.

▶ noun CORROSION, oxidation.

rustic ▶ adjective **1** *a rustic setting* RURAL, country, countryside, countrified, pastoral, bucolic; agricultural, agrarian; *literary* sylvan, georgic. **2** *rustic wooden tables* PLAIN, simple, homely, unsophisticated; rough, rude, crude. **3** *rustic peasants* UNSOPHISTICATED, uncultured, unrefined, simple; artless, unassuming, guileless, naive, ingenuous; coarse, rough, uncouth, boorish; *informal* hillbilly, hick.
— OPPOSITES: urban, ornate, sophisticated.

▶ noun *the rustics were carousing* PEASANT, countryman, countrywoman, bumpkin, yokel, country cousin; *informal* hillbilly, hayseed, hick; *(Nfld)* baywop ♣, bayman ♣, noddy ♣; *archaic* swain, cottier.

rustle ▶ verb **1** *her dress rustled as she moved* SWISH, whoosh, swoosh, whisper, sigh. **2** *he was rustling cattle* STEAL, thieve, take; abduct, kidnap; *informal* swipe.

▶ noun *the rustle of the leaves* SWISH, whisper, rustling; *literary* susurration, susurrus.

■ **rustle something up** (*informal*) PREPARE HASTILY, throw together, make; *informal* fix.

rusty ▶ **adjective 1** *rusty wire* RUSTED, rust-covered, corroded, oxidized; tarnished, discoloured. **2** *rusty hair* REDDISH-BROWN, rust-coloured, chestnut, auburn, tawny, russet, coppery, copper, Titian, red, ginger, gingery. **3** *my French is a little rusty* OUT OF PRACTICE, below par; unpractised, deficient, impaired, weak.

rut ▶ **noun 1** *the car bumped across the ruts* FURROW, groove, trough, ditch, hollow, pothole, crater. **2** *he was stuck in a rut* BORING ROUTINE, humdrum existence, habit, dead end.

ruthless ▶ **adjective** MERCILESS, pitiless, cruel, heartless, hard-hearted, cold-hearted, cold-blooded, harsh, callous, unmerciful, unforgiving, uncaring, unsympathetic, uncharitable; remorseless, unbending, inflexible, implacable; brutal, inhuman, inhumane, barbarous, barbaric, savage, sadistic, vicious; *informal* take no prisoners.
– OPPOSITES: merciful.

Ss

sable ▶ adjective BLACK, jet-black, pitch-black, ebony, raven, sooty, dusky, inky, coal-black.

sabotage ▶ noun VANDALISM, wrecking, destruction, impairment, incapacitation, damage; subversion, obstruction, disruption, spoiling, undermining; *informal* a wrench in the works.
▶ verb VANDALIZE, wreck, damage, destroy, cripple, impair, incapacitate; obstruct, disrupt, spoil, ruin, undermine, threaten, subvert.

saccharine ▶ adjective SENTIMENTAL, sickly, mawkish, cloying, sugary, sickening, nauseating; *informal* mushy, slushy, schmaltzy, weepy, gooey, drippy, cheesy, corny, soppy, twee, cornball, sappy.

sack¹ ▶ noun **1** *she carried her supplies in a sack* BAG, pouch, pack, satchel; knapsack, backpack, rucksack, packsack, day pack, bookbag, (Nfld) nunny bag ♣, tote bag. **2** (*informal*) *work hard or you'll get the sack* DISMISSAL, discharge; *informal* the boot, the axe, the heave-ho, one's marching orders, the pink slip. **3** (*informal*) *she stayed in the sack* BED.
▶ verb (*informal*) *she was sacked for stealing* DISMISS, discharge, lay off, make redundant, let go, terminate, sack, get rid of; *Military* cashier; *informal* fire, give the sack, give someone their marching orders, give someone the boot, show someone the door, send packing, pink-slip.
■ **hit the sack** (*informal*) GO TO BED, retire, go to sleep; *informal* turn in, hit the hay.

sack² ▶ verb *raiders sacked the town* RAVAGE, lay waste, devastate, raid, ransack, strip, plunder, despoil, pillage, loot, rob.

sackcloth ▶ noun HESSIAN, sacking, hopsack, burlap; (Nfld) brin ♣, gunny.
■ **wearing sackcloth and ashes** PENITENT, contrite, regretful, sorrowful, rueful, remorseful, apologetic, ashamed, guilt-ridden, chastened, shamefaced, guilty.

sacred ▶ adjective **1** *the priest entered the sacred place* HOLY, hallowed, blessed, consecrated, sanctified, venerated, revered; *archaic* blest. **2** *sacred music* RELIGIOUS, spiritual, devotional, church, ecclesiastical. **3** *the hill is sacred to the tribe* SACROSANCT, inviolable, inviolate, invulnerable, untouchable, protected, defended, secure.
− RELATED TERMS: hiero-.
− OPPOSITES: secular, profane.

sacrifice ▶ noun **1** *the sacrifice of animals* RITUAL SLAUGHTER, offering, oblation, immolation. **2** *the calf was a sacrifice* (VOTIVE) OFFERING, burnt offering, gift, oblation. **3** *the sacrifice of sovereignty* SURRENDER, giving up, abandonment, renunciation, forfeiture, relinquishment, resignation, abdication.
▶ verb **1** *two goats were sacrificed* OFFER UP, immolate, slaughter. **2** *he sacrificed his principles* GIVE UP, abandon, surrender, forgo, renounce, forfeit, relinquish, resign, abdicate; betray.

sacrificial ▶ adjective VOTIVE, expiatory, propitiatory.

sacrilege ▶ noun DESECRATION, profanity, blasphemy, impiety, irreligion, unholiness, irreverence, disrespect, profanation.
− OPPOSITES: piety.

sacrilegious ▶ adjective PROFANE, blasphemous, impious, sinful, irreverent, irreligious, unholy, disrespectful.

sacrosanct ▶ adjective SACRED, hallowed, respected, inviolable, inviolate, unimpeachable, invulnerable, untouchable, inalienable; protected, defended, secure, safe.

sad ▶ adjective **1** *we felt sad when we left* UNHAPPY, sorrowful, dejected, depressed, downcast, miserable, down, despondent, despairing, disconsolate, desolate, wretched, glum, gloomy, doleful, dismal, melancholy, mournful, woebegone, forlorn, crestfallen, heartbroken, inconsolable; *informal* blue, down in the mouth, down in the dumps, blah. **2** *they knew her sad story* TRAGIC, unhappy, unfortunate, awful, miserable, wretched, sorry, pitiful, pathetic, traumatic, heartbreaking, heart-rending, harrowing. **3** *a sad state of affairs* UNFORTUNATE, regrettable, sorry, deplorable, lamentable, pitiful, shameful, disgraceful.
− OPPOSITES: happy, cheerful, fortunate.

sadden ▶ verb DEPRESS, dispirit, deject, dishearten, grieve, desolate, discourage, upset, get down, bring down, break someone's heart.

saddle ▶ verb *they were saddled with the children* BURDEN, encumber, land, charge; impose something on, thrust something on, fob something off on to.

sadistic ▶ adjective CRUEL, barbarous, vicious, brutal, callous, fiendish, cold-blooded, inhuman, ruthless, heartless; perverted.

sadness ▶ noun UNHAPPINESS, sorrow, dejection, depression, misery, despondency, despair, desolation, wretchedness, gloom, gloominess, dolefulness, melancholy, mournfulness, woe, heartache, grief; *informal* the blues.

safe ▶ adjective **1** *the jewels are safe in the bank* SECURE, protected, shielded, sheltered, guarded, out of harm's way. **2** *the lost children are all safe* UNHARMED, unhurt, uninjured, unscathed, all right, well, in one piece, out of danger, home free; *informal* OK. **3** *a safe place to hide* SECURE, sound, impregnable, unassailable, invulnerable. **4** *a safe driver* CAUTIOUS, circumspect, prudent, attentive; unadventurous, conservative, unenterprising. **5** *the drug is safe* HARMLESS, innocuous, benign, non-toxic, non-poisonous.
− OPPOSITES: insecure, dangerous, reckless, harmful.
▶ noun *I keep the ring in a safe* STRONGBOX, safety-deposit box, safe-deposit box, coffer, strongroom, vault.

safeguard ▶ noun *a safeguard against terrorism* PROTECTION, defence, guard, screen, buffer, preventive, precaution, provision, security; surety, cover, insurance, indemnity.
▶ verb *the contract will safeguard 1000 jobs* PROTECT, preserve, conserve, save, secure, shield, guard, keep

safe.
— OPPOSITES: jeopardize.

safety ▶ noun **1** *the safety of the residents* WELFARE, well-being, protection, security. **2** *she worried about the safety of planes* SECURITY, soundness, dependability, reliability. **3** *we reached the safety of the shore* SHELTER, sanctuary, refuge.

sag ▶ verb **1** *she sagged in his arms* SINK, slump, loll, flop, crumple. **2** *the floors all sag* DIP, droop; bulge, bag. **3** *the markets sagged as the day wore on* DECLINE, fall, drop, slump, plummet; *informal* nosedive.

saga ▶ noun **1** *Celtic tribal sagas* EPIC, chronicle, legend, folk tale, romance, history, narrative, adventure, myth, fairy story. **2** *the saga of how they met* LONG STORY, rigmarole; chain of events; *informal* spiel.

sagacious ▶ adjective WISE, clever, intelligent, knowledgeable, sensible, sage; discerning, judicious, canny, perceptive, astute, shrewd, prudent, thoughtful, insightful, perspicacious; *informal* streetwise, savvy; *formal* sapient.
— OPPOSITES: foolish.

sage ▶ noun *the Chinese sage Confucius* WISE MAN/WOMAN, learned person, philosopher, thinker, scholar, savant; authority, expert, guru.
▶ adjective *some very sage comments* WISE, learned, clever, intelligent, having/showing great knowledge, knowledgeable, sensible, intellectual, scholarly, sagacious, erudite; discerning, judicious, canny, penetrating, perceptive, acute, astute, shrewd, prudent, politic, thoughtful, insightful, percipient, perspicacious, philosophical, profound, deep.

sail ▶ noun *the ship's sails* canvas, sailcloth.
▶ verb **1** *we sailed across the Atlantic* VOYAGE, travel by water, steam, navigate, cruise. **2** *you can learn to sail here* YACHT, boat, go sailing; crew, helm. **3** *we sail tonight* SET SAIL, put to sea, leave port, weigh anchor, shove off. **4** *he is sailing the ship* STEER, pilot, navigate, con, helm, captain; *informal* skipper. **5** *clouds were sailing past* GLIDE, drift, float, flow, sweep, skim, coast, flit. **6** *a pencil sailed past his ear* WHIZ, speed, streak, shoot, whip, buzz, zoom, flash; fly, wing, soar, zip.
■ **sail through** SUCCEED EASILY AT, pass easily, romp through, walk through.

sailing ship ▶ noun. *See table.*

Sailing Vessels

barque	ketch
barquentine	knockabout
brig	lateen
brigantine	longboat
bully ♣	motorsailer
caique	sailboat
catamaran	schooner
catboat	skiff
clipper	skipjack
cutter	sloop
dhow	smack
felucca	tall ship
frigate	tartan
galleon	trimaran
gallery	windjammer
hermaphrodite brig	xebec
hoy	yacht
junk	yawl
	See also SHIPS.

sailor ▶ noun SEAMAN, seafarer, mariner; boatman, yachtsman, hand; *informal* (old) salt, sea dog, rating, bluejacket, matelot, shellback.

saintly ▶ adjective HOLY, godly, pious, religious, devout, spiritual, prayerful; virtuous, righteous, good, moral, innocent, sinless, guiltless, irreproachable, spotless, uncorrupted, pure, angelic.
— OPPOSITES: ungodly.

sake ▶ noun **1** *this is simplified for the sake of clarity* PURPOSE, reason, aim, end, objective, object, goal, motive. **2** *she had to be brave for her daughter's sake* BENEFIT, advantage, good, well-being, welfare, interest, profit.

salacious ▶ adjective **1** *salacious writing* PORNOGRAPHIC, obscene, indecent, crude, lewd, vulgar, dirty, filthy; erotic, titillating, arousing, suggestive, sexy, risqué, ribald, smutty, bawdy; X-rated; *informal* porn, porno, blue, XXX; *euphemistic* adult. **2** *salacious women* LUSTFUL, lecherous, licentious, lascivious, libidinous, prurient, lewd; debauched, wanton, loose, fast, impure, unchaste, degenerate, sinful, depraved, promiscuous; *informal* randy, horny, hot to trot.

salary ▶ noun PAY, wages, earnings, payment, remuneration, fee(s), stipend, income, *Parliament* indemnity ♣; *informal* take-home; *formal* emolument.

sale ▶ noun **1** *the sale of firearms* SELLING, vending; dealing, trading. **2** *they make a sale every minute* DEAL, transaction. **3** *there's a sale on* MARKDOWN, discount, blowout, clearance (sale), fire sale, sell-off, liquidation (sale).
— OPPOSITES: purchase.
■ **for sale** ON THE MARKET, on sale, available, purchasable, obtainable.

salesperson ▶ noun SALES ASSISTANT, sales associate, salesman, saleswoman, shop assistant, seller, agent, (sales) clerk; shopkeeper, trader, merchant, retailer, dealer, peddler, hawker, hustler; *informal* (sales) rep.

salient ▶ adjective IMPORTANT, main, principal, major, chief, primary; notable, noteworthy, outstanding, conspicuous, striking, noticeable, obvious, remarkable, prominent, predominant, dominant; key, crucial, vital, essential, pivotal, prime, central, paramount.
— OPPOSITES: minor.

saliva ▶ noun SPIT, spittle, dribble, drool, slaver, slobber, gob, sputum.

sallow ▶ adjective YELLOWISH, jaundiced, pallid, wan, pale, anemic, bloodless, pasty; unhealthy, sickly, washed out, peaky; *informal* like death warmed over; *Medicine* icteric.

sally ▶ noun **1** *the garrison made a sally against us* SORTIE, charge, foray, thrust, drive, offensive, attack, assault, raid, incursion, invasion, onset, onslaught. **2** *a fruitless sally into the city* EXPEDITION, excursion, trip, outing, jaunt, visit. **3** *he was delighted with his sally* WITTICISM, smart remark, quip, barb, pleasantry; joke, pun, jest, bon mot; retort, riposte, counter, rejoinder; *informal* gag, wisecrack, comeback.

salmon ▶ noun grilse, kelt, parr, fry, alevin, smolt, blackfish, kipper. *See table.*

salon ▶ noun **1** *a hairdressing salon* SHOP, parlour, establishment, premises; boutique, store. **2** *the chateau's mirrored salon* DRAWING ROOM, sitting room, living room, lounge; *dated* parlour. **3** *he showed his artwork in a salon* EXHIBITION, (public) display, show, showing, showcase, exhibit.

saloon ▶ noun *See* TAVERN.

Salmon, Trout & Related Fishes

Arctic char	keta
Arctic grayling	king salmon
Atlantic salmon	kokanee
aurora trout	lake trout
blueback	Mackinaw trout
brookie	mud trout ✣
brook trout	ouananiche ✣
brown trout	Pacific salmon
bull trout	pink salmon
char	rainbow trout
chinook salmon	red salmon
chum salmon	Restigouche salmon
cisco	silver salmon
coho salmon	sockeye salmon
cutthroat trout	speckled trout
dog salmon	splake
Dolly Varden	spring salmon ✣
grayling	steelhead
humpback salmon	tullibee
inconnu	tyee ✣
Kamloops trout ✣	whitefish

salt ▶ noun **1** *the potatoes need salt* SODIUM CHLORIDE. **2** (*literary*) *he added salt to the conversation* ZEST, spice, piquancy, bite, edge; vitality, liveliness, spirit, sparkle; *informal* zing, punch.
— RELATED TERMS: saline.
▶ adjective *salt water* SALTY, salted, saline, briny, brackish.
■ **salt something away** (*informal*) SAVE, put aside, put by, set aside, reserve, keep, store, stockpile, hoard, stow away; *informal* squirrel away, stash away.
■ **with a pinch of salt** WITH RESERVATIONS, with misgivings, skeptically, cynically, doubtfully, doubtingly, suspiciously, quizzically, incredulously.

salty ▶ adjective **1** *salty water* SALT, salted, saline, briny, brackish. **2** *a salty sense of humour* EARTHY, colourful, spicy, racy, risqué, naughty, vulgar, rude; piquant, biting.

salubrious ▶ adjective **1** *I found the climate salubrious* HEALTHY, health-giving, healthful, beneficial, wholesome; *archaic* salutary. **2** *a salubrious Sunday afternoon* PLEASANT, agreeable, pleasing, enjoyable, pleasurable, nice, delightful; select, high-class, upscale, upmarket; *informal* posh, swanky, classy, swank.
— OPPOSITES: unhealthy, unpleasant.

salutary ▶ adjective **1** *a salutary lesson on the fragility of nature* BENEFICIAL, advantageous, good, profitable, productive, helpful, useful, valuable, worthwhile; timely. **2** (*archaic*) *the salutary Atlantic air. See* SALUBRIOUS sense 1.
— OPPOSITES: unwelcome, unhealthy.

salutation ▶ noun GREETING, salute, address, welcome.

salute ▶ noun **1** *he gave the Captain a salute* GREETING, salutation, gesture of respect, obeisance, acknowledgement, welcome, address. **2** *she raised her hands in salutation* TRIBUTE, testimonial, homage, toast, honour, eulogy; celebration of, acknowledgement of.
▶ verb **1** *he saluted the ambassadors* GREET, address, hail, welcome, acknowledge, toast; make obeisance to. **2** *we salute a great photographer* PAY TRIBUTE TO, pay homage to, honour, celebrate, acknowledge, take one's hat off to.

salvage ▶ verb **1** *an attempt to salvage the vessel* RESCUE, save, recover, retrieve, raise, reclaim. **2** *he tried to salvage his reputation* RETAIN, preserve, conserve; regain, recoup, redeem, snatch.
▶ noun **1** *the salvage is taking place off the coast* RESCUE, recovery, reclamation. **2** *she sifted through the salvage* REMAINS, debris, wreckage, rubble, remnants, flotsam and jetsam, scrap.

salvation ▶ noun **1** *salvation by way of repentance* REDEMPTION, deliverance, reclamation. **2** *that conviction was her salvation* LIFELINE, preservation; means of escape, help, saving, saviour.
— OPPOSITES: damnation.

salve ▶ noun *lip salve* OINTMENT, cream, balm, unguent, emollient; embrocation, liniment.
▶ verb *she did it to salve her conscience* SOOTHE, assuage, ease, allay, lighten, alleviate, comfort, mollify.

salver ▶ noun *See* TRAY.

same ▶ adjective **1** *we stayed at the same hotel* IDENTICAL, selfsame, very same, one and the same. **2** *they had the same symptoms* MATCHING, identical, alike, duplicate, carbon-copy, twin; indistinguishable, interchangeable, corresponding, equivalent, parallel, like, comparable, similar, congruent, concordant, consonant. **3** *it happened that same month* SELFSAME; aforesaid, aforementioned. **4** *they provide the same menu worldwide* UNCHANGING, unvarying, unvaried, invariable, consistent, uniform, regular.
— RELATED TERMS: homo-.
— OPPOSITES: another, different, dissimilar, varying.
▶ noun *Louise said the same* THE SAME THING, the aforementioned, the aforesaid, the above-mentioned.
■ **all the same 1** *I was frightened all the same* IN SPITE OF EVERYTHING, despite that, nevertheless, nonetheless, even so, however, but, still, yet, though, be that as it may, just the same, at the same time, in any event, notwithstanding, regardless, anyway, anyhow; *informal* still and all. **2** *it's all the same to me* IMMATERIAL, of no importance, of no consequence, inconsequential, unimportant, of little account, irrelevant, insignificant, trivial, petty.

sample ▶ noun **1** *a sample of the fabric* SPECIMEN, example, bit, snippet, swatch, representative piece, exemplification; prototype, test piece, dummy, pilot, trial, taste, taster, tester. **2** *a sample of 10,000 people nationwide* CROSS SECTION, variety, sampling, test.
▶ verb *we sampled the culinary offerings* TRY (OUT), taste, test, put to the test, experiment with; appraise, evaluate, test drive; *informal* check out.
▶ adjective **1** *the sample group is small* REPRESENTATIVE, illustrative, selected, specimen, test, trial, typical. **2** *a sample copy can be obtained* SPECIMEN, test, trial, pilot, dummy.

sanatorium ▶ noun INFIRMARY, clinic, hospital, medical centre, hospice; sick bay, sickroom.

sanctify ▶ verb **1** *he came to sanctify the site* CONSECRATE, bless, make holy, hallow, make sacred, dedicate to God. **2** *they sanctified themselves* PURIFY, cleanse, free from sin, absolve, unburden, redeem. **3** *we must not sanctify this outrage* APPROVE, sanction, condone, vindicate, endorse, support, back, permit, allow, authorize, legitimize.

sanctimonious ▶ adjective SELF-RIGHTEOUS, holier-than-thou, pious, pietistic, churchy, moralizing, preachy, smug, superior, priggish, hypocritical, insincere; *informal* goody-goody.

sanction ▶ noun **1** *trade sanctions* PENALTY, punishment, deterrent; punitive action, discipline, restriction; embargo, ban, prohibition, boycott. **2** *the scheme has the sanction of the court* AUTHORIZATION, consent, leave, permission, authority, warrant, licence, dispensation, assent, acquiescence, agreement, approval, approbation, endorsement, accreditation, ratification, validation, blessing, imprimatur; *informal* the go-ahead, the OK, the green light.
– OPPOSITES: reward, prohibition.
▶ verb **1** *the rally was sanctioned by the government* AUTHORIZE, permit, allow, warrant, accredit, license, endorse, approve, accept, back, support; *informal* OK. **2** *the penalties available to sanction crime* PUNISH, discipline someone for.
– OPPOSITES: prohibit.

sanctity ▶ noun **1** *the sanctity of St. Francis* HOLINESS, godliness, blessedness, saintliness, spirituality, piety, piousness, devoutness, righteousness, goodness, virtue, purity; *formal* sanctitude. **2** *the sanctity of the family meal* INVIOLABILITY; importance, paramountcy.

sanctuary ▶ noun **1** *the sanctuary at Delphi. See* SANCTUM sense 1. **2** *the island is our sanctuary* REFUGE, haven, harbour, port in a storm, oasis, shelter, retreat, bolthole, hideaway, hideout, fastness. **3** *he was given sanctuary in the embassy* SAFETY, protection, shelter, immunity, asylum. **4** *a bird sanctuary* RESERVE, park, reservation, preserve.

sanctum ▶ noun **1** *the sanctum in the temple* HOLY PLACE, shrine, sanctuary, temple, holy of holies, sanctum sanctorum, sanctuary. **2** *a private sanctum for the bar's regulars* REFUGE, retreat, bolthole, hideout, hideaway, den.

sand ▶ noun *she ran across the sand* BEACH, sands, shore, seashore; (sand) dunes; *literary* strand.

sandwich ▶ noun *See table.*

Sandwiches

BLT	hero US
clubhouse sandwich ✦	panino
club sandwich	Reuben
croque monsieur	sloppy joe
Denver	sub
falafel	submarine
grilled cheese	western sandwich
gyro	wrap

sane ▶ adjective **1** *the accused is presumed to be sane* OF SOUND MIND, in one's right mind, compos mentis, lucid, rational, balanced, stable, normal; *informal* all there, together. **2** *it isn't sane to use nuclear weapons* SENSIBLE, practical, advisable, responsible, realistic, prudent, wise, reasonable, rational, level-headed, commonsensical, judicious, politic.
– OPPOSITES: mad, foolish.

sang-froid ▶ noun COMPOSURE, equanimity, self-possession, equilibrium, aplomb, poise, self-assurance, self-control, nerve, calm, presence of mind; *informal* cool, unflappability.

sanguine ▶ adjective **1** *he is sanguine about the advance of technology* OPTIMISTIC, bullish, hopeful, buoyant, positive, confident, cheerful, cheery; *informal* upbeat. **2** (*archaic*) *a sanguine complexion. See* FLORID sense 1.
– OPPOSITES: gloomy.

sanitary ▶ adjective HYGIENIC, clean, antiseptic,

aseptic, sterile, uninfected, disinfected, unpolluted, uncontaminated; salubrious, healthy, wholesome.

sanitize ▶ verb **1** *the best way to sanitize a bottle* STERILIZE, disinfect, clean, cleanse, purify, fumigate, decontaminate. **2** *the diaries have not been sanitized* MAKE PRESENTABLE, make acceptable, make palatable, clean up; expurgate, bowdlerize, censor.

sanity ▶ noun **1** *she was losing her sanity* MENTAL HEALTH, faculties, reason, rationality, saneness, stability, lucidity; sense, wits, mind. **2** *sanity has prevailed* (COMMON) SENSE, wisdom, prudence, judiciousness, rationality, soundness, sensibleness.

sap¹ ▶ noun **1** *sap from the roots of trees* JUICE, secretion, fluid, liquid. **2** *they're full of youthful sap* VIGOUR, energy, drive, dynamism, life, spirit, liveliness, sparkle, verve, ebullience, enthusiasm, gusto, vitality, vivacity, fire, zest, zeal, exuberance; *informal* get-up-and-go, oomph, vim.
▶ verb *they sapped the will of the troops* ERODE, wear away/down, deplete, reduce, lessen, attenuate, undermine, exhaust, drain, bleed.

sap² ▶ noun (*informal*) *he fell for it – what a sap! See* IDIOT.

sappy ▶ adjective *See* SACCHARINE.

sarcasm ▶ noun DERISION, mockery, scorn, sneering, scoffing; irony; cynicism.

sarcastic ▶ adjective SARDONIC, ironic, ironical, derisive, snide, scornful, contemptuous, mocking, sneering, jeering; caustic, scathing, trenchant, cutting, biting, sharp, acerbic; *informal* snarky, smart-alecky.

sardonic ▶ adjective MOCKING, satirical, sarcastic, ironical, ironic; cynical, scornful, contemptuous, derisive, derisory, sneering, jeering; scathing, caustic, trenchant, cutting, sharp, acerbic.

sash ▶ noun BELT, cummerbund, waistband, girdle, obi; arrow sash ✦, ceinture fléchée ✦, voyageur sash ✦, Assomption sash ✦; *literary* cincture.

sass ▶ noun *See* SAUCE sense 2.

Satan ▶ noun. *See* DEVIL sense 1.

satanic ▶ adjective DIABOLICAL, fiendish, devilish, demonic, demoniacal, ungodly, hellish, infernal, wicked, evil, sinful, iniquitous, nefarious, vile, foul, abominable, unspeakable, loathsome, monstrous, heinous, hideous, horrible, horrifying, shocking, appalling, dreadful, awful, terrible, ghastly, abhorrent, despicable, damnable.

sate ▶ verb *See* SATIATE.

satellite ▶ noun **1** *the satellite orbited the earth* SPACE STATION, space capsule, spacecraft; Sputnik. **2** *the two small satellites of Mars* MOON, secondary planet. **3** *Bulgaria was then a Russian satellite* BRANCH, colony, protectorate, puppet state, possession, holding; *historical* fief, vassal; *informal* offshoot.
▶ adjective *a satellite state* DEPENDENT, subordinate, subsidiary.

satiate ▶ verb FILL, satisfy, sate; slake, quench; gorge, stuff, surfeit, glut, cloy, sicken, nauseate.

satiny ▶ adjective SMOOTH, shiny, glossy, shining, gleaming, lustrous, sleek, silky.

satire ▶ noun **1** *a satire on Canadian politics* PARODY, burlesque, caricature, lampoon, skit; *informal* spoof, takeoff, send-up. **2** *he has become the subject of satire* MOCKERY, ridicule, derision, scorn, caricature; irony, sarcasm.

satirical ▶ adjective MOCKING, ironic, ironical, satiric, sarcastic, sardonic; caustic, trenchant, mordant, biting, cutting, stinging, acerbic; critical, irreverent, disparaging, disrespectful.

satirize ▶ verb MOCK, ridicule, deride, make fun of, poke fun at, parody, lampoon, burlesque, caricature, take off; criticize; *informal* send up.

satisfaction ▶ noun **1** *he derived great satisfaction from his work* CONTENTMENT, pleasure, gratification, fulfillment, enjoyment, happiness, pride; self-satisfaction, smugness, complacency. **2** *the satisfaction of consumer needs* FULFILLMENT, gratification; appeasement, assuaging. **3** *investors turned to the courts for satisfaction* COMPENSATION, recompense, redress, reparation, restitution, repayment, payment, settlement, reimbursement, indemnification, indemnity.

satisfactory ▶ adjective ADEQUATE, all right, acceptable, good enough, sufficient, reasonable, quite good, competent, fair, decent, average, passable; fine, in order, up to scratch, up to the mark, up to standard, up to par; *informal* OK, jake, hunky-dory, so-so, {comme ci, comme ça}.
– OPPOSITES: inadequate, poor.

satisfied ▶ adjective **1** *a satisfied smile* PLEASED, well pleased, content, contented, happy, proud, triumphant; smug, self-satisfied, pleased with oneself, complacent. **2** *the pleasure of satisfied desire* FULFILLED, gratified. **3** *I am satisfied that she understands* CONVINCED, certain, sure, positive, persuaded, easy in one's mind.
– OPPOSITES: discontented, unhappy.

satisfy ▶ verb **1** *a last chance to satisfy his hunger for romance* FULFILL, gratify, meet, fill; indulge, cater to, pander to; appease, assuage; quench, slake, satiate, sate, take the edge off. **2** *she satisfied herself that it had been an accident* CONVINCE, persuade, assure; reassure, put someone's mind at rest. **3** *products which satisfy the criteria* COMPLY WITH, meet, fulfill, answer, conform to; measure up to, come up to; suffice, be good enough, fit/fill the bill. **4** *there was insufficient collateral to satisfy the loan* REPAY, pay (off), settle, make good, discharge, square, liquidate, clear.
– OPPOSITES: frustrate.

saturate ▶ verb **1** *heavy rain saturated the ground* SOAK, drench, waterlog, wet through; souse, steep, douse. **2** *the air was saturated with the stench of incense* PERMEATE, suffuse, imbue, pervade, charge, infuse, fill. **3** *the company has saturated the market* FLOOD, glut, oversupply, overload.

saturnine ▶ adjective **1** *a saturnine temperament* GLOOMY, sombre, melancholy, moody, lugubrious, dour, glum, morose, unsmiling, humourless. **2** *his saturnine good looks* SWARTHY, dark, dark-skinned, dark-complexioned; mysterious, mercurial, moody, brooding.
– OPPOSITES: cheerful.

sauce ▶ noun **1** *a piquant sauce* RELISH, condiment, ketchup; dip, dressing. *See table.* **2** *(informal)* 'I'll have less of your sauce,' said Aunt Edie IMPUDENCE, impertinence, cheek, cheekiness, sauciness, effrontery, forwardness, brazenness; insolence, rudeness, disrespect; *informal* mouth, lip, sass, sassiness. **3** *Uncle Reg was into the sauce again* ALCOHOL, drink, spirits, liquor; *informal* booze, hooch, the hard stuff, firewater, rotgut, moonshine, moose milk ♣, grog, tipple, the demon drink, the bottle, juice.

saucepan ▶ noun PAN, pot, casserole, skillet, stockpot, stewpot, Dutch oven, double boiler, (*Nfld & PEI*) dipper ♣; billy, billycan.

Sauces, Condiments, and Dressings

alfredo	mint sauce
applesauce	mole
arrabbiata	mornay
avgolemono	mousseline
barbecue sauce	mustard
Béarnaise	nam pla
béchamel	nuoc mam
beurre blanc	oyster sauce
bolognese	pesto
bourguignon	piccalilli
brandy butter	piri piri
bread sauce	pistou
carbonara	plum sauce
chili sauce	ranch dressing
chutney	relish
coady ♣(*Nfld*)	remoulade
coulis	Roquefort dressing
cream sauce	rouille
crème anglaise	Russian dressing
custard	salad dressing
dip	salsa
dressing	salsa verde
duxelles	sweet and sour sauce
fish sauce	tartar sauce (sauce
French dressing	tartare)
gravy	skordalia
guacamole	soy sauce
hard sauce	Tabasco*
hoisin sauce	tahini
hollandaise	tamari
horseradish	tapenade
hot sauce	teriyaki
hummus	Thousand Island
jus	dressing
ketchup	velouté
marinara	vinaigrette
mayonnaise	white sauce
	Worcestershire sauce
	*Proprietary term.

saucy ▶ adjective *(informal)* **1** *you saucy girl!* CHEEKY, impudent, impertinent, irreverent, forward, disrespectful, bold, as bold as brass, brazen, pert; *informal* fresh, lippy, mouthy, sassy. **2** *the cap sat at a saucy angle* JAUNTY, rakish, sporty, raffish.
– OPPOSITES: demure, polite.

saunter ▶ verb STROLL, amble, wander, meander, drift, walk; stretch one's legs, take the air; *informal* mosey, tootle; *formal* promenade.

sausage ▶ noun *See table.*

savage ▶ adjective **1** *savage dogs* FEROCIOUS, fierce; wild, untamed, untameable, undomesticated, feral. **2** *a savage assault* VICIOUS, brutal, cruel, sadistic, ferocious, fierce, violent, bloody, murderous, homicidal, bloodthirsty; *literary* fell; *archaic* sanguinary. **3** *a savage attack on free-trade policy* FIERCE, blistering, scathing, searing, stinging, devastating, mordant, trenchant, caustic, cutting, biting, withering, virulent, vitriolic. **4** *a savage race* PRIMITIVE, uncivilized, unenlightened, non-literate. **5** *a savage landscape* RUGGED, rough, wild, inhospitable, uninhabitable. **6** *a savage blow for the town* SEVERE, crushing, devastating, crippling, terrible, awful, dreadful, dire, catastrophic, calamitous, ruinous.
– OPPOSITES: tame, mild, civilized.
▶ noun **1** *she'd expected mud huts and savages* BARBARIAN,

Sausages and Hot Dogs

all-dressed ✤	kielbasa
andouille	knackwurst
banger (Brit.)	kolbassa
bierwurst	kubasa
blood sausage (black	liverwurst
pudding)	pig in a blanket
bratwurst	Pogo* ✤
chili dog	Polish sausage
chorizo	saveloy
chub	smokie ✤
corn dog	steamie ✤(Que.)
dog	summer sausage
farmer's sausage ✤	wiener
frankfurter	wurst
	*Proprietary term.

wild man, wild woman, primitive. **2** *she described her son's assailants as savages* BRUTE, beast, monster, barbarian, sadist, animal.
▶ **verb 1** *he was savaged by a dog* MAUL, attack, tear to pieces, lacerate, claw, bite. **2** *critics savaged the film* CRITICIZE SEVERELY, attack, lambaste, condemn, denounce, pillory, revile; *informal* pan, tear to pieces, hammer, slam, do a hatchet job on, crucify, trash; *formal* excoriate.

savant ▶ **noun** INTELLECTUAL, scholar, sage, philosopher, thinker, wise/learned person; guru, master, pandit.
— OPPOSITES: ignoramus.

save ▶ **verb 1** *the captain was saved by his crew* RESCUE, come to someone's rescue, save someone's life; set free, free, liberate, deliver, extricate; bail out; *informal* save someone's bacon/neck/skin. **2** *the farmhouse has been saved from demolition* PRESERVE, keep safe, keep, protect, safeguard; salvage, retrieve, reclaim, rescue. **3** *start saving money* PUT ASIDE, set aside, put by, put to one side, save up, keep, retain, reserve, conserve, stockpile, store, hoard, save for a rainy day; *informal* salt away, squirrel away, stash away, hang on to. **4** *asking me first would have saved a lot of trouble* PREVENT, obviate, forestall, spare; stop; avoid, avert.
▶ **preposition & conjunction** (*formal*) *no one needed to know save herself* EXCEPT, apart from, but, other than, besides, aside from, bar, barring, excluding, leaving out, saving; *informal* outside of.

saving ▶ **noun 1** *a considerable saving in development costs* REDUCTION, cut, decrease, economy. **2** *I'll have to use some of my savings* NEST EGG, money for a rainy day, life savings, RRSP; capital, assets, funds, resources, reserves.

saving grace ▶ **noun** REDEEMING QUALITY, good point, thing in its/one's favour, advantage, asset, selling point.

saviour ▶ **noun** *the country's saviour* RESCUER, liberator, deliverer, emancipator; champion, knight in shining armour, friend in need, good Samaritan.

savoir faire ▶ **noun** SOCIAL SKILL, social grace(s), urbanity, suavity, finesse, sophistication, poise, aplomb, adroitness, polish, style, smoothness, tact, tactfulness, diplomacy, discretion, delicacy, sensitivity; *informal* savvy.
— OPPOSITES: gaucheness.

savour ▶ **verb 1** *she wanted to savour every moment* RELISH, enjoy (to the full), appreciate, delight in, revel in, luxuriate in, bask in. **2** *such a declaration savoured of*

immodesty SUGGEST, smack of, have the hallmarks of, seem like, have the air of, show signs of.
▶ **noun 1** *the subtle savour of wood smoke* SMELL, aroma, fragrance, scent, perfume, bouquet; TASTE, flavour, tang, smack. **2** *a savour of bitterness seasoned my feelings for him* TRACE, hint, suggestion, touch, smack. **3** *her usual diversions had lost their savour* PIQUANCY, interest, attraction, flavour, spice, zest, excitement, enjoyment, shine; *informal* zing, pizzazz, sparkle.

savoury ▶ **adjective 1** *sweet or savoury dishes* SALTY, spicy, piquant, tangy. **2** *a rich, savoury aroma* APPETIZING, mouth-watering, delicious, delectable, luscious; tasty, flavourful, full of flavour, palatable, toothsome; *informal* scrumptious, finger-licking, lip-smacking, melt-in-your/the-mouth, yummy. **3** *one of the less savoury aspects of the affair* ACCEPTABLE, pleasant, respectable, wholesome, honourable, proper, seemly.
— OPPOSITES: sweet, unappetizing.

savvy (*informal*) ▶ **noun** *his political savvy* SHREWDNESS, astuteness, sharp-wittedness, sharpness, acuteness, acumen, acuity, intelligence, wit, canniness, common sense, discernment, insight, understanding, penetration, perception, perceptiveness, perspicacity, knowledge, sagacity; *informal* horse sense, know-how, (street) smarts; *rare* sapience.
▶ **adjective** *a savvy investor* SHREWD, astute, sharp-witted, sharp, acute, adroit, intelligent, clever, canny, perceptive, perspicacious, sagacious, sage, wise; *informal* on the ball, quick on the uptake, smart, streetwise, pawky, heads-up.

saw ▶ **noun 1** *an old rusty saw. See table.* **2** *the old saw about when the going gets tough* SAYING, maxim, proverb, aphorism, axiom, adage, epigram.

Types of Saw

backsaw	fretsaw
band saw	hacksaw
bench saw	handsaw
bowsaw	jig saw
bucksaw	mitre saw
buzz saw	radial arm saw
chainsaw	ripsaw
circular saw	sabre saw
compass saw	scroll saw
coping saw	slasher
crosscut saw	swede saw ✤
cylinder saw	table saw
dovetail saw	whipsaw

say ▶ **verb 1** *she felt her stomach flutter as he said her name* SPEAK, utter, voice, pronounce, give voice to, vocalize. **2** *'I must go,' she said* DECLARE, state, announce, remark, observe, mention, comment, note, add; reply, respond, answer, rejoin; *informal* come out with. **3** *Newall says he's innocent* CLAIM, maintain, assert, hold, insist, contend; allege, profess; *formal* opine, aver. **4** *I can't conjure up the words to say how I feel* EXPRESS, put into words, phrase, articulate, communicate, make known, put/get across, convey, verbalize; reveal, divulge, impart, disclose; imply, suggest. **5** *they sang hymns and said a prayer* RECITE, repeat, utter, deliver, perform, declaim, orate. **6** *the clock said one twenty* INDICATE, show, read. **7** *I'd say it's about five kilometres* ESTIMATE, judge, guess, hazard a guess, predict, speculate, surmise, conjecture, venture; *informal* reckon. **8** *let's* *say you'd just won a million dollars* SUPPOSE, assume, imagine, presume, hypothesize, postulate, posit.

▶ **noun 1** *everyone is entitled to their say* CHANCE TO SPEAK, turn to speak, opinion, view, voice; *informal* two cents, two cents' worth. **2** *don't I have any say in the matter?* INFLUENCE, sway, weight, voice, input, share, part.

■ **that is to say** IN OTHER WORDS, to put it another way; i.e., that is, to wit, viz, namely.

■ **to say the least** TO PUT IT MILDLY, putting it mildly, without any exaggeration, at the very least.

saying ▶ **noun** PROVERB, maxim, aphorism, axiom, adage, saw, tag, motto, epigram, dictum, expression, phrase, formula; slogan, catchphrase, mantra; platitude, cliché, commonplace, truism, chestnut.

■ **it goes without saying** OF COURSE, naturally, needless to say, it's taken for granted, it's understood/ assumed, it's taken as read, it's an accepted fact; obviously, self-evidently, manifestly; *informal* natch.

say-so ▶ **noun** *(informal)* **1** *they could not act without Parliament's say-so* AUTHORIZATION, (seal of) approval, agreement, consent, assent, permission, endorsement, sanction, ratification, approbation, acquiescence, blessing, leave; *informal* the OK, the go-ahead, the green light, the thumbs up, the rubber stamp. **2** *we wouldn't proceed merely on his say-so* ASSERTION, declaration, opinion.

− OPPOSITES: refusal, denial.

scalawag ▶ **noun** RASCAL, scamp, monkey, imp, devil, rogue; *informal* hellion, rapscallion, monster, terror, horror, tyke, varmint, *Nfld & Irish* sleeveen ❖.

scalding ▶ **adjective** EXTREMELY HOT, burning, blistering, searing, red-hot; piping hot; *informal* boiling (hot), sizzling.

scale[1] ▶ **noun 1** *the reptile's scales* plate; *technical* lamella, lamina, squama, scute. **2** *scales on the skin* FLAKE; **(scales)** scurf, dandruff. **3** *scale in kettles* BUILDUP, deposit, incrustation.

scale[2] ▶ **noun 1** *the Richter scale* CALIBRATED SYSTEM, graduated system, system of measurement. **2** *opposite ends of the social scale* HIERARCHY, ladder, ranking, pecking order, order, spectrum; succession, sequence, series. **3** *the scale of the map* RATIO, proportion, relative size. **4** *no one foresaw the scale of the disaster* EXTENT, size, scope, magnitude, dimensions, range, breadth, compass, degree, reach.

▶ **verb** *thieves scaled the fence* CLIMB, ascend, clamber up, shin (up), scramble up, mount, shinny (up).

■ **scale something down** REDUCE, cut down, cut back, cut, decrease, lessen, lower, trim, slim down, prune.

■ **scale something up** INCREASE, expand, augment, build up, add to; step up, boost, escalate.

scaly ▶ **adjective 1** *the dragon's scaly hide* technical squamous, squamate, lamellate. **2** *scaly patches of dead skin* DRY, flaky, flaking, scurfy, rough, scabrous, mangy, scabious.

scam ▶ **noun** *(informal)* FRAUD, swindle, racket, trick; *informal* con, hustle, bunco.

▶ **verb** SWINDLE, cheat, deceive, trick, dupe, hoodwink, double-cross, gull; *informal* rip off, con, fleece, shaft, hose, sting, bilk, diddle, rook, gyp, finagle, bamboozle, flim-flam, put one over on, pull a fast one on, sucker, stiff, hornswoggle.

scamp ▶ **noun** *(informal)* RASCAL, monkey, devil, imp, wretch, mischief-maker; *informal* scalawag, horror, monster, tyke, varmint, rapscallion; *archaic* scapegrace.

scamper ▶ **verb** SCURRY, scuttle, dart, run, rush, race, dash, hurry, hasten, scoot; skip, play, frolic, romp.

scan ▶ **verb 1** *Adam scanned the horizon* SCRUTINIZE, examine, study, inspect, survey, search, scour, sweep, look at, stare at, gaze at, eye, watch; *informal* check out, scope (out). **2** *I scanned the papers* GLANCE THROUGH, look through, have a look at, run/cast one's eye over, skim through, flick through, flip through, leaf through, thumb through.

▶ **noun 1** *a careful scan of the terrain* INSPECTION, scrutiny, examination, survey. **2** *a quick scan through the report* GLANCE, look, flick, browse. **3** *a brain scan* EXAMINATION, screening, MRI, ultrasound.

scandal ▶ **noun 1** *revelation of the sex scandal forced him to resign* WRONGDOING, impropriety, misconduct, immoral behaviour, unethical behaviour; offence, transgression, crime, sin; skeleton in the closet; *informal* -gate. **2** *it's a scandal that the disease is not adequately treated* DISGRACE, outrage, injustice; (crying) shame. **3** *no scandal attached to her name* MALICIOUS GOSSIP, malicious rumour(s), slander, libel, calumny, defamation, aspersions, muckraking; *informal* dirt.

scandalize ▶ **verb** SHOCK, appall, outrage, horrify, disgust; offend, affront, insult.

− OPPOSITES: impress.

scandalous ▶ **adjective 1** *a scandalous waste of taxpayers' money* DISGRACEFUL, shocking, outrageous, monstrous, criminal, wicked, shameful, appalling, deplorable, reprehensible, inexcusable, intolerable, insupportable, unforgivable, unconscionable, unpardonable. **2** *a series of scandalous liaisons* DISCREDITABLE, disreputable, dishonourable, improper, unseemly, sordid. **3** *scandalous rumours* SCURRILOUS, malicious, slanderous, libellous, defamatory.

scant ▶ **adjective** LITTLE, little or no, minimal, limited, negligible, meagre; insufficient, inadequate, deficient; *formal* exiguous.

− OPPOSITES: abundant, ample.

scanty ▶ **adjective 1** *their scanty wages* MEAGRE, scant, minimal, limited, modest, restricted, sparse; tiny, small, paltry, negligible, insufficient, inadequate, deficient; scarce, in short supply, thin on the ground, few and far between; *informal* measly, piddling, mingy, pathetic; *formal* exiguous. **2** *scanty clothing* SKIMPY, revealing, short, brief, low, low-cut; indecent.

− OPPOSITES: ample, plentiful.

scapegoat ▶ **noun** WHIPPING BOY; *informal* fall guy, patsy.

scar ▶ **noun 1** *the scar on his left cheek* CICATRIX, mark, blemish, disfigurement, discoloration; pockmark, pock, pit; lesion, stigma; birthmark, nevus. **2** *deep psychological scars* TRAUMA, damage, injury.

▶ **verb 1** *he's likely to be scarred for life* DISFIGURE, mark, blemish; pockmark, pit; stigmatize. **2** *a landscape which has been scarred by strip mining* DAMAGE, spoil, mar, deface, injure. **3** *she was profoundly scarred by the incident* TRAUMATIZE, damage, injure; distress, disturb, upset.

scarce ▶ **adjective 1** *food was scarce* IN SHORT SUPPLY, scant, scanty, meagre, sparse, hard to find, hard to come by, insufficient, deficient, inadequate; at a premium, paltry, negligible; *informal* not to be had for love or money; *formal* exiguous. **2** *birds that prefer dense forest are becoming scarce* RARE, few and far between, thin on the ground; uncommon, unusual.

− OPPOSITES: plentiful.

scarcely ▶ adverb **1** *she could scarcely hear what he was saying* HARDLY, barely, only just; almost not. **2** *I scarcely ever see him* RARELY, seldom, infrequently, not often, hardly ever, every once in a while; *informal* once in a blue moon. **3** *this could scarcely be accidental* SURELY NOT, not, hardly, certainly not, not at all, on no account, under no circumstances, by no means, noway.
— OPPOSITES: often.

scarcity ▶ noun SHORTAGE, dearth, lack, insufficiency, paucity, scantness, meagreness, sparseness, poverty; deficiency, inadequacy; unavailability, absence.

scare ▶ verb *stop it, you're scaring me* FRIGHTEN, startle, alarm, terrify, petrify, unnerve, intimidate, terrorize, cow; strike terror into, put the fear of God into, chill someone to the bone/marrow, make someone's blood run cold; *informal* frighten/scare the living daylights out of, scare stiff, scarify, frighten/scare someone out of their wits, scare witless, frighten/scare to death, scare the pants off, make someone's hair stand on end, make someone jump out of their skin, make someone's hair curl, spook, scare the bejesus out of, give someone the heebie-jeebies.
▶ noun *you gave me a scare — how did you get here?* FRIGHT, shock, start, turn, jump; *informal* heart attack.

scared ▶ adjective FRIGHTENED, afraid, fearful, nervous, panicky; terrified, petrified, horrified, panic-stricken, scared stiff, frightened/scared out of one's wits, scared witless, frightened/scared to death; *informal* in a cold sweat, spooked.

scaremonger ▶ noun ALARMIST, prophet of doom, Cassandra, voice of doom, doom-monger; *informal* Chicken Little.

scarf ▶ noun *she wore a scarf* MUFFLER, head scarf, mantilla, stole, tippet, babushka.
■ **scarf down** *he scarfed down his supper. See* GOBBLE.

scary ▶ adjective (*informal*) FRIGHTENING, alarming, terrifying, hair-raising, spine-chilling, blood-curdling, bone-chilling, white-knuckle, horrifying, nerve-racking, unnerving; eerie, sinister; *informal* creepy, spine-tingling, spooky, hairy.

scathing ▶ adjective WITHERING, blistering, searing, devastating, fierce, ferocious, savage, severe, stinging, biting, cutting, mordant, trenchant, virulent, caustic, vitriolic, scornful, sharp, bitter, harsh, unsparing.
— OPPOSITES: mild.

scatter ▶ verb **1** *scatter the seeds as evenly as possible* THROW, strew, toss, fling; sprinkle, spread, distribute, sow, broadcast, disseminate. **2** *the crowd scattered | onlookers were scattered in all directions* DISPERSE, break up, disband, separate, go separate ways, dissolve; drive, send, put to flight, chase.
— OPPOSITES: gather, assemble.

scatterbrain ▶ noun ABSENT-MINDED PERSON; *informal* airhead, flake, ditz, space cadet.

scatterbrained ▶ adjective ABSENT-MINDED, forgetful, disorganized; dreamy, with one's head in the clouds, feather-brained, giddy; *informal* scatty, with a mind/memory like a sieve, dizzy, dippy, ditzy, flaky.

scavenge ▶ verb SEARCH, hunt, look, forage, rummage, root about/around, grub about/around.

scenario ▶ noun **1** *Walt wrote scenarios for a major Hollywood studio* PLOT, outline, synopsis, storyline, framework; screenplay, script, libretto; *formal* diegesis. **2** *every possible scenario must be explored* SEQUENCE OF EVENTS, course of events, chain of events, situation. **3** *this film has a more contemporary scenario* SETTING, background, context, scene, milieu.

scene ▶ noun **1** *the scene of the accident* LOCATION, site, place, position, point, spot; locale, whereabouts; *technical* locus. **2** *the scene is Montreal, in the late 1890s* BACKGROUND, setting, context, milieu, backdrop, mise en scène. **3** *terrible scenes of violence* INCIDENT, event, episode, happening. **4** *an impressive mountain scene* VIEW, vista, outlook, panorama, sight; landscape, scenery. **5** *she created a scene* FUSS, exhibition of oneself, performance, tantrum, commotion, disturbance, upset, furor, brouhaha; *informal* to-do. **6** *the political scene* ARENA, stage, sphere, world, milieu, realm, domain; area of interest, field, province, preserve. **7** *a scene from a Laurel and Hardy film* CLIP, section, segment, part, sequence.
■ **behind the scenes** SECRETLY, in secret, privately, in private, behind closed doors, surreptitiously; *informal* on the quiet, on the q.t.; *formal* sub rosa.

scenery ▶ noun **1** *the beautiful scenery of the Rockies* LANDSCAPE, countryside, country, terrain, topography, setting, surroundings, environment; view, vista, panorama. **2** *we all helped with the scenery and costumes* STAGE SET, set, mise en scène, backdrop, drop curtain.

scenic ▶ adjective PICTURESQUE, pretty, pleasing, attractive, lovely, beautiful, charming, pretty as a picture, easy on the eye; impressive, striking, spectacular, breathtaking; panoramic.

scent ▶ noun **1** *the scent of freshly cut hay* SMELL, fragrance, aroma, perfume, redolence, savour, odour; bouquet, nose. **2** *the hounds picked up the scent of a hare* SPOOR, trail, track; *Hunting* foil, wind.
▶ verb **1** *a shark can scent blood from over half a kilometre away* SMELL, detect the smell of, get a whiff of. **2** *Rose looked at him, scenting a threat* SENSE, become aware of, detect, discern, recognize, get wind of.

scented ▶ adjective PERFUMED, fragranced, perfumy; sweet-smelling, fragrant, aromatic.

schedule ▶ noun **1** *we need to draw up a production schedule* PLAN, program, timetable, scheme. **2** *I have a very busy schedule* TIMETABLE, agenda, diary, calendar, timeline; itinerary.
▶ verb *another meeting was scheduled for April 20* ARRANGE, organize, plan, program, timetable, set up, line up, slate.
■ **behind schedule** LATE, running late, overdue, behind time, behind, behindhand.

scheme ▶ noun **1** *crazy fundraising schemes* PLAN, project, plan of action, program, strategy, stratagem, tactic, game plan, course/line of action; system, procedure, design, formula, recipe. **2** *Uncle Fred uncovered a scheme to steal the paintings* PLOT, intrigue, conspiracy; ruse, ploy, stratagem, manoeuvre, subterfuge; machinations; *informal* game, racket, con, scam. **3** *the sonnet's rhyme scheme* ARRANGEMENT, system, organization, configuration, pattern, format; *technical* schema.
▶ verb *he schemed to bring about the collapse of the government* PLOT, hatch a plot, conspire, intrigue, connive, manoeuvre, plan.

scheming ▶ adjective CUNNING, crafty, calculating, devious, designing, conniving, wily, sly, tricky, artful, guileful, slippery, slick, manipulative, Machiavellian, unscrupulous, disingenuous, duplicitous, deceitful, underhanded, treacherous.
— OPPOSITES: ingenuous, honest.

schism ▶ noun DIVISION, split, rift, breach, rupture,

break, separation, severance; chasm, gulf; discord, disagreement, dissension.

schmaltzy ▶ adjective. *See* SENTIMENTAL sense 2.

schmooze ▶ verb TALK, chat (up), converse, mingle, mix, hobnob, network; *informal* work the room.

scholar ▶ noun **1** *a leading biblical scholar* ACADEMIC, intellectual, learned person, man/woman of letters, mind, intellect, savant, polymath, highbrow, bluestocking; authority, expert; *informal* egghead. **2** (*archaic*) *the school had 28 scholars* PUPIL, student, schoolchild, schoolboy, schoolgirl.

scholarly ▶ adjective **1** *an earnest, scholarly man* LEARNED, erudite, academic, well-read, widely read, intellectual, literary, lettered, educated, knowledgeable, highbrow; studious, bookish, donnish, bluestocking, cerebral; *informal* pointy-headed. **2** *a scholarly career* ACADEMIC, scholastic, pedagogic.
— OPPOSITES: uneducated, illiterate.

scholarship ▶ noun **1** *a centre of medieval scholarship* LEARNING, book learning, knowledge, erudition, education, letters, culture, academic study, academic achievement. **2** *a scholarship of $200 per term* GRANT, award, endowment, payment, bursary.

scholastic ▶ adjective ACADEMIC, educational, school, scholarly.

Schools

academy	junior college ✦(*Que.*)
Bible school	junior high school
boarding school	kindergarten
CEGEP ✦(*Que.*)	law school
charm school	library school
charter school	lycée (*France*)
cheder	magnet school
choir school	middle school
church school	Montessori school
college	night school
collège classique ✦(*Que.*)	nursery school
hist.	parochial school
collegiate institute ✦	pre-law
community college	pre-med
composite high	prep school
school ✦(*Alta.*)	preparatory school
comprehensive high	preschool
school ✦	private school
conservatory	public school
consolidated school ✦	reform school
convent school	regional school ✦
correspondence school	residential school
day school	secondary school
district high school ✦	seminary
divinity school	senior high school
elementary school	separate school
finishing school	summer school
grade school	Sunday school
graduate school	teachers' college
grammar school	technical school
high school	university
integrated school ✦(*Nfld*)	vocational school
juku (*Japan*)	Waldorf school
	yeshiva

school ▶ noun **1** *their children went to the local school* EDUCATIONAL INSTITUTION; academy, college, university; seminary; alma mater. **2** *the university's School of Law* DEPARTMENT, faculty, division. **3** *the Barbizon school* GROUP, set, circle; followers, following, disciples,

apostles, admirers, devotees, votaries; proponents, adherents. **4** *that school of thought* WAY OF THINKING, persuasion, creed, credo, doctrine, belief, faith, opinion, point of view; approach, method, style. **5** *a school of fish* shoal, (*Nfld*) scull ✦; pod, gam.
— RELATED TERMS: scholastic.

▶ verb **1** *he was born in Paris and schooled in Lyon* EDUCATE, teach, instruct. **2** *he schooled her in horsemanship* TRAIN, teach, tutor, coach, instruct, drill, discipline, direct, guide, prepare, groom; prime, verse.

schooling ▶ noun **1** *his parents paid for his schooling* EDUCATION, teaching, tuition, instruction, tutoring, tutelage; lessons; (*book*) learning. **2** *the schooling of horses* TRAINING, coaching, instruction, drill, drilling, discipline, disciplining.

schoolteacher ▶ noun TEACHER, schoolmaster, schoolmistress, tutor, educationist; *informal* schoolmarm; *formal* pedagogue.

science ▶ noun **1** *a science teacher* physics, chemistry, biology; physical sciences, life sciences. **2** *the science of criminology* BRANCH OF KNOWLEDGE, body of knowledge/information, area of study, discipline, field.

scientific ▶ adjective **1** *scientific research* technological, technical; research-based, knowledge-based, empirical. **2** *you need to approach it in a more scientific way* SYSTEMATIC, methodical, organized, well-organized, ordered, orderly, meticulous, rigorous; exact, precise, accurate, mathematical; analytical, rational.

scintilla ▶ noun PARTICLE, iota, jot, whit, atom, speck, bit, trace, ounce, shred, crumb, fragment, grain, drop, spot, modicum, hint, touch, suggestion, whisper, suspicion; *informal* smidgen, tad.

scintillating ▶ adjective **1** *a scintillating diamond necklace* SPARKLING, shining, bright, brilliant, gleaming, glittering, twinkling, shimmering, glistening; *literary* glistering. **2** *a scintillating performance* BRILLIANT, dazzling, exciting, exhilarating, stimulating; sparkling, lively, vivacious, vibrant, animated, ebullient, effervescent; witty, clever; *literary* coruscating.
— OPPOSITES: dull, boring.

scion ▶ noun **1** *a scion of the tree* CUTTING, graft, slip; shoot, offshoot, twig. **2** *the scion of an aristocratic family* DESCENDANT; heir, successor; child, offspring; *Law* issue.

scoff ▶ verb *they scoffed at her article* MOCK, deride, ridicule, sneer at, jeer at, jibe at, taunt, make fun of, poke fun at, laugh at, scorn, laugh to scorn, dismiss, make light of, belittle; *informal* pooh-pooh.

scold ▶ verb *Mom took Anna away, scolding her for her bad behaviour* REBUKE, reprimand, reproach, reprove, admonish, remonstrate with, chastise, chide, upbraid, berate, take to task, read someone the riot act, give someone a piece of one's mind, rake someone over the coals; *informal* tell off, dress down, give someone an earful, rap over the knuckles, let someone have it, bawl out, give someone hell, tear a strip off someone, chew out, give someone what for, ream out, light into; *formal* castigate.
— OPPOSITES: praise.

▶ noun (*archaic*) *she is turning into a scold* NAG, shrew, fishwife, harpy, termagant, harridan; complainer, moaner, grumbler; *informal* kvetch.

scolding ▶ noun REBUKE, reprimand, reproach, reproof, admonishment, remonstration, lecture, upbraiding; *informal* talking-to, rap over the knuckles, dressing-down, earful, roasting; *formal* castigation.

scoop ▶ noun **1** *a measuring scoop* SPOON, ladle, dipper; bailer, (*Nfld*) spudgel ✦. **2** *a scoop of vanilla ice cream* SPOONFUL, ladleful, portion, lump, ball; *informal* dollop. **3** (*informal*) *he got the scoop on the new CEO* EXCLUSIVE (STORY), inside story, exposé, revelation, information.
▶ verb **1** *a hole was scooped out in the floor* HOLLOW OUT, gouge out, dig, excavate, cut out. **2** *cut the tomatoes in half and scoop out the flesh* REMOVE, take out, spoon out, scrape out. **3** *she scooped up armfuls of clothes* PICK UP, gather up, lift, take up; snatch up, grab.

scoot ▶ verb (*informal*). *See* SCURRY verb.

scope ▶ noun **1** *the scope of the investigation* EXTENT, range, breadth, width, reach, sweep, purview, span, horizon; area, sphere, field, realm, compass, orbit, ambit, terms/field of reference, jurisdiction; confine, limit; gamut. **2** *the scope for change is limited by political realities* OPPORTUNITY, freedom, latitude, leeway, capacity, liberty, room (to manoeuvre), elbow room; possibility, chance.

scorch ▶ verb **1** *the buildings were scorched by the fire* BURN, sear, singe, char, blacken, discolour. **2** *grass scorched by the sun* DRY UP, desiccate, parch, wither, shrivel; burn, bake.

scorching ▶ adjective **1** *the scorching July sun* EXTREMELY HOT, red-hot, blazing, flaming, fiery, burning, blistering, searing, sweltering, torrid, broiling; *informal* boiling (hot), baking (hot), sizzling. **2** *scorching criticism* FIERCE, savage, scathing, withering, blistering, searing, devastating, stringent, severe, harsh, stinging, biting, mordant, trenchant, caustic, virulent, vitriolic.
— OPPOSITES: freezing, mild.

score ▶ noun **1** *the final score was 4–3* RESULT, outcome; total, sum total, tally, count. **2** *an IQ score of 161* RATING, grade, mark, percentage. **3** *I've got a score to settle with you* GRIEVANCE, bone to pick, axe to grind, grudge, complaint; dispute, bone of contention. **4** (*informal*) *he knew the score before he got here* THE SITUATION, the position, the facts, the truth of the matter, the (true) state of affairs, the picture, how things stand, the lay of the land; *informal* what's what. **5** *scores of complaints* A GREAT MANY, a lot, a great/good deal, large quantities, plenty; *informal* lots, umpteen, a slew, loads, masses, stacks, scads, heaps, piles, bags, tons, oodles, dozens, hundreds, thousands, millions, billions, gazillions, a bunch.
▶ verb **1** *Lou's already scored 13 goals this season* NET, bag, rack up, chalk up, tally, notch, record; get, gain, achieve, make. **2** (*informal*) *his new movie really scored* BE SUCCESSFUL, be a success, triumph, make an impression, go down well; *informal* be a hit, be a winner, be a sell-out. **3** *the piece was scored for flute, violin, and continuo* ORCHESTRATE, arrange, set, adapt; write, compose. **4** *score the wood in criss-cross patterns* SCRATCH, cut, notch, incise, scrape, nick, chip, gouge; mark. **5** *he was hoping to score on his date tonight* GET LUCKY, have sex, go all the way, do it.
■ **score points off** GET THE BETTER OF, gain the advantage over, outdo, best, have the edge over; have the last laugh on, make a fool of, humiliate; *informal* get/be one up on, get one over on.

scorn ▶ noun *he was unable to hide the scorn in his voice* CONTEMPT, derision, contemptuousness, disdain, derisiveness, mockery, sneering.
— OPPOSITES: admiration, respect.
▶ verb **1** *critics scorned the painting* DERIDE, hold in

contempt, treat with contempt, pour/heap scorn on, look down on, look down one's nose at, disdain, curl one's lip at, mock, scoff at, sneer at, jeer at, laugh at, laugh out of court; disparage, slight; dismiss, thumb one's nose at; *informal* turn one's nose up at. **2** *'I am a woman scorned,' she thought* SPURN, rebuff, reject, ignore, shun, snub. **3** *she would have scorned to stoop to such tactics* REFUSE TO, refrain from, not lower oneself to; be above, consider it beneath one.
— OPPOSITES: admire, respect.

scornful ▶ adjective CONTEMPTUOUS, derisive, withering, mocking, scoffing, sneering, jeering, scathing, snide, disparaging, supercilious, disdainful, superior; *archaic* contumelious.
— OPPOSITES: admiring, respectful.

scotch ▶ verb PUT AN END TO, put a stop to, nip in the bud, put the lid on; ruin, wreck, destroy, smash, shatter, demolish, frustrate, thwart; *informal* put paid to, put the kibosh on, scupper, scuttle.

scot-free ▶ adverb UNPUNISHED, without punishment; unscathed, unhurt, unharmed, without a scratch; safely.

scoundrel ▶ noun ROGUE, rascal, miscreant, good-for-nothing, reprobate; cheat, swindler, scam artist, fraudster, trickster, charlatan; *informal* villain, bastard, beast, son of a bitch, SOB, rat, louse, swine, dog, skunk, heel, snake (in the grass), wretch, scumbag, scum-bucket, scuzzball, sleazeball, sleazebag, *Nfld & Irish* sleeveen ✦, rat fink; *informal, dated* hound; *dated* cad; *archaic* blackguard, knave, varlet, whoreson, picaroon.

scour¹ ▶ verb *she scoured the oven and cleaned out the cupboards* SCRUB, rub, clean, wash, cleanse, wipe; polish, buff (up), shine, burnish; abrade.

scour² ▶ verb *Christine scoured the shops for a gift* SEARCH, comb, hunt through, rummage through, go through with a fine-tooth comb, root through, rake through, leave no stone unturned, look high and low in; ransack, turn upside-down.

scourge ▶ noun **1** (*historical*) *he was beaten with a scourge* WHIP, horsewhip, lash, strap, birch, switch, bullwhip, rawhide; *historical* cat-o'-nine-tails. **2** *inflation was the scourge of the mid-1970s* AFFLICTION, bane, curse, plague, menace, evil, misfortune, burden, cross to bear; blight, cancer, canker.
— OPPOSITES: blessing, godsend.
▶ verb **1** (*historical*) *he was publicly scourged* FLOG, whip, beat, horsewhip, lash, flagellate, strap, birch, cane, thrash, belt, leather; *informal* tan someone's hide, take a strap to. **2** *a disease which scourged North America* AFFLICT, plague, torment, torture, curse, oppress, burden, bedevil, beset.

scout ▶ noun **1** *scouts reported the enemy's position* LOOKOUT, outrider, advance guard, vanguard; spy. **2** *a lengthy scout round the area* RECONNAISSANCE, reconnoitre; exploration, search, expedition; *informal* recon. **3** *a scout for a major-league team* TALENT SPOTTER, talent scout; *informal* bird dog.
▶ verb **1** *I scouted around for some logs* SEARCH, look, hunt, ferret about/around, root about/around. **2** *a night patrol was sent to scout out the area* RECONNOITRE, explore, make a reconnaissance of, inspect, investigate, spy out, survey; examine, scan, study, observe; *informal* check out, case.

scowl ▶ verb GLOWER, frown, glare, grimace, lower, look daggers at, give someone a black look; make a face, pull a face, turn the corner's of one's mouth down, pout; *informal* give someone a dirty look.
— OPPOSITES: smile, grin.

scrabble ▶ verb SCRATCH, grope, rummage, root, grub, scavenge, fumble, feel, clamber, scramble, scravel ✤.

scraggy ▶ adjective SCRAWNY, thin, as thin as a rake, skinny, skin-and-bones, gaunt, bony, angular, gawky, raw-boned.
– OPPOSITES: fat.

scram ▶ verb (informal) scram or I'll call the police GO AWAY, leave, get out; go, get moving, be off (with you); shoo; informal skedaddle, split, scat, run along, beat it, get lost, shove off, buzz off, push off, clear off, bug off, take a powder, take a hike; literary begone.

scramble ▶ verb 1 we scrambled over the boulders CLAMBER, climb, crawl, claw one's way, scrabble, grope one's way, scravel ✤, struggle, shinny. 2 small children scrambled for the scattered coins JOSTLE, scuffle, tussle, struggle, strive, compete, contend, vie, jockey. 3 the alcohol has scrambled his brains MUDDLE, confuse, mix up, jumble (up), disarrange, disorganize, disorder, disturb, mess up.
▶ noun 1 a short scramble over the rocks CLAMBER, climb, trek. 2 I lost Tommy in the scramble for a seat TUSSLE, jostle, scrimmage, scuffle, struggle, free-for-all, competition, contention, vying, jockeying; muddle, confusion, melee.

scrap¹ ▶ noun 1 a scrap of paper FRAGMENT, piece, bit, snippet, shred; offcut, oddment, remnant. 2 there wasn't a scrap of evidence BIT, speck, iota, particle, ounce, whit, jot, atom, shred, scintilla, tittle, jot or tittle; informal smidgen, tad. 3 he slept in the streets and lived on scraps LEFTOVERS, leavings, crumbs, scrapings, remains, remnants, residue, odds and ends, bits and pieces. 4 the whole thing was made from bits of scrap WASTE, rubbish, refuse, litter, debris, detritus; flotsam and jetsam, garbage, trash; informal junk.
▶ verb 1 old cars which are due to be scrapped THROW AWAY, throw out, dispose of, get rid of, toss out, throw on the scrap heap, discard, remove, dispense with, lose, decommission, recycle, break up, demolish; informal chuck (away/out), ditch, dump, junk, get shut of, trash, deep-six. 2 campaigners called for the plans to be scrapped ABANDON, drop, abolish, withdraw, throw out, do away with, put an end to, cancel, axe, jettison; informal ditch, dump, junk, can.
– OPPOSITES: keep, preserve.

scrap² (informal) ▶ noun he and Joe had several scraps QUARREL, argument, row, fight, disagreement, difference of opinion, falling-out, blow-up, dispute, squabble, contretemps, clash, altercation, brawl, tussle, conflict, shouting match; informal tiff, set-to, run-in, slanging match, shindy, spat, dust-up, ruction, bust-up.
▶ verb the older boys started scrapping with me QUARREL, argue, row, fight, squabble, brawl, bicker, spar, wrangle, lock horns, be at each other's throats.

scrape ▶ verb 1 we scraped all the paint off the windows ABRADE, grate, sand, sandpaper, scour, scratch, rub, file, rasp. 2 their boots scraped along the floor GRATE, creak, rasp, grind, scratch. 3 she scraped her hair back behind her ears RAKE, drag, pull, tug, draw. 4 he scraped a hole in the ground SCOOP OUT, hollow out, dig (out), excavate, gouge out. 5 Ellen had scraped her shins on the wall GRAZE, scratch, abrade, scuff, rasp, skin, rub raw, cut, lacerate, bark, chafe; Medicine excoriate.
▶ noun 1 the scrape of her key in the lock GRATING, creaking, grinding, rasp, rasping, scratch, scratching. 2 there was a long scrape on his shin GRAZE, scratch, abrasion, cut, laceration, wound. 3 (informal) he's always getting into scrapes PREDICAMENT, plight, tight

corner/spot, ticklish/tricky situation, problem, crisis, mess, muddle; informal jam, fix, stew, bind, hole, hot water, a pretty/fine kettle of fish.
■ **scrape by** MANAGE, cope, survive, muddle through/along, make ends meet, get by/along, make do, keep the wolf from the door, keep one's head above water, eke out a living; informal make out.

scrappy ▶ adjective 1 scrappy bits of paper DISORGANIZED, untidy, disjointed, unsystematic, uneven, bitty, sketchy; piecemeal; fragmentary, incomplete, unfinished. 2 a scrappy kid of sixteen FEISTY, tenacious, determined, persistent, dogged, aggressive, forceful; argumentative, confrontational, combative, antagonistic, bellicose, belligerent, combative, pugnacious, chippy; informal spoiling for a fight.

scratch ▶ verb 1 the paintwork was scratched SCORE, abrade, scrape, scuff. 2 thorns scratched her skin GRAZE, scrape, abrade, skin, rub raw, cut, lacerate, bark, chafe; wound; Medicine excoriate. 3 many names had been scratched out CROSS OUT, strike out, score out, delete, erase, remove, eliminate, expunge, obliterate. 4 she was forced to scratch from the race WITHDRAW, pull out of, back out of, bow out of, stand down.
▶ noun 1 he had two scratches on his cheek GRAZE, scrape, abrasion, cut, laceration, wound. 2 a scratch on the paintwork SCORE, mark, line, scrape.
■ **up to scratch** GOOD ENOUGH, up to the mark, up to standard, up to par, satisfactory, acceptable, adequate, passable, sufficient, all right; informal OK, jake, up to snuff.

scrawl ▶ verb he scrawled his name at the bottom of the page SCRIBBLE, write hurriedly, write untidily, dash off.
▶ noun his writing was a scrawl SCRIBBLE, chicken scratch, squiggle(s), hieroglyphics.

scrawny ▶ adjective SKINNY, thin, lean, as thin as a rake, skin-and-bones, gaunt, bony, angular, gawky, scraggy, raw-boned, anorexic.
– OPPOSITES: fat.

scream ▶ verb he screamed in pain SHRIEK, screech, yell, howl, shout, bellow, bawl, cry out, call out, yelp, squeal, wail, squawk; informal holler.
▶ noun 1 a scream of pain SHRIEK, screech, yell, howl, shout, bellow, bawl, cry, yelp, squeal, wail, squawk; informal holler. 2 (informal) the whole thing's a scream LAUGH, hoot; informal gas, giggle, riot, laff riot, bundle of fun/laughs, blast. 3 (informal) he's an absolute scream WIT, hoot, comedian, comic, entertainer, joker, clown, character; informal gas, giggle, riot; informal, dated caution, card.

screech ▶ verb. See SCREAM verb.

screen ▶ noun 1 he dressed hurriedly behind the screen PARTITION, (room) divider. 2 a computer with a 15-inch screen DISPLAY, monitor, video display terminal, VDT, cathode-ray tube, CRT. 3 every window has a screen because of mosquitoes MESH, net, netting. 4 the hedge acts as a screen against the wind BUFFER, protection, shield, shelter, guard, windbreak. 5 sift the dirt through a screen SIEVE, riddle, strainer, colander, filter.
▶ verb 1 the end of the hall had been screened off PARTITION OFF, divide off, separate off, curtain off. 2 the cottage was screened by the trees CONCEAL, hide, veil; shield, shelter, shade, protect, guard, safeguard. 3 the prospective candidates will have to be screened VET, check, check up on, investigate; informal check out. 4 all donated blood is screened for the virus CHECK, test, examine, investigate. 5 coal used to be screened by hand SIEVE, riddle, sift, strain, filter, winnow. 6 the program

is screened on Thursday evenings SHOW, broadcast, transmit, air, televise, telecast, put on the air.

screw ▶ noun **1** *stainless steel screws* BOLT, fastener; nail, pin, tack, spike, rivet, brad. **2** *the handle needs a couple of screws to tighten it* TURN, twist, wrench. **3** *the ship's twin screws* PROPELLER, rotor.

▶ verb **1** *he screwed the lid back on the jar* TIGHTEN, turn, twist, wind. **2** *the bracket was screwed in place* FASTEN, secure, fix, attach. **3** (*informal*) *she intended to screw money out of them* EXTORT, force, extract, wrest, wring, squeeze; *informal* bleed. **4** *he realized he had been screwed* CHEAT, trick, deceive, swindle, con, scam, dupe, fool; *informal* rip off, hose, gyp, bamboozle, stiff.

■ **put the screws on** (*informal*) PRESSURE, put pressure on, coerce, browbeat, use strong-arm tactics on, strong-arm; hold a gun to someone's head; *informal* turn the heat on, lean on, bulldoze.

■ **screw something up 1** *Christina screwed up her face in disgust* WRINKLE (UP), pucker, crumple, crease, furrow, contort, distort, twist, purse. **2** (*informal*) *they'll screw up the whole economy* WRECK, ruin, destroy, wreak havoc on, damage, spoil, mar; dash, shatter, scotch, make a mess of, mess up; *informal* louse up, foul up, put the kibosh on, scupper, scuttle, do for, nix.

scribble ▶ verb *he scribbled a few lines on a piece of paper* SCRAWL, write hurriedly, write untidily, scratch, dash off, jot (down); doodle.

▶ noun *a page of scribble* SCRAWL, squiggle(s), jottings; doodle, doodlings.

scribe ▶ noun **1** (*historical*) *a medieval scribe* CLERK, secretary, copyist, transcriber, amanuensis; *historical* penman, scrivener. **2** (*informal*) *a local scribe* WRITER, author, penman; journalist, reporter; *informal* hack, pencil-pusher.

scrimmage ▶ noun FIGHT, tussle, brawl, struggle, fracas, free-for-all, rough-and-tumble; *informal* scrap, dust-up, punch-up, set-to, shindy, scrum, roughhouse.

scrimp ▶ verb ECONOMIZE, skimp, scrimp and save, save; be thrifty, be frugal, tighten one's belt, cut back, husband one's resources, watch one's pennies, pinch (the) pennies.

script ▶ noun **1** *her neat, tidy script* HANDWRITING, writing, hand, penmanship, calligraphy. **2** *the script of the play* TEXT, screenplay; libretto, score; lines, dialogue, words.

scripture ▶ noun HOLY BOOK, sacred text(s). *See table.*

Scriptures

Christianity	Bible, New Testament
Confucianism	Analects
Hinduism	Bhagavad-Gita, Vedas
Islam	Koran
Judaism	Bible, Torah
Sikhism	Adi Granth
Taoism	Tao-te Ching

Scrooge ▶ noun MISER, penny-pincher, pinchpenny; *informal* skinflint, money-grubber, cheapskate, tightwad.

— OPPOSITES: spendthrift.

scrounge ▶ verb BEG, borrow; *informal* cadge, sponge, bum, touch someone for, mooch.

scrounger ▶ noun BEGGAR, borrower, parasite, cadger; *informal* sponger, freeloader, mooch, moocher, bum, bottom-feeder, schnorrer.

scrub[1] ▶ verb **1** *he scrubbed the kitchen floor* SCOUR,

rub; clean, cleanse, wash, wipe. **2** (*informal*) *the plans were scrubbed. See* SCRAP[1] *verb* sense 2.

scrub[2] ▶ noun *there the buildings ended and the scrub began* BRUSH, brushwood, (*Nfld*) tuckamore ✤, scrubland, underbrush, krummholz, undergrowth.

scruffy ▶ adjective SHABBY, worn, down-at-(the)-heel, ragged, tattered, mangy, dirty; untidy, unkempt, bedraggled, messy, dishevelled, ill-groomed; *informal* tatty, the worse for wear, ratty, raggedy, scuzzy.

— OPPOSITES: smart, tidy.

scrumptious ▶ adjective (*informal*) DELICIOUS, delectable, mouth-watering, tasty, appetizing, rich, savoury, flavourful, toothsome; succulent, luscious; *informal* yummy, lip-smacking, finger-licking, melt-in-your/the-mouth, nummy.

— OPPOSITES: unpalatable.

scrunch ▶ verb CRUMPLE, crunch, crush, rumple, screw up, squash, squeeze, compress.

scruple ▶ verb *she would not scruple to ask them for money* HESITATE, be reluctant, be loath, have qualms, have scruples, have misgivings, have reservations, think twice, balk, demur; recoil from, shrink from, shy away from, flinch from.

scruples ▶ plural noun *he had no scruples about eavesdropping* QUALMS, compunction, pangs/twinges of conscience, hesitation, reservations, second thoughts, doubt(s), misgivings, uneasiness, reluctance.

scrupulous ▶ adjective **1** *scrupulous attention to detail* CAREFUL, meticulous, painstaking, thorough, assiduous, sedulous, attentive, conscientious, punctilious, searching, close, minute, rigorous, particular, strict. **2** *a scrupulous man* HONEST, honourable, upright, upstanding, high-minded, right-minded, moral, ethical, good, virtuous, principled, incorruptible.

— OPPOSITES: careless, dishonest.

scrutinize ▶ verb EXAMINE, inspect, survey, study, look at, peruse; investigate, explore, probe, inquire into, go into, check; *informal* eyeball.

scrutiny ▶ noun EXAMINATION, inspection, survey, study, perusal; investigation, exploration, probe, inquiry; *informal* going-over.

scud ▶ verb SPEED, race, rush, sail, shoot, sweep, skim, whip, whiz, flash, fly, scurry, flit, scutter, scuttle.

scuff ▶ verb SCRAPE, scratch, rub, abrade; mark.

scuffle ▶ noun *there was a scuffle outside the pub* FIGHT, struggle, tussle, brawl, fracas, free-for-all, rough-and-tumble, scrimmage; *informal* scrap, dust-up, punch-up, set-to, shindy, roughhouse.

▶ verb *demonstrators scuffled with police* FIGHT, struggle, tussle, exchange blows, come to blows, brawl, clash; *informal* scrap.

sculpt ▶ verb CARVE, model, chisel, sculpture, fashion, form, shape, cast, cut, hew.

sculpture ▶ noun *a bronze sculpture* MODEL, carving, statue, statuette, figure, figurine, effigy, bust, head, likeness.

▶ verb *the choir stalls were carefully sculptured. See* SCULPT.

scum ▶ noun **1** *the water was covered with a thick green scum* FILM, layer, covering, froth; filth, dross, dirt. **2** (*informal*) *drug dealers are scum* DESPICABLE PEOPLE, the lowest of the low, the dregs of society, vermin, riff-raff, low-lifes; *informal* the scum of the earth, dirt.

scupper ▶ verb **1** *the captain decided to scupper the ship* SINK, scuttle, submerge, send to the bottom. **2** (*informal*) *he denied trying to scupper the agreement* RUIN, wreck, destroy, sabotage, torpedo, spoil, mess up; *informal* screw up, foul up, put the kibosh on; *archaic* bring to naught.

scurrilous ▶ adjective DEFAMATORY, slanderous, libellous, scandalous, insulting, offensive, gross; abusive, vituperative, malicious; *informal* bitchy.

scurry ▶ verb *pedestrians scurried for cover* HURRY, hasten, run, rush, dash; scamper, scuttle, scramble, scutter; *informal* scoot, beetle; *dated* make haste.
— OPPOSITES: amble.
▶ noun *there was a scurry to get out* RUSH, race, dash, run, hurry; scramble, bustle.

scuttle ▶ verb. *See* SCURRY *verb.*

sea ▶ noun **1** *the sea sparkled in the sun* (THE) OCEAN, the waves; *informal* the drink, the briny; *West* the chuck, (the) saltchuck; *literary* the deep, the main, the foam. *See table.* **2** *the boat overturned in the heavy seas* WAVES, swell, breakers, rollers, combers. **3** *a sea of roofs and turrets* EXPANSE, stretch, area, tract, sweep, blanket, sheet, carpet, mass; multitude, host, profusion, abundance, plethora.
— RELATED TERMS: marine, maritime, nautical.
▶ adjective *sea creatures* MARINE, ocean, oceanic; saltwater, seawater; ocean-going, seagoing, seafaring; maritime, naval, nautical; *technical* pelagic.
■ **at sea** CONFUSED, perplexed, puzzled, baffled, mystified, bemused, bewildered, nonplussed, disconcerted, disoriented, dumbfounded, at a loss, at sixes and sevens; *informal* flummoxed, bamboozled, fazed, discombobulated; *archaic* mazed.

Seas & Oceans

Adriatic Sea	Indian Ocean
Aegean Sea	Inland Sea
Antarctic Ocean	Ionian Sea
Arabian Sea	Irish Sea
Arafura Sea	Japan, Sea of
Aral Sea	Java Sea
Arctic Ocean	Kara Sea
Atlantic Ocean	Labrador Sea
Azov, Sea of	Laptev Sea
Baltic Sea	Ligurian Sea
Banda Sea	Marmara, Sea of
Barents Sea	Mediterranean Sea
Beaufort Sea	North Sea
Bellingshausen Sea	Okhotsk, Sea of
Bering Sea	Pacific Ocean
Bismarck Sea	Red Sea
Black Sea	Ross Sea
Caribbean Sea	Sargasso Sea
Caspian Sea	Savu Sea
Celebes Sea	South China Sea
Celtic Sea	Sulu Sea
China Sea	Tasman Sea
Chukchi Sea	Timor Sea
Coral Sea	Tyrrhenian Sea
Dead Sea	Weddell Sea
East China Sea	White Sea
East Siberian Sea	Yellow Sea
Galilee, Sea of	

seafaring ▶ adjective MARITIME, nautical, naval, seagoing, sea.

seal¹ ▶ noun **1** *the seal round the bath* SEALANT, sealer, adhesive, caulking. **2** *the king put his seal on the letter* EMBLEM, symbol, insignia, device, badge, crest, coat of arms, mark, monogram, stamp. **3** *the Minister gave his seal of approval to the project* RATIFICATION, approval,

blessing, consent, agreement, permission, sanction, endorsement, clearance.
▶ verb **1** *she quietly sealed the door behind her* FASTEN, secure, shut, close, lock, bolt. **2** *seal each bottle while it is hot* STOP UP, seal up, make airtight/watertight, cork, stopper, plug. **3** *police sealed off the block* CLOSE OFF, shut off, cordon off, fence off, isolate. **4** *that seals it* CLINCH, secure, settle, conclude, determine, complete, establish, set the seal on, confirm, guarantee; *informal* sew up.

seal² ▶ noun *seals were basking in the water* bull, cow. *See table.*
— RELATED TERMS: phocine.

Seals

bearded seal	sea lion
California sea lion	square-flipper seal
common seal	Steller's sea lion
elephant seal	walrus
fur seal	
grey seal	**Young seals**
harbour seal	beater
harp seal	bedlamer
hooded seal	blueback
northern sea lion	calf
ringed seal	pup
sea dog	raggedy-jacket
sea elephant	whelp
	whitecoat

seam ▶ noun **1** *the seam was coming undone* JOIN, stitching; *Surgery* suture. **2** *a seam of coal* LAYER, stratum, vein, lode. **3** *the seams of his face* WRINKLE, line, crow's foot, furrow, crease, corrugation, crinkle, pucker, groove, ridge.

seaman ▶ noun SAILOR, seafarer, mariner, boatman; hand; *informal* (old) salt, sea dog, rating, bluejacket, matelot, shellback.
— OPPOSITES: landlubber.

seamy ▶ adjective SORDID, disreputable, degenerate, seedy, sleazy, squalid, insalubrious, unwholesome, unsavoury, rough, unpleasant.
— OPPOSITES: salubrious.

sear ▶ verb **1** *the heat of the blast seared his face* SCORCH, burn, singe, char. **2** *sear the meat before adding the other ingredients* FLASH-FRY, seal, brown. **3** *his betrayal had seared her terribly* HURT, wound, pain, cut to the quick, sting; distress, grieve, upset, trouble, harrow, torment, torture.

search ▶ verb **1** *I searched for the key in my handbag* HUNT, look, seek, forage, fish about/around, look high and low, cast about/around, ferret about/around, root about/around, rummage about/around. **2** *he searched the house thoroughly* LOOK THROUGH, hunt through, explore, scour, rifle through, go through, sift through, comb, go through with a fine-tooth comb; turn upside down, turn inside out, leave no stone unturned in. **3** *the guards searched him for weapons* EXAMINE, inspect, check, frisk.
▶ noun *the police continued their search* HUNT, look, quest; pursuit, manhunt.
■ **in search of** SEARCHING FOR, hunting for, seeking, looking for, on the lookout for, in pursuit of.
■ **search me!** (*informal*) I DON'T KNOW, how should I know?, it's a mystery, I haven't a clue, I haven't the least idea, I've no idea, who knows; *informal* (I) dunno, don't ask me, I haven't the faintest/foggiest (idea/ notion), (it) beats me, ask me another, you got me.

searching ▶ **adjective** PENETRATING, piercing, probing, penetrative, keen, shrewd, sharp, intent.

searing ▶ **adjective 1** *the searing heat* SCORCHING, blistering, sweltering, blazing (hot), burning, fiery, torrid; *informal* boiling (hot), baking (hot), sizzling, roasting. **2** *searing pain* INTENSE, excruciating, agonizing, sharp, stabbing, shooting, stinging, severe, extreme, racking. **3** *a searing attack* FIERCE, savage, blistering, scathing, stinging, devastating, mordant, trenchant, caustic, cutting, biting, withering.

seaside ▶ **noun** COAST, shore, seashore, waterside; beach, sand, sands; *literary* strand.
— RELATED TERMS: littoral.

season ▶ **noun** *the rainy season* PERIOD, time, time of year, spell, term.
▶ **verb 1** *season the casserole to taste* FLAVOUR, add flavouring to, add salt/pepper to, spice. **2** *his answers were seasoned with wit* ENLIVEN, leaven, spice (up), liven up; *informal* pep up.
■ **in season** AVAILABLE, obtainable, to be had, on the market; plentiful, abundant.

seasonable ▶ **adjective** USUAL, expected, predictable, normal for the time of year.

seasoned ▶ **adjective** EXPERIENCED, practised, well versed, knowledgeable, established, habituated, veteran, hardened, battle-scarred, battle-weary.
— OPPOSITES: inexperienced.

seasoning ▶ **noun** FLAVOURING, salt and pepper, herbs, spices, condiments.

seat ▶ **noun 1** *a wooden seat* CHAIR, bench, stool, settle, stall; (**seats**) seating, room; pew. **2** *the seat of government* HEADQUARTERS, base, centre, nerve centre, hub, heart; location, site, whereabouts, place.
▶ **verb 1** *they seated themselves around the table* POSITION, put, place; ensconce, install, settle; *informal* plonk, park. **2** *the hall seats 500* HAVE ROOM FOR, contain, take, sit, hold, accommodate.

seating ▶ **noun** SEATS, room, places, chairs, accommodation.

secede ▶ **verb** *the southern states seceded from the Union, precipitating the Civil War* WITHDRAW FROM, break away from, break with, separate (oneself) from, leave, split with, split off from, disaffiliate from, resign from, pull out of; *informal* quit.
— OPPOSITES: join.

secluded ▶ **adjective** SHELTERED, private, concealed, hidden, unfrequented, sequestered, tucked away.
— OPPOSITES: busy.

seclusion ▶ **noun** ISOLATION, solitude, retreat, privacy, retirement, withdrawal, purdah, concealment, hiding, secrecy.

second¹ ▶ **adjective 1** *the second day of the trial* NEXT, following, subsequent, succeeding. **2** *he keeps a second pair of glasses in his office* ADDITIONAL, extra, alternative, another, spare, backup, fallback, alternate. **3** *he played second fiddle* SECONDARY, lower, subordinate, subsidiary, lesser, inferior. **4** *the conflict could turn into a second Vietnam* ANOTHER, new; repeat of, copy of, carbon copy of.
— OPPOSITES: first.
▶ **noun 1** *Eva had been working as his second. See* SECOND-IN-COMMAND. **2** (*informal*) *he enjoyed the pie and asked for seconds* A SECOND HELPING, a further helping, more.
▶ **verb** *the backbenchers seconded the motion* FORMALLY SUPPORT, give one's support to, vote for, back, approve, endorse.
■ **second to none** INCOMPARABLE, matchless,

unrivalled, inimitable, beyond compare/comparison, unparalleled, without parallel, unequalled, without equal, in a class of its own, peerless, unsurpassed, unsurpassable, nonpareil, unique; perfect, consummate, transcendent, surpassing, superlative, supreme; *formal* unexampled.

second² ▶ **noun** *I'll only be gone for a second* MOMENT, bit, little while, short time, instant, split second, eyeblink, heartbeat; *informal* sec, jiffy, the blink of an eye.
■ **in a second** VERY SOON, in a minute, in a moment, in a trice, shortly, any minute (now), in the twinkling of an eye, in (less than) no time, in no time at all, momentarily; *informal* in a jiffy, in two shakes (of a lamb's tail), in the blink of an eye, in a snap; *literary* ere long.

second³ ▶ **verb** *he was seconded to my department* ASSIGN TEMPORARILY, lend; transfer, move, shift, relocate, assign, reassign, send.

secondary ▶ **adjective 1** *a secondary issue* LESS IMPORTANT, subordinate, lesser, minor, peripheral, incidental, ancillary, subsidiary, non-essential, inessential, of little account, unimportant. **2** *secondary infections* ACCOMPANYING, attendant, concomitant, consequential, resulting, resultant.
— OPPOSITES: primary, main.

second-class ▶ **adjective** SECOND-RATE, second-best, inferior, lesser, unimportant.

second-hand ▶ **adjective 1** *second-hand clothes* USED, old, worn, pre-owned, handed-down, hand-me-down, cast-off. **2** *second-hand information* INDIRECT, derivative; vicarious.
— OPPOSITES: new, direct.
▶ **adverb** *I ignore anything I hear second-hand* INDIRECTLY, at second-hand, (esp. *North*) on the moccasin telegraph ✦; *informal* on the grapevine.
— OPPOSITES: directly.

second-in-command ▶ **noun** DEPUTY, number two, subordinate, right-hand man/woman, second; understudy; *informal* sidekick, second banana.

second-last ▶ **adjective** PENULTIMATE, next-to-last.

secondly ▶ **adverb** FURTHERMORE, also, moreover, likewise; second, in the second place, next; secondarily.

second-rate ▶ **adjective** INFERIOR, substandard, low-quality, below par, bad, poor, deficient, defective, faulty, imperfect, shoddy, chintzy, inadequate, insufficient, unacceptable; *informal* crummy, not up to scratch/snuff, rinky-dink.
— OPPOSITES: first-rate, excellent.

secrecy ▶ **noun 1** *the secrecy of the material* CONFIDENTIALITY, classified nature. **2** *a government which thrived on secrecy* SECRETIVENESS, covertness, furtiveness, surreptitiousness, stealth, stealthiness; *informal* hugger-mugger.

secret ▶ **adjective 1** *a secret plan* CONFIDENTIAL, top secret, classified, undisclosed, unknown, private, under wraps; *informal* hush-hush; *formal* sub rosa. **2** *a secret drawer in the table* HIDDEN, concealed, disguised; invisible. **3** *a secret operation to infiltrate terrorist groups* CLANDESTINE, covert, undercover, underground, surreptitious, stealthy, furtive, cloak-and-dagger, hole-and-corner, closet; *informal* hush-hush. **4** *a secret message | a secret code* CRYPTIC, encoded, coded; mysterious, abstruse, recondite, arcane, esoteric, cabbalistic. **5** *a secret place* SECLUDED, private, concealed, hidden, unfrequented, out of the way,

tucked away. **6** *a very secret person. See* SECRETIVE.
– OPPOSITES: public, open.
▶ **noun 1** *he just can't keep a secret* CONFIDENTIAL MATTER, confidence, private affair; skeleton in the closet. **2** *the secrets of the universe* MYSTERY, enigma, paradox, puzzle, conundrum, poser, riddle. **3** *the secret of their success* RECIPE, (magic) formula, blueprint, key, answer, solution.
■ **in secret** *See* SECRETLY sense 1.

secret agent ▶ **noun** SPY, double agent, counterspy, undercover agent, operative, plant, mole, sleeper, informant; *informal* spook.

secretary ▶ **noun** ASSISTANT, executive assistant, administrative assistant, personal assistant, clerical assistant, administrator, amanuensis, girl/man Friday, clerk.

secrete[1] ▶ **verb** *a substance secreted by the prostate gland* PRODUCE, discharge, emit, excrete, release, send out.
– OPPOSITES: absorb.

secrete[2] ▶ **verb** *we secreted ourselves in the bushes* CONCEAL, hide, cover up, veil, shroud, screen, stow away; bury, cache; *informal* stash away.
– OPPOSITES: reveal.

secretive ▶ **adjective** UNCOMMUNICATIVE, secret, unforthcoming, playing one's cards close to one's chest, reticent, reserved, silent, non-communicative, quiet, tight-lipped, close-mouthed, taciturn.
– OPPOSITES: open, communicative.

secretly ▶ **adverb 1** *they met secretly for a year* IN SECRET, in private, privately, behind closed doors, in camera, behind the scenes, under cover, under the counter, behind someone's back, furtively, stealthily, on the sly, on the quiet, conspiratorially, covertly, clandestinely, on the side; *informal* on the q.t., off the record, hush-hush; *formal* sub rosa. **2** *he was secretly jealous of Bartholomew* PRIVATELY, in one's heart (of hearts), deep down.

sect ▶ **noun** (RELIGIOUS) CULT, religious group, denomination, persuasion, religious order; splinter group, faction.

sectarian ▶ **adjective** FACTIONAL, separatist, partisan, parti pris; doctrinaire, dogmatic, extreme, fanatical, rigid, inflexible, bigoted, hidebound, narrow-minded.
– OPPOSITES: tolerant, liberal.

section ▶ **noun 1** *the separate sections of a train* PART, piece, bit, segment, component, division, portion, element, unit, constituent. **2** *the last section of the questionnaire* SUBDIVISION, part, subsection, division, portion, bit, chapter, passage, clause. **3** *the reference section of the library* DEPARTMENT, area, part, division. **4** *a residential section of the city. See* SECTOR sense 2.

sector ▶ **adjective 1** *every sector of the industry is affected* PART, branch, arm, division, area, department, field, sphere. **2** *the north-eastern sector of the town* DISTRICT, quarter, part, section, zone, region, area, belt.

secular ▶ **adjective** NON-RELIGIOUS, lay, temporal, worldly, earthly, profane; *formal* laic.
– OPPOSITES: holy, religious.

secure ▶ **adjective 1** *check to ensure that all bolts are secure* FASTENED, fixed, secured, done up; closed, shut, locked. **2** *an environment in which children can feel secure* SAFE, protected from harm/danger, out of danger, sheltered, safe and sound, out of harm's way, in a safe place, in safe hands, invulnerable; at ease, unworried, relaxed, happy, confident. **3** *a secure*

investment CERTAIN, assured, reliable, dependable, settled, fixed.
– OPPOSITES: loose, vulnerable, uncertain.
▶ **verb 1** *pins secure the handle to the main body* FIX, attach, fasten, affix, connect, couple. **2** *the doors had not been properly secured* FASTEN, close, shut, lock, bolt, chain, seal. **3** *he leapt out to secure the boat* TIE UP, moor, make fast; anchor. **4** *they sought to secure the country against attack* PROTECT, make safe, fortify, strengthen; undergird. **5** *a written constitution would secure the rights of the individual* ASSURE, ensure, guarantee, protect, confirm, establish. **6** *the division secured a major contract* OBTAIN, acquire, gain, get, get possession of; *informal* get hold of, land.

security ▶ **noun 1** *the security of the nation's citizens* SAFETY, freedom from danger, protection, invulnerability. **2** *he could give her the security she needed* PEACE OF MIND, feeling of safety, stability, certainty, happiness, confidence. **3** *security at the court was tight* SAFETY MEASURES, safeguards, surveillance, defence, protection. **4** *additional security for your loan may be required* GUARANTEE, collateral, surety, pledge, bond.
– OPPOSITES: vulnerability, danger.

sedate[1] ▶ **verb** *the patient had to be sedated* TRANQUILIZE, put under sedation, drug.

sedate[2] ▶ **adjective 1** *a sedate pace* SLOW, steady, dignified, unhurried, relaxed, measured, leisurely, slow-moving, easy, easygoing, gentle. **2** *he had lived a sedate and straightforward life* CALM, placid, tranquil, quiet, uneventful; boring, dull.
– OPPOSITES: exciting, fast.

sedative ▶ **adjective** *sedative drugs* TRANQUILIZING, calming, calmative, relaxing, soporific, narcotic; depressant; *Medicine* neuroleptic.
▶ **noun** *the doctor gave him a sedative* TRANQUILIZER, calmative, sleeping pill, narcotic, opiate; depressant; *informal* trank, downer.

sedentary ▶ **adjective** SITTING, seated, desk-bound, stationary; inactive, lethargic, lazy, idle.
– OPPOSITES: active.

sediment ▶ **noun** DREGS, lees, precipitate, deposit, grounds; residue, remains; silt, alluvium; *technical* residuum.

sedition ▶ **noun** RABBLE-ROUSING, incitement to rebel, subversion, troublemaking, provocation; rebellion, insurrection, mutiny, insurgence, civil disorder.

seditious ▶ **adjective** RABBLE-ROUSING, provocative, inflammatory, subversive, troublemaking; rebellious, insurrectionist, mutinous, insurgent.

seduce ▶ **verb 1** *he took her to his hotel room and tried to seduce her* persuade to have sex; *euphemistic* have one's (wicked) way with, take advantage of; *dated* debauch. **2** *she was seduced by the smell of coffee* ATTRACT, allure, lure, tempt, entice, beguile, inveigle, manoeuvre.

seducer ▶ **noun** WOMANIZER, philanderer, Romeo, Don Juan, Lothario, Casanova, playboy, ladies' man; *informal* lady-killer, wolf, skirt chaser.

seductive ▶ **adjective** SEXY, alluring, tempting, irresistible, exciting, provocative, sultry, slinky; coquettish, flirtatious; *informal* vampish, come-hither.

seductress ▶ **noun** TEMPTRESS, siren, femme fatale, Mata Hari, home wrecker, man-eater; flirt, coquette; *informal* vamp.

sedulous ▶ **adjective** DILIGENT, careful, meticulous, thorough, assiduous, attentive, industrious, conscientious, ultra-careful, punctilious, scrupulous, painstaking, minute, rigorous, particular.

see ▶ verb **1** *he saw her running across the road* DISCERN, spot, notice, catch sight of, glimpse, catch/get a glimpse of, make out, pick out, spy, distinguish, detect, perceive, note; *informal* clap/lay/set eyes on, clock; *literary* behold, descry, espy. **2** *I saw a documentary about it last week* WATCH, look at, view; catch. **3** *would you like to see the house?* INSPECT, view, look round, tour, survey, examine, scrutinize; *informal* give something a/the once-over. **4** *I finally saw what she meant* UNDERSTAND, grasp, comprehend, follow, take in, realize, appreciate, recognize, work out, get the drift of, perceive, fathom; *informal* get, latch on to, cotton on to, catch on to, savvy, figure out, get a fix on; *twig, suss* (out). **5** *I must go and see what Victor is up to* FIND OUT, discover, learn, ascertain, determine, establish. **6** *see that no harm comes to him* ENSURE, make sure/certain, see to it, take care, mind. **7** *I see trouble ahead* FORESEE, predict, forecast, prophesy, anticipate, envisage, picture, visualize. **8** *about a year later, I saw him in town* ENCOUNTER, meet, run into/across, come across, stumble on/across, happen on, chance on; *informal* bump into. **9** *they see each other from time to time* MEET, meet up with, get together with, socialize with. **10** *you'd better see a doctor* CONSULT, confer with, talk to, speak to, have recourse to, call on, call in, turn to, ask. **11** *he's seeing someone else now* GO OUT WITH, date, take out, be involved with; *informal* go steady with; *dated* court. **12** *he saw her to her car* ESCORT, accompany, show, walk, conduct, lead, take, usher, attend.

■ **see through** UNDERSTAND, get/have the measure of, read like a book; *informal* be wise to, have someone's number, know someone's (little) game.

■ **see someone through** SUSTAIN, encourage, buoy up, keep going, support, be a tower of strength to, comfort, help (out), stand by, stick by.

■ **see something through** PERSEVERE WITH, persist with, continue (with), carry on with, keep at, follow through, stay with; *informal* stick to, stick it out, hang in there.

■ **see to** ATTEND TO, deal with, see about, take care of, look after, sort out, fix, organize, arrange.

seed ▶ noun **1** *apple seeds* pip, stone, kernel; ovule. **2** *each war contains within it the seeds of a fresh war* GENESIS, source, origin, root, starting point, germ, beginnings, potential (for); cause, reason, motivation, motive, grounds. **3** *Abraham and his seed* DESCENDANTS, heirs, successors, scions; offspring, children, sons and daughters, progeny, family; *Law* issue; *derogatory* spawn; *archaic* fruit of someone's loins.
— RELATED TERMS: seminal.

■ **go/run to seed** DETERIORATE, degenerate, decline, decay, fall into decay, go to rack and ruin, go downhill, moulder, rot; *informal* go to pot, go to the dogs, go down the toilet.

seedy ▶ adjective **1** *the seedy world of prostitution* SORDID, disreputable, seamy, sleazy, squalid, unwholesome, unsavoury. **2** *a seedy strip* DILAPIDATED, tumbledown, ramshackle, falling to pieces, decrepit, gone to rack and ruin, run-down, down-at-the-heel, shabby, dingy, slummy, insalubrious, squalid; *informal* crummy; grotty, scuzzy.
— OPPOSITES: high-class.

seek ▶ verb **1** *they sought shelter from the winter snows* SEARCH FOR, try to find, look for, be on the lookout for, be after, hunt for, be in quest of. **2** *the company is*

seeking *a judicial review of the decision* TRY TO OBTAIN, work towards, be intent on, aim at/for. **3** *he sought help from the police* ASK FOR, request, solicit, call for, entreat, beg for, petition for, appeal for, apply for, put in for. **4** *we constantly seek to improve the service* TRY, attempt, endeavour, strive, work, do one's best; *formal* essay.

seem ▶ verb APPEAR (TO BE), have the appearance/air of being, give the impression of being, look, look as though one is, look like, show signs of, look to be; come across as, strike someone as, sound.

seeming ▶ adjective APPARENT, ostensible, supposed, outward, surface, superficial; pretended, feigned.
— OPPOSITES: actual, genuine.

seemingly ▶ adverb APPARENTLY, on the face of it, to all appearances, as far as one can see/tell, on the surface, to all intents and purposes, outwardly, superficially, supposedly.

seemly ▶ adjective DECOROUS, proper, decent, becoming, fitting, suitable, appropriate, apt, apposite, in good taste, genteel, polite, the done thing, right, correct, acceptable, comme il faut.
— OPPOSITES: unseemly, unbecoming.

seep ▶ verb OOZE, trickle, exude, drip, dribble, flow, issue, escape, leak, drain, bleed, filter, percolate, soak.

seer ▶ noun SOOTHSAYER, oracle, prophet(ess), augur, prognosticator, diviner, visionary, fortune teller, crystal-gazer, clairvoyant, psychic, medium; *literary* sibyl.

see-saw ▶ verb FLUCTUATE, swing, go up and down, rise and fall, oscillate, alternate, yo-yo, vary.
▶ noun TEETER-TOTTER.

seethe ▶ verb **1** *the brew seethed* BOIL, bubble, simmer, foam, froth, fizz, effervesce. **2** *the water was seething with fish* TEEM, swarm, boil, swirl, churn, surge. **3** *I seethed at the injustice of it all* BE ANGRY, be furious, be enraged, be incensed, be beside oneself, boil, simmer, rage, rant, rave, storm, fume, smoulder; *informal* be livid, be wild, foam at the mouth, be steamed up, be hot under the collar.

see-through ▶ adjective TRANSPARENT, translucent, clear, limpid, pellucid; thin, lightweight, flimsy, sheer, diaphanous, filmy, gossamer, chiffony, gauzy.
— OPPOSITES: opaque.

segment ▶ noun **1** *orange segments* PIECE, bit, section, part, chunk, portion, division, slice; fragment, wedge, lump. **2** *all segments of society* PART, section, sector, division, portion, constituent, element, unit, compartment; branch, wing.
▶ verb *they plan to segment their market share* DIVIDE (UP), subdivide, separate, split, cut up, carve up, slice up, break up; segregate, divorce, partition, section.
— OPPOSITES: amalgamate.

segregate ▶ verb SEPARATE, set apart, keep apart, isolate, quarantine, closet; partition, divide, detach, disconnect, sever, dissociate; marginalize, ghettoize.
— OPPOSITES: amalgamate.

seize ▶ verb **1** *she seized the microphone* GRAB, grasp, snatch, take hold of, get one's hands on; grip, clutch; nab. **2** *rebels seized the air base* CAPTURE, take, overrun, occupy, conquer, take over. **3** *the drugs were seized by customs* CONFISCATE, impound, commandeer, requisition, appropriate, expropriate, take away; *Law* distrain. **4** *terrorists seized his wife* KIDNAP, abduct, take captive, take prisoner, take hostage, hold to ransom; *informal* snatch.
— OPPOSITES: relinquish, release.

■ **seize on** *they seized on the opportunity* TAKE ADVANTAGE OF, exploit, grasp with both hands, leap at, jump at, pounce on.

seizure ▸ noun **1** *Napoleon's seizure of Spain* CAPTURE, takeover, annexation, invasion, occupation, colonization. **2** *the seizure of property* CONFISCATION, appropriation, expropriation, sequestration; *Law* distraint. **3** *the seizure of UN staff by rebels* KIDNAPPING, kidnap, abduction. **4** *the baby suffered a seizure* CONVULSION, fit, spasm, paroxysm; *Medicine* ictus; *dated* apoplexy.

seldom ▸ adverb RARELY, infrequently, hardly (ever), scarcely (ever), almost never; now and then, occasionally, sporadically; *informal* once in a blue moon.
– OPPOSITES: often.

select ▸ verb *select the correct tool for the job* CHOOSE, pick (out), single out, sort out, take; opt for, decide on, settle on, determine, nominate, appoint, elect.
▸ adjective **1** *a select group of players* CHOICE, hand-picked, prime, first-rate, first-class, superior, finest, best, top-class, blue-ribbon, supreme, superb, excellent; *informal* A1, top-notch. **2** *a select clientele* EXCLUSIVE, elite, favoured, privileged; wealthy; *informal* posh.
– OPPOSITES: inferior.

selection ▸ noun **1** *Jim made his selection of toys* CHOICE, pick; option, preference. **2** *a wide selection of dishes* RANGE, array, diversity, variety, assortment, mixture. **3** *a selection of his poems* ANTHOLOGY, assortment, collection, assemblage, compilation; miscellany, medley, potpourri.

selective ▸ adjective DISCERNING, discriminating, discriminatory, critical, exacting, demanding, particular; fussy, fastidious; *informal* choosy, persnickety, picky, finicky.

self ▸ noun EGO, I, oneself, persona, person, identity, character, personality, psyche, soul, spirit, mind, inner self, inner being.
– OPPOSITES: other.

self-assurance ▸ noun SELF-CONFIDENCE, confidence, assertiveness, self-reliance, composure, self-possession, presence of mind, aplomb.
– OPPOSITES: diffidence.

self-assured ▸ adjective SELF-CONFIDENT, confident, assertive, assured, authoritative, commanding, self-reliant, self-possessed, poised.

self-centred ▸ adjective EGOCENTRIC, egotistic, egotistical, egomaniacal, self-absorbed, self-obsessed, self-seeking, self-interested, self-serving; narcissistic, vain; inconsiderate, thoughtless; *informal* looking after number one.

self-confidence ▸ noun MORALE, confidence, self-assurance, assurance, assertiveness, self-reliance, self-possession, composure.

self-conscious ▸ adjective EMBARRASSED, uncomfortable, uneasy, nervous; unnatural, inhibited, gauche, awkward; modest, shy, diffident, bashful, retiring, shrinking.
– OPPOSITES: confident.

self-contained ▸ adjective **1** *each train was a self-contained unit* COMPLETE, independent, separate, free-standing, enclosed. **2** *a very self-contained child* INDEPENDENT, self-sufficient, self-reliant; introverted, quiet, private, aloof, insular, reserved, reticent, secretive.

self-control ▸ noun SELF-DISCIPLINE, restraint, self-possession, willpower, composure, coolness;

moderation, temperance, abstemiousness; *informal* cool.

self-denial ▸ noun SELF-SACRIFICE, selflessness, unselfishness; self-discipline, asceticism, self-deprivation, abstemiousness, abstinence, abstention; moderation, temperance.
– OPPOSITES: self-indulgence.

self-discipline ▸ noun SELF-CONTROL; restraint, self-restraint; willpower, purposefulness, strong-mindedness, resolve, moral fibre; doggedness, persistence, determination, grit.

self-employed ▸ adjective FREELANCE, independent, casual; consultant, consulting; temporary, jobbing, contract, visiting, outside, external, extramural.

self-esteem ▸ noun SELF-RESPECT, pride, dignity, self-regard, faith in oneself; morale, self-confidence, confidence, self-assurance.

self-evident ▸ adjective OBVIOUS, clear, plain, evident, apparent, manifest, patent, axiomatic; distinct, transparent, overt, conspicuous, palpable, unmistakable, undeniable.
– OPPOSITES: unclear.

self-explanatory ▸ adjective EASILY UNDERSTOOD, comprehensible, intelligible, straightforward, unambiguous, accessible, crystal clear, user-friendly, simple, self-evident, obvious.
– OPPOSITES: impenetrable.

self-government ▸ noun INDEPENDENCE, self-rule, home rule, self-determination, sovereignty, autonomy, non-alignment, freedom.
– OPPOSITES: hegemony, colonialism.

self-important ▸ adjective CONCEITED, arrogant, bumptious, full of oneself, puffed up, pompous, overbearing, opinionated, cocky, presumptuous, sententious, vain, overweening, proud, egotistical; *informal* snooty, uppity, uppish.
– OPPOSITES: humble.

self-indulgent ▸ adjective HEDONISTIC, pleasure-seeking, sybaritic, indulgent, luxurious, lotus-eating, epicurean; intemperate, immoderate, overindulgent, excessive, extravagant, licentious, dissolute, decadent.
– OPPOSITES: abstemious.

self-interested ▸ adjective SELF-SEEKING, self-serving, self-obsessed, self-absorbed, wrapped up in oneself, egocentric, egotistic, egotistical, egomaniacal, selfish; *informal* looking after number one.

selfish ▸ adjective EGOCENTRIC, egotistic, egotistical, egomaniacal, self-centred, self-absorbed, self-obsessed, self-seeking, self-serving, wrapped up in oneself; inconsiderate, thoughtless, unthinking, uncaring, uncharitable; mean, miserly, grasping, greedy, mercenary, acquisitive, opportunistic; *informal* looking after number one.
– OPPOSITES: altruistic.

selfless ▸ adjective UNSELFISH, altruistic, self-sacrificing, self-denying; considerate, compassionate, kind, noble, generous, magnanimous, ungrudging, charitable, benevolent, open-handed.
– OPPOSITES: inconsiderate.

self-possessed ▸ adjective ASSURED, self-assured, calm, cool, composed, at ease, unperturbed, unruffled, confident, self-confident, poised, imperturbable; *informal* together, unfazed,

nonplussed, unflappable.
— OPPOSITES: unsure.

self-possession ▶ noun COMPOSURE, assurance, self-assurance, self-control, imperturbability, impassivity, equanimity, nonchalance, confidence, self-confidence, poise, aplomb, presence of mind, nerve, sang-froid; *informal* cool.

self-reliant ▶ adjective SELF-SUFFICIENT, self-supporting, self-sustaining, able to stand on one's own two feet; independent, autarkic.

self-respect ▶ noun SELF-ESTEEM, self-regard, amour propre, faith in oneself, pride, dignity, morale, self-confidence.

self-restraint ▶ noun SELF-CONTROL, restraint, self-discipline, self-possession, willpower, moderation, temperance, abstemiousness, abstention.
— OPPOSITES: self-indulgence.

self-righteous ▶ adjective SANCTIMONIOUS, holier-than-thou, self-satisfied, smug, priggish, complacent, pious, moralizing, preachy, superior, hypocritical; *informal* goody-goody.
— OPPOSITES: humble.

self-sacrifice ▶ noun SELF-DENIAL, selflessness, unselfishness; self-discipline, abstinence, asceticism, abnegation, self-deprivation, moderation, austerity, temperance, abstention.

self-satisfied ▶ adjective COMPLACENT, self-congratulatory, smug, superior, puffed up, pleased with oneself; *informal* goody-goody.

self-seeking ▶ adjective SELF-INTERESTED, self-serving, selfish, egocentric, egotistic, egotistical, self-obsessed, self-absorbed; inconsiderate, thoughtless, unthinking; *informal* looking after number one.
— OPPOSITES: altruistic.

self-styled ▶ adjective WOULD-BE, so-called, self-appointed, self-titled, professed, self-confessed, soi-disant.

self-sufficient ▶ adjective SELF-SUPPORTING, self-reliant, self-sustaining, able to stand on one's own two feet; independent, autarkic.

self-willed ▶ adjective WILFUL, contrary, perverse, uncooperative, wayward, headstrong, stubborn, obstinate, obdurate, pigheaded, mulish, intransigent, recalcitrant, intractable; *informal* bloody-minded; *formal* refractory.
— OPPOSITES: biddable.

sell ▶ verb **1** *they are selling their house* PUT UP FOR SALE, offer for sale, put on sale, dispose of, vend, auction (off); trade, barter. **2** *he sells cakes* TRADE IN, deal in, traffic in, stock, carry, offer for sale, peddle, hawk, retail, market. **3** *the book should sell well* GO, be bought, be purchased; move, be in demand. **4** *it sells for $79.95* COST, be priced at, retail at, go for, be. **5** *he still has to sell his plan to management* PROMOTE; persuade someone to accept, talk someone into, bring someone round to, win someone over to, win approval for.
— OPPOSITES: buy.
■ **sell someone down the river** (*informal*). See BETRAY verb sense 1.
■ **sell out 1** *we've sold out of chocolate* HAVE NONE LEFT, be out of stock, have run out; *informal* be fresh out, be cleaned out. **2** *the edition sold out quickly* BE BOUGHT UP, be bedelled, be exhausted. **3** *they say he has sold out as an artist* ABANDON ONE'S PRINCIPLES, prostitute oneself, sell one's soul, betray one's ideals, be untrue to oneself; debase oneself, degrade oneself, demean oneself.
■ **sell someone out** BETRAY, inform on; be disloyal to, be unfaithful to, double-cross, break faith with, stab in the back; *informal* tell on, sell down the river, blow the whistle on, squeal on, peach on, finger.
■ **sell someone short** UNDERVALUE, underrate, underestimate, disparage, deprecate, belittle; *formal* derogate.

seller ▶ noun VENDOR, retailer, purveyor, supplier, trader, merchant, dealer; shopkeeper, salesperson, salesman, saleswoman, sales assistant, sales associate, clerk, shop assistant, travelling salesperson, peddler, hawker; auctioneer.

semblance ▶ noun (OUTWARD) APPEARANCE, air, show, facade, front, veneer, guise, pretense.

seminal ▶ adjective INFLUENTIAL, formative, groundbreaking, pioneering, original, innovative; major, important.

seminar ▶ noun **1** *a seminar for education officials* CONFERENCE, symposium, meeting, convention, forum, summit, discussion, consultation. **2** *teaching in the form of seminars* STUDY GROUP, workshop, tutorial, class, lesson.

seminary ▶ noun THEOLOGICAL COLLEGE, rabbinical college, Talmudical college, Bible school/college, divinity school; academy, training college, training institute, school.

send ▶ verb **1** *they sent a message to HQ* DISPATCH, post, mail, address, consign, direct, forward; transmit, convey, communicate; telephone, phone, broadcast, radio, fax, email; *dated* telegraph, wire, cable. **2** *we sent for a doctor* CALL, summon, contact; ask for, request, order. **3** *the pump sent out a jet of steam* PROPEL, project, eject, deliver, discharge, spout, fire, shoot, release; throw, let fly; *informal* chuck.
— OPPOSITES: receive.
■ **send someone off** (*Sport*) ORDER OFF, dismiss; show someone the red card; *informal* red-card.
■ **send someone/something up** (*informal*) SATIRIZE, ridicule, make fun of, parody, lampoon, mock, caricature, imitate, ape; *informal* take off, spoof.

send-off ▶ noun FAREWELL, goodbye, adieu, leave-taking, valediction; *archaic* vale.
— OPPOSITES: welcome.

send-up ▶ noun (*informal*) SATIRE, burlesque, lampoon, pastiche, caricature, imitation, impression, impersonation; mockery, mimicry, travesty; *informal* spoof, takeoff.

senile ▶ adjective DODDERING, doddery, decrepit, senescent, declining, infirm, feeble; aged, long in the tooth, in one's dotage; mentally confused, having Alzheimer's (disease), having senile dementia; *informal* past it, gaga.

senior ▶ adjective **1** *senior school students* OLDER, elder. **2** *a senior officer* SUPERIOR, higher-ranking, high-ranking, more important; top, chief, ranking. **3** *Albert Stone Senior* THE ELDER, I.
— OPPOSITES: junior, subordinate.

senior citizen ▶ noun RETIRED PERSON, (old-age) pensioner; old person, elderly person, senior, geriatric, dotard, Methuselah, retiree, golden ager; *informal* old-timer, oldie, oldster, geezer, blue-hair.

seniority ▶ noun RANK, superiority, standing, primacy, precedence, priority; age, experience.

sensation ▶ noun **1** *a sensation of light* FEELING, sense, awareness, consciousness, perception, impression. **2** *he caused a sensation by donating $1m*

COMMOTION, stir, uproar, furor, scandal, impact; interest, excitement; *informal* splash, to-do, hullabaloo, hoopla. **3** *the film became an instant sensation* TRIUMPH, success, sell-out; talking point; *informal* smash (hit), hit, winner, crowd-pleaser, knockout, blockbuster.

sensational ▶ adjective **1** *a sensational murder trial* SHOCKING, scandalous, appalling; amazing, startling, astonishing, staggering; stirring, exciting, thrilling, electrifying, red-hot; fascinating, interesting, noteworthy, significant, remarkable, momentous, historic, newsworthy. **2** *sensational stories* OVER-DRAMATIZED, dramatic, melodramatic, exaggerated, sensationalist, sensationalistic; graphic, explicit, lurid; *informal* juicy. **3** (*informal*) *she looked sensational* GORGEOUS, stunning, wonderful, exquisite, lovely, radiant, delightful, charming, enchanting, captivating; striking, spectacular, remarkable, outstanding, arresting, eye-catching; marvellous, superb, excellent, fine, first-class; *informal* great, terrific, tremendous, super, fantastic, fabulous, fab, heavenly, divine, knockout, hot, red-hot, delectable, scrumptious, awesome, magic, wicked, killer, out of this world, smashing, brilliant.
− OPPOSITES: dull, understated, unremarkable.

sense ▶ noun **1** *the sense of touch* SENSORY FACULTY, feeling, sensation, perception; sight, hearing, touch, taste, smell. **2** *a sense of guilt* FEELING, awareness, sensation, consciousness, recognition. **3** *a sense of humour* APPRECIATION, awareness, understanding, comprehension, discernment; *informal* nose. **4** *she had the sense to press the panic button* WISDOM, common sense, sagacity, discernment, perception; wit, intelligence, cleverness, shrewdness, judgment, reason, logic, brain(s); *informal* gumption, horse sense, savvy, (street) smarts. **5** *I can't see the sense in this* PURPOSE, point, reason, object, motive; use, value, advantage, benefit. **6** *the different senses of 'well'* MEANING, definition, import, signification, significance, purport, implication, nuance; drift, gist, thrust, tenor, message.
− OPPOSITES: stupidity.
▶ verb *she sensed their hostility* DISCERN, feel, observe, notice, recognize, pick up, be aware of, distinguish, make out, identify; comprehend, apprehend, see, appreciate, realize; suspect, have a funny feeling about, have a hunch, divine, intuit; *informal* catch on to, twig.

senseless ▶ adjective **1** *they found him senseless on the floor* UNCONSCIOUS, stunned, insensible, insensate, comatose, knocked out, out cold, out for the count; numb; *informal* KO'd, dead to the world, passed out. **2** *a senseless waste* POINTLESS, futile, useless, needless, unavailing, in vain, purposeless, meaningless, unprofitable; absurd, foolish, insane, stupid, idiotic, ridiculous, ludicrous, mindless, illogical.
− OPPOSITES: conscious, wise.

sensibility ▶ noun **1** *develop your sensibility* SENSITIVITY, finer feelings, delicacy, taste, discrimination, discernment; understanding, insight, empathy, appreciation; feeling, intuition, responsiveness, receptiveness, perceptiveness, awareness. **2** *the wording might offend their sensibilities* (FINER) FEELINGS, emotions, sensitivities, moral sense.

sensible ▶ adjective PRACTICAL, realistic, responsible, reasonable, commonsensical, rational, logical, sound, balanced, sober, no-nonsense, pragmatic, level-headed, thoughtful, down-to-earth, wise, prudent, judicious, sagacious, shrewd.
− OPPOSITES: foolish.

sensitive ▶ adjective **1** *she's sensitive to changes in temperature* RESPONSIVE TO, reactive to, sentient of, sensitized to; aware of, conscious of, alive to; susceptible to, affected by, vulnerable to; attuned to. **2** *sensitive skin* DELICATE, fragile; tender, sore, raw. **3** *the matter needs sensitive handling* TACTFUL, careful, thoughtful, diplomatic, delicate, subtle, kid-glove; sympathetic, compassionate, understanding, intuitive, responsive, insightful. **4** *he's sensitive about his bald patch* TOUCHY, over-sensitive, hypersensitive, easily offended, easily upset, easily hurt, thin-skinned, defensive; paranoid, neurotic; *informal* uptight. **5** *a sensitive issue* DIFFICULT, delicate, tricky, awkward, problematic, ticklish, precarious; controversial, emotive; *informal* sticky.
− OPPOSITES: impervious, resilient, clumsy, thick-skinned, uncontroversial.

sensitivity ▶ noun **1** *the sensitivity of the skin* RESPONSIVENESS, sensitiveness, reactivity; susceptibility, vulnerability. **2** *the job calls for sensitivity* CONSIDERATION, care, thoughtfulness, tact, diplomacy, delicacy, subtlety, finer feelings; understanding, empathy, sensibility, feeling, intuition, responsiveness, receptiveness; perception, discernment, insight; savoir faire. **3** *her sensitivity on the subject of marriage* TOUCHINESS, oversensitivity, hypersensitivity, defensiveness. **4** *the sensitivity of the issue* DELICACY, trickiness, awkwardness, ticklishness.

sensual ▶ adjective **1** *sensual pleasure* PHYSICAL, carnal, bodily, fleshly, animal; hedonistic, epicurean, sybaritic, voluptuary. **2** *a beautiful, sensual woman* SEXUALLY ATTRACTIVE, sexy, voluptuous, sultry, seductive, passionate; sexually arousing, erotic, sexual.
− OPPOSITES: spiritual, passionless.

sensuality ▶ noun SEXINESS, sexual attractiveness, sultriness, seductiveness; sexuality, eroticism; physicality, carnality.

sensuous ▶ adjective **1** *big sensuous images* AESTHETICALLY PLEASING, gratifying, rich, sumptuous, luxurious; sensory, sensorial. **2** *sensuous lips* SEXUALLY ATTRACTIVE, sexy, seductive, voluptuous, luscious, lush.

sentence ▶ noun PRISON TERM, prison sentence; punishment; *informal* time, stretch, stint.
▶ verb *they were sentenced to death* PASS JUDGMENT ON, punish, convict; condemn, doom.

sententious ▶ adjective MORALISTIC, moralizing, sanctimonious, self-righteous, pietistic, pious, priggish, judgmental; pompous, pontifical, self-important; *informal* preachy.

sentient ▶ adjective (CAPABLE OF) FEELING, living, live; conscious, aware, responsive, reactive.

sentiment ▶ noun **1** *the comments echo my own sentiments* VIEW, feeling, attitude, thought, opinion, belief. **2** *there's no room for sentiment in sport* SENTIMENTALITY, sentimentalism, mawkishness, emotionalism; emotion, sensibility, soft-heartedness; tender-heartedness; *informal* schmaltz, mush, slushiness, corniness, cheese, soppiness, sappiness.

sentimental ▶ adjective **1** *she kept the vase for sentimental reasons* NOSTALGIC, tender, emotional, affectionate. **2** *the film is too sentimental* MAWKISH, over-emotional, cloying, sickly, saccharine, sugary; romantic, touching, twee; *informal* slushy, mushy, weepy, tear-jerking, schmaltzy, lovey-dovey, gooey, drippy, cheesy, corny, soppy, cornball, sappy, hokey.

3 *she is sentimental about animals* SOFT-HEARTED, tender-hearted, soft; *informal* soppy.
– OPPOSITES: practical, gritty.

sentry ▶ noun GUARD, sentinel, lookout, watch, watchman, patrol.

separable ▶ adjective DIVISIBLE, distinct, independent, distinguishable; detachable; removable, pull-off.

separate ▶ adjective **1** *his personal life was separate from his job* UNCONNECTED, unrelated, different, distinct, discrete; detached, divorced, disconnected, independent, autonomous. **2** *the infirmary was separate from the school* SET APART, detached, fenced off, cut off, segregated, isolated; free-standing, self-contained.
– OPPOSITES: linked, attached.
▶ verb **1** *they separated two rioting mobs* SPLIT (UP), break up, part, pull apart, divide; *literary* sunder. **2** *the connectors can be separated* DISCONNECT, detach, disengage, uncouple, unyoke, disunite, disjoin; split, divide, sever; disentangle. **3** *the wall that separated the two properties* PARTITION, divide, come between, keep apart; bisect, intersect. **4** *the south aisle was separated off* ISOLATE, partition off, section off; close off, shut off, cordon off, fence off, screen off. **5** *they separated at the airport* PART (COMPANY), go their separate ways, split up; say goodbye; disperse, disband, scatter. **6** *the road separated* FORK, divide, branch, bifurcate, diverge. **7** *her parents separated* SPLIT UP, break up, part, be estranged, divorce. **8** *separate fact from fiction* ISOLATE, set apart, segregate; distinguish, differentiate, dissociate; sort out, sift out, filter out, remove, weed out. **9** *those who separate themselves from society* BREAK AWAY FROM, break with, secede from, withdraw from, leave, quit, dissociate oneself from, resign from, drop out of, repudiate, reject.
– OPPOSITES: unite, join, link, meet, merge, marry.

separately ▶ adverb INDIVIDUALLY, one by one, one at a time, singly, severally; apart, independently, alone, by oneself, on one's own.

separation ▶ noun **1** *the separation of the two companies* DISCONNECTION, detachment, severance, dissociation, disunion, disaffiliation, segregation, partition. **2** *her parents' separation* BREAKUP, split, parting (of the ways), estrangement, rift, rupture, breach; divorce. **3** *the separation between art and life* DISTINCTION, difference, differentiation, division, dividing line; gulf, gap, chasm.

separatist ▶ noun sovereignist ✦ (or sovereigntist ✦), indépendantiste ✦, Péquiste ✦.

septic ▶ adjective INFECTED, festering, suppurating, pus-filled, putrid, putrefying, poisoned, diseased; *Medicine* purulent.

sepulchral ▶ adjective GLOOMY, lugubrious, sombre, melancholy, melancholic, sad, sorrowful, mournful, doleful, dismal; *literary* dolorous.
– OPPOSITES: cheerful.

sepulchre ▶ noun TOMB, vault, burial chamber, mausoleum, crypt, undercroft, catacomb; grave.

sequel ▶ noun **1** *the film inspired a sequel* FOLLOW-UP, continuation. **2** *the immediate sequel to the coup was an armed uprising* CONSEQUENCE, result, upshot, outcome, development, issue, postscript; effect, after-effect, aftermath, by-product; *informal* payoff.

sequence ▶ noun **1** *the sequence of events* SUCCESSION, order, course, series, chain, train, string, progression, chronology, timeline; pattern, flow;

formal concatenation. **2** *a sequence from his film* EXCERPT, clip, extract, episode, section.

sequester ▶ verb **1** *he sequestered himself from the world* ISOLATE ONESELF, hide away, shut oneself away, seclude oneself, cut oneself off, segregate oneself; closet oneself, cloister oneself, withdraw, retire. **2** *the government sequestered his property* CONFISCATE, seize, sequestrate, take, appropriate, expropriate, impound, commandeer.

seraphic ▶ adjective BLISSFUL, beatific, sublime, rapturous, ecstatic, joyful, rapt; serene, ethereal; cherubic, saintly, angelic.

serendipitous ▶ adjective CHANCE, accidental, coincidental; lucky, fluky, fortuitous; unexpected, unforeseen.

serendipity ▶ noun (HAPPY) CHANCE, (happy) accident, fluke; luck, good luck, good fortune, fortuity, providence; happy coincidence.

serene ▶ adjective **1** *on the surface she seemed serene* CALM, composed, tranquil, peaceful, untroubled, relaxed, at ease, unperturbed, unruffled, unworried; placid, equable, centered; *informal* together, unflappable. **2** *serene valleys* PEACEFUL, tranquil, quiet, still, restful, relaxing, undisturbed.
– OPPOSITES: agitated, turbulent.

series ▶ noun **1** *a series of lectures* SUCCESSION, sequence, string, chain, run, round; spate, wave, rash; set, course, cycle; row, line; *formal* concatenation. **2** *a new TV series* SERIAL, program, show, drama; soap opera; *informal* soap, sitcom, miniseries.

serious ▶ adjective **1** *a serious expression* SOLEMN, earnest, grave, sombre, sober, unsmiling, poker-faced, stern, grim, dour, humourless, stony-faced; thoughtful, preoccupied, pensive. **2** *serious decisions* IMPORTANT, significant, consequential, momentous, weighty, far-reaching, major, grave; urgent, pressing, crucial, critical, vital, life-and-death, high-priority. **3** *give serious consideration to this* CAREFUL, detailed, in-depth, deep, profound, meaningful. **4** *a serious play* INTELLECTUAL, highbrow, heavyweight, deep, profound, literary, learned, scholarly; *informal* heavy. **5** *serious injuries* SEVERE, grave, bad, critical, acute, terrible, dire, dangerous, perilous, parlous; *formal* grievous. **6** *we're serious about equality* IN EARNEST, earnest, sincere, wholehearted, genuine; committed, resolute, determined.
– OPPOSITES: light-hearted, trivial, superficial, lowbrow, minor, half-hearted.

seriously ▶ adverb **1** *Faye nodded seriously* SOLEMNLY, earnestly, gravely, soberly, sombrely, sternly, grimly, dourly, humourlessly; pensively, thoughtfully. **2** *she was seriously injured* SEVERELY, gravely, badly, critically, acutely, dangerously; *formal* grievously. **3** *do you seriously expect me to come?* REALLY, actually, honestly. **4** *seriously, I'm very pleased* JOKING ASIDE, to be serious, honestly, truthfully, truly, I mean it; *informal* scout's honour. **5** (*informal*) *'I've resigned.' 'Seriously?'* REALLY, is that so, is that a fact, you're joking, well I never, go on, you don't say; *informal* you're kidding. **6** (*informal*) *he was seriously rich. See* EXTREMELY.

sermon ▶ noun **1** *he preached a sermon* HOMILY, address, speech, talk, discourse, oration; lesson. **2** *her mother gave her a sermon on personal hygiene* LECTURE, tirade, harangue, diatribe; speech, disquisition, monologue; reprimand, reproach, reproof, admonishment, admonition, remonstration, criticism; *informal* talking-to, dressing-down, earful; *formal* castigation.

serpentine ▸ adjective **1** *a serpentine form* SERPENT-LIKE, snake-like. **2** *a serpentine path* WINDING, windy, zigzag, twisty, twisting and turning, labyrinthine, meandering, sinuous, snaky, tortuous. **3** *serpentine sentences* COMPLICATED, complex, intricate, involved, tortuous, convoluted, elaborate, knotty, confusing, bewildering, baffling, impenetrable.
– OPPOSITES: straight, simple.

serrated ▸ adjective JAGGED, sawtoothed, sawtooth, zigzag, notched, indented, toothed; *Botany* serrate; *technical* crenulated.
– OPPOSITES: smooth.

serried ▸ adjective CLOSE TOGETHER, packed together, close-set, dense, tight, compact.

servant ▸ noun **1** *servants were cleaning the hall* ATTENDANT, retainer; domestic (worker), (hired) help, cleaner; lackey, flunky, minion; maid, housemaid, footman, page (boy), valet, butler, manservant; housekeeper, steward; drudge, joe-boy, menial, slave, water boy; *archaic* scullion. **2** *a servant of the people* HELPER, supporter, follower.

serve ▸ verb **1** *they served their masters faithfully* WORK FOR, be in the service of, be employed by; obey. **2** *this job serves the community* BE OF SERVICE TO, be of use to, help, assist, aid, make a contribution to, do one's bit for, do something for, benefit. **3** *she served on the committee for years* BE A MEMBER OF, work on, be on, sit on, have a place on. **4** *he served his apprenticeship in the North* CARRY OUT, perform, do, fulfill, complete, discharge; spend. **5** *serve the soup hot* DISH UP/OUT, give out, distribute; present, provide, supply; eat. **6** *she served another customer* ATTEND TO, deal with, see to; ASSIST, help, look after. **7** *they served him with a writ* PRESENT, deliver, give, hand over. **8** *a plate serving as an ashtray* ACT AS, function as, do the work of, be a substitute for. **9** *official forms will serve in most cases* SUFFICE, be adequate, be good enough, fit/fill the bill, do, answer, be useful, meet requirements, suit.

server ▸ noun WAITER/WAITRESS, attendant, garçon, waitperson; busboy; hostess, host, maître d'; wait staff.

service ▸ noun **1** *your conditions of service* WORK, employment, employ, labour. **2** *he has done us a service* FAVOUR, kindness, good turn, helping hand; (**services**) ASSISTANCE, help, aid, offices, ministrations. **3** *the food and service were excellent* WAITING, waitressing, serving, attendance. **4** *products which give reliable service* USE, usage; functioning. **5** *he took his car in for a service* tune-up, maintenance check, servicing. **6** *a marriage service* CEREMONY, ritual, rite, observance; liturgy, sacrament; *formal* ordinance. **7** *a range of local services* AMENITY, facility, resource, utility. **8** *soldiers leaving the services* (ARMED) FORCES, armed services, military; army, navy, air force.
▸ verb *the appliances are serviced regularly* OVERHAUL, check, go over, maintain; repair, mend, recondition.
■ **be of service** HELP, assist, benefit, be of assistance, be beneficial, serve, be useful, be of use, be valuable; do someone a good turn.
■ **out of service** OUT OF ORDER, broken, broken-down, out of commission, unserviceable, faulty, defective, inoperative, in disrepair; down; *informal* conked out, bust, kaput, on the blink, on the fritz, acting up, shot.

serviceable ▸ adjective **1** *a serviceable heating system* IN WORKING ORDER, working, functioning,

functional, operational, operative; usable, workable, viable. **2** *serviceable lace-up shoes* FUNCTIONAL, utilitarian, sensible, practical; HARD-WEARING, durable, tough, robust.
– OPPOSITES: unusable, impractical.

service station ▸ noun GAS STATION, garage, gas bar ✦, filling station, gasoline station, self-serve, truck stop.

servile ▸ adjective OBSEQUIOUS, sycophantic, deferential, subservient, fawning, ingratiating, unctuous, grovelling, toadyish, slavish, humble, self-abasing; *informal* slimy, bootlicking, smarmy, sucky.
– OPPOSITES: assertive.

serving ▸ noun PORTION, helping, plateful, plate, bowlful; amount, quantity, ration.

servitude ▸ noun SLAVERY, enslavement, bondage, subjugation, subjection, domination; *historical* serfdom.
– OPPOSITES: liberty.

session ▸ noun **1** *a special session of the committee* MEETING, sitting, *Law* assize ✦, assembly, conclave, plenary; hearing; conference, discussion, forum, symposium, caucus. **2** *training sessions* PERIOD, time, spell, stretch, bout. **3** *the next school session begins in August* ACADEMIC YEAR, school year; term, semester.

set[1] ▸ verb **1** *Beth set the bag on the table* PUT (DOWN), place, lay, deposit, position, settle, leave, stand, plant, posit; *informal* stick, dump, park, plonk, plunk. **2** *the cottage is set on a hill* BE SITUATED, be located, lie, stand, be sited, be perched. **3** *the fence is set in concrete* FIX, embed, insert; mount. **4** *a ring set with precious stones* ADORN, ornament, decorate, embellish; *literary* bejewel. **5** *I'll go and set the table* LAY, prepare, arrange. **6** *we set them some easy tasks* ASSIGN, allocate, give, allot, prescribe. **7** *just set your mind to it* APPLY, address, direct, aim, turn, focus, concentrate. **8** *they set a date for the election* DECIDE ON, select, choose, arrange, schedule; fix (on), settle on, determine, designate, name, appoint, specify, stipulate. **9** *he set his horse towards her* DIRECT, steer, orientate, point, aim, train. **10** *his jump set a national record* ESTABLISH, create, institute. **11** *he set his watch* ADJUST, regulate, synchronize; calibrate; put right, correct; program, activate, turn on. **12** *the adhesive will set in an hour* SOLIDIFY, harden, stiffen, thicken, jell, cake, congeal, coagulate, clot; freeze, crystallize. **13** *the sun was setting* GO DOWN, sink, dip; vanish, disappear.
– OPPOSITES: melt, rise.
■ **set about** *Mike set about raising $5000* BEGIN, start, commence, go about, get to work on, get down to, embark on, tackle, address oneself to, undertake.
■ **set someone against someone else** ALIENATE FROM, estrange from; drive a wedge between, sow dissension, set at odds.
■ **set someone apart** DISTINGUISH, differentiate, mark out, single out, separate, demarcate.
■ **set something apart** ISOLATE, separate, segregate, put to one side.
■ **set something aside 1** *set aside some money each month* SAVE, put by, put aside, put away, lay by, keep, reserve; store, stockpile, hoard, stow away, cache, withhold; *informal* salt away, squirrel away, stash away. **2** *he set aside his cup* PUT DOWN, cast aside, discard, abandon, dispense with. **3** *set aside your differences* DISREGARD, put aside, ignore, forget, discount, shrug off, bury. **4** *the Supreme Court set aside the decision* OVERRULE, overturn, reverse, revoke, countermand,

nullify, annul, cancel, quash, dismiss, reject, repudiate; *Law* disaffirm; *formal* abrogate.

■ **set someone/something back** DELAY, hold up, hold back, slow down/up, retard, check, decelerate; hinder, impede, hobble, obstruct, hamper, inhibit, frustrate, thwart.

■ **set something down 1** *he set down his thoughts* WRITE DOWN, put in writing, jot down, note down, make a note of; record, register, log. **2** *we set down some rules* FORMULATE, draw up, establish, frame; lay down, determine, fix, stipulate, specify, prescribe, impose, ordain. **3** *I set it down to the fact that he was drunk* ATTRIBUTE, put down, ascribe, assign, chalk up; blame on, impute.

■ **set something forth** PRESENT, describe, set out, detail, delineate, explain, expound; state, declare, announce; submit, offer, put forward, advance, propose, propound.

■ **set someone free** RELEASE, free, let go, turn loose, let out, liberate, deliver, emancipate.

■ **set in** *bad weather set in* BEGIN, start, arrive, come, develop.

■ **set off** SET OUT, start out, sally forth, leave, depart, embark, set sail; *informal* hit the road.

■ **set something off 1** *the bomb was set off* DETONATE, explode, blow up, touch off, trigger; ignite. **2** *it set off a wave of protest* GIVE RISE TO, cause, lead to, set in motion, occasion, bring about, initiate, precipitate, prompt, trigger (off), spark (off), touch off, provoke, incite. **3** *the blue dress set off her auburn hair* ENHANCE, bring out, emphasize, show off, throw into relief; complement.

■ **set on/upon** ATTACK, assail, assault, hit, strike, beat, thrash, pummel, wallop, set about, fall on; *informal* lay into, lace into, let someone have it, work over, rough up, knock about/around, have a go at, beat up on, light into.

■ **set one's heart on** WANT DESPERATELY, wish for, desire, long for, yearn for, hanker after, ache for, hunger for, thirst for, burn for; *informal* be itching for, be dying for.

■ **set out 1** *he set out early. See* SET OFF. **2** *you've done what you set out to do* AIM, intend, mean, seek; hope, aspire, want.

■ **set something out 1** *the gifts were set out on tables* ARRANGE, lay out, put out, array, dispose, display, exhibit. **2** *they set out some guidelines* PRESENT, set forth, detail; state, declare, announce; submit, put forward, advance, propose, propound.

■ **set someone up 1** *his father set him up in business* ESTABLISH, finance, fund, back, subsidize. **2** *(informal) she set him up for Newley's murder* FALSELY INCRIMINATE, frame, entrap.

■ **set something up 1** *a monument to her memory was set up* ERECT, put up, construct, build, raise, elevate. **2** *she set up her own business* ESTABLISH, start, begin, initiate, institute, found, create. **3** *set up a meeting* ARRANGE, organize, fix (up), schedule, timetable, line up. **4** *set up a committee* ESTABLISH, form, strike ♣.

set² ▶ noun **1** *a set of colour postcards* GROUP, collection, series; assortment, selection, compendium, batch, number; arrangement, array. **2** *the literary set* CLIQUE, coterie, circle, crowd, group, crew, band, company, ring, camp, fraternity, school, faction, league; *informal* gang, bunch. **3** *a chemistry set* KIT, apparatus, equipment, outfit. **4** *a set of china* SERVICE. **5** *the set of his shoulders* POSTURE, position, cast, attitude; bearing, carriage. **6** *a set for the play* SCENERY, setting, backdrop, flats; mise en scène. **7** *the*

band *played two sets* SESSION, time; stretch, bout, round.

set³ ▶ adjective **1** *a set routine* FIXED, established, predetermined, hard and fast, pre-arranged, prescribed, specified, defined; unvarying, unchanging, invariable, unvaried, rigid, inflexible, cast-iron, strict, ironclad, settled, predictable; routine, standard, customary, regular, usual, habitual, accustomed, wonted. **2** *she had set ideas* INFLEXIBLE, rigid, fixed, firm, deep-rooted, deep-seated, ingrained, entrenched. **3** *he had a set speech for such occasions* STOCK, standard, routine, rehearsed, well-worn, formulaic, conventional. **4** *I was all set for the evening* READY, prepared, organized, equipped, primed; *informal* geared up, psyched up. **5** *he's set on marrying her* DETERMINED TO, intent on, bent on, hell-bent on, resolute about, insistent about. **6** *you were dead set against the idea* OPPOSED TO, averse to, hostile to, resistant to, antipathetic to, unsympathetic to; *informal* anti.

– OPPOSITES: variable, flexible, original, unprepared, uncertain.

setback ▶ noun PROBLEM, difficulty, hitch, complication, upset, disappointment, misfortune, mishap, reversal; blow, stumbling block, hurdle, hindrance, impediment, obstruction; delay, holdup; *informal* glitch, hiccup.

– OPPOSITES: breakthrough.

settee ▶ noun SOFA, couch, divan, chaise longue, chesterfield, davenport, daybed.

setting ▶ noun **1** *a rural setting* SURROUNDINGS, position, situation, environment, background, backdrop, milieu, environs, habitat; spot, place, location, locale, site, scene; area, region, district. **2** *a garnet in a gold setting* MOUNT, fixture, surround.

settle ▶ verb **1** *they settled the dispute* RESOLVE, sort out, solve, clear up, end, fix, work out, iron out, straighten out, set right, rectify, remedy, reconcile; *informal* patch up. **2** *she settled their affairs* PUT IN ORDER, sort out, tidy up, arrange, organize, order, clear up. **3** *they settled on a date for the wedding* DECIDE ON, set, fix, agree on, name, establish, arrange, appoint, designate, assign; choose, select, pick. **4** *she went down to the lobby to settle her bill* PAY, settle up, square, clear, defray. **5** *they settled for a 4.2% raise* ACCEPT, agree to, assent to; *formal* accede to. **6** *he settled in Oshawa* MAKE ONE'S HOME, set up home, take up residence, put down roots, establish oneself; live, move to, emigrate to. **7** *immigrants settled much of Australia* COLONIZE, occupy, inhabit, people, populate. **8** *Catherine settled down to her work* APPLY ONESELF TO, get down to, set about, attack; concentrate on, focus on, devote oneself to. **9** *the class wouldn't settle down* CALM DOWN, quieten down, be quiet, be still; *informal* shut up. **10** *a brandy will settle your nerves* CALM, quieten, quiet, soothe, pacify, quell, sedate, tranquilize. **11** *he settled into an armchair* SIT DOWN, seat oneself, install oneself, ensconce oneself, plant oneself; *informal* park oneself, plonk oneself. **12** *a butterfly settled on the flower* LAND, come to rest, alight, descend, perch; *archaic* light. **13** *sediment settles at the bottom* SINK, subside, fall, gravitate.

– OPPOSITES: agitate, rise.

settlement ▶ noun **1** *a pay settlement* AGREEMENT, deal, arrangement, resolution, bargain, understanding, pact. **2** *the settlement of the dispute* RESOLUTION, settling, solution, reconciliation. **3** *a frontier settlement* COMMUNITY, colony, outpost, encampment, post; village, commune; *historical* plantation, clearing ♣. **4** *the settlement of the area* COLONIZATION, settling, populating; *historical* plantation. **5** *the settlement of their debts* PAYMENT, discharge, liquidation, clearance.

settler ▶ **noun** COLONIST, colonizer, frontiersman, frontierswoman, pioneer, bushwhacker; immigrant, newcomer; *historical* homesteader.
– OPPOSITES: native.

set-up ▶ **noun 1** *a complicated set-up* SYSTEM, structure, organization, arrangement, framework, layout, configuration. **2** *a set-up called Film International* ORGANIZATION, group, body, agency, association, operation; company, firm; *informal* outfit. **3** *(informal) the whole thing was a set-up* TRICK, trap; conspiracy; *informal* put-up job, frame-up.

seven ▶ **cardinal number** SEPTET, septuplets; *technical* heptad.
– RELATED TERMS: hepta-, septi-.

sever ▶ **verb 1** *the head was severed from the body* CUT OFF, chop off, detach, disconnect, dissever, separate, part; amputate; *literary* sunder. **2** *a knife had severed the artery* CUT (THROUGH), rupture, split, pierce. **3** *they severed diplomatic relations* BREAK OFF, discontinue, suspend, end, terminate, cease, dissolve.
– OPPOSITES: join, maintain.

several ▶ **adjective 1** *several people* SOME, a number of, a few; various, assorted, sundry, diverse; *literary* divers. **2** *they sorted out their several responsibilities* RESPECTIVE, individual, own, particular, specific; separate, different, disparate, distinct; various.

severe ▶ **adjective 1** *severe injuries* ACUTE, very bad, serious, grave, critical, dreadful, terrible, awful; dangerous, parlous, life-threatening; *formal* grievous. **2** *severe storms* FIERCE, violent, strong, powerful, intense; tempestuous, strong. **3** *a severe winter* HARSH, bitter, cold, bleak, freezing, icy, arctic, extreme; *informal* brutal. **4** *a severe headache* EXCRUCIATING, agonizing, intense, dreadful, awful, terrible, unbearable, intolerable; *informal* splitting, pounding, screaming. **5** *a severe test of their stamina* DIFFICULT, demanding, tough, arduous, formidable, exacting, rigorous, punishing, onerous, gruelling. **6** *severe criticism* HARSH, scathing, sharp, strong, fierce, savage, scorching, devastating, trenchant, caustic, biting, withering. **7** *severe tax penalties* EXTORTIONATE, excessive, unreasonable, inordinate, outrageous, sky-high, harsh, stiff; punitive. **8** *they received severe treatment* HARSH, stern, hard, inflexible, uncompromising, unrelenting, merciless, pitiless, ruthless, draconian, oppressive, repressive, punitive; brutal, cruel, savage. **9** *his severe expression* STERN, dour, grim, forbidding, disapproving, unsmiling, unfriendly, sombre, grave, serious, stony, steely; cold, frosty. **10** *a severe style of architecture* PLAIN, simple, austere, unadorned, unembellished, unornamented, stark, Spartan, ascetic; clinical, uncluttered.
– OPPOSITES: minor, gentle, mild, easy, lenient, friendly, ornate.

severely ▶ **adjective 1** *he was severely injured* BADLY, seriously, critically; fatally; *formal* grievously. **2** *she was severely criticized* SHARPLY, roundly, soundly, fiercely, savagely. **3** *murderers should be treated more severely* HARSHLY, strictly, sternly, rigorously, mercilessly, pitilessly, roughly, sharply; with a rod of iron; brutally, cruelly, savagely. **4** *she looked severely at Harriet* STERNLY, grimly, dourly, disapprovingly; coldly, frostily. **5** *she dressed severely in black* PLAINLY, simply, austerely, starkly.

sew ▶ **verb** *she sewed the seams of the tunic* STITCH, tack, baste, seam, hem; embroider.
■ **sew something up 1** *the tear was sewn up* DARN, mend, repair, patch. **2** *(informal) the company sewed up a deal with IBM* SECURE, clinch, pull off, bring off, settle, conclude, complete, finalize, tie up; *informal* swing.

sewing ▶ **noun** STITCHING, needlework, needlecraft, fancy-work. See table.

Sewing Techniques and Stitches

appliqué	mitring
backstitch	needlepoint
baste	overcasting
blanket stitch	oversewing
blindstitch	patchwork
braid	petit point
broderie anglaise	pintuck
buttonhole stitch	pleating
chain stitch	quilting
crewel work	running stitch
crocheting	satin stitch
cross-stitch	selvage
cutwork	shirring
darning	slipstitch
drawnwork	smocking
embroidery	staystitch
faggoting	straight stitch
fancy-work	tack
feather stitch	tent stitch
French knot	topstitch
gros point	tucking
hemstitch	tufting
herringbone stitch	whipstitch
lock stitch	

sex ▶ **noun 1** *they talked about sex* SEXUAL INTERCOURSE, intercourse, lovemaking, making love, sex act, (sexual) relations; mating, copulation; *informal* nookie, whoopee, bonking, boinking, the horizontal mambo, a roll in the hay, quickie; *formal* fornication; *technical* coitus, coition; *dated* carnal knowledge. **2** *teach your children about sex* THE FACTS OF LIFE, reproduction; *informal* the birds and the bees. **3** *adults of both sexes* GENDER.
■ **have sex** HAVE SEXUAL INTERCOURSE, make love, sleep with, go to bed; mate, copulate; seduce, rape; *informal* do it, go all the way, know in the biblical sense; bonk, boink, get it on; *euphemistic* be intimate; *literary* ravish; *formal* fornicate.

sex appeal ▶ **noun** SEXINESS, seductiveness, sexual attractiveness, desirability, sensuality, sexuality; *informal* it, SA.

sexism ▶ **noun** SEXUAL DISCRIMINATION, chauvinism, prejudice, bias.

sexless ▶ **adjective** ASEXUAL, non-sexual, neuter; androgynous, epicene.

sex symbol ▶ **noun** SEXUALLY ATTRACTIVE PERSON, sex object, sexpot, sex kitten.

sexual ▶ **adjective 1** *the sexual organs* REPRODUCTIVE, genital, sex, procreative. **2** *sexual activity* CARNAL, erotic; *formal* venereal; *technical* coital.

sexual intercourse ▶ **noun**. See SEX sense 1.

sexuality ▶ **noun 1** *she had a powerful sexuality* SENSUALITY, sexiness, seductiveness, desirability, eroticism, physicality; sexual appetite, passion, desire, lust. **2** *I'm open about my sexuality* SEXUAL

ORIENTATION, sexual preference, leaning, persuasion; heterosexuality, homosexuality, lesbianism, bisexuality.

sexy ► adjective **1** *he's so sexy* SEXUALLY ATTRACTIVE, seductive, desirable, alluring, toothsome, sensual, sultry, slinky, provocative, tempting, tantalizing; nubile, voluptuous, luscious, lush, hot, beddable, foxy, cute. **2** *sexy videos* EROTIC, sexually explicit, arousing, exciting, stimulating, hot, titillating, racy, naughty, risqué, adult, X-rated; rude, pornographic, crude, lewd; *informal* raunchy, steamy, porno, blue, skin, XXX. **3** *they weren't feeling sexy* (SEXUALLY) AROUSED, sexually excited, amorous, lustful, passionate; *informal* horny, hot, turned on, sexed up, randy. **4** *(informal) a sexy sales promotion* EXCITING, stimulating, interesting, appealing, intriguing, slick, red-hot.

sh ► exclamation BE QUIET, keep quiet, quieten down, be silent, silence, stop talking, hold your tongue; *informal* shut up, hush (up), shut your mouth, shut your face, shut your trap, button your lip, pipe down, put a sock in it, give it a rest, save it, not another word.

shabby ► adjective **1** *a shabby little bar* RUN-DOWN, down-at-the-heel, scruffy, dilapidated, ramshackle, tumbledown; seedy, slummy, insalubrious, squalid, sordid, flea-bitten; *informal* crummy, scuzzy, grotty, shacky. **2** *a shabby grey coat* SCRUFFY, old, worn out, threadbare, ragged, frayed, tattered, battered, faded, moth-eaten, mangy; *informal* tatty, ratty, the worse for wear, raggedy. **3** *her shabby treatment of Bill* CONTEMPTIBLE, despicable, dishonourable, discreditable, mean, low, dirty, hateful, shameful, sorry, ignoble, unfair, unworthy, unkind, shoddy, nasty; *informal* rotten, lowdown; beastly.
— OPPOSITES: smart, honourable.

shack ► noun HUT, shanty, cabin, lean-to, shed, caboose ✦; hovel; fish hut ✦, *(Nfld)* tilt ✦, ice-fishing hut ✦, ice hut ✦.
■ **shack up with** *(informal)* COHABIT, live with; *informal, dated* live in sin.

shackle ► verb **1** *he was shackled to the wall* CHAIN, fetter, manacle; secure, tie (up), bind, tether, hobble; put in chains, clap in irons, handcuff. **2** *journalists were shackled by a new law* RESTRAIN, restrict, limit, constrain, handicap, hamstring, hamper, hinder, impede, obstruct, inhibit, check, curb.

shackles ► plural noun **1** *shackles of iron* CHAINS, fetters, irons, leg irons, manacles, handcuffs; bonds; *informal* cuffs, bracelets. **2** *the shackles of bureaucracy* RESTRICTIONS, restraints, constraints, impediments, hindrances, obstacles, barriers, obstructions, checks, curbs; *literary* trammels.

shade ► noun **1** *they sat in the shade* SHADOW(S), shadiness, shelter, cover; cool. **2** *shades of blue* COLOUR, hue, tone, tint, tinge. **3** *shades of meaning* NUANCE, gradation, degree, difference, variation, variety; nicety, subtlety; undertone, overtone. **4** *her skirt was a shade too short* A LITTLE, a bit, a trace, a touch, a modicum, a tinge; slightly, rather, somewhat; *informal* a tad, a smidgen, a titch, a hair. **5** *the window shade* BLIND, curtain, screen, cover, covering; awning, canopy. **6** *(informal) he was wearing shades* SUNGLASSES, dark glasses.
— OPPOSITES: light.
► verb **1** *vines shaded the garden* CAST A SHADOW OVER, shadow, shelter, cover, screen; darken. **2** *she shaded in the picture* DARKEN, colour in, pencil in, block in, fill in; cross-hatch. **3** *the sky shaded from turquoise to blue*

CHANGE, transmute, turn, go; merge, blend, graduate.
■ **put someone/something in the shade** SURPASS, outshine, outclass, overshadow, eclipse, transcend, cap, top, outstrip, outdo, put to shame, beat, outperform, upstage; *informal* run rings around, be a cut above.
■ **shades of** ECHOES OF, a reminder of, memories of, suggestions of, hints of.

shadow ► noun **1** *he saw her shadow in the doorway* SILHOUETTE, outline, shape, contour, profile. **2** *he emerged from the shadows* SHADE, darkness, twilight; gloom, murkiness. **3** *the shadow of war* (BLACK) CLOUD, pall; gloom, blight; threat. **4** *she knew without any shadow of doubt* TRACE, scrap, shred, crumb, iota, scintilla, jot, whit, grain; *informal* smidgen, smidge, tad. **5** *a shadow of a smile* TRACE, hint, suggestion, suspicion, ghost, glimmer. **6** *he's a shadow of his former self* INFERIOR VERSION, poor imitation, apology, travesty; remnant. **7** *the dog became her shadow* CONSTANT COMPANION, alter ego, second self; close friend, bosom friend; *informal* Siamese twin, bosom buddy.
► verb **1** *the market is shadowed by the church* OVERSHADOW, shade; darken, dim. **2** *he is shadowing a poacher* FOLLOW, trail, track, stalk, pursue, hunt; *informal* tail, keep tabs on.

shadowy ► adjective **1** *a shadowy corridor* DARK, dim, gloomy, murky, crepuscular, shady, shaded; *literary* tenebrous. **2** *a shadowy figure* INDISTINCT, hazy, indefinite, vague, nebulous, ill-defined, faint, blurred, blurry, unclear, indistinguishable, unrecognizable; ghostly, spectral, wraithlike.
— OPPOSITES: bright, clear.

shady ► adjective **1** *a shady garden* SHADED, shadowy, dim, dark; sheltered, screened, shrouded; leafy; *literary* bosky, tenebrous. **2** *(informal) shady deals* SUSPICIOUS, suspect, questionable, dubious, doubtful, disreputable, untrustworthy, dishonest, devious, dishonourable, underhanded, unscrupulous, irregular, unethical; *informal* fishy, murky.
— OPPOSITES: bright, honest.

shaft ► noun **1** *the shaft of a golf club* POLE, shank, stick, rod, staff; handle, hilt, stem. **2** *the shaft of a feather* QUILL; *Ornithology* rachis. **3** *shafts of sunlight* RAY, beam, gleam, streak, finger. **4** *a ventilation shaft* MINESHAFT, tunnel, passage, pit, adit, downcast, upcast; borehole, bore; duct, well, flue, vent.
► verb DECEIVE, delude, trick, hoodwink, mislead, take in, dupe, fool, double-cross, cheat, defraud, swindle, fleece, catch out, gull, hoax, bamboozle, con, diddle, rook, put one over on, pull a fast one on, pull the wool over someone's eyes, take for a ride, shanghai, flim-flam, sucker, snooker.

shaggy ► adjective HAIRY, bushy, thick, woolly; tangled, tousled, unkempt, dishevelled, untidy, matted; *formal* hirsute.
— OPPOSITES: sleek.

shake ► verb **1** *the whole building shook* VIBRATE, tremble, quiver, quake, shiver, shudder, judder, jiggle, wobble, rock, sway; convulse. **2** *she shook the bottle* JIGGLE, joggle, agitate; *informal* waggle. **3** *he shook his stick at them* BRANDISH, flourish, swing, wield; *informal* waggle. **4** *the look in his eyes really shook her* UPSET, distress, disturb, unsettle, disconcert, discompose, disquiet, unnerve, trouble, throw off balance, agitate, fluster; shock, alarm, frighten, scare, worry; *informal* rattle. **5** *this will shake their confidence* WEAKEN, undermine, damage, impair,

harm; reduce, diminish, decrease.
— OPPOSITES: soothe, strengthen.
▶ **noun 1** *he gave his coat a shake* JIGGLE, joggle; *informal* waggle. **2** *a shake of his fist* FLOURISH, brandish, wave. **3** *it gives me the shakes* TREMORS, delirium tremens; *informal* DTs, jitters, the creeps, the shivers, willies, heebie-jeebies, the jim-jams.
■ **in two shakes (of a lamb's tail)** (*informal*). See IN A MOMENT at MOMENT.
■ **no great shakes** (*informal*) NOT VERY GOOD, unexceptional, unmemorable, forgettable, uninspired, uninteresting, indifferent, unimpressive, lacklustre; *informal* nothing to write home about, nothing special.
■ **shake a leg** (*informal*). See HURRY *verb* sense 1.
■ **shake someone off** GET AWAY FROM, escape, elude, dodge, lose, leave behind, get rid of, give someone the slip, throw off the scent.
■ **shake something off** RECOVER FROM, get over; get rid of, free oneself from; *informal* shuck off.
■ **shake someone/something up 1** *the accident shook him up.* See SHAKE *verb* sense 4. **2** *plans to shake up the legal profession* REORGANIZE, restructure, revolutionize, alter, change, transform, reform, overhaul.

shake-up ▶ **noun** (*informal*) REORGANIZATION, restructuring, reshuffle, change, overhaul, makeover; upheaval, shakedown, housecleaning.

shaky ▶ **adjective 1** *shaky legs* TREMBLING, shaking, tremulous, quivering, quivery, unsteady, wobbly, weak; tottering, tottery, teetering, doddery; *informal* trembly. **2** *I feel a bit shaky* FAINT, dizzy, light-headed, giddy; weak, wobbly, quivery, groggy, muzzy; *informal* trembly, woozy. **3** *a shaky table* UNSTEADY, unstable, wobbly, precarious, rocky, rickety, ramshackle, wonky. **4** *the evidence is shaky* UNRELIABLE, untrustworthy, questionable, dubious, doubtful, tenuous, suspect, flimsy, weak, unsound, unsupported, unsubstantiated, unfounded; *informal* iffy.
— OPPOSITES: steady, stable, sound.

shallow ▶ **adjective** SUPERFICIAL, facile, simplistic, oversimplified; flimsy, insubstantial, lightweight, empty, trivial, trifling; surface, skin-deep, two-dimensional; frivolous, foolish, silly, Mickey Mouse.
— OPPOSITES: profound.

sham ▶ **noun 1** *his tenderness had been a sham* PRETENSE, fake, act, fiction, simulation, fraud, feint, lie, counterfeit; humbug. **2** *the doctor was a sham* CHARLATAN, fake, fraud, imposter, pretender; quack, mountebank; *informal* phony.
▶ **adjective** *sham togetherness* FAKE, pretended, feigned, simulated, false, artificial, bogus, insincere, contrived, affected, make-believe, fictitious; imitation, mock, counterfeit, fraudulent; *informal* pretend, put-on, phony, pseudo.
— OPPOSITES: genuine.

shaman ▶ **noun** medicine man/woman, (*North*) angakok ♣, healer, kahuna.

shamble ▶ **verb** SHUFFLE, drag one's feet, lumber, totter, dodder; hobble, limp.

shambles ▶ **plural noun 1** *we have to sort out this shambles* CHAOS, mess, muddle, confusion, disorder, havoc, mare's nest, dog's breakfast. **2** *the room was a shambles* MESS, pigsty; *informal* disaster area.

shame ▶ **noun 1** *her face was scarlet with shame* HUMILIATION, mortification, chagrin, ignominy, embarrassment, indignity, discomfort. **2** *I felt shame at telling a lie* GUILT, remorse, contrition, compunction. **3** *he brought shame on the family* DISGRACE, dishonour, discredit, degradation, ignominy, disrepute, infamy, scandal, opprobrium, contempt; *dated* disesteem. **4** *it's a shame she never married* PITY, misfortune, sad thing; bad luck; *informal* bummer, crime, sin, crying shame.
— OPPOSITES: pride, honour.
▶ **verb 1** *you shamed your family's name* DISGRACE, dishonour, discredit, degrade, debase; stigmatize, taint, sully, tarnish, besmirch, blacken, drag through the mud. **2** *he was shamed in public* HUMILIATE, mortify, chagrin, embarrass, abash, chasten, humble, take down a peg or two, cut down to size; *informal* show up, make someone eat crow.
— OPPOSITES: honour.
■ **put someone/something to shame** OUTSHINE, outclass, eclipse, surpass, excel, outstrip, outdo, put in the shade, upstage; *informal* run rings around.

shamefaced ▶ **adjective** ASHAMED, abashed, sheepish, guilty, conscience-stricken, guilt-ridden, contrite, sorry, remorseful, repentant, penitent, regretful, rueful, apologetic; embarrassed, mortified, red-faced, chagrined, humiliated; *informal* with one's tail between one's legs.
— OPPOSITES: unrepentant.

shameful ▶ **adjective 1** *shameful behaviour* DISGRACEFUL, deplorable, despicable, contemptible, dishonourable, discreditable, reprehensible, low, unworthy, ignoble, shabby; shocking, scandalous, outrageous, abominable, atrocious, appalling, vile, odious, heinous, egregious, loathsome, bad; inexcusable, unforgivable; *informal* lowdown, hateful. **2** *a shameful secret* EMBARRASSING, mortifying, humiliating, degrading, ignominious.
— OPPOSITES: admirable.

shameless ▶ **adjective** FLAGRANT, blatant, barefaced, overt, brazen, brash, audacious, outrageous, undisguised, unconcealed, transparent; immodest, indecorous; unabashed, unashamed, unblushing, unrepentant.
— OPPOSITES: modest.

shanty ▶ **noun** SHACK, hut, (log) cabin, lean-to, shed, caboose ♣; hovel.

shape ▶ **noun 1** *the shape of the dining table* FORM, appearance, configuration, formation, structure; figure, build, physique, body; contours, lines, outline, silhouette, profile. **2** *a spirit in the shape of a fox* GUISE, likeness, semblance, form, appearance, image. **3** *you're in pretty good shape* CONDITION, health, fettle, order.
— RELATED TERMS: morpho-.
▶ **verb 1** *the metal is shaped into tools* FORM, fashion, make, mould, model, cast; sculpt, sculpture, carve, cut, whittle. **2** *attitudes were shaped by his report* DETERMINE, form, fashion, mould, define, develop; influence, affect.
■ **shape up** *her work is shaping up nicely* IMPROVE, get better, progress, show promise; develop, take shape, come on, come along.
■ **take shape** BECOME CLEAR, become definite, become tangible, crystallize, come together, fall into place.

shapeless ▶ **adjective 1** *shapeless lumps* FORMLESS, amorphous, unformed, indefinite. **2** *a shapeless dress* BAGGY, saggy, ill-fitting, sack-like, oversized, unshapely, formless.

shapely ▶ **adjective** WELL-PROPORTIONED,

clean-limbed; curvaceous, voluptuous, Junoesque; attractive, sexy; *informal* curvy; *archaic* comely.

shard ▶ **noun** FRAGMENT, sliver, splinter, shiver, chip, piece, bit, particle.

share ▶ **noun** *her share of the profits* PORTION, part, division, quota, quantum, allowance, ration, allocation, measure, due; percentage, commission, dividend; helping, serving; *informal* cut, slice, rake-off. ▶ **verb** 1 *we share the bills* SPLIT, divide, go halves on; *informal* go fifty-fifty, go Dutch. 2 *they shared out the peanuts* APPORTION, divide up, allocate, portion out, ration out, parcel out, measure out; carve up, divvy up. 3 *we all share in the learning process* PARTICIPATE IN, take part in, play a part in, be involved in, contribute to, have a hand in, partake in.

shark ▶ **noun**. *See table.*

Sharks

angel shark	monkfish
basking shark	nurse shark
blue shark	porbeagle
dogfish	requiem shark
great white shark	shovelhead
hammerhead	thresher shark
mackerel shark	tope
mako	whale shark

sharp ▶ **adjective** 1 *a sharp knife* KEEN, razor-edged; sharpened, honed. 2 *a sharp pain* EXCRUCIATING, agonizing, intense, stabbing, shooting, severe, acute, keen, fierce, searing; exquisite. 3 *a sharp taste* TANGY, piquant, strong; ACIDIC, acid, sour, tart, pungent, acrid, bitter, acidulous. 4 *a sharp cry of pain* LOUD, piercing, shrill, high-pitched, penetrating, harsh, strident, ear-splitting, deafening. 5 *a sharp wind* COLD, chilly, chill, brisk, keen, penetrating, biting, icy, bitter, freezing, raw; *informal* nippy, wicked. 6 *sharp words* HARSH, bitter, cutting, scathing, caustic, barbed, trenchant, acrimonious, acerbic, sarcastic, sardonic, spiteful, venomous, malicious, vitriolic, vicious, hurtful, nasty, cruel, abrasive; *informal* bitchy, catty. 7 *a sharp sense of loss* INTENSE, acute, keen, strong, bitter, fierce, heartfelt, overwhelming. 8 *the lens brings it into sharp focus* DISTINCT, clear, crisp; stark, obvious, marked, definite, pronounced. 9 *a sharp increase* SUDDEN, abrupt, rapid; steep, precipitous. 10 *a sharp corner* HAIRPIN, tight. 11 *a sharp drop* STEEP, sheer, abrupt, precipitous, vertical. 12 *sharp eyes* KEEN, perceptive, observant, acute, beady, hawklike. 13 *she was sharp and witty* PERCEPTIVE, percipient, perspicacious, incisive, sensitive, keen, acute, quick-witted, clever, shrewd, canny, astute, intelligent, intuitive, bright, alert, smart, quick off the mark, insightful, knowing; *informal* on the ball, quick on the uptake, savvy, pawky, heads-up. 14 *(informal) a sharp suit* SMART, stylish, fashionable, chic, modish, elegant; *informal* trendy, cool, hip, snazzy, classy, snappy, styling/stylin', natty, nifty, fly, spiffy. — OPPOSITES: blunt, mild, sweet, soft, kind, indistinct, gradual, slow, weak, stupid, naive, untidy. ▶ **adverb** 1 *nine o'clock sharp* PRECISELY, exactly, on the dot; promptly, prompt, punctually, dead on; *informal* on the nose, on the button. 2 *the recession pulled people up sharp* ABRUPTLY, suddenly, sharply, unexpectedly. — OPPOSITES: roughly.

sharpen ▶ **verb** 1 *sharpen the carving knife* HONE, whet, strop, grind, file. 2 *the players are sharpening up*

their skills IMPROVE, brush up, polish up, better, enhance; hone, fine-tune, perfect.

sharp-eyed ▶ **adjective** OBSERVANT, perceptive, eagle-eyed, hawk-eyed, gimlet-eyed; watchful, vigilant, alert, on the lookout; *informal* beady-eyed.

sharp-tongued ▶ **adjective** SCOLDING, shrill, shrewish; harsh, cutting, caustic, abrasive; *literary* trenchant.

shatter ▶ **verb** 1 *the glasses shattered* SMASH, break, splinter, crack, fracture, fragment, disintegrate, shiver; *informal* bust. 2 *the announcement shattered their hopes* DESTROY, wreck, ruin, dash, crush, devastate, demolish, torpedo, scotch; *informal* put the kibosh on, put paid to, scupper, scuttle. 3 *we were shattered by the news* DEVASTATE, shock, stun, daze, traumatize, crush, distress.

shave ▶ **verb** 1 *he shaved his beard* CUT OFF, snip off; crop, trim, barber. 2 *shave off excess wood* PLANE, pare, whittle, scrape. 3 *he shaved the MP's majority to 2,000* REDUCE, cut, lessen, decrease, pare down, shrink. 4 *the shot just shaved my arm* GRAZE, brush, touch, glance off, kiss.

sheaf ▶ **noun** BUNDLE, bunch, stack, pile, heap, mass.

sheath ▶ **noun** 1 *put the sword in its sheath* SCABBARD, case. 2 *the wire has a plastic sheath* COVERING, cover, case, casing, envelope, sleeve, wrapper, capsule. 3 *a contraceptive sheath*. *See* CONDOM.

shed[1] ▶ **noun** *the rabbit lives in the shed* HUT, lean-to, outhouse, outbuilding; shack; potting shed, woodshed, tool shed, garden shed; (*Ont.*) drive shed ✦, (*Nfld*) linny ✦, (*West*) machine shed ✦.

shed[2] ▶ **verb** 1 *the trees shed their leaves* DROP, scatter, spill. 2 *the caterpillar shed its skin* SLOUGH OFF, cast off, moult. 3 *we shed our jackets* TAKE OFF, remove, shrug off, discard, doff, climb out of, slip out of, divest oneself of, peel off. 4 *much blood has been shed* SPILL, discharge. 5 *she shed 20 pounds* LOSE, get rid of, discard. 6 *they must shed their illusions* DISCARD, get rid of, dispose of, do away with, drop, abandon, jettison, scrap, cast aside, dump, reject, repudiate; *informal* ditch, junk. 7 *the moon shed a watery light* CAST, radiate, diffuse, disperse, give out. — OPPOSITES: don, keep.

■ **shed tears** WEEP, cry, sob; lament, grieve, mourn; *informal* blubber, boo-hoo.

sheen ▶ **noun** SHINE, lustre, gloss, patina, shininess, burnish, polish, shimmer, brilliance, radiance.

sheep ▶ **noun** ram, ewe, lamb, wether, bellwether. — RELATED TERMS: ovine.

sheepish ▶ **adjective** EMBARRASSED, uncomfortable, hangdog, self-conscious; shamefaced, ashamed, abashed, mortified, chastened, remorseful, contrite, apologetic, rueful, regretful, penitent, repentant.

sheer[1] ▶ **adjective** 1 *the sheer audacity of the plan* UTTER, complete, absolute, total, pure, downright, out-and-out, arrant, thorough, thoroughgoing, patent, veritable, unmitigated, plain. 2 *a sheer drop* PRECIPITOUS, steep, vertical, perpendicular, abrupt, bluff, sharp. 3 *a sheer dress* DIAPHANOUS, gauzy, filmy, floaty, gossamer, thin, translucent, transparent, see-through, insubstantial. — OPPOSITES: gradual, thick.

sheer[2] ▶ **verb** 1 *the boat sheered off along the coast* SWERVE, veer, slew, skew, swing, change course. 2 *her mind sheered away from his image* TURN AWAY, flinch, recoil, shy away; avoid.

sheet ▶ **noun** 1 *she changed the sheets* BED LINEN, linen, bedclothes. 2 *a sheet of ice* LAYER, stratum, covering, blanket, coating, coat, film, skin. **3** *a sheet of glass* PANE, panel, piece, plate; slab. **4** *she put a fresh sheet in the typewriter* PIECE OF PAPER, leaf, page, folio. **5** *a sheet of water* EXPANSE, area, stretch, sweep.

shelf ▶ noun **1** *the plant on the shelf* LEDGE, sill, bracket, rack; mantelpiece; shelving. **2** *an ocean shelf* SANDBANK, sandbar, bank, bar, reef, shoal.

shell ▶ noun **1** *a crab shell* CARAPACE, exterior; armour; *Zoology* exoskeleton. **2** *peanut shells* POD, husk, hull, casing, case, covering, integument, shuck. **3** *shells passing overhead* PROJECTILE, bomb, explosive; grenade; bullet, cartridge. **4** *the metal shell of the car* FRAMEWORK, frame, chassis, skeleton; hull, exterior.
— RELATED TERMS: conchoidal, concho-.
▶ verb **1** *they were shelling peas* HULL, pod, husk, shuck. **2** *rebel artillery shelled the city* BOMBARD, fire on, shoot at, attack, bomb, blitz, strafe.
■ **shell out** (*informal*). *See* PAY *verb* sense 2.

shellfish ▶ noun CRUSTACEAN, bivalve, mollusc. *See tables at* CRAB *and* MOLLUSC.

shelter ▶ noun **1** *the trees provide shelter for animals* PROTECTION, cover, screening, shade; safety, security, refuge, sanctuary, asylum. **2** *a shelter for abused women* SANCTUARY, refuge, home, haven, safe house, interval house ✤, transition house ✤; harbour, port in a storm.
— OPPOSITES: exposure.
▶ verb **1** *the hut sheltered him from the wind* PROTECT, shield, screen, cover, shade, save, safeguard, preserve, defend, cushion, guard, insulate. **2** *the anchorage where the convoy sheltered* TAKE SHELTER, take refuge, seek sanctuary, take cover; *informal* hole up.
— OPPOSITES: expose.

sheltered ▶ adjective **1** *a sheltered stretch of water* PROTECTED, screened, shielded, covered; shady; cozy. **2** *she led a sheltered life* SECLUDED, cloistered, isolated, protected, withdrawn, sequestered, reclusive; privileged, secure, safe, quiet.

shelve ▶ verb POSTPONE, put off, delay, defer, put back, reschedule, hold over/off, put to one side, suspend, stay, keep in abeyance, mothball; abandon, drop, give up, stop, cancel, jettison, axe, put over, table, take a rain check on; *informal* put on ice, put on the back burner, put in cold storage, ditch, dump, junk.
— OPPOSITES: execute.

shepherd ▶ noun *he worked as a shepherd* shepherdess, herdsman, herder, sheepman.
▶ verb *we shepherded them away* USHER, steer, herd, lead, take, escort, guide, conduct, marshal, walk; show, see, chaperone.

shield ▶ noun **1** *he used his shield to fend off blows* *Heraldry* escutcheon; *historical* buckler, target. **2** *a shield against dirt* PROTECTION, guard, defence, cover, screen, security, shelter, safeguard, protector.
▶ verb *he shielded his eyes* PROTECT, cover, screen, shade; save, safeguard, preserve, defend, secure, guard; cushion, insulate.
— OPPOSITES: expose.

shift ▶ verb **1** *he shifted some chairs* MOVE, carry, transfer, transport, convey, lug, haul, fetch, switch, relocate, reposition, rearrange; *informal* cart. **2** *she shifted her position* CHANGE, alter, adjust, vary; modify, revise, reverse, retract; do a U-turn. **3** *the cargo has shifted* MOVE, slide, slip, be displaced. **4** *the wind shifted* VEER, alter, change, turn, swing round.
— OPPOSITES: keep.
▶ noun **1** *the southward shift of people* MOVEMENT, move, transference, transport, transposition, relocation.

2 *a shift in public opinion* CHANGE, alteration, adjustment, amendment, variation, modification, revision, reversal, retraction, U-turn. **3** *they worked three shifts* STINT, stretch, spell of work. **4** *the night shift went home* WORKERS, crew, gang, team, squad, patrol.
■ **shift for oneself** COPE, manage, survive, make it, fend for oneself, take care of oneself, make do, get by/along, scrape by/along, muddle through; stand on one's own two feet; *informal* make out.

shiftless ▶ adjective LAZY, idle, indolent, slothful, lethargic, lackadaisical; spiritless, apathetic, feckless, good-for-nothing, worthless; unambitious, unenterprising.

shifty ▶ adjective (*informal*) DEVIOUS, evasive, slippery, duplicitous, false, deceitful, underhanded, untrustworthy, dishonest, shady, wily, crafty, tricky, sneaky, treacherous, artful, sly, scheming, snide.
— OPPOSITES: honest.

shilly-shally ▶ verb DITHER, be indecisive, be irresolute, vacillate, waver, hesitate, blow hot and cold, falter, drag one's feet, hem and haw, hum and haw; *informal* dilly-dally.

shimmer ▶ verb *the lake shimmered* GLINT, glisten, twinkle, sparkle, flash, scintillate, gleam, glow, glimmer, glitter, wink; *literary* coruscate.
▶ noun *the shimmer of lights from the traffic* GLINT, twinkle, sparkle, flash, gleam, glow, glimmer, lustre, glitter; *literary* coruscation.

shindig ▶ noun SOCIAL EVENT, party, social occasion, affair, function, gathering, reception, soiree, jamboree, gala, meet-and-greet, levee; *informal* do, bash, shindy, (*Atlantic*) time ✤.

shine ▶ verb **1** *the sun shone* EMIT LIGHT, beam, radiate, gleam, glow, glint, glimmer, sparkle, twinkle, glitter, glisten, shimmer, flash, flare, glare, fluoresce; *literary* glister, coruscate. **2** *she shone his shoes* POLISH, burnish, buff, wax, gloss. **3** *they shone at university* EXCEL, be outstanding, be brilliant, be successful, stand out.
▶ noun **1** *the shine of the moon on her face* LIGHT, brightness, gleam, glow, glint, glimmer, sparkle, twinkle, glitter, glisten, shimmer, beam, glare, radiance, illumination, luminescence, luminosity, incandescence. **2** *linseed oil restores the shine* POLISH, burnish, gleam, gloss, lustre, sheen, patina.

shining ▶ adjective **1** *a shining expanse of water* GLEAMING, bright, brilliant, illuminated, lustrous, glowing, glinting, sparkling, twinkling, glittering, glistening, shimmering, dazzling, luminous, luminescent, incandescent; *literary* glistering, coruscating. **2** *a shining face* GLOWING, beaming, radiant, happy. **3** *shining chromium tubes* SHINY, bright, polished, gleaming, glossy, sheeny, lustrous.
■ **a shining example** PARAGON, model, epitome, archetype, ideal, exemplar, nonpareil, paradigm, quintessence, the crème de la crème, beau ideal; acme, jewel, flower, treasure; *informal* one in a million, the bee's knees.

shinny ▶ verb CLIMB, clamber, scramble, go; mount, ascend, scale; descend.

shiny ▶ adjective GLOSSY, glassy, bright, polished, gleaming, satiny, sheeny, lustrous.
— OPPOSITES: matte.

ship ▶ noun *they travelled by ship* BOAT, vessel, craft. *See table.*
— RELATED TERMS: marine, maritime, naval.
▶ verb *he shipped me the package* SEND, post, mail, dispatch, courier, forward, express.

Ships

aircraft carrier	factory ship
barge	freighter
battle cruiser	frigate
battleship	galleon
bulk carrier	galley
capital ship	ice-breaker
caravel	laker
cargo ship	liner
carrack	merchant ship
coal ship	oil tanker
container ship	passenger ship
corvette	pirate ship
cruise ship	schooner
cutter	steamship
destroyer	supertanker
dreadnought	tall ship
	tanker

See also SAILING VESSELS.

shirk ▶ verb **1** *she didn't shirk any task* EVADE, dodge, avoid, get out of, sidestep, shrink from, shun, skip, miss; neglect; *informal* duck (out of), cop out of, cut. **2** *no one shirked* AVOID ONE'S DUTY, be remiss, be negligent, play truant, swing the lead, slack off; *informal* goof off, play hooky.

shirker ▶ noun DODGER, truant, absentee, layabout, good-for-nothing, loafer, idler; *informal* slacker, bum, lazybones.

shirt ▶ noun. *See table.*

Shirts & Tops

aloha shirt	middy
blouse	muscle shirt
button-down shirt	overblouse
camisole	overshirt
dashiki	Oxford shirt
dress shirt	polo shirt
golf shirt	rugby shirt
hair shirt	sports shirt
halter top	tank top
Hawaiian shirt	T-shirt
jersey	tube top
kurta	turtleneck
lumberjack shirt	undershirt

shiver¹ ▶ verb *she was shivering with fear* TREMBLE, quiver, shake, shudder, quaver, quake.
▶ noun *she gave a shiver as the door opened* TREMBLE, quiver, shake, shudder, quaver, quake, tremor, twitch.

shiver² ▶ noun *a shiver of glass* SPLINTER, sliver, shard, fragment, chip, shaving, smithereen, particle, bit, piece.
▶ verb *the window shivered into thousands of pieces* SHATTER, splinter, smash, fragment, crack, break.

shivery ▶ adjective TREMBLING, trembly, quivery, shaky, shuddering, shuddery, quavery, quaking; cold, chilly.

shoal ▶ noun SANDBANK, bank, mudbank, bar, sandbar, (*Nfld*) sunker ✦, tombolo, shelf, cay.

shock¹ ▶ noun **1** *the news came as a shock* BLOW, upset, disturbance; surprise, revelation, a bolt from the blue, thunderbolt, bombshell, rude awakening, eye-opener; *informal* whammy, wake-up call. **2** *you gave me a shock* FRIGHT, scare, jolt, start; *informal* turn. **3** *she*

was suffering from shock TRAUMA, prostration; collapse, breakdown. **4** *the first shock of the earthquake* VIBRATION, reverberation, shake, jolt, jar, jerk; impact, blow.
▶ verb *the murder shocked the nation* APPALL, horrify, outrage, revolt, disgust, nauseate, sicken; traumatize, distress, upset, disturb, disquiet, unsettle; stun, rock, stagger, astound, astonish, amaze, startle, surprise, dumbfound, shake, take aback, throw, unnerve.

shock² ▶ noun *a shock of red hair* MASS, mane, mop, thatch, head, crop, bush, frizz, tangle, cascade, halo.

shocking ▶ adjective APPALLING, horrifying, horrific, dreadful, awful, frightful, terrible; scandalous, outrageous, disgraceful, vile, abominable, abhorrent, atrocious; odious, repugnant, disgusting, nauseating, sickening, loathsome; distressing, upsetting, disturbing, disquieting, unsettling; staggering, amazing, astonishing, startling, surprising.

shoddy ▶ adjective **1** *shoddy goods* POOR-QUALITY, inferior, second-rate, third-rate, tinpot, cheap, cheapjack, trashy, jerry-built; *informal* tacky, chintzy, rubbishy, junky, cheapo, cheesy, schlocky. **2** *shoddy workmanship* CARELESS, slapdash, sloppy, slipshod, crude; negligent, cursory.
— OPPOSITES: quality, careful.

shoe ▶ noun *he laced up his shoe* (**shoes**) footwear. *See table.*

Shoes

alligator shoes	overshoes
aerobic shoes	oxfords
athletic shoes	patent leather
boat shoes	pattens
brogans	penny loafers
brogues	platform shoes
chappals	pointe shoes
cleats	pumps
clodhoppers	runners
clogs	running shoes
court shoes	sabots
creepers	saddle shoes
crocodile	sandals
Cuban heels	slingbacks
deck shoes	slip-ons
Doctor Martens*	slippers
dress shoes	sneakers
elevator shoes	spectator pumps
espadrille	spike heels
flip-flops	spikes
galoshes	square-toed
gym shoes	stiletto heels
high heels	tennis shoes
high-tops	thongs
huaraches	toe rubbers ✦
jellies	toeshoes
joggers	Topsiders*
kilties	track shoes
lace-ups	training shoes
loafers	walking shoes
low-cut	wedgies
Mary Janes	wingtips
moccasins	winkle-pickers
open-toe	zoris

See also the table at BOOT.

*Proprietary term.

shoemaker ▶ noun COBBLER, bootmaker.

shoot ▸ verb **1** *they shot him in the street* GUN DOWN, mow down, hit, wound, injure; put a bullet in, pick off, bag, fell, kill; *informal* pot, blast, pump full of lead, plug. **2** *they shot at the enemy* FIRE, open fire, aim, snipe, let fly; bombard, shell. **3** *faster than a gun can shoot bullets* DISCHARGE, fire, launch, loose off, let fly, emit. **4** *a car shot past* RACE, speed, flash, dash, dart, rush, hurtle, career, streak, whiz, go like lightning, go hell(-bent) for leather, zoom, charge; career, sweep, fly, wing; *informal* belt, scoot, scorch, tear, zip, whip, step on it, burn rubber, bomb, hightail it, barrel. **5** *the plant failed to shoot* SPROUT, bud, burgeon, germinate. **6** *the film was shot in Toronto* FILM, photograph, take, snap, capture, record, tape; videotape, video.
▸ noun *nip off the new shoots* SPROUT, bud, offshoot, scion, sucker, spear, runner, tendril, sprig.

shop ▸ noun **1** *a shop selling clothes* STORE, (retail) outlet, boutique, emporium, department store, big box store, supermarket, superstore, chain store, market, mart, trading post, minimart, convenience store, *(Que)* depanneur ♣. **2** *he works in the machine shop* WORKSHOP, workroom, plant, factory, works, mill, yard.
▸ verb *he was shopping for spices* GO SHOPPING, buy, purchase, get, acquire, obtain, pick up, snap up, procure, stock up on.

shopkeeper ▸ noun SHOP-OWNER, storekeeper, vendor, retailer, dealer, seller, merchant, trader, wholesaler, salesperson, sales assistant, sales associate, clerk, shop assistant; distributor.

shopper ▸ noun BUYER, purchaser, customer, consumer, client, patron; *Law* vendee.

shopping centre ▸ noun (SHOPPING) MALL, shopping complex, megamall, mini-mall, strip mall, power centre, galleria, marketplace, plaza.

shore¹ ▸ noun *he swam out from the shore* SEASHORE, lakeshore, lakefront, bayfront, beach, foreshore, sand(s), shoreline, waterside, front, coast, seaboard; *literary* strand.
— RELATED TERMS: littoral.

shore² ▸ verb *we had to shore up the building* PROP UP, hold up, bolster, support, brace, buttress, strengthen, fortify, reinforce, underpin.

short ▸ adjective **1** *a short piece of string* SMALL, little, tiny; *informal* teeny. **2** *short people* SMALL, little, petite, tiny, diminutive, stubby, elfin, dwarfish, midget, pygmy, Lilliputian, minuscule, miniature; *informal* pint-sized, teeny, knee-high to a grasshopper; *Scottish* wee. **3** *a short report* CONCISE, brief, succinct, compact, summary, economical, crisp, pithy, epigrammatic, laconic, thumbnail, capsule, abridged, abbreviated, condensed, synoptic, summarized, contracted, truncated; *formal* compendious. **4** *a short time* BRIEF, momentary, temporary, short-lived, impermanent, cursory, fleeting, passing, fugitive, lightning, transitory, transient, ephemeral, quick. **5** *money is a bit short* SCARCE, in short supply, scant, meagre, sparse, insufficient, deficient, inadequate, lacking, wanting, tight. **6** *he was rather short with her* CURT, sharp, abrupt, blunt, brusque, terse, offhand, gruff, surly, testy, rude, uncivil; *informal* snappy, snappish.
— OPPOSITES: long, tall, plentiful, courteous.
▸ adverb *she stopped short* ABRUPTLY, suddenly, sharply, all of a sudden, all at once, unexpectedly, without warning, out of the blue.
■ **in short** BRIEFLY, in a word, in a nutshell, in précis, in essence, to come to the point; in conclusion, in summary, to sum up.

■ **short of 1** *we are short of nurses* DEFICIENT IN, lacking, wanting, in need of, low on, short on, missing; *informal* strapped for, pushed for, minus. **2** *short of searching everyone, there is nothing we can do* APART FROM, other than, aside from, besides, except (for), excepting, without, excluding, not counting, save (for).

shortage ▸ noun SCARCITY, sparseness, sparsity, dearth, paucity, poverty, insufficiency, deficiency, inadequacy, famine, lack, want, deficit, shortfall, rarity.
— OPPOSITES: abundance.

shortcoming ▸ noun DEFECT, fault, flaw, imperfection, deficiency, limitation, failing, drawback, weakness, weak point, foible, frailty, vice.
— OPPOSITES: strength.

shorten ▸ verb MAKE SHORTER, abbreviate, abridge, condense, précis, synopsize, contract, compress, reduce, shrink, diminish, cut (down); dock, trim, crop, pare down, prune; curtail, truncate.
— OPPOSITES: extend.

short-lived ▸ adjective BRIEF, short, momentary, temporary, impermanent, cursory, fleeting, passing, fugitive, lightning, transitory, transient, ephemeral, quick.

shortly ▸ adverb **1** *she will be with you shortly* SOON, presently, momentarily, in a little while, at any moment, in a minute, in next to no time, before long, by and by; *informal* anon, any time now, pretty soon, in a jiffy; *dated* directly. **2** *'I know,' he replied shortly* CURTLY, sharply, abruptly, bluntly, brusquely, tersely, gruffly, snappily, testily, rudely.

short-sighted ▸ adjective **1** *I'm a little short-sighted* MYOPIC, near-sighted; *informal* as blind as a bat. **2** *short-sighted critics* NARROW-MINDED, unimaginative, small-minded, insular, parochial, provincial, improvident.
— OPPOSITES: far-sighted, imaginative.

short-staffed ▸ adjective UNDERSTAFFED, short-handed, undermanned, below strength.

short-tempered ▸ adjective IRRITABLE, irascible, hot-tempered, quick-tempered, snappish, fiery, touchy, volatile; cross, crabby, crotchety, cantankerous, grumpy, ill-tempered, bad-tempered, testy, tetchy, prickly, choleric; *informal* snappy, chippy, grouchy, cranky, on a short fuse, bitchy.
— OPPOSITES: placid.

shot¹ ▸ noun **1** *a shot rang out* report of a gun, crack, bang, blast; **(shots)** gunfire. **2** *the cannons have run out of shot* BULLETS, cannonballs, pellets, ammunition. **3** *the winning shot* STROKE, hit, strike; kick, throw, pitch, lob. **4** *Mike was an excellent shot* MARKSMAN, markswoman, shooter. **5** *a shot of us on holiday* PHOTOGRAPH, photo, snap, snapshot, picture, print, slide, still. **6** *(informal) it's nice to get a shot at driving* ATTEMPT, try; turn, chance, opportunity; *informal* go, stab, crack, kick at the can/cat ♣; *formal* essay. **7** *tetanus shots* INJECTION, inoculation, immunization, vaccination, booster; *informal* jab, needle.
■ **a shot in the arm** *(informal)* BOOST, tonic, stimulus, spur, impetus, encouragement.
■ **a shot in the dark** (WILD) GUESS, surmise, supposition, conjecture, speculation.
■ **like a shot** *(informal)* WITHOUT HESITATION, unhesitatingly, eagerly, enthusiastically; immediately, at once, right away/now, straight away, instantly, instantaneously, without delay; *informal* in/like a flash.
■ **not by a long shot** BY NO (MANNER OF) MEANS, not at

all, in no way, certainly not, absolutely not, definitely not.

shot² ▶ adjective *shot silk* VARIEGATED, mottled; multicoloured, varicoloured; iridescent, opalescent.

shoulder ▶ verb **1** *he shouldered the burden* TAKE ON (ONESELF), undertake, accept, assume; bear, carry. **2** *another kid shouldered him aside* PUSH, shove, thrust, jostle, force, bulldoze, elbow.
■ **give someone the cold shoulder** SNUB, shun, cold-shoulder, ignore, rebuff, spurn, ostracize, cut out; *informal* freeze out.
■ **put one's shoulder to the wheel** GET (DOWN) TO WORK, apply oneself, set to work, buckle down, roll up one's sleeves; work hard, be diligent, be industrious, exert oneself.
■ **shoulder to shoulder 1** *the regiment lined up shoulder to shoulder* SIDE BY SIDE, abreast, alongside (each other). **2** *he fought shoulder to shoulder with the others* UNITED, (working) together, jointly, in partnership, in collaboration, in co-operation, side by side, in alliance.

shout ▶ verb *'Help,' he shouted* YELL, cry (out), call (out), roar, howl, bellow, bawl, call at the top of one's voice, clamour, shriek, scream; raise one's voice, vociferate; *informal* holler.
— OPPOSITES: whisper.
▶ noun *a shout of pain* YELL, cry, call, roar, howl, bellow, bawl, clamour, vociferation, shriek, scream; *informal* holler.

shove ▶ verb **1** *she shoved him back into the chair* PUSH, thrust, propel, drive, force, ram, knock, elbow, shoulder; jostle, hustle, manhandle. **2** *she shoved past him* PUSH (ONE'S WAY), force one's way, barge (one's way), elbow (one's way), shoulder one's way.
▶ noun *a hefty shove* PUSH, thrust, bump, jolt.
■ **shove off** (*informal*) GO AWAY, get out (of my sight); get going, take oneself off, be off (with you), shoo; *informal* scram, make yourself scarce, be on your way, beat it, get lost, push off, buzz off, clear off, go (and) jump in the lake, bug off, haul it, take a hike; *literary* begone.

shovel ▶ noun *a pick and shovel* SPADE.
▶ verb *shovelling snow* SCOOP (UP), dig, excavate.

show ▶ verb **1** *the stitches do not show* BE VISIBLE, be seen, be in view, be obvious. **2** *he wouldn't show the picture* DISPLAY, exhibit, put on show/display, put on view, parade, uncover, reveal. **3** *Frank showed his frustration* MANIFEST, exhibit, reveal, convey, communicate, make known; express, proclaim, make plain, make obvious, disclose, betray; *formal* evince. **4** *I'll show you how to make a daisy chain* DEMONSTRATE, explain, describe, illustrate; teach, instruct, give instructions. **5** *recent events show this to be true* PROVE, demonstrate, confirm, show beyond doubt; substantiate, corroborate, verify, establish, attest, certify, testify, bear out; *formal* evince. **6** *a young woman showed them to their seats* ESCORT, accompany, take, conduct, lead, usher, guide, direct, steer, shepherd. **7** (*informal*) *they never showed* APPEAR, arrive, come, get here/there, put in an appearance, materialize, turn up; *informal* show up.
— OPPOSITES: conceal.
▶ noun **1** *a spectacular show of fireworks* DISPLAY, array, exhibition, presentation, exposition, spectacle. **2** *the motor show* EXHIBITION, exposition, fair, extravaganza, spectacle, exhibit. **3** *they took in a show* (THEATRICAL) PERFORMANCE, musical, play, opera, ballet. **4** *she's only doing it for show* APPEARANCE, display, impression, ostentation, image. **5** *Drew made a show of looking busy*

PRETENSE, outward appearance, (false) front, guise, semblance, pose, parade. **6** (*informal*) *I don't run the show* UNDERTAKING, affair, operation, proceedings, enterprise, business, venture.
■ **show off** (*informal*) BEHAVE AFFECTEDLY, put on airs, put on an act, swagger around, swank, strut, strike an attitude, posture; draw attention to oneself; *informal* cop an attitude.
■ **show something off** DISPLAY, show to advantage, exhibit, demonstrate, parade, draw attention to, flaunt.
■ **show up 1** *cancers show up on X-rays* BE VISIBLE, be obvious, be seen, be revealed. **2** (*informal*) *only two waitresses showed up.* See SHOW verb sense 7.
■ **show someone/something up 1** *the sun showed up the shabbiness of the room* EXPOSE, reveal, make visible, make obvious, highlight. **2** (*informal*) *they showed him up in front of his friends.* See HUMILIATE.

showdown ▶ noun CONFRONTATION, clash, faceoff.

shower ▶ noun **1** *a shower of rain* (LIGHT) FALL, drizzle, sprinkling, misting. **2** *a shower of arrows* VOLLEY, hail, salvo, bombardment, barrage, fusillade, cannonade. **3** *a shower of awards* AVALANCHE, deluge, flood, spate, flurry; profusion, abundance, plethora.
▶ verb **1** *confetti showered down on us* RAIN, fall, hail. **2** *she showered them with gifts* DELUGE, flood, inundate, swamp, engulf; overwhelm, overload, snow under. **3** *showering praise on his cronies* LAVISH, heap, bestow freely.

showing ▶ noun **1** *another showing of the series* PRESENTATION, broadcast, airing, televising, screening. **2** *the party's present showing* PERFORMANCE, (track) record, results, success, achievement.

showman ▶ noun **1** *a travelling showman* IMPRESARIO, stage manager; ringmaster, host, master of ceremonies, MC; presenter; *informal* emcee. **2** *Jack is a great showman* ENTERTAINER, performer, virtuoso.

show-off ▶ noun (*informal*) EXHIBITIONIST, extrovert, poser, poseur, peacock, swaggerer, self-publicist, braggart; *informal* showboat, blowhard, grandstander.

showy ▶ adjective OSTENTATIOUS, conspicuous, pretentious, flamboyant, gaudy, garish, brash, vulgar, loud, extravagant, fancy, ornate, over-elaborate, kitsch, kitschy; *informal* flash, flashy, glitzy, ritzy, swanky, fancy-dancy, fancy-schmancy.
— OPPOSITES: restrained.

shred ▶ noun **1** *her dress was torn to shreds* TATTER, scrap, strip, ribbon, rag, fragment, sliver, (tiny) bit/piece. **2** *not a shred of evidence* SCRAP, bit, speck, iota, particle, ounce, whit, jot, crumb, morsel, fragment, grain, drop, trace, scintilla, spot; *informal* smidgen.
▶ verb *shredding vegetables* CHOP FINELY, cut up, tear up, grate, mince, macerate, grind.

shrew ▶ noun VIRAGO, dragon, termagant, fishwife, witch, tartar, hag; *informal* battleaxe, old bag, old bat; *archaic* scold.

shrewd ▶ adjective ASTUTE, sharp-witted, sharp, smart, acute, intelligent, clever, canny, perceptive, perspicacious, sagacious, wise; *informal* on the ball, savvy, heads-up; *formal* sapient.
— OPPOSITES: stupid.

shrewdness ▶ noun ASTUTENESS, sharp-wittedness, acuteness, acumen, acuity, intelligence, cleverness, smartness, wit, canniness, common sense, discernment, insight, understanding, perception, perceptiveness, perspicacity, discrimination, sagacity, sageness; *informal* horse sense, savvy, (street) smarts; *formal* sapience.

shrewish ▶ **adjective** BAD-TEMPERED, quarrelsome, spiteful, sharp-tongued, scolding, nagging; venomous, rancorous, bitchy.

shriek ▶ **verb** *she shrieked with laughter* SCREAM, screech, squeal, squawk, roar, howl, shout, yelp; *informal* holler.
▶ **noun** *a shriek of laughter* SCREAM, screech, squeal, squawk, roar, howl, shout, yelp; *informal* holler.

shrill ▶ **adjective** HIGH-PITCHED, piercing, high, sharp, ear-piercing, ear-splitting, penetrating, screeching, shrieking, screechy.

shrine ▶ **noun 1** *the shrine of St. James* HOLY PLACE, temple, church, chapel, tabernacle, sanctuary, sanctum. **2** *a shrine to the Beatles* MEMORIAL, monument.

shrink ▶ **verb 1** *the number of competitors shrank* GET SMALLER, become/grow smaller, contract, diminish, lessen, reduce, decrease, dwindle, decline, fall off, drop off. **2** *he shrank back against the wall* DRAW BACK, recoil, back away, retreat, withdraw, cringe, cower, quail. **3** *he doesn't shrink from naming names* RECOIL, shy away, demur, flinch, have scruples, have misgivings, have qualms, be loath, be reluctant, be unwilling, be averse, fight shy of, be hesitant, be afraid, hesitate, balk at.
— OPPOSITES: expand, increase.

shrivel ▶ **verb** WITHER, shrink, wilt; dry up, desiccate, dehydrate, parch, frazzle.

shroud ▶ **noun 1** *the Turin Shroud* WINDING SHEET; *historical* cerements. **2** *a shroud of mist | a shroud of secrecy* COVERING, cover, cloak, mantle, blanket, layer, cloud, veil.
▶ **verb** *a mist shrouded the shore* COVER, envelop, veil, cloak, blanket, screen, conceal, hide, mask, obscure; *literary* enshroud.

shrub ▶ **noun** BUSH, woody plant.

shrug
■ **shrug something off** DISREGARD, dismiss, take no notice of, ignore, pay no heed to, play down, make light of.

shudder ▶ **verb** *she shuddered at the thought* SHAKE, shiver, tremble, quiver, vibrate, palpitate.
▶ **noun** *a shudder racked his body* SHAKE, shiver, tremor, tremble, trembling, quiver, quivering, vibration, palpitation, spasm.

shuffle ▶ **verb 1** *they shuffled along the passage* SHAMBLE, drag one's feet, totter, dodder. **2** *she shuffled her feet* SCRAPE, drag, scuffle, scuff. **3** *he shuffled the cards* MIX (UP), mingle, rearrange, jumble.

shun ▶ **verb** AVOID, evade, eschew, steer clear of, shy away from, fight shy of, keep one's distance from, give a wide berth to, have nothing to do with; snub, give someone the cold shoulder, cold-shoulder, ignore, look through, reject, rebuff, spurn, ostracize; *informal* give someone the brush-off, freeze out, give someone the bum's rush, give someone the brush off.
— OPPOSITES: welcome.

shut ▶ **verb** *please shut the door* CLOSE, pull/push to, slam, fasten; put the lid on, bar, lock, secure.
— OPPOSITES: open, unlock.
■ **shut down** CEASE ACTIVITY, close (down), cease operating, cease trading, be shut (down); turn off, switch off; *informal* fold; power down.
■ **shut something in** CONFINE, enclose, impound, shut up, pen (in/up), fence in, immure, lock up/in, cage, imprison, intern, incarcerate, corral.
■ **shut someone/something out 1** *he shut me out of the house* LOCK OUT, keep out, refuse entrance to. **2** *she shut out the memories* BLOCK, suppress. **3** *the bamboo shut out the light* KEEP OUT, block out, screen, veil. **4** *they shut out the opposition in three straight games* PREVENT FROM SCORING, blank.
■ **shut up** (*informal*) BE QUIET, keep quiet, hold one's tongue, keep one's lips sealed; stop talking, quieten (down); *informal* keep mum, button it, hush up, cut the crap, shut it, shut your face/mouth/trap, put a sock in it, give it a rest, save it.
■ **shut someone/something up 1** *I haven't shut the hens up yet. See* SHUT SOMETHING IN. **2** (*informal*) *that should shut them up* QUIETEN (DOWN), silence, hush, shush, quiet, gag, muzzle.

shutdown ▶ **noun** CLOSURE, termination, closing down, winding up; turning off, switching off, powering down.

shuttle ▶ **verb** PLY, run, commute, go/travel back and forth, go/travel to and fro; ferry.

shy ▶ **adjective** *I was painfully shy* BASHFUL, diffident, farouche, timid, sheepish, reserved, reticent, introverted, retiring, self-effacing, withdrawn, timorous, mousy, nervous, insecure, unconfident, inhibited, repressed, self-conscious, embarrassed.
— OPPOSITES: confident.
■ **shy away from** FLINCH, demur, recoil, hang back, have scruples, have misgivings, have qualms, be chary, be diffident, be bashful, fight shy, be coy; be loath, be reluctant, be unwilling, be disinclined, be hesitant, hesitate, balk at; *informal* boggle at.

shyness ▶ **noun** BASHFULNESS, diffidence, sheepishness, reserve, reservedness, introversion, reticence, timidity, timidness, timorousness, mousiness, lack of confidence, self-consciousness, embarrassment, coyness, demureness.

sibling ▶ **noun** brother, sister; *Zoology* sib.

sick ▶ **adjective 1** *the children are sick* ILL, unwell, poorly, ailing, indisposed, not oneself; off; *informal* laid up, under the weather. **2** *he was feeling sick* NAUSEOUS, nauseated, queasy, bilious, green around/at the gills; seasick, carsick, airsick, travel-sick; *informal* about to throw up. **3** (*informal*) *we're just sick about it* DISAPPOINTED, depressed, dejected, despondent, downcast, unhappy; angry, cross, annoyed, displeased, disgruntled, fed up, cheesed off. **4** *I'm sick of this music* FED UP, bored, tired, weary. **5** (*informal*) *a sick joke* MACABRE, black, ghoulish, morbid, perverted, gruesome, sadistic, cruel.
— OPPOSITES: well.
■ **be sick** VOMIT, throw up, retch, heave, gag; *informal* chuck up, hurl, spew, spit up, barf, upchuck, toss one's cookies.

sicken ▶ **verb 1** *the stench sickened him* CAUSE TO FEEL SICK/NAUSEOUS, make sick, turn someone's stomach, revolt, disgust; *informal* make someone want to throw up, gross out. **2** *she sickened and died* BECOME ILL, fall ill, be taken ill/sick, catch something.
— OPPOSITES: recover.

sickening ▶ **adjective** NAUSEATING, stomach-turning, stomach-churning, repulsive, revolting, disgusting, repellent, repugnant, appalling, obnoxious, nauseous, vile, nasty, foul, loathsome, offensive, objectionable, off-putting, distasteful, obscene, gruesome, grisly, vomitous; *informal* gross; *formal* rebarbative.

sickly ▶ **adjective 1** *a sickly child* UNHEALTHY, in poor health, delicate, frail, weak. **2** *sickly faces* PALE, wan, pasty, sallow, pallid, ashen, anemic. **3** *a sickly green* INSIPID, pale, light, light-coloured, washed out, faded.

4 *sickly love songs* SENTIMENTAL, mawkish, cloying, sugary, syrupy, saccharine; *informal* mushy, slushy, schmaltzy, weepy, lovey-dovey, corny, soppy, cornball, sappy, hokey, three-hankie.
— OPPOSITES: healthy.

sickness ▶ noun **1** *she was absent through sickness* ILLNESS, disease, ailment, complaint, infection, malady, infirmity, indisposition; *informal* bug, virus. **2** *a wave of sickness* NAUSEA, biliousness, queasiness. **3** *he suffered sickness and diarrhea* VOMITING, retching, gagging; travel-sickness, seasickness, carsickness, airsickness, motion sickness; *informal* throwing up, puking, barfing.

side ▶ noun **1** *the side of the road* EDGE, border, verge, boundary, margin, fringe(s), flank, bank, perimeter, extremity, periphery, (outer) limit, limits, bounds; *literary* marge, bourn. **2** *the wrong side of the road* HALF, part; lane. **3** *the east side of the city* DISTRICT, quarter, area, region, part, neighbourhood, sector, section, zone, ward. **4** *one side of the paper* SURFACE, face, plane. **5** *his side of the argument* POINT OF VIEW, viewpoint, perspective, opinion, way of thinking, standpoint, position, outlook, slant, angle. **6** *the losing side in the war* FACTION, camp, bloc, party, wing. **7** *the players on their side* TEAM, squad, lineup.
— RELATED TERMS: lateral.
— OPPOSITES: centre, end.
▶ adjective **1** *elaborate side pieces* LATERAL, wing, flanking. **2** *a side issue* SUBORDINATE, lesser, lower-level, secondary, minor, peripheral, incidental, ancillary, subsidiary, of little account, extraneous.
— OPPOSITES: front, central.
▶ verb *siding with the underdog.* See TAKE SOMEONE'S SIDE.
■ **side by side** *they worked side by side* ALONGSIDE (EACH OTHER), beside each other, abreast, shoulder to shoulder, close together; in collaboration, in solidarity.
■ **take someone's side** SUPPORT, take someone's part, side with, be on someone's side, stand by, back, give someone one's backing, be loyal to, defend, champion, ally (oneself) with, sympathize with, favour.

sideline ▶ noun *he founded the company as a sideline* SECONDARY OCCUPATION, second job; hobby, leisure activity/pursuit, recreation.
▶ verb **1** *the injury sidelined their top defenceman* REMOVE, take out, bench. **2** *we've sidelined plans to build a house* POSTPONE, suspend, delay, defer, shelve; *informal* put on the back burner.
■ **on the sidelines** WITHOUT TAKING PART, without getting involved.

sidelong ▶ adjective *a sidelong glance* INDIRECT, oblique, sideways, sideward; surreptitious, furtive, covert, sly.
— OPPOSITES: overt.
▶ adverb *he looked sidelong at her* INDIRECTLY, obliquely, sideways, out of the corner of one's eye; surreptitiously, furtively, covertly, slyly.

side-splitting ▶ adjective *(informal).* See HILARIOUS.

sidestep ▶ verb AVOID, evade, dodge, circumvent, skirt around, bypass; *informal* duck, pussyfoot around.

sidetrack ▶ verb DISTRACT, divert, deflect, draw away.

sidewalk ▶ noun WALKWAY, walk, pedway, path.

sideways ▶ adverb **1** *I slid off sideways* TO THE SIDE, laterally. **2** *the expansion slots are mounted sideways* EDGEWISE, sidewards, side first, edgeways, end on, broadside. **3** *he looked sideways at her* OBLIQUELY,

indirectly, sidelong; covertly, furtively, surreptitiously, slyly.
▶ adjective **1** *sideways force* LATERAL, sideward, on the side, side to side. **2** *a sideways look* OBLIQUE, indirect, sidelong; covert, furtive, sly, surreptitious.

siding ▶ noun *applying some new siding to the house* cladding, clapboard, Insulbrick ✦, board and batten, shiplap; facade.

sidle ▶ verb CREEP, sneak, slink, slip, slide, steal, edge, inch, move furtively.

siege ▶ noun BLOCKADE, encirclement.
— OPPOSITES: relief.

siesta ▶ noun AFTERNOON SLEEP, nap, catnap, doze, rest; *informal* snooze, lie-down, forty winks, a bit of shut-eye.

sieve ▶ noun *use a sieve to strain the mixture* STRAINER, sifter, filter, riddle, screen.
▶ verb **1** *sieve the mixture into a bowl.* See SIFT sense 1. **2** *the coins were sieved from the ash.* See SIFT sense 2.

sift ▶ verb **1** *sift the flour into a large bowl* SIEVE, strain, screen, filter, riddle; *archaic* bolt. **2** *we sift out unsuitable applications* SEPARATE OUT, filter out, sort out, put to one side, weed out, get rid of, remove. **3** *investigators are sifting through the wreckage* SEARCH THROUGH, look through, examine, inspect, scrutinize, pore over, investigate, analyze, dissect, review.

sigh ▶ verb **1** *she sighed with relief* BREATHE OUT, exhale; groan, moan. **2** *the wind sighed in the trees* RUSTLE, whisper, murmur, sough. **3** *he sighed for days gone by* YEARN, long, pine, ache, grieve, cry for/over, weep for/over, rue, miss, mourn, lament, hanker for/after.

sight ▶ noun **1** *she has excellent sight* EYESIGHT, vision, eyes, faculty of sight, visual perception. **2** *her first sight of it* VIEW, glimpse, glance, look. **3** *within sight of the enemy* RANGE OF VISION, field of vision, view. **4** *(dated) we are all equal in the sight of God* PERCEPTION, judgment, belief, opinion, point of view, view, viewpoint, mind, perspective, standpoint. **5** *historic sights* LANDMARK, place of interest, monument, spectacle, view, marvel, wonder. **6** *(informal) I must look a sight* EYESORE, spectacle, mess; *informal* fright.
— RELATED TERMS: optical, visual.
▶ verb *one of the helicopters sighted wreckage* GLIMPSE, catch/get a glimpse of, catch sight of, see, spot, spy, notice, observe; *literary* espy, descry.
■ **catch sight of** GLIMPSE, catch/get a glimpse of, see, spot, spy, make out, pick out, have sight of; *literary* espy, descry.
■ **set one's sights on** ASPIRE TO, aim at/for, try for, strive for/towards, work towards.

sightseer ▶ noun *sightseers to the city* TOURIST, visitor, holidaymaker, tripper, day tripper.

sign ▶ noun **1** *a sign of affection* INDICATION, signal, symptom, pointer, suggestion, intimation, mark, manifestation, demonstration, token, evidence; *literary* sigil. **2** *a sign of things to come* PORTENT, omen, warning, forewarning, augury, presage; promise, threat. **3** *at his sign the soldiers followed* GESTURE, signal, wave, gesticulation, cue, nod. **4** *he read the sign on the wall* NOTICE, signpost, signboard, warning sign, road sign, traffic sign, guidepost, marquee. **5** *the dancers were daubed with signs* SYMBOL, mark, cipher, letter, character, figure, hieroglyph, ideogram, rune, emblem, device, logo.
▶ verb **1** *he signed the letter* WRITE ONE'S NAME ON, autograph, endorse, initial, countersign, ink; *formal* subscribe. **2** *the government signed the agreement* ENDORSE, validate, certify, authenticate, sanction,

authorize; agree to, approve, ratify, adopt, give one's approval to; *informal* give something the go-ahead, give something the green light, give something the thumbs up. **3** *he signed his name* WRITE, inscribe, pen. **4** *we have signed a new player* RECRUIT, hire, engage, employ, take on, appoint, sign on/up, enlist. **5** *she signed to Susan to leave. See* SIGNAL¹ *verb* sense 1.
■ **sign on/up** ENLIST, take a job, join (up), enrol, register, volunteer.
■ **sign someone on/up.** *See* SIGN *verb* sense 4.
■ **sign something over** TRANSFER, make over, hand over, bequeath, pass on, transmit, cede; *Law* devolve, convey.

signal¹ ▶ **noun 1** *a signal to stop* GESTURE, sign, wave, gesticulation, cue, indication, warning, motion. **2** *a clear signal that the company is in trouble* INDICATION, sign, symptom, hint, pointer, intimation, clue, demonstration, evidence, proof. **3** *the encroaching dark is a signal for people to emerge* CUE, prompt, impetus, stimulus; *informal* go-ahead.
▶ **verb 1** *the driver signalled to her to cross* GESTURE, sign, give a sign to, direct, motion; wave, beckon, nod. **2** *they signalled displeasure by refusing to co-operate* INDICATE, show, express, communicate, proclaim, declare. **3** *his death signals the end of an era* MARK, signify, mean, be a sign of, be evidence of, herald; *literary* betoken, foretoken.

signal² ▶ **adjective** *a signal victory. See* SIGNIFICANT.

signature ▶ **noun** AUTOGRAPH, inscription; *informal* John Hancock.

significance ▶ **noun 1** *a matter of considerable significance* IMPORTANCE, import, consequence, seriousness, gravity, weight, magnitude, momentousness; *formal* moment. **2** *the significance of his remarks* MEANING, sense, signification, import, thrust, drift, gist, implication, message, essence, substance, point.

significant ▶ **adjective 1** *a significant increase* NOTABLE, noteworthy, worthy of attention, remarkable, important, of importance, of consequence; serious, crucial, weighty, momentous, epoch-making, uncommon, unusual, rare, extraordinary, exceptional, special; *formal* of moment. **2** *a significant look* MEANINGFUL, expressive, eloquent, suggestive, knowing, telling.

significantly ▶ **adverb 1** *significantly better* NOTABLY, remarkably, outstandingly, importantly, crucially, materially, appreciably; markedly, considerably, obviously, conspicuously, strikingly, signally. **2** *he paused significantly* MEANINGFULLY, expressively, eloquently, revealingly, suggestively, knowingly.

signify ▶ **verb 1** *this signified a fundamental change* BE EVIDENCE OF, be a sign of, mark, signal, mean, spell, be symptomatic of, herald, indicate; *literary* betoken. **2** *the egg signifies life* MEAN, denote, designate, represent, symbolize, stand for; *literary* betoken. **3** *signify your agreement by signing below* EXPRESS, indicate, show, proclaim, declare. **4** *the locked door doesn't signify* MEAN ANYTHING, be of importance, be important, be significant, be of significance, be of account, count, matter, be relevant.

silence ▶ **noun 1** *the silence of the night* QUIETNESS, quiet, quietude, still, stillness, hush, tranquility, noiselessness, soundlessness, peacefulness, peace (and quiet). **2** *she was reduced to silence* SPEECHLESSNESS, wordlessness, dumbness, muteness, taciturnity. **3** *the politicians kept their silence* SECRETIVENESS, secrecy, reticence, taciturnity, uncommunicativeness.
− OPPOSITES: sound.
▶ **verb 1** *he silenced her with a kiss* QUIETEN, quiet, hush, shush; gag, muzzle, censor. **2** *silencing outside noises* MUFFLE, deaden, soften, mute, smother, dampen, damp down, mask, suppress, reduce. **3** *this would silence their complaints* STOP, put an end to, put a stop to.

silent ▶ **adjective 1** *the night was silent* COMPLETELY QUIET, still, hushed, inaudible, noiseless, soundless. **2** *the right to remain silent* SPEECHLESS, quiet, unspeaking, dumb, mute, taciturn, uncommunicative, tight-lipped; *informal* mum. **3** *silent thanks* UNSPOKEN, wordless, unsaid, unexpressed, unvoiced, tacit, implicit, understood.
− OPPOSITES: audible, noisy.

silently ▶ **adverb 1** *Nancy crept silently up the stairs* QUIETLY, inaudibly, noiselessly, soundlessly, in silence. **2** *they drove on silently* WITHOUT A WORD, saying nothing, in silence. **3** *I silently said goodbye* WITHOUT WORDS, wordlessly, in one's head, tacitly, implicitly.
− OPPOSITES: audibly, out loud.

silhouette ▶ **noun** *the silhouette of the dome* OUTLINE, contour(s), profile, form, shape, figure, shadow.
▶ **verb** *the castle was silhouetted against the sky* OUTLINE, delineate, define; stand out.

silky ▶ **adjective** SMOOTH, soft, sleek, fine, glossy, satiny, silken.

silly ▶ **adjective 1** *don't be so silly* FOOLISH, stupid, unintelligent, idiotic, brainless, mindless, witless, imbecilic, doltish; imprudent, thoughtless, rash, reckless, foolhardy, irresponsible; mad, scatterbrained, feather-brained; frivolous, giddy, inane, immature, childish, puerile, empty-headed; *informal* crazy, dotty, scatty, loopy, wingy ♣, ditzy, spinny ♣, screwy, thick, thick-headed, birdbrained, pea-brained, dopey, dim, dim-witted, halfwitted, dippy, blockheaded, boneheaded, lamebrained; daft, chowderhead; *dated* tomfool. **2** *that was a silly thing to do* UNWISE, imprudent, thoughtless, foolish, stupid, idiotic, senseless, mindless; rash, reckless, foolhardy, irresponsible, injudicious, misguided, irrational; *informal* crazy; daft. **3** *he would brood about silly things* TRIVIAL, trifling, frivolous, footling, petty, small, insignificant, unimportant; *informal* piffling, piddling, small-bore. **4** *he drank himself silly* SENSELESS, insensible, unconscious, stupid, into a stupor, into senselessness, stupefied.
− OPPOSITES: sensible.
▶ **noun** (*informal*) *you're such a silly! See* FOOL *noun* sense 1.

silt ▶ **noun** *the flooding brought more silt* SEDIMENT, deposit, alluvium, mud.
▶ **verb** *the harbour had silted up* BECOME BLOCKED, become clogged, fill up (with silt).

silver ▶ **noun 1** *freshly polished silver* SILVERWARE, (silver) plate; cutlery, {knives, forks, and spoons}. **2** *a handful of silver* COINS, coinage, specie; (small) change, loose change. **3** *she won three silvers* SILVER MEDAL, second prize.
▶ **adjective 1** *silver hair* GREY, greyish, white. **2** *the silver water* SILVERY, shining, lustrous, gleaming; *literary* argent.

silviculture ▶ **noun** *See* FORESTRY.

similar ▶ **adjective 1** *you two are very similar* ALIKE, (much) the same, indistinguishable, almost identical, homogeneous, homologous; *informal* much of a muchness. **2** *northern India and similar areas* COMPARABLE, like, corresponding, homogeneous,

equivalent, analogous. **3** *other towns were similar to this one* LIKE, much the same as, comparable to.
— OPPOSITES: different, unlike.
■ **be similar to** RESEMBLE, look like, have the appearance of.

similarity ▶ noun RESEMBLANCE, likeness, sameness, similitude, comparability, correspondence, parallel, equivalence, homogeneity, indistinguishability, uniformity; *archaic* semblance.

similarly ▶ adverb LIKEWISE, in similar fashion, in like manner, comparably, correspondingly, uniformly, indistinguishably, analogously, homogeneously, equivalently, in the same way, the same, identically.

similitude ▶ noun RESEMBLANCE, similarity, likeness, sameness, similar nature, comparability, correspondence, comparison, analogy, parallel, parallelism, equivalence; interchangeability, closeness, nearness, affinity, homogeneity, agreement, indistinguishability, uniformity; community, kinship, relatedness; *archaic* semblance.

simmer ▶ verb **1** *the soup was simmering on the stove* BOIL GENTLY, cook gently, bubble, stew. **2** *she was simmering with resentment* BE FURIOUS, be enraged, be angry, be incensed, be infuriated, seethe, fume, brim, smoulder; *informal* be steamed up, be hot under the collar, stew.
■ **simmer down** BECOME LESS ANGRY, cool off/down, be placated, control oneself, become calmer, calm down, become quieter, quieten down; *informal* chill out.

simper ▶ verb SMILE AFFECTEDLY, smile coquettishly, look coy.

simple ▶ adjective **1** *it's really pretty simple* STRAIGHTFORWARD, easy, uncomplicated, uninvolved, effortless, painless, undemanding, elementary, child's play; *informal* as easy as pie, as easy as ABC, a piece of cake, a cinch, no sweat, a pushover, kids' stuff, a breeze, duck soup, a snap. **2** *simple language* CLEAR, plain, straightforward, intelligible, comprehensible, uncomplicated, accessible; *informal* user-friendly. **3** *a simple white blouse* PLAIN, unadorned, undecorated, unembellished, unornamented, unelaborate, basic, unsophisticated, no-frills; classic, understated, uncluttered, restrained. **4** *the simple truth* CANDID, frank, honest, sincere, plain, absolute, unqualified, bald, stark, unadorned, unvarnished, unembellished. **5** *simple country people* UNPRETENTIOUS, unsophisticated, ordinary, unaffected, unassuming, natural, honest-to-goodness, cracker-barrel. **6** *he's a bit simple* HAVING LEARNING DIFFICULTIES, having special (educational) needs; of low intelligence, simple-minded, unintelligent, backward, (mentally) retarded. **7** *simple chemical substances* NON-COMPOUND, non-complex, uncombined, unblended, unalloyed, pure, single.
— OPPOSITES: difficult, complex, fancy, compound.

simpleton ▶ noun. *See* FOOL *noun* sense 1.

simplicity ▶ noun **1** *the simplicity of the recipes* STRAIGHTFORWARDNESS, ease, easiness, simpleness, effortlessness. **2** *the simplicity of the language* CLARITY, clearness, plainness, simpleness, intelligibility, comprehensibility, understandability, accessibility, straightforwardness. **3** *the building's simplicity* PLAINNESS, lack/absence of adornment, lack/absence of decoration, austerity, spareness, clean lines. **4** *the simplicity of their lifestyle* UNPRETENTIOUSNESS, ordinariness, lack of sophistication, lack of affectation, naturalness.

simplify ▶ verb MAKE SIMPLE/SIMPLER, make easy/ easier to understand, make plainer, clarify, make more comprehensible/intelligible; paraphrase.
— OPPOSITES: complicate.

simplistic ▶ adjective FACILE, superficial, oversimple, oversimplified; shallow, jejune, naive.

simply ▶ adverb **1** *he spoke simply and forcefully* STRAIGHTFORWARDLY, directly, clearly, plainly, intelligibly, lucidly, unambiguously. **2** *she was dressed simply* PLAINLY, without adornment, without decoration, without ornament/ornamentation, soberly, unfussily, unelaborately, classically. **3** *they lived simply* UNPRETENTIOUSLY, modestly, quietly. **4** *they are welcomed simply because they have plenty of money* MERELY, just, purely, solely, only. **5** *Mrs. Marks was simply livid* UTTERLY, absolutely, completely, positively, really; *informal* plain. **6** *it's simply the best thing ever written* WITHOUT DOUBT, unquestionably, undeniably, incontrovertibly, certainly, categorically.

simulate ▶ verb **1** *they simulated pleasure* FEIGN, pretend, fake, sham, affect, put on, give the appearance of. **2** *simulating conditions in space* IMITATE, reproduce, replicate, duplicate, mimic.

simulated ▶ adjective **1** *simulated fear* FEIGNED, fake, mock, affected, sham, insincere, false, bogus; *informal* pretend, put-on, phony. **2** *simulated leather* ARTIFICIAL, imitation, fake, mock, synthetic, man-made, ersatz.
— OPPOSITES: real.

simultaneous ▶ adjective CONCURRENT, happening at the same time, contemporaneous, concomitant, coinciding, coincident, synchronous, synchronized.

simultaneously ▶ adverb AT (ONE AND) THE SAME TIME, at the same instant/moment, at once, concurrently, concomitantly; (all) together, in unison, in concert, in chorus.

sin ▶ noun **1** *a sin in the eyes of God* IMMORAL ACT, wrong, wrongdoing, act of evil/wickedness, transgression, crime, offence, misdeed, misdemeanour; *archaic* trespass. **2** *the human capacity for sin* WICKEDNESS, wrongdoing, wrong, evil, evildoing, sinfulness, immorality, iniquity, vice, crime. **3** *(informal) they've cut the school music program — it's a sin* SCANDAL, crime, disgrace, outrage.
— OPPOSITES: virtue.
▶ verb *I have sinned* COMMIT A SIN, commit an offence, transgress, do wrong, commit a crime, break the law, misbehave, go astray; *archaic* trespass.

since ▶ conjunction BECAUSE, as, inasmuch, for the reason that, seeing that/as.

sincere ▶ adjective **1** *our sincere gratitude* HEARTFELT, wholehearted, profound, deep; genuine, real, unfeigned, unaffected, true, honest, bona fide. **2** *a sincere person* HONEST, genuine, truthful, unhypocritical, straightforward, direct, frank, candid; *informal* straight, upfront, on the level, on the up and up.

sincerely ▶ adverb GENUINELY, honestly, really, truly, truthfully, wholeheartedly, earnestly, fervently.

sincerity ▶ noun HONESTY, genuineness, truthfulness, integrity, probity, trustworthiness; straightforwardness, openness, candour, candidness.

sinecure ▶ noun EASY JOB, cushy job, soft option; *informal* picnic, cinch, easy money, free ride, gravy train.

sinewy ▶ adjective MUSCULAR, muscly, brawny, powerfully built, burly, strapping, sturdy, rugged,

strong, powerful, athletic, muscle-bound; *informal* hunky, beefy; *dated* stalwart; *literary* thewy.
— OPPOSITES: puny.

sinful ▸ adjective **1** *sinful conduct* IMMORAL, wicked, (morally) wrong, wrongful, evil, bad, iniquitous, corrupt, criminal, nefarious, depraved, degenerate. **2** *a sinful waste of money* REPREHENSIBLE, scandalous, disgraceful, deplorable, shameful, criminal.
— OPPOSITES: virtuous.

sinfulness ▸ noun IMMORALITY, wickedness, sin, wrongdoing, evil, evil-doing, iniquitousness, corruption, depravity, degeneracy, vice; *formal* turpitude.
— OPPOSITES: virtue.

sing ▸ verb **1** *the choir began to sing* croon, carol, trill, chant, intone, chorus; *informal* belt out. **2** *the birds were singing* WARBLE, trill, chirp, chirrup, cheep, peep. **3** *Rudy sang out a greeting* CALL (OUT), cry (out), shout, yell; *informal* holler. **4** (*informal*) *he's going to sing to the police* INFORM (ON SOMEONE), confess; *informal* squeal, rat on someone, blow the whistle on someone, peach (on someone), snitch (on someone), narc (on someone), finger someone, fink on someone.

singe ▸ verb SCORCH, burn, sear, char.

singer ▸ noun VOCALIST, soloist, songster, songstress, cantor, chorister, cantor; *informal* songbird, siren, diva, chanteuse, chansonnier; *literary* troubadour, minstrel.

single ▸ adjective **1** *a single red rose* ONE (ONLY), sole, lone, solitary, by itself/oneself, unaccompanied, alone. **2** *she wrote down every single word* INDIVIDUAL, separate, distinct, particular, last. **3** *is she single?* UNMARRIED, unwed, unwedded, unattached, free, a bachelor, a spinster; partnerless, husbandless, wifeless; separated, divorced, widowed; *informal* solo.
— OPPOSITES: double, married.

■ **single someone/something out** SELECT, pick out, choose, decide on; target, earmark, mark out, separate out, set apart/aside.

single-handed ▸ adverb BY ONESELF, alone, on one's own, solo, unaided, unassisted, without help.

single-minded ▸ adjective DETERMINED, committed, unswerving, unwavering, resolute, purposeful, devoted, dedicated, uncompromising, tireless, tenacious, persistent, indefatigable, dogged; *formal* pertinacious.
— OPPOSITES: half-hearted.

singly ▸ adverb ONE BY ONE, one at a time, one after the other, individually, separately, by oneself, on one's own.
— OPPOSITES: together.

singular ▸ adjective **1** *the gallery's singular capacity to attract sponsors* REMARKABLE, extraordinary, exceptional, outstanding, signal, notable, noteworthy, rare, unique, unparalleled, unprecedented, amazing, astonishing, phenomenal, astounding; *informal* fantastic, terrific. **2** *why was Betty behaving in so singular a fashion?* STRANGE, unusual, odd, peculiar, funny, curious, extraordinary, bizarre, eccentric, weird, queer, unexpected, unfamiliar, abnormal, atypical, unconventional, out of the ordinary, untypical, puzzling, mysterious, perplexing, baffling, unaccountable.

singularity ▸ noun **1** *the singularity of their concerns* UNIQUENESS, distinctiveness. **2** *his singularities* IDIOSYNCRASY, quirk, foible, peculiarity, oddity, eccentricity.

singularly ▸ adverb REMARKABLY, extraordinarily, exceptionally, very, extremely, really, outstandingly,

signally, particularly, incredibly, decidedly, supremely, distinctly, tremendously; *informal* awfully, terribly, terrifically, powerful.

sinister ▸ adjective **1** *there was a sinister undertone in his words* MENACING, threatening, ominous, forbidding, baleful, frightening, alarming, disturbing, disquieting, dark, black; *formal* minatory; *literary* direful. **2** *a sinister motive* EVIL, wicked, criminal, corrupt, nefarious, villainous, base, vile, malevolent, malicious; *informal* shady.
— OPPOSITES: innocent.

sink ▸ verb **1** *the coffin sank below the waves* BECOME SUBMERGED, be engulfed, go down, drop, fall, descend. **2** *the cruise liner sank yesterday* FOUNDER, go under, submerge. **3** *they sank their ships* SCUTTLE, send to the bottom; scupper. **4** *the announcement sank hopes of a recovery* DESTROY, ruin, wreck, put an end to, demolish, smash, shatter, dash; *informal* put the kibosh on, put paid to; *informal* scupper; *archaic* bring to naught. **5** *they agreed to sink their differences* IGNORE, overlook, disregard, forget, put aside, set aside, bury. **6** *I sank myself in student life* IMMERSE, submerge, plunge, lose, bury. **7** *the plane sank towards the airstrip* DESCEND, drop, go down/downwards. **8** *the sun was sinking* SET, go down/downwards. **9** *Loretta sank into an armchair* LOWER ONESELF, flop, collapse, fall, drop down, slump; *informal* plonk oneself. **10** *her voice sank to a whisper* FALL, drop, become/get quieter, become/ get softer. **11** *she would never sink to your level* STOOP, lower oneself, descend. **12** *he was sinking fast* DETERIORATE, decline, fade, grow weak, flag, waste away; be at death's door, be on one's deathbed, be slipping away; *informal* go downhill, be on one's last legs, be giving up the ghost. **13** *sink the pots into the ground* EMBED, insert, drive, plant. **14** *sinking a gold mine* DIG, excavate, bore, drill. **15** *they sank their life savings into the company* INVEST, venture, risk.
— OPPOSITES: float, rise.
▸ noun *he washed himself at the sink* BASIN, wash basin; *dated* lavabo.

■ **sink in** REGISTER, be understood, be comprehended, be grasped, get through.

sinless ▸ adjective INNOCENT, pure, virtuous, as pure as the driven snow, uncorrupted, faultless, blameless, guiltless, immaculate.
— OPPOSITES: wicked.

sinner ▸ noun WRONGDOER, evildoer, transgressor, miscreant, offender, criminal; *archaic* trespasser.

sinuous ▸ adjective **1** *a sinuous river* WINDING, windy, serpentine, curving, twisting, meandering, snaking, zigzag, curling, coiling. **2** *she moved with sinuous grace* LITHE, supple, agile, graceful, loose-limbed, limber, lissome.

sip ▸ verb *Amanda sipped her coffee* DRINK (SLOWLY).
▸ noun *a sip of whisky* MOUTHFUL, swallow, drink, drop, dram, nip, taste; *informal* swig.

siren ▸ noun **1** *a fire engine's siren* ALARM (BELL), warning bell, danger signal; *archaic* tocsin. **2** *the siren's allure* SEDUCTRESS, temptress, tease, femme fatale, flirt, coquette; *informal* man-eater, home wrecker, vamp.

sissy (*informal*) ▸ noun *he's a real sissy* COWARD, weakling, milksop, namby-pamby, baby, wimp; *informal* softie, chicken, milquetoast; mama's boy, pantywaist, twinkie, sook, (*Atlantic*) sooky baby ✦, crybaby, powder puff.
▸ adjective *sissy manners* effeminate, effete, unmanly.

sister ▸ noun **1** *Amy and Julie are sisters* SIBLING; sis. **2** *our sisters in the struggle* COMRADE, partner, colleague. **3** *the sisters in the convent* NUN, novice, abbess, prioress.

— RELATED TERMS: sororal.

sit ▶ **verb 1** *you'd better sit down* TAKE A SEAT, seat oneself, be seated, perch, ensconce oneself, plump oneself, flop; *informal* take the load/weight off one's feet, plonk oneself, take a load off. **2** *she sat the package on the table* PUT (DOWN), place, set (down), lay, deposit, rest, stand; *informal* stick, dump, park, plonk. **3** *the church sat about 3,000 people* HOLD, seat, have seats for, have space/room for, accommodate. **4** *she sat for Picasso* POSE, model. **5** *a hotel sitting on the mountain* BE SITUATED, be located, be sited, stand. **6** *the committee sits on Saturday* BE IN SESSION, meet, be convened. **7** *women jurists sit on the tribunal* SERVE ON, have a seat on, be a member of. **8** *his shyness doesn't sit easily with Hollywood tradition* BE HARMONIOUS, go, fit in, harmonize. **9** *Mrs. Hillman will sit for us* BABYSIT.

— OPPOSITES: stand.

■ **sit back** RELAX, unwind, lie back; *informal* let it all hang out, veg out, hang loose, chill (out), take a load off.

■ **sit in for** STAND IN FOR, fill in for, cover for, substitute for; *informal* sub for.

■ **sit in on** ATTEND, be present at, be an observer at, observe, audit.

■ **sit tight** (*informal*) **1** *just sit tight* STAY PUT, wait there, remain in one's place. **2** *we're advising our clients to sit tight* TAKE NO ACTION, wait, hold back, bide one's time; *informal* hold one's horses.

site ▶ **noun** *the site of the battle* LOCATION, place, position, situation, locality, whereabouts; *technical* locus.
▶ **verb** *garbage cans sited along the street* PLACE, put, position, situate, locate.

sit-in ▶ **noun** DEMONSTRATION, protest, strike, rally, lobby.

sitting ▶ **noun** *all-night sittings* SESSION, meeting, assembly; hearing.
▶ **adjective** *a sitting position* SEDENTARY, seated.

— OPPOSITES: standing.

sitting room ▶ **noun** LIVING ROOM, lounge, front room, drawing room, family room, den; *dated* parlour.

situate ▶ **verb** LOCATE, site, position, place, station, build.

situation ▶ **noun 1** *their financial situation* CIRCUMSTANCES, (state of) affairs, state, condition. **2** *I'll fill you in on the situation* THE FACTS, how things stand, the lay of the land, what's going on; *informal* the score, the scoop. **3** *the hotel's pleasant situation* LOCATION, position, spot, site, setting, environment; *technical* locus. **4** *he was offered a situation in Britain* JOB, post, position, appointment; employment.

six ▶ **cardinal number** SEXTET, sextuplets; *technical* hexad.

— RELATED TERMS: hexa-, sexi-.

size ▶ **noun** *the room was of medium size* DIMENSIONS, measurements, proportions, magnitude, largeness, bigness, area, expanse; breadth, width, length, height, depth; immensity, hugeness, vastness.
▶ **verb** *the drills are sized in millimetres* SORT, categorize, classify.

■ **size someone/something up** (*informal*) ASSESS, appraise, form an estimate of, take the measure of, judge, take stock of, evaluate, suss out.

sizeable ▶ **adjective** FAIRLY LARGE, substantial,

considerable, respectable, significant, largish, biggish, goodly.

— OPPOSITES: small.

sizzle ▶ **verb** CRACKLE, frizzle, sputter, spit.

sizzling ▶ **adjective** (*informal*) **1** *sizzling temperatures* EXTREMELY HOT, unbearably hot, blazing, burning, scorching, sweltering, broiling, blistering; *informal* boiling (hot), baking (hot). **2** *a sizzling affair* PASSIONATE, torrid, ardent, lustful, erotic; *informal* steamy, hot.

— OPPOSITES: freezing.

skate ▶ **noun** ICE SKATE, hockey skate, figure skate, goalie skate, bobskate, cheese cutter ♣, tube skate ♣, speedskate, clap skate.

skating ▶ **noun** ICE SKATING, figure skating, speed skating, power skating ♣, ice dancing; crack the whip. *See also the table at* FIGURE SKATING.

skedaddle ▶ **verb** (*informal*). *See* RUN *verb* sense 2.

skeletal ▶ **adjective 1** *a skeletal man* EMACIATED, very thin, as thin as a rake, cadaverous, skin-and-bones, skinny, bony, gaunt; *informal* anorexic. **2** *a skeletal account* LACKING IN DETAIL, incomplete, outline, fragmentary, sketchy; thumbnail.

— OPPOSITES: fat, detailed.

skeleton ▶ **noun 1** *the human skeleton* BONES. **2** *she was no more than a skeleton* SKIN AND BONE; *informal* bag of bones. **3** *a concrete skeleton* FRAMEWORK, frame, shell. **4** *the skeleton of a report* OUTLINE, (rough) draft, abstract, (bare) bones.
▶ **adjective** *a skeleton staff* MINIMUM, minimal, basic; essential.

skeptic ▶ **noun 1** *skeptics said the marriage wouldn't last* CYNIC, doubter; pessimist, prophet of doom. **2** *skeptics who have found faith* AGNOSTIC, atheist, unbeliever, non-believer, disbeliever, doubting Thomas.

skeptical ▶ **adjective** DUBIOUS, doubtful, taking something with a pinch of salt, doubting; cynical, distrustful, mistrustful, suspicious, disbelieving, unconvinced, incredulous, scoffing, pessimistic, defeatist.

— OPPOSITES: certain, convinced.

skepticism ▶ **noun 1** *his ideas were met with skepticism* DOUBT, doubtfulness, a pinch of salt; disbelief, cynicism, distrust, mistrust, suspicion, incredulity; pessimism, defeatism; *formal* dubiety. **2** *he passed from skepticism to religious belief* AGNOSTICISM, doubt; atheism, unbelief, non-belief.

sketch ▶ **noun 1** *a sketch of the proposed design* (PRELIMINARY) DRAWING, outline; diagram, design, plan; *informal* rough. **2** *she gave a rough sketch of what had happened* OUTLINE, brief description, rundown, main points, thumbnail sketch, (bare) bones; summary, synopsis, summarization, précis, resumé, wrap-up. **3** *a biographical sketch* DESCRIPTION, portrait, profile, portrayal, depiction. **4** *a hilarious sketch* SKIT, scene, piece, act, item, routine.
▶ **verb 1** *he sketched the garden* DRAW, make a drawing of, draw a picture of, pencil, rough out, outline. **2** *the company sketched out its plans* DESCRIBE, outline, give a brief idea of, rough out; summarize, précis.

sketchily ▶ **adverb** PERFUNCTORILY, cursorily, incompletely, patchily, vaguely, imprecisely; hastily, hurriedly.

sketchy ▶ **adjective** INCOMPLETE, patchy, fragmentary, cursory, perfunctory, scanty, vague, imprecise, imperfect; hurried, hasty.

— OPPOSITES: detailed.

skew ▶ verb DISTORT, misrepresent, pervert, twist, falsify, bias, alter, change; *informal* doctor, put a spin on.

skilful ▶ adjective EXPERT, accomplished, skilled, masterly, master, virtuoso, consummate, proficient, talented, gifted, adept, adroit, deft, dexterous, able, good, competent, capable, brilliant, handy; *informal* mean, wicked, crack, ace, wizard, crackerjack, pro.

skill ▶ noun **1** *his skill as a politician* EXPERTISE, skilfulness, expertness, adeptness, adroitness, deftness, dexterity, ability, prowess, mastery, competence, capability, aptitude, artistry, virtuosity, talent. **2** *bringing up a family gives you many skills* ACCOMPLISHMENT, strength, gift.
− OPPOSITES: incompetence.

skilled ▶ adjective EXPERIENCED, trained, qualified, proficient, practised, accomplished, expert, skilful, talented, gifted, adept, adroit, deft, dexterous, able, good, competent; *informal* crack, crackerjack.
− OPPOSITES: inexperienced.

skim ▶ verb **1** *skim off the scum* REMOVE, cream off, scoop off. **2** *the boat skimmed over the water* GLIDE, move lightly, slide, sail, skate, float. **3** *he skimmed the pebble across the water* THROW, toss, cast, pitch; bounce. **4** *she skimmed through the newspaper* GLANCE, flick, flip, leaf, riffle, thumb, read quickly, scan, run one's eye over. **5** *Hannah skimmed over this part of the story* MENTION BRIEFLY, pass over quickly, skate over, gloss over.
− OPPOSITES: elaborate on.

skimp ▶ verb **1** *don't skimp on the quantity* STINT ON, scrimp on, economize on, cut back on, be sparing, be frugal, be mean, be parsimonious, cut corners; *informal* be stingy, be mingy, be tight. **2** *the process cannot be skimped* DO HASTILY, do carelessly.

skimpy ▶ adjective **1** *a skimpy black dress* REVEALING, short, low, low-cut; flimsy, thin, see-through, indecent. **2** *my information is rather skimpy* MEAGRE, scanty, sketchy, limited, paltry, deficient, sparse.

skin ▶ noun **1** *these chemicals could damage the skin* EPIDERMIS, dermis, derma. **2** *Mary's fair skin* COMPLEXION, colouring, skin colour/tone, pigmentation. **3** *leopard skins* HIDE, pelt, fleece, *hist.* plew; *archaic* fell. **4** *a banana skin* PEEL, rind, integument. **5** *milk with a skin on it* FILM, layer, membrane. **6** *the plane's skin was damaged* CASING, exterior.
− RELATED TERMS: cutaneous.
▶ verb **1** *skin the tomatoes* PEEL, pare, hull; *technical* decorticate. **2** *he skinned his knee* GRAZE, scrape, abrade, bark, rub something raw, chafe; *Medicine* excoriate. **3** (*informal*) *Dad would skin me alive if I forgot it* PUNISH SEVERELY; *informal* murder, come down on someone (like a ton of bricks), give someone what for.
■ **by the skin of one's teeth** (ONLY) JUST, narrowly, barely, by a hair's breadth, by a very small margin; *informal* by a whisker.
■ **get under someone's skin** (*informal*) **1** *the children really got under my skin. See* IRRITATE sense 1. **2** *she got under my skin* OBSESS, intrigue, captivate, charm; enthrall, enchant, entrance.
■ **it's no skin off my nose** (*informal*) I DON'T CARE, I don't mind, I'm not bothered, it doesn't bother me, it doesn't matter to me; *informal* I don't give a damn, I couldn't/could care less.

skin-deep ▶ adjective SUPERFICIAL, (on the) surface, external, outward, shallow.

skinflint ▶ noun (*informal*) MISER, penny-pincher, Scrooge, pinchpenny; *informal* money-grubber, cheapskate, tightwad, piker, greedhead.

skinny ▶ adjective THIN, scrawny, scraggy, bony, angular, raw-boned, hollow-cheeked, gaunt, as thin as a rake, skin-and-bones, stick-like, emaciated, waiflike, skeletal, pinched, undernourished, underfed; SLIM, lean, slender, rangy; lanky, spindly, gangly, gangling, gawky; *informal* looking like a bag of bones, anorexic; *dated* spindle-shanked.
▶ noun (*informal*) GOSSIP, (inside) information, intelligence, news, the inside story; *informal* the lowdown, info, the dope, the dirt, the scoop, the poop.

skip ▶ verb **1** *skipping down the path* CAPER, prance, trip, dance, bound, bounce, gambol, frisk, romp, cavort. **2** *we skipped the boring stuff* OMIT, leave out, miss out, dispense with, pass over, skim over, disregard; *informal* give something a miss. **3** *I skipped school* PLAY TRUANT FROM, miss, cut, (*Ont.*) skip off ✦, (*West*) skip out ✦; *informal* play hooky from, ditch. **4** (*informal*) *they skipped off again* RUN OFF/AWAY, take off; *informal* beat it, clear off, cut and run, light out, cut out.

skirmish ▶ noun **1** *the unit was caught up in a skirmish* FIGHT, battle, clash, conflict, encounter, engagement, fray, combat. **2** *there was a skirmish over the budget* ARGUMENT, quarrel, squabble, contretemps, disagreement, difference of opinion, falling-out, dispute, blow-up, clash, altercation; *informal* tiff, spat; row.
▶ verb *they skirmished with enemy soldiers* FIGHT, (do) battle with, engage with, close with, combat, clash with.

skirt ▶ noun. *See table.*
▶ verb **1** *he skirted the city* GO ROUND, walk round, circle. **2** *the fields that skirt the highway* BORDER, edge, flank, line, lie alongside. **3** *he carefully skirted the subject* AVOID, evade, sidestep, dodge, pass over, gloss over; *informal* duck.

Skirts

A-line	kilt
crinoline	miniskirt
dirndl skirt	overskirt
grass skirt	petticoat
hobble skirt	prairie skirt

skit ▶ noun COMEDY SKETCH, comedy act, parody, pastiche, burlesque, satire; *informal* spoof, takeoff, send-up.

skittish ▶ adjective NERVOUS, anxious, on edge, excitable, restive, skittery, jumpy, jittery, high-strung.

skulduggery ▶ noun TRICKERY, fraudulence, sharp practice, underhandedness, chicanery; *informal* shenanigans, funny business, monkey business, monkeyshines.

skulk ▶ verb LURK, loiter, hide; creep, sneak, slink, prowl, pussyfoot.

skull ▶ noun CRANIUM, braincase; *informal* brainpan.
− RELATED TERMS: cranial.

sky ▶ noun *the sun was shining in the sky* the upper atmosphere; *literary* the heavens, the firmament, the blue, the (wide) blue yonder, the welkin, the azure, the empyrean.
− RELATED TERMS: celestial.
■ **to the skies** EFFUSIVELY, profusely, very highly, very enthusiastically, unreservedly, fervently, fulsomely, extravagantly.

slab ▶ noun PIECE, block, hunk, chunk, lump; cake, tablet, brick.

slack ▶ adjective **1** *the rope went slack* LOOSE, limp, hanging, flexible. **2** *slack skin* FLACCID, flabby, loose, sagging, saggy. **3** *business is slack* SLUGGISH, slow, quiet, slow-moving, flat, depressed, stagnant. **4** *slack accounting procedures* LAX, negligent, remiss, careless, slapdash, slipshod, lackadaisical, inefficient, casual; *informal* sloppy, slap-happy.
— OPPOSITES: tight, taut.
▶ noun **1** *the rope had some slack in it* LOOSENESS, play, give. **2** *foreign demand will help pick up the slack* SURPLUS, excess, residue, spare capacity. **3** *a little slack in the daily routine* LULL, pause, respite, break, hiatus, breathing space; *informal* let-up, breather.
▶ verb *(informal) no slacking!* IDLE, shirk, be lazy, be indolent, waste time, lounge about; *informal* goof off.
■ **slack off 1** *the rain has slacked off* DECREASE, subside, let up, ease off, abate, diminish, die down, fall off. **2** *you deserve to slack off a bit* RELAX, take things easy, let up, ease up/off, loosen up, slow down; *informal* hang loose, chill (out).
■ **slack up** *he doesn't slack up until he gets there* SLOW (DOWN), decelerate, reduce speed.

slacken ▶ verb **1** *he slackened his grip* LOOSEN, release, relax, loose, lessen, weaken. **2** *he slackened his pace* SLOW (DOWN), become/get/make slower, decelerate, slack (up). **3** *the rain is slackening* DECREASE, lessen, subside, ease up/off, let up, abate, slack off, diminish, die down.
— OPPOSITES: tighten.

slacker ▶ noun *(informal)* LAYABOUT, idler, shirker, malingerer, sluggard, laggard; *informal* lazybones, bum, flâneur, goof-off, *(Atlantic)* hangashore ♣.

slag ▶ verb *everyone's always slagging the coach.* See CRITICIZE.

slake ▶ verb QUENCH, satisfy, sate, satiate, relieve, assuage.

slam ▶ verb **1** *he slammed the door behind him* BANG, shut/close with a bang, shut/close noisily, shut/close with force. **2** *the car slammed into a lamp post* CRASH INTO, smash into, collide with, hit, strike, ram, plow into, run into, bump into, impact. **3** *(informal) he was slammed by the critics.* See CRITICIZE.

slander ▶ noun *he could sue us for slander* DEFAMATION (OF CHARACTER), character assassination, calumny, libel; scandalmongering, malicious gossip, disparagement, aspersions, vilification, traducement, obloquy; lie, slur, smear, false accusation; *informal* mud-slinging, badmouthing; *archaic* contumely.
▶ verb *they were accused of slandering the minister* DEFAME (SOMEONE'S CHARACTER), blacken someone's name, tell lies about, speak ill/evil of, sully someone's reputation, libel, smear, cast aspersions on, spread scandal about, besmirch, tarnish, taint; malign, traduce, vilify, disparage, denigrate, run down, slur; *informal* badmouth, dis, trash; *formal* derogate.

slanderous ▶ adjective DEFAMATORY, denigratory, disparaging, libellous, pejorative, false, misrepresentative, scurrilous, scandalous, malicious, abusive, insulting; *informal* mud-slinging.
— OPPOSITES: complimentary.

slang ▶ noun INFORMAL LANGUAGE, colloquialisms, patois, argot, cant, jargon.

slanging match ▶ noun *(informal).* See QUARREL *noun.*

slant ▶ verb **1** *the floor was slanting* SLOPE, tilt, incline, be at an angle, tip, cant, lean, dip, pitch, shelve, list,

bank. **2** *their findings were slanted in our favour* BIAS, distort, twist, skew, weight, give a bias to.
▶ noun **1** *the slant of the roof* SLOPE, incline, tilt, gradient, pitch, angle, cant, camber, inclination. **2** *a feminist slant* POINT OF VIEW, viewpoint, standpoint, stance, angle, perspective, approach, view, attitude, position; bias, leaning.

slanting ▶ adjective OBLIQUE, sloping, at an angle, on an incline, inclined, tilting, tilted, slanted, aslant, diagonal, canted, cambered.

slap ▶ verb **1** *he slapped her hard* HIT, strike, smack, clout, cuff, thump, punch, spank; *informal* whack, thwack, wallop, bash, boff, slug, bust; *archaic* smite. **2** *he slapped down a $10 bill* FLING, throw, toss, slam, bang; *informal* plonk. **3** *slap on a coat of paint* DAUB, plaster, spread. **4** *(informal) they slapped a huge tax on imports* IMPOSE, levy, put on.
▶ noun *a slap across the cheek* SMACK, blow, thump, cuff, clout, punch, spank; *informal* whack, thwack, wallop, clip, bash.
■ **a slap in the face** REBUFF, rejection, snub, insult, put-down, humiliation.
■ **a slap on the back** CONGRATULATIONS, commendation, approbation, approval, accolades, compliments, tributes, a pat on the back, praise, acclaim, acclamation.
■ **a slap on the wrist** REPRIMAND, rebuke, reproof, scolding, admonishment; *informal* rap on/over the knuckles, dressing-down.

slapdash ▶ adjective CARELESS, slipshod, hurried, haphazard, unsystematic, untidy, messy, hit-or-miss, negligent, neglectful, lax; *informal* sloppy, slap-happy, shambolic.
— OPPOSITES: meticulous.

slap-happy ▶ adverb *(informal)* **1** *his slap-happy friend* HAPPY-GO-LUCKY, devil-may-care, carefree, easygoing, nonchalant, insouciant, blithe, airy, casual. **2** *slap-happy work.* See SLAPDASH. **3** *she's a bit slap-happy after such a narrow escape* DAZED, stupefied, punch-drunk.

slash ▶ verb **1** *her tires had been slashed* CUT (OPEN), gash, slit, split open, lacerate, knife, make an incision in. **2** *(informal) the company slashed prices* REDUCE, cut, lower, bring down, mark down. **3** *(informal) they have slashed 10,000 jobs* GET RID OF, axe, cut, shed, make redundant.
▶ noun **1** *a slash across his arm* CUT, gash, laceration, slit, incision; wound. **2** *sentence breaks are indicated by slashes* SOLIDUS, oblique, backslash.

slate ▶ verb PLAN, schedule, book; organize, arrange.

slatternly ▶ adjective SLOVENLY, untidy, messy, scruffy, unkempt, ill-groomed, dishevelled, frowzy, bedraggled; *informal* raggedy, grubby, scuzzy.

slaughter ▶ verb **1** *the animals were slaughtered* KILL, butcher. **2** *innocent civilians are being slaughtered* MASSACRE, murder, butcher, kill (off), annihilate, exterminate, liquidate, eliminate, destroy, decimate, wipe out, put to death; *literary* slay. **3** *(informal) their team was slaughtered.* See DEFEAT *verb* sense 1.
▶ noun **1** *the slaughter of 20 demonstrators* MASSACRE, murdering, (mass) murder, mass killing, mass execution, annihilation, extermination, liquidation, decimation, carnage, butchery, genocide; *literary* slaying. **2** *a scene of slaughter* CARNAGE, bloodshed, bloodletting, bloodbath. **3** *(informal) their electoral slaughter.* See DEFEAT *noun* sense 1.

slave ▶ noun **1** *the work was done by slaves* *historical* serf, vassal, thrall; *archaic* bondsman, bondswoman. **2** *Anna was his willing slave* DRUDGE, servant, lackey,

joe-boy; *informal* gofer. **3** *a slave to fashion* DEVOTEE, worshipper, adherent; fan, lover, aficionado; *informal* fanatic, freak, nut, addict.
— RELATED TERMS: servile.
— OPPOSITES: freeman, master.

▶ **verb** *slaving away for a pittance* TOIL, labour, grind, sweat, work one's fingers to the bone, work like a Trojan/dog; *informal* kill oneself, sweat blood, slog away; *literary* travail; *archaic* drudge, moil.

slave-driver ▶ **noun** (HARD) TASKMASTER, (hard) taskmistress, tyrant, dictator.

slaver ▶ **verb** DROOL, slobber, dribble, salivate.

slavery ▶ **noun** **1** *thousands were sold into slavery* BONDAGE, enslavement, servitude, thraldom, thrall, serfdom, vassalage. **2** *this work is sheer slavery* DRUDGERY, toil, (hard) slog, hard labour, grind; *literary* travail; *archaic* moil.
— OPPOSITES: freedom.

slavish ▶ **adjective** **1** *slavish lackeys of the government* SERVILE, subservient, fawning, obsequious, sycophantic, toadying, unctuous; *informal* bootlicking, forelock-tugging. **2** *slavish copying* UNORIGINAL, uninspired, unimaginative, imitative.

slay ▶ **verb 1** (*literary*) *8,000 men were slain* KILL, murder, put to death, butcher, cut down, cut to pieces, slaughter, massacre, shoot down, gun down, mow down, eliminate, annihilate, exterminate, liquidate; *informal* wipe out, bump off, do in. **2** (*informal*) *you slay me, you really do* AMUSE GREATLY, entertain greatly, make someone laugh; *informal* have people rolling in the aisles, kill, knock dead, be a hit with.

slaying ▶ **noun** (*literary*) MURDER, killing, butchery, slaughter, massacre, extermination, liquidation.

sleazy ▶ **adjective 1** *sleazy arms dealers* CORRUPT, immoral, unsavoury, disreputable; *informal* shady, sleazoid. **2** *a sleazy bar* SQUALID, seedy, seamy, sordid, insalubrious, mean, cheap, low-class, run-down; *informal* scruffy, scuzzy, crummy, skanky, flea-bitten, grotty. **3** *a sleazy outfit* REVEALING, skimpy; *informal* slutty, whorish.
— OPPOSITES: reputable, upmarket.

sled ▶ **noun** toboggan, sledge, basket sled, bobsled, luge, coaster; crazy carpet; dogsled, komatik, alliak, pulk; sleigh, cutter, carriole, troika; (*Nfld*) catamaran ♣, (*North*) cat/sled/tractor train ♣, stoneboat.

sleek ▶ **adjective 1** *his sleek dark hair* SMOOTH, glossy, shiny, shining, lustrous, silken, silky. **2** *the car's sleek lines* STREAMLINED, trim, elegant, graceful. **3** *sleek young men in city suits* WELL-GROOMED, stylish, wealthy-looking, suave, sophisticated, debonair.

sleep ▶ **noun** go and have a sleep NAP, doze, siesta, catnap, beauty sleep; *informal* snooze, forty winks, a bit of shut-eye, power nap; *literary* slumber.
▶ **verb** *she slept for about an hour* BE ASLEEP, doze, take a siesta, take a nap, catnap, sleep like a log; *informal* snooze, catch/snatch forty winks, get some shut-eye, put one's head down, catch some zees; *humorous* be in the land of Nod, be in the arms of Morpheus; *literary* slumber.
— OPPOSITES: wake up.
■ **go to sleep** FALL ASLEEP, get to sleep; *informal* drop off, nod off, drift off, crash out, flake out, sack out.
■ **put an animal to sleep** PUT DOWN, destroy, euthanize.

sleepiness ▶ **noun** DROWSINESS, tiredness, somnolence, languor, languidness, doziness; lethargy, sluggishness, lassitude, enervation.

sleepless ▶ **adjective** WAKEFUL, restless, without sleep, insomniac; (wide) awake, unsleeping, tossing and turning.

sleepwalker ▶ **noun** SOMNAMBULIST.

sleepy ▶ **adjective 1** *she felt very sleepy* DROWSY, tired, somnolent, languid, languorous, heavy-eyed, asleep on one's feet; lethargic, sluggish, enervated, torpid; *informal* dopey; *literary* slumberous. **2** *the sleepy heat of the afternoon* SOPORIFIC, sleep-inducing, somnolent. **3** *a sleepy little village* QUIET, peaceful, tranquil, placid, slow-moving; dull, boring.
— OPPOSITES: awake, alert.

sleight of hand ▶ **noun 1** *impressive sleight of hand* DEXTERITY, adroitness, deftness, skill. **2** *financial sleight of hand* DECEPTION, deceit, dissimulation, chicanery, trickery, sharp practice.

slender ▶ **adjective 1** *her tall slender figure* SLIM, lean, willowy, sylphlike, svelte, lissome, graceful; slight, slightly built, thin, skinny. **2** *slender evidence* MEAGRE, limited, slight, scanty, scant, sparse, paltry, insubstantial, insufficient, deficient, negligible; *formal* exiguous. **3** *we had a slender chance of making it* FAINT, remote, flimsy, tenuous, fragile, slim; unlikely, improbable.
— OPPOSITES: plump.

sleuth ▶ **noun** (*informal*) (PRIVATE) DETECTIVE, (private) investigator; *informal* private eye, snoop, shamus, gumshoe, (private) dick, PI.

slice ▶ **noun 1** *a slice of fruitcake* PIECE, portion, slab, sliver, wafer, shaving. **2** *a huge slice of public spending* SHARE, part, portion, tranche, piece, proportion, allocation, percentage.
▶ **verb 1** *slice the cheese thinly* CUT (UP), shave, carve, julienne, section. **2** *one man had his ear sliced off* CUT OFF, sever, chop off, shear off.

slick ▶ **adjective 1** *a slick advertising campaign* EFFICIENT, smooth, smooth-running, polished, well-organized, well run, streamlined. **2** *his slick use of words* GLIB, smooth, fluent, plausible. **3** *a slick salesman* SUAVE, urbane, polished, assured, self-assured, smooth-talking, glib; *informal* smarmy. **4** *her slick brown hair* SHINY, glossy, shining, sleek, smooth, oiled. **5** *the sidewalks were slick with rain* SLIPPERY, wet, greasy; *informal* slippy.
▶ **verb** *his hair was slicked down* SMOOTH, sleek, grease, oil, gel.

slide ▶ **verb 1** *the glass slid across the table* GLIDE, move smoothly, slip, slither, skim, skate; skid, slew. **2** *tears slid down her cheeks* TRICKLE, run, flow, pour, stream. **3** *four men slid out of the shadows* CREEP, steal, slink, slip, tiptoe, sidle. **4** *the country is sliding into recession* SINK, fall, drop, descend; decline, degenerate.
▶ **noun 1** *the current slide in house prices* FALL, decline, drop, slump, downturn, downswing. **2** *a slide show* TRANSPARENCY.
— OPPOSITES: rise.
■ **let things slide** NEGLECT, pay little/no attention to, not attend to, be remiss about, let something go downhill.

slight ▶ **adjective 1** *the chance of success is slight* SMALL, modest, tiny, minute, inappreciable, negligible, insignificant, minimal, remote, slim, faint; *informal* minuscule; *formal* exiguous. **2** *the book is of slight consequence* MINOR, inconsequential, trivial, unimportant, lightweight, superficial, shallow. **3** *Elizabeth's slight figure* SLIM, slender, petite, diminutive, small, delicate, dainty.
— OPPOSITES: considerable.
▶ **verb** *he had been slighted* INSULT, snub, rebuff, repulse,

spurn, treat disrespectfully, give someone the cold shoulder, scorn; *informal* give someone the brush-off, freeze out.
— OPPOSITES: respect.

▶ **noun** *an unintended slight* INSULT, affront, snub, rebuff; *informal* put-down, dig.
— OPPOSITES: compliment.

slighting ▶ adjective INSULTING, disparaging, derogatory, disrespectful, denigratory, pejorative, abusive, offensive, defamatory, slanderous, scurrilous; disdainful, scornful, contemptuous; *archaic* contumelious.

slightly ▶ adverb A LITTLE, a bit, somewhat, rather, moderately, to a certain extent, faintly, vaguely, a shade, a touch.
— OPPOSITES: very.

slim ▶ adjective **1** *she was tall and slim* SLENDER, lean, thin, willowy, sylphlike, svelte, lissome, trim, slight, slightly built. **2** *a slim silver bracelet* NARROW, slender, slimline. **3** *a slim chance of escape* SLIGHT, small, slender, faint, poor, remote, unlikely, improbable.
— OPPOSITES: plump.

▶ **verb 1** *I'm trying to slim down* LOSE WEIGHT, get thinner, lose some pounds/inches, diet, get into shape, slenderize. **2** *the number of staff had been slimmed down* REDUCE, cut (down/back), scale down, decrease, diminish, pare down.

slime ▶ noun OOZE, sludge, muck, mud, mire; *informal* goo, gunk, gook, gloop, (*Nfld*) slub ♣, gunge, guck, glop; *humorous* ectoplasm.

slimy ▶ adjective **1** *the floor was slimy* SLIPPERY, greasy, muddy, mucky, sludgy, wet, sticky; *informal* slippy, gunky, gooey. **2** (*informal*) *her slimy press agent* OBSEQUIOUS, sycophantic, excessively deferential, subservient, fawning, toadying, ingratiating, unctuous, oily, oleaginous, greasy, toadyish, slavish; *informal* bootlicking, smarmy, forelock-tugging.

sling ▶ noun **1** *she had her arm in a sling* (SUPPORT) BANDAGE, support, strap. **2** *armed only with a sling* CATAPULT, slingshot.

▶ **verb 1** *a hammock was slung between two trees* HANG, suspend, string, swing. **2** (*informal*) *she slung her jacket on the sofa. See* THROW *verb sense 1.*

slink ▶ verb CREEP, sneak, steal, slip, slide, sidle, tiptoe, pussyfoot.

slinky ▶ adjective (*informal*) *a slinky black dress* TIGHT-FITTING, close-fitting, form-fitting, figure-hugging, sexy.

slip¹ ▶ verb **1** *she slipped on the ice* SLIDE, skid, glide; fall (over), lose one's balance, tumble. **2** *the envelope slipped through Luke's fingers* FALL, drop, slide. **3** *we slipped out by a back door* CREEP, steal, sneak, slide, sidle, slope, slink, tiptoe. **4** *standards have slipped* DECLINE, deteriorate, degenerate, worsen, get worse, fall (off), drop; *informal* go downhill, go to the dogs, go to pot. **5** *the TSX slipped 30 points* DROP, go down, sink, slump, decrease, depreciate. **6** *the hours slipped by* PASS, elapse, go by/past, roll by/past, fly by/past, tick by/past. **7** *she slipped the map into her pocket* PUT, tuck, shove; *informal* pop, stick, stuff. **8** *Sarah slipped into a black skirt* PUT ON, pull on, don, dress/clothe oneself in; change into. **9** *she slipped out of her clothes* TAKE OFF, remove, pull off, doff, peel off. **10** *he slipped the knot of his tie* UNTIE, unfasten, undo.

▶ **noun 1** *a single slip could send them plummeting downwards* FALSE STEP, misstep, slide, skid, fall, tumble. **2** *a careless slip* MISTAKE, error, blunder, gaffe, slip of the tongue/pen; oversight, omission, lapse,

inaccuracy; *informal* slip-up, boo-boo, howler, goof, blooper. **3** *a silk slip* UNDERSKIRT, petticoat.

■ **give someone the slip** (*informal*) ESCAPE FROM, get away from, evade, dodge, elude, lose, shake off, throw off (the scent), get clear of.

■ **let something slip** REVEAL, disclose, divulge, let out, give away, blurt out; give the game away; *informal* let on, blab, let the cat out of the bag, spill the beans.

■ **slip away 1** *they managed to slip away* ESCAPE, get away, break free; *informal* fly the coop, take a powder. **2** *she slipped away in her sleep. See* DIE *sense 1.*

■ **slip up** (*informal*) MAKE A MISTAKE, (make a) blunder, get something wrong, make an error, err; *informal* make a boo-boo, goof up.

slip² ▶ noun **1** *a slip of paper* PIECE OF PAPER, scrap of paper, sheet, note; *informal* sticky; *proprietary* Post-it. **2** *they took slips from rare plants* CUTTING, graft; scion, shoot, offshoot.

■ **a slip of a** —— SMALL, slender, slim, slight, slightly built, petite, little, tiny, diminutive; *informal* pint-sized.

slipper ▶ noun **1** *he pulled on his slippers* carpet slipper, bedroom slipper, house shoe, slipper sock, moccasin. **2** *satin slippers* pump, mule.

slippery ▶ adjective **1** *the roads are slippery* ICY, greasy, oily, glassy, smooth, slimy, wet; *informal* slippy, glib. **2** *a slippery customer* EVASIVE, unreliable, unpredictable; devious, crafty, cunning, unscrupulous, wily, tricky, artful, slick, sly, sneaky, scheming, untrustworthy, deceitful, duplicitous, dishonest, treacherous, two-faced, snide; *informal* shady, shifty.

slipshod ▶ adjective CARELESS, lackadaisical, slapdash, disorganized, haphazard, hit-or-miss, untidy, messy, unsystematic, unmethodical, casual, negligent, neglectful, remiss, lax, slack; *informal* sloppy, slap-happy.
— OPPOSITES: meticulous.

slip-up ▶ noun (*informal*) MISTAKE, slip, error, blunder, oversight, omission, gaffe, slip of the tongue/pen, inaccuracy; *informal* boo-boo, howler, goof, blooper, boner.

slit ▶ noun **1** *three diagonal slits* CUT, incision, split, slash, gash, laceration. **2** *a slit in the curtains* OPENING, gap, chink, crack, aperture, slot.

▶ **verb** *he threatened to slit her throat* CUT, slash, split open, slice open, gash, lacerate, make an incision in.

slither ▶ verb SLIDE, slip, glide, wriggle, crawl; skid.

sliver ▶ noun SPLINTER, shard, shiver, chip, flake, shred, scrap, shaving, paring, piece, fragment.

slob ▶ noun (*informal*) LAYABOUT, good-for-nothing, sluggard, laggard, (*Atlantic*) hangashore ♣; *informal* slacker, lazybones, bum, couch potato; *archaic* sloven.

slobber ▶ verb DROOL, slaver, dribble, salivate.

slog ▶ verb **1** *they were all slogging away* WORK HARD, toil, labour, work one's fingers to the bone, work like a Trojan/dog, exert oneself, grind, slave, grub, plow, plod, peg; *informal* beaver, work one's guts out, put one's nose to the grindstone, sweat blood; *literary* travail; *archaic* drudge, moil. **2** *they slogged around the streets* TRUDGE, tramp, tromp, traipse, toil, plod, trek, footslog.
— OPPOSITES: relax.

▶ **noun 1** *10 months' hard slog* HARD WORK, toil, toiling, labour, effort, exertion, grind, drudgery; *informal* sweat; *literary* travail; *archaic* moil. **2** *a steady uphill slog* TRUDGE, tramp, traipse, plod, trek, footslog.
— OPPOSITES: leisure.

slogan ▶ noun CATCHPHRASE, jingle, byword, motto; *informal* tag line, buzzword, mantra.

slop ▶ verb *water slopped over the edge* SPILL, flow, overflow, run, slosh, splash.

■ **slop around/about** (*informal*) LAZE (AROUND/ABOUT), lounge (around/about), loll (around/about), loaf (around/about), slouch (about/around); *informal* hang around, bum around, lallygag.

slope ▶ noun **1** *the slope of the roof* GRADIENT, incline, angle, slant, inclination, pitch, decline, ascent, declivity, rise, fall, tilt, tip, downslope, upslope, grade, downgrade, upgrade. **2** *a grassy slope* HILL, hillside, hillock, bank, sidehill, escarpment, scarp; *literary* steep. **3** *the ski slopes* PISTE, run, trail.
▶ verb *the garden sloped down to a stream* SLANT, incline, tilt; drop away, fall away, decline, descend, shelve, lean; rise, ascend, climb.

sloping ▶ adjective AT A SLANT, on a slant, at an angle, slanting, slanted, leaning, inclining, inclined, angled, cambered, canted, tilting, tilted, dipping.
— OPPOSITES: level.

sloppy ▶ adjective **1** *their defence was sloppy* CARELESS, slapdash, slipshod, lackadaisical, haphazard, lax, slack, slovenly; *informal* slap-happy, shambolic. **2** *sloppy T-shirts* BAGGY, loose-fitting, loose, generously cut; shapeless, sack-like, oversized. **3** *a sloppy dish* RUNNY, watery, thin, liquid, semi-liquid, mushy, gloppy. **4** *sloppy letters* SENTIMENTAL, mawkish, cloying, saccharine, sugary, syrupy; *romantic*; *informal* slushy, schmaltzy, lovey-dovey, soppy, cornball, corny, sappy, hokey, three-hankie.

slosh ▶ verb **1** *beer sloshed over the side of the glass* SPILL, slop, splash, flow, overflow. **2** *workers sloshed around in boots* SPLASH, squelch, wade; *informal* splosh. **3** *she sloshed more wine into her glass* POUR, slop, splash.

slot ▶ noun **1** *he slid a coin into the slot* APERTURE, slit, crack, hole, opening. **2** *I have an early time slot* SPOT, time, period, niche, space; *informal* window.
▶ verb *he slotted a cassette into the machine* INSERT, put, place, slide, slip.

sloth ▶ noun LAZINESS, idleness, indolence, slothfulness, inactivity, inertia, sluggishness, shiftlessness, apathy, acedia, listlessness, lassitude, lethargy, languor, torpidity; *literary* hebetude.
— OPPOSITES: industriousness.

slothful ▶ adjective LAZY, idle, indolent, inactive, sluggish, apathetic, lethargic, listless, languid, torpid; *archaic* otiose.

slouch ▶ verb **1** *sit up straight–don't slouch!* SLUMP, hunch; loll, droop. **2** *he just slouched, pretending to work* LOUNGE, loaf, laze, loll, idle, do nothing.
▶ noun *she's no slouch* INCOMPETENT, amateur, bumbler, bungler.

slovenly ▶ adjective **1** *his slovenly appearance* SCRUFFY, untidy, messy, unkempt, ill-groomed, slatternly, dishevelled, bedraggled, tousled, rumpled, frowzy; *informal* slobbish, slobby, raggedy, scuzzy. **2** *his work is slovenly* CARELESS, slapdash, slipshod, haphazard, hit-or-miss, untidy, messy, negligent, lax, lackadaisical, slack; *informal* sloppy, slap-happy.
— OPPOSITES: tidy, careful.

slow ▶ adjective **1** *their slow walk home* UNHURRIED, leisurely, steady, sedate, slow-moving, plodding, dawdling, sluggish, sluggardly, lead-footed. **2** *a slow process* LONG-DRAWN-OUT, time-consuming, lengthy, protracted, prolonged, gradual. **3** *he can be so slow* OBTUSE, stupid, unperceptive, insensitive, bovine,

stolid, slow-witted, dull-witted, unintelligent, doltish, witless; *informal* dense, dim, dim-witted, thick, slow on the uptake, dumb, dopey, boneheaded, dozy, logy, chowderheaded. **4** *they were slow to voice their opinions* RELUCTANT, unwilling, disinclined, loath, hesitant, afraid, chary, shy. **5** *the slow season* SLUGGISH, slack, quiet, inactive, flat, depressed, stagnant, dead. **6** *a slow movie* DULL, boring, uninteresting, unexciting, uneventful, tedious, tiresome, wearisome, monotonous, dreary, lacklustre.
— OPPOSITES: fast.
▶ verb **1** *the traffic forced him to slow down* REDUCE SPEED, go slower, decelerate, brake. **2** *you need to slow down* TAKE IT EASY, relax, ease up/off, take a break, slack off, let up; *informal* chill (out), hang loose. **3** *this would slow down economic growth* HOLD BACK/UP, delay, retard, set back; restrict, check, curb, inhibit, impede, obstruct, hinder, hamper; *archaic* stay.
— OPPOSITES: accelerate.

slowly ▶ adverb **1** *Tom walked off slowly* AT A SLOW PACE, without hurrying, unhurriedly, steadily, at a leisurely pace, at a snail's pace; *Music* adagio, lento, largo. **2** *her health is improving slowly* GRADUALLY, bit by bit, little by little, slowly but surely, step by step.
— OPPOSITES: quickly.

sludge ▶ noun MUD, muck, mire, ooze, silt, alluvium; *informal* gunk, crud, gloop, gook, goo, gunge, guck, glop.

slug ▶ verb *he started slugging the other patrons. See* HIT verb sense 1.
▶ noun **1** *don't be such a slug. See* SLUGGARD. **2** *he put three slugs into him* BULLET, shot, cartridge.

sluggard ▶ noun NE'ER-DO-WELL, layabout, do-nothing, idler, loafer, lounger, good-for-nothing, shirker, underachiever; *informal* slacker, slug, lazybones, bum, couch potato.

sluggish ▶ adjective **1** *Alex felt tired and sluggish* LETHARGIC, listless, lacking in energy, lifeless, inert, inactive, slow, torpid, languid, apathetic, weary, tired, fatigued, sleepy, drowsy, enervated; lazy, idle, indolent, slothful, sluggardly, logy; *Medicine* asthenic; *informal* dozy, dopey. **2** *the economy is sluggish* INACTIVE, quiet, slow, slack, flat, depressed, stagnant.
— OPPOSITES: vigorous.

sluice ▶ verb **1** *crews sluiced down the decks* WASH (DOWN), rinse, clean, cleanse. **2** *the water sluiced out* POUR, flow, run, gush, stream, course, flood, surge, spill.

slum ▶ noun HOVEL, rathole; (**slums**) ghetto, shantytown, favela, bustee, shacktown, skid row.

slumber (*literary*) ▶ verb *the child slumbered fitfully. See* SLEEP verb.
▶ noun *an uneasy slumber. See* SLEEP noun.

slummy ▶ adjective SEEDY, insalubrious, squalid, sleazy, run-down, down-at-the-heel, shabby, dilapidated; *informal* scruffy, skanky, flea-bitten; grotty, shacky.
— OPPOSITES: upmarket.

slump ▶ verb **1** *he slumped into a chair* SIT HEAVILY, flop, flump, collapse, sink, fall; *informal* plonk oneself. **2** *housing prices slumped* FALL STEEPLY, plummet, tumble, drop, go down; *informal* crash, nosedive. **3** *reading standards have slumped* DECLINE, deteriorate, degenerate, worsen, slip; *informal* go downhill.
▶ noun **1** *a slump in profits* STEEP FALL, drop, tumble, downturn, downswing, slide, *informal* toboggan slide ✦, decline, decrease, nosedive. **2** *an economic*

slump RECESSION, economic decline, depression, slowdown, stagnation.
– OPPOSITES: rise, boom.

slur ▶ verb *she was slurring her words* MUMBLE, speak unclearly, garble.
▶ noun *a gross slur* INSULT, slight, slander, slanderous statement, aspersion, smear, allegation.

slush ▶ noun **1** *he wiped the slush off his shoes* MELTING SNOW, wet snow, mush, sludge. **2** (*informal*) *the slush of romantic films* SENTIMENTALITY, mawkishness, sentimentalism; *informal* schmaltz, mush, slushiness, corniness, soppiness, sappiness, hokeyness.

slut ▶ noun PROMISCUOUS WOMAN, prostitute, whore; *informal* tart, floozie, tramp, hooker, hustler; *dated* scarlet woman, loose woman, hussy, trollop; *archaic* harlot, strumpet, wanton.

sly ▶ adjective **1** *she's rather sly* CUNNING, crafty, clever, wily, artful, guileful, tricky, scheming, devious, deceitful, duplicitous, dishonest, underhanded, sneaky; *archaic* subtle. **2** *a sly grin* ROGUISH, mischievous, impish, playful, wicked, arch, knowing. **3** *she took a sly sip of water* SURREPTITIOUS, furtive, stealthy, covert.
■ **on the sly** IN SECRET, secretly, furtively, surreptitiously, covertly, clandestinely, on the quiet, behind someone's back; *informal* on the q.t.

smack¹ ▶ noun **1** *she gave him a smack* SLAP, clout, cuff, blow, spank, rap, swat, crack, thump, punch, karate chop; *informal* whack, thwack, clip, wallop, swipe, bop, belt, bash, sock. **2** *the parcel landed with a smack* BANG, crash, crack, thud, thump. **3** (*informal*) *a smack on the lips* KISS, peck, smooch; *informal* smacker.
▶ verb **1** *he tried to smack her* SLAP, hit, strike, spank, cuff, clout, thump, punch, swat; box someone's ears; *informal* whack, clip, wallop, swipe, bop, belt, bash, sock, boff, slug, bust. **2** *the waiter smacked a plate down* BANG, slam, crash, thump; sling, fling; *informal* plonk, plunk.
▶ adverb (*informal*) *smack in the middle* EXACTLY, precisely, straight, right, directly, squarely, dead, plumb, point-blank; *informal* slap, bang, smack dab.

smack² ▶ noun **1** *the beer has a smack of hops* TASTE, flavour, savour. **2** *a smack of bitterness in his words* TRACE, tinge, touch, suggestion, hint, overtone, suspicion, whisper.
■ **smack of 1** *the tea smacked of tannin* TASTE OF, have the flavour of. **2** *the plan smacked of self-promotion* SUGGEST, hint at, have overtones of, give the impression of, have the stamp of, seem like; smell of, reek of.

smack³ ▶ noun *they were shooting smack in the alley.* See HEROIN.

small ▶ adjective **1** *a small apartment* LITTLE, compact, bijou, tiny, miniature, mini; minute, microscopic, minuscule; toy, baby; poky, cramped, boxy; *informal* teeny, teensy, itsy-bitsy, itty-bitty, pocket-sized, half-pint, little-bitty; *Scottish* wee. **2** *a very small man* SHORT, little, petite, diminutive, elfin, tiny; puny, undersized, stunted, dwarfish, midget, pygmy, Lilliputian; *Scottish* wee; *informal* teeny, pint-sized. **3** *a few small changes* SLIGHT, minor, unimportant, trifling, trivial, insignificant, inconsequential, negligible, nugatory, infinitesimal; *informal* minuscule, piffling, piddling. **4** *small helpings* INADEQUATE, meagre, insufficient, ungenerous; *informal* measly, stingy, mingy, pathetic. **5** *they made him feel small* FOOLISH, stupid, insignificant, unimportant, embarrassed, humiliated, uncomfortable, mortified,

ashamed; crushed. **6** *a small business* SMALL-SCALE, modest, unpretentious, humble.
– RELATED TERMS: micro-, mini-, nano-.
– OPPOSITES: big, tall, major, ample, substantial.

small change ▶ noun COINS, change, coppers, silver, cash, specie.

small-minded ▶ adjective NARROW-MINDED, petty, mean-spirited, uncharitable; close-minded, short-sighted, myopic, blinkered, inward-looking, unimaginative, parochial, provincial, insular, small-town; intolerant, illiberal, conservative, hidebound, dyed-in-the-wool, set in one's ways, inflexible; prejudiced, bigoted.
– OPPOSITES: tolerant.

small-time ▶ adjective MINOR, small-scale; petty, unimportant, insignificant, inconsequential, minor-league; *informal* penny-ante, piddling, two-bit, bush-league, picayune.
– OPPOSITES: major.

smarmy ▶ adjective (*informal*) UNCTUOUS, ingratiating, slick, oily, greasy, obsequious, sycophantic, fawning; *informal* slimy, sucky.

smart ▶ adjective **1** *you look very smart* WELL-DRESSED, stylish, chic, fashionable, modish, elegant, neat, spruce, trim, dapper; *informal* snazzy, natty, snappy, sharp, cool, spiffy, fly, kicky. **2** *a smart restaurant* FASHIONABLE, stylish, high-class, exclusive, chic, fancy, upscale, upmarket, high-toned; *informal* trendy, posh, ritzy, plush, classy, swanky, glitzy, swank. **3** (*informal*) *he's the smart one* CLEVER, bright, intelligent, sharp-witted, quick-witted, shrewd, astute, able, perceptive, percipient; *informal* brainy, savvy, quick on the uptake. **4** *a smart pace* BRISK, quick, fast, rapid, swift, lively, spanking, energetic, vigorous; *informal* snappy, cracking. **5** *a smart blow on the snout* SHARP, severe, forceful, violent.
– OPPOSITES: untidy, stupid, slow, gentle.
▶ verb **1** *her eyes were smarting* STING, burn, tingle, prickle; hurt, ache. **2** *she smarted at the accusations* FEEL ANNOYED, feel upset, take offence, feel aggrieved, feel indignant, be put out, feel hurt.

smash ▶ verb **1** *he smashed a window* BREAK, shatter, splinter, crack, shiver; *informal* bust. **2** *she's smashed the car* CRASH, wreck, write off; *informal* total. **3** *they smashed into a wall* CRASH INTO, collide with, hit, strike, ram, smack into, slam into, plow into, run into, bump into, impact. **4** *Don smashed him over the head* HIT, strike, thump, punch, smack; *informal* whack, schmuck ✤, bash, bop, clout, wallop, crown, slug. **5** *he smashed their hopes of glory* DESTROY, wreck, ruin, shatter, dash, crush, devastate, demolish, overturn, scotch; *informal* put the kibosh on, put paid to, scupper, scuttle.
▶ noun **1** *the smash of glass* BREAKING, shattering, crash. **2** *he had a smash* CRASH, collision, accident, wreck; *informal* pileup, smash-up. **3** (*informal*) *a box-office smash* SUCCESS, sensation, sell-out, triumph; *informal* (smash) hit, blockbuster, winner, knockout, wow, barnburner, biggie.

smattering ▶ noun BIT, little, modicum, touch, soupçon; nodding acquaintance; rudiments, basics; *informal* smidgen, smidge, tad, titch.

smear ▶ verb **1** *the table was smeared with grease* STREAK, smudge, mark, soil, dirty; *informal* splotch; *literary* besmear. **2** *smear the meat with olive oil* COVER, coat, grease; *literary* bedaub. **3** *she smeared sunblock on her skin* SPREAD, rub, daub, slap, slather, smother, plaster, slick; apply; *literary* besmear. **4** *they are trying to smear our reputation* SULLY, tarnish, blacken, drag through the mud, taint, damage, defame, discredit, malign, slander, libel, slur; *informal* do a hatchet job on; *formal* calumniate, impugn; *literary* besmirch.

▶ **noun 1** *smears of blood* STREAK, smudge, daub, dab, spot, patch, blotch, mark; *informal* splotch. **2** *press smears about his closest aides* FALSE ACCUSATION, lie, untruth, slur, slander, libel, defamation, calumny.

smell ▶ **noun** *the smell of the kitchen* ODOUR, aroma, fragrance, scent, perfume, redolence; bouquet, nose; stench, fetor, stink, reek, whiff, hum; *informal* funk; *literary* miasma.

– RELATED TERMS: osmic, olfactory.

▶ **verb 1** *he smelled her perfume* SCENT, get a sniff of, detect. **2** *the dogs smelled each other* SNIFF, nose. **3** *the cellar smells* STINK, reek, have a bad smell, whiff. **4** *it smells like a hoax to me* SMACK OF, have the hallmarks of, seem like, have the air of, suggest.

smelly ▶ **adjective** FOUL-SMELLING, stinking, reeking, fetid, malodorous, pungent, rank, noxious, mephitic; off, gamy, high; musty, fusty; *informal* stinky, humming, funky; *literary* miasmic, noisome.

smile ▶ **verb** *he smiled at her* BEAM, grin (from ear to ear), dimple, twinkle; smirk, simper; leer.

– OPPOSITES: frown.

▶ **noun** *the smile on Sara's face* BEAM, grin, twinkle; smirk, simper; leer.

smirk ▶ **verb** SMILE SMUGLY, simper, snicker, snigger; leer.

smite ▶ **verb** *See* HIT *verb* sense 1.

smitten ▶ **adjective 1** *he was smitten with cholera* STRUCK DOWN, laid low, suffering, affected, afflicted, plagued, stricken. **2** *Jane's smitten with you* INFATUATED, besotted, in love, obsessed, head over heels; enamoured of, attracted to, taken with; captivated, enchanted, under someone's spell, moonstruck; *informal* bowled over, swept off one's feet, crazy about, mad about, keen on, hot on/for, gone on, sweet on, gaga for.

smog ▶ **noun** FOG, haze; fumes, smoke, pollution.

smoke ▶ **verb 1** *the fire was smoking* SMOULDER, emit smoke; *archaic* reek. **2** *he smoked his cigarette* PUFF ON, draw on, pull on; inhale; light; *informal* drag on, toke. **3** *they smoked their salmon* CURE, preserve, dry.

▶ **noun** *the smoke from the bonfire* FUMES, exhaust, gas, vapour; smog.

smoky ▶ **adjective 1** *the smoky atmosphere* SMOKE-FILLED, sooty, smoggy, hazy, foggy, murky, thick. **2** *her smoky eyes* GREY, sooty, dark, black.

smooth ▶ **adjective 1** *the smooth flat rocks* EVEN, level, flat, plane; unwrinkled, featureless; glassy, glossy, silky, polished. **2** *his face was smooth* CLEAN-SHAVEN, hairless. **3** *a smooth sauce* CREAMY, velvety, blended. **4** *a smooth sea* CALM, still, tranquil, undisturbed, unruffled, even, flat, waveless, like a millpond. **5** *the smooth running of the equipment* STEADY, regular, uninterrupted, unbroken, fluid, fluent; straightforward, easy, effortless, trouble-free, seamless. **6** *a smooth wine* MELLOW, mild, agreeable, pleasant. **7** *the smooth tone of the clarinet* DULCET, soft, soothing, mellow, sweet, silvery, honeyed, mellifluous, melodious, lilting, lyrical, harmonious. **8** *a smooth, confident man* SUAVE, urbane, sophisticated, polished, debonair; courteous, gracious, glib, slick, ingratiating, unctuous; *informal* smarmy.

– OPPOSITES: uneven, rough, hairy, lumpy, irregular, raucous, gauche.

▶ **verb 1** *she smoothed the soil* FLATTEN, level (out/off),

even out/off; press, roll, steamroll, iron, plane. **2** *a plan to smooth the way for the agreement* EASE, facilitate, clear the way for, pave the way for, expedite, assist, aid, help, oil the wheels of, lubricate.

smoothly ▶ **adverb 1** *her hair was combed smoothly back* EVENLY, level, flat, flush. **2** *the door closed smoothly* FLUIDLY, fluently, steadily, frictionlessly, easily; quietly. **3** *the plan had gone smoothly* WITHOUT A HITCH, like clockwork, without difficulty, easily, effortlessly, according to plan, swimmingly, satisfactorily, very well; *informal* like a dream.

smooth-talking ▶ **adjective** (*informal*) PERSUASIVE, glib, plausible, silver-tongued, slick, eloquent, fast-talking; ingratiating, flattering, unctuous, obsequious, sycophantic; *informal* smarmy.

– OPPOSITES: blunt.

smother ▶ **verb 1** *she tried to smother her baby* SUFFOCATE, asphyxiate, stifle, choke. **2** *we smothered the flames* EXTINGUISH, put out, snuff out, dampen, douse, stamp out, choke. **3** *we smothered ourselves with sunscreen* SMEAR, daub, spread, cover; *literary* besmear, bedaub. **4** *their granny always smothers them with affection* OVERWHELM, inundate, envelop, cocoon. **5** *she smothered a sigh* STIFLE, muffle, strangle, repress, suppress, hold back, fight back, bite back, swallow, contain, bottle up, conceal, hide; bite one's lip; *informal* keep a/the lid on.

smoulder ▶ **verb 1** *the bonfire still smouldered* SMOKE, glow, burn. **2** *she was smouldering with resentment* SEETHE, boil, fume, burn, simmer, be boiling over, be beside oneself; *informal* be livid.

smudge ▶ **noun** *a smudge of ink* STREAK, smear, mark, stain, blotch, stripe, blob, dab; *informal* splotch.

▶ **verb 1** *her face was smudged with dust* STREAK, mark, dirty, soil, blotch, blacken, smear, blot, daub, stain; *informal* splotch; *literary* bedaub, besmirch. **2** *she smudged her makeup* SMEAR, streak, mess up.

smug ▶ **adjective** SELF-SATISFIED, self-congratulatory, complacent, superior, pleased with oneself, self-approving.

smuggle ▶ **verb** IMPORT/EXPORT ILLEGALLY, traffic in, run, bootleg.

smuggler ▶ **noun** TRAFFICKER, runner, courier; *informal* mule, moonshiner, rum-runner.

smutty ▶ **adjective** VULGAR, rude, crude, dirty, filthy, salacious, coarse, obscene, lewd, pornographic, X-rated; risqué, racy, earthy, bawdy, suggestive, naughty, ribald, off-colour; *informal* blue, raunchy, saucy; *euphemistic* adult.

snack ▶ **noun** *she made herself a snack* LIGHT MEAL, collation, treat, refreshments, lunch, nibbles, tidbit(s); *informal* bite (to eat).

▶ **verb** *don't snack on sugary foods* EAT BETWEEN MEALS, nibble, munch; *informal* graze, nosh.

snack bar ▶ **noun** concession (stand), kiosk, snack counter, luncheonette, casse-croûte ♣.

snaffle ▶ **verb** (*informal*). *See* STEAL *verb* sense 1.

snafu ▶ **noun** MUDDLE, mess, tangle, jumble, confusion; misunderstanding, misinterpretation, misconception; mistake, mix-up, bungle; *informal* hash, foul-up, screw-up.

snag ▶ **noun 1** *the snag is that this might affect inflation* COMPLICATION, difficulty, catch, hitch, hiccup, obstacle, stumbling block, pitfall, problem, impediment, hindrance, inconvenience, setback, hurdle, disadvantage, downside, drawback. **2** *smooth rails with no snags* SHARP PROJECTION, jag; thorn, spur. **3** *a snag in her stocking* TEAR, rip, hole, gash, slash; run.

▶ verb **1** *she snagged her stockings* TEAR, rip. **2** *the zipper snagged on the fabric* CATCH, get caught, hook.

snake ▶ noun *the snake shed its skin* literary serpent; Zoology ophidian. *See table.*
— RELATED TERMS: colubrine, serpentine.
▶ verb *the road snakes inland* TWIST, wind, meander, zigzag, curve.
■ **snake in the grass** TRAITOR, turncoat, betrayer, informer, backstabber, double-crosser, quisling, Judas; fraudster, trickster, charlatan, scam artist; informal two-timer, rat.

Snakes

adder	horned viper
anaconda	king cobra
asp	krait
boa	mamba
boa constrictor	massasauga
bull snake	milk snake
bushmaster	pit viper
cobra	puff adder
constrictor	python
copperhead	rattlesnake
coral snake	rock python
cottonmouth	sidewinder
death adder	spitting cobra
diamondback	taipan
fer-de-lance	viper
garter snake	water moccasin
grass snake	water snake
hamadryad	whip snake
hognose snake	

snap ▶ verb **1** *the ruler snapped* BREAK, fracture, splinter, come apart, split, crack; informal bust. **2** *she snapped after years of violence* FLARE UP, lose one's self-control, freak out, go to pieces, get worked up; informal crack up, lose one's cool, blow one's top, fly off the handle. **3** *a dog was snapping at his heels* BITE; gnash its teeth. **4** *'shut up!' Anna snapped* SAY ROUGHLY, say brusquely, say abruptly, say angrily, bark, snarl, growl; retort, rejoin, retaliate; round on someone; informal jump down someone's throat.
▶ noun **1** *she closed her purse with a snap* CLICK, crack, pop. **2** *a cold snap* PERIOD, spell, time, interval, stretch, patch. **3** (informal) *holiday snaps* PHOTOGRAPH, picture, photo, shot, snapshot, print, slide, frame, still; informal mug shot. **4** *it's a snap to put together* EASY TASK; informal a piece of cake, cinch, breeze, child's play, kid's stuff, duck soup.
■ **snap out of it** (informal) RECOVER, get a grip, pull oneself together, get over it, get better, cheer up, perk up; informal buck up.
■ **snap something up** BUY EAGERLY, accept eagerly, jump at, take advantage of, grab, seize (on), grasp with both hands, pounce on.

snappy ▶ adjective (informal) **1** *a snappy mood* IRRITABLE, irascible, short-tempered, hot-tempered, quick-tempered, snappish, fiery, touchy, volatile; cross, crabby, crotchety, cantankerous, grumpy, bad-tempered, testy, tetchy; informal chippy, grouchy, cranky, on a short fuse. **2** *a snappy catchphrase* CONCISE, succinct, memorable, catchy, neat, clever, crisp, pithy, witty, incisive, brief, short. **3** *a snappy dresser* SMART, fashionable, stylish, chic, modish, elegant, neat, spruce, trim, dapper; informal snazzy, natty, sharp, nifty, cool, hip, styling, spiffy, fly.
— OPPOSITES: peaceable, long-winded, slovenly.

■ **make it snappy** HURRY (UP), be quick (about it), get a move on, look lively, speed up; informal get cracking, step on it, move it, buck up, shake a leg; dated make haste.

snare ▶ noun **1** *the hare was caught in a snare* TRAP, gin, net, noose. **2** *avoid the snares of the new law* PITFALL, trap, catch, danger, hazard, peril; web, mesh.
▶ verb **1** *game birds were snared* TRAP, catch, net, bag, ensnare, entrap. **2** *he managed to snare an heiress* ENSNARE, catch, get hold of, bag, hook, land.

snarl¹ ▶ verb **1** *the wolves are snarling* GROWL, gnash one's teeth. **2** *'Shut up!' he snarled* SAY ROUGHLY, say brusquely, say nastily, bark, snap, growl; informal jump down someone's throat.

snarl² ▶ verb **1** *the rope got snarled up in a bush* TANGLE, entangle, entwine, enmesh, ravel, knot, foul. **2** *this case has snarled up the court process* COMPLICATE, confuse, muddle, jumble; informal mess up.

snatch ▶ verb **1** *she snatched the sandwich* GRAB, seize, take hold of, get one's hands on, take, pluck; grasp at, scravel ♣, clutch at. **2** (informal) *someone snatched my bag. See* STEAL *verb sense 1.* **3** (informal) *she snatched the newborn from the hospital. See* ABDUCT. **4** *he snatched victory* SEIZE, pluck, wrest, achieve, secure, obtain; scrape.
▶ noun **1** *brief snatches of sleep* PERIOD, spell, time, fit, bout, interval, stretch. **2** *a snatch of conversation* FRAGMENT, snippet, bit, scrap, part, extract, excerpt, portion.

snazzy ▶ adjective (informal). *See* STYLISH.

sneak ▶ verb **1** *I sneaked out* CREEP, slink, steal, slip, slide, sidle, edge, move furtively, tiptoe, pussyfoot, pad, prowl. **2** *she sneaked a camera in* SMUGGLE, bring/take surreptitiously, bring/take secretly, bring/take illicitly, spirit, slip. **3** *he sneaked a doughnut* STEAL, take furtively, take surreptitiously; informal snatch.
▶ adjective **1** *a sneak attack* FURTIVE, secret, stealthy, sly, surreptitious, clandestine, covert. **2** *a sneak preview* EXCLUSIVE, private, quick.

sneaking ▶ adjective **1** *she had a sneaking admiration for him* SECRET, private, hidden, concealed, unvoiced, undisclosed, undeclared, unavowed. **2** *a sneaking feeling* NIGGLING, nagging, lurking, insidious, lingering, gnawing, persistent.

sneaky ▶ adjective SLY, crafty, cunning, wily, artful, scheming, devious, guileful, deceitful, duplicitous, underhanded, unscrupulous; furtive, secretive, secret, stealthy, surreptitious, clandestine, covert; informal foxy, shifty, dirty.
— OPPOSITES: honest.

sneer ▶ noun **1** *she had a sneer on her face* SMIRK, curl of the lip, disparaging smile, contemptuous smile, cruel smile. **2** *the sneers of others* JIBE, barb, jeer, taunt, insult, slight, affront, slur; informal dig.
▶ verb **1** *he looked at me and sneered* SMIRK, curl one's lip, smile disparagingly, smile contemptuously, smile cruelly. **2** *it is easy to sneer at them* SCOFF AT, scorn, disdain, mock, jeer at, hold in contempt, deride, insult, slight, slur.

snicker ▶ verb *they all snickered at her* GIGGLE, titter, snigger, chortle, simper, laugh.
▶ noun *he could not suppress a snicker* GIGGLE, titter, snigger, chortle, simper.

snide ▶ adjective DISPARAGING, derogatory, deprecating, denigratory, insulting, contemptuous; mocking, taunting, sneering, scornful, derisive, sarcastic, spiteful, nasty, mean.

sniff¹ ▶ verb **1** *she sniffed and blew her nose* INHALE, breathe in; snuffle. **2** *Sandra sniffed the socks and grimaced* SMELL, scent, get a whiff of.

▶ **noun 1** *she gave a loud sniff* SNUFFLE, inhalation. **2** *a sniff of fresh air* SMELL, scent, whiff; lungful. **3** (*informal*) *the first sniff of trouble* INDICATION, hint, whiff, inkling, suggestion, whisper, trace, sign, suspicion.

■ **sniff at** SCORN, disdain, hold in contempt, look down one's nose at, treat as inferior, look down on, sneer at, scoff at; *informal* turn one's nose up at.

■ **sniff something out** (*informal*) DETECT, find, discover, bring to light, track down, dig up, hunt out, ferret out, root out, uncover, unearth.

snigger ▶ **verb & noun** See SNICKER.

snip ▶ **verb 1** *an usher snipped our tickets* CUT, clip, slit, nick, notch. **2** *snip off the faded flowers* CUT OFF, trim (off), clip, prune, chop off, lop (off), dock, crop, sever, detach, remove, take off.

▶ **noun 1** *make snips along the edge* CUT, slit, nick, notch, incision. **2** *snips of wallpaper* SCRAP, snippet, cutting, shred, remnant, fragment, sliver, bit, piece.

snippet ▶ **noun** PIECE, bit, scrap, fragment, particle, shred; excerpt, extract.

snit ▶ **noun** STATE, temper, bad mood, fit of pique, huff, hissy fit.

snivel ▶ **verb 1** *he slumped in a chair, snivelling* SNIFFLE, snuffle, whimper, whine, weep, cry; *informal* blubber, boo-hoo. **2** *don't snivel about what you get* COMPLAIN, mutter, grumble, grouse, groan, carp, bleat, whine; *informal* gripe, moan, grouch, beef, bellyache, whinge, sound off, kvetch.

snobbery ▶ **noun** AFFECTATION, pretension, pretentiousness, arrogance, haughtiness, airs and graces, elitism; disdain, condescension, superciliousness; *informal* snootiness, uppitiness.

snobbish ▶ **adjective** ELITIST, snobby, superior, supercilious; arrogant, haughty, disdainful, condescending; pretentious, affected; *informal* snooty, uppity, high and mighty, la-di-da, stuck-up, hoity-toity, snotty.

snoop (*informal*) ▶ **verb 1** *don't snoop into our affairs* PRY, inquire, be inquisitive, be curious, poke about/around, be a busybody, poke one's nose into; interfere (in/with), meddle (in/with), intrude (on); *informal* be nosy. **2** *they snooped around the building* INVESTIGATE, explore, search, nose, have a good look; prowl around.

▶ **noun** *he went for a snoop around* SEARCH, nose, look, prowl, ferret, poke, investigation.

snooper ▶ **noun** MEDDLER, busybody, eavesdropper; investigator, detective; *informal* nosy parker, snoop, private eye, PI, sleuth, gumshoe.

snooty ▶ **adjective** (*informal*) ARROGANT, proud, haughty, conceited, aloof, superior, self-important, disdainful, supercilious, snobbish, snobby, patronizing, condescending; *informal* uppity, high and mighty, la-di-da, stuck-up, hoity-toity.

— OPPOSITES: modest.

snooze (*informal*) ▶ **noun** *a good place for a snooze* NAP, doze, sleep, rest, siesta, catnap; *informal* forty winks; *literary* slumber.

▶ **verb** *she gently snoozed* NAP, doze, sleep, rest, take a siesta, catnap, drop off; *informal* snatch forty winks, get some shut-eye, put one's head down, catch some zees; *literary* slumber.

snout ▶ **noun** MUZZLE, nose, proboscis, trunk.

snow ▶ **noun** SNOWFLAKES, flakes, snowfall, white stuff, (*Nfld*) batch of snow ♣, (*Nfld*) Sheila's brush ♣;

snowdrift, snowbank, snowpack; avalanche. *See table.*

— RELATED TERMS: niveous, nival.

Types and Conditions of Snow

blizzard	packing snow
blowing snow	powder
corn snow	skiff
drift	sleet
dusting	slush
flurry	snow devil
freezing rain	snow squall
frozen granular	snowstorm
hard packed	soft packed
icy	wet granular
lake effect	wet packed
loose granular	wet snow
machine groomed	whiteout
névé	windblown
packed powder	

snowbound ▶ **adjective** *snowbound skiers* SNOWED-IN, (*Maritimes & Ont.*) storm-stayed ♣.

snowmobile ▶ **noun** *proprietary* Ski-Doo, snow machine; snowcat; *proprietary* Bombardier ♣; *informal* sled, scooter ♣.

snowshoe ▶ **noun** bearpaw, racquet, Algonquin, beavertail.

snub ▶ **verb** *they snubbed their hosts* REBUFF, spurn, repulse, cold-shoulder, brush off, give the cold shoulder to, keep at arm's length; ignore; insult, slight, affront, humiliate; *informal* freeze out, stiff.

▶ **noun** *a very public snub* REBUFF, repulse, slap in the face; humiliation, insult, slight, affront; *informal* brush-off, kiss-off, put-down.

snuff ▶ **verb** EXTINGUISH, put out, douse, smother, choke, blow out, quench, stub out.

snug ▶ **adjective 1** *our tents were snug* COZY, comfortable, warm, welcoming, restful, reassuring, intimate, sheltered, secure; *informal* comfy. **2** *a snug dress* TIGHT, skin-tight, close-fitting, form-fitting, figure-hugging, slinky.

— OPPOSITES: bleak, loose.

snuggle ▶ **verb** NESTLE, curl up, huddle (up), cuddle up, nuzzle, settle.

soak ▶ **verb 1** *soak the beans in water* IMMERSE, steep, submerge, submerse, dip, dunk, bathe, douse, marinate, souse. **2** *we got soaked outside* DRENCH, wet through, saturate, waterlog, deluge, inundate, submerge, drown, swamp. **3** *the sweat soaked through his clothes* PERMEATE, penetrate, percolate, seep into, spread through, infuse, impregnate. **4** *use towels to soak up the water* ABSORB, suck up, blot (up), mop (up), sponge up, sop up.

soaking ▶ **adjective** DRENCHED, wet (through), soaked (through), sodden, soggy, waterlogged, saturated, sopping wet, dripping wet, wringing wet.

— OPPOSITES: parched.

soar ▶ **verb 1** *the bird soared into the air* FLY, wing, ascend, climb, rise; take off, take flight. **2** *the gulls soared on the winds* GLIDE, plane, float, drift, wheel, hover. **3** *the cost of living soared* INCREASE, escalate, shoot up, rise, spiral; *informal* go through the roof, skyrocket.

— OPPOSITES: plummet.

sob ▶ **verb** WEEP, cry, shed tears, snivel, whimper; howl, bawl; *informal* blubber, boo-hoo.

sober ▶ adjective **1** *the driver was clearly sober* NOT DRUNK, clear-headed; teetotal, abstinent, abstemious, dry; *informal* on the wagon. **2** *a sober view of life* SERIOUS, solemn, sensible, thoughtful, grave, sombre, staid, level-headed, businesslike, down-to-earth, commonsensical, pragmatic, conservative; unemotional, dispassionate, objective, matter-of-fact, no-nonsense, rational, logical, straightforward. **3** *a sober suit* SOMBRE, subdued, severe; conventional, traditional, quiet, drab, plain.
— OPPOSITES: drunk, frivolous, sensational, flamboyant.
▶ verb **1** *I ought to sober up* QUIT DRINKING, dry out, become sober. **2** *his expression sobered her* MAKE SERIOUS, subdue, calm down, quieten, steady; bring down to earth, make someone stop and think, give someone pause for thought.

sobriety ▶ noun **1** *she noted his sobriety* SOBERNESS, clear-headedness; abstinence, teetotalism, non-indulgence, abstemiousness, temperance. **2** *the mayor is a model of sobriety* SERIOUSNESS, solemnity, gravity, gravitas, dignity, level-headedness, common sense, pragmatism, practicality, self-control, self-restraint, conservatism.

so-called ▶ adjective INAPPROPRIATELY NAMED, supposed, alleged, presumed, ostensible, reputed; nominal, titular, self-styled, professed, would-be, self-appointed, soi-disant.

sociable ▶ adjective FRIENDLY, affable, companionable, gregarious, convivial, amicable, cordial, warm, genial; communicative, responsive, forthcoming, open, outgoing, extrovert, hail-fellow-well-met, approachable; *informal* chummy, clubby.
— OPPOSITES: unfriendly.

social ▶ adjective **1** *a major social problem* COMMUNAL, community, collective, group, general, popular, civil, public, societal. **2** *a social club* RECREATIONAL, leisure, entertainment, amusement. **3** *a uniquely social animal* GREGARIOUS, interactional; organized.
— OPPOSITES: individual.
▶ noun *the club has a social once a month* PARTY, gathering, function, get-together, soiree; celebration, reunion, jamboree; *informal* bash, shindig, (*Atlantic*) time ✦, do, bunfight.

socialism ▶ noun LEFTISM, welfarism; radicalism, progressivism, social democracy; communism, Marxism, labour movement.

socialist ▶ adjective *the socialist movement* LEFT-WING, progressive, leftist, labour, CCF/NDP ✦, anti-corporate, anti-globalization; radical, revolutionary, militant; communist; *informal* lefty, red.
— OPPOSITES: conservative.
▶ noun *a well-known socialist* LEFT-WINGER, leftist, progressive, progressivist, NDPer ✦; radical, revolutionary; communist, Marxist; *informal* lefty, red.
— OPPOSITES: conservative.

socialize ▶ verb INTERACT, converse, be sociable, mix, mingle, get together, meet, fraternize, consort; entertain, go out; *informal* hobnob.

society ▶ noun **1** *a danger to society* THE COMMUNITY, the (general) public, the people, the population; civilization, humankind, mankind, humanity. **2** *an industrial society* CULTURE, community, civilization, nation, population. **3** *Sir Paul will help you enter society* HIGH SOCIETY, polite society, the upper classes, the elite, the smart set, the beautiful people, the beau monde, the haut monde; *informal* the upper crust, the

top drawer. **4** *a local history society* ASSOCIATION, club, group, circle, fellowship, guild, lodge, fraternity, brotherhood, sisterhood, sorority, league, union, alliance. **5** *the society of others* COMPANY, companionship, fellowship, friendship, comradeship, camaraderie.

socket ▶ noun *she plugged the toaster into the wall socket* POWER OUTLET, jack, port; *informal* plug.

soda ▶ noun POP, fizzy drink, soft drink; soda water, club soda.

sodden ▶ adjective **1** *his clothes were sodden* SOAKING, soaked (through), wet (through), saturated, drenched, sopping wet, wringing wet. **2** *sodden fields* WATERLOGGED, soggy, saturated, boggy, swampy, miry, marshy; heavy, squelchy, soft.
— OPPOSITES: arid.

sofa ▶ noun. *See table.*

Sofas & Couches

button-back	loveseat
camelback	pullout
canapé	settee
chesterfield	sleeper
davenport	sofa bed
daybed	studio couch
divan	tête-à-tête
futon	Winnipeg couch ✦
Hide-A-Bed*	*See also* CHAIRS.
	*Proprietary term.

soft ▶ adjective **1** *soft fruit* MUSHY, squashy, pulpy, pappy, slushy, squelchy, squishy, doughy; *informal* gooey. **2** *soft ground* SWAMPY, marshy, boggy, miry, oozy; heavy, squelchy. **3** *a soft cushion* SQUASHY, spongy, compressible, supple, springy, pliable, pliant, resilient, malleable. **4** *soft fabric* VELVETY, smooth, fleecy, downy, furry, silky, silken, satiny. **5** *a soft wind* GENTLE, light, mild, moderate. **6** *soft light* DIM, low, faint, subdued, muted, mellow. **7** *soft colours* PALE, pastel, muted, understated, restrained, subdued, subtle. **8** *soft voices* QUIET, low, faint, muted, subdued, muffled, hushed, whispered, stifled, murmured, gentle, dulcet; indistinct, inaudible. **9** *soft outlines* BLURRED, vague, hazy, misty, foggy, nebulous, fuzzy, blurry, indistinct, unclear. **10** *he seduced her with soft words* KIND, gentle, sympathetic, soothing, tender, sensitive, affectionate, loving, amorous, warm, sweet, sentimental, pretty; *informal* mushy, slushy, schmaltzy, sappy. **11** *she's too soft with her pupils* LENIENT, easygoing, tolerant, forgiving, forbearing, indulgent, clement, permissive, liberal, lax. **12** (*informal*) *he's soft in the head* FOOLISH, stupid, simple, brainless, mindless; mad, scatterbrained, feather-brained; slow, weak, feeble; *informal* dopey, dippy, scatty, loopy, flaky.
— OPPOSITES: hard, firm, rough, strong, harsh, lurid, strident, sharp, strict, sensible.

soften ▶ verb **1** *she tried to soften the blow of new service cuts* ALLEVIATE, ease, relieve, soothe, take the edge off, assuage, cushion, moderate, mitigate, palliate, diminish, blunt, deaden. **2** *the winds softened* DIE DOWN, abate, subside, moderate, let up, calm, diminish, slacken, weaken.
■ **soften someone up** CHARM, win over, persuade, influence, weaken, disarm, sweeten, butter up, soft-soap.

soft-hearted ▶ adjective KIND, kindly,

tender-hearted, tender, gentle, sympathetic, compassionate, humane; generous, indulgent, lenient, merciful, benevolent.

soft-pedal ▶ verb *the major candidates wish to soft-pedal the immigration issue* PLAY DOWN, make light of, make little/nothing of, set little/no store by, gloss over, de-emphasize, underemphasize, downplay, understate, underplay, minimize, shrug off.
– OPPOSITES: emphasize, exaggerate.

soggy ▶ adjective MUSHY, squashy, pulpy, slushy, squelchy, squishy; swampy, marshy, boggy, miry; soaking, soaked through, wet, saturated, drenched.

soil[1] ▶ noun **1** *acid soil* EARTH, loam, dirt, clay, gumbo; ground. **2** *Canadian soil* TERRITORY, land, domain, dominion, region, country.

soil[2] ▶ verb **1** *he soiled his tie* DIRTY, stain, splash, spot, spatter, splatter, smear, smudge, sully, spoil, foul; *informal* muck up; *literary* begrime. **2** *our reputation is being soiled* DISHONOUR, damage, sully, stain, blacken, tarnish, taint, blemish, defile, blot, smear, drag through the mud; *literary* besmirch.

sojourn (*formal*) ▶ noun *a sojourn in France* STAY, visit, stop, stopover; holiday, vacation.
▶ verb *they sojourned in the monastery* STAY, live, put up, stop (over), lodge, room, board; holiday, vacation.

solace ▶ noun *they found solace in each other* COMFORT, consolation, cheer, support, relief.
▶ verb *she was solaced with tea and sympathy* COMFORT, console, cheer, support, soothe, calm.

soldier ▶ noun FIGHTER, trooper, serviceman, servicewoman; warrior; *US* GI; peacekeeper, blue helmet/beret; *archaic* man-at-arms.
■ **soldier on** (*informal*). See PERSEVERE.

sole ▶ adjective ONLY, one (and only), single, solitary, lone, unique, exclusive, isolated.

solecism ▶ noun **1** *a poem marred by solecisms* (GRAMMATICAL) MISTAKE, error, blunder; *informal* howler, blooper. **2** *it would have been a solecism to answer* FAUX PAS, gaffe, impropriety, social indiscretion, infelicity, slip, error, blunder, lapse; *informal* slip-up, boo-boo, goof, blooper, flub.

solely ▶ adverb ONLY, simply, just, merely, uniquely, exclusively, entirely, wholly; alone.

solemn ▶ adjective **1** *a solemn occasion* DIGNIFIED, ceremonious, ceremonial, stately, formal, courtly, majestic, imposing, awe-inspiring, splendid, magnificent, grand. **2** *he looked very solemn* SERIOUS, grave, sober, sombre, unsmiling, stern, grim, dour, humourless; pensive, meditative, thoughtful. **3** *a solemn promise* SINCERE, earnest, honest, genuine, firm, heartfelt, wholehearted, sworn.
– OPPOSITES: frivolous, light-hearted, insincere.

solemnize ▶ verb PERFORM, celebrate; formalize, officiate at.

solicit ▶ verb **1** *Phil tried to solicit his help* ASK FOR, request, seek, apply for, put in for, call for, press for, beg, plead for. **2** *they are solicited for their opinions* ASK, petition, importune, implore, plead with, entreat, appeal to, lobby, beg, supplicate, call on, press; *literary* beseech.

solicitous ▶ adjective CONCERNED, caring, considerate, attentive, mindful, thoughtful, interested; anxious, worried.

solid ▶ adjective **1** *the ice cream was solid* HARD, rock-hard, rigid, firm, solidified, set, frozen, concrete. **2** *solid gold* PURE, 24-carat, unalloyed, unadulterated, genuine. **3** *a solid line* CONTINUOUS, uninterrupted, unbroken, non-stop, undivided.

4 *solid houses* WELL-BUILT, sound, substantial, strong, sturdy, durable. **5** *a solid argument* WELL-FOUNDED, valid, sound, reasonable, logical, authoritative, convincing, cogent, plausible, credible, reliable. **6** *a solid friendship* DEPENDABLE, reliable, firm, unshakeable, trustworthy, stable, steadfast, staunch, constant, rock-steady. **7** *solid citizens* SENSIBLE, dependable, trustworthy, decent, law-abiding, upright, upstanding, worthy. **8** *the company is very solid* FINANCIALLY SOUND, secure, creditworthy, profit-making, solvent, in credit, in the black. **9** *solid support from their colleagues* UNANIMOUS, united, consistent, undivided, wholehearted.
– OPPOSITES: liquid, alloyed, broken, flimsy, untenable, unreliable.

solidarity ▶ noun UNANIMITY, unity, like-mindedness, agreement, accord, harmony, consensus, concurrence, co-operation, cohesion, fraternity, mutual support; *formal* concord.

solidify ▶ verb HARDEN, set, freeze, thicken, stiffen, congeal, cake, dry, bake; ossify, calcify, fossilize, petrify.
– OPPOSITES: liquefy.

soliloquy ▶ noun MONOLOGUE, speech, address, lecture, oration, sermon, homily, aside.

solitary ▶ adjective **1** *a solitary life* LONELY, companionless, unaccompanied, by oneself, on one's own, alone, friendless; anti-social, unsociable, withdrawn, reclusive, cloistered, hermitic, incommunicado, lonesome. **2** *solitary farmsteads* ISOLATED, remote, lonely, out of the way, in the back of beyond, outlying, off the beaten track, godforsaken, obscure, inaccessible, cut-off; secluded, private, sequestered, desolate, in the backwoods; *informal* in the sticks, in the middle of nowhere, in the boondocks, in the back woods, in the back concessions ◆; *literary* lone. **3** *a solitary piece of evidence* SINGLE, lone, sole, unique; only, one, individual; odd.
– OPPOSITES: sociable, accessible.

solitude ▶ noun **1** *she savoured her solitude* LONELINESS, solitariness, isolation, seclusion, sequestration, withdrawal, privacy, peace. **2** *solitudes in the north of the province* WILDERNESS, rural area, wilds, backwoods, desert, emptiness, wasteland; the bush, backcountry; *informal* the sticks, the boondocks.

solo ▶ adjective *a solo flight* UNACCOMPANIED, single-handed, companionless, unescorted, unattended, unchaperoned, independent, solitary; alone, on one's own, by oneself.
– OPPOSITES: accompanied.
▶ adverb *he went solo to the party* UNACCOMPANIED, alone, on one's own, single-handed(ly), by oneself, unescorted, unattended, unchaperoned, unaided, independently; *informal* stag.
– OPPOSITES: accompanied.

solution ▶ noun **1** *an easy solution to the problem* ANSWER, result, resolution, way out, fix, panacea; key, formula, explanation, interpretation. **2** *a solution of ammonia in water* MIXTURE, mix, blend, compound, suspension, tincture, infusion, emulsion.

solve ▶ verb RESOLVE, answer, work out, find a solution to, find the key to, puzzle out, fathom, decipher, decode, clear up, straighten out, get to the bottom of, unravel, piece together, explain; *informal* figure out, crack.

solvent ▶ adjective FINANCIALLY SOUND, debt-free, in

the black, in credit, creditworthy, solid, secure, profit-making; *Finance* unlevered.

sombre ▶ **adjective 1** *sombre clothes* DARK, drab, dull, dingy; restrained, subdued, sober, funereal. **2** *a sombre expression* SOLEMN, earnest, serious, grave, sober, unsmiling, stern, grim, dour, humourless; gloomy, depressed, sad, melancholy, dismal, doleful, mournful, lugubrious.
— OPPOSITES: bright, cheerful.

somebody ▶ **noun** *she wanted to be a somebody* IMPORTANT PERSON, VIP, public figure, notable, dignitary, worthy; someone, (big/household) name, celebrity, star, superstar; grandee, luminary, leading light; *informal* celeb, bigwig, big shot, big cheese, hotshot, megastar.
— OPPOSITES: nonentity, no-name.

some day ▶ **adverb** SOMETIME, one (fine) day, one of these days, at a future date, sooner or later, by and by, in due course, in the fullness of time, in the long run.
— OPPOSITES: never.

somehow ▶ **adverb** BY SOME MEANS, by any means, in some way, one way or another, no matter how, by fair means or foul, by hook or by crook, come what may.

sometime ▶ **adverb 1** *I'll visit sometime* SOME DAY, one day, one of these (fine) days, at a future date, sooner or later, by and by, in due course, in the fullness of time, in the long run. **2** *it happened sometime on Sunday* AT SOME TIME, at some point; during, in the course of.
— OPPOSITES: never.
▶ **adjective** *the sometime editor of the paper* FORMER, past, previous, prior, foregoing, late, erstwhile, one-time, ex-; *formal* quondam.

sometimes ▶ **adverb** OCCASIONALLY, from time to time, now and then, every so often, once in a while, on occasion, at times, off and on, at intervals, periodically, sporadically, spasmodically, intermittently.

somewhat ▶ **adverb 1** *matters have improved somewhat* A LITTLE, a bit, to some extent, (up) to a point, in some measure, rather, quite, some; *informal* kind of, kinda, sort of. **2** *a somewhat thicker book* SLIGHTLY, relatively, comparatively, moderately, fairly, rather, quite, marginally.
— OPPOSITES: greatly.

somewhere ▶ **adverb** SOMEPLACE, somewheres.

somnolent ▶ **adjective 1** *he felt somnolent after lunch* SLEEPY, drowsy, tired, languid, dozy, groggy, lethargic, sluggish, enervated, torpid; *informal* snoozy, dopey, yawny; *literary* slumberous. **2** *a somnolent village* QUIET, restful, tranquil, calm, peaceful, relaxing, soothing, undisturbed, untroubled.

son ▶ **noun** MALE CHILD, boy, heir; descendant, offspring, scion; *informal* lad.
— RELATED TERMS: filial.

song ▶ **noun 1** *a beautiful song* AIR, strain, ditty, melody, tune, number, track, anthem, hymn, shanty, ballad, aria. **2** *the song of the birds* CALL(S), chirping, cheeping, peeping, chirruping, warble(s), warbling, trilling, twitter; birdsong.
■ **song and dance** (*informal*). *See* FUSS *noun* sense 1.

songster, songstress ▶ **noun** SINGER, vocalist, soloist, crooner, chorister, choirboy, choirgirl, songbird, diva, chansonnier, chanteuse; alto, bass, basso profundo, baritone, contralto, tenor, soprano, mezzo (soprano); balladeer; *informal* warbler, popster, soulster, folkie; *historical* minstrel, troubadour; *archaic* melodist.

sonorous ▶ **adjective 1** *a sonorous voice* RESONANT, rich, full, round, booming, deep, clear, mellow, orotund, fruity, strong, resounding, reverberant. **2** *sonorous words of condemnation* IMPRESSIVE, imposing, grandiloquent, magniloquent, high-flown, lofty, orotund, bombastic, grandiose, pompous, pretentious, overblown, turgid; oratorical, rhetorical; *informal* highfalutin.

soon ▶ **adverb 1** *we'll be there soon* SHORTLY, presently, in the near future, before long, in a little while, in a minute, in a moment, in an instant, in a bit, in the twinkling of an eye, in no time, before you know it, any minute (now), any day (now), by and by; *informal* pronto, in a jiffy; *dated* directly, anon. **2** *how soon can you get here?* EARLY, quickly, promptly, speedily, punctually.

sooner ▶ **adverb 1** *he should have done it sooner* EARLIER, before, beforehand, in advance, ahead of time; already. **2** *I would sooner stay* RATHER, preferably, by preference, by choice, more willingly, more readily.

soothe ▶ **verb 1** *Rachel tried to soothe him* CALM (DOWN), pacify, comfort, hush, quiet, subdue (down), lull, tranquilize; appease, conciliate, mollify. **2** *an anaesthetic to soothe the pain* ALLEVIATE, ease, relieve, take the edge off, assuage, allay, lessen, palliate, diminish, decrease, dull, blunt, deaden.
— OPPOSITES: agitate, aggravate.

soother ▶ **noun** *babies sucking on soothers* PACIFIER, dummy, plug, rubber nipple.

soothing ▶ **adjective 1** *soothing music* RELAXING, restful, calm, calming, tranquil, peaceful, reposeful, tranquilizing, soporific. **2** *soothing ointment* PALLIATIVE, pain-relieving, analgesic, mild, calmative.

soothsayer ▶ **noun** SEER, oracle, augur, prophet(ess), sage, prognosticator, diviner, fortune teller, crystal-gazer, clairvoyant, psychic; *literary* sibyl.

sop ▶ **noun** CONCESSION, bribe.

sophisticated ▶ **adjective 1** *sophisticated techniques* ADVANCED, modern, state of the art, the latest, new, up-to-the-minute; innovative, trail-blazing, revolutionary, futuristic, avant-garde; complex, complicated, intricate, highly evolved. **2** *a sophisticated woman* WORLDLY, worldly-wise, experienced, enlightened, cosmopolitan, knowledgeable; urbane, cultured, cultivated, civilized, polished, refined; elegant, stylish; *informal* cool.
— OPPOSITES: crude, naive.

sophistication ▶ **noun** WORLDLINESS, experience; urbanity, culture, civilization, polish, refinement; elegance, style, poise, finesse, savoir faire; *informal* cool.

sophistry ▶ **noun 1** *to claim this is pure sophistry* SPECIOUS REASONING, fallacy, sophism, casuistry. **2** *a speech full of sophistries* FALLACIOUS ARGUMENT, sophism, fallacy; *Logic* paralogism.

soporific ▶ **adjective 1** *soporific drugs* SLEEP-INDUCING, sedative, somnolent, calmative, tranquilizing, narcotic, opiate; drowsy, sleepy, somniferous; *Medicine* hypnotic. **2** *a soporific TV drama* BORING, tedious, tired, dreary, turgid, dry, mind-numbing.
— OPPOSITES: invigorating.
▶ **noun** *she was given a soporific* SLEEPING PILL, sedative, calmative, tranquilizer, narcotic, opiate; *Medicine* hypnotic.
— OPPOSITES: stimulant.

soppy ▶ **adjective** *See* SENTIMENTAL sense 2.

sorcerer, sorceress ▶ noun WIZARD, witch, magician, warlock, enchanter, enchantress, magus; witch doctor; *archaic* mage.

sorcery ▶ noun (BLACK) MAGIC, the black arts, witchcraft, wizardry, enchantment, spells, incantation, witching, witchery, thaumaturgy.

sordid ▶ adjective **1** *a sordid love affair* SLEAZY, dirty, seedy, seamy, unsavoury, tawdry, cheap, debased, degenerate, dishonourable, disreputable, discreditable, contemptible, ignominious, shameful, abhorrent. **2** *a sordid little street* SQUALID, slummy, insalubrious, dirty, filthy, mucky, grimy, shabby, messy, soiled, scummy, unclean; *informal* cruddy, grungy, crummy, scuzzy; grotty.
— OPPOSITES: respectable, immaculate.

sore ▶ adjective **1** *a sore leg* PAINFUL, hurting, hurt, aching, throbbing, smarting, stinging, agonizing, excruciating; inflamed, sensitive, tender, raw, bruised, wounded, injured. **2** *we are in sore need of you* DIRE, urgent, pressing, desperate, parlous, critical, crucial, acute, grave, serious, drastic, extreme, life-and-death, great, terrible; *formal* exigent. **3** *(informal) they were sore at us* UPSET, angry, annoyed, cross, furious, vexed, displeased, disgruntled, dissatisfied, exasperated, irritated, galled, irked, put out, aggrieved, offended, affronted, piqued, nettled; *informal* aggravated, miffed, peeved, riled, cheesed off, teed off, ticked off, hacked off.
▶ noun *a sore on his leg* INFLAMMATION, swelling, lesion; wound, scrape, abrasion, cut, laceration, graze, contusion, bruise; ulcer, boil, abscess, carbuncle.

sorrow ▶ noun **1** *he felt sorrow at her death* SADNESS, unhappiness, misery, despondency, regret, depression, despair, desolation, dejection, wretchedness, gloom, dolefulness, melancholy, woe, heartache, grief; *literary* dolour. **2** *the sorrows of life* TROUBLE, difficulty, problem, adversity, misery, woe, affliction, trial, tribulation, misfortune, pain, setback, reverse, blow, failure, tragedy.
— OPPOSITES: joy.
▶ verb *they sorrowed over her grave* MOURN, lament, grieve, be sad, be miserable, be despondent, despair, suffer, ache, agonize, anguish, pine, weep, wail.
— OPPOSITES: rejoice.

sorrowful ▶ adjective **1** *sorrowful eyes* SAD, unhappy, dejected, regretful, downcast, miserable, downhearted, despondent, despairing, disconsolate, desolate, glum, gloomy, doleful, dismal, melancholy, mournful, woeful, woebegone, forlorn, crestfallen, heartbroken; *informal* blue, down in the mouth, down in the dumps. **2** *sorrowful news* TRAGIC, sad, unhappy, awful, miserable, sorry, pitiful; traumatic, upsetting, depressing, distressing, dispiriting, heartbreaking, harrowing; *formal* grievous.

sorry ▶ adjective **1** *I was sorry to hear about his accident* SAD, unhappy, sorrowful, distressed, upset, downcast, downhearted, disheartened, despondent; heartbroken, inconsolable, grief-stricken. **2** *he felt sorry for her* FULL OF PITY, sympathetic, compassionate, moved, consoling, empathetic, concerned. **3** *I'm sorry if I was brusque* REGRETFUL, remorseful, contrite, repentant, rueful, penitent, apologetic, abject, guilty, ashamed, sheepish, shamefaced. **4** *he looks a sorry sight* PITIFUL, pitiable, heart-rending, distressing; unfortunate, unhappy, wretched, unlucky, shameful, regrettable, awful.
— OPPOSITES: glad, unsympathetic, unrepentant.
▶ exclamation APOLOGIES, excuse me, pardon me, forgive me, my mistake; *informal* my bad.

sort ▶ noun **1** *what sort of book is it?* TYPE, kind, nature, manner, variety, class, category, style; calibre, quality, form, group, set, bracket, genre, species, family, order, generation, vintage, make, model, brand, stamp, stripe, ilk, cast, grain, mould. **2** *(informal) he's a good sort* PERSON, individual, soul, creature, human being; character, customer; *informal* fellow, type, cookie, dog.
▶ verb *they sorted things of similar size* CLASSIFY, class, categorize, catalogue, grade, group; organize, arrange, order, marshal, assemble, systematize, systemize, pigeonhole, sort out.
■ **out of sorts 1** *I'm feeling out of sorts* UNWELL, ill, poorly, sick, queasy, nauseous, peaky, run-down, below par; *informal* under the weather, funny, rough, lousy, rotten, awful, crappy, off. **2** *he's out of sorts because she turned him down* GRUMPY, irritable, crabby; unhappy, sad, miserable, down, depressed, gloomy, glum, forlorn, low, in a blue funk; *informal* blue, down in the dumps.
■ **sort of** *(informal)* **1** *you look sort of familiar* SLIGHTLY, faintly, remotely, vaguely; somewhat, moderately, quite, rather, fairly, reasonably, relatively; *informal* pretty, kind of, kinda. **2** *he sort of pirouetted* AS IT WERE, kind of, somehow.
■ **sort something out 1** *she sorted out the clothes.* See SORT verb sense 1. **2** *they must sort out their problems* RESOLVE, settle, solve, fix, work out, straighten out, deal with, put right, set right, rectify, iron out; answer, explain, fathom, unravel, clear up; *informal* sew up, hammer out, thrash out, patch up, figure out.

sortie ▶ noun **1** *a sortie against their besiegers* FORAY, sally, charge, offensive, attack, assault, onset, onslaught, thrust, drive. **2** *a bomber sortie* RAID, flight, mission, operation, op.

so-so ▶ adjective *(informal)* MEDIOCRE, indifferent, average, middle-of-the-road, middling, moderate, ordinary, adequate, fair; uninspired, undistinguished, unexceptional, unremarkable, run-of-the-mill, lacklustre, {comme ci, comme ca}; *informal* no great shakes, not up to much, okay.

soul ▶ noun **1** *seeing the soul through the eyes* SPIRIT, psyche, (inner) self, inner being, life force, vital force; individuality, makeup, subconscious, anima; *Philosophy* pneuma; *Hinduism* atman. **2** *he is the soul of discretion* EMBODIMENT, personification, incarnation, epitome, quintessence, essence; model, exemplification, exemplar, image, manifestation. **3** *not a soul in sight* PERSON, human being, individual, man, woman, mortal, creature. **4** *their music lacked soul* INSPIRATION, feeling, emotion, passion, animation, intensity, fervour, ardour, enthusiasm, warmth, energy, vitality, spirit.

soulful ▶ adjective EMOTIONAL, deep, profound, fervent, heartfelt, sincere, passionate; meaningful, significant, eloquent, expressive; moving, stirring; sad, mournful, doleful.

soulless ▶ adjective **1** *a soulless room* CHARACTERLESS, featureless, bland, dull, colourless, lacklustre, dreary, drab, uninspiring, undistinguished, anemic, insipid. **2** *it was soulless work* BORING, dull, tedious, dreary, humdrum, tiresome, wearisome, uninteresting, uninspiring, unexciting, soul-destroying, mind-numbing, dry; monotonous, repetitive.
— OPPOSITES: exciting.

sound¹ ▶ noun **1** *the sound of the car* NOISE, note; din, racket, row, hubbub; resonance, reverberation. **2** *she*

did not make a sound UTTERANCE, cry, word, noise, peep. **3** *the sound of the flute* MUSIC, tone, notes. **4** *I don't like the sound of that* IDEA, thought, concept, prospect, description.
– RELATED TERMS: acoustic, sonic, aural, audio-, sono-.
– OPPOSITES: silence.
▶ **verb 1** *the buzzer sounded* MAKE A NOISE, resonate, resound, reverberate, go off, blare; ring, chime, peal. **2** *drivers must sound their horns* BLOW, blast, toot, blare; operate, set off; ring. **3** *do you sound the 'h'?* PRONOUNCE, verbalize, voice, enunciate, articulate, vocalize, say. **4** *she sounded a warning* UTTER, voice, deliver, express, speak, announce, pronounce. **5** *it sounds like a crazy idea* APPEAR, look (like), seem, strike someone as being, give every indication of being, come across as.

sound² ▶ **adjective 1** *your heart is sound* HEALTHY, in good condition, in good shape, fit, hale and hearty, in fine fettle; undamaged, unimpaired. **2** *a sound building* WELL-BUILT, solid, substantial, strong, sturdy, durable, stable, intact, unimpaired. **3** *sound advice* WELL-FOUNDED, valid, reasonable, logical, weighty, authoritative, reliable, well-grounded. **4** *a sound judge of character* RELIABLE, dependable, trustworthy, fair; good, sensible, wise, judicious, sagacious, shrewd, perceptive. **5** *financially sound* SOLVENT, debt-free, in the black, in credit, creditworthy, secure, solid. **6** *a sound sleep* DEEP, undisturbed, uninterrupted, untroubled, peaceful.
– OPPOSITES: unhealthy, unsafe, unreliable, insolvent, light.

sound³ ▶ **verb** *sound the depth of the river* MEASURE, gauge, determine, test, investigate, survey, plumb, fathom, probe.
■ **sound someone/something out** INVESTIGATE, test, check, examine, probe, research, look into; canvass, survey, poll, question, interview, sample; *informal* pump.

sound⁴ ▶ **noun** *an oil spill in Clayoquot Sound* CHANNEL, (sea) passage, strait(s), (*Atlantic*) tickle ✦, narrows, waterway; inlet, arm (of the sea), fjord, creek, bay; estuary.

soup ▶ **noun** BROTH, potage, consommé, bouillon, chowder, bisque. *See table.*

Soups

alphabet soup	minestrone
bird's nest soup	miso soup
bisque	mock turtle soup
borscht	mulligatawny
bouillon	oxtail
broth	pea soup
burgoo	pistou
callaloo	pot-au-feu
chicken noodle	potage
chowder	Scotch broth
cock-a-leekie	shchi
congee	soup du jour
consommé	stracciatella
egg drop soup	tomato
gazpacho	turtle soup
gumbo	vichyssoise
hot and sour soup	won ton soup
Manhattan clam chowder	zuppa

sour ▶ **adjective 1** *sour wine* ACID, acidic, acidy, acidulated, tart, bitter, sharp, vinegary, pungent; *technical* acerbic. **2** *sour milk* BAD, off, turned, curdled, rancid, high, rank, foul, fetid; (of beer) skunky ✦. **3** *a sour old man* EMBITTERED, resentful, rancorous, jaundiced, bitter; nasty, spiteful, irritable, peevish, fractious, cross, crabby, crotchety, cantankerous, disagreeable, petulant, querulous, grumpy, bad-tempered, ill-humoured, sullen, surly, sulky, churlish; *informal* snappy, grouchy, shirty, cranky.
– OPPOSITES: sweet, fresh, amiable.
▶ **verb 1** *the war had soured him* EMBITTER, disillusion, disenchant, poison, alienate; dissatisfy, frustrate. **2** *the dispute soured relations* SPOIL, mar, damage, harm, impair, wreck, upset, poison, blight, tarnish.
– OPPOSITES: improve.

source ▶ **noun 1** *the source of the river* SPRING, origin, headspring, headwater(s); *literary* wellspring. **2** *the source of the rumour* ORIGIN, birthplace, spring, fountainhead, fount, starting point, ground zero; history, provenance, derivation, root, beginning, genesis, start, rise; author, originator, initiator, inventor. **3** *a historian uses primary and secondary sources* REFERENCE, authority, material, document, informant.

souse ▶ **verb** DRENCH, douse, soak, steep, saturate, plunge, immerse, submerge, dip, sink, dunk.

soused ▶ **adjective 1** *a soused herring* PICKLED, marinated, soaked, steeped. **2** (*informal*) *he was well and truly soused. See* DRUNK *adjective.*

south ▶ **adjective** SOUTHERN, southerly, meridional, austral.

souvenir ▶ **noun** MEMENTO, keepsake, reminder, remembrance, token, memorial; bomboniere; trophy, relic.

sovereign ▶ **noun** RULER, monarch, crowned head, head of state, potentate, suzerain, overlord, dynast, leader; king, queen, emperor, empress, prince, princess, czar, royal duke, regent, mogul, emir, sheikh, sultan, maharaja, raja.
– RELATED TERMS: regal.
▶ **adjective 1** *sovereign control* SUPREME, absolute, unlimited, unrestricted, boundless, ultimate, total, unconditional, full; principal, chief, dominant, predominant, ruling; royal, regal, monarchical. **2** *a sovereign state* INDEPENDENT, autonomous, self-governing, self-determining; non-aligned, free.

sovereignty ▶ **noun 1** *their sovereignty over the islands* JURISDICTION, rule, supremacy, dominion, power, ascendancy, suzerainty, hegemony, domination, authority, control, influence. **2** *the colony demanded full sovereignty* AUTONOMY, independence, self-government, self-rule, home rule, self-determination, freedom.

sow ▶ **verb 1** *sow the seeds in rows* PLANT, scatter, spread, disperse, strew, disseminate, distribute, broadcast; drill, seed. **2** *the new policy has sown confusion* CAUSE, bring about, occasion, create, lead to, produce, spread, engender, generate, prompt, initiate, precipitate, trigger, provoke; culminate in, entail, necessitate; foster, foment; *literary* beget.

spa ▶ **noun 1** *she spent her money at a luxury spa* HEALTH CLUB, health farm, watering place, beauty parlour. **2** *the healing spa waters* MINERAL SPRING, source; *literary* wellspring, fount.

space ▶ **noun 1** *there was not enough space* ROOM, capacity, area, volume, expanse, extent, scope, latitude, margin, leeway, play, clearance. **2** *green spaces in the city* AREA, expanse, stretch, sweep, tract.

3 *the space between the timbers* GAP, interval, opening, aperture, cavity, cranny, fissure, crack, interstice, lacuna. **4** *write your name in the appropriate space* BLANK, gap, box; place. **5** *a space of seven years* PERIOD, span, time, duration, stretch, course, interval. **6** *the first woman in space* OUTER SPACE, deep space; the universe, the galaxy, the solar system; infinity.
▶ verb *the chairs were spaced widely* POSITION, arrange, range, array, dispose, lay out, locate, situate, set, stand.

spaceman, spacewoman ▶ noun ASTRONAUT, cosmonaut, space traveller.

spaceship ▶ noun SPACECRAFT, space shuttle, rocket ship.

spacious ▶ adjective ROOMY, capacious, palatial, airy, sizable, generous, large, big, vast, immense; extensive, expansive, sweeping, rolling, rambling, open; *formal* commodious.
– OPPOSITES: cramped.

spadework ▶ noun GROUNDWORK, preliminary work, preliminaries, preparatory measures, preparations, planning, foundations; hard work, donkey work, labour, drudgery, toil; *informal* grind.

span ▶ noun **1** *a six-foot wing span* EXTENT, length, width, reach, stretch, spread, distance, range. **2** *the span of one working day* PERIOD, space, time, duration, course, interval.
▶ verb **1** *an arch spanned the stream* BRIDGE, cross, traverse, pass over. **2** *his career spanned twenty years* LAST, cover, extend, spread over, comprise.

spank ▶ verb SMACK, slap, hit, cuff; *informal* wallop, belt, whack, give someone a hiding.

spar ▶ verb QUARREL, argue, fight, disagree, differ, be at odds, be at variance, fall out, dispute, squabble, wrangle, bandy words, cross swords, lock horns, be at loggerheads; *informal* scrap, spat.

spare ▶ adjective **1** *a spare set of keys* EXTRA, supplementary, additional, second, other, alternative, alternate; emergency, reserve, backup, relief, fallback, substitute; fresh. **2** *they sold off the spare land* SURPLUS, superfluous, excessive, extra; redundant, unnecessary, inessential, unessential, unneeded, uncalled for, dispensable, disposable, expendable, unwanted; *informal* going begging. **3** *your spare time* FREE, leisure, own.
▶ verb **1** *sorry, I can't spare a quarter* AFFORD, do without, manage without, dispense with, part with, give, provide. **2** *they were spared by their captors* PARDON, let off, forgive, reprieve, release, free; leave uninjured, leave unhurt; be merciful to, show mercy to, have mercy on, be lenient to, have pity on.

sparing ▶ adjective THRIFTY, economical, frugal, canny, careful, prudent, cautious; mean, miserly, niggardly, parsimonious, close-fisted, penny-pinching, cheese-paring, ungenerous, close, grasping; *informal* stingy, cheap, tight-fisted, tight, mingy, money-grubbing.
– OPPOSITES: lavish.

spark ▶ noun **1** *a spark from the fire* (Nfld) flanker ♣. **2** *a spark of light* FLASH, glint, twinkle, flicker, flare, pinprick. **3** *not a spark of truth in the story* PARTICLE, iota, jot, whit, glimmer, atom, bit, trace, vestige, ounce, shred, crumb, grain, mite, hint, touch, suggestion, whisper, scintilla; *informal* smidgen, tad.
▶ verb *the trial sparked a furious debate* CAUSE, give rise to, lead to, occasion, bring about, start, initiate, precipitate, prompt, trigger (off), provoke, stimulate, stir up.

sparkle ▶ verb **1** *her earrings sparkled* GLITTER, glint, glisten, twinkle, flash, blink, wink, shimmer, shine, gleam; *literary* coruscate, glister. **2** *she sparkled as the hostess* BE LIVELY, be vivacious, be animated, be ebullient, be exuberant, be bubbly, be effervescent, be witty, be full of life.
▶ noun *the sparkle of the pool* GLITTER, glint, twinkle, flicker, shimmer, flash, shine, gleam; *literary* coruscation.

sparkling ▶ adjective **1** *sparkling wine* EFFERVESCENT, fizzy, carbonated, aerated, gassy, bubbly, frothy; spumante. **2** *a sparkling performance* BRILLIANT, dazzling, scintillating, exciting, exhilarating, stimulating, invigorating; vivacious, lively, vibrant, animated.
– OPPOSITES: still, dull.

sparse ▶ adjective SCANT, scanty, scattered, scarce, infrequent, few and far between; meagre, paltry, skimpy, limited, in short supply.
– OPPOSITES: abundant.

Spartan ▶ adjective AUSTERE, harsh, hard, frugal, stringent, rigorous, strict, stern, severe; ascetic, abstemious; bleak, joyless, grim, bare, stark, plain.
– OPPOSITES: luxurious.

spasm ▶ noun **1** *a muscle spasm* CONTRACTION, convulsion, cramp; twitch, jerk, tic, shudder, shiver, tremor. **2** *a spasm of coughing* FIT, paroxysm, attack, burst, bout, seizure, outburst, outbreak, access.

spasmodic ▶ adjective INTERMITTENT, fitful, irregular, sporadic, erratic, occasional, infrequent, scattered, patchy, isolated, periodic, periodical, on and off; *informal* herky-jerky.

spate ▶ noun SERIES, succession, run, cluster, string, rash, epidemic, outbreak, wave, flurry, rush, flood, deluge, torrent.

spatter ▶ verb SPLASH, bespatter, splatter, spray, sprinkle, shower, speck, speckle, fleck, mottle, blotch, mark, cover; *informal* splotch.

spawn ▶ verb GIVE RISE TO, bring about, occasion, generate, engender, originate; lead to, result in, effect, induce, initiate, start, set off, precipitate, trigger; breed, bear; *literary* beget.

speak ▶ verb **1** *she refused to speak about it* TALK, say anything/something; utter, state, declare, tell, voice, express, pronounce, articulate, enunciate, vocalize, verbalize. **2** *we spoke the other day* CONVERSE, have a conversation, talk, communicate, chat, pass the time of day, have a word, gossip; *informal* have a confab, chew the fat; natter, shoot the breeze; *formal* confabulate. **3** *the Minister spoke for two hours* GIVE A SPEECH, talk, lecture, hold forth, discourse, expound, expatiate, orate, sermonize, pontificate, declaim; *informal* spout, spiel, speechify, jaw, sound off. **4** *he was spoken of as a promising student* MENTION, talk about, discuss, refer to, remark on, allude to, describe. **5** *her expression spoke disbelief* INDICATE, show, display, register, reveal, betray, exhibit, manifest, express, convey, impart, bespeak, communicate, evidence; suggest, denote, reflect; *formal* evince. **6** *you must speak to him about his rudeness* REPRIMAND, rebuke, admonish, chastise, chide, upbraid, reprove, reproach, scold, remonstrate with, take to task, pull up; *informal* tell off, dress down, rap over the knuckles, come down on, tear a strip off, give someone what for; *formal* castigate.
■ **speak for 1** *she speaks for the CNIB* REPRESENT, act for, appear for, express the views of, be spokesperson for. **2** *I spoke for the motion* ADVOCATE, champion,

uphold, defend, support, promote, recommend, back, endorse, sponsor, espouse.

■ **speak out** SPEAK PUBLICLY, speak openly, speak frankly, speak one's mind, sound off, stand up and be counted.

■ **speak up** SPEAK LOUDLY, speak clearly, raise one's voice; shout, yell, bellow; *informal* holler.

speaker ▶ noun SPEECH-MAKER, lecturer, talker, speechifier, orator, declaimer, rhetorician; spokesperson, spokesman/woman, mouthpiece; reader, lector, commentator, broadcaster, narrator; *informal* tub-thumper, spieler; *historical* demagogue, rhetor.

spear ▶ noun JAVELIN, lance, assegai, harpoon, bayonet; gaff, leister; *historical* pike.

spearhead ▶ noun 1 *a Bronze Age spearhead* SPEAR TIP, spear point. 2 *the spearhead of the struggle against Fascism* LEADER(S), driving force; forefront, front-runner(s), front line, vanguard, van, cutting edge.
▶ verb *she spearheaded the campaign* LEAD, head, front; lead the way, be in the van, be in the vanguard.

special ▶ adjective 1 *a very special person* EXCEPTIONAL, unusual, singular, uncommon, notable, noteworthy, remarkable, outstanding, unique. 2 *our town's special character* DISTINCTIVE, distinct, individual, particular, characteristic, specific, peculiar, idiosyncratic. 3 *a special occasion* MOMENTOUS, significant, memorable, signal, important, historic, festive, gala, red-letter. 4 *a special tool for cutting tiles* SPECIFIC, particular, purpose-built, tailor-made, custom-built/made.
— OPPOSITES: ordinary, general.

specialist ▶ noun EXPERT, authority, pundit, professional; connoisseur; master, maestro, adept, virtuoso; *informal* pro, buff, ace, whiz, hotshot, maven.
— OPPOSITES: amateur.

specialty ▶ noun 1 *his specialty was watercolours* FORTE, strong point, strength, métier, strong suit, talent, skill, bent, gift, speciality; *informal* bag, thing, cup of tea. 2 *a specialty of the region* DELICACY, speciality, fine food/product, traditional food/product.

species ▶ noun TYPE, kind, sort; genus, family, order, breed, strain, variety, class, classification, category, set, bracket; style, manner, form, genre; generation, vintage.

specific ▶ adjective 1 *a specific purpose* PARTICULAR, specified, fixed, set, determined, distinct, definite; single, individual, peculiar, discrete, express, precise. 2 *I gave specific instructions* DETAILED, explicit, express, clear-cut, unequivocal, precise, exact, meticulous, strict, definite.
— OPPOSITES: general, vague.

specification ▶ noun 1 *clear specification of objectives* STATEMENT, identification, definition, description, setting out, framing, designation, detailing, enumeration; stipulation, prescription. 2 *a shelter built to their specifications* INSTRUCTIONS, guidelines, parameters, stipulations, requirements, conditions, provisions, restrictions, order; description, details; *informal* specs.

specify ▶ verb STATE, name, identify, define, describe, set out, frame, itemize, detail, list, spell out, enumerate, particularize, cite, instance; stipulate, prescribe.

specimen ▶ noun SAMPLE, example, instance, illustration, demonstration, exemplification; bit,

snippet; model, prototype, pattern, dummy, pilot, trial, taster, tester.

specious ▶ adjective MISLEADING, deceptive, false, fallacious, unsound, spurious, casuistic, sophistic.

speck ▶ noun 1 *a mere speck in the distance* DOT, pinprick, spot, fleck, speckle. 2 *a speck of dust* PARTICLE, grain, atom, molecule; bit, trace.

speckled ▶ adjective FLECKED, speckly, specked, freckled, freckly, spotted, spotty, dotted, mottled, dappled.

spectacle ▶ noun 1 *a spectacle fit for a monarch* DISPLAY, show, pageant, parade, performance, exhibition, extravaganza, spectacular. 2 *they were rather an odd spectacle* SIGHT, vision, scene, prospect, vista, picture. 3 *don't make a spectacle of yourself* EXHIBITION, laughingstock, fool, curiosity.

spectacles ▶ plural noun GLASSES, eyewear, eyeglasses; *informal* specs; bifocals.

spectacular ▶ adjective 1 *a spectacular victory* IMPRESSIVE, magnificent, splendid, dazzling, sensational, dramatic, remarkable, outstanding, memorable, unforgettable. 2 *a spectacular view* STRIKING, picturesque, eye-catching, breathtaking, arresting, glorious; *informal* out of this world.
— OPPOSITES: unimpressive, dull.

spectator ▶ noun WATCHER, viewer, observer, onlooker, looker-on, bystander, witness; commentator, reporter, monitor; *literary* beholder.
— OPPOSITES: participant.

spectral ▶ adjective GHOSTLY, phantom, wraithlike, shadowy, incorporeal, insubstantial, disembodied, unearthly, otherworldly; *informal* spooky.

spectre ▶ noun 1 *the spectres in the crypt* GHOST, phantom, apparition, spirit, wraith, shadow, presence; *informal* spook; *literary* phantasm, shade. 2 *the looming spectre of war* THREAT, menace, shadow, cloud; prospect; danger, peril, fear, dread.

spectrum ▶ noun RANGE, gamut, sweep, extent, scope, span; compass, orbit, ambit.

speculate ▶ verb 1 *they speculated about my private life* CONJECTURE, theorize, hypothesize, guess, surmise; think, wonder, muse. 2 *investors speculate on the stock market* GAMBLE, take a risk, venture, wager; invest, play the market.

speculative ▶ adjective 1 *any discussion is largely speculative* CONJECTURAL, suppositional, theoretical, hypothetical, putative, academic, notional, abstract; tentative, unproven, unfounded, groundless, unsubstantiated. 2 *a speculative investment* RISKY, hazardous, unsafe, uncertain, unpredictable; *informal* chancy, dicey, iffy.

speech ▶ noun 1 *he doesn't have the power of speech* SPEAKING, talking, verbal expression, verbal communication. 2 *her speech was slurred* DICTION, elocution, articulation, enunciation, pronunciation; utterance, words. 3 *an after-dinner speech* TALK, address, lecture, discourse, oration, disquisition, peroration, deliverance, presentation; sermon, homily; monologue, soliloquy; *informal* spiel. 4 *Spanish popular speech* LANGUAGE, tongue, parlance, idiom, dialect, vernacular, patois; *informal* lingo, patter, -speak, -ese.
— RELATED TERMS: lingual, oral, phono-, -phone, -phasia.

speechless ▶ adjective LOST FOR WORDS, at a loss (for words), dumbstruck, dumbfounded, bereft of speech, tongue-tied, inarticulate, mute, dumb,

voiceless, silent; *informal* mum.
— OPPOSITES: verbose.

speed ▶ noun **1** *the speed of their progress* RATE, pace, tempo, momentum. **2** *the speed with which they responded* RAPIDITY, swiftness, speediness, quickness, dispatch, promptness, immediacy, briskness, sharpness; haste, hurry, precipitateness; acceleration, velocity; *informal* lick, clip; *literary* celerity.
— RELATED TERMS: tacho-, tachy-.
▶ verb **1** *I sped home* HURRY, rush, dash, run, race, sprint, bolt, dart, gallop, career, charge, shoot, hurtle, career, hare, fly, zoom, scurry, scuttle, scamper, hasten; *informal* tear, belt, pelt, scoot, zip, zap, whip, hotfoot it, bomb, hightail it. **2** *he was caught speeding* DRIVE TOO FAST, exceed the speed limit. **3** *a holiday will speed his recovery* HASTEN, expedite, speed up, accelerate, advance, further, promote, boost, stimulate, aid, assist, facilitate.
— OPPOSITES: slow, hinder.
■ **speed up** HURRY UP, accelerate, go faster, get a move on, pick up speed, gather speed, gear up; *informal* get cracking, get moving, step on it, shake a leg.

speedily ▶ adverb RAPIDLY, swiftly, quickly, fast, post-haste, at the speed of light, at full tilt; promptly, immediately, briskly; hastily, hurriedly, precipitately; *informal* PDQ (pretty damn quick), hell for leather, at the double, like the wind, like (greased) lightning, lickety-split; *literary* apace.

speedy ▶ adjective **1** *a speedy reply* RAPID, swift, quick, fast; prompt, immediate, expeditious, express, brisk, sharp; whirlwind, lightning, meteoric; hasty, hurried, precipitate, breakneck, rushed; *informal* PDQ (pretty damn quick), snappy, quickie. **2** *a speedy little car* FAST, high-speed; *informal* nippy, zippy, peppy; *literary* fleet.
— OPPOSITES: slow.

spell¹ ▶ verb *the drought spelled disaster for them* SIGNAL, signify, mean, amount to, add up to, constitute; portend, augur, herald, bode, promise; involve; *literary* betoken, foretoken, forebode.
■ **spell something out** EXPLAIN, make clear, make plain, elucidate, clarify; specify, itemize, detail, enumerate, list, expound, particularize, catalogue.

spell² ▶ noun **1** *the witch recited a spell* INCANTATION, charm, conjuration, formula; (**spells**) magic, sorcery, witchcraft, hex, curse. **2** *he surrendered to his spell* INFLUENCE, (animal) magnetism, charisma, allure, lure, charm, attraction, enticement; magic, romance, mystique.
■ **cast a spell on** BEWITCH, enchant, entrance; curse, jinx, witch, hex.

spell³ ▶ noun **1** *a spell of dry weather* PERIOD, time, interval, season, stretch, run, course, streak, patch. **2** *a spell of dizziness* BOUT, fit, attack.

spellbinding ▶ adjective FASCINATING, enthralling, entrancing, bewitching, captivating, riveting, engrossing, gripping, absorbing, compelling, compulsive, mesmerizing, hypnotic; *informal* unputdownable.
— OPPOSITES: boring.

spellbound ▶ adjective ENTHRALLED, fascinated, rapt, riveted, transfixed, gripped, captivated, bewitched, enchanted, mesmerized, hypnotized; *informal* hooked.

spend ▶ verb **1** *she spent $185 on shoes* PAY OUT, dish out, expend, disburse; squander, waste, fritter away; lavish; *informal* fork out, lay out, shell out, cough up, drop, blow, splurge, pony up. **2** *the morning was spent gardening* PASS, occupy, fill, take up, while away. **3** *I've

spent hours on this essay* PUT IN, devote; waste. **4** *the storm had spent its force* USE UP, consume, exhaust, deplete, drain.

spendthrift ▶ noun *he is such a spendthrift* PROFLIGATE, prodigal, squanderer, waster; *informal* big spender.
— OPPOSITES: miser.
▶ adjective *his spendthrift father* PROFLIGATE, improvident, thriftless, wasteful, extravagant, prodigal.
— OPPOSITES: frugal.

spent ▶ adjective **1** *a spent force* USED UP, consumed, exhausted, finished, depleted, drained; *informal* burnt out. **2** *that's enough — I'm spent* EXHAUSTED, tired (out), weary, worn out, dog-tired, on one's last legs, drained, fatigued, ready to drop; *informal* done in, all in, dead on one's feet, dead beat, bushed, wiped out, frazzled, whacked, pooped, tuckered out.

spew ▶ verb **1** *factories spewed out yellow smoke* EMIT, discharge, eject, expel, belch out, pour out, spout, gush, spurt, disgorge. **2** (*informal*) *he wanted to spew*. See VOMIT verb sense 1.

sphere ▶ noun **1** *a glass sphere* GLOBE, ball, orb, spheroid, globule, round; bubble. **2** *our sphere of influence* AREA, field, compass, orbit; range, scope, extent. **3** *the sphere of foreign affairs* DOMAIN, realm, province, field, area, territory, arena, department.

spherical ▶ adjective ROUND, globular, globose, globoid, globe-shaped, spheroidal, spheric.

spic and span ▶ adjective NEAT, tidy, orderly, well-kept, shipshape, in apple-pie order; immaculate, uncluttered, trim, spruce; spotless.
— OPPOSITES: untidy.

spice ▶ noun **1** *the spices in curry powder* SEASONING, flavouring, condiment. *See* table. **2** *the risk added spice to their affair* EXCITEMENT, interest, colour, piquancy, zest; an edge; *informal* a kick; *literary* salt.
■ **spice something up** ENLIVEN, make more exciting, vitalize, perk up, put some life into, ginger up, galvanize, electrify, boost; *informal* pep up, jazz up, buck up.

Spices

allspice	ginseng
black pepper	grains of paradise
caraway seeds	juniper berries
cardamom	mace
cayenne pepper	mustard
celery salt	nutmeg
chili pepper	paprika
chili powder	pepper
cinnamon	peppercorn
cloves	saffron
coriander	star anise
cumin	turmeric
curcuma	white pepper
fennel seeds	curry powder
fenugreek	garam masala
five-spice powder	pickling spice
garlic powder	poultry seasoning
garlic salt	pumpkin pie spice
ginger	

spicy ▶ adjective **1** *a spicy casserole* HOT, peppery, piquant, picante; spiced, seasoned; strong, pungent. **2** *spicy stories* ENTERTAINING, colourful, lively, spirited, exciting, piquant, zesty; risqué, racy, scandalous, ribald, titillating, bawdy, naughty, salacious, dirty, smutty; *informal* raunchy, juicy, saucy.

— OPPOSITES: bland, boring.

spider ▶ noun. *See table.*

— RELATED TERMS: arachnoid.

Spiders and other Arachnids

black widow	spider mite
chigger	tarantula
daddy-long-legs	tick
deer tick	trap door spider
harvest mite	whip scorpion
mite	wolf spider
scorpion	wood tick
spider	

spiel ▶ noun (*informal*) SPEECH, patter, (sales) pitch, blurb, talk; monologue; rigmarole, story, saga.

spiffy ▶ adjective FASHIONABLE, well-dressed, elegant, trendy, stylish, chic, sharp, snazzy.

spike ▶ noun **1** *a metal spike* PRONG, barb, point; skewer, stake, spit; tine, pin; spur; *Mountaineering* piton. **2** *the spikes of a cactus* THORN, spine, prickle, bristle; *Zoology* spicule.
▶ verb **1** *she spiked an oyster* IMPALE, spear, skewer; pierce, penetrate, perforate, stab, stick, transfix; *literary* transpierce. **2** (*informal*) *his drink was spiked with drugs* ADULTERATE, contaminate, drug, lace; *informal* dope, doctor, cut.

spill ▶ verb **1** *Kevin spilled his drink* KNOCK OVER, tip over, upset, overturn. **2** *the bath water spilled on to the floor* OVERFLOW, flow, pour, run, slop, slosh, splash; leak, escape; *archaic* overbrim. **3** *students spilled out of the building* STREAM, pour, surge, swarm, flood, throng, crowd. **4** *the horse spilled his rider* UNSEAT, throw, dislodge, unhorse. **5** (*informal*) *he's spilling out his troubles to her* REVEAL, disclose, divulge, blurt out, babble, betray, tell; *informal* blab.
▶ noun **1** *an oil spill* SPILLAGE, leak, leakage, overflow, flood. **2** *she took a spill in the opening race* FALL, tumble; *informal* header, cropper, nosedive.
■ **spill the beans** (*informal*) REVEAL ALL, tell all, give the game away, talk; *informal* let the cat out of the bag, blab, come clean.

spin ▶ verb **1** *the bike wheels are spinning* REVOLVE, rotate, turn, go round, whirl, gyrate, circle. **2** *she spun round to face him* WHIRL, wheel, twirl, turn, swing, twist, swivel, pirouette, pivot. **3** *her head was spinning* REEL, whirl, go round, swim. **4** *she spun me a yarn* TELL, recount, relate, narrate; weave, concoct, invent, fabricate, make up.
— RELATED TERMS: rotary.
▶ noun **1** *a spin of the wheel* ROTATION, revolution, turn, whirl, twirl, gyration. **2** *a positive spin on the campaign* SLANT, angle, twist, bias. **3** *a spin in the car* TRIP, jaunt, outing, excursion, journey; drive, ride, run, turn, airing, joyride.
■ **spin something out** PROLONG, protract, draw out, drag out, string out, extend, carry on, continue; fill out, pad out.

spindle ▶ noun pivot, pin, rod, axle, capstan; axis.

spindly ▶ adjective **1** *he was pale and spindly* LANKY, thin, skinny, lean, spare, gangling, gangly, scrawny, bony, rangy, angular; *dated* spindle-shanked. **2** *spindly chairs* RICKETY, flimsy, wobbly, shaky.
— OPPOSITES: stocky.

spine ▶ noun **1** *he injured his spine* BACKBONE, spinal column, vertebral column; back; *technical* rachis. **2** *the spine of his philosophy* CORE, centre, cornerstone, foundation, basis. **3** *the spines of a porcupine* NEEDLE, quill, bristle, barb, spike, prickle; thorn; *technical* spicule.
— RELATED TERMS: vertebral.

spine-chilling ▶ adjective TERRIFYING, blood-curdling, petrifying, hair-raising, frightening, scaring, chilling, horrifying, fearsome; eerie, sinister, bone-chilling, ghostly; eldritch; *informal* scary, creepy, spooky.
— OPPOSITES: comforting, reassuring.

spineless ▶ adjective WEAK, weak-willed, weak-kneed, feeble, soft, ineffectual, irresolute, indecisive; COWARDLY, timid, timorous, fearful, faint-hearted, pusillanimous, craven, unmanly, namby-pamby, lily-livered, chicken-hearted; *informal* wimpish, wimpy, sissy, wussy, chicken, yellow, yellow-bellied, gutless.
— OPPOSITES: bold, brave, strong-willed.

spiny ▶ adjective PRICKLY, spiky, thorny, bristly, bristled, spiked, barbed, scratchy, sharp; *technical* spinose, spinous.

spiral ▶ adjective *a spiral column of smoke* COILED, helical, corkscrew, curling, winding, twisting, whorled; *technical* voluted, helicoid, helicoidal.
▶ noun *a spiral of smoke* COIL, helix, corkscrew, curl, twist, gyre, whorl, scroll; *technical* volute, volution.
▶ verb **1** *smoke spiralled up* COIL, wind, swirl, twist, wreathe, snake, gyrate; *literary* gyre. **2** *prices spiralled* SOAR, shoot up, rocket, increase rapidly, rise rapidly, escalate, climb; *informal* skyrocket, go through the roof. **3** *the economy is spiralling downward* DETERIORATE, decline, degenerate, worsen, get worse; *informal* go downhill, take a nosedive, go to pot, go to the dogs, hit the skids, go down the tubes.
— OPPOSITES: fall, improve.

spire ▶ noun STEEPLE, flèche.

spirit ▶ noun **1** *harmony between body and spirit* SOUL, psyche, (inner) self, inner being, inner man/woman, mind, ego, id; *Philosophy* pneuma. **2** *a spirit haunts the island* GHOST, phantom, spectre, apparition, wraith, presence; *informal* spook; *literary* shade. *See table.* **3** *that's the spirit* ATTITUDE, frame of mind, way of thinking, point of view, outlook, thoughts, ideas. **4** *she was in good spirits when I left* MOOD, frame of mind, state of mind, emotional state, humour, temper. **5** *team spirit* MORALE, esprit de corps. **6** *the spirit of the age* ETHOS, prevailing tendency, motivating force, essence, quintessence; atmosphere, mood, feeling, climate; attitudes, beliefs, principles, standards, ethics. **7** *his spirit never failed him* COURAGE, bravery, pluck, valour, strength of character, fortitude, backbone, mettle, stout-heartedness; determination, resolution, resolve, fight, grit; *informal* guts, spunk, sand, moxie. **8** *they played with great spirit* ENTHUSIASM, eagerness, keenness, liveliness, vivacity, vivaciousness, animation, energy, verve, vigour, dynamism, zest, dash, élan, panache, sparkle, exuberance, gusto, brio, pep, fervour, zeal, fire, passion; *informal* get-up-and-go. **9** *the spirit of the law* REAL/TRUE MEANING, true intention, essence, substance. **10** *he drinks spirits* STRONG LIQUOR/DRINK; *informal* hard stuff, firewater, hooch. *See tables at* ALCOHOL *and* COCKTAIL.
— OPPOSITES: body, flesh.
■ **spirit someone/something away** WHISK AWAY/OFF, vanish with, make off with, make someone/something disappear, run away with, abscond with,

carry off, steal someone/something away, abduct, kidnap, snatch, seize.

Spirits

angel	jinni
banshee	jumbie
bibe ♣(Nfld)	kachina
bogey	kelpie
bogeyman	kobold
brownie	manes
cacodemon	manitou
demon	nature spirit
devil	numen
dybbuk	phantom
eidolon	poltergeist
familiar spirit	shade
fiend	skookum ♣(BC)
genie	spectre
ghost	succubus
ghoul	sylph
hobgoblin	undine
imp	wraith
incubus	

spirited ▶ adjective LIVELY, vivacious, vibrant, full of life, vital, animated, high-spirited, sparkling, sprightly, energetic, active, vigorous, dynamic, dashing, enthusiastic, passionate; determined, resolute, purposeful; informal feisty, spunky, take-charge, gutsy, peppy.
– OPPOSITES: timid, apathetic, lifeless.

spiritless ▶ adjective APATHETIC, passive, unenthusiastic, lifeless, listless, weak, feeble, spineless, languid, bloodless, insipid, characterless, submissive, meek, irresolute, indecisive; lacklustre, flat, colourless, passionless, uninspired, wooden, dry, anemic, vapid, dull, boring, wishy-washy.
– OPPOSITES: spirited, lively.

spiritual ▶ adjective **1** your spiritual self NON-MATERIAL, incorporeal, intangible; inner, mental, psychological; transcendent, ethereal, otherworldly, mystic, mystical, metaphysical; rare extramundane. **2** spiritual writings RELIGIOUS, sacred, divine, holy, non-secular, church, ecclesiastical, devotional.
– OPPOSITES: physical, secular.

spit[1] ▶ verb **1** Cranston coughed and spat EXPECTORATE; informal hawk, hork, gob. **2** 'Go to hell,' she spat SNAP, say angrily, hiss. **3** the fat began to spit SIZZLE, hiss; crackle, sputter. **4** it began to spit RAIN LIGHTLY, drizzle, sprinkle.
▶ noun SPITTLE, saliva, sputum, slobber, dribble, gob.

spit[2] ▶ noun chicken cooked on a spit SKEWER, brochette, rotisserie.

spite ▶ noun he said it out of spite MALICE, malevolence, ill will, vindictiveness, vengefulness, revenge, malignity, evil intentions, animus, enmity; informal bitchiness, cattiness; literary maleficence.
– OPPOSITES: benevolence.
▶ verb he did it to spite me UPSET, hurt, make miserable, grieve, distress, wound, pain, torment, injure.
– OPPOSITES: please.
■ **in spite of** DESPITE, notwithstanding, regardless of, for all; undeterred by, in defiance of, in the face of; even though, although.

spiteful ▶ adjective MALICIOUS, malevolent, evil-intentioned, vindictive, vengeful, malign, mean, nasty, hurtful, mischievous, wounding, cruel,

unkind; informal bitchy, catty; literary malefic, maleficent.
– OPPOSITES: benevolent.

splash ▶ verb **1** splash your face with cool water SPRINKLE, spray, shower, splatter, slosh, slop, squirt; daub; wet. **2** his boots were splashed with mud SPATTER, bespatter, splatter, speck, speckle, blotch, smear, stain, mark; informal splotch. **3** waves splashed on the beach SWASH, wash, break, lap; dash, beat, lash, batter, crash, buffet; literary plash. **4** children splashed in the water PADDLE, wade, slosh; wallow; informal splosh. **5** the story was splashed across the front pages BLAZON, display, spread, plaster, trumpet, publicize; informal splatter.
▶ noun **1** a splash of fat on his shirt SPOT, blob, dab, daub, smudge, smear, speck, fleck; mark, stain; informal splotch. **2** a splash of soda water DROP, dash, bit, spot, soupçon, dribble, driblet. **3** a splash of colour PATCH, burst, streak.
■ **make a splash** (informal) CAUSE A SENSATION, cause a stir, attract attention, draw attention to oneself/ itself, get noticed, make an impression, make an impact.

splashy ▶ adjective OSTENTATIOUS, sensational, attention-grabbing, showy, eye-catching, flashy, glitzy.

spleen ▶ noun BAD TEMPER, bad mood, ill temper, ill humour, anger, wrath, vexation, annoyance, irritation, displeasure, dissatisfaction, resentment, rancour; spite, ill feeling, malice, maliciousness, bitterness, animosity, antipathy, hostility, malevolence, venom, gall, malignance, malignity, acrimony, bile, hatred, hate; literary ire, choler.
– OPPOSITES: good humour.

splendid ▶ adjective **1** splendid costumes MAGNIFICENT, sumptuous, grand, impressive, imposing, superb, spectacular, resplendent, opulent, luxurious, deluxe, rich, fine, costly, expensive, lavish, ornate, gorgeous, glorious, dazzling, elegant, regal, handsome, beautiful, stately, majestic, princely, noble, proud, palatial; informal plush, posh, swanky, spiffy, ritzy, splendiferous, swank; literary brave. **2** (informal) we had a splendid holiday EXCELLENT, wonderful, marvellous, superb, glorious, sublime, lovely, delightful, first-class, first-rate, blue-chip; informal super, great, amazing, fantastic, terrific, tremendous, phenomenal, sensational, heavenly, gorgeous, dreamy, grand, fabulous, fab, awesome, magic, ace, cool, mean, wicked, far out, A1, out of this world, killer; smashing, dandy, neat, divine, swell; archaic goodly.
– OPPOSITES: modest, awful.

splendour ▶ noun MAGNIFICENCE, sumptuousness, grandeur, impressiveness, resplendence, opulence, luxury, richness, fineness, lavishness, ornateness, glory, beauty, elegance; majesty, stateliness; informal ritziness, splendiferousness.
– OPPOSITES: ordinariness, simplicity, modesty.

splenetic ▶ adjective BAD-TEMPERED, ill-tempered, angry, cross, peevish, petulant, pettish, irritable, irascible, choleric, dyspeptic, testy, tetchy, snappish, waspish, crotchety, crabby, querulous, resentful, rancorous, bilious; SPITEFUL, malicious, ill-natured, hostile, acrimonious, sour, bitter, malevolent, malignant, malign; informal bitchy.
– OPPOSITES: good-humoured.

splice ▶ verb **1** the ropes are spliced together INTERWEAVE, braid, plait, entwine, intertwine, interlace, knit, mesh; Nautical marry. **2** we had to splice *the two sections* JOIN, attach, stick together, unite; blend, mix together.

splinter ▶ noun *a splinter of wood* SLIVER, shiver, chip, shard; fragment, piece, bit, shred; (**splinters**) matchwood, flinders.

▶ **verb** *the windshield splintered* SHATTER, break into tiny pieces, smash, smash into smithereens, fracture, split, crack, disintegrate, crumble.

split ▶ verb 1 *the axe split the wood* BREAK, chop, cut, hew, lop, cleave; snap, crack. **2** *the ice cracked and split* BREAK APART, fracture, rupture, fissure, snap, come apart, splinter. **3** *her dress was split* TEAR, rip, slash, slit; *literary* rend. **4** *the issue could split the party* DIVIDE, disunite, separate, sever; bisect, partition; *literary* tear asunder. **5** *they split the money between them* SHARE (OUT), divide (up), apportion, allocate, allot, distribute, dole out, parcel out, measure out; carve up, slice up; *informal* divvy up. **6** *the path split* FORK, divide, bifurcate, diverge, branch. **7** *they split up last year* BREAK UP, separate, part, part company, become estranged; divorce, get divorced. **8** (*informal*) *let's split.* See LEAVE[1] sense 1.
— RELATED TERMS: fissile, schizo-.
— OPPOSITES: mend, join, unite, pool, converge, get together, marry.
▶ **noun 1** *a split in the rock face* CRACK, fissure, cleft, crevice, break, fracture, breach. **2** *a split in the curtain* RIP, tear, cut, rent, slash, slit. **3** *a split in the governing party* DIVISION, rift, breach, schism, rupture, partition, separation, severance, scission, breakup. **4** *the acrimonious split with his wife* BREAKUP, split-up, separation, parting, estrangement, rift; divorce.
— OPPOSITES: marriage.
■ **split hairs** QUIBBLE, cavil, carp, niggle, chop logic; *informal* nitpick; *archaic* pettifog.

spoil ▶ verb 1 *too much sun spoils the complexion* MAR, damage, impair, blemish, disfigure, blight, flaw, deface, scar, injure, harm; ruin, destroy, wreck; be a blot on the landscape. **2** *rain spoiled my plans* RUIN, wreck, destroy, upset, undo, mess up, make a mess of, dash, sabotage, scotch, torpedo; *informal* foul up, louse up, muck up, screw up, put the kibosh on, scupper, scuttle, do for, throw a wrench in the works of, deep-six; *archaic* bring to naught. **3** *his sisters spoil him* OVERINDULGE, pamper, indulge, mollycoddle, cosset, coddle, baby, wait on hand and foot, kill with kindness; nanny. **4** *stockpiled food may spoil* GO BAD, go off, go rancid, turn, go sour, go mouldy, go rotten, rot, perish.
— OPPOSITES: improve, enhance, further, help, neglect, be strict with, keep.
■ **spoiling for** EAGER FOR, itching for, looking for, keen to have, after, bent on, longing for.

spoils ▶ plural noun 1 *the spoils of war* BOOTY, loot, stolen goods, plunder, ill-gotten gains, haul, pickings; *informal* swag, boodle. **2** *the spoils of office* BENEFITS, advantages, perks, prize; *formal* perquisites.

spoilsport ▶ noun KILLJOY, misery, damper; *informal* wet blanket, party-pooper.

spoken ▶ adjective *spoken communication* VERBAL, oral, vocal, viva voce, uttered, said, stated; unwritten; by word of mouth.
— OPPOSITES: non-verbal, written.
■ **spoken for 1** *the money is spoken for* RESERVED, set aside, claimed, owned, booked. **2** *Claudine is spoken for* ATTACHED, going out with someone, in a relationship; *informal* going steady, taken.

spokesman, spokeswoman ▶ noun

SPOKESPERSON, representative, agent, mouthpiece, voice, official; *informal* spin doctor, PR person.

sponge ▶ verb 1 *I'll sponge your face* WASH, clean, wipe, swab; mop, rinse, sluice, swill. **2** (*informal*) *he lived by sponging off others* SCROUNGE, be a parasite, beg; live off; *informal* freeload, cadge, bum, mooch.

sponger ▶ noun (*informal*) PARASITE, hanger-on, leech, scrounger, beggar; *informal* freeloader, cadger, bum, bloodsucker, mooch, moocher, bottom-feeder, schnorrer.

spongy ▶ adjective SOFT, squashy, cushioned, cushiony, compressible, yielding; springy, resilient, elastic; porous, absorbent, permeable; *technical* spongiform.
— OPPOSITES: hard, solid.

sponsor ▶ noun *the money came from sponsors* BACKER, patron, promoter, benefactor, benefactress, supporter, partner, contributor, subscriber, friend, guarantor, underwriter; *informal* angel.
▶ **verb** *a bank sponsored the event* FINANCE, put up the money for, fund, subsidize, back, promote, support, contribute to, be a patron of, guarantee, underwrite; *informal* foot the bill for, pick up the tab for, bankroll.

sponsorship ▶ noun BACKING, support, promotion, patronage, subsidy, funding, financing, aid, financial assistance.

spontaneous ▶ adjective 1 *a spontaneous display of affection* UNPLANNED, unpremeditated, unrehearsed, impulsive, impetuous, unstudied, impromptu, spur-of-the-moment, extempore, extemporaneous; unforced, voluntary, unconstrained, unprompted, unbidden, unsolicited; *informal* off-the-cuff. **2** *a spontaneous reaction to danger* REFLEX, automatic, mechanical, natural, knee-jerk, involuntary, unthinking, unconscious, instinctive, instinctual, visceral; *informal* gut. **3** *a spontaneous kind of person* NATURAL, uninhibited, relaxed, unselfconscious, unaffected, open, genuine, easy, free and easy; impulsive, impetuous.
— OPPOSITES: planned, calculated, conscious, voluntary, inhibited.

spontaneously ▶ adverb 1 *they applauded spontaneously* WITHOUT BEING ASKED, of one's own accord, voluntarily, on impulse, impulsively, on the spur of the moment, extempore, extemporaneously; *informal* off the cuff. **2** *he reacted spontaneously* WITHOUT THINKING, automatically, mechanically, unthinkingly, involuntarily, instinctively, naturally, by oneself/itself.

spooky ▶ adjective (*informal*) EERIE, sinister, ghostly, uncanny, weird, unearthly, mysterious; FRIGHTENING, spine-chilling, hair-raising; *informal* creepy, scary, spine-tingling.

spool ▶ noun REEL, bobbin.

sporadic ▶ adjective OCCASIONAL, infrequent, irregular, periodic, scattered, patchy, isolated, odd; intermittent, spasmodic, fitful, desultory, erratic, unpredictable.
— OPPOSITES: frequent, steady, continuous.

sport ▶ noun 1 *we did a lot of sports* (COMPETITIVE) GAME(S), physical recreation, physical activity, physical exercise, athletics; pastime. **2** (*dated*) *they were rogues out for a bit of sport* FUN, pleasure, enjoyment, entertainment, amusement, diversion.
▶ **verb** *he sported a beard* WEAR, have on, dress in; DISPLAY, exhibit, show off, flourish, parade, flaunt.

sporting ▶ adjective SPORTSMANLIKE, generous,

gentlemanly, considerate; fair, just, honourable, decent.
— OPPOSITES: dirty, unfair.

sporty ▶ adjective (*informal*) **1** *he's quite a sporty type* ATHLETIC, fit, active, energetic. **2** *a sporty outfit* STYLISH, smart, jaunty; CASUAL, informal; *informal* trendy, cool, snazzy, sassy, spiffy. **3** *a sporty car* FAST, speedy; *informal* nippy, zippy, peppy.
— OPPOSITES: unfit, lazy, formal, sloppy, slow.

spot ▶ noun **1** *a grease spot on the wall* MARK, patch, dot, fleck, smudge, smear, stain, blotch, blot, splash; *informal* splotch. **2** *a secluded spot* PLACE, location, site, position, point, situation, scene, setting, locale, locality, area, neighbourhood, region; venue; *technical* locus. **3** *social policy has a regular spot on the agenda* POSITION, place, slot, space. **4** (*informal*) *in a tight spot* PREDICAMENT, mess, difficulty, trouble, plight, corner, quandary, dilemma; *informal* fix, jam, hole, sticky situation, can of worms, pickle, scrape, hot water, Catch-22.
▶ verb **1** *she spotted him in his car* NOTICE, see, observe, note, discern, detect, perceive, make out, recognize, identify, locate; catch sight of, glimpse; *literary* behold, espy. **2** *her clothes were spotted with grease* STAIN, mark, fleck, speckle, smudge, streak, splash, spatter; *informal* splotch.
■ **on the spot** IMMEDIATELY, at once, straight away, right away, without delay, without hesitation, that instant, directly, there and then, then and there, forthwith, instantly, summarily, in short order; *archaic* straightway.

spot check ▶ noun *drivers stopped at random spot checks* checkpoint, roadblock, (*Ont.*) RIDE ✦, (*Alta.*) checkstop ✦.

spotless ▶ adjective **1** *the kitchen was spotless* PERFECTLY CLEAN, ultra-clean, pristine, immaculate, shining, shiny, gleaming, spic and span. **2** *a spotless reputation* UNBLEMISHED, unsullied, untarnished, untainted, unstained, pure, whiter than white, innocent, impeccable, blameless, irreproachable, above reproach; *informal* squeaky clean.
— OPPOSITES: dirty, tarnished, impure.

spotlight ▶ noun *she was constantly in the spotlight* PUBLIC EYE, glare of publicity, limelight, centre stage; focus of public/media attention.
▶ verb *this article spotlights the problem* FOCUS ATTENTION ON, highlight, point up, draw/call attention to, give prominence to, throw into relief, turn the spotlight on, bring to the fore.

spotted ▶ adjective **1** *the spotted leaves* MOTTLED, dappled, speckled, flecked, freckled, freckly, dotted, stippled, brindle(d); *informal* splotchy. **2** *a black-and-white spotted dress* POLKA-DOT, spotty, dotted.
— OPPOSITES: plain.

spotty ▶ adjective *a spotty dog* SPOTTED, mottled, speckled, speckly, flecked, specked, stippled; *informal* splotchy.

spouse ▶ noun (LIFE) PARTNER, mate, consort; *informal* better half, other half. *See also* HUSBAND, WIFE.

spout ▶ verb **1** *lava was spouting from the crater* SPURT, gush, spew, erupt, shoot, squirt, spray; disgorge, discharge, emit, belch forth. **2** *he spouts on about foreign affairs* HOLD FORTH, sound off, go on, talk at length, expatiate; *informal* mouth off, speechify, spiel.
▶ noun *a can with a spout* NOZZLE, lip.

sprawl ▶ verb **1** *he sprawled on a sofa* STRETCH OUT, lounge, loll, lie, recline, drape oneself, slump, flop, slouch. **2** *the town sprawled ahead of them* SPREAD,

stretch, extend, be strung out, be scattered, straggle, spill.

spray¹ ▶ noun **1** *a spray of water* SHOWER, sprinkling, sprinkle, jet, mist, drizzle; spume, spindrift; foam, froth. **2** *a perfume spray* ATOMIZER, vaporizer, aerosol, sprinkler; nebulizer.
▶ verb **1** *water was sprayed around* SPRINKLE, shower, spatter, scatter, disperse, diffuse; mist; douche; *literary* besprinkle. **2** *water sprayed into the air* SPOUT, jet, gush, spurt, shoot, squirt.

spray² ▶ noun **1** *a spray of holly* SPRIG, twig. **2** *a spray of flowers* BOUQUET, bunch, posy, nosegay; corsage.

spread ▶ verb **1** *he spread the map out* LAY OUT, open out, unfurl, unroll, roll out; straighten out, fan out; stretch out, extend; *literary* outspread. **2** *the landscape spread out below* EXTEND, stretch, open out, be displayed, be exhibited, be on show; sprawl. **3** *papers were spread all over his desk* SCATTER, strew, disperse, distribute. **4** *he's been spreading rumours* DISSEMINATE, circulate, pass on, put about, communicate, diffuse, make public, make known, purvey, broadcast, publicize, propagate, promulgate; repeat; *literary* bruit about/abroad. **5** *she spread cold cream on her face* SMEAR, daub, plaster, slather, lather, apply, put; smooth, rub. **6** *he spread the toast with butter* COVER, coat, layer, daub, smother; butter.
— OPPOSITES: fold up, suppress.
▶ noun **1** *the spread of learning* EXPANSION, proliferation, extension, growth; dissemination, diffusion, transmission, propagation. **2** *a spread of six feet* SPAN, width, extent, stretch, reach. **3** *the immense spread of the heavens* EXPANSE, area, sweep, stretch. **4** *a wide spread of subjects* RANGE, span, spectrum, sweep; variety. **5** (*informal*) *the caterers laid on a huge spread* LARGE/ELABORATE MEAL, feast, banquet; *informal* blowout, nosh.

spree ▶ noun BINGE, bout, orgy, splurge, session.

sprig ▶ noun SMALL STEM, spray, twig.

sprightly ▶ adjective SPRY, lively, agile, nimble, energetic, active, full of energy, vigorous, spirited, animated, vivacious, frisky; *informal* full of vim and vigour.
— OPPOSITES: doddery, lethargic.

spring ▶ verb **1** *the cat sprang off her lap* LEAP, jump, bound, vault, hop. **2** *the branch sprang back* FLY, whip, flick, whisk, kick, bounce. **3** *all art springs from feelings* ORIGINATE, derive, arise, stem, emanate, proceed, issue, evolve, come. **4** *fifty men sprang from nowhere* APPEAR SUDDENLY, appear unexpectedly, materialize, pop up, shoot up, sprout, develop quickly; proliferate, mushroom. **5** *he sprang the truth on me* ANNOUNCE SUDDENLY/UNEXPECTEDLY, reveal suddenly/unexpectedly, surprise someone with.
▶ noun **1** *with a sudden spring he leapt on to the table* LEAP, jump, bound, vault, hop; pounce. **2** *the mattress has lost its spring* SPRINGINESS, bounciness, bounce, resilience, elasticity, flexibility, stretch, stretchiness, give. **3** *there was a spring in his step* BUOYANCY, bounce, energy, liveliness, jauntiness, sprightliness, confidence. **4** *a mineral spring* SOURCE, geyser; *literary* wellspring, fount. **5** *the spring from which all her emotions poured* ORIGIN, source, fountainhead, root, roots, basis; *informal* ground zero.
— RELATED TERMS: vernal.

springy ▶ adjective ELASTIC, stretchy, stretchable, tensile; flexible, pliant, pliable, whippy; bouncy, resilient, spongy.
— OPPOSITES: rigid, squashy.

sprinkle ▶ verb **1** *he sprinkled water over the towel*

SPLASH, trickle, spray, shower; spatter. **2** *sprinkle sesame seeds over the top* SCATTER, strew; drizzle, pepper. **3** *sprinkle the cake with icing sugar* DREDGE, dust. **4** *the sky was sprinkled with stars* DOT, stipple, stud, fleck, speckle, spot, pepper; scatter, cover.

sprinkling ▶ noun **1** *a sprinkling of nutmeg* SCATTERING, sprinkle, scatter, dusting; pinch, dash. **2** *mainly women, but a sprinkling of men* FEW, one or two, couple, handful, small number, trickle, scattering.

sprint ▶ verb RUN, race, dart, rush, dash, hasten, hurry, scurry, scamper, hare, bolt, fly, gallop, career, charge, shoot, hurtle, speed, zoom, go like lightning, go hell for leather, go like the wind; jog, trot; *informal* tear, pelt, scoot, hotfoot it, belt, zip, whip, bomb, hightail it, barrel.
– OPPOSITES: walk.

sprite ▶ noun FAIRY, elf, pixie, imp, brownie, puck, peri, leprechaun; nymph, sylph, naiad.

sprout ▶ verb **1** *the weeds begin to sprout* GERMINATE, put/send out shoots, bud, burgeon. **2** *he had sprouted a beard* GROW, develop, put/send out. **3** *parsley sprouted from the pot* SPRING UP, shoot up, come up, grow, burgeon, develop, appear.

spruce ▶ adjective *the Captain looked very spruce* NEAT, well-groomed, well-turned-out, well-dressed, smart, trim, dapper, elegant, chic; *informal* natty, snazzy, spiffy.
– OPPOSITES: untidy.
▶ verb **1** *the cottage had been spruced up* SMARTEN, tidy, neaten, put in order, clean, upgrade, renovate; *informal* do up, gussy up. **2** *Sarah had spruced herself up* GROOM, tidy, smarten, preen, primp; *informal* titivate, doll up, tart up.

spry ▶ adjective SPRIGHTLY, lively, agile, nimble, energetic, active, full of energy, full of vim and vigour, vigorous, spirited, animated, vivacious, frisky, peppy.
– OPPOSITES: doddery, lethargic.

spume ▶ noun FOAM, froth, surf, spindrift, bubbles.

spunk ▶ noun (*informal*) COURAGE, bravery, valour, nerve, confidence, daring, audacity, pluck, spirit, grit, mettle, spine, backbone; *informal* guts, gumption, moxie; *humorous* derring-do.

spur ▶ noun **1** *competition can be a spur* STIMULUS, incentive, encouragement, inducement, impetus, prod, motivation, inspiration, catalyst, springboard; *informal* kick up the backside, shot in the arm. **2** *a spur of bone* PROJECTION, spike, point; *technical* process.
– OPPOSITES: disincentive, discouragement.
▶ verb *the thought spurred him into action* STIMULATE, encourage, prompt, propel, prod, induce, impel, motivate, move, galvanize, inspire, incentivize, urge, drive, egg on, stir; incite, goad, provoke, prick, sting, light a fire under.
– OPPOSITES: discourage.
■ **on the spur of the moment** IMPULSIVELY, on impulse, impetuously, without thinking, without premeditation, unpremeditatedly, impromptu, extempore, spontaneously; *informal* off the cuff.

spurious ▶ adjective BOGUS, fake, false, counterfeit, forged, fraudulent, sham, artificial, imitation, simulated, feigned, deceptive, specious; *informal* phony, pretend.
– OPPOSITES: genuine.

spurn ▶ verb REJECT, rebuff, scorn, turn down, treat with contempt, disdain, look down one's nose at, despise; snub, slight, jilt, dismiss, brush off, turn one's back on; give someone the cold shoulder,

cold-shoulder; *informal* turn one's nose up at, give someone the brush-off, kick in the teeth, give someone the bum's rush.
– OPPOSITES: welcome, accept.

spurt ▶ verb *water spurted from the tap* SQUIRT, shoot, jet, erupt, gush, pour, stream, pump, surge, spew, course, well, spring, burst; disgorge, discharge, emit, belch forth, expel, eject.
▶ noun **1** *a spurt of water* SQUIRT, jet, spout, gush, stream, rush, surge, flood, cascade, torrent. **2** *a spurt of courage* BURST, fit, bout, rush, spate, surge, attack, outburst, blaze. **3** *the sprinter put on a spurt* BURST OF SPEED, turn of speed, sprint, rush, burst of energy.

spy ▶ noun *a foreign spy* SECRET AGENT, intelligence agent, double agent, undercover agent, counterspy, mole, sleeper, plant, scout; *informal* snooper, spook; *archaic* intelligencer.
▶ verb **1** *she spied for the West* BE A SPY, gather intelligence, work for the secret service; *informal* snoop. **2** *investigators spied on them* OBSERVE FURTIVELY, keep under surveillance/observation, watch, keep a watch on, keep an eye on. **3** *she spied a coffee shop* NOTICE, observe, see, spot, sight, catch sight of, glimpse, make out, discern, detect; *informal* clap/lay/set eyes on; *literary* espy, behold, descry.

spying ▶ noun ESPIONAGE, intelligence gathering, surveillance, infiltration, undercover work, cloak-and-dagger activities.

squabble ▶ noun *there was a squabble over which way they should go* QUARREL, disagreement, row, argument, contretemps, falling-out, dispute, clash, blow-up, altercation, shouting match, exchange, war of words; *informal* tiff, set-to, run-in, slanging match, shindig, shindy, spat, scrap, dust-up, rhubarb.
▶ verb *the boys were squabbling over a ball* QUARREL, row, argue, bicker, fall out, disagree, have words, dispute, spar, cross swords, lock horns, be at loggerheads; *informal* scrap.

squad ▶ noun **1** *an assassination squad* TEAM, crew, gang, band, cell, body, mob, outfit, force. **2** *a firing squad* DETACHMENT, detail, unit, platoon, battery, troop, patrol, squadron, cadre, commando.

squalid ▶ adjective **1** *a squalid prison* DIRTY, filthy, grubby, grimy, mucky, slummy, foul, vile, poor, sorry, wretched, miserable, mean, seedy, shabby, sordid, insalubrious, NEGLECTED, uncared-for, broken-down, run-down, down-at-the-heel, depressed, dilapidated, ramshackle, tumbledown, gone to rack and ruin, crumbling, decaying; *informal* scruffy, crummy, ratty, flea-bitten, grotty, shacky. **2** *a squalid deal with the opposition* IMPROPER, sordid, unseemly, unsavoury, sleazy, seedy, seamy, shoddy, cheap, base, low, corrupt, dishonest, dishonourable, disreputable, despicable, discreditable, disgraceful, contemptible, shameful, underhanded; *informal* sleazoid.
– OPPOSITES: clean, pleasant, smart, upmarket, proper, decent.

squall ▶ noun GUST, storm, blast, flurry, shower, gale, blow, rush.

squally ▶ adjective STORMY, gusty, gusting, blustery, blustering, windy, blowy; wild, tempestuous, rough.

squalor ▶ noun DIRT, filth, grubbiness, grime, muck, foulness, vileness, poverty, wretchedness, meanness, seediness, shabbiness, sordidness, sleaziness, NEGLECT, decay, dilapidation; *informal* scruffiness, crumminess, grunge, rattiness, grottiness.
– OPPOSITES: cleanliness, pleasantness, smartness.

squander ▶ verb WASTE, misspend, misuse, throw away, fritter away, spend recklessly, spend unwisely, spend like water; *informal* blow, go through, splurge, drop, pour down the drain.
– OPPOSITES: manage, make good use of, save.

square ▶ noun **1** *a shop in the square* MARKET SQUARE, marketplace, plaza, piazza. **2** *(informal) you're such a square!* (OLD) FOGEY, conservative, traditionalist, conformist, bourgeois, fossil; *informal* stick-in-the-mud, fuddy-duddy, prig, stuffed shirt.
– OPPOSITES: trendy.
▶ adjective **1** *a square table* QUADRILATERAL, rectangular, oblong, right-angled, at right angles, perpendicular; straight, level, parallel, horizontal, upright, vertical, true, plane. **2** *the sides were square at halftime* LEVEL, even, drawn, equal, tied; neck and neck, nip and tuck, side by side, evenly matched; *informal* even-steven(s). **3** *I'm going to be square with you* FAIR, honest, just, equitable, straight, true, upright, above board, ethical, decent, proper; *informal* on the level. **4** *(informal) don't be square!* OLD-FASHIONED, behind the times, out of date, conservative, traditionalist, conventional, fit, conformist, bourgeois, straitlaced, fogeyish, stuffy; *informal* stick-in-the-mud, fuddy-duddy.
– OPPOSITES: crooked, uneven, underhanded, trendy.
▶ verb **1** *the theory does not square with the data* AGREE, tally, be in agreement, be consistent, match up, correspond, fit, coincide, accord, conform, be compatible. **2** *his goal squared the match 1–1* LEVEL, even, make equal. **3** *would you square up the bill?* PAY, settle, discharge, clear, meet. **4** *(informal) they tried to square the press* BRIBE, buy off, buy, corrupt, suborn; *informal* grease someone's palm. **5** *Bob squared things with his boss* RESOLVE, sort out, settle, clear up, work out, iron out, smooth over, straighten out, deal with, put right, set right, put to rights, rectify, remedy; *informal* patch up.

squash ▶ verb **1** *the fruit got squashed* CRUSH, squeeze, flatten, compress, press, smash, distort, pound, trample, stamp on; pulp, mash, cream, liquidize, beat, pulverize; *informal* squish, squoosh. **2** *she squashed her clothes inside the bag* FORCE, ram, thrust, push, cram, jam, stuff, pack, compress, squeeze, wedge, press. **3** *the proposal was immediately squashed* REJECT, block, cancel, scotch, frustrate, thwart, suppress, put a stop to, nip in the bud, put the lid on; *informal* put paid to, put the kibosh on, stymie, scupper, scuttle, deep-six.
▶ noun acorn squash, buttercup squash, butternut squash, crookneck squash, Hubbard squash, pepper squash ✤, scallop squash, spaghetti squash, summer squash, winter squash, zucchini, pumpkin, (vegetable) marrow.

squashy ▶ adjective **1** *a squashy pillow* SPRINGY, resilient, spongy, soft, pliant, pliable, yielding, elastic, cushiony, compressible. **2** *squashy pears* MUSHY, pulpy, pappy, slushy, squelchy, squishy, oozy, doughy, soft.
– OPPOSITES: firm, hard.

squat ▶ verb **1** *I was squatting on the floor* CROUCH (DOWN), hunker (down), sit on one's haunches, sit on one's heels. **2** *they are squatting on private land* OCCUPY ILLEGALLY, set up residence, dwell, settle, live.
▶ adjective *he was muscular and squat* STOCKY, thickset, dumpy, stubby, stumpy, short, small.
▶ noun **1** *an overcrowded squat* PROPERTY, dwelling; slum, hovel. **2** *they gave me squat.* See DIDDLY-SQUAT.

squawk ▶ verb & noun *a pheasant squawked | the gull gave a squawk* SCREECH, squeal, shriek, scream, croak, crow, caw, cluck, cackle, hoot, cry, call.

squeak ▶ noun & verb **1** *the vole's dying squeak | the rat squeaked* PEEP, cheep, pipe, piping, squeal, tweet, yelp, whimper. **2** *the squeak of the hinge | the hinges of the gate squeaked* SCREECH, creak, scrape, grate, rasp, jar, groan.

squeaker ▶ noun NAIL-BITER, tight game, close game.

squeal ▶ noun *the harsh squeal of a fox* SCREECH, scream, shriek, squawk.
▶ verb **1** *a dog squealed* SCREECH, scream, shriek, squawk. **2** *the bookies only squealed because we beat them* COMPLAIN, protest, object, grouse, grumble, whine, wail, carp, squawk; *informal* kick up a fuss, gripe, grouch, bellyache, moan, bitch, beef, whinge. **3** *(informal) he squealed on the rest of the gang to the police* INFORM, tell tales, sneak; report, give away, be disloyal, sell out, stab in the back; *informal* rat, rat out, peach, snitch, put the finger on, finger, sell down the river.

squeamish ▶ adjective **1** *I'm too squeamish to gut fish* EASILY NAUSEATED, nervous; **(be squeamish about)** BE PUT OFF BY, cannot stand the sight of, —— makes one feel sick. **2** *less squeamish nations will sell them arms* SCRUPULOUS, principled, fastidious, particular, punctilious, honourable, upright, upstanding, high-minded, righteous, right-minded, moral, ethical.

squeeze ▶ verb **1** *I squeezed the bottle* COMPRESS, press, crush, squash, pinch, nip, grasp, grip, clutch, flatten. **2** *squeeze the juice from both oranges* EXTRACT, press, force, express. **3** *Sally squeezed her feet into the sandals* FORCE, thrust, cram, ram, jam, stuff, pack, wedge, press, squash. **4** *we all squeezed into Steve's van* CROWD, crush, cram, pack, jam, squash, wedge oneself, shove, push, force one's way. **5** *he would squeeze more money out of Bill* EXTORT, force, extract, wrest, wring, milk; *informal* bleed someone of something.
▶ noun **1** *he gave her hand a squeeze* PRESS, pinch, nip; grasp, grip, clutch, hug, clasp; compression. **2** *it was a tight squeeze in the tiny hall* CRUSH, jam, squash, press, huddle; congestion. **3** *a squeeze of lemon juice* FEW DROPS, dash, splash, dribble, trickle, spot, hint, touch.

squiggle ▶ noun WAVY LINE, doodle.
▶ verb SCRAWL, scribble.

squint ▶ verb **1** *the sun made them squint* SCREW UP ONE'S EYES, narrow one's eyes, peer, blink. **2** *he has squinted from birth* BE CROSS-EYED, have a squint, suffer from strabismus.
▶ noun **1** *(informal) we must have another squint at his record card* LOOK, glance, peep, peek, glimpse; view, examination, study, inspection, scan, sight; *informal* eyeful, gander, look-see, once-over. **2** *does he have a squint?* CROSS-EYES, strabismus.

squire ▶ noun **1** *the squire of the village* LANDOWNER, landholder, landlord, lord of the manor, country gentleman. **2** *(historical) his squire carried a banner* ATTENDANT, courtier, equerry, aide, steward, page boy.

squirm ▶ verb **1** *I tried to squirm away* WRIGGLE, wiggle, writhe, twist, slide, slither, turn, shift, fidget, jiggle, twitch, thresh, flounder, flail, toss and turn. **2** *he squirmed as everyone laughed* WINCE, shudder, feel embarrassed, feel ashamed.

squirrel ▶ noun. See table at RODENT.
– RELATED TERMS: sciurine.
■ **squirrel something away** SAVE, put aside, put

by, lay by, set aside, lay aside, keep in reserve, stockpile, accumulate, stock up with/on, hoard; *informal* salt away, stash away.

squirt ▶ verb 1 *a jet of ink squirted out of the tube* SPURT, shoot, spray, fountain, jet, erupt; gush, rush, pump, surge, stream, spew, well, spring, burst, issue, emanate; emit, belch forth, expel, eject. **2** *she squirted me with scent* SPLASH, wet, spray, shower, spatter, splatter, sprinkle; *literary* besprinkle.
▶ **noun 1** *a squirt of water* SPURT, jet, spray, fountain, gush, stream, surge. **2** *(informal) he was just a little squirt* IMPUDENT PERSON, insignificant person, gnat, insect; *informal* pipsqueak, whippersnapper, picayune.

stab ▶ verb 1 *the soldier stabbed the civilian in the stomach* KNIFE, run through, skewer, spear, bayonet, gore, spike, stick, impale, transfix, pierce, prick, puncture; *literary* transpierce. **2** *she stabbed at the earth with a fork* LUNGE, thrust, jab, poke, prod, dig.
▶ **noun 1** *a stab in the leg* KNIFE WOUND, puncture, incision, prick, cut, perforation. **2** *they made stabs into the air* LUNGE, thrust, jab, poke, prod, dig, punch. **3** *a stab of pain* TWINGE, pang, throb, spasm, cramp, dart, prick, flash, thrill. **4** *(informal) he took a stab at writing* ATTEMPT, try, effort, endeavour; guess; *informal* go, shot, crack, bash, whack; *formal* essay.
■ **stab someone in the back** BETRAY, be disloyal to, be unfaithful to, desert, break one's promise to, double-cross, break faith with, sell out, play false, inform on/against; *informal* tell on, sell down the river, squeal on, peach on, rat out, finger.

stability ▶ noun 1 *the stability of play equipment* FIRMNESS, solidity, steadiness, strength, security, safety. **2** *his mental stability* BALANCE OF MIND, mental health, sanity, normality, soundness, rationality, reason, sense. **3** *the stability of their relationship* STEADINESS, firmness, solidity, strength, durability, lasting nature, enduring nature, permanence, changelessness, invariability, immutability, indestructibility, reliability, dependability.

stable ▶ adjective 1 *a stable tent* FIRM, solid, steady, secure, fixed, fast, safe, moored, anchored, stuck down, immovable. **2** *a stable person* WELL-BALANCED, of sound mind, compos mentis, sane, normal, right in the head, rational, steady, reasonable, sensible, sober, down-to-earth, matter-of-fact, having both one's feet on the ground; *informal* all there. **3** *a stable relationship* SECURE, solid, strong, steady, firm, sure, steadfast, unwavering, unvarying, unfaltering, unfluctuating; established, abiding, durable, enduring, lasting, permanent, reliable, dependable.
— OPPOSITES: loose, wobbly, unbalanced, rocky, lasting, changeable.

stack ▶ noun 1 *a stack of boxes* HEAP, pile, mound, mountain, pyramid, tower. **2** *a stack of hay* HAYSTACK, rick, hayrick, stook, mow, shock, coil ♣, haycock; *dated* cock. **3** *(informal) a stack of money. See* LOT *noun sense 1.* **4** CHIMNEY, smokestack, funnel, exhaust pipe.
— OPPOSITES: few, little.
▶ **verb 1** *Leo was stacking plates* HEAP (UP), pile (up), make a heap/pile/stack of; assemble, put together, collect, hoard, store, stockpile. **2** *they stacked the shelves* LOAD, fill (up), lade, pack, charge, stuff, cram; stock.
— OPPOSITES: empty.

stadium ▶ noun ARENA, field, ground, pitch; bowl, amphitheatre, coliseum, ring, dome, manège; track, course, racetrack, racecourse, raceway, speedway, velodrome, sportsplex.

staff ▶ noun 1 *there is a reluctance to take on new staff* EMPLOYEES, workers, workforce, personnel, human

resources, manpower, labour. **2** *he carried a wooden staff* STICK, stave, pole, crook. **3** *a staff of office* ROD, tipstaff, cane, mace, wand, sceptre, crozier, verge; *Greek Mythology* caduceus.
▶ **verb** *the centre is staffed by teachers* MAN, people, crew, work, operate, occupy.

stage ▶ noun 1 *this stage of the development* PHASE, period, juncture, step, point, time, moment, instant, level. **2** *the last stage of the race* PART, section, portion, stretch, leg, lap, circuit. **3** *a theatre stage* PLATFORM, dais, stand, grandstand, staging, apron, rostrum, podium; bandstand, bandshell; catwalk. **4** *she has written for the stage* THEATRE, drama, dramatics, dramatic art, thespianism; *informal* the boards. **5** *the political stage* SCENE, setting; context, frame, sphere, field, realm, arena, backdrop; affairs.
▶ **verb 1** *they staged two plays* PUT ON, put before the public, present, produce, mount, direct; perform, act, give. **2** *workers staged a protest* ORGANIZE, arrange, coordinate, lay on, put together, get together, set up; orchestrate, choreograph, mastermind, engineer; take part in, participate in, join in.

stagger ▶ verb 1 *he staggered to the door* LURCH, walk unsteadily, reel, sway, teeter, totter, stumble, wobble. **2** *I was absolutely staggered* AMAZE, astound, astonish, surprise, startle, stun, confound, dumbfound, stupefy, daze, take aback, leave open-mouthed, leave aghast; *informal* flabbergast, bowl over. **3** *meetings are staggered throughout the day* SPREAD (OUT), space (out), time at intervals.

stagnant ▶ adjective 1 *stagnant water* STILL, motionless, static, stationary, standing, dead, slack; FOUL, stale, putrid, smelly. **2** *a stagnant economy* INACTIVE, sluggish, slow-moving, lethargic, static, flat, depressed, declining, moribund, dying, dead, dormant.
— OPPOSITES: flowing, fresh, active, vibrant.

stagnate ▶ verb 1 *obstructions allow water to stagnate* STOP FLOWING, become stagnant, become trapped; stand; become foul, become stale; fester, putrefy. **2** *exports stagnated* LANGUISH, decline, deteriorate, fall, become stagnant, do nothing, stand still, tread water, be sluggish.
— OPPOSITES: flow, rise, boom.

staid ▶ adjective SEDATE, respectable, quiet, serious, serious-minded, steady, conventional, traditional, unadventurous, unenterprising, set in one's ways, sober, proper, decorous, formal, stuffy, stiff, priggish; *informal* starchy, buttoned-down, stick-in-the-mud.
— OPPOSITES: frivolous, daring, informal.

stain ▶ verb 1 *her clothing was stained with blood* DISCOLOUR, blemish, soil, mark, muddy, spot, spatter, splatter, smear, splash, smudge, blotch, blacken; *literary* imbrue. **2** *the report stained his reputation* DAMAGE, injure, harm, sully, blacken, tarnish, taint, smear, bring discredit to, dishonour, drag through the mud; *literary* besmirch. **3** *the wood was stained* COLOUR, tint, dye, tinge, pigment, colour-wash.
▶ **noun 1** *a mud stain* MARK, spot, spatter, splatter, blotch, smudge, smear. **2** *a stain on his character* BLEMISH, injury, taint, blot, smear, discredit, dishonour; damage. **3** *dark wood stain* TINT, colour, dye, tinge, pigment, colourant, colour wash.

stake¹ ▶ noun *a stake in the ground* POST, pole, stick, spike, upright, support, prop, strut, pale, paling, picket, pile, piling, cane.
▶ **verb 1** *the plants have to be staked* PROP UP, tie up, tether, support, hold up, brace, truss. **2** *he staked his*

claim ASSERT, declare, proclaim, state, make, lay, put in.

■ **stake something out 1** *builders staked out the plot* MARK OFF/OUT, demarcate, measure out, delimit, fence off, section off, close off, shut off, cordon off. **2** *(informal) the police staked out his apartment* OBSERVE, watch, keep an eye on, keep under observation, keep watch on, monitor, keep under surveillance, surveil; *informal* keep tabs on, keep a tab on, case.

stake² ▶ noun **1** *playing dice for high stakes* BET, wager, ante. **2** *they are racing for record stakes* PRIZE MONEY, purse, pot, winnings. **3** *low down in the popularity stakes* COMPETITION, contest, battle, challenge, rivalry, race, running, struggle, scramble. **4** *a 40-per-cent stake in the business* SHARE, interest, ownership, involvement.
▶ verb *he staked all his week's pay* BET, wager, lay, put on, gamble, chance, venture, risk, hazard.

stale ▶ adjective **1** *stale food* OLD, past its best, off, dry, hard, musty, rancid. **2** *stale air* STUFFY, close, musty, fusty, stagnant, frowzy. **3** *stale beer* FLAT, turned, spoiled, off, insipid, tasteless. **4** *stale jokes* HACKNEYED, tired, worn out, overworked, threadbare, warmed-up, banal, trite, clichéd, platitudinous, unoriginal, unimaginative, uninspired, flat; out of date, outdated, outmoded, passé, archaic, obsolete; warmed-over; *informal* old hat, corny, unfunny, played out.
– OPPOSITES: fresh, original.

stalemate ▶ noun DEADLOCK, impasse, standoff; draw, tie, saw-off ♣, dead heat.

stalk¹ ▶ noun *the stalk of a plant* STEM, shoot, trunk, stock, cane, bine, bent, haulm, straw, reed.
– RELATED TERMS: cauline.

stalk² ▶ verb **1** *a cat was stalking a rabbit* CREEP UP ON, trail, follow, shadow, track down, go after, be after, course, hunt; *informal* tail, still-hunt. **2** *she stalked out* STRUT, stride, march, flounce, storm, stomp, sweep.

stall ▶ noun **1** *a market stall* STAND, table, counter, booth, kiosk. **2** *stalls for larger animals* PEN, coop, sty, corral, enclosure, compartment.
▶ verb **1** *the Government has stalled the project* OBSTRUCT, impede, interfere with, hinder, hamper, block, interrupt, hold up, hold back, thwart, balk, sabotage, delay, stonewall, check, stop, halt, derail, put a brake on; *informal* stymie. **2** *the project has stalled* STOP, fizzle, flatline, die, reach an impasse, hit a roadblock. **3** *quit stalling* USE DELAYING TACTICS, play for time, temporize, gain time, procrastinate, hedge, beat around the bush, drag one's feet, delay, filibuster, stonewall, give someone the runaround. **4** *stall him for a bit* DELAY, divert, distract; HOLD OFF, stave off, fend off, keep off, ward off, keep at bay.

stalwart ▶ adjective STAUNCH, loyal, faithful, committed, devoted, dedicated, dependable, reliable, steady, constant, trusty, solid, hard-working, steadfast, redoubtable, unwavering.
– OPPOSITES: disloyal, unfaithful, unreliable.

stamina ▶ noun ENDURANCE, staying power, tirelessness, fortitude, strength, energy, toughness, determination, tenacity, perseverance, grit.

stammer ▶ verb *he began to stammer* STUTTER, stumble over one's words, hesitate, falter, pause, halt, splutter.
▶ noun *he had a stammer* STUTTER, speech impediment, speech defect.

stamp ▶ verb **1** *he stamped on my toe* TRAMPLE, step, tread, tramp, stomp; CRUSH, squash, flatten. **2** *John*

stamped off, muttering STOMP, stump, clomp, clump. **3** *the name is stamped on the cover* IMPRINT, print, impress, punch, inscribe, emboss, brand, frank. **4** *his face was stamped on Martha's memory* FIX, inscribe, etch, carve, imprint, impress. **5** *his style stamps him as a player to watch* IDENTIFY, characterize, brand, distinguish, classify, mark out, set apart, single out.
▶ noun **1** *the stamp of authority* MARK, hallmark, indication, sign, seal, sure sign, telltale sign, quality, smack, smell, savour, air. **2** *he was of a very different stamp* TYPE, kind, sort, variety, class, category, classification, style, description, condition, calibre, status, quality, nature, ilk, kidney, cast, grain, mould, stripe.

■ **stamp something out** PUT AN END/STOP TO, end, stop, crush, put down, crack down on, curb, nip in the bud, scotch, squash, quash, quell, subdue, suppress, extinguish, stifle, abolish, get rid of, eliminate, eradicate, beat, overcome, defeat, destroy, wipe out; *informal* put the kibosh on, clean house.

stamp collecting ▶ noun PHILATELY.

stampede ▶ noun *the noise caused a stampede* CHARGE, panic, rush, flight, rout.
▶ verb *the sheep stampeded* BOLT, charge, flee, take flight; race, rush, career, sweep, run.

stance ▶ noun **1** *a natural golfer's stance* POSTURE, body position, pose, attitude. **2** *a liberal stance* ATTITUDE, stand, point of view, viewpoint, opinion, way of thinking, outlook, standpoint, position, angle, perspective, approach, line, policy.

stand ▶ verb **1** *Lionel stood in the doorway* BE ON ONE'S FEET, be upright, be erect, be vertical. **2** *the men stood up* RISE, get/rise to one's feet, get up, straighten up, pick oneself up, find one's feet, be upstanding; *formal* arise. **3** *today a house stands on the site* BE, exist, be situated, be located, be positioned, be sited, have been built. **4** *he stood the book on the shelf* PUT, set, set up, erect, up-end, place, position, locate, prop, lean, stick, install, arrange; *informal* park. **5** *my decision stands* REMAIN IN FORCE, remain valid/effective/ operative, remain in operation, hold, hold good, apply, be the case, exist. **6** *her heart could not stand the strain* WITHSTAND, endure, bear, put up with, take, cope with, handle, sustain, resist, stand up to. **7** *(informal) I can't stand arrogance* ENDURE, tolerate, bear, put up with, take, abide, support, countenance; *informal* swallow, stomach; *formal* brook.
– OPPOSITES: sit, lie, sit down, lie down.
▶ noun **1** *the party's stand on immigration* ATTITUDE, stance, point of view, viewpoint, opinion, way of thinking, outlook, standpoint, position, approach, thinking, policy, line. **2** *a stand against tyranny* OPPOSITION, resistance, objection, hostility, animosity. **3** *a large mirror on a stand* BASE, support, mounting, platform, rest, plinth, bottom; tripod, rack, trivet. **4** *a beer stand* STALL, counter, booth, kiosk, tent. **5** *a taxi stand* RANK, station, park, bay. **6** *the train drew to a stand* STOP, halt, standstill, dead stop. **7** *a stand of trees* COPSE, thicket, grove, bush, woodlot, *(Prairies)* bluff ♣.

■ **stand by** WAIT, be prepared, be in (a state of) readiness, be ready for action, be on full alert, wait in the wings.

■ **stand by someone/something 1** *she stood by her husband* REMAIN/BE LOYAL TO, stick with/by, remain/be true to, stand up for, support, back up, defend, stick up for. **2** *the government must stand by its pledges* ABIDE BY, keep (to), adhere to, hold to, stick to, observe, comply with.

■ **stand down** RELAX, stand easy, come off full alert.

■ **stand for 1** *BC stands for British Columbia* MEAN, be an abbreviation of, represent, signify, denote, indicate, symbolize. **2** (*informal*) *I won't stand for any nonsense* PUT UP WITH, endure, tolerate, accept, take, abide, support, countenance; *informal* swallow, stomach; *formal* brook. **3** *we stand for animal welfare* ADVOCATE, champion, uphold, defend, stand up for, support, back, endorse, be in favour of, promote, recommend, urge.

■ **stand in** DEPUTIZE, act, act as deputy, substitute, fill in, sit in, do duty, take over, act as locum, be a proxy, cover, hold the fort, step into the breach; replace, relieve, take over from; *informal* sub, fill someone's shoes, step into someone's shoes, pinch-hit.

■ **stand out 1** *his veins stood out* PROJECT, stick out, bulge (out), be proud, jut (out). **2** *she stood out in the crowd* BE NOTICEABLE, be visible, be obvious, be conspicuous, stick out, be striking, be distinctive, be prominent, attract attention, catch the eye, leap out, show up; *informal* stick/stand out like a sore thumb.

■ **stand up** REMAIN/BE VALID, be sound, be plausible, hold water, hold up, stand questioning, survive investigation, bear examination, be verifiable.

■ **stand someone up** FAIL TO KEEP A DATE WITH, fail to meet, fail to keep an appointment with, jilt.

■ **stand up for someone/something** SUPPORT, defend, back, back up, stick up for, champion, promote, uphold, take someone's part, take the side of, side with.

■ **stand up to someone/something 1** *she stood up to her parents* DEFY, confront, challenge, resist, take on, put up a fight against, argue with, take a stand against. **2** *the old house has stood up to the war* WITHSTAND, survive, come through (unscathed), outlast, outlive, weather, ride out, ward off.

standard ▶ noun **1** *the standard of her work* QUALITY, level, grade, calibre, merit, excellence. **2** *a safety standard* GUIDELINE, norm, yardstick, benchmark, measure, criterion, guide, touchstone, model, pattern, example, exemplar. **3** *a standard to live by* PRINCIPLE, ideal; (**standards**) code of behaviour, code of honour, morals, scruples, ethics. **4** *the regiment's standard* FLAG, banner, pennant, ensign, colour(s), banderole, guidon; *Nautical* burgee.

▶ adjective **1** *the standard way of doing it* NORMAL, usual, typical, stock, common, ordinary, customary, conventional, wonted, established, settled, set, fixed, traditional, prevailing. **2** *the standard work on the subject* DEFINITIVE, established, classic, recognized, accepted, authoritative, most reliable, exhaustive.

— OPPOSITES: unusual, special.

standardize ▶ verb SYSTEMATIZE, make consistent, make uniform, make comparable, regulate, normalize, bring into line, equalize, homogenize, regiment.

stand-in ▶ noun *a stand-in for the minister* SUBSTITUTE, replacement, deputy, surrogate, proxy, understudy, locum, supply, fill-in, cover, relief, stop-gap; *informal* temp, pinch-hitter; (*body*) double, stuntman.

▶ adjective *a stand-in goaltender* SUBSTITUTE, replacement, deputy, fill-in, stop-gap, supply, surrogate, relief, acting, temporary, provisional, caretaker; *informal* pinch-hitting.

standing ▶ noun **1** *his standing in the community* STATUS, rank, ranking, position; reputation, estimation, stature; *dated* station. **2** *a person of some standing* SENIORITY, rank, eminence, prominence,

prestige, repute, stature, esteem, importance, account, consequence, influence, distinction; *informal* clout. **3** *a squabble of long standing* DURATION, existence, continuance, endurance, life, history.

▶ adjective **1** *standing stones* UPRIGHT, erect, vertical, plumb, upended, on end, perpendicular; on one's feet. **2** *standing water* STAGNANT, still, motionless, static, stationary, dead, slack. **3** *a standing invitation* PERMANENT, perpetual, everlasting, continuing, abiding, indefinite, open-ended; regular, repeated.

— OPPOSITES: flat, lying down, seated, flowing, temporary, occasional.

standoff ▶ noun DEADLOCK, stalemate, impasse, saw-off ♣; draw, tie, dead heat; suspension of hostilities, lull.

standoffish ▶ adjective (*informal*) ALOOF, distant, remote, detached, withdrawn, reserved, uncommunicative, unforthcoming, unapproachable, unresponsive, unfriendly, unsociable, introspective, introverted.

— OPPOSITES: friendly, approachable, sociable.

standpoint ▶ noun POINT OF VIEW, viewpoint, vantage point, attitude, stance, view, opinion, position, way of thinking, outlook, perspective.

standstill ▶ noun HALT, stop, dead stop, stand, gridlock.

staple ▶ adjective MAIN, principal, chief, major, primary, leading, foremost, first, most important, predominant, dominant, (most) prominent, basic, standard, prime, premier; *informal* number-one.

star ▶ noun **1** *the sky was full of stars* CELESTIAL BODY, heavenly body, sun; asteroid, planet. *See table.* **2** *the stars of the film* PRINCIPAL, leading lady/man, lead, female/male lead, hero, heroine. **3** *a star of the world of chess* CELEBRITY, superstar, big name, famous name, household name, someone, somebody, lion, leading light, VIP, personality, personage, luminary; *informal* celeb, big shot, megastar.

— RELATED TERMS: astral, astro-, sidereal, sidero-, stellar.

— OPPOSITES: nobody.

▶ adjective **1** *a star pupil* BRILLIANT, talented, gifted, able, exceptional, outstanding, bright, clever, masterly, consummate, precocious, prodigious. **2** *the star attraction* TOP, leading, best, greatest, foremost, major, pre-eminent, champion.

— OPPOSITES: poor, minor.

starchy ▶ adjective (*informal*). *See* STAID.

stare ▶ verb GAZE, gape, goggle, glare, ogle, peer; *informal* gawk, rubberneck.

stark ▶ adjective **1** *a stark silhouette* SHARP, sharply defined, well-focused, crisp, distinct, obvious, evident, clear, clear-cut, graphic, striking. **2** *a stark landscape* DESOLATE, bare, barren, arid, vacant, empty, forsaken, godforsaken, bleak, sombre, depressing, cheerless, joyless; *literary* drear. **3** *a stark room* AUSTERE, severe, bleak, plain, simple, bare, unadorned, unembellished, undecorated. **4** *stark terror* SHEER, utter, complete, absolute, total, pure, downright, out-and-out, outright; rank, thorough, consummate, unqualified, unmitigated, unalloyed. **5** *the stark facts* BLUNT, bald, bare, simple, basic, plain, unvarnished, harsh, grim.

— OPPOSITES: fuzzy, indistinct, pleasant, ornate, disguised.

▶ adverb *stark naked* COMPLETELY, totally, utterly, absolutely, downright, dead, entirely, wholly, fully, quite, altogether, thoroughly, truly, one hundred per cent.

The Brightest Stars (apparent visual magnitude)

Star	Constellation
Sirius	Canis Major
Canopus*	Carina
Alpha Centauri*	Centaurus
Arcturus	Boötes
Vega	Lyra
Capella	Auriga
Rigel	Orion
Procyon	Canis Minor
Achernar*	Eridanus
Betelgeuse	Orion
Hadar*	Centaurus
Altair	Aquila
Aldebaran	Taurus
Acrux*	Crux
Antares	Scorpius
Spica	Virgo
Pollux	Gemini
Fomalhaut	Piscis Austrinus
Deneb	Cygnus
Mimosa*	Crux
Regulus	Leo
Adhara	Canis Major
Castor	Gemini
Gamma Crucis*	Crux
Bellatrix	Orion

* Stars not visible from Canadian territory

start ▶ verb **1** *the meeting starts at 7:45* BEGIN, commence, get underway, go ahead, get going; *informal* kick off. **2** *this was how her illness had started* ARISE, come into being, begin, commence, be born, come into existence, appear, arrive, come forth, establish oneself, emerge, erupt, burst out, originate, develop. **3** *she started her own charity* ESTABLISH, set up, found, create, bring into being, institute, initiate, inaugurate, introduce, open, launch, float, kick-start, jump-start, get something off the ground, pioneer, organize, mastermind; *informal* kick something off. **4** *we had better start on the work* COMMENCE, make a start, begin, take the first step, make the first move, get going, go ahead, set things moving, start/get/set the ball rolling, buckle to/down, turn to; *informal* get moving, get cracking, get down to it, get to it, get down to business, get the show on the road, take the plunge, kick off, get off one's backside, fire away. **5** *he started across the field* SET OFF, set out, start out, set forth, begin one's journey, get on the road, depart, leave, get underway, make a start, sally forth, embark, sail; *informal* hit the road. **6** *you can start the machine* ACTIVATE, set in motion, switch on, start up, turn on, fire up; energize, actuate, set off, start off, set something going/moving. **7** *the machine started* BEGIN WORKING, start up, get going, spring into life. **8** *'Oh my!' she said, starting* FLINCH, jerk, jump, twitch, recoil, shy, shrink, blench, wince.
— OPPOSITES: finish, stop, clear up, wind up, give up, arrive, stay, close down.
▶ noun **1** *the start of the event* BEGINNING, commencement, inception. **2** *the start of her illness* ONSET, commencement, emergence, (first) appearance, arrival, eruption, dawn, birth; *informal* square one. **3** *a quarter of an hour's start* LEAD, head start, advantage. **4** *a start in life* ADVANTAGEOUS

BEGINNING, flying start, helping hand, lift, assistance, support, encouragement, boost, kick-start; *informal* break, leg up. **5** *she awoke with a start* JERK, twitch, flinch, wince, spasm, convulsion, jump.
— OPPOSITES: end, finish, handicap.

startle ▶ verb SURPRISE, frighten, scare, alarm, give someone a shock/fright/jolt, make someone jump; PERTURB, unsettle, agitate, disturb, disconcert, disquiet; *informal* give someone a turn, make someone jump out of their skin, freak someone out.
— OPPOSITES: put at ease.

startling ▶ adjective SURPRISING, astonishing, amazing, unexpected, unforeseen, staggering, shocking, stunning; extraordinary, remarkable, dramatic; disturbing, unsettling, perturbing, disconcerting, disquieting; frightening, alarming, scary.
— OPPOSITES: predictable, ordinary.

starvation ▶ noun EXTREME HUNGER, lack of food, famine, undernourishment, malnourishment, fasting; deprivation of food; death from lack of food.

starving ▶ adjective DYING OF HUNGER, deprived of food, undernourished, malnourished, starved, half-starved; very hungry, ravenous, famished, empty, hollow; fasting.
— OPPOSITES: full.

stash (*informal*) ▶ verb *he stashed his things away* STORE, stow, pack, load, cache, hide, conceal, secrete; hoard, save, stockpile; *informal* salt away, squirrel away.
▶ noun *a stash of money* CACHE, hoard, stock, stockpile, store, supply, accumulation, collection, reserve.

state¹ ▶ noun **1** *the state of the economy* CONDITION, shape, situation, circumstances, position; predicament, plight. **2** (*informal*) *don't get into a state* FLUSTER, frenzy, fever, fret, panic, state of agitation/ anxiety; *informal* flap, tizzy, dither, stew, sweat. **3** (*informal*) *your room is in a state* MESS, chaos, disorder, disarray, confusion, muddle, heap, shambles; clutter, untidiness, disorganization, imbroglio. **4** *an autonomous state* COUNTRY, nation, land, sovereign state, nation state, kingdom, realm, power, republic, confederation, federation. *See table at* COUNTRY. **5** *the country is divided into thirty-two states* PROVINCE, federal state, region, territory, canton, department, county, district, shire. **6** *the power of the state* GOVERNMENT, parliament, administration, regime, authorities.
▶ adjective *a state visit to China* CEREMONIAL, official, formal, governmental, national, public.
— OPPOSITES: unofficial, private, informal.

state² ▶ verb *I stated my views* EXPRESS, voice, utter, put into words, declare, affirm, assert, announce, make known, put across/over, communicate, air, reveal, disclose, divulge, proclaim, present, expound; set out, set down; *informal* come out with.

stated ▶ adjective SPECIFIED, fixed, settled, set, agreed, declared, designated, laid down.
— OPPOSITES: undefined, irregular, tacit.

stately ▶ adjective DIGNIFIED, majestic, ceremonious, courtly, imposing, impressive, solemn, awe-inspiring, regal, elegant, grand, glorious, splendid, magnificent, resplendent; slow-moving, measured, deliberate.

statement ▶ noun DECLARATION, expression of views/ facts, affirmation, assertion, announcement, utterance, communication, proclamation, presentation, expounding; account, testimony, evidence, report, bulletin, communiqué.

state-of-the-art ▶ adjective MODERN,

ultra-modern, the latest, new, the newest, up-to-the-minute, cutting-edge; advanced, highly developed, innovative, trail-blazing, revolutionary; sophisticated.

statesman, stateswoman ▶ noun SENIOR POLITICIAN, respected political figure, elder statesman, political leader, national leader.

static ▶ adjective **1** *static prices* UNCHANGED, fixed, stable, steady, unchanging, changeless, unvarying, invariable, constant, consistent. **2** *a static display* STATIONARY, motionless, immobile, unmoving, still, stock-still, at a standstill, at rest, not moving a muscle, like a statue, rooted to the spot, frozen, inactive, inert, lifeless, inanimate.
− OPPOSITES: variable, mobile, active, dynamic.

station ▶ noun **1** *a railway station* STOPPING PLACE, stop, halt, stage; terminus, terminal, depot. **2** *a research station* ESTABLISHMENT, base, camp; post, depot; mission; site, facility, installation, yard. **3** *a police station* OFFICE, depot, base, headquarters, precinct, station house, detachment ♣; *informal* cop shop. **4** *a radio station* CHANNEL, broadcasting organization; wavelength. **5** *the watchman resumed his station* POST, position, place. **6** *(dated) Karen was getting ideas above her station* RANK, place, status, position in society, social class, stratum, level, grade; caste; *archaic* condition, degree.
▶ verb *the regiment was stationed at Camp Borden* PUT ON DUTY, post, position, place; establish, install; deploy, base, garrison.

stationary ▶ adjective **1** *a stationary car* STATIC, parked, stopped, motionless, immobile, unmoving, still, stock-still, at a standstill, at rest; not moving a muscle, like a statue, rooted to the spot, frozen, inactive, inert, lifeless, inanimate. **2** *a stationary population* UNCHANGING, unvarying, invariable, constant, consistent, unchanged, changeless, fixed, stable, steady.
− OPPOSITES: moving, shifting.

statistics ▶ noun DATA, facts and figures, numbers, information, details; *informal* stats.

statue ▶ noun SCULPTURE, figure, effigy, statuette, figurine, idol; carving, bronze, graven image, model; bust, head.

statuesque ▶ adjective TALL AND DIGNIFIED, imposing, striking, stately, majestic, noble, magnificent, splendid, impressive, regal.

stature ▶ noun **1** *she was small in stature* HEIGHT, tallness; size, build. **2** *an architect of international stature* REPUTATION, repute, standing, status, position, prestige, distinction, eminence, pre-eminence, prominence, importance, influence, note, fame, celebrity, renown, acclaim.

status ▶ noun **1** *the status of women* STANDING, rank, ranking, position, social position, level, place, estimation; *dated* station. **2** *wealth and status* PRESTIGE, kudos, cachet, standing, stature, regard, fame, note, renown, honour, esteem, image, importance, prominence, consequence, distinction, influence, authority, eminence. **3** *the current status of the project* STATE, position, condition, shape, stage.

statute ▶ noun LAW, regulation, enactment, act, bill, decree, edict, rule, ruling, resolution, dictum, command, order, directive, order-in-council, pronouncement, proclamation, dictate, diktat, fiat, bylaw, ordinance.

staunch[1] ▶ adjective *a staunch supporter* STALWART, loyal, faithful, committed, devoted, dedicated,

dependable, reliable, steady, constant, trusty, hard-working, steadfast, redoubtable, unwavering, tireless.
− OPPOSITES: disloyal, unfaithful, unreliable.

staunch[2] ▶ verb *she tried to staunch the flow of blood* STEM, stop, halt, check, hold back, restrain, restrict, control, contain, curb; block, dam; slow, lessen, reduce, diminish, retard, stanch; *archaic* stay.

stave
■ **stave something in** BREAK IN, smash in, put a hole in, push in, kick in, cave in.
■ **stave something off** AVERT, prevent, avoid, counter, preclude, forestall, nip in the bud; ward off, fend off, head off, keep off, keep at bay.

stay[1] ▶ verb **1** *he stayed where he was* REMAIN (BEHIND), stay behind, stay put; wait, linger, stick, be left, hold on, hang on, lodge; *informal* hang around/round; *archaic* bide, tarry. **2** *they won't stay hidden* CONTINUE (TO BE), remain, keep, persist in being, carry on being, go on being. **3** *our aunt is staying with us* VISIT, spend time, put up, stop (off/over); holiday; lodge, room, board, have rooms, be housed, be accommodated, be quartered, be billeted, vacation; *formal* sojourn; *archaic* bide. **4** *legal proceedings were stayed* POSTPONE, put off, delay, defer, put back, hold over/off; adjourn, suspend, prorogue, put over, table, lay on the table, take a rain check on; *US Law* continue; *informal* put on ice, put on the back burner. **5** *(literary) we must stay the enemy's advance* DELAY, slow down/up, hold back/up, set back, keep back, put back, put a brake on, retard; hinder, hamper, obstruct, inhibit, impede, curb, check, restrain, restrict, arrest; *informal* throw a wrench in the works of.
− OPPOSITES: leave, advance, promote.
▶ noun **1** *a stay at a hotel* VISIT, stop, stop-off, stopover, overnight, break, holiday, vacation; *formal* sojourn. **2** *a stay of judgment* POSTPONEMENT, putting off, delay, deferment, deferral, putting back; adjournment, suspension, prorogation, tabling.

stay[2] ▶ noun *the stays holding up the mast* STRUT, WIRE, brace, tether, guy, prop, rod, support, truss; *Nautical* shroud.
▶ verb *her masts were well stayed* BRACE, tether, strut, wire, guy, prop, support, truss.

steadfast ▶ adjective **1** *a steadfast friend* LOYAL, faithful, committed, devoted, dedicated, dependable, reliable, steady, true, constant, staunch, solid, trusty. **2** *a steadfast policy* FIRM, determined, resolute, relentless, implacable, single-minded; unchanging, unwavering, unhesitating, unfaltering, unswerving, unyielding, unflinching, uncompromising.
− OPPOSITES: disloyal, irresolute.

steady ▶ adjective **1** *the ladder must be steady* STABLE, firm, fixed, secure, fast, safe, immovable, unshakeable, dependable; anchored, moored, jammed, rooted, braced. **2** *keep the camera steady* MOTIONLESS, still, unshaking, static, stationary, unmoving. **3** *a steady gaze* FIXED, intent, unwavering, unfaltering. **4** *a steady young student* SENSIBLE, level-headed, rational, settled, mature, down-to-earth, full of common sense, reliable, dependable, sound, sober, serious-minded, responsible, serious. **5** *a steady income* CONSTANT, unchanging, regular, consistent, invariable, continuous, continual, unceasing, ceaseless, perpetual, unremitting, unvarying, unfaltering, unending, endless, round-the-clock, all-year-round. **6** *a steady boyfriend* REGULAR, usual, established, settled, firm, devoted, faithful.

- OPPOSITES: unstable, loose, shaky, darting, flighty, immature, fluctuating, sporadic, occasional.
▶ **verb 1** *he steadied the rifle* STABILIZE, hold steady; brace, support; balance, poise; secure, fix, make fast. **2** *she needed to steady her nerves* CALM, soothe, quieten, compose, settle; subdue, quell, control, get a grip on.

steal ▶ **verb 1** *the raiders stole a fax machine* PURLOIN, thieve, take, take for oneself, help oneself to, loot, pilfer, run off with, abscond with, carry off, shoplift; embezzle, misappropriate; have one's fingers/hand in the till; *informal* walk off with, rob, swipe, snatch, (Nfld) buck ✿, nab, nick, rip off, lift, 'liberate', 'borrow', filch, snaffle, snitch, pinch, heist; *formal* peculate. **2** *his work was stolen by his tutor* PLAGIARIZE, copy, pass off as one's own, poach, borrow; *informal* rip off, lift, pinch, nick, crib. **3** *he stole a kiss* SNATCH, sneak, get stealthily/surreptitiously. **4** *he stole out of the room* CREEP, sneak, slink, slip, slide, glide, tiptoe, sidle, slope, edge.
▶ **noun** *(informal) at $30 it's a steal.* See BARGAIN noun sense 2.

stealing ▶ **noun** THEFT, thieving, thievery, robbery, larceny, burglary, shoplifting, pilfering, pilferage, looting, misappropriation; embezzlement; *formal* peculation.

stealth ▶ **noun** FURTIVENESS, secretiveness, secrecy, surreptitiousness, sneakiness, slyness.
- OPPOSITES: openness.

stealthy ▶ **adjective** FURTIVE, secretive, secret, surreptitious, sneaking, sly, clandestine, covert, conspiratorial.
- OPPOSITES: open.

steam ▶ **noun 1** *steam from the kettle* WATER VAPOUR, condensation, mist, haze, fog, moisture. **2** *he ran out of steam* ENERGY, vigour, vitality, stamina, enthusiasm; MOMENTUM, impetus, force, strength, thrust, impulse, push, drive; speed, pace.
■ **steamed up** *(informal)* **1** *he got steamed up about forgetting his papers.* See AGITATED. **2** *they get steamed up about the media.* See ANGRY sense 1.
■ **let off steam** *(informal)* GIVE VENT TO ONE'S FEELINGS, speak one's mind, speak out, sound off, lose one's inhibitions, let oneself go; use up surplus energy.
■ **steam up** MIST (UP/OVER), fog (up), become misty/misted.

steamy ▶ **adjective 1** *the steamy jungle* HUMID, muggy, sticky, dripping, moist, damp, clammy, sultry, sweaty, steaming. **2** *(informal) a steamy love scene.* See EROTIC. **3** *(informal) they had a steamy affair* PASSIONATE, torrid, amorous, ardent, lustful; *informal* sizzling, hot, red-hot.

steel
■ **steel oneself** BRACE ONESELF, nerve oneself, summon (up) one's courage, screw up one's courage, gear oneself up, prepare oneself, get in the right frame of mind; fortify oneself, harden oneself; *informal* psych oneself up; *literary* gird (up) one's loins.

steely ▶ **adjective 1** *steely light* BLUE-GREY, grey, steel-coloured, steel-grey, iron-grey. **2** *steely muscles* HARD, firm, toned, rigid, stiff, tense, tensed, taut. **3** *steely eyes* CRUEL, unfeeling, merciless, ruthless, pitiless, heartless, hard-hearted, hard, stony, cold-blooded, cold-hearted, harsh, callous, severe, unrelenting, unpitying, unforgiving, uncaring, unsympathetic; *literary* adamantine. **4** *steely determination* RESOLUTE, firm, steadfast, dogged, single-minded; bitter, burning, ferocious, fanatical; ruthless, iron, grim, gritty; unquenchable, unflinching, unswerving, unfaltering, untiring,

unwavering.
- OPPOSITES: flabby, kind, half-hearted.

steep[1] ▶ **adjective 1** *steep cliffs* PRECIPITOUS, sheer, abrupt, sharp, perpendicular, vertical, bluff, vertiginous. **2** *a steep increase* SHARP, sudden, precipitate, precipitous, rapid. **3** *(informal) steep prices* EXPENSIVE, costly, high, stiff; unreasonable, excessive, exorbitant, extortionate, outrageous, prohibitive, dear.
- OPPOSITES: gentle, gradual, reasonable.

steep[2] ▶ **verb 1** *the ham is then steeped in brine* MARINADE, marinate, soak, souse, macerate; pickle. **2** *winding sheets were steeped in mercury sulphate* SOAK, saturate, immerse, wet through, drench; *technical* ret. **3** *a city steeped in history* IMBUE WITH, fill with, permeate with, pervade with, suffuse with, infuse with, soak in.

steeple ▶ **noun** SPIRE, tower; bell tower, belfry, campanile; minaret.

steer ▶ **verb 1** *he steered the boat* GUIDE, direct, manoeuvre, drive, pilot, navigate; *Nautical* con, helm. **2** *steering our plans through various levels of government* manoeuvre, stickhandle ✿. **3** *Luke steered her down the path* GUIDE, conduct, direct, lead, take, usher, shepherd, marshal, herd.
■ **steer clear of** KEEP AWAY FROM, keep one's distance from, keep at arm's length, give a wide berth to, avoid, avoid dealing with, have nothing to do with, shun, eschew.

stellar ▶ **adjective 1** *an estimate of stellar ages* ASTRAL, sidereal. **2** *a stellar cast* ALL-STAR, star-studded. **3** *a stellar performance* MARVELLOUS, outstanding, superb, first-rate, out of this world, heavenly, dazzling.

stem[1] ▶ **noun** *a plant stem* STALK, shoot, trunk, stock, cane, bine.
- RELATED TERMS: cauline.
■ **stem from** HAVE ITS ORIGINS IN, arise from, originate from, spring from, derive from, come from, emanate from, flow from, proceed from; BE CAUSED BY, be brought on/about by, be produced by.

stem[2] ▶ **verb** *he stemmed the flow of blood* STAUNCH, stop, halt, check, hold back, restrict, control, contain, curb; block, dam; slow, lessen, reduce, diminish, stanch; *archaic* stay.

stench ▶ **noun** STINK, reek, whiff, fetor, funk; *literary* miasma.

stentorian ▶ **adjective** LOUD, thundering, thunderous, ear-splitting, deafening; powerful, strong, carrying; booming, resonant; strident.
- OPPOSITES: quiet, soft.

step ▶ **noun 1** *Frank took a step forward* PACE, stride. **2** *she heard a step on the stairs* FOOTSTEP, footfall, tread. **3** *she left the room with a springy step* GAIT, walk, tread. **4** *it is only a step to the river* SHORT DISTANCE, stone's throw, spitting distance; *informal* {a hop, skip, and jump}. **5** *the top step* STAIR, tread; (**steps**) STAIRS, staircase, stairway. **6** *each step of the ladder* RUNG, tread. **7** *resigning is a very serious step* COURSE OF ACTION, measure, move, act, action, initiative, manoeuvre, operation, tactic. **8** *a significant step towards a ceasefire* ADVANCE, development, move, movement, breakthrough. **9** *the first step on the managerial ladder* STAGE, level, grade, rank, degree; notch, rung.
▶ **verb 1** *she stepped gingerly through the snow* WALK, move, tread, pace, stride. **2** *the bull stepped on the farmer's foot* TREAD, stamp, trample; squash, crush, flatten.
■ **in step** *he is in step with mainstream thinking* IN

ACCORD, in accordance, in harmony, in agreement, in tune, in line, in keeping, in conformity, compatible with.

■ **mind/watch one's step** BE CAREFUL, take care, step/tread carefully, exercise care/caution, mind how one goes, look out, watch out, be wary, be on one's guard, be on the qui vive.

■ **out of step** *the paper was often out of step with public opinion* AT ODDS, at variance, in disagreement, out of tune, out of line, not in keeping, out of harmony.

■ **step by step** ONE STEP AT A TIME, bit by bit, gradually, in stages, by degrees, slowly, steadily.

■ **step down** RESIGN, quit, stand down, give up one's post/job, bow out, abdicate; *informal* pack it in, call it quits, hang up one's skates ✦.

■ **step in 1** *nobody stepped in to save the bank* INTERVENE, intercede, involve oneself, become/get involved, take a hand. **2** *I stepped in for a sick colleague* STAND IN, sit in, fill in, cover, substitute, take over; replace, take someone's place; *informal* sub.

■ **step on it** (*informal*) HURRY UP, get a move on, speed up, go faster, be quick; *informal* get cracking, get moving, step on the gas; *dated* make haste.

■ **step something up 1** *the army stepped up its offensive* INCREASE, intensify, strengthen, augment, escalate; *informal* up, crank up. **2** *I stepped up my pace* SPEED UP, increase, accelerate, quicken, hasten.

stereo ▸ noun *we bought a new stereo* SOUND SYSTEM, ghetto blaster, radio, CD player, tape deck, eight-track, boom box, beat box, hi-fi.

stereotype ▸ noun *the stereotype of the rancher* STANDARD/CONVENTIONAL IMAGE, received idea, cliché, hackneyed idea, formula.
▸ verb *women in detective novels are often stereotyped as femmes fatales* TYPECAST, pigeonhole, conventionalize, categorize, label, tag.

stereotyped ▸ adjective STOCK, conventional, stereotypical, standard, formulaic, predictable; hackneyed, clichéd, cliché-ridden, banal, trite, unoriginal; typecast; *informal* corny, old hat.
– OPPOSITES: unconventional, original.

sterile ▸ adjective **1** *mules are sterile* INFERTILE, unable to reproduce/conceive, unable to have children/young; *archaic* barren. **2** *sterile desert* UNPRODUCTIVE, infertile, unfruitful, uncultivatable, barren. **3** *a sterile debate* POINTLESS, unproductive, unfruitful, unrewarding, useless, unprofitable, profitless, futile, vain, idle; *archaic* bootless. **4** *sterile academicism* UNIMAGINATIVE, uninspired, uninspiring, unoriginal, stale, lifeless, musty, phlegmatic. **5** *sterile conditions* ASEPTIC, sterilized, germ-free, antiseptic, disinfected; uncontaminated, unpolluted, pure, clean; sanitary, hygienic.
– OPPOSITES: fertile, productive, creative, original, septic.

sterilize ▸ verb **1** *the scalpel was first sterilized* DISINFECT, fumigate, decontaminate, sanitize; pasteurize; clean, cleanse, purify; *technical* autoclave. **2** *over 6.5 million people were sterilized* MAKE UNABLE TO HAVE CHILDREN, make infertile, hysterectomize, vasectomize, have one's tubes tied, have a tubal ligation, have a salpingectomy. **3** *stray pets are usually sterilized* NEUTER, castrate, spay, geld, cut, fix, desex, alter, doctor.
– OPPOSITES: contaminate.

sterling ▸ adjective EXCELLENT, first-rate, first-class, exceptional, outstanding, splendid, superlative, praiseworthy, laudable, commendable, admirable,

valuable, worthy, deserving.
– OPPOSITES: poor, unexceptional.

stern¹ ▸ adjective **1** *a stern expression* SERIOUS, unsmiling, frowning, severe, forbidding, grim, unfriendly, austere, dour, stony, flinty, steely, unrelenting, unforgiving, unbending, unsympathetic, disapproving. **2** *stern measures* STRICT, severe, stringent, harsh, drastic, hard, tough, extreme, rigid, ruthless, rigorous, exacting, demanding, uncompromising, unsparing, inflexible, authoritarian, draconian.
– OPPOSITES: genial, friendly, lenient, lax.

stern² ▸ noun *the stern of the ship* REAR (END), back, after end, poop, transom, tail.
– OPPOSITES: bow.

stew ▸ noun **1** *we ate a hearty stew. See table.* **2** (*informal*) *she's in a stew about that parking ticket* MOOD, flap, panic, fluster, fret, fuss, sweat, lather, tizzy, dither, twitter, state; *literary* pother.
▸ verb **1** *stew the meat for an hour* BRAISE, simmer, boil. **2** (*informal*) *there's no point stewing over it. See* WORRY *verb* sense 1. **3** (*informal*) *the girls sat stewing in the heat* SWELTER, be very hot, perspire, sweat; *informal* roast, bake, cook, be boiling.

Stews and Casseroles

bake	Jiggs' dinner ✦(*Nfld*)
beef bourguignon	korma
beef stroganoff	kugel
blanquette	lasagna
bouillabaisse	lobster thermidor
Brunswick stew	macaroni and cheese
cabbage rolls	Madras
callaloo	manicotti
cannelloni	moussaka
carbonnade	mulligan
cassoulet	navarin
chicken cacciatore	olio
chili (con carne)	olla podrida
colcannon	osso bucco
coq au vin	paella
couscous	paprikash
curry	pot-au-feu
daube	ragoût des
dhansak	pattes ✦(*Que.*)
finnan haddie	ragout
fish and brewis ✦(*Nfld*)	rappie pie ✦(*Maritimes*)
fricassee	ratatouille
fricot ✦(*Maritimes*)	rogan josh
goulash	salmi
gratin	sauté
gumbo	scallop
holubtsi	strata
hotpot	tajine
Irish stew	tsimmes
jambalaya	tetrazzini
	vindaloo

steward ▸ noun **1** *an air steward* FLIGHT ATTENDANT, cabin attendant; stewardess, air hostess, purser. **2** *the race stewards* OFFICIAL, marshal, organizer. **3** *the steward of the estate* (ESTATE) MANAGER, agent, overseer, custodian, caretaker; *historical* reeve.

stick¹ ▸ noun **1** *a fire made of sticks* PIECE OF WOOD, twig, small branch. **2** *he walks with a stick* WALKING STICK, cane, staff, alpenstock, crook, crutch. **3** *the plants need supporting on sticks* CANE, pole, post, stake, upright. **4** *he beat me with a stick* CLUB, cudgel,

bludgeon, shillelagh; truncheon, baton; cane, birch, switch, rod.
− OPPOSITES: praise, commendation.
■ **the sticks** (*informal*) THE COUNTRY, the countryside, rural areas, the provinces; the backwoods, (*Ont. & Que.*) the back concessions ✦, the back of beyond, the wilds, the hinterland, moose pasture ✦, a backwater, the backcountry, the backland, the middle of nowhere, the boondocks, the boonies, hicksville.

stick² ▶ verb **1** *he stuck his fork into the sausage* THRUST, push, insert, jab, poke, dig, plunge. **2** *the bristles stuck into her skin* PIERCE, penetrate, puncture, prick, stab. **3** *the cup stuck to its saucer* ADHERE, cling, be fixed, be glued. **4** *stick the stamp there* AFFIX, attach, fasten, fix; paste, glue, gum, tape, Scotch-tape, pin, tack. **5** *the wheels stuck fast* BECOME TRAPPED, become jammed, jam, catch, become wedged, become lodged, become fixed, become embedded. **6** *that sticks in his mind* REMAIN, stay, linger, dwell, persist, continue, last, endure, burn. **7** *the charges won't stick* BE UPHELD, hold, be believed; *informal* hold water. **8** (*informal*) *just stick that sandwich on my desk* PUT (DOWN), place, set (down), lay (down), deposit, position; leave, stow; *informal* dump, park, pop, plonk, plunk.
■ **stick at** PERSEVERE WITH, persist with, keep at, work at, continue with, carry on with, not give up with, hammer away at, stay with; go the distance, stay the course; *informal* soldier on with, hang in there.
■ **stick by** BE LOYAL TO, be faithful to, be true to, stand by, keep faith with, keep one's promise to.
■ **stick it out** PUT UP WITH IT, grin and bear it, keep at it, keep going, stay with it, see it through; persevere, persist, carry on, struggle on; *informal* hang in there, soldier on, tough it out, nail one's colours to the mast.
■ **stick out 1** *his front teeth stuck out* PROTRUDE, jut (out), project, stand out, extend, poke out; bulge, overhang. **2** *they stuck out in their strange clothes* BE NOTICEABLE, be visible, be obvious, be conspicuous, stand out, be obtrusive, be prominent, attract attention, catch the eye, leap out, show up; *informal* stick/stand out like a sore thumb.
■ **stick to** *he stuck to his promise* ABIDE BY, keep, adhere to, hold to, comply with, fulfill, make good, stand by.
■ **stick up for** SUPPORT, take someone's side, side with, be on the side of, stand by, stand up for, take someone's part, defend, come to the defence of, champion, speak up for, fight for.

sticker ▶ noun LABEL, adhesive, decal, (price) tag.

stickhandle ▶ verb deke, carry the puck, dipsy-doodle; rag the puck; manoeuvre.

stick-in-the-mud ▶ noun (*informal*) (OLD) FOGEY, conservative, fossil, troglodyte, museum piece, fuddy-duddy, square, stuffed shirt, dinosaur, throwback.

stickler ▶ noun PERFECTIONIST, pedant, nitpicker, purist, diehard, hard-liner, fanatic.

sticky ▶ adjective **1** *sticky tape* (SELF-)ADHESIVE, gummed; *technical* adherent. **2** *sticky clay* GLUTINOUS, viscous, viscid, gluey, tacky, gummy, treacly, syrupy; mucilaginous; *informal* gooey, icky, gloppy. **3** *sticky weather* HUMID, muggy, close, sultry, steamy, sweaty, oppressive, heavy. **4** *a sticky situation* AWKWARD, difficult, tricky, ticklish, problematic, delicate, touch-and-go, touchy, embarrassing, sensitive, uncomfortable; *informal* hairy.
− OPPOSITES: dry, fresh, cool, easy.

stiff ▶ adjective **1** *stiff cardboard* RIGID, hard, firm, inelastic, inflexible. **2** *a stiff paste* SEMI-SOLID, viscous,

viscid, thick, stiffened, firm. **3** *I'm stiff all over* ACHING, achy, painful; arthritic, rheumatic; *informal* creaky, rusty. **4** *a rather stiff manner* FORMAL, reserved, unfriendly, chilly, cold, frigid, icy, austere, wooden, forced, strained, stilted; *informal* starchy, uptight, standoffish. **5** *a stiff fine* HARSH, severe, heavy, crippling, punishing, stringent, drastic, draconian. **6** *stiff resistance* VIGOROUS, determined, full of determination, strong, spirited, resolute, tenacious, steely, four-square, unflagging, unyielding, dogged, stubborn, obdurate, rock-ribbed. **7** *a stiff climb* DIFFICULT, hard, arduous, tough, strenuous, laborious, uphill, exacting, tiring, demanding, formidable, challenging, punishing, gruelling; *informal* killing, hellish. **8** *a stiff breeze* STRONG, fresh, brisk. **9** *a stiff drink* STRONG, potent, alcoholic.
− OPPOSITES: flexible, plastic, limp, runny, supple, limber, relaxed, informal, lenient, mild, half-hearted, easy, gentle, weak.

stiffen ▶ verb **1** *stir until the mixture stiffens* BECOME STIFF, thicken; set, become solid, solidify, harden, jell, congeal, coagulate, clot. **2** *she stiffened her muscles | without exercise, joints will stiffen* MAKE/BECOME STIFF, tense (up), tighten, tauten. **3** *intimidation stiffened their resolve* STRENGTHEN, harden, toughen, fortify, reinforce, give a boost to.
− OPPOSITES: soften, liquefy, relax, weaken.

stifle ▶ verb **1** *she stifled him with a bolster* SUFFOCATE, choke, asphyxiate, smother, gag. **2** *Eleanor stifled a giggle* SUPPRESS, smother, restrain, fight back, choke back, gulp back, check, swallow, curb, silence. **3** *cartels stifle competition* CONSTRAIN, hinder, hamper, impede, hold back, curb, check, restrain, prevent, inhibit, suppress.
− OPPOSITES: let out, encourage.

stifling ▶ adjective AIRLESS, suffocating, oppressive; very hot, sweltering; humid, close, muggy; *informal* boiling.
− OPPOSITES: fresh, airy, cold.

stigma ▶ noun SHAME, disgrace, dishonour, ignominy, opprobrium, humiliation, (bad) reputation.
− OPPOSITES: honour, credit.

stigmatize ▶ verb CONDEMN, denounce; brand, label, mark out; disparage, vilify, pillory, pour scorn on, defame.

still ▶ adjective **1** *the parrot lay still* MOTIONLESS, unmoving, not moving a muscle, stock-still, immobile, inanimate, like a statue, as if turned to stone, rooted to the spot, transfixed, static, stationary. **2** *a still night* QUIET, silent, hushed, soundless, noiseless, undisturbed; CALM, peaceful, serene, windless; *literary* stilly. **3** *the lake was still* CALM, flat, even, smooth, placid, tranquil, pacific, waveless, glassy, like a millpond, unruffled, stagnant.
− OPPOSITES: moving, active, noisy, rough.
▶ noun *the still of the night* QUIETNESS, quiet, quietude, silence, stillness, hush, soundlessness; calm, tranquility, peace, serenity.
− OPPOSITES: noise, disturbance, hubbub.
▶ adverb **1** *she's still running in circles* UP TO THIS TIME, up to the present time, until now, even now, yet. **2** *He's crazy. Still, he's good for dinner conversation* NEVERTHELESS, nonetheless, regardless, all the same, just the same, anyway, anyhow, even so, yet, but, however, notwithstanding, despite that, in spite of that, for all that, be that as it may, in any event, at any rate; *informal* still and all, anyhoo.
▶ verb **1** *she stilled the crowd* QUIETEN, quiet, silence,

hush; calm, settle, pacify, soothe, lull, allay, subdue. **2** *the wind stilled* ABATE, die down, lessen, subside, ease up/off, let up, moderate, slacken, weaken.
— OPPOSITES: stir up, get stronger, get up.

stilted ▶ adjective STRAINED, forced, contrived, constrained, laboured, stiff, self-conscious, awkward, unnatural, wooden.
— OPPOSITES: natural, effortless, spontaneous.

stimulant ▶ noun **1** *caffeine is a stimulant* TONIC, restorative; antidepressant; *informal* pep pill, upper, pick-me-up, bracer, happy pill; *Medicine* analeptic. **2** *a stimulant to discussion* STIMULUS, incentive, encouragement, impetus, inducement, boost, spur, prompt; *informal* shot in the arm.
— OPPOSITES: sedative, downer, deterrent.

stimulate ▶ verb ENCOURAGE, act as a stimulus/incentive/impetus/spur to, prompt, prod, move, motivate, trigger, spark, spur on, galvanize, activate, kindle, fire, fire with enthusiasm, fuel, whet, nourish; inspire, incentivize, inspirit, rouse, excite, animate, electrify, jump-start, light a fire under.
— OPPOSITES: discourage.

stimulating ▶ adjective **1** *a stimulating effect on the circulation* RESTORATIVE, tonic, invigorating, bracing, energizing, reviving, refreshing, revitalizing, revivifying; *Medicine* analeptic. **2** *a stimulating lecture* THOUGHT-PROVOKING, interesting, fascinating, inspiring, inspirational, lively, sparkling, exciting, stirring, rousing, intriguing, giving one food for thought, refreshing; provocative, challenging.
— OPPOSITES: sedative, uninspiring, uninteresting, boring.

stimulus ▶ noun SPUR, stimulant, encouragement, impetus, boost, prompt, prod, incentive, inducement, inspiration; motivation, impulse; *informal* shot in the arm.
— OPPOSITES: deterrent, discouragement.

sting ▶ noun **1** *a bee sting* PRICK, wound, injury, puncture. **2** *this cream will take the sting away* SMART, pricking; pain, soreness, hurt, irritation. **3** *the sting of his betrayal* HEARTACHE, heartbreak, agony, torture, torment, hurt, pain, anguish. **4** *there was a sting in her words* SHARPNESS, severity, bite, edge, pointedness, asperity; sarcasm, acrimony, malice, spite, venom. **5** *(informal) the victim of a sting* SWINDLE, fraud, deception; trickery, sharp practice; *informal* rip-off, con, con trick, fiddle, bunco.
▶ verb **1** *she was stung by a scorpion* PRICK, wound, bite; poison. **2** *the smoke made her eyes sting* SMART, burn, hurt, be irritated, be sore. **3** *the criticism stung her* UPSET, wound, cut to the quick, sear, grieve, hurt, pain, torment, mortify. **4** *he was stung into action* PROVOKE, goad, incite, spur, prick, prod, rouse, drive, galvanize. **5** *(informal) they stung a bank for thousands* SWINDLE, defraud, cheat, fleece, gull; *informal* rip off, screw, shaft, bilk, do, rook, diddle, take for a ride, chisel, gouge.
— OPPOSITES: deter.

stingy ▶ adjective *(informal)* MEAN, miserly, niggardly, close-fisted, parsimonious, penny-pinching, cheese-paring, Scrooge-like; *informal* tight-fisted, cheap, tight, mingy, money-grubbing.
— OPPOSITES: generous, liberal.

stink ▶ verb **1** *his clothes stank of sweat* REEK, smell (foul/bad/disgusting), stink/smell to high heaven; *informal* hum. **2** *(informal) the whole idea stinks* BE VERY UNPLEASANT, be abhorrent, be despicable, be contemptible, be disgusting, be vile, be foul; *informal* suck. **3** *(informal) the whole affair stinks of a set-up* SMACK,

reek, give the impression, have all the hallmarks; strongly suggest.
▶ noun **1** *the stink of sweat* STENCH, reek, fetor, foul/bad smell; *informal* funk; *literary* miasma. **2** *(informal) a big stink about the new proposals* FUSS, commotion, rumpus, ruckus, trouble, outcry, uproar, brouhaha, furor; *informal* song and dance, to-do, kerfuffle, hoo-ha.

stinking ▶ adjective **1** *stinking garbage* FOUL-SMELLING, smelly, reeking, fetid, malodorous, rank, putrid, noxious; *informal* stinky, humming, funky; *literary* miasmic, noisome. **2** *(informal) this stinking tax* HORRIBLE, nasty, foul, dreadful, awful, terrible, frightful, ghastly, vile, rotten.
— OPPOSITES: sweet-smelling, aromatic.

stint ▶ verb *we saved by stinting on food* SKIMP, scrimp, be economical, economize, be sparing, hold back, be frugal; be mean, be parsimonious; limit, restrict; *informal* be stingy, be mingy, be tight.
▶ noun *a two-week stint in the office* SPELL, stretch, turn, session, term, shift, tour of duty.

stipulate ▶ verb SPECIFY, set down, set out, lay down; demand, require, insist on, make a condition of, prescribe, impose; *Law* provide.

stipulation ▶ noun CONDITION, precondition, proviso, provision, prerequisite, specification; demand, requirement; rider, caveat, qualification.

stir ▶ verb **1** *stir the mixture well* MIX, blend, agitate; beat, whip, whisk, fold in. **2** *Travis stirred in his sleep* MOVE SLIGHTLY, change one's position, shift. **3** *a breeze stirred the leaves* DISTURB, rustle, shake, move, flutter, agitate. **4** *she finally stirred at ten o'clock* GET UP, get out of bed, rouse oneself, rise; WAKE (UP), awaken; *informal* rise and shine, surface, show signs of life; *formal* arise; *literary* waken. **5** *I never stirred from here* MOVE, budge, make a move, shift, go away; leave. **6** *symbolism can stir the imagination* AROUSE, rouse, fire, kindle, inspire, stimulate, excite, awaken, quicken; *literary* waken. **7** *the war stirred him to action* SPUR, drive, rouse, prompt, propel, prod, motivate, encourage, urge, impel; provoke, goad, prick, sting, incite, light a fire under.
— OPPOSITES: go to bed, retire, go to sleep, stultify, stay, stay put.
▶ noun *the news caused a stir* COMMOTION, disturbance, fuss, excitement, turmoil, sensation; *informal* to-do, hoo-ha, hullabaloo, flap, splash.
■ **stir something up** WHIP UP, work up, foment, fan the flames of, trigger, spark off, precipitate, excite, provoke, incite, ignite.

stirring ▶ adjective EXCITING, thrilling, rousing, stimulating, moving, inspiring, inspirational, passionate, impassioned, emotional, heady.
— OPPOSITES: boring, pedestrian.

stitch ▶ noun *he was panting and had a stitch* SHARP PAIN, stabbing pain, shooting pain, stab of pain, pang, twinge, spasm.
▶ verb *the seams are stitched by hand* SEW, baste, tack; seam, hem; darn.

stock ▶ noun **1** *the shop carries little stock* MERCHANDISE, goods, wares, items/articles for sale, inventory. **2** *a stock of fuel* STORE, supply, stockpile, reserve, hoard, cache, bank, accumulation, quantity, collection. **3** *farm stock* ANIMALS, livestock, beasts; flocks, herds. **4** *blue-chip stocks* SHARES, securities, equities, bonds. **5** *her stock is low with most voters* POPULARITY, favour, regard, estimation, standing, status, reputation, name, prestige. **6** *his mother was of French stock* DESCENT, ancestry, origin(s), parentage, pedigree, lineage, line (of descent), heritage, birth, extraction, family, blood, bloodline. **7** *chicken stock* BOUILLON, broth, consommé. **8** *the stock of a weapon* HANDLE, butt, haft, grip, shaft, shank.

▶ **adjective 1** *a stock size* STANDARD, regular, normal, established, set; common, readily/widely available; staple. **2** *the stock response* USUAL, routine, predictable, set, standard, staple, customary, familiar, conventional, traditional, stereotyped, clichéd, hackneyed, unoriginal, formulaic.
 − OPPOSITES: non-standard, original, unusual.

▶ **verb 1** *we stock organic food* SELL, carry, keep (in stock), offer, have (for sale), retail, supply. **2** *the fridge was well stocked with milk* SUPPLY, provide, furnish, provision, equip, fill, load.

■ **in stock** FOR/ON SALE, (immediately) available, on the shelf.

■ **stock up on/with** AMASS SUPPLIES OF, stockpile, hoard, cache, lay in, buy up/in, put away/by, put/set aside, collect, accumulate, save; *informal* squirrel away, salt away, stash away.

■ **take stock of** REVIEW, assess, appraise, evaluate; *informal* size up.

stockings ▶ **plural noun** NYLONS, pantyhose, tights; hosiery, hose, stay-ups, leotards.

stockpile ▶ **noun** *a stockpile of weapons* STOCK, store, supply, accumulation, collection, reserve, hoard, cache; *informal* stash.

▶ **verb** *food had been stockpiled* STORE UP, amass, accumulate, store (up), stock up on, hoard, cache, collect, lay in, put away, put/set aside, put by, put away for a rainy day, stow away, save; *informal* salt away, stash away.

stock-still ▶ **adjective** MOTIONLESS, completely still, unmoving, not moving a muscle, immobile, like a statue/stone, rooted to the spot, transfixed, paralyzed, petrified, static, stationary.
 − OPPOSITES: moving, active.

stocky ▶ **adjective** THICKSET, sturdy, heavily built, chunky, burly, strapping, brawny, solid, heavy, heavy-set, hefty, beefy, blocky.
 − OPPOSITES: slender, skinny.

stodgy ▶ **adjective 1** *a stodgy pudding* SOLID, substantial, filling, hearty, heavy, starchy, indigestible. **2** *stodgy writing* BORING, dull, uninteresting, dreary, turgid, tedious, dry, unimaginative, uninspired, unexciting, unoriginal, monotonous, humdrum, prosaic, staid, heavy going; *informal* deadly, square.
 − OPPOSITES: light, interesting, lively.

stoic ▶ **adjective** LONG-SUFFERING, uncomplaining, patient, forbearing, accepting, tolerant, resigned, phlegmatic, philosophical.
 − OPPOSITES: complaining, intolerant.

stoicism ▶ **noun** PATIENCE, forbearance, resignation, fortitude, endurance, acceptance, tolerance, phlegm.
 − OPPOSITES: intolerance.

stoke ▶ **verb** ADD FUEL TO, mend, keep burning, tend.

stolid ▶ **adjective** IMPASSIVE, phlegmatic, unemotional, cool, calm, placid, unexcitable; dependable; unimaginative, dull.
 − OPPOSITES: emotional, lively, imaginative.

stomach ▶ **noun 1** *a stomach pain* ABDOMEN, belly, gut, middle; *informal* tummy, tum, breadbasket, insides. **2** *his fat stomach* PAUNCH, pot-belly, beer belly, Molson muscle ♣, girth; *informal* beer gut, pot, tummy, spare tire, middle-aged spread. **3** *he had no*

stomach for it APPETITE, taste, hunger, thirst; inclination, desire, relish, fancy.
 − RELATED TERMS: gastric.

▶ **verb 1** *I can't stomach butter* DIGEST, keep down, manage to eat/consume, tolerate, take. **2** *they couldn't stomach the sight* TOLERATE, put up with, take, stand, endure, bear; *informal* hack, abide.

stomach ache ▶ **noun** INDIGESTION, dyspepsia; colic, gripe, cramps; *informal* bellyache, tummy ache, gut ache, collywobbles.

stone ▶ **noun 1** *someone threw a stone at me* ROCK, pebble, boulder. **2** *a commemorative stone* TABLET, monument, monolith, obelisk; gravestone, headstone, tombstone. **3** *paving stones* SLAB, flagstone, flag, cobble. **4** *a precious stone* GEM, gemstone, jewel, semi-precious stone, brilliant; *informal* rock, sparkler. **5** *a peach stone* KERNEL, seed, pip, pit.
 − RELATED TERMS: lithic, lapidary.

stony ▶ **adjective 1** *a stony path* ROCKY, pebbly, gravelly, shingly; rough, hard. **2** *a stony stare* UNFRIENDLY, hostile, cold, chilly, frosty, icy; flinty, steely, stern, severe; fixed, expressionless, blank, poker-faced, deadpan; unfeeling, uncaring, unsympathetic, indifferent, cold-hearted, callous, heartless, hard-hearted, stony-hearted, merciless, pitiless.
 − OPPOSITES: smooth, friendly, sympathetic.

stooge ▶ **noun 1** *a government stooge* UNDERLING, minion, lackey, subordinate; henchman; PUPPET, pawn, cat's paw; *informal* sidekick. **2** *a comedian's stooge* BUTT, foil, straight man.

stoop ▶ **verb 1** *she stooped to pick up the pen* BEND (OVER/DOWN), lean over/down, crouch (down). **2** *he stooped his head* LOWER, bend, incline, bow, duck. **3** *he stoops when he walks* HUNCH ONE'S SHOULDERS, walk with a stoop, be round-shouldered. **4** *Davis would stoop to crime* LOWER ONESELF, sink, descend, resort; go as far as, sink as low as.

▶ **noun 1** *a man with a stoop* HUNCH, round shoulders; curvature of the spine; *Medicine* kyphosis. **2** *we sat on the front stoop and watched the passers-by* PORCH, steps, platform, veranda, terrace.

stop ▶ **verb 1** *we can't stop the decline* PUT AN END/STOP/ HALT TO, bring to an end/stop/halt/close/standstill, end, halt; finish, terminate, wind up, discontinue, cut short, interrupt, nip in the bud; deactivate, shut down. **2** *he stopped running* CEASE, discontinue, desist from, break off; give up, abandon, abstain from, cut out; *informal* quit, leave off, knock off, pack in, lay off, give over. **3** *the car stopped* PULL UP, draw up, come to a stop/halt, come to rest, pull in, pull over; park. **4** *the music stopped* CONCLUDE, come to an end/stop/ standstill, cease, end, finish, draw to a close, be over, terminate; pause, break off; peter out, fade away. **5** *divers stopped the flow of oil* STEM, staunch, hold back, check, curb, block, dam; *archaic* stay. **6** *the police stopped her leaving* PREVENT, hinder, obstruct, impede, block, bar, preclude; dissuade from. **7** *the council stopped the housing project* THWART, balk, foil, frustrate, stand in the way of; scotch, derail; *informal* put paid to, put the kibosh on, put a stop to, do for, stymie, scupper, scuttle, deep-six. **8** *just stop the bottle with your thumb* BLOCK (UP), plug, close (up), fill (up); seal, caulk, bung up; *technical* occlude.
 − OPPOSITES: start, begin, continue, allow, encourage, expedite, open.

▶ **noun 1** *all business came to a stop* HALT, end, finish, close, standstill; cessation, conclusion, stoppage, discontinuation. **2** *a brief stop in the town* BREAK,

stopover, stop-off, stay, visit; *formal* sojourn. **3** *the next stop is Neville Park* STOPPING PLACE, halt, station.
— OPPOSITES: start, beginning, continuation.
■ **put a stop to.** See STOP verb senses 1, 7.
■ **stop off/over** BREAK ONE'S JOURNEY, take a break, pause, linger; stay, remain, put up, lodge, rest; *formal* sojourn.

stop-gap ► noun *that old plane was merely a stop-gap* TEMPORARY SOLUTION/FIX, expedient, makeshift; substitute, stand-in, pinch-hitter.
► adjective *a stop-gap measure* TEMPORARY, provisional, interim, pro tem, short-term, working, makeshift, emergency; caretaker, acting, stand-in, fill-in.
— OPPOSITES: permanent.

stopover ► noun BREAK, stop, stop-off, layover, overnight, visit, stay; *formal* sojourn.

stoppage ► noun **1** *the stoppage of production* DISCONTINUATION, stopping, halting, cessation, termination, end, finish; interruption, suspension, breaking off. **2** *a stoppage of the blood supply* OBSTRUCTION, blocking, blockage, block; *Medicine* occlusion, stasis. **3** *a stoppage over pay* STRIKE, walkout; industrial action.
— OPPOSITES: start, continuation.

stopper ► noun BUNG, plug, cork, spigot, spile, seal.

store ► noun **1** *a store of money* STOCK, supply, stockpile, hoard, cache, reserve, bank, pool; *informal* war chest, pork barrel. **2** *a grain store* STOREROOM, storehouse, repository, depository, stockroom, depot, warehouse, magazine; *informal* lock-up. **3** *ship's stores* SUPPLIES, provisions, stocks, necessities; food, rations, provender; materials, equipment, hardware; *Military* matériel, accoutrements; *Nautical* chandlery. **4** *a hardware store* SHOP, (retail) outlet, boutique, department store, chain store, emporium; supermarket, hypermarket, superstore, megastore, big box store. *See also* CONVENIENCE STORE.
► verb *rabbits don't store food* KEEP, keep in reserve, stockpile, lay in, put/set aside, put away/by, put away for a rainy day, save, collect, accumulate, hoard, cache; *informal* squirrel away, salt away, stash away.
— OPPOSITES: use, discard.
■ **set (great) store by** VALUE, attach great importance to, put a high value on, put a premium on; THINK HIGHLY OF, hold in (high) regard, have a high opinion of; *informal* rate.

storehouse ► noun WAREHOUSE, depository, repository, store, storeroom, depot, storage.

storey ► noun FLOOR, level, deck.

storm ► noun **1** *battered by a storm* TEMPEST, squall; gale, hurricane, tornado, cyclone, typhoon; thunderstorm, thundershower, rainstorm, monsoon, hailstorm, snowstorm, blizzard; dust storm, black blizzard, windstorm. **2** *a storm of bullets* VOLLEY, salvo, fusillade, barrage, cannonade; shower, spray, hail, rain. **3** *there was a storm over his remarks* UPROAR, outcry, fuss, furor, brouhaha, rumpus, trouble, hue and cry, controversy; *informal* to-do, hoo-ha, hullabaloo, ballyhoo, stink, row. **4** *a storm of protest* OUTBURST, outbreak, explosion, eruption, outpouring, surge, blaze, flare-up, wave.
► verb **1** *she stormed out* STRIDE ANGRILY, stomp, march, stalk, flounce, stamp, fling. **2** *his mother stormed at him* RANT, rave, shout, bellow, roar, thunder, rage. **3** *police stormed the building* ATTACK, charge, rush, assail, descend on, swoop on.

stormy ► adjective **1** *stormy weather* BLUSTERY, squally, windy, gusty, blowy; rainy, thundery, snowy; wild, tempestuous, turbulent, violent, rough, foul.

2 *a stormy debate* ANGRY, heated, fiery, fierce, furious, passionate, lively.
— OPPOSITES: calm, fine, peaceful.

story ► noun **1** *an adventure story* TALE, narrative, anecdote; *informal* yarn, spiel. See table. **2** *the novel has a good story* PLOT, storyline, scenario, libretto. **3** *the story appeared in the papers* NEWS ITEM, news report, article, feature, piece. **4** *there have been a lot of stories going round* RUMOUR, piece of gossip, whisper; speculation. **5** *Harper changed his story* TESTIMONY, statement, report, account, version. **6** *Ellie never told stories.* See FALSEHOOD sense 1.

Types of Story

adventure story	gothic novel
allegory	historical novel
bedtime story	horror story
black comedy	just-so story
cliffhanger	legend
cock-and-bull story	mystery
comedy	myth
conte	parable
crime story	romance
detective story	saga
epic	shaggy-dog story
exemplum	short story
fable	tearjerker
fairy tale	thriller
fantasy	tragedy
fish story	traveller's tale
folk tale	true story
ghost story	urban myth

storyteller ► noun NARRATOR, teller of tales, raconteur, raconteuse, fabulist, anecdotalist.

stout ► adjective **1** *a short stout man* FAT, plump, portly, rotund, dumpy, chunky, corpulent; stocky, burly, bulky, hefty, heavy-set, solidly built, thickset; *informal* tubby, pudgy, zaftig, corn-fed. **2** *stout leather shoes* STRONG, sturdy, solid, substantial, robust, tough, durable, hard-wearing. **3** *stout resistance* DETERMINED, vigorous, forceful, spirited; staunch, steadfast, stalwart, firm, resolute, unyielding, dogged; brave, bold, courageous, valiant, valorous, gallant, fearless, doughty, intrepid; *informal* gutsy, spunky.
— OPPOSITES: thin, flimsy, feeble.

stout-hearted ► adjective BRAVE, determined, courageous, bold, plucky, spirited, valiant, valorous, gallant, fearless, doughty, intrepid, stalwart; *informal* gutsy, spunky.

stove ► noun OVEN, range, cooker, wood stove, wood-burning stove, wood-burner, pot-bellied stove, Franklin stove, camp stove, hot plate; *proprietary* Coleman stove, cookstove; *proprietary* Primus, Quebec heater ♣, airtight, (*North*) Yukon stove ♣, salamander.

stow ► verb *Barney stowed her bags in the trunk* PACK, load, store, place, put (away), deposit, stash.
— OPPOSITES: unload.
■ **stow away** HIDE, conceal oneself, travel secretly.

straddle ► verb **1** *she straddled the motorbike* SIT/STAND ASTRIDE, bestride, mount, get on. **2** *a mountain range straddling the border* LIE ON BOTH SIDES OF, extend across, span. **3** *he straddled the issue of taxes* BE EQUIVOCAL ABOUT, be undecided about, equivocate about, vacillate about, waver about, waffle on; *informal* sit on the fence regarding.

strafe ▶ verb BOMB, shell, bombard, fire on, machine-gun, rake with gunfire, enfilade; *archaic* fusillade.

straggle ▶ verb TRAIL, lag, dawdle, walk slowly, dally, lallygag; fall behind, bring up the rear.

straggly ▶ adjective UNTIDY, messy, unkempt, straggling, dishevelled.

straight ▶ adjective **1** *a long, straight road* UNSWERVING, undeviating, linear, as straight as an arrow, uncurving, unbending. **2** *that picture isn't straight* LEVEL, even, in line, aligned, square; vertical, upright, perpendicular; horizontal. **3** *we must get the place straight* IN ORDER, (neat and) tidy, neat, shipshape, orderly, spic and span, organized, arranged, sorted out, straightened out. **4** *a straight answer* HONEST, direct, frank, candid, truthful, sincere, forthright, straightforward, plain-spoken, blunt, straight from the shoulder, unequivocal, unambiguous; *informal* upfront. **5** *straight thinking* LOGICAL, rational, clear, lucid, sound, coherent. **6** *three straight wins* SUCCESSIVE, in succession, consecutive, in a row, running. **7** *straight brandy* UNDILUTED, neat, pure, straight up. **8** (*informal*) *she's very straight* RESPECTABLE, conventional, conservative, traditional, old-fashioned, straitlaced; *informal* stuffy, square, fuddy-duddy.
− OPPOSITES: winding, crooked, untidy, evasive.
▶ adverb **1** *he looked me straight in the eyes* RIGHT, directly, squarely, full; *informal* smack, bang, spang, smack dab. **2** *she drove straight home* DIRECTLY, right, by a direct route. **3** *I'll call you straight back* RIGHT AWAY, straight away, immediately, directly, at once; *archaic* straightway. **4** *I told her straight* FRANKLY, directly, candidly, honestly, forthrightly, plainly, point-blank, bluntly, flatly, straight from the shoulder, without beating about the bush, without mincing words, unequivocally, unambiguously, in plain English, to someone's face, straight up. **5** *he can't think straight* LOGICALLY, rationally, clearly, lucidly, coherently, cogently.
■ **go straight** REFORM, mend one's ways, turn over a new leaf, get back on the straight and narrow.
■ **straight away** AT ONCE, right away, (right) now, this/that (very) minute, this/that instant, immediately, instantly, directly, forthwith, without further/more ado, promptly, quickly, without delay, then and there, here and now, as soon as possible, ASAP, as quickly as possible, in short order; *informal* straight off, PDQ, pretty damn quick, pronto, lickety-split; *archaic* straightway.
■ **straight from the shoulder.** See STRAIGHT adverb sense 4.

straighten ▶ verb **1** *Rory straightened his tie* MAKE STRAIGHT, adjust, arrange, rearrange, (make) tidy, spruce up. **2** *we must straighten things out with Viola* PUT/SET RIGHT, sort out, clear up, settle, resolve, put in order, regularize, rectify, remedy; *informal* patch up. **3** *he straightened up* STAND UP (STRAIGHT), stand upright.

straightforward ▶ adjective **1** *the process was remarkably straightforward* UNCOMPLICATED, simple, easy, effortless, painless, undemanding, plain sailing, child's play; *informal* as easy as pie, a piece of cake, a cinch, a snip, a breeze, a cakewalk, duck soup, a snap. **2** *a straightforward man* HONEST, frank, candid, open, truthful, sincere, on the level; forthright, plain-speaking, direct, unambiguous; *informal* upfront, on the up and up.
− OPPOSITES: complicated.

strain¹ ▶ verb **1** *take care that you don't strain yourself* OVERTAX, overwork, overextend, overreach, drive too far, overdo it; exhaust, wear out; *informal* knock oneself out. **2** *you have strained a muscle* INJURE, damage, pull, wrench, twist, sprain. **3** *we strained to haul the guns up the slope* STRUGGLE, labour, toil, make every effort, try very hard, break one's back, push/ drive oneself to the limit; *informal* pull out all the stops, go all out, bust a gut. **4** *the flood of refugees is straining the relief services* MAKE EXCESSIVE DEMANDS ON, overtax, be too much for, test, tax, put a strain on. **5** *the bear strained at the chain* PULL, tug, heave, haul, jerk; *informal* yank. **6** (*archaic*) *she strained the infant to her bosom* CLASP, press, clutch, hold tight; embrace, hug, enfold, envelop. **7** *strain the mixture* SIEVE, sift, filter, screen, riddle; *rare* filtrate.
▶ noun **1** *the rope snapped under the strain* TENSION, tightness, tautness. **2** *muscle strain* INJURY, sprain, wrench, twist. **3** *the strain of her job* PRESSURE, demands, burdens; stress; *informal* hassle. **4** *Nancy was showing signs of strain* STRESS, (nervous) tension; exhaustion, fatigue, pressure of work, overwork. **5** *the strains of Brahms's lullaby* SOUND, music; melody, tune.

strain² ▶ noun **1** *a different strain of flu* VARIETY, kind, type, sort; breed, genus. **2** *McCallum was of Puritan strain* DESCENT, ancestry, origin(s), parentage, lineage, extraction, family, roots. **3** *there was a strain of insanity in the family* TENDENCY, susceptibility, propensity, proneness; trait, disposition. **4** *a strain of solemnity* ELEMENT, strand, vein, note, trace, touch, suggestion, hint.

strained ▶ adjective **1** *relations between them were strained* AWKWARD, tense, uneasy, uncomfortable, edgy, difficult, troubled. **2** *Jean's strained face* DRAWN, careworn, worn, pinched, tired, exhausted, drained, haggard. **3** *a strained smile* FORCED, constrained, unnatural; artificial, insincere, false, affected, put-on.
− OPPOSITES: friendly.

strainer ▶ noun SIEVE, colander, filter, sifter, riddle, screen; *archaic* griddle.

strait ▶ noun **1** *a strait about six miles wide* CHANNEL, sound, (*Atlantic*) tickle ❧, inlet, stretch of water. **2** *the company is in desperate straits* A BAD/DIFFICULT SITUATION, difficulty, trouble, crisis, a mess, a predicament, a plight; *informal* hot/deep water, a jam, a hole, a bind, a fix, a scrape.

straitened ▶ adjective IMPOVERISHED, poverty-stricken, poor, destitute, penniless, as poor as a church mouse, in penury, impecunious, unable to make ends meet, in reduced circumstances; *informal* (flat) broke, strapped (for cash); *formal* penurious.

straitlaced ▶ adjective PRIM (AND PROPER), prudish, puritanical, prissy, conservative, old-fashioned, stuffy, staid, narrow-minded; *informal* starchy, square, fuddy-duddy.
− OPPOSITES: broad-minded.

strand¹ ▶ noun **1** *strands of wool* THREAD, filament, fibre; length, ply. **2** *the various strands of the ecological movement* ELEMENT, component, factor, ingredient, aspect, feature, strain.

strand² ▶ noun (*literary*) *a walk along the strand* SEASHORE, shore, beach, sands, foreshore, shoreline, seaside, waterfront, front, waterside.

stranded ▶ adjective **1** *a stranded ship* BEACHED, grounded, run aground, high and dry; shipwrecked, wrecked, marooned. **2** *she was stranded in a strange city* HELPLESS, without resources, in difficulties; in the lurch, abandoned, deserted.

strange ▶ adjective **1** *strange things have been happening* UNUSUAL, odd, curious, peculiar, funny, bizarre, weird, uncanny, queer, unexpected, unfamiliar, atypical, anomalous, out of the ordinary, extraordinary, puzzling, mystifying, mysterious, perplexing, baffling, unaccountable, inexplicable, singular, freakish; suspicious, questionable; eerie, unnatural; *informal* fishy, creepy, spooky. **2** *strange clothes* WEIRD, eccentric, odd, peculiar, funny, bizarre, unusual; unconventional, outlandish, freakish, quirky, zany; *informal* wacky, way out, freaky, kooky, offbeat, off the wall, screwy, wacko. **3** *visiting a strange house* UNFAMILIAR, unknown, new. **4** *Jean was feeling strange* ILL, unwell, poorly, peaky; *informal* under the weather, funny, peculiar, lousy, off; *dated* queer. **5** *she felt strange with him* ILL AT EASE, uneasy, uncomfortable, awkward, self-conscious. **6** (*archaic*) *I am strange to the work. See* A STRANGER TO *at* STRANGER.
– OPPOSITES: ordinary, familiar.

strangeness ▶ noun ODDITY, eccentricity, peculiarity, curiousness, bizarreness, weirdness, queerness, unusualness, abnormality, unaccountability, inexplicability, incongruousness, outlandishness, singularity.

stranger ▶ noun NEWCOMER, new arrival, visitor, outsider, newbie.
■ **a stranger to** UNACCUSTOMED TO, unfamiliar with, unused to, new to, fresh to, inexperienced in; *archaic* strange to.

strangle ▶ verb **1** *the victim was strangled with a scarf* THROTTLE, choke, garrotte; *informal* strangulate. **2** *she strangled a sob* SUPPRESS, smother, stifle, repress, restrain, fight back, choke back. **3** *bureaucracy is strangling commercial activity* HAMPER, hinder, impede, restrict, inhibit, curb, check, constrain, squash, crush, suppress, repress.

strap ▶ noun *thick leather straps* THONG, tie, band, belt. ▶ verb **1** *a bag was strapped to the bicycle* FASTEN, secure, tie, bind, make fast, lash, truss. **2** *his knee was strapped up* BANDAGE, bind. **3** *his father strapped him. See* LASH *verb* sense 1.

strapping ▶ adjective BIG, strong, well-built, brawny, burly, broad-shouldered, muscular, rugged; *informal* hunky, beefy; *dated* stalwart.
– OPPOSITES: weedy.

stratagem ▶ noun PLAN, scheme, tactic, manoeuvre, ploy, device, trick, ruse, plot, machination, dodge; subterfuge, artifice, wile; *archaic* shift.

strategic ▶ adjective PLANNED, calculated, tactical, politic, judicious, prudent, shrewd.

strategy ▶ noun **1** *the government's economic strategy* MASTER PLAN, grand design, game plan, plan (of action), action plan, policy, program; tactics. **2** *military strategy* THE ART OF WAR, (military) tactics.

stratum ▶ noun **1** *a stratum of flint* LAYER, vein, seam, lode, bed. **2** *this stratum of society* LEVEL, class, echelon, rank, grade, group, set; caste; *dated* station, estate.

stray ▶ verb **1** *the gazelle had strayed from the herd* WANDER OFF, go astray, get separated, get lost. **2** *we strayed from our original topic* DIGRESS, deviate, wander, get sidetracked, go off at a tangent, veer off; get off the subject. **3** *the young men were likely to stray* BE UNFAITHFUL, have affairs, cheat, philander; *informal* play around, play the field. **4** *he strayed from the path of righteousness* SIN, transgress, err, go astray; *archaic* trespass. ▶ adjective **1** *a stray dog* HOMELESS, lost, strayed, gone astray, abandoned. **2** *a stray bullet* RANDOM, chance, freak, unexpected, isolated, lone, single. ▶ noun *she adopted three strays* HOMELESS ANIMAL, stray dog/cat, waif.

streak ▶ noun **1** *a streak of orange light* BAND, line, strip, stripe, vein, slash, ray. **2** *green streaks on her legs* MARK, smear, smudge, stain, blotch; *informal* splotch. **3** *a streak of self-destructiveness* ELEMENT, vein, touch, strain; trait, characteristic. **4** *a winning streak* PERIOD, spell, stretch, run, patch. ▶ verb **1** *the sky was streaked with red* STRIPE, band, fleck. **2** *overalls streaked with paint* MARK, daub, smear; *informal* splotch.

streaky ▶ adjective STRIPED, stripy, streaked, banded, veined.

stream ▶ noun **1** *a mountain stream* CREEK, river, rivulet, rill, runnel, streamlet, freshet; tributary; bourn; brook. **2** *a stream of boiling water* JET, flow, rush, gush, surge, torrent, flood, cascade, outpouring, outflow; *technical* efflux. **3** *a steady stream of visitors* SUCCESSION, flow, series, string. ▶ verb **1** *tears were streaming down her face* FLOW, pour, course, run, gush, surge, flood, cascade, spill. **2** *children streamed out of the classrooms* POUR, surge, charge, flood, swarm, pile, crowd. **3** *a flag streamed from the mast* FLUTTER, float, flap, fly, blow, waft, wave.

streamer ▶ noun PENNANT, pennon, flag, banderole, banner.

streamlined ▶ adjective **1** *streamlined cars* AERODYNAMIC, smooth, sleek. **2** *a streamlined organization* EFFICIENT, smooth-running, well run, slick; time-saving, labour-saving.

street ▶ noun *Amsterdam's narrow cobbled streets* ROAD, thoroughfare, avenue, drive, crescent, boulevard; side street/road, lane, highway.
■ **the man/woman in the street** AN ORDINARY PERSON, Mr./Ms. Average; *informal* Joe Public, John Q. Public, Joe Blow, Joe Schmoe, schmo; John Doe, Joe Sixpack.
■ **on the streets** HOMELESS, down and out.

street hockey (*Cdn*) ▶ noun ball hockey ✦, road hockey ✦.

street smarts ▶ noun COMMON SENSE, acumen, savvy, shrewdness, wisdom, know-how, horse sense.

streetwise ▶ adjective WORLDLY, savvy, street smart, experienced, seasoned.

strength ▶ noun **1** *enormous physical strength* POWER, brawn, muscle, muscularity, burliness, sturdiness, robustness, toughness, hardiness, vigour, force, might; *informal* beef; *literary* thew. **2** *Oliver began to regain his strength* HEALTH, fitness, vigour, stamina. **3** *her great inner strength* FORTITUDE, resilience, spirit, backbone, strength of character; courage, bravery, pluck, pluckiness, courageousness, grit, mettle; *informal* guts, spunk. **4** *the strength of the retaining wall* ROBUSTNESS, sturdiness, firmness, toughness, soundness, solidity, durability. **5** *China's military strength* POWER, influence, dominance, ascendancy, supremacy; *informal* clout; *literary* puissance. **6** *the strength of feeling against the president* INTENSITY, vehemence, force, forcefulness, depth, ardour, fervour. **7** *the strength of their argument* COGENCY, forcefulness, force, weight, power, potency, persuasiveness, soundness, validity. **8** *what are your strengths?* STRONG POINT, advantage, asset, forte, aptitude, talent, skill; specialty. **9** *the strength of the*

army SIZE, extent, magnitude.
– OPPOSITES: weakness.
■ **on the strength of** BECAUSE OF, by virtue of, on the basis of.

strengthen ▶ verb **1** *calcium strengthens growing bones* FORTIFY, make strong/stronger, build up, give strength to. **2** *engineers strengthened the walls* REINFORCE, make stronger, buttress, shore up, underpin. **3** *strengthened glass* TOUGHEN, temper, anneal. **4** *the wind had strengthened* BECOME STRONG/ STRONGER, gain strength, intensify, pick up. **5** *his insistence strengthened her determination* FORTIFY, bolster, make stronger, boost, reinforce, harden, stiffen, toughen, fuel. **6** *they strengthened their efforts* REDOUBLE, step up, increase, escalate; *informal* up, crank up, beef up. **7** *the argument is strengthened by this evidence* REINFORCE, lend more weight to; support, substantiate, back up, confirm, bear out, corroborate.
– OPPOSITES: weaken.

strenuous ▶ adjective **1** *a strenuous climb* ARDUOUS, difficult, hard, tough, taxing, demanding, exacting, exhausting, tiring, gruelling, back-breaking; *informal* killing; *archaic* toilsome. **2** *strenuous efforts* VIGOROUS, energetic, zealous, forceful, strong, spirited, intense, determined, resolute, tenacious, tireless, indefatigable, dogged; *formal* pertinacious.
– OPPOSITES: easy, half-hearted.

stress ▶ noun **1** *he's under a lot of stress* STRAIN, pressure, (nervous) tension, worry, anxiety, trouble, difficulty; *informal* hassle. **2** *laying greater stress on education* EMPHASIS, importance, weight. **3** *the stress falls on the first syllable* EMPHASIS, accent, accentuation; beat; *Prosody* ictus. **4** *the stress is uniform across the bar* PRESSURE, tension, strain.
▶ verb **1** *they stressed the need for reform* EMPHASIZE, draw attention to, underline, underscore, point up, place emphasis on, lay stress on, highlight, accentuate, press home. **2** *the last syllable is stressed* PLACE THE EMPHASIS ON, emphasize, place the accent on. **3** *all the staff were stressed* OVERSTRETCH, overtax, push to the limit, pressure, make tense, worry, harass; *informal* hassle.
– OPPOSITES: play down.

stressful ▶ adjective DEMANDING, trying, taxing, difficult, hard, tough; fraught, traumatic, pressured, tense, frustrating.
– OPPOSITES: relaxing.

stretch ▶ verb **1** *this material stretches* BE ELASTIC, be stretchy, be tensile. **2** *he stretched the elastic* PULL (OUT), draw out, extend, lengthen, elongate, expand. **3** *stretch your weekend into a vacation* PROLONG, lengthen, make longer, extend, spin out. **4** *my budget won't stretch to a new car* BE SUFFICIENT FOR, be enough for, cover; afford, have the money for. **5** *the court case stretched their finances* PUT A STRAIN ON, overtax, overextend, drain, sap. **6** *stretching the truth* BEND, strain, distort, exaggerate, embellish. **7** *she stretched out her hand to him* REACH OUT, hold out, extend, outstretch, proffer; *literary* outreach. **8** *he stretched his arms* EXTEND, straighten (out). **9** *she stretched out on the sofa* LIE DOWN, recline, lean back, be recumbent, sprawl, lounge, loll. **10** *the desert stretches for miles* EXTEND, spread, continue.
– OPPOSITES: shorten.
▶ noun **1** *magnificent stretches of forest* EXPANSE, area, tract, belt, sweep, extent. **2** *a four-hour stretch* PERIOD, time, spell, run, stint, session, shift. **3** *(informal) a*

ten-year stretch (PRISON) SENTENCE, rap.
▶ **adjective** *stretch fabrics* STRETCHY, stretchable, elastic.

strew ▶ verb SCATTER, spread, disperse, litter, toss; *literary* bestrew.

stricken ▶ adjective TROUBLED, (deeply) affected, afflicted, struck, hit.

strict ▶ adjective **1** *a strict interpretation of the law* PRECISE, exact, literal, faithful, accurate, rigorous, careful, meticulous, pedantic. **2** *strict controls on spending* STRINGENT, rigorous, severe, harsh, hard, rigid, tough, ironclad. **3** *strict parents* STERN, severe, harsh, uncompromising, authoritarian, firm, austere. **4** *this will be treated in strict confidence* ABSOLUTE, utter, complete, total. **5** *a strict Roman Catholic* ORTHODOX, devout, conscientious.
– OPPOSITES: loose, liberal.

strictness ▶ noun **1** *the strictness of the laws* SEVERITY, harshness, rigidity, rigidness, stringency, rigorousness, sternness. **2** *the provision has been interpreted with strictness* PRECISION, preciseness, accuracy, exactness, faithfulness; meticulousness, scrupulousness.
– OPPOSITES: imprecision.

stricture ▶ noun **1** *the constant strictures of the nuns* CRITICISM, censure, condemnation, reproof, reproach, admonishment, animadversion. **2** *the strictures on Victorian women* CONSTRAINT, restriction, limitation, restraint, curb, impediment, barrier, obstacle. **3** *an intestinal stricture* NARROWING, constriction.
– OPPOSITES: praise, freedom.

stride ▶ verb *she came striding down the path* MARCH, pace, step.
▶ **noun** *long swinging strides* (LONG/LARGE) STEP, pace.
■ **take something in one's stride** DEAL WITH EASILY, cope with easily, not bat an eyelid, absorb.

strident ▶ adjective HARSH, raucous, rough, grating, rasping, jarring, loud, shrill, screeching, piercing, ear-piercing.
– OPPOSITES: soft.

strife ▶ noun CONFLICT, friction, discord, disagreement, dissension, dispute, argument, quarrelling, wrangling, bickering, controversy; ill/ bad feeling, falling-out, bad blood, hostility, animosity.
– OPPOSITES: peace.

strike ▶ verb **1** *the teacher struck Mary* HIT, slap, smack, beat, thrash, spank, thump, punch, cuff; cane, lash, whip, club; *informal* clout, schmuck, wallop, belt, whack, thwack, bash, clobber, bop, cold-cock; *literary* smite. **2** *he struck the gong* BANG, beat, hit; *informal* bash, wallop. **3** *the car struck a tree* CRASH INTO, collide with, hit, run into, bump into, smash into, impact. **4** *Jennifer struck the ball* HIT, drive, propel; *informal* clout, wallop, swipe. **5** *he struck a match* IGNITE, light. **6** *she was asleep when the killer struck* ATTACK, set upon someone, fall on someone, assault someone. **7** *the disease is striking 3,000 people a year* AFFECT, afflict, attack, hit. **8** *striking a balance* ACHIEVE, reach, arrive at, find, attain, establish. **9** *we have struck a bargain* AGREE (ON), come to an agreement on, settle on; *informal* clinch. **10** *he struck a heroic pose* ASSUME, adopt, take on/up, affect, cop. **11** *they have struck oil* DISCOVER, find, come upon, hit. **12** *a thought struck her* OCCUR TO, come to (mind), dawn on one, hit, spring to mind, enter one's head. **13** *you strike me as intelligent* SEEM TO, appear to, come across as, give the impression of. **14** *train drivers are striking* TAKE INDUSTRIAL ACTION, go on strike, down tools, walk out, hit the bricks. **15** *they struck the big tent* TAKE DOWN, pull down. **16** *Lord Black struck his flag* LOWER, take down, bring down. **17** *we should strike south* GO, make one's way, head, forge.

▶ **noun 1** *a 48-hour strike* INDUSTRIAL ACTION, walkout, job action, stoppage. **2** *a military strike* (AIR) ATTACK, assault, bombing, raid. **3** *a gold strike* FIND, discovery.

■ **strike something out** DELETE, cross out, erase, rub out.

■ **strike something up 1** *the band struck up another tune* BEGIN TO PLAY, start playing. **2** *we struck up a friendship* BEGIN, start, commence, embark on, establish.

striking ▶ **adjective 1** *Lizzie bears a striking resemblance to her sister* NOTICEABLE, obvious, conspicuous, evident, marked, notable, unmistakable, strong; remarkable, extraordinary, incredible, amazing, astounding, astonishing, staggering. **2** *Kenya's striking landscape* IMPRESSIVE, imposing, grand, splendid, magnificent, spectacular, breathtaking, superb, marvellous, wonderful, stunning, staggering, sensational, dramatic. **3** *striking good looks* STUNNING, attractive, good-looking, beautiful, glamorous, gorgeous, prepossessing, ravishing, handsome, pretty; *informal* knockout, drop-dead gorgeous; *archaic* fair, comely.
– OPPOSITES: unremarkable.

string ▶ **noun 1** *a knotted piece of string* TWINE, cord, yarn, thread, strand. **2** *a string of brewers* CHAIN, group, firm, company. **3** *a string of convictions* SERIES, succession, chain, sequence, run, streak. **4** *a string of wagons* LINE, train, procession, queue, file, column, convoy, cavalcade. **5** *a string of pearls* STRAND, rope, necklace. **6** *a guaranteed loan with no strings* CONDITION, qualification, provision, proviso, caveat, stipulation, rider, prerequisite, limitation, limit, constraint, restriction; *informal* catch.
▶ **verb 1** *lights were strung across the promenade* HANG, suspend, sling, stretch, run; thread, loop, festoon. **2** *beads strung on a silver chain* THREAD, loop, link.

■ **string along** GO ALONG, come too, accompany, join (up with).

■ **string someone along** (*informal*) MISLEAD, deceive, take advantage of, dupe, hoax, fool, make a fool of, play with, toy with, dally with, trifle with; *informal* lead up the garden path, take for a ride.

■ **string something out 1** *stringing out a story* SPIN OUT, drag out, lengthen. **2** *airfields strung out along the Gulf* SPREAD OUT, space out, distribute, scatter.

■ **string someone up** (*informal*) HANG, lynch, gibbet.

stringent ▶ **adjective** STRICT, firm, rigid, rigorous, severe, harsh, tough, tight, exacting, demanding, inflexible, hard and fast.

stringy ▶ **adjective 1** *stringy hair* STRAGGLY, lank, thin. **2** *a stringy brunette* LANKY, gangling, gangly, rangy, wiry, bony, skinny, scrawny, thin, spare, gaunt. **3** *stringy meat* FIBROUS, gristly, sinewy, chewy, tough, leathery.

strip¹ ▶ **verb 1** *he stripped and got into bed* UNDRESS, strip off, take one's clothes off, unclothe, disrobe, strip naked. **2** *stripping off paint* PEEL, remove, take off, scrape, rub, clean. **3** *they stripped her of her doctorate* TAKE AWAY FROM, dispossess, deprive, confiscate, divest, relieve. **4** *they stripped down my engine* DISMANTLE, disassemble, take to bits/pieces, take apart. **5** *the house had been stripped* EMPTY, clear, clean out, plunder, rob, burgle, burglarize, loot, pillage, ransack, despoil, sack.
– OPPOSITES: dress.

strip² ▶ **noun** *a strip of paper* (NARROW) PIECE, bit, band, belt, ribbon, slip, shred.

stripe ▶ **noun** LINE, band, strip, belt, bar, streak, vein, flash, blaze; *technical* stria, striation.

striped ▶ **adjective**. See STRIPY.

stripling ▶ **noun** YOUTH, adolescent, youngster, boy, schoolboy, lad, teenager, juvenile, minor, young man; *informal* kid, young 'un, whippersnapper, shaver, laddie.

stripper ▶ **noun** EXOTIC DANCER, lap dancer, peeler.

stripy ▶ **adjective** STRIPED, barred, lined, banded; streaky, variegated; *technical* striated.

strive ▶ **verb 1** *I shall strive to be virtuous* TRY (HARD), attempt, endeavour, aim, venture, make an effort, exert oneself, do one's best, do all one can, do one's utmost, labour, work; *informal* go all out, give it one's best shot, pull out all the stops; *formal* essay. **2** *scholars must strive against bias* STRUGGLE, fight, battle, combat; campaign, crusade.

stroke ▶ **noun 1** *five strokes of the axe* BLOW, hit, thump, punch, slap, smack, cuff, knock; *informal* wallop, clout, whack, thwack, bash, swipe; *archaic* smite. **2** *she hit the green in three strokes* SHOT, hit, strike. **3** *light upward strokes* MOVEMENT, action, motion. **4** *a stroke of genius* FEAT, accomplishment, achievement, master stroke. **5** *broad brush strokes* MARK, line. **6** *the budget was full of bold strokes* DETAIL, touch, point. **7** *he suffered a stroke* THROMBOSIS, seizure; *Medicine* ictus.
▶ **verb** *she stroked the cat* CARESS, fondle, pat, pet, touch, rub, massage, soothe.

stroll ▶ **verb** *they strolled along the river* SAUNTER, amble, wander, meander, ramble, promenade, walk, go for a walk, stretch one's legs, get some air; *informal* mosey; *formal* perambulate.
▶ **noun** *a stroll in the park* SAUNTER, amble, wander, walk, turn, promenade; *informal* mosey; *dated* constitutional; *formal* perambulation.

strong ▶ **adjective 1** *Ben is a strong lad* POWERFUL, muscular, brawny, powerfully built, strapping, sturdy, burly, meaty, robust, athletic, tough, rugged, lusty, strong as an ox/horse; *informal* beefy, hunky, husky; *dated* stalwart. **2** *a strong character* FORCEFUL, determined, spirited, self-assertive, tough, tenacious, indomitable, formidable, redoubtable, strong-minded; *informal* gutsy, feisty. **3** *a strong fortress* SECURE, well-built, indestructible, well fortified, well protected, impregnable, solid. **4** *strong cotton bags* DURABLE, hard-wearing, heavy-duty, industrial-strength, tough, sturdy, well-made, long-lasting. **5** *the current is very strong* FORCEFUL, powerful, vigorous, fierce, intense. **6** *a strong interest in literature* KEEN, eager, passionate, fervent. **7** *strong feelings* INTENSE, forceful, passionate, ardent, fervent, fervid, deep-seated; *literary* perfervid. **8** *a strong supporter* KEEN, eager, enthusiastic, dedicated, staunch, loyal, steadfast. **9** *strong arguments* COMPELLING, cogent, forceful, powerful, potent, weighty, convincing, sound, valid, well-founded, persuasive, influential. **10** *a need for strong action* FIRM, forceful, drastic, extreme. **11** *she bore a very strong resemblance to Vera* MARKED, striking, noticeable, pronounced, distinct, definite, unmistakable, notable. **12** *a strong voice* LOUD, powerful, forceful, resonant, sonorous, rich, deep, booming. **13** *strong language* BAD, foul, obscene, profane. **14** *a strong blue colour* INTENSE, deep, rich, bright, brilliant, vivid. **15** *strong lights* BRIGHT, brilliant, dazzling, glaring. **16** *strong black coffee* CONCENTRATED, undiluted, potent. **17** *strong cheese* HIGHLY FLAVOURED, flavourful,

piquant, tangy, spicy. **18** *strong drink* ALCOHOLIC, intoxicating, hard, stiff; *formal* spirituous.
— OPPOSITES: weak, gentle, mild.

strong-arm ▶ adjective AGGRESSIVE, forceful, bullying, coercive, threatening, intimidatory.

strongbox ▶ noun SAFE, safety deposit box, cash/money box.

stronghold ▶ noun **1** *the enemy stronghold* FORTRESS, fort, castle, citadel, garrison. **2** *a Liberal stronghold* BASTION, centre, hotbed, safe seat.

strong-minded ▶ adjective DETERMINED, firm, resolute, purposeful, strong-willed, uncompromising, unbending, forceful, persistent, tenacious, dogged; *informal* gutsy, spunky.

strong point ▶ noun STRENGTH, strong suit, forte, specialty.
— OPPOSITES: weakness.

strong-willed ▶ adjective DETERMINED, resolute, stubborn, obstinate, wilful, headstrong, strong-minded, self-willed, unbending, unyielding, intransigent, intractable, obdurate, recalcitrant; *formal* refractory.

structure ▶ noun **1** *a vast Gothic structure* BUILDING, edifice, construction, erection, pile. **2** *the structure of local government* CONSTRUCTION, form, formation, shape, composition, anatomy, makeup, constitution; organization, system, arrangement, design, framework, configuration, pattern.
▶ verb *the program is structured around periods of home study* ARRANGE, organize, design, shape, construct, build, put together.

struggle ▶ verb **1** *they struggled to do better* STRIVE, try hard, endeavour, make every effort, do one's best/utmost, bend over backwards, put oneself out; *informal* go all out, give it one's best shot; *formal* essay. **2** *James struggled with the raiders* FIGHT, grapple, wrestle, scuffle, brawl, spar; *informal* scrap. **3** *the teams struggled to be first* COMPETE, contend, vie, fight, battle, jockey. **4** *she struggled over the dunes* SCRAMBLE, flounder, stumble, fight/battle one's way, labour.
▶ noun **1** *the struggle for justice* ENDEAVOUR, striving, effort, exertion, labour; campaign, battle, crusade, drive, push. **2** *they were arrested without a struggle* FIGHT, scuffle, brawl, tussle, wrestling bout, skirmish, fracas, melee; breach of the peace; *informal* scrap, dust-up, punch-up, bust-up. **3** *many perished in the struggle* CONFLICT, fight, battle, confrontation, clash, skirmish; hostilities, fighting, war, warfare, campaign. **4** *a struggle within the leadership* CONTEST, competition, fight, clash; rivalry, friction, feuding, conflict, tug-of-war, turf war. **5** *life has been a struggle for me* EFFORT, trial, trouble, stress, strain, battle; *informal* grind, hassle.

strumpet ▶ noun *(archaic)*. See PROSTITUTE *noun*.

strut ▶ verb SWAGGER, swank, parade, stride, sweep, sashay.

stub ▶ noun **1** *a cigarette stub* BUTT, (tail) end. **2** *a ticket stub* COUNTERFOIL, ticket slip, tab. **3** *a stub of pencil* STUMP, remnant, (tail) end.

stubble ▶ noun **1** *a field of stubble* STALKS, straw. **2** *grey stubble* BRISTLES, whiskers, facial hair; *informal* five o'clock shadow.

stubbly ▶ adjective BRISTLY, unshaven, whiskered; prickly, rough, coarse, scratchy.

stubborn ▶ adjective **1** *you're too stubborn to admit it* OBSTINATE, headstrong, wilful, strong-willed, pigheaded, obdurate, difficult, contrary, perverse, recalcitrant, inflexible, iron-willed,

uncompromising, unbending; *informal* stiff-necked, bloody-minded, balky; *formal* pertinacious, refractory, contumacious. **2** *stubborn stains* INDELIBLE, permanent, persistent, tenacious, resistant.
— OPPOSITES: compliant.

stubby ▶ adjective DUMPY, stocky, chunky, chubby, squat; short, stumpy, dwarfish.
— OPPOSITES: slender, tall.

stuck ▶ adjective **1** *a message was stuck to his screen* FIXED, fastened, attached, glued, pinned. **2** *the gate was stuck* IMMOVABLE, stuck fast, jammed. **3** *if you get stuck, leave a blank* BAFFLED, beaten, at a loss, at one's wits' end; *informal* stumped, bogged down, flummoxed, fazed, bamboozled.
■ **stuck on** (*informal*) INFATUATED WITH, besotted with, smitten with, (head over heels) in love with, obsessed with; *informal* struck on, crazy about, mad about, wild about, carrying a torch for.
■ **stuck with** LUMBERED WITH, left with, made responsible for.

stuck-up ▶ adjective (*informal*). See CONCEITED.

stud ▶ noun **1** *he's a real stud* HUNK, ladies' man, lady-killer, Romeo, Don Juan, Casanova, Lothario, womanizer, playboy, gigolo, lover, chick/babe magnet, studmuffin. **2** *a jacket with silver studs* BUTTON, fastener; knob, boss; ornament, jewel.

studded ▶ adjective DOTTED, scattered, sprinkled, covered, spangled; *literary* bespangled, bejewelled.

student ▶ noun **1** *a university student* SCHOLAR, undergraduate, graduate, grad student, post-doctoral fellow; freshman, frosh, sophomore. **2** *high school student* PUPIL, schoolchild, schoolboy, schoolgirl, scholar. **3** *a nursing student* TRAINEE, apprentice, probationer, recruit, intern, novice; *informal* rookie.

studied ▶ adjective DELIBERATE, careful, considered, conscious, calculated, intentional; affected, forced, strained, artificial.

studio ▶ noun WORKSHOP, workroom, atelier, workspace.

studious ▶ adjective **1** *a studious nature* SCHOLARLY, academic, bookish, intellectual, erudite, learned, donnish. **2** *studious attention* DILIGENT, careful, attentive, assiduous, painstaking, thorough, meticulous. **3** *his studious absence from public view* DELIBERATE, wilful, conscious, intentional.

study ▶ noun **1** *two years of study* LEARNING, education, schooling, academic work, scholarship, tuition, research; *informal* cramming. **2** *a study of global warming* INVESTIGATION, inquiry, examination, analysis, review, survey. **3** *Father was in his study* OFFICE, workroom, studio. **4** *a critical study* ESSAY, article, work, review, paper, dissertation, disquisition.
▶ verb **1** *Anne studied hard* WORK, review; *informal* cram, hit the books. **2** *he studied electronics* LEARN, read, be taught. **3** *Thomas was studying child development* INVESTIGATE, inquire into, research, look into, examine, analyze, explore, review, appraise, conduct a survey of. **4** *she studied her friend thoughtfully* SCRUTINIZE, examine, inspect, consider, regard, look at, eye, observe, watch, survey; *informal* check out, eyeball.
■ **in a brown study** LOST IN THOUGHT, in a reverie, musing, ruminating, cogitating, dreaming, daydreaming; *informal* miles away.

stuff ▶ noun **1** *suede is tough stuff* MATERIAL, fabric, cloth, textile; matter, substance. **2** *first-aid stuff* ITEMS,

articles, objects, goods, equipment; *informal* things, bits and pieces, odds and ends. **3** *all my stuff is in the suitcase* BELONGINGS, (personal) possessions, effects, goods (and chattels), paraphernalia; *informal* gear, things. **4** *he knows his stuff* FACTS, information, data, subject.
▶ **verb 1** *stuffing pillows* FILL, pack, pad, upholster. **2** *Robyn stuffed her clothes into a bag* SHOVE, thrust, push, ram, cram, squeeze, force, jam, pack, pile, stick. **3** (*informal*) *they stuffed themselves with chocolate* FILL, gorge, overindulge; gobble, devour, wolf; *informal* pig out, make a pig of oneself. **4** *my nose was stuffed up* BLOCK, bung, congest, obstruct.

stuffing ▶ **noun 1** *the stuffing is coming out of the armchair* PADDING, wadding, filling, upholstery, packing, filler. **2** *sage and onion stuffing* dressing, filling, forcemeat, salpicon.
■ **knock the stuffing out of** (*informal*) DEVASTATE, shatter, crush, shock.

stuffy ▶ **adjective 1** *a stuffy atmosphere* AIRLESS, close, musty, stale. **2** *a stuffy young man* STAID, sedate, sober, prim, priggish, straitlaced, conformist, conservative, old-fashioned; *informal* square, straight, starchy, fuddy-duddy. **3** *a stuffy nose* BLOCKED, stuffed up, bunged up.
− OPPOSITES: airy, clear.

stultify ▶ **verb 1** *social welfare was stultified by international trade regulations* HAMPER, impede, thwart, frustrate, foil, suppress, smother. **2** *he stultifies her with too much gentleness* BORE, make bored, dull, numb, benumb, stupefy.

stumble ▶ **verb 1** *she stumbled and fell heavily* TRIP (OVER/UP), lose one's balance, lose/miss one's footing, slip. **2** *he stumbled back home* STAGGER, totter, teeter, dodder, blunder, hobble, move clumsily. **3** *she stumbled through her speech* STAMMER, stutter, hesitate, falter, speak haltingly; *informal* fluff/flub one's lines.
■ **stumble across/on** COME ACROSS/UPON, chance on, happen on, bump into, light on; discover, find, unearth, uncover; *informal* dig up.

stumbling block ▶ **noun** OBSTACLE, hurdle, barrier, bar, hindrance, impediment, handicap, disadvantage; snag, hitch, catch, drawback, difficulty, problem, weakness, defect, pitfall; *informal* fly in the ointment, hiccup.

stump ▶ **verb** BAFFLE, perplex, puzzle, confuse, confound, defeat, put at a loss; *informal* flummox, fox, throw, floor, discombobulate.

stumpy ▶ **adjective** SHORT, stubby, squat, stocky, chunky.
− OPPOSITES: long, thin.

stun ▶ **verb 1** *a glancing blow stunned Gary* DAZE, stupefy, knock unconscious, knock out, lay out. **2** *she was stunned by the news* ASTOUND, amaze, astonish, dumbfound, stupefy, stagger, shock, take aback; *informal* flabbergast, bowl over.

stunner ▶ **noun** (*informal*). See BEAUTY sense 2.

stunning ▶ **adjective 1** *a stunning win* REMARKABLE, extraordinary, staggering, incredible, outstanding, amazing, astonishing, marvellous, phenomenal, splendid; *informal* fabulous, fantastic, tremendous, jaw-dropping. **2** *she was looking stunning.* See BEAUTIFUL.
− OPPOSITES: ordinary.

stunt[1] ▶ **verb** *a disease that stunts growth* INHIBIT, impede, hamper, hinder, restrict, retard, slow, curb, check.
− OPPOSITES: encourage.

stunt[2] ▶ **noun** *acrobatic stunts* FEAT, exploit, trick.

stunted ▶ **adjective** SMALL, undersize(d), diminutive.

stupefaction ▶ **noun 1** *alcoholic stupefaction* OBLIVION, obliviousness, unconsciousness, insensibility, stupor, daze. **2** *Don shook his head in stupefaction* BEWILDERMENT, confusion, perplexity, wonder, amazement, astonishment.

stupefy ▶ **verb 1** *the blow had stupefied her* STUN, daze, knock unconscious, knock out, lay out. **2** *they were stupefied* DRUG, sedate, tranquilize, intoxicate, inebriate; *informal* dope. **3** *the amount stupefied us* SHOCK, stun, astound, dumbfound, overwhelm, stagger, amaze, astonish, take aback, take someone's breath away; *informal* flabbergast, bowl over, floor.

stupendous ▶ **adjective 1** *stupendous achievements* AMAZING, astounding, astonishing, extraordinary, remarkable, phenomenal, staggering, breathtaking; *informal* fantastic, mind-boggling, awesome; *literary* wondrous. **2** *a building of stupendous size* COLOSSAL, immense, vast, gigantic, massive, mammoth, huge, enormous.
− OPPOSITES: ordinary.

stupid ▶ **adjective 1** *they're rather stupid* UNINTELLIGENT, ignorant, dense, foolish, dull-witted, stunned ✧, slow, simple-minded, vacuous, vapid, idiotic, imbecilic, imbecile, obtuse, doltish; *informal* thick (as two short planks), dim, dim-witted, dumb, dopey, dozy, moronic, cretinous, pea-brained, halfwitted, soft in the head, brain-dead, boneheaded, thick-headed, wooden-headed, muttonheaded, daft. **2** *a stupid mistake* FOOLISH, silly, unintelligent, idiotic, scatterbrained, nonsensical, senseless, unthinking, ill-advised, ill-considered, unwise, injudicious; inane, absurd, ludicrous, ridiculous, laughable, risible, fatuous, asinine, mad, insane, lunatic; *informal* crazy, dopey, cracked, half-baked, dim-witted, cockeyed, hare-brained, lamebrained, nutty, batty, cuckoo, loony, loopy. **3** *he drank himself stupid* INTO A STUPOR, into a daze, into oblivion; stupefied, dazed, unconscious.
− OPPOSITES: intelligent, sensible.

stupidity ▶ **noun 1** *he cursed their stupidity* LACK OF INTELLIGENCE, foolishness, denseness, brainlessness, ignorance, dull-wittedness, slow-wittedness, doltishness, slowness; *informal* thickness, dimness, dopiness, doziness. **2** *the stupidity of the question* FOOLISHNESS, folly, silliness, idiocy, brainlessness, senselessness, injudiciousness, ineptitude, inaneness, inanity, absurdity, ludicrousness, ridiculousness, fatuousness, madness, insanity, lunacy; *informal* craziness.

stupor ▶ **noun** DAZE, state of unconsciousness, torpor, insensibility, oblivion.

sturdy ▶ **adjective 1** *a sturdy lad* STRAPPING, well-built, muscular, athletic, strong, hefty, brawny, powerful, solid, burly, rugged, robust, tough, hardy, lusty; *informal* husky, beefy, meaty; *dated* stalwart; *literary* thewy. **2** *sturdy boots* ROBUST, strong, strongly made, well built, solid, stout, tough, resilient, durable, long-lasting, hard-wearing. **3** *sturdy resistance* VIGOROUS, strong, stalwart, firm, determined, resolute, staunch, steadfast.
− OPPOSITES: weak.

stutter ▶ **verb** *he stuttered over a word* STAMMER, stumble, falter.
▶ **noun** *a bad stutter* STAMMER, speech impediment, speech defect.

Stygian ▶ **adjective** (*literary*). See DARK adjective sense 1.

style ▶ **noun 1** *differing styles of management* MANNER,

way, technique, method, methodology, approach, system, mode, form, modus operandi; *informal* MO. **2** *a non-directive style of counselling* TYPE, kind, variety, sort, genre, school, brand, pattern, model. **3** *wearing clothes with style* FLAIR, stylishness, elegance, grace, gracefulness, poise, polish, suaveness, sophistication, urbanity, chic, dash, panache, élan; *informal* class, pizzazz. **4** *Laura travelled in style* COMFORT, luxury, elegance, opulence, lavishness. **5** *modern styles* FASHION, trend, vogue, mode.
▶ **verb 1** *sportswear styled by Karl* DESIGN, fashion, tailor. **2** *men who were styled 'knight'* CALL, name, title, entitle, dub, designate, term, label, tag, nickname; *formal* denominate.

stylish ▶ **adjective** FASHIONABLE, modish, voguish, modern, up to date; smart, sophisticated, elegant, chic, dapper, dashing; *informal* trendy, natty, classy, nifty, ritzy, snazzy, fly, kicky, tony, spiffy.
– OPPOSITES: unfashionable.

stymie ▶ **verb** (*informal*). See HAMPER².

suave ▶ **adjective** CHARMING, sophisticated, debonair, urbane, polished, refined, poised, self-possessed, dignified, civilized, gentlemanly, gallant; smooth, blow-dried, polite, well-mannered, civil, courteous, affable, tactful, diplomatic.
– OPPOSITES: unsophisticated.

suavity ▶ **noun** CHARM, sophistication, polish, urbanity, suaveness, refinement, poise; politeness, courtesy, courteousness, civility, tact.

subconscious ▶ **adjective** *subconscious desires* UNCONSCIOUS, latent, suppressed, repressed, subliminal, dormant, underlying, innermost; *informal* bottled up.
▶ **noun** *the creative powers of the subconscious* (UNCONSCIOUS) MIND, imagination, inner(most) self, psyche.

subdue ▶ **verb 1** *he subdued all his enemies* CONQUER, defeat, vanquish, overcome, overwhelm, crush, quash, beat, trounce, subjugate, suppress, bring someone to their knees; *informal* lick, thrash, hammer. **2** *she could not subdue her longing* CURB, restrain, hold back, constrain, contain, repress, suppress, stifle, smother, keep in check, rein in, control, master, quell; *informal* keep a/the lid on.

subdued ▶ **adjective 1** *Lewis's subdued air* SOMBRE, low-spirited, downcast, sad, dejected, depressed, gloomy, despondent, dispirited, disheartened, forlorn, woebegone; withdrawn, preoccupied; *informal* down in the mouth, down in the dumps, in the doldrums, in a blue funk. **2** *subdued voices* HUSHED, muted, quiet, low, soft, faint, muffled, indistinct. **3** *subdued light* DIM, muted, softened, soft, lowered, subtle.
– OPPOSITES: cheerful, bright.

subject ▶ **noun 1** *the subject of this chapter* THEME, subject matter, topic, issue, question, concern, point; substance, essence, gist. **2** *popular university subjects* BRANCH OF STUDY, discipline, field. **3** *six subjects did the trials* PARTICIPANT, volunteer; *informal* guinea pig. **4** *Her Majesty's subjects* CITIZEN, national; taxpayer, voter. **5** *a loyal subject* LIEGE, liegeman, vassal, henchman, follower.
▶ **verb** *they were subjected to violence* PUT THROUGH, treat with, expose to.
■ **subject to 1** *it is subject to budgetary approval* CONDITIONAL ON, contingent on, dependent on. **2** *horses are subject to coughs* SUSCEPTIBLE TO, liable to, prone to, vulnerable to, predisposed to, at risk of. **3** *we are all*

subject to the law BOUND BY, constrained by, accountable to.

subjection ▶ **noun** SUBJUGATION, domination, oppression, mastery, repression, suppression.

subjective ▶ **adjective** PERSONAL, individual, emotional, instinctive, intuitive.
– OPPOSITES: objective.

subjugate ▶ **verb** CONQUER, vanquish, defeat, crush, quash, bring someone to their knees, enslave, subdue, suppress.
– OPPOSITES: liberate.

sublimate ▶ **verb** CHANNEL, control, divert, transfer, redirect, convert.

sublime ▶ **adjective 1** *sublime music* EXALTED, elevated, noble, lofty, awe-inspiring, majestic, magnificent, glorious, superb, wonderful, marvellous, splendid; *informal* fantastic, fabulous, terrific, heavenly, divine, out of this world. **2** *the sublime confidence of youth* SUPREME, total, complete, utter, consummate.

subliminal ▶ **adjective** SUBCONSCIOUS, unconscious; hidden, concealed.
– OPPOSITES: explicit.

submerge ▶ **verb 1** *the U-boat submerged* GO UNDER WATER, dive, sink. **2** *submerge the bowl in water* IMMERSE, plunge, sink. **3** *the farmland was submerged* FLOOD, inundate, deluge, swamp. **4** *she was submerged in work* OVERWHELM, inundate, deluge, swamp, bury, engulf, snow under.
– OPPOSITES: surface.

submission ▶ **noun 1** *submission to authority* YIELDING, capitulation, acceptance, consent, compliance. **2** *Tim raised his hands in submission* SURRENDER, capitulation, resignation, defeat. **3** *he wanted her total submission* COMPLIANCE, submissiveness, acquiescence, passivity, obedience, docility, deference, subservience, servility, subjection. **4** *a report for submission to the Board* PRESENTATION, presenting, proffering, tendering, proposal, proposing. **5** *his original submission* PROPOSAL, suggestion, proposition, recommendation. **6** *the judge rejected her submission* ARGUMENT, assertion, contention, statement, claim, allegation.
– OPPOSITES: defiance, resistance.

submissive ▶ **adjective** COMPLIANT, yielding, acquiescent, unassertive, passive, obedient, biddable, dutiful, docile, pliant; *informal* under someone's thumb.

submit ▶ **verb 1** *she submitted under duress* GIVE IN/WAY, yield, back down, cave in, capitulate; surrender, knuckle under. **2** *he refused to submit to their authority* BE GOVERNED BY, abide by, be regulated by, comply with, accept, adhere to, be subject to, agree to, consent to, conform to. **3** *we submitted an unopposed bid* PUT FORWARD, present, offer, proffer, tender, propose, suggest, float; put in, send in, register. **4** *they submitted that the judgment was inappropriate* CONTEND, assert, argue, state, claim, posit, postulate.
– OPPOSITES: resist, withdraw.

subnormal ▶ **adjective** BELOW AVERAGE, below normal, low, poor, subpar.

subordinate ▶ **adjective 1** *subordinate staff* LOWER-RANKING, junior, lower, supporting. **2** *a subordinate rule* SECONDARY, lesser, minor, subsidiary, subservient, ancillary, auxiliary, peripheral, marginal; supplementary, accessory.
– OPPOSITES: senior.

▶ **noun** *the manager and his subordinates* JUNIOR, assistant, second (in command), number two, right-hand man/woman, deputy, aide, underling, minion; *informal* sidekick, second banana.
— OPPOSITES: superior.

subordination ▶ **noun** INFERIORITY, subjection, subservience, submission, servitude.

sub rosa ▶ **adverb** (*formal*) IN SECRET, secretly, in private, privately, behind closed doors, in camera.
— OPPOSITES: openly.

subscribe ▶ **verb 1** *we subscribe to 'Western Living'* PAY A SUBSCRIPTION, take, buy regularly. **2** *I subscribe to the ballet* HAVE SEASON TICKETS, have a subscription. **3** *I can't subscribe to that theory* AGREE WITH, accept, believe in, endorse, back, support, champion, buy into; *formal* accede to. **4** (*formal*) *he subscribed the document* SIGN, countersign, initial, autograph, witness.

subscriber ▶ **noun** (regular) reader, member, patron, supporter, backer, contributor, season-ticket holder, subscription holder.

subscription ▶ **noun 1** *the club's subscription* MEMBERSHIP FEE, dues, annual payment, charge. **2** *their subscription to capitalism* AGREEMENT, belief, endorsement, backing, support. **3** (*formal*) *the subscription was witnessed* SIGNATURE, initials; addition, appendage.

subsequent ▶ **adjective** *the subsequent months* FOLLOWING, ensuing, succeeding, later, future, coming, to come, next.
— OPPOSITES: previous.
■ **subsequent to** FOLLOWING, after, at the close/end of.

subsequently ▶ **adverb** LATER (ON), at a later date, afterwards, in due course, following this/that, eventually; *informal* after a bit; *formal* thereafter.

subservient ▶ **adjective 1** *subservient women* SUBMISSIVE, deferential, compliant, obedient, dutiful, biddable, docile, passive, unassertive, subdued, downtrodden; *informal* under someone's thumb. **2** *individual rights are subservient to the interests of the state* SUBORDINATE, secondary, subsidiary, peripheral, ancillary, auxiliary, less important.
— OPPOSITES: independent.

subset ▶ **noun** SUBCATEGORY, branch, subdivision, subsection, subsidiary.

subside ▶ **verb 1** *wait until the storm subsides* ABATE, let up, quieten down, calm, slacken (off), ease (up), relent, die down, recede, lessen, soften, diminish, decline, dwindle, weaken, fade, wane, ebb. **2** *the flood has subsided* RECEDE, ebb, fall, go down, get lower, abate. **3** *the volcano is gradually subsiding* SINK, settle, cave in, collapse, crumple, give way. **4** *Sarah subsided into a chair* SLUMP, flop, sink, collapse; *informal* flump, plonk oneself.
— OPPOSITES: intensify, rise.

subsidiary ▶ **adjective** *a subsidiary company* SUBORDINATE, secondary, ancillary, auxiliary, subservient, supplementary, peripheral.
— OPPOSITES: principal.
▶ **noun** *two major subsidiaries* SUBORDINATE COMPANY, branch, branch plant, division, subdivision, derivative, subset, offshoot.

subsidize ▶ **verb** GIVE MONEY TO, pay a subsidy to, contribute to, invest in, sponsor, support, fund, finance, underwrite; *informal* shell out for, fork out for, cough up for; bankroll.

subsidy ▶ **noun** GRANT, allowance, endowment, contribution, donation, bursary, handout; backing,

support, sponsorship, finance, funding; *formal* benefaction.

subsist ▶ **verb 1** *he subsists on his pension* SURVIVE, live, stay alive, exist, eke out an existence; support oneself, manage, get along/by, make (both) ends meet. **2** *the tenant's rights of occupation subsist* CONTINUE, last, persist, endure, prevail, carry on, remain.

subsistence ▶ **noun 1** *they depend on fish for subsistence* SURVIVAL, existence, living, life, sustenance, nourishment. **2** *the money needed for his subsistence* MAINTENANCE, keep, upkeep, livelihood, board (and lodging), nourishment, food.

substance ▶ **noun 1** *an organic substance* MATERIAL, matter, stuff. **2** *ghostly figures with no substance* SOLIDITY, body, corporeality; density, mass, weight, shape, structure. **3** *none of the objections has any substance* MEANINGFULNESS, significance, importance, import, validity, foundation; *formal* moment. **4** *the substance of the tale is very thin* CONTENT, subject matter, theme, message, essence. **5** *the Leafs are a team of substance* CHARACTER, backbone, mettle. **6** *independent men of substance* WEALTH, fortune, riches, affluence, prosperity, money, means.

substandard ▶ **adjective** INFERIOR, second-rate, low-quality, poor, below par, subpar, imperfect, faulty, defective, shoddy, shabby, unsound, unsatisfactory, third-rate, crummy, lousy.

substantial ▶ **adjective 1** *substantial beings* REAL, true, actual; physical, solid, material, concrete, corporeal. **2** *substantial progress had been made* CONSIDERABLE, real, significant, important, notable, major, valuable, useful. **3** *substantial damages* SIZEABLE, considerable, significant, large, ample, appreciable, goodly. **4** *substantial oak beams* STURDY, solid, stout, thick, strong, well built, durable, long-lasting, hard-wearing. **5** *rugby players with substantial builds* HEFTY, stout, sturdy, large, solid, bulky, burly, well built, portly. **6** *substantial landowners* SUCCESSFUL, profitable, prosperous, wealthy, affluent, moneyed, well-to-do, rich; *informal* loaded, stinking rich. **7** *substantial agreement* FUNDAMENTAL, essential, basic.

substantially ▶ **adverb 1** *the cost has fallen substantially* CONSIDERABLY, significantly, to a great/large extent, greatly, markedly, appreciably. **2** *the draft was substantially accepted* LARGELY, for the most part, by and large, on the whole, in the main, mainly, in essence, basically, fundamentally, to all intents and purposes.
— OPPOSITES: slightly.

substantiate ▶ **verb** PROVE, show to be true, give substance to, support, uphold, bear out, justify, vindicate, validate, corroborate, verify, authenticate, confirm, endorse, give credence to.
— OPPOSITES: disprove.

substitute ▶ **noun** *substitutes for permanent employees* REPLACEMENT, deputy, relief, proxy, reserve, surrogate, cover, stand-in, locum (tenens), understudy; *informal* sub, pinch-hitter.
▶ **adjective** *a substitute teacher* ACTING, supply, replacement, deputy, relief, reserve, surrogate, stand-in, temporary, caretaker, interim, provisional.
— OPPOSITES: permanent.
▶ **verb 1** *cottage cheese can be substituted for yogourt* EXCHANGE, replace, use instead of, use as an alternative to, use in place of, swap. **2** *the Senate was empowered to substitute for the President* DEPUTIZE, act as deputy, act as a substitute, stand in, cover; replace,

relieve, take over from; *informal* sub, fill someone's boots/shoes.

substitution ▶ noun EXCHANGE, change; replacement, replacing, swapping, switching; *informal* switcheroo.

subterfuge ▶ noun 1 *the use of subterfuge by journalists* TRICKERY, intrigue, deviousness, deceit, deception, dishonesty, cheating, duplicity, guile, cunning, craftiness, chicanery, pretense, fraud, fraudulence. 2 *a disreputable subterfuge* TRICK, hoax, ruse, wile, ploy, stratagem, artifice, dodge, bluff, pretense, deception, fraud, blind, smokescreen; *informal* con, scam.

subtle ▶ adjective 1 *subtle colours* UNDERSTATED, muted, subdued; delicate, faint, pale, soft, indistinct. 2 *subtle distinctions* FINE, fine-drawn, nice, hair-splitting. 3 *a subtle mind* ASTUTE, keen, quick, fine, acute, sharp, shrewd, perceptive, discerning, discriminating, penetrating, sagacious, wise, clever, intelligent. 4 *a subtle plan* INGENIOUS, clever, cunning, crafty, wily, artful, devious.

subtlety ▶ noun 1 *the subtlety of the flavour* DELICACY, delicateness, subtleness; understatedness, mutedness, softness. 2 *classification is fraught with subtlety* FINENESS, subtleness, niceness, nicety, nuance. 3 *the subtlety of the human mind* ASTUTENESS, keenness, acuteness, sharpness, canniness, shrewdness, perceptiveness, discernment, discrimination, percipience, perspicacity, wisdom, cleverness, intelligence. 4 *the subtlety of their tactics* INGENUITY, cleverness, skilfulness, adroitness, cunning, guile, craftiness, wiliness, artfulness, deviousness.

subtract ▶ verb TAKE AWAY/OFF, deduct, debit, dock; *informal* knock off, minus.
— OPPOSITES: add.

suburb ▶ noun RESIDENTIAL AREA, dormitory area, bedroom community, commutershed, commuter belt, exurb; suburbia, the burbs.

suburban ▶ adjective 1 *a suburban area* RESIDENTIAL, commuter, dormitory. 2 *her drab suburban existence* DULL, boring, uninteresting, conventional, ordinary, commonplace, unremarkable, unexceptional; provincial, unsophisticated, parochial, bourgeois, middle-class, white-picket-fence.

subversive ▶ adjective *subversive activities* DISRUPTIVE, troublemaking, inflammatory, insurrectionary; seditious, revolutionary, rebellious, rebel, renegade, dissident.
▶ noun *a dangerous subversive* TROUBLEMAKER, dissident, agitator, revolutionary, renegade, rebel.

subvert ▶ verb 1 *a plot to subvert the state* DESTABILIZE, unsettle, overthrow, overturn; bring down, topple, depose, oust; disrupt, wreak havoc on, sabotage, ruin, undermine, weaken, damage. 2 *attempts to subvert Soviet youth* CORRUPT, pervert, deprave, contaminate, poison, embitter.

subway ▶ noun 1 *Tokyo's subway* UNDERGROUND (RAILWAY), metro. 2 *he walked through the subway* UNDERPASS, (pedestrian) tunnel.

succeed ▶ verb 1 *Darwin succeeded where others had failed* TRIUMPH, achieve success, be successful, do well, flourish, thrive; *informal* make it, make the grade, make a name for oneself. 2 *the plan succeeded* BE SUCCESSFUL, turn out well, work (out), be effective; *informal* come off, pay off. 3 *Campbell succeeded Mulroney as Prime Minister* REPLACE, take the place of, take over from, follow, supersede; *informal* step into someone's

shoes. 4 *he succeeded to the throne* INHERIT, assume, acquire, attain; *formal* accede to. 5 *embarrassment was succeeded by fear* FOLLOW, come after, follow after.
— OPPOSITES: fail, precede.

succeeding ▶ adjective SUBSEQUENT, successive, following, ensuing, later, future, coming.

success ▶ noun 1 *the success of the scheme* FAVOURABLE OUTCOME, successfulness, successful result, triumph. 2 *the trappings of success* PROSPERITY, affluence, wealth, riches, opulence. 3 *a box-office success* TRIUMPH, bestseller, blockbuster, sell-out; *informal* (smash) hit, megahit, winner. 4 *an overnight success* STAR, superstar, celebrity, big name, household name; *informal* celeb, megastar.
— OPPOSITES: failure.

successful ▶ adjective 1 *a successful campaign* VICTORIOUS, triumphant; fortunate, lucky; effective; *informal* socko. 2 *a successful designer* PROSPEROUS, affluent, wealthy, rich; doing well, famous, eminent, top. 3 *successful companies* FLOURISHING, thriving, booming, buoyant, doing well, profitable, money-making, lucrative.

succession ▶ noun 1 *a succession of exciting events* SEQUENCE, series, progression, chain, cycle, round, string, train, line, run, flow, stream. 2 *his succession to the throne* ACCESSION, elevation, assumption.
■ **in succession** ONE AFTER THE OTHER, in a row, consecutively, successively, in sequence; running.

successive ▶ adjective CONSECUTIVE, in a row, straight, sequential, in succession, running.

successor ▶ noun HEIR (APPARENT), inheritor, next-in-line.
— OPPOSITES: predecessor.

succinct ▶ adjective CONCISE, short (and sweet), brief, compact, condensed, crisp, laconic, terse, to the point, pithy, epigrammatic, synoptic, gnomic; *formal* compendious.
— OPPOSITES: verbose.

succour ▶ noun *providing succour in times of need* AID, help, a helping hand, assistance; comfort, ease, relief, support, TLC.
▶ verb *the prisoners were succoured* HELP, aid, bring aid to, give/render assistance to, assist, lend a (helping) hand to; minister to, care for, comfort, bring relief to, support, take care of, look after, attend to.

succulent ▶ adjective JUICY, moist, luscious, soft, tender; choice, mouth-watering, appetizing, tasty, delicious; *informal* scrumptious.
— OPPOSITES: dry.

succumb ▶ verb 1 *she succumbed to temptation* YIELD, give in/way, submit, surrender, capitulate, cave in. 2 *he succumbed to the disease* DIE FROM/OF; catch, develop, contract, fall ill with; *informal* come down with.
— OPPOSITES: resist.

suck ▶ verb 1 *they sucked orange juice through straws* SIP, sup, siphon, slurp, draw, drink. 2 *Fran sucked in a deep breath* DRAW, pull, breathe, gasp; inhale, inspire. 3 *they got sucked into petty crime* IMPLICATE IN, involve in, draw into; *informal* mix up in. 4 (*informal*) *the weather sucks* BE VERY BAD, be awful, be terrible, be dreadful, be horrible; *informal* stink.
■ **suck up** (*informal*) *they suck up to him, hanging on to his every word* GROVEL, creep, toady, be obsequious, be sycophantic, kowtow, bow and scrape, truckle; fawn on; *informal* lick someone's boots, be all over, brown-nose.

suckle ▶ verb BREASTFEED, feed, nurse.

sudden ▶ **adjective** UNEXPECTED, unforeseen, unanticipated, unlooked-for; immediate, instantaneous, instant, precipitous, precipitate, abrupt, rapid, swift, quick.

suddenly ▶ **adverb** IMMEDIATELY, instantaneously, instantly, straight away, all of a sudden, all at once, promptly, abruptly, swiftly; unexpectedly, without warning, without notice, out of the blue; *informal* straight off, in a flash, like a shot.
— OPPOSITES: gradually.

suds ▶ **plural noun** LATHER, foam, froth, bubbles, soap.

sue ▶ **verb 1** *he sued for negligence* TAKE LEGAL ACTION, take to court, bring an action/suit, proceed against, litigate (against). **2** *suing for peace* APPEAL, petition, ask, solicit, request, seek.

suffer ▶ **verb 1** *I hate to see him suffer* HURT, ache, be in pain, feel pain; be in distress, be upset, be miserable. **2** *she suffers from asthma* BE AFFLICTED BY, be affected by, be troubled with, have. **3** *Brazil suffered a humiliating defeat* UNDERGO, experience, be subjected to, receive, endure, face. **4** *the school's reputation has suffered* BE IMPAIRED, be damaged, deteriorate, decline. **5** (*archaic*) *he was obliged to suffer her intimate proximity* TOLERATE, put up with, bear, stand, abide, endure; *formal* brook. **6** (*archaic*) *my conscience would not suffer me to accept* ALLOW, permit, let, give leave to, sanction.

suffering ▶ **noun** HARDSHIP, distress, misery, wretchedness, adversity, tribulation; pain, agony, anguish, trauma, torment, torture, hurt, affliction, sadness, unhappiness, sorrow, grief, woe, angst, heartache, heartbreak, stress; *literary* dolour.

suffice ▶ **verb** BE ENOUGH, be sufficient, be adequate, do, serve, meet requirements, satisfy demands, answer/meet one's needs, answer/serve the purpose; *informal* fit/fill the bill.

sufficient ▶ **adjective** ENOUGH, plenty of, ample; adequate, satisfactory.
— OPPOSITES: inadequate.

suffocate ▶ **verb** SMOTHER, asphyxiate, stifle; choke, strangle.

suffrage ▶ **noun** FRANCHISE, right to vote, the vote, enfranchisement, ballot.

suffuse ▶ **verb** PERMEATE, spread over, spread throughout, cover, bathe, pervade, wash, saturate, imbue.

sugar *See table.*
— RELATED TERMS: saccharine, glyco-.

Sugar

beet sugar	icing sugar
berry sugar ✤	maple sugar
brown sugar	powdered sugar
cane sugar	vanilla sugar
caster sugar (*Brit.*)	white sugar
confectioner's	fruit sugar (fructose)
sugar (*US*)	grape sugar (dextrose)
demerara sugar	milk sugar (lactose)
granulated sugar	

sugar shack ▶ **noun** sugar house, (*Que.*) cabane à sucre ✤.

sugary ▶ **adjective 1** *sugary snacks* SWEET, sugared, candied, sickly. **2** *sugary romance* SENTIMENTAL, mawkish, cloying, sickly (sweet), saccharine, syrupy; *informal* sappy, schmaltzy, slushy, mushy, sloppy, cutesy, corny.
— OPPOSITES: sour.

suggest ▶ **verb 1** *Ruth suggested a holiday* PROPOSE, put forward, recommend, advocate; advise, urge, encourage, counsel. **2** *evidence suggests that teenagers are responsive to price increases* INDICATE, lead to the belief, argue, demonstrate, show; *formal* evince. **3** *sources suggest that the Prime Minister will change his cabinet* HINT, insinuate, imply, intimate, indicate; *informal* put ideas into one's head. **4** *the seduction scenes suggest his guilt and her loneliness* CONVEY, express, communicate, impart, imply, intimate, smack of, evoke, conjure up; *formal* evince.

suggestion ▶ **noun 1** *some suggestions for tackling this problem* PROPOSAL, proposition, motion, submission, recommendation; advice, counsel, hint, tip, clue, idea, trial balloon. **2** *the suggestion of a smirk* HINT, trace, touch, suspicion, dash, soupçon, tinge; ghost, semblance, shadow, glimmer, impression, whisper. **3** *there is no suggestion that he was party to a conspiracy* INSINUATION, hint, implication, intimation, innuendo, imputation.

suggestive ▶ **adjective 1** *suggestive remarks* INDECENT, indelicate, improper, unseemly, sexual, sexy, smutty, dirty, ribald, bawdy, racy, risqué, lewd, vulgar, coarse, salacious. **2** *an odour suggestive of a brewery* REDOLENT, evocative, reminiscent; characteristic, indicative, typical.

suicide ▶ **noun** SELF-DESTRUCTION, taking one's own life, killing oneself, self-murder; *informal* topping oneself.

suit ▶ **noun 1** *a pinstriped suit* OUTFIT, set of clothes, ensemble. **2** (*informal*) *suits in faraway boardrooms* BUSINESSMAN, BUSINESSWOMAN, executive, bureaucrat, administrator, manager. **3** *a medical malpractice suit* LEGAL ACTION, lawsuit, (court) case, action, (legal/judicial) proceedings, litigation. **4** *they spurned his suit* ENTREATY, request, plea, appeal, petition, supplication, application. **5** *his suit came to nothing* COURTSHIP, wooing, attentions.
▶ **verb 1** *blue really suits you* BECOME, work for, look good on, look attractive on, flatter. **2** *savings plans to suit all customers* BE CONVENIENT FOR, be acceptable to, be suitable for, meet the requirements of; *informal* fit the bill. **3** *recipes ideally suited to students* MAKE APPROPRIATE TO/FOR, tailor, fashion, adjust, adapt, modify, fit, gear, design.

suitable ▶ **adjective 1** *suitable employment opportunities* ACCEPTABLE, satisfactory, fitting; *informal* right up someone's alley/street. **2** *a drama suitable for all ages* APPROPRIATE, fitting, fit, acceptable, right. **3** *music suitable for a lively dinner party* APPROPRIATE, suited, befitting, in keeping with; *informal* cut out for. **4** *they treated him with suitable respect* PROPER, seemly, decent, appropriate, fitting, befitting, correct, due. **5** *suitable candidates* WELL QUALIFIED, well-suited, appropriate, fitting.
— OPPOSITES: inappropriate.

suitcase ▶ **noun** TRAVELLING BAG, travel bag, case, valise, overnight case, portmanteau, vanity case, garment bag, backpack; (**suitcases**) luggage, baggage.

suite ▶ **noun** APARTMENT, flat, (set of) rooms.

suitor ▶ **noun** ADMIRER, wooer, boyfriend, sweetheart, lover, beau; *literary* swain.

sulk ▶ **verb** *Dad was sulking* MOPE, brood, be sullen, have a long face, be in a bad mood, be in a huff, be grumpy, be moody; *informal* be down in the dumps.
▶ **noun** *she sank into a deep sulk* (BAD) MOOD, fit of ill humour, fit of pique, pet, huff, (bad) temper, the sulks, the blues.

sulky ▶ adjective *sulky faces* SULLEN, surly, moping, pouting, moody, sour, piqued, petulant, brooding, broody, disgruntled, ill-humoured, in a bad mood, out of humour, fed up, put out; bad-tempered, grumpy, huffy, glum, gloomy, morose; *informal* grouchy, crabby, cranky.
– OPPOSITES: cheerful.

sullen ▶ adjective SURLY, sulky, pouting, sour, morose, resentful, glum, moody, gloomy, grumpy, bad-tempered, ill-tempered; unresponsive, uncommunicative, farouche, uncivil, unfriendly.
– OPPOSITES: cheerful.

sully ▶ verb TAINT, defile, soil, tarnish, stain, blemish, pollute, spoil, mar; *literary* besmirch, befoul.

sultry ▶ adjective **1** *a sultry day* HUMID, close, airless, stifling, oppressive, muggy, sticky, sweltering, tropical, heavy; hot; *informal* boiling, roasting. **2** *a sultry film star* PASSIONATE, attractive, sensual, sexy, voluptuous, erotic, seductive.
– OPPOSITES: refreshing.

sum ▶ noun **1** *a large sum of money* AMOUNT, quantity, volume. **2** *just a small sum* AMOUNT OF MONEY, price, charge, fee, cost. **3** *the sum of two numbers* (SUM) TOTAL, grand total, tally, aggregate, summation. **4** *the sum of his wisdom* ENTIRETY, totality, total, whole, aggregate, summation, beginning and end. **5** *we did sums at school* (ARITHMETICAL) PROBLEM, calculation; (**sums**) arithmetic, mathematics, math, computation.
– OPPOSITES: difference.
■ **sum up** SUMMARIZE THE EVIDENCE, review the evidence, give a summing-up.
■ **sum someone/something up 1** *one reviewer summed it up as 'compelling'* EVALUATE, assess, appraise, rate, gauge, judge, deem, adjudge, estimate, form an opinion of. **2** *he summed up his reasons* SUMMARIZE, make/give a summary of, précis, outline, give an outline of, recapitulate, review; *informal* recap.

summarily ▶ adverb IMMEDIATELY, instantly, right away, straight away, at once, on the spot, promptly; speedily, swiftly, rapidly, without delay; arbitrarily, without formality, peremptorily, without due process.

summarize ▶ verb SUM UP, abridge, condense, encapsulate, outline, give an outline of, put in a nutshell, recapitulate, give/make a summary of, give a synopsis of, précis, synopsize, give the gist of; *informal* recap.

summary ▶ noun *a summary of the findings* SYNOPSIS, précis, resumé, abstract, digest, encapsulation, abbreviated version; outline, sketch, rundown, review, summing-up, overview, recapitulation, epitome; *informal* recap.
▶ adjective **1** *a summary financial statement* ABRIDGED, abbreviated, shortened, condensed, concise, capsule, succinct, short, brief, pithy; *formal* compendious. **2** *summary execution* IMMEDIATE, instant, instantaneous, on-the-spot; speedy, swift, rapid, without delay, sudden; arbitrary, without formality, peremptory.

summer
– RELATED TERMS: aestival.

summer house ▶ noun GAZEBO, pavilion, belvedere; cottage, cabin; *literary* bower.

summit ▶ noun **1** *the summit of Mount Washington* (MOUNTAIN) TOP, peak, crest, crown, apex, tip, cap, hilltop. **2** *the summits of world literature* ACME, peak, height, pinnacle, zenith, climax, high point/spot, highlight, crowning glory, capstone, best, finest,

nonpareil. **3** *the next superpower summit* MEETING, negotiation, conference, talk(s), discussion.
– OPPOSITES: base, nadir.

summon ▶ verb **1** *she was summoned to the Embassy* SEND FOR, call for, request the presence of; ask, invite. **2** *they were summoned as witnesses* SERVE WITH A SUMMONS, summons, subpoena, cite, serve with a citation. **3** *the chair summoned a meeting* CONVENE, assemble, order, call, announce; *formal* convoke. **4** *he summoned the courage to move closer* MUSTER, gather, collect, rally, screw up. **5** *summoning up their memories of home* CALL TO MIND, call up/forth, conjure up, evoke, recall, revive, arouse, kindle, awaken, spark (off), invoke. **6** *they summoned spirits of the dead* CONJURE UP, call up, invoke.

summons ▶ noun **1** *the court issued a summons* WRIT, subpoena, warrant, court order; *Law* citation. **2** *a summons to go to the boss's office* ORDER, directive, command, instruction, demand, decree, injunction, edict, call, request.
▶ verb *he was summonsed to appear in court* SERVE WITH A SUMMONS, summon, subpoena, cite, serve with a citation.

sumptuous ▶ adjective LAVISH, luxurious, opulent, magnificent, resplendent, gorgeous, splendid, grand, lavishly appointed, palatial, rich; *informal* plush, ritzy.
– OPPOSITES: plain.

sun ▶ noun SUNSHINE, sunlight, daylight, light, warmth; beams, rays.
– RELATED TERMS: solar, helio-.
■ **sun oneself**. See SUNBATHE.

sunbathe ▶ verb SUN ONESELF, bask, get a tan, tan; *informal* catch/bag some rays.

sunburnt ▶ adjective **1** *his sunburnt shoulders* BURNT, sunburned, red, scarlet. **2** *a handsome sunburnt face* TANNED, suntanned, brown, bronzed, bronze.
– OPPOSITES: pale.

sunder ▶ verb (*literary*) DIVIDE, split, cleave, separate, rend, sever, rive.

sundry ▶ adjective VARIOUS, varied, miscellaneous, assorted, mixed, diverse, diversified; several, numerous, many, manifold, multifarious, multitudinous; *literary* divers.

sunken ▶ adjective **1** *sunken eyes* HOLLOWED, hollow, depressed, deep-set, concave, indented. **2** *a sunken garden* BELOW GROUND LEVEL, at a lower level, lowered.

sunless ▶ adjective **1** *a cold sunless day* DARK, overcast, cloudy, grey, gloomy, dismal, murky, dull. **2** *the sunless side of the house* SHADY, shadowy, dark, gloomy.

sunlight ▶ noun DAYLIGHT, sun, sunshine, sun's rays, (natural) light.

sunny ▶ adjective **1** *a sunny day* BRIGHT, sunshiny, sunlit, clear, fine, cloudless, without a cloud in the sky, sun-drenched. **2** *a sunny disposition* CHEERFUL, cheery, happy, light-hearted, bright, merry, joyful, bubbly, blithe, jolly, jovial, animated, buoyant, ebullient, upbeat, vivacious. **3** *look on the sunny side* OPTIMISTIC, rosy, bright, hopeful, auspicious, favourable.
– OPPOSITES: dull, miserable.

sunrise ▶ noun (CRACK OF) DAWN, daybreak, break of day, first light, (early) morning, cock crow, sun-up; *literary* aurora.

sunset ▶ noun NIGHTFALL, sundown, close of day, twilight, dusk, evening; *literary* eventide, gloaming.

sunshine ▶ noun **1** *relaxing in the sunshine* SUNLIGHT, sun, sun's rays, daylight, (natural) light. **2** *his smile was all sunshine* HAPPINESS, cheerfulness, cheer, gladness, laughter, gaiety, merriment, joy, joyfulness, blitheness, joviality, jollity.

super ► adjective (*informal*) EXCELLENT, superb, superlative, first-class, outstanding, marvellous, magnificent, wonderful, splendid, glorious; *informal* great, fantastic, fabulous, terrific, ace, divine, A1, wicked, cool, killer; smashing, brilliant.
— OPPOSITES: rotten.

superannuated ► adjective **1** *a superannuated civil servant* PENSIONED (OFF), retired; elderly, old. **2** *superannuated computing equipment* OLD, old-fashioned, antiquated, out of date, outmoded, broken-down, obsolete, disused, defunct.

superb ► adjective **1** *he scored a superb goal* EXCELLENT, superlative, first-rate, first-class, outstanding, remarkable, marvellous, magnificent, wonderful, splendid, admirable, noteworthy, impressive, fine, exquisite, exceptional, glorious; *informal* great, fantastic, fabulous, terrific, super, awesome, ace, cool, A1, brilliant, killer. **2** *a superb diamond necklace* MAGNIFICENT, majestic, splendid, grand, impressive, imposing, awe-inspiring, breathtaking; gorgeous.
— OPPOSITES: poor, inferior.

supercilious ► adjective ARROGANT, haughty, conceited, disdainful, overbearing, pompous, condescending, superior, patronizing, imperious, proud, snobbish, snobby, smug, scornful, sneering; *informal* hoity-toity, high and mighty, uppity, snooty, stuck-up, snotty, snot-nosed, jumped up, too big for one's britches/boots.

superficial ► adjective **1** *superficial burns* SURFACE, exterior, external, outer, outside, slight. **2** *a superficial friendship* SHALLOW, surface, skin-deep, artificial; empty, hollow, meaningless. **3** *a superficial investigation* CURSORY, perfunctory, casual, sketchy, desultory, token, slapdash, offhand, rushed, hasty, hurried. **4** *a superficial resemblance* APPARENT, seeming, outward, ostensible, cosmetic, slight. **5** *a superficial biography* TRIVIAL, lightweight, two-dimensional. **6** *a superficial person* FACILE, shallow, flippant, empty-headed, trivial, frivolous, silly, inane.
— OPPOSITES: deep, thorough.

superficially ► adverb APPARENTLY, seemingly, ostensibly, outwardly, on the surface, on the face of it, at first glance, to the casual eye.

superfluity ► noun SURPLUS, excess, overabundance, glut, surfeit, profusion, plethora.
— OPPOSITES: shortage.

superfluous ► adjective **1** *superfluous material* SURPLUS (TO REQUIREMENTS), redundant, unneeded, excess, extra, (to) spare, remaining, unused, left over, in excess, waste. **2** *words seemed superfluous* UNNECESSARY, unneeded, redundant, uncalled for, unwarranted.
— OPPOSITES: necessary.

superhuman ► adjective **1** *a superhuman effort* EXTRAORDINARY, phenomenal, prodigious, stupendous, exceptional, immense, heroic. **2** *superhuman power* DIVINE, holy, heavenly. **3** *superhuman beings* SUPERNATURAL, preternatural, paranormal, otherworldly, unearthly; *rare* extramundane.
— OPPOSITES: mundane.

superintend ► verb SUPERVISE, oversee, be in charge of, be in control of, preside over, direct, administer, manage, run, be responsible for.

superintendent ► noun **1** *the superintendent of the museum* MANAGER, director, administrator, supervisor, overseer, controller, chief, head, governor; *informal* boss. **2** *the building's superintendent* CARETAKER, janitor, warden, porter.

superior ► adjective **1** *a superior officer* HIGHER-RANKING, higher-level, senior, higher, higher-up. **2** *the superior candidate* BETTER, more expert, more skilful; worthier, fitter, preferred. **3** *superior workmanship* FINER, better, higher-grade, of higher quality, greater; accomplished, expert. **4** *superior chocolate* GOOD-QUALITY, high-quality, first-class, first-rate, top-quality; choice, select, exclusive, prime, prize, fine, excellent, best, choicest, finest. **5** *a superior hotel* HIGH-CLASS, upper-class, select, exclusive, upscale, upmarket, five-star; *informal* classy, posh. **6** *Hamish regarded her with superior amusement* CONDESCENDING, supercilious, patronizing, haughty, disdainful, pompous, snobbish; *informal* high and mighty, hoity-toity, snooty, stuck-up.
— OPPOSITES: junior, inferior.
► noun *my immediate superior* MANAGER, chief, supervisor, senior, controller, foreman; *informal* boss.
— OPPOSITES: subordinate.

superiority ► noun SUPREMACY, advantage, lead, dominance, primacy, ascendancy, eminence.

superlative ► adjective EXCELLENT, magnificent, wonderful, marvellous, supreme, consummate, outstanding, remarkable, fine, choice, first-rate, first-class, premier, prime, unsurpassed, unequalled, unparalleled, unrivalled, pre-eminent; *informal* crack, ace, wicked, brilliant.
— OPPOSITES: mediocre.

supernatural ► adjective **1** *supernatural powers* PARANORMAL, psychic, magic, magical, occult, mystic, mystical, superhuman, supernormal; *rare* extramundane. **2** *a supernatural being* GHOSTLY, phantom, spectral, otherworldly, unearthly, unnatural.

supersede ► verb REPLACE, take the place of, take over from, succeed; supplant, displace, oust, overthrow, remove, unseat; *informal* fill someone's shoes/boots.

superstition ► noun **1** *the old superstitions held by sailors* MYTH, belief, old wives' tale; legend, story. **2** *medicine was riddled with superstition* UNFOUNDED BELIEF, credulity, fallacy, delusion, illusion; magic, sorcery; *informal* humbug, hooey.

superstitious ► adjective **1** *superstitious beliefs* MYTHICAL, irrational, illusory, groundless, unfounded; traditional. **2** *he's incredibly superstitious* CREDULOUS, naive, gullible.
— OPPOSITES: factual, skeptical.

supervise ► verb **1** *he had to supervise the loading* OVERSEE, superintend, be in charge of, preside over, direct, manage, run, look after, be responsible for, govern, organize, handle, micromanage. **2** *you may need to supervise the patient* WATCH, oversee, keep an eye on, observe, monitor, mind; invigilate.

supervision ► noun **1** *the supervision of the banking system* ADMINISTRATION, management, control, charge; superintendence, regulation, government, governance. **2** *keep your children under supervision* OBSERVATION, guidance, custody, charge, safekeeping, care, guardianship; control.

supervisor ► noun MANAGER, director, overseer, controller, superintendent, governor, chief, head; steward, foreman; *informal* boss.

supine ▶ adjective **1** *she lay supine on the sand* FLAT ON ONE'S BACK, face upwards, flat, horizontal, recumbent, stretched out. **2** *the supine media* WEAK, spineless, yielding, effete; docile, acquiescent, pliant, submissive, passive, inert, spiritless.
— OPPOSITES: prostrate, strong.

supper ▶ noun DINNER, evening meal, main meal; snack, mealtime; *formal* repast; *literary* refection.

supplant ▶ verb **1** *paved highways supplanted the network of dirt roads* REPLACE, supersede, displace, take over from, substitute for, override. **2** *the man he supplanted as Prime Minister* OUST, usurp, overthrow, remove, topple, unseat, depose, dethrone; succeed, come after; *informal* fill someone's shoes/boots.

supple ▶ adjective **1** *her supple body* LITHE, limber, lissome, willowy, flexible, loose-limbed, agile, acrobatic, nimble, double-jointed. **2** *supple leather* PLIANT, pliable, flexible, soft, bendable, workable, malleable, stretchy, elastic, springy, yielding, rubbery.
— OPPOSITES: stiff, rigid.

supplement ▶ noun **1** *a mouse is a keyboard supplement* ADDITION, accessory, supplementation, supplementary, extra, add-on, adjunct, appendage; *Computing* peripheral. **2** *a single room supplement* SURCHARGE, addition, increase. **3** *a supplement to the essay* APPENDIX, addendum, adhesion ✦, end matter, tailpiece, codicil, postscript, addition, coda. **4** *a special supplement with today's paper* PULL-OUT, insert, extra section.
▶ verb *they supplemented their incomes by busking* AUGMENT, increase, add to, boost, swell, amplify, enlarge, top up.

supplementary ▶ adjective **1** *supplementary income* ADDITIONAL, supplemental, extra, further; add-on, subsidiary, auxiliary, ancillary. **2** *a supplementary index* APPENDED, attached, added, extra, accompanying.

suppliant ▶ noun *they were not mere suppliants* PETITIONER, supplicant, pleader, beggar, applicant.
▶ adjective *those around her were suppliant* PLEADING, begging, imploring, entreating, supplicating; on bended knee.

supplicate ▶ verb ENTREAT, beg, plead with, implore, petition, appeal to, call on, urge, enjoin, importune, sue, ask, request; *literary* beseech.

supply ▶ verb **1** *they supplied money to rebels* GIVE, contribute, provide, furnish, donate, bestow, grant, endow, impart; dispense, disburse, allocate, assign; *informal* fork out, shell out. **2** *the lake supplies the city with water* PROVIDE, furnish, endow, serve, confer; equip, arm. **3** *windmills supply their power needs* SATISFY, meet, fulfill, cater for.
▶ noun **1** *a limited supply of food* STOCK, store, reserve, reservoir, stockpile, hoard, cache; storehouse, repository; fund, mine, bank. **2** *the supply of alcoholic liquor* PROVISION, dissemination, distribution, serving. **3** *go to a grocery store for supplies* PROVISIONS, stores, stocks, rations, food, foodstuffs, produce, necessities; *informal* eats; *formal* comestibles.

support ▶ verb **1** *a roof supported by pillars* HOLD UP, bear, carry, prop up, keep up, brace, shore up, underpin, buttress, reinforce, undergird. **2** *he struggled to support his family* PROVIDE FOR, maintain, sustain, keep, take care of, look after. **3** *she supported him to the end* COMFORT, encourage, sustain, buoy up, hearten, fortify, console, solace, reassure; *informal* buck up. **4** *evidence to support the argument* SUBSTANTIATE, back up, bear out, corroborate,

confirm, attest to, verify, prove, validate, authenticate, endorse, ratify, undergird. **5** *the money supports charitable projects* HELP, aid, assist; contribute to, back, subsidize, fund, finance; *informal* bankroll. **6** *an independent candidate supported by locals* BACK, champion, help, assist, aid, abet, favour, encourage; vote for, stand behind, defend; sponsor, second, promote, endorse, sanction; *informal* throw one's weight behind. **7** *they support human rights* ADVOCATE, promote, champion, back, espouse, be in favour of, recommend, defend, subscribe to.
— OPPOSITES: neglect, contradict, oppose.
▶ noun **1** *bridge supports* PILLAR, post, prop, upright, crutch, plinth, brace, buttress; base, substructure, foundation, underpinning. **2** *he pays support for his wife* MAINTENANCE, keep, sustenance, subsistence; alimony. **3** *I was lucky to have their support* ENCOURAGEMENT, friendship, strength, consolation, solace, succour, relief. **4** *he was a great support* COMFORT, help, assistance, tower of strength, prop, mainstay. **5** *support for community services* CONTRIBUTIONS, backing, donations, money, subsidy, funding, funds, finance, capital. **6** *they voiced their support for him* BACKING, help, assistance, aid, endorsement, approval, endorsation ✦; votes, patronage. **7** *a surge in support for decentralization* ADVOCACY, backing, promotion, championship, espousal, defence, recommendation.

supporter ▶ noun **1** *supporters of gun control* ADVOCATE, backer, adherent, promoter, champion, defender, upholder, crusader, proponent, campaigner, apologist; *informal* cheerleader. **2** *Liberal supporters* BACKER, helper, adherent, follower, ally, voter, disciple; member. **3** *the charity relies on its supporters* CONTRIBUTOR, donor, benefactor, sponsor, backer, patron, well-wisher. **4** *the team's supporters* FAN, follower, enthusiast, devotee, admirer; *informal* buff, addict, groupie.

supportive ▶ adjective **1** *a supportive teacher* ENCOURAGING, caring, sympathetic, reassuring, understanding, concerned, helpful, kind, kindly. **2** *we are supportive of the proposal* IN FAVOUR OF, favourable to, pro, on the side of, sympathetic to, well-disposed to, receptive to.

suppose ▶ verb **1** *I suppose he's used to this* ASSUME, presume, expect, dare say, take it (as read); believe, think, fancy, suspect, sense, trust; guess, surmise, reckon, conjecture, deduce, infer, gather; *formal* opine. **2** *suppose you had a spacecraft* ASSUME, imagine, (let's) say; hypothesize, theorize, speculate. **3** *the theory supposes rational players* REQUIRE, presuppose, imply, assume; call for, need.

supposed ▶ adjective **1** *the supposed phenomena* APPARENT, ostensible, seeming, alleged, putative, reputed, rumoured, claimed, purported; professed, declared, assumed, presumed. **2** *I'm supposed to meet him at 8:30* MEANT, intended, expected; required, obliged.

supposition ▶ noun BELIEF, surmise, idea, notion, suspicion, conjecture, speculation, inference, theory, hypothesis, postulation, guess, feeling, hunch, assumption, presumption.

suppress ▶ verb **1** *they could suppress the rebellion* SUBDUE, repress, crush, quell, quash, squash, stamp out; defeat, conquer, overpower, put down, crack down on; end, stop, terminate, halt. **2** *he suppressed her irritation* CONCEAL, restrain, stifle, smother, bottle up, hold back, control, check, curb, contain, bridle, inhibit, keep a rein on, put a lid on. **3** *the report was*

suppressed CENSOR, keep secret, conceal, hide, hush up, gag, withhold, cover up, stifle; ban, proscribe, outlaw; sweep under the carpet.
— OPPOSITES: incite, reveal.

suppurate ▶ verb FESTER, form pus, discharge, run, weep, become septic.

supremacy ▶ noun ASCENDANCY, predominance, primacy, dominion, hegemony, authority, mastery, control, power, rule, sovereignty, influence; dominance, superiority, advantage, the upper hand, the whip hand, the edge; distinction, greatness.

supreme ▶ adjective **1** *the supreme commander* HIGHEST RANKING, chief, head, top, foremost, principal, superior, premier, first, prime; greatest, dominant, predominant, pre-eminent. **2** *a supreme achievement* EXTRAORDINARY, remarkable, incredible, phenomenal, rare, exceptional, outstanding, great, incomparable, unparalleled, peerless. **3** *the supreme sacrifice* ULTIMATE, final, last; utmost, extreme, greatest, highest.
— OPPOSITES: subordinate, insignificant.

sure ▶ adjective **1** *I am sure that they didn't* CERTAIN, positive, convinced, confident, definite, assured, satisfied, persuaded; unhesitating, unwavering, unshakeable. **2** *someone was sure to be blamed* BOUND, likely, destined, fated. **3** *a sure winner with the children* GUARANTEED, unfailing, infallible, unerring, assured, certain, inevitable; *informal* sure-fire. **4** *he entered in the sure knowledge that he would win* UNQUESTIONABLE, indisputable, irrefutable, incontrovertible, undeniable, indubitable, undoubted, absolute, categorical, true, certain; obvious, evident, plain, clear, conclusive, definite. **5** *a sure sign that he's worried* RELIABLE, dependable, trustworthy, unfailing, infallible, certain, unambiguous, true, foolproof, established, effective; *informal* sure-fire; *formal* efficacious. **6** *the sure hand of the soloist* FIRM, steady, stable, secure, confident, steadfast, unfaltering, unwavering.
— OPPOSITES: uncertain, unlikely.

▶ exclamation *'Can I come too?' 'Sure.'* YES, all right, of course, indeed, certainly, absolutely, agreed; *informal* OK, yeah, yep, uh-huh, you bet, I'll say, sure thing.
■ **be sure to** REMEMBER TO, don't forget to, see that you, mind that you, take care to, be certain to.
■ **for sure** (*informal*) DEFINITELY, surely, certainly, without doubt, without question, undoubtedly, indubitably, absolutely, undeniably, unmistakably.
■ **make sure** CHECK, confirm, make certain, ensure, assure; verify, corroborate, substantiate.

surely ▶ adverb **1** *surely you remembered?* IT MUST BE THE CASE THAT, assuredly, without question. **2** *I will surely die* CERTAINLY, for sure, definitely, undoubtedly, without doubt, doubtless, indubitably, unquestionably, without fail, inevitably. **3** *slowly but surely manipulating the public* FIRMLY, steadily, confidently, assuredly, unhesitatingly, unfalteringly, unswervingly, determinedly, doggedly, tenaciously.

surety ▶ noun **1** *she's a surety for his obligations* GUARANTOR, sponsor. **2** *a $10,000 surety* PLEDGE, collateral, guaranty, guarantee, bond, assurance, insurance, deposit; security, indemnity, indemnification; earnest.

surface ▶ noun **1** *the surface of the door* OUTSIDE, exterior; top, side; finish, veneer. **2** *the surface of police culture* OUTWARD APPEARANCE, facade. **3** *a floured surface* counter, table.
— OPPOSITES: inside, interior.

▶ adjective *surface appearances* SUPERFICIAL, external,

exterior, outward, ostensible, apparent, cosmetic, skin deep.
— OPPOSITES: underlying.

▶ verb **1** *a submarine surfaced* COME TO THE SURFACE, come up, rise. **2** *the idea first surfaced in the sixties* EMERGE, arise, appear, come to light, crop up, materialize, spring up. **3** (*informal*) *she eventually surfaces for breakfast* GET UP, get out of bed, rise, wake, awaken, appear.
— OPPOSITES: dive.
■ **on the surface** AT FIRST GLANCE, to the casual eye, outwardly, to all appearances, apparently, ostensibly, superficially, externally.

surfeit ▶ noun *a surfeit of apples* EXCESS, surplus, abundance, oversupply, superabundance, superfluity, glut, avalanche, deluge; overdose; *informal* bellyful.
— OPPOSITES: lack.

▶ verb *we'll all be surfeited with food* SATIATE, sate, gorge, overfeed, overfill, glut, cram, stuff, overindulge, fill; saturate.

surfer ▶ noun INTERNET USER, netizen, nethead, power user.

surge ▶ noun **1** *a surge of water* GUSH, rush, outpouring, stream, flow. **2** *a surge in public support* INCREASE, rise, growth, upswing, upsurge, groundswell, escalation, leap. **3** *a sudden surge of anger* RUSH, uprush, storm, torrent, blaze, outburst, eruption. **4** *the surge of sea* SWELL, heaving, rolling, roll, swirling; tide.

▶ verb **1** *the water surged into people's homes* GUSH, rush, stream, flow, burst, pour, cascade, spill, overflow, sweep, roll. **2** *the TSX surged 47.63 points* INCREASE, rise, grow, escalate, leap. **3** *the sea surged* SWELL, heave, rise, roll.

surly ▶ adjective SULLEN, sulky, moody, sour, unfriendly, unpleasant, scowling, unsmiling; bad-tempered, grumpy, crotchety, prickly, cantankerous, irascible, testy, short-tempered; abrupt, brusque, curt, gruff, churlish, ill-humoured, crabby, cranky, uncivil; *informal* grouchy.
— OPPOSITES: pleasant.

surmise ▶ verb GUESS, conjecture, suspect, deduce, infer, conclude, theorize, speculate, divine; assume, presume, suppose, understand, gather, feel, sense, think, believe, imagine, fancy, reckon; *formal* opine.

surmount ▶ verb **1** *his reputation surmounts language barriers* OVERCOME, conquer, prevail over, triumph over, beat, vanquish; clear, cross, pass over; resist, endure. **2** *they surmounted the ridge* CLIMB OVER, top, ascend, scale, mount. **3** *the dome is surmounted by a statue* CAP, top, crown, finish.
— OPPOSITES: descend.

surname ▶ noun FAMILY NAME, last name; patronymic.

surpass ▶ verb EXCEL, exceed, transcend; outdo, outshine, outstrip, outclass, overshadow, eclipse; improve on, top, trump, cap, beat, better, outperform; *informal* leapfrog.

surplus ▶ noun *a surplus of grain* EXCESS, surfeit, superabundance, superfluity, oversupply, glut, profusion, plethora; remainder, residue, remains, leftovers.
— OPPOSITES: dearth.

▶ adjective *surplus adhesive* EXCESS, leftover, unused, remaining, extra, additional, spare; superfluous, redundant, unwanted, unneeded, dispensable, expendable.
— OPPOSITES: insufficient.

surprise ▸ noun **1** *Kate looked at me in surprise* ASTONISHMENT, amazement, wonder, incredulity, bewilderment, stupefaction, disbelief. **2** *the test came as a big surprise* SHOCK, bolt from the blue, bombshell, revelation, rude awakening, eye-opener, wake-up call; *informal* shocker.
▸ verb **1** *I was so surprised that I dropped it* ASTONISH, amaze, startle, astound, stun, stagger, shock; leave open-mouthed, take someone's breath away, dumbfound, stupefy, daze, take aback, shake up; *informal* bowl over, floor, flabbergast. **2** *she surprised a burglar* TAKE BY SURPRISE, catch unawares, catch off guard, catch red-handed, catch in the act, catch out.

surprised ▸ adjective ASTONISHED, amazed, astounded, startled, stunned, staggered, nonplussed, shocked, taken aback, stupefied, dumbfounded, dumbstruck, speechless, thunderstruck, confounded, shaken up; *informal* bowled over, flabbergasted, floored, flummoxed.

surprising ▸ adjective UNEXPECTED, unforeseen, unpredictable; astonishing, amazing, startling, astounding, staggering, incredible, extraordinary, breathtaking, remarkable; *informal* mind-blowing.

surreal ▸ adjective UNREAL, bizarre, unusual, weird, strange, freakish, unearthly, uncanny, dreamlike, phantasmagorical.

surrender ▸ verb **1** *the army surrendered* CAPITULATE, give in, give (oneself) up, give way, yield, concede (defeat), submit, climb down, back down, cave in, relent, crumble; lay down one's arms, raise the white flag, throw in the towel/sponge. **2** *they surrendere power to the workers* GIVE UP, relinquish, renounce forgo, forswear; cede, abdicate, waive, forfeit, sacrifice; hand over, turn over, yield, resign, transfer, grant. **3** *don't surrender all hope of changing things* ABANDON, give up, cast aside.
— OPPOSITES: resist, seize.
▸ noun CAPITULATION, submission, yielding, succumbing, acquiescence; fall, defeat, resignation.

surreptitious ▸ adjective SECRET, secretive, stealthy, clandestine, sneaky, sly, furtive; concealed, hidden, undercover, covert, veiled, cloak-and-dagger.
— OPPOSITES: blatant.

surrogate ▸ noun SUBSTITUTE, proxy, replacement; deputy, representative, stand-in, standby, stop-gap, relief, pinch-hitter, understudy.

surround ▸ verb *we were surrounded by cops* ENCIRCLE, enclose, encompass, ring; fence in, hem in, confine, bound, circumscribe, cut off; besiege, trap.
▸ noun *a fireplace with a wood surround* BORDER, edging, edge, perimeter, boundary, margin, skirting, fringe.

surrounding ▸ adjective NEIGHBOURING, nearby, near, neighbourhood, local; adjoining, adjacent, bordering, abutting; encircling, encompassing.

surroundings ▸ plural noun ENVIRONMENT, setting, milieu, background, backdrop; conditions, circumstances, situation, context; vicinity, locality, habitat.

surveillance ▸ noun OBSERVATION, scrutiny, watch, view, inspection, supervision; spying, espionage, infiltration, reconnaissance; *informal* bugging, wiretapping, recon.

survey ▸ verb **1** *he surveyed his work* LOOK AT, look over, observe, view, contemplate, regard, gaze at, stare at, eye; scrutinize, examine, inspect, scan, study, consider, review, take stock of; *informal* size up; *literary* behold. **2** *they surveyed 4000 drug users* INTERVIEW,

question, canvass, poll, cross-examine, investigate, research, study, probe, sample.
▸ noun **1** *a survey of the current literature* STUDY, review, consideration, overview; scrutiny, examination, inspection, appraisal. **2** *a survey of sexual behaviour* POLL, review, investigation, inquiry, study, probe, questionnaire, census, research.

survive ▸ verb **1** *he survived by escaping through a hole* REMAIN ALIVE, live, sustain oneself, pull through, get through, hold on/out, make it, keep body and soul together. **2** *the theatre must survive* CONTINUE, remain, persist, endure, live on, persevere, abide, go on, carry on, be extant, exist. **3** *he was survived by his sons* OUTLIVE, outlast; live longer than.

susceptible ▸ adjective **1** *susceptible children* IMPRESSIONABLE, credulous, gullible, innocent, ingenuous, naive, easily led; defenceless, vulnerable; persuadable, tractable; sensitive, responsive, thin-skinned. **2** *people susceptible to blackmail* OPEN TO, receptive to, vulnerable to; an easy target for. **3** *he is susceptible to ulcers* LIABLE TO, prone to, subject to, inclined to, predisposed to, disposed to, given to, at risk of.
— OPPOSITES: skeptical, immune, resistant.

suspect ▸ verb **1** *I suspected she'd made a mistake* HAVE A SUSPICION, have a feeling, feel, (be inclined to) think, fancy, reckon, guess, surmise, conjecture, conclude, have a hunch; suppose, presume, deduce, infer, sense, imagine; fear. **2** *he had no reason to suspect my honesty* DOUBT, distrust, mistrust, have misgivings about, be skeptical about, have qualms about, be suspicious of, be wary of, harbour reservations about.
▸ noun *a murder suspect* SUSPECTED PERSON, accused, defendant.
▸ adjective *a suspect package* SUSPICIOUS, dubious, doubtful, untrustworthy; odd, queer; *informal* fishy, funny, shady.

suspend ▸ verb **1** *the court case was suspended* ADJOURN, interrupt, break off, postpone, delay, defer, shelve, put off, intermit, prorogue, hold over, hold in abeyance; cut short, discontinue, dissolve, disband, terminate, table; *informal* put on ice, put on the back burner, mothball, take a rain check on. **2** *he was suspended from his duties* EXCLUDE, debar, remove, eliminate, expel, eject. **3** *lights were suspended from the ceiling* HANG, sling, string; swing, dangle.

suspenders ▸ plural noun braces; *dated* galluses.

suspense ▸ noun *I can't bear the suspense* TENSION, uncertainty, doubt, anticipation, expectation, expectancy, excitement, anxiety, apprehension, strain.
■ **in suspense** EAGERLY, agog, with bated breath, on tenterhooks; on edge, anxious, edgy, jumpy, keyed up, uneasy, antsy, uptight, jittery.

suspension ▸ noun **1** *the suspension of army operations* ADJOURNMENT, interruption, postponement, delay, deferral, deferment, stay, prorogation; armistice; cessation, end, halt, stoppage, dissolution, disbandment, termination. **2** *his suspension from school* EXCLUSION, debarment, removal, elimination, expulsion, ejection.

suspicion ▸ noun **1** *she had a suspicion that he didn't like her* INTUITION, feeling, impression, inkling, hunch, fancy, notion, supposition, belief, idea, theory; presentiment, premonition; *informal* gut feeling, sixth sense. **2** *I confronted him with my suspicions* MISGIVING, doubt, qualm, reservation, hesitation, question; skepticism, uncertainty, distrust, mistrust. **3** *wine with a suspicion of soda* TRACE, touch, suggestion, hint, soupçon, tinge, shade, whiff, bit, drop, dash, taste, jot, mite.

suspicious ► adjective **1** *she gave him a suspicious look* DOUBTFUL, unsure, dubious, wary, chary, skeptical, distrustful, mistrustful, disbelieving, cynical. **2** *a highly suspicious character* DISREPUTABLE, unsavoury, dubious, suspect, dishonest-looking, funny-looking, slippery; *informal* shifty, shady. **3** *she disappeared in suspicious circumstances* QUESTIONABLE, odd, strange, dubious, irregular, queer, funny, doubtful, mysterious, murky; *informal* fishy.
— OPPOSITES: trusting, honest, innocent.

sustain ► verb **1** *the balcony might not sustain the weight* BEAR, support, carry, stand, keep up, prop up, shore up, underpin. **2** *her memories sustained her* COMFORT, help, assist, encourage, succour, support, give strength to, buoy up, carry, cheer up, hearten; *informal* buck up. **3** *they were unable to sustain a coalition* CONTINUE, carry on, keep up, keep alive, maintain, preserve, conserve, perpetuate, retain. **4** *she had bread and cheese to sustain her* NOURISH, feed, nurture; maintain, preserve, keep alive, keep going, provide for. **5** *she sustained slight injuries* UNDERGO, experience, suffer, endure. **6** *the allegation was not sustained* UPHOLD, validate, ratify, vindicate, confirm, endorse; verify, corroborate, substantiate, bear out, prove, authenticate, back up, evidence, justify.

sustained ► adjective CONTINUOUS, ongoing, steady, continual, constant, prolonged, persistent, non-stop, perpetual, unabating, relentless, unrelieved, unbroken, never-ending, incessant, unceasing, ceaseless, round the clock.
— OPPOSITES: sporadic.

sustenance ► noun **1** *the creature needs sustenance* NOURISHMENT, food, nutriment, nutrition, provisions, provender, rations; *informal* grub, chow, scoff; *formal* comestibles; *literary* viands; *dated* victuals. **2** *the sustenance of his family* SUPPORT, maintenance, keep, living, livelihood, subsistence, income.

svelte ► adjective SLENDER, slim, graceful, elegant, willowy, sylphlike.

swagger ► verb **1** *we swaggered into the arena* STRUT, parade, stride; walk confidently; *informal* sashay. **2** *he likes to swagger about his kindness* BOAST, brag, bluster, crow, gloat; strut, posture, blow one's own horn, lord it; *informal* show off, swank.
► noun **1** *a slight swagger in his stride* STRUT; confidence, arrogance, ostentation. **2** *he was full of swagger* BLUSTER, braggadocio, bumptiousness, vainglory; *informal* swank.

swallow ► verb **1** *she couldn't swallow anything* EAT, gulp down, consume, devour, put away; ingest, assimilate; drink, guzzle, quaff, imbibe, sup, slug; *informal* polish off, swig, chug, (*Nfld*) glutch ♣, swill, down, scoff. **2** *I can't swallow any more of your insults* TOLERATE, endure, stand, put up with, bear, abide, countenance, stomach, take, accept; *informal* hack; *formal* brook. **3** *he swallowed my story* BELIEVE, credit, accept, trust; *informal* fall for, buy, go for, {swallow hook, line, and sinker}. **4** *she swallowed her pride* RESTRAIN, repress, suppress, hold back, fight back; overcome, check, control, curb, rein in; silence, muffle, stifle, smother, hide, bottle up; *informal* keep a/the lid on.
■ **swallow someone/something up 1** *the darkness swallowed them up* ENGULF, swamp, devour, overwhelm, overcome. **2** *the colleges were swallowed up by universities* TAKE OVER, engulf, absorb, assimilate, incorporate.

swamp ► noun *her horse got stuck in a swamp* MARSH, bog, muskeg, quagmire, mire, morass, fen; quicksand, bayou; *archaic* quag.
► verb **1** *the rain was swamping the dry roads* FLOOD, inundate, deluge, immerse; soak, drench, saturate. **2** *he was swamped by media attention* OVERWHELM, inundate, flood, deluge, engulf, snow under, overload, overpower, weigh down, besiege, beset.

swampy ► adjective MARSHY, boggy, fenny, miry; soft, soggy, muddy, spongy, heavy, squelchy, waterlogged, sodden, wet; *archaic* quaggy.

swan ► noun *male:* cob; *female:* pen; *young:* cygnet. See table at DUCK.

swap ► verb **1** *I swapped my stereo for some hockey equipment* EXCHANGE, trade, barter, interchange, bargain; switch, change, replace. **2** *we swapped jokes* BANDY, exchange, trade, reciprocate.
► noun *a job swap* EXCHANGE, interchange, trade, switch, trade-off, substitution; *informal* switcheroo.

swarm ► noun **1** *a swarm of bees* HIVE, flock, collection. **2** *a swarm of gendarmes* CROWD, multitude, horde, host, mob, gang, throng, mass, army, troop, herd, pack; *literary* myriad.
► verb *reporters were swarming all over the place* FLOCK, crowd, throng, surge, stream.
■ **be swarming with** BE CROWDED WITH, be thronged with, be overrun with, be full of, abound in, be teeming with, be aswarm with, bristle with, be alive with, be crawling with, be infested with, overflow with, be prolific in, be abundant in; *informal* be thick with.

swarthy ► adjective DARK-SKINNED, olive-skinned, dusky, tanned, saturnine, black; *archaic* swart.
— OPPOSITES: pale.

swashbuckling ► adjective DARING, heroic, daredevil, dashing, adventurous, bold, valiant, valorous, fearless, lion-hearted, dauntless, devil-may-care; gallant, chivalrous, romantic.
— OPPOSITES: timid.

swathe ► verb WRAP, envelop, bind, swaddle, bandage, cover, shroud, drape, wind, enfold, sheathe.

sway ► verb **1** *the curtains swayed in the breeze* SWING, shake, oscillate, undulate, move to and fro, move back and forth. **2** *she swayed on her feet* STAGGER, wobble, rock, lurch, reel, roll, list, stumble, pitch. **3** *we are swayed by the media* INFLUENCE, affect, bias, persuade, talk round, win over; manipulate, bend, mould. **4** *you must not be swayed by emotion* RULE, govern, dominate, control, guide.
► noun **1** *the sway of her hips* SWING, roll, shake, oscillation, undulation. **2** *his opinions have a lot of sway* CLOUT, influence, power, weight, authority, control.
■ **hold sway** HOLD POWER, wield power, exercise power, have jurisdiction, have authority, have dominion, rule, be in control, predominate; have the upper hand, have the edge, have the whip hand, have mastery; *informal* run the show, be in the driver's seat, be in the saddle.

swear ► verb **1** *they swore to marry each other* PROMISE, vow, pledge, give one's word, take an oath, undertake, guarantee; *Law* depose; *formal* aver. **2** *she swore she would never go back* INSIST, avow, pronounce, declare, proclaim, assert, profess, maintain, contend, emphasize, stress; *formal* aver. **3** *Kate spilled wine and swore* CURSE, blaspheme, utter profanities, utter oaths, use bad language, take the Lord's name in vain; *informal* cuss; *archaic* execrate.
■ **swear by** (*informal*) EXPRESS CONFIDENCE IN, have

faith in, trust, believe in; set store by, value; *informal* rate.

■ **swear off** (*informal*) RENOUNCE, forswear, forgo, abstain from, go without, shun, avoid, eschew, steer clear of; give up, dispense with, stop, discontinue, drop; *informal* kick, quit.

swearing ▶ noun BAD LANGUAGE, strong language, cursing, blaspheming, blasphemy; profanities, obscenities, curses, oaths, expletives, swear words; *informal* cussing, four-letter words; *formal* imprecation.

sweat ▶ noun **1** *he was drenched with sweat* PERSPIRATION, moisture, dampness, wetness; *Medicine* diaphoresis. **2** (*informal*) *he got into such a sweat about that girl* FLUSTER, panic, frenzy, fever, pother; *informal* state, flap, tizzy, dither, stew, lather. **3** (*informal*) *the sweat of the working classes* LABOUR, hard work, toil(s), effort(s), exertion(s), industry, drudgery, slog; *informal* grind, elbow grease.
— RELATED TERMS: sudatory.
▶ verb **1** *she was sweating heavily* PERSPIRE, swelter, glow; be damp, be wet; secrete. **2** *I've sweated over this for six months* WORK (HARD), work like a Trojan, labour, toil, slog, slave, work one's fingers to the bone; *informal* plug away; *archaic* drudge. **3** *he sweated over his mistakes* WORRY, agonize, fuss, panic, fret, lose sleep; *informal* be on pins and needles, be in a state, be in a flap, be in a stew, torture oneself, torment oneself.

sweater ▶ noun PULLOVER, Cowichan sweater ♣, Siwash sweater ♣; jersey; sweatshirt, (*Sask.*) bunny hug ♣, kangaroo jacket ♣; cardigan; *informal* woolly; turtleneck, V-neck, crewneck.

sweaty ▶ adjective PERSPIRING, sweating, clammy, sticky, glowing; moist, damp.

sweep ▶ verb **1** *she swept the floor* BRUSH, clean, scrub, wipe, mop, dust, scour; *informal* do. **2** *I swept the crumbs off* REMOVE, brush, clean, clear, whisk. **3** *he was swept out to sea* CARRY, pull, drag, tow. **4** *riots swept the country* ENGULF, overwhelm, flood. **5** *he swept down the stairs* GLIDE, sail, breeze, drift, flit, flounce; stride, stroll, swagger. **6** *a limousine swept past* GLIDE, sail, rush, race, streak, speed, fly, zoom, whiz, hurtle; *informal* tear, whip. **7** *police swept the conference room* SEARCH, probe, check, explore, go through, scour, comb.
▶ noun **1** *a great sweep of his hand* GESTURE, stroke, wave, movement. **2** *a security sweep* SEARCH, hunt, exploration, probe. **3** *a long sweep of golden sand* EXPANSE, tract, stretch, extent, plain. **4** *the broad sweep of our interests* RANGE, span, scope, compass, reach, spread, ambit, gamut, spectrum, extent.

■ **sweep something aside** DISREGARD, ignore, take no notice of, dismiss, shrug off, forget about, brush aside.

■ **sweep something under the carpet** HIDE, conceal, suppress, hush up, keep quiet about, censor, gag, withhold, cover up, stifle.

sweeping ▶ adjective **1** *sweeping changes* EXTENSIVE, wide-ranging, global, broad, comprehensive, all-inclusive, all-embracing, far-reaching, across the board; thorough, radical; *informal* wall-to-wall. **2** *a sweeping victory* OVERWHELMING, decisive, thorough, complete, total, absolute, out-and-out, unqualified, landslide. **3** *sweeping statements* WHOLESALE, blanket, generalized, all-inclusive, unqualified, indiscriminate, universal, oversimplified, imprecise. **4** *sweeping banks of flowers* BROAD, extensive, expansive, vast, spacious, boundless, panoramic.
— OPPOSITES: limited, narrow, focused, small.

sweet ▶ adjective **1** *sweet cakes* SUGARY, sweetened,

saccharine; sugared, honeyed, candied, glacé; sickly, cloying. **2** *the sweet scent of roses* FRAGRANT, aromatic, perfumed; *literary* ambrosial. **3** *her sweet voice* DULCET, melodious, lyrical, mellifluous, musical, tuneful, soft, harmonious, silvery, honeyed, mellow, rich, golden. **4** *life was still sweet* PLEASANT, pleasing, pleasurable, agreeable, delightful, nice, satisfying, gratifying, good, acceptable, fine; *informal* lovely, great. **5** *the sweet April air* PURE, wholesome, fresh, clean, clear. **6** *she has a sweet nature* LIKEABLE, appealing, engaging, amiable, pleasant, agreeable, genial, friendly, nice, kind, thoughtful, considerate; charming, enchanting, captivating, delightful, lovely. **7** *she looks quite sweet* CUTE, lovable, adorable, endearing, charming, attractive, dear. **8** *my sweet Lydia* DEAR, dearest, darling, beloved, loved, cherished, precious, treasured.
— OPPOSITES: sour, savoury, harsh, disagreeable.
▶ noun **1** *trying to cut back on sweets* DESSERT, treat, dainty, cake, cookie, pastry. **2** *happy birthday my sweet!* DEAR, darling, dearest, love, sweetheart, beloved, honey, hon, pet, treasure, angel, babe.

■ **sweet on** (*informal*) FOND OF, taken with, attracted to, in love with, enamoured of, captivated by, infatuated with, keen on, devoted to, smitten with, moonstruck by; *informal* mad about, bowled over by.

sweeten ▶ verb **1** *sweeten the milk with honey* MAKE SWEET, add sugar to, sugar, sugar-coat. **2** *he chewed gum to sweeten his breath* FRESHEN, refresh, purify, deodorize, perfume. **3** *try to sweeten the bad news* SOFTEN, ease, alleviate, mitigate, temper, cushion; embellish, embroider. **4** (*informal*) *a bigger dividend to sweeten shareholders* MOLLIFY, placate, soothe, soften up, pacify, appease, win over.

sweetheart ▶ noun **1** *you look lovely, sweetheart* DARLING, dear, dearest, love, beloved, sweet; *informal* honey, hon, sweetie, sugar, baby, babe, poppet. **2** *my high-school sweetheart* LOVER, love, girlfriend, boyfriend, beloved, significant other, main squeeze, lady love, loved one, suitor, admirer; *informal* steady, flame; valentine; *literary* swain; *dated* beau; *archaic* paramour.

swell ▶ verb **1** *her lip swelled up* EXPAND, bulge, distend, inflate, dilate, bloat, puff up, balloon, fatten, fill out, tumefy. **2** *the population swelled* GROW, enlarge, increase, expand, rise, escalate, multiply, proliferate, snowball, mushroom. **3** *she swelled with pride* BE FILLED, be bursting, brim, overflow. **4** *the program swelled enrolments* INCREASE, enlarge, augment, boost, top up, step up, multiply. **5** *the music swelled to fill the house* GROW LOUD, grow louder, amplify, crescendo, intensify, heighten.
— OPPOSITES: shrink, decrease, quieten.
▶ noun **1** *a brief swell in the volume* INCREASE, rise, escalation, surge, boost. **2** *a heavy swell on the sea* SURGE, wave, undulation, roll.
— OPPOSITES: decrease, dip.
▶ adjective (*informal, dated*) *a swell idea* EXCELLENT, marvellous, wonderful, splendid, magnificent, superb; *informal* super, great, fantastic.
— OPPOSITES: bad.

swelling ▶ noun BUMP, lump, bulge, protuberance, enlargement, distension, prominence, protrusion, node, nodule, tumescence; boil, blister, bunion, carbuncle.

sweltering ▶ adjective HOT, stifling, humid, sultry, sticky, muggy, close, stuffy; tropical, torrid, searing, blistering; *informal* boiling (hot), baking, roasting, sizzling.

— OPPOSITES: freezing.

swerve ▶ **verb** *a car swerved into her path* VEER, deviate, skew, diverge, sheer, weave, zigzag, change direction; *Sailing* tack.

▶ **noun** *the bowler regulated his swerve* CURVE, curl, deviation, twist.

swift ▶ **adjective 1** *a swift decision* PROMPT, rapid, sudden, immediate, instant, instantaneous; abrupt, hasty, hurried, precipitate, headlong. **2** *swift runners* FAST, rapid, quick, speedy, high-speed, fast-paced, brisk, lively; express, breakneck; fleet-footed; *informal* nippy, supersonic.

— OPPOSITES: slow, leisurely.

swill ▶ **verb** (*informal*) *she was swilling pints* DRINK, quaff, swallow, down, gulp, drain, imbibe, sup, slurp, consume, slug; *informal* swig, knock back, toss off, put away, chug, chugalug.

▶ **noun 1** (*informal*) *she took a swill of coffee* GULP, swallow, drink, draft, mouthful, slug; *informal* swig. **2** *swill for the pigs* PIGSWILL, mash, slops, scraps, refuse, scourings, leftovers; *archaic* hogwash.

swim ▶ **verb 1** *they swam in the pool* BATHE, take a dip, splash around; float, tread water, paddle. **2** *his food was swimming in gravy* BE SATURATED IN, be drenched in, be soaked in, be steeped in, be immersed in, be covered in, be drowning in, be full of.

swimming ▶ **noun**. *See table.*

Swimming Strokes & Kicks

Australian crawl	freestyle
backstroke	side stroke
breaststroke	flutter kick
butterfly	frog kick
crawl	scissor kick
dog-paddle	whip kick
elementary backstroke	

swimmingly ▶ **adverb** WELL, smoothly, easily, effortlessly, like clockwork, without a hitch, as planned, to plan; *informal* like a dream, like magic.

swimming pool ▶ **noun** POOL, baths, lap pool, natatorium.

swimsuit ▶ **noun** BATHING SUIT, (swimming) trunks, bikini; swimwear.

swindle ▶ **verb** *I was swindled out of money* DEFRAUD, cheat, trick, dupe, deceive, fool, hoax, hoodwink, bilk, bamboozle; *informal* fleece, con, sting, hose, diddle, rip off, take for a ride, pull a fast one on, put one over on, take to the cleaners, gull, stiff, euchre, hornswoggle; *literary* cozen.

▶ **noun** *an insurance swindle* FRAUD, trick, deception, deceit, cheat, sham, artifice, ruse, dodge, racket, wile; sharp practice; *informal* con, fiddle, diddle, rip-off, flim-flam, bunco.

swindler ▶ **noun** FRAUDSTER, fraud, (confidence) trickster, cheat, rogue, mountebank, charlatan, imposter, hoaxer; *informal* con man, con artist, scam artist, shyster, goniff, shark, sharp, hustler, phony, crook, snake oil salesman.

swing ▶ **verb 1** *the sign swung in the wind* SWAY, oscillate, move back and forth, move to and fro, wave, wag, rock, flutter, flap. **2** *Helen swung the bottle* BRANDISH, wave, flourish, wield, shake, wag, twirl. **3** *this road swings off to the north* CURVE, bend, veer, turn, bear, wind, twist, deviate, slew, skew, drift, head. **4** *the balance swung from one party to the other* CHANGE, fluctuate, shift, alter, oscillate, waver, alternate, see-saw, yo-yo, vary. **5** (*informal*) *if we keep trying we can swing this deal* ACCOMPLISH, achieve, obtain, acquire, get, secure, net, win, attain, bag, hook; *informal* wangle, land.

▶ **noun 1** *a swing of the pendulum* OSCILLATION, sway, wave. **2** *a swing to the New Democrats in this constituency* CHANGE, move; turnaround, turnabout, reversal, about face, volte face, change of heart, U-turn, sea change. **3** *a swing towards plain food* TREND, tendency, drift, movement. **4** *a mood swing* FLUCTUATION, change, shift, variation, oscillation.

swipe (*informal*) ▶ **verb 1** *he swiped at her head* SWING, lash out; strike, hit, slap, cuff; *informal* belt, wallop, sock, clout. **2** *they're always swiping candy* STEAL, thieve, take, pilfer, purloin, (*Nfld*) buck ♣, snatch, shoplift; *informal* filch, lift, snaffle, rob, nab, pinch, glom.

▶ **noun** *she took a swipe at his face* SWING, stroke, strike, hit, slap, cuff, clip; *informal* belt, wallop.

swirl ▶ **verb** WHIRL, eddy, billow, spiral, circulate, revolve, spin, twist; flow, stream, surge, seethe.

switch ▶ **noun 1** *the switch on top of the telephone* BUTTON, lever, control, dial, rocker. **2** *a switch from direct to indirect taxation* CHANGE, move, shift, transition, transformation; reversal, turnaround, U-turn, changeover, transfer, conversion; substitution, exchange. **3** *a switch of willow* BRANCH, twig, stick, rod.

▶ **verb 1** *he switched sides* CHANGE, shift; reverse; *informal* chop and change. **2** *he managed to switch envelopes* EXCHANGE, swap, interchange, trade, substitute, replace, rotate.

■ **switch something on** TURN ON, put on, flick on, activate, start, power up, set going, set in motion, operate, initiate, actuate, initialize, energize; toggle, flip, throw.

■ **switch something off** TURN OFF, shut off, flick off, power down, stop, cut, halt, deactivate; toggle, flip.

swivel ▶ **verb** TURN, rotate, revolve, pivot, swing; spin, twirl, whirl, wheel, gyrate, pirouette.

swollen ▶ **adjective** DISTENDED, expanded, enlarged, bulging, inflated, dilated, bloated, puffed up, puffy, tumescent, tumid; inflamed, varicose.

swoop ▶ **verb 1** *pigeons swooped down after the grain* DIVE, descend, sweep, pounce, plunge, pitch, nosedive; rush, dart, speed, zoom. **2** *police swooped on the building* RAID, pounce on, attack, assault, assail, charge, bust.

■ **at one fell swoop** *See* FELL.

sword ▶ **noun** *a ceremonial sword* BLADE, foil, broadsword, épée, cutlass, rapier, sabre, scimitar; *literary* brand.

■ **cross swords** QUARREL, disagree, dispute, wrangle, bicker, be at odds, be at loggerheads, lock horns; fight, contend; *informal* scrap.

sybarite ▶ **noun** HEDONIST, sensualist, voluptuary, libertine, pleasure-seeker, epicure, bon vivant, bon viveur.

— OPPOSITES: puritan.

sybaritic ▶ **adjective** LUXURIOUS, extravagant, lavish, self-indulgent, pleasure-seeking, sensual, voluptuous, hedonistic, epicurean, lotus-eating, libertine, debauched, decadent.

— OPPOSITES: ascetic.

sycophant ▶ **noun** bootlicker, brown-noser, browner ♣, toady, lickspittle, flatterer, flunky, lackey, yes-man, spaniel, doormat, stooge, cringer, suck ♣, suck-up.

sycophantic ▶ adjective OBSEQUIOUS, servile, subservient, deferential, grovelling, toadying, fawning, flattering, ingratiating, cringing, unctuous, slavish; *informal* smarmy, bootlicking, brown-nosing.

syllabus ▶ noun CURRICULUM, course (of study), program of study, course outline; timetable, schedule, calendar.

symbol ▶ noun **1** *the lotus is the symbol of purity* EMBLEM, token, sign, representation, figure, image; metaphor, allegory; icon. **2** *the chemical symbol for helium* SIGN, character, mark, letter, ideogram. **3** *the Red Cross symbol* LOGO, emblem, badge, stamp, trademark, crest, insignia, coat of arms, seal, device, monogram, hallmark, flag, motif, icon.

symbolic ▶ adjective **1** *the Colosseum is symbolic of the Roman Empire* EMBLEMATIC, representative, typical, characteristic, symptomatic. **2** *symbolic language* FIGURATIVE, representative, illustrative, emblematic, metaphorical, allegorical, parabolic, allusive, suggestive; meaningful, significant.
– OPPOSITES: literal.

symbolize ▶ verb REPRESENT, stand for, be a sign of, exemplify; denote, signify, mean, indicate, convey, express, imply, suggest, allude to; embody, epitomize, encapsulate, personify, typify; *literary* betoken.

symmetrical ▶ adjective REGULAR, uniform, consistent; evenly shaped, aligned, equal; mirror-image; balanced, proportional, even.

symmetry ▶ noun REGULARITY, evenness, uniformity, consistency, conformity, correspondence, equality; balance, proportions; *formal* concord.

sympathetic ▶ adjective **1** *a sympathetic listener* COMPASSIONATE, caring, concerned, solicitous, empathetic, understanding, sensitive; commiserative, pitying, consoling, comforting, supportive, encouraging; considerate, kind, tender-hearted. **2** *the most sympathetic character in the book* LIKEABLE, pleasant, agreeable, congenial, friendly, genial, simpatico. **3** *I was sympathetic to his cause* IN FAVOUR OF, in sympathy with, pro, on the side of, supportive of, encouraging of; well-disposed to, favourably disposed to, receptive to.
– OPPOSITES: unfeeling, opposed.

sympathize ▶ verb **1** *I do sympathize with the poor creature* PITY, feel sorry for, show compassion for, commiserate, offer condolences to, feel for, show concern, show interest; console, comfort, solace, soothe, support, encourage; empathize with, identify with, understand, relate to. **2** *they sympathize with the critique* AGREE WITH, support, be in favour of, go along with, favour, approve of, back, side with.

sympathizer ▶ noun SUPPORTER, backer, well-wisher, advocate, ally, partisan; collaborator, fraternizer, conspirator, quisling.

sympathy ▶ noun **1** *he shows sympathy for the poor* COMPASSION, caring, concern, solicitude, empathy; commiseration, pity, condolence, comfort, solace, support, encouragement; consideration, kindness. **2** *sympathy with a fellow journalist* RAPPORT, fellow feeling, affinity, empathy, harmony, accord, compatibility; fellowship, camaraderie. **3** *their sympathy with the Communists* AGREEMENT, favour, approval, approbation, support, encouragement, partiality; association, alignment, affiliation.
– OPPOSITES: indifference, hostility.

symptom ▶ noun **1** *the symptoms of the disease* MANIFESTATION, indication, indicator, sign, mark, feature, trait; *Medicine* prodrome. **2** *a symptom of the country's present turmoil* EXPRESSION, sign, indication, mark, token, manifestation; portent, warning, clue, hint; testimony, evidence, proof; result, consequence, product.

symptomatic ▶ adjective INDICATIVE, characteristic, suggestive, typical, representative, symbolic.

syndrome ▶ noun CONDITION, illness, complex, disorder, affliction, sickness.

synonym ▶ noun ALTERNATE, substitute, alternative, equivalent, euphemism.

synopsis ▶ noun SUMMARY, summarization, précis, abstract, outline, digest, rundown, roundup, abridgement.

synthesis ▶ noun COMBINATION, union, amalgam, blend, mixture, compound, fusion, composite, alloy; unification, amalgamation, marrying.

synthesizer ▶ noun KEYBOARD, keys, synth, vocoder, sampler, MIDI device.

synthetic ▶ adjective ARTIFICIAL, fake, imitation, faux, mock, simulated, ersatz, substitute; pseudo, so-called; man-made, manufactured, fabricated; *informal* phony, pretend.
– OPPOSITES: natural.

syrupy ▶ adjective **1** *syrupy medicine* OVERSWEET, sweet, sugary, treacly, honeyed, saccharine; thick, sticky, gluey, viscid, glutinous; *informal* gooey. **2** *syrupy romantic drivel* SENTIMENTAL, mawkish, cloying, sickly, saccharine, trite; *informal* soppy, schmaltzy, mushy, slushy, sloppy, lovey-dovey, cheesy, corny.

system ▶ noun **1** *a system of canals* STRUCTURE, organization, arrangement, complex, network; *informal* set-up. **2** *a system for regulating sales* METHOD, methodology, technique, process, procedure, approach, practice; means, way, mode, framework, modus operandi; scheme, plan, policy, program, regimen, formula, routine. **3** *there was no system in his work* ORDER, method, orderliness, systematization, planning, logic, routine. **4** *youngsters have no faith in the system* THE ESTABLISHMENT, the administration, the authorities, the powers that be; bureaucracy, officialdom; the status quo.

systematic ▶ adjective STRUCTURED, methodical, organized, orderly, planned, systematized, regular, routine, standardized, standard; logical, coherent, consistent; efficient, businesslike, practical.
– OPPOSITES: disorganized.

Tt

tab ▶ noun **1** *his name is on the tab of his jacket* TAG, label, flap. **2** (*informal*) *the company will pick up the tab* BILL, invoice, account, charge, check, expense, cost.

table ▶ noun **1** *put the plates on the table* bench, buffet, stand, counter, work surface; desk, bar. **2** *he provides an excellent table* MEAL, food, fare, menu, nourishment; eatables, provisions; *informal* spread, grub, chow, eats, nosh; *literary* viands; *dated* victuals. **3** *the report has numerous tables* CHART, diagram, figure, graph, plan; list, tabulation, index.
▶ verb **1** *she tabled a question in parliament* SUBMIT, put forward, propose, suggest, move, lodge, file, introduce, air, moot. **2** *the council tabled the rezoning until April* POSTPONE, delay, defer, sideline, put on the back burner.

tableau ▶ noun **1** *mythic tableaux* PICTURE, painting, representation, illustration, image. **2** *the first act consists of a series of tableaux* PAGEANT, tableau vivant, parade, diorama, scene. **3** *a domestic tableau around the fireplace* SCENE, arrangement, grouping, group; picture, spectacle, image, vignette.

tablet ▶ noun **1** *a carved tablet* SLAB, stone, panel, plaque, plate, sign. **2** *a headache tablet* PILL, capsule, lozenge, caplet, pastille, drop, pilule; *informal* tab. **3** *a tablet of soap* BAR, cake, slab, brick, block, chunk, piece.

taboo ▶ noun *the taboo against healing on the Sabbath* PROHIBITION, proscription, veto, interdiction, interdict, ban, restriction.
▶ adjective *taboo subjects* FORBIDDEN, prohibited, banned, proscribed, interdicted, outlawed, illegal, illicit, unlawful, restricted, off limits; unmentionable, unspeakable, unutterable, unsayable, ineffable; rude, impolite.
— OPPOSITES: acceptable.

tabulate ▶ verb CHART, arrange, order, organize, systematize, systemize, catalogue, list, index, classify, class, codify; compile, group, log, grade, rate.

tacit ▶ adjective IMPLICIT, understood, implied, hinted, suggested; unspoken, unstated, unsaid, unexpressed, unvoiced; taken for granted, taken as read, inferred.
— OPPOSITES: explicit.

taciturn ▶ adjective UNTALKATIVE, uncommunicative, reticent, unforthcoming, quiet, secretive, tight-lipped, close-mouthed; silent, mute, dumb, inarticulate; reserved, withdrawn.
— OPPOSITES: talkative.

tack ▶ noun **1** *tacks held the carpet down* PIN, thumbtack, pushpin, nail, staple, rivet, stud. **2** *the boat bowled past on the opposite tack* HEADING, bearing, course, track, path, line. **3** *the defender changed his tack* APPROACH, way, method; policy, procedure, technique, tactic, plan, strategy, stratagem; path, line, angle, direction, course.
▶ verb **1** *a photo tacked to the wall* PIN, nail, staple, fix, fasten, attach, secure, affix. **2** *the dress was roughly tacked together* STITCH, baste, sew, bind. **3** *the yachts tacked back and forth* ZIGZAG, change direction, change course, swerve, veer; *Nautical* go/come about, beat.

4 *poems tacked on at the end of the book* ADD, append, join, tag, stick.

tackle ▶ noun **1** *fishing tackle* GEAR, equipment, apparatus, kit, hardware; implements, instruments, accoutrements, paraphernalia, trappings, appurtenances; *informal* things, stuff, bits and pieces; *archaic* equipage. **2** *lifting tackle* PULLEYS, gear, hoist, crane, winch, davit, windlass, sheave. **3** *a tackle by the linebacker* BLOCK, interception, challenge, attack.
▶ verb **1** *we must tackle environmental problems* COME TO GRIPS WITH, address, get to work on, set one's hand to, approach, take on, attend to, see to, try to sort out; deal with, take care of, handle, manage; *informal* have a crack at, have a go at. **2** *he tackled a masked intruder* CONFRONT, face up to, take on, contend with, challenge, attack; seize, grab, grapple with, intercept, block, stop; bring down, floor, fell; *informal* have a go at.

tacky¹ ▶ adjective *the paint was still tacky* STICKY, wet, gluey, gummy, adhesive, viscous, viscid, treacly; *informal* gooey.

tacky² ▶ adjective *a tacky game show* TAWDRY, tasteless, kitsch, kitschy, (*Que.*) kétaine ♣, vulgar, crude, garish, gaudy, showy, trashy, cheesy, cheap, common, second-rate.
— OPPOSITES: tasteful.

tact ▶ noun DIPLOMACY, tactfulness, sensitivity, understanding, thoughtfulness, consideration, delicacy, discretion, prudence, judiciousness, subtlety, savoir faire; *informal* savvy.

tactful ▶ adjective DIPLOMATIC, discreet, considerate, sensitive, understanding, thoughtful, delicate, judicious, politic, perceptive, subtle; courteous, polite, decorous, respectful; *informal* savvy.

tactic ▶ noun **1** *a tax-saving tactic* STRATEGY, scheme, stratagem, plan, manoeuvre; method, expedient, gambit, move, approach, tack; device, trick, ploy, dodge, ruse, machination, contrivance; *informal* wangle; *archaic* shift. **2** *our fleet's superior tactics* STRATEGY, policy, campaign, battle plans, game plans, manoeuvres, logistics; generalship, organization, planning, direction, orchestration.

tactical ▶ adjective CALCULATED, planned, strategic; prudent, politic, diplomatic, judicious, shrewd, cunning, artful.

tactless ▶ adjective INSENSITIVE, inconsiderate, thoughtless, indelicate, undiplomatic, impolitic, indiscreet, unsubtle, clumsy, heavy-handed, graceless, awkward, inept, gauche; blunt, frank, outspoken, abrupt, gruff, rough, crude, coarse; imprudent, injudicious, unwise; rude, impolite, uncouth, discourteous, crass, tasteless, disrespectful, boorish.

tad ▶ noun BIT, whit, mite, touch, modicum, iota, hint, soupçon, fraction, titch.

tag ▶ noun **1** *a price tag* LABEL, ticket, badge, mark, marker, tab, sticker, stub, counterfoil, flag. **2** *he gained a 'bad boy' tag* DESIGNATION, label, description, characterization, identity; nickname, name, epithet, title, sobriquet; *informal* handle, moniker; *formal* denomination, appellation. **3** *tags from Shakespeare* QUOTATION, quote, tag line, phrase, platitude, cliché, excerpt; saying, proverb, maxim, adage, aphorism, motto, epigram; slogan, catchphrase.

▶ **verb 1** *bottles tagged with coloured stickers* LABEL, mark, ticket, identify, flag, indicate. **2** *she is tagged as a 'thinking' actor* LABEL, class, categorize, characterize, designate, describe, identify, classify; mark, stamp, brand, pigeonhole, stereotype, typecast, compartmentalize, typify; name, call, title, entitle, dub, term, style. **3** *a poem tagged on as an afterthought* ADD, tack, join; attach, append, stick. **4** *he was tagging along behind her* FOLLOW, trail; come after, go after, shadow, dog; accompany, attend, escort; *informal* tail.

tail ▶ **noun 1** *the dog's tail* brush, scut, dock; tail feathers; hindquarters. **2** *the tail of the plane* REAR, end, back, extremity; bottom. **3** *the tail of the hunting season* CLOSE, end, conclusion, tail end. **4** (*informal*) *put a tail on that suspect* DETECTIVE, investigator, shadow; *informal* sleuth, private eye, gumshoe.

– RELATED TERMS: caudal
– OPPOSITES: head, front, start.

▶ **verb** (*informal*) *the paparazzi tailed them* FOLLOW, shadow, stalk, trail, track, hunt, hound, dog, pursue, chase.

■ **on someone's tail** CLOSE BEHIND, following closely, (hard) on someone's heels.

■ **tail off/away** FADE, wane, ebb, dwindle, decrease, lessen, diminish, decline, subside, abate, drop off, peter out, taper off; let up, ease off, die away, die down, come to an end.

■ **turn tail** RUN AWAY, flee, bolt, make off, take to one's heels, cut and run, beat a (hasty) retreat; *informal* scram, skedaddle, vamoose.

tailor ▶ **noun** OUTFITTER, dressmaker, couturier, (fashion) designer; clothier, costumier, seamstress.
– RELATED TERMS: sartorial.

▶ **verb** *services can be tailored to customer requirements* CUSTOMIZE, adapt, adjust, modify, change, convert, alter, attune, mould, gear, fit, cut, shape, tune.

tailspin ▶ **noun** NOSEDIVE, dive, plummet, plunge, fall, rapid descent, sharp decline.

taint ▶ **noun** *the taint of corruption* TRACE, touch, suggestion, hint, tinge; stain, blot, blemish, stigma, black mark, discredit, dishonour, disgrace, shame.

▶ **verb 1** *the wilderness is tainted by pollution* CONTAMINATE, pollute, adulterate, infect, blight, spoil, soil, ruin, destroy; *literary* befoul. **2** *those fraudsters taint the reputation of legitimate claimants* TARNISH, sully, blacken, stain, blot, blemish, stigmatize, mar, corrupt, defile, soil, muddy, damage, harm, hurt; drag through the mud; *literary* besmirch.
– OPPOSITES: clean, improve.

take ▶ **verb 1** *she took his hand* LAY HOLD OF, get hold of; grasp, grip, clasp, clutch, grab. **2** *he took an envelope from his pocket* REMOVE, pull, draw, withdraw, extract, fish. **3** *a passage taken from my book* EXTRACT, quote, cite, excerpt, derive, abstract, copy, cull. **4** *she took a little wine* DRINK, imbibe; consume, swallow, eat, ingest. **5** *many prisoners were taken* CAPTURE, seize, catch, arrest, apprehend, take into custody; carry off, abduct. **6** *someone's taken my car* STEAL, remove, appropriate, make off with, pilfer, purloin, (*Nfld*) buck ✤; *informal* filch, swipe, snaffle, pinch. **7** *take four from the total* SUBTRACT, deduct, remove; discount; *informal* knock off, minus. **8** *all the seats had been taken* OCCUPY, use, utilize, fill, hold; reserve, engage; *informal* bag. **9** *I have taken a room nearby* RENT, lease, hire,

charter; reserve, book, engage. **10** *I took the job* ACCEPT, undertake. **11** *I'd take this over the other option* PICK, choose, select; prefer, favour, opt for, vote for. **12** *take, for instance, Alberta* CONSIDER, contemplate, ponder, think about, mull over, examine, study, meditate over, ruminate about. **13** *she took his temperature* ASCERTAIN, determine, establish, measure, find out, discover; calculate, compute, evaluate, rate, assess, appraise, gauge. **14** *he took notes* WRITE, note (down), jot (down), scribble, scrawl, record, register, document, minute. **15** *I took the package to Whitehorse* BRING, carry, bear, transport, convey, move, transfer, shift, ferry; *informal* cart, tote. **16** *the police took her home* ESCORT, accompany, help, assist, show, lead, guide, see, usher, convey. **17** *he took the train* TRAVEL ON/BY, journey on, go via; use. **18** *the town takes its name from the lake* DERIVE, get, obtain, come by, acquire, pick up. **19** *she took the prize for best speaker* RECEIVE, obtain, gain, get, acquire, collect, accept, be awarded; secure, come by, win, earn, pick up, carry off; *informal* land, bag, net, scoop. **20** *I took the chance to postpone it* ACT ON, take advantage of, capitalize on, use, exploit, make the most of, leap at, jump at, pounce on, seize, grasp, grab, accept. **21** *he took great pleasure in painting* DERIVE, draw, acquire, obtain, get, gain, extract, procure; experience, undergo, feel. **22** *Liz took the news badly* RECEIVE, respond to, react to, meet, greet; deal with, cope with. **23** *do you take me for a fool?* REGARD AS, consider to be, view as, see as, believe to be, reckon to be, imagine to be, deem to be. **24** *I take it that you are hungry* ASSUME, presume, suppose, imagine, expect, reckon, gather, dare say, trust, surmise, deduce, guess, conjecture, fancy, suspect. **25** *I take your point* UNDERSTAND, grasp, get, comprehend, apprehend, see, follow; accept, appreciate, acknowledge, sympathize with, agree with. **26** *Shirley was very taken with him* CAPTIVATE, enchant, charm, delight, attract, beguile, enthrall, entrance, infatuate, dazzle; amuse, divert, entertain; *informal* tickle someone's fancy. **27** *I can't take much more* ENDURE, bear, tolerate, stand, put up with, abide, stomach, accept, allow, countenance, support, shoulder; *formal* brook; *archaic* suffer. **28** *applicants must take a test* CARRY OUT, do, complete, write ✤, conduct, perform, execute, discharge, accomplish, fulfil. **29** *I took Drama and History of Art* STUDY, learn, have lessons in; take up, pursue; *informal* do. **30** *the journey took six hours* LAST, continue for, go on for, carry on for; require, call for, need, necessitate, entail, involve. **31** *it would take an expert to know that* REQUIRE, need, necessitate, demand, call for, entail, involve. **32** *I take size six shoes* WEAR, use; require, need. **33** *the dye did not take* BE EFFECTIVE, take effect, hold, root, be productive, be effectual, be useful; work, operate, succeed, function; *formal* be efficacious.
– OPPOSITES: give, free, add, refuse, miss.

▶ **noun 1** *the whalers' commercial take* CATCH, haul, bag, yield, net. **2** *the state's tax take* REVENUE, income, gain, profit; takings, proceeds, returns, receipts, winnings, pickings, earnings, spoils; purse. **3** *a clapperboard for the start of each take* SCENE, sequence, (film) clip. **4** *a fresh take on gender issues* VIEW OF, reading of, version of, interpretation of, understanding of, account of, analysis of, approach to.

■ **take after** RESEMBLE, look like; remind one of, make one think of, recall, conjure up, suggest, evoke; *informal* favour, be a chip off the old block.

■ **take something apart 1** *we took the machine apart* DISMANTLE, pull to pieces, pull apart, disassemble, break up; tear down, demolish, destroy, wreck. **2** (*informal*) *the scene was taken apart by the director. See* CRITICIZE.

■ **take someone back 1** *the dream took me back to Vienna* EVOKE, remind one of, conjure up, summon up; echo, suggest. **2** *I will never take her back* BE RECONCILED TO, forgive, pardon, excuse, exonerate, absolve; let bygones be bygones, bury the hatchet.

■ **take something back 1** *I take back every word* RETRACT, withdraw, renounce, disclaim, unsay, disavow, recant, repudiate; *formal* abjure. **2** *I must take the keys back* RETURN, bring back, give back, restore.

■ **take something down** WRITE DOWN, note down, jot down, set down, record, commit to paper, register, draft, document, minute, pen.

■ **take someone in 1** *she took in paying guests* ACCOMMODATE, board, house, feed, put up, admit, receive; harbour. **2** *you were taken in by a hoax* DECEIVE, delude, hoodwink, mislead, trick, dupe, fool, cheat, defraud, swindle, outwit, gull, hoax, bamboozle; *informal* con, put one over on.

■ **take something in 1** *she could hardly take in the news* COMPREHEND, understand, grasp, follow, absorb; *informal* get. **2** *this route takes in some great scenery* INCLUDE, encompass, embrace, contain, comprise, cover, incorporate, comprehend, hold.

■ **take someone in hand** CONTROL, be in charge of, dominate, master; reform, improve, correct, change, rehabilitate.

■ **take something in hand** DEAL WITH, apply oneself to, come to grips with, set one's hand to, grapple with, take on, attend to, see to, sort out, take care of, handle, manage.

■ **take it out of someone** EXHAUST, drain, enervate, tire, fatigue, wear out, weary, debilitate; *informal* poop.

■ **take off 1** *the horse took off at great speed* RUN AWAY/OFF, flee, abscond, take flight, decamp, leave, go, depart, make off, bolt, take to one's heels, escape; *informal* split, clear off, skedaddle, vamoose. **2** *the plane took off* BECOME AIRBORNE, take to the air, take wing; lift off, blast off. **3** *the idea really took off* SUCCEED, do well, become popular, catch on, prosper, flourish, thrive, boom.

■ **take someone off** MIMIC, impersonate, imitate, ape, parody, mock, caricature, satirize, burlesque, lampoon, ridicule; *informal* spoof, send up.

■ **take someone on 1** *there was no challenger to take him on* COMPETE AGAINST, oppose, challenge, confront, face, fight, vie with, contend with, stand up to. **2** *we took on extra staff* ENGAGE, hire, employ, enrol, enlist, sign up; *informal* take on board.

■ **take something on 1** *he took on more responsibility* UNDERTAKE, accept, assume, shoulder, acquire, carry, bear. **2** *the study took on political meaning* ACQUIRE, assume, come to have.

■ **take one's time** GO SLOWLY, dally, dawdle, delay, linger, drag one's feet, waste time, kill time; *informal* dilly-dally, lallygag; *archaic* tarry.

■ **take someone out 1** *he asked if he could take her out* GO OUT WITH, escort, partner, accompany, go with; romance, woo; *informal* date, see, go steady with; *dated* court. **2** (*informal*) *the sniper took them all out* KILL, murder, assassinate, dispatch, execute, finish off, eliminate, exterminate, terminate; *informal* do in, do away with, bump off, rub out, mow down. *literary* slay.

■ **take something over** ASSUME CONTROL OF, take charge of, take command of.

■ **take to 1** *he took to carrying his money in his sock* MAKE A HABIT OF, resort to, turn to, have recourse to; start, commence. **2** *Ruth took to the cat instantly* LIKE, get on

with, be friendly towards; *informal* take a shine to. **3** *the dog has really taken to racing* BECOME GOOD AT, develop an ability for; like, enjoy.

■ **take something up 1** *she took up abstract painting* ENGAGE IN, practise; begin, start, commence. **2** *the meetings took up all her time* CONSUME, fill, absorb, use, occupy; waste, squander. **3** *her cousin took up the story* RESUME, recommence, restart, carry on, continue, pick up, return to. **4** *he took up their offer of a job* ACCEPT, say yes to, agree to, adopt; *formal* accede to. **5** *take the skirt up an inch* SHORTEN, turn up; raise, lift.

■ **take up with** BECOME FRIENDS WITH, go around with, fall in with, string along with, get involved with, start seeing; *informal* knock around with, hang out with.

takeoff ▶ **noun 1** *the plane performed a safe takeoff* DEPARTURE, liftoff, launch, blast-off; ascent, flight. **2** (*informal*) *a takeoff of a talent show* PARODY, pastiche, mockery, caricature, travesty, satire, lampoon, mimicry, imitation, impersonation, impression; *informal* send-up, spoof.
— OPPOSITES: touchdown.

takeover ▶ **noun** BUYOUT, merger, amalgamation; purchase, acquisition.

takings ▶ **plural noun** PROCEEDS, returns, receipts, earnings, winnings, pickings, spoils; profit, gain, income, revenue; gate, purse.

tale ▶ **noun 1** *a tale of witches* STORY, narrative, anecdote, report, account, history; legend, fable, myth, parable, allegory, saga; *informal* yarn. **2** *she told tales to her mother* LIE, fib, falsehood, story, untruth, fabrication, fiction; *informal* tall story, fairy tale/story, cock-and-bull story.

talent ▶ **noun** FLAIR, aptitude, facility, gift, knack, technique, touch, bent, ability, expertise, capacity, faculty; strength, forte, genius, brilliance; dexterity, skill, artistry.

talented ▶ **adjective** GIFTED, skilful, skilled, accomplished, brilliant, expert, consummate, masterly, adroit, dexterous, able, competent, apt, capable, deft, adept, proficient; *informal* crack, ace.
— OPPOSITES: inept.

talisman ▶ **noun** (LUCKY) CHARM, fetish, amulet, mascot, totem, buffalo stone, beaver bundle, medicine bundle, juju.

talk ▶ **verb 1** *I was talking to a friend* SPEAK, chat, chatter, gossip, prattle, babble, rattle on, blather; *informal* yak, gab, jaw, chew the fat, natter, rap. **2** *you're talking garbage* UTTER, speak, say, voice, express, articulate, pronounce, verbalize, vocalize. **3** *they were able to talk in peace* CONVERSE, communicate, speak, confer, consult; negotiate, parley; *informal* have a confab, chew the fat, rap; *formal* confabulate. **4** *he talked of suicide* MENTION, refer to, speak about, discuss. **5** *he learned to talk Cree* SPEAK (IN), talk in, communicate in, converse in, express oneself in; use. **6** *nothing would make her talk* CONFESS, speak out/up, reveal all, tell tales, give the game away, open one's mouth; *informal* come clean, blab, squeal, let the cat out of the bag, spill the beans, sing, rat. **7** *the others will talk* GOSSIP, pass comment, make remarks; criticize.
▶ **noun 1** *he was bored with all this talk* CHATTER, gossip, prattle, jabbering, babbling, gabbling; *informal* yakking, gabbing, nattering. **2** *she needed a talk with Jim* CONVERSATION, chat, discussion, tête-à-tête, heart-to-heart, dialogue, parley, powwow, consultation, conference, meeting; *informal* confab, jaw, chit-chat, gossip; *formal* colloquy, confabulation. **3** *peace talks* NEGOTIATIONS, discussions; conference,

summit, meeting, consultation, dialogue, symposium, seminar, conclave, parley; mediation, arbitration; *informal* powwow. **4** *she gave a talk on her travels* LECTURE, speech, address, discourse, oration, presentation, report, sermon; *informal* spiel, chalk talk. **5** *there was talk of a takeover* GOSSIP, rumour, hearsay, tittle-tattle; news, report. **6** (*informal*) *he's all talk* BOASTING, bragging, idle talk, bombast, braggadocio; *informal* hot air, mouth. **7** *baby talk* SPEECH, language, slang, idiom, idiolect; words; *informal* lingo, -ese.

■ **talk back** ANSWER BACK, be impertinent, be cheeky, be rude; contradict, argue with, disagree with.

■ **talk big** (*informal*). See BOAST *verb* sense 1.

■ **talk down to** CONDESCEND TO, patronize, look down one's nose at, put down.

■ **talk someone into something** PERSUADE INTO, argue into, cajole into, coax into, bring round to, inveigle into, wheedle into, sweet-talk into, prevail on someone to; *informal* hustle, fast-talk.

talkative ▶ adjective CHATTY, loquacious, garrulous, voluble, conversational, communicative; gossipy, babbling, blathering; long-winded, wordy, verbose, prolix; *informal* gabby, mouthy, motor-mouthed, talky.
— OPPOSITES: taciturn.

talker ▶ noun CONVERSATIONALIST, speaker, communicator; chatterbox, motormouth, gossip, flibbertigibbet.

talking-to ▶ noun (*informal*). See REPRIMAND *noun*.

tall ▶ adjective **1** *a tall man* BIG, large, huge, towering, colossal, gigantic, giant, monstrous; leggy; *informal* long. **2** *tall buildings* HIGH, big, lofty, towering, elevated, sky-high; multi-storey. **3** *she's five feet tall* IN HEIGHT, high, from head to toe; from top to bottom. **4** *a tall tale* UNLIKELY, improbable, exaggerated, far-fetched, implausible, dubious, unbelievable, incredible, absurd, untrue; *informal* cock-and-bull. **5** *a tall order* DEMANDING, exacting, difficult; unreasonable, impossible.
— OPPOSITES: short, low, wide, credible, easy.

tally ▶ noun **1** *he keeps a tally of the score* RUNNING TOTAL, count, record, reckoning, register, account, roll; census, poll. **2** *her tally of 22 victories* TOTAL, score, count, sum.
▶ verb **1** *these statistics tally with government figures* CORRESPOND, agree, accord, concur, coincide, match, fit, be consistent, conform, equate, harmonize, be in tune, dovetail, correlate, parallel; *informal* square, jibe. **2** *votes were tallied with abacuses* COUNT, calculate, add up, total, compute; figure out, work out, reckon, measure, quantify, tot up; *formal* enumerate.
— OPPOSITES: disagree.

tame ▶ adjective **1** *a tame elephant* DOMESTICATED, domestic, docile, tamed, broken, trained; gentle, mild; pet, housebroken, house-trained. **2** (*informal*) *he has a tame lawyer* AMENABLE, biddable, co-operative, willing, obedient, tractable, acquiescent, docile, submissive, compliant, meek. **3** *it was a pretty tame affair* UNEXCITING, uninteresting, uninspiring, dull, bland, flat, insipid, spiritless, pedestrian, colourless, run-of-the-mill, mediocre, ordinary, humdrum, boring; harmless, safe, inoffensive.
— OPPOSITES: wild, uncooperative, exciting.

▶ verb **1** *wild rabbits can be tamed* DOMESTICATE, break, train, master, subdue. **2** *she learned to tame her emotions* SUBDUE, curb, control, calm, master, moderate, overcome, discipline, suppress, repress, mellow, temper, soften, bridle, get a grip on; *informal* lick.

tamper ▶ verb **1** *she saw them tampering with her car* INTERFERE, monkey around, meddle, tinker, fiddle, fool around, play around; doctor, alter, change, adjust, damage, deface, vandalize; *informal* mess around, muck about/around. **2** *the defendant tampered with the jury* INFLUENCE, get at, rig, manipulate, bribe, corrupt, bias; *informal* fix.

tan ▶ adjective *a tan waistcoat* YELLOWISH-BROWN, light brown, pale brown, tawny.
▶ verb **1** *use a sunscreen to help you tan* BECOME SUNTANNED, get a suntan, (go) brown, bronze. **2** (*informal*) *I'll tan his hide*. See THRASH sense 1.

tang ▶ noun FLAVOUR, taste, savour; sharpness, zest, bite, edge, smack, piquancy, spice; smell, odour, aroma, fragrance, perfume, redolence; *informal* kick, pep.

tangible ▶ adjective TOUCHABLE, palpable, material, physical, real, substantial, corporeal, solid, concrete; visible, noticeable; actual, definite, clear, clear-cut, distinct, manifest, evident, unmistakable, perceptible, discernible.
— OPPOSITES: abstract.

tangle ▶ verb **1** *the wool got tangled up* ENTANGLE, snarl, catch, entwine, twist, ravel, knot, enmesh, coil, mat, jumble, muddle. **2** *he tangled with his old rival* COME INTO CONFLICT, dispute, argue, quarrel, fight, wrangle, squabble, contend, cross swords, lock horns.
▶ noun **1** *a tangle of branches* SNARL, mass, knot, mesh, mishmash. **2** *the defence got into an awful tangle* MUDDLE, jumble, mix-up, confusion, shambles.

tangled ▶ adjective **1** *tangled hair* KNOTTED, knotty, ravelled, entangled, snarled (up), twisted, matted, tangly, messy; tousled, unkempt; *informal* mussed up. **2** *a tangled bureaucratic mess* CONFUSED, jumbled, mixed up, messy, chaotic, complicated, involved, complex, intricate, knotty, tortuous.
— OPPOSITES: simple.

tangy ▶ adjective ZESTY, sharp, acid, acidic, tart, sour, bitter, piquant, spicy, tasty, pungent.
— OPPOSITES: bland.

tank ▶ noun **1** *a hot water tank* CONTAINER, receptacle, vat, cistern, repository, reservoir, basin. **2** *a tank full of fish* AQUARIUM, bowl. **3** *the army's use of tanks* ARMOURED VEHICLE, armoured car, combat vehicle; panzer.

tantalize ▶ verb TEASE, torment, torture, bait; tempt, entice, lure, allure, beguile; excite, fascinate, titillate, intrigue.

tantamount ▶ adjective *this is tantamount to mutiny* EQUIVALENT TO, equal to, as good as, more or less, much the same as, comparable to, on a par with, commensurate with.

tantrum ▶ noun FIT OF TEMPER, fit of rage, fit, outburst, pet, paroxysm, frenzy, (bad) mood, huff, scene; *informal* hissy fit.

tap¹ ▶ noun **1** *she turned the tap on* FAUCET, valve, stopcock, cock, spout, spigot, spile. **2** *a phone tap in the embassy* LISTENING DEVICE, wiretap, wire, bug, bugging device, microphone, mic, recorder.
▶ verb **1** *several barrels were tapped* DRAIN, bleed, milk; broach, open. **2** *butlers were tapping ale* POUR (OUT), draw off, siphon off, pump out, decant. **3** *their telephones were tapped* BUG, wiretap, monitor, overhear, eavesdrop on, spy on. **4** *the resources were to be tapped for our benefit* DRAW ON, exploit, milk, mine, use, utilize, turn to account.

■ **on tap 1** *beers on tap* ON DRAFT, cask-conditioned, from barrels. **2** (*informal*) *trained staff are on tap* ON HAND, at hand, available, ready, handy, accessible, standing by.

tap² ▸ **verb 1** *she tapped on the door* KNOCK, rap, strike, beat, drum. **2** *Dad tapped me on the knee* PAT, hit, strike, slap, jab, poke, dig.
▸ **noun 1** *a sharp tap at the door* KNOCK, rap, drumming. **2** *a tap on the shoulder* PAT, blow, slap, jab, poke, dig.

tape ▸ **noun 1** *a package tied with tape* BINDING, ribbon, string, braid. **2** *secure the bandage with tape* ADHESIVE TAPE, sticky tape, masking tape, duct tape; *proprietary* Scotch Tape. **3** *they recorded the interview on tape* (AUDIO/VIDEO) CASSETTE, (tape) recording, reel, spool; video, VHS.
▸ **verb 1** *a card was taped to the box* BIND, stick, fix, fasten, secure, attach; tie, strap. **2** *they taped off the area* CORDON, seal, close, shut, mark, fence; isolate, segregate. **3** *police taped his confession* RECORD, tape-record, capture on tape; video. **4** *tape your ankle* BIND, wrap, bandage.

taper ▸ **verb 1** *the leaves taper at the tip* NARROW, thin (out), come to a point, attenuate. **2** *the meetings soon tapered off* DECREASE, lessen, dwindle, diminish, reduce, decline, die down, peter out, wane, ebb, slacken (off), fall off, let up, thin out.
− OPPOSITES: thicken, increase.
▸ **noun** *a lighted taper* CANDLE, spill, sconce; *historical* rushlight.

tardy ▸ **adjective** LATE, unpunctual, behind schedule, running late; behind, overdue, belated, delayed; slow, dilatory.
− OPPOSITES: punctual.

target ▸ **noun 1** *targets at a range of 200 metres* MARK, bull's eye, goal. **2** *eagles can spot their targets from half a mile* PREY, quarry, game, kill. **3** *their profit target* OBJECTIVE, goal, aim, end; plan, intention, intent, design, aspiration, ambition, ideal, desire, wish. **4** *she was the target for a wave of abuse* VICTIM, butt, recipient, focus, object, subject.
▸ **verb 1** *he was targeted by a gunman* PICK OUT, single out, earmark, fix on; attack, aim at, fire at. **2** *the product is targeted at a specific market* AIM, direct, level, intend, focus.
■ **on target 1** *the shot was on target* ACCURATE, precise, unerring, sure, on the mark. **2** *the project was on target* ON SCHEDULE, on track, on course, on time.

tariff ▸ **noun** TAX, duty, toll, excise, levy, charge, rate, fee, countervail ✦; price list.

tarnish ▸ **verb 1** *gold does not tarnish easily* DISCOLOUR, rust, oxidize, corrode, stain, dull, blacken. **2** *it tarnished his reputation* SULLY, blacken, stain, blemish, blot, taint, soil, ruin, disgrace, mar, damage, harm, hurt, undermine, dishonour, stigmatize; *literary* besmirch.
− OPPOSITES: polish, enhance.
▸ **noun 1** *the tarnish on the candlesticks* DISCOLORATION, oxidation, rust; film. **2** *the tarnish on his reputation* SMEAR, stain, blemish, blot, taint, stigma.

tarry ▸ **verb** (*archaic*) LINGER, loiter, procrastinate, delay, wait, dawdle; *informal* hang around.
− OPPOSITES: hurry.

tart¹ ▸ **noun** *a jam tart* PASTRY, flan, tartlet, quiche, pie. *See also the box at* PIE.

tart² (*informal*) ▸ **noun** *a tart on a street corner. See* PROSTITUTE *noun.*
▸ **verb 1** *she tarted herself up* DRESS UP, make up, smarten up, preen oneself, beautify oneself, groom oneself; *informal* doll oneself up, titivate oneself. **2** *we must tart this place up a bit* DECORATE, renovate,

refurbish, redecorate; smarten up; *informal* do up, fix up.

tart³ ▸ **adjective 1** *a tart apple* SOUR, sharp, acid, acidic, zesty, tangy, piquant; lemony, acetic. **2** *a tart reply* ACERBIC, sharp, biting, cutting, astringent, caustic, trenchant, incisive, barbed, scathing, sarcastic, acrimonious, nasty, rude, vicious, spiteful, venomous.
− OPPOSITES: sweet, kind.

task ▸ **noun** *a daunting task* JOB, duty, chore, charge, assignment, detail, mission, engagement, occupation, undertaking, exercise, business, responsibility, burden, endeavour, enterprise, venture.
■ **take someone to task** REBUKE, reprimand, reprove, reproach, remonstrate with, upbraid, scold, berate, castigate, lecture, censure, criticize, admonish, chide, chasten, arraign; *informal* tell off, bawl out, give someone a dressing-down.

taste ▸ **noun 1** *a distinctive sharp taste* FLAVOUR, savour, relish, tang, smack. **2** *he was dying for a taste of brandy* MOUTHFUL, drop, bit, sip, nip, swallow, touch, soupçon, dash, modicum. **3** *it's too sweet for my taste* PALATE, taste buds, appetite, stomach. **4** *a taste for adventure* LIKING, love, fondness, fancy, desire, preference, penchant, predilection, inclination, partiality; hankering, appetite, hunger, thirst, relish. **5** *my first taste of prison* EXPERIENCE, impression; exposure to, contact with, involvement with. **6** *the house was furnished with taste* JUDGMENT, discrimination, discernment, tastefulness, refinement, finesse, elegance, grace, style. **7** *the photo was rejected on grounds of taste* DECORUM, propriety, etiquette, politeness, delicacy, nicety, sensitivity, discretion, tastefulness.
− RELATED TERMS: gustative, gustatory.
− OPPOSITES: dislike.
▸ **verb 1** *Adam tasted the wine* SAMPLE, test, try, savour; sip, sup. **2** *he could taste blood on his lip* PERCEIVE, discern, make out, distinguish. **3** *a beer that tasted of pumpkin* HAVE A FLAVOUR, savour, smack, be reminiscent; suggest. **4** *it'll be good to taste real coffee again* CONSUME, drink, partake of; eat, devour. **5** *he tasted defeat* EXPERIENCE, encounter, come face to face with, come up against, undergo; know.

tasteful ▸ **adjective** *the decor is simple and tasteful* AESTHETICALLY PLEASING, in good taste, refined, cultured, elegant, stylish, smart, chic, attractive, exquisite.
− OPPOSITES: tasteless.

tasteless ▸ **adjective 1** *the vegetables are tasteless* FLAVOURLESS, bland, insipid, unappetizing, savourless, watery, weak. **2** *tasteless leather panelling* VULGAR, crude, tawdry, garish, gaudy, loud, trashy, showy, ostentatious, cheap, chintzy, inelegant, tacky, kitsch, (Que.) kétaine ✦. **3** *a tasteless remark* CRUDE, vulgar, indelicate, uncouth, crass, tactless, gauche, undiplomatic, indiscreet, inappropriate, offensive.
− OPPOSITES: tasty, tasteful, seemly.

tasty ▸ **adjective** DELICIOUS, palatable, luscious, mouth-watering, delectable, ambrosial, toothsome, dainty, flavourful; appetizing, tempting; *informal* yummy, scrumptious, finger-licking, lip-smacking, melt-in-your/the-mouth.
− OPPOSITES: bland.

tatters ▸ **plural noun** *the satin had frayed to tatters* RAGS, scraps, shreds, bits, pieces, ribbons.
■ **in tatters 1** *his clothes were in tatters* RAGGED, tattered, torn, ripped, frayed, in pieces, worn out,

moth-eaten, falling to pieces, threadbare. **2** *her marriage is in tatters* IN RUINS, on the rocks, destroyed, finished, devastated.

tattle ▶ **verb 1** *we were tattling about him* GOSSIP, chatter, chat, prattle, babble, jabber, gabble, rattle on; *informal* chinwag, jaw, yak, gab, natter, tittle-tattle, chit-chat. **2** *I would tattle on her if I had evidence* INFORM; report, talk, tell all, spill the beans; *informal* squeal, sing, let the cat out of the bag.
▶ **noun** *tabloid tattle* GOSSIP, rumour, tittle-tattle, hearsay, scandal.

taunt ▶ **noun** *the taunts of his classmates* JEER, jibe, sneer, insult, barb, catcall; (**taunts**) teasing, provocation, goading, derision, mockery; *informal* dig, put-down.
▶ **verb** *she taunted him about his job* JEER AT, sneer at, scoff at, poke fun at, make fun of, get at, insult, tease, chaff, torment, goad, ridicule, deride, mock, heckle, ride; *informal* rib, needle.

taut ▶ **adjective 1** *the rope was pulled taut* TIGHT, stretched, rigid. **2** *her muscles remained taut* FLEXED, tense, hard, solid, firm, rigid, stiff. **3** *a taut expression* FRAUGHT, strained, stressed, tense; *informal* uptight.
— OPPOSITES: slack, relaxed.

tautology ▶ **noun** PLEONASM, repetition, reiteration, redundancy, superfluity, duplication.

tavern ▶ **noun** BAR, booze can ✖, watering hole, pub, cocktail lounge, beer parlour ✖, beverage room ✖, taproom, (*Que.*) brasserie ✖, gin mill, after-hours (club), lounge, parlour ✖, nightclub, brew pub, speakeasy, blind pig, barrelhouse, roadhouse, beer cellar, boîte, club, dive, hotel, inn, nineteenth hole, rathskeller, estaminet, public house; *historical* saloon; *historical* alehouse.

tawdry ▶ **adjective** GAUDY, flashy, showy, garish, loud; tasteless, vulgar, trashy, kétaine ✖, junky, cheapjack, shoddy, shabby, gimcrack, chintzy; *informal* tacky, cheesy, kitschy, schlocky.
— OPPOSITES: tasteful.

tax ▶ **noun 1** *they have to pay tax on the interest* DUTY, excise, customs, dues; levy, tariff, toll, impost, tithe, charge, fee. **2** *a heavy tax on one's attention* BURDEN, load, weight, demand, strain, pressure, stress, drain, imposition.
— RELATED TERMS: fiscal.
— OPPOSITES: rebate.
▶ **verb 1** *they tax foreign companies more harshly* CHARGE (DUTY ON), tithe; *formal* mulct. **2** *his whining taxed her patience* STRAIN, stretch, overburden, overload, encumber, push too far; overwhelm, try, wear out, exhaust, sap, drain, weary, weaken.

taxi ▶ **noun** CAB, taxicab, hack; rickshaw, calèche ✖, trishaw, pedicab, water taxi.

taxing ▶ **adjective** DEMANDING, exacting, challenging, burdensome, arduous, onerous, difficult, hard, tough, laborious, back-breaking, strenuous, rigorous, punishing; tiring, exhausting, enervating, wearing, stressful; *informal* murderous.
— OPPOSITES: easy.

tea ▶ **noun**. *See table.*

teach ▶ **verb 1** *Alison teaches small children* EDUCATE, instruct, school, tutor, coach, train; enlighten, illuminate, verse, edify, indoctrinate; drill, discipline. **2** *I taught yoga* GIVE LESSONS IN, lecture in, be a teacher of; demonstrate, instill, inculcate. **3** *she taught me how to love* TRAIN, show, guide, instruct, explain, demonstrate to.
— RELATED TERMS: didactic, pedagogic.

Types of Tea

Assam	iced tea
black tea	jasmine tea
blueberry tea	Labrador tea
bubble tea	Lapsang tea
Ceylon tea	oolong
chai	orange pekoe
China tea	pekoe
Darjeeling	sage tea
Earl Grey	souchong
English Breakfast	switchel ✖(*Nfld*) *hist.*
green tea	tisane
herbal tea	

teacher ▶ **noun** EDUCATOR, tutor, instructor, master, mistress, governess, educationist, preceptor; coach, trainer; lecturer, professor, don; guide, mentor, guru, counsellor; substitute teacher, sub, supply teacher ✖; *informal* teach; *formal* pedagogue; *historical* schoolman, schoolmarm.

team ▶ **noun 1** *the sales team* GROUP, squad, company, party, crew, troupe, band, side, lineup, phalanx; *informal* bunch, gang, posse. **2** *a team of horses* PAIR, span, yoke, duo, set, tandem.
▶ **verb 1** *the horses are teamed in pairs* HARNESS, yoke, hitch, couple. **2** *team up with another artist for an exhibition* JOIN (FORCES), collaborate, get together, work together; unite, combine, co-operate, link, ally, associate.

tear¹ ▶ **verb 1** *I tore up the letter* RIP UP, rip in two, pull to pieces, shred. **2** *his flesh was torn* LACERATE, cut (open), gash, slash, scratch, hack, pierce, stab; injure, wound. **3** *the traumas tore her family apart* DIVIDE, split, sever, break up, disunite, rupture; *literary* rend, sunder, cleave. **4** *Gina tore the book from his hands* SNATCH, grab, seize, rip, wrench, wrest, pull, pluck; *informal* yank. **5** (*informal*) *Jack tore down the street* SPRINT, race, run, dart, rush, dash, hasten, hurry, hare, bolt, fly, career, charge, shoot, hurtle, careen, speed, whiz, zoom, go like lightning, go like the wind; *informal* pelt, scoot, hotfoot it, belt, zip, whip, bomb, hightail it.
— OPPOSITES: unite.
▶ **noun** *a tear in her dress* RIP, hole, split, slash, slit; ladder, snag.
■ **tear something down** DEMOLISH, knock down, raze (to the ground), flatten, level, bulldoze; dismantle, disassemble.

tear² ▶ **noun** *tears in her eyes* TEARDROP.
— RELATED TERMS: lachrymal, lachrymose.
■ **in tears** CRYING, weeping, sobbing, wailing, howling, bawling, whimpering; tearful, upset; *informal* weepy, teary, blubbing, blubbering.

tearful ▶ **adjective 1** *Betty-May was tearful* CLOSE TO TEARS, emotional, upset, distressed, sad, unhappy; in tears, with tears in one's eyes, choked up, crying, weeping, sobbing, snivelling; *informal* weepy, teary, misty-eyed; *formal* lachrymose. **2** *a tearful farewell* EMOTIONAL, upsetting, distressing, sad, heartbreaking, sorrowful; poignant, moving, touching, tear-jerking; *literary* dolorous.
— OPPOSITES: cheerful.

tease ▶ **verb** MAKE FUN OF, poke fun at, chaff, laugh at, guy, make a monkey (out) of; taunt, bait, goad, pick on; deride, mock, ridicule; *informal* give someone the gears ✖, send up, rib, josh, have on, pull someone's leg, pull someone's chain, razz.

teaser ▶ **noun 1** *a difficult teaser to answer* QUESTION, problem, quandary, poser. **2** *teasers point readers to the main features* ADVERTISEMENT, hook, taster.

technical ▶ **adjective 1** *an important technical achievement* practical, scientific, technological, high-tech. **2** *this might seem very technical* SPECIALIST, specialized, scientific; complex, complicated, esoteric. **3** *a technical fault* MECHANICAL.

technique ▶ **noun 1** *different techniques for solving the problem* METHOD, approach, procedure, system, modus operandi, MO, way; means, strategy, tack, tactic, line; routine, practice. **2** *I was impressed with his technique* SKILL, ability, proficiency, expertise, mastery, talent, genius, artistry, craftsmanship; aptitude, adroitness, deftness, dexterity, facility, competence; performance, delivery; *informal* know-how.

technology ▶ **noun** SCIENCE, know-how, sophistication, invention, high-tech, mechanics, engineering.

tedious ▶ **adjective** BORING, dull, monotonous, repetitive, unrelieved, unvaried, uneventful; characterless, colourless, lifeless, insipid, uninteresting, unexciting, uninspiring, flat, bland, dry, stale, tired, lacklustre, stodgy, dreary, mundane; mind-numbing, soul-destroying, wearisome, tiring, tiresome, irksome, trying, frustrating; *informal* deadly, not up to much, samey, humdrum, ho-hum, blah, dullsville, {same old, same old}.
— OPPOSITES: exciting.

tedium ▶ **noun** MONOTONY, boredom, ennui, uniformity, routine, dreariness, dryness, banality, vapidity, insipidity.
— OPPOSITES: variety.

teem¹ ▶ **verb** *the pond was teeming with fish* BE FULL OF, be filled with, be alive with, be brimming with, abound in, be swarming with, be aswarm with; be packed with, be crawling with, be overrun by, bristle with, seethe with, be thick with; be jam-packed with, be chockablock with, be chock full of.

teem² ▶ **verb** *the rain was teeming down* POUR, pelt, beat, lash, sheet; come down in torrents, rain cats and dogs, bucket down.

teenage ▶ **adjective** ADOLESCENT, teenaged, youthful, young, juvenile, teen.

teenager ▶ **noun** ADOLESCENT, youth, young person, minor, juvenile, teen, teeny-bopper.

teeny ▶ **adjective** (*informal*). See TINY.

teeter ▶ **verb 1** *Daisy teetered towards them* TOTTER, wobble, toddle, sway, stagger, stumble, reel, lurch, pitch. **2** *the situation teetered between tragedy and farce* SEE-SAW, veer, fluctuate, oscillate, swing, alternate, waver.

teeter-totter ▶ **noun** SEE-SAW.

teetotal ▶ **adjective** ABSTINENT, abstemious; sober, dry; *informal* on the wagon.
— OPPOSITES: alcoholic.

telegram ▶ **noun** telex; *informal* wire; *dated* radiogram; *historical* cable, cablegram.

telepathic ▶ **adjective** PSYCHIC, clairvoyant.

telepathy ▶ **noun** MIND-READING, thought transference; extrasensory perception, ESP; clairvoyance, sixth sense; psychometry.

telephone ▶ **noun** *she picked up the telephone* PHONE, cellphone, cell; handset; receiver; *informal* blower, horn.
▶ **verb** *he telephoned me last night* PHONE, call, dial; get, reach; *informal* call up, give someone a buzz, get on the blower to, get someone on the horn.

telescope ▶ **noun** SPYGLASS; *informal* scope.
▶ **verb 1** *the front of the car was telescoped* CONCERTINA, compact, compress, crush, squash. **2** *his experience can be telescoped into a paragraph* CONDENSE, shorten, reduce, abbreviate, abridge, summarize, précis, abstract, shrink, consolidate; truncate, curtail.

televise ▶ **verb** BROADCAST, screen, air, telecast; transmit, relay.

television ▶ **noun** TV; *informal* the small screen, idiot box, the tube, boob tube, the box.

tell ▶ **verb 1** *why didn't you tell me before?* INFORM, notify, apprise, let know, make aware, acquaint with, advise, put in the picture, brief, fill in; alert, warn; *informal* clue in/up. **2** *she told the story slowly* RELATE, recount, narrate, unfold, report, recite, describe, sketch, weave, spin; utter, voice, state, declare, communicate, impart, divulge. **3** *she told him to leave* INSTRUCT, order, command, direct, charge, enjoin, call on, require; *literary* bid. **4** *I tell you, I did nothing wrong* ASSURE, promise, give one's word, swear, guarantee. **5** *the figures tell a different story* REVEAL, show, indicate, be evidence of, disclose, convey, signify. **6** *promise you won't tell?* GIVE THE GAME AWAY, talk, tell tales, tattle; *informal* spill the beans, let the cat out of the bag, blab. **7** *she was bound to tell on him* INFORM ON, tell tales on, give away, denounce, sell out; *informal* blow the whistle on, rat on, peach on, squeal on, finger. **8** *it was hard to tell what he said* ASCERTAIN, determine, work out, make out, deduce, discern, perceive, see, identify, recognize, understand, comprehend; *informal* figure out, suss out. **9** *he couldn't tell one from the other* DISTINGUISH, differentiate, discriminate. **10** *the strain began to tell on him* TAKE ITS TOLL, leave its mark; affect.
■ **tell someone off** (*informal*). See REPRIMAND *verb*.

teller ▶ **noun 1** *a bank teller* CASHIER, clerk. **2** *a teller of tales* NARRATOR, raconteur; storyteller, anecdotalist.

telling ▶ **adjective** REVEALING, significant, weighty, important, meaningful, influential, striking, potent, powerful, compelling.
— OPPOSITES: insignificant.

telltale ▶ **adjective** *the telltale blush on her face* REVEALING, revelatory, suggestive, meaningful, significant, meaning; *informal* giveaway.

temerity ▶ **noun** AUDACITY, nerve, effrontery, impudence, impertinence, cheek, gall, presumption; daring; *informal* face, front, neck, chutzpah.

temper ▶ **noun 1** *he walked out in a temper* (FIT OF) RAGE, fury, fit of pique, tantrum, (bad) mood, sulk, huff; *informal* grump, snit, hissy fit. **2** *a display of temper* ANGER, fury, rage, annoyance, vexation, irritation, irritability, ill humour, spleen, pique, petulance, testiness, tetchiness, crabbiness; *literary* ire, choler. **3** *she struggled to keep her temper* COMPOSURE, equanimity, self-control, self-possession, sang-froid, calm, good humour; *informal* cool.
▶ **verb 1** *the steel is tempered by heat* HARDEN, strengthen, toughen, fortify, anneal. **2** *their idealism is tempered with realism* MODERATE, modify, modulate, mitigate, alleviate, reduce, weaken, lighten, soften.
■ **lose one's temper** GET ANGRY, fly into a rage, erupt, lose control, go berserk, breathe fire, flare up, boil over; *informal* go mad, go crazy, go bananas, have a fit, see red, fly off the handle, blow one's top, hit the roof, go off the deep end, go ape, flip, freak out.

temperament ▶ **noun** DISPOSITION, nature, character, personality, makeup, constitution, mind, spirit; stamp, mettle, mould; mood, frame of mind, attitude, outlook, humour.

temperamental ▶ adjective **1** *a temperamental chef* VOLATILE, excitable, emotional, mercurial, capricious, erratic, unpredictable, changeable, inconsistent; hot-headed, fiery, quick-tempered, irritable, irascible, impatient; touchy, moody, sensitive, over-sensitive, high-strung, neurotic, melodramatic. **2** *a temperamental dislike of conflict* INHERENT, innate, natural, inborn, constitutional, deep-rooted, ingrained, congenital.
– OPPOSITES: placid.

temperance ▶ noun TEETOTALISM, abstinence, abstention, sobriety, self-restraint; prohibition.
– OPPOSITES: alcoholism.

temperate ▶ adjective **1** *temperate climates* MILD, clement, benign, gentle, balmy. **2** *he was temperate in his consumption* SELF-RESTRAINED, restrained, moderate, self-controlled, disciplined; abstemious, self-denying, austere, ascetic; teetotal, abstinent.
– OPPOSITES: extreme.

tempest ▶ noun STORM, gale, hurricane; tornado, whirlwind, cyclone, typhoon.

tempestuous ▶ adjective **1** *the day was tempestuous* STORMY, blustery, squally, wild, turbulent, windy, gusty, blowy, rainy; foul, nasty, inclement. **2** *the tempestuous political environment* TURBULENT, stormy, tumultuous, wild, lively, heated, explosive, feverish, frenetic, frenzied. **3** *a tempestuous woman* EMOTIONAL, passionate, impassioned, fiery, intense; temperamental, volatile, excitable, mercurial, capricious, unpredictable, quick-tempered.
– OPPOSITES: calm, peaceful, placid.

template ▶ noun MODEL, example, guide, mould, blueprint, pattern.

temple ▶ noun HOUSE OF GOD, house of worship, shrine, sanctuary; church, cathedral, mosque, synagogue, shul; *archaic* fane.

tempo ▶ noun **1** *the tempo of the music* SPEED, cadence, rhythm, beat, time, pulse; measure, metre. **2** *the tempo of life in Western society* PACE, rate, speed, velocity.

temporal ▶ adjective SECULAR, non-spiritual, worldly, profane, material, mundane, earthly, terrestrial; non-religious, lay.
– OPPOSITES: spiritual.

temporarily ▶ adverb **1** *the girl was temporarily placed with a foster family* FOR THE TIME BEING, for the moment, for now, for the present, in the interim, for the nonce, in/for the meantime, in the meanwhile; provisionally, pro tem; *informal* for the minute. **2** *he was temporarily blinded by the light* BRIEFLY, for a short time, momentarily, fleetingly.
– OPPOSITES: permanently.

temporary ▶ adjective **1** *temporary accommodation* | *the temporary captain* NON-PERMANENT, short-term, interim; provisional, pro tem, makeshift, stop-gap; acting, fill-in, stand-in, caretaker. **2** *a temporary loss of self-control* BRIEF, short-lived, momentary, fleeting, passing.
– OPPOSITES: permanent, lasting.

temporize ▶ verb EQUIVOCATE, procrastinate, play for time, play a waiting game, stall, use delaying tactics, give someone the runaround, delay, hang back, prevaricate, hem and haw; *rare* tergiversate.

tempt ▶ verb **1** *the manager tried to tempt him to stay* ENTICE, persuade, convince, inveigle, induce, cajole, coax, woo; *informal* sweet-talk. **2** *more customers are being tempted by credit* ALLURE, attract, appeal to, whet the appetite of; lure, seduce, beguile, tantalize, draw.
– OPPOSITES: discourage, deter.

temptation ▶ noun **1** *Mary resisted the temptation to answer back* DESIRE, urge, itch, impulse, inclination. **2** *the temptations of Montreal* LURE, allurement, enticement, seduction, attraction, draw, pull; siren song. **3** *the temptation of travel to exotic locations* ALLURE, appeal, attraction, fascination.

tempting ▶ adjective **1** *a tempting opportunity* ENTICING, alluring, attractive, appealing, inviting, captivating, seductive, beguiling, fascinating, tantalizing; irresistible. **2** *a plate of tempting cakes* APPETIZING, mouth-watering, delicious, toothsome; *informal* scrumptious, yummy, lip-smacking.
– OPPOSITES: off-putting, uninviting.

temptress ▶ noun SEDUCTRESS, siren, femme fatale, Mata Hari; *informal* vamp, home wrecker, man-eater.

ten ▶ cardinal number DECADE.
– RELATED TERMS: decimal, deca-, deci-.

tenable ▶ adjective DEFENSIBLE, justifiable, supportable, sustainable, arguable, able to hold water, reasonable, sensible, rational, sound, viable, plausible, credible, believable, conceivable.
– OPPOSITES: indefensible.

tenacious ▶ adjective **1** *his tenacious grip* FIRM, tight, fast, clinging; strong, forceful, powerful, unshakeable, immovable, iron. **2** *a tenacious opponent* PERSEVERING, persistent, determined, dogged, strong-willed, tireless, indefatigable, resolute, patient, unflagging, staunch, steadfast, untiring, unwavering, unswerving, unshakeable, unyielding, insistent; stubborn, intransigent, obstinate, obdurate, stiff-necked; rock-ribbed; pertinacious.
– OPPOSITES: weak, irresolute.

tenacity ▶ noun PERSISTENCE, determination, perseverance, doggedness, strength of purpose, tirelessness, indefatigability, resolution, resoluteness, resolve, firmness, patience, purposefulness, staunchness, steadfastness, staying power, endurance, stamina, stubbornness, intransigence, obstinacy, obduracy, pertinacity.

tenant ▶ noun OCCUPANT, resident, inhabitant; renter, leaseholder, lessee, lodger, roomer, squatter.
– OPPOSITES: owner, freeholder.

tend¹ ▶ verb **1** *I tend to get very involved in my work* BE INCLINED, be apt, be disposed, be prone, be liable, have a tendency, have a propensity. **2** *younger voters tended towards the tabloid press* INCLINE, lean, gravitate, move; prefer, favour, trend.

tend² ▶ verb *she tended her garden* LOOK AFTER, take care of, care for, minister to, attend to, see to, wait on; watch over, keep an eye on, mind, protect, watch, guard, supervise; nurse, nurture, cherish.
– OPPOSITES: neglect.

tendency ▶ noun **1** *his tendency to take the law into his own hands* PROPENSITY, proclivity, proneness, aptness, likelihood, inclination, disposition, predisposition, bent, leaning, penchant, predilection, susceptibility, liability; readiness; habit. **2** *this tendency towards cohabitation* TREND, movement, drift, swing, gravitation, direction, course; orientation, bias.

tender¹ ▶ adjective **1** *a gentle, tender man* CARING, kind, kindly, kind-hearted, soft-hearted, tender-hearted, compassionate, sympathetic, warm, warm-hearted, solicitous, fatherly, motherly, maternal, gentle, mild, benevolent, generous, giving, humane. **2** *a tender kiss* AFFECTIONATE, fond, loving, emotional, warm, gentle, soft; amorous, adoring;

informal lovey-dovey. **3** *simmer until the meat is tender* EASILY CHEWED, chewable, soft; succulent, juicy; tenderized, fork-tender. **4** *tender plants* DELICATE, easily damaged, fragile, vulnerable. **5** *her ankle was swollen and tender* SORE, painful, sensitive, inflamed, raw, red, chafed, bruised, irritated; hurting, aching, throbbing, smarting. **6** *the tender age of fifteen* YOUNG, youthful, early; impressionable, inexperienced, immature, unseasoned, juvenile, callow, green, raw, unripe, wet behind the ears. **7** *the issue of conscription was a particularly tender one* DIFFICULT, delicate, touchy, tricky, awkward, problematic, troublesome, thorny, ticklish, sticky; controversial, emotive.
— OPPOSITES: hard-hearted, callous, tough.

tender² ▶ verb *she tendered her resignation* OFFER, proffer, present, put forward, propose, suggest, advance, submit, extend, give, render; hand in. **2** *firms of interior decorators tendered for the work* PUT IN A BID, bid, quote, give an estimate.
▶ noun *six contractors were invited to submit tenders* BID, offer, quotation, quote, estimate, price; proposal, submission, pitch.

tender-hearted ▶ adjective. See TENDER¹ sense 1.

tenderness ▶ noun **1** *I felt an enormous tenderness for her* AFFECTION, fondness, love, devotion, loving kindness, emotion, sentiment. **2** *with unexpected tenderness, he told her what had happened* KINDNESS, kindliness, kind-heartedness, tender-heartedness, compassion, care, concern, sympathy, humanity, warmth, fatherliness, motherliness, gentleness, benevolence, generosity. **3** *abdominal tenderness* SORENESS, pain, inflammation, irritation, bruising; ache, aching, smarting, throbbing.

tenement ▶ noun APARTMENT BUILDING, apartment block/complex; condominium.

tenet ▶ noun PRINCIPLE, belief, doctrine, precept, creed, credo, article of faith, axiom, dogma, canon; theory, thesis, premise, conviction, idea, view, opinion, position; (**tenets**) ideology, code of belief, teaching(s).

tennis ▶ noun. *See table.*

Tennis Terms

ace	game point
advantage	grand slam
alley	grass court
backcourt	clay court
backhand	groundstroke
ballboy	half court
ballgirl	half-volley
baseline	let
break	match point
break point	mixed doubles
chop	net
court	overhand
cross-court	passing shot
deuce	rally
double fault	serve
doubles	service break
drop shot	set
fault	set point
foot-fault	slice
forecourt	smash
forehand	topspin
game	volley

tenor ▶ noun **1** *the general tenor of his speech* SENSE, meaning, theme, drift, thread, import, purport, intent, intention, burden, thrust, significance, message; gist, tone, essence, substance, spirit, feel. **2** *the even tenor of life in the village* COURSE, direction, movement, drift, current, trend.

tense ▶ adjective **1** *the tense muscles of his neck* TAUT, tight, rigid, stretched, strained, stiff. **2** *Loretta was feeling tense and irritable* ANXIOUS, nervous, on edge, edgy, antsy, strained, stressed (out), under pressure, agitated, uptight, ill at ease, fretful, uneasy, restless, strung out, worked up, wound up, het up, keyed up, overwrought, jumpy, on tenterhooks, with one's stomach in knots, worried, apprehensive; panicky, jittery, twitchy, spooky, squirrelly, a bundle of nerves. **3** *a tense moment* NERVE-RACKING, stressful, anxious, worrying, fraught, charged, strained, nail-biting, white-knuckle, suspenseful, uneasy, difficult, uncomfortable; exciting, cliffhanging, knife-edge.
— OPPOSITES: slack, calm.
▶ verb *Hebden tensed his muscles* TIGHTEN, tauten, tense up, flex, contract, brace, stiffen; screw up, knot, strain, stretch, squinch up.
— OPPOSITES: relax.

tension ▶ noun **1** *the tension of the rope* TIGHTNESS, tautness, rigidity; pull, traction. **2** *the tension was unbearable* STRAIN, stress, anxiety, pressure; worry, apprehensiveness, apprehension, agitation, nerves, nervousness, jumpiness, edginess, restlessness; suspense, uncertainty, anticipation, excitement; *informal* heebie-jeebies, butterflies (in one's stomach), collywobbles. **3** *months of tension between the military and the government* STRAINED RELATIONS, strain; ill feeling, friction, antagonism, antipathy, hostility, enmity.

tent ▶ noun marquee, big top; dome tent, pup tent; tupik, teepee, wigwam.

tentative ▶ adjective **1** *tentative arrangements* | *a tentative conclusion* PROVISIONAL, unconfirmed, pencilled in, iffy, preliminary, to be confirmed, subject to confirmation; speculative, conjectural, sketchy, untried, unproven, exploratory, experimental, trial, test, pilot. **2** *he took a few tentative steps* HESITANT, uncertain, cautious, timid, hesitating, faltering, shaky, unsteady, halting; wavering, unsure.
— OPPOSITES: definite, confident.

tenterhooks
■ **on tenterhooks** IN SUSPENSE, waiting with bated breath; anxious, nervous, apprehensive, worried, worried sick, on edge, edgy, antsy, tense, strained, stressed, agitated, restless, worked up, keyed up, het up, jumpy, with one's stomach in knots, with one's heart in one's mouth; *informal* with butterflies in one's stomach, jittery, twitchy, in a state, uptight; spooky, squirrelly.

tenuous ▶ adjective **1** *a tenuous connection* SLIGHT, insubstantial, meagre, flimsy, weak, doubtful, dubious, questionable, suspect; vague, nebulous, hazy. **2** *a tenuous thread* FINE, thin, slender, delicate, wispy, gossamer, fragile.
— OPPOSITES: convincing, strong.

tenure ▶ noun INCUMBENCY, term (of office), period (of/in office), time (in office), stint.

tepid ▶ adjective **1** *tepid water* LUKEWARM, warmish, slightly warm; at room temperature. **2** *a tepid response* UNENTHUSIASTIC, apathetic, muted, half-hearted, so-so, {comme ci, comme ça}, indifferent, subdued, cool, lukewarm, uninterested,

unenthused.
— OPPOSITES: hot, cold, enthusiastic.

term ▶ noun **1** *scientific and technical terms* WORD, expression, phrase, turn of phrase, idiom, locution; name, title, designation, label, moniker; *formal* appellation, denomination, descriptor. **2** *a protest in the strongest terms* LANGUAGE, mode of expression, manner of speaking, phraseology, terminology; words, expressions. **3** *the terms of the contract* CONDITIONS, stipulations, specifications, provisions, provisos, qualifications, particulars, small print, details, points. **4** *a policy offering more favourable terms* RATES, prices, charges, costs, fees; tariff. **5** *the director is elected for a two-year term* PERIOD, period of time, time, length of time, spell, stint, duration; stretch, run; period of office, mandate ♣, incumbency. **6** (*archaic*) *the whole term of your natural life* DURATION, length, span. **7** *the summer term* SESSION, semester, trimester, quarter; intersession.
▶ verb *he has been termed the saviour of Canadian unions* CALL, name, entitle, title, style, designate, describe as, dub, label, brand, tag, bill, nickname; *formal* denominate.
■ **come to terms 1** *the two sides came to terms* REACH AN AGREEMENT/UNDERSTANDING, make a deal, reach a compromise, meet each other halfway. **2** *she eventually came to terms with her situation* ACCEPT, come to accept, reconcile oneself to, learn to live with, become resigned to, make the best of; face up to.

terminal ▶ adjective **1** *a terminal illness* INCURABLE, untreatable, inoperable; fatal, mortal, deadly; *Medicine* immedicable. **2** *terminal patients* INCURABLE, dying; near death, on one's deathbed, on one's last legs, with one foot in the grave. **3** *a terminal bonus may be payable when a policy matures* FINAL, last, concluding, closing, end.
▶ noun **1** *a railway terminal* STATION, last stop, end of the line; depot, terminus. **2** *a computer terminal* WORKSTATION, VDT, visual display terminal.

terminate ▶ verb **1** *the project was terminated* BRING TO AN END, end, abort, curtail, bring to a close/conclusion, close, conclude, finish, stop, put an end to, wind up/down, wrap up, discontinue, cease, kill, cut short, axe, can; *informal* pull the plug on. **2** *ten employees were terminated* FIRE, downsize; *informal* can, cut. **3** *this bus terminates at Granville Street* END ITS JOURNEY, finish up, stop.
— OPPOSITES: begin, start, continue.

termination ▶ noun ENDING, end, closing, close, conclusion, finish, stopping, winding up, discontinuance, discontinuation; cancellation, dissolution; *informal* wind-up.
— OPPOSITES: start, beginning.

terminology ▶ noun PHRASEOLOGY, terms, expressions, words, language, lexicon, parlance, vocabulary, wording, nomenclature; usage, idiom; jargon, cant, argot; *informal* lingo, -speak, -ese.

terminus ▶ noun STATION, last stop, end of the line, end point, destination, terminal, depot.

terrace ▶ noun PATIO, sundeck, platform, porch, stoop, veranda, balcony.

terrain ▶ noun LAND, ground, territory; topography, landscape, countryside, country.

terrestrial ▶ adjective EARTHLY, worldly, mundane, earthbound, land; *literary* sublunary.

terrible ▶ adjective **1** *a terrible crime* | *terrible injuries* DREADFUL, awful, appalling, horrific, horrifying, horrible, horrendous, atrocious, abominable, deplorable, abhorrent, frightful, shocking, hideous, ghastly, grim, dire, unspeakable, gruesome, monstrous, sickening, heinous, vile; serious, grave, acute; *formal* grievous. **2** *a terrible smell* REPULSIVE, disgusting, awful, dreadful, ghastly, horrid, horrible, vile, foul, abominable, frightful, loathsome, revolting, nasty, odious, nauseating, repellent, horrendous, hideous, appalling, offensive, objectionable, obnoxious, gruesome, putrid, noisome, yucky, godawful, gross. **3** *he was in terrible pain* SEVERE, extreme, intense, acute, excruciating, agonizing, unbearable, intolerable, unendurable. **4** *that's a terrible thing to say* UNKIND, nasty, unpleasant, foul, obnoxious, vile, contemptible, despicable, wretched, shabby; spiteful, mean, malicious, poisonous, mean-spirited, cruel, hateful, hurtful; unfair, uncharitable, uncalled for, below the belt, unwarranted. **5** *the film was terrible* VERY BAD, dreadful, awful, deplorable, atrocious, hopeless, worthless, useless, poor, pathetic, pitiful, lamentable, appalling, abysmal; *informal* lame, lousy, dire, brutal, painful, crappy. **6** *I feel terrible. I've been in bed all day* ILL, sick, queasy, poorly, unwell, nauseous, nauseated, green at/around the gills, groggy, lousy, awful, dreadful, dead. **7** *she still feels terrible about what she did to John* GUILTY, conscience-stricken, remorseful, guilt-ridden, ashamed, chastened, contrite, sorry, sick, bad, awful.
— OPPOSITES: minor, slight, pleasant, wonderful.

terribly ▶ adverb **1** *she's not terribly upset* VERY, extremely, particularly, hugely, intensely, really, terrifically, tremendously, immensely, dreadfully, incredibly, remarkably, extraordinarily, seriously; *informal* real, mighty, awful, majorly. **2** *he played terribly* VERY BADLY, atrociously, deplorably, awfully, dreadfully, appallingly, execrably, abysmally, pitifully. **3** *I shall miss you terribly* VERY MUCH, greatly, a great deal, a lot; *informal* tons, loads, big time.

terrific ▶ adjective **1** *a terrific all-star cast* MARVELLOUS, wonderful, sensational, outstanding, great, superb, excellent, first-rate, first-class, dazzling, out of this world, breathtaking; fantastic, fabulous, super, blue-ribbon, magic; *informal* cool, wicked, awesome, bang-up, skookum, dandy, mean. **2** *a terrific bang* TREMENDOUS, huge, massive, enormous, gigantic, colossal, mighty, great, prodigious, formidable, monstrous, sizeable, considerable; intense, extreme, extraordinary; *informal* whopping, humongous; deafening.

terrify ▶ verb PETRIFY, horrify, frighten, scare, scare stiff, scare/frighten to death, scare/frighten the living daylights out of, scare/frighten the life out of, scare/frighten someone out of their wits, scare witless, strike terror into, put the fear of God into; terrorize, paralyze, transfix, scare the pants off, scare the bejesus out of.

territorial ▶ adjective **1** *the two nations have engaged in territorial disputes* GEOGRAPHICAL, jurisdictional, regional, land-related. **2** *she gets territorial about her clients* DEFENSIVE, possessive, protective, jealous.

territory ▶ noun **1** *First Nations territory* AREA, area of land, region, enclave; country, state, land, colony, dominion, protectorate, fief, dependency, possession, jurisdiction, holding; section, turf. **2** *mountainous territory* TERRAIN, land, ground, countryside. **3** *linguistic puzzles are Sarah's territory* DOMAIN, area of concern/interest/knowledge, province, department, field, preserve, bailiwick, sphere, arena, realm, world.

terror ► noun **1** *she screamed in terror* EXTREME FEAR, dread, horror, fear and trembling, fright, alarm, panic. **2** *(informal) that child is a little terror* RASCAL, rogue, rapscallion, devil, imp, monkey, sleeveen, mischief-maker, trouble-maker, scalawag, scamp, horror.

terrorist ► noun EXTREMIST, fanatic; revolutionary, radical, insurgent, guerrilla, anarchist, freedom fighter; bomber, gunman, assassin, hijacker, arsonist, incendiary.

terrorize ► verb PERSECUTE, victimize, torment, harass, tyrannize, intimidate, menace, threaten, bully, browbeat; scare, frighten, terrify, petrify.

terse ► adjective BRIEF, short, to the point, concise, succinct, crisp, pithy, incisive, trenchant, short and sweet, laconic, elliptical; BRUSQUE, abrupt, curt, clipped, blunt, pointed, ungracious, gruff.
— OPPOSITES: long-winded, polite.

test ► noun **1** *a series of scientific tests* TRIAL, experiment, test case, case study, pilot study, trial run, tryout, dry run; check, examination, assessment, evaluation, appraisal, investigation, inspection, analysis, scrutiny, study, probe, exploration; screening; *technical* assay. **2** *candidates may be required to take a test* EXAM, examination, quiz.
► verb **1** *a small-scale prototype was tested* TRY OUT, put to the test, put through its paces, experiment with, pilot; check, examine, assess, evaluate, appraise, investigate, analyze, scrutinize, study, probe, explore, trial; sample; screen; *technical* assay. **2** *such behaviour would test any marriage* PUT A STRAIN ON, strain, tax, try; make demands on, stretch, challenge.

testament ► noun *an achievement which is a testament to his professionalism and dedication* TESTIMONY, witness, evidence, proof, attestation; demonstration, indication, symbol, exemplification; monument, tribute.

testicles ► plural noun gonads, testes; *informal* prairie oysters, mountain oysters, cojones, family jewels; *vulgar slang* BALLS, nuts; *Brit.* bollocks.

testify ► verb **1** *you may be required to testify in court* GIVE EVIDENCE, bear witness, be a witness, give one's testimony, attest; *Law* make a deposition. **2** *he testified that he had been threatened by a fellow officer* ATTEST, swear, state on oath, state, declare, assert, affirm; allege, submit, claim; *Law* depose. **3** *the exhibits testify to the talents of the local sculptors* BE EVIDENCE/PROOF OF, attest to, confirm, prove, corroborate, substantiate, bear out; show, demonstrate, bear witness to, speak to, indicate, reveal, bespeak.

testimonial ► noun RECOMMENDATION, (character) reference, letter of recommendation, commendation, endorsement, blurb.

testimony ► noun **1** *Smith was in court to hear her testimony* EVIDENCE, sworn statement, attestation, affidavit; statement, declaration, assertion, affirmation; allegation, submission, claim; *Law* deposition. **2** *the work is a testimony to his professional commitment* TESTAMENT, proof, evidence, attestation, witness; confirmation, verification, corroboration; demonstration, illustration, indication.

testy ► adjective IRRITABLE, tetchy, cranky, ornery, cantankerous, irascible, bad-tempered, grumpy, grouchy, crotchety, petulant, crabby, crusty, curmudgeonly, ill-tempered, ill-humoured, peevish, cross, fractious, pettish, prickly, short-fused, waspish, snappish, snippy, snarky.
— OPPOSITES: good-humoured.

tetchy ► adjective See TESTY.

tête-à-tête ► noun CONVERSATION, dialogue, chat, chit-chat, talk, heart-to-heart, one-on-one, confab; *formal* confabulation.

tether ► verb *the horse had been tethered to a post* TIE (UP), hitch, rope, chain; fasten, bind, fetter, secure.
— OPPOSITES: unleash.
► noun *a dog on a tether* ROPE, chain, cord, leash, lead; restraint, fetter; halter.
■ **at the end of one's tether** AT ONE'S WITS' END, desperate, not knowing which way to turn, unable to cope; at the end of one's rope.

text ► noun **1** *a text which explores pain and grief* BOOK, work, written/printed work, document. **2** *the pictures are clear and relate well to the text* WORDS, wording, writing; content, body, main body; narrative, story. **3** *academic texts* TEXTBOOK, book, material. **4** *a text from the First Book of Samuel* PASSAGE, extract, excerpt, quotation, verse, line; reading.

textiles ► plural noun FABRICS, cloths, materials. See *table at* FABRIC.

texture ► noun FEEL, touch; appearance, finish, surface, grain; quality, consistency; weave, nap.

thank ► verb EXPRESS (ONE'S) GRATITUDE TO, express one's thanks to, offer/extend thanks to, say thank you to, show one's appreciation to, credit, recognize, bless.

thankful ► adjective GRATEFUL, appreciative, filled with gratitude, relieved.

thankless ► adjective **1** *a thankless task* UNENVIABLE, difficult, unpleasant, unrewarding; unappreciated, unrecognized, unacknowledged. **2** *her thankless children* UNGRATEFUL, unappreciative, unthankful, ingrate.
— OPPOSITES: rewarding, grateful.

thanks ► plural noun *they expressed their thanks and wished her well* GRATITUDE, appreciation; acknowledgement, recognition, credit.
► exclamation *thanks for being so helpful* THANK YOU, many thanks, thanks very much, thanks a lot, thank you kindly, much obliged, much appreciated, bless you; *informal* thanks a million.
■ **thanks to** AS A RESULT OF, owing to, due to, because of, through, as a consequence of, on account of, by virtue of, by dint of, by reason of.

thaw ► verb MELT, unfreeze, soften, liquefy, dissolve; defrost, warm.
— OPPOSITES: freeze.
► noun **1** *spring thaw* RUNOFF, (spring) breakup ✦, debacle, ice-out. **2** *a thaw in relations* IMPROVEMENT, relaxation, coming-to-terms, rapprochement.

theatre ► noun **1** *the local theatre* PLAYHOUSE, auditorium, amphitheatre; cinema, movie theatre/house, *proprietary* Cineplex; *dated* nickelodeon. **2** *what made you want to go into the theatre?* ACTING, performing, the stage; drama, the dramatic arts, dramaturgy, the thespian art; show business, Broadway; *informal* the boards, show biz. **3** *the lecture theatre* HALL, room, auditorium. **4** *the theatre of war* SCENE, arena, field/sphere/place of action.

theatrical ► adjective **1** *a theatrical career* STAGE, dramatic, thespian, dramaturgical; show-business; *informal* showbiz; *formal* histrionic. **2** *Henry looked over his shoulder with theatrical caution* EXAGGERATED, ostentatious, stagy, showy, melodramatic, overacted, overdone, histrionic, over-the-top, artificial, affected, mannered; *informal* hammy, ham, camp.

theft ► noun ROBBERY, stealing, thieving, larceny,

thievery, shoplifting, burglary, misappropriation, appropriation, embezzlement; raid, holdup; *informal* smash and grab, heist, stickup; five-finger discount, rip-off; *formal* peculation.
− RELATED TERMS: kleptomania.

theme ▶ noun **1** *the theme of her speech* SUBJECT, topic, subject matter, matter, thesis, argument, text, burden, concern, thrust, message; thread, motif, keynote. **2** *the first violin takes up the theme* MELODY, tune, air; motif, leitmotif. **3** *the band played the Beachcombers theme* SONG, theme tune, jingle.

then ▶ adverb **1** *I was living in Cairo then* AT THAT TIME, in those days; at that point (in time), at that moment, on that occasion. **2** *she won the first and then the second game* NEXT, after that, afterwards, subsequently, later. **3** *and then there's another problem* IN ADDITION, also, besides, as well, additionally, on top of that, over and above that, moreover, furthermore, what's more, to boot; too. **4** *well, if that's what he wants, then he should leave* IN THAT CASE, that being so, it follows that.

theological ▶ adjective RELIGIOUS, scriptural, ecclesiastical, doctrinal; divine, holy.

theoretical ▶ adjective HYPOTHETICAL, abstract, conjectural, academic, suppositional, speculative, notional, postulatory, what-if, assumed, presumed, untested, unproven, unsubstantiated.
− OPPOSITES: actual, real.

theorize ▶ verb SPECULATE, conjecture, hypothesize, philosophize, postulate, propose, posit, suppose.

theory ▶ noun **1** *I reckon that confirms my theory* HYPOTHESIS, thesis, conjecture, supposition, speculation, postulation, postulate, proposition, premise, surmise, assumption, presupposition; opinion, view, belief, contention. **2** *modern economic theory* PRINCIPLES, ideas, concepts; philosophy, ideology, system of ideas, science.
■ **in theory** IN PRINCIPLE, on paper, in the abstract, all things being equal, in an ideal world; hypothetically, theoretically, supposedly.

therapeutic ▶ adjective HEALING, curative, remedial, medicinal, restorative, salubrious, health-giving, tonic, reparative, corrective, beneficial, good, salutary.
− OPPOSITES: harmful.

therapist ▶ noun PSYCHOLOGIST, psychotherapist, analyst, counsellor, psychoanalyst, psychiatrist; *informal* shrink.

therapy ▶ noun **1** *a wide range of complementary therapies* TREATMENT, remedy, cure. **2** *he's currently in therapy* PSYCHOTHERAPY, psychoanalysis, analysis, counselling.

thereabouts ▶ adverb **1** *the land thereabouts* NEAR THERE, around there, in that area. **2** *they sold it for five million or thereabouts* APPROXIMATELY, roughly, or so, give or take, plus or minus, in round numbers, in the ballpark of.

thereafter ▶ adverb AFTER THAT, following that, afterwards, subsequently, then, next.

therefore ▶ adverb CONSEQUENTLY, so, as a result, hence, thus, accordingly, for that reason, ergo, that being the case, on that account; *formal* whence; *archaic* wherefore.

thesaurus ▶ noun WORDFINDER, wordbook, synonym dictionary/lexicon; *rare* synonymy.

thesis ▶ noun **1** *the central thesis of his lecture* THEORY, contention, argument, line of argument, proposal, proposition, idea, claim, premise, assumption, hypothesis, postulation, supposition. **2** *a doctoral thesis* DISSERTATION, essay, paper, treatise, disquisition, composition, monograph, study.

thick ▶ adjective **1** *the walls are five feet thick* IN EXTENT/ DIAMETER, across, wide, broad, deep. **2** *his short, thick legs* STOCKY, sturdy, stubby, chunky, blocky, hefty, thickset, burly, beefy, meaty, big, solid; fat, stout, plump. **3** *a thick Aran sweater* CHUNKY, bulky, heavy; cable-knit, woolly. **4** *the arena was thick with skaters* CROWDED, swarming, full, filled, packed, teeming, seething, buzzing, crawling, crammed, solid, overflowing, choked, jammed, congested; *informal* jam-packed, chockablock, stuffed. **5** *the thick summer vegetation* PLENTIFUL, abundant, profuse, luxuriant, bushy, rich, riotous, exuberant; rank, rampant; dense, impenetrable, impassable; serried; *informal* jungly. **6** *a thick paste* VISCOUS, gooey, syrupy, firm, stiff, heavy; clotted, coagulated, viscid, semi-solid, gelatinous; concentrated. **7** *thick fog* DENSE, heavy, opaque, impenetrable, soupy, murky. **8** *(informal)* he's a bit thick. *See* STUPID sense 1. **9** *Guy's voice was thick with desire* HUSKY, hoarse, throaty, guttural, gravelly, rough. **10** *a thick Scottish accent* OBVIOUS, pronounced, marked, broad, strong, rich, decided, distinct.
− OPPOSITES: thin, slender, sparse.
▶ noun *in the thick of the crisis* MIDST, centre, hub, middle, core, heart.

thicken ▶ verb BECOME THICK/THICKER, stiffen, condense; solidify, firm up, set, jell, congeal, clot, coagulate, cake, inspissate.

thicket ▶ noun COPSE, coppice, grove, (*Prairies*) bluff ♣, (*Nfld*) droke ♣, brake, covert, clump; wood, woodlot, bush.

thickness ▶ noun **1** *the wall is several feet in thickness* WIDTH, breadth, depth, diameter. **2** *several thicknesses of limestone* LAYER, stratum, stratification, seam, vein; sheet, lamina.

thickset ▶ adjective STOCKY, sturdy, big-boned, heavily built, well-built, chunky, burly, strapping, brawny, solid, blocky, heavy, hefty, beefy, meaty.
− OPPOSITES: slight.

thick-skinned ▶ adjective INSENSITIVE, unfeeling, tough, hardened, callous, case-hardened; *informal* hard-boiled.
− OPPOSITES: sensitive.

thief ▶ noun ROBBER, burglar, housebreaker, cat burglar, rustler, shoplifter, pickpocket, purse snatcher, sneak thief, mugger; embezzler, swindler, plunderer; criminal, villain; kleptomaniac; bandit, pirate, highwayman; *informal* crook; *literary* brigand.

thieve ▶ verb STEAL, take, purloin, help oneself to, snatch, pilfer; embezzle, misappropriate; have one's fingers/hand in the till, rob; swipe, make off with, finagle, lift, 'liberate', 'borrow', filch, snaffle, pinch, heist; *formal* peculate.

thievery ▶ noun. *See* THEFT.

thieving ▶ noun. *See* THEFT.

thin ▶ adjective **1** *a thin white line* NARROW, fine, attenuated. **2** *a thin cotton nightdress* LIGHTWEIGHT, light, fine, delicate, floaty, flimsy, diaphanous, gossamer, insubstantial; sheer, gauzy, filmy, transparent, see-through; paper-thin. **3** *a tall, thin woman* SLIM, lean, slender, rangy, willowy, svelte, sylphlike, spare, slight; SKINNY, underweight, scrawny, waiflike, scraggy, bony, angular, raw-boned, hollow-cheeked, gaunt, skin-and-bones, emaciated, skeletal, wasted, pinched, undernourished, underfed; lanky, spindly, gangly, gangling, weedy; *informal* anorexic, like a bag of bones. **4** *his thin grey*

hair SPARSE, scanty, wispy, thinning. **5** *a bowl of thin soup* WATERY, weak, dilute, diluted; runny. **6** *her thin voice* WEAK, faint, feeble, small, soft; reedy. **7** *the plot is very thin* INSUBSTANTIAL, flimsy, slight, feeble, lame, poor, weak, tenuous, inadequate, insufficient, unconvincing, unbelievable, implausible.
— OPPOSITES: thick, broad, fat, abundant.
▶ verb **1** *some paint must be thinned down before use* DILUTE, water down, weaken. **2** *the crowds were beginning to thin out* DISPERSE, dissipate, scatter; become less dense/numerous, decrease, diminish, dwindle.

thing ▶ noun **1** *the room was full of strange things* OBJECT, article, item, artifact, commodity; device, gadget, instrument, utensil, tool, implement; entity, body; *informal* whatsit, whatchamacallit, thingummy, thingy, thingamabob, thingamajig, doohickey, doodad, dingus. **2** *I'll come back tomorrow to collect my things* BELONGINGS, possessions, stuff, property, worldly goods, (personal) effects, trappings, paraphernalia, bits and pieces, luggage, baggage, bags; *informal* gear, junk; *Law* goods and chattels. **3** *his gardening things* EQUIPMENT, apparatus, gear, kit, tackle, stuff; implements, tools, utensils; accoutrements. **4** *I've got several things to do today* ACTIVITY, act, action, deed, undertaking, exploit, feat; task, job, chore. **5** *I've got other things on my mind just now* THOUGHT, notion, idea; concern, matter, worry, preoccupation. **6** *I keep remembering things he said* REMARK, statement, comment, utterance, observation, declaration, pronouncement. **7** *quite a few odd things happened* INCIDENT, episode, event, happening, occurrence, phenomenon. **8** *how are things with you?* MATTERS, affairs, circumstances, conditions, relations; state of affairs, situation, life. **9** *one of the things I like about you is your optimism* CHARACTERISTIC, quality, attribute, property, trait, feature, point, aspect, facet, quirk. **10** *there's another thing you should know* FACT, piece of information, point, detail, particular, factor. **11** *the thing is, I'm not sure if it's what I want* FACT OF THE MATTER, fact, point, issue, problem. **12** *you lucky thing!* PERSON, soul, creature, wretch; *informal* devil, bastard. **13** *Twylla developed a thing about noise* PHOBIA, fear, dislike, aversion, problem; obsession, fixation; complex, neurosis; *informal* hang-up. **14** *she had a thing about men who wore glasses* PENCHANT, preference, taste, inclination, partiality, predilection, soft spot, weakness, fondness, fancy, liking, love; fetish, obsession, fixation. **15** *books aren't really my thing* WHAT ONE LIKES, what interests one; *informal* one's cup of tea, one's bag, what turns one on. **16** *it's the latest thing* FASHION, trend, rage.

think ▶ verb **1** *I think he's gone home* BELIEVE, be of the opinion, be of the view, be under the impression; expect, imagine, anticipate; surmise, suppose, conjecture, guess, fancy; conclude, determine, reason; *informal* reckon, figure; *formal* opine. **2** *his family was thought to be enormously rich* DEEM, judge, hold, reckon, consider, presume, estimate; regard as, view as. **3** *Jack thought for a moment* PONDER, reflect, deliberate, consider, meditate, contemplate, muse, ruminate, be lost in thought, be in a brown study, brood; concentrate, brainstorm, rack one's brains; put on one's thinking cap, sleep on it; *formal* cogitate. **4** *she thought of all the visits she had made to her father* RECALL, remember, recollect, call to mind, think back to. **5** *she forced herself to think of how he must be feeling* IMAGINE, picture, visualize, envisage, consider; dream about, fantasize about.

■ **think better of** HAVE SECOND THOUGHTS ABOUT, think twice about, think again about, change one's mind about; reconsider, decide against; *informal* get cold feet about.
■ **think something over** CONSIDER, contemplate, deliberate about, mull over, ponder, chew over, chew on, reflect on, muse on, ruminate on.
■ **think something up** DEVISE, dream up, conjure up, come up with, invent, create, concoct, make up; hit on.

thinker ▶ noun THEORIST, philosopher, scholar, savant, sage, intellectual, intellect, ideologist, ideologue; mind, brain, brainiac, genius.

thinking ▶ adjective *he seemed a thinking man* INTELLIGENT, sensible, reasonable, rational; logical, analytical; thoughtful, reflective, meditative, contemplative, pensive, shrewd, philosophical, sagacious.
— OPPOSITES: stupid, irrational.
▶ noun *the thinking behind the campaign* REASONING, logic, idea(s), theory, line of thought, philosophy, beliefs; opinion(s), view(s), thoughts, position, judgment, assessment, evaluation.

thinner ▶ noun TURPENTINE, mineral spirits, paint thinner; *proprietary* Varsol ♣.

thin-skinned ▶ adjective SENSITIVE, over-sensitive, hypersensitive, easily offended/hurt, touchy, defensive.
— OPPOSITES: insensitive.

third-rate ▶ adjective SUBSTANDARD, bad, inferior, poor, poor-quality, low-grade, inadequate, unsatisfactory, unacceptable, not up to snuff/scratch; appalling, abysmal, atrocious, awful, terrible, dreadful, execrable, godawful, miserable, pitiful; jerry-built, shoddy, chintzy, tinpot, trashy; cheapjack; *informal* lousy, rotten, dire, bum, crummy, rubbishy.
— OPPOSITES: excellent.

thirst ▶ noun **1** *I need a drink — I'm dying of thirst* THIRSTINESS, dryness; dehydration. **2** *his thirst for knowledge* CRAVING, desire, longing, yearning, hunger, hankering, keenness, eagerness, lust, appetite; *informal* yen, itch.
▶ verb *she thirsted for power* CRAVE, want, covet, desire, hunger for, burn for, lust after, hanker after, have one's heart set on; wish, long.

thirsty ▶ adjective **1** *the boys were hot and thirsty* LONGING FOR A DRINK, dry, dehydrated; *informal* parched, gasping. **2** *the thirsty soil* DRY, arid, dried up/out, bone-dry, parched, baked, desiccated. **3** *she was thirsty for power* EAGER, hungry, greedy, thirsting, craving, longing, yearning, lusting, burning, desirous, hankering; *informal* itching, dying.

thong ▶ noun STRIP, band, cord, string, lash, tie, belt, strap, tape, rope, tether; babiche ♣, *(West)* shaganappi ♣.

thorn ▶ noun PRICKLE, spike, barb, spine; snag.

thorny ▶ adjective **1** *dense thorny undergrowth* PRICKLY, spiky, barbed, spiny, sharp; *technical* spinose, spinous. **2** *the thorny subject of confidentiality* PROBLEMATIC, tricky, ticklish, touchy, delicate, controversial, awkward, difficult, knotty, tough, taxing, trying, troublesome; complicated, complex, involved, intricate; vexed, sticky.

thorough ▶ adjective **1** *a thorough investigation* RIGOROUS, in-depth, exhaustive, thoroughgoing, minute, detailed, close, meticulous, methodical, careful, complete, comprehensive, full, extensive,

widespread, sweeping, all-embracing, all-inclusive. **2** *he is slow but thorough* METICULOUS, scrupulous, assiduous, conscientious, painstaking, methodical, careful, diligent, industrious, hard-working. **3** *the child is being a thorough nuisance* UTTER, downright, thoroughgoing, absolute, complete, total, out-and-out, arrant, real, perfect, sheer, unqualified, unmitigated.
– OPPOSITES: superficial, cursory, careless.

thoroughbred ▶ adjective PUREBRED, pedigree, pure, pure-blooded, blooded.

thoroughfare ▶ noun ROUTE, passageway, waterway, throughway; main road, highway, freeway, autoroute, street, road, roadway, avenue, trail, boulevard.

thoroughly ▶ adverb **1** *we will investigate all complaints thoroughly* RIGOROUSLY, in depth, exhaustively, minutely, closely, in detail, meticulously, scrupulously, assiduously, conscientiously, painstakingly, methodically, carefully, comprehensively, fully, from A to Z, from soup to nuts. **2** *she is thoroughly spoiled* UTTERLY, downright, absolutely, completely, totally, entirely, one-hundred-per-cent, really, perfectly, positively, in every respect, through and through; *informal* plain, to the hilt.

though ▶ conjunction *though she smiled bravely, she looked pale and tired* ALTHOUGH, even though/if, in spite of the fact that, despite the fact that, notwithstanding (the fact) that, for all that.
▶ adverb *You can't always do that. You can try, though* NEVERTHELESS, nonetheless, even so, however, be that as it may, for all that, despite that, having said that; *informal* still and all.

thought ▶ noun **1** *what are your thoughts on the matter?* IDEA, notion, opinion, view, impression, feeling, theory; judgment, assessment, conclusion. **2** *he gave up any thought of getting a degree* HOPE, aspiration, ambition, dream; intention, idea, plan, design, aim. **3** *it only took a moment's thought* THINKING, contemplation, musing, pondering, consideration, reflection, introspection, deliberation, rumination, meditation, brooding, reverie, concentration; *formal* cogitation.

thoughtful ▶ adjective **1** *a thoughtful expression* PENSIVE, reflective, contemplative, musing, meditative, introspective, philosophical, ruminative, absorbed, engrossed, rapt, preoccupied, deep/lost in thought, in a brown study, brooding; *formal* cogitative. **2** *how very thoughtful of you!* CONSIDERATE, caring, attentive, understanding, sympathetic, solicitous, concerned, helpful, obliging, neighbourly, unselfish, kind, compassionate, charitable.
– OPPOSITES: vacant, inconsiderate.

thoughtless ▶ adjective **1** *I'm so sorry—how thoughtless of me* INCONSIDERATE, uncaring, insensitive, uncharitable, unkind, flippant, tactless, undiplomatic, indiscreet, remiss. **2** *a few minutes of thoughtless pleasure* UNTHINKING, heedless, careless, unmindful, unguarded, absent-minded, injudicious, ill-advised, ill-considered, imprudent, unwise, foolish, frivolous, silly, stupid, reckless, rash, precipitate, negligent, neglectful.
– OPPOSITES: considerate, careful.

thought-provoking ▶ adjective INTERESTING, provocative, stimulating, intriguing, inspiring, meaty.

thousand ▶ cardinal number *informal* K, thou.
– RELATED TERMS: millenary, kilo-, milli-.

thrall ▶ noun POWER, clutches, hands, control, grip, yoke, tyranny.
■ **in thrall** ENSLAVED, subjected, subjugated.

thrash ▶ verb **1** *she thrashed him across the head and shoulders* HIT, beat, strike, batter, thump, hammer, pound, rain blows on; assault, attack; cudgel, club; *informal* wallop, belt, bash, whup, whack, thwack, clout, clobber, pummel, slug, tan, sock, beat the living daylights out of, give someone a good hiding. **2** *he was thrashing around in pain* FLAIL, writhe, thresh, jerk, toss, twist, twitch.
■ **thrash something out 1** *thrash out a problem* RESOLVE, settle, sort out, work out, straighten out, iron out, clear up; talk through, discuss, debate. **2** *thrash out an agreement* WORK OUT, negotiate, agree on, bring about, hammer out, hammer together, hash out, produce, effect.

thread ▶ noun **1** *a needle and thread* cotton, filament, fibre; yarn, string, twine. **2** *(literary)* *the Fraser was a thread of silver below them* STREAK, strand, stripe, line, strip, seam, vein. **3** *she lost the thread of the conversation* GIST, train of thought, drift, direction; theme, motif, tenor; storyline, plot.
▶ verb **1** *he threaded the rope through a pulley* PASS, string, work, ease, push, poke. **2** *she threaded her way through the tables* WEAVE ONE'S WAY, inch one's way, wind one's way, squeeze one's way, make one's way.

threadbare ▶ adjective WORN, well-worn, old, thin, worn out, holey, moth-eaten, mangy, ragged, frayed, tattered, battered; decrepit, shabby, scruffy, unkempt; having seen better days, falling apart at the seams, falling to pieces, tatty, ratty, the worse for wear, raggedy, dog-eared.

threat ▶ noun **1** *Maggie ignored his threats* THREATENING REMARK, warning, ultimatum. **2** *a possible threat to aircraft* DANGER, peril, hazard, menace, risk. **3** *the company faces the threat of liquidation proceedings* POSSIBILITY, prospect, chance, probability, likelihood, risk.

threaten ▶ verb **1** *how dare you threaten me?* MENACE, intimidate, browbeat, bully, blackmail, terrorize; make/issue threats to. **2** *these events could threaten the stability of Europe* ENDANGER, be a danger/threat to, jeopardize, imperil, put at risk, put in jeopardy. **3** *the grey skies threatened snow* FORESHADOW, bode, warn of, presage, augur, portend, herald, be a harbinger of, indicate, point to, be a sign of, signal, spell; *literary* foretoken. **4** *as rain threatened, the party moved indoors* SEEM LIKELY, seem imminent, be on the horizon, be brewing, be gathering, be looming, be on the way, be impending; hang over someone.

threatening ▶ adjective **1** *a threatening letter* MENACING, intimidating, bullying, frightening, hostile; *formal* minatory. **2** *banks of threatening clouds* OMINOUS, sinister, menacing, alarming, portentous, dark, black, thunderous.

three ▶ cardinal number TRIO, threesome, triple, triad, trinity, troika, triumvirate, trilogy, triptych, trefoil, three-piece, triplets.
– RELATED TERMS: triple, treble, ter-, tri-.

three-dimensional ▶ adjective **1** *three-dimensional art* SOLID, concrete, sculptural, perspectival, stereoscopic, stereographic, stereo-, pop-up. **2** *three-dimensional characters* VIVID, realistic, rounded, concrete.
– OPPOSITES: flat.

three-sixty ▶ noun SPIN, rotation, turn, revolution, twirl.

threesome ▶ noun TRIO, triumvirate, triad, trinity, troika; triplets.

threshold ▶ noun **1** *the threshold of the church* DOORSTEP, doorway, entrance, entry, door, gate, gateway, portal, doorsill. **2** *the threshold of a new era* START, beginning, commencement, brink, verge, cusp, dawn, inception, day one, opening, debut; *informal* kickoff. **3** *the human threshold of pain* LOWER LIMIT, minimum.
— RELATED TERMS: liminal.

thrift ▶ noun FRUGALITY, economy, economizing, thriftiness, providence, prudence, good management/husbandry, saving, scrimping and saving, abstemiousness; parsimony, penny-pinching, austerity.
— OPPOSITES: extravagance.

thrifty ▶ adjective FRUGAL, economical, sparing, careful with money, penny-wise, provident, prudent, abstemious; parsimonious, penny-pinching, cheap.
— OPPOSITES: extravagant.

thrill ▶ noun **1** *the thrill of jumping out of an airplane* (FEELING OF) EXCITEMENT, stimulation, adrenaline rush, pleasure, tingle; fun, enjoyment, amusement, delight, joy; *informal* buzz, high, rush, kick, charge. **2** *a thrill of excitement ran through her* WAVE, frisson, shiver, rush, surge, flash, blaze, tremor, quiver, flutter, shudder.
▶ verb **1** *his words thrilled her* EXCITE, stimulate, arouse, rouse, inspire, delight, exhilarate, intoxicate, stir, charge up, electrify, galvanize, move, fire (with enthusiasm), fire someone's imagination; *informal* give someone a buzz, give someone a kick, give someone a charge. **2** *he thrilled at the sound of her voice* BE/FEEL EXCITED, tingle, quiver; *informal* get a buzz/kick/ charge out of.
— OPPOSITES: bore.

thrilling ▶ adjective EXCITING, stirring, action-packed, breathtaking, rip-roaring, spine-tingling, gripping, riveting, fascinating, dramatic, hair-raising, mind-blowing; rousing, stimulating, moving, inspiring, inspirational, electrifying, heady.
— OPPOSITES: boring.

thrive ▶ verb FLOURISH, prosper, burgeon, bloom, blossom, mushroom, do well, advance, succeed, boom.
— OPPOSITES: decline, wither.

thriving ▶ adjective FLOURISHING, prosperous, prospering, growing, developing, burgeoning, blooming, healthy, successful, booming, mushrooming, profitable, expanding; *informal* going strong, going from strength to strength.
— OPPOSITES: moribund.

throat ▶ noun GULLET, esophagus; windpipe, trachea, gorge; maw, neck, jowl.
— RELATED TERMS: guttural, jugular.

throaty ▶ adjective GRAVELLY, husky, rough, guttural, deep, thick, smoky, gruff, growly, growling, hoarse, croaky, croaking; rasping, raspy.
— OPPOSITES: pure, crystal-clear.

throb ▶ verb *her arms and legs throbbed with tiredness* PULSATE, beat, pulse, palpitate, pound, thud, thump, drum, thrum, trip-hammer, pitter-patter, go pit-a-pat, quiver.
▶ noun *the throb of the ship's engines* PULSATION, beat, beating, pulse, palpitation, pounding, thudding, thumping, drumming, thrumming.

throes ▶ plural noun *the throes of childbirth* AGONY, pain, pangs, spasms, torment, suffering, torture; *literary* travail.
■ **in the throes of** IN THE MIDDLE OF, in the process of, in the midst of, busy with, occupied with, taken up with/by, involved in, dealing with; struggling with, wrestling with, grappling with.

throne ▶ noun *the czar risked losing his throne* SOVEREIGN POWER, sovereignty, rule, dominion.

throng ▶ noun *throngs of people blocked her way* CROWD, horde, mass, multitude, host, army, herd, flock, drove, swarm, mob, sea, troop, pack, crush; collection, company, gathering, assembly, congregation; *informal* gaggle, bunch, gang.
▶ verb **1** *people thronged to see the play* FLOCK, stream, swarm, troop, pour in. **2** *visitors thronged round him* CROWD, cluster, mill, swarm, surge, congregate, gather.

throttle ▶ verb **1** *he tried to throttle her* CHOKE, strangle, strangulate, garrotte, gag. **2** *attempts to throttle the criminal supply of drugs* SUPPRESS, inhibit, stifle, control, restrain, check, contain, choke off, put a/the lid on; stop, put an end to, end, stamp out.

through ▶ preposition **1** *we drove through the tunnel* INTO AND OUT OF, to the other/far side of, from one side to the other of. **2** *he got the job through an advertisement* BY MEANS OF, by way of, by dint of, via, using, thanks to, by virtue of, as a result of, as a consequence of, on account of, owing to, because of. **3** *he worked through the night* THROUGHOUT, all through, for the whole of, for the duration of, until/to the end of.
▶ adverb *as soon as we opened the gate they came streaming through* FROM ONE SIDE TO THE OTHER, from one end to another, in and out the other side.
▶ adjective *a through train* DIRECT, non-stop.
■ **through and through** IN EVERY RESPECT, to the core; thoroughly, utterly, absolutely, completely, totally, wholly, fully, entirely, unconditionally, unreservedly, altogether, out-and-out.

throughout ▶ preposition **1** *it had repercussions throughout the Middle East* ALL OVER, across, in every part of, everywhere in, all through, right through, all around. **2** *she remained fit throughout her life* ALL THROUGH, all, for the duration of, for the whole of, until the end of.

throw ▶ verb **1** *she threw the ball back* HURL, toss, fling, huck ✦, pitch, cast, lob, launch, catapult, project, propel; bowl; *informal* chuck, heave, sling, peg, let fly with. **2** *he threw another punch* DELIVER, give, land. **3** *she threw a withering glance at him* DIRECT, cast, send, dart, shoot. **4** *the horse threw his rider* UNSEAT, dislodge. **5** *her question threw me* DISCONCERT, unnerve, fluster, ruffle, agitate, discomfit, put off, throw off balance, discountenance, unsettle, confuse; *informal* rattle, faze, flummox, baffle, befuddle, discombobulate. **6** *he threw a farewell party for them* GIVE, host, hold, have, provide, put on, lay on, arrange, organize. **7** *books were thrown all over her desk* STREW, cast, scatter, disperse. **8** *he threw his keys on the table* TOSS, deposit, throw down, put down, dump, drop, plunk, plonk, plump.
▶ noun **1** *we were allowed two throws each* LOB, pitch; go, turn; bowl, ball. **2** *the loveseat was decorated with a red throw* RUG, blanket, covering, fabric; shawl, afghan.
■ **throw something away 1** *she hated throwing old clothes away* DISCARD, throw out, dispose of, get rid of, do away with, toss out, scrap, clear out, dump, jettison; *informal* chuck (away/out), deep-six, ditch, get shut of. **2** *the Leafs threw away a 3-0 lead* SQUANDER,

waste, fritter away, fail to exploit, lose, let slip; *informal* blow, throw something down the drain.

■ **throw someone out** EXPEL, eject, evict, drive out, force out, oust, remove; get rid of, depose, topple, unseat, overthrow, bring down, overturn, dislodge, displace, supplant, show someone the door; banish, deport, exile; *informal* boot out, kick out, give someone the boot, turf out.

■ **throw something out 1** *throw out food that's past its best-before date.* See THROW SOMETHING AWAY sense 1. **2** *his case was thrown out* REJECT, dismiss, turn down, refuse, disallow, veto; *informal* give the thumbs down to.

■ **throw up** (*informal*). See VOMIT *verb* sense 1.

throwaway ▶ **adjective 1** *throwaway packaging* DISPOSABLE, single-use, non-returnable, unrecyclable. **2** *throwaway remarks* CASUAL, passing, careless, unthinking, unstudied, unconsidered, offhand; underemphasized.

thrust ▶ **verb 1** *she thrust her hands into her pockets* SHOVE, push, force, plunge, stick, drive, propel, ram, poke, jam. **2** *fame had been thrust on him* FORCE, foist, impose, inflict. **3** *he thrust his way past her* PUSH, shove, force, elbow, shoulder, barge, bulldoze.
▶ **noun 1** *a hard thrust* SHOVE, push, lunge, poke. **2** *a thrust led by Canadian forces* ADVANCE, push, drive, attack, assault, onslaught, offensive, charge, sortie, foray, raid, sally, invasion, incursion. **3** *only one engine is producing thrust* FORCE, propulsive force, propulsion, power, impetus, momentum. **4** *the thrust of the speech* GIST, substance, drift, burden, meaning, sense, theme, message, import, tenor.

thud ▶ **noun & verb** THUMP, thunk, whump, clunk, clonk, crash, smack, bang; stomp, stamp, clump, clomp, wham.

thug ▶ **noun** RUFFIAN, goon, hooligan, bully boy, vandal, hoodlum, gangster, villain, criminal; tough, bruiser, heavy, enforcer, lout, hired gun, hood.

thumb ▶ **noun** *technical* pollex, opposable digit.
▶ **verb 1** *he thumbed through his notebook* LEAF, flick, flip, riffle, skim, browse, look. **2** *his dictionaries were thumbed and ink-stained* SOIL, mark, make dog-eared. **3** *he was thumbing his way across Mexico* HITCHHIKE; *informal* hitch, hitch/thumb a lift.

■ **all thumbs** CLUMSY, klutzy, awkward, maladroit, inept, unskilful, heavy-handed, inexpert, butterfingered, ham-fisted.

■ **thumbs down** (*informal*) REJECTION, refusal, veto, no, negation, rebuff; *informal* red light.

■ **thumbs up** (*informal*) APPROVAL, seal of approval, endorsement; permission, authorization, consent, yes, leave, authority, sanction, ratification, licence, dispensation, nod, assent, blessing, rubber stamp, clearance; *informal* go-ahead, OK, A-OK, green light, say-so.

thumbnail ▶ **adjective** CONCISE, short, brief, succinct, potted, to the point, compact, crisp, short and sweet, quick, rapid; miniature, mini, small.

thump ▶ **verb 1** *the two men kicked and thumped him* HIT, strike, smack, cuff, punch; beat, slug, thrash, thwack, batter, knock, belabour, lash, pound, pummel, box someone's ears, whack, wallop, bash, bop, clout, clobber, sock, swipe, beat the living daylights out of, give someone a (good) hiding, belt, tan, lay into, let someone have it, boff; *literary* smite. **2** *her heart thumped with fright* THROB, pound, thud, hammer, pulsate, pulse, pump, palpitate, race, beat heavily.
▶ **noun** *she put the box down with a thump* THUD, thunk, clunk, clonk, crash, smack, bang.

thunder ▶ **noun 1** *thunder and lightning* THUNDERCLAP, peal of thunder, roll/rumble of thunder, crack/crash of thunder; *literary* thunderbolt. **2** *the ceaseless thunder of the traffic* RUMBLE, rumbling, boom, booming, roar, roaring, pounding, thud, thudding, crash, crashing, reverberation.
▶ **verb 1** *below me the surf thrashed and thundered* RUMBLE, boom, roar, pound, thud, thump, bang; resound, reverberate, beat. **2** *she thundered against the evils of the age* RAIL, fulminate, inveigh, rage, rant; condemn, denounce. **3** *'Answer me!' he thundered* ROAR, bellow, bark, yell, shout, bawl; *informal* holler.

thundering ▶ **adjective** *a thundering noise.* See THUNDEROUS.

thunderous ▶ **adjective** VERY LOUD, tumultuous, booming, roaring, resounding, reverberating, reverberant, ringing, deafening, ear-splitting, noisy, stentorian, thundering.

thunderstruck ▶ **adjective** ASTONISHED, amazed, astounded, staggered, surprised, startled, stunned, shocked, aghast, taken aback, dumbfounded, floored, blown away, dumbstruck, stupefied, dazed, speechless; *informal* flabbergasted.

thus ▶ **adverb 1** *the studio handled production, thus cutting its costs* CONSEQUENTLY, as a consequence, in consequence, thereby, so, that being so, therefore, ergo, accordingly, hence, as a result, for that reason, ipso facto, because of that, on that account. **2** *all decent aristocrats act thus* LIKE THAT, in that way, so, like so.

■ **thus far** SO FAR, (up) until now, up to now, up to this point, hitherto.

thwack ▶ **noun** SLAP, whack, smack, wallop.
▶ **verb** See THUMP *verb*.

thwart ▶ **verb** FOIL, frustrate, stand in the way of, forestall, derail, dash; stop, check, block, stonewall, prevent, defeat, impede, hinder, obstruct, snooker; *informal* put paid to, put a crimp in, put the kibosh on, scotch, scupper, spike, scuttle, do for, stymie.
— OPPOSITES: facilitate.

tic ▶ **noun** TWITCH, spasm, jerk, tremor; quirk.

tick ▶ **noun 1** *the tick of his watch* TICKING, tick-tock, click, clicking, tap, tapping. **2** *put a tick against the item of your choice* CHECK MARK, check, stroke, mark. **3** *a bloodsucking tick* LOUSE, flea, parasite; *informal* insect; *technical* acarid, arachnid.
▶ **verb 1** *the clock ticks* CLICK, tock, tick-tock, tap. **2** *time is ticking away* PASS, elapse, go, continue, advance, wear on, roll on, fly, run out, vanish.

■ **tick off 1** *that really ticked me off* ANNOY, irritate, rile, rattle, anger, antagonize, cheese off, make someone mad, get on someone's nerves, get to, get someone's back up. **2** *tick off a list* CHECK OFF; count off, cross off.

ticket ▶ **noun** PASS, authorization, permit, token, coupon, voucher; transfer.

tickle ▶ **noun 1** *a tickle in her throat* TINGLE, itch, irritation. **2** *Cdn (Atlantic) we navigated the tickle* CHANNEL, strait, sound.
▶ **verb 1** *he tried to tickle her under the chin* STROKE, pet, tease, chuck. **2** *she found something that tickled her imagination* STIMULATE, interest, appeal to, arouse, titillate, excite.

■ **tickled pink** OVER THE MOON, tickled to death, jumping for joy, high as a kite, pleased as punch, delighted, thrilled.

ticklish ▶ **adjective** DIFFICULT, problematic, tricky, touchy, delicate, sensitive, tender, awkward, prickly, thorny, tough; vexed, sticky.

tidal wave ▸ noun TSUNAMI.

tidbit ▸ noun **1** *a tidbit of information* MORSEL, piece, scrap, item, bit, nugget. **2** *tasty tidbits* DELICACY, dainty, snack, nibble, appetizer, hors d'oeuvre, goody, dipper, finger food, nibbly.

tide ▸ noun **1** *ships come up the river with the tide* TIDEWATER, ebb and flow, tidal flow. **2** *the tide of history* COURSE, movement, direction, trend, current, drift, run, turn, tendency, tenor.
■ **tide someone over** SUSTAIN, keep someone going, keep someone afloat, keep someone's head above water, see someone through; keep the wolf from the door; help out, assist, aid.

tidings ▸ plural noun *(literary)* NEWS, information, intelligence, word, reports, dispatches, notification, communication, the latest; *informal* info, the scuttlebutt, the lowdown, the scoop.

tidy ▸ adjective **1** *a tidy room* NEAT, neat and tidy, orderly, well-ordered, in (good) order, well-kept, shipshape, in apple-pie order, immaculate, spic and span, uncluttered, straight, trim, spruce. **2** *he's a very tidy person* NEAT, trim, spruce, dapper, well-groomed, organized, well-organized, methodical, meticulous; fastidious; *informal* natty. **3** *(informal) a tidy sum* LARGE, sizeable, considerable, substantial, generous, significant, appreciable, handsome, respectable, ample, decent, goodly.
− OPPOSITES: messy.
▸ verb **1** *I'd better tidy up the living room* PUT IN ORDER, clear up, sort out, straighten (up), clean up, spruce up. **2** *she tidied herself up in the bathroom* GROOM ONESELF, spruce oneself up, freshen oneself up, smarten oneself up; *informal* titivate oneself.

tie ▸ verb **1** *they tied Max to a chair* BIND, tie up, tether, hitch, strap, truss, fetter, rope, chain, make fast, moor, lash, attach, fasten, fix, secure, join, connect, link, couple. **2** *he bent to tie his shoelaces* DO UP, lace, knot. **3** *a pay deal tied to a productivity agreement* LINK, connect, couple, relate, join, marry; make conditional on, bind up with. **4** *they tied for second place* DRAW, be equal, be even, be neck and neck.
▸ noun **1** *he tightened the ties of his robe* LACE, string, cord, fastening, fastener. **2** *a collar and tie* NECKTIE, bow tie, string tie, bolo tie. **3** *family ties* BOND, connection, link, relationship, attachment, affiliation, allegiance, friendship; kinship, interdependence. **4** *there was a tie for first place* DRAW, dead heat, deadlock, saw-off ♣.
■ **tie someone down** *she was afraid of getting tied down* RESTRICT, restrain, limit, constrain, trammel, confine, cramp, hamper, handicap, hamstring, encumber, shackle, inhibit.
■ **tie in** BE CONSISTENT, tally, agree, be in agreement, accord, concur, fit in, harmonize, be in tune, dovetail, correspond, match; square, jibe.
■ **tie someone/something up 1** *robbers tied her up and ransacked her home* BIND, bind hand and foot, fasten together, truss (up), fetter, chain up. **2** *he is tied up in meetings all morning* OCCUPY, engage, keep busy. **3** *her capital is tied up in GICs* LOCK, bind up, trap; entangle.
■ **have one's hands tied** HAVE NO CHOICE, be held hostage to, be forced, be compelled, be constrained, be obliged.

tiebreaker ▸ noun RUBBER MATCH, deciding game/round, playoff; game-decider, golden goal; overtime, OT, sudden death.

tie-in ▸ noun **1** *a tie-in to the Expo theme* CONNECTION, link, association, correlation, relation, relationship;

parallel, similarity. **2** *a movie tie-in* JOINT PROMOTION, spinoff.

tier ▸ noun **1** *tiers of empty seats* ROW, line; layer; level; balcony. **2** *the most senior tier of management* GRADE, gradation, echelon, rank, stratum, level, rung on the ladder.

tiff ▸ noun QUARREL, squabble, argument, disagreement, fight, falling-out, rift, difference of opinion, dispute, row, wrangle, altercation, contretemps, disputation, shouting match, blow-up, slanging match, duel, run-in, spat, scrap, bust-up, set-to.

tight ▸ adjective **1** *a tight grip* FIRM, fast, secure, fixed, clenched. **2** *the rope was pulled tight* TAUT, rigid, stiff, tense, stretched, strained. **3** *tight jeans* TIGHT-FITTING, close-fitting, form-fitting, narrow, figure-hugging, skin-tight; ill-fitting. **4** *a tight mass of fibres* COMPACT, compacted, compressed, dense, solid. **5** *a tight space* SMALL, tiny, narrow, limited, restricted, confined, cramped, constricted, uncomfortable. **6** *tight control* STRICT, rigorous, stringent, tough, rigid, firm, uncompromising. **7** *a tight schedule* BUSY, rigorous, packed, non-stop. **8** *he's in a tight spot* DIFFICULT, tricky, delicate, awkward, problematic, worrying, precarious, sticky. **9** *a tight piece of writing* SUCCINCT, concise, pithy, incisive, crisp, condensed, well structured, clean, to the point. **10** *a tight race* CLOSE, even, evenly matched, well-matched; hard-fought, neck and neck. **11** *money is tight these days* LIMITED, restricted, in short supply, scarce, depleted, diminished, low, inadequate, insufficient. **12** *she is tight with the big movie stars* CLOSE, friendly, intimate, connected, close-knit, tight-knit, on good terms, buddy-buddy.
− OPPOSITES: slack, loose, generous.

tighten ▸ verb **1** *she tightened the rope* PULL TAUT, tauten, pull tight, stretch, tense. **2** *he tightened his lips* NARROW, constrict, contract, compress, screw up, pucker, purse, squinch up. **3** *security in the area has been tightened* INCREASE, make stricter, toughen up, heighten, scale up.
− OPPOSITES: loosen, slacken, relax.

tight-fisted ▸ adjective CHEAP, miserly, parsimonious, niggardly, penny-pinching, cheese-paring, Scrooge-like, close; *informal* stingy, mingy, tight, mean; *formal* penurious.
− OPPOSITES: generous.

tight-lipped ▸ adjective RETICENT, uncommunicative, unforthcoming, quiet, secretive, cagey, playing one's cards close to one's chest, close-mouthed, silent, taciturn; *informal* mum.
− OPPOSITES: forthcoming.

tightwad ▸ noun MISER, cheapskate, penny-pincher, skinflint, Scrooge.

till[1] ▸ noun *she counted the money in the till* CASH REGISTER, cash box, strongbox; checkout, cash ♣.

till[2] ▸ verb *he went back to tilling the land* CULTIVATE, work, farm, plow, dig, hoe, turn over, prepare.

tilt ▸ verb SLOPE, tip, lean, list, bank, slant, incline, pitch, cant, angle.
■ **(at) full tilt** (AT) FULL SPEED, at top speed, full bore, as fast as one's legs can carry one, at a gallop, helter-skelter, headlong, pell-mell, at breakneck speed, hell for leather, a mile a minute, like the wind, like a bat out of hell, like (greased) lightning, lickety-split; *literary* apace, with great force, with full force, full blast, with all the stops out, all out, with a vengeance; *informal* like crazy, like mad.

timber ▶ noun WOOD, lumber, logs; trees, sawlogs; hardwood, softwood; beam, spar, plank, batten, lath, board, joist, rafter.

timbre ▶ noun TONE, sound, sound quality, voice, voice quality, colour, tone colour, tonality, resonance.

time ▶ noun **1** *what time is it?* HOUR. **2** *late at night was the best time to leave* MOMENT, point (in time), occasion, hour, minute, second, instant, juncture, stage. **3** *he worked there for a time* WHILE, spell, stretch, stint, span, season, interval, period (of time), length of time, duration, space, phase, stage, term, patch. **4** *the time of the dinosaurs* ERA, age, epoch, period, years, days; generation, date. **5** *I've known a lot of cats in my time* LIFETIME, life, life span, days, time on earth, existence. **6** *he had been a professional actor in his time* HEYDAY, day, best days/years, glory days, prime, peak, Golden Age. **7** *the times are a-changing* CONDITIONS, circumstances; life, state of affairs, way of the world. **8** *tunes in waltz time* RHYTHM, tempo, beat; metre, measure, pattern.
– RELATED TERMS: chronological, temporal.
▶ verb **1** *the events were timed perfectly* SCHEDULE, set, set up, arrange, organize, co-ordinate, fix, line up, slot in, pre-arrange, timetable, plan; slate. **2** *we timed ourselves to prepare for the race* MEASURE, clock, record one's time.
■ **ahead of time** EARLY, in good time, with time to spare, in advance.
■ **ahead of one's/its time** REVOLUTIONARY, avant-garde, futuristic, innovatory, innovative, trail-blazing, pioneering, groundbreaking, advanced, cutting edge.
■ **all the time** CONSTANTLY, the entire time, around the clock, day and night, night and day, {morning, noon, and night}, {day in, day out}, at all times, always, without a break, ceaselessly, endlessly, unfailingly, incessantly, perpetually, permanently, interminably, continuously, continually, eternally, unremittingly, remorselessly, relentlessly, unrelentingly, without surcease, 24-7, non-stop.
■ **at one time** FORMERLY, previously, once, in the past, at one point, once upon a time, time was when, one fine day, in days/times gone by, in times past, in the (good) old days, long ago, back in the day; *literary* in days/times of yore; *archaic* erstwhile, whilom.
■ **at the same time 1** *they arrived at the same time* SIMULTANEOUSLY, at the same instant/moment, together, all together, as a group, at once, at one and the same time; in unison, in concert, in chorus, in synchrony, as one, in tandem. **2** *I can't really explain it, but at the same time I'm not convinced* NONETHELESS, even so, however, but, still, yet, though, on the other hand; in spite of that, despite that, be that as it may, for all that, that said; notwithstanding, regardless, anyway, anyhow, still and all.
■ **at times** OCCASIONALLY, sometimes, from time to time, now and then, every so often, once in a while, on occasion, off and on, at intervals, periodically, sporadically.
■ **behind the times** OLD-FASHIONED, out of date, outmoded, outdated, dated, old, passé; *informal* square, not with it, old-school, horse-and-buggy, fusty.
■ **for the time being** FOR NOW, for the moment, for the present, in the interim, for the nonce, in/for the meantime, in the meanwhile, for a short time, briefly; temporarily, provisionally, pro tem.
■ **from time to time** See AT TIMES.
■ **in no time** (VERY) SOON, in a second, in an instant, in a minute, in a moment, in a trice, in a flash,

shortly, any second, any minute (now), momentarily, in a jiffy, in two shakes of a lamb's tail, in a snap; *formal* directly.
■ **in good time** PUNCTUALLY, on time, early, with time to spare, ahead of time/schedule.
■ **in time 1** *I came back in time for the party* EARLY ENOUGH, in good time, punctually, on time, not too late, with time to spare, on schedule. **2** *in time, she forgot about it* EVENTUALLY, in the end, in due course, by and by, finally, after a while; one day, some day, sometime, sooner or later.
■ **many a time** FREQUENTLY, regularly, often, very often, all the time, habitually, customarily, routinely; again and again, time and again, over and over again, repeatedly, recurrently, continually, oftentimes; *literary* oft, oft-times.
■ **on time** PUNCTUALLY, in good time, to/on schedule, when expected, on the dot.
■ **take time off** book off ↓.
■ **time after time** REPEATEDLY, frequently, often, again and again, over and over (again), time and (time) again, many times, many a time; persistently, recurrently, constantly, continually, oftentimes; *literary* oft, oft-times.

time-consuming ▶ adjective LABORIOUS, tedious, drawn-out, prolonged, protracted, lengthy, labour-intensive, time-wasting.

time-honoured ▶ adjective TRADITIONAL, established, long-established, long-standing, long-lived, time-tested, age-old, enduring, lasting, tried and tested, tried and true.

timeless ▶ adjective LASTING, enduring, classic, ageless, permanent, perennial, abiding, unfailing, unchanging, unvarying, never-changing, changeless, unfading, unending, undying, immortal, eternal, everlasting, immutable.
– OPPOSITES: ephemeral.

timely ▶ adjective OPPORTUNE, well-timed, at the right time, convenient, appropriate, expedient, seasonable, felicitous.
– OPPOSITES: ill-timed.

time out ▶ noun PAUSE, break, rest; stoppage, intermission, recess.

timetable ▶ noun *a bus timetable | I have a very full timetable* SCHEDULE, program, agenda, calendar; list, itinerary, timeline.

time-worn ▶ adjective **1** *the carpet was old and time-worn* WORN OUT, worn, well-worn, old, threadbare, moth-eaten, tattered, battered, dog-eared, well-thumbed, well-used, shabby, having seen better days, tatty, dilapidated. **2** *time-worn faces* OLD, aged, weathered, lined, wrinkled, hoary, bedraggled. **3** *a time-worn aphorism* HACKNEYED, trite, banal, platitudinous, clichéd, stock, conventional, unoriginal, overused, overworked, tired, stale; antiquated, old hat.
– OPPOSITES: new, fresh.

timid ▶ adjective APPREHENSIVE, fearful, easily frightened, afraid, faint-hearted, timorous, nervous, scared, frightened, cowardly, pusillanimous, spineless; shy, diffident, self-effacing; *informal* wimpish, wimpy, yellow, chicken, mousy, gutless, sissy, lily-livered, nebbishy, candy-assed, weak-kneed.
– OPPOSITES: bold.

timorous ▶ adjective. See TIMID.

tin ▶ noun CONTAINER, box, can, tin can.

tincture ▶ noun **1** *tincture of iodine* SOLUTION,

suspension, infusion, elixir. **2** *a tincture of bitterness.* See TINGE *noun* sense 2.

tinder ▸ **noun** KINDLING, fire starter, (*Nfld*) splits ♣, feathersticks ♣, brush, splints.

tinderbox ▸ **noun** *the issue became a political tinderbox* POWDER KEG, time bomb, ticking bomb, explosive situation, hot button, flashpoint, minefield, disaster waiting to happen, can of worms.

tinge ▸ **verb** **1** *a mass of white blossom tinged with pink* TINT, colour, stain, shade, wash. **2** *his optimism is tinged with realism* INFLUENCE, affect, touch, flavour, colour, modify; taint.
▸ **noun** **1** *the light had a blue tinge to it* TINT, colour, shade, tone, hue. **2** *a tinge of cynicism* TRACE, note, touch, suggestion, hint, bit, scintilla, savour, flavour, element, modicum, streak, vein, suspicion, soupçon, tincture.

tingle ▸ **verb** *her flesh still tingled from the shock* PRICKLE, sting; tremble, quiver, shiver.
▸ **noun** *she felt a tingle of anticipation* THRILL, buzz, quiver, shiver, tingling, sting, stinging; tremor.

tinker ▸ **verb** *a mechanic was tinkering with the engine* FIDDLE WITH, adjust, fix, try to mend, play about with, fool with, futz with; tamper with, interfere with, mess about with, meddle with.

tinkle ▸ **verb** **1** *the bell tinkled* RING, jingle, jangle, chime, peal, ding, ping. **2** *cool water tinkled in the stone fountain* SPLASH, purl, babble, burble; *literary* plash.
▸ **noun** RING, chime, ding, ping, jingle, jangle, tintinnabulation.

tinny ▸ **adjective** JANGLY, jangling, jingling, jingly; thin, metallic.

tinsel ▸ **noun** *the tinsel of Hollywood* OSTENTATION, showiness, show, glitter, flamboyance, gaudiness; attractiveness, glamour; *informal* flashiness, ritz, glitz, garishness, razzle-dazzle, razzmatazz, eye candy.

tint ▸ **noun** **1** *the sky was taking on an apricot tint* SHADE, colour, tone, hue, pigmentation, tinge, cast, tincture, flush, blush, wash. **2** *a hair tint* DYE, colouring, rinse, highlights, lowlights.

tiny ▸ **adjective** MINUTE, minuscule, microscopic, infinitesimal, very small, little, mini, diminutive, miniature, scaled down, baby, toy, dwarf, pygmy, peewee, Lilliputian; *informal* teeny, teeny-weeny, teensy, teensy-weensy, itty-bitty, itsy-bitsy, eensy, eensy-weensy, little-bitty, bite-sized, pint-sized; *Scottish* wee.
— OPPOSITES: huge.

tip¹ ▸ **noun** POINT, end, extremity, head, sharp end, spike, prong, tine, nib; top, summit, apex, cusp, crown, crest, pinnacle, vertex.

tip² ▸ **verb** **1** *the boat tipped over* OVERTURN, turn over, topple (over), fall (over); keel over, capsize, flip, turn turtle; *Nautical* pitchpole. **2** *a whale could tip over a small boat* UPSET, overturn, topple over, turn over, knock over, push over, upend, capsize, roll, flip. **3** *the car tipped to one side* LEAN, tilt, list, slope, bank, slant, incline, pitch, cant, heel, careen.

tip³ ▸ **noun** **1** *a generous tip* GRATUITY, baksheesh; present, gift, reward. **2** *useful tips* PIECE OF ADVICE, suggestion, word of advice, pointer, recommendation; clue, hint, steer, tipoff; word to the wise.

tipoff ▸ **noun** PIECE OF INFORMATION, warning, lead, forewarning; hint, clue; advice, information, notification.

tipsy ▸ **adjective** MERRY, half-drunk, light-headed,
woozy, mellow, slightly drunk, lubricated.
— OPPOSITES: sober.

tirade ▸ **noun** DIATRIBE, harangue, rant, onslaught, attack, polemic, denunciation, broadside, fulmination, condemnation, censure, invective, criticism, tongue-lashing; blast; lecture; *literary* philippic.

tire ▸ **verb** **1** *he began to tire as the ascent grew steeper* WEAKEN, grow weak, flag, wilt, droop; deteriorate. **2** *the journey had tired her* FATIGUE, tire out, exhaust, wear out, drain, weary, frazzle, overtire, enervate; *informal* knock out, do in, wear to a frazzle. **3** *we are tired of your difficult behaviour* WEARY, get fed up, get sick, get bored, get impatient; *informal* have had it up to here, have had enough.

tired ▸ **adjective** **1** *you're just tired from travelling* EXHAUSTED, worn out, weary, fatigued, dog-tired, dead beat, bone-tired, ready to drop, drained, zonked, wasted, enervated, jaded; *informal* done in, bushed, whipped, bagged, knocked out, wiped out, pooped, tuckered out. **2** *are you tired of having him here?* FED UP WITH, weary of, bored with/by, sick (to death) of; *informal* up to here with. **3** *tired jokes* HACKNEYED, overused, overworked, worn out, stale, clichéd, hoary, stock, stereotyped, predictable, unimaginative, unoriginal, uninspired, dull, boring, routine; *informal* old hat, corny.
— OPPOSITES: energetic, lively, fresh.

tiredness ▸ **noun** FATIGUE, weariness, exhaustion, burnout, enervation, inertia, inanition; sleepiness, drowsiness, somnolence.
— OPPOSITES: energy.

tireless ▸ **adjective** INDEFATIGABLE, energetic, vigorous, industrious, hard-working, determined, enthusiastic, keen, zealous, spirited, dynamic, dogged, tenacious, persevering, untiring, unwearying, unremitting, unflagging, indomitable.
— OPPOSITES: lazy.

tiresome ▸ **adjective** BORING, dull, tedious, insipid, wearisome, wearing, uninteresting, uneventful, humdrum, monotonous, mind-numbing; annoying, irritating, trying, irksome, vexing, troublesome, bothersome, nettlesome; *informal* aggravating, pesky.
— OPPOSITES: interesting, pleasant.

tiring ▸ **adjective** EXHAUSTING, wearying, taxing, fatiguing, wearing, enervating, draining; hard, heavy, arduous, strenuous, onerous, uphill, demanding, gruelling; *informal* murderous.

tissue ▸ **noun** **1** *living tissue* MATTER, material, substance; flesh. **2** *a box of tissues* PAPER HANDKERCHIEF; *proprietary* Kleenex.

titanic ▸ **adjective** HUGE, great, enormous, gigantic, massive, colossal, monumental, mammoth, immense, tremendous, mighty, stupendous, prodigious, gargantuan, ginormous, Herculean, Brobdingnagian; *informal* humongous, whopping.

tit for tat ▸ **noun** RETALIATION, reprisal, counter-attack, comeback; revenge; vengeance, retribution, an eye for an eye, a tooth for a tooth, payback; *informal* a taste of someone's own medicine; *Latin* lex talionis, quid pro quo.

titillate ▸ **verb** AROUSE, excite, tantalize, stimulate, stir, thrill, interest, attract, fascinate; *informal* turn on.
— OPPOSITES: bore.

titillating ▸ **adjective** AROUSING, exciting, stimulating, sexy, thrilling, provocative, tantalizing, interesting, fascinating; suggestive, salacious, erotic.
— OPPOSITES: boring.

titivate ▶ verb *she titivated herself in front of the hall mirror* GROOM, smarten (up), spruce up, freshen up, preen, primp, tidy, arrange, gussy up, doll up.

title ▶ noun **1** *the title of the work* NAME, heading, legend, label, caption, inscription. **2** *the company publishes 400 titles a year* PUBLICATION, work, book, newspaper, paper, magazine, periodical. **3** *the title of Governor General* DESIGNATION, name, form of address, honorific; epithet, rank, office, position, job title; *informal* moniker, handle, tag; *formal* appellation, denomination; sobriquet. **4** *an Olympic title* CHAMPIONSHIP, crown, first place; laurels, palm. **5** *the landlord is obliged to prove his title to the land* OWNERSHIP, proprietorship, possession, holding, freehold, entitlement, right, claim.
▶ verb *a paper titled 'Immigration Today'* CALL, entitle, name, dub, designate, style, term; *formal* denominate.

titter ▶ verb & noun GIGGLE, snicker, twitter, tee-hee, chuckle, laugh, chortle.

tittle-tattle *See* GOSSIP.

titular ▶ adjective **1** *the titular head of a university* NOMINAL, in title/name only, ceremonial, honorary, so-called; token, puppet. **2** *the book's titular hero* EPONYMOUS, identifying.

tizzy ▶ noun FRENZY, state of anxiety, state of agitation, nervous state, panic, fret, hysteria; *informal* flap, state, sweat.

toady ▶ noun *a conniving little toady* SYCOPHANT, bootlicker, brown-noser, browner ♣, lickspittle, flatterer, flunky, lackey, yes-man, trained seal, doormat, stooge, cringer, suck ♣, suck-up, kiss-ass, ass-kisser.
▶ verb *she imagined him toadying to his rich clients* GROVEL TO, ingratiate oneself with, be obsequious to, kowtow to, pander to, crawl to, truckle to, bow and scrape to, curry favour with, make up to, fawn on/over, slaver over, flatter, adulate, suck up to, lick someone's boots, butter up.

toast ▶ noun **1** *he raised his glass in a toast* TRIBUTE, salute, salutation; *archaic* pledge. **2** *he was the toast of Toronto* DARLING, favourite, pet, heroine, hero; talk; fair-haired boy/girl.
▶ verb **1** *she toasted her hands in front of the fire* WARM (UP), heat, heat (up). **2** *we toasted the couple with champagne* DRINK (TO) THE HEALTH OF, drink to, salute, honour, pay tribute to.

toboggan ▶ noun SLED, bobsled, sledge, luge, coaster, pulk, crazy carpet.

today ▶ adverb **1** *the work must be finished today* THIS (VERY) DAY, this morning, this afternoon, this evening. **2** *the complex tasks demanded of computers today* NOWADAYS, these days, at the present time, in these times, in this day and age, now, currently, at the moment, at present, at this moment in time; in the present climate, presently.

toddle ▶ verb **1** *the child toddled towards him* TOTTER, teeter, wobble, falter, waddle, stumble. **2** *(informal) I toddled down to the quay* AMBLE, wander, meander, stroll, saunter; mosey, toodle, tootle, putter.

toddler ▶ noun SMALL CHILD, infant, moppet, munchkin, tot, tyke, rug rat, terrible two, young 'un.

to-do ▶ noun *(informal)* COMMOTION, fuss, ado, excitement, agitation, stir, palaver, confusion, disturbance, brouhaha, fracas, uproar, furor, tempest in a teapot, much ado about nothing; hoo-ha, ballyhoo, hullabaloo, kerfuffle.

toehold ▶ noun FOOTHOLD, foot in the door, jumping-off point, beachhead.

together ▶ adverb **1** *friends who work together* WITH EACH OTHER, in conjunction, jointly, in co-operation, in collaboration, in partnership, in combination, in league, in tandem, side by side, hand in hand, shoulder to shoulder, cheek by jowl; in collusion, hand in glove; *informal* in cahoots. **2** *they both spoke together* SIMULTANEOUSLY, at the same time, at one and the same time, at once, all together, as a group, in unison, in concert, in chorus, as one, with one accord.
— OPPOSITES: separately.
▶ adjective *(informal) a very together young woman.* See LEVEL-HEADED.

togetherness ▶ noun COHESION, cohesiveness, harmony, fellowship, camaraderie, close bond.

toil ▶ verb **1** *she toiled all night* WORK HARD, labour, exert oneself, slave (away), grind away, strive, work one's fingers to the bone, put one's nose to the grindstone; *informal* slog away, plug away, beaver away, work one's butt off, sweat blood; *literary* travail; *archaic* moil. **2** *she began to toil up the cliff path* STRUGGLE, trudge, tramp, tromp, traipse, slog, plod, trek, drag oneself, tug; *informal* schlep.
— OPPOSITES: rest, relax.
▶ noun *a life of toil* HARD WORK, labour, exertion, slaving, drudgery, effort, industry, {blood, sweat, and tears}; slogging, elbow grease; *literary* travail; *archaic* moil.

toilet ▶ noun WASHROOM, bathroom, powder room, urinal, stall, privy, lavatory, latrine, throne room, restroom, men's/women's/ladies' room, facilities, can, john, biffy, commode, comfort station, porta-potty, outhouse, honey bucket; little girls'/boys' room, loo; *(vulgar slang)* crapper; *Nautical* head.

toilet paper ▶ noun BATHROOM TISSUE, toilet tissue, *(vulgar slang)* bumwad.

toke ▶ noun & verb DRAG, puff, smoke, draw, pull.

token ▶ noun **1** *a token of our appreciation* SYMBOL, sign, emblem, badge, representation, indication, mark, manifestation, expression, pledge, demonstration, recognition; evidence, proof. **2** *he kept the menu as a token of their wedding anniversary* MEMENTO, souvenir, keepsake, reminder, remembrance, memorial.
▶ adjective *token resistance* SYMBOLIC, emblematic; perfunctory, slight, nominal, minimal, minor, mild, superficial, inconsequential.

tolerable ▶ adjective **1** *a tolerable noise level* BEARABLE, endurable, supportable, acceptable. **2** *he had a tolerable voice* FAIRLY GOOD, passable, adequate, all right, acceptable, satisfactory, not (too) bad, average, fair; mediocre, middling, ordinary, indifferent, unremarkable, unexceptional; *informal* OK, so-so, {comme ci, comme ça}, nothing to write home about, no great shakes.
— OPPOSITES: unacceptable.

tolerance ▶ noun **1** *an attitude of tolerance towards other people* ACCEPTANCE, toleration; open-mindedness, broad-mindedness, forbearance, liberality, liberalism; patience, charity, indulgence, understanding. **2** *the plant's tolerance of pollution* ENDURANCE, resilience, resistance, immunity.

tolerant ▶ adjective OPEN-MINDED, forbearing, broad-minded, liberal, unprejudiced, unbiased; patient, long-suffering, understanding, forgiving, charitable, lenient, indulgent, permissive, easygoing, lax, laid-back, loosey-goosey.
— OPPOSITES: intolerant.

tolerate ▶ verb **1** *a regime unwilling to tolerate serious dissent* ALLOW, permit, condone, accept, swallow, countenance; *formal* brook; *archaic* suffer. **2** *he couldn't tolerate her moods any longer* ENDURE, put up with, bear, take, stand, support, stomach, deal with; abide.

toleration ▶ noun ACCEPTANCE, tolerance, endurance; forbearance, sufferance, liberality, open-mindedness, broad-mindedness, liberalism; patience, charity, indulgence, understanding.

toll¹ ▶ noun **1** *a highway toll* CHARGE, fee, payment, levy, tariff, tax. **2** *the toll of dead and injured* NUMBER, count, tally, total, sum total, grand total, sum; record, list. **3** *the toll on the environment has been high* ADVERSE EFFECT(S), detriment, harm, damage, injury, impact, hurt; cost, price, loss, disadvantage, suffering, penalty.

toll² ▶ verb *I heard the bell toll* RING (OUT), chime, strike, peal; sound, ding, dong, clang, bong, resound, reverberate; *literary* knell.

tomb ▶ noun BURIAL CHAMBER, sepulchre, mausoleum, vault, crypt, catacomb; last/final resting place, grave, barrow, burial mound; *historical* charnel house.
— RELATED TERMS: sepulchral.

tombstone ▶ noun GRAVESTONE, headstone, stone; memorial, monument.

tome ▶ noun VOLUME, book, work, opus, publication, title.

tomfoolery ▶ noun SILLINESS, fooling around, clowning, shenanigans, capers, antics, pranks, tricks, buffoonery, skylarking, nonsense, horseplay, monkey business, mischief, foolishness, foolery, fandango.

tone ▶ noun **1** *the tone of the tuba* TIMBRE, sound, sound quality, voice, voice quality, colour, tonality. **2** *the somewhat impatient tone of his letter* MOOD, air, spirit, feel, sound, flavour, note, attitude, character, nature, manner, temper; tenor, vein, drift, gist. **3** *a dial tone* NOTE, signal, beep, bleep. **4** *tones of burgundy and firebrick red* SHADE, colour, hue, tint, tinge.
■ **tone something down** SOFTEN, lighten, mute, subdue, mellow; MODERATE, modify, modulate, mitigate, temper, dampen.

tongue ▶ noun **1** *a foreign tongue* LANGUAGE, dialect, patois, vernacular, mother tongue, native tongue, heritage language ✦, lingua franca; *informal* lingo. **2** *her sharp tongue* WAY/MANNER OF SPEAKING, speech, parlance.

tongue-tied ▶ adjective LOST FOR WORDS, speechless, unable to get a word out, struck dumb, dumbstruck; mute, dumb, silent; *informal* mum.
— OPPOSITES: loquacious.

tonic ▶ noun **1** *ginseng can be used as a natural tonic* STIMULANT, restorative, refresher, medicine; *informal* pick-me-up; *Medicine* analeptic. **2** *we found the change of scene a tonic* STIMULANT, boost, fillip; *informal* shot in the arm, pick-me-up.

tony ▶ adjective STYLISH, fashionable, high-class, affluent, yuppie, posh, rich, uptown; salubrious.

too ▶ adverb **1** *invasion would be too risky* EXCESSIVELY, overly, over, unduly, immoderately, inordinately, unreasonably, extremely, exorbitantly, very; *informal* too-too. **2** *he was unhappy, too, you know* ALSO, as well, in addition, additionally, into the bargain, besides, furthermore, moreover, on top of that, to boot, likewise.

tool ▶ noun **1** *garden tools* IMPLEMENT, utensil, instrument, device, apparatus, gadget, appliance, machine, contrivance, contraption; *informal* gizmo.

2 *the beautiful Estella is Miss Havisham's tool* PUPPET, pawn, creature, cat's paw; minion, lackey, instrument, organ; *informal* stooge.
▶ verb *tool leather into a saddle* WORK, fashion, shape, cut; ornament, embellish, decorate, chase.

toot ▶ verb BLOW, sound.
■ **toot one's own horn** BOAST, brag, sing one's own praises, show off, congratulate oneself.

tooth ▶ noun FANG, tusk, molar, incisor; *Zoology* denticle; *informal* pearly white.
— RELATED TERMS: dental.

toothsome ▶ adjective TASTY, delicious, luscious, mouth-watering, delectable, succulent; tempting, appetizing, inviting; *informal* scrumptious, yummy, nummy, finger-licking, melt-in-your/the-mouth, lip-smacking.

top ▶ noun **1** *the top of the cliff* SUMMIT, peak, pinnacle, crest, crown, brow, head, tip, apex, vertex. **2** *the top of the table* UPPER PART, upper surface, upper layer. **3** *the carrots' green tops* LEAVES, shoots, stem, stalk. **4** *the top of the coffee jar* LID, cap, cover, stopper, cork. **5** *a short-sleeved top* SWEATER, jersey, sweatshirt, vest, pullover; T-shirt, tank top, shirt; blouse. *See also the table at* SHIRT. **6** *by 1981 he was at the top of his profession* HIGH POINT, height, peak, pinnacle, zenith, acme, culmination, climax, prime.
— OPPOSITES: bottom, base.
▶ adjective **1** *the top floor* HIGHEST, topmost, uppermost. **2** *the world's top scientists* FOREMOST, leading, principal, pre-eminent, greatest, best, finest, elite; *informal* top-notch, number one, blue-ribbon, blue-chip. **3** *the organization's top management* UPPER, chief, principal, main, leading, highest, highest-ranking, ruling, commanding, most powerful, most important. **4** *a top Paris hotel* PRIME, excellent, superb, superior, choice, select, top-quality, top-grade, first-rate, first-class, grade A, best, finest, premier, superlative, second to none, nonpareil; *informal* A1, top-notch, blue-ribbon, blue-chip, number one. **5** *they are travelling at top speed* MAXIMUM, maximal, greatest, utmost.
— OPPOSITES: bottom, lowest, minimum.
▶ verb **1** *sales are expected to top $1.3 billion* EXCEED, surpass, go beyond, better, best, beat, outstrip, outdo, outshine, eclipse, go one better than, cap. **2** *their debut CD is currently topping the charts* LEAD, head, be at the top of. **3** *chocolate mousse topped with cream* COVER, cap, coat, smother; finish, garnish.
■ **over the top** EXCESSIVE, immoderate, inordinate, extreme, exaggerated, extravagant, overblown, too much, unreasonable, hyperbolic, disproportionate, undue, unwarranted, uncalled for, unnecessary, going too far.
■ **top something up** FILL, refill, refresh, freshen, replenish, recharge, resupply; supplement, add to, augment.

topic ▶ noun SUBJECT, subject matter, theme, issue, matter, point, talking point, question, concern, argument, thesis, text, keynote.

topical ▶ adjective CURRENT, up-to-date, up-to-the-minute, contemporary, recent, relevant; newsworthy, in the news.
— OPPOSITES: out of date.

topless ▶ adjective HALF-NAKED, bare-breasted, bare-chested, semi-nude, shirtless.

topmost *See* UPPERMOST.

top-notch ▶ adjective (*informal*) FIRST-CLASS, first-rate, top-quality, five-star; superior, prime, premier, premium, grade A, blue-chip, blue-ribbon, superlative, best, finest, select, exclusive, excellent, superb, outstanding, unbeatable, splendid, of the highest order, top-of-the-line, top-flight, top-grade; *informal* bang-up, skookum, A1.

topple ▸ verb **1** *she toppled over* FALL, tumble, overbalance, overturn, tip, keel over, collapse; lose one's balance. **2** *protesters toppled a huge statue* KNOCK OVER, upset, push over, tip over, fell, upend. **3** *a plot to topple the government* OVERTHROW, oust, unseat, overturn, bring down, defeat, get rid of, dislodge, unhorse, eject.

topsy-turvy ▸ adjective **1** *a topsy-turvy flag* UPSIDE DOWN, the wrong way/side up, inverted; *informal* bass-ackwards, ass-backwards. **2** *everything in the apartment was topsy-turvy* IN DISARRAY, in a mess, in a muddle, in disorder, disordered, jumbled, in chaos, chaotic, disorganized, awry, upside down, at sixes and sevens; *informal* every which way, higgledy-piggledy.
— OPPOSITES: neat.

toque See table at HAT.

torch ▸ noun LIGHT, flame, cresset, flambeau, lantern.
▸ verb *one of the shops had been torched* BURN, set fire to, set on fire, set alight, incinerate, put a match to.

torment ▸ noun **1** *months of mental and emotional torment* AGONY, suffering, torture, pain, anguish, misery, distress, affliction, trauma, wretchedness; hell, purgatory. **2** *it was a torment to see him like that* ORDEAL, affliction, scourge, curse, plague, bane, thorn in someone's side/flesh, cross to bear; sorrow, tribulation, trouble.
▸ verb **1** *she was tormented by shame* TORTURE, afflict, rack, harrow, plague, haunt, bedevil, distress, agonize. **2** *she began to torment the two younger boys* TEASE, taunt, bait, harass, provoke, goad, plague, bother, trouble, persecute; *informal* needle.

torn ▸ adjective **1** *a torn shirt* RIPPED, rent, cut, slit; ragged, tattered, in tatters, in ribbons. **2** *she was torn between the two options* WAVERING, vacillating, irresolute, dithering, uncertain, unsure, undecided, split, of two minds.

tornado ▸ noun WHIRLWIND, twister, dust devil; cyclone, typhoon, storm, windstorm, hurricane.

torpid ▸ adjective LETHARGIC, sluggish, inert, inactive, slow, lifeless; languid, listless, lazy, idle, indolent, slothful, supine, passive, apathetic, phlegmatic, somnolent, sleepy, weary, tired.
— OPPOSITES: energetic.

torpor ▸ noun LETHARGY, sluggishness, inertia, inactivity, lifelessness, listlessness, languor, lassitude, laziness, idleness, indolence, sloth, acedia, passivity, somnolence, weariness, sleepiness.

torrent ▸ noun **1** *a torrent of water* FLOOD, deluge, inundation, spate, cascade, cataract, rush, stream, current, flow, overflow, tide. **2** *a torrent of abuse* OUTBURST, outpouring, stream, flood, volley, barrage, tide, spate.
— OPPOSITES: trickle.

torrential ▸ adjective COPIOUS, heavy, teeming, pelting, severe, relentless, violent.

torrid ▸ adjective **1** *a torrid summer* HOT, dry, scorching, searing, blazing, blistering, sweltering, burning, sultry; *informal* boiling (hot), baking (hot), sizzling. **2** *a torrid affair* PASSIONATE, ardent, lustful, amorous; *informal* steamy, sultry, sizzling, hot.
— OPPOSITES: cold.

torso ▸ noun BODY, upper body, trunk, chest.

tortuous ▸ adjective **1** *a tortuous route* TWISTING, twisty, twisting and turning, winding, windy, zigzag, sinuous, snaky, serpentine, meandering, circuitous. **2** *a tortuous argument* CONVOLUTED, complicated, complex, labyrinthine, tangled, tangly, involved, confusing, difficult to follow, involuted, lengthy, overlong, circuitous.
— OPPOSITES: straight, straightforward.

torture ▸ noun **1** *acts of torture* INFLICTION OF PAIN, abuse, ill-treatment, maltreatment, persecution; sadism. **2** *the torture of losing a loved one* TORMENT, agony, suffering, pain, anguish, misery, distress, heartbreak, affliction, scourge, trauma, wretchedness; hell, purgatory.
▸ verb **1** *the security forces routinely tortured suspects* INFLICT PAIN ON, ill-treat, abuse, mistreat, maltreat, persecute. **2** *he was tortured by grief* TORMENT, rack, afflict, harrow, plague, agonize, scourge, crucify.

toss ▸ verb **1** *he tossed the ball over the fence* THROW, hurl, fling, sling, cast, pitch, lob, project, heave, huck ♣, chuck. **2** *he tossed a coin and it landed heads* FLIP, flick. **3** *the ship tossed about on the waves* PITCH, lurch, rock, roll, plunge, reel, list, keel, sway, wallow, flounder. **4** *she tossed about in her sleep* THRASH, squirm, wriggle, writhe, fidget, turn. **5** *toss the salad ingredients together* SHAKE, stir, turn, mix, combine.

toss-up ▸ noun COIN TOSS, anyone's guess.

total ▸ adjective **1** *the total cost* ENTIRE, complete, whole, full, comprehensive, combined, aggregate, gross, overall, final. **2** *a total success* COMPLETE, utter, absolute, thorough, out-and-out, outright, all-out, sheer, perfect, consummate, arrant, positive, rank, unmitigated, unqualified, unreserved, categorical.
— OPPOSITES: partial.
▸ noun *a total of $160,000* SUM, sum total, grand total, aggregate, result; whole, entirety, totality.
▸ verb **1** *the prize money totalled $33,050* ADD UP TO, amount to, come to, run to, make, work out to. **2** *she totalled up her score* ADD (UP), count, reckon, tot up, tally up, compute, work out.

totalitarian ▸ adjective AUTOCRATIC, undemocratic, one-party, dictatorial, tyrannical, despotic, fascist, oppressive, repressive, illiberal; authoritarian, autarchic, absolute, absolutist; dystopian.
— OPPOSITES: democratic.

totality ▸ noun ENTIRETY, whole, total, aggregate, sum, sum total; all, everything; *informal* kit and caboodle, the whole enchilada, the whole ball of wax.

totally ▸ adverb COMPLETELY, entirely, wholly, thoroughly, fully, utterly, absolutely, perfectly, unreservedly, unconditionally, quite, altogether, downright; in every way, in every respect, one hundred per cent, every inch, to the hilt, flat out, to the max.
— OPPOSITES: partly.

tote ▸ verb CARRY, move, take, bring, bear, lug, fetch, cart.

totter ▸ verb **1** *he tottered off down the road* TEETER, dodder, walk unsteadily, stagger, wobble, stumble, shuffle, shamble, toddle; reel, sway, roll, lurch. **2** *the foundations began to heave and totter* SHAKE, sway, tremble, quiver, teeter, shudder, judder, rock, quake.

touch ▸ verb **1** *his shoes were touching the end of the bed* BE IN CONTACT WITH, come into contact with, meet, join, connect with, converge with, be contiguous with, be against. **2** *he touched her cheek* PRESS LIGHTLY, tap, pat; feel, stroke, fondle, caress, pet; brush, graze, put a hand to. **3** *nobody can touch her when she's on her* *game* COMPARE WITH, rival, compete with, come/get close to, be on a par with, equal, match, be a match for, be in the same class/league as, measure up to; better, beat; *informal* hold a candle to. **4** *you're not supposed to touch the computer* HANDLE, hold, pick up, move; meddle with, play about with, fiddle with, interfere with, tamper with, disturb, lay a finger on; use, employ, make use of. **5** *people whose lives have been touched by the recession* AFFECT, impact, have an effect/impact on, make a difference to, change. **6** *Lisa felt touched by the farmer's kindness* AFFECT, move, tug at someone's heartstrings; leave an impression on, have an effect on.

▶ **noun 1** *he felt her touch on his shoulder* TAP, pat; stroke, caress; brush; graze; hand. **2** *his political touch* SKILL, skilfulness, expertise, dexterity, deftness, adroitness, adeptness, ability, talent, flair, facility, proficiency, mastery, knack, technique, approach, style. **3** *a touch of sadness* TRACE, bit, grain, hint, suggestion, suspicion, scintilla, tinge, overtone, undertone, note; dash, taste, drop, dab, dribble, pinch, speck, soupçon. **4** *the gas lights are a nice touch* DETAIL, feature, point; addition, accessory. **5** *have you been in touch with him?* CONTACT, communication, correspondence; connection, association, interaction.

– RELATED TERMS: tactile.

■ **touch down** LAND, alight, come down, put down, arrive.

■ **touch something off** *the action touched off a string of protests* CAUSE, spark, trigger, start, set in motion, ignite, stir up, provoke, give rise to, lead to, generate, set off.

■ **touch on/upon** REFER TO, mention, comment on, speak on, remark on, bring up, raise, broach, allude to; cover, deal with.

■ **touch something up 1** *these paints are handy for touching up small areas* REPAINT, retouch, patch, fix; renovate, refurbish, revamp. **2** *the editor touched up my prose* IMPROVE, enhance, make better, refine, give the finishing touches to; *informal* tweak.

touch-and-go ▶ **adjective** UNCERTAIN, precarious, dicey, risky, chancy, hazardous, dangerous, critical, suspenseful, cliffhanging, hanging by a thread.

– OPPOSITES: certain.

touching ▶ **adjective** MOVING, affecting, heart-warming, emotional, emotive, tender, sentimental; poignant, sad, tear-jerking.

touchstone ▶ **noun** CRITERION, standard, yardstick, benchmark, barometer, bellwether, litmus test; measure, point of reference, norm, gauge, test, guide, exemplar, model, pattern.

touchy ▶ **adjective 1** *she can be so touchy* SENSITIVE, over-sensitive, hypersensitive, easily offended, thin-skinned, high-strung, tense; irritable, dyspeptic, tetchy, testy, crotchety, peevish, waspish, querulous, bad-tempered, petulant, pettish, cranky, fractious, choleric. **2** *a touchy subject* DELICATE, sensitive, tricky, ticklish, thorny, prickly, embarrassing, awkward, difficult; contentious, controversial.

– OPPOSITES: affable.

touchy-feely ▶ **adjective 1** *a touchy-feely person* DEMONSTRATIVE, huggy, huggy-kissy, affectionate, tender. **2** *a touchy-feely political initiative* FEEL-GOOD, warm and fuzzy, sentimental, soft-hearted, saccharine; ingratiating, toadying.

tough ▶ **adjective 1** *tough leather gloves* DURABLE, strong, resilient, sturdy, rugged, solid, stout, long-lasting, heavy-duty, industrial-strength, well-built, made to last. **2** *the steak was tough* CHEWY, leathery, gristly, stringy, fibrous. **3** *she'll survive — she's tough* ROBUST, resilient, strong, hardy, rugged, flinty, fit; stalwart, tough as nails. **4** *another tough report from the auditor-general* STRICT, stern, severe, stringent, rigorous, hard, firm, hard-hitting, uncompromising; unsentimental, unsympathetic. **5** *that exercise sure was tough* ARDUOUS, onerous, strenuous, gruelling, exacting, difficult, demanding, hard, taxing, tiring, exhausting, punishing, laborious, stressful, back-breaking, Herculean; *archaic* toilsome. **6** *these are tough questions for Ottawa's policy-makers* DIFFICULT, hard, heavy, knotty, thorny, tricky.

– OPPOSITES: soft, weak, easy.

▶ **noun** *a gang of toughs* RUFFIAN, thug, goon, hoodlum, hooligan, bully boy; roughneck, heavy, bruiser, yahoo.

toughen ▶ **verb 1** *the process toughens the wood fibres* STRENGTHEN, fortify, reinforce, harden, temper, anneal. **2** *measures to toughen up prison discipline* MAKE STRICTER, make more severe, stiffen, tighten up; *informal* beef up.

tour ▶ **noun 1** *we enjoyed a two-week tour of Italy* TRIP, excursion, journey, expedition, jaunt, outing; trek, safari; *archaic* peregrination. **2** *a tour of the factory* VISIT, inspection, guided tour. **3** *his tour of duty in Afghanistan* STINT, stretch, spell, turn, assignment, period of service.

▶ **verb 1** *this hotel is well placed for touring the Cariboo* TRAVEL ROUND, explore, discover, vacation in, holiday in. **2** *the Prime Minister toured the factory* VISIT, go round, walk round, inspect; *informal* check out.

tour de force ▶ **noun** TRIUMPH, masterpiece, achievement, success, masterful performance, magnum opus.

tourist ▶ **noun** VACATIONER, traveller, sightseer, visitor, backpacker, globetrotter, day tripper, out-of-towner.

– OPPOSITES: local.

tournament ▶ **noun 1** *a golf tournament* COMPETITION, contest, championship, meeting, tourney, meet, event, match, round robin. **2** *(historical) a knight preparing for a tournament* JOUST, tilt; the lists.

tousled ▶ **adjective** UNTIDY, dishevelled, wind-blown, messy, disordered, disarranged, messed up, rumpled, uncombed, ungroomed, tangled, wild, unkempt; *informal* mussed up.

– OPPOSITES: neat, tidy.

tout ▶ **verb 1** *street merchants were touting their wares* PEDDLE, sell, hawk, offer for sale, promote; *informal* flog. **2** *cab drivers were touting for business* SOLICIT, seek, drum up; ask, petition, appeal. **3** *she's being touted as the next party leader* RECOMMEND, speak of, extol, advocate, talk of; predict.

tow ▶ **verb** *the car was towed back to the garage* PULL, haul, drag, draw, tug, lug.

■ **in tow** *he arrived with his new girlfriend in tow* IN ATTENDANCE, by one's side, alongside, in one's charge; accompanying, following, tagging along.

toward(s) ▶ **preposition 1** *they were driving towards her apartment* IN THE DIRECTION OF, to; on the way to, on the road to, en route to. **2** *toward evening dark clouds gathered* JUST BEFORE, shortly before, near, around, approaching, close to, coming to, getting on for. **3** *her attitude towards politics* WITH REGARD TO, as regards, regarding, in/with regard to, respecting, in relation to, concerning, about, apropos, vis-à-vis. **4** *some money toward the cost of a new house* AS A CONTRIBUTION TO, for, to help with.

tower ▶ **noun** *a church tower* STEEPLE, spire; minaret; turret; bell tower, belfry, campanile; skyscraper, high-rise, edifice; office tower; hydro tower ✦, transmission tower.
▶ **verb 1** *snow-capped peaks towered over the valley* SOAR, rise, rear, loom; overshadow, overhang, hang over, dominate. **2** *she towered over most other theologians of her generation* ECLIPSE, overshadow, outshine, outclass, surpass, dominate, be head and shoulders above, put someone/something in the shade.

towering ▶ **adjective 1** *a towering skyscraper* HIGH, tall, lofty, soaring, sky-high, multi-storey; giant, gigantic, enormous, huge, massive; *informal* ginormous. **2** *a towering intellect* OUTSTANDING, pre-eminent, leading, foremost, finest, top, surpassing, supreme, great, incomparable, unrivalled, unsurpassed, peerless.

town ▶ **noun** MUNICIPALITY, conurbation, urban area, township; city, capital, metropolis, megalopolis, megacity, burg; small town, whistle stop.
— RELATED TERMS: municipal, urban.
— OPPOSITES: country.

toxic ▶ **adjective** POISONOUS, virulent, noxious, deadly, dangerous, harmful, injurious, pernicious.
— OPPOSITES: harmless.

toy ▶ **noun** PLAYTHING, game; gadget; device; trinket, knick-knack, gizmo.
▶ **adjective 1** *a toy gun* MODEL, imitation, replica, fake; miniature. **2** *a toy poodle* MINIATURE, small, tiny, diminutive, dwarf, midget, pygmy.
■ **toy with 1** *I was toying with the idea of writing a book* THINK ABOUT, consider, flirt with, entertain the possibility of; kick around. **2** *Adam toyed with his glasses* FIDDLE WITH, play with, fidget with, twiddle; finger. **3** *she toyed with her food* NIBBLE, pick at, peck at, eat listlessly, eat like a bird. **4** *you are toying with my emotions* TRIFLE WITH, play with, play havoc with, amuse oneself with, mess with, be flippant with.

trace ▶ **verb 1** *police hope to trace the owner of the vehicle* TRACK DOWN, find, discover, detect, unearth, turn up, hunt down, ferret out. **2** *she traced a pattern in the sand with her toe* DRAW, outline, mark, sketch. **3** *the analysis traces the origins of cowboy poetry* OUTLINE, map out, follow, sketch out, delineate, depict, show, indicate.
▶ **noun 1** *no trace had been found of the runaways* VESTIGE, sign, mark, indication, evidence, clue; trail, tracks, marks, prints, footprints, spoor; remains, remnant, relic. **2** *a trace of bitterness crept into her voice* BIT, touch, hint, suggestion, suspicion, shadow, whiff; drop, dash, tinge, speck, shred, iota; smidgen, tad.

track ▶ **noun 1** *a gravel track* PATH, pathway, footpath, lane, trail, (*West*) monkey trail ✦, route, portage trail, way, course. **2** *the final lap of the track* COURSE, racetrack, raceway; velodrome. **3** *he found the tracks of a wolverine* TRACES, marks, prints, footprints, trail, spoor. **4** *we followed the track of the hurricane* COURSE, path, line, route, way, trajectory, wake. **5** *railway tracks* RAIL, line, railway line, steel ✦. **6** *the album's title track* SONG, recording, number, piece.
▶ **verb** *he tracked a bear for 40 km* FOLLOW, trail, trace, pursue, shadow, stalk, keep an eye on, keep in sight; *informal* tail.
■ **keep track of** MONITOR, follow, keep up with, keep an eye on; keep in touch with, keep up to date with; *informal* keep tabs on.
■ **track someone/something down** DISCOVER, find, sketch out, hunt down/out, unearth, uncover, turn up, dig up, ferret out, bring to light.
■ **on track** ON COURSE, on an even keel, on schedule.

track and field ▶ *See table.*

Athletic/Track and Field Events

biathlon	marathon
cross-country run	modern pentathlon
decathlon	pole vault
discus throw	relay
hammer throw	shot put
heptathlon	steeplechase
high jump	triathlon
hurdles	triple jump
javelin throw	walk
long jump	

tract[1] ▶ **noun** *large tracts of land* AREA, region, expanse, sweep, stretch, extent, belt, swathe, zone.

tract[2] ▶ **noun** *a political tract* TREATISE, essay, article, paper, work, monograph, disquisition, dissertation, thesis, homily, tractate; pamphlet, booklet, chapbook, leaflet.

tractable ▶ **adjective** MALLEABLE, manageable, amenable, pliable, governable, yielding, complaisant, compliant, game, persuadable, accommodating, docile, biddable, obliging, obedient, submissive, meek.
— OPPOSITES: recalcitrant.

traction ▶ **noun** GRIP, purchase, friction, adhesion.

trade ▶ **noun 1** *the illicit trade in stolen cattle* COMMERCE, buying and selling, dealing, traffic, trafficking, business, marketing, merchandising; dealings, transactions, deal-making. **2** *we shook hands as we made the trade* EXCHANGE, transaction, swap, handover. **3** *the glazier's trade* CRAFT, occupation, job, career, profession, business, line (of work), métier, vocation, calling, walk of life, field; work, employment, livelihood.
— RELATED TERMS: mercantile.
▶ **verb 1** *he made his fortune trading in beaver pelts* DEAL, buy and sell, traffic, market, merchandise, peddle, vend, hawk, flog. **2** *the business is trading at a loss* OPERATE, run, do business. **3** *I traded the old machine for a newer model* SWAP, exchange, switch; barter, trade in.
■ **trade on** EXPLOIT, take advantage of, capitalize on, profit from, use, make use of; milk; *informal* cash in on.

trademark ▶ **noun 1** *the company's trademark* LOGO, brand, emblem, sign, mark, stamp, symbol, badge, crest, monogram, colophon; brand name, trade name, proprietary name. **2** *it had all the trademarks of a Mafia hit* CHARACTERISTIC, hallmark, calling card, sign, trait, quality, attribute, feature, peculiarity, idiosyncrasy, quirk.

trader ▶ **noun** DEALER, merchant, buyer, seller, buyer and seller, marketeer, merchandiser, broker, agent; distributor, vendor, purveyor, monger, supplier, trafficker; shopkeeper, retailer, wholesaler; wheeler-dealer.

tradesman, tradeswoman ▶ **noun** *a qualified tradesman* CRAFTSMAN, craftsperson, workman, artisan.

trading post ▶ **noun** *historical* factory ✦, trading station, store, fort, house ✦, post.

tradition ▶ **noun 1** *during a maiden speech, by tradition, everyone keeps absolutely silent* HISTORICAL CONVENTION, unwritten law, mores; oral history, lore, folklore. **2** *an age-old tradition* CUSTOM, practice, convention, ritual, observance, way, usage, habit, institution; *formal* praxis.

traditional ▶ adjective **1** *traditional Christmas fare* LONG-ESTABLISHED, customary, time-honoured, established, classic, accustomed, standard, regular, normal, conventional, usual, orthodox, habitual, set, fixed, routine, ritual; old, age-old, ancestral. **2** *traditional beliefs* HANDED-DOWN, folk, unwritten, oral.

traduce ▶ verb DEFAME, slander, speak ill of, misrepresent, malign, vilify, denigrate, disparage, slur, impugn, smear, besmirch, run down, blacken the name of, cast aspersions on; *informal* badmouth, dis.

traffic ▶ noun **1** *the bridge is not open to traffic* VEHICLES; cars, trucks. **2** *they might be stuck in traffic* TRAFFIC JAMS, congestion, gridlock, holdups, stoppages, bottlenecks, tie-ups, snarl-ups, log-jams. **3** *the illegal traffic in stolen art* TRADE, trading, trafficking, dealing, commerce, business, buying and selling; smuggling, bootlegging, black market; dealings, transactions.
▶ verb *he confessed to trafficking in narcotics* TRADE, deal, do business, buy and sell; smuggle, bootleg; *informal* run, push.

tragedy ▶ noun DISASTER, calamity, catastrophe, cataclysm, misfortune, mishap, blow, trial, tribulation, affliction, adversity.

tragic ▶ adjective **1** *a tragic accident* DISASTROUS, calamitous, catastrophic, cataclysmic, devastating, terrible, dreadful, awful, appalling, dismal, horrendous; fatal, deadly, mortal, lethal. **2** *a tragic tale* SAD, unhappy, pathetic, moving, distressing, depressing, painful, harrowing, heart-rending, piteous, wretched, sorry; melancholy, doleful, mournful, miserable, gut-wrenching. **3** *a tragic waste of talent* REGRETTABLE, shameful, terrible, horrible, awful, deplorable, lamentable, piteous, dreadful, grievous.
— OPPOSITES: fortunate, happy.

trail ▶ noun **1** *he left a trail of clues | a trail of devastation* SERIES, string, chain, succession, sequence; aftermath, wake. **2** *wolves on the trail of their prey* TRACK, spoor, path, scent; traces, marks, signs, prints, footprints. **3** *the airplane's vapour trail* WAKE, contrail, tail, stream. **4** *a trail of ants* LINE, column, train, file, procession, string, chain, convoy; lineup. **5** *provincial parks with nature trails* PATH, pathway, way, footpath, walk, (*West*) monkey trail ✚, track, portage trail, course, route.
▶ verb **1** *her robe trailed along the ground* DRAG, sweep, swish, be drawn; dangle, hang (down), droop. **2** *the roses grew wild, their stems trailing over the banks* HANG, droop, fall, spill, cascade. **3** *Filteau suspected that they were trailing him* FOLLOW, pursue, track, shadow, stalk, hunt (down); *informal* tail. **4** *the defending champions were trailing 3–1 in the second period* LOSE, be down, be behind, lag behind. **5** *her voice trailed off* FADE, tail off/away, grow faint, die away, dwindle, taper off, subside, peter out, fizzle out.

trailblazer ▶ noun PIONEER, innovator, ground-breaker, spearhead, trend-setter; explorer, bushwhacker.

trail-blazing ▶ adjective INNOVATIVE, cutting-edge, leading-edge, groundbreaking, pioneering, state-of-the-art, avant-garde, trend-setting, unprecedented, experimental, original, inventive, new.

trailer ▶ noun CAMPER, recreational vehicle, RV;

proprietary Winnebago, house trailer, motorhome, tent trailer, fifth wheel (trailer).

trail mix ▶ noun GORP, cereal, granola, nuts and raisins, good ol' raisins and peanuts.

train ▶ verb **1** *an engineer trained in remote-sensing techniques* INSTRUCT, teach, coach, tutor, school, educate, prime, drill, ground; inculcate, indoctrinate, initiate, break in. **2** *she's training to be a hairdresser* STUDY, learn, prepare, take instruction. **3** *with the Olympics in mind, athletes are training hard* EXERCISE, do exercises, work out, get into shape, practise, prepare. **4** *she trained the gun on his chest* AIM, point, direct, level, focus; take aim, zero in on.
▶ noun **1** *the train for Oshawa* locomotive, railway train, subway, LRT, monorail; *informal* iron horse; *baby talk* choo choo. **2** *a minister and his train of attendants* RETINUE, entourage, cortège, following, staff, household. **3** *a train of elephants* PROCESSION, line, file, column, convoy, cavalcade, caravan, string, succession, trail. **4** *a bizarre train of events* CHAIN, string, series, sequence, succession, set, course, cycle, concatenation.

trainee ▶ noun APPRENTICE, new employee, new hire, newbie, intern; cadet, rookie, novice, student.

trainer ▶ noun COACH, instructor, teacher, tutor; handler.

training ▶ noun **1** *in-house training for staff* INSTRUCTION, teaching, coaching, tuition, tutoring, guidance, schooling, education, orientation; indoctrination, inculcation, initiation. **2** *four months' hard training before the tournament* EXERCISE, exercises, working out, conditioning; practice, preparation.

traipse ▶ verb TRUDGE, trek, tramp, tromp, trail, plod, drag oneself, slog, schlep.

trait ▶ noun CHARACTERISTIC, attribute, feature, quality, property; habit, custom, mannerism, idiosyncrasy, peculiarity, quirk, oddity, foible.

traitor ▶ noun BETRAYER, backstabber, double-crosser, renegade, Judas, quisling, fifth columnist; turncoat, defector, deserter; collaborator, informer, fink, mole, snitch, double agent; *informal* snake in the grass, two-timer.

traitorous ▶ adjective TREACHEROUS, disloyal, treasonous, renegade, backstabbing; double-crossing, double-dealing, faithless, unfaithful, two-faced, duplicitous, deceitful, false; *informal* two-timing; *literary* perfidious.
— OPPOSITES: loyal.

trajectory ▶ noun COURSE, path, route, track, line, orbit.

trammel (*literary*) ▶ noun *the trammels of domesticity* RESTRAINT, constraint, curb, check, impediment, obstacle, barrier, handicap, bar, hindrance, encumbrance, disadvantage, drawback, shackles, fetters, bonds.
▶ verb *those less trammelled by convention than himself* RESTRICT, restrain, constrain, hamper, confine, hinder, handicap, obstruct, impede, hold back, tie down, hamstring, shackle, fetter.

tramp ▶ verb TRUDGE, tromp, plod, galumph, stamp, trample, lumber, clump, clomp, stump, stomp; trek, slog, schlep, drag oneself, walk, hike, march, traipse.
▶ noun **1** *a wandering old tramp* VAGRANT, vagabond, street person, hobo, homeless person, down-and-out; traveller, drifter, derelict, beggar, mendicant, bag lady, bum. **2** *the regular tramp of the sentry's boots* FOOTSTEP, tromp, step, footfall, tread, stamp, stomp.

trample ▶ verb **1** *someone had trampled on the tulips*

TREAD, tramp, stamp, stomp, walk over; squash, crush, flatten. **2** *we do nothing but trample over their feelings* TREAT WITH CONTEMPT, disregard, show no consideration for, abuse; encroach on, infringe.

trance ▸ **noun** DAZE, stupor, hypnotic state, half-conscious state, dream, reverie, fugue state.

tranquil ▸ **adjective 1** *the lake's tranquil waters* PEACEFUL, calm, calming, still, serene, placid, restful, quiet, relaxing, undisturbed, limpid, pacific. **2** *Martha smiled, perfectly tranquil* CALM, serene, relaxed, unruffled, unperturbed, unflustered, untroubled, composed, {calm, cool, and collected}; equable, even-tempered, placid, unflappable.
– OPPOSITES: busy, excitable.

tranquility ▸ **noun 1** *the tranquility of a Gulf Island* PEACE, peacefulness, restfulness, repose, calm, calmness, quiet, quietness, stillness. **2** *the incident jolted her out of her tranquility* COMPOSURE, calmness, serenity, peace; equanimity, equability, placidity; *informal* cool, unflappability.

tranquilize ▸ **verb** SEDATE, put under sedation, narcotize, anaesthetize, etherize, drug.

tranquilizer ▸ **noun** SEDATIVE, barbiturate, calmative, sleeping pill, depressant, narcotic, opiate; *informal* trank, downer.
– OPPOSITES: stimulant.

transact ▸ **verb** CONDUCT, carry out, negotiate, do, perform, execute, take care of, discharge; settle, conclude, finish, clinch, accomplish.

transaction ▸ **noun 1** *property transactions* DEAL, business deal, undertaking, arrangement, bargain, negotiation, agreement, settlement; proceedings. *See also* TRADE (*sense 2*). **2** *the bank statement records your transactions* DEBIT, credit, deposit or withdrawal. **3** *the transaction of government business* CONDUCT, carrying out, negotiation, performance, execution.

transcend ▸ **verb** *an issue that transcended party politics* GO BEYOND, rise above, cut across. **2** *his exploits far transcended those of his predecessors* SURPASS, exceed, beat, cap, tower above, outdo, outclass, outstrip, leave behind, outshine, eclipse, overshadow, throw into the shade, upstage, top.

transcendence ▸ **noun** EXCELLENCE, supremacy, incomparability, matchlessness, peerlessness, magnificence.

transcendent ▸ **adjective 1** *the search for a transcendent level of knowledge* MYSTICAL, mystic, transcendental, spiritual, divine; metaphysical. **2** *a transcendent genius* INCOMPARABLE, matchless, peerless, unrivalled, inimitable, beyond compare/comparison, unparalleled, unequalled, without equal, second to none, unsurpassed, unsurpassable, nonpareil; exceptional, consummate, unique, perfect, rare, surpassing, magnificent.

transcendental ▸ **adjective.** *See* TRANSCENDENT *sense 1.*

transcribe ▸ **verb 1** *each interview was taped and transcribed* WRITE OUT, write down, copy out/down, put in writing, put on paper, render. **2** *a person who can take and transcribe shorthand* TRANSLITERATE, interpret, translate.

transcript ▸ **noun 1** *a radio transcript* WRITTEN VERSION, printed version, script, text, transliteration, record, reproduction. **2** *university transcript* STUDENT RECORD, grades, report card.

transfer ▸ **verb 1** *the hostages were transferred to a safe house* MOVE, convey, take, bring, shift, remove, carry, transport; transplant, relocate, resettle. **2** *the property*

was transferred to his wife HAND OVER, pass on, make over, turn over, sign over, consign, devolve, assign, delegate.
▸ **noun 1** *he died shortly after his transfer to hospital* MOVE, conveyance, transferral, transference, shift, relocation, removal, switch, transplantation. **2** *keep your bus transfer in your pocket* TICKET, pass; receipt, proof of purchase.

transfigure ▸ **verb** TRANSFORM, transmute, change, alter, metamorphose; *informal* transmogrify.

transfix ▸ **verb 1** *she was transfixed by the images on the screen* MESMERIZE, hypnotize, spellbind, bewitch, captivate, entrance, enthrall, fascinate, absorb, enrapture, grip, hook, rivet, paralyze. **2** *a field mouse is transfixed by the owl's curved talons* IMPALE, stab, spear, pierce, spike, skewer, gore, stick, run through.

transform ▸ **verb** CHANGE, alter, convert, metamorphose, transfigure, transmute, mutate; revolutionize, overhaul; remodel, reshape, redo, reconstruct, rebuild, reorganize, rearrange, rework, renew, revamp, remake, retool; *informal* transmogrify, morph.

transformation ▸ **noun** CHANGE, alteration, mutation, conversion, metamorphosis, transfiguration, transmutation, sea change; revolution, overhaul; remodelling, reshaping, redoing, reconstruction, rebuilding, reorganization, rearrangement, reworking, renewal, revamp, remaking, remake; *informal* transmogrification, morphing.

transgress ▸ **verb 1** *if they transgress, the punishment is harsh* MISBEHAVE, behave badly, break the law, err, fall from grace, stray from the straight and narrow, sin, do wrong, go astray; *archaic* trespass. **2** *she had transgressed an unwritten social law* INFRINGE, breach, contravene, disobey, defy, violate, break, flout.

transgression ▸ **noun 1** *a punishment for past transgressions* OFFENCE, crime, sin, wrong, wrongdoing, misdemeanour, impropriety, infraction, misdeed, law-breaking; error, lapse, peccadillo, fault; *archaic* trespass. **2** *Adam's transgression of God's law* INFRINGEMENT, breach, contravention, violation, defiance, disobedience, non-observance.

transgressor ▸ **noun** OFFENDER, miscreant, lawbreaker, criminal, villain, felon, malefactor, guilty party, culprit; sinner, evildoer; *archaic* trespasser.

transient ▸ **adjective** TRANSITORY, temporary, short-lived, short-term, ephemeral, impermanent, brief, short, momentary, fleeting, passing, here today and gone tomorrow; *literary* evanescent, fugitive.
▸ **noun** HOBO, vagrant, vagabond, street person, homeless person, down-and-out; traveller, drifter, derelict.
– OPPOSITES: permanent.

transit ▸ **noun 1** *public transit* TRANSPORTATION, transport, mass transit, bus system, subway system. **2** *the transit of goods between states* TRANSPORTATION, transport, movement, flow, conveyance, shipping, shipment, trucking, carriage, transfer.
■ **in transit** EN ROUTE, on the journey, on the way, along/on the road.

transition ▸ **noun** CHANGE, passage, move, transformation, conversion, metamorphosis, alteration, handover, changeover; segue, shift, switch, jump, leap, progression; progress, development, evolution, flux.

transitional ▸ adjective **1** *a transitional period* CHANGEOVER, interim; changing, fluid, in flux, unsettled, intermediate, liminal. **2** *the transitional government* INTERIM, temporary, provisional, pro tem, acting, caretaker.

transitory ▸ adjective TRANSIENT, temporary, brief, short, short-lived, short-term, impermanent, ephemeral, momentary, fleeting, passing, here today and gone tomorrow; *literary* evanescent, fugitive.
— OPPOSITES: permanent.

translate ▸ verb **1** *the German original had been translated into English* RENDER, put, express, convert, change; transcribe, transliterate. **2** *be prepared to translate plenty of jargon* RENDER, paraphrase, reword, rephrase, convert, decipher, decode, gloss, explain. **3** *interesting ideas cannot always be translated into effective movies* ADAPT, change, convert, transform, alter, turn, transmute; *informal* transmogrify, morph.

translation ▸ noun *the translation of the Bible into English* RENDITION, rendering, conversion; transcription, transliteration.

translucent ▸ adjective SEMI-TRANSPARENT, semi-opaque, pellucid, limpid, clear; diaphanous, gossamer, sheer.
— OPPOSITES: opaque.

transmission ▸ noun **1** *the transmission of ideas* SPREAD, transferral, communication, conveyance; dissemination, circulation, transference. **2** *a live transmission* BROADCAST, program, show, airing. **3** *her car had a faulty transmission* POWERTRAIN, drivetrain.

transmit ▸ verb **1** *the use of computers to transmit information* TRANSFER, pass on, hand on, communicate, convey, impart, channel, carry, relay, forward, dispatch; disseminate, spread, circulate. **2** *the program will be transmitted on Sunday* BROADCAST, relay, send out, air, televise.

transmute ▸ verb CHANGE, alter, adapt, transform, convert, metamorphose, morph, translate; *humorous* transmogrify.

transparency ▸ noun **1** *the transparency of the glass* TRANSLUCENCY, limpidity, clearness, clarity. **2** *colour transparencies* SLIDE, acetate. **3** *the new government aims for better transparency* OPENNESS, accountability, straightforwardness, candour.

transparent ▸ adjective **1** *transparent blue water* CLEAR, crystal clear, see-through, translucent, pellucid, limpid, glassy, vitreous. **2** *fine transparent fabrics* SEE-THROUGH, sheer, filmy, gauzy, diaphanous, translucent. **3** *a transparent attempt to win favour* OBVIOUS, evident, self-evident, undisguised, unconcealed, conspicuous, patent, clear, crystal clear, plain, (as) plain as the nose on your face, apparent, unmistakable, easily discerned, manifest, palpable, indisputable, unambiguous, unequivocal.
— OPPOSITES: opaque, obscure.

transpire ▸ verb **1** *it transpired that her family had moved away* BECOME KNOWN, emerge, come to light, be revealed, turn out, come out, be discovered, prove to be the case, unfold. **2** *I'm going to find out exactly what transpired* HAPPEN, occur, take place, arise, come about, materialize, turn up, chance, befall, ensue; *literary* come to pass.

transplant ▸ verb **1** *our headquarters will be transplanted to Calgary* TRANSFER, move, remove, shift, relocate, take. **2** *the seedlings should be transplanted in larger pots* REPLANT, repot, relocate. **3** *kidneys must be transplanted within 48 hours of removal* TRANSFER, implant.

transport ▸ verb CONVEY, carry, take, transfer, move, shift, send, deliver, bear, ship, ferry, haul; *informal* cart.
▸ noun *alternative forms of transport.* See TRANSPORTATION sense 1.

transportation ▸ noun **1** *alternative forms of transportation* TRANSIT, transport, conveyance, travel; getting around; vehicle, car, truck, train. **2** *the transportation of crude oil* TRANSPORT, conveyance, movement, carriage, haulage, freight, shipment, shipping.

transpose ▸ verb **1** *the blue and black plates were transposed* INTERCHANGE, exchange, switch, swap (round), reverse, invert, flip. **2** *the themes are transposed from the sphere of love to that of work* TRANSFER, shift, relocate, transplant, move, displace.

transsexual ▸ noun HERMAPHRODITE, androgyne, epicene, intersex, transgendered person; *informal* trannie.

transverse ▸ adjective CROSSWISE, crossways, cross, horizontal, diagonal, oblique, slanted.

transvestite ▸ noun DRAG QUEEN, cross-dresser, female impersonator, gender-bender, trannie.

trap ▸ noun **1** *an animal caught in a trap* SNARE, net, mesh, deadfall, leghold (trap), pitfall. **2** *the question was set as a trap* TRICK, ploy, ruse, deception, subterfuge; booby trap, ambush, set-up. **3** (*informal*) *shut your trap!* See MOUTH noun sense 1.
▸ verb **1** *police trapped the two men and arrested them* SNARE, entrap, ensnare, lay a trap for; capture, catch, bag, corner, ambush. **2** *a rat trapped in a barn* CONFINE, cut off, corner, shut in, pen in, hem in; imprison, hold captive. **3** *I hoped to trap him into an admission* TRICK, dupe, deceive, lure, inveigle, beguile, fool, hoodwink; catch out, trip up.

trappings ▸ plural noun ACCESSORIES, accoutrements, appurtenances, trimmings, frills, accompaniments, extras, ornamentation, adornment, decoration; regalia, panoply, paraphernalia, apparatus, finery, equipment, gear, effects, things, bits and pieces.

trash ▸ noun **1** *the subway entrance was blocked with trash* GARBAGE, refuse, waste, litter, junk, debris, detritus, rubbish. **2** *if they read at all, they read trash* JUNK, dross, dreck, drivel, nonsense, trivia, pulp (fiction), pap, garbage, rubbish; *informal* crap, schlock. **3** (*informal*) *that family is trash* SCUM, vermin, the dregs of society, the scum of the earth, the lowest of the low; *informal* dirt.
▸ verb **1** *the apartment had been totally trashed* WRECK, ruin, destroy, wreak havoc on, devastate; vandalize, tear up, bust up, smash; *informal* total. **2** *his play was trashed by the critics* CRITICIZE, LAMBASTE, censure, attack, insult, abuse, malign, give a bad press to, condemn, flay, savage, pan, knock, take to pieces, take/pull apart, crucify, hammer, slam, bash, trash talk, roast, maul, rubbish, badmouth, pummel; *informal* bitch about.

trashy ▸ adjective WORTHLESS, substandard, rubbishy, inferior, tawdry, kitschy, second-rate, third-rate, poor-quality, lousy, cheap, shoddy, tinpot, bad, poor, dreadful, awful, terrible, crummy, appalling, dire, tacky, chintzy, garish, meretricious.

trauma ▸ noun **1** *the trauma of divorce* SHOCK, upheaval, distress, stress, strain, pain, anguish, suffering, upset, agony, misery, sorrow, grief, heartache, heartbreak, torture; ordeal, trial, tribulation, trouble, worry, anxiety; nightmare, hell, hellishness. **2** *the trauma to the liver* INJURY, damage, wound; cut, laceration, lesion, abrasion, contusion.

traumatic ▶ adjective DISTURBING, shocking, distressing, upsetting, heartbreaking, painful, scarring, jolting, agonizing, hurtful, stressful, damaging, injurious, harmful, awful, terrible, devastating, harrowing.

travail (*literary*) ▶ noun ORDEAL, trial, tribulation, trial and tribulation, trouble, hardship, privation, stress; drudgery, toil, slog, effort, exertion, labour, work, endeavour, sweat, struggle.

travel ▶ verb **1** *Tim spent much of his time travelling abroad* JOURNEY, tour, take a trip, voyage, explore, go sightseeing, globe-trot, backpack, gallivant; *archaic* peregrinate. **2** *we travelled the length and breadth of the island* JOURNEY THROUGH, cross, traverse, cover; roam, wander, rove, range, trek. **3** *light travels faster than sound* MOVE, be transmitted.
▶ noun *she amassed great wealth during her travels* JOURNEYS, expeditions, trips, tours, excursions, voyages, treks, safaris, explorations, wanderings, odysseys, pilgrimages, jaunts, junkets; travelling, touring, sightseeing, backpacking, globe-trotting, gallivanting; *archaic* peregrinations.

traveller ▶ noun *thousands of travellers were left stranded* TOURIST, vacationer, tripper, holidaymaker, sightseer, visitor, globetrotter, backpacker; pilgrim, wanderer, drifter, nomad, migrant; passenger, commuter, fare.

travelling ▶ adjective NOMADIC, itinerant, peripatetic, wandering, roaming, saddlebag ♣, roving, wayfaring, migrant, vagrant, of no fixed address.

traverse ▶ verb **1** *he traversed the deserts of Iran* TRAVEL OVER/ACROSS, cross, journey over/across, pass over; cover; ply; wander, roam, range. **2** *a ditch traversed by a wooden bridge* CROSS, bridge, span; extend across, lie across, stretch across.

travesty ▶ noun *a travesty of justice* PERVERSION, distortion, corruption, misrepresentation, poor imitation, poor substitute, mockery, parody, caricature; farce, charade, pantomime, sham, spoof; *informal* apology for, excuse for.

trawl ▶ verb FISH, seine, drag a net; sift, troll, hunt, search, look.

tray ▶ noun PLATTER, salver, plate, dish, box, basket.

treacherous ▶ adjective **1** *her treacherous brother betrayed her* TRAITOROUS, disloyal, faithless, unfaithful, duplicitous, deceitful, deceptive, false, backstabbing, double-crossing, double-dealing, two-faced, weaselly, untrustworthy, unreliable; apostate, renegade, two-timing; *literary* perfidious. **2** *treacherous driving conditions* DANGEROUS, hazardous, perilous, unsafe, precarious, risky, deceptive, unreliable; *informal* dicey, hairy.
– OPPOSITES: loyal, faithful, reliable.

treachery ▶ noun BETRAYAL, disloyalty, faithlessness, unfaithfulness, infidelity, breach of trust, duplicity, dirty tricks, deceit, deception, chicanery, stab in the back, backstabbing, double-dealing, untrustworthiness; treason, two-timing; *literary* perfidy.

tread ▶ verb **1** *he trod purposefully down the hall* WALK, step, stride, pace, go; march, tramp, plod, thump, stomp, trudge. **2** *the snow had been trodden down by the* horses CRUSH, flatten, press down, squash; trample on, tramp on, stamp on, stomp on.
▶ noun *we heard her heavy tread on the stairs* STEP, footfall, footfall, tramp, thump; clip-clop.

treason ▶ noun TREACHERY, disloyalty, betrayal, faithlessness; sedition, subversion, mutiny, rebellion; high treason, lèse-majesté; apostasy; *literary* perfidy.
– OPPOSITES: allegiance, loyalty.

treasonable ▶ adjective TRAITOROUS, treasonous, treacherous, disloyal; seditious, subversive, mutinous, rebellious; *literary* perfidious.
– OPPOSITES: loyal.

treasure ▶ noun **1** *a casket of treasure* RICHES, valuables, jewels, gems, gold, silver, precious metals, money, cash; wealth, fortune; treasure trove. **2** *art treasures* VALUABLE OBJECT, valuable, work of art, masterpiece, precious item. **3** (*informal*) *she's a real treasure* PARAGON, gem, angel, find, star, one of a kind, one in a million.
▶ verb *I treasure the photographs I took of Jack* CHERISH, hold dear, prize, value greatly; adore, dote on, love, be devoted to, worship, venerate.

treasury ▶ noun **1** *the provincial treasury* COFFERS, purse, finance department; bank, revenues, finances, funds, moneys. **2** *the area is a treasury of early fossils* RICH SOURCE, repository, storehouse, treasure house; fund, mine, bank, treasure trove. **3** *a treasury of stories* ANTHOLOGY, collection, miscellany, compilation, compendium.

treat ▶ verb **1** *Charlotte treated him very badly* BEHAVE TOWARDS, act towards; deal with, handle; *literary* use. **2** *police are treating the fires as arson* REGARD, consider, view, look upon, think of. **3** *the book treats its subject with insight and responsibility* TACKLE, deal with, handle, discuss, present, explore, investigate, approach; consider, study, analyze. **4** *she was treated at St. Paul's Hospital* GIVE MEDICAL CARE TO, nurse, care for, tend, help, give treatment to, attend to, administer to; medicate. **5** *the plants may prove useful in treating cancer* CURE, heal, remedy; fight, combat. **6** *she treated him to an expensive meal* BUY, take out for, give; pay for; entertain, wine and dine; foot the bill for, pick up the tab for. **7** *delegates were treated to an Indonesian dance show* REGALE WITH, entertain with/by, fete with, amuse with, divert with.
▶ noun **1** *a birthday treat* CELEBRATION, entertainment, amusement; surprise; party, excursion, outing, special event. **2** *I bought you some chocolate as a treat* PRESENT, gift; delicacy, luxury, indulgence, extravagance, guilty pleasure; *informal* goodie. **3** *it was a real treat to see them* PLEASURE, delight, boon, thrill, joy.

treatise ▶ noun DISQUISITION, essay, paper, work, exposition, discourse, dissertation, thesis, monograph, opus, oeuvre, study, critique; tract, pamphlet, account.

treatment ▶ noun **1** *the company's treatment of its workers* BEHAVIOUR TOWARDS, conduct towards; handling of, dealings with, management of. **2** *she's responding well to treatment* MEDICAL CARE, therapy, nursing, ministrations; medication, drugs, medicaments; cure, remedy. **3** *her treatment of the topic* DISCUSSION, handling, investigation, exploration, consideration, study, analysis, critique; approach, methodology.

treaty ▶ noun AGREEMENT, settlement, pact, deal, entente, concordat, accord, protocol, convention, contract, covenant, bargain, pledge; concord, compact.

tree ▶ noun sapling, conifer, evergreen. *See table.*
— RELATED TERMS: arboreal.

Types of Tree

acacia	hemlock
alder	hickory
apple	hornbeam
arborvitae	juniper
ash	larch
aspen	linden
banyan	magnolia
baobab	maple
basswood	mulberry
beech	oak
birch	olive
cascara	peach
cedar	pear
cherry	pine
chestnut	plum
cottonwood	poplar
cypress	redbud
dogwood	redwood
elm	sequoia
eucalyptus	spruce
fig	sumac
fir	sycamore
ginkgo	tulip tree
hackberry	walnut
hawthorn	willow
hazel	yew

trek ▶ noun *a three-day trek across the desert* JOURNEY, trip, expedition, safari, odyssey, voyage; hike, march, slog, tramp, walk; long haul.
▶ verb *we trekked through the jungle* HIKE, tramp, march, slog, footslog, trudge, traipse, walk; travel, journey, hoof it.

trellis ▶ noun LATTICE, framework, espalier, arbour; network, mesh; grille, grid, grating; latticework; *technical* reticulation.

tremble ▶ verb **1** *Joe's hands were trembling* SHAKE, shake like a leaf, quiver, twitch, jerk; quaver, waver. **2** *the entire building trembled* SHAKE, shudder, judder, quake, wobble, rock, vibrate, move, sway, totter, teeter. **3** *she trembled at the thought of what he had in store for her* BE AFRAID, be frightened, be apprehensive, worry, shake in one's boots; quail, quake, shrink, blench.
▶ noun *the slight tremble in her hands* TREMOR, shake, shakiness, trembling, quiver, quaking, twitch, vibration, unsteadiness.
— OPPOSITES: steadiness.

tremendous ▶ adjective **1** *tremendous sums of money* HUGE, enormous, immense, colossal, massive, prodigious, stupendous, monumental, mammoth, vast, gigantic, giant, mighty, epic, titanic, towering, king-size(d), jumbo, gargantuan, Herculean; substantial, considerable, Brobdingnagian; whopping, astronomical, humongous, ginormous. **2** *a tremendous explosion* VERY LOUD, deafening, ear-splitting, booming, thundering, thunderous, resounding. **3** *I've seen him play and he's tremendous* EXCELLENT, splendid, wonderful, marvellous, magnificent, superb, sublime, lovely, delightful, too good to be true; super, great, amazing, fantastic, terrific, sensational, heavenly, divine, fabulous,

awesome, to die for, magic, wicked, mind-blowing, splendiferous, far out, out of this world, brilliant, boss, swell.
— OPPOSITES: tiny, small, poor.

tremor ▶ noun **1** *the sudden tremor of her hands* TREMBLING, shaking, shakiness, tremble, shake, quivering, quiver, twitching, twitch, tic; quavering, quaver, quake, palpitation. **2** *a tremor of fear ran through her* FRISSON, shiver, spasm, thrill, tingle, stab, dart, wave, surge, rush, ripple. **3** *the epicentre of the tremor* EARTHQUAKE, earth tremor, shock; *informal* quake.

tremulous ▶ adjective **1** *a tremulous voice* SHAKY, trembling, shaking, unsteady, quavering, wavering, quivering, quivery, quaking, weak, warbly, trembly. **2** *a tremulous smile* TIMID, diffident, shy, hesitant, uncertain, nervous, jittery, timorous, frightened, scared, anxious, apprehensive.
— OPPOSITES: steady, confident.

trench ▶ noun DITCH, channel, trough, excavation, furrow, rut, conduit, cut, drain, duct, waterway, watercourse; entrenchment, moat; *Archaeology* fosse.

trenchant ▶ adjective INCISIVE, penetrating, sharp, keen, insightful, acute, focused, shrewd, razor-sharp; piercing; vigorous, forceful, strong, potent, telling, emphatic, forthright; mordant, cutting, biting, acerbic, pungent.
— OPPOSITES: vague.

trend ▶ noun **1** *an upward trend in unemployment* TENDENCY, movement, drift, swing, shift, course, current, direction, progression, inclination, leaning; bias, bent. **2** *the latest trend in dance music* FASHION, vogue, style, mode, craze, mania, rage; *informal* fad, thing, flavour of the month.
▶ verb *interest rates are trending up* MOVE, go, head, drift, gravitate, swing, shift, turn, incline, tend, lean, veer.

trendoid ▶ noun TREND-SETTER, slave to fashion, fashion victim, fop.
▶ adjective *See* TRENDY.

trendy ▶ adjective FASHIONABLE, in fashion, in vogue, popular, up to date, au courant, modern, all the rage, du jour, modish, à la mode, trend-setting; stylish, chic, designer; cool, funky, in, the in thing, hot, big, hip, now, happening, sharp, groovy, snazzy, with it, trendoid, tony.
— OPPOSITES: unfashionable.

trepidation ▶ noun FEAR, apprehension, dread, fearfulness, fright, agitation, anxiety, worry, nervousness, tension, misgivings, unease, uneasiness, foreboding, disquiet, dismay, consternation, alarm, panic; *informal* butterflies, jitteriness, the jitters, the creeps, the shivers, a cold sweat, the heebie-jeebies, the willies, the shakes, jim-jams, collywobbles, cold feet.
— OPPOSITES: equanimity, composure.

trespass ▶ verb **1** *there is no excuse for trespassing on railway property* INTRUDE ON, encroach on, enter without permission, invade. **2** *I must not trespass on your good nature* TAKE ADVANTAGE OF, impose on, play on, exploit, abuse; encroach on, infringe. **3** *(archaic) he would be the last among us to trespass* SIN, transgress, offend, do wrong, err, go astray, fall from grace, stray from the straight and narrow.
▶ noun **1** *his alleged trespass on private land* UNLAWFUL ENTRY, intrusion, encroachment, invasion. **2** *(archaic) he asked forgiveness for his trespasses* SIN, wrong, wrongdoing, transgression, crime, offence, misdeed, misdemeanour, error, lapse, fall from grace.

trespasser ▶ noun INTRUDER, interloper, unwelcome visitor, encroacher.

tresses ▶ plural noun HAIR, head of hair, mane, mop of hair, shock of hair, shag of hair; locks, curls, ringlets.

trial ▶ noun **1** *the trial is expected to last several weeks* COURT CASE, case, assize ✦, lawsuit, suit, hearing, inquiry, tribunal, litigation, (legal/judicial) proceedings, legal action; court martial; appeal, retrial. **2** *the product is undergoing clinical trials* TEST, tryout, experiment, pilot study; examination, check, assessment, evaluation, check, trial/test run, beta test, dry run. **3** *she could be a bit of a trial at times* NUISANCE, pest, irritant, problem, ordeal, inconvenience, plague, thorn in one's side, one's cross to bear; bore, pain, pain in the neck/backside/ butt, headache, drag, bother, nightmare, albatross; nudnik, burr under/in someone's saddle. **4** *a long account of her trials and tribulations* TROUBLE, anxiety, worry, burden, affliction, ordeal, tribulation, adversity, hardship, trying time, tragedy, trauma, setback, difficulty, problem, misfortune, bad luck, mishap, hiccup, misadventure; *informal* hassle; *literary* travails.
▶ adjective *a three-month trial period* TEST, experimental, pilot, exploratory, probationary, provisional.

tribalism ▶ noun SECTARIANISM, chauvinism; esprit de corps.

tribe ▶ noun ETHNIC GROUP, people, band, nation; family, dynasty, house, clan, sept.

tribulation ▶ noun **1** *the tribulations of her personal life* TROUBLE, difficulty, problem, worry, hassle, anxiety, burden, cross to bear, ordeal, trial, adversity, hardship, tragedy, sorrow, trauma, affliction; setback, blow. **2** *his time of tribulation was just beginning* SUFFERING, distress, trouble, misery, wretchedness, unhappiness, sadness, heartache, woe, grief, sorrow, pain, anguish, agony; *literary* travail.

tribunal ▶ noun ARBITRATION BOARD/PANEL, board, panel, committee, jury, forum; COURT, court of justice, court of law, law court.

tributary ▶ noun HEADWATER, creek, branch, fork, feeder, side stream, side channel, snye ✦.

tribute ▶ noun **1** *tributes flooded in from friends and colleagues* ACCOLADE, praise, commendation, salute, testimonial, homage, eulogy, paean, panegyric; congratulations, compliments, plaudits, appreciation; gift, present, offering; bouquet; *formal* encomium. **2** *it is a tribute to his courage that he ever played again* TESTIMONY, indication, manifestation, testament, evidence, proof, attestation.
− OPPOSITES: criticism, condemnation.
■ **pay tribute to** PRAISE, sing the praises of, speak highly of, commend, acclaim, tip one's hat to, applaud, salute, honour, show appreciation of, recognize, acknowledge, pay homage to, extol; *formal* laud.

trice
■ **in a trice** VERY SOON, in a moment/second/instant, shortly, ASAP, pronto, any minute (now), in a short time, in (less than) no time, in a flash, before you know it, before long; momentarily, anon, forthwith, in a jiffy, in the twinkling of an eye, in two shakes (of a lamb's tail), in a snap, directly.

trick ▶ noun **1** *he's capable of any mean trick* STRATAGEM, ploy, ruse, scheme, device, manoeuvre, contrivance, machination, artifice, wile, dodge; deceit, deception,

trickery, subterfuge, shenanigan, chicanery, swindle, hoax, fraud, confidence trick, con (trick), set-up, rip-off, game, scam, sting, flim-flam, bunco. **2** *I think she's playing a trick on us* PRACTICAL JOKE, joke, prank, jape, spoof, gag, put-on. **3** *conjuring tricks* FEAT, stunt; **(tricks)** SLEIGHT OF HAND, legerdemain, prestidigitation; magic. **4** *it was probably a trick of the light* ILLUSION, optical illusion, figment of the imagination; mirage. **5** *the tricks of the trade* KNACK, art, skill, technique; secret, short cut.
▶ verb *many people have been tricked by con artists with false identity cards* DECEIVE, delude, hoodwink, mislead, take in, dupe, fool, double-cross, cheat, defraud, swindle, catch out, gull, hoax, bamboozle, con, diddle, rook, put one over on, pull a fast one on, pull the wool over someone's eyes, take for a ride, shanghai, shaft, flim-flam, sucker, snooker; *literary* cozen.
■ **do the trick** *(informal)* BE EFFECTIVE, work, solve the problem, fill/fit the bill.
■ **trick or treat!** *(Prairies)* Halloween apples! ✦

trickery ▶ noun DECEPTION, deceit, dishonesty, cheating, duplicity, double-dealing, legerdemain, sleight of hand, guile, craftiness, deviousness, subterfuge, skulduggery, chicanery, fraud, fraudulence, swindling; *formal* pettifoggery; *informal* monkey business, funny business.
− OPPOSITES: honesty.

trickle ▶ verb *blood was trickling from two cuts in his lip* DRIP, dribble, ooze, leak, seep, percolate, spill.
− OPPOSITES: pour, gush.
▶ noun *trickles of water* DRIBBLE, drip, thin stream, rivulet.

trickster ▶ noun SWINDLER, cheat, fraud, fraudster; charlatan, mountebank, quack, imposter, sham, hoaxer; rogue, villain, shyster, scoundrel, con man, shark, flim-flammer, grifter, grafter, scam artist, bunco artist.

tricky ▶ adjective **1** *a tricky situation* DIFFICULT, awkward, problematic, delicate, ticklish, sensitive, embarrassing, touchy; risky, uncertain, precarious, touch-and-go; thorny, knotty, sticky, dicey. **2** *a tricky and unscrupulous politician* CUNNING, crafty, wily, guileful, artful, devious, sly, scheming, calculating, designing, sharp, shrewd, astute, canny; duplicitous, dishonest, deceitful.
− OPPOSITES: straightforward, honest.

tried and true ▶ adjective RELIABLE, dependable, trustworthy, trusted, certain, sure; proven, tested, tried and tested, established, traditional, good old-fashioned, fail-safe; reputable.

trifle ▶ noun **1** *we needn't bother the principal over such trifles* UNIMPORTANT THING, trivial thing, triviality, thing of no importance/consequence, bagatelle, inessential, nothing; technicality, non-issue; trinket, knick-knack, gimcrack, gewgaw, toy; **(trifles)** trivia, minutiae, flummery, small potatoes. **2** *he bought it for a trifle* NEXT TO NOTHING, very small amount; pittance; *informal* peanuts, chump change.
■ **a trifle** A LITTLE, a bit, somewhat, a touch, a mite, a whit; *informal* a tad, a titch.
■ **trifle with** PLAY WITH, amuse oneself with, toy with, dally with, be flippant with, flirt with, play fast and loose with, mess about with; *dated* sport with.

trifling ▶ adjective TRIVIAL, unimportant, insignificant, inconsequential, petty, minor, of little/ no account, of little/no consequence, footling, pettifogging, incidental, silly, idle, insipid, superficial, small, tiny, inconsiderable, nominal, negligible, nugatory; *informal* piddling; *formal* exiguous.

— OPPOSITES: important.

trigger ▶ verb **1** *the incident triggered an acrimonious debate* PRECIPITATE, prompt, elicit, trigger off, set off, spark (off), touch off, provoke, stir up; cause, give rise to, launch, lead to, set in motion, occasion, bring about, generate, engender, begin, start, initiate; *literary* enkindle. **2** *thieves triggered the alarm* ACTIVATE, set off, set going, trip.

trill ▶ verb WARBLE, sing, chirp, chirrup, tweet, twitter, cheep, peep.

trim ▶ verb **1** *his hair had been washed and trimmed* CUT, crop, bob, shorten, clip, snip, shear, barber; neaten, shape, tidy up. **2** *trim off the lower leaves using a sharp knife* CUT OFF, remove, take off, chop off, lop off; prune. **3** *production costs need to be trimmed* REDUCE, decrease, cut down, cut back on, scale down, prune, slim down, pare down, dock. **4** *the story was severely trimmed for the movie version* SHORTEN, abridge, condense, abbreviate, telescope, truncate. **5** *a pair of black leather gloves trimmed with fake fur* DECORATE, adorn, ornament, embellish; edge, pipe, border, hem, fringe.

▶ noun **1** *white curtains with a tasteful blue trim* DECORATION, trimming, ornamentation, adornment; embellishment; border, edging, piping, rickrack, hem, fringe, frill, frippery. **2** *an unruly mop in need of a trim* HAIRCUT, cut, barbering, clip, snip; pruning, tidying up.

▶ adjective **1** *a trim little villa* NEAT, tidy, neat and tidy, orderly, in (good) order, uncluttered, well-kept, well-maintained, shipshape, spruce, in apple-pie order, immaculate, spic and span. **2** *she does Pilates to stay trim* SLIM, in shape, slender, lean, sleek, willowy, lissome, svelte; streamlined.

— OPPOSITES: untidy, messy.

trimming ▶ noun **1** *a black dress with lace trimming.* See TRIM. noun sense 1. **2** *roast turkey with all the trimmings* ACCOMPANIMENTS, extras, frills, fixings, accessories, accoutrements, trappings, paraphernalia; garnishing, garnish.

trinket ▶ noun KNICK-KNACK, bauble, ornament, bibelot, curio, trifle, toy, novelty, doohickey, gimcrack, gewgaw, tchotchke; kickshaw, whim-wham.

trio ▶ noun THREESOME, triumvirate, triad, trinity, troika; triplets.

trip ▶ verb **1** *he tripped on the loose stones* STUMBLE, lose one's footing, catch one's foot, slip, lose one's balance, fall (down), tumble, topple, take a spill, wipe out. **2** *students often trip up by forgetting to add a bibliography* MAKE A MISTAKE, miscalculate, make a blunder, blunder, go wrong, make an error, err; *informal* slip up, screw up, make a boo-boo, goof up, mess up, fluff. **3** *the question was intended to trip him up* CATCH OUT, trick, outwit, outsmart; throw off balance, disconcert, unsettle, discountenance, discomfit, throw, wrong-foot. **4** *they tripped merrily along the path* SKIP, run, dance, prance, bound, spring, scamper. **5** *Hoffman tripped the alarm* SET OFF, activate, trigger; turn on.

▶ noun **1** *a trip to Winnipeg* EXCURSION, outing, jaunt, HOLIDAY, visit, tour, journey, expedition, voyage; drive, run, day out, day trip, road trip, cruise, junket, spin; peregrination. **2** *trips and falls cause nearly half such accidents* STUMBLE, slip, misstep, false step; fall, tumble, spill.

triple ▶ adjective **1** *a triple alliance* THREE-WAY,

tripartite; threefold. **2** *they paid her triple the standard fee* THREE TIMES, treble.

tripper ▶ noun EXPLORER, canoe tripper, day tripper, traveller, visitor, vacationer, holidaymaker.

trite ▶ adjective BANAL, hackneyed, clichéd, platitudinous, vapid, commonplace, stock, conventional, stereotyped, overused, overdone, overworked, stale, worn out, time-worn, tired, hoary, hack, unimaginative, unoriginal, uninteresting, dull; *informal* old hat, corny, cornball, cheesy, boilerplate.

— OPPOSITES: original, imaginative.

triumph ▶ noun **1** *Gretzky's many triumphs* VICTORY, win, conquest, success; achievement, feat, accomplishment. **2** *his eyes shone with triumph* JUBILATION, exultation, elation, delight, joy, happiness, glee, pride, satisfaction. **3** *a triumph of Frontier ingenuity* TOUR DE FORCE, masterpiece, coup, wonder, sensation, master stroke, feat.

— OPPOSITES: defeat, disappointment.

▶ verb **1** *she triumphed in the tournament* WIN, succeed, come first, clinch first place, be victorious, carry the day, prevail, take the honours, come out on top. **2** *they had no chance of triumphing over the Francophone majority* DEFEAT, beat, conquer, trounce, vanquish, overcome, overpower, overwhelm, get the better of; bring someone to their knees, prevail against, subdue, subjugate; *informal* lick, best.

— OPPOSITES: lose.

triumphant ▶ adjective **1** *the triumphant Canadian team* VICTORIOUS, successful, winning, conquering, all-conquering; undefeated, unbeaten. **2** *a triumphant expression* JUBILANT, exultant, elated, rejoicing, joyful, joyous, delighted, gleeful, proud, gloating.

— OPPOSITES: unsuccessful, despondent.

trivia ▶ plural noun MINUTIAE, minor details, niceties, technicalities, trivialities, trifles, trumpery, non-essentials, ephemera, small potatoes, peanuts.

trivial ▶ adjective **1** *trivial problems* UNIMPORTANT, banal, trite, commonplace, insignificant, inconsequential, minor, of no account, of no consequence, of no importance; incidental, inessential, non-essential, petty, trifling, trumpery, pettifogging, footling, small, slight, little, inconsiderable, negligible, paltry, nugatory, piddling, picayune, nickel-and-dime, penny-ante; *proprietary* Mickey Mouse. **2** *I used to be quite a trivial person* FRIVOLOUS, superficial, shallow, unthinking, airheaded, feather-brained, lightweight, foolish, silly, trite.

— OPPOSITES: important, significant, serious.

triviality ▶ noun **1** *the triviality of the subject matter* UNIMPORTANCE, insignificance, inconsequence, inconsequentiality, pettiness, banality. **2** *he need not concern himself with such trivialities* MINOR DETAIL, minutiae, thing of no importance/consequence, trifle, non-essential, nothing; technicality; (**trivialities**) trivia.

trivialize ▶ verb TREAT AS UNIMPORTANT, minimize, play down, underestimate, make light of, treat lightly, dismiss, underplay, downplay, diminish, belittle; pooh-pooh.

troll ▶ noun GOBLIN, hobgoblin, gnome, demon, monster, bugaboo, ogre. *See also table at* MONSTER.

troops ▶ plural noun *Canadian troops were stationed here* SOLDIERS, armed forces, servicemen, servicewomen, infantry, peacekeepers, blue helmets; guards, escorts; the services, the army, the military.

▶ verb *we trooped out of the hall* WALK, march, file,

proceed; flock, crowd, throng, stream, swarm, surge, spill.

trophy ▸ noun **1** *a swimming trophy* CUP, medal, pennant; prize, award. **2** *a cabinet full of trophies from his travels* SOUVENIR, memento, keepsake; spoils, booty.

tropical ▸ adjective *tropical weather* VERY HOT, sweltering, boiling, scorching, humid, sultry, steamy, sticky, oppressive, stifling, suffocating, heavy, equatorial.
– OPPOSITES: cold, arctic.

trot ▸ verb *Trigger trotted across the patio* RUN, jog, jogtrot, dogtrot; scuttle, scurry, bustle, scamper.
■ **trot something out** RECITE, repeat, regurgitate, rattle off, churn out; come out with, produce.

troubadour ▸ noun (*historical*) MINSTREL, singer, balladeer, poet, bard; *historical* jongleur.

trouble ▸ noun **1** *you've caused enough trouble already* PROBLEMS, difficulty, bother, inconvenience, worry, concern, anxiety, distress, stress, strife, agitation, harassment, hassle, unpleasantness. **2** *she poured out all her troubles* PROBLEM, misfortune, difficulty, trial, tribulation, trauma, burden, pain, woe, grief, heartache, misery, affliction, vexation, suffering. **3** *he's gone to a lot of trouble to help you* EFFORT, inconvenience, fuss, bother, exertion, work, labour; pains, care, attention, thought. **4** *Rodney has been no trouble at all* NUISANCE, bother, inconvenience, irritation, irritant, problem, trial, pest, thorn in someone's flesh/side, headache, pain, pain in the neck/backside, drag; *informal* pain in the butt, burr in/under someone's saddle, nudnik. **5** *you're too gullible, that's your trouble* SHORTCOMING, flaw, weakness, weak point, failing, fault, imperfection, defect, blemish; problem, difficulty. **6** *he had a history of heart trouble* DISEASE, illness, sickness, ailments, complaints, problems; disorder, disability. **7** *the crash was due to engine trouble* MALFUNCTION, dysfunction, failure, breakdown. **8** *a game marred by serious crowd trouble* DISTURBANCE, disorder, unrest, unruliness, fighting, fracas, breach of the peace.
▸ verb **1** *this matter had been troubling her for some time* WORRY, bother, concern, disturb, upset, agitate, distress, perturb, annoy, irritate, vex, irk, nag, niggle, prey on someone's mind, weigh down, burden, bug. **2** *he was troubled by bouts of ill health* BE AFFLICTED BY, be burdened with; suffer from, be cursed with, be plagued by. **3** *there is nothing you need trouble about* WORRY, upset oneself, fret, be anxious, be concerned, concern oneself. **4** *don't trouble to see me out* BOTHER, take the trouble, go to the trouble, exert oneself, go out of one's way. **5** *I'm sorry to trouble you* INCONVENIENCE, bother, impose on, disturb, put out, pester, hassle; *formal* discommode.
■ **in trouble** IN DIFFICULTY, in difficulties, in a mess, in a bad way, in a predicament, in a fix, in a pickle, in dire straits, in a tight corner/spot, in a hole, in hot water, in the soup, up against it, toast.

troubled ▸ adjective **1** *Joanna looked troubled* ANXIOUS, worried, concerned, perturbed, disturbed, bothered, ill at ease, uneasy, unsettled, agitated; distressed, upset, dismayed, hag-ridden, haunted. **2** *we live in troubled times* DIFFICULT, problematic, full of problems, unsettled, hard, tough, stressful, dark.

troublemaker ▸ noun RABBLE-ROUSER, rogue, scourge, agitator, agent provocateur, ringleader; incendiary, firebrand, demagogue; scandalmonger, gossipmonger, meddler, nuisance, mischief-maker; hellraiser; *informal* badass.

troubleshooting ▸ noun FIXING, problem-solving, repairing, debugging, technical support; crisis management.

troublesome ▸ adjective **1** *a troublesome problem* ANNOYING, irritating, exasperating, maddening, infuriating, irksome, pesky, vexatious, vexing, bothersome, nettlesome, tiresome, worrying, worrisome, disturbing, upsetting, niggling, nagging; difficult, awkward, problematic, taxing; *informal* aggravating. **2** *a troublesome child* DIFFICULT, awkward, trying, demanding, uncooperative, rebellious, unmanageable, unruly, obstreperous, disruptive, badly behaved, disobedient, naughty, recalcitrant; *formal* refractory.
– OPPOSITES: simple, co-operative.

trough ▸ noun **1** *a large feeding trough* MANGER, feeder, bunk, rack, crib, feed box; waterer. **2** *a thirty-metre trough* CHANNEL, conduit, trench, ditch, gully, drain, culvert, cut, flume, gutter; eavestrough ♣, rain gutter.

trounce ▸ verb DEFEAT CONVINCINGLY, beat hollow, rout, crush, overwhelm; *informal* hammer, clobber, thrash, whip, drub, shellac, cream, skunk, pulverize, massacre, crucify, demolish, destroy, blow away, annihilate, make mincemeat of, wipe the floor with, walk over, murder.

troupe ▸ noun GROUP, company, band, ensemble, set; cast.

trousers See PANTS.

truancy ▸ noun ABSENTEEISM, non-attendance, playing truant, truanting, playing hooky, skipping.

truant ▸ noun ABSENTEE, runaway.
■ **play truant** skip school, skip, (*Ont.*) skip off ♣, (*West*) skip out ♣, stay away from school, play hooky.

truce ▸ noun CEASEFIRE, armistice, suspension of hostilities, peace, entente; respite, lull; *informal* let-up.

truck ▸ noun *a heavily laden truck* RIG, eighteen-wheeler, transport (truck), tractor-trailer, flatbed; pickup, van.

trucker ▸ noun TRUCK DRIVER, teamster.

truckle ▸ verb *an ambitious woman who truckled to no man* KOWTOW, submit, defer, yield, back down, bow and scrape, be obsequious, be subordinate, pander, toady, prostrate oneself, grovel; dance attendance on, curry favour with, ingratiate oneself with; *informal* suck up to, crawl, lick someone's boots.

truculent ▸ adjective DEFIANT, aggressive, antagonistic, combative, belligerent, pugnacious, confrontational, ready for a fight, obstreperous, argumentative, quarrelsome, uncooperative; bad-tempered, ornery, short-tempered, cross, snappish, cranky; feisty, spoiling for a fight.
– OPPOSITES: co-operative, amiable.

trudge ▸ verb PLOD, tramp, tromp, drag oneself, walk heavily/slowly, plow, slog, toil, trek, traipse, galumph.

true ▸ adjective **1** *you'll see that what I say is true* CORRECT, accurate, right, verifiable, in accordance with the facts, what actually/really happened, well-documented, the case, so; literal, factual, unelaborated, unvarnished. **2** *people are still willing to pay for true craftsmanship* GENUINE, authentic, real, actual, bona fide, proper; honest-to-goodness, kosher, legit, pukka, the real McCoy. **3** *the true owner of the goods* RIGHTFUL, legitimate, legal, lawful, authorized, bona fide, de jure. **4** *the necessity for true repentance* SINCERE, genuine, real, unfeigned, heartfelt, hearty, from the heart. **5** *a true friend* LOYAL,

faithful, constant, devoted, staunch, steadfast, true-blue, unswerving, unwavering; trustworthy, trusty, reliable, dependable. **6** *a true reflection of life in the 50s* ACCURATE, true to life, faithful, telling it like it is, fact-based, realistic, close, lifelike.
— OPPOSITES: untrue, false, disloyal, inaccurate.

true-blue ▶ adjective STAUNCH, loyal, faithful, stalwart, committed, card-carrying, confirmed, dyed-in-the-wool, devoted, dedicated, firm, steadfast, unswerving, unwavering, unfaltering.

truism ▶ noun PLATITUDE, commonplace, cliché, stock phrase, banality, old chestnut, old saw, bromide.

truly ▶ adverb **1** *tell me truly what you want* TRUTHFULLY, honestly, frankly, sincerely, candidly, openly, to someone's face, laying one's cards on the table; *informal* pulling no punches. **2** *I'm truly grateful to them* SINCERELY, genuinely, really, indeed, from the bottom of one's heart, heartily, profoundly; very, surely, extremely, immensely, thoroughly, positively, completely, tremendously, totally, incredibly, awfully; *formal* most; *informal* sure. **3** *this is truly a miracle* WITHOUT (A) DOUBT, unquestionably, undoubtedly, certainly, surely, definitely, beyond doubt/question, indubitably, undeniably, beyond the shadow of a doubt; in truth, really, in reality, actually, in fact; *archaic* forsooth, verily. **4** *exams do not truly reflect children's ability* ACCURATELY, correctly, exactly, precisely, faithfully; *informal* to a T.

trump ▶ verb *by wearing the simplest of dresses, she had trumped them all* OUTSHINE, outclass, upstage, put in the shade, eclipse, surpass, outdo, outperform; beat, better, top, cap; *informal* be a cut above, be head and shoulders above, leave standing.

trumped-up ▶ adjective BOGUS, spurious, specious, false, fabricated, invented, manufactured, contrived, made-up, falsified, fake, factitious; *informal* phony, cooked-up.
— OPPOSITES: genuine.

trumpet ▶ verb **1** *the elephant trumpeted* call out, bellow, roar, yell, cry out, toot, bugle, holler. **2** *companies trumpeted their success* PROCLAIM, announce, declare, herald, celebrate, shout from the rooftops.

truncate ▶ verb SHORTEN, cut, cut short, curtail, bring to an untimely end; abbreviate, condense, reduce, prune.
— OPPOSITES: lengthen, extend.

truncheon ▶ noun See BLUDGEON noun.

trunk ▶ noun **1** *the trunk of a tree* MAIN STEM, bole. **2** *the trunk of her car* LUGGAGE COMPARTMENT, back. **3** *his powerful trunk* TORSO, body, upper body. **4** *an elephant's trunk* PROBOSCIS, nose, snout. **5** *a steamer trunk* CHEST, box, crate, coffer; case.

truss ▶ noun SUPPORT, buttress, joist, brace, beam, prop, strut, stay, stanchion, pier.
▶ verb TIE UP, bind, chain up; pinion, fetter, tether, secure; swaddle, wrap.

trust ▶ noun **1** *good relationships are built on trust* CONFIDENCE, belief, faith, certainty, assurance, conviction, credence; reliance. **2** *a position of trust* RESPONSIBILITY, duty, obligation. **3** *the money is to be held in trust for his son* SAFEKEEPING, protection, charge, care, custody; trusteeship.
— OPPOSITES: distrust, mistrust, doubt.

▶ verb **1** *I should never have trusted her* PUT ONE'S TRUST IN, have faith in, have (every) confidence in, believe in, pin one's hopes/faith on, confide in. **2** *he can be trusted to carry out an impartial investigation* RELY ON, depend

on, bank on, count on, be sure of. **3** *I trust we shall meet again* HOPE, expect, take it, assume, presume, suppose. **4** *they don't like to trust their money to anyone outside the family* ENTRUST, consign, commit, give, hand over, turn over, assign.
— OPPOSITES: distrust, mistrust, doubt.

trustee ▶ noun ADMINISTRATOR, agent; custodian, keeper, steward, depositary; executor, executrix; board member; *Law* fiduciary.

trusting ▶ adjective TRUSTFUL, unsuspecting, unquestioning, unguarded, unwary; naive, innocent, childlike, ingenuous, wide-eyed, credulous, gullible, easily taken in.
— OPPOSITES: distrustful, suspicious.

trustworthy ▶ adjective RELIABLE, dependable, honest, honourable, upright, principled, true, truthful, as good as one's word, ethical, virtuous, incorruptible, unimpeachable, above suspicion; responsible, sensible, level-headed; loyal, faithful, staunch, steadfast, trusty; safe, sound, reputable, discreet; *informal* on the level, straight-up.
— OPPOSITES: unreliable.

trusty ▶ adjective RELIABLE, dependable, trustworthy, unfailing, fail-safe, trusted, tried and true; loyal, faithful, true, staunch, steadfast, constant, unswerving, unwavering.
— OPPOSITES: unreliable.

truth ▶ noun **1** *he doubted the truth of her statement* VERACITY, truthfulness, verity, sincerity, candour, honesty; accuracy, correctness, validity, factuality, authenticity. **2** *it's the truth, I swear* WHAT ACTUALLY HAPPENED, the case, so; gospel (truth), the honest truth. **3** *truth is stranger than fiction* FACT(S), reality, real life, actuality. **4** *scientific truths* FACT, verity, certainty, certitude; law, principle.
— OPPOSITES: lies, fiction, falsehood.

■ **in truth** IN (ACTUAL) FACT, as it happens, in point of fact, in reality, really, actually, to tell the truth, if truth be told.

truthful ▶ adjective **1** *truthful behaviour* HONEST, sincere, trustworthy, genuine; candid, frank, straight-shooting, open, forthright, straight, upfront, on the level, on the up and up. **2** *a truthful account* TRUE, accurate, correct, factual, faithful, reliable; unvarnished, unembellished, unidealized; *formal* veracious, veridical.
— OPPOSITES: deceitful, untrue.

try ▶ verb **1** *try to help him* ATTEMPT, endeavour, venture, make an effort, exert oneself, strive, do one's best, do one's utmost, move heaven and earth; undertake, aim, take it upon oneself, have a go, give it one's best shot, bend over backwards, bust a gut, do one's damnedest, pull out all the stops, go all out, knock oneself out; *formal* essay. **2** *try it and see what you think* TEST, put to the test, sample, taste, inspect, investigate, examine, appraise, evaluate, assess; *informal* check out, give something a whirl, test drive. **3** *Mary tried everyone's patience* TAX, strain, test, stretch, sap, drain, exhaust, wear out. **4** *the case is to be tried by a jury* ADJUDICATE, consider, hear, adjudge, examine.
▶ noun *I'll have one last try* ATTEMPT, effort, endeavour; *informal* go, shot, crack, stab; *formal* essay.

■ **try something out** TEST, trial, experiment with, pilot; put through its paces; assess, evaluate.

trying ▶ adjective **1** *a trying day* STRESSFUL, taxing, demanding, difficult, tough, hard, pressured, frustrating, fraught; arduous, gruelling, tiring, exhausting; *informal* hellish. **2** *Steve was very trying* ANNOYING, irritating, exasperating, maddening,

infuriating; tiresome, irksome, troublesome, bothersome, vexing; *informal* aggravating.
— OPPOSITES: easy, accommodating.

tryout ▶ noun TRIAL, mini-camp, training camp, audition, test.

tryst ▶ noun MEETING, rendezvous, date, appointment, assignation; love affair.

tub ▶ noun **1** *a wooden tub* CONTAINER, barrel, cask, drum, keg. **2** *a tub of yogourt* POT, carton. **3** *a soak in the tub* BATH, bathtub; hot tub, Jacuzzi.

tubby *See* CHUBBY.

tube ▶ noun CYLINDER, pipe, piping, conduit, line, flue, hose, cannula, catheter, siphon, pipette, funnel, duct, pipeline, *North* utilidor ♣, drain.

tuck ▶ verb **1** *he tucked his shirt into his pants* PUSH, insert, slip, fold; thrust, stuff, stick, cram. **2** *the dress was tucked all over* PLEAT, gather, fold, ruffle. **3** *he tucked the knife behind his seat* HIDE, conceal, secrete; store, stow, stash.
▶ noun *a dress with tucks* PLEAT, gather, fold, ruffle.
■ **tuck someone in** MAKE COMFORTABLE, settle down, cover up; put to bed.
■ **tuck in** EAT HEARTILY, devour, consume, munch, gobble up, wolf down; *informal* dispose of, polish off, put away, scarf (down/up).

tuft ▶ noun CLUMP, bunch, knot, cluster, tussock, tuffet; lock, wisp; crest, topknot; tassel.

tug ▶ verb **1** *Ben tugged at her sleeve* PULL, pluck, tweak, twitch, jerk, wrench; catch hold of, yank. **2** *she tugged him towards the door* DRAG, pull, lug, draw, haul, heave, tow.
▶ noun *one good tug would loosen it* PULL, jerk, wrench, heave, yank.

tug-of-war ▶ noun STRUGGLE, battle, conflict, fight, altercation, duel, tussle, wrangle, dispute, rivalry.

tuition ▶ noun **1** *students go broke paying the increased tuition* FEES, charges, bill. **2** *her skill improved with tuition* INSTRUCTION, teaching, coaching, tutoring, tutelage, lessons, education, schooling; training, drill, preparation, guidance.

tumble ▶ verb **1** *he tumbled over* FALL (OVER/DOWN), topple over, lose one's balance, keel over, take a spill, go headlong, go head over heels, trip (up), stumble; *informal* come a cropper. **2** *they all tumbled from the room* HURRY, rush, scramble, scurry, bound, pile, bundle. **3** *a creek tumbled over the rocks* CASCADE, fall, flow, pour, spill, stream. **4** *oil prices tumbled* PLUMMET, plunge, fall, dive, nosedive, drop, slump, slide, decrease, decline, crash.
— OPPOSITES: rise.
▶ noun **1** *I took a tumble in the nettles* FALL, trip, spill; *informal* nosedive. **2** *a tumble in share prices* DROP, fall, plunge, dive, nosedive, slump, decline, *informal* toboggan slide ♣, collapse, crash.
— OPPOSITES: rise.

tumbledown ▶ adjective DILAPIDATED, ramshackle, decrepit, neglected, beat-up, run down, falling to pieces, decaying, derelict, crumbling; rickety, shaky, shacky.

tummy ▶ noun (*informal*) STOMACH, abdomen, belly, gut, middle, midriff, paunch, breadbasket; *informal* insides.

tummy tuck ▶ noun COSMETIC SURGERY, plastic surgery.

tumour ▶ noun CANCEROUS GROWTH, malignant growth, cancer, malignancy; lump, growth, swelling, fibroid; *Medicine* carcinoma, sarcoma.
— RELATED TERMS: onco-, -oma.

tumult ▶ noun **1** *she added her voice to the tumult* CLAMOUR, din, noise, racket, uproar, hue and cry, commotion, ruckus, maelstrom, rumpus, hubbub, pandemonium, babel, bedlam, brouhaha, furor, fracas, melee, frenzy; *informal* hullabaloo. **2** *years of political tumult* TURMOIL, confusion, disorder, disarray, unrest, chaos, turbulence, mayhem, maelstrom, havoc, upheaval, ferment, agitation, trouble.
— OPPOSITES: tranquility.

tumultuous ▶ adjective **1** *tumultuous applause* LOUD, deafening, thunderous, uproarious, noisy, clamorous, vociferous, vehement. **2** *a tumultuous crowd* DISORDERLY, unruly, rowdy, turbulent, boisterous, excited, agitated, restless, wild, riotous, frenzied.
— OPPOSITES: soft, orderly.

tundra ▶ noun the Barrens ♣, Barren lands ♣, Barren grounds ♣; fellfield.

tune ▶ noun *she hummed a cheerful tune* MELODY, air, strain, theme; song, jingle, ditty.
▶ verb **1** *they tuned their guitars* ADJUST, fine-tune, tune up. **2** *a body clock tuned to the lunar cycle* ATTUNE, adapt, adjust, fine-tune; regulate, modulate.
■ **change one's tune** CHANGE ONE'S MIND, do a U-turn, pull a U-ey, do a one-eighty, have a change of heart; do an about-face.
■ **in tune** IN ACCORD, in keeping, in accordance, in agreement, in harmony, in step, in line, in sympathy, compatible.
■ **tune up** TWEAK, adjust, fine-tune, calibrate, maintain, improve, ameliorate, enhance.

tuneful ▶ adjective MELODIOUS, melodic, musical, mellifluous, dulcet, euphonious, harmonious, lyrical, lilting, sweet.
— OPPOSITES: discordant.

tuneless ▶ adjective DISCORDANT, unmelodious, dissonant, harsh, cacophonous; monotonous, dull.
— OPPOSITES: melodious.

tune-up ▶ noun SERVICE, maintenance, repairs, fine-tuning, tweaking.

tunnel ▶ noun *a tunnel under the hills* UNDERGROUND PASSAGE, underpass, subway; shaft; burrow, hole; *historical* mine.
▶ verb *he tunnelled under the fence* DIG, burrow, mine, bore, drill.

tunnel vision ▶ noun NARROW FOCUS, concentration, fixation, narrow-mindedness, single-mindedness, closed-mindedness.

tuque ▶ noun See table at HAT.

turbid ▶ adjective MURKY, opaque, cloudy, unclear, muddy, thick, milky, roily.
— OPPOSITES: clear.

turbulent ▶ adjective **1** *the country's turbulent past* TEMPESTUOUS, stormy, unstable, unsettled, tumultuous, chaotic; violent, anarchic, lawless. **2** *turbulent seas* ROUGH, stormy, tempestuous, storm-tossed, heavy, violent, wild, roiling, raging, seething, choppy, agitated, boisterous.
— OPPOSITES: peaceful, calm.

turd ▶ noun STOOL, dung, scat, dropping; excrement, feces, fecal matter; *informal* poo, doo-doo.

turf ▶ noun **1** *they walked over a patch of turf* GRASS, lawn, sod. **2** *she was keen to protect her turf* TERRITORY, domain, province, preserve, sphere of influence; stomping ground; bailiwick.
■ **turf someone/something out** *See* EJECT sense 3.

turgid ▶ adjective **1** *his turgid prose* BOMBASTIC, pompous, overblown, inflated, tumid, high-flown,

puffed up, affected, pretentious, grandiose, florid, ornate, grandiloquent, orotund; *informal* highfalutin, purple. **2** *the tissues become turgid* SWOLLEN, distended, tumescent, engorged, bloated, tumid.
— OPPOSITES: simple.

turmoil ▶ noun *political turmoil* CONFUSION, upheaval, turbulence, tumult, disorder, disturbance, agitation, ferment, unrest, disquiet, trouble, disruption, chaos, mayhem; uncertainty.
— OPPOSITES: peace.

■ **in turmoil** CONFUSED, chaotic, in chaos, topsy-turvy, at sixes and sevens; reeling, disorientated; *informal* all over the place.

turn ▶ verb **1** *the wheels were still turning* GO AROUND, revolve, rotate, spin, roll, circle, wheel, whirl, twirl, gyrate, swivel, pivot. **2** *I turned and headed back* CHANGE DIRECTION, change course, make a U-turn, about-face, turn about/round, pull a U-ey, do a one-eighty. **3** *the car turned the corner* GO ROUND, round, negotiate, take. **4** *the path turned to right and left* BEND, curve, wind, veer, twist, meander, snake, zigzag. **5** *he turned his gun on Lenny* AIM AT, point at, level at, direct at, train on. **6** *he turned his ankle* SPRAIN, twist, wrench; hurt. **7** *their honeymoon turned into a nightmare* BECOME, develop into, turn out to be; be transformed into, metamorphose into, descend into, grow into. **8** *Emma turned red* BECOME, go, grow, get. **9** *he turned the house into apartments* CONVERT, change, transform, make; adapt, modify, rebuild, reconstruct. **10** *I've just turned forty* REACH, get to, become, hit. **11** *she turned to politics* TAKE UP, become involved in, go into, enter, undertake. **12** *we can now turn to another topic* MOVE ON TO, go on to, proceed to, consider, attend to, address; take up, switch to.
▶ noun **1** *a turn of the wheel* ROTATION, revolution, spin, whirl, gyration, swivel. **2** *a turn to the left* CHANGE OF DIRECTION, veer, divergence. **3** *we're approaching the turn* BEND, corner, turning, turnoff, junction, crossroads. **4** *you'll get your turn in a minute* OPPORTUNITY, chance, say; stint, time; try, go, shot, kick at the can/cat ♣, stab, crack. **5** *she did me some good turns* SERVICE, deed, act; favour, kindness.

■ **at every turn** REPEATEDLY, recurrently, all the time, always, constantly, again and again.

■ **in turn** ONE AFTER THE OTHER, one by one, one at a time, in succession, successively, sequentially.

■ **take a turn for the better** IMPROVE, pick up, look up, perk up, rally, turn the corner; recover, revive.

■ **take a turn for the worse** DETERIORATE, worsen, decline; *informal* go downhill.

■ **turn of events** DEVELOPMENT, incident, occurrence, happening, circumstance, surprise.

■ **turn against someone** BECOME HOSTILE TO, take a dislike to, betray, double-cross.

■ **turn someone away** SEND AWAY, reject, rebuff, repel, cold-shoulder; *informal* send packing.

■ **turn back** RETRACE ONE'S STEPS, go back, return; retreat.

■ **turn someone/something down 1** *his novel was turned down* REJECT, refuse, decline, spurn, rebuff. **2** *Pete turned the sound down* REDUCE, lower, decrease, lessen; muffle, mute.

■ **turn someone in** BETRAY, inform on, denounce, sell out, stab someone in the back; blow the whistle on, rat on, squeal on, finger.

■ **turn something in** HAND IN/OVER/BACK, give in, submit, surrender, give up; deliver, return.

■ **turn of mind** DISPOSITION, inclination, tendency, propensity, bias, bent.

■ **turn someone off** PUT OFF, leave cold, repel,

disgust, revolt, offend; disenchant, alienate; bore, gross out.

■ **turn something off** SWITCH OFF, shut off, turn out, flick off, extinguish, (*Nfld*) dout ♣, deactivate; *informal* kill, cut, power down.

■ **turn on** *the decision turned on the law* DEPEND ON, rest on, hinge on, be contingent on, be decided by.

■ **turn someone on** See AROUSE sense 3.

■ **turn someone on to** INTRODUCE SOMEONE TO, get someone into, pique someone's interest in.

■ **turn something on** SWITCH ON, start up, activate, trip, power up.

■ **turn on someone** ATTACK, set on, fall on, let fly at, lash out at, hit out at, round on; *informal* lay into, tear into, let someone have it, bite someone's head off, jump down someone's throat; light into.

■ **turn out 1** *a huge crowd turned out* COME, be present, attend, appear, turn up, arrive; assemble, gather, show up. **2** *it turned out that she had been abroad* TRANSPIRE, emerge, come to light, become apparent, become clear. **3** *things didn't turn out as I'd intended* HAPPEN, occur, come about; develop, proceed; work out, come out, end up, pan out, result; *formal* eventuate.

■ **turn someone out** THROW OUT, eject, evict, expel, oust, drum out, banish; *informal* kick out, send packing, boot out, show someone the door, turf out.

■ **turn something out 1** *turn out the light.* See TURN SOMETHING OFF. **2** *they turn out a million engines a year* PRODUCE, make, manufacture, fabricate, generate, put out, churn out.

■ **turn over** OVERTURN, upturn, capsize, keel over, flip, turn turtle, be upended, tip.

■ **turn something over 1** *I turned over a few pages* FLIP OVER, flick through, leaf through. **2** *she turned the proposal over in her mind* THINK ABOUT/OVER, consider, ponder, contemplate, reflect on, chew over, mull over, muse on, ruminate on. **3** *he turned over the business to his brother* TRANSFER, hand over, pass on, consign, commit.

■ **turn of phrase** EXPRESSION, idiom, phrase, term, word, aphorism.

■ **turn someone's stomach** NAUSEATE, sicken.

■ **turn to someone/something** SEEK HELP FROM, have recourse to, approach, apply to, appeal to; take to, resort to.

■ **turn up 1** *the missing documents turned up* BE FOUND, be discovered, be located, reappear. **2** *the police turned up* ARRIVE, appear, present oneself, show (up), show one's face. **3** *something better will turn up* PRESENT ITSELF, offer itself, occur, happen, crop up, appear.

■ **turn something up 1** *she turned up the volume* INCREASE, raise, amplify, intensify. **2** *they turned up lots of information* DISCOVER, uncover, unearth, find, dig up, ferret out, root out, expose.

turnaround ▶ noun REVERSAL, change, sea change, turnabout, volte-face, about-face, one-eighty.

turncoat ▶ noun TRAITOR, renegade, defector, deserter, betrayer, Judas; fifth columnist, quisling; *informal* rat, fink.

turning point ▶ noun CROSSROADS, critical moment, decisive moment, moment of truth, watershed, crisis, landmark.

turnoff ▶ noun **1** *I missed my turnoff* TURN, turning, exit, junction, off-ramp. **2** *narrow-mindedness is a real turnoff for me* PEEVE, bugbear, bête noire, anti-aphrodisiac, disincentive, no-no, blemish, gross-out.

turn-on ▶ noun ATTRACTION, aphrodisiac, thrill, stimulant, rush, inducement, incentive.

turnout ▶ noun ATTENDANCE, audience, crowd, gathering, showing, throng, assembly, assemblage, congregation, number; participation.

turnover ▶ noun **1** *an annual turnover of $2.25 million* (GROSS) REVENUE, income, yield; sales, gross. **2** *a high turnover of staff* rate of replacement, change, movement.

turpitude ▶ noun *(formal).* See DEPRAVITY.

tussle ▶ noun *his glasses were smashed in the tussle* SCUFFLE, fight, struggle, skirmish, brawl, scrum, rough-and-tumble, free-for-all, fracas, fray, rumpus, melee; dust-up, punch-up, bust-up, spat, scrap, tug-of-war.
▶ verb *demonstrators tussled with police* SCUFFLE, fight, struggle, brawl, grapple, wrestle, clash; *informal* scrap, roughhouse.

tutor ▶ noun *a history tutor* TEACHER, instructor, educator, lecturer, trainer, mentor; *formal* pedagogue.
▶ verb *he was tutored at home* TEACH, instruct, educate, school, coach, train, drill.

tutorial ▶ noun LESSON, class, seminar, training session; *Computing* wizard.

tuxedo ▶ noun FORMAL WEAR, penguin suit, monkey suit, tux.

TV ▶ noun *See* TELEVISION.

twaddle ▶ noun *(informal).* See NONSENSE sense 1.

tweak ▶ verb **1** *she tweaked his nose* PULL, jerk, tug, twist, twitch, pinch, squeeze. **2** *the product can be tweaked to suit your needs* ADJUST, modify, alter, change, adapt; refine.
▶ noun **1** *he gave her hair a tweak* PULL, jerk, tug, twist, pinch, twitch, squeeze. **2** *a few minor tweaks were required* ADJUSTMENT, modification, alteration, change; refinement.

twee ▶ adjective CUTESY, sickly sweet, dainty, pretty, quaint, cute; sentimental, precious, affected, pretentious.

tweet ▶ verb *See* CHIRP.

tweeze ▶ verb PINCH, tweezer, pluck, extract.

tweezers ▶ noun PINCERS, pliers, needle-nose pliers.

twelve ▶ cardinal number DOZEN.
— RELATED TERMS: duodecimal, dodeca-.

twenty ▶ cardinal number SCORE.
— RELATED TERMS: icos-.

twerp ▶ noun IDIOT, ass, halfwit, blockhead, jughead, dunce, dolt, ignoramus, simpleton; dope, ninny, nincompoop, chump, dim-wit, dim-bulb, dumbo, dummy, loon, dork, jackass, bonehead, knucklehead, fathead, numbskull, numbnuts, dumb-ass, doofus, dunderhead, lummox, thickhead, airhead, pinhead, lamebrain, cretin, moron, imbecile, pea-brain, birdbrain, jerk, nerd, donkey, nitwit, dipstick, twit, boob, schmuck, bozo, hoser ♣, turkey, chowderhead, dingbat.

twiddle ▶ verb *she twiddled the dials* TURN, twist, swivel, twirl; adjust, move, jiggle; fiddle with, play with.
■ **twiddle one's thumbs** BE IDLE, do nothing, kill time, waste time, futz around, hang around, stand/sit around.

twig ▶ noun *leafy twigs* STICK, sprig, shoot, stem, branchlet.
▶ verb *she twigged to the fact immediately* REALIZE, understand, figure out, grasp, comprehend, take in, fathom, see, notice, recognize; latch on to, cotton on

to, become conscious of, become aware of, get, get wise to.

twilight ▶ noun **1** *we arrived at twilight* DUSK, sunset, sundown, nightfall, evening, close of day, *(Nfld)* duckish ♣; *literary* eventide, gloaming. **2** *it was scarcely visible in the twilight* HALF-LIGHT, semi-darkness, gloom. **3** *the twilight of his career* DECLINE, waning, ebb; autumn, final years, tail end.
— OPPOSITES: dawn.
▶ adjective *a twilight world* SHADOWY, dark, shady, dim, gloomy, obscure, crepuscular, twilit.

twin ▶ noun *a sitting room that was the twin of her own* DUPLICATE, double, carbon-copy, exact likeness, mirror image, replica, look-alike, doppelgänger, clone; counterpart, match, pair; *informal* dead ringer, spitting image.
▶ adjective **1** *twin peaks* MATCHING, identical, matched, paired. **2** *the twin aims of conservation and recreation* TWOFOLD, double, dual; related, linked, connected; corresponding, parallel, complementary, equivalent.
▶ verb *the company twinned its brewing with distilling* COMBINE, join, link, couple, pair.

twine ▶ noun *a ball of twine* STRING, cord, thread, yarn; *(Nfld)* linnet ♣, binder twine, baler twine.
▶ verb **1** *she twined her arms around him* WIND, entwine, wrap, wreathe. **2** *ivy twined around the tree* ENTWINE ITSELF, coil, loop, twist, spiral, curl; weave, interlace, intertwine, braid.

twinge ▶ noun **1** *twinges in her stomach* PAIN, spasm, ache, throb; cramp, stitch. **2** *a twinge of guilt* PANG, prick, qualm, scruple, misgiving.

twinkle ▶ noun & verb GLITTER, sparkle, shine, glimmer, shimmer, glint, gleam, flicker, flash, wink; *literary* glister.

twinkling ▶ adjective SPARKLING, glistening, glittering, glimmering, glinting, gleaming, flickering, winking, shining, scintillating, lambent; *literary* coruscating.

twirl ▶ verb **1** *he twirled the gun around* SPIN, whirl, turn, pivot, swivel, twist, revolve, rotate. **2** *she twirled her hair around her finger* WIND, twist, coil, curl, wrap.
▶ noun *she did a quick twirl* PIROUETTE, spin, whirl, turn, twist, rotation, revolution, twizzle, gyration.

twist ▶ verb **1** *the impact twisted the chassis* CRUMPLE, crush, buckle, mangle, warp, deform, distort. **2** *her face twisted with rage* CONTORT, screw up. **3** *Ma anxiously twisted a handkerchief* WRING, squeeze. **4** *he twisted around in his seat* TURN (AROUND), swivel (around), spin (around), pivot, rotate, revolve. **5** *she twisted out of his grasp* WRIGGLE, squirm, worm one's way, wiggle. **6** *I twisted my ankle* SPRAIN, wrench, turn. **7** *you are twisting my words* DISTORT, misrepresent, change, alter, pervert, falsify, warp, skew, misinterpret, misconstrue, misstate, misquote; garble. **8** *he twisted the radio knob* TWIDDLE, adjust, turn, rotate, swivel. **9** *she twisted her hair round her finger* WIND, twirl, coil, curl, wrap. **10** *the wires were twisted together* INTERTWINE, twine, interlace, weave, plait, braid, coil, wind. **11** *the road twisted and turned* WIND, curve, turn, meander, weave, zigzag, swerve, snake.
▶ noun **1** *a twist of the wrist* TURN, twirl, spin, rotation; flick. **2** *the twists of the road* BEND, curve, turn, zigzag, kink. **3** *the twists of the plot* CONVOLUTION, complication, complexity, intricacy; surprise, revelation. **4** *a modern twist on an old theme* INTERPRETATION, slant, outlook, angle, approach, treatment; variation, change, difference.
■ **twist someone's arm** PRESSURIZE, coerce, force;

persuade; *informal* lean on, browbeat, strong-arm, bulldoze, railroad, put the screws on.

twisted ▶ **adjective 1** *twisted metal* CRUMPLED, bent, crushed, buckled, warped, misshapen, distorted, deformed. **2** *his twisted mind* PERVERTED, warped, deviant, depraved, corrupt, abnormal, unhealthy, aberrant, distorted, corrupted, debauched, debased, disturbed; *informal* sick, kinky.

twisty ▶ **adjective** WINDING, windy, twisting, bendy, zigzag, meandering, curving, sinuous, snaky.
— OPPOSITES: straight.

twit ▶ **noun** (*informal*). See FOOL *noun* sense 1.

twitch ▶ **verb** *he twitched and then lay still* JERK, convulse, have a spasm, quiver, tremble, shiver, shudder.
▶ **noun 1** *a twitch of her lips* SPASM, convulsion, quiver, tremor, shiver, shudder, small movement; tic. **2** *he gave a twitch at his moustache* PULL, tug, tweak, yank, jerk. **3** *he felt a twitch of annoyance* PANG, twinge, dart, stab, prick.

twitter ▶ **verb 1** *sparrows twittered under the eaves* CHIRP, chirrup, cheep, tweet, peep, chatter, trill, warble, sing. **2** *stop twittering about Francis* BLATHER, jabber, blabber, chatter, chitter, gabble, go on, blab, rattle, waffle, yap, prattle, natter, babble, blither, ramble, yak, quack, yabber, talk someone's ear off.
▶ **noun 1** *a bird's twitter* CHIRP, chirrup, cheep, tweet, peep, trill, warble, song. **2** *her non-stop twitter* PRATTLE, chatter, babble, talk, gabble, blabber, yakking, nattering.

two ▶ **cardinal number** PAIR, duo, duet, double, dyad, duplet, tandem; *archaic* twain.
— RELATED TERMS: binary, dual, bi-, di-, duo-.

two-faced ▶ **adjective** DECEITFUL, insincere, double-dealing, hypocritical, backstabbing, false, fickle, untrustworthy, duplicitous, deceiving, dissembling, dishonest; disloyal, treacherous, faithless, traitorous, cheating, lying, weaselly; *literary* perfidious.
— OPPOSITES: sincere.

twosome ▶ **noun** COUPLE, pair, duo.

two-timing ▶ **adjective** ADULTEROUS, unfaithful, fickle, untrue, unchaste, inconstant; cheating, philandering.

tycoon ▶ **noun** MAGNATE, mogul, industrialist, businessman, financier, entrepreneur, captain of industry, millionaire, multi-millionaire, merchant prince; *informal* big shot, bigwig, honcho, supremo, big wheel, kahuna; *derogatory* fat cat, robber baron.

tyke ▶ **noun** SMALL CHILD, infant, moppet, munchkin, tot, toddler, rug rat, terrible two, ankle-biter, young 'un.

type ▶ **noun 1** *a curate of the old-fashioned type* KIND, sort, variety, class, category, set, genre, species, order, breed, race; style, nature, manner, rank; generation, vintage; stamp, ilk, cast, grain, mould, stripe, brand, flavour. **2** *sporty types* PERSON, individual, character, sort. **3** *italic type* PRINT, font, typeface, face, characters, lettering, letters.

typecast ▶ **verb** LABEL, tag; characterize, style; stereotype, pigeonhole.

typhoon ▶ **noun** CYCLONE, tropical storm, storm, hurricane, twister, tornado, whirlwind.

typical ▶ **adjective 1** *a typical example of art deco* REPRESENTATIVE, classic, quintessential, archetypal, model, prototypical, stereotypical, paradigmatic. **2** *a fairly typical day* NORMAL, average, ordinary, standard, regular, routine, run-of-the-mill, conventional, unremarkable, unsurprising, unexceptional, blah. **3** *it's typical of him to forget* CHARACTERISTIC, in keeping, usual, normal, par for the course, predictable, true to form; customary, habitual.
— OPPOSITES: atypical, unusual, exceptional, uncharacteristic.

typify ▶ **verb** EPITOMIZE, exemplify, characterize, be representative of; personify, embody, be emblematic of.

tyrannical ▶ **adjective** DICTATORIAL, despotic, autocratic, oppressive, repressive, totalitarian, undemocratic, illiberal; authoritarian, high-handed, imperious, harsh, strict, iron-handed, iron-fisted, severe, cruel, brutal, ruthless.
— OPPOSITES: liberal.

tyrannize ▶ **verb** DOMINATE, dictate to, browbeat, intimidate, bully, lord it over; persecute, victimize, torment, terrorize; oppress, repress, crush, subjugate; *informal* push around.

tyranny ▶ **noun** DESPOTISM, absolute power, autocracy, dictatorship, totalitarianism, Fascism; oppression, repression, subjugation, enslavement; authoritarianism, bullying, severity, cruelty, brutality, ruthlessness.

tyrant ▶ **noun** DICTATOR, despot, autocrat, authoritarian, oppressor; slave-driver, martinet, bully, megalomaniac.

tyro ▶ **noun** NOVICE, beginner, learner, neophyte, newcomer, initiate, fledgling; apprentice, trainee, probationer, tenderfoot, rookie, newbie, greenhorn.
— OPPOSITES: veteran.

Uu

ubiquitous ▶ adjective OMNIPRESENT, ever-present, everywhere, all over the place, pervasive, universal, worldwide, global; rife, prevalent, far-reaching, inescapable.
— OPPOSITES: rare.

UFO ▶ noun FLYING SAUCER, alien spacecraft/spaceship, unidentified flying object.

ugly ▶ adjective **1** *an ugly face* UNATTRACTIVE, unappealing, unpleasant, hideous, unlovely, unprepossessing, unsightly, horrible, frightful, awful, ghastly, vile, revolting, repellent, repulsive, repugnant; grotesque, disgusting, monstrous, reptilian, misshapen, deformed, disfigured, plug-ugly, butt-ugly; homely, plain, not much to look at. **2** *things got pretty ugly* UNPLEASANT, nasty, disagreeable, alarming, tense, charged, serious, grave; dangerous, perilous, threatening, menacing, hostile, ominous, sinister. **3** *an ugly rumour* HORRIBLE, despicable, reprehensible, nasty, appalling, objectionable, offensive, obnoxious, vile, dishonourable, rotten, vicious, spiteful.
— OPPOSITES: beautiful, pleasant.

uh-oh ▶ exclamation YIKES, oh dear, cripes, mercy, holy moly, alas, dear me, {oh me, oh my}, whoops.

ulcer ▶ noun SORE, ulceration, abscess, boil, carbuncle, blister, gumboil, cyst; *Medicine* aphtha, chancre, furuncle.

ulterior ▶ adjective UNDERLYING, undisclosed, undivulged, concealed, hidden, covert, secret, personal, private, selfish.
— OPPOSITES: overt.

ultimate ▶ adjective **1** *the ultimate collapse of their empire* EVENTUAL, final, concluding, terminal, end; resulting, ensuing, consequent, subsequent. **2** *ultimate truths about civilization* FUNDAMENTAL, basic, primary, elementary, elemental, absolute, central, key, crucial, essential, pivotal. **3** *the ultimate gift for cat lovers* BEST, ideal, perfect, greatest, supreme, paramount, superlative, highest, utmost, optimum, quintessential.
▶ noun *the ultimate in bohemian chic* UTMOST, optimum, last word, height, epitome, peak, pinnacle, acme, zenith, nonpareil, dernier cri, ne plus ultra; *informal* the granddaddy, the bee's knees, the cat's pyjamas/whiskers/meow/ass, da bomb.

ultimately ▶ adverb **1** *the money will ultimately belong to us* EVENTUALLY, in the end, in the long run, at length, finally, sooner or later, in time, in the fullness of time, when all is said and done, one day, some day, sometime, over the long haul; *informal* when push comes to shove. **2** *two ultimately contradictory reasons* FUNDAMENTALLY, basically, primarily, essentially, at heart, deep down.

ultimatum ▶ noun FINAL OFFER, final demand, take-it-or-leave-it deal; threat.

ultra- ▶ combining form *an ultra-conservative view* EXTREMELY, uber-, exceedingly, excessively, immensely, especially, exceptionally; mega, mucho, majorly, oh-so, real.

ultrasound ▶ noun SONOGRAM, echocardiogram; tomography.

umbrage
■ **take umbrage** TAKE OFFENCE, take exception, be aggrieved, be affronted, be annoyed, be angry, be indignant, be put out, be insulted, be hurt, be piqued, be resentful, be disgruntled, go into a huff, be miffed, have one's nose put out of joint, chafe.

umbrella ▶ noun **1** *they huddled under the umbrella* PARASOL, sunshade. **2** *the groups worked under the umbrella of the Liberal Party* AEGIS, auspices, patronage, protection, guardianship, support, backing, agency, guidance, care, charge, responsibility, cover.

umpire ▶ noun *the umpire reversed his decision* REFEREE, linesman, adjudicator, arbitrator, judge, moderator, official; ref, ump.
▶ verb *he umpired a boat race* REFEREE, adjudicate, arbitrate, judge, moderate, oversee, officiate; *informal* ref, ump.

umpteen ▶ adjective See COUNTLESS.

unabashed ▶ adjective UNASHAMED, shameless, unembarrassed, brazen, audacious, blatant, flagrant, bold, barefaced, cocky, unrepentant, undaunted, unconcerned, fearless.
— OPPOSITES: sheepish.

unable ▶ adjective POWERLESS, impotent, at a loss, inadequate, incompetent, unfit, unqualified, incapable.

unabridged ▶ adjective COMPLETE, entire, whole, full-length, intact, uncut, unshortened, unexpurgated.

unacceptable ▶ adjective INTOLERABLE, insufferable, unsatisfactory, inadmissible, inappropriate, unsuitable, undesirable, unreasonable, insupportable; offensive, obnoxious, disagreeable, disgraceful, deplorable, beyond the pale, bad; a bit much, too much, not on.
— OPPOSITES: satisfactory.

unaccompanied ▶ adjective ALONE, on one's own, by oneself, solo, lone, solitary, single-handed; unescorted, unattended, unchaperoned; *informal* by one's lonesome.

unaccountable ▶ adjective **1** *for some unaccountable reason* INEXPLICABLE, insoluble, incomprehensible, unfathomable, impenetrable, puzzling, perplexing, baffling, bewildering, mystifying, mysterious, inscrutable, peculiar, strange, queer, odd, obscure; *informal* weird, freaky. **2** *the private company unaccountable to voters* NOT ANSWERABLE, not liable, not responsible; free, exempt, immune; unsupervised.

unaccustomed ▶ adjective **1** *she was unaccustomed to being bossed around* UNUSED, new, fresh; unfamiliar with, inexperienced in, unconversant with, unacquainted with. **2** *he showed unaccustomed emotion* UNUSUAL, unfamiliar, uncommon, unwonted, exceptional, unprecedented, extraordinary, rare, surprising, abnormal, atypical.
— OPPOSITES: habitual.

unacknowledged ▶ adjective UNSUNG, unstated, uncelebrated, unrewarded, neglected, unrecognized, unheeded, overlooked, forgotten, ignored; uncredited.

unacquainted ▶ adjective UNFAMILIAR, unaccustomed, unused; inexperienced, ignorant, uninformed, unenlightened, not conversant; *informal* in the dark.
– OPPOSITES: familiar.

unadorned ▶ adjective UNEMBELLISHED, unornamented, undecorated, unvarnished, unfussy, no-nonsense, no-frills; plain, basic, restrained; bare, simple, austere, stark, Spartan, clinical, chaste.
– OPPOSITES: ornate.

unadulterated ▶ adjective PURE, unalloyed, unsullied, untainted, virgin, untouched; absolute, downright, solid, utter.

unadventurous ▶ adjective CAUTIOUS, careful, circumspect, wary, hesitant, timid; conservative, conventional, unenterprising, unexciting, unimaginative, myopic; boring, straitlaced, stuffy, narrow-minded; *informal* square, straight, stick-in-the-mud.
– OPPOSITES: enterprising.

unaffected ▶ adjective 1 *they are unaffected by the cabinet reshuffle* UNCHANGED, unaltered, uninfluenced; untouched, unmoved, unresponsive to; proof against, impervious to, immune to. 2 *his manner was unaffected* UNASSUMING, unpretentious, down-to-earth, natural, easy, uninhibited, open, artless, guileless, ingenuous, unsophisticated, genuine, real, sincere, honest, earnest, wholehearted, heartfelt, true, bona fide, frank; *informal* upfront.
– OPPOSITES: influenced, pretentious, false.

unafraid ▶ adjective UNDAUNTED, unabashed, fearless, brave, courageous, plucky, intrepid, stout-hearted, bold, valiant, daring, confident, audacious, unshrinking; *informal* gutsy, spunky.
– OPPOSITES: timid.

unalterable See UNCHANGEABLE.

unanimous ▶ adjective 1 *doctors were unanimous about the effects* UNITED, in agreement, in accord, of one mind, of the same mind, in harmony, concordant, undivided, as one. 2 *a unanimous vote* UNIFORM, consistent, united, concerted, congruent.
– OPPOSITES: divided.

unanswerable ▶ adjective 1 *an unanswerable case* IRREFUTABLE, indisputable, undeniable, incontestable, incontrovertible, irrefragable; conclusive, absolute, positive. 2 *unanswerable questions* INSOLUBLE, unsolvable, inexplicable, unexplainable.
– OPPOSITES: weak, obvious.

unanswered ▶ adjective UNRESOLVED, undecided, unsettled, undetermined; pending, open to question, up in the air, doubtful, disputed.

unappetizing ▶ adjective UNPALATABLE, uninviting, unappealing, unpleasant, off-putting, disagreeable, distasteful, unsavoury, insipid, tasteless, flavourless, dull; inedible, uneatable, revolting; *informal* yucky, gross.
– OPPOSITES: tempting.

unappreciated ▶ adjective UNACKNOWLEDGED, unthanked, uncredited, unrecognized, taken for granted, overlooked; undervalued, underpaid.

unapproachable ▶ adjective 1 *unapproachable islands* INACCESSIBLE, unreachable, remote, out of the way, isolated, far-flung; *informal* off the beaten track,

in the middle of nowhere, in the sticks, in the boondocks. 2 *her boss appeared unapproachable* ALOOF, distant, remote, detached, reserved, withdrawn, uncommunicative, guarded, unresponsive, unforthcoming, unfriendly, unsympathetic, unsociable; cool, cold, frosty, stiff, haughty, superior, formal, intimidating; *informal* standoffish, stuck-up.
– OPPOSITES: accessible, friendly.

unarmed ▶ adjective DEFENCELESS, weaponless; unprotected, undefended, unguarded, unshielded, vulnerable, exposed, assailable, open to attack.

unasked-for See UNBIDDEN.

unassailable ▶ adjective 1 *an unassailable fortress* IMPREGNABLE, invulnerable, impenetrable, inviolable, invincible, unconquerable; secure, safe, strong, indestructible. 2 *his logic was unassailable* INDISPUTABLE, undeniable, unquestionable, incontestable, incontrovertible, irrefutable, indubitable, watertight, sound, rock-solid, good, sure, manifest, patent, obvious.
– OPPOSITES: defenceless.

unassertive ▶ adjective PASSIVE, retiring, submissive, unassuming, self-effacing, modest, humble, meek, unconfident, diffident, shy, timid, feeble, insecure; *informal* mousy.
– OPPOSITES: bold.

unassisted ▶ adjective *an unassisted effort* INDIVIDUAL, unaided, unsupported, single-handed, lone, solo.
▶ adverb *she achieved it all unassisted* ALONE, individually, single-handedly, by oneself, on one's own, without help.

unassuming ▶ adjective MODEST, self-effacing, humble, meek, bashful, reserved, diffident; unobtrusive, unostentatious, low-key, unpretentious, unaffected, natural, artless, ingenuous.

unattached ▶ adjective 1 *they were both unattached* SINGLE, unmarried, unwed, uncommitted, available, at large, footloose and fancy free, on one's own; unloved. 2 *we are unattached to any organization* UNAFFILIATED, unallied; autonomous, independent, non-aligned, self-governing, neutral, separate, unconnected, detached.
– OPPOSITES: married.

unattended ▶ adjective 1 *his cries went unattended* IGNORED, disregarded, neglected, passed over, unheeded. 2 *an unattended vehicle* UNGUARDED, unwatched, alone, solitary; abandoned. 3 *she had to walk there unattended* UNACCOMPANIED, unescorted, partnerless, unchaperoned, alone, on one's own, by oneself, solo; *informal* by one's lonesome.

unattractive ▶ adjective PLAIN, ugly, unappealing, unpleasant, hideous, unlovely, unprepossessing, unsightly, ghastly, revolting, repellent, repulsive, repugnant; grotesque, disgusting, misshapen, plug-ugly; homely, not much to look at.
– OPPOSITES: beautiful.

unauthorized ▶ adjective UNOFFICIAL, unsanctioned, unaccredited, unlicensed, unwarranted, unapproved, bootleg, pirated; wildcat; disallowed, prohibited, out of bounds, banned, barred, forbidden, outlawed, illegal, illegitimate, illicit, proscribed.
– OPPOSITES: official.

unavoidable ▶ adjective INESCAPABLE, inevitable, inexorable, assured, certain, predestined, predetermined, fated, ineluctable; necessary, compulsory, required, obligatory, mandatory.

unaware ▶ adjective IGNORANT, unknowing, unconscious, heedless, unmindful, oblivious, incognizant, unsuspecting, uninformed, unenlightened, unwitting, innocent; inattentive, unobservant, unperceptive, blind; *informal* in the dark; *literary* nescient.
– OPPOSITES: conscious.

unawares ▶ adverb **1** *brigands caught them unawares* BY SURPRISE, unexpectedly, without warning, suddenly, abruptly, unprepared, off-guard; *informal* with one's pants down, napping. **2** *the chipmunk, unawares, approached the waiting cat* UNKNOWINGLY, unwittingly, unconsciously; unintentionally, inadvertently, accidentally, by mistake.
– OPPOSITES: prepared, knowingly.

unbalanced ▶ adjective **1** *he is unbalanced and dangerous* UNSTABLE, mentally ill, deranged, demented, disturbed, unhinged, insane, mad, out of one's mind; *informal* crazy, loopy, loony, nuts, nutso, nutty, cracked, bushed ♣, screwy, batty, dotty, cuckoo, bonkers, squirrelly; *dated* touched. **2** *a most unbalanced article* BIASED, prejudiced, one-sided, partisan, inequitable, unjust, unfair, parti pris.
– OPPOSITES: sane, unbiased.

unbearable ▶ adjective INTOLERABLE, insufferable, insupportable, unendurable, unacceptable, unmanageable, overpowering; *informal* too much.
– OPPOSITES: tolerable.

unbeatable ▶ adjective INVINCIBLE, unstoppable, unassailable, indomitable, unconquerable, unsurpassable, matchless, peerless, nonpareil; supreme.

unbeaten ▶ adjective UNDEFEATED, unconquered, unsurpassed, unequalled, unrivalled; triumphant, victorious, supreme, second to none.

unbecoming ▶ adjective **1** *an unbecoming sundress* UNFLATTERING, unattractive, unsightly, plain, ugly, homely, hideous; unsuitable, ill-fitting. **2** *conduct unbecoming to the Senate* INAPPROPRIATE, unfitting, unbefitting, unsuitable, unsuited, inapt, indecorous, out of keeping, untoward, incorrect, unacceptable; unworthy, improper, unseemly, undignified.
– OPPOSITES: flattering, appropriate.

unbelievable ▶ adjective INCREDIBLE, beyond belief, inconceivable, unthinkable, unimaginable; unconvincing, far-fetched, dubious, implausible, improbable, unrealistic; *informal* hard to swallow.
– OPPOSITES: credible.

unbeliever ▶ noun *a Holy War against the unbelievers* INFIDEL, heretic, heathen, non-believer, atheist, agnostic, pagan, nihilist, apostate, freethinker, dissenter, nonconformist; disbeliever, skeptic, cynic, doubter, doubting Thomas, questioner, scoffer.
– OPPOSITES: believer.

unbending ▶ adjective INFLEXIBLE, rigid, strict, austere, stern, tough, firm, uncompromising, unyielding, hardline, resolute, determined, unrelenting, relentless, inexorable, intransigent, immovable; unfeeling, unemotional, stiff, forbidding, unfriendly.

unbiased ▶ adjective IMPARTIAL, unprejudiced, neutral, non-partisan, disinterested, detached, dispassionate, objective, value-free, open-minded, equitable, even-handed, fair.
– OPPOSITES: prejudiced.

unbidden ▶ adjective **1** *an unbidden guest* UNINVITED,

unasked-for, unsolicited; unwanted, unwelcome. **2** *unbidden excitement* SPONTANEOUS, unprompted, voluntary, unforced, unplanned, unpremeditated; *informal* off-the-cuff.

unblemished ▶ adjective IMPECCABLE, flawless, faultless, perfect, pure, virgin, clean, spotless, immaculate, unsullied, unspoiled, undefiled, untouched, untarnished, unpolluted; guiltless, sinless, innocent, blameless; *informal* squeaky clean.
– OPPOSITES: flawed.

unblinking ▶ adjective STEADY, unflinching, steadfast, dauntless; stolid, cool; open-eyed.

unborn ▶ adjective EMBRYONIC, fetal, in utero; expected.

unbounded ▶ adjective UNLIMITED, boundless, limitless, illimitable; unrestrained, unrestricted, unconstrained, uncontrolled, unchecked, unbridled, rampant; untold, immeasurable, endless, unending, interminable, everlasting, infinite, inexhaustible.
– OPPOSITES: limited.

unbreakable ▶ adjective INDESTRUCTIBLE, shatterproof, durable, long-lasting; reinforced, sturdy, tough, stout, resistant, infrangible, heavy-duty, industrial-strength.
– OPPOSITES: fragile.

unbridled ▶ adjective UNRESTRAINED, unconstrained, uncontrolled, uninhibited, unrestricted, unchecked, uncurbed, rampant, runaway, irrepressible, unstoppable, intemperate, immoderate.
– OPPOSITES: restrained.

unbroken ▶ adjective **1** *the last unbroken window* UNDAMAGED, unimpaired, unharmed, unscathed, untouched, sound, intact, whole, perfect. **2** *an unbroken horse* UNTAMED, undomesticated, untrained, wild, feral. **3** *an unbroken chain of victories* UNINTERRUPTED, continuous, endless, constant, unremitting, perpetual; unobstructed. **4** *his record is still unbroken* UNBEATEN, undefeated, unsurpassed, unrivalled, unmatched, supreme, intact.

unburden ▶ verb *she had a sudden wish to unburden herself* OPEN ONE'S HEART, confess, confide, tell all; *informal* come clean, fess up, spill one's guts, let it all out.

uncalled
■ **uncalled for** GRATUITOUS, unnecessary, needless, inessential; undeserved, unmerited, unwarranted, unjustified, unreasonable, unfair, inappropriate, inapt, pointless; unasked, unsolicited, unrequested, unprompted, unprovoked, unwelcome.

uncanny ▶ adjective **1** *the silence was uncanny* EERIE, unnatural, unearthly, preternatural, supernatural, otherworldly, ghostly, mysterious, strange, unsettling, abnormal, weird, bizarre, surreal, eldritch; *informal* creepy, spooky, freakish, freaky. **2** *an uncanny resemblance* STRIKING, remarkable, extraordinary, exceptional, incredible, noteworthy, notable, arresting.

unceasing ▶ adjective INCESSANT, ceaseless, constant, continual, unabating, interminable, endless, unending, never-ending, everlasting, eternal, perpetual, continuous, non-stop, uninterrupted, unbroken, unremitting, persistent, relentless, unrelenting, unrelieved, sustained.

uncensored ▶ adjective UNCUT, complete, raw, whole, unexpurgated, unedited.

unceremonious ▶ adjective **1** *an unceremonious dismissal* ABRUPT, sudden, hasty, hurried, summary, perfunctory, undignified; rude, impolite,

discourteous, offhand. **2** *an unceremonious man* INFORMAL, casual, relaxed, easygoing, familiar, natural, laid-back.
— OPPOSITES: formal.

uncertain ▶ adjective **1** *the outcome is uncertain* UNKNOWN, debatable, open to question, in doubt, undetermined, unsure, in the balance, up in the air; unpredictable, unforeseeable, incalculable; risky, chancy, dicey; *informal* iffy. **2** *its origin is uncertain* VAGUE, unclear, fuzzy, ambiguous, unknown, unascertainable, obscure, arcane. **3** *uncertain weather* CHANGEABLE, variable, irregular, unpredictable, unreliable, unsettled, erratic, fluctuating. **4** *Ed was uncertain about the decision* UNSURE, doubtful, dubious, undecided, irresolute, hesitant, blowing hot and cold, vacillating, vague, unclear, ambivalent, of two minds. **5** *an uncertain smile* HESITANT, tentative, faltering, unsure, unconfident.
— OPPOSITES: predictable, sure, confident.

uncertainty ▶ noun **1** *the uncertainty of the future* UNPREDICTABILITY, unreliability, riskiness, chanciness, precariousness, changeability, variability, inconstancy, fickleness, caprice. **2** *uncertainty about the future is always bad for morale* DOUBT, lack of certainty, indecision, irresolution, hesitancy, unsureness, doubtfulness, wavering, vacillation, equivocation, vagueness, haziness, ambivalence, lack of conviction, disquiet, wariness, chariness, leeriness, skepticism; queries, questions; *formal* dubiety. **3** *she pushed the anxious uncertainties out of her mind* DOUBT, qualm, misgiving, apprehension, quandary, reservation, scruple, second thought, query, question, question mark, suspicion. **4** *there was uncertainty in his voice* HESITANCY, hesitation, tentativeness, unsureness, lack of confidence, diffidence, doubtfulness, doubt.
— OPPOSITES: certainty, predictability, confidence.

unchangeable ▶ adjective UNALTERABLE, immutable, invariable, changeless, fixed, hard and fast, cast-iron, ironclad, set/cast/carved in stone, dyed-in-the-wool, established, permanent, enduring, abiding, lasting, indestructible, ineradicable, irreversible.
— OPPOSITES: variable.

unchanging ▶ adjective CONSISTENT, constant, regular, unvarying, predictable, stable, steady, fixed, rigid, abiding, permanent, perpetual, eternal, enduring; sustained, lasting, persistent.

uncharitable ▶ adjective MEAN, mean-spirited, unkind, selfish, self-centred, inconsiderate, thoughtless, insensitive, unfriendly, unsympathetic, hard-hearted, uncaring, unfeeling, ungenerous, ungracious, unfair.

uncharted ▶ adjective UNEXPLORED, undiscovered, unmapped, untravelled, unfamiliar, untrodden, unplumbed, unknown.

uncivil ▶ adjective IMPOLITE, rude, discourteous, disrespectful, unmannerly, bad-mannered, impertinent, impudent, ungracious; brusque, sharp, curt, offhand, gruff, churlish, snippy.
— OPPOSITES: polite.

uncivilized ▶ adjective UNCOUTH, coarse, rough, boorish, vulgar, philistine, uneducated, uncultured, uncultivated, benighted, unsophisticated, unpolished; ill-bred, ill-mannered, thuggish, loutish, redneck; barbarian, primitive, savage, brutish; *archaic* rude.

unclean ▶ adjective **1** *unclean premises* DIRTY, filthy, grubby, grimy, mucky, foul, impure, tainted, grungy,

sullied, soiled, unwashed; polluted, contaminated, infected, unsanitary, unhygienic, unhealthy, disease-ridden. **2** *an unclean meat* IMPURE; forbidden, taboo.
— OPPOSITES: pure, halal, kosher.

unclear ▶ adjective UNCERTAIN, unsure, unsettled, up in the air, debatable, open to question, in doubt, doubtful; ambiguous, equivocal, indefinite, vague, mysterious, obscure, hazy, foggy, nebulous; *informal* iffy.
— OPPOSITES: evident.

unclothed ▶ adjective NAKED, bare, nude, stripped, undressed, undraped, unclad; *informal* in one's birthday suit, in the buff, in the raw, in the altogether, au naturel, starkers, buck-naked, butt-naked, mother-naked, buck.
— OPPOSITES: dressed.

uncomfortable ▶ adjective **1** *an uncomfortable chair* PAINFUL, disagreeable, intolerable, unbearable, confining, cramped. **2** *I felt uncomfortable in her presence* UNEASY, awkward, nervous, tense, ill-at-ease, strained, edgy, restless, embarrassed, troubled, worried, anxious, fraught, rattled, twitchy, discombobulated, antsy.
— OPPOSITES: relaxed.

uncommitted ▶ adjective **1** *uncommitted voters* FLOATING, undecided, non-partisan, unaffiliated, neutral, non-aligned, impartial, independent, undeclared, uncertain; *informal* sitting on the fence. **2** *the uncommitted male* UNMARRIED, unattached, unwed, partnerless; footloose and fancy free, available, single, lone.
— OPPOSITES: aligned, attached.

uncommon ▶ adjective **1** *an uncommon occurrence* UNUSUAL, abnormal, rare, atypical, unconventional, unfamiliar, strange, odd, curious, extraordinary, outlandish, novel, singular, peculiar, bizarre; alien, weird, oddball, offbeat; scarce, few and far between, exceptional, isolated, infrequent, irregular, seldom seen. **2** *an uncommon capacity for hard work* REMARKABLE, extraordinary, exceptional, singular, particular, marked, outstanding, noteworthy, significant, especial, special, signal, superior, unique, unparalleled, prodigious, unearthly; *informal* mind-boggling.

uncommonly ▶ adverb UNUSUALLY, remarkably, extraordinarily, exceptionally, singularly, particularly, especially, decidedly, notably, eminently, extremely, very.

uncommunicative ▶ adjective TACITURN, quiet, unforthcoming, reserved, reticent, laconic, tongue-tied, mute, silent, tight-lipped, close-mouthed; guarded, secretive, close, private; distant, remote, aloof, curt, withdrawn, unsociable, farouche; *informal* mum, standoffish.
— OPPOSITES: talkative.

uncomplicated ▶ adjective SIMPLE, straightforward, clear, accessible, basic, undemanding, unchallenging, unsophisticated, trouble-free, painless, effortless, easy, elementary, foolproof, idiot-proof, goof-proof; *informal* a piece of cake, child's play, a cinch, a breeze.
— OPPOSITES: complex.

uncompromising ▶ adjective INFLEXIBLE, unbending, unyielding, unshakeable, resolute, rigid, hard-line, immovable, intractable, inexorable, firm, determined, obstinate, stubborn, adamant, obdurate, intransigent, headstrong, stiff-necked,

pigheaded, single-minded, bloody-minded.
— OPPOSITES: flexible.

unconcerned ▸ adjective **1** *she is unconcerned about their responses* INDIFFERENT, unmoved, apathetic, uninterested, incurious, dispassionate, heedless, impassive, unmindful. **2** *he tried to look unconcerned* UNTROUBLED, unworried, unruffled, insouciant, nonchalant, blasé, carefree, casual, blithe, relaxed, at ease, {calm, cool, and collected}; *informal* laid-back, poker-faced.
— OPPOSITES: interested, anxious.

unconditional ▸ adjective WHOLEHEARTED, unqualified, unreserved, unlimited, unrestricted, unmitigated, unquestioning; complete, total, entire, full, absolute, out-and-out, unequivocal.

unconnected ▸ adjective **1** *the ground wire was unconnected* DETACHED, disconnected, loose. **2** *unconnected tasks* UNRELATED, dissociated, separate, independent, distinct, different, disparate, discrete. **3** *unconnected chains of thought* DISJOINTED, incoherent, disconnected, rambling, wandering, diffuse, disorderly, haphazard, disorganized, garbled, mixed, muddled, aimless.
— OPPOSITES: attached, related, coherent.

unconscionable ▸ adjective **1** *the unconscionable use of test animals* UNETHICAL, amoral, immoral, unprincipled, indefensible, unforgivable, wrong; unscrupulous, unfair, underhanded, dishonourable. **2** *we waited an unconscionable length of time* EXCESSIVE, unreasonable, unwarranted, uncalled for, unfair, inordinate, immoderate, undue, inexcusable, unforgivable, unnecessary, needless; *informal* over the top.
— OPPOSITES: ethical, acceptable.

unconscious ▸ adjective **1** *she made sure he was unconscious* INSENSIBLE, senseless, insentient, insensate, comatose, inert, knocked out, stunned; motionless, immobile, prostrate; *informal* out cold, out like a light, out of it, down for the count, passed out, dead to the world. **2** *she was unconscious of the pain* HEEDLESS, unmindful, disregarding, oblivious to, insensible to, impervious to, unaffected by, unconcerned by, indifferent to; unaware, unknowing, ignorant of, incognizant of. **3** *an unconscious desire* SUBCONSCIOUS, latent, suppressed, subliminal, sleeping, dormant, inherent, instinctive, involuntary, uncontrolled, spontaneous; unintentional, unthinking, unwitting, inadvertent; *informal* gut.
— OPPOSITES: aware, voluntary.
▸ noun *fantasies raging in the unconscious* SUBCONSCIOUS, psyche, ego, id, inner self.

uncontrollable ▸ adjective **1** *the crowds were uncontrollable* UNMANAGEABLE, out of control, ungovernable, wild, unruly, disorderly, recalcitrant, turbulent, disobedient, delinquent, defiant, undisciplined; *formal* refractory. **2** *an uncontrollable rage* UNSTOPPABLE, irrepressible, ungovernable, unquenchable; wild, violent, frenzied, furious, mad, hysterical, passionate, out of control.
— OPPOSITES: compliant.

unconventional ▸ adjective UNUSUAL, irregular, unorthodox, unfamiliar, uncommon, unwonted, out of the ordinary, atypical, singular, alternative, different; new, novel, innovative, groundbreaking, pioneering, original, unprecedented; eccentric, idiosyncratic, quirky, odd, strange, bizarre, weird, outlandish, curious; abnormal, anomalous, aberrant, extraordinary; nonconformist, bohemian,

avant-garde; *informal* far out, offbeat, off the wall, wacky, madcap, oddball, zany, hippie, kooky, wacko.
— OPPOSITES: orthodox.

unconvincing ▸ adjective IMPROBABLE, unlikely, implausible, incredible, unbelievable, questionable, dubious, doubtful; strained, laboured, far-fetched, unrealistic, fanciful, fantastic; feeble, flimsy, weak, transparent, poor, lame, ineffectual, half-baked; *informal* hard to swallow.
— OPPOSITES: persuasive.

uncool ▸ adjective **1** *those shoes are uncool* SQUARE, unhip, boring, unfashionable, unstylish, untrendy, behind the times; conformist, straitlaced, goody-goody. **2** *it was so uncool of her to pick on Joffrey* LAME, unpleasant, unfair, unimpressive; *informal* sucky, crappy.

uncooperative ▸ adjective UNHELPFUL, awkward, recalcitrant, perverse, contrary, stubborn, stiff-necked, unyielding, unbending, inflexible, immovable, obstructive, difficult, obstreperous, cussed, disobedient, disobliging, bloody-minded.
— OPPOSITES: obliging.

uncoordinated ▸ adjective CLUMSY, awkward, blundering, bumbling, lumbering, flat-footed, heavy-handed, graceless, gawky, ungainly, ungraceful; inept, unhandy, unskilful, inexpert, maladroit, bungling; *informal* klutzy, butterfingered, ham-fisted, ham-handed, all thumbs.
— OPPOSITES: dexterous.

uncouth ▸ adjective UNCIVILIZED, uncultured, uncultivated, unrefined, unpolished, unsophisticated, bush-league, common, plebeian, low, rough, rough-hewn, coarse, loutish, boorish, oafish, troglodyte; churlish, uncivil, rude, impolite, discourteous, disrespectful, unmannerly, bad-mannered, ill-bred, indecorous, crass, indelicate; vulgar, crude, raunchy.
— OPPOSITES: refined.

uncover ▸ verb **1** *she uncovered the new artwork* EXPOSE, reveal, lay bare; unwrap, unveil; strip, denude. **2** *they uncovered a money-laundering plot* DETECT, discover, come across, stumble on, chance on, find, turn up, unearth, dig up; expose, unveil, unmask, disclose, reveal, lay bare, make known, make public, bring to light, blow the lid off, blow the whistle on, pull the plug on.

unctuous ▸ adjective SYCOPHANTIC, ingratiating, obsequious, fawning, servile, grovelling, subservient, cringing, humble, hypocritical, insincere, gushing, effusive; glib, smooth, slick, slippery, oily, greasy; smarmy, slimy, sucky.

undaunted ▸ adjective UNAFRAID, undismayed, unflinching, unshrinking, unabashed, fearless, dauntless, intrepid, bold, valiant, brave, courageous, plucky, gritty, indomitable, confident, audacious, daring; *informal* gutsy, spunky.
— OPPOSITES: fearful.

undead ▸ noun LIVING DEAD, zombies, vampires.

undecided ▸ adjective UNRESOLVED, uncertain, unsure, unclear, unsettled, indefinite, undetermined, unknown, in the balance, up in the air, debatable, arguable, moot, open to question, doubtful, dubious, borderline, ambiguous, vague; indecisive, irresolute, hesitant, tentative, wavering, vacillating, uncommitted, ambivalent, of two minds, torn, fence-sitting, on the fence; *informal* iffy, wishy-washy, waffly.
— OPPOSITES: certain.

undefined ▶ adjective **1** *some matters are still undefined* UNSPECIFIED, unexplained, unspecific, indeterminate, unsettled; unclear, woolly, imprecise, inexact, indefinite, vague, fuzzy. **2** *undefined shapes* INDISTINCT, indefinite, formless, indistinguishable, vague, amorphous, hazy, misty, shadowy, nebulous, blurred, blurry.
— OPPOSITES: definite, distinct.

undemanding ▶ adjective EASY, accessible, manageable, straightforward, painless, unchallenging; easygoing, obliging.

undeniable ▶ adjective INDISPUTABLE, indubitable, unquestionable, beyond doubt, beyond question, undebatable, incontrovertible, incontestable, irrefutable, unassailable; certain, sure, definite, positive, conclusive, plain, obvious, unmistakable, self-evident, patent, emphatic, categorical, unequivocal.
— OPPOSITES: questionable.

under ▶ preposition **1** *they hid under a bush* BENEATH, below, underneath. **2** *the rent is under $450* LESS THAN, lower than, below. **3** *branch managers are under the retail director* SUBORDINATE TO, junior to, inferior to, subservient to, answerable to, responsible to, subject to, controlled by. **4** *the town was under water* FLOODED BY, immersed in, submerged by, sunk in, engulfed by, inundated by. **5** *forty homes are under construction* UNDERGOING, in the process of. **6** *our finances are under pressure* SUBJECT TO, liable to, at the mercy of.
— OPPOSITES: above, over.
▶ adverb *coughing and spluttering she went under* DOWN, lower, below, underneath, beneath; underwater.

underachiever ▶ noun UNDERPERFORMER, slacker, disappointment, failure, loser.

underarm ▶ noun ARMPIT, pit; *technical* axilla.

undercooked ▶ adjective UNDERDONE, half-cooked, half-baked, uncooked; rare, raw.

undercover ▶ adjective COVERT, secret, clandestine, incognito, underground, surreptitious, furtive, cloak-and-dagger, stealthy, hidden, concealed, backstairs, closet; *informal* hush-hush, sneaky, on the q.t.
— OPPOSITES: overt.

undercurrent ▶ noun **1** *dangerous undercurrents in the cove* UNDERTOW, underflow; riptide. **2** *the undercurrent of despair in his words* UNDERTONE, overtone, suggestion, connotation, intimation, hint, nuance, trace, suspicion, whisper, tinge; feeling, atmosphere, aura, echo; *informal* vibes.

undercut ▶ verb **1** *the firm undercut their rivals* CHARGE LESS THAN, undersell, underprice, underbid. **2** *his authority was being undercut* UNDERMINE, weaken, impair, sap, threaten, subvert, sabotage, ruin, destabilize, wreck.

underdog ▶ noun LONG SHOT, dark horse, weaker one, little guy, David; downtrodden, victim, loser, fall guy.

underestimate ▶ verb UNDERRATE, undervalue, lowball, do an injustice to, be wrong about, sell short, play down, understate; minimize, de-emphasize, underemphasize, diminish, gloss over, trivialize; miscalculate, misjudge, misconstrue, misread.
— OPPOSITES: exaggerate.

underfoot ▶ adverb UNDERNEATH, beneath one's feet, on the ground.

underfunded ▶ adjective UNDERCAPITALIZED, cash-starved, starved for funds, neglected.

undergarment ▶ noun *See table at* UNDERWEAR.

undergo ▶ verb GO THROUGH, experience, undertake, face, submit to, be subjected to, come in for, receive, sustain, endure, brave, bear, tolerate, stand, withstand, weather.

undergraduate ▶ noun STUDENT, undergrad, scholar, freshman; *informal* frosh.

underground ▶ adjective **1** *an underground parking garage* SUBTERRANEAN, buried, sunken, subsurface, basement. **2** *underground trade* CLANDESTINE, secret, surreptitious, covert, undercover, closet, cloak-and-dagger, back-alley, backstairs, black-market, hidden, sneaky, furtive; resistance, subversive; *informal* hush-hush. **3** *the underground art scene* ALTERNATIVE, radical, revolutionary, unconventional, unorthodox, avant-garde, counterculture, experimental, innovative.
▶ adverb **1** *the insects live underground* BELOW GROUND, in the earth, subterraneously. **2** *the rebels went underground* INTO HIDING, into seclusion, undercover, to earth, to ground.

undergrowth ▶ noun SHRUBBERY, vegetation, underbrush, greenery, ground cover, underwood, brushwood, *(Nfld)* tuckamore ♣, brush, scrub, bush, covert, thicket, copse; bushes, plants, brambles, herbage; *technical* herbaceous layer.

underhanded ▶ adjective DECEITFUL, deceptive, dishonest, dishonourable, disreputable, unethical, unprincipled, immoral, unscrupulous, fraudulent, dubious, unfair, snide; treacherous, lowdown, duplicitous, double-dealing; devious, artful, crooked, shady, crafty, conniving, scheming, sly, wily, not above board; clandestine, backstairs, secret, surreptitious, sneaky, furtive, covert, cloak-and-dagger.
— OPPOSITES: honest.

underline ▶ verb **1** *she underlined a phrase* UNDERSCORE, mark, pick out, emphasize, highlight. **2** *the program underlines the benefits of exercise* EMPHASIZE, stress, highlight, accentuate, accent, focus on, spotlight, point up, play up; *informal* rub in.

underling ▶ noun SUBORDINATE, inferior, junior, minion, lackey, subaltern, flunky, menial, vassal, subject, hireling, servant, henchman, factotum; *informal* gofer.
— OPPOSITES: boss.

underlying ▶ adjective **1** *the underlying aims of the research* FUNDAMENTAL, basic, primary, prime, central, principal, root, chief, cardinal, key, elementary, intrinsic, essential. **2** *an underlying feeling of irritation* LATENT, repressed, suppressed, unrevealed, undisclosed, unexpressed, concealed, hidden, masked.

undermine ▶ verb **1** *their integrity is being undermined* SUBVERT, undercut, sabotage, threaten, weaken, compromise, diminish, reduce, impair, mar, spoil, ruin, damage, hurt, injure, cripple, sap, shake; *informal* drag through the mud. **2** *rivers undermined their banks* ERODE, wear away, eat away at.
— OPPOSITES: strengthen, support.

underneath ▶ adjective & adverb BELOW, beneath, under, underfoot, lower down.

underpants ▶ plural noun UNDERWEAR, boxers, panties, undershorts, undergarments, underthings, lingerie; *informal* undies, skivvies, gaunch ♣, gitch ♣, gotch ♣, gotchies ♣, frillies; *proprietary* Jockey shorts.

underpin ▶ verb *See* REINFORCE.

underprivileged ▶ adjective NEEDY, deprived, disadvantaged, poor, destitute, in need, in straitened

circumstances, impoverished, poverty-stricken, on the poverty line, indigent, lower-class; *formal* penurious.
— OPPOSITES: wealthy.

underrate ▶ verb UNDERVALUE, underestimate, do an injustice to, sell short, play down, understate, minimize, diminish, downgrade, trivialize.
— OPPOSITES: exaggerate.

undersized ▶ adjective UNDERDEVELOPED, stunted, small, short, little, tiny, petite, slight, compact, miniature, mini, diminutive, dwarfish, pygmy, pint-sized, pocket-sized, baby, teeny-weeny, itsy-bitsy, itty-bitty.
— OPPOSITES: overgrown.

understand ▶ verb 1 *he couldn't understand anything we said* COMPREHEND, grasp, take in, see, apprehend, follow, make sense of, fathom; unravel, decipher, interpret; *informal* work out, figure out, make head or tail of, get one's head around, get the drift of, catch on to, get, twig. 2 *she understood how hard he'd worked* APPRECIATE, recognize, realize, acknowledge, know, be aware of, be conscious of; *informal* be wise to; *formal* be cognizant of. 3 *I understand that you wish to go* BELIEVE, gather, take it, hear (tell), notice, see, learn; conclude, infer, assume, surmise, fancy.
▶ exclamation *I want out, understand?* CAPISCE, comprende, get it, get the picture, see, right, eh, know what I mean, get my drift.

understandable ▶ adjective 1 *make it understandable to the beginner* COMPREHENSIBLE, intelligible, coherent, clear, explicit, unambiguous, transparent, plain, straightforward, digestible, accessible, user-friendly. 2 *an understandable desire to be happy* UNSURPRISING, expected, predictable, inevitable; reasonable, acceptable, logical, rational, normal, natural; justifiable, justified, defensible, excusable, pardonable, forgivable.

understanding ▶ noun 1 *test your understanding of the language* COMPREHENSION, apprehension, grasp, mastery, appreciation, assimilation, absorption; knowledge, awareness, insight, skill, expertise, proficiency; *informal* know-how; *formal* cognizance. 2 *it was my understanding that this was free* BELIEF, perception, view, conviction, feeling, opinion, intuition, impression, assumption, supposition, inference, interpretation. 3 *she treated me with understanding* COMPASSION, sympathy, pity, feeling, concern, consideration, kindness, sensitivity, decency, humanity, charity, goodwill, mercy, tolerance. 4 *we had a tacit understanding* AGREEMENT, arrangement, deal, bargain, settlement, pledge, pact, compact, contract, covenant, bond, meeting of minds.
— OPPOSITES: ignorance, indifference.
▶ adjective *an understanding friend* COMPASSIONATE, sympathetic, sensitive, considerate, tender, kind, thoughtful, tolerant, patient, forbearing, lenient, merciful, forgiving, humane; approachable, supportive, perceptive.

understate ▶ verb PLAY DOWN, downplay, underrate, underplay, de-emphasize, trivialize, minimize, diminish, downgrade, brush aside, gloss over, put it mildly; *informal* soft-pedal, sell short.
— OPPOSITES: exaggerate.

understatement ▶ noun MINIMIZATION, trivialization, euphemism; understatedness, restraint, reserve, underplaying, underemphasis; *technical* litotes, meiosis.
— OPPOSITES: overstatement, exaggeration.

understood ▶ adjective ACCEPTED, agreed-upon, acknowledged, assumed, established, unwritten, unspoken, taken for granted, tacit.

understudy ▶ noun STAND-IN, substitute, replacement, reserve, fill-in, locum, proxy, backup, relief, standby, stop-gap; *informal* sub, pinch-hitter.

undertake ▶ verb TACKLE, take on, assume, shoulder, handle, manage, deal with, be responsible for; engage in, take part in, go about, set about, get down to, come to grips with, embark on; attempt, try, endeavour; *informal* have a go at; *formal* essay.

undertaker ▶ noun FUNERAL DIRECTOR, mortician.

undertaking ▶ noun 1 *a risky undertaking* ENTERPRISE, venture, project, campaign, scheme, plan, operation, endeavour, effort, task, deed, activity, pursuit, exploit, business, affair, procedure; mission, quest. 2 *make an undertaking to comply with the rules* PLEDGE, agreement, promise, oath, covenant, vow, commitment, guarantee, assurance, contract.

undertone ▶ noun 1 *he said something in an undertone* LOW VOICE, murmur, whisper, mutter. 2 *the story's dark undertones* UNDERCURRENT, overtone, suggestion, nuance, vein, atmosphere, aura, tenor, flavour, tinge; vibrations.

undervalue ▶ verb UNDERRATE, underestimate, play down, understate, underemphasize, diminish, minimize, downgrade, reduce, brush aside, gloss over, trivialize, underprice; *informal* sell short.

underwater ▶ adjective SUBMERGED, immersed, sunken, subaqueous, subsurface; undersea, subsea, submarine.

underwear ▶ noun. See table.

Underwear

bicycle shorts	lingerie
bikini briefs	long johns
bloomers	panties
boxer shorts	shorts
bra	skivvies
brassiere	slip
briefs	Stanfields* ♣
camisole	tanga
chemise	tap pants
corset	teddy
drawers	thermals
foundation garments	thong
frillies	underclothes
gaunch ♣(BC & Alta)	undergarments
girdle	underpants
gitch ♣	undershorts
gotch ♣	underthings
gotchies ♣	undies
Jockey shorts*	unmentionables
	*Proprietary term.

underworld ▶ noun 1 *Osiris, god of the underworld* THE NETHERWORLD, the nether regions, hell, the abyss; eternal damnation; Gehenna, Tophet, Sheol, Hades; *informal* the other place; *literary* the pit. 2 *the city's violent underworld* CRIMINAL WORLD, gangland; criminals, gangsters; *informal* mobsters.
— OPPOSITES: heaven.

underwrite ▶ verb SPONSOR, support, back, insure, guarantee, indemnify, subsidize, pay for, finance, fund; *informal* foot the bill for, bankroll.

undesirable ▶ adjective 1 *undesirable side effects* UNPLEASANT, disagreeable, objectionable, nasty,

unwelcome, unwanted, unfortunate, inconvenient, infelicitous. **2** *some very undesirable people* UNPLEASANT, disagreeable, obnoxious, nasty, vile, unsavoury, awful, repulsive, repellent, objectionable, abhorrent, loathsome, hateful, detestable, deplorable, appalling, insufferable, intolerable, despicable, contemptible, odious, terrible, dreadful, frightful, ghastly, horrible, horrid.
– OPPOSITES: pleasant, agreeable.
▶ noun *the bar was full of undesirables* OUTCAST, low-life, misfit, deviant, unsavoury character, pariah, leper, untouchable, freak.

undetectable ▶ adjective UNNOTICEABLE, imperceptible, invisible, inaudible, odourless, subtle, faint, obscure; tiny, minute, infinitesimal.

undignified ▶ adjective UNSEEMLY, demeaning, unbecoming, unworthy, unbefitting, degrading, shameful, dishonourable, ignominious, discreditable, ignoble, untoward, unsuitable; scandalous, disgraceful, indelicate, indecent, low, base.

undisciplined ▶ adjective UNRULY, disorderly, disobedient, badly behaved, recalcitrant, restive, wayward, delinquent, rebellious, refractory, insubordinate, disruptive, errant, out of control, uncontrollable, wild, naughty; disorganized, unsystematic, unmethodical, lax, slapdash, slipshod, sloppy.

undisguised ▶ adjective OBVIOUS, evident, patent, manifest, transparent, overt, unconcealed, unhidden, unmistakable, undeniable, plain, clear, clear-cut, explicit, naked, visible; blatant, flagrant, glaring, bold.

undisputed ▶ adjective UNCONTESTED, indubitable, undoubted, incontestable, unchallenged, incontrovertible, unequivocal, undeniable, irrefutable, unmistakable, sure, certain, definite, accepted, acknowledged, recognized.
– OPPOSITES: doubtful.

undistinguished ▶ adjective UNEXCEPTIONAL, indifferent, run-of-the-mill, middle-of-the-road, ordinary, average, commonplace, mediocre, humdrum, lacklustre, forgettable, uninspired, uneventful, unremarkable, inconsequential, featureless, nondescript, middling, moderate; *informal* garden-variety, by-the-numbers, nothing special, no great shakes, nothing to write home about, OK, so-so, {comme ci, comme ça}, bush-league, blah, plain-vanilla.
– OPPOSITES: extraordinary.

undivided ▶ adjective COMPLETE, full, total, whole, entire, absolute, whole-hearted, unqualified, unreserved, unmitigated, unbroken, consistent, thorough, exclusive, dedicated; focused, engrossed, absorbed, attentive, committed.

undo ▶ verb **1** *he undid another button* UNFASTEN, unbutton, unhook, untie, unlace; unlock, unbolt; loosen, disentangle, extricate, release, detach, free, open; disconnect, disengage, separate. **2** *they will undo a decision by the provincial court* REVOKE, overrule, overturn, repeal, rescind, reverse, retract, countermand, cancel, annul, nullify, invalidate, void, negate; *Law* vacate; *formal* abrogate. **3** *she undid much of the good work done* RUIN, undermine, subvert, overturn, scotch, sabotage, spoil, impair, mar, destroy, wreck, eradicate, obliterate; cancel out, neutralize, thwart, foil, frustrate, hamper, hinder, obstruct; *informal* blow, put the kibosh on, foul up,

scupper, scuttle, muck up.
– OPPOSITES: fasten, ratify, enhance.

undoing ▶ noun **1** *she plotted the emperor's undoing* DOWNFALL, defeat, conquest, deposition, overthrow, ruin, ruination, elimination, end, collapse, failure, fall, fall from grace, debasement; Waterloo. **2** *their complacency was their undoing* FATAL FLAW, Achilles' heel, weakness, weak point, failing, nemesis, affliction, curse.

undone ▶ adjective **1** *some work was left undone* UNFINISHED, incomplete, half-done, unaccomplished, unfulfilled, unconcluded; omitted, neglected, disregarded, ignored; remaining, outstanding, deferred, pending, on ice; *informal* on the back burner. **2** (*formal*) *she had lost and was utterly undone* DONE FOR, finished, ruined, destroyed, doomed, lost, defeated, beaten; *informal* washed up, toast.
– OPPOSITES: finished, successful.

undoubted ▶ adjective UNDISPUTED, unchallenged, unquestioned, indubitable, incontrovertible, irrefutable, incontestable, sure, certain, unmistakable; definite, accepted, acknowledged, recognized.

undoubtedly ▶ adverb DOUBTLESS, indubitably, doubtlessly, no doubt, without (a) doubt, unquestionably, without question, indisputably, undeniably, incontrovertibly, clearly, obviously, patently, certainly, definitely, surely, of course, indeed.

undress ▶ verb *he undressed and got into bed* STRIP (OFF), disrobe, take off one's clothes, peel down.
■ **undressed/in a state of undress** NAKED, (in the) nude, bare, stripped, unclothed, undressed, unclad; *informal* in one's birthday suit, in the raw, in the buff, au naturel, starkers, buck-naked, butt-naked, mother-naked, buck.

undue ▶ adjective EXCESSIVE, immoderate, intemperate, inordinate, disproportionate; uncalled for, unneeded, unnecessary, needless, unwarranted, unjustified, unreasonable; inappropriate, unmerited, unsuitable, improper.
– OPPOSITES: appropriate.

undulate ▶ verb RISE AND FALL, surge, swell, heave, ripple, billow, flow, roll; wind, wobble, oscillate, fluctuate.

unduly ▶ adverb See EXCESSIVELY.

undying ▶ adjective ABIDING, lasting, enduring, permanent, constant, infinite; unceasing, perpetual, ceaseless, incessant, unending, never-ending, unfading, amaranthine; immortal, eternal, deathless.

unearth ▶ verb **1** *workers unearthed an artillery shell* DIG UP, excavate, exhume, disinter, root out, unbury. **2** *I unearthed an interesting fact* DISCOVER, uncover, find, come across, stumble upon, hit on, bring to light, expose, turn up, hunt out.

unearthly ▶ adjective *an unearthly chill in the air* OTHERWORLDLY, supernatural, preternatural, alien; ghostly, spectral, phantom, mysterious, spine-chilling, hair-raising; uncanny, eerie, strange, weird, unnatural, bizarre, surreal; eldritch; *informal* spooky, creepy, scary.
– OPPOSITES: normal.

uneasy ▶ adjective **1** *the doctor made him feel uneasy* WORRIED, anxious, troubled, disturbed, agitated, rattled, nervous, tense, overwrought, edgy, jumpy, apprehensive, restless, discomfited, perturbed, fearful, uncomfortable, unsettled; *informal* jittery,

antsy. **2** *he had an uneasy feeling* WORRYING, disturbing, troubling, alarming, disquieting, unsettling, disconcerting, upsetting, nagging, niggling. **3** *the victory ensured an uneasy peace* TENSE, awkward, strained, fraught; precarious, unstable, insecure.
— OPPOSITES: calm, stable.

uneconomic, uneconomical ► adjective UNPROFITABLE, uncommercial, money-losing, not viable, unviable, unsustainable, worthless; wasteful, inefficient, improvident.

uneducated ► adjective UNTAUGHT, unschooled, untutored, untrained, unread, unscholarly, illiterate, unlettered, ignorant, ill-informed, uninformed; uncouth, unsophisticated, uncultured, unaccomplished, unenlightened, philistine, benighted, backward, redneck.
— OPPOSITES: learned.

unemotional ► adjective RESERVED, undemonstrative, sober, restrained, passionless, perfunctory, emotionless, unsentimental, unexcitable, impassive, apathetic, phlegmatic, stoical, equable; cool, cold, frigid, unfeeling, callous.

unemployed ► adjective JOBLESS, out-of-work, between jobs, unwaged, unoccupied, redundant, laid off, idle; on welfare, on pogey ♣, on EI ♣.

unending ► adjective ENDLESS, never-ending, interminable, perpetual, eternal, amaranthine, ceaseless, incessant, unceasing, non-stop, uninterrupted, continuous, continual, constant, persistent, recurring, unbroken, unabating, unremitting, relentless.

unendurable ► adjective INTOLERABLE, unbearable, insufferable, insupportable, too much to bear.

unenthusiastic ► adjective INDIFFERENT, apathetic, half-hearted, lukewarm, tepid, casual, cool, lacklustre, subdued, unmoved; cursory, perfunctory; *informal* so-so, {comme ci, comme ça}.
— OPPOSITES: keen.

unenviable ► adjective DISAGREEABLE, nasty, unpleasant, undesirable, unfortunate, unlucky, horrible, thankless; unwanted.

unequal ► adjective **1** *they are unequal in length* DIFFERENT, dissimilar, unalike, unlike, disparate, unmatched, uneven, irregular, varying, variable, asymmetrical. **2** *the unequal distribution of wealth* UNFAIR, unjust, disproportionate, inequitable, biased, askew. **3** *an unequal contest* ONE-SIDED, uneven, unfair, ill-matched, unbalanced, lopsided, skewed. **4** *she felt unequal to the task* INADEQUATE FOR, incapable of, unqualified for, unsuited to, incompetent at, not up to; *informal* not cut out for.
— OPPOSITES: identical, fair.

unequalled ► adjective UNBEATEN, matchless, unmatched, unrivalled, unsurpassed, unparalleled, peerless, incomparable, inimitable, unique, second to none, in a class of its/one's own.

unequivocal ► adjective UNAMBIGUOUS, unmistakable, indisputable, incontrovertible, indubitable, undeniable; clear, clear-cut, plain, plain-spoken, explicit, specific, categorical, straightforward, blunt, candid, emphatic, manifest.
— OPPOSITES: ambiguous.

unerring ► adjective UNFAILING, infallible, perfect, flawless, faultless, error-free, impeccable, unimpeachable; sure, accurate, true, assured, sure-fire, sure-footed; *Theology* inerrant.

unethical ► adjective IMMORAL, amoral, unprincipled, unscrupulous, dishonourable,

dishonest, wrong, deceitful, unconscionable, unfair, fraudulent, underhanded, wicked, evil, sneaky, corrupt; unprofessional, improper.

uneven ► adjective **1** *uneven ground* BUMPY, rough, lumpy, stony, rocky, rugged, potholed, rutted, pitted, jagged. **2** *uneven teeth* IRREGULAR, unequal, unbalanced, misaligned, lopsided, askew, crooked, wonky, asymmetrical, unsymmetrical. **3** *uneven quality* INCONSISTENT, variable, varying, fluctuating, irregular, erratic, patchy; choppy, unsteady. **4** *an uneven contest* ONE-SIDED, unequal, unfair, unjust, inequitable, ill-matched, unbalanced, David and Goliath.
— OPPOSITES: flat, regular, equal.

uneventful ► adjective UNEXCITING, uninteresting, monotonous, boring, dull, tedious, humdrum, routine, unvaried, ordinary, run-of-the-mill, pedestrian, mundane, predictable; *informal* blah.
— OPPOSITES: exciting.

unexceptional ► adjective ORDINARY, average, typical, everyday, mediocre, run-of-the-mill, middle-of-the-road, indifferent; *informal* OK, blah, so-so, {comme ci, comme ça}, nothing special, no great shakes, fair-to-middling.

unexpected ► adjective UNFORESEEN, unanticipated, unpredicted, unlooked-for, sudden, abrupt, surprising, unannounced.

unexpectedly ► adverb OUT OF THE BLUE, out of nowhere, out of left field, without warning, unannounced, surprisingly.

unfailing ► adjective CONSTANT, reliable, dependable, steadfast, steady; endless, undying, unfading, inexhaustible, indefatigable, boundless, tireless, ceaseless.

unfair ► adjective **1** *the trial was unfair* UNJUST, inequitable, prejudiced, biased, discriminatory; one-sided, unequal, uneven, unbalanced, partisan, partial, skewed. **2** *his comments were unfair* UNDESERVED, unmerited, uncalled for, unreasonable, unjustified. **3** *unfair play* UNSPORTSMANLIKE, unsporting, dirty, below the belt, underhanded, dishonourable. **4** *you're being very unfair* INCONSIDERATE, thoughtless, insensitive, selfish, spiteful, mean, unkind, unreasonable; hypercritical, overcritical.
— OPPOSITES: just, justified.

unfaithful ► adjective **1** *her husband had been unfaithful* ADULTEROUS, faithless, fickle, untrue, inconstant; unchaste, cheating, philandering, two-timing. **2** *an unfaithful friend* DISLOYAL, treacherous, traitorous, untrustworthy, unreliable, undependable, fair-weather, false, two-faced, double-crossing, deceitful; *literary* perfidious.
— OPPOSITES: loyal.

unfaltering ► adjective STEADY, resolute, resolved, firm, steadfast, fixed, decided, unswerving, unwavering, tireless, indefatigable, persistent, unyielding, relentless, unremitting, unrelenting, rock-steady.
— OPPOSITES: unsteady.

unfamiliar ► adjective **1** *an unfamiliar part of the city* UNKNOWN, new, strange, foreign, alien; unexplored, uncharted. **2** *the unfamiliar sounds* UNUSUAL, uncommon, unconventional, novel, different, exotic, unorthodox, odd, peculiar, curious, uncharacteristic, anomalous, abnormal, out of the ordinary. **3** *investors unfamiliar with the stock market* UNACQUAINTED, unused, unaccustomed, unconversant, unversed, inexperienced, uninformed, unschooled, unenlightened, ignorant, not cognizant, new to, a stranger to.

unfashionable ▶ adjective OUT, out of date, outdated, old-fashioned, outmoded, out of style, dated, unstylish, passé, démodé, unhip, uncool, nerdy, dowdy, frumpy, lame, unsexy, old hat, square.

unfasten ▶ verb UNDO, open, disconnect, remove, untie, unbutton, unzip, unlash, loose, loosen, free, unlock, unbolt.

unfathomable ▶ adjective INSCRUTABLE, incomprehensible, enigmatic, indecipherable, impenetrable, obscure, esoteric, mysterious, mystifying, deep, profound.
– OPPOSITES: penetrable.

unfavourable ▶ adjective 1 *unfavourable comment* ADVERSE, critical, hostile, inimical, unfriendly, unsympathetic, negative, scathing; discouraging, disapproving, uncomplimentary, unflattering. 2 *the unfavourable economic climate* GLOOMY, adverse, inauspicious, unpropitious, disadvantageous; unsuitable, inappropriate, inopportune.
– OPPOSITES: positive.

unfazed ▶ adjective CALM, unruffled, unperturbed, untroubled, poised, relaxed, self-possessed, nonplussed, together, laid-back.

unfeeling ▶ adjective UNCARING, unsympathetic, unemotional, uncharitable; heartless, hard-hearted, hard, harsh, austere, cold, cold-hearted, cold-blooded, insensitive, callous.
– OPPOSITES: compassionate.

unfeigned ▶ adjective SINCERE, genuine, real, true, honest, unaffected, unforced, heartfelt, wholehearted, bona fide.
– OPPOSITES: insincere.

unfettered ▶ adjective UNRESTRAINED, unrestricted, unconstrained, uninhibited, free, rampant, unbridled, unchecked, uncontrolled.
– OPPOSITES: restricted.

unfinished ▶ adjective 1 *an unfinished essay* INCOMPLETE, uncompleted; partial, undone, half-done, in progress; imperfect, unpolished, unrefined, sketchy, fragmentary, rough. 2 *the door can be supplied unfinished* UNPAINTED, unvarnished, untreated.
– OPPOSITES: complete.

unfit ▶ adjective 1 *that party is unfit to govern* UNQUALIFIED, unsuitable, unsuited, inappropriate, unequipped, inadequate, not designed; incapable of, unable to, not up to, not equal to, unworthy of; *informal* not cut out for, not up to scratch. 2 *unfit and overweight children* UNHEALTHY, out of shape, in poor condition/shape.
– OPPOSITES: suitable.

unflagging ▶ adjective TIRELESS, persistent, dogged, tenacious, determined, indefatigable, resolute, steadfast, staunch, single-minded, unrelenting, unfaltering, unfailing.
– OPPOSITES: inconstant.

unflappable ▶ adjective (*informal*) IMPERTURBABLE, unexcitable, cool, calm, {calm, cool, and collected}, self-controlled, cool-headed, level-headed; *informal* laid-back, Type-B.
– OPPOSITES: excitable.

unflattering ▶ adjective 1 *an unflattering review* UNFAVOURABLE, uncomplimentary, harsh, unsympathetic, critical, negative, hostile, scathing.

2 *an unflattering dress* UNATTRACTIVE, unbecoming, unsightly, ugly, homely, plain, ill-fitting.
– OPPOSITES: complimentary, becoming.

unflinching ▶ adjective RESOLUTE, determined, single-minded, dogged, steadfast, solid, resolved, firm, committed, steady, unwavering, unflagging, unswerving, unfaltering, untiring, undaunted, fearless.

unfold ▶ verb 1 *May unfolded the map* OPEN OUT, spread out, flatten, straighten out, unroll, unfurl. 2 *I watched the events unfold* DEVELOP, evolve, happen, take place, occur, transpire, progress, play out.

unforeseen ▶ adjective UNPREDICTED, unexpected, unanticipated, unplanned, not bargained for, surprising.
– OPPOSITES: expected.

unforgettable ▶ adjective MEMORABLE, not/never to be forgotten, haunting, catchy; striking, impressive, outstanding, extraordinary, exceptional.
– OPPOSITES: unexceptional.

unforgivable ▶ adjective INEXCUSABLE, unpardonable, unjustifiable, indefensible.
– OPPOSITES: venial.

unfortunate ▶ adjective 1 *unfortunate people* UNLUCKY, hapless, jinxed, out of luck, luckless, wretched, miserable, forlorn, poor, pitiful; *informal* down on one's luck. 2 *an unfortunate start to our holiday* ADVERSE, disadvantageous, unfavourable, unlucky, unwelcome, unpromising, inauspicious, unpropitious, bad; *formal* grievous. 3 *an unfortunate remark* REGRETTABLE, inappropriate, unsuitable, infelicitous, unbecoming, inopportune, tactless, injudicious.
– OPPOSITES: lucky, auspicious.

unfortunately ▶ adverb UNLUCKILY, sadly, regrettably, unhappily, alas, sad to say; *informal* worse luck.

unfounded ▶ adjective GROUNDLESS, baseless, unsubstantiated, unproven, unsupported, uncorroborated, unconfirmed, unverified, unattested, unjustified, without basis, without foundation; specious, speculative, conjectural, idle; false, untrue.
– OPPOSITES: proven.

unfriendly ▶ adjective 1 *an unfriendly look* HOSTILE, disagreeable, antagonistic, aggressive; ill-natured, unpleasant, surly, sour, uncongenial; inhospitable, unneighbourly, unwelcoming, unkind, unsympathetic; unsociable, anti-social; aloof, stiff, cold, cool, frosty, distant, unapproachable; *informal* standoffish, starchy. 2 *an unfriendly wind* UNFAVOURABLE, unhelpful, disadvantageous, unpropitious, inauspicious, hostile. 3 *environmentally unfriendly* HARMFUL, damaging, destructive, disrespectful.
– OPPOSITES: amiable, favourable.

unfunny ▶ adjective UNAMUSING, bad, lame, stupid, pathetic, stale, flat.

ungainly ▶ adjective AWKWARD, clumsy, klutzy, ungraceful, graceless, inelegant, gawky, maladroit, gauche, uncoordinated; *archaic* lubberly.
– OPPOSITES: graceful.

ungodly ▶ adjective 1 *ungodly behaviour* UNHOLY, godless, irreligious, impious, blasphemous, sacrilegious, profane; immoral, corrupt, depraved, sinful, wicked, evil, iniquitous. 2 *he called at an ungodly hour* UNREASONABLE, unsocial, anti-social, unearthly, godforsaken.

ungovernable ▶ adjective UNCONTROLLABLE, unmanageable, anarchic, intractable; unruly, disorderly, rebellious, riotous, restive, refractory, wild, mutinous, undisciplined.

ungracious ▶ adjective RUDE, impolite, uncivil, discourteous, ill-mannered, bad-mannered, curt, brusque, uncouth, disrespectful, insolent, impertinent, offhand.
– OPPOSITES: polite.

ungrateful ▶ adjective UNAPPRECIATIVE, unthankful, thankless, ungracious, churlish.
– OPPOSITES: thankful.

unguarded ▶ adjective **1** *an unguarded frontier* UNDEFENDED, unprotected, unfortified; vulnerable, insecure, open to attack. **2** *an unguarded remark* CARELESS, indiscreet, incautious, thoughtless, rash, reckless, foolhardy, foolish, imprudent, injudicious, ill-considered, ill-judged, insensitive; unwary, inattentive, off guard, distracted, absent-minded; candid, open; *literary* temerarious.

unhappiness ▶ noun SADNESS, sorrow, dejection, depression, misery, wretchedness, despondency, despair, desolation, glumness, gloom, gloominess, dolefulness; melancholy, low spirits, mournfulness, woe, malaise, heartache, distress, chagrin, grief, pain, agony, anguish, torment, suffering, tribulation; *informal* the blues.

unhappy ▶ adjective **1** *the unhappy boy cried all night* SAD, miserable, sorrowful, dejected, despondent, disconsolate, morose, broken-hearted, heartbroken, hurting, down, downcast, dispirited, downhearted, depressed, melancholy, mournful, gloomy, glum, lugubrious, despairing, doleful, forlorn, woebegone, woeful, long-faced, joyless, cheerless; *informal* down in the dumps/mouth, blue. **2** *in the unhappy event of litigation* UNFORTUNATE, unlucky, luckless; ill-starred, ill-fated, doomed; regrettable, lamentable; *informal* jinxed; *literary* star-crossed. **3** *I was unhappy with the service I received* DISSATISFIED, displeased, discontented, disappointed, disgruntled, angry; *informal* PO'd.
– OPPOSITES: cheerful.

unharmed ▶ adjective UNINJURED, unhurt, unscathed, safe (and sound), alive and well, in one piece, without a scratch; undamaged, unbroken, unmarred, unspoiled, unsullied, unmarked; sound, intact, perfect, unblemished, pristine.
– OPPOSITES: injured, damaged.

unhealthy ▶ adjective **1** *an unhealthy lifestyle* HARMFUL, detrimental, destructive, injurious, damaging, deleterious; malign, noxious, poisonous, insalubrious, baleful. **2** *an unhealthy pallor* SICKLY, ill, unwell, in poor health, ailing, sick, indisposed, weak, wan, sallow, frail, delicate, infirm, washed out, run-down. **3** *an unhealthy obsession with toenails* UNWHOLESOME, morbid, macabre, twisted, abnormal, warped, depraved, unnatural; *informal* sick, wrong.

unheard of ▶ adjective UNPRECEDENTED, exceptional, extraordinary, out of the ordinary, unthought of, undreamed of, unbelievable, inconceivable, unimaginable, unthinkable; UNKNOWN, unfamiliar, new.
– OPPOSITES: common, well-known.

unheeded ▶ adjective DISREGARDED, ignored, neglected, overlooked, unnoted, unrecognized.

unheralded ▶ adjective OVERLOOKED, unhyped, unannounced, unnoticed, underrated, underestimated, disregarded.

unhinged ▶ adjective DERANGED, demented, unbalanced, unglued, crazed, mad, insane, disturbed, out of one's mind, out of one's tree; *informal* crazy, mental, nutso, bonkers, batty, bushed ♣, loopy, loco, postal, wingy ♣, bananas, touched.
– OPPOSITES: sane.

unholy ▶ adjective **1** *a grin of unholy amusement* UNGODLY, godless, irreligious, impious, blasphemous, sacrilegious, profane, irreverent; wicked, evil, immoral, corrupt, depraved, sinful. **2** *an unholy alliance* UNNATURAL, unusual, improbable, made in Hell.

unhurried ▶ adjective LEISURELY, easy, easygoing, relaxed, slow, deliberate, measured, calm.
– OPPOSITES: hasty.

unhygienic ▶ adjective UNSANITARY, dirty, filthy, contaminated, unhealthy, unwholesome, insalubrious, polluted, foul.
– OPPOSITES: sanitary.

unidentified ▶ adjective UNKNOWN, unnamed, anonymous, incognito, nameless, unfamiliar, strange, mysterious.
– OPPOSITES: known.

unification ▶ noun UNION, merger, fusion, fusing, amalgamation, coalition, combination, confederation, federation, synthesis, joining.

uniform ▶ adjective **1** *a uniform temperature* CONSTANT, consistent, steady, invariable, unvarying, unfluctuating, unchanging, stable, static, regular, fixed, even, equal. **2** *pieces of uniform size* IDENTICAL, matching, similar, equal; same, like, homogeneous, consistent.
– OPPOSITES: variable.
▶ noun *a soldier in uniform* COSTUME, livery, regalia, suit, ensemble, outfit; colours; *informal* getup, monkey suit, rig, gear; *archaic* habit.

uniformity ▶ noun **1** *uniformity in tax law* CONSTANCY, consistency, conformity, invariability, stability, regularity, evenness, homogeneity, equality, harmony. **2** *a dull uniformity* MONOTONY, tedium, tediousness, dullness, dreariness, flatness, sameness.
– OPPOSITES: variation, variety.

unify ▶ verb UNITE, bring together, join (together), marry, merge, fuse, amalgamate, integrate, coalesce, combine, blend, mix, meld, bind, consolidate.
– OPPOSITES: separate.

unilateral ▶ adjective INDEPENDENT, autonomous, solitary, solo, go-it-alone, single-handed, self-determined, maverick, isolationist.

unimaginable ▶ adjective UNTHINKABLE, inconceivable, indescribable, incredible, unbelievable, unheard of, unthought of, untold, mind-boggling, undreamed of, beyond one's wildest dreams.

unimaginative ▶ adjective UNINSPIRED, uninventive, unoriginal, uncreative, commonplace, pedestrian, mundane, institutional, ordinary, routine, matter-of-fact, humdrum, workaday, run-of-the-mill, by-the-numbers, hackneyed, trite, hoary.

unimpeachable ▶ adjective TRUSTWORTHY, reliable, dependable, above suspicion, irreproachable; *informal* squeaky clean.
– OPPOSITES: unreliable.

unimpeded ▶ adjective UNRESTRICTED, unhindered, unblocked, unhampered, free, clear.

unimportant ▶ adjective INSIGNIFICANT, inconsequential, insubstantial, immaterial, trivial, minor, venial, trifling, of little/no importance, of little/no consequence, of no account, no-account, irrelevant, peripheral, extraneous, petty, paltry, derisory, weightless, small; *informal* piddling.

uninhabited ▶ adjective UNPOPULATED, unpeopled, unsettled, vacant, empty, unoccupied; unlived-in, untenanted.

uninhibited ▶ adjective **1** *uninhibited dancing* UNRESTRAINED, unrepressed, abandoned, wild, reckless; unrestricted, uncontrolled, unchecked, intemperate, wanton, loose; *informal* gung-ho. **2** *I'm pretty uninhibited* UNRESERVED, unrepressed, liberated, unselfconscious, free and easy, free-spirited, relaxed, informal, open, outgoing, extrovert, outspoken, candid, frank, forthright; *informal* upfront.
— OPPOSITES: repressed.

uninitiated ▶ adjective UNTRAINED, uninstructed, unschooled, untaught, untutored, uneducated, unknowledgeable, unprepared, unfamiliar.
▶ noun OUTSIDERS, beginners, novices, newcomers, neophytes, newbies.

uninspired ▶ adjective UNIMAGINATIVE, uninventive, pedestrian, mundane, unoriginal, commonplace, ordinary, routine, humdrum, run-of-the-mill, hackneyed, trite; spiritless, passionless, stolid, prosaic.

uninspiring ▶ adjective BORING, dull, dreary, unexciting, unstimulating; dry, colourless, bland, lacklustre, tedious, flaccid, formulaic, humdrum, run-of-the-mill, by-the-numbers.

unintelligent ▶ adjective STUPID, ignorant, dense, brainless, mindless, slow, dull-witted, feeble-minded, stunned ♣, simple-minded, vacuous, obtuse, vapid, irrational, idiotic; *informal* thick, knuckleheaded, bubbleheaded, lunkheaded, dim, dumb, dopey, halfwitted, dozy.

unintelligible ▶ adjective **1** *unintelligible sounds* INCOMPREHENSIBLE, indiscernible, mumbled, indistinct, unclear, slurred, inarticulate, incoherent, garbled. **2** *unintelligible logic* IMPENETRABLE, baffling, perplexing, inscrutable, opaque, cryptic, abstruse, unfathomable, incoherent, incomprehensible, as clear as mud, impossible to follow. **3** *unintelligible graffiti* ILLEGIBLE, indecipherable, unreadable, hieroglyphic.

unintentional ▶ adjective UNINTENDED, accidental, inadvertent, involuntary, unwitting, unthinking, unpremeditated, unconscious; random, fortuitous, serendipitous, fluky.
— OPPOSITES: deliberate.

uninterested ▶ adjective INDIFFERENT, unconcerned, incurious, uninvolved, apathetic, lukewarm, unenthusiastic, bored.

uninteresting ▶ adjective UNEXCITING, boring, dull, tiresome, wearisome, soporific, tedious, jejune, lifeless, lacklustre, humdrum, colourless, soulless, bland, insipid, banal, dry, dreary, drab, pedestrian, lacking; *informal* blah, samey.
— OPPOSITES: exciting.

uninterrupted ▶ adjective UNBROKEN, continuous, continual, constant, non-stop, ceaseless; undisturbed, untroubled.
— OPPOSITES: intermittent.

uninvited ▶ adjective **1** *an uninvited guest* UNASKED, unexpected; unwelcome, unwanted. **2** *uninvited suggestions* UNSOLICITED, unrequested, unsought.

uninviting ▶ adjective UNAPPEALING, unattractive, unappetizing, off-putting; bleak, cheerless, dreary,

dismal, depressing, grim, inhospitable, forbidding.
— OPPOSITES: tempting.

union ▶ noun **1** *the union of art and nature* UNIFICATION, uniting, joining, merging, merger, fusion, fusing, amalgamation, coalition, combination, synthesis, blend, blending, mingling; MARRIAGE, wedding, alliance; coupling. **2** *the workers joined a union* ASSOCIATION, labour union, trade union, league, guild, confederation, federation, brotherhood, organization.
— OPPOSITES: separation, parting.

unionize ▶ verb ORGANIZE, unite; join forces, band together, gang up.

unique ▶ adjective **1** *each site is unique* DISTINCTIVE, distinct, individual, special, idiosyncratic; single, sole, lone, unrepeated, unrepeatable, solitary, exclusive, rare, uncommon, unusual, sui generis; *informal* one-off, one-of-a-kind, once-in-a-lifetime, one-shot. **2** *a unique insight* REMARKABLE, special, singular, noteworthy, notable, extraordinary; unequalled, unparalleled, unmatched, unsurpassed, unrivalled, peerless, nonpareil, incomparable; *formal* unexampled. **3** *species unique to the island* PECULIAR, specific, limited.

unisex ▶ adjective GENDER-NEUTRAL, androgynous, epicene; coed, mixed.

unison
■ **in unison** SIMULTANEOUSLY, at (one and) the same time, (all) at once, (all) together.

unit ▶ noun **1** *the family is the fundamental unit of society* COMPONENT, element, building block, constituent; subdivision. **2** *a unit of currency* QUANTITY, measure, denomination. **3** *a guerrilla unit* DETACHMENT, contingent, division, company, squadron, corps, regiment, brigade, platoon, battalion; cell, faction.

unite ▶ verb **1** *uniting the municipalities* UNIFY, join, link, connect, combine, amalgamate, fuse, weld, bond, wed, marry, bring together, knit together, splice. **2** *environmentalists and activists united* JOIN TOGETHER, join forces, combine, band together, ally, co-operate, collaborate, work together, pull together, team up, hitch up, hook up, twin.
— OPPOSITES: divide.

united ▶ adjective **1** *a united Germany* UNIFIED, integrated, amalgamated, joined, merged; federal, confederate. **2** *a united response* COMMON, shared, joint, combined, communal, co-operative, collective, collaborative, concerted. **3** *they were united in their views* UNANIMOUS, in agreement, agreed, in unison, of the same opinion, like-minded, as one, in accord, in harmony, in unity.

United States of America ▶ noun USA, US, America; *informal* the States, the US of A, Uncle Sam, south of the border, (*Atlantic*) the Boston States ♣.

unity ▶ noun **1** *European unity* UNION, unification, integration, amalgamation; coalition, federation, confederation. **2** *unity between alliance members* HARMONY, accord, co-operation, collaboration, agreement, consensus, solidarity; *formal* concord, concordance. **3** *the organic unity of the universe* ONENESS, singleness, wholeness, uniformity, homogeneity.
— OPPOSITES: division, discord.

universal ▶ adjective GENERAL, ubiquitous, comprehensive, common, omnipresent, all-inclusive, all-embracing, across-the-board; global, worldwide, international, widespread; *formal* catholic.

universally ▶ adverb GENERALLY, widely, commonly, across the board, all over.

universe ▶ noun **1** *the physical universe* COSMOS, macrocosm, totality; infinity, all existence, Creation; space, outer space, firmament. **2** *the universe of computer hardware* WORLD, sphere, domain, preserve, milieu, province.
– RELATED TERMS: cosmic.

university ▶ noun SCHOOL, college, post-secondary institution, academy, institute, polytechnic, alma mater, graduate school.
▶ adjective POST-SECONDARY, undergraduate, college, graduate, academic, ivory-tower; varsity.

unjust ▶ adjective **1** *the assessment was unjust* UNFAIR, prejudiced, prejudicial, biased, inequitable, discriminatory, partisan, partial, one-sided, jaundiced. **2** *an unjust attack* WRONGFUL, unfair, undeserved, unmerited, unwarranted, uncalled for, unreasonable, unjustifiable, undue, gratuitous.
– OPPOSITES: fair.

unjustifiable ▶ adjective **1** *an unjustifiable extravagance* INDEFENSIBLE, inexcusable, unforgivable, unpardonable, uncalled for, gratuitous, without justification, unwarrantable; excessive, immoderate. **2** *an unjustifiable slur on his character* GROUNDLESS, unfounded, baseless, unsubstantiated, unconfirmed, uncorroborated, indefensible, irrational.
– OPPOSITES: reasonable.

unkempt ▶ adjective UNTIDY, messy, scruffy, straggly, disordered, dishevelled, disarranged, rumpled, wind-blown, ungroomed, bedraggled, in a mess, mussed, messed up; tousled, uncombed.
– OPPOSITES: tidy.

unkind ▶ adjective UNCHARITABLE, unpleasant, disagreeable, nasty, mean, mean-spirited, cruel, vindictive, vicious, spiteful, malicious, callous, unsympathetic, unfeeling, uncaring, unsparing, hurtful, ill-natured, hard-hearted, cold-hearted; unfriendly, uncivil, inconsiderate, insensitive, hostile; *informal* bitchy, catty.

unknown ▶ adjective **1** *the future is unknown* UNCERTAIN, undisclosed, unrevealed, secret; undetermined, undecided, unresolved, unsettled, unsure, unascertained. **2** *unknown country* UNEXPLORED, uncharted, unmapped, untravelled, undiscovered, unfamiliar, unheard of, new, novel, strange. **3** *persons unknown* UNIDENTIFIED, anonymous, unnamed, nameless; faceless, hidden. **4** *unknown artists* OBSCURE, unrecognized, unheard of, unsung, overlooked, unheralded, minor, insignificant, unimportant.
– OPPOSITES: familiar.
▶ noun *the overseas ballots are a big unknown* MYSTERY, unknown quantity, uncertainty, ambiguity, variable, anyone's guess; *informal* crapshoot.

unlawful ▶ adjective ILLEGAL, illicit, illegitimate, against the law; criminal, felonious; prohibited, banned, outlawed, proscribed, forbidden.
– OPPOSITES: legal.

unleash ▶ verb LET LOOSE, release, (set) free, unloose, untie, unchain.

unlettered ▶ adjective ILLITERATE, uneducated, poorly educated, unschooled, unlearned, untutored, ignorant.
– OPPOSITES: educated.

unlike ▶ preposition **1** *Montreal is totally unlike Wawa* DIFFERENT FROM, dissimilar to. **2** *unlike Bob, Regis*

enjoyed swing dancing IN CONTRAST TO, as opposed to.
– OPPOSITES: similar too.
▶ adjective *a meeting of unlike minds* DISSIMILAR, unalike, disparate, contrasting, antithetical, different, diverse, incongruous, heterogeneous, mismatched, divergent, at variance, varying, at odds; *informal* poles apart, like night and day, like apples and oranges.

unlikely ▶ adjective **1** *it is unlikely they will ever recover* IMPROBABLE, doubtful, dubious. **2** *an unlikely story* IMPLAUSIBLE, improbable, questionable, unconvincing, far-fetched, unrealistic, incredible, unbelievable, inconceivable, unimaginable; absurd, preposterous; *informal* tall.
– OPPOSITES: probable, believable.

unlimited ▶ adjective **1** *unlimited supplies of water* INEXHAUSTIBLE, limitless, illimitable, boundless, immeasurable, incalculable, untold, infinite, endless, bottomless, never-ending. **2** *unlimited travel* UNRESTRICTED, unconstrained, unrestrained, unchecked, unbridled, uncurbed. **3** *unlimited power* TOTAL, unqualified, unconditional, unrestricted, absolute, supreme.
– OPPOSITES: finite, restricted.

unload ▶ verb **1** *we unloaded the van* UNPACK, empty. **2** *they unloaded the cases from the truck* REMOVE, off-load, discharge. **3** *the government unloaded its 20 per cent stake* SELL, discard, jettison, off-load, get rid of, dispose of; palm something off on someone, foist something on someone, fob something off on someone; *informal* dump, ditch, get shut of. **4** *she unloaded her troubles* DIVULGE, talk about, open up about, pour out, vent, give vent to, get (something) off one's chest.

unlock ▶ verb UNBOLT, unlatch, unbar, unfasten, open.

unloved ▶ adjective UNWANTED, uncared-for, friendless, unvalued; rejected, unwelcome, shunned, spurned, neglected, abandoned.

unlucky ▶ adjective **1** *he was unlucky not to score* UNFORTUNATE, luckless, out of luck, jinxed, hapless, ill-fated, ill-starred, unhappy; *informal* down on one's luck; *literary* star-crossed. **2** *an unlucky number* UNFAVOURABLE, inauspicious, unpropitious, ominous, cursed, ill-fated, ill-omened, disadvantageous, unfortunate.
– OPPOSITES: fortunate, favourable.

unmanageable ▶ adjective **1** *the huge project was unmanageable* TROUBLESOME, awkward, inconvenient; cumbersome, bulky, unwieldy. **2** *his behaviour was becoming unmanageable* UNCONTROLLABLE, ungovernable, unruly, disorderly, out of hand, difficult, disruptive, undisciplined, wayward, refractory, restive; *archaic* contumacious.

unmanly ▶ adjective EFFEMINATE, effete, unmasculine, womanish, epicene; weak, limp-wristed, soft, timid, timorous; *informal* sissy, swishy, wimpish, wimpy, nancy, pansy, camp.
– OPPOSITES: virile.

unmanned ▶ adjective **1** *an unmanned spacecraft* AUTOMATIC, computerized, remote-controlled, robotic. **2** *he was unmanned by her response* TAKEN ABACK, gobsmacked, shell-shocked, devastated.

unmarried ▶ adjective UNWED(DED), single; spinster, bachelor; unattached, available, eligible, free.

unmask ▶ verb REVEAL, uncover, expose, bring to light, lay bare.

unmatched ▶ adjective UNEQUALLED, unrivalled, unparalleled, unsurpassed, peerless, matchless, without equal, nonpareil, without parallel, incomparable, inimitable, superlative, second to none, in a class of its own.

unmentionable ► adjective TABOO, censored, forbidden, banned, proscribed, prohibited, not to be spoken of, ineffable, unspeakable, unutterable, unprintable, off limits; *informal* no go.

unmercifully ► adjective RUTHLESSLY, cruelly, harshly, mercilessly, pitilessly, cold-bloodedly, hard-heartedly, callously, brutally, severely, unforgivingly, inhumanely, inhumanly, heartlessly, unsympathetically, unfeelingly, unsparingly.

unmistakable ► adjective DISTINCTIVE, distinct, telltale, indisputable, indubitable, undoubted, unambiguous, unequivocal; plain, clear, clear-cut, definite, obvious, unmissable, evident, self-evident, manifest, patent, pronounced, as plain as the nose on your face, as clear as day.

unmitigated ► adjective ABSOLUTE, unqualified, categorical, complete, total, downright, outright, utter, out-and-out, undiluted, unequivocal, untempered, veritable, perfect, consummate, pure, sheer.

unmoved ► adjective **1** *he was totally unmoved by her outburst* UNAFFECTED, untouched, unimpressed, aloof, cool, cold, dry-eyed; unconcerned, uncaring, unsympathetic, unreceptive, indifferent, impassive, unemotional, stoical, phlegmatic, equable, nonchalant; impervious (to), oblivious (to), heedless (of), deaf to. **2** *he remained unmoved on the crucial issues* STEADFAST, firm, unwavering, unswerving, resolved, resolute, decided, unswayed, uninfluenced, inflexible, unbending, intransigent, implacable, adamant.

unnatural ► adjective **1** *the life of a circus bear is completely unnatural* ABNORMAL, unusual, uncommon, extraordinary, strange, odd, peculiar, unorthodox, exceptional, irregular, atypical, untypical; freakish, freaky, uncanny. **2** *a flash of unnatural colour* ARTIFICIAL, man-made, synthetic, manufactured, inorganic, genetically engineered. **3** *unnatural vice* PERVERTED, warped, aberrant, twisted, deviant, depraved, degenerate; *informal* kinky, sick. **4** *her voice sounded unnatural* AFFECTED, artificial, mannered, stilted, forced, laboured, strained, false, fake, theatrical, insincere, ersatz; *informal* put on, phony.
– OPPOSITES: normal, genuine.

unnecessary ► adjective UNNEEDED, inessential, not required, uncalled for, useless, unwarranted, unwanted, undesired, dispensable, unimportant, optional, extraneous, gratuitous, expendable, disposable, redundant, pointless, purposeless.
– OPPOSITES: essential.

unnerve ► verb DEMORALIZE, discourage, dishearten, dispirit, daunt, alarm, frighten, dismay, disconcert, discompose, perturb, upset, discomfit, take aback, unsettle, disquiet, fluster, agitate, shake, ruffle, throw off balance; *informal* rattle, faze, shake up, discombobulate.
– OPPOSITES: hearten.

unobtrusive ► adjective INCONSPICUOUS, unnoticeable, low-key, discreet, circumspect, understated, unostentatious.
– OPPOSITES: extrovert, conspicuous.

unoccupied ► adjective **1** *an unoccupied house* VACANT, empty, uninhabited, unlived-in, untenanted, abandoned; free, available. **2** *an unoccupied territory* UNINHABITED, unpopulated, unpeopled, unsettled. **3** *many young people were unoccupied* AT LEISURE, idle,

free, with time on one's hands, at a loose end; unemployed, without work.
– OPPOSITES: inhabited, populated, busy.

unofficial ► adjective **1** *unofficial figures* UNCONFIRMED, unauthenticated, uncorroborated, unsubstantiated, provisional, off the record. **2** *an unofficial committee* INFORMAL, casual; unauthorized, unsanctioned, unaccredited.
– OPPOSITES: confirmed, formal.

unoriginal ► adjective CONVENTIONAL, uninspired, overdone, tired, clichéd, hackneyed; recycled, stock, paint-by-number.

unorthodox ► adjective UNCONVENTIONAL, unusual, radical, nonconformist, avant-garde, eccentric, maverick, strange, idiosyncratic; heterodox, heretical, dissenting; *informal* off-the-wall, way out, offbeat, kooky.
– OPPOSITES: conventional.

unpaid ► adjective **1** *unpaid bills* UNSETTLED, outstanding, due, overdue, owing, owed, payable, undischarged, delinquent, past due. **2** *unpaid charity work* VOLUNTARY, volunteer, honorary, unsalaried, unremunerative, unwaged, pro bono (publico).

unpalatable ► adjective **1** *unpalatable food* UNAPPETIZING, unappealing, unsavoury, inedible, uneatable; disgusting, rancid, revolting, nauseating, tasteless, flavourless, gross. **2** *the unpalatable truth* DISAGREEABLE, unpleasant, regrettable, unwelcome, lamentable, hard to swallow, hard to take.
– OPPOSITES: tasty.

unparalleled ► adjective EXCEPTIONAL, unique, singular, rare, unequalled, unprecedented, without parallel, without equal, nonpareil, matchless, peerless, unrivalled, unsurpassed, unexcelled, incomparable, second to none; *formal* unexampled.

unperturbed ► adjective UNTROUBLED, undisturbed, unworried, unconcerned, unmoved, unflustered, unruffled, undismayed, impassive; calm, composed, cool, collected, unemotional, self-possessed, self-assured, level-headed, unfazed, nonplussed, laid-back.

unplanned ► adjective UNPREMEDITATED, unscheduled, accidental, unexpected, surprise; spontaneous, impromptu, impulsive, sudden.

unpleasant ► adjective **1** *a very unpleasant situation* DISAGREEABLE, irksome, troublesome, annoying, irritating, vexatious, displeasing, distressing, nasty, horrible, terrible, awful, dreadful, hateful, miserable, invidious, objectionable, offensive, obnoxious, repugnant, repulsive, repellent, revolting, disgusting, distasteful, nauseating, unsavoury. **2** *an unpleasant man* UNLIKABLE, unlovable, disagreeable; unfriendly, rude, impolite, obnoxious, nasty, spiteful, mean, mean-spirited; insufferable, unbearable, annoying, irritating.
– OPPOSITES: agreeable, likable.

unpolished ► adjective **1** *unpolished wood* UNVARNISHED, unfinished, untreated, natural. **2** *his unpolished ways* UNSOPHISTICATED, unrefined, uncultured, uncultivated, inelegant, coarse, vulgar, crude, rough (and ready), awkward, clumsy, gauche. **3** *an unpolished performance* SLIPSHOD, rough, loose, crude, uneven; amateurish; unprepared, unrehearsed, inchoate.
– OPPOSITES: varnished, sophisticated.

unpopular ► adjective DISLIKED, friendless, unliked, unloved, loathed, despised; unwelcome, avoided, ignored, rejected, outcast, shunned, spurned, cold-shouldered, ostracized; unfashionable, unhip, out.

unprecedented ▶ adjective UNHEARD OF, unknown, new, novel, groundbreaking, revolutionary, pioneering, epoch-making; unparalleled, unequalled, unmatched, unrivalled, without parallel, without equal, out of the ordinary, unusual, exceptional, singular, unique; *formal* unexampled.

unpredictable ▶ adjective **1** *unpredictable results* UNFORESEEABLE, uncertain, unsure, doubtful, dubious, iffy, dicey, in the balance, up in the air. **2** *unpredictable behaviour* ERRATIC, moody, volatile, unstable, capricious, temperamental, mercurial, changeable, variable; {on-again, off-again}.

unprejudiced ▶ adjective **1** *unprejudiced observation* OBJECTIVE, impartial, unbiased, neutral, value-free, non-partisan, detached, disinterested. **2** *unprejudiced attitudes* UNBIASED, tolerant, non-discriminatory, politically correct, liberal, broad-minded.
– OPPOSITES: partisan, intolerant.

unpremeditated ▶ adjective UNPLANNED, spontaneous, unprepared, impromptu, spur-of-the-moment, unrehearsed, ad lib, improvised, extemporaneous; *informal* off-the-cuff, off the top of one's head.
– OPPOSITES: planned.

unprepared ▶ adjective **1** *we were unprepared for the PST hike* UNREADY, off (one's) guard, surprised, taken aback; caught napping, caught flat-footed, caught with one's pants down. **2** *they are unprepared to support the reforms* UNWILLING, disinclined, loath, reluctant, resistant, opposed. **3** *the pianist's recital sounded unprepared. See* UNPOLISHED *sense 3.*
– OPPOSITES: ready, willing.

unpretentious ▶ adjective **1** *he was thoroughly unpretentious* UNAFFECTED, modest, unassuming, without airs, natural, straightforward, open, honest, sincere, frank, ingenuous. **2** *an unpretentious hotel* SIMPLE, plain, modest, humble, unostentatious, unsophisticated, folksy, no-frills.

unprincipled ▶ adjective IMMORAL, unethical, amoral, unscrupulous, Machiavellian, dishonourable, dishonest, deceitful, devious, corrupt, crooked, wicked, evil, villainous, shameless, base, low; libertine, licentious.
– OPPOSITES: ethical.

unproductive ▶ adjective **1** *unproductive soil* INFERTILE, sterile, barren, arid, unfruitful, poor. **2** *unproductive meetings* FRUITLESS, futile, vain, idle, useless, worthless, valueless, pointless, ineffective, ineffectual, unprofitable, unrewarding.
– OPPOSITES: fruitful.

unprofessional ▶ adjective IMPROPER, unethical, unprincipled, unscrupulous, dishonourable, disreputable, unseemly, unbecoming, indecorous; AMATEURISH, amateur, unskilled, unskilful, inexpert, unqualified, inexperienced, incompetent, second-rate, inefficient.

unpromising ▶ adjective INAUSPICIOUS, unfavourable, unpropitious, discouraging, disheartening, gloomy, bleak, black, portentous, ominous, ill-omened.
– OPPOSITES: auspicious.

unprotected ▶ adjective VULNERABLE, defenceless, undefended, unguarded, helpless, wide open, exposed.

unqualified ▶ adjective **1** *an unqualified accountant* UNTRAINED, inexperienced; unlicensed, quack. **2** *those*

unqualified to look after children UNSUITABLE, unsuited, unfit, ineligible, incompetent, unable, incapable, unprepared, ill-equipped, ill-prepared. **3** *unqualified support* UNCONDITIONAL, unreserved, unlimited, without reservations, categorical, unequivocal, unambiguous, wholehearted; complete, absolute, downright, undivided, total, utter.

unquestionable ▶ adjective INDUBITABLE, undoubted, beyond question, beyond doubt, indisputable, undeniable, irrefutable, incontestable, incontrovertible, unequivocal; certain, sure, definite, self-evident, evident, manifest, obvious, apparent, patent.

unravel ▶ verb **1** *he unravelled the strands* UNTANGLE, disentangle, separate out, unwind, untwist, unsnarl, unthread. **2** *detectives are trying to unravel the mystery* SOLVE, resolve, clear up, puzzle out, unscramble, get to the bottom of, explain, clarify, make head or tail of; figure out, dope out. **3** *society is starting to unravel* FALL APART, fail, collapse, go wrong, deteriorate, go downhill, fray.
– OPPOSITES: entangle.

unreadable ▶ adjective **1** *unreadable writing* ILLEGIBLE, hard to read, indecipherable, unintelligible, hieroglyphic, scrawled, crabbed, chicken-scratchy. **2** *heavy, unreadable novels* DULL, tedious, boring, uninteresting, dry, wearisome, stodgy, turgid, difficult, indigestible, impenetrable, heavy, ponderous. **3** *Tyler's expression was unreadable* INSCRUTABLE, enigmatic, impenetrable, cryptic, mysterious, deadpan; *informal* poker-faced.
– OPPOSITES: legible, accessible.

unready ▶ *See* UNPREPARED *sense 1.*

unreal ▶ adjective **1** *an unreal world of monsters and fairies* IMAGINARY, fictitious, pretend, make-believe, made-up, dreamed-up, mock, false, illusory, chimerical, mythical, fanciful; hypothetical, theoretical; *informal* phony. **2** *informal that roller coaster was totally unreal* INCREDIBLE, fantastic, unbelievable, out of this world.

unrealistic ▶ adjective **1** *unrealistic expectations* IMPRACTICAL, impracticable, unfeasible, non-viable; unreasonable, irrational, illogical, senseless, silly, foolish, fanciful, idealistic, quixotic, romantic, starry-eyed, airy-fairy, blue-sky, pie in the sky. **2** *unrealistic images* UNLIFELIKE, non-realistic, unnatural, non-representational, abstract; unbelievable, implausible.
– OPPOSITES: pragmatic, lifelike.

unreasonable ▶ adjective **1** *an unreasonable officer* UNCOOPERATIVE, unhelpful, disobliging, unaccommodating, awkward, contrary, difficult; obstinate, obdurate, wilful, headstrong, pigheaded, cussed, intractable, intransigent, inflexible; irrational, illogical, prejudiced, intolerant. **2** *unreasonable demands* UNACCEPTABLE, preposterous, outrageous, ridiculous; excessive, impossible, immoderate, disproportionate, undue, inordinate, intolerable, unjustified, unwarranted, uncalled for.

unrecognizable ▶ adjective UNIDENTIFIABLE, unknowable; disguised, beyond recognition.

unrefined ▶ adjective **1** *unrefined clay* UNPROCESSED, untreated, crude, raw, natural, unprepared, unfinished. **2** *unrefined people* UNCULTURED, uncultivated, uncivilized, uneducated, unsophisticated; boorish, lumpen, oafish, loutish, coarse, vulgar, rude, rough, uncouth.
– OPPOSITES: processed.

unrelated ▶ adjective **1** *unrelated incidents* SEPARATE, unconnected, independent, unassociated, distinct, discrete, disparate, random. **2** *a reason unrelated to my work* IRRELEVANT, immaterial, inapplicable, extraneous, unconcerned, off the topic, beside the point, not pertinent, not germane.

unrelenting ▶ adjective **1** *the unrelenting heat* CONTINUAL, constant, continuous, relentless, unremitting, unabating, unflagging, uninterrupted, unrelieved, incessant, unceasing, ceaseless, endless, unending, persistent, non-stop. **2** *an unrelenting opponent* IMPLACABLE, inflexible, uncompromising, unyielding, unbending, relentless, determined, dogged, tenacious, steadfast, tireless, indefatigable, unflagging, unshakeable, unswerving, unwavering.
— OPPOSITES: intermittent.

unreliable ▶ adjective **1** *unreliable volunteers* UNDEPENDABLE, untrustworthy, irresponsible, fickle, fair-weather, capricious, erratic, unpredictable, inconstant, faithless, temperamental. **2** *an unreliable indicator* QUESTIONABLE, open to doubt, doubtful, dubious, suspect, unsound, tenuous, uncertain, fallible; risky, chancy, inaccurate; *informal* iffy, dicey.

unremitting ▶ adjective RELENTLESS, incessant, unrelenting, continual, constant, continuous, unabating, uninterrupted, unbroken, unrelieved, sustained, unshakeable, unceasing, ceaseless, endless, unending, persistent, perpetual, interminable; merciless.

unrepentant ▶ adjective REMORSELESS, unrepenting, impenitent, unashamed, shameless, unapologetic, unabashed.

unreported ▶ adjective *See* UNTOLD sense 2.

unrequited ▶ adjective UNRECIPROCATED, unreturned; vain, spurned, rejected, unsatisfied.

unreserved ▶ adjective **1** *unreserved support* UNCONDITIONAL, unqualified, without reservations, unlimited, categorical, unequivocal, unambiguous; absolute, complete, thorough, wholehearted, full, total, utter, undivided. **2** *unreserved seats* NOT BOOKED, unallocated, unoccupied, free, empty, vacant, available.
— OPPOSITES: qualified, booked.

unresolved ▶ adjective UNDECIDED, unsettled, undetermined, uncertain, open, pending, open to debate/question, moot, doubtful, on the table, in play, in doubt, up in the air.
— OPPOSITES: decided.

unrest ▶ noun DISRUPTION, disturbance, trouble, turmoil, turbulence, disorder, chaos, anarchy; discord, disquiet, dissension, dissent, strife, protest, rebellion, uprising, rioting.
— OPPOSITES: peace.

unrestrained ▶ adjective UNCONTROLLED, rampant, runaway, unconstrained, unrestricted, unreserved, unchecked, unbridled, unlimited, unfettered, uninhibited, full on, unbounded, undisciplined.

unrestricted ▶ adjective UNLIMITED, open, free, freewheeling, clear, unhindered, unimpeded, unhampered, unchecked, unqualified, unrestrained, unconstrained, unblocked, unbounded, unconfined, rampant.
— OPPOSITES: limited.

unripe ▶ adjective IMMATURE, unready, green, sour; incipient, in development.

unrivalled ▶ adjective UNEQUALLED, without equal, unparalleled, without parallel, unmatched,

unsurpassed, unexcelled, incomparable, beyond compare, inimitable, second to none, nonpareil.

unruffled ▶ adjective CALM, composed, self-controlled, self-possessed, untroubled, unperturbed, at ease, relaxed, serene, cool, poised, placid, cool-headed, unemotional, equanimous, equable, stoical; *informal* unfazed, nonplussed, laid-back, loosey-goosey.

unruly ▶ adjective DISORDERLY, rowdy, wild, unmanageable, uncontrollable, disobedient, disruptive, undisciplined, restive, wayward, wilful, headstrong, irrepressible, obstreperous, difficult, intractable, out of hand, recalcitrant; boisterous, lively, rambunctious, refractory; *archaic* contumacious.
— OPPOSITES: disciplined.

unsafe ▶ adjective **1** *the building was unsafe* DANGEROUS, risky, perilous, hazardous, life-threatening, high-risk, treacherous, hairy, insecure, unsound; harmful, injurious, toxic, contaminated. **2** *an unsafe assumption* UNRELIABLE, insecure, unsound, questionable, open to question/doubt, doubtful, dubious, suspect, fallible; *informal* iffy.
— OPPOSITES: harmless, secure.

unsaid ▶ adjective UNSPOKEN, unuttered, unstated, unexpressed, unvoiced, suppressed; tacit, implicit, not spelled out, implied; understood, inferred.

unsanitary ▶ adjective UNHYGIENIC, unhealthy, contaminated, germ-ridden, disease-ridden, unclean, insalubrious, squalid, dirty, filthy, polluted, unsafe; *informal* germy.

unsatisfactory ▶ adjective DISAPPOINTING, dissatisfying, undesirable, disagreeable, displeasing; inadequate, unacceptable, poor, bad, substandard, weak, mediocre, no good, not good enough, lacking, wanting, subpar, defective, deficient, insufficient, imperfect, inferior; *informal* leaving a lot to be desired, no great shakes.

unsavoury ▶ adjective **1** *unsavoury portions of food* UNPALATABLE, unappetizing, distasteful, disagreeable, unappealing, repugnant, off-putting, unattractive; inedible, uneatable, disgusting, revolting, nauseating, sickening, foul, raunchy, nasty, vile; tasteless, bland, flavourless; *informal* yucky. **2** *an unsavoury character* DISREPUTABLE, unpleasant, undesirable, disagreeable, nasty, mean, rough; immoral, degenerate, dishonourable, dishonest, unprincipled, unscrupulous, low, villainous; *informal* shady, crooked.
— OPPOSITES: tasty, appetizing.

unscathed ▶ adjective UNHARMED, unhurt, uninjured, undamaged, in one piece, intact, safe (and sound), unmarked, untouched, without a scratch.
— OPPOSITES: harmed, injured.

unscrupulous ▶ adjective UNPRINCIPLED, unethical, immoral, conscienceless, shameless, reprobate, exploitative, corrupt, dishonest, dishonourable, deceitful, devious, underhanded, unsavoury, disreputable, evil, wicked, villainous, Machiavellian; *informal* crooked, shady; *dated* dastardly.

unseat ▶ verb **1** *the horse unseated his rider* DISLODGE, throw, dismount, upset, unhorse. **2** *an attempt to unseat the party leader* DEPOSE, oust, remove from office, topple, overthrow, bring down, overturn, eject, dislodge, supplant; usurp.

unseemly ▶ adjective IMPROPER, unbecoming,

unfitting, unbefitting, unworthy, undignified, indiscreet, indelicate, indecorous, ungentlemanly, unladylike.
— OPPOSITES: decorous.

unseen ▶ adjective HIDDEN, concealed, obscured, camouflaged, out of sight, invisible, imperceptible, undetectable, unnoticeable, unnoticed, unobserved; mysterious.

unselfish ▶ adjective ALTRUISTIC, selfless, self-denying, self-sacrificing; generous, giving, magnanimous, philanthropic, public-spirited, charitable, benevolent, caring, kind, considerate, thoughtful, noble.

unsettle ▶ verb UNNERVE, upset, disturb, disquiet, perturb, discomfit, disconcert, alarm, dismay, trouble, bother, agitate, fluster, ruffle, shake (up), throw, unbalance, destabilize; *informal* rattle, faze, pull the rug (out) from under.

unsettled ▶ adjective **1** *an unsettled life* AIMLESS, directionless, purposeless, without purpose; rootless, nomadic. **2** *an unsettled child* RESTLESS, restive, fidgety, anxious, worried, troubled, fretful; agitated, ruffled, uneasy, disconcerted, discomposed, unnerved, ill at ease, edgy, on edge, tense, nervous, apprehensive, disturbed, perturbed, unstrung; *informal* rattled, fazed. **3** *unsettled weather* CHANGEABLE, changing, variable, varying, inconstant, inconsistent, ever-changing, erratic, unstable, undependable, unreliable, uncertain, unpredictable, protean. **4** *the question remains unsettled* UNDECIDED, to be decided, unresolved, undetermined, moot, uncertain, open to debate, doubtful, in doubt, up in the air, in a state of uncertainty. **5** *the debt remains unsettled* UNPAID, payable, outstanding, owing, owed, to be paid, due, undischarged, delinquent, past due. **6** *unsettled areas* UNINHABITED, unpopulated, unpeopled, unoccupied, desolate, lonely.

unshakeable ▶ adjective STEADFAST, resolute, staunch, firm, decided, determined, unswerving, unwavering; unyielding, inflexible, dogged, obstinate, obdurate, tenacious, persistent, indefatigable, tireless, unflagging, unremitting, unrelenting, relentless.

unsightly ▶ adjective UGLY, unattractive, unprepossessing, unlovely, disagreeable, displeasing, hideous, horrible, repulsive, revolting, offensive, grotesque, monstrous, gross, ghastly.
— OPPOSITES: attractive.

unskilful ▶ adjective INEXPERT, incompetent, inept, unskilled, amateurish, hack, unprofessional, inexperienced, untrained, unpractised; uncoordinated; *informal* ham-fisted, ham-handed.

unskilled ▶ adjective UNTRAINED, unqualified; manual, blue-collar, labouring, menial; inexpert, inexperienced, unpractised, amateurish, unprofessional.

unsociable ▶ adjective UNFRIENDLY, uncongenial, unneighbourly, unapproachable, introverted, reticent, reserved, withdrawn, aloof, distant, remote, detached, unsocial, anti-social, asocial, taciturn, silent, quiet; *informal* standoffish.
— OPPOSITES: friendly.

unsolicited ▶ adjective UNINVITED, unsought, unasked-for, unrequested.

unsophisticated ▶ adjective **1** *she seemed a bit unsophisticated* UNWORLDLY, naive, unrefined, simple, innocent, ignorant, green, immature, callow, inexperienced, childlike, artless, guileless,

ingenuous, natural, unaffected, unassuming, unpretentious; *informal* cheesy. **2** *unsophisticated software* SIMPLE, crude, low-tech, basic, rudimentary, primitive, rough and ready, homespun, bush-league; straightforward, uncomplicated, uninvolved.

unsound ▶ adjective **1** *structurally unsound* WEAK, rickety, flimsy, wobbly, unstable, crumbling, damaged, rotten, ramshackle, shoddy, insubstantial, unsafe, dangerous. **2** *this submission appears unsound* UNTENABLE, flawed, defective, faulty, ill-founded, flimsy, unreliable, questionable, dubious, tenuous, suspect, fallacious, fallible; *informal* iffy. **3** *of unsound mind* DISORDERED, deranged, disturbed, demented, unstable, unbalanced, unhinged, addled, insane.
— OPPOSITES: strong.

unsparing ▶ adjective **1** *he is unsparing in his criticism* MERCILESS, pitiless, ruthless, relentless, remorseless, unmerciful, unforgiving, implacable, uncompromising; stern, strict, severe, harsh, tough, rigorous. **2** *unsparing approval* UNGRUDGING, unstinting, willingly given, free, ready; lavish, liberal, generous, magnanimous, open-handed.

unspeakable ▶ adjective **1** *unspeakable delights* INDESCRIBABLE, beyond description, inexpressible, unutterable, indefinable, unimaginable, inconceivable. **2** *an unspeakable crime* HORRIFIC, awful, appalling, dreadful, horrifying, horrendous, abominable, frightful, fearful, shocking, ghastly, gruesome, monstrous, heinous, egregious, deplorable, despicable, execrable, vile.

unspecified ▶ adjective UNNAMED, unstated, unidentified, undesignated, undefined, unfixed, undecided, undetermined, uncertain; nameless, unknown, indefinite, indeterminate, vague, t.b.a.

unspectacular ▶ adjective UNREMARKABLE, unexceptional, undistinguished, unmemorable, ordinary, average, commonplace, mediocre, run-of-the-mill, indifferent.
— OPPOSITES: remarkable.

unspoiled ▶ adjective IMMACULATE, perfect, pristine, virgin, unimpaired, unblemished, unharmed, unflawed, undamaged, untouched, unmarked, untainted, as good as new/before.

unspoken ▶ adjective UNSTATED, unexpressed, unuttered, unsaid, unvoiced, unarticulated, undeclared, not spelt out; tacit, implicit, implied, understood, unwritten.
— OPPOSITES: explicit.

unsportsmanlike ▶ adjective DISHONOURABLE, unfair, underhanded, below the belt, improper, unseemly, foul, mean.

unstable ▶ adjective **1** *that old ladder looks unstable* UNSTEADY, rocky, wobbly, tippy; rickety, shaky, unsafe, insecure, precarious. **2** *unstable coffee prices* CHANGEABLE, volatile, variable, fluctuating, irregular, unpredictable, capricious, erratic, {on-again, off-again}. **3** *he was mentally unstable* UNBALANCED, of unsound mind, mentally ill, deranged, demented, disturbed, unhinged, volatile; *informal* kooky.
— OPPOSITES: steady, firm.

unsteady ▶ adjective **1** *she was unsteady on her feet* UNSTABLE, rocky, wobbly, rickety, shaky, tottery, doddery, insecure. **2** *an unsteady flow* IRREGULAR, uneven, varying, variable, erratic, spasmodic, changeable, changing, fluctuating, inconstant, intermittent, fitful, stop-and-go; *informal* herky-jerky.
— OPPOSITES: stable, regular.

unstinting ▶ adjective UNGRUDGING, unsparing, free,

ready, benevolent, big-hearted, kind-hearted, kind, unselfish; lavish, liberal, generous, magnanimous, open-handed, freely given, munificent, beneficent, bountiful; profuse, abundant, ample, gushing; *literary* plenteous, bounteous.

unstoppable ▶ adjective INDOMITABLE, unbeatable, invincible, supreme; *informal* on fire; irrepressible, inextinguishable, inexorable, uncontrollable.

unstudied ▶ adjective NATURAL, easy, spontaneous, unaffected, unforced, uncontrived, unstilted, unpretentious, ingenuous, without airs, artless.

unsubstantiated ▶ adjective UNCONFIRMED, unsupported, uncorroborated, unverified, unattested, unproven; unfounded, groundless, baseless, without foundation, unjustified.

unsuccessful ▶ adjective **1** *an unsuccessful attempt* FAILED, ineffective, fruitless, profitless, unproductive, abortive; vain, futile, useless, pointless, worthless, luckless. **2** *an unsuccessful business* UNPROFITABLE, loss-making. **3** *an unsuccessful candidate* FAILED, losing, beaten; unlucky, out of luck.

unsuitable ▶ adjective **1** *the product is unsuitable for your needs* INAPPROPRIATE, unsuited, wrong, ill-suited, inapt, inapplicable, unacceptable, unfitting, unbefitting, incompatible, out of place/keeping, misplaced; *formal* inapposite. **2** *an unsuitable moment for belching* INOPPORTUNE, infelicitous, inappropriate, wrong, unfortunate; *formal* malapropos.
— OPPOSITES: appropriate, opportune.

unsullied ▶ adjective SPOTLESS, untarnished, unblemished, unspoiled, untainted, impeccable, undamaged, unimpaired, stainless, immaculate, flawless, unflawed.
— OPPOSITES: tarnished.

unsung ▶ adjective UNACKNOWLEDGED, uncelebrated, unacclaimed, unapplauded, unhailed, unheralded; neglected, unrecognized, overlooked, forgotten.
— OPPOSITES: celebrated.

unsure ▶ adjective **1** *she felt very unsure* UNCONFIDENT, unassertive, insecure, hesitant, diffident, anxious, apprehensive. **2** *Sally was unsure what to do* UNDECIDED, irresolute, dithering, equivocating, vacillating, of two minds, wishy-washy, in a quandary. **3** *some teachers are unsure about the proposed strike* DUBIOUS, doubtful, skeptical, uncertain, unconvinced. **4** *the date is unsure* NOT FIXED, undecided, uncertain.
— OPPOSITES: confident.

unsurpassed ▶ adjective UNMATCHED, unrivalled, unparalleled, unequalled, matchless, peerless, without equal, nonpareil, inimitable, incomparable, unsurpassable; *formal* unexampled.

unsurprising ▶ adjective PREDICTABLE, foreseeable, to be expected, foreseen, anticipated, routine, par for the course; *informal* inevitable, in the cards.

unsuspecting ▶ adjective UNSUSPICIOUS, unwary, unaware, unconscious, ignorant, unwitting; trusting, gullible, credulous, ingenuous, naive, wide-eyed.
— OPPOSITES: wary.

unswerving ▶ adjective UNWAVERING, unfaltering, steadfast, unshakeable, staunch, firm, resolute, stalwart, dedicated, committed, constant, single-minded, dogged, indefatigable, unyielding, unbending, indomitable.

unsympathetic ▶ adjective **1** *unsympathetic staff* UNCARING, unconcerned, unfriendly, unfeeling, apathetic, insensitive, indifferent, unkind, pitiless, thoughtless, heartless, hard-hearted, stony, callous.

2 *the government was unsympathetic to these views* OPPOSED, against, (dead) set against, antagonistic, ill-disposed; *informal* anti. **3** *an unsympathetic character* UNLIKEABLE, dislikable, disagreeable, unpleasant, unappealing, off-putting, objectionable, unsavoury; unfriendly.
— OPPOSITES: caring.

unsystematic ▶ adjective UNMETHODICAL, uncoordinated, disorganized, unplanned, indiscriminate; random, inconsistent, irregular, erratic, casual, haphazard, chaotic.

untamed ▶ adjective WILD, feral, undomesticated, unbroken.

untangle ▶ verb **1** *I untangled the fishing tackle* DISENTANGLE, unravel, unsnarl, straighten out, untwist, untwine, unknot. **2** *untangling a mystery* SOLVE, find the/an answer to, resolve, puzzle out, work out, fathom, clear up, clarify, get to the bottom of; *informal* figure out.

untarnished ▶ adjective UNSULLIED, unblemished, untainted, impeccable, undamaged, unspoiled, unimpaired, spotless, stainless, pristine, perfect; *informal* squeaky clean.

untenable ▶ adjective INDEFENSIBLE, insupportable, unsustainable, unjustified, unjustifiable, flimsy, weak, shaky.

untested ▶ adjective *See* UNTRIED.

unthinkable ▶ adjective UNIMAGINABLE, inconceivable, unbelievable, incredible, beyond belief, implausible, preposterous.

unthinking ▶ adjective **1** *an unthinking lout* THOUGHTLESS, inconsiderate, insensitive; tactless, undiplomatic, indiscreet. **2** *an unthinking remark* ABSENT-MINDED, heedless, thoughtless, careless, injudicious, imprudent, unwise, foolish, reckless, rash, precipitate; involuntary, inadvertent, unintentional, spontaneous, impulsive, unpremeditated.
— OPPOSITES: thoughtful, intentional.

untidy ▶ adjective **1** *untidy hair* SCRUFFY, tousled, dishevelled, unkempt, messy, disordered, disarranged, messed up, rumpled, bedraggled, uncombed, ungroomed, straggly, ruffled, tangled, matted, wind-blown, raddled; *informal* mussed up, raggedy. **2** *the room was untidy* DISORDERED, messy, in a mess, disorderly, disorganized, in disorder, cluttered, in a muddle, muddled, in chaos, chaotic, haywire, topsy-turvy, in disarray, at sixes and sevens; *informal* higgledy-piggledy.
— OPPOSITES: neat, orderly.

untie ▶ verb UNDO, unknot, unbind, unfasten, unlace, untether, unhitch, unmoor; (turn) loose, (set) free, release, let go, unshackle.

until ▶ preposition & conjunction **1** *I work until Thursday* (UP) TILL, to, up to, through (to), up until, as late as. **2** *this did not happen until 1998* BEFORE, prior to, previous to, up to, up until, (up) till, earlier than.

untimely ▶ adjective **1** *an untimely interruption* ILL-TIMED, badly timed, mistimed; inopportune, inappropriate, unseasonable; inconvenient, unwelcome, infelicitous; *formal* malapropos. **2** *his untimely death* PREMATURE, (too) early, too soon, before time.
— OPPOSITES: opportune.

untiring ▶ adjective VIGOROUS, energetic, determined, resolute, enthusiastic, keen, zealous, spirited, dogged, tenacious, persistent, persevering, staunch; tireless, unflagging, unfailing, unfaltering, unwavering, indefatigable, unrelenting, unswerving; *formal* pertinacious.

untold ▶ **adjective 1** *untold quantities* BOUNDLESS, immeasurable, incalculable, limitless, unlimited, infinite, measureless; countless, innumerable, endless, numberless, uncountable; numerous, many, multiple; *literary* multitudinous, myriad. **2** *the untold story* UNREPORTED, overlooked, ignored; hidden, secret, unrecounted, unrevealed, undisclosed, undivulged, unpublished.
– OPPOSITES: limited.

untouched ▶ **adjective 1** *the food was untouched* UNEATEN, unconsumed, undrunk, untasted; ignored. **2** *one of the few untouched areas* UNSPOILED, unmarked, unblemished, unsullied, undefiled, undamaged, unharmed; pristine, natural, immaculate, virgin, in perfect condition, unaffected, unchanged, unaltered.

untoward ▶ **adjective 1** *an untoward occurrence* INCONVENIENT, unlucky, unexpected, unforeseen, surprising, unusual; unwelcome, unfavourable, adverse, unfortunate, infelicitous; *formal* malapropos. **2** *untoward behaviour* IMPROPER, unseemly; perverse.

untrained ▶ **adjective** UNSKILLED, untaught, unschooled, untutored, unpractised, amateur, inexperienced, ill-equipped, ill-prepared; unqualified, unlicensed, amateur, non-professional.

untried ▶ **adjective** UNTESTED, unestablished, new, experimental, unattempted, trial, test, pilot, unproven.
– OPPOSITES: established.

untroubled ▶ **adjective** UNWORRIED, unperturbed, unconcerned, unruffled, undismayed, unbothered, unalarmed, unflustered; insouciant, nonchalant, composed, blasé, carefree, calm, serene, tranquil, relaxed, halcyon, comfortable, at ease, happy-go-lucky, blissful, laid-back, mellow; *informal* supercool.

untrue ▶ **adjective 1** *these suggestions are totally untrue* FALSE, untruthful, fabricated, made up, invented, concocted, trumped up; erroneous, wrong, incorrect, inaccurate; fallacious, fictitious, unsound, unfounded, baseless, misguided. **2** *he was untrue to his friends* UNFAITHFUL, disloyal, faithless, false, treacherous, traitorous, deceitful, deceiving, duplicitous, double-dealing, insincere, unreliable, undependable, inconstant; *informal* two-timing; *literary* perfidious.
– OPPOSITES: correct, faithful.

untrustworthy ▶ **adjective** DISHONEST, deceitful, double-dealing, treacherous, fickle, traitorous, two-faced, duplicitous, mendacious, dishonourable, unprincipled, unscrupulous, corrupt, slippery; unreliable, undependable, fly-by-night, capricious.
– OPPOSITES: reliable.

untruth ▶ **noun 1** *a patent untruth* LIE, falsehood, fib, fabrication, invention, falsification, half-truth, exaggeration; story, myth, piece of fiction; *informal* tall story, fairy tale, cock-and-bull story, whopper. **2** *the total untruth of the story* FALSITY, falsehood, falseness, untruthfulness, fictitiousness; fabrication, dishonesty, deceit, deceitfulness, inaccuracy, unreliability.

untruthful ▶ **adjective 1** *the answers may be untruthful* FALSE, untrue, fabricated, made up, invented, trumped up; erroneous, wrong, incorrect, inaccurate; fallacious, fictitious. **2** *an untruthful person* LYING, mendacious, dishonest, deceitful, duplicitous, false, double-dealing, two-faced,

untrustworthy, dishonourable; *informal* crooked; *literary* perfidious.
– OPPOSITES: honest.

untutored ▶ **adjective** UNEDUCATED, untaught, unschooled, ignorant, unsophisticated, uncultured, unenlightened, unlettered, uninitiated.
– OPPOSITES: educated.

untwist ▶ **verb** UNDO, untwine, disentangle, unravel, unsnarl, unwind, unroll, uncoil, unfurl, open (out), straighten (out).

unused ▶ **adjective 1** *unused supplies* UNUTILIZED, unemployed, unexploited, spare, surplus; left over, extra, untouched, remaining, uneaten, unopened, unconsumed, unneeded, not required, not in service. **2** *he was unused to such directness* UNACCUSTOMED, new, unfamiliar, unconversant, unacquainted; a stranger.
– OPPOSITES: accustomed.

unusual ▶ **adjective** UNCOMMON, abnormal, atypical, unexpected, surprising, unfamiliar, different; strange, odd, curious, out of the ordinary, extraordinary, unorthodox, unconventional, outlandish, singular, special, unique, peculiar, bizarre; rare, scarce, few and far between, thin on the ground, exceptional, isolated, occasional, infrequent; *informal* weird, offbeat, out there, freaky.
– OPPOSITES: common.

unutterable *See* UNSPEAKABLE.

unvarnished ▶ **adjective 1** *unvarnished wood* BARE, plain, unpainted, unpolished, unfinished, untreated. **2** *the unvarnished truth* STRAIGHTFORWARD, plain, simple, stark, blunt, straight-up, raw, undiluted; truthful, realistic, candid, honest, frank, forthright, direct.

unveil ▶ **verb** REVEAL, present, display, show, exhibit, put on display; release, launch, bring out; disclose, divulge, make known, make public, publish, broadcast, communicate.

unwanted ▶ **adjective 1** *an unwanted development* UNWELCOME, undesirable, undesired, unpopular; unpleasant, disagreeable, displeasing, distasteful, objectionable; regrettable, deplorable, lamentable; unacceptable, intolerable, awful. **2** *an unwanted guest* UNINVITED, unbidden, unasked, unrequested, unsolicited. **3** *many people feel unwanted* FRIENDLESS, unloved, uncared-for, forsaken, rejected, shunned, ostracized; superfluous, useless, unnecessary, unneeded. **4** *unwanted food* UNUSED, left over, surplus, excess, uneaten, unconsumed, untouched.
– OPPOSITES: welcome.

unwarranted ▶ **adjective 1** *the criticism is unwarranted* UNJUSTIFIED, uncalled for, unnecessary, unreasonable, unjust, groundless, excessive, gratuitous, immoderate, disproportionate, undue, unconscionable, unjustifiable, indefensible, inexcusable, unforgivable, unpardonable. **2** *an unwarranted invasion of privacy* UNAUTHORIZED, unsanctioned, unapproved, uncertified, unlicensed; illegal, unlawful, illicit, illegitimate.
– OPPOSITES: justified.

unwary ▶ **adjective** INCAUTIOUS, careless, thoughtless, heedless, inattentive, unwatchful, off one's guard.

unwavering ▶ **adjective** STEADY, fixed, resolute, resolved, firm, constant, steadfast, enduring, abiding, unswerving, unfaltering, untiring, tireless, indefatigable, unyielding, relentless, unremitting, unrelenting, sustained.
– OPPOSITES: unsteady.

unwelcome ► **adjective 1** *I was made to feel unwelcome* UNWANTED, uninvited, unaccepted, excluded, rejected. **2** *even a small increase is unwelcome* UNDESIRABLE, undesired, unpopular, unfortunate, disappointing, upsetting, distressing, disagreeable, displeasing; regrettable, deplorable, objectionable, lamentable.

unwell ► **adjective** ILL, sick, indisposed, ailing, not (very) well, not too good, lousy, bad, rough, not oneself, under/below par, groggy, peaky, queasy, woozy, nauseous, nauseated; off, poorly, wretched, dead; under the weather; funny, weird; *informal* crappy, pukey.

unwholesome ► **adjective 1** *unwholesome air* UNHEALTHY, noxious, poisonous; insalubrious, unhygienic, unsanitary; harmful, injurious, detrimental, destructive, damaging, deleterious, baleful. **2** *unwholesome websites* IMPROPER, immoral, indecent, depraved, corrupting, salacious. — OPPOSITES: healthy, seemly.

unwieldy ► **adjective** CUMBERSOME, unmanageable, unmanoeuvrable; awkward, clumsy, massive, heavy, hefty, ponderous, bulky, weighty. — OPPOSITES: manageable.

unwilling ► **adjective 1** *unwilling conscripts* RELUCTANT, unenthusiastic, hesitant, resistant, grudging, involuntary, forced. **2** *he was unwilling to take on that responsibility* DISINCLINED, reluctant, averse, loath; **(be unwilling to do something)** not have the heart to, balk at, refuse to, demur at, shy away from, flinch from, shrink from, have qualms about, have misgivings about, have reservations about. — OPPOSITES: keen.

unwillingness ► **adjective** DISINCLINATION, reluctance, hesitation, diffidence, wavering, vacillation, resistance, foot-dragging, objection, opposition, doubts, second thoughts, scruples, qualms, misgivings.

unwind ► **verb 1** *Ella unwound the scarf from her neck* UNROLL, uncoil, unravel, untwine, untwist, disentangle, open (out), straighten (out). **2** *he liked to unwind after work* RELAX, loosen up, ease up/off, slow down, de-stress, unbend, rest, put one's feet up, sit back, take it easy, take a load off; *informal* wind down, mellow (out), let it all hang out, veg, hang loose, chill (out).

unwise ► **adjective** INJUDICIOUS, ill-advised, ill-judged, imprudent, inexpedient, foolish, silly, inadvisable, impolitic, misguided, foolhardy, irresponsible, impetuous, rash, hasty, overhasty, reckless. — OPPOSITES: sensible.

unwitting ► **adjective 1** *an unwitting accomplice* UNKNOWING, unconscious, unsuspecting, oblivious, unaware, innocent, in the dark. **2** *an unwitting mistake* UNINTENTIONAL, unintended, inadvertent, involuntary, unconscious, accidental. — OPPOSITES: conscious.

unworkable ► **adjective** IMPRACTICABLE, unfeasible, non-viable, unrealizable, impossible.

unworldly ► **adjective 1** *a gauche, unworldly girl* NAIVE, simple, inexperienced, innocent, green, raw, callow, immature, ignorant, gullible, ingenuous, artless, guileless, childlike, trusting, credulous; non-materialistic. **2** *unworldly beauty* UNEARTHLY, otherworldly, ethereal, ghostly, preternatural, supernatural, paranormal, mystical.

unworthy ► **adjective 1** *he was unworthy of trust* UNDESERVING, ineligible, unqualified, unfit. **2** *unworthy behaviour* UNBECOMING, unsuitable, inappropriate, unbefitting, unfitting, unseemly, improper; discreditable, shameful, dishonourable, despicable, ignoble, contemptible, reprehensible. — OPPOSITES: deserving, becoming.

unwritten ► **adjective** TACIT, implicit, unvoiced, taken for granted, accepted, recognized, understood; traditional, customary, conventional; oral, verbal, spoken, vocal, word-of-mouth.

unyielding ► **adjective 1** *an unyielding oak door* STIFF, inflexible, unbending, rigid, firm, hard, solid, tough, tight, compact, compressed, dense. **2** *an unyielding taskmaster* RESOLUTE, inflexible, uncompromising, unbending, unshakeable, unwavering, immovable, intractable, intransigent, rigid, stiff, firm, determined, dogged, iron, obstinate, stubborn, adamant, obdurate, tenacious, insistent, relentless, implacable, single-minded; *formal* pertinacious.

up ► **adverb** See UPWARDS.
► **adjective 1** *she was up early today* AWAKE, wide awake, out of bed, about, conscious, alert, functioning. **2** *he was up for some fun* READY, eager, willing, open, prepared. **3** *I'm not up on the latest news* INFORMED, up-to-date, versed, cognizant, familiar, briefed, in touch, plugged in, savvy.

up-and-coming ► **adjective** PROMISING, budding, emerging, rising, with potential, to watch, upwardly-mobile; talented, gifted, able.

upbeat ► **adjective** OPTIMISTIC, cheerful, cheery, positive, confident, hopeful, sanguine, bullish, buoyant, gung-ho. — OPPOSITES: pessimistic, negative.

upbraid ► **verb** REPRIMAND, rebuke, admonish, chastise, chide, reprove, reproach, scold, berate, take to task, lambaste, give someone a piece of one's mind, give someone a tongue-lashing, rake/haul over the coals, lecture; *informal* tell off, give someone a talking-to, tear a strip off (of), dress down, give someone an earful, rap over the knuckles, bawl out, lay into, chew out, ream out; *formal* castigate; *rare* reprehend.

upbringing ► **noun** CHILDHOOD, early life, formative years, teaching, education, instruction, tutelage, care, rearing, raising, breeding.

upcoming ► **adjective** FORTHCOMING, coming, impending, future, imminent, approaching, looming, ahead, in the pipeline, in the offing, on the horizon, coming down the pike.

update ► **verb 1** *security measures are continually updated* MODERNIZE, upgrade, bring up to date, improve, overhaul. **2** *I'll update him on today's developments* BRIEF, bring up to date, inform, fill in, tell, notify, apprise, keep posted; *informal* clue in, put in the picture, bring/keep up to speed.

upend ► **verb** OVERTURN, invert, turn over, turn upside down; capsize, flip, tip, keel over, turn turtle; trip, take the legs out from under.

upfront ► **adjective** FRANK, open, honest, candid, forthright, plain-spoken, direct, unequivocal.

upgrade ► **verb 1** *there are plans to upgrade the rail system* IMPROVE, modernize, update, bring up to date, make better, ameliorate, reform; rehabilitate, recondition, refurbish, spruce up, renovate, rejuvenate, overhaul; bring up to code. **2** *he was upgraded to a seat in the cabinet* PROMOTE, give promotion to, elevate, move up, raise. — OPPOSITES: downgrade, demote.

upheaval ▶ noun DISRUPTION, disturbance, trouble, turbulence, disorder, confusion, turmoil, pandemonium, chaos, mayhem, cataclysm, shakeup, debacle; revolution, change, craziness.

uphill ▶ adjective **1** *an uphill path* UPWARD, rising, ascending, climbing. **2** *an uphill struggle* ARDUOUS, difficult, hard, taxing, demanding, exacting, stiff, formidable, exhausting, tiring, wearisome, laborious, gruelling, back-breaking, punishing, burdensome, onerous, Herculean; *informal* no picnic, killing; *archaic* toilsome.
– OPPOSITES: downhill.

uphold ▶ verb **1** *the court upheld his claim for damages* CONFIRM, endorse, sustain, approve, agree to, support; champion, defend. **2** *they've a tradition to uphold* MAINTAIN, sustain, continue, preserve, protect, champion, defend, keep, hold to, keep alive, keep going, back (up), stand by.
– OPPOSITES: overturn, oppose.

upkeep ▶ noun MAINTENANCE, repair(s), service, servicing, preservation, conservation; running; care, support, keep, subsistence.

uplift ▶ verb *she needs something to uplift her spirits* BOOST, raise, buoy up, lift, cheer up, perk up, enliven, brighten up, lighten, stimulate, inspire, revive, restore; *informal* buck up.

uplifted ▶ adjective RAISED, upraised, elevated, upthrust; held high, erect, proud.

uplifting ▶ adjective INSPIRING, stirring, inspirational, rousing, moving, touching, affecting, cheering, heartening, heartwarming, encouraging; *formal* numinous.

upload ▶ verb TRANSFER, send, transmit.

upper ▶ adjective **1** *the upper floor* HIGHER, superior; top; *informal* nosebleed. **2** *the upper echelons of the party* SENIOR, superior, higher-level, higher-ranking, top, loftier.
– OPPOSITES: lower.
■ **the upper hand** AN ADVANTAGE, the edge, the whip hand, a lead, a head start, ascendancy, superiority, supremacy, sway, control, power, mastery, dominance, command, leverage.

upper-class ▶ adjective ARISTOCRATIC, noble, of noble birth, patrician, titled, blue-blooded, high-born, well-born, elite, born with a silver spoon in one's mouth; rich, wealthy; upscale, upmarket, upper-crust, high-class, tony, top-drawer, classy, posh, uptown; landowning, landed; *archaic* gentle, of gentle birth.

uppermost ▶ adjective **1** *the uppermost branches* HIGHEST, top, topmost. **2** *their own problems remained uppermost in their minds* PREDOMINANT, of greatest importance, to the fore, foremost, first, primary, dominant, principal, chief, main, paramount, supreme, preponderant, major.

uppity ▶ adjective ARROGANT, snobbish, hoity-toity, snooty, pretentious, bumptious, full of oneself, puffed up, conceited, pompous, self-assertive, overbearing, throwing one's weight about, cocky, cocksure, impertinent, haughty, self-important, superior, presumptuous, overweening, uppish, high and mighty, too big for one's britches/boots.

upright ▶ adjective **1** *an upright position* VERTICAL, perpendicular, plumb, straight (up), straight up and down, standing, bolt upright, erect, on end; on one's feet. **2** *an upright member of the community* HONEST, honourable, upstanding, respectable, high-minded, law-abiding, right-minded, worthy, moral, ethical,

righteous, decent, scrupulous, conscientious, good, virtuous, principled, of principle, noble, incorruptible.
– OPPOSITES: horizontal, dishonourable.

uprising ▶ noun REBELLION, revolt, insurrection, mutiny, revolution, insurgence, intifada, rioting, riot; civil disobedience, unrest, anarchy, coup, coup d'état, putsch.

uproar ▶ noun **1** *the uproar in the kitchen continued for some time* TURMOIL, disorder, confusion, chaos, commotion, disturbance, rumpus, ruckus, tumult, turbulence, mayhem, pandemonium, bedlam, noise, din, clamour, hubbub, racket; shouting, yelling, babel; *informal* hullaballoo, hoo-ha, brouhaha. **2** *there was an uproar when she was dismissed* OUTCRY, furor, protest; fuss, reaction, backlash, commotion, hue and cry; *informal* hullabaloo, stink, kerfuffle, rhubarb, firestorm.
– OPPOSITES: calm.

uproarious ▶ adjective **1** *an uproarious party* RIOTOUS, rowdy, noisy, loud, wild, unrestrained, unruly, rip-roaring, rollicking, boisterous, rambunctious, knockabout. **2** *an uproarious joke* HILARIOUS, hysterical, rib-tickling, gut-busting, priceless, side-splitting, knee-slapping, thigh-slapping.
– OPPOSITES: quiet.

uproot ▶ verb **1** *don't uproot wild flowers* PULL UP, root out, rip out; *literary* deracinate. **2** *hundreds of families were uprooted* DISPLACE, expel, drive out, evict, deport.
– OPPOSITES: plant.

upscale ▶ adjective DELUXE, posh, ritzy, upper-class, classy, chi-chi; high-end, expensive, high-priced.

upset ▶ verb **1** *the accusation upset her* DISTRESS, trouble, perturb, dismay, disturb, discompose, unsettle, disconcert, disquiet, worry, bother, agitate, fluster, throw, ruffle, unnerve, shake; hurt, sadden, grieve. **2** *he upset a tureen of soup* KNOCK OVER, overturn, upend, tip over, flip, topple (over); spill. **3** *the dam will upset the ecological balance* DISRUPT, interfere with, disturb, throw out, throw into confusion, throw off balance, mess with/up. **4** *the Flames upset the Canucks 3-0* DEFEAT, beat, topple; surprise, embarrass.
▶ noun **1** *a stomach upset* COMPLAINT, disorder, ailment, illness, sickness, malady; *informal* bug. **2** *the Oilers' victory was a remarkable upset* SURPRISE WIN, shocker.
▶ adjective **1** *the loss made Jane upset* DISTRESSED, troubled, perturbed, dismayed, disturbed, unsettled, disconcerted, worried, bothered, anxious, agitated, flustered, ruffled, unnerved, shaken, unstrung; hurt, saddened, grieved; *informal* cut up, choked. **2** *an upset stomach* DISTURBED, unsettled, queasy, bad, hurting, poorly.
– OPPOSITES: unperturbed, calm.

upshot ▶ noun RESULT, end result, consequence, outcome, conclusion; effect, repercussion, reverberations, ramification, after-effect, payoff.
– OPPOSITES: cause.

upside down ▶ adjective **1** *an upside-down canoe* UPTURNED, upended, inverted, wrong side up, overturned; capsized, flipped. **2** *the apartment was turned upside-down* IN DISARRAY, in disorder, jumbled up, in a mess, in a muddle, untidy, disorganized, chaotic, all over the place, in chaos, in confusion, topsy-turvy, at sixes and sevens; *informal* higgledy-piggledy.

upstage ▶ verb OUTSHINE, outclass, eclipse, overshadow, trump, put someone in the shade, put to shame.

upstanding ▶ adjective *an upstanding citizen* HONEST, honourable, upright, respectable, high-minded, law-abiding, right-minded, worthy, trustworthy, moral, ethical, righteous, decent, good, virtuous, principled, of principle, noble, incorruptible, straightforward.
– OPPOSITES: dishonourable.

upstart ▶ noun PARVENU, arriviste, nouveau riche, status seeker, social climber, a jumped-up——, johnny-come-lately.

upsurge ▶ noun See SURGE.

upswing ▶ noun See SURGE sense 2.

uptight ▶ adjective TENSE, nervous, anxious, on edge, high-strung, hypersensitive, defensive, worked up, impatient, angry; straightlaced, rigid, prim, priggish, anal-retentive, anal.

up to date ▶ adjective **1** *up-to-date equipment* MODERN, contemporary, the latest, state-of-the-art, cutting-edge, leading-edge, new, present-day, up-to-the-minute; advanced; mod. **2** *the newsletter will keep you up to date* INFORMED, up to speed, in the picture, in touch, au fait, au courant, conversant, familiar, knowledgeable, acquainted, aware, clued in.
– OPPOSITES: out of date, old-fashioned.

upturn ▶ noun IMPROVEMENT, upswing, turn for the better; recovery, revival, rally, resurgence, increase, rise, hike, jump, leap, upsurge, boost, escalation.
– OPPOSITES: fall, slump.

upward ▶ adjective *an upward trend* RISING, on the rise, ascending, climbing, mounting; uphill.
– OPPOSITES: downward.
▶ adverb *the smoke drifts upward. See* UPWARDS.

upwards ▶ adverb *he inched his way upwards* UP, upward, higher, uphill, upslope; to the top, skyward, heavenward.
– OPPOSITES: downward.
■ **upward(s) of** MORE THAN, above, over, in excess of, exceeding, beyond, greater than.

urban ▶ adjective TOWN, city, municipal, civic, metropolitan, built-up, inner-city, downtown, suburban; urbanized, citified, townie.
– OPPOSITES: rural.

urbane ▶ adjective SUAVE, sophisticated, debonair, worldly, cultivated, cultured, civilized, cosmopolitan; smooth, polished, refined, self-possessed; courteous, polite, well-mannered, mannerly, civil, charming, gentlemanly, gallant.
– OPPOSITES: uncouth, unsophisticated.

urchin ▶ noun RAGAMUFFIN, waif, stray; imp, rascal, street urchin; *derogatory* guttersnipe; scapegrace; *dated* gamin.

urge ▶ verb **1** *she urged him to try again* ENCOURAGE, exhort, enjoin, press, entreat, implore, call on, appeal to, beg, plead with, coax; egg on, prod, prompt, spur, goad, incite, push, pressure, pressurize; *formal* adjure; *literary* beseech. **2** *she urged her horse down the lane* SPUR (ON), force, drive, impel, propel. **3** *I urge caution in interpreting these results* ADVISE, counsel, advocate, recommend, suggest, advance.
▶ noun *his urge to travel* DESIRE, wish, need, compulsion, longing, yearning, hankering, craving, appetite, hunger, thirst; fancy, impulse, impetus; *informal* yen, itch.

urgent ▶ adjective **1** *the urgent need for more funding* ACUTE, pressing, dire, desperate, critical, serious, grave, intense, crying, burning, compelling, extreme,

exigent, high-priority, top-priority; life-and-death. **2** *an urgent whisper* INSISTENT, persistent, importunate, earnest, pleading, begging.

urinate ▶ verb PEE, relieve oneself, pass water, make water, have/take a leak, piddle, have a tinkle, take a whiz; *informal* piss; *formal* micturate.

URL ▶ noun ADDRESS, IP address, link, alias.

usability ▶ noun ERGONOMICS, ease of use, user-friendliness, accessibility, convenience, intuitiveness.

usable ▶ adjective READY/FIT FOR USE, able to be used, at someone's disposal, disposable; working, in working order, functioning, functional, serviceable, operational, up and running, accessible.

usage ▶ noun **1** *energy usage* USE, consumption, utilization. **2** *the usage of equipment* USE, utilization, operation, manipulation, running, handling. **3** *the intricacies of English usage* PHRASEOLOGY, parlance, idiom, way of speaking/writing, mode of expression, style; idiolect. **4** *the usages of polite society* CUSTOM, practice, habit, tradition, convention, rule, observance; way, procedure, form, wont; *formal* praxis; (**usages**) mores.

use ▶ verb **1** *she used her key to open the front door* UTILIZE, make use of, avail oneself of, employ, work, operate, wield, ply, apply, manoeuvre, manipulate, put to use, put/press into service. **2** *the court will use its discretion in making an order* EXERCISE, employ, bring into play, practise, apply, exert, bring to bear. **3** *he just felt used* TAKE ADVANTAGE OF, exploit, manipulate, take liberties with, impose on, abuse; capitalize on, profit from, trade on, milk; *informal* walk all over. **4** *we have used all the available funds* CONSUME, get/go through, exhaust, deplete, expend, spend; waste, fritter away, squander, dissipate, run out of.
▶ noun **1** *the use of such weapons* UTILIZATION, usage, application, employment, operation, manipulation. **2** *what is the use of that?* ADVANTAGE, benefit, service, utility, usefulness, help, good, gain, avail, profit, value, worth, point, object, purpose, sense, reason. **3** *composers have not found much use for the device* NEED, necessity, call, demand, requirement.

used ▶ adjective *a used car* SECOND-HAND, pre-owned, nearly new, old; worn, hand-me-down, cast-off, recycled, warmed-over.
– OPPOSITES: new.
■ **used to** ACCUSTOMED TO, no stranger to, familiar with, at home with, in the habit of, an old hand at, experienced in, versed in, conversant with, acquainted with.

useful ▶ adjective **1** *a useful multi-purpose tool* FUNCTIONAL, practical, handy, convenient, utilitarian, serviceable, of use, of service. **2** *a useful experience* BENEFICIAL, advantageous, helpful, worthwhile, profitable, rewarding, productive, constructive, valuable, fruitful.
– OPPOSITES: useless, disadvantageous.

useless ▶ adjective **1** *useless attempts* FUTILE, to no avail, (in) vain, pointless, to no purpose, unavailing, hopeless, ineffectual, ineffective, to no effect, fruitless, unprofitable, profitless, unproductive; *archaic* bootless. **2** *useless machines* UNUSABLE, broken, kaput, defunct, dud, faulty. **3** (*informal*) *he was a useless worker* INCOMPETENT, inept, ineffective, incapable, unemployable, inadequate, hopeless, no-account, bad; *informal* pathetic.
– OPPOSITES: useful, beneficial, competent.

user ▶ noun CUSTOMER, consumer, client; operator.

user-defined ▸ adjective ADJUSTABLE, changeable, editable, customizable.

user-friendly ▸ adjective EASY-TO-USE, accessible, intuitive, usable, practical, ergonomic, simple, idiot-proof, goof-proof.

usher ▸ verb *she ushered him to a window seat* ESCORT, accompany, take, show, see, lead, conduct, guide, steer, shepherd, marshal.

▸ noun *ushers showed them to their seats* GUIDE, attendant, escort, sidesman.

■ **usher something in** HERALD, mark the start of, signal, ring in, show in, set the scene for, pave the way for; start, begin, introduce, open the door to, get going, set in motion, get underway, kick off, launch.

usual ▸ adjective HABITUAL, customary, accustomed, wonted, normal, routine, regular, standard, typical, established, set, settled, stock, conventional, traditional, expected, predictable, familiar; average, general, ordinary, everyday.

— OPPOSITES: exceptional.

usually ▸ adverb NORMALLY, generally, habitually, customarily, routinely, typically, ordinarily, commonly, conventionally, traditionally; as a rule, in general, more often than not, in the main, mainly, mostly, for the most part, nine times out of ten.

usurp ▸ verb **1** *Richard usurped the throne* SEIZE, take over, take possession of, take, commandeer, wrest, assume, expropriate. **2** *the Hanoverian dynasty had usurped the Stuarts* OUST, overthrow, remove, topple, unseat, depose, dethrone; supplant, replace.

utensil ▸ noun IMPLEMENT, tool, instrument, device, apparatus, gadget, appliance, contrivance, contraption, aid; *informal* gizmo.

utilitarian ▸ adjective PRACTICAL, functional, pragmatic, serviceable, useful, sensible, efficient, utility, workaday, no-frills; plain, unadorned, undecorative.

— OPPOSITES: decorative.

utility ▸ noun **1** *we have increased the machine's utility* USEFULNESS, use, benefit, value, advantage, advantageousness, help, helpfulness, effectiveness, avail; *formal* efficacy. **2** *an important public utility* SERVICE, service provider, organization, corporation, institution.

utilize ▸ verb USE, make use of, put to use, employ, avail oneself of, bring/press into service, bring into play, deploy, draw on, exploit, harness.

utmost ▸ adjective *a matter of the utmost importance* GREATEST, highest, maximum, most, uttermost; extreme, supreme, paramount.

▸ noun *a plot that stretches credulity to the utmost* MAXIMUM, uttermost, limit; *informal* max.

Utopia ▸ noun PARADISE, heaven (on earth), Eden, Garden of Eden, Shangri-La, Elysium; idyll, nirvana, God's country; *literary* Arcadia.

Utopian ▸ adjective IDEALISTIC, visionary, romantic, starry-eyed, fanciful, unrealistic, pie-in-the-sky; ideal, perfect, paradisal, heavenly, idyllic, blissful, Elysian; *literary* Arcadian.

utter¹ ▸ adjective *that's utter garbage* COMPLETE, total, absolute, thorough, perfect, downright, out-and-out, outright, thoroughgoing, all-out, sheer, arrant, wholesale, rank, pure, real, veritable, consummate, categorical, unmitigated, unqualified, unadulterated, unalloyed.

utter² ▸ verb **1** *he uttered an exasperated snort* EMIT, let out, give, produce. **2** *he hardly uttered a word* SAY, speak, voice, express, articulate, pronounce, enunciate, verbalize, vocalize.

utterance ▸ noun REMARK, comment, word, statement, observation, declaration, pronouncement; exclamation, assertion.

utterly ▸ adverb COMPLETELY, totally, absolutely, entirely, wholly, fully, thoroughly, quite, altogether, one hundred per cent, downright, outright, in all respects, unconditionally, perfectly, really, to the hilt, to the core; dead.

uttermost ▸ adjective & noun. *See* UTMOST.

U-turn ▸ noun *a complete U-turn in economic policy* VOLTE-FACE, turnaround, about-face, reversal, shift, change of heart, change of mind, backtracking, change of plan, flip-flop; one-eighty, U-ey.

Vv

vacancy ▶ noun **1** *there are vacancies for computer technicians* OPENING, position, post, job, opportunity, place. **2** *a hotel vacancy* ROOM AVAILABLE, space for rent.

vacant ▶ adjective **1** *a vacant house* EMPTY, unoccupied, available, not in use, free, unfilled; uninhabited, untenanted. **2** *a vacant look* BLANK, expressionless, unresponsive, emotionless, impassive, uninterested, vacuous, empty, absent, glazed, glassy; unintelligent, dull-witted, dense, brainless, empty-headed, zombified, lobotomized.
— OPPOSITES: full, occupied, expressive.

vacate ▶ verb **1** *he was forced to vacate the premises* LEAVE, move out of, evacuate, quit, free, depart from; abandon, desert. **2** *she will be vacating his post next year* RESIGN FROM, leave, stand down from, give up, bow out of, relinquish, retire from, quit.
— OPPOSITES: occupy, take up.

vacation ▶ noun *their summer vacations in Hawaii* HOLIDAY, trip, tour, break, leave, leave of absence, time off, recess, furlough, sabbatical; *formal* sojourn.

vaccination ▶ noun INOCULATION, immunization; injection; *informal* jab, shot; vaccine.

vacillate ▶ verb DITHER, waver, be indecisive, be undecided, be ambivalent, hesitate, be of two minds, blow hot and cold, keep changing one's mind; fluctuate, oscillate, hem and haw; *informal* dilly-dally, shilly-shally, be conflicted.

vacuous ▶ adjective SILLY, inane, unintelligent, insipid, foolish, stupid, fatuous, idiotic, brainless, witless, vapid, vacant, empty-headed; *informal* dumb, moronic, brain-dead, fluffy, fluffball.
— OPPOSITES: intelligent.

vacuum ▶ noun **1** *people longing to fill the spiritual vacuum in their lives* EMPTINESS, void, nothingness, vacancy, absence, black hole. **2** *the political vacuum left by the Emperor's death* GAP, space, lacuna, void. **3** (*informal*) *I use the vacuum for cleaning the rug* VACUUM CLEANER, vac; *proprietary* Dustbuster.

vagabond ▶ noun. See VAGRANT *noun*.

vagary ▶ noun CHANGE, fluctuation, variation, quirk, peculiarity, oddity, eccentricity, unpredictability, caprice, foible, whim, whimsy, fancy.

vagrant ▶ noun *a temporary home for vagrants* STREET PERSON, tramp, drifter, down-and-out, derelict, beggar, itinerant, wanderer, nomad, traveller, vagabond, transient, homeless person, hobo; *informal* bag lady, bum; *literary* wayfarer.
▶ adjective *vagrant beggars* HOMELESS, drifting, transient, roving, roaming, itinerant, wandering, nomadic, travelling, vagabond, rootless, of no fixed address/abode.

vague ▶ adjective **1** *a vague shape* INDISTINCT, indefinite, indeterminate, unclear, ill-defined; hazy, fuzzy, misty, blurred, blurry, out of focus, faint, shadowy, dim, obscure, nebulous, amorphous, diaphanous. **2** *a vague description* IMPRECISE, rough, approximate, inexact, non-specific, generalized, ambiguous, equivocal, hazy, woolly. **3** *they had only vague plans* HAZY, uncertain, undecided, unsure, unclear, unsettled, indefinite, indeterminate, unconfirmed, up in the air, speculative, sketchy. **4** *she was so vague in everyday life* ABSENT-MINDED, forgetful, dreamy, abstracted, with one's head in the clouds, scatty, scattered, not with it.
— OPPOSITES: clear, precise, certain.

vaguely ▶ adverb **1** *she looks vaguely familiar* SLIGHTLY, a little, a bit, somewhat, rather, in a way; faintly, obscurely; *informal* sort of, kind of, kinda. **2** *he fired his rifle vaguely in our direction* ROUGHLY, more or less, approximately. **3** *he smiled vaguely* ABSENT-MINDEDLY, abstractedly, vacantly.
— OPPOSITES: very, exactly.

vain ▶ adjective **1** *he was vain about his looks* CONCEITED, narcissistic, self-loving, in love with oneself, self-admiring, self-regarding, self-obsessed, egocentric, egotistic, egotistical; proud, arrogant, boastful, cocky, cocksure, immodest, swaggering; *informal* big-headed; *literary* vainglorious. **2** *a vain attempt* FUTILE, useless, pointless, to no purpose, hopeless, in vain; ineffective, ineffectual, inefficacious, impotent, unavailing, to no avail, fruitless, profitless, unrewarding, unproductive, unsuccessful, failed, abortive, for nothing; thwarted, frustrated, foiled; *archaic* bootless.
— OPPOSITES: modest, successful.
■ **in vain 1** *they tried in vain to save him* UNSUCCESSFULLY, without success, to no avail, to no purpose, fruitlessly. **2** *his efforts were in vain. See* VAIN *sense 2.* **3** *she took his name in vain* IRREVERENTLY, casually, disrespectfully, flippantly.

valediction ▶ noun FAREWELL, goodbye, adieu, leave-taking; parting words.

valedictory ▶ noun SPEECH, address, lecture, declamation.
▶ adjective FAREWELL, goodbye, leaving, parting; last, final.

valet ▶ noun MANSERVANT, man, personal attendant, personal servant, page, servant, flunky; hotel attendant, parking attendant, concierge.

valiant ▶ adjective BRAVE, courageous, valorous, intrepid, heroic, gallant, lion-hearted, bold, fearless, daring, audacious; unflinching, unshrinking, unafraid, dauntless, undaunted, doughty, tough, indomitable, mettlesome, stout-hearted, spirited, plucky; *informal* game, gutsy, spunky.
— OPPOSITES: cowardly.

valid ▶ adjective **1** *a valid criticism* WELL-FOUNDED, sound, reasonable, rational, logical, justifiable, defensible, viable, bona fide; cogent, effective, powerful, potent, convincing, credible, forceful, strong, solid, weighty. **2** *a valid contract* LEGALLY BINDING, lawful, legal, legitimate, official, signed and sealed, contractual; in force, current, in effect, effective; *informal* legit. **3** *valid information* LEGITIMATE, authentic, authoritative, reliable, bona fide.

validate ▶ verb **1** *clinical trials now exist to validate this claim* PROVE, substantiate, corroborate, verify, support, back up, bear out, lend force to, confirm, justify, vindicate, authenticate. **2** *250 certificates need*

to be validated RATIFY, endorse, approve, agree to, accept, authorize, legalize, legitimate, warrant, license, certify, recognize.
– OPPOSITES: disprove.

valley ▶ noun DALE, vale; hollow, basin, hanging valley, gully, gorge, ravine, coulee, trough, (Atlantic) droke ♣, canyon, rift; glen; literary dell, dingle.

valour ▶ noun BRAVERY, courage, pluck, nerve, daring, fearlessness, audacity, boldness, dauntlessness, stout-heartedness, heroism, backbone, spirit; informal guts, true grit, spunk; moxie, mojo.
– OPPOSITES: cowardice.

valuable ▶ adjective **1** a valuable watch PRECIOUS, costly, pricey, expensive, dear, high-priced, high-cost, high-end, upscale, big-ticket; worth its weight in gold, priceless. **2** a valuable contribution USEFUL, helpful, beneficial, invaluable, crucial, productive, constructive, effective, advantageous, worthwhile, worthy, important.
– OPPOSITES: cheap, worthless, useless.

valuation ▶ noun PRICE, evaluation, assessment, appraisal, costing, quotation, estimate.

value ▶ noun **1** houses exceeding $250,000 in value PRICE, cost, worth; market price, monetary value, face value. **2** the value of adequate preparation cannot be understated WORTH, usefulness, advantage, benefit, gain, profit, good, help, merit, helpfulness, avail; importance, significance. **3** society's values are passed on to us as children PRINCIPLES, ethics, moral code, morals, standards, code of behaviour.
▶ verb **1** his estate was valued at $345,000 EVALUATE, assess, estimate, appraise, price, put/set a price on. **2** she valued his opinion THINK HIGHLY OF, have a high opinion of, hold in high regard, rate highly, esteem, set (great) store by, put stock in, appreciate, respect; prize, cherish, treasure.

valued ▶ adjective CHERISHED, treasured, dear, prized; esteemed, respected, highly regarded, appreciated, important.

valueless ▶ adjective WORTHLESS, of no value, useless, to no purpose, (of) no use, profitless, futile, pointless, vain, in vain, to no avail, to no effect, fruitless, unproductive, idle, meretricious, ineffective, unavailing; archaic bootless.

valve ▶ noun GATE, flap, inlet, tap, faucet, stopcock.

vamoose ▶ exclamation See BUZZ OFF at BUZZ.

vamp ▶ noun (informal) a tawny-haired vamp SEDUCTRESS, temptress, siren, femme fatale, sex kitten, trollop, home wrecker, man-eater; flirt, coquette, tease.
▶ verb FLIRT.

vandal ▶ noun HOODLUM, barbarian, thug, hooligan, delinquent, despoiler, desecrator, saboteur.

vandalize ▶ verb DESTROY, desecrate, despoil, deface, disfigure, mutilate, damage, sabotage, wreck, ruin.

vanguard ▶ noun FOREFRONT, advance guard, spearhead, front, front line, fore, van, lead, cutting edge; avant-garde, leaders, founders, founding fathers, pioneers, trailblazers, trend-setters, innovators, ground-breakers.
– OPPOSITES: rear.

vanish ▶ verb **1** he vanished into the darkness DISAPPEAR, be lost to sight/view, become invisible, vanish into thin air, recede from view, dematerialize. **2** all hope of freedom vanished FADE (AWAY), evaporate,

vaporize, melt away, come to an end, end, cease to exist, pass away, die out, be no more.
– OPPOSITES: appear, materialize.

vanity ▶ noun **1** she had none of the vanity often associated with beautiful women CONCEIT, narcissism, self-love, self-admiration, self-absorption, self-regard, egotism; pride, arrogance, boastfulness, cockiness, swagger, rodomontade; informal big-headedness; literary vainglory. **2** the vanity of all desires of the will FUTILITY, uselessness, pointlessness, worthlessness, fruitlessness.
– OPPOSITES: modesty.

vanquish ▶ verb CONQUER, defeat, beat, trounce, rout, triumph over, be victorious over, get the better of, worst, upset; overcome, overwhelm, overpower, overthrow, subdue, subjugate, quell, quash, crush, bring someone to their knees, tear someone apart; informal lick, hammer, clobber, thrash, smash, demolish, wipe the floor with, make mincemeat of, massacre, slaughter, annihilate, cream, skunk, shellac.

vapid ▶ adjective INSIPID, uninspired, colourless, uninteresting, feeble, flat, dull, boring, tedious, tired, unexciting, uninspiring, unimaginative, lifeless, tame, vacuous, bland, trite, jejune.
– OPPOSITES: lively, colourful.

vapour ▶ noun HAZE, mist, steam, condensation, moisture; fumes, exhalation, fog, smog, smoke.

variable ▶ adjective CHANGEABLE, changing, varying, shifting, fluctuating, irregular, inconstant, inconsistent, fluid, unsteady, unstable, unsettled, fitful, mutable, protean, wavering, vacillating, capricious, fickle, volatile, unpredictable, mercurial, unreliable; informal up and down.
– OPPOSITES: constant.
▶ noun FACTOR, element, ingredient, (unknown) quantity, condition.

variance ▶ noun DIFFERENCE, variation, discrepancy, dissimilarity, disagreement, conflict, divergence, deviation, contrast, contradiction, imbalance, incongruity.
■ **at variance** INCONSISTENT, at odds, not in keeping, out of keeping, out of line, out of step, in conflict, in disagreement, different, differing, divergent, discrepant, dissimilar, contrary, incompatible, contradictory, irreconcilable, incongruous; at cross purposes, at loggerheads, in dispute, quarrelling.

variant ▶ noun there are a number of variants of the same idea VARIATION, form, alternative, adaptation, alteration, modification, permutation, version, analogue.
▶ adjective a variant spelling ALTERNATIVE, other, different, substitute, divergent, derived, modified.

variation ▶ noun **1** regional variations in farming practice DIFFERENCE, dissimilarity; disparity, contrast, discrepancy, imbalance; technical differential. **2** opening times are subject to variation CHANGE, alteration, modification; diversification. **3** there was very little variation from an understood pattern DEVIATION, variance, divergence, departure, fluctuation. **4** hurling is an Irish variation of field hockey VARIANT, form, alternative form; development, adaptation, alteration, mutation, transformation, diversification, modification.

varied ▶ adjective DIVERSE, assorted, miscellaneous, mixed, sundry, heterogeneous, wide-ranging, manifold, multifarious; disparate, motley.

variegated ▶ adjective MULTICOLOURED,

Vegetables

acorn squash	cauliflower	kidney bean	rhubarb
adzuki	celeriac	kohlrabi	rocket
alfalfa sprouts	celery	lamb's lettuce	romaine lettuce
artichoke	chard	leaf lettuce	romano bean
arugula	chayote	leek	rutabaga
asparagus	chicory	lentil	samphire
avocado	chickpea	lettuce	scallop squash
bamboo shoots	Chinese cabbage	lima bean	scorzonera
bean	corn	mâche	seakale
bean sprouts	cowpea	mung bean	snap bean
beet	crookneck squash	napa	snow pea
Belgian endive	cucumber	navy bean	spinach
bibb lettuce	eggplant	oakleaf lettuce	squash
black bean	endive	okra	string bean
black-eyed pea	escarole	onion	sweet corn
bok choy	fava bean	parsnip	sweet potato
Boston lettuce	fennel	pea	tomato
broad bean	french bean	pepper	turnip
broccoflower	garden cress	pepper squash ✤	turnip top
broccoli	green bean	pinto bean	water chestnut
Brussels sprouts	green onion	potato	watercress
buffalo bean	green pepper	pumpkin	wax bean
buttercup squash	haricot	purslane	yam
butternut squash	head lettuce	radicchio	yellow pepper
cabbage	Hubbard squash	radish	zucchini
cardoon	Jerusalem artichoke	rampion	
carrot	kale	red pepper	

multicolour, many-coloured, many-hued, polychromatic, varicoloured, colourful, prismatic, rainbow, kaleidoscopic; mottled, striated, marbled, streaked, speckled, flecked, dappled; *informal* splotchy.
— OPPOSITES: plain, monochrome.

variety ▸ noun **1** *the lack of variety in the curriculum* DIVERSITY, variation, diversification, heterogeneity, multifariousness, change, choice, difference. **2** *a wide variety of flowers and shrubs* ASSORTMENT, miscellany, range, array, collection, selection, mixture, medley, multiplicity; mixed bag, motley collection, potpourri, hodgepodge. **3** *fifty varieties of pasta* SORT, kind, type, class, category, style, form; make, model, brand; strain, breed, genus.
— OPPOSITES: uniformity.

variety store ▸ noun CONVENIENCE STORE, corner store, general store, (*Que.*) dep ✤ (depanneur ✤), milk store ✤, (*Ont.*) jug milk ✤, mini-mart, smoke shop, (*Cape Breton*) dairy ✤, confectionery.

various ▸ adjective DIVERSE, different, differing, varied, varying, a variety of, assorted, mixed, myriad, sundry, miscellaneous, heterogeneous, disparate, motley; several, a number of; *literary* divers.

varnish ▸ noun & verb LACQUER, shellac, finish, japan, enamel, glaze; polish, wax.

varsity ▸ adjective UNIVERSITY-LEVEL, college-level.

vary ▸ verb **1** *estimates of the development cost vary* DIFFER, be different, be dissimilar, conflict. **2** *rates of interest can vary over time* FLUCTUATE, rise and fall, go up and down, change, alter, shift, swing, deviate, differ. **3** *the diaphragm is used for varying the aperture of the lens* MODIFY, change, alter, transform, adjust, regulate, control, tweak, set; diversify, reshape.

vase ▸ noun VESSEL, urn, amphora, jar.

vassal ▸ noun (*historical*) SERF, dependant, servant, slave, subject, bondsman, thrall, villein; *rare* vavasour, helot.

vast ▸ adjective HUGE, extensive, expansive, broad, wide, sweeping, boundless, immeasurable, limitless, infinite; enormous, immense, great, massive, colossal, tremendous, mighty, prodigious, gigantic, gargantuan, mammoth, monumental; giant, towering, mountainous, titanic, Brobdingnagian; *informal* jumbo, mega, monster, whopping, humongous, astronomical, ginormous.
— OPPOSITES: tiny.

vat ▸ noun TUB, tank, cistern, barrel, cask, tun, drum, basin; vessel, receptacle, container, holder, reservoir.

vault ▸ noun **1** *the highest Gothic vault in Europe* ARCHED ROOF, dome, arch. **2** *the vault under the church* CELLAR, basement, underground chamber; crypt, catacomb, burial chamber. **3** *valuables stored in the vault* STRONGROOM, repository, coffer, safe/safety deposit box.
▸ verb *he vaulted over the gate* JUMP OVER, leap over, spring over, bound over; hurdle, clear.

vaunt ▸ verb BOAST ABOUT, brag about, make much of, crow about, parade, flaunt; acclaim, trumpet, praise, extol, celebrate; *informal* show off about, hype; *formal* laud.

veer ▸ verb TURN, swerve, curve, swing, sheer, career, weave, wheel; change direction/course, go off course, deviate.

veg ▸ verb RELAX, chill (out), do nothing, unwind, de-stress, unbend, rest, put one's feet up, take a load off, take it easy; *informal* wind down, mellow (out), let it all hang out, veg out, hang loose.

vegetable ▸ noun. *See table.*

vegetarian ▸ adjective *vegetarian food* MEATLESS, meat-free, no-meat, veggie; vegan.

vegetate ▸ verb DO NOTHING, relax, rest, idle, languish, laze, lounge, loll; stagnate; *informal* veg, bum around, hang out, zone out, lallygag.

vegetation ▸ noun PLANTS, flora; greenery, foliage, herbage, verdure.

vehemence ▶ noun PASSION, force, forcefulness, ardour, fervour, violence, urgency, strength, vigour, intensity, keenness, feeling, enthusiasm, zeal.

vehement ▶ adjective PASSIONATE, forceful, ardent, impassioned, heated, spirited, urgent, fervent, violent, fierce, fiery, strong, forcible, powerful, emphatic, vigorous, intense, earnest, keen, enthusiastic, zealous.
− OPPOSITES: mild, apathetic.

vehicle ▶ noun **1** *a stolen vehicle* MEANS OF TRANSPORT, conveyance, motor vehicle. *See table at* CAR. **2** *a vehicle for the communication of original ideas* CHANNEL, medium, conduit, means (of expression), agency, agent, instrument, mechanism, organ, apparatus.

veil ▶ noun **1** *a thin veil of high cloud made the sun hazy* COVERING, cover, screen, curtain, mantle, cloak, mask, blanket, shroud, canopy, cloud, pall. **2** *the women wore black veils* MASK, scarf, kerchief, head covering, headdress; dupatta, purdah, mantilla, chador, hijab, yashmak.
▶ verb *the peak was veiled in mist* ENVELOP, surround, swathe, enfold, cover, conceal, hide, screen, shield, cloak, blanket, shroud; obscure; *literary* enshroud, mantle.

veiled ▶ adjective *veiled threats* DISGUISED, camouflaged, masked, covert, hidden, concealed, suppressed, underlying, implicit, implied, indirect.
− OPPOSITES: overt.

vein ▶ noun **1** *a vein in his neck pulsed* BLOOD VESSEL, Medicine (*informal*) mainline. **2** *the mineral veins in the rock* LAYER, lode, seam, stratum, stratification, deposit, pipe. **3** *white marble with grey veins* STREAK, marking, mark, line, stripe, strip, band, thread, strand; *technical* stria, striation. **4** *he closes the article in a humorous vein* MOOD, humour, frame of mind, temper, disposition, attitude, tenor, tone, key, spirit, character, fashion, feel, flavour, quality, atmosphere; manner, mode, way, style.
− RELATED TERMS: vascular.

velocity ▶ noun SPEED, pace, rate, tempo, momentum, impetus; swiftness, rapidity; *literary* fleetness, celerity.

velvety ▶ adjective SOFT, furry, downy, fleecy, creamy, strokable; velvet.

venal ▶ adjective CORRUPT, corruptible, bribable, open to bribery; dishonest, dishonourable, untrustworthy, unscrupulous, unprincipled; mercenary, greedy; *informal* crooked.
− OPPOSITES: honourable, honest.

vend ▶ verb *See* SELL.

vendetta ▶ noun FEUD, blood feud, quarrel, argument, falling-out, dispute, fight, war; bad blood, enmity, rivalry, conflict, strife.

vending machine ▶ noun COIN-OPERATED MACHINE, dispenser, vendor.

vendor ▶ noun RETAILER, seller, dealer, trader, purveyor, storekeeper, shopkeeper, merchant, salesperson, supplier, huckster, peddler, hawker, scalper, trafficker.

veneer ▶ noun **1** *American cherry wood with a maple veneer* SURFACE, lamination, layer, overlay; *proprietary* Arborite ♣, facing, covering, finish, exterior, cladding, laminate. **2** *a veneer of sophistication* FACADE, front, false front, show, outward display, appearance, impression, semblance, guise, disguise, mask, masquerade, pretense, camouflage, cover, window dressing.

venerable ▶ adjective RESPECTED, venerated, revered, honoured, esteemed, hallowed, august, distinguished, eminent, great, grand.

venerate ▶ verb REVERE, regard highly, reverence, worship, hallow, hold sacred, exalt, vaunt, adore, honour, respect, esteem.

vengeance ▶ noun REVENGE, retribution, retaliation, payback, requital, reprisal, satisfaction, an eye for an eye (and a tooth for a tooth).
■ **with a vengeance** VIGOROUSLY, strenuously, energetically, with a will, with all the stops out, for all one is worth, all out, flat out, at full tilt; *informal* hammer and tongs, like crazy, like mad, like gangbusters.

vengeful ▶ adjective VINDICTIVE, revengeful, out for revenge, unforgiving, on the warpath.
− OPPOSITES: forgiving.

venial ▶ adjective FORGIVABLE, pardonable, excusable, allowable, permissible; slight, minor, unimportant, insignificant, trivial, trifling.
− OPPOSITES: unforgivable, mortal.

venom ▶ noun **1** *snake venom* POISON, toxin; *archaic* bane. **2** *his voice was full of venom* RANCOUR, malevolence, vitriol, spite, vindictiveness, malice, maliciousness, ill will, acrimony, animosity, animus, bitterness, antagonism, hostility, bile, hate, hatred; *informal* bitchiness, cattiness.

venomous ▶ adjective **1** *a venomous snake* | *the spider's venomous bite* POISONOUS, toxic; dangerous, deadly, lethal, fatal, mortal. **2** *venomous remarks* VICIOUS, spiteful, rancorous, malevolent, vitriolic, vindictive, malicious, poisonous, virulent, bitter, acidic, acrimonious, caustic, antagonistic, hostile, cruel; *informal* bitchy, catty; *literary* malefic, maleficent.
− OPPOSITES: harmless, benevolent.

vent ▶ noun *an air vent* DUCT, flue, shaft, well, passage, airway; outlet, inlet, opening, aperture, hole, gap, orifice.
▶ verb *the crowd vented their fury on the police* RELEASE, air, give vent to, give free rein to, let out, pour out, express, give expression to, voice, give voice to, verbalize, ventilate, discuss, talk over, communicate.

ventilate ▶ verb AIR, aerate, air out, oxygenate, air-condition, fan; freshen, cool.

venture ▶ noun *a business venture* ENTERPRISE, undertaking, project, initiative, scheme, operation, endeavour, speculation, plunge, gamble, gambit, experiment.
▶ verb **1** *we ventured across the country* SET OUT, go, travel, journey. **2** *may I venture an opinion?* PUT FORWARD, advance, proffer, offer, volunteer, air, suggest, submit, propose, moot, **3** *I ventured to ask her to come and dine with me* DARE, be/make so bold as, presume; take the liberty of, stick one's neck out, go out on a limb.

veracious ▶ adjective (*formal*). *See* TRUTHFUL senses 1, 2.

veracity ▶ noun TRUTHFULNESS, truth, accuracy, correctness, faithfulness, fidelity; reputability, honesty, sincerity, trustworthiness, reliability, dependability, scrupulousness, ethics, morality, righteousness, virtuousness, decency, straightforwardness, goodness, probity.

veranda ▶ noun PORCH, gallery, balcony, lanai, sun porch, stoop.

verbal ▶ adjective ORAL, spoken, stated, said, verbalized, expressed; unwritten, word-of-mouth.

verbatim ▶ adverb WORD FOR WORD, letter for letter, line for line, to the letter, literally, exactly, precisely, accurately, closely, faithfully.

verbiage ▸ noun VERBOSITY, padding, wordiness, prolixity, long-windedness, loquacity, rigmarole, circumlocution, superfluity, periphrasis, waffle; *humorous* verbal diarrhea.

verbose ▸ adjective WORDY, loquacious, garrulous, talkative, voluble; long-winded, flatulent, lengthy, prolix, tautological, pleonastic, periphrastic, circumlocutory, circuitous, wandering, discursive, digressive, rambling; *informal* mouthy, gabby, waffly, motor-mouthed.
− OPPOSITES: succinct, laconic.

verdant ▸ adjective GREEN, leafy, grassy; lush, rich; *literary* verdurous.

verdict ▸ noun JUDGMENT, adjudication, decision, finding, ruling, decree, resolution, pronouncement, conclusion, opinion; *Law* determination.

verge ▸ noun **1** *the verge of the lake* EDGE, border, margin, side, brink, rim, lip; fringe, boundary, perimeter, outskirts; *literary* skirt. **2** *Spain was on the verge of an economic crisis* BRINK, threshold, edge, point.
▸ verb *a degree of caution that verged on the obsessive* APPROACH, border on, come close/near to, be tantamount to; tend towards, approximate to, resemble.

verification ▸ noun CONFIRMATION, substantiation, proof, corroboration, support, attestation, validation, authentication, endorsement.

verify ▸ verb **1** *the evidence verifies my claim* SUBSTANTIATE, confirm, prove, corroborate, back up, bear out, justify, support, uphold, attest to, testify to, validate, authenticate, endorse, certify. **2** *we need to verify those figures* TEST, double-check, check out, establish the truth of.
− OPPOSITES: refute.

verisimilitude ▸ noun REALISM, believability, plausibility, authenticity, credibility, lifelikeness.

veritable ▸ adjective REAL, bona fide, authentic, genuine, indubitable, utter; *informal* sure as shootin'.

vermin ▸ plural noun PESTS, parasites; infestations; undesirables, low-life.

vernacular ▸ noun **1** *he wrote in the vernacular to reach a wider audience* EVERYDAY LANGUAGE, colloquial language, conversational language, common parlance, demotic, lay terms. **2** *(informal) the vernacular of Vancouver's ski bums* LANGUAGE, dialect, regional language, regionalisms, patois, parlance; idiom, slang, jargon; *informal* lingo, -speak, -ese.

versatile ▸ adjective ADAPTABLE, flexible, all around, multi-faceted, multitalented, resourceful; adjustable, multi-purpose, all-purpose, handy.

verse ▸ noun **1** *Elizabethan verse* POETRY, versification, poetic form; poems, balladry, lyrics, lines, doggerel; *literary* poesy. *See also the table at* POETRY. **2** *a verse he'd composed to mark my anniversary* POEM, lyric, ballad, sonnet, ode, limerick, rhyme, ditty, lay. **3** *a poem with sixty verses* STANZA, canto, couplet; strophe.
− OPPOSITES: prose.

versed ▸ adjective *See* INFORMED.

version ▸ noun **1** *his version of events* ACCOUNT, report, statement, description, record, story, rendering, interpretation, explanation, understanding, reading, impression, side, take. **2** *the Japanese version will be published next year* EDITION, translation, impression. **3** *they replaced coal-burning furnaces with gas versions* FORM, sort, kind, type, variety, variant, model.

versus ▸ preposition AGAINST, facing, confronting, v., vs.; as opposed to, in contrast with.

vertex ▸ noun APEX, peak, pinnacle, zenith, crown, crest, tip, top.

vertical ▸ adjective UPRIGHT, erect, perpendicular, plumb, straight up and down, on end, standing, upstanding, bolt upright.
− OPPOSITES: horizontal.

vertigo ▸ noun DIZZINESS, giddiness, light-headedness, loss of balance.

verve ▸ noun ENTHUSIASM, vigour, energy, pep, dynamism, élan, vitality, vivacity, buoyancy, liveliness, animation, zest, sparkle, charisma, spirit, ebullience, exuberance, life, brio, gusto, eagerness, keenness, passion, zeal, relish, feeling, ardour, fire; *informal* zing, zip, vim, pizzazz, oomph, mojo, moxie, get-up-and-go.

very ▸ adverb *that's very kind of you* EXTREMELY, exceedingly, exceptionally, extraordinarily, tremendously, immensely, hugely, intensely, acutely, abundantly, singularly, uncommonly, decidedly, particularly, supremely, highly, remarkably, really, truly, mightily, ever so; *informal* terrifically, awfully, fearfully, terribly, devilishly, majorly, seriously, mega, ultra, damn, damned; dead, real, way, mighty, awful, darned; *archaic* exceeding.
− OPPOSITES: slightly.
▸ adjective **1** *those were his very words* EXACT, actual, precise. **2** *the very thought of food made her feel ill* MERE, simple, pure; sheer.

vessel ▸ noun **1** *a fishing vessel* BOAT, ship, craft, watercraft; *literary* barque. **2** *pour the mixture into a heatproof vessel* CONTAINER, receptacle; basin, bowl, pan, pot; urn, tank, cask, barrel, drum, vat.

vest ▸ verb *executive power is vested in the President* CONFER ON, entrust to, invest in, bestow on, grant to, give to, put in the hands of; endow, lodge, lay, place.

vestibule ▸ noun ENTRANCE HALL, hall, hallway, entrance, porch, mud room, portico, foyer, lobby, anteroom, narthex, antechamber, waiting room.

vestige ▸ noun **1** *the last vestiges of colonialism* REMNANT, fragment, relic, echo, indication, sign, trace, residue, mark, legacy, reminder; remains. **2** *she showed no vestige of emotion* BIT, touch, hint, suggestion, suspicion, shadow, scrap, tinge, speck, shred, jot, iota, whit, scintilla, glimmer; *informal* smidgen, tad, titch.

vestigial ▸ adjective **1** *vestigial limbs* RUDIMENTARY, undeveloped; non-functional; *Biology* primitive. **2** *he felt a vestigial flicker of anger from last night* REMAINING, surviving, residual, leftover, lingering.

vet ▸ verb *press releases are vetted by an executive council* CHECK, examine, scrutinize, investigate, inspect, look over, screen, assess, evaluate, appraise; *informal* check out.
▸ noun *I took the cat to the vet* VETERINARIAN, animal doctor, horse doctor.

veteran ▸ noun *a veteran of 16 political campaigns* OLD HAND, old sweat, past master, doyen, vet; *informal* old-timer, old stager, old warhorse.
− OPPOSITES: novice.
▸ adjective *a veteran diplomat* LONG-SERVING, seasoned, old, hardened; adept, expert, well trained, practised, experienced, senior; *informal* battle-scarred.

veto ▸ noun *parliament's right of veto* REJECTION, dismissal; prohibition, proscription, embargo, ban,

interdict, check; *informal* thumbs down, red light.
— OPPOSITES: approval.

▶ verb *China vetoed the proposal* REJECT, turn down, throw out, dismiss; prohibit, forbid, interdict, proscribe, disallow, embargo, ban, rule out, say no to; *informal* kill, put the kibosh on, give the thumbs down to, give the red light to.
— OPPOSITES: approve.

vex ▶ verb ANNOY, irritate, anger, infuriate, exasperate, irk, gall, pique, put out, antagonize, get on someone's nerves, ruffle someone's feathers, rattle someone's cage, make someone's hackles rise, rub the wrong way, aggravate, peeve, miff, rile, nettle, needle, get (to), bug, get someone's goat, get someone's back up, get someone's dander up, tee off, tick off, burn up, rankle.

vexation ▶ noun ANNOYANCE, irritation, exasperation, indignation, anger, crossness, displeasure, pique, bile, disgruntlement, bad mood; *informal* aggravation.

vexed ▶ adjective 1 *a vexed expression* ANNOYED, irritated, cross, angry, infuriated, exasperated, irked, piqued, displeased, put out, disgruntled; *informal* aggravated, peeved, nettled, miffed, riled, hacked off, hot under the collar, teed off, ticked off, sore, bent out of shape; PO'd; *archaic* wroth. 2 *the vexed issue of immigration* DISPUTED, in dispute, contested, in contention, contentious, debated, at issue, controversial, moot; problematic, difficult, knotty, thorny, ticklish, tense.

via ▶ preposition THROUGH, by way of; by means of, with the aid of, by virtue of.

viable ▶ adjective FEASIBLE, workable, practicable, practical, usable, possible, realistic, achievable, attainable, realizable; *informal* doable.
— OPPOSITES: impracticable.

vibe ▶ noun VIBRATION, feeling, atmosphere, sensation, energy.

vibrant ▶ adjective 1 *a vibrant and passionate woman* SPIRITED, lively, full of life, energetic, vigorous, vital, full of vim and vigour, animated, sparkling, effervescent, vivacious, dynamic, stimulating, exciting, passionate, fiery; *informal* peppy, feisty. 2 *vibrant colours* VIVID, bright, striking, brilliant, strong, rich, colourful, bold. 3 *his vibrant voice* RESONANT, sonorous, reverberant, resounding, ringing, echoing; strong, rich, full, round.
— OPPOSITES: lifeless, pale.

vibrate ▶ verb 1 *the floor beneath them vibrated* QUIVER, shake, tremble, shiver, shudder, judder, throb, pulsate, rattle; rock, wobble, oscillate, waver, swing, sway, move to and fro. 2 *a low rumbling sound began to vibrate through the car* REVERBERATE, resonate, resound, ring, echo.

vibration ▶ noun TREMOR, shaking, quivering, quaking, judder, juddering, shuddering, throb, throbbing, pulsation.

vicarious ▶ adjective INDIRECT, second-hand, secondary, derivative, derived, surrogate, substitute; empathetic, empathic.

vice ▶ noun 1 *youngsters may be driven to vice* IMMORALITY, wrongdoing, wickedness, badness, evil, iniquity, villainy, corruption, misconduct, misdeeds; sin, sinfulness, ungodliness; depravity, degeneracy, dissolution, dissipation, debauchery, decadence, lechery, perversion; crime, transgression; *formal* turpitude; *archaic* trespass. 2 *smoking is my only vice* SHORTCOMING, failing, flaw, fault, bad habit, defect,

weakness, deficiency, limitation, imperfection, blemish, foible, frailty.
— OPPOSITES: virtue.

viceroy ▶ noun GOVERNOR, deputy, representative, proconsul; regent, steward.

vice versa ▶ adverb CONVERSELY, inversely, contrariwise; reciprocally, the other way round.

vicinity ▶ noun NEIGHBOURHOOD, surrounding area, locality, locale, (local) area, district, region, quarter, zone; environs, surroundings, precincts; *informal* neck of the woods.
■ **in the vicinity of** AROUND, about, nearly, circa, approaching, roughly, approximating, approximately, something like, more or less; in the region of, in the neighbourhood of, near to, close to.

vicious ▶ adjective 1 *a vicious killer* BRUTAL, ferocious, savage, violent, dangerous, ruthless, remorseless, merciless, heartless, callous, cruel, harsh, cold-blooded, inhuman, fierce, barbarous, barbaric, brutish, bloodthirsty, fiendish, sadistic, monstrous, murderous, homicidal. 2 *a vicious hate campaign* MALICIOUS, malevolent, malignant, malign, spiteful, hateful, vindictive, venomous, poisonous, rancorous, mean, cruel, bitter, cutting, acrimonious, hostile, nasty; defamatory, slanderous; *informal* catty.
— OPPOSITES: gentle, kindly.

vicious circle ▶ noun DILEMMA, vicious cycle, downward spiral, vortex, no-win situation, Catch-22, chicken-and-egg situation.

vicissitude ▶ noun CHANGE, alteration, shift, reversal, twist, turn, downturn, variation; inconstancy, instability, uncertainty, chanciness, unpredictability, fickleness, variability, changeability, fluctuation, vacillation; ups and downs.

victim ▶ noun 1 *a victim of crime* SUFFERER, injured party, casualty; fatality, loss; loser. 2 *the victim of a confidence trick* TARGET, object, subject, focus, recipient, butt. 3 *a born victim* LOSER, prey, stooge, dupe, sucker, quarry, fool, fall guy, chump; *informal* patsy, sap. 4 *a sacrificial victim* SACRIFICE, (burnt) offering, scapegoat.
■ **fall victim to** FALL ILL WITH, be stricken with, catch, develop, contract, pick up; succumb to.

victimize ▶ verb PERSECUTE, pick on, push around, bully, abuse, discriminate against, ill-treat, mistreat, maltreat, terrorize, hector; exploit, prey on, take advantage of, dupe, cheat, double-cross, get at, have it in for, give someone a hard time, hassle, lean on, gang up on.

victor ▶ verb WINNER, champion, conqueror, conquering hero, vanquisher, hero; prizewinner, gold medallist; *informal* champ, top dog.
— OPPOSITES: loser.

victorious ▶ adjective TRIUMPHANT, conquering, vanquishing, winning, champion, successful, top, first.

victory ▶ noun SUCCESS, triumph, conquest, win, favourable result, landslide, coup; mastery, superiority, supremacy; *informal* walkover, laugher, thrashing, trouncing.
— OPPOSITES: defeat.

victuals ▶ plural noun (*dated*) See FOOD sense 1.

video ▶ noun *we recorded it on video* TAPE, videotape, proprietary VHS.

video game ▶ noun COMPUTER GAME, arcade game; entertainment software.

vie ▶ verb COMPETE, contend, contest, struggle, fight,

battle, cross swords, lock horns, buck, jockey; war, feud.

view ▶ noun **1** *the view from her apartment* OUTLOOK, prospect, panorama, vista, scene, aspect, perspective, spectacle, sight; scenery, landscape. **2** *we agree with this view* OPINION, point of view, viewpoint, belief, judgment, thinking, notion, idea, conviction, persuasion, attitude, feeling, sentiment, concept, hypothesis, theory; stance, standpoint, philosophy, doctrine, dogma, approach, take. **3** *the church came into view* SIGHT, perspective, vision, visibility.
▶ verb **1** *they viewed the landscape* LOOK AT, eye, observe, gaze at, stare at, ogle, contemplate, watch, scan, regard, take in, survey, inspect, scrutinize; *informal* check out, get a load of, eyeball; *literary* espy, behold. **2** *the law was viewed as a last resort* CONSIDER, regard, look upon, see, perceive, judge, deem, reckon.
■ **in view of** CONSIDERING, bearing in mind, taking into account, on account of, in the light of, owing to, because of, as a result of, given.
■ **on view** ON DISPLAY, on exhibition, on show.

viewer ▶ noun WATCHER, spectator, onlooker, looker-on, observer; (**viewers**) audience, crowd; *literary* beholder.

viewpoint ▶ noun **1** *I understand your viewpoint. See* VIEW *noun* sense 2. **2** *a short hike to the viewpoint* VANTAGE POINT, look-off, lookout, scenic spot.

vigilant ▶ adjective WATCHFUL, observant, attentive, alert, eagle-eyed, hawk-eyed, on the lookout, on one's toes, on the qui vive; wide awake, wakeful, unwinking, on one's guard, cautious, wary, circumspect, heedful, mindful; *informal* beady-eyed.
— OPPOSITES: inattentive.

vigorous ▶ adjective **1** *the child was vigorous* ROBUST, healthy, hale and hearty, strong, sturdy, fit; hardy, tough, athletic; bouncing, thriving, flourishing, blooming; energetic, lively, active, perky, spirited, vibrant, vital, zestful; *informal* peppy, bouncy, in the pink. **2** *a vigorous defence of policy* STRENUOUS, powerful, forceful, spirited, mettlesome, determined, aggressive, two-fisted, driving, eager, zealous, ardent, fervent, vehement, passionate; tough, robust, thorough, blunt, hard-hitting; *informal* punchy.
— OPPOSITES: weak, feeble.

vigorously ▶ adverb STRENUOUSLY, strongly, powerfully, forcefully, energetically, heartily, vehemently, for dear life, for all one is worth, all out, fiercely, hard; *informal* like mad, like crazy, like gangbusters.

vigour ▶ noun ROBUSTNESS, health, hardiness, strength, sturdiness, toughness; bloom, radiance, energy, life, vitality, virility, verve, spirit; zeal, passion, determination, dynamism, zest, pep, drive, force; *informal* oomph, get-up-and-go, zing, piss and vinegar.
— OPPOSITES: lethargy.

vile ▶ adjective FOUL, nasty, unpleasant, bad, disagreeable, horrid, horrible, dreadful, abominable, atrocious, offensive, obnoxious, odious, unsavoury, repulsive, disgusting, distasteful, loathsome, hateful, nauseating, sickening; disgraceful, appalling, shocking, sorry, shabby, shameful, dishonourable, execrable, heinous, abhorrent, deplorable, monstrous, wicked, evil, iniquitous, nefarious, depraved, debased; contemptible, despicable, reprehensible; *informal* gross, godawful, lowdown, lousy; *archaic* scurvy.
— OPPOSITES: pleasant.

vilify ▶ verb DISPARAGE, denigrate, defame, run down, revile, abuse, speak ill of, criticize, condemn, denounce; malign, slander, libel, slur; *informal* tear apart/into, lay into, slam, badmouth, dis, crucify; *formal* derogate, calumniate.
— OPPOSITES: commend.

village ▶ noun SMALL TOWN, hamlet, (*Nfld*) outport ✤ (outharbour ✤); (*Sask.*) resort village ✤; hicksville, nowheresville, whistle stop, settlement.

villain ▶ noun CRIMINAL, lawbreaker, offender, felon, convict, malefactor, wrongdoer; gangster, gunman, thief, robber; rogue, reprobate, ruffian, hoodlum; miscreant, scoundrel, sleeveen; *Law* malfeasant; *informal* crook, con, baddy, bad guy, low-life; *dated* cad, knave; *archaic* blackguard.

villainous ▶ adjective WICKED, evil, iniquitous, sinful, nefarious, vile, foul, monstrous, outrageous, atrocious, abominable, reprehensible, hateful, odious, contemptible, horrible, heinous, egregious, diabolical, flagitious, fiendish, vicious, murderous; criminal, illicit, unlawful, illegal, lawless; immoral, corrupt, degenerate, sordid, depraved, dishonest, dishonourable, unscrupulous, unprincipled; *informal* crooked, bent, lowdown, dirty, shady; *dated* dastardly.
— OPPOSITES: virtuous.

vindicate ▶ verb **1** *he was vindicated by the jury* ACQUIT, clear, absolve, exonerate; discharge, liberate, free; *informal* let off (the hook); *formal* exculpate. **2** *I had fully vindicated my contention* JUSTIFY, warrant, substantiate, ratify, authenticate, verify, confirm, corroborate, prove, defend, support, back up, bear out, evidence, endorse.

vindictive ▶ adjective VENGEFUL, revengeful, unforgiving, resentful, acrimonious, bitter; spiteful, mean, rancorous, venomous, malicious, malevolent, nasty, mean-spirited, cruel, unkind; *informal* catty.
— OPPOSITES: forgiving.

vine ▶ noun *See* CREEPER.

vineyard ▶ noun VINERY, domaine, cru; winery, microwinery.

vintage ▶ noun **1** *1986 was a classic vintage* YEAR. **2** *furniture of Louis XV vintage* PERIOD, era, epoch, time, origin; genre, style, kind, sort, type.
▶ adjective **1** *vintage French wine* HIGH-QUALITY, quality, choice, select, prime, superior, best. **2** *vintage motor vehicles* CLASSIC, ageless, timeless; old, antique, heritage, historic. **3** *his reaction was vintage Humphrey* CHARACTERISTIC, typical, pure, prime, trademark.

violate ▶ verb **1** *this violates fundamental human rights* CONTRAVENE, breach, infringe, break, transgress, overstep, disobey, defy, flout; disregard, ignore, trample on. **2** *they felt their privacy had been violated* INVADE, trespass upon, encroach upon, intrude upon; disrespect. **3** *the tomb was violated* DESECRATE, profane, defile, degrade, debase; damage, vandalize, deface, destroy. **4** *he drugged and then violated her* RAPE, (sexually) assault, force oneself on, abuse, attack, molest, interfere with; *archaic* defile, deflower, dishonour, ruin; *literary* ravish.
— OPPOSITES: respect.

violence ▶ noun **1** *violence against women* BRUTALITY, brute force, ferocity, savagery, cruelty, sadism, barbarity, brutishness. **2** *the protest ended in violence* FIGHTS, bloodshed, brawling, disorder, rioting, hostility, turbulence, mayhem; *informal* punch-ups. **3** *the violence of the blow* FORCEFULNESS, force, power, strength, might, savagery, ferocity, brutality. **4** *the violence of his passion* INTENSITY, severity, strength, force, vehemence, power, potency, fervency, ferocity, fury, fire.

violent ▶ adjective **1** *he gets violent when drunk* BRUTAL, vicious, savage, rough, aggressive, (physically) abusive, threatening, fierce, physical, wild, ferocious; barbarous, barbaric, thuggish, pugnacious, cutthroat, homicidal, murderous, cruel. **2** *a violent blow* POWERFUL, forceful, hard, sharp, smart, strong, vigorous, mighty, hefty; savage, ferocious, brutal, vicious. **3** *violent jealousy* INTENSE, extreme, strong, powerful, vehement, intemperate, unbridled, uncontrollable, ungovernable, inordinate, consuming, passionate. **4** *a violent movie* GORY, gruesome, grisly, full of violence.
− OPPOSITES: gentle, weak, mild.

VIP ▶ noun CELEBRITY, famous person, very important person, personality, big name, star, superstar; dignitary, luminary, leading light, worthy, grandee, lion, notable, personage; *informal* heavyweight, celeb, bigwig, big shot, big cheese, honcho, top dog, megastar, big wheel, (big) kahuna, mucky-muck, high muckamuck.

virago ▶ noun HARRIDAN, shrew, dragon, termagant, vixen; fishwife, witch, hellcat, she-devil, tartar, martinet, ogress; *informal* battleaxe; *archaic* scold.

virgin ▶ noun *she remained a virgin* chaste woman/man, celibate; *literary* maiden, maid, vestal, ingenue.
▶ adjective **1** *virgin forest* UNTOUCHED, unspoiled, untainted, immaculate, pristine, flawless; spotless, unsullied, unpolluted, undefiled, perfect; unchanged, intact; unexplored, uncharted, unmapped. **2** *virgin girls* CHASTE, virginal, celibate, abstinent; maiden, maidenly; pure, uncorrupted, undefiled, unsullied, innocent; *literary* vestal.

virginal ▶ adjective. *See* VIRGIN *adjective sense 2.*

virginity ▶ noun CHASTITY, maidenhood, maidenhead, honour, purity, innocence; celibacy, abstinence; *informal* cherry; *archaic* virtue.

virile ▶ adjective MANLY, masculine, male; strong, tough, vigorous, robust, muscular, muscly, brawny, rugged, sturdy, lusty, husky; red-blooded, fertile; *informal* macho, butch, beefy, hunky.
− OPPOSITES: effeminate.

virtual ▶ adjective **1** *a virtual guarantee* EFFECTIVE, in effect, near (enough), essential, practical, to all intents and purposes. **2** *a virtual shopping environment* SIMULATED, artificial, imitation, make-believe; computer-generated, online, virtual reality.

virtually ▶ adverb EFFECTIVELY, in effect, all but, more or less, practically, almost, nearly, close to, verging on, just about, as good as, essentially, to all intents and purposes, roughly, approximately; *informal* pretty much, pretty well; *literary* well-nigh, nigh on.

virtue ▶ noun **1** *the simple virtue of peasant life* GOODNESS, virtuousness, righteousness, morality, integrity, dignity, rectitude, honour, decency, respectability, nobility, worthiness, purity; principles, ethics. **2** *promptness was not one of his virtues* STRONG POINT, good point, good quality, asset, forte, attribute, strength, talent, feature. **3** *(archaic) she lost her virtue in the city. See* VIRGINITY. **4** *I can see no virtue in this* MERIT, advantage, benefit, usefulness, strength, efficacy, plus, point.
− OPPOSITES: vice, failing, disadvantage.
■ **by virtue of** BECAUSE OF, on account of, by dint of, by means of, by way of, via, through, as a result of, as

a consequence of, on the strength of, owing to, thanks to, due to, by reason of.

virtuosity ▶ noun SKILL, skilfulness, mastery, expertise, prowess, proficiency, ability, aptitude; excellence, brilliance, talent, genius, artistry, flair, panache, finesse, wizardry; *informal* know-how, chops.

virtuoso ▶ noun *the pianist is clearly a virtuoso* GENIUS, expert, (past) master, maestro, artist, prodigy, marvel, adept, professional, doyen, veteran; star, champion; *informal* hotshot, wizard, magician, pro, ace.
− OPPOSITES: duffer.
▶ adjective *a virtuoso violinist* SKILFUL, expert, accomplished, masterly, master, consummate, proficient, talented, gifted, adept, good, capable; impressive, outstanding, exceptional, magnificent, supreme, first-rate, stellar, brilliant, excellent; *informal* superb, mean, ace.
− OPPOSITES: incompetent.

virtuous ▶ adjective RIGHTEOUS, good, pure, whiter than white, saintly, angelic, moral, ethical, upright, upstanding, high-minded, principled, exemplary; law-abiding, irreproachable, blameless, guiltless, unimpeachable, immaculate, honest, honourable, reputable, laudable, decent, respectable, noble, worthy, meritorious; *informal* squeaky clean.

virulent ▶ adjective **1** *virulent herbicides* POISONOUS, toxic, venomous, noxious, deadly, lethal, fatal, dangerous, harmful, injurious, pernicious, damaging, destructive; *literary* deathly. **2** *a virulent epidemic* INFECTIOUS, infective, contagious, communicable, transmittable, transmissible, spreading, pestilential; *informal* catching. **3** *a virulent attack on morals* VITRIOLIC, malicious, malevolent, hostile, spiteful, venomous, vicious, vindictive, bitter, sharp, rancorous, acrimonious, scathing, caustic, withering, nasty, savage, harsh.
− OPPOSITES: harmless, amicable.

virus ▶ noun **1** *the child caught a virus* DISEASE, bug, infection; *dated* contagion. **2** *a computer virus* WORM, Trojan Horse.

visage ▶ noun FACE, countenance, look, (facial) features, (facial) expression.

vis-à-vis ▶ preposition REGARDING, concerning, apropos, towards, relating to, compared with, with respect to; *informal* re.

visceral ▶ adjective INSTINCTIVE, instinctual, gut, deep-down, deep-seated, deep-rooted, inward; emotional; animal.

viscosity ▶ noun THICKNESS, gooeyness, viscidity; consistency, texture.

viscous ▶ adjective GLUTINOUS, gelatinous, thick, viscid, mucous, mucoid, mucilaginous, gummy, gluey, adhesive, tacky, adherent, treacly, syrupy; *technical* viscoelastic; *informal* gooey, gloppy.

visible ▶ adjective PERCEPTIBLE, perceivable, seeable, observable, noticeable, detectable, discernible; in sight, in/on view, on display; evident, apparent, manifest, transparent, plain, clear, conspicuous, obvious, patent, unmistakable, unconcealed, undisguised, prominent, salient, striking, glaring.
■ **visible minority** ETHNIC MINORITY, ethnic group, racial minority, subculture.

vision ▶ noun **1** *her vision was blurred by tears* EYESIGHT, sight, observation, (visual) perception; eyes; view, perspective. **2** *the psychic was troubled by visions of the dead* APPARITION, hallucination, illusion, mirage, spectre, phantom, ghost, wraith, manifestation;

literary phantasm, shade. **3** *visions of a better future* DREAM, daydream, reverie; plan, hope; fantasy, pipe dream, delusion. **4** *his speech lacked vision* IMAGINATION, creativity, inventiveness, innovation, inspiration, intuition, perception, insight, foresight, prescience. **5** *Melissa was a vision in lilac* BEAUTIFUL SIGHT, feast for the eyes, pleasure to behold, delight, dream, beauty, picture, joy, marvel; *informal* sight for sore eyes, stunner, knockout, looker, eye-catcher, peach.

visionary ► **adjective 1** *a visionary person* INSPIRED, imaginative, creative, inventive, ingenious, enterprising, innovative; insightful, perceptive, intuitive, prescient, discerning, shrewd, wise, clever, resourceful; idealistic, romantic, quixotic, dreamy; *informal* starry-eyed. **2** *(archaic) a visionary image. See* IMAGINARY.
► **noun** *a visionary pictured him in hell* SEER, mystic, oracle, prophet(ess), soothsayer, augur, diviner, clairvoyant, crystal-gazer, medium; *literary* sibyl.

visit ► **verb 1** *I visited my dear uncle* CALL ON, pay a visit to, go to see, look in on; stay with, holiday with; stop by, drop by; *informal* go see; pop in on, drop in on, look up. **2** *Alex was visiting the Yukon* STAY IN, stop over in, spend time in, holiday in, vacation in; tour, explore, see.
► **noun 1** *she paid a visit to her mom* (SOCIAL) CALL, visitation. **2** *a visit to the museum* TRIP TO, tour of, look round; stopover, stay; holiday, break, vacation; *formal* sojourn.

visitation ► **noun 1** *the bishop's pastoral visitations* (OFFICIAL) VISIT, tour of inspection, survey, examination. **2** *a visitation from God* APPARITION, vision, appearance, manifestation, materialization. **3** *Jehovah punished them by visitations* AFFLICTION, scourge, bane, curse, plague, blight, disaster, tragedy, catastrophe; punishment, retribution, vengeance.

visitor ► **noun 1** *I am expecting a visitor* GUEST, caller, house guest; company; *archaic* visitant. **2** *the monument attracts foreign visitors* TOURIST, traveller, holidaymaker, day tripper, tripper, vacationer, vacationist, sightseer; pilgrim, habitué; foreigner, outsider, stranger, alien.

visor ► **noun** BRIM, peak, eyeshade; bill.

vista ► **noun** VIEW, prospect, panorama, aspect, perspective, spectacle, sight, outlook; scenery, landscape.

visual ► **adjective 1** *visual defects* OPTICAL, optic, ocular, eye; vision, sight. **2** *a visual indication that the alarm works* VISIBLE, perceptible, perceivable, discernible.
► **noun** *the speaker employed excellent visuals* GRAPHIC, visual aid, image, illustration, diagram, display, show and tell.

visualize ► **verb** ENVISAGE, envision, conjure up, picture, call to mind, see, imagine, evoke, dream up, fantasize about, conceptualize, contemplate, conceive of.

vital ► **adjective 1** *it is vital that action be taken soon* ESSENTIAL, of the essence, critical, crucial, key, indispensable, integral, all-important, imperative, mandatory, requisite, urgent, pressing, burning, compelling, high-priority, life-and-death. **2** *the vital organs* MAJOR, main, chief; essential, necessary. **3** *he is young and vital* LIVELY, energetic, active, sprightly, spry, spirited, vivacious, exuberant, bouncy, enthusiastic, vibrant, zestful, sparkling, dynamic, virile, vigorous, lusty, hale and hearty; *informal* peppy,

spunky, full of beans, bright-eyed and bushy-tailed.
— OPPOSITES: unimportant, minor, listless.

vitality ► **noun** LIVELINESS, life, energy, spirit, vivacity, exuberance, buoyancy, bounce, élan, verve, vim, pep, brio, zest, sparkle, dynamism, passion, fire, vigour, drive, punch; get-up-and-go.

vitamin *See table.*

Vitamins	
A	retinol
B₁	thiamine
B₂	riboflavin
B₃	niacin
B₅	pantothenic acid
B₆	pyridoxine
B₇/Bw/H	biotin
B₈/Bh	inositol
B₉/Bc/M	folic acid
B₁₂	cyanocobalamin
C	ascorbic acid
D₂	calciferol
D₃	cholecalciferol
E	tocopherol
K₁	phylloquinone
K₂	menaquinone

vitriolic ► **adjective** ACRIMONIOUS, rancorous, bitter, caustic, mordant, acerbic, trenchant, virulent, spiteful, savage, venomous, poisonous, malicious, splenetic; nasty, mean, cruel, unkind, harsh, hostile, vindictive, vicious, scathing, barbed, wounding, sharp, cutting, withering, sarcastic; *informal* bitchy, catty.

vituperation ► **noun** INVECTIVE, condemnation, opprobrium, scolding, criticism, disapprobation, fault-finding; blame, abuse, insults, vilification, denunciation, obloquy, denigration, disparagement, slander, libel, defamation, slurs, aspersions; vitriol, venom; *informal* flak; *formal* castigation.
— OPPOSITES: praise.

vivacious ► **adjective** LIVELY, spirited, bubbly, ebullient, buoyant, sparkling, light-hearted, jaunty, merry, happy, jolly, full of fun, cheery, cheerful, perky, sunny, breezy, enthusiastic, irrepressible, vibrant, vital, zestful, energetic, effervescent, dynamic; *informal* peppy, bouncy, upbeat, chirpy.
— OPPOSITES: dull.

vivid ► **adjective 1** *a vivid blue sea* BRIGHT, colourful, brilliant, radiant, vibrant, glaring, strong, bold, deep, intense, rich, warm. **2** *a vivid account of urban poverty* GRAPHIC, evocative, realistic, lifelike, faithful, authentic, clear, detailed, lucid, eloquent, striking, arresting, impressive, colourful, rich, dramatic, lively, stimulating, interesting, fascinating, scintillating; memorable, powerful, stirring, moving, telling, haunting.
— OPPOSITES: dull, vague.

viz. ► **adverb** NAMELY, that is to say, in other words, to wit, specifically, i.e.; *formal* videlicet.

vocabulary ► **noun 1** *technical vocabulary* LANGUAGE, lexicon, lexis, words; diction, terminology, phraseology, nomenclature, terms, expressions, parlance, idiom, jargon, vernacular, argot, cant; *informal* vocab, lingo, -speak, -ese. **2** *she is improving her vocabulary* WORD POWER, lexicon, command of language; *informal* vocab.

vocal ▶ **adjective 1** *vocal sounds* VOCALIZED, voiced, uttered, articulated, oral; spoken, viva voce, said. **2** *a vocal critic of the government* VOCIFEROUS, outspoken, forthright, plain-spoken, expressive, blunt, frank, candid, open; vehement, strident, vigorous, emphatic, insistent, forceful, zealous, clamorous, loud-mouthed.
▶ (**vocals**) **plural noun** VOICES, singing; harmonies.

vocal cords ▶ **plural noun** VOICE BOX, vocal folds, larynx; *informal* pipe.

vocalist ▶ **noun** SINGER, songster, diva, songbird, prima donna, chanteuse, chansonnier, melodist.

vocation ▶ **noun** CALLING, life's work, mission, purpose, function, avocation; profession, occupation, career, job, employment, trade, craft, business, line (of work), métier.

vociferous ▶ **adjective.** *See* VOCAL *sense 2.*

vogue ▶ **noun** *the skirt is enjoying a new vogue* FASHION, trend, fad, craze, rage, enthusiasm, passion, obsession, mania; fashionableness, popularity, currency, favour; *informal* trendiness.
■ **in vogue** FASHIONABLE, voguish, stylish, modish, up-to-date, up-to-the-minute, du jour, modern, current; prevalent, popular, in favour, in demand, sought-after, all the rage; chic, chi-chi, smart, tony, kicky, le dernier cri; trendy, hip, cool, big, happening, now, in, with it.

voice ▶ **noun 1** *she lost her voice* POWER OF SPEECH. **2** *he gave voice to his anger* EXPRESSION, utterance, verbalization, vocalization. **3** *the voice of the people* OPINION, view, feeling, wish, desire, will, vox populi, vox pop. **4** *citizens must have a voice in this* SAY, influence, vote, input, role, representation, seat at the table. **5** *a powerful voice for conservation* SPOKESPERSON, speaker, champion, representative, mouthpiece, intermediary; forum, vehicle, instrument, channel, organ, agent.
▶ **verb** *they voiced their opposition* EXPRESS, vocalize, communicate, articulate, declare, state, assert, reveal, proclaim, announce, publish, publicize, make public, make known, table, air, vent; utter, say, speak; *informal* come out with.

voice mail ▶ **noun** VOICE MESSAGING; answering machine, answering service, call answer.

void ▶ **noun** *the void of space* VACUUM, emptiness, nothingness, nullity, blankness, vacuity; (empty) space, gap, cavity, chasm, abyss, gulf, pit, black hole.
▶ **verb** *the contract was voided* INVALIDATE, annul, nullify; negate, quash, cancel, countermand, repeal, revoke, rescind, retract, withdraw, reverse, undo, abolish; *Law* vacate; *formal* abrogate.
— OPPOSITES: validate.
▶ **adjective 1** *vast void spaces* EMPTY, vacant, blank, bare, clear, free, unfilled, unoccupied, uninhabited. **2** *a country void of man or beast* DEVOID OF, empty of, vacant of, bereft of, free from; lacking, wanting, without, with nary a. **3** *the election was void* INVALID, null, ineffective, non-viable, useless, worthless, nugatory.
— OPPOSITES: full, occupied, valid.

voila ▶ **exclamation** ta-dah, lookit, looky here; here you are, here you go, hey presto.

volatile ▶ **adjective 1** *a volatile personality* UNPREDICTABLE, changeable, variable, inconstant, inconsistent, erratic, irregular, unstable, turbulent, blowing hot and cold, varying, shifting, fluctuating, fluid, mutable; mercurial, capricious, whimsical, fickle, flighty, impulsive, temperamental, high-strung, excitable, emotional, fiery, moody,

tempestuous. **2** *the atmosphere is too volatile for an election* TENSE, strained, fraught, uneasy, uncomfortable, charged, explosive, inflammatory, turbulent; *informal* nail-biting, ready to blow. **3** *a volatile organic compound* EVAPORATIVE, vaporous; explosive, inflammable; unstable, labile.
— OPPOSITES: stable, calm.

volition
■ **of one's own volition** OF ONE'S OWN FREE WILL, of one's own accord, by choice, by preference; voluntarily, willingly, readily, freely, intentionally, consciously, deliberately, on purpose, purposely; gladly, with pleasure.

volley ▶ **noun** BARRAGE, cannonade, battery, bombardment, salvo, discharge, fusillade; storm, hail, shower, deluge, torrent; *historical* broadside.

volte-face ▶ *See* ABOUT-FACE.

voluble ▶ **adjective** TALKATIVE, loquacious, garrulous, verbose, wordy, chatty, gossipy, effusive, gushing, forthcoming, conversational, communicative, expansive; articulate, fluent; *informal* mouthy, motor-mouthed, gabby, gassy, windy, talky.
— OPPOSITES: taciturn.

volume ▶ **noun 1** *a volume from the library* BOOK, publication, tome, hardback, paperback, title; manual, almanac, compendium. **2** *a glass syringe of known volume* CAPACITY, cubic measure, size, magnitude, mass, bulk, extent; dimensions, proportions, measurements. **3** *a huge volume of water* QUANTITY, amount, proportion, measure, mass, bulk. **4** *she turned the volume down* LOUDNESS, sound, amplification; *informal* decibels.

voluminous ▶ **adjective** CAPACIOUS, roomy, spacious, ample, full, big, large, bulky, extensive, sizeable, generous; billowing, baggy, loose-fitting; *formal* commodious.

voluntarily ▶ **adverb** FREELY, of one's own free will, of one's own accord, of one's own volition, by choice, by preference; willingly, readily, intentionally, deliberately, on purpose, purposely, spontaneously; gladly, with pleasure.

voluntary ▶ **adjective 1** *attendance is voluntary* OPTIONAL, discretionary, elective, non-compulsory, volitional; *Law* permissive. **2** *voluntary work* UNPAID, unsalaried, unwaged, for free, without charge, for nothing; honorary, volunteer; *Law* pro bono (publico).
— OPPOSITES: compulsory, paid.

volunteer ▶ **verb 1** *I volunteered my services* OFFER, tender, proffer, put forward, put up, venture. **2** *he volunteered as a driver* OFFER ONE'S SERVICES, present oneself, make oneself available, sign up.
▶ **noun** *each volunteer was tested three times* SUBJECT, participant, case, patient; *informal* guinea pig.

voluptuous ▶ **adjective 1** *a voluptuous model* CURVACEOUS, shapely, ample, buxom, full-figured; seductive, alluring, comely, sultry, sensuous, sexy, womanly; *informal* bodacious, hot, curvy, busty, stacked, built, slinky; *formal* Junoesque, Rubenesque. **2** *she was voluptuous by nature* HEDONISTIC, sybaritic, epicurean, pleasure-loving, self-indulgent; decadent, intemperate, immoderate, dissolute, sensual, licentious.
— OPPOSITES: scrawny, ascetic.

vomit ▶ **verb 1** *he needed to vomit* BE SICK, spew, heave, retch, gag, get sick; *informal* throw up, puke, purge, hurl, barf, upchuck, ralph. **2** *I vomited my breakfast* REGURGITATE, bring up, spew up, cough up, lose; throw up, puke, spit up.

▶ **noun** *a coat stained with vomit* VOMITUS; *informal* puke, spew, barf.

voodoo ▶ **noun** WITCHCRAFT, magic, black magic, sorcery, wizardry, dark arts, devilry, hoodoo, necromancy, mojo.

voracious ▶ **adjective** INSATIABLE, unquenchable, unappeasable, prodigious, uncontrollable, compulsive, gluttonous, greedy, esurient, rapacious; enthusiastic, eager, keen, avid, desirous, hungry, ravenous; *informal* piggish.

vortex ▶ **noun** WHIRLWIND, cyclone, whirlpool, gyre, maelstrom, eddy, swirl, spiral; black hole.

vote ▶ **noun 1** *a rigged vote* BALLOT, poll, election, referendum, plebiscite; show of hands. **2** *women finally got the vote* SUFFRAGE, voting rights, franchise, enfranchisement; voice, say.
▶ **verb 1** *only half of them voted* GO TO THE POLLS, cast one's vote/ballot. **2** *I vote we have one more game* SUGGEST, propose, recommend, advocate, move, table, submit.
■ **vote someone in** ELECT, return, select, choose, pick, adopt, appoint, designate, opt for, decide on.

vouch
■ **vouch for** ATTEST TO, confirm, affirm, verify, swear to, testify to, bear out, back up, support, stick up for, go to bat for, corroborate, substantiate, prove, uphold, sponsor, give credence to, endorse, certify, warrant, validate.

voucher ▶ **noun** COUPON, token, ticket, licence, permit, pass; chit, slip, stub; *informal* ducat, comp.

vow ▶ **noun** *a vow of silence* OATH, pledge, promise, bond, covenant, commitment, avowal, profession, affirmation, attestation, assurance, guarantee; word (of honour); *formal* troth.
— RELATED TERMS: votive.
▶ **verb** *I vowed to do better* SWEAR, pledge, promise, avow, undertake, engage, make a commitment, give one's word, guarantee; *archaic* plight.

voyage ▶ **noun** *the voyage lasted 120 days* JOURNEY, trip, expedition, excursion, tour; hike, trek, travels;

pilgrimage, quest, crusade, odyssey; cruise, passage, flight, drive, road trip.
▶ **verb** *he voyaged through Peru* TRAVEL, journey, tour, globe-trot; sail, steam, cruise, fly, jetset, drive; *informal* gallivant; *archaic* peregrinate.

voyageur (*Cdn*) ▶ **noun** riverman ✦, canoeman ✦, homme du nord ✦, Northman ✦, engagé ✦, coureur de bois ✦.

voyageur sash (*Cdn*) ▶ **noun** ceinture fléchée ✦, arrow sash ✦, Assomption sash ✦.

voyeur ▶ **noun** PEEPING TOM, pervert, watcher; *informal* perv.

vulgar ▶ **adjective 1** *a vulgar joke* RUDE, indecent, indelicate, offensive, distasteful, coarse, crude, ribald, risqué, naughty, suggestive, racy, earthy, off-colour, bawdy, obscene, profane, lewd, salacious, smutty, dirty, filthy, pornographic, X-rated; *informal* sleazy, raunchy, blue, locker-room; saucy, salty; *euphemistic* adult. **2** *the decor was lavish but vulgar* TASTELESS, crass, tawdry, ostentatious, flamboyant, overdone, showy, gaudy, garish, brassy, kitsch, tinselly, loud; *informal* flash, flashy, tacky, (*Que.*) kétaine ✦. **3** *it was vulgar for a lady to belch* IMPOLITE, ill-mannered, unmannerly, rude, indecorous, unseemly, ill-bred, boorish, uncouth, crude, rough; unsophisticated, unrefined, common, low-minded; unladylike, ungentlemanly.
— OPPOSITES: tasteful, decorous.

vulnerable ▶ **adjective 1** *a vulnerable city* IN DANGER, in peril, in jeopardy, at risk, endangered, unsafe, unprotected, unguarded; open to attack, assailable, exposed, wide open; undefended, unfortified, unarmed, defenceless, helpless, pregnable. **2** *he is vulnerable to criticism* EXPOSED TO, open to, liable to, prone to, prey to, susceptible to, subject to, an easy target for.
— OPPOSITES: resilient.

vulture ▶ **noun** *lawyers can be absolute vultures* PREDATOR, shark, vampire, bloodsucker, profiteer, racketeer, opportunist, extortionist.

Ww

wacky ► adjective (*informal*). See ECCENTRIC *adjective*.

wad ► noun **1** *a wad of cotton* LUMP, clump, mass, pad, swab, hunk, wedge, ball, cake, nugget; bit, piece, plug. **2** *a wad of $20 bills* BUNDLE, roll, pile, stack, sheaf, bankroll. **3** *a wad of tobacco* QUID, twist, plug, chew, chaw.
► verb *he wadded up his napkins* CRUMPLE, stuff, press, gather, pack, wrap.

wadding ► noun STUFFING, filling, filler, packing, padding, cushioning, quilting; (cotton) batting, (cotton) batten.

waddle ► verb TODDLE, dodder, totter, wobble, shuffle; duckwalk.

wade ► verb **1** *they waded in the icy water* PADDLE, wallow, dabble; *informal* splosh. **2** *I had to wade through some hefty documents* PLOW, plod, trawl, labour, toil; study, browse; *informal* slog.
■ **wade in** (*informal*) SET TO WORK, buckle down, go to it, put one's shoulder to the wheel; *informal* plunge in, dive in, jump in, get cracking.

waffle ► verb **1** *faced with this commitment, she waffled* WAVER, vacillate, equivocate, sit on the fence. **2** *the lecturer waffled on* BABBLE, chatter, prattle, ramble, jabber, gibber, gabble, prate, drivel, blather, natter, yak.
► noun *my panic reduced the interview to waffle* PRATTLE, drivel, nonsense, twaddle, gibberish, mumbo-jumbo, verbiage; *informal* hot air, poppycock, hogwash, gobbledegook.

waft ► verb **1** *smoke wafted through the air* DRIFT, float, glide, whirl, travel. **2** *a breeze wafted the smell towards us* CONVEY, carry, transport, bear; blow, puff.

wag[1] ► verb **1** *the dog's tail wagged frantically* SWING, swish, switch, sway, shake, quiver, twitch, whip, bob; *informal* waggle. **2** *he wagged his stick at them* SHAKE, wave, wiggle, flourish, brandish.

wag[2] ► noun (*informal*) *he's a bit of a wag.* See JOKER.

wage ► noun **1** *the farm workers' wages* PAY, payment, remuneration, salary, stipend, fee, honorarium; income, revenue, profit, gain, reward; earnings, paycheque, pay packet; *formal* emolument. **2** *the wages of sin is death* REWARD, recompense, retribution; returns, deserts.
► verb *they waged war on the guerrillas* ENGAGE IN, carry on, conduct, execute, pursue, prosecute, proceed with.

wager ► noun *a wager of $100* BET, gamble, speculation; stake, pledge, ante.
► verb *I'll wager ten bucks on the home team* BET, gamble, lay odds, put money on; stake, pledge, risk, venture, hazard, chance.

waggle ► verb (*informal*). See WAG[1] verb senses 1, 2.

wagon ► noun. See table at CARRIAGE.

waif ► noun **1** *a homeless waif* RAGAMUFFIN, urchin; foundling, orphan, stray; *derogatory* guttersnipe; *dated* gamin. **2** *only waifs could wear pants that small* BEANPOLE, string bean, anorexic, hardbody, scrag, wisp; *proprietary* Barbie.

wail ► noun *a wail of anguish* HOWL, bawl, yowl, cry, moan, groan; shriek, scream, holler, yelp.
► verb *the children began to wail* HOWL, weep, cry, sob, moan, groan, keen, lament, yowl, snivel, whimper, whine, bawl, shriek, scream, yelp, caterwaul; *informal* blubber.

waist ► noun MIDDLE, midriff, abdomen, waistline.

wait ► verb **1** *Jill waited while Jack fetched the water* STAY (PUT), remain, rest, stop, halt, pause; linger, loiter, dally; *informal* stick around, hang out, hang around, kill time, waste time, kick one's heels, twiddle one's thumbs; *archaic* tarry. **2** *Jack waited until she nodded* HOLD ON, hold back, bide one's time, hang fire, mark time, stand by, sit tight, hold one's horses. **3** *they were waiting for the kettle to boil* AWAIT; anticipate, look forward, long, pine, yearn, expect, be ready. **4** *the tea will have to wait* BE POSTPONED, be delayed, be put off, be deferred; *informal* be put on the back burner, be put on ice.
► noun *a long wait* DELAY, holdup, interval, interlude, intermission, pause, break, stay, cessation, suspension, stoppage, halt, interruption, lull, respite, recess, moratorium, hiatus, gap, rest.
■ **wait on someone** SERVE, attend to, tend, cater for/to; minister to, take care of, look after, see to.
■ **wait up 1** *she waited up for him every night* STAY AWAKE, stay up, keep vigil. **2** *wait up!* STOP, slow down, hold on, wait for me.

waiter, waitress ► noun SERVER, stewardess, steward, attendant, garçon, waitperson; busboy; hostess, host, maître d'; butler, servant, page; carhop; wait staff.

wait-list ► noun LINEUP, queue, waiting list, backlog.

waive ► verb **1** *he waived his right to a hearing* RELINQUISH, renounce, give up, abandon, surrender, cede, sign away, yield, reject, dispense with, abdicate, sacrifice, refuse, turn down, spurn. **2** *the manager waived the rules* DISREGARD, ignore, overlook, set aside, forgo, drop.

wake[1] ► verb **1** *at 4:30 am Mark woke up* AWAKE, waken, awaken, rouse oneself, stir, come to, come round, bestir oneself; get up, get out of bed; *formal* arise. **2** *she woke her husband* ROUSE, arouse, waken. **3** *a shock woke him up a bit* ACTIVATE, stimulate, galvanize, enliven, animate, stir up, spur on, ginger up, buoy, invigorate, revitalize; *informal* perk up, pep up. **4** *they woke up to what we were saying* REALIZE, become aware of, become conscious of, become mindful of, clue in to. **5** *the name woke an old memory* EVOKE, conjure up, rouse, stir, revive, awaken, rekindle, stimulate.
— OPPOSITES: sleep.
► noun *a mourner at a wake* VIGIL, watch; funeral.

wake[2] ► noun *the cruiser's wake* BACKWASH, wash, slipstream, trail, path.
■ **in the wake of** IN THE AFTERMATH OF, after, subsequent to, following, as a result of, as a consequence of, on account of, because of, owing to.

wakeful ► adjective **1** *he had been wakeful all night* AWAKE, restless, restive, tossing and turning. **2** *I was*

suddenly wakeful ALERT, watchful, vigilant, on the lookout, on one's guard, attentive, heedful, wary.
— OPPOSITES: asleep, inattentive.

waken ▶ **verb.** *See* WAKE[1] *verb senses 1, 2.*

walk ▶ **verb 1** *they walked along the road* STROLL, saunter, amble, trudge, plod, dawdle, hike, tramp, tromp, slog, stomp, trek, march, stride, sashay, glide, troop, patrol, wander, ramble, tread, prowl, promenade, roam, traipse; stretch one's legs; *informal* mosey, hoof it; *formal* perambulate. **2** *he walked her home* ACCOMPANY, escort, guide, show, see, usher, take, chaperone, steer, shepherd.
▶ **noun 1** *their country walks* STROLL, saunter, amble, promenade; ramble, hike, tramp, march; turn; *dated* constitutional. **2** *the map shows several nature walks. See* TRAIL *noun sense 5.* **3** *he shovelled the front walk* PATH, pathway, drive, driveway, walkway, sidewalk. **4** *her elegant walk* GAIT, step, stride, tread.
■ **walk all over someone** (*informal*) **1** *be firm or he'll walk all over you* TAKE ADVANTAGE OF, impose on, exploit, use, abuse, misuse, manipulate, take liberties with; *informal* take for a ride, run rings around. **2** *we walked all over the home team. See* TROUNCE.
■ **walk off/away with 1** (*informal*) *she walked off with my car keys. See* STEAL *verb sense 1.* **2** *he walked off with four awards* WIN EASILY, win hands down, attain, earn, gain, garner, receive, acquire, secure, collect, pick up, net; *informal* bag.
■ **walk of life** CLASS, status, rank, caste, sphere, arena; profession, career, vocation, job, occupation, employment, business, trade, craft; province, field.
■ **walk out 1** *he walked out in a temper* LEAVE, depart, get up and go, storm off/out, flounce out, absent oneself; *informal* take off. **2** *teachers walked out in protest* (GO ON) STRIKE, stop work; protest, mutiny, revolt.
■ **walk out on someone** DESERT, abandon, leave, betray, throw over, jilt, run out on; *informal* chuck, dump, ditch.

walker ▶ **noun 1** *a vigorous walker* HIKER, rambler, traveller, roamer, rover, pedestrian; *literary* wayfarer. **2** *she used a walker for balance* WALKING FRAME.

walkie-talkie ▶ **noun** RADIO, CB, transmitter, marconi.

walkout ▶ **noun** STRIKE, stoppage, industrial action, job action, revolt, rebellion.

walkover ▶ **noun** EASY VICTORY, rout, landslide; *informal* piece of cake, pushover, cinch, breeze, picnic, laugher, whitewash; *informal* duck soup.

wall ▶ **noun 1** *brick walls* BARRIER, partition, enclosure, screen, panel, divider; bulkhead. **2** *an ancient city wall* FORTIFICATION, rampart, barricade, bulwark, stockade. **3** *break down the walls that stop world trade* OBSTACLE, barrier, fence; impediment, hindrance, block, roadblock, check.
— RELATED TERMS: mural.
▶ **verb 1** *tenements walled in the courtyard* ENCLOSE, bound, encircle, confine, hem, close in, shut in, fence in. **2** *the doorway had been walled up* BLOCK, seal, close, brick up.
■ **go to the wall for** (*informal*) RISK EVERYTHING FOR, do anything for, put one's life on the line for.
■ **off the wall** (*informal*). *See* UNCONVENTIONAL.

wallet ▶ **noun** PURSE, change purse; billfold, pocketbook, fanny pack.

wallop ▶ **verb** (*informal*). *See* THUMP *verb sense 1.*

wallow ▶ **verb 1** *pigs wallow in the mud* LOLL ABOUT/AROUND, roll about/around, lie about/around, splash about/around; slosh, wade, paddle; *informal* splosh. **2** *a*

ship wallowing in stormy seas ROLL, lurch, toss, plunge, pitch, reel, rock, flounder, keel, list; labour. **3** *she seems to wallow in self-pity* LUXURIATE, bask, take pleasure, take satisfaction, indulge (oneself), delight, revel, glory; enjoy, like, love, relish, savour; *informal* get a kick out of, get off on.

wan ▶ **adjective 1** *she looked so wan and frail* PALE, pallid, ashen, white, grey; anemic, colourless, bloodless, waxen, chalky, pasty, peaky, peaked, sickly, washed out, drained, drawn, ghostly. **2** *the wan light of the moon* DIM, faint, weak, feeble, pale, watery, washy.
— OPPOSITES: flushed, bright.

wand ▶ **noun** BATON, stick, staff, bar, dowel, rod; twig, cane, birch, switch; *historical* caduceus.

wander ▶ **verb 1** *I wandered around the mansion* STROLL, amble, saunter, walk, dawdle, potter, ramble, meander; roam, rove, range, drift, prowl; *informal* traipse, mosey, tootle, mooch. **2** *we are wandering from the point* STRAY, depart, diverge, veer, swerve, deviate, digress, drift, get sidetracked.

wanderer ▶ **noun** TRAVELLER, rambler, hiker, migrant, globetrotter, roamer, rover; itinerant, rolling stone, nomad; tramp, transient, drifter, vagabond, vagrant; *informal* hobo, bum; *literary* wayfarer.

wane ▶ **verb** DECLINE, diminish, decrease, dwindle, shrink, tail off, ebb, fade (away), lessen, peter out, fall off, recede, slump, flag, weaken, give way, wither, crumble, evaporate, disintegrate, die out; *literary* evanesce.
— OPPOSITES: wax, grow.

wangle ▶ **verb** (*informal*). *See* CONTRIVE.

want ▶ **verb 1** *do you want more coffee?* DESIRE, wish for, hope for, aspire to, fancy, care for, like; long for, yearn for, crave, hanker after, hunger for, thirst for, cry out for, covet; need; *informal* have a yen for, have a jones for, be dying for. **2** (*informal*) *you want to be more careful* SHOULD, ought, need, must. **3** *this mollycoddled generation wants for nothing* LACK, be without, have need of, be devoid of, be bereft of, be missing.
▶ **noun 1** *his want of vigilance* LACK, absence, non-existence, unavailability; dearth, deficiency, inadequacy, insufficiency; paucity, shortage, scarcity, deficit. **2** *a time of want* NEED, neediness, austerity, privation, deprivation, poverty, impoverishment, penury, destitution; famine, drought. **3** *all her wants would be taken care of* WISH, desire, demand, longing, yearning, fancy, craving, hankering; need, requirement; *informal* yen.

wanting ▶ **adjective 1** *the defences were found wanting* DEFICIENT, inadequate, lacking, insufficient, imperfect, unacceptable, unsatisfactory, flawed, faulty, defective, unsound, substandard, inferior, second-rate, poor, shoddy. **2** *millions were left wanting for food* WITHOUT, lacking, deprived of, devoid of, bereft of, in need of, out of; deficient in, short on; *informal* minus.
— OPPOSITES: sufficient.

wanton ▶ **adjective 1** *wanton destruction* DELIBERATE, wilful, malicious, spiteful, wicked, cruel; gratuitous, unprovoked, motiveless, arbitrary, groundless, unjustifiable, needless, unnecessary, uncalled for, senseless, pointless, purposeless, meaningless, empty, random; capricious. **2** *a wanton seductress* PROMISCUOUS, immoral, immodest, indecent, shameless, unchaste, fast, loose, impure, abandoned, lustful, lecherous, lascivious, libidinous, licentious,

dissolute, debauched, degenerate, corrupt, whorish, disreputable.
– OPPOSITES: justifiable, chaste.

war ► noun **1** *the Napoleonic wars* CONFLICT, warfare, combat, fighting, (military) action, bloodshed, struggle; battle, skirmish, fight, clash, engagement, encounter; offensive, attack, campaign; hostilities; jihad, crusade. *See also the table at* BATTLE. **2** *the war against drugs* CAMPAIGN, crusade, battle, fight, struggle, movement, drive.
– RELATED TERMS: belligerent, martial.
– OPPOSITES: peace.
► verb *rival Emperors warred against each other* FIGHT, battle, combat, wage war, take up arms; feud, quarrel, struggle, contend, wrangle, cross swords; attack, engage, take on, skirmish with.

warble ► verb *larks warbled in the sky* TRILL, sing, chirp, chirrup, cheep, twitter, tweet, chatter, peep, call.

ward ► noun **1** *the surgical ward* ROOM, department, unit, area, wing. **2** *the most marginal ward in Victoria* DISTRICT, constituency, division, quarter, zone, parish. **3** *the boy is my ward* DEPENDANT, charge, protege.
■ **ward someone off** FEND OFF, repel, repulse, beat back, chase away; *informal* send packing.
■ **ward something off 1** *she warded off the blow* PARRY, avert, deflect, block; evade, avoid, dodge. **2** *garlic is worn to ward off evil spirits* REBUFF, avert, keep at bay, fend off, stave off, turn away, repel, resist, prevent, obstruct, foil, frustrate, thwart, check, stop.

warden ► noun **1** *a park warden* RANGER, parks officer ✦; custodian, keeper, guardian, protector; superintendent, caretaker, supervisor. **2** *he was hauled before the prison warden* GOVERNOR, executive, president, official; jailer, keeper; *informal* screw.

wardrobe ► noun **1** *she opened the wardrobe* CUPBOARD, cabinet, locker, (clothes) closet, armoire. **2** *she bought new shirts to expand his wardrobe* COLLECTION OF CLOTHES; garments, attire, outfits; trousseau.

warehouse ► noun DEPOT, distribution centre, storehouse, store, storeroom, depository, storage, entrepôt, stockroom; granary; *Military* magazine.

wares ► plural noun MERCHANDISE, goods, products, produce, stock, commodities; lines, range; *informal* stuff.

warfare ► noun FIGHTING, war, combat, conflict, (military) action, hostilities; bloodshed, battles, skirmishes.

warlike ► adjective AGGRESSIVE, belligerent, warring, bellicose, pugnacious, combative, bloodthirsty, jingoistic, hostile, threatening, quarrelsome; militaristic, militant, warmongering.

warlock ► noun SORCERER, wizard, magus, (black) magician, enchanter; *archaic* mage.

warm ► adjective **1** *a warm kitchen* HOT, cozy, snug; *informal* toasty. **2** *a warm day in spring* BALMY, summery, sultry, hot, mild, temperate; sunny, fine. **3** *warm water* HEATED, tepid, lukewarm. **4** *a warm sweater* THICK, chunky, thermal, winter, woolly. **5** *a warm welcome* FRIENDLY, cordial, amiable, genial, kind, pleasant, fond; welcoming, hospitable, benevolent, benign, charitable; sincere, genuine, wholehearted, heartfelt, enthusiastic, eager, hearty.
– OPPOSITES: cold, chilly, light, hostile.
► verb *warm the soup in that pan* HEAT (UP), reheat, cook;

thaw (out), melt, warm over, microwave; *informal* zap, nuke.
– OPPOSITES: chill.
■ **warm to/towards 1** *everyone warmed to him* LIKE, take to, get on (well) with, hit it off with, be on good terms with. **2** *he couldn't warm to the notion* BE ENTHUSIASTIC ABOUT, be supportive of, be excited about, get into.
■ **warm up** LIMBER UP, loosen up, stretch, work out, exercise; prepare, rehearse.
■ **warm someone up** *the MC warmed up the crowd* ENLIVEN, liven, stimulate, animate, rouse, stir, excite; *informal* get going.

warm-blooded ► adjective **1** *mammals are warm-blooded* HOMEOTHERMIC, homeothermal. **2** *a warm-blooded woman* PASSIONATE, ardent, red-blooded, emotional, intense, impetuous, lively, lusty, spirited, fiery, tempestuous.
– OPPOSITES: poikilothermic, reserved.

warmed-over ► adjective **1** *a warmed-over meal* REHEATED; warmed-up. **2** *warmed-over ideas* UNORIGINAL, derivative, imitative, uninspired; copied, plagiarized, rehashed; hackneyed, stale, tired, banal; *informal* old hat.

warmed-up *See* WARMED-OVER.

warm-hearted ► adjective KIND, warm, big-hearted, tender-hearted, tender, loving, caring, feeling, unselfish, selfless, benevolent, humane, good-natured; friendly, sympathetic, understanding, compassionate, charitable, generous.

warmonger ► noun MILITARIST, hawk, jingoist, aggressor, belligerent.

warmth ► noun **1** *the warmth of the fire* HEAT, warmness, hotness, fieriness; coziness. **2** *the warmth of their welcome* FRIENDLINESS, amiability, geniality, cordiality, kindness, tenderness, fondness; benevolence, charity; enthusiasm, eagerness, ardour, fervour, energy, effusiveness.

warn ► verb **1** *David warned her about the cat* NOTIFY, alert, apprise, inform, tell, make someone aware, forewarn, remind, give notice; *informal* tip off. **2** *police are warning galleries to be alert* ADVISE, exhort, urge, counsel, caution.

warning ► noun **1** *the earthquake came without warning* ADVANCE NOTICE, forewarning, alert; hint, signal, sign, alarm bells; *informal* tipoff, heads-up, red flag. **2** *a health warning* CAUTION, advisory, notification, information; exhortation, injunction; advice. **3** *a warning of things to come* OMEN, premonition, foreboding, prophecy, prediction, forecast, token, portent, signal, sign; *literary* foretoken. **4** *his sentence is a warning to other drunk drivers* EXAMPLE, deterrent, lesson, caution, exemplar, message, moral. **5** *a written warning* ADMONITION, caution, remonstrance, reprimand, censure; *informal* dressing-down, talking-to.

warp ► verb **1** *timber that is too dry will warp* BUCKLE, twist, bend, distort, deform, misshape, skew, curve, bow, contort. **2** *he warped the mind of her child* CORRUPT, twist, pervert, deprave, lead astray.
– OPPOSITES: straighten.

warrant ► noun **1** *a warrant for his arrest* AUTHORIZATION, order, licence, permit, document; writ, summons, subpoena; mandate, decree, fiat, edict. **2** *a travel warrant* VOUCHER, slip, ticket, coupon, pass.
► verb **1** *the charges warranted a severe sentence* JUSTIFY, vindicate, call for, sanction, validate; permit,

authorize; deserve, excuse, account for, legitimize; support, license, approve of; merit, qualify for, rate, be worthy of, be deserving of. **2** *we warrant that the texts do not infringe copyright* GUARANTEE, affirm, swear, promise, vow, pledge, undertake, state, assert, declare, profess, attest; vouch, testify, bear witness; *formal* aver.

warranty ▶ noun GUARANTEE, assurance, promise, commitment, undertaking, agreement.

warring ▶ adjective OPPOSING, conflicting, at war, fighting, battling, quarrelling; competing, hostile, rival.

warrior ▶ noun FIGHTER, soldier, serviceman, combatant, mercenary.

wart ▶ noun GROWTH, lump, swelling, protuberance, carbuncle, boil, blister, verruca, corn, tumour, excrescence, blemish.

war-torn ▶ adjective WAR-RAVAGED, war-weary, devastated, racked.

wary ▶ adjective **1** *he was trained to be wary* CAUTIOUS, careful, circumspect, on one's guard, chary, alert, on the lookout, on one's toes, on the qui vive; attentive, heedful, watchful, vigilant, observant; *informal* wide awake. **2** *we are wary of strangers* SUSPICIOUS, chary, leery, careful, distrustful, mistrustful, skeptical, doubtful, dubious.
— OPPOSITES: inattentive, trustful.

wash ▶ verb **1** *he washed in the bath* CLEAN ONESELF; bathe, bath, shower, soak, freshen up; *formal* perform one's ablutions. **2** *he washed her socks* CLEAN, cleanse, rinse, launder, scour; shampoo, lather, sponge, scrub, wipe; sluice, douse, swab, disinfect; *literary* lave. **3** *waves washed against the hull* SPLASH, lap, splosh, dash, crash, break, beat, surge, ripple, roll. **4** *the wreckage was washed downriver* SWEEP, carry, convey, transport. **5** IT WASHED UP ON MY FRONT LAWN, land, come to rest, be deposited, be beached. **6** *guilt washed over her* SURGE THROUGH, rush through, course through, flood over, flow over; affect, overcome. **7** (*informal*) *this story just won't wash* BE ACCEPTED, be acceptable, be plausible, be convincing, hold up, hold water, stand up, bear scrutiny; do.
— OPPOSITES: dirty, soil.
▶ noun **1** *she needs a wash* CLEAN, shower, dip, bath, soak; *formal* ablutions. **2** *that shirt should go in the wash* LAUNDRY, washing. **3** *antiseptic skin wash* LOTION, salve, preparation, rinse, liquid; liniment. **4** *the wash of a motor boat* BACKWASH, wake, trail, path. **5** *the wash of the waves on the beach* SURGE, flow, swell, sweep, rise and fall, roll, splash. **6** *a light watercolour wash* PAINT, stain, film, coat, coating; tint, glaze.

■ **wash something away** ERODE, abrade, wear away, eat away, undermine.

■ **wash one's hands of** DISOWN, renounce, reject, forswear, disavow, give up on, turn one's back on, cast aside, abandon; *formal* abjure.

■ **wash up** WASH THE DISHES, do the dishes, clean up.

washcloth ▶ noun face cloth, terry cloth, washrag.

washed out ▶ adjective **1** *a washed-out denim jacket* FADED, bleached, decolorized, stonewashed; pale, light, drab, muted. **2** *he looked washed out after his exams* EXHAUSTED, tired, worn out, weary, fatigued, spent, drained, enervated, run-down; *informal* done in, dog-tired, bushed, beat, zonked, pooped, tuckered out.
— OPPOSITES: bold, energetic.

washout ▶ noun (*informal*). See FAILURE senses 2, 3.

washroom ▶ noun TOILET, bathroom, powder room,

urinal, stall, privy, lavatory, latrine, throne room, restroom, men's/women's/ladies' room, facilities, can, john, biffy, commode, comfort station, porta-potty, outhouse, honey bucket; little girls'/boys' room, loo; (*vulgar slang*) crapper; *Nautical* head.

waspish ▶ adjective IRRITABLE, touchy, testy, cross, snappish, cantankerous, splenetic, short-tempered, bad-tempered, moody, ornery, crotchety, crabby; *informal* grouchy.

waste ▶ verb **1** *he doesn't like to waste money* SQUANDER, misspend, misuse, fritter away, throw away, lavish, dissipate, throw around; *informal* blow, splurge. **2** *kids are wasting away in the streets* GROW WEAK, grow thin, shrink, decline, wilt, fade, flag, deteriorate, degenerate, languish. **3** *the disease wasted his legs* EMACIATE, atrophy, wither, debilitate, shrivel, shrink, weaken, enfeeble. **4** (*informal*) *I saw them waste the guy. See* MURDER *verb* sense 1.
— OPPOSITES: conserve, thrive.
▶ adjective **1** *waste material* UNWANTED, excess, superfluous, left over, scrap, useless, worthless; unusable, unprofitable. **2** *waste ground* UNCULTIVATED, barren, desert, arid, bare; desolate, void, uninhabited, unpopulated; wild.
▶ noun **1** *a waste of money* MISUSE, misapplication, misemployment, abuse; extravagance, wastefulness, lavishness. **2** *household waste* GARBAGE, rubbish, trash, refuse, litter, debris, flotsam and jetsam, dross, junk, detritus, scrap; dregs; scraps; sewage, effluent. **3** *the frozen wastes of the Arctic* DESERT, wasteland, the Barrens ♣, the Barren Lands ♣, wilderness, wilds, emptiness.

■ **lay waste. See** LAY[1].

wasted ▶ adjective **1** *a wasted effort* SQUANDERED, misspent, misdirected, misused, dissipated; pointless, useless, needless, unnecessary; vain, fruitless. **2** *a wasted opportunity* MISSED, lost, forfeited, neglected, squandered, bungled; *informal* down the drain. **3** *I'm wasted in this job* UNDEREMPLOYED, underused, too good for, above. **4** *his wasted legs* EMACIATED, atrophied, withered, shrivelled, weak, frail, shrunken, skeletal, rickety, scrawny, wizened. **5** (*informal*) *everybody at the party was wasted. See* DRUNK.

wasteful ▶ adjective PRODIGAL, profligate, uneconomical, inefficient, extravagant, lavish, excessive, imprudent, improvident, intemperate; thriftless, spendthrift; needless, useless.
— OPPOSITES: frugal.

wasteland ▶ noun WILDERNESS, desert; wilds, wastes, badlands, moose pasture ♣.

wastrel ▶ noun See DEADBEAT.

watch ▶ verb **1** *she watched him as he spoke* OBSERVE, view, look at, eye, gaze at, stare at, peer at; contemplate, survey, keep an eye on; inspect, scrutinize, scan, examine, study, ogle, gawk at, regard, mark; *informal* check out, get a load of, eyeball; *literary* behold. **2** *he was being watched by the police* SPY ON, keep in sight, track, monitor, survey, follow, keep under surveillance; *informal* keep tabs on, stake out. **3** *will you watch the kids?* LOOK AFTER, mind, keep an eye on, take care of, supervise, tend, attend to; guard, safeguard, protect, babysit. **4** *we stayed to watch the boat* GUARD, protect, shield, defend, safeguard; cover, patrol, police. **5** *watch what you say* BE CAREFUL, mind, be aware of, pay attention to, consider, pay heed to.
— OPPOSITES: ignore, neglect.
▶ noun **1** *Bill looked at his watch* TIMEPIECE, chronometer; wristwatch, pocket watch, stopwatch. **2** *we kept watch*

on the yacht GUARD, vigil, lookout, an eye; observation, surveillance, vigilance.

■ **watch out/it/yourself** BE CAREFUL, be watchful, be on your guard, beware, be wary, be cautious, look out, pay attention, take heed, take care, keep an eye open/out, keep one's eyes peeled, be vigilant.

watchdog ▶ noun 1 *they use watchdogs to ward off trespassers* GUARD DOG. 2 *a consumer watchdog* OMBUDSMAN, monitor, scrutineer, inspector, supervisor; custodian, guardian, protector.

watcher ▶ noun ONLOOKER, spectator, observer, viewer, fly on the wall; witness, bystander, looker-on; spy; *informal* rubberneck; *literary* beholder.

watchful ▶ adjective OBSERVANT, alert, vigilant, attentive, awake, aware, heedful, sharp-eyed, eagle-eyed, hawk-eyed; on the lookout, on the qui vive, wary, cautious, careful, canny, chary.

watchman ▶ noun SECURITY GUARD, custodian, warden; sentry, guard, patrolman, lookout, sentinel, scout, watch.

watchword ▶ noun GUIDING PRINCIPLE, motto, slogan, maxim, mantra, catchphrase, byword, shibboleth; *informal* buzzword.

water ▶ noun 1 *a glass of water* H_2O; *dated* Adam's ale. 2 *a house down by the water* SEA, ocean; lake, river; drink; (*West*) *informal* chuck.
— RELATED TERMS: aqueous, aqua-.
▶ verb 1 *water the plants* SPRINKLE, moisten, dampen, wet, spray, splash; soak, douse, souse, drench, saturate; hose (down). 2 *my mouth watered* MOISTEN, become wet, salivate; *informal* drool.
■ **hold water** BE TENABLE, ring true, bear scrutiny, make sense, stand up, hold up, be convincing, be plausible, be sound.
■ **water something down** 1 *staff had watered down the drinks* DILUTE, thin (out), weaken; adulterate, doctor, mix; *informal* cut. 2 *the proposals were watered down* MODERATE, temper, tone down, soften, tame; understate, play down, soft-pedal.

water cooler ▶ noun FOUNTAIN, tap, water fountain, drinking fountain, water filter.

waterfall ▶ noun CASCADE, cataract, falls, chute.

waterfront ▶ noun SHORE, lakefront, lakeshore, harbourfront, riverfront, riverside, esplanade, docks, quay, beach, foreshore, shoreline, embankment.

waterlogged ▶ adjective SATURATED, sodden, soaked, soggy, wet through.

waterproof ▶ adjective *a waterproof jacket* WATERTIGHT, water-repellent, water-resistant, weathertight, rainproof, impermeable, impervious; rubberized, waxed.

watershed ▶ noun 1 *the Mackenzie River watershed* divide, height of land ✦. 2 *a watershed in the party's history* turning point, milestone, landmark.

watertight ▶ adjective 1 *a watertight container* IMPERMEABLE, impervious, (hermetically) sealed; waterproof, water-repellent, water-resistant. 2 *a watertight alibi* INDISPUTABLE, unquestionable, incontrovertible, irrefutable, unassailable, impregnable; foolproof, sound, flawless, airtight, bulletproof, conclusive.
— OPPOSITES: leaky, flawed.

waterway ▶ noun CHANNEL, water route, watercourse, canal, river, seaway.

watery ▶ adjective 1 *a watery discharge* LIQUID, fluid, aqueous; *technical* hydrous. 2 *a watery meadow* WET, damp, moist, sodden, soggy, squelchy, slushy, soft; saturated, waterlogged; boggy, marshy, swampy,

miry, muddy. 3 *watery porridge* THIN, runny, weak, sloppy, dilute, diluted; tasteless, flavourless, insipid, bland. 4 *the light was watery and grey* PALE, wan, faint, weak, feeble; *informal* wishy-washy, washy. 5 *watery eyes* TEARFUL, teary, weepy, moist, rheumy; *formal* lachrymose.
— OPPOSITES: dry, thick, bright.

wave ▶ verb 1 *he waved his flag in triumph* BRANDISH, shake, swish, move to and fro, move up and down, wag, sweep, swing, flourish, wield; flick, flutter; *informal* waggle. 2 *the grass waved in the breeze* RIPPLE, flutter, undulate, stir, flap, sway, billow, shake, quiver, move. 3 *the waiter waved them closer* GESTURE, gesticulate, signal, beckon, motion.
▶ noun 1 *she gave him a friendly wave* GESTURE, gesticulation; signal, sign, motion; salute. 2 *he surfs the big waves* BREAKER, roller, comber, boomer, ripple, white horse, bore, big kahuna; (**waves**) swell, surf, froth; backwash. 3 *a wave of emigration* FLOW, rush, surge, flood, stream, tide, deluge, spate. 4 *a wave of self-pity* SURGE, rush, stab, dart, upsurge, groundswell; thrill, frisson; feeling. 5 *his hair grew in thick waves* CURL, kink, corkscrew, twist, ringlet, coil. 6 *electromagnetic waves* ripple, vibration, oscillation.
■ **make waves** (*informal*) CAUSE TROUBLE, be disruptive, be troublesome; make an impression, get noticed.
■ **wave something aside** DISMISS, reject, brush aside, shrug off, disregard, ignore, discount, play down; *informal* pooh-pooh.
■ **wave someone/something down** FLAG DOWN, hail, stop, summon, call, accost.

waver ▶ verb 1 *the candlelight wavered in the draft* FLICKER, quiver, twinkle, glimmer, wink, blink. 2 *his voice wavered* FALTER, wobble, tremble, quaver, shake. 3 *he wavered between the choices* BE UNDECIDED, be irresolute, hesitate, dither, equivocate, vacillate, waffle, fluctuate; think twice, change one's mind, blow hot and cold; *informal* shilly-shally, sit on the fence.

wavy ▶ adjective CURLY, curvy, curved, undulating, squiggly, rippled, crinkly, kinked, zigzag.

wax ▶ verb *the moon is waxing* GET BIGGER, increase, enlarge.
— OPPOSITES: wane.
■ **wax lyrical** BE ENTHUSIASTIC, enthuse, eulogize, rave, gush, get carried away.

waxen ▶ adjective PALLID, pale, pasty, wan, ashen, colourless, anemic, bloodless, washed out, white, grey, whitish, waxy, drained, sickly.
— OPPOSITES: ruddy.

waxy ▶ adjective. See WAXEN.

way ▶ noun 1 *a way of reducing the damage* METHOD, process, procedure, technique, system; plan, strategy, scheme; means, mechanism, approach. 2 *she kissed him in her brisk way* MANNER, style, fashion, mode; modus operandi, MO. 3 *I've changed my ways* PRACTICE, wont, habit, custom, policy, procedure, convention, routine, modus vivendi; trait, attribute, peculiarity, idiosyncrasy; conduct, behaviour, manner, style, nature, personality, temperament, disposition, character. 4 *which way leads home?* ROUTE, course, direction; road, street, track, path. 5 *I'll go out the back way* DOOR, gate, exit, entrance, entry; route. 6 *a short way downstream* DISTANCE, length, stretch, journey; space, interval, span. 7 *April is a long way away* TIME, stretch, term, span, duration. 8 *a car coming the other way* DIRECTION, bearing, course, orientation, line, tack. 9 *in some ways, he may be better off* RESPECT, regard, aspect, facet, sense, angle; detail, point, particular. **10** *the country is in a bad way* STATE, condition, situation, circumstances, position; predicament, plight; *informal* shape.

■ **by the way** INCIDENTALLY, by the by, in passing, en passant, as an aside.

■ **give way 1** *the government gave way and passed the bill* YIELD, back down, surrender, capitulate, concede defeat, give in, submit, succumb; acquiesce, agree, assent; *informal* throw in the towel/sponge, cave in. **2** *the door gave way* COLLAPSE, give, cave in, fall in, come apart, crumple, buckle. **3** *grief gave way to guilt* BE REPLACED BY, be succeeded by, be followed by, be supplanted by.

■ **on the way** COMING, imminent, forthcoming, approaching, impending, close, near, on us; proceeding, en route, in transit.

wayfarer ▶ noun *(literary).* See WANDERER.

waylay ▶ verb **1** *we were waylaid and robbed* AMBUSH, hold up, attack, assail, rob; *informal* mug, stick up. **2** *several people waylaid her for an interview* ACCOST, detain, intercept, take aside, pounce on, importune; *informal* buttonhole.

way-out ▶ adjective *(informal)* UNCONVENTIONAL, avant-garde, outlandish, eccentric, quirky, unusual, bizarre, strange, peculiar, odd, uncommon, offbeat; *informal* far-out, oddball, off the wall.
— OPPOSITES: ordinary.

wayward ▶ adjective WILFUL, headstrong, stubborn, obstinate, obdurate, perverse, contrary, disobedient, insubordinate, undisciplined; rebellious, defiant, uncooperative, recalcitrant, unruly, wild, unmanageable, erratic; difficult, impossible; *formal* refractory.
— OPPOSITES: docile.

weak ▶ adjective **1** *they are too weak to move* FRAIL, feeble, delicate, fragile; infirm, sick, sickly, debilitated, incapacitated, ailing, indisposed, decrepit; tired, fatigued, exhausted, anemic; *informal* weedy. **2** *weak eyesight* INADEQUATE, poor, feeble; defective, faulty, deficient, imperfect, substandard. **3** *a weak excuse* UNCONVINCING, untenable, tenuous, implausible, unsatisfactory, poor, inadequate, feeble, flimsy, lame, hollow; *informal* pathetic. **4** *I was too weak to be a rebel* SPINELESS, craven, cowardly, pusillanimous, timid; irresolute, indecisive, ineffectual, inept, effete, meek, tame, ineffective, impotent, soft, faint-hearted; *informal* yellow, weak-kneed, gutless, chicken. **5** *a weak light* DIM, pale, wan, faint, feeble, muted. **6** *a weak voice* INDISTINCT, muffled, muted, hushed, low, faint, thready, thin. **7** *weak coffee* WATERY, diluted, dilute, watered down, thin, tasteless, flavourless, bland, insipid, wishy-washy. **8** *a weak smile* UNENTHUSIASTIC, feeble, half-hearted, lame.
— OPPOSITES: strong, powerful, convincing, resolute, bright, loud.

weaken ▶ verb **1** *the virus weakened him terribly* ENFEEBLE, debilitate, incapacitate, sap, enervate, tire, exhaust, wear out; wither, cripple, disable, emasculate. **2** *she tried to weaken the blow for him* REDUCE, decrease, diminish, soften, lessen, moderate, temper, dilute, blunt, mitigate. **3** *our morale weakened* DECREASE, dwindle, diminish, wane, ebb, subside, peter out, fizzle out, tail off, decline, falter. **4** *the move weakened her authority* IMPAIR, undermine, erode, eat away at, compromise; invalidate, negate, discredit.

weakling ▶ noun PUSHOVER, namby-pamby, coward, milksop; *informal* wimp, weed, sissy, twinkie, drip,

softie, doormat, chicken, yellow-belly, scaredy-cat, wuss.

weakness ▶ noun **1** *with old age came weakness* FRAILTY, feebleness, enfeeblement, fragility, delicacy; infirmity, sickness, sickliness, debility, incapacity, impotence, indisposition, decrepitude, vulnerability. **2** *he has worked on his weaknesses* FAULT, flaw, defect, deficiency, weak point, failing, shortcoming, weak link, imperfection, Achilles' heel, foible. **3** *a weakness for champagne* FONDNESS, liking, partiality, preference, love, penchant, soft spot, predilection, inclination, taste, eye; enthusiasm, appetite; susceptibility. **4** *the President was accused of weakness* TIMIDITY, cowardliness, pusillanimity; indecision, irresolution, ineffectuality, ineptitude, impotence, meekness, powerlessness, ineffectiveness. **5** *the weakness of this argument* UNTENABILITY, implausibility, poverty, inadequacy, transparency; flimsiness, hollowness. **6** *the weakness of the sound* INDISTINCTNESS, muteness, faintness, feebleness, lowness; dimness, paleness.

weak-willed ▶ adjective SPINELESS, weak, irresolute, indecisive, weak-minded; impressionable, persuadable, submissive, unassertive, compliant, pusillanimous; *informal* wimpish, chicken.

wealth ▶ noun **1** *a gentleman of wealth* AFFLUENCE, prosperity, riches, means, substance, fortune; money, cash, lucre, capital, treasure, finance; assets, possessions, resources, funds; property, stock, reserves, securities, holdings; *informal* wherewithal, dough, moolah. **2** *a wealth of information* ABUNDANCE, profusion, plethora, mine, store, treasury, bounty, bonanza, cornucopia, myriad; *informal* lot, load, heap, mass, mountain, stack, whack, ton; *formal* plenitude.
— OPPOSITES: poverty, dearth.

wealthy ▶ adjective RICH, affluent, moneyed, well off, well-to-do, prosperous, comfortable, propertied, of substance; *informal* well-heeled, rolling in it, in the money, made of money, filthy rich, stinking rich, loaded, flush.
— OPPOSITES: poor.

wean ▶ verb **1** *they weaned him off the habit* DISENGAGE; accustom, train; guide, encourage. **2** *she was weaned on sitcoms* RAISE, fed, nourish, expose to.

wear ▶ verb **1** *he wore a suit* DRESS IN, be clothed in, have on, sport, model; put on, don. **2** *Barbara wore a smile* BEAR, have (on one's face), show, display, exhibit; give, put on, assume. **3** *the bricks have been worn down* ERODE, abrade, rub away, grind away, wash away, crumble (away), wear down; corrode, eat away (at), dissolve. **4** *the tires are wearing well* LAST, endure, hold up, bear up, prove durable.
▶ noun **1** *you won't get much wear out of that* USE, wearing, service, utility, value; *informal* mileage. **2** *evening wear* CLOTHES, clothing, garments, dress, attire, garb, wardrobe; *informal* getup, gear, togs, duds, kit; *formal* apparel; *literary* array. **3** *the varnish which will withstand wear* DAMAGE, friction, erosion, attrition, abrasion; weathering.

■ **wear something down** *he wore down her resistance* GRADUALLY OVERCOME, slowly reduce, erode, wear away, exhaust, undermine.

■ **wear off** *the novelty soon wore off* FADE, diminish, lessen, dwindle, decrease, wane, ebb, peter out, fizzle out, pall, disappear, run out.

■ **wear on** *the afternoon wore on* PASS, elapse, proceed, advance, progress, go by, roll by, march on, slip by/away, fly by/past.

■ **wear out** DETERIORATE, become worn, wear thin, fray, become threadbare, wear through.

■ **wear something out** USE UP, consume, go through.

■ **wear someone out** FATIGUE, tire out, weary, exhaust, drain, sap, overtax, enervate, debilitate, jade, prostrate; *informal* poop, frazzle, do in.

wearing ▶ adjective. *See* WEARISOME.

wearisome ▶ adjective TIRING, exhausting, wearying, fatiguing, enervating, draining, sapping, stressful, wearing, crushing; demanding, exacting, taxing, trying, challenging, burdensome, arduous, gruelling, punishing, grinding, onerous, difficult, hard, tough, heavy, laborious, back-breaking, crippling, strenuous, rigorous, uphill; tiresome, irksome, weary, boring, dull, tedious, monotonous, humdrum, prosaic, unexciting, uninteresting.

weary ▶ adjective **1** *he was weary after cycling* TIRED, worn out, exhausted, fatigued, sapped, burnt-out, dog-tired, spent, drained, prostrate, enervated; *informal* all in, done in, beat, ready to drop, bushed, worn to a frazzle, pooped, bagged, tuckered out. **2** *she was weary of the arguments* TIRED OF, fed up with, bored by, sick of, burnt-out on; *informal* have had it up to here with. **3** *a weary journey* TIRING, exhausting, wearying, fatiguing, enervating, draining, sapping, wearing, trying, demanding, taxing, arduous, gruelling, difficult, hard, tough.

— OPPOSITES: fresh, keen, refreshing.

wearying ▶ adjective. *See* WEARISOME.

weasel ▶ noun *he was a double-crossing weasel* SCOUNDREL, wretch, rogue; *informal* swine, bastard, creep, louse, rat, rat fink, toad, snake, snake in the grass, serpent, viper, skunk, dog, cur, scumbag, scum-bucket, scuzzball, sleazeball, sleazebag, slimeball, sneak, backstabber, heel, nogoodnik, nasty piece of work, sleeveen; *dated* cad; *archaic* blackguard, knave, varlet.

weather ▶ noun *what's the weather like?* FORECAST, outlook; meteorological conditions, climate, atmospheric pressure, temperature; elements.
▶ verb *we weathered the recession* SURVIVE, come through, ride out, pull through; withstand, endure, rise above, surmount, overcome, resist, brave; *informal* stick out.
■ **under the weather** (*informal*). *See* ILL adjective sense 1.

weathered ▶ adjective WEATHER-BEATEN, worn; tanned, bronzed; lined, creased, wrinkled, gnarled, gnarly.

weave ▶ verb **1** *flowers were woven into their hair* ENTWINE, lace, twist, knit, intertwine, braid, plait, loop. **2** *he weaves colourful plots* INVENT, make up, fabricate, construct, create, contrive, spin; tell, recount, relate. **3** *he had to weave his way through the crowds* THREAD, wind, wend; dodge, deke, zigzag.

web ▶ noun **1** *a spider's web* MESH, net, lattice, latticework, lacework, webbing; gauze, gossamer. **2** *a web of friendships* NETWORK, nexus, complex, set, chain; tissue. **3** *visit us on the Web* INTERNET, World Wide Web, information superhighway, Infobahn, cyberspace, Net.
▶ adjective *a web environment* ONLINE, Internet, virtual, digital, cyber, web-based, e-.

weblog ▶ noun BLOG, online journal/diary.

web page ▶ noun WEBSITE, home page, hypertext document.

wed ▶ verb **1** *they are old enough to wed* MARRY, get married, become husband and wife; *informal* tie the knot, walk down the aisle, get hitched, take the plunge. **2** *he will wed his girlfriend* MARRY, take as one's wife/husband, lead to the altar; *informal* make an honest woman of; *archaic* espouse. **3** *she wedded the two forms of spirituality* UNITE, unify, join, combine, amalgamate, fuse, integrate, bond, merge, meld, splice.

— OPPOSITES: divorce, separate.

wedded ▶ adjective **1** *wedded bliss* MARRIED, matrimonial, marital, conjugal, nuptial; *Law* spousal; *literary* connubial. **2** *she is wedded to her work* DEDICATED TO, devoted to, attached to, fixated on, single-minded about.

wedding ▶ noun MARRIAGE (SERVICE/CEREMONY/RITES), nuptials, union, commitment ceremony; *archaic* espousal.

— RELATED TERMS: nuptial.

wedge ▶ noun **1** *the door was secured by a wedge* DOORSTOP, chock, block, stop. **2** *a wedge of cheese* HUNK, segment, triangle, slice, section; chunk, lump, slab, block, piece.
▶ verb *she wedged her case between two bags* SQUEEZE, cram, jam, ram, force, push, shove; *informal* stuff.

wedlock ▶ noun MARRIAGE, (holy) matrimony, married state, union.

wee ▶ adjective *See* LITTLE.

weed
■ **weed something/someone out** ISOLATE, separate out, sort out, sift out, winnow out, filter out, set apart, segregate; eliminate, get rid of, remove, cut, chop; *informal* lose.

weedy ▶ adjective (*informal*) PUNY, feeble, weak, frail, undersized, slight, skinny; *informal* pint-sized, pantywaist.

weekly ▶ adjective *weekly instalments* ONCE A WEEK; lasting a week; *formal* hebdomadal.
▶ adverb *the directors meet weekly* ONCE A WEEK, every week, each week, on a weekly basis; by the week, per week, a week.

weep ▶ verb *even the toughest soldiers wept* CRY, shed tears, sob, snivel, whimper, whine, wail, bawl, boo-hoo, blubber.

weepy ▶ adjective TEARFUL, close to tears, upset, distressed, sad, unhappy; in tears, crying, weeping, snivelling; *informal* teary, misty-eyed, choked-up; *formal* lachrymose.

weigh ▶ verb **1** *she weighs the fruit* MEASURE THE WEIGHT OF, put on the scales; heft. **2** *he weighed 170 lbs* HAVE A WEIGHT OF, tip the scales at, weigh in at. **3** *the situation weighed heavily on him* OPPRESS, lie heavy on, burden, hang over, gnaw at, prey on (one's mind); trouble, worry, bother, disturb, get down, depress, haunt, nag, torment, plague. **4** *he has to weigh his options* CONSIDER, contemplate, think about, mull over, chew over, reflect on, ruminate about, muse on; assess, appraise, analyze, investigate, inquire into, look into, examine, review, explore, take stock of. **5** *they need to weigh benefit against risk* BALANCE, evaluate, compare, juxtapose, contrast, measure.
■ **weigh someone down** *my fishing gear weighed me down* BURDEN, saddle, overload, overburden, encumber, hamper, handicap.

weight ▶ noun **1** *the weight of the book* HEAVINESS, mass, load, burden, pressure, force; poundage, tonnage. **2** *his recommendation will carry great weight* INFLUENCE, force, leverage, sway, pull, importance, significance, consequence, value, substance, power, authority; *informal* clout. **3** *a weight off her mind* BURDEN, load, millstone, albatross, encumbrance; trouble, worry, pressure, strain. **4** *the weight of the evidence is against him* PREPONDERANCE, majority, bulk, body, lion's share, predominance; most, almost all.

weighty ▶ adjective **1** *a weighty tome* HEAVY, thick, bulky, hefty, cumbersome, ponderous. **2** *a weighty subject* IMPORTANT, significant, momentous, consequential, far-reaching, key, major, big, vital, critical, crucial; serious, grave, solemn. **3** *a weighty responsibility* BURDENSOME, onerous, heavy, oppressive, taxing, troublesome, solemn. **4** *weighty arguments* COMPELLING, cogent, strong, forceful, powerful, beefy, potent, effective, sound, valid, telling; impressive, persuasive, convincing, influential, authoritative.
— OPPOSITES: light, trivial, weak.

weird ▶ adjective **1** *weird apparitions* UNCANNY, eerie, unnatural, supernatural, unearthly, otherworldly, ghostly, mysterious, strange, abnormal, unusual; eldritch; *informal* creepy, spooky, freaky. **2** *a weird sense of humour* BIZARRE, quirky, outlandish, eccentric, unconventional, unorthodox, idiosyncratic, surreal, crazy, peculiar, odd, strange, queer, freakish, zany, madcap, outré; *informal* wacky, freaky, way-out, offbeat, off the wall, wacko.
■ **weird out** DISTURB, freak out, unnerve, unsettle, alarm, alienate.
— OPPOSITES: normal, conventional.

weirdo ▶ noun (*informal*). See ECCENTRIC *noun*.

welcome ▶ noun *a welcome from the vicar* GREETING, salutation; reception, hospitality; the red carpet.
▶ verb **1** *welcome your guests in their own language* GREET, salute, receive, meet, usher in. **2** *we welcomed their decision* BE PLEASED BY, be glad about, approve of, appreciate, embrace; *informal* give the thumbs up to.
▶ adjective *welcome news* PLEASING, agreeable, encouraging, gratifying, heartening, promising, favourable, pleasant, refreshing; gladly received, wanted, appreciated, popular, desirable.

weld ▶ verb FUSE, bond, stick, join, attach, seal, splice, melt, solder, cement.

welfare ▶ noun **1** *the welfare of children* WELL-BEING, health, comfort, security, safety, protection, prosperity, success, fortune; interest, good. **2** *we cannot claim welfare* SOCIAL ASSISTANCE, social security, benefit, public assistance; pension, credit, support; sick pay, unemployment benefit; *informal* the dole, pogey ♣.

well¹ ▶ adverb **1** *he behaves well* SATISFACTORILY, nicely, correctly, properly, fittingly, suitably, appropriately; decently, fairly, kindly, generously, honestly. **2** *they get on well together* HARMONIOUSLY, agreeably, pleasantly, nicely, happily, amicably, amiably, peaceably; *informal* famously. **3** *he plays the piano well* SKILFULLY, ably, competently, proficiently, adeptly, deftly, expertly, admirably, excellently. **4** *I know her quite well* INTIMATELY, thoroughly, deeply, profoundly, personally. **5** *they studied the recipe well* CAREFULLY, closely, attentively, rigorously, in depth, exhaustively, in detail, meticulously, scrupulously, conscientiously, methodically, completely, comprehensively, fully, extensively, thoroughly, effectively. **6** *they speak well of him* ADMIRINGLY, highly, approvingly, favourably, appreciatively, warmly, enthusiastically, positively, glowingly. **7** *she makes enough money to live well* COMFORTABLY, in (the lap of) luxury, prosperously. **8** *you may well be right* QUITE POSSIBLY, conceivably, probably; undoubtedly, certainly, unquestionably. **9** *he is well over forty* CONSIDERABLY, very much, a great deal, substantially,

easily, comfortably, significantly. **10** *she could well afford it* EASILY, comfortably, readily, effortlessly.
— OPPOSITES: badly, negligently, disparagingly, barely.
■ **well done** CONGRATULATIONS, bravo, right on, congrats, my compliments, good work, three cheers, felicitations.
▶ adjective **1** *she was completely well again* HEALTHY, fine, fit, robust, strong, vigorous, blooming, thriving, hale and hearty, in good shape, in good condition, in fine fettle; *informal* in the pink. **2** *all is not well* SATISFACTORY, all right, fine, in order, as it should be, acceptable; *informal* OK, hunky-dory, jake. **3** *it would be well to tell us in advance* ADVISABLE, sensible, prudent, politic, commonsensical, wise, judicious, expedient, recommended, advantageous, beneficial, profitable, desirable; a good idea.
— OPPOSITES: poorly, unsatisfactory, inadvisable.
■ **as well** TOO, also, in addition, additionally, into the bargain, besides, furthermore, moreover, likewise, to boot.
■ **as well as** TOGETHER WITH, along with, besides, plus, and, with, on top of, not to mention, to say nothing of, let alone.

well² ▶ noun **1** *she drew water from the well* BOREHOLE, bore, spring, water hole. **2** *he's a bottomless well of forgiveness* SOURCE, supply, fount, reservoir, wellspring, mine, fund, treasury.
▶ verb *tears welled from her eyes* FLOW, spill, stream, run, rush, gush, roll, cascade, flood, spout; seep, trickle; burst, issue, upwell.

well-advised ▶ adjective WISE, prudent, sensible.

well-balanced ▶ adjective. See BALANCED.

well-behaved ▶ adjective ORDERLY, obedient, disciplined, peaceable, docile, controlled, restrained, co-operative, compliant, law-abiding; mannerly, polite, civil, courteous, respectful, proper, decorous, refined, polished.
— OPPOSITES: naughty.

well-being ▶ noun. See WELFARE sense 1.

well-bred ▶ adjective WELL BROUGHT UP, polite, civil, mannerly, courteous, respectful; ladylike, gentlemanly, genteel, cultivated, urbane, proper, refined, patrician, polished, well-behaved.

well-built ▶ adjective STURDY, strapping, brawny, burly, hefty, muscular, muscly, strong, rugged, lusty, Herculean; *informal* hunky, beefy, husky, hulking.
— OPPOSITES: puny.

well-dressed ▶ adjective SMART, fashionable, stylish, chic, chi-chi, modish, elegant, neat, spruce, trim, dapper; snazzy, natty, snappy, sharp, spiffy, fly, preppy.
— OPPOSITES: scruffy.

well-founded ▶ adjective JUSTIFIABLE, justified, warranted, legitimate, defensible, valid, admissible, allowable, understandable, excusable, acceptable, reasonable, sensible, sound, well-grounded.
— OPPOSITES: groundless.

well-heeled ▶ adjective (*informal*). See WEALTHY.

well-known ▶ adjective **1** *well-known principles* FAMILIAR, widely known, popular, common, everyday, established. **2** *a well-known family of architects* FAMOUS, famed, prominent, notable, renowned, distinguished, eminent, illustrious, celebrated, acclaimed, recognized, important; notorious.
— OPPOSITES: obscure.

well-mannered ▶ adjective POLITE, courteous, civil, mannerly, genteel, decorous, debonair, respectful, refined, polished, civilized, urbane, well-behaved, well-bred.

well-nigh ▶ adverb ALMOST, nearly, just about, more or less, practically, virtually, all but, as good as, nearing, close to, approaching; roughly, approximately; *informal* pretty much, nigh on.

well off ▶ adjective **1** *her family's very well off. See* WELL-TO-DO. **2** *the prisoners were relatively well off* FORTUNATE, lucky, comfortable; *informal* sitting pretty. **3** *the island is not well off for harbours* WELL SUPPLIED WITH, well stocked with, well furnished with, well equipped with; well situated for.

well-read ▶ adjective KNOWLEDGEABLE, well-informed, well versed, erudite, scholarly, literate, educated, cultured, bookish, studious; *dated* lettered.
— OPPOSITES: ignorant.

well-spoken ▶ adjective ARTICULATE, eloquent, coherent, nicely spoken; refined, polite.

well-to-do ▶ adjective WEALTHY, rich, affluent, moneyed, well off, prosperous, comfortable, propertied; *informal* rolling in it, in the money, loaded, well-heeled, flush, made of money, on easy street.

welt ▶ noun SWELLING, lump, bump; mark, pimple, blister, bruise, contusion, *Medicine* bleb.

welter ▶ noun CONFUSION, jumble, tangle, mess, hodgepodge, mishmash, mass; *informal* rat's nest.

wend ▶ verb MEANDER, wind one's way, wander, amble, stroll, saunter, drift, roam, traipse, walk; journey, travel; *informal* mosey, tootle.

west ▶ adjective WESTERN, westerly, occidental; Pacific.
▶ noun *commercialism in the West* THE OCCIDENT, Western nations.

wet ▶ adjective **1** *wet clothes* DAMP, moist, soaked, drenched, saturated, sopping, dripping, soggy; waterlogged, squelchy. **2** *it was cold and wet* RAINY, raining, pouring, teeming, inclement, showery, drizzly, drizzling; damp; humid, muggy. **3** *the paint is still wet* STICKY, tacky; fresh. **4** *a wet mortar mix* AQUEOUS, watery, sloppy.
— OPPOSITES: dry, fine.
▶ verb *wet the clothes before ironing them* DAMPEN, damp, moisten; sprinkle, spray, splash, spritz; soak, saturate, flood, douse, souse, drench.
— OPPOSITES: dry.
▶ noun **1** *the wet of his tears* WETNESS, damp, moisture, moistness, sogginess; wateriness. **2** *the race was held in the wet* RAIN, drizzle, precipitation; spray, dew, damp.

wetland ▶ noun MARSH, bogland, bog, swamp, morass, (*NB & NS*) barren ✤, quagmire, muskeg, slough, fen, fenland, bayou.

whack (*informal*) ▶ verb *she whacked him on the head. See* STRIKE verb sense 1.
▶ noun **1** *he got a whack with a stick. See* BLOW noun sense 1. **2** *a whole whack of information. See* LOAD sense 2.

whale ▶ noun CETACEAN, leviathan. *See table.*

wharf ▶ noun QUAY, pier, dock, berth, landing, jetty; harbour, dockyard, marina; (*Nfld*) head ✤.

what-if ▶ noun SPECULATION, conjecture, fancy, thought experiment.
▶ adjective HYPOTHETICAL, speculative, theoretical, notional; imagined.

whatsit ▶ noun (*informal*) THING, so-and-so, whatever it's called; *informal* whatnot, whatchamacallit, whatchacallit, what-d'you-call-it, what's-its-name, thingy, thingummy, thingamabob, thingamajig, doodad, doohickey.

Whales & Dolphins

beluga	killer whale
blue whale	minke
bottlenose dolphin	narwhal
bowhead whale	orca
cachalot	pilot whale
dolphin	porpoise
fin whale	pothead
finback	right whale
grampus	rorqual
grey whale	sei
humpback whale	sperm whale
	white whale

---

whatsoever ▶ adjective AT ALL, of any kind, whatever, in the least, {in any way, shape or form}.

wheat ▶ noun cracked wheat, hulled wheat, whole wheat, soft wheat, hard wheat. *See table at* CEREAL.

wheedle ▶ verb COAX, cajole, inveigle, induce, entice, charm, tempt, beguile, blandish, flatter, persuade, influence, win someone over, bring someone round, convince, prevail on, get round; *informal* sweet-talk, soft-soap.

wheel ▶ noun *a wagon wheel* disc, hoop, ring, circle.
▶ verb **1** *she wheeled the trolley away* PUSH, trundle, roll. **2** *the flock of doves wheeled round* TURN, go round, circle, orbit.
■ **at/behind the wheel** DRIVING, steering, in the driver's seat.

wheelbarrow ▶ noun CART, barrow.

wheeze ▶ verb BREATHE NOISILY, gasp, whistle, hiss, rasp, croak, pant, cough.

whereabouts ▶ noun LOCATION, position, site, place, situation, spot, point, vicinity; home, address, locale, neighbourhood; bearings, orientation.

wherewithal ▶ noun MONEY, cash, capital, finance(s), funds; resources, means, ability, capability; *informal* dough, loot, the necessary, boodle, bucks.

whet ▶ verb **1** *he whetted his knife on a stone* SHARPEN, hone, strop, grind, file. **2** *something to whet your appetite* STIMULATE, excite, arouse, rouse, kindle, trigger, spark, quicken, stir, inspire, animate, waken, fuel, fire, activate, tempt, galvanize.
— OPPOSITES: blunt.

whew ▶ exclamation PHEW, thank goodness, thank God, what a relief.

whiff ▶ noun **1** *I caught a whiff of perfume* FAINT SMELL, trace, sniff, scent, odour, aroma. **2** *the faintest whiff of irony* TRACE, hint, suggestion, impression, suspicion, soupçon, smidgen, nuance, intimation, tinge, vein, shred, whisper, air, element, overtone. **3** *whiffs of smoke from the boiler* PUFF, gust, flurry, breath, draft, waft.

while ▶ noun *we chatted for a while* TIME, spell, stretch, stint, span, interval, period; duration, phase, patch.
▶ verb *tennis helped to while away the time* PASS, spend, occupy, use up, fritter, kill.

whim ▶ noun **1** *she bought it on a whim* IMPULSE, urge, notion, fancy, foible, caprice, conceit, vagary, inclination, megrim. **2** *human whim* CAPRICIOUSNESS, whimsy, caprice, volatility, fickleness, idiosyncrasy.

whimper ▶ noun & verb WHINE, cry, sob, moan, snivel, wail, groan; mewl, bleat.

whimsical ▶ adjective **1** *a whimsical sense of humour* FANCIFUL, playful, mischievous, waggish, quaint, quizzical, curious, droll; eccentric, quirky, idiosyncratic, unconventional, outlandish, queer, fey; *informal* offbeat, freaky. **2** *the whimsical arbitrariness of autocracy* VOLATILE, capricious, fickle, changeable, unpredictable, variable, erratic, mercurial, mutable, inconstant, inconsistent, unstable, protean.

whine ▶ noun & verb **1** *she heard an animal whine* WHIMPER, cry, mewl, howl, yowl. **2** *the motor whined* | *the motor's whine* HUM, drone. **3** *we listened to the orderly whine* COMPLAIN(T), grouse, grumble, murmur; *informal* gripe, moan, grouch, whinge, bellyache, beef.

whip ▶ noun *he would use a whip on his dogs* LASH, scourge, strap, belt, rod, bullwhip; *historical* cat-o'-nine-tails.

▶ verb **1** *he whipped the boy* FLOG, scourge, flagellate, lash, strap, belt, thrash, beat, tan someone's hide. **2** *whip the cream* WHISK, beat. **3** *she whipped her listeners into a frenzy* ROUSE, stir up, excite, galvanize, electrify, stimulate, inspire, fire up, get someone going, inflame, agitate, goad, provoke. **4** (*informal*) *he whipped round the corner.* See DASH *verb* sense 1. **5** (*informal*) *then she whipped out a revolver* PULL, whisk, snatch, pluck, jerk.

whippersnapper ▶ noun (*informal*) UPSTART, stripling; *informal* pipsqueak, squirt.

whirl ▶ verb **1** *leaves whirled in eddies* ROTATE, circle, wheel, turn, revolve, orbit, spin, twirl. **2** *they whirled past* HURRY, race, dash, rush, run, sprint, bolt, dart, gallop, career, charge, shoot, hurtle, fly, speed, scurry; *informal* tear, belt, pelt, scoot, bomb, hightail it. **3** *his mind was whirling* SPIN, reel, swim.

▶ noun **1** *a whirl of dust* SWIRL, flurry, eddy. **2** *the mad social whirl* HURLY-BURLY, activity, bustle, rush, flurry, fuss, turmoil, merry-go-round. **3** *Laura's mind was in a whirl* SPIN, daze, stupor, muddle, jumble; confusion; *informal* dither.

whirlpool ▶ noun **1** *a river full of whirlpools* EDDY, vortex, maelstrom. **2** *the health club has a whirlpool* HOT TUB; *proprietary* Jacuzzi.

whirlwind ▶ noun **1** *the building was hit by a whirlwind* TORNADO, hurricane, typhoon, cyclone, vortex, twister, dust devil. **2** *a whirlwind of activity* MAELSTROM, welter, bedlam, mayhem, babel, swirl, tumult, hurly-burly, commotion, confusion; *informal* madhouse, three-ring circus.

▶ adjective *a whirlwind romance* RAPID, lightning, headlong, impulsive, breakneck, meteoric, sudden, swift, fast, quick, speedy, dizzying; *informal* quickie.

whisk ▶ verb **1** *the cable car will whisk you to the top* SPEED, hurry, rush, sweep, hurtle, shoot. **2** *she whisked the cloth away* PULL, snatch, pluck, tug, jerk; *informal* whip, yank. **3** *he whisked out of sight* DASH, rush, race, bolt, dart, gallop, career, charge, shoot, hurtle, fly, speed, zoom, scurry, scuttle, scamper; *informal* tear, belt, pelt, scoot, zip, whip. **4** *she whisked the hair from her face* FLICK, brush, sweep, wave. **5** *whisk the egg yolks* WHIP, beat, mix.

whisker ▶ noun FACIAL HAIR, moustache, beard, mustachios, goatee, mutton chop; stubble, five o'clock shadow.

whisper ▶ verb **1** *Alison whispered in his ear* MURMUR, mutter, mumble, speak softly, breathe; hiss; *formal* susurrate. **2** (*literary*) *the wind whispered in the grass* RUSTLE, murmur, sigh, moan, whoosh, whirr, swish, blow, breathe.

— OPPOSITES: roar.

▶ noun **1** *she spoke in a whisper* MURMUR, mutter, mumble, low voice, undertone; *rare* sibilation, susurration. **2** (*literary*) *the wind died to a whisper* RUSTLE, murmur, sigh, whoosh, swish. **3** *I heard a whisper that he's left town* RUMOUR, story, report, speculation,

insinuation, suggestion, hint; *informal* buzz. **4** *not a whisper of interest.* See WHIT.

whit ▶ noun SCRAP, bit, speck, iota, jot, atom, crumb, shred, grain, mite, touch, trace, shadow, suggestion, whisper, suspicion, scintilla, modicum; *informal* smidgen, smidge.

white ▶ adjective **1** *a clean white bandage* COLOURLESS, unpigmented, bleached, natural; snowy, milky, chalky, ivory. **2** *her face was white with fear* PALE, pallid, wan, ashen, bloodless, waxen, chalky, pasty, washed out, drained, drawn, ghostly, deathly. **3** *white hair* SNOWY, grey, silver, silvery, hoary, grizzled. **4** *the early white settlers* CAUCASIAN, European.

white-collar ▶ adjective CLERICAL, administrative, professional, executive, salaried, office.

whiten ▶ verb MAKE WHITE, make pale, bleach, blanch, lighten, fade.

whitewash ▶ noun **1** *the report was a whitewash* COVER-UP, camouflage, deception, facade, veneer, pretext. **2** *a four-game whitewash* WALKOVER, rout, landslide, laugher; *informal* pushover, cinch, breeze.

▶ verb *don't whitewash what happened* COVER UP, sweep under the carpet, hush up, suppress, draw a veil over, conceal, veil, obscure, keep secret; gloss over, downplay, soft-pedal.

— OPPOSITES: expose.

whittle ▶ verb **1** *he sat whittling a piece of wood* PARE, shave, trim, carve, shape, model. **2** *his powers were whittled away* ERODE, wear away, eat away, reduce, diminish, undermine, weaken, subvert, compromise, impair, impede, hinder, cripple, disable, enfeeble, sap. **3** *the ten teams have been whittled down to six* REDUCE, cut down, cut back, prune, trim, slim down, pare down, shrink, decrease, diminish.

whiz ▶ noun GENIUS, virtuoso, ace, master, prodigy, hotshot, wizard, magician.

▶ verb ZOOM, flash, zip, whip, hurtle, fly.

whoa ▶ exclamation **1** *whoa, boy* STOP, easy, slow down, hold your horses. **2** *whoa, man!* See WOW.

whole ▶ adjective **1** *the whole report* ENTIRE, complete, full, unabridged, uncut. **2** *he was swallowed whole* INTACT, in one piece, unbroken; undamaged, unmarked, perfect.

— OPPOSITES: incomplete.

▶ noun **1** *a single whole* ENTITY, unit, body, discrete item, ensemble. **2** *the whole of the year* ALL, every part, the lot, the sum (total), the entirety.

■ **on the whole** OVERALL, all in all, all things considered, for the most part, in the main, in general, generally (speaking), as a (general) rule, by and large; normally, usually, more often than not, almost always, most of the time, typically, ordinarily.

wholehearted ▶ adjective COMMITTED, positive, emphatic, devoted, dedicated, enthusiastic, unshakeable, unswerving; unqualified, unstinting, unreserved, without reservations, unconditional, unequivocal, unmitigated; complete, full, total, absolute.

— OPPOSITES: half-hearted.

wholesale ▶ adverb *the images were removed wholesale* EXTENSIVELY, on a large scale, comprehensively; indiscriminately, without exception, across the board.

— OPPOSITES: selectively.

▶ adjective *wholesale destruction* EXTENSIVE, widespread, large-scale, wide-ranging, comprehensive, total,

mass; indiscriminate.
— OPPOSITES: partial.

wholesome ► adjective **1** *wholesome food* HEALTHY, health-giving, healthful, good (for one), nutritious, nourishing; natural, uncontaminated, organic. **2** *wholesome fun* GOOD, ethical, moral, clean, virtuous, pure, innocent, chaste; uplifting, edifying, proper, correct, decent, harmless; *informal* squeaky clean.

wholly ► adverb **1** *the measures were wholly inadequate* COMPLETELY, totally, absolutely, entirely, fully, thoroughly, utterly, quite, perfectly, downright, in every respect, in all respects; *informal* one hundred per cent, lock, stock and barrel. **2** *they rely wholly on you* EXCLUSIVELY, only, solely, purely, alone.

whoop ► noun & verb SHOUT, cry, call, yell, roar, scream, shriek, screech, cheer, hoot; *informal* holler.

whoop-de-do ► exclamation (*sarcastic*) BIG DEAL, big whoop, whoopee, stop the presses; so what, so, who cares, and...?.

whoops ► exclamation OOPS, oh dear, oh no, eek, ack, yikes, uh-oh, sorry, silly me, doh, damn, argh, aiyee, whoopsy, oopsy daisy.

whopper ► noun (*informal*) **1** *what a whopper!* GIANT, monster, colossus, mammoth, monstrosity, brute; *informal* jumbo. **2** *Joseph's story is a whopper.* See LIE[1] noun.

whopping ► adjective (*informal*). See HUGE.

whore ► noun *the whores on the street.* See PROSTITUTE noun.
► verb **1** *she spent her life whoring* WORK AS A PROSTITUTE, sell one's body, sell oneself, be on the streets. **2** *the men whored and drank* USE PROSTITUTES; *archaic* wench.

whorehouse ► noun. See BROTHEL.

whorl ► noun LOOP, coil, hoop, ring, curl, twirl, twist, spiral, helix, arabesque.

why ► adverb HOW COME, for what reason/purpose, what for, to what end; *archaic* wherefore.

wicked ► adjective **1** *wicked deeds* EVIL, sinful, immoral, (morally) wrong, wrongful, bad, iniquitous, corrupt, base, mean, vile; villainous, nefarious, erring, foul, monstrous, shocking, outrageous, atrocious, abominable, depraved, reprehensible, hateful, detestable, despicable, odious, contemptible, horrible, heinous, egregious, execrable, fiendish, vicious, murderous, black-hearted, barbarous; criminal, illicit, unlawful, illegal, lawless, felonious, dishonest, unscrupulous; *Law* malfeasant; *informal* crooked; *dated* dastardly. **2** *the wind was wicked* NASTY, harsh, formidable, unpleasant, foul, bad, disagreeable, irksome, troublesome, displeasing, uncomfortable, annoying, irritating, hateful, detestable. **3** *a wicked sense of humour* MISCHIEVOUS, playful, naughty, impish, roguish, arch, puckish, cheeky. **4** (*informal*) *Sophie makes wicked cakes.* See EXCELLENT.
— OPPOSITES: virtuous.

wickedness ► noun EVIL, sin, evildoing, sinfulness, iniquity, vileness, baseness, badness, wrongdoing, dishonesty, unscrupulousness, roguery, villainy, viciousness, degeneracy, depravity, immorality, vice, corruption, corruptness, devilry, fiendishness; *Law* malfeasance; *informal* crookedness; *formal* turpitude.

wide ► adjective **1** *a wide river* BROAD, extensive, spacious, vast, spread out. **2** *their eyes were wide with shock* FULLY OPEN, dilated, gaping, staring, wide open. **3** *a wide range of opinion* COMPREHENSIVE, broad, extensive, diverse, full, ample, large, large-scale, wide-ranging, exhaustive, general, all-inclusive. **4** *her shot was wide* OFF TARGET, off the mark, inaccurate.
— OPPOSITES: narrow.
► adverb **1** *he opened his eyes wide* FULLY, to the fullest/furthest extent, as far/much as possible. **2** *he shot wide* OFF TARGET, inaccurately.
■ **wide open 1** *their mouths were wide open* AGAPE, yawning, open wide, fully open. **2** *the championship is wide open* UNDECIDED, uncertain, unsure, in the balance, up in the air; *informal* anyone's guess. **3** *they were wide open to attacks* VULNERABLE, exposed, unprotected, defenceless, undefended, at risk, in danger.

wide-eyed ► adjective **1** *the onlookers were wide-eyed as the spaceship descended* SURPRISED, flabbergasted, amazed, astonished, astounded, stunned, staggered, goggle-eyed, pop-eyed, open-mouthed, dumbstruck; enthralled, fascinated, gripped. **2** *a wide-eyed youth in a wicked world* INNOCENT, naive, impressionable, ingenuous, childlike, credulous, trusting, unquestioning, unsophisticated, gullible.

widen ► verb **1** *a proposal to widen the highway* BROADEN, make/become wider, open up/out, expand, extend, enlarge. **2** *the society must widen its support* INCREASE, augment, boost, swell, enlarge.

widespread ► adjective GENERAL, extensive, universal, common, global, worldwide, international, omnipresent, ubiquitous, across the board, blanket, sweeping, wholesale; predominant, prevalent, rife, broad, rampant, pervasive.
— OPPOSITES: limited.

width ► noun **1** *the width of the river* BREADTH, broadness, wideness, thickness, span, diameter, girth. **2** *the width of experience required* RANGE, breadth, compass, scope, span, spectrum, scale, extent, extensiveness, comprehensiveness.
— OPPOSITES: length, narrowness.

wield ► verb **1** *he was wielding a sword* BRANDISH, flourish, wave, swing; use, employ, handle. **2** *he has wielded power since 1972* EXERCISE, exert, hold, maintain, command, control.

wiener ► noun See table at SAUSAGE.

wife ► noun SPOUSE, (life) partner, mate, consort, woman, helpmate, helpmeet, bride; *informal* old lady, wifey, better half, other half, missus, ball and chain, significant other.
— RELATED TERMS: uxorial.

wiggle ► verb JIGGLE, wriggle, twitch, shimmy, joggle, wag, wobble, shake, twist, squirm, writhe; *informal* waggle, bump and grind.

wild ► adjective **1** *wild animals* UNTAMED, undomesticated, feral; fierce, ferocious, savage, untameable. **2** *wild flowers* UNCULTIVATED, native, indigenous. **3** *wild tribes* PRIMITIVE, uncivilized, uncultured; savage, barbarous, barbaric. **4** *wild country* UNINHABITED, unpopulated, uncultivated; rugged, rough, inhospitable, desolate, barren. **5** *wild weather* STORMY, squally, tempestuous, turbulent. **6** *her wild black hair* DISHEVELLED, tousled, tangled, windswept, untidy, unkempt, mussed up. **7** *wild behaviour* UNCONTROLLED, unrestrained, out of control, undisciplined, unruly, rowdy, disorderly, riotous, corybantic. **8** *wild with excitement* VERY EXCITED, delirious, in a frenzy; tumultuous, passionate, vehement, unrestrained. **9** (*informal*) *I was wild with jealousy* DISTRAUGHT, frantic, beside oneself, in a frenzy, hysterical, deranged, berserk; *informal* mad, crazy. **10** (*informal*) *Hank went wild when he found out.* See FURIOUS sense 1. **11** (*informal*) *his family wasn't wild about me* ENAMOURED, very enthusiastic, very keen,

infatuated, smitten; *informal* crazy, blown away, mad, nuts. **12** *Bill's wild schemes* MADCAP, ridiculous, ludicrous, foolish, rash, stupid, foolhardy, idiotic, absurd, silly, ill-considered, senseless, nonsensical; impractical, impracticable, unworkable; *informal* crazy, crackpot, cockeyed, hare-brained, cockamamie, loopy. **13** *a wild guess* RANDOM, arbitrary, haphazard, uninformed.
— OPPOSITES: tame, cultivated, calm, disciplined.
■ **run wild 1** *the garden had run wild* GROW UNCHECKED, grow profusely, run riot. **2** *the children are running wild* RUN AMOK, run riot, get out of control, be undisciplined.

wilderness ► noun **1** *the Siberian wilderness* WILDS, wastes, bush, bush country, bushland, inhospitable region; desert, backcountry, boondocks, boonies, outback, moose pasture ♣; the great outdoors, the Barrens ♣, the Barren Lands ♣. **2** *an urban wilderness* WASTELAND, no man's land.
► adjective *wilderness activities* OUTDOOR RECREATION, ecotourism, adventure, backcountry.

wildlife ► noun (WILD) ANIMALS, fauna.

wilds ► plural noun *See* WILDERNESS.

wiles ► plural noun TRICKS, ruses, ploys, schemes, dodges, manoeuvres, subterfuges, shenanigans, artifices; guile, artfulness, cunning, craftiness.

wilful ► adjective **1** *wilful destruction* DELIBERATE, intentional, done on purpose, premeditated, planned, conscious. **2** *a wilful child* HEADSTRONG, strong-willed, obstinate, stubborn, pigheaded, recalcitrant, uncooperative, obstreperous, ungovernable, unmanageable; balky; *formal* refractory, contumacious.
— OPPOSITES: accidental, amenable.

will¹ ► verb *accidents will happen* TEND TO, have a tendency to, are bound to, do, are going to, must.

will² ► noun **1** *the will to succeed* DETERMINATION, willpower, strength of character, resolution, resolve, resoluteness, single-mindedness, purposefulness, drive, commitment, dedication, doggedness, tenacity, tenaciousness, staying power. **2** *they stayed against their will* DESIRE, wish, preference, inclination, intention, intent, volition. **3** *God's will* WISH, desire, decision, choice; decree, command. **4** *the dead man's will* (LAST WILL AND) TESTAMENT, bequest.
► verb **1** *do what you will* WANT, wish, please, see/think fit, think best, like, choose, prefer. **2** *God willed it* DECREE, order, ordain, command. **3** *she willed the money to her husband* BEQUEATH, leave, hand down, pass on, settle on; *Law* devise.
■ **at will** AS ONE PLEASES, as one thinks fit, to suit oneself, at whim.

willing ► adjective **1** *I'm willing to give it a try* READY, prepared, disposed, inclined, of a mind, minded; happy, glad, pleased, agreeable, amenable; *informal* game. **2** *willing help* READILY GIVEN, willingly given, ungrudging, volunteered.
— OPPOSITES: reluctant.

willingly ► adverb VOLUNTARILY, of one's own free will, of one's own accord; readily, without reluctance, ungrudgingly, cheerfully, happily, gladly, with pleasure.

willingness ► noun READINESS, inclination, will, wish, desire, alacrity.

willowy ► adjective TALL, SLIM, slender, svelte, lissome, sylphlike, long-limbed, graceful, lithe; *informal* slinky.

willpower ► noun. *See* WILL² *noun* sense 1.

willy-nilly ► adverb **1** *cars were parked willy-nilly* HAPHAZARDLY, at random, randomly. **2** *we are, willy-nilly, in a new situation* WHETHER ONE LIKES IT OR NOT, of necessity; *informal* like it or lump it; *formal* perforce, nolens volens.

wilt ► verb **1** *the roses had begun to wilt* DROOP, sag, become limp, flop; wither, shrivel (up). **2** *we wilted in the heat* LANGUISH, flag, droop, become listless, tire, wane.
— OPPOSITES: flourish.

wily ► adjective SHREWD, clever, sharp, sharp-witted, astute, canny, smart; crafty, cunning, artful, sly, scheming, calculating, devious; *informal* tricky, foxy; *archaic* subtle.
— OPPOSITES: naive.

wimp ► noun (*informal*) COWARD, namby-pamby, pantywaist, milksop, weakling; drip, sissy, weed, wuss, milquetoast, pansy, candy-ass, scaredy-cat, chicken, twinkie, cupcake, sook, (*Atlantic*) sooky baby ♣; *archaic* poltroon.

win ► verb **1** *he won the race* TAKE, be the victor in, be the winner of, come first in, take first prize in, triumph in, be successful in. **2** *Claire knew he would win* COME FIRST, be the winner, be victorious, carry/win the day, come out on top, succeed, triumph, prevail. **3** *he won a cash prize* SECURE, gain, garner, collect, pick up, walk away/off with, carry off; *informal* land, net, bag, scoop. **4** *she won his heart* CAPTIVATE, steal, snare, capture.
► noun *a 1–0 win* VICTORY, triumph, conquest.
— OPPOSITES: defeat.
■ **win someone round/over** PERSUADE, talk round, convince, sway, prevail on; seduce.

wince ► verb *he winced at the pain* GRIMACE, pull a face, flinch, blench, start.
► noun *a wince of pain* GRIMACE, flinch, start.

wind¹ ► noun **1** *the trees were swaying in the wind* BREEZE, current of air; gale, hurricane; *informal* blow; *literary* zephyr. *See table.* **2** *Jez got his wind back* BREATH; *informal* puff. **3** FLATULENCE, gas; *formal* flatus.
— RELATED TERMS: aeolian.
■ **get wind of** (*informal*) HEAR ABOUT/OF, learn of, find out about, pick up on, be told about, be informed of; *informal* hear something on the grapevine, hear something on the moccasin telegraph ♣.
■ **in the wind** ON THE WAY, coming, about to happen, in the offing, in the air, on the horizon, approaching, looming, brewing, afoot; *informal* in the cards.

Beaufort Wind Scale

Force	Description	Wind Speed in knots
0	Calm	<1
1	Light air	1-3
2	Light breeze	4-6
3	Gentle breeze	7-10
4	Moderate breeze	11-16
5	Fresh breeze	17-21
6	Strong breeze	22-27
7	Near gale	28-33
8	Gale	34-40
9	Strong gale	41-47
10	Storm	48-55
11	Violent storm	56-63
12	Hurricane	≥64

wind² ► verb **1** *this road winds dangerously* TWIST (AND

TURN), bend, curve, loop, zigzag, weave, snake. **2** *she wound a towel around her waist* WRAP, furl, entwine, lace, loop. **3** *he wound the wool into a ball* COIL, roll, twist, twine.

■ **wind down 1** (*informal*) *they needed to wind down* RELAX, unwind, calm down, cool down/off, ease up/off, take it easy, rest, put one's feet up, take a load off, hang loose, chill (out). **2** *the summer was winding down* DRAW TO A CLOSE, come to an end, tail off, taper off, slack(en) off, slow down, die.

■ **wind something down** BRING TO A CLOSE/END, wind up, close down, phase out.

■ **wind up** (*informal*) END UP, finish up, find oneself, fetch up.

■ **wind someone up** ANNOY, anger, irritate, irk, exasperate, get on someone's nerves, provoke, goad; *informal* aggravate, rile, niggle, rankle, bug, get someone's back up, give someone the gears ♣, ride.

■ **wind something up** CONCLUDE, bring to an end/close, end, terminate; *informal* wrap up.

winded ► adjective OUT OF BREATH, breathless, gasping for breath, panting, puffing, puffed out, hyperventilating.

windfall ► noun BONANZA, jackpot, pennies from heaven, piece of luck.

winding ► noun *the windings of the stream* TWIST, turn, turning, bend, loop, curve, zigzag, meander.
► adjective *the winding country roads* TWISTING AND TURNING, meandering, windy, twisty, bending, curving, zigzag, zigzagging, serpentine, sinuous, snaking, tortuous; *rare* flexuous.
— OPPOSITES: straight.

window ► noun casement, opening, aperture. *See table.*
— RELATED TERMS: fenestral.

Windows

bay window	low-E
bow window	Palladian window
bull's eye	picture window
casement	porthole
Catherine wheel	rose window
dormer	sash window
double-hung	sidelight
double-paned	stained glass window
fanlight	store window
French window	storm window
judas	transom window
lattice window	Venetian window
leaded window	

windpipe ► noun TRACHEA, pharynx; throat.

windsurfing ► noun SAILBOARDING, boardsailing.

windswept ► adjective **1** *the windswept prairies* EXPOSED, bleak, bare, desolate. **2** *his windswept hair* DISHEVELLED, tousled, unkempt, wind-blown, untidy, mussed up.

windy ► adjective **1** *a windy day* BREEZY, blowy, fresh, blustery, gusty; wild, stormy, squally, tempestuous, boisterous. **2** *a windy hillside* WINDSWEPT, exposed, open to the elements, bare, bleak.
— OPPOSITES: still, sheltered.

wine ► noun *informal* plonk, vino, the grape; *literary* vintage. *See table.*
— RELATED TERMS: vinous, oeno-.

Wines

White Wine	Red Wine
Asti (Spumante)	Amarone
Auslese	Barolo
Barsac	Beaujolais
blanc de blancs	Beaune
(white) Bordeaux	(red) Bordeaux
catawba	Burgundy
Chablis	Cabernet Franc
champagne	Cabernet Sauvignon
Chardonnay	Chianti
Chenin Blanc	claret
Entre-Deux-Mers	Côtes du Rhône
frascati	Gamay
Gewürztraminer	Malbec
Liebfraumilch	Merlot
Meursault	mourvèdre
Montrachet	Nebbiolo
moselle	Pinot Noir
Muscadet	(red) Rioja
Orvieto	Saint-Émilion
Pedro Ximenez	sangiovese
Pinot Blanc	Syrah
Pinot Grigio	Tempranillo
Prosecco	
Riesling	**Fortified Wine and**
(white) Rioja	**Dessert Wine**
Sancerre	Cinzano*
Sauvignon (Blanc)	Dubonnet*
sekt	Grenache
Sémillon	icewine ♣
Soave	Madeira
Spätlese	Malaga
Tocai Friulano	malmsey
Trebbiano	Marsala
	muscat
Pink Wine	port
blush	Sauternes
rosé	sherry
white Zinfandel	Tokay
	vermouth
	*Proprietary term.

wing ► noun **1** *a bird's wings* *literary* pinion. **2** *the east wing of the house* PART, section, side; annex, extension, ell. **3** *the radical wing of the party* FACTION, camp, arm, branch, group, section, set, coterie, cabal; side, end.
► verb **1** *a seagull winged its way over the sea* FLY, glide, soar. **2** *the bomb winged past* HURTLE, speed, shoot, whiz, zoom, streak, fly. **3** *the hunter only winged the hawk* WOUND, graze, hit.

■ **wing it** (*informal*) IMPROVISE, play it by ear, extemporize, ad lib, fly by the seat of one's pants, fake it.

wink ► verb **1** *he winked an eye at her* BLINK, flutter, bat. **2** *the diamond winked in the moonlight* SPARKLE, twinkle, flash, glitter, gleam, shine, scintillate.

■ **wink at** TURN A BLIND EYE TO, close one's eyes to, ignore, overlook, disregard; connive at, condone, tolerate.

winkle
■ **winkle something out** WORM OUT, prise out, dig out, extract, draw out, obtain, get.

winner ► noun VICTOR, champion, conqueror, vanquisher, hero; medallist; *informal* champ, top dog, world-beater.
— OPPOSITES: loser.

winning ► adjective **1** *the winning team* VICTORIOUS, successful, triumphant, vanquishing, conquering; first, first-place, top, leading. **2** *a winning smile* ENGAGING, charming, appealing, endearing, sweet, cute, winsome, attractive, pretty, prepossessing, fetching, lovely, lovable, adorable, delightful, disarming, captivating, bewitching.

winnings ▶ plural noun PRIZE MONEY, gains, prize, booty, spoils, loot; proceeds, profits, earnings, takings, purse.

winnow ▶ verb SEPARATE (OUT), divide, segregate, sort out, sift out, filter out; isolate, find, identify, narrow down; remove, get rid of.

winsome ▶ adjective. *See* WINNING sense 2.

winter ▶ noun.
— RELATED TERMS: hibernal.

Winter Sports

alpine skiing	hockey
barrel jumping ♣	luge
biathlon	moguls
bobsleigh	nordic combined
cross-country skiing	skating
curling	skeleton
dog racing	ski jumping
downhill skiing	slalom
figure skating	snowboarding
freestyle skiing	speed skating
giant slalom	super-G

wintry ▶ adjective **1** *wintry weather* BLEAK, cold, chilly, chill, frosty, freezing, icy, snowy, blizzardy, arctic, glacial, bitter, raw, hypothermic; *informal* nippy. **2** *a wintry smile* UNFRIENDLY, unwelcoming, cool, cold, frosty, frigid, dismal, cheerless.
— OPPOSITES: summery, warm.

wipe ▶ verb **1** *Beth wiped the table* RUB, mop, sponge, swab; clean, dry, polish, towel. **2** *he wiped the marks off the window* RUB OFF, clean off, clear up, remove, get rid of, take off, erase, efface. **3** *she wiped the memory from her mind* OBLITERATE, expunge, erase, blot out. **4** *I wiped the file accidentally* ERASE, delete, trash, zap, kill, nuke.
▶ noun *he gave the table a wipe* RUB, mop, sponge, swab; clean, polish.
■ **wipe someone/something out** DESTROY, annihilate, eradicate, eliminate; slaughter, massacre, kill, exterminate; demolish, raze to the ground; *informal* take out, zap, waste; *literary* slay.

wire ▶ noun CABLE, lead, cord; power line, hydro line ♣, transmission line.

wired ▶ adjective **1** *she's totally wired* HYPER, buzzing, excited high, manic, tense, strung out, antsy. **2** *get your company wired* ONLINE, hooked up, connected, web-enabled.

wiry ▶ adjective **1** *a wiry man* SINEWY, tough, athletic, strong; lean, spare, thin, stringy, skinny. **2** *wiry hair* COARSE, rough, strong; curly, wavy.
— OPPOSITES: flabby, smooth.

wisdom ▶ noun **1** *we questioned the wisdom of the decision* SAGACITY, intelligence, sense, common sense, shrewdness, astuteness, smartness, judiciousness, judgment, prudence, circumspection; logic, rationale, rationality, soundness, advisability. **2** *the wisdom of the East* KNOWLEDGE, learning, erudition, sophistication, scholarship, philosophy; lore.
— OPPOSITES: folly.

wise ▶ adjective **1** *a wise old man* SAGE, sagacious,

intelligent, clever, learned, knowledgeable, enlightened; astute, smart, shrewd, sharp-witted, canny, knowing; sensible, prudent, discerning, discriminating, sophisticated, judicious, perceptive, insightful, perspicacious; rational, logical, sound, sane; *formal* sapient. **2** *wise course of action. See* SENSIBLE.
— OPPOSITES: foolish.
■ **wise to** (*informal*) AWARE OF, familiar with, acquainted with; *formal* cognizant of.

wisecrack ▶ noun (*informal*) JOKE, witticism, quip, jest, sally, thrust; pun, bon mot; *informal* crack, gag, funny, one-liner, zinger.

wish ▶ verb **1** *I wished for power* DESIRE, want, hope for, covet, dream of, long for, yearn for, crave, hunger for, lust after; aspire to, set one's heart on, seek, fancy, hanker after; *informal* have a yen for, itch for; *archaic* be desirous of. **2** *they can do as they wish* WANT, desire, feel inclined, feel like, care; choose, please, think fit. **3** *I wish you to send them a message* WANT, desire, require. **4** *I wished him farewell* BID.
▶ noun **1** *his wish to own a Mercedes* DESIRE, longing, yearning, inclination, urge, whim, craving, hunger; hope, aspiration, aim, ambition, dream; *informal* hankering, yen, itch. **2** *her parents' wishes* REQUEST, requirement, bidding, instruction, direction, demand, entreaty, order, command; want, desire; will; *literary* behest.

wishy-washy ▶ adjective **1** *he's so wishy-washy* FEEBLE, ineffectual, weak, vapid, effete, gutless, spineless, limp, namby-pamby, spiritless, indecisive, characterless; pathetic. **2** *wishy-washy soup* WATERY, weak, thin; tasteless, flavourless, insipid. **3** *a wishy-washy colour* PALE, insipid, pallid, muted, pastel.
— OPPOSITES: strong, tasty, vibrant.

wisp ▶ noun STRAND, tendril, lock; scrap, shred, thread.

wispy ▶ adjective THIN, fine, feathery, fly-away.

wistful ▶ adjective NOSTALGIC, yearning, longing; plaintive, regretful, rueful, melancholy, mournful, elegiac; pensive, reflective, contemplative.

wit ▶ noun **1** *he needed all his wits to escape* INTELLIGENCE, shrewdness, astuteness, cleverness, canniness, (common) sense, wisdom, sagacity, judgment, acumen, insight; brains, mind; *informal* gumption, savvy, horse sense, (street) smarts. **2** *my sparkling wit* WITTINESS, humour, funniness, drollery, esprit; repartee, badinage, banter, wordplay; jokes, witticisms, quips, puns. **3** *she's such a wit* COMEDIAN, humorist, comic, joker, jokester; *informal* wag, funnyman; *informal, dated* card.

witch ▶ noun **1** *the witch cast a spell* SORCERESS, enchantress, hex; *archaic* pythoness. **2** (*informal*) *she's a nasty old witch* HAG, crone, harpy, harridan, she-devil; *informal* battleaxe.

witchcraft ▶ noun SORCERY, (black) magic, witching, witchery, wizardry, thaumaturgy, spells, incantations; Wicca.

with ▶ preposition ACCOMPANIED BY, escorted by; alongside, in addition to, as well as.

withdraw ▶ verb **1** *she withdrew her hand from his* REMOVE, extract, pull out, take out; take back, take away. **2** *the ban on advertising was withdrawn* ABOLISH, cancel, lift, set aside, end, stop, remove, reverse, revoke, rescind, repeal, annul, void. **3** *she withdrew the allegation* RETRACT, take back, go back on, recant, disavow, disclaim, repudiate, renounce, abjure; back down, climb down, backtrack, backpedal, do a U-turn, eat one's words. **4** *the troops withdrew from the*

city LEAVE, pull out of, evacuate, quit, (beat a) retreat from. **5** *his partner withdrew from the project* PULL OUT OF, back out of, bow out of; get cold feet. **6** *they withdrew to their rooms* RETIRE, retreat, adjourn, decamp; leave, depart, absent oneself; *formal* repair; *dated* remove; *literary* betake oneself.
— OPPOSITES: insert, introduce, deposit, enter.

withdrawal ► noun **1** *the withdrawal of subsidies* REMOVAL, abolition, cancellation, discontinuation, termination, elimination. **2** *the withdrawal of the troops* DEPARTURE, pull-out, exit, exodus, evacuation, retreat. **3** *she's suffering the effects of withdrawal* DETOXIFICATION, detox, cold turkey.

withdrawn ► adjective INTROVERTED, unsociable, inhibited, uncommunicative, unforthcoming, quiet, taciturn, reticent, reserved, retiring, private, reclusive; shy, timid; aloof, indrawn; *informal* standoffish.
— OPPOSITES: outgoing.

wither ► verb **1** *the flowers withered in the sun* SHRIVEL (UP), dry up; wilt, droop, go limp, fade, perish; shrink, waste away, atrophy. **2** *her confidence withered* DIMINISH, dwindle, shrink, lessen, fade, ebb, wane; evaporate, disappear.
— OPPOSITES: thrive, grow.

withering ► adjective SCORNFUL, contemptuous, scathing, stinging, devastating; humiliating, mortifying.
— OPPOSITES: admiring.

withhold ► verb **1** *he withheld the information* HOLD BACK, keep back, refuse to give; retain, hold on to; hide, conceal, keep secret; *informal* sit on. **2** *she could not withhold her tears* SUPPRESS, repress, hold back, fight back, choke back, control, check, restrain, contain.

within ► preposition **1** *within the prison walls* INSIDE, in, enclosed by, surrounded by; within the bounds of, within the confines of. **2** *within a few hours* IN LESS THAN, in under, in no more than, after only.
— OPPOSITES: outside.

without ► preposition **1** *thousands were without food* LACKING, short of, deprived of, in need of, wanting, needing, requiring. **2** *I don't want to go without you* UNACCOMPANIED BY, unescorted by; in the absence of; *informal* sans, minus.

withstand ► verb RESIST, weather, survive, endure, cope with, stand, tolerate, bear, stomach, defy, brave, hold out against, tough out, bear up against; stand up to, face, confront.

witless ► adjective FOOLISH, stupid, unintelligent, idiotic, brainless, mindless; fatuous, inane, half-baked, empty-headed, slow-witted; *informal* thick, birdbrained, pea-brained, dopey, doltish, dim-witted, halfwitted, dippy, spinny ♣, dumb-ass, lamebrained, wooden-headed, daft.

witness ► noun **1** *witnesses claimed that he started the fight* OBSERVER, onlooker, eyewitness, spectator, viewer, watcher; bystander, passerby. **2** *she cross-examined the witness* DEPONENT.
► verb **1** *who witnessed the incident?* SEE, observe, watch, view, notice, spot; be present at, attend; *literary* behold; *informal* get a look at. **2** *Canada witnessed a cultural explosion* UNDERGO, experience, go through, see; enjoy; suffer. **3** *the will is correctly witnessed* COUNTERSIGN, sign, endorse, validate; notarize.
■ **bear witness to** ATTEST TO, testify to, confirm, evidence, prove, verify, corroborate, substantiate; show, demonstrate, indicate, reveal, bespeak.

witticism ► noun JOKE, quip, jest, pun, play on words, bon mot; *informal* one-liner, gag, funny, crack, wisecrack, zinger.

witty ► adjective HUMOROUS, amusing, droll, funny, comic, comical; jocular, facetious, waggish, tongue-in-cheek; sparkling, scintillating, entertaining; clever, quick-witted.

wizard ► noun **1** *the wizard cast a spell over them* SORCERER, warlock, magus, (black) magician, enchanter; *archaic* mage. **2** *a financial wizard* GENIUS, expert, master, virtuoso, maestro, marvel, Wunderkind, guru; *informal* hotshot, demon, whiz kid, buff, pro, ace; maven.

wizardry ► noun SORCERY, witchcraft, witchery, witching, (black) magic, enchantment; spells, charms.

wizened ► adjective WRINKLED, lined, creased, shrivelled (up), withered, weather-beaten, shrunken, gnarled, aged.

wobble ► verb **1** *the table wobbled* ROCK, teeter, jiggle, sway, see-saw, shake. **2** *he wobbled across to the door* TEETER, totter, stagger, lurch. **3** *her voice wobbled* TREMBLE, shake, quiver, quaver, waver. **4** *for a few days the minister wobbled* HESITATE, vacillate, waver, dither, fluctuate, shilly-shally, blow hot and cold.
► noun **1** *she stood up with a wobble* TOTTER, teeter, sway. **2** *the operatic wobble in her voice* TREMOR, quiver, quaver, trembling, vibrato.

wobbly ► adjective **1** *a wobbly table* UNSTEADY, unstable, shaky, rocky, rickety; unsafe, precarious; uneven, unbalanced; *informal* wonky. **2** *her legs were a bit wobbly* SHAKY, quivery, weak, unsteady; *informal* trembly, like jelly.
— OPPOSITES: stable.

woe ► noun **1** *a tale of woe* MISERY, sorrow, distress, wretchedness, sadness, unhappiness, heartache, heartbreak, despondency, despair, depression, regret, gloom, melancholy; adversity, misfortune, disaster, suffering, hardship; *literary* dolour. **2** *financial woes* TROUBLE, difficulty, problem, trial, tribulation, misfortune, setback, reverse.
— OPPOSITES: joy.

woebegone ► adjective SAD, unhappy, miserable, dejected, disconsolate, forlorn, crestfallen, downcast, glum, gloomy, doleful, downhearted, heavy-hearted, despondent, melancholy, sorrowful, mournful, woeful, plaintive, depressed, wretched, desolate; *informal* down in the mouth, down in the dumps, blue.
— OPPOSITES: cheerful.

woeful ► adjective **1** *her face was woeful. See* WOEBEGONE. **2** *a woeful tale* TRAGIC, sad, miserable, cheerless, gloomy, sorry, pitiful, pathetic, traumatic, depressing, heartbreaking, heart-rending, tear-jerking, gut-wrenching. **3** *the team's woeful performance* LAMENTABLE, awful, terrible, atrocious, disgraceful, deplorable, shameful, hopeless, dreadful; substandard, poor, inadequate, inferior, unsatisfactory; *informal* rotten, appalling, crummy, pathetic, pitiful, lousy, abysmal, dire, crappy, lame, brutal.
— OPPOSITES: cheerful, excellent.

wolf ► noun. *See table.*
► verb DEVOUR, gobble (up), guzzle, gulp down, bolt; *informal* put away, demolish, shovel down, scoff (down), scarf (down/up), snarf (down/up), gorp.

Wild Dogs

Arctic fox	jackal
Arctic wolf	prairie wolf
brush wolf	red fox
coyote	silver fox
cross fox	swift fox
dingo	timber wolf
fox	tundra wolf
grey wolf	wolf

wolfish ▸ **adjective** (*informal*) LASCIVIOUS, lecherous, lustful; predatory, rapacious.

woman ▸ **noun 1** *a woman got out of the car* LADY, girl, female; matron; *Scottish* lass, lassie; *informal* chick, girlie, biddy, baba, plain-Jane, sister, dame, broad, gal; grrrl; *literary* maid, maiden, damsel; *archaic* wench, gentlewoman; (**women**) womenfolk. **2** *he found himself a new woman* GIRLFRIEND, sweetheart, partner, significant other, inamorata, lover, mistress; fiancée; wife, spouse; *informal* missus, better half, main squeeze, squeeze, babe, baby; *dated* lady friend, lady love.
— RELATED TERMS: female, gyneco-.

womanhood ▸ **noun** FEMININITY; adulthood, maturity.

womanish ▸ **adjective** EFFEMINATE, girlish, girly, unmanly, unmasculine, epicene.
— OPPOSITES: manly.

womanizer ▸ **noun** PHILANDERER, Casanova, Don Juan, Romeo, Lothario, ladies' man, playboy, seducer, rake, roué, libertine, lecher; *informal* skirt chaser, lady-killer, lech, wolf.

womankind ▸ **noun** WOMEN; woman, the female sex, womenkind, womanhood, womenfolk; womyn, wimmin.

womanly ▸ **adjective 1** *womanly virtues* FEMININE, female; *archaic* feminal. **2** *her womanly figure* VOLUPTUOUS, curvaceous, shapely, ample, buxom, full-figured, Junoesque, Rubenesque; *informal* curvy, busty.
— OPPOSITES: masculine, boyish.

womb ▸ **noun** UTERUS.

wonder ▸ **noun 1** *she was speechless with wonder* AWE, admiration, wonderment, fascination; surprise, astonishment, stupefaction, amazement. **2** *the wonders of nature* MARVEL, miracle, phenomenon, sensation, spectacle, beauty; curiosity; *informal* humdinger.
▸ **verb 1** *I wondered what was on her mind* PONDER, think about, meditate on, reflect on, muse on, puzzle over, speculate about, conjecture; be curious about. **2** *people wondered at such bravery* MARVEL, be amazed, be astonished, stand in awe, be dumbfounded, gape, goggle; *informal* be flabbergasted.

wonderful ▸ **adjective** MARVELLOUS, magnificent, superb, glorious, sublime, lovely, delightful; *informal* super, great, fantastic, terrific, tremendous, sensational, incredible, fabulous, fab, out of this world, awesome, magic, ace, wicked, far out, killer, brilliant, peachy, dandy, neat, swell.
— OPPOSITES: awful.

wonky ▸ **adjective** (*informal*) **1** *a wonky picture*. See CROOKED sense 3. **2** *wonky stools*. See WOBBLY sense 1.

wont ▸ **adjective** *he was wont to arise at 5:30* ACCUSTOMED, used, given, inclined.
▸ **noun** *Paul drove fast, as was his wont* CUSTOM, habit, way, practice, convention, rule.

wonted ▸ **adjective** CUSTOMARY, habitual, usual, accustomed, familiar, normal, conventional, routine, common.

woo ▸ **verb 1** *Richard wooed Joan* PAY COURT TO, pursue, chase (after); *dated* court, romance, seek the hand of, set one's cap at, make love to. **2** *the party wooed voters with promises* SEEK, pursue, curry favour with, try to win, try to attract, try to cultivate. **3** *an attempt to woo him out of retirement* ENTICE, tempt, coax, persuade, wheedle; *informal* sweet-talk.

wood ▸ **noun 1** *polished wood* TIMBER, lumber, planks, planking; logs, sawlogs. **2** *a walk through the woods* FOREST, woodland, trees; copse, coppice, grove, bush, woodlot, (*Prairies*) bluff ✦, (*Atlantic*) droke ✦.
— RELATED TERMS: ligneous.

wood-burning ▸ **adjective** WOOD-FIRED.

wooded ▸ **adjective** FORESTED, treed, tree-covered, woody; *literary* sylvan, bosky.

wooden ▸ **adjective 1** *a wooden door* WOOD, timber, woody; ligneous. **2** *wooden acting* STILTED, stiff, unnatural, awkward, leaden; dry, flat, stodgy, lifeless, passionless, spiritless, soulless. **3** *her face was wooden* EXPRESSIONLESS, impassive, poker-faced, emotionless, blank, vacant, unresponsive.

woodland ▸ **noun** WOODS, wood, forest, trees; *archaic* greenwood.

woodlot ▸ **noun** bush ✦, bushlot ✦, copse, wood.

woodwork ▸ **noun** CARPENTRY, joinery.

woof ▸ **noun & verb** See BARK[1] sense 1.

wool ▸ **noun 1** *sheep's wool* FLEECE, hair, coat; floccus. **2** *a sweater made of cream wool* YARN.
■ **pull the wool over someone's eyes** (*informal*) DECEIVE, fool, trick, hoodwink, dupe, deke, delude; *informal* lead up the garden path, put one over on, bamboozle, con.

woolgathering ▸ **noun** DAYDREAMING, reverie, dreaming, musing, abstraction, preoccupation; absent-mindedness, forgetfulness.

woolly ▸ **adjective 1** *a woolly hat* WOOLLEN, wool, fleecy. **2** *a sheep's woolly coat* FLEECY, shaggy, hairy, fluffy, flocculent. **3** *woolly generalizations* VAGUE, ill-defined, hazy, unclear, fuzzy, blurry, foggy, nebulous, imprecise, inexact, indefinite; confused, muddled.

woozy ▸ **adjective** (*informal*). See GROGGY.

word ▸ **noun 1** *the Italian word for 'ham'* TERM, name, expression, designation, locution, vocable; *formal* appellation. **2** *his words were meant kindly* REMARK, comment, observation, statement, utterance, pronouncement. **3** *I've got three weeks to learn the words* SCRIPT, lyrics, libretto. **4** *I give you my word* PROMISE, word of honour, assurance, guarantee, undertaking; pledge, vow, oath, bond; *formal* troth. **5** *I want a word with you* TALK, conversation, chat, tête-à-tête, heart-to-heart, one-to-one, man-to-man; discussion, consultation; *informal* confab, powwow; *formal* confabulation. **6** *there's no word from the hospital* NEWS, information, communication, intelligence; message, report, communiqué, dispatch, bulletin; *informal* info, dope; *literary* tidings. **7** *word has it he's turned over a new leaf* RUMOUR, hearsay, talk, gossip; *informal* the grapevine, the word on the street, (*esp. North*) the moccasin telegraph ✦. **8** *I'm waiting for the word from HQ* INSTRUCTION, order, command; signal, prompt, cue, tip-off; *informal* go-ahead, thumbs up, green light. **9** *Heather's word was law* COMMAND, order, decree, edict; bidding, will. **10** *our word now must be success*

MOTTO, watchword, slogan, catchword, buzz word.
− RELATED TERMS: verbal, lexical.
▶ **verb** *the question was carefully worded* PHRASE, express, put, couch, frame, formulate, style; say, utter.
■ **have words** QUARREL, argue, disagree, squabble, bicker, fight, wrangle, dispute, fall out, clash, row.
■ **in a word** BRIEFLY, to be brief, in short, in a nutshell, to come to the point, to cut a long story short, not to put too fine a point on it; to sum up, to summarize, in summary.
■ **word for word 1** *they took down the speeches word for word* VERBATIM, letter for letter, to the letter; exactly, faithfully. **2** *a word-for-word translation* VERBATIM, literal, exact, direct, accurate, faithful; unadulterated, unabridged.

wording ▶ **noun** PHRASING, words, phraseology, language, expression, terminology.

wordplay ▶ **noun** PUNNING, puns, play on words; wit, witticisms, repartee.

wordy ▶ **adjective** LONG-WINDED, verbose, prolix, lengthy, protracted, long-drawn-out, overlong, rambling, circumlocutory, periphrastic, pleonastic; loquacious, garrulous, voluble; *informal* windy.
− OPPOSITES: succinct.

work ▶ **noun 1** *a day's work in the fields* LABOUR, toil, slog, drudgery, exertion, effort, industry, service; *informal* grind, sweat, elbow grease; *literary* travail. **2** *I'm looking for work* EMPLOYMENT, a job, a post, a position, a situation; occupation, profession, career, vocation, calling; wage labour; tasks, jobs, duties, assignments, projects; chores. **3** *works of literature* COMPOSITION, piece, creation; opus, oeuvre. **4** *the complete works of Shakespeare* WRITINGS, oeuvre, canon, output. **5** *this is the work of a radical faction* HANDIWORK, doing, act, deed. **6** *a lifetime spent doing good works* DEEDS, acts, actions. **7** (*informal*) *for only $60 you can get the works* EVERYTHING, the full treatment; *informal* the lot, the whole shebang, the full nine yards, the whole kaboodle.
− OPPOSITES: leisure.
▶ **verb 1** *staff worked late into the night* TOIL, labour, exert oneself, slave (away); keep at it, put one's nose to the grindstone; *informal* slog (away), beaver away, plug away, put one's back into it, knock oneself out, sweat blood; *literary* travail. **2** *he worked in education for years* BE EMPLOYED, have a job, earn one's living, do business. **3** *farmers worked the land* CULTIVATE, farm, till, plow. **4** *his car was working perfectly* FUNCTION, go, run, operate; *informal* behave. **5** *how do I work this machine?* OPERATE, use, handle, control, manipulate, run. **6** *their ploy worked* SUCCEED, work out, turn out well, go as planned, get results, be effective; *informal* come off, pay off, do/turn the trick. **7** *makeup can work miracles* BRING ABOUT, accomplish, achieve, produce, perform, create, engender, contrive, effect. **8** (*informal*) *the chairman was prepared to work it for Jim* ARRANGE, manipulate, contrive; pull strings, pull wires, fix, swing, wangle. **9** *he worked the crowd into a frenzy* STIR (UP), excite, drive, move, rouse, fire, galvanize; whip up, agitate. **10** *work the mixture into a paste* KNEAD, squeeze, form; mix, stir, blend. **11** *he worked the blade into the padlock* MANOEUVRE, manipulate, guide, edge. **12** *her mouth worked furiously* TWITCH, quiver, convulse. **13** *he worked his way through the crowd* MANOEUVRE, make, thread, wind, weave, wend.
− OPPOSITES: rest, fail.
■ **work on someone** PERSUADE, manipulate, influence; coax, cajole, wheedle, soften up, sweet-talk; *informal* twist someone's arm, lean on.
■ **work out 1** *the bill works out at $50* AMOUNT TO, add

up to, come to, total. **2** *my idea worked out. See* WORK *verb* sense 6. **3** *things didn't work out the way she planned* END UP, turn out, go, come out, develop; happen, occur; *informal* pan out. **4** *he works out at the local gym* EXERCISE, train.
■ **work something out 1** *work out what you can afford* CALCULATE, compute, reckon up, determine. **2** *I'm trying to work out what she meant* UNDERSTAND, comprehend, puzzle out, sort out, make sense of, get to the bottom of, make head or tail of, unravel, decipher, decode; *informal* figure out; suss out. **3** *they worked out a plan* DEVISE, formulate, draw up, put together, develop, construct, arrange, organize, contrive, concoct; hammer out, negotiate.
■ **work something up** STIMULATE, rouse, raise, arouse, awaken, excite.

workable ▶ **adjective** PRACTICABLE, feasible, viable, possible, achievable; realistic, reasonable, sensible, practical; *informal* doable.
− OPPOSITES: impracticable.

workaday ▶ **adjective** ORDINARY, average, run-of-the-mill, middle-of-the-road, conventional, unremarkable, unexceptional, humdrum, undistinguished, commonplace, mundane, pedestrian; routine, common or garden, everyday, day-to-day, garden-variety, standard; *informal* nothing to write home about, a dime a dozen.
− OPPOSITES: exceptional.

workbook ▶ **noun** EXERCISE BOOK, school book; notebook, scribbler ♣.

worker ▶ **noun 1** *a strike by 500 workers* EMPLOYEE, member of staff; workman, labourer, hand, operative, operator; proletarian; artisan, craftsman, craftswoman; wage earner, breadwinner. **2** (*informal*) *I got a reputation for being a worker* HARD WORKER, toiler, workhorse; grinder, mucker, digger; busy bee, eager beaver, workaholic, wheelhorse.

workforce ▶ **noun** EMPLOYEES, staff, personnel, workers, labour force, human resources, manpower.

working ▶ **adjective 1** *working mothers* EMPLOYED, in (gainful) employment, in work, waged. **2** *a working water wheel* FUNCTIONING, operating, running, active, operational, functional, serviceable; *informal* up and running. **3** *a working knowledge of contract law* SUFFICIENT, adequate, viable; useful, effective.
− OPPOSITES: unemployed, faulty.
▶ **noun 1** *the working of a carburetor* FUNCTIONING, operation, running, action, performance. **2** *the workings of a watch* MECHANISM, machinery, parts, movement, action, works; *informal* insides.

workman ▶ **noun** (MANUAL) WORKER, labourer, hand, operative, operator; employee, journeyman, artisan.

workmanlike ▶ **adjective** EFFICIENT, competent, professional, proficient, skilful, adept, masterly.

workmanship ▶ **noun** CRAFTSMANSHIP, artistry, craft, art, artisanship, handiwork; skill, expertise, technique.

workout ▶ **noun** EXERCISE SESSION/CLASS, training session, drill; warm-up; exercises, aerobics; *informal, dated* daily dozen.

workshop ▶ **noun 1** *the craftsmen had a chilly workshop* WORKROOM, studio, atelier; factory, plant. **2** *a workshop on combating stress* STUDY GROUP, discussion group, seminar, class.

world ▶ **noun 1** *he travelled the world* EARTH, globe, planet, sphere. **2** *life on other worlds* PLANET, moon, star, heavenly body, orb. **3** *the academic world* SPHERE, society, circle, arena, milieu, province, domain, orbit, preserve, realm, field, discipline, area, sector. **4** *she would show the world that she was strong* EVERYONE, everybody, people, mankind, humankind, humanity, the (general) public, the population, the populace, all and sundry, {every Tom, Dick, and Harry}, every man jack. **5** *a world of difference* HUGE AMOUNT, good deal, great deal, abundance, wealth, profusion, mountain; plenty; *informal* heap, lot, load, ton, masses. **6** *she renounced the world* SOCIETY, secular interests, temporal concerns, earthly concerns.

■ **on top of the world** (*informal*). See OVERJOYED.

■ **out of this world** (*informal*). See WONDERFUL.

worldly ▶ adjective **1** *his youth was wasted on worldly pursuits* EARTHLY, terrestrial, temporal, mundane; mortal, human, material, materialistic, physical, carnal, fleshly, bodily, corporeal, sensual. **2** *a worldly woman* SOPHISTICATED, experienced, worldly-wise, knowledgeable, knowing, enlightened, shrewd, mature, seasoned, cosmopolitan, streetwise, street-smart, urbane, cultivated, cultured.
— OPPOSITES: spiritual, naive.

worldly-wise ▶ adjective. See WORLDLY sense 2.

worldwide ▶ adjective GLOBAL, international, intercontinental, universal; ubiquitous, extensive, widespread, far-reaching, wide-ranging, all-embracing.
— OPPOSITES: local.

worn ▶ adjective **1** *his hat was worn* SHABBY, worn out, threadbare, tattered, in tatters, holey, falling to pieces, ragged, frayed, well-used, well-thumbed, moth-eaten, scruffy, having seen better days; *informal* tatty, ratty, the worse for wear, raggedy, dog-eared. **2** *her face looked worn.* See WORN OUT sense 2.
— OPPOSITES: smart, fresh.

worn out ▶ adjective **1** *a worn-out shirt.* See WORN sense 1. **2** *by evening they looked worn out* EXHAUSTED, fatigued, tired (out), weary, drained, worn, drawn, wan, sapped, spent, burned out; careworn, haggard, hollow-eyed, pale, peaky; *informal* all in, done in, dog-tired, dead beat, fit to drop, pooped, bagged, tuckered out. **3** *worn-out ideas* OBSOLETE, antiquated, stale, hackneyed, trite, tired, old, hoary, overused, overworked, clichéd, unoriginal, commonplace, pedestrian, prosaic, stock, conventional; old hat.
— OPPOSITES: smart, fresh.

worried ▶ adjective ANXIOUS, perturbed, troubled, bothered, concerned, upset, distressed, distraught, disquieted, uneasy, fretful, agitated, nervous, edgy, on edge, tense, overwrought, worked up, keyed up, jumpy, stressed, strung out; apprehensive, fearful, afraid, frightened, scared, uptight, a bundle of nerves, on tenterhooks, jittery, twitchy, in a stew, in a flap, in a sweat, het up, rattled, antsy, squirrelly.
— OPPOSITES: carefree.

worrisome ▶ adjective. See WORRYING.

worry ▶ verb **1** *she worries about his health* FRET, be concerned, be anxious, agonize, brood, panic, lose sleep, get worked up, get stressed, get in a flap, get in a state, stew, torment oneself. **2** *is something worrying you?* TROUBLE, bother, make anxious, disturb, distress, upset, concern, disquiet, fret, agitate, unsettle, perturb, scare, fluster, stress, tax, torment, plague, bedevil; prey on one's mind, weigh down, gnaw at, rattle, bug, get to, dig at, nag. **3** *a dog worried his sheep* ATTACK, savage, maul, mutilate, mangle, go for; molest, torment, persecute.

▶ noun **1** *I'm beside myself with worry* ANXIETY, perturbation, distress, concern, uneasiness, unease, disquiet, fretfulness, restlessness, nervousness,

nerves, agitation, edginess, tension, stress; apprehension, fear, dread, trepidation, misgiving, angst; *informal* butterflies (in the stomach), the willies, the heebie-jeebies, the jim-jams. **2** *the rats are a worry* PROBLEM, cause for concern, issue; nuisance, pest, plague, trial, trouble, vexation, bane, bugbear; *informal* pain (in the neck), headache, hassle, stress.

worrying ▶ adjective ALARMING, worrisome, daunting, perturbing, niggling, nagging, bothersome, troublesome, unsettling, nerve-racking; distressing, disquieting, upsetting, traumatic, problematic; *informal* scary, hairy.

worsen ▶ verb **1** *insomnia can worsen a patient's distress* AGGRAVATE, exacerbate, compound, add to, intensify, increase, magnify, heighten, inflame, augment; *informal* add fuel to the fire. **2** *the recession worsened* DETERIORATE, degenerate, decline, regress; *informal* go downhill, go to pot, go to the dogs, hit the skids, nosedive.
— OPPOSITES: improve.

worship ▶ noun **1** *the worship of idols* REVERENCE, veneration, adoration, glorification, glory, exaltation; devotion, praise, thanksgiving, homage, honour; *archaic* magnification. **2** *morning worship* SERVICE, religious rite, prayer, praise, devotion, religious observance. **3** *he contemplated her with worship* ADMIRATION, adulation, idolization, lionization, hero-worship.
▶ verb *they worship pagan gods* REVERE, reverence, venerate, pay homage to, honour, adore, praise, pray to, glorify, exalt, extol; hold dear, cherish, treasure, esteem, adulate, idolize, deify, hero-worship, lionize; follow, look up to; *informal* put on a pedestal; *formal* laud; *archaic* magnify.

worst ▶ verb DEFEAT, beat, prevail over, triumph over, trounce, rout, vanquish, conquer, master, overcome, overwhelm, overpower, crush; outdo, outclass, outstrip, surpass; *informal* thrash, smash, lick, best, clobber, drub, slaughter, murder, wipe out, crucify, demolish, wipe the floor with, take to the cleaners, walk all over, make mincemeat of, shellac, cream, whup.

worth ▶ noun **1** *evidence of the rug's worth* VALUE, price, cost; valuation, quotation, estimate. **2** *the intrinsic worth of education* BENEFIT, advantage, use, value, virtue, utility, service, profit, help, aid; desirability, appeal; significance, sense; *informal* mileage, percentage; *archaic* behoof. **3** *a sense of personal worth* WORTHINESS, merit, value, excellence, calibre, quality, stature, eminence, consequence, importance, significance, distinction.

worthless ▶ adjective **1** *the item was worthless* VALUELESS; poor quality, inferior, second-rate, third-rate, low-grade, cheap, shoddy, tawdry, cheesy; *informal* crummy, rubbishy, nickel-and-dime. **2** *his conclusions are worthless* USELESS, no use, ineffective, ineffectual, fruitless, unproductive, unavailing, pointless, nugatory, valueless, inadequate, deficient, meaningless, senseless, insubstantial, empty, hollow, trifling, petty, inconsequential, lame, paltry, pathetic, no-account. **3** *his worthless son* GOOD-FOR-NOTHING, ne'er-do-well, useless, despicable, contemptible, low, ignominious, corrupt, villainous, degenerate, shiftless, feckless; *informal* no-good, lousy, crappy.
— OPPOSITES: valuable, useful.

worthwhile ▶ adjective VALUABLE, useful, of use, of service, beneficial, rewarding, advantageous, positive, helpful, profitable, gainful, fruitful, productive, lucrative, constructive, effective, effectual, meaningful, worthy.

worthy ▶ adjective *a worthy citizen* VIRTUOUS, righteous, good, moral, ethical, upright, upstanding, high-minded, principled, exemplary; law-abiding, irreproachable, blameless, guiltless, unimpeachable, honest, honourable, reputable, decent, respectable, noble, meritorious; pure, saintly, angelic; *informal* squeaky clean.
— OPPOSITES: disreputable.
▶ noun *local worthies* DIGNITARY, personage, grandee, VIP, notable, notability, pillar of society, luminary, leading light, big name; *informal* heavyweight, bigwig, top dog, big shot, big cheese, big wheel, big kahuna.
— OPPOSITES: nobody.
■ **be worthy of** DESERVE, merit, warrant, rate, justify, earn, be entitled to, qualify for.

would-be ▶ adjective ASPIRING, budding, promising, prospective, potential, hopeful, keen, eager, ambitious; *informal* wannabe.

wound ▶ noun **1** *a chest wound* INJURY, lesion, cut, gash, laceration, tear, slash; graze, scratch, abrasion; bruise, contusion; *Medicine* trauma. **2** *the wounds inflicted by the media* INSULT, blow, slight, offence, affront; hurt, damage, injury, pain, distress, grief, anguish, torment.
▶ verb **1** *he was critically wounded* INJURE, hurt, harm; maim, mutilate, disable, incapacitate, cripple; lacerate, cut, graze, gash, stab, slash. **2** *her words had wounded him* HURT, scar, damage, injure; insult, slight, offend, affront, distress, disturb, upset, trouble; grieve, sadden, pain, cut, sting, shock, traumatize, torment.

wow! ▶ exclamation HOLY COW! holy mackerel! holy moly! holy jumpin'! ✤ caramba! cool! whoa! wild! amazing! awesome! hot damn! ye gods! far out! *dated* golly! gosh! gadzooks!

wraith ▶ noun GHOST, spectre, spirit, phantom, apparition, manifestation; *informal* spook; *literary* shade, phantasm.

wrangle ▶ noun *a wrangle over money* ARGUMENT, dispute, disagreement, quarrel, falling-out, fight, squabble, turf war, altercation, war of words, shouting match, tiff, tug-of-war; *informal* set-to, run-in, slanging match, row, bust-up.
▶ verb *we wrangled over the details* ARGUE, quarrel, bicker, squabble, fall out, have words, disagree, be at odds, fight, battle, feud, clash; *informal* scrap.

wrap ▶ verb **1** *she wrapped herself in a towel* SWATHE, bundle, swaddle, muffle, cloak, enfold, envelop, encase, cover, fold, wind. **2** *I wrapped the vase carefully* PARCEL (UP), package, pack (up), bundle (up); gift-wrap.
▶ noun *he put a wrap around her* SHAWL, stole, cloak, cape, mantle, scarf, poncho, serape; *historical* pelisse.
■ **wrap up** *wrap up well — it's cold* DRESS WARMLY, bundle up.
■ **wrap something up** (*informal*) CONCLUDE, finish, end, wind up, round off, terminate, stop, cease, finalize, complete, tie up; *informal* sew up.

wrapper ▶ noun *a candy wrapper* WRAPPING, wrap, packaging, paper, cover, covering; jacket, sheath.

wrath ▶ noun ANGER, rage, fury, outrage, spleen, vexation, (high) dudgeon, crossness, displeasure, annoyance, irritation; *literary* ire, choler.
— OPPOSITES: happiness.

wreak ▶ verb INFLICT, bestow, mete out, administer, deliver, impose, exact, create, cause, result in, effect,

engender, bring about, perpetrate, unleash, let loose, vent; *formal* effectuate.

wreath ▶ noun GARLAND, circlet, chaplet, crown, festoon, lei; ring, loop, circle.

wreathe ▶ verb **1** *a pulpit wreathed in holly* FESTOON, garland, drape, cover, bedeck, deck, decorate, ornament, adorn. **2** *blue smoke wreathed upwards* SPIRAL, coil, loop, wind, curl, twist, snake, curve.

wreck ▶ noun **1** *salvage teams landed on the wreck* SHIPWRECK, sunken ship, derelict; shell, hull. **2** *the wreck of a stolen car* WRECKAGE, debris, remainder, ruins, remains.
▶ verb **1** *he had wrecked her car* DEMOLISH, crash, smash up, damage, destroy; vandalize, deface, desecrate, write off, trash, total. **2** *his ship was wrecked* SHIPWRECK, sink, capsize, run aground. **3** *the crisis wrecked his plans* RUIN, spoil, disrupt, undo, put a stop to, frustrate, blight, crush, quash, dash, destroy, scotch, shatter, devastate, sabotage; *informal* mess up, screw up, foul up, put paid to, scupper, scuttle, stymie, put the kibosh on, nix.

wreckage ▶ noun. See WRECK noun senses 1, 2.

wrench ▶ noun **1** *she felt a wrench on her shoulders* TUG, pull, jerk, jolt, heave; *informal* yank. **2** *hold the piston with a wrench* monkey wrench. **3** *leaving was an immense wrench* PAINFUL PARTING, traumatic event; pang, trauma.
▶ verb **1** *he wrenched the gun from her hand* TUG, pull, wrest, heave, twist, pluck, grab, seize, snatch, force, pry, jimmy; *informal* yank. **2** *she wrenched her ankle* SPRAIN, twist, turn, strain, crick, pull; injure, hurt.

wrest ▶ verb WRENCH, snatch, seize, grab, pry, pluck, tug, pull, jerk, dislodge, remove; *informal* yank.

wrestle ▶ verb GRAPPLE, fight, struggle, contend, vie, battle, wrangle; scuffle, tussle, brawl; *informal* scrap, wrassle, rassle.

wretch ▶ noun **1** *the wretches killed themselves* POOR CREATURE, poor soul, poor thing, poor unfortunate; *informal* poor devil. **2** *I wouldn't trust the old wretch* SCOUNDREL, villain, ruffian, rogue, rascal, reprobate, criminal, miscreant, good-for-nothing; *informal* heel, creep, louse, rat, swine, dog, low-life, scumbag, scum-bucket, scuzzball, sleazeball, sleazebag; *informal*, *archaic* blackguard, picaroon.

wretched ▶ adjective **1** *I felt so wretched without you* MISERABLE, unhappy, sad, heartbroken, grief-stricken, sorrowful, sorry for oneself, distressed, desolate, devastated, despairing, disconsolate, downcast, dejected, crestfallen, cheerless, depressed, melancholy, morose, gloomy, mournful, doleful, dismal, forlorn, woebegone; *informal* blue; *literary* dolorous. **2** *I feel wretched* ILL, unwell, poorly, sick, below par, rough; *informal* under the weather, out of sorts. **3** *their living conditions are wretched* HARSH, hard, grim, stark, difficult; poor, impoverished, pitiful, pathetic, miserable, cheerless, sordid, shabby, seedy, unhealthy, insalubrious, dilapidated; *informal* scummy. **4** *the wretched dweller in the shanty town* UNFORTUNATE, unlucky, luckless, ill-starred, blighted, hapless, poor, pitiable, downtrodden, oppressed; *literary* star-crossed. **5** *he's a wretched coward* DESPICABLE, contemptible, reprehensible, base, vile, loathsome, hateful, detestable, odious, ignoble, shameful, shabby, worthless; *informal* dirty, rotten, lowdown, lousy. **6** *wretched weather* TERRIBLE, awful, dire, atrocious, dreadful, bad, poor, lamentable, deplorable; *informal* godawful. **7** *I don't want the*

wretched money informal damn, damned, blessed, cursed, flaming, confounded, rotten, blasted, bloody.
— OPPOSITES: cheerful, well, comfortable, fortunate, excellent.

wriggle ▶ verb **1** *she tried to hug him but he wriggled* SQUIRM, writhe, wiggle, jiggle, jerk, thresh, flounder, flail, twitch, twist and turn; snake, worm, slither. **2** *he wriggled out of his responsibilities* AVOID, shirk, dodge, evade, elude, sidestep; escape from; *informal* duck.

wring ▶ verb **1** *wring out the clothes* TWIST, squeeze, screw, scrunch, knead, press, mangle. **2** *concessions were wrung from the government* EXTRACT, elicit, force, exact, wrest, wrench, squeeze, milk; *informal* bleed. **3** *his expression wrung her heart* REND, tear at, harrow, pierce, stab, wound, rack; distress, pain, hurt.

wrinkle ▶ noun **1** *fine wrinkles around her mouth* CREASE, fold, pucker, line, crinkle, furrow, ridge, groove; *informal* crow's feet, laugh line. **2** *the project has some wrinkles to iron out* DIFFICULTY, snag, hitch, drawback, imperfection, problem.
▶ verb *his coat tails wrinkled up* CREASE, pucker, gather, line, crinkle, crimp, crumple, rumple, ruck up, scrunch up.

writ ▶ noun SUMMONS, subpoena, warrant, arraignment, indictment, citation, court order.

write ▶ verb **1** *he wrote her name in the book* NOTE (DOWN), write down, jot down, put down, put in writing, take down, record, register, log, list; inscribe, sign, scribble, scrawl, pencil. **2** *Jacqueline wrote a poem* COMPOSE, draft, think up, formulate, compile, pen, dash off, produce. **3** *he had her address and promised to write* CORRESPOND, write a letter, communicate, get/stay in touch, keep in contact, email; *informal* drop someone a line.
■ **write someone/something off 1** *they have had to write off loans* FORGET ABOUT, disregard, give up on, cancel, annul. **2** *he wrote off his car in an accident* WRECK, total, smash up, crash, destroy, demolish, ruin. **3** *she wrote off the cost of the computer* DEDUCT, claim. **4** *who would write off a player of his stature?* DISREGARD, dismiss, ignore.

writer ▶ noun AUTHOR, wordsmith, man/woman of letters, penman; novelist, essayist, biographer; journalist, columnist, correspondent; scriptwriter, playwright, dramatist, dramaturge, tragedian; poet; *informal* scribbler, scribe, pencil-pusher, hack.

writhe ▶ verb SQUIRM, wriggle, thrash, flail, toss, toss and turn, twist, twist and turn, struggle.

writing ▶ noun **1** *I can't read his writing* HANDWRITING, hand, script, print; penmanship, calligraphy, chirography; *informal* scribble, scrawl, chicken scratch. **2** *the writings of Bronwen Wallace* WORKS, compositions, books, publications, oeuvre; papers, articles, essays.

wrong ▶ adjective **1** *the wrong answer* INCORRECT, mistaken, in error, erroneous, inaccurate, inexact, imprecise, fallacious, wide of the mark, off target, unsound, faulty; *informal* out. **2** *he knew he had said the wrong thing* INAPPROPRIATE, unsuitable, inapt, inapposite, undesirable; ill-advised, ill-considered, ill-judged, impolitic, injudicious, infelicitous, unfitting, out of keeping, improper; *informal* out of order. **3** *I've done nothing wrong* ILLEGAL, unlawful, illicit, criminal, dishonest, dishonourable, corrupt; unethical, immoral, bad, wicked, sinful, iniquitous, nefarious, blameworthy, reprehensible; *informal* crooked. **4** *there's something wrong with the engine* AMISS, awry, out of order, not right, faulty, flawed, defective.
— OPPOSITES: right, correct, appropriate, legal.
▶ adverb *she guessed wrong* INCORRECTLY, wrongly, inaccurately, erroneously, mistakenly, in error.
▶ noun **1** *the difference between right and wrong* IMMORALITY, sin, sinfulness, wickedness, evil; unlawfulness, crime, corruption, villainy, dishonesty, injustice, wrongdoing, misconduct, transgression. **2** *an attempt to make up for past wrongs* MISDEED, offence, injury, crime, transgression, violation, peccadillo, sin; injustice, outrage, atrocity; *Law* tort; *archaic* trespass.
— OPPOSITES: right.
▶ verb **1** *she was determined to forget the man who had wronged her* ILL-USE, mistreat, do an injustice to, do wrong to, ill-treat, abuse, harm, hurt, injure. **2** *perhaps I am wronging him* MALIGN, misrepresent, do a disservice to, impugn, defame, slander, libel.
■ **get someone/something wrong** MISUNDERSTAND, misinterpret, misconstrue, mistake, misread, take amiss; get the wrong idea/impression; *informal* be barking up the wrong tree.
■ **go wrong 1** *I've gone wrong somewhere* MAKE A MISTAKE, make an error, make a blunder, blunder, miscalculate, trip up, slip up, goof, screw up, make a boo-boo, fluff, flub. **2** *their plans went wrong* GO AWRY, go amiss, go off course, fail, be unsuccessful, fall through, come to nothing; backfire, misfire, rebound; *informal* come to grief, come a cropper, go up in smoke, go adrift. **3** *the radio's gone wrong* BREAK DOWN, malfunction, fail, stop working, crash, give out; *informal* be on the blink, conk out, go kaput, go on the fritz.
■ **in the wrong** TO BLAME, blameworthy, at fault, reprehensible, responsible, culpable, answerable, guilty; *archaic* peccant.

wrongdoer ▶ noun OFFENDER, lawbreaker, criminal, felon, delinquent, villain, culprit, evildoer, sinner, transgressor, malefactor, miscreant, rogue, scoundrel; *informal* crook, *Law* malfeasant, *archaic* trespasser.

wrongdoing ▶ noun CRIME, law-breaking, lawlessness, criminality, misconduct, misbehaviour, malpractice, corruption, immorality, sin, sinfulness, wickedness, evil, vice, iniquity, villainy; offence, felony, wrong, misdeed, misdemeanour, fault, peccadillo, transgression; *Law* malfeasance, tort; *formal* malversation; *archaic* trespass.

wrongful ▶ adjective UNJUSTIFIED, unwarranted, unjust, unfair, undue, undeserved, unreasonable, groundless, indefensible, inappropriate, improper, unlawful, illegal, illegitimate.
— OPPOSITES: rightful.

wrought ▶ adjective *skilfully wrought works of art* MADE, created, built, crafted, fashioned, worked, moulded, formed, manufactured.
■ **wrought up** AGITATED, tense, stressed, overwrought, nervous, on edge, edgy, keyed up, worked up, jumpy, antsy, anxious, flustered, fretful, upset; *informal* in a state, in a stew, het up, wound up, uptight, in a tizz/tizzy, spooky, squirrelly.

wry ▶ adjective **1** *his wry humour* IRONIC, sardonic, satirical, mocking, sarcastic; dry, droll, witty, humorous. **2** *a wry expression* UNIMPRESSED, displeased, annoyed, irritated, irked, vexed, piqued, disgruntled, dissatisfied; *informal* peeved.

Xx

xenophobic ▶ adjective chauvinistic, flag-waving, anti-foreigner, excessively nationalistic, isolationist, jingoistic; prejudiced, bigoted, intolerant.

X-rated ▶ adjective ADULT, hard-core, pornographic, blue, triple-X, XXX.

X-ray ▶ noun RADIOGRAM, X-ray image/picture/photograph, roentgenogram, radiograph.
— RELATED TERMS: radiography

Yy

yahoo ▶ noun REDNECK, boor, lout, oaf, thug, barbarian, Neanderthal, knuckle-dragger, brute, bully boy; *informal* clod, roughneck, bruiser.
▶ exclamation WAHOO, yippee, hooray, hurrah, hallelujah, bravo, cowabunga, hot dog, whoopee, yay, yee-haw.

yank ▶ verb *(informal)* JERK, pull, tug, wrench; snatch, seize.

yap ▶ verb **1** *the dogs yapped about his heels* BARK, woof, yelp. **2** *(informal) what are they yapping on about? See* BABBLE *verb* sense 1.

yard ▶ noun **1** *they kicked a soccer ball around the yard* BACKYARD, garden, lawn, grounds; courtyard, court, quadrangle, enclosure, cloister, quad. **2** *a boat-building yard* WORKSHOP, works, factory, garage, plant, foundry, mill, shipyard; *archaic* manufactory.

yard sale ▶ noun LAWN SALE, garage sale, street sale, rummage sale.

yardstick ▶ noun STANDARD, measure, gauge, scale, guide, guideline, indicator, test, touchstone, barometer, criterion, benchmark, point of reference, model, pattern, template.

yardwork ▶ noun GARDENING, (lawn) maintenance.

yarn ▶ noun **1** *you need to use a fine yarn* THREAD, cotton, wool, fibre, filament; ply. **2** *(informal) a far-fetched yarn* STORY, tale, anecdote, saga, narrative; *informal* tall tale/story, fish story, cock-and-bull story, shaggy-dog story, spiel.

yawning ▶ adjective GAPING, wide open, wide, cavernous, deep; huge, great, big.

year ▶ noun ANNUM, twelve-month period; *archaic* twelvemonth.
— RELATED TERMS: annual.
■ **year in, year out** REPEATEDLY, again and again, time and (time) again, time after time, over and over (again), {week in, week out}, {day in, day out}, inexorably, recurrently, continuously, continually, constantly, non-stop, habitually, regularly, without a break, unfailingly, always.

Animals of the Chinese Calendar

rat	1996	horse	2002
ox	1997	goat/sheep	2003
tiger	1998	monkey	2004
rabbit	1999	rooster	2005
dragon	2000	dog	2006
snake	2001	pig	2007

(Chinese New Year occurs in late January or early February.)

---

yearly ▶ adjective *a yearly payment* ANNUAL, once a year, every year, each year, per annum.
▶ adverb *the guide is published yearly* ANNUALLY, once a year, per annum, by the year, every year, each year.

yearn ▶ verb LONG, pine, crave, desire, want, wish, hanker, covet, lust, pant, hunger, burn, thirst, ache, eat one's heart out, have one's heart set on; *informal* have a yen, have a jones, itch.

yearning ▶ noun LONGING, craving, desire, want, wish, hankering, urge, hunger, thirst, appetite, lust, ache; *informal* yen, itch.

yell ▶ verb *he yelled in agony* CRY OUT, call out, shout, howl, yowl, wail, scream, shriek, screech, yelp, squeal; roar, bawl; *informal* holler.
▶ noun *a yell of rage* CRY, shout, howl, yowl, scream, shriek, screech, yelp, squeal; roar; *informal* holler.

yellow ▶ adjective **1** *yellow hair | a yellow shirt* FLAXEN, golden, gold, blond, fair; lemon, cadmium yellow, daffodil, mustard, primrose yellow. **2** *(informal) he'll have to prove he's not yellow. See* COWARDLY.

yelp ▶ noun & verb SQUEAL, shriek, howl, yowl, yell, cry, shout, yawp; *informal* holler.

yen ▶ noun *(informal)* HANKERING, yearning, longing, craving, urge, desire, want, wish, hunger, thirst, lust, appetite, ache; fancy, inclination; *informal* itch.

yes ▶ adverb ALL RIGHT, very well, of course, by all means, sure, certainly, absolutely, indeed, right, affirmative, in the affirmative, agreed, roger; *Nautical*

aye aye; *informal* yeah, yep, yup, ya, uh-huh, okay, OK, okey-dokey, okey-doke; surely; *archaic* yea, aye.
— OPPOSITES: no.

yes-man ▶ noun (*informal*) SYCOPHANT, toady, creep, fawner, flatterer, lickspittle, doormat, trained seal; *informal* bootlicker, suck-up, brown-noser, browner ✦; henchman, stooge.

yet ▶ adverb **1** *he hasn't made up his mind yet* SO FAR, thus far, as yet, up till/to now, until now. **2** *don't celebrate just yet* NOW, right now, at this time; already, so soon. **3** *he was doing nothing, yet he appeared purposeful* NEVERTHELESS, nonetheless, even so, but, however, still, notwithstanding, despite that, in spite of that, for all that, all the same, just the same, at the same time, be that as it may; *archaic* natheless. **4** *he supplied yet more unsolicited advice* EVEN, still, further, in addition, additionally, besides, into the bargain, to boot, on top (of that).

yield ▶ verb **1** *too many projects yield poor returns* PRODUCE, bear, give, supply, provide, afford, return, bring in, earn, realize, generate, deliver, offer, pay out. **2** *the nobility yielded power to the capitalists* RELINQUISH, surrender, cede, remit, part with, hand over; make over, bequeath, leave. **3** *the Duke was forced to yield* SURRENDER, capitulate, submit, relent, admit defeat, back down, climb down, give in, give up the struggle, lay down one's arms, raise/show the white flag, throw in the towel/sponge. **4** *he yielded to her demands* GIVE IN TO, give way to, submit to, bow down to, comply with, agree to, consent to, go along with; grant, permit, allow; *informal* cave in to; *formal* accede to. **5** *the floorboards yielded underfoot* BEND, give, give way.
— OPPOSITES: withhold, resist, defy.
▶ noun *risky investments usually have higher yields* PROFIT, gain, return, dividend, earnings.

yoke ▶ noun **1** *the horses were loosened from the yoke* HARNESS, collar, coupling. **2** *countries struggling under the yoke of imperialism* TYRANNY, oppression, domination, hegemony, enslavement, servitude, subjugation, subjection, bondage, thrall; bonds, chains, fetters, shackles. **3** *the yoke of marriage* BOND, tie, connection, link.

▶ verb **1** *a pair of oxen were yoked together* HARNESS, hitch, couple, tether, fasten, attach, join. **2** *their aim of yoking biology and mechanics* UNITE, join, marry, link, connect; tie, bind, bond.

yokel ▶ noun BUMPKIN, peasant, provincial, rustic, country cousin, countryman/woman; hayseed, hillbilly, hick, rube; (*Nfld*) baywop ✦, bayman ✦, noddy ✦.

young ▶ adjective **1** *young people* YOUTHFUL, juvenile; junior, adolescent, teenage; in the springtime of life, in one's salad days. **2** *she's very young for her age* IMMATURE, childish, inexperienced, unsophisticated, naive, unworldly; *informal* wet behind the ears. **3** *the young microbrewery industry* FLEDGLING, developing, budding, in its infancy, emerging.
— OPPOSITES: old, elderly, mature.
▶ noun **1** *a robin feeding its young* OFFSPRING, progeny, family, babies. **2** *the young don't care nowadays* YOUNG PEOPLE, children, kids, boys and girls, youngsters, youth, the younger generation, juveniles, minors; young 'uns.

youngster ▶ noun CHILD, teenager, adolescent, youth, juvenile, minor, junior; boy, girl, lass, lad; kid, whippersnapper, stripling, young 'un, teen.

youth ▶ noun **1** *he had been a keen sportsman in his youth* EARLY YEARS, young days, salad days, teens, teenage years, adolescence, boyhood, girlhood, childhood; minority; *formal* juvenescence. **2** *she had kept her youth and beauty* YOUTHFULNESS, freshness, bloom, vigour, energy. **3** *local youths* YOUNG PERSON/MAN/WOMAN, boy, girl, juvenile, teenager, adolescent, junior, minor, kid. **4** *the youth of the nation* YOUNG PEOPLE, young, younger generation, next generation; kids, children.
— OPPOSITES: adulthood, old age.

youthful ▶ adjective YOUNG-LOOKING, spry, sprightly, vigorous, active; young, boyish, girlish; fresh-faced, in the springtime of life, in one's salad days.
— OPPOSITES: old, elderly.

yuck ▶ exclamation BLECH, ugh, yech, ick, phew, eeew, barf, gag.

Zz

Zamboni ▶ noun ICE RESURFACER.

zany ▶ adjective ECCENTRIC, peculiar, odd, unconventional, strange, bizarre, weird; mad, crazy, comic, madcap, funny, quirky, idiosyncratic; *informal* wacky, screwy, nutty, oddball, off the wall; daft; kooky, wacko.
— OPPOSITES: conventional, sensible.

zap ▶ verb (*informal*) **1** *they were zapped by anti-radar missiles.* See DESTROY sense 5. **2** *racing cars zapped past.* See SPEED verb sense 1. **3** *she zapped a chicken burger for lunch* NUKE, microwave.

zeal ▶ noun PASSION, ardour, love, fervour, fire, avidity, devotion, enthusiasm, eagerness, keenness, appetite, relish, gusto, vigour, energy, intensity; fanaticism.
— OPPOSITES: apathy.

zealot ▶ noun FANATIC, enthusiast, extremist, radical, young Turk, diehard, true believer, activist, militant; bigot, dogmatist, sectarian, partisan; *informal* fiend, maniac, ultra, nut; keener ♣, eager beaver.

zealous ▶ adjective FERVENT, ardent, fervid, fanatical, passionate, impassioned, devout, devoted, committed, dedicated, enthusiastic, eager, keen, avid, card-carrying, vigorous, energetic, intense, fierce; *literary* perfervid.
— OPPOSITES: apathetic.

zenith ▶ noun HIGHEST POINT, high point, crowning point, height, top, acme, peak, pinnacle, apex, apogee, crown, crest, summit, climax, culmination, prime, meridian.
— OPPOSITES: nadir.

zero ▶ noun *I rated my chances at zero* NOTHING (AT ALL), nil, none; *informal* zilch, nix, zip, nada, diddly-squat; *archaic* naught, nought.
■ **zero in on** FOCUS ON, focus attention on, centre on, concentrate on, home in on, fix on, pinpoint, highlight, spotlight; *informal* zoom in on.

zero hour ▶ noun THE APPOINTED TIME, the critical moment, the moment of truth, the point/moment of decision, the Rubicon, the crux; *informal* the crunch.

zest ▶ noun **1** *she had a great zest for life* ENTHUSIASM, gusto, relish, appetite, eagerness, keenness, avidity, zeal, fervour, ardour, passion; verve, vigour, liveliness, sparkle, fire, animation, vitality, dynamism, energy, brio, pep, spirit, exuberance, high spirits, joie de vivre; *informal* zing, zip, oomph, vim, pizzazz, get-up-and-go. **2** *he wanted to add some zest to his life* PIQUANCY, tang, flavour, savour, taste,

spice, spiciness, relish, bite; excitement, interest, an edge; *informal* kick, punch, zing, oomph. **3** *the zest of an orange* RIND, peel, skin.
— OPPOSITES: apathy, indifference, blandness.

zigzag ▶ adjective TWISTING, twisty, full of twists and turns, serpentine, meandering, snaking, snaky, winding, crooked.
— OPPOSITES: straight.

zing ▶ noun (*informal*). See ZEST sense 1.

zinger ▶ noun WITTICISM, quip, joke; criticism, dig, poke.

zip (*informal*) ▶ noun *he's full of zip.* See ENERGY.
▶ verb *I zipped back along the 401.* See SPEED verb sense 1.

zodiac See table.

Signs of the Zodiac

Aries	21 Mar. - 19 Apr.	Ram
Taurus	20 Apr. - 20 May	Bull
Gemini	21 May - 21 June	Twins
Cancer	22 June - 22 July	Crab
Leo	23 July - 22 Aug.	Lion
Virgo	23 Aug. - 22 Sept.	Virgin
Libra	23 Sept. - 23 Oct.	Scales
Scorpio	24 Oct. - 21 Nov.	Scorpion
Sagittarius	22 Nov. - 21 Dec.	Archer
Capricorn	22 Dec. - 19 Jan.	Goat
Aquarius	20 Jan. - 18 Feb.	Water Carrier
Pisces	19 Feb. - 20 Mar.	Fish

zombie ▶ noun See UNDEAD.

zone ▶ noun AREA, sector, section, belt, stretch, region, territory, district, quarter, precinct, locality, neighbourhood, province.

zonked ▶ adjective See EXHAUSTED.

zoo ▶ noun **1** PARK, menagerie, game farm, wildlife park, safari park, zoological park. **2** *it's an absolute zoo in here* CIRCUS, madhouse, maelstrom, hullabaloo, kerfuffle, free-for-all; pandemonium, chaos, bedlam.

zoom ▶ verb (*informal*) **1** *she zoomed off into the distance* WHIZ, zip, zap, whip, buzz, hurtle, speed, rush, streak, shoot, race, bolt, dash, run, flash, blast, charge, fly, pelt, careen, career, go like the wind, belt, scoot, tear, go like a bat out of hell, bomb, hightail, hare, clip. **2** *zoom in on the rabbit in the background* ENLARGE, magnify, close in on, focus in on.
▶ noun *you need to increase the zoom to see it* MAGNIFICATION.